The
DAILY
BIBLE®

NEW INTERNATIONAL VERSION

With Devotional Insights
to Guide You Through God's Word

Commentary by

F. LaGard Smith

Guideposts
New York, New York

To my father,
Frank L. Smith,
who gave his life to the ministry of the gospel
and first suggested the idea for this book

and

to my mother,
Mary Faye Smith,
who taught me to love God's Word.

This Guideposts edition is published by special arrangement with Harvest House Publishers and the Zondervan Corporation.

THE DAILY BIBLE is a registered trademark of The Hawkins Children's LLC. Harvest House Publishers, Inc., is the exclusive licensee of the federally registered trademark THE DAILY BIBLE.

The DAILY BIBLE®

Cover by Koechel Peterson & Associates, Inc., Minneapolis, Minnesota

Copyright © 1984 by Harvest House Publishers
Eugene, Oregon 97402
www.harvesthousepublishers.com

Library of Congress Catalog Number 83-83372

	ISBN-10:	ISBN-13:
Hardcover	0-7369-0124-8	978-0-7369-0124-6
(first published 1996)		
Softcover	0-7369-0198-1	978-0-7369-0198-7
Milano Softone™	0-7369-1733-0	978-0-7369-1733-9
Compact Hardcover	0-7369-1581-8	978-0-7369-1581-6
Compact Softcover	0-7369-1582-6	978-0-7369-1582-3

Printed in the United States of America   15 14 13 12 11 10 9

Dear Guideposts Friend,

The original idea for the volume you have in your hand came from my father, a gospel preacher. When I was still a teenager, he said to me once: "Somebody ought to put the Bible in the right order!" I don't remember the context of his statement, nor did he elaborate any further. But I intuitively knew what he was thinking, and why it would be so helpful if a chronologically arranged Bible could be produced. When he died suddenly at the age of sixty-three, I felt that the torch was being passed down to the next generation. Again and again, his idea from so many years before kept coming to mind.

About that same time, I had a close friend who—reading the Bible pretty much for the first time—was having great difficulty putting it all together. It occurred to me how valuable it would be for readers to have "Dad's Bible." In fact, I myself kept thinking how great it would be to have such a Bible! There being none in existence at the time, I finally felt called to attempt such a presentation of Scripture as a tribute to my father.

My dream for *The Daily Bible* has always been that people could read the *entire* Bible, from cover to cover, making sense of it along the way. How many folks have resolved to read the Bible, say in a year, but have become discouraged some-where in the middle of Leviticus? How many readers have wondered just where the prophets fit in the history of Israel, or tried in vain to consolidate the four different Gospel accounts? Here, at last, is a presentation of Scripture that can take you from start to finish with relative ease and, hopefully, far deeper insight than ever.

I hope you agree that my father was right, and that this chronological presentation of God's Word makes it easier for you to read and enjoy Scripture.

Sincerely,

F. LaGard Smith

As You Begin . . .

*T*HE DAILY BIBLE is conveniently presented for your daily reading so that you may read through the entire Bible in one year. But this is not just another yearly Bible. In fact, it is unlike any other Bible you have ever read. In *The Daily Bible*, you will read the Scriptures in chronological order, just as the events they portray happened in history. Instead of reading portions of the Old Testament and New Testament at random, in *The Daily Bible* you will see the events unfold before you like an epic novel. Along the way, you will be led from one passage to another by informative, interesting narrative which sets the scene for what you are about to read.

If you have never read the Bible from cover to cover, this is the one Bible that will help you to do that. It takes you by the hand and leads you gently into "the whole counsel of God." Seeing the big picture, and every separate part in its proper context, you will sometimes be pleasantly surprised, always edified, and greatly challenged. Reading the Bible on a daily basis throughout an entire year will not be a burdensome commitment but a joyous daily renewal of your faith. If your Bible study has taken on a certain sameness over the years, you will discover through *The Daily Bible* that God really is speaking to you with wonderful words of life!

Unique, Topical Presentations

As you read, you will find exciting differences between your traditional Bible and *The Daily Bible*. For the first time, you will have all of the Laws of Moses gathered together in a single, unified presentation by subject matter. You will gain a new appreciation for the history of Israel when you see the ceremonial laws, the dietary and health laws, and the various civil and criminal laws in one place. You will also enjoy the Psalms even more than ever now that they are grouped together by themes: Psalms of the Troubled Soul, Psalms of Joy and Praise, Psalms of the Messiah. And, unique to *The Daily Bible*, you will discover new insights for your life in the topical arrangement of Proverbs and Ecclesiastes.

For all those who have ever wondered where the writings of the prophets fit into the history of the people of Israel, *The Daily Bible* sorts it out for you. With the dust blown off the writings of these great men of God, you will find yourself at the very threshold of God's presence. Their sermons decrying materialism, injustice, and religious hypocrisy ring out to a dying nation and draw each of us to a more committed response to God.

The Harmonized Gospels

Many attempts have been made to harmonize the four Gospels or to present them in parallel columns for easy comparison. But *The Daily Bible* gives you, for the first time, a totally integrated account of the life of Christ in chronological order. You will come to know Jesus as perhaps never before—intimately! And Paul's various epistles bristle with new meaning when you read them in the context of the Book of Acts, into which they are placed. No other Bible so completely organizes the Scriptures in a way that brings them so easily to life for you.

The Daily Bible has been divided into 365 easily readable sections. Based on logical content, the readings will vary somewhat in length. On the average, however, each daily reading section is less than five pages. The sections are identified by this reading symbol ![symbol] which will appear at the beginning of each day's reading.

Descriptive Narration—
Guides You Smoothly Though the Scriptures

The Daily Bible is neither a retranslation nor a paraphrase. The central text is composed entirely of Scripture, using the widely acclaimed New International Version. Thoughtful and reflective narrative commentary has been set apart by a screened background, but is written to integrate with the Scriptures in such a way as to be part of an unfolding story. For the most part, the narrative is written in the present tense in order to heighten your own sense of involvement in the lives of those who have sought to know God.

Throughout this presentation of Scripture, chapter and verse designations are placed in the margin for easy reference. Boldface references indicate passages which are actually shown in the text. Lightface references indicate parallel passages which are duplications of the text presented. Where repetitive text is mixed together, every scriptural thought is preserved in at least one of the passages actually shown. In addition, by the use of elevated book abbreviations, the text itself will indicate which book is being presented at the time. Where verses are rearranged in chronological order, the punctuation and format of the New International Version has been left unaltered.

The Daily Bible will become your second Bible and constant reading companion for years to come. Giving you a greater appreciation of context and a love for reading God's revelation, it will make Bible reading a refreshing personal experience. To that end, may God richly bless your life and your reading of His Word.

—F. LaGard Smith

DAILY BIBLE READING SCHEDULE

For those who may wish to follow a daily Bible reading schedule, *The Daily Bible* has been divided into 365 easily readable sections. Because the daily reading sections have been determined on the basis of logical content, the reading will vary somewhat in length. On the average, however, each daily reading section is less than five pages. The sections are identified by this daily reading symbol ![symbol] which will appear at the beginning of each day's reading.

Day	Pages	Day	Pages	Day	Pages
January 1	1-6	February 5	157-162	March 12	322-328
2	6-10	6	162-166	13	328-333
3	11-16	7	166-170	14	333-338
4	17-22	8	170-174	15	338-343
5	23-28	9	174-179	16	343-346
6	29-34	10	179-183	17	346-349
7	34-39	11	184-190	18	349-353
8	39-44	12	190-194	19	353-357
9	44-47	13	194-198	20	357-361
10	47-50	14	198-203	21	361-364
11	50-55	15	203-210	22	365-369
12	55-59	16	210-214	23	369-375
13	59-63	17	214-218	24	375-378
14	63-68	18	219-223	25	378-383
15	68-71	19	223-228	26	384-388
16	71-74	20	228-236	27	388-392
17	74-78	21	236-240	28	392-398
18	78-82	22	240-245	29	398-402
19	82-87	23	245-248	30	402-405
20	87-91	24	248-252	31	405-409
21	91-96	25	252-256		
22	97-102	26	256-261	April 1	409-414
23	103-107	27	261-263	2	414-419
24	107-110	28	263-267	3	419-424
25	110-113			4	424-431
26	113-117	March 1	267-274	5	431-434
27	117-121	2	274-280	6	434-439
28	121-126	3	280-285	7	439-443
29	126-131	4	285-288	8	443-448
30	131-135	5	288-292	9	448-451
31	135-139	6	292-295	10	451-456
		7	296-302	11	456-460
February 1	140-145	8	303-308	12	460-464
2	145-147	9	308-312	13	464-467
3	147-151	10	312-317	14	467-471
4	152-157	11	317-322	15	471-475

DAILY READING SCHEDULE

Day	Pages	Day	Pages	Day	Pages
April 16	475-480	June 1	690-694	July 17	902-907
17	480-485	2	694-698	18	908-911
18	485-490	3	698-704	19	911-916
19	490-495	4	704-709	20	916-923
20	495-500	5	709-715	21	923-928
21	500-504	6	715-719	22	929-933
22	505-508	7	720-724	23	934-935
23	508-513	8	724-726	24	935-941
24	513-517	9	727-729	25	941-947
25	517-520	10	729-734	26	947-953
26	521-526	11	734-738	27	953-957
27	526-531	12	738-741	28	957-963
28	531-536	13	741-748	29	963-968
29	536-540	14	748-752	30	968-973
30	540-546	15	752-755	31	973-978
		16	755-758		
May 1	546-550	17	758-762	August 1	978-983
2	550-554	18	762-769	2	983-987
3	554-562	19	770-776	3	987-991
4	562-566	20	776-782	4	991-994
5	566-569	21	782-788	5	994-999
6	570-574	22	788-790	6	999-1033
7	574-578	23	791-797	7	1033-1055
8	578-580	24	798-803	8	1006-1010
9	580-584	25	803-806	9	1010-1018
10	584-587	26	806-810	10	1018-1020
11	587-591	27	810-813	11	1020-1024
12	591-595	28	813-815	12	1024-1026
13	596-602	29	815-819	13	1026-1030
14	602-606	30	819-825	14	1030-1038
15	606-613			15	1038-1045
16	613-619	July 1	825-829	16	1045-1049
17	619-624	2	829-833	17	1049-1053
18	624-630	3	834-839	18	1053-1060
19	630-634	4	839-843	19	1060-1067
20	634-639	5	844-849	20	1067-1070
21	639-642	6	850-855	21	1070-1072
22	643-646	7	855-859	22	1072-1077
23	647-652	8	859-862	23	1077-1082
24	652-657	9	863-869	24	1082-1085
25	657-661	10	870-877	25	1085-1091
26	661-672	11	877-878	26	1091-1096
27	672-674	12	878-883	27	1097-1099
28	674-678	13	883-887	28	1100-1103
29	678-684	14	887-893	29	1103-1109
30	684-687	15	893-898	30	1109-1115
31	687-689	16	898-902	31	1115-1120

Day	Pages	Day	Pages	Day	Pages
September 1	1121-1126	October 11	1309-1314	November 21	1488-1493
2	1126-1130	12	1315-1318	22	1493-1496
3	1130-1134	13	1318-1326	23	1496-1500
4	1134-1136	14	1326-1336	24	1500-1506
5	1136-1143	15	1337-1339	25	1506-1512
6	1143-1150	16	1339-1343	26	1513-1519
7	1150-1154	17	1343-1348	27	1519-1523
8	1155-1159	18	1349-1352	28	1524-1527
9	1159-1164	19	1353-1355	29	1527-1531
10	1164-1168	20	1355-1361	30	1531-1535
11	1168-1173	21	1361-1363		
12	1173-1176	22	1364-1367	December 1	1535-1542
13	1176-1182	23	1367-1373	2	1542-1546
14	1182-1185	24	1373-1376	3	1546-1550
15	1185-1193	25	1376-1380	4	1550-1557
16	1193-1202	26	1381-1386	5	1557-1561
17	1202-1209	27	1386-1390	6	1561-1565
18	1209-1217	28	1390-1394	7	1565-1571
19	1217-1221	29	1394-1397	8	1571-1575
20	1221-1225	30	1397-1400	9	1576-1581
21	1225-1229	31	1400-1403	10	1581-1583
22	1230-1232			11	1583-1587
23	1233-1238	November 1	1403-1408	12	1587-1592
24	1238-1242	2	1408-1410	13	1592-1596
25	1243-1246	3	1410-1415	14	1596-1601
26	1247-1250	4	1415-1418	15	1601-1607
27	1250-1254	5	1418-1422	16	1608-1612
28	1255-1257	6	1422-1426	17	1613-1618
29	1258-1261	7	1427-1433	18	1618-1620
30	1261-1266	8	1433-1435	19	1620-1624
		9	1435-1440	20	1624-1630
		10	1440-1443	21	1631-1636
October 1	1266-1269	11	1443-1449	22	1636-1640
2	1269-1276	12	1449-1453	23	1640-1646
3	1276-1281	13	1453-1457	24	1646-1650
4	1281-1285	14	1457-1461	25	1650-1656
5	1286-1290	15	1462-1465	26	1656-1663
6	1290-1293	16	1465-1469	27	1663-1667
7	1293-1296	17	1470-1473	28	1667-1672
8	1297-1300	18	1473-1477	29	1672-1677
9	1300-1304	19	1477-1484	30	1677-1683
10	1304-1309	20	1485-1488	31	1683-1688

OLD TESTAMENT CONTENTS

Contents

CONTENTS

NEW TESTAMENT CONTENTS

BEGINNINGS OF EARLY MANKIND

(Creation to ca. 2100 B.C.)

The Beginning

*I*s it possible to imagine a time when nothing existed? Take away the brilliance of the sun, for example, and the moon and stars at night. What would life be like without them? Take away the clouds and sky and rivers and oceans. Imagine the earth without any human beings, animals, fish, birds, grass, trees, or plants of any kind. What would it be like with the earth completely bare? Indeed, what would it be like if there were no earth at all, no universe—nothing? Has the universe existed forever? Was there never a time when it had a beginning? Surely it must have had a beginning. But when would that have been? How would it all have happened? What made it happen? For what purpose, if any, did it happen? Who am I? Where did I come from? Why am I here?

Since recorded history began, men and women of every generation, culture, and place have searched for the answers to those questions. Some say it all happened by chance, without any reason or purpose whatever. But given what appears to be intelligent design and order throughout the universe, an origin by chance seems hard to accept. And life without meaning seems clearly contrary to the very mind which searches for meaning. So what are the answers? Where did I come from, and why am I here? How did it all begin?

ACCOUNT OF CREATION.   In the beginning God created the heavens and the earth. Now the earth was[a] formless and empty, darkness was over the surface of the deep, and the Spirit of God was hovering over the waters.

Gen. 1:1,2

And God said, "Let there be light," and there was light. God saw that the light was good, and he separated the light from the darkness. God called the light "day," and the darkness he called "night." And there was evening, and there was morning—the first day.

Gen. 1:3-5

And God said, "Let there be an expanse between the waters to separate water from water." So God made the expanse and separated the water under the expanse from the water above it. And it was so. God called the expanse "sky." And there was evening, and there was morning—the second day.

Gen. 1:6-8

[a]Or possibly *became*

Gen.
1:9-13

And God said, "Let the water under the sky be gathered to one place, and let dry ground appear." And it was so. God called the dry ground "land," and the gathered waters he called "seas." And God saw that it was good.

Then God said, "Let the land produce vegetation: seed-bearing plants and trees on the land that bear fruit with seed in it, according to their various kinds." And it was so. The land produced vegetation: plants bearing seed according to their kinds and trees bearing fruit with seed in it according to their kinds. And God saw that it was good. And there was evening, and there was morning—the third day.

Gen.
1:14-19

And God said, "Let there be lights in the expanse of the sky to separate the day from the night, and let them serve as signs to mark seasons and days and years, and let them be lights in the expanse of the sky to give light on the earth." And it was so. God made two great lights—the greater light to govern the day and the lesser light to govern the night. He also made the stars. God set them in the expanse of the sky to give light on the earth, to govern the day and the night, and to separate light from darkness. And God saw that it was good. And there was evening, and there was morning—the fourth day.

Gen.
1:20-23

And God said, "Let the water teem with living creatures, and let birds fly above the earth across the expanse of the sky." So God created the great creatures of the sea and every living and moving thing with which the water teems, according to their kinds, and every winged bird according to its kind. And God saw that it was good. God blessed them and said, "Be fruitful and increase in number and fill the water in the seas, and let the birds increase on the earth." And there was evening, and there was morning—the fifth day.

Gen.
1:24,25

And God said, "Let the land produce living creatures according to their kinds: livestock, creatures that move along the ground, and wild animals, each according to its kind." And it was so. God made the wild animals according to their kinds, the livestock according to their kinds, and all the creatures that move along the ground according to their kinds. And God saw that it was good.

Gen.
1:26-30

Then God said, "Let us make man in our image, in our likeness, and let them rule over the fish of the sea and the birds of the air, over the livestock, over all the earth,[b] and over all the creatures that move along the ground."

> So God created man in his own image,
>   in the image of God he created him;
>   male and female he created them.

God blessed them and said to them, "Be fruitful and increase in number; fill the earth and subdue it. Rule over the fish of the sea and the birds of the air and over every living creature that moves on the ground."

Then God said, "I give you every seed-bearing plant on the face of the whole earth and every tree that has fruit with seed in it. They will be yours for food. And to all the beasts of the earth and all the birds of the air and all the creatures that move on the ground—everything

[b]Hebrew; Syriac *all the wild animals*

that has the breath of life in it—I give every green plant for food." And it was so.

God saw all that he had made, and it was very good. And there was evening, and there was morning—the sixth day.

Thus the heavens and the earth were completed in all their vast array.

Gen.
1:31-2:1

By the seventh day God had finished the work he had been doing; so on the seventh day he rested^c from all his work. And God blessed the seventh day and made it holy, because on it he rested from all the work of creating that he had done.

This is the account of the heavens and the earth when they were created.

Gen.
2:2-4a

Adam and Eve

*T*he answer is God. God is the Creator of all things. God existed before the universe came into being, and it was God who made it all happen. What power and majesty must accompany this God! The Genesis account of the beginnings of all things is a revelation which ascribes creation to an all-powerful, all-knowing, and purposeful Supreme Being—a living Creator and spiritual God acting with meaningful deliberation. In documenting the creation of man, the account suggests that God speaks with more than one voice in bringing about his creation. The implication is that there is a fullness to this divine personality, a fullness which will be more completely revealed as the biblical text unfolds.

Of even more significance is the statement that, in some way distinctly different from all other creatures, mankind has been created in the very likeness of God. Surely this cannot mean that the likeness is a physical resemblance, since God existed before anything physical came into being. Therefore it probably suggests that, like God, human beings are essentially spiritual beings, having intelligence, moral consciousness, and freedom of choice. Though limited by human form, mankind is given creativity and permitted to exercise a degree of dominion over God's creation and the lesser creatures within it. What an amazing thought, that mankind, both male and female, should be so honored by the Creator!

As if to underscore the significance of mankind's creation, the Genesis revelation gives a special account of the first man and woman, known as Adam and Eve. Adam is formed first from elements of the earth, as if God, working like a potter, fashions him from a lump of clay. Then Eve is formed from part of Adam's own body, suggesting a wholeness and unity between man and woman, particularly when the two are joined in the marriage relationship, which is instituted with this first couple. Both Adam and Eve share in the uniqueness of having received a divine inbreathing of God's Spirit which sets them apart from all other living creatures. They are given dominion over the other creatures and are set in a garden of lush vegetation in a place called Eden, an area associated with the Tigris and Euphrates rivers, just east of the Arabian Desert in the Middle East.

^{c}Or *ceased*

Here in Eden, Adam and Eve live in a time of innocence until both are tempted by a serpent to eat of a particular fruit which God has forbidden them to touch or taste. Although a complete explanation is lacking, it appears that the serpent is being used on this occasion by Satan, or the Devil, who will subsequently be identified as God's adversary in the spirit realm and the great Tempter of mankind to do evil.

The effect of Adam and Eve's disobedience to God is a new acquaintance with sin and the reality of punishment. Their sin not only produces feelings of shame, fear, and blame but also results in more specific consequences to all mankind, who will be seen in each subsequent generation to participate in their own disobedience to God's will. The ultimate punishment, as far as Adam and Eve are personally concerned, is banishment from the garden, with all its ease and pleasure. They, like all generations thereafter, must face the hardships and struggles which life on the earth imposes.

Gen. 2:4b-7

CREATION OF MAN. When the LORD God made the earth and the heavens—and no shrub of the field had yet appeared on the earth[d] and no plant of the field had yet sprung up, for the LORD God had not sent rain on the earth[d] and there was no man to work the ground, but streams[e] came up from the earth and watered the whole surface of the ground—the LORD God formed the man[f] from the dust of the ground and breathed into his nostrils the breath of life, and the man became a living being.

Gen. 2:8-17 Mesopotamia

GARDEN OF EDEN. Now the LORD God had planted a garden in the east, in Eden; and there he put the man he had formed. And the LORD God made all kinds of trees grow out of the ground—trees that were pleasing to the eye and good for food. In the middle of the garden were the tree of life and the tree of the knowledge of good and evil.

A river watering the garden flowed from Eden; from there it was separated into four headwaters. The name of the first is the Pishon; it winds through the entire land of Havilah, where there is gold. (The gold of that land is good; aromatic resin[g] and onyx are also there.) The name of the second river is the Gihon; it winds through the entire land of Cush.[h] The name of the third river is the Tigris; it runs along the east side of Asshur. And the fourth river is the Euphrates.

The LORD God took the man and put him in the Garden of Eden to work it and take care of it. And the LORD God commanded the man, "You are free to eat from any tree in the garden; but you must not eat from the tree of the knowledge of good and evil, for when you eat of it you will surely die."

Gen. 2:18-22

CREATION OF WOMAN. The LORD God said, "It is not good for the man to be alone. I will make a helper suitable for him."

Now the LORD God had formed out of the ground all the beasts of the field and all the birds of the air. He brought them to the man to see what he would name them; and whatever the man called each living creature, that was its name. So the man gave names to all the livestock, the birds of the air and all the beasts of the field.

---

[d]Or land   [e]Or mist   [f]The Hebrew for man (adam) sounds like and may be related to the Hebrew for ground (adamah); it is also the name Adam (see Gen. 2:20).   [g]Or good; pearls   [h]Possibly southeast Mesopotamia

But for Adam[i] no suitable helper was found. So the LORD God caused the man to fall into a deep sleep; and while he was sleeping, he took one of the man's ribs[j] and closed up the place with flesh. Then the LORD God made a woman from the rib[k] he had taken out of the man, and he brought her to the man.

UNION OF MAN AND WOMAN.   The man said,

> "This is now bone of my bones
>   and flesh of my flesh;
> she shall be called 'woman,[l]'
>   for she was taken out of man."

Gen. 2:23-25

For this reason a man will leave his father and mother and be united to his wife, and they will become one flesh.

The man and his wife were both naked, and they felt no shame.

TEMPTATION TO SIN.   Now the serpent was more crafty than any of the wild animals the LORD God had made. He said to the woman, "Did God really say, 'You must not eat from any tree in the garden'?"

Gen. 3:1-5

The woman said to the serpent, "We may eat fruit from the trees in the garden, but God did say, 'You must not eat fruit from the tree that is in the middle of the garden, and you must not touch it, or you will die.' "

"You will not surely die," the serpent said to the woman. "For God knows that when you eat of it your eyes will be opened, and you will be like God, knowing good and evil."

SIN PRODUCES SHAME.   When the woman saw that the fruit of the tree was good for food and pleasing to the eye, and also desirable for gaining wisdom, she took some and ate it. She also gave some to her husband, who was with her, and he ate it. Then the eyes of both of them were opened, and they realized they were naked; so they sewed fig leaves together and made coverings for themselves.

Gen. 3:6,7

SIN PRODUCES FEAR.   Then the man and his wife heard the sound of the LORD God as he was walking in the garden in the cool of the day, and they hid from the LORD God among the trees of the garden. But the LORD God called to the man, "Where are you?"

Gen. 3:8-10

He answered, "I heard you in the garden, and I was afraid because I was naked; so I hid."

SIN PRODUCES BLAME.   And he said, "Who told you that you were naked? Have you eaten from the tree that I commanded you not to eat from?"

Gen. 3:11-13

The man said, "The woman you put here with me—she gave me some fruit from the tree, and I ate it."

Then the LORD God said to the woman, "What is this you have done?"

The woman said, "The serpent deceived me, and I ate."

CURSE ON THE TEMPTER.   So the LORD God said to the serpent, "Because you have done this,

Gen. 3:14,15

> "Cursed are you above all the livestock
>   and all the wild animals!
> You will crawl on your belly

[i]Or *the man*   [j]Or *took part of the man's side*   [k]Or *part*   [l]The Hebrew for *woman* sounds like the Hebrew for *man*.

> and you will eat dust
>> all the days of your life.
> And I will put enmity
>> between you and the woman,
>> and between your offspring[m] and hers;
> he will crush[n] your head,
>> and you will strike his heel."

Gen. 3:16 CONSEQUENCES FOR WOMAN. To the woman he said,

> "I will greatly increase your pains in childbearing;
>> with pain you will give birth to children.
> Your desire will be for your husband,
>> and he will rule over you."

Gen. 3:17-19 CONSEQUENCES FOR MAN. To Adam he said, "Because you listened to your wife and ate from the tree about which I commanded you, 'You must not eat of it,'

> "Cursed is the ground because of you;
>> through painful toil you will eat of it
>> all the days of your life.
> It will produce thorns and thistles for you,
>> and you will eat the plants of the field.
> By the sweat of your brow
>> you will eat your food
> until you return to the ground,
>> since from it you were taken;
> for dust you are
>> and to dust you will return."

Gen. 3:20 WOMAN NAMED. Adam[o] named his wife Eve,[p] because she would become the mother of all the living.

Gen. 3:21 SHAME HIDDEN. The LORD God made garments of skin for Adam and his wife and clothed them.

Gen. 3:22-24 BANISHMENT FROM GARDEN. And the LORD God said, "The man has now become like one of us, knowing good and evil. He must not be allowed to reach out his hand and take also from the tree of life and eat, and live forever." So the LORD God banished him from the Garden of Eden to work the ground from which he had been taken. After he drove the man out, he placed on the east side[q] of the Garden of Eden cherubim and a flaming sword flashing back and forth to guard the way to the tree of life.

First Three Sons of Adam and Eve

In a continuing succession of beginnings, the Genesis account records the beginning of the first family. Adam and Eve give birth to two sons, named Cain and Abel, and later to a third, named Seth. The text will subsequently indicate that over a period of many years the family will include numerous sons and daughters. As there is no indication of other created

[m]Or seed   [n]Or strike   [o]Or The man   [p]Eve probably means living.   [q]Or placed in front

human beings, it is altogether likely that these first brothers and sisters enter into marriages with each other, despite the sense of inappropriateness which would be felt should that occur in following generations.

Still another "first" is the Genesis record of mankind's earliest formal worship of God. Both Cain and Abel offer sacrifices to God by devoting the fruits of their individual labors. As a farmer, Cain brings a portion of his crops, while Abel, a herdsman, offers up some of the best of his flock to God. Although the text is silent as to what prompts God's response, it is evident that God is not pleased with Cain's offering. Whether this is because God has specifically commanded the brothers to offer animal sacrifices, or whether perhaps Cain's character is already known by God to be evil, is unclear. In any event Cain's pride is dashed and his anger toward Abel is so great that in an act of premeditated murder Cain kills Abel. The murder is then compounded when Cain lies to God concerning Abel's whereabouts.

Although God punishes Cain for his wrongdoing, the text gives some interesting insight into the character of God by indicating that, despite Cain's great sin, God nevertheless shows mercy to him. This is not to be a unique act of grace. God's mercy will be seen time and again. Unfortunately, Cain apparently does not respond favorably to God's mercy, at least if his descendants are any reflection of Cain's continued character. In contrast, when Seth is born it appears that Seth takes on the righteous character of Abel and instills a respect for God in his children as well.

CAIN AND ABEL BORN.   Adam[r] lay with his wife Eve, and she became pregnant and gave birth to Cain.[s] She said, "With the help of the LORD I have brought forth[t] a man." Later she gave birth to his brother Abel.

Gen. 4:1,2a Eden

BROTHERS BRING OFFERINGS.   Now Abel kept flocks, and Cain worked the soil. In the course of time Cain brought some of the fruits of the soil as an offering to the LORD. But Abel brought fat portions from some of the firstborn of his flock. The LORD looked with favor on Abel and his offering, but on Cain and his offering he did not look with favor. So Cain was very angry, and his face was downcast.

Then the LORD said to Cain, "Why are you angry? Why is your face downcast? If you do what is right, will you not be accepted? But if you do not do what is right, sin is crouching at your door; it desires to have you, but you must master it."

Gen. 4:2b-7

CAIN KILLS ABEL.   Now Cain said to his brother Abel, "Let's go out to the field."[u] And while they were in the field, Cain attacked his brother Abel and killed him.

Then the LORD said to Cain, "Where is your brother Abel?"

"I don't know," he replied. "Am I my brother's keeper?"

Gen. 4:8,9

CAIN PUNISHED.   The LORD said, "What have you done? Listen! Your brother's blood cries out to me from the ground. Now you are under a curse and driven from the ground, which opened its mouth to receive your brother's blood from your hand. When you work the ground, it will no

Gen. 4:10-16

[r]Or The man   [s]Cain sounds like the Hebrew for brought forth or acquired.   [t]Or have acquired   [u]Samaritan Pentateuch, Septuagint, Vulgate and Syriac; Masoretic Text does not have "Let's go out to the field."

longer yield its crops for you. You will be a restless wanderer on the earth."

Cain said to the LORD, "My punishment is more than I can bear. Today you are driving me from the land, and I will be hidden from your presence; I will be a restless wanderer on the earth, and whoever finds me will kill me."

But the LORD said to him, "Not so*v*; if anyone kills Cain, he will suffer vengeance seven times over." Then the LORD put a mark on Cain so that no one who found him would kill him. So Cain went out from the LORD's presence and lived in the land of Nod,*w* east of Eden.

Gen. 4:17-22 Nod, east of Eden

CAIN'S DESCENDANTS.   Cain lay with his wife, and she became pregnant and gave birth to Enoch. Cain was then building a city, and he named it after his son Enoch. To Enoch was born Irad, and Irad was the father of Mehujael, and Mehujael was the father of Methushael, and Methushael was the father of Lamech.

Lamech married two women, one named Adah and the other Zillah. Adah gave birth to Jabal; he was the father of those who live in tents and raise livestock. His brother's name was Jubal; he was the father of all who play the harp and flute. Zillah also had a son, Tubal-Cain, who forged all kinds of tools out of*x* bronze and iron. Tubal-Cain's sister was Naamah.

Gen. 4:23,24

LAMECH CONFESSES KILLING.   Lamech said to his wives,

> "Adah and Zillah, listen to me;
>   wives of Lamech, hear my words.
> I have killed*y* a man for wounding me,
>   a young man for injuring me.
> If Cain is avenged seven times,
>   then Lamech seventy-seven times."

Gen. 4:25,26

SETH BORN.   Adam lay with his wife again, and she gave birth to a son and named him Seth,*z* saying, "God has granted me another child in place of Abel, since Cain killed him." Seth also had a son, and he named him Enosh.

At that time men began to call on*a* the name of the LORD.

Descendants from Adam to Noah

*W*hat follows is a simple chronology of ten generations from Adam through Seth to Noah. Yet this brief family record is full of surprises. For one thing, the men who are named each live for hundreds of years and have children when they are from 65 to 500 years old! Much speculation has been generated as to the cause of this longevity. Some have even rejected the historical accuracy of the account, saying that the "years" are merely representative periods of time, perhaps shorter than modern years. However, the original language allows no such interpretation. In support of the historic credibility of the account, others have explained the unusual longevity on a variety of bases, including the effect of the fruit of the

*v*Septuagint, Vulgate and Syriac; Hebrew *Very well* 12 and 14).   *x*Or *who instructed all who work in* means *granted.*   *a*Or *to proclaim*   *w*Nod means *wandering* (see verses *y*Or *I will kill*   *z*Seth probably means *granted.*

Tree of Life in the Garden of Eden; the original immortality of man feeling only the slightest consequences of sin at this early stage in man's development; or the superiority of the food, atmosphere, and other living conditions during this period. One can only speculate, but acknowledging a creative Being powerful enough to bring the universe into existence certainly allows the option for such a Creator to permit unusually lengthy lives for whatever purpose might suit his comprehensive plan for mankind. A number of possible purposes immediately present themselves, including the need to quickly populate the earth and the need to promulgate basic moral principles throughout the beginnings of mankind.

Promulgating morality throughout the early generations is made easier due to the fact that Adam and Seth continue to live as contemporaries with their offspring several generations removed. By living 930 years, for example, Adam is still alive during the days of Lamech, father of Noah, toward the end of the first millennium from creation. One can almost see Adam gathering the early patriarchs together and telling them over and over how God created the world, how he directed mankind to live, and how he showed both punishment and mercy when Adam and Eve, and even Cain, had been disobedient.

Still another surprise is that one of Adam's descendants, Enoch, does not die—ever! After 365 years of what is apparently an exceptionally righteous life, Enoch is taken from the world in some manner other than death. The accounts of the other patriarchs each record the year in which they die, but the account of Enoch indicates that "he was no more." What is even more noteworthy than one's being translated out of this life without experiencing death is the exciting suggestion that mankind is immortal—that there is actually life beyond death!

It is altogether possible that this genealogical listing and others to follow may not list every successive generation, and therefore may omit hundreds of years of mankind's history. Such would be the case, for example, if "son" were used in reference to a grandson or an even more remote descendant, as is sometimes seen in later historical records. Should that be the case, there would be great difficulty in assigning specific dates to such major events as the creation of the first man and woman, or the great flood which will come in the days of Noah. Because there is no indication to the contrary, this narrative proceeds on the assumption that the genealogies list father-to-son progressions without omission of intervening generations, but leaves the matter as an open question.

Early dating will be shown as A.C., After Creation (of mankind), as calculated from the information supplied in the Genesis record, until such time as more positive dating in the B.C. era can be utilized. Even then, the dates indicated are usually only approximate and should not be considered unquestionable. Dates are supplied where reasonably believed to be accurate in order to aid the reader's understanding of the historical context.

RECORD OF MANKIND.   This is the written account of Adam's line.   Gen. 5:1,2
    When God created man, he made him in the likeness of God. He created

them male and female and blessed them. And when they were created, he called them "man.*b*"

Gen. 5:3-5
(130 A.C.)

SETH. When Adam had lived 130 years, he had a son in his own likeness, in his own image; and he named him Seth. After Seth was born, Adam lived 800 years and had other sons and daughters. Altogether, Adam lived 930 years, and then he died.

Gen. 5:6-8
(235 A.C.)

ENOSH. When Seth had lived 105 years, he became the father*c* of Enosh. And after he became the father of Enosh, Seth lived 807 years and had other sons and daughters. Altogether, Seth lived 912 years, and then he died.

Gen. 5:9-11
(325 A.C.)

KENAN. When Enosh had lived 90 years, he became the father of Kenan. And after he became the father of Kenan, Enosh lived 815 years and had other sons and daughters. Altogether, Enosh lived 905 years, and then he died.

Gen. 5:12-14
(395 A.C.)

MAHALALEL. When Kenan had lived 70 years, he became the father of Mahalalel. And after he became the father of Mahalalel, Kenan lived 840 years and had other sons and daughters. Altogether, Kenan lived 910 years, and then he died.

Gen. 5:15-17
(460 A.C.)

JARED. When Mahalalel had lived 65 years, he became the father of Jared. And after he became the father of Jared, Mahalalel lived 830 years and had other sons and daughters. Altogether, Mahalalel lived 895 years, and then he died.

Gen. 5:18-20
(622 A.C.)

ENOCH. When Jared had lived 162 years, he became the father of Enoch. And after he became the father of Enoch, Jared lived 800 years and had other sons and daughters. Altogether, Jared lived 962 years, and then he died.

Gen. 5:21-24
(687 A.C.)

METHUSELAH. When Enoch had lived 65 years, he became the father of Methuselah. And after he became the father of Methuselah, Enoch walked with God 300 years and had other sons and daughters. Altogether, Enoch lived 365 years. Enoch walked with God; then he was no more, because God took him away.

Gen. 5:25-27
(874 A.C.)

LAMECH. When Methuselah had lived 187 years, he became the father of Lamech. And after he became the father of Lamech, Methuselah lived 782 years and had other sons and daughters. Altogether, Methuselah lived 969 years, and then he died.

Gen. 5:28-31
(1056 A.C.)

NOAH. When Lamech had lived 182 years, he had a son. He named him Noah*d* and said, "He will comfort us in the labor and painful toil of our hands caused by the ground the LORD has cursed." After Noah was born, Lamech lived 595 years and had other sons and daughters. Altogether, Lamech lived 777 years, and then he died.

Gen. 5:32
(1556 A.C.)

SHEM, HAM, AND JAPHETH. After Noah was 500 years old, he became the father of Shem, Ham and Japheth.

---

*b*Hebrew *adam*   *c*Father* may mean *ancestor*; also in verses 7-26.   *d*Noah* sounds like the Hebrew for *comfort*.

Mankind's Degeneration into Wickedness

*I*n the accounts of Seth, Cain, and their descendants is a hint that two distinct groups of people have been developing. Those descending from Seth—for example, Enoch—were apparently people who lived righteously before God. On the other hand, those descending from Cain, as typified by Lamech the murderer, appear to have degenerated into unrighteousness. Therefore, although undoubtedly individual exceptions might be found within each of the two extended families, it can generally be assumed that the Sethites were godly people and the Cainites ungodly. At this point, however, the record seems to indicate that the "sons of God," perhaps referring to the Sethites, or in any event to those who have had a God-fearing heritage, now begin to intermarry with the "daughters of men," not because they are righteous women but only because they are physically attractive. The apparent result is that such mixture of the godly and ungodly leads to an obliteration of moral distinctions and righteous living. The situation is so bad, in fact, that terribly wicked men, known as Nephilim, have become heroes among the people.

Only ten generations have lived since Adam was first created in God's own image, and they have all sinned, to one extent or another, by being disobedient to God's moral law. With each generation has come rejection of God's sovereignty and love. As it now begins to appear that more and more of mankind has turned to wickedness, God is inclined to destroy his creation. Yet there is a handful of people, including Noah, who still walk with God, so God mercifully postpones destruction of the world for 120 years.

INTERMARRIAGE BRINGS DECAY.   When men began to increase in number on the earth and daughters were born to them, the sons of God saw that the daughters of men were beautiful, and they married any of them they chose.   *Gen. 6:1,2*

MANKIND GIVEN GRACE PERIOD.   Then the LORD said, "My Spirit will not contend with*e* man forever, for he is mortal*f*; his days will be a hundred and twenty years."   *Gen. 6:3*

WICKED CONSIDERED HEROES.   The Nephilim were on the earth in those days—and also afterward—when the sons of God went to the daughters of men and had children by them. They were the heroes of old, men of renown.   *Gen. 6:4*

GOD GRIEVED BY MANKIND.   The LORD saw how great man's wickedness on the earth had become, and that every inclination of the thoughts of his heart was only evil all the time. The LORD was grieved that he had made man on the earth, and his heart was filled with pain. So the LORD said, "I will wipe mankind, whom I have created, from the face of the earth—men and animals, and creatures that move along the ground, and birds of the air—for I am grieved that I have made them." But Noah found favor in the eyes of the LORD.   *Gen. 6:5-8*

eOr My spirit will not remain in   *fOr corrupt*

Noah and the Flood

ecause of the degradation of the human race, God has reluctantly decided to destroy mankind from the earth. Yet there is a remnant of righteous men and women who comprise the family of Noah, and God looks upon them with mercy. God warns Noah that he will soon unleash a flood of waters upon the earth that will destroy all living creatures. Noah is instructed to build an ark, or ship, in which he and his family, plus pairs of each kind of living creature, will be saved from destruction. Despite undoubted ridicule from curious onlookers, Noah and his sons act in faith and construct the ark. As the rains begin to fall and the springs pour forth water, Noah's family enters into the ark with the various animals and prepares for the most cataclysmic event in the history of the earth—the great flood.

The flood comes 1656 years after the creation and will last for the better part of a year. After 40 days and nights of constant rain, the waters will cover the mountaintops by more than 20 feet before beginning to diminish on the 150th day. The mountains will once again be seen on the 224th day, and a raven will be sent out 40 days later in an unsuccessful attempt to find evidence of life. Then, apparently after a lapse of seven more days, a dove will be released once each week for three weeks. On the second week the dove will return with an olive branch, which gives Noah evidence of new life on the earth, and on its third release the dove will disappear altogether. Still, Noah will remain in the ark until the ground is completely dry. Finally, after 370 days inside this unusual vessel of human and animal cargo, Noah and his family will emerge to a new life of promise with God's blessings.

Gen. 6:9,10 NOAH FOUND RIGHTEOUS.   This is the account of Noah.

Noah was a righteous man, blameless among the people of his time, and he walked with God. Noah had three sons: Shem, Ham and Japheth.

Gen. 6:11-16 INSTRUCTIONS FOR ARK.   Now the earth was corrupt in God's sight and was full of violence. God saw how corrupt the earth had become, for all the people on earth had corrupted their ways. So God said to Noah, "I am going to put an end to all people, for the earth is filled with violence because of them. I am surely going to destroy both them and the earth. So make yourself an ark of cypressg wood; make rooms in it and coat it with pitch inside and out. This is how you are to build it: The ark is to be 450 feet long, 75 feet wide and 45 feet high.ʰ Make a roof for it and finishⁱ the ark to within 18 inchesʲ of the top. Put a door in the side of the ark and make lower, middle and upper decks.

Gen. 6:17-21 PLAN FOR SAVING NOAH.   I am going to bring floodwaters on the earth to destroy all life under the heavens, every creature that has the breath of life in it. Everything on earth will perish. But I will establish my covenant with you, and you will enter the ark—you and your sons and your wife and your sons' wives with you. You are to bring into the ark

gThe meaning of the Hebrew for this word is uncertain.   hHebrew *300 cubits long, 50 cubits wide and 30 cubits high* (about 140 meters long, 23 meters wide and 13.5 meters high)   iOr *Make an opening for light by finishing*   jHebrew *a cubit* (about 0.5 meter)

two of all living creatures, male and female, to keep them alive with you. Two of every kind of bird, of every kind of animal and of every kind of creature that moves along the ground will come to you to be kept alive. You are to take every kind of food that is to be eaten and store it away as food for you and for them."

NOAH BUILDS ARK. Noah did everything just as God commanded him.   Gen. 6:22

GOD'S LAST INSTRUCTIONS.   The LORD then said to Noah, "Go into   Gen. 7:1-5
the ark, you and your whole family, because I have found you righteous in this generation. Take with you seven[k] of every kind of clean animal, a male and its mate, and two of every kind of unclean animal, a male and its mate, and also seven of every kind of bird, male and female, to keep their various kinds alive throughout the earth. Seven days from now I will send rain on the earth for forty days and forty nights, and I will wipe from the face of the earth every living creature I have made."
    And Noah did all that the LORD commanded him.

FINAL WEEK'S PREPARATIONS.   Noah was six hundred years old   Gen.
when the floodwaters came on the earth. And Noah and his sons and his   7:6-10
wife and his sons' wives entered the ark to escape the waters of the flood. Pairs of clean and unclean animals, of birds and of all creatures that move along the ground, male and female, came to Noah and entered the ark, as God had commanded Noah. And after the seven days the floodwaters came on the earth.

FLOODWATERS BEGIN.   In the six hundredth year of Noah's life, on the   Gen.
seventeenth day of the second month—on that day all the springs of the   7:11,12
great deep burst forth, and the floodgates of the heavens were opened.   (Ca.
And rain fell on the earth forty days and forty nights,   3000-2500
                                                                            B.C.?)

NOAH'S FAMILY ENTERS ARK.   On that very day Noah and his sons,   Gen.
Shem, Ham and Japheth, together with his wife and the wives of his three   7:13-16
sons, entered the ark. They had with them every wild animal according to its kind, all livestock according to their kinds, every creature that moves along the ground according to its kind and every bird according to its kind, everything with wings. Pairs of all creatures that have the breath of life in them came to Noah and entered the ark. The animals going in were male and female of every living thing, as God had commanded Noah. Then the LORD shut him in.

DESTRUCTION BENEATH WATERS. For forty days the flood kept com-   Gen.
ing on the earth, and as the waters increased they lifted the ark high above   7:17-23
the earth. The waters rose and increased greatly on the earth, and the ark floated on the surface of the water. They rose greatly on the earth, and all the high mountains under the entire heavens were covered. The waters rose and covered the mountains to a depth of more than twenty feet.[l] [m] Every living thing that moved on the earth perished—birds, livestock, wild animals, all the creatures that swarm over the earth, and all mankind. Everything on dry land that had the breath of life in its nostrils died. Every living thing on the face of the earth was wiped out; men and animals and the creatures that move along the ground and the birds of the air were wiped from the earth. Only Noah was left, and those with him in the ark.

[k]Or seven pairs   [l]Hebrew fifteen cubits (about 6.9 meters)   [m]Or rose more than twenty
feet, and the mountains were covered

Gen. 7:24-8:4 Mountains of Ararat	**WATERS RECEDE IN 150 DAYS.** The waters flooded the earth for a hundred and fifty days. But God remembered Noah and all the wild animals and the livestock that were with him in the ark, and he sent a wind over the earth, and the waters receded. Now the springs of the deep and the floodgates of the heavens had been closed, and the rain had stopped falling from the sky. The water receded steadily from the earth. At the end of the hundred and fifty days the water had gone down, and on the seventeenth day of the seventh month the ark came to rest on the mountains of Ararat.
Gen. 8:5	**MOUNTAINS SEEN ON 224TH DAY.** The waters continued to recede until the tenth month, and on the first day of the tenth month the tops of the mountains became visible.
Gen. 8:6,7	**RAVEN SENT OUT ON 264TH DAY.** After forty days Noah opened the window he had made in the ark and sent out a raven, and it kept flying back and forth until the water had dried up from the earth.
Gen. 8:8,9	**DOVE SENT OUT ON 271ST DAY.** Then he sent out a dove to see if the water had receded from the surface of the ground. But the dove could find no place to set its feet because there was water over all the surface of the earth; so it returned to Noah in the ark. He reached out his hand and took the dove and brought it back to himself in the ark.
Gen. 8:10-11	**BRANCH BROUGHT ON 278TH DAY.** He waited seven more days and again sent out the dove from the ark. When the dove returned to him in the evening, there in its beak was a freshly plucked olive leaf! Then Noah knew that the water had receded from the earth.
Gen. 8:12	**DOVE DEPARTS ON 285TH DAY.** He waited seven more days and sent the dove out again, but this time it did not return to him.
Gen. 8:13	**SURFACE DRY BY 314TH DAY.** By the first day of the first month of Noah's six hundred and first year, the water had dried up from the earth. Noah then removed the covering from the ark and saw that the surface of the ground was dry.

Gen.
8:14-19
	NOAH CALLED AFTER 370 DAYS. By the twenty-seventh day of the second month the earth was completely dry.
	    Then God said to Noah, "Come out of the ark, you and your wife and your sons and their wives. Bring out every kind of living creature that is with you—the birds, the animals, and all the creatures that move along the ground—so they can multiply on the earth and be fruitful and increase in number upon it."
	    So Noah came out, together with his sons and his wife and his sons' wives. All the animals and all the creatures that move along the ground and all the birds—everything that moves on the earth—came out of the ark, one kind after another.

Gen. 8:20	**NOAH OFFERS SACRIFICE.** Then Noah built an altar to the LORD and, taking some of all the clean animals and clean birds, he sacrificed burnt offerings on it.
Gen. 8:21,22	**GOD MAKES VOW.** The LORD smelled the pleasing aroma and said in his heart: "Never again will I curse the ground because of man, even

though[n] every inclination of his heart is evil from childhood. And never again will I destroy all living creatures, as I have done.

> "As long as the earth endures,
>   seedtime and harvest,
>   cold and heat,
>   summer and winter,
>   day and night
>   will never cease."

MANKIND'S REGENERATION.   Then God blessed Noah and his sons, saying to them, "Be fruitful and increase in number and fill the earth. The fear and dread of you will fall upon all the beasts of the earth and all the birds of the air, upon every creature that moves along the ground, and upon all the fish of the sea; they are given into your hands.

Gen. 9:1,2

DIETARY INSTRUCTIONS. Everything that lives and moves will be food for you. Just as I gave you the green plants, I now give you everything.
   "But you must not eat meat that has its lifeblood still in it.

Gen. 9:3,4

LAW OF LIFE FOR LIFE.   And for your lifeblood I will surely demand an accounting. I will demand an accounting from every animal. And from each man, too, I will demand an accounting for the life of his fellow man.

Gen. 9:5-7

> "Whoever sheds the blood of man,
>   by man shall his blood be shed;
>   for in the image of God
>   has God made man.

As for you, be fruitful and increase in number; multiply on the earth and increase upon it."

GOD'S COVENANT.   Then God said to Noah and to his sons with him: "I now establish my covenant with you and with your descendants after you and with every living creature that was with you—the birds, the livestock and all the wild animals, all those that came out of the ark with you—every living creature on earth. I establish my covenant with you: Never again will all life be cut off by the waters of a flood; never again will there be a flood to destroy the earth."

Gen. 9:8-11

RAINBOW AS SIGN OF COVENANT.   And God said, "This is the sign of the covenant I am making between me and you and every living creature with you, a covenant for all generations to come: I have set my rainbow in the clouds, and it will be the sign of the covenant between me and the earth. Whenever I bring clouds over the earth and the rainbow appears in the clouds, I will remember my covenant between me and you and all living creatures of every kind. Never again will the waters become a flood to destroy all life. Whenever the rainbow appears in the clouds, I will see it and remember the everlasting covenant between God and all living creatures of every kind on the earth."
   So God said to Noah, "This is the sign of the covenant I have established between me and all life on the earth."

Gen. 9:12-17

[n]Or *man, for*

Human Condition Remains Sinful

*W*hat God accomplished in the flood was the eradication of a corrupt and degenerate human race. Even such ancient traditions as the "Gilgamesh Epic" of ancient Babylon confirm early acceptance of such an extraordinary deluge. Beyond its own historical context, the flood stands as a symbol of the destructiveness of sin and the grace of God in saving those who would act in faith through righteous living.

But the human condition even among the righteous remnant of Noah's family is such that sin soon finds its way back into the lives of even those who were saved in the flood. To document man's continued fallen state, the Genesis account records an incident in which Noah drinks himself into a drunken stupor, and Ham shows great disrespect for his father, Noah, whom he finds not only drunk but naked.

Noah's response upon learning of Ham's disrespect is to utter a curse against Ham's son, Canaan—a curse presumably intended as a prediction of servitude on the part of Ham's descendants. As the biblical text unfolds, it will appear that the descendants of Canaan, who are known as Canaanites, will be of the same ethnic stock as the people known as Israelites, and indeed at times will be in servitude to the descendants of Shem and Japheth.

Gen. 9:18,19 NOAH'S SONS. The sons of Noah who came out of the ark were Shem, Ham and Japheth. (Ham was the father of Canaan.) These were the three sons of Noah, and from them came the people who were scattered over the earth.

Gen. 9:20-23 HAM DISRESPECTFUL OF NOAH. Noah, a man of the soil, proceeded[o] to plant a vineyard. When he drank some of its wine, he became drunk and lay uncovered inside his tent. Ham, the father of Canaan, saw his father's nakedness and told his two brothers outside. But Shem and Japheth took a garment and laid it across their shoulders; then they walked in backward and covered their father's nakedness. Their faces were turned the other way so that they would not see their father's nakedness.

Gen. 9:24-27 CURSE ON HAM'S DESCENDANTS. When Noah awoke from his wine and found out what his youngest son had done to him, he said,

> "Cursed be Canaan!
> The lowest of slaves
> will he be to his brothers."

He also said,

> "Blessed be the LORD, the God of Shem!
> May Canaan be the slave of Shem.[p]
> May God extend the territory of Japheth[q];
> may Japheth live in the tents of Shem,
> and may Canaan be his[r] slave."

Gen. 9:28,29 NOAH DIES. After the flood Noah lived 350 years. Altogether, Noah lived 950 years, and then he died.

[o]Or soil, was the first   [p]Or be his slave   [q]Japheth sounds like the Hebrew for extend.
[r]Or their

Dispersion of the Human Family

*A*long with this account of Noah's own sin and that of his son, Ham, the Genesis record also shows mankind's continued decadence as it focuses upon the now-regenerating human family in the Plain of Shinar, an area more familiarly known as Babylon. Somewhere around 2500 B.C. the people ambitiously decide to build a great city, known as Babel, together with a tower so high that, in figurative terms, it will "reach to the heavens." This is by no means the first city ever to be built, and the tower itself is probably designed in very similar fashion to the Babylonian ziggurat temples, the ruins of which will still be found centuries later. But God is displeased with these grandiose plans, apparently because the people's motive is characterized by a defiant and self-assertive pride in rebellion against God.

In light of this situation God determines to remind mankind once again of their human limitations. Until this time everyone has been part of one rapidly multiplying extended family, and therefore everyone has been speaking the same language. In order to break the self-willed strength found in this unity, God intervenes with his creative and divine power to confuse their language and to scatter mankind throughout the earth. It is the beginning not only of diverse languages but also diverse peoples. For the first time mankind is divided into clans, nations, and even various ethnic stocks. Although the Genesis record makes no specific reference in this regard, it is possible that this supernatural event also sets in motion the separation of human beings into different races. And the implication would be significant: despite the external differences, there is a commonness of background which compels brotherhood by creation and equality among all mankind regardless of race, nation, or tongue.

COMMONNESS OF MANKIND.   Now the whole world had one language and a common speech. As men moved eastward,[s] they found a plain in Shinar[t] and settled there.

Gen. 11:1,2

PLAN TO BUILD CITY.   They said to each other, "Come, let's make bricks and bake them thoroughly." They used brick instead of stone, and tar for mortar. Then they said, "Come, let us build ourselves a city, with a tower that reaches to the heavens, so that we may make a name for ourselves and not be scattered over the face of the whole earth."

Gen. 11:3,4

ATTITUDE DISPLEASES GOD.   But the LORD came down to see the city and the tower that the men were building. The LORD said, "If as one people speaking the same language they have begun to do this, then nothing they plan to do will be impossible for them. Come, let us go down and confuse their language so they will not understand each other."

Gen. 11:5-7

LANGUAGE CONFUSED.   So the LORD scattered them from there over all the earth, and they stopped building the city. That is why it was called Babel[u]—because there the LORD confused the language of the whole

Gen. 11:8,9 Babel (Ca. 2400 B.C.?)

[s]Or *from the east*; or *in the east*   [t]That is, Babylonia   [u]That is, Babylon; *Babel* sounds like the Hebrew for *confused*.

world. From there the LORD scattered them over the face of the whole earth.

Beginning of Nations

*A*s mankind begins to disperse throughout the earth, families begin to divide into clans, and the clans develop into nations. The earliest known account of the geographical, national, and dialectical divisions among the human family is contained in the Genesis record. This tabulation begins with Shem, Ham, and Japheth, three generations before the great division at Babel. In this record there is first of all a brief tracing of Japheth's seven sons and seven grandsons, particularly the descendants through Japheth's son Javan, whose people begin to spread north to the coastal areas of the Caspian, Black, and Mediterranean seas. The reference to the Japhethites may be as brief as it is because these Indo-Europeans will be among the latest to develop and will have the least contact with the theocratic concerns of the Hebrew people, upon whom the biblical text will soon focus.

The table of nations gives more attention to the descendants of Ham, perhaps because they will develop early and be founders of the first empires, and perhaps also because it is with these peoples that the Hebrew nation will have both its closest association and many of its conflicts. Ham's descendants will settle in the warmer climates of the southern portions of the earth and will populate the Egyptian, Canaanite, and Arabian nations. Of particular note among Ham's descendants is the great warrior Nimrod, who is the first leader of record to establish a monarchy. His rule over several tribes apparently comes through the power of conquest and not because he is their natural patriarchal head. It is Nimrod who establishes Babylon (from the city of Babel) in southern Mesopotamia, and later the city of Nineveh, further north in Assyria.

Of great historical significance is the record of Ham's descendants through Canaan, Ham's son upon whom Noah pronounced a curse. The land which will eventually be occupied by the Canaanites is known as the land of Canaan or, more modernly, Israel. Its original Canaanite inhabitants, including the Hittites, Jebusites, and Amorites, will come into conflict with the descendants of Shem, principally those of the Hebrew nation. That conflict, bearing out the prophetic nature of Noah's curse on Canaan, will continue even to modern times.

As for Shem's descendants, the table of nations concentrates on the lineage through Shem's son Arphaxad. The principal reason undoubtedly lies in the theological significance of the descent through Arphaxad. It is through his branch of the Shemites that (after eight generations) the father of the Hebrew nation, Abraham, will come. The Shemites, later to be known as Semites, will initially settle primarily in the region of Mesopotamia, between the Tigris and Euphrates rivers. From the earliest Semite descendants will eventually come the Syrians, Assyrians, Joktanite Arabs and, most importantly, the Hebrews.

NATIONS FROM NOAH'S SONS.   This is the account of Shem, Ham and   Gen. 10:1
Japheth, Noah's sons, who themselves had sons after the flood.

DESCENDANTS OF JAPHETH.   Gen.
   The sons[v] of Japheth: 10:2-5
   Gomer, Magog, Madai, Javan, Tubal, Meshech and Tiras.
   The sons of Gomer:
   Ashkenaz, Riphath and Togarmah.
   The sons of Javan:
   Elishah, Tarshish, the Kittim and the Rodanim.[w] (From these the
      maritime peoples spread out into their territories by their clans
      within their nations, each with its own language.)

DESCENDANTS OF HAM.   Gen.
   The sons of Ham: 10:6-20
   Cush, Mizraim,[x] Put and Canaan.
   The sons of Cush:
   Seba, Havilah, Sabtah, Raamah and Sabteca.
   The sons of Raamah:
   Sheba and Dedan.

Cush was the father[y] of Nimrod, who grew to be a mighty warrior on
the earth. He was a mighty hunter before the LORD; that is why it is said,
"Like Nimrod, a mighty hunter before the LORD." The first centers of his
kingdom were Babylon, Erech, Akkad and Calneh, in[z] Shinar.[a] From that
land he went to Assyria, where he built Nineveh, Rehoboth Ir,[b] Calah and
Resen, which is between Nineveh and Calah; that is the great city.

   Mizraim was the father of
      the Ludites, Anamites, Lehabites, Naphtuhites, Pathrusites, Caslu-
      hites (from whom the Philistines came) and Caphtorites.
   Canaan was the father of
      Sidon his firstborn,[c] and of the Hittites, Jebusites, Amorites, Girga-
         shites, Hivites, Arkites, Sinites, Arvadites, Zemarites and Ha-
         mathites.

   Later the Canaanite clans scattered and the borders of Canaan reached
from Sidon toward Gerar as far as Gaza, and then toward Sodom, Gomorrah, Admah and Zeboiim, as far as Lasha.
   These are the sons of Ham by their clans and languages, in their territories and nations.

DESCENDANTS OF SHEM.   Sons were also born to Shem, whose older   Gen.
brother was[d] Japheth; Shem was the ancestor of all the sons of Eber.   10:21-31

   The sons of Shem:
   Elam, Asshur, Arphaxad, Lud and Aram.
   The sons of Aram:
   Uz, Hul, Gether and Meshech.[e]

[v]*Sons* may mean *descendants* or *successors* or *nations*.   [w]Some manuscripts of the
Masoretic Text and Samaritan Pentateuch (see also Septuagint and 1 Chron. 1:7); most
manuscripts of the Masoretic Text *Dodanim*   [x]That is, Egypt   [y]*Father* may mean
ancestor or *predecessor* or *founder*; also in verses 13, 15, 24 and 26.   [z]Or *Erech and
Akkad—all of them in*   [a]That is, Babylonia   [b]Or *Nineveh with its city squares*   [c]Or
of the Sidonians, the foremost   [d]Or *Shem, the older brother of*   [e]See Septuagint and
1 Chron. 1:17; Hebrew *Mash*

Arphaxad was the father of*f* Shelah,
and Shelah the father of Eber.
Two sons were born to Eber:
One was named Peleg,*g* because in his time the earth was divided;
his brother was named Joktan.
Joktan was the father of
Almodad, Sheleph, Hazarmaveth, Jerah, Hadoram, Uzal, Diklah,
Obal, Abimael, Sheba, Ophir, Havilah and Jobab. All these were
sons of Joktan.

The region where they lived stretched from Mesha toward Sephar, in the
eastern hill country.
These are the sons of Shem by their clans and languages, in their territories and nations.

Gen. 10:32   PEOPLE DISPERSE.   These are the clans of Noah's sons, according to
their lines of descent, within their nations. From these the nations spread
out over the earth after the flood.

Descendants from Shem to Abram_____

*F*ollowing this tabulation of the nations, the Genesis record falls mostly
silent upon the earth's inhabitants except for the descendants of Shem
through Arphaxad: Shelah, Eber, Peleg, and others down to Abram,
who, known later as Abraham, will become the father of the Hebrews. This is
the family of promise through whom God will preserve religious and moral
truth. It will be through the Hebrew nation that God will ultimately speak to
the whole world. Therefore it is important for the Genesis record to trace
Abram's ancestry back to Shem, who through his father, Noah, descends from
the first man, Adam.

Gen.
11:10a   SHEM.   This is the account of Shem.

Gen.
11:10b,11   ARPHAXAD.   Two years after the flood, when Shem was 100 years old,
(1659   he became the father*h* of Arphaxad. And after he became the father of
A.C.)   Arphaxad, Shem lived 500 years and had other sons and daughters.

Gen.
11:12,13   SHELAH.   When Arphaxad had lived 35 years, he became the father of
(1694   Shelah. And after he became the father of Shelah, Arphaxad lived 403
A.C.)   years and had other sons and daughters.*i*

Gen.
11:14,15   EBER.   When Shelah had lived 30 years, he became the father of Eber.
(1724   And after he became the father of Eber, Shelah lived 403 years and had
A.C.)   other sons and daughters.

Gen.
11:16,17   PELEG.   When Eber had lived 34 years, he became the father of Peleg.
(1758   And after he became the father of Peleg, Eber lived 430 years and had
A.C.)   other sons and daughters.

*f*Hebrew; Septuagint *father of Cainan, and Cainan was the father of*   *g*Peleg means
division.   *h*Father *may mean* ancestor.   *i*Hebrew; Septuagint (see also Luke 3:35, 36
and note at Gen. 10:24) *35 years, he became the father of Cainan.* *13And after he became the*
father of Cainan, Arphaxad lived 430 years and had other sons and daughters, and then he died.
When Cainan had lived 130 years, he became the father of Shelah. And after he became the father of
Shelah, Cainan lived 330 years and had other sons and daughters

REU.   When Peleg had lived 30 years, he became the father of Reu. And after he became the father of Reu, Peleg lived 209 years and had other sons and daughters.

Gen. 11:18,19 (1788 A.C.)

SERUG.   When Reu had lived 32 years, he became the father of Serug. And after he became the father of Serug, Reu lived 207 years and had other sons and daughters.

Gen. 11:20,21 (1820 A.C.)

NAHOR.   When Serug had lived 30 years, he became the father of Nahor. And after he became the father of Nahor, Serug lived 200 years and had other sons and daughters.

Gen. 11:22,23 (1850 A.C.)

TERAH.   When Nahor had lived 29 years, he became the father of Terah. And after he became the father of Terah, Nahor lived 119 years and had other sons and daughters.

Gen. 11:24,25 (1879 A.C.)

ABRAM, NAHOR, AND HARAN.   After Terah had lived 70 years, he became the father of Abram, Nahor and Haran.

Gen. 11:26 (1949-2009 A.C.)

It is interesting to observe in this account that there is a gradual decline in the longevity of Shem's descendants. Shem himself will live for 600 years, but by the time of Abram the typical age at death is about 200. Also noteworthy is the fact that the first child is born much earlier than ever before. Except for Shem and Abram, most of the men in this lineage are in their thirties when their first son is born.

The combined result of earlier longevity and now-decreasing lifespans is that there are surprisingly few links in the chain from Adam to Abram. Adam lived even beyond Methuselah's birth, and Methuselah was still living when Shem was born. Assuming that Abram was not Terah's firstborn son but, as other Scripture seems to indicate, was born when Terah was 130 years old, Shem will predecease Abram by only 25 years. So the ties between Adam and Abram in the first 2000 years from creation are indeed close ones.

The Genesis record pauses briefly at this point to give a special account of Terah's family. Included in the account is an introduction to Abram's nephew, Lot, who will become a central character in events to follow. Equally significant is the fact that Abram's wife, Sarai, has not yet given birth to a child. Amidst a culture in which the woman's role in bearing children, especially sons, is of vital importance, Sarai's barrenness will take on increased significance.

Of major importance at this point is the record of Terah's journey from Ur of the Chaldeans, located somewhere south of the lower Euphrates, to the city of Haran, some 600 miles north. Taking Abram, Sarai, and Lot, Terah sets out from Ur toward the land of Canaan by the route of the Fertile Crescent, which would bypass the Arabian Desert. Why Terah leaves Ur is a matter of some speculation as far as the Genesis record is concerned. Later Scripture provides a more complete answer when it records that Abram, and presumably Terah, were directed by God to leave Ur for a land that God would show them. Therefore this account of Terah and his journey to Haran is important in that it sets the stage for an even more significant journey for Abram in fulfilling the purpose that God has in mind.

Gen. 11:27a	TERAH. This is the account of Terah.
Gen. 11:27b,28 Ur of the Chaldeans	LOT BORN; HARAN DIES. Terah became the father of Abram, Nahor and Haran. And Haran became the father of Lot. While his father Terah was still alive, Haran died in Ur of the Chaldeans, in the land of his birth.
Gen. 11:29,30	ABRAM AND NAHOR TAKE WIVES. Abram and Nahor both married. The name of Abram's wife was Sarai, and the name of Nahor's wife was Milcah; she was the daughter of Haran, the father of both Milcah and Iscah. Now Sarai was barren; she had no children.
Gen. 11:31,32 From Ur to Haran	TERAH MOVES FAMILY TO HARAN. Terah took his son Abram, his grandson Lot son of Haran, and his daughter-in-law Sarai, the wife of his son Abram, and together they set out from Ur of the Chaldeans to go to Canaan. But when they came to Haran, they settled there. Terah lived 205 years, and he died in Haran.

Job, the Righteous Sufferer

*A*lthough there is no scriptural reference to Job during this period of time, there is compelling evidence to believe that an important historical figure named Job should be included here among the ancients. His home is in the land of Uz, which is probably in the northern Arabian desert in a territory which will come to be known as Edom, or Idumea. Job is unusually blessed with prosperity and holds his family very dear to him. Above all things, Job is a righteous man, esteemed among his peers and even those who serve him. However, disaster strikes Job when all his flocks, herds, and possessions are taken from him through a series of adversities. Even worse, all his children are killed, and he himself is stricken with a terrible, painful disease. Although he questions why such disaster should beset him, Job nevertheless maintains his faith in God. As a result, his wealth is restored to double its original worth, more children are born to him, and he dies a happy man.

The story of his great faith, and of his apparently successful struggle with the reason for his suffering, will be handed down over the generations to come. Several centuries later, at a time when a whole nation will be struggling with the problem of suffering, Job's life will become the basis for a literary masterpiece dealing with suffering and the issue of its causes. Little does this humble man know how his very personal adversity will be a source of comfort to multitudes of fellow-sufferers for centuries to come. That fact alone might well have something to do with why he is called upon to experience such adversity. The book of Job will be presented later at the time of its writing.

PERIOD OF THE PATRIARCHS

(Ca. 2100-1525 B.C.)

The Call of Abram

ith the life of Abram a new chapter in the history of God's dealings with mankind begins. God's presence in Abram's life does not appear to be based upon any special meritorious qualities that Abram himself might possess, but simply because God chooses him as the man through whom he will bless all of mankind.

Abram lives at a time when in the western part of the Fertile Crescent the Egyptian Empire is in its golden age during the Twelfth Dynasty. In the eastern part of the crescent, the Sumerians have controlled the area from their capital at Ur. Somewhere around 1950 B.C., however, the Sumerians are overthrown by the Elamites, who come from east of the Tigris River. The Elamite invasion causes such confusion and turmoil in this once-stable area that hordes of people from the Arabian desert are drawn into the more fertile area. These descendants of Ham from the west (or Amorites, as they are known) decisively take over the land and establish various capitals, the most notable of which is at Mari on the northern Euphrates River. This Amorite culture will flourish until about 1700 B.C., when it will be overrun by King Hammurabi of the Babylonians, who is remembered principally because of the code of laws which bears his name.

It is this Amorite culture with which Abram is most closely associated while in Haran. However, Abram himself is an Aramean and a descendant of Shem. Although the details are sketchy, it appears that Abram belongs to a rootless, unsettled, and seminomadic people who wander about among more settled people in search of food and water for the flocks which they tend. As the Genesis record continues, Abram and his clan will be seen wandering throughout Canaan in this very fashion.

The life of Abram, however, is more than a historical narrative about a Semitic Aramean wandering throughout Canaan. It is a life which will later be praised as an outstanding example of faith in God. With his father, Terah, now dead, and himself middle-aged, Abram is called by God to leave his homeland, his tribe, and his father's family in order to journey 300 miles to a land about which he knows very little. Once Abram arrives in the land, God promises Abram that he will give the land not to Abram but to his offspring; and this is promised despite the fact that the land is already occupied by the

Canaanites. Yet Abram believes God's promise and continually worships God.

As the Genesis record continues, it appears that God had already called Abram at an earlier time, which other Scripture indicates had taken place when Abram was still in his former homeland. But here God reaffirms the call and covenants a sevenfold promise both to Abram and, through him, to all peoples of the world.

Gen. 12:1 GOD'S CALL TO ABRAM.   The LORD had said to Abram, "Leave your country, your people and your father's household and go to the land I will show you.

Gen. 12:2,3 GOD'S PROMISE TO ABRAM.

> "I will make you into a great nation
>   and I will bless you;
> I will make your name great,
>   and you will be a blessing.
> I will bless those who bless you,
>   and whoever curses you I will curse;
> and all peoples on earth
>   will be blessed through you."

Gen. 12:4,5 To Canaan (Ca. 2091 B.C.) ABRAM LEAVES FOR CANAAN.   So Abram left, as the LORD had told him; and Lot went with him. Abram was seventy-five years old when he set out from Haran. He took his wife Sarai, his nephew Lot, all the possessions they had accumulated and the people they had acquired in Haran, and they set out for the land of Canaan, and they arrived there.

Gen. 12:6,7 Shechem LAND PROMISED TO OFFSPRING.   Abram traveled through the land as far as the site of the great tree of Moreh at Shechem. At that time the Canaanites were in the land. The LORD appeared to Abram and said, "To your offspring[a] I will give this land." So he built an altar there to the LORD, who had appeared to him.

Gen. 12:8,9 Between Bethel and Ai WORSHIP NEAR BETHEL.   From there he went on toward the hills east of Bethel and pitched his tent, with Bethel on the west and Ai on the east. There he built an altar to the LORD and called on the name of the LORD. Then Abram set out and continued toward the Negev.

Abram Dishonors Himself in Egypt

*H*aving seen that Abram is a man of great faith, who trusted God enough to move to an unknown land, it comes as somewhat of a disappointment to learn that Abram can also be a man of great moral weakness. This insight comes out of an incident which takes place in Egypt, where Abram will take his family because of a famine in Canaan. Even at 65 years of age, Abram's wife, Sarai, is less than middle-aged and still beautiful, especially in the eyes of the Egyptians, who would be attracted by Sarai's presumably fair complexion. Fearful that the Egyptian men will be attracted enough by her beauty to kill him in order to have Sarai, Abram asks Sarai to represent herself as his sister, if necessary. Sarai is in fact a half-sister

[a]Or *seed*

to Abram, since both have the same father. But asking Sarai to join him in a deception which could result in a sacrifice of her honor is clearly an indication of weakness in Abram's character. And Abram's failure to trust God to deliver him out of any trouble that might result from his being completely truthful shows that Abram's faith is still a matter of personal struggle.

ABRAM LEAVES FOR EGYPT. Now there was a famine in the land, and Abram went down to Egypt to live there for a while because the famine was severe.

Gen. 12:10

ABRAM PLANS DECEPTION. As he was about to enter Egypt, he said to his wife Sarai, "I know what a beautiful woman you are. When the Egyptians see you, they will say, 'This is his wife.' Then they will kill me but will let you live. Say you are my sister, so that I will be treated well for your sake and my life will be spared because of you."

Gen. 12:11-13

SARAI TAKEN BY PHARAOH. When Abram came to Egypt, the Egyptians saw that she was a very beautiful woman. And when Pharaoh's officials saw her, they praised her to Pharaoh, and she was taken into his palace. He treated Abram well for her sake, and Abram acquired sheep and cattle, male and female donkeys, menservants and maidservants, and camels.

Gen. 12:14-16

GOD DELIVERS SARAI. But the LORD inflicted serious diseases on Pharaoh and his household because of Abram's wife Sarai. So Pharaoh summoned Abram. "What have you done to me?" he said. "Why didn't you tell me she was your wife? Why did you say, 'She is my sister,' so that I took her to be my wife? Now then, here is your wife. Take her and go!" Then Pharaoh gave orders about Abram to his men, and they sent him on his way, with his wife and everything he had.

Gen. 12:17-20

Separation of Abram and Lot

*A*bram has dishonored himself in Egypt, but he is not destined to remain in this valley of self-defeat and moral failure. As he and his nephew, Lot, come out of Egypt once again into Canaan, the renewal of Abram's moral character will become evident. When grazing land becomes scarce and trouble develops between their herdsmen, Abram is put in a position where, as the elder patriarch, he can insist on his right to whatever territory he might choose. Rather than being self-assertive, however, Abram gives Lot first choice and accepts the consequences when Lot chooses the then-lush valley of the Jordan River instead of the less fertile hill country of Canaan.

The solution to his conflict with Lot is not only both practical and gracious on Abram's part but also further evidence of Abram's faith in God. He had come to this area at God's call and had been promised that his descendants would someday inherit the land. Yet despite the fact that his decision could well affect that inheritance, Abram sacrifices personal gain in favor of maintaining an important family relationship. While this incident gives reassuring insight into Abram's depth of commitment to God, it also hints of a serious character flaw in Lot which will become more and more evident.

The Genesis record begins the account of this incident as Abram and Lot bring their large clan of people, as well as herds of cattle and flocks of sheep, out of Egypt and into the Negev, or southern part of Canaan.

Gen. 13:1,2	**ABRAM AND LOT LEAVE EGYPT.** So Abram went up from Egypt to the Negev, with his wife and everything he had, and Lot went with him. Abram had become very wealthy in livestock and in silver and gold.
Gen. 13:3-4	**RETURN TO BETHEL.** From the Negev he went from place to place until he came to Bethel, to the place between Bethel and Ai where his tent had been earlier and where he had first built an altar. There Abram called on the name of the LORD.
Gen. 13:5-7	**TROUBLE BETWEEN HERDSMEN.** Now Lot, who was moving about with Abram, also had flocks and herds and tents. But the land could not support them while they stayed together, for their possessions were so great that they were not able to stay together. And quarreling arose between Abram's herdsmen and the herdsmen of Lot. The Canaanites and Perizzites were also living in the land at that time.
Gen. 13:8-9	**ABRAM PROPOSES SEPARATION.** So Abram said to Lot, "Let's not have any quarreling between you and me, or between your herdsmen and mine, for we are brothers. Is not the whole land before you? Let's part company. If you go to the left, I'll go to the right; if you go to the right, I'll go to the left."
Gen. 13:10-13	**LOT CHOOSES LAND NEAR SODOM.** Lot looked up and saw that the whole plain of the Jordan was well watered, like the garden of the LORD, like the land of Egypt, toward Zoar. (This was before the LORD destroyed Sodom and Gomorrah.) So Lot chose for himself the whole plain of the Jordan and set out toward the east. The two men parted company: Abram lived in the land of Canaan, while Lot lived among the cities of the plain and pitched his tents near Sodom. Now the men of Sodom were wicked and were sinning greatly against the LORD.
Gen. 13:14-17	**PROMISE REPEATED TO ABRAM.** The LORD said to Abram after Lot had parted from him, "Lift up your eyes from where you are and look north and south, east and west. All the land that you see I will give to you and your offspring[b] forever. I will make your offspring like the dust of the earth, so that if anyone could count the dust, then your offspring could be counted. Go, walk through the length and breadth of the land, for I am giving it to you."
Gen. 13:18 Hebron	**ABRAM SETTLES IN HEBRON.** So Abram moved his tents and went to live near the great trees of Mamre at Hebron, where he built an altar to the LORD.

◇

[b]Or *seed*; also in verse 16

Defeat of the Kings

*W*ith Lot settling near Sodom, a city of the Jordan Plain near the Dead Sea, and Abram settling to the west in Hebron, not far south of modern Jerusalem, the Genesis record shows the transformation of Abram from a wandering Hebrew patriarch, concerned mostly with finding sustenance for his people and herds, into a courageous warrior. It all happens in the context of political and military turmoil to the east of Hebron—rather far removed from Abram in both distance and seeming importance.

For some 12 to 15 years a power struggle has been taking place among various kings of the East, among whom King Kedorlaomer of Elam has remained the strongest. When five kings in the Dead Sea region join to oppose the eastern federation, Kedorlaomer gathers his three allies for a punitive foray into the Valley of Siddim, which surrounds the Dead Sea. Not only do the kings of the eastern federation defeat the local kings, but they also sack Sodom and Gomorrah and take away the inhabitants of those cities. Among the hostages are Abram's nephew, Lot, and his family, who by this time have taken up residence in Sodom.

When word of Lot's capture reaches Abram, he responds quickly and unselfishly by gathering a small force of men and setting out to rescue his captive relatives. Daring to challenge a much larger force of trained soldiers, Abram and his men execute a surprise attack during the night, completely routing the enemy and liberating Lot and his family.

As Abram is returning from this exciting venture, he is met and welcomed by King Melchizedek of Salem, probably the ancient name of the city known today as Jerusalem. When Melchizedek pays honor to Abram's heroism by feeding Abram and his men, Abram responds by giving Melchizedek a tenth of all they are carrying. This act will be more fully explained by subsequent text, but suffice it to say now that Abram recognizes Melchizedek not only as a king but also as a priest in the service of the same true and living God which Abram himself worships.

The Genesis record begins now with the background leading to Abram's dramatic rescue of Lot.

WAR AMONG EASTERN KINGS.   At this time Amraphel king of Shinar,[c] Arioch king of Ellasar, Kedorlaomer king of Elam and Tidal king of Goiim went to war against Bera king of Sodom, Birsha king of Gomorrah, Shinab king of Admah, Shemeber king of Zeboiim, and the king of Bela (that is, Zoar). All these latter kings joined forces in the Valley of Siddim (the Salt Sea[d]).

Gen.
14:1-3
East of the
Jordan

HISTORY OF THE CONFLICT.   For twelve years they had been subject to Kedorlaomer, but in the thirteenth year they rebelled.

Gen.
14:4-7

In the fourteenth year, Kedorlaomer and the kings allied with him went out and defeated the Rephaites in Ashteroth Karnaim, the Zuzites in Ham, the Emites in Shaveh Kiriathaim and the Horites in the hill country of Seir, as far as El Paran near the desert. Then they turned back and went to En Mishpat (that is, Kadesh), and they conquered the whole territory of the

[c]That is, Babylonia   [d]That is, the Dead Sea

Amalekites, as well as the Amorites who were living in Hazazon Tamar.

Gen.
14:8-10
Valley of
Siddim

DEFEAT OF DEAD SEA KINGS.   Then the king of Sodom, the king of Gomorrah, the king of Admah, the king of Zeboiim and the king of Bela (that is, Zoar) marched out and drew up their battle lines in the Valley of Siddim against Kedorlaomer king of Elam, Tidal king of Goiim, Amraphel king of Shinar and Arioch king of Ellasar—four kings against five. Now the Valley of Siddim was full of tar pits, and when the kings of Sodom and Gomorrah fled, some of the men fell into them and the rest fled to the hills.

Gen.
14:11,12
Sodom

LOT TAKEN CAPTIVE. The four kings seized all the goods of Sodom and Gomorrah and all their food; then they went away. They also carried off Abram's nephew Lot and his possessions, since he was living in Sodom.

Gen.
14:13-16
At Dan

ABRAM RESCUES LOT.   One who had escaped came and reported this to Abram the Hebrew. Now Abram was living near the great trees of Mamre the Amorite, a brother[e] of Eshcol and Aner, all of whom were allied with Abram. When Abram heard that his relative had been taken captive, he called out the 318 trained men born in his household and went in pursuit as far as Dan. During the night Abram divided his men to attack them and he routed them, pursuing them as far as Hobah, north of Damascus. He recovered all the goods and brought back his relative Lot and his possessions, together with the women and the other people.

Gen.
14:17,21-24
Valley of
Shaveh

ABRAM REFUSES REWARD.   After Abram returned from defeating Kedorlaomer and the kings allied with him, the king of Sodom came out to meet him in the Valley of Shaveh (that is, the King's Valley).

The king of Sodom said to Abram, "Give me the people and keep the goods for yourself."

But Abram said to the king of Sodom, "I have raised my hand to the LORD, God Most High, Creator of heaven and earth, and have taken an oath that I will accept nothing belonging to you, not even a thread or the thong of a sandal, so that you will never be able to say, 'I made Abram rich.' I will accept nothing but what my men have eaten and the share that belongs to the men who went with me—to Aner, Eshcol and Mamre. Let them have their share."

Gen.
14:18-20
Near
Jerusalem?

MELCHIZEDEK BLESSES ABRAM.   Then Melchizedek king of Salem[f] brought out bread and wine. He was priest of God Most High, and he blessed Abram, saying,

> "Blessed be Abram by God Most High,
>   Creator[g] of heaven and earth.
> And blessed be[h] God Most High,
>   who delivered your enemies into your hand."

Then Abram gave him a tenth of everything.

◆

[e]Or *a relative*; or *an ally*   [f]That is, Jerusalem   [g]Or *Possessor*; also in verse 22   [h]Or *And praise be to*

God's Covenant with Abram_____

With the passing of time Abram begins to be concerned that he and Sarai still have no children. How can his offspring inherit the land if there are no children? Must the inheritance come only through the children of his headservant, Eliezer, whom he could adopt in order to preserve his line of inheritance? Abram is genuinely puzzled. So God reassures Abram that he himself will have children, who in turn will multiply exceedingly. When God also restates his earlier promise that Abram's descendants would inherit the land, Abram asks God for a sign that his promise is true.

God graciously overlooks Abram's insecurity and instructs Abram to prepare for a covenant after the manner in which agreements are commonly sealed during this time. By the prevailing custom the covenanting parties pass between the split carcasses of animals which have been specially killed for the ceremony, as if the covenantors are saying, "This same fate be to all my herds and flocks should I not keep my promise." God's passage through the pieces of slain animals comes in the appearance of a blazing torch, whereupon the promise is sealed. Interestingly, God alone passes through the carcasses, indicating the unique one-sidedness of this covenant.

Just before this covenanting takes place, God appears to Abram in his sleep and tells him that his descendants will serve as slaves in a foreign land before returning to possess the land of Canaan. Subsequent text bears out the detailed accuracy of God's prophetic vision to Abram when the Hebrew nation is later enslaved in Egypt for some 400 years.

Perhaps the most significant statement at this point in the record of Abram is the fact that, when God promises Abram children, Abram believes God. As will soon be evident, Abram is still not so sure that children will come through himself and Sarai, but never again will he fail to trust that by God's power he will somehow have offspring.

As the account of God's covenanting with Abram begins, God may also be addressing Abram's fear of revenge from the Eastern kings whom Abram has recently defeated.

ABRAM'S CONCERN ABOUT HEIR.   After this, the word of the LORD   Gen.
came to Abram in a vision: 15:1-3

> "Do not be afraid, Abram.
>   I am your shield,[i]
>   your very great reward.[j]"

But Abram said, "O Sovereign LORD, what can you give me since I remain childless and the one who will inherit[k] my estate is Eliezer of Damascus?" And Abram said, "You have given me no children; so a servant in my household will be my heir."

GOD PROMISES ABRAM CHILDREN.   Then the word of the LORD   Gen.
came to him: "This man will not be your heir, but a son coming from your   15:4-6

[i]Or sovereign   [j]Or shield; / your reward will be very great   [k]The meaning of the Hebrew for this phrase is uncertain.

own body will be your heir." He took him outside and said, "Look up at the heavens and count the stars—if indeed you can count them." Then he said to him, "So shall your offspring be."

Abram believed the LORD, and he credited it to him as righteousness.

| Gen.
15:7,8 | ABRAM ASKS FOR SIGN.   He also said to him, "I am the LORD, who brought you out of Ur of the Chaldeans to give you this land to take possession of it." |

But Abram said, "O Sovereign LORD, how can I know that I will gain possession of it?"

| Gen.
15:9-11 | PREPARATION FOR COVENANT.   So the LORD said to him, "Bring me a heifer, a goat and a ram, each three years old, along with a dove and a young pigeon." |

Abram brought all these to him, cut them in two and arranged the halves opposite each other; the birds, however, he did not cut in half. Then birds of prey came down on the carcasses, but Abram drove them away.

| Gen.
15:12-16 | PREDICTION OF SLAVERY.   As the sun was setting, Abram fell into a deep sleep, and a thick and dreadful darkness came over him. Then the LORD said to him, "Know for certain that your descendants will be strangers in a country not their own, and they will be enslaved and mistreated four hundred years. But I will punish the nation they serve as slaves, and afterward they will come out with great possessions. You, however, will go to your fathers in peace and be buried at a good old age. In the fourth generation your descendants will come back here, for the sin of the Amorites has not yet reached its full measure." |

| Gen.
15:17-21 | GOD PROMISES ABRAM LAND.   When the sun had set and darkness had fallen, a smoking firepot with a blazing torch appeared and passed between the pieces. On that day the LORD made a covenant with Abram and said, "To your descendants I give this land, from the river[1] of Egypt to the great river, the Euphrates—the land of the Kenites, Kenizzites, Kadmonites, Hittites, Perizzites, Rephaites, Amorites, Canaanites, Girgashites and Jebusites." |

Birth of Ishmael Through Hagar

*A*lmost ten years have passed since God renewed his promise that Abram would have children. Although both Abram and Sarai continue to believe that it will happen, Sarai apparently begins to wonder if the promise specifically includes her as the mother of Abram's offspring. Despite her faith in the promise, Sarai finally convinces herself that she is not a part of God's plan and comes up with an idea to help make the promise come true. She suggests that Abram take as a secondary wife her Egyptian maidservant, Hagar. By the custom of the times it is altogether proper, even if somewhat personally humiliating, for a woman of Sarai's position to give her servant to her husband for the purpose of bearing children. Children born under such an arrangement may inherit as natural children. Therefore, when viewed from a strictly human perspective, Sarai's

[1]Or Wadi

suggestion is both unselfish and ostensibly designed to bring about God's promise to Abram.

   With Hagar's pregnancy, however, it soon becomes clear that the plan is
fraught with problems. Pride, jealousy, and alienation of affections naturally
arise in such a mixture of relationships, and in the end Hagar runs away from
her mistress. However, Hagar is instructed to return and be submissive. God
promises Hagar that the descendants of her son, Ishmael, will be countless, but
prophesies that Ishmael and his offspring will be characterized by hostility, particularly against his brothers. (It is noteworthy that in centuries to follow there
will be conflict in the Middle East between the Arabs, who descend from
Ishmael, and the Jews, who are descendants from Ishmael's half-brother, a son
soon to be born.)

SARAI SUGGESTS SECOND WIFE.   Now Sarai, Abram's wife, had
borne him no children. But she had an Egyptian maidservant named
Hagar; so she said to Abram, "The LORD has kept me from having children. Go, sleep with my maidservant; perhaps I can build a family
through her."
   Abram agreed to what Sarai said.

ABRAM TAKES HAGAR AS WIFE.   So after Abram had been living in
Canaan ten years, Sarai his wife took her Egyptian maidservant Hagar and
gave her to her husband to be his wife. He slept with Hagar, and she conceived.

TROUBLE BETWEEN WIVES.   When she knew she was pregnant, she
began to despise her mistress. Then Sarai said to Abram, "You are responsible for the wrong I am suffering. I put my servant in your arms, and now
that she knows she is pregnant, she despises me. May the LORD judge
between you and me."
   "Your servant is in your hands," Abram said. "Do with her whatever
you think best." Then Sarai mistreated Hagar; so she fled from her.

ANGEL TALKS WITH HAGAR.   The angel of the LORD found Hagar near
a spring in the desert; it was the spring that is beside the road to Shur. And
he said, "Hagar, servant of Sarai, where have you come from, and where
are you going?"
   "I'm running away from my mistress Sarai," she answered.
   Then the angel of the LORD told her, "Go back to your mistress and submit to her." The angel added, "I will so increase your descendants that
they will be too numerous to count."
   The angel of the LORD also said to her:

> "You are now with child
>   and you will have a son.
> You shall name him Ishmael,[m]
>   for the LORD has heard of your misery.
> He will be a wild donkey of a man;
>   his hand will be against everyone
>   and everyone's hand against him,
> and he will live in hostility
>   toward[n] all his brothers."

Gen.
16:1,2
Hebron
(Ca. 2081
B.C.)

Gen.
16:3,4a

Gen.
16:4b-6

Gen.
16:7-12
Near
Beer-
sheba?

---

[m]Ishmael means God hears.   [n]Or live to the east / of

Gen. 16:13,14	HAGAR NAMES THE ANGEL. She gave this name to the LORD who spoke to her: "You are the God who sees me," for she said, "I have now seen[o] the One who sees me." That is why the well was called Beer Lahai Roi[p]; it is still there, between Kadesh and Bered.
Gen. 16:15,16 (Ca. 2080 B.C.)	ISHMAEL IS BORN. So Hagar bore Abram a son, and Abram gave the name Ishmael to the son she had borne. Abram was eighty-six years old when Hagar bore him Ishmael.

Names and Circumcision As Signs of Covenant _____

The Genesis record is silent as to what events transpire over the next few years. However, the door to history is once again opened some 13 years after Ishmael's birth. At this time God appears once again to Abram in order to restate his promises and to confirm his prior covenant with Abram. Two signs are given to mark the occasion. The first involves the changing of Abram's and Sarai's names. Whereas "Abram" has meant exalted father, his new name, "Abraham," signifies the father of many. And whereas "Sarai" has meant princess, God adds a dignity befitting a princess who is the mother of many in making the slight change to "Sarah." A happy part of God's appearance to Abraham is the surprise announcement that Sarah herself will bear the son of promise.

Abraham's response to that announcement has been viewed by many to be one of skepticism in which Abraham pleads with God to let Ishmael, instead, be the honored son. However, the text seems to indicate quite to the contrary— that in fact Abraham laughs in joyous amazement that after all these years he and Sarah will actually have a child of their own just as promised, despite the increasing human odds against it. Even the son's name, "Isaac" (which means "he laughs"), will memorialize this outburst of Abraham's happiness. Although Abraham is overjoyed at the prospect of fathering a son through Sarah, nevertheless it is obvious that Abraham has become attached to his son Ishmael. Therefore Abraham asks that Ishmael be able to share in God's blessings. God assures Abraham that Ishmael, as well as Isaac, will have many descendants, but makes it clear that it will be through Isaac's lineage that the covenant will be honored.

As a second sign of God's covenant with his chosen people, God institutes the rite of circumcision for all the males in Abraham's household, including servants and others not naturally a part of the family by birth. With this inclusion of those who are not direct descendants of Abraham there is even now a striking affirmation of God's promise to bless "all peoples on earth." The rite of circumcision is not itself a novel practice in these times. Evidence points to such a custom among Ethiopians, Syrians, Phoenicians, and even some Egyptians. However, in those societies the rite is normally associated with the child's coming of age at puberty and being accepted into the community. The circumcision commanded by God is distinct in that it takes place in early infancy and is imbued with great religious significance.

---

[o]Or seen the back of   [p]Beer Lahai Roi means well of the Living One who sees me.

The act of cutting off the male foreskin is not to be thought of as merely, or even primarily, hygienic. Rather, this symbolic ritual represents consecration and dedication as well as spiritual purity. Circumcision of the young males is to be a sign of God's covenant with all of the descendants of Abraham, both male and female, and a reminder of the obligation of righteousness therein. Perhaps most importantly, circumcision foreshadows the purity of lineage through which all the world will someday be blessed.

CONFIRMATION OF COVENANT.   When Abram was ninety-nine years old, the LORD appeared to him and said, "I am God Almighty[q]; walk before me and be blameless. I will confirm my covenant between me and you and will greatly increase your numbers." *(Gen. 17:1,2 (Ca. 2067 B.C.))*

ABRAM'S NAME CHANGED.   Abram fell facedown, and God said to him, "As for me, this is my covenant with you: You will be the father of many nations. No longer will you be called Abram[r]; your name will be Abraham,[s] for I have made you a father of many nations. I will make you very fruitful; I will make nations of you, and kings will come from you. I will establish my covenant as an everlasting covenant between me and you and your descendants after you for the generations to come, to be your God and the God of your descendants after you. *(Gen. 17:3-7)*

LAND PROMISE RENEWED.   The whole land of Canaan, where you are now an alien, I will give as an everlasting possession to you and your descendants after you; and I will be their God." *(Gen. 17:8)*

CIRCUMCISION AS SIGN.   Then God said to Abraham, "As for you, you must keep my covenant, you and your descendants after you for the generations to come. This is my covenant with you and your descendants after you, the covenant you are to keep: Every male among you shall be circumcised. You are to undergo circumcision, and it will be the sign of the covenant between me and you. For the generations to come every male among you who is eight days old must be circumcised, including those born in your household or bought with money from a foreigner—those who are not your offspring. Whether born in your household or bought with your money, they must be circumcised. My covenant in your flesh is to be an everlasting covenant. Any uncircumcised male, who has not been circumcised in the flesh, will be cut off from his people; he has broken my covenant." *(Gen. 17:9-14)*

SARAI'S NAME CHANGED.   God also said to Abraham, "As for Sarai your wife, you are no longer to call her Sarai; her name will be Sarah. I will bless her and will surely give you a son by her. I will bless her so that she will be the mother of nations; kings of peoples will come from her." *(Gen. 17:15,16)*

ABRAHAM AMAZED.   Abraham fell facedown; he laughed and said to himself, "Will a son be born to a man a hundred years old? Will Sarah bear a child at the age of ninety?" *(Gen. 17:17)*

BLESSINGS FOR ISHMAEL.   And Abraham said to God, "If only Ishmael might live under your blessing!" *(Gen. 17:18-22)*
Then God said, "Yes, but your wife Sarah will bear you a son, and you will call him Isaac.[t] I will establish my covenant with him as an everlasting

[q]Hebrew *El-Shaddai*   [r]*Abram* means *exalted father.*   [s]*Abraham* means *father of many.*
[t]*Isaac* means *he laughs.*

covenant for his descendants after him. And as for Ishmael, I have heard you: I will surely bless him; I will make him fruitful and will greatly increase his numbers. He will be the father of twelve rulers, and I will make him into a great nation. But my covenant I will establish with Isaac, whom Sarah will bear to you by this time next year." When he had finished speaking with Abraham, God went up from him.

**Gen.
17:23-27**

MALES CIRCUMCISED. On that very day Abraham took his son Ishmael and all those born in his household or bought with his money, every male in his household, and circumcised them, as God told him. Abraham was ninety-nine years old when he was circumcised, and his son Ishmael was thirteen; Abraham and his son Ishmael were both circumcised on that same day. And every male in Abraham's household, including those born in his household or bought from a foreigner, was circumcised with him.

Appearance of Heavenly Visitors

Not long after Abraham has responded to God's instructions regarding circumcision, God appears to Abraham in the form of a human visitor. With this manifestation of God are two created angels, also in human form. It is not clear whether Abraham immediately recognizes his Lord as being more than simply a personage of superior authority. If not, the Visitor's divine nature begins to unfold to Abraham when the Visitor seems to know not only Sarah's name but also the innermost thoughts of her heart.

When God announces that Sarah will soon bear a son, Sarah, who has been listening from the tent, laughs with disbelief, though perhaps with hopeful anticipation as well. When God questions her laugh, Sarah impulsively denies any expression of doubt. But when God insists that she is not telling the truth, Sarah stands silent and fearful in recognition that this heavenly Visitor has correctly perceived her disbelief.

The incarnation of God on this occasion, and his announcement of a clearly supernatural birth, are both predictive of the promised spiritual heir to Abraham. And the freedom and joy of fellowship between God and man is witnessed in Abraham's hospitality to his heavenly guests, who now appear to Abraham as he relaxes in his tent, probably after his own midday meal.

**Gen.
18:1-8
Mamre
(Hebron)**

HOSPITALITY TOWARD VISITORS. The LORD appeared to Abraham near the great trees of Mamre while he was sitting at the entrance to his tent in the heat of the day. Abraham looked up and saw three men standing nearby. When he saw them, he hurried from the entrance of his tent to meet them and bowed low to the ground.

He said, "If I have found favor in your eyes, my lord,ᵘ do not pass your servant by. Let a little water be brought, and then you may all wash your feet and rest under this tree. Let me get you something to eat, so you can be refreshed and then go on your way—now that you have come to your servant."

"Very well," they answered, "do as you say."

ᵘOr O Lord

So Abraham hurried into the tent to Sarah. "Quick," he said, "get three seahs^v of fine flour and knead it and bake some bread."

Then he ran to the herd and selected a choice, tender calf and gave it to a servant, who hurried to prepare it. He then brought some curds and milk and the calf that had been prepared, and set these before them. While they ate, he stood near them under a tree.

SARAH LAUGHS ABOUT BIRTH.   "Where is your wife Sarah?" they asked him.

    Gen.
18:9-15

"There, in the tent," he said.

Then the LORD^w said, "I will surely return to you about this time next year, and Sarah your wife will have a son."

Now Sarah was listening at the entrance to the tent, which was behind him. Abraham and Sarah were already old and well advanced in years, and Sarah was past the age of childbearing. So Sarah laughed to herself as she thought, "After I am worn out and my master^x is old, will I now have this pleasure?"

Then the LORD said to Abraham, "Why did Sarah laugh and say, 'Will I really have a child, now that I am old?' Is anything too hard for the LORD? I will return to you at the appointed time next year and Sarah will have a son."

Sarah was afraid, so she lied and said, "I did not laugh."

But he said, "Yes, you did laugh."

Destruction of Sodom and Gomorrah

*I*f God is perturbed by Sarah's impulsive deception, it is nothing to compare with the righteous wrath he is soon to display against the wicked cities of Sodom and Gomorrah in the Jordan Plain, presumably near what is today known as the Dead Sea. It is in Sodom that Abraham's nephew, Lot, lives with his wife and two daughters. So it is understandable that, when God tells Abraham he is going to destroy Sodom, Abraham should plead that at least the righteous in Sodom be saved. But Abraham's humble, yet bold, intercession with God extends to even those outside Lot's family, should they be found righteous. God's response to Abraham's calculated bargaining reveals God's sublime righteousness and mercy.

God's extraordinary judgment against Sodom is apparently prompted by an uncommon wickedness, made all the more repulsive because of the unnaturalness, violence, and presumptuousness with which its inhabitants' lives are filled. An example of their wickedness is found in the way in which the two angels are received as they arrive in Sodom after their visit with Abraham. When Lot shares with them the hospitality and protection of his home, the men of Sodom demand that Lot release to them the angels, whom they presume to be normal men, so that they might use the angels for sexual perversion. It is because of this incident that the practice of homosexuality has ever since been associated with the Sodomites, although this particular depravity is not the only one in which they engaged.

---

^{v}That is, probably about 20 quarts (about 22 liters) ^{w}Hebrew *Then he* ^{x}Or *husband*

Even Lot seems not to have escaped the influence of Sodom's wickedness. Although Lot here extends hospitality to strangers and defends them courageously when they are threatened, his character is impugned when he offers to give his own daughters to the Sodomites for their pleasure in exchange for the safety of his guests. And when the angels tell of the impending destruction, Lot is hesitant to leave Sodom, perhaps because of undue attachment to his material possessions.

After being practically dragged out of the city by the angels, Lot, his wife, and their two daughters are told by God to run for their lives and not to look back. However, Lot's wife, who is apparently convinced but not converted, turns to view the destruction of the cities in the plain and is herself destroyed. Whereas Sodom and Gomorrah are consumed with a rain of what may have been burning pitch or sulfur, Lot's wife turns into a pillar of salt.

This account of the destruction of Sodom and Gomorrah contains a wealth of insight into man's sinful state, as well as God's judgment and mercy. It shows that God's judgment, although markedly righteous, is catastrophic, unexpected, and certainly complete. Thus it calls sinful man to flee from his own unrighteousness, without turning back to inevitable moral destruction, but persevering until he has reached the safety of God's promised rest.

It is perhaps with these lessons in mind that, as the three heavenly visitors now set out for Sodom, God anticipates the need to tell Abraham what he is about to do. As the one who is to become the father of God's chosen nation, Abraham needs to witness for himself the awesome judgment of God upon those who practice wickedness, and pass on to future generations how terrible the consequences of sin really are.

Gen. 18:16-21 Mamre (Hebron)

GOD TELLS ABOUT SODOM.   When the men got up to leave, they looked down toward Sodom, and Abraham walked along with them to see them on their way. Then the LORD said, "Shall I hide from Abraham what I am about to do? Abraham will surely become a great and powerful nation, and all nations on earth will be blessed through him. For I have chosen him, so that he will direct his children and his household after him to keep the way of the LORD by doing what is right and just, so that the LORD will bring about for Abraham what he has promised him."

Then the LORD said, "The outcry against Sodom and Gomorrah is so great and their sin so grievous that I will go down and see if what they have done is as bad as the outcry that has reached me. If not, I will know."

Gen. 18:22-33

ABRAHAM INTERCEDES.   The men turned away and went toward Sodom, but Abraham remained standing before the LORD.[y] Then Abraham approached him and said: "Will you sweep away the righteous with the wicked? What if there are fifty righteous people in the city? Will you really sweep it away and not spare[z] the place for the sake of the fifty righteous people in it? Far be it from you to do such a thing—to kill the righteous with the wicked, treating the righteous and the wicked alike. Far be it from you! Will not the Judge[a] of all the earth do right?"

[y]Masoretic Text; an ancient Hebrew scribal tradition *but the LORD remained standing before Abraham*   [z]Or *forgive*   [a]Or *Ruler*

The LORD said, "If I find fifty righteous people in the city of Sodom, I will spare the whole place for their sake."

Then Abraham spoke up again: "Now that I have been so bold as to speak to the Lord, though I am nothing but dust and ashes, what if the number of the righteous is five less than fifty? Will you destroy the whole city because of five people?"

"If I find forty-five there," he said, "I will not destroy it."

Once again he spoke to him, "What if only forty are found there?"

He said, "For the sake of forty, I will not do it."

Then he said, "May the Lord not be angry, but let me speak. What if only thirty can be found there?"

He answered, "I will not do it if I find thirty there."

Abraham said, "Now that I have been so bold as to speak to the Lord, what if only twenty can be found there?"

He said, "For the sake of twenty, I will not destroy it."

Then he said, "May the Lord not be angry, but let me speak just once more. What if only ten can be found there?"

He answered, "For the sake of ten, I will not destroy it."

When the LORD had finished speaking with Abraham, he left, and Abraham returned home.

LOT HOSPITABLE TO ANGELS.   The two angels arrived at Sodom in the evening, and Lot was sitting in the gateway of the city. When he saw them, he got up to meet them and bowed down with his face to the ground. "My lords," he said, "please turn aside to your servant's house. You can wash your feet and spend the night and then go on your way early in the morning."

Gen. 19:1-3 Sodom

"No," they answered, "we will spend the night in the square."

But he insisted so strongly that they did go with him and entered his house. He prepared a meal for them, baking bread without yeast, and they ate.

SODOMITES DEMAND ANGELS.   Before they had gone to bed, all the men from every part of the city of Sodom—both young and old—surrounded the house. They called to Lot, "Where are the men who came to you tonight? Bring them out to us so that we can have sex with them."

Gen. 19:4-11

Lot went outside to meet them and shut the door behind him and said, "No, my friends. Don't do this wicked thing. Look, I have two daughters who have never slept with a man. Let me bring them out to you, and you can do what you like with them. But don't do anything to these men, for they have come under the protection of my roof."

"Get out of our way," they replied. And they said, "This fellow came here as an alien, and now he wants to play the judge! We'll treat you worse than them." They kept bringing pressure on Lot and moved forward to break down the door.

But the men inside reached out and pulled Lot back into the house and shut the door. Then they struck the men who were at the door of the house, young and old, with blindness so that they could not find the door.

LOT WARNED OF DESTRUCTION.   The two men said to Lot, "Do you have anyone else here—sons-in-law, sons or daughters, or anyone else in the city who belongs to you? Get them out of here, because we are going to destroy this place. The outcry to the LORD against its people is so great that he has sent us to destroy it."

Gen. 19:12-14

So Lot went out and spoke to his sons-in-law, who were pledged to marry[b] his daughters. He said, "Hurry and get out of this place, because the LORD is about to destroy the city!" But his sons-in-law thought he was joking.

Gen. 19:15-17

LOT LED FROM SODOM.   With the coming of dawn, the angels urged Lot, saying, "Hurry! Take your wife and your two daughters who are here, or you will be swept away when the city is punished."

When he hesitated, the men grasped his hand and the hands of his wife and of his two daughters and led them safely out of the city, for the LORD was merciful to them. As soon as they had brought them out, one of them said, "Flee for your lives! Don't look back, and don't stop anywhere in the plain! Flee to the mountains or you will be swept away!"

Gen. 19:18-23 Zoar

LOT SEEKS REFUGE IN ZOAR.   But Lot said to them, "No, my lords,[c] please! Your[d] servant has found favor in your[d] eyes, and you[d] have shown great kindness to me in sparing my life. But I can't flee to the mountains; this disaster will overtake me, and I'll die. Look, here is a town near enough to run to, and it is small. Let me flee to it—it is very small, isn't it? Then my life will be spared."

He said to him, "Very well, I will grant this request too; I will not overthrow the town you speak of. But flee there quickly, because I cannot do anything until you reach it." (That is why the town was called Zoar.[e])

By the time Lot reached Zoar, the sun had risen over the land.

Gen. 19:24-25, 29,26

SODOM DESTROYED.   Then the LORD rained down burning sulfur on Sodom and Gomorrah—from the LORD out of the heavens. Thus he overthrew those cities and the entire plain, including all those living in the cities—and also the vegetation in the land.

So when God destroyed the cities of the plain, he remembered Abraham, and he brought Lot out of the catastrophe that overthrew the cities where Lot had lived. But Lot's wife looked back, and she became a pillar of salt.

Gen. 19:27,28

ABRAHAM VIEWS DESTRUCTION.   Early the next morning Abraham got up and returned to the place where he had stood before the LORD. He looked down toward Sodom and Gomorrah, toward all the land of the plain, and he saw dense smoke rising from the land, like smoke from a furnace.

The Scheme of Lot's Daughters

As Abraham looks out from the heights of Hebron over the now-desolate Jordan Plain—undoubtedly with awe, and with obvious concern for Lot—he apparently has no way of knowing whether Lot was sufficiently righteous to be saved. There is no record that Abraham ever again sees Lot, or even learns of his escape. Perhaps it is best that Abraham never knows of Lot's end in life, which is characterized by haunting fear, reclusion, and apparent dissoluteness. That God had ever saved Lot in the first place may have been a monument to his everlasting mercy, or perhaps a testimony to the high regard in which God held Abraham.

---

[b]Or *were married to*   [c]Or *No, Lord;* or *No, my lord*   [d]The Hebrew is singular.
[e]*Zoar* means *small*.

What follows is the last historical record of Lot. Strangely, it involves a somewhat bizarre scheme on the part of Lot's two daughters to bear children by their father. The motive for their scheme appears to be legitimate enough, but under normal circumstances their acts of incest would be unquestionably immoral. And although the record indicates that Lot was unaware of his involvement in the plan, it is all made possible by his apparent willingness to let his daughters get him drunk.

Of continuing historical significance are the two sons born as a result of this incestuous relationship and the people who descend from them. Moab will become father of the Moabites, who will first settle northeast of the Dead Sea between the Jabbok and the Arnon rivers, but will later be driven out by the Amorites to an area south of the Arnon. Ben-Ammi (Ammon) will become father of the Ammonites, who will be migratory and marauding Molech-worshipers in the land between the Jabbok and the Arnon. Both nations will come into conflict repeatedly with Abraham's descendants, all as a result of the events which now unfold.

LOT SETTLES IN CAVE.   Lot and his two daughters left Zoar and settled in the mountains, for he was afraid to stay in Zoar. He and his two daughters lived in a cave.   Gen. 19:30

DAUGHTERS COMMIT INCEST.   One day the older daughter said to the younger, "Our father is old, and there is no man around here to lie with us, as is the custom all over the earth. Let's get our father to drink wine and then lie with him and preserve our family line through our father."   Gen. 19:31-38

That night they got their father to drink wine, and the older daughter went in and lay with him. He was not aware of it when she lay down or when she got up.

The next day the older daughter said to the younger, "Last night I lay with my father. Let's get him to drink wine again tonight, and you go in and lie with him so we can preserve our family line through our father." So they got their father to drink wine that night also, and the younger daughter went and lay with him. Again he was not aware of it when she lay down or when she got up.

So both of Lot's daughters became pregnant by their father. The older daughter had a son, and she named him Moab*f*; he is the father of the Moabites of today. The younger daughter also had a son, and she named him Ben-Ammi*g*; he is the father of the Ammonites of today.

Abraham Deceives Abimelech

*T*he human condition is always surprising. It has been 20 years since Abraham was in Egypt and lied to the Pharaoh about Sarah's being his sister and not his wife. In the intervening two decades Abraham has been reassured repeatedly that God will continue to bless him and keep his promises. Abraham has been honored with the very presence of God and made to witness the destructive power of God's judgment against Sodom and

---

*f*Moab sounds like the Hebrew for *from father.*   *g*Ben-Ammi means *son of my people.*

Gomorrah. Yet almost unbelievably the Genesis account records that Abraham once again lies about his true relationship with Sarah—this time to a pre-Philistine father-king whose titular name is Abimelech.

Abimelech may desire to marry Sarah in order to form an alliance with Abraham, whom he undoubtedly regards as a powerful nomad prince. Fortunately, God intervenes before any doubt can be cast upon the paternity of the son whom Sarah will soon bear to Abraham. Not so fortunately, there continues to be doubt cast upon the character of this great man of faith. Despite all his outstanding qualities, Abraham appears to have a tendency toward deception. Interestingly enough, that same character flaw will be seen again in his son and grandsons. It simply stands as a warning that even men and women of faith can lapse into great sin.

If there is any encouragement, however, it is in knowing that while there is bad in the best of mankind, there is also good in the worst. As a Canaanite, Abimelech is not a believer in the true God, and undoubtedly engages in common heathen practices. Yet he asserts in his defense to God that he has acted in good conscience, even if he is somehow still guilty in God's eyes; then he responds to divine rebuke with repentance, generosity, and kindness.

Why Abraham is in the territory of Gerar in the first place is unknown. Perhaps it is at the direction of God, or simply because Abraham's herds and flocks need more pastureland than he can find for them in Mamre.

Gen.
20:1,2
Gerar

ABRAHAM LIES TO ABIMELECH.   Now Abraham moved on from there into the region of the Negev and lived between Kadesh and Shur. For a while he stayed in Gerar, and there Abraham said of his wife Sarah, "She is my sister." Then Abimelech king of Gerar sent for Sarah and took her.

Gen.
20:3-7

GOD APPEARS IN DREAM.   But God came to Abimelech in a dream one night and said to him, "You are as good as dead because of the woman you have taken; she is a married woman."

Now Abimelech had not gone near her, so he said, "Lord, will you destroy an innocent nation? Did he not say to me, 'She is my sister,' and didn't she also say, 'He is my brother'? I have done this with a clear conscience and clean hands."

Then God said to him in the dream, "Yes, I know you did this with a clear conscience, and so I have kept you from sinning against me. That is why I did not let you touch her. Now return the man's wife, for he is a prophet, and he will pray for you and you will live. But if you do not return her, you may be sure that you and all yours will die."

Gen.
20:8-13

ABRAHAM OFFERS DEFENSE.   Early the next morning Abimelech summoned all his officials, and when he told them all that had happened, they were very much afraid. Then Abimelech called Abraham in and said, "What have you done to us? How have I wronged you that you have brought such great guilt upon me and my kingdom? You have done things to me that should not be done." And Abimelech asked Abraham, "What was your reason for doing this?"

Abraham replied, "I said to myself, 'There is surely no fear of God in this place, and they will kill me because of my wife.' Besides, she really is my sister, the daughter of my father though not of my mother; and she became my wife. And when God had me wander from my father's household, I said to her, 'This is how you can show your love to me: Everywhere we go, say of me, "He is my brother." ' "

ABIMELECH SHOWS FORGIVENESS.   Then Abimelech brought sheep and cattle and male and female slaves and gave them to Abraham, and he returned Sarah his wife to him. And Abimelech said, "My land is before you; live wherever you like."
   To Sarah he said, "I am giving your brother a thousand shekels*h* of silver. This is to cover the offense against you before all who are with you; you are completely vindicated."

Gen.
20:14-16

PRAYER FOR ABIMELECH.   Then Abraham prayed to God, and God healed Abimelech, his wife and his slave girls so they could have children again, for the LORD had closed up every womb in Abimelech's household because of Abraham's wife Sarah.

Gen.
20:17,18

The Birth of Isaac

*I*t cannot be long after this bittersweet experience with Abimelech that Sarah conceives a child by Abraham. Even during a period of extended lifespans, with Abraham at 100 and Sarah at 90 years of age, in human terms childbirth would have been impossible. Sarah herself is clearly astonished, for she and Abraham have waited 25 years for this promised son—sometimes fully believing, sometimes filled with doubt and outright disbelief.

ISAAC BORN TO SARAH.   Now the LORD was gracious to Sarah as he had said, and the LORD did for Sarah what he had promised. Sarah became pregnant and bore a son to Abraham in his old age, at the very time God had promised him. Abraham gave the name Isaac*i* to the son Sarah bore him. When his son Isaac was eight days old, Abraham circumcised him, as God commanded him. Abraham was a hundred years old when his son Isaac was born to him.

Gen.
21:1-5
(Ca. 2066
B.C.)

SARAH EXPRESSES JOY.   Sarah said, "God has brought me laughter, and everyone who hears about this will laugh with me." And she added, "Who would have said to Abraham that Sarah would nurse children? Yet I have borne him a son in his old age."

Gen.
21:6,7

   The song of joy which Sarah sings at Isaac's birth is a happy prelude to what a much younger Hebrew mother in another age to come will sing in joyous anticipation of her promised son—the true spiritual heir to Abraham.

◇

---

*h*That is, about 25 pounds (about 11.5 kilograms)   *i*Isaac means *he laughs.*

Abraham and Abimelech Settle Dispute_____

*J*n the time which has passed since Abraham came into the land ruled by
Abimelech, Abraham has greatly prospered, not only in having a son
born in his old age, but also in the increase of his flocks and herds. It is
only natural, then, that Abimelech should become concerned about Abraham's
growing power. The Genesis account records Abimelech's diplomatic move to
protect his own political position by entering into a treaty of mutual peace with
Abraham.

A brief account follows of how Abraham and Abimelech implement the
spirit of the treaty in resolving a dispute over a well. The significance of the
agreement lies in the extreme importance of water sources in such a desert area.

Gen.
21:22-24
Beersheba

ENTRY OF TREATY.   At that time Abimelech and Phicol the commander of his forces said to Abraham, "God is with you in everything you do.
Now swear to me here before God that you will not deal falsely with me
or my children or my descendants. Show to me and the country where
you are living as an alien the same kindness I have shown to you."
Abraham said, "I swear it."

Gen.
21:25-34

DISPUTE RESOLVED. . Then Abraham complained to Abimelech about
a well of water that Abimelech's servants had seized. But Abimelech said,
"I don't know who has done this. You did not tell me, and I heard about
it only today."
So Abraham brought sheep and cattle and gave them to Abimelech, and
the two men made a treaty. Abraham set apart seven ewe lambs from the
flock, and Abimelech asked Abraham, "What is the meaning of these
seven ewe lambs you have set apart by themselves?"
He replied, "Accept these seven lambs from my hand as a witness that
I dug this well."
So that place was called Beersheba,ʲ because the two men swore an
oath there.
After the treaty had been made at Beersheba, Abimelech and Phicol the
commander of his forces returned to the land of the Philistines. Abraham
planted a tamarisk tree in Beersheba, and there he called upon the name
of the LORD, the Eternal God. And Abraham stayed in the land of the
Philistines for a long time.

Even in modern times the city of Beersheba, meaning Well of Seven or Well
of the Oath, stands as a tribute to the amicable attitude with which these two
men defused a potentially explosive situation.

◇

ʲBeersheba can mean *well of seven* or *well of the oath*.

Expulsion of Hagar and Ishmael_____

*P*robably three years have passed since Isaac was born, and it is the time of Isaac's weaning. The customary feast at the time of a child's weaning is normally an occasion for celebration. But the feast for Isaac becomes an occasion for resentment. Sarah knows that Ishmael, now a lad of 17, is mocking young Isaac, and that he also represents a threat to Isaac's right of inheritance. It is therefore Sarah's wish that Abraham cast out Ishmael, along with his mother, Hagar. Naturally Abraham is reluctant to do this, not only because of his natural ties to Ishmael, but also because of the customary law of his day which forbids the expulsion of a slave wife and her children. But God, for his own reasons, instructs Abraham to do as Sarah has requested, and Abraham makes the painful separation.

As Ishmael and his mother wander through the desert region, and their supply of water finally runs out, Hagar lapses into despair. Although 17 years old, Ishmael evidently is still immature and very much dependent upon Hagar. The picture is that both Hagar and the boy are sitting in the desert, sobbing at their imminent death. But God responds to Ishmael's crying by providing a well of water, and he reassures Hagar that Ishmael will be the father of a nation. The account begins as Isaac grows from infancy into early childhood.

ISHMAEL AND HAGAR SENT AWAY. The child grew and was weaned, and on the day Isaac was weaned Abraham held a great feast. But Sarah saw that the son whom Hagar the Egyptian had borne to Abraham was mocking, and she said to Abraham, "Get rid of that slave woman and her son, for that slave woman's son will never share in the inheritance with my son Isaac."

Gen.
21:8-14
(Ca. 2063
B.C.)
Beersheba

The matter distressed Abraham greatly because it concerned his son. But God said to him, "Do not be so distressed about the boy and your maidservant. Listen to whatever Sarah tells you, because it is through Isaac that your offspring[k] will be reckoned. I will make the son of the maidservant into a nation also, because he is your offspring."

Early the next morning Abraham took some food and a skin of water and gave them to Hagar. He set them on her shoulders and then sent her off with the boy. She went on her way and wandered in the desert of Beersheba.

GOD PROVIDES WATER. When the water in the skin was gone, she put the boy under one of the bushes. Then she went off and sat down nearby, about a bowshot away, for she thought, "I cannot watch the boy die." And as she sat there nearby, she[l] began to sob.

Gen.
21:15-19

God heard the boy crying, and the angel of God called to Hagar from heaven and said to her, "What is the matter, Hagar? Do not be afraid; God has heard the boy crying as he lies there. Lift the boy up and take him by the hand, for I will make him into a great nation."

Then God opened her eyes and she saw a well of water. So she went and filled the skin with water and gave the boy a drink.

[k]Or *seed*   [l]Hebrew; Septuagint *the child*

<table>
<tr><td>Gen.
21:20,21</td><td>ISHMAEL GROWS INTO MANHOOD.   God was with the boy as he grew up. He lived in the desert and became an archer. While he was living in the Desert of Paran, his mother got a wife for him from Egypt.</td></tr>
</table>

Abraham's Ultimate Test of Faith

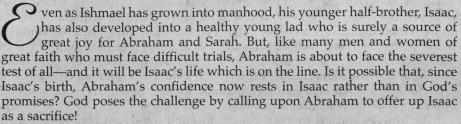

*E*ven as Ishmael has grown into manhood, his younger half-brother, Isaac, has also developed into a healthy young lad who is surely a source of great joy for Abraham and Sarah. But, like many men and women of great faith who must face difficult trials, Abraham is about to face the severest test of all—and it will be Isaac's life which is on the line. Is it possible that, since Isaac's birth, Abraham's confidence now rests in Isaac rather than in God's promises? God poses the challenge by calling upon Abraham to offer up Isaac as a sacrifice!

Although human sacrifice is not unusual among the surrounding Canaanites and Chaldeans, this request of God's must strike Abraham at the very foundation of his faith. It not only causes Abraham to wonder about God's righteousness, but, more importantly, it threatens the fulfillment of God's promise to bring about an entire nation through the descendants of Isaac. In such a dilemma, how can Abraham reconcile his faith? How should he respond?

Gen. 22:1,2 Beersheba	ABRAHAM TO SACRIFICE ISAAC. Some time later God tested Abraham. He said to him, "Abraham!" "Here I am," he replied. Then God said, "Take your son, your only son, Isaac, whom you love, and go to the region of Moriah. Sacrifice him there as a burnt offering on one of the mountains I will tell you about."
Gen. 22:3-8 Region of Moriah	ABRAHAM RESPONDS. Early the next morning Abraham got up and saddled his donkey. He took with him two of his servants and his son Isaac. When he had cut enough wood for the burnt offering, he set out for the place God had told him about. On the third day Abraham looked up and saw the place in the distance. He said to his servants, "Stay here with the donkey while I and the boy go over there. We will worship and then we will come back to you." Abraham took the wood for the burnt offering and placed it on his son Isaac, and he himself carried the fire and the knife. As the two of them went on together, Isaac spoke up and said to his father Abraham, "Father?" "Yes, my son?" Abraham replied. "The fire and wood are here," Isaac said, "but where is the lamb for the burnt offering?" Abraham answered, "God himself will provide the lamb for the burnt offering, my son." And the two of them went on together.
Gen. 22:9-14	GOD SUBSTITUTES RAM. When they reached the place God had told him about, Abraham built an altar there and arranged the wood on it. He bound his son Isaac and laid him on the altar, on top of the wood. Then he reached out his hand and took the knife to slay his son. But the angel of the LORD called out to him from heaven, "Abraham! Abraham!" "Here I am," he replied.

"Do not lay a hand on the boy," he said. "Do not do anything to him. Now I know that you fear God, because you have not withheld from me your son, your only son."

Abraham looked up and there in a thicket he saw a ram[m] caught by its horns. He went over and took the ram and sacrificed it as a burnt offering instead of his son. So Abraham called that place The LORD Will Provide. And to this day it is said, "On the mountain of the LORD it will be provided."

PROMISE OF BLESSINGS.   The angel of the LORD called to Abraham from heaven a second time and said, "I swear by myself, declares the LORD, that because you have done this and have not withheld your son, your only son, I will surely bless you and make your descendants as numerous as the stars in the sky and as the sand on the seashore. Your descendants will take possession of the cities of their enemies, and through your offspring[n] all nations on earth will be blessed, because you have obeyed me."

Then Abraham returned to his servants, and they set off together for Beersheba. And Abraham stayed in Beersheba.

Gen.
22:15-19
Beersheba

Abraham's feelings throughout this encounter must have been beyond adequate description. Yet he evidently believed that God would raise Isaac from the dead, if necessary, in order to fulfill his promise. In the midst of his own personal struggle to obey God's extraordinary request, little could Abraham know that God was asking no more of him than at a future time God would ask of himself. When Abraham's ultimate heir (Jesus) eventually appears on the canvas of history, the prophetic nature of Isaac's sacrifice will be repeated with much similarity and with strikingly parallel significance.

News Regarding Nahor's Family

Sometime after Abraham's return to Beersheba from his brief trip with Isaac to the land of Moriah, Abraham receives word regarding his brother Nahor, whom Abraham has not seen since he left Ur of the Chaldeans some 40 years ago. The good news is that Nahor now has eight children by his wife and four by his concubine. The historical significance of Nahor's family record is found in Nahor's youngest son, Bethuel, and more importantly in Bethuel's daughter, Rebekah, who will soon become an important figure in Abraham's own lineage.

NEWS FROM NAHOR.   Some time later Abraham was told, "Milcah is also a mother; she has borne sons to your brother Nahor: Uz the firstborn, Buz his brother, Kemuel (the father of Aram), Kesed, Hazo, Pildash, Jidlaph and Bethuel." Bethuel became the father of Rebekah. Milcah bore these eight sons to Abraham's brother Nahor. His concubine, whose name was Reumah, also had sons: Tebah, Gaham, Tahash and Maacah.

Gen.
22:20-24

[m]Many manuscripts of the Masoretic Text, Samaritan Pentateuch, Septuagint and Syriac; most manuscripts of the Masoretic Text *a ram behind him*   [n]Or *seed*

Sarah's Death and Burial

The years have passed and Abraham is now 137 years old. Isaac, a century behind his father, is a relatively young 37. Sarah, who has the distinction of being the only woman in all of Scripture whose age is mentioned, has reached 127. The Genesis account now abruptly records Sarah's death, in the region of Hebron in the land of Canaan, to which Abraham has returned sometime during the last 40 years.

That Scripture would pause to take note of Abraham's mourning over the loss of his beloved companion is a touching memorial to this woman of faith who would become the mother of a great nation. Of some curiosity, however, is the attention which the text gives to a transaction between Abraham and a man named Ephron who owns a cave which Abraham wishes to purchase as a burial site for Sarah's remains. The transaction itself is an interesting introduction to Oriental bargaining, in which an apparent offer of a gift is nothing more than a subtle way of setting a price. But the true significance of the account may be its further evidence of Abraham's faith that God will one day give this land to Abraham's descendants. It is as if Abraham wants to guarantee that, even in death, he and Sarah will be a part of this promised land.

Gen. 23:1,2 (Ca. 2029 B.C.)	ABRAHAM MOURNS SARAH'S DEATH. Sarah lived to be a hundred and twenty-seven years old. She died at Kiriath Arba (that is, Hebron) in the land of Canaan, and Abraham went to mourn for Sarah and to weep over her.
Gen. 23:3-18	CAVE PURCHASED FOR TOMB. Then Abraham rose from beside his dead wife and spoke to the Hittites.º He said, "I am an alien and a stranger among you. Sell me some property for a burial site here so I can bury my dead."

The Hittites replied to Abraham, "Sir, listen to us. You are a mighty prince among us. Bury your dead in the choicest of our tombs. None of us will refuse you his tomb for burying your dead."

Then Abraham rose and bowed down before the people of the land, the Hittites. He said to them, "If you are willing to let me bury my dead, then listen to me and intercede with Ephron son of Zohar on my behalf so he will sell me the cave of Machpelah, which belongs to him and is at the end of his field. Ask him to sell it to me for the full price as a burial site among you."

Ephron the Hittite was sitting among his people and he replied to Abraham in the hearing of all the Hittites who had come to the gate of his city. "No, my lord," he said. "Listen to me; I giveᴾ you the field, and I giveᴾ you the cave that is in it. I giveᴾ it to you in the presence of my people. Bury your dead."

Again Abraham bowed down before the people of the land and he said to Ephron in their hearing, "Listen to me, if you will. I will pay the price of the field. Accept it from me so I can bury my dead there."

Ephron answered Abraham, "Listen to me, my lord; the land is worth

ºOr *the sons of Heth*; also in verses 5, 7, 10, 16, 18 and 20   ᴾOr *sell*

four hundred shekels*q* of silver, but what is that between me and you? Bury your dead."

Abraham agreed to Ephron's terms and weighed out for him the price he had named in the hearing of the Hittites: four hundred shekels of silver, according to the weight current among the merchants.

So Ephron's field in Machpelah near Mamre—both the field and the cave in it, and all the trees within the borders of the field—was deeded to Abraham as his property in the presence of all the Hittites who had come to the gate of the city.

SARAH BURIED.   Afterward Abraham buried his wife Sarah in the cave in the field of Machpelah near Mamre (which is at Hebron) in the land of Canaan. So the field and the cave in it were deeded to Abraham by the Hittites as a burial site.

Gen.
23:19,20

Abraham Arranges a Wife for Isaac

*T*he death of Sarah must have caused Abraham to reflect on the few years remaining in his own life and to be concerned about preserving his lineage. So Abraham makes preparations for Isaac to marry a woman from among his own kinsmen back in the Mesopotamian region, from which he had emigrated some 60 years earlier. Perhaps Abraham is fearful that if Isaac marries a woman from among the local Canaanites he might be drawn into the worship of their pagan gods. Therefore, using an ancient custom for confirming a solemn oath, Abraham commissions a trusted servant, probably Eliezer of Damascus, to go to Mesopotamia to find Isaac a wife. The servant invokes God's intervention in the selection process and thereby meets Rebekah, the daughter of Bethuel, one of Abraham's nephews.

ABRAHAM INSTRUCTS SERVANT.   Abraham was now old and well advanced in years, and the LORD had blessed him in every way. He said to the chief*r* servant in his household, the one in charge of all that he had, "Put your hand under my thigh. I want you to swear by the LORD, the God of heaven and the God of earth, that you will not get a wife for my son from the daughters of the Canaanites, among whom I am living, but will go to my country and my own relatives and get a wife for my son Isaac."

Gen.
24:1-9

The servant asked him, "What if the woman is unwilling to come back with me to this land? Shall I then take your son back to the country you came from?"

"Make sure that you do not take my son back there," Abraham said. "The LORD, the God of heaven, who brought me out of my father's household and my native land and who spoke to me and promised me on oath, saying, 'To your offspring*s* I will give this land'—he will send his angel before you so that you can get a wife for my son from there. If the woman is unwilling to come back with you, then you will be released from this oath of mine. Only do not take my son back there." So the servant put his hand under the thigh of his master Abraham and swore an oath to him concerning this matter.

---

*q*That is, about 10 pounds (about 4.5 kilograms)   *r*Or *oldest*   *s*Or *seed*

Gen.
24:10-14
Nahor

SERVANT PRAYS FOR GUIDANCE.   Then the servant took ten of his master's camels and left, taking with him all kinds of good things from his master. He set out for Aram Naharaim[t] and made his way to the town of Nahor. He had the camels kneel down near the well outside the town; it was toward evening, the time the women go out to draw water.

Then he prayed, "O LORD, God of my master Abraham, give me success today, and show kindness to my master Abraham. See, I am standing beside this spring, and the daughters of the townspeople are coming out to draw water. May it be that when I say to a girl, 'Please let down your jar that I may have a drink,' and she says, 'Drink, and I'll water your camels too'—let her be the one you have chosen for your servant Isaac. By this I will know that you have shown kindness to my master."

Gen.
24:15-21

SERVANT MEETS REBEKAH.   Before he had finished praying, Rebekah came out with her jar on her shoulder. She was the daughter of Bethuel son of Milcah, who was the wife of Abraham's brother Nahor. The girl was very beautiful, a virgin; no man had ever lain with her. She went down to the spring, filled her jar and came up again.

The servant hurried to meet her and said, "Please give me a little water from your jar."

"Drink, my lord," she said, and quickly lowered the jar to her hands and gave him a drink.

After she had given him a drink, she said, "I'll draw water for your camels too, until they have finished drinking." So she quickly emptied her jar into the trough, ran back to the well to draw more water, and drew enough for all his camels. Without saying a word, the man watched her closely to learn whether or not the LORD had made his journey successful.

Gen.
24:22-27

REBEKAH IS DAUGHTER OF KIN.   When the camels had finished drinking, the man took out a gold nose ring weighing a beka[u] and two gold bracelets weighing ten shekels.[v] Then he asked, "Whose daughter are you? Please tell me, is there room in your father's house for us to spend the night?"

She answered him, "I am the daughter of Bethuel, the son that Milcah bore to Nahor." And she added, "We have plenty of straw and fodder, as well as room for you to spend the night."

Then the man bowed down and worshiped the LORD, saying, "Praise be to the LORD, the God of my master Abraham, who has not abandoned his kindness and faithfulness to my master. As for me, the LORD has led me on the journey to the house of my master's relatives."

Gen.
24:28-32

LABAN OFFERS HOSPITALITY.   The girl ran and told her mother's household about these things. Now Rebekah had a brother named Laban, and he hurried out to the man at the spring. As soon as he had seen the nose ring, and the bracelets on his sister's arms, and had heard Rebekah tell what the man said to her, he went out to the man and found him standing by the camels near the spring. "Come, you who are blessed by the LORD," he said. "Why are you standing out here? I have prepared the house and a place for the camels."

So the man went to the house, and the camels were unloaded. Straw

---

[t]That is, Northwest Mesopotamia   [u]That is, about 1/5 ounce (about 5.5 grams)
[v]That is, about 4 ounces (about 110 grams)

and fodder were brought for the camels, and water for him and his men to
wash their feet.

SERVANT TELLS OF MISSION.   Then food was set before him, but he
said, "I will not eat until I have told you what I have to say."

Gen.
24:33-41

"Then tell us," ⌐Laban⌐ said.

So he said, "I am Abraham's servant. The LORD has blessed my master
abundantly, and he has become wealthy. He has given him sheep and cattle, silver and gold, menservants and maidservants, and camels and donkeys. My master's wife Sarah has borne him a son in her*w* old age, and he
has given him everything he owns. And my master made me swear an
oath, and said, 'You must not get a wife for my son from the daughters of
the Canaanites, in whose land I live, but go to my father's family and to
my own clan, and get a wife for my son.'

"Then I asked my master, 'What if the woman will not come back with
me?'

"He replied, 'The LORD, before whom I have walked, will send his angel
with you and make your journey a success, so that you can get a wife for
my son from my own clan and from my father's family. Then, when you
go to my clan, you will be released from my oath even if they refuse to give
her to you—you will be released from my oath.'

SERVANT RELATES PRAYER.   "When I came to the spring today, I said,
'O LORD, God of my master Abraham, if you will, please grant success to
the journey on which I have come. See, I am standing beside this spring; if
a maiden comes out to draw water and I say to her, "Please let me drink a
little water from your jar," and if she says to me, "Drink, and I'll draw
water for your camels too," let her be the one the LORD has chosen for my
master's son.'

Gen.
24:42-48

"Before I finished praying in my heart, Rebekah came out, with her jar
on her shoulder. She went down to the spring and drew water, and I said
to her, 'Please give me a drink.'

"She quickly lowered her jar from her shoulder and said, 'Drink, and I'll
water your camels too.' So I drank, and she watered the camels also.

"I asked her, 'Whose daughter are you?'

"She said, 'The daughter of Bethuel son of Nahor, whom Milcah bore to
him.'

"Then I put the ring in her nose and the bracelets on her arms, and I
bowed down and worshiped the LORD. I praised the LORD, the God of my
master Abraham, who had led me on the right road to get the granddaughter of my master's brother for his son.

BETHUEL AGREES TO MARRIAGE.   Now if you will show kindness
and faithfulness to my master, tell me; and if not, tell me, so I may know
which way to turn."

Gen.
24:49-51

Laban and Bethuel answered, "This is from the LORD; we can say nothing to you one way or the other. Here is Rebekah; take her and go, and let
her become the wife of your master's son, as the LORD has directed."

REBEKAH GOES WITH SERVANT.   When Abraham's servant heard
what they said, he bowed down to the ground before the LORD. Then the
servant brought out gold and silver jewelry and articles of clothing and

Gen.
24:52-61

*w*Or *his*

gave them to Rebekah; he also gave costly gifts to her brother and to her mother. Then he and the men who were with him ate and drank and spent the night there.

When they got up the next morning, he said, "Send me on my way to my master."

But her brother and her mother replied, "Let the girl remain with us ten days or so; then you[x] may go."

But he said to them, "Do not detain me, now that the LORD has granted success to my journey. Send me on my way so I may go to my master."

Then they said, "Let's call the girl and ask her about it." So they called Rebekah and asked her, "Will you go with this man?"

"I will go," she said.

So they sent their sister Rebekah on her way, along with her nurse and Abraham's servant and his men. And they blessed Rebekah and said to her,

> "Our sister, may you increase
> to thousands upon thousands;
> may your offspring possess
> the gates of their enemies."

Then Rebekah and her maids got ready and mounted their camels and went back with the man. So the servant took Rebekah and left.

**Gen.
24:62-67
Beer Lahai
Roi**

ISAAC MARRIES REBEKAH.   Now Isaac had come from Beer Lahai Roi, for he was living in the Negev. He went out to the field one evening to meditate, [y] and as he looked up, he saw camels approaching. Rebekah also looked up and saw Isaac. She got down from her camel and asked the servant, "Who is that man in the field coming to meet us?"

"He is my master," the servant answered. So she took her veil and covered herself.

Then the servant told Isaac all he had done. Isaac brought her into the tent of his mother Sarah, and he married Rebekah. So she became his wife, and he loved her; and Isaac was comforted after his mother's death.

Abraham Marries Keturah

*J*ust as Isaac is comforted after his mother's death by taking a wife, so Abraham is comforted after Sarah's passing by taking a wife named Keturah. However, all of Abraham's sons other than Isaac are eventually sent away, presumably to insure preeminence to Isaac and his descendants. The record of Abraham's offspring by Keturah lists six sons, seven grandsons, and three great-grandsons, regarding whom any future reference is uncertain.

**Gen.
25:1-6**

OFFSPRING BY KETURAH.   Abraham took[z] another wife, whose name was Keturah. She bore him Zimran, Jokshan, Medan, Midian, Ishbak and Shuah. Jokshan was the father of Sheba and Dedan; the descendants of Dedan were the Asshurites, the Letushites and the Leummites. The sons of Midian were Ephah, Epher, Hanoch, Abida and Eldaah. All these were descendants of Keturah.

---

[x]Or *she*   [y]The meaning of the Hebrew for this word is uncertain.   [z]Or *had taken*

Abraham left everything he owned to Isaac. But while he was still living, he gave gifts to the sons of his concubines and sent them away from
his son Isaac to the land of the east.

Death of Abraham

*T*he Genesis record closes its account of Abraham's life with a brief
account of his death and burial. Significantly, Ishmael and Isaac bury
not only their father, but also (at least temporarily) any hostility which
may have come between them over the years. All evidence from this point forward, however, indicates that the descendants of these two half-brothers will
have virtually nothing in common with each other. The single known exception will come when Isaac's son, Esau, will take wives from the daughters of
Ishmael.

For now, one of the most significant characters in the unfolding story of
God's dealings with mankind is laid to rest. But Abraham will be remembered
throughout history as one of the most outstanding men of faith ever to have
lived.

ABRAHAM BURIED.   Altogether, Abraham lived a hundred and seventy-five years. Then Abraham breathed his last and died at a good old age,
an old man and full of years; and he was gathered to his people. His sons
Isaac and Ishmael buried him in the cave of Machpelah near Mamre, in the
field of Ephron son of Zohar the Hittite, the field Abraham had bought
from the Hittites.[a] There Abraham was buried with his wife Sarah.

Gen.
25:7-10
(Ca. 1991
B.C.)

Last Account of Ishmael

*I*shmael is 89 years old when his father, Abraham, dies, and he will
live for another 48 years. He will have 12 sons and presumably many
daughters. Because the Genesis record will soon concentrate exclusively on the life of Isaac and his descendants, a last account of Ishmael and his sons
is given at this point.

ISHMAEL'S DESCENDANTS.   This is the account of Abraham's son Ishmael, whom Sarah's maidservant, Hagar the Egyptian, bore to Abraham.

Gen.
25:12-18

These are the names of the sons of Ishmael, listed in the order of their
birth: Nebaioth the firstborn of Ishmael, Kedar, Adbeel, Mibsam, Mishma,
Dumah, Massa, Hadad, Tema, Jetur, Naphish and Kedemah. These were
the sons of Ishmael, and these are the names of the twelve tribal rulers
according to their settlements and camps. Altogether, Ishmael lived a
hundred and thirty-seven years. He breathed his last and died, and he was
gathered to his people. His descendants settled in the area from Havilah
to Shur, near the border of Egypt, as you go toward Asshur. And they lived
in hostility toward[b] all their brothers.

---

[a]Or *the sons of Heth*   [b]Or *lived to the east of*

Esau and Jacob_____

With the death of Abraham, the Genesis record begins to provide increasing detail regarding the lives of Abraham's descendants, and events are recorded at briefer intervals. Whereas major events of the first 2500 years have been chronicled as only a brief outline, the remainder of the Genesis record provides an in-depth look at Isaac's children and grandchildren. For the most part, the events speak for themselves. The people whose lives are recorded exhibit both the best and worst of human nature, typifying the moral struggles which encompass the human predicament and pointing up the need for a God who can lift mankind above its own circumstances.

The scene for the next 150 years is set when Rebekah gives birth to twins and is told prophetically that these two sons will be the fathers of nations which will in time struggle with each other for dominance. The account picks up immediately following the death of Isaac's father.

Gen. 25:11	**GOD PROSPERS ISAAC.** After Abraham's death, God blessed his son Isaac, who then lived near Beer Lahai Roi.
Gen. 25:19-21	**CONCERN ABOUT DESCENDANTS.** This is the account of Abraham's son Isaac.

Abraham became the father of Isaac, and Isaac was forty years old when he married Rebekah daughter of Bethuel the Aramean from Paddan Aram[c] and sister of Laban the Aramean.

Isaac prayed to the LORD on behalf of his wife, because she was barren. The LORD answered his prayer, and his wife Rebekah became pregnant.

Gen. 25:22,23	**PROPHECY REGARDING CHILDREN.** The babies jostled each other within her, and she said, "Why is this happening to me?" So she went to inquire of the LORD.

The LORD said to her,

"Two nations are in your womb,
    and two peoples from within you will be separated;
one people will be stronger than the other,
    and the older will serve the younger."

Gen. 25:24-26 (Ca. 2006 B.C.)	**ESAU AND JACOB BORN.** When the time came for her to give birth, there were twin boys in her womb. The first to come out was red, and his whole body was like a hairy garment; so they named him Esau.[d] After this, his brother came out, with his hand grasping Esau's heel; so he was named Jacob.[e] Isaac was sixty years old when Rebekah gave birth to them.

As Esau and Jacob grow into manhood, they take on individual characteristics and become especially favored: Esau, by Isaac; Jacob, by Rebekah.

Gen. 25:27,28	**ESAU AND JACOB GROW UP.** The boys grew up, and Esau became a skillful hunter, a man of the open country, while Jacob was a quiet man,

---

[c]That is, Northwest Mesopotamia   [d]*Esau* may mean *hairy*; he was also called Edom, which means *red*.   [e]*Jacob* means *he grasps the heel* (figuratively, *he deceives*).

staying among the tents. Isaac, who had a taste for wild game, loved Esau, but Rebekah loved Jacob.

A Birthright Is Sold

*A*n incident having extraordinary consequences is now recorded which not only gives insight into the character of each man, but also has important implications for the further descent of the people through whom God has chosen to reveal himself. The event involves the transfer of the birthright belonging to Esau, the firstborn of the twins. By that birthright Esau would stand to receive a double part of Isaac's estate, and take over leadership of the family upon Isaac's death.

ESAU SELLS HIS BIRTHRIGHT.   Once when Jacob was cooking some stew, Esau came in from the open country, famished. He said to Jacob, "Quick, let me have some of that red stew! I'm famished!" (That is why he was also called Edom.*f*)

Gen. 25:29-34

Jacob replied, "First sell me your birthright."

"Look, I am about to die," Esau said. "What good is the birthright to me?"

But Jacob said, "Swear to me first." So he swore an oath to him, selling his birthright to Jacob.

Then Jacob gave Esau some bread and some lentil stew. He ate and drank, and then got up and left.

So Esau despised his birthright.

Careless, and apparently disinterested in the benefits and responsibilities attendant to the birthright, Esau unknowingly forfeits his opportunity to be the one in his generation through whom the blessings promised to his grandfather Abraham would pass. Esau's descendants will never be God's special people. In fact, pursuant to the prophecy given to Rebekah, in future years Esau's descendants will indeed be subservient to the Hebrews, who will be the direct descendants of Jacob. With reference to the redness associated with Esau's birth, Esau's descendants will bear the name "Edomites" and be a continuing source of friction for the Hebrew nation.

Isaac Follows in Abraham's Footsteps

*A*s his two sons engage in fraternal conflict, Isaac himself experiences moral conflict in a series of situations which are amazingly parallel to situations experienced by his father, Abraham. First Isaac encounters a famine and is forced to migrate to Gerar, where he lies about Rebekah exactly as Abraham lied about Sarah. He is then blessed with great wealth, as was Abraham, and finally has similar disputes over the same wells previously dug by his father. It is interesting to note the influence of a parent and, in a more general sense, the cycles of human behavior which one can observe throughout history.

f Edom means *red*.

Gen.
26:1-5

PROMISES REAFFIRMED.   Now there was a famine in the land—
besides the earlier famine of Abraham's time—and Isaac went to Abimelech king of the Philistines in Gerar. The LORD appeared to Isaac and said,
"Do not go down to Egypt; live in the land where I tell you to live. Stay
in this land for a while, and I will be with you and will bless you. For to
you and your descendants I will give all these lands and will confirm the
oath I swore to your father Abraham. I will make your descendants as
numerous as the stars in the sky and will give them all these lands, and
through your offspring[g] all nations on earth will be blessed, because
Abraham obeyed me and kept my requirements, my commands, my
decrees and my laws."

Gen.
26:6-11
Gerar

ISAAC LIES ABOUT REBEKAH.   So Isaac stayed in Gerar.
    When the men of that place asked him about his wife, he said, "She is
my sister," because he was afraid to say, "She is my wife." He thought,
"The men of this place might kill me on account of Rebekah, because she
is beautiful."
    When Isaac had been there a long time, Abimelech king of the Phi-
listines looked down from a window and saw Isaac caressing his wife
Rebekah. So Abimelech summoned Isaac and said, "She is really your
wife! Why did you say, 'She is my sister'?"
    Isaac answered him, "Because I thought I might lose my life on account
of her."
    Then Abimelech said, "What is this you have done to us? One of the
men might well have slept with your wife, and you would have brought
guilt upon us."
    So Abimelech gave orders to all the people: "Anyone who molests this
man or his wife shall surely be put to death."

Gen.
26:12-14

GOD BLESSES ISAAC.   Isaac planted crops in that land and the same
year reaped a hundredfold, because the LORD blessed him. The man
became rich, and his wealth continued to grow until he became very
wealthy. He had so many flocks and herds and servants that the Philistines
envied him.

Gen.
26:15-22

QUARRELS OVER WELLS.   So all the wells that his father's servants had
dug in the time of his father Abraham, the Philistines stopped up, filling
them with earth.
    Then Abimelech said to Isaac, "Move away from us; you have become
too powerful for us."
    So Isaac moved away from there and encamped in the Valley of Gerar
and settled there. Isaac reopened the wells that had been dug in the time
of his father Abraham, which the Philistines had stopped up after
Abraham died, and he gave them the same names his father had given
them.
    Isaac's servants dug in the valley and discovered a well of fresh water
there. But the herdsmen of Gerar quarreled with Isaac's herdsmen and
said, "The water is ours!" So he named the well Esek,[h] because they
disputed with him. Then they dug another well, but they quarreled over
that one also; so he named it Sitnah.[i] He moved on from there and dug
another well, and no one quarreled over it. He named it Rehoboth,[j] saying, "Now the LORD has given us room and we will flourish in the land."

<hr>

[g]Or seed   [h]Esek means dispute.   [i]Sitnah means opposition.   [j]Rehoboth means room.

GOD REASSURES ISAAC. From there he went up to Beersheba. That night the LORD appeared to him and said, "I am the God of your father Abraham. Do not be afraid, for I am with you; I will bless you and will increase the number of your descendants for the sake of my servant Abraham."

    Isaac built an altar there and called on the name of the LORD. There he pitched his tent, and there his servants dug a well.

Gen. 26:23-25

ABIMELECH COVENANTS. Meanwhile, Abimelech had come to him from Gerar, with Ahuzzath his personal adviser and Phicol the commander of his forces. Isaac asked them, "Why have you come to me, since you were hostile to me and sent me away?"

    They answered, "We saw clearly that the LORD was with you; so we said, 'There ought to be a sworn agreement between us'—between us and you. Let us make a treaty with you that you will do us no harm, just as we did not molest you but always treated you well and sent you away in peace. And now you are blessed by the LORD."

    Isaac then made a feast for them, and they ate and drank. Early the next morning the men swore an oath to each other. Then Isaac sent them on their way, and they left him in peace.

    That day Isaac's servants came and told him about the well they had dug. They said, "We've found water!" He called it Shibah,*k* and to this day the name of the town has been Beersheba.*l*

Gen. 26:26-33

Trouble Between Jacob and Esau

*I*n several respects the differences and difficulties between Jacob and Esau are not unlike those between Cain and Abel centuries earlier. Like their predecessors, Jacob and Esau are of different occupations, temperament, and moral character. Esau, like Cain, appears to be the rebellious sort, as may be demonstrated by his marriages to two women from among the local heathen population. Yet Jacob himself is not without fault. Prompted by his doting mother's scheming, Jacob conspires with Rebekah to deceive Isaac, who in his old age wishes to bestow a special blessing upon his own favorite son, Esau. With the birthright already his, Jacob would have received the greater part of Isaac's inheritance in any event, but, despite this fact, he consents to perpetrate the fraud. A long period of exile in future years may well be the consequent penalty for this sin against his father. Rebekah's own involvement evidently stems from dissension with Esau's two wives, whose Canaanite background undoubtedly clashes with her own.

ESAU MARRIES HEATHEN WIVES. When Esau was forty years old, he married Judith daughter of Beeri the Hittite, and also Basemath daughter of Elon the Hittite. They were a source of grief to Isaac and Rebekah.

Gen. 26:34,35

ISAAC PREPARES BLESSING. When Isaac was old and his eyes were so weak that he could no longer see, he called for Esau his older son and said to him, "My son."

    "Here I am," he answered.

    Isaac said, "I am now an old man and don't know the day of my death.

Gen 27:1-4

---

*k*Shibah can mean *oath* or *seven*.   *l*Beersheba can mean *well of the oath* or *well of seven*.

Now then, get your weapons—your quiver and bow—and go out to the open country to hunt some wild game for me. Prepare me the kind of tasty food I like and bring it to me to eat, so that I may give you my blessing before I die."

Gen.
27:5-17

REBEKAH AND JACOB CONSPIRE.   Now Rebekah was listening as Isaac spoke to his son Esau. When Esau left for the open country to hunt game and bring it back, Rebekah said to her son Jacob, "Look, I overheard your father say to your brother Esau, 'Bring me some game and prepare me some tasty food to eat, so that I may give you my blessing in the presence of the LORD before I die.' Now, my son, listen carefully and do what I tell you: Go out to the flock and bring me two choice young goats, so I can prepare some tasty food for your father, just the way he likes it. Then take it to your father to eat, so that he may give you his blessing before he dies."

Jacob said to Rebekah his mother, "But my brother Esau is a hairy man, and I'm a man with smooth skin. What if my father touches me? I would appear to be tricking him and would bring down a curse on myself rather than a blessing."

His mother said to him, "My son, let the curse fall on me. Just do what I say; go and get them for me."

So he went and got them and brought them to his mother, and she prepared some tasty food, just the way his father liked it. Then Rebekah took the best clothes of Esau her older son, which she had in the house, and put them on her younger son Jacob. She also covered his hands and the smooth part of his neck with the goatskins. Then she handed to her son Jacob the tasty food and the bread she had made.

Gen.
27:18-25

JACOB DECEIVES ISAAC.   He went to his father and said, "My father."

"Yes, my son," he answered. "Who is it?"

Jacob said to his father, "I am Esau your firstborn. I have done as you told me. Please sit up and eat some of my game so that you may give me your blessing."

Isaac asked his son, "How did you find it so quickly, my son?"

"The LORD your God gave me success," he replied.

Then Isaac said to Jacob, "Come near so I can touch you, my son, to know whether you really are my son Esau or not."

Jacob went close to his father Isaac, who touched him and said, "The voice is the voice of Jacob, but the hands are the hands of Esau." He did not recognize him, for his hands were hairy like those of his brother Esau; so he blessed him. "Are you really my son Esau?" he asked.

"I am," he replied.

Then he said, "My son, bring me some of your game to eat, so that I may give you my blessing."

Jacob brought it to him and he ate; and he brought some wine and he drank.

Gen.
27:26-29

ISAAC BLESSES JACOB.   Then his father Isaac said to him, "Come here, my son, and kiss me."

So he went to him and kissed him. When Isaac caught the smell of his clothes, he blessed him and said,

> "Ah, the smell of my son
>   is like the smell of a field

that the LORD has blessed.
May God give you of heaven's dew
    and of earth's richness—
        an abundance of grain and new wine.
May nations serve you
    and peoples bow down to you.
Be lord over your brothers,
    and may the sons of your mother bow down to you.
May those who curse you be cursed
    and those who bless you be blessed."

ESAU LEARNS OF DECEPTION.   After Isaac finished blessing him and Jacob had scarcely left his father's presence, his brother Esau came in from hunting. He too prepared some tasty food and brought it to his father. Then he said to him, "My father, sit up and eat some of my game, so that you may give me your blessing."

Gen. 27:30-36a

His father Isaac asked him, "Who are you?"

"I am your son," he answered, "your firstborn, Esau."

Isaac trembled violently and said, "Who was it, then, that hunted game and brought it to me? I ate it just before you came and I blessed him—and indeed he will be blessed!"

When Esau heard his father's words, he burst out with a loud and bitter cry and said to his father, "Bless me—me too, my father!"

But he said, "Your brother came deceitfully and took your blessing."

Esau said, "Isn't he rightly named Jacob[m]? He has deceived me these two times: He took my birthright, and now he's taken my blessing!"

ESAU ANGERED.   Then he asked, "Haven't you reserved any blessing for me?"

Gen. 27:36b-41

Isaac answered Esau, "I have made him lord over you and have made all his relatives his servants, and I have sustained him with grain and new wine. So what can I possibly do for you, my son?"

Esau said to his father, "Do you have only one blessing, my father? Bless me too, my father!" Then Esau wept aloud.

His father Isaac answered him,

> "Your dwelling will be
>   away from the earth's richness,
>   away from the dew of heaven above.
> You will live by the sword
>   and you will serve your brother.
> But when you grow restless,
>   you will throw his yoke
>   from off your neck."

Esau held a grudge against Jacob because of the blessing his father had given him. He said to himself, "The days of mourning for my father are near; then I will kill my brother Jacob."

———◇———

[m]*Jacob* means *he grasps the heel* (figuratively, *he deceives*).

Jacob Leaves for Haran

*A*s a result of Esau's threat, Jacob follows his mother's suggestion, as well as patriarchal mandate, and leaves for Haran, the region from which Rebekah herself had come. Isaac seems to have reconciled himself to the fact that it is Jacob through whom God's promises to Abraham will be fulfilled, so he sends Jacob away with his blessing. To this Esau reacts with typical rebellion.

As he begins his journey, Jacob has a dream in which God reaffirms that it will indeed be Jacob through whose descendants the promises given to Abraham will be fulfilled. At the place where his dream occurs, Jacob makes a vow which at first appears to be a bargain with God, but which is actually a customary manner of expressing thanksgiving. The account begins when news of Esau's threat reaches Rebekah.

Gen.
27:42-45

REBEKAH PLANS JACOB'S EXILE.   When Rebekah was told what her older son Esau had said, she sent for her younger son Jacob and said to him, "Your brother Esau is consoling himself with the thought of killing you. Now then, my son, do what I say: Flee at once to my brother Laban in Haran. Stay with him for a while until your brother's fury subsides. When your brother is no longer angry with you and forgets what you did to him, I'll send word for you to come back from there. Why should I lose both of you in one day?"

Gen.
27:46-28:5

ISAAC BLESSES MISSION.   Then Rebekah said to Isaac, "I'm disgusted with living because of these Hittite women. If Jacob takes a wife from among the women of this land, from Hittite women like these, my life will not be worth living." So Isaac called for Jacob and blessed[n] him and commanded him: "Do not marry a Canaanite woman. Go at once to Paddan Aram,[o] to the house of your mother's father Bethuel. Take a wife for yourself there, from among the daughters of Laban, your mother's brother. May God Almighty[p] bless you and make you fruitful and increase your numbers until you become a community of peoples. May he give you and your descendants the blessing given to Abraham, so that you may take possession of the land where you now live as an alien, the land God gave to Abraham." Then Isaac sent Jacob on his way, and he went to Paddan Aram, to Laban son of Bethuel the Aramean, the brother of Rebekah, who was the mother of Jacob and Esau.

Gen.
28:6-9

ESAU TAKES WIFE FOR SPITE.   Now Esau learned that Isaac had blessed Jacob and had sent him to Paddan Aram to take a wife from there, and that when he blessed him he commanded him, "Do not marry a Canaanite woman," and that Jacob had obeyed his father and mother and had gone to Paddan Aram. Esau then realized how displeasing the Canaanite women were to his father Isaac; so he went to Ishmael and married Mahalath, the sister of Nebaioth and daughter of Ishmael son of Abraham, in addition to the wives he already had.

Gen.
28:10-17

JACOB HAS DREAM.   Jacob left Beersheba and set out for Haran. When he reached a certain place, he stopped for the night because the sun had set. Taking one of the stones there, he put it under his head and lay down

---

[n]Or *greeted*   [o]That is, Northwest Mesopotamia   [p]Hebrew *El-Shaddai*

to sleep. He had a dream in which he saw a stairway[q] resting on the earth, with its top reaching to heaven, and the angels of God were ascending and descending on it. There above it[r] stood the LORD, and he said: "I am the LORD, the God of your father Abraham and the God of Isaac. I will give you and your descendants the land on which you are lying. Your descendants will be like the dust of the earth, and you will spread out to the west and to the east, to the north and to the south. All peoples on earth will be blessed through you and your offspring. I am with you and will watch over you wherever you go, and I will bring you back to this land. I will not leave you until I have done what I have promised you."

When Jacob awoke from his sleep, he thought, "Surely the LORD is in this place, and I was not aware of it." He was afraid and said, "How awesome is this place! This is none other than the house of God; this is the gate of heaven."

JACOB ERECTS PILLAR.   Early the next morning Jacob took the stone he had placed under his head and set it up as a pillar and poured oil on top of it. He called that place Bethel,[s] though the city used to be called Luz.

Then Jacob made a vow, saying, "If God will be with me and will watch over me on this journey I am taking and will give me food to eat and clothes to wear so that I return safely to my father's house, then the LORD[t] will be my God and[u] this stone that I have set up as a pillar will be God's house, and of all that you give me I will give you a tenth."

*Gen.
28:18-22
Bethel*

Jacob Marries and Has Children

As he returns to his mother's country, Jacob meets his uncle Laban and agrees to work for Laban in exchange for his daughter Rachel. But Laban deceives Jacob, giving him his older daughter, Leah, instead of Rachel. Ultimately Jacob gets both Rachel and Leah, but Laban's deception must surely have reminded Jacob of his own deception which forced his flight to Haran in the first place.

As might be expected, rivalry emerges between the two sisters, and childbearing quickly becomes the focus of their rivalry. Jacob fathers 12 sons and a daughter, some by his two wives and some by their maids, Zilpah and Bilhah, who are given to Jacob as part of the contest to give Jacob children. The account begins as Jacob nears the land of his kinsmen.

JACOB MEETS MEN OF HARAN.   Then Jacob continued on his journey and came to the land of the eastern peoples. There he saw a well in the field, with three flocks of sheep lying near it because the flocks were watered from that well. The stone over the mouth of the well was large. When all the flocks were gathered there, the shepherds would roll the stone away from the well's mouth and water the sheep. Then they would return the stone to its place over the mouth of the well.

*Gen.
29:1-8
Paddan
Aram*

Jacob asked the shepherds, "My brothers, where are you from?"

"We're from Haran," they replied.

He said to them, "Do you know Laban, Nahor's grandson?"

"Yes, we know him," they answered.

[q]Or *ladder*   [r]Or *There beside him*   [s]*Bethel* means *house of God.*   [t]Or *Since God . . .
father's house, the* LORD   [u]Or *house, and the* LORD *will be my God,* [22]*then*

Then Jacob asked them, "Is he well?"

"Yes, he is," they said, "and here comes his daughter Rachel with the sheep."

"Look," he said, "the sun is still high; it is not time for the flocks to be gathered. Water the sheep and take them back to pasture."

"We can't," they replied, "until all the flocks are gathered and the stone has been rolled away from the mouth of the well. Then we will water the sheep."

Gen.
29:9-14

JACOB MEETS RACHEL.   While he was still talking with them, Rachel came with her father's sheep, for she was a shepherdess. When Jacob saw Rachel daughter of Laban, his mother's brother, and Laban's sheep, he went over and rolled the stone away from the mouth of the well and watered his uncle's sheep. Then Jacob kissed Rachel and began to weep aloud. He had told Rachel that he was a relative of her father and a son of Rebekah. So she ran and told her father.

As soon as Laban heard the news about Jacob, his sister's son, he hurried to meet him. He embraced him and kissed him and brought him to his home, and there Jacob told him all these things. Then Laban said to him, "You are my own flesh and blood."

After Jacob had stayed with him for a whole month,

Gen.
29:15-20

JACOB WORKS TO GET RACHEL.   Laban said to him, "Just because you are a relative of mine, should you work for me for nothing? Tell me what your wages should be."

Now Laban had two daughters; the name of the older was Leah, and the name of the younger was Rachel. Leah had weak^v eyes, but Rachel was lovely in form, and beautiful. Jacob was in love with Rachel and said, "I'll work for you seven years in return for your younger daughter Rachel."

Laban said, "It's better that I give her to you than to some other man. Stay here with me." So Jacob served seven years to get Rachel, but they seemed like only a few days to him because of his love for her.

Gen.
29:21-30

LABAN TRICKS JACOB.   Then Jacob said to Laban, "Give me my wife. My time is completed, and I want to lie with her."

So Laban brought together all the people of the place and gave a feast. But when evening came, he took his daughter Leah and gave her to Jacob, and Jacob lay with her. And Laban gave his servant girl Zilpah to his daughter as her maidservant.

When morning came, there was Leah! So Jacob said to Laban, "What is this you have done to me? I served you for Rachel, didn't I? Why have you deceived me?"

Laban replied, "It is not our custom here to give the younger daughter in marriage before the older one. Finish this daughter's bridal week; then we will give you the younger one also, in return for another seven years of work."

And Jacob did so. He finished the week with Leah, and then Laban gave him his daughter Rachel to be his wife. Laban gave his servant girl Bilhah to his daughter Rachel as her maidservant. Jacob lay with Rachel also, and he loved Rachel more than Leah. And he worked for Laban another seven years.

^{v}Or *delicate*

LEAH HAS FOUR SONS.   When the LORD saw that Leah was not loved, he opened her womb, but Rachel was barren. Leah became pregnant and gave birth to a son. She named him Reuben,[w] for she said, "It is because the LORD has seen my misery. Surely my husband will love me now."

Gen.
29:31-35

She conceived again, and when she gave birth to a son she said, "Because the LORD heard that I am not loved, he gave me this one too." So she named him Simeon.[x]

Again she conceived, and when she gave birth to a son she said, "Now at last my husband will become attached to me, because I have borne him three sons." So he was named Levi.[y]

She conceived again, and when she gave birth to a son she said, "This time I will praise the LORD." So she named him Judah.[z] Then she stopped having children.

BILHAH HAS TWO SONS.   When Rachel saw that she was not bearing Jacob any children, she became jealous of her sister. So she said to Jacob, "Give me children, or I'll die!"

Gen.
30:1-8

Jacob became angry with her and said, "Am I in the place of God, who has kept you from having children?"

Then she said, "Here is Bilhah, my maidservant. Sleep with her so that she can bear children for me and that through her I too can build a family."

So she gave him her servant Bilhah as a wife. Jacob slept with her, and she became pregnant and bore him a son. Then Rachel said, "God has vindicated me; he has listened to my plea and given me a son." Because of this she named him Dan.[a]

Rachel's servant Bilhah conceived again and bore Jacob a second son. Then Rachel said, "I have had a great struggle with my sister, and I have won." So she named him Naphtali.[b]

ZILPAH HAS TWO SONS.   When Leah saw that she had stopped having children, she took her maidservant Zilpah and gave her to Jacob as a wife. Leah's servant Zilpah bore Jacob a son. Then Leah said, "What good fortune!"[c] So she named him Gad.[d]

Gen.
30:9-13

Leah's servant Zilpah bore Jacob a second son. Then Leah said, "How happy I am! The women will call me happy." So she named him Asher.[e]

LEAH HAS TWO SONS, DAUGHTER.   During wheat harvest, Reuben went out into the fields and found some mandrake plants, which he brought to his mother Leah. Rachel said to Leah, "Please give me some of your son's mandrakes."

Gen.
30:14-21

But she said to her, "Wasn't it enough that you took away my husband? Will you take my son's mandrakes too?"

"Very well," Rachel said, "he can sleep with you tonight in return for your son's mandrakes."

So when Jacob came in from the fields that evening, Leah went out to meet him. "You must sleep with me," she said. "I have hired you with my son's mandrakes." So he slept with her that night.

God listened to Leah, and she became pregnant and bore Jacob a fifth

---

[w]*Reuben* sounds like the Hebrew for *he has seen my misery*; the name means *see, a son*.
[x]*Simeon* probably means *one who hears*.   [y]*Levi* sounds like and may be derived from the Hebrew for *attached*.   [z]*Judah* sounds like and may be derived from the Hebrew for *praise*.   [a]*Dan* here means *he has vindicated*.   [b]*Naphtali* means *my struggle*.   [c]Or "A troop is coming!"   [d]*Gad* can mean *good fortune* or *a troop*.   [e]*Asher* means *happy*.

son. Then Leah said, "God has rewarded me for giving my maidservant to my husband." So she named him Issachar.*f*

Leah conceived again and bore Jacob a sixth son. Then Leah said, "God has presented me with a precious gift. This time my husband will treat me with honor, because I have borne him six sons." So she named him Zebulun.*g*

Some time later she gave birth to a daughter and named her Dinah.

Gen.
30:22-24
(Ca. 1915
B.C.)

JOSEPH BORN TO RACHEL.   Then God remembered Rachel; he listened to her and opened her womb. She became pregnant and gave birth to a son and said, "God has taken away my disgrace." She named him Joseph,*h* and said, "May the LORD add to me another son."

Laban and Jacob Outsmart Each Other

Sometime after Joseph is born, Jacob decides to return to Canaan. When he agrees with Laban as to appropriate wages for his many years of service, Laban once again deceives Jacob. Not to be outdone, Jacob devises a scheme of his own to increase the flocks which are rightfully his by their agreement. Apparently Jacob holds an early belief that whatever objects sheep happen to view while mating will affect the genetic characteristics of their young.

Gen.
30:25-34

BARGAIN FOR SEVERANCE PAY.   After Rachel gave birth to Joseph, Jacob said to Laban, "Send me on my way so I can go back to my own homeland. Give me my wives and children, for whom I have served you, and I will be on my way. You know how much work I've done for you."

But Laban said to him, "If I have found favor in your eyes, please stay. I have learned by divination that*i* the LORD has blessed me because of you." He added, "Name your wages, and I will pay them."

Jacob said to him, "You know how I have worked for you and how your livestock has fared under my care. The little you had before I came has increased greatly, and the LORD has blessed you wherever I have been. But now, when may I do something for my own household?"

"What shall I give you?" he asked.

"Don't give me anything," Jacob replied. "But if you will do this one thing for me, I will go on tending your flocks and watching over them: Let me go through all your flocks today and remove from them every speckled or spotted sheep, every dark-colored lamb and every spotted or speckled goat. They will be my wages. And my honesty will testify for me in the future, whenever you check on the wages you have paid me. Any goat in my possession that is not speckled or spotted, or any lamb that is not dark-colored, will be considered stolen."

"Agreed," said Laban. "Let it be as you have said."

Gen.
30:35,36

LABAN DECEIVES JACOB.   That same day he removed all the male goats that were streaked or spotted, and all the speckled or spotted female goats (all that had white on them) and all the dark-colored lambs, and he placed them in the care of his sons. Then he put a three-day journey between himself and Jacob, while Jacob continued to tend the rest of Laban's flocks.

---

*f*Issachar sounds like the Hebrew for *reward*.   *g*Zebulun probably means *honor*.
*h*Joseph means *may he add*.   *i*Or possibly *have become rich and*

JACOB TRICKS LABAN. Jacob, however, took fresh-cut branches from poplar, almond and plane trees and made white stripes on them by peeling the bark and exposing the white inner wood of the branches. Then he placed the peeled branches in all the watering troughs, so that they would be directly in front of the flocks when they came to drink. When the flocks were in heat and came to drink, they mated in front of the branches. And they bore young that were streaked or speckled or spotted. Jacob set apart the young of the flock by themselves, but made the rest face the streaked and dark-colored animals that belonged to Laban. Thus he made separate flocks for himself and did not put them with Laban's animals. Whenever the stronger females were in heat, Jacob would place the branches in the troughs in front of the animals so they would mate near the branches, but if the animals were weak, he would not place them there. So the weak animals went to Laban and the strong ones to Jacob. In this way the man grew exceedingly prosperous and came to own large flocks, and maidservants and menservants, and camels and donkeys.

Gen. 30:37-43

Jacob Leaves Laban

*I*f there is one lapse in moral character which besets early man—including God's special people—it is dishonesty and trickery. Fearful that Laban might not let him leave, Jacob secretly steals away with his family and flocks. To make matters worse, Rachel takes some household gods belonging to her father and later covers up her theft by lying to him. After Jacob and Laban exchange hostile accusations, they resolve their differences by establishing a mutual treaty of peace. In all of the dealings between Jacob and Laban, and again in the reprehensible conduct of Rachel, there is a reminder that God can work his will even through men and women who share in the frailties of moral character.

JACOB PLANS TO LEAVE. Jacob heard that Laban's sons were saying, "Jacob has taken everything our father owned and has gained all this wealth from what belonged to our father." And Jacob noticed that Laban's attitude toward him was not what it had been.

Gen. 31:1-13

Then the LORD said to Jacob, "Go back to the land of your fathers and to your relatives, and I will be with you."

So Jacob sent word to Rachel and Leah to come out to the fields where his flocks were. He said to them, "I see that your father's attitude toward me is not what it was before, but the God of my father has been with me. You know that I've worked for your father with all my strength, yet your father has cheated me by changing my wages ten times. However, God has not allowed him to harm me. If he said, 'The speckled ones will be your wages,' then all the flocks gave birth to speckled young; and if he said, 'The streaked ones will be your wages,' then all the flocks bore streaked young. So God has taken away your father's livestock and has given them to me.

"In breeding season I once had a dream in which I looked up and saw that the male goats mating with the flock were streaked, speckled or spotted. The angel of God said to me in the dream, 'Jacob.' I answered, 'Here I am.' And he said, 'Look up and see that all the male goats mating with the flock are streaked, speckled or spotted, for I have seen all that

Laban has been doing to you. I am the God of Bethel, where you anointed a pillar and where you made a vow to me. Now leave this land at once and go back to your native land.' "

Gen.
31:14-16

RACHEL AND LEAH AGREE.   Then Rachel and Leah replied, "Do we still have any share in the inheritance of our father's estate? Does he not regard us as foreigners? Not only has he sold us, but he has used up what was paid for us. Surely all the wealth that God took away from our father belongs to us and our children. So do whatever God has told you."

Gen.
31:17-21

JACOB LEAVES SECRETLY.   Then Jacob put his children and his wives on camels, and he drove all his livestock ahead of him, along with all the goods he had accumulated in Paddan Aram,[j] to go to his father Isaac in the land of Canaan.

When Laban had gone to shear his sheep, Rachel stole her father's household gods. Moreover, Jacob deceived Laban the Aramean by not telling him he was running away. So he fled with all he had, and crossing the River,[k] he headed for the hill country of Gilead.

Gen.
31:22-24

LABAN PURSUES JACOB.   On the third day Laban was told that Jacob had fled. Taking his relatives with him, he pursued Jacob for seven days and caught up with him in the hill country of Gilead. Then God came to Laban the Aramean in a dream at night and said to him, "Be careful not to say anything to Jacob, either good or bad."

Gen.
31:25-29

LABAN DENOUNCES FLIGHT.   Jacob had pitched his tent in the hill country of Gilead when Laban overtook him, and Laban and his relatives camped there too. Then Laban said to Jacob, "What have you done? You've deceived me, and you've carried off my daughters like captives in war. Why did you run off secretly and deceive me? Why didn't you tell me, so I could send you away with joy and singing to the music of tambourines and harps? You didn't even let me kiss my grandchildren and my daughters good-by. You have done a foolish thing. I have the power to harm you; but last night the God of your father said to me, 'Be careful not to say anything to Jacob, either good or bad.'

Gen.
31:30-32

LABAN COMPLAINS OF THEFT.   Now you have gone off because you longed to return to your father's house. But why did you steal my gods?"

Jacob answered Laban, "I was afraid, because I thought you would take your daughters away from me by force. But if you find anyone who has your gods, he shall not live. In the presence of our relatives, see for yourself whether there is anything of yours here with me; and if so, take it." Now Jacob did not know that Rachel had stolen the gods.

Gen.
31:33-35

RACHEL HIDES STOLEN GODS.   So Laban went into Jacob's tent and into Leah's tent and into the tent of the two maidservants, but he found nothing. After he came out of Leah's tent, he entered Rachel's tent. Now Rachel had taken the household gods and put them inside her camel's saddle and was sitting on them. Laban searched through everything in the tent but found nothing.

Rachel said to her father, "Don't be angry, my lord, that I cannot stand up in your presence; I'm having my period." So he searched but could not find the household gods.

[j]That is, Northwest Mesopotamia   [k]That is, the Euphrates

JACOB REBUFFS LABAN.   Jacob was angry and took Laban to task.   **Gen.**
"What is my crime?" he asked Laban. "What sin have I committed that   **31:36-42**
you hunt me down? Now that you have searched through all my goods,
what have you found that belongs to your household? Put it here in front
of your relatives and mine, and let them judge between the two of us.

"I have been with you for twenty years now. Your sheep and goats have
not miscarried, nor have I eaten rams from your flocks. I did not bring you
animals torn by wild beasts; I bore the loss myself. And you demanded
payment from me for whatever was stolen by day or night. This was my
situation: The heat consumed me in the daytime and the cold at night, and
sleep fled from my eyes. It was like this for the twenty years I was in your
household. I worked for you fourteen years for your two daughters and
six years for your flocks, and you changed my wages ten times. If the God
of my father, the God of Abraham and the Fear of Isaac, had not been with
me, you would surely have sent me away empty-handed. But God has
seen my hardship and the toil of my hands, and last night he rebuked
you."

LABAN SUGGESTS COVENANT.   Laban answered Jacob, "The women   **Gen.**
are my daughters, the children are my children, and the flocks are my   **31:43,44**
flocks. All you see is mine. Yet what can I do today about these daughters
of mine, or about the children they have borne? Come now, let's make a
covenant, you and I, and let it serve as a witness between us."

JACOB SETS UP PILLAR.   So Jacob took a stone and set it up as a pillar.   **Gen.**
He said to his relatives, "Gather some stones." So they took stones and   **31:45-50**
piled them in a heap, and they ate there by the heap. Laban called it Jegar
Sahadutha,*l* and Jacob called it Galeed.*m*

Laban said, "This heap is a witness between you and me today." That is
why it was called Galeed. It was also called Mizpah,*n* because he said,
"May the LORD keep watch between you and me when we are away from
each other. If you mistreat my daughters or if you take any wives besides
my daughters, even though no one is with us, remember that God is a witness between you and me."

LABAN MAKES OATH.   Laban also said to Jacob, "Here is this heap, and   **Gen.**
here is this pillar I have set up between you and me. This heap is a witness,   **31:51-55**
and this pillar is a witness, that I will not go past this heap to your side to
harm you and that you will not go past this heap and pillar to my side to
harm me. May the God of Abraham and the God of Nahor, the God of
their father, judge between us."

So Jacob took an oath in the name of the Fear of his father Isaac. He
offered a sacrifice there in the hill country and invited his relatives to a
meal. After they had eaten, they spent the night there.

Early the next morning Laban kissed his grandchildren and his daughters and blessed them. Then he left and returned home.

---

*l*The Aramaic *Jegar Sahadutha* means *witness heap.*   *m*The Hebrew *Galeed* means *witness
heap.*   *n*Mizpah means *watchtower.*

Jacob Returns to Canaan

*R*ealizing that he is going to pass through territory occupied by Esau, and apprehensive about the threat under which he has left Canaan, Jacob makes careful preparation in anticipation of encountering Esau. While he waits in uncertainty, Jacob is found rather mysteriously wrestling with God. In some way God presents himself to Jacob as a human being. Why Jacob is wrestling is not given in this account, but his physical struggle is not unlike the spiritual struggle of a person facing potential conflict or perhaps death. In any event, there are two rather important consequences: one relates to a dietary law which Jacob's descendants will observe, and the other suggests that Jacob's name will be changed.

As Jacob leaves on this journey from Gilead to Canaan, he is met by messengers from God who give renewed assurance that God will be with him on his journey.

Gen.
32:1,2
(Ca. 1905
B.C.)

ANGELS GIVE REASSURANCE.   Jacob also went on his way, and the angels of God met him. When Jacob saw them, he said, "This is the camp of God!" So he named that place Mahanaim.*o*

Gen.
32:3-5

MESSENGERS SENT TO ESAU.   Jacob sent messengers ahead of him to his brother Esau in the land of Seir, the country of Edom. He instructed them: "This is what you are to say to my master Esau: 'Your servant Jacob says, I have been staying with Laban and have remained there till now. I have cattle and donkeys, sheep and goats, menservants and maidservants. Now I am sending this message to my lord, that I may find favor in your eyes.' "

Gen.
32:6-8

JACOB FEARS MEETING ESAU.   When the messengers returned to Jacob, they said, "We went to your brother Esau, and now he is coming to meet you, and four hundred men are with him."

In great fear and distress Jacob divided the people who were with him into two groups,*p* and the flocks and herds and camels as well. He thought, "If Esau comes and attacks one group,*q* the group*q* that is left may escape."

Gen.
32:9-12

JACOB PRAYS TO GOD.   Then Jacob prayed, "O God of my father Abraham, God of my father Isaac, O LORD, who said to me, 'Go back to your country and your relatives, and I will make you prosper,' I am unworthy of all the kindness and faithfulness you have shown your servant. I had only my staff when I crossed this Jordan, but now I have become two groups. Save me, I pray, from the hand of my brother Esau, for I am afraid he will come and attack me, and also the mothers with their children. But you have said, 'I will surely make you prosper and will make your descendants like the sand of the sea, which cannot be counted.' "

Gen.
32:13-21

PRESENTS ARE SENT AHEAD.   He spent the night there, and from what he had with him he selected a gift for his brother Esau: two hundred female goats and twenty male goats, two hundred ewes and twenty rams, thirty female camels with their young, forty cows and ten bulls, and twenty female donkeys and ten male donkeys. He put them in the care

oMahanaim means *two camps.*   *pOr camps*   *qOr camp*

of his servants, each herd by itself, and said to his servants, "Go ahead of me, and keep some space between the herds."

He instructed the one in the lead: "When my brother Esau meets you and asks, 'To whom do you belong, and where are you going, and who owns all these animals in front of you?' then you are to say, 'They belong to your servant Jacob. They are a gift sent to my lord Esau, and he is coming behind us.' "

He also instructed the second, the third and all the others who followed the herds: "You are to say the same thing to Esau when you meet him. And be sure to say, 'Your servant Jacob is coming behind us.' " For he thought, "I will pacify him with these gifts I am sending on ahead; later, when I see him, perhaps he will receive me." So Jacob's gifts went on ahead of him, but he himself spent the night in the camp.

PARTY CROSSES JABBOK.   That night Jacob got up and took his two wives, his two maidservants and his eleven sons and crossed the ford of the Jabbok. After he had sent them across the stream, he sent over all his possessions.

Gen.
32:22,23

JACOB WRESTLES WITH GOD.   So Jacob was left alone, and a man wrestled with him till daybreak. When the man saw that he could not overpower him, he touched the socket of Jacob's hip so that his hip was wrenched as he wrestled with the man. Then the man said, "Let me go, for it is daybreak."

Gen.
32:24-32
At Jabbok

But Jacob replied, "I will not let you go unless you bless me."

The man asked him, "What is your name?"

"Jacob," he answered.

Then the man said, "Your name will no longer be Jacob, but Israel,ʳ because you have struggled with God and with men and have overcome."

Jacob said, "Please tell me your name."

But he replied, "Why do you ask my name?" Then he blessed him there.

So Jacob called the place Peniel,ˢ saying, "It is because I saw God face to face, and yet my life was spared."

The sun rose above him as he passed Peniel,ᵗ and he was limping because of his hip. Therefore to this day the Israelites do not eat the tendon attached to the socket of the hip, because the socket of Jacob's hip was touched near the tendon.

FORWARD TO MEET ESAU.   Jacob looked up and there was Esau, coming with his four hundred men; so he divided the children among Leah, Rachel and the two maidservants. He put the maidservants and their children in front, Leah and her children next, and Rachel and Joseph in the rear. He himself went on ahead and bowed down to the ground seven times as he approached his brother.

Gen.
33:1-3

ESAU ACCEPTS JACOB.   But Esau ran to meet Jacob and embraced him; he threw his arms around his neck and kissed him. And they wept. Then Esau looked up and saw the women and children. "Who are these with you?" he asked.

Gen.
33:4-11

Jacob answered, "They are the children God has graciously given your servant."

Then the maidservants and their children approached and bowed

---

ʳIsrael means *he struggles with God.*   ˢPeniel means *face of God.*   ᵗHebrew *Penuel,* a variant of *Peniel*

down. Next, Leah and her children came and bowed down. Last of all came Joseph and Rachel, and they too bowed down.

Esau asked, "What do you mean by all these droves I met?"

"To find favor in your eyes, my lord," he said.

But Esau said, "I already have plenty, my brother. Keep what you have for yourself."

"No, please!" said Jacob. "If I have found favor in your eyes, accept this gift from me. For to see your face is like seeing the face of God, now that you have received me favorably. Please accept the present that was brought to you, for God has been gracious to me and I have all I need." And because Jacob insisted, Esau accepted it.

Gen.
33:12-17

BROTHERS SEPARATE PEACEFULLY.　Then Esau said, "Let us be on our way; I'll accompany you."

But Jacob said to him, "My lord knows that the children are tender and that I must care for the ewes and cows that are nursing their young. If they are driven hard just one day, all the animals will die. So let my lord go on ahead of his servant, while I move along slowly at the pace of the droves before me and that of the children, until I come to my lord in Seir."

Esau said, "Then let me leave some of my men with you."

"But why do that?" Jacob asked. "Just let me find favor in the eyes of my lord."

So that day Esau started on his way back to Seir. Jacob, however, went to Succoth, where he built a place for himself and made shelters for his livestock. That is why the place is called Succoth.[u]

Gen.
33:18-20
Shechem

JACOB SETTLES IN SHECHEM.　After Jacob came from Paddan Aram,[v] he arrived safely at the[w] city of Shechem in Canaan and camped within sight of the city. For a hundred pieces of silver,[x] he bought from the sons of Hamor, the father of Shechem, the plot of ground where he pitched his tent. There he set up an altar and called it El Elohe Israel.[y]

Dinah and the Men of Shechem

As Jacob and his family come again into Canaan, they cross the Jordan River and settle at a place somewhere near Mount Gerizim, north of Jerusalem. Jacob's daughter, Dinah, becomes a central character in a story of violence turned to love, followed by treachery and revenge. The other main characters are Shechem, son of the local prince; Hamor, his father; and Simeon and Levi, two of Dinah's brothers.

Gen.
34:1-4
Shechem

SHECHEM RAPES DINAH.　Now Dinah, the daughter Leah had borne to Jacob, went out to visit the women of the land. When Shechem son of Hamor the Hivite, the ruler of that area, saw her, he took her and violated her. His heart was drawn to Dinah daughter of Jacob, and he loved the girl and spoke tenderly to her. And Shechem said to his father Hamor, "Get me this girl as my wife."

---

[u]*Succoth* means *shelters*.　[v]That is, Northwest Mesopotamia　[w]Or *arrived at Shalem, a*
[x]Hebrew *hundred kesitahs*; a kesitah was a unit of money of unknown weight and value.
[y]*El Elohe Israel* can mean *God, the God of Israel* or *mighty is the God of Israel*.

JACOB AND SONS FIND OUT.   When Jacob heard that his daughter Dinah had been defiled, his sons were in the fields with his livestock; so he kept quiet about it until they came home.

Gen. 34:5-7

Then Shechem's father Hamor went out to talk with Jacob. Now Jacob's sons had come in from the fields as soon as they heard what had happened. They were filled with grief and fury, because Shechem had done a disgraceful thing in[z] Israel by lying with Jacob's daughter—a thing that should not be done.

MARRIAGE IS SOUGHT.   But Hamor said to them, "My son Shechem has his heart set on your daughter. Please give her to him as his wife. Intermarry with us; give us your daughters and take our daughters for yourselves. You can settle among us; the land is open to you. Live in it, trade[a] in it, and acquire property in it."

Gen. 34:8-12

Then Shechem said to Dinah's father and brothers, "Let me find favor in your eyes, and I will give you whatever you ask. Make the price for the bride and the gift I am to bring as great as you like, and I'll pay whatever you ask me. Only give me the girl as my wife."

CIRCUMCISION AS CONDITION.   Because their sister Dinah had been defiled, Jacob's sons replied deceitfully as they spoke to Shechem and his father Hamor. They said to them, "We can't do such a thing; we can't give our sister to a man who is not circumcised. That would be a disgrace to us. We will give our consent to you on one condition only: that you become like us by circumcising all your males. Then we will give you our daughters and take your daughters for ourselves. We'll settle among you and become one people with you. But if you will not agree to be circumcised, we'll take our sister[b] and go."

Gen. 34:13-17

MEN OF SHECHEM CIRCUMCISED.   Their proposal seemed good to Hamor and his son Shechem. The young man, who was the most honored of all his father's household, lost no time in doing what they said, because he was delighted with Jacob's daughter. So Hamor and his son Shechem went to the gate of their city to speak to their fellow townsmen. "These men are friendly toward us," they said. "Let them live in our land and trade in it; the land has plenty of room for them. We can marry their daughters and they can marry ours. But the men will consent to live with us as one people only on the condition that our males be circumcised, as they themselves are. Won't their livestock, their property and all their other animals become ours? So let us give our consent to them, and they will settle among us."

Gen. 34:18-24

All the men who went out of the city gate agreed with Hamor and his son Shechem, and every male in the city was circumcised.

BROTHERS TAKE REVENGE.   Three days later, while all of them were still in pain, two of Jacob's sons, Simeon and Levi, Dinah's brothers, took their swords and attacked the unsuspecting city, killing every male. They put Hamor and his son Shechem to the sword and took Dinah from Shechem's house and left. The sons of Jacob came upon the dead bodies and looted the city where[c] their sister had been defiled. They seized their flocks and herds and donkeys and everything else of theirs in the city and

Gen. 34:25-31

---

[z]Or *against*   [a]Or *move about freely*; also in verse 21   [b]Hebrew *daughter*   [c]Or *because*

out in the fields. They carried off all their wealth and all their women and children, taking as plunder everything in the houses.

Then Jacob said to Simeon and Levi, "You have brought trouble on me by making me a stench to the Canaanites and Perizzites, the people living in this land. We are few in number, and if they join forces against me and attack me, I and my household will be destroyed."

But they replied, "Should he have treated our sister like a prostitute?"

Jacob's Journey Continues

*J*acob's sons may have saved some sense of honor for the family, but Jacob knows that the slaughter of Shechem's men has made them enemies in the region. At God's direction Jacob moves southward to Bethel, where Jacob had made a covenant with God on his way to exile in Haran. Perhaps this is more than a simple call to changed circumstances; perhaps God wants also to draw Jacob's sons away from worshiping the false gods of the area. And just as God had done with Jacob's grandfather Abraham, God gives Jacob a new name—Israel. It is a name by which an entire nation will be known, and it bears great significance even to the present time. As Jacob is moving still further south, Rachel bears her second son, but dies in giving him life. Sometime later, Jacob also buries his father, Isaac, in Hebron.

Gen. 35:1   JACOB DIRECTED TO BETHEL.   Then God said to Jacob, "Go up to Bethel and settle there, and build an altar there to God, who appeared to you when you were fleeing from your brother Esau."

Gen. 35:2-4   FOREIGN GODS TAKEN.   So Jacob said to his household and to all who were with him, "Get rid of the foreign gods you have with you, and purify yourselves and change your clothes. Then come, let us go up to Bethel, where I will build an altar to God, who answered me in the day of my distress and who has been with me wherever I have gone." So they gave Jacob all the foreign gods they had and the rings in their ears, and Jacob buried them under the oak at Shechem.

Gen. 35:5-8 Bethel   SAFE ARRIVAL IN BETHEL.   Then they set out, and the terror of God fell upon the towns all around them so that no one pursued them.

Jacob and all the people with him came to Luz (that is, Bethel) in the land of Canaan. There he built an altar, and he called the place El Bethel,[d] because it was there that God revealed himself to him when he was fleeing from his brother.

Now Deborah, Rebekah's nurse, died and was buried under the oak below Bethel. So it was named Allon Bacuth.[e]

Gen. 35:9,10   JACOB RENAMED ISRAEL.   After Jacob returned from Paddan Aram,[f] God appeared to him again and blessed him. God said to him, "Your name is Jacob,[g] but you will no longer be called Jacob; your name will be Israel.[h]" So he named him Israel.

[d]*El Bethel* means *God of Bethel.*   [e]*Allon Bacuth* means *oak of weeping.*   [f]That is, Northwest Mesopotamia   [g]*Jacob* means *he grasps the heel* (figuratively, *he deceives*). [h]*Israel* means *he struggles with God.*

DRINK OFFERING.   And God said to him, "I am God Almighty[i]; be fruitful and increase in number. A nation and a community of nations will
come from you, and kings will come from your body. The land I gave to
Abraham and Isaac I also give to you, and I will give this land to your
descendants after you." Then God went up from him at the place where
he had talked with him.

Gen.
35:11-15

Jacob set up a stone pillar at the place where God had talked with him,
and he poured out a drink offering on it; he also poured oil on it. Jacob
called the place where God had talked with him Bethel. [j]

BENJAMIN BORN TO RACHEL.   Then they moved on from Bethel.
While they were still some distance from Ephrath, Rachel began to give
birth and had great difficulty. And as she was having great difficulty in
childbirth, the midwife said to her, "Don't be afraid, for you have another
son." As she breathed her last—for she was dying—she named her son
Ben-Oni.[k] But his father named him Benjamin.[l]

Gen.
35:16-18
Near
Bethlehem

RECOUNTING THE TWELVE SONS.   Jacob had twelve sons:
    The sons of Leah:
        Reuben the firstborn of Jacob,
        Simeon, Levi, Judah, Issachar and Zebulun.
    The sons of Rachel:
        Joseph and Benjamin.
    The sons of Rachel's maidservant Bilhah:
        Dan and Naphtali.
    The sons of Leah's maidservant Zilpah:
        Gad and Asher.
    These were the sons of Jacob, who were born to him in Paddan Aram.

Gen.
35:22b-26

RACHEL DIES AND IS BURIED.   So Rachel died and was buried on the
way to Ephrath (that is, Bethlehem). Over her tomb Jacob set up a pillar,
and to this day that pillar marks Rachel's tomb.

Gen.
35:19-21

Israel moved on again and pitched his tent beyond Migdal Eder.

REUBEN SINS WITH BILHAH.   While Israel was living in that region,
Reuben went in and slept with his father's concubine Bilhah, and Israel
heard of it.

Gen.
35:22a

ISAAC DIES AND IS BURIED.   Jacob came home to his father Isaac in
Mamre, near Kiriath Arba (that is, Hebron), where Abraham and Isaac had
stayed. Isaac lived a hundred and eighty years. Then he breathed his last
and died and was gathered to his people, old and full of years. And his
sons Esau and Jacob buried him.

Gen.
35:27-29
(Ca. 1886
B.C.)

Record of the Edomites

*B*efore continuing with the history of the people descending through
Jacob, the Genesis record pauses to give final mention to Esau
(Edom) and his descendants. The Edomites, as they will soon be
called, will live in the hill country of Seir, which lies southeast of the Dead
Sea. They will become constant enemies of Jacob's descendants, the Israel-
ites, and their opposition to God's chosen people will be so bitter over

[i]Hebrew *El-Shaddai*   [l]*Bethel* means *house of God.*   [k]*Ben-Oni* means *son of my trouble.*
[l]*Benjamin* means *son of my right hand.*

the years that Edom will become a symbol of unbelief and hostility to God. In the last days they will be singled out as a special object of God's punishment.

This nation will spring from Esau and his three wives, whose names have already been cited in the Genesis record. In this account, additional names of two of his three wives are given: Adah (Mahalath), Oholibamah (Judith), and Basemath (as earlier given). The sheer length of this listing of Esau's descendants attests to how numerous and powerful the Edomites will become.

Gen.
36:1-5

SONS OF ESAU.   This is the account of Esau (that is, Edom).

Esau took his wives from the women of Canaan: Adah daughter of Elon the Hittite, and Oholibamah daughter of Anah and granddaughter of Zibeon the Hivite—also Basemath daughter of Ishmael and sister of Nebaioth.

Adah bore Eliphaz to Esau, Basemath bore Reuel, and Oholibamah bore Jeush, Jalam and Korah. These were the sons of Esau, who were born to him in Canaan.

Gen.
36:6-8

EDOMITES INHABIT SEIR.   Esau took his wives and sons and daughters and all the members of his household, as well as his livestock and all his other animals and all the goods he had acquired in Canaan, and moved to a land some distance from his brother Jacob. Their possessions were too great for them to remain together; the land where they were staying could not support them both because of their livestock. So Esau (that is, Edom) settled in the hill country of Seir.

Gen.
36:9-14

ESAU'S GRANDSONS.   This is the account of Esau the father of the Edomites in the hill country of Seir.

These are the names of Esau's sons:
  Eliphaz, the son of Esau's wife Adah, and Reuel, the son of Esau's wife Basemath.
The sons of Eliphaz:
  Teman, Omar, Zepho, Gatam and Kenaz.
  Esau's son Eliphaz also had a concubine named Timna, who bore him Amalek. These were grandsons of Esau's wife Adah.
The sons of Reuel:
  Nahath, Zerah, Shammah and Mizzah. These were grandsons of Esau's wife Basemath.
The sons of Esau's wife Oholibamah daughter of Anah and granddaughter of Zibeon, whom she bore to Esau:
  Jeush, Jalam and Korah.

Gen.
36:15-19

THE CHIEFS OF EDOM.   These were the chiefs among Esau's descendants:
The sons of Eliphaz the firstborn of Esau:
  Chiefs Teman, Omar, Zepho, Kenaz, Korah,[m] Gatam and Amalek. These were the chiefs descended from Eliphaz in Edom; they were grandsons of Adah.

[m]Masoretic Text; Samaritan Pentateuch (see also Gen. 36:11 and 1 Chron. 1:36) does not have *Korah*.

The sons of Esau's son Reuel:
>Chiefs Nahath, Zerah, Shammah and Mizzah. These were the chiefs
>descended from Reuel in Edom; they were grandsons of Esau's
>wife Basemath.

The sons of Esau's wife Oholibamah:
>Chiefs Jeush, Jalam and Korah. These were the chiefs descended
>from Esau's wife Oholibamah daughter of Anah.

These were the sons of Esau (that is, Edom), and these were their chiefs.

PREDECESSORS IN SEIR. These were the sons of Seir the Horite, who were living in the region: Gen.
36:20-30
>Lotan, Shobal, Zibeon, Anah, Dishon, Ezer and Dishan. These sons
>of Seir in Edom were Horite chiefs.

The sons of Lotan:
>Hori and Homam.[n] Timna was Lotan's sister.

The sons of Shobal:
>Alvan, Manahath, Ebal, Shepho and Onam.

The sons of Zibeon:
>Aiah and Anah. This is the Anah who discovered the hot springs[o]
>in the desert while he was grazing the donkeys of his father
>Zibeon.

The children of Anah:
>Dishon and Oholibamah daughter of Anah.

The sons of Dishon[p]:
>Hemdan, Eshban, Ithran and Keran.

The sons of Ezer:
>Bilhan, Zaavan and Akan.

The sons of Dishan:
>Uz and Aran.

These were the Horite chiefs:
>Lotan, Shobal, Zibeon, Anah, Dishon, Ezer and Dishan. These were
>the Horite chiefs, according to their divisions, in the land of Seir.

KINGS IN SEIR.   These were the kings who reigned in Edom before any Israelite king reigned[q]:   Gen.
36:31-39
>Bela son of Beor became king of Edom. His city was named
>Dinhabah.

>When Bela died, Jobab son of Zerah from Bozrah succeeded him as
>king.

>When Jobab died, Husham from the land of the Temanites succeeded
>him as king.

>When Husham died, Hadad son of Bedad, who defeated Midian in
>the country of Moab, succeeded him as king. His city was named
>Avith.

>When Hadad died, Samlah from Masrekah succeeded him as king.

>When Samlah died, Shaul from Rehoboth on the river[r] succeeded him
>as king.

>When Shaul died, Baal-Hanan son of Acbor succeeded him as king.

---

[n]Hebrew *Hemam*, a variant of *Homam* (see 1 Chron. 1:39)   [o]Vulgate; Syriac *discovered water*; the meaning of the Hebrew for this word is uncertain.   [p]Hebrew *Dishan*, a variant of *Dishon*   [q]Or *before an Israelite king reigned over them*   [r]Possibly the Euphrates

> When Baal-Hanan son of Acbor died, Hadad[s] succeeded him as king. His city was named Pau, and his wife's name was Mehetabel daughter of Matred, the daughter of Me-Zahab.

Gen. 36:40-43   CHIEFS BY DWELLING PLACES.   These were the chiefs descended from Esau, by name, according to their clans and regions:

> Timna, Alvah, Jetheth, Oholibamah, Elah, Pinon, Kenaz, Teman, Mibzar, Magdiel and Iram. These were the chiefs of Edom, according to their settlements in the land they occupied.

This was Esau the father of the Edomites.

Joseph's Early Years

ollowing this basically genealogical account of Esau's family, the Genesis record focuses with greater detail upon Jacob and his descendants, for it is through the descendants of Jacob (now called Israel) that the promised blessings are to come. Taking a leading role in the continuing saga is Israel's son Joseph. Israel's special fondness for Joseph, and perhaps Joseph's own attitude, lead to envy and hatred by Joseph's brothers. Their behavior toward Joseph, and toward their own father, is hardly worthy of the important positions they will later occupy as the heads of the tribes which together form the nation of God's people.

Gen. 37:1,2a Canaan   HISTORY OF JACOB'S FAMILY.   Jacob lived in the land where his father had stayed, the land of Canaan.

This is the account of Jacob.

Gen. 37:2b   JOSEPH TELLS ON BROTHERS.   Joseph, a young man of seventeen, was tending the flocks with his brothers, the sons of Bilhah and the sons of Zilpah, his father's wives, and he brought their father a bad report about them.

Gen. 37:3,4   BROTHERS HATE JOSEPH.   Now Israel loved Joseph more than any of his other sons, because he had been born to him in his old age; and he made a richly ornamented[t] robe for him. When his brothers saw that their father loved him more than any of them, they hated him and could not speak a kind word to him.

Gen. 37:5-8   JOSEPH DREAMS OF SHEAVES.   Joseph had a dream, and when he told it to his brothers, they hated him all the more. He said to them, "Listen to this dream I had: We were binding sheaves of grain out in the field when suddenly my sheaf rose and stood upright, while your sheaves gathered around mine and bowed down to it."

His brothers said to him, "Do you intend to reign over us? Will you actually rule us?" And they hated him all the more because of his dream and what he had said.

Gen. 37:9-11   JOSEPH DREAMS OF STARS.   Then he had another dream, and he told it to his brothers. "Listen," he said, "I had another dream, and this time the sun and moon and eleven stars were bowing down to me."

[s]Many manuscripts of the Masoretic Text, Samaritan Pentateuch and Syriac (see also 1 Chron. 1:50); most manuscripts of the Masoretic Text *Hadar*   [t]The meaning of the Hebrew for *richly ornamented* is uncertain.

When he told his father as well as his brothers, his father rebuked him and said, "What is this dream you had? Will your mother and I and your brothers actually come and bow down to the ground before you?" His brothers were jealous of him, but his father kept the matter in mind.

JOSEPH SENT TO BROTHERS.   Now his brothers had gone to graze their father's flocks near Shechem, and Israel said to Joseph, "As you know, your brothers are grazing the flocks near Shechem. Come, I am going to send you to them."

Gen.
37:12-17

"Very well," he replied.

So he said to him, "Go and see if all is well with your brothers and with the flocks, and bring word back to me." Then he sent him off from the Valley of Hebron.

When Joseph arrived at Shechem, a man found him wandering around in the fields and asked him, "What are you looking for?"

He replied, "I'm looking for my brothers. Can you tell me where they are grazing their flocks?"

"They have moved on from here," the man answered. "I heard them say, 'Let's go to Dothan.' "

So Joseph went after his brothers and found them near Dothan.

BROTHERS PUT JOSEPH INTO PIT.   But they saw him in the distance, and before he reached them, they plotted to kill him.

Gen.
37:18-24
Dothan

"Here comes that dreamer!" they said to each other. "Come now, let's kill him and throw him into one of these cisterns and say that a ferocious animal devoured him. Then we'll see what comes of his dreams."

When Reuben heard this, he tried to rescue him from their hands. "Let's not take his life," he said. "Don't shed any blood. Throw him into this cistern here in the desert, but don't lay a hand on him." Reuben said this to rescue him from them and take him back to his father.

So when Joseph came to his brothers, they stripped him of his robe—the richly ornamented robe he was wearing—and they took him and threw him into the cistern. Now the cistern was empty; there was no water in it.

JOSEPH SOLD TO TRADERS.   As they sat down to eat their meal, they looked up and saw a caravan of Ishmaelites coming from Gilead. Their camels were loaded with spices, balm and myrrh, and they were on their way to take them down to Egypt.

Gen.
37:25-28

Judah said to his brothers, "What will we gain if we kill our brother and cover up his blood? Come, let's sell him to the Ishmaelites and not lay our hands on him; after all, he is our brother, our own flesh and blood." His brothers agreed.

So when the Midianite merchants came by, his brothers pulled Joseph up out of the cistern and sold him for twenty shekels[u] of silver to the Ishmaelites, who took him to Egypt.

REUBEN UPSET AT LOSS.   When Reuben returned to the cistern and saw that Joseph was not there, he tore his clothes. He went back to his brothers and said, "The boy isn't there! Where can I turn now?"

Gen.
37:29,30

ISRAEL MOURNS SUPPOSED DEATH.   Then they got Joseph's robe, slaughtered a goat and dipped the robe in the blood. They took the

Gen.
37:31-35

[u]That is, about 8 ounces (about 0.2 kilogram)

ornamented robe back to their father and said, "We found this. Examine it to see whether it is your son's robe."

He recognized it and said, "It is my son's robe! Some ferocious animal has devoured him. Joseph has surely been torn to pieces."

Then Jacob tore his clothes, put on sackcloth and mourned for his son many days. All his sons and daughters came to comfort him, but he refused to be comforted. "No," he said, "in mourning will I go down to the grave[v] to my son." So his father wept for him.

Gen. 37:36 **JOSEPH SOLD TO POTIPHAR.**   Meanwhile, the Midianites[w] sold Joseph
Egypt   in Egypt to Potiphar, one of Pharaoh's officials, the captain of the guard.

Judah and Tamar

As Joseph becomes a slave in an Egyptian household, a most fascinating story is unfolding back in Canaan involving Judah, one of Israel's sons by Leah. It concerns the ancient custom of estates—quite foreign to modern thinking—in which the brother of a deceased man having no children marries the brother's wife so that the brother's lineage, and property as well, may continue through a proper line of succession. Disgrace comes when Onan, one of Judah's sons, goes through the sexual act with his brother's wife, Tamar, but purposely prevents any offspring from being born. There follows a rather curious story of Tamar, who resolves to bear a child by Judah himself.

Gen.   **JUDAH'S MARRIAGE.**   At that time, Judah left his brothers and went
38:1-5   down to stay with a man of Adullam named Hirah. There Judah met the
Canaan   daughter of a Canaanite man named Shua. He married her and lay with
            her; she became pregnant and gave birth to a son, who was named Er. She
            conceived again and gave birth to a son and named him Onan. She gave
            birth to still another son and named him Shelah. It was at Kezib that she
            gave birth to him.

Gen.   **ONAN BREAKS LEVIRATE LAW.**   Judah got a wife for Er, his firstborn,
38:6-10   and her name was Tamar. But Er, Judah's firstborn, was wicked in the
            LORD's sight; so the LORD put him to death.

Then Judah said to Onan, "Lie with your brother's wife and fulfill your duty to her as a brother-in-law to produce offspring for your brother." But Onan knew that the offspring would not be his; so whenever he lay with his brother's wife, he spilled his semen on the ground to keep from producing offspring for his brother. What he did was wicked in the LORD's sight; so he put him to death also.

Gen. 38:11 **TAMAR PROMISED A HUSBAND.**   Judah then said to his daughter-in-
            law Tamar, "Live as a widow in your father's house until my son Shelah
            grows up." For he thought, "He may die too, just like his brothers." So
            Tamar went to live in her father's house.

Gen.   **TAMAR DECEIVES JUDAH.**   After a long time Judah's wife, the daugh-
38:12-19   ter of Shua, died. When Judah had recovered from his grief, he went up to

[v]Hebrew *Sheol*   [w]Samaritan Pentateuch, Septuagint, Vulgate and Syriac (see also verse 28); Masoretic Text *Medanites*

Timnah, to the men who were shearing his sheep, and his friend Hirah the Adullamite went with him.

When Tamar was told, "Your father-in-law is on his way to Timnah to shear his sheep," she took off her widow's clothes, covered herself with a veil to disguise herself, and then sat down at the entrance to Enaim, which is on the road to Timnah. For she saw that, though Shelah had now grown up, she had not been given to him as his wife.

When Judah saw her, he thought she was a prostitute, for she had covered her face. Not realizing that she was his daughter-in-law, he went over to her by the roadside and said, "Come now, let me sleep with you."

"And what will you give me to sleep with you?" she asked.

"I'll send you a young goat from my flock," he said.

"Will you give me something as a pledge until you send it?" she asked. He said, "What pledge should I give you?"

"Your seal and its cord, and the staff in your hand," she answered. So he gave them to her and slept with her, and she became pregnant by him. After she left, she took off her veil and put on her widow's clothes again.

JUDAH UNABLE TO FIND HARLOT.   Meanwhile Judah sent the young goat by his friend the Adullamite in order to get his pledge back from the woman, but he did not find her. He asked the men who lived there, "Where is the shrine prostitute who was beside the road at Enaim?"

Gen.
38:20-23

"There hasn't been any shrine prostitute here," they said.

So he went back to Judah and said, "I didn't find her. Besides, the men who lived there said, 'There hasn't been any shrine prostitute here.'"

Then Judah said, "Let her keep what she has, or we will become a laughingstock. After all, I did send her this young goat, but you didn't find her."

JUDAH LEARNS IT WAS TAMAR.   About three months later Judah was told, "Your daughter-in-law Tamar is guilty of prostitution, and as a result she is now pregnant."

Gen.
38:24-26

Judah said, "Bring her out and have her burned to death!"

As she was being brought out, she sent a message to her father-in-law. "I am pregnant by the man who owns these," she said. And she added, "See if you recognize whose seal and cord and staff these are."

Judah recognized them and said, "She is more righteous than I, since I wouldn't give her to my son Shelah." And he did not sleep with her again.

TAMAR HAS TWINS.   When the time came for her to give birth, there were twin boys in her womb. As she was giving birth, one of them put out his hand; so the midwife took a scarlet thread and tied it on his wrist and said, "This one came out first." But when he drew back his hand, his brother came out, and she said, "So this is how you have broken out!" And he was named Perez.[x] Then his brother, who had the scarlet thread on his wrist, came out and he was given the name Zerah.[y]

Gen.
38:27-30

The most important aspect of this seemingly insignificant story will come to light only after many centuries have passed. At that time it will become

[x]*Perez* means *breaking out.*   [y]*Zerah* can mean *scarlet* or *brightness.*

evident that a descendant of Judah (through Perez) will become God's messenger to all mankind—the Messiah.

Joseph the Egyptian Ruler

While Judah has been dealing with his various personal problems, his younger brother Joseph has been making the best of one disastrous situation after another. The story of his rise from being an imprisoned slave to being a ruler second only to Egypt's Pharaoh himself is wonderfully captivating. Equally fascinating is the account of how Joseph ultimately brings his father and brothers to live in Egypt, a move which Joseph sees as the clear culmination of a long series of events brought about by God's providence. The narrative begins when Joseph is first sold as a slave to an Egyptian military leader.

Gen. 39:1-6a Egypt

POTIPHAR PROMOTES JOSEPH.   Now Joseph had been taken down to Egypt. Potiphar, an Egyptian who was one of Pharaoh's officials, the captain of the guard, bought him from the Ishmaelites who had taken him there.

The LORD was with Joseph and he prospered, and he lived in the house of his Egyptian master. When his master saw that the LORD was with him and that the LORD gave him success in everything he did, Joseph found favor in his eyes and became his attendant. Potiphar put him in charge of his household, and he entrusted to his care everything he owned. From the time he put him in charge of his household and of all that he owned, the LORD blessed the household of the Egyptian because of Joseph. The blessing of the LORD was on everything Potiphar had, both in the house and in the field. So he left in Joseph's care everything he had; with Joseph in charge, he did not concern himself with anything except the food he ate.

Gen. 39:6b-10

JOSEPH REFUSES ADVANCES.   Now Joseph was well-built and handsome, and after a while his master's wife took notice of Joseph and said, "Come to bed with me!"

But he refused. "With me in charge," he told her, "my master does not concern himself with anything in the house; everything he owns he has entrusted to my care. No one is greater in this house than I am. My master has withheld nothing from me except you, because you are his wife. How then could I do such a wicked thing and sin against God?" And though she spoke to Joseph day after day, he refused to go to bed with her or even be with her.

Gen. 39:11-18

JOSEPH FALSELY ACCUSED.   One day he went into the house to attend to his duties, and none of the household servants was inside. She caught him by his cloak and said, "Come to bed with me!" But he left his cloak in her hand and ran out of the house.

When she saw that he had left his cloak in her hand and had run out of the house, she called her household servants. "Look," she said to them, "this Hebrew has been brought to us to make sport of us! He came in here to sleep with me, but I screamed. When he heard me scream for help, he left his cloak beside me and ran out of the house."

She kept his cloak beside her until his master came home. Then she told

him this story: "That Hebrew slave you brought us came to me to make
sport of me. But as soon as I screamed for help, he left his cloak beside me
and ran out of the house."

JOSEPH PUT INTO PRISON.   When his master heard the story his wife   Gen.
told him, saying, "This is how your slave treated me," he burned with   39:19,20a
anger. Joseph's master took him and put him in prison, the place where the
king's prisoners were confined.

PRISON IN JOSEPH'S CARE.   But while Joseph was there in the prison,   Gen.
the LORD was with him; he showed him kindness and granted him favor in   39:20b-23
the eyes of the prison warden. So the warden put Joseph in charge of all
those held in the prison, and he was made responsible for all that was done
there. The warden paid no attention to anything under Joseph's care,
because the LORD was with Joseph and gave him success in whatever he did.

BUTLER AND BAKER IMPRISONED.   Some time later, the cupbearer   Gen.
and the baker of the king of Egypt offended their master, the king of   40:1-4a
Egypt. Pharaoh was angry with his two officials, the chief cupbearer and
the chief baker, and put them in custody in the house of the captain of the
guard, in the same prison where Joseph was confined. The captain of the
guard assigned them to Joseph, and he attended them.

JOSEPH TO INTERPRET DREAMS.   After they had been in custody for   Gen.
some time, each of the two men—the cupbearer and the baker of the king   40:4b-8
of Egypt, who were being held in prison—had a dream the same night,
and each dream had a meaning of its own.
   When Joseph came to them the next morning, he saw that they were
dejected. So he asked Pharaoh's officials who were in custody with him in
his master's house, "Why are your faces so sad today?"
   "We both had dreams," they answered, "but there is no one to interpret
them."
   Then Joseph said to them, "Do not interpretations belong to God? Tell
me your dreams."

THE BUTLER'S DREAM.   So the chief cupbearer told Joseph his dream.   Gen.
He said to him, "In my dream I saw a vine in front of me, and on the vine   40:9-15
were three branches. As soon as it budded, it blossomed, and its clusters
ripened into grapes. Pharaoh's cup was in my hand, and I took the grapes,
squeezed them into Pharaoh's cup and put the cup in his hand."
   "This is what it means," Joseph said to him. "The three branches are
three days. Within three days Pharaoh will lift up your head and restore
you to your position, and you will put Pharaoh's cup in his hand, just as
you used to do when you were his cupbearer. But when all goes well with
you, remember me and show me kindness; mention me to Pharaoh and
get me out of this prison. For I was forcibly carried off from the land of the
Hebrews, and even here I have done nothing to deserve being put in a
dungeon."

THE BAKER'S DREAM.   When the chief baker saw that Joseph had given   Gen.
a favorable interpretation, he said to Joseph, "I too had a dream: On my   40:16-19
head were three baskets of bread.z In the top basket were all kinds of

zOr three wicker baskets

baked goods for Pharaoh, but the birds were eating them out of the basket on my head."

"This is what it means," Joseph said. "The three baskets are three days. Within three days Pharaoh will lift off your head and hang you on a tree.[a] And the birds will eat away your flesh."

Gen.
40:20-23

INTERPRETATIONS FULFILLED.   Now the third day was Pharaoh's birthday, and he gave a feast for all his officials. He lifted up the heads of the chief cupbearer and the chief baker in the presence of his officials: He restored the chief cupbearer to his position, so that he once again put the cup into Pharaoh's hand, but he hanged[b] the chief baker, just as Joseph had said to them in his interpretation.

The chief cupbearer, however, did not remember Joseph; he forgot him.

Gen.
41:1-8

PHARAOH HAS DREAM.   When two full years had passed, Pharaoh had a dream: He was standing by the Nile, when out of the river there came up seven cows, sleek and fat, and they grazed among the reeds. After them, seven other cows, ugly and gaunt, came up out of the Nile and stood beside those on the riverbank. And the cows that were ugly and gaunt ate up the seven sleek, fat cows. Then Pharaoh woke up.

He fell asleep again and had a second dream: Seven heads of grain, healthy and good, were growing on a single stalk. After them, seven other heads of grain sprouted—thin and scorched by the east wind. The thin heads of grain swallowed up the seven healthy, full heads. Then Pharaoh woke up; it had been a dream.

In the morning his mind was troubled, so he sent for all the magicians and wise men of Egypt. Pharaoh told them his dreams, but no one could interpret them for him.

Gen.
41:9-13

BUTLER REMEMBERS JOSEPH.   Then the chief cupbearer said to Pharaoh, "Today I am reminded of my shortcomings. Pharaoh was once angry with his servants, and he imprisoned me and the chief baker in the house of the captain of the guard. Each of us had a dream the same night, and each dream had a meaning of its own. Now a young Hebrew was there with us, a servant of the captain of the guard. We told him our dreams, and he interpreted them for us, giving each man the interpretation of his dream. And things turned out exactly as he interpreted them to us: I was restored to my position, and the other man was hanged.[b]"

Gen.
41:14-16

PHARAOH CALLS FOR JOSEPH.   So Pharaoh sent for Joseph, and he was quickly brought from the dungeon. When he had shaved and changed his clothes, he came before Pharaoh.

Pharaoh said to Joseph, "I had a dream, and no one can interpret it. But I have heard it said of you that when you hear a dream you can interpret it."

"I cannot do it," Joseph replied to Pharaoh, "but God will give Pharaoh the answer he desires."

Gen.
41:17-24

PHARAOH RECOUNTS DREAM.   Then Pharaoh said to Joseph, "In my dream I was standing on the bank of the Nile, when out of the river there came up seven cows, fat and sleek, and they grazed among the reeds. After them, seven other cows came up—scrawny and very ugly and lean. I had never seen such ugly cows in all the land of Egypt. The lean, ugly

[a]Or *and impale you on a pole*   [b]Or *impaled*

cows ate up the seven fat cows that came up first. But even after they ate them, no one could tell that they had done so; they looked just as ugly as before. Then I woke up.

"In my dreams I also saw seven heads of grain, full and good, growing on a single stalk. After them, seven other heads sprouted—withered and thin and scorched by the east wind. The thin heads of grain swallowed up the seven good heads. I told this to the magicians, but none could explain it to me."

PLENTY AND FAMINE FORECAST.   Then Joseph said to Pharaoh, "The dreams of Pharaoh are one and the same. God has revealed to Pharaoh what he is about to do. The seven good cows are seven years, and the seven good heads of grain are seven years; it is one and the same dream. The seven lean, ugly cows that came up afterward are seven years, and so are the seven worthless heads of grain scorched by the east wind: They are seven years of famine.

Gen. 41:25-32

"It is just as I said to Pharaoh: God has shown Pharaoh what he is about to do. Seven years of great abundance are coming throughout the land of Egypt, but seven years of famine will follow them. Then all the abundance in Egypt will be forgotten, and the famine will ravage the land. The abundance in the land will not be remembered, because the famine that follows it will be so severe. The reason the dream was given to Pharaoh in two forms is that the matter has been firmly decided by God, and God will do it soon.

JOSEPH SUGGESTS PLAN.   "And now let Pharaoh look for a discerning and wise man and put him in charge of the land of Egypt. Let Pharaoh appoint commissioners over the land to take a fifth of the harvest of Egypt during the seven years of abundance. They should collect all the food of these good years that are coming and store up the grain under the authority of Pharaoh, to be kept in the cities for food. This food should be held in reserve for the country, to be used during the seven years of famine that will come upon Egypt, so that the country may not be ruined by the famine."

Gen. 41:33-36

JOSEPH MADE RULER.   The plan seemed good to Pharaoh and to all his officials. So Pharaoh asked them, "Can we find anyone like this man, one in whom is the spirit of God*c*?"

Gen. 41:37-46a (Ca. 1885 B.C.)

Then Pharaoh said to Joseph, "Since God has made all this known to you, there is no one so discerning and wise as you. You shall be in charge of my palace, and all my people are to submit to your orders. Only with respect to the throne will I be greater than you."

So Pharaoh said to Joseph, "I hereby put you in charge of the whole land of Egypt." Then Pharaoh took his signet ring from his finger and put it on Joseph's finger. He dressed him in robes of fine linen and put a gold chain around his neck. He had him ride in a chariot as his second-in-command,*d* and men shouted before him, "Make way*e*!" Thus he put him in charge of the whole land of Egypt.

Then Pharaoh said to Joseph, "I am Pharaoh, but without your word no one will lift hand or foot in all Egypt." Pharaoh gave Joseph the name Zaphenath-Paneah and gave him Asenath daughter of Potiphera, priest

---

*c*Or *of the gods*   *d*Or *in the chariot of his second-in-command; or in his second chariot*
*e*Or *Bow down*

of On,^{f} to be his wife. And Joseph went throughout the land of Egypt.

Joseph was thirty years old when he entered the service of Pharaoh king of Egypt.

**Gen.
41:46b-49**

JOSEPH STORES ABUNDANCE.   And Joseph went out from Pharaoh's presence and traveled throughout Egypt. During the seven years of abundance the land produced plentifully. Joseph collected all the food produced in those seven years of abundance in Egypt and stored it in the cities. In each city he put the food grown in the fields surrounding it. Joseph stored up huge quantities of grain, like the sand of the sea; it was so much that he stopped keeping records because it was beyond measure.

**Gen.
41:50-52**

MANASSEH AND EPHRAIM BORN.   Before the years of famine came, two sons were born to Joseph by Asenath daughter of Potiphera, priest of On. Joseph named his firstborn Manasseh^g and said, "It is because God has made me forget all my trouble and all my father's household." The second son he named Ephraim^h and said, "It is because God has made me fruitful in the land of my suffering."

**Gen.
41:53-57**

GRAIN SAVES FROM FAMINE.   The seven years of abundance in Egypt came to an end, and the seven years of famine began, just as Joseph had said. There was famine in all the other lands, but in the whole land of Egypt there was food. When all Egypt began to feel the famine, the people cried to Pharaoh for food. Then Pharaoh told all the Egyptians, "Go to Joseph and do what he tells you."

When the famine had spread over the whole country, Joseph opened the storehouses and sold grain to the Egyptians, for the famine was severe throughout Egypt. And all the countries came to Egypt to buy grain from Joseph, because the famine was severe in all the world.

**Gen.
42:1-5
Beersheba**

ISRAEL SENDS SONS TO EGYPT.   When Jacob learned that there was grain in Egypt, he said to his sons, "Why do you just keep looking at each other?" He continued, "I have heard that there is grain in Egypt. Go down there and buy some for us, so that we may live and not die."

Then ten of Joseph's brothers went down to buy grain from Egypt. But Jacob did not send Benjamin, Joseph's brother, with the others, because he was afraid that harm might come to him. So Israel's sons were among those who went to buy grain, for the famine was in the land of Canaan also.

**Gen.
42:6-12
Egypt**

JOSEPH FEIGNS UNAWARENESS.   Now Joseph was the governor of the land, the one who sold grain to all its people. So when Joseph's brothers arrived, they bowed down to him with their faces to the ground. As soon as Joseph saw his brothers, he recognized them, but he pretended to be a stranger and spoke harshly to them. "Where do you come from?" he asked.

"From the land of Canaan," they replied, "to buy food."

Although Joseph recognized his brothers, they did not recognize him. Then he remembered his dreams about them and said to them, "You are spies! You have come to see where our land is unprotected."

"No, my lord," they answered. "Your servants have come to buy food. We are all the sons of one man. Your servants are honest men, not spies."

---

^{f} That is, Heliopolis ^{g}Manasseh sounds like and may be derived from the Hebrew for *forget*. ^{h}Ephraim sounds like the Hebrew for *twice fruitful*.

"No!" he said to them. "You have come to see where our land is unprotected."

JOSEPH PLANS SCHEME.   But they replied, "Your servants were twelve brothers, the sons of one man, who lives in the land of Canaan. The youngest is now with our father, and one is no more."

Gen. 42:13-17

Joseph said to them, "It is just as I told you: You are spies! And this is how you will be tested: As surely as Pharaoh lives, you will not leave this place unless your youngest brother comes here. Send one of your number to get your brother; the rest of you will be kept in prison, so that your words may be tested to see if you are telling the truth. If you are not, then as surely as Pharaoh lives, you are spies!" And he put them all in custody for three days.

SCHEME IS ALTERED.   On the third day, Joseph said to them, "Do this and you will live, for I fear God: If you are honest men, let one of your brothers stay here in prison, while the rest of you go and take grain back for your starving households. But you must bring your youngest brother to me, so that your words may be verified and that you may not die." This they proceeded to do.

Gen. 42:18-20

REUBEN'S SUPPORT INDICATED.   They said to one another, "Surely we are being punished because of our brother. We saw how distressed he was when he pleaded with us for his life, but we would not listen; that's why this distress has come upon us."

Gen. 42:21-24a

Reuben replied, "Didn't I tell you not to sin against the boy? But you wouldn't listen! Now we must give an accounting for his blood." They did not realize that Joseph could understand them, since he was using an interpreter.

He turned away from them and began to weep, but then turned back and spoke to them again.

BROTHERS LEAVE.   He had Simeon taken from them and bound before their eyes.

Gen. 42:24b-26

Joseph gave orders to fill their bags with grain, to put each man's silver back in his sack, and to give them provisions for their journey. After this was done for them, they loaded their grain on their donkeys and left.

MONEY DISCOVERED IN SACK.   At the place where they stopped for the night one of them opened his sack to get feed for his donkey, and he saw his silver in the mouth of his sack. "My silver has been returned," he said to his brothers. "Here it is in my sack."

Gen. 42:27,28

Their hearts sank and they turned to each other trembling and said, "What is this that God has done to us?"

ISRAEL TOLD OF CONDITIONS.   When they came to their father Jacob in the land of Canaan, they told him all that had happened to them. They said, "The man who is lord over the land spoke harshly to us and treated us as though we were spying on the land. But we said to him, 'We are honest men; we are not spies. We were twelve brothers, sons of one father. One is no more, and the youngest is now with our father in Canaan.'

Gen. 42:29-34 Beersheba

"Then the man who is lord over the land said to us, 'This is how I will know whether you are honest men: Leave one of your brothers here with me, and take food for your starving households and go. But bring your youngest brother to me so I will know that you are not spies but honest men. Then I will give your brother back to you, and you can trade[i] in the land.'"

Gen. 42:35   MONEY IN ALL SACKS.   As they were emptying their sacks, there in each man's sack was his pouch of silver! When they and their father saw the money pouches, they were frightened.

Gen. 42:36-38   ISRAEL FEARFUL.   Their father Jacob said to them, "You have deprived me of my children. Joseph is no more and Simeon is no more, and now you want to take Benjamin. Everything is against me!"

Then Reuben said to his father, "You may put both of my sons to death if I do not bring him back to you. Entrust him to my care, and I will bring him back."

But Jacob said, "My son will not go down there with you; his brother is dead and he is the only one left. If harm comes to him on the journey you are taking, you will bring my gray head down to the grave[j] in sorrow."

Gen. 43:1-10   JUDAH CONVINCES ISRAEL.   Now the famine was still severe in the land. So when they had eaten all the grain they had brought from Egypt, their father said to them, "Go back and buy us a little more food."

But Judah said to him, "The man warned us solemnly, 'You will not see my face again unless your brother is with you.' If you will send our brother along with us, we will go down and buy food for you. But if you will not send him, we will not go down, because the man said to us, 'You will not see my face again unless your brother is with you.'"

Israel asked, "Why did you bring this trouble on me by telling the man you had another brother?"

They replied, "The man questioned us closely about ourselves and our family. 'Is your father still living?' he asked us. 'Do you have another brother?' We simply answered his questions. How were we to know he would say, 'Bring your brother down here'?"

Then Judah said to Israel his father, "Send the boy along with me and we will go at once, so that we and you and our children may live and not die. I myself will guarantee his safety; you can hold me personally responsible for him. If I do not bring him back to you and set him here before you, I will bear the blame before you all my life. As it is, if we had not delayed, we could have gone and returned twice."

Gen. 43:11-15   SONS TAKE GIFTS.   Then their father Israel said to them, "If it must be, then do this: Put some of the best products of the land in your bags and take them down to the man as a gift—a little balm and a little honey, some spices and myrrh, some pistachio nuts and almonds. Take double the amount of silver with you, for you must return the silver that was put back into the mouths of your sacks. Perhaps it was a mistake. Take your brother also and go back to the man at once. And may God Almighty[k] grant you mercy before the man so that he will let your other brother and Benjamin come back with you. As for me, if I am bereaved, I am bereaved."

So the men took the gifts and double the amount of silver, and Benjamin also. They hurried down to Egypt and presented themselves to Joseph.

_____

[i]Or _move about freely_   [j]Hebrew _Sheol_   [k]Hebrew _El-Shaddai_

JOSEPH PLANS DINNER.   When Joseph saw Benjamin with them, he
said to the steward of his house, "Take these men to my house, slaughter
an animal and prepare dinner; they are to eat with me at noon."
    The man did as Joseph told him and took the men to Joseph's house.

BROTHERS REASSURED.   Now the men were frightened when they
were taken to his house. They thought, "We were brought here because of
the silver that was put back into our sacks the first time. He wants to attack
us and overpower us and seize us as slaves and take our donkeys."
    So they went up to Joseph's steward and spoke to him at the entrance to
the house. "Please, sir," they said, "we came down here the first time to buy
food. But at the place where we stopped for the night we opened our sacks
and each of us found his silver—the exact weight—in the mouth of his
sack. So we have brought it back with us. We have also brought additional
silver with us to buy food. We don't know who put our silver in our sacks."
    "It's all right," he said. "Don't be afraid. Your God, the God of your
father, has given you treasure in your sacks; I received your silver." Then
he brought Simeon out to them.

GIFTS GIVEN TO JOSEPH.   The steward took the men into Joseph's
house, gave them water to wash their feet and provided fodder for their
donkeys. They prepared their gifts for Joseph's arrival at noon, because
they had heard that they were to eat there.
    When Joseph came home, they presented to him the gifts they had
brought into the house, and they bowed down before him to the ground.

JOSEPH OVERCOME BY JOY.   He asked them how they were, and then
he said, "How is your aged father you told me about? Is he still living?"
    They replied, "Your servant our father is still alive and well." And they
bowed low to pay him honor.
    As he looked about and saw his brother Benjamin, his own mother's
son, he asked, "Is this your youngest brother, the one you told me about?"
And he said, "God be gracious to you, my son." Deeply moved at the sight
of his brother, Joseph hurried out and looked for a place to weep. He went
into his private room and wept there.

THE BROTHERS FEAST.   After he had washed his face, he came out and,
controlling himself, said, "Serve the food."
    They served him by himself, the brothers by themselves, and the
Egyptians who ate with him by themselves, because Egyptians could not
eat with Hebrews, for that is detestable to Egyptians. The men had been
seated before him in the order of their ages, from the firstborn to the
youngest; and they looked at each other in astonishment. When portions
were served to them from Joseph's table, Benjamin's portion was five
times as much as anyone else's. So they feasted and drank freely with him.

JOSEPH SCHEMES AGAIN.   Now Joseph gave these instructions to the
steward of his house: "Fill the men's sacks with as much food as they can
carry, and put each man's silver in the mouth of his sack. Then put my cup,
the silver one, in the mouth of the youngest one's sack, along with the silver for his grain." And he did as Joseph said.
    As morning dawned, the men were sent on their way with their don-
keys. They had not gone far from the city when Joseph said to his steward,
"Go after those men at once, and when you catch up with them, say to

them, 'Why have you repaid good with evil? Isn't this the cup my master
drinks from and also uses for divination? This is a wicked thing you have
done.' "

Gen.
44:6-13

BENJAMIN HAS SILVER CUP.   When he caught up with them, he repeated these words to them. But they said to him, "Why does my lord say such
things? Far be it from your servants to do anything like that! We even
brought back to you from the land of Canaan the silver we found inside
the mouths of our sacks. So why would we steal silver or gold from your
master's house? If any of your servants is found to have it, he will die; and
the rest of us will become my lord's slaves."

"Very well, then," he said, "let it be as you say. Whoever is found to
have it will become my slave; the rest of you will be free from blame."

Each of them quickly lowered his sack to the ground and opened it.
Then the steward proceeded to search, beginning with the oldest and ending with the youngest. And the cup was found in Benjamin's sack. At this,
they tore their clothes. Then they all loaded their donkeys and returned to
the city.

Gen.
44:14-17

JOSEPH CONFRONTS BROTHERS.   Joseph was still in the house when
Judah and his brothers came in, and they threw themselves to the ground
before him. Joseph said to them, "What is this you have done? Don't you
know that a man like me can find things out by divination?"

"What can we say to my lord?" Judah replied. "What can we say? How
can we prove our innocence? God has uncovered your servants' guilt. We
are now my lord's slaves—we ourselves and the one who was found to
have the cup."

But Joseph said, "Far be it from me to do such a thing! Only the man
who was found to have the cup will become my slave. The rest of you, go
back to your father in peace."

Gen.
44:18-34

JUDAH PLEADS FOR BENJAMIN.   Then Judah went up to him and said:
"Please, my lord, let your servant speak a word to my lord. Do not be
angry with your servant, though you are equal to Pharaoh himself. My
lord asked his servants, 'Do you have a father or a brother?' And we
answered, 'We have an aged father, and there is a young son born to him
in his old age. His brother is dead, and he is the only one of his mother's
sons left, and his father loves him.'

"Then you said to your servants, 'Bring him down to me so I can see him
for myself.' And we said to my lord, 'The boy cannot leave his father; if he
leaves him, his father will die.' But you told your servants, 'Unless your
youngest brother comes down with you, you will not see my face again.'
When we went back to your servant my father, we told him what my lord
had said.

"Then our father said, 'Go back and buy a little more food.' But we said,
'We cannot go down. Only if our youngest brother is with us will we go.
We cannot see the man's face unless our youngest brother is with us.'

"Your servant my father said to us, 'You know that my wife bore me two
sons. One of them went away from me, and I said, "He has surely been
torn to pieces." And I have not seen him since. If you take this one from
me too and harm comes to him, you will bring my gray head down to the
grave[l] in misery.'

[l]Hebrew *Sheol*; also in verse 31

"So now, if the boy is not with us when I go back to your servant my father and if my father, whose life is closely bound up with the boy's life, sees that the boy isn't there, he will die. Your servants will bring the gray head of our father down to the grave in sorrow. Your servant guaranteed the boy's safety to my father. I said, 'If I do not bring him back to you, I will bear the blame before you, my father, all my life!'

"Now then, please let your servant remain here as my lord's slave in place of the boy, and let the boy return with his brothers. How can I go back to my father if the boy is not with me? No! Do not let me see the misery that would come upon my father."

JOSEPH REVEALS IDENTITY.   Then Joseph could no longer control himself before all his attendants, and he cried out, "Have everyone leave my presence!" So there was no one with Joseph when he made himself known to his brothers. And he wept so loudly that the Egyptians heard him, and Pharaoh's household heard about it.

Gen.
45:1-3

Joseph said to his brothers, "I am Joseph! Is my father still living?" But his brothers were not able to answer him, because they were terrified at his presence.

GOD'S PROVIDENCE EXPLAINED.   Then Joseph said to his brothers, "Come close to me." When they had done so, he said, "I am your brother Joseph, the one you sold into Egypt! And now, do not be distressed and do not be angry with yourselves for selling me here, because it was to save lives that God sent me ahead of you. For two years now there has been famine in the land, and for the next five years there will not be plowing and reaping. But God sent me ahead of you to preserve for you a remnant on earth and to save your lives by a great deliverance.*m*

Gen.
45:4-8

"So then, it was not you who sent me here, but God. He made me father to Pharaoh, lord of his entire household and ruler of all Egypt.

BROTHERS TO TELL ISRAEL.   Now hurry back to my father and say to him, 'This is what your son Joseph says: God has made me lord of all Egypt. Come down to me; don't delay. You shall live in the region of Goshen and be near me—you, your children and grandchildren, your flocks and herds, and all you have. I will provide for you there, because five years of famine are still to come. Otherwise you and your household and all who belong to you will become destitute.'

Gen.
45:9-15

"You can see for yourselves, and so can my brother Benjamin, that it is really I who am speaking to you. Tell my father about all the honor accorded me in Egypt and about everything you have seen. And bring my father down here quickly."

Then he threw his arms around his brother Benjamin and wept, and Benjamin embraced him, weeping. And he kissed all his brothers and wept over them. Afterward his brothers talked with him.

PHARAOH EXTENDS INVITATION.   When the news reached Pharaoh's palace that Joseph's brothers had come, Pharaoh and all his officials were pleased. Pharaoh said to Joseph, "Tell your brothers, 'Do this: Load your animals and return to the land of Canaan, and bring your father and your families back to me. I will give you the best of the land of Egypt and you can enjoy the fat of the land.'

Gen.
45:16-20

"You are also directed to tell them, 'Do this: Take some carts from Egypt

*m*Or *save you as a great band of survivors*

for your children and your wives, and get your father and come. Never mind about your belongings, because the best of all Egypt will be yours.'"

Gen.
45:21-24

JOSEPH SENDS GIFTS.   So the sons of Israel did this. Joseph gave them carts, as Pharaoh had commanded, and he also gave them provisions for their journey. To each of them he gave new clothing, but to Benjamin he gave three hundred shekels[n] of silver and five sets of clothes. And this is what he sent to his father: ten donkeys loaded with the best things of Egypt, and ten female donkeys loaded with grain and bread and other provisions for his journey. Then he sent his brothers away, and as they were leaving he said to them, "Don't quarrel on the way!"

Gen.
45:25-28
Beersheba

ISRAEL TOLD ABOUT JOSEPH.   So they went up out of Egypt and came to their father Jacob in the land of Canaan. They told him, "Joseph is still alive! In fact, he is ruler of all Egypt." Jacob was stunned; he did not believe them. But when they told him everything Joseph had said to them, and when he saw the carts Joseph had sent to carry him back, the spirit of their father Jacob revived. And Israel said, "I'm convinced! My son Joseph is still alive. I will go and see him before I die."

Gen.
46:1-4

GOD GIVES ISRAEL ASSURANCE.   So Israel set out with all that was his, and when he reached Beersheba, he offered sacrifices to the God of his father Isaac.
        And God spoke to Israel in a vision at night and said, "Jacob! Jacob!"
        "Here I am," he replied.
        "I am God, the God of your father," he said. "Do not be afraid to go down to Egypt, for I will make you into a great nation there. I will go down to Egypt with you, and I will surely bring you back again. And Joseph's own hand will close your eyes."

Gen.
46:5-7
To Egypt

ISRAEL AND SONS IMMIGRATE.   Then Jacob left Beersheba, and Israel's sons took their father Jacob and their children and their wives in the carts that Pharaoh had sent to transport him. They also took with them their livestock and the possessions they had acquired in Canaan, and Jacob and all his offspring went to Egypt. He took with him to Egypt his sons and grandsons and his daughters and granddaughters—all his offspring.

Gen.
46:8-27

LIST OF THE IMMIGRANTS.   These are the names of the sons of Israel (Jacob and his descendants) who went to Egypt:

> Reuben the firstborn of Jacob.
>   The sons of Reuben:
>   Hanoch, Pallu, Hezron and Carmi.
>   The sons of Simeon:
>   Jemuel, Jamin, Ohad, Jakin, Zohar and Shaul the son of a Canaanite
>   woman.
>   The sons of Levi:
>   Gershon, Kohath and Merari.
>   The sons of Judah:
>   Er, Onan, Shelah, Perez and Zerah (but Er and Onan had died in the
>   land of Canaan).
>   The sons of Perez:
>   Hezron and Hamul.
>   The sons of Issachar:

[n]That is, about 7 1/2 pounds (about 3.5 kilograms)

Tola, Puah,[o] Jashub[p] and Shimron.
The sons of Zebulun:
    Sered, Elon and Jahleel.
These were the sons Leah bore to Jacob in Paddan Aram,[q] besides his
daughter Dinah. These sons and daughters of his were thirty-three in all.

The sons of Gad:
    Zephon,[r] Haggi, Shuni, Ezbon, Eri, Arodi and Areli.
The sons of Asher:
    Imnah, Ishvah, Ishvi and Beriah.
    Their sister was Serah.
The sons of Beriah:
    Heber and Malkiel.
These were the children born to Jacob by Zilpah, whom Laban had
given to his daughter Leah—sixteen in all.

The sons of Jacob's wife Rachel:
    Joseph and Benjamin. In Egypt, Manasseh and Ephraim were born
    to Joseph by Asenath daughter of Potiphera, priest of On.[s]
The sons of Benjamin:
    Bela, Beker, Ashbel, Gera, Naaman, Ehi, Rosh, Muppim, Huppim
    and Ard.
These were the sons of Rachel who were born to Jacob—fourteen in all.

The son of Dan:
    Hushim.
The sons of Naphtali:
    Jahziel, Guni, Jezer and Shillem.
These were the sons born to Jacob by Bilhah, whom Laban had given to
his daughter Rachel—seven in all.

All those who went to Egypt with Jacob—those who were his direct
descendants, not counting his sons' wives—numbered sixty-six persons.
With the two sons[t] who had been born to Joseph in Egypt, the members of
Jacob's family, which went to Egypt, were seventy[u] in all.

JOSEPH REUNITED WITH FATHER.   Now Jacob sent Judah ahead of   **Gen.**
him to Joseph to get directions to Goshen. When they arrived in the region   **46:28-30**
of Goshen, Joseph had his chariot made ready and went to Goshen to meet
his father Israel. As soon as Joseph appeared before him, he threw his arms
around his father[v] and wept for a long time.

Israel said to Joseph, "Now I am ready to die, since I have seen for
myself that you are still alive."

JOSEPH SUGGESTS OCCUPATION.   Then Joseph said to his brothers   **Gen.**
and to his father's household, "I will go up and speak to Pharaoh and will   **46:31-34**
say to him, 'My brothers and my father's household, who were living in
the land of Canaan, have come to me. The men are shepherds; they tend
livestock, and they have brought along their flocks and herds and everything

[o]Samaritan Pentateuch and Syriac (see also 1 Chron. 7:1); Masoretic Text *Puvah*
[p]Samaritan Pentateuch and some Septuagint manuscripts (see also Num. 26:24 and 1 Chron.
7:1); Masoretic Text *Iob*   [q]That is, Northwest Mesopotamia   [r]Samaritan Pentateuch and
Septuagint (see also Num. 26:15); Masoretic Text *Ziphion*   [s]That is, Heliopolis
[t]Hebrew; Septuagint *the nine children*   [u]Hebrew (see also Exodus 1:5 and footnote);
Septuagint (see also Acts 7:14) *seventy-five*   [v]Hebrew *around him*

they own.' When Pharaoh calls you in and asks, 'What is your occupation?' you should answer, 'Your servants have tended livestock from our boyhood on, just as our fathers did.' Then you will be allowed to settle in the region of Goshen, for all shepherds are detestable to the Egyptians."

BROTHERS TO KEEP CATTLE.   Joseph went and told Pharaoh, "My father and brothers, with their flocks and herds and everything they own, have come from the land of Canaan and are now in Goshen." He chose five of his brothers and presented them before Pharaoh.

Gen.
47:1-6

Pharaoh asked the brothers, "What is your occupation?"

"Your servants are shepherds," they replied to Pharaoh, "just as our fathers were." They also said to him, "We have come to live here awhile, because the famine is severe in Canaan and your servants' flocks have no pasture. So now, please let your servants settle in Goshen."

Pharaoh said to Joseph, "Your father and your brothers have come to you, and the land of Egypt is before you; settle your father and your brothers in the best part of the land. Let them live in Goshen. And if you know of any among them with special ability, put them in charge of my own livestock."

ISRAEL BLESSES PHARAOH.   Then Joseph brought his father Jacob in and presented him before Pharaoh. After Jacob blessed[w] Pharaoh, Pharaoh asked him, "How old are you?"

Gen.
47:7-10
(Ca. 1876
B.C.)

And Jacob said to Pharaoh, "The years of my pilgrimage are a hundred and thirty. My years have been few and difficult, and they do not equal the years of the pilgrimage of my fathers." Then Jacob blessed[x] Pharaoh and went out from his presence.

SETTLEMENT IN GOSHEN.   So Joseph settled his father and his brothers in Egypt and gave them property in the best part of the land, the district of Rameses, as Pharaoh directed. Joseph also provided his father and his brothers and all his father's household with food, according to the number of their children.

Gen.
47:11,12
Goshen

CATTLE GIVEN FOR FOOD.   There was no food, however, in the whole region because the famine was severe; both Egypt and Canaan wasted away because of the famine. Joseph collected all the money that was to be found in Egypt and Canaan in payment for the grain they were buying, and he brought it to Pharaoh's palace. When the money of the people of Egypt and Canaan was gone, all Egypt came to Joseph and said, "Give us food. Why should we die before your eyes? Our money is used up."

Gen.
47:13-17

"Then bring your livestock," said Joseph. "I will sell you food in exchange for your livestock, since your money is gone." So they brought their livestock to Joseph, and he gave them food in exchange for their horses, their sheep and goats, their cattle and donkeys. And he brought them through that year with food in exchange for all their livestock.

EGYPTIANS OFFER LAND.   When that year was over, they came to him the following year and said, "We cannot hide from our lord the fact that since our money is gone and our livestock belongs to you, there is nothing left for our lord except our bodies and our land. Why should we perish before your eyes—we and our land as well? Buy us and our land in

Gen.
47:18,19

---

[w]Or *greeted*   [x]Or *said farewell to*

exchange for food, and we with our land will be in bondage to Pharaoh. Give us seed so that we may live and not die, and that the land may not become desolate."

PHARAOH ACQUIRES ALL.   So Joseph bought all the land in Egypt for Pharaoh. The Egyptians, one and all, sold their fields, because the famine was too severe for them. The land became Pharaoh's, and Joseph reduced the people to servitude,y from one end of Egypt to the other. However, he did not buy the land of the priests, because they received a regular allotment from Pharaoh and had food enough from the allotment Pharaoh gave them. That is why they did not sell their land.

Gen.
47:20-22

PEOPLE TAXED ONE-FIFTH.   Joseph said to the people, "Now that I have bought you and your land today for Pharaoh, here is seed for you so you can plant the ground. But when the crop comes in, give a fifth of it to Pharaoh. The other four-fifths you may keep as seed for the fields and as food for yourselves and your households and your children."

Gen.
47:23-26

"You have saved our lives," they said.."May we find favor in the eyes of our lord; we will be in bondage to Pharaoh."

So Joseph established it as a law concerning land in Egypt—still in force today—that a fifth of the produce belongs to Pharaoh. It was only the land of the priests that did not become Pharaoh's.

ISRAELITES PROSPER.   Now the Israelites settled in Egypt in the region of Goshen. They acquired property there and were fruitful and increased greatly in number.

Gen.
47:27,28
(Ca. 1859
B.C.)

Jacob lived in Egypt seventeen years, and the years of his life were a hundred and forty-seven.

Jacob's and Joseph's Last Days

Seventeen years have passed since Israel (Jacob) brought his family into Egypt. Nearing death, Israel is anxious to pronounce final blessings upon his sons and grandsons, and to insure his burial in the tomb where Abraham and Isaac were buried. Israel's death marks the end of the early patriarchs, and attention begins to focus more broadly upon the nation which bears Israel's name. Joseph's death is also recorded after the third generation of Israelites is born in Egypt.

ISRAEL REQUESTS CANAAN BURIAL.   When the time drew near for Israel to die, he called for his son Joseph and said to him, "If I have found favor in your eyes, put your hand under my thigh and promise that you will show me kindness and faithfulness. Do not bury me in Egypt, but when I rest with my fathers, carry me out of Egypt and bury me where they are buried."

Gen.
47:29-31

"I will do as you say," he said.

"Swear to me," he said. Then Joseph swore to him, and Israel worshiped as he leaned on the top of his staff.z

JOSEPH'S INHERITANCE ASSURED.   Some time later Joseph was told, "Your father is ill." So he took his two sons Manasseh and Ephraim along

Gen.
48:1-7

ySamaritan Pentateuch and Septuagint (see also Vulgate); Masoretic Text *and he moved the people into the cities*   zOr *Israel bowed down at the head of his bed*

with him. When Jacob was told, "Your son Joseph has come to you," Israel rallied his strength and sat up on the bed.

Jacob said to Joseph, "God Almighty[a] appeared to me at Luz in the land of Canaan, and there he blessed me and said to me, 'I am going to make you fruitful and will increase your numbers. I will make you a community of peoples, and I will give this land as an everlasting possession to your descendants after you.'

"Now then, your two sons born to you in Egypt before I came to you here will be reckoned as mine; Ephraim and Manasseh will be mine, just as Reuben and Simeon are mine. Any children born to you after them will be yours; in the territory they inherit they will be reckoned under the names of their brothers. As I was returning from Paddan,[b] to my sorrow Rachel died in the land of Canaan while we were still on the way, a little distance from Ephrath. So I buried her there beside the road to Ephrath" (that is, Bethlehem).

Gen.
48:8-13

SONS BROUGHT TO ISRAEL   When Israel saw the sons of Joseph, he asked, "Who are these?"

"They are the sons God has given me here," Joseph said to his father.

Then Israel said, "Bring them to me so I may bless them."

Now Israel's eyes were failing because of old age, and he could hardly see. So Joseph brought his sons close to him, and his father kissed them and embraced them.

Israel said to Joseph, "I never expected to see your face again, and now God has allowed me to see your children too."

Then Joseph removed them from Israel's knees and bowed down with his face to the ground. And Joseph took both of them, Ephraim on his right toward Israel's left hand and Manasseh on his left toward Israel's right hand, and brought them close to him.

Gen.
48:14-16

ISRAEL BLESSES SONS.   But Israel reached out his right hand and put it on Ephraim's head, though he was the younger, and crossing his arms, he put his left hand on Manasseh's head, even though Manasseh was the firstborn.

Then he blessed Joseph and said,

"May the God before whom my fathers
  Abraham and Isaac walked,
the God who has been my shepherd
  all my life to this day,
the Angel who has delivered me from all harm
  —may he bless these boys.
May they be called by my name
  and the names of my fathers Abraham and Isaac,
and may they increase greatly
  upon the earth."

Gen.
48:17-20

EPHRAIM OVER MANASSEH.   When Joseph saw his father placing his right hand on Ephraim's head he was displeased; so he took hold of his father's hand to move it from Ephraim's head to Manasseh's head. Joseph said to him, "No, my father, this one is the firstborn; put your right hand on his head."

[a]Hebrew *El-Shaddai*   [b]That is, Northwest Mesopotamia

But his father refused and said, "I know, my son, I know. He too will become a people, and he too will become great. Nevertheless, his younger brother will be greater than he, and his descendants will become a group of nations." He blessed them that day and said,

> "In your[c] name will Israel pronounce this blessing:
> 'May God make you like Ephraim and Manasseh.'"

So he put Ephraim ahead of Manasseh.

SPECIAL LAND FOR JOSEPH. Then Israel said to Joseph, "I am about to die, but God will be with you[d] and take you[d] back to the land of your[d] fathers. And to you, as one who is over your brothers, I give the ridge of land[e] I took from the Amorites with my sword and my bow."

Gen.
48:21,22

ISRAEL PRONOUNCES BLESSINGS. Then Jacob called for his sons and said: "Gather around so I can tell you what will happen to you in days to come.

Gen.
49:1,2

> "Assemble and listen, sons of Jacob;
> listen to your father Israel.

REUBEN THE UNSTABLE.

Gen.
49:3,4

> "Reuben, you are my firstborn,
> my might, the first sign of my strength,
> excelling in honor, excelling in power.
> Turbulent as the waters, you will no longer excel,
> for you went up onto your father's bed,
> onto my couch and defiled it.

SIMEON AND LEVI THE WRATHFUL.

Gen.
49:5-7

> "Simeon and Levi are brothers—
> their swords[f] are weapons of violence.
> Let me not enter their council,
> let me not join their assembly,
> for they have killed men in their anger
> and hamstrung oxen as they pleased.
> Cursed be their anger, so fierce,
> and their fury, so cruel!
> I will scatter them in Jacob
> and disperse them in Israel.

JUDAH THE RULER.

Gen.
49:8-12

> "Judah,[g] your brothers will praise you;
> your hand will be on the neck of your enemies;
> your father's sons will bow down to you.
> You are a lion's cub, O Judah;
> you return from the prey, my son.
> Like a lion he crouches and lies down,
> like a lioness—who dares to rouse him?
> The scepter will not depart from Judah,

[c]The Hebrew is singular.   [d]The Hebrew is plural.   [e]Or *And to you I give one portion more than to your brothers—the portion*   [f]The meaning of the Hebrew for this word is uncertain.   [g]*Judah* sounds like and may be derived from the Hebrew for *praise*.

> nor the ruler's staff from between his feet,
> until he comes to whom it belongs[h]
>   and the obedience of the nations is his.
> He will tether his donkey to a vine,
>   his colt to the choicest branch;
> he will wash his garments in wine,
>   his robes in the blood of grapes.
> His eyes will be darker than wine,
>   his teeth whiter than milk.[i]

Gen. 49:13   ZEBULUN THE SEAMAN.

> "Zebulun will live by the seashore
>   and become a haven for ships;
>   his border will extend toward Sidon.

Gen. 49:14,15   ISSACHAR THE INDOLENT.

> "Issachar is a rawboned[j] donkey
>   lying down between two saddlebags.[k]
> When he sees how good is his resting place
>   and how pleasant is his land,
> he will bend his shoulder to the burden
>   and submit to forced labor.

Gen. 49:16-18   DAN THE JUDGE.

> "Dan[l] will provide justice for his people
>   as one of the tribes of Israel.
> Dan will be a serpent by the roadside,
>   a viper along the path,
> that bites the horse's heels
>   so that its rider tumbles backward.

> "I look for your deliverance, O LORD.

Gen. 49:19   GAD THE HARASSED.

> "Gad[m] will be attacked by a band of raiders,
>   but he will attack them at their heels.

Gen. 49:20   ASHER THE FARMER.

> "Asher's food will be rich;
>   he will provide delicacies fit for a king.

Gen. 49:21   NAPHTALI THE ELOQUENT.

> "Naphtali is a doe set free
>   that bears beautiful fawns.[n]

Gen. 49:22-26   JOSEPH THE BLESSED.

> "Joseph is a fruitful vine,
>   a fruitful vine near a spring,

---

[h]Or until Shiloh comes; or until he comes to whom tribute belongs
wine, / his teeth white from milk   [j]Or strong   [k]Or campfires
provides justice.   [m]Gad can mean attack and band of raiders.
beautiful words

[i]Or will be dull from
[l]Dan here means he
[n]Or free; / he utters

> whose branches climb over a wall.[o]
> With bitterness archers attacked him;
>> they shot at him with hostility.
> But his bow remained steady,
>> his strong arms stayed[p] limber,
> because of the hand of the Mighty One of Jacob,
>> because of the Shepherd, the Rock of Israel,
> because of your father's God, who helps you,
>> because of the Almighty,[q] who blesses you
> with blessings of the heavens above,
>> blessings of the deep that lies below,
>> blessings of the breast and womb.
> Your father's blessings are greater
>> than the blessings of the ancient mountains,
>> than[r] the bounty of the age-old hills.
> Let all these rest on the head of Joseph,
>> on the brow of the prince among[s] his brothers.

BENJAMIN THE AGGRESSOR.   Gen. 49:27

> "Benjamin is a ravenous wolf;
>> in the morning he devours the prey,
>> in the evening he divides the plunder."

BURIAL DIRECTIONS GIVEN. All these are the twelve tribes of Israel,   Gen.
and this is what their father said to them when he blessed them, giving   49:28-32
each the blessing appropriate to him.

Then he gave them these instructions: "I am about to be gathered to my
people. Bury me with my fathers in the cave in the field of Ephron the
Hittite, the cave in the field of Machpelah, near Mamre in Canaan, which
Abraham bought as a burial place from Ephron the Hittite, along with the
field. There Abraham and his wife Sarah were buried, there Isaac and his
wife Rebekah were buried, and there I buried Leah. The field and the cave
in it were bought from the Hittites.[t]"

ISRAEL (JACOB) DIES. When Jacob had finished giving instructions to his   Gen. 49:33
sons, he drew his feet up into the bed, breathed his last and was gathered   (Ca. 1859
to his people.   B.C.)

ISRAEL EMBALMED. Joseph threw himself upon his father and wept   Gen.
over him and kissed him. Then Joseph directed the physicians in his ser-   50:1-3
vice to embalm his father Israel. So the physicians embalmed him, taking
a full forty days, for that was the time required for embalming. And the
Egyptians mourned for him seventy days.

PROCESSION TO BURIAL. When the days of mourning had passed,   Gen.
Joseph said to Pharaoh's court, "If I have found favor in your eyes, speak   50:4-9
to Pharaoh for me. Tell him, 'My father made me swear an oath and said,   By the
"I am about to die; bury me in the tomb I dug for myself in the land of   Jordan
Canaan." Now let me go up and bury my father; then I will return.'"

Pharaoh said, "Go up and bury your father, as he made you swear to
do."

[o]Or Joseph is a wild colt, / a wild colt near a spring, / a wild donkey on a terraced hill   [p]Or
archers will attack . . . will shoot . . . will remain . . . will stay   [q]Hebrew Shaddai   [r]Or of my
progenitors, / as great as   [s]Or the one separated from   [t]Or the sons of Heth

So Joseph went up to bury his father. All Pharaoh's officials accompanied him—the dignitaries of his court and all the dignitaries of Egypt—besides all the members of Joseph's household and his brothers and those belonging to his father's household. Only their children and their flocks and herds were left in Goshen. Chariots and horsemen[u] also went up with him. It was a very large company.

Gen.
50:10-14
Mamre
(Hebron)

MOURNING AND BURIAL.   When they reached the threshing floor of Atad, near the Jordan, they lamented loudly and bitterly; and there Joseph observed a seven-day period of mourning for his father. When the Canaanites who lived there saw the mourning at the threshing floor of Atad, they said, "The Egyptians are holding a solemn ceremony of mourning." That is why that place near the Jordan is called Abel Mizraim.[v]

So Jacob's sons did as he had commanded them: They carried him to the land of Canaan and buried him in the cave in the field of Machpelah, near Mamre, which Abraham had bought as a burial place from Ephron the Hittite, along with the field. After burying his father, Joseph returned to Egypt, together with his brothers and all the others who had gone with him to bury his father.

Gen.
50:15-21
Egypt

JOSEPH ALLAYS FEARS.   When Joseph's brothers saw that their father was dead, they said, "What if Joseph holds a grudge against us and pays us back for all the wrongs we did to him?" So they sent word to Joseph, saying, "Your father left these instructions before he died: 'This is what you are to say to Joseph: I ask you to forgive your brothers the sins and the wrongs they committed in treating you so badly.' Now please forgive the sins of the servants of the God of your father." When their message came to him, Joseph wept.

His brothers then came and threw themselves down before him. "We are your slaves," they said.

But Joseph said to them, "Don't be afraid. Am I in the place of God? You intended to harm me, but God intended it for good to accomplish what is now being done, the saving of many lives. So then, don't be afraid. I will provide for you and your children." And he reassured them and spoke kindly to them.

Gen.
50:22,23

JOSEPH'S GREAT-GRANDCHILDREN.   Joseph stayed in Egypt, along with all his father's family. He lived a hundred and ten years and saw the third generation of Ephraim's children. Also the children of Makir son of Manasseh were placed at birth on Joseph's knees.[w]

Gen. 50:24

JOSEPH ARRANGES RETURN.   Then Joseph said to his brothers, "I am about to die. But God will surely come to your aid and take you up out of this land to the land he promised on oath to Abraham, Isaac and Jacob."

Gen.
50:25,26
(Ca. 1805
B.C.)

JOSEPH DIES.   And Joseph made the sons of Israel swear an oath and said, "God will surely come to your aid, and then you must carry my bones up from this place."

So Joseph died at the age of a hundred and ten. And after they embalmed him, he was placed in a coffin in Egypt.

---

[u]Or *charioteers*   [v]*Abel Mizraim* means *mourning of the Egyptians.*   [w]That is, were
counted as his

ESTABLISHMENT OF A NATION

(Ca. 1525-1400 B.C.)

Moses Emerges As Leader

With the death of Joseph, the Genesis record comes to an end, and some 400 years apparently pass before another scriptural account focuses back on the descendants of Israel in Egypt. In the years covered by the Genesis record, the outstanding man of God was Abraham. It was Abraham who fathered the nation which would become God's chosen people. It was Abraham whose belief and trust in God's promises made him an example of faith for all times. As the Exodus record begins, a new spiritual leader emerges from among God's people. For a more sophisticated age, Moses will be a man of education, training, and royal upbringing. He will be an author, lawgiver, builder, and military leader. Most importantly, he, like Abraham, will be a man of faith in God and an intermediary between God and his people.

The story of Moses' ascension to a place of leadership over the Israelites is a fascinating one in which the providential hand of God can be seen to lift Moses from his lowly birth as a Hebrew to a place of honor in the very household of the ruling Pharaoh. Then, during a time of exile in the land of Midian, just east of the Sinai Peninsula and across from the Gulf of Aqaba, Moses takes a wife by the name of Zipporah. Zipporah's father is known as both Reuel and Jethro.

It is in Midian that Moses is called by God to lead the Hebrew nation out of the oppressive bondage into which they have fallen since the days of Joseph. It is clear that Moses is reluctant to take on the responsibility of leadership, and therefore God must demonstrate the power that will be given to Moses in order to accomplish the mission which God has assigned him. It is near Mount Horeb, also known as Mount Sinai, that God confronts Moses, and it will be on this same mountain that one of the most important events in the history of the Hebrew nation will later take place.

The Exodus record now begins where the Genesis record ended, with a last recital of the sons of Israel who had first emigrated to Egypt.

DESCENDANTS MULTIPLY.   These are the names of the sons of Israel who went to Egypt with Jacob, each with his family: Reuben, Simeon, Levi and Judah; Issachar, Zebulun and Benjamin; Dan and Naphtali; Gad and

Ex. 1:1-7
Goshen

Asher. The descendants of Jacob numbered seventy[a] in all; Joseph was already in Egypt.

Now Joseph and all his brothers and all that generation died, but the Israelites were fruitful and multiplied greatly and became exceedingly numerous, so that the land was filled with them.

Ex. 1:8-14   ISRAELITES OPPRESSED BY KING.   Then a new king, who did not know about Joseph, came to power in Egypt. "Look," he said to his people, "the Israelites have become much too numerous for us. Come, we must deal shrewdly with them or they will become even more numerous and, if war breaks out, will join our enemies, fight against us and leave the country."

So they put slave masters over them to oppress them with forced labor, and they built Pithom and Rameses as store cities for Pharaoh. But the more they were oppressed, the more they multiplied and spread; so the Egyptians came to dread the Israelites and worked them ruthlessly. They made their lives bitter with hard labor in brick and mortar and with all kinds of work in the fields; in all their hard labor the Egyptians used them ruthlessly.

Ex. 1:15-22   ATTEMPT TO KILL BOYS.   The king of Egypt said to the Hebrew midwives, whose names were Shiphrah and Puah, "When you help the Hebrew women in childbirth and observe them on the delivery stool, if it is a boy, kill him; but if it is a girl, let her live." The midwives, however, feared God and did not do what the king of Egypt had told them to do; they let the boys live. Then the king of Egypt summoned the midwives and asked them, "Why have you done this? Why have you let the boys live?"

The midwives answered Pharaoh, "Hebrew women are not like Egyptian women; they are vigorous and give birth before the midwives arrive."

So God was kind to the midwives and the people increased and became even more numerous. And because the midwives feared God, he gave them families of their own.

Then Pharaoh gave this order to all his people: "Every boy that is born[b] you must throw into the Nile, but let every girl live."

Ex. 2:1-4
(Ca. 1526   MOSES BORN AND HIDDEN.   Now a man of the house of Levi married
B.C.)   a Levite woman, and she became pregnant and gave birth to a son. When she saw that he was a fine child, she hid him for three months. But when she could hide him no longer, she got a papyrus basket for him and coated it with tar and pitch. Then she placed the child in it and put it among the reeds along the bank of the Nile. His sister stood at a distance to see what would happen to him.

Ex. 2:5-10   PHARAOH'S DAUGHTER FINDS MOSES.   Then Pharaoh's daughter went down to the Nile to bathe, and her attendants were walking along the river bank. She saw the basket among the reeds and sent her slave girl to get it. She opened it and saw the baby. He was crying, and she felt sorry for him. "This is one of the Hebrew babies," she said.

Then his sister asked Pharaoh's daughter, "Shall I go and get one of the Hebrew women to nurse the baby for you?"

"Yes, go," she answered. And the girl went and got the baby's mother.

[a]Masoretic Text (see also Gen. 46:27); Dead Sea Scrolls and Septuagint (see also Acts 7:14 and note at Gen. 46:27) *seventy-five*   [b]Masoretic Text; Samaritan Pentateuch, Septuagint and Targums *born to the Hebrews*

Pharaoh's daughter said to her, "Take this baby and nurse him for me, and I will pay you." So the woman took the baby and nursed him. When the child grew older, she took him to Pharaoh's daughter and he became her son. She named him Moses,[c] saying, "I drew him out of the water."

MOSES KILLS AN EGYPTIAN.   One day, after Moses had grown up, he went out to where his own people were and watched them at their hard labor. He saw an Egyptian beating a Hebrew, one of his own people. Glancing this way and that and seeing no one, he killed the Egyptian and hid him in the sand. The next day he went out and saw two Hebrews fighting. He asked the one in the wrong, "Why are you hitting your fellow Hebrew?"   Ex. 2:11-15

The man said, "Who made you ruler and judge over us? Are you thinking of killing me as you killed the Egyptian?" Then Moses was afraid and thought, "What I did must have become known."

When Pharaoh heard of this, he tried to kill Moses, but Moses fled from Pharaoh and went to live in Midian, where he sat down by a well.

MOSES FLEES TO MIDIAN.   Now a priest of Midian had seven daughters, and they came to draw water and fill the troughs to water their father's flock. Some shepherds came along and drove them away, but Moses got up and came to their rescue and watered their flock.   Ex. 2:16-20 (Ca. 1486 B.C.) Midian

When the girls returned to Reuel their father, he asked them, "Why have you returned so early today?"

They answered, "An Egyptian rescued us from the shepherds. He even drew water for us and watered the flock."

"And where is he?" he asked his daughters. "Why did you leave him? Invite him to have something to eat."

MOSES MARRIES ZIPPORAH.   Moses agreed to stay with the man, who gave his daughter Zipporah to Moses in marriage. Zipporah gave birth to a son, and Moses named him Gershom,[d] saying, "I have become an alien in a foreign land."   Ex. 2:21,22

GOD PREPARES DELIVERANCE.   During that long period, the king of Egypt died. The Israelites groaned in their slavery and cried out, and their cry for help because of their slavery went up to God. God heard their groaning and he remembered his covenant with Abraham, with Isaac and with Jacob. So God looked on the Israelites and was concerned about them.   Ex. 2:23-25

THE BURNING BUSH.   Now Moses was tending the flock of Jethro his father-in-law, the priest of Midian, and he led the flock to the far side of the desert and came to Horeb, the mountain of God. There the angel of the LORD appeared to him in flames of fire from within a bush. Moses saw that though the bush was on fire it did not burn up. So Moses thought, "I will go over and see this strange sight—why the bush does not burn up."   Ex. 3:1-6

When the LORD saw that he had gone over to look, God called to him from within the bush, "Moses! Moses!"

And Moses said, "Here I am."

"Do not come any closer," God said. "Take off your sandals, for the

---

[c]*Moses* sounds like the Hebrew for *draw out.*   [d]*Gershom* sounds like the Hebrew for *an alien there.*

place where you are standing is holy ground." Then he said, "I am the God of your father, the God of Abraham, the God of Isaac and the God of Jacob." At this, Moses hid his face, because he was afraid to look at God.

Ex. 3:7-9   GOD'S PLAN REVEALED.   The LORD said, "I have indeed seen the misery of my people in Egypt. I have heard them crying out because of their slave drivers, and I am concerned about their suffering. So I have come down to rescue them from the hand of the Egyptians and to bring them up out of that land into a good and spacious land, a land flowing with milk and honey—the home of the Canaanites, Hittites, Amorites, Perizzites, Hivites and Jebusites. And now the cry of the Israelites has reached me, and I have seen the way the Egyptians are oppressing them.

Ex. 3:10-12   MOSES RELUCTANT TO SERVE.   So now, go. I am sending you to Pharaoh to bring my people the Israelites out of Egypt."

But Moses said to God, "Who am I, that I should go to Pharaoh and bring the Israelites out of Egypt?"

And God said, "I will be with you. And this will be the sign to you that it is I who have sent you: When you have brought the people out of Egypt, you[e] will worship God on this mountain."

Ex. 3:13-15   GOD THE "I AM."   Moses said to God, "Suppose I go to the Israelites and say to them, 'The God of your fathers has sent me to you,' and they ask me, 'What is his name?' Then what shall I tell them?"

God said to Moses, "I AM WHO I AM.[f] This is what you are to say to the Israelites: 'I AM has sent me to you.'"

God also said to Moses, "Say to the Israelites, 'The LORD,[g] the God of your fathers—the God of Abraham, the God of Isaac and the God of Jacob—has sent me to you.' This is my name forever, the name by which I am to be remembered from generation to generation.

Ex. 3:16-22   OUTLINE OF MISSION.   "Go, assemble the elders of Israel and say to them, 'The LORD, the God of your fathers—the God of Abraham, Isaac and Jacob—appeared to me and said: I have watched over you and have seen what has been done to you in Egypt. And I have promised to bring you up out of your misery in Egypt into the land of the Canaanites, Hittites, Amorites, Perizzites, Hivites and Jebusites—a land flowing with milk and honey.'

"The elders of Israel will listen to you. Then you and the elders are to go to the king of Egypt and say to him, 'The LORD, the God of the Hebrews, has met with us. Let us take a three-day journey into the desert to offer sacrifices to the LORD our God.' But I know that the king of Egypt will not let you go unless a mighty hand compels him. So I will stretch out my hand and strike the Egyptians with all the wonders that I will perform among them. After that, he will let you go.

"And I will make the Egyptians favorably disposed toward this people, so that when you leave you will not go empty-handed. Every woman is to ask her neighbor and any woman living in her house for articles of silver and gold and for clothing, which you will put on your sons and daughters. And so you will plunder the Egyptians."

---

[e]The Hebrew is plural.   [f]Or I WILL BE WHAT I WILL BE   [g]The Hebrew for LORD sounds like and may be derived from the Hebrew for I AM in verse 14.

GOD'S POWER DEMONSTRATED.   Moses answered, "What if they do   Ex. 4:1-9
not believe me or listen to me and say, 'The LORD did not appear to you'?"
    Then the LORD said to him, "What is that in your hand?"
    "A staff," he replied.
    The LORD said, "Throw it on the ground."
    Moses threw it on the ground and it became a snake, and he ran from it.
Then the LORD said to him, "Reach out your hand and take it by the tail."
So Moses reached out and took hold of the snake and it turned back into
a staff in his hand. "This," said the LORD, "is so that they may believe that
the LORD, the God of their fathers—the God of Abraham, the God of Isaac
and the God of Jacob—has appeared to you."
    Then the LORD said, "Put your hand inside your cloak." So Moses put
his hand into his cloak, and when he took it out, it was leprous,[h] like snow.
    "Now put it back into your cloak," he said. So Moses put his hand back
into his cloak, and when he took it out, it was restored, like the rest of his
flesh.
    Then the LORD said, "If they do not believe you or pay attention to the
first miraculous sign, they may believe the second. But if they do not
believe these two signs or listen to you, take some water from the Nile and
pour it on the dry ground. The water you take from the river will become
blood on the ground."

AARON TO BE SPOKESMAN.   Moses said to the LORD, "O Lord, I have   Ex. 4:10-17
never been eloquent, neither in the past nor since you have spoken to your
servant. I am slow of speech and tongue."
    The LORD said to him, "Who gave man his mouth? Who makes him deaf
or mute? Who gives him sight or makes him blind? Is it not I, the LORD?
Now go; I will help you speak and will teach you what to say."
    But Moses said, "O Lord, please send someone else to do it."
    Then the LORD's anger burned against Moses and he said, "What about
your brother, Aaron the Levite? I know he can speak well. He is already on
his way to meet you, and his heart will be glad when he sees you. You shall
speak to him and put words in his mouth; I will help both of you speak
and will teach you what to do. He will speak to the people for you, and it
will be as if he were your mouth and as if you were God to him. But take
this staff in your hand so you can perform miraculous signs with it."

MOSES LEAVES FOR EGYPT.   Then Moses went back to Jethro his   Ex. 4:18-20
father-in-law and said to him, "Let me go back to my own people in Egypt
to see if any of them are still alive."
    Jethro said, "Go, and I wish you well."
    Now the LORD had said to Moses in Midian, "Go back to Egypt, for all
the men who wanted to kill you are dead." So Moses took his wife and
sons, put them on a donkey and started back to Egypt. And he took the
staff of God in his hand.

PREDICTION ABOUT PHARAOH.   The LORD said to Moses, "When   Ex. 4:21-23
you return to Egypt, see that you perform before Pharaoh all the wonders
I have given you the power to do. But I will harden his heart so that he

---

[h]The Hebrew word was used for various diseases affecting the skin—not necessarily
leprosy.

will not let the people go. Then say to Pharaoh, 'This is what the LORD says: Israel is my firstborn son, and I told you, "Let my son go, so he may worship me." But you refused to let him go; so I will kill your firstborn son.'"

Ex. 4:24-26 MOSES' SON CIRCUMCISED.   At a lodging place on the way, the LORD met ⌊Moses⌋[i] and was about to kill him. But Zipporah took a flint knife, cut off her son's foreskin and touched ⌊Moses'⌋ feet with it.[j] "Surely you are a bridegroom of blood to me," she said. So the LORD let him alone. (At that time she said "bridegroom of blood," referring to circumcision.)

Ex. 4:27,28 AARON MEETS MOSES.   The LORD said to Aaron, "Go into the desert
Wilder- to meet Moses." So he met Moses at the mountain of God and kissed him.
ness Then Moses told Aaron everything the LORD had sent him to say, and also about all the miraculous signs he had commanded him to perform.

Ex. 4:29-31 ISRAELITES TOLD OF PLAN.   Moses and Aaron brought together all
Egypt the elders of the Israelites, and Aaron told them everything the LORD had said to Moses. He also performed the signs before the people, and they believed. And when they heard that the LORD was concerned about them and had seen their misery, they bowed down and worshiped.

Ex. 6:14-27 LINEAGE OF MOSES AND AARON.   These were the heads of their families[k]:

The sons of Reuben the firstborn son of Israel were Hanoch and Pallu, Hezron and Carmi. These were the clans of Reuben.

The sons of Simeon were Jemuel, Jamin, Ohad, Jakin, Zohar and Shaul the son of a Canaanite woman. These were the clans of Simeon.

These were the names of the sons of Levi according to their records: Gershon, Kohath and Merari. Levi lived 137 years.

The sons of Gershon, by clans, were Libni and Shimei.

The sons of Kohath were Amram, Izhar, Hebron and Uzziel. Kohath lived 133 years.

The sons of Merari were Mahli and Mushi.

These were the clans of Levi according to their records.

Amram married his father's sister Jochebed, who bore him Aaron and Moses. Amram lived 137 years.

The sons of Izhar were Korah, Nepheg and Zicri.

The sons of Uzziel were Mishael, Elzaphan and Sithri.

Aaron married Elisheba, daughter of Amminadab and sister of Nahshon, and she bore him Nadab and Abihu, Eleazar and Ithamar.

The sons of Korah were Assir, Elkanah and Abiasaph. These were the Korahite clans.

Eleazar son of Aaron married one of the daughters of Putiel, and she bore him Phinehas.

These were the heads of the Levite families, clan by clan.

It was this same Aaron and Moses to whom the LORD said, "Bring the Israelites out of Egypt by their divisions." They were the ones who spoke to Pharaoh king of Egypt about bringing the Israelites out of Egypt. It was the same Moses and Aaron.

[i]Or ⌊Moses' son⌋; Hebrew *him*   [j]Or *and drew near* ⌊Moses'⌋ *feet*   [k]The Hebrew for *families* here and in verse 25 refers to units larger than clans.

Plagues on the Egyptians

One of the classic confrontations between God and man is about to take place. Pharaoh, a heathen king, knows little about the true and living God of Creation. Yet he will soon learn about this God, perhaps more than he may want to know. God has promised Moses that Pharaoh's heart will be hardened against letting the people of Israel go out of Egypt. At first this seems to be a curious way to deliver his people from their bondage, and it also appears to be a rather inconsistent act on the part of a righteous God. But God knows both the stubborn will of Pharaoh and the need to demonstrate the divine power of deliverance to his own chosen people. Therefore God will take direct advantage of Pharaoh's own disposition in working out his divine plan to save the Israelites.

The struggle between God and Pharaoh is classic because it demonstrates how all men and women tend to struggle with God. Pharaoh will first reject God altogether, then respond to the initial demonstrations of God's power by believing in the artificial manifestations of power which human trickery can devise. When even the tricks of his magicians cannot duplicate the plagues brought against his people and property, Pharaoh will try to avoid God through procrastination, compromise, and insincere repentance. With each attempt at resisting God, Pharaoh's heart gets harder, until he is unmoved by even the threat of death to his people.

The period of time during which these dramatic events will take place is not clearly indicated. However, it appears that weeks or even months may elapse between each of the ten plagues which God will bring against Egypt. This can be seen, for example, in the time which presumably must pass between the plague of dead animals and the plague of hail.

As the confrontation begins, Pharaoh's tough response and vindictive actions against the Israelites cause them to question Moses' leadership.

PHARAOH REFUSES PLEA.   Afterward Moses and Aaron went to   Ex. 5:1-5
Pharaoh and said, "This is what the LORD, the God of Israel, says: 'Let my people go, so that they may hold a festival to me in the desert.'"

Pharaoh said, "Who is the LORD, that I should obey him and let Israel go? I do not know the LORD and I will not let Israel go."

Then they said, "The God of the Hebrews has met with us. Now let us take a three-day journey into the desert to offer sacrifices to the LORD our God, or he may strike us with plagues or with the sword."

But the king of Egypt said, "Moses and Aaron, why are you taking the people away from their labor? Get back to your work!" Then Pharaoh said, "Look, the people of the land are now numerous, and you are stopping them from working."

BURDENS INCREASED.   That same day Pharaoh gave this order to the   Ex. 5:6-14
slave drivers and foremen in charge of the people: "You are no longer to supply the people with straw for making bricks; let them go and gather their own straw. But require them to make the same number of bricks as before; don't reduce the quota. They are lazy; that is why they are crying out, 'Let us go and sacrifice to our God.' Make the work harder for the men so that they keep working and pay no attention to lies."

Then the slave drivers and the foremen went out and said to the people, "This is what Pharaoh says: 'I will not give you any more straw. Go and get your own straw wherever you can find it, but your work will not be reduced at all.' " So the people scattered all over Egypt to gather stubble to use for straw. The slave drivers kept pressing them, saying, "Complete the work required of you for each day, just as when you had straw." The Israelite foremen appointed by Pharaoh's slave drivers were beaten and were asked, "Why didn't you meet your quota of bricks yesterday or today, as before?"

Ex. 5:15-21 FOREMEN BLAME MOSES.   Then the Israelite foremen went and appealed to Pharaoh: "Why have you treated your servants this way? Your servants are given no straw, yet we are told, 'Make bricks!' Your servants are being beaten, but the fault is with your own people."

Pharaoh said, "Lazy, that's what you are—lazy! That is why you keep saying, 'Let us go and sacrifice to the LORD.' Now get to work. You will not be given any straw, yet you must produce your full quota of bricks."

The Israelite foremen realized they were in trouble when they were told, "You are not to reduce the number of bricks required of you for each day." When they left Pharaoh, they found Moses and Aaron waiting to meet them, and they said, "May the LORD look upon you and judge you! You have made us a stench to Pharaoh and his officials and have put a sword in their hand to kill us."

Ex. 5:22-6:1 MOSES ENTREATS GOD.   Moses returned to the LORD and said, "O Lord, why have you brought trouble upon this people? Is this why you sent me? Ever since I went to Pharaoh to speak in your name, he has brought trouble upon this people, and you have not rescued your people at all." Then the LORD said to Moses, "Now you will see what I will do to Pharaoh: Because of my mighty hand he will let them go; because of my mighty hand he will drive them out of his country."

Ex. 6:2-9 GOD TO FULFILL PROMISES.   God also said to Moses, "I am the LORD. I appeared to Abraham, to Isaac and to Jacob as God Almighty,[l] but by my name the LORD[m] I did not make myself known to them.[n] I also established my covenant with them to give them the land of Canaan, where they lived as aliens. Moreover, I have heard the groaning of the Israelites, whom the Egyptians are enslaving, and I have remembered my covenant.

"Therefore, say to the Israelites: 'I am the LORD, and I will bring you out from under the yoke of the Egyptians. I will free you from being slaves to them, and I will redeem you with an outstretched arm and with mighty acts of judgment. I will take you as my own people, and I will be your God. Then you will know that I am the LORD your God, who brought you out from under the yoke of the Egyptians. And I will bring you to the land I swore with uplifted hand to give to Abraham, to Isaac and to Jacob. I will give it to you as a possession. I am the LORD.' "

Moses reported this to the Israelites, but they did not listen to him because of their discouragement and cruel bondage.

Ex. 6:10-13
6:28-30 MOSES DOUBTS SUCCESS.   Then the LORD said to Moses, "Go, tell Pharaoh king of Egypt to let the Israelites go out of his country."

---

[l]Hebrew *El-Shaddai*   [m]See note at Exodus 3:15.   [n]Or *Almighty, and by my name the* LORD *did I not let myself be known to them?*

But Moses said to the LORD, "If the Israelites will not listen to me, why would Pharaoh listen to me, since I speak with faltering lips[o]?"

Now the LORD spoke to Moses and Aaron about the Israelites and Pharaoh king of Egypt, and he commanded them to bring the Israelites out of Egypt.

GOD REASSURES MOSES.   Then the LORD said to Moses, "See, I have made you like God to Pharaoh, and your brother Aaron will be your prophet. You are to say everything I command you, and your brother Aaron is to tell Pharaoh to let the Israelites go out of his country. But I will harden Pharaoh's heart, and though I multiply my miraculous signs and wonders in Egypt, he will not listen to you. Then I will lay my hand on Egypt and with mighty acts of judgment I will bring out my divisions, my people the Israelites. And the Egyptians will know that I am the LORD when I stretch out my hand against Egypt and bring the Israelites out of it."

Ex. 7:1-7
(Ca. 1446
B.C.)

Moses and Aaron did just as the LORD commanded them. Moses was eighty years old and Aaron eighty-three when they spoke to Pharaoh.

RODS BECOME SNAKES.   The LORD said to Moses and Aaron, "When Pharaoh says to you, 'Perform a miracle,' then say to Aaron, 'Take your staff and throw it down before Pharaoh,' and it will become a snake."

Ex. 7:8-13

So Moses and Aaron went to Pharaoh and did just as the LORD commanded. Aaron threw his staff down in front of Pharaoh and his officials, and it became a snake. Pharaoh then summoned wise men and sorcerers, and the Egyptian magicians also did the same things by their secret arts: Each one threw down his staff and it became a snake. But Aaron's staff swallowed up their staffs. Yet Pharaoh's heart became hard and he would not listen to them, just as the LORD had said.

PLAGUE OF WATER TO BLOOD.   Then the LORD said to Moses, "Pharaoh's heart is unyielding; he refuses to let the people go. Go to Pharaoh in the morning as he goes out to the water. Wait on the bank of the Nile to meet him, and take in your hand the staff that was changed into a snake. Then say to him, 'The LORD, the God of the Hebrews, has sent me to say to you: Let my people go, so that they may worship me in the desert. But until now you have not listened. This is what the LORD says: By this you will know that I am the LORD: With the staff that is in my hand I will strike the water of the Nile, and it will be changed into blood. The fish in the Nile will die, and the river will stink; the Egyptians will not be able to drink its water.'"

Ex. 7:14-24

The LORD said to Moses, "Tell Aaron, 'Take your staff and stretch out your hand over the waters of Egypt—over the streams and canals, over the ponds and all the reservoirs'—and they will turn to blood. Blood will be everywhere in Egypt, even in the wooden buckets and stone jars."

Moses and Aaron did just as the LORD had commanded. He raised his staff in the presence of Pharaoh and his officials and struck the water of the Nile, and all the water was changed into blood. The fish in the Nile died, and the river smelled so bad that the Egyptians could not drink its water. Blood was everywhere in Egypt.

But the Egyptian magicians did the same things by their secret arts, and Pharaoh's heart became hard; he would not listen to Moses and Aaron,

[o]Hebrew *I am uncircumcised of lips*

just as the LORD had said. Instead, he turned and went into his palace, and did not take even this to heart. And all the Egyptians dug along the Nile to get drinking water, because they could not drink the water of the river.

Ex.
7:25-8:15

PLAGUE OF FROGS.   Seven days passed after the LORD struck the Nile. Then the LORD said to Moses, "Go to Pharaoh and say to him, 'This is what the LORD says: Let my people go, so that they may worship me. If you refuse to let them go, I will plague your whole country with frogs. The Nile will teem with frogs. They will come up into your palace and your bedroom and onto your bed, into the houses of your officials and on your people, and into your ovens and kneading troughs. The frogs will go up on you and your people and all your officials.' "

Then the LORD said to Moses, "Tell Aaron, 'Stretch out your hand with your staff over the streams and canals and ponds, and make frogs come up on the land of Egypt.' "

So Aaron stretched out his hand over the waters of Egypt, and the frogs came up and covered the land. But the magicians did the same things by their secret arts; they also made frogs come up on the land of Egypt.

Pharaoh summoned Moses and Aaron and said, "Pray to the LORD to take the frogs away from me and my people, and I will let your people go to offer sacrifices to the LORD."

Moses said to Pharaoh, "I leave to you the honor of setting the time for me to pray for you and your officials and your people that you and your houses may be rid of the frogs, except for those that remain in the Nile."

"Tomorrow," Pharaoh said.

Moses replied, "It will be as you say, so that you may know there is no one like the LORD our God. The frogs will leave you and your houses, your officials and your people; they will remain only in the Nile."

After Moses and Aaron left Pharaoh, Moses cried out to the LORD about the frogs he had brought on Pharaoh. And the LORD did what Moses asked. The frogs died in the houses, in the courtyards and in the fields. They were piled into heaps, and the land reeked of them. But when Pharaoh saw that there was relief, he hardened his heart and would not listen to Moses and Aaron, just as the LORD had said.

Ex. 8:16-19

PLAGUE OF GNATS.   Then the LORD said to Moses, "Tell Aaron, 'Stretch out your staff and strike the dust of the ground,' and throughout the land of Egypt the dust will become gnats." They did this, and when Aaron stretched out his hand with the staff and struck the dust of the ground, gnats came upon men and animals. All the dust throughout the land of Egypt became gnats. But when the magicians tried to produce gnats by their secret arts, they could not. And the gnats were on men and animals.

The magicians said to Pharaoh, "This is the finger of God." But Pharaoh's heart was hard and he would not listen, just as the LORD had said.

Ex. 8:20-24

PLAGUE OF FLIES.   Then the LORD said to Moses, "Get up early in the morning and confront Pharaoh as he goes to the water and say to him, 'This is what the LORD says: Let my people go, so that they may worship me. If you do not let my people go, I will send swarms of flies on you and your officials, on your people and into your houses. The houses of the Egyptians will be full of flies, and even the ground where they are.

" 'But on that day I will deal differently with the land of Goshen, where my people live; no swarms of flies will be there, so that you will know that

I, the LORD, am in this land. I will make a distinction[p] between my people and your people. This miraculous sign will occur tomorrow.'"

And the LORD did this. Dense swarms of flies poured into Pharaoh's palace and into the houses of his officials, and throughout Egypt the land was ruined by the flies.

LOCAL SACRIFICE AGREED.   Then Pharaoh summoned Moses and Aaron and said, "Go, sacrifice to your God here in the land."

Ex. 8:25-32

But Moses said, "That would not be right. The sacrifices we offer the LORD our God would be detestable to the Egyptians. And if we offer sacrifices that are detestable in their eyes, will they not stone us? We must take a three-day journey into the desert to offer sacrifices to the LORD our God, as he commands us."

Pharaoh said, "I will let you go to offer sacrifices to the LORD your God in the desert, but you must not go very far. Now pray for me."

Moses answered, "As soon as I leave you, I will pray to the LORD, and tomorrow the flies will leave Pharaoh and his officials and his people. Only be sure that Pharaoh does not act deceitfully again by not letting the people go to offer sacrifices to the LORD."

Then Moses left Pharaoh and prayed to the LORD, and the LORD did what Moses asked: The flies left Pharaoh and his officials and his people; not a fly remained. But this time also Pharaoh hardened his heart and would not let the people go.

PLAGUE OF DEAD ANIMALS.   Then the LORD said to Moses, "Go to Pharaoh and say to him, 'This is what the LORD, the God of the Hebrews, says: "Let my people go, so that they may worship me." If you refuse to let them go and continue to hold them back, the hand of the LORD will bring a terrible plague on your livestock in the field—on your horses and donkeys and camels and on your cattle and sheep and goats. But the LORD will make a distinction between the livestock of Israel and that of Egypt, so that no animal belonging to the Israelites will die.'"

Ex. 9:1-7

The LORD set a time and said, "Tomorrow the LORD will do this in the land." And the next day the LORD did it: All the livestock of the Egyptians died, but not one animal belonging to the Israelites died. Pharaoh sent men to investigate and found that not even one of the animals of the Israelites had died. Yet his heart was unyielding and he would not let the people go.

PLAGUE OF BOILS.   Then the LORD said to Moses and Aaron, "Take handfuls of soot from a furnace and have Moses toss it into the air in the presence of Pharaoh. It will become fine dust over the whole land of Egypt, and festering boils will break out on men and animals throughout the land."

Ex. 9:8-12

So they took soot from a furnace and stood before Pharaoh. Moses tossed it into the air, and festering boils broke out on men and animals. The magicians could not stand before Moses because of the boils that were on them and on all the Egyptians. But the LORD hardened Pharaoh's heart and he would not listen to Moses and Aaron, just as the LORD had said to Moses.

PLAGUE OF HAIL.   Then the LORD said to Moses, "Get up early in the morning, confront Pharaoh and say to him, 'This is what the LORD, the

Ex. 9:13-26

[p]Septuagint and Vulgate; Hebrew *will put a deliverance*

God of the Hebrews, says: Let my people go, so that they may worship me, or this time I will send the full force of my plagues against you and against your officials and your people, so you may know that there is no one like me in all the earth. For by now I could have stretched out my hand and struck you and your people with a plague that would have wiped you off the earth. But I have raised you up[q] for this very purpose, that I might show you my power and that my name might be proclaimed in all the earth. You still set yourself against my people and will not let them go. Therefore, at this time tomorrow I will send the worst hailstorm that has ever fallen on Egypt, from the day it was founded till now. Give an order now to bring your livestock and everything you have in the field to a place of shelter, because the hail will fall on every man and animal that has not been brought in and is still out in the field, and they will die.' "

Those officials of Pharaoh who feared the word of the LORD hurried to bring their slaves and their livestock inside. But those who ignored the word of the LORD left their slaves and livestock in the field.

Then the LORD said to Moses, "Stretch out your hand toward the sky so that hail will fall all over Egypt—on men and animals and on everything growing in the fields of Egypt." When Moses stretched out his staff toward the sky, the LORD sent thunder and hail, and lightning flashed down to the ground. So the LORD rained hail on the land of Egypt; hail fell and lightning flashed back and forth. It was the worst storm in all the land of Egypt since it had become a nation. Throughout Egypt hail struck everything in the fields—both men and animals; it beat down everything growing in the fields and stripped every tree. The only place it did not hail was the land of Goshen, where the Israelites were.

Ex. 9:27-35 **PHARAOH RENEGES AGAIN.** Then Pharaoh summoned Moses and Aaron. "This time I have sinned," he said to them. "The LORD is in the right, and I and my people are in the wrong. Pray to the LORD, for we have had enough thunder and hail. I will let you go; you don't have to stay any longer."

Moses replied, "When I have gone out of the city, I will spread out my hands in prayer to the LORD. The thunder will stop and there will be no more hail, so you may know that the earth is the LORD's. But I know that you and your officials still do not fear the LORD God."

(The flax and barley were destroyed, since the barley had headed and the flax was in bloom. The wheat and spelt, however, were not destroyed, because they ripen later.)

Then Moses left Pharaoh and went out of the city. He spread out his hands toward the LORD; the thunder and hail stopped, and the rain no longer poured down on the land. When Pharaoh saw that the rain and hail and thunder had stopped, he sinned again: He and his officials hardened their hearts. So Pharaoh's heart was hard and he would not let the Israelites go, just as the LORD had said through Moses.

Ex. 10:1,2 **PURPOSE OF THE PLAGUES.** Then the LORD said to Moses, "Go to Pharaoh, for I have hardened his heart and the hearts of his officials so that I may perform these miraculous signs of mine among them that you may tell your children and grandchildren how I dealt harshly with the

q Or *have spared you*

Egyptians and how I performed my signs among them, and that you may know that I am the LORD."

MOSES WARNS PHARAOH.   So Moses and Aaron went to Pharaoh and said to him, "This is what the LORD, the God of the Hebrews, says: 'How long will you refuse to humble yourself before me? Let my people go, so that they may worship me. If you refuse to let them go, I will bring locusts into your country tomorrow. They will cover the face of the ground so that it cannot be seen. They will devour what little you have left after the hail, including every tree that is growing in your fields. They will fill your houses and those of all your officials and all the Egyptians—something neither your fathers nor your forefathers have ever seen from the day they settled in this land till now.' " Then Moses turned and left Pharaoh. *Ex. 10:3-6*

PHARAOH AGREES MEN CAN GO.   Pharaoh's officials said to him, "How long will this man be a snare to us? Let the people go, so that they may worship the LORD their God. Do you not yet realize that Egypt is ruined?" *Ex. 10:7-11*

Then Moses and Aaron were brought back to Pharaoh. "Go, worship the LORD your God," he said. "But just who will be going?"

Moses answered, "We will go with our young and old, with our sons and daughters, and with our flocks and herds, because we are to celebrate a festival to the LORD."

Pharaoh said, "The LORD be with you—if I let you go, along with your women and children! Clearly you are bent on evil.*r* No! Have only the men go; and worship the LORD, since that's what you have been asking for." Then Moses and Aaron were driven out of Pharaoh's presence.

PLAGUE OF LOCUSTS.   And the LORD said to Moses, "Stretch out your hand over Egypt so that locusts will swarm over the land and devour everything growing in the fields, everything left by the hail." *Ex. 10:12-20*

So Moses stretched out his staff over Egypt, and the LORD made an east wind blow across the land all that day and all that night. By morning the wind had brought the locusts; they invaded all Egypt and settled down in every area of the country in great numbers. Never before had there been such a plague of locusts, nor will there ever be again. They covered all the ground until it was black. They devoured all that was left after the hail— everything growing in the fields and the fruit on the trees. Nothing green remained on tree or plant in all the land of Egypt.

Pharaoh quickly summoned Moses and Aaron and said, "I have sinned against the LORD your God and against you. Now forgive my sin once more and pray to the LORD your God to take this deadly plague away from me."

Moses then left Pharaoh and prayed to the LORD. And the LORD changed the wind to a very strong west wind, which caught up the locusts and carried them into the Red Sea.*s* Not a locust was left anywhere in Egypt. But the LORD hardened Pharaoh's heart, and he would not let the Israelites go.

PLAGUE OF DARKNESS.   Then the LORD said to Moses, "Stretch out your hand toward the sky so that darkness will spread over Egypt—darkness that can be felt." So Moses stretched out his hand toward the sky, and total darkness covered all Egypt for three days. No one could see *Ex. 10:21-23*

*r*Or *Be careful, trouble is in store for you!*   *s*Hebrew *Yam Suph*; that is, Sea of Reeds

anyone else or leave his place for three days. Yet all the Israelites had light in the places where they lived.

Ex.
10:24-29

PHARAOH PARTIALLY AGREES.   Then Pharaoh summoned Moses and said, "Go, worship the LORD. Even your women and children may go with you; only leave your flocks and herds behind."

But Moses said, "You must allow us to have sacrifices and burnt offerings to present to the LORD our God. Our livestock too must go with us; not a hoof is to be left behind. We have to use some of them in worshiping the LORD our God, and until we get there we will not know what we are to use to worship the LORD."

But the LORD hardened Pharaoh's heart, and he was not willing to let them go. Pharaoh said to Moses, "Get out of my sight! Make sure you do not appear before me again! The day you see my face you will die."

"Just as you say," Moses replied, "I will never appear before you again."

Ex. 11:1-3

GOLD AND SILVER GIVEN.   Now the LORD had said to Moses, "I will bring one more plague on Pharaoh and on Egypt. After that, he will let you go from here, and when he does, he will drive you out completely. Tell the people that men and women alike are to ask their neighbors for articles of silver and gold."   (The LORD made the Egyptians favorably disposed toward the people, and Moses himself was highly regarded in Egypt by Pharaoh's officials and by the people.)

Ex. 11:4-10

MOSES WARNS OF DEATH.   So Moses said, "This is what the LORD says: 'About midnight I will go throughout Egypt. Every firstborn son in Egypt will die, from the firstborn son of Pharaoh, who sits on the throne, to the firstborn son of the slave girl, who is at her hand mill, and all the firstborn of the cattle as well. There will be loud wailing throughout Egypt—worse than there has ever been or ever will be again. But among the Israelites not a dog will bark at any man or animal.' Then you will know that the LORD makes a distinction between Egypt and Israel. All these officials of yours will come to me, bowing down before me and saying, 'Go, you and all the people who follow you!' After that I will leave." Then Moses, hot with anger, left Pharaoh. .

The LORD had said to Moses, "Pharaoh will refuse to listen to you—so that my wonders may be multiplied in Egypt." Moses and Aaron performed all these wonders before Pharaoh, but the LORD hardened Pharaoh's heart, and he would not let the Israelites go out of his country.

Passover and the Exodus

Negotiations with Pharaoh have failed. Pharaoh has taken a clearly intractable position which only the severest of divine intervention can overcome. Therefore God makes preparation to bring his people out of their Egyptian bondage by a devastating demonstration of power in which the firstborn of all living things throughout Egypt will meet with death—all, that is, except the Israelites, whom God will spare through a plan involving the sacrifice of lambs and the use of their blood to identify those who are God's people. Death throughout Egypt and the passing over of the Israelites will herald a mass exodus of the Hebrew people from the country of their bondage.

The significance of the event is nothing less than the implementation of God's promises to Abraham, Isaac, and Jacob. It is the deliverance of God's people from their bondage in a heathen land, and a prelude to the establishment of the nation of Israel through which all nations will one day be blessed. Wanting this significant occasion to be remembered and symbolically reenacted by generations to follow, God here institutes the Passover celebration.

INSTRUCTION ABOUT PASSOVER.   The LORD said to Moses and Aaron in Egypt, "This month is to be for you the first month, the first month of your year. Tell the whole community of Israel that on the tenth day of this month each man is to take a lamb† for his family, one for each household. If any household is too small for a whole lamb, they must share one with their nearest neighbor, having taken into account the number of people there are. You are to determine the amount of lamb needed in accordance with what each person will eat. The animals you choose must be year-old males without defect, and you may take them from the sheep or the goats. Take care of them until the fourteenth day of the month, when all the people of the community of Israel must slaughter them at twilight. Then they are to take some of the blood and put it on the sides and tops of the doorframes of the houses where they eat the lambs. That same night they are to eat the meat roasted over the fire, along with bitter herbs, and bread made without yeast. Do not eat the meat raw or cooked in water, but roast it over the fire—head, legs and inner parts. Do not leave any of it till morning; if some is left till morning, you must burn it. This is how you are to eat it: with your cloak tucked into your belt, your sandals on your feet and your staff in your hand. Eat it in haste; it is the LORD's Passover.

"On that same night I will pass through Egypt and strike down every firstborn—both men and animals—and I will bring judgment on all the gods of Egypt. I am the LORD. The blood will be a sign for you on the houses where you are; and when I see the blood, I will pass over you. No destructive plague will touch you when I strike Egypt.

Ex. 12:1-13

TO BE ANNUAL CELEBRATION.   "This is a day you are to commemorate; for the generations to come you shall celebrate it as a festival to the LORD—a lasting ordinance. For seven days you are to eat bread made without yeast. On the first day remove the yeast from your houses, for whoever eats anything with yeast in it from the first day through the seventh must be cut off from Israel. On the first day hold a sacred assembly, and another one on the seventh day. Do no work at all on these days, except to prepare food for everyone to eat—that is all you may do.

"Celebrate the Feast of Unleavened Bread, because it was on this very day that I brought your divisions out of Egypt. Celebrate this day as a lasting ordinance for the generations to come. In the first month you are to eat bread made without yeast, from the evening of the fourteenth day until the evening of the twenty-first day. For seven days no yeast is to be found in your houses. And whoever eats anything with yeast in it must be cut off from the community of Israel, whether he is an alien or native-born.

Ex. 12:14-20

†The Hebrew word can mean *lamb* or *kid*; also in verse 4.

Eat nothing made with yeast. Wherever you live, you must eat unleavened bread."

Ex.
12:43-49

RULES FOR FOREIGNERS. The LORD said to Moses and Aaron, "These are the regulations for the Passover:

"No foreigner is to eat of it. Any slave you have bought may eat of it after you have circumcised him, but a temporary resident and a hired worker may not eat of it.

"It must be eaten inside one house; take none of the meat outside the house. Do not break any of the bones. The whole community of Israel must celebrate it.

"An alien living among you who wants to celebrate the LORD's Passover must have all the males in his household circumcised; then he may take part like one born in the land. No uncircumcised male may eat of it. The same law applies to the native-born and to the alien living among you."

Ex.
12:21-28
12:50

PEOPLE GIVEN INSTRUCTIONS. Then Moses summoned all the elders of Israel and said to them, "Go at once and select the animals for your families and slaughter the Passover lamb. Take a bunch of hyssop, dip it into the blood in the basin and put some of the blood on the top and on both sides of the doorframe. Not one of you shall go out the door of his house until morning. When the LORD goes through the land to strike down the Egyptians, he will see the blood on the top and sides of the doorframe and will pass over that doorway, and he will not permit the destroyer to enter your houses and strike you down.

"Obey these instructions as a lasting ordinance for you and your descendants. When you enter the land that the LORD will give you as he promised, observe this ceremony. And when your children ask you, 'What does this ceremony mean to you?' then tell them, 'It is the Passover sacrifice to the LORD, who passed over the houses of the Israelites in Egypt and spared our homes when he struck down the Egyptians.'" Then the people bowed down and worshiped. The Israelites did just what the LORD commanded Moses and Aaron.

Ex.
12:29-32

PHARAOH LETS ISRAELITES GO. At midnight the LORD struck down all the firstborn in Egypt, from the firstborn of Pharaoh, who sat on the throne, to the firstborn of the prisoner, who was in the dungeon, and the firstborn of all the livestock as well. Pharaoh and all his officials and all the Egyptians got up during the night, and there was loud wailing in Egypt, for there was not a house without someone dead.

During the night Pharaoh summoned Moses and Aaron and said, "Up! Leave my people, you and the Israelites! Go, worship the LORD as you have requested. Take your flocks and herds, as you have said, and go. And also bless me."

Ex.
12:33-36

EGYPTIANS GIVE AID. The Egyptians urged the people to hurry and leave the country. "For otherwise," they said, "we will all die!" So the people took their dough before the yeast was added, and carried it on their shoulders in kneading troughs wrapped in clothing. The Israelites did as Moses instructed and asked the Egyptians for articles of silver and gold and for clothing. The LORD had made the Egyptians favorably disposed toward the people, and they gave them what they asked for; so they plundered the Egyptians.

THE EXODUS BEGINS.   And on that very day the LORD brought the
Israelites out of Egypt by their divisions. The Israelites journeyed from
Rameses to Succoth. There were about six hundred thousand men on foot,
besides women and children. Many other people went up with them, as
well as large droves of livestock, both flocks and herds. With the dough
they had brought from Egypt, they baked cakes of unleavened bread. The
dough was without yeast because they had been driven out of Egypt and
did not have time to prepare food for themselves.

Ex. 12:51
12:37-39
(Ca. 1446
B.C.)

IMPORTANCE OF THE EXODUS.   Now the length of time the Israelite
people lived in Egypt[u] was 430 years. At the end of the 430 years, to the
very day, all the LORD's divisions left Egypt. Because the LORD kept vigil
that night to bring them out of Egypt, on this night all the Israelites are to
keep vigil to honor the LORD for the generations to come.

Ex.
12:40-42

GOD DEMANDS FIRSTBORN.   The LORD said to Moses, "Consecrate to
me every firstborn male. The first offspring of every womb among the
Israelites belongs to me, whether man or animal."

Ex. 13:1,2

FEAST OF UNLEAVENED BREAD.   Then Moses said to the people,
"Commemorate this day, the day you came out of Egypt, out of the land
of slavery, because the LORD brought you out of it with a mighty hand. Eat
nothing containing yeast. Today, in the month of Abib, you are leaving.
When the LORD brings you into the land of the Canaanites, Hittites,
Amorites, Hivites and Jebusites—the land he swore to your forefathers to
give you, a land flowing with milk and honey—you are to observe this
ceremony in this month: For seven days eat bread made without yeast and
on the seventh day hold a festival to the LORD. Eat unleavened bread during those seven days; nothing with yeast in it is to be seen among you, nor
shall any yeast be seen anywhere within your borders. On that day tell
your son, 'I do this because of what the LORD did for me when I came out
of Egypt.' This observance will be for you like a sign on your hand and a
reminder on your forehead that the law of the LORD is to be on your lips.
For the LORD brought you out of Egypt with his mighty hand. You must
keep this ordinance at the appointed time year after year.

Ex. 13:3-10

LAW OF FIRSTBORN ENJOINED.   "After the LORD brings you into the
land of the Canaanites and gives it to you, as he promised on oath to you
and your forefathers, you are to give over to the LORD the first offspring of
every womb. All the firstborn males of your livestock belong to the LORD.
Redeem with a lamb every firstborn donkey, but if you do not redeem it,
break its neck. Redeem every firstborn among your sons.

Ex.
13:11-16

"In days to come, when your son asks you, 'What does this mean?' say
to him, 'With a mighty hand the LORD brought us out of Egypt, out of the
land of slavery. When Pharaoh stubbornly refused to let us go, the LORD
killed every firstborn in Egypt, both man and animal. This is why I sacrifice to the LORD the first male offspring of every womb and redeem each
of my firstborn sons.' And it will be like a sign on your hand and a symbol on your forehead that the LORD brought us out of Egypt with his
mighty hand."

CLOUD AND FIRE LEAD EXODUS.   When Pharaoh let the people go,
God did not lead them on the road through the Philistine country, though

Ex.
13:17-22

[u]Masoretic Text; Samaritan Pentateuch and Septuagint *Egypt and Canaan*

that was shorter. For God said, "If they face war, they might change their minds and return to Egypt." So God led the people around by the desert road toward the Red Sea.^{v} The Israelites went up out of Egypt armed for battle.

Moses took the bones of Joseph with him because Joseph had made the sons of Israel swear an oath. He had said, "God will surely come to your aid, and then you must carry my bones up with you from this place."^{w}

After leaving Succoth they camped at Etham on the edge of the desert. By day the LORD went ahead of them in a pillar of cloud to guide them on their way and by night in a pillar of fire to give them light, so that they could travel by day or night. Neither the pillar of cloud by day nor the pillar of fire by night left its place in front of the people.

Ex. 14:1-4 **CAMP BY RED SEA.** Then the LORD said to Moses, "Tell the Israelites to turn back and encamp near Pi Hahiroth, between Migdol and the sea. They are to encamp by the sea, directly opposite Baal Zephon. Pharaoh will think, 'The Israelites are wandering around the land in confusion, hemmed in by the desert.' And I will harden Pharaoh's heart, and he will pursue them. But I will gain glory for myself through Pharaoh and all his army, and the Egyptians will know that I am the LORD." So the Israelites did this.

Ex. 14:5-9 **PHARAOH PURSUES ISRAELITES.** When the king of Egypt was told that the people had fled, Pharaoh and his officials changed their minds about them and said, "What have we done? We have let the Israelites go and have lost their services!" So he had his chariot made ready and took his army with him. He took six hundred of the best chariots, along with all the other chariots of Egypt, with officers over all of them. The LORD hardened the heart of Pharaoh king of Egypt, so that he pursued the Israelites, who were marching out boldly. The Egyptians—all Pharaoh's horses and chariots, horsemen^x and troops—pursued the Israelites and overtook them as they camped by the sea near Pi Hahiroth, opposite Baal Zephon.

Ex. 14:10-14 **PEOPLE FEAR DEATH.** As Pharaoh approached, the Israelites looked up, and there were the Egyptians, marching after them. They were terrified and cried out to the LORD. They said to Moses, "Was it because there were no graves in Egypt that you brought us to the desert to die? What have you done to us by bringing us out of Egypt? Didn't we say to you in Egypt, 'Leave us alone; let us serve the Egyptians'? It would have been better for us to serve the Egyptians than to die in the desert!"

Moses answered the people, "Do not be afraid. Stand firm and you will see the deliverance the LORD will bring you today. The Egyptians you see today you will never see again. The LORD will fight for you; you need only to be still."

Ex. 14:15-18 **MOSES ASSURED OF ESCAPE.** Then the LORD said to Moses, "Why are you crying out to me? Tell the Israelites to move on. Raise your staff and stretch out your hand over the sea to divide the water so that the Israelites can go through the sea on dry ground. I will harden the hearts of the Egyptians so that they will go in after them. And I will gain glory through Pharaoh and all his army, through his chariots and his horsemen. The

^{v}Hebrew *Yam Suph*; that is, Sea of Reeds ^{w}See Gen. 50:25. ^{x}Or *charioteers*; also in verses 17, 18, 23, 26 and 28

Egyptians will know that I am the LORD when I gain glory through Pharaoh, his chariots and his horsemen."

CLOUD SEPARATES FORCES.   Then the angel of God, who had been traveling in front of Israel's army, withdrew and went behind them. The pillar of cloud also moved from in front and stood behind them, coming between the armies of Egypt and Israel. Throughout the night the cloud brought darkness to the one side and light to the other side; so neither went near the other all night long. Ex. 14:19,20

ISRAELITES PASS THROUGH SEA.   Then Moses stretched out his hand over the sea, and all that night the LORD drove the sea back with a strong east wind and turned it into dry land. The waters were divided, and the Israelites went through the sea on dry ground, with a wall of water on their right and on their left. Ex. 14:21-25

The Egyptians pursued them, and all Pharaoh's horses and chariots and horsemen followed them into the sea. During the last watch of the night the LORD looked down from the pillar of fire and cloud at the Egyptian army and threw it into confusion. He made the wheels of their chariots come off[y] so that they had difficulty driving. And the Egyptians said, "Let's get away from the Israelites! The LORD is fighting for them against Egypt."

EGYPTIANS DESTROYED.   Then the LORD said to Moses, "Stretch out your hand over the sea so that the waters may flow back over the Egyptians and their chariots and horsemen." Moses stretched out his hand over the sea, and at daybreak the sea went back to its place. The Egyptians were fleeing toward[z] it, and the LORD swept them into the sea. The water flowed back and covered the chariots and horsemen—the entire army of Pharaoh that had followed the Israelites into the sea. Not one of them survived. Ex. 14:26-29

But the Israelites went through the sea on dry ground, with a wall of water on their right and on their left.

FAITH BY ISRAELITES.   That day the LORD saved Israel from the hands of the Egyptians, and Israel saw the Egyptians lying dead on the shore. And when the Israelites saw the great power the LORD displayed against the Egyptians, the people feared the LORD and put their trust in him and in Moses his servant. Ex. 14:30,31

THE SONG OF MOSES. Then Moses and the Israelites sang this song to the LORD: Ex. 15:1-18

> "I will sing to the LORD,
>   for he is highly exalted.
> The horse and its rider
>   he has hurled into the sea.
> The LORD is my strength and my song;
>   he has become my salvation.
> He is my God, and I will praise him,
>   my father's God, and I will exalt him.
> The LORD is a warrior;
>   the LORD is his name.

---

[y]Or *He jammed the wheels of their chariots* (see Samaritan Pentateuch, Septuagint and Syriac)
[z]Or *from*

Pharaoh's chariots and his army
    he has hurled into the sea.
The best of Pharaoh's officers
    are drowned in the Red Sea.[a]
The deep waters have covered them;
    they sank to the depths like a stone.

"Your right hand, O Lord,
    was majestic in power.
Your right hand, O Lord,
    shattered the enemy.
In the greatness of your majesty
    you threw down those who opposed you.
You unleashed your burning anger;
    it consumed them like stubble.
By the blast of your nostrils
    the waters piled up.
The surging waters stood firm like a wall;
    the deep waters congealed in the heart of the sea.

"The enemy boasted,
    'I will pursue, I will overtake them.
I will divide the spoils;
    I will gorge myself on them.
I will draw my sword
    and my hand will destroy them.'
But you blew with your breath,
    and the sea covered them.
They sank like lead
    in the mighty waters.

"Who among the gods is like you, O Lord?
    Who is like you—
        majestic in holiness,
        awesome in glory,
        working wonders?
You stretched out your right hand
    and the earth swallowed them.

"In your unfailing love you will lead
    the people you have redeemed.
In your strength you will guide them
    to your holy dwelling.
The nations will hear and tremble;
    anguish will grip the people of Philistia.
The chiefs of Edom will be terrified,
    the leaders of Moab will be seized with trembling,
the people[b] of Canaan will melt away;
    terror and dread will fall upon them.
By the power of your arm
    they will be as still as a stone—
until your people pass by, O Lord,

---

[a]Hebrew *Yam Suph*; that is, Sea of Reeds   [b]Or *rulers*

until the people you bought[c] pass by.
You will bring them in and plant them
    on the mountain of your inheritance—
the place, O LORD, you made for your dwelling,
    the sanctuary, O Lord, your hands established.
The LORD will reign
    for ever and ever."

THE SONG OF MIRIAM.   When Pharaoh's horses, chariots and horsemen[d] went into the sea, the LORD brought the waters of the sea back over
them, but the Israelites walked through the sea on dry ground. Then
Miriam the prophetess, Aaron's sister, took a tambourine in her hand, and
all the women followed her, with tambourines and dancing. Miriam sang
to them:

Ex.
15:19-21

"Sing to the LORD,
    for he is highly exalted.
The horse and its rider
    he has hurled into the sea."

Journey to Sinai _____

The thrill of victory and the praising of God for salvation have hardly
    subsided when fear, doubt, and murmuring set in among the Israelites.
    As they face the wilderness without food and water, they quickly forget
the miracles which have brought them out of Egypt and begin to complain that
Moses has brought them out of Egypt only to face certain death in the desert.
But they have overlooked the possibility that God is able to miraculously provide for their needs, which of course he does.

During the next three months the Israelites will move eastward from the
Red Sea. In this period of time they will defend themselves against the
Amalekites, a nomadic people of the Sinai and Negev region who are naturally resentful of the Israelites' intrusion into their territory. Here Moses will be
reunited with his wife and children, who had returned to be with Moses'
father-in-law, Jethro, while Moses was locked in the struggle with Pharaoh.
While the two are together Jethro gives Moses some excellent advice which
leads to the establishment of a system of judges to settle disputes among the
Israelites.

The account begins as the people leave the banks of the Red Sea, in which
Pharaoh's army has just been destroyed.

BITTER WATER MADE SWEET.   Then Moses led Israel from the Red Sea
and they went into the Desert of Shur. For three days they traveled in the
desert without finding water. When they came to Marah, they could not
drink its water because it was bitter. (That is why the place is called
Marah.[e]) So the people grumbled against Moses, saying, "What are we to
drink?"

Ex.
15:22-25a

Then Moses cried out to the LORD, and the LORD showed him a piece of
wood. He threw it into the water, and the water became sweet.

_____
[c]Or *created*   [d]Or *charioteers*   [e]*Marah* means *bitter.*

Ex.
15:25b,26

PROTECTION FROM DISEASES. There the LORD made a decree and a law for them, and there he tested them. He said, "If you listen carefully to the voice of the LORD your God and do what is right in his eyes, if you pay attention to his commands and keep all his decrees, I will not bring on you any of the diseases I brought on the Egyptians, for I am the LORD, who heals you."

Ex.
15:27-16:3

MURMURING FOR FOOD. Then they came to Elim, where there were twelve springs and seventy palm trees, and they camped there near the water. The whole Israelite community set out from Elim and came to the Desert of Sin, which is between Elim and Sinai, on the fifteenth day of the second month after they had come out of Egypt. In the desert the whole community grumbled against Moses and Aaron. The Israelites said to them, "If only we had died by the LORD's hand in Egypt! There we sat around pots of meat and ate all the food we wanted, but you have brought us out into this desert to starve this entire assembly to death."

Ex. 16:4-12

MEAT AND BREAD PROMISED. Then the LORD said to Moses, "I will rain down bread from heaven for you. The people are to go out each day and gather enough for that day. In this way I will test them and see whether they will follow my instructions. On the sixth day they are to prepare what they bring in, and that is to be twice as much as they gather on the other days."

So Moses and Aaron said to all the Israelites, "In the evening you will know that it was the LORD who brought you out of Egypt, and in the morning you will see the glory of the LORD, because he has heard your grumbling against him. Who are we, that you should grumble against us?" Moses also said, "You will know that it was the LORD when he gives you meat to eat in the evening and all the bread you want in the morning, because he has heard your grumbling against him. Who are we? You are not grumbling against us, but against the LORD."

Then Moses told Aaron, "Say to the entire Israelite community, 'Come before the LORD, for he has heard your grumbling.'"

While Aaron was speaking to the whole Israelite community, they looked toward the desert, and there was the glory of the LORD appearing in the cloud.

The LORD said to Moses, "I have heard the grumbling of the Israelites. Tell them, 'At twilight you will eat meat, and in the morning you will be filled with bread. Then you will know that I am the LORD your God.'"

Ex.
16:13-21

QUAIL AND MANNA SENT. That evening quail came and covered the camp, and in the morning there was a layer of dew around the camp. When the dew was gone, thin flakes like frost on the ground appeared on the desert floor. When the Israelites saw it, they said to each other, "What is it?" For they did not know what it was.

Moses said to them, "It is the bread the LORD has given you to eat. This is what the LORD has commanded: 'Each one is to gather as much as he needs. Take an omer[f] for each person you have in your tent.'"

The Israelites did as they were told; some gathered much, some little. And when they measured it by the omer, he who gathered much did not have too much, and he who gathered little did not have too little. Each one gathered as much as he needed.

[f] That is, probably about 2 quarts (about 2 liters)

Then Moses said to them, "No one is to keep any of it until morning."

However, some of them paid no attention to Moses; they kept part of it until morning, but it was full of maggots and began to smell. So Moses was angry with them.

Each morning everyone gathered as much as he needed, and when the sun grew hot, it melted away.

SABBATH REST INSTITUTED.   On the sixth day, they gathered twice as much—two omers^g for each person—and the leaders of the community came and reported this to Moses. He said to them, "This is what the LORD commanded: 'Tomorrow is to be a day of rest, a holy Sabbath to the LORD. So bake what you want to bake and boil what you want to boil. Save whatever is left and keep it until morning.'"

Ex.
16:22-30

So they saved it until morning, as Moses commanded, and it did not stink or get maggots in it. "Eat it today," Moses said, "because today is a Sabbath to the LORD. You will not find any of it on the ground today. Six days you are to gather it, but on the seventh day, the Sabbath, there will not be any."

Nevertheless, some of the people went out on the seventh day to gather it, but they found none. Then the LORD said to Moses, "How long will you^h refuse to keep my commands and my instructions? Bear in mind that the LORD has given you the Sabbath; that is why on the sixth day he gives you bread for two days. Everyone is to stay where he is on the seventh day; no one is to go out." So the people rested on the seventh day.

MANNA KEPT FOR MEMORIAL.   The people of Israel called the bread manna.ⁱ It was white like coriander seed and tasted like wafers made with honey. Moses said, "This is what the LORD has commanded: 'Take an omer of manna and keep it for the generations to come, so they can see the bread I gave you to eat in the desert when I brought you out of Egypt.'"

Ex.
16:31-36

So Moses said to Aaron, "Take a jar and put an omer of manna in it. Then place it before the LORD to be kept for the generations to come."

As the LORD commanded Moses, Aaron put the manna in front of the Testimony, that it might be kept. The Israelites ate manna forty years, until they came to a land that was settled; they ate manna until they reached the border of Canaan.

(An omer is one tenth of an ephah.)

WATER FROM ROCK.   The whole Israelite community set out from the Desert of Sin, traveling from place to place as the LORD commanded. They camped at Rephidim, but there was no water for the people to drink. So they quarreled with Moses and said, "Give us water to drink."

Ex. 17:1-7

Moses replied, "Why do you quarrel with me? Why do you put the LORD to the test?"

But the people were thirsty for water there, and they grumbled against Moses. They said, "Why did you bring us up out of Egypt to make us and our children and livestock die of thirst?"

Then Moses cried out to the LORD, "What am I to do with these people? They are almost ready to stone me."

The LORD answered Moses, "Walk on ahead of the people. Take with

^gThat is, probably about 4 quarts (about 4.5 liters)   ^hThe Hebrew is plural.   ⁱManna means What is it? (see verse 15).

you some of the elders of Israel and take in your hand the staff with which you struck the Nile, and go. I will stand there before you by the rock at Horeb. Strike the rock, and water will come out of it for the people to drink." So Moses did this in the sight of the elders of Israel. And he called the place Massah[j] and Meribah[k] because the Israelites quarreled and because they tested the LORD saying, "Is the LORD among us or not?"

Ex. 17:8-13 DEFEAT OF AMALEKITES.   The Amalekites came and attacked the Israelites at Rephidim. Moses said to Joshua, "Choose some of our men and go out to fight the Amalekites. Tomorrow I will stand on top of the hill with the staff of God in my hands."

So Joshua fought the Amalekites as Moses had ordered, and Moses, Aaron and Hur went to the top of the hill. As long as Moses held up his hands, the Israelites were winning, but whenever he lowered his hands, the Amalekites were winning. When Moses' hands grew tired, they took a stone and put it under him and he sat on it. Aaron and Hur held his hands up—one on one side, one on the other—so that his hands remained steady till sunset. So Joshua overcame the Amalekite army with the sword.

Ex.
17:14-16 AMALEK TO BE DESTROYED.   Then the LORD said to Moses, "Write this on a scroll as something to be remembered and make sure that Joshua hears it, because I will completely blot out the memory of Amalek from under heaven."

Moses built an altar and called it The LORD is my Banner. He said, "For hands were lifted up to the throne of the LORD. The[l] LORD will be at war against the Amalekites from generation to generation."

Ex. 18:1-9 REUNION OF MOSES AND JETHRO. Now Jethro, the priest of Midian and father-in-law of Moses, heard of everything God had done for Moses and for his people Israel, and how the LORD had brought Israel out of Egypt.

After Moses had sent away his wife Zipporah, his father-in-law Jethro received her and her two sons. One son was named Gershom,[m] for Moses said, "I have become an alien in a foreign land"; and the other was named Eliezer,[n] for he said, "My father's God was my helper; he saved me from the sword of Pharaoh."

Jethro, Moses' father-in-law, together with Moses' sons and wife, came to him in the desert, where he was camped near the mountain of God. Jethro had sent word to him, "I, your father-in-law Jethro, am coming to you with your wife and her two sons."

So Moses went out to meet his father-in-law and bowed down and kissed him. They greeted each other and then went into the tent. Moses told his father-in-law about everything the LORD had done to Pharaoh and the Egyptians for Israel's sake and about all the hardships they had met along the way and how the LORD had saved them.

Jethro was delighted to hear about all the good things the LORD had done for Israel in rescuing them from the hand of the Egyptians.

Ex.
18:10-12 JETHRO WORSHIPS GOD. He said, "Praise be to the LORD, who rescued you from the hand of the Egyptians and of Pharaoh, and who rescued the people from the hand of the Egyptians. Now I know that the LORD is

[j]Massah means testing.   [k]Meribah means quarreling.   [l]Or "Because a hand was against the throne of the LORD, the   [m]Gershom sounds like the Hebrew for an alien there. [n]Eliezer means my God is helper.

greater than all other gods, for he did this to those who had treated Israel arrogantly." Then Jethro, Moses' father-in-law, brought a burnt offering and other sacrifices to God, and Aaron came with all the elders of Israel to eat bread with Moses' father-in-law in the presence of God.

JETHRO SUGGESTS JUDICIARY.   The next day Moses took his seat to serve as judge for the people, and they stood around him from morning till evening. When his father-in-law saw all that Moses was doing for the people, he said, "What is this you are doing for the people? Why do you alone sit as judge, while all these people stand around you from morning till evening?" Ex. 18:13-23

Moses answered him, "Because the people come to me to seek God's will. Whenever they have a dispute, it is brought to me, and I decide between the parties and inform them of God's decrees and laws."

Moses' father-in-law replied, "What you are doing is not good. You and these people who come to you will only wear yourselves out. The work is too heavy for you; you cannot handle it alone. Listen now to me and I will give you some advice, and may God be with you. You must be the people's representative before God and bring their disputes to him. Teach them the decrees and laws, and show them the way to live and the duties they are to perform. But select capable men from all the people—men who fear God, trustworthy men who hate dishonest gain—and appoint them as officials over thousands, hundreds, fifties and tens. Have them serve as judges for the people at all times, but have them bring every difficult case to you; the simple cases they can decide themselves. That will make your load lighter, because they will share it with you. If you do this and God so commands, you will be able to stand the strain, and all these people will go home satisfied."

JUDGES APPOINTED.   Moses listened to his father-in-law and did everything he said. He chose capable men from all Israel and made them leaders of the people, officials over thousands, hundreds, fifties and tens. They served as judges for the people at all times. The difficult cases they brought to Moses, but the simple ones they decided themselves. Ex. 18:24-27

Then Moses sent his father-in-law on his way, and Jethro returned to his own country.

The Israelites Covenant with God

*J*t has been some 635 years since God promised Abraham that he would make a great nation of Abraham's descendants and bless that nation as his chosen people. Abraham's part in the covenant was minimal, as God simply asked for Abraham's belief and trust in that promise. Now, however, the time to fulfill God's promise has come, and God approaches the Israelites to covenant with them as his special people. Naturally the Israelites are enthusiastic and excited, yet it soon becomes clear that they have not anticipated the full impact of their part of the covenant. In agreeing to covenant, the people will be pledging their faith and allegiance to an invisible king, their very Creator, and promising to obey the many stringent laws which are part of the covenant.

The solemnity of this historically unprecedented occasion begins with God's proposal of the covenant and the need for all the people to purify themselves in anticipation of their formal acceptance.

Ex. 19:1,2
(Ca. 1445 B.C.)

ARRIVAL AT SINAI.   In the third month after the Israelites left Egypt—on the very day—they came to the Desert of Sinai. After they set out from Rephidim, they entered the Desert of Sinai, and Israel camped there in the desert in front of the mountain.

Ex. 19:3-6

GOD PROPOSES COVENANT.   Then Moses went up to God, and the LORD called to him from the mountain and said, "This is what you are to say to the house of Jacob and what you are to tell the people of Israel: 'You yourselves have seen what I did to Egypt, and how I carried you on eagles' wings and brought you to myself. Now if you obey me fully and keep my covenant, then out of all nations you will be my treasured possession. Although the whole earth is mine, you° will be for me a kingdom of priests and a holy nation.' These are the words you are to speak to the Israelites."

Ex. 19:7-9

ISRAELITES AGREE TO COVENANT.   So Moses went back and summoned the elders of the people and set before them all the words the LORD had commanded him to speak. The people all responded together, "We will do everything the LORD has said." So Moses brought their answer back to the LORD.

The LORD said to Moses, "I am going to come to you in a dense cloud, so that the people will hear me speaking with you and will always put their trust in you." Then Moses told the LORD what the people had said.

Ex. 19:10-15

CONSECRATION OF THE PEOPLE.   And the LORD said to Moses, "Go to the people and consecrate them today and tomorrow. Have them wash their clothes and be ready by the third day, because on that day the LORD will come down on Mount Sinai in the sight of all the people. Put limits for the people around the mountain and tell them, 'Be careful that you do not go up the mountain or touch the foot of it. Whoever touches the mountain shall surely be put to death. He shall surely be stoned or shot with arrows; not a hand is to be laid on him. Whether man or animal, he shall not be permitted to live.' Only when the ram's horn sounds a long blast may they go up to the mountain."

After Moses had gone down the mountain to the people, he consecrated them, and they washed their clothes. Then he said to the people, "Prepare yourselves for the third day. Abstain from sexual relations."

Ex. 19:16-25

MOSES MEETS GOD ON MOUNTAIN.   On the morning of the third day there was thunder and lightning, with a thick cloud over the mountain, and a very loud trumpet blast. Everyone in the camp trembled. Then Moses led the people out of the camp to meet with God, and they stood at the foot of the mountain. Mount Sinai was covered with smoke, because the LORD descended on it in fire. The smoke billowed up from it like smoke from a furnace, the whole mountain^p trembled violently, and the sound of the trumpet grew louder and louder. Then Moses spoke and the voice of God answered him.^q

---

°Or *possession, for the whole earth is mine.* ⁶You   ^pMost Hebrew manuscripts; a few Hebrew manuscripts and Septuagint *all the people*   ^qOr *and God answered him with thunder*

The LORD descended to the top of Mount Sinai and called Moses to the top of the mountain. So Moses went up and the LORD said to him, "Go down and warn the people so they do not force their way through to see the LORD and many of them perish. Even the priests, who approach the LORD, must consecrate themselves, or the LORD will break out against them."

Moses said to the LORD, "The people cannot come up Mount Sinai, because you yourself warned us, 'Put limits around the mountain and set it apart as holy.'"

The LORD replied, "Go down and bring Aaron up with you. But the priests and the people must not force their way through to come up to the LORD, or he will break out against them."

So Moses went down to the people and told them.

THE TEN COMMANDMENTS GIVEN. And God spoke all these words: Ex. 20:1-17

"I am the LORD your God, who brought you out of Egypt, out of the
        land of slavery.
"You shall have no other gods before[r] me.
"You shall not make for yourself an idol in the form of anything in
        heaven above or on the earth beneath or in the waters below.
        You shall not bow down to them or worship them; for I, the
        LORD your God, am a jealous God, punishing the children for
        the sin of the fathers to the third and fourth generation of those
        who hate me, but showing love to a thousand ⌊generations⌋ of
        those who love me and keep my commandments.
"You shall not misuse the name of the LORD your God, for the LORD will
        not hold anyone guiltless who misuses his name.
"Remember the Sabbath day by keeping it holy. Six days you shall
        labor and do all your work, but the seventh day is a Sabbath to
        the LORD your God. On it you shall not do any work, neither
        you, nor your son or daughter, nor your manservant or maid-
        servant, nor your animals, nor the alien within your gates. For
        in six days the LORD made the heavens and the earth, the sea,
        and all that is in them, but he rested on the seventh day.
        Therefore the LORD blessed the Sabbath day and made it holy.
"Honor your father and your mother, so that you may live long in the
        land the LORD your God is giving you.
"You shall not murder.
"You shall not commit adultery.
"You shall not steal.
"You shall not give false testimony against your neighbor.
"You shall not covet your neighbor's house. You shall not covet your
        neighbor's wife, or his manservant or maidservant, his ox or
        donkey, or anything that belongs to your neighbor."

PEOPLE AFRAID OF GOD. When the people saw the thunder and light-   Ex.
ning and heard the trumpet and saw the mountain in smoke, they trem-   20:18-20
bled with fear. They stayed at a distance and said to Moses, "Speak to us
yourself and we will listen. But do not have God speak to us or we will
die."

[r]Or *besides*

Moses said to the people, "Do not be afraid. God has come to test you, so that the fear of God will be with you to keep you from sinning."

Ex.
20:21-26

INSTRUCTIONS FOR ALTAR.   The people remained at a distance, while Moses approached the thick darkness where God was.

Then the LORD said to Moses, "Tell the Israelites this: 'You have seen for yourselves that I have spoken to you from heaven: Do not make any gods to be alongside me; do not make for yourselves gods of silver or gods of gold.

" 'Make an altar of earth for me and sacrifice on it your burnt offerings and fellowship offerings,ˢ your sheep and goats and your cattle. Wherever I cause my name to be honored, I will come to you and bless you. If you make an altar of stones for me, do not build it with dressed stones, for you will defile it if you use a tool on it. And do not go up to my altar on steps, lest your nakedness be exposed on it.'

At this point the Exodus record lists the first of many laws which God will set forth for his people to follow. The nation of Israel is to be a theocracy, under the direct rule of God himself. Whereas other nations around them are governed by customs, rules, and laws of the king or other human authority figures, the Israelites will be governed by divine laws which they must observe in keeping with the very covenant which they are now making with God.

The laws spoken to Moses on this occasion amplify the first ten commandments, which form the constitutional framework for all the other laws which follow. On this occasion God gives Moses a wide variety of laws, ranging from proper altar worship to proper treatment of slaves; from laws relating to crimes against persons and property to other offenses, punishable by death, such as sorcery, bestiality, and idolatry.

In addition, various duties are imposed relative to strangers, creditors, the firstborn, and other matters. Numerous ethical instructions are also promulgated to encourage honesty, justice, and mutual assistance in emergencies. Finally, several laws are given regarding Sabbath rests and the three yearly festivals which are instituted—the Feast of Unleavened Bread, the Feast of Harvest, and the Feast of Ingathering.

So as to avoid the repetition found in the records of Exodus, Leviticus, Numbers, and Deuteronomy, all the laws will be presented later in a single collection organized by subject. Now, however, attention turns back to God's final instructions and the promises which he makes as his part of the covenant with the people of Israel.

Ex.
23:20-22

ANGEL SENT FOR GUIDANCE.   "See, I am sending an angel ahead of you to guard you along the way and to bring you to the place I have prepared. Pay attention to him and listen to what he says. Do not rebel against him; he will not forgive your rebellion, since my Name is in him. If you listen carefully to what he says and do all that I say, I will be an enemy to your enemies and will oppose those who oppose you.

ˢTradionally *peace offerings*

PROMISES AND BLESSINGS.   My angel will go ahead of you and bring   Ex.
you into the land of the Amorites, Hittites, Perizzites, Canaanites, Hivites   23:23-33
and Jebusites, and I will wipe them out. Do not bow down before their
gods or worship them or follow their practices. You must demolish them
and break their sacred stones to pieces. Worship the LORD your God, and
his blessing will be on your food and water. I will take away sickness from
among you, and none will miscarry or be barren in your land. I will give
you a full life span.

"I will send my terror ahead of you and throw into confusion every
nation you encounter. I will make all your enemies turn their backs and
run. I will send the hornet ahead of you to drive the Hivites, Canaanites
and Hittites out of your way. But I will not drive them out in a single year,
because the land would become desolate and the wild animals too numerous for you. Little by little I will drive them out before you, until you have
increased enough to take possession of the land.

"I will establish your borders from the Red Sea[t] to the Sea of the
Philistines,[u] and from the desert to the River.[v] I will hand over to you the
people who live in the land and you will drive them out before you. Do
not make a covenant with them or with their gods. Do not let them live in
your land, or they will cause you to sin against me, because the worship
of their gods will certainly be a snare to you."

ELDERS SUMMONED TO WORSHIP.   Then he said to Moses, "Come up   Ex. 24:1,2
to the LORD, you and Aaron, Nadab and Abihu, and seventy of the elders
of Israel. You are to worship at a distance, but Moses alone is to approach
the LORD; the others must not come near. And the people may not come up
with him."

ISRAELITES ACCEPT COVENANT.   When Moses went and told the   Ex. 24:3,4
people all the LORD's words and laws, they responded with one voice,
"Everything the LORD has said we will do." Moses then wrote down
everything the LORD had said.

He got up early the next morning and built an altar at the foot of the
mountain and set up twelve stone pillars representing the twelve tribes of
Israel.

ISRAELITES PROMISE OBEDIENCE.   Then he sent young Israelite men,   Ex. 24:5-8
and they offered burnt offerings and sacrificed young bulls as fellowship
offerings[w] to the LORD. Moses took half of the blood and put it in bowls,
and the other half he sprinkled on the altar. Then he took the Book of the
Covenant and read it to the people. They responded, "We will do everything the LORD has said; we will obey."

Moses then took the blood, sprinkled it on the people and said, "This is
the blood of the covenant that the LORD has made with you in accordance
with all these words."

ELDERS SEE GOD'S GLORY.   Moses and Aaron, Nadab and Abihu, and   Ex. 24:9-11
the seventy elders of Israel went up and saw the God of Israel. Under his
feet was something like a pavement made of sapphire,[x] clear as the sky
itself. But God did not raise his hand against these leaders of the Israelites;
they saw God, and they ate and drank.

[t]Hebrew *Yam Suph*; that is, Sea of Reeds   [u]That is, the Mediterranean   [v]That is, the
Euphrates   [w]Traditionally *peace offerings*   [x]Or *lapis lazuli*

Ex. 24:12-14	MOSES CALLED TO MOUNTAIN. The LORD said to Moses, "Come up to me on the mountain and stay here, and I will give you the tablets of stone, with the law and commands I have written for their instruction." Then Moses set out with Joshua his aide, and Moses went up on the mountain of God. He said to the elders, "Wait here for us until we come back to you. Aaron and Hur are with you, and anyone involved in a dispute can go to them."
Ex. 24:15-18	FORTY DAYS ON MOUNTAIN. When Moses went up on the mountain, the cloud covered it, and the glory of the LORD settled on Mount Sinai. For six days the cloud covered the mountain, and on the seventh day the LORD called to Moses from within the cloud. To the Israelites the glory of the LORD looked like a consuming fire on top of the mountain. Then Moses entered the cloud as he went on up the mountain. And he stayed on the mountain forty days and forty nights.

Instructions for the Tabernacle

While Moses communes with God upon Mount Sinai, God gives Moses lengthy instructions for the design and construction of a place of worship. It is called a tabernacle, or a tent of meeting, and can be moved along with the Israelites as they migrate about the Sinai region. The tabernacle will be filled with God's holy presence and will contain an altar to be presided over by priests, with the assistance from men of the tribe of Levi. Those who minister will wear special clothes in their times of service. Within the tabernacle various offerings will be made, and other ceremonies will take place as God instructs.

Of particular importance will be various items of national and religious significance which are to be kept within the tabernacle, including an ark, or chest, of wood which eventually will contain Aaron's rod, a pot of manna, and two tablets of the law. The ark itself is to be about four feet long, two feet wide, and two feet deep. Above the ark is to be a mercy seat decorated with two cherubs. There is also to be a special table of acacia wood, a golden lampstand of specific ornate design, and the altar of incense.

The tabernacle itself is to be constructed of the very finest materials. Using 18 inches as a cubit, the court of the tabernacle will extend approximately 150 feet long and 75 feet wide, with walls just over seven feet high. A special part of the tabernacle is to be called the "holy of holies," and only the high priest will enter it, once each year, to seek atonement for the people's sins.

The details of the blueprints given to Moses, as well as the descriptions of priestly garments, not only arouse one's fascination but also suggest that no detail of man's worship of God is too small for God's concern.

Ex. 25:1-9	OFFERING FOR TABERNACLE The LORD said to Moses, "Tell the Israelites to bring me an offering. You are to receive the offering for me from each man whose heart prompts him to give. These are the offerings you are to receive from them: gold, silver and bronze; blue, purple and scarlet yarn and fine linen; goat hair; ram skins dyed red and hides of sea

cows[y]; acacia wood; olive oil for the light; spices for the anointing oil and for the fragrant incense; and onyx stones and other gems to be mounted on the ephod and breastpiece.

"Then have them make a sanctuary for me, and I will dwell among them. Make this tabernacle and all its furnishings exactly like the pattern I will show you.

THE ARK.   "Have them make a chest of acacia wood—two and a half cubits long, a cubit and a half wide, and a cubit and a half high.[z] Overlay it with pure gold, both inside and out, and make a gold molding around it. Cast four gold rings for it and fasten them to its four feet, with two rings on one side and two rings on the other. Then make poles of acacia wood and overlay them with gold. Insert the poles into the rings on the sides of the chest to carry it. The poles are to remain in the rings of this ark; they are not to be removed. Then put in the ark the Testimony, which I will give you.

Ex.
25:10-16

THE MERCY SEAT.   "Make an atonement cover[a] of pure gold—two and a half cubits long and a cubit and a half wide.[b] And make two cherubim out of hammered gold at the ends of the cover. Make one cherub on one end and the second cherub on the other; make the cherubim of one piece with the cover, at the two ends. The cherubim are to have their wings spread upward, overshadowing the cover with them. The cherubim are to face each other, looking toward the cover. Place the cover on top of the ark and put in the ark the Testimony, which I will give you. There, above the cover between the two cherubim that are over the ark of the Testimony, I will meet with you and give you all my commands for the Israelites.

Ex.
25:17-22

THE TABLE.   "Make a table of acacia wood—two cubits long, a cubit wide and a cubit and a half high.[c] Overlay it with pure gold and make a gold molding around it. Also make around it a rim a handbreadth[d] wide and put a gold molding on the rim. Make four gold rings for the table and fasten them to the four corners, where the four legs are. The rings are to be close to the rim to hold the poles used in carrying the table. Make the poles of acacia wood, overlay them with gold and carry the table with them. And make its plates and dishes of pure gold, as well as its pitchers and bowls for the pouring out of offerings. Put the bread of the Presence on this table to be before me at all times.

Ex.
25:23-30

THE LAMPSTAND.   "Make a lampstand of pure gold and hammer it out, base and shaft; its flowerlike cups, buds and blossoms shall be of one piece with it. Six branches are to extend from the sides of the lampstand—three on one side and three on the other. Three cups shaped like almond flowers with buds and blossoms are to be on one branch, three on the next branch, and the same for all six branches extending from the lampstand. And on the lampstand there are to be four cups shaped like almond flowers with buds and blossoms. One bud shall be under the first pair of branches extending from the lampstand, a second bud under the second pair, and a

Ex.
25:31-40

[y]That is, dugongs   [z]That is, about 3 3/4 feet (about 1.1 meters) long and 2 1/4 feet (about 0.7 meter) wide and high   [a]Traditionally a mercy seat   [b]That is, about 3 3/4 feet (about 1.1 meters) long and 2 1/4 feet (about 0.7 meter) wide   [c]That is, about 3 feet (about 0.9 meter) long and 1 1/2 feet (about 0.5 meter) wide and 2 1/4 feet (about 0.7 meter) high   [d]That is, about 3 inches (about 8 centimeters)

third bud under the third pair—six branches in all. The buds and branches shall all be of one piece with the lampstand, hammered out of pure gold.

"Then make its seven lamps and set them up on it so that they light the space in front of it. Its wick trimmers and trays are to be of pure gold. A talent[e] of pure gold is to be used for the lampstand and all these accessories. See that you make them according to the pattern shown you on the mountain.

Ex. 26:1-30   THE TABERNACLE.   "Make the tabernacle with ten curtains of finely twisted linen and blue, purple and scarlet yarn, with cherubim worked into them by a skilled craftsman. All the curtains are to be the same size— twenty-eight cubits long and four cubits wide.[f] Join five of the curtains together, and do the same with the other five. Make loops of blue material along the edge of the end curtain in one set, and do the same with the end curtain in the other set. Make fifty loops on one curtain and fifty loops on the end curtain of the other set, with the loops opposite each other. Then make fifty gold clasps and use them to fasten the curtains together so that the tabernacle is a unit.

"Make curtains of goat hair for the tent over the tabernacle—eleven altogether. All eleven curtains are to be the same size—thirty cubits long and four cubits wide.[g] Join five of the curtains together into one set and the other six into another set. Fold the sixth curtain double at the front of the tent. Make fifty loops along the edge of the end curtain in one set and also along the edge of the end curtain in the other set. Then make fifty bronze clasps and put them in the loops to fasten the tent together as a unit. As for the additional length of the tent curtains, the half curtain that is left over is to hang down at the rear of the tabernacle. The tent curtains will be a cubit[h] longer on both sides; what is left will hang over the sides of the tabernacle so as to cover it. Make for the tent a covering of ram skins dyed red, and over that a covering of hides of sea cows.[i]

"Make upright frames of acacia wood for the tabernacle. Each frame is to be ten cubits long and a cubit and a half wide,[j] with two projections set parallel to each other. Make all the frames of the tabernacle in this way. Make twenty frames for the south side of the tabernacle and make forty silver bases to go under them—two bases for each frame, one under each projection. For the other side, the north side of the tabernacle, make twenty frames and forty silver bases—two under each frame. Make six frames for the far end, that is, the west end of the tabernacle, and make two frames for the corners at the far end. At these two corners they must be double from the bottom all the way to the top, and fitted into a single ring; both shall be like that. So there will be eight frames and sixteen silver bases—two under each frame.

"Also make crossbars of acacia wood: five for the frames on one side of the tabernacle, five for those on the other side, and five for the frames on the west, at the far end of the tabernacle. The center crossbar is to extend from end to end at the middle of the frames. Overlay the frames with gold

[e]That is, about 75 pounds (about 34 kilograms)   [f]That is, about 42 feet (about 12.5 meters) long and 6 feet (about 1.8 meters) wide   [g]That is, about 45 feet (about 13.5 meters) long and 6 feet (about 1.8 meters) wide   [h]That is, about 1 1/2 feet (about 0.5 meter)   [i]That is, dugongs   [j]That is, about 15 feet (about 4.5 meters) long and 2 1/4 feet (about 0.7 meter) wide

and make gold rings to hold the crossbars. Also overlay the crossbars with gold.

"Set up the tabernacle according to the plan shown you on the mountain.

VEIL AND MOST HOLY PLACE. "Make a curtain of blue, purple and scarlet yarn and finely twisted linen, with cherubim worked into it by a skilled craftsman. Hang it with gold hooks on four posts of acacia wood overlaid with gold and standing on four silver bases. Hang the curtain from the clasps and place the ark of the Testimony behind the curtain. The curtain will separate the Holy Place from the Most Holy Place. Put the atonement cover on the ark of the Testimony in the Most Holy Place. Place the table outside the curtain on the north side of the tabernacle and put the lampstand opposite it on the south side.

Ex.
26:31-37

"For the entrance to the tent make a curtain of blue, purple and scarlet yarn and finely twisted linen—the work of an embroiderer. Make gold hooks for this curtain and five posts of acacia wood overlaid with gold. And cast five bronze bases for them.

ALTAR OF BURNT OFFERINGS. "Build an altar of acacia wood, three cubits[k] high; it is to be square, five cubits long and five cubits wide.[l] Make a horn at each of the four corners, so that the horns and the altar are of one piece, and overlay the altar with bronze. Make all its utensils of bronze—its pots to remove the ashes, and its shovels, sprinkling bowls, meat forks and firepans. Make a grating for it, a bronze network, and make a bronze ring at each of the four corners of the network. Put it under the ledge of the altar so that it is halfway up the altar. Make poles of acacia wood for the altar and overlay them with bronze. The poles are to be inserted into the rings so they will be on two sides of the altar when it is carried. Make the altar hollow, out of boards. It is to be made just as you were shown on the mountain.

Ex. 27:1-8

OUTER COURT. "Make a courtyard for the tabernacle. The south side shall be a hundred cubits[m] long and is to have curtains of finely twisted linen, with twenty posts and twenty bronze bases and with silver hooks and bands on the posts. The north side shall also be a hundred cubits long and is to have curtains, with twenty posts and twenty bronze bases and with silver hooks and bands on the posts.

Ex. 27:9-19

"The west end of the courtyard shall be fifty cubits[n] wide and have curtains, with ten posts and ten bases. On the east end, toward the sunrise, the courtyard shall also be fifty cubits wide. Curtains fifteen cubits[o] long are to be on one side of the entrance, with three posts and three bases, and curtains fifteen cubits long are to be on the other side, with three posts and three bases.

"For the entrance to the courtyard, provide a curtain twenty cubits[p] long, of blue, purple and scarlet yarn and finely twisted linen—the work of an embroiderer—with four posts and four bases. All the posts around the courtyard are to have silver bands and hooks, and bronze bases. The courtyard shall be a hundred cubits long and fifty cubits wide,[q] with

---

[k]That is, about 4 1/2 feet (about 1.3 meters)   [l]That is, about 7 1/2 feet (about 2.3 meters) long and wide   [m]That is, about 150 feet (about 46 meters)   [n]That is, about 75 feet (about 23 meters)   [o]That is, about 22 1/2 feet (about 6.9 meters)   [p]That is, about 30 feet (about 9 meters)   [q]That is, about 150 feet (about 46 meters) long and 75 feet (about 23 meters) wide

curtains of finely twisted linen five cubits[r] high, and with bronze bases. All the other articles used in the service of the tabernacle, whatever their function, including all the tent pegs for it and those for the courtyard, are to be of bronze.

Ex.
27:20,21

OIL FOR LAMP.   "Command the Israelites to bring you clear oil of pressed olives for the light so that the lamps may be kept burning. In the Tent of Meeting, outside the curtain that is in front of the Testimony, Aaron and his sons are to keep the lamps burning before the LORD from evening till morning. This is to be a lasting ordinance among the Israelites for the generations to come.

Ex. 28:1-43

GARMENTS FOR PRIESTS.   "Have Aaron your brother brought to you from among the Israelites, along with his sons Nadab and Abihu, Eleazar and Ithamar, so they may serve me as priests. Make sacred garments for your brother Aaron, to give him dignity and honor. Tell all the skilled men to whom I have given wisdom in such matters that they are to make garments for Aaron, for his consecration, so he may serve me as priest. These are the garments they are to make: a breastpiece, an ephod, a robe, a woven tunic, a turban and a sash. They are to make these sacred garments for your brother Aaron and his sons, so they may serve me as priests. Have them use gold, and blue, purple and scarlet yarn, and fine linen.

"Make the ephod of gold, and of blue, purple and scarlet yarn, and of finely twisted linen—the work of a skilled craftsman. It is to have two shoulder pieces attached to two of its corners, so it can be fastened. Its skillfully woven waistband is to be like it—of one piece with the ephod and made with gold, and with blue, purple and scarlet yarn, and with finely twisted linen.

"Take two onyx stones and engrave on them the names of the sons of Israel in the order of their birth—six names on one stone and the remaining six on the other. Engrave the names of the sons of Israel on the two stones the way a gem cutter engraves a seal. Then mount the stones in gold filigree settings and fasten them on the shoulder pieces of the ephod as memorial stones for the sons of Israel. Aaron is to bear the names on his shoulders as a memorial before the LORD. Make gold filigree settings and two braided chains of pure gold, like a rope, and attach the chains to the settings.

"Fashion a breastpiece for making decisions—the work of a skilled craftsman. Make it like the ephod: of gold, and of blue, purple and scarlet yarn, and of finely twisted linen. It is to be square—a span[s] long and a span wide—and folded double. Then mount four rows of precious stones on it. In the first row there shall be a ruby, a topaz and a beryl; in the second row a turquoise, a sapphire[t] and an emerald; in the third row a jacinth, an agate and an amethyst; in the fourth row a chrysolite, an onyx and a jasper.[u] Mount them in gold filigree settings. There are to be twelve stones, one for each of the names of the sons of Israel, each engraved like a seal with the name of one of the twelve tribes.

"For the breastpiece make braided chains of pure gold, like a rope. Make

[r]That is, about 7 1/2 feet (about 2.3 meters)   [s]That is, about 9 inches (about 22 centimeters)   [t]Or lapis lazuli   [u]The precise identification of some of these precious stones is uncertain.

two gold rings for it and fasten them to two corners of the breastpiece. Fasten the two gold chains to the rings at the corners of the breastpiece, and the other ends of the chains to the two settings, attaching them to the shoulder pieces of the ephod at the front. Make two gold rings and attach them to the other two corners of the breastpiece on the inside edge next to the ephod. Make two more gold rings and attach them to the bottom of the shoulder pieces on the front of the ephod, close to the seam just above the waistband of the ephod. The rings of the breastpiece are to be tied to the rings of the ephod with blue cord, connecting it to the waistband, so that the breastpiece will not swing out from the ephod.

"Whenever Aaron enters the Holy Place, he will bear the names of the sons of Israel over his heart on the breastpiece of decision as a continuing memorial before the LORD. Also put the Urim and the Thummim in the breastpiece, so they may be over Aaron's heart whenever he enters the presence of the LORD. Thus Aaron will always bear the means of making decisions for the Israelites over his heart before the LORD.

"Make the robe of the ephod entirely of blue cloth, with an opening for the head in its center. There shall be a woven edge like a collar[v] around this opening, so that it will not tear. Make pomegranates of blue, purple and scarlet yarn around the hem of the robe, with gold bells between them. The gold bells and the pomegranates are to alternate around the hem of the robe. Aaron must wear it when he ministers. The sound of the bells will be heard when he enters the Holy Place before the LORD and when he comes out, so that he will not die.

"Make a plate of pure gold and engrave on it as on a seal: HOLY TO THE LORD. Fasten a blue cord to it to attach it to the turban; it is to be on the front of the turban. It will be on Aaron's forehead, and he will bear the guilt involved in the sacred gifts the Israelites consecrate, whatever their gifts may be. It will be on Aaron's forehead continually so that they will be acceptable to the LORD.

"Weave the tunic of fine linen and make the turban of fine linen. The sash is to be the work of an embroiderer. Make tunics, sashes and headbands for Aaron's sons, to give them dignity and honor. After you put these clothes on your brother Aaron and his sons, anoint and ordain them. Consecrate them so they may serve me as priests.

"Make linen undergarments as a covering for the body, reaching from the waist to the thigh. Aaron and his sons must wear them whenever they enter the Tent of Meeting or approach the altar to minister in the Holy Place, so that they will not incur guilt and die.

"This is to be a lasting ordinance for Aaron and his descendants.

ORDINATION OF PRIESTS.   "This is what you are to do to consecrate them, so they may serve me as priests: Take a young bull and two rams without defect. And from fine wheat flour, without yeast, make bread, and cakes mixed with oil, and wafers spread with oil. Put them in a basket and present them in it—along with the bull and the two rams. Then bring Aaron and his sons to the entrance to the Tent of Meeting and wash them with water. Take the garments and dress Aaron with the tunic, the robe of the ephod, the ephod itself and the breastpiece. Fasten the ephod on him by its skillfully woven waistband. Put the turban on his head and attach

Ex. 29:1-9

---

[v]The meaning of the Hebrew for this word is uncertain.

the sacred diadem to the turban. Take the anointing oil and anoint him by pouring it on his head. Bring his sons and dress them in tunics and put headbands on them. Then tie sashes on Aaron and his sons.^{w} The priesthood is theirs by a lasting ordinance. In this way you shall ordain Aaron and his sons.

Ex.
29:10-14

SPECIAL SIN OFFERING.   "Bring the bull to the front of the Tent of Meeting, and Aaron and his sons shall lay their hands on its head. Slaughter it in the LORD's presence at the entrance to the Tent of Meeting. Take some of the bull's blood and put it on the horns of the altar with your finger, and pour out the rest of it at the base of the altar. Then take all the fat around the inner parts, the covering of the liver, and both kidneys with the fat on them, and burn them on the altar. But burn the bull's flesh and its hide and its offal outside the camp. It is a sin offering.

Ex.
29:15-18

SPECIAL BURNT OFFERING.   "Take one of the rams, and Aaron and his sons shall lay their hands on its head. Slaughter it and take the blood and sprinkle it against the altar on all sides. Cut the ram into pieces and wash the inner parts and the legs, putting them with the head and the other pieces. Then burn the entire ram on the altar. It is a burnt offering to the LORD, a pleasing aroma, an offering made to the LORD by fire.

Ex.
29:19-34

RAM OF ORDINATION.   "Take the other ram, and Aaron and his sons shall lay their hands on its head. Slaughter it, take some of its blood and put it on the lobes of the right ears of Aaron and his sons, on the thumbs of their right hands, and on the big toes of their right feet. Then sprinkle blood against the altar on all sides. And take some of the blood on the altar and some of the anointing oil and sprinkle it on Aaron and his garments and on his sons and their garments. Then he and his sons and their garments will be consecrated.

"Take from this ram the fat, the fat tail, the fat around the inner parts, the covering of the liver, both kidneys with the fat on them, and the right thigh. (This is the ram for the ordination.) From the basket of bread made without yeast, which is before the LORD, take a loaf, and a cake made with oil, and a wafer. Put all these in the hands of Aaron and his sons and wave them before the LORD as a wave offering. Then take them from their hands and burn them on the altar along with the burnt offering for a pleasing aroma to the LORD, an offering made to the LORD by fire. After you take the breast of the ram for Aaron's ordination, wave it before the LORD as a wave offering, and it will be your share.

"Consecrate those parts of the ordination ram that belong to Aaron and his sons: the breast that was waved and the thigh that was presented. This is always to be the regular share from the Israelites for Aaron and his sons. It is the contribution the Israelites are to make to the LORD from their fellowship offerings.^{x}

"Aaron's sacred garments will belong to his descendants so that they can be anointed and ordained in them. The son who succeeds him as priest and comes to the Tent of Meeting to minister in the Holy Place is to wear them seven days.

"Take the ram for the ordination and cook the meat in a sacred place. At the entrance to the Tent of Meeting, Aaron and his sons are to eat the meat of the ram and the bread that is in the basket. They are to eat these

---

^{w}Hebrew; Septuagint *on them* ^{x}Traditionally *peace offerings*

offerings by which atonement was made for their ordination and conse-cration. But no one else may eat them, because they are sacred. And if any of the meat of the ordination ram or any bread is left over till morning, burn it up. It must not be eaten, because it is sacred.

ORDINATION WEEK ACTIVITIES. "Do for Aaron and his sons every-thing I have commanded you, taking seven days to ordain them. Sacrifice a bull each day as a sin offering to make atonement. Purify the altar by making atonement for it, and anoint it to consecrate it. For seven days make atonement for the altar and consecrate it. Then the altar will be most holy, and whatever touches it will be holy.   Ex. 29:35-37

CONTINUOUS BURNT OFFERINGS. "This is what you are to offer on the altar regularly each day: two lambs a year old. Offer one in the morn-ing and the other at twilight. With the first lamb offer a tenth of an ephah^y of fine flour mixed with a quarter of a hin^z of oil from pressed olives, and a quarter of a hin of wine as a drink offering. Sacrifice the other lamb at twilight with the same grain offering and its drink offering as in the morn-ing—a pleasing aroma, an offering made to the LORD by fire.   Ex. 29:38-46

"For the generations to come this burnt offering is to be made regularly at the entrance to the Tent of Meeting before the LORD. There I will meet you and speak to you; there also I will meet with the Israelites, and the place will be consecrated by my glory.

"So I will consecrate the Tent of Meeting and the altar and will conse-crate Aaron and his sons to serve me as priests. Then I will dwell among the Israelites and be their God. They will know that I am the LORD their God, who brought them out of Egypt so that I might dwell among them. I am the LORD their God.

ALTAR OF INCENSE. "Make an altar of acacia wood for burning incense. It is to be square, a cubit long and a cubit wide, and two cubits high^a—its horns of one piece with it. Overlay the top and all the sides and the horns with pure gold, and make a gold molding around it. Make two gold rings for the altar below the molding—two on opposite sides—to hold the poles used to carry it. Make the poles of acacia wood and overlay them with gold. Put the altar in front of the curtain that is before the ark of the Testimony—before the atonement cover that is over the Testi-mony—where I will meet with you.   Ex. 30:1-10

"Aaron must burn fragrant incense on the altar every morning when he tends the lamps. He must burn incense again when he lights the lamps at twilight so incense will burn regularly before the LORD for the generations to come. Do not offer on this altar any other incense or any burnt offering or grain offering, and do not pour a drink offering on it. Once a year Aaron shall make atonement on its horns. This annual atonement must be made with the blood of the atoning sin offering for the generations to come. It is most holy to the LORD."

CENSUS OFFERING. Then the LORD said to Moses, "When you take a census of the Israelites to count them, each one must pay the LORD a ransom for his life at the time he is counted. Then no plague will come on them when you number them. Each one who crosses over to those   Ex. 30:11-16

^{y}That is, probably about 2 quarts (about 2 liters) ^{z}That is, probably about 1 quart (about 1 liter) ^{a}That is, about 1 1/2 feet (about 0.5 meter) long and wide and about 3 feet (about 0.9 meter) high

already counted is to give a half shekel,[b] according to the sanctuary shekel, which weighs twenty gerahs. This half shekel is an offering to the LORD. All who cross over, those twenty years old or more, are to give an offering to the LORD. The rich are not to give more than a half shekel and the poor are not to give less when you make the offering to the LORD to atone for your lives. Receive the atonement money from the Israelites and use it for the service of the Tent of Meeting. It will be a memorial for the Israelites before the LORD, making atonement for your lives."

Ex.
30:17-21

BRONZE LAVER.   Then the LORD said to Moses, "Make a bronze basin, with its bronze stand, for washing. Place it between the Tent of Meeting and the altar, and put water in it. Aaron and his sons are to wash their hands and feet with water from it. Whenever they enter the Tent of Meeting, they shall wash with water so that they will not die. Also, when they approach the altar to minister by presenting an offering made to the LORD by fire, they shall wash their hands and feet so that they will not die. This is to be a lasting ordinance for Aaron and his descendants for the generations to come."

Ex.
30:22-33

ANOINTING OIL.   Then the LORD said to Moses, "Take the following fine spices: 500 shekels[c] of liquid myrrh, half as much (that is, 250 shekels) of fragrant cinnamon, 250 shekels of fragrant cane, 500 shekels of cassia— all according to the sanctuary shekel—and a hin[d] of olive oil. Make these into a sacred anointing oil, a fragrant blend, the work of a perfumer. It will be the sacred anointing oil. Then use it to anoint the Tent of Meeting, the ark of the Testimony, the table and all its articles, the lampstand and its accessories, the altar of incense, the altar of burnt offering and all its utensils, and the basin with its stand. You shall consecrate them so they will be most holy, and whatever touches them will be holy.

"Anoint Aaron and his sons and consecrate them so they may serve me as priests. Say to the Israelites, 'This is to be my sacred anointing oil for the generations to come. Do not pour it on men's bodies and do not make any oil with the same formula. It is sacred, and you are to consider it sacred. Whoever makes perfume like it and whoever puts it on anyone other than a priest must be cut off from his people.'"

Ex.
30:34-38

INCENSE.   Then the LORD said to Moses, "Take fragrant spices—gum resin, onycha and galbanum—and pure frankincense, all in equal amounts, and make a fragrant blend of incense, the work of a perfumer. It is to be salted and pure and sacred. Grind some of it to powder and place it in front of the Testimony in the Tent of Meeting, where I will meet with you. It shall be most holy to you. Do not make any incense with this formula for yourselves; consider it holy to the LORD. Whoever makes any like it to enjoy its fragrance must be cut off from his people."

Ex. 31:1-11

WORKMEN NAMED.   Then the LORD said to Moses, "See, I have chosen Bezalel son of Uri, the son of Hur, of the tribe of Judah, and I have filled him with the Spirit of God, with skill, ability and knowledge in all kinds of crafts—to make artistic designs for work in gold, silver and bronze, to cut and set stones, to work in wood, and to engage in all kinds of craftsmanship. Moreover, I have appointed Oholiab son of Ahisamach, of the tribe of Dan, to help him. Also I have given skill to all the craftsmen to

[b]That is, about 1/5 ounce (about 6 grams)   [c]That is, about 12 1/2 pounds (about 6 kilograms)   [d]That is, probably about 4 quarts (about 4 liters)

make everything I have commanded you: the Tent of Meeting, the ark of the Testimony with the atonement cover on it, and all the other furnishings of the tent—the table and its articles, the pure gold lampstand and all its accessories, the altar of incense, the altar of burnt offering and all its utensils, the basin with its stand—and also the woven garments, both the sacred garments for Aaron the priest and the garments for his sons when they serve as priests, and the anointing oil and fragrant incense for the Holy Place. They are to make them just as I commanded you."

MOSES GIVEN STONE TABLETS.   When the LORD finished speaking to   Ex. 31:18
Moses on Mount Sinai, he gave him the two tablets of the Testimony, the tablets of stone inscribed by the finger of God.

These detailed instructions indicate how strongly God feels about the purity of his people, the constancy of their worship, the need for sacrifice and offerings, and the value of all that is dedicated to God's service. The plans also indicate the distance which must be kept between deity and humanity, yet the closeness of God to those who would worship him. And once again the remarkable detail makes a strong statement about how specifically God is involved in the lives of his people and what great expectations he has for precise obedience to whatever commands he gives.

But the tabernacle is more than just a temporary place for the Israelites to worship God: it foreshadows a more permanent temple to be built in future years, and later a spiritual temple to be known as the church. Therefore its symbolism is rich indeed. The mercy seat above the ark, for example, suggests the grace which will be given to cover all law. The blood of the animal sacrifice looks forward to a future time when the Messiah will be slain as the Lamb of God. The veil which separates man from God will one day be torn apart by this spiritual High Priest who will enter that holiest of holies—heaven itself—and there atone for the sins of all mankind. And all who believe in God and obey the laws of his covenant will become as priests, wearing the priestly garments of righteous character and offering up their very lives to God's service.

The Covenant Broken and Renewed

*I*t has been only a brief time since the Israelites enthusiastically accepted the terms of God's covenant and vowed obedience to his laws. Yet their commitment was apparently more a matter of emotion than of sincere dedication, for with Moses gone up into the mountain only a month, the people ask Aaron to give them a tangible god to worship—an idol. God, of course, has specifically forbidden such worship. Nevertheless Aaron is persuaded and builds a golden calf, which the Israelites worship. God's response is one of anger, and Moses must intercede on behalf of the people. Moses' own reaction is also one of anger, as is witnessed by his responses to this disheartening turn of events. Yet God is forgiving and, with firm repetition of his laws, he agrees to renew the covenant.

AARON MAKES GOLDEN CALF.   When the people saw that Moses was   Ex. 32:1-6
so long in coming down from the mountain, they gathered around Aaron

and said, "Come, make us gods^e who will go before us. As for this fellow Moses who brought us up out of Egypt, we don't know what has happened to him."

Aaron answered them, "Take off the gold earrings that your wives, your sons and your daughters are wearing, and bring them to me." So all the people took off their earrings and brought them to Aaron. He took what they handed him and made it into an idol cast in the shape of a calf, fashioning it with a tool. Then they said, "These are your gods,^f O Israel, who brought you up out of Egypt."

When Aaron saw this, he built an altar in front of the calf and announced, "Tomorrow there will be a festival to the LORD." So the next day the people rose early and sacrificed burnt offerings and presented fellowship offerings.^g Afterward they sat down to eat and drink and got up to indulge in revelry.

Ex. 32:7-10 GOD EXPRESSES ANGER. Then the LORD said to Moses, "Go down, because your people, whom you brought up out of Egypt, have become corrupt. They have been quick to turn away from what I commanded them and have made themselves an idol cast in the shape of a calf. They have bowed down to it and sacrificed to it and have said, 'These are your gods, O Israel, who brought you up out of Egypt.'

"I have seen these people," the LORD said to Moses, "and they are a stiff-necked people. Now leave me alone so that my anger may burn against them and that I may destroy them. Then I will make you into a great nation."

Ex. 32:11-14 MOSES INTERCEDES. But Moses sought the favor of the LORD his God. "O LORD," he said, "why should your anger burn against your people, whom you brought out of Egypt with great power and a mighty hand? Why should the Egyptians say, 'It was with evil intent that he brought them out, to kill them in the mountains and to wipe them off the face of the earth'? Turn from your fierce anger; relent and do not bring disaster on your people. Remember your servants Abraham, Isaac and Israel, to whom you swore by your own self: 'I will make your descendants as numerous as the stars in the sky and I will give your descendants all this land I promised them, and it will be their inheritance forever.'" Then the LORD relented and did not bring on his people the disaster he had threatened.

Ex. 32:15-20 CALF DESTROYED; TABLETS BROKEN. Moses turned and went down the mountain with the two tablets of the Testimony in his hands. They were inscribed on both sides, front and back. The tablets were the work of God; the writing was the writing of God, engraved on the tablets.

When Joshua heard the noise of the people shouting, he said to Moses, "There is the sound of war in the camp."

Moses replied:

> "It is not the sound of victory,
>   it is not the sound of defeat;
>   it is the sound of singing that I hear."

When Moses approached the camp and saw the calf and the dancing, his anger burned and he threw the tablets out of his hands, breaking them

---

^eOr *a god*   ^fOr *This is your god*; also in verse 8   ^gTraditionally *peace offerings*

to pieces at the foot of the mountain. And he took the calf they had made and burned it in the fire; then he ground it to powder, scattered it on the water and made the Israelites drink it.

AARON DENIES RESPONSIBILITY.   He said to Aaron, "What did these people do to you, that you led them into such great sin?"

"Do not be angry, my lord," Aaron answered. "You know how prone these people are to evil. They said to me, 'Make us gods who will go before us. As for this fellow Moses who brought us up out of Egypt, we don't know what has happened to him.' So I told them, 'Whoever has any gold jewelry, take it off.' Then they gave me the gold, and I threw it into the fire, and out came this calf!"

Ex. 32:21-24

EXECUTIONS BY LEVITES.   Moses saw that the people were running wild and that Aaron had let them get out of control and so become a laughing-stock to their enemies. So he stood at the entrance to the camp and said, "Whoever is for the LORD, come to me." And all the Levites rallied to him.

Then he said to them, "This is what the LORD, the God of Israel, says: 'Each man strap a sword to his side. Go back and forth through the camp from one end to the other, each killing his brother and friend and neighbor.'" The Levites did as Moses commanded, and that day about three thousand of the people died. Then Moses said, "You have been set apart to the LORD today, for you were against your own sons and brothers, and he has blessed you this day."

Ex. 32:25-29

MOSES INTERCEDES AGAIN.   The next day Moses said to the people, "You have committed a great sin. But now I will go up to the LORD; perhaps I can make atonement for your sin."

So Moses went back to the LORD and said, "Oh, what a great sin these people have committed! They have made themselves gods of gold. But now, please forgive their sin—but if not, then blot me out of the book you have written."

The LORD replied to Moses, "Whoever has sinned against me I will blot out of my book. Now go, lead the people to the place I spoke of, and my angel will go before you. However, when the time comes for me to punish, I will punish them for their sin."

And the LORD struck the people with a plague because of what they did with the calf Aaron had made.

Ex. 32:30-35

GOD MANIFESTS DISPLEASURE.   Then the LORD said to Moses, "Leave this place, you and the people you brought up out of Egypt, and go up to the land I promised on oath to Abraham, Isaac and Jacob, saying, 'I will give it to your descendants.' I will send an angel before you and drive out the Canaanites, Amorites, Hittites, Perizzites, Hivites and Jebusites. Go up to the land flowing with milk and honey. But I will not go with you, because you are a stiff-necked people and I might destroy you on the way."

Ex. 33:1-3

ORNAMENTS REMOVED.   When the people heard these distressing words, they began to mourn and no one put on any ornaments. For the LORD had said to Moses, "Tell the Israelites, 'You are a stiff-necked people. If I were to go with you even for a moment, I might destroy you. Now take off your ornaments and I will decide what to do with you.'" So the Israelites stripped off their ornaments at Mount Horeb.

Ex. 33:4-6

Ex. 33:7-11   THE TENT OF MEETING. Now Moses used to take a tent and pitch it outside the camp some distance away, calling it the "tent of meeting." Anyone inquiring of the LORD would go to the tent of meeting outside the camp. And whenever Moses went out to the tent, all the people rose and stood at the entrances to their tents, watching Moses until he entered the tent. As Moses went into the tent, the pillar of cloud would come down and stay at the entrance, while the LORD spoke with Moses. Whenever the people saw the pillar of cloud standing at the entrance to the tent, they all stood and worshiped, each at the entrance to his tent. The LORD would speak to Moses face to face, as a man speaks with his friend. Then Moses would return to the camp, but his young aide Joshua son of Nun did not leave the tent.

Ex. 33:12-16   GOD PROMISES PRESENCE. Moses said to the LORD, "You have been telling me, 'Lead these people,' but you have not let me know whom you will send with me. You have said, 'I know you by name and you have found favor with me.' If you are pleased with me, teach me your ways so I may know you and continue to find favor with you. Remember that this nation is your people."

The LORD replied, "My Presence will go with you, and I will give you rest."

Then Moses said to him, "If your Presence does not go with us, do not send us up from here. How will anyone know that you are pleased with me and with your people unless you go with us? What else will distinguish me and your people from all the other people on the face of the earth?"

Ex. 33:17-23   MOSES SEES GOD'S GLORY. And the LORD said to Moses, "I will do the very thing you have asked, because I am pleased with you and I know you by name."

Then Moses said, "Now show me your glory."

And the LORD said, "I will cause all my goodness to pass in front of you, and I will proclaim my name, the LORD, in your presence. I will have mercy on whom I will have mercy, and I will have compassion on whom I will have compassion. But," he said, "you cannot see my face, for no one may see me and live."

Then the LORD said, "There is a place near me where you may stand on a rock. When my glory passes by, I will put you in a cleft in the rock and cover you with my hand until I have passed by. Then I will remove my hand and you will see my back; but my face must not be seen."

Ex. 34:1-7   GOD REVEALS CHARACTER. The LORD said to Moses, "Chisel out two stone tablets like the first ones, and I will write on them the words that were on the first tablets, which you broke. Be ready in the morning, and then come up on Mount Sinai. Present yourself to me there on top of the mountain. No one is to come with you or be seen anywhere on the mountain; not even the flocks and herds may graze in front of the mountain."

So Moses chiseled out two stone tablets like the first ones and went up Mount Sinai early in the morning, as the LORD had commanded him; and he carried the two stone tablets in his hands. Then the LORD came down in the cloud and stood there with him and proclaimed his name, the LORD. And he passed in front of Moses, proclaiming, "The LORD, the LORD, the compassionate and gracious God, slow to anger, abounding in love and faithfulness, maintaining love to thousands, and forgiving wickedness, rebellion and sin. Yet he does not leave the guilty unpunished; he punishes the children and their children for the sin of the fathers to the third and fourth generation."

GOD RENEWS COVENANT.   Moses bowed to the ground at once and worshiped. "O Lord, if I have found favor in your eyes," he said, "then let the Lord go with us. Although this is a stiff-necked people, forgive our wickedness and our sin, and take us as your inheritance."

Ex. 34:8-10

Then the LORD said: "I am making a covenant with you. Before all your people I will do wonders never before done in any nation in all the world. The people you live among will see how awesome is the work that I, the LORD, will do for you.

WARNING AGAINST TREATIES.   Obey what I command you today. I will drive out before you the Amorites, Canaanites, Hittites, Perizzites, Hivites and Jebusites. Be careful not to make a treaty with those who live in the land where you are going, or they will be a snare among you. Break down their altars, smash their sacred stones and cut down their Asherah poles.[h] Do not worship any other god, for the LORD, whose name is Jealous, is a jealous God.

Ex. 34:11-16

"Be careful not to make a treaty with those who live in the land; for when they prostitute themselves to their gods and sacrifice to them, they will invite you and you will eat their sacrifices. And when you choose some of their daughters as wives for your sons and those daughters prostitute themselves to their gods, they will lead your sons to do the same.

SECOND TABLETS WRITTEN.   Then the LORD said to Moses, "Write down these words, for in accordance with these words I have made a covenant with you and with Israel." Moses was there with the LORD forty days and forty nights without eating bread or drinking water. And he wrote on the tablets the words of the covenant—the Ten Commandments.

Ex. 34:27,28

MOSES VEILS HIS FACE.   When Moses came down from Mount Sinai with the two tablets of the Testimony in his hands, he was not aware that his face was radiant because he had spoken with the LORD. When Aaron and all the Israelites saw Moses, his face was radiant, and they were afraid to come near him. But Moses called to them; so Aaron and all the leaders of the community came back to him, and he spoke to them. Afterward all the Israelites came near him, and he gave them all the commands the LORD had given him on Mount Sinai.

Ex. 34:29-35

When Moses finished speaking to them, he put a veil over his face. But whenever he entered the LORD's presence to speak with him, he removed the veil until he came out. And when he came out and told the Israelites what he had been commanded, they saw that his face was radiant. Then Moses would put the veil back over his face until he went in to speak with the LORD.

—————————◇—————————

[h]That is, symbols of the goddess Asherah

Construction of the Tabernacle

*W*ith the Israelites chastised for their breach of the covenant, and with God's reaffirmation of his part in the covenant, the stage is now set for actual construction of the tabernacle. This new "tent of meeting" will replace Moses' own tent which he had set outside the camp. Now every direction must be followed to the smallest detail, from the gathering of the proper materials to the use of the right tools in the tabernacle's assembly. Moreover, the garments of the priests must be made with careful attention to accuracy. Here, then, the Exodus account records the beginning and completion of the project, and the dedication of the tabernacle's use in the service of God.

Ex. 35:4-9   CALL FOR MATERIALS.   Moses said to the whole Israelite community, "This is what the LORD has commanded: From what you have, take an offering for the LORD. Everyone who is willing is to bring to the LORD an offering of gold, silver and bronze; blue, purple and scarlet yarn and fine linen; goat hair; ram skins dyed red and hides of sea cows[i]; acacia wood; olive oil for the light; spices for the anointing oil and for the fragrant incense; and onyx stones and other gems to be mounted on the ephod and breastpiece.

Ex. 35:10-19   CALL FOR WORKERS.   "All who are skilled among you are to come and make everything the LORD has commanded: the tabernacle with its tent and its covering, clasps, frames, crossbars, posts and bases; the ark with its poles and the atonement cover and the curtain that shields it; the table with its poles and all its articles and the bread of the Presence; the lampstand that is for light with its accessories, lamps and oil for the light; the altar of incense with its poles, the anointing oil and the fragrant incense; the curtain for the doorway at the entrance to the tabernacle; the altar of burnt offering with its bronze grating, its poles and all its utensils; the bronze basin with its stand; the curtains of the courtyard with its posts and bases, and the curtain for the entrance to the courtyard; the tent pegs for the tabernacle and for the courtyard, and their ropes; the woven garments worn for ministering in the sanctuary—both the sacred garments for Aaron the priest and the garments for his sons when they serve as priests."

Ex. 35:20-29   OFFERING OF MATERIALS.   Then the whole Israelite community withdrew from Moses' presence, and everyone who was willing and whose heart moved him came and brought an offering to the LORD for the work on the Tent of Meeting, for all its service, and for the sacred garments. All who were willing, men and women alike, came and brought gold jewelry of all kinds: brooches, earrings, rings and ornaments. They all presented their gold as a wave offering to the LORD. Everyone who had blue, purple or scarlet yarn or fine linen, or goat hair, ram skins dyed red or hides of sea cows brought them. Those presenting an offering of silver or bronze brought it as an offering to the LORD, and everyone who had acacia wood for any part of the work brought it. Every skilled woman spun with her hands and brought what she had spun—blue, purple or scarlet yarn or

[i]That is, dugongs

fine linen. And all the women who were willing and had the skill spun the goat hair. The leaders brought onyx stones and other gems to be mounted on the ephod and breastpiece. They also brought spices and olive oil for the light and for the anointing oil and for the fragrant incense. All the Israelite men and women who were willing brought to the LORD freewill offerings for all the work the LORD through Moses had commanded them to do.

ARTISTS APPOINTED.   Then Moses said to the Israelites, "See, the LORD has chosen Bezalel son of Uri, the son of Hur, of the tribe of Judah, and he has filled him with the Spirit of God, with skill, ability and knowledge in all kinds of crafts—to make artistic designs for work in gold, silver and bronze, to cut and set stones, to work in wood and to engage in all kinds of artistic craftsmanship. And he has given both him and Oholiab son of Ahisamach, of the tribe of Dan, the ability to teach others. He has filled them with skill to do all kinds of work as craftsmen, designers, embroiderers in blue, purple and scarlet yarn and fine linen, and weavers—all of them master craftsmen and designers. So Bezalel, Oholiab and every skilled person to whom the LORD has given skill and ability to know how to carry out all the work of constructing the sanctuary are to do the work just as the LORD has commanded."

Ex. 35:30-36:1

TOO MANY OFFERINGS.   Then Moses summoned Bezalel and Oholiab and every skilled person to whom the LORD had given ability and who was willing to come and do the work. They received from Moses all the offerings the Israelites had brought to carry out the work of constructing the sanctuary. And the people continued to bring freewill offerings morning after morning. So all the skilled craftsmen who were doing all the work on the sanctuary left their work and said to Moses, "The people are bringing more than enough for doing the work the LORD commanded to be done."

Ex. 36:2-7

Then Moses gave an order and they sent this word throughout the camp: "No man or woman is to make anything else as an offering for the sanctuary." And so the people were restrained from bringing more, because what they already had was more than enough to do all the work.

CURTAIN AND COVERINGS.   All the skilled men among the workmen made the tabernacle with ten curtains of finely twisted linen and blue, purple and scarlet yarn, with cherubim worked into them by a skilled craftsman. All the curtains were the same size—twenty-eight cubits long and four cubits wide.ʲ They joined five of the curtains together and did the same with the other five. Then they made loops of blue material along the edge of the end curtain in one set, and the same was done with the end curtain in the other set. They also made fifty loops on one curtain and fifty loops on the end curtain of the other set, with the loops opposite each other. Then they made fifty gold clasps and used them to fasten the two sets of curtains together so that the tabernacle was a unit.

Ex. 36:8-19

They made curtains of goat hair for the tent over the tabernacle—eleven altogether. All eleven curtains were the same size—thirty cubits long and four cubits wide.ᵏ They joined five of the curtains into one set and the other six into another set. Then they made fifty loops along the edge of the end curtain in one set and also along the edge of the end curtain in

ʲThat is, about 42 feet (about 12.5 meters) long and 6 feet (about 1.8 meters) wide
ᵏThat is, about 45 feet (about 13.5 meters) long and 6 feet (about 1.8 meters) wide

the other set. They made fifty bronze clasps to fasten the tent together as a unit. Then they made for the tent a covering of ram skins dyed red, and over that a covering of hides of sea cows.[l]

Ex.
36:20-34

FRAMEWORK BUILT.   They made upright frames of acacia wood for the tabernacle. Each frame was ten cubits long and a cubit and a half wide,[m] with two projections set parallel to each other. They made all the frames of the tabernacle in this way. They made twenty frames for the south side of the tabernacle and made forty silver bases to go under them—two bases for each frame, one under each projection. For the other side, the north side of the tabernacle, they made twenty frames and forty silver bases— two under each frame. They made six frames for the far end, that is, the west end of the tabernacle, and two frames were made for the corners of the tabernacle at the far end. At these two corners the frames were double from the bottom all the way to the top and fitted into a single ring; both were made alike. So there were eight frames and sixteen silver bases—two under each frame.

They also made crossbars of acacia wood: five for the frames on one side of the tabernacle, five for those on the other side, and five for the frames on the west, at the far end of the tabernacle. They made the center crossbar so that it extended from end to end at the middle of the frames. They overlaid the frames with gold and made gold rings to hold the crossbars. They also overlaid the crossbars with gold.

Ex.
36:35-38

VEIL MADE.   They made the curtain of blue, purple and scarlet yarn and finely twisted linen, with cherubim worked into it by a skilled craftsman. They made four posts of acacia wood for it and overlaid them with gold. They made gold hooks for them and cast their four silver bases. For the entrance to the tent they made a curtain of blue, purple and scarlet yarn and finely twisted linen—the work of an embroiderer; and they made five posts with hooks for them. They overlaid the tops of the posts and their bands with gold and made their five bases of bronze.

Ex. 37:1-9

ARK AND MERCY SEAT.   Bezalel made the ark of acacia wood—two and a half cubits long, a cubit and a half wide, and a cubit and a half high.[n] He overlaid it with pure gold, both inside and out, and made a gold molding around it. He cast four gold rings for it and fastened them to its four feet, with two rings on one side and two rings on the other. Then he made poles of acacia wood and overlaid them with gold. And he inserted the poles into the rings on the sides of the ark to carry it.

He made the atonement cover of pure gold—two and a half cubits long and a cubit and a half wide.[o] Then he made two cherubim out of hammered gold at the ends of the cover. He made one cherub on one end and the second cherub on the other; at the two ends he made them of one piece with the cover. The cherubim had their wings spread upward, overshadowing the cover with them. The cherubim faced each other, looking toward the cover.

[l]That is, dugongs   [m]That is, about 15 feet (about 4.5 meters) long and 2 1/4 feet (about 0.7 meter) wide   [n]That is, about 3 3/4 feet (about 1.1 meters) long and 2 1/4 feet (about 0.7 meter) wide and high   [o]That is, about 3 3/4 feet (about 1.1 meters) long and 2 1/4 feet (about 0.7 meter) wide

TABLE BUILT.   They[p] made the table of acacia wood—two cubits long, a cubit wide, and a cubit and a half high.[q] Then they overlaid it with pure gold and made a gold molding around it. They also made around it a rim a handbreadth[r] wide and put a gold molding on the rim. They cast four gold rings for the table and fastened them to the four corners, where the four legs were. The rings were put close to the rim to hold the poles used in carrying the table. The poles for carrying the table were made of acacia wood and were overlaid with gold. And they made from pure gold the articles for the table—its plates and dishes and bowls and its pitchers for the pouring out of drink offerings.

Ex.
37:10-16

LAMPSTAND FASHIONED.   They made the lampstand of pure gold and hammered it out, base and shaft; its flowerlike cups, buds and blossoms were of one piece with it. Six branches extended from the sides of the lampstand—three on one side and three on the other. Three cups shaped like almond flowers with buds and blossoms were on one branch, three on the next branch and the same for all six branches extending from the lampstand. And on the lampstand were four cups shaped like almond flowers with buds and blossoms. One bud was under the first pair of branches extending from the lampstand, a second bud under the second pair, and a third bud under the third pair—six branches in all. The buds and the branches were all of one piece with the lampstand, hammered out of pure gold.
   They made its seven lamps, as well as its wick trimmers and trays, of pure gold. They made the lampstand and all its accessories from one talent[s] of pure gold.

Ex.
37:17-24

ALTAR OF INCENSE.   They made the altar of incense out of acacia wood. It was square, a cubit long and a cubit wide, and two cubits high[t]—its horns of one piece with it. They overlaid the top and all the sides and the horns with pure gold, and made a gold molding around it. They made two gold rings below the molding—two on opposite sides—to hold the poles used to carry it. They made the poles of acacia wood and overlaid them with gold.

Ex.
37:25-28

OIL AND INCENSE BLENDED.   They also made the sacred anointing oil and the pure, fragrant incense—the work of a perfumer.

Ex. 37:29

ALTAR OF SACRIFICE.   They[u] built the altar of burnt offering of acacia wood, three cubits[v] high; it was square, five cubits long and five cubits wide.[w] They made a horn at each of the four corners, so that the horns and the altar were of one piece, and they overlaid the altar with bronze. They made all its utensils of bronze—its pots, shovels, sprinkling bowls, meat forks and firepans. They made a grating for the altar, a bronze network, to be under its ledge, halfway up the altar. They cast bronze rings to hold the poles for the four corners of the bronze grating. They made the poles of acacia wood and overlaid them with bronze. They inserted the poles into

Ex. 38:1-7

[p]Or He; also in verses 11-29   [q]That is, about 3 feet (about 0.9 meter) long, 1 1/2 feet (about 0.5 meter) wide, and 2 1/4 feet (about 0.7 meter) high   [r]That is, about 3 inches (about 8 centimeters)   [s]That is, about 75 pounds (about 34 kilograms)   [t]That is, about 1 1/2 feet (about 0.5 meter) long and wide, and about 3 feet (about 0.9 meter) high   [u]Or He; also in verses 2-9   [v]That is, about 4 1/2 feet (about 1.3 meters)   [w]That is, about 7 1/2 feet (about 2.3 meters) long and wide

the rings so they would be on the sides of the altar for carrying it. They made it hollow, out of boards.

Ex. 38:8   LAVER BRAZED.   They made the bronze basin and its bronze stand from the mirrors of the women who served at the entrance to the Tent of Meeting.

Ex. 38:9-20   COURT CONSTRUCTED.   Next they made the courtyard. The south side was a hundred cubits[x] long and had curtains of finely twisted linen, with twenty posts and twenty bronze bases, and with silver hooks and bands on the posts. The north side was also a hundred cubits long and had twenty posts and twenty bronze bases, with silver hooks and bands on the posts.

The west end was fifty cubits[y] wide and had curtains, with ten posts and ten bases, with silver hooks and bands on the posts. The east end, toward the sunrise, was also fifty cubits wide. Curtains fifteen cubits[z] long were on one side of the entrance, with three posts and three bases, and curtains fifteen cubits long were on the other side of the entrance to the courtyard, with three posts and three bases. All the curtains around the courtyard were of finely twisted linen. The bases for the posts were bronze. The hooks and bands on the posts were silver, and their tops were overlaid with silver; so all the posts of the courtyard had silver bands.

The curtain for the entrance to the courtyard was of blue, purple and scarlet yarn and finely twisted linen—the work of an embroiderer. It was twenty cubits[a] long and, like the curtains of the courtyard, five cubits[b] high, with four posts and four bronze bases. Their hooks and bands were silver, and their tops were overlaid with silver. All the tent pegs of the tabernacle and of the surrounding courtyard were bronze.

Ex. 38:21-31   VALUE OF MATERIALS USED.   These are the amounts of the materials used for the tabernacle, the tabernacle of the Testimony, which were recorded at Moses' command by the Levites under the direction of Ithamar son of Aaron, the priest. (Bezalel son of Uri, the son of Hur, of the tribe of Judah, made everything the LORD commanded Moses; with him was Oholiab son of Ahisamach, of the tribe of Dan—a craftsman and designer, and an embroiderer in blue, purple and scarlet yarn and fine linen.) The total amount of the gold from the wave offering used for all the work on the sanctuary was 29 talents and 730 shekels,[c] according to the sanctuary shekel.

The silver obtained from those of the community who were counted in the census was 100 talents and 1,775 shekels,[d] according to the sanctuary shekel—one beka per person, that is, half a shekel,[e] according to the sanctuary shekel, from everyone who had crossed over to those counted, twenty years old or more, a total of 603,550 men. The 100 talents[f] of silver were used to cast the bases for the sanctuary and for the curtain—100 bases from the 100 talents, one talent for each base. They used the 1,775 shekels[g]

---

[x]That is, about 150 feet (about 46 meters)   [y]That is, about 75 feet (about 23 meters)   [z]That is, about 22 1/2 feet (about 6.9 meters)   [a]That is, about 30 feet (about 9 meters)   [b]That is, about 7 1/2 feet (about 2.3 meters)   [c]The weight of the gold was a little over one ton (about 1 metric ton).   [d]The weight of the silver was a little over 3 3/4 tons (about 3.4 metric tons).   [e]That is, about 1/5 ounce (about 5.5 grams)   [f]That is, about 3 3/4 tons (about 3.4 metric tons)   [g]That is, about 45 pounds (about 20 kilograms)

to make the hooks for the posts, to overlay the tops of the posts, and to make their bands.

The bronze from the wave offering was 70 talents and 2,400 shekels.[h] They used it to make the bases for the entrance to the Tent of Meeting, the bronze altar with its bronze grating and all its utensils, the bases for the surrounding courtyard and those for its entrance and all the tent pegs for the tabernacle and those for the surrounding courtyard.

PRIESTLY GARMENTS SEWN.   From the blue, purple and scarlet yarn they made woven garments for ministering in the sanctuary. They also made sacred garments for Aaron, as the LORD commanded Moses.

Ex. 39:1

EPHOD MADE.   They[i] made the ephod of gold, and of blue, purple and scarlet yarn, and of finely twisted linen. They hammered out thin sheets of gold and cut strands to be worked into the blue, purple and scarlet yarn and fine linen—the work of a skilled craftsman. They made shoulder pieces for the ephod, which were attached to two of its corners, so it could be fastened. Its skillfully woven waistband was like it—of one piece with the ephod and made with gold, and with blue, purple and scarlet yarn, and with finely twisted linen, as the LORD commanded Moses.

They mounted the onyx stones in gold filigree settings and engraved them like a seal with the names of the sons of Israel. Then they fastened them on the shoulder pieces of the ephod as memorial stones for the sons of Israel, as the LORD commanded Moses.

Ex. 39:2-7

BREASTPIECE MADE.   They fashioned the breastpiece—the work of a skilled craftsman. They made it like the ephod: of gold, and of blue, purple and scarlet yarn, and of finely twisted linen. It was square—a span[j] long and a span wide—and folded double. Then they mounted four rows of precious stones on it. In the first row there was a ruby, a topaz and a beryl; in the second row a turquoise, a sapphire[k] and an emerald; in the third row a jacinth, an agate and an amethyst; in the fourth row a chryso-lite, an onyx and a jasper.[l] They were mounted in gold filigree settings. There were twelve stones, one for each of the names of the sons of Israel, each engraved like a seal with the name of one of the twelve tribes.

For the breastpiece they made braided chains of pure gold, like a rope. They made two gold filigree settings and two gold rings, and fastened the rings to two of the corners of the breastpiece. They fastened the two gold chains to the rings at the corners of the breastpiece, and the other ends of the chains to the two settings, attaching them to the shoulder pieces of the ephod at the front. They made two gold rings and attached them to the other two corners of the breastpiece on the inside edge next to the ephod. Then they made two more gold rings and attached them to the bottom of the shoulder pieces on the front of the ephod, close to the seam just above the waistband of the ephod. They tied the rings of the breastpiece to the rings of the ephod with blue cord, connecting it to the waistband so that the breastpiece would not swing out from the ephod—as the LORD commanded Moses.

Ex. 39:8-21

ROBE WOVEN.   They made the robe of the ephod entirely of blue cloth— the work of a weaver—with an opening in the center of the robe like the

Ex. 39:22-26

---

[h]The weight of the bronze was about 2 1/2 tons (about 2.4 metric tons).   [i]Or *He*; also in verses 7, 8 and 22   [j]That is, about 9 inches (about 22 centimeters)   [k]Or *lapis lazuli*   [l]The precise identification of some of these precious stones is uncertain.

opening of a collar,[m] and a band around this opening, so that it would not tear. They made pomegranates of blue, purple and scarlet yarn and finely twisted linen around the hem of the robe. And they made bells of pure gold and attached them around the hem between the pomegranates. The bells and pomegranates alternated around the hem of the robe to be worn for ministering, as the LORD commanded Moses.

Ex.
39:27-31

OTHER CLOTHES MADE.   For Aaron and his sons, they made tunics of fine linen—the work of a weaver—and the turban of fine linen, the linen headbands and the undergarments of finely twisted linen. The sash was of finely twisted linen and blue, purple and scarlet yarn—the work of an embroiderer—as the LORD commanded Moses.

They made the plate, the sacred diadem, out of pure gold and engraved on it, like an inscription on a seal: HOLY TO THE LORD. Then they fastened a blue cord to it to attach it to the turban, as the LORD commanded Moses.

Ex.
39:32-43

MOSES BLESSES COMPLETION.   So all the work on the tabernacle, the Tent of Meeting, was completed. The Israelites did everything just as the LORD commanded Moses. Then they brought the tabernacle to Moses: the tent and all its furnishings, its clasps, frames, crossbars, posts and bases; the covering of ram skins dyed red, the covering of hides of sea cows[n] and the shielding curtain; the ark of the Testimony with its poles and the atonement cover; the table with all its articles and the bread of the Presence; the pure gold lampstand with its row of lamps and all its accessories, and the oil for the light; the gold altar, the anointing oil, the fragrant incense, and the curtain for the entrance to the tent; the bronze altar with its bronze grating, its poles and all its utensils; the basin with its stand; the curtains of the courtyard with its posts and bases, and the curtain for the entrance to the courtyard; the ropes and tent pegs for the courtyard; all the furnishings for the tabernacle, the Tent of Meeting; and the woven garments worn for ministering in the sanctuary, both the sacred garments for Aaron the priest and the garments for his sons when serving as priests.

The Israelites had done all the work just as the LORD had commanded Moses. Moses inspected the work and saw that they had done it just as the LORD had commanded. So Moses blessed them.

Ex. 40:1-11

TABERNACLE ASSEMBLY ORDERED.   Then the LORD said to Moses: "Set up the tabernacle, the Tent of Meeting, on the first day of the first month. Place the ark of the Testimony in it and shield the ark with the curtain. Bring in the table and set out what belongs on it. Then bring in the lampstand and set up its lamps. Place the gold altar of incense in front of the ark of the Testimony and put the curtain at the entrance to the tabernacle.

"Place the altar of burnt offering in front of the entrance to the tabernacle, the Tent of Meeting; place the basin between the Tent of Meeting and the altar and put water in it. Set up the courtyard around it and put the curtain at the entrance to the courtyard.

"Take the anointing oil and anoint the tabernacle and everything in it; consecrate it and all its furnishings, and it will be holy. Then anoint the altar of burnt offering and all its utensils; consecrate the altar, and it will be most holy. Anoint the basin and its stand and consecrate them.

[m]The meaning of the Hebrew for this word is uncertain.   [n]That is, dugongs

PRIESTS TO BE ANOINTED. "Bring Aaron and his sons to the entrance to the Tent of Meeting and wash them with water. Then dress Aaron in the sacred garments, anoint him and consecrate him so he may serve me as priest. Bring his sons and dress them in tunics. Anoint them just as you anointed their father, so they may serve me as priests. Their anointing will be to a priesthood that will continue for all generations to come."

Ex. 40:12-15

TABERNACLE ERECTED. Moses did everything just as the LORD commanded him.

So the tabernacle was set up on the first day of the first month in the second year. When Moses set up the tabernacle, he put the bases in place, erected the frames, inserted the crossbars and set up the posts. Then he spread the tent over the tabernacle and put the covering over the tent, as the LORD commanded him.

He took the Testimony and placed it in the ark, attached the poles to the ark and put the atonement cover over it. Then he brought the ark into the tabernacle and hung the shielding curtain and shielded the ark of the Testimony, as the LORD commanded him.

Moses placed the table in the Tent of Meeting on the north side of the tabernacle outside the curtain and set out the bread on it before the LORD, as the LORD commanded him.

He placed the lampstand in the Tent of Meeting opposite the table on the south side of the tabernacle and set up the lamps before the LORD, as the LORD commanded him.

Moses placed the gold altar in the Tent of Meeting in front of the curtain and burned fragrant incense on it, as the LORD commanded him. Then he put up the curtain at the entrance to the tabernacle.

He set the altar of burnt offering near the entrance to the tabernacle, the Tent of Meeting, and offered on it burnt offerings and grain offerings, as the LORD commanded him.

He placed the basin between the Tent of Meeting and the altar and put water in it for washing, and Moses and Aaron and his sons used it to wash their hands and feet. They washed whenever they entered the Tent of Meeting or approached the altar, as the LORD commanded Moses.

Then Moses set up the courtyard around the tabernacle and altar and put up the curtain at the entrance to the courtyard. And so Moses finished the work.

Ex. 40:16-33 1st day of 2nd year (Ca. 1445 B.C.) Sinai

GLORY FILLS TABERNACLE. Then the cloud covered the Tent of Meeting, and the glory of the LORD filled the tabernacle. Moses could not enter the Tent of Meeting because the cloud had settled upon it, and the glory of the LORD filled the tabernacle.

Ex. 40:34,35

Ordination of the Priests

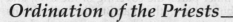

Now that the tabernacle is dedicated, it is time for Aaron and his sons to be ordained as priests to perform service in the tabernacle. Aaron and his four sons are to be ordained with special offerings and sacrifices during a week of dedication. The Leviticus record contains the account of Moses implementing God's instructions on this auspicious occasion.

The fact that Aaron is permitted to become high priest despite his sin in making the golden calf (and later trying to avoid responsibility for it) is testimony to the forgiving nature of God, as well as perhaps to the need for the one who will intercede on behalf of his people to be thoroughly acquainted with temptations and moral failure.

Following the week of ordination, although perhaps not immediately, Leviticus records that two of Aaron's sons make their own fire instead of using the fire which God sends for the sacrifices. There is reason to speculate that their mistake may be caused by drunkenness, because a special instruction is later imposed regarding use of wine during the temple service.

Lev. 8:1-4	CONGREGATION ASSEMBLED. The LORD said to Moses, "Bring Aaron and his sons, their garments, the anointing oil, the bull for the sin offering, the two rams and the basket containing bread made without yeast, and gather the entire assembly at the entrance to the Tent of Meeting." Moses did as the LORD commanded him, and the assembly gathered at the entrance to the Tent of Meeting.
Lev. 8:5-9	AARON CLOTHED. Moses said to the assembly, "This is what the LORD has commanded to be done." Then Moses brought Aaron and his sons forward and washed them with water. He put the tunic on Aaron, tied the sash around him, clothed him with the robe and put the ephod on him. He also tied the ephod to him by its skillfully woven waistband; so it was fastened on him. He placed the breastpiece on him and put the Urim and Thummim in the breastpiece. Then he placed the turban on Aaron's head and set the gold plate, the sacred diadem, on the front of it, as the LORD commanded Moses.
Lev. 8:10-12	AARON, TABERNACLE ANOINTED. Then Moses took the anointing oil and anointed the tabernacle and everything in it, and so consecrated them. He sprinkled some of the oil on the altar seven times, anointing the altar and all its utensils and the basin with its stand, to consecrate them. He poured some of the anointing oil on Aaron's head and anointed him to consecrate him.
Lev. 8:13	AARON'S SONS CLOTHED. Then he brought Aaron's sons forward, put tunics on them, tied sashes around them and put headbands on them, as the LORD commanded Moses.
Lev. 8:14-17	SIN OFFERING MADE. He then presented the bull for the sin offering, and Aaron and his sons laid their hands on its head. Moses slaughtered the bull and took some of the blood, and with his finger he put it on all the horns of the altar to purify the altar. He poured out the rest of the blood at the base of the altar. So he consecrated it to make atonement for it. Moses also took all the fat around the inner parts, the covering of the liver, and both kidneys and their fat, and burned it on the altar. But the bull with its hide and its flesh and its offal he burned up outside the camp, as the LORD commanded Moses.
Lev. 8:18-21	BURNT OFFERING MADE. He then presented the ram for the burnt offering, and Aaron and his sons laid their hands on its head. Then Moses slaughtered the ram and sprinkled the blood against the altar on all sides. He cut the ram into pieces and burned the head, the pieces and the fat. He washed the inner parts and the legs with water and burned the whole ram

on the altar as a burnt offering, a pleasing aroma, an offering made to the LORD by fire, as the LORD commanded Moses.

RAM OF ORDINATION.   He then presented the other ram, the ram for the ordination, and Aaron and his sons laid their hands on its head. Moses slaughtered the ram and took some of its blood and put it on the lobe of Aaron's right ear, on the thumb of his right hand and on the big toe of his right foot. Moses also brought Aaron's sons forward and put some of the blood on the lobes of their right ears, on the thumbs of their right hands and on the big toes of their right feet. Then he sprinkled blood against the altar on all sides. He took the fat, the fat tail, all the fat around the inner parts, the covering of the liver, both kidneys and their fat and the right thigh. Then from the basket of bread made without yeast, which was before the LORD, he took a cake of bread, and one made with oil, and a wafer; he put these on the fat portions and on the right thigh. He put all these in the hands of Aaron and his sons and waved them before the LORD as a wave offering. Then Moses took them from their hands and burned them on the altar on top of the burnt offering as an ordination offering, a pleasing aroma, an offering made to the LORD by fire. He also took the breast—Moses' share of the ordination ram—and waved it before the LORD as a wave offering, as the LORD commanded Moses.

Lev. 8:22-29

PRIESTS CONSECRATED.   Then Moses took some of the anointing oil and some of the blood from the altar and sprinkled them on Aaron and his garments and on his sons and their garments. So he consecrated Aaron and his garments and his sons and their garments.

Lev. 8:30

SEVEN DAYS IN TABERNACLE.   Moses then said to Aaron and his sons, "Cook the meat at the entrance to the Tent of Meeting and eat it there with the bread from the basket of ordination offerings, as I commanded, saying,[o] 'Aaron and his sons are to eat it.' Then burn up the rest of the meat and the bread. Do not leave the entrance to the Tent of Meeting for seven days, until the days of your ordination are completed, for your ordination will last seven days. What has been done today was commanded by the LORD to make atonement for you. You must stay at the entrance to the Tent of Meeting day and night for seven days and do what the LORD requires, so you will not die; for that is what I have been commanded." So Aaron and his sons did everything the LORD commanded through Moses.

Lev. 8:31-36

MOSES CALLS FOR ANIMALS.   On the eighth day Moses summoned Aaron and his sons and the elders of Israel. He said to Aaron, "Take a bull calf for your sin offering and a ram for your burnt offering, both without defect, and present them before the LORD. Then say to the Israelites: 'Take a male goat for a sin offering, a calf and a lamb—both a year old and without defect—for a burnt offering, and an ox[p] and a ram for a fellowship offering[q] to sacrifice before the LORD, together with a grain offering mixed with oil. For today the LORD will appear to you.'"

They took the things Moses commanded to the front of the Tent of Meeting, and the entire assembly came near and stood before the LORD. Then Moses said, "This is what the LORD has commanded you to do, so that the glory of the LORD may appear to you."

Moses said to Aaron, "Come to the altar and sacrifice your sin offering

Lev. 9:1-7

---

[o]Or *I was commanded:*   [p]The Hebrew word can include both male and female.
[q]Traditionally *peace offering*

and your burnt offering and make atonement for yourself and the people; sacrifice the offering that is for the people and make atonement for them, as the LORD has commanded."

Lev. 9:8-11 SIN OFFERING FOR AARON. So Aaron came to the altar and slaughtered the calf as a sin offering for himself. His sons brought the blood to him, and he dipped his finger into the blood and put it on the horns of the altar; the rest of the blood he poured out at the base of the altar. On the altar he burned the fat, the kidneys and the covering of the liver from the sin offering, as the LORD commanded Moses; the flesh and the hide he burned up outside the camp.

Lev. 9:12-14 PEOPLE'S BURNT OFFERING. Then he slaughtered the burnt offering. His sons handed him the blood, and he sprinkled it against the altar on all sides. They handed him the burnt offering piece by piece, including the head, and he burned them on the altar. He washed the inner parts and the legs and burned them on top of the burnt offering on the altar.

Lev. 9:15-17 PEOPLE'S SIN OFFERING. Aaron then brought the offering that was for the people. He took the goat for the people's sin offering and slaughtered it and offered it for a sin offering as he did with the first one.

He brought the burnt offering and offered it in the prescribed way. He also brought the grain offering, took a handful of it and burned it on the altar in addition to the morning's burnt offering.

Lev. 9:18-21 PEOPLE'S PEACE OFFERING. He slaughtered the ox and the ram as the fellowship offering for the people. His sons handed him the blood, and he sprinkled it against the altar on all sides. But the fat portions of the ox and the ram—the fat tail, the layer of fat, the kidneys and the covering of the liver—these they laid on the breasts, and then Aaron burned the fat on the altar. Aaron waved the breasts and the right thigh before the LORD as a wave offering, as Moses commanded.

Lev. 9:22,23 PEOPLE BLESSED. Then Aaron lifted his hands toward the people and blessed them. And having sacrificed the sin offering, the burnt offering and the fellowship offering, he stepped down.

Moses and Aaron then went into the Tent of Meeting. When they came out, they blessed the people; and the glory of the LORD appeared to all the people.

Lev. 9:24 FIRE ASTOUNDS ISRAELITES. Fire came out from the presence of the LORD and consumed the burnt offering and the fat portions on the altar. And when all the people saw it, they shouted for joy and fell facedown.

Lev. 10:1-3 NADAB AND ABIHU DIE. Aaron's sons Nadab and Abihu took their censers, put fire in them and added incense; and they offered unauthorized fire before the LORD, contrary to his command. So fire came out from the presence of the LORD and consumed them, and they died before the LORD. Moses then said to Aaron, "This is what the LORD spoke of when he said:

" 'Among those who approach me
I will show myself holy;
in the sight of all the people
I will be honored.' "

Aaron remained silent.

BODIES CARRIED OUT.   Moses summoned Mishael and Elzaphan, sons   Lev. 10:4-7
of Aaron's uncle Uzziel, and said to them, "Come here; carry your cousins
outside the camp, away from the front of the sanctuary." So they came and
carried them, still in their tunics, outside the camp, as Moses ordered.

Then Moses said to Aaron and his sons Eleazar and Ithamar, "Do not let
your hair become unkempt,[r] and do not tear your clothes, or you will die
and the LORD will be angry with the whole community. But your relatives,
all the house of Israel, may mourn for those the LORD has destroyed by fire.
Do not leave the entrance to the Tent of Meeting or you will die, because
the LORD's anointing oil is on you." So they did as Moses said.

NO WINE DURING SERVICE.   Then the LORD said to Aaron, "You and   Lev. 10:8-11
your sons are not to drink wine or other fermented drink whenever you
go into the Tent of Meeting, or you will die. This is a lasting ordinance for
the generations to come. You must distinguish between the holy and the
common, between the unclean and the clean, and you must teach the
Israelites all the decrees the LORD has given them through Moses."

EATING OF THE HOLY FOOD.   Moses said to Aaron and his remaining   Lev. 10:12-15
sons, Eleazar and Ithamar, "Take the grain offering left over from the offerings made to the LORD by fire and eat it prepared without yeast beside the
altar, for it is most holy. Eat it in a holy place, because it is your share and
your sons' share of the offerings made to the LORD by fire; for so I have
been commanded. But you and your sons and your daughters may eat the
breast that was waved and the thigh that was presented. Eat them in a
ceremonially clean place; they have been given to you and your children
as your share of the Israelites' fellowship offerings.[s] The thigh that was
presented and the breast that was waved must be brought with the fat
portions of the offerings made by fire, to be waved before the LORD as a
wave offering. This will be the regular share for you and your children, as
the LORD has commanded."

REBUKE FOR ABUSING FOOD.   When Moses inquired about the goat of   Lev. 10:16-20
the sin offering and found that it had been burned up, he was angry with
Eleazar and Ithamar, Aaron's remaining sons, and asked, "Why didn't you
eat the sin offering in the sanctuary area? It is most holy; it was given to you
to take away the guilt of the community by making atonement for them
before the LORD. Since its blood was not taken into the Holy Place, you
should have eaten the goat in the sanctuary area, as I commanded."

Aaron replied to Moses, "Today they sacrificed their sin offering and
their burnt offering before the LORD, but such things as this have happened to me. Would the LORD have been pleased if I had eaten the sin
offering today?" When Moses heard this, he was satisfied.

[r]Or *Do not uncover your heads*   [s]Traditionally *peace offerings*

The Levites Chosen for Service

*T*he task of maintaining the tabernacle service is clearly too great for Aaron and his two remaining sons to bear alone. So it becomes necessary to choose others for this special religious duty. God could very naturally choose the firstborn of each family, since they are already specially dedicated to him. Instead, God selects the single tribe of Levi to assist Aaron in the priesthood and tabernacle service. No reason is given explicitly as to why the Levites are chosen, but it could well be because they are the smallest of the tribes, and thus easily supported with the offerings available; or possibly because they had already demonstrated their allegiance to God in taking punitive action against those who had worshiped the golden calf; or simply because they are one with Moses and Aaron as descendants of Levi.

The book of Numbers contains an account of the Levites' selection, beginning with a preface regarding Aaron and his sons.

Num. 3:1-4   SONS OF AARON. This is the account of the family of Aaron and Moses at the time the LORD talked with Moses on Mount Sinai.

The names of the sons of Aaron were Nadab the firstborn and Abihu, Eleazar and Ithamar. Those were the names of Aaron's sons, the anointed priests, who were ordained to serve as priests. Nadab and Abihu, however, fell dead before the LORD when they made an offering with unauthorized fire before him in the Desert of Sinai. They had no sons; so only Eleazar and Ithamar served as priests during the lifetime of their father Aaron.

Num. 3:5-10   LEVITES CHOSEN FOR SERVICE. The LORD said to Moses, "Bring the tribe of Levi and present them to Aaron the priest to assist him. They are to perform duties for him and for the whole community at the Tent of Meeting by doing the work of the tabernacle. They are to take care of all the furnishings of the Tent of Meeting, fulfilling the obligations of the Israelites by doing the work of the tabernacle. Give the Levites to Aaron and his sons; they are the Israelites who are to be given wholly to him.[t] Appoint Aaron and his sons to serve as priests; anyone else who approaches the sanctuary must be put to death."

Num. 3:11-13 8:16-18   FIRSTBORN NOT CHOSEN. The LORD also said to Moses, "I have taken the Levites from among the Israelites in place of the first male offspring of every Israelite woman. The Levites are mine, for all the firstborn are mine. When I struck down all the firstborn in Egypt, I set apart for myself every firstborn in Israel, whether man or animal. They are to be mine. I am the LORD."

Num. 8:5-13   PURIFICATION FOR LEVITES. The LORD said to Moses: "Take the Levites from among the other Israelites and make them ceremonially clean. To purify them, do this: Sprinkle the water of cleansing on them; then have them shave their whole bodies and wash their clothes, and so purify themselves. Have them take a young bull with its grain offering of fine flour mixed with oil; then you are to take a second young bull for a sin

---

[t]Most manuscripts of the Masoretic Text; some manuscripts of the Masoretic Text, Samaritan Pentateuch and Septuagint (see also Num. 8:16) *to me*

offering. Bring the Levites to the front of the Tent of Meeting and assemble the whole Israelite community. You are to bring the Levites before the LORD, and the Israelites are to lay their hands on them. Aaron is to present the Levites before the LORD as a wave offering from the Israelites, so that they may be ready to do the work of the LORD.

"After the Levites lay their hands on the heads of the bulls, use the one for a sin offering to the LORD and the other for a burnt offering, to make atonement for the Levites. Have the Levites stand in front of Aaron and his sons and then present them as a wave offering to the LORD.

COMMISSION FOR SERVICE.   In this way you are to set the Levites apart from the other Israelites, and the Levites will be mine.

Num. 8:14,15,19

"After you have purified the Levites and presented them as a wave offering, they are to come to do their work at the Tent of Meeting. Of all the Israelites, I have given the Levites as gifts to Aaron and his sons to do the work at the Tent of Meeting on behalf of the Israelites and to make atonement for them so that no plague will strike the Israelites when they go near the sanctuary."

AGE OF DUTY.   The LORD said to Moses, "This applies to the Levites: Men twenty-five years old or more shall come to take part in the work at the Tent of Meeting, but at the age of fifty, they must retire from their regular service and work no longer. They may assist their brothers in performing their duties at the Tent of Meeting, but they themselves must not do the work. This, then, is how you are to assign the responsibilities of the Levites."

Num. 8:23-26

LEVITES BEGIN SERVICES.   Moses, Aaron and the whole Israelite community did with the Levites just as the LORD commanded Moses. The Levites purified themselves and washed their clothes. Then Aaron presented them as a wave offering before the LORD and made atonement for them to purify them. After that, the Levites came to do their work at the Tent of Meeting under the supervision of Aaron and his sons. They did with the Levites just as the LORD commanded Moses.

Num. 8:20-22

Offerings from the Tribes

*T*he book of Numbers also records the many offerings which are brought by the leaders of each tribe as part of the dedication of the tabernacle and the altar. The first offerings are brought on the day the tabernacle is erected, then more are given each day for 12 days, according to each of the tribes. The prince of each tribe brings the offering on behalf of his people.

LEADERS BRING OFFERINGS.   When Moses finished setting up the tabernacle, he anointed it and consecrated it and all its furnishings. He also anointed and consecrated the altar and all its utensils. Then the leaders of Israel, the heads of families who were the tribal leaders in charge of those who were counted, made offerings. They brought as their gifts before the LORD six covered carts and twelve oxen—an ox from each leader and a cart from every two. These they presented before the tabernacle.

The LORD said to Moses, "Accept these from them, that they may be

Num. 7:1-5

used in the work at the Tent of Meeting. Give them to the Levites as each man's work requires."

Num. 7:6-9   OFFERINGS GIVEN TO LEVITES.   So Moses took the carts and oxen and gave them to the Levites. He gave two carts and four oxen to the Gershonites, as their work required, and he gave four carts and eight oxen to the Merarites, as their work required. They were all under the direction of Ithamar son of Aaron, the priest. But Moses did not give any to the Kohathites, because they were to carry on their shoulders the holy things, for which they were responsible.

Num. 7:10,11   OFFERINGS FOR ALTAR.   When the altar was anointed, the leaders brought their offerings for its dedication and presented them before the altar. For the LORD had said to Moses, "Each day one leader is to bring his offering for the dedication of the altar."

Num. 7:12-17   NAHSHON OF JUDAH.   The one who brought his offering on the first day was Nahshon son of Amminadab of the tribe of Judah.

His offering was one silver plate weighing a hundred and thirty shekels,[u] and one silver sprinkling bowl weighing seventy shekels,[v] both according to the sanctuary shekel, each filled with fine flour mixed with oil as a grain offering; one gold dish weighing ten shekels,[w] filled with incense; one young bull, one ram and one male lamb a year old, for a burnt offering; one male goat for a sin offering; and two oxen, five rams, five male goats and five male lambs a year old, to be sacrificed as a fellowship offering.[x] This was the offering of Nahshon son of Amminadab.

Num. 7:18-23   NETHANEL OF ISSACHAR.   On the second day Nethanel son of Zuar, the leader of Issachar, brought his offering.

The offering he brought was one silver plate weighing a hundred and thirty shekels, and one silver sprinkling bowl weighing seventy shekels, both according to the sanctuary shekel, each filled with fine flour mixed with oil as a grain offering; one gold dish weighing ten shekels, filled with incense; one young bull, one ram and one male lamb a year old, for a burnt offering; one male goat for a sin offering; and two oxen, five rams, five male goats and five male lambs a year old, to be sacrificed as a fellowship offering. This was the offering of Nethanel son of Zuar.

Num. 7:24-29   ELIAB OF ZEBULUN.   On the third day, Eliab son of Helon, the leader of the people of Zebulun, brought his offering.

His offering was one silver plate weighing a hundred and thirty shekels, and one silver sprinkling bowl weighing seventy shekels, both according to the sanctuary shekel, each filled with fine flour mixed with oil as a grain offering; one gold dish weighing ten shekels, filled with incense; one young bull, one ram and one male lamb a year old, for a burnt offering; one male goat for a sin offering; and two oxen, five rams, five male goats and five male lambs a year old, to be sacrificed as a fellowship offering. This was the offering of Eliab son of Helon.

Num. 7:30-35   ELIZUR OF REUBEN.   On the fourth day Elizur son of Shedeur, the leader of the people of Reuben, brought his offering.

[u]That is, about 3 1/4 pounds (about 1.5 kilograms)   [v]That is, about 1 3/4 pounds (about 0.8 kilogram)   [w]That is, about 4 ounces (about 110 grams)   [x]Traditionally *peace offering*

His offering was one silver plate weighing a hundred and thirty shekels, and one silver sprinkling bowl weighing seventy shekels, both according to the sanctuary shekel, each filled with fine flour mixed with oil as a grain offering; one gold dish weighing ten shekels, filled with incense; one young bull, one ram and one male lamb a year old, for a burnt offering; one male goat for a sin offering; and two oxen, five rams, five male goats and five male lambs a year old, to be sacrificed as a fellowship offering. This was the offering of Elizur son of Shedeur.

SHELUMIEL OF SIMEON.   On the fifth day Shelumiel son of Zurishaddai, the leader of the people of Simeon, brought his offering. *Num. 7:36-41*
His offering was one silver plate weighing a hundred and thirty shekels, and one silver sprinkling bowl weighing seventy shekels, both according to the sanctuary shekel, each filled with fine flour mixed with oil as a grain offering; one gold dish weighing ten shekels, filled with incense; one young bull, one ram and one male lamb a year old, for a burnt offering; one male goat for a sin offering; and two oxen, five rams, five male goats and five male lambs a year old, to be sacrificed as a fellowship offering. This was the offering of Shelumiel son of Zurishaddai.

ELIASAPH OF GAD.   On the sixth day Eliasaph son of Deuel, the leader of the people of Gad, brought his offering. *Num. 7:42-47*
His offering was one silver plate weighing a hundred and thirty shekels, and one silver sprinkling bowl weighing seventy shekels, both according to the sanctuary shekel, each filled with fine flour mixed with oil as a grain offering; one gold dish weighing ten shekels, filled with incense; one young bull, one ram and one male lamb a year old, for a burnt offering; one male goat for a sin offering; and two oxen, five rams, five male goats and five male lambs a year old, to be sacrificed as a fellowship offering. This was the offering of Eliasaph son of Deuel.

ELISHAMA OF EPHRAIM.   On the seventh day Elishama son of Ammihud, the leader of the people of Ephraim, brought his offering. *Num. 7:48-53*
His offering was one silver plate weighing a hundred and thirty shekels, and one silver sprinkling bowl weighing seventy shekels, both according to the sanctuary shekel, each filled with fine flour mixed with oil as a grain offering; one gold dish weighing ten shekels, filled with incense; one young bull, one ram and one male lamb a year old, for a burnt offering; one male goat for a sin offering; and two oxen, five rams, five male goats and five male lambs a year old, to be sacrificed as a fellowship offering. This was the offering of Elishama son of Ammihud.

GAMALIEL OF MANASSEH.   On the eighth day Gamaliel son of Pedahzur, the leader of the people of Manasseh, brought his offering. *Num. 7:54-59*
His offering was one silver plate weighing a hundred and thirty shekels, and one silver sprinkling bowl weighing seventy shekels, both according to the sanctuary shekel, each filled with fine flour mixed with oil as a grain offering; one gold dish weighing ten shekels, filled with incense; one young bull, one ram and one male lamb a year old, for a burnt offering; one male goat for a sin offering; and two oxen, five rams, five male goats and five male lambs a year old, to be sacrificed as a fellowship offering. This was the offering of Gamaliel son of Pedahzur.

Num.
7:60-65

ABIDAN OF BENJAMIN.   On the ninth day Abidan son of Gideoni, the leader of the people of Benjamin, brought his offering.

His offering was one silver plate weighing a hundred and thirty shekels, and one silver sprinkling bowl weighing seventy shekels, both according to the sanctuary shekel, each filled with fine flour mixed with oil as a grain offering; one gold dish weighing ten shekels, filled with incense; one young bull, one ram and one male lamb a year old, for a burnt offering; one male goat for a sin offering; and two oxen, five rams, five male goats and five male lambs a year old, to be sacrificed as a fellowship offering. This was the offering of Abidan son of Gideoni.

Num.
7:66-71

AHIEZER OF DAN.   On the tenth day Ahiezer son of Ammishaddai, the leader of the people of Dan, brought his offering.

His offering was one silver plate weighing a hundred and thirty shekels, and one silver sprinkling bowl weighing seventy shekels, both according to the sanctuary shekel, each filled with fine flour mixed with oil as a grain offering; one gold dish weighing ten shekels, filled with incense; one young bull, one ram and one male lamb a year old, for a burnt offering; one male goat for a sin offering; and two oxen, five rams, five male goats and five male lambs a year old, to be sacrificed as a fellowship offering. This was the offering of Ahiezer son of Ammishaddai.

Num.
7:72-77

PAGIEL OF ASHER.   On the eleventh day Pagiel son of Ocran, the leader of the people of Asher, brought his offering.

His offering was one silver plate weighing a hundred and thirty shekels, and one silver sprinkling bowl weighing seventy shekels, both according to the sanctuary shekel, each filled with fine flour mixed with oil as a grain offering; one gold dish weighing ten shekels, filled with incense; one young bull, one ram and one male lamb a year old, for a burnt offering; one male goat for a sin offering; and two oxen, five rams, five male goats and five male lambs a year old, to be sacrificed as a fellowship offering. This was the offering of Pagiel son of Ocran.

Num.
7:78-83

AHIRA OF NAPHTALI.   On the twelfth day Ahira son of Enan, the leader of the people of Naphtali, brought his offering.

His offering was one silver plate weighing a hundred and thirty shekels, and one silver sprinkling bowl weighing seventy shekels, both according to the sanctuary shekel, each filled with fine flour mixed with oil as a grain offering; one gold dish weighing ten shekels, filled with incense; one young bull, one ram and one male lamb a year old, for a burnt offering; one male goat for a sin offering; and two oxen, five rams, five male goats and five male lambs a year old, to be sacrificed as a fellowship offering. This was the offering of Ahira son of Enan.

Num.
7:84-88

SUMMARY OF OFFERING.   These were the offerings of the Israelite leaders for the dedication of the altar when it was anointed: twelve silver plates, twelve silver sprinkling bowls and twelve gold dishes. Each silver plate weighed a hundred and thirty shekels, and each sprinkling bowl seventy shekels. Altogether, the silver dishes weighed two thousand four hundred shekels,ʸ according to the sanctuary shekel. The twelve gold dishes filled with incense weighed ten shekels each, according to the sanctuary shekel. Altogether, the gold ladles weighed a hundred and

ʸThat is, about 60 pounds (about 28 kilograms)

twenty shekels.^z The total number of animals for the burnt offering came
to twelve young bulls, twelve rams and twelve male lambs a year old,
together with their grain offering. Twelve male goats were used for the sin
offering. The total number of animals for the sacrifice of the fellowship
offering came to twenty-four oxen, sixty rams, sixty male goats and sixty
male lambs a year old. These were the offerings for the dedication of the
altar after it was anointed.

VOICE FROM MERCY SEAT.   When Moses entered the Tent of Meeting   Num. 7:89
to speak with the LORD, he heard the voice speaking to him from between
the two cherubim above the atonement cover on the ark of the Testimony.
And he spoke with him.

LAMPS LIT BEFORE LAMPSTAND.   The LORD said to Moses, "Speak to   Num. 8:1-4
Aaron and say to him, 'When you set up the seven lamps, they are to light
the area in front of the lampstand.'"
   Aaron did so; he set up the lamps so that they faced forward on the
lampstand, just as the LORD commanded Moses. This is how the lampstand was made: It was made of hammered gold—from its base to its blossoms. The lampstand was made exactly like the pattern the LORD had
shown Moses.

A Nation Under Law

*W*ith the tabernacle now constructed, and the priests ready to serve at its
altars, the Israelites are about to begin a new phase in the history of
their young nation. They are going to begin functioning as a nation
under covenant relationship, with virtually every daily action influenced, if not
directly prescribed, by law. During the next four decades God will give to
Moses scores of laws—laws affecting their religious and ceremonial duties;
laws regulating diet and hygiene; laws of dedication and religious symbolism;
civil laws and laws affecting political leaders, the army, and the court system;
criminal laws and offenses against religion, society, and morality; and various
family and estate laws.
   The many laws within Israel's code are recorded in Exodus, Leviticus,
Numbers, and Deuteronomy. Often the same laws are repeated on different
occasions and in varying contexts. Sometimes a law will be further expanded
or more completely explained. In anticipation of the Israelites becoming less
nomadic and more settled, the laws will appropriately reflect the changing circumstances. In an effort to avoid unnecessary duplication, and in order to get a
more understandable overview of the laws of Israel, all of the various laws will
be brought together in one compendium at a later point in this volume, in the
context of events to take place some 40 years later. Therefore the book of
Leviticus, which takes up where the Exodus record leaves off, will be left largely to later inclusion. Suffice it to say at this point that, as the name suggests,
Leviticus pertains principally to the Levites and their priestly duties. Yet the
fact that Leviticus also contains so many laws is not at all surprising in view of
its theme: ". . .you shall therefore be holy, for I am holy."

First Passover After Egypt

*T*he book of Numbers records briefly that here in the wilderness near Sinai the Israelites observe their first Passover celebration since the actual passover of death which took place a year earlier in Egypt. It must be a time of mixed emotions—joy in having been freed from their bondage, and excitement at having become an independent nation, yet uncertainty about what the future holds.

Even in this first celebration is an indication that the Israelites are already concerned about God's laws and how he might interpret them in light of exceptional circumstances. Here they learn that, along with the strictness in his laws, God has provided measures of grace as well.

Num. 9:1-5
1st month,
14th day
(Ca. 1445
B.C.)

PASSOVER CELEBRATED.   The LORD spoke to Moses in the Desert of Sinai in the first month of the second year after they came out of Egypt. He said, "Have the Israelites celebrate the Passover at the appointed time. Celebrate it at the appointed time, at twilight on the fourteenth day of this month, in accordance with all its rules and regulations."

So Moses told the Israelites to celebrate the Passover, and they did so in the Desert of Sinai at twilight on the fourteenth day of the first month. The Israelites did everything just as the LORD commanded Moses.

Num.
9:6-12

PROBLEM OF THE UNCLEAN.   But some of them could not celebrate the Passover on that day because they were ceremonially unclean on account of a dead body. So they came to Moses and Aaron that same day and said to Moses, "We have become unclean because of a dead body, but why should we be kept from presenting the LORD's offering with the other Israelites at the appointed time?"

Moses answered them, "Wait until I find out what the LORD commands concerning you."

Then the LORD said to Moses, "Tell the Israelites: 'When any of you or your descendants are unclean because of a dead body or are away on a journey, they may still celebrate the LORD's Passover. They are to celebrate it on the fourteenth day of the second month at twilight. They are to eat the lamb, together with unleavened bread and bitter herbs. They must not leave any of it till morning or break any of its bones. When they celebrate the Passover, they must follow all the regulations.

Numbering of the Israelites

A month has passed since the tabernacle was erected, the priesthood ordained, the first laws of Moses given, and the nation of Israel truly established in fulfillment of the ancient promise to Abraham. Still, another part of God's covenant with Abraham has yet to be fulfilled—the occupation of Canaan, the promised land. God has never said that the land will simply be handed over to the Israelites without struggle. On the contrary, God has told the Israelites that they will have to fight for the land. Yet God has also promised to be with them and make them victorious, so long as they keep their faith in him as the only true God, and remain obedient to his laws. Now, in preparation for the taking of the promised land, God orders a numbering of the people of Israel—at least those of fighting age, 20 years old or older. The numbering is more than a census or even a military draft. In fact it is a national registration from which the Jewish people in centuries to come will trace their ancestry. One interesting feature of the numbering is that the descendants of Joseph are counted as two separate tribes through his sons, Ephraim and Manasseh, in accordance with Jacob's own words. Of a nation of approximately two million strong, 603,550 men are found to be of the age to fight. In addition to the numbering, the tribes are also assigned areas of encampment and given their order of march.

Noticeably missing from the numbering of the fighting men is the tribe of Levi. It is clear that the nation will be strong in battle only as long as it is religiously dedicated to the service of God, so the Levites will be responsible for maintaining the people's spiritual service. Therefore the numbering of the Levites will be done separately from the other tribes and on two different bases—once for all males at least a month old (22,000), and once for all males between 30 and 50 years old who are ready to serve in the tabernacle (8,580). The places of encampment and the specific items to be carried by each family are also assigned.

PEOPLE TO BE NUMBERED.   The LORD spoke to Moses in the Tent of Meeting in the Desert of Sinai on the first day of the second month of the second year after the Israelites came out of Egypt. He said: "Take a census of the whole Israelite community by their clans and families, listing every man by name, one by one. You and Aaron are to number by their divisions all the men in Israel twenty years old or more who are able to serve in the army.

Num. 1:1-3
2nd month,
2nd year
(Ca. 1445 B.C.)
Wilderness

PRINCES TO HELP COUNT.   One man from each tribe, each the head of his family, is to help you. These are the names of the men who are to assist you:

Num. 1:4-16

from Reuben, Elizur son of Shedeur;
from Simeon, Shelumiel son of Zurishaddai;
from Judah, Nahshon son of Amminadab;
from Issachar, Nethanel son of Zuar;
from Zebulun, Eliab son of Helon;
from the sons of Joseph:
    from Ephraim, Elishama son of Ammihud;
    from Manasseh, Gamaliel son of Pedahzur;
from Benjamin, Abidan son of Gideoni;
from Dan, Ahiezer son of Ammishaddai;
from Asher, Pagiel son of Ocran;
from Gad, Eliasaph son of Deuel;
from Naphtali, Ahira son of Enan."

These were the men appointed from the community, the leaders of their ancestral tribes. They were the heads of the clans of Israel.

TRIBES REGISTER.   Moses and Aaron took these men whose names had been given, and they called the whole community together on the first day of the second month. The people indicated their ancestry by their clans and families, and the men twenty years old or more were listed by name,

Num. 1:17-19

one by one, as the LORD commanded Moses. And so he counted them in the Desert of Sinai:

Num.
1:20,21

TRIBE OF REUBEN.   From the descendants of Reuben the firstborn son of Israel:
>All the men twenty years old or more who were able to serve in the army were listed by name, one by one, according to the records of their clans and families. The number from the tribe of Reuben was 46,500.

Num.
1:22,23

TRIBE OF SIMEON.   From the descendants of Simeon:
>All the men twenty years old or more who were able to serve in the army were counted and listed by name, one by one, according to the records of their clans and families. The number from the tribe of Simeon was 59,300.

Num.
1:24,25

TRIBE OF GAD.   From the descendants of Gad:
>All the men twenty years old or more who were able to serve in the army were listed by name, according to the records of their clans and families. The number from the tribe of Gad was 45,650.

Num.
1:26,27

TRIBE OF JUDAH.   From the descendants of Judah:
>All the men twenty years old or more who were able to serve in the army were listed by name, according to the records of their clans and families. The number from the tribe of Judah was 74,600.

Num.
1:28,29

TRIBE OF ISSACHAR.   From the descendants of Issachar:
>All the men twenty years old or more who were able to serve in the army were listed by name, according to the records of their clans and families. The number from the tribe of Issachar was 54,400.

Num.
1:30,31

TRIBE OF ZEBULUN.   From the descendants of Zebulun:
>All the men twenty years old or more who were able to serve in the army were listed by name, according to the records of their clans and families. The number from the tribe of Zebulun was 57,400.

Num.
1:32,33

TRIBE OF EPHRAIM (JOSEPH).   From the sons of Joseph:
From the descendants of Ephraim:
>All the men twenty years old or more who were able to serve in the army were listed by name, according to the records of their clans and families. The number from the tribe of Ephraim was 40,500.

Num.
1:34,35

TRIBE OF MANASSEH (JOSEPH).   From the descendants of Manasseh:
>All the men twenty years old or more who were able to serve in the army were listed by name, according to the records of their clans and families. The number from the tribe of Manasseh was 32,200.

Num.
1:36,37

TRIBE OF BENJAMIN.   From the descendants of Benjamin:
>All the men twenty years old or more who were able to serve in the army were listed by name, according to the records of their clans and families. The number from the tribe of Benjamin was 35,400.

Num.
1:38,39

TRIBE OF DAN.   From the descendants of Dan:
>All the men twenty years old or more who were able to serve in the army were listed by name, according to the records of their clans and families. The number from the tribe of Dan was 62,700.

TRIBE OF ASHER.   From the descendants of Asher: Num.
  All the men twenty years old or more who were able to serve in the   1:40,41
    army were listed by name, according to the records of their clans
    and families. The number from the tribe of Asher was 41,500.

TRIBE OF NAPHTALI.   From the descendants of Naphtali: Num.
  All the men twenty years old or more who were able to serve in the   1:42,43
    army were listed by name, according to the records of their clans
    and families. The number from the tribe of Naphtali was 53,400.

NUMBER OF FIGHTING MEN.   These were the men counted by Moses   Num.
and Aaron and the twelve leaders of Israel, each one representing his fam-   1:44-46
ily. All the Israelites twenty years old or more who were able to serve in
Israel's army were counted according to their families. The total number
was 603,550.

LEVITES NOT NUMBERED.   The families of the tribe of Levi, however,   Num.
were not counted along with the others. The LORD had said to Moses: "You   1:47-54
must not count the tribe of Levi or include them in the census of the other
Israelites. Instead, appoint the Levites to be in charge of the tabernacle of
the Testimony—over all its furnishings and everything belonging to it.
They are to carry the tabernacle and all its furnishings; they are to take care
of it and encamp around it. Whenever the tabernacle is to move, the
Levites are to take it down, and whenever the tabernacle is to be set up,
the Levites shall do it. Anyone else who goes near it shall be put to death.
The Israelites are to set up their tents by divisions, each man in his own
camp under his own standard. The Levites, however, are to set up their
tents around the tabernacle of the Testimony so that wrath will not fall on
the Israelite community. The Levites are to be responsible for the care of
the tabernacle of the Testimony."
  The Israelites did all this just as the LORD commanded Moses.

TRIBES TO CAMP EASTWARD.   The LORD said to Moses and Aaron: Num. 2:1-9
"The Israelites are to camp around the Tent of Meeting some distance from
it, each man under his standard with the banners of his family."

  On the east, toward the sunrise, the divisions of the camp of Judah are
to encamp under their standard. The leader of the people of Judah is
Nahshon son of Amminadab. His division numbers 74,600.
  The tribe of Issachar will camp next to them. The leader of the people of
Issachar is Nethanel son of Zuar. His division numbers 54,400.
  The tribe of Zebulun will be next. The leader of the people of Zebulun
is Eliab son of Helon. His division numbers 57,400.
  All the men assigned to the camp of Judah, according to their divisions,
number 186,400. They will set out first.

TRIBES TO CAMP SOUTHWARD.   On the south will be the divisions of   Num.
the camp of Reuben under their standard. The leader of the people of   2:10-16
Reuben is Elizur son of Shedeur. His division numbers 46,500.
  The tribe of Simeon will camp next to them. The leader of the people of
Simeon is Shelumiel son of Zurishaddai. His division numbers 59,300.

The tribe of Gad will be next. The leader of the people of Gad is Eliasaph son of Deuel.[a] His division numbers 45,650.

All the men assigned to the camp of Reuben, according to their divisions, number 151,450. They will set out second.

Num. 2:17   LEVITES TO CAMP IN CENTER.   Then the Tent of Meeting and the camp of the Levites will set out in the middle of the camps. They will set out in the same order as they encamp, each in his own place under his standard.

Num. 2:18-24   TRIBES TO CAMP WESTWARD.   On the west will be the divisions of the camp of Ephraim under their standard. The leader of the people of Ephraim is Elishama son of Ammihud. His division numbers 40,500.

The tribe of Manasseh will be next to them. The leader of the people of Manasseh is Gamaliel son of Pedahzur. His division numbers 32,200.

The tribe of Benjamin will be next. The leader of the people of Benjamin is Abidan son of Gideoni. His division numbers 35,400.

All the men assigned to the camp of Ephraim, according to their divisions, number 108,100. They will set out third.

Num. 2:25-31   TRIBES TO CAMP NORTHWARD.   On the north will be the divisions of the camp of Dan, under their standard. The leader of the people of Dan is Ahiezer son of Ammishaddai. His division numbers 62,700.

The tribe of Asher will camp next to them. The leader of the people of Asher is Pagiel son of Ocran. His division numbers 41,500.

The tribe of Naphtali will be next. The leader of the people of Naphtali is Ahira son of Enan. His division numbers 53,400.

All the men assigned to the camp of Dan number 157,600. They will set out last, under their standards.

Num. 2:32-34   CONCLUSION TO ORDERS.   These are the Israelites, counted according to their families. All those in the camps, by their divisions, number 603,550. The Levites, however, were not counted along with the other Israelites, as the LORD commanded Moses.

So the Israelites did everything the LORD commanded Moses; that is the way they encamped under their standards, and that is the way they set out, each with his clan and family.

Num. 3:14-20   LEVITES NUMBERED.   The LORD said to Moses in the Desert of Sinai, "Count the Levites by their families and clans. Count every male a month old or more." So Moses counted them, as he was commanded by the word of the LORD.

These were the names of the sons of Levi:
Gershon, Kohath and Merari.
These were the names of the Gershonite clans:
Libni and Shimei.
The Kohathite clans:
Amram, Izhar, Hebron and Uzziel.
The Merarite clans:
Mahli and Mushi.
These were the Levite clans, according to their families.

---

[a]Many manuscripts of the Masoretic Text, Samaritan Pentateuch and Vulgate (see also Num. 1:14); most manuscripts of the Masoretic Text *Reuel*

FAMILY OF GERSHON. To Gershon belonged the clans of the Libnites and Shimeites; these were the Gershonite clans. The number of all the males a month old or more who were counted was 7,500. The Gershonite clans were to camp on the west, behind the tabernacle. The leader of the families of the Gershonites was Eliasaph son of Lael. At the Tent of Meeting the Gershonites were responsible for the care of the tabernacle and tent, its coverings, the curtain at the entrance to the Tent of Meeting, the curtains of the courtyard, the curtain at the entrance to the courtyard surrounding the tabernacle and altar, and the ropes—and everything related to their use.

Num. 3:21-26

FAMILY OF KOHATH. To Kohath belonged the clans of the Amramites, Izharites, Hebronites and Uzzielites; these were the Kohathite clans. The number of all the males a month old or more was 8,600.[b] The Kohathites were responsible for the care of the sanctuary. The Kohathite clans were to camp on the south side of the tabernacle. The leader of the families of the Kohathite clans was Elizaphan son of Uzziel. They were responsible for the care of the ark, the table, the lampstand, the altars, the articles of the sanctuary used in ministering, the curtain, and everything related to their use. The chief leader of the Levites was Eleazar son of Aaron, the priest. He was appointed over those who were responsible for the care of the sanctuary.

Num. 3:27-32

FAMILY OF MERARI. To Merari belonged the clans of the Mahlites and the Mushites; these were the Merarite clans. The number of all the males a month old or more who were counted was 6,200. The leader of the families of the Merarite clans was Zuriel son of Abihail; they were to camp on the north side of the tabernacle. The Merarites were appointed to take care of the frames of the tabernacle, its crossbars, posts, bases, all its equipment, and everything related to their use, as well as the posts of the surrounding courtyard with their bases, tent pegs and ropes.

Num. 3:33-37

MOSES AND AARON. Moses and Aaron and his sons were to camp to the east of the tabernacle, toward the sunrise, in front of the Tent of Meeting. They were responsible for the care of the sanctuary on behalf of the Israelites. Anyone else who approached the sanctuary was to be put to death.

Num. 3:38,39

The total number of Levites counted at the LORD's command by Moses and Aaron according to their clans, including every male a month old or more, was 22,000.

DUTIES OF KOHATHITES. The LORD said to Moses and Aaron: "Take a census of the Kohathite branch of the Levites by their clans and families. Count all the men from thirty to fifty years of age who come to serve in the work in the Tent of Meeting.

Num. 4:1-15

"This is the work of the Kohathites in the Tent of Meeting: the care of the most holy things. When the camp is to move, Aaron and his sons are to go in and take down the shielding curtain and cover the ark of the Testimony

---

[b]Hebrew; some Septuagint manuscripts 8,300

with it. Then they are to cover this with hides of sea cows,^{c} spread a cloth of solid blue over that and put the poles in place.

"Over the table of the Presence they are to spread a blue cloth and put on it the plates, dishes and bowls, and the jars for drink offerings; the bread that is continually there is to remain on it. Over these they are to spread a scarlet cloth, cover that with hides of sea cows and put its poles in place.

"They are to take a blue cloth and cover the lampstand that is for light, together with its lamps, its wick trimmers and trays, and all its jars for the oil used to supply it. Then they are to wrap it and all its accessories in a covering of hides of sea cows and put it on a carrying frame.

"Over the gold altar they are to spread a blue cloth and cover that with hides of sea cows and put its poles in place.

"They are to take all the articles used for ministering in the sanctuary, wrap them in a blue cloth, cover that with hides of sea cows and put them on a carrying frame.

"They are to remove the ashes from the bronze altar and spread a purple cloth over it. Then they are to place on it all the utensils used for ministering at the altar, including the firepans, meat forks, shovels and sprinkling bowls. Over it they are to spread a covering of hides of sea cows and put its poles in place.

"After Aaron and his sons have finished covering the holy furnishings and all the holy articles, and when the camp is ready to move, the Kohathites are to come to do the carrying. But they must not touch the holy things or they will die. The Kohathites are to carry those things that are in the Tent of Meeting.

Num. 4:16   ELEAZAR'S RESPONSIBILITIES. "Eleazar son of Aaron, the priest, is to have charge of the oil for the light, the fragrant incense, the regular grain offering and the anointing oil. He is to be in charge of the entire tabernacle and everything in it, including its holy furnishings and articles."

Num. 4:17-20   CAUTION FOR KOHATHITES. The LORD said to Moses and Aaron, "See that the Kohathite tribal clans are not cut off from the Levites. So that they may live and not die when they come near the most holy things, do this for them: Aaron and his sons are to go into the sanctuary and assign to each man his work and what he is to carry. But the Kohathites must not go in to look at the holy things, even for a moment, or they will die."

Num. 4:21-28   DUTIES OF GERSHONITES. The LORD said to Moses, "Take a census also of the Gershonites by their families and clans. Count all the men from thirty to fifty years of age who come to serve in the work at the Tent of Meeting.

"This is the service of the Gershonite clans as they work and carry burdens: They are to carry the curtains of the tabernacle, the Tent of Meeting, its covering and the outer covering of hides of sea cows, the curtains for the entrance to the Tent of Meeting, the curtains of the courtyard surrounding the tabernacle and altar, the curtain for the entrance, the ropes and all the equipment used in its service. The Gershonites are to do all that needs to be done with these things. All their service, whether carrying or doing other work, is to be done under the direction of Aaron and his sons. You shall assign to them as their responsibility all they are to carry. This is

^{c}That is, dugongs

the service of the Gershonite clans at the Tent of Meeting. Their duties are to be under the direction of Ithamar son of Aaron, the priest.

DUTIES OF MERARITES. "Count the Merarites by their clans and families. Count all the men from thirty to fifty years of age who come to serve in the work at the Tent of Meeting. This is their duty as they perform service at the Tent of Meeting: to carry the frames of the tabernacle, its crossbars, posts and bases, as well as the posts of the surrounding courtyard with their bases, tent pegs, ropes, all their equipment and everything related to their use. Assign to each man the specific things he is to carry. This is the service of the Merarite clans as they work at the Tent of Meeting under the direction of Ithamar son of Aaron, the priest."

Num.
4:29-33

KOHATHITE SERVANTS. Moses, Aaron and the leaders of the community counted the Kohathites by their clans and families. All the men from thirty to fifty years of age who came to serve in the work in the Tent of Meeting, counted by clans, were 2,750. This was the total of all those in the Kohathite clans who served in the Tent of Meeting. Moses and Aaron counted them according to the LORD's command through Moses.

Num.
4:34-37

GERSHONITE SERVANTS. The Gershonites were counted by their clans and families. All the men from thirty to fifty years of age who came to serve in the work at the Tent of Meeting, counted by their clans and families, were 2,630. This was the total of those in the Gershonite clans who served at the Tent of Meeting. Moses and Aaron counted them according to the LORD's command.

Num.
4:38-41

MERARI SERVANTS. The Merarites were counted by their clans and families. All the men from thirty to fifty years of age who came to serve in the work at the Tent of Meeting, counted by their clans, were 3,200. This was the total of those in the Merarite clans. Moses and Aaron counted them according to the LORD's command through Moses.

Num.
4:42-45

TOTAL LEVITES IN SERVICE. So Moses, Aaron and the leaders of Israel counted all the Levites by their clans and families. All the men from thirty to fifty years of age who came to do the work of serving and carrying the Tent of Meeting numbered 8,580. At the LORD's command through Moses, each was assigned his work and told what to carry.

Thus they were counted, as the LORD commanded Moses.

Num.
4:46-49

NUMBERING OF FIRSTBORN. The LORD said to Moses, "Count all the firstborn Israelite males who are a month old or more and make a list of their names. Take the Levites for me in place of all the firstborn of the Israelites, and the livestock of the Levites in place of all the firstborn of the livestock of the Israelites. I am the LORD."

So Moses counted all the firstborn of the Israelites, as the LORD commanded him. The total number of firstborn males a month old or more, listed by name, was 22,273.

Num.
3:40-43

REDEMPTION OF FIRSTBORN. The LORD also said to Moses, "Take the Levites in place of all the firstborn of Israel, and the livestock of the Levites in place of their livestock. The Levites are to be mine. I am the LORD. To redeem the 273 firstborn Israelites who exceed the number of the Levites, collect five shekels*d* for each one, according to the sanctuary shekel, which

Num.
3:44-51

*d*That is, about 2 ounces (about 55 grams)

weighs twenty gerahs. Give the money for the redemption of the additional Israelites to Aaron and his sons."

So Moses collected the redemption money from those who exceeded the number redeemed by the Levites. From the firstborn of the Israelites he collected silver weighing 1,365 shekels,[e] according to the sanctuary shekel. Moses gave the redemption money to Aaron and his sons, as he was commanded by the word of the LORD.

The Journey Begins

The people have been numbered and their duties have been assigned, so God now gives the Israelites their marching orders. Moses asks a relative named Hobab to be a guide for the Israelites, and Hobab apparently agrees to do so. But the real guide is God himself, manifested in the movement of the cloud of his presence over the ark and tabernacle. There is one final preparation, and then the journey begins.

Num. 10:1-10

SILVER TRUMPETS ORDERED. The LORD said to Moses: "Make two trumpets of hammered silver, and use them for calling the community together and for having the camps set out. When both are sounded, the whole community is to assemble before you at the entrance to the Tent of Meeting. If only one is sounded, the leaders—the heads of the clans of Israel—are to assemble before you. When a trumpet blast is sounded, the tribes camping on the east are to set out. At the sounding of a second blast, the camps on the south are to set out. The blast will be the signal for setting out. To gather the assembly, blow the trumpets, but not with the same signal.

"The sons of Aaron, the priests, are to blow the trumpets. This is to be a lasting ordinance for you and the generations to come. When you go into battle in your own land against an enemy who is oppressing you, sound a blast on the trumpets. Then you will be remembered by the LORD your God and rescued from your enemies. Also at your times of rejoicing—your appointed feasts and New Moon festivals—you are to sound the trumpets over your burnt offerings and fellowship offerings,[f] and they will be a memorial for you before your God. I am the LORD your God."

Num. 10:11-16 2nd month, 2nd year (Ca. 1445 B.C.)

ISRAELITES SET OUT. On the twentieth day of the second month of the second year, the cloud lifted from above the tabernacle of the Testimony. Then the Israelites set out from the Desert of Sinai and traveled from place to place until the cloud came to rest in the Desert of Paran. They set out, this first time, at the LORD's command through Moses.

The divisions of the camp of Judah went first, under their standard. Nahshon son of Amminadab was in command. Nethanel son of Zuar was over the division of the tribe of Issachar, and Eliab son of Helon was over the division of the tribe of Zebulun.

Num. 10:17-20

TABERNACLE TAKEN DOWN. Then the tabernacle was taken down, and the Gershonites and Merarites, who carried it, set out.

The divisions of the camp of Reuben went next, under their standard.

---

[e]That is, about 35 pounds (about 15.5 kilograms)   [f]Traditionally *peace offering*

Elizur son of Shedeur was in command. Shelumiel son of Zurishaddai was over the division of the tribe of Simeon, and Eliasaph son of Deuel was over the division of the tribe of Gad.

HOLY THINGS CARRIED.   Then the Kohathites set out, carrying the holy things. The tabernacle was to be set up before they arrived.

Num.
10:21-24

The divisions of the camp of Ephraim went next, under their standard. Elishama son of Ammihud was in command. Gamaliel son of Pedahzur was over the division of the tribe of Manasseh, and Abidan son of Gideoni was over the division of the tribe of Benjamin.

REAR GUARD MOVES.   Finally, as the rear guard for all the units, the divisions of the camp of Dan set out, under their standard. Ahiezer son of Ammishaddai was in command. Pagiel son of Ocran was over the division of the tribe of Asher, and Ahira son of Enan was over the division of the tribe of Naphtali. This was the order of march for the Israelite divisions as they set out.

Num.
10:25-28

HOBAB ASKED TO BE GUIDE.   Now Moses said to Hobab son of Reuel the Midianite, Moses' father-in-law, "We are setting out for the place about which the LORD said, 'I will give it to you.' Come with us and we will treat you well, for the LORD has promised good things to Israel."

Num.
10:29-32

He answered, "No, I will not go; I am going back to my own land and my own people."

But Moses said, "Please do not leave us. You know where we should camp in the desert, and you can be our eyes. If you come with us, we will share with you whatever good things the LORD gives us."

THREE DAYS' JOURNEY.   So they set out from the mountain of the LORD and traveled for three days. The ark of the covenant of the LORD went before them during those three days to find them a place to rest. The cloud of the LORD was over them by day when they set out from the camp.

Num.
10:33,34

CLOUD OF GUIDANCE.   On the day the tabernacle, the Tent of the Testimony, was set up, the cloud covered it. From evening till morning the cloud above the tabernacle looked like fire. That is how it continued to be; the cloud covered it, and at night it looked like fire. Whenever the cloud lifted from above the Tent, the Israelites set out; wherever the cloud settled, the Israelites encamped. At the LORD's command the Israelites set out, and at his command they encamped. As long as the cloud stayed over the tabernacle, they remained in camp. When the cloud remained over the tabernacle a long time, the Israelites obeyed the LORD's order and did not set out. Sometimes the cloud was over the tabernacle only a few days; at the LORD's command they would encamp, and then at his command they would set out. Sometimes the cloud stayed only from evening till morning, and when it lifted in the morning, they set out. Whether by day or by night, whenever the cloud lifted, they set out. Whether the cloud stayed over the tabernacle for two days or a month or a year, the Israelites would remain in camp and not set out; but when it lifted, they would set out. At the LORD's command they encamped, and at the LORD's command they set out. They obeyed the LORD's order, in accordance with his command through Moses.

Num.
9:15-23
Ex.
40:36-38

BLESSINGS GO WITH ARK.   Whenever the ark set out, Moses said,

Num.
10:35,36

"Rise up, O LORD!

> May your enemies be scattered;
> may your foes flee before you."

Whenever it came to rest, he said,

> "Return, O LORD,
> to the countless thousands of Israel."

Doubts and Murmurs

*T*he journey has hardly begun when the people of Israel begin to complain to Moses, just as they had done when first liberated from Egypt. The troubles come first when misfortunes arise, then later when certain people of apparently mixed ancestry complain about the absence of meat. Moses' touching prayer to God for help could be the prayer of many a spiritual leader emotionally exhausted by the responsibilities which he bears. God responds to Moses' prayer by calling for the appointment of 70 elders to share the administrative burden which Moses has borne thus far. The council of seventy will set a pattern of Jewish administration for centuries to come. As a sign of their authority, the Holy Spirit descends upon the seventy and causes them to prophesy, apparently in ecstatic utterances. This unusual glorification of the elders does not seem to be repeated, perhaps because of the jealousy which is aroused when two others also receive the divine gift in a special manifestation.

**Num.
11:1-3
Taberah**

COMPLAINING AT TABERAH.   Now the people complained about their hardships in the hearing of the LORD, and when he heard them his anger was aroused. Then fire from the LORD burned among them and consumed some of the outskirts of the camp. When the people cried out to Moses, he prayed to the LORD and the fire died down. So that place was called Taberah,*8* because fire from the LORD had burned among them.

**Num.
11:4-6**

CRY FOR MEAT.   The rabble with them began to crave other food, and again the Israelites started wailing and said, "If only we had meat to eat! We remember the fish we ate in Egypt at no cost—also the cucumbers, melons, leeks, onions and garlic. But now we have lost our appetite; we never see anything but this manna!"

**Num.
11:7-9**

DESCRIPTION OF MANNA.   The manna was like coriander seed and looked like resin. The people went around gathering it, and then ground it in a handmill or crushed it in a mortar. They cooked it in a pot or made it into cakes. And it tasted like something made with olive oil. When the dew settled on the camp at night, the manna also came down.

**Num.
11:10-15**

MOSES PRAYS FOR HELP.   Moses heard the people of every family wailing, each at the entrance to his tent. The LORD became exceedingly angry, and Moses was troubled. He asked the LORD, "Why have you brought this trouble on your servant? What have I done to displease you that you put the burden of all these people on me? Did I conceive all these people? Did I give them birth? Why do you tell me to carry them in my arms, as a nurse carries an infant, to the land you promised on oath to their forefathers? Where can I get meat for all these people? They keep wailing to me, 'Give us meat to eat!' I cannot carry all these people by myself; the burden is too

8Taberah means burning.

heavy for me. If this is how you are going to treat me, put me to death right now—if I have found favor in your eyes—and do not let me face my own ruin."

SEVENTY TO BE APPOINTED.   The LORD said to Moses: "Bring me seventy of Israel's elders who are known to you as leaders and officials among the people. Have them come to the Tent of Meeting, that they may stand there with you. I will come down and speak with you there, and I will take of the Spirit that is on you and put the Spirit on them. They will help you carry the burden of the people so that you will not have to carry it alone.

Num.
11:16,17

MEAT TO BE GIVEN.   "Tell the people: 'Consecrate yourselves in preparation for tomorrow, when you will eat meat. The LORD heard you when you wailed, "If only we had meat to eat! We were better off in Egypt!" Now the LORD will give you meat, and you will eat it. You will not eat it for just one day, or two days, or five, ten or twenty days, but for a whole month—until it comes out of your nostrils and you loathe it—because you have rejected the LORD, who is among you, and have wailed before him, saying, "Why did we ever leave Egypt?" ' "

Num.
11:18-20

MOSES DOUBTS SUFFICIENCY.   But Moses said, "Here I am among six hundred thousand men on foot, and you say, 'I will give them meat to eat for a whole month!' Would they have enough if flocks and herds were slaughtered for them? Would they have enough if all the fish in the sea were caught for them?"

The LORD answered Moses, "Is the LORD's arm too short? You will now see whether or not what I say will come true for you."

Num.
11:21-23

SPIRIT ON THE SEVENTY.   So Moses went out and told the people what the LORD had said. He brought together seventy of their elders and had them stand around the Tent. Then the LORD came down in the cloud and spoke with him, and he took of the Spirit that was on him and put the Spirit on the seventy elders. When the Spirit rested on them, they prophesied, but they did not do so again.[h]

Num.
11:24,25

TWO OTHERS PROPHESYING.   However, two men, whose names were Eldad and Medad, had remained in the camp. They were listed among the elders, but did not go out to the Tent. Yet the Spirit also rested on them, and they prophesied in the camp. A young man ran and told Moses, "Eldad and Medad are prophesying in the camp."

Joshua son of Nun, who had been Moses' aide since youth, spoke up and said, "Moses, my lord, stop them!"

But Moses replied, "Are you jealous for my sake? I wish that all the LORD's people were prophets and that the LORD would put his Spirit on them!" Then Moses and the elders of Israel returned to the camp.

Num.
11:26-30

QUAIL GIVEN FOR MEAT.   Now a wind went out from the LORD and drove quail in from the sea. It brought them[i] down all around the camp to about three feet[j] above the ground, as far as a day's walk in any direction. All that day and night and all the next day the people went out and gathered quail. No one gathered less than ten homers.[k] Then they spread them out all around the camp. But while the meat was still between their teeth

Num.
11:31-35

---

[h]Or prophesied and continued to do so   [i]Or They flew   [j]Hebrew two cubits (about 1 meter)   [k]That is, probably about 60 bushels (about 2.2 kiloliters)

and before it could be consumed, the anger of the LORD burned against the people, and he struck them with a severe plague. Therefore the place was named Kibroth Hattaavah,[1] because there they buried the people who had craved other food.

From Kibroth Hattaavah the people traveled to Hazeroth and stayed there.

Moses Rebuked by Miriam

While the Israelites are encamped at Hazeroth, it appears that Moses has married a Cushite woman, perhaps a dark-skinned offspring of the Hamites. Whether Moses' first wife, Zipporah, has died or whether this is a second wife is not given. But Moses' sister, Miriam, who had saved Moses in the river back in Egypt and has since become an influential prophetess among the Israelites, is clearly upset by Moses' choice of a spouse. Her reasons are not stated and do not appear to be of any particular religious significance, but her opposition to Moses draws God's judgment nevertheless. Aaron once again seems to demonstrate a certain weakness of character in going along with his sister, somewhat as he had done with the Israelites in making the golden calf. His lack of punishment may indicate only a secondary role in the dispute against his brother and co-leader.

Num. 12:1,2 Hazeroth

MOSES REBUKED. Miriam and Aaron began to talk against Moses because of his Cushite wife, for he had married a Cushite. "Has the LORD spoken only through Moses?" they asked. "Hasn't he also spoken through us?" And the LORD heard this.

Num. 12:3-8

GOD REAFFIRMS MOSES. (Now Moses was a very humble man, more humble than anyone else on the face of the earth.)

At once the LORD said to Moses, Aaron and Miriam, "Come out to the Tent of Meeting, all three of you." So the three of them came out. Then the LORD came down in a pillar of cloud; he stood at the entrance to the Tent and summoned Aaron and Miriam. When both of them stepped forward, he said, "Listen to my words:

"When a prophet of the LORD is among you,
I reveal myself to him in visions,
I speak to him in dreams.
But this is not true of my servant Moses;
he is faithful in all my house.
With him I speak face to face,
clearly and not in riddles;
he sees the form of the LORD.
Why then were you not afraid
to speak against my servant Moses?"

Num. 12:9-16

MIRIAM BECOMES LEPER. The anger of the LORD burned against them, and he left them.

When the cloud lifted from above the Tent, there stood Miriam—

[1]Kibroth Hattaavah means graves of craving.

leprous,[m] like snow. Aaron turned toward her and saw that she had leprosy; and he said to Moses, "Please, my lord, do not hold against us the sin
we have so foolishly committed. Do not let her be like a stillborn infant
coming from its mother's womb with its flesh half eaten away."

So Moses cried out to the LORD, "O God, please heal her!"

The LORD replied to Moses, "If her father had spit in her face, would she
not have been in disgrace for seven days? Confine her outside the camp
for seven days; after that she can be brought back." So Miriam was confined outside the camp for seven days, and the people did not move on till
she was brought back.

After that, the people left Hazeroth and encamped in the Desert of
Paran.

The People Lack Courage

One of the most significant events in the early history of Israel comes just
as the Israelites are preparing to enter into the land of Canaan. When
spies are sent out to determine the strength of the Canaanites, they find
impressive armies and fortifications. After ten of the 12 spies bring back a dis-
mal report, the Israelites become discouraged.

When two of the spies encourage them to put their faith in God, the people
become vocally antagonistic. For their disbelief, the judgment of God is that
none of the fearful Israelites will enter into the promised land, and that the
nation of Israel will wander in the wilderness for 40 years, letting death take its
natural toll.

SPIES TO BE SENT.   The LORD said to Moses, "Send some men to explore
the land of Canaan, which I am giving to the Israelites. From each ancestral tribe send one of its leaders."

So at the LORD's command Moses sent them out from the Desert of
Paran. All of them were leaders of the Israelites.

Num.
13:1-3

THE 12 SPIES.   These are their names:

from the tribe of Reuben, Shammua son of Zaccur;
from the tribe of Simeon, Shaphat son of Hori;
from the tribe of Judah, Caleb son of Jephunneh;
from the tribe of Issachar, Igal son of Joseph;
from the tribe of Ephraim, Hoshea son of Nun;
from the tribe of Benjamin, Palti son of Raphu;
from the tribe of Zebulun, Gaddiel son of Sodi;
from the tribe of Manasseh (a tribe of Joseph), Gaddi son of Susi;
from the tribe of Dan, Ammiel son of Gemalli;
from the tribe of Asher, Sethur son of Michael;
from the tribe of Naphtali, Nahbi son of Vophsi;
from the tribe of Gad, Geuel son of Maki.

Num.
13:4-16

These are the names of the men Moses sent to explore the land. (Moses
gave Hoshea son of Nun the name Joshua.)

---

[m]The Hebrew word was used for various diseases affecting the skin—not necessarily
leprosy.

Num.
13:17-20

SPIES COMMISSIONED.   When Moses sent them to explore Canaan, he said, "Go up through the Negev and on into the hill country. See what the land is like and whether the people who live there are strong or weak, few or many. What kind of land do they live in? Is it good or bad? What kind of towns do they live in? Are they unwalled or fortified? How is the soil? Is it fertile or poor? Are there trees on it or not? Do your best to bring back some of the fruit of the land." (It was the season for the first ripe grapes.)

Num.
13:21-24

SPIES GO OUT.   So they went up and explored the land from the Desert of Zin as far as Rehob, toward Lebo[n] Hamath. They went up through the Negev and came to Hebron, where Ahiman, Sheshai and Talmai, the descendants of Anak, lived. (Hebron had been built seven years before Zoan in Egypt.) When they reached the Valley of Eshcol,[o] they cut off a branch bearing a single cluster of grapes. Two of them carried it on a pole between them, along with some pomegranates and figs. That place was called the Valley of Eshcol because of the cluster of grapes the Israelites cut off there.

Num.
13:25-29

REPORT OF THE SPIES.   At the end of forty days they returned from exploring the land.

They came back to Moses and Aaron and the whole Israelite community at Kadesh in the Desert of Paran. There they reported to them and to the whole assembly and showed them the fruit of the land. They gave Moses this account: "We went into the land to which you sent us, and it does flow with milk and honey! Here is its fruit. But the people who live there are powerful, and the cities are fortified and very large. We even saw descendants of Anak there. The Amalekites live in the Negev; the Hittites, Jebusites and Amorites live in the hill country; and the Canaanites live near the sea and along the Jordan."

Num.
13:30-33

CALEB DISPUTES REPORT.   Then Caleb silenced the people before Moses and said, "We should go up and take possession of the land, for we can certainly do it."

But the men who had gone up with him said, "We can't attack those people; they are stronger than we are." And they spread among the Israelites a bad report about the land they had explored. They said, "The land we explored devours those living in it. All the people we saw there are of great size. We saw the Nephilim there (the descendants of Anak come from the Nephilim). We seemed like grasshoppers in our own eyes, and we looked the same to them."

Num.
14:1-3

ISRAELITES MURMUR.   That night all the people of the community raised their voices and wept aloud. All the Israelites grumbled against Moses and Aaron, and the whole assembly said to them, "If only we had died in Egypt! Or in this desert! Why is the LORD bringing us to this land only to let us fall by the sword? Our wives and children will be taken as plunder. Wouldn't it be better for us to go back to Egypt?"

Num.
14:4-10a

JOSHUA AND CALEB PLEAD.   And they said to each other, "We should choose a leader and go back to Egypt."

Then Moses and Aaron fell facedown in front of the whole Israelite assembly gathered there. Joshua son of Nun and Caleb son of Jephunneh,

---

[n]Or *toward the entrance to*   [o]*Eshcol* means *cluster*; also in verse 24.

who were among those who had explored the land, tore their clothes and said to the entire Israelite assembly, "The land we passed through and explored is exceedingly good. If the LORD is pleased with us, he will lead us into that land, a land flowing with milk and honey, and will give it to us. Only do not rebel against the LORD. And do not be afraid of the people of the land, because we will swallow them up. Their protection is gone, but the LORD is with us. Do not be afraid of them."

But the whole assembly talked about stoning them.

GOD'S ANGER KINDLED. Then the glory of the LORD appeared at the Tent of Meeting to all the Israelites. The LORD said to Moses, "How long will these people treat me with contempt? How long will they refuse to believe in me, in spite of all the miraculous signs I have performed among them? I will strike them down with a plague and destroy them, but I will make you into a nation greater and stronger than they."

Num. 14:10b-12

MOSES PLEADS FOR MERCY. Moses said to the LORD, "Then the Egyptians will hear about it! By your power you brought these people up from among them. And they will tell the inhabitants of this land about it. They have already heard that you, O LORD, are with these people and that you, O LORD, have been seen face to face, that your cloud stays over them, and that you go before them in a pillar of cloud by day and a pillar of fire by night. If you put these people to death all at one time, the nations who have heard this report about you will say, 'The LORD was not able to bring these people into the land he promised them on oath; so he slaughtered them in the desert.'

Num. 14:13-19

"Now may the Lord's strength be displayed, just as you have declared: 'The LORD is slow to anger, abounding in love and forgiving sin and rebellion. Yet he does not leave the guilty unpunished; he punishes the children for the sin of the fathers to the third and fourth generation.' In accordance with your great love, forgive the sin of these people, just as you have pardoned them from the time they left Egypt until now."

JUDGMENT ON ISRAEL. The LORD replied, "I have forgiven them, as you asked. Nevertheless, as surely as I live and as surely as the glory of the LORD fills the whole earth, not one of the men who saw my glory and the miraculous signs I performed in Egypt and in the desert but who disobeyed me and tested me ten times—not one of them will ever see the land I promised on oath to their forefathers. No one who has treated me with contempt will ever see it. But because my servant Caleb has a different spirit and follows me wholeheartedly, I will bring him into the land he went to, and his descendants will inherit it. Since the Amalekites and Canaanites are living in the valleys, turn back tomorrow and set out toward the desert along the route to the Red Sea.ᵖ"

Num. 14:20-25

TO WANDER 40 YEARS. The LORD said to Moses and Aaron: "How long will this wicked community grumble against me? I have heard the complaints of these grumbling Israelites. So tell them, 'As surely as I live, declares the LORD, I will do to you the very things I heard you say: In this desert your bodies will fall—every one of you twenty years old or more who was counted in the census and who has grumbled against me. Not one of you will enter the land I swore with uplifted hand to make your home, except Caleb son of Jephunneh and Joshua son of Nun. As for your

Num. 14:26-35

ᵖHebrew *Yam Suph*; that is, Sea of Reeds

children that you said would be taken as plunder, I will bring them in to enjoy the land you have rejected. But you—your bodies will fall in this desert. Your children will be shepherds here for forty years, suffering for your unfaithfulness, until the last of your bodies lies in the desert. For forty years—one year for each of the forty days you explored the land—you will suffer for your sins and know what it is like to have me against you.' I, the LORD, have spoken, and I will surely do these things to this whole wicked community, which has banded together against me. They will meet their end in this desert; here they will die."

Num.
14:36-38

SPIES DIE.   So the men Moses had sent to explore the land, who returned and made the whole community grumble against him by spreading a bad report about it—these men responsible for spreading the bad report about the land were struck down and died of a plague before the LORD. Of the men who went to explore the land, only Joshua son of Nun and Caleb son of Jephunneh survived.

Num.
14:39-43

PEOPLE LEAVE CAMP.   When Moses reported this to all the Israelites, they mourned bitterly. Early the next morning they went up toward the high hill country. "We have sinned," they said. "We will go up to the place the LORD promised."

But Moses said, "Why are you disobeying the LORD's command? This will not succeed! Do not go up, because the LORD is not with you. You will be defeated by your enemies, for the Amalekites and Canaanites will face you there. Because you have turned away from the LORD, he will not be with you and you will fall by the sword."

Num.
14:44,45

PEOPLE ARE DEFEATED.   Nevertheless, in their presumption they went up toward the high hill country, though neither Moses nor the ark of the LORD's covenant moved from the camp. Then the Amalekites and Canaanites who lived in that hill country came down and attacked them and beat them down all the way to Hormah.

Challenge to Leadership

*P*ostponement of the advance into Canaan and defeat by the foreign armies has a calamitous effect on the Israelites. During the next 40 years they will become bitter, quarrelsome, and openly rebellious. Trouble reaches a peak when Korah, himself a Levite, and two men of the tribe of Reuben lead 250 others in what amounts to a mutiny. After they are miraculously destroyed for their rebellion, thousands of other Israelites who stand in sympathy with them are also stricken by plague and die. The issue is not simply one of political leadership. Despite what may have been a sincere conviction on Korah's part, this is an assault against God's chosen priesthood. To make his selection of Aaron as priest perfectly clear, God directs Moses to perform a test involving the collection of rods from each tribe. Only Aaron's rod proves to be God's choice.

To further instruct the Israelites regarding the proper position of the priesthood, and the Levites who serve with them, God declares that the priests and the Levites will have no inheritance in the promised land, but will rather be supported through the practice of tithing.

LEADERSHIP CHALLENGED.   Korah son of Izhar, the son of Kohath, the son of Levi, and certain Reubenites—Dathan and Abiram, sons of Eliab, and On son of Peleth—became insolent*q* and rose up against Moses. With them were 250 Israelite men, well-known community leaders who had been appointed members of the council. They came as a group to oppose Moses and Aaron and said to them, "You have gone too far! The whole community is holy, every one of them, and the LORD is with them. Why then do you set yourselves above the LORD's assembly?"

Num. 16:1-3 Wilderness

MOSES PROPOSES TEST.   When Moses heard this, he fell facedown. Then he said to Korah and all his followers: "In the morning the LORD will show who belongs to him and who is holy, and he will have that person come near him. The man he chooses he will cause to come near him. You, Korah, and all your followers are to do this: Take censers and tomorrow put fire and incense in them before the LORD. The man the LORD chooses will be the one who is holy. You Levites have gone too far!"

Num. 16:4-7

MOSES REBUKES KORAH.   Moses also said to Korah, "Now listen, you Levites! Isn't it enough for you that the God of Israel has separated you from the rest of the Israelite community and brought you near himself to do the work at the LORD's tabernacle and to stand before the community and minister to them? He has brought you and all your fellow Levites near himself, but now you are trying to get the priesthood too. It is against the LORD that you and all your followers have banded together. Who is Aaron that you should grumble against him?"

Num. 16:8-11

MOSES TAUNTED.   Then Moses summoned Dathan and Abiram, the sons of Eliab. But they said, "We will not come! Isn't it enough that you have brought us up out of a land flowing with milk and honey to kill us in the desert? And now you also want to lord it over us? Moreover, you haven't brought us into a land flowing with milk and honey or given us an inheritance of fields and vineyards. Will you gouge out the eyes of*r* these men? No, we will not come!"

Num. 16:12-14

CENSERS BROUGHT.   Then Moses became very angry and said to the LORD, "Do not accept their offering. I have not taken so much as a donkey from them, nor have I wronged any of them."

Moses said to Korah, "You and all your followers are to appear before the LORD tomorrow—you and they and Aaron. Each man is to take his censer and put incense in it—250 censers in all—and present it before the LORD. You and Aaron are to present your censers also." So each man took his censer, put fire and incense in it, and stood with Moses and Aaron at the entrance to the Tent of Meeting. When Korah had gathered all his followers in opposition to them at the entrance to the Tent of Meeting, the glory of the LORD appeared to the entire assembly.

Num. 16:15-19

PEOPLE SEPARATED FROM REBELS.   The LORD said to Moses and Aaron, "Separate yourselves from this assembly so I can put an end to them at once."

But Moses and Aaron fell facedown and cried out, "O God, God of the spirits of all mankind, will you be angry with the entire assembly when only one man sins?"

Num. 16:20-26

*q*Or *Peleth—took* ⌊*men*⌋   *r*Or *you make slaves of;* or *you deceive*

Then the LORD said to Moses, "Say to the assembly, 'Move away from the tents of Korah, Dathan and Abiram.'"

Moses got up and went to Dathan and Abiram, and the elders of Israel followed him. He warned the assembly, "Move back from the tents of these wicked men! Do not touch anything belonging to them, or you will be swept away because of all their sins."

Num.
16:27-30

MOSES PREDICTS DEATH.   So they moved away from the tents of Korah, Dathan and Abiram. Dathan and Abiram had come out and were standing with their wives, children and little ones at the entrances to their tents.

Then Moses said, "This is how you will know that the LORD has sent me to do all these things and that it was not my idea: If these men die a natural death and experience only what usually happens to men, then the LORD has not sent me. But if the LORD brings about something totally new, and the earth opens its mouth and swallows them, with everything that belongs to them, and they go down alive into the grave,ˢ then you will know that these men have treated the LORD with contempt."

Num.
16:31-35

REBELS SWALLOWED UP.   As soon as he finished saying all this, the ground under them split apart and the earth opened its mouth and swallowed them, with their households and all Korah's men and all their possessions. They went down alive into the grave, with everything they owned; the earth closed over them, and they perished and were gone from the community. At their cries, all the Israelites around them fled, shouting, "The earth is going to swallow us too!"

And fire came out from the LORD and consumed the 250 men who were offering the incense.

Num.
16:36-40

CENSERS BECOME ALTAR COVER.   The LORD said to Moses, "Tell Eleazar son of Aaron, the priest, to take the censers out of the smoldering remains and scatter the coals some distance away, for the censers are holy—the censers of the men who sinned at the cost of their lives. Hammer the censers into sheets to overlay the altar, for they were presented before the LORD and have become holy. Let them be a sign to the Israelites."

So Eleazar the priest collected the bronze censers brought by those who had been burned up, and he had them hammered out to overlay the altar, as the LORD directed him through Moses. This was to remind the Israelites that no one except a descendant of Aaron should come to burn incense before the LORD, or he would become like Korah and his followers.

Num.
16:41-45

GOD READY TO PUNISH.   The next day the whole Israelite community grumbled against Moses and Aaron. "You have killed the LORD's people," they said.

But when the assembly gathered in opposition to Moses and Aaron and turned toward the Tent of Meeting, suddenly the cloud covered it and the glory of the LORD appeared. Then Moses and Aaron went to the front of the Tent of Meeting, and the LORD said to Moses, "Get away from this assembly so I can put an end to them at once." And they fell facedown.

Num.
16:46-50

14,700 DIE OF PLAGUE.   Then Moses said to Aaron, "Take your censer and put incense in it, along with fire from the altar, and hurry to the

ˢHebrew Sheol

assembly to make atonement for them. Wrath has come out from the LORD; the plague has started." So Aaron did as Moses said, and ran into the midst of the assembly. The plague had already started among the people, but Aaron offered the incense and made atonement for them. He stood between the living and the dead, and the plague stopped. But 14,700 people died from the plague, in addition to those who had died because of Korah. Then Aaron returned to Moses at the entrance to the Tent of Meeting, for the plague had stopped.

GOD CALLS FOR RODS.   The LORD said to Moses, "Speak to the Israelites and get twelve staffs from them, one from the leader of each of their ancestral tribes. Write the name of each man on his staff. On the staff of Levi write Aaron's name, for there must be one staff for the head of each ancestral tribe. Place them in the Tent of Meeting in front of the Testimony, where I meet with you. The staff belonging to the man I choose will sprout, and I will rid myself of this constant grumbling against you by the Israelites."
Num.
17:1-7

So Moses spoke to the Israelites, and their leaders gave him twelve staffs, one for the leader of each of their ancestral tribes, and Aaron's staff was among them. Moses placed the staffs before the LORD in the Tent of the Testimony.

ONLY AARON'S ROD BUDS.   The next day Moses entered the Tent of the Testimony and saw that Aaron's staff, which represented the house of Levi, had not only sprouted but had budded, blossomed and produced almonds. Then Moses brought out all the staffs from the LORD's presence to all the Israelites. They looked at them, and each man took his own staff.
Num.
17:8-11

The LORD said to Moses, "Put back Aaron's staff in front of the Testimony, to be kept as a sign to the rebellious. This will put an end to their grumbling against me, so that they will not die." Moses did just as the LORD commanded him.

THE PEOPLE FEAR.   The Israelites said to Moses, "We will die! We are lost, we are all lost! Anyone who even comes near the tabernacle of the LORD will die. Are we all going to die?"
Num.
17:12,13

AARON'S PRIESTHOOD ASSURED.   The LORD said to Aaron, "You, your sons and your father's family are to bear the responsibility for offenses against the sanctuary, and you and your sons alone are to bear the responsibility for offenses against the priesthood. Bring your fellow Levites from your ancestral tribe to join you and assist you when you and your sons minister before the Tent of the Testimony. They are to be responsible to you and are to perform all the duties of the Tent, but they must not go near the furnishings of the sanctuary or the altar, or both they and you will die. They are to join you and be responsible for the care of the Tent of Meeting—all the work at the Tent—and no one else may come near where you are.
Num.
18:1-7

"You are to be responsible for the care of the sanctuary and the altar, so that wrath will not fall on the Israelites again. I myself have selected your fellow Levites from among the Israelites as a gift to you, dedicated to the LORD to do the work at the Tent of Meeting. But only you and your sons may serve as priests in connection with everything at the altar and inside the curtain. I am giving you the service of the priesthood as a gift. Anyone else who comes near the sanctuary must be put to death."

<table>
<tr><td>Num.
18:8-19</td><td>

OFFERINGS BELONG TO PRIESTS.   Then the LORD said to Aaron, "I myself have put you in charge of the offerings presented to me; all the holy offerings the Israelites give me I give to you and your sons as your portion and regular share. You are to have the part of the most holy offerings that is kept from the fire. From all the gifts they bring me as most holy offerings, whether grain or sin or guilt offerings, that part belongs to you and your sons. Eat it as something most holy; every male shall eat it. You must regard it as holy.

"This also is yours: whatever is set aside from the gifts of all the wave offerings of the Israelites. I give this to you and your sons and daughters as your regular share. Everyone in your household who is ceremonially clean may eat it.

"I give you all the finest olive oil and all the finest new wine and grain they give the LORD as the firstfruits of their harvest. All the land's firstfruits that they bring to the LORD will be yours. Everyone in your household who is ceremonially clean may eat it.

"Everything in Israel that is devoted[t] to the LORD is yours. The first offspring of every womb, both man and animal, that is offered to the LORD is yours. But you must redeem every firstborn son and every firstborn male of unclean animals. When they are a month old, you must redeem them at the redemption price set at five shekels[u] of silver, according to the sanctuary shekel, which weighs twenty gerahs.

"But you must not redeem the firstborn of an ox, a sheep or a goat; they are holy. Sprinkle their blood on the altar and burn their fat as an offering made by fire, an aroma pleasing to the LORD. Their meat is to be yours, just as the breast of the wave offering and the right thigh are yours. Whatever is set aside from the holy offerings the Israelites present to the LORD I give to you and your sons and daughters as your regular share. It is an everlasting covenant of salt before the LORD for both you and your offspring."

</td></tr>

<tr><td>Num.
18:20</td><td>

AARON TO HAVE NO LAND.   The LORD said to Aaron, "You will have no inheritance in their land, nor will you have any share among them; I am your share and your inheritance among the Israelites.

</td></tr>

<tr><td>Num.
18:21-24</td><td>

LEVITES GET TITHES.   "I give to the Levites all the tithes in Israel as their inheritance in return for the work they do while serving at the Tent of Meeting. From now on the Israelites must not go near the Tent of Meeting, or they will bear the consequences of their sin and will die. It is the Levites who are to do the work at the Tent of Meeting and bear the responsibility for offenses against it. This is a lasting ordinance for the generations to come. They will receive no inheritance among the Israelites. Instead, I give to the Levites as their inheritance the tithes that the Israelites present as an offering to the LORD. That is why I said concerning them: 'They will have no inheritance among the Israelites.' "

</td></tr>

<tr><td>Num.
18:25-32</td><td>

LEVITES TO GIVE TITHES.   The LORD said to Moses, "Speak to the Levites and say to them: 'When you receive from the Israelites the tithe I give you as your inheritance, you must present a tenth of that tithe as the LORD's offering. Your offering will be reckoned to you as grain from the threshing floor or juice from the winepress. In this way you also will

</td></tr>
</table>

---

[t]The Hebrew term refers to the irrevocable giving over of things or persons to the LORD.
[u]That is, about 2 ounces (about 55 grams)

present an offering to the LORD from all the tithes you receive from the Israelites. From these tithes you must give the LORD's portion to Aaron the priest. You must present as the LORD's portion the best and holiest part of everything given to you.'

"Say to the Levites: 'When you present the best part, it will be reckoned to you as the product of the threshing floor or the winepress. You and your households may eat the rest of it anywhere, for it is your wages for your work at the Tent of Meeting. By presenting the best part of it you will not be guilty in this matter; then you will not defile the holy offerings of the Israelites, and you will not die.' "

From Kadesh to Moab

he account of the Israelites wandering in the wilderness as recorded in the book of Numbers skips over virtually all of the 40 years in the wilderness except for the foregoing account of the people's rebellion and for the events of the final year to come. With the beginning of the last year of their probationary wanderings, the Israelites return once again to Kadesh in the Wilderness of Zin, west of Edom and south of Canaan. Here Miriam will die, and her brothers, Moses and Aaron, will so displease God that they too will be denied entrance into the promised land. Apparently their sin involves not simply failure to follow God's specific directions, but manifestations of pride and self-importance which minimize God's power—a potential danger for all who would be spiritual leaders.

As Israel begins to mobilize for the march to Canaan, a request is made for safe passage through the territory of Edom. The Edomites' refusal is the first of many conflicts which will fulfill the prophecy of antagonism between the descendants of Jacob (Israel) and Esau (Edom).

After God calls Aaron to his death, the people will mourn for a month and then set out for a series of military victories. This will finally bring them out of the wilderness and into the territory of Moab, east of the Dead (Salt) Sea, and as far north as Bashan, east of the Sea of Galilee (Chinnereth).

DEATH OF MIRIAM.   In the first month the whole Israelite community arrived at the Desert of Zin, and they stayed at Kadesh. There Miriam died and was buried.

Num. 20:1
(Ca. 1406
B.C.)

PEOPLE CRY FOR WATER.   Now there was no water for the community, and the people gathered in opposition to Moses and Aaron. They quarreled with Moses and said, "If only we had died when our brothers fell dead before the LORD! Why did you bring the LORD's community into this desert, that we and our livestock should die here? Why did you bring us up out of Egypt to this terrible place? It has no grain or figs, grapevines or pomegranates. And there is no water to drink!"

Num.
20:2-5

MOSES GIVEN INSTRUCTIONS.   Moses and Aaron went from the assembly to the entrance to the Tent of Meeting and fell facedown, and the glory of the LORD appeared to them. The LORD said to Moses, "Take the staff, and you and your brother Aaron gather the assembly together. Speak to that rock before their eyes and it will pour out its water. You will bring

Num.
20:6-9

water out of the rock for the community so they and their livestock can drink."

So Moses took the staff from the LORD's presence, just as he commanded him.

Num.
20:10,11

MOSES STRIKES ROCK.   He and Aaron gathered the assembly together in front of the rock and Moses said to them, "Listen, you rebels, must we bring you water out of this rock?" Then Moses raised his arm and struck the rock twice with his staff. Water gushed out, and the community and their livestock drank.

Num.
20:12,13

MOSES AND AARON PUNISHED.   But the LORD said to Moses and Aaron, "Because you did not trust in me enough to honor me as holy in the sight of the Israelites, you will not bring this community into the land I give them."

These were the waters of Meribah,*v* where the Israelites quarreled with the LORD and where he showed himself holy among them.

Num.
20:14-17

PASSAGE REQUESTED OF EDOM.   Moses sent messengers from Kadesh to the king of Edom, saying:

"This is what your brother Israel says: You know about all the hardships that have come upon us. Our forefathers went down into Egypt, and we lived there many years. The Egyptians mistreated us and our fathers, but when we cried out to the LORD, he heard our cry and sent an angel and brought us out of Egypt.

"Now we are here at Kadesh, a town on the edge of your territory. Please let us pass through your country. We will not go through any field or vineyard, or drink water from any well. We will travel along the king's highway and not turn to the right or to the left until we have passed through your territory."

Num.
20:18-21

EDOMITES REFUSE REQUESTS.   But Edom answered:

"You may not pass through here; if you try, we will march out and attack you with the sword."

The Israelites replied:

"We will go along the main road, and if we or our livestock drink any of your water, we will pay for it. We only want to pass through on foot— nothing else."

Again they answered:

"You may not pass through."

Then Edom came out against them with a large and powerful army. Since Edom refused to let them go through their territory, Israel turned away from them.

Num.
20:22-29
Mount
Hor

DEATH OF AARON.   The whole Israelite community set out from Kadesh and came to Mount Hor. At Mount Hor, near the border of Edom, the LORD said to Moses and Aaron, "Aaron will be gathered to his people. He will not enter the land I give the Israelites, because both of you rebelled against my command at the waters of Meribah. Get Aaron and his son Eleazar and take them up Mount Hor. Remove Aaron's garments and put

*v*Meribah means *quarreling.*

them on his son Eleazar, for Aaron will be gathered to his people; he will die there."

Moses did as the LORD commanded: They went up Mount Hor in the sight of the whole community. Moses removed Aaron's garments and put them on his son Eleazar. And Aaron died there on top of the mountain. Then Moses and Eleazar came down from the mountain, and when the whole community learned that Aaron had died, the entire house of Israel mourned for him thirty days.

VICTORY OVER KING ARAD.   When the Canaanite king of Arad, who lived in the Negev, heard that Israel was coming along the road to Atharim, he attacked the Israelites and captured some of them. Then Israel made this vow to the LORD: "If you will deliver these people into our hands, we will totally destroy[w] their cities." The LORD listened to Israel's plea and gave the Canaanites over to them. They completely destroyed them and their towns; so the place was named Hormah.[x]

Num.
21:1-3
Hormah

SNAKES BITE MURMURERS.   They traveled from Mount Hor along the route to the Red Sea,[y] to go around Edom. But the people grew impatient on the way; they spoke against God and against Moses, and said, "Why have you brought us up out of Egypt to die in the desert? There is no bread! There is no water! And we detest this miserable food!"

Then the LORD sent venomous snakes among them; they bit the people and many Israelites died.

Num.
21:4-6
Wilder-
ness

BRONZE SNAKE ERECTED.   The people came to Moses and said, "We sinned when we spoke against the LORD and against you. Pray that the LORD will take the snakes away from us." So Moses prayed for the people.

The LORD said to Moses, "Make a snake and put it up on a pole; anyone who is bitten can look at it and live." So Moses made a bronze snake and put it up on a pole. Then when anyone was bitten by a snake and looked at the bronze snake, he lived.

Num.
21:7-9

FROM OBOTH TO THE ARNON.   The Israelites moved on and camped at Oboth. Then they set out from Oboth and camped in Iye Abarim, in the desert that faces Moab toward the sunrise. From there they moved on and camped in the Zered Valley. They set out from there and camped alongside the Arnon, which is in the desert extending into Amorite territory. The Arnon is the border of Moab, between Moab and the Amorites.

Num.
21:10-13

BOOK OF WARS DESCRIPTION.   That is why the Book of the Wars of the LORD says:

Num.
21:14,15

> ". . . Waheb in Suphah[z] and the ravines,
>   the Arnon and[a] the slopes of the ravines
>   that lead to the site of Ar
>   and lie along the border of Moab."

THE WELL AT BEER.   From there they continued on to Beer, the well where the LORD said to Moses, "Gather the people together and I will give them water."

Then Israel sang this song:

Num.
21:16-18a

[w]The Hebrew term refers to the irrevocable giving over of things or persons to the LORD, often by totally destroying them.   [x]*Hormah* means *destruction*.   [y]Hebrew *Yam Suph*; that is, Sea of Reeds   [z]The meaning of the Hebrew for this phrase is uncertain.
[a]Or "*I have been given from Suphah and the ravines / of the Arnon* [15]to

> "Spring up, O well!
>   Sing about it,
>   about the well that the princes dug,
>   that the nobles of the people sank—
>   the nobles with scepters and staffs."

Num.
21:18b-20

FROM WILDERNESS TO PISGAH.   Then they went from the desert to Mattanah, from Mattanah to Nahaliel, from Nahaliel to Bamoth, and from Bamoth to the valley in Moab where the top of Pisgah overlooks the wasteland.

Num.
21:21-26

SIHON AND AMORITES DEFEATED.   Israel sent messengers to say to Sihon king of the Amorites:

"Let us pass through your country. We will not turn aside into any field or vineyard, or drink water from any well. We will travel along the king's highway until we have passed through your territory."

But Sihon would not let Israel pass through his territory. He mustered his entire army and marched out into the desert against Israel. When he reached Jahaz, he fought with Israel. Israel, however, put him to the sword and took over his land from the Arnon to the Jabbok, but only as far as the Ammonites, because their border was fortified. Israel captured all the cities of the Amorites and occupied them, including Heshbon and all its surrounding settlements. Heshbon was the city of Sihon king of the Amorites, who had fought against the former king of Moab and had taken from him all his land as far as the Arnon.

Num.
21:27-30

VICTORY BALLAD.   That is why the poets say:

> "Come to Heshbon and let it be rebuilt;
>   let Sihon's city be restored.
>
> "Fire went out from Heshbon,
>   a blaze from the city of Sihon.
> It consumed Ar of Moab,
>   the citizens of Arnon's heights.
> Woe to you, O Moab!
>   You are destroyed, O people of Chemosh!
> He has given up his sons as fugitives
>   and his daughters as captives
>   to Sihon king of the Amorites.
>
> "But we have overthrown them;
>   Heshbon is destroyed all the way to Dibon.
> We have demolished them as far as Nophah,
>   which extends to Medeba."

Num.
21:31-35

OG AND BASHANITES DEFEATED.   So Israel settled in the land of the Amorites.

After Moses had sent spies to Jazer, the Israelites captured its surrounding settlements and drove out the Amorites who were there. Then they turned and went up along the road toward Bashan, and Og king of Bashan and his whole army marched out to meet them in battle at Edrei.

The Lord said to Moses, "Do not be afraid of him, for I have handed him over to you, with his whole army and his land. Do to him what you did to Sihon king of the Amorites, who reigned in Heshbon."

So they struck him down, together with his sons and his whole army, leaving them no survivors. And they took possession of his land.

Moses' Journal of Israel's Trek_____

Now that Israel has finally come out of its wilderness wanderings and into the more habitable land of Moab, the book of Numbers gives a retrospective overview of the places where Israel has camped during the previous 40 years. At God's direction, Moses has been keeping a detailed journal of the exodus from Egypt. The following passages come from that journal.

INTRODUCTION TO JOURNAL.   Here are the stages in the journey of the Israelites when they came out of Egypt by divisions under the leadership of Moses and Aaron. At the LORD's command Moses recorded the stages in their journey. This is their journey by stages: | Num. 33:1,2

RECOUNTING THE EXODUS.   The Israelites set out from Rameses on the fifteenth day of the first month, the day after the Passover. They marched out boldly in full view of all the Egyptians, who were burying all their firstborn, whom the LORD had struck down among them; for the LORD had brought judgment on their gods. | Num. 33:3,4

FROM RAMESES TO SINAI.   The Israelites left Rameses and camped at Succoth. | Num. 33:5-15

They left Succoth and camped at Etham, on the edge of the desert.

They left Etham, turned back to Pi Hahiroth, to the east of Baal Zephon, and camped near Migdol.

They left Pi Hahiroth[b] and passed through the sea into the desert, and when they had traveled for three days in the Desert of Etham, they camped at Marah.

They left Marah and went to Elim, where there were twelve springs and seventy palm trees, and they camped there.

They left Elim and camped by the Red Sea.[c]

They left the Red Sea and camped in the Desert of Sin.

They left the Desert of Sin and camped at Dophkah.

They left Dophkah and camped at Alush.

They left Alush and camped at Rephidim, where there was no water for the people to drink.

They left Rephidim and camped in the Desert of Sinai.

FROM SINAI TO MOUNT HOR.   They left the Desert of Sinai and camped at Kibroth Hattaavah. | Num. 33:16-37

They left Kibroth Hattaavah and camped at Hazeroth.

They left Hazeroth and camped at Rithmah.

They left Rithmah and camped at Rimmon Perez.

They left Rimmon Perez and camped at Libnah.

They left Libnah and camped at Rissah.

They left Rissah and camped at Kehelathah.

They left Kehelathah and camped at Mount Shepher.

[b]Many manuscripts of the Masoretic Text, Samaritan Pentateuch and Vulgate; most manuscripts of the Masoretic Text *left from before Hahiroth*   [c]Hebrew *Yam Suph*; that is, Sea of Reeds

They left Mount Shepher and camped at Haradah.
They left Haradah and camped at Makheloth.
They left Makheloth and camped at Tahath.
They left Tahath and camped at Terah.
They left Terah and camped at Mithcah.
They left Mithcah and camped at Hashmonah.
They left Hashmonah and camped at Moseroth.
They left Moseroth and camped at Bene Jaakan.
They left Bene Jaakan and camped at Hor Haggidgad.
They left Hor Haggidgad and camped at Jotbathah.
They left Jotbathah and camped at Abronah.
They left Abronah and camped at Ezion Geber.
They left Ezion Geber and camped at Kadesh, in the Desert of Zin.
They left Kadesh and camped at Mount Hor, on the border of Edom.

Num.
33:38,39

RECOUNTING AARON'S DEATH. At the LORD's command Aaron the priest went up Mount Hor, where he died on the first day of the fifth month of the fortieth year after the Israelites came out of Egypt. Aaron was a hundred and twenty-three years old when he died on Mount Hor.

Num.
33:40-49

FROM MOUNT HOR TO MOAB. The Canaanite king of Arad, who lived in the Negev of Canaan, heard that the Israelites were coming.
They left Mount Hor and camped at Zalmonah.
They left Zalmonah and camped at Punon.
They left Punon and camped at Oboth.
They left Oboth and camped at Iye Abarim, on the border of Moab.
They left Iyim*d* and camped at Dibon Gad.
They left Dibon Gad and camped at Almon Diblathaim.
They left Almon Diblathaim and camped in the mountains of Abarim, near Nebo.
They left the mountains of Abarim and camped on the plains of Moab by the Jordan across from Jericho.*e* There on the plains of Moab they camped along the Jordan from Beth Jeshimoth to Abel Shittim.

Blessings and Prophecy of Balaam

*A*s the Israelites move into the land east of the Jordan River (from which they plan to enter Canaan), the inhabitants of Moab are naturally apprehensive of their presence. Moab's ruler, King Balak, is so convinced that he cannot win a military victory over the Israelites that he decides to summon a soothsayer by the name of Balaam to curse the invaders. Although he is a spiritualist, Balaam is by no means a good man. He is a diviner from the region of the upper Euphrates, near Carchemish, and one who uses pagan ritual to search for omens. On this occasion, however, God allows Balaam to speak on behalf of the Almighty.

After receiving God's direction not to curse the Israelites, Balaam at first refuses to help King Balak. But when Balaam is told that he can become a wealthy man by helping King Balak, he once again seeks God's counsel. Balaam obviously knows God's will, but he is so intrigued by the possibility of

---

*d*That is, Iye Abarim   *e*Hebrew *Jordan of Jericho*; possibly an ancient name for the Jordan River

wealth that he hopes God will change his mind. To Balaam's surprise and delight, God permits him to go to Balak. But it is soon clear that God has allowed Balaam to go for the sole purpose of teaching Balak how wrong it is to put God's will to the test in hope of personal gain.

The final prophecy which Balaam is given concerning Israel's eventual conquests contains a secondary prophecy about the Messiah and offspring of Jacob, whose kingdom will one day be established throughout the earth. Balaam, of course, is unaware of the significance of the words he is uttering. Otherwise he would not be party to the scheming which will soon take place against the Israelites on the part of the Midianites. The account begins with Balak's call for Balaam's help.

BALAK FEARS ISRAEL.   Then the Israelites traveled to the plains of Moab and camped along the Jordan across from Jericho./   Num. 22:1-3 Moab

Now Balak son of Zippor saw all that Israel had done to the Amorites, and Moab was terrified because there were so many people. Indeed, Moab was filled with dread because of the Israelites.

BALAK WANTS BALAAM'S HELP.   The Moabites said to the elders of Midian, "This horde is going to lick up everything around us, as an ox licks up the grass of the field."   Num. 22:4-6

So Balak son of Zippor, who was king of Moab at that time, sent messengers to summon Balaam son of Beor, who was at Pethor, near the River,^{g} in his native land. Balak said:

"A people has come out of Egypt; they cover the face of the land and have settled next to me. Now come and put a curse on these people, because they are too powerful for me. Perhaps then I will be able to defeat them and drive them out of the country. For I know that those you bless are blessed, and those you curse are cursed."

BALAAM REFUSES TO HELP.   The elders of Moab and Midian left, taking with them the fee for divination. When they came to Balaam, they told him what Balak had said.   Num. 22:7-14

"Spend the night here," Balaam said to them, "and I will bring you back the answer the LORD gives me." So the Moabite princes stayed with him.

God came to Balaam and asked, "Who are these men with you?"

Balaam said to God, "Balak son of Zippor, king of Moab, sent me this message: 'A people that has come out of Egypt covers the face of the land. Now come and put a curse on them for me. Perhaps then I will be able to fight them and drive them away.'"

But God said to Balaam, "Do not go with them. You must not put a curse on those people, because they are blessed."

The next morning Balaam got up and said to Balak's princes, "Go back to your own country, for the LORD has refused to let me go with you."

So the Moabite princes returned to Balak and said, "Balaam refused to come with us."

BALAAM TESTS GOD.   Then Balak sent other princes, more numerous and more distinguished than the first. They came to Balaam and said: Num. 22:15-20 East of Moab

---

/Hebrew *Jordan of Jericho*; possibly an ancient name for the Jordan River   gThat is, the Euphrates

This is what Balak son of Zippor says: Do not let anything keep you from coming to me, because I will reward you handsomely and do whatever you say. Come and put a curse on these people for me."

But Balaam answered them, "Even if Balak gave me his palace filled with silver and gold, I could not do anything great or small to go beyond the command of the LORD my God. Now stay here tonight as the others did, and I will find out what else the LORD will tell me."

That night God came to Balaam and said, "Since these men have come to summon you, go with them, but do only what I tell you."

Num.
22:21-27

ANGEL CONFRONTS DONKEY.   Balaam got up in the morning, saddled his donkey and went with the princes of Moab. But God was very angry when he went, and the angel of the LORD stood in the road to oppose him. Balaam was riding on his donkey, and his two servants were with him. When the donkey saw the angel of the LORD standing in the road with a drawn sword in his hand, she turned off the road into a field. Balaam beat her to get her back on the road.

Then the angel of the LORD stood in a narrow path between two vineyards, with walls on both sides. When the donkey saw the angel of the LORD, she pressed close to the wall, crushing Balaam's foot against it. So he beat her again.

Then the angel of the LORD moved on ahead and stood in a narrow place where there was no room to turn, either to the right or to the left. When the donkey saw the angel of the LORD, she lay down under Balaam, and he was angry and beat her with his staff.

Num.
22:28-30

DONKEY REBUKES BALAAM.   Then the LORD opened the donkey's mouth, and she said to Balaam, "What have I done to you to make you beat me these three times?"

Balaam answered the donkey, "You have made a fool of me! If I had a sword in my hand, I would kill you right now."

The donkey said to Balaam, "Am I not your own donkey, which you have always ridden, to this day? Have I been in the habit of doing this to you?"

"No," he said.

Num.
22:31-33

ANGEL REBUKES BALAAM.   Then the LORD opened Balaam's eyes, and he saw the angel of the LORD standing in the road with his sword drawn. So he bowed low and fell facedown.

The angel of the LORD asked him, "Why have you beaten your donkey these three times? I have come here to oppose you because your path is a reckless one before me.[h] The donkey saw me and turned away from me these three times. If she had not turned away, I would certainly have killed you by now, but I would have spared her."

Num.
22:34,35

BALAAM PERMITTED TO GO.   Balaam said to the angel of the LORD, "I have sinned. I did not realize you were standing in the road to oppose me. Now if you are displeased, I will go back."

The angel of the LORD said to Balaam, "Go with the men, but speak only what I tell you." So Balaam went with the princes of Balak.

Num.
22:36-41
Moab

BALAAM MEETS BALAK.   When Balak heard that Balaam was coming, he went out to meet him at the Moabite town on the Arnon border, at the

[h]The meaning of the Hebrew for this clause is uncertain.

edge of his territory. Balak said to Balaam, "Did I not send you an urgent summons? Why didn't you come to me? Am I really not able to reward you?"

"Well, I have come to you now," Balaam replied. "But can I say just anything? I must speak only what God puts in my mouth."

Then Balaam went with Balak to Kiriath Huzoth. Balak sacrificed cattle and sheep, and gave some to Balaam and the princes who were with him. The next morning Balak took Balaam up to Bamoth Baal, and from there he saw part of the people.

BALAAM SEEKS OMEN. Balaam said, "Build me seven altars here, and prepare seven bulls and seven rams for me." Balak did as Balaam said, and the two of them offered a bull and a ram on each altar.

Num. 23:1-5

Then Balaam said to Balak, "Stay here beside your offering while I go aside. Perhaps the LORD will come to meet with me. Whatever he reveals to me I will tell you." Then he went off to a barren height.

God met with him, and Balaam said, "I have prepared seven altars, and on each altar I have offered a bull and a ram."

The LORD put a message in Balaam's mouth and said, "Go back to Balak and give him this message."

BALAAM BLESSES ISRAEL. So he went back to him and found him standing beside his offering, with all the princes of Moab. Then Balaam uttered his oracle:

Num. 23:6-10

"Balak brought me from Aram,
the king of Moab from the eastern mountains.
'Come,' he said, 'curse Jacob for me;
come, denounce Israel.'
How can I curse
those whom God has not cursed?
How can I denounce
those whom the LORD has not denounced?
From the rocky peaks I see them,
from the heights I view them.
I see a people who live apart
and do not consider themselves one of the nations.
Who can count the dust of Jacob
or number the fourth part of Israel?
Let me die the death of the righteous,
and may my end be like theirs!"

BALAK ASKS SECOND TRY. Balak said to Balaam, "What have you done to me? I brought you to curse my enemies, but you have done nothing but bless them!"

Num. 23:11-16

He answered, "Must I not speak what the LORD puts in my mouth?"

Then Balak said to him, "Come with me to another place where you can see them; you will see only a part but not all of them. And from there, curse them for me." So he took him to the field of Zophim on the top of Pisgah, and there he built seven altars and offered a bull and a ram on each altar.

Balaam said to Balak, "Stay here beside your offering while I meet with him over there."

The LORD met with Balaam and put a message in his mouth and said, "Go back to Balak and give him this message."

Num.
23:17-24

BALAAM'S SECOND BLESSING.   So he went to him and found him standing beside his offering, with the princes of Moab. Balak asked him, "What did the LORD say?"

Then he uttered his oracle:

> "Arise, Balak, and listen;
> > hear me, son of Zippor.
> God is not a man, that he should lie,
> > nor a son of man, that he should change his mind.
> Does he speak and then not act?
> > Does he promise and not fulfill?
> I have received a command to bless;
> > he has blessed, and I cannot change it.

> "No misfortune is seen in Jacob,
> > no misery observed in Israel.[i]
> The LORD their God is with them;
> > the shout of the King is among them.
> God brought them out of Egypt;
> > they have the strength of a wild ox.
> There is no sorcery against Jacob,
> > no divination against Israel.
> It will now be said of Jacob
> > and of Israel, 'See what God has done!'
> The people rise like a lioness;
> > they rouse themselves like a lion
> that does not rest till he devours his prey
> > and drinks the blood of his victims."

Num.
23:25-30

BALAK ASKS THIRD TRY.   Then Balak said to Balaam, "Neither curse them at all nor bless them at all!"

Balaam answered, "Did I not tell you I must do whatever the LORD says?"

Then Balak said to Balaam, "Come, let me take you to another place. Perhaps it will please God to let you curse them for me from there." And Balak took Balaam to the top of Peor, overlooking the wasteland.

Balaam said, "Build me seven altars here, and prepare seven bulls and seven rams for me." Balak did as Balaam had said, and offered a bull and a ram on each altar.

Num.
24:1-9

BALAAM'S THIRD BLESSING.   Now when Balaam saw that it pleased the LORD to bless Israel, he did not resort to sorcery as at other times, but turned his face toward the desert. When Balaam looked out and saw Israel encamped tribe by tribe, the Spirit of God came upon him and he uttered his oracle:

> "The oracle of Balaam son of Beor,
> > the oracle of one whose eye sees clearly,
> > the oracle of one who hears the words of God,

---

[i]Or *He has not looked on Jacob's offenses / or on the wrongs found in Israel.*

who sees a vision from the Almighty,[j]
who falls prostrate, and whose eyes are opened:

"How beautiful are your tents, O Jacob,
    your dwelling places, O Israel!

"Like valleys they spread out,
    like gardens beside a river,
  like aloes planted by the LORD,
    like cedars beside the waters.
Water will flow from their buckets;
    their seed will have abundant water.

"Their king will be greater than Agag;
    their kingdom will be exalted.

"God brought them out of Egypt;
    they have the strength of a wild ox.
They devour hostile nations
    and break their bones in pieces;
    with their arrows they pierce them.
Like a lion they crouch and lie down,
    like a lioness—who dares to rouse them?

"May those who bless you be blessed
    and those who curse you be cursed!"

BALAK ANGRY AT BALAAM. Then Balak's anger burned against Balaam. He struck his hands together and said to him, "I summoned you to curse my enemies, but you have blessed them these three times. Now leave at once and go home! I said I would reward you handsomely, but the LORD has kept you from being rewarded."   *Num. 24:10-13*

Balaam answered Balak, "Did I not tell the messengers you sent me, 'Even if Balak gave me his palace filled with silver and gold, I could not do anything of my own accord, good or bad, to go beyond the command of the LORD—and I must say only what the LORD says'?

ISRAEL TO DEFEAT NATIONS. Now I am going back to my people, but come, let me warn you of what this people will do to your people in days to come."   *Num. 24:14-25*

Then he uttered his oracle:

"The oracle of Balaam son of Beor,
    the oracle of one whose eye sees clearly,
  the oracle of one who hears the words of God,
    who has knowledge from the Most High,
who sees a vision from the Almighty,
    who falls prostrate, and whose eyes are opened:

"I see him, but not now;
    I behold him, but not near.
A star will come out of Jacob;
    a scepter will rise out of Israel.
He will crush the foreheads of Moab,

[j]Hebrew *Shaddai*

the skulls[k] of[l] all the sons of Sheth.[m]
Edom will be conquered;
  Seir, his enemy, will be conquered,
  but Israel will grow strong.
A ruler will come out of Jacob
  and destroy the survivors of the city."

Then Balaam saw Amalek and uttered his oracle:

"Amalek was first among the nations,
  but he will come to ruin at last."

Then he saw the Kenites and uttered his oracle:

"Your dwelling place is secure,
  your nest is set in a rock;
yet you Kenites will be destroyed
  when Asshur takes you captive."

Then he uttered his oracle:

"Ah, who can live when God does this?[n]
  Ships will come from the shores of Kittim;
they will subdue Asshur and Eber,
  but they too will come to ruin."

Then Balaam got up and returned home and Balak went his own way.

Israel Sins in Moab

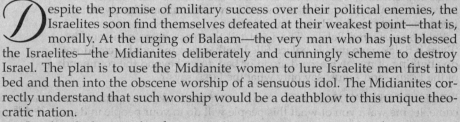

Despite the promise of military success over their political enemies, the Israelites soon find themselves defeated at their weakest point—that is, morally. At the urging of Balaam—the very man who has just blessed the Israelites—the Midianites deliberately and cunningly scheme to destroy Israel. The plan is to use the Midianite women to lure Israelite men first into bed and then into the obscene worship of a sensuous idol. The Midianites correctly understand that such worship would be a deathblow to this unique theocratic nation.

It takes little time for the men of Israel to be attracted by the Midianite women in Moab, and equally little time to be seduced into worshiping Baal-Peor, the fertility god which the women worship. Israel's seduction serves as a good example of how personal relationships—particularly wrong ones—can easily influence religious preferences, and why the Israelites are so severely restricted from mixing with foreigners.

The impudence of one Israelite in flaunting a foreign woman before the congregation of God's people is met with a forceful response by Eleazar's son, Phinehas. And God's own wrath against the idolatrous Israelites results in thousands dying of the plague for their transgressions.

---

[k]Samaritan Pentateuch (see also Jer. 48:45); the meaning of the word in the Masoretic Text is uncertain.   [l]Or possibly *Moab, / batter*   [m]Or *all the noisy boasters*
[n]Masoretic Text; with a different word division of the Hebrew *A people will gather from the north.*

SEDUCTION TO IDOLATRY.   While Israel was staying in Shittim, the **Num.**
men began to indulge in sexual immorality with Moabite women, who **25:1-5**
invited them to the sacrifices to their gods. The people ate and bowed
down before these gods. So Israel joined in worshiping the Baal of Peor.
And the LORD's anger burned against them.

The LORD said to Moses, "Take all the leaders of these people, kill them
and expose them in broad daylight before the LORD, so that the LORD's
fierce anger may turn away from Israel."

So Moses said to Israel's judges, "Each of you must put to death those
of your men who have joined in worshiping the Baal of Peor."

MAN WITH MIDIANITE WOMAN.   Then an Israelite man brought to **Num.**
his family a Midianite woman right before the eyes of Moses and the **25:6-8a**
whole assembly of Israel while they were weeping at the entrance to the
Tent of Meeting. When Phinehas son of Eleazar, the son of Aaron, the
priest, saw this, he left the assembly, took a spear in his hand and followed
the Israelite into the tent. He drove the spear through both of them—
through the Israelite and into the woman's body.

24,000 DIE.   Then the plague against the Israelites was stopped; but those **Num.**
who died in the plague numbered 24,000. **25:8b,9**

PHINEHAS PRAISED.   The LORD said to Moses, "Phinehas son of Elea- **Num.**
zar, the son of Aaron, the priest, has turned my anger away from the **25:10-13**
Israelites; for he was as zealous as I am for my honor among them, so that
in my zeal I did not put an end to them. Therefore tell him I am making
my covenant of peace with him. He and his descendants will have a
covenant of a lasting priesthood, because he was zealous for the honor of
his God and made atonement for the Israelites."

NAMES OF DEAD COUPLE.   The name of the Israelite who was killed **Num.**
with the Midianite woman was Zimri son of Salu, the leader of a **25:14,15**
Simeonite family. And the name of the Midianite woman who was put to
death was Cozbi daughter of Zur, a tribal chief of a Midianite family.

MIDIANITES TARGETED.   The LORD said to Moses, "Treat the Midian- **Num.**
ites as enemies and kill them, because they treated you as enemies when **25:16-18**
they deceived you in the affair of Peor and their sister Cozbi, the daughter
of a Midianite leader, the woman who was killed when the plague came
as a result of Peor."

Destruction of the Midianites

God is clearly incensed by the insidious moral attack brought against his
people by the Midianites, but he is also incensed by the Israelites
themselves. Because of their willful disobedience, and pursuant to his
promise, he sends a plague which claims 24,000 lives. Having dealt with the
Israelites, God then confronts the Midianites. That God should punish the
Midianites for their great wickedness is understandable, but the account of that
punishment is difficult for some to accept.

FORCES AGAINST MIDIANITES. The LORD said to Moses, "Take ven- **Num.**
geance on the Midianites for the Israelites. After that, you will be gathered **31:1-6**
to your people."

So Moses said to the people, "Arm some of your men to go to war against the Midianites and to carry out the LORD's vengeance on them. Send into battle a thousand men from each of the tribes of Israel." So twelve thousand men armed for battle, a thousand from each tribe, were supplied from the clans of Israel. Moses sent them into battle, a thousand from each tribe, along with Phinehas son of Eleazar, the priest, who took with him articles from the sanctuary and the trumpets for signaling.

Num. 31:7-12

VICTORY AND TOTAL CONQUEST.   They fought against Midian, as the LORD commanded Moses, and killed every man. Among their victims were Evi, Rekem, Zur, Hur and Reba—the five kings of Midian. They also killed Balaam son of Beor with the sword. The Israelites captured the Midianite women and children and took all the Midianite herds, flocks and goods as plunder. They burned all the towns where the Midianites had settled, as well as all their camps. They took all the plunder and spoils, including the people and animals, and brought the captives, spoils and plunder to Moses and Eleazar the priest and the Israelite assembly at their camp on the plains of Moab, by the Jordan across from Jericho.[o]

Num. 31:13-16

WOMEN SPARED.   Moses, Eleazar the priest and all the leaders of the community went to meet them outside the camp. Moses was angry with the officers of the army—the commanders of thousands and commanders of hundreds—who returned from the battle.

"Have you allowed all the women to live?" he asked them. "They were the ones who followed Balaam's advice and were the means of turning the Israelites away from the LORD in what happened at Peor, so that a plague struck the LORD's people.

Num. 31:17,18

WOMEN AND BOYS TO DIE.   Now kill all the boys. And kill every woman who has slept with a man, but save for yourselves every girl who has never slept with a man.

Num. 31:19-24

PURIFICATION INSTRUCTIONS.   "All of you who have killed anyone or touched anyone who was killed must stay outside the camp seven days. On the third and seventh days you must purify yourselves and your captives. Purify every garment as well as everything made of leather, goat hair or wood."

Then Eleazar the priest said to the soldiers who had gone into battle, "This is the requirement of the law that the LORD gave Moses: Gold, silver, bronze, iron, tin, lead and anything else that can withstand fire must be put through the fire, and then it will be clean. But it must also be purified with the water of cleansing. And whatever cannot withstand fire must be put through that water. On the seventh day wash your clothes and you will be clean. Then you may come into the camp."

Num. 31:25-54

DIVIDING THE SPOILS.   The LORD said to Moses, "You and Eleazar the priest and the family heads of the community are to count all the people and animals that were captured. Divide the spoils between the soldiers who took part in the battle and the rest of the community. From the soldiers who fought in the battle, set apart as tribute for the LORD one out of every five hundred, whether persons, cattle, donkeys, sheep or goats. Take this tribute from their half share and give it to Eleazar the priest as the LORD's part. From the Israelites' half, select one out of every fifty, whether persons, cattle, donkeys, sheep, goats or other animals. Give them to the

---

[o]Hebrew *Jordan of Jericho*; possibly an ancient name for the Jordan River

Levites, who are responsible for the care of the LORD's tabernacle." So Moses and Eleazar the priest did as the LORD commanded Moses.

The plunder remaining from the spoils that the soldiers took was 675,000 sheep, 72,000 cattle, 61,000 donkeys and 32,000 women who had never slept with a man.

The half share of those who fought in the battle was:

337,500 sheep, 37of which the tribute for the LORD was 675;
36,000 cattle, of which the tribute for the LORD was 72;
30,500 donkeys, of which the tribute for the LORD was 61;
16,000 people, of which the tribute for the LORD was 32.

Moses gave the tribute to Eleazar the priest as the LORD's part, as the LORD commanded Moses.

The half belonging to the Israelites, which Moses set apart from that of the fighting men—the community's half—was 337,500 sheep, 36,000 cattle, 30,500 donkeys and 16,000 people. From the Israelites' half, Moses selected one out of every fifty persons and animals, as the LORD commanded him, and gave them to the Levites, who were responsible for the care of the LORD's tabernacle.

Then the officers who were over the units of the army—the commanders of thousands and commanders of hundreds—went to Moses and said to him, "Your servants have counted the soldiers under our command, and not one is missing. So we have brought as an offering to the LORD the gold articles each of us acquired—armlets, bracelets, signet rings, earrings and necklaces—to make atonement for ourselves before the LORD."

Moses and Eleazar the priest accepted from them the gold—all the crafted articles. All the gold from the commanders of thousands and commanders of hundreds that Moses and Eleazar presented as a gift to the LORD weighed 16,750 shekels. Each soldier had taken plunder for himself. Moses and Eleazar the priest accepted the gold from the commanders of thousands and commanders of hundreds and brought it into the Tent of Meeting as a memorial for the Israelites before the LORD.

One might like to believe that the orders to kill were those of Moses acting on his own, but there is every reason to believe that Moses acted at God's direction. The question then arises: how can a loving God either direct or condone such action? The answer is undoubtedly very complex. As for the women, it was they who turned the Israelites away from the Lord at Peor. As for the young boys, perhaps they would have presented a continuing threat to Israel as they grew into manhood. (Such a threat will indeed be confirmed some years later when Midianites from other areas engage in war against Israel.) The young girls, on the other hand, were to be taken as slaves into the homes of the Israelites, where they would at least be spared inevitable spiritual enslavement of the sensuous worship of Baal-Peor. (There is no suggestion that Moses meant for the Israelites to take them as wives or concubines.)

But even these possible explanations are not easy to accept. In order to appreciate more fully God's actions, it is necessary to understand the level of moral consciousness of the times. Among the nations of this era, wars of revenge involving total destruction or confiscation of property, and either extermination or enslavement of men, women, and children, are commonplace and expected. (That is doubtless why there is no hint that the Israelites felt the slightest discomfort in carrying out Moses' orders.) In raising the moral consciousness of first a nation, and then the world, God must take his people as he finds them and introduce principles of righteousness within a moral framework with which the people can identify.

The fact that the women and children were saved from death initially may indicate that an exception was made to the customary practices of such a war of revenge. If so, the reason for the exception becomes important. Quite possibly the men of Israel were still enticed by the Midianite women and did not understand the continuing moral threat which the women posed. Viewed in that light, Moses' action takes on greatly increased respectability.

It also appears that God is teaching a vitally important lesson about the attitude which his people must have regarding the various human lusts which war against the soul. Even the weakest of lusts (perhaps represented here by the women and young boys) must be resisted as completely and early as possible in order to prevent their success in moments of moral vulnerability.

The account of the Midianites' destruction concludes with various directions concerning the booty which was taken in the conquest. And even from this part of the account profitable lessons can be learned—particularly about the rewards accruing to those who wage war against sin.

Israel's Second Numbering

Twenty-four thousand Israelites have recently died of the plague, and others have undoubtedly been killed in the conquest of Moab. Natural death has also taken its toll over the last 40 years. Therefore, in anticipation of conquering the land of Canaan, it is once again a good time for Israel to determine its military strength by taking a census. It will be learned that since the last census there are approximately 1,800 fewer men above the age of 20 (601,730), but an increase of some 700 Levites (23,000) to perform the religious service. Five of the tribes have fewer men than in the first census, while seven tribes have increased in number.

The census will also provide the basis for dividing the land of Canaan once it is occupied by the Israelites.

Num.
26:1-4
Moab

CENSUS COMMANDED. After the plague the LORD said to Moses and Eleazar son of Aaron, the priest, "Take a census of the whole Israelite community by families—all those twenty years old or more who are able to serve in the army of Israel." So on the plains of Moab by the Jordan across from Jericho,[p] Moses and Eleazar the priest spoke with them and said, "Take a census of the men twenty years old or more, as the LORD commanded Moses."

These were the Israelites who came out of Egypt:

Num.
26:5-11

REUBEN'S TRIBE FEWER. The descendants of Reuben, the firstborn son of Israel, were:
through Hanoch, the Hanochite clan;

[p]Hebrew *Jordan of Jericho*; possibly an ancient name for the Jordan River

through Pallu, the Palluite clan;
through Hezron, the Hezronite clan;
through Carmi, the Carmite clan.
These were the clans of Reuben; those numbered were 43,730.

The son of Pallu was Eliab, and the sons of Eliab were Nemuel, Dathan and Abiram. The same Dathan and Abiram were the community officials who rebelled against Moses and Aaron and were among Korah's followers when they rebelled against the LORD. The earth opened its mouth and swallowed them along with Korah, whose followers died when the fire devoured the 250 men. And they served as a warning sign. The line of Korah, however, did not die out.

SIMEON'S TRIBE FEWER. The descendants of Simeon by their clans were:
through Nemuel, the Nemuelite clan;
through Jamin, the Jaminite clan;
through Jakin, the Jakinite clan;
through Zerah, the Zerahite clan;
through Shaul, the Shaulite clan.
These were the clans of Simeon; there were 22,200 men.

Num.
26:12-14

GAD'S TRIBE FEWER. The descendants of Gad by their clans were:
through Zephon, the Zephonite clan;
through Haggi, the Haggite clan;
through Shuni, the Shunite clan;
through Ozni, the Oznite clan;
through Eri, the Erite clan;
through Arodi,[q] the Arodite clan;
through Areli, the Arelite clan.
These were the clans of Gad; those numbered were 40,500.

Num.
26:15-18

JUDAH'S TRIBE GREATER. Er and Onan were sons of Judah, but they died in Canaan.
The descendants of Judah by their clans were:
through Shelah, the Shelanite clan;
through Perez, the Perezite clan;
through Zerah, the Zerahite clan.
The descendants of Perez were:
through Hezron, the Hezronite clan;
through Hamul, the Hamulite clan.
These were the clans of Judah; those numbered were 76,500.

Num.
26:19-22

ISAACHAR'S TRIBE GREATER. The descendants of Issachar by their clans were:
through Tola, the Tolaite clan;
through Puah, the Puite[r] clan;
through Jashub, the Jashubite clan;
through Shimron, the Shimronite clan.
These were the clans of Issachar; those numbered were 64,300.

Num.
26:23-25

ZEBULUN'S TRIBE GREATER. The descendants of Zebulun by their clans were:

Num.
26:26,27

[q]Samaritan Pentateuch and Syriac (see also Gen. 46:16); Masoretic Text *Arod*
[r]Samaritan Pentateuch, Septuagint, Vulgate and Syriac (see also 1 Chron. 7:1); Masoretic Text *through Puvah, the Punite*

through Sered, the Seredite clan;
through Elon, the Elonite clan;
through Jahleel, the Jahleelite clan.
These were the clans of Zebulun; those numbered were 60,500.

Num.
26:28-34

MANASSEH'S TRIBE GREATER.   The descendants of Joseph by their clans through Manasseh and Ephraim were:

The descendants of Manasseh:
through Makir, the Makirite clan (Makir was the father of Gilead);
through Gilead, the Gileadite clan.
These were the descendants of Gilead:
through Iezer, the Iezerite clan;
through Helek, the Helekite clan;
through Asriel, the Asrielite clan;
through Shechem, the Shechemite clan;
through Shemida, the Shemidaite clan;
through Hepher, the Hepherite clan.
(Zelophehad son of Hepher had no sons; he had only daughters, whose names were Mahlah, Noah, Hoglah, Milcah and Tirzah.)
These were the clans of Manasseh; those numbered were 52,700.

Num.
26:35-37

EPHRAIM'S TRIBE FEWER.   These were the descendants of Ephraim by their clans:
through Shuthelah, the Shuthelahite clan;
through Beker, the Bekerite clan;
through Tahan, the Tahanite clan.
These were the descendants of Shuthelah:
through Eran, the Eranite clan.
These were the clans of Ephraim; those numbered were 32,500.

These were the descendants of Joseph by their clans.

Num.
26:38-41

BENJAMIN'S TRIBE GREATER.   The descendants of Benjamin by their clans were:
through Bela, the Belaite clan;
through Ashbel, the Ashbelite clan;
through Ahiram, the Ahiramite clan;
through Shupham,[s] the Shuphamite clan;
through Hupham, the Huphamite clan.
The descendants of Bela through Ard and Naaman were:
through Ard,[t] the Ardite clan;
through Naaman, the Naamite clan.
These were the clans of Benjamin; those numbered were 45,600.

Num.
26:42,43

DAN'S TRIBE GREATER.   These were the descendants of Dan by their clans:
through Shuham, the Shuhamite clan.
These were the clans of Dan: All of them were Shuhamite clans; and those numbered were 64,400.

---

[s]A few manuscripts of the Masoretic Text, Samaritan Pentateuch, Vulgate and Syriac (see also Septuagint); most manuscripts of the Masoretic Text *Shephupham*   [t]Samaritan Pentateuch and Vulgate (see also Septuagint); Masoretic Text does not have *through Ard*.

ASHER'S TRIBE GREATER.   The descendants of Asher by their clans
were:

> through Imnah, the Imnite clan;
> through Ishvi, the Ishvite clan;
> through Beriah, the Beriite clan;
> and through the descendants of Beriah:
>> through Heber, the Heberite clan;
>> through Malkiel, the Malkielite clan.
>
> (Asher had a daughter named Serah.)

These were the clans of Asher; those numbered were 53,400.

Num.
26:44-47

NAPHTALI'S TRIBE FEWER.   The descendants of Naphtali by their clans
were:

> through Jahzeel, the Jahzeelite clan;
> through Guni, the Gunite clan;
> through Jezer, the Jezerite clan;
> through Shillem, the Shillemite clan.

These were the clans of Naphtali; those numbered were 45,400.

Num.
26:48-50

TOTAL FIGHTING FORCE.   The total number of the men of Israel was
601,730.

Num.
26:51

DIVISION OF LAND.   The LORD said to Moses, "The land is to be allotted
to them as an inheritance based on the number of names. To a larger group
give a larger inheritance, and to a smaller group a smaller one; each is to
receive its inheritance according to the number of those listed. Be sure that
the land is distributed by lot. What each group inherits will be according
to the names for its ancestral tribe. Each inheritance is to be distributed by
lot among the larger and smaller groups."

Num.
26:52-56

LEVITES NUMBERED SEPARATELY.   These were the Levites who were
counted by their clans:

> through Gershon, the Gershonite clan;
> through Kohath, the Kohathite clan;
> through Merari, the Merarite clan.
> These also were Levite clans:
> the Libnite clan,
> the Hebronite clan,
> the Mahlite clan,
> the Mushite clan,
> the Korahite clan.

(Kohath was the forefather of Amram; the name of Amram's wife was
Jochebed, a descendant of Levi, who was born to the Levites[u] in Egypt. To
Amram she bore Aaron, Moses and their sister Miriam. Aaron was the
father of Nadab and Abihu, Eleazar and Ithamar. But Nadab and Abihu
died when they made an offering before the LORD with unauthorized fire.)

All the male Levites a month old or more numbered 23,000. They were not
counted along with the other Israelites because they received no inheritance among them.

Num.
26:57-62

[u]Or *Jochebed, a daughter of Levi, who was born to Levi*

Num.
26:63-65

ORIGINAL DISBELIEVERS DEAD. These are the ones counted by Moses and Eleazar the priest when they counted the Israelites on the plains of Moab by the Jordan across from Jericho. Not one of them was among those counted by Moses and Aaron the priest when they counted the Israelites in the Desert of Sinai. For the LORD had told those Israelites they would surely die in the desert, and not one of them was left except Caleb son of Jephunneh and Joshua son of Nun.

Joshua Named As Successor

God has already told Moses that because of his earlier sin he will not be able to enter the promised land. Aware that his death is imminent, Moses is quite naturally concerned about the future leadership of Israel and asks for God's guidance in the selection of his replacement. It must be gratifying for Moses to learn that God has chosen Joshua, who has been Moses' faithful protégé, for over 40 years. The investiture of Joshua will take place before the people of Israel and in the presence of Eleazar the Priest.

Num.
27:15-17

MOSES ASKS FOR SUCCESSOR. Moses said to the LORD, "May the LORD, the God of the spirits of all mankind, appoint a man over this community to go out and come in before them, one who will lead them out and bring them in, so the LORD's people will not be like sheep without a shepherd."

Num.
27:18-21

JOSHUA NAMED FUTURE LEADER. So the LORD said to Moses, "Take Joshua son of Nun, a man in whom is the spirit,^{v} and lay your hand on him. Have him stand before Eleazar the priest and the entire assembly and commission him in their presence. Give him some of your authority so the whole Israelite community will obey him. He is to stand before Eleazar the priest, who will obtain decisions for him by inquiring of the Urim before the LORD. At his command he and the entire community of the Israelites will go out, and at his command they will come in."

Num.
27:22,23

JOSHUA INVESTED. Moses did as the LORD commanded him. He took Joshua and had him stand before Eleazar the priest and the whole assembly. Then he laid his hands on him and commissioned him, as the LORD instructed through Moses.

Two-and-a-Half Tribes East of Jordan

While preparations are being made for the invasion of Canaan, Moses is approached by the men of Gad and Reuben, who have decided that they prefer to settle east of the Jordan River, an area which they believe will afford especially good pasturage for their many cattle. Moses is at first skeptical, thinking that perhaps the men are making the request in order to avoid fighting for Canaan. When assured that the men will help conquer the promised land, Moses agrees to their request. Apparently half of the tribe of Manasseh also likes the plan and is permitted to settle on the east bank along with the other two tribes. Anticipating the need for cities of refuge, as detailed

^{v}Or *Spirit*

more fully under Israel's criminal statutes, Moses designates a city of refuge for each of the eastern tribes.

REUBEN AND GAD SEEK LAND.   The Reubenites and Gadites, who had very large herds and flocks, saw that the lands of Jazer and Gilead were suitable for livestock. So they came to Moses and Eleazar the priest and to the leaders of the community, and said, "Ataroth, Dibon, Jazer, Nimrah, Heshbon, Elealeh, Sebam, Nebo and Beon—the land the LORD subdued before the people of Israel—are suitable for livestock, and your servants have livestock. If we have found favor in your eyes," they said, "let this land be given to your servants as our possession. Do not make us cross the Jordan."

Num. 32:1-5

MOSES FEARS COWARDICE.   Moses said to the Gadites and Reubenites, "Shall your countrymen go to war while you sit here? Why do you discourage the Israelites from going over into the land the LORD has given them? This is what your fathers did when I sent them from Kadesh Barnea to look over the land. After they went up to the Valley of Eshcol and viewed the land, they discouraged the Israelites from entering the land the LORD had given them. The LORD's anger was aroused that day and he swore this oath: 'Because they have not followed me wholeheartedly, not one of the men twenty years old or more who came up out of Egypt will see the land I promised on oath to Abraham, Isaac and Jacob—not one except Caleb son of Jephunneh the Kenizzite and Joshua son of Nun, for they followed the LORD wholeheartedly.' The LORD's anger burned against Israel and he made them wander in the desert forty years, until the whole generation of those who had done evil in his sight was gone.

Num. 32:6-15

"And here you are, a brood of sinners, standing in the place of your fathers and making the LORD even more angry with Israel. If you turn away from following him, he will again leave all this people in the desert, and you will be the cause of their destruction."

OFFER TO AID FIGHT.   Then they came up to him and said, "We would like to build pens here for our livestock and cities for our women and children. But we are ready to arm ourselves and go ahead of the Israelites until we have brought them to their place. Meanwhile our women and children will live in fortified cities, for protection from the inhabitants of the land. We will not return to our homes until every Israelite has received his inheritance. We will not receive any inheritance with them on the other side of the Jordan, because our inheritance has come to us on the east side of the Jordan."

Num. 32:16-19

MOSES ACCEPTS OFFER.   Then Moses said to them, "If you will do this—if you will arm yourselves before the LORD for battle, and if all of you will go armed over the Jordan before the LORD until he has driven his enemies out before him—then when the land is subdued before the LORD, you may return and be free from your obligation to the LORD and to Israel. And this land will be your possession before the LORD.

Num. 32:20-27

"But if you fail to do this, you will be sinning against the LORD; and you may be sure that your sin will find you out. Build cities for your women and children, and pens for your flocks, but do what you have promised."

The Gadites and Reubenites said to Moses, "We your servants will do as our lord commands. Our children and wives, our flocks and herds will remain here in the cities of Gilead. But your servants, every man armed for battle, will cross over to fight before the LORD, just as our lord says."

Num.
32:28-32

AGREEMENT ANNOUNCED.   Then Moses gave orders about them to Eleazar the priest and Joshua son of Nun and to the family heads of the Israelite tribes. He said to them, "If the Gadites and Reubenites, every man armed for battle, cross over the Jordan with you before the LORD, then when the land is subdued before you, give them the land of Gilead as their possession. But if they do not cross over with you armed, they must accept their possession with you in Canaan."

The Gadites and Reubenites answered, "Your servants will do what the LORD has said. We will cross over before the LORD into Canaan armed, but the property we inherit will be on this side of the Jordan."

Num.
32:33-42

MANASSEH ALSO IN GILEAD.   Then Moses gave to the Gadites, the Reubenites and the half-tribe of Manasseh son of Joseph the kingdom of Sihon king of the Amorites and the kingdom of Og king of Bashan—the whole land with its cities and the territory around them.

The Gadites built up Dibon, Ataroth, Aroer, Atroth Shophan, Jazer, Jogbehah, Beth Nimrah and Beth Haran as fortified cities, and built pens for their flocks. And the Reubenites rebuilt Heshbon, Elealeh and Kiriathaim, as well as Nebo and Baal Meon (these names were changed) and Sibmah. They gave names to the cities they rebuilt.

The descendants of Makir son of Manasseh went to Gilead, captured it and drove out the Amorites who were there. So Moses gave Gilead to the Makirites, the descendants of Manasseh, and they settled there. Jair, descendant of Manasseh, captured their settlements and called them Havvoth Jair.[w] And Nobah captured Kenath and its surrounding settlements and called it Nobah after himself.

Deut.
4:41-43

CITIES OF REFUGE.   Then Moses set aside three cities east of the Jordan, to which anyone who had killed a person could flee if he had unintentionally killed his neighbor without malice aforethought. He could flee into one of these cities and save his life. The cities were these: Bezer in the desert plateau, for the Reubenites; Ramoth in Gilead, for the Gadites; and Golan in Bashan, for the Manassites.

*Preparations for Conquest and Settlement*_____

*L*est the Israelites forget the lesson which God had to teach them through the horrible destruction of the Midianites, God warns them in advance that when they enter Canaan they must drive out all of its inhabitants and completely destroy the idolatry rampant in the land. (Almost needless to say in light of their past experience, the Israelites will not wholly comply with God's directive and will therefore fall repeatedly into religious apostasy.)

The land which God has for centuries promised to give to his people is the land of Canaan, the borders of which God carefully delineates. From the Mediterranean Sea on the west, the land will stretch eastward across the plains and over the mountains to a line running north and south from the eastern shore of the Sea of Galilee, down the Jordan River to the Dead Sea.

_____

wOr them the settlements of Jair

The northernmost border will be in the upper Galilee region, near a mountain called Hor, which should not be confused with the Mount Hor upon which Aaron died. (Ironically, that Mount Hor is near what is to be the southern border of Canaan, down near Kadesh-barnea in the northern Sinai Peninsula, south of the Dead Sea and east of Edom.)

TOTAL CONQUEST ORDERED.   On the plains of Moab by the Jordan across from Jericho the LORD said to Moses, "Speak to the Israelites and say to them: 'When you cross the Jordan into Canaan, drive out all the inhabitants of the land before you. Destroy all their carved images and their cast idols, and demolish all their high places. Take possession of the land and settle in it, for I have given you the land to possess. Distribute the land by lot, according to your clans. To a larger group give a larger inheritance, and to a smaller group a smaller one. Whatever falls to them by lot will be theirs. Distribute it according to your ancestral tribes.

   " 'But if you do not drive out the inhabitants of the land, those you allow to remain will become barbs in your eyes and thorns in your sides. They will give you trouble in the land where you will live. And then I will do to you what I plan to do to them.' "

*Num.
33:50-56*

AMALEKITES TO BE DESTROYED.   Remember what the Amalekites did to you along the way when you came out of Egypt. When you were weary and worn out, they met you on your journey and cut off all who were lagging behind; they had no fear of God. When the LORD your God gives you rest from all the enemies around you in the land he is giving you to possess as an inheritance, you shall blot out the memory of Amalek from under heaven. Do not forget!

*Deut.
25:17-19*

SOUTHERN BOUNDARIES.   The LORD said to Moses, "Command the Israelites and say to them: 'When you enter Canaan, the land that will be allotted to you as an inheritance will have these boundaries:

   " 'Your southern side will include some of the Desert of Zin along the border of Edom. On the east, your southern boundary will start from the end of the Salt Sea,ˣ cross south of Scorpionʸ Pass, continue on to Zin and go south of Kadesh Barnea. Then it will go to Hazar Addar and over to Azmon, where it will turn, join the Wadi of Egypt and end at the Sea.ᶻ

*Num.
34:1-5*

WESTERN BOUNDARY.   " 'Your western boundary will be the coast of the Great Sea. This will be your boundary on the west.

Num. 34:6

NORTHERN BOUNDARIES.   " 'For your northern boundary, run a line from the Great Sea to Mount Hor and from Mount Hor to Leboᵃ Hamath. Then the boundary will go to Zedad, continue to Ziphron and end at Hazar Enan. This will be your boundary on the north.

*Num.
34:7-9*

EASTERN BOUNDARIES.   " 'For your eastern boundary, run a line from Hazar Enan to Shepham. The boundary will go down from Shepham to Riblah on the east side of Ain and continue along the slopes east of the Sea of Kinnereth.ᵇ Then the boundary will go down along the Jordan and end at the Salt Sea.

   " 'This will be your land, with its boundaries on every side.' "

*Num.
34:10-12*

ˣThat is, the Dead Sea   ʸHebrew *Akrabbim*   ᶻThat is, the Mediterranean   ᵃOr *to
the entrance to*   ᵇThat is, Galilee

Num.
34:13-15

CANAAN FOR REMAINING TRIBES. Moses commanded the Israelites: "Assign this land by lot as an inheritance. The LORD has ordered that it be given to the nine and a half tribes, because the families of the tribe of Reuben, the tribe of Gad and the half-tribe of Manasseh have received their inheritance. These two and a half tribes have received their inheritance on the east side of the Jordan of Jericho,[c] toward the sunrise."

Num.
34:16-29

MEN TO DIVIDE THE LAND. The LORD said to Moses, "These are the names of the men who are to assign the land for you as an inheritance: Eleazar the priest and Joshua son of Nun. And appoint one leader from each tribe to help assign the land. These are their names:

> Caleb son of Jephunneh,
>   from the tribe of Judah;
> Shemuel son of Ammihud,
>   from the tribe of Simeon;
> Elidad son of Kislon,
>   from the tribe of Benjamin;
> Bukki son of Jogli,
>   the leader from the tribe of Dan;
> Hanniel son of Ephod,
>   the leader from the tribe of Manasseh son of Joseph;
> Kemuel son of Shiphtan,
>   the leader from the tribe of Ephraim son of Joseph;
> Elizaphan son of Parnach,
>   the leader from the tribe of Zebulun;
> Paltiel son of Azzan,
>   the leader from the tribe of Issachar;
> Ahihud son of Shelomi,
>   the leader from the tribe of Asher;
> Pedahel son of Ammihud,
>   the leader from the tribe of Naphtali."

These are the men the LORD commanded to assign the inheritance to the Israelites in the land of Canaan.

Num.
35:1-8

CITIES FOR THE LEVITES. On the plains of Moab by the Jordan across from Jericho,[d] the LORD said to Moses, "Command the Israelites to give the Levites towns to live in from the inheritance the Israelites will possess. And give them pasturelands around the towns. Then they will have towns to live in and pasturelands for their cattle, flocks and all their other livestock.

"The pasturelands around the towns that you give the Levites will extend out fifteen hundred feet[e] from the town wall. Outside the town, measure three thousand feet[f] on the east side, three thousand on the south side, three thousand on the west and three thousand on the north, with the town in the center. They will have this area as pastureland for the towns.

"Six of the towns you give the Levites will be cities of refuge, to which a person who has killed someone may flee. In addition, give them forty-two other towns. In all you must give the Levites forty-eight towns,

---

[c]*Jordan of Jericho* was possibly an ancient name for the Jordan River.   [d]Hebrew *Jordan of Jericho*; possibly an ancient name for the Jordan River   [e]Hebrew *a thousand cubits* (about 450 meters)   [f]Hebrew *two thousand cubits* (about 900 meters)

together with their pasturelands. The towns you give the Levites from the land the Israelites possess are to be given in proportion to the inheritance of each tribe: Take many towns from a tribe that has many, but few from one that has few."

Moses Reviews History and Purpose

*P*reparations now nearly completed, and aware that his own life is very near an end, Moses addresses his people as would an aging head of state before transfer of leadership. Moses feels keenly the responsibility for orienting a new generation to the history of their young nation, its unique relationship to God, and their purpose in the conquest which will begin shortly—in fact, just over a month from this very week in which Moses himself will die.

In this first of two final addresses, Moses will include some surprising and interesting details not included in any previous accounts. Especially touching are Moses' personal feelings about some of the incidents which have occurred, and repeated references to his own sin which keeps him from entering into the promised land personally.

FIRST ADDRESS.   These are the words Moses spoke to all Israel in the desert east of the Jordan—that is, in the Arabah—opposite Suph, between Paran and Tophel, Laban, Hazeroth and Dizahab. (It takes eleven days to go from Horeb to Kadesh Barnea by the Mount Seir road.) **Deut. 1:1-4**

In the fortieth year, on the first day of the eleventh month, Moses proclaimed to the Israelites all that the LORD had commanded him concerning them. This was after he had defeated Sihon king of the Amorites, who reigned in Heshbon, and at Edrei had defeated Og king of Bashan, who reigned in Ashtaroth.

BEGINNING FROM SINAI.   East of the Jordan in the territory of Moab, Moses began to expound this law, saying: **Deut. 1:5-8**

The LORD our God said to us at Horeb, "You have stayed long enough at this mountain. Break camp and advance into the hill country of the Amorites; go to all the neighboring peoples in the Arabah, in the mountains, in the western foothills, in the Negev and along the coast, to the land of the Canaanites and to Lebanon, as far as the great river, the Euphrates. See, I have given you this land. Go in and take possession of the land that the LORD swore he would give to your fathers—to Abraham, Isaac and Jacob—and to their descendants after them."

EARLY ADMINISTRATION.   At that time I said to you, "You are too heavy a burden for me to carry alone. The LORD your God has increased your numbers so that today you are as many as the stars in the sky. May the LORD, the God of your fathers, increase you a thousand times and bless you as he has promised! But how can I bear your problems and your burdens and your disputes all by myself? Choose some wise, understanding and respected men from each of your tribes, and I will set them over you." **Deut. 1:9-18**

You answered me, "What you propose to do is good."

So I took the leading men of your tribes, wise and respected men, and appointed them to have authority over you—as commanders of thousands, of hundreds, of fifties and of tens and as tribal officials. And I charged your judges at that time: Hear the disputes between your brothers and judge fairly, whether the case is between brother Israelites or between one of them and an alien. Do not show partiality in judging; hear both small and great alike. Do not be afraid of any man, for judgment belongs to God. Bring me any case too hard for you, and I will hear it. And at that time I told you everything you were to do.

**Deut.
1:19-25**

SENDING OF THE SPIES.   Then, as the LORD our God commanded us, we set out from Horeb and went toward the hill country of the Amorites through all that vast and dreadful desert that you have seen, and so we reached Kadesh Barnea. Then I said to you, "You have reached the hill country of the Amorites, which the LORD our God is giving us. See, the LORD your God has given you the land. Go up and take possession of it as the LORD, the God of your fathers, told you. Do not be afraid; do not be discouraged."

Then all of you came to me and said, "Let us send men ahead to spy out the land for us and bring back a report about the route we are to take and the towns we will come to."

The idea seemed good to me; so I selected twelve of you, one man from each tribe. They left and went up into the hill country, and came to the Valley of Eshcol and explored it. Taking with them some of the fruit of the land, they brought it down to us and reported, "It is a good land that the LORD our God is giving us."

**Deut.
1:26-33**

COWARDICE IN FACE OF REPORT.   But you were unwilling to go up; you rebelled against the command of the LORD your God. You grumbled in your tents and said, "The LORD hates us; so he brought us out of Egypt to deliver us into the hands of the Amorites to destroy us. Where can we go? Our brothers have made us lose heart. They say, 'The people are stronger and taller than we are; the cities are large, with walls up to the sky. We even saw the Anakites there.'"

Then I said to you, "Do not be terrified; do not be afraid of them. The LORD your God, who is going before you, will fight for you, as he did for you in Egypt, before your very eyes, and in the desert. There you saw how the LORD your God carried you, as a father carries his son, all the way you went until you reached this place."

In spite of this, you did not trust in the LORD your God, who went ahead of you on your journey, in fire by night and in a cloud by day, to search out places for you to camp and to show you the way you should go.

**Deut.
1:34-40**

PENALTY FOR COWARDICE.   When the LORD heard what you said, he was angry and solemnly swore: "Not a man of this evil generation shall see the good land I swore to give your forefathers, except Caleb son of Jephunneh. He will see it, and I will give him and his descendants the land he set his feet on, because he followed the LORD wholeheartedly."

Because of you the LORD became angry with me also and said, "You shall not enter it, either. But your assistant, Joshua son of Nun, will enter it. Encourage him, because he will lead Israel to inherit it. And the little ones that you said would be taken captive, your children who do not yet know good from bad—they will enter the land. I will give it to them and they will take possession of it. But as for you, turn around and set out toward the desert along the route to the Red Sea.8"

UNSUCCESSFUL INVASION.   Then you replied, "We have sinned against the LORD. We will go up and fight, as the LORD our God commanded us." So every one of you put on his weapons, thinking it easy to go up into the hill country.

Deut.
1:41-46

But the LORD said to me, "Tell them, 'Do not go up and fight, because I will not be with you. You will be defeated by your enemies.'"

So I told you, but you would not listen. You rebelled against the LORD's command and in your arrogance you marched up into the hill country. The Amorites who lived in those hills came out against you; they chased you like a swarm of bees and beat you down from Seir all the way to Hormah. You came back and wept before the LORD, but he paid no attention to your weeping and turned a deaf ear to you. And so you stayed in Kadesh many days—all the time you spent there.

EDOMITES LEFT ALONE.   Then we turned back and set out toward the desert along the route to the Red Sea,8 as the LORD had directed me. For a long time we made our way around the hill country of Seir.

Deut.
2:1-8a

Then the LORD said to me, "You have made your way around this hill country long enough; now turn north. Give the people these orders: 'You are about to pass through the territory of your brothers the descendants of Esau, who live in Seir. They will be afraid of you, but be very careful. Do not provoke them to war, for I will not give you any of their land, not even enough to put your foot on. I have given Esau the hill country of Seir as his own. You are to pay them in silver for the food you eat and the water you drink.'"

The LORD your God has blessed you in all the work of your hands. He has watched over your journey through this vast desert. These forty years the LORD your God has been with you, and you have not lacked anything.

So we went on past our brothers the descendants of Esau, who live in Seir.

WAITING FOR DOUBTERS' DEATHS.   We turned from the Arabah road, which comes up from Elath and Ezion Geber, and traveled along the desert road of Moab.

Deut.
2:8b-15

Then the LORD said to me, "Do not harass the Moabites or provoke them to war, for I will not give you any part of their land. I have given Ar to the descendants of Lot as a possession."

(The Emites used to live there—a people strong and numerous, and as tall as the Anakites. Like the Anakites, they too were considered Rephaites, but the Moabites called them Emites. Horites used to live in Seir, but the descendants of Esau drove them out. They destroyed the Horites from before them and settled in their place, just as Israel did in the land the LORD gave them as their possession.)

And the LORD said, "Now get up and cross the Zered Valley." So we crossed the valley.

Thirty-eight years passed from the time we left Kadesh Barnea until we crossed the Zered Valley. By then, that entire generation of fighting men had perished from the camp, as the LORD had sworn to them. The LORD's

8Hebrew *Yam Suph*; that is, Sea of Reeds

hand was against them until he had completely eliminated them from the camp.

Deut.
2:16-25

AMMONITES LEFT ALONE.   Now when the last of these fighting men among the people had died, the LORD said to me, "Today you are to pass by the region of Moab at Ar. When you come to the Ammonites, do not harass them or provoke them to war, for I will not give you possession of any land belonging to the Ammonites. I have given it as a possession to the descendants of Lot."

(That too was considered a land of the Rephaites, who used to live there; but the Ammonites called them Zamzummites. They were a people strong and numerous, and as tall as the Anakites. The LORD destroyed them from before the Ammonites, who drove them out and settled in their place. The LORD had done the same for the descendants of Esau, who lived in Seir, when he destroyed the Horites from before them. They drove them out and have lived in their place to this day. And as for the Avvites who lived in villages as far as Gaza, the Caphtorites coming out from Caphtor[h] destroyed them and settled in their place.)

"Set out now and cross the Arnon Gorge. See, I have given into your hand Sihon the Amorite, king of Heshbon, and his country. Begin to take possession of it and engage him in battle. This very day I will begin to put the terror and fear of you on all the nations under heaven. They will hear reports of you and will tremble and be in anguish because of you."

Deut.
2:26-37

DEFEAT OF AMORITES.   From the desert of Kedemoth I sent messengers to Sihon king of Heshbon offering peace and saying, "Let us pass through your country. We will stay on the main road; we will not turn aside to the right or to the left. Sell us food to eat and water to drink for their price in silver. Only let us pass through on foot—as the descendants of Esau, who live in Seir, and the Moabites, who live in Ar, did for us— until we cross the Jordan into the land the LORD our God is giving us." But Sihon king of Heshbon refused to let us pass through. For the LORD your God had made his spirit stubborn and his heart obstinate in order to give him into your hands, as he has now done.

The LORD said to me, "See, I have begun to deliver Sihon and his country over to you. Now begin to conquer and possess his land."

When Sihon and all his army came out to meet us in battle at Jahaz, the LORD our God delivered him over to us and we struck him down, together with his sons and his whole army. At that time we took all his towns and completely destroyed[i] them—men, women and children. We left no survivors. But the livestock and the plunder from the towns we had captured we carried off for ourselves. From Aroer on the rim of the Arnon Gorge, and from the town in the gorge, even as far as Gilead, not one town was too strong for us. The LORD our God gave us all of them. But in accordance with the command of the LORD our God, you did not encroach on any of the land of the Ammonites, neither the land along the course of the Jabbok nor that around the towns in the hills.

Deut.
3:1-11

DEFEAT OF BASHONITES.   Next we turned and went up along the road toward Bashan, and Og king of Bashan with his whole army marched out to meet us in battle at Edrei. The LORD said to me, "Do not be afraid of him,

[h]That is, Crete   [i]The Hebrew term refers to the irrevocable giving over of things or persons to the LORD, often by totally destroying them.

for I have handed him over to you with his whole army and his land. Do to him what you did to Sihon king of the Amorites, who reigned in Heshbon."

So the LORD our God also gave into our hands Og king of Bashan and all his army. We struck them down, leaving no survivors. At that time we took all his cities. There was not one of the sixty cities that we did not take from them—the whole region of Argob, Og's kingdom in Bashan. All these cities were fortified with high walls and with gates and bars, and there were also a great many unwalled villages. We completely destroyed*j* them, as we had done with Sihon king of Heshbon, destroying*j* every city—men, women and children. But all the livestock and the plunder from their cities we carried off for ourselves.

So at that time we took from these two kings of the Amorites the territory east of the Jordan, from the Arnon Gorge as far as Mount Hermon. (Hermon is called Sirion by the Sidonians; the Amorites call it Senir.) We took all the towns on the plateau, and all Gilead, and all Bashan as far as Salecah and Edrei, towns of Og's kingdom in Bashan. (Only Og king of Bashan was left of the remnant of the Rephaites. His bed*k* was made of iron and was more than thirteen feet long and six feet wide.*l* It is still in Rabbah of the Ammonites.)

TRANS-JORDAN TRIBES.   Of the land that we took over at that time, I gave the Reubenites and the Gadites the territory north of Aroer by the Arnon Gorge, including half the hill country of Gilead, together with its towns. The rest of Gilead and also all of Bashan, the kingdom of Og, I gave to the half-tribe of Manasseh. (The whole region of Argob in Bashan used to be known as a land of the Rephaites. Jair, a descendant of Manasseh, took the whole region of Argob as far as the border of the Geshurites and the Maacathites; it was named after him, so that to this day Bashan is called Havvoth Jair.*m*) And I gave Gilead to Makir. But to the Reubenites and the Gadites I gave the territory extending from Gilead down to the Arnon Gorge (the middle of the gorge being the border) and out to the Jabbok River, which is the border of the Ammonites. Its western border was the Jordan in the Arabah, from Kinnereth to the Sea of the Arabah (the Salt Sea*n*), below the slopes of Pisgah.

Deut. 3:12-17

AGREEMENT FOR COOPERATION.   I commanded you at that time: "The LORD your God has given you this land to take possession of it. But all your able-bodied men, armed for battle, must cross over ahead of your brother Israelites. However, your wives, your children and your livestock (I know you have much livestock) may stay in the towns I have given you, until the LORD gives rest to your brothers as he has to you, and they too have taken over the land that the LORD your God is giving them, across the Jordan. After that, each of you may go back to the possession I have given you."

Deut. 3:18-22

At that time I commanded Joshua: "You have seen with your own eyes all that the LORD your God has done to these two kings. The LORD will do the same to all the kingdoms over there where you are going. Do not be afraid of them; the LORD your God himself will fight for you."

*j*The Hebrew term refers to the irrevocable giving over of things or persons to the LORD, often by totally destroying them.   *k*Or *sarcophagus*   *l*Hebrew *nine cubits long and four cubits wide* (about 4 meters long and 1.8 meters wide)   *m*Or *called the settlements of Jair*   *n*That is, the Dead Sea

Deut. 3:23-29	**WHY LEADERSHIP CHANGED.** At that time I pleaded with the LORD: "O Sovereign LORD, you have begun to show to your servant your greatness and your strong hand. For what god is there in heaven or on earth who can do the deeds and mighty works you do? Let me go over and see the good land beyond the Jordan—that fine hill country and Lebanon."

But because of you the LORD was angry with me and would not listen to me. "That is enough," the LORD said. "Do not speak to me anymore about this matter. Go up to the top of Pisgah and look west and north and south and east. Look at the land with your own eyes, since you are not going to cross this Jordan. But commission Joshua, and encourage and strengthen him, for he will lead this people across and will cause them to inherit the land that you will see." So we stayed in the valley near Beth Peor.

Deut. 4:1-8   **CALL TO OBEY LAWS.**   Hear now, O Israel, the decrees and laws I am about to teach you. Follow them so that you may live and may go in and take possession of the land that the LORD, the God of your fathers, is giving you. Do not add to what I command you and do not subtract from it, but keep the commands of the LORD your God that I give you.

You saw with your own eyes what the LORD did at Baal Peor. The LORD your God destroyed from among you everyone who followed the Baal of Peor, but all of you who held fast to the LORD your God are still alive today.

See, I have taught you decrees and laws as the LORD my God commanded me, so that you may follow them in the land you are entering to take possession of it. Observe them carefully, for this will show your wisdom and understanding to the nations, who will hear about all these decrees and say, "Surely this great nation is a wise and understanding people." What other nation is so great as to have their gods near them the way the LORD our God is near us whenever we pray to him? And what other nation is so great as to have such righteous decrees and laws as this body of laws I am setting before you today?

Deut.
4:9-14   **IMPORTANCE OF DIVINE SOURCE.**   Only be careful, and watch yourselves closely so that you do not forget the things your eyes have seen or let them slip from your heart as long as you live. Teach them to your children and to their children after them. Remember the day you stood before the LORD your God at Horeb, when he said to me, "Assemble the people before me to hear my words so that they may learn to revere me as long as they live in the land and may teach them to their children." You came near and stood at the foot of the mountain while it blazed with fire to the very heavens, with black clouds and deep darkness. Then the LORD spoke to you out of the fire. You heard the sound of words but saw no form; there was only a voice. He declared to you his covenant, the Ten Commandments, which he commanded you to follow and then wrote them on two stone tablets. And the LORD directed me at that time to teach you the decrees and laws you are to follow in the land that you are crossing the Jordan to possess.

Deut.
4:15-24   **IDOLATRY AS GREATEST EVIL.**   You saw no form of any kind the day the LORD spoke to you at Horeb out of the fire. Therefore watch yourselves very carefully, so that you do not become corrupt and make for yourselves an idol, an image of any shape, whether formed like a man or a woman, or like any animal on earth or any bird that flies in the air, or like any creature that moves along the ground or any fish in the waters below. And

when you look up to the sky and see the sun, the moon and the stars—all the heavenly array—do not be enticed into bowing down to them and worshiping things the LORD your God has apportioned to all the nations under heaven. But as for you, the LORD took you and brought you out of the iron-smelting furnace, out of Egypt, to be the people of his inheritance, as you now are.

The LORD was angry with me because of you, and he solemnly swore that I would not cross the Jordan and enter the good land the LORD your God is giving you as your inheritance. I will die in this land; I will not cross the Jordan; but you are about to cross over and take possession of that good land. Be careful not to forget the covenant of the LORD your God that he made with you; do not make for yourselves an idol in the form of anything the LORD your God has forbidden. For the LORD your God is a consuming fire, a jealous God.

IDOLATRY AS GREATEST THREAT.   After you have had children and grandchildren and have lived in the land a long time—if you then become corrupt and make any kind of idol, doing evil in the eyes of the LORD your God and provoking him to anger, I call heaven and earth as witnesses against you this day that you will quickly perish from the land that you are crossing the Jordan to possess. You will not live there long but will certainly be destroyed. The LORD will scatter you among the peoples, and only a few of you will survive among the nations to which the LORD will drive you. There you will worship man-made gods of wood and stone, which cannot see or hear or eat or smell. But if from there you seek the LORD your God, you will find him if you look for him with all your heart and with all your soul. When you are in distress and all these things have happened to you, then in later days you will return to the LORD your God and obey him. For the LORD your God is a merciful God; he will not abandon or destroy you or forget the covenant with your forefathers, which he confirmed to them by oath.

Deut. 4:25-31

HONOR AS CHOSEN NATION.   Ask now about the former days, long before your time, from the day God created man on the earth; ask from one end of the heavens to the other. Has anything so great as this ever happened, or has anything like it ever been heard of? Has any other people heard the voice of God[o] speaking out of fire, as you have, and lived? Has any god ever tried to take for himself one nation out of another nation, by testings, by miraculous signs and wonders, by war, by a mighty hand and an outstretched arm, or by great and awesome deeds, like all the things the LORD your God did for you in Egypt before your very eyes?

Deut. 4:32-40

You were shown these things so that you might know that the LORD is God; besides him there is no other. From heaven he made you hear his voice to discipline you. On earth he showed you his great fire, and you heard his words from out of the fire. Because he loved your forefathers and chose their descendants after them, he brought you out of Egypt by his Presence and his great strength, to drive out before you nations greater and stronger than you and to bring you into their land to give it to you for your inheritance, as it is today.

Acknowledge and take to heart this day that the LORD is God in heaven above and on the earth below. There is no other. Keep his decrees and

[o]Or of a god

commands, which I am giving you today, so that it may go well with you and your children after you and that you may live long in the land the LORD your God gives you for all time.

The Lawgiver Urges Obedience

*J*n his second address within a few days, Moses emphasizes even more forcefully the need for obedience to God's laws and statutes. Moses, the great lawgiver, stresses that, while he has been the spokesman through whom the laws have been delivered, it is God alone who has determined the laws and legislated the nation's statures. Moses reminds the people of the law's twofold purpose: to bring them into a proper relationship with God, and to regulate their conduct toward orderly and beneficial living. He is mindful of the need to promulgate the law in future generations and therefore entrusts the parents with the responsibility for teaching the laws to their children.

In an attempt to foster increased respect for God's laws, Moses recounts several examples of how the Israelites have suffered both indirect consequences and direct punishment when they have failed or refused to follow the law. Because many of the Israelites are too young to remember, Moses reminds the people that God's covenant is as much with them as with their parents. He also speaks to the older ones who personally witnessed or experienced the events to which he refers. In all, it is a forceful and sobering address from the man whose name, even until modern times, will be the name most often associated with law and lawkeeping.

Deut. 4:44-49 SECOND ADDRESS. This is the law Moses set before the Israelites. These are the stipulations, decrees and laws Moses gave them when they came out of Egypt and were in the valley near Beth Peor east of the Jordan, in the land of Sihon king of the Amorites, who reigned in Heshbon and was defeated by Moses and the Israelites as they came out of Egypt. They took possession of his land and the land of Og king of Bashan, the two Amorite kings east of the Jordan. This land extended from Aroer on the rim of the Arnon Gorge to Mount Siyon*p* (that is, Hermon), and included all the Arabah east of the Jordan, as far as the Sea of the Arabah,*q* below the slopes of Pisgah.

Deut. 5:1-3 COVENANT WITH ALL ISRAELITES. Moses summoned all Israel and said:

Hear, O Israel, the decrees and laws I declare in your hearing today. Learn them and be sure to follow them. The LORD our God made a covenant with us at Horeb. It was not with our fathers that the LORD made this covenant, but with us, with all of us who are alive here today.

Deut. 5:4,5a LAW CAME FROM GOD. The LORD spoke to you face to face out of the fire on the mountain. (At that time I stood between the LORD and you to declare to you the word of the LORD, because you were afraid of the fire and did not go up the mountain.)

*p*Hebrew; Syriac (see also Deut. 3:9) *Sirion*   *q*That is, the Dead Sea

MOSES DELEGATED FOR LAWS.   These are the commandments the LORD proclaimed in a loud voice to your whole assembly there on the mountain from out of the fire, the cloud and the deep darkness; and he added nothing more. Then he wrote them on two stone tablets and gave them to me.

Deut. 5:22-27

When you heard the voice out of the darkness, while the mountain was ablaze with fire, all the leading men of your tribes and your elders came to me. And you said, "The LORD our God has shown us his glory and his majesty, and we have heard his voice from the fire. Today we have seen that a man can live even if God speaks with him. But now, why should we die? This great fire will consume us, and we will die if we hear the voice of the LORD our God any longer. For what mortal man has ever heard the voice of the living God speaking out of fire, as we have, and survived? Go near and listen to all that the LORD our God says. Then tell us whatever the LORD our God tells you. We will listen and obey."

GOD APPROVES MOSES' ROLE.   The LORD heard you when you spoke to me and the LORD said to me, "I have heard what this people said to you. Everything they said was good. Oh, that their hearts would be inclined to fear me and keep all my commands always, so that it might go well with them and their children forever!

Deut. 5:28-33

"Go, tell them to return to their tents. But you stay here with me so that I may give you all the commands, decrees and laws you are to teach them to follow in the land I am giving them to possess."

So be careful to do what the LORD your God has commanded you; do not turn aside to the right or to the left. Walk in all the way that the LORD your God has commanded you, so that you may live and prosper and prolong your days in the land that you will possess.

PURPOSE OF THE LAW.   These are the commands, decrees and laws the LORD your God directed me to teach you to observe in the land that you are crossing the Jordan to possess, so that you, your children and their children after them may fear the LORD your God as long as you live by keeping all his decrees and commands that I give you, and so that you may enjoy long life. Hear, O Israel, and be careful to obey so that it may go well with you and that you may increase greatly in a land flowing with milk and honey, just as the LORD, the God of your fathers, promised you.

Deut. 6:1-3

THE PREMIER COMMANDMENT.   Hear, O Israel: The LORD our God, the LORD is one.*r* Love the LORD your God with all your heart and with all your soul and with all your strength.

Deut. 6:4,5

REMEMBERING THE LAWS.   These commandments that I give you today are to be upon your hearts. Impress them on your children. Talk about them when you sit at home and when you walk along the road, when you lie down and when you get up. Tie them as symbols on your hands and bind them on your foreheads. Write them on the doorframes of your houses and on your gates.

Deut. 6:6-9

MOTIVATION FOR OBEDIENCE.   When the LORD your God brings you into the land he swore to your fathers, to Abraham, Isaac and Jacob, to give you—a land with large, flourishing cities you did not build, houses filled

Deut. 6:10-15

r Or The LORD our God is one LORD; or The LORD is our God, the LORD is one; or The LORD is our God, the LORD alone with all kinds of good things you did not provide, wells you did not dig, and vineyards and olive groves you did not plant—then when you eat and are satisfied, be careful that you do not forget the LORD, who brought you out of Egypt, out of the land of slavery.

Fear the LORD your God, serve him only and take your oaths in his name. Do not follow other gods, the gods of the peoples around you; for the LORD your God, who is among you, is a jealous God and his anger will burn against you, and he will destroy you from the face of the land.

Deut. 6:16-19

NOT TO TEST GOD.   Do not test the LORD your God as you did at Massah. Be sure to keep the commands of the LORD your God and the stipulations and decrees he has given you. Do what is right and good in the LORD's sight, so that it may go well with you and you may go in and take over the good land that the LORD promised on oath to your forefathers, thrusting out all your enemies before you, as the LORD said.

Deut. 6:20-25

TO TEACH LAW'S HISTORY.   In the future, when your son asks you, "What is the meaning of the stipulations, decrees and laws the LORD our God has commanded you?" tell him: "We were slaves of Pharaoh in Egypt, but the LORD brought us out of Egypt with a mighty hand. Before our eyes the LORD sent miraculous signs and wonders—great and terrible—upon Egypt and Pharaoh and his whole household. But he brought us out from there to bring us in and give us the land that he promised on oath to our forefathers. The LORD commanded us to obey all these decrees and to fear the LORD our God, so that we might always prosper and be kept alive, as is the case today. And if we are careful to obey all this law before the LORD our God, as he has commanded us, that will be our righteousness."

Deut. 7:1-5

IDOLATRY TO BE DESTROYED.   When the LORD your God brings you into the land you are entering to possess and drives out before you many nations—the Hittites, Girgashites, Amorites, Canaanites, Perizzites, Hivites and Jebusites, seven nations larger and stronger than you—and when the LORD your God has delivered them over to you and you have defeated them, then you must destroy them totally.[s] Make no treaty with them, and show them no mercy. Do not intermarry with them. Do not give your daughters to their sons or take their daughters for your sons, for they will turn your sons away from following me to serve other gods, and the LORD's anger will burn against you and will quickly destroy you. This is what you are to do to them: Break down their altars, smash their sacred stones, cut down their Asherah poles[t] and burn their idols in the fire.

Deut. 7:6-11

ISRAEL'S UNIQUE STATUS.   For you are a people holy to the LORD your God. The LORD your God has chosen you out of all the peoples on the face of the earth to be his people, his treasured possession.

The LORD did not set his affection on you and choose you because you were more numerous than other peoples, for you were the fewest of all peoples. But it was because the LORD loved you and kept the oath he swore to your forefathers that he brought you out with a mighty hand and redeemed you from the land of slavery, from the power of Pharaoh king of Egypt. Know therefore that the LORD your God is God; he is the faithful

---

[s]The Hebrew term refers to the irrevocable giving over of things or persons to the LORD, often by totally destroying them.   [t]That is, symbols of the goddess Asherah; here and elsewhere in Deuteronomy

God, keeping his covenant of love to a thousand generations of those who love him and keep his commands. But

> those who hate him he will repay to their face by destruction;
> he will not be slow to repay to their face those who hate him.

Therefore, take care to follow the commands, decrees and laws I give you today.

BLESSINGS FOR OBEDIENCE.   If you pay attention to these laws and are careful to follow them, then the LORD your God will keep his covenant of love with you, as he swore to your forefathers. He will love you and bless you and increase your numbers. He will bless the fruit of your womb, the crops of your land—your grain, new wine and oil—the calves of your herds and the lambs of your flocks in the land that he swore to your forefathers to give you. You will be blessed more than any other people; none of your men or women will be childless, nor any of your livestock without young. The LORD will keep you free from every disease. He will not inflict on you the horrible diseases you knew in Egypt, but he will inflict them on all who hate you. You must destroy all the peoples the LORD your God gives over to you. Do not look on them with pity and do not serve their gods, for that will be a snare to you.
Deut. 7:12-16

GOD TO BE WITH FAITHFUL.   You may say to yourselves, "These nations are stronger than we are. How can we drive them out?" But do not be afraid of them; remember well what the LORD your God did to Pharaoh and to all Egypt. You saw with your own eyes the great trials, the miraculous signs and wonders, the mighty hand and outstretched arm, with which the LORD your God brought you out. The LORD your God will do the same to all the peoples you now fear. Moreover, the LORD your God will send the hornet among them until even the survivors who hide from you have perished. Do not be terrified by them, for the LORD your God, who is among you, is a great and awesome God. The LORD your God will drive out those nations before you, little by little. You will not be allowed to eliminate them all at once, or the wild animals will multiply around you. But the LORD your God will deliver them over to you, throwing them into great confusion until they are destroyed. He will give their kings into your hand, and you will wipe out their names from under heaven. No one will be able to stand up against you; you will destroy them.
Deut. 7:17-24

IDOLATRY AN ABOMINATION.   The images of their gods you are to burn in the fire. Do not covet the silver and gold on them, and do not take it for yourselves, or you will be ensnared by it, for it is detestable to the LORD your God. Do not bring a detestable thing into your house or you, like it, will be set apart for destruction. Utterly abhor and detest it, for it is set apart for destruction.
Deut. 7:25,26

LAW IS FOR DISCIPLINE.   Be careful to follow every command I am giving you today, so that you may live and increase and may enter and possess the land that the LORD promised on oath to your forefathers. Remember how the LORD your God led you all the way in the desert these forty years, to humble you and to test you in order to know what was in your heart, whether or not you would keep his commands. He humbled
Deut. 8:1-5

you, causing you to hunger and then feeding you with manna, which neither you nor your fathers had known, to teach you that man does not live on bread alone but on every word that comes from the mouth of the LORD. Your clothes did not wear out and your feet did not swell during these forty years. Know then in your heart that as a man disciplines his son, so the LORD your God disciplines you.

**Deut.
8:6-10**

YET GOD WILL BLESS. Observe the commands of the LORD your God, walking in his ways and revering him. For the LORD your God is bringing you into a good land—a land with streams and pools of water, with springs flowing in the valleys and hills; a land with wheat and barley, vines and fig trees, pomegranates, olive oil and honey; a land where bread will not be scarce and you will lack nothing; a land where the rocks are iron and you can dig copper out of the hills.

When you have eaten and are satisfied, praise the LORD your God for the good land he has given you.

**Deut.
8:11-20**

BEWARE OF PRIDE. Be careful that you do not forget the LORD your God, failing to observe his commands, his laws and his decrees that I am giving you this day. Otherwise, when you eat and are satisfied, when you build fine houses and settle down, and when your herds and flocks grow large and your silver and gold increase and all you have is multiplied, then your heart will become proud and you will forget the LORD your God, who brought you out of Egypt, out of the land of slavery. He led you through the vast and dreadful desert, that thirsty and waterless land, with its venomous snakes and scorpions. He brought you water out of hard rock. He gave you manna to eat in the desert, something your fathers had never known, to humble and to test you so that in the end it might go well with you. You may say to yourself, "My power and the strength of my hands have produced this wealth for me." But remember the LORD your God, for it is he who gives you the ability to produce wealth, and so confirms his covenant, which he swore to your forefathers, as it is today.

If you ever forget the LORD your God and follow other gods and worship and bow down to them, I testify against you today that you will surely be destroyed. Like the nations the LORD destroyed before you, so you will be destroyed for not obeying the LORD your God.

Deut. 9:1-3

VICTORY PROMISED. Hear, O Israel. You are now about to cross the Jordan to go in and dispossess nations greater and stronger than you, with large cities that have walls up to the sky. The people are strong and tall—Anakites! You know about them and have heard it said: "Who can stand up against the Anakites?" But be assured today that the LORD your God is the one who goes across ahead of you like a devouring fire. He will destroy them; he will subdue them before you. And you will drive them out and annihilate them quickly, as the LORD has promised you.

Deut. 9:4,5

VICTORY NOT MERITED. After the LORD your God has driven them out before you, do not say to yourself, "The LORD has brought me here to take possession of this land because of my righteousness." No, it is on account of the wickedness of these nations that the LORD is going to drive them out before you. It is not because of your righteousness or your integrity that you are going in to take possession of their land; but on account of the wickedness of these nations, the LORD your God will drive them out before you, to accomplish what he swore to your fathers, to Abraham, Isaac and Jacob.

REMINDER OF GOLDEN CALF.   Understand, then, that it is not because of your righteousness that the LORD your God is giving you this good land to possess, for you are a stiff-necked people. Deut. 9:6-14

Remember this and never forget how you provoked the LORD your God to anger in the desert. From the day you left Egypt until you arrived here, you have been rebellious against the LORD. At Horeb you aroused the LORD's wrath so that he was angry enough to destroy you. When I went up on the mountain to receive the tablets of stone, the tablets of the covenant that the LORD had made with you, I stayed on the mountain forty days and forty nights; I ate no bread and drank no water. The LORD gave me two stone tablets inscribed by the finger of God. On them were all the commandments the LORD proclaimed to you on the mountain out of the fire, on the day of the assembly.

At the end of the forty days and forty nights, the LORD gave me the two stone tablets, the tablets of the covenant. Then the LORD told me, "Go down from here at once, because your people whom you brought out of Egypt have become corrupt. They have turned away quickly from what I commanded them and have made a cast idol for themselves."

And the LORD said to me, "I have seen this people, and they are a stiff-necked people indeed! Let me alone, so that I may destroy them and blot out their name from under heaven. And I will make you into a nation stronger and more numerous than they."

MOSES HAD TO INTERCEDE.   So I turned and went down from the mountain while it was ablaze with fire. And the two tablets of the covenant were in my hands.[u] When I looked, I saw that you had sinned against the LORD your God; you had made for yourselves an idol cast in the shape of a calf. You had turned aside quickly from the way that the LORD had commanded you. So I took the two tablets and threw them out of my hands, breaking them to pieces before your eyes. Deut. 9:15-21

Then once again I fell prostrate before the LORD for forty days and forty nights; I ate no bread and drank no water, because of all the sin you had committed, doing what was evil in the LORD's sight and so provoking him to anger. I feared the anger and wrath of the LORD, for he was angry enough with you to destroy you. But again the LORD listened to me. And the LORD was angry enough with Aaron to destroy him, but at that time I prayed for Aaron too. Also I took that sinful thing of yours, the calf you had made, and burned it in the fire. Then I crushed it and ground it to powder as fine as dust and threw the dust into a stream that flowed down the mountain.

OTHER REBELLIOUS INCIDENTS.   You also made the LORD angry at Taberah, at Massah and at Kibroth Hattaavah. Deut. 9:22-24

And when the LORD sent you out from Kadesh Barnea, he said, "Go up and take possession of the land I have given you." But you rebelled against the command of the LORD your God. You did not trust him or obey him. You have been rebellious against the LORD ever since I have known you.

MOSES HAD TO PRAY.   I lay prostrate before the LORD those forty days and forty nights because the LORD had said he would destroy you. I Deut. 9:25-29

[u]Or *And I had the two tablets of the covenant with me, one in each hand*

prayed to the LORD and said, "O Sovereign LORD, do not destroy your people, your own inheritance that you redeemed by your great power and brought out of Egypt with a mighty hand. Remember your servants Abraham, Isaac and Jacob. Overlook the stubbornness of this people, their wickedness and their sin. Otherwise, the country from which you brought us will say, 'Because the LORD was not able to take them into the land he had promised them, and because he hated them, he brought them out to put them to death in the desert.' But they are your people, your inheritance that you brought out by your great power and your outstretched arm."

Deut.
10:1-5

SECOND TABLETS OF LAW.   At that time the LORD said to me, "Chisel out two stone tablets like the first ones and come up to me on the mountain. Also make a wooden chest.^{v} I will write on the tablets the words that were on the first tablets, which you broke. Then you are to put them in the chest."

So I made the ark out of acacia wood and chiseled out two stone tablets like the first ones, and I went up on the mountain with the two tablets in my hands. The LORD wrote on these tablets what he had written before, the Ten Commandments he had proclaimed to you on the mountain, out of the fire, on the day of the assembly. And the LORD gave them to me. Then I came back down the mountain and put the tablets in the ark I had made, as the LORD commanded me, and they are there now.

Deut.
10:6-9

PARENTHETICAL NOTES.   (The Israelites traveled from the wells of the Jaakanites to Moserah. There Aaron died and was buried, and Eleazar his son succeeded him as priest. From there they traveled to Gudgodah and on to Jotbathah, a land with streams of water. At that time the LORD set apart the tribe of Levi to carry the ark of the covenant of the LORD, to stand before the LORD to minister and to pronounce blessings in his name, as they still do today. That is why the Levites have no share or inheritance among their brothers; the LORD is their inheritance, as the LORD your God told them.)

Deut.
10:10,11

MOSES SOUGHT GOD'S MERCY.   Now I had stayed on the mountain forty days and nights, as I did the first time, and the LORD listened to me at this time also. It was not his will to destroy you. "Go," the LORD said to me, "and lead the people on their way, so that they may enter and possess the land that I swore to their fathers to give them."

Deut.
10:12,13

SUMMARY OF GOD'S WILL.   And now, O Israel, what does the LORD your God ask of you but to fear the LORD your God, to walk in all his ways, to love him, to serve the LORD your God with all your heart and with all your soul, and to observe the LORD's commands and decrees that I am giving you today for your own good?

Deut.
10:14-11:1

GOD'S LOVE FOR ISRAEL.   To the LORD your God belong the heavens, even the highest heavens, the earth and everything in it. Yet the LORD set his affection on your forefathers and loved them, and he chose you, their descendants, above all the nations, as it is today. Circumcise your hearts, therefore, and do not be stiff-necked any longer. For the LORD your God is God of gods and Lord of lords, the great God, mighty and awesome, who shows no partiality and accepts no bribes. He defends the cause of the

^{v}That is, an ark

fatherless and the widow, and loves the alien, giving him food and clothing. And you are to love those who are aliens, for you yourselves were aliens in Egypt. Fear the LORD your God and serve him. Hold fast to him and take your oaths in his name. He is your praise; he is your God, who performed for you those great and awesome wonders you saw with your own eyes. Your forefathers who went down into Egypt were seventy in all, and now the LORD your God has made you as numerous as the stars in the sky. Love the LORD your God and keep his requirements, his decrees, his laws and his commands always.

DEMONSTRATIONS OF POWER.   Remember today that your children were not the ones who saw and experienced the discipline of the LORD your God: his majesty, his mighty hand, his outstretched arm; the signs he performed and the things he did in the heart of Egypt, both to Pharaoh king of Egypt and to his whole country; what he did to the Egyptian army, to its horses and chariots, how he overwhelmed them with the waters of the Red Sea[w] as they were pursuing you, and how the LORD brought lasting ruin on them. It was not your children who saw what he did for you in the desert until you arrived at this place, and what he did to Dathan and Abiram, sons of Eliab the Reubenite, when the earth opened its mouth right in the middle of all Israel and swallowed them up with their households, their tents and every living thing that belonged to them. But it was your own eyes that saw all these great things the LORD has done.

Deut.
11:2-7

OBLIGATION OF OBEDIENCE.   Observe therefore all the commands I am giving you today, so that you may have the strength to go in and take over the land that you are crossing the Jordan to possess, and so that you may live long in the land that the LORD swore to your forefathers to give to them and their descendants, a land flowing with milk and honey. The land you are entering to take over is not like the land of Egypt, from which you have come, where you planted your seed and irrigated it by foot as in a vegetable garden. But the land you are crossing the Jordan to take possession of is a land of mountains and valleys that drinks rain from heaven. It is a land the LORD your God cares for; the eyes of the LORD your God are continually on it from the beginning of the year to its end.

Deut.
11:8-12

BLESSINGS ARE CONTINGENT.   So if you faithfully obey the commands I am giving you today—to love the LORD your God and to serve him with all your heart and with all your soul—then I will send rain on your land in its season, both autumn and spring rains, so that you may gather in your grain, new wine and oil. I will provide grass in the fields for your cattle, and you will eat and be satisfied.

Be careful, or you will be enticed to turn away and worship other gods and bow down to them. Then the LORD's anger will burn against you, and he will shut the heavens so that it will not rain and the ground will yield no produce, and you will soon perish from the good land the LORD is giving you.

Deut.
11:13-17

VARIOUS EXHORTATIONS.   Fix these words of mine in your hearts and minds; tie them as symbols on your hands and bind them on your foreheads. Teach them to your children, talking about them when you sit at home and when you walk along the road, when you lie down and when you get up. Write them on the doorframes of your houses and on your

Deut.
11:18-25

[w]Hebrew *Yam Suph*; that is, Sea of Reeds

gates, so that your days and the days of your children may be many in the land that the LORD swore to give your forefathers, as many as the days that the heavens are above the earth.

If you carefully observe all these commands I am giving you to follow—to love the LORD your God, to walk in all his ways and to hold fast to him—then the LORD will drive out all these nations before you, and you will dispossess nations larger and stronger than you. Every place where you set your foot will be yours: Your territory will extend from the desert to Lebanon, and from the Euphrates River to the western sea.ˣ No man will be able to stand against you. The LORD your God, as he promised you, will put the terror and fear of you on the whole land, wherever you go.

**Deut.
11:26-32**

A BLESSING AND A CURSE.   See, I am setting before you today a blessing and a curse—the blessing if you obey the commands of the LORD your God that I am giving you today; the curse if you disobey the commands of the LORD your God and turn from the way that I command you today by following other gods, which you have not known. When the LORD your God has brought you into the land you are entering to possess, you are to proclaim on Mount Gerizim the blessings, and on Mount Ebal the curses. As you know, these mountains are across the Jordan, west of the road,ʸ toward the setting sun, near the great trees of Moreh, in the territory of those Canaanites living in the Arabah in the vicinity of Gilgal. You are about to cross the Jordan to enter and take possession of the land the LORD your God is giving you. When you have taken it over and are living there, be sure that you obey all the decrees and laws I am setting before you today.

ˣThat is, the Mediterranean   ʸOr *Jordan, westward*

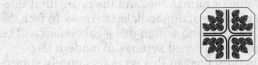

THE LAWS OF MOSES
(Ca. 1450-1400 B.C.)

Introduction to the Laws

*A*t this point in his second address Moses begins an exposition of principal laws, some of which he gives here for the first time—or at least they are recorded here for the first time—and some of which he has already given but now further explains or reemphasizes. (As indicated earlier, all the laws previously given have been held in abeyance until this section in order to bring the total together in one collection organized by subject matter.) Although these laws are traditionally known as the Laws of Moses, it is of course God who is their source. However, because there will be other laws of Israel as the nation becomes more fully developed, it is appropriate to distinguish these early commandments by referring to them as Moses' laws.

Most of the laws are set forth in the form of statutes. Others are in the nature of case decisions or ethical duties. Some of the laws are given to meet only temporary or immediate needs, while others are intended to last for centuries. The laws are to be read to the people at regular times throughout each year in order that each person can learn them and have no excuse for not obeying them.

The explicit purpose for each law is rarely given. However, most of the laws are ultimately designed to teach the Israelites to respect and honor God, to make them holy and aware of their separateness as a specially chosen people, and to learn respect for the rights of their neighbors. Laws regulating personal injury, or even diet, are no less significant than those regulating offerings and sacrifices, for all laws are essentially religious laws. All are given by a personal God and Lawgiver to whom the people have sworn allegiance and promised obedience.

The laws of Israel may sometimes appear to be cruel or unnecessarily harsh, particularly the penalties which accompany given offenses. Yet what may appear to be cruel and unusual in modern times must be viewed in the context of the life and times in which the Israelites are living. Death and suffering are very much a reality to all people of this time, and in the surrounding nations wicked kings practice unspeakable cruelties in ruling their people. Thus the laws given to Moses are designed to lift the national consciousness and impose a high level of ethical conduct. Even the death penalty is an elevating concept in teaching the value of human life, and the procedural safe-guards which are imposed insure a measure of unparalleled fairness. In fact, the concepts of due process and equal justice found within this legal system will be incorporated even centuries later into enlightened systems of modern law.

The organization of the laws as presented in this section is purely subjec-tive, and therefore should not be taken as an authoritative structuring. Be-cause of the fact that in a theocratic legal system all laws are basically religious in nature, any categorization necessarily involves a certain amount of over-lapping coverage. For example, laws pertaining to health and quarantine over-lap with purification rites, which properly belong with other rules of religious ceremony. Therefore, as often as possible, such overlapping will be indicated.

I. Religious and Ceremonial Laws

At the cornerstone of all the laws is the first commandment.

Deut.
5:5b-7

OTHER GODS PROHIBITED.   And he said:

"I am the LORD your God, who brought you out of Egypt, out of the land of slavery.
"You shall have no other gods before[a] me.

The second commandment insures allegiance to the one true and living God.

Deut.
5:8-10

IDOLATRY PROHIBITED.
"You shall not make for yourself an idol in the form of anything in heaven above or on the earth beneath or in the waters below. You shall not bow down to them or worship them; for I, the LORD your God, am a jealous God, punishing the children for the sin of the fathers to the third and fourth generation of those who hate me, but showing love to a thousand ˌgenerationsˌ of those who love me and keep my commandments.

A. Laws Against Idolatry and Paganism

Ex. 22:20

SACRIFICING TO GODS.   "Whoever sacrifices to any god other than the LORD must be destroyed.[b]

Ex. 23:13

REFERRING TO GODS.   "Be careful to do everything I have said to you. Do not invoke the names of other gods; do not let them be heard on your lips.

Ex. 34:17
Lev. 19:4

MAKING MOLTEN GODS.   " 'Do not turn to idols or make gods of cast metal for yourselves. I am the LORD your God.

Lev. 26:1

MAKING OTHER IMAGES.   " 'Do not make idols or set up an image or a sacred stone for yourselves, and do not place a carved stone in your land to bow down before it. I am the LORD your God.

---

[a]Or *besides*   [b]The Hebrew term refers to the irrevocable giving over of things or persons to the LORD, often by totally destroying them.

WOODEN PILLARS.   Do not set up any wooden Asherah pole[c] beside the altar you build to the LORD your God, and do not erect a sacred stone, for these the LORD your God hates.

Deut. 16:21,22

CHILDREN TO MOLECH.   The LORD said to Moses, "Say to the Israelites: 'Any Israelite or any alien living in Israel who gives[d] any of his children to Molech must be put to death. The people of the community are to stone him. I will set my face against that man and I will cut him off from his people; for by giving his children to Molech, he has defiled my sanctuary and profaned my holy name. If the people of the community close their eyes when that man gives one of his children to Molech and they fail to put him to death, I will set my face against that man and his family and will cut off from their people both him and all who follow him in prostituting themselves to Molech.

Lev. 20:1-5 18:21

SEPARATION FROM PAGANS.   You are the children of the LORD your God. Do not cut yourselves or shave the front of your heads for the dead, for you are a people holy to the LORD your God. Out of all the peoples on the face of the earth, the LORD has chosen you to be his treasured possession.

Deut. 14:1,2

MOURNING PRACTICES.   " 'Do not cut the hair at the sides of your head or clip off the edges of your beard.
" 'Do not cut your bodies for the dead or put tattoo marks on yourselves. I am the LORD.

Lev. 19:27,28

AVOIDING ENTICEMENT.   The LORD your God will cut off before you the nations you are about to invade and dispossess. But when you have driven them out and settled in their land, and after they have been destroyed before you, be careful not to be ensnared by inquiring about their gods, saying, "How do these nations serve their gods? We will do the same." You must not worship the LORD your God in their way, because in worshiping their gods, they do all kinds of detestable things the LORD hates. They even burn their sons and daughters in the fire as sacrifices to their gods.

Deut. 12:29-31

SOLICITORS OF IDOLATRY.   If your very own brother, or your son or daughter, or the wife you love, or your closest friend secretly entices you, saying, "Let us go and worship other gods" (gods that neither you nor your fathers have known, gods of the peoples around you, whether near or far, from one end of the land to the other), do not yield to him or listen to him. Show him no pity. Do not spare him or shield him. You must certainly put him to death. Your hand must be the first in putting him to death, and then the hands of all the people. Stone him to death, because he tried to turn you away from the LORD your God, who brought you out of Egypt, out of the land of slavery. Then all Israel will hear and be afraid, and no one among you will do such an evil thing again.

Deut. 13:6-11

IDOLATROUS CITIES.   If you hear it said about one of the towns the LORD your God is giving you to live in that wicked men have arisen among you and have led the people of their town astray, saying, "Let us go and worship other gods" (gods you have not known), then you must inquire, probe and investigate it thoroughly. And if it is true and it has been proved that this detestable thing has been done among you, you

Deut. 13:12-18

---

[c]Or *Do not plant any tree dedicated to Asherah*   [d]Or *sacrifices*; also in verses 3 and 4

must certainly put to the sword all who live in that town. Destroy it completely,*e* both its people and its livestock. Gather all the plunder of the town into the middle of the public square and completely burn the town and all its plunder as a whole burnt offering to the LORD your God. It is to remain a ruin forever, never to be rebuilt. None of those condemned things*e* shall be found in your hands, so that the LORD will turn from his fierce anger; he will show you mercy, have compassion on you, and increase your numbers, as he promised on oath to your forefathers, because you obey the LORD your God, keeping all his commands that I am giving you today and doing what is right in his eyes.

Deut.
17:2-7

PUNISHMENT FOR IDOLATRY.   If a man or woman living among you in one of the towns the LORD gives you is found doing evil in the eyes of the LORD your God in violation of his covenant, and contrary to my command has worshiped other gods, bowing down to them or to the sun or the moon or the stars of the sky, and this has been brought to your attention, then you must investigate it thoroughly. If it is true and it has been proved that this detestable thing has been done in Israel, take the man or woman who has done this evil deed to your city gate and stone that person to death. On the testimony of two or three witnesses a man shall be put to death, but no one shall be put to death on the testimony of only one witness. The hands of the witnesses must be the first in putting him to death, and then the hands of all the people. You must purge the evil from among you.

Deut.
12:1-15,
17-22,
26-28

ONLY ONE PLACE OF WORSHIP.   These are the decrees and laws you must be careful to follow in the land that the LORD, the God of your fathers, has given you to possess—as long as you live in the land. Destroy completely all the places on the high mountains and on the hills and under every spreading tree where the nations you are dispossessing worship their gods. Break down their altars, smash their sacred stones and burn their Asherah poles in the fire; cut down the idols of their gods and wipe out their names from those places.

You must not worship the LORD your God in their way. But you are to seek the place the LORD your God will choose from among all your tribes to put his Name there for his dwelling. To that place you must go; there bring your burnt offerings and sacrifices, your tithes and special gifts, what you have vowed to give and your freewill offerings, and the firstborn of your herds and flocks. There, in the presence of the LORD your God, you and your families shall eat and shall rejoice in everything you have put your hand to, because the LORD your God has blessed you.

You are not to do as we do here today, everyone as he sees fit, since you have not yet reached the resting place and the inheritance the LORD your God is giving you. But you will cross the Jordan and settle in the land the LORD your God is giving you as an inheritance, and he will give you rest from all your enemies around you so that you will live in safety. Then to the place the LORD your God will choose as a dwelling for his Name— there you are to bring everything I command you: your burnt offerings and sacrifices, your tithes and special gifts, and all the choice possessions you have vowed to the LORD. And there rejoice before the LORD your God,

---

*e*The Hebrew term refers to the irrevocable giving over of things or persons to the LORD, often by totally destroying them.

you, your sons and daughters, your menservants and maidservants, and the Levites from your towns, who have no allotment or inheritance of their own. Be careful not to sacrifice your burnt offerings anywhere you please. Offer them only at the place the LORD will choose in one of your tribes, and there observe everything I command you.

Nevertheless, you may slaughter your animals in any of your towns and eat as much of the meat as you want, as if it were gazelle or deer, according to the blessing the LORD your God gives you. Both the ceremonially unclean and the clean may eat it. You must not eat in your own towns the tithe of your grain and new wine and oil, or the firstborn of your herds and flocks, or whatever you have vowed to give, or your freewill offerings or special gifts. Instead, you are to eat them in the presence of the LORD your God at the place the LORD your God will choose—you, your sons and daughters, your menservants and maidservants, and the Levites from your towns—and you are to rejoice before the LORD your God in everything you put your hand to. Be careful not to neglect the Levites as long as you live in your land.

When the LORD your God has enlarged your territory as he promised you, and you crave meat and say, "I would like some meat," then you may eat as much of it as you want. If the place where the LORD your God chooses to put his Name is too far away from you, you may slaughter animals from the herds and flocks the LORD has given you, as I have commanded you, and in your own towns you may eat as much of them as you want. Eat them as you would gazelle or deer. Both the ceremonially unclean and the clean may eat.

But take your consecrated things and whatever you have vowed to give, and go to the place the LORD will choose. Present your burnt offerings on the altar of the LORD your God, both the meat and the blood. The blood of your sacrifices must be poured beside the altar of the LORD your God, but you may eat the meat. Be careful to obey all these regulations I am giving you, so that it may always go well with you and your children after you, because you will be doing what is good and right in the eyes of the LORD your God.

B. Laws Against False Spiritualists

WITCHCRAFT AND DIVINATION.   When you enter the land the LORD your God is giving you, do not learn to imitate the detestable ways of the nations there. Let no one be found among you who sacrifices his son or daughter in^f the fire, who practices divination or sorcery, interprets omens, engages in witchcraft, or casts spells, or who is a medium or spiritist or who consults the dead. Anyone who does these things is detestable to the LORD, and because of these detestable practices the LORD your God will drive out those nations before you. You must be blameless before the LORD your God.

The nations you will dispossess listen to those who practice sorcery or divination. But as for you, the LORD your God has not permitted you to do so.

Lev.
19:26b
19:31
20:6-8
**Deut.
18:9-14**

^{f}Or *who makes his son or daughter pass through*

Ex. 22:18	**DEATH FOR SORCERY.** "Do not allow a sorceress to live.

Lev. 20:27	**DEATH FOR SPIRITUALISTS.** " 'A man or woman who is a medium or spiritist among you must be put to death. You are to stone them; their blood will be on their own heads.' "

Deut. 13:1-5	**FALSE PROPHETS AND DREAMERS.** If a prophet, or one who foretells by dreams, appears among you and announces to you a miraculous sign or wonder, and if the sign or wonder of which he has spoken takes place, and he says, "Let us follow other gods" (gods you have not known) "and let us worship them," you must not listen to the words of that prophet or dreamer. The LORD your God is testing you to find out whether you love him with all your heart and with all your soul. It is the LORD your God you must follow, and him you must revere. Keep his commands and obey him; serve him and hold fast to him. That prophet or dreamer must be put to death, because he preached rebellion against the LORD your God, who brought you out of Egypt and redeemed you from the land of slavery; he has tried to turn you from the way the LORD your God commanded you to follow. You must purge the evil from among you.

Deut. 18:15-19	**MESSIAH TO BE TRUE PROPHET.** The LORD your God will raise up for you a prophet like me from among your own brothers. You must listen to him. For this is what you asked of the LORD your God at Horeb on the day of the assembly when you said, "Let us not hear the voice of the LORD our God nor see this great fire anymore, or we will die." The LORD said to me: "What they say is good. I will raise up for them a prophet like you from among their brothers; I will put my words in his mouth, and he will tell them everything I command him. If anyone does not listen to my words that the prophet speaks in my name, I myself will call him to account.

Deut. 18:20-22	**TEST OF FALSE PROPHETS.** But a prophet who presumes to speak in my name anything I have not commanded him to say, or a prophet who speaks in the name of other gods, must be put to death." You may say to yourselves, "How can we know when a message has not been spoken by the LORD?" If what a prophet proclaims in the name of the LORD does not take place or come true, that is a message the LORD has not spoken. That prophet has spoken presumptuously. Do not be afraid of him.

C. Laws Regarding Blasphemy

Respect for the Sovereign of the universe is of utmost importance.

Deut. 5:11	**REVERENCE FOR GOD COMMANDED.** "You shall not misuse the name of the LORD your God, for the LORD will not hold anyone guiltless who misuses his name.

Ex. 22:28a	**REVILING GOD.** "Do not blaspheme God8 . . .

Lev. 24:10-16,23	**CASE OF BLASPHEMY.** Now the son of an Israelite mother and an Egyptian father went out among the Israelites, and a fight broke out in the camp between him and an Israelite. The son of the Israelite woman blasphemed the Name with a curse; so they brought him to Moses. (His

8Or *Do not revile the judges*

mother's name was Shelomith, the daughter of Dibri the Danite.) They put him in custody until the will of the LORD should be made clear to them.

Then the LORD said to Moses: "Take the blasphemer outside the camp. All those who heard him are to lay their hands on his head, and the entire assembly is to stone him. Say to the Israelites: 'If anyone curses his God, he will be held responsible; anyone who blasphemes the name of the LORD must be put to death. The entire assembly must stone him. Whether an alien or native-born, when he blasphemes the Name, he must be put to death.

Then Moses spoke to the Israelites, and they took the blasphemer outside the camp and stoned him. The Israelites did as the LORD commanded Moses.

D. Laws Requiring Dedications

To instill a proper sense of priorities and gratitude, God gives various laws demanding gifts of both the first and the best things. These gifts are to be used to support the spiritual work of the priests and Levites, and to assist in benevolence for those who have special needs.

FIRSTBORN FOR GOD.   "You must give me the firstborn of your sons. Do the same with your cattle and your sheep. Let them stay with their mothers for seven days, but give them to me on the eighth day.   Ex. 22:29b,30

PROPER SUBSTITUTES.   "The first offspring of every womb belongs to me, including all the firstborn males of your livestock, whether from herd or flock. Redeem the firstborn donkey with a lamb, but if you do not redeem it, break its neck. Redeem all your firstborn sons.   Ex. 34:19,20

"No one is to appear before me empty-handed.

FIRST CROPS FOR GOD.   Do not hold back offerings from your granaries or your vats.[h]   Ex. 22:29a

FIRSTFRUITS FOR GOD.   "Bring the best of the firstfruits of your soil to the house of the LORD your God.   Ex. 23:19a 34:26a

FIRSTBORN ANIMALS.   Set apart for the LORD your God every firstborn male of your herds and flocks. Do not put the firstborn of your oxen to work, and do not shear the firstborn of your sheep. Each year you and your family are to eat them in the presence of the LORD your God at the place he will choose. If an animal has a defect, is lame or blind, or has any serious flaw, you must not sacrifice it to the LORD your God. You are to eat it in your own towns. Both the ceremonially unclean and the clean may eat it, as if it were gazelle or deer. But you must not eat the blood; pour it out on the ground like water.   Deut. 15:19-23

E. Laws Requiring Tithing

TITHES FOR PRIESTS.   The priests, who are Levites—indeed the whole tribe of Levi—are to have no allotment or inheritance with Israel. They shall live on the offerings made to the LORD by fire, for that is their inheritance. They shall have no inheritance among their brothers; the LORD is their inheritance, as he promised them.   Deut. 18:1-5

This is the share due the priests from the people who sacrifice a bull or a sheep: the shoulder, the jowls and the inner parts. You are to give them

[h]The meaning of the Hebrew for this phrase is uncertain.

the firstfruits of your grain, new wine and oil, and the first wool from the shearing of your sheep, for the LORD your God has chosen them and their descendants out of all your tribes to stand and minister in the LORD's name always.

Deut.
18:6-8

PORTION FOR LEVITES.   If a Levite moves from one of your towns anywhere in Israel where he is living, and comes in all earnestness to the place the LORD will choose, he may minister in the name of the LORD his God like all his fellow Levites who serve there in the presence of the LORD. He is to share equally in their benefits, even though he has received money from the sale of family possessions.

Deut.
14:22-27

YEARLY PRODUCE TITHE.   Be sure to set aside a tenth of all that your fields produce each year. Eat the tithe of your grain, new wine and oil, and the firstborn of your herds and flocks in the presence of the LORD your God at the place he will choose as a dwelling for his Name, so that you may learn to revere the LORD your God always. But if that place is too distant and you have been blessed by the LORD your God and cannot carry your tithe (because the place where the LORD will choose to put his Name is so far away), then exchange your tithe for silver, and take the silver with you and go to the place the LORD your God will choose. Use the silver to buy whatever you like: cattle, sheep, wine or other fermented drink, or anything you wish. Then you and your household shall eat there in the presence of the LORD your God and rejoice. And do not neglect the Levites living in your towns, for they have no allotment or inheritance of their own.

Deut.
14:28,29

TRIENNIAL PRODUCE TITHE.   At the end of every three years, bring all the tithes of that year's produce and store it in your towns, so that the Levites (who have no allotment or inheritance of their own) and the aliens, the fatherless and the widows who live in your towns may come and eat and be satisfied, and so that the LORD your God may bless you in all the work of your hands.

F. Special Instructions for Conquest

Deut.
26:1-4

SPECIAL DEDICATION OF FRUITS.   When you have entered the land the LORD your God is giving you as an inheritance and have taken possession of it and settled in it, take some of the firstfruits of all that you produce from the soil of the land the LORD your God is giving you and put them in a basket. Then go to the place the LORD your God will choose as a dwelling for his Name and say to the priest in office at the time, "I declare today to the LORD your God that I have come to the land the LORD swore to our forefathers to give us." The priest shall take the basket from your hands and set it down in front of the altar of the LORD your God.

Deut.
26:5-11

DEDICATION FOR REMEMBRANCE.   Then you shall declare before the LORD your God: "My father was a wandering Aramean, and he went down into Egypt with a few people and lived there and became a great nation, powerful and numerous. But the Egyptians mistreated us and made us suffer, putting us to hard labor. Then we cried out to the LORD, the God of our fathers, and the LORD heard our voice and saw our misery, toil and oppression. So the LORD brought us out of Egypt with a mighty hand and an outstretched arm, with great terror and with miraculous signs and wonders. He brought us to this place and gave us this land, a land flowing with milk and honey; and now I bring the firstfruits of the soil that you, O LORD, have given me." Place the basket before the LORD your God and bow down before him. And you and the Levites and the aliens among you shall rejoice in all the good things the LORD your God has given to you and your household.

PRAYER OF THANKSGIVING.   When you have finished setting aside a tenth of all your produce in the third year, the year of the tithe, you shall give it to the Levite, the alien, the fatherless and the widow, so that they may eat in your towns and be satisfied. Then say to the LORD your God: "I have removed from my house the sacred portion and have given it to the Levite, the alien, the fatherless and the widow, according to all you commanded. I have not turned aside from your commands nor have I forgotten any of them. I have not eaten any of the sacred portion while I was in mourning, nor have I removed any of it while I was unclean, nor have I offered any of it to the dead. I have obeyed the LORD my God; I have done everything you commanded me. Look down from heaven, your holy dwelling place, and bless your people Israel and the land you have given us as you promised on oath to our forefathers, a land flowing with milk and honey."

Deut. 26:12-15

REGARDING FRUIT TREES.   " 'When you enter the land and plant any kind of fruit tree, regard its fruit as forbidden.[i] For three years you are to consider it forbidden[i]; it must not be eaten. In the fourth year all its fruit will be holy, an offering of praise to the LORD. But in the fifth year you may eat its fruit. In this way your harvest will be increased. I am the LORD your God.

Lev. 19:23-25

G. Law of the Sabbath

To promote continual remembrance, and to provide periodic occasions for formal worship of God, various special days, months, and years are set aside for national celebration and individual devotion.

The first and foremost day of worship, the Sabbath, is commanded no less than 12 times throughout the giving of the laws. It is symbolic of the day upon which God rested after creation, and a reminder that no day of rest was permitted when the Israelites were in Egyptian bondage. It is the one day each week when all attention can be focused upon God and his blessings. And, although the Sabbath falls on the last day of each week, it foreshadows a time when the first day of each week will be observed in memory of the greatest event which will have happened since creation.

SABBATH REST COMMANDED.
"Observe the Sabbath day by keeping it holy, as the LORD your God has commanded you. Six days you shall labor and do all your work, but the seventh day is a Sabbath to the LORD your God. On it you shall not do any work, neither you, nor your son or daughter, nor your manservant or maidservant, nor your ox, your donkey or any of your animals, nor the alien within your gates, so that your manservant and maidservant may rest, as you do. Remember that you were slaves in Egypt and that the

Ex. 23:12 35:1,2 Lev. 19:3b Deut. 5:12-15

---

[i]Hebrew *uncircumcised*

LORD your God brought you out of there with a mighty hand and an outstretched arm. Therefore the LORD your God has commanded you to observe the Sabbath day.

Ex. 31:16,17   SYMBOL OF COVENANT. The Israelites are to observe the Sabbath, celebrating it for the generations to come as a lasting covenant. It will be a sign between me and the Israelites forever, for in six days the LORD made the heavens and the earth, and on the seventh day he abstained from work and rested.'"

Lev. 19:30 26:2   DAY TO HONOR SANCTUARY. " 'Observe my Sabbaths and have reverence for my sanctuary. I am the LORD.

Lev. 23:1-3   DAY FOR HOLY CONVOCATION. The LORD said to Moses, "Speak to the Israelites and say to them: 'These are my appointed feasts, the appointed feasts of the LORD, which you are to proclaim as sacred assemblies.

" 'There are six days when you may work, but the seventh day is a Sabbath of rest, a day of sacred assembly. You are not to do any work; wherever you live, it is a Sabbath to the LORD.

Ex. 35:3   NO FIRE ON SABBATH. Do not light a fire in any of your dwellings on the Sabbath day."

Ex. 34:21   PLOWING AND HARVEST. "Six days you shall labor, but on the seventh day you shall rest; even during the plowing season and harvest you must rest.

Ex. 31:12-15   DEATH FOR BREACH OF SABBATH. Then the LORD said to Moses, "Say to the Israelites, 'You must observe my Sabbaths. This will be a sign between me and you for the generations to come, so you may know that I am the LORD, who makes you holy.*j*

" 'Observe the Sabbath, because it is holy to you. Anyone who desecrates it must be put to death; whoever does any work on that day must be cut off from his people. For six days, work is to be done, but the seventh day is a Sabbath of rest, holy to the LORD. Whoever does any work on the Sabbath day must be put to death.

Num. 15:32-36   CASE OF PUNISHMENT. While the Israelites were in the desert, a man was found gathering wood on the Sabbath day. Those who found him gathering wood brought him to Moses and Aaron and the whole assembly, and they kept him in custody, because it was not clear what should be done to him. Then the LORD said to Moses, "The man must die. The whole assembly must stone him outside the camp." So the assembly took him outside the camp and stoned him to death, as the LORD commanded Moses.

H. The Special Feast

Ex. 23:14-17 34:23   THREE FEASTS APPOINTED. "Three times a year you are to celebrate a festival to me.

"Celebrate the Feast of Unleavened Bread; for seven days eat bread made without yeast, as I commanded you. Do this at the appointed time in the month of Abib, for in that month you came out of Egypt.

"No one is to appear before me empty-handed.

---

*j*Or *who sanctifies you;* or *who sets you apart as holy*

"Celebrate the Feast of Harvest with the firstfruits of the crops you sow in your field.

"Celebrate the Feast of Ingathering at the end of the year, when you gather in your crops from the field.

"Three times a year all the men are to appear before the Sovereign LORD.

ALTERNATE NAMES FOR FEASTS.   Three times a year all your men must appear before the LORD your God at the place he will choose: at the Feast of Unleavened Bread, the Feast of Weeks and the Feast of Tabernacles. No man should appear before the LORD empty-handed: Each of you must bring a gift in proportion to the way the LORD your God has blessed you.

Deut. 16:16,17

PROMISE FOR OBSERVANCE.   I will drive out nations before you and enlarge your territory, and no one will covet your land when you go up three times each year to appear before the LORD your God.

Ex. 34:24

With these passages the three major feasts are made "pilgrim" events: each year all male Israelites will be required to travel to the designated place of worship to offer the required sacrifices.

1. Passover and Feast of Unleavened Bread
1st Month, 14th-21st Days (March-April)

Passover memorializes the freeing of the Israelites from their Egyptian bondage, when death passed over the land and killed the firstborn of all but the Israelites. The weeklong Feast of Unleavened Bread which follows is a commemoration of the exodus itself. The Passover meal includes lamb, representing the passover lamb; unleavened bread, representing purity; and bitter herbs, representing the horrors of bondage. Cleansing of sins is seen in the blood of the lamb.

WHAT PASSOVER SIGNIFIES.   Observe the month of Abib and celebrate the Passover of the LORD your God, because in the month of Abib he brought you out of Egypt by night. Sacrifice as the Passover to the LORD your God an animal from your flock or herd at the place the LORD will choose as a dwelling for his Name. Do not eat it with bread made with yeast, but for seven days eat unleavened bread, the bread of affliction, because you left Egypt in haste—so that all the days of your life you may remember the time of your departure from Egypt. Let no yeast be found in your possession in all your land for seven days. Do not let any of the meat you sacrifice on the evening of the first day remain until morning.

Ex. 34:18
Deut. 16:1-7

You must not sacrifice the Passover in any town the LORD your God gives you except in the place he will choose as a dwelling for his Name. There you must sacrifice the Passover in the evening, when the sun goes down, on the anniversary[k] of your departure from Egypt. Roast it and eat it at the place the LORD your God will choose. Then in the morning return to your tents.

PENALTY FOR NOT OBSERVING.   But if a man who is ceremonially clean and not on a journey fails to celebrate the Passover, that person must be cut off from his people because he did not present the LORD's offering

Num. 9:13

[k]Or down, at the time of day

at the appointed time. That man will bear the consequences of his sin.

Num. 9:14 APPLICATION TO GUESTS. " 'An alien living among you who wants to celebrate the LORD's Passover must do so in accordance with its rules and regulations. You must have the same regulations for the alien and the native-born.' "

Lev. 23:4-8
Num.
28:16,17
Deut. 16:8
OBSERVING UNLEAVENED BREAD. " 'These are the LORD's appointed feasts, the sacred assemblies you are to proclaim at their appointed times: The LORD's Passover begins at twilight on the fourteenth day of the first month. On the fifteenth day of that month the LORD's Feast of Unleavened Bread begins; for seven days you must eat bread made without yeast. On the first day hold a sacred assembly and do no regular work. For seven days present an offering made to the LORD by fire. And on the seventh day hold a sacred assembly and do no regular work.' "

Num.
28:18-25
OFFERINGS. On the first day hold a sacred assembly and do no regular work. Present to the LORD an offering made by fire, a burnt offering of two young bulls, one ram and seven male lambs a year old, all without defect. With each bull prepare a grain offering of three-tenths of an ephah of fine flour mixed with oil; with the ram, two-tenths; and with each of the seven lambs, one-tenth. Include one male goat as a sin offering to make atonement for you. Prepare these in addition to the regular morning burnt offering. In this way prepare the food for the offering made by fire every day for seven days as an aroma pleasing to the LORD; it is to be prepared in addition to the regular burnt offering and its drink offering. On the seventh day hold a sacred assembly and do no regular work.

2. Feast of Weeks (Harvest or Firstfruits)
3rd Month, 6th Day (May-June)

The second major feast takes place seven weeks following the Feast of Unleavened Bread, on the fiftieth day. Hence the name by which it is presently called, the Feast of Weeks, and the name by which it will one day be called, Pentecost (meaning 50). Because it falls at the time of the wheat harvest and the offering for firstfruits, it is also referred to by those names. Although closely associated with a time of agricultural harvest, it foreshadows various spiritual "firstfruits" in which believers in God will be "harvested."

Deut.
16:9-12
TIME FOR FEAST. Count off seven weeks from the time you begin to put the sickle to the standing grain. Then celebrate the Feast of Weeks to the LORD your God by giving a freewill offering in proportion to the blessings the LORD your God has given you. And rejoice before the LORD your God at the place he will choose as a dwelling for his Name—you, your sons and daughters, your menservants and maidservants, the Levites in your towns, and the aliens, the fatherless and the widows living among you. Remember that you were slaves in Egypt, and follow carefully these decrees.

Lev.
23:9-14
Ex. 34:22
WAVE OFFERING. The LORD said to Moses, "Speak to the Israelites and say to them: 'When you enter the land I am going to give you and you reap its harvest, bring to the priest a sheaf of the first grain you harvest. He is to wave the sheaf before the LORD so it will be accepted on your behalf; the priest is to wave it on the day after the Sabbath. On the day you wave the

sheaf, you must sacrifice as a burnt offering to the LORD a lamb a year old without defect, together with its grain offering of two-tenths of an ephah[l] of fine flour mixed with oil—an offering made to the LORD by fire, a pleasing aroma—and its drink offering of a quarter of a hin[m] of wine. You must not eat any bread, or roasted or new grain, until the very day you bring this offering to your God. This is to be a lasting ordinance for the generations to come, wherever you live.

OFFERINGS FROM LEVITICUS.   " 'From the day after the Sabbath, the day you brought the sheaf of the wave offering, count off seven full weeks. Count off fifty days up to the day after the seventh Sabbath, and then present an offering of new grain to the LORD. From wherever you live, bring two loaves made of two-tenths of an ephah of fine flour, baked with yeast, as a wave offering of firstfruits to the LORD. Present with this bread seven male lambs, each a year old and without defect, one young bull and two rams. They will be a burnt offering to the LORD, together with their grain offerings and drink offerings—an offering made by fire, an aroma pleasing to the LORD. Then sacrifice one male goat for a sin offering and two lambs, each a year old, for a fellowship offering.[n] The priest is to wave the two lambs before the LORD as a wave offering, together with the bread of the firstfruits. They are a sacred offering to the LORD for the priest. On that same day you are to proclaim a sacred assembly and do no regular work. This is to be a lasting ordinance for the generations to come, wherever you live.

Lev.
23:15-21

OFFERINGS FROM NUMBERS.   " 'On the day of firstfruits, when you present to the LORD an offering of new grain during the Feast of Weeks, hold a sacred assembly and do no regular work. Present a burnt offering of two young bulls, one ram and seven male lambs a year old as an aroma pleasing to the LORD. With each bull there is to be a grain offering of three-tenths of an ephah of fine flour mixed with oil; with the ram, two-tenths; and with each of the seven lambs, one-tenth. Include one male goat to make atonement for you. Prepare these together with their drink offerings, in addition to the regular burnt offering and its grain offering. Be sure the animals are without defect.

Num.
28:26-31

3. Feast of Trumpets
7th Month, 1st Day (September-October)

Shortly before the third major feast, the Israelites are to celebrate one of less significance, known as the Feast of Trumpets. It takes place on the first day of the seventh month according to the religious calendar, in association with the institution of the Sabbath. And because that month is the first month on the civil calendar, it is a new year's celebration as well, modernly called Rosh Hashanah.

FEAST AND OFFERINGS.   " 'On the first day of the seventh month hold a sacred assembly and do no regular work. It is a day for you to sound the trumpets. As an aroma pleasing to the LORD, prepare a burnt offering of one young bull, one ram and seven male lambs a year old, all without

Lev.
23:23-25
Num.
29:1-6

---

[l]That is, probably about 4 quarts (about 4.5 liters)   [m]That is, probably about 1 quart (about 1 liter)   [n]Traditionally *peace offering*

defect. With the bull prepare a grain offering of three-tenths of an ephah[o] of fine flour mixed with oil; with the ram, two-tenths[p]; and with each of the seven lambs, one-tenth.[q] Include one male goat as a sin offering to make atonement for you. These are in addition to the monthly and daily burnt offerings with their grain offerings and drink offerings as specified. They are offerings made to the LORD by fire—a pleasing aroma.

4. Day of Atonement

7th Month, 10th Day (September-October)

In addition to the required feasts, God called for an annual Day of Atonement, just before the Feast of Tabernacles or Booths. The Day of Atonement was established when Aaron was the high priest, but will continue until even modern times, in which it is celebrated as Yom Kippur. It is the only day upon which the Israelites are commanded to fast. Its great significance lies in the confession of sins and the sending out of the scapegoat for atonement.

Lev. 16:1-5 PRIEST IN HOLY PLACE: The LORD spoke to Moses after the death of the two sons of Aaron who died when they approached the LORD. The LORD said to Moses: "Tell your brother Aaron not to come whenever he chooses into the Most Holy Place behind the curtain in front of the atonement cover on the ark, or else he will die, because I appear in the cloud over the atonement cover.

"This is how Aaron is to enter the sanctuary area: with a young bull for a sin offering and a ram for a burnt offering. He is to put on the sacred linen tunic, with linen undergarments next to his body; he is to tie the linen sash around him and put on the linen turban. These are sacred garments; so he must bathe himself with water before he puts them on. From the Israelite community he is to take two male goats for a sin offering and a ram for a burnt offering.

Lev. 16:6-10 TWO GOATS. "Aaron is to offer the bull for his own sin offering to make atonement for himself and his household. Then he is to take the two goats and present them before the LORD at the entrance to the Tent of Meeting. He is to cast lots for the two goats—one lot for the LORD and the other for the scapegoat.[r] Aaron shall bring the goat whose lot falls to the LORD and sacrifice it for a sin offering. But the goat chosen by lot as the scapegoat shall be presented alive before the LORD to be used for making atonement by sending it into the desert as a scapegoat.

Lev. 16:11-14 SIN OFFERING FOR PRIEST. "Aaron shall bring the bull for his own sin offering to make atonement for himself and his household, and he is to slaughter the bull for his own sin offering. He is to take a censer full of burning coals from the altar before the LORD and two handfuls of finely ground fragrant incense and take them behind the curtain. He is to put the incense on the fire before the LORD, and the smoke of the incense will conceal the atonement cover above the Testimony, so that he will not die. He is to take some of the bull's blood and with his finger sprinkle it on the

[o]That is, probably about 6 quarts (about 6.5 liters) [p]That is, probably about 4 quarts (about 4.5 liters) [q]That is, probably about 2 quarts (about 2 liters) [r]That is, the goat of removal; Hebrew *azazel*; also in verses 10 and 26

front of the atonement cover; then he shall sprinkle some of it with his finger seven times before the atonement cover.

SIN OFFERING FOR PEOPLE. "He shall then slaughter the goat for the sin offering for the people and take its blood behind the curtain and do with it as he did with the bull's blood: He shall sprinkle it on the atonement cover and in front of it. In this way he will make atonement for the Most Holy Place because of the uncleanness and rebellion of the Israelites, whatever their sins have been. He is to do the same for the Tent of Meeting, which is among them in the midst of their uncleanness. No one is to be in the Tent of Meeting from the time Aaron goes in to make atonement in the Most Holy Place until he comes out, having made atonement for himself, his household and the whole community of Israel.

Lev. 16:15-17

BLOOD OF BULL AND GOAT. "Then he shall come out to the altar that is before the LORD and make atonement for it. He shall take some of the bull's blood and some of the goat's blood and put it on all the horns of the altar. He shall sprinkle some of the blood on it with his finger seven times to cleanse it and to consecrate it from the uncleanness of the Israelites.

Lev. 16:18,19

CONFESSION OVER SCAPEGOAT. "When Aaron has finished making atonement for the Most Holy Place, the Tent of Meeting and the altar, he shall bring forward the live goat. He is to lay both hands on the head of the live goat and confess over it all the wickedness and rebellion of the Israelites—all their sins—and put them on the goat's head. He shall send the goat away into the desert in the care of a man appointed for the task. The goat will carry on itself all their sins to a solitary place; and the man shall release it in the desert.

Lev. 16:20-22

PURIFICATION FOLLOWING RITE. "Then Aaron is to go into the Tent of Meeting and take off the linen garments he put on before he entered the Most Holy Place, and he is to leave them there. He shall bathe himself with water in a holy place and put on his regular garments. Then he shall come out and sacrifice the burnt offering for himself and the burnt offering for the people, to make atonement for himself and for the people. He shall also burn the fat of the sin offering on the altar.

"The man who releases the goat as a scapegoat must wash his clothes and bathe himself with water; afterward he may come into the camp. The bull and the goat for the sin offerings, whose blood was brought into the Most Holy Place to make atonement, must be taken outside the camp; their hides, flesh and offal are to be burned up. The man who burns them must wash his clothes and bathe himself with water; afterward he may come into the camp.

Lev. 16:23-28

DAY TO BE ANNUAL. "This is to be a lasting ordinance for you: On the tenth day of the seventh month you must deny yourselves^s and not do any work—whether native-born or an alien living among you—because on this day atonement will be made for you, to cleanse you. Then, before the LORD, you will be clean from all your sins. It is a sabbath of rest, and you must deny yourselves; it is a lasting ordinance. The priest who is anointed and ordained to succeed his father as high priest is to make atonement. He is to put on the sacred linen garments and make atonement for the Most

Lev. 16:29-34

^sOr *must fast*

Holy Place, for the Tent of Meeting and the altar, and for the priests and all the people of the community.

"This is to be a lasting ordinance for you: Atonement is to be made once a year for all the sins of the Israelites."

And it was done, as the LORD commanded Moses.

Lev.
23:26-32

TO BE DAY OF FASTING.   The LORD said to Moses, "The tenth day of this seventh month is the Day of Atonement. Hold a sacred assembly and deny yourselves,[t] and present an offering made to the LORD by fire. Do no work on that day, because it is the Day of Atonement, when atonement is made for you before the LORD your God. Anyone who does not deny himself on that day must be cut off from his people. I will destroy from among his people anyone who does any work on that day. You shall do no work at all. This is to be a lasting ordinance for the generations to come, wherever you live. It is a sabbath of rest for you, and you must deny yourselves. From the evening of the ninth day of the month until the following evening you are to observe your sabbath."

Num.
29:7-11

SPECIAL OFFERING.   " 'On the tenth day of this seventh month hold a sacred assembly. You must deny yourselves[u] and do no work. Present as an aroma pleasing to the LORD a burnt offering of one young bull, one ram and seven male lambs a year old, all without defect. With the bull prepare a grain offering of three-tenths of an ephah of fine flour mixed with oil; with the ram, two-tenths; and with each of the seven lambs, one-tenth. Include one male goat as a sin offering, in addition to the sin offering for atonement and the regular burnt offering with its grain offering, and their drink offerings.

5. Feast of Tabernacles (Booths or Ingathering)
7th Month, 15th-21st Days (September-October)

The final feast is known as the Feast of Tabernacles (or Booths) as a solemn reminder of Israel's wandering in the wilderness in punishment for its sin of disbelief. During the week of celebration the Israelites are to live in tents or booths made of tree branches. As with the Feast of Weeks, this feast is also associated with a time of harvest and thus is alternately known as the Feast of Ingathering.

Lev.
23:33-36

SEVEN-DAY FEAST.   The LORD said to Moses, "Say to the Israelites: 'On the fifteenth day of the seventh month the LORD's Feast of Tabernacles begins, and it lasts for seven days. The first day is a sacred assembly; do no regular work. For seven days present offerings made to the LORD by fire, and on the eighth day hold a sacred assembly and present an offering made to the LORD by fire. It is the closing assembly; do no regular work.

Lev.
23:39-41

TAKING OF BRANCHES.   " 'So beginning with the fifteenth day of the seventh month, after you have gathered the crops of the land, celebrate the festival to the LORD for seven days; the first day is a day of rest, and the eighth day also is a day of rest. On the first day you are to take choice fruit from the trees, and palm fronds, leafy branches and poplars, and rejoice before the LORD your God for seven days. Celebrate this as a festival to the

[t]Or _and fast_; also in verses 29 and 32   [u]Or _must fast_

LORD for seven days each year. This is to be a lasting ordinance for the generations to come; celebrate it in the seventh month.

DWELLING IN BOOTHS.   Live in booths for seven days: All native-born Israelites are to live in booths so your descendants will know that I had the Israelites live in booths when I brought them out of Egypt. I am the LORD your God.'"

Lev.
23:42,43

OFFERINGS FOR FEAST.   " 'On the fifteenth day of the seventh month, hold a sacred assembly and do no regular work. Celebrate a festival to the LORD for seven days. Present an offering made by fire as an aroma pleasing to the LORD, a burnt offering of thirteen young bulls, two rams and fourteen male lambs a year old, all without defect. With each of the thirteen bulls prepare a grain offering of three-tenths of an ephah of fine flour mixed with oil; with each of the two rams, two-tenths; and with each of the fourteen lambs, one-tenth. Include one male goat as a sin offering, in addition to the regular burnt offering with its grain offering and drink offering.

Num.
29:12-38

" 'On the second day prepare twelve young bulls, two rams and fourteen male lambs a year old, all without defect. With the bulls, rams and lambs, prepare their grain offerings and drink offerings according to the number specified. Include one male goat as a sin offering, in addition to the regular burnt offering with its grain offering, and their drink offerings.

" 'On the third day prepare eleven bulls, two rams and fourteen male lambs a year old, all without defect. With the bulls, rams and lambs, prepare their grain offerings and drink offerings according to the number specified. Include one male goat as a sin offering, in addition to the regular burnt offering with its grain offering and drink offering.

" 'On the fourth day prepare ten bulls, two rams and fourteen male lambs a year old, all without defect. With the bulls, rams and lambs, prepare their grain offerings and drink offerings according to the number specified. Include one male goat as a sin offering, in addition to the regular burnt offering with its grain offering and drink offering.

" 'On the fifth day prepare nine bulls, two rams and fourteen male lambs a year old, all without defect. With the bulls, rams and lambs, prepare their grain offerings and drink offerings according to the number specified. Include one male goat as a sin offering, in addition to the regular burnt offering with its grain offering and drink offering.

" 'On the sixth day prepare eight bulls, two rams and fourteen male lambs a year old, all without defect. With the bulls, rams and lambs, prepare their grain offerings and drink offerings according to the number specified. Include one male goat as a sin offering, in addition to the regular burnt offering with its grain offering and drink offering.

" 'On the seventh day prepare seven bulls, two rams and fourteen male lambs a year old, all without defect. With the bulls, rams and lambs, prepare their grain offerings and drink offerings according to the number specified. Include one male goat as a sin offering, in addition to the regular burnt offering with its grain offering and drink offering.

" 'On the eighth day hold an assembly and do no regular work. Present an offering made by fire as an aroma pleasing to the LORD, a burnt offering of one bull, one ram and seven male lambs a year old, all without defect. With the bull, the ram and the lambs, prepare their grain offerings and drink offerings according to the number specified. Include one male goat as a sin offering, in addition to the regular burnt offering with its grain offering and drink offering.

Deut.
16:13-15

FEAST TO BE JOYFUL.   Celebrate the Feast of Tabernacles for seven days after you have gathered the produce of your threshing floor and your winepress. Be joyful at your Feast—you, your sons and daughters, your menservants and maidservants, and the Levites, the aliens, the fatherless and the widows who live in your towns. For seven days celebrate the Feast to the LORD your God at the place the LORD will choose. For the LORD your God will bless you in all your harvest and in all the work of your hands, and your joy will be complete.

These four major feasts are to be celebrated in addition to all the other gifts, sacrifices, and offerings required of the Israelites.

Lev.
23:37,38,44
Num.
29:39,40

CONCLUSION TO THE FEASTS.   (" 'These are the LORD's appointed feasts, which you are to proclaim as sacred assemblies for bringing offerings made to the LORD by fire—the burnt offerings and grain offerings, sacrifices and drink offerings required for each day. These offerings are in addition to those for the LORD's Sabbaths and^v in addition to your gifts and whatever you have vowed and all the freewill offerings you give to the LORD.)

So Moses announced to the Israelites the appointed feasts of the LORD.

I. Sacrifices and Offerings

While the feasts are principally times of celebration, remembrance, and thanksgiving, the sacrifices and offerings are designed to bring the removal of guilt (expiation) or the obtaining of God's favor (propitiation). The Day of Atonement has already been presented as a special day of sacrifice for the sins of the people, and it is by far the most important. In addition, there are five major offerings required, and numerous special ones besides.

1. Burnt Offerings

Burnt offerings are continuous sacrifices of unblemished animals which are completely burned and never eaten. After the worshiper lays his hands on the animal and it is killed, its blood is sprinkled around the altar in atonement for the worshiper's sins.

Lev. 1:1-9

OFFERINGS FROM HERD.   The LORD called to Moses and spoke to him from the Tent of Meeting. He said, "Speak to the Israelites and say to them: 'When any of you brings an offering to the LORD, bring as your offering an animal from either the herd or the flock.

" 'If the offering is a burnt offering from the herd, he is to offer a male without defect. He must present it at the entrance to the Tent of Meeting so that it^w will be acceptable to the LORD. He is to lay his hand on the head of the burnt offering, and it will be accepted on his behalf to make atonement for him. He is to slaughter the young bull before the LORD, and then Aaron's sons the priests shall bring the blood and sprinkle it against the

^{v}Or *These feasts are in addition to the* LORD's *Sabbaths, and these offerings are* ^{w}Or he

altar on all sides at the entrance to the Tent of Meeting. He is to skin the burnt offering and cut it into pieces. The sons of Aaron the priest are to put fire on the altar and arrange wood on the fire. Then Aaron's sons the priests shall arrange the pieces, including the head and the fat, on the burning wood that is on the altar. He is to wash the inner parts and the legs with water, and the priest is to burn all of it on the altar. It is a burnt offering, an offering made by fire, an aroma pleasing to the LORD.

OFFERINGS FROM FLOCK.   " 'If the offering is a burnt offering from the flock, from either the sheep or the goats, he is to offer a male without defect. He is to slaughter it at the north side of the altar before the LORD, and Aaron's sons the priests shall sprinkle its blood against the altar on all sides. He is to cut it into pieces, and the priest shall arrange them, including the head and the fat, on the burning wood that is on the altar. He is to wash the inner parts and the legs with water, and the priest is to bring all of it and burn it on the altar. It is a burnt offering, an offering made by fire, an aroma pleasing to the LORD.

Lev. 1:10-13

OFFERINGS FROM BIRDS.   " 'If the offering to the LORD is a burnt offering of birds, he is to offer a dove or a young pigeon. The priest shall bring it to the altar, wring off the head and burn it on the altar; its blood shall be drained out on the side of the altar. He is to remove the crop with its contents^x and throw it to the east side of the altar, where the ashes are. He shall tear it open by the wings, not severing it completely, and then the priest shall burn it on the wood that is on the fire on the altar. It is a burnt offering, an offering made by fire, an aroma pleasing to the LORD.

Lev. 1:14-17

INSTRUCTIONS FOR PRIESTS.   The LORD said to Moses: "Give Aaron and his sons this command: 'These are the regulations for the burnt offering: The burnt offering is to remain on the altar hearth throughout the night, till morning, and the fire must be kept burning on the altar. The priest shall then put on his linen clothes, with linen undergarments next to his body, and shall remove the ashes of the burnt offering that the fire has consumed on the altar and place them beside the altar. Then he is to take off these clothes and put on others, and carry the ashes outside the camp to a place that is ceremonially clean. The fire on the altar must be kept burning; it must not go out. Every morning the priest is to add firewood and arrange the burnt offering on the fire and burn the fat of the fellowship offerings^y on it. The fire must be kept burning on the altar continuously; it must not go out.

Lev. 6:8-13

CONTINUOUS DAILY OFFERINGS.   The LORD said to Moses, "Give this command to the Israelites and say to them: 'See that you present to me at the appointed time the food for my offerings made by fire, as an aroma pleasing to me.' Say to them: 'This is the offering made by fire that you are to present to the LORD: two lambs a year old without defect, as a regular burnt offering each day. Prepare one lamb in the morning and the other at twilight, together with a grain offering of a tenth of an ephah^z of fine flour mixed with a quarter of a hin^a of oil from pressed olives. This is the regular burnt offering instituted at Mount Sinai as a pleasing aroma, an offering made to the LORD by fire. The accompanying drink offering is to be a quarter of a hin of fermented drink with each lamb. Pour out the drink offering to the LORD at the sanctuary. Prepare the second lamb at twilight,

Num. 28:1-8

^{x}Or *crop and the feathers*; the meaning of the Hebrew for this word is uncertain.
^{y}Traditionally *peace offerings* ^{z}That is, probably about 2 quarts (about 2 liters)
^{a}That is, probably about 1 quart (about 1 liters)

along with the same kind of grain offering and drink offering that you prepare in the morning. This is an offering made by fire, an aroma pleasing to
the LORD.

Lev. 17:8-9   MUST BE AT TABERNACLE.   "Say to them: 'Any Israelite or any alien
living among them who offers a burnt offering or sacrifice and does not
bring it to the entrance to the Tent of Meeting to sacrifice it to the LORD—
that man must be cut off from his people.

2. Cereal Offerings

Cereal offerings are given, perhaps as an expression of devotion. They are
made of vegetables or other crops and cooked according to specific instructions,
but never mixed with either honey or leaven, which would make the meal spoil.
The offering of grain is to bring special blessings upon the entire crop.

Lev. 2:1-3   FLOUR, OIL, AND FRANKINCENSE.   " 'When someone brings a grain
offering to the LORD, his offering is to be of fine flour. He is to pour oil on
it, put incense on it and take it to Aaron's sons the priests. The priest shall
take a handful of the fine flour and oil, together with all the incense, and
burn this as a memorial portion on the altar, an offering made by fire, an
aroma pleasing to the LORD. The rest of the grain offering belongs to Aaron
and his sons; it is a most holy part of the offerings made to the LORD by fire.

Lev. 2:4-10   UNLEAVENED CAKES.   " 'If you bring a grain offering baked in an
oven, it is to consist of fine flour: cakes made without yeast and mixed
with oil, or[b] wafers made without yeast and spread with oil. If your grain
offering is prepared on a griddle, it is to be made of fine flour mixed with
oil, and without yeast. Crumble it and pour oil on it; it is a grain offering.
If your grain offering is cooked in a pan, it is to be made of fine flour and
oil. Bring the grain offering made of these things to the LORD; present it to
the priest, who shall take it to the altar. He shall take out the memorial portion from the grain offering and burn it on the altar as an offering made by
fire, an aroma pleasing to the LORD. The rest of the grain offering belongs
to Aaron and his sons; it is a most holy part of the offerings made to the
LORD by fire.

Lev.
2:11-13   SALT OF THE COVENANT.   " 'Every grain offering you bring to the
LORD must be made without yeast, for you are not to burn any yeast or
honey in an offering made to the LORD by fire. You may bring them to the
LORD as an offering of the firstfruits, but they are not to be offered on the
altar as a pleasing aroma. Season all your grain offerings with salt. Do not
leave the salt of the covenant of your God out of your grain offerings; add
salt to all your offerings.

Lev.
2:14-16   GRAIN FOR FIRSTFRUITS.   " 'If you bring a grain offering of firstfruits
to the LORD, offer crushed heads of new grain roasted in the fire. Put oil
and incense on it; it is a grain offering. The priest shall burn the memorial
portion of the crushed grain and the oil, together with all the incense, as
an offering made to the LORD by fire.

[b]Or and

INSTRUCTIONS FOR PRIESTS. " 'These are the regulations for the grain offering: Aaron's sons are to bring it before the LORD, in front of the altar. The priest is to take a handful of fine flour and oil, together with all the incense on the grain offering, and burn the memorial portion on the altar as an aroma pleasing to the LORD. Aaron and his sons shall eat the rest of it, but it is to be eaten without yeast in a holy place; they are to eat it in the courtyard of the Tent of Meeting. It must not be baked with yeast; I have given it as their share of the offerings made to me by fire. Like the sin offering and the guilt offering, it is most holy. Any male descendant of Aaron may eat it. It is his regular share of the offerings made to the LORD by fire for the generations to come. Whatever touches them will become holy.[c] "

Lev.
6:14-23

The LORD also said to Moses, "This is the offering Aaron and his sons are to bring to the LORD on the day he[d] is anointed: a tenth of an ephah[e] of fine flour as a regular grain offering, half of it in the morning and half in the evening. Prepare it with oil on a griddle; bring it well-mixed and present the grain offering broken[f] in pieces as an aroma pleasing to the LORD. The son who is to succeed him as anointed priest shall prepare it. It is the LORD's regular share and is to be burned completely. Every grain offering of a priest shall be burned completely; it must not be eaten."

TYPE FOR EACH ANIMAL.   The LORD said to Moses, "Speak to the Israelites and say to them: 'After you enter the land I am giving you as a home and you present to the LORD offerings made by fire, from the herd or the flock, as an aroma pleasing to the LORD—whether burnt offerings or sacrifices, for special vows or freewill offerings or festival offerings—then the one who brings his offering shall present to the LORD a grain offering of a tenth of an ephah[e] of fine flour mixed with a quarter of a hin[g] of oil. With each lamb for the burnt offering or the sacrifice, prepare a quarter of a hin of wine as a drink offering.

Num.
15:1-12

" 'With a ram prepare a grain offering of two-tenths of an ephah[h] of fine flour mixed with a third of a hin[i] of oil, and a third of a hin of wine as a drink offering. Offer it as an aroma pleasing to the LORD.

" 'When you prepare a young bull as a burnt offering or sacrifice, for a special vow or a fellowship offering[j] to the LORD, bring with the bull a grain offering of three-tenths of an ephah[k] of fine flour mixed with half a hin[l] of oil. Also bring half a hin of wine as a drink offering. It will be an offering made by fire, an aroma pleasing to the LORD. Each bull or ram, each lamb or young goat, is to be prepared in this manner. Do this for each one, for as many as you prepare.

LAWS SAME FOR GUESTS.   " 'Everyone who is native-born must do these things in this way when he brings an offering made by fire as an aroma pleasing to the LORD. For the generations to come, whenever an alien or anyone else living among you presents an offering made by fire as an aroma pleasing to the LORD, he must do exactly as you do. The community is to have the same rules for you and for the alien living among

Num.
15:13-16

---

[c]Or *Whoever touches them must be holy*; similarly in verse 27   [d]Or *each*   [e]That is, probably about 2 quarts (about 2 liters)   [f]The meaning of the Hebrew for this word is uncertain.   [g]That is, probably about 1 quart (about 1 liter)   [h]That is, probably about 4 quarts (about 4.5 liters)   [i]That is, probably about 1 1/4 quarts (about 1.2 liters) [j]Traditionally *peace offering*   [k]That is, probably about 6 quarts (about 6.5 liters)   [l]That is, probably about 2 quarts (about 2 liters); also in verse 10

you; this is a lasting ordinance for the generations to come. You and the alien shall be the same before the LORD: The same laws and regulations will apply both to you and to the alien living among you.'"

**Num.
15:17-21** COARSE MEAL OFFERING.   The LORD said to Moses, "Speak to the Israelites and say to them: 'When you enter the land to which I am taking you and you eat the food of the land, present a portion as an offering to the LORD. Present a cake from the first of your ground meal and present it as an offering from the threshing floor. Throughout the generations to come you are to give this offering to the LORD from the first of your ground meal.

3. Peace Offerings

Unlike the burnt and cereal offerings, the peace offerings—whether animals or unleavened cakes—are only partially burned and the rest eaten. Nor does it matter whether the animal is male or female. If the offering is required, then only the priests are to eat of it; but if it is a freewill offering, then the worshiper may also partake. Peace offerings are given for thanksgiving and praise, and are considered meals of fellowship between God and man.

Lev. 3:1-5 REGARDING CATTLE.   " 'If someone's offering is a fellowship offering,[m] and he offers an animal from the herd, whether male or female, he is to present before the LORD an animal without defect. He is to lay his hand on the head of his offering and slaughter it at the entrance to the Tent of Meeting. Then Aaron's sons the priests shall sprinkle the blood against the altar on all sides. From the fellowship offering he is to bring a sacrifice made to the LORD by fire: all the fat that covers the inner parts or is connected to them, both kidneys with the fat on them near the loins, and the covering of the liver, which he will remove with the kidneys. Then Aaron's sons are to burn it on the altar on top of the burnt offering that is on the burning wood, as an offering made by fire, an aroma pleasing to the LORD.

Lev. 3:6-11 REGARDING SHEEP.   " 'If he offers an animal from the flock as a fellowship offering to the LORD, he is to offer a male or female without defect. If he offers a lamb, he is to present it before the LORD. He is to lay his hand on the head of his offering and slaughter it in front of the Tent of Meeting. Then Aaron's sons shall sprinkle its blood against the altar on all sides. From the fellowship offering he is to bring a sacrifice made to the LORD by fire: its fat, the entire fat tail cut off close to the backbone, all the fat that covers the inner parts or is connected to them, both kidneys with the fat on them near the loins, and the covering of the liver, which he will remove with the kidneys. The priest shall burn them on the altar as food, an offering made to the LORD by fire.

**Lev.
3:12-17** REGARDING GOATS.   " 'If his offering is a goat, he is to present it before the LORD. He is to lay his hand on its head and slaughter it in front of the Tent of Meeting. Then Aaron's sons shall sprinkle its blood against the altar on all sides. From what he offers he is to make this offering to the LORD by fire: all the fat that covers the inner parts or is connected to them,

[m]Traditionally *peace offering*

both kidneys with the fat on them near the loins, and the covering of the liver, which he will remove with the kidneys. The priest shall burn them on the altar as food, an offering made by fire, a pleasing aroma. All the fat is the LORD's.

" 'This is a lasting ordinance for the generations to come, wherever you live: You must not eat any fat or any blood.' "

OFFERINGS OF THANKSGIVING.   " 'These are the regulations for the fellowship offering[n] a person may present to the LORD:

    " 'If he offers it as an expression of thankfulness, then along with this thank offering he is to offer cakes of bread made without yeast and mixed with oil, wafers made without yeast and spread with oil, and cakes of fine flour well-kneaded and mixed with oil. Along with his fellowship offering of thanksgiving he is to present an offering with cakes of bread made with yeast. He is to bring one of each kind as an offering, a contribution to the LORD; it belongs to the priest who sprinkles the blood of the fellowship offerings. The meat of his fellowship offering of thanksgiving must be eaten on the day it is offered; he must leave none of it till morning.

Lev. 7:11-15

FREEWILL OFFERINGS.   " 'If, however, his offering is the result of a vow or is a freewill offering, the sacrifice shall be eaten on the day he offers it, but anything left over may be eaten on the next day. Any meat of the sacrifice left over till the third day must be burned up. If any meat of the fellowship offering is eaten on the third day, it will not be accepted. It will not be credited to the one who offered it, for it is impure; the person who eats any of it will be held responsible.

Lev. 7:16-18 19:5-8

CLEANNESS REQUIRED.   " 'Meat that touches anything ceremonially unclean must not be eaten; it must be burned up. As for other meat, anyone ceremonially clean may eat it. But if anyone who is unclean eats any meat of the fellowship offering belonging to the LORD, that person must be cut off from his people. If anyone touches something unclean—whether human uncleanness or an unclean animal or any unclean, detestable thing—and then eats any of the meat of the fellowship offering belonging to the LORD, that person must be cut off from his people.' "

Lev. 7:19-21

PORTION FOR PRIESTS.   The LORD said to Moses, "Say to the Israelites: 'Anyone who brings a fellowship offering to the LORD is to bring part of it as his sacrifice to the LORD. With his own hands he is to bring the offering made to the LORD by fire; he is to bring the fat, together with the breast, and wave the breast before the LORD as a wave offering. The priest shall burn the fat on the altar, but the breast belongs to Aaron and his sons. You are to give the right thigh of your fellowship offerings to the priest as a contribution. The son of Aaron who offers the blood and the fat of the fellowship offering shall have the right thigh as his share. From the fellowship offerings of the Israelites, I have taken the breast that is waved and the thigh that is presented and have given them to Aaron the priest and his sons as their regular share from the Israelites.' "

    This is the portion of the offerings made to the LORD by fire that were allotted to Aaron and his sons on the day they were presented to serve the LORD as priests. On the day they were anointed, the LORD commanded that the Israelites give this to them as their regular share for the generations to come.

Lev. 7:28-36

[n]Traditionally *peace offering*

Lev. 17:1-7   MUST BE AT TABERNACLE.   The LORD said to Moses, "Speak to Aaron and his sons and to all the Israelites and say to them: 'This is what the LORD has commanded: Any Israelite who sacrifices an ox,[o] a lamb or a goat in the camp or outside of it instead of bringing it to the entrance to the Tent of Meeting to present it as an offering to the LORD in front of the tabernacle of the LORD—that man shall be considered guilty of bloodshed; he has shed blood and must be cut off from his people. This is so the Israelites will bring to the LORD the sacrifices they are now making in the open fields. They must bring them to the priest, that is, to the LORD, at the entrance to the Tent of Meeting and sacrifice them as fellowship offerings.[p] The priest is to sprinkle the blood against the altar of the LORD at the entrance to the Tent of Meeting and burn the fat as an aroma pleasing to the LORD. They must no longer offer any of their sacrifices to the goat idols[q] to whom they prostitute themselves. This is to be a lasting ordinance for them and for the generations to come.'

4. Sin Offerings

When any unintentional omissions or transgressions are discovered, various sin offerings are to be made. Included for special offerings are the high priest himself, the entire congregation, leaders of the congregation, and ordinary worshipers. It is noteworthy by these offerings that ignorance is no excuse under the law.

Lev. 4:1-12   FOR THE PRIEST.   The LORD said to Moses, "Say to the Israelites: 'When anyone sins unintentionally and does what is forbidden in any of the LORD's commands—

" 'If the anointed priest sins, bringing guilt on the people, he must bring to the LORD a young bull without defect as a sin offering for the sin he has committed. He is to present the bull at the entrance to the Tent of Meeting before the LORD. He is to lay his hand on its head and slaughter it before the LORD. Then the anointed priest shall take some of the bull's blood and carry it into the Tent of Meeting. He is to dip his finger into the blood and sprinkle some of it seven times before the LORD, in front of the curtain of the sanctuary. The priest shall then put some of the blood on the horns of the altar of fragrant incense that is before the LORD in the Tent of Meeting. The rest of the bull's blood he shall pour out at the base of the altar of burnt offering at the entrance to the Tent of Meeting. He shall remove all the fat from the bull of the sin offering—the fat that covers the inner parts or is connected to them, both kidneys with the fat on them near the loins, and the covering of the liver, which he will remove with the kidneys—just as the fat is removed from the ox[o] sacrificed as a fellowship offering.[r] Then the priest shall burn them on the altar of burnt offering. But the hide of the bull and all its flesh, as well as the head and legs, the inner parts and offal—that is, all the rest of the bull—he must take outside the camp to a place ceremonially clean, where the ashes are thrown, and burn it in a wood fire on the ash heap.

Lev. 4:13-21 Num. 15:22-26   FOR THE CONGREGATION.   " 'If the whole Israelite community sins unintentionally and does what is forbidden in any of the LORD's commands,

[o]The Hebrew word can include both male and female.   [p]Traditionally *peace offerings*
[q]Or *demons*   [r]Traditionally *peace offering*

even though the community is unaware of the matter, they are guilty. When they become aware of the sin they committed, the assembly must bring a young bull as a sin offering and present it before the Tent of Meeting. The elders of the community are to lay their hands on the bull's head before the LORD, and the bull shall be slaughtered before the LORD. Then the anointed priest is to take some of the bull's blood into the Tent of Meeting. He shall dip his finger into the blood and sprinkle it before the LORD seven times in front of the curtain. He is to put some of the blood on the horns of the altar that is before the LORD in the Tent of Meeting. The rest of the blood he shall pour out at the base of the altar of burnt offering at the entrance to the Tent of Meeting. He shall remove all the fat from it and burn it on the altar, and do with this bull just as he did with the bull for the sin offering. In this way the priest will make atonement for them, and they will be forgiven. Then he shall take the bull outside the camp and burn it as he burned the first bull. This is the sin offering for the community.

FOR LEADERS. " 'When a leader sins unintentionally and does what is forbidden in any of the commands of the LORD his God, he is guilty. When he is made aware of the sin he committed, he must bring as his offering a male goat without defect. He is to lay his hand on the goat's head and slaughter it at the place where the burnt offering is slaughtered before the LORD. It is a sin offering. Then the priest shall take some of the blood of the sin offering with his finger and put it on the horns of the altar of burnt offering and pour out the rest of the blood at the base of the altar. He shall burn all the fat on the altar as he burned the fat of the fellowship offering. In this way the priest will make atonement for the man's sin, and he will be forgiven.

*Lev.
4:22-26*

FOR ORDINARY WORSHIPERS. " 'If a member of the community sins unintentionally and does what is forbidden in any of the LORD's commands, he is guilty. When he is made aware of the sin he committed, he must bring as his offering for the sin he committed a female goat without defect. He is to lay his hand on the head of the sin offering and slaughter it at the place of the burnt offering. Then the priest is to take some of the blood with his finger and put it on the horns of the altar of burnt offering and pour out the rest of the blood at the base of the altar. He shall remove all the fat, just as the fat is removed from the fellowship offering, and the priest shall burn it on the altar as an aroma pleasing to the LORD. In this way the priest will make atonement for him, and he will be forgiven.
 " 'If he brings a lamb as his sin offering, he is to bring a female without defect. He is to lay his hand on its head and slaughter it for a sin offering at the place where the burnt offering is slaughtered. Then the priest shall take some of the blood of the sin offering with his finger and put it on the horns of the altar of burnt offering and pour out the rest of the blood at the base of the altar. He shall remove all the fat, just as the fat is removed from the lamb of the fellowship offering, and the priest shall burn it on the altar on top of the offerings made to the LORD by fire. In this way the priest will make atonement for him for the sin he has committed, and he will be forgiven.

*Lev.
4:27-35
Num.
15:27,28*

Lev. 5:1-6   ACTS REQUIRING OFFERING.   " 'If a person sins because he does not speak up when he hears a public charge to testify regarding something he has seen or learned about, he will be held responsible.

" 'Or if a person touches anything ceremonially unclean—whether the carcasses of unclean wild animals or of unclean livestock or of unclean creatures that move along the ground—even though he is unaware of it, he has become unclean and is guilty.

" 'Or if he touches human uncleanness—anything that would make him unclean—even though he is unaware of it, when he learns of it he will be guilty.

" 'Or if a person thoughtlessly takes an oath to do anything, whether good or evil—in any matter one might carelessly swear about—even though he is unaware of it, in any case when he learns of it he will be guilty.

" 'When anyone is guilty in any of these ways, he must confess in what way he has sinned and, as a penalty for the sin he has committed, he must bring to the LORD a female lamb or goat from the flock as a sin offering; and the priest shall make atonement for him for his sin.

Lev. 5:7-10   BIRD OFFERING FOR POOR.   " 'If he cannot afford a lamb, he is to bring two doves or two young pigeons to the LORD as a penalty for his sin—one for a sin offering and the other for a burnt offering. He is to bring them to the priest, who shall first offer the one for the sin offering. He is to wring its head from its neck, not severing it completely, and is to sprinkle some of the blood of the sin offering against the side of the altar; the rest of the blood must be drained out at the base of the altar. It is a sin offering. The priest shall then offer the other as a burnt offering in the prescribed way and make atonement for him for the sin he has committed, and he will be forgiven.

Lev.   CEREAL OFFERING FOR POOR.   " 'If, however, he cannot afford two
5:11-13   doves or two young pigeons, he is to bring as an offering for his sin a tenth of an ephah[s] of fine flour for a sin offering. He must not put oil or incense on it, because it is a sin offering. He is to bring it to the priest, who shall take a handful of it as a memorial portion and burn it on the altar on top of the offerings made to the LORD by fire. It is a sin offering. In this way the priest will make atonement for him for any of these sins he has committed, and he will be forgiven. The rest of the offering will belong to the priest, as in the case of the grain offering.' "

Lev.   INSTRUCTIONS FOR PRIESTS.   The LORD said to Moses, "Say to Aaron
6:24-30   and his sons: 'These are the regulations for the sin offering: The sin offering is to be slaughtered before the LORD in the place the burnt offering is slaughtered; it is most holy. The priest who offers it shall eat it; it is to be eaten in a holy place, in the courtyard of the Tent of Meeting. Whatever touches any of the flesh will become holy, and if any of the blood is spattered on a garment, you must wash it in a holy place. The clay pot the meat is cooked in must be broken; but if it is cooked in a bronze pot, the pot is to be scoured and rinsed with water. Any male in a priest's family may eat it; it is most holy. But any sin offering whose blood is brought into the Tent of Meeting to make atonement in the Holy Place must not be eaten; it must be burned.

[s]That is, probably about 2 quarts (about 2 liters)

LAW FOR GUESTS.   One and the same law applies to everyone who sins unintentionally, whether he is a native-born Israelite or an alien.

Num. 15:29

NOT FOR INTENTIONAL SIN.   " 'But anyone who sins defiantly, whether native-born or alien, blasphemes the LORD, and that person must be cut off from his people. Because he has despised the LORD's word and broken his commands, that person must surely be cut off; his guilt remains on him.' "

Num. 15:30,31

5. Guilt Offerings

In any case of sin or offense a guilt (or trespass) offering is to be made to atone for the sin. Where monetary damages can be assessed, there is also the idea of restitution, in which value is given over and above the damage inflicted. In effect it is an offering of money or of value equivalent.

SINS OF OMISSION.   The LORD said to Moses: "When a person commits a violation and sins unintentionally in regard to any of the LORD's holy things, he is to bring to the LORD as a penalty a ram from the flock, one without defect and of the proper value in silver, according to the sanctuary shekel.[t] It is a guilt offering. He must make restitution for what he has failed to do in regard to the holy things, add a fifth of the value to that and give it all to the priest, who will make atonement for him with the ram as a guilt offering, and he will be forgiven.

Lev. 5:14-16

SINS OF COMMISSION.   "If a person sins and does what is forbidden in any of the LORD's commands, even though he does not know it, he is guilty and will be held responsible. He is to bring to the priest as a guilt offering a ram from the flock, one without defect and of the proper value. In this way the priest will make atonement for him for the wrong he has committed unintentionally, and he will be forgiven. It is a guilt offering; he has been guilty of[u] wrongdoing against the LORD."

Lev. 5:17-19

FRAUD OR THEFT.   The LORD said to Moses: "If anyone sins and is unfaithful to the LORD by deceiving his neighbor about something entrusted to him or left in his care or stolen, or if he cheats him, or if he finds lost property and lies about it, or if he swears falsely, or if he commits any such sin that people may do—when he thus sins and becomes guilty, he must return what he has stolen or taken by extortion, or what was entrusted to him, or the lost property he found, or whatever it was he swore falsely about. He must make restitution in full, add a fifth of the value to it and give it all to the owner on the day he presents his guilt offering. And as a penalty he must bring to the priest, that is, to the LORD, his guilt offering, a ram from the flock, one without defect and of the proper value. In this way the priest will make atonement for him before the LORD, and he will be forgiven for any of these things he did that made him guilty."

Lev. 6:1-7

INSTRUCTIONS FOR PRIESTS.   " 'These are the regulations for the guilt offering, which is most holy: The guilt offering is to be slaughtered in the place where the burnt offering is slaughtered, and its blood is to be sprinkled against the altar on all sides. All its fat shall be offered: the fat tail and the fat that covers the inner parts, both kidneys with the fat on them near the loins, and the covering of the liver, which is to be removed with the

Lev. 7:1-10

---

[t]That is, about 2/5 ounce (about 11.5 grams)   [u]Or *has made full expiation for his*

kidneys. The priest shall burn them on the altar as an offering made to the LORD by fire. It is a guilt offering. Any male in a priest's family may eat it, but it must be eaten in a holy place; it is most holy.

" 'The same law applies to both the sin offering and the guilt offering: They belong to the priest who makes atonement with them. The priest who offers a burnt offering for anyone may keep its hide for himself. Every grain offering baked in an oven or cooked in a pan or on a griddle belongs to the priest who offers it, and every grain offering, whether mixed with oil or dry, belongs equally to all the sons of Aaron.

Lev.
7:37,38
CONCLUSION TO MAIN OFFERINGS.   These, then, are the regulations for the burnt offering, the grain offering, the sin offering, the guilt offering, the ordination offering and the fellowship offering, which the LORD gave Moses on Mount Sinai on the day he commanded the Israelites to bring their offerings to the LORD, in the Desert of Sinai.

6. Special Offerings

In addition to the five main offerings, there are other special offerings.

Num.
28:9,10
OFFERING ON THE SABBATH.   " 'On the Sabbath day, make an offering of two lambs a year old without defect, together with its drink offering and a grain offering of two-tenths of an ephah^v of fine flour mixed with oil. This is the burnt offering for every Sabbath, in addition to the regular burnt offering and its drink offering.

Num.
28:11-15
OFFERING ON EACH MONTH.   " 'On the first of every month, present to the LORD a burnt offering of two young bulls, one ram and seven male lambs a year old, all without defect. With each bull there is to be a grain offering of three-tenths of an ephah^w of fine flour mixed with oil; with the ram, a grain offering of two-tenths of an ephah of fine flour mixed with oil; and with each lamb, a grain offering of a tenth of an ephah of fine flour mixed with oil. This is for a burnt offering, a pleasing aroma, an offering made to the LORD by fire. With each bull there is to be a drink offering of half a hin^x of wine; with the ram, a third of a hin^y; and with each lamb, a quarter of a hin. This is the monthly burnt offering to be made at each new moon during the year. Besides the regular burnt offering with its drink offering, one male goat is to be presented to the LORD as a sin offering.

Deut.
21:1-9
OFFERING FOR UNKNOWN MURDERER.   If a man is found slain, lying in a field in the land the LORD your God is giving you to possess, and it is not known who killed him, your elders and judges shall go out and measure the distance from the body to the neighboring towns. Then the elders of the town nearest the body shall take a heifer that has never been worked and has never worn a yoke and lead her down to a valley that has not been plowed or planted and where there is a flowing stream. There in the valley they are to break the heifer's neck. The priests, the sons of Levi, shall step forward, for the LORD your God has chosen them to minister and to pronounce blessings in the name of the LORD and to decide all cases of dispute and assault. Then all the elders of the town nearest the body shall

---

^{v}That is, probably about 4 quarts (about 4.5 liters) ^{w}That is, probably about 6 quarts (about 6.5 liters) ^{x}That is, probably about 2 quarts (about 2 liters) ^{y}That is, probably about 1 1/4 quarts (about 1.2 liters)

wash their hands over the heifer whose neck was broken in the valley, and they shall declare: "Our hands did not shed this blood, nor did our eyes see it done. Accept this atonement for your people Israel, whom you have redeemed, O LORD, and do not hold your people guilty of the blood of an innocent man." And the bloodshed will be atoned for. So you will purge from yourselves the guilt of shedding innocent blood, since you have done what is right in the eyes of the LORD.

7. Rules Pertaining to Offerings

ACCEPTABLE OFFERINGS.   The LORD said to Moses, "Speak to Aaron and his sons and to all the Israelites and say to them: 'If any of you—either an Israelite or an alien living in Israel—presents a gift for a burnt offering to the LORD, either to fulfill a vow or as a freewill offering, you must present a male without defect from the cattle, sheep or goats in order that it may be accepted on your behalf. Do not bring anything with a defect, because it will not be accepted on your behalf. When anyone brings from the herd or flock a fellowship offering^z to the LORD to fulfill a special vow or as a freewill offering, it must be without defect or blemish to be acceptable. Do not offer to the LORD the blind, the injured or the maimed, or anything with warts or festering or running sores. Do not place any of these on the altar as an offering made to the LORD by fire. You may, however, present as a freewill offering an ox,^a or a sheep that is deformed or stunted, but it will not be accepted in fulfillment of a vow. You must not offer to the LORD an animal whose testicles are bruised, crushed, torn or cut. You must not do this in your own land, and you must not accept such animals from the hand of a foreigner and offer them as the food of your God. They will not be accepted on your behalf, because they are deformed and have defects.'"

Lev.
22:17-25
Deut. 17:1

CONCERN FOR ANIMALS.   The LORD said to Moses, "When a calf, a lamb or a goat is born, it is to remain with its mother for seven days. From the eighth day on, it will be acceptable as an offering made to the LORD by fire. Do not slaughter a cow or a sheep and its young on the same day.

Lev.
22:26-28

PERIOD OF EATING.   "When you sacrifice a thank offering to the LORD, sacrifice it in such a way that it will be accepted on your behalf. It must be eaten that same day; leave none of it till morning. I am the LORD.

Lev.
22:29,30

NO LEAVENED BREAD.   "Do not offer the blood of a sacrifice to me along with anything containing yeast.
    "The fat of my festival offerings must not be kept until morning.

Ex. 23:18
34:25

J. Other Rituals

OIL FOR LAMPS CONTINUALLY.   The LORD said to Moses, "Command the Israelites to bring you clear oil of pressed olives for the light so that the lamps may be kept burning continually. Outside the curtain of the Testimony in the Tent of Meeting, Aaron is to tend the lamps before the LORD from evening till morning, continually. This is to be a lasting ordinance for the generations to come. The lamps on the pure gold lampstand before the LORD must be tended continually.

Lev. 24:1-4

---

^zTraditionally *peace offering*   ^aThe Hebrew word can include both male and female.

Lev. 24:5-9	SHOWBREAD ON SABBATH. "Take fine flour and bake twelve loaves of bread, using two-tenths of an ephah[b] for each loaf. Set them in two rows, six in each row, on the table of pure gold before the LORD. Along each row put some pure incense as a memorial portion to represent the bread and to be an offering made to the LORD by fire. This bread is to be set out before the LORD regularly, Sabbath after Sabbath, on behalf of the Israelites, as a lasting covenant. It belongs to Aaron and his sons, who are to eat it in a holy place, because it is a most holy part of their regular share of the offerings made to the LORD by fire."
Num. 6:22-27	AARONIC BENEDICTION. The LORD said to Moses, "Tell Aaron and his sons, 'This is how you are to bless the Israelites. Say to them:

> " ' "The LORD bless you
> and keep you;
> the LORD make his face shine upon you
> and be gracious to you;
> the LORD turn his face toward you
> and give you peace." '

"So they will put my name on the Israelites, and I will bless them."

K. Rules for the Priests

At the heart of the worship rituals is the office of priest. In order that the many sacrifices and offerings be holy unto God, the priests themselves must be holy.

Lev. 21:1-4	DEFILEMENT FOR DEAD. The LORD said to Moses, "Speak to the priests, the sons of Aaron, and say to them: 'A priest must not make himself ceremonially unclean for any of his people who die, except for a close relative, such as his mother or father, his son or daughter, his brother, or an unmarried sister who is dependent on him since she has no husband— for her he may make himself unclean. He must not make himself unclean for people related to him by marriage,[c] and so defile himself.
Lev. 21:5,6	HOLY APPEARANCE. " 'Priests must not shave their heads or shave off the edges of their beards or cut their bodies. They must be holy to their God and must not profane the name of their God. Because they present the offerings made to the LORD by fire, the food of their God, they are to be holy.
Lev. 21:7,8	NONAPPROVED MARRIAGES. " 'They must not marry women defiled by prostitution or divorced from their husbands, because priests are holy to their God. Regard them as holy, because they offer up the food of your God. Consider them holy, because I the LORD am holy—I who make you holy.[d]
Lev. 21:9	HARLOT DAUGHTERS. " 'If a priest's daughter defiles herself by becoming a prostitute, she disgraces her father; she must be burned in the fire.

[b] That is, probably about 4 quarts (about 4.5 liters)   [c] Or *unclean as a leader among his people*   [d] Or *who sanctify you;* or *who set you apart as holy*

RULES FOR HIGH PRIEST.   " 'The high priest, the one among his broth-   Lev.
21:10-15
ers who has had the anointing oil poured on his head and who has been
ordained to wear the priestly garments, must not let his hair become
unkempt*e* or tear his clothes. He must not enter a place where there is a
dead body. He must not make himself unclean, even for his father or
mother, nor leave the sanctuary of his God or desecrate it, because he has
been dedicated by the anointing oil of his God. I am the LORD.

" 'The woman he marries must be a virgin. He must not marry a widow,
a divorced woman, or a woman defiled by prostitution, but only a virgin
from his own people, so he will not defile his offspring among his people.
I am the LORD, who makes him holy.*f* "

BLEMISHED NOT TO SERVE.   The LORD said to Moses, "Say to Aaron: Lev.
21:16-24
'For the generations to come none of your descendants who has a defect
may come near to offer the food of his God. No man who has any defect
may come near: no man who is blind or lame, disfigured or deformed; no
man with a crippled foot or hand, or who is hunchbacked or dwarfed, or
who has any eye defect, or who has festering or running sores or damaged
testicles. No descendant of Aaron the priest who has any defect is to come
near to present the offerings made to the LORD by fire. He has a defect; he
must not come near to offer the food of his God. He may eat the most holy
food of his God, as well as the holy food; yet because of his defect, he must
not go near the curtain or approach the altar, and so desecrate my sanctuary. I am the LORD, who makes them holy.*g* "

So Moses told this to Aaron and his sons and to all the Israelites.

UNCLEAN NOT TO TOUCH HOLY.   The LORD said to Moses, "Tell   Lev. 22:1-9
Aaron and his sons to treat with respect the sacred offerings the Israelites
consecrate to me, so they will not profane my holy name. I am the LORD.

"Say to them: 'For the generations to come, if any of your descendants
is ceremonially unclean and yet comes near the sacred offerings that the
Israelites consecrate to the LORD, that person must be cut off from my presence. I am the LORD.

" 'If a descendant of Aaron has an infectious skin disease*h* or a bodily
discharge, he may not eat the sacred offerings until he is cleansed. He will
also be unclean if he touches something defiled by a corpse or by anyone
who has an emission of semen, or if he touches any crawling thing that
makes him unclean, or any person who makes him unclean, whatever the
uncleanness may be. The one who touches any such thing will be unclean
till evening. He must not eat any of the sacred offerings unless he has
bathed himself with water. When the sun goes down, he will be clean, and
after that he may eat the sacred offerings, for they are his food. He must
not eat anything found dead or torn by wild animals, and so become
unclean through it. I am the LORD.

" 'The priests are to keep my requirements so that they do not become
guilty and die for treating them with contempt. I am the LORD, who makes
them holy.*i*

---

*e*Or *not uncover his head*   *f*Or *who sanctifies him; or who sets him apart as holy*   *g*Or *who
sanctifies them; or who sets them apart as holy*   *h*Traditionally *leprosy*; the Hebrew word
was used for various diseases affecting the skin—not necessarily leprosy.   *i*Or *who
sanctifies them; or who sets them apart as holy*; also in verse 16

Lev.
22:10-16

OUTSIDER NOT TO EAT. " 'No one outside a priest's family may eat the sacred offering, nor may the guest of a priest or his hired worker eat it. But if a priest buys a slave with money, or if a slave is born in his household, that slave may eat his food. If a priest's daughter marries anyone other than a priest, she may not eat any of the sacred contributions. But if a priest's daughter becomes a widow or is divorced, yet has no children, and she returns to live in her father's house as in her youth, she may eat of her father's food. No unauthorized person, however, may eat any of it.

" 'If anyone eats a sacred offering by mistake, he must make restitution to the priest for the offering and add a fifth of the value to it. The priests must not desecrate the sacred offerings the Israelites present to the LORD by allowing them to eat the sacred offerings and so bring upon them guilt requiring payment. I am the LORD, who makes them holy.' "

L. The Sabbatical Year

In addition to the weekly Sabbath for rest and worship, there is also to be a rest for the land on each seventh year.

Lev. 25:1-7

SABBATH REST FOR LAND. The LORD said to Moses on Mount Sinai, "Speak to the Israelites and say to them: 'When you enter the land I am going to give you, the land itself must observe a sabbath to the LORD. For six years sow your fields, and for six years prune your vineyards and gather their crops. But in the seventh year the land is to have a sabbath of rest, a sabbath to the LORD. Do not sow your fields or prune your vineyards. Do not reap what grows of itself or harvest the grapes of your untended vines. The land is to have a year of rest. Whatever the land yields during the sabbath year will be food for you—for yourself, your manservant and maidservant, and the hired worker and temporary resident who live among you, as well as for your livestock and the wild animals in your land. Whatever the land produces may be eaten.

Ex.
23:10,11

PROVISION FOR POOR AND ANIMALS. "For six years you are to sow your fields and harvest the crops, but during the seventh year let the land lie unplowed and unused. Then the poor among your people may get food from it, and the wild animals may eat what they leave. Do the same with your vineyard and your olive grove.

M. Year of Jubilee

Every 50 years there is to be a special yearlong Jubilee, beginning on the Day of Atonement with the solemn blowing of trumpets. It is to be a holy year, like the Sabbatical years, in which the land is to lie fallow. One of the most remarkable features of the Jubilee is the concept of redemption, in which inheritances are restored, slaves are set free, and property formerly sold may be either repurchased or automatically returned. It is both a nobly humanitarian provision and a foretaste of even greater spiritual redemption in the era of the Messiah.

Lev.
25:8-10

FIFTIETH YEAR FOR LIBERTY. " 'Count off seven sabbaths of years— seven times seven years—so that the seven sabbaths of years amount to a period of forty-nine years. Then have the trumpet sounded everywhere on the tenth day of the seventh month; on the Day of Atonement sound the trumpet throughout your land. Consecrate the fiftieth year and proclaim liberty throughout the land to all its inhabitants. It shall be a jubilee for you; each one of you is to return to his family property and each to his own clan.

TO BE HOLY YEAR. The fiftieth year shall be a jubilee for you; do not sow and do not reap what grows of itself or harvest the untended vines. For it is a jubilee and is to be holy for you; eat only what is taken directly from the fields.

Lev. 25:11,12

PURCHASE OF PROPERTY. " 'In this Year of Jubilee everyone is to return to his own property.

Lev. 25:13-17

" 'If you sell land to one of your countrymen or buy any from him, do not take advantage of each other. You are to buy from your countryman on the basis of the number of years since the Jubilee. And he is to sell to you on the basis of the number of years left for harvesting crops. When the years are many, you are to increase the price, and when the years are few, you are to decrease the price, because what he is really selling you is the number of crops. Do not take advantage of each other, but fear your God. I am the LORD your God.

BOUNTIFUL SIXTH YEAR. " 'Follow my decrees and be careful to obey my laws, and you will live safely in the land. Then the land will yield its fruit, and you will eat your fill and live there in safety. You may ask, "What will we eat in the seventh year if we do not plant or harvest our crops?" I will send you such a blessing in the sixth year that the land will yield enough for three years. While you plant during the eighth year, you will eat from the old crop and will continue to eat from it until the harvest of the ninth year comes in.

Lev. 25:18-22

NO LAND IN PERPETUITY. " 'The land must not be sold permanently, because the land is mine and you are but aliens and my tenants. Throughout the country that you hold as a possession, you must provide for the redemption of the land.

Lev. 25:23,24

REDEMPTION OF PROPERTY. " 'If one of your countrymen becomes poor and sells some of his property, his nearest relative is to come and redeem what his countryman has sold. If, however, a man has no one to redeem it for him but he himself prospers and acquires sufficient means to redeem it, he is to determine the value for the years since he sold it and refund the balance to the man to whom he sold it; he can then go back to his own property. But if he does not acquire the means to repay him, what he sold will remain in the possession of the buyer until the Year of Jubilee. It will be returned in the Jubilee, and he can then go back to his property.

Lev. 25:25-28

REGARDING HOUSES. " 'If a man sells a house in a walled city, he retains the right of redemption a full year after its sale. During that time he may redeem it. If it is not redeemed before a full year has passed, the house in the walled city shall belong permanently to the buyer and his descendants. It is not to be returned in the Jubilee. But houses in villages without walls around them are to be considered as open country. They can be redeemed, and they are to be returned in the Jubilee.

Lev. 25:29-31

RULES FOR LEVITES. " 'The Levites always have the right to redeem their houses in the Levitical towns, which they possess. So the property of the Levites is redeemable—that is, a house sold in any town they hold—

Lev. 25:32-34

and is to be returned in the Jubilee, because the houses in the towns of the Levites are their property among the Israelites. But the pastureland belonging to their towns must not be sold; it is their permanent possession.

Lev.
25:39-43

RELEASE OF SERVANTS. " 'If one of your countrymen becomes poor among you and sells himself to you, do not make him work as a slave. He is to be treated as a hired worker or a temporary resident among you; he is to work for you until the Year of Jubilee. Then he and his children are to be released, and he will go back to his own clan and to the property of his forefathers. Because the Israelites are my servants, whom I brought out of Egypt, they must not be sold as slaves. Do not rule over them ruthlessly, but fear your God.

Lev.
25:47-55

REDEMPTION OF SERVANTS. " 'If an alien or a temporary resident among you becomes rich and one of your countrymen becomes poor and sells himself to the alien living among you or to a member of the alien's clan, he retains the right of redemption after he has sold himself. One of his relatives may redeem him: An uncle or a cousin or any blood relative in his clan may redeem him. Or if he prospers, he may redeem himself. He and his buyer are to count the time from the year he sold himself up to the Year of Jubilee. The price for his release is to be based on the rate paid to a hired man for that number of years. If many years remain, he must pay for his redemption a larger share of the price paid for him. If only a few years remain until the Year of Jubilee, he is to compute that and pay for his redemption accordingly. He is to be treated as a man hired from year to year; you must see to it that his owner does not rule over him ruthlessly.

" 'Even if he is not redeemed in any of these ways, he and his children are to be released in the Year of Jubilee, for the Israelites belong to me as servants. They are my servants, whom I brought out of Egypt. I am the LORD your God.

N. Purification

Partially for purposes of maintaining proper health conditions, and partially for teaching proper personal conduct, but primarily for promoting the idea of holiness, the Laws of Moses designate certain types of ceremonial uncleanness. These various types of uncleanness are associated with diet, childbirth, bodily emissions and discharges, numerous diseases, and contact with the dead. In normal law codes the regulations would most properly fit within a health-and-general-welfare section. However, in a theocratic code such as this, there are religious and ceremonial aspects which more properly fit within the present section. Therefore a certain amount of overlapping must take place at this point. Regulations pertaining primarily to ceremonial purification for uncleanness will be listed here, while other related regulations will be presented in other sections.

1. After Childbirth

Each woman is required to purify her uncleanness after childbirth. This may be associated with the sin of Eve and its consequence of pain for all women giving birth. Or it may be that in order to bring a new child into the human family without sin, the "vessel" through which it comes must itself be made clean. Certainly there is no hint that either the child, or even the act which brought about the birth, is itself unclean.

UNCLEANNESS AFTER CHILDBIRTH.   The Lord said to Moses, "Say   Lev. 12:1-5
to the Israelites: 'A woman who becomes pregnant and gives birth to a son will be ceremonially unclean for seven days, just as she is unclean during her monthly period. On the eighth day the boy is to be circumcised. Then the woman must wait thirty-three days to be purified from her bleeding. She must not touch anything sacred or go to the sanctuary until the days of her purification are over. If she gives birth to a daughter, for two weeks the woman will be unclean, as during her period. Then she must wait sixty-six days to be purified from her bleeding.

OFFERING FOR ATONEMENT.   " 'When the days of her purification for   Lev. 12:6-8
a son or daughter are over, she is to bring to the priest at the entrance to the Tent of Meeting a year-old lamb for a burnt offering and a young pigeon or a dove for a sin offering. He shall offer them before the Lord to make atonement for her, and then she will be ceremonially clean from her flow of blood.
    " 'These are the regulations for the woman who gives birth to a boy or a girl. If she cannot afford a lamb, she is to bring two doves or two young pigeons, one for a burnt offering and the other for a sin offering. In this way the priest will make atonement for her, and she will be clean.' "

2. For Leprosy

The term "leprosy" is used generically to refer to any number of skin diseases, molds, or defects in people, garments, or even houses. While specific diagnosis and treatment is regulated in the health section, the various means of purifying the ceremonial uncleanness are now given.

WEEK OF CLEANSING.   The Lord said to Moses, "These are the regu-   Lev. 14:1-9
lations for the diseased person at the time of his ceremonial cleansing, when he is brought to the priest: The priest is to go outside the camp and examine him. If the person has been healed of his infectious skin disease,[j] the priest shall order that two live clean birds and some cedar wood, scarlet yarn and hyssop be brought for the one to be cleansed. Then the priest shall order that one of the birds be killed over fresh water in a clay pot. He is then to take the live bird and dip it, together with the cedar wood, the scarlet yarn and the hyssop, into the blood of the bird that was killed over the fresh water. Seven times he shall sprinkle the one to be cleansed of the infectious disease and pronounce him clean. Then he is to release the live bird in the open fields.
    "The person to be cleansed must wash his clothes, shave off all his hair and bathe with water; then he will be ceremonially clean. After this he may come into the camp, but he must stay outside his tent for seven days. On the seventh day he must shave off all his hair; he must shave his head, his beard, his eyebrows and the rest of his hair. He must wash his clothes and bathe himself with water, and he will be clean.

[j]Traditionally *leprosy*; the Hebrew word was used for various diseases affecting the skin—not necessarily leprosy.

Lev.
14:10-20

OFFERINGS FOR ATONEMENT.   "On the eighth day he must bring two male lambs and one ewe lamb a year old, each without defect, along with three-tenths of an ephah^k of fine flour mixed with oil for a grain offering, and one log^l of oil. The priest who pronounces him clean shall present both the one to be cleansed and his offerings before the LORD at the entrance to the Tent of Meeting.

"Then the priest is to take one of the male lambs and offer it as a guilt offering, along with the log of oil; he shall wave them before the LORD as a wave offering. He is to slaughter the lamb in the holy place where the sin offering and the burnt offering are slaughtered. Like the sin offering, the guilt offering belongs to the priest; it is most holy. The priest is to take some of the blood of the guilt offering and put it on the lobe of the right ear of the one to be cleansed, on the thumb of his right hand and on the big toe of his right foot. The priest shall then take some of the log of oil, pour it in the palm of his own left hand, dip his right forefinger into the oil in his palm, and with his finger sprinkle some of it before the LORD seven times. The priest is to put some of the oil remaining in his palm on the lobe of the right ear of the one to be cleansed, on the thumb of his right hand and on the big toe of his right foot, on top of the blood of the guilt offering. The rest of the oil in his palm the priest shall put on the head of the one to be cleansed and make atonement for him before the LORD.

"Then the priest is to sacrifice the sin offering and make atonement for the one to be cleansed from his uncleanness. After that, the priest shall slaughter the burnt offering and offer it on the altar, together with the grain offering, and make atonement for him, and he will be clean.

Lev.
14:21-32

OFFERINGS IF POOR.   "If, however, he is poor and cannot afford these, he must take one male lamb as a guilt offering to be waved to make atonement for him, together with a tenth of an ephah^m of fine flour mixed with oil for a grain offering, a log of oil, and two doves or two young pigeons, which he can afford, one for a sin offering and the other for a burnt offering.

"On the eighth day he must bring them for his cleansing to the priest at the entrance to the Tent of Meeting, before the LORD. The priest is to take the lamb for the guilt offering, together with the log of oil, and wave them before the LORD as a wave offering. He shall slaughter the lamb for the guilt offering and take some of its blood and put it on the lobe of the right ear of the one to be cleansed, on the thumb of his right hand and on the big toe of his right foot. The priest is to pour some of the oil into the palm of his own left hand, and with his right forefinger sprinkle some of the oil from his palm seven times before the LORD. Some of the oil in his palm he is to put on the same places he put the blood of the guilt offering—on the lobe of the right ear of the one to be cleansed, on the thumb of his right hand and on the big toe of his right foot. The rest of the oil in his palm the priest shall put on the head of the one to be cleansed, to make atonement for him before the LORD. Then he shall sacrifice the doves or the young pigeons, which the person can afford, one^n as a sin offering and the other as a burnt offering, together with the grain offering. In this way the priest will make atonement before the LORD on behalf of the one to be cleansed."

---

^{k}That is, probably about 6 quarts (about 6.5 liters) ^{l}That is, probably about 2/3 pint (about 0.3 liter) ^{m}That is, probably about 2 quarts (about 2 liters) ^{n}Septuagint and Syriac; Hebrew ^{31}*such as the person can afford, one*

These are the regulations for anyone who has an infectious skin disease and who cannot afford the regular offerings for his cleansing.

3. For Discharges

Bodily discharges and emissions are set forth as forms of uncleanness, even if they issue involuntarily. They may or may not have a direct relation to moral impurity, though many diseases are in fact the result of sin. Of more importance is any perceived uncleanness and the need for purity of the body as well as of the soul. While specific regulations pertaining to various secretions are included in the health section, the methods of ceremonial cleansing which require action by a priest are set forth at this point.

FOR MAN'S DISCHARGE.   " 'When a man is cleansed from his discharge, he is to count off seven days for his ceremonial cleansing; he must wash his clothes and bathe himself with fresh water, and he will be clean. On the eighth day he must take two doves or two young pigeons and come before the LORD to the entrance to the Tent of Meeting and give them to the priest. The priest is to sacrifice them, the one for a sin offering and the other for a burnt offering. In this way he will make atonement before the LORD for the man because of his discharge.

Lev. 15:13-15

FOR WOMAN'S DISCHARGE.   " 'When she is cleansed from her discharge, she must count off seven days, and after that she will be ceremonially clean. On the eighth day she must take two doves or two young pigeons and bring them to the priest at the entrance to the Tent of Meeting. The priest is to sacrifice one for a sin offering and the other for a burnt offering. In this way he will make atonement for her before the LORD for the uncleanness of her discharge.

Lev. 15:28-30

4. Concerning Death

Death has almost universally been associated with sin, so it is no surprise to find regulations defining uncleanness and requirements for sacrifices when one has come into contact with the dead. Physical contact with the dead has great significance for a nation whose God is not merely a piece of stone or wood: Death must not be permitted to contaminate worship of a living God who has given life to all living things.

CONTACT WITH DEAD BODY.   "Whoever touches the dead body of anyone will be unclean for seven days. He must purify himself with the water on the third day and on the seventh day; then he will be clean. But if he does not purify himself on the third and seventh days, he will not be clean. Whoever touches the dead body of anyone and fails to purify himself defiles the LORD's tabernacle. That person must be cut off from Israel. Because the water of cleansing has not been sprinkled on him, he is unclean; his uncleanness remains on him.

Num. 19:11-13

(REGARDING THE PASSOVER)

(Num. 9:10)

CONTACT WITH ENVIRONMENT.   "This is the law that applies when a person dies in a tent: Anyone who enters the tent and anyone who is in

Num. 19:14-19

it will be unclean for seven days, and every open container without a lid fastened on it will be unclean.

"Anyone out in the open who touches someone who has been killed with a sword or someone who has died a natural death, or anyone who touches a human bone or a grave, will be unclean for seven days.

"For the unclean person, put some ashes from the burned purification offering into a jar and pour fresh water over them. Then a man who is ceremonially clean is to take some hyssop, dip it in the water and sprinkle the tent and all the furnishings and the people who were there. He must also sprinkle anyone who has touched a human bone or a grave or someone who has been killed or someone who has died a natural death. The man who is clean is to sprinkle the unclean person on the third and seventh days, and on the seventh day he is to purify him. The person being cleansed must wash his clothes and bathe with water, and that evening he will be clean.

Num.
19:20-22

CLEANSING MANDATORY.   But if a person who is unclean does not purify himself, he must be cut off from the community, because he has defiled the sanctuary of the LORD. The water of cleansing has not been sprinkled on him, and he is unclean. This is a lasting ordinance for them.

"The man who sprinkles the water of cleansing must also wash his clothes, and anyone who touches the water of cleansing will be unclean till evening. Anything that an unclean person touches becomes unclean, and anyone who touches it becomes unclean till evening."

Num.
19:1-10

ASHES AND WATER FOR IMPURITY.   The LORD said to Moses and Aaron: "This is a requirement of the law that the LORD has commanded: Tell the Israelites to bring you a red heifer without defect or blemish and that has never been under a yoke. Give it to Eleazar the priest; it is to be taken outside the camp and slaughtered in his presence. Then Eleazar the priest is to take some of its blood on his finger and sprinkle it seven times toward the front of the Tent of Meeting. While he watches, the heifer is to be burned—its hide, flesh, blood and offal. The priest is to take some cedar wood, hyssop and scarlet wool and throw them onto the burning heifer. After that, the priest must wash his clothes and bathe himself with water. He may then come into the camp, but he will be ceremonially unclean till evening. The man who burns it must also wash his clothes and bathe with water, and he too will be unclean till evening.

"A man who is clean shall gather up the ashes of the heifer and put them in a ceremonially clean place outside the camp. They shall be kept by the Israelite community for use in the water of cleansing; it is for purification from sin. The man who gathers up the ashes of the heifer must also wash his clothes, and he too will be unclean till evening. This will be a lasting ordinance both for the Israelites and for the aliens living among them.

O. Persons Excluded from the Congregation

Not only are individuals to keep themselves pure, but the whole congregation must also be without blemish. It is a chosen nation, a holy people. Therefore certain persons are specifically excluded from the spiritual congregation, though they are apparently permitted to enjoy covenant relationship and to observe the Sabbaths in personal worship. Among the ones excluded are those whose genitals are mutilated (perhaps in response to pagan practices of self-mutilation) and the children of certain forbidden relationships, such as prostitution and incest. These seemingly harsh exclusions are undoubtedly aimed at denouncing and preventing the practices which cause them.

MUTILATED GENITALS.   No one who has been emasculated by crush- Deut. 23:1
ing or cutting may enter the assembly of the LORD.

CHILDREN OF FORBIDDEN UNIONS.   No one born of a forbidden Deut. 23:2
marriage*o* nor any of his descendants may enter the assembly of the LORD, even down to the tenth generation.

MOABITES AND AMMONITES.   No Ammonite or Moabite or any of his Deut. 23:3-6
descendants may enter the assembly of the LORD, even down to the tenth generation. For they did not come to meet you with bread and water on your way when you came out of Egypt, and they hired Balaam son of Beor from Pethor in Aram Naharaim*p* to pronounce a curse on you. However, the LORD your God would not listen to Balaam but turned the curse into a blessing for you, because the LORD your God loves you. Do not seek a treaty of friendship with them as long as you live.

EDOMITES.   Do not abhor an Edomite, for he is your brother. Do not Deut. 23:7,8
abhor an Egyptian, because you lived as an alien in his country. The third generation of children born to them may enter the assembly of the LORD.

P. The Nazirite Vow

Just as there are individuals whom the congregation must set apart in a negative sense for the sake of maintaining purity, so there are those who have been set apart in a positive sense for work within the congregation. The priests are set apart by heredity, and the prophets are chosen directly by God. But there are also men and women who, for a given time, feel a special calling to be set apart or separated for particular devotion to God. Although acting in no official capacity, and usually for personal spiritual enrichment, these individuals characteristically refrain from certain worldly pleasures and abase themselves with deprivation or service to others. Apparently it is already customary among the Israelites for a special vow to be taken when one wishes to begin such a period of separation, and the religious code now formally recognizes and regulates the practice. The Nazirite vow refers specifically to the fact of being set apart, and will be taken by at least three important historical figures in years to come.

ABSTENTION FROM GRAPES.   The LORD said to Moses, "Speak to the Num. 6:1-4
Israelites and say to them: 'If a man or woman wants to make a special vow, a vow of separation to the LORD as a Nazirite, he must abstain from wine and other fermented drink and must not drink vinegar made from wine or from other fermented drink. He must not drink grape juice or eat grapes or raisins. As long as he is a Nazirite, he must not eat anything that comes from the grapevine, not even the seeds or skins.

HAIR NOT TO BE CUT.   " 'During the entire period of his vow of separa- Num. 6:5
tion no razor may be used on his head. He must be holy until the period

---

*o*Or *one of illegitimate birth*   *p*That is, Northwest Mesopotamia

of his separation to the LORD is over; he must let the hair of his head grow long.

Num. 6:6-8 | NO CONTACT WITH DEAD. Throughout the period of his separation to the LORD he must not go near a dead body. Even if his own father or mother or brother or sister dies, he must not make himself ceremonially unclean on account of them, because the symbol of his separation to God is on his head. Throughout the period of his separation he is consecrated to the LORD.

Num. 6:9-12 | INVOLUNTARY CONTACT. " 'If someone dies suddenly in his presence, thus defiling the hair he has dedicated, he must shave his head on the day of his cleansing—the seventh day. Then on the eighth day he must bring two doves or two young pigeons to the priest at the entrance to the Tent of Meeting. The priest is to offer one as a sin offering and the other as a burnt offering to make atonement for him because he sinned by being in the presence of the dead body. That same day he is to consecrate his head. He must dedicate himself to the LORD for the period of his separation and must bring a year-old male lamb as a guilt offering. The previous days do not count, because he became defiled during his separation.

Num. 6:13-21 | COMPLETION OF VOW. " 'Now this is the law for the Nazirite when the period of his separation is over. He is to be brought to the entrance to the Tent of Meeting. There he is to present his offerings to the LORD: a year-old male lamb without defect for a burnt offering, a year-old ewe lamb without defect for a sin offering, a ram without defect for a fellowship offering,*q* together with their grain offerings and drink offerings, and a basket of bread made without yeast—cakes made of fine flour mixed with oil, and wafers spread with oil.

" 'The priest is to present them before the LORD and make the sin offering and the burnt offering. He is to present the basket of unleavened bread and is to sacrifice the ram as a fellowship offering to the LORD, together with its grain offering and drink offering.

" 'Then at the entrance to the Tent of Meeting, the Nazirite must shave off the hair that he dedicated. He is to take the hair and put it in the fire that is under the sacrifice of the fellowship offering.

" 'After the Nazirite has shaved off the hair of his dedication, the priest is to place in his hands a boiled shoulder of the ram, and a cake and a wafer from the basket, both made without yeast. The priest shall then wave them before the LORD as a wave offering; they are holy and belong to the priest, together with the breast that was waved and the thigh that was presented. After that, the Nazirite may drink wine.

" 'This is the law of the Nazirite who vows his offering to the LORD in accordance with his separation, in addition to whatever else he can afford. He must fulfill the vow he has made, according to the law of the Nazirite.' "

Q. Vows of Dedication

Although one might never take a Nazirite vow of self-abasement, he might voluntarily dedicate himself or his possessions for the Lord's work as a means of helping to support the financial needs of the tabernacle. This is done

qTraditionally peace offering

through an act of redemption by placing a value upon the person or thing dedicated and giving the value as a donation. The following rules pertain to such vows and gifts.

VALUATION OF PERSONS. The LORD said to Moses, "Speak to the Israelites and say to them: 'If anyone makes a special vow to dedicate persons to the LORD by giving equivalent values, set the value of a male between the ages of twenty and sixty at fifty shekels[r] of silver, according to the sanctuary shekel[s]; and if it is a female, set her value at thirty shekels.[t] If it is a person between the ages of five and twenty, set the value of a male at twenty shekels[u] and of a female at ten shekels.[v] If it is a person between one month and five years, set the value of a male at five shekels[w] of silver and that of a female at three shekels[x] of silver. If it is a person sixty years old or more, set the value of a male at fifteen shekels[y] and of a female at ten shekels. If anyone making the vow is too poor to pay the specified amount, he is to present the person to the priest, who will set the value for him according to what the man making the vow can afford.

Lev. 27:1-8

VALUATION OF ANIMALS. " 'If what he vowed is an animal that is acceptable as an offering to the LORD, such an animal given to the LORD becomes holy. He must not exchange it or substitute a good one for a bad one, or a bad one for a good one; if he should substitute one animal for another, both it and the substitute become holy. If what he vowed is a ceremonially unclean animal—one that is not acceptable as an offering to the LORD—the animal must be presented to the priest, who will judge its quality as good or bad. Whatever value the priest then sets, that is what it will be. If the owner wishes to redeem the animal, he must add a fifth to its value.

Lev. 27:9-13

VALUATION OF HOUSES. " 'If a man dedicates his house as something holy to the LORD, the priest will judge its quality as good or bad. Whatever value the priest then sets, so it will remain. If the man who dedicates his house redeems it, he must add a fifth to its value, and the house will again become his.

Lev. 27:14,15

VALUATION OF LAND. " 'If a man dedicates to the LORD part of his family land, its value is to be set according to the amount of seed required for it—fifty shekels of silver to a homer[z] of barley seed. If he dedicates his field during the Year of Jubilee, the value that has been set remains. But if he dedicates his field after the Jubilee, the priest will determine the value according to the number of years that remain until the next Year of Jubilee, and its set value will be reduced. If the man who dedicates the field wishes to redeem it, he must add a fifth to its value, and the field will again become his. If, however, he does not redeem the field, or if he has sold it to someone else, it can never be redeemed. When the field is released in the Jubilee, it will become holy, like a field devoted to the LORD; it will become the property of the priests.[a]

Lev. 27:16-25

[r]That is, about 1 1/4 pounds (about 0.6 kilogram)   [s]That is, about 2/5 ounce (about 11.5 grams)   [t]That is, about 12 ounces (about 0.3 kilogram)   [u]That is, about 8 ounces (about 0.2 kilogram)   [v]That is, about 4 ounces (about 110 grams)   [w]That is, about 2 ounces (about 55 grams)   [x]That is, about 1 1/4 ounces (about 35 grams)   [y]That is, about 6 ounces (about 170 grams)   [z]That is, probably about 6 bushels (about 220 liters)
[a]Or *priest*

" 'If a man dedicates to the LORD a field he has bought, which is not part of his family land, the priest will determine its value up to the Year of Jubilee, and the man must pay its value on that day as something holy to the LORD. In the Year of Jubilee the field will revert to the person from whom he bought it, the one whose land it was. Every value is to be set according to the sanctuary shekel, twenty gerahs to the shekel.

Lev.
27:26,27

NO VOW OF FIRST THINGS.   " 'No one, however, may dedicate the firstborn of an animal, since the firstborn already belongs to the LORD; whether an ox[b] or a sheep, it is the LORD's. If it is one of the unclean animals, he may buy it back at its set value, adding a fifth of the value to it. If he does not redeem it, it is to be sold at its set value.

Lev.
27:28,29

NO VOW OF DEVOTED THINGS.   " 'But nothing that a man owns and devotes[c] to the LORD—whether man or animal or family land—may be sold or redeemed; everything so devoted is most holy to the LORD.
" 'No person devoted to destruction[d] may be ransomed; he must be put to death.

Lev.
27:30-34

NO VOW OF TITHES.   " 'A tithe of everything from the land, whether grain from the soil or fruit from the trees, belongs to the LORD; it is holy to the LORD. If a man redeems any of his tithe, he must add a fifth of the value to it. The entire tithe of the herd and flock—every tenth animal that passes under the shepherd's rod—will be holy to the LORD. He must not pick out the good from the bad or make any substitution. If he does make a substitution, both the animal and its substitute become holy and cannot be redeemed.' "

These are the commands the LORD gave Moses on Mount Sinai for the Israelites.

Deut.
23:21-23

FULFILLING VOWS.   If you make a vow to the LORD your God, do not be slow to pay it, for the LORD your God will certainly demand it of you and you will be guilty of sin. But if you refrain from making a vow, you will not be guilty. Whatever your lips utter you must be sure to do, because you made your vow freely to the LORD your God with your own mouth.

(Num.
30:1-16)

(POSSIBLE RENUNCIATIONS)

R. Laws of Separation

In all things the Israelites are to be holy, pure, and set apart from the people and practices of the nations around them. To emphasize the idea of separateness, the Israelites are forbidden certain mixtures.

Lev. 19:1,2

PEOPLE TO BE HOLY.   The LORD said to Moses, "Speak to the entire assembly of Israel and say to them: 'Be holy because I, the LORD your God, am holy.

Lev.
19:19b
Deut. 22:9

MIXTURE OF SEED.   Do not plant two kinds of seed in your vineyard; if you do, not only the crops you plant but also the fruit of the vineyard will be defiled.[e]

[b]The Hebrew word can include both male and female.   [c]The Hebrew term refers to the irrevocable giving over of things or persons to the LORD.   [d]The Hebrew term refers to the irrevocable giving over of things or persons to the LORD, often by totally destroying them.   [e]Or *be forfeited to the sanctuary*

MIXTURE IN PLOWING.   Do not plow with an ox and a donkey yoked together.

Deut. 22:10

MIXTURE OF MATERIAL.   Do not wear clothes of wool and linen woven together.

Lev. 19:19c
Deut. 22:11

MIXTURE IN BREEDING.   " 'Keep my decrees.
" 'Do not mate different kinds of animals.

Lev. 19:19a

II. Laws of Government

Normally the most important laws of any nation are those which provide the base of government, upon which all other laws depend. In a theocracy, however, there is a minimum of legislative or administrative function. The ruler is God, and it is he who determines the nation's laws, as well as the people's direction—politically, militarily, and economically.

For over four decades Moses has served as Israel's leader. Under the direct control of God himself, Moses has taught as a prophet, interceded as a priest, and legislated as a lawgiver. The high priests, Aaron and Eleazar, have shared Moses' responsibilities in leading the religious activities, which constitute such a vital part of the Israelites' daily life. In addition, a council of 70 elders has been appointed to assist in the administration of national affairs. And not to be forgotten is the continuing patriarchal leadership provided by the chiefs and leaders within each tribe.

In light of such a structure, it is of great interest that God should anticipate the people's desire for a king in future years and actually provide certain guidelines at this early time.

A. Concerning a King

SELECTION OF KING.   When you enter the land the LORD your God is giving you and have taken possession of it and settled in it, and you say, "Let us set a king over us like all the nations around us," be sure to appoint over you the king the LORD your God chooses. He must be from among your own brothers. Do not place a foreigner over you, one who is not a brother Israelite.

Deut. 17:14,15

RESTRICTIONS ON KING.   The king, moreover, must not acquire great numbers of horses for himself or make the people return to Egypt to get more of them, for the LORD has told you, "You are not to go back that way again." He must not take many wives, or his heart will be led astray. He must not accumulate large amounts of silver and gold.

Deut. 17:16,17

KING TO SERVE UNDER LAW.   When he takes the throne of his kingdom, he is to write for himself on a scroll a copy of this law, taken from that of the priests, who are Levites. It is to be with him, and he is to read it all the days of his life so that he may learn to revere the LORD his God and follow carefully all the words of this law and these decrees and not consider himself better than his brothers and turn from the law to the right or to the left. Then he and his descendants will reign a long time over his kingdom in Israel.

Deut. 17:18-20

B. Respect for Rulers

Whether it be a future king or a present leader at any lesser level, the people are to show proper respect for God's chosen representatives.

Ex. 22:28b   ATTITUDE TOWARD RULERS.   [Do not] . . . curse the ruler of your people.

C. The Judicial System

A nation of laws must have courts, judges, and established rules of procedure. Moses had acted alone as a judge until the burden became too great for one man. At the suggestion of his father-in-law (Jethro), Moses made judges of men who were rulers over their tribes and families, and retained only the responsibility for deciding difficult cases. As the nation moves toward a more stabilized government God provides for a more formal judicial structure.

1. Establishment of Courts

Deut. 16:18   APPOINTMENT OF JUDGES.   Appoint judges and officials for each of your tribes in every town the LORD your God is giving you, and they shall judge the people fairly.

Deut. 17:8,9   COURTS OF APPEALS.   If cases come before your courts that are too difficult for you to judge—whether bloodshed, lawsuits or assaults—take them to the place the LORD your God will choose. Go to the priests, who are Levites, and to the judge who is in office at that time. Inquire of them and they will give you the verdict.

Deut. 17:10-13   CONTEMPT OF COURT.   You must act according to the decisions they give you at the place the LORD will choose. Be careful to do everything they direct you to do. Act according to the law they teach you and the decisions they give you. Do not turn aside from what they tell you, to the right or to the left. The man who shows contempt for the judge or for the priest who stands ministering there to the LORD your God must be put to death. You must purge the evil from Israel. All the people will hear and be afraid, and will not be contemptuous again.

(Deut. 1:9-18)   (LEADERS AS JUDGES)

2. Fairness and Justice

Ex. 23:8   BRIBES.   "Do not accept a bribe, for a bribe blinds those who see and twists the words of the righteous.

Ex. 23:3,6   PARTIALITY.   Do not pervert justice; do not show partiality to the poor
Lev. 19:15   or favoritism to the great, but judge your neighbor fairly.

Deut. 24:17,18   JUSTICE FOR DISADVANTAGED.   Do not deprive the alien or the fatherless of justice, or take the cloak of the widow as a pledge. Remember that you were slaves in Egypt and the LORD your God redeemed you from there. That is why I command you to do this.

Deut. 16:19,20   IMPORTANCE OF JUSTICE.   Do not pervert justice or show partiality. Do not accept a bribe, for a bribe blinds the eyes of the wise and twists the words of the righteous. Follow justice and justice alone, so that you may live and possess the land the LORD your God is giving you.

3. Witnesses

The truthfulness of those who would testify against others is so central to honesty and justice that it is required as one of the ten basic commandments.

PERJURY PROHIBITED.   "You shall not give false testimony against your neighbor.   Deut. 5:20

FAIR TESTIMONY.   "Do not spread false reports. Do not help a wicked man by being a malicious witness.   Ex. 23:1,2
"Do not follow the crowd in doing wrong. When you give testimony in a lawsuit, do not pervert justice by siding with the crowd,

FALSE CHARGES.   Have nothing to do with a false charge and do not put an innocent or honest person to death, for I will not acquit the guilty.   Ex. 23:7

PENALTY FOR FALSE CHARGES.   If a malicious witness takes the stand to accuse a man of a crime, the two men involved in the dispute must stand in the presence of the LORD before the priests and the judges who are in office at the time. The judges must make a thorough investigation, and if the witness proves to be a liar, giving false testimony against his brother, then do to him as he intended to do to his brother. You must purge the evil from among you. The rest of the people will hear of this and be afraid, and never again will such an evil thing be done among you. Show no pity: life for life, eye for eye, tooth for tooth, hand for hand, foot for foot.   Deut. 19:16-21

NUMBER OF WITNESSES.   One witness is not enough to convict a man accused of any crime or offense he may have committed. A matter must be established by the testimony of two or three witnesses.   Deut. 19:15

4. Punishment

PERSONAL RESPONSIBILITY.   Fathers shall not be put to death for their children, nor children put to death for their fathers; each is to die for his own sin.   Deut. 24:16

LIMIT TO BEATINGS.   When men have a dispute, they are to take it to court and the judges will decide the case, acquitting the innocent and condemning the guilty. If the guilty man deserves to be beaten, the judge shall make him lie down and have him flogged in his presence with the number of lashes his crime deserves, but he must not give him more than forty lashes. If he is flogged more than that, your brother will be degraded in your eyes.   Deut. 25:1-3

BURYING HANGED CRIMINAL.   If a man guilty of a capital offense is put to death and his body is hung on a tree, you must not leave his body on the tree overnight. Be sure to bury him that same day, because anyone who is hung on a tree is under God's curse. You must not desecrate the land the LORD your God is giving you as an inheritance.   Deut. 21:22,23

III. Laws of Special Crimes

Crimes are normally defined as offenses against society (in contrast to civil wrongs, which affect only individuals). Crimes are typically punished by fines, imprisonment, and even death, whereas civil wrongs are remedied by various forms of restitution—usually monetary. In the theocracy of Israel, there are many offenses punishable by death which do not fall within traditional crime categories, and offenses which fall within traditional crime categories which are not punishable by death. There is no punishment by imprisonment at all. Theft, for example, is punished by a form of fine and restitution. (Therefore the special crimes category set forth below is arbitrarily based upon more traditional classifications of offenses.)

To insure respect for human life, the most basic moral principle of life is given.

Deut. 5:17 MURDER PROHIBITED. "You shall not murder.

A. Crimes Against the Person

1. Homicide

Ex. 21:12-14
Lev. 24:17
24:21b PREMEDITATED MURDER. "Anyone who strikes a man and kills him shall surely be put to death. However, if he does not do it intentionally, but God lets it happen, he is to flee to a place I will designate. But if a man schemes and kills another man deliberately, take him away from my altar and put him to death.

Num. 35:20,21 INTENTIONAL MURDER. If anyone with malice aforethought shoves another or throws something at him intentionally so that he dies or if in hostility he hits him with his fist so that he dies, that person shall be put to death; he is a murderer. The avenger of blood shall put the murderer to death when he meets him.

Num. 35:16-19 MURDER BY INSTRUMENT. " 'If a man strikes someone with an iron object so that he dies, he is a murderer; the murderer shall be put to death. Or if anyone has a stone in his hand that could kill, and he strikes someone so that he dies, he is a murderer; the murderer shall be put to death. Or if anyone has a wooden object in his hand that could kill, and he hits someone so that he dies, he is a murderer; the murderer shall be put to death.

Num. 35:29,30 ONE WITNESS INSUFFICIENT. " 'These are to be legal requirements for you throughout the generations to come, wherever you live.

" 'Anyone who kills a person is to be put to death as a murderer only on the testimony of witnesses. But no one is to be put to death on the testimony of only one witness.

Num. 35:31 NO RANSOM FOR MURDERER. " 'Do not accept a ransom for the life of a murderer, who deserves to die. He must surely be put to death.

Num. 35:33,34 REASON FOR DEATH PENALTY. " 'Do not pollute the land where you are. Bloodshed pollutes the land, and atonement cannot be made for the land on which blood has been shed, except by the blood of the one who shed it. Do not defile the land where you live and where I dwell, for I, the LORD, dwell among the Israelites.' "

Ex. 22:2,3a CRIME PREVENTION DEFENSE. "If a thief is caught breaking in and is struck so that he dies, the defender is not guilty of bloodshed; but if it happens^f after sunrise, he is guilty of bloodshed.

ᶠOr *if he strikes him*

MANSLAUGHTER.   " 'But if without hostility someone suddenly shoves another or throws something at him unintentionally or, without seeing him, drops a stone on him that could kill him, and he dies, then since he was not his enemy and he did not intend to harm him, the assembly must judge between him and the avenger of blood according to these regulations. The assembly must protect the one accused of murder from the avenger of blood and send him back to the city of refuge to which he fled. He must stay there until the death of the high priest, who was anointed with the holy oil.

Num. 35:22-25

INNOCENT HOMICIDE.   This is the rule concerning the man who kills another and flees there to save his life—one who kills his neighbor unintentionally, without malice aforethought. For instance, a man may go into the forest with his neighbor to cut wood, and as he swings his ax to fell a tree, the head may fly off and hit his neighbor and kill him. That man may flee to one of these cities and save his life. Otherwise, the avenger of blood might pursue him in a rage, overtake him if the distance is too great, and kill him even though he is not deserving of death, since he did it to his neighbor without malice aforethought.

Deut. 19:4-6

CITIES OF REFUGE.   Then the LORD said to Moses: "Speak to the Israelites and say to them: 'When you cross the Jordan into Canaan, select some towns to be your cities of refuge, to which a person who has killed someone accidentally may flee. They will be places of refuge from the avenger, so that a person accused of murder may not die before he stands trial before the assembly. These six towns you give will be your cities of refuge. Give three on this side of the Jordan and three in Canaan as cities of refuge. These six towns will be a place of refuge for Israelites, aliens and any other people living among them, so that anyone who has killed another accidentally can flee there.

Num. 35:9-15

THREE CITIES IN CANAAN.   When the LORD your God has destroyed the nations whose land he is giving you, and when you have driven them out and settled in their towns and houses, then set aside for yourselves three cities centrally located in the land the LORD your God is giving you to possess. Build roads to them and divide into three parts the land the LORD your God is giving you as an inheritance, so that anyone who kills a man may flee there.

Deut. 19:1-3

PROVISION FOR MORE CITIES.   This is why I command you to set aside for yourselves three cities.
    If the LORD your God enlarges your territory, as he promised on oath to your forefathers, and gives you the whole land he promised them, because you carefully follow all these laws I command you today—to love the LORD your God and to walk always in his ways—then you are to set aside three more cities. Do this so that innocent blood will not be shed in your land, which the LORD your God is giving you as your inheritance, and so that you will not be guilty of bloodshed.

Deut. 19:7-10

RISK OUTSIDE CITIES.   " 'But if the accused ever goes outside the limits of the city of refuge to which he has fled and the avenger of blood finds him outside the city, the avenger of blood may kill the accused without being guilty of murder. The accused must stay in his city of refuge until the death of the high priest; only after the death of the high priest may he return to his own property.

Num. 35:26-28

Deut.
19:11-13   CITIES NOT FOR MURDERERS.   But if a man hates his neighbor and lies in wait for him, assaults and kills him, and then flees to one of these cities, the elders of his town shall send for him, bring him back from the city, and hand him over to the avenger of blood to die. Show him no pity. You must purge from Israel the guilt of shedding innocent blood, so that it may go well with you.

Num.
35:32   NO RANSOM FOR MANSLAYER.   " 'Do not accept a ransom for anyone who has fled to a city of refuge and so allow him to go back and live on his own land before the death of the high priest.

2. Feticide

Ex. 21:22   MISCARRIAGE ITSELF.   "If men who are fighting hit a pregnant woman and she gives birth prematurely[g] but there is no serious injury, the offender must be fined whatever the woman's husband demands and the court allows.

Ex.
21:23-25   HARM TO MOTHER.   But if there is serious injury, you are to take life for life, eye for eye, tooth for tooth, hand for hand, foot for foot, burn for burn, wound for wound, bruise for bruise.

3. Kidnapping

Ex. 21:16   KIDNAPPING PROHIBITED.   "Anyone who kidnaps another and either sells him or still has him when he is caught must be put to death.

Deut. 24:7   SPECIAL REGULATION.   If a man is caught kidnapping one of his brother Israelites and treats him as a slave or sells him, the kidnapper must die. You must purge the evil from among you.

4. Mayhem

Lev.
24:19,20   DISFIGUREMENT.   If anyone injures his neighbor, whatever he has done must be done to him: fracture for fracture, eye for eye, tooth for tooth. As he has injured the other, so he is to be injured.

Ex.
21:26,27   MAIMING OF SLAVE.   If a man hits a manservant or maidservant in the eye and destroys it, he must let the servant go free to compensate for the eye. And if he knocks out the tooth of a manservant or maidservant, he must let the servant go free to compensate for the tooth.

5. Rape

Deut.
22:25-27   RAPE OF BETROTHED.   But if out in the country a man happens to meet a girl pledged to be married and rapes her, only the man who has done this shall die. Do nothing to the girl; she has committed no sin deserving death. This case is like that of someone who attacks and murders his neighbor, for the man found the girl out in the country, and though the betrothed girl screamed, there was no one to rescue her.

Deut.
22:28,29   WHEN NOT BETROTHED.   If a man happens to meet a virgin who is not pledged to be married and rapes her and they are discovered, he shall pay the girl's father fifty shekels of silver.[h] He must marry the girl, for he has violated her. He can never divorce her as long as he lives.

gOr she has a miscarriage   _hThat is, about 1 1/4 pounds (about 0.6 kilogram)_

6. Assault

STRIKING PARENTS. "Anyone who attacks[i] his father or his mother must be put to death. Ex. 21:15

PERMANENT INJURY. "If men quarrel and one hits the other with a stone or with his fist[j] and he does not die but is confined to bed, the one who struck the blow will not be held responsible if the other gets up and walks around outside with his staff; however, he must pay the injured man for the loss of his time and see that he is completely healed. Ex. 21:18,19

SURVIVING SLAVE. "If a man beats his male or female slave with a rod and the slave dies as a direct result, he must be punished, but he is not to be punished if the slave gets up after a day or two, since the slave is his property. Ex. 21:20,21

INTERFERENCE BY WOMAN. If two men are fighting and the wife of one of them comes to rescue her husband from his assailant, and she reaches out and seizes him by his private parts, you shall cut off her hand. Show her no pity. Deut. 25:11,12

B. Crimes Against Property

A person's property is also to be respected.

STEALING PROHIBITED. "You shall not steal. Deut. 5:19

1. Theft of Personal Property

PENALTY. "A thief must certainly make restitution, but if he has nothing, he must be sold to pay for his theft. Ex. 22:3b

THEFT OF ANIMALS. "If a man steals an ox or a sheep and slaughters it or sells it, he must pay back five head of cattle for the ox and four sheep for the sheep. Ex. 22:1,4
   "If the stolen animal is found alive in his possession—whether ox or donkey or sheep—he must pay back double.

2. Theft of Real Property

REMOVING LANDMARKS. Do not move your neighbor's boundary stone set up by your predecessors in the inheritance you receive in the land the LORD your God is giving you to possess. Deut. 19:14

IV. Personal Rights and Remedies

Personal injuries, economic losses, and matters of inheritance are among the many matters of personal rights and responsibilities included in this section of various civil laws. Some regulations are merely directory in nature while others set forth specific remedies. These civil laws are designed to regulate daily activities in a fair manner for each citizen and to instill a sense of order throughout society.

[i]Or kills   [j]Or with a tool

A. Restitution for Loss

Num.
5:5-10
WRONGFUL TAKING.   The LORD said to Moses, "Say to the Israelites: 'When a man or woman wrongs another in any way[k] and so is unfaithful to the LORD, that person is guilty and must confess the sin he has committed. He must make full restitution for his wrong, add one fifth to it and give it all to the person he has wronged. But if that person has no close relative to whom restitution can be made for the wrong, the restitution belongs to the LORD and must be given to the priest, along with the ram with which atonement is made for him. All the sacred contributions the Israelites bring to a priest will belong to him. Each man's sacred gifts are his own, but what he gives to the priest will belong to the priest.'"

Ex. 22:9
DISPUTED LOST PROPERTY.   In all cases of illegal possession of an ox, a donkey, a sheep, a garment, or any other lost property about which somebody says, 'This is mine,' both parties are to bring their cases before the judges. The one whom the judges declare[l] guilty must pay back double to his neighbor.

Ex. 22:7,8
BAILEE OF MONEY OR GOODS.   "If a man gives his neighbor silver or goods for safekeeping and they are stolen from the neighbor's house, the thief, if he is caught, must pay back double. But if the thief is not found, the owner of the house must appear before the judges[m] to determine whether he has laid his hands on the other man's property.

Ex.
22:10-13
BAILEE OF ANIMALS.   "If a man gives a donkey, an ox, a sheep or any other animal to his neighbor for safekeeping and it dies or is injured or is taken away while no one is looking, the issue between them will be settled by the taking of an oath before the LORD that the neighbor did not lay hands on the other person's property. The owner is to accept this, and no restitution is required. But if the animal was stolen from the neighbor, he must make restitution to the owner. If it was torn to pieces by a wild animal, he shall bring in the remains as evidence and he will not be required to pay for the torn animal.

Ex.
22:14,15
BORROWER'S RESPONSIBILITY.   "If a man borrows an animal from his neighbor and it is injured or dies while the owner is not present, he must make restitution. But if the owner is with the animal, the borrower will not have to pay. If the animal was hired, the money paid for the hire covers the loss.

B. Seduction

In addition to the impropriety involved, there is an economic aspect to cases of seduction.

Ex.
22:16,17
COMPENSATION FOR VIRGIN.   "If a man seduces a virgin who is not pledged to be married and sleeps with her, he must pay the bride-price, and she shall be his wife. If her father absolutely refuses to give her to him, he must still pay the bride-price for virgins.

---

[k]Or woman commits any wrong common to mankind   [l]Or whom God declares   [m]Or before God; also in verse 9

C. Injuries and Damages

OPEN PITS.   "If a man uncovers a pit or digs one and fails to cover it and an ox or a donkey falls into it, the owner of the pit must pay for the loss; he must pay its owner, and the dead animal will be his.   *Ex. 21:33,34*

DESTRUCTION BY FIRE.   "If a fire breaks out and spreads into thorn-bushes so that it burns shocks of grain or standing grain or the whole field, the one who started the fire must make restitution.   *Ex. 22:6*

CROP DAMAGE BY ANIMALS.   "If a man grazes his livestock in a field or vineyard and lets them stray and they graze in another man's field, he must make restitution from the best of his own field or vineyard.   *Ex. 22:5*

OX GORING PERSONS.   "If a bull gores a man or a woman to death, the bull must be stoned to death, and its meat must not be eaten. But the owner of the bull will not be held responsible.   *Ex. 21:28*

KNOWN DANGEROUS PROPENSITIES.   If, however, the bull has had the habit of goring and the owner has been warned but has not kept it penned up and it kills a man or woman, the bull must be stoned and the owner also must be put to death. However, if payment is demanded of him, he may redeem his life by paying whatever is demanded. This law also applies if the bull gores a son or daughter. If the bull gores a male or female slave, the owner must pay thirty shekels[n] of silver to the master of the slave, and the bull must be stoned.   *Ex. 21:29-32*

OX GORING ANIMALS.   "If a man's bull injures the bull of another and it dies, they are to sell the live one and divide both the money and the dead animal equally. However, if it was known that the bull had the habit of goring, yet the owner did not keep it penned up, the owner must pay, animal for animal, and the dead animal will be his.   *Ex. 21:35,36*

KILLING ANIMAL.   Anyone who takes the life of someone's animal must make restitution—life for life.   *Lev. 24:18 24:21a*

PREVENTION OF INJURY.   When you build a new house, make a parapet around your roof so that you may not bring the guilt of bloodshed on your house if someone falls from the roof.   *Deut. 22:8*

D. Masters and Servants

PROMPT PAYMENT.   Do not take advantage of a hired man who is poor and needy, whether he is a brother Israelite or an alien living in one of your towns. Pay him his wages each day before sunset, because he is poor and is counting on it. Otherwise he may cry to the LORD against you, and you will be guilty of sin.   *Lev. 19:13 Deut. 24:14,15*

ACQUIRING SLAVES.   " 'Your male and female slaves are to come from the nations around you; from them you may buy slaves. You may also buy some of the temporary residents living among you and members of their clans born in your country, and they will become your property. You can will them to your children as inherited property and can make them slaves for life, but you must not rule over your fellow Israelites ruthlessly.   *Lev. 25:44-46*

[n]That is, about 12 ounces (about 0.3 kilogram)

Deut. 23:15,16	ESCAPED SLAVES. If a slave has taken refuge with you, do not hand him over to his master. Let him live among you wherever he likes and in whatever town he chooses. Do not oppress him.
Deut. 15:12-18	SEVEN-YEAR RELEASE. If a fellow Hebrew, a man or a woman, sells himself to you and serves you six years, in the seventh year you must let him go free. And when you release him, do not send him away empty-handed. Supply him liberally from your flock, your threshing floor and your winepress. Give to him as the LORD your God has blessed you. Remember that you were slaves in Egypt and the LORD your God redeemed you. That is why I give you this command today.

But if your servant says to you, "I do not want to leave you," because he loves you and your family and is well off with you, then take an awl and push it through his ear lobe into the door, and he will become your servant for life. Do the same for your maidservant.

Do not consider it a hardship to set your servant free, because his service to you these six years has been worth twice as much as that of a hired hand. And the LORD your God will bless you in everything you do.

Ex. 21:1-6	RELEASE WITH FAMILY. "These are the laws you are to set before them:

"If you buy a Hebrew servant, he is to serve you for six years. But in the seventh year, he shall go free, without paying anything. If he comes alone, he is to go free alone; but if he has a wife when he comes, she is to go with him. If his master gives him a wife and she bears him sons or daughters, the woman and her children shall belong to her master, and only the man shall go free.

"But if the servant declares, 'I love my master and my wife and children and do not want to go free,' then his master must take him before the judges.[o] He shall take him to the door or the doorpost and pierce his ear with an awl. Then he will be his servant for life.

Ex. 21:7-11	RELEASE OF WOMEN SLAVES. "If a man sells his daughter as a servant, she is not to go free as menservants do. If she does not please the master who has selected her for himself,[p] he must let her be redeemed. He has no right to sell her to foreigners, because he has broken faith with her. If he selects her for his son, he must grant her the rights of a daughter. If he marries another woman, he must not deprive the first one of her food, clothing and marital rights. If he does not provide her with these three things, she is to go free, without any payment of money.
(Ex. 21:26,27)	(RELEASE AFTER MAIMING)

E. Credit, Interest, and Collateral

Deut. 23:19,20	CHARGING INTEREST. Do not charge your brother interest, whether on money or food or anything else that may earn interest. You may charge a foreigner interest, but not a brother Israelite, so that the LORD your God may bless you in everything you put your hand to in the land you are entering to possess.
Ex. 22:25-27 Deut. 24:12,13	POOR PROTECTED. If you lend money to one of my people among you who is needy, do not be like a moneylender; charge him no interest.[q] If you take your neighbor's cloak as a pledge, return it to him by sunset, because his cloak is the only covering he has for his body. What else will he sleep

oOr before God   pOr master so that he does not choose her   qOr excessive interest

in? When he cries out to me, I will hear, for I am compassionate.

NO MILL FOR PLEDGE.   Do not take a pair of millstones—not even the upper one—as security for a debt, because that would be taking a man's livelihood as security. — *Deut. 24:6*

RETRIEVAL OF PLEDGE.   When you make a loan of any kind to your neighbor, do not go into his house to get what he is offering as a pledge. Stay outside and let the man to whom you are making the loan bring the pledge out to you. — *Deut. 24:10,11*

(PLEDGE FROM WIDOW) — *(Deut. 24:17)*

SEVEN-YEAR RELEASE.   At the end of every seven years you must cancel debts. This is how it is to be done: Every creditor shall cancel the loan he has made to his fellow Israelite. He shall not require payment from his fellow Israelite or brother, because the LORD's time for canceling debts has been proclaimed. You may require payment from a foreigner, but you must cancel any debt your brother owes you. However, there should be no poor among you, for in the land the LORD your God is giving you to possess as your inheritance, he will richly bless you, if only you fully obey the LORD your God and are careful to follow all these commands I am giving you today. — *Deut. 15:1-5*

LENDING TO OTHER NATIONS.   For the LORD your God will bless you as he has promised, and you will lend to many nations but will borrow from none. You will rule over many nations but none will rule over you. — *Deut. 15:6*

OBLIGATION TO POOR.   If there is a poor man among your brothers in any of the towns of the land that the LORD your God is giving you, do not be hardhearted or tightfisted toward your poor brother. Rather be openhanded and freely lend him whatever he needs. Be careful not to harbor this wicked thought: "The seventh year, the year for canceling debts, is near," so that you do not show ill will toward your needy brother and give him nothing. He may then appeal to the LORD against you, and you will be found guilty of sin. Give generously to him and do so without a grudging heart; then because of this the LORD your God will bless you in all your work and in everything you put your hand to. There will always be poor people in the land. Therefore I command you to be openhanded toward your brothers and toward the poor and needy in your land. — *Deut. 15:7-11*

F. Contracts and Agreements

OATHS TO BE KEPT.   " 'Do not swear falsely by my name and so profane the name of your God. I am the LORD. — *Lev. 19:12*

AGREEMENTS TO BE HONORED.   Moses said to the heads of the tribes of Israel: "This is what the LORD commands: When a man makes a vow to the LORD or takes an oath to obligate himself by a pledge, he must not break his word but must do everything he said. — *Num. 30:1,2*

VOW OF DAUGHTER.   "When a young woman still living in her father's house makes a vow to the LORD or obligates herself by a pledge and her father hears about her vow or pledge but says nothing to her, then all her vows and every pledge by which she obligated herself will stand. But if her father forbids her when he hears about it, none of her vows or the pledges by which she obligated herself will stand; the LORD will release her because her father has forbidden her. — *Num. 30:3-5*

Num.
30:6-8

VOW OF WIFE.   "If she marries after she makes a vow or after her lips utter a rash promise by which she obligates herself and her husband hears about it but says nothing to her, then her vows or the pledges by which she obligated herself will stand. But if her husband forbids her when he hears about it, he nullifies the vow that obligates her or the rash promise by which she obligates herself, and the LORD will release her.

Num.
30:9-12

VOW OF WIDOW OR DIVORCEE.   "Any vow or obligation taken by a widow or divorced woman will be binding on her.

"If a woman living with her husband makes a vow or obligates herself by a pledge under oath and her husband hears about it but says nothing to her and does not forbid her, then all her vows or the pledges by which she obligated herself will stand. But if her husband nullifies them when he hears about them, then none of the vows or pledges that came from her lips will stand. Her husband has nullified them, and the LORD will release her.

Num.
30:13-16

HUSBAND'S LIABILITY.   Her husband may confirm or nullify any vow she makes or any sworn pledge to deny herself. But if her husband says nothing to her about it from day to day, then he confirms all her vows or the pledges binding on her. He confirms them by saying nothing to her when he hears about them. If, however, he nullifies them some time after he hears about them, then he is responsible for her guilt."

These are the regulations the LORD gave Moses concerning relationships between a man and his wife, and between a father and his young daughter still living in his house.

G. Weights and Measures

Lev. 19:11

DEALINGS TO BE HONEST.   " 'Do not steal.

" 'Do not lie.

" 'Do not deceive one another.

Lev.
19:35-37

PROPER MEASUREMENTS.   " 'Do not use dishonest standards when measuring length, weight or quantity. Use honest scales and honest weights, an honest ephah[r] and an honest hin.[s] I am the LORD your God, who brought you out of Egypt.

" 'Keep all my decrees and all my laws and follow them. I am the LORD.' "

Deut.
25:13-16

PROPER WEIGHTS.   Do not have two differing weights in your bag— one heavy, one light. Do not have two differing measures in your house— one large, one small. You must have accurate and honest weights and measures, so that you may live long in the land the LORD your God is giving you. For the LORD your God detests anyone who does these things, anyone who deals dishonestly.

H. Inheritance

1. Right of Firstborn

Deut.
21:15-17

DOUBLE PORTION DUE.   If a man has two wives, and he loves one but not the other, and both bear him sons but the firstborn is the son of the wife he does not love, when he wills his property to his sons, he must not

---

[r]An ephah was a dry measure.   [s]A hin was a liquid measure.

give the rights of the firstborn to the son of the wife he loves in preference to his actual firstborn, the son of the wife he does not love. He must acknowledge the son of his unloved wife as the firstborn by giving him a double share of all he has. That son is the first sign of his father's strength. The right of the firstborn belongs to him.

2. Levirate Marriage

A custom of the ages is incorporated into the Laws of Moses, presumably to preserve the right of inheritance. When a man dies childless, his brother is to take the widow as a wife and to father a child in his brother's name. That first child will receive the deceased brother's inheritance, while any other children of the union will inherit through their natural father. (The marriage itself receives its more modern name of "levirate" from the Latin word for a husband's brother.) An example of the custom was seen in the account of Tamar and Judah (Genesis 38).

BROTHER'S OBLIGATION.   If brothers are living together and one of them dies without a son, his widow must not marry outside the family. Her husband's brother shall take her and marry her and fulfill the duty of a brother-in-law to her. The first son she bears shall carry on the name of the dead brother so that his name will not be blotted out from Israel.

Deut. 25:5,6

IF BROTHER REFUSES.   However, if a man does not want to marry his brother's wife, she shall go to the elders at the town gate and say, "My husband's brother refuses to carry on his brother's name in Israel. He will not fulfill the duty of a brother-in-law to me." Then the elders of his town shall summon him and talk to him. If he persists in saying, "I do not want to marry her," his brother's widow shall go up to him in the presence of the elders, take off one of his sandals, spit in his face and say, "This is what is done to the man who will not build up his brother's family line." That man's line shall be known in Israel as The Family of the Unsandaled.

Deut. 25:7-10

3. Case of Zelophehad's Daughters

In anticipation of the settlement of Canaan and the assignment of territory to each tribe and family, Moses is approached by the daughters of a man who had died without any sons to inherit a portion of the promised land. Concerned about loss of family possessions, the daughters ask that land be assigned to the family through them. Moses agrees, but limits their marriages to men within the same tribe so that their inheritance will not be transferred to another tribe. Why a levirate marriage is not involved is not indicated. Perhaps the man had no brothers. But the case does indicate something of the status of women in a predominantly male-oriented society.

DAUGHTERS SEEK INHERITANCE.   The daughters of Zelophehad son of Hepher, the son of Gilead, the son of Makir, the son of Manasseh, belonged to the clans of Manasseh son of Joseph. The names of the daughters were Mahlah, Noah, Hoglah, Milcah and Tirzah. They approached the entrance to the Tent of Meeting and stood before Moses, Eleazar the priest, the leaders and the whole assembly, and said, "Our father died in the desert. He was not among Korah's followers, who banded together

Num. 27:1-4

against the LORD, but he died for his own sin and left no sons. Why should our father's name disappear from his clan because he had no son? Give us property among our father's relatives."

**Num.
27:5-11**

ORDER OF INHERITANCE.   So Moses brought their case before the LORD and the LORD said to him, "What Zelophehad's daughters are saying is right. You must certainly give them property as an inheritance among their father's relatives and turn their father's inheritance over to them.

"Say to the Israelites, 'If a man dies and leaves no son, turn his inheritance over to his daughter. If he has no daughter, give his inheritance to his brothers. If he has no brothers, give his inheritance to his father's brothers. If his father had no brothers, give his inheritance to the nearest relative in his clan, that he may possess it. This is to be a legal requirement for the Israelites, as the LORD commanded Moses.'"

**Num.
36:1-4**

PROBLEM IF DAUGHTERS MARRY.   The family heads of the clan of Gilead son of Makir, the son of Manasseh, who were from the clans of the descendants of Joseph, came and spoke before Moses and the leaders, the heads of the Israelite families. They said, "When the LORD commanded my lord to give the land as an inheritance to the Israelites by lot, he ordered you to give the inheritance of our brother Zelophehad to his daughters. Now suppose they marry men from other Israelite tribes; then their inheritance will be taken from our ancestral inheritance and added to that of the tribe they marry into. And so part of the inheritance allotted to us will be taken away. When the Year of Jubilee for the Israelites comes, their inheritance will be added to that of the tribe into which they marry, and their property will be taken from the tribal inheritance of our forefathers."

**Num.
36:5-9**

MUST MARRY WITHIN TRIBE.   Then at the LORD's command Moses gave this order to the Israelites: "What the tribe of the descendants of Joseph is saying is right. This is what the LORD commands for Zelophehad's daughters: They may marry anyone they please as long as they marry within the tribal clan of their father. No inheritance in Israel is to pass from tribe to tribe, for every Israelite shall keep the tribal land inherited from his forefathers. Every daughter who inherits land in any Israelite tribe must marry someone in her father's tribal clan, so that every Israelite will possess the inheritance of his fathers. No inheritance may pass from tribe to tribe, for each Israelite tribe is to keep the land it inherits."

**Num.
36:10-13**

DAUGHTERS COMPLY.   So Zelophehad's daughters did as the LORD commanded Moses. Zelophehad's daughters—Mahlah, Tirzah, Hoglah, Milcah and Noah—married their cousins on their father's side. They married within the clans of the descendants of Manasseh son of Joseph, and their inheritance remained in their father's clan and tribe.

These are the commands and regulations the LORD gave through Moses to the Israelites on the plains of Moab by the Jordan across from Jericho.[f]

V. Marriage, Divorce, and Sexual Relations

A. Marriage

Modern notions of proper marriage relations do not necessarily reflect the custom and laws of the Israelites. Most noticeable is the tacitly permitted

---

[f]Hebrew *Jordan of Jericho*; possibly an ancient name for the Jordan River

practice of polygamy in the ancient law. In centuries to come most societies, both religious and secular, will generally disapprove of the practice.

Nothing is said in the Laws of Moses regarding any prerequisites for marriage, or regarding any required formalities. The marriage relationship is assumed to be permanent in nature and necessary for the establishment of certain rights and for the legitimacy of sexual relations (and for having offspring therefrom). Only the following special laws relating to marriage are given.

MARRYING A CAPTIVE WOMAN.   When you go to war against your enemies and the LORD your God delivers them into your hands and you take captives, if you notice among the captives a beautiful woman and are attracted to her, you may take her as your wife. Bring her into your home and have her shave her head, trim her nails and put aside the clothes she was wearing when captured. After she has lived in your house and mourned her father and mother for a full month, then you may go to her and be her husband and she shall be your wife. If you are not pleased with her, let her go wherever she wishes. You must not sell her or treat her as a slave, since you have dishonored her.

Deut. 21:10-14

FIRST-YEAR FREEDOM.   If a man has recently married, he must not be sent to war or have any other duty laid on him. For one year he is to be free to stay at home and bring happiness to the wife he has married.

Deut. 24:5

IF VIRGINITY DOUBTED.   If a man takes a wife and, after lying with her, dislikes her and slanders her and gives her a bad name, saying, "I married this woman, but when I approached her, I did not find proof of her virginity," then the girl's father and mother shall bring proof that she was a virgin to the town elders at the gate. The girl's father will say to the elders, "I gave my daughter in marriage to this man, but he dislikes her. Now he has slandered her and said, 'I did not find your daughter to be a virgin.' But here is the proof of my daughter's virginity." Then her parents shall display the cloth before the elders of the town, and the elders shall take the man and punish him. They shall fine him a hundred shekels of silver[u] and give them to the girl's father, because this man has given an Israelite virgin a bad name. She shall continue to be his wife; he must not divorce her as long as he lives.

Deut. 22:13-21

If, however, the charge is true and no proof of the girl's virginity can be found, she shall be brought to the door of her father's house and there the men of her town shall stone her to death. She has done a disgraceful thing in Israel by being promiscuous while still in her father's house. You must purge the evil from among you.

B. Divorce

Although scholars have long debated whether the Laws of Moses permit divorce for seemingly any cause, unlike in other nations the Israelites are at least taught the seriousness and finality of a dissolved marriage. Later Scripture indicates that any ease of divorce under the Laws of Moses may be merely a concession on God's part at this time.

[u] That is, about 2 1/2 pounds (about 1 kilogram)

Deut.
24:1-4
FINALITY OF DIVORCE. If a man marries a woman who becomes displeasing to him because he finds something indecent about her, and he writes her a certificate of divorce, gives it to her and sends her from his house, and if after she leaves his house she becomes the wife of another man, and her second husband dislikes her and writes her a certificate of divorce, gives it to her and sends her from his house, or if he dies, then her first husband, who divorced her, is not allowed to marry her again after she has been defiled. That would be detestable in the eyes of the LORD. Do not bring sin upon the land the LORD your God is giving you as an inheritance.

C. Sexual Violations

1. Introduction

Lev. 18:1-5
CONTRAST WITH PAGANS. The LORD said to Moses, "Speak to the Israelites and say to them: 'I am the LORD your God. You must not do as they do in Egypt, where you used to live, and you must not do as they do in the land of Canaan, where I am bringing you. Do not follow their practices. You must obey my laws and be careful to follow my decrees. I am the LORD your God. Keep my decrees and laws, for the man who obeys them will live by them. I am the LORD.

2. Adultery

At the heart of the marriage relationship is the idea of faithfulness to the vows of commitment. Faithfulness is important both in marriage and in the people's relationship with God. Their unfaithfulness to God is considered spiritual adultery. Breach of the marriage vow by sexual relations with a person other than one's spouse is so serious that it is prohibited by one of the ten basic commandments.

Deut. 5:18
ADULTERY PROHIBITED. "You shall not commit adultery.

Lev. 18:20
LAW AGAINST ADULTERY. " 'Do not have sexual relations with your neighbor's wife and defile yourself with her.

Lev. 20:10
Deut.
22:22
PENALTY FOR ADULTERY. If a man is found sleeping with another man's wife, both the man who slept with her and the woman must die. You must purge the evil from Israel.

Deut.
22:23,24
ADULTERY WITH ONE BETROTHED. If a man happens to meet in a town a virgin pledged to be married and he sleeps with her, you shall take both of them to the gate of that town and stone them to death—the girl because she was in a town and did not scream for help, and the man because he violated another man's wife. You must purge the evil from among you.

Lev.
19:20-22
WHERE BETROTHED IS SLAVE. " 'If a man sleeps with a woman who is a slave girl promised to another man but who has not been ransomed or given her freedom, there must be due punishment. Yet they are not to be put to death, because she had not been freed. The man, however, must bring a ram to the entrance to the Tent of Meeting for a guilt offering to the LORD. With the ram of the guilt offering the priest is to make atonement for him before the LORD for the sin he has committed, and his sin will be forgiven.

TEST OF ADULTERY.   Then the LORD said to Moses, "Speak to the   Num.
Israelites and say to them: 'If a man's wife goes astray and is unfaithful to   5:11-31
him by sleeping with another man, and this is hidden from her husband
and her impurity is undetected (since there is no witness against her and
she has not been caught in the act), and if feelings of jealousy come over
her husband and he suspects his wife and she is impure—or if he is jealous and suspects her even though she is not impure—then he is to take his
wife to the priest. He must also take an offering of a tenth of an ephah^v of
barley flour on her behalf. He must not pour oil on it or put incense on it,
because it is a grain offering for jealousy, a reminder offering to draw
attention to guilt.

" 'The priest shall bring her and have her stand before the LORD. Then
he shall take some holy water in a clay jar and put some dust from the tabernacle floor into the water. After the priest has had the woman stand
before the LORD, he shall loosen her hair and place in her hands the
reminder offering, the grain offering for jealousy, while he himself holds
the bitter water that brings a curse. Then the priest shall put the woman
under oath and say to her, "If no other man has slept with you and you
have not gone astray and become impure while married to your husband,
may this bitter water that brings a curse not harm you. But if you have
gone astray while married to your husband and you have defiled yourself
by sleeping with a man other than your husband"— here the priest is to
put the woman under this curse of the oath— "may the LORD cause your
people to curse and denounce you when he causes your thigh to waste
away and your abdomen to swell.^{w} May this water that brings a curse
enter your body so that your abdomen swells and your thigh wastes
away.^{x}"

" 'Then the woman is to say, "Amen. So be it."

" 'The priest is to write these curses on a scroll and then wash them off
into the bitter water. He shall have the woman drink the bitter water that
brings a curse, and this water will enter her and cause bitter suffering. The
priest is to take from her hands the grain offering for jealousy, wave it
before the LORD and bring it to the altar. The priest is then to take a handful of the grain offering as a memorial offering and burn it on the altar;
after that, he is to have the woman drink the water. If she has defiled herself and been unfaithful to her husband, then when she is made to drink
the water that brings a curse, it will go into her and cause bitter suffering;
her abdomen will swell and her thigh waste away,^{y} and she will become
accursed among her people. If, however, the woman has not defiled herself and is free from impurity, she will be cleared of guilt and will be able
to have children.

" 'This, then, is the law of jealousy when a woman goes astray and
defiles herself while married to her husband, or when feelings of jealousy
come over a man because he suspects his wife. The priest is to have her
stand before the LORD and is to apply this entire law to her. The husband
will be innocent of any wrongdoing, but the woman will bear the consequences of her sin.' "

---

^{v}That is, probably about 2 quarts (about 2 liters) ^{w}Or *causes you to have a miscarrying*
womb and barrenness ^{x}Or *body and cause you to be barren and have a miscarrying womb*
^{y}Or *suffering; she will have barrenness and a miscarrying womb*

3. Fornication

Sexual relations between unmarried persons may result in certain adverse consequences. As noted previously, the woman's lack of virginity at the time of marriage can subject her to punishment. (See Deut. 22:13-21.)

4. Prostitution

Prohibition of sexual relations given in exchange for money concerns not only the unapproved sexual activity itself, but also forbidden participation in pagan cult worship, in which prostitution by both men and women is commonplace.

Lev. 19:29	EVIL OF PROSTITUTION. " 'Do not degrade your daughter by making her a prostitute, or the land will turn to prostitution and be filled with wickedness.
Deut. 23:17,18	NO CULT PROSTITUTION. No Israelite man or woman is to become a shrine prostitute. You must not bring the earnings of a female prostitute or of a male prostitute[z] into the house of the LORD your God to pay any vow, because the LORD your God detests them both.

5. Incest

Sexual activity between blood relatives and other near relatives is prohibited. This is therefore the formal end of the early period during which extremely close relatives married each other, presumably for more rapid propagation of the human family.

Lev. 18:6-8 Deut. 22:30	PARENTS. " 'No one is to approach any close relative to have sexual relations. I am the LORD. " 'Do not dishonor your father by having sexual relations with your mother. She is your mother; do not have relations with her. " 'Do not have sexual relations with your father's wife; that would dishonor your father.
Lev. 20:11	PENALTY. " 'If a man sleeps with his father's wife, he has dishonored his father. Both the man and the woman must be put to death; their blood will be on their own heads.
Lev. 18:9	SISTER. " 'Do not have sexual relations with your sister, either your father's daughter or your mother's daughter, whether she was born in the same home or elsewhere.
Lev. 18:11	HALF-SISTER. " 'Do not have sexual relations with the daughter of your father's wife, born to your father; she is your sister.
Lev. 20:17	PENALTY. " 'If a man marries his sister, the daughter of either his father or his mother, and they have sexual relations, it is a disgrace. They must be cut off before the eyes of their people. He has dishonored his sister and will be held responsible.
Lev. 18:10	GRANDDAUGHTER. " 'Do not have sexual relations with your son's daughter or your daughter's daughter; that would dishonor you.

[z]Hebrew *of a dog*

AUNT OR UNCLE.   " 'Do not have sexual relations with your father's   Lev.
sister; she is your father's close relative.   18:12-14
    " 'Do not have sexual relations with your mother's sister, because she is
your mother's close relative.
    " 'Do not dishonor your father's brother by approaching his wife to
have sexual relations; she is your aunt.

PENALTY.   " 'Do not have sexual relations with the sister of either your   Lev.
mother or your father, for that would dishonor a close relative; both of you   20:19,20
would be held responsible.
    " 'If a man sleeps with his aunt, he has dishonored his uncle. They will
be held responsible; they will die childless.

DAUGHTER-IN-LAW.   " 'Do not have sexual relations with your daugh-   Lev. 18:15
ter-in-law. She is your son's wife; do not have relations with her.

PENALTY.   " 'If a man sleeps with his father's wife, he has dishonored   Lev. 20:12
his father. Both the man and the woman must be put to death; their blood
will be on their own heads.

SISTER-IN-LAW.   " 'Do not have sexual relations with your brother's   Lev. 18:16
wife; that would dishonor your brother.

PENALTY.   " 'If a man marries his brother's wife, it is an act of impurity;   Lev. 20:21
he has dishonored his brother. They will be childless.

MOTHER AND DAUGHTER.   " 'Do not have sexual relations with both   Lev. 18:17
a woman and her daughter. Do not have sexual relations with either her
son's daughter or her daughter's daughter; they are her close relatives.
That is wickedness.

PENALTY.   " 'If a man marries both a woman and her mother, it is   Lev. 20:14
wicked. Both he and they must be burned in the fire, so that no wickedness will be among you.

TWO SISTERS.   " 'Do not take your wife's sister as a rival wife and have   Lev. 18:18
sexual relations with her while your wife is living.

6. Violation of Uncleanness

    Because a woman is considered ceremonially unclean during her menstru-
al period, sexual relations during that time are prohibited.

MENSTRUAL INTERCOURSE.   " 'Do not approach a woman to have sex-   Lev. 18:19
ual relations during the uncleanness of her monthly period.

PENALTY.   " 'If a man lies with a woman during her monthly period and   Lev. 20:18
has sexual relations with her, he has exposed the source of her flow, and
she has also uncovered it. Both of them must be cut off from their people.

7. Homosexual Practices

HOMOSEXUAL CONDUCT PROHIBITED.   " 'Do not lie with a man as   Lev. 18:22
one lies with a woman; that is detestable.

PENALTY.   " 'If a man lies with a man as one lies with a woman, both of   Lev. 20:13
them have done what is detestable. They must be put to death; their blood
will be on their own heads.

8. Bestiality

Lev. 18:23 BESTIALITY PROHIBITED. " 'Do not have sexual relations with an animal and defile yourself with it. A woman must not present herself to an animal to have sexual relations with it; that is a perversion.

Ex. 22:19 PENALTY. " 'If a man has sexual relations with an animal, he must be
Lev. put to death, and you must kill the animal.
20:15,16
" 'If a woman approaches an animal to have sexual relations with it, kill both the woman and the animal. They must be put to death; their blood will be on their own heads.

9. Conclusion

Lev. WARNING ABOUT SEXUAL SINS. " 'Do not defile yourselves in any of
18:24-30 these ways, because this is how the nations that I am going to drive out
20:22,23 before you became defiled. Even the land was defiled; so I punished it for its sin, and the land vomited out its inhabitants. But you must keep my decrees and my laws. The native-born and the aliens living among you must not do any of these detestable things, for all these things were done by the people who lived in the land before you, and the land became defiled. And if you defile the land, it will vomit you out as it vomited out the nations that were before you.
" 'Everyone who does any of these detestable things—such persons must be cut off from their people. Keep my requirements and do not follow any of the detestable customs that were practiced before you came and do not defile yourselves with them. I am the LORD your God.' "

Lev. 20:24 PEOPLE TO BE SEPARATE. But I said to you, "You will possess their land; I will give it to you as an inheritance, a land flowing with milk and honey." I am the LORD your God, who has set you apart from the nations.

D. Separation of Sexes

Deut. 22:5 CLOTHES OF OPPOSITE SEX. A woman must not wear men's clothing, nor a man wear women's clothing, for the LORD your God detests anyone who does this.

VI. Health and Dietary Laws

A. Health Regulations

In the Laws of Moses there is a close relationship between cleanliness and godliness. Persons suffering from various bodily discharges and other illnesses—especially involving blemishes of the skin called leprosy—are considered ceremonially unclean as well. The religious and ceremonial laws noted earlier contain rites of purification for such persons. Regulations for diagnosis and treatment are set out separately in this section.

1. Leprosy

Lev. 13:1-8 DIAGNOSIS OF LEPROSY. The LORD said to Moses and Aaron, "When anyone has a swelling or a rash or a bright spot on his skin that may become an infectious skin disease,[a] he must be brought to Aaron the priest or to one of his sons[b] who is a priest. The priest is to examine the sore on his skin, and if the hair in the sore has turned white and the sore appears to be more than skin deep,[c] it is an infectious skin disease. When the priest examines him, he shall pronounce him ceremonially unclean. If the spot on his skin is white but does not appear to be more than skin deep and the hair in it has not turned white, the priest is to put the infected person in isolation for seven days. On the seventh day the priest is to examine him, and if he sees that the sore is unchanged and has not spread in the skin, he is to keep him in isolation another seven days. On the seventh day the priest is to examine him again, and if the sore has faded and has not spread in the skin, the priest shall pronounce him clean; it is only a rash. The man must wash his clothes, and he will be clean. But if the rash does spread in his skin after he has shown himself to the priest to be pronounced clean, he must appear before the priest again. The priest is to examine him, and if the rash has spread in the skin, he shall pronounce him unclean; it is an infectious disease.

NONCONTAGIOUS LEPROSY. "When anyone has an infectious skin disease, he must be brought to the priest. The priest is to examine him, and if there is a white swelling in the skin that has turned the hair white and if there is raw flesh in the swelling, it is a chronic skin disease and the priest shall pronounce him unclean. He is not to put him in isolation, because he is already unclean.

Lev.
13:9-17

"If the disease breaks out all over his skin and, so far as the priest can see, it covers all the skin of the infected person from head to foot, the priest is to examine him, and if the disease has covered his whole body, he shall pronounce that person clean. Since it has all turned white, he is clean. But whenever raw flesh appears on him, he will be unclean. When the priest sees the raw flesh, he shall pronounce him unclean. The raw flesh is unclean; he has an infectious disease. Should the raw flesh change and turn white, he must go to the priest. The priest is to examine him, and if the sores have turned white, the priest shall pronounce the infected person clean; then he will be clean.

DIAGNOSIS OF BOILS. "When someone has a boil on his skin and it heals, and in the place where the boil was, a white swelling or reddish-white spot appears, he must present himself to the priest. The priest is to examine it, and if it appears to be more than skin deep and the hair in it has turned white, the priest shall pronounce him unclean. It is an infectious skin disease that has broken out where the boil was. But if, when the priest examines it, there is no white hair in it and it is not more than skin deep and has faded, then the priest is to put him in isolation for seven days. If it is spreading in the skin, the priest shall pronounce him unclean; it is infectious. But if the spot is unchanged and has not spread, it is only a scar from the boil, and the priest shall pronounce him clean.

Lev.
13:18-23

DIAGNOSIS OF BURNS. "When someone has a burn on his skin and a reddish-white or white spot appears in the raw flesh of the burn, the priest is to examine the spot, and if the hair in it has turned white, and it appears

Lev.
13:24-28

---

[a]Traditionally *leprosy*; the Hebrew word was used for various diseases affecting the skin—not necessarily leprosy.   [b]Or *descendants*   [c]Or *be lower than the rest of the skin*; also elsewhere in this chapter

to be more than skin deep, it is an infectious disease that has broken out in the burn. The priest shall pronounce him unclean; it is an infectious skin disease. But if the priest examines it and there is no white hair in the spot and if it is not more than skin deep and has faded, then the priest is to put him in isolation for seven days. On the seventh day the priest is to examine him, and if it is spreading in the skin, the priest shall pronounce him unclean; it is an infectious skin disease. If, however, the spot is unchanged and has not spread in the skin but has faded, it is a swelling from the burn, and the priest shall pronounce him clean; it is only a scar from the burn.

Lev.
13:29-37

DIAGNOSIS OF ITCH.   "If a man or woman has a sore on the head or on the chin, the priest is to examine the sore, and if it appears to be more than skin deep and the hair in it is yellow and thin, the priest shall pronounce that person unclean; it is an itch, an infectious disease of the head or chin. But if, when the priest examines this kind of sore, it does not seem to be more than skin deep and there is no black hair in it, then the priest is to put the infected person in isolation for seven days. On the seventh day the priest is to examine the sore, and if the itch has not spread and there is no yellow hair in it and it does not appear to be more than skin deep, he must be shaved except for the diseased area, and the priest is to keep him in isolation another seven days. On the seventh day the priest is to examine the itch, and if it has not spread in the skin and appears to be no more than skin deep, the priest shall pronounce him clean. He must wash his clothes, and he will be clean. But if the itch does spread in the skin after he is pronounced clean, the priest is to examine him, and if the itch has spread in the skin, the priest does not need to look for yellow hair; the person is unclean. If, however, in his judgment it is unchanged and black hair has grown in it, the itch is healed. He is clean, and the priest shall pronounce him clean.

Lev.
13:38,39

DIAGNOSIS OF SPOTS.   "When a man or woman has white spots on the skin, the priest is to examine them, and if the spots are dull white, it is a harmless rash that has broken out on the skin; that person is clean.

Lev.
13:40-44

DIAGNOSIS OF BALDNESS.   "When a man has lost his hair and is bald, he is clean. If he has lost his hair from the front of his scalp and has a bald forehead, he is clean. But if he has a reddish-white sore on his bald head or forehead, it is an infectious disease breaking out on his head or forehead. The priest is to examine him, and if the swollen sore on his head or forehead is reddish-white like an infectious skin disease, the man is diseased and is unclean. The priest shall pronounce him unclean because of the sore on his head.

Lev.
13:45,46

RULES FOR THE SICK.   "The person with such an infectious disease must wear torn clothes, let his hair be unkempt,[d] cover the lower part of his face and cry out, 'Unclean! Unclean!' As long as he has the infection he remains unclean. He must live alone; he must live outside the camp.

Lev.
13:47-59

MOLD IN GARMENTS.   "If any clothing is contaminated with mildew— any woolen or linen clothing, any woven or knitted material of linen or wool, any leather or anything made of leather—and if the contamination in the clothing, or leather, or woven or knitted material, or any leather

---

[d]Or *clothes, uncover his head*

article, is greenish or reddish, it is a spreading mildew and must be shown to the priest. The priest is to examine the mildew and isolate the affected article for seven days. On the seventh day he is to examine it, and if the mildew has spread in the clothing, or the woven or knitted material, or the leather, whatever its use, it is a destructive mildew; the article is unclean. He must burn up the clothing, or the woven or knitted material of wool or linen, or any leather article that has the contamination in it, because the mildew is destructive; the article must be burned up.

"But if, when the priest examines it, the mildew has not spread in the clothing, or the woven or knitted material, or the leather article, he shall order that the contaminated article be washed. Then he is to isolate it for another seven days. After the affected article has been washed, the priest is to examine it, and if the mildew has not changed its appearance, even though it has not spread, it is unclean. Burn it with fire, whether the mildew has affected one side or the other. If, when the priest examines it, the mildew has faded after the article has been washed, he is to tear the contaminated part out of the clothing, or the leather, or the woven or knitted material. But if it reappears in the clothing, or in the woven or knitted material, or in the leather article, it is spreading, and whatever has the mildew must be burned with fire. The clothing, or the woven or knitted material, or any leather article that has been washed and is rid of the mildew, must be washed again, and it will be clean."

These are the regulations concerning contamination by mildew in woolen or linen clothing, woven or knitted material, or any leather article, for pronouncing them clean or unclean.

MOLD IN HOUSE.   The LORD said to Moses and Aaron, "When you enter the land of Canaan, which I am giving you as your possession, and I put a spreading mildew in a house in that land, the owner of the house must go and tell the priest, 'I have seen something that looks like mildew in my house.' The priest is to order the house to be emptied before he goes in to examine the mildew, so that nothing in the house will be pronounced unclean. After this the priest is to go in and inspect the house. He is to examine the mildew on the walls, and if it has greenish or reddish depressions that appear to be deeper than the surface of the wall, the priest shall go out the doorway of the house and close it up for seven days. On the seventh day the priest shall return to inspect the house. If the mildew has spread on the walls, he is to order that the contaminated stones be torn out and thrown into an unclean place outside the town. He must have all the inside walls of the house scraped and the material that is scraped off dumped into an unclean place outside the town. Then they are to take other stones to replace these and take new clay and plaster the house.

Lev.
14:33-42

DESTRUCTION OF HOUSE.   "If the mildew reappears in the house after the stones have been torn out and the house scraped and plastered, the priest is to go and examine it and, if the mildew has spread in the house, it is a destructive mildew; the house is unclean. It must be torn down—its stones, timbers and all the plaster—and taken out of the town to an unclean place.

"Anyone who goes into the house while it is closed up will be unclean till evening. Anyone who sleeps or eats in the house must wash his clothes.

Lev.
14:43-47

Lev. 14:48-53	**CLEANSING OF HOUSE.** "But if the priest comes to examine it and the mildew has not spread after the house has been plastered, he shall pronounce the house clean, because the mildew is gone. To purify the house he is to take two birds and some cedar wood, scarlet yarn and hyssop. He shall kill one of the birds over fresh water in a clay pot. Then he is to take the cedar wood, the hyssop, the scarlet yarn and the live bird, dip them into the blood of the dead bird and the fresh water, and sprinkle the house seven times. He shall purify the house with the bird's blood, the fresh water, the live bird, the cedar wood, the hyssop and the scarlet yarn. Then he is to release the live bird in the open fields outside the town. In this way he will make atonement for the house, and it will be clean."
Lev. 14:54-57	**CONCLUSION.** These are the regulations for any infectious skin disease, for an itch, for mildew in clothing or in a house, and for a swelling, a rash or a bright spot, to determine when something is clean or unclean. These are the regulations for infectious skin diseases and mildew.
Deut. 24:8,9	**WARNING.** In cases of leprous[e] diseases be very careful to do exactly as the priests, who are Levites, instruct you. You must follow carefully what I have commanded them. Remember what the LORD your God did to Miriam along the way after you came out of Egypt.

2. Discharges

Lev. 15:1-12	**UNCLEANNESS OF MAN.** The LORD said to Moses and Aaron, "Speak to the Israelites and say to them: 'When any man has a bodily discharge, the discharge is unclean. Whether it continues flowing from his body or is blocked, it will make him unclean. This is how his discharge will bring about uncleanness: " 'Any bed the man with a discharge lies on will be unclean, and anything he sits on will be unclean. Anyone who touches his bed must wash his clothes and bathe with water, and he will be unclean till evening. Whoever sits on anything that the man with a discharge sat on must wash his clothes and bathe with water, and he will be unclean till evening. " 'Whoever touches the man who has a discharge must wash his clothes and bathe with water, and he will be unclean till evening. " 'If the man with the discharge spits on someone who is clean, that person must wash his clothes and bathe with water, and he will be unclean till evening. " 'Everything the man sits on when riding will be unclean, and whoever touches any of the things that were under him will be unclean till evening; whoever picks up those things must wash his clothes and bathe with water, and he will be unclean till evening. " 'Anyone the man with a discharge touches without rinsing his hands with water must wash his clothes and bathe with water, and he will be unclean till evening. " 'A clay pot that the man touches must be broken, and any wooden article is to be rinsed with water.
Lev. 15:16-18	**EMISSION OF SEMEN.** " 'When a man has an emission of semen, he must bathe his whole body with water, and he will be unclean till evening. Any clothing or leather that has semen on it must be washed with water,

[e]The Hebrew word was used for various diseases affecting the skin—not necessarily leprosy.

and it will be unclean till evening. When a man lies with a woman and there is an emission of semen, both must bathe with water, and they will be unclean till evening.

WOMAN'S MENSTRUAL DISCHARGE.   " 'When a woman has her regular flow of blood, the impurity of her monthly period will last seven days, and anyone who touches her will be unclean till evening.

Lev.
15:19-24

   " 'Anything she lies on during her period will be unclean, and anything she sits on will be unclean. Whoever touches her bed must wash his clothes and bathe with water, and he will be unclean till evening. Whoever touches anything she sits on must wash his clothes and bathe with water, and he will be unclean till evening. Whether it is the bed or anything she was sitting on, when anyone touches it, he will be unclean till evening.

   " 'If a man lies with her and her monthly flow touches him, he will be unclean for seven days; any bed he lies on will be unclean.

WOMAN'S OTHER DISCHARGES.   " 'When a woman has a discharge of blood for many days at a time other than her monthly period or has a discharge that continues beyond her period, she will be unclean as long as she has the discharge, just as in the days of her period. Any bed she lies on while her discharge continues will be unclean, as is her bed during her monthly period, and anything she sits on will be unclean, as during her period. Whoever touches them will be unclean; he must wash his clothes and bathe with water, and he will be unclean till evening.

Lev.
15:25-27

CONCLUSION.   These are the regulations for a man with a discharge, for anyone made unclean by an emission of semen, for a woman in her monthly period, for a man or a woman with a discharge, and for a man who lies with a woman who is ceremonially unclean.

Lev.
15:32,33

3. Isolation

UNCLEAN TO BE OUTSIDE CAMP.   The LORD said to Moses, "Command the Israelites to send away from the camp anyone who has an infectious skin disease f or a discharge of any kind, or who is ceremonially unclean because of a dead body. Send away male and female alike; send them outside the camp so they will not defile their camp, where I dwell among them." The Israelites did this; they sent them outside the camp. They did just as the LORD had instructed Moses.

Num. 5:1-4

CLEANLINESS AND GODLINESS.   " 'You must keep the Israelites separate from things that make them unclean, so they will not die in their uncleanness for defiling my dwelling place, g which is among them.' "

Lev. 15:31

B. Dietary Regulations

   Dietary regulations may reflect both health and religious concerns. Animals, fish, birds, insects, and creatures of the ground are divided into categories of "clean" and "unclean," indicating whether or not it is acceptable for the Israelites to eat them. A creature may be "unclean" because it has unsanitary contact with that which is putrefied; because it is associated with objectionable living habits; because it is unhealthful for human consumption; or perhaps because it is a creature typically used in pagan worship. The eating of blood is

f Traditionally *leprosy*; the Hebrew word was used for various diseases affecting the skin—
not necessarily leprosy.   g Or *my tabernacle*

particularly prohibited because blood represents all life, and because it is used to seek atonement for sin.

1. Clean and Unclean Creatures

Lev.
11:46,47

UNCLEANNESS PROHIBITS EATING. " 'These are the regulations concerning animals, birds, every living thing that moves in the water and every creature that moves about on the ground. You must distinguish between the unclean and the clean, between living creatures that may be eaten and those that may not be eaten.' "

Lev. 11:1-3
Deut.
14:3-5

CLEAN ANIMALS.   Do not eat any detestable thing. These are the animals you may eat: the ox, the sheep, the goat, the deer, the gazelle, the roe deer, the wild goat, the ibex, the antelope and the mountain sheep.[h]

Lev. 11:4-8
Deut.
14:6-8

UNCLEAN ANIMALS.   " 'There are some that only chew the cud or only have a split hoof, but you must not eat them. The camel, though it chews the cud, does not have a split hoof; it is ceremonially unclean for you. The coney,[i] though it chews the cud, does not have a split hoof; it is unclean for you. The rabbit, though it chews the cud, does not have a split hoof; it is unclean for you. And the pig, though it has a split hoof completely divided, does not chew the cud; it is unclean for you. You must not eat their meat or touch their carcasses; they are unclean for you.

Lev.
11:9-12
Deut.
14:9,10

FISH.   " 'Of all the creatures living in the water of the seas and the streams, you may eat any that have fins and scales. But all creatures in the seas or streams that do not have fins and scales—whether among all the swarming things or among all the other living creatures in the water—you are to detest. And since you are to detest them, you must not eat their meat and you must detest their carcasses. Anything living in the water that does not have fins and scales is to be detestable to you.

Lev.
11:13-19
Deut.
14:11-18

BIRDS.   " 'These are the birds you are to detest and not eat because they are detestable: the eagle, the vulture, the black vulture, the red kite, any kind of black kite, any kind of raven, the horned owl, the screech owl, the gull, any kind of hawk, the little owl, the cormorant, the great owl, the white owl, the desert owl, the osprey, the stork, any kind of heron, the hoopoe and the bat.[j]

Lev.
11:20-23
Deut.
14:19,20

INSECTS.   " 'All flying insects that walk on all fours are to be detestable to you. There are, however, some winged creatures that walk on all fours that you may eat: those that have jointed legs for hopping on the ground. Of these you may eat any kind of locust, katydid, cricket or grasshopper. But all other winged creatures that have four legs you are to detest.

Lev.
11:41-45

GROUND CREATURES.   " 'Every creature that moves about on the ground is detestable; it is not to be eaten. You are not to eat any creature that moves about on the ground, whether it moves on its belly or walks on all fours or on many feet; it is detestable. Do not defile yourselves by any of these creatures. Do not make yourselves unclean by means of them or be made unclean by them. I am the LORD your God; consecrate yourselves and be holy, because I am holy. Do not make yourselves unclean by any creature that moves about on the ground. I am the LORD who

---

[h]The precise identification of some of the birds and animals in this chapter is uncertain.
[i]That is, the hyrax or rock badger   [j]The precise identification of some of the birds, insects and animals in this chapter is uncertain.

brought you up out of Egypt to be your God; therefore be holy, because I am holy.

CONTACT WITH UNCLEAN. " 'You will make yourselves unclean by these; whoever touches their carcasses will be unclean till evening. Whoever picks up one of their carcasses must wash his clothes, and he will be unclean till evening.

Lev. 11:24-28

" 'Every animal that has a split hoof not completely divided or that does not chew the cud is unclean for you; whoever touches [the carcass of] any of them will be unclean. Of all the animals that walk on all fours, those that walk on their paws are unclean for you; whoever touches their carcasses will be unclean till evening. Anyone who picks up their carcasses must wash his clothes, and he will be unclean till evening. They are unclean for you.

CONTACT WITH GROUND CREATURES. " 'Of the animals that move about on the ground, these are unclean for you: the weasel, the rat, any kind of great lizard, the gecko, the monitor lizard, the wall lizard, the skink and the chameleon. Of all those that move along the ground, these are unclean for you. Whoever touches them when they are dead will be unclean till evening. When one of them dies and falls on something, that article, whatever its use, will be unclean, whether it is made of wood, cloth, hide or sackcloth. Put it in water; it will be unclean till evening, and then it will be clean. If one of them falls into a clay pot, everything in it will be unclean, and you must break the pot. Any food that could be eaten but has water on it from such a pot is unclean, and any liquid that could be drunk from it is unclean. Anything that one of their carcasses falls on becomes unclean; an oven or cooking pot must be broken up. They are unclean, and you are to regard them as unclean. A spring, however, or a cistern for collecting water remains clean, but anyone who touches one of these carcasses is unclean. If a carcass falls on any seeds that are to be planted, they remain clean. But if water has been put on the seed and a carcass falls on it, it is unclean for you.

Lev. 11:29-38

CALL FOR HOLINESS. " 'You must therefore make a distinction between clean and unclean animals and between unclean and clean birds. Do not defile yourselves by any animal or bird or anything that moves along the ground—those which I have set apart as unclean for you. You are to be holy to me[k] because I, the LORD, am holy, and I have set you apart from the nations to be my own.

Lev. 20:25,26

2. Dead Animals

DEAD ANIMALS UNCLEAN. " 'If an animal that you are allowed to eat dies, anyone who touches the carcass will be unclean till evening. Anyone who eats some of the carcass must wash his clothes, and he will be unclean till evening. Anyone who picks up the carcass must wash his clothes, and he will be unclean till evening.

Lev. 11:39,40

EATING PROHIBITED. Do not eat anything you find already dead. You may give it to an alien living in any of your towns, and he may eat it, or you may sell it to a foreigner. But you are a people holy to the LORD your God.

Deut. 14:21a

[k] Or be my holy ones

3. Killed Animals

Lev.
17:15,16

KILLED ANIMALS UNCLEAN. " 'Anyone, whether native-born or alien, who eats anything found dead or torn by wild animals must wash his clothes and bathe with water, and he will be ceremonially unclean till evening; then he will be clean. But if he does not wash his clothes and bathe himself, he will be held responsible.' "

Ex. 22:31

EATING PROHIBITED. "You are to be my holy people. So do not eat the meat of an animal torn by wild beasts; throw it to the dogs.

4. Blood and Fat

Lev.
17:10-14
7:26,27
19:26a
Deut.
12:16
12:23-25

BLOOD PROHIBITED. " 'Any Israelite or any alien living among them who eats any blood—I will set my face against that person who eats blood and will cut him off from his people. For the life of a creature is in the blood, and I have given it to you to make atonement for yourselves on the altar; it is the blood that makes atonement for one's life. Therefore I say to the Israelites, "None of you may eat blood, nor may an alien living among you eat blood."

" 'Any Israelite or any alien living among you who hunts any animal or bird that may be eaten must drain out the blood and cover it with earth, because the life of every creature is its blood. That is why I have said to the Israelites, "You must not eat the blood of any creature, because the life of every creature is its blood; anyone who eats it must be cut off."

Lev.
7:22-25

FAT PROHIBITED. The LORD said to Moses, "Say to the Israelites: 'Do not eat any of the fat of cattle, sheep or goats. The fat of an animal found dead or torn by wild animals may be used for any other purpose, but you must not eat it. Anyone who eats the fat of an animal from which an offering by fire may be[1] made to the LORD must be cut off from his people.

5. Meat and Milk

Ex. 23:19b
34:26b
Deut. 14:21b

BOILING GOAT IN MILK. "Do not cook a young goat in its mother's milk.

VII. General Welfare Laws

One feature of the Laws of Moses which sets them apart from the laws of nontheocratic nations is the attention given to protection of the weak, the poor, and the stranger. For example, a common provision throughout the code is that, for the most part, each law is applicable to citizens and noncitizens alike. (There is in this a reminder that the Israelites themselves were once persecuted as foreigners in the land of Egypt.) In addition to the general principles of fairness and equal protection found throughout all the laws, there are various specific laws calling for acts of benevolence, special respect for particular persons, and care for human and animal life.

A. Requirements for Benevolence

Lev.
19:9,10
23:22

EXCESS CROPS FOR POOR. " 'When you reap the harvest of your land, do not reap to the very edges of your field or gather the gleanings of your harvest. Do not go over your vineyard a second time or pick up the grapes

[1]Or fire is

that have fallen. Leave them for the poor and the alien. I am the LORD your God.

EXCESS CROPS FOR OTHERS.   When you are harvesting in your field and you overlook a sheaf, do not go back to get it. Leave it for the alien, the fatherless and the widow, so that the LORD your God may bless you in all the work of your hands. When you beat the olives from your trees, do not go over the branches a second time. Leave what remains for the alien, the fatherless and the widow. When you harvest the grapes in your vineyard, do not go over the vines again. Leave what remains for the alien, the fatherless and the widow. Remember that you were slaves in Egypt. That is why I command you to do this.

Deut. 24:19-22

LIMITATION ON RECIPIENT.   If you enter your neighbor's vineyard, you may eat all the grapes you want, but do not put any in your basket. If you enter your neighbor's grainfield, you may pick kernels with your hands, but you must not put a sickle to his standing grain.

Deut. 23:24,25

MAINTAINING THE POOR.   " 'If one of your countrymen becomes poor and is unable to support himself among you, help him as you would an alien or a temporary resident, so he can continue to live among you. Do not take interest of any kind[m] from him, but fear your God, so that your countryman may continue to live among you. You must not lend him money at interest or sell him food at a profit. I am the LORD your God, who brought you out of Egypt to give you the land of Canaan and to be your God.

Lev. 25:35-38

B. Duties of Respect and Support

1. Parents

At the heart of any society is the family, and at the heart of the family is the parent-child relationship. In order to insure both financial support and proper attitudes in this important family responsibility, children are commanded to honor their parents.

PARENTAL HONOR COMMANDED.
"Honor your father and your mother, as the LORD your God has commanded you, so that you may live long in the land the LORD your God is giving you.

Deut. 5:16

RESPECT FOR PARENTS.   " 'Each of you must respect his mother and father. . .

Lev. 19:3a

PARENT CURSED.   " 'If anyone curses his father or mother, he must be put to death. He has cursed his father or his mother, and his blood will be on his own head.

Ex. 21:17
Lev. 20:9

REBELLIOUS SON.   If a man has a stubborn and rebellious son who does not obey his father and mother and will not listen to them when they discipline him, his father and mother shall take hold of him and bring him to the elders at the gate of his town. They shall say to the elders, "This son of ours is stubborn and rebellious. He will not obey us. He is a profligate and a drunkard." Then all the men of his town shall stone him to death. You

Deut. 21:18-21

[m] *Or* take excessive interest; similarly in verse 37

must purge the evil from among you. All Israel will hear of it and be afraid.

2. Elderly

Lev. 19:32   RESPECT FOR AGED.   " 'Rise in the presence of the aged, show respect for the elderly and revere your God. I am the LORD.

3. Widows and Orphans

Ex. 22:22-24   CARE FOR SURVIVORS.   "Do not take advantage of a widow or an orphan. If you do and they cry out to me, I will certainly hear their cry. My anger will be aroused, and I will kill you with the sword; your wives will become widows and your children fatherless.

4. Strangers

Ex. 22:21
23:9
Lev.
19:33:34   CONCERN FOR FOREIGNERS.   " 'When an alien lives with you in your land, do not mistreat him. The alien living with you must be treated as one of your native-born. Love him as yourself, for you were aliens in Egypt. I am the LORD your God.

Lev. 24:22   LAW SAME FOR FOREIGNERS.   You are to have the same law for the alien and the native-born. I am the LORD your God.' "

5. Deaf and Blind

Lev. 19:14   RESPECT FOR HANDICAPPED.   " 'Do not curse the deaf or put a stumbling block in front of the blind, but fear your God. I am the LORD.

6. Neighbors

Lev. 19:16   SLANDER PROHIBITED.   " 'Do not go about spreading slander among your people.
     " 'Do not do anything that endangers your neighbor's life. I am the LORD.

Lev.
19:17,18   SECOND LAW OF LOVE.   " 'Do not hate your brother in your heart. Rebuke your neighbor frankly so you will not share in his guilt.
     " 'Do not seek revenge or bear a grudge against one of your people, but love your neighbor as yourself. I am the LORD.

Ex. 23:4,5
Deut.
22:1-4   EMERGENCY ASSISTANCE.   If you see your brother's ox or sheep straying, do not ignore it but be sure to take it back to him. If the brother does not live near you or if you do not know who he is, take it home with you and keep it until he comes looking for it. Then give it back to him. Do the same if you find your brother's donkey or his cloak or anything he loses. Do not ignore it.
     If you see your brother's donkey or his ox fallen on the road, do not ignore it. Help him get it to its feet.

To insure respect for all that belongs to one's neighbor, the last of the Ten Commandments prohibits even the kind of attitude which would lead to any wrongful acquisition from a neighbor.

Deut. 5:21   COVETING PROHIBITED.
     "You shall not covet your neighbor's wife. You shall not set your desire on your neighbor's house or land, his manservant or

maidservant, his ox or donkey, or anything that belongs to your neighbor."

C. Treatment of Animals

PROPER FEEDING.   Do not muzzle an ox while it is treading out the grain.

Deut. 25:4

RESPECT FOR BIRDS.   If you come across a bird's nest beside the road, either in a tree or on the ground, and the mother is sitting on the young or on the eggs, do not take the mother with the young. You may take the young, but be sure to let the mother go, so that it may go well with you and you may have a long life.

Deut. 22:6,7

VIII. Rules of Warfare

A. Preparation for Battles

PRIEST TO GIVE COURAGE.   When you go to war against your enemies and see horses and chariots and an army greater than yours, do not be afraid of them, because the LORD your God, who brought you up out of Egypt, will be with you. When you are about to go into battle, the priest shall come forward and address the army. He shall say: "Hear, O Israel, today you are going into battle against your enemies. Do not be faint-hearted or afraid; do not be terrified or give way to panic before them. For the LORD your God is the one who goes with you to fight for you against your enemies to give you victory."

Deut. 20:1-4

SELECTING THE SINGLE-MINDED.   The officers shall say to the army: "Has anyone built a new house and not dedicated it? Let him go home, or he may die in battle and someone else may dedicate it. Has anyone plant-ed a vineyard and not begun to enjoy it? Let him go home, or he may die in battle and someone else enjoy it. Has anyone become pledged to a woman and not married her? Let him go home, or he may die in battle and someone else marry her." Then the officers shall add, "Is any man afraid or fainthearted? Let him go home so that his brothers will not become dis-heartened too." When the officers have finished speaking to the army, they shall appoint commanders over it.

Deut. 20:5-9

B. Rules of Siege

DISTANT CITIES.   When you march up to attack a city, make its people an offer of peace. If they accept and open their gates, all the people in it shall be subject to forced labor and shall work for you. If they refuse to make peace and they engage you in battle, lay siege to that city. When the LORD your God delivers it into your hand, put to the sword all the men in it. As for the women, the children, the livestock and everything else in the city, you may take these as plunder for yourselves. And you may use the plunder the LORD your God gives you from your enemies. This is how you are to treat all the cities that are at a distance from you and do not belong to the nations nearby.

Deut. 20:10-15

CANAANITE CITIES.   However, in the cities of the nations the LORD your God is giving you as an inheritance, do not leave alive anything that

Deut. 20:16-18

breathes. Completely destroy[n] them—the Hittites, Amorites, Canaanites, Perizzites, Hivites and Jebusites—as the LORD your God has commanded you. Otherwise, they will teach you to follow all the detestable things they do in worshiping their gods, and you will sin against the LORD your God.

Deut. 20:19,20 TREES TO BE SPARED.   When you lay siege to a city for a long time, fighting against it to capture it, do not destroy its trees by putting an ax to them, because you can eat their fruit. Do not cut them down. Are the trees of the field people, that you should besiege them?[o] However, you may cut down trees that you know are not fruit trees and use them to build siege works until the city at war with you falls.

C. Camp Regulations

Deut. 23:9 PURITY IN CAMP.   When you are encamped against your enemies, keep away from everything impure.

Deut. 23:10,11 NOCTURNAL UNCLEANNESS.   If one of your men is unclean because of a nocturnal emission, he is to go outside the camp and stay there. But as evening approaches he is to wash himself, and at sunset he may return to the camp.

Deut. 23:12-14 SANITARY REGULATIONS.   Designate a place outside the camp where you can go to relieve yourself. As part of your equipment have something to dig with, and when you relieve yourself, dig a hole and cover up your excrement. For the LORD your God moves about in your camp to protect you and to deliver your enemies to you. Your camp must be holy, so that he will not see among you anything indecent and turn away from you.

D. Soldiers and Marriage

(Deut. 24:5) (EXEMPTION FROM SERVICE)

(Deut. 21:10-14) (MARRYING CAPTIVES)

IX. Responsibilities Under the Laws

A. Obedience Enjoined

Lev. 22:31-33 BASIS FOR OBEDIENCE.   "Keep my commands and follow them. I am the LORD. Do not profane my holy name. I must be acknowledged as holy by the Israelites. I am the LORD, who makes[p] you holy[q] and who brought you out of Egypt to be your God. I am the LORD."

Deut. 12:32 LAW NOT TO BE CHANGED.   See that you do all I command you; do not add to it or take away from it.

B. Duty to Promulgate

Num. 15:37-41 Deut. 22:12 TASSELS OF REMEMBRANCE. The LORD said to Moses, "Speak to the Israelites and say to them: 'Throughout the generations to come you are to make tassels on the corners of your garments, with a blue cord on each tassel. You will have these tassels to look at and so you will remember all

---

[n]The Hebrew term refers to the irrevocable giving over of things or persons to the LORD, often by totally destroying them.   [o]Or *down to use in the siege, for the fruit trees are for the benefit of man*   [p]Or *made*   [q]Or *who sanctifies you; or who sets you apart as holy*

the commands of the LORD, that you may obey them and not prostitute yourselves by going after the lusts of your own hearts and eyes. Then you will remember to obey all my commands and will be consecrated to your God. I am the LORD your God, who brought you out of Egypt to be your God. I am the LORD your God.'"

READING OF LAW REQUIRED. So Moses wrote down this law and gave it to the priests, the sons of Levi, who carried the ark of the covenant of the LORD, and to all the elders of Israel. Then Moses commanded them: "At the end of every seven years, in the year for canceling debts, during the Feast of Tabernacles, when all Israel comes to appear before the LORD your God at the place he will choose, you shall read this law before them in their hearing. Assemble the people—men, women and children, and the aliens living in your towns—so they can listen and learn to fear the LORD your God and follow carefully all the words of this law. Their children, who do not know this law, must hear it and learn to fear the LORD your God as long as you live in the land you are crossing the Jordan to possess."

Deut.
31:9-13

C. Blessings of Obedience

BLESSINGS ENUMERATED. " 'If you follow my decrees and are careful to obey my commands, I will send you rain in its season, and the ground will yield its crops and the trees of the field their fruit. Your threshing will continue until grape harvest and the grape harvest will continue until planting, and you will eat all the food you want and live in safety in your land.

" 'I will grant peace in the land, and you will lie down and no one will make you afraid. I will remove savage beasts from the land, and the sword will not pass through your country. You will pursue your enemies, and they will fall by the sword before you. Five of you will chase a hundred, and a hundred of you will chase ten thousand, and your enemies will fall by the sword before you.

" 'I will look on you with favor and make you fruitful and increase your numbers, and I will keep my covenant with you. You will still be eating last year's harvest when you will have to move it out to make room for the new. I will put my dwelling place[r] among you, and I will not abhor you. I will walk among you and be your God, and you will be my people. I am the LORD your God, who brought you out of Egypt so that you would no longer be slaves to the Egyptians; I broke the bars of your yoke and enabled you to walk with heads held high.

Lev.
26:3-13

D. Punishments for Disobedience

PUNISHMENTS ENUMERATED. " 'But if you will not listen to me and carry out all these commands, and if you reject my decrees and abhor my laws and fail to carry out all my commands and so violate my covenant, then I will do this to you: I will bring upon you sudden terror, wasting diseases and fever that will destroy your sight and drain away your life. You will plant seed in vain, because your enemies will eat it. I will set my face against you so that you will be defeated by your enemies; those who hate

Lev.
26:14-17

[r]Or *my tabernacle*

you will rule over you, and you will flee even when no one is pursuing you.

Lev.
26:18-22
" 'If after all this you will not listen to me, I will punish you for your sins seven times over. I will break down your stubborn pride and make the sky above you like iron and the ground beneath you like bronze. Your strength will be spent in vain, because your soil will not yield its crops, nor will the trees of the land yield their fruit.

" 'If you remain hostile toward me and refuse to listen to me, I will multiply your afflictions seven times over, as your sins deserve. I will send wild animals against you, and they will rob you of your children, destroy your cattle and make you so few in number that your roads will be deserted.

Lev.
26:23-26
" 'If in spite of these things you do not accept my correction but continue to be hostile toward me, I myself will be hostile toward you and will afflict you for your sins seven times over. And I will bring the sword upon you to avenge the breaking of the covenant. When you withdraw into your cities, I will send a plague among you, and you will be given into enemy hands. When I cut off your supply of bread, ten women will be able to bake your bread in one oven, and they will dole out the bread by weight. You will eat, but you will not be satisfied.

Lev.
26:27-35
" 'If in spite of this you still do not listen to me but continue to be hostile toward me, then in my anger I will be hostile toward you, and I myself will punish you for your sins seven times over. You will eat the flesh of your sons and the flesh of your daughters. I will destroy your high places, cut down your incense altars and pile your dead bodies on the lifeless forms of your idols, and I will abhor you. I will turn your cities into ruins and lay waste your sanctuaries, and I will take no delight in the pleasing aroma of your offerings. I will lay waste the land, so that your enemies who live there will be appalled. I will scatter you among the nations and will draw out my sword and pursue you. Your land will be laid waste, and your cities will lie in ruins. Then the land will enjoy its sabbath years all the time that it lies desolate and you are in the country of your enemies; then the land will rest and enjoy its sabbaths. All the time that it lies desolate, the land will have the rest it did not have during the sabbaths you lived in it.

Lev.
26:36-39
" 'As for those of you who are left, I will make their hearts so fearful in the lands of their enemies that the sound of a windblown leaf will put them to flight. They will run as though fleeing from the sword, and they will fall, even though no one is pursuing them. They will stumble over one another as though fleeing from the sword, even though no one is pursuing them. So you will not be able to stand before your enemies. You will perish among the nations; the land of your enemies will devour you. Those of you who are left will waste away in the lands of their enemies because of their sins; also because of their fathers' sins they will waste away.

Lev.
26:40-42
EFFECTS OF REPENTANCE. " 'But if they will confess their sins and the sins of their fathers—their treachery against me and their hostility toward me, which made me hostile toward them so that I sent them into the land of their enemies—then when their uncircumcised hearts are humbled and they pay for their sin, I will remember my covenant with Jacob and my covenant with Isaac and my covenant with Abraham, and I will remember the land.

CONCERN IN CAPTIVITY.   For the land will be deserted by them and will enjoy its sabbaths while it lies desolate without them. They will pay for their sins because they rejected my laws and abhorred my decrees. Yet in spite of this, when they are in the land of their enemies, I will not reject them or abhor them so as to destroy them completely, breaking my covenant with them. I am the LORD their God. But for their sake I will remember the covenant with their ancestors whom I brought out of Egypt in the sight of the nations to be their God. I am the LORD.' "

Lev.
26:43-45

E. Conclusion

EPILOGUE.   These are the decrees, the laws and the regulations that the LORD established on Mount Sinai between himself and the Israelites through Moses.

Lev. 26:46

CONQUERING A LAND
(Ca. 1400-1100 B.C.)

*Renewal of the Covenant*_____

ith this restatement of the laws completed, it is an appropriate time for the Israelites to reaffirm their covenant with God, just as they had done at Mount Sinai when the law was first given. It is not a covenant to be taken lightly, for along with God's promised blessings go the promised curses which will be imposed for breach of the covenant. Breach of the covenant will occur when breach of the law occurs; and breach of the law can easily occur, for the law handed down from God through Moses is the most comprehensive, radically different, and morally demanding law that any nation of people has seen to this time.

Deut.
26:16-19
THE COVENANT RENEWED.   The LORD your God commands you this day to follow these decrees and laws; carefully observe them with all your heart and with all your soul. You have declared this day that the LORD is your God and that you will walk in his ways, that you will keep his decrees, commands and laws, and that you will obey him. And the LORD has declared this day that you are his people, his treasured possession as he promised, and that you are to keep all his commands. He has declared that he will set you in praise, fame and honor high above all the nations he has made and that you will be a people holy to the LORD your God, as he promised.

Deut.
28:1-4
BLESSINGS OF FRUITFULNESS.   If you fully obey the LORD your God and carefully follow all his commands I give you today, the LORD your God will set you high above all the nations on earth. All these blessings will come upon you and accompany you if you obey the LORD your God:

You will be blessed in the city and blessed in the country.
The fruit of your womb will be blessed, and the crops of your land and the young of your livestock—the calves of your herds and the lambs of your flocks.

Deut.
28:5-14
BLESSINGS OF PROSPERITY.   Your basket and your kneading trough will be blessed.
You will be blessed when you come in and blessed when you go out.

The LORD will grant that the enemies who rise up against you will be defeated before you. They will come at you from one direction but flee from you in seven.

The LORD will send a blessing on your barns and on everything you put your hand to. The LORD your God will bless you in the land he is giving you.

The LORD will establish you as his holy people, as he promised you on oath, if you keep the commands of the LORD your God and walk in his ways. Then all the peoples on earth will see that you are called by the name of the LORD, and they will fear you. The LORD will grant you abundant prosperity—in the fruit of your womb, the young of your livestock and the crops of your ground—in the land he swore to your forefathers to give you.

The LORD will open the heavens, the storehouse of his bounty, to send rain on your land in season and to bless all the work of your hands. You will lend to many nations but will borrow from none. The LORD will make you the head, not the tail. If you pay attention to the commands of the LORD your God that I give you this day and carefully follow them, you will always be at the top, never at the bottom. Do not turn aside from any of the commands I give you today, to the right or to the left, following other gods and serving them.

CURSES OF UNFRUITFULNESS.   However, if you do not obey the LORD your God and do not carefully follow all his commands and decrees I am giving you today, all these curses will come upon you and overtake you:

Deut. 28:15-19

You will be cursed in the city and cursed in the country.
Your basket and your kneading trough will be cursed.
The fruit of your womb will be cursed, and the crops of your land, and the calves of your herds and the lambs of your flocks.
You will be cursed when you come in and cursed when you go out.

CURSES OF PLAGUES.   The LORD will send on you curses, confusion and rebuke in everything you put your hand to, until you are destroyed and come to sudden ruin because of the evil you have done in forsaking him.ᵃ The LORD will plague you with diseases until he has destroyed you from the land you are entering to possess. The LORD will strike you with wasting disease, with fever and inflammation, with scorching heat and drought, with blight and mildew, which will plague you until you perish. The sky over your head will be bronze, the ground beneath you iron. The LORD will turn the rain of your country into dust and powder; it will come down from the skies until you are destroyed.

Deut. 28:20-24

CURSES OF OPPRESSION.   The LORD will cause you to be defeated before your enemies. You will come at them from one direction but flee from them in seven, and you will become a thing of horror to all the kingdoms on earth. Your carcasses will be food for all the birds of the air and the beasts of the earth, and there will be no one to frighten them away. The LORD will afflict you with the boils of Egypt and with tumors, festering sores and the itch, from which you cannot be cured. The LORD will afflict you with madness, blindness and confusion of mind. At midday you will grope about like a blind man in the dark. You will be unsuccessful in everything you do; day after day you will be oppressed and robbed, with no one to rescue you.

Deut. 28:25-35

You will be pledged to be married to a woman, but another will take her

ᵃHebrew *me*

and ravish her. You will build a house, but you will not live in it. You will plant a vineyard, but you will not even begin to enjoy its fruit. Your ox will be slaughtered before your eyes, but you will eat none of it. Your donkey will be forcibly taken from you and will not be returned. Your sheep will be given to your enemies, and no one will rescue them. Your sons and daughters will be given to another nation, and you will wear out your eyes watching for them day after day, powerless to lift a hand. A people that you do not know will eat what your land and labor produce, and you will have nothing but cruel oppression all your days. The sights you see will drive you mad. The LORD will afflict your knees and legs with painful boils that cannot be cured, spreading from the soles of your feet to the top of your head.

**Deut.
28:36-46**

CURSES OF RUIN.   The LORD will drive you and the king you set over you to a nation unknown to you or your fathers. There you will worship other gods, gods of wood and stone. You will become a thing of horror and an object of scorn and ridicule to all the nations where the LORD will drive you.

You will sow much seed in the field but you will harvest little, because locusts will devour it. You will plant vineyards and cultivate them but you will not drink the wine or gather the grapes, because worms will eat them. You will have olive trees throughout your country but you will not use the oil, because the olives will drop off. You will have sons and daughters but you will not keep them, because they will go into captivity. Swarms of locusts will take over all your trees and the crops of your land.

The alien who lives among you will rise above you higher and higher, but you will sink lower and lower. He will lend to you, but you will not lend to him. He will be the head, but you will be the tail.

All these curses will come upon you. They will pursue you and overtake you until you are destroyed, because you did not obey the LORD your God and observe the commands and decrees he gave you. They will be a sign and a wonder to you and your descendants forever.

**Deut.
28:47-57**

CURSES OF CAPTIVITY.   Because you did not serve the LORD your God joyfully and gladly in the time of prosperity, therefore in hunger and thirst, in nakedness and dire poverty, you will serve the enemies the LORD sends against you. He will put an iron yoke on your neck until he has destroyed you.

The LORD will bring a nation against you from far away, from the ends of the earth, like an eagle swooping down, a nation whose language you will not understand, a fierce-looking nation without respect for the old or pity for the young. They will devour the young of your livestock and the crops of your land until you are destroyed. They will leave you no grain, new wine or oil, nor any calves of your herds or lambs of your flocks until you are ruined. They will lay siege to all the cities throughout your land until the high fortified walls in which you trust fall down. They will besiege all the cities throughout the land the LORD your God is giving you.

Because of the suffering that your enemy will inflict on you during the siege, you will eat the fruit of the womb, the flesh of the sons and daughters the LORD your God has given you. Even the most gentle and sensitive man among you will have no compassion on his own brother or the wife he loves or his surviving children, and he will not give to one of them any of the flesh of his children that he is eating. It will be all he has left because of the suffering your enemy will inflict on you during the siege of all your cities. The most gentle and sensitive woman among you—so sensitive and gentle that she would not venture to touch the ground with the sole of her foot—will begrudge the husband she loves and her own son or daughter the afterbirth from her womb and the children she bears. For she intends to eat them secretly during the siege and in the distress that your enemy will inflict on you in your cities.

CURSES OF DISEASE. If you do not carefully follow all the words of this law, which are written in this book, and do not revere this glorious and awesome name—the LORD your God—the LORD will send fearful plagues on you and your descendants, harsh and prolonged disasters, and severe and lingering illnesses. He will bring upon you all the diseases of Egypt that you dreaded, and they will cling to you. The LORD will also bring on you every kind of sickness and disaster not recorded in this Book of the Law, until you are destroyed.

Deut. 28:58-61

CURSES OF DISPERSION. You who were as numerous as the stars in the sky will be left but few in number, because you did not obey the LORD your God. Just as it pleased the LORD to make you prosper and increase in number, so it will please him to ruin and destroy you. You will be uprooted from the land you are entering to possess.

Deut. 28:62-68

Then the LORD will scatter you among all nations, from one end of the earth to the other. There you will worship other gods—gods of wood and stone, which neither you nor your fathers have known. Among those nations you will find no repose, no resting place for the sole of your foot. There the LORD will give you an anxious mind, eyes weary with longing, and a despairing heart. You will live in constant suspense, filled with dread both night and day, never sure of your life. In the morning you will say, "If only it were evening!" and in the evening, "If only it were morning!"—because of the terror that will fill your hearts and the sights that your eyes will see. The LORD will send you back in ships to Egypt on a journey I said you should never make again. There you will offer yourselves for sale to your enemies as male and female slaves, but no one will buy you.

HOW GOD HAS KEPT COVENANT. Moses summoned all the Israelites and said to them:

Deut. 29:2-9

Your eyes have seen all that the LORD did in Egypt to Pharaoh, to all his officials and to all his land. With your own eyes you saw those great trials, those miraculous signs and great wonders. But to this day the LORD has not given you a mind that understands or eyes that see or ears that hear. During the forty years that I led you through the desert, your clothes did not wear out, nor did the sandals on your feet. You ate no bread and drank no wine or other fermented drink. I did this so that you might know that I am the LORD your God.

When you reached this place, Sihon king of Heshbon and Og king of Bashan came out to fight against us, but we defeated them. We took their land and gave it as an inheritance to the Reubenites, the Gadites and the half-tribe of Manasseh.

Carefully follow the terms of this covenant, so that you may prosper in everything you do.

**Deut.
29:10-15**

COVENANT IS PERPETUAL. All of you are standing today in the presence of the LORD your God—your leaders and chief men, your elders and officials, and all the other men of Israel, together with your children and your wives, and the aliens living in your camps who chop your wood and carry your water. You are standing here in order to enter into a covenant with the LORD your God, a covenant the LORD is making with you this day and sealing with an oath, to confirm you this day as his people, that he may be your God as he promised you and as he swore to your fathers, Abraham, Isaac and Jacob. I am making this covenant, with its oath, not only with you who are standing here with us today in the presence of the LORD our God but also with those who are not here today.

**Deut.
29:16-29**

WARNING AGAINST FORSAKING. You yourselves know how we lived in Egypt and how we passed through the countries on the way here. You saw among them their detestable images and idols of wood and stone, of silver and gold. Make sure there is no man or woman, clan or tribe among you today whose heart turns away from the LORD our God to go and worship the gods of those nations; make sure there is no root among you that produces such bitter poison.

When such a person hears the words of this oath, he invokes a blessing on himself and therefore thinks, "I will be safe, even though I persist in going my own way." This will bring disaster on the watered land as well as the dry.[b] The LORD will never be willing to forgive him; his wrath and zeal will burn against that man. All the curses written in this book will fall upon him, and the LORD will blot out his name from under heaven. The LORD will single him out from all the tribes of Israel for disaster, according to all the curses of the covenant written in this Book of the Law.

Your children who follow you in later generations and foreigners who come from distant lands will see the calamities that have fallen on the land and the diseases with which the LORD has afflicted it. The whole land will be a burning waste of salt and sulfur—nothing planted, nothing sprouting, no vegetation growing on it. It will be like the destruction of Sodom and Gomorrah, Admah and Zeboiim, which the LORD overthrew in fierce anger. All the nations will ask: "Why has the LORD done this to this land? Why this fierce, burning anger?"

And the answer will be: "It is because this people abandoned the covenant of the LORD, the God of their fathers, the covenant he made with them when he brought them out of Egypt. They went off and worshiped other gods and bowed down to them, gods they did not know, gods he had not given them. Therefore the LORD's anger burned against this land, so that he brought on it all the curses written in this book. In furious anger and in great wrath the LORD uprooted them from their land and thrust them into another land, as it is now."

The secret things belong to the LORD our God, but the things revealed belong to us and to our children forever, that we may follow all the words of this law.

**Deut.
30:1-10**

FORGIVENESS FOR REPENTANCE. When all these blessings and curses I have set before you come upon you and you take them to heart wherever the LORD your God disperses you among the nations, and when you and your children return to the LORD your God and obey him with all your

---

[b]Or way, in order to add drunkenness to thirst."

heart and with all your soul according to everything I command you today, then the LORD your God will restore your fortunes[c] and have compassion on you and gather you again from all the nations where he scattered you. Even if you have been banished to the most distant land under the heavens, from there the LORD your God will gather you and bring you back. He will bring you to the land that belonged to your fathers, and you will take possession of it. He will make you more prosperous and numerous than your fathers. The LORD your God will circumcise your hearts and the hearts of your descendants, so that you may love him with all your heart and with all your soul, and live. The LORD your God will put all these curses on your enemies who hate and persecute you. You will again obey the LORD and follow all his commands I am giving you today. Then the LORD your God will make you most prosperous in all the work of your hands and in the fruit of your womb, the young of your livestock and the crops of your land. The LORD will again delight in you and make you prosperous, just as he delighted in your fathers, if you obey the LORD your God and keep his commands and decrees that are written in this Book of the Law and turn to the LORD your God with all your heart and with all your soul.

COVENANT NOT TOO DIFFICULT.   Now what I am commanding you today is not too difficult for you or beyond your reach. It is not up in heaven, so that you have to ask, "Who will ascend into heaven to get it and proclaim it to us so we may obey it?" Nor is it beyond the sea, so that you have to ask, "Who will cross the sea to get it and proclaim it to us so we may obey it?" No, the word is very near you; it is in your mouth and in your heart so you may obey it.

Deut.
30:11-14

LIFE AND DEATH IN COVENANT.   See, I set before you today life and prosperity, death and destruction. For I command you today to love the LORD your God, to walk in his ways, and to keep his commands, decrees and laws; then you will live and increase, and the LORD your God will bless you in the land you are entering to possess.

Deut.
30:15-20

But if your heart turns away and you are not obedient, and if you are drawn away to bow down to other gods and worship them, I declare to you this day that you will certainly be destroyed. You will not live long in the land you are crossing the Jordan to enter and possess.

This day I call heaven and earth as witnesses against you that I have set before you life and death, blessings and curses. Now choose life, so that you and your children may live and that you may love the LORD your God, listen to his voice, and hold fast to him. For the LORD is your life, and he will give you many years in the land he swore to give to your fathers, Abraham, Isaac and Jacob.

CONCLUSION TO COVENANT.   These are the terms of the covenant the LORD commanded Moses to make with the Israelites in Moab, in addition to the covenant he had made with them at Horeb.

Deut. 29:1

ALTAR TO BE BUILT.   Moses and the elders of Israel commanded the people: "Keep all these commands that I give you today. When you have crossed the Jordan into the land the LORD your God is giving you, set up some large stones and coat them with plaster. Write on them all the words of this law when you have crossed over to enter the land the LORD your

Deut.
27:1-8

[c]Or *will bring you back from captivity*

God is giving you, a land flowing with milk and honey, just as the LORD, the God of your fathers, promised you. And when you have crossed the Jordan, set up these stones on Mount Ebal, as I command you today, and coat them with plaster. Build there an altar to the LORD your God, an altar of stones. Do not use any iron tool upon them. Build the altar of the LORD your God with fieldstones and offer burnt offerings on it to the LORD your God. Sacrifice fellowship offerings[d] there, eating them and rejoicing in the presence of the LORD your God. And you shall write very clearly all the words of this law on these stones you have set up."

Deut.
27:9,10

COVENANT CONFIRMED. Then Moses and the priests, who are Levites, said to all Israel, "Be silent, O Israel, and listen! You have now become the people of the LORD your God. Obey the LORD your God and follow his commands and decrees that I give you today."

Deut.
27:11-26

CEREMONY OF REMINDER. On the same day Moses commanded the people:

When you have crossed the Jordan, these tribes shall stand on Mount Gerizim to bless the people: Simeon, Levi, Judah, Issachar, Joseph and Benjamin. And these tribes shall stand on Mount Ebal to pronounce curses: Reuben, Gad, Asher, Zebulun, Dan and Naphtali.

The Levites shall recite to all the people of Israel in a loud voice:

"Cursed is the man who carves an image or casts an idol—a thing detestable to the LORD, the work of the craftsman's hands—and sets it up in secret."

Then all the people shall say, "Amen!"

"Cursed is the man who dishonors his father or his mother."

Then all the people shall say, "Amen!"

"Cursed is the man who moves his neighbor's boundary stone."

Then all the people shall say, "Amen!"

"Cursed is the man who leads the blind astray on the road."

Then all the people shall say, "Amen!"

"Cursed is the man who withholds justice from the alien, the fatherless or the widow."

Then all the people shall say, "Amen!"

"Cursed is the man who sleeps with his father's wife, for he dishonors his father's bed."

Then all the people shall say, "Amen!"

"Cursed is the man who has sexual relations with any animal."

Then all the people shall say, "Amen!"

"Cursed is the man who sleeps with his sister, the daughter of his father or the daughter of his mother."

Then all the people shall say, "Amen!"

"Cursed is the man who sleeps with his mother-in-law."

Then all the people shall say, "Amen!"

"Cursed is the man who kills his neighbor secretly."

Then all the people shall say, "Amen!"

"Cursed is the man who accepts a bribe to kill an innocent person."

Then all the people shall say, "Amen!"

"Cursed is the man who does not uphold the words of this law by carrying them out."

Then all the people shall say, "Amen!"

[d] Traditionally *peace offerings*

Transfer of Leadership to Joshua

*M*oses has had a busy final week as the temporal and spiritual leader of his people. He has reminded the Israelites of their history and unique status; he has instructed them in the law; and he has brought them into a renewed covenant relationship with God. Now it is time to step down and turn the leadership over to Joshua, his successor. There is little fanfare, for Moses has not been a typical ruler. He has not been dependent upon political power or process. He has been merely a servant of the nation's true ruler, God himself—and so shall Joshua be.

MOSES URGES COURAGE. Then Moses went out and spoke these words to all Israel: "I am now a hundred and twenty years old and I am no longer able to lead you. The LORD has said to me, 'You shall not cross the Jordan.' The LORD your God himself will cross over ahead of you. He will destroy these nations before you, and you will take possession of their land. Joshua also will cross over ahead of you, as the LORD said. And the LORD will do to them what he did to Sihon and Og, the kings of the Amorites, whom he destroyed along with their land. The LORD will deliver them to you, and you must do to them all that I have commanded you. Be strong and courageous. Do not be afraid or terrified because of them, for the LORD your God goes with you; he will never leave you nor forsake you." *Deut. 31:1-6*

MOSES ENCOURAGES JOSHUA. Then Moses summoned Joshua and said to him in the presence of all Israel, "Be strong and courageous, for you must go with this people into the land that the LORD swore to their fore-fathers to give them, and you must divide it among them as their inheritance. The LORD himself goes before you and will be with you; he will never leave you nor forsake you. Do not be afraid; do not be discouraged." *Deut. 31:7,8*

GOD COMMISSIONS JOSHUA. The LORD said to Moses, "Now the day of your death is near. Call Joshua and present yourselves at the Tent of Meeting, where I will commission him." So Moses and Joshua came and presented themselves at the Tent of Meeting. *Deut. 31:14,15,23*

Then the LORD appeared at the Tent in a pillar of cloud, and the cloud stood over the entrance to the Tent.

The LORD gave this command to Joshua son of Nun: "Be strong and courageous, for you will bring the Israelites into the land I promised them on oath, and I myself will be with you."

A Song of Unfaithfulness

*A*nticipating the fact that, despite their recently renewed covenant, the Israelites will soon breach their vows of commitment to him, God asks Moses to teach the Israelites a song, and to command its transmission from one generation to the next. It is a song about unfaithfulness in which God's own faithfulness stands in sharp contrast. The song contains a recital of promised punishments and a reminder of the mercy which awaits Israel's timely repentance, as well as the vengeance which God will bring against Israel's enemies. In short, it is a call to law-keeping—yet a promise of divine grace where human efforts fail.

Until the time when God gave Moses this song, Moses had personally written the account which is now known as the book of Deuteronomy (a name referring to the restatement of law which it contains). Yet at this point, before assembling the congregation to teach them God's song, there is an indication that Moses gives over his book to the Levites so that it may be kept with the ark.

**Deut.
31:16-18**
GOD FORESEES UNFAITHFULNESS.   And the LORD said to Moses: "You are going to rest with your fathers, and these people will soon prostitute themselves to the foreign gods of the land they are entering. They will forsake me and break the covenant I made with them. On that day I will become angry with them and forsake them; I will hide my face from them, and they will be destroyed. Many disasters and difficulties will come upon them, and on that day they will ask, 'Have not these disasters come upon us because our God is not with us?' And I will certainly hide my face on that day because of all their wickedness in turning to other gods.

**Deut.
31:19-22**
GOD GIVES MOSES A SONG.   "Now write down for yourselves this song and teach it to the Israelites and have them sing it, so that it may be a witness for me against them. When I have brought them into the land flowing with milk and honey, the land I promised on oath to their forefathers, and when they eat their fill and thrive, they will turn to other gods and worship them, rejecting me and breaking my covenant. And when many disasters and difficulties come upon them, this song will testify against them, because it will not be forgotten by their descendants. I know what they are disposed to do, even before I bring them into the land I promised them on oath." So Moses wrote down this song that day and taught it to the Israelites.

**Deut.
31:24-26**
BOOK TO BE KEPT WITH ARK.   After Moses finished writing in a book the words of this law from beginning to end, he gave this command to the Levites who carried the ark of the covenant of the LORD: "Take this Book of the Law and place it beside the ark of the covenant of the LORD your God. There it will remain as a witness against you.

**Deut.
31:27-29**
MOSES CALLS FOR ASSEMBLY.   For I know how rebellious and stiff-necked you are. If you have been rebellious against the LORD while I am still alive and with you, how much more will you rebel after I die! Assemble before me all the elders of your tribes and all your officials, so that I can speak these words in their hearing and call heaven and earth to testify against them. For I know that after my death you are sure to become utterly corrupt and to turn from the way I have commanded you. In days to come, disaster will fall upon you because you will do evil in the sight of the LORD and provoke him to anger by what your hands have made."

**Deut.
31:30-32:6**
MOSES PRESENTS THE SONG. And Moses recited the words of this song from beginning to end in the hearing of the whole assembly of Israel:

> Listen, O heavens, and I will speak;
>   hear, O earth, the words of my mouth.
> Let my teaching fall like rain

and my words descend like dew,
like showers on new grass,
   like abundant rain on tender plants.

I will proclaim the name of the LORD.
   Oh, praise the greatness of our God!
He is the Rock, his works are perfect,
   and all his ways are just.
A faithful God who does no wrong,
   upright and just is he.

They have acted corruptly toward him;
   to their shame they are no longer his children,
   but a warped and crooked generation.*e*
Is this the way you repay the LORD,
   O foolish and unwise people?
Is he not your Father, your Creator,*f*
   who made you and formed you?

Remember the days of old;
   consider the generations long past.
Ask your father and he will tell you,
   your elders, and they will explain to you.
When the Most High gave the nations their inheritance,
   when he divided all mankind,
he set up boundaries for the peoples
   according to the number of the sons of Israel.*g*
For the LORD's portion is his people,
   Jacob his allotted inheritance.

**Deut.
32:7-14**

In a desert land he found him,
   in a barren and howling waste.
He shielded him and cared for him;
   he guarded him as the apple of his eye,
like an eagle that stirs up its nest
   and hovers over its young,
that spreads its wings to catch them
   and carries them on its pinions.
The LORD alone led him;
   no foreign god was with him.

He made him ride on the heights of the land
   and fed him with the fruit of the fields.
He nourished him with honey from the rock,
   and with oil from the flinty crag,
with curds and milk from herd and flock
   and with fattened lambs and goats,
with choice rams of Bashan
   and the finest kernels of wheat.
You drank the foaming blood of the grape.

---

*e*Or *Corrupt are they and not his children, / a generation warped and twisted to their shame*
*f*Or *Father, who bought you*   *g*Masoretic Text; Dead Sea Scrolls (see also Septuagint)
sons of God

Deut.
32:15-22

Jeshurun[h] grew fat and kicked;
  filled with food, he became heavy and sleek.
He abandoned the God who made him
  and rejected the Rock his Savior.
They made him jealous with their foreign gods
  and angered him with their detestable idols.
They sacrificed to demons, which are not God—
  gods they had not known,
  gods that recently appeared,
  gods your fathers did not fear.
You deserted the Rock, who fathered you;
  you forgot the God who gave you birth.

The LORD saw this and rejected them
  because he was angered by his sons and daughters.
"I will hide my face from them," he said,
  "and see what their end will be;
for they are a perverse generation,
  children who are unfaithful.
They made me jealous by what is no god
  and angered me with their worthless idols.
I will make them envious by those who are not a people;
  I will make them angry by a nation that has no
    understanding.
For a fire has been kindled by my wrath,
  one that burns to the realm of death[i] below.
It will devour the earth and its harvests
  and set afire the foundations of the mountains.

Deut.
32:23-27

"I will heap calamities upon them
  and spend my arrows against them.
I will send wasting famine against them,
  consuming pestilence and deadly plague;
I will send against them the fangs of wild beasts,
  the venom of vipers that glide in the dust.
In the street the sword will make them childless;
  in their homes terror will reign.
Young men and young women will perish,
  infants and gray-haired men.
I said I would scatter them
  and blot out their memory from mankind,
but I dreaded the taunt of the enemy,
  lest the adversary misunderstand
and say, 'Our hand has triumphed;
  the LORD has not done all this.'"

Deut.
32:28-33

They are a nation without sense,
  there is no discernment in them.
If only they were wise and would understand this
  and discern what their end will be!
How could one man chase a thousand,

[h]Jeshurun means *the upright one*, that is, Israel.   [i]Hebrew *to Sheol*

or two put ten thousand to flight,
unless their Rock had sold them,
    unless the LORD had given them up?
For their rock is not like our Rock,
    as even our enemies concede.
Their vine comes from the vine of Sodom
    and from the fields of Gomorrah.
Their grapes are filled with poison,
    and their clusters with bitterness.
Their wine is the venom of serpents,
    the deadly poison of cobras.

"Have I not kept this in reserve
    and sealed it in my vaults?
It is mine to avenge; I will repay.
    In due time their foot will slip;
their day of disaster is near
    and their doom rushes upon them."

Deut. 32:34-38

The LORD will judge his people
    and have compassion on his servants
when he sees their strength is gone
    and no one is left, slave or free.
He will say: "Now where are their gods,
    the rock they took refuge in,
the gods who ate the fat of their sacrifices
    and drank the wine of their drink offerings?
Let them rise up to help you!
    Let them give you shelter!

"See now that I myself am He!
    There is no god besides me.
I put to death and I bring to life,
    I have wounded and I will heal,
    and no one can deliver out of my hand.
I lift my hand to heaven and declare:
    As surely as I live forever,
when I sharpen my flashing sword
    and my hand grasps it in judgment,
I will take vengeance on my adversaries
    and repay those who hate me.
I will make my arrows drunk with blood,
    while my sword devours flesh:
the blood of the slain and the captives,
    the heads of the enemy leaders."

Deut. 32:39-43

Rejoice, O nations, with his people,^{j} ^{k}
    for he will avenge the blood of his servants;
he will take vengeance on his enemies
    and make atonement for his land and people.

---

^{j}Or *Make his people rejoice, O nations* ^{k}Masoretic Text; Dead Sea Scrolls (see also
Septuagint) *people, / and let all the angels worship him /*

Deut.
32:44-47

IMPORTANCE OF THE SONG.   Moses came with Joshua[l] son of Nun
and spoke all the words of this song in the hearing of the people. When
Moses finished reciting all these words to all Israel, he said to them, "Take
to heart all the words I have solemnly declared to you this day, so that you
may command your children to obey carefully all the words of this law.
They are not just idle words for you—they are your life. By them you will
live long in the land you are crossing the Jordan to possess."

Moses Blesses the Tribes

*J*n contrast to the urgent warnings against unfaithfulness, Moses' last
recorded words are optimistic blessings for each of the tribes of Israel
as they prepare to take over the land which was promised to their
forefathers. Although the exact interpretation of each blessing is sometimes
obscure, it is clear that Moses is caught up in the excitement of pending conquests and uses the occasion for giving encouragement and hope.

Prior to giving these blessings, Moses is told that he is to go up on a mountain to view the land of Canaan and then die soon thereafter.

Num.
27:12-14
Deut.
32:48-52

MOSES SUMMONED BEFORE DEATH.   On that same day the LORD told
Moses, "Go up into the Abarim Range to Mount Nebo in Moab, across from
Jericho, and view Canaan, the land I am giving the Israelites as their own
possession. There on the mountain that you have climbed you will die and
be gathered to your people, just as your brother Aaron died on Mount Hor
and was gathered to his people. This is because both of you broke faith
with me in the presence of the Israelites at the waters of Meribah Kadesh
in the Desert of Zin and because you did not uphold my holiness among
the Israelites. Therefore, you will see the land only from a distance; you
will not enter the land I am giving to the people of Israel."

Deut.
33:1-6

MOSES BLESSES THE TRIBES.   This is the blessing that Moses the man
of God pronounced on the Israelites before his death. He said:

"The LORD came from Sinai
       and dawned over them from Seir;
       he shone forth from Mount Paran.
He came with[m] myriads of holy ones
       from the south, from his mountain slopes.[n]
Surely it is you who love the people;
       all the holy ones are in your hand.
At your feet they all bow down,
       and from you receive instruction,
the law that Moses gave us,
       the possession of the assembly of Jacob.
He was king over Jeshurun[o]
       when the leaders of the people assembled,
       along with the tribes of Israel.

"Let Reuben live and not die,
       nor[p] his men be few."

[l]Hebrew *Hoshea*, a variant of *Joshua*   [m]Or *from*   [n]The meaning of the Hebrew for
this phrase is uncertain.   [o]*Jeshurun* means *the upright one*, that is, Israel.   [p]Or *but let*

And this he said about Judah:

Deut. 33:7

> "Hear, O LORD, the cry of Judah;
>   bring him to his people.
> With his own hands he defends his cause.
>   Oh, be his help against his foes!"

About Levi he said:

Deut. 33:8-11

> "Your Thummim and Urim belong
>   to the man you favored.
> You tested him at Massah;
>   you contended with him at the waters of Meribah.
> He said of his father and mother,
>   'I have no regard for them.'
> He did not recognize his brothers
>   or acknowledge his own children,
> but he watched over your word
>   and guarded your covenant.
> He teaches your precepts to Jacob
>   and your law to Israel.
> He offers incense before you
>   and whole burnt offerings on your altar.
> Bless all his skills, O LORD,
>   and be pleased with the work of his hands.
> Smite the loins of those who rise up against him;
>   strike his foes till they rise no more."

About Benjamin he said:

Deut. 33:12

> "Let the beloved of the LORD rest secure in him,
>   for he shields him all day long,
>   and the one the LORD loves rests between his shoulders."

About Joseph he said:

Deut. 33:13-17

> "May the LORD bless his land
>   with the precious dew from heaven above
>   and with the deep waters that lie below;
> with the best the sun brings forth
>   and the finest the moon can yield;
> with the choicest gifts of the ancient mountains
>   and the fruitfulness of the everlasting hills;
> with the best gifts of the earth and its fullness
>   and the favor of him who dwelt in the burning bush.
> Let all these rest on the head of Joseph,
>   on the brow of the prince among⁹ his brothers.
> In majesty he is like a firstborn bull;
>   his horns are the horns of a wild ox.
> With them he will gore the nations,
>   even those at the ends of the earth.
> Such are the ten thousands of Ephraim;
>   such are the thousands of Manasseh."

⁹Or *of the one separated from*

Deut.
33:18,19

About Zebulun he said:

> "Rejoice, Zebulun, in your going out,
>   and you, Issachar, in your tents.
> They will summon peoples to the mountain
>   and there offer sacrifices of righteousness;
> they will feast on the abundance of the seas,
>   on the treasures hidden in the sand."

Deut.
33:20,21

About Gad he said:

> "Blessed is he who enlarges Gad's domain!
>   Gad lives there like a lion,
>   tearing at arm or head.
> He chose the best land for himself;
>   the leader's portion was kept for him.
> When the heads of the people assembled,
>   he carried out the LORD's righteous will,
>   and his judgments concerning Israel."

Deut.
33:22

About Dan he said:

> "Dan is a lion's cub,
>   springing out of Bashan."

Deut.
33:23

About Naphtali he said:

> "Naphtali is abounding with the favor of the LORD
>   and is full of his blessing;
> he will inherit southward to the lake."

Deut.
33:24-29

About Asher he said:

> "Most blessed of sons is Asher;
>   let him be favored by his brothers,
>   and let him bathe his feet in oil.
> The bolts of your gates will be iron and bronze,
>   and your strength will equal your days.
>
> "There is no one like the God of Jeshurun,
>   who rides on the heavens to help you
>   and on the clouds in his majesty.
> The eternal God is your refuge,
>   and underneath are the everlasting arms.
> He will drive out your enemy before you,
>   saying, 'Destroy him!'
> So Israel will live in safety alone;
>   Jacob's spring is secure
> in a land of grain and new wine,
>   where the heavens drop dew.
> Blessed are you, O Israel!
>   Who is like you,
>   a people saved by the LORD?
> He is your shield and helper
>   and your glorious sword.
> Your enemies will cower before you,
>   and you will trample down their high places.ʳ"

ʳOr *will tread upon their bodies*

Moses' Death and Burial

*T*he tribes having been blessed, and all things set in order, Moses prepares to ascend Mount Nebo for a long-awaited view of the promised land. It must be with mixed emotions that he climbs that last step and looks down over "the land that flows with milk and honey." The land is rich and fertile. There is room for a nation, and roots at last for a wandering people. The long journey has been worth it, and the God who has promised it all is indeed faithful. But the land must still be conquered. While Moses has every confidence that God can deliver the land, he knows that territorial conquest is nothing compared to the struggle which the Israelites will face in trying to maintain their covenant relationship with God. So Moses must be both excited and concerned (not to mention apprehensive about his own impending death).

MOSES VIEWS PROMISED LAND.   Then Moses climbed Mount Nebo from the plains of Moab to the top of Pisgah, across from Jericho. There the LORD showed him the whole land—from Gilead to Dan, all of Naphtali, the territory of Ephraim and Manasseh, all the land of Judah as far as the western sea,[s] the Negev and the whole region from the Valley of Jericho, the City of Palms, as far as Zoar. Then the LORD said to him, "This is the land I promised on oath to Abraham, Isaac and Jacob when I said, 'I will give it to your descendants.' I have let you see it with your eyes, but you will not cross over into it."

Deut. 34:1-4 Mount Nebo (Ca. 1406 B.C.)

MOSES DIES.   And Moses the servant of the LORD died there in Moab, as the LORD had said. He buried him[t] in Moab, in the valley opposite Beth Peor, but to this day no one knows where his grave is. Moses was a hundred and twenty years old when he died, yet his eyes were not weak nor his strength gone.

Deut. 34:5-7 Moab

ISRAEL MOURNS.   The Israelites grieved for Moses in the plains of Moab thirty days, until the time of weeping and mourning was over.

Deut. 34:8

JOSHUA LEADS.   Now Joshua son of Nun was filled with the spirit[u] of wisdom because Moses had laid his hands on him. So the Israelites listened to him and did what the LORD had commanded Moses.

Deut. 34:9

TRIBUTE TO MOSES.   Since then, no prophet has risen in Israel like Moses, whom the LORD knew face to face, who did all those miraculous signs and wonders the LORD sent him to do in Egypt—to Pharaoh and to all his officials and to his whole land. For no one has ever shown the mighty power or performed the awesome deeds that Moses did in the sight of all Israel.

Deut. 34:10-12

So ends the life of the greatest man of God since Abraham. As Abraham had taught a family about faith, Moses had taught a nation about law. And in

---

[s]That is, the Mediterranean   [t]Or *He was buried*   [u]Or *Spirit*

centuries to come, One greater than them both will teach the whole world about love and grace.

Preparation for Conquest

*W*ith the burial of Moses, the focus of leadership falls upon Joshua, who will lead the Israelites west across the Jordan River into Canaan—the land first promised to Abraham some 685 years previously. Over the next six years the Israelites will conquer the land and begin to occupy it. However, it will take many more years for the tribes to assume full control, and even then many of the local inhabitants will never be driven out.

But for now the time has come for Joshua to mobilize the nation. Preparations for the conquest include not only the formulation of military strategy but also rededication to God and the holy purposes for which battles will soon be fought.

In the midst of all the activity of a nation preparing for war is the fascinating account of a woman in Canaan whose faith in the God of the Israelites leads her to play a key role in the initial invasion.

The historical record of Joshua reveals that God has chosen a righteous and courageous leader for his people. Joshua is in almost every respect a forerunner of One who will one day come to lead all true believers into an even greater promised land. That ultimate spiritual Leader will even bear the Greek name which is equivalent to the Hebrew name Joshua (meaning "God is salvation"). As Joshua is a savior of the nation, this Messiah will be the Savior of the world.

The record begins with God's final instructions to Joshua.

Josh. 1:1-9
Jordan's east bank
(Ca. 1406 B.C.)

GOD INSTRUCTS JOSHUA. After the death of Moses the servant of the LORD, the LORD said to Joshua son of Nun, Moses' aide: "Moses my servant is dead. Now then, you and all these people, get ready to cross the Jordan River into the land I am about to give to them—to the Israelites. I will give you every place where you set your foot, as I promised Moses. Your territory will extend from the desert to Lebanon, and from the great river, the Euphrates—all the Hittite country—to the Great Sea*v* on the west. No one will be able to stand up against you all the days of your life. As I was with Moses, so I will be with you; I will never leave you nor forsake you.

"Be strong and courageous, because you will lead these people to inherit the land I swore to their forefathers to give them. Be strong and very courageous. Be careful to obey all the law my servant Moses gave you; do not turn from it to the right or to the left, that you may be successful wherever you go. Do not let this Book of the Law depart from your mouth; meditate on it day and night, so that you may be careful to do everything written in it. Then you will be prosperous and successful. Have I not commanded you? Be strong and courageous. Do not be terrified; do not be discouraged, for the LORD your God will be with you wherever you go."

*v*That is, the Mediterranean

ENCAMPMENT BY JORDAN.   Early in the morning Joshua and all the Israelites set out from Shittim and went to the Jordan, where they camped before crossing over.

Josh. 3:1

SPIES SENT TO JERICHO.   Then Joshua son of Nun secretly sent two spies from Shittim. "Go, look over the land," he said, "especially Jericho." So they went and entered the house of a prostitute^w named Rahab and stayed there.

Josh. 2:1
Jericho

RAHAB SAVES SPIES.   The king of Jericho was told, "Look! Some of the Israelites have come here tonight to spy out the land." So the king of Jericho sent this message to Rahab: "Bring out the men who came to you and entered your house, because they have come to spy out the whole land."

Josh. 2:2-7

But the woman had taken the two men and hidden them. She said, "Yes, the men came to me, but I did not know where they had come from. At dusk, when it was time to close the city gate, the men left. I don't know which way they went. Go after them quickly. You may catch up with them." (But she had taken them up to the roof and hidden them under the stalks of flax she had laid out on the roof.) So the men set out in pursuit of the spies on the road that leads to the fords of the Jordan, and as soon as the pursuers had gone out, the gate was shut.

PROMISE OF SAFETY.   Before the spies lay down for the night, she went up on the roof and said to them, "I know that the LORD has given this land to you and that a great fear of you has fallen on us, so that all who live in this country are melting in fear because of you. We have heard how the LORD dried up the water of the Red Sea^x for you when you came out of Egypt, and what you did to Sihon and Og, the two kings of the Amorites east of the Jordan, whom you completely destroyed.^y When we heard of it, our hearts melted and everyone's courage failed because of you, for the LORD your God is God in heaven above and on the earth below. Now then, please swear to me by the LORD that you will show kindness to my family, because I have shown kindness to you. Give me a sure sign that you will spare the lives of my father and mother, my brothers and sisters, and all who belong to them, and that you will save us from death."

Josh.
2:8-16

"Our lives for your lives!" the men assured her. "If you don't tell what we are doing, we will treat you kindly and faithfully when the LORD gives us the land."

So she let them down by a rope through the window, for the house she lived in was part of the city wall. Now she had said to them, "Go to the hills so the pursuers will not find you. Hide yourselves there three days until they return, and then go on your way."

THE SCARLET CORD.   The men said to her, "This oath you made us swear will not be binding on us unless, when we enter the land, you have tied this scarlet cord in the window through which you let us down, and unless you have brought your father and mother, your brothers and all your family into your house. If anyone goes outside your house into the street, his blood will be on his own head; we will not be responsible. As for anyone who is in the house with you, his blood will be on our head if a

Josh.
2:17-21

^wOr possibly *an innkeeper*   ^xHebrew *Yam Suph*; that is, Sea of Reeds   ^yThe Hebrew term refers to the irrevocable giving over of things or persons to the LORD, often by totally destroying them.

hand is laid on him. But if you tell what we are doing, we will be released from the oath you made us swear."

"Agreed," she replied. "Let it be as you say." So she sent them away and they departed. And she tied the scarlet cord in the window.

Josh.
2:22-24

SPIES RETURN.   When they left, they went into the hills and stayed there three days, until the pursuers had searched all along the road and returned without finding them. Then the two men started back. They went down out of the hills, forded the river and came to Joshua son of Nun and told him everything that had happened to them. They said to Joshua, "The LORD has surely given the whole land into our hands; all the people are melting in fear because of us."

Josh.
1:10,11

MOBILIZATION ORDERED.   So Joshua ordered the officers of the people: "Go through the camp and tell the people, 'Get your supplies ready. Three days from now you will cross the Jordan here to go in and take possession of the land the LORD your God is giving you for your own.'"

Josh.
1:12-15

REMINDER TO THREE TRIBES.   But to the Reubenites, the Gadites and the half-tribe of Manasseh, Joshua said, "Remember the command that Moses the servant of the LORD gave you: 'The LORD your God is giving you rest and has granted you this land.' Your wives, your children and your livestock may stay in the land that Moses gave you east of the Jordan, but all your fighting men, fully armed, must cross over ahead of your brothers. You are to help your brothers until the LORD gives them rest, as he has done for you, and until they too have taken possession of the land that the LORD your God is giving them. After that, you may go back and occupy your own land, which Moses the servant of the LORD gave you east of the Jordan toward the sunrise."

Josh.
1:16-18

COMMITMENT AFFIRMED.   Then they answered Joshua, "Whatever you have commanded us we will do, and wherever you send us we will go. Just as we fully obeyed Moses, so we will obey you. Only may the LORD your God be with you as he was with Moses. Whoever rebels against your word and does not obey your words, whatever you may command them, will be put to death. Only be strong and courageous!"

Josh. 3:2-6

ARK TO LEAD WAY.   After three days the officers went throughout the camp, giving orders to the people: "When you see the ark of the covenant of the LORD your God, and the priests, who are Levites, carrying it, you are to move out from your positions and follow it. Then you will know which way to go, since you have never been this way before. But keep a distance of about a thousand yards[z] between you and the ark; do not go near it."

Joshua told the people, "Consecrate yourselves, for tomorrow the LORD will do amazing things among you."

Joshua said to the priests, "Take up the ark of the covenant and pass on ahead of the people." So they took it up and went ahead of them.

Josh.
3:7-13

A MIRACULOUS CROSSING.   And the LORD said to Joshua, "Today I will begin to exalt you in the eyes of all Israel, so they may know that I am with you as I was with Moses. Tell the priests who carry the ark of the

---

[z]Hebrew *about two thousand cubits* (about 900 meters)

covenant: 'When you reach the edge of the Jordan's waters, go and stand in the river.'"

Joshua said to the Israelites, "Come here and listen to the words of the LORD your God. This is how you will know that the living God is among you and that he will certainly drive out before you the Canaanites, Hittites, Hivites, Perizzites, Girgashites, Amorites and Jebusites. See, the ark of the covenant of the Lord of all the earth will go into the Jordan ahead of you. Now then, choose twelve men from the tribes of Israel, one from each tribe. And as soon as the priests who carry the ark of the LORD— the Lord of all the earth—set foot in the Jordan, its waters flowing downstream will be cut off and stand up in a heap."

THE JORDAN PARTED.   So when the people broke camp to cross the Jordan, the priests carrying the ark of the covenant went ahead of them. Now the Jordan is at flood stage all during harvest. Yet as soon as the priests who carried the ark reached the Jordan and their feet touched the water's edge, the water from upstream stopped flowing. It piled up in a heap a great distance away, at a town called Adam in the vicinity of Zarethan, while the water flowing down to the Sea of the Arabah (the Salt Sea*a*) was completely cut off. So the people crossed over opposite Jericho. The priests who carried the ark of the covenant of the LORD stood firm on dry ground in the middle of the Jordan, while all Israel passed by until the whole nation had completed the crossing on dry ground.

Josh.
3:14-17

EASTERN TRIBES CROSS.   The men of Reuben, Gad and the half-tribe of Manasseh crossed over, armed, in front of the Israelites, as Moses had directed them. About forty thousand armed for battle crossed over before the LORD to the plains of Jericho for war.

Josh.
4:12,13

MEMORIAL TO CROSSING.   Joshua set up the twelve stones that had been*b* in the middle of the Jordan at the spot where the priests who carried the ark of the covenant had stood. And they are there to this day.

Now the priests who carried the ark remained standing in the middle of the Jordan until everything the LORD had commanded Joshua was done by the people, just as Moses had directed Joshua. The people hurried over, and as soon as all of them had crossed, the ark of the LORD and the priests came to the other side while the people watched.

Josh.
4:9-11

CROSSING COMPLETED.   Then the LORD said to Joshua, "Command the priests carrying the ark of the Testimony to come up out of the Jordan."

So Joshua commanded the priests, "Come up out of the Jordan."

And the priests came up out of the river carrying the ark of the covenant of the LORD. No sooner had they set their feet on the dry ground than the waters of the Jordan returned to their place and ran at flood stage as before.

Josh.
4:15-18

STONES TAKEN FROM JORDAN.   When the whole nation had finished crossing the Jordan, the LORD said to Joshua, "Choose twelve men from among the people, one from each tribe, and tell them to take up twelve stones from the middle of the Jordan from right where the priests stood and to carry them over with you and put them down at the place where you stay tonight."

So Joshua called together the twelve men he had appointed from the

Josh.
4:1-8

---

*a*That is, the Dead Sea   *b*Or *Joshua also set up twelve stones*

Israelites, one from each tribe, and said to them, "Go over before the ark of the LORD your God into the middle of the Jordan. Each of you is to take up a stone on his shoulder, according to the number of the tribes of the Israelites to serve as a sign among you. In the future, when your children ask you, 'What do these stones mean?' tell them that the flow of the Jordan was cut off before the ark of the covenant of the LORD. When it crossed the Jordan, the waters of the Jordan were cut off. These stones are to be a memorial to the people of Israel forever."

So the Israelites did as Joshua commanded them. They took twelve stones from the middle of the Jordan, according to the number of the tribes of the Israelites, as the LORD had told Joshua; and they carried them over with them to their camp, where they put them down.

Josh.
4:19-24

MONUMENT TO MIRACLE.   On the tenth day of the first month the people went up from the Jordan and camped at Gilgal on the eastern border of Jericho. And Joshua set up at Gilgal the twelve stones they had taken out of the Jordan. He said to the Israelites, "In the future when your descendants ask their fathers, 'What do these stones mean?' tell them, 'Israel crossed the Jordan on dry ground.' For the LORD your God dried up the Jordan before you until you had crossed over. The LORD your God did to the Jordan just what he had done to the Red Sea^c when he dried it up before us until we had crossed over. He did this so that all the peoples of the earth might know that the hand of the LORD is powerful and so that you might always fear the LORD your God."

Josh. 4:14

JOSHUA EXALTED.   That day the LORD exalted Joshua in the sight of all Israel; and they revered him all the days of his life, just as they had revered Moses.

Josh. 5:1

CANAANITES FEAR.   Now when all the Amorite kings west of the Jordan and all the Canaanite kings along the coast heard how the LORD had dried up the Jordan before the Israelites until we had crossed over, their hearts melted and they no longer had the courage to face the Israelites.

Josh. 5:2-9
Gilgal

CIRCUMCISION AT GILGAL.   At that time the LORD said to Joshua, "Make flint knives and circumcise the Israelites again." So Joshua made flint knives and circumcised the Israelites at Gibeath Haaraloth.^d

Now this is why he did so: All those who came out of Egypt—all the men of military age—died in the desert on the way after leaving Egypt. All the people that came out had been circumcised, but all the people born in the desert during the journey from Egypt had not. The Israelites had moved about in the desert forty years until all the men who were of military age when they left Egypt had died, since they had not obeyed the LORD. For the LORD had sworn to them that they would not see the land that he had solemnly promised their fathers to give us, a land flowing with milk and honey. So he raised up their sons in their place, and these were the ones Joshua circumcised. They were still uncircumcised because they had not been circumcised on the way. And after the whole nation had been circumcised, they remained where they were in camp until they were healed.

Then the LORD said to Joshua, "Today I have rolled away the reproach

^cHebrew *Yam Suph*; that is, Sea of Reeds   ^d*Gibeath Haaraloth* means *hill of foreskins*.

of Egypt from you." So the place has been called Gilgal*e* to this day.

PASSOVER OBSERVED.   On the evening of the fourteenth day of the
month, while camped at Gilgal on the plains of Jericho, the Israelites
celebrated the Passover. The day after the Passover, that very day, they
ate some of the produce of the land: unleavened bread and roasted
grain.

*Josh.
5:10,11*

LAST OF MANNA.   The manna stopped the day after*f* they ate this food
from the land; there was no longer any manna for the Israelites, but that
year they ate of the produce of Canaan.

Josh. 5:12

DIVINE COMMANDER APPEARS.   Now when Joshua was near Jericho,
he looked up and saw a man standing in front of him with a drawn sword
in his hand. Joshua went up to him and asked, "Are you for us or for our
enemies?"

*Josh.
5:13-15*

"Neither," he replied, "but as commander of the army of the LORD I have
now come." Then Joshua fell facedown to the ground in reverence, and
asked him, "What message does my Lord*g* have for his servant?"

The commander of the LORD's army replied, "Take off your sandals, for
the place where you are standing is holy." And Joshua did so.

The Taking of Jericho and Ai

*T*he first victory in Canaan will be no real battle at all. God will once
again demonstrate his power by giving over the city of Jericho to the
Israelites in a miraculous fashion. But the joy of victory will turn into
surprise defeat at the city of Ai, because one of the Israelites has taken forbidden plunder from Jericho. However, once the sin in the camp has been eradi-
cated, God will again lead his people to win the battle for Ai. Following that
victory, the Israelites will honor their divine Commander by reading his laws
and erecting the altar which God had commanded through Moses.

GOD'S JERICHO STRATEGY.   Now Jericho was tightly shut up because
of the Israelites. No one went out and no one came in.

Then the LORD said to Joshua, "See, I have delivered Jericho into your
hands, along with its king and its fighting men. March around the city
once with all the armed men. Do this for six days. Have seven priests carry
trumpets of rams' horns in front of the ark. On the seventh day, march
around the city seven times, with the priests blowing the trumpets. When
you hear them sound a long blast on the trumpets, have all the people give
a loud shout; then the wall of the city will collapse and the people will go
up, every man straight in."

*Josh. 6:1-5
Jericho*

THE PLAN IMPLEMENTED.   So Joshua son of Nun called the priests
and said to them, "Take up the ark of the covenant of the LORD and have
seven priests carry trumpets in front of it." And he ordered the people,
"Advance! March around the city, with the armed guard going ahead of
the ark of the LORD."

*Josh.
6:6-11*

When Joshua had spoken to the people, the seven priests carrying the
seven trumpets before the LORD went forward, blowing their trumpets,
and the ark of the LORD's covenant followed them. The armed guard

eGilgal sounds like the Hebrew for roll.   *fOr the day*   *gOr lord*

marched ahead of the priests who blew the trumpets, and the rear guard
followed the ark. All this time the trumpets were sounding. But Joshua
had commanded the people, "Do not give a war cry, do not raise your
voices, do not say a word until the day I tell you to shout. Then shout!" So
he had the ark of the LORD carried around the city, circling it once. Then
the people returned to camp and spent the night there.

**Josh.
6:12-14**

MARCHING AROUND JERICHO.   Joshua got up early the next morning and the priests took up the ark of the LORD. The seven priests carrying
the seven trumpets went forward, marching before the ark of the LORD and
blowing the trumpets. The armed men went ahead of them and the rear
guard followed the ark of the LORD, while the trumpets kept sounding. So
on the second day they marched around the city once and returned to the
camp. They did this for six days.

**Josh.
6:15-19**

FINAL INSTRUCTIONS.   On the seventh day, they got up at daybreak
and marched around the city seven times in the same manner, except that
on that day they circled the city seven times. The seventh time around,
when the priests sounded the trumpet blast, Joshua commanded the people, "Shout! For the LORD has given you the city! The city and all that is in
it are to be devoted[h] to the LORD. Only Rahab the prostitute[i] and all who
are with her in her house shall be spared, because she hid the spies we
sent. But keep away from the devoted things, so that you will not bring
about your own destruction by taking any of them. Otherwise you will
make the camp of Israel liable to destruction and bring trouble on it. All
the silver and gold and the articles of bronze and iron are sacred to the
LORD and must go into his treasury."

**Josh.
6:20,21**

JERICHO'S WALLS FALL.   When the trumpets sounded, the people
shouted, and at the sound of the trumpet, when the people gave a loud
shout, the wall collapsed; so every man charged straight in, and they took
the city. They devoted the city to the LORD and destroyed with the sword
every living thing in it—men and women, young and old, cattle, sheep
and donkeys.

**Josh.
6:22-25**

RESCUE OF RAHAB.   Joshua said to the two men who had spied out the
land, "Go into the prostitute's house and bring her out and all who belong
to her, in accordance with your oath to her." So the young men who had
done the spying went in and brought out Rahab, her father and mother
and brothers and all who belonged to her. They brought out her entire
family and put them in a place outside the camp of Israel.

Then they burned the whole city and everything in it, but they put the
silver and gold and the articles of bronze and iron into the treasury of the
LORD's house. But Joshua spared Rahab the prostitute, with her family and
all who belonged to her, because she hid the men Joshua had sent as spies
to Jericho—and she lives among the Israelites to this day.

**Josh.
6:26,27**

CURSE ON JERICHO.   At that time Joshua pronounced this solemn oath:
"Cursed before the LORD is the man who undertakes to rebuild this city,
Jericho:

> "At the cost of his firstborn son
>   will he lay its foundations;

[h]The Hebrew term refers to the irrevocable giving over of things or persons to the LORD,
often by totally destroying them.   [i]Or possibly *innkeeper*; also in verses 22 and 25

> at the cost of his youngest
> will he set up its gates."

So the LORD was with Joshua, and his fame spread throughout the land.

ACHAN TAKES DEVOTED THINGS.   But the Israelites acted unfaith- Josh. 7:1
fully in regard to the devoted things[j]; Achan son of Carmi, the son of
Zimri,[k] the son of Zerah, of the tribe of Judah, took some of them. So the
LORD's anger burned against Israel.

ROUT BY MEN OF AI.   Now Joshua sent men from Jericho to Ai, which   Josh. 7:2-5
is near Beth Aven to the east of Bethel, and told them, "Go up and spy out   Ai
the region." So the men went up and spied out Ai.

When they returned to Joshua, they said, "Not all the people will have
to go up against Ai. Send two or three thousand men to take it and do not
weary all the people, for only a few men are there." So about three thousand men went up; but they were routed by the men of Ai, who killed
about thirty-six of them. They chased the Israelites from the city gate as far
as the stone quarries[l] and struck them down on the slopes. At this the
hearts of the people melted and became like water.

JOSHUA'S PRAYER.   Then Joshua tore his clothes and fell facedown to   Josh. 7:6-9
the ground before the ark of the LORD, remaining there till evening. The
elders of Israel did the same, and sprinkled dust on their heads. And
Joshua said, "Ah, Sovereign LORD, why did you ever bring this people
across the Jordan to deliver us into the hands of the Amorites to destroy
us? If only we had been content to stay on the other side of the Jordan! O
Lord, what can I say, now that Israel has been routed by its enemies? The
Canaanites and the other people of the country will hear about this and
they will surround us and wipe out our name from the earth. What then
will you do for your own great name?"

JOSHUA TOLD OF SIN.   The LORD said to Joshua, "Stand up! What are   Josh.
you doing down on your face? Israel has sinned; they have violated my   7:10-15
covenant, which I commanded them to keep. They have taken some of the
devoted things; they have stolen, they have lied, they have put them with
their own possessions. That is why the Israelites cannot stand against their
enemies; they turn their backs and run because they have been made liable
to destruction. I will not be with you anymore unless you destroy whatever among you is devoted to destruction.

"Go, consecrate the people. Tell them, 'Consecrate yourselves in preparation for tomorrow; for this is what the LORD, the God of Israel, says: That
which is devoted is among you, O Israel. You cannot stand against your
enemies until you remove it.

" 'In the morning, present yourselves tribe by tribe. The tribe that the
LORD takes shall come forward clan by clan; the clan that the LORD takes
shall come forward family by family; and the family that the LORD takes
shall come forward man by man. He who is caught with the devoted
things shall be destroyed by fire, along with all that belongs to him. He has
violated the covenant of the LORD and has done a disgraceful thing
in Israel!' "

[j]The Hebrew term refers to the irrevocable giving over of things or persons to the LORD,
often by totally destroying them   [k]See Septuagint and 1 Chronicles 2:6; Hebrew *Zabdi*;
also in verses 17 and 18.   [l]Or *as far as Shebarim*

Josh.
7:16-21
ACHAN CONFESSES GUILT.   Early the next morning Joshua had Israel come forward by tribes, and Judah was taken. The clans of Judah came forward, and he took the Zerahites. He had the clan of the Zerahites come forward by families, and Zimri was taken. Joshua had his family come forward man by man, and Achan son of Carmi, the son of Zimri, the son of Zerah, of the tribe of Judah, was taken.

Then Joshua said to Achan, "My son, give glory to the LORD,^m the God of Israel, and give him the praise.ⁿ Tell me what you have done; do not hide it from me."

Achan replied, "It is true! I have sinned against the LORD, the God of Israel. This is what I have done: When I saw in the plunder a beautiful robe from Babylonia,^o two hundred shekels^p of silver and a wedge of gold weighing fifty shekels,^q I coveted them and took them. They are hidden in the ground inside my tent, with the silver underneath."

Josh.
7:22-26
ACHAN STONED.   So Joshua sent messengers, and they ran to the tent, and there it was, hidden in his tent, with the silver underneath. They took the things from the tent, brought them to Joshua and all the Israelites and spread them out before the LORD.

Then Joshua, together with all Israel, took Achan son of Zerah, the silver, the robe, the gold wedge, his sons and daughters, his cattle, donkeys and sheep, his tent and all that he had, to the Valley of Achor. Joshua said, "Why have you brought this trouble on us? The LORD will bring trouble on you today."

Then all Israel stoned him, and after they had stoned the rest, they burned them. Over Achan they heaped up a large pile of rocks, which remains to this day. Then the LORD turned from his fierce anger. Therefore that place has been called the Valley of Achor^r ever since.

Josh. 8:1,2
GOD PROMISES AI.   Then the LORD said to Joshua, "Do not be afraid; do not be discouraged. Take the whole army with you, and go up and attack Ai. For I have delivered into your hands the king of Ai, his people, his city and his land. You shall do to Ai and its king as you did to Jericho and its king, except that you may carry off their plunder and livestock for yourselves. Set an ambush behind the city."

Josh. 8:3-9
JOSHUA PLANS AMBUSH.   So Joshua and the whole army moved out to attack Ai. He chose thirty thousand of his best fighting men and sent them out at night with these orders: "Listen carefully. You are to set an ambush behind the city. Don't go very far from it. All of you be on the alert. I and all those with me will advance on the city, and when the men come out against us, as they did before, we will flee from them. They will pursue us until we have lured them away from the city, for they will say, 'They are running away from us as they did before.' So when we flee from them, you are to rise up from ambush and take the city. The LORD your God will give it into your hand. When you have taken the city, set it on fire. Do what the LORD has commanded. See to it; you have my orders."

Then Joshua sent them off, and they went to the place of ambush and lay in wait between Bethel and Ai, to the west of Ai—but Joshua spent that night with the people.

---

^mA solemn charge to tell the truth   ⁿOr *and confess to him*   ^oHebrew *Shinar*
^pThat is, about 5 pounds (about 2.3 kilograms)   ^qThat is, about 1 1/4 pounds (about 0.6 kilogram)   ^r*Achor* means *trouble.*

THE TRAP IS SET.   Early the next morning Joshua mustered his men, and he and the leaders of Israel marched before them to Ai. The entire force that was with him marched up and approached the city and arrived in front of it. They set up camp north of Ai, with the valley between them and the city. Joshua had taken about five thousand men and set them in ambush between Bethel and Ai, to the west of the city. They had the soldiers take up their positions—all those in the camp to the north of the city and the ambush to the west of it. That night Joshua went into the valley.

Josh.
8:10-17

When the king of Ai saw this, he and all the men of the city hurried out early in the morning to meet Israel in battle at a certain place overlooking the Arabah. But he did not know that an ambush had been set against him behind the city. Joshua and all Israel let themselves be driven back before them, and they fled toward the desert. All the men of Ai were called to pursue them, and they pursued Joshua and were lured away from the city. Not a man remained in Ai or Bethel who did not go after Israel. They left the city open and went in pursuit of Israel.

THE TRAP IS SPRUNG.   Then the LORD said to Joshua, "Hold out toward Ai the javelin that is in your hand, for into your hand I will deliver the city." So Joshua held out his javelin toward Ai. As soon as he did this, the men in the ambush rose quickly from their position and rushed forward. They entered the city and captured it and quickly set it on fire.

Josh.
8:18-23

The men of Ai looked back and saw the smoke of the city rising against the sky, but they had no chance to escape in any direction, for the Israelites who had been fleeing toward the desert had turned back against their pursuers. For when Joshua and all Israel saw that the ambush had taken the city and that smoke was going up from the city, they turned around and attacked the men of Ai. The men of the ambush also came out of the city against them, so that they were caught in the middle, with Israelites on both sides. Israel cut them down, leaving them neither survivors nor fugitives. But they took the king of Ai alive and brought him to Joshua.

INHABITANTS DESTROYED.   When Israel had finished killing all the men of Ai in the fields and in the desert where they had chased them, and when every one of them had been put to the sword, all the Israelites returned to Ai and killed those who were in it. Twelve thousand men and women fell that day—all the people of Ai. For Joshua did not draw back the hand that held out his javelin until he had destroyed[s] all who lived in Ai. But Israel did carry off for themselves the livestock and plunder of this city, as the LORD had instructed Joshua.

Josh.
8:24-29

So Joshua burned Ai and made it a permanent heap of ruins, a desolate place to this day. He hung the king of Ai on a tree and left him there until evening. At sunset, Joshua ordered them to take his body from the tree and throw it down at the entrance of the city gate. And they raised a large pile of rocks over it, which remains to this day.

ALTAR AT MOUNT EBAL.   Then Joshua built on Mount Ebal an altar to the LORD, the God of Israel, as Moses the servant of the LORD had commanded the Israelites. He built it according to what is written in the Book of the Law of Moses—an altar of uncut stones, on which no iron tool had

Josh.
8:30-33

---

[s]The Hebrew term refers to the irrevocable giving over of things or persons to the LORD, often by totally destroying them.

been used. On it they offered to the LORD burnt offerings and sacrificed fellowship offerings.[t] There, in the presence of the Israelites, Joshua copied on stones the law of Moses, which he had written. All Israel, aliens and citizens alike, with their elders, officials and judges, were standing on both sides of the ark of the covenant of the LORD, facing those who carried it—the priests, who were Levites. Half of the people stood in front of Mount Gerizim and half of them in front of Mount Ebal, as Moses the servant of the LORD had formerly commanded when he gave instructions to bless the people of Israel.

Josh. 8:34,35   Afterward, Joshua read all the words of the law—the blessings and the curses—just as it is written in the Book of the Law. There was not a word of all that Moses had commanded that Joshua did not read to the whole assembly of Israel, including the women and children, and the aliens who lived among them.

General Conquest of Canaan

*T*he initial invasion successfully completed, the Israelites will now engage in two sweeping campaigns—first against an alliance of southern kings, then against a confederation of kings in the north. In battle against the Amorites in the south, Israel receives miraculous support from God. God not only causes hailstones to fall on enemy forces, but, upon Joshua's request, God also miraculously prolongs the day so that the fleeing enemy may be pursued. In commemoration of "the sun's standing still," a song is quoted from the Book of the Righteous, which is a collection of odes to Jewish heroes.

The record seems to indicate that the conquest of Canaan is complete following these two campaigns, yet at this point the Israelites will have achieved only a general conquest, with much fighting still to come under leaders to follow Joshua. Even now the cost in Canaanite lives is shocking, and once again a moral issue is raised, particularly because the Israelites themselves are the invaders. Though it affords little comfort to the modern mind, it must be remembered that extermination of defeated enemies is expected of victorious armies at this time. The record further hints that God is using the Israelites as his instrument in punishing the pagan Canaanites for their continual wickedness. Some of this wickedness is seen when the men of Gibeon trick Joshua into making a forbidden covenant with them, and thus play upon Joshua's failure to consult God in the matter.

Josh. 9:1,2   ALLIANCE OF KINGS. Now when all the kings west of the Jordan heard about these things—those in the hill country, in the western foothills, and along the entire coast of the Great Sea[u] as far as Lebanon (the kings of the Hittites, Amorites, Canaanites, Perizzites, Hivites and Jebusites)—they came together to make war against Joshua and Israel.

Josh. 9:3-15   GIBEONITES TRICK JOSHUA. However, when the people of Gibeon heard what Joshua had done to Jericho and Ai, they resorted to a ruse:

[t] Traditionally *peace offerings*   [u] That is, the Mediterranean

They went as a delegation whose donkeys were loaded[v] with worn-out sacks and old wineskins, cracked and mended. The men put worn and patched sandals on their feet and wore old clothes. All the bread of their food supply was dry and moldy. Then they went to Joshua in the camp at Gilgal and said to him and the men of Israel, "We have come from a distant country; make a treaty with us."

The men of Israel said to the Hivites, "But perhaps you live near us. How then can we make a treaty with you?"

"We are your servants," they said to Joshua.

But Joshua asked, "Who are you and where do you come from?"

They answered: "Your servants have come from a very distant country because of the fame of the LORD your God. For we have heard reports of him: all that he did in Egypt, and all that he did to the two kings of the Amorites east of the Jordan—Sihon king of Heshbon, and Og king of Bashan, who reigned in Ashtaroth. And our elders and all those living in our country said to us, 'Take provisions for your journey; go and meet them and say to them, "We are your servants; make a treaty with us." ' This bread of ours was warm when we packed it at home on the day we left to come to you. But now see how dry and moldy it is. And these wineskins that we filled were new, but see how cracked they are. And our clothes and sandals are worn out by the very long journey."

The men of Israel sampled their provisions but did not inquire of the LORD. Then Joshua made a treaty of peace with them to let them live, and the leaders of the assembly ratified it by oath.

OATH PREVENTS KILLING.   Three days after they made the treaty with the Gibeonites, the Israelites heard that they were neighbors, living near them. So the Israelites set out and on the third day came to their cities: Gibeon, Kephirah, Beeroth and Kiriath Jearim. But the Israelites did not attack them, because the leaders of the assembly had sworn an oath to them by the LORD, the God of Israel.

Josh. 9:16-21

The whole assembly grumbled against the leaders, but all the leaders answered, "We have given them our oath by the LORD, the God of Israel, and we cannot touch them now. This is what we will do to them: We will let them live, so that wrath will not fall on us for breaking the oath we swore to them." They continued, "Let them live, but let them be wood-cutters and water carriers for the entire community." So the leaders' promise to them was kept.

GIBEONITES MADE SLAVES.   Then Joshua summoned the Gibeonites and said, "Why did you deceive us by saying, 'We live a long way from you,' while actually you live near us? You are now under a curse: You will never cease to serve as woodcutters and water carriers for the house of my God."

Josh. 9:22-27

They answered Joshua, "Your servants were clearly told how the LORD your God had commanded his servant Moses to give you the whole land and to wipe out all its inhabitants from before you. So we feared for our lives because of you, and that is why we did this. We are now in your hands. Do to us whatever seems good and right to you."

So Joshua saved them from the Israelites, and they did not kill them.

[v]Most Hebrew manuscripts; some Hebrew manuscripts, Vulgate and Syriac (see also Septuagint) *They prepared provisions and loaded their donkeys*

That day he made the Gibeonites woodcutters and water carriers for the community and for the altar of the LORD at the place the LORD would choose. And that is what they are to this day.

Josh.
10:1-5

CONFEDERATION AGAINST GIBEON.   Now Adoni-Zedek king of Jerusalem heard that Joshua had taken Ai and totally destroyed^w it, doing to Ai and its king as he had done to Jericho and its king, and that the people of Gibeon had made a treaty of peace with Israel and were living near them. He and his people were very much alarmed at this, because Gibeon was an important city, like one of the royal cities; it was larger than Ai, and all its men were good fighters. So Adoni-Zedek king of Jerusalem appealed to Hoham king of Hebron, Piram king of Jarmuth, Japhia king of Lachish and Debir king of Eglon. "Come up and help me attack Gibeon," he said, "because it has made peace with Joshua and the Israelites."

Then the five kings of the Amorites—the kings of Jerusalem, Hebron, Jarmuth, Lachish and Eglon—joined forces. They moved up with all their troops and took up positions against Gibeon and attacked it.

Josh.
10:6-11

GOD SENDS HAILSTONES.   The Gibeonites then sent word to Joshua in the camp at Gilgal: "Do not abandon your servants. Come up to us quickly and save us! Help us, because all the Amorite kings from the hill country have joined forces against us."

So Joshua marched up from Gilgal with his entire army, including all the best fighting men. The LORD said to Joshua, "Do not be afraid of them; I have given them into your hand. Not one of them will be able to withstand you."

After an all-night march from Gilgal, Joshua took them by surprise. The LORD threw them into confusion before Israel, who defeated them in a great victory at Gibeon. Israel pursued them along the road going up to Beth Horon and cut them down all the way to Azekah and Makkedah. As they fled before Israel on the road down from Beth Horon to Azekah, the LORD hurled large hailstones down on them from the sky, and more of them died from the hailstones than were killed by the swords of the Israelites.

Josh.
10:12-14

SUN STANDS STILL.   On the day the LORD gave the Amorites over to Israel, Joshua said to the LORD in the presence of Israel:

> "O sun, stand still over Gibeon,
>   O moon, over the Valley of Aijalon."
>   So the sun stood still,
>   and the moon stopped,
>   till the nation avenged itself on^x its enemies,

as it is written in the Book of Jashar.

The sun stopped in the middle of the sky and delayed going down about a full day. There has never been a day like it before or since, a day when the LORD listened to a man. Surely the LORD was fighting for Israel!

Josh.
10:15-21
Makkedah

FIVE KINGS HIDE.   Then Joshua returned with all Israel to the camp at Gilgal.

Now the five kings had fled and hidden in the cave at Makkedah. When Joshua was told that the five kings had been found hiding in the cave at

---

^{w}The Hebrew term refers to the irrevocable giving over of things or persons to the LORD, often by totally destroying them. ^{x}Or *nation triumphed over*

Makkedah, he said, "Roll large rocks up to the mouth of the cave, and post some men there to guard it. But don't stop! Pursue your enemies, attack them from the rear and don't let them reach their cities, for the LORD your God has given them into your hand."

So Joshua and the Israelites destroyed them completely—almost to a man—but the few who were left reached their fortified cities. The whole army then returned safely to Joshua in the camp at Makkedah, and no one uttered a word against the Israelites.

FIVE KINGS HANGED.   Joshua said, "Open the mouth of the cave and bring those five kings out to me." So they brought the five kings out of the cave—the kings of Jerusalem, Hebron, Jarmuth, Lachish and Eglon. When they had brought these kings to Joshua, he summoned all the men of Israel and said to the army commanders who had come with him, "Come here and put your feet on the necks of these kings." So they came forward and placed their feet on their necks.

Josh.
10:22-27

Joshua said to them, "Do not be afraid; do not be discouraged. Be strong and courageous. This is what the LORD will do to all the enemies you are going to fight." Then Joshua struck and killed the kings and hung them on five trees, and they were left hanging on the trees until evening.

At sunset Joshua gave the order and they took them down from the trees and threw them into the cave where they had been hiding. At the mouth of the cave they placed large rocks, which are there to this day.

SOUTHERN CAMPAIGN.   That day Joshua took Makkedah. He put the city and its king to the sword and totally destroyed everyone in it. He left no survivors. And he did to the king of Makkedah as he had done to the king of Jericho.

Josh.
10:28-43

Then Joshua and all Israel with him moved on from Makkedah to Libnah and attacked it. The LORD also gave that city and its king into Israel's hand. The city and everyone in it Joshua put to the sword. He left no survivors there. And he did to its king as he had done to the king of Jericho.

Then Joshua and all Israel with him moved on from Libnah to Lachish; he took up positions against it and attacked it. The LORD handed Lachish over to Israel, and Joshua took it on the second day. The city and everyone in it he put to the sword, just as he had done to Libnah. Meanwhile, Horam king of Gezer had come up to help Lachish, but Joshua defeated him and his army—until no survivors were left.

Then Joshua and all Israel with him moved on from Lachish to Eglon; they took up positions against it and attacked it. They captured it that same day and put it to the sword and totally destroyed everyone in it, just as they had done to Lachish.

Then Joshua and all Israel with him went up from Eglon to Hebron and attacked it. They took the city and put it to the sword, together with its king, its villages and everyone in it. They left no survivors. Just as at Eglon, they totally destroyed it and everyone in it.

Then Joshua and all Israel with him turned around and attacked Debir. They took the city, its king and its villages, and put them to the sword. Everyone in it they totally destroyed. They left no survivors. They did to Debir and its king as they had done to Libnah and its king and to Hebron.

So Joshua subdued the whole region, including the hill country, the Negev, the western foothills and the mountain slopes, together with all their kings. He left no survivors. He totally destroyed all who breathed, just as the LORD, the God of Israel, had commanded. Joshua subdued them from Kadesh Barnea to Gaza and from the whole region of Goshen to Gibeon. All these kings and their lands Joshua conquered in one campaign, because the LORD, the God of Israel, fought for Israel.

Then Joshua returned with all Israel to the camp at Gilgal.

Josh. 11:1-5

NORTHERN CONFEDERATION.   When Jabin king of Hazor heard of this, he sent word to Jobab king of Madon, to the kings of Shimron and Acshaph, and to the northern kings who were in the mountains, in the Arabah south of Kinnereth, in the western foothills and in Naphoth Dor[y] on the west; to the Canaanites in the east and west; to the Amorites, Hittites, Perizzites and Jebusites in the hill country; and to the Hivites below Hermon in the region of Mizpah. They came out with all their troops and a large number of horses and chariots—a huge army, as numerous as the sand on the seashore. All these kings joined forces and made camp together at the Waters of Merom, to fight against Israel.

Josh. 11:6-9 Merom

CONFEDERATION DEFEATED.   The LORD said to Joshua, "Do not be afraid of them, because by this time tomorrow I will hand all of them over to Israel, slain. You are to hamstring their horses and burn their chariots."

So Joshua and his whole army came against them suddenly at the Waters of Merom and attacked them, and the LORD gave them into the hand of Israel. They defeated them and pursued them all the way to Greater Sidon, to Misrephoth Maim, and to the Valley of Mizpah on the east, until no survivors were left. Joshua did to them as the LORD had directed: He hamstrung their horses and burned their chariots.

Josh. 11:10-15 Hazor

DESTRUCTION OF HAZOR.   At that time Joshua turned back and captured Hazor and put its king to the sword. (Hazor had been the head of all these kingdoms.) Everyone in it they put to the sword. They totally destroyed[z] them, not sparing anything that breathed, and he burned up Hazor itself.

Joshua took all these royal cities and their kings and put them to the sword. He totally destroyed them, as Moses the servant of the LORD had commanded. Yet Israel did not burn any of the cities built on their mounds—except Hazor, which Joshua burned. The Israelites carried off for themselves all the plunder and livestock of these cities, but all the people they put to the sword until they completely destroyed them, not sparing anyone that breathed. As the LORD commanded his servant Moses, so Moses commanded Joshua, and Joshua did it; he left nothing undone of all that the LORD commanded Moses.

Josh. 11:16-23 14:15b

FIRST PHASE COMPLETED.   So Joshua took this entire land: the hill country, all the Negev, the whole region of Goshen, the western foothills, the Arabah and the mountains of Israel with their foothills, from Mount Halak, which rises toward Seir, to Baal Gad in the Valley of Lebanon below Mount Hermon. He captured all their kings and struck them down, putting them to death. Joshua waged war against all these kings for a long time. Except for the Hivites living in Gibeon, not one city made a treaty of peace with the Israelites, who took them all in battle. For it was the LORD himself who hardened their hearts to wage war against Israel, so that he

---

[y]Or *in the heights of Dor*   [z]The Hebrew term refers to the irrevocable giving over of things or persons to the LORD, often by totally destroying them.

might destroy them totally, exterminating them without mercy, as the LORD had commanded Moses.

At that time Joshua went and destroyed the Anakites from the hill country: from Hebron, Debir and Anab, from all the hill country of Judah, and from all the hill country of Israel. Joshua totally destroyed them and their towns. No Anakites were left in Israelite territory; only in Gaza, Gath and Ashdod did any survive. So Joshua took the entire land, just as the LORD had directed Moses, and he gave it as an inheritance to Israel according to their tribal divisions.

Then the land had rest from war.

KINGS DEFEATED BY MOSES.   These are the kings of the land whom the Israelites had defeated and whose territory they took over east of the Jordan, from the Arnon Gorge to Mount Hermon, including all the eastern side of the Arabah:

Josh. 12:1-6

Sihon king of the Amorites,
who reigned in Heshbon. He ruled from Aroer on the rim of the Arnon Gorge—from the middle of the gorge—to the Jabbok River, which is the border of the Ammonites. This included half of Gilead. He also ruled over the eastern Arabah from the Sea of Kinnereth*a* to the Sea of the Arabah (the Salt Sea*b*), to Beth Jeshimoth, and then southward below the slopes of Pisgah.

And the territory of Og king of Bashan,
one of the last of the Rephaites, who reigned in Ashtaroth and Edrei. He ruled over Mount Hermon, Salecah, all of Bashan to the border of the people of Geshur and Maacah, and half of Gilead to the border of Sihon king of Heshbon.

Moses, the servant of the LORD, and the Israelites conquered them. And Moses the servant of the LORD gave their land to the Reubenites, the Gadites and the half-tribe of Manasseh to be their possession.

KINGS DEFEATED BY JOSHUA.   These are the kings of the land that Joshua and the Israelites conquered on the west side of the Jordan, from Baal Gad in the Valley of Lebanon to Mount Halak, which rises toward Seir (their lands Joshua gave as an inheritance to the tribes of Israel according to their tribal divisions—the hill country, the western foothills, the Arabah, the mountain slopes, the desert and the Negev—the lands of the Hittites, Amorites, Canaanites, Perizzites, Hivites and Jebusites):

Josh. 12:7-24

the king of Jericho	one
the king of Ai (near Bethel)	one
the king of Jerusalem	one
the king of Hebron	one
the king of Jarmuth	one
the king of Lachish	one
the king of Eglon	one
the king of Gezer	one
the king of Debir	one
the king of Geder	one
the king of Hormah	one

*a*That is, Galilee   *b*That is, the Dead Sea

the king of Arad	one
the king of Libnah	one
the king of Adullam	one
the king of Makkedah	one
the king of Bethel	one
the king of Tappuah	one
the king of Hepher	one
the king of Aphek	one
the king of Lasharon	one
the king of Madon	one
the king of Hazor	one
the king of Shimron Meron	one
the king of Acshaph	one
the king of Taanach	one
the king of Megiddo	one
the king of Kedesh	one
the king of Jokneam in Carmel	one
the king of Dor (in Naphoth Dor[c])	one
the king of Goyim in Gilgal	one
the king of Tirzah	one

thirty-one kings in all.

Division of the Promised Land

Now that the general conquest of Canaan is complete, it is time to partition the promised land among the remaining 9 1/2 tribes who will be occupying the land west of the Jordan River. For some unknown reason, the tribes of Judah and Ephraim, and the remaining half-tribe of Manasseh, are given a preferential portion of the land, along with a special grant for Caleb, the former faithful spy. Thereafter the remaining land will be surveyed and divided by lot among the other tribes.

Josh. 13:1-7 (Ca. 1400 B.C.) PARTITION OF LAND. When Joshua was old and well advanced in years, the LORD said to him, "You are very old, and there are still very large areas of land to be taken over.

"This is the land that remains: all the regions of the Philistines and Geshurites: from the Shihor River on the east of Egypt to the territory of Ekron on the north, all of it counted as Canaanite (the territory of the five Philistine rulers in Gaza, Ashdod, Ashkelon, Gath and Ekron—that of the Avvites); from the south, all the land of the Canaanites, from Arah of the Sidonians as far as Aphek, the region of the Amorites, the area of the Gebalites[d]; and all Lebanon to the east, from Baal Gad below Mount Hermon to Lebo[e] Hamath.

"As for all the inhabitants of the mountain regions from Lebanon to Misrephoth Maim, that is, all the Sidonians, I myself will drive them out before the Israelites. Be sure to allocate this land to Israel for an inheritance, as I have instructed you, and divide it as an inheritance among the nine tribes and half of the tribe of Manasseh."

[c]Or *in the heights of Dor*   [d]That is, the area of Byblos   [e]Or *to the entrance to*

DIVISION OF EAST CANAAN.   The other half of Manasseh,*f* the Reu-   Josh.
benites and the Gadites had received the inheritance that Moses had given   13:8-12,14
them east of the Jordan, as he, the servant of the LORD, had assigned it to
them.

It extended from Aroer on the rim of the Arnon Gorge, and from the town
in the middle of the gorge, and included the whole plateau of Medeba as
far as Dibon, and all the towns of Sihon king of the Amorites, who ruled
in Heshbon, out to the border of the Ammonites. It also included Gilead,
the territory of the people of Geshur and Maacah, all of Mount Hermon
and all Bashan as far as Salecah—that is, the whole kingdom of Og in
Bashan, who had reigned in Ashtaroth and Edrei and had survived as one
of the last of the Rephaites. Moses had defeated them and taken over their
land.
     But to the tribe of Levi he gave no inheritance, since the offerings made
by fire to the LORD, the God of Israel, are their inheritance, as he promised
them.

INHERITANCE OF REUBENITES.   This is what Moses had given to the   Josh.
tribe of Reuben, clan by clan: 13:15-23

The territory from Aroer on the rim of the Arnon Gorge, and from the town
in the middle of the gorge, and the whole plateau past Medeba to Heshbon
and all its towns on the plateau, including Dibon, Bamoth Baal, Beth Baal
Meon, Jahaz, Kedemoth, Mephaath, Kiriathaim, Sibmah, Zereth Shahar on
the hill in the valley, Beth Peor, the slopes of Pisgah, and Beth Jeshimoth—
all the towns on the plateau and the entire realm of Sihon king of the
Amorites, who ruled at Heshbon. Moses had defeated him and the
Midianite chiefs, Evi, Rekem, Zur, Hur and Reba—princes allied with
Sihon—who lived in that country. In addition to those slain in battle, the
Israelites had put to the sword Balaam son of Beor, who practiced divina-
tion. The boundary of the Reubenites was the bank of the Jordan. These
towns and their villages were the inheritance of the Reubenites, clan by clan.

INHERITANCE OF GADITES.   This is what Moses had given to the tribe   Josh.
of Gad, clan by clan: 13:24-28

The territory of Jazer, all the towns of Gilead and half the Ammonite country as far as Aroer, near Rabbah; and from Heshbon to Ramath Mizpah
and Betonim, and from Mahanaim to the territory of Debir; and in the valley, Beth Haram, Beth Nimrah, Succoth and Zaphon with the rest of the
realm of Sihon king of Heshbon (the east side of the Jordan, the territory
up to the end of the Sea of Kinnereth*g*). These towns and their villages
were the inheritance of the Gadites, clan by clan.

HALF OF MANASSEH'S LAND.   This is what Moses had given to the   Josh.
half-tribe of Manasseh, that is, to half the family of the descendants of   13:29-31
Manasseh, clan by clan:

The territory extending from Mahanaim and including all of Bashan, the
entire realm of Og king of Bashan—all the settlements of Jair in Bashan,
sixty towns, half of Gilead, and Ashtaroth and Edrei (the royal cities of Og

*f*Hebrew *With it* (that is, with the other half of Manasseh)   *g*That is, Galilee in Bashan). This was for the descendants of Makir son of Manasseh—for half of the sons of Makir, clan by clan.

Josh.
13:32,33

NO INHERITANCE FOR LEVITES.   This is the inheritance Moses had given when he was in the plains of Moab across the Jordan east of Jericho. But to the tribe of Levi, Moses had given no inheritance; the LORD, the God of Israel, is their inheritance, as he promised them.

Josh.
14:1-5

DIVISION OF THE WEST.   Now these are the areas the Israelites received as an inheritance in the land of Canaan, which Eleazar the priest, Joshua son of Nun and the heads of the tribal clans of Israel allotted to them. Their inheritances were assigned by lot to the nine-and-a-half tribes, as the LORD had commanded through Moses. Moses had granted the two-and-a-half tribes their inheritance east of the Jordan but had not granted the Levites an inheritance among the rest, for the sons of Joseph had become two tribes—Manasseh and Ephraim. The Levites received no share of the land but only towns to live in, with pasturelands for their flocks and herds. So the Israelites divided the land, just as the LORD had commanded Moses.

Josh.
14:6-12
Gilgal

CALEB REQUESTS HEBRON.   Now the men of Judah approached Joshua at Gilgal, and Caleb son of Jephunneh the Kenizzite said to him, "You know what the LORD said to Moses the man of God at Kadesh Barnea about you and me. I was forty years old when Moses the servant of the LORD sent me from Kadesh Barnea to explore the land. And I brought him back a report according to my convictions, but my brothers who went up with me made the hearts of the people melt with fear. I, however, followed the LORD my God wholeheartedly. So on that day Moses swore to me, 'The land on which your feet have walked will be your inheritance and that of your children forever, because you have followed the LORD my God wholeheartedly.'[h]

"Now then, just as the LORD promised, he has kept me alive for forty-five years since the time he said this to Moses, while Israel moved about in the desert. So here I am today, eighty-five years old! I am still as strong today as the day Moses sent me out; I'm just as vigorous to go out to battle now as I was then. Now give me this hill country that the LORD promised me that day. You yourself heard then that the Anakites were there and their cities were large and fortified, but, the LORD helping me, I will drive them out just as he said."

Josh.
14:13-15a
Judges
1:20a

CALEB'S REQUEST GRANTED.   Then Joshua blessed Caleb son of Jephunneh and gave him Hebron as his inheritance. So Hebron has belonged to Caleb son of Jephunneh the Kenizzite ever since, because he followed the LORD, the God of Israel, wholeheartedly. (Hebron used to be called Kiriath Arba after Arba, who was the greatest man among the Anakites.)

Josh.
15:1-12

JUDAH BETWEEN THE SEAS.   The allotment for the tribe of Judah, clan by clan, extended down to the territory of Edom, to the Desert of Zin in the extreme south.

Their southern boundary started from the bay at the southern end of the Salt Sea,[i] crossed south of Scorpion[j] Pass, continued on to Zin and went over to the south of Kadesh Barnea. Then it ran past Hezron up to Addar and curved around to Karka. It then passed along to Azmon and joined

[h]Deut. 1:36   [i]That is, the Dead Sea   [j]Hebrew *Akrabbim*

the Wadi of Egypt, ending at the sea. This is their[k] southern boundary.

The eastern boundary is the Salt Sea as far as the mouth of the Jordan.

The northern boundary started from the bay of the sea at the mouth of the Jordan, went up to Beth Hoglah and continued north of Beth Arabah to the Stone of Bohan son of Reuben. The boundary then went up to Debir from the Valley of Achor and turned north to Gilgal, which faces the Pass of Adummim south of the gorge. It continued along to the waters of En Shemesh and came out at En Rogel. Then it ran up the Valley of Ben Hinnom along the southern slope of the Jebusite city (that is, Jerusalem). From there it climbed to the top of the hill west of the Hinnom Valley at the northern end of the Valley of Rephaim. From the hilltop the boundary headed toward the spring of the waters of Nephtoah, came out at the towns of Mount Ephron and went down toward Baalah (that is, Kiriath Jearim). Then it curved westward from Baalah to Mount Seir, ran along the northern slope of Mount Jearim (that is, Kesalon), continued down to Beth Shemesh and crossed to Timnah. It went to the northern slope of Ekron, turned toward Shikkeron, passed along to Mount Baalah and reached Jabneel. The boundary ended at the sea.

The western boundary is the coastline of the Great Sea.[l]

These are the boundaries around the people of Judah by their clans.

CITIES OF JUDAH.   This is the inheritance of the tribe of Judah, clan by clan:

Josh. 15:20-62

The southernmost towns of the tribe of Judah in the Negev toward the boundary of Edom were:

Kabzeel, Eder, Jagur, Kinah, Dimonah, Adadah, Kedesh, Hazor, Ithnan, Ziph, Telem, Bealoth, Hazor Hadattah, Kerioth Hezron (that is, Hazor), Amam, Shema, Moladah, Hazar Gaddah, Heshmon, Beth Pelet, Hazar Shual, Beersheba, Biziothiah, Baalah, Iim, Ezem, Eltolad, Kesil, Hormah, Ziklag, Madmannah, Sansannah, Lebaoth, Shilhim, Ain and Rimmon—a total of twenty-nine towns and their villages.

In the western foothills:

Eshtaol, Zorah, Ashnah, Zanoah, En Gannim, Tappuah, Enam, Jarmuth, Adullam, Socoh, Azekah, Shaaraim, Adithaim and Gederah (or Gederothaim)[m]—fourteen towns and their villages.

Zenan, Hadashah, Migdal Gad, Dilean, Mizpah, Joktheel, Lachish, Bozkath, Eglon, Cabbon, Lahmas, Kitlish, Gederoth, Beth Dagon, Naamah and Makkedah—sixteen towns and their villages.

Libnah, Ether, Ashan, Iphtah, Ashnah, Nezib, Keilah, Aczib and Mareshah—nine towns and their villages.

Ekron, with its surrounding settlements and villages; west of Ekron, all that were in the vicinity of Ashdod, together with their villages; Ashdod, its surrounding settlements and villages; and Gaza, its settlements and villages, as far as the Wadi of Egypt and the coastline of the Great Sea.

In the hill country:

Shamir, Jattir, Socoh, Dannah, Kiriath Sannah (that is, Debir), Anab, Eshtemoh, Anim, Goshen, Holon and Giloh—eleven towns and their villages.

[k]Hebrew your   [l]That is, the Mediterranean   [m]Or Gederah and Gederothaim

Arab, Dumah, Eshan, Janim, Beth Tappuah, Aphekah, Humtah, Kiriath
Arba (that is, Hebron) and Zior—nine towns and their villages.

Maon, Carmel, Ziph, Juttah, Jezreel, Jokdeam, Zanoah, Kain, Gibeah
and Timnah—ten towns and their villages.

Halhul, Beth Zur, Gedor, Maarath, Beth Anoth and Eltekon—six towns
and their villages.

Kiriath Baal (that is, Kiriath Jearim) and Rabbah—two towns and their
villages.

In the desert:

Beth Arabah, Middin, Secacah, Nibshan, the City of Salt and En Gedi—
six towns and their villages.

Josh.
16:1-4

JOSEPH'S DESCENDANTS.   The allotment for Joseph began at the Jordan of Jericho,[n] east of the waters of Jericho, and went up from there
through the desert into the hill country of Bethel. It went on from Bethel
(that is, Luz),[o] crossed over to the territory of the Arkites in Ataroth,
descended westward to the territory of the Japhletites as far as the region
of Lower Beth Horon and on to Gezer, ending at the sea.

So Manasseh and Ephraim, the descendants of Joseph, received their
inheritance.

Josh.
16:5-9

EPHRAIM, CENTRAL CANAAN.   This was the territory of Ephraim,
clan by clan:

The boundary of their inheritance went from Ataroth Addar in the east
to Upper Beth Horon and continued to the sea. From Micmethath on the
north it curved eastward to Taanath Shiloh, passing by it to Janoah on the
east. Then it went down from Janoah to Ataroth and Naarah, touched
Jericho and came out at the Jordan. From Tappuah the border went west
to the Kanah Ravine and ended at the sea. This was the inheritance of the
tribe of the Ephraimites, clan by clan. It also included all the towns and
their villages that were set aside for the Ephraimites within the inheritance
of the Manassites.

Josh.
17:1,2

MANASSEH'S OTHER HALF.   This was the allotment for the tribe of
Manasseh as Joseph's firstborn, that is, for Makir, Manasseh's firstborn.
Makir was the ancestor of the Gileadites, who had received Gilead and
Bashan because the Makirites were great soldiers. So this allotment was
for the rest of the people of Manasseh—the clans of Abiezer, Helek, Asriel,
Shechem, Hepher and Shemida. These are the other male descendants of
Manasseh son of Joseph by their clans.

Josh.
17:3-6

INHERITANCE OF DAUGHTERS.   Now Zelophehad son of Hepher, the
son of Gilead, the son of Makir, the son of Manasseh, had no sons but only
daughters, whose names were Mahlah, Noah, Hoglah, Milcah and Tirzah.
They went to Eleazar the priest, Joshua son of Nun, and the leaders and
said, "The LORD commanded Moses to give us an inheritance among our
brothers." So Joshua gave them an inheritance along with the brothers of
their father, according to the LORD's command. Manasseh's share consisted of ten tracts of land besides Gilead and Bashan east of the Jordan,
because the daughters of the tribe of Manasseh received an inheritance

[n] *Jordan of Jericho* was possibly an ancient name for the Jordan River.   [o]*Septuagint;*
Hebrew *Bethel to Luz*

among the sons. The land of Gilead belonged to the rest of the descendants
of Manasseh.

MANASSEH, COAST TO JORDAN.   The territory of Manasseh extend-   Josh.
ed from Asher to Micmethath east of Shechem. The boundary ran south-   17:7-10
ward from there to include the people living at En Tappuah. (Manasseh
had the land of Tappuah, but Tappuah itself, on the boundary of
Manasseh, belonged to the Ephraimites.) Then the boundary continued
south to the Kanah Ravine. There were towns belonging to Ephraim lying
among the towns of Manasseh, but the boundary of Manasseh was the
northern side of the ravine and ended at the sea. On the south the land
belonged to Ephraim, on the north to Manasseh. The territory of Manasseh
reached the sea and bordered Asher on the north and Issachar on the east.

JOSEPH'S LAND INCREASED.   The people of Joseph said to Joshua,   Josh.
"Why have you given us only one allotment and one portion for an in-   17:14-18
heritance? We are a numerous people and the LORD has blessed us
abundantly."
    "If you are so numerous," Joshua answered, "and if the hill country of
Ephraim is too small for you, go up into the forest and clear land for yourselves there in the land of the Perizzites and Rephaites."
    The people of Joseph replied, "The hill country is not enough for us, and
all the Canaanites who live in the plain have iron chariots, both those in
Beth Shan and its settlements and those in the Valley of Jezreel."
    But Joshua said to the house of Joseph—to Ephraim and Manasseh—
"You are numerous and very powerful. You will have not only one allotment but the forested hill country as well. Clear it, and its farthest limits
will be yours; though the Canaanites have iron chariots and though they
are strong, you can drive them out."

REMAINING LAND SURVEYED.   The whole assembly of the Israelites   Josh.
gathered at Shiloh and set up the Tent of Meeting there. The country was   18:1-7
brought under their control, but there were still seven Israelite tribes who   Shiloh
had not yet received their inheritance.
    So Joshua said to the Israelites: "How long will you wait before you
begin to take possession of the land that the LORD, the God of your fathers,
has given you? Appoint three men from each tribe. I will send them out to
make a survey of the land and to write a description of it, according to the
inheritance of each. Then they will return to me. You are to divide the land
into seven parts. Judah is to remain in its territory on the south and the
house of Joseph in its territory on the north. After you have written
descriptions of the seven parts of the land, bring them here to me and I
will cast lots for you in the presence of the LORD our God. The Levites,
however, do not get a portion among you, because the priestly service of
the LORD is their inheritance. And Gad, Reuben and the half-tribe of
Manasseh have already received their inheritance on the east side of the
Jordan. Moses the servant of the LORD gave it to them."

LOTS CAST FOR LAND.   As the men started on their way to map out the   Josh.
land, Joshua instructed them, "Go and make a survey of the land and   18:8-10
write a description of it. Then return to me, and I will cast lots for you here
at Shiloh in the presence of the LORD." So the men left and went through
the land. They wrote its description on a scroll, town by town, in seven

parts, and returned to Joshua in the camp at Shiloh. Joshua then cast lots for them in Shiloh in the presence of the LORD, and there he distributed the land to the Israelites according to their tribal divisions.

<table>
<tr><td>Josh.
18:11-20</td><td></td></tr>
</table>

BENJAMIN IN MIDDLE. The lot came up for the tribe of Benjamin, clan by clan. Their allotted territory lay between the tribes of Judah and Joseph:

On the north side their boundary began at the Jordan, passed the northern slope of Jericho and headed west into the hill country, coming out at the desert of Beth Aven. From there it crossed to the south slope of Luz (that is, Bethel) and went down to Ataroth Addar on the hill south of Lower Beth Horon.

From the hill facing Beth Horon on the south the boundary turned south along the western side and came out at Kiriath Baal (that is, Kiriath Jearim), a town of the people of Judah. This was the western side.

The southern side began at the outskirts of Kiriath Jearim on the west, and the boundary came out at the spring of the waters of Nephtoah. The boundary went down to the foot of the hill facing the Valley of Ben Hinnom, north of the Valley of Rephaim. It continued down the Hinnom Valley along the southern slope of the Jebusite city and so to En Rogel. It then curved north, went to En Shemesh, continued to Geliloth, which faces the Pass of Adummim, and ran down to the Stone of Bohan son of Reuben. It continued to the northern slope of Beth Arabah*p* and on down into the Arabah. It then went to the northern slope of Beth Hoglah and came out at the northern bay of the Salt Sea,*q* at the mouth of the Jordan in the south. This was the southern boundary.

The Jordan formed the boundary on the eastern side.

These were the boundaries that marked out the inheritance of the clans of Benjamin on all sides.

CITIES OF BENJAMIN. The tribe of Benjamin, clan by clan, had the following cities:

Jericho, Beth Hoglah, Emek Keziz, Beth Arabah, Zemaraim, Bethel, Avvim, Parah, Ophrah, Kephar Ammoni, Ophni and Geba—twelve towns and their villages.

Gibeon, Ramah, Beeroth, Mizpah, Kephirah, Mozah, Rekem, Irpeel, Taralah, Zelah, Haeleph, the Jebusite city (that is, Jerusalem), Gibeah and Kiriath—fourteen towns and their villages. This was the inheritance of Benjamin for its clans.

SIMEON, IN SOUTHERN JUDAH. The second lot came out for the tribe of Simeon, clan by clan. Their inheritance lay within the territory of Judah. It included:

Beersheba (or Sheba),*r* Moladah, Hazar Shual, Balah, Ezem, Eltolad, Bethul, Hormah, Ziklag, Beth Marcaboth, Hazar Susah, Beth Lebaoth and Sharuhen—thirteen towns and their villages;

Ain, Rimmon, Ether and Ashan—four towns and their villages—and all the villages around these towns as far as Baalath Beer (Ramah in the Negev).

This was the inheritance of the tribe of the Simeonites, clan by clan. The inheritance of the Simeonites was taken from the share of Judah, because

The side notes on the left:

Josh.
18:21-28

Josh.
19:1-9

---

p Septuagint; Hebrew *slope facing the Arabah*   *q* That is, the Dead Sea   *r* Or *Beersheba, Sheba;* 1 Chron. 4:28 does not have *Sheba.*

Judah's portion was more than they needed. So the Simeonites received their inheritance within the territory of Judah.

ZEBULUN, NORTH CENTRAL. The third lot came up for Zebulun, clan by clan:

Josh. 19:10-16

The boundary of their inheritance went as far as Sarid. Going west it ran to Maralah, touched Dabbesheth, and extended to the ravine near Jokneam. It turned east from Sarid toward the sunrise to the territory of Kisloth Tabor and went on to Daberath and up to Japhia. Then it continued eastward to Gath Hepher and Eth Kazin; it came out at Rimmon and turned toward Neah. There the boundary went around on the north to Hannathon and ended at the Valley of Iphtah El. Included were Kattath, Nahalal, Shimron, Idalah and Bethlehem. There were twelve towns and their villages.

These towns and their villages were the inheritance of Zebulun, clan by clan.

ISSACHAR, EAST OF ZEBULUN. The fourth lot came out for Issachar, clan by clan. Their territory included:

Josh. 19:17-23

Jezreel, Kesulloth, Shunem, Hapharaim, Shion, Anaharath, Rabbith, Kishion, Ebez, Remeth, En Gannim, En Haddah and Beth Pazzez. The boundary touched Tabor, Shahazumah and Beth Shemesh, and ended at the Jordan. There were sixteen towns and their villages.

These towns and their villages were the inheritance of the tribe of Issachar, clan by clan.

ASHER, NORTHWEST COAST. The fifth lot came out for the tribe of Asher, clan by clan. Their territory included:

Josh. 19:24-31

Helkath, Hali, Beten, Acshaph, Allammelech, Amad and Mishal. On the west the boundary touched Carmel and Shihor Libnath. It then turned east toward Beth Dagon, touched Zebulun and the Valley of Iphtah El, and went north to Beth Emek and Neiel, passing Cabul on the left. It went to Abdon,[s] Rehob, Hammon and Kanah, as far as Greater Sidon. The boundary then turned back toward Ramah and went to the fortified city of Tyre, turned toward Hosah and came out at the sea in the region of Aczib, Ummah, Aphek and Rehob. There were twenty-two towns and their villages.

These towns and their villages were the inheritance of the tribe of Asher, clan by clan.

NAPHTALI, NORTHEAST. The sixth lot came out for Naphtali, clan by clan:

Josh. 19:32-39

Their boundary went from Heleph and the large tree in Zaanannim, passing Adami Nekeb and Jabneel to Lakkum and ending at the Jordan. The boundary ran west through Aznoth Tabor and came out at Hukkok. It touched Zebulun on the south, Asher on the west and the Jordan[t] on the east. The fortified cities were Ziddim, Zer, Hammath, Rakkath, Kinnereth, Adamah, Ramah, Hazor, Kedesh, Edrei, En Hazor, Iron, Migdal El, Horem, Beth Anath and Beth Shemesh. There were nineteen towns and their villages.

These towns and their villages were the inheritance of the tribe of Naphtali, clan by clan.

[s]Some Hebrew manuscripts (see also Joshua 21:30); most Hebrew manuscripts *Ebron*
[t]Septuagint; Hebrew *west, and Judah, the Jordan,*

Josh.
19:40-48

DAN, CENTRAL COAST.   The seventh lot came out for the tribe of Dan, clan by clan. The territory of their inheritance included:

Zorah, Eshtaol, Ir Shemesh, Shaalabbin, Aijalon, Ithlah, Elon, Timnah, Ekron, Eltekeh, Gibbethon, Baalath, Jehud, Bene Berak, Gath Rimmon, Me Jarkon and Rakkon, with the area facing Joppa.

(But the Danites had difficulty taking possession of their territory, so they went up and attacked Leshem, took it, put it to the sword and occupied it. They settled in Leshem and named it Dan after their forefather.)

These towns and their villages were the inheritance of the tribe of Dan, clan by clan.

Josh.
19:49,50

CITY FOR JOSHUA.   When they had finished dividing the land into its allotted portions, the Israelites gave Joshua son of Nun an inheritance among them, as the LORD had commanded. They gave him the town he asked for—Timnath Serah[u] in the hill country of Ephraim. And he built up the town and settled there.

Josh. 19:51

END OF PARTITION.   These are the territories that Eleazar the priest, Joshua son of Nun and the heads of the tribal clans of Israel assigned by lot at Shiloh in the presence of the LORD at the entrance to the Tent of Meeting. And so they finished dividing the land.

Josh.
20:1-6

CITIES OF REFUGE.   Then the LORD said to Joshua: "Tell the Israelites to designate the cities of refuge, as I instructed you through Moses, so that anyone who kills a person accidentally and unintentionally may flee there and find protection from the avenger of blood.

"When he flees to one of these cities, he is to stand in the entrance of the city gate and state his case before the elders of that city. Then they are to admit him into their city and give him a place to live with them. If the avenger of blood pursues him, they must not surrender the one accused, because he killed his neighbor unintentionally and without malice aforethought. He is to stay in that city until he has stood trial before the assembly and until the death of the high priest who is serving at that time. Then he may go back to his own home in the town from which he fled."

Josh.
20:7-9

SIX CITIES NAMED.   So they set apart Kedesh in Galilee in the hill country of Naphtali, Shechem in the hill country of Ephraim, and Kiriath Arba (that is, Hebron) in the hill country of Judah. On the east side of the Jordan of Jericho[v] they designated Bezer in the desert on the plateau in the tribe of Reuben, Ramoth in Gilead in the tribe of Gad, and Golan in Bashan in the tribe of Manasseh. Any of the Israelites or any alien living among them who killed someone accidentally could flee to these designated cities and not be killed by the avenger of blood prior to standing trial before the assembly.

Josh.
21:1-7

DISTRIBUTION OF LEVITES.   Now the family heads of the Levites approached Eleazar the priest, Joshua son of Nun, and the heads of the other tribal families of Israel at Shiloh in Canaan and said to them, "The LORD commanded through Moses that you give us towns to live in, with pasturelands for our livestock." So, as the LORD had commanded, the

---

[u]Also known as *Timnath Heres* (see Judges 2:9)   [v]*Jordan of Jericho* was possibly an ancient name for the Jordan River.

Israelites gave the Levites the following towns and pasturelands out of their own inheritance:

The first lot came out for the Kohathites, clan by clan. The Levites who were descendants of Aaron the priest were allotted thirteen towns from the tribes of Judah, Simeon and Benjamin. The rest of Kohath's descendants were allotted ten towns from the clans of the tribes of Ephraim, Dan and half of Manasseh.

The descendants of Gershon were allotted thirteen towns from the clans of the tribes of Issachar, Asher, Naphtali and the half-tribe of Manasseh in Bashan.

The descendants of Merari, clan by clan, received twelve towns from the tribes of Reuben, Gad and Zebulun.

DESCENDANTS OF AARON.   So the Israelites allotted to the Levites these towns and their pasturelands, as the LORD had commanded through Moses.

Josh.
21:8-19

From the tribes of Judah and Simeon they allotted the following towns by name (these towns were assigned to the descendants of Aaron who were from the Kohathite clans of the Levites, because the first lot fell to them):

They gave them Kiriath Arba (that is, Hebron), with its surrounding pastureland, in the hill country of Judah. (Arba was the forefather of Anak.) But the fields and villages around the city they had given to Caleb son of Jephunneh as his possession.

So to the descendants of Aaron the priest they gave Hebron (a city of refuge for one accused of murder), Libnah, Jattir, Eshtemoa, Holon, Debir, Ain, Juttah and Beth Shemesh, together with their pasturelands—nine towns from these two tribes.

And from the tribe of Benjamin they gave them Gibeon, Geba, Anathoth and Almon, together with their pasturelands—four towns.

All the towns for the priests, the descendants of Aaron, were thirteen, together with their pasturelands.

OTHER KOHATHITES.   The rest of the Kohathite clans of the Levites were allotted towns from the tribe of Ephraim:

Josh.
21:20-26

In the hill country of Ephraim they were given Shechem (a city of refuge for one accused of murder) and Gezer, Kibzaim and Beth Horon, together with their pasturelands—four towns.

Also from the tribe of Dan they received Eltekeh, Gibbethon, Aijalon and Gath Rimmon, together with their pasturelands—four towns.

From half the tribe of Manasseh they received Taanach and Gath Rimmon, together with their pasturelands—two towns.

All these ten towns and their pasturelands were given to the rest of the Kohathite clans.

GERSHONITES.   The Levite clans of the Gershonites were given:
from the half-tribe of Manasseh,

Josh.
21:27-33

Golan in Bashan (a city of refuge for one accused of murder) and Be Eshtarah, together with their pasturelands—two towns;
from the tribe of Issachar,
Kishion, Daberath, Jarmuth and En Gannim, together with their pasturelands—four towns;
from the tribe of Asher,

Mishal, Abdon, Helkath and Rehob, together with their pasturelands—four towns;

from the tribe of Naphtali,

Kedesh in Galilee (a city of refuge for one accused of murder), Hammoth Dor and Kartan, together with their pasturelands—three towns.

All the towns of the Gershonite clans were thirteen, together with their pasturelands.

Josh.
21:34-40

MERARITES.   The Merarite clans (the rest of the Levites) were given:
  from the tribe of Zebulun,

Jokneam, Kartah, Dimnah and Nahalal, together with their pasturelands—four towns;

from the tribe of Reuben,

Bezer, Jahaz, Kedemoth and Mephaath, together with their pasturelands—four towns;

from the tribe of Gad,

Ramoth in Gilead (a city of refuge for one accused of murder), Mahanaim, Heshbon and Jazer, together with their pasturelands—four towns in all.

All the towns allotted to the Merarite clans, who were the rest of the Levites, were twelve.

Josh.
21:41,42

TOTAL LEVITE CITIES.   The towns of the Levites in the territory held by the Israelites were forty-eight in all, together with their pasturelands. Each of these towns had pasturelands surrounding it; this was true for all these towns.

Josh.
21:43-45

PROMISE FULFILLED.   So the LORD gave Israel all the land he had sworn to give their forefathers, and they took possession of it and settled there. The LORD gave them rest on every side, just as he had sworn to their forefathers. Not one of their enemies withstood them; the LORD handed all their enemies over to them. Not one of all the LORD's good promises to the house of Israel failed; every one was fulfilled.

Joshua's Farewell Addresses

*T*he initial phase of the conquest now complete, Joshua turns his thoughts to the ongoing need for Israel's spiritual commitment to God.

In a manner reminiscent of Moses, Joshua addresses his people on three separate occasions. The first is a farewell to the soldiers of the eastern tribes who have joined the western tribes in taking Canaan. Joshua blesses them and exhorts them to remain faithful to God and his laws. Great concern arises when the rest of Israel learns that the eastern tribes have built an altar on their way back across the Jordan, but all ends well when it is learned that no rebellion was intended, as some had feared.

Joshua's second address, to the western tribes, is a review of God's blessings and a stern warning against involvement with pagan people and their idolatry.

The last address calls the people to renew their covenant with God, as each generation must do for itself. The people vow to be faithful, but Joshua knows that it is easier said than done. In order to encourage their faithfulness, Joshua constructs a memorial of this third covenant between Israel and God.

ADDRESS TO EASTERN TRIBES.   Then Joshua summoned the Reuben-   Josh. 22:1-6
ites, the Gadites and the half-tribe of Manasseh and said to them, "You
have done all that Moses the servant of the LORD commanded, and you
have obeyed me in everything I commanded. For a long time now—to this
very day—you have not deserted your brothers but have carried out the
mission the LORD your God gave you. Now that the LORD your God has
given your brothers rest as he promised, return to your homes in the land
that Moses the servant of the LORD gave you on the other side of the
Jordan. But be very careful to keep the commandment and the law that
Moses the servant of the LORD gave you: to love the LORD your God, to
walk in all his ways, to obey his commands, to hold fast to him and to
serve him with all your heart and all your soul."
      Then Joshua blessed them and sent them away, and they went to their
homes.

TRIBES RETURN TO GILEAD.   (To the half-tribe of Manasseh Moses had   Josh. 22:7-9 Gilead
given land in Bashan, and to the other half of the tribe Joshua gave land
on the west side of the Jordan with their brothers.) When Joshua sent them
home, he blessed them, saying, "Return to your homes with your great
wealth—with large herds of livestock, with silver, gold, bronze and iron,
and a great quantity of clothing—and divide with your brothers the plunder from your enemies."
      So the Reubenites, the Gadites and the half-tribe of Manasseh left the
Israelites at Shiloh in Canaan to return to Gilead, their own land, which
they had acquired in accordance with the command of the LORD through
Moses.

TRIBES BUILD ALTAR.   When they came to Geliloth near the Jordan in   Josh. 22:10-12
the land of Canaan, the Reubenites, the Gadites and the half-tribe of
Manasseh built an imposing altar there by the Jordan. And when the
Israelites heard that they had built the altar on the border of Canaan at
Geliloth near the Jordan on the Israelite side, the whole assembly of Israel
gathered at Shiloh to go to war against them.

WESTERN TRIBES ANGERED.   So the Israelites sent Phinehas son of   Josh. 22:13-20
Eleazar, the priest, to the land of Gilead—to Reuben, Gad and the half-
tribe of Manasseh. With him they sent ten of the chief men, one for each of
the tribes of Israel, each the head of a family division among the Israelite
clans.
      When they went to Gilead—to Reuben, Gad and the half-tribe of
Manasseh—they said to them: "The whole assembly of the LORD says:
'How could you break faith with the God of Israel like this? How could
you turn away from the LORD and build yourselves an altar in rebellion
against him now? Was not the sin of Peor enough for us? Up to this very
day we have not cleansed ourselves from that sin, even though a plague
fell on the community of the LORD! And are you now turning away from
the LORD?
      " 'If you rebel against the LORD today, tomorrow he will be angry with
the whole community of Israel. If the land you possess is defiled, come
over to the LORD's land, where the LORD's tabernacle stands, and share
the land with us. But do not rebel against the LORD or against us by
building an altar for yourselves, other than the altar of the LORD our God.
When Achan son of Zerah acted unfaithfully regarding the devoted

things, *w* did not wrath come upon the whole community of Israel? He was not the only one who died for his sin.'"

Josh.
22:21-29

EASTERN TRIBES EXPLAIN.   Then Reuben, Gad and the half-tribe of Manasseh replied to the heads of the clans of Israel: "The Mighty One, God, the LORD! The Mighty One, God, the LORD! He knows! And let Israel know! If this has been in rebellion or disobedience to the LORD, do not spare us this day. If we have built our own altar to turn away from the LORD and to offer burnt offerings and grain offerings, or to sacrifice fellowship offerings*x* on it, may the LORD himself call us to account.

"No! We did it for fear that some day your descendants might say to ours, 'What do you have to do with the LORD, the God of Israel? The LORD has made the Jordan a boundary between us and you—you Reubenites and Gadites! You have no share in the LORD.' So your descendants might cause ours to stop fearing the LORD.

"That is why we said, 'Let us get ready and build an altar—but not for burnt offerings or sacrifices.' On the contrary, it is to be a witness between us and you and the generations that follow, that we will worship the LORD at his sanctuary with our burnt offerings, sacrifices and fellowship offerings. Then in the future your descendants will not be able to say to ours, 'You have no share in the LORD.'

"And we said, 'If they ever say this to us, or to our descendants, we will answer: Look at the replica of the LORD's altar, which our fathers built, not for burnt offerings and sacrifices, but as a witness between us and you.'

"Far be it from us to rebel against the LORD and turn away from him today by building an altar for burnt offerings, grain offerings and sacrifices, other than the altar of the LORD our God that stands before his tabernacle."

Josh.
22:30-34

JOY IN UNITY.   When Phinehas the priest and the leaders of the community—the heads of the clans of the Israelites—heard what Reuben, Gad and Manasseh had to say, they were pleased. And Phinehas son of Eleazar, the priest, said to Reuben, Gad and Manasseh, "Today we know that the LORD is with us, because you have not acted unfaithfully toward the LORD in this matter. Now you have rescued the Israelites from the LORD's hand."

Then Phinehas son of Eleazar, the priest, and the leaders returned to Canaan from their meeting with the Reubenites and Gadites in Gilead and reported to the Israelites. They were glad to hear the report and praised God. And they talked no more about going to war against them to devastate the country where the Reubenites and the Gadites lived.

And the Reubenites and the Gadites gave the altar this name: A Witness Between Us that the LORD is God.

Josh.
23:1-16

ADDRESS TO WESTERN TRIBES.   After a long time had passed and the LORD had given Israel rest from all their enemies around them, Joshua, by then old and well advanced in years, summoned all Israel—their elders, leaders, judges and officials—and said to them: "I am old and well advanced in years. You yourselves have seen everything the LORD your God has done to all these nations for your sake; it was the LORD your God who fought for you. Remember how I have allotted as an inheritance for

---

*w*The Hebrew term refers to the irrevocable giving over of things or persons to the LORD, often by totally destroying them.   *x*Traditionally *peace offerings*; also in verse 27

your tribes all the land of the nations that remain—the nations I conquered—between the Jordan and the Great Sea[y] in the west. The LORD your God himself will drive them out of your way. He will push them out before you, and you will take possession of their land, as the LORD your God promised you.

"Be very strong; be careful to obey all that is written in the Book of the Law of Moses, without turning aside to the right or to the left. Do not associate with these nations that remain among you; do not invoke the names of their gods or swear by them. You must not serve them or bow down to them. But you are to hold fast to the LORD your God, as you have until now.

"The LORD has driven out before you great and powerful nations; to this day no one has been able to withstand you. One of you routs a thousand, because the LORD your God fights for you, just as he promised. So be very careful to love the LORD your God.

"But if you turn away and ally yourselves with the survivors of these nations that remain among you and if you intermarry with them and associate with them, then you may be sure that the LORD your God will no longer drive out these nations before you. Instead, they will become snares and traps for you, whips on your backs and thorns in your eyes, until you perish from this good land, which the LORD your God has given you.

"Now I am about to go the way of all the earth. You know with all your heart and soul that not one of all the good promises the LORD your God gave you has failed. Every promise has been fulfilled; not one has failed. But just as every good promise of the LORD your God has come true, so the LORD will bring on you all the evil he has threatened, until he has destroyed you from this good land he has given you. If you violate the covenant of the LORD your God, which he commanded you, and go and serve other gods and bow down to them, the LORD's anger will burn against you, and you will quickly perish from the good land he has given you."

ADDRESS AT SHECHEM. Then Joshua assembled all the tribes of Israel at Shechem. He summoned the elders, leaders, judges and officials of Israel, and they presented themselves before God.

Josh.
24:1-13
Shechem

Joshua said to all the people, "This is what the LORD, the God of Israel, says: 'Long ago your forefathers, including Terah the father of Abraham and Nahor, lived beyond the River[z] and worshiped other gods. But I took your father Abraham from the land beyond the River and led him throughout Canaan and gave him many descendants. I gave him Isaac, and to Isaac I gave Jacob and Esau. I assigned the hill country of Seir to Esau, but Jacob and his sons went down to Egypt.

" 'Then I sent Moses and Aaron, and I afflicted the Egyptians by what I did there, and I brought you out. When I brought your fathers out of Egypt, you came to the sea, and the Egyptians pursued them with chariots and horsemen[a] as far as the Red Sea.[b] But they cried to the LORD for help, and he put darkness between you and the Egyptians; he brought the sea over them and covered them. You saw with your own eyes what I did to the Egyptians. Then you lived in the desert for a long time.

---

[y]That is, the Mediterranean   [z]That is, the Euphrates   [a]Or *charioteers*   [b]Hebrew *Yam Suph*; that is, Sea of Reeds

" 'I brought you to the land of the Amorites who lived east of the Jordan. They fought against you, but I gave them into your hands. I destroyed them from before you, and you took possession of their land. When Balak son of Zippor, the king of Moab, prepared to fight against Israel, he sent for Balaam son of Beor to put a curse on you. But I would not listen to Balaam, so he blessed you again and again, and I delivered you out of his hand.

" 'Then you crossed the Jordan and came to Jericho. The citizens of Jericho fought against you, as did also the Amorites, Perizzites, Canaanites, Hittites, Girgashites, Hivites and Jebusites, but I gave them into your hands. I sent the hornet ahead of you, which drove them out before you—also the two Amorite kings. You did not do it with your own sword and bow. So I gave you a land on which you did not toil and cities you did not build; and you live in them and eat from vineyards and olive groves that you did not plant.'

Josh.
24:14,15

CHALLENGE TO COMMITMENT. "Now fear the LORD and serve him with all faithfulness. Throw away the gods your forefathers worshiped beyond the River and in Egypt, and serve the LORD. But if serving the LORD seems undesirable to you, then choose for yourselves this day whom you will serve, whether the gods your forefathers served beyond the River, or the gods of the Amorites, in whose land you are living. But as for me and my household, we will serve the LORD."

Josh.
24:16-18

ISRAEL'S THIRD COVENANT. Then the people answered, "Far be it from us to forsake the LORD to serve other gods! It was the LORD our God himself who brought us and our fathers up out of Egypt, from that land of slavery, and performed those great signs before our eyes. He protected us on our entire journey and among all the nations through which we traveled. And the LORD drove out before us all the nations, including the Amorites, who lived in the land. We too will serve the LORD, because he is our God."

Josh.
24:19-24

JOSHUA TESTS COMMITMENT. Joshua said to the people, "You are not able to serve the LORD. He is a holy God; he is a jealous God. He will not forgive your rebellion and your sins. If you forsake the LORD and serve foreign gods, he will turn and bring disaster on you and make an end of you, after he has been good to you."

But the people said to Joshua, "No! We will serve the LORD."

Then Joshua said, "You are witnesses against yourselves that you have chosen to serve the LORD."

"Yes, we are witnesses," they replied.

"Now then," said Joshua, "throw away the foreign gods that are among you and yield your hearts to the LORD, the God of Israel."

And the people said to Joshua, "We will serve the LORD our God and obey him."

Josh.
24:25-27

MONUMENT TO COVENANT. On that day Joshua made a covenant for the people, and there at Shechem he drew up for them decrees and laws. And Joshua recorded these things in the Book of the Law of God. Then he took a large stone and set it up there under the oak near the holy place of the LORD.

"See!" he said to all the people. "This stone will be a witness against us.

It has heard all the words the LORD has said to us. It will be a witness against you if you are untrue to your God."

ACQUISITION OF TERRITORY.   Then Joshua sent the people away, each to his own inheritance.

Josh. 24:28
Judges 2:6

*Three Burials*_____

*H*aving led the Israelites into Canaan, and having completed the general conquest and partition of the promised land, Joshua now faces the end of his life. He is called to be with his fathers, knowing that over the years he has proved himself to be a man of great faith and courage. And with Joshua goes the high priest, Eleazar, who has served the people's spiritual needs throughout the conquest. With the passing of these two men of God, the last immediate links with Moses and Aaron will be severed, and a new era will soon find the Israelites in spiritual eclipse. Never again will the Israelites as a nation be this closely united, either among themselves or with their God.

About the same time as Joshua's and Eleazar's deaths, the people also bury the 400-year-old bones of Joseph, which were brought out of Egypt during the exodus, in keeping with Joseph's deathbed request. It is an appropriate tie with the early patriarchs, to whom God first promised this land.

DEATH OF JOSHUA.   Joshua son of Nun, the servant of the LORD, died at the age of a hundred and ten. And they buried him in the land of his inheritance, at Timnath Heres[c] in the hill country of Ephraim, north of Mount Gaash.

Judges
2:8,9
Josh.
24:29,30
(Ca. 1390
B.C.?)

DEATH OF ELEAZAR.   And Eleazar son of Aaron died and was buried at Gibeah, which had been allotted to his son Phinehas in the hill country of Ephraim.

Josh. 24:33

JOSEPH'S BONES BURIED.   And Joseph's bones, which the Israelites had brought up from Egypt, were buried at Shechem in the tract of land that Jacob bought for a hundred pieces of silver[d] from the sons of Hamor, the father of Shechem. This became the inheritance of Joseph's descendants.

Josh. 24:32

*Additional Conquests*_____

*T*he fact that territory has been given to a tribe or individual does not mean that the land can be immediately occupied. The inhabitants living in the land must first be driven out. While some of the territorial conquests occurred when Joshua was still living, the following additional conquests are made after Joshua's death.

JUDAH AND SIMEON JOIN FORCES.   After the death of Joshua, the Israelites asked the LORD, "Who will be the first to go up and fight for us against the Canaanites?"

Judges
1:1-10,16-19

---

[c]Also known as *Timnath Serah* (see Joshua 19:50 and 24:30)   [d]Hebrew *hundred kesitahs*;
a kesitah was a unit of money of unknown weight and value.

The LORD answered, "Judah is to go; I have given the land into their hands."

Then the men of Judah said to the Simeonites their brothers, "Come up with us into the territory allotted to us, to fight against the Canaanites. We in turn will go with you into yours." So the Simeonites went with them.

When Judah attacked, the LORD gave the Canaanites and Perizzites into their hands and they struck down ten thousand men at Bezek. It was there that they found Adoni-Bezek and fought against him, putting to rout the Canaanites and Perizzites. Adoni-Bezek fled, but they chased him and caught him, and cut off his thumbs and big toes.

Then Adoni-Bezek said, "Seventy kings with their thumbs and big toes cut off have picked up scraps under my table. Now God has paid me back for what I did to them." They brought him to Jerusalem, and he died there.

The men of Judah attacked Jerusalem also and took it. They put the city to the sword and set it on fire.

After that, the men of Judah went down to fight against the Canaanites living in the hill country, the Negev and the western foothills. They advanced against the Canaanites living in Hebron (formerly called Kiriath Arba) and defeated Sheshai, Ahiman and Talmai.

The descendants of Moses' father-in-law, the Kenite, went up from the City of Palms[e] with the men of Judah to live among the people of the Desert of Judah in the Negev near Arad.

Then the men of Judah went with the Simeonites their brothers and attacked the Canaanites living in Zephath, and they totally destroyed[f] the city. Therefore it was called Hormah.[g] The men of Judah also took[h] Gaza, Ashkelon and Ekron—each city with its territory.

The LORD was with the men of Judah. They took possession of the hill country, but they were unable to drive the people from the plains, because they had iron chariots.

Josh.
15:13,14
Judges
1:20b

CALEB TAKES TERRITORY. In accordance with the LORD's command to him, Joshua gave to Caleb son of Jephunneh a portion in Judah—Kiriath Arba, that is, Hebron. (Arba was the forefather of Anak.) From Hebron Caleb drove out the three Anakites—Sheshai, Ahiman and Talmai—descendants of Anak.

Judges
1:11-15
Josh.
15:15-19

GIFT TO CALEB'S DAUGHTER. From there they advanced against the people living in Debir (formerly called Kiriath Sepher). And Caleb said, "I will give my daughter Acsah in marriage to the man who attacks and captures Kiriath Sepher." Othniel son of Kenaz, Caleb's younger brother, took it; so Caleb gave his daughter Acsah to him in marriage.

One day when she came to Othniel, she urged him[i] to ask her father for a field. When she got off her donkey, Caleb asked her, "What can I do for you?"

She replied, "Do me a special favor. Since you have given me land in the Negev, give me also springs of water." So Caleb gave her the upper and lower springs.

[e]That is, Jericho   [f]The Hebrew term refers to the irrevocable giving over of things or persons to the LORD, often by totally destroying them.   [g]*Hormah* means *destruction.*
[h]Hebrew; Septuagint *Judah did not take*   [i]Hebrew; Septuagint and Vulgate *Othniel, he urged her*

EPHRAIM CAPTURES BETHEL.   Now the house of Joseph attacked   Judges
Bethel, and the LORD was with them. When they sent men to spy out   1:22-26
Bethel (formerly called Luz), the spies saw a man coming out of the city
and they said to him, "Show us how to get into the city and we will see
that you are treated well." So he showed them, and they put the city to the
sword but spared the man and his whole family. He then went to the land
of the Hittites, where he built a city and called it Luz, which is its name to
this day.

Failure to Complete Conquests

*D*espite all the conquests which have been made, there are still sections of unclaimed territory and, more importantly, still inhabitants
who have not been driven out, contrary to God's specific orders.
The danger of an incomplete conquest is the lingering presence of pagan
influence. As long as the Canaanites remain, the Israelites will inevitably
intermarry with them, and, just as inevitably, turn to worship their pagan
gods.

Failure to drive out the inhabitants may indicate not only the softness
of Israel's resolve but also a certain fascination with the pagan culture
about them. Whatever the reasons for their failure, God considers it a
breach of covenant and knows that widespread idolatry is soon to follow.

A number of lands and peoples are never conquered. Interestingly
enough, neither Judah nor Benjamin is able to completely drive out the
Jebusites from the city of Jerusalem, which is within the region of their
common boundary (even despite the fact that Judah has already attacked
the city once and put it to the torch).

FAILURE OF EASTERN TRIBES.   But the Israelites did not drive out the   Josh. 13:13
people of Geshur and Maacah, so they continue to live among the
Israelites to this day.

FAILURE OF EPHRAIM.   They did not dislodge the Canaanites living in   Josh. 16:10
Gezer; to this day the Canaanites live among the people of Ephraim but   Judges
are required to do forced labor.   1:29

FAILURE OF MANASSEH.   Within Issachar and Asher, Manasseh also   Josh.
had Beth Shan, Ibleam and the people of Dor, Endor, Taanach and Megid-   17:11-13
do, together with their surrounding settlements (the third in the list is   Judges
Naphoth*j*).   1:27,28

Yet the Manassites were not able to occupy these towns, for the
Canaanites were determined to live in that region. However, when the
Israelites grew stronger, they subjected the Canaanites to forced labor but
did not drive them out completely.

FAILURE OF JUDAH.   Judah could not dislodge the Jebusites, who were   Josh. 15:63
living in Jerusalem; to this day the Jebusites live there with the people of
Judah.

j That is, Naphoth Dor

MARCH 17

Judges 1:21	**FAILURE OF BENJAMIN.** The Benjamites, however, failed to dislodge the Jebusites, who were living in Jerusalem; to this day the Jebusites live there with the Benjamites.
Judges 1:30	**FAILURE OF ZEBULUN.** Neither did Zebulun drive out the Canaanites living in Kitron or Nahalol, who remained among them; but they did subject them to forced labor.
Judges 1:31,32	**FAILURE OF ASHER.** Nor did Asher drive out those living in Acco or Sidon or Ahlab or Aczib or Helbah or Aphek or Rehob, and because of this the people of Asher lived among the Canaanite inhabitants of the land.
Judges 1:33	**FAILURE OF NAPHTALI.** Neither did Naphtali drive out those living in Beth Shemesh or Beth Anath; but the Naphtalites too lived among the Canaanite inhabitants of the land, and those living in Beth Shemesh and Beth Anath became forced laborers for them.
Judges 1:34-36	**FAILURE OF DANITES.** The Amorites confined the Danites to the hill country, not allowing them to come down into the plain. And the Amorites were determined also to hold out in Mount Heres, Aijalon and Shaalbim, but when the power of the house of Joseph increased, they too were pressed into forced labor. The boundary of the Amorites was from Scorpion[k] Pass to Sela and beyond.
Judges 2:1-5	**FAILURES BREACH COVENANT.** The angel of the LORD went up from Gilgal to Bokim and said, "I brought you up out of Egypt and led you into the land that I swore to give to your forefathers. I said, 'I will never break my covenant with you, and you shall not make a covenant with the people of this land, but you shall break down their altars.' Yet you have disobeyed me. Why have you done this? Now therefore I tell you that I will not drive them out before you; they will be ˌthornsˌ in your sides and their gods will be a snare to you." When the angel of the LORD had spoken these things to all the Israelites, the people wept aloud, and they called that place Bokim.[l] There they offered sacrifices to the LORD.

Apostasy and the Judges

*P*oliticaly and militarily, there is need for a more complete conquest of the promised land. Spiritually, there is still a great lesson for a new generation of Israelites to learn—namely, that with obedience comes prosperity; with disobedience, adversity. It is a lesson which the older Israelites had learned through the wilderness wanderings and the initial conquest of Canaan, but the passing of the older generation leaves a vacuum of any real dedication to God or his laws. From this point forward, Israel heads into both spiritual and political decline.

The incomplete conquests have left Israel vulnerable to the pagan influences around them. As they begin to evolve into a more agricultural society, the Israelites will become increasingly attracted by the Canaanite cult of Baal, which is associated with fertility and crops. A strong spirit of compromise leads to intermarriage, idolatry, and immorality. The combination of national sin and unconquered inhabitants results in dominance and oppression by various

[k]Hebrew *Akrabbim*   [l]*Bokim* means *weepers*.

pagan peoples, just as God predicted. During this time the Israelites go through repeated cycles of sin and oppression, but, fortunately, of repentance as well. And for each time the people come to their senses God raises up a leader to deliver them. Each of these "judges" leads only a few tribes within the now-loose federation of Israel. Although the total time of their collective leadership amounts to some 450 years, the overlapping of their individual leadership probably puts the figure closer to 335 years.

PERIOD OF THE ELDERS.   The people served the LORD throughout the lifetime of Joshua and of the elders who outlived him and who had seen all the great things the LORD had done for Israel.

Judges 2:7
Josh. 24:31
(1400-1380
B.C.?)

A NEW GENERATION.   After that whole generation had been gathered to their fathers, another generation grew up, who knew neither the LORD nor what he had done for Israel.

Judges
2:10

FROM GOD TO IDOLATRY.   Then the Israelites did evil in the eyes of the LORD and served the Baals. They forsook the LORD, the God of their fathers, who had brought them out of Egypt. They followed and wor-shiped various gods of the peoples around them. They provoked the LORD to anger because they forsook him and served Baal and the Ashtoreths.

Judges
2:11-13

SIN BRINGS DEFEAT.   In his anger against Israel the LORD handed them over to raiders who plundered them. He sold them to their enemies all around, whom they were no longer able to resist. Whenever Israel went out to fight, the hand of the LORD was against them to defeat them, just as he had sworn to them. They were in great distress.

Judges
2:14,15

RESCUE THROUGH JUDGES.   Then the LORD raised up judges,[m] who saved them out of the hands of these raiders. Yet they would not listen to their judges but prostituted themselves to other gods and worshiped them. Unlike their fathers, they quickly turned from the way in which their fathers had walked, the way of obedience to the LORD's commands. Whenever the LORD raised up a judge for them, he was with the judge and saved them out of the hands of their enemies as long as the judge lived; for the LORD had compassion on them as they groaned under those who oppressed and afflicted them. But when the judge died, the people returned to ways even more corrupt than those of their fathers, following other gods and serving and worshiping them. They refused to give up their evil practices and stubborn ways.

Judges
2:16-19

ISRAEL'S FAITH TESTED.   Therefore the LORD was very angry with Israel and said, "Because this nation has violated the covenant that I laid down for their forefathers and has not listened to me, I will no longer drive out before them any of the nations Joshua left when he died. I will use them to test Israel and see whether they will keep the way of the LORD and walk in it as their forefathers did." The LORD had allowed those nations to remain; he did not drive them out at once by giving them into the hands of Joshua.

Judges
2:20-23

ENEMIES GOD USES.   These are the nations the LORD left to test all those Israelites who had not experienced any of the wars in Canaan (he did this only to teach warfare to the descendants of the Israelites who had not had previous battle experience): the five rulers of the Philistines, all the

Judges
3:1-4

m Or *leaders*; similarly in verses 17-19

Canaanites, the Sidonians, and the Hivites living in the Lebanon mountains from Mount Baal Hermon to Lebo[n] Hamath. They were left to test
the Israelites to see whether they would obey the LORD's commands,
which he had given their forefathers through Moses.

Judges
3:5,6

ISRAEL FAILS TESTS.   The Israelites lived among the Canaanites, Hittites, Amorites, Perizzites, Hivites and Jebusites. They took their daughters in marriage and gave their own daughters to their sons, and served
their gods.

Othniel, Ehud, and Shamgar

*I*n the first century of Israel's decline, various tribes are oppressed by the
Mesopotamites, Moabites, and Philistines. Othniel, a nephew of Caleb,
leads Judah and Simeon in victory over the Mesopotamites. Ehud personally assassinates the leader of the Moabites (who have been enemies of
Israel ever since King Balak tried to get Balaam to pronounce a curse on the
Israelites). It is by Ehud's courageous act that the tribes of Ephraim and
Benjamin are thus liberated from occupation by a nation which Israel had once
defeated soundly. Finally, brief mention is given to Shamgar, who will be the
first of several Israelites to do battle with the warlike Philistines in the southern
coastal area of Canaan.

Judges
3:7,8
(1380-1367
B.C.?)

OPPRESSION BY MESOPOTAMITES.   The Israelites did evil in the eyes
of the LORD; they forgot the LORD their God and served the Baals and the
Asherahs. The anger of the LORD burned against Israel so that he sold them
into the hands of Cushan-Rishathaim king of Aram Naharaim,[o] to whom
the Israelites were subject for eight years.

Judges
3:9-11
(1367-1327
B.C.?)

DELIVERANCE BY OTHNIEL.   But when they cried out to the LORD, he
raised up for them a deliverer, Othniel son of Kenaz, Caleb's younger
brother, who saved them. The Spirit of the LORD came upon him, so that
he became Israel's judge[p] and went to war. The LORD gave Cushan-
Rishathaim king of Aram into the hands of Othniel, who overpowered
him. So the land had peace for forty years, until Othniel son of Kenaz died.

Judges
3:12-14
(1327-1304
B.C.?)

OPPRESSION BY MOABITES.   Once again the Israelites did evil in the
eyes of the LORD, and because they did this evil the LORD gave Eglon king
of Moab power over Israel. Getting the Ammonites and Amalekites to join
him, Eglon came and attacked Israel, and they took possession of the City
of Palms.[q] The Israelites were subject to Eglon king of Moab for eighteen
years.

Judges
3:15-25

EHUD KILLS EGLON.   Again the Israelites cried out to the LORD, and he
gave them a deliverer—Ehud, a left-handed man, the son of Gera the
Benjamite. The Israelites sent him with tribute to Eglon king of Moab.
Now Ehud had made a double-edged sword about a foot and a half[r] long,
which he strapped to his right thigh under his clothing. He presented the
tribute to Eglon king of Moab, who was a very fat man. After Ehud had
presented the tribute, he sent on their way the men who had carried it.

---

[n]Or *to the entrance to*   [o]That is, Northwest Mesopotamia   [p]Or *leader*   [q]That is,
Jericho   [r]Hebrew *a cubit* (about 0.5 meter)

At the idols[s] near Gilgal he himself turned back and said, "I have a secret message for you, O king."

The king said, "Quiet!" And all his attendants left him.

Ehud then approached him while he was sitting alone in the upper room of his summer palace[t] and said, "I have a message from God for you." As the king rose from his seat, Ehud reached with his left hand, drew the sword from his right thigh and plunged it into the king's belly. Even the handle sank in after the blade, which came out his back. Ehud did not pull the sword out, and the fat closed in over it. Then Ehud went out to the porch[u]; he shut the doors of the upper room behind him and locked them.

After he had gone, the servants came and found the doors of the upper room locked. They said, "He must be relieving himself in the inner room of the house." They waited to the point of embarrassment, but when he did not open the doors of the room, they took a key and unlocked them. There they saw their lord fallen to the floor, dead.

DELIVERANCE FROM MOABITES.   While they waited, Ehud got away. He passed by the idols and escaped to Seirah. When he arrived there, he blew a trumpet in the hill country of Ephraim, and the Israelites went down with him from the hills, with him leading them.

Judges 3:26-30 (1304-1224 B.C.?)

"Follow me," he ordered, "for the LORD has given Moab, your enemy, into your hands." So they followed him down and, taking possession of the fords of the Jordan that led to Moab, they allowed no one to cross over. At that time they struck down about ten thousand Moabites, all vigorous and strong; not a man escaped. That day Moab was made subject to Israel, and the land had peace for eighty years.

DELIVERANCE BY SHAMGAR.   After Ehud came Shamgar son of Anath, who struck down six hundred Philistines with an oxgoad. He too saved Israel.

Judges 3:31

Deborah and Barak

*O*ne of the areas which Joshua's forces had never been able to fully take over was the Plain of Esdraelon (Jezreel) in the north-central region between Manasseh, Issachar, Zebulun, and Asher. When local Canaanite forces now unite under Jabin and Sisera, it falls to a courageous woman named Deborah to take the initiative in repelling the Canaanites. Deborah is able to persuade a cautious general named Barak to lead the northern tribes to victory. Another woman (Jael) also shares in the glory of victory when she bravely kills Sisera.

OPPRESSION BY CANAANITES.   After Ehud died, the Israelites once again did evil in the eyes of the LORD. So the LORD sold them into the hands of Jabin, a king of Canaan, who reigned in Hazor. The commander of his army was Sisera, who lived in Harosheth Haggoyim. Because he had nine hundred iron chariots and had cruelly oppressed the Israelites for twenty years, they cried to the LORD for help.

Judges 4:1-3 (1253-1224 B.C.?)

[s]Or *the stone quarries*   [t]The meaning of the Hebrew for this phrase is uncertain.
[u]The meaning of the Hebrew for this word is uncertain.

Judges
4:4-10
Hill country
of Ephraim

DEBORAH PLANS ATTACK. Deborah, a prophetess, the wife of Lappidoth, was leading*v* Israel at that time. She held court under the Palm of Deborah between Ramah and Bethel in the hill country of Ephraim, and the Israelites came to her to have their disputes decided. She sent for Barak son of Abinoam from Kedesh in Naphtali and said to him, "The LORD, the God of Israel, commands you: 'Go, take with you ten thousand men of Naphtali and Zebulun and lead the way to Mount Tabor. I will lure Sisera, the commander of Jabin's army, with his chariots and his troops to the Kishon River and give him into your hands.'"

Barak said to her, "If you go with me, I will go; but if you don't go with me, I won't go."

"Very well," Deborah said, "I will go with you. But because of the way you are going about this,*w* the honor will not be yours, for the LORD will hand Sisera over to a woman." So Deborah went with Barak to Kedesh, where he summoned Zebulun and Naphtali. Ten thousand men followed him, and Deborah also went with him.

Judges
4:12-16

SISERA DEFEATED BY BARAK. When they told Sisera that Barak son of Abinoam had gone up to Mount Tabor, Sisera gathered together his nine hundred iron chariots and all the men with him, from Harosheth Haggoyim to the Kishon River.

Then Deborah said to Barak, "Go! This is the day the LORD has given Sisera into your hands. Has not the LORD gone ahead of you?" So Barak went down Mount Tabor, followed by ten thousand men. At Barak's advance, the LORD routed Sisera and all his chariots and army by the sword, and Sisera abandoned his chariot and fled on foot. But Barak pursued the chariots and army as far as Harosheth Haggoyim. All the troops of Sisera fell by the sword; not a man was left.

Judges
4:17,11,18-22

JAEL KILLS SISERA. Sisera, however, fled on foot to the tent of Jael, the wife of Heber the Kenite, because there were friendly relations between Jabin king of Hazor and the clan of Heber the Kenite.

Now Heber the Kenite had left the other Kenites, the descendants of Hobab, Moses' brother-in-law,*x* and pitched his tent by the great tree in Zaanannim near Kedesh.

Jael went out to meet Sisera and said to him, "Come, my lord, come right in. Don't be afraid." So he entered her tent, and she put a covering over him.

"I'm thirsty," he said. "Please give me some water." She opened a skin of milk, gave him a drink, and covered him up.

"Stand in the doorway of the tent," he told her. "If someone comes by and asks you, 'Is anyone here?' say 'No.'"

But Jael, Heber's wife, picked up a tent peg and a hammer and went quietly to him while he lay fast asleep, exhausted. She drove the peg through his temple into the ground, and he died.

Barak came by in pursuit of Sisera, and Jael went out to meet him. "Come," she said, "I will show you the man you're looking for." So he went in with her, and there lay Sisera with the tent peg through his temple—dead.

---

*v*Traditionally *judging*   *w*Or *But on the expedition you are undertaking*   *x*Or
father-in-law

JABIN DESTROYED.   On that day God subdued Jabin, the Canaanite Judges 4:23,24
king, before the Israelites. And the hand of the Israelites grew stronger and
stronger against Jabin, the Canaanite king, until they destroyed him.

SONG OF DEBORAH AND BARAK.   On that day Deborah and Barak Judges 5:1-3 (1224-1184 B.C.?)
son of Abinoam sang this song:

> "When the princes in Israel take the lead,
>> when the people willingly offer themselves—
>> praise the LORD!

> "Hear this, you kings! Listen, you rulers!
>> I will sing to[y] the LORD, I will sing;
>> I will make music to[z] the LORD, the God of Israel.

> "O LORD, when you went out from Seir, Judges 5:4-9
>> when you marched from the land of Edom,
> the earth shook, the heavens poured,
>> the clouds poured down water.
> The mountains quaked before the LORD, the One of Sinai,
>> before the LORD, the God of Israel.

> "In the days of Shamgar son of Anath,
>> in the days of Jael, the roads were abandoned;
>> travelers took to winding paths.
> Village life[a] in Israel ceased,
>> ceased until I,[b] Deborah, arose,
>> arose a mother in Israel.
> When they chose new gods,
>> war came to the city gates,
> and not a shield or spear was seen
>> among forty thousand in Israel.
> My heart is with Israel's princes,
>> with the willing volunteers among the people.
>> Praise the LORD!

> "You who ride on white donkeys, Judges 5:10-12
>> sitting on your saddle blankets,
>> and you who walk along the road,
> consider the voice of the singers[c] at the watering places.
>> They recite the righteous acts of the LORD,
>> the righteous acts of his warriors[d] in Israel.

> "Then the people of the LORD
>> went down to the city gates.
> 'Wake up, wake up, Deborah!
>> Wake up, wake up, break out in song!
> Arise, O Barak!
>> Take captive your captives, O son of Abinoam.'

> "Then the men who were left Judges 5:13-18
>> came down to the nobles;
> the people of the LORD

[y] Or of   [z] Or / with song I will praise   [a] Or Warriors   [b] Or you   [c] Or archers; the
meaning of the Hebrew for this word is uncertain.   [d] Or villagers

came to me with the mighty.
Some came from Ephraim, whose roots were in Amalek;
    Benjamin was with the people who followed you.
From Makir captains came down,
    from Zebulun those who bear a commander's staff.
The princes of Issachar were with Deborah;
    yes, Issachar was with Barak,
    rushing after him into the valley.
In the districts of Reuben
    there was much searching of heart.
Why did you stay among the campfires[e]
    to hear the whistling for the flocks?
In the districts of Reuben
    there was much searching of heart.
Gilead stayed beyond the Jordan.
    And Dan, why did he linger by the ships?
Asher remained on the coast
    and stayed in his coves.
The people of Zebulun risked their very lives;
    so did Naphtali on the heights of the field.

**Judges
5:19-23**

"Kings came, they fought;
    the kings of Canaan fought
at Taanach by the waters of Megiddo,
    but they carried off no silver, no plunder.
From the heavens the stars fought,
    from their courses they fought against Sisera.
The river Kishon swept them away,
    the age-old river, the river Kishon.
    March on, my soul; be strong!
Then thundered the horses' hoofs—
    galloping, galloping go his mighty steeds.
'Curse Meroz,' said the angel of the LORD.
    'Curse its people bitterly,
because they did not come to help the LORD,
    to help the LORD against the mighty.'

**Judges
5:24-27**

"Most blessed of women be Jael,
    the wife of Heber the Kenite,
    most blessed of tent-dwelling women.
He asked for water, and she gave him milk;
    in a bowl fit for nobles she brought him curdled milk.
Her hand reached for the tent peg,
    her right hand for the workman's hammer.
She struck Sisera, she crushed his head,
    she shattered and pierced his temple.
At her feet he sank,
    he fell; there he lay.
At her feet he sank, he fell;
    where he sank, there he fell—dead.

[e]Or saddlebags

"Through the window peered Sisera's mother;
    behind the lattice she cried out,
'Why is his chariot so long in coming?
    Why is the clatter of his chariots delayed?'
The wisest of her ladies answer her;
    indeed, she keeps saying to herself,
'Are they not finding and dividing the spoils:
    a girl or two for each man,
    colorful garments as plunder for Sisera,
    colorful garments embroidered,
    highly embroidered garments for my neck—
all this as plunder?'

Judges 5:28-30

"So may all your enemies perish, O LORD!
    But may they who love you be like the sun
    when it rises in its strength."

Judges 5:31

Then the land had peace forty years.

Gideon and His Son

As if traditional military warfare were not difficult enough, the people of Ephraim, and the people of Manasseh on both sides of the Jordan, are the object of attack by Midianites from the east, who are the first people known to use camels in battle. With the mobility provided by the camels, the Midianites are able to force many of the Israelites to live in caves, away from their crops (which are being destroyed). God raises up Gideon, an unlikely leader who only reluctantly takes command of the outnumbered forces. Gideon's initial battle with the Midianites is an exciting example of the power of God which is available whenever one is overwhelmed by an enemy. Gideon is well aware that his victories are really God's; therefore he refuses to allow the people to make him their king. Even when he makes a golden ephod, which some of the people later use in an idolatrous manner, Gideon does so to honor the true God of Israel.

One of Gideon's sons, Abimelech, does not have the same strength of character as his father, and actively seeks to be a king. In the process, Abimelech kills his many brothers. Although he manages for a time to reign over some of the people of Manasseh near Shechem, he is neither one of the judges raised up by God nor a true king of Israel. Abimelech is but a sorry example of a son who refuses to follow in the steps of a righteous father.

OPPRESSION BY MIDIANITES.   Again the Israelites did evil in the eyes of the LORD, and for seven years he gave them into the hands of the Midianites. Because the power of Midian was so oppressive, the Israelites prepared shelters for themselves in mountain clefts, caves and strongholds. Whenever the Israelites planted their crops, the Midianites, Amalekites and other eastern peoples invaded the country. They camped on the land and ruined the crops all the way to Gaza and did not spare a living thing for Israel, neither sheep nor cattle nor donkeys. They came up with their livestock and their tents like swarms of locusts. It was impossible to count the men and their camels; they invaded the land to ravage it. Midian

Judges 6:1-6 (1184-1177 B.C.?)

so impoverished the Israelites that they cried out to the LORD for help.

Judges 6:7-10

PROPHET REBUKES ISRAEL.   When the Israelites cried to the LORD because of Midian, he sent them a prophet, who said, "This is what the LORD, the God of Israel, says: I brought you up out of Egypt, out of the land of slavery. I snatched you from the power of Egypt and from the hand of all your oppressors. I drove them from before you and gave you their land. I said to you, 'I am the LORD your God; do not worship the gods of the Amorites, in whose land you live.' But you have not listened to me."

Judges 6:11-18 Ophrah

GOD CALLS GIDEON.   The angel of the LORD came and sat down under the oak in Ophrah that belonged to Joash the Abiezrite, where his son Gideon was threshing wheat in a winepress to keep it from the Midianites. When the angel of the LORD appeared to Gideon, he said, "The LORD is with you, mighty warrior."

"But sir," Gideon replied, "if the LORD is with us, why has all this happened to us? Where are all his wonders that our fathers told us about when they said, 'Did not the LORD bring us up out of Egypt?' But now the LORD has abandoned us and put us into the hand of Midian."

The LORD turned to him and said, "Go in the strength you have and save Israel out of Midian's hand. Am I not sending you?"

"But Lord,*f*" Gideon asked, "how can I save Israel? My clan is the weakest in Manasseh, and I am the least in my family."

The LORD answered, "I will be with you, and you will strike down all the Midianites together."

Gideon replied, "If now I have found favor in your eyes, give me a sign that it is really you talking to me. Please do not go away until I come back and bring my offering and set it before you."

And the LORD said, "I will wait until you return."

Judges 6:19-21

ANGEL GIVES SIGN.   Gideon went in, prepared a young goat, and from an ephah*g* of flour he made bread without yeast. Putting the meat in a basket and its broth in a pot, he brought them out and offered them to him under the oak.

The angel of God said to him, "Take the meat and the unleavened bread, place them on this rock, and pour out the broth." And Gideon did so. With the tip of the staff that was in his hand, the angel of the LORD touched the meat and the unleavened bread. Fire flared from the rock, consuming the meat and the bread. And the angel of the LORD disappeared.

Judges 6:22-24

GIDEON FEARS GOD.   When Gideon realized that it was the angel of the LORD, he exclaimed, "Ah, Sovereign LORD! I have seen the angel of the LORD face to face!"

But the LORD said to him, "Peace! Do not be afraid. You are not going to die."

So Gideon built an altar to the LORD there and called it The LORD is Peace. To this day it stands in Ophrah of the Abiezrites.

Judges 6:25-27

GIDEON DESTROYS ALTAR.   That same night the LORD said to him, "Take the second bull from your father's herd, the one seven years old.*h* Tear down your father's altar to Baal and cut down the Asherah pole*i* beside it. Then build a proper kind of*j* altar to the LORD your God on the

*f*Or *sir*   *g*That is, probably about 3/5 bushel (about 22 liters)   *h*Or *Take a full-grown, mature bull from your father's herd*   *i*That is, a symbol of the goddess Asherah; here and elsewhere in Judges   *j*Or *build with layers of stone an*

top of this height. Using the wood of the Asherah pole that you cut down, offer the second^k bull as a burnt offering."

So Gideon took ten of his servants and did as the LORD told him. But because he was afraid of his family and the men of the town, he did it at night rather than in the daytime.

JOASH SAVES GIDEON. In the morning when the men of the town got up, there was Baal's altar, demolished, with the Asherah pole beside it cut down and the second bull sacrificed on the newly built altar!

Judges
6:28-32

They asked each other, "Who did this?"

When they carefully investigated, they were told, "Gideon son of Joash did it."

The men of the town demanded of Joash, "Bring out your son. He must die, because he has broken down Baal's altar and cut down the Asherah pole beside it."

But Joash replied to the hostile crowd around him, "Are you going to plead Baal's cause? Are you trying to save him? Whoever fights for him shall be put to death by morning! If Baal really is a god, he can defend himself when someone breaks down his altar." So that day they called Gideon "Jerub-Baal,^l" saying, "Let Baal contend with him," because he broke down Baal's altar.

PREPARATION FOR BATTLE. Now all the Midianites, Amalekites and other eastern peoples joined forces and crossed over the Jordan and camped in the Valley of Jezreel. Then the Spirit of the LORD came upon Gideon, and he blew a trumpet, summoning the Abiezrites to follow him. He sent messengers throughout Manasseh, calling them to arms, and also into Asher, Zebulun and Naphtali, so that they too went up to meet them.

Judges
6:33-35
Valley of
Jezreel

TESTS WITH FLEECE. Gideon said to God, "If you will save Israel by my hand as you have promised—look, I will place a wool fleece on the threshing floor. If there is dew only on the fleece and all the ground is dry, then I will know that you will save Israel by my hand, as you said." And that is what happened. Gideon rose early the next day; he squeezed the fleece and wrung out the dew—a bowlful of water.

Judges
6:36-40

Then Gideon said to God, "Do not be angry with me. Let me make just one more request. Allow me one more test with the fleece. This time make the fleece dry and the ground covered with dew." That night God did so. Only the fleece was dry; all the ground was covered with dew.

FEARFUL LET GO. Early in the morning, Jerub-Baal (that is, Gideon) and all his men camped at the spring of Harod. The camp of Midian was north of them in the valley near the hill of Moreh. The LORD said to Gideon, "You have too many men for me to deliver Midian into their hands. In order that Israel may not boast against me that her own strength has saved her, announce now to the people, 'Anyone who trembles with fear may turn back and leave Mount Gilead.'" So twenty-two thousand men left, while ten thousand remained.

Judges
7:1-3

THREE HUNDRED CHOSEN. But the LORD said to Gideon, "There are still too many men. Take them down to the water, and I will sift them for you there. If I say, 'This one shall go with you,' he shall go; but if I say, 'This one shall not go with you,' he shall not go."

Judges
7:4-8

^kOr *full-grown*   ^lJerub-Baal means *let Baal contend.*

So Gideon took the men down to the water. There the LORD told him, "Separate those who lap the water with their tongues like a dog from those who kneel down to drink." Three hundred men lapped with their hands to their mouths. All the rest got down on their knees to drink.

The LORD said to Gideon, "With the three hundred men that lapped I will save you and give the Midianites into your hands. Let all the other men go, each to his own place." So Gideon sent the rest of the Israelites to their tents but kept the three hundred, who took over the provisions and trumpets of the others.

Now the camp of Midian lay below him in the valley.

Judges 7:9-14

GIDEON HEARS PROPHECY.   During that night the LORD said to Gideon, "Get up, go down against the camp, because I am going to give it into your hands. If you are afraid to attack, go down to the camp with your servant Purah and listen to what they are saying. Afterward, you will be encouraged to attack the camp." So he and Purah his servant went down to the outposts of the camp. The Midianites, the Amalekites and all the other eastern peoples had settled in the valley, thick as locusts. Their camels could no more be counted than the sand on the seashore.

Gideon arrived just as a man was telling a friend his dream. "I had a dream," he was saying. "A round loaf of barley bread came tumbling into the Midianite camp. It struck the tent with such force that the tent overturned and collapsed."

His friend responded, "This can be nothing other than the sword of Gideon son of Joash, the Israelite. God has given the Midianites and the whole camp into his hands."

Judges 7:15-18

PLAN FOR SURPRISE.   When Gideon heard the dream and its interpretation, he worshiped God. He returned to the camp of Israel and called out, "Get up! The LORD has given the Midianite camp into your hands." Dividing the three hundred men into three companies, he placed trumpets and empty jars in the hands of all of them, with torches inside.

"Watch me," he told them. "Follow my lead. When I get to the edge of the camp, do exactly as I do. When I and all who are with me blow our trumpets, then from all around the camp blow yours and shout, 'For the LORD and for Gideon.'"

Judges 7:19-23

MIDIANITES FLEE.   Gideon and the hundred men with him reached the edge of the camp at the beginning of the middle watch, just after they had changed the guard. They blew their trumpets and broke the jars that were in their hands. The three companies blew the trumpets and smashed the jars. Grasping the torches in their left hands and holding in their right hands the trumpets they were to blow, they shouted, "A sword for the LORD and for Gideon!" While each man held his position around the camp, all the Midianites ran, crying out as they fled.

When the three hundred trumpets sounded, the LORD caused the men throughout the camp to turn on each other with their swords. The army fled to Beth Shittah toward Zererah as far as the border of Abel Meholah near Tabbath. Israelites from Naphtali, Asher and all Manasseh were called out, and they pursued the Midianites.

Judges 7:24,25

TWO PRINCES KILLED.   Gideon sent messengers throughout the hill country of Ephraim, saying, "Come down against the Midianites and seize the waters of the Jordan ahead of them as far as Beth Barah."

So all the men of Ephraim were called out and they took the waters of the Jordan as far as Beth Barah. They also captured two of the Midianite leaders, Oreb and Zeeb. They killed Oreb at the rock of Oreb, and Zeeb at the winepress of Zeeb. They pursued the Midianites and brought the heads of Oreb and Zeeb to Gideon, who was by the Jordan.

GIDEON CALMS DISPUTE.   Now the Ephraimites asked Gideon, "Why have you treated us like this? Why didn't you call us when you went to fight Midian?" And they criticized him sharply.

> Judges
> 8:1-3

But he answered them, "What have I accomplished compared to you? Aren't the gleanings of Ephraim's grapes better than the full grape harvest of Abiezer? God gave Oreb and Zeeb, the Midianite leaders, into your hands. What was I able to do compared to you?" At this, their resentment against him subsided.

CITIES REFUSE AID.   Gideon and his three hundred men, exhausted yet keeping up the pursuit, came to the Jordan and crossed it. He said to the men of Succoth, "Give my troops some bread; they are worn out, and I am still pursuing Zebah and Zalmunna, the kings of Midian."

> Judges
> 8:4-9
> Succoth

But the officials of Succoth said, "Do you already have the hands of Zebah and Zalmunna in your possession? Why should we give bread to your troops?"

Then Gideon replied, "Just for that, when the LORD has given Zebah and Zalmunna into my hand, I will tear your flesh with desert thorns and briers."

From there he went up to Peniel[m] and made the same request of them, but they answered as the men of Succoth had. So he said to the men of Peniel, "When I return in triumph, I will tear down this tower."

MIDIANITE KINGS TAKEN.   Now Zebah and Zalmunna were in Karkor with a force of about fifteen thousand men, all that were left of the armies of the eastern peoples; a hundred and twenty thousand swordsmen had fallen. Gideon went up by the route of the nomads east of Nobah and Jogbehah and fell upon the unsuspecting army. Zebah and Zalmunna, the two kings of Midian, fled, but he pursued them and captured them, routing their entire army.

> Judges
> 8:10-12

CITIES PUNISHED.   Gideon son of Joash then returned from the battle by the Pass of Heres. He caught a young man of Succoth and questioned him, and the young man wrote down for him the names of the seventy-seven officials of Succoth, the elders of the town. Then Gideon came and said to the men of Succoth, "Here are Zebah and Zalmunna, about whom you taunted me by saying, 'Do you already have the hands of Zebah and Zalmunna in your possession? Why should we give bread to your exhausted men?'" He took the elders of the town and taught the men of Succoth a lesson by punishing them with desert thorns and briers. He also pulled down the tower of Peniel and killed the men of the town.

> Judges
> 8:13-17

MIDIANITE KINGS KILLED.   Then he asked Zebah and Zalmunna, "What kind of men did you kill at Tabor?"

> Judges
> 8:18-21

"Men like you," they answered, "each one with the bearing of a prince."

Gideon replied, "Those were my brothers, the sons of my own mother.

---

[m]Hebrew *Penuel*, a variant of *Peniel*; also in verses 9 and 17

As surely as the LORD lives, if you had spared their lives, I would not kill you." Turning to Jether, his oldest son, he said, "Kill them!" But Jether did not draw his sword, because he was only a boy and was afraid.

Zebah and Zalmunna said, "Come, do it yourself. 'As is the man, so is his strength.'" So Gideon stepped forward and killed them, and took the ornaments off their camels' necks.

Judges
8:22,23

GIDEON REFUSES KINGSHIP. The Israelites said to Gideon, "Rule over us—you, your son and your grandson—because you have saved us out of the hand of Midian."

But Gideon told them, "I will not rule over you, nor will my son rule over you. The LORD will rule over you."

Judges
8:24-27

GIDEON MAKES EPHOD. And he said, "I do have one request, that each of you give me an earring from your share of the plunder." (It was the custom of the Ishmaelites to wear gold earrings.)

They answered, "We'll be glad to give them." So they spread out a garment, and each man threw a ring from his plunder onto it. The weight of the gold rings he asked for came to seventeen hundred shekels,[n] not counting the ornaments, the pendants and the purple garments worn by the kings of Midian or the chains that were on their camels' necks. Gideon made the gold into an ephod, which he placed in Ophrah, his town. All Israel prostituted themselves by worshiping it there, and it became a snare to Gideon and his family.

Judges
8:28
(1177-1137
B.C.?)

ISRAEL AT PEACE. Thus Midian was subdued before the Israelites and did not raise its head again. During Gideon's lifetime, the land enjoyed peace forty years.

Judges
8:29-32

GIDEON DIES. Jerub-Baal son of Joash went back home to live. He had seventy sons of his own, for he had many wives. His concubine, who lived in Shechem, also bore him a son, whom he named Abimelech. Gideon son of Joash died at a good old age and was buried in the tomb of his father Joash in Ophrah of the Abiezrites.

Judges
8:33-35

ISRAEL SINS AGAIN. No sooner had Gideon died than the Israelites again prostituted themselves to the Baals. They set up Baal-Berith as their god and did not remember the LORD their God, who had rescued them from the hands of all their enemies on every side. They also failed to show kindness to the family of Jerub-Baal (that is, Gideon) for all the good things he had done for them.

Judges
9:1-6
Shechem

ABIMELECH KILLS BROTHERS. Abimelech son of Jerub-Baal went to his mother's brothers in Shechem and said to them and to all his mother's clan, "Ask all the citizens of Shechem, 'Which is better for you: to have all seventy of Jerub-Baal's sons rule over you, or just one man?' Remember, I am your flesh and blood."

When the brothers repeated all this to the citizens of Shechem, they were inclined to follow Abimelech, for they said, "He is our brother." They gave him seventy shekels[o] of silver from the temple of Baal-Berith, and Abimelech used it to hire reckless adventurers, who became his followers. He went to his father's home in Ophrah and on one stone murdered his seventy brothers, the sons of Jerub-Baal. But Jotham, the youngest son of

[n]That is, about 43 pounds (about 19.5 kilograms)   [o]That is, about 1 3/4 pounds (about 0.8 kilogram)

Jerub-Baal, escaped by hiding. Then all the citizens of Shechem and Beth Millo gathered beside the great tree at the pillar in Shechem to crown Abimelech king.

JOTHAM'S PARABLE.   When Jotham was told about this, he climbed up on the top of Mount Gerizim and shouted to them, "Listen to me, citizens of Shechem, so that God may listen to you. One day the trees went out to anoint a king for themselves. They said to the olive tree, 'Be our king.'

"But the olive tree answered, 'Should I give up my oil, by which both gods and men are honored, to hold sway over the trees?'

"Next, the trees said to the fig tree, 'Come and be our king.'

"But the fig tree replied, 'Should I give up my fruit, so good and sweet, to hold sway over the trees?'

"Then the trees said to the vine, 'Come and be our king.'

"But the vine answered, 'Should I give up my wine, which cheers both gods and men, to hold sway over the trees?'

"Finally all the trees said to the thornbush, 'Come and be our king.'

"The thornbush said to the trees, 'If you really want to anoint me king over you, come and take refuge in my shade; but if not, then let fire come out of the thornbush and consume the cedars of Lebanon!'

Judges 9:7-15

PARABLE EXPLAINED.   "Now if you have acted honorably and in good faith when you made Abimelech king, and if you have been fair to Jerub-Baal and his family, and if you have treated him as he deserves—and to think that my father fought for you, risked his life to rescue you from the hand of Midian (but today you have revolted against my father's family, murdered his seventy sons on a single stone, and made Abimelech, the son of his slave girl, king over the citizens of Shechem because he is your brother)—if then you have acted honorably and in good faith toward Jerub-Baal and his family today, may Abimelech be your joy, and may you be his, too! But if you have not, let fire come out from Abimelech and consume you, citizens of Shechem and Beth Millo, and let fire come out from you, citizens of Shechem and Beth Millo, and consume Abimelech!"

Judges 9:16-20

JOTHAM FLEES.   Then Jotham fled, escaping to Beer, and he lived there because he was afraid of his brother Abimelech.

Judges 9:21

ABIMELECH LOSES SUPPORT.   After Abimelech had governed Israel three years, God sent an evil spirit between Abimelech and the citizens of Shechem, who acted treacherously against Abimelech. God did this in order that the crime against Jerub-Baal's seventy sons, the shedding of their blood, might be avenged on their brother Abimelech and on the citizens of Shechem, who had helped him murder his brothers. In opposition to him these citizens of Shechem set men on the hilltops to ambush and rob everyone who passed by, and this was reported to Abimelech.

Judges 9:22-25

GAAL TALKS REVOLT.   Now Gaal son of Ebed moved with his brothers into Shechem, and its citizens put their confidence in him. After they had gone out into the fields and gathered the grapes and trodden them, they held a festival in the temple of their god. While they were eating and drinking, they cursed Abimelech. Then Gaal son of Ebed said, "Who is Abimelech, and who is Shechem, that we should be subject to him? Isn't he Jerub-Baal's son, and isn't Zebul his deputy? Serve the men of Hamor, Shechem's father! Why should we serve Abimelech? If only this people

Judges 9:26-29

were under my command! Then I would get rid of him. I would say to Abimelech, 'Call out your whole army!' "[p]

Judges 9:30-33

ZEBUL INFORMS ABIMELECH. When Zebul the governor of the city heard what Gaal son of Ebed said, he was very angry. Under cover he sent messengers to Abimelech, saying, "Gaal son of Ebed and his brothers have come to Shechem and are stirring up the city against you. Now then, during the night you and your men should come and lie in wait in the fields. In the morning at sunrise, advance against the city. When Gaal and his men come out against you, do whatever your hand finds to do."

Judges 9:34-41

GAAL DRIVEN OUT. So Abimelech and all his troops set out by night and took up concealed positions near Shechem in four companies. Now Gaal son of Ebed had gone out and was standing at the entrance to the city gate just as Abimelech and his soldiers came out from their hiding place.

When Gaal saw them, he said to Zebul, "Look, people are coming down from the tops of the mountains!"

Zebul replied, "You mistake the shadows of the mountains for men."

But Gaal spoke up again: "Look, people are coming down from the center of the land, and a company is coming from the direction of the soothsayers' tree."

Then Zebul said to him, "Where is your big talk now, you who said, 'Who is Abimelech that we should be subject to him?' Aren't these the men you ridiculed? Go out and fight them!"

So Gaal led out[q] the citizens of Shechem and fought Abimelech. Abimelech chased him, and many fell wounded in the flight—all the way to the entrance to the gate. Abimelech stayed in Arumah, and Zebul drove Gaal and his brothers out of Shechem.

Judges 9:42-45

SHECHEM RAZED. The next day the people of Shechem went out to the fields, and this was reported to Abimelech. So he took his men, divided them into three companies and set an ambush in the fields. When he saw the people coming out of the city, he rose to attack them. Abimelech and the companies with him rushed forward to a position at the entrance to the city gate. Then two companies rushed upon those in the fields and struck them down. All that day Abimelech pressed his attack against the city until he had captured it and killed its people. Then he destroyed the city and scattered salt over it.

Judges 9:46-49

TOWER BURNED. On hearing this, the citizens in the tower of Shechem went into the stronghold of the temple of El-Berith. When Abimelech heard that they had assembled there, he and all his men went up Mount Zalmon. He took an ax and cut off some branches, which he lifted to his shoulders. He ordered the men with him, "Quick! Do what you have seen me do!" So all the men cut branches and followed Abimelech. They piled them against the stronghold and set it on fire over the people inside. So all the people in the tower of Shechem, about a thousand men and women, also died.

Judges 9:50-54

ABIMELECH KILLED. Next Abimelech went to Thebez and besieged it and captured it. Inside the city, however, was a strong tower, to which

---

[p]Septuagint; Hebrew *him." Then he said to Abimelech, "Call out your whole army!"*   [q]Or *Gaal went out in the sight of*

all the men and women—all the people of the city—fled. They locked themselves in and climbed up on the tower roof. Abimelech went to the tower and stormed it. But as he approached the entrance to the tower to set it on fire, a woman dropped an upper millstone on his head and cracked his skull.

Hurriedly he called to his armor-bearer, "Draw your sword and kill me, so that they can't say, 'A woman killed him.'" So his servant ran him through, and he died.

WICKED PUNISHED.   When the Israelites saw that Abimelech was dead, they went home.

Judges 9:55-57

Thus God repaid the wickedness that Abimelech had done to his father by murdering his seventy brothers. God also made the men of Shechem pay for all their wickedness. The curse of Jotham son of Jerub-Baal came on them.

Jephthah and Five Others _____

*J*n contrast to Abimelech, who despised his righteous family background, Jephthah overcomes an embarrassing beginning to become one of the next six "judges" in Israel. Leader of a band of ruffians, Jephthah is called upon to liberate Israel from various enemies, principally the Ammonites, who have oppressed the area east of the Jordan River near Gilead, and parts of Canaan belonging to Ephraim, Benjamin, and Judah. Jephthah's greatest personal tragedy is the sacrificing of his own daughter pursuant to a rash oath.

During the period of these six leaders, it is apparent that the fabric of Israel's unity has worn thin. Intertribal jealousy finally leads to war between the Ephraimites and the men of Manasseh in Gilead (with 42,000 men of Ephraim killed). It is also apparent that, among the various tribes, different dialects are beginning to develop by this time, to the point of becoming a strategic factor in the civil conflict.

The record of Jephthah's leadership is couched between brief accounts of five other leaders, beginning with Tola.

LEADERSHIP OF TOLA.   After the time of Abimelech a man of Issachar, Tola son of Puah, the son of Dodo, rose to save Israel. He lived in Shamir, in the hill country of Ephraim. He led[r] Israel twenty-three years; then he died, and was buried in Shamir.

Judges 10:1,2 (1134-1111 B.C.?) Shamir

LEADERSHIP OF JAIR.   He was followed by Jair of Gilead, who led Israel twenty-two years. He had thirty sons, who rode thirty donkeys. They controlled thirty towns in Gilead, which to this day are called Havvoth Jair.[s] When Jair died, he was buried in Kamon.

Judges 10:3-5 (1111-1089 B.C.?) Gilead

OPPRESSION BY AMMONITES.   Again the Israelites did evil in the eyes of the LORD. They served the Baals and the Ashtoreths, and the gods of Aram, the gods of Sidon, the gods of Moab, the gods of the Ammonites and the gods of the Philistines. And because the Israelites forsook the LORD and no longer served him, he became angry with them. He sold them into the hands of the Philistines and the Ammonites, who that year shattered

Judges 10:6-9

[r] Traditionally *judged*; also in verse 3   [s] Or *called the settlements of Jair*

and crushed them. For eighteen years they oppressed all the Israelites on the east side of the Jordan in Gilead, the land of the Amorites. The Ammonites also crossed the Jordan to fight against Judah, Benjamin and the house of Ephraim; and Israel was in great distress.

Judges 10:10-16 PEOPLE CRY IN VAIN.   Then the Israelites cried out to the LORD, "We have sinned against you, forsaking our God and serving the Baals."

The LORD replied, "When the Egyptians, the Amorites, the Ammonites, the Philistines, the Sidonians, the Amalekites and the Maonites[t] oppressed you and you cried to me for help, did I not save you from their hands? But you have forsaken me and served other gods, so I will no longer save you. Go and cry out to the gods you have chosen. Let them save you when you are in trouble!"

But the Israelites said to the LORD, "We have sinned. Do with us whatever you think best, but please rescue us now." Then they got rid of the foreign gods among them and served the LORD. And he could bear Israel's misery no longer.

Judges 10:17,18 LEADER SOUGHT.   When the Ammonites were called to arms and camped in Gilead, the Israelites assembled and camped at Mizpah. The leaders of the people of Gilead said to each other, "Whoever will launch the attack against the Ammonites will be the head of all those living in Gilead."

Judges 11:1-3 JEPHTHAH'S BACKGROUND.   Jephthah the Gileadite was a mighty warrior. His father was Gilead; his mother was a prostitute. Gilead's wife also bore him sons, and when they were grown up, they drove Jephthah away. "You are not going to get any inheritance in our family," they said, "because you are the son of another woman." So Jephthah fled from his brothers and settled in the land of Tob, where a group of adventurers gathered around him and followed him.

Judges 11:4-11 (Ca. 1089 B.C.?) JEPHTHAH CHOSEN. Some time later, when the Ammonites made war on Israel, the elders of Gilead went to get Jephthah from the land of Tob. "Come," they said, "be our commander, so we can fight the Ammonites."

Jephthah said to them, "Didn't you hate me and drive me from my father's house? Why do you come to me now, when you're in trouble?"

The elders of Gilead said to him, "Nevertheless, we are turning to you now; come with us to fight the Ammonites, and you will be our head over all who live in Gilead."

Jephthah answered, "Suppose you take me back to fight the Ammonites and the LORD gives them to me—will I really be your head?"

The elders of Gilead replied, "The LORD is our witness; we will certainly do as you say." So Jephthah went with the elders of Gilead, and the people made him head and commander over them. And he repeated all his words before the LORD in Mizpah.

Judges 11:12,13 AMMONITES WANT EAST CANAAN.   Then Jephthah sent messengers to the Ammonite king with the question: "What do you have against us that you have attacked our country?"

The king of the Ammonites answered Jephthah's messengers, "When Israel came up out of Egypt, they took away my land from the Arnon to the Jabbok, all the way to the Jordan. Now give it back peaceably."

---

[t]Hebrew; some Septuagint manuscripts *Midianites*

JEPHTHAH'S RESPONSE.   Jephthah sent back messengers to the Am-   Judges
11:14-28
monite king, saying:

"This is what Jephthah says: Israel did not take the land of Moab or the
land of the Ammonites. But when they came up out of Egypt, Israel went
through the desert to the Red Sea[u] and on to Kadesh. Then Israel sent messengers to the king of Edom, saying, 'Give us permission to go through
your country,' but the king of Edom would not listen. They sent also to the
king of Moab, and he refused. So Israel stayed at Kadesh.

"Next they traveled through the desert, skirted the lands of Edom and
Moab, passed along the eastern side of the country of Moab, and camped
on the other side of the Arnon. They did not enter the territory of Moab,
for the Arnon was its border.

"Then Israel sent messengers to Sihon king of the Amorites, who ruled
in Heshbon, and said to him, 'Let us pass through your country to our own
place.' Sihon, however, did not trust Israel[v] to pass through his territory. He
mustered all his men and encamped at Jahaz and fought with Israel.

"Then the LORD, the God of Israel, gave Sihon and all his men into
Israel's hands, and they defeated them. Israel took over all the land of the
Amorites who lived in that country, capturing all of it from the Arnon to
the Jabbok and from the desert to the Jordan.

"Now since the LORD, the God of Israel, has driven the Amorites out
before his people Israel, what right have you to take it over? Will you not
take what your god Chemosh gives you? Likewise, whatever the LORD our
God has given us, we will possess. Are you better than Balak son of
Zippor, king of Moab? Did he ever quarrel with Israel or fight with them?
For three hundred years Israel occupied Heshbon, Aroer, the surrounding
settlements and all the towns along the Arnon. Why didn't you retake
them during that time? I have not wronged you, but you are doing me
wrong by waging war against me. Let the LORD, the Judge,[w] decide the
dispute this day between the Israelites and the Ammonites."

The king of Ammon, however, paid no attention to the message Jephthah
sent him.

JEPHTHAH MAKES VOW.   Then the Spirit of the LORD came upon   Judges
11:29-31
Jephthah. He crossed Gilead and Manasseh, passed through Mizpah of
Gilead, and from there he advanced against the Ammonites. And Jephthah
made a vow to the LORD: "If you give the Ammonites into my hands,
whatever comes out of the door of my house to meet me when I return in
triumph from the Ammonites will be the LORD's, and I will sacrifice it as a
burnt offering."

AMMONITES DESTROYED.   Then Jephthah went over to fight the Am-   Judges
11:32,33
monites, and the LORD gave them into his hands. He devastated twenty
towns from Aroer to the vicinity of Minnith, as far as Abel Keramim. Thus
Israel subdued Ammon.

JEPHTHAH SACRIFICES DAUGHTER.   When Jephthah returned to his   Judges
11:34-40
Mizpah
home in Mizpah, who should come out to meet him but his daughter,
dancing to the sound of tambourines! She was an only child. Except for
her he had neither son nor daughter. When he saw her, he tore his clothes

<hr>

[u]Hebrew *Yam Suph*; that is, Sea of Reeds   [v]Or *however, would not make an agreement for
Israel*   [w]Or *Ruler*

and cried, "Oh! My daughter! You have made me miserable and wretched, because I have made a vow to the LORD that I cannot break."

"My father," she replied, "you have given your word to the LORD. Do to me just as you promised, now that the LORD has avenged you of your enemies, the Ammonites. But grant me this one request," she said. "Give me two months to roam the hills and weep with my friends, because I will never marry."

"You may go," he said. And he let her go for two months. She and the girls went into the hills and wept because she would never marry. After the two months, she returned to her father and he did to her as he had vowed. And she was a virgin.

From this comes the Israelite custom that each year the young women of Israel go out for four days to commemorate the daughter of Jephthah the Gileadite.

Judges 12:1-3   **EPHRAIM UPSET AGAIN.** The men of Ephraim called out their forces, crossed over to Zaphon and said to Jephthah, "Why did you go to fight the Ammonites without calling us to go with you? We're going to burn down your house over your head."

Jephthah answered, "I and my people were engaged in a great struggle with the Ammonites, and although I called, you didn't save me out of their hands. When I saw that you wouldn't help, I took my life in my hands and crossed over to fight the Ammonites, and the LORD gave me the victory over them. Now why have you come up today to fight me?"

Judges 12:4-6   **SHIBBOLETH OR SIBBOLETH.** Jephthah then called together the men of Gilead and fought against Ephraim. The Gileadites struck them down because the Ephraimites had said, "You Gileadites are renegades from Ephraim and Manasseh." The Gileadites captured the fords of the Jordan leading to Ephraim, and whenever a survivor of Ephraim said, "Let me cross over," the men of Gilead asked him, "Are you an Ephraimite?" If he replied, "No," they said, "All right, say 'Shibboleth.'" If he said, "Sibboleth," because he could not pronounce the word correctly, they seized him and killed him at the fords of the Jordan. Forty-two thousand Ephraimites were killed at that time.

Judges 12:7 (Ca. 1083 B.C.?)   **JEPHTHAH DIES.** Jephthah led[x] Israel six years. Then Jephthah the Gileadite died, and was buried in a town in Gilead.

Judges 12:8-10 (1083-1076 B.C.?)   **LEADERSHIP OF IBZAN.** After him, Ibzan of Bethlehem led Israel. He had thirty sons and thirty daughters. He gave his daughters away in marriage to those outside his clan, and for his sons he brought in thirty young women as wives from outside his clan. Ibzan led Israel seven years. Then Ibzan died, and was buried in Bethlehem.

Judges 12:11,12 (1076-1066 B.C.?)   **LEADERSHIP OF ELON.** After him, Elon the Zebulunite led Israel ten years. Then Elon died, and was buried in Aijalon in the land of Zebulun.

Judges 12:13-15 (1066-1058 B.C.?)   **LEADERSHIP OF ABDON.** After him, Abdon son of Hillel, from Pirathon, led Israel. He had forty sons and thirty grandsons, who rode on seventy donkeys. He led Israel eight years. Then Abdon son of Hillel died, and was buried at Pirathon in Ephraim, in the hill country of the Amalekites.

[x]Traditionally *judged*; also in verses 8-14

The Story of Ruth

*I*n the midst of all the wars, violence, and bloodshed of these times, life proceeds rather normally for many Israelites. Like all people, the Israelites are primarily concerned with family relations and the eking out of a daily living. In sharp contrast to the national breach of faith in God on the part of the Israelites comes the account of personal faithfulness on the part of a woman toward her widowed mother-in-law. Of great interest is the fact that the woman is a Gentile—in fact one of the hated Moabites. When her own husband dies, Ruth chooses to be with her mother-in-law, Naomi, and with the Israelites and their God. Her choice brings her the blessings of both a new husband and a son, through whom Ruth becomes the great-grandmother of David, who will be king of all Israel.

This beautiful love story shows the law of levirate marriage in a far better light than the similar story of Judah and Tamar centuries before, and foreshadows the grace which one day will extend to Jews and Gentiles alike through still another Descendant of this godly Gentile woman named Ruth.

NAOMI LOSES FAMILY.   In the days when the judges ruled,[y] there was a famine in the land, and a man from Bethlehem in Judah, together with his wife and two sons, went to live for a while in the country of Moab. The man's name was Elimelech, his wife's name Naomi, and the names of his two sons were Mahlon and Kilion. They were Ephrathites from Bethlehem, Judah. And they went to Moab and lived there.

Now Elimelech, Naomi's husband, died, and she was left with her two sons. They married Moabite women, one named Orpah and the other Ruth. After they had lived there about ten years, both Mahlon and Kilion also died, and Naomi was left without her two sons and her husband.

Ruth 1:1-5
Moab
(Ca. 1100
B.C.)

FAREWELL TO DAUGHTERS-IN-LAW.   When she heard in Moab that the LORD had come to the aid of his people by providing food for them, Naomi and her daughters-in-law prepared to return home from there. With her two daughters-in-law she left the place where she had been living and set out on the road that would take them back to the land of Judah.

Ruth
1:6-14

Then Naomi said to her two daughters-in-law, "Go back, each of you, to your mother's home. May the LORD show kindness to you, as you have shown to your dead and to me. May the LORD grant that each of you will find rest in the home of another husband."

Then she kissed them and they wept aloud and said to her, "We will go back with you to your people."

But Naomi said, "Return home, my daughters. Why would you come with me? Am I going to have any more sons, who could become your husbands? Return home, my daughters; I am too old to have another husband. Even if I thought there was still hope for me—even if I had a husband tonight and then gave birth to sons—would you wait until they grew up? Would you remain unmarried for them? No, my daughters. It is more bitter for me than for you, because the LORD's hand has gone out against me!"

[y] Traditionally *judged*

At this they wept again. Then Orpah kissed her mother-in-law good-by, but Ruth clung to her.

Ruth 1:15-18

RUTH EXPRESSES BOND. "Look," said Naomi, "your sister-in-law is going back to her people and her gods. Go back with her."

But Ruth replied, "Don't urge me to leave you or to turn back from you. Where you go I will go, and where you stay I will stay. Your people will be my people and your God my God. Where you die I will die, and there I will be buried. May the LORD deal with me, be it ever so severely, if anything but death separates you and me." When Naomi realized that Ruth was determined to go with her, she stopped urging her.

Ruth 1:19-22 Bethlehem

RETURN TO BETHLEHEM. So the two women went on until they came to Bethlehem. When they arrived in Bethlehem, the whole town was stirred because of them, and the women exclaimed, "Can this be Naomi?"

"Don't call me Naomi,^{z}" she told them. "Call me Mara,^{a} because the Almighty^b has made my life very bitter. I went away full, but the LORD has brought me back empty. Why call me Naomi? The LORD has afflicted^c me; the Almighty has brought misfortune upon me."

So Naomi returned from Moab accompanied by Ruth the Moabitess, her daughter-in-law, arriving in Bethlehem as the barley harvest was beginning.

Ruth 2:1-7

BOAZ SEES RUTH. Now Naomi had a relative on her husband's side, from the clan of Elimelech, a man of standing, whose name was Boaz.

And Ruth the Moabitess said to Naomi, "Let me go to the fields and pick up the leftover grain behind anyone in whose eyes I find favor."

Naomi said to her, "Go ahead, my daughter." So she went out and began to glean in the fields behind the harvesters. As it turned out, she found herself working in a field belonging to Boaz, who was from the clan of Elimelech.

Just then Boaz arrived from Bethlehem and greeted the harvesters, "The LORD be with you!"

"The LORD bless you!" they called back.

Boaz asked the foreman of his harvesters, "Whose young woman is that?"

The foreman replied, "She is the Moabitess who came back from Moab with Naomi. She said, 'Please let me glean and gather among the sheaves behind the harvesters.' She went into the field and has worked steadily from morning till now, except for a short rest in the shelter."

Ruth 2:8-16

BOAZ GRACIOUS TO RUTH. So Boaz said to Ruth, "My daughter, listen to me. Don't go and glean in another field and don't go away from here. Stay here with my servant girls. Watch the field where the men are harvesting, and follow along after the girls. I have told the men not to touch you. And whenever you are thirsty, go and get a drink from the water jars the men have filled."

At this, she bowed down with her face to the ground. She exclaimed, "Why have I found such favor in your eyes that you notice me—a foreigner?"

Boaz replied, "I've been told all about what you have done for your mother-in-law since the death of your husband—how you left your father

---

^{z}*Naomi* means *pleasant.* ^{a}*Mara* means *bitter.* ^{b}Hebrew *Shaddai*; also in verse 21
^{c}Or *has testified against*

and mother and your homeland and came to live with a people you did not know before. May the LORD repay you for what you have done. May you be richly rewarded by the LORD, the God of Israel, under whose wings you have come to take refuge."

"May I continue to find favor in your eyes, my lord," she said. "You have given me comfort and have spoken kindly to your servant—though I do not have the standing of one of your servant girls."

At mealtime Boaz said to her, "Come over here. Have some bread and dip it in the wine vinegar."

When she sat down with the harvesters, he offered her some roasted grain. She ate all she wanted and had some left over. As she got up to glean, Boaz gave orders to his men, "Even if she gathers among the sheaves, don't embarrass her. Rather, pull out some stalks for her from the bundles and leave them for her to pick up, and don't rebuke her."

RUTH TELLS NAOMI. So Ruth gleaned in the field until evening. Then she threshed the barley she had gathered, and it amounted to about an ephah.[d] She carried it back to town, and her mother-in-law saw how much she had gathered. Ruth also brought out and gave her what she had left over after she had eaten enough.

Her mother-in-law asked her, "Where did you glean today? Where did you work? Blessed be the man who took notice of you!"

Then Ruth told her mother-in-law about the one at whose place she had been working. "The name of the man I worked with today is Boaz," she said.

"The LORD bless him!" Naomi said to her daughter-in-law. "He has not stopped showing his kindness to the living and the dead." She added, "That man is our close relative; he is one of our kinsman-redeemers."

Then Ruth the Moabitess said, "He even said to me, 'Stay with my workers until they finish harvesting all my grain.'"

Naomi said to Ruth her daughter-in-law, "It will be good for you, my daughter, to go with his girls, because in someone else's field you might be harmed."

So Ruth stayed close to the servant girls of Boaz to glean until the barley and wheat harvests were finished. And she lived with her mother-in-law.

Ruth 2:17-23

NAOMI PLANS ENCOUNTER. One day Naomi her mother-in-law said to her, "My daughter, should I not try to find a home[e] for you, where you will be well provided for? Is not Boaz, with whose servant girls you have been, a kinsman of ours? Tonight he will be winnowing barley on the threshing floor. Wash and perfume yourself, and put on your best clothes. Then go down to the threshing floor, but don't let him know you are there until he has finished eating and drinking. When he lies down, note the place where he is lying. Then go and uncover his feet and lie down. He will tell you what to do."

"I will do whatever you say," Ruth answered.

Ruth 3:1-5

BOAZ AGREES TO DUTY. So she went down to the threshing floor and did everything her mother-in-law told her to do.

When Boaz had finished eating and drinking and was in good spirits, he went over to lie down at the far end of the grain pile. Ruth approached quietly, uncovered his feet and lay down. In the middle of the night

Ruth 3:6-13

---

[d]That is, probably about 3/5 bushel (about 22 liters)   [e]Hebrew *find rest* (see Ruth 1:9)

something startled the man, and he turned and discovered a woman lying at his feet.

"Who are you?" he asked.

"I am your servant Ruth," she said. "Spread the corner of your garment over me, since you are a kinsman-redeemer."

"The LORD bless you, my daughter," he replied. "This kindness is greater than that which you showed earlier: You have not run after the younger men, whether rich or poor. And now, my daughter, don't be afraid. I will do for you all you ask. All my fellow townsmen know that you are a woman of noble character. Although it is true that I am near of kin, there is a kinsman-redeemer nearer than I. Stay here for the night, and in the morning if he wants to redeem, good; let him redeem. But if he is not willing, as surely as the LORD lives I will do it. Lie here until morning."

Ruth 3:14-18

NAOMI AND RUTH WAIT.   So she lay at his feet until morning, but got up before anyone could be recognized; and he said, "Don't let it be known that a woman came to the threshing floor."

He also said, "Bring me the shawl you are wearing and hold it out." When she did so, he poured into it six measures of barley and put it on her. Then he*f* went back to town.

When Ruth came to her mother-in-law, Naomi asked, "How did it go, my daughter?"

Then she told her everything Boaz had done for her and added, "He gave me these six measures of barley, saying, 'Don't go back to your mother-in-law empty-handed.'"

Then Naomi said, "Wait, my daughter, until you find out what happens. For the man will not rest until the matter is settled today."

Ruth 4:1-6

KINSMAN DECLINES DUTY.   Meanwhile Boaz went up to the town gate and sat there. When the kinsman-redeemer he had mentioned came along, Boaz said, "Come over here, my friend, and sit down." So he went over and sat down.

Boaz took ten of the elders of the town and said, "Sit here," and they did so. Then he said to the kinsman-redeemer, "Naomi, who has come back from Moab, is selling the piece of land that belonged to our brother Elimelech. I thought I should bring the matter to your attention and suggest that you buy it in the presence of these seated here and in the presence of the elders of my people. If you will redeem it, do so. But if you*g* will not, tell me, so I will know. For no one has the right to do it except you, and I am next in line."

"I will redeem it," he said.

Then Boaz said, "On the day you buy the land from Naomi and from Ruth the Moabitess, you acquire*h* the dead man's widow, in order to maintain the name of the dead with his property."

At this, the kinsman-redeemer said, "Then I cannot redeem it because I might endanger my own estate. You redeem it yourself. I cannot do it."

Ruth 4:7-12

TRANSACTION MADE LEGAL.   (Now in earlier times in Israel, for the redemption and transfer of property to become final, one party took off his

---

*f*Most Hebrew manuscripts; many Hebrew manuscripts, Vulgate and Syriac *she*
*g*Many Hebrew manuscripts, Septuagint, Vulgate and Syriac; most Hebrew manuscripts *he*
*h*Hebrew; Vulgate and Syriac *Naomi, you acquire Ruth the Moabitess,*

sandal and gave it to the other. This was the method of legalizing transactions in Israel.)

So the kinsman-redeemer said to Boaz, "Buy it yourself." And he removed his sandal.

Then Boaz announced to the elders and all the people, "Today you are witnesses that I have bought from Naomi all the property of Elimelech, Kilion and Mahlon. I have also acquired Ruth the Moabitess, Mahlon's widow, as my wife, in order to maintain the name of the dead with his property, so that his name will not disappear from among his family or from the town records. Today you are witnesses!"

Then the elders and all those at the gate said, "We are witnesses. May the LORD make the woman who is coming into your home like Rachel and Leah, who together built up the house of Israel. May you have standing in Ephrathah and be famous in Bethlehem. Through the offspring the LORD gives you by this young woman, may your family be like that of Perez, whom Tamar bore to Judah."

BOAZ MARRIES RUTH.   So Boaz took Ruth and she became his wife.   **Ruth 4:13**
Then he went to her, and the LORD enabled her to conceive, and she gave birth to a son.

SON NAMED OBED.   The women said to Naomi: "Praise be to the LORD,   **Ruth**
who this day has not left you without a kinsman-redeemer. May he   **4:14-17**
become famous throughout Israel! He will renew your life and sustain you in your old age. For your daughter-in-law, who loves you and who is better to you than seven sons, has given him birth."

Then Naomi took the child, laid him in her lap and cared for him. The women living there said, "Naomi has a son." And they named him Obed. He was the father of Jesse, the father of David.

GENEALOGY OF OBED.   This, then, is the family line of Perez: **Ruth**
    4:18-22

Perez was the father of Hezron,
Hezron the father of Ram,
Ram the father of Amminadab,
Amminadab the father of Nahshon,
Nahshon the father of Salmon,[i]
Salmon the father of Boaz,
Boaz the father of Obed,
Obed the father of Jesse,
and Jesse the father of David.

Samson the Strong Man

*T*he simple purity and love of Ruth is only a quiet interlude in the violent era of the "judges." While the average Israelite seeks to till his land peaceably, it is still necessary to contend with the marauding Philistines. From their highly civilized coastal cities, the Philistines have moved throughout Canaan with ease, perhaps due to their prolific use of iron, both in farming tools and weapons of war. Their unusually strong military arms seem to call for an unusually strong response, and it comes in the form of a Danite

---

[i]A few Hebrew manuscripts, some Septuagint manuscripts and Vulgate (see also verse 21 and Septuagint of 1 Chron. 2:11); most Hebrew manuscripts *Salma*

named Samson. Samson is unique among the "judges" in that he does not lead armies, but rather acts on his own, using a superhuman strength which God has given him. But he is an unlikely savior of his people. Despite being bound by a Nazirite vow, even from birth, Samson is extremely carnal and of tempestuous temperament—hardly the righteous leader one might expect. Nevertheless God uses him through exciting personal exploits to harass and destroy thousands of the Philistines. Unfortunately, because of his weakness for pagan women, Samson himself will finally come to a tragic end.

Judges 13:1 (1090-1050 B.C.?)	OPPRESSION BY PHILISTINES. Again the Israelites did evil in the eyes of the LORD, so the LORD delivered them into the hands of the Philistines for forty years.
Judges 13:2-5	NAZIRITE CHILD PROMISED. A certain man of Zorah, named Manoah, from the clan of the Danites, had a wife who was sterile and remained childless. The angel of the LORD appeared to her and said, "You are sterile and childless, but you are going to conceive and have a son. Now see to it that you drink no wine or other fermented drink and that you do not eat anything unclean, because you will conceive and give birth to a son. No razor may be used on his head, because the boy is to be a Nazirite, set apart to God from birth, and he will begin the deliverance of Israel from the hands of the Philistines."
Judges 13:6,7	WIFE TELLS MANOAH. Then the woman went to her husband and told him, "A man of God came to me. He looked like an angel of God, very awesome. I didn't ask him where he came from, and he didn't tell me his name. But he said to me, 'You will conceive and give birth to a son. Now then, drink no wine or other fermented drink and do not eat anything unclean, because the boy will be a Nazirite of God from birth until the day of his death.'"
Judges 13:8-14	ANGEL GIVES DIRECTION. Then Manoah prayed to the LORD: "O Lord, I beg you, let the man of God you sent to us come again to teach us how to bring up the boy who is to be born." God heard Manoah, and the angel of God came again to the woman while she was out in the field; but her husband Manoah was not with her. The woman hurried to tell her husband, "He's here! The man who appeared to me the other day!" Manoah got up and followed his wife. When he came to the man, he said, "Are you the one who talked to my wife?" "I am," he said. So Manoah asked him, "When your words are fulfilled, what is to be the rule for the boy's life and work?" The angel of the LORD answered, "Your wife must do all that I have told her. She must not eat anything that comes from the grapevine, nor drink any wine or other fermented drink nor eat anything unclean. She must do everything I have commanded her."
Judges 13:15-23	ANGEL DEPARTS MIRACULOUSLY. Manoah said to the angel of the LORD, "We would like you to stay until we prepare a young goat for you." The angel of the LORD replied, "Even though you detain me, I will not eat any of your food. But if you prepare a burnt offering, offer it to the LORD." (Manoah did not realize that it was the angel of the LORD.)

Then Manoah inquired of the angel of the LORD, "What is your name, so that we may honor you when your word comes true?"

He replied, "Why do you ask my name? It is beyond understanding.*j*" Then Manoah took a young goat, together with the grain offering, and sacrificed it on a rock to the LORD. And the LORD did an amazing thing while Manoah and his wife watched: As the flame blazed up from the altar toward heaven, the angel of the LORD ascended in the flame. Seeing this, Manoah and his wife fell with their faces to the ground. When the angel of the LORD did not show himself again to Manoah and his wife, Manoah realized that it was the angel of the LORD.

"We are doomed to die!" he said to his wife. "We have seen God!"

But his wife answered, "If the LORD had meant to kill us, he would not have accepted a burnt offering and grain offering from our hands, nor shown us all these things or now told us this."

SAMSON BORN AND RAISED. The woman gave birth to a boy and named him Samson. He grew and the LORD blessed him, and the Spirit of the LORD began to stir him while he was in Mahaneh Dan, between Zorah and Eshtaol.

Judges
13:24,25

SAMSON REQUESTS WIFE. Samson went down to Timnah and saw there a young Philistine woman. When he returned, he said to his father and mother, "I have seen a Philistine woman in Timnah; now get her for me as my wife."

Judges
14:1-4
Timnah

His father and mother replied, "Isn't there an acceptable woman among your relatives or among all our people? Must you go to the uncircumcised Philistines to get a wife?"

But Samson said to his father, "Get her for me. She's the right one for me." (His parents did not know that this was from the LORD, who was seeking an occasion to confront the Philistines; for at that time they were ruling over Israel.)

SAMSON KILLS LION. Samson went down to Timnah together with his father and mother. As they approached the vineyards of Timnah, suddenly a young lion came roaring toward him. The Spirit of the LORD came upon him in power so that he tore the lion apart with his bare hands as he might have torn a young goat. But he told neither his father nor his mother what he had done. Then he went down and talked with the woman, and he liked her.

Judges
14:5-9

Some time later, when he went back to marry her, he turned aside to look at the lion's carcass. In it was a swarm of bees and some honey, which he scooped out with his hands and ate as he went along. When he rejoined his parents, he gave them some, and they too ate it. But he did not tell them that he had taken the honey from the lion's carcass.

RIDDLE AT WEDDING FEAST. Now his father went down to see the woman. And Samson made a feast there, as was customary for bridegrooms. When he appeared, he was given thirty companions.

Judges
14:10-14

"Let me tell you a riddle," Samson said to them. "If you can give me the answer within the seven days of the feast, I will give you thirty linen garments and thirty sets of clothes. If you can't tell me the answer, you must give me thirty linen garments and thirty sets of clothes."

"Tell us your riddle," they said. "Let's hear it."

*j*Or *is wonderful*

He replied,

> "Out of the eater, something to eat;
> out of the strong, something sweet."

For three days they could not give the answer.

Judges 14:15-17

WIFE PRESSES ANSWER.   On the fourth[k] day, they said to Samson's wife, "Coax your husband into explaining the riddle for us, or we will burn you and your father's household to death. Did you invite us here to rob us?"

Then Samson's wife threw herself on him, sobbing, "You hate me! You don't really love me. You've given my people a riddle, but you haven't told me the answer."

"I haven't even explained it to my father or mother," he replied, "so why should I explain it to you?" She cried the whole seven days of the feast. So on the seventh day he finally told her, because she continued to press him. She in turn explained the riddle to her people.

Judges 14:18-20

SAMSON KILLS 30 MEN.   Before sunset on the seventh day the men of the town said to him,

> "What is sweeter than honey?
> What is stronger than a lion?"

Samson said to them,

> "If you had not plowed with my heifer,
> you would not have solved my riddle."

Then the Spirit of the LORD came upon him in power. He went down to Ashkelon, struck down thirty of their men, stripped them of their belongings and gave their clothes to those who had explained the riddle. Burning with anger, he went up to his father's house. And Samson's wife was given to the friend who had attended him at his wedding.

Judges 15:1-5

FOXTAILS AND FIRE.   Later on, at the time of wheat harvest, Samson took a young goat and went to visit his wife. He said, "I'm going to my wife's room." But her father would not let him go in.

"I was so sure you thoroughly hated her," he said, "that I gave her to your friend. Isn't her younger sister more attractive? Take her instead."

Samson said to them, "This time I have a right to get even with the Philistines; I will really harm them." So he went out and caught three hundred foxes and tied them tail to tail in pairs. He then fastened a torch to every pair of tails, lit the torches and let the foxes loose in the standing grain of the Philistines. He burned up the shocks and standing grain, together with the vineyards and olive groves.

Judges 15:6-8

SAMSON'S WIFE BURNED.   When the Philistines asked, "Who did this?" they were told, "Samson, the Timnite's son-in-law, because his wife was given to his friend."

So the Philistines went up and burned her and her father to death. Samson said to them, "Since you've acted like this, I won't stop until I get my revenge on you." He attacked them viciously and slaughtered many of them. Then he went down and stayed in a cave in the rock of Etam.

---

[k]Some Septuagint manuscripts and Syriac; Hebrew *seventh*

SAMSON BOUND WITH ROPES.   The Philistines went up and camped in Judah, spreading out near Lehi. The men of Judah asked, "Why have you come to fight us?"

"We have come to take Samson prisoner," they answered, "to do to him as he did to us."

Then three thousand men from Judah went down to the cave in the rock of Etam and said to Samson, "Don't you realize that the Philistines are rulers over us? What have you done to us?"

He answered, "I merely did to them what they did to me."

They said to him, "We've come to tie you up and hand you over to the Philistines."

Samson said, "Swear to me that you won't kill me yourselves."

"Agreed," they answered. "We will only tie you up and hand you over to them. We will not kill you." So they bound him with two new ropes and led him up from the rock.

Judges
15:9-13
Lehi

SAMSON SLAYS A THOUSAND.   As he approached Lehi, the Philistines came toward him shouting. The Spirit of the LORD came upon him in power. The ropes on his arms became like charred flax, and the bindings dropped from his hands. Finding a fresh jawbone of a donkey, he grabbed it and struck down a thousand men.

Then Samson said,

Judges
15:14-17

> "With a donkey's jawbone
> I have made donkeys of them.[l]
> With a donkey's jawbone
> I have killed a thousand men."

When he finished speaking, he threw away the jawbone; and the place was called Ramath Lehi.[m]

GOD QUENCHES THIRST.   Because he was very thirsty, he cried out to the LORD, "You have given your servant this great victory. Must I now die of thirst and fall into the hands of the uncircumcised?" Then God opened up the hollow place in Lehi, and water came out of it. When Samson drank, his strength returned and he revived. So the spring was called En Hakkore,[n] and it is still there in Lehi.

Samson led[o] Israel for twenty years in the days of the Philistines.

Judges
15:18-20
(1080-1060
B.C.?)

SAMSON LIFTS CITY GATES.   One day Samson went to Gaza, where he saw a prostitute. He went in to spend the night with her. The people of Gaza were told, "Samson is here!" So they surrounded the place and lay in wait for him all night at the city gate. They made no move during the night, saying, "At dawn we'll kill him."

But Samson lay there only until the middle of the night. Then he got up and took hold of the doors of the city gate, together with the two posts, and tore them loose, bar and all. He lifted them to his shoulders and carried them to the top of the hill that faces Hebron.

Judges
16:1-3
Gaza

DELILAH ASKED TO PRY.   Some time later, he fell in love with a woman in the Valley of Sorek whose name was Delilah. The rulers of the Philistines went to her and said, "See if you can lure him into showing you

Judges
16:4,5
Valley of
Sorek

[l]Or *made a heap or two*; the Hebrew for *donkey* sounds like the Hebrew for *heap*.
[m]*Ramath Lehi* means *jawbone hill*.   [n]*En Hakkore* means *caller's spring*.   [o]Traditionally *judged*

the secret of his great strength and how we can overpower him so we may tie him up and subdue him. Each one of us will give you eleven hundred shekels[p] of silver."

Judges 16:6-9

BOWSTRINGS FAIL.   So Delilah said to Samson, "Tell me the secret of your great strength and how you can be tied up and subdued."

Samson answered her, "If anyone ties me with seven fresh thongs[q] that have not been dried, I'll become as weak as any other man."

Then the rulers of the Philistines brought her seven fresh thongs that had not been dried, and she tied him with them. With men hidden in the room, she called to him, "Samson, the Philistines are upon you!" But he snapped the thongs as easily as a piece of string snaps when it comes close to a flame. So the secret of his strength was not discovered.

Judges 16:10-12

NEW ROPES FAIL.   Then Delilah said to Samson, "You have made a fool of me; you lied to me. Come now, tell me how you can be tied."

He said, "If anyone ties me securely with new ropes that have never been used, I'll become as weak as any other man."

So Delilah took new ropes and tied him with them. Then, with men hidden in the room, she called to him, "Samson, the Philistines are upon you!" But he snapped the ropes off his arms as if they were threads.

Judges 16:13,14

HAIRLOCKS FAIL.   Delilah then said to Samson, "Until now, you have been making a fool of me and lying to me. Tell me how you can be tied."

He replied, "If you weave the seven braids of my head into the fabric ⌊on the loom⌋ and tighten it with the pin, I'll become as weak as any other man." So while he was sleeping, Delilah took the seven braids of his head, wove them into the fabric and[r] tightened it with the pin.

Again she called to him, "Samson, the Philistines are upon you!" He awoke from his sleep and pulled up the pin and the loom, with the fabric.

Judges 16:15-17

SAMSON REVEALS SECRET.   Then she said to him, "How can you say, 'I love you,' when you won't confide in me? This is the third time you have made a fool of me and haven't told me the secret of your great strength." With such nagging she prodded him day after day until he was tired to death.

So he told her everything. "No razor has ever been used on my head," he said, "because I have been a Nazirite set apart to God since birth. If my head were shaved, my strength would leave me, and I would become as weak as any other man."

Judges 16:18-22

SAMSON'S HAIR IS CUT.   When Delilah saw that he had told her everything, she sent word to the rulers of the Philistines, "Come back once more; he has told me everything." So the rulers of the Philistines returned with the silver in their hands. Having put him to sleep on her lap, she called a man to shave off the seven braids of his hair, and so began to subdue him.[s] And his strength left him.

Then she called, "Samson, the Philistines are upon you!"

He awoke from his sleep and thought, "I'll go out as before and shake myself free." But he did not know that the LORD had left him.

Then the Philistines seized him, gouged out his eyes and took him down

[p]That is, about 28 pounds (about 13 kilograms)   [q]Or *bowstrings*; also in verses 8 and 9   [r]Some Septuagint manuscripts; Hebrew "⌊*I can⌋ if you weave the seven braids of my head into the fabric ⌊on the loom⌋." 14So she*   [s]Hebrew; some Septuagint manuscripts *and he began to weaken*

to Gaza. Binding him with bronze shackles, they set him to grinding in the prison. But the hair on his head began to grow again after it had been shaved.

SAMSON'S FINAL REVENGE. Now the rulers of the Philistines assembled to offer a great sacrifice to Dagon their god and to celebrate, saying, "Our god has delivered Samson, our enemy, into our hands."
When the people saw him, they praised their god, saying,

> "Our god has delivered our enemy
> into our hands,
> the one who laid waste our land
> and multiplied our slain."

Judges
16:23-30
Gaza

While they were in high spirits, they shouted, "Bring out Samson to entertain us." So they called Samson out of the prison, and he performed for them.
When they stood him among the pillars, Samson said to the servant who held his hand, "Put me where I can feel the pillars that support the temple, so that I may lean against them." Now the temple was crowded with men and women; all the rulers of the Philistines were there, and on the roof were about three thousand men and women watching Samson perform. Then Samson prayed to the LORD, "O Sovereign LORD, remember me. O God, please strengthen me just once more, and let me with one blow get revenge on the Philistines for my two eyes." Then Samson reached toward the two central pillars on which the temple stood. Bracing himself against them, his right hand on the one and his left hand on the other, Samson said, "Let me die with the Philistines!" Then he pushed with all his might, and down came the temple on the rulers and all the people in it. Thus he killed many more when he died than while he lived.

SAMSON BURIED. Then his brothers and his father's whole family went down to get him. They brought him back and buried him between Zorah and Eshtaol in the tomb of Manoah his father. He had led[t] Israel twenty years.

Judges
16:31
(Ca. 1060
B.C.?)

Micah and the Danites

*E*ven while God is working wonders through his specially chosen leaders, there are many Israelites who continue to be attracted by pagan idols and practices. What follows is an account of one such Israelite who compromises and perverts true worship, and even manages to persuade a Levite to participate. Perhaps the greater significance of the account lies in the fact that one man's sin eventually leads to the practice of pagan idolatry by an entire tribe. The power of individual influence shouts aloud in this seemingly well-motivated and innocent deviation from God's directed pattern.

MICAH MAKES IDOLS. Now a man named Micah from the hill country of Ephraim said to his mother, "The eleven hundred shekels[u] of silver that were taken from you and about which I heard you utter a curse—I have that silver with me; I took it."

Judges
17:1-6
Ephraim

[t]Traditionally *judged*   [u]That is, about 28 pounds (about 13 kilograms)

Then his mother said, "The LORD bless you, my son!"

When he returned the eleven hundred shekels of silver to his mother, she said, "I solemnly consecrate my silver to the LORD for my son to make a carved image and a cast idol. I will give it back to you."

So he returned the silver to his mother, and she took two hundred shekels[v] of silver and gave them to a silversmith, who made them into the image and the idol. And they were put in Micah's house.

Now this man Micah had a shrine, and he made an ephod and some idols and installed one of his sons as his priest. In those days Israel had no king; everyone did as he saw fit.

Judges 17:7-13

MICAH HIRES LEVITE.   A young Levite from Bethlehem in Judah, who had been living within the clan of Judah, left that town in search of some other place to stay. On his way[w] he came to Micah's house in the hill country of Ephraim.

Micah asked him, "Where are you from?"

"I'm a Levite from Bethlehem in Judah," he said, "and I'm looking for a place to stay."

Then Micah said to him, "Live with me and be my father and priest, and I'll give you ten shekels[x] of silver a year, your clothes and your food." So the Levite agreed to live with him, and the young man was to him like one of his sons. Then Micah installed the Levite, and the young man became his priest and lived in his house. And Micah said, "Now I know that the LORD will be good to me, since this Levite has become my priest."

Judges 18:1-6

DANITE SPIES MEET LEVITE.   In those days Israel had no king.

And in those days the tribe of the Danites was seeking a place of their own where they might settle, because they had not yet come into an inheritance among the tribes of Israel. So the Danites sent five warriors from Zorah and Eshtaol to spy out the land and explore it. These men represented all their clans. They told them, "Go, explore the land."

The men entered the hill country of Ephraim and came to the house of Micah, where they spent the night. When they were near Micah's house, they recognized the voice of the young Levite; so they turned in there and asked him, "Who brought you here? What are you doing in this place? Why are you here?"

He told them what Micah had done for him, and said, "He has hired me and I am his priest."

Then they said to him, "Please inquire of God to learn whether our journey will be successful."

The priest answered them, "Go in peace. Your journey has the LORD's approval."

Judges 18:7-10

SPIES BRING GOOD REPORT.   So the five men left and came to Laish, where they saw that the people were living in safety, like the Sidonians, unsuspecting and secure. And since their land lacked nothing, they were prosperous.[y] Also, they lived a long way from the Sidonians and had no relationship with anyone else.[z]

When they returned to Zorah and Eshtaol, their brothers asked them, "How did you find things?"

---

[v]That is, about 5 pounds (about 2.3 kilograms)   [w]Or *To carry on his profession*
[x]That is, about 4 ounces (about 110 grams)   [y]The meaning of the Hebrew for this
clause is uncertain.   [z]Hebrew; some Septuagint manuscripts *with the Arameans*

They answered, "Come on, let's attack them! We have seen that the land is very good. Aren't you going to do something? Don't hesitate to go there and take it over. When you get there, you will find an unsuspecting people and a spacious land that God has put into your hands, a land that lacks nothing whatever."

DANITES MOVE FORCES.   Then six hundred men from the clan of the Danites, armed for battle, set out from Zorah and Eshtaol. On their way they set up camp near Kiriath Jearim in Judah. This is why the place west of Kiriath Jearim is called Mahaneh Dan[a] to this day. From there they went on to the hill country of Ephraim and came to Micah's house.   *Judges 18:11-13*

MICAH'S IDOLS TAKEN.   Then the five men who had spied out the land of Laish said to their brothers, "Do you know that one of these houses has an ephod, other household gods, a carved image and a cast idol? Now you know what to do." So they turned in there and went to the house of the young Levite at Micah's place and greeted him. The six hundred Danites, armed for battle, stood at the entrance to the gate. The five men who had spied out the land went inside and took the carved image, the ephod, the other household gods and the cast idol while the priest and the six hundred armed men stood at the entrance to the gate.   *Judges 18:14-20*

When these men went into Micah's house and took the carved image, the ephod, the other household gods and the cast idol, the priest said to them, "What are you doing?"

They answered him, "Be quiet! Don't say a word. Come with us, and be our father and priest. Isn't it better that you serve a tribe and clan in Israel as priest rather than just one man's household?" Then the priest was glad. He took the ephod, the other household gods and the carved image and went along with the people.

RECAPTURE ATTEMPT FAILS.   Putting their little children, their livestock and their possessions in front of them, they turned away and left.   *Judges 18:21-26*

When they had gone some distance from Micah's house, the men who lived near Micah were called together and overtook the Danites. As they shouted after them, the Danites turned and said to Micah, "What's the matter with you that you called out your men to fight?"

He replied, "You took the gods I made, and my priest, and went away. What else do I have? How can you ask, 'What's the matter with you?'"

The Danites answered, "Don't argue with us, or some hot-tempered men will attack you, and you and your family will lose your lives." So the Danites went their way, and Micah, seeing that they were too strong for him, turned around and went back home.

LAISH RENAMED DAN.   Then they took what Micah had made, and his priest, and went on to Laish, against a peaceful and unsuspecting people. They attacked them with the sword and burned down their city. There was no one to rescue them because they lived a long way from Sidon and had no relationship with anyone else. The city was in a valley near Beth Rehob.   *Judges 18:27-29 Laish*

The Danites rebuilt the city and settled there. They named it Dan after their forefather Dan, who was born to Israel—though the city used to be called Laish.

---

[a]*Mahaneh Dan* means *Dan's camp.*

MARCH 25

Judges 18:30,31	**GRAVEN IMAGE SET UP.** There the Danites set up for themselves the idols, and Jonathan son of Gershom, the son of Moses,[b] and his sons were priests for the tribe of Dan until the time of the captivity of the land. They continued to use the idols Micah had made, all the time the house of God was in Shiloh.

Civil War with Benjamin

*R*eligious apostasy is somewhat understandable in an age of idolatry and pagan practices, so it is not surprising to see the Israelites repeatedly lapse into spiritual unfaithfulness. What is surprising, however, is the extent to which immorality has grown, particularly among the Benjamites. A grim example is seen when certain lewd men demand that a hospitable old man turn over a visiting Levite so that they can have homosexual relations with him. In a response reminiscent of Lot and the two angels—and yet even more repugnant—the Levite instead sends out his concubine to be sexually abused. When the Levite discovers his concubine dead the next morning, he suddenly feels resentment and sends a part of his concubine's body to each tribe. At this, Israel also becomes incensed and, after several defeats, almost annihilates the tribe of Benjamin.

Thus, once again, sin leads to broken relationships and civil strife. Yet there is a remnant of goodness remaining, and it manifests itself in the concern which Israel feels when it realizes that part of their national family has almost been destroyed. A valuable lesson in family forgiveness, and acceptance despite sin, is seen in the lengths to which Israel goes to restore the wayward tribe of Benjamin.

Judges 19:1,2a,b Ephraim	**LEVITE AND CONCUBINE.** In those days Israel had no king. Now a Levite who lived in a remote area in the hill country of Ephraim took a concubine from Bethlehem in Judah. But she was unfaithful to him. She left him and went back to her father's house in Bethlehem, Judah.
Judges 19:2c-9 Bethlehem	**LEVITE AND FATHER-IN-LAW.** After she had been there four months, her husband went to her to persuade her to return. He had with him his servant and two donkeys. She took him into her father's house, and when her father saw him, he gladly welcomed him. His father-in-law, the girl's father, prevailed upon him to stay; so he remained with him three days, eating and drinking, and sleeping there. On the fourth day they got up early and he prepared to leave, but the girl's father said to his son-in-law, "Refresh yourself with something to eat; then you can go." So the two of them sat down to eat and drink together. Afterward the girl's father said, "Please stay tonight and enjoy yourself." And when the man got up to go, his father-in-law persuaded him, so he stayed there that night. On the morning of the fifth day, when he rose to go, the girl's father said, "Refresh yourself. Wait till afternoon!" So the two of them ate together. Then when the man, with his concubine and his servant, got up to leave, his father-in-law, the girl's father, said, "Now look, it's almost evening.

[b]An ancient Hebrew scribal tradition, some Septuagint manuscripts and Vulgate; Masoretic Text *Manasseh*

Spend the night here; the day is nearly over. Stay and enjoy yourself. Early tomorrow morning you can get up and be on your way home."

JOURNEY TO GIBEAH.   But, unwilling to stay another night, the man left and went toward Jebus (that is, Jerusalem), with his two saddled donkeys and his concubine.

Judges 19:10-15

When they were near Jebus and the day was almost gone, the servant said to his master, "Come, let's stop at this city of the Jebusites and spend the night."

His master replied, "No. We won't go into an alien city, whose people are not Israelites. We will go on to Gibeah." He added, "Come, let's try to reach Gibeah or Ramah and spend the night in one of those places." So they went on, and the sun set as they neared Gibeah in Benjamin. There they stopped to spend the night. They went and sat in the city square, but no one took them into his home for the night.

OLD MAN'S HOSPITALITY.   That evening an old man from the hill country of Ephraim, who was living in Gibeah (the men of the place were Benjamites), came in from his work in the fields. When he looked and saw the traveler in the city square, the old man asked, "Where are you going? Where did you come from?"

Judges 19:16-21 Gibeah

He answered, "We are on our way from Bethlehem in Judah to a remote area in the hill country of Ephraim where I live. I have been to Bethlehem in Judah and now I am going to the house of the LORD. No one has taken me into his house. We have both straw and fodder for our donkeys and bread and wine for ourselves your servants—me, your maidservant, and the young man with us. We don't need anything."

"You are welcome at my house," the old man said. "Let me supply whatever you need. Only don't spend the night in the square." So he took him into his house and fed his donkeys. After they had washed their feet, they had something to eat and drink.

BENJAMITES SEEK EVIL.   While they were enjoying themselves, some of the wicked men of the city surrounded the house. Pounding on the door, they shouted to the old man who owned the house, "Bring out the man who came to your house so we can have sex with him."

Judges 19:22-25a

The owner of the house went outside and said to them, "No, my friends, don't be so vile. Since this man is my guest, don't do this disgraceful thing. Look, here is my virgin daughter, and his concubine. I will bring them out to you now, and you can use them and do to them whatever you wish. But to this man, don't do such a disgraceful thing."

But the men would not listen to him.

CONCUBINE RAPED.   So the man took his concubine and sent her outside to them, and they raped her and abused her throughout the night, and at dawn they let her go. At daybreak the woman went back to the house where her master was staying, fell down at the door and lay there until daylight.

Judges 19:25b,26

BODY SENT TO TRIBES.   When her master got up in the morning and opened the door of the house and stepped out to continue on his way, there lay his concubine, fallen in the doorway of the house, with her hands on the threshold. He said to her, "Get up; let's go." But there was no answer. Then the man put her on his donkey and set out for home.

Judges 19:27-30

When he reached home, he took a knife and cut up his concubine, limb by limb, into twelve parts and sent them into all the areas of Israel. Everyone who saw it said, "Such a thing has never been seen or done, not since the day the Israelites came up out of Egypt. Think about it! Consider it! Tell us what to do!"

**Judges
20:1-3a
Mizpah**

ISRAEL MARSHALS FORCES.   Then all the Israelites from Dan to Beersheba and from the land of Gilead came out as one man and assembled before the LORD in Mizpah. The leaders of all the people of the tribes of Israel took their places in the assembly of the people of God, four hundred thousand soldiers armed with swords.   (The Benjamites heard that the Israelites had gone up to Mizpah.)

**Judges
20:3b-7**

LEVITE RECOUNTS INCIDENT.   Then the Israelites said, "Tell us how this awful thing happened."

So the Levite, the husband of the murdered woman, said, "I and my concubine came to Gibeah in Benjamin to spend the night. During the night the men of Gibeah came after me and surrounded the house, intending to kill me. They raped my concubine, and she died. I took my concubine, cut her into pieces and sent one piece to each region of Israel's inheritance, because they committed this lewd and disgraceful act in Israel. Now, all you Israelites, speak up and give your verdict."

**Judges
20:8-11**

DECISION TO PUNISH GIBEAH.   All the people rose as one man, saying, "None of us will go home. No, not one of us will return to his house. But now this is what we'll do to Gibeah: We'll go up against it as the lot directs. We'll take ten men out of every hundred from all the tribes of Israel, and a hundred from a thousand, and a thousand from ten thousand, to get provisions for the army. Then, when the army arrives at Gibeah^c in Benjamin, it can give them what they deserve for all this vileness done in Israel." So all the men of Israel got together and united as one man against the city.

**Judges
20:12-18**

PREPARATIONS FOR BATTLE.   The tribes of Israel sent men throughout the tribe of Benjamin, saying, "What about this awful crime that was committed among you? Now surrender those wicked men of Gibeah so that we may put them to death and purge the evil from Israel."

But the Benjamites would not listen to their fellow Israelites. From their towns they came together at Gibeah to fight against the Israelites. At once the Benjamites mobilized twenty-six thousand swordsmen from their towns, in addition to seven hundred chosen men from those living in Gibeah. Among all these soldiers there were seven hundred chosen men who were left-handed, each of whom could sling a stone at a hair and not miss.

Israel, apart from Benjamin, mustered four hundred thousand swordsmen, all of them fighting men.

The Israelites went up to Bethel^d and inquired of God. They said, "Who of us shall go first to fight against the Benjamites?"

The LORD replied, "Judah shall go first."

**Judges
20:19-23
Gibeah**

BENJAMITES WIN FIRST.   The next morning the Israelites got up and pitched camp near Gibeah. The men of Israel went out to fight the

---

^{c}One Hebrew manuscript; most Hebrew manuscripts *Geba*, a variant of *Gibeah* ^{d}Or *to the house of God*; also in verse 26

Benjamites and took up battle positions against them at Gibeah. The
Benjamites came out of Gibeah and cut down twenty-two thousand
Israelites on the battlefield that day. But the men of Israel encouraged one
another and again took up their positions where they had stationed themselves the first day. The Israelites went up and wept before the LORD until
evening, and they inquired of the LORD. They said, "Shall we go up again
to battle against the Benjamites, our brothers?"

The LORD answered, "Go up against them."

ISRAEL AGAIN DEFEATED.   Then the Israelites drew near to Benjamin
the second day. This time, when the Benjamites came out from Gibeah to
oppose them, they cut down another eighteen thousand Israelites, all of
them armed with swords.

Then the Israelites, all the people, went up to Bethel, and there they sat
weeping before the LORD. They fasted that day until evening and presented burnt offerings and fellowship offerings[e] to the LORD. And the Israelites
inquired of the LORD. (In those days the ark of the covenant of God was
there, with Phinehas son of Eleazar, the son of Aaron, ministering before
it.) They asked, "Shall we go up again to battle with Benjamin our brother, or not?"

The LORD responded, "Go, for tomorrow I will give them into your
hands."

Judges 20:24-28

ISRAEL FINALLY VICTORIOUS.   Then Israel set an ambush around
Gibeah. They went up against the Benjamites on the third day and took up
positions against Gibeah as they had done before. The Benjamites came
out to meet them and were drawn away from the city. They began to inflict
casualties on the Israelites as before, so that about thirty men fell in the
open field and on the roads—the one leading to Bethel and the other to
Gibeah.

While the Benjamites were saying, "We are defeating them as before,"
the Israelites were saying, "Let's retreat and draw them away from the city
to the roads."

All the men of Israel moved from their places and took up positions at
Baal Tamar, and the Israelite ambush charged out of its place on the west[f]
of Gibeah.[g] Then ten thousand of Israel's finest men made a frontal attack
on Gibeah. The fighting was so heavy that the Benjamites did not realize
how near disaster was. The LORD defeated Benjamin before Israel, and on
that day the Israelites struck down 25,100 Benjamites, all armed with
swords. Then the Benjamites saw that they were beaten.

Judges 20:29-36a

DETAILS OF THE VICTORY.   Now the men of Israel had given way
before Benjamin, because they relied on the ambush they had set near
Gibeah. The men who had been in ambush made a sudden dash into
Gibeah, spread out and put the whole city to the sword. The men of Israel
had arranged with the ambush that they should send up a great cloud of
smoke from the city, and then the men of Israel would turn in the battle.

The Benjamites had begun to inflict casualties on the men of Israel
(about thirty), and they said, "We are defeating them as in the first battle."
But when the column of smoke began to rise from the city, the Benjamites
turned and saw the smoke of the whole city going up into the sky. Then

Judges 20:36b-46

---

[e] Traditionally *peace offerings*   [f] Some Septuagint manuscripts and Vulgate; the meaning
of the Hebrew for this word is uncertain.   [g] Hebrew *Geba*, a variant of *Gibeah*

the men of Israel turned on them, and the men of Benjamin were terrified, because they realized that disaster had come upon them. So they fled before the Israelites in the direction of the desert, but they could not escape the battle. And the men of Israel who came out of the towns cut them down there. They surrounded the Benjamites, chased them and easily[h] overran them in the vicinity of Gibeah on the east. Eighteen thousand Benjamites fell, all of them valiant fighters. As they turned and fled toward the desert to the rock of Rimmon, the Israelites cut down five thousand men along the roads. They kept pressing after the Benjamites as far as Gidom and struck down two thousand more.

On that day twenty-five thousand Benjamite swordsmen fell, all of them valiant fighters.

Judges 20:47,48

LAST RESISTANCE QUELLED.   But six hundred men turned and fled into the desert to the rock of Rimmon, where they stayed four months. The men of Israel went back to Benjamin and put all the towns to the sword, including the animals and everything else they found. All the towns they came across they set on fire.

Judges 21:1-7

CONCERN FOR BENJAMIN.   The men of Israel had taken an oath at Mizpah: "Not one of us will give his daughter in marriage to a Benjamite."

The people went to Bethel[i], where they sat before God until evening, raising their voices and weeping bitterly. "O LORD, the God of Israel," they cried, "why has this happened to Israel? Why should one tribe be missing from Israel today?"

Early the next day the people built an altar and presented burnt offerings and fellowship offerings.[j]

Then the Israelites asked, "Who from all the tribes of Israel has failed to assemble before the LORD?" For they had taken a solemn oath that anyone who failed to assemble before the LORD at Mizpah should certainly be put to death.

Now the Israelites grieved for their brothers, the Benjamites. "Today one tribe is cut off from Israel," they said. "How can we provide wives for those who are left, since we have taken an oath by the LORD not to give them any of our daughters in marriage?"

Judges 21:8-12 Jabesh Gilead

VIRGINS FROM JABESH GILEAD.   Then they asked, "Which one of the tribes of Israel failed to assemble before the LORD at Mizpah?" They discovered that no one from Jabesh Gilead had come to the camp for the assembly. For when they counted the people, they found that none of the people of Jabesh Gilead were there.

So the assembly sent twelve thousand fighting men with instructions to go to Jabesh Gilead and put to the sword those living there, including the women and children. "This is what you are to do," they said. "Kill every male and every woman who is not a virgin." They found among the people living in Jabesh Gilead four hundred young women who had never slept with a man, and they took them to the camp at Shiloh in Canaan.

Judges 21:13-15

NOT ENOUGH WOMEN.   Then the whole assembly sent an offer of peace to the Benjamites at the rock of Rimmon. So the Benjamites returned at that time and were given the women of Jabesh Gilead who had been spared. But there were not enough for all of them.

[h]The meaning of the Hebrew for this word is uncertain.   [i]Or *to the house of God*
[j]Traditionally *peace offerings*

The people grieved for Benjamin, because the LORD had made a gap in the tribes of Israel.

PLAN TO EVADE VOW.   And the elders of the assembly said, "With the women of Benjamin destroyed, how shall we provide wives for the men who are left? The Benjamite survivors must have heirs," they said, "so that a tribe of Israel will not be wiped out. We can't give them our daughters as wives, since we Israelites have taken this oath: 'Cursed be anyone who gives a wife to a Benjamite.' But look, there is the annual festival of the LORD in Shiloh, to the north of Bethel, and east of the road that goes from Bethel to Shechem, and to the south of Lebonah."

So they instructed the Benjamites, saying, "Go and hide in the vineyards and watch. When the girls of Shiloh come out to join in the dancing, then rush from the vineyards and each of you seize a wife from the girls of Shiloh and go to the land of Benjamin. When their fathers or brothers complain to us, we will say to them, 'Do us a kindness by helping them, because we did not get wives for them during the war, and you are innocent, since you did not give your daughters to them.'"

So that is what the Benjamites did. While the girls were dancing, each man caught one and carried her off to be his wife. Then they returned to their inheritance and rebuilt the towns and settled in them.

At that time the Israelites left that place and went home to their tribes and clans, each to his own inheritance.

Judges 21:16-24 Shiloh

Period of Judges Summarized

It seems that Israel's moral decline has so affected the people that even honest attempts at goodness are blemished. Even in the sincere efforts made to forgive and restore the Benjamites, there is an indication that the Israelites have exercised extremely questionable moral judgment as far as their methods were concerned. This entire period of the Canaan conflict is a sad testimony to the relationship between God and man. From a pinnacle of adherence to law under Moses (as imperfect as their obedience was, even then), the nation of Israel has sunk to a low ebb in which moral authority is no higher than self-will. The inspired record sums it up with a disappointing epitaph.

SELF-RULE IN ISRAEL.   In those days Israel had no king; everyone did as he saw fit.

Judges 21:25 (Ca. 1380-1043 B.C.)

ISRAEL AS A MONARCHY

(Ca. 1100-930 B.C.)

Samuel Brings About Transition

*W*ith the period of the judges coming to a close, attention now focuses upon a person of unique status. Born in response to his barren mother's prayers, Samuel is the last of Israel's judges, one of its many prophets, and the anointer of its first king. As seen even in the laws given to Moses, God has already anticipated his people's desire to have a human king just as the nations around them, and the time is drawing near for God to grant that which he knows will only be destructive to the nation of Israel. With the land of Canaan substantially under Israel's control, it is time for the inevitable transition from a theocracy to a monarchy.

The record of this 465-year period of the kings is contained principally in the books of 1 and 2 Samuel, 1 and 2 Kings, and 1 and 2 Chronicles. As this record unfolds, the monarchy will both thrive and suffer under three major kings, then divide into two smaller kingdoms ruled by a succession of kings— some good, but many more bad—before God's people are overthrown and taken into captivity by foreign powers.

1 Sam. 1:1-8 (Ca. 1100-1050 B.C.) Shiloh — HANNAH MOURNS BARRENNESS. There was a certain man from Ramathaim, a Zuphite[a] from the hill country of Ephraim, whose name was Elkanah son of Jeroham, the son of Elihu, the son of Tohu, the son of Zuph, an Ephraimite. He had two wives; one was called Hannah and the other Peninnah. Peninnah had children, but Hannah had none.

Year after year this man went up from his town to worship and sacrifice to the LORD Almighty at Shiloh, where Hophni and Phinehas, the two sons of Eli, were priests of the LORD. Whenever the day came for Elkanah to sacrifice, he would give portions of the meat to his wife Peninnah and to all her sons and daughters. But to Hannah he gave a double portion because he loved her, and the LORD had closed her womb. And because the LORD had closed her womb, her rival kept provoking her in order to irritate her. This went on year after year. Whenever Hannah went up to the house of the LORD, her rival provoked her till she wept and would not eat. Elkanah her husband would say to her, "Hannah, why are you weeping? Why don't you eat? Why are you downhearted? Don't I mean more to you than ten sons?"

---

aOr from Ramathaim Zuphim

A PRAYER AND A VOW. Once when they had finished eating and drinking in Shiloh, Hannah stood up. Now Eli the priest was sitting on a chair by the doorpost of the LORD's temple.[b] In bitterness of soul Hannah wept much and prayed to the LORD. And she made a vow, saying, "O LORD Almighty, if you will only look upon your servant's misery and remember me, and not forget your servant but give her a son, then I will give him to the LORD for all the days of his life, and no razor will ever be used on his head."

As she kept on praying to the LORD, Eli observed her mouth. Hannah was praying in her heart, and her lips were moving but her voice was not heard. Eli thought she was drunk and said to her, "How long will you keep on getting drunk? Get rid of your wine."

"Not so, my lord," Hannah replied, "I am a woman who is deeply troubled. I have not been drinking wine or beer; I was pouring out my soul to the LORD. Do not take your servant for a wicked woman; I have been praying here out of my great anguish and grief."

Eli answered, "Go in peace, and may the God of Israel grant you what you have asked of him."

She said, "May your servant find favor in your eyes." Then she went her way and ate something, and her face was no longer downcast.

1 Sam. 1:9-18

SAMUEL BORN. Early the next morning they arose and worshiped before the LORD and then went back to their home at Ramah. Elkanah lay with Hannah his wife, and the LORD remembered her. So in the course of time Hannah conceived and gave birth to a son. She named him Samuel,[c] saying, "Because I asked the LORD for him."

1 Sam. 1:19,20 Ramah

SAMUEL DEDICATED. When the man Elkanah went up with all his family to offer the annual sacrifice to the LORD and to fulfill his vow, Hannah did not go. She said to her husband, "After the boy is weaned, I will take him and present him before the LORD, and he will live there always."

"Do what seems best to you," Elkanah her husband told her. "Stay here until you have weaned him; only may the LORD make good his[d] word." So the woman stayed at home and nursed her son until she had weaned him.

After he was weaned, she took the boy with her, young as he was, along with a three-year-old bull,[e] an ephah[f] of flour and a skin of wine, and brought him to the house of the LORD at Shiloh. When they had slaughtered the bull, they brought the boy to Eli, and she said to him, "As surely as you live, my lord, I am the woman who stood here beside you praying to the LORD. I prayed for this child, and the LORD has granted me what I asked of him. So now I give him to the LORD. For his whole life he will be given over to the LORD." And he worshiped the LORD there.

1 Sam. 1:21-28 Shiloh

HANNAH PRAISES GOD. Then Hannah prayed and said:

1 Sam. 2:1-11

> "My heart rejoices in the LORD;
>   in the LORD my horn[g] is lifted high.
> My mouth boasts over my enemies,

---

[b]That is, tabernacle   [c]*Samuel* sounds like the Hebrew for *heard of God.*   [d]Masoretic Text; Dead Sea Scrolls, Septuagint and Syriac *your*   [e]Dead Sea Scrolls, Septuagint and Syriac; Masoretic Text *with three bulls*   [f]That is, probably about 3/5 bushel (about 22 liters)   [g]*Horn* here symbolizes strength.

for I delight in your deliverance.

"There is no one holy[h] like the LORD;
    there is no one besides you;
    there is no Rock like our God.

"Do not keep talking so proudly
    or let your mouth speak such arrogance,
for the LORD is a God who knows,
    and by him deeds are weighed.

"The bows of the warriors are broken,
    but those who stumbled are armed with strength.
Those who were full hire themselves out for food,
    but those who were hungry hunger no more.
She who was barren has borne seven children,
    but she who has had many sons pines away.

"The LORD brings death and makes alive;
    he brings down to the grave[i] and raises up.
The LORD sends poverty and wealth;
    he humbles and he exalts.
He raises the poor from the dust
    and lifts the needy from the ash heap;
he seats them with princes
    and has them inherit a throne of honor.

"For the foundations of the earth are the LORD's;
    upon them he has set the world.
He will guard the feet of his saints,
    but the wicked will be silenced in darkness.

"It is not by strength that one prevails;
    those who oppose the LORD will be shattered.
He will thunder against them from heaven;
    the LORD will judge the ends of the earth.

"He will give strength to his king
    and exalt the horn of his anointed."

Then Elkanah went home to Ramah, but the boy ministered before the LORD under Eli the priest.

1 Sam. 2:12-17   ELI'S WICKED SONS.   Eli's sons were wicked men; they had no regard for the LORD. Now it was the practice of the priests with the people that whenever anyone offered a sacrifice and while the meat was being boiled, the servant of the priest would come with a three-pronged fork in his hand. He would plunge it into the pan or kettle or caldron or pot, and the priest would take for himself whatever the fork brought up. This is how they treated all the Israelites who came to Shiloh. But even before the fat was burned, the servant of the priest would come and say to the man who was sacrificing, "Give the priest some meat to roast; he won't accept boiled meat from you, but only raw."

If the man said to him, "Let the fat be burned up first, and then take

[h]Or *no Holy One*   [i]Hebrew *Sheol*

whatever you want," the servant would then answer, "No, hand it over now; if you don't, I'll take it by force."

This sin of the young men was very great in the LORD's sight, for they[j] were treating the LORD's offering with contempt.

SAMUEL'S FAMILY BLESSED.   But Samuel was ministering before the LORD—a boy wearing a linen ephod. Each year his mother made him a little robe and took it to him when she went up with her husband to offer the annual sacrifice. Eli would bless Elkanah and his wife, saying, "May the LORD give you children by this woman to take the place of the one she prayed for and gave to the LORD." Then they would go home. And the LORD was gracious to Hannah; she conceived and gave birth to three sons and two daughters. Meanwhile, the boy Samuel grew up in the presence of the LORD.

1 Sam.
2:18-21

ELI REBUKES SONS.   Now Eli, who was very old, heard about everything his sons were doing to all Israel and how they slept with the women who served at the entrance to the Tent of Meeting. So he said to them, "Why do you do such things? I hear from all the people about these wicked deeds of yours. No, my sons; it is not a good report that I hear spreading among the LORD's people. If a man sins against another man, God[k] may mediate for him; but if a man sins against the LORD, who will intercede for him?" His sons, however, did not listen to their father's rebuke, for it was the LORD's will to put them to death.

And the boy Samuel continued to grow in stature and in favor with the LORD and with men.

1 Sam.
2:22-26

JUDGMENT OF ELI'S HOUSE.   Now a man of God came to Eli and said to him, "This is what the LORD says: 'Did I not clearly reveal myself to your father's house when they were in Egypt under Pharaoh? I chose your father out of all the tribes of Israel to be my priest, to go up to my altar, to burn incense, and to wear an ephod in my presence. I also gave your father's house all the offerings made with fire by the Israelites. Why do you[l] scorn my sacrifice and offering that I prescribed for my dwelling? Why do you honor your sons more than me by fattening yourselves on the choice parts of every offering made by my people Israel?'

"Therefore the LORD, the God of Israel, declares: 'I promised that your house and your father's house would minister before me forever.' But now the LORD declares: 'Far be it from me! Those who honor me I will honor, but those who despise me will be disdained. The time is coming when I will cut short your strength and the strength of your father's house, so that there will not be an old man in your family line and you will see distress in my dwelling. Although good will be done to Israel, in your family line there will never be an old man. Every one of you that I do not cut off from my altar will be spared only to blind your eyes with tears and to grieve your heart, and all your descendants will die in the prime of life.

" 'And what happens to your two sons, Hophni and Phinehas, will be a sign to you—they will both die on the same day. I will raise up for myself a faithful priest, who will do according to what is in my heart and mind. I will firmly establish his house, and he will minister before my anointed one always. Then everyone left in your family line will come and bow

1 Sam.
2:27-36

---

[j]Or men   [k]Or the judges   [l]The Hebrew is plural.

down before him for a piece of silver and a crust of bread and plead, "Appoint me to some priestly office so I can have food to eat.'"'"

1 Sam. 3:1-18

GOD CALLS SAMUEL. The boy Samuel ministered before the LORD under Eli. In those days the word of the LORD was rare; there were not many visions.

One night Eli, whose eyes were becoming so weak that he could barely see, was lying down in his usual place. The lamp of God had not yet gone out, and Samuel was lying down in the temple*m* of the LORD, where the ark of God was. Then the LORD called Samuel.

Samuel answered, "Here I am." And he ran to Eli and said, "Here I am; you called me."

But Eli said, "I did not call; go back and lie down." So he went and lay down.

Again the LORD called, "Samuel!" And Samuel got up and went to Eli and said, "Here I am; you called me."

"My son," Eli said, "I did not call; go back and lie down."

Now Samuel did not yet know the LORD: The word of the LORD had not yet been revealed to him.

The LORD called Samuel a third time, and Samuel got up and went to Eli and said, "Here I am; you called me."

Then Eli realized that the LORD was calling the boy. So Eli told Samuel, "Go and lie down, and if he calls you, say, 'Speak, LORD, for your servant is listening.'" So Samuel went and lay down in his place.

The LORD came and stood there, calling as at the other times, "Samuel! Samuel!"

Then Samuel said, "Speak, for your servant is listening."

And the LORD said to Samuel: "See, I am about to do something in Israel that will make the ears of everyone who hears of it tingle. At that time I will carry out against Eli everything I spoke against his family—from beginning to end. For I told him that I would judge his family forever because of the sin he knew about; his sons made themselves contemptible,*n* and he failed to restrain them. Therefore, I swore to the house of Eli, 'The guilt of Eli's house will never be atoned for by sacrifice or offering.'"

Samuel lay down until morning and then opened the doors of the house of the LORD. He was afraid to tell Eli the vision, but Eli called him and said, "Samuel, my son."

Samuel answered, "Here I am."

"What was it he said to you?" Eli asked. "Do not hide it from me. May God deal with you, be it ever so severely, if you hide from me anything he told you." So Samuel told him everything, hiding nothing from him. Then Eli said, "He is the LORD; let him do what is good in his eyes."

1 Sam. 3:19-21

SAMUEL KNOWN AS PROPHET. The LORD was with Samuel as he grew up, and he let none of his words fall to the ground. And all Israel from Dan to Beersheba recognized that Samuel was attested as a prophet of the LORD. The LORD continued to appear at Shiloh, and there he revealed himself to Samuel through his word.

---

m That is, tabernacle   *n* Masoretic Text; an ancient Hebrew scribal tradition and Septuagint *sons blasphemed God*

DEFEAT BY PHILISTINES.   And Samuel's word came to all Israel.

Now the Israelites went out to fight against the Philistines. The Israelites camped at Ebenezer, and the Philistines at Aphek. The Philistines deployed their forces to meet Israel, and as the battle spread, Israel was defeated by the Philistines, who killed about four thousand of them on the battlefield.

1 Sam.
4:1,2
Ebenezer

ARK BROUGHT FROM SHILOH.   When the soldiers returned to camp, the elders of Israel asked, "Why did the LORD bring defeat upon us today before the Philistines? Let us bring the ark of the LORD's covenant from Shiloh, so that it *o* may go with us and save us from the hand of our enemies."

So the people sent men to Shiloh, and they brought back the ark of the covenant of the LORD Almighty, who is enthroned between the cherubim. And Eli's two sons, Hophni and Phinehas, were there with the ark of the covenant of God.

When the ark of the LORD's covenant came into the camp, all Israel raised such a great shout that the ground shook.

1 Sam.
4:3-5

PHILISTINES CAPTURE ARK.   Hearing the uproar, the Philistines asked, "What's all this shouting in the Hebrew camp?"

When they learned that the ark of the LORD had come into the camp, the Philistines were afraid. "A god has come into the camp," they said. "We're in trouble! Nothing like this has happened before. Woe to us! Who will deliver us from the hand of these mighty gods? They are the gods who struck the Egyptians with all kinds of plagues in the desert. Be strong, Philistines! Be men, or you will be subject to the Hebrews, as they have been to you. Be men, and fight!"

So the Philistines fought, and the Israelites were defeated and every man fled to his tent. The slaughter was very great; Israel lost thirty thousand foot soldiers. The ark of God was captured, and Eli's two sons, Hophni and Phinehas, died.

1 Sam.
4:6-11

DEATH OF ELI.   That same day a Benjamite ran from the battle line and went to Shiloh, his clothes torn and dust on his head. When he arrived, there was Eli sitting on his chair by the side of the road, watching, because his heart feared for the ark of God. When the man entered the town and told what had happened, the whole town sent up a cry.

Eli heard the outcry and asked, "What is the meaning of this uproar?"

The man hurried over to Eli, who was ninety-eight years old and whose eyes were set so that he could not see. He told Eli, "I have just come from the battle line; I fled from it this very day."

Eli asked, "What happened, my son?"

The man who brought the news replied, "Israel fled before the Philistines, and the army has suffered heavy losses. Also your two sons, Hophni and Phinehas, are dead, and the ark of God has been captured."

When he mentioned the ark of God, Eli fell backward off his chair by the side of the gate. His neck was broken and he died, for he was an old man and heavy. He had led *p* Israel forty years.

1 Sam.
4:12-18

ICHABOD BORN.   His daughter-in-law, the wife of Phinehas, was pregnant and near the time of delivery. When she heard the news that the ark of God had been captured and that her father-in-law and her husband

1 Sam.
4:19-22

*o*Or *he*   *p*Traditionally *judged*

were dead, she went into labor and gave birth, but was overcome by her labor pains. As she was dying, the women attending her said, "Don't despair; you have given birth to a son." But she did not respond or pay any attention.

She named the boy Ichabod,*q* saying, "The glory has departed from Israel"— because of the capture of the ark of God and the deaths of her father-in-law and her husband. She said, "The glory has departed from Israel, for the ark of God has been captured."

1 Sam.
5:1-12
Philistine
territory

ARK BRINGS TROUBLE. After the Philistines had captured the ark of God, they took it from Ebenezer to Ashdod. Then they carried the ark into Dagon's temple and set it beside Dagon. When the people of Ashdod rose early the next day, there was Dagon, fallen on his face on the ground before the ark of the LORD! They took Dagon and put him back in his place. But the following morning when they rose, there was Dagon, fallen on his face on the ground before the ark of the LORD! His head and hands had been broken off and were lying on the threshold; only his body remained. That is why to this day neither the priests of Dagon nor any others who enter Dagon's temple at Ashdod step on the threshold.

The LORD's hand was heavy upon the people of Ashdod and its vicinity; he brought devastation upon them and afflicted them with tumors.*r* When the men of Ashdod saw what was happening, they said, "The ark of the god of Israel must not stay here with us, because his hand is heavy upon us and upon Dagon our god." So they called together all the rulers of the Philistines and asked them, "What shall we do with the ark of the god of Israel?"

They answered, "Have the ark of the god of Israel moved to Gath." So they moved the ark of the God of Israel.

But after they had moved it, the LORD's hand was against that city, throwing it into a great panic. He afflicted the people of the city, both young and old, with an outbreak of tumors.*s* So they sent the ark of God to Ekron.

As the ark of God was entering Ekron, the people of Ekron cried out, "They have brought the ark of the god of Israel around to us to kill us and our people." So they called together all the rulers of the Philistines and said, "Send the ark of the god of Israel away; let it go back to its own place, or it*t* will kill us and our people." For death had filled the city with panic; God's hand was very heavy upon it. Those who did not die were afflicted with tumors, and the outcry of the city went up to heaven.

1 Sam.
6:1-12

ARK RETURNED. When the ark of the LORD had been in Philistine territory seven months, the Philistines called for the priests and the diviners and said, "What shall we do with the ark of the LORD? Tell us how we should send it back to its place."

They answered, "If you return the ark of the god of Israel, do not send it away empty, but by all means send a guilt offering to him. Then you will be healed, and you will know why his hand has not been lifted from you."

The Philistines asked, "What guilt offering should we send to him?"

---

qIchabod means *no glory.*   *r*Hebrew; Septuagint and Vulgate *tumors. And rats appeared in their land, and death and destruction were throughout the city*   *sOr with tumors in the groin* (see Septuagint)   *tOr he*

They replied, "Five gold tumors and five gold rats, according to the number of the Philistine rulers, because the same plague has struck both you and your rulers. Make models of the tumors and of the rats that are destroying the country, and pay honor to Israel's god. Perhaps he will lift his hand from you and your gods and your land. Why do you harden your hearts as the Egyptians and Pharaoh did? When he[u] treated them harshly, did they not send the Israelites out so they could go on their way?

"Now then, get a new cart ready, with two cows that have calved and have never been yoked. Hitch the cows to the cart, but take their calves away and pen them up. Take the ark of the LORD and put it on the cart, and in a chest beside it put the gold objects you are sending back to him as a guilt offering. Send it on its way, but keep watching it. If it goes up to its own territory, toward Beth Shemesh, then the LORD has brought this great disaster on us. But if it does not, then we will know that it was not his hand that struck us and that it happened to us by chance."

So they did this. They took two such cows and hitched them to the cart and penned up their calves. They placed the ark of the LORD on the cart and along with it the chest containing the gold rats and the models of the tumors. Then the cows went straight up toward Beth Shemesh, keeping on the road and lowing all the way; they did not turn to the right or to the left. The rulers of the Philistines followed them as far as the border of Beth Shemesh.

ARK CAUSES FEAR.   Now the people of Beth Shemesh were harvesting their wheat in the valley, and when they looked up and saw the ark, they rejoiced at the sight. The cart came to the field of Joshua of Beth Shemesh, and there it stopped beside a large rock. The people chopped up the wood of the cart and sacrificed the cows as a burnt offering to the LORD. The Levites took down the ark of the LORD, together with the chest containing the gold objects, and placed them on the large rock. On that day the people of Beth Shemesh offered burnt offerings and made sacrifices to the LORD. The five rulers of the Philistines saw all this and then returned that same day to Ekron.

> 1 Sam.
> 6:13-7:1
> Beth
> Shemesh

These are the gold tumors the Philistines sent as a guilt offering to the LORD—one each for Ashdod, Gaza, Ashkelon, Gath and Ekron. And the number of the gold rats was according to the number of Philistine towns belonging to the five rulers—the fortified towns with their country villages. The large rock, on which[v] they set the ark of the LORD, is a witness to this day in the field of Joshua of Beth Shemesh.

But God struck down some of the men of Beth Shemesh, putting seventy[w] of them to death because they had looked into the ark of the LORD. The people mourned because of the heavy blow the LORD had dealt them, and the men of Beth Shemesh asked, "Who can stand in the presence of the LORD, this holy God? To whom will the ark go up from here?"

Then they sent messengers to the people of Kiriath Jearim, saying, "The Philistines have returned the ark of the LORD. Come down and take it up to your place." So the men of Kiriath Jearim came and took up the ark of the LORD. They took it to Abinadab's house on the hill and consecrated Eleazar his son to guard the ark of the LORD.

[u]That is, God   [v]A few Hebrew manuscripts (see also Septuagint); most Hebrew manuscripts *villages as far as Greater Abel, where*   [w]A few Hebrew manuscripts; most Hebrew manuscripts and Septuagint *50,070*

| 1 Sam. 7:2-6 Kiriath Jearim |

CALL FOR REDEDICATION. It was a long time, twenty years in all, that the ark remained at Kiriath Jearim, and all the people of Israel mourned and sought after the LORD. And Samuel said to the whole house of Israel, "If you are returning to the LORD with all your hearts, then rid yourselves of the foreign gods and the Ashtoreths and commit yourselves to the LORD and serve him only, and he will deliver you out of the hand of the Philistines." So the Israelites put away their Baals and Ashtoreths, and served the LORD only.

Then Samuel said, "Assemble all Israel at Mizpah and I will intercede with the LORD for you." When they had assembled at Mizpah, they drew water and poured it out before the LORD. On that day they fasted and there they confessed, "We have sinned against the LORD." And Samuel was leader[x] of Israel at Mizpah.

| 1 Sam. 7:7-14 Mizpah |

ISRAEL DEFEATS PHILISTINES. When the Philistines heard that Israel had assembled at Mizpah, the rulers of the Philistines came up to attack them. And when the Israelites heard of it, they were afraid because of the Philistines. They said to Samuel, "Do not stop crying out to the LORD our God for us, that he may rescue us from the hand of the Philistines." Then Samuel took a suckling lamb and offered it up as a whole burnt offering to the LORD. He cried out to the LORD on Israel's behalf, and the LORD answered him.

While Samuel was sacrificing the burnt offering, the Philistines drew near to engage Israel in battle. But that day the LORD thundered with loud thunder against the Philistines and threw them into such a panic that they were routed before the Israelites. The men of Israel rushed out of Mizpah and pursued the Philistines, slaughtering them along the way to a point below Beth Car.

Then Samuel took a stone and set it up between Mizpah and Shen. He named it Ebenezer, [y] saying, "Thus far has the LORD helped us." So the Philistines were subdued and did not invade Israelite territory again.

Throughout Samuel's lifetime, the hand of the LORD was against the Philistines. The towns from Ekron to Gath that the Philistines had captured from Israel were restored to her, and Israel delivered the neighboring territory from the power of the Philistines. And there was peace between Israel and the Amorites.

| 1 Sam. 7:15-17 Ramah |

SAMUEL LEADS AS JUDGE. Samuel continued as judge over Israel all the days of his life. From year to year he went on a circuit from Bethel to Gilgal to Mizpah, judging Israel in all those places. But he always went back to Ramah, where his home was, and there he also judged Israel. And he built an altar there to the LORD.

Saul Appointed King

Although Israel is soon to have a king, the Scriptures make it clear that God will have a hand in choosing the kings and in regulating their conduct. Unlike other kings, Israel's kings will not rule by their own power. The first king, like so many of the leaders of God's people, would seem to be a rather unlikely choice, due to serious flaws in his character, In fact, he is

---

[x] Traditionally *judge*　　[y] *Ebenezer* means *stone of help.*

of the tribe of Benjamin, which not many years earlier had engaged in spiritual rebellion. Nevertheless God uses Saul to bring about his will in the unification of the Kingdom. Samuel here records the details of the first selection process and tells about the role that he himself plays.

ISRAEL ASKS FOR KING.   When Samuel grew old, he appointed his sons as judges for Israel. The name of his firstborn was Joel and the name of his second was Abijah, and they served at Beersheba. But his sons did not walk in his ways. They turned aside after dishonest gain and accepted bribes and perverted justice.

1 Sam.
8:1-5

So all the elders of Israel gathered together and came to Samuel at Ramah. They said to him, "You are old, and your sons do not walk in your ways; now appoint a king to lead^z us, such as all the other nations have."

GOD GIVES PERMISSION.   But when they said, "Give us a king to lead us," this displeased Samuel; so he prayed to the LORD. And the LORD told him: "Listen to all that the people are saying to you; it is not you they have rejected, but they have rejected me as their king. As they have done from the day I brought them up out of Egypt until this day, forsaking me and serving other gods, so they are doing to you. Now listen to them; but warn them solemnly and let them know what the king who will reign over them will do."

1 Sam.
8:6-9

SAMUEL WARNS ISRAEL.   Samuel told all the words of the LORD to the people who were asking him for a king. He said, "This is what the king who will reign over you will do: He will take your sons and make them serve with his chariots and horses, and they will run in front of his chariots. Some he will assign to be commanders of thousands and commanders of fifties, and others to plow his ground and reap his harvest, and still others to make weapons of war and equipment for his chariots. He will take your daughters to be perfumers and cooks and bakers. He will take the best of your fields and vineyards and olive groves and give them to his attendants. He will take a tenth of your grain and of your vintage and give it to his officials and attendants. Your menservants and maidservants and the best of your cattle^a and donkeys he will take for his own use. He will take a tenth of your flocks, and you yourselves will become his slaves. When that day comes, you will cry out for relief from the king you have chosen, and the LORD will not answer you in that day."

1 Sam.
8:10-18

ISRAEL DISREGARDS WARNING.   But the people refused to listen to Samuel. "No!" they said. "We want a king over us. Then we will be like all the other nations, with a king to lead us and to go out before us and fight our battles."

1 Sam.
8:19-22

When Samuel heard all that the people said, he repeated it before the LORD. The LORD answered, "Listen to them and give them a king."

Then Samuel said to the men of Israel, "Everyone go back to his town."

SAUL SEEKS FATHER'S DONKEYS.   There was a Benjamite, a man of standing, whose name was Kish son of Abiel, the son of Zeror, the son of Becorath, the son of Aphiah of Benjamin. He had a son named Saul, an impressive young man without equal among the Israelites—a head taller than any of the others.

1 Sam.
9:1-5

Now the donkeys belonging to Saul's father Kish were lost, and Kish

^zTraditionally *judge*   ^aSeptuagint; Hebrew *young men*

said to his son Saul, "Take one of the servants with you and go and look for the donkeys." So he passed through the hill country of Ephraim and through the area around Shalisha, but they did not find them. They went on into the district of Shaalim, but the donkeys were not there. Then he passed through the territory of Benjamin, but they did not find them.

When they reached the district of Zuph, Saul said to the servant who was with him, "Come, let's go back, or my father will stop thinking about the donkeys and start worrying about us."

1 Sam.
9:6-14

ATTEMPT TO FIND SEER.   But the servant replied, "Look, in this town there is a man of God; he is highly respected, and everything he says comes true. Let's go there now. Perhaps he will tell us what way to take."

Saul said to his servant, "If we go, what can we give the man? The food in our sacks is gone. We have no gift to take to the man of God. What do we have?"

The servant answered him again. "Look," he said, "I have a quarter of a shekel[b] of silver. I will give it to the man of God so that he will tell us what way to take." (Formerly in Israel, if a man went to inquire of God, he would say, "Come, let us go to the seer," because the prophet of today used to be called a seer.)

"Good," Saul said to his servant. "Come, let's go." So they set out for the town where the man of God was.

As they were going up the hill to the town, they met some girls coming out to draw water, and they asked them, "Is the seer here?"

"He is," they answered. "He's ahead of you. Hurry now; he has just come to our town today, for the people have a sacrifice at the high place. As soon as you enter the town, you will find him before he goes up to the high place to eat. The people will not begin eating until he comes, because he must bless the sacrifice; afterward, those who are invited will eat. Go up now; you should find him about this time."

They went up to the town, and as they were entering it, there was Samuel, coming toward them on his way up to the high place.

1 Sam.
9:15-17

GOD TALKS TO SAMUEL.   Now the day before Saul came, the LORD had revealed this to Samuel: "About this time tomorrow I will send you a man from the land of Benjamin. Anoint him leader over my people Israel; he will deliver my people from the hand of the Philistines. I have looked upon my people, for their cry has reached me."

When Samuel caught sight of Saul, the LORD said to him, "This is the man I spoke to you about; he will govern my people."

1 Sam.
9:18-27

SAMUEL ENTERTAINS SAUL.   Saul approached Samuel in the gateway and asked, "Would you please tell me where the seer's house is?"

"I am the seer," Samuel replied. "Go up ahead of me to the high place, for today you are to eat with me, and in the morning I will let you go and will tell you all that is in your heart. As for the donkeys you lost three days ago, do not worry about them; they have been found. And to whom is all the desire of Israel turned, if not to you and all your father's family?"

Saul answered, "But am I not a Benjamite, from the smallest tribe of Israel, and is not my clan the least of all the clans of the tribe of Benjamin? Why do you say such a thing to me?"

[b]That is, about 1/10 ounce (about 3 grams)

Then Samuel brought Saul and his servant into the hall and seated them at the head of those who were invited—about thirty in number. Samuel said to the cook, "Bring the piece of meat I gave you, the one I told you to lay aside."

So the cook took up the leg with what was on it and set it in front of Saul. Samuel said, "Here is what has been kept for you. Eat, because it was set aside for you for this occasion, from the time I said, 'I have invited guests.'" And Saul dined with Samuel that day.

After they came down from the high place to the town, Samuel talked with Saul on the roof of his house. They rose about daybreak and Samuel called to Saul on the roof, "Get ready, and I will send you on your way." When Saul got ready, he and Samuel went outside together. As they were going down to the edge of the town, Samuel said to Saul, "Tell the servant to go on ahead of us"—and the servant did so—"but you stay here awhile, so that I may give you a message from God."

SIGNS FOR SAUL'S ASSURANCE.   Then Samuel took a flask of oil and poured it on Saul's head and kissed him, saying, "Has not the LORD anointed you leader over his inheritance? ᶜ When you leave me today, you will meet two men near Rachel's tomb, at Zelzah on the border of Benjamin. They will say to you, 'The donkeys you set out to look for have been found. And now your father has stopped thinking about them and is worried about you. He is asking, "What shall I do about my son?"'

"Then you will go on from there until you reach the great tree of Tabor. Three men going up to God at Bethel will meet you there. One will be carrying three young goats, another three loaves of bread, and another a skin of wine. They will greet you and offer you two loaves of bread, which you will accept from them.

"After that you will go to Gibeah of God, where there is a Philistine outpost. As you approach the town, you will meet a procession of prophets coming down from the high place with lyres, tambourines, flutes and harps being played before them, and they will be prophesying. The Spirit of the LORD will come upon you in power, and you will prophesy with them; and you will be changed into a different person. Once these signs are fulfilled, do whatever your hand finds to do, for God is with you.

"Go down ahead of me to Gilgal. I will surely come down to you to sacrifice burnt offerings and fellowship offerings,ᵈ but you must wait seven days until I come to you and tell you what you are to do."

1 Sam.
10:1-8

SAUL PROPHESIES.   As Saul turned to leave Samuel, God changed Saul's heart, and all these signs were fulfilled that day. When they arrived at Gibeah, a procession of prophets met him; the Spirit of God came upon him in power, and he joined in their prophesying. When all those who had formerly known him saw him prophesying with the prophets, they asked each other, "What is this that has happened to the son of Kish? Is Saul also among the prophets?"

A man who lived there answered, "And who is their father?" So it became a saying: "Is Saul also among the prophets?" After Saul stopped prophesying, he went to the high place.

1 Sam.
10:9-13
Gibeah

ᶜHebrew; Septuagint and Vulgate *over his people Israel? You will reign over the* LORD's *people and save them from the power of their enemies round about. And this will be a sign to you that the* LORD *has anointed you leader over his inheritance:*   ᵈTraditionally *peace offerings*

1 Sam.
10:14-16

KINGSHIP PLANS UNDISCLOSED. Now Saul's uncle asked him and his servant, "Where have you been?"

"Looking for the donkeys," he said. "But when we saw they were not to be found, we went to Samuel."

Saul's uncle said, "Tell me what Samuel said to you."

Saul replied, "He assured us that the donkeys had been found." But he did not tell his uncle what Samuel had said about the kingship.

1 Sam.
10:17-25
(1043
B.C.?)
Mizpah

SAUL CHOSEN AS KING. Samuel summoned the people of Israel to the LORD at Mizpah and said to them, "This is what the LORD, the God of Israel, says: 'I brought Israel up out of Egypt, and I delivered you from the power of Egypt and all the kingdoms that oppressed you.' But you have now rejected your God, who saves you out of all your calamities and distresses. And you have said, 'No, set a king over us.' So now present yourselves before the LORD by your tribes and clans."

When Samuel brought all the tribes of Israel near, the tribe of Benjamin was chosen. Then he brought forward the tribe of Benjamin, clan by clan, and Matri's clan was chosen. Finally Saul son of Kish was chosen. But when they looked for him, he was not to be found. So they inquired further of the LORD, "Has the man come here yet?"

And the LORD said, "Yes, he has hidden himself among the baggage."

They ran and brought him out, and as he stood among the people he was a head taller than any of the others. Samuel said to all the people, "Do you see the man the LORD has chosen? There is no one like him among all the people."

Then the people shouted, "Long live the king!"

Samuel explained to the people the regulations of the kingship. He wrote them down on a scroll and deposited it before the LORD. Then Samuel dismissed the people, each to his own home.

1 Sam.
10:26,27
Gibeah

MIXED ACCEPTANCE. Saul also went to his home in Gibeah, accompanied by valiant men whose hearts God had touched. But some troublemakers said, "How can this fellow save us?" They despised him and brought him no gifts. But Saul kept silent.

1 Sam.
11:1-11

SAUL SHOWS LEADERSHIP. Nahash the Ammonite went up and besieged Jabesh Gilead. And all the men of Jabesh said to him, "Make a treaty with us, and we will be subject to you."

But Nahash the Ammonite replied, "I will make a treaty with you only on the condition that I gouge out the right eye of every one of you and so bring disgrace on all Israel."

The elders of Jabesh said to him, "Give us seven days so we can send messengers throughout Israel; if no one comes to rescue us, we will surrender to you."

When the messengers came to Gibeah of Saul and reported these terms to the people, they all wept aloud. Just then Saul was returning from the fields, behind his oxen, and he asked, "What is wrong with the people? Why are they weeping?" Then they repeated to him what the men of Jabesh had said.

When Saul heard their words, the Spirit of God came upon him in power, and he burned with anger. He took a pair of oxen, cut them into pieces, and sent the pieces by messengers throughout Israel, proclaiming, "This is what will be done to the oxen of anyone who does not follow Saul and Samuel." Then the terror of the LORD fell on the people, and they turned out as one man. When Saul mustered them at Bezek, the men of Israel numbered three hundred thousand and the men of Judah thirty thousand.

They told the messengers who had come, "Say to the men of Jabesh Gilead, 'By the time the sun is hot tomorrow, you will be delivered.'" When the messengers went and reported this to the men of Jabesh, they were elated. They said to the Ammonites, "Tomorrow we will surrender to you, and you can do to us whatever seems good to you."

The next day Saul separated his men into three divisions; during the last watch of the night they broke into the camp of the Ammonites and slaughtered them until the heat of the day. Those who survived were scattered, so that no two of them were left together.

SAUL'S KINGSHIP CONFIRMED.   The people then said to Samuel, "Who was it that asked, 'Shall Saul reign over us?' Bring these men to us and we will put them to death."

1 Sam.
11:12-15
Gilgal

But Saul said, "No one shall be put to death today, for this day the LORD has rescued Israel."

Then Samuel said to the people, "Come, let us go to Gilgal and there reaffirm the kingship." So all the people went to Gilgal and confirmed Saul as king in the presence of the LORD. There they sacrificed fellowship offerings[e] before the LORD, and Saul and all the Israelites held a great celebration.

SAMUEL'S FAREWELL ADDRESS. Samuel said to all Israel, "I have listened to everything you said to me and have set a king over you. Now you have a king as your leader. As for me, I am old and gray, and my sons are here with you. I have been your leader from my youth until this day. Here I stand. Testify against me in the presence of the LORD and his anointed. Whose ox have I taken? Whose donkey have I taken? Whom have I cheated? Whom have I oppressed? From whose hand have I accepted a bribe to make me shut my eyes? If I have done any of these, I will make it right."

1 Sam.
12:1-7

"You have not cheated or oppressed us," they replied. "You have not taken anything from anyone's hand."

Samuel said to them, "The LORD is witness against you, and also his anointed is witness this day, that you have not found anything in my hand."

"He is witness," they said.

Then Samuel said to the people, "It is the LORD who appointed Moses and Aaron and brought your forefathers up out of Egypt. Now then, stand here, because I am going to confront you with evidence before the LORD as to all the righteous acts performed by the LORD for you and your fathers.

"After Jacob entered Egypt, they cried to the LORD for help, and the LORD sent Moses and Aaron, who brought your forefathers out of Egypt and settled them in this place.

1 Sam.
12:8-15

"But they forgot the LORD their God; so he sold them into the hand of Sisera, the commander of the army of Hazor, and into the hands of the Philistines and the king of Moab, who fought against them. They cried out to the LORD and said, 'We have sinned; we have forsaken the LORD and served the Baals and the Ashtoreths. But now deliver us from the hands of

_____
[e]Traditionally *peace offerings*

our enemies, and we will serve you.' Then the LORD sent Jerub-Baal, *f* Barak, *g* Jephthah and Samuel, *h* and he delivered you from the hands of your enemies on every side, so that you lived securely.

"But when you saw that Nahash king of the Ammonites was moving against you, you said to me, 'No, we want a king to rule over us'—even though the LORD your God was your king. Now here is the king you have chosen, the one you asked for; see, the LORD has set a king over you. If you fear the LORD and serve and obey him and do not rebel against his commands, and if both you and the king who reigns over you follow the LORD your God—good! But if you do not obey the LORD, and if you rebel against his commands, his hand will be against you, as it was against your fathers.

1 Sam. 12:16-18

"Now then, stand still and see this great thing the LORD is about to do before your eyes! Is it not wheat harvest now? I will call upon the LORD to send thunder and rain. And you will realize what an evil thing you did in the eyes of the LORD when you asked for a king."

Then Samuel called upon the LORD, and that same day the LORD sent thunder and rain. So all the people stood in awe of the LORD and of Samuel.

The people all said to Samuel, "Pray to the LORD your God for your servants so that we will not die, for we have added to all our other sins the evil of asking for a king."

1 Sam. 12:19-25

"Do not be afraid," Samuel replied. "You have done all this evil; yet do not turn away from the LORD, but serve the LORD with all your heart. Do not turn away after useless idols. They can do you no good, nor can they rescue you, because they are useless. For the sake of his great name the LORD will not reject his people, because the LORD was pleased to make you his own. As for me, far be it from me that I should sin against the LORD by failing to pray for you. And I will teach you the way that is good and right. But be sure to fear the LORD and serve him faithfully with all your heart; consider what great things he has done for you. Yet if you persist in doing evil, both you and your king will be swept away."

The Reign of Saul

s the first king of Israel, Saul proves to be a courageous leader, but it is clear that he is only human and therefore fallible. Although a sovereign king, Saul is not above rebuke by God's prophet, Samuel. Saul's disobedience to God will in fact lead ultimately to his rejection as king. In sharp contrast to his father, Saul's son Jonathan shows himself to be a man of great character. His military exploits show a courage and strength not seen in Saul himself.

1 Sam. 13:1; 14:49-51

SAUL'S FAMILY.   Saul was ⌞thirty⌟ *i* years old when he became king, and he reigned over Israel ⌞forty-⌟ *j* two years.

Saul's sons were Jonathan, Ishvi and Malki-Shua. The name of his older daughter was Merab, and that of the younger was Michal. His wife's name

f Also called *Gideon*   *g* Some Septuagint manuscripts and Syriac; Hebrew *Bedan*
h Hebrew; some Septuagint manuscripts and Syriac *Samson*   *i* A few late manuscripts of the Septuagint; Hebrew does not have *thirty*.   *j* See the round number in Acts 13:21; Hebrew does not have *forty-*.

was Ahinoam daughter of Ahimaaz. The name of the commander of Saul's
army was Abner son of Ner, and Ner was Saul's uncle. Saul's father Kish
and Abner's father Ner were sons of Abiel.

HOUSE OF SAUL.   1 Chron.
   Jeiel the father ^k of Gibeon lived in Gibeon.   9:35-44
     His wife's name was Maacah, and his firstborn son was Abdon,
      followed by Zur, Kish, Baal, Ner, Nadab, Gedor, Ahio, Zeker and
      Mikloth, who was the father of Shimeam. They too lived near
      their relatives in Jerusalem.
   Ner was the father of Kish, Kish the father of Saul, and Saul the father
     of Jonathan, Malki-Shua, Abinadab and Esh-Baal. ^l
   The son of Jonathan:
     Merib-Baal, ^m who was the father of Micah.
   The sons of Micah:
     Pithon, Melech, Tahrea and Ahaz. ⁿ
     Ahaz was the father of Jadah, Jadah ^o was the father of Alemeth,
      Azmaveth and Zimri, and Zimri was the father of Moza. Moza
      was the father of Binea; Rephaiah was his son, Eleasah his son
      and Azel his son.
   Azel had six sons, and these were their names:
     Azrikam, Bokeru, Ishmael, Sheariah, Obadiah and Hanan. All these
     were the sons of Azel.

SAMUEL REBUKES SAUL.   Saul ^p chose three thousand men from Israel;   1 Sam.
two thousand were with him at Micmash and in the hill country of Bethel,   13:2-15
and a thousand were with Jonathan at Gibeah in Benjamin. The rest of the   Gilgal
men he sent back to their homes.
   Jonathan attacked the Philistine outpost at Geba, and the Philistines
heard about it. Then Saul had the trumpet blown throughout the land and
said, "Let the Hebrews hear!" So all Israel heard the news: "Saul has
attacked the Philistine outpost, and now Israel has become a stench to the
Philistines." And the people were summoned to join Saul at Gilgal.
   The Philistines assembled to fight Israel, with three thousand^q chariots,
six thousand charioteers, and soldiers as numerous as the sand on the
seashore. They went up and camped at Micmash, east of Beth Aven. When
the men of Israel saw that their situation was critical and that their army
was hard pressed, they hid in caves and thickets, among the rocks, and in
pits and cisterns. Some Hebrews even crossed the Jordan to the land of
Gad and Gilead.
   Saul remained at Gilgal, and all the troops with him were quaking with
fear. He waited seven days, the time set by Samuel; but Samuel did not
come to Gilgal, and Saul's men began to scatter. So he said, "Bring me the
burnt offering and the fellowship offerings."^r And Saul offered up the
burnt offering. Just as he finished making the offering, Samuel arrived,
and Saul went out to greet him.
   "What have you done?" asked Samuel.

^k*Father* may mean *civic leader* or *military leader.*   ^lAlso known as *Ish-Bosheth*   ^mAlso
known as *Mephibosheth*   ⁿVulgate and Syriac (see also Septuagint and 1 Chron. 8:35);
Hebrew does not have *and Ahaz.*   ^oSome Hebrew manuscripts and Septuagint (see
also 1 Chron. 8:36); most Hebrew manuscripts *Jarah, Jarah*   ^pOr *and when he had
reigned over Israel two years,* ²*he*   ^qSome Septuagint manuscripts and Syriac; Hebrew
thirty thousand   ^rTraditionally *peace offerings*

Saul replied, "When I saw that the men were scattering, and that you did not come at the set time, and that the Philistines were assembling at Micmash, I thought, 'Now the Philistines will come down against me at Gilgal, and I have not sought the LORD's favor.' So I felt compelled to offer the burnt offering."

"You acted foolishly," Samuel said. "You have not kept the command the LORD your God gave you; if you had, he would have established your kingdom over Israel for all time. But now your kingdom will not endure; the LORD has sought out a man after his own heart and appointed him leader of his people, because you have not kept the LORD's command."

Then Samuel left Gilgal[s] and went up to Gibeah in Benjamin, and Saul counted the men who were with him. They numbered about six hundred.

1 Sam. 13:16-22 Gibeah

PHILISTINES' WEAPON STRATEGY.   Saul and his son Jonathan and the men with them were staying in Gibeah[t] in Benjamin, while the Philistines camped at Micmash. Raiding parties went out from the Philistine camp in three detachments. One turned toward Ophrah in the vicinity of Shual, another toward Beth Horon, and the third toward the borderland overlooking the Valley of Zeboim facing the desert.

Not a blacksmith could be found in the whole land of Israel, because the Philistines had said, "Otherwise the Hebrews will make swords or spears!" So all Israel went down to the Philistines to have their plowshares, mattocks, axes and sickles [u] sharpened. The price was two thirds of a shekel[v] for sharpening plowshares and mattocks, and a third of a shekel[w] for sharpening forks and axes and for repointing goads.

So on the day of the battle not a soldier with Saul and Jonathan had a sword or spear in his hand; only Saul and his son Jonathan had them.

1 Sam. 14:1-13

JONATHAN ATTACKS PHILISTINES.   One day Jonathan son of Saul said to the young man bearing his armor, "Come, let's go over to the Philistine outpost on the other side." But he did not tell his father.

Saul was staying on the outskirts of Gibeah under a pomegranate tree in Migron. With him were about six hundred men, among whom was Ahijah, who was wearing an ephod. He was a son of Ichabod's brother Ahitub son of Phinehas, the son of Eli, the LORD's priest in Shiloh. No one was aware that Jonathan had left.

On each side of the pass that Jonathan intended to cross to reach the Philistine outpost was a cliff; one was called Bozez, and the other Seneh. One cliff stood to the north toward Micmash, the other to the south toward Geba.

Jonathan said to his young armor-bearer, "Come, let's go over to the outpost of those uncircumcised fellows. Perhaps the LORD will act in our behalf. Nothing can hinder the LORD from saving, whether by many or by few."

"Do all that you have in mind," his armor-bearer said. "Go ahead; I am with you heart and soul."

Jonathan said, "Come, then; we will cross over toward the men and let them see us. If they say to us, 'Wait there until we come to you,' we will

[s] Hebrew; Septuagint *Gilgal and went his way; the rest of the people went after Saul to meet the army, and they went out of Gilgal*   [t] Two Hebrew manuscripts; most Hebrew manuscripts *Geba*, a variant of *Gibeah*   [u] Septuagint; Hebrew *plowshares*   [v] Hebrew *pim*; that is, about 1/4 ounce (about 8 grams)   [w] That is, about 1/8 ounce (about 4 grams)

stay where we are and not go up to them. But if they say, 'Come up to us,' we will climb up, because that will be our sign that the LORD has given them into our hands."

So both of them showed themselves to the Philistine outpost. "Look!" said the Philistines. "The Hebrews are crawling out of the holes they were hiding in." The men of the outpost shouted to Jonathan and his armor-bearer, "Come up to us and we'll teach you a lesson."

So Jonathan said to his armor-bearer, "Climb up after me; the LORD has given them into the hand of Israel."

Jonathan climbed up, using his hands and feet, with his armor-bearer right behind him. The Philistines fell before Jonathan, and his armor-bearer followed and killed behind him.

PHILISTINES ARE ROUTED.   In that first attack Jonathan and his armor-bearer killed some twenty men in an area of about half an acre.^{x} 1 Sam.
14:14-23

Then panic struck the whole army—those in the camp and field, and those in the outposts and raiding parties—and the ground shook. It was a panic sent by God.^{y}

Saul's lookouts at Gibeah in Benjamin saw the army melting away in all directions. Then Saul said to the men who were with him, "Muster the forces and see who has left us." When they did, it was Jonathan and his armor-bearer who were not there.

Saul said to Ahijah, "Bring the ark of God." (At that time it was with the Israelites.)^z While Saul was talking to the priest, the tumult in the Philistine camp increased more and more. So Saul said to the priest, "Withdraw your hand."

Then Saul and all his men assembled and went to the battle. They found the Philistines in total confusion, striking each other with their swords. Those Hebrews who had previously been with the Philistines and had gone up with them to their camp went over to the Israelites who were with Saul and Jonathan. When all the Israelites who had hidden in the hill country of Ephraim heard that the Philistines were on the run, they joined the battle in hot pursuit. So the LORD rescued Israel that day, and the battle moved on beyond Beth Aven.

JONATHAN VIOLATES SAUL'S ORDER.   Now the men of Israel were in distress that day, because Saul had bound the people under an oath, saying, "Cursed be any man who eats food before evening comes, before I have avenged myself on my enemies!" So none of the troops tasted food.   1 Sam.
14:24-30

The entire army^a entered the woods, and there was honey on the ground. When they went into the woods, they saw the honey oozing out, yet no one put his hand to his mouth, because they feared the oath. But Jonathan had not heard that his father had bound the people with the oath, so he reached out the end of the staff that was in his hand and dipped it into the honeycomb. He raised his hand to his mouth, and his eyes brightened.^{b} Then one of the soldiers told him, "Your father bound the army under a strict oath, saying, 'Cursed be any man who eats food today!' That is why the men are faint."

Jonathan said, "My father has made trouble for the country. See how

---

^{x}Hebrew *half a yoke*; a "yoke" was the land plowed by a yoke of oxen in one day.
^{y}Or *a terrible panic* ^{z}Hebrew; Septuagint *"Bring the ephod." (At that time he wore the ephod before the Israelites.)* ^{a}Or *Now all the people of the land* ^{b}Or *his strength was renewed.*

my eyes brightened[c] when I tasted a little of this honey. How much better it would have been if the men had eaten today some of the plunder they took from their enemies. Would not the slaughter of the Philistines have been even greater?"

1 Sam. 14:31-39

That day, after the Israelites had struck down the Philistines from Micmash to Aijalon, they were exhausted. They pounced on the plunder and, taking sheep, cattle and calves, they butchered them on the ground and ate them, together with the blood. Then someone said to Saul, "Look, the men are sinning against the LORD by eating meat that has blood in it."

"You have broken faith," he said. "Roll a large stone over here at once." Then he said, "Go out among the men and tell them, 'Each of you bring me your cattle and sheep, and slaughter them here and eat them. Do not sin against the LORD by eating meat with blood still in it.'"

So everyone brought his ox that night and slaughtered it there. Then Saul built an altar to the LORD; it was the first time he had done this.

Saul said, "Let us go down after the Philistines by night and plunder them till dawn, and let us not leave one of them alive."

"Do whatever seems best to you," they replied.

But the priest said, "Let us inquire of God here."

So Saul asked God, "Shall I go down after the Philistines? Will you give them into Israel's hand?" But God did not answer him that day.

1 Sam. 14:40-45

Saul therefore said, "Come here, all you who are leaders of the army, and let us find out what sin has been committed today. As surely as the LORD who rescues Israel lives, even if it lies with my son Jonathan, he must die." But not one of the men said a word.

Saul then said to all the Israelites, "You stand over there; I and Jonathan my son will stand over here."

"Do what seems best to you," the men replied.

Then Saul prayed to the LORD, the God of Israel, "Give me the right answer."[d] And Jonathan and Saul were taken by lot, and the men were cleared. Saul said, "Cast the lot between me and Jonathan my son." And Jonathan was taken.

Then Saul said to Jonathan, "Tell me what you have done."

So Jonathan told him, "I merely tasted a little honey with the end of my staff. And now must I die?"

Saul said, "May God deal with me, be it ever so severely, if you do not die, Jonathan."

But the men said to Saul, "Should Jonathan die—he who has brought about this great deliverance in Israel? Never! As surely as the LORD lives, not a hair of his head will fall to the ground, for he did this today with God's help." So the men rescued Jonathan, and he was not put to death.

1 Sam. 14:46-48,52

SAUL A SUCCESSFUL LEADER.   Then Saul stopped pursuing the Philistines, and they withdrew to their own land.

After Saul had assumed rule over Israel, he fought against their enemies on every side: Moab, the Ammonites, Edom, the kings[e] of Zobah, and the Philistines. Wherever he turned, he inflicted punishment on them.[f] He

---

[c]Or *my strength was renewed*   [d]Hebrew; Septuagint *"Why have you not answered your servant today? If the fault is in me or my son Jonathan, respond with Urim, but if the men of Israel are at fault, respond with Thummim."*   [e]Masoretic Text; Dead Sea Scrolls and Septuagint *king*   [f]Hebrew; Septuagint *he was victorious*

fought valiantly and defeated the Amalekites, delivering Israel from the hands of those who had plundered them.

All the days of Saul there was bitter war with the Philistines, and whenever Saul saw a mighty or brave man, he took him into his service.

EASTERN TRIBES FIGHT HAGRITES.   During Saul's reign they waged war against the Hagrites, who were defeated at their hands; they occupied the dwellings of the Hagrites throughout the entire region east of Gilead.

1 Chron.
5:10,18-22

The Reubenites, the Gadites and the half-tribe of Manasseh had 44,760 men ready for military service—able-bodied men who could handle shield and sword, who could use a bow, and who were trained for battle. They waged war against the Hagrites, Jetur, Naphish and Nodab. They were helped in fighting them, and God handed the Hagrites and all their allies over to them, because they cried out to him during the battle. He answered their prayers, because they trusted in him. They seized the livestock of the Hagrites—fifty thousand camels, two hundred fifty thousand sheep and two thousand donkeys. They also took one hundred thousand people captive, and many others fell slain, because the battle was God's. And they occupied the land until the exile.

MISSION AGAINST AMALEKITES.   Samuel said to Saul, "I am the one the LORD sent to anoint you king over his people Israel; so listen now to the message from the LORD. This is what the LORD Almighty says: 'I will punish the Amalekites for what they did to Israel when they waylaid them as they came up from Egypt. Now go, attack the Amalekites and totally destroy[g] everything that belongs to them. Do not spare them; put to death men and women, children and infants, cattle and sheep, camels and donkeys.'"

1 Sam.
15:1-9
Amalek

So Saul summoned the men and mustered them at Telaim—two hundred thousand foot soldiers and ten thousand men from Judah. Saul went to the city of Amalek and set an ambush in the ravine. Then he said to the Kenites, "Go away, leave the Amalekites so that I do not destroy you along with them; for you showed kindness to all the Israelites when they came up out of Egypt." So the Kenites moved away from the Amalekites.

Then Saul attacked the Amalekites all the way from Havilah to Shur, to the east of Egypt. He took Agag king of the Amalekites alive, and all his people he totally destroyed with the sword. But Saul and the army spared Agag and the best of the sheep and cattle, the fat calves[h] and lambs— everything that was good. These they were unwilling to destroy completely, but everything that was despised and weak they totally destroyed.

SAUL REJECTED AS KING.   Then the word of the LORD came to Samuel: "I am grieved that I have made Saul king, because he has turned away from me and has not carried out my instructions." Samuel was troubled, and he cried out to the LORD all that night.

1 Sam.
15:10-21
Gilgal

Early in the morning Samuel got up and went to meet Saul, but he was told, "Saul has gone to Carmel. There he has set up a monument in his own honor and has turned and gone on down to Gilgal."

When Samuel reached him, Saul said, "The LORD bless you! I have carried out the LORD's instructions."

---

[g]The Hebrew term refers to the irrevocable giving over of things or persons to the LORD, often by totally destroying them.   [h]Or the grown bulls; the meaning of the Hebrew for this phrase is uncertain.

But Samuel said, "What then is this bleating of sheep in my ears? What is this lowing of cattle that I hear?"

Saul answered, "The soldiers brought them from the Amalekites; they spared the best of the sheep and cattle to sacrifice to the LORD your God, but we totally destroyed the rest."

"Stop!" Samuel said to Saul. "Let me tell you what the LORD said to me last night."

"Tell me," Saul replied.

Samuel said, "Although you were once small in your own eyes, did you not become the head of the tribes of Israel? The LORD anointed you king over Israel. And he sent you on a mission, saying, 'Go and completely destroy those wicked people, the Amalekites; make war on them until you have wiped them out.' Why did you not obey the LORD? Why did you pounce on the plunder and do evil in the eyes of the LORD?"

"But I did obey the LORD," Saul said. "I went on the mission the LORD assigned me. I completely destroyed the Amalekites and brought back Agag their king. The soldiers took sheep and cattle from the plunder, the best of what was devoted to God, in order to sacrifice them to the LORD your God at Gilgal."

1 Sam. 15:22,23   But Samuel replied:

> "Does the LORD delight in burnt offerings and sacrifices
>   as much as in obeying the voice of the LORD?
> To obey is better than sacrifice,
>   and to heed is better than the fat of rams.
> For rebellion is like the sin of divination,
>   and arrogance like the evil of idolatry.
> Because you have rejected the word of the LORD,
>   he has rejected you as king."

1 Sam. 15:24-29   Then Saul said to Samuel, "I have sinned. I violated the LORD's command and your instructions. I was afraid of the people and so I gave in to them. Now I beg you, forgive my sin and come back with me, so that I may worship the LORD."

But Samuel said to him, "I will not go back with you. You have rejected the word of the LORD, and the LORD has rejected you as king over Israel!"

As Samuel turned to leave, Saul caught hold of the hem of his robe, and it tore. Samuel said to him, "The LORD has torn the kingdom of Israel from you today and has given it to one of your neighbors—to one better than you. He who is the Glory of Israel does not lie or change his mind; for he is not a man, that he should change his mind."

1 Sam. 15:30-33   AGAG KILLED.   Saul replied, "I have sinned. But please honor me before the elders of my people and before Israel; come back with me, so that I may worship the LORD your God." So Samuel went back with Saul, and Saul worshiped the LORD.

Then Samuel said, "Bring me Agag king of the Amalekites."

Agag came to him confidently,[i] thinking, "Surely the bitterness of death is past."

But Samuel said,

> "As your sword has made women childless,

[i]Or *him trembling, yet*

so will your mother be childless among women."

And Samuel put Agag to death before the LORD at Gilgal.

SAMUEL GRIEVES OVER SAUL.   Then Samuel left for Ramah, but Saul   1 Sam.
went up to his home in Gibeah of Saul. Until the day Samuel died, he did   15:34,35
not go to see Saul again, though Samuel mourned for him. And the LORD
was grieved that he had made Saul king over Israel.

David's Rise to Power

*T*he die is cast, but the time for Saul to be replaced is not yet at hand.
Over the next several years his successor, David, will become a powerful figure in Israel and take on increased influence. Saul is well aware
of David's growing popularity as somewhat of a folk hero, and this causes
resentment and jealousy in Saul. The repeated incidents of rage which arise out
of his insecurity reveal still another defect in character in addition to his previous disobedience to God's commands.

In sharp contrast, David is seen repeatedly as a gentle, forgiving servant of
his king. Instead of retaliating for undeserved threats, David responds with
mercy and avoidance. (Even when David seemingly aligns himself with Israel's
archenemies, the Philistines, it is apparently only a practical means of avoiding
violent conflict with Saul.)

Throughout this period of confrontation, David reveals himself as a deeply
sensitive and expressive man of God. In times of trouble David rises above his
inner fears and feelings of helplessness to express himself through poetic songs,
known as psalms. Virtually every important encounter he faces becomes
memorialized in his petitions to God. David often identifies the specific incident to which he refers in a given psalm, and those psalms are therefore included at the appropriate place in the historical narrative. Other psalms are also
included where they reflect the events David is experiencing, although their
relation to the particular historical context is only speculative.

Woven throughout the story of Saul's pursuit of David is the close friendship enjoyed by David and Jonathan. It is a touching relief from the animosity
of Saul, yet it comes to a tragic end.

One of the most interesting incidents recorded during this period is an
encounter in which Saul asks a witch to consult the spirit of Samuel for him. Of
course God has severely condemned witches as deceivers and pretenders, and
the witch herself surely does not expect Samuel's real spirit to appear. When
God intervenes to call Samuel from the dead, no one is more surprised and
frightened than the witch. Saul's resort to the heathen practice of divination,
along with his previous disobedience to God's commands, may well contribute
to his downfall and untimely death.

DAVID NAMED AS SUCCESSOR.   The LORD said to Samuel, "How long   1 Sam.
will you mourn for Saul, since I have rejected him as king over Israel? Fill   16:1-5
your horn with oil and be on your way; I am sending you to Jesse of   Bethlehem
Bethlehem. I have chosen one of his sons to be king."

But Samuel said, "How can I go? Saul will hear about it and kill me."

The LORD said, "Take a heifer with you and say, 'I have come to sacrifice to the LORD.' Invite Jesse to the sacrifice, and I will show you what to do. You are to anoint for me the one I indicate."

Samuel did what the LORD said. When he arrived at Bethlehem, the elders of the town trembled when they met him. They asked, "Do you come in peace?"

Samuel replied, "Yes, in peace; I have come to sacrifice to the LORD. Consecrate yourselves and come to the sacrifice with me." Then he consecrated Jesse and his sons and invited them to the sacrifice.

1 Sam.
16:6-13
When they arrived, Samuel saw Eliab and thought, "Surely the LORD's anointed stands here before the LORD."

But the LORD said to Samuel, "Do not consider his appearance or his height, for I have rejected him. The LORD does not look at the things man looks at. Man looks at the outward appearance, but the LORD looks at the heart."

Then Jesse called Abinadab and had him pass in front of Samuel. But Samuel said, "The LORD has not chosen this one either." Jesse then had Shammah pass by, but Samuel said, "Nor has the LORD chosen this one." Jesse had seven of his sons pass before Samuel, but Samuel said to him, "The LORD has not chosen these." So he asked Jesse, "Are these all the sons you have?"

"There is still the youngest," Jesse answered, "but he is tending the sheep."

Samuel said, "Send for him; we will not sit down^j until he arrives."

So he sent and had him brought in. He was ruddy, with a fine appearance and handsome features.

Then the LORD said, "Rise and anoint him; he is the one."

So Samuel took the horn of oil and anointed him in the presence of his brothers, and from that day on the Spirit of the LORD came upon David in power. Samuel then went to Ramah.

1 Sam.
16:14-23
DAVID IS SAUL'S SERVANT.   Now the Spirit of the LORD had departed from Saul, and an evil^k spirit from the LORD tormented him.

Saul's attendants said to him, "See, an evil spirit from God is tormenting you. Let our lord command his servants here to search for someone who can play the harp. He will play when the evil spirit from God comes upon you, and you will feel better."

So Saul said to his attendants, "Find someone who plays well and bring him to me."

One of the servants answered, "I have seen a son of Jesse of Bethlehem who knows how to play the harp. He is a brave man and a warrior. He speaks well and is a fine-looking man. And the LORD is with him."

Then Saul sent messengers to Jesse and said, "Send me your son David, who is with the sheep." So Jesse took a donkey loaded with bread, a skin of wine and a young goat and sent them with his son David to Saul.

David came to Saul and entered his service. Saul liked him very much, and David became one of his armor-bearers. Then Saul sent word to Jesse, saying, "Allow David to remain in my service, for I am pleased with him."

Whenever the spirit from God came upon Saul, David would take his harp and play. Then relief would come to Saul; he would feel better, and the evil spirit would leave him.

---

^{j}Some Septuagint manuscripts; Hebrew *not gather around* ^{k}Or *injurious*; also in verses 15, 16 and 23

DAVID KILLS GOLIATH.   Now the Philistines gathered their forces for war and assembled at Socoh in Judah. They pitched camp at Ephes Dammim, between Socoh and Azekah. Saul and the Israelites assembled and camped in the Valley of Elah and drew up their battle line to meet the Philistines. The Philistines occupied one hill and the Israelites another, with the valley between them.

1 Sam. 17:1-3 Socoh

A champion named Goliath, who was from Gath, came out of the Philistine camp. He was over nine feet[l] tall. He had a bronze helmet on his head and wore a coat of scale armor of bronze weighing five thousand shekels[m]; on his legs he wore bronze greaves, and a bronze javelin was slung on his back. His spear shaft was like a weaver's rod, and its iron point weighed six hundred shekels.[n] His shield bearer went ahead of him.

1 Sam. 17:4-11

Goliath stood and shouted to the ranks of Israel, "Why do you come out and line up for battle? Am I not a Philistine, and are you not the servants of Saul? Choose a man and have him come down to me. If he is able to fight and kill me, we will become your subjects; but if I overcome him and kill him, you will become our subjects and serve us." Then the Philistine said, "This day I defy the ranks of Israel! Give me a man and let us fight each other." On hearing the Philistine's words, Saul and all the Israelites were dismayed and terrified.

Now David was the son of an Ephrathite named Jesse, who was from Bethlehem in Judah. Jesse had eight sons, and in Saul's time he was old and well advanced in years. Jesse's three oldest sons had followed Saul to the war: The firstborn was Eliab; the second, Abinadab; and the third, Shammah. David was the youngest. The three oldest followed Saul, but David went back and forth from Saul to tend his father's sheep at Bethlehem.

1 Sam. 17:12-24

For forty days the Philistine came forward every morning and evening and took his stand.

Now Jesse said to his son David, "Take this ephah[o] of roasted grain and these ten loaves of bread for your brothers and hurry to their camp. Take along these ten cheeses to the commander of their unit.[p] See how your brothers are and bring back some assurance[q] from them. They are with Saul and all the men of Israel in the Valley of Elah, fighting against the Philistines."

Early in the morning David left the flock with a shepherd, loaded up and set out, as Jesse had directed. He reached the camp as the army was going out to its battle positions, shouting the war cry. Israel and the Philistines were drawing up their lines facing each other. David left his things with the keeper of supplies, ran to the battle lines and greeted his brothers. As he was talking with them, Goliath, the Philistine champion from Gath, stepped out from his lines and shouted his usual defiance, and David heard it. When the Israelites saw the man, they all ran from him in great fear.

Now the Israelites had been saying, "Do you see how this man keeps coming out? He comes out to defy Israel. The king will give great wealth

1 Sam. 17:25-31

---

[l]Hebrew *was six cubits and a span* (about 3 meters)   [m]That is, about 125 pounds (about 57 kilograms)   [n]That is, about 15 pounds (about 7 kilograms)   [o]That is, probably about 3/5 bushel (about 22 liters)   [p]Hebrew *thousand*   [q]Or *some token*; or *some pledge of spoils*

to the man who kills him. He will also give him his daughter in marriage and will exempt his father's family from taxes in Israel."

David asked the men standing near him, "What will be done for the man who kills this Philistine and removes this disgrace from Israel? Who is this uncircumcised Philistine that he should defy the armies of the living God?"

They repeated to him what they had been saying and told him, "This is what will be done for the man who kills him."

When Eliab, David's oldest brother, heard him speaking with the men, he burned with anger at him and asked, "Why have you come down here? And with whom did you leave those few sheep in the desert? I know how conceited you are and how wicked your heart is; you came down only to watch the battle."

"Now what have I done?" said David. "Can't I even speak?" He then turned away to someone else and brought up the same matter, and the men answered him as before. What David said was overheard and reported to Saul, and Saul sent for him.

1 Sam. 17:32-37

David said to Saul, "Let no one lose heart on account of this Philistine; your servant will go and fight him."

Saul replied, "You are not able to go out against this Philistine and fight him; you are only a boy, and he has been a fighting man from his youth."

But David said to Saul, "Your servant has been keeping his father's sheep. When a lion or a bear came and carried off a sheep from the flock, I went after it, struck it and rescued the sheep from its mouth. When it turned on me, I seized it by its hair, struck it and killed it. Your servant has killed both the lion and the bear; this uncircumcised Philistine will be like one of them, because he has defied the armies of the living God. The LORD who delivered me from the paw of the lion and the paw of the bear will deliver me from the hand of this Philistine."

Saul said to David, "Go, and the LORD be with you."

1 Sam. 17:38-40

Then Saul dressed David in his own tunic. He put a coat of armor on him and a bronze helmet on his head. David fastened on his sword over the tunic and tried walking around, because he was not used to them.

"I cannot go in these," he said to Saul, "because I am not used to them." So he took them off. Then he took his staff in his hand, chose five smooth stones from the stream, put them in the pouch of his shepherd's bag and, with his sling in his hand, approached the Philistine.

1 Sam. 17:41-47

Meanwhile, the Philistine, with his shield bearer in front of him, kept coming closer to David. He looked David over and saw that he was only a boy, ruddy and handsome, and he despised him. He said to David, "Am I a dog, that you come at me with sticks?" And the Philistine cursed David by his gods. "Come here," he said, "and I'll give your flesh to the birds of the air and the beasts of the field!"

David said to the Philistine, "You come against me with sword and spear and javelin, but I come against you in the name of the LORD Almighty, the God of the armies of Israel, whom you have defied. This day the LORD will hand you over to me, and I'll strike you down and cut off your head. Today I will give the carcasses of the Philistine army to the birds of the air and the beasts of the earth, and the whole world will know that there is a God in Israel. All those gathered here will know that it is not by sword or spear that the LORD saves; for the battle is the LORD's, and he will give all of you into our hands."

As the Philistine moved closer to attack him, David ran quickly toward the battle line to meet him. Reaching into his bag and taking out a stone, he slung it and struck the Philistine on the forehead. The stone sank into his forehead, and he fell facedown on the ground.

1 Sam.
17:48-51a

So David triumphed over the Philistine with a sling and a stone; without a sword in his hand he struck down the Philistine and killed him.

David ran and stood over him. He took hold of the Philistine's sword and drew it from the scabbard. After he killed him, he cut off his head with the sword.

When the Philistines saw that their hero was dead, they turned and ran. Then the men of Israel and Judah surged forward with a shout and pursued the Philistines to the entrance of Gath[r] and to the gates of Ekron. Their dead were strewn along the Shaaraim road to Gath and Ekron. When the Israelites returned from chasing the Philistines, they plundered their camp. David took the Philistine's head and brought it to Jerusalem, and he put the Philistine's weapons in his own tent.

1 Sam.
17:51b-58

As Saul watched David going out to meet the Philistine, he said to Abner, commander of the army, "Abner, whose son is that young man?"

Abner replied, "As surely as you live, O king, I don't know."

The king said, "Find out whose son this young man is."

As soon as David returned from killing the Philistine, Abner took him and brought him before Saul, with David still holding the Philistine's head.

"Whose son are you, young man?" Saul asked him.

David said, "I am the son of your servant Jesse of Bethlehem."

JONATHAN BEFRIENDS DAVID. After David had finished talking with Saul, Jonathan became one in spirit with David, and he loved him as himself. From that day Saul kept David with him and did not let him return to his father's house. And Jonathan made a covenant with David because he loved him as himself. Jonathan took off the robe he was wearing and gave it to David, along with his tunic, and even his sword, his bow and his belt.

1 Sam.
18:1-4

DAVID'S INFLUENCE INCREASES. Whatever Saul sent him to do, David did it so successfully[s] that Saul gave him a high rank in the army. This pleased all the people, and Saul's officers as well.

1 Sam.
18:5

SAUL BECOMES JEALOUS. When the men were returning home after David had killed the Philistine, the women came out from all the towns of Israel to meet King Saul with singing and dancing, with joyful songs and with tambourines and lutes. As they danced, they sang:

1 Sam.
18:6-11

"Saul has slain his thousands,
and David his tens of thousands."

Saul was very angry; this refrain galled him. "They have credited David with tens of thousands," he thought, "but me with only thousands. What more can he get but the kingdom?" And from that time on Saul kept a jealous eye on David.

The next day an evil[t] spirit from God came forcefully upon Saul. He was prophesying in his house, while David was playing the harp, as he

[r]Some Septuagint manuscripts; Hebrew *a valley*   [s]Or *wisely*   [t]Or *injurious*

usually did. Saul had a spear in his hand and he hurled it, saying to himself, "I'll pin David to the wall." But David eluded him twice.

1 Sam.
18:12-16

DAVID A GOOD COMMANDER.   Saul was afraid of David, because the LORD was with David but had left Saul. So he sent David away from him and gave him command over a thousand men, and David led the troops in their campaigns. In everything he did he had great success,^{u} because the LORD was with him. When Saul saw how successful^v he was, he was afraid of him. But all Israel and Judah loved David, because he led them in their campaigns.

1 Sam.
18:17-27

MARRIAGE TO SAUL'S DAUGHTER.   Saul said to David, "Here is my older daughter Merab. I will give her to you in marriage; only serve me bravely and fight the battles of the LORD." For Saul said to himself, "I will not raise a hand against him. Let the Philistines do that!"

But David said to Saul, "Who am I, and what is my family or my father's clan in Israel, that I should become the king's son-in-law?" So^w when the time came for Merab, Saul's daughter, to be given to David, she was given in marriage to Adriel of Meholah.

Now Saul's daughter Michal was in love with David, and when they told Saul about it, he was pleased. "I will give her to him," he thought, "so that she may be a snare to him and so that the hand of the Philistines may be against him." So Saul said to David, "Now you have a second opportunity to become my son-in-law."

Then Saul ordered his attendants: "Speak to David privately and say, 'Look, the king is pleased with you, and his attendants all like you; now become his son-in-law.'"

They repeated these words to David. But David said, "Do you think it is a small matter to become the king's son-in-law? I'm only a poor man and little known."

When Saul's servants told him what David had said, Saul replied, "Say to David, 'The king wants no other price for the bride than a hundred Philistine foreskins, to take revenge on his enemies.'" Saul's plan was to have David fall by the hands of the Philistines.

When the attendants told David these things, he was pleased to become the king's son-in-law. So before the allotted time elapsed, David and his men went out and killed two hundred Philistines. He brought their foreskins and presented the full number to the king so that he might become the king's son-in-law. Then Saul gave him his daughter Michal in marriage.

1 Sam.
18:28-30

SAUL HARDENS ATTITUDE.   When Saul realized that the LORD was with David and that his daughter Michal loved David, Saul became still more afraid of him, and he remained his enemy the rest of his days.

The Philistine commanders continued to go out to battle, and as often as they did, David met with more success^x than the rest of Saul's officers, and his name became well known.

1 Sam.
19:1-7

JONATHAN INTERCEDES.   Saul told his son Jonathan and all the attendants to kill David. But Jonathan was very fond of David and warned him, "My father Saul is looking for a chance to kill you. Be on your guard tomorrow morning; go into hiding and stay there. I will go out and stand

---

^{u}Or *he was very wise* ^{v}Or *wise* ^{w}Or *However,* ^{x}Or *David acted more wisely*

with my father in the field where you are. I'll speak to him about you and will tell you what I find out."

Jonathan spoke well of David to Saul his father and said to him, "Let not the king do wrong to his servant David; he has not wronged you, and what he has done has benefited you greatly. He took his life in his hands when he killed the Philistine. The LORD won a great victory for all Israel, and you saw it and were glad. Why then would you do wrong to an innocent man like David by killing him for no reason?"

Saul listened to Jonathan and took this oath: "As surely as the LORD lives, David will not be put to death."

So Jonathan called David and told him the whole conversation. He brought him to Saul, and David was with Saul as before.

SAUL RENEWS JEALOUSY.   Once more war broke out, and David went out and fought the Philistines. He struck them with such force that they fled before him.

> 1 Sam.
> 19:8-10

But an evil[y] spirit from the LORD came upon Saul as he was sitting in his house with his spear in his hand. While David was playing the harp, Saul tried to pin him to the wall with his spear, but David eluded him as Saul drove the spear into the wall. That night David made good his escape.

WIFE AIDS IN ESCAPE.   Saul sent men to David's house to watch it and to kill him in the morning. But Michal, David's wife, warned him, "If you don't run for your life tonight, tomorrow you'll be killed." So Michal let David down through a window, and he fled and escaped. Then Michal took an idol[z] and laid it on the bed, covering it with a garment and putting some goats' hair at the head.

> 1 Sam.
> 19:11-18
> Naioth

When Saul sent the men to capture David, Michal said, "He is ill."

Then Saul sent the men back to see David and told them, "Bring him up to me in his bed so that I may kill him." But when the men entered, there was the idol in the bed, and at the head was some goats' hair.

Saul said to Michal, "Why did you deceive me like this and send my enemy away so that he escaped?"

Michal told him, "He said to me, 'Let me get away. Why should I kill you?'"

When David had fled and made his escape, he went to Samuel at Ramah and told him all that Saul had done to him. Then he and Samuel went to Naioth and stayed there.

David prays for God's strength.

> Psa. 59

For the director of music. ⌊To the tune of⌋ "Do Not Destroy." Of David. A *miktam.*[a]
When Saul had sent men to watch David's house in order to kill him.

> Deliver me from my enemies, O God;
>   protect me from those who rise up against me.
> Deliver me from evildoers
>   and save me from bloodthirsty men.
>
> See how they lie in wait for me!
>   Fierce men conspire against me
>   for no offense or sin of mine, O LORD.
> I have done no wrong, yet they are ready to attack me.

[y]Or *injurious*   [z]Hebrew *teraphim*; also in verse 16   [a]Title: Probably a literary or musical term

Arise to help me; look on my plight!
O Lord God Almighty, the God of Israel,
rouse yourself to punish all the nations;
show no mercy to wicked traitors.   *Selah*

They return at evening,
snarling like dogs,
and prowl about the city.
See what they spew from their mouths—
they spew out swords from their lips,
and they say, "Who can hear us?"
But you, O Lord, laugh at them;
you scoff at all those nations.

O my Strength, I watch for you;
you, O God, are my fortress, my loving God.

God will go before me
and will let me gloat over those who slander me.
But do not kill them, O Lord our shield,[b]
or my people will forget.
In your might make them wander about,
and bring them down.
For the sins of their mouths,
for the words of their lips,
let them be caught in their pride.
For the curses and lies they utter,
consume them in wrath,
consume them till they are no more.
Then it will be known to the ends of the earth
that God rules over Jacob.   *Selah*

They return at evening,
snarling like dogs,
and prowl about the city.
They wander about for food
and howl if not satisfied.
But I will sing of your strength,
in the morning I will sing of your love;
for you are my fortress,
my refuge in times of trouble.

O my Strength, I sing praise to you;
you, O God, are my fortress, my loving God.

1 Sam.
19:19-24
Naioth
PROPHESYING THWARTS HARM.   Word came to Saul: "David is in Naioth at Ramah"; so he sent men to capture him. But when they saw a group of prophets prophesying, with Samuel standing there as their leader, the Spirit of God came upon Saul's men and they also prophesied. Saul was told about it, and he sent more men, and they prophesied too. Saul sent men a third time, and they also prophesied. Finally, he himself left for Ramah and went to the great cistern at Secu. And he asked, "Where are Samuel and David?"

[b]Or *sovereign*

"Over in Naioth at Ramah," they said.

So Saul went to Naioth at Ramah. But the Spirit of God came even upon him, and he walked along prophesying until he came to Naioth. He stripped off his robes and also prophesied in Samuel's presence. He lay that way all that day and night. This is why people say, "Is Saul also among the prophets?"

DAVID AND JONATHAN COVENANT.   Then David fled from Naioth at Ramah and went to Jonathan and asked, "What have I done? What is my crime? How have I wronged your father, that he is trying to take my life?"

1 Sam.
20:1-17

"Never!" Jonathan replied. "You are not going to die! Look, my father doesn't do anything, great or small, without confiding in me. Why would he hide this from me? It's not so!"

But David took an oath and said, "Your father knows very well that I have found favor in your eyes, and he has said to himself, 'Jonathan must not know this or he will be grieved.' Yet as surely as the LORD lives and as you live, there is only a step between me and death."

Jonathan said to David, "Whatever you want me to do, I'll do for you."

So David said, "Look, tomorrow is the New Moon festival, and I am supposed to dine with the king; but let me go and hide in the field until the evening of the day after tomorrow. If your father misses me at all, tell him, 'David earnestly asked my permission to hurry to Bethlehem, his hometown, because an annual sacrifice is being made there for his whole clan.' If he says, 'Very well,' then your servant is safe. But if he loses his temper, you can be sure that he is determined to harm me. As for you, show kindness to your servant, for you have brought him into a covenant with you before the LORD. If I am guilty, then kill me yourself! Why hand me over to your father?"

"Never!" Jonathan said. "If I had the least inkling that my father was determined to harm you, wouldn't I tell you?"

David asked, "Who will tell me if your father answers you harshly?"

"Come," Jonathan said, "let's go out into the field." So they went there together.

Then Jonathan said to David: "By the LORD, the God of Israel, I will surely sound out my father by this time the day after tomorrow! If he is favorably disposed toward you, will I not send you word and let you know? But if my father is inclined to harm you, may the LORD deal with me, be it ever so severely, if I do not let you know and send you away safely. May the LORD be with you as he has been with my father. But show me unfailing kindness like that of the LORD as long as I live, so that I may not be killed, and do not ever cut off your kindness from my family—not even when the LORD has cut off every one of David's enemies from the face of the earth."

So Jonathan made a covenant with the house of David, saying, "May the LORD call David's enemies to account." And Jonathan had David reaffirm his oath out of love for him, because he loved him as he loved himself.

A PLAN FOR WARNING.   Then Jonathan said to David: "Tomorrow is the New Moon festival. You will be missed, because your seat will be empty. The day after tomorrow, toward evening, go to the place where you hid when this trouble began, and wait by the stone Ezel. I will shoot

1 Sam.
20:18-23

three arrows to the side of it, as though I were shooting at a target. Then I will send a boy and say, 'Go, find the arrows.' If I say to him, 'Look, the arrows are on this side of you; bring them here,' then come, because, as surely as the LORD lives, you are safe; there is no danger. But if I say to the boy, 'Look, the arrows are beyond you,' then you must go, because the LORD has sent you away. And about the matter you and I discussed— remember, the LORD is witness between you and me forever."

1 Sam.
20:24-34

SAUL DISCLOSES INTENTIONS.   So David hid in the field, and when the New Moon festival came, the king sat down to eat. He sat in his customary place by the wall, opposite Jonathan,^{c} and Abner sat next to Saul, but David's place was empty. Saul said nothing that day, for he thought, "Something must have happened to David to make him ceremonially unclean—surely he is unclean." But the next day, the second day of the month, David's place was empty again. Then Saul said to his son Jonathan, "Why hasn't the son of Jesse come to the meal, either yesterday or today?"

Jonathan answered, "David earnestly asked me for permission to go to Bethlehem. He said, 'Let me go, because our family is observing a sacrifice in the town and my brother has ordered me to be there. If I have found favor in your eyes, let me get away to see my brothers.' That is why he has not come to the king's table."

Saul's anger flared up at Jonathan and he said to him, "You son of a perverse and rebellious woman! Don't I know that you have sided with the son of Jesse to your own shame and to the shame of the mother who bore you? As long as the son of Jesse lives on this earth, neither you nor your kingdom will be established. Now send and bring him to me, for he must die!"

"Why should he be put to death? What has he done?" Jonathan asked his father. But Saul hurled his spear at him to kill him. Then Jonathan knew that his father intended to kill David.

Jonathan got up from the table in fierce anger; on that second day of the month he did not eat, because he was grieved at his father's shameful treatment of David.

1 Sam.
20:35-42

DAVID AND JONATHAN PART.   In the morning Jonathan went out to the field for his meeting with David. He had a small boy with him, and he said to the boy, "Run and find the arrows I shoot." As the boy ran, he shot an arrow beyond him. When the boy came to the place where Jonathan's arrow had fallen, Jonathan called out after him, "Isn't the arrow beyond you?" Then he shouted, "Hurry! Go quickly! Don't stop!" The boy picked up the arrow and returned to his master. (The boy knew nothing of all this; only Jonathan and David knew.) Then Jonathan gave his weapons to the boy and said, "Go, carry them back to town."

After the boy had gone, David got up from the south side ⌊of the stone⌋ and bowed down before Jonathan three times, with his face to the ground. Then they kissed each other and wept together—but David wept the most.

Jonathan said to David, "Go in peace, for we have sworn friendship with each other in the name of the LORD, saying, 'The LORD is witness between you and me, and between your descendants and my descendants forever.'" Then David left, and Jonathan went back to the town.

---

^{c}Septuagint; Hebrew *wall. Jonathan arose*

CONSECRATED BREAD EATEN. David went to Nob, to Ahimelech the priest. Ahimelech trembled when he met him, and asked, "Why are you alone? Why is no one with you?"

1 Sam.
21:1-6
Nob

David answered Ahimelech the priest, "The king charged me with a certain matter and said to me, 'No one is to know anything about your mission and your instructions.' As for my men, I have told them to meet me at a certain place. Now then, what do you have on hand? Give me five loaves of bread, or whatever you can find."

But the priest answered David, "I don't have any ordinary bread on hand; however, there is some consecrated bread here—provided the men have kept themselves from women."

David replied, "Indeed women have been kept from us, as usual whenever[d] I set out. The men's things[e] are holy even on missions that are not holy. How much more so today!" So the priest gave him the consecrated bread, since there was no bread there except the bread of the Presence that had been removed from before the LORD and replaced by hot bread on the day it was taken away.

GOLIATH'S SWORD TAKEN. Now one of Saul's servants was there that day, detained before the LORD; he was Doeg the Edomite, Saul's head shepherd.

1 Sam.
21:7-9

David asked Ahimelech, "Don't you have a spear or a sword here? I haven't brought my sword or any other weapon, because the king's business was urgent."

The priest replied, "The sword of Goliath the Philistine, whom you killed in the Valley of Elah, is here; it is wrapped in a cloth behind the ephod. If you want it, take it; there is no sword here but that one."

David said, "There is none like it; give it to me."

PHILISTINES THREATEN. That day David fled from Saul and went to Achish king of Gath. But the servants of Achish said to him, "Isn't this David, the king of the land? Isn't he the one they sing about in their dances:

1 Sam.
21:10-12
Gath

" 'Saul has slain his thousands,
and David his tens of thousands'?"

David took these words to heart and was very much afraid of Achish king of Gath.

David prays for confidence.

Psa. 56

For the director of music. To the tune of "A Dove on Distant Oaks." Of David. A
    miktam.[f] When the Philistines had seized him in Gath.

Be merciful to me, O God, for men hotly pursue me;
    all day long they press their attack.
My slanderers pursue me all day long;
    many are attacking me in their pride.

When I am afraid,
    I will trust in you.
In God, whose word I praise,
    in God I trust; I will not be afraid.

[d] Or *from us in the past few days since*   [e] Or *bodies*   [f] Title: Probably a literary or musical term

What can mortal man do to me?

All day long they twist my words;
>they are always plotting to harm me.
They conspire, they lurk,
>they watch my steps,
>eager to take my life.

On no account let them escape;
>in your anger, O God, bring down the nations.
Record my lament;
>list my tears on your scroll[g]—
>are they not in your record?

Then my enemies will turn back
>when I call for help.
>By this I will know that God is for me.
In God, whose word I praise,
>in the LORD, whose word I praise—
in God I trust; I will not be afraid.
>What can man do to me?

I am under vows to you, O God;
>I will present my thank offerings to you.
For you have delivered me[h] from death
>and my feet from stumbling,
that I may walk before God
>in the light of life.[i]

1 Sam. 21:13-15   DAVID FEIGNS INSANITY.   So he pretended to be insane in their presence; and while he was in their hands he acted like a madman, making marks on the doors of the gate and letting saliva run down his beard.

Achish said to his servants, "Look at the man! He is insane! Why bring him to me? Am I so short of madmen that you have to bring this fellow here to carry on like this in front of me? Must this man come into my house?"

Psa. 34   ### David gives thanks for God's encouragement.

Of David. When he pretended to be insane before Abimelech, who drove him away, and he left.

I[j] will extol the LORD at all times;
>his praise will always be on my lips.
My soul will boast in the LORD;
>let the afflicted hear and rejoice.
Glorify the LORD with me;
>let us exalt his name together.

I sought the LORD, and he answered me;
>he delivered me from all my fears.
Those who look to him are radiant;
>their faces are never covered with shame.

---

[g]Or / put my tears in your wineskin   [h]Or my soul   [i]Or the land of the living   [j]This psalm is an acrostic poem, the verses of which begin with the successive letters of the Hebrew alphabet.

This poor man called, and the LORD heard him;
    he saved him out of all his troubles.
The angel of the LORD encamps around those who fear him,
    and he delivers them.

Taste and see that the LORD is good;
    blessed is the man who takes refuge in him.
Fear the LORD, you his saints,
    for those who fear him lack nothing.
The lions may grow weak and hungry,
    but those who seek the LORD lack no good thing.

Come, my children, listen to me;
    I will teach you the fear of the LORD.
Whoever of you loves life
    and desires to see many good days,
keep your tongue from evil
    and your lips from speaking lies.
Turn from evil and do good;
    seek peace and pursue it.

The eyes of the LORD are on the righteous
    and his ears are attentive to their cry;
the face of the LORD is against those who do evil,
    to cut off the memory of them from the earth.

The righteous cry out, and the LORD hears them;
    he delivers them from all their troubles.
The LORD is close to the brokenhearted
    and saves those who are crushed in spirit.

A righteous man may have many troubles,
    but the LORD delivers him from them all;
he protects all his bones,
    not one of them will be broken.

Evil will slay the wicked;
    the foes of the righteous will be condemned.
The LORD redeems his servants;
    no one will be condemned who takes refuge in him.

SUPPORTERS ASSEMBLE.   David left Gath and escaped to the cave of
Adullam. When his brothers and his father's household heard about it,
they went down to him there. All those who were in distress or in debt or
discontented gathered around him, and he became their leader. About
four hundred men were with him.

*1 Sam.
22:1,2
Adullam*

David prays for refuge from his enemies.

Psa. 142

A *maskil* [k] of David. When he was in the cave. A prayer.

I cry aloud to the LORD;
    I lift up my voice to the LORD for mercy.
I pour out my complaint before him;
    before him I tell my trouble.

[k] Title: Probably a literary or musical term

When my spirit grows faint within me,
  it is you who know my way.
In the path where I walk
  men have hidden a snare for me.
Look to my right and see;
  no one is concerned for me.
I have no refuge;
  no one cares for my life.

I cry to you, O LORD;
  I say, "You are my refuge,
  my portion in the land of the living."
Listen to my cry,
  for I am in desperate need;
rescue me from those who pursue me,
  for they are too strong for me.
Set me free from my prison,
  that I may praise your name.

Then the righteous will gather about me
  because of your goodness to me.

1 Chron. 12:8-18 Wilderness   WARRIORS JOIN DAVID. Some Gadites defected to David at his stronghold in the desert. They were brave warriors, ready for battle and able to handle the shield and spear. Their faces were the faces of lions, and they were as swift as gazelles in the mountains.
  Ezer was the chief,
  Obadiah the second in command, Eliab the third,
  Mishmannah the fourth, Jeremiah the fifth,
  Attai the sixth, Eliel the seventh,
  Johanan the eighth, Elzabad the ninth,
  Jeremiah the tenth and Macbannai the eleventh.
These Gadites were army commanders; the least was a match for a hundred, and the greatest for a thousand. It was they who crossed the Jordan in the first month when it was overflowing all its banks, and they put to flight everyone living in the valleys, to the east and to the west.

Other Benjamites and some men from Judah also came to David in his stronghold. David went out to meet them and said to them, "If you have come to me in peace, to help me, I am ready to have you unite with me. But if you have come to betray me to my enemies when my hands are free from violence, may the God of our fathers see it and judge you."
Then the Spirit came upon Amasai, chief of the Thirty, and he said:

  "We are yours, O David!
  We are with you, O son of Jesse!
  Success, success to you,
    and success to those who help you,
    for your God will help you."

So David received them and made them leaders of his raiding bands.

1 Sam. 22:3-5 Mizpah   PARENTS LEFT IN MOAB. From there David went to Mizpah in Moab and said to the king of Moab, "Would you let my father and mother come and stay with you until I learn what God will do for me?" So he left them with the king of Moab, and they stayed with him as long as David was in the stronghold.

But the prophet Gad said to David, "Do not stay in the stronghold. Go into the land of Judah." So David left and went to the forest of Hereth.

DOEG KILLS PRIESTS OF NOB.   Now Saul heard that David and his men had been discovered. And Saul, spear in hand, was seated under the tamarisk tree on the hill at Gibeah, with all his officials standing around him. Saul said to them, "Listen, men of Benjamin! Will the son of Jesse give all of you fields and vineyards? Will he make all of you commanders of thousands and commanders of hundreds? Is that why you have all con-spired against me? No one tells me when my son makes a covenant with the son of Jesse. None of you is concerned about me or tells me that my son has incited my servant to lie in wait for me, as he does today."

1 Sam.
22:6-19
Nob

But Doeg the Edomite, who was standing with Saul's officials, said, "I saw the son of Jesse come to Ahimelech son of Ahitub at Nob. Ahimelech inquired of the LORD for him; he also gave him provisions and the sword of Goliath the Philistine."

Then the king sent for the priest Ahimelech son of Ahitub and his father's whole family, who were the priests at Nob, and they all came to the king. Saul said, "Listen now, son of Ahitub."

"Yes, my lord," he answered.

Saul said to him, "Why have you conspired against me, you and the son of Jesse, giving him bread and a sword and inquiring of God for him, so that he has rebelled against me and lies in wait for me, as he does today?"

Ahimelech answered the king, "Who of all your servants is as loyal as David, the king's son-in-law, captain of your bodyguard and highly respected in your household? Was that day the first time I inquired of God for him? Of course not! Let not the king accuse your servant or any of his father's family, for your servant knows nothing at all about this whole affair."

But the king said, "You will surely die, Ahimelech, you and your father's whole family."

Then the king ordered the guards at his side: "Turn and kill the priests of the LORD, because they too have sided with David. They knew he was fleeing, yet they did not tell me."

But the king's officials were not willing to raise a hand to strike the priests of the LORD.

The king then ordered Doeg, "You turn and strike down the priests." So Doeg the Edomite turned and struck them down. That day he killed eighty-five men who wore the linen ephod. He also put to the sword Nob, the town of the priests, with its men and women, its children and infants, and its cattle, donkeys and sheep.

DAVID LEARNS OF SLAUGHTER.   But Abiathar, a son of Ahimelech son of Ahitub, escaped and fled to join David. He told David that Saul had killed the priests of the LORD. Then David said to Abiathar: "That day, when Doeg the Edomite was there, I knew he would be sure to tell Saul. I am responsible for the death of your father's whole family. Stay with me; don't be afraid; the man who is seeking your life is seeking mine also. You will be safe with me."

1 Sam.
22:20-23

Psa. 52   **David upbraids the evildoer.**

> For the director of music. A *maskil[1]* of David. When Doeg the Edomite had gone to
> Saul and told him: "David has gone to the house of Ahimelech."

Why do you boast of evil, you mighty man?
  Why do you boast all day long,
    you who are a disgrace in the eyes of God?
Your tongue plots destruction;
  it is like a sharpened razor,
    you who practice deceit.
You love evil rather than good,
  falsehood rather than speaking the truth.   *Selah*
You love every harmful word,
  O you deceitful tongue!

Surely God will bring you down to everlasting ruin:
  He will snatch you up and tear you from your tent;
    he will uproot you from the land of the living.   *Selah*
The righteous will see and fear;
  they will laugh at him, saying,
"Here now is the man
  who did not make God his stronghold
but trusted in his great wealth
  and grew strong by destroying others!"

But I am like an olive tree
  flourishing in the house of God;
I trust in God's unfailing love
  for ever and ever.
I will praise you forever for what you have done;
  in your name I will hope, for your name is good.
  I will praise you in the presence of your saints.

1 Sam.   DAVID SAVES KEILAH.   When David was told, "Look, the Philistines
23:1-6   are fighting against Keilah and are looting the threshing floors," he
Keilah   inquired of the LORD, saying, "Shall I go and attack these Philistines?"
         The LORD answered him, "Go, attack the Philistines and save Keilah."
         But David's men said to him, "Here in Judah we are afraid. How much
         more, then, if we go to Keilah against the Philistine forces!"
         Once again David inquired of the LORD, and the LORD answered him,
         "Go down to Keilah, for I am going to give the Philistines into your hand."
         So David and his men went to Keilah, fought the Philistines and carried
         off their livestock. He inflicted heavy losses on the Philistines and saved
         the people of Keilah. (Now Abiathar son of Ahimelech had brought the
         ephod down with him when he fled to David at Keilah.)

1 Sam.   DAVID SEEKS GOD'S GUIDANCE.   Saul was told that David had gone
23:7-12   to Keilah, and he said, "God has handed him over to me, for David has
         imprisoned himself by entering a town with gates and bars." And Saul
         called up all his forces for battle, to go down to Keilah to besiege David
         and his men.
         When David learned that Saul was plotting against him, he said to
         Abiathar the priest, "Bring the ephod." David said, "O LORD, God of Israel,

[1]Title: Probably a literary or musical term

your servant has heard definitely that Saul plans to come to Keilah and destroy the town on account of me. Will the citizens of Keilah surrender me to him? Will Saul come down, as your servant has heard? O Lord, God of Israel, tell your servant."

And the Lord said, "He will."

Again David asked, "Will the citizens of Keilah surrender me and my men to Saul?"

And the Lord said, "They will."

IN DESERT OF JUDAH.   So David and his men, about six hundred in number, left Keilah and kept moving from place to place. When Saul was told that David had escaped from Keilah, he did not go there.

1 Sam.
23:13,14
Desert of
Ziph

David stayed in the desert strongholds and in the hills of the Desert of Ziph. Day after day Saul searched for him, but God did not give David into his hands.

David expresses gratitude for God's protection.

Psa. 63

A psalm of David. When he was in the Desert of Judah.

O God, you are my God,
    earnestly I seek you;
my soul thirsts for you,
    my body longs for you,
in a dry and weary land
    where there is no water.

I have seen you in the sanctuary
    and beheld your power and your glory.
Because your love is better than life,
    my lips will glorify you.
I will praise you as long as I live,
    and in your name I will lift up my hands.
My soul will be satisfied as with the richest of foods;
    with singing lips my mouth will praise you.

On my bed I remember you;
    I think of you through the watches of the night.
Because you are my help,
    I sing in the shadow of your wings.
My soul clings to you;
    your right hand upholds me.

They who seek my life will be destroyed;
    they will go down to the depths of the earth.
They will be given over to the sword
    and become food for jackals.

But the king will rejoice in God;
    all who swear by God's name will praise him,
    while the mouths of liars will be silenced.

JONATHAN COVENANTS AGAIN.   While David was at Horesh in the Desert of Ziph, he learned that Saul had come out to take his life. And Saul's son Jonathan went to David at Horesh and helped him find strength in God. "Don't be afraid," he said. "My father Saul will not lay a hand on you. You will be king over Israel, and I will be second to you. Even my

1 Sam.
23:15-18
Horesh

father Saul knows this." The two of them made a covenant before the LORD. Then Jonathan went home, but David remained at Horesh.

1 Sam.
23:19-25

ZIPHITES PLOT WITH SAUL.   The Ziphites went up to Saul at Gibeah and said, "Is not David hiding among us in the strongholds at Horesh, on the hill of Hakilah, south of Jeshimon? Now, O king, come down whenever it pleases you to do so, and we will be responsible for handing him over to the king."

Saul replied, "The LORD bless you for your concern for me. Go and make further preparation. Find out where David usually goes and who has seen him there. They tell me he is very crafty. Find out about all the hiding places he uses and come back to me with definite information.[m] Then I will go with you; if he is in the area, I will track him down among all the clans of Judah."

So they set out and went to Ziph ahead of Saul. Now David and his men were in the Desert of Maon, in the Arabah south of Jeshimon. Saul and his men began the search, and when David was told about it, he went down to the rock and stayed in the Desert of Maon. When Saul heard this, he went into the Desert of Maon in pursuit of David.

Psa. 54

Reaction to those who inform against David.

For the director of music. With stringed instruments. A *maskil*[n] of David. When the Ziphites had gone to Saul and said, "Is not David hiding among us?"

> Save me, O God, by your name;
> vindicate me by your might.
> Hear my prayer, O God;
> listen to the words of my mouth.

> Strangers are attacking me;
> ruthless men seek my life—
> men without regard for God.   *Selah*

> Surely God is my help;
> the Lord is the one who sustains me.

> Let evil recoil on those who slander me;
> in your faithfulness destroy them.

> I will sacrifice a freewill offering to you;
> I will praise your name, O LORD,
> for it is good.
> For he has delivered me from all my troubles,
> and my eyes have looked in triumph on my foes.

1 Sam.
23:26-29

DAVID BARELY ESCAPES.   Saul was going along one side of the mountain, and David and his men were on the other side, hurrying to get away from Saul. As Saul and his forces were closing in on David and his men to capture them, a messenger came to Saul, saying, "Come quickly! The Philistines are raiding the land." Then Saul broke off his pursuit of David and went to meet the Philistines. That is why they call this place Sela

---

[m]Or *me at Nacon*   [n]Title: Probably a literary or musical term

Hammahlekoth.[o] And David went up from there and lived in the strong-holds of En Gedi.

DAVID SPARES SAUL'S LIFE.   After Saul returned from pursuing the Philistines, he was told, "David is in the Desert of En Gedi." So Saul took three thousand chosen men from all Israel and set out to look for David and his men near the Crags of the Wild Goats.

1 Sam.
24:1-7
Desert of
En Gedi

He came to the sheep pens along the way; a cave was there, and Saul went in to relieve himself. David and his men were far back in the cave. The men said, "This is the day the LORD spoke of when he said[p] to you, 'I will give your enemy into your hands for you to deal with as you wish.'" Then David crept up unnoticed and cut off a corner of Saul's robe.

Afterward, David was conscience-stricken for having cut off a corner of his robe. He said to his men, "The LORD forbid that I should do such a thing to my master, the LORD's anointed, or lift my hand against him; for he is the anointed of the LORD." With these words David rebuked his men and did not allow them to attack Saul. And Saul left the cave and went his way.

Then David went out of the cave and called out to Saul, "My lord the king!" When Saul looked behind him, David bowed down and prostrated himself with his face to the ground. He said to Saul, "Why do you listen when men say, 'David is bent on harming you'? This day you have seen with your own eyes how the LORD delivered you into my hands in the cave. Some urged me to kill you, but I spared you; I said, 'I will not lift my hand against my master, because he is the LORD's anointed.' See, my father, look at this piece of your robe in my hand! I cut off the corner of your robe but did not kill you. Now understand and recognize that I am not guilty of wrongdoing or rebellion. I have not wronged you, but you are hunting me down to take my life. May the LORD judge between you and me. And may the LORD avenge the wrongs you have done to me, but my hand will not touch you. As the old saying goes, 'From evildoers come evil deeds,' so my hand will not touch you.

1 Sam.
24:8-15

"Against whom has the king of Israel come out? Whom are you pursuing? A dead dog? A flea? May the LORD be our judge and decide between us. May he consider my cause and uphold it; may he vindicate me by delivering me from your hand."

SAUL ASKS COVENANT.   When David finished saying this, Saul asked, "Is that your voice, David my son?" And he wept aloud. "You are more righteous than I," he said. "You have treated me well, but I have treated you badly. You have just now told me of the good you did to me; the LORD delivered me into your hands, but you did not kill me. When a man finds his enemy, does he let him get away unharmed? May the LORD reward you well for the way you treated me today. I know that you will surely be king and that the kingdom of Israel will be established in your hands. Now swear to me by the LORD that you will not cut off my descendants or wipe out my name from my father's family."

1 Sam.
24:16-22

So David gave his oath to Saul. Then Saul returned home, but David and his men went up to the stronghold.

---

[o]Sela Hammahlekoth means rock of parting.   [p]Or "Today the LORD is saying

Psa. 57 **David praises God for giving safety.**

For the director of music. To the tune of "Do Not Destroy." Of David. A *miktam.*[q]
When he had fled from Saul into the cave.

Have mercy on me, O God, have mercy on me,
    for in you my soul takes refuge.
I will take refuge in the shadow of your wings
    until the disaster has passed.

I cry out to God Most High,
    to God, who fulfills his purpose for me.
He sends from heaven and saves me,
    rebuking those who hotly pursue me;   *Selah*
God sends his love and his faithfulness.

I am in the midst of lions;
    I lie among ravenous beasts—
men whose teeth are spears and arrows,
    whose tongues are sharp swords.

Be exalted, O God, above the heavens;
    let your glory be over all the earth.

They spread a net for my feet—
    I was bowed down in distress.
They dug a pit in my path—
    but they have fallen into it themselves.   *Selah*

My heart is steadfast, O God,
    my heart is steadfast;
I will sing and make music.
Awake, my soul!
    Awake, harp and lyre!
    I will awaken the dawn.

I will praise you, O Lord, among the nations;
    I will sing of you among the peoples.
For great is your love, reaching to the heavens;
    your faithfulness reaches to the skies.

Be exalted, O God, above the heavens;
    let your glory be over all the earth.

1 Sam.
25:1a
Ramah **DEATH OF SAMUEL.** Now Samuel died, and all Israel assembled and mourned for him; and they buried him at his home in Ramah.

1 Sam.
25:1b-8
Carmel **ABIGAIL PLEADS FOR MERCY.** Then David moved down into the Desert of Maon.[r] A certain man in Maon, who had property there at Carmel, was very wealthy. He had a thousand goats and three thousand sheep, which he was shearing in Carmel. His name was Nabal and his wife's name was Abigail. She was an intelligent and beautiful woman, but her husband, a Calebite, was surly and mean in his dealings.

    While David was in the desert, he heard that Nabal was shearing sheep. So he sent ten young men and said to them, "Go up to Nabal at Carmel

[q]Title: Probably a literary or musical term   [r]Some Septuagint manuscripts; Hebrew *Paran*

and greet him in my name. Say to him: 'Long life to you! Good health to you and your household! And good health to all that is yours!

" 'Now I hear that it is sheep-shearing time. When your shepherds were with us, we did not mistreat them, and the whole time they were at Carmel nothing of theirs was missing. Ask your own servants and they will tell you. Therefore be favorable toward my young men, since we come at a festive time. Please give your servants and your son David whatever you can find for them.' "

When David's men arrived, they gave Nabal this message in David's name. Then they waited.

1 Sam. 25:9-13

Nabal answered David's servants, "Who is this David? Who is this son of Jesse? Many servants are breaking away from their masters these days. Why should I take my bread and water, and the meat I have slaughtered for my shearers, and give it to men coming from who knows where?"

David's men turned around and went back. When they arrived, they reported every word. David said to his men, "Put on your swords!" So they put on their swords, and David put on his. About four hundred men went up with David, while two hundred stayed with the supplies.

One of the servants told Nabal's wife Abigail: "David sent messengers from the desert to give our master his greetings, but he hurled insults at them. Yet these men were very good to us. They did not mistreat us, and the whole time we were out in the fields near them nothing was missing. Night and day they were a wall around us all the time we were herding our sheep near them. Now think it over and see what you can do, because disaster is hanging over our master and his whole household. He is such a wicked man that no one can talk to him."

1 Sam. 25:14-22

Abigail lost no time. She took two hundred loaves of bread, two skins of wine, five dressed sheep, five seahs[s] of roasted grain, a hundred cakes of raisins and two hundred cakes of pressed figs, and loaded them on donkeys. Then she told her servants, "Go on ahead; I'll follow you." But she did not tell her husband Nabal.

As she came riding her donkey into a mountain ravine, there were David and his men descending toward her, and she met them. David had just said, "It's been useless—all my watching over this fellow's property in the desert so that nothing of his was missing. He has paid me back evil for good. May God deal with David,[t] be it ever so severely, if by morning I leave alive one male of all who belong to him!"

When Abigail saw David, she quickly got off her donkey and bowed down before David with her face to the ground. She fell at his feet and said: "My lord, let the blame be on me alone. Please let your servant speak to you; hear what your servant has to say. May my lord pay no attention to that wicked man Nabal. He is just like his name—his name is Fool, and folly goes with him. But as for me, your servant, I did not see the men my master sent.

1 Sam. 25:23-31

"Now since the LORD has kept you, my master, from bloodshed and from avenging yourself with your own hands, as surely as the LORD lives and as you live, may your enemies and all who intend to harm my master be like Nabal. And let this gift, which your servant has brought to my master, be given to the men who follow you. Please forgive your servant's

---

[s]That is, probably about a bushel (about 37 liters) Hebrew *with David's enemies*   [t]Some Septuagint manuscripts;

offense, for the LORD will certainly make a lasting dynasty for my master, because he fights the LORD's battles. Let no wrongdoing be found in you as long as you live. Even though someone is pursuing you to take your life, the life of my master will be bound securely in the bundle of the living by the LORD your God. But the lives of your enemies he will hurl away as from the pocket of a sling. When the LORD has done for my master every good thing he promised concerning him and has appointed him leader over Israel, my master will not have on his conscience the staggering burden of needless bloodshed or of having avenged himself. And when the LORD has brought my master success, remember your servant."

1 Sam.
25:32-35

David said to Abigail, "Praise be to the LORD, the God of Israel, who has sent you today to meet me. May you be blessed for your good judgment and for keeping me from bloodshed this day and from avenging myself with my own hands. Otherwise, as surely as the LORD, the God of Israel, lives, who has kept me from harming you, if you had not come quickly to meet me, not one male belonging to Nabal would have been left alive by daybreak."

Then David accepted from her hand what she had brought him and said, "Go home in peace. I have heard your words and granted your request."

1 Sam.
25:36-39a

When Abigail went to Nabal, he was in the house holding a banquet like that of a king. He was in high spirits and very drunk. So she told him nothing until daybreak. Then in the morning, when Nabal was sober, his wife told him all these things, and his heart failed him and he became like a stone. About ten days later, the LORD struck Nabal and he died.

When David heard that Nabal was dead, he said, "Praise be to the LORD, who has upheld my cause against Nabal for treating me with contempt. He has kept his servant from doing wrong and has brought Nabal's wrongdoing down on his own head."

1 Sam.
25:39b-44

NEW AND FORMER WIVES.   Then David sent word to Abigail, asking her to become his wife. His servants went to Carmel and said to Abigail, "David has sent us to you to take you to become his wife."

She bowed down with her face to the ground and said, "Here is your maidservant, ready to serve you and wash the feet of my master's servants." Abigail quickly got on a donkey and, attended by her five maids, went with David's messengers and became his wife. David had also married Ahinoam of Jezreel, and they both were his wives. But Saul had given his daughter Michal, David's wife, to Paltiel[u] son of Laish, who was from Gallim.

1 Sam.
26:1-20
Desert of
Ziph

DAVID TAKES SAUL'S SPEAR.   The Ziphites went to Saul at Gibeah and said, "Is not David hiding on the hill of Hakilah, which faces Jeshimon?"

So Saul went down to the Desert of Ziph, with his three thousand chosen men of Israel, to search there for David. Saul made his camp beside the road on the hill of Hakilah facing Jeshimon, but David stayed in the desert. When he saw that Saul had followed him there, he sent out scouts and learned that Saul had definitely arrived.[v]

Then David set out and went to the place where Saul had camped. He saw where Saul and Abner son of Ner, the commander of the army, had

---

[u]Hebrew Palti, a variant of Paltiel   [v]Or had come to Nacon

lain down. Saul was lying inside the camp, with the army encamped around him.

David then asked Ahimelech the Hittite and Abishai son of Zeruiah, Joab's brother, "Who will go down into the camp with me to Saul?"

"I'll go with you," said Abishai.

So David and Abishai went to the army by night, and there was Saul, lying asleep inside the camp with his spear stuck in the ground near his head. Abner and the soldiers were lying around him.

Abishai said to David, "Today God has delivered your enemy into your hands. Now let me pin him to the ground with one thrust of my spear; I won't strike him twice."

But David said to Abishai, "Don't destroy him! Who can lay a hand on the LORD's anointed and be guiltless? As surely as the LORD lives," he said, "the LORD himself will strike him; either his time will come and he will die, or he will go into battle and perish. But the LORD forbid that I should lay a hand on the LORD's anointed. Now get the spear and water jug that are near his head, and let's go."

So David took the spear and water jug near Saul's head, and they left. No one saw or knew about it, nor did anyone wake up. They were all sleeping, because the LORD had put them into a deep sleep.

Then David crossed over to the other side and stood on top of the hill some distance away; there was a wide space between them. He called out to the army and to Abner son of Ner, "Aren't you going to answer me, Abner?"

Abner replied, "Who are you who calls to the king?"

David said, "You're a man, aren't you? And who is like you in Israel? Why didn't you guard your lord the king? Someone came to destroy your lord the king. What you have done is not good. As surely as the LORD lives, you and your men deserve to die, because you did not guard your master, the LORD's anointed. Look around you. Where are the king's spear and water jug that were near his head?"

Saul recognized David's voice and said, "Is that your voice, David my son?"

David replied, "Yes it is, my lord the king." And he added, "Why is my lord pursuing his servant? What have I done, and what wrong am I guilty of? Now let my lord the king listen to his servant's words. If the LORD has incited you against me, then may he accept an offering. If, however, men have done it, may they be cursed before the LORD! They have now driven me from my share in the LORD's inheritance and have said, 'Go, serve other gods.' Now do not let my blood fall to the ground far from the presence of the LORD. The king of Israel has come out to look for a flea—as one hunts a partridge in the mountains."

SAUL APOLOGIZES AGAIN. Then Saul said, "I have sinned. Come back, David my son. Because you considered my life precious today, I will not try to harm you again. Surely I have acted like a fool and have erred greatly."

"Here is the king's spear," David answered. "Let one of your young men come over and get it. The LORD rewards every man for his righteousness and faithfulness. The LORD delivered you into my hands today, but I would not lay a hand on the LORD's anointed. As surely as I valued your life today, so may the LORD value my life and deliver me from all trouble."

1 Sam.
26:21-25

Then Saul said to David, "May you be blessed, my son David; you will do great things and surely triumph."

So David went on his way, and Saul returned home.

1 Sam.
27:1-7
Ziklag

DAVID AMONG PHILISTINES.   But David thought to himself, "One of these days I will be destroyed by the hand of Saul. The best thing I can do is to escape to the land of the Philistines. Then Saul will give up searching for me anywhere in Israel, and I will slip out of his hand."

So David and the six hundred men with him left and went over to Achish son of Maoch king of Gath. David and his men settled in Gath with Achish. Each man had his family with him, and David had his two wives: Ahinoam of Jezreel and Abigail of Carmel, the widow of Nabal. When Saul was told that David had fled to Gath, he no longer searched for him.

Then David said to Achish, "If I have found favor in your eyes, let a place be assigned to me in one of the country towns, that I may live there. Why should your servant live in the royal city with you?"

So on that day Achish gave him Ziklag, and it has belonged to the kings of Judah ever since. David lived in Philistine territory a year and four months.

1 Chron.
12:1-7

WARRIORS CAME TO DAVID.   These were the men who came to David at Ziklag, while he was banished from the presence of Saul son of Kish (they were among the warriors who helped him in battle; they were armed with bows and were able to shoot arrows or to sling stones right-handed or left-handed; they were kinsmen of Saul from the tribe of Benjamin):

Ahiezer their chief and Joash the sons of Shemaah the Gibeathite; Jeziel and Pelet the sons of Azmaveth; Beracah, Jehu the Anathothite, and Ishmaiah the Gibeonite, a mighty man among the Thirty, who was a leader of the Thirty; Jeremiah, Jahaziel, Johanan, Jozabad the Gederathite, Eluzai, Jerimoth, Bealiah, Shemariah and Shephatiah the Haruphite; Elkanah, Isshiah, Azarel, Joezer and Jashobeam the Korahites; and Joelah and Zebadiah the sons of Jeroham from Gedor.

1 Sam.
27:8-28:2

VARIOUS RAIDS.   Now David and his men went up and raided the Geshurites, the Girzites and the Amalekites. (From ancient times these peoples had lived in the land extending to Shur and Egypt.) Whenever David attacked an area, he did not leave a man or woman alive, but took sheep and cattle, donkeys and camels, and clothes. Then he returned to Achish.

When Achish asked, "Where did you go raiding today?" David would say, "Against the Negev of Judah" or "Against the Negev of Jerahmeel" or "Against the Negev of the Kenites." He did not leave a man or woman alive to be brought to Gath, for he thought, "They might inform on us and say, 'This is what David did.'" And such was his practice as long as he lived in Philistine territory. Achish trusted David and said to himself, "He has become so odious to his people, the Israelites, that he will be my servant forever." In those days the Philistines gathered their forces to fight against Israel. Achish said to David, "You must understand that you and your men will accompany me in the army."

David said, "Then you will see for yourself what your servant can do."

Achish replied, "Very well, I will make you my bodyguard for life."

1 Sam.
29:1-11

ACHISH REFUSES HELP.   The Philistines gathered all their forces at Aphek, and Israel camped by the spring in Jezreel. As the Philistine rulers marched with their units of hundreds and thousands, David and his men were marching at the rear with Achish. The commanders of the Philistines asked, "What about these Hebrews?"

Achish replied, "Is this not David, who was an officer of Saul king of Israel? He has already been with me for over a year, and from the day he left Saul until now, I have found no fault in him."

But the Philistine commanders were angry with him and said, "Send the man back, that he may return to the place you assigned him. He must not go with us into battle, or he will turn against us during the fighting. How better could he regain his master's favor than by taking the heads of our own men? Isn't this the David they sang about in their dances:

> " 'Saul has slain his thousands,
>   and David his tens of thousands'?"

So Achish called David and said to him, "As surely as the LORD lives, you have been reliable, and I would be pleased to have you serve with me in the army. From the day you came to me until now, I have found no fault in you, but the rulers don't approve of you. Turn back and go in peace; do nothing to displease the Philistine rulers."

"But what have I done?" asked David. "What have you found against your servant from the day I came to you until now? Why can't I go and fight against the enemies of my lord the king?"

Achish answered, "I know that you have been as pleasing in my eyes as an angel of God; nevertheless, the Philistine commanders have said, 'He must not go up with us into battle.' Now get up early, along with your master's servants who have come with you, and leave in the morning as soon as it is light."

So David and his men got up early in the morning to go back to the land of the Philistines, and the Philistines went up to Jezreel.

DEFECTORS AID DAVID.   Some of the men of Manasseh defected to David when he went with the Philistines to fight against Saul. (He and his men did not help the Philistines because, after consultation, their rulers sent him away. They said, "It will cost us our heads if he deserts to his master Saul.") When David went to Ziklag, these were the men of Manasseh who defected to him: Adnah, Jozabad, Jediael, Michael, Jozabad, Elihu and Zillethai, leaders of units of a thousand in Manasseh. They helped David against raiding bands, for all of them were brave warriors, and they were commanders in his army. Day after day men came to help David, until he had a great army, like the army of God.^{w}

1 Chron.
12:19-22

AMALEKITES TAKE WOMAN.   David and his men reached Ziklag on the third day. Now the Amalekites had raided the Negev and Ziklag. They had attacked Ziklag and burned it, and had taken captive the women and all who were in it, both young and old. They killed none of them, but carried them off as they went on their way.

When David and his men came to Ziklag, they found it destroyed by fire and their wives and sons and daughters taken captive. So David and his men wept aloud until they had no strength left to weep. David's two wives had been captured—Ahinoam of Jezreel and Abigail, the widow of Nabal of Carmel. David was greatly distressed because the men were

1 Sam.
30:1-8

^{w}Or *a great and mighty army*

talking of stoning him; each one was bitter in spirit because of his sons and daughters. But David found strength in the LORD his God.

Then David said to Abiathar the priest, the son of Ahimelech, "Bring me the ephod." Abiathar brought it to him, and David inquired of the LORD, "Shall I pursue this raiding party? Will I overtake them?"

"Pursue them," he answered. "You will certainly overtake them and succeed in the rescue."

1 Sam.
30:9-20

WOMEN RECAPTURED.   David and the six hundred men with him came to the Besor Ravine, where some stayed behind, for two hundred men were too exhausted to cross the ravine. But David and four hundred men continued the pursuit.

They found an Egyptian in a field and brought him to David. They gave him water to drink and food to eat—part of a cake of pressed figs and two cakes of raisins. He ate and was revived, for he had not eaten any food or drunk any water for three days and three nights.

David asked him, "To whom do you belong, and where do you come from?"

He said, "I am an Egyptian, the slave of an Amalekite. My master abandoned me when I became ill three days ago. We raided the Negev of the Kerethites and the territory belonging to Judah and the Negev of Caleb. And we burned Ziklag."

David asked him, "Can you lead me down to this raiding party?"

He answered, "Swear to me before God that you will not kill me or hand me over to my master, and I will take you down to them."

He led David down, and there they were, scattered over the countryside, eating, drinking and reveling because of the great amount of plunder they had taken from the land of the Philistines and from Judah. David fought them from dusk until the evening of the next day, and none of them got away, except four hundred young men who rode off on camels and fled. David recovered everything the Amalekites had taken, including his two wives. Nothing was missing: young or old, boy or girl, plunder or anything else they had taken. David brought everything back. He took all the flocks and herds, and his men drove them ahead of the other livestock, saying, "This is David's plunder."

1 Sam.
30:21-25

RULE OF PLUNDER ESTABLISHED.   Then David came to the two hundred men who had been too exhausted to follow him and who were left behind at the Besor Ravine. They came out to meet David and the people with him. As David and his men approached, he greeted them. But all the evil men and troublemakers among David's followers said, "Because they did not go out with us, we will not share with them the plunder we recovered. However, each man may take his wife and children and go."

David replied, "No, my brothers, you must not do that with what the LORD has given us. He has protected us and handed over to us the forces that came against us. Who will listen to what you say? The share of the man who stayed with the supplies is to be the same as that of him who went down to the battle. All will share alike." David made this a statute and ordinance for Israel from that day to this.

1 Sam.
30:26-31

PLUNDER SHARED WITH JUDAH.   When David arrived in Ziklag, he sent some of the plunder to the elders of Judah, who were his friends, saying, "Here is a present for you from the plunder of the LORD's enemies."

He sent it to those who were in Bethel, Ramoth Negev and Jattir; to those in Aroer, Siphmoth, Eshtemoa and Racal; to those in the towns of the Jerahmeelites and the Kenites; to those in Hormah, Bor Ashan, Athach and Hebron; and to those in all the other places where David and his men had roamed.

WITCH CALLS UP SAMUEL. The Philistines assembled and came and set up camp at Shunem, while Saul gathered all the Israelites and set up camp at Gilboa. When Saul saw the Philistine army, he was afraid; terror filled his heart. He inquired of the LORD, but the LORD did not answer him by dreams or Urim or prophets. Saul then said to his attendants, "Find me a woman who is a medium, so I may go and inquire of her."

1 Sam.
28:4-7,3,8-14
Endor

"There is one in Endor," they said.

Now Samuel was dead, and all Israel had mourned for him and buried him in his own town of Ramah. Saul had expelled the mediums and spiritists from the land.

So Saul disguised himself, putting on other clothes, and at night he and two men went to the woman. "Consult a spirit for me," he said, "and bring up for me the one I name."

But the woman said to him, "Surely you know what Saul has done. He has cut off the mediums and spiritists from the land. Why have you set a trap for my life to bring about my death?"

Saul swore to her by the LORD, "As surely as the LORD lives, you will not be punished for this."

Then the woman asked, "Whom shall I bring up for you?"

"Bring up Samuel," he said.

When the woman saw Samuel, she cried out at the top of her voice and said to Saul, "Why have you deceived me? You are Saul!"

The king said to her, "Don't be afraid. What do you see?"

The woman said, "I see a spirit[x] coming up out of the ground."

"What does he look like?" he asked.

"An old man wearing a robe is coming up," she said.

Then Saul knew it was Samuel, and he bowed down and prostrated himself with his face to the ground.

SAMUEL'S SPIRIT PROPHESIES. Samuel said to Saul, "Why have you disturbed me by bringing me up?"

1 Sam.
28:15-25

"I am in great distress," Saul said. "The Philistines are fighting against me, and God has turned away from me. He no longer answers me, either by prophets or by dreams. So I have called on you to tell me what to do."

Samuel said, "Why do you consult me, now that the LORD has turned away from you and become your enemy? The LORD has done what he predicted through me. The LORD has torn the kingdom out of your hands and given it to one of your neighbors—to David. Because you did not obey the LORD or carry out his fierce wrath against the Amalekites, the LORD has done this to you today. The LORD will hand over both Israel and you to the Philistines, and tomorrow you and your sons will be with me. The LORD will also hand over the army of Israel to the Philistines."

Immediately Saul fell full length on the ground, filled with fear because of Samuel's words. His strength was gone, for he had eaten nothing all that day and night.

[x]Or see spirits; or see gods

When the woman came to Saul and saw that he was greatly shaken, she said, "Look, your maidservant has obeyed you. I took my life in my hands and did what you told me to do. Now please listen to your servant and let me give you some food so you may eat and have the strength to go on your way."

He refused and said, "I will not eat."

But his men joined the woman in urging him, and he listened to them. He got up from the ground and sat on the couch.

The woman had a fattened calf at the house, which she butchered at once. She took some flour, kneaded it and baked bread without yeast. Then she set it before Saul and his men, and they ate. That same night they got up and left.

1 Sam. 31:1-10 1 Chron. 10:1-12 (Ca. 1011 B.C.)

DEATHS OF SAUL AND JONATHAN.   Now the Philistines fought against Israel; the Israelites fled before them, and many fell slain on Mount Gilboa. The Philistines pressed hard after Saul and his sons, and they killed his sons Jonathan, Abinadab and Malki-Shua. The fighting grew fierce around Saul, and when the archers overtook him, they wounded him critically.

Saul said to his armor-bearer, "Draw your sword and run me through, or these uncircumcised fellows will come and run me through and abuse me."

But his armor-bearer was terrified and would not do it; so Saul took his own sword and fell on it. When the armor-bearer saw that Saul was dead, he too fell on his sword and died with him. So Saul and his three sons and his armor-bearer and all his men died together that same day.

When the Israelites along the valley and those across the Jordan saw that the Israelite army had fled and that Saul and his sons had died, they abandoned their towns and fled. And the Philistines came and occupied them.

The next day, when the Philistines came to strip the dead, they found Saul and his three sons fallen on Mount Gilboa. They cut off his head and stripped off his armor, and they sent messengers throughout the land of the Philistines to proclaim the news in the temple of their idols and among their people. They put his armor in the temple of the Ashtoreths and fastened his body to the wall of Beth Shan.

1 Sam. 31:11-13

BODIES BURIED.   When the people of Jabesh Gilead heard of what the Philistines had done to Saul, all their valiant men journeyed through the night to Beth Shan. They took down the bodies of Saul and his sons from the wall of Beth Shan and went to Jabesh, where they burned them. Then they took their bones and buried them under a tamarisk tree at Jabesh, and they fasted seven days.

1 Chron. 10:13,14

REASON FOR SAUL'S DEATH.   Saul died because he was unfaithful to the LORD; he did not keep the word of the LORD and even consulted a medium for guidance, and did not inquire of the LORD. So the LORD put him to death and turned the kingdom over to David son of Jesse.

2 Sam. 4:4

NEWS INJURES JONATHAN'S SON.   (Jonathan son of Saul had a son who was lame in both feet. He was five years old when the news about Saul and Jonathan came from Jezreel. His nurse picked him up and fled, but as she hurried to leave, he fell and became crippled. His name was Mephibosheth.)

DAVID LEARNS OF DEATHS.   After the death of Saul, David returned   2 Sam.
from defeating the Amalekites and stayed in Ziklag two days. On the third   1:1-11
day a man arrived from Saul's camp, with his clothes torn and with dust
on his head. When he came to David, he fell to the ground to pay him
honor.

"Where have you come from?" David asked him.

He answered, "I have escaped from the Israelite camp."

"What happened?" David asked. "Tell me."

He said, "The men fled from the battle. Many of them fell and died. And
Saul and his son Jonathan are dead."

Then David said to the young man who brought him the report, "How
do you know that Saul and his son Jonathan are dead?"

"I happened to be on Mount Gilboa," the young man said, "and there
was Saul, leaning on his spear, with the chariots and riders almost upon
him. When he turned around and saw me, he called out to me, and I said,
'What can I do?'

"He asked me, 'Who are you?'

" 'An Amalekite,' I answered.

"Then he said to me, 'Stand over me and kill me! I am in the throes of
death, but I'm still alive.'

"So I stood over him and killed him, because I knew that after he had
fallen he could not survive. And I took the crown that was on his head and
the band on his arm and have brought them here to my lord."

Then David and all the men with him took hold of their clothes and tore
them.

MESSENGER IS KILLED.   They mourned and wept and fasted till eve-   2 Sam.
ning for Saul and his son Jonathan, and for the army of the LORD and the   1:12-16
house of Israel, because they had fallen by the sword.

David said to the young man who brought him the report, "Where are
you from?"

"I am the son of an alien, an Amalekite," he answered.

David asked him, "Why were you not afraid to lift your hand to destroy
the LORD's anointed?"

Then David called one of his men and said, "Go, strike him down!" So
he struck him down, and he died. For David had said to him, "Your blood
be on your own head. Your own mouth testified against you when you
said, 'I killed the LORD's anointed.' "

DAVID'S LAMENT.   David took up this lament concerning Saul and his   2 Sam.
son Jonathan, and ordered that the men of Judah be taught this lament of   1:17-27
the bow (it is written in the Book of Jashar):

> "Your glory, O Israel, lies slain on your heights.
>   How the mighty have fallen!
>
> "Tell it not in Gath,
>   proclaim it not in the streets of Ashkelon,
> lest the daughters of the Philistines be glad,
>   lest the daughters of the uncircumcised rejoice.
>
> "O mountains of Gilboa,
>   may you have neither dew nor rain,
>   nor fields that yield offerings ˻of grain˼.
> For there the shield of the mighty was defiled,

the shield of Saul—no longer rubbed with oil.
From the blood of the slain,
from the flesh of the mighty,
the bow of Jonathan did not turn back,
the sword of Saul did not return unsatisfied.

"Saul and Jonathan—
in life they were loved and gracious,
and in death they were not parted.
They were swifter than eagles,
they were stronger than lions.

"O daughters of Israel,
weep for Saul,
who clothed you in scarlet and finery,
who adorned your garments with ornaments of gold.

"How the mighty have fallen in battle!
Jonathan lies slain on your heights.
I grieve for you, Jonathan my brother;
you were very dear to me.
Your love for me was wonderful,
more wonderful than that of women.

"How the mighty have fallen!
The weapons of war have perished!"

David Becomes King

*D*avid must surely have mixed emotions as he considers the future. He is obviously relieved to be free of Saul's constant threats, but the mantle of responsibility is now his. (His kingship over all Israel is still some seven years away. He must rule over Judah alone until civil conflict is resolved and he is accepted by all the people.)

The most significant move which David will make as king of Israel is the capture and occupation of Jerusalem, known even until this day as the City of David. To that city he will also return the sacred ark of God and make initial plans for the building of a permanent temple. For all his efforts, David is assured by God that he and his family will be blessed.

The account of these initial years begins with David seeking God's guidance—one of the many traits which makes David such a special leader for God's people.

2 Sam.
2:1-4a
(Ca. 1011
B.C.)

DAVID KING OVER JUDAH.   In the course of time, David inquired of the LORD. "Shall I go up to one of the towns of Judah?" he asked.

The LORD said, "Go up."

David asked, "Where shall I go?"

"To Hebron," the LORD answered.

So David went up there with his two wives, Ahinoam of Jezreel and Abigail, the widow of Nabal of Carmel. David also took the men who were with him, each with his family, and they settled in Hebron and its towns. Then the men of Judah came to Hebron and there they anointed David king over the house of Judah.

KINDNESS TO MEN OF JABESH.   When David was told that it was the men of Jabesh Gilead who had buried Saul, he sent messengers to the men of Jabesh Gilead to say to them, "The LORD bless you for showing this kindness to Saul your master by burying him. May the LORD now show you kindness and faithfulness, and I too will show you the same favor because you have done this. Now then, be strong and brave, for Saul your master is dead, and the house of Judah has anointed me king over them." 2 Sam. 2:4b-7

ISH-BOSHETH KING OF ISRAEL.   Meanwhile, Abner son of Ner, the commander of Saul's army, had taken Ish-Bosheth son of Saul and brought him over to Mahanaim. He made him king over Gilead, Ashuriʸ and Jezreel, and also over Ephraim, Benjamin and all Israel. 2 Sam. 2:8-10 (Ca. 1011 B.C.) Mahanaim

Ish-Bosheth son of Saul was forty years old when he became king over Israel, and he reigned two years. The house of Judah, however, followed David.

CIVIL WAR ERUPTS.   Abner son of Ner, together with the men of Ish-Bosheth son of Saul, left Mahanaim and went to Gibeon. Joab son of Zeruiah and David's men went out and met them at the pool of Gibeon. One group sat down on one side of the pool and one group on the other side. 2 Sam. 2:12-17 Gibeon

Then Abner said to Joab, "Let's have some of the young men get up and fight hand to hand in front of us."

"All right, let them do it," Joab said.

So they stood up and were counted off—twelve men for Benjamin and Ish-Bosheth son of Saul, and twelve for David. Then each man grabbed his opponent by the head and thrust his dagger into his opponent's side, and they fell down together. So that place in Gibeon was called Helkath Hazzurim.ᶻ

The battle that day was very fierce, and Abner and the men of Israel were defeated by David's men.

The three sons of Zeruiah were there: Joab, Abishai and Asahel. Now Asahel was as fleet-footed as a wild gazelle. He chased Abner, turning neither to the right nor to the left as he pursued him. Abner looked behind him and asked, "Is that you, Asahel?" 2 Sam. 2:18-23

"It is," he answered.

Then Abner said to him, "Turn aside to the right or to the left; take on one of the young men and strip him of his weapons." But Asahel would not stop chasing him.

Again Abner warned Asahel, "Stop chasing me! Why should I strike you down? How could I look your brother Joab in the face?"

But Asahel refused to give up the pursuit; so Abner thrust the butt of his spear into Asahel's stomach, and the spear came out through his back. He fell there and died on the spot. And every man stopped when he came to the place where Asahel had fallen and died.

But Joab and Abishai pursued Abner, and as the sun was setting, they came to the hill of Ammah, near Giah on the way to the wasteland of Gibeon. Then the men of Benjamin rallied behind Abner. They formed themselves into a group and took their stand on top of a hill. 2 Sam. 2:24-29

Abner called out to Joab, "Must the sword devour forever? Don't you

ʸOr Asher   ᶻHelkath Hazzurim means *field of daggers* or *field of hostilities.*

realize that this will end in bitterness? How long before you order your men to stop pursuing their brothers?"

Joab answered, "As surely as God lives, if you had not spoken, the men would have continued the pursuit of their brothers until morning.[a]"

So Joab blew the trumpet, and all the men came to a halt; they no longer pursued Israel, nor did they fight anymore.

All that night Abner and his men marched through the Arabah. They crossed the Jordan, continued through the whole Bithron[b] and came to Mahanaim.

2 Sam.
2:30-3:1

Then Joab returned from pursuing Abner and assembled all his men. Besides Asahel, nineteen of David's men were found missing. But David's men had killed three hundred and sixty Benjamites who were with Abner. They took Asahel and buried him in his father's tomb at Bethlehem. Then Joab and his men marched all night and arrived at Hebron by daybreak. The war between the house of Saul and the house of David lasted a long time. David grew stronger and stronger, while the house of Saul grew weaker and weaker.

2 Sam.
3:2-5
1 Chron.
3:1-4a
Hebron

DAVID'S SONS IN HEBRON.

Sons were born to David in Hebron:

His firstborn was Amnon the son of Ahinoam of Jezreel;

his second, Kileab the son of Abigail the widow of Nabal of Carmel;

the third, Absalom the son of Maacah daughter of Talmai king of Geshur;

the fourth, Adonijah the son of Haggith;

the fifth, Shephatiah the son of Abital;

and the sixth, Ithream the son of David's wife Eglah.

These were born to David in Hebron.

2 Sam.
3:6-11
(Ca. 1004
B.C.)

ISH-BOSHETH ANGERS ABNER.

During the war between the house of Saul and the house of David, Abner had been strengthening his own position in the house of Saul. Now Saul had had a concubine named Rizpah daughter of Aiah. And Ish-Bosheth said to Abner, "Why did you sleep with my father's concubine?"

Abner was very angry because of what Ish-Bosheth said and he answered, "Am I a dog's head—on Judah's side? This very day I am loyal to the house of your father Saul and to his family and friends. I haven't handed you over to David. Yet now you accuse me of an offense involving this woman! May God deal with Abner, be it ever so severely, if I do not do for David what the LORD promised him on oath and transfer the kingdom from the house of Saul and establish David's throne over Israel and Judah from Dan to Beersheba." Ish-Bosheth did not dare to say another word to Abner, because he was afraid of him.

2 Sam.
3:12,13

ABNER OFFERS ALLIANCE.

Then Abner sent messengers on his behalf to say to David, "Whose land is it? Make an agreement with me, and I will help you bring all Israel over to you."

"Good," said David. "I will make an agreement with you. But I demand one thing of you: Do not come into my presence unless you bring Michal daughter of Saul when you come to see me."

---

[a]Or *spoken this morning, the men would not have taken up the pursuit of their brothers;* or *spoken, the men would have given up the pursuit of their brothers by morning*   [b]Or *morning;* or *ravine; the meaning of the Hebrew for this word is uncertain.*

DAVID GETS MICHAL BACK.   Then David sent messengers to Ish-Bosheth son of Saul, demanding, "Give me my wife Michal, whom I betrothed to myself for the price of a hundred Philistine foreskins."

    So Ish-Bosheth gave orders and had her taken away from her husband Paltiel son of Laish. Her husband, however, went with her, weeping behind her all the way to Bahurim. Then Abner said to him, "Go back home!" So he went back.

2 Sam. 3:14-16

ABNER ARRANGES FOR UNION.   Abner conferred with the elders of Israel and said, "For some time you have wanted to make David your king. Now do it! For the LORD promised David, 'By my servant David I will rescue my people Israel from the hand of the Philistines and from the hand of all their enemies.'"

    Abner also spoke to the Benjamites in person. Then he went to Hebron to tell David everything that Israel and the whole house of Benjamin wanted to do.

2 Sam. 3:17-19

ABNER AND DAVID MEET.   When Abner, who had twenty men with him, came to David at Hebron, David prepared a feast for him and his men. Then Abner said to David, "Let me go at once and assemble all Israel for my lord the king, so that they may make a compact with you, and that you may rule over all that your heart desires." So David sent Abner away, and he went in peace.

2 Sam. 3:20,21

JOAB TAKES REVENGE ON ABNER.   Just then David's men and Joab returned from a raid and brought with them a great deal of plunder. But Abner was no longer with David in Hebron, because David had sent him away, and he had gone in peace. When Joab and all the soldiers with him arrived, he was told that Abner son of Ner had come to the king and that the king had sent him away and that he had gone in peace.

    So Joab went to the king and said, "What have you done? Look, Abner came to you. Why did you let him go? Now he is gone! You know Abner son of Ner; he came to deceive you and observe your movements and find out everything you are doing."

    Joab then left David and sent messengers after Abner, and they brought him back from the well of Sirah. But David did not know it. Now when Abner returned to Hebron, Joab took him aside into the gateway, as though to speak with him privately. And there, to avenge the blood of his brother Asahel, Joab stabbed him in the stomach, and he died.

2 Sam. 3:22-27

DAVID ANGRY AND SAD.   Later, when David heard about this, he said, "I and my kingdom are forever innocent before the LORD concerning the blood of Abner son of Ner. May his blood fall upon the head of Joab and upon all his father's house! May Joab's house never be without someone who has a running sore or leprosy^c or who leans on a crutch or who falls by the sword or who lacks food."

    (Joab and his brother Abishai murdered Abner because he had killed their brother Asahel in the battle at Gibeon.)

    Then David said to Joab and all the people with him, "Tear your clothes and put on sackcloth and walk in mourning in front of Abner." King David himself walked behind the bier. They buried Abner in Hebron, and the king wept aloud at Abner's tomb. All the people wept also.

2 Sam. 3:28-29

^cThe Hebrew word was used for various diseases affecting the skin—not necessarily leprosy.

The king sang this lament for Abner:

> "Should Abner have died as the lawless die?
>   Your hands were not bound,
>   your feet were not fettered.
>   You fell as one falls before wicked men."

And all the people wept over him again.

Then they all came and urged David to eat something while it was still day; but David took an oath, saying, "May God deal with me, be it ever so severely, if I taste bread or anything else before the sun sets!"

All the people took note and were pleased; indeed, everything the king did pleased them. So on that day all the people and all Israel knew that the king had no part in the murder of Abner son of Ner.

Then the king said to his men, "Do you not realize that a prince and a great man has fallen in Israel this day? And today, though I am the anointed king, I am weak, and these sons of Zeruiah are too strong for me. May the LORD repay the evildoer according to his evil deeds!"

2 Sam.
4:1-3,5,6

ISH-BOSHETH MURDERED.   When Ish-Bosheth son of Saul heard that Abner had died in Hebron, he lost courage, and all Israel became alarmed. Now Saul's son had two men who were leaders of raiding bands. One was named Baanah and the other Recab; they were sons of Rimmon the Beerothite from the tribe of Benjamin—Beeroth is considered part of Benjamin, because the people of Beeroth fled to Gittaim and have lived there as aliens to this day.

Now Recab and Baanah, the sons of Rimmon the Beerothite, set out for the house of Ish-Bosheth, and they arrived there in the heat of the day while he was taking his noonday rest. They went into the inner part of the house as if to get some wheat, and they stabbed him in the stomach. Then Recab and his brother Baanah slipped away.

2 Sam.
4:7-12

MURDERERS EXECUTED.   They had gone into the house while he was lying on the bed in his bedroom. After they stabbed and killed him, they cut off his head. Taking it with them, they traveled all night by way of the Arabah. They brought the head of Ish-Bosheth to David at Hebron and said to the king, "Here is the head of Ish-Bosheth son of Saul, your enemy, who tried to take your life. This day the LORD has avenged my lord the king against Saul and his offspring."

David answered Recab and his brother Baanah, the sons of Rimmon the Beerothite, "As surely as the LORD lives, who has delivered me out of all trouble, when a man told me, 'Saul is dead,' and thought he was bringing good news, I seized him and put him to death in Ziklag. That was the reward I gave him for his news! How much more—when wicked men have killed an innocent man in his own house and on his own bed—should I not now demand his blood from your hand and rid the earth of you!"

So David gave an order to his men, and they killed them. They cut off their hands and feet and hung the bodies by the pool in Hebron. But they took the head of Ish-Bosheth and buried it in Abner's tomb at Hebron.

2 Sam.
5:1-3
1 Chron.
11:1-3
(Ca. 1004
B.C.)
Hebron

DAVID KING OVER ISRAEL.   All Israel came together to David at Hebron and said, "We are your own flesh and blood. In the past, even while Saul was king, you were the one who led Israel on their military campaigns. And the LORD your God said to you, 'You will shepherd my people Israel, and you will become their ruler.'"

When all the elders of Israel had come to King David at Hebron, he made a compact with them at Hebron before the LORD, and they anointed David king over Israel, as the LORD had promised through Samuel.

RECORD OF DAVID'S REIGN.   David was thirty years old when he became king, and he reigned forty years. In Hebron he reigned over Judah seven years and six months, and in Jerusalem he reigned over all Israel and Judah thirty-three years.

2 Sam.
2:11
5:4,5
1 Kgs. 2:11
1 Chron.
3:4b
29:26,27

WARRIORS WHO MAKE DAVID KING.   These are the numbers of the men armed for battle who came to David at Hebron to turn Saul's kingdom over to him, as the LORD had said:

1 Chron.
12:23-40

　men of Judah, carrying shield and spear—6,800 armed for battle;
　men of Simeon, warriors ready for battle—7,100;
　men of Levi—4,600, including Jehoiada, leader of the family of Aaron, with 3,700 men, and Zadok, a brave young warrior, with 22 officers from his family;
　men of Benjamin, Saul's kinsmen—3,000, most of whom had remained loyal to Saul's house until then;
　men of Ephraim, brave warriors, famous in their own clans—20,800;
　men of half the tribe of Manasseh, designated by name to come and make David king—18,000;
　men of Issachar, who understood the times and knew what Israel should do—200 chiefs, with all their relatives under their command;
　men of Zebulun, experienced soldiers prepared for battle with every type of weapon, to help David with undivided loyalty—50,000;
　men of Naphtali—1,000 officers, together with 37,000 men carrying shields and spears;
　men of Dan, ready for battle—28,600;
　men of Asher, experienced soldiers prepared for battle—40,000;
　and from east of the Jordan, men of Reuben, Gad and the half-tribe of Manasseh, armed with every type of weapon—120,000.

All these were fighting men who volunteered to serve in the ranks. They came to Hebron fully determined to make David king over all Israel. All the rest of the Israelites were also of one mind to make David king. The men spent three days there with David, eating and drinking, for their families had supplied provisions for them. Also, their neighbors from as far away as Issachar, Zebulun and Naphtali came bringing food on donkeys, camels, mules and oxen. There were plentiful supplies of flour, fig cakes, raisin cakes, wine, oil, cattle and sheep, for there was joy in Israel.

DAVID CAPTURES JERUSALEM.   The king and his men marched to Jerusalem to attack the Jebusites, who lived there. The Jebusites said to David, "You will not get in here; even the blind and the lame can ward you off." They thought, "David cannot get in here." Nevertheless, David captured the fortress of Zion, the City of David.

2 Sam.
5:6-8
1 Chron.
11:4,5
Jerusalem

On that day, David said, "Anyone who conquers the Jebusites will have to use the water shaft[d] to reach those 'lame and blind' who are David's enemies.[e]" That is why they say, "The 'blind and lame' will not enter the palace."

---

[d]Or *use scaling hooks*　　　[e]Or *are hated by David*

2 Sam. 5:9,10 1 Chron. 11:6-9	**THE CITY OF DAVID.** David had said, "Whoever leads the attack on the Jebusites will become commander-in-chief." Joab son of Zeruiah went up first, and so he received the command. David then took up residence in the fortress, and so it was called the City of David. He built up the city around it, from the supporting terraces*f* to the surrounding wall, while Joab restored the rest of the city. And David became more and more powerful, because the LORD Almighty was with him.
2 Sam. 5:11,12 1 Chron. 14:1,2	**HIRAM BUILDS DAVID'S HOUSE.** Now Hiram king of Tyre sent messengers to David, along with cedar logs, stonemasons and carpenters to build a palace for him. And David knew that the LORD had established him as king over Israel and that his kingdom had been highly exalted for the sake of his people Israel.
2 Sam. 6:1-5 1 Chron. 13:1-8	**DAVID GOES FOR ARK.** David conferred with each of his officers, the commanders of thousands and commanders of hundreds. He then said to the whole assembly of Israel, "If it seems good to you and if it is the will of the LORD our God, let us send word far and wide to the rest of our brothers throughout the territories of Israel, and also to the priests and Levites who are with them in their towns and pasturelands, to come and join us. Let us bring the ark of our God back to us, for we did not inquire of*g* it*h* during the reign of Saul." The whole assembly agreed to do this, because it seemed right to all the people. So David assembled all the Israelites, from the Shihor River in Egypt to Lebo*i* Hamath, to bring the ark of God from Kiriath Jearim. David and all the Israelites with him went to Baalah of Judah (Kiriath Jearim) to bring up from there the ark of God the LORD, who is enthroned between the cherubim—the ark that is called by the Name. They moved the ark of God from Abinadab's house on a new cart, with Uzzah and Ahio guiding it. David and all the Israelites were celebrating with all their might before God, with songs and with harps, lyres, tambourines, cymbals and trumpets.
2 Sam. 6:6-11 1 Chron. 13:9-14	**UZZAH IS KILLED.** When they came to the threshing floor of Kidon, Uzzah reached out his hand to steady the ark, because the oxen stumbled. The LORD's anger burned against Uzzah, and he struck him down because he had put his hand on the ark. So he died there before God. Then David was angry because the LORD's wrath had broken out against Uzzah, and to this day that place is called Perez Uzzah.*j* David was afraid of God that day and asked, "How can I ever bring the ark of God to me?" He did not take the ark to be with him in the City of David. Instead, he took it aside to the house of Obed-Edom the Gittite. The ark of God remained with the family of Obed-Edom in his house for three months, and the LORD blessed his household and everything he had.
2 Sam. 5:17-25 1 Chron. 14:8-17 Baal Perazim	**DEFENSE AGAINST PHILISTINES.** When the Philistines heard that David had been anointed king over all Israel, they went up in full force to search for him, but David heard about it and went out to meet them. Now the Philistines had come and raided the Valley of Rephaim; so David inquired of God: "Shall I go and attack the Philistines? Will you hand them over to me?"

*f*Or *the Millo*   *g*Or *we neglected*   *h*Or *him*   *i*Or *to the entrance to*   *j*Perez Uzzah
means *outbreak against Uzzah.*

The Lord answered him, "Go, I will hand them over to you."

So David and his men went up to Baal Perazim, and there he defeated them. He said, "As waters break out, God has broken out against my enemies by my hand." So that place was called Baal Perazim.*k* The Philistines had abandoned their gods there, and David gave orders to burn them in the fire.

Once more the Philistines raided the valley; so David inquired of God again, and God answered him, "Do not go straight up, but circle around them and attack them in front of the balsam trees. As soon as you hear the sound of marching in the tops of the balsam trees, move out to battle, because that will mean God has gone out in front of you to strike the Philistine army." So David did as God commanded him, and they struck down the Philistine army, all the way from Gibeon to Gezer.

So David's fame spread throughout every land, and the Lord made all the nations fear him.

A SONG OF DELIVERANCE.

2 Sam.
22:1-51
Psa. 18

Ps For the director of music. Of David the servant of the Lord. He sang to the Lord the words of this song when the Lord delivered him from the hand of all his enemies and from the hand of Saul. He said:

> I love you, O Lord, my strength.
>
> The Lord is my rock, my fortress and my deliverer;
>> my God is my rock, in whom I take refuge.
>> He is my shield and the horn*l* of my salvation, my
>>> stronghold.
> I call to the Lord, who is worthy of praise,
>> and I am saved from my enemies.
>
> *Sa* "The waves of death swirled about me;
>> the torrents of destruction overwhelmed me.
> The cords of the grave*m* coiled around me;
>> the snares of death confronted me.
> In my distress I called to the Lord;
>> I called out to my God.
> From his temple he heard my voice;
>> my cry came to his ears.
>
> "The earth trembled and quaked,
>> the foundations of the heavens*n* shook;
>> they trembled because he was angry.
> Smoke rose from his nostrils;
>> consuming fire came from his mouth,
>> burning coals blazed out of it.
> He parted the heavens and came down;
>> dark clouds were under his feet.
> He mounted the cherubim and flew;
>> he soared*o* on the wings of the wind.
> He made darkness his canopy around him—

---

*k*Baal Perazim means *the lord who breaks out.*   *l*Horn here symbolizes strength.
*m*Hebrew *Sheol*   *n*Hebrew; Vulgate and Syriac (see also Psalm 18:7) *mountains*
*o*Many Hebrew manuscripts (see also Psalm 18:10); most Hebrew manuscripts *appeared*

the dark[p] rain clouds of the sky.
Out of the brightness of his presence
    bolts of lightning blazed forth.
The LORD thundered from heaven;
    the voice of the Most High resounded.
He shot arrows and scattered the enemies,
    bolts of lightning and routed them.
The valleys of the sea were exposed
    and the foundations of the earth laid bare
at the rebuke of the LORD,
    at the blast of breath from his nostrils.

"He reached down from on high and took hold of me;
    he drew me out of deep waters.
He rescued me from my powerful enemy,
    from my foes, who were too strong for me.
They confronted me in the day of my disaster,
    but the LORD was my support.
He brought me out into a spacious place;
    he rescued me because he delighted in me.

"The LORD has dealt with me according to my righteousness;
    according to the cleanness of my hands he has
        rewarded me.
For I have kept the ways of the LORD;
    I have not done evil by turning from my God.
All his laws are before me;
    I have not turned away from his decrees.
I have been blameless before him
    and have kept myself from sin.
The LORD has rewarded me according to my righteousness,
    according to my cleanness[q] in his sight.

"To the faithful you show yourself faithful,
    to the blameless you show yourself blameless,
to the pure you show yourself pure,
    but to the crooked you show yourself shrewd.
You save the humble,
    but your eyes are on the haughty to bring them low.
You are my lamp, O LORD;
    the LORD turns my darkness into light.
With your help I can advance against a troop[r];
    with my God I can scale a wall.

"As for God, his way is perfect;
    the word of the LORD is flawless.
He is a shield
    for all who take refuge in him.
For who is God besides the LORD?
    And who is the Rock except our God?

[p]Septuagint and Vulgate (see also Psalm 18:11); Hebrew *massed*   [q]Hebrew; Septuagint and Vulgate (see also Psalm 18:24) *to the cleanness of my hands*   [r]Or *can run through a barricade*

It is God who arms me with strength[s]
  and makes my way perfect.
He makes my feet like the feet of a deer;
  he enables me to stand on the heights.
He trains my hands for battle;
  my arms can bend a bow of bronze.
You give me your shield of victory,
  and your right hand sustains me;
  you stoop down to make me great.
You broaden the path beneath me,
  so that my ankles do not turn.

Ps I pursued my enemies and overtook them;
  I did not turn back till they were destroyed.
I crushed them so that they could not rise;
  they fell beneath my feet.
You armed me with strength for battle;
  you made my adversaries bow at my feet.
You made my enemies turn their backs in flight,
  and I destroyed my foes.
They cried for help, but there was no one to save them—
  to the LORD, but he did not answer.
I beat them as fine as dust borne on the wind;
  I poured them out like mud in the streets.

You have delivered me from the attacks of the people;
  you have made me the head of nations;
  people I did not know are subject to me.
As soon as they hear me, they obey me;
  foreigners cringe before me.
They all lose heart;
  they come trembling from their strongholds.

The LORD lives! Praise be to my Rock!
  Exalted be God my Savior!
He is the God who avenges me,
  who subdues nations under me,
  who saves me from my enemies.
You exalted me above my foes;
  from violent men you rescued me.
Therefore I will praise you among the nations, O LORD;
  I will sing praises to your name.
He gives his king great victories;
  he shows unfailing kindness to his anointed,
  to David and his descendants forever.

DAVID REMINDED OF ARK.   Now King David was told, "The LORD has blessed the household of Obed-Edom and everything he has, because of the ark of God."

2 Sam.
6:12a

ARRANGEMENTS FOR RETURN.   After David had constructed buildings for himself in the City of David, he prepared a place for the ark of

1 Chron.
15:1-10
Jerusalem

[s]Dead Sea Scrolls, some Septuagint manuscripts, Vulgate and Syriac (see also Psalm 18:32); Masoretic Text *who is my strong refuge*

God and pitched a tent for it. Then David said, "No one but the Levites may carry the ark of God, because the LORD chose them to carry the ark of the LORD and to minister before him forever."

David assembled all Israel in Jerusalem to bring up the ark of the LORD to the place he had prepared for it. He called together the descendants of Aaron and the Levites:

From the descendants of Kohath,
     Uriel the leader and 120 relatives;
from the descendants of Merari,
     Asaiah the leader and 220 relatives;
from the descendants of Gershon,[t]
     Joel the leader and 130 relatives;
from the descendants of Elizaphan,
     Shemaiah the leader and 200 relatives;
from the descendants of Hebron,
     Eliel the leader and 80 relatives;
from the descendants of Uzziel,
     Amminadab the leader and 112 relatives.

1 Chron. 15:11-16 Then David summoned Zadok and Abiathar the priests, and Uriel, Asaiah, Joel, Shemaiah, Eliel and Amminadab the Levites. He said to them, "You are the heads of the Levitical families; you and your fellow Levites are to consecrate yourselves and bring up the ark of the LORD, the God of Israel, to the place I have prepared for it. It was because you, the Levites, did not bring it up the first time that the LORD our God broke out in anger against us. We did not inquire of him about how to do it in the prescribed way." So the priests and Levites consecrated themselves in order to bring up the ark of the LORD, the God of Israel. And the Levites carried the ark of God with the poles on their shoulders, as Moses had commanded in accordance with the word of the LORD.

David told the leaders of the Levites to appoint their brothers as singers to sing joyful songs, accompanied by musical instruments: lyres, harps and cymbals.

1 Chron. 15:17-24 So the Levites appointed Heman son of Joel; from his brothers, Asaph son of Berekiah; and from their brothers the Merarites, Ethan son of Kushaiah; and with them their brothers next in rank: Zechariah,[u] Jaaziel, Shemiramoth, Jehiel, Unni, Eliab, Benaiah, Maaseiah, Mattithiah, Eliphelehu, Mikneiah, Obed-Edom and Jeiel,[v] the gatekeepers.

The musicians Heman, Asaph and Ethan were to sound the bronze cymbals; Zechariah, Aziel, Shemiramoth, Jehiel, Unni, Eliab, Maaseiah and Benaiah were to play the lyres according to *alamoth*,[w] and Mattithiah, Eliphelehu, Mikneiah, Obed-Edom, Jeiel and Azaziah were to play the harps, directing according to *sheminith*.[w] Kenaniah the head Levite was in charge of the singing; that was his responsibility because he was skillful at it.

Berekiah and Elkanah were to be doorkeepers for the ark. Shebaniah, Joshaphat, Nethanel, Amasai, Zechariah, Benaiah and Eliezer the priests

---

[t]Hebrew *Gershom*, a variant of *Gershon*   [u]Three Hebrew manuscripts and most Septuagint manuscripts (see also verse 20 and 1 Chron. 16:5); most Hebrew manuscripts *Zechariah son and* or *Zechariah, Ben and*   [v]Hebrew; Septuagint (see also verse 21) *Jeiel and Azaziah*   [w]Probably a musical term

were to blow trumpets before the ark of God. Obed-Edom and Jehiah were also to be doorkeepers for the ark.

TRIUMPHANT RETURN OF ARK.   So David and the elders of Israel and the commanders of units of a thousand went to bring up the ark of the covenant of the LORD from the house of Obed-Edom, with rejoicing. Because God had helped the Levites who were carrying the ark of the covenant of the LORD, seven bulls and seven rams were sacrificed. Now David was clothed in a robe of fine linen, as were all the Levites who were carrying the ark, and as were the singers, and Kenaniah, who was in charge of the singing of the choirs. David also wore a linen ephod. So all Israel brought up the ark of the covenant of the LORD with shouts, with the sounding of rams' horns and trumpets, and of cymbals, and the playing of lyres and harps.

2 Sam.
6:12b-15
1 Chron.
15:25-28

MICHAL DESPISES DAVID.   As the ark of the covenant of the LORD was entering the City of David, Michal daughter of Saul watched from a window. And when she saw King David dancing and celebrating, she despised him in her heart.

2 Sam.
6:16
1 Chron.
15:29

CELEBRATION IN JERUSALEM.   They brought the ark of God and set it inside the tent that David had pitched for it, and they presented burnt offerings and fellowship offerings[x] before God. After David had finished sacrificing the burnt offerings and fellowship offerings, he blessed the people in the name of the LORD. Then he gave a loaf of bread, a cake of dates and a cake of raisins to each Israelite man and woman.

2 Sam.
6:17-19
1 Chron.
16:1-3

LEVITES APPOINTED MINISTERS.   He appointed some of the Levites to minister before the ark of the LORD, to make petition, to give thanks, and to praise the LORD, the God of Israel: Asaph was the chief, Zechariah second, then Jeiel, Shemiramoth, Jehiel, Mattithiah, Eliab, Benaiah, Obed-Edom and Jeiel. They were to play the lyres and harps, Asaph was to sound the cymbals, and Benaiah and Jahaziel the priests were to blow the trumpets regularly before the ark of the covenant of God.

1 Chron.
16:4-6

SONGS OF PRAISE.   Ch That day David first committed to Asaph and his associates this psalm of thanks to the LORD:

1 Chron.
16:7-36
Psa. 105
Psa. 96

> Give thanks to the LORD, call on his name;
>   make known among the nations what he has done.
> Sing to him, sing praise to him;
>   tell of all his wonderful acts.
> Glory in his holy name;
>   let the hearts of those who seek the LORD rejoice.
> Look to the LORD and his strength;
>   seek his face always.
> Remember the wonders he has done,
>   his miracles, and the judgments he pronounced,
> O descendants of Israel his servant,
>   O sons of Jacob, his chosen ones.
>
> He is the LORD our God;
>   his judgments are in all the earth.

x Traditionally *peace offerings;* also in verse 2

He remembers[y] his covenant forever,
　　the word he commanded, for a thousand generations,
the covenant he made with Abraham,
　　the oath he swore to Isaac.
He confirmed it to Jacob as a decree,
　　to Israel as an everlasting covenant:
"To you I will give the land of Canaan
　　as the portion you will inherit."

When they were but few in number,
　　few indeed, and strangers in it,
they[z] wandered from nation to nation,
　　from one kingdom to another.
He allowed no one to oppress them;
　　for their sake he rebuked kings:
"Do not touch my anointed ones;
　　do my prophets no harm."

Ps He called down famine on the land
　　and destroyed all their supplies of food;
and he sent a man before them—
　　Joseph, sold as a slave.
They bruised his feet with shackles,
　　his neck was put in irons,
till what he foretold came to pass,
　　till the word of the LORD proved him true.
The king sent and released him,
　　the ruler of peoples set him free.
He made him master of his household,
　　ruler over all he possessed,
to instruct his princes as he pleased
　　and teach his elders wisdom.

Then Israel entered Egypt;
　　Jacob lived as an alien in the land of Ham.
The LORD made his people very fruitful;
　　he made them too numerous for their foes,
whose hearts he turned to hate his people,
　　to conspire against his servants.
He sent Moses his servant,
　　and Aaron, whom he had chosen.
They performed his miraculous signs among them,
　　his wonders in the land of Ham.
He sent darkness and made the land dark—
　　for had they not rebelled against his words?
He turned their waters into blood,
　　causing their fish to die.
Their land teemed with frogs,
　　which went up into the bedrooms of their rulers.

[y]Some Septuagint manuscripts (see also Psalm 105:8); Hebrew *Remember*   [z]One
Hebrew manuscript, Septuagint and Vulgate (see also Psalm 105:12); most Hebrew
manuscripts *inherit, | 19though you are but few in number, | few indeed, and strangers in it." |
20They*

He spoke, and there came swarms of flies,
  and gnats throughout their country.
He turned their rain into hail,
  with lightning throughout their land;
he struck down their vines and fig trees
  and shattered the trees of their country.
He spoke, and the locusts came,
  grasshoppers without number;
they ate up every green thing in their land,
  ate up the produce of their soil.
Then he struck down all the firstborn in their land,
  the firstfruits of all their manhood.

He brought out Israel, laden with silver and gold,
  and from among their tribes no one faltered.
Egypt was glad when they left,
  because dread of Israel had fallen on them.
He spread out a cloud as a covering,
  and a fire to give light at night.
They asked, and he brought them quail
  and satisfied them with the bread of heaven.
He opened the rock, and water gushed out;
  like a river it flowed in the desert.

For he remembered his holy promise
  given to his servant Abraham.
He brought out his people with rejoicing,
  his chosen ones with shouts of joy;
he gave them the lands of the nations,
  and they fell heir to what others had toiled for—
that they might keep his precepts
  and observe his laws.

Praise the LORD.[a]

Ch Sing to the LORD, all the earth;
  proclaim his salvation day after day.
Declare his glory among the nations,
  his marvelous deeds among all peoples.
For great is the LORD and most worthy of praise;
  he is to be feared above all gods.
For all the gods of the nations are idols,
  but the LORD made the heavens.
Splendor and majesty are before him;
  strength and joy in his dwelling place.
Ascribe to the LORD, O families of nations,
  ascribe to the LORD glory and strength,
  ascribe to the LORD the glory due his name.
Bring an offering and come before him;
  worship the LORD in the splendor of his[b] holiness.
Tremble before him, all the earth!
  The world is firmly established; it cannot be moved.

[a]Hebrew *Hallelu Yah*   [b]Or LORD *with the splendor of*

> Let the heavens rejoice, let the earth be glad;
>> let them say among the nations, "The LORD reigns!"
> Let the sea resound, and all that is in it;
>> let the fields be jubilant, and everything in them!
> Then the trees of the forest will sing,
>> they will sing for joy before the LORD,
>> for he comes to judge the earth.

> Ps He will judge the world in righteousness
>> and the peoples in his truth.

> Ch Give thanks to the LORD, for he is good;
>> his love endures forever.
> Cry out, "Save us, O God our Savior;
>> gather us and deliver us from the nations,
> that we may give thanks to your holy name,
>> that we may glory in your praise."
> Praise be to the LORD, the God of Israel,
>> from everlasting to everlasting.

Then all the people said "Amen" and "Praise the LORD."

1 Chron.
16:37-43
Jerusalem

REGULAR WORSHIP ESTABLISHED.   David left Asaph and his associates before the ark of the covenant of the LORD to minister there regularly, according to each day's requirements. He also left Obed-Edom and his sixty-eight associates to minister with them. Obed-Edom son of Jeduthun, and also Hosah, were gatekeepers.

David left Zadok the priest and his fellow priests before the tabernacle of the LORD at the high place in Gibeon to present burnt offerings to the LORD on the altar of burnt offering regularly, morning and evening, in accordance with everything written in the Law of the LORD, which he had given Israel. With them were Heman and Jeduthun and the rest of those chosen and designated by name to give thanks to the LORD, "for his love endures forever." Heman and Jeduthun were responsible for the sounding of the trumpets and cymbals and for the playing of the other instruments for sacred song. The sons of Jeduthun were stationed at the gate.

Then all the people left, each for his own home, and David returned home to bless his family.

2 Sam.
6:20-23

MICHAL REBUKES DAVID.   When David returned home to bless his household, Michal daughter of Saul came out to meet him and said, "How the king of Israel has distinguished himself today, disrobing in the sight of the slave girls of his servants as any vulgar fellow would!"

David said to Michal, "It was before the LORD, who chose me rather than your father or anyone from his house when he appointed me ruler over the LORD's people Israel—I will celebrate before the LORD. I will become even more undignified than this, and I will be humiliated in my own eyes. But by these slave girls you spoke of, I will be held in honor."

And Michal daughter of Saul had no children to the day of her death.

2 Sam.
8:15-18
1 Chron.
18:14-17

DAVID'S OFFICIALS.   David reigned over all Israel, doing what was just and right for all his people. Joab son of Zeruiah was over the army; Jehoshaphat son of Ahilud was recorder; Zadok son of Ahitub and Ahimelech son of Abiathar were priests; Seraiah was secretary; Benaiah son of

Jehoiada was over the Kerethites and Pelethites; and David's sons were royal advisers.[c]

JONATHAN'S SON HONORED.   David asked, "Is there anyone still left of the house of Saul to whom I can show kindness for Jonathan's sake?"

Now there was a servant of Saul's household named Ziba. They called him to appear before David, and the king said to him, "Are you Ziba?"

"Your servant," he replied.

The king asked, "Is there no one still left of the house of Saul to whom I can show God's kindness?"

Ziba answered the king, "There is still a son of Jonathan; he is crippled in both feet."

"Where is he?" the king asked.

Ziba answered, "He is at the house of Makir son of Ammiel in Lo Debar."

So King David had him brought from Lo Debar, from the house of Makir son of Ammiel.

When Mephibosheth son of Jonathan, the son of Saul, came to David, he bowed down to pay him honor.

David said, "Mephibosheth!"

"Your servant," he replied.

"Don't be afraid," David said to him, "for I will surely show you kindness for the sake of your father Jonathan. I will restore to you all the land that belonged to your grandfather Saul, and you will always eat at my table."

Mephibosheth bowed down and said, "What is your servant, that you should notice a dead dog like me?"

Then the king summoned Ziba, Saul's servant, and said to him, "I have given your master's grandson everything that belonged to Saul and his family. You and your sons and your servants are to farm the land for him and bring in the crops, so that your master's grandson may be provided for. And Mephibosheth, grandson of your master, will always eat at my table." (Now Ziba had fifteen sons and twenty servants.)

Then Ziba said to the king, "Your servant will do whatever my lord the king commands his servant to do." So Mephibosheth ate at David's[d] table like one of the king's sons.

Mephibosheth had a young son named Mica, and all the members of Ziba's household were servants of Mephibosheth. And Mephibosheth lived in Jerusalem, because he always ate at the king's table, and he was crippled in both feet.

PLAN TO BUILD A TEMPLE.   After David was settled in his palace, he said to Nathan the prophet, "Here I am, living in a palace of cedar, while the ark of the covenant of the LORD is under a tent."

Nathan replied to David, "Whatever you have in mind, do it, for God is with you."

GOD'S RESPONSE BY NATHAN.   That night the word of God came to Nathan, saying:

"Go and tell my servant David, 'This is what the LORD says: Are you the one to build me a house to dwell in? I have not dwelt in a house from the

2 Sam.
9:1-13

2 Sam.
7:1-3
1 Chron.
17:1,2

2 Sam.
7:4-17
1 Chron.
17:3-15

[c]Or *were priests*   [d]Septuagint; Hebrew *my*

day I brought the Israelites up out of Egypt to this day. I have been moving from place to place with a tent as my dwelling. Wherever I have moved with all the Israelites, did I ever say to any of their rulers whom I commanded to shepherd my people Israel, "Why have you not built me a house of cedar?" '

"Now then, tell my servant David, 'This is what the LORD Almighty says: I took you from the pasture and from following the flock to be ruler over my people Israel. I have been with you wherever you have gone, and I have cut off all your enemies from before you. Now I will make your name great, like the names of the greatest men of the earth. And I will provide a place for my people Israel and will plant them so that they can have a home of their own and no longer be disturbed. Wicked people will not oppress them anymore, as they did at the beginning and have done ever since the time I appointed leaders*e* over my people Israel. I will also give you rest from all your enemies.

" 'The LORD declares to you that the LORD himself will establish a house for you: When your days are over and you rest with your fathers, I will raise up your offspring to succeed you, who will come from your own body, and I will establish his kingdom. He is the one who will build a house for my Name, and I will establish the throne of his kingdom forever. I will be his father, and he will be my son. When he does wrong, I will punish him with the rod of men, with floggings inflicted by men. But my love will never be taken away from him, as I took it away from Saul, whom I removed from before you. Your house and your kingdom will endure forever before me*f*; your throne will be established forever.' "

Nathan reported to David all the words of this entire revelation.

2 Sam. 7:18-29 1 Chron. 17:16-27

DAVID'S THANKSGIVING.   Then King David went in and sat before the LORD, and he said:

"Who am I, O Sovereign LORD, and what is my family, that you have brought me this far? And as if this were not enough in your sight, O Sovereign LORD, you have also spoken about the future of the house of your servant. Is this your usual way of dealing with man, O Sovereign LORD?

"What more can David say to you? For you know your servant, O Sovereign LORD. For the sake of your word and according to your will, you have done this great thing and made it known to your servant.

"How great you are, O Sovereign LORD! There is no one like you, and there is no God but you, as we have heard with our own ears. And who is like your people Israel—the one nation on earth that God went out to redeem as a people for himself, and to make a name for himself, and to perform great and awesome wonders by driving out nations and their gods from before your people, whom you redeemed from Egypt?*g* You have established your people Israel as your very own forever, and you, O LORD, have become their God.

"And now, LORD God, keep forever the promise you have made concerning your servant and his house. Do as you promised, so that your name will be great forever. Then men will say, 'The LORD Almighty is God

*e*Traditionally *judges*   *f*Some Hebrew manuscripts and Septuagint; most Hebrew manuscripts *you*   *g*See Septuagint and 1 Chron. 17:21; Hebrew *wonders for your land and before your people, whom you redeemed from Egypt, from the nations and their gods*

over Israel!' And the house of your servant David will be established before you.

"O LORD Almighty, God of Israel, you have revealed this to your servant, saying, 'I will build a house for you.' So your servant has found courage to offer you this prayer. O Sovereign LORD, you are God! Your words are trustworthy, and you have promised these good things to your servant. Now be pleased to bless the house of your servant, that it may continue forever in your sight; for you, O Sovereign LORD, have spoken, and with your blessing the house of your servant will be blessed forever."

Period of the Wars

Although David's position as king is secure in God's sight, David will have to fight for his kingdom in order to make it secure in the eyes of men. David battles almost constantly with Israel's enemies, including the Philistines, Moabites, Edomites, and Ammonites. (Perhaps this period of the wars suggests the constant need for God's people of all times to combat God's enemies in order to preserve the blessings which are promised to his people.) Yet in the midst of defending his kingdom and spreading its borders offensively, David falls victim to his own lust and becomes both an adulterer and a murderer. (Here again may be a warning that God's people must be on guard against both external and internal enemies.) David's subsequent repentance and upright attitude show why, despite such serious offenses, he will later be called a man after God's own heart.

FIRST PHILISTINE BATTLE.   Once again there was a battle between the Philistines and Israel. David went down with his men to fight against the Philistines, and he became exhausted. And Ishbi-Benob, one of the descendants of Rapha, whose bronze spearhead weighed three hundred shekels[h] and who was armed with a new sword , said he would kill David. But Abishai son of Zeruiah came to David's rescue; he struck the Philistine down and killed him.

2 Sam.
21:15-17a

DAVID LEAVES ACTIVE SERVICE.   Then David's men swore to him, saying, "Never again will you go out with us to battle, so that the lamp of Israel will not be extinguished."

2 Sam.
21:17b

OTHER PHILISTINE BATTLES.   In the course of time, there was another battle with the Philistines, at Gob. At that time Sibbecai the Hushathite killed Saph, one of the descendants of Rapha.

In another battle with the Philistines at Gob, Elhanan son of Jaare-Oregim[i] the Bethlehemite killed Goliath[j] the Gittite, who had a spear with a shaft like a weaver's rod.

In still another battle, which took place at Gath, there was a huge man with six fingers on each hand and six toes on each foot—twenty-four in all. He also was descended from Rapha. When he taunted Israel, Jonathan son of Shimeah, David's brother, killed him.

2 Sam.
21:18-22
1 Chron.
20:4-8

[h]That is, about 7 1/2 pounds (about 3.5 kilograms)   [i]Or son of Jair the weaver
[j]Hebrew and Septuagint; 1 Chron. 20:5 son of Jair killed Lahmi the brother of Goliath

These four were descendants of Rapha in Gath, and they fell at the hands of David and his men.

2 Sam. 8:1
1 Chron.
18:1

SUMMARY OF DEFEATS.   In the course of time, David defeated the Philistines and subdued them, and he took Gath and its surrounding villages from the control of the Philistines.

2 Sam.
10:1-5
1 Chron.
19:1-5

AMMONITES DEGRADE AMBASSADORS.   In the course of time, Nahash king of the Ammonites died, and his son succeeded him as king. David thought, "I will show kindness to Hanun son of Nahash, because his father showed kindness to me." So David sent a delegation to express his sympathy to Hanun concerning his father.

When David's men came to Hanun in the land of the Ammonites to express sympathy to him, the Ammonite nobles said to Hanun, "Do you think David is honoring your father by sending men to you to express sympathy? Haven't his men come to you to explore and spy out the country and overthrow it?" So Hanun seized David's men, shaved them, cut off their garments in the middle at the buttocks, and sent them away.

When someone came and told David about the men, he sent messengers to meet them, for they were greatly humiliated. The king said, "Stay at Jericho till your beards have grown, and then come back."

2 Sam.
10:6-14
1 Chron.
19:6-15

AMMONITES AND ARAMEANS ROUTED.   When the Ammonites realized that they had become a stench in David's nostrils, Hanun and the Ammonites sent a thousand talents^k of silver to hire chariots and charioteers from Aram Naharaim,^{l} Aram Maacah and Zobah. They hired thirty-two thousand chariots and charioteers, as well as the king of Maacah with his troops, who came and camped near Medeba, while the Ammonites were mustered from their towns and moved out for battle.

On hearing this, David sent Joab out with the entire army of fighting men. The Ammonites came out and drew up in battle formation at the entrance to their city, while the kings who had come were by themselves in the open country.

Joab saw that there were battle lines in front of him and behind him; so he selected some of the best troops in Israel and deployed them against the Arameans. He put the rest of the men under the command of Abishai his brother, and they were deployed against the Ammonites. Joab said, "If the Arameans are too strong for me, then you are to rescue me; but if the Ammonites are too strong for you, then I will rescue you. Be strong and let us fight bravely for our people and the cities of our God. The LORD will do what is good in his sight."

Then Joab and the troops with him advanced to fight the Arameans, and they fled before him. When the Ammonites saw that the Arameans were fleeing, they too fled before his brother Abishai and went inside the city. So Joab went back to Jerusalem.

2 Sam.
10:15-19
1 Chron.
19:16-19

ARAMEANS TOTALLY DEFEATED.   After the Arameans saw that they had been routed by Israel, they sent messengers and had Arameans brought from beyond the River,^{m} with Shophach the commander of Hadadezer's army leading them.

When David was told of this, he gathered all Israel and crossed the Jordan; he advanced against them and formed his battle lines opposite

---

^{k}That is, about 37 tons (about 34 metric tons) ^{l}That is, Northwest Mesopotamia
^{m}That is, the Euphrates

them. David formed his lines to meet the Arameans in battle, and they fought against him. But they fled before Israel, and David killed seven thousand of their charioteers and forty thousand of their foot soldiers. He also killed Shophach the commander of their army.

When the vassals of Hadadezer saw that they had been defeated by Israel, they made peace with David and became subject to him.

So the Arameans were not willing to help the Ammonites anymore.

David prays for restoration.   Psa. 60

For the director of music. To the tune of, "The Lily of the Covenant." A *miktam*[n] of David. For teaching. When he fought Aram Naharaim[o] and Aram Zobah,[p] and when Joab returned and struck down twelve thousand Edomites in the Valley of Salt.

You have rejected us, O God, and burst forth upon us;
　　you have been angry—now restore us!
You have shaken the land and torn it open;
　　mend its fractures, for it is quaking.
You have shown your people desperate times;
　　you have given us wine that makes us stagger.

But for those who fear you, you have raised a banner
　　to be unfurled against the bow.   *Selah*

Save us and help us with your right hand,
　　that those you love may be delivered.
God has spoken from his sanctuary:
　　"In triumph I will parcel out Shechem
　　and measure off the Valley of Succoth.
Gilead is mine, and Manasseh is mine;
　　Ephraim is my helmet,
　　Judah my scepter.
Moab is my washbasin,
　　upon Edom I toss my sandal;
　　over Philistia I shout in triumph."

Who will bring me to the fortified city?
　　Who will lead me to Edom?
Is it not you, O God, you who have rejected us
　　and no longer go out with our armies?
Give us aid against the enemy,
　　for the help of man is worthless.
With God we will gain the victory,
　　and he will trample down our enemies.

SIEGE OF RABBAH.   In the spring, at the time when kings go off to war, David sent Joab out with the king's men and the whole Israelite army. They destroyed the Ammonites and besieged Rabbah. But David remained in Jerusalem.

2 Sam.
11:2
1 Chron.
20:1a

ADULTERY WITH BATHSHEBA.   One evening David got up from his bed and walked around on the roof of the palace. From the roof he saw a woman bathing. The woman was very beautiful, and David sent someone to find out about her. The man said, "Isn't this Bathsheba, the daughter of

2 Sam.
11:2-5
Jerusalem

[n]Title: Probably a literary or musical term   [o]Title: That is, Arameans of Northwest Mesopotamia   [p]Title: That is, Arameans of central Syria

Eliam and the wife of Uriah the Hittite?" Then David sent messengers to get her. She came to him, and he slept with her. (She had purified herself from her uncleanness.) Then [q] she went back home. The woman conceived and sent word to David, saying, "I am pregnant."

2 Sam.
11:6-13

ATTEMPT TO COVER UP.   So David sent this word to Joab: "Send me Uriah the Hittite." And Joab sent him to David. When Uriah came to him, David asked him how Joab was, how the soldiers were and how the war was going. Then David said to Uriah, "Go down to your house and wash your feet." So Uriah left the palace, and a gift from the king was sent after him. But Uriah slept at the entrance to the palace with all his master's servants and did not go down to his house.

When David was told, "Uriah did not go home," he asked him, "Haven't you just come from a distance? Why didn't you go home?"

Uriah said to David, "The ark and Israel and Judah are staying in tents, and my master Joab and my lord's men are camped in the open fields. How could I go to my house to eat and drink and lie with my wife? As surely as you live, I will not do such a thing!"

Then David said to him, "Stay here one more day, and tomorrow I will send you back." So Uriah remained in Jerusalem that day and the next. At David's invitation, he ate and drank with him, and David made him drunk. But in the evening Uriah went out to sleep on his mat among his master's servants; he did not go home.

2 Sam.
11:14-21

URIAH IS KILLED.   In the morning David wrote a letter to Joab and sent it with Uriah. In it he wrote, "Put Uriah in the front line where the fighting is fiercest. Then withdraw from him so he will be struck down and die."

So while Joab had the city under siege, he put Uriah at a place where he knew the strongest defenders were. When the men of the city came out and fought against Joab, some of the men in David's army fell; moreover, Uriah the Hittite died.

Joab sent David a full account of the battle. He instructed the messenger: "When you have finished giving the king this account of the battle, the king's anger may flare up, and he may ask you, 'Why did you get so close to the city to fight? Didn't you know they would shoot arrows from the wall? Who killed Abimelech son of Jerub-Besheth [r]? Didn't a woman throw an upper millstone on him from the wall, so that he died in Thebez? Why did you get so close to the wall?' If he asks you this, then say to him, 'Also, your servant Uriah the Hittite is dead.'"

2 Sam.
11:22-25

DAVID TOLD OF DEATH.   The messenger set out, and when he arrived he told David everything Joab had sent him to say. The messenger said to David, "The men overpowered us and came out against us in the open, but we drove them back to the entrance to the city gate. Then the archers shot arrows at your servants from the wall, and some of the king's men died. Moreover, your servant Uriah the Hittite is dead."

David told the messenger, "Say this to Joab: 'Don't let this upset you; the sword devours one as well as another. Press the attack against the city and destroy it.' Say this to encourage Joab."

2 Sam.
11:26,27

DAVID MARRIES BATHSHEBA.   When Uriah's wife heard that her husband was dead, she mourned for him. After the time of mourning was

---

[q] Or *with her. When she purified herself from her uncleanness,*   [r] Also known as *Jerub-Baal* (that is, Gideon)

over, David had her brought to his house, and she became his wife and bore him a son. But the thing David had done displeased the LORD.

NATHAN REBUKES DAVID.   The LORD sent Nathan to David. When he came to him, he said, "There were two men in a certain town, one rich and the other poor. The rich man had a very large number of sheep and cattle, but the poor man had nothing except one little ewe lamb he had bought. He raised it, and it grew up with him and his children. It shared his food, drank from his cup and even slept in his arms. It was like a daughter to him.

2 Sam.
12:1-12

"Now a traveler came to the rich man, but the rich man refrained from taking one of his own sheep or cattle to prepare a meal for the traveler who had come to him. Instead, he took the ewe lamb that belonged to the poor man and prepared it for the one who had come to him."

David burned with anger against the man and said to Nathan, "As surely as the LORD lives, the man who did this deserves to die! He must pay for that lamb four times over, because he did such a thing and had no pity."

Then Nathan said to David, "You are the man! This is what the LORD, the God of Israel, says: 'I anointed you king over Israel, and I delivered you from the hand of Saul. I gave your master's house to you, and your master's wives into your arms. I gave you the house of Israel and Judah. And if all this had been too little, I would have given you even more. Why did you despise the word of the LORD by doing what is evil in his eyes? You struck down Uriah the Hittite with the sword and took his wife to be your own. You killed him with the sword of the Ammonites. Now, therefore, the sword will never depart from your house, because you despised me and took the wife of Uriah the Hittite to be your own.'

"This is what the LORD says: 'Out of your own household I am going to bring calamity upon you. Before your very eyes I will take your wives and give them to one who is close to you, and he will lie with your wives in broad daylight. You did it in secret, but I will do this thing in broad daylight before all Israel.'"

DAVID ACKNOWLEDGES SIN.   Then David said to Nathan, "I have sinned against the LORD."

2 Sam.
12:13a

David prays for forgiveness.

Psa. 51

For the director of music. A psalm of David. When the prophet Nathan came to him after David had committed adultery with Bathsheba.

Have mercy on me, O God,
    according to your unfailing love;
according to your great compassion
    blot out my transgressions.
Wash away all my iniquity
    and cleanse me from my sin.

For I know my transgressions,
    and my sin is always before me.
Against you, you only, have I sinned
    and done what is evil in your sight,
so that you are proved right when you speak
    and justified when you judge.
Surely I was sinful at birth,

sinful from the time my mother conceived me.
Surely you desire truth in the inner parts[s];
   you teach[t] me wisdom in the inmost place.

Cleanse me with hyssop, and I will be clean;
   wash me, and I will be whiter than snow.
Let me hear joy and gladness;
   let the bones you have crushed rejoice.
Hide your face from my sins
   and blot out all my iniquity.

Create in me a pure heart, O God,
   and renew a steadfast spirit within me.
Do not cast me from your presence
   or take your Holy Spirit from me.
Restore to me the joy of your salvation
   and grant me a willing spirit, to sustain me.

Then I will teach transgressors your ways,
   and sinners will turn back to you.
Save me from bloodguilt, O God,
   the God who saves me,
   and my tongue will sing of your righteousness.
O Lord, open my lips,
   and my mouth will declare your praise.
You do not delight in sacrifice, or I would bring it;
   you do not take pleasure in burnt offerings.
The sacrifices of God are[u] a broken spirit;
   a broken and contrite heart,
   O God, you will not despise.

In your good pleasure make Zion prosper;
   build up the walls of Jerusalem.
Then there will be righteous sacrifices,
   whole burnt offerings to delight you;
   then bulls will be offered on your altar.

2 Sam.
12:13b-17

DAVID MOURNS AND PRAYS.   Nathan replied, "The LORD has taken away your sin. You are not going to die. But because by doing this you have made the enemies of the LORD show utter contempt,[v] the son born to you will die."

After Nathan had gone home, the LORD struck the child that Uriah's wife had borne to David, and he became ill. David pleaded with God for the child. He fasted and went into his house and spent the nights lying on the ground. The elders of his household stood beside him to get him up from the ground, but he refused, and he would not eat any food with them.

2 Sam.
12:18-23

FAST ENDS UPON DEATH.   On the seventh day the child died. David's servants were afraid to tell him that the child was dead, for they thought, "While the child was still living, we spoke to David but he would not

---

[s]The meaning of the Hebrew for this phrase is uncertain.   [t]Or you desired…; / you taught
[u]Or My sacrifice, O God, is   [v]Masoretic Text; an ancient Hebrew scribal tradition this you have shown utter contempt for the LORD

listen to us. How can we tell him the child is dead? He may do something desperate."

David noticed that his servants were whispering among themselves and he realized the child was dead. "Is the child dead?" he asked.

"Yes," they replied, "he is dead."

Then David got up from the ground. After he had washed, put on lotions and changed his clothes, he went into the house of the LORD and worshiped. Then he went to his own house, and at his request they served him food, and he ate.

His servants asked him, "Why are you acting this way? While the child was alive, you fasted and wept, but now that the child is dead, you get up and eat!"

He answered, "While the child was still alive, I fasted and wept. I thought, 'Who knows? The LORD may be gracious to me and let the child live.' But now that he is dead, why should I fast? Can I bring him back again? I will go to him, but he will not return to me."

CAPTURE OF RABBAH.   Meanwhile Joab fought against Rabbah of the Ammonites and captured the royal citadel. Joab then sent messengers to David, saying, "I have fought against Rabbah and taken its water supply. Now muster the rest of the troops and besiege the city and capture it. Otherwise I will take the city, and it will be named after me."

So David mustered the entire army and went to Rabbah, and attacked and captured it. He took the crown from the head of their king[w]—its weight was a talent[x] of gold, and it was set with precious stones—and it was placed on David's head. He took a great quantity of plunder from the city and brought out the people who were there, consigning them to labor with saws and with iron picks and axes, and he made them work at brick-making.[y] He did this to all the Ammonite towns. Then David and his entire army returned to Jerusalem.

1 Sam. 12:26-31
1 Chron. 20:1b-3

MOAB FALLS TO DAVID.   David also defeated the Moabites. He made them lie down on the ground and measured them off with a length of cord. Every two lengths of them were put to death, and the third length was allowed to live. So the Moabites became subject to David and brought tribute.

2 Sam. 8:2
1 Chron. 18:2

DAVID DEFEATS HADADEZER.   Moreover, David fought Hadadezer son of Rehob, king of Zobah, when he went to restore his control along the Euphrates River. David captured a thousand of his chariots, seven thousand charioteers[z] and twenty thousand foot soldiers. He hamstrung all but a hundred of the chariot horses.

David took the gold shields that belonged to the officers of Hadadezer and brought them to Jerusalem. From Tebah[a] and Berothai, towns that belonged to Hadadezer, King David took a great quantity of bronze.

2 Sam. 8:3,4,7,8
1 Chron. 18:3,4,7,8

DAMASCUS SUBJUGATED.   When the Arameans of Damascus came to help Hadadezer king of Zobah, David struck down twenty-two thousand of them. He put garrisons in the Aramean kingdom of Damascus, and the

2 Sam. 8:5,6
1 Chron. 18:5,6

---

[w]Or *of Milcom*, that is, Molech)   [x]That is, about 75 pounds (about 34 kilograms)
[y]The meaning of the Hebrew for this clause is uncertain.   [z]Septuagint (see also Dead Sea Scrolls and 1 Chron. 18:4); Masoretic Text *captured seventeen hundred of his charioteers*
[a]See some Septuagint manuscripts (see also 1 Chron. 18:8); Hebrew *Betah*

Arameans became subject to him and brought tribute. The LORD gave David victory wherever he went.

2 Sam.
8:13,14
1 Chron.
18:12,13

EDOM DEFEATED.   Abishai son of Zeruiah struck down eighteen thousand Edomites in the Valley of Salt.

He put garrisons in Edom, and all the Edomites became subject to David. The LORD gave David victory everywhere he went.

2 Sam.
8:9,10
1 Chron.
18:9,10

HAMATH SUBMITS ALLEGIANCE.   When Tou^b king of Hamath heard that David had defeated the entire army of Hadadezer, he sent his son Joram^c to King David to greet him and congratulate him on his victory in battle over Hadadezer, who had been at war with Tou. Joram brought with him articles of silver and gold and bronze.

2 Sam.
8:11,12
1 Chron.
18:11

PLUNDER DEDICATED TO GOD.   King David dedicated these articles to the LORD, as he had done with the silver and gold from all the nations he had subdued: Edom^d and Moab, the Ammonites and the Philistines, and Amalek. He also dedicated the plunder taken from Hadadezer son of Rehob, king of Zobah.

1 Chron.
11:10

CHIEFS OF THE MIGHTY MEN.   These were the chiefs of David's mighty men—they, together with all Israel, gave his kingship strong support to extend it over the whole land, as the LORD had promised—

2 Sam.
23:8
1 Chron.
11:11

JASHOBEAM.   [T]his is the list of David's mighty men:

Jashobeam,^{e} a Hacmonite, was chief of the officers^f; he raised his spear against three hundred men, whom he killed in one encounter.

2 Sam.
23:9,10
1 Chron.
11:12-14

ELEAZAR.   Next to him was Eleazar son of Dodai the Ahohite. As one of the three mighty men, he was with David when they taunted the Philistines gathered ⌊at Pas Dammim⌋ ^{g} for battle. Then the men of Israel retreated, but he stood his ground and struck down the Philistines till his hand grew tired and froze to the sword. The LORD brought about a great victory that day. The troops returned to Eleazar, but only to strip the dead.

2 Sam.
23:11,12

SHAMMAH.   Next to him was Shammah son of Agee the Hararite. When the Philistines banded together at a place where there was a field full of lentils, Israel's troops fled from them. But Shammah took his stand in the middle of the field. He defended it and struck the Philistines down, and the LORD brought about a great victory.

2 Sam.
23:13-17
1 Chron.
11:15-19

CHIEFS' BRAVERY.   During harvest time, three of the thirty chief men came down to David at the cave of Adullam, while a band of Philistines was encamped in the Valley of Rephaim. At that time David was in the stronghold, and the Philistine garrison was at Bethlehem. David longed for water and said, "Oh, that someone would get me a drink of water from the well near the gate of Bethlehem!" So the three mighty men broke through the Philistine lines, drew water from the well near the gate of Bethlehem and carried it back to David. But he refused to drink it; instead, he poured it out before the LORD. "Far be it from me, O LORD, to do this!" he said. "Is it not the blood of men who went at the risk of their lives?" And David would not drink it.

---

^{b}Hebrew *Toi*, a variant of *Tou* ^{c}A variant of *Hadoram* ^{d}Some Hebrew manuscripts, Septuagint and Syriac (see also 1 Chron. 18:11); most Hebrew manuscripts *Aram* ^{e}Possibly a variant of *Jashob-Baal* ^{f}Or *Thirty*; some Septuagint manuscripts *Three* (see also 2 Samuel 23:8) ^{g}See 1 Chron. 11:13; Hebrew *gathered there.*

Such were the exploits of the three mighty men.

ABISHAI.   Abishai the brother of Joab was chief of the Three. He raised
his spear against three hundred men, whom he killed, and so he became
as famous as the Three. He was doubly honored above the Three and
became their commander, even though he was not included among them.

2 Sam.
23:18,19
1 Chron.
11:20,21

BENAIAH.   Benaiah son of Jehoiada was a valiant fighter from Kabzeel,
who performed great exploits. He struck down two of Moab's best men.
He also went down into a pit on a snowy day and killed a lion. And he
struck down an Egyptian who was seven and a half feet[h] tall. Although the
Egyptian had a spear like a weaver's rod in his hand, Benaiah went
against him with a club. He snatched the spear from the Egyptian's hand
and killed him with his own spear. Such were the exploits of Benaiah son
of Jehoiada; he too was as famous as the three mighty men. He was held
in greater honor than any of the Thirty, but he was not included among the
Three. And David put him in charge of his bodyguard.

2 Sam.
23:20-23
1 Chron.
11:22-25

OTHER MIGHTY MEN.
    The mighty men were:
        Asahel the brother of Joab,
        Elhanan son of Dodo from Bethlehem,
        Shammoth the Harorite,
        Helez the Pelonite,
        Ira son of Ikkesh from Tekoa,
        Abiezer from Anathoth,
        Sibbecai the Hushathite,
        Ilai the Ahohite,
        Maharai the Netophathite,
        Heled son of Baanah the Netophathite,
        Ithai son of Ribai from Gibeah in Benjamin,
        Benaiah the Pirathonite,
        Hurai from the ravines of Gaash,
        Abiel the Arbathite,
        Azmaveth the Baharumite,
        Eliahba the Shaalbonite,
        the sons of Hashem the Gizonite,
        Jonathan son of Shagee the Hararite,
        Ahiam son of Sacar the Hararite,
        Eliphal son of Ur,
        Hepher the Mekerathite,
        Ahijah the Pelonite,
        Hezro the Carmelite,
        Naarai son of Ezbai,
        Joel the brother of Nathan,
        Mibhar son of Hagri,
        Zelek the Ammonite,
        Naharai the Berothite, the armor-bearer of Joab son of Zeruiah,
        Ira the Ithrite,
        Gareb the Ithrite,
        Uriah the Hittite,
        Zabad son of Ahlai,

2 Sam.
23:24-39
1 Chron.
11:26-47

[h]Hebrew *five cubits* (about 2.3 meters)

Adina son of Shiza the Reubenite, who was chief of the Reubenites,
    and the thirty with him,
Hanan son of Maacah,
Joshaphat the Mithnite,
Uzzia the Ashterathite,
Shama and Jeiel the sons of Hotham the Aroerite,
Jediael son of Shimri,
    his brother Joha the Tizite,
Eliel the Mahavite,
Jeribai and Joshaviah the sons of Elnaam,
Ithmah the Moabite,
Eliel, Obed and Jaasiel the Mezobaite.

Absalom's Rebellion

*P*erhaps nothing is sadder for a righteous father than to be burdened with a rebellious son—a son who so envies his father's power that he is willing to oppose him openly and to disgrace him in every possible way. David has been blessed abundantly, but not with the loyalty of his son Absalom. The account of Absalom's rebellion provides an insight into the political intrigue of David's time and a further insight into the heart of this extraordinary king.

As the historical record of this period begins, there is the record of the birth of David's son Solomon. Solomon will prove to be of an altogether different character from that of his brother, and will one day succeed his father on the throne.

2 Sam.
12:24,25
Jerusalem

SOLOMON BORN.   Then David comforted his wife Bathsheba, and he went to her and lay with her. She gave birth to a son, and they named him Solomon. The LORD loved him; and because the LORD loved him, he sent word through Nathan the prophet to name him Jedidiah.[i]

2 Sam.
5:13-16
1 Chron.
3:4c-9
1 Chron.
14:3-7

DAVID'S FAMILY INCREASES. David reigned in Jerusalem thirty-three years, and these were the children born to him there:
    Shammua,[j] Shobab, Nathan and Solomon. These four were by Bathsheba[k] daughter of Ammiel. There were also Ibhar, Elishua,[l] Eliphelet, Nogah, Nepheg, Japhia, Elishama, Eliada and Eliphelet—nine in all. All these were the sons of David, besides his sons by his concubines. And Tamar was their sister.

2 Sam.
13:1-14

AMNON RAPES TAMAR.   In the course of time, Amnon son of David fell in love with Tamar, the beautiful sister of Absalom son of David.
    Amnon became frustrated to the point of illness on account of his sister Tamar, for she was a virgin, and it seemed impossible for him to do anything to her.
    Now Amnon had a friend named Jonadab son of Shimeah, David's brother. Jonadab was a very shrewd man. He asked Amnon, "Why do

---

[i]Jedidiah means *loved by the LORD*.   [j]Hebrew *Shimea*, a variant of *Shammua*   [k]One Hebrew manuscript and Vulgate (see also Septuagint and 2 Samuel 11:3); most Hebrew manuscripts *Bathshua*   [l]Two Hebrew manuscripts (see also 2 Samuel 5:15 and 1 Chron. 14:5); most Hebrew manuscripts *Elishama*

you, the king's son, look so haggard morning after morning? Won't you tell me?"

Amnon said to him, "I'm in love with Tamar, my brother Absalom's sister."

"Go to bed and pretend to be ill," Jonadab said. "When your father comes to see you, say to him, 'I would like my sister Tamar to come and give me something to eat. Let her prepare the food in my sight so I may watch her and then eat it from her hand.'"

So Amnon lay down and pretended to be ill. When the king came to see him, Amnon said to him, "I would like my sister Tamar to come and make some special bread in my sight, so I may eat from her hand."

David sent word to Tamar at the palace: "Go to the house of your brother Amnon and prepare some food for him." So Tamar went to the house of her brother Amnon, who was lying down. She took some dough, kneaded it, made the bread in his sight and baked it. Then she took the pan and served him the bread, but he refused to eat.

"Send everyone out of here," Amnon said. So everyone left him. Then Amnon said to Tamar, "Bring the food here into my bedroom so I may eat from your hand." And Tamar took the bread she had prepared and brought it to her brother Amnon in his bedroom. But when she took it to him to eat, he grabbed her and said, "Come to bed with me, my sister."

"Don't, my brother!" she said to him. "Don't force me. Such a thing should not be done in Israel! Don't do this wicked thing. What about me? Where could I get rid of my disgrace? And what about you? You would be like one of the wicked fools in Israel. Please speak to the king; he will not keep me from being married to you." But he refused to listen to her, and since he was stronger than she, he raped her.

Then Amnon hated her with intense hatred. In fact, he hated her more than he had loved her. Amnon said to her, "Get up and get out!" 2 Sam.
13:15-22

"No!" she said to him. "Sending me away would be a greater wrong than what you have already done to me."

But he refused to listen to her. He called his personal servant and said, "Get this woman out of here and bolt the door after her." So his servant put her out and bolted the door after her. She was wearing a richly ornamented[m] robe, for this was the kind of garment the virgin daughters of the king wore. Tamar put ashes on her head and tore the ornamented[n] robe she was wearing. She put her hand on her head and went away, weeping aloud as she went.

Her brother Absalom said to her, "Has that Amnon, your brother, been with you? Be quiet now, my sister; he is your brother. Don't take this thing to heart." And Tamar lived in her brother Absalom's house, a desolate woman.

When King David heard all this, he was furious. Absalom never said a word to Amnon, either good or bad; he hated Amnon because he had disgraced his sister Tamar.

ABSALOM KILLS AMNON.   Two years later, when Absalom's sheepshearers were at Baal Hazor near the border of Ephraim, he invited all the king's sons to come there. Absalom went to the king and said, "Your 2 Sam.
13:23-29
Baal Hazor

---

[m]The meaning of the Hebrew for this phrase is uncertain.   [n]The meaning of the Hebrew for this word is uncertain.

servant has had shearers come. Will the king and his officials please join me?"

"No, my son," the king replied. "All of us should not go; we would only be a burden to you." Although Absalom urged him, he still refused to go, but gave him his blessing.

Then Absalom said, "If not, please let my brother Amnon come with us."

The king asked him, "Why should he go with you?" But Absalom urged him, so he sent with him Amnon and the rest of the king's sons.

Absalom ordered his men, "Listen! When Amnon is in high spirits from drinking wine and I say to you, 'Strike Amnon down,' then kill him. Don't be afraid. Have not I given you this order? Be strong and brave." So Absalom's men did to Amnon what Absalom had ordered. Then all the king's sons got up, mounted their mules and fled.

2 Sam.
13:30-39

ABSALOM FLEES AMID RUMORS.   While they were on their way, the report came to David: "Absalom has struck down all the king's sons; not one of them is left." The king stood up, tore his clothes and lay down on the ground; and all his servants stood by with their clothes torn.

But Jonadab son of Shimeah, David's brother, said, "My lord should not think that they killed all the princes; only Amnon is dead. This has been Absalom's expressed intention ever since the day Amnon raped his sister Tamar. My lord the king should not be concerned about the report that all the king's sons are dead. Only Amnon is dead."

Meanwhile, Absalom had fled.

Now the man standing watch looked up and saw many people on the road west of him, coming down the side of the hill. The watchman went and told the king, "I see men in the direction of Horonaim, on the side of the hill."*o*

Jonadab said to the king, "See, the king's sons are here; it has happened just as your servant said."

As he finished speaking, the king's sons came in, wailing loudly. The king, too, and all his servants wept very bitterly.

Absalom fled and went to Talmai son of Ammihud, the king of Geshur. But King David mourned for his son every day.

After Absalom fled and went to Geshur, he stayed there three years. And the spirit of the king*p* longed to go to Absalom, for he was consoled concerning Amnon's death.

2 Sam.
14:1-3

JOAB SCHEMES.   Joab son of Zeruiah knew that the king's heart longed for Absalom. So Joab sent someone to Tekoa and had a wise woman brought from there. He said to her, "Pretend you are in mourning. Dress in mourning clothes, and don't use any cosmetic lotions. Act like a woman who has spent many days grieving for the dead. Then go to the king and speak these words to him." And Joab put the words in her mouth.

2 Sam.
14:4-11

When the woman from Tekoa went*q* to the king, she fell with her face to the ground to pay him honor, and she said, "Help me, O king!"

The king asked her, "What is troubling you?"

She said, "I am indeed a widow; my husband is dead. I your servant had

---

*o*Septuagint; Hebrew does not have this sentence.   *p*Dead Sea Scrolls and some
Septuagint manuscripts; Masoretic Text *But ⸤the spirit of⸥ David the king*   *q*Many
Hebrew manuscripts, Septuagint, Vulgate and Syriac; most Hebrew manuscripts *spoke*

two sons. They got into a fight with each other in the field, and no one was there to separate them. One struck the other and killed him. Now the whole clan has risen up against your servant; they say, 'Hand over the one who struck his brother down, so that we may put him to death for the life of his brother whom he killed; then we will get rid of the heir as well.' They would put out the only burning coal I have left, leaving my husband neither name nor descendant on the face of the earth."

The king said to the woman, "Go home, and I will issue an order in your behalf."

But the woman from Tekoa said to him, "My lord the king, let the blame rest on me and on my father's family, and let the king and his throne be without guilt."

The king replied, "If anyone says anything to you, bring him to me, and he will not bother you again."

She said, "Then let the king invoke the LORD his God to prevent the avenger of blood from adding to the destruction, so that my son will not be destroyed."

"As surely as the LORD lives," he said, "not one hair of your son's head will fall to the ground."

Then the woman said, "Let your servant speak a word to my lord the king."

"Speak," he replied.

The woman said, "Why then have you devised a thing like this against the people of God? When the king says this, does he not convict himself, for the king has not brought back his banished son? Like water spilled on the ground, which cannot be recovered, so we must die. But God does not take away life; instead, he devises ways so that a banished person may not remain estranged from him.

2 Sam.
14:12-17

"And now I have come to say this to my lord the king because the people have made me afraid. Your servant thought, 'I will speak to the king; perhaps he will do what his servant asks. Perhaps the king will agree to deliver his servant from the hand of the man who is trying to cut off both me and my son from the inheritance God gave us.'

"And now your servant says, 'May the word of my lord the king bring me rest, for my lord the king is like an angel of God in discerning good and evil. May the LORD your God be with you.'"

Then the king said to the woman, "Do not keep from me the answer to what I am going to ask you."

2 Sam.
14:18-24

"Let my lord the king speak," the woman said.

The king asked, "Isn't the hand of Joab with you in all this?"

The woman answered, "As surely as you live, my lord the king, no one can turn to the right or to the left from anything my lord the king says. Yes, it was your servant Joab who instructed me to do this and who put all these words into the mouth of your servant. Your servant Joab did this to change the present situation. My lord has wisdom like that of an angel of God—he knows everything that happens in the land."

The king said to Joab, "Very well, I will do it. Go, bring back the young man Absalom."

Joab fell with his face to the ground to pay him honor, and he blessed the king. Joab said, "Today your servant knows that he has found favor in your eyes, my lord the king, because the king has granted his servant's request."

Then Joab went to Geshur and brought Absalom back to Jerusalem. But the king said, "He must go to his own house; he must not see my face." So Absalom went to his own house and did not see the face of the king.

**2 Sam.
14:25-28
Jerusalem**

TWO YEARS PASS.   In all Israel there was not a man so highly praised for his handsome appearance as Absalom. From the top of his head to the sole of his foot there was no blemish in him. Whenever he cut the hair of his head—he used to cut his hair from time to time when it became too heavy for him—he would weigh it, and its weight was two hundred shekels[r] by the royal standard.

Three sons and a daughter were born to Absalom. The daughter's name was Tamar, and she became a beautiful woman.

Absalom lived two years in Jerusalem without seeing the king's face.

**2 Sam.
14:29-33**

DAVID AND ABSALOM RECONCILE.   Then Absalom sent for Joab in order to send him to the king, but Joab refused to come to him. So he sent a second time, but he refused to come. Then he said to his servants, "Look, Joab's field is next to mine, and he has barley there. Go and set it on fire." So Absalom's servants set the field on fire.

Then Joab did go to Absalom's house and he said to him, "Why have your servants set my field on fire?"

Absalom said to Joab, "Look, I sent word to you and said, 'Come here so I can send you to the king to ask, "Why have I come from Geshur? It would be better for me if I were still there!"' Now then, I want to see the king's face, and if I am guilty of anything, let him put me to death."

So Joab went to the king and told him this. Then the king summoned Absalom, and he came in and bowed down with his face to the ground before the king. And the king kissed Absalom.

**2 Sam.
15:1-6**

ABSALOM POLITICS.   In the course of time, Absalom provided himself with a chariot and horses and with fifty men to run ahead of him. He would get up early and stand by the side of the road leading to the city gate. Whenever anyone came with a complaint to be placed before the king for a decision, Absalom would call out to him, "What town are you from?" He would answer, "Your servant is from one of the tribes of Israel." Then Absalom would say to him, "Look, your claims are valid and proper, but there is no representative of the king to hear you." And Absalom would add, "If only I were appointed judge in the land! Then everyone who has a complaint or case could come to me and I would see that he gets justice."

Also, whenever anyone approached him to bow down before him, Absalom would reach out his hand, take hold of him and kiss him. Absalom behaved in this way toward all the Israelites who came to the king asking for justice, and so he stole the hearts of the men of Israel.

**2 Sam.
15:7-12
Hebron**

FORMATION OF CONSPIRACY.   At the end of four[s] years, Absalom said to the king, "Let me go to Hebron and fulfill a vow I made to the LORD. While your servant was living at Geshur in Aram, I made this vow: 'If the LORD takes me back to Jerusalem, I will worship the LORD in Hebron.[t]' "

The king said to him, "Go in peace." So he went to Hebron.

Then Absalom sent secret messengers throughout the tribes of Israel to say, "As soon as you hear the sound of the trumpets, then say, 'Absalom is

---

[r]That is, about 5 pounds (about 2.3 kilograms)   [s]Some Septuagint manuscripts, Syriac and Josephus; Hebrew *forty*   [t]Some Septuagint manuscripts; Hebrew does not have *in Hebron.*

king in Hebron.'" Two hundred men from Jerusalem had accompanied Absalom. They had been invited as guests and went quite innocently, knowing nothing about the matter. While Absalom was offering sacrifices, he also sent for Ahithophel the Gilonite, David's counselor, to come from Giloh, his hometown. And so the conspiracy gained strength, and Absalom's following kept on increasing.

DAVID GOES INTO EXILE.   A messenger came and told David, "The hearts of the men of Israel are with Absalom."   2 Sam. 15:13-18

Then David said to all his officials who were with him in Jerusalem, "Come! We must flee, or none of us will escape from Absalom. We must leave immediately, or he will move quickly to overtake us and bring ruin upon us and put the city to the sword."

The king's officials answered him, "Your servants are ready to do whatever our lord the king chooses."

The king set out, with his entire household following him; but he left ten concubines to take care of the palace. So the king set out, with all the people following him, and they halted at a place some distance away. All his men marched past him, along with all the Kerethites and Pelethites; and all the six hundred Gittites who had accompanied him from Gath marched before the king.

ITTAI JOINS DAVID.   The king said to Ittai the Gittite, "Why should you come along with us? Go back and stay with King Absalom. You are a foreigner, an exile from your homeland. You came only yesterday. And today shall I make you wander about with us, when I do not know where I am going? Go back, and take your countrymen. May kindness and faithfulness be with you."   2 Sam. 15:19-22

But Ittai replied to the king, "As surely as the LORD lives, and as my lord the king lives, wherever my lord the king may be, whether it means life or death, there will your servant be."

David said to Ittai, "Go ahead, march on." So Ittai the Gittite marched on with all his men and the families that were with him.

ARK RETURNED TO JERUSALEM.   The whole countryside wept aloud as all the people passed by. The king also crossed the Kidron Valley, and all the people moved on toward the desert.   2 Sam. 15:23-29 Kidron Valley

Zadok was there, too, and all the Levites who were with him were carrying the ark of the covenant of God. They set down the ark of God, and Abiathar offered sacrifices[u] until all the people had finished leaving the city.

Then the king said to Zadok, "Take the ark of God back into the city. If I find favor in the LORD's eyes, he will bring me back and let me see it and his dwelling place again. But if he says, 'I am not pleased with you,' then I am ready; let him do to me whatever seems good to him."

The king also said to Zadok the priest, "Aren't you a seer? Go back to the city in peace, with your son Ahimaaz and Jonathan son of Abiathar. You and Abiathar take your two sons with you. I will wait at the fords in the desert until word comes from you to inform me." So Zadok and Abiathar took the ark of God back to Jerusalem and stayed there.

SCHEME TO GIVE BAD ADVICE.   But David continued up the Mount of Olives, weeping as he went; his head was covered and he was barefoot.   2 Sam. 15:30-37 Mt. of Olives

[u]Or Abiathar went up

All the people with him covered their heads too and were weeping as they went up. Now David had been told, "Ahithophel is among the conspirators with Absalom." So David prayed, "O LORD, turn Ahithophel's counsel into foolishness."

When David arrived at the summit, where people used to worship God, Hushai the Arkite was there to meet him, his robe torn and dust on his head. David said to him, "If you go with me, you will be a burden to me. But if you return to the city and say to Absalom, 'I will be your servant, O king; I was your father's servant in the past, but now I will be your servant,' then you can help me by frustrating Ahithophel's advice. Won't the priests Zadok and Abiathar be there with you? Tell them anything you hear in the king's palace. Their two sons, Ahimaaz son of Zadok and Jonathan son of Abiathar, are there with them. Send them to me with anything you hear."

So David's friend Hushai arrived at Jerusalem as Absalom was entering the city.

2 Sam. 16:1-4

ZIBA FEIGNS GIFT.   When David had gone a short distance beyond the summit, there was Ziba, the steward of Mephibosheth, waiting to meet him. He had a string of donkeys saddled and loaded with two hundred loaves of bread, a hundred cakes of raisins, a hundred cakes of figs and a skin of wine.

The king asked Ziba, "Why have you brought these?"

Ziba answered, "The donkeys are for the king's household to ride on, the bread and fruit are for the men to eat, and the wine is to refresh those who become exhausted in the desert."

The king then asked, "Where is your master's grandson?"

Ziba said to him, "He is staying in Jerusalem, because he thinks, 'Today the house of Israel will give me back my grandfather's kingdom.'"

Then the king said to Ziba, "All that belonged to Mephibosheth is now yours."

"I humbly bow," Ziba said. "May I find favor in your eyes, my lord the king."

2 Sam. 16:5-14 Bahurim

SHIMEI CURSES DAVID.   As King David approached Bahurim, a man from the same clan as Saul's family came out from there. His name was Shimei son of Gera, and he cursed as he came out. He pelted David and all the king's officials with stones, though all the troops and the special guard were on David's right and left. As he cursed, Shimei said, "Get out, get out, you man of blood, you scoundrel! The LORD has repaid you for all the blood you shed in the household of Saul, in whose place you have reigned. The LORD has handed the kingdom over to your son Absalom. You have come to ruin because you are a man of blood!"

Then Abishai son of Zeruiah said to the king, "Why should this dead dog curse my lord the king? Let me go over and cut off his head."

But the king said, "What do you and I have in common, you sons of Zeruiah? If he is cursing because the LORD said to him, 'Curse David,' who can ask, 'Why do you do this?'"

David then said to Abishai and all his officials, "My son, who is of my own flesh, is trying to take my life. How much more, then, this Benjamite! Leave him alone; let him curse, for the LORD has told him to. It may be that the LORD will see my distress and repay me with good for the cursing I am receiving today."

So David and his men continued along the road while Shimei was going along the hillside opposite him, cursing as he went and throwing stones at him and showering him with dirt. The king and all the people with him arrived at their destination exhausted. And there he refreshed himself.

David prays in desperation.   Psa. 3

A psalm of David. When he fled from his son Absalom.

> O LORD, how many are my foes!
>   How many rise up against me!
> Many are saying of me,
>   "God will not deliver him."   *Selah*[v]
>
> But you are a shield around me, O LORD;
>   you bestow glory on me and lift[w] up my head.
> To the LORD I cry aloud,
>   and he answers me from his holy hill.   *Selah*
>
> I lie down and sleep;
>   I wake again, because the LORD sustains me.
> I will not fear the tens of thousands
>   drawn up against me on every side.
>
> Arise, O LORD!
>   Deliver me, O my God!
> Strike all my enemies on the jaw;
>   break the teeth of the wicked.
>
> From the LORD comes deliverance.
>   May your blessing be on your people.   *Selah*

HUSHAI FEIGNS LOYALTY.   Meanwhile, Absalom and all the men of Israel came to Jerusalem, and Ahithophel was with him. Then Hushai the Arkite, David's friend, went to Absalom and said to him, "Long live the king! Long live the king!"
   Absalom asked Hushai, "Is this the love you show your friend? Why didn't you go with your friend?"
   Hushai said to Absalom, "No, the one chosen by the LORD, by these people, and by all the men of Israel—his I will be, and I will remain with him.

2 Sam.
16:15-18
Jerusalem

ABSALOM DEFILES CONCUBINES.   Furthermore, whom should I serve? Should I not serve the son? Just as I served your father, so I will serve you."
   Absalom said to Ahithophel, "Give us your advice. What should we do?"
   Ahithophel answered, "Lie with your father's concubines whom he left to take care of the palace. Then all Israel will hear that you have made yourself a stench in your father's nostrils, and the hands of everyone with you will be strengthened." So they pitched a tent for Absalom on the roof, and he lay with his father's concubines in the sight of all Israel.

2 Sam.
16:19-22

AHITHOPHEL'S ADVICE.   Now in those days the advice Ahithophel gave was like that of one who inquires of God. That was how both David

2 Sam.
16:23-17:4

[v]A word of uncertain meaning, occurring frequently in the Psalms; possibly a musical term
[w]Or LORD, / my Glorious One, who lifts

and Absalom regarded all of Ahithophel's advice. Ahithophel said to Absalom, "I would^x choose twelve thousand men and set out tonight in pursuit of David. I would^y attack him while he is weary and weak. I would^y strike him with terror, and then all the people with him will flee. I would^y strike down only the king and bring all the people back to you. The death of the man you seek will mean the return of all; all the people will be unharmed." This plan seemed good to Absalom and to all the elders of Israel.

2 Sam.
17:5-14

HUSHAI'S ADVICE.   But Absalom said, "Summon also Hushai the Arkite, so we can hear what he has to say." When Hushai came to him, Absalom said, "Ahithophel has given this advice. Should we do what he says? If not, give us your opinion."

Hushai replied to Absalom, "The advice Ahithophel has given is not good this time. You know your father and his men; they are fighters, and as fierce as a wild bear robbed of her cubs. Besides, your father is an experienced fighter; he will not spend the night with the troops. Even now, he is hidden in a cave or some other place. If he should attack your troops first,^{z} whoever hears about it will say, 'There has been a slaughter among the troops who follow Absalom.' Then even the bravest soldier, whose heart is like the heart of a lion, will melt with fear, for all Israel knows that your father is a fighter and that those with him are brave.

"So I advise you: Let all Israel, from Dan to Beersheba—as numerous as the sand on the seashore—be gathered to you, with you yourself leading them into battle. Then we will attack him wherever he may be found, and we will fall on him as dew settles on the ground. Neither he nor any of his men will be left alive. If he withdraws into a city, then all Israel will bring ropes to that city, and we will drag it down to the valley until not even a piece of it can be found."

Absalom and all the men of Israel said, "The advice of Hushai the Arkite is better than that of Ahithophel." For the LORD had determined to frustrate the good advice of Ahithophel in order to bring disaster on Absalom.

2 Sam.
17:15-22

MESSAGE SENT TO DAVID.   Hushai told Zadok and Abiathar, the priests, "Ahithophel has advised Absalom and the elders of Israel to do such and such, but I have advised them to do so and so. Now send a message immediately and tell David, 'Do not spend the night at the fords in the desert; cross over without fail, or the king and all the people with him will be swallowed up.'"

Jonathan and Ahimaaz were staying at En Rogel. A servant girl was to go and inform them, and they were to go and tell King David, for they could not risk being seen entering the city. But a young man saw them and told Absalom. So the two of them left quickly and went to the house of a man in Bahurim. He had a well in his courtyard, and they climbed down into it. His wife took a covering and spread it out over the opening of the well and scattered grain over it. No one knew anything about it.

When Absalom's men came to the woman at the house, they asked, "Where are Ahimaaz and Jonathan?"

The woman answered them, "They crossed over the brook."^{a} The men searched but found no one, so they returned to Jerusalem.

---

^{x}Or *Let me* ^{y}Or *will* ^{z}Or *When some of the men fall at the first attack* ^{a}Or *"They passed by the sheep pen toward the water."*

After the men had gone, the two climbed out of the well and went to inform King David. They said to him, "Set out and cross the river at once; Ahithophel has advised such and such against you." So David and all the people with him set out and crossed the Jordan. By daybreak, no one was left who had not crossed the Jordan.

AHITHOPHEL COMMITS SUICIDE.   When Ahithophel saw that his advice had not been followed, he saddled his donkey and set out for his house in his hometown. He put his house in order and then hanged himself. So he died and was buried in his father's tomb.

2 Sam.
17:23

PREPARATIONS FOR BATTLE.   David went to Mahanaim, and Absalom crossed the Jordan with all the men of Israel. Absalom had appointed Amasa over the army in place of Joab. Amasa was the son of a man named Jether,[b] an Israelite[c] who had married Abigail,[d] the daughter of Nahash and sister of Zeruiah the mother of Joab. The Israelites and Absalom camped in the land of Gilead.

2 Sam.
17:24-29
Mahanaim

When David came to Mahanaim, Shobi son of Nahash from Rabbah of the Ammonites, and Makir son of Ammiel from Lo Debar, and Barzillai the Gileadite from Rogelim brought bedding and bowls and articles of pottery. They also brought wheat and barley, flour and roasted grain, beans and lentils,[e] honey and curds, sheep, and cheese from cows' milk for David and his people to eat. For they said, "The people have become hungry and tired and thirsty in the desert."

DAVID SENDS OUT TROOPS.   David mustered the men who were with him and appointed over them commanders of thousands and commanders of hundreds. David sent the troops out—a third under the command of Joab, a third under Joab's brother Abishai son of Zeruiah, and a third under Ittai the Gittite. The king told the troops, "I myself will surely march out with you."

2 Sam.
18:1-5

But the men said, "You must not go out; if we are forced to flee, they won't care about us. Even if half of us die, they won't care; but you are worth ten thousand of us.[f] It would be better now for you to give us support from the city."

The king answered, "I will do whatever seems best to you."

So the king stood beside the gate while all the men marched out in units of hundreds and of thousands. The king commanded Joab, Abishai and Ittai, "Be gentle with the young man Absalom for my sake." And all the troops heard the king giving orders concerning Absalom to each of the commanders.

DAVID'S WARRIORS PREVAIL.   The army marched into the field to fight Israel, and the battle took place in the forest of Ephraim. There the army of Israel was defeated by David's men, and the casualties that day were great—twenty thousand men. The battle spread out over the whole countryside, and the forest claimed more lives that day than the sword.

2 Sam.
18:6-8
Forest of
Ephraim

ABSALOM IS KILLED.   Now Absalom happened to meet David's men. He was riding his mule, and as the mule went under the thick branches of

2 Sam.
18:9-18

[b]Hebrew *Ithra*, a variant of *Jether*   [c]Hebrew and some Septuagint manuscripts; other Septuagint manuscripts (see also 1 Chron. 2:17) *Ishmaelite* or *Jezreelite*   [d]Hebrew *Abigal*, a variant of *Abigail*   [e]Most Septuagint manuscripts and Syriac; Hebrew *lentils, and roasted grain*   [f]Two Hebrew manuscripts, some Septuagint manuscripts and Vulgate; most Hebrew manuscripts *care; for now there are ten thousand like us*

a large oak, Absalom's head got caught in the tree. He was left hanging in midair, while the mule he was riding kept on going.

When one of the men saw this, he told Joab, "I just saw Absalom hanging in an oak tree."

Joab said to the man who had told him this, "What! You saw him? Why didn't you strike him to the ground right there? Then I would have had to give you ten shekels^g of silver and a warrior's belt."

But the man replied, "Even if a thousand shekels^h were weighed out into my hands, I would not lift my hand against the king's son. In our hearing the king commanded you and Abishai and Ittai, 'Protect the young man Absalom for my sake.$^{i'}$ And if I had put my life in jeopardy^j— and nothing is hidden from the king—you would have kept your distance from me."

Joab said, "I'm not going to wait like this for you." So he took three javelins in his hand and plunged them into Absalom's heart while Absalom was still alive in the oak tree. And ten of Joab's armor-bearers surrounded Absalom, struck him and killed him.

Then Joab sounded the trumpet, and the troops stopped pursuing Israel, for Joab halted them. They took Absalom, threw him into a big pit in the forest and piled up a large heap of rocks over him. Meanwhile, all the Israelites fled to their homes.

During his lifetime Absalom had taken a pillar and erected it in the King's Valley as a monument to himself, for he thought, "I have no son to carry on the memory of my name." He named the pillar after himself, and it is called Absalom's Monument to this day.

2 Sam.
18:19-23
DAVID TOLD OF DEATH.   Now Ahimaaz son of Zadok said, "Let me run and take the news to the king that the LORD has delivered him from the hand of his enemies."

"You are not the one to take the news today," Joab told him. "You may take the news another time, but you must not do so today, because the king's son is dead."

Then Joab said to a Cushite, "Go, tell the king what you have seen." The Cushite bowed down before Joab and ran off.

Ahimaaz son of Zadok again said to Joab, "Come what may, please let me run behind the Cushite."

But Joab replied, "My son, why do you want to go? You don't have any news that will bring you a reward."

He said, "Come what may, I want to run."

So Joab said, "Run!" Then Ahimaaz ran by way of the plain^k and outran the Cushite.

2 Sam.
18:24-28
While David was sitting between the inner and outer gates, the watchman went up to the roof of the gateway by the wall. As he looked out, he saw a man running alone. The watchman called out to the king and reported it.

The king said, "If he is alone, he must have good news." And the man came closer and closer.

---

^{g}That is, about 4 ounces (about 115 grams) ^{h}That is, about 25 pounds (about 11 kilograms) ^{i}A few Hebrew manuscripts, Septuagint, Vulgate and Syriac; most Hebrew manuscripts may be translated *Absalom, whoever you may be.* ^{j}Or *Otherwise, if I had acted treacherously toward him* ^{k}That is, the plain of the Jordan

Then the watchman saw another man running, and he called down to the gatekeeper, "Look, another man running alone!"

The king said, "He must be bringing good news, too."

The watchman said, "It seems to me that the first one runs like Ahimaaz son of Zadok."

"He's a good man," the king said. "He comes with good news."

Then Ahimaaz called out to the king, "All is well!" He bowed down before the king with his face to the ground and said, "Praise be to the LORD your God! He has delivered up the men who lifted their hands against my lord the king."

The king asked, "Is the young man Absalom safe?"

Ahimaaz answered, "I saw great confusion just as Joab was about to send the king's servant and me, your servant, but I don't know what it was."

2 Sam. 18:29-33

The king said, "Stand aside and wait here." So he stepped aside and stood there.

Then the Cushite arrived and said, "My lord the king, hear the good news! The LORD has delivered you today from all who rose up against you."

The king asked the Cushite, "Is the young man Absalom safe?"

The Cushite replied, "May the enemies of my lord the king and all who rise up to harm you be like that young man."

The king was shaken. He went up to the room over the gateway and wept. As he went, he said: "O my son Absalom! My son, my son Absalom! If only I had died instead of you—O Absalom, my son, my son!"

DAVID MOURNS FOR ABSALOM.   Joab was told, "The king is weeping and mourning for Absalom." And for the whole army the victory that day was turned into mourning, because on that day the troops heard it said, "The king is grieving for his son." The men stole into the city that day as men steal in who are ashamed when they flee from battle. The king covered his face and cried aloud, "O my son Absalom! O Absalom, my son, my son!"

2 Sam. 19:1-4

JOAB ADVISES DISCRETION.   Then Joab went into the house to the king and said, "Today you have humiliated all your men, who have just saved your life and the lives of your sons and daughters and the lives of your wives and concubines. You love those who hate you and hate those who love you. You have made it clear today that the commanders and their men mean nothing to you. I see that you would be pleased if Absalom were alive today and all of us were dead. Now go out and encourage your men. I swear by the LORD that if you don't go out, not a man will be left with you by nightfall. This will be worse for you than all the calamities that have come upon you from your youth till now."

2 Sam. 19:5-8

So the king got up and took his seat in the gateway. When the men were told, "The king is sitting in the gateway," they all came before him.

Meanwhile, the Israelites had fled to their homes.

KINGDOM IN CONFUSION.   Throughout the tribes of Israel, the people were all arguing with each other, saying, "The king delivered us from the hand of our enemies; he is the one who rescued us from the hand of the Philistines. But now he has fled the country because of Absalom; and Absalom, whom we anointed to rule over us, has died in battle. So why do you say nothing about bringing the king back?"

2 Sam. 19:9,10

2 Sam.
19:11-14

DAVID PREPARES HIS RETURN.   King David sent this message to Zadok and Abiathar, the priests: "Ask the elders of Judah, 'Why should you be the last to bring the king back to his palace, since what is being said throughout Israel has reached the king at his quarters? You are my brothers, my own flesh and blood. So why should you be the last to bring back the king?' And say to Amasa, 'Are you not my own flesh and blood? May God deal with me, be it ever so severely, if from now on you are not the commander of my army in place of Joab.'"

He won over the hearts of all the men of Judah as though they were one man. They sent word to the king, "Return, you and all your men."

2 Sam.
19:15-23
At the
Jordan

SHIMEI GRANTED MERCY.   Then the king returned and went as far as the Jordan.

Now the men of Judah had come to Gilgal to go out and meet the king and bring him across the Jordan. Shimei son of Gera, the Benjamite from Bahurim, hurried down with the men of Judah to meet King David. With him were a thousand Benjamites, along with Ziba, the steward of Saul's household, and his fifteen sons and twenty servants. They rushed to the Jordan, where the king was. They crossed at the ford to take the king's household over and to do whatever he wished.

When Shimei son of Gera crossed the Jordan, he fell prostrate before the king and said to him, "May my lord not hold me guilty. Do not remember how your servant did wrong on the day my lord the king left Jerusalem. May the king put it out of his mind. For I your servant know that I have sinned, but today I have come here as the first of the whole house of Joseph to come down and meet my lord the king."

Then Abishai son of Zeruiah said, "Shouldn't Shimei be put to death for this? He cursed the LORD's anointed."

David replied, "What do you and I have in common, you sons of Zeruiah? This day you have become my adversaries! Should anyone be put to death in Israel today? Do I not know that today I am king over Israel?" So the king said to Shimei, "You shall not die." And the king promised him on oath.

2 Sam.
19:24-30

MEPHIBOSHETH MEETS DAVID.   Mephibosheth, Saul's grandson, also went down to meet the king. He had not taken care of his feet or trimmed his mustache or washed his clothes from the day the king left until the day he returned safely. When he came from Jerusalem to meet the king, the king asked him, "Why didn't you go with me, Mephibosheth?"

He said, "My lord the king, since I your servant am lame, I said, 'I will have my donkey saddled and will ride on it, so I can go with the king.' But Ziba my servant betrayed me. And he has slandered your servant to my lord the king. My lord the king is like an angel of God; so do whatever pleases you. All my grandfather's descendants deserved nothing but death from my lord the king, but you gave your servant a place among those who eat at your table. So what right do I have to make any more appeals to the king?"

The king said to him, "Why say more? I order you and Ziba to divide the fields."

Mephibosheth said to the king, "Let him take everything, now that my lord the king has arrived home safely."

2 Sam.
19:31-40

DAVID FAVORS BARZILLAI.   Barzillai the Gileadite also came down from Rogelim to cross the Jordan with the king and to send him on his way from there. Now Barzillai was a very old man, eighty years of age. He had provided for the king during his stay in Mahanaim, for he was a very wealthy man. The king said to Barzillai, "Cross over with me and stay with me in Jerusalem, and I will provide for you."

But Barzillai answered the king, "How many more years will I live, that I should go up to Jerusalem with the king? I am now eighty years old. Can I tell the difference between what is good and what is not? Can your servant taste what he eats and drinks? Can I still hear the voices of men and women singers? Why should your servant be an added burden to my lord the king? Your servant will cross over the Jordan with the king for a short distance, but why should the king reward me in this way? Let your servant return, that I may die in my own town near the tomb of my father and mother. But here is your servant Kimham. Let him cross over with my lord the king. Do for him whatever pleases you."

The king said, "Kimham shall cross over with me, and I will do for him whatever pleases you. And anything you desire from me I will do for you."

So all the people crossed the Jordan, and then the king crossed over. The king kissed Barzillai and gave him his blessing, and Barzillai returned to his home.

When the king crossed over to Gilgal, Kimham crossed with him. All the troops of Judah and half the troops of Israel had taken the king over.

SHEBA REBELS AGAINST DAVID.   Soon all the men of Israel were coming to the king and saying to him, "Why did our brothers, the men of Judah, steal the king away and bring him and his household across the Jordan, together with all his men?"

2 Sam.
19:41-20:2

All the men of Judah answered the men of Israel, "We did this because the king is closely related to us. Why are you angry about it? Have we eaten any of the king's provisions? Have we taken anything for ourselves?"

Then the men of Israel answered the men of Judah, "We have ten shares in the king; and besides, we have a greater claim on David than you have. So why do you treat us with contempt? Were we not the first to speak of bringing back our king?"

But the men of Judah responded even more harshly than the men of Israel. Now a troublemaker named Sheba son of Bicri, a Benjamite, happened to be there. He sounded the trumpet and shouted,

> "We have no share in David,
>   no part in Jesse's son!
> Every man to his tent, O Israel!"

So all the men of Israel deserted David to follow Sheba son of Bicri. But the men of Judah stayed by their king all the way from the Jordan to Jerusalem.

RETURN TO JERUSALEM.   When David returned to his palace in Jerusalem, he took the ten concubines he had left to take care of the palace and put them in a house under guard. He provided for them, but did not lie with them. They were kept in confinement till the day of their death, living as widows.

2 Sam.
20:3
Jerusalem

JOAB KILLS AMASA.   Then the king said to Amasa, "Summon the men of Judah to come to me within three days, and be here yourself." But

2 Sam.
20:4-13
Gibeon

when Amasa went to summon Judah, he took longer than the time the king had set for him.

David said to Abishai, "Now Sheba son of Bicri will do us more harm than Absalom did. Take your master's men and pursue him, or he will find fortified cities and escape from us." So Joab's men and the Kerethites and Pelethites and all the mighty warriors went out under the command of Abishai. They marched out from Jerusalem to pursue Sheba son of Bicri.

While they were at the great rock in Gibeon, Amasa came to meet them. Joab was wearing his military tunic, and strapped over it at his waist was a belt with a dagger in its sheath. As he stepped forward, it dropped out of its sheath.

Joab said to Amasa, "How are you, my brother?" Then Joab took Amasa by the beard with his right hand to kiss him. Amasa was not on his guard against the dagger in Joab's hand, and Joab plunged it into his belly, and his intestines spilled out on the ground. Without being stabbed again, Amasa died. Then Joab and his brother Abishai pursued Sheba son of Bicri.

One of Joab's men stood beside Amasa and said, "Whoever favors Joab, and whoever is for David, let him follow Joab!" Amasa lay wallowing in his blood in the middle of the road, and the man saw that all the troops came to a halt there. When he realized that everyone who came up to Amasa stopped, he dragged him from the road into a field and threw a garment over him. After Amasa had been removed from the road, all the men went on with Joab to pursue Sheba son of Bicri.

2 Sam.
20:14-22
Abel Beth
Maacah

SHEBA EXCHANGED FOR CITY. Sheba passed through all the tribes of Israel to Abel Beth Maacah[l] and through the entire region of the Berites, who gathered together and followed him. All the troops with Joab came and besieged Sheba in Abel Beth Maacah. They built a siege ramp up to the city, and it stood against the outer fortifications. While they were battering the wall to bring it down, a wise woman called from the city, "Listen! Listen! Tell Joab to come here so I can speak to him." He went toward her, and she asked, "Are you Joab?"

"I am," he answered.

She said, "Listen to what your servant has to say."

"I'm listening," he said.

She continued, "Long ago they used to say, 'Get your answer at Abel,' and that settled it. We are the peaceful and faithful in Israel. You are trying to destroy a city that is a mother in Israel. Why do you want to swallow up the LORD's inheritance?"

"Far be it from me!" Joab replied, "Far be it from me to swallow up or destroy! That is not the case. A man named Sheba son of Bicri, from the hill country of Ephraim, has lifted up his hand against the king, against David. Hand over this one man, and I'll withdraw from the city."

The woman said to Joab, "His head will be thrown to you from the wall."

Then the woman went to all the people with her wise advice, and they cut off the head of Sheba son of Bicri and threw it to Joab. So he sounded the trumpet, and his men dispersed from the city, each returning to his home. And Joab went back to the king in Jerusalem.

[l]Or *Abel, even Beth Maacah*

GOVERNMENT OFFICIALS.   Joab was over Israel's entire army; Benaiah   2 Sam.
son of Jehoiada was over the Kerethites and Pelethites; Adoniram^m was in   20:23-26
charge of forced labor; Jehoshaphat son of Ahilud was recorder; Sheva was
secretary; Zadok and Abiathar were priests; and Ira the Jairite was David's
priest.

Two Major Calamities

Two major calamities strike Israel during David's reign, though it is not
clear exactly when either occurs. The first calamity—a famine—befalls
Israel as a consequence of the late King Saul's attempt to exterminate
the Gibeonites—a violation of the agreement of protection made years earlier
by Joshua and the nation of Israel. Seeking to make atonement for this national sin, David executes several innocent descendants of Saul—a response which
raises some difficult questions regarding corporate sin, vicarious punishment,
and deferred retribution. On a simpler level, the incident teaches something
about the relationship between moral and physical evil and also the significance in God's eyes of sins long forgotten by man.

The second calamity is a death-causing pestilence brought on by David's
decision (somehow incited by Satan) to number his army. The wrong in this
act does not readily appear, since God himself had commanded such a numbering on two prior occasions. But those times of census-taking occurred as
Israel prepared to conquer the promised land of Canaan. With the nation of
Israel basically secure at this point, David's motive for ordering such a count
could perhaps be seen as selfish ambition for aggressive expansionism.
Perhaps in his older years the heady wine of power and influence has greatly changed David from the humble shepherd boy who once felt total security
in having only five small stones to fling against his adversary. And yet, even
now, David's redeeming quality is his genuine sorrow for his sins and his
willingness to confess them. It should also be noted that God forgives David
in the same way that David has forgiven Saul and the many others who have
wronged him.

REASON FOR FAMINE.   During the reign of David, there was a famine   2 Sam.
for three successive years; so David sought the face of the LORD. The LORD   21:1
said, "It is on account of Saul and his blood-stained house; it is because he
put the Gibeonites to death."

WRONG TO GIBEONITES AVENGED.   The king summoned the Gibe-   2 Sam.
onites and spoke to them. (Now the Gibeonites were not a part of Israel   21:2-9
but were survivors of the Amorites; the Israelites had sworn to ⸢spare⸥
them, but Saul in his zeal for Israel and Judah had tried to annihilate
them.) David asked the Gibeonites, "What shall I do for you? How shall I
make amends so that you will bless the LORD's inheritance?"

The Gibeonites answered him, "We have no right to demand silver or
gold from Saul or his family, nor do we have the right to put anyone in
Israel to death."

"What do you want me to do for you?" David asked.

^mSome Septuagint manuscripts (see also 1 Kings 4:6 and 5:14); Hebrew *Adoram*

They answered the king, "As for the man who destroyed us and plotted against us so that we have been decimated and have no place anywhere in Israel, let seven of his male descendants be given to us to be killed and exposed before the LORD at Gibeah of Saul—the LORD's chosen one."

So the king said, "I will give them to you."

The king spared Mephibosheth son of Jonathan, the son of Saul, because of the oath before the LORD between David and Jonathan son of Saul. But the king took Armoni and Mephibosheth, the two sons of Aiah's daughter Rizpah, whom she had borne to Saul, together with the five sons of Saul's daughter Merab,[n] whom she had borne to Adriel son of Barzillai the Meholathite. He handed them over to the Gibeonites, who killed and exposed them on a hill before the LORD. All seven of them fell together; they were put to death during the first days of the harvest, just as the barley harvest was beginning.

2 Sam.
21:10-14

BONES BURIED. Rizpah daughter of Aiah took sackcloth and spread it out for herself on a rock. From the beginning of the harvest till the rain poured down from the heavens on the bodies, she did not let the birds of the air touch them by day or the wild animals by night. When David was told what Aiah's daughter Rizpah, Saul's concubine, had done, he went and took the bones of Saul and his son Jonathan from the citizens of Jabesh Gilead. (They had taken them secretly from the public square at Beth Shan, where the Philistines had hung them after they struck Saul down on Gilboa.) David brought the bones of Saul and his son Jonathan from there, and the bones of those who had been killed and exposed were gathered up.

They buried the bones of Saul and his son Jonathan in the tomb of Saul's father Kish, at Zela in Benjamin, and did everything the king commanded. After that, God answered prayer in behalf of the land.

2 Sam.
24:1-9
1 Chron.
21:1-6

DAVID COUNTS SOLDIERS. [Ch]Satan rose up against Israel and incited David to take a census of Israel. So David said to Joab and the commanders of the troops, "Go and count the Israelites from Beersheba to Dan. Then report back to me so that I may know how many there are."

But Joab replied, "May the LORD multiply his troops a hundred times over. My lord the king, are they not all my lord's subjects? Why does my lord want to do this? Why should he bring guilt on Israel?" [Sa]The king's word, however, overruled Joab and the army commanders; so they left the presence of the king to enroll the fighting men of Israel.

After crossing the Jordan, they camped near Aroer, south of the town in the gorge, and then went through Gad and on to Jazer. They went to Gilead and the region of Tahtim Hodshi, and on to Dan Jaan and around toward Sidon. Then they went toward the fortress of Tyre and all the towns of the Hivites and Canaanites. Finally, they went on to Beersheba in the Negev of Judah.

After they had gone through the entire land, they came back to Jerusalem at the end of nine months and twenty days. [Ch]Joab reported the number of the fighting men to David: In all Israel there were one million one hundred thousand men who could handle a sword, including four hundred and seventy thousand in Judah.

[n]Two Hebrew manuscripts, some Septuagint manuscripts and Syriac (see also 1 Samuel 18:19); most Hebrew and Septuagint manuscripts *Michal*

But Joab did not include Levi and Benjamin in the numbering, because the king's command was repulsive to him.

DAVID SEES THE WRONG.   This command was also evil in the sight of God; so he punished Israel.

Then David said to God, "I have sinned greatly by doing this. Now, I beg you, take away the guilt of your servant. I have done a very foolish thing."

The LORD said to Gad, David's seer, "Go and tell David, 'This is what the LORD says: I am giving you three options. Choose one of them for me to carry out against you.'"

So Gad went to David and said to him, "This is what the LORD says: 'Take your choice: three years of famine, three months of being swept away[o] before your enemies, with their swords overtaking you, or three days of the sword of the LORD—days of plague in the land, with the angel of the LORD ravaging every part of Israel.' Now then, decide how I should answer the one who sent me."

David said to Gad, "I am in deep distress. Let me fall into the hands of the LORD, for his mercy is very great; but do not let me fall into the hands of men."

2 Sam.
24:10-14
1 Chron.
21:7-13

PLAGUE OF DEATH.   So the LORD sent a plague on Israel, and seventy thousand men of Israel fell dead. And God sent an angel to destroy Jerusalem. But as the angel was doing so, the LORD saw it and was grieved because of the calamity and said to the angel who was destroying the people, "Enough! Withdraw your hand." The angel of the LORD was then standing at the threshing floor of Araunah[p] the Jebusite.

David looked up and saw the angel of the LORD standing between heaven and earth, with a drawn sword in his hand extended over Jerusalem. Then David and the elders, clothed in sackcloth, fell facedown.

David said to God, "Was it not I who ordered the fighting men to be counted? I am the one who has sinned and done wrong. These are but sheep. What have they done? O LORD my God, let your hand fall upon me and my family, but do not let this plague remain on your people."

2 Sam.
24:15-17
1 Chron.
21:14-17

DAVID BUILDS AN ALTAR.   Then the angel of the LORD ordered Gad to tell David to go up and build an altar to the LORD on the threshing floor of Araunah the Jebusite. So David went up in obedience to the word that Gad had spoken in the name of the LORD.

While Araunah was threshing wheat, he turned and saw the angel; his four sons who were with him hid themselves. Then David approached, and when Araunah looked and saw him, he left the threshing floor and bowed down before David with his face to the ground.

David said to him, "Let me have the site of your threshing floor so I can build an altar to the LORD, that the plague on the people may be stopped. Sell it to me at the full price."

Araunah said to David, "Take it! Let my lord the king do whatever pleases him. Look, I will give the oxen for the burnt offerings, the threshing sledges for the wood, and the wheat for the grain offering. I will give all this."

But King David replied to Araunah, "No, I insist on paying the full

2 Sam.
24:18-25
1 Chron.
21:18-30

[o]Hebrew; Septuagint and Vulgate (see also 2 Samuel 24:13) *of fleeing*   [p]Hebrew *Ornan*, a variant of *Araunah*

price. I will not take for the LORD what is yours, or sacrifice a burnt offering that costs me nothing."

So David paid Araunah six hundred shekels*q* of gold for the site. David built an altar to the LORD there and sacrificed burnt offerings and fellowship offerings.*r* He called on the LORD, and the LORD answered him with fire from heaven on the altar of burnt offering.

Then the LORD spoke to the angel, and he put his sword back into its sheath. At that time, when David saw that the LORD had answered him on the threshing floor of Araunah the Jebusite, he offered sacrifices there. The tabernacle of the LORD, which Moses had made in the desert, and the altar of burnt offering were at that time on the high place at Gibeon. But David could not go before it to inquire of God, because he was afraid of the sword of the angel of the LORD.

Preparations for Building the Temple

*H*aving just built an altar to God, and knowing that the old tabernacle and altar of burnt offerings are at Gibeon, David now makes preparation for the building of a permanent temple. The site he chooses, a simple threshing floor, is not a surprising one in view of his most recent experience. It must grieve David to realize that he himself will not erect this magnificent edifice of worship. Yet he cannot help but play some part in its inception, and thus he begins to organize the project. He then gives his son Solomon the responsibility for completing the work and enlists the aid of his princes in the construction of this national symbol of commitment to God.

1 Chron. 22:1

TEMPLE SITE DESIGNATED.   Then David said, "The house of the LORD God is to be here, and also the altar of burnt offering for Israel."

1 Chron. 22:2-5

MATERIALS ORDERED.   So David gave orders to assemble the aliens living in Israel, and from among them he appointed stonecutters to prepare dressed stone for building the house of God. He provided a large amount of iron to make nails for the doors of the gateways and for the fittings, and more bronze than could be weighed. He also provided more cedar logs than could be counted, for the Sidonians and Tyrians had brought large numbers of them to David.

David said, "My son Solomon is young and inexperienced, and the house to be built for the LORD should be of great magnificence and fame and splendor in the sight of all the nations. Therefore I will make preparations for it." So David made extensive preparations before his death.

1 Chron. 22:6-16

SOLOMON GIVEN TASK.   Then he called for his son Solomon and charged him to build a house for the LORD, the God of Israel. David said to Solomon: "My son, I had it in my heart to build a house for the Name of the LORD my God. But this word of the LORD came to me: 'You have shed much blood and have fought many wars. You are not to build a house for my Name, because you have shed much blood on the earth in my sight. But you will have a son who will be a man of peace and rest, and I will give him rest from all his enemies on every side. His name will be

---

*q*That is, about 15 pounds (about 7 kilograms)   *r*Traditionally *peace offerings*

Solomon,[s] and I will grant Israel peace and quiet during his reign. He is the one who will build a house for my Name. He will be my son, and I will be his father. And I will establish the throne of his kingdom over Israel forever.'

"Now, my son, the LORD be with you, and may you have success and build the house of the LORD your God, as he said you would. May the LORD give you discretion and understanding when he puts you in command over Israel, so that you may keep the law of the LORD your God. Then you will have success if you are careful to observe the decrees and laws that the LORD gave Moses for Israel. Be strong and courageous. Do not be afraid or discouraged.

"I have taken great pains to provide for the temple of the LORD a hundred thousand talents[t] of gold, a million talents[u] of silver, quantities of bronze and iron too great to be weighed, and wood and stone. And you may add to them. You have many workmen: stonecutters, masons and carpenters, as well as men skilled in every kind of work in gold and silver, bronze and iron—craftsmen beyond number. Now begin the work, and the LORD be with you."

LEADERS TO ASSIST.   Then David ordered all the leaders of Israel to help his son Solomon. He said to them, "Is not the LORD your God with you? And has he not granted you rest on every side? For he has handed the inhabitants of the land over to me, and the land is subject to the LORD and to his people. Now devote your heart and soul to seeking the LORD your God. Begin to build the sanctuary of the LORD God, so that you may bring the ark of the covenant of the LORD and the sacred articles belonging to God into the temple that will be built for the Name of the LORD."

1 Chron. 22:17-19

David writes a song of dedication for the temple.

Psa. 30

A psalm. A song. For the dedication of the temple.[v] Of David.

I will exalt you, O LORD,
for you lifted me out of the depths
and did not let my enemies gloat over me.
O LORD my God, I called to you for help
and you healed me.
O LORD, you brought me up from the grave[w];
you spared me from going down into the pit.

Sing to the LORD, you saints of his;
praise his holy name.
For his anger lasts only a moment,
but his favor lasts a lifetime;
weeping may remain for a night,
but rejoicing comes in the morning.

When I felt secure, I said,
"I will never be shaken."
O LORD, when you favored me,
you made my mountain[x] stand firm;
but when you hid your face,

[s]*Solomon* sounds like and may be derived from the Hebrew for *peace*.   [t]That is, about 3,750 tons (about 3,450 metric tons)   [u]That is, about 37,500 tons (about 34,500 metric tons)   [v]Title: Or *palace*   [w]Hebrew *Sheol*   [x]Or *hill country*

I was dismayed.

To you, O LORD, I called;
  to the Lord I cried for mercy:
"What gain is there in my destruction, [y]
  in my going down into the pit?
Will the dust praise you?
  Will it proclaim your faithfulness?
Hear, O LORD, and be merciful to me;
  O LORD, be my help."

You turned my wailing into dancing;
  you removed my sackcloth and clothed me with joy,
that my heart may sing to you and not be silent.
  O LORD my God, I will give you thanks forever.

The National Convention

*I*n his last years as king, David moves to provide a smooth transition of government from himself to Solomon. Realizing Solomon's youth and inexperience, David takes great pains to organize his governmental officials and religious leaders. Once the necessary appointments are settled, David calls all the leaders together for a national convention, where he addresses them regarding the need for unity and mutual support, particularly in the building of the temple. At both the beginning and the end of the convention, Solomon is presented as the king-designate to follow his father on the royal throne.

1 Chron.
23:1a,2-6

LEVITES ASSEMBLED.   When David was old and full of years...
     He also gathered together all the leaders of Israel, as well as the priests and Levites. The Levites thirty years old or more were counted, and the total number of men was thirty-eight thousand. David said, "Of these, twenty-four thousand are to supervise the work of the temple of the LORD and six thousand are to be officials and judges. Four thousand are to be gatekeepers and four thousand are to praise the LORD with the musical instruments I have provided for that purpose."
     David divided the Levites into groups corresponding to the sons of Levi: Gershon, Kohath and Merari.

1 Chron.
23:7-11

GERSHONITES.   Belonging to the Gershonites:
     Ladan and Shimei.
     The sons of Ladan:
     Jehiel the first, Zetham and Joel—three in all.
     The sons of Shimei:
     Shelomoth, Haziel and Haran—three in all.
     These were the heads of the families of Ladan.
     And the sons of Shimei:
     Jahath, Ziza,[z] Jeush and Beriah.
     These were the sons of Shimei—four in all.
     Jahath was the first and Ziza the second, but Jeush and Beriah did

y Or *there if I am silenced*   z One Hebrew manuscript, Septuagint and Vulgate (see also
verse 11); most Hebrew manuscripts *Zina*

not have many sons; so they were counted as one family with one assignment.

KOHATHITES.   The sons of Kohath:
   Amram, Izhar, Hebron and Uzziel—four in all.
   The sons of Amram:
   Aaron and Moses.
   Aaron was set apart, he and his descendants forever, to consecrate the most holy things, to offer sacrifices before the LORD, to minister before him and to pronounce blessings in his name forever. The sons of Moses the man of God were counted as part of the tribe of Levi.
   The sons of Moses:
   Gershom and Eliezer.
   The descendants of Gershom:
   Shubael was the first.
   The descendants of Eliezer:
   Rehabiah was the first.
   Eliezer had no other sons, but the sons of Rehabiah were very numerous.
   The sons of Izhar:
   Shelomith was the first.
   The sons of Hebron:
   Jeriah the first, Amariah the second, Jahaziel the third and Jekameam the fourth.
   The sons of Uzziel:
   Micah the first and Isshiah the second.

1 Chron.
23:12-20
24:20-25

MERARITES.   The sons of Merari:
   Mahli and Mushi.
   The sons of Mahli:
   Eleazar and Kish.
   Eleazar died without having sons: he had only daughters. Their cousins, the sons of Kish, married them.
   The sons of Mushi:
   Mahli, Eder and Jerimoth—three in all.

1 Chron.
23:21-23
24:26-30a

LEVITES' DUTIES CHANGED.   These were the descendants of Levi by their families—the heads of families as they were registered under their names and counted individually, that is, the workers twenty years old or more who served in the temple of the LORD. For David had said, "Since the LORD, the God of Israel, has granted rest to his people and has come to dwell in Jerusalem forever, the Levites no longer need to carry the tabernacle or any of the articles used in its service." According to the last instructions of David, the Levites were counted from those twenty years old or more.

1 Chron.
23:24-27
24:30b

HOW LEVITES SERVED.   The duty of the Levites was to help Aaron's descendants in the service of the temple of the LORD: to be in charge of the courtyards, the side rooms, the purification of all sacred things and the performance of other duties at the house of God. They were in charge of the bread set out on the table, the flour for the grain offerings, the unleavened wafers, the baking and the mixing, and all measurements of quantity and size. They were also to stand every morning to thank and praise the

1 Chron.
23:28-32
24:31

LORD. They were to do the same in the evening and whenever burnt offerings were presented to the LORD on Sabbaths and at New Moon festivals and at appointed feasts. They were to serve before the LORD regularly in the proper number and in the way prescribed for them.

And so the Levites carried out their responsibilities for the Tent of Meeting, for the Holy Place and, under their brothers the descendants of Aaron, for the service of the temple of the LORD. They also cast lots, just as their brothers the descendants of Aaron did, in the presence of King David and of Zadok, Ahimelech, and the heads of families of the priests and of the Levites. The families of the oldest brother were treated the same as those of the youngest.

1 Chron. 24:1-5

PRIESTS DIVIDED BY LOT.   These were the divisions of the sons of Aaron:

The sons of Aaron were Nadab, Abihu, Eleazar and Ithamar. But Nadab and Abihu died before their father did, and they had no sons; so Eleazar and Ithamar served as the priests. With the help of Zadok a descendant of Eleazar and Ahimelech a descendant of Ithamar, David separated them into divisions for their appointed order of ministering. A larger number of leaders were found among Eleazar's descendants than among Ithamar's, and they were divided accordingly: sixteen heads of families from Eleazar's descendants and eight heads of families from Ithamar's descendants. They divided them impartially by drawing lots, for there were officials of the sanctuary and officials of God among the descendants of both Eleazar and Ithamar.

1 Chron. 24:6-19

TWENTY-FOUR DIVISIONS.   The scribe Shemaiah son of Nethanel, a Levite, recorded their names in the presence of the king and of the officials: Zadok the priest, Ahimelech son of Abiathar and the heads of families of the priests and of the Levites—one family being taken from Eleazar and then one from Ithamar.

> The first lot fell to Jehoiarib,
> the second to Jedaiah,
> the third to Harim,
> the fourth to Seorim,
> the fifth to Malkijah,
> the sixth to Mijamin,
> the seventh to Hakkoz,
> the eighth to Abijah,
> the ninth to Jeshua,
> the tenth to Shecaniah,
> the eleventh to Eliashib,
> the twelfth to Jakim,
> the thirteenth to Huppah,
> the fourteenth to Jeshebeab,
> the fifteenth to Bilgah,
> the sixteenth to Immer,
> the seventeenth to Hezir,
> the eighteenth to Happizzez,
> the nineteenth to Pethahiah,
> the twentieth to Jehezkel,
> the twenty-first to Jakin,

the twenty-second to Gamul,
the twenty-third to Delaiah
and the twenty-fourth to Maaziah.

This was their appointed order of ministering when they entered the temple of the LORD, according to the regulations prescribed for them by their forefather Aaron, as the LORD, the God of Israel, had commanded him.

APPOINTMENT OF SINGERS.   David, together with the commanders of the army, set apart some of the sons of Asaph, Heman and Jeduthun for the ministry of prophesying, accompanied by harps, lyres and cymbals. Here is the list of the men who performed this service:

1 Chron.
25:1-5

From the sons of Asaph:
Zaccur, Joseph, Nethaniah and Asarelah. The sons of Asaph were under the supervision of Asaph, who prophesied under the king's supervision.
As for Jeduthun, from his sons:
Gedaliah, Zeri, Jeshaiah, Shimei,[a] Hashabiah and Mattithiah, six in all, under the supervision of their father Jeduthun, who prophesied, using the harp in thanking and praising the LORD.
As for Heman, from his sons:
Bukkiah, Mattaniah, Uzziel, Shubael and Jerimoth; Hananiah, Hanani, Eliathah, Giddalti and Romamti-Ezer; Joshbekashah, Mallothi, Hothir and Mahazioth. All these were sons of Heman the king's seer. They were given him through the promises of God to exalt him.[b] God gave Heman fourteen sons and three daughters.

TWENTY-FOUR CLASSES.   All these men were under the supervision of their fathers for the music of the temple of the LORD, with cymbals, lyres and harps, for the ministry at the house of God. Asaph, Jeduthun and Heman were under the supervision of the king. Along with their relatives—all of them trained and skilled in music for the LORD—they numbered 288. Young and old alike, teacher as well as student, cast lots for their duties.

1 Chron.
25:6-31

The first lot, which was for Asaph, fell to Joseph,
  his sons and relatives,[c]   12[d]
the second to Gedaliah,
  he and his relatives and sons,   12
the third to Zaccur,
  his sons and relatives,   12
the fourth to Izri,[e]
  his sons and relatives,   12
the fifth to Nethaniah,
  his sons and relatives,   12
the sixth to Bukkiah,
  his sons and relatives,   12
the seventh to Jesarelah,[f]
  his sons and relatives,   12

[a]One Hebrew manuscript and some Septuagint manuscripts (see also verse 17); most Hebrew manuscripts do not have *Shimei*.   [b]Hebrew *exalt the horn*   [c]See Septuagint; Hebrew does not have *his sons and relatives*.   [d]See the total in verse 7; Hebrew does not have *twelve*.   [e]A variant of *Zeri*   [f]A variant of *Asarelah*

the eighth to Jeshaiah,	
his sons and relatives,	12
the ninth to Mattaniah,	
his sons and relatives,	12
the tenth to Shimei,	
his sons and relatives,	12
the eleventh to Azarel,[8]	
his sons and relatives,	12
the twelfth to Hashabiah,	
his sons and relatives,	12
the thirteenth to Shubael,	
his sons and relatives,	12
the fourteenth to Mattithiah,	
his sons and relatives,	12
the fifteenth to Jerimoth,	
his sons and relatives,	12
the sixteenth to Hananiah,	
his sons and relatives,	12
the seventeenth to Joshbekashah,	
his sons and relatives,	12
the eighteenth to Hanani,	
his sons and relatives,	12
the nineteenth to Mallothi,	
his sons and relatives,	12
the twentieth to Eliathah,	
his sons and relatives,	12
the twenty-first to Hothir,	
his sons and relatives,	12
the twenty-second to Giddalti,	
his sons and relatives,	12
the twenty-third to Mahazioth,	
his sons and relatives,	12
the twenty-fourth to Romamti-Ezer,	
his sons and relatives,	12

1 Chron.
26:1-11

GATEKEEPERS APPOINTED. The divisions of the gatekeepers:

From the Korahites: Meshelemiah son of Kore, one of the sons of
Asaph.
Meshelemiah had sons:
Zechariah the firstborn,
Jediael the second,
Zebadiah the third,
Jathniel the fourth,
Elam the fifth,
Jehohanan the sixth
and Eliehoenai the seventh.
Obed-Edom also had sons:
Shemaiah the firstborn,
Jehozabad the second,
Joah the third,

8A variant of *Uzziel*

Sacar the fourth,
Nethanel the fifth,
Ammiel the sixth,
Issachar the seventh
and Peullethai the eighth.
(For God had blessed Obed-Edom.)

His son Shemaiah also had sons, who were leaders in their father's family because they were very capable men. The sons of Shemaiah: Othni, Rephael, Obed and Elzabad; his relatives Elihu and Semakiah were also able men. All these were descendants of Obed-Edom; they and their sons and their relatives were capable men with the strength to do the work—descendants of Obed-Edom, 62 in all.
Meshelemiah had sons and relatives, who were able men—18 in all.

Hosah the Merarite had sons: Shimri the first (although he was not the firstborn, his father had appointed him the first), Hilkiah the second, Tabaliah the third and Zechariah the fourth. The sons and relatives of Hosah were 13 in all.

RESPONSIBILITIES DIVIDED.   These divisions of the gatekeepers, through their chief men, had duties for ministering in the temple of the LORD, just as their relatives had. Lots were cast for each gate, according to their families, young and old alike.

1 Chron.
26:12-19

The lot for the East Gate fell to Shelemiah.[h] Then lots were cast for his son Zechariah, a wise counselor, and the lot for the North Gate fell to him. The lot for the South Gate fell to Obed-Edom, and the lot for the storehouse fell to his sons. The lots for the West Gate and the Shalleketh Gate on the upper road fell to Shuppim and Hosah.

Guard was alongside of guard: There were six Levites a day on the east, four a day on the north, four a day on the south and two at a time at the storehouse. As for the court to the west, there were four at the road and two at the court itself.

These were the divisions of the gatekeepers who were descendants of Korah and Merari.

APPOINTMENT OF TREASURERS.   Their fellow Levites were[i] in charge of the treasuries of the house of God and the treasuries for the dedicated things.

1 Chron.
26:20-28

The descendants of Ladan, who were Gershonites through Ladan and who were heads of families belonging to Ladan the Gershonite, were Jehieli, the sons of Jehieli, Zetham and his brother Joel. They were in charge of the treasuries of the temple of the LORD.

From the Amramites, the Izharites, the Hebronites and the Uzzielites:

Shubael, a descendant of Gershom son of Moses, was the officer in charge of the treasuries. His relatives through Eliezer: Rehabiah his son, Jeshaiah his son, Joram his son, Zicri his son and Shelomith his son. Shelomith and his relatives were in charge of all the treasuries for the things dedicated by King David, by the heads of families who were the commanders of thousands and commanders of hundreds, and by the other army commanders. Some

[h]A variant of *Meshelemiah*   [i]Septuagint; Hebrew *As for the Levites, Ahijah was*

of the plunder taken in battle they dedicated for the repair of the temple of the LORD. And everything dedicated by Samuel the seer and by Saul son of Kish, Abner son of Ner and Joab son of Zeruiah, and all the other dedicated things were in the care of Shelomith and his relatives.

1 Chron.
26:29-32

OTHER OFFICIALS AND JUDGES.
From the Izharites: Kenaniah and his sons were assigned duties away from the temple, as officials and judges over Israel.

From the Hebronites: Hashabiah and his relatives—seventeen hundred able men—were responsible in Israel west of the Jordan for all the work of the LORD and for the king's service. As for the Hebronites, Jeriah was their chief according to the genealogical records of their families. In the fortieth year of David's reign a search was made in the records, and capable men among the Hebronites were found at Jazer in Gilead. Jeriah had twenty-seven hundred relatives, who were able men and heads of families, and King David put them in charge of the Reubenites, the Gadites and the half-tribe of Manasseh for every matter pertaining to God and for the affairs of the king.

1 Chron.
27:1-15

TWELVE MILITARY COMMANDERS. This is the list of the Israelites—heads of families, commanders of thousands and commanders of hundreds, and their officers, who served the king in all that concerned the army divisions that were on duty month by month throughout the year. Each division consisted of 24,000 men.

In charge of the first division, for the first month, was Jashobeam son of Zabdiel. There were 24,000 men in his division. He was a descendant of Perez and chief of all the army officers for the first month.

In charge of the division for the second month was Dodai the Ahohite; Mikloth was the leader of his division. There were 24,000 men in his division.

The third army commander, for the third month, was Benaiah son of Jehoiada the priest. He was chief and there were 24,000 men in his division. This was the Benaiah who was a mighty man among the Thirty and was over the Thirty. His son Ammizabad was in charge of his division.

The fourth, for the fourth month, was Asahel the brother of Joab; his son Zebadiah was his successor. There were 24,000 men in his division.

The fifth, for the fifth month, was the commander Shamhuth the Izrahite. There were 24,000 men in his division.

The sixth, for the sixth month, was Ira the son of Ikkesh the Tekoite. There were 24,000 men in his division.

The seventh, for the seventh month, was Helez the Pelonite, an Ephraimite. There were 24,000 men in his division.

The eighth, for the eighth month, was Sibbecai the Hushathite, a Zerahite. There were 24,000 men in his division.

The ninth, for the ninth month, was Abiezer the Anathothite, a Benjamite. There were 24,000 men in his division.

The tenth, for the tenth month, was Maharai the Netophathite, a Zerahite. There were 24,000 men in his division.

The eleventh, for the eleventh month, was Benaiah the Pirathonite, an Ephraimite. There were 24,000 men in his division.

The twelfth, for the twelfth month, was Heldai the Netophathite, from the family of Othniel. There were 24,000 men in his division.

OFFICERS OF EACH TRIBE.   The officers over the tribes of Israel:

1 Chron. 27:16-22

over the Reubenites: Eliezer son of Zicri;
over the Simeonites: Shephatiah son of Maacah;
over Levi: Hashabiah son of Kemuel;
over Aaron: Zadok;
over Judah: Elihu, a brother of David;
over Issachar: Omri son of Michael;
over Zebulun: Ishmaiah son of Obadiah;
over Naphtali: Jerimoth son of Azriel;
over the Ephraimites: Hoshea son of Azaziah;
over half the tribe of Manasseh: Joel son of Pedaiah;
over the half-tribe of Manasseh in Gilead: Iddo son of Zechariah;
over Benjamin: Jaasiel son of Abner;
over Dan: Azarel son of Jeroham.
These were the officers over the tribes of Israel.

CAUTION IN NUMBERING.   David did not take the number of the men twenty years old or less, because the LORD had promised to make Israel as numerous as the stars in the sky. Joab son of Zeruiah began to count the men but did not finish. Wrath came on Israel on account of this numbering, and the number was not entered in the book*j* of the annals of King David.

1 Chron. 27:23,24

OVERSEERS OF POSSESSIONS.   Azmaveth son of Adiel was in charge of the royal storehouses.

1 Chron. 27:25-31

Jonathan son of Uzziah was in charge of the storehouses in the outlying districts, in the towns, the villages and the watchtowers.

Ezri son of Kelub was in charge of the field workers who farmed the land.

Shimei the Ramathite was in charge of the vineyards.

Zabdi the Shiphmite was in charge of the produce of the vineyards for the wine vats.

Baal-Hanan the Gederite was in charge of the olive and sycamore-fig trees in the western foothills.

Joash was in charge of the supplies of olive oil.

Shitrai the Sharonite was in charge of the herds grazing in Sharon.

Shaphat son of Adlai was in charge of the herds in the valleys.

Obil the Ishmaelite was in charge of the camels.

Jehdeiah the Meronothite was in charge of the donkeys.

Jaziz the Hagrite was in charge of the flocks.

All these were the officials in charge of King David's property.

CLOSEST ADVISORS.   Jonathan, David's uncle, was a counselor, a man of insight and a scribe. Jehiel son of Hacmoni took care of the king's sons.

1 Chron. 27:32-34

Ahithophel was the king's counselor.

*j*Septuagint; Hebrew *number*

Hushai the Arkite was the king's friend. Ahithophel was succeeded by Jehoiada son of Benaiah and by Abiathar.

Joab was the commander of the royal army.

1 Chron. 28:1

ASSEMBLY CONVENED.   David summoned all the officials of Israel to assemble at Jerusalem: the officers over the tribes, the commanders of the divisions in the service of the king, the commanders of thousands and commanders of hundreds, and the officials in charge of all the property and livestock belonging to the king and his sons, together with the palace officials, the mighty men and all the brave warriors.

1 Chron. 23:1b

SOLOMON'S SUCCESSION TOLD.   [David] . . . made his son Solomon king over Israel.

1 Chron. 28:2-8

DAVID'S KEYNOTE ADDRESS.   King David rose to his feet and said: "Listen to me, my brothers and my people. I had it in my heart to build a house as a place of rest for the ark of the covenant of the LORD, for the footstool of our God, and I made plans to build it. But God said to me, 'You are not to build a house for my Name, because you are a warrior and have shed blood.'

"Yet the LORD, the God of Israel, chose me from my whole family to be king over Israel forever. He chose Judah as leader, and from the house of Judah he chose my family, and from my father's sons he was pleased to make me king over all Israel. Of all my sons—and the LORD has given me many—he has chosen my son Solomon to sit on the throne of the kingdom of the LORD over Israel. He said to me: 'Solomon your son is the one who will build my house and my courts, for I have chosen him to be my son, and I will be his father. I will establish his kingdom forever if he is unswerving in carrying out my commands and laws, as is being done at this time.'

"So now I charge you in the sight of all Israel and of the assembly of the LORD, and in the hearing of our God: Be careful to follow all the commands of the LORD your God, that you may possess this good land and pass it on as an inheritance to your descendants forever.

1 Chron. 28:9,10

ADMONITION TO SOLOMON.   "And you, my son Solomon, acknowledge the God of your father, and serve him with wholehearted devotion and with a willing mind, for the LORD searches every heart and understands every motive behind the thoughts. If you seek him, he will be found by you; but if you forsake him, he will reject you forever. Consider now, for the LORD has chosen you to build a temple as a sanctuary. Be strong and do the work."

1 Chron. 28:11-19

TEMPLE PLANS DELIVERED.   Then David gave his son Solomon the plans for the portico of the temple, its buildings, its storerooms, its upper parts, its inner rooms and the place of atonement. He gave him the plans of all that the Spirit had put in his mind for the courts of the temple of the LORD and all the surrounding rooms, for the treasuries of the temple of God and for the treasuries for the dedicated things. He gave him instructions for the divisions of the priests and Levites, and for all the work of serving in the temple of the LORD, as well as for all the articles to be used in its service. He designated the weight of gold for all the gold articles to be used in various kinds of service, and the weight of silver for all the silver articles to be used in various kinds of service: the weight of gold for the gold lampstands and their lamps, with the weight for each lampstand

and its lamps; and the weight of silver for each silver lampstand and its lamps, according to the use of each lampstand; the weight of gold for each table for consecrated bread; the weight of silver for the silver tables; the weight of pure gold for the forks, sprinkling bowls and pitchers; the weight of gold for each gold dish; the weight of silver for each silver dish; and the weight of the refined gold for the altar of incense. He also gave him the plan for the chariot, that is, the cherubim of gold that spread their wings and shelter the ark of the covenant of the LORD.

"All this," David said, "I have in writing from the hand of the LORD upon me, and he gave me understanding in all the details of the plan."

ENCOURAGEMENT FOR SOLOMON.   David also said to Solomon his son, "Be strong and courageous, and do the work. Do not be afraid or discouraged, for the LORD God, my God, is with you. He will not fail you or forsake you until all the work for the service of the temple of the LORD is finished. The divisions of the priests and Levites are ready for all the work on the temple of God, and every willing man skilled in any craft will help you in all the work. The officials and all the people will obey your every command."

1 Chron. 28:20,21

CONTRIBUTIONS SOLICITED. Then King David said to the whole assembly: "My son Solomon, the one whom God has chosen, is young and inexperienced. The task is great, because this palatial structure is not for man but for the LORD God. With all my resources I have provided for the temple of my God—gold for the gold work, silver for the silver, bronze for the bronze, iron for the iron and wood for the wood, as well as onyx for the settings, turquoise,[k] stones of various colors, and all kinds of fine stone and marble—all of these in large quantities. Besides, in my devotion to the temple of my God I now give my personal treasures of gold and silver for the temple of my God, over and above everything I have provided for this holy temple: three thousand talents[l] of gold (gold of Ophir) and seven thousand talents[m] of refined silver, for the overlaying of the walls of the buildings, for the gold work and the silver work, and for all the work to be done by the craftsmen. Now, who is willing to consecrate himself today to the LORD?"

1 Chron. 29:1-5

A GENEROUS RESPONSE.   Then the leaders of families, the officers of the tribes of Israel, the commanders of thousands and commanders of hundreds, and the officials in charge of the king's work gave willingly. They gave toward the work on the temple of God five thousand talents[n] and ten thousand darics[o] of gold, ten thousand talents[p] of silver, eighteen thousand talents[q] of bronze and a hundred thousand talents[r] of iron. Any who had precious stones gave them to the treasury of the temple of the LORD in the custody of Jehiel the Gershonite. The people rejoiced at the willing response of their leaders, for they had given freely and wholeheartedly to the LORD. David the king also rejoiced greatly.

1 Chron. 29:6-9

PRAYER AND PRAISE.   David praised the LORD in the presence of the whole assembly, saying,

1 Chron. 29:10-20

[k]The meaning of the Hebrew for this word is uncertain.   [l]That is, about 110 tons (about 100 metric tons)   [m]That is, about 260 tons (about 240 metric tons)   [n]That is, about 190 tons (about 170 metric tons)   [o]That is, about 185 pounds (about 84 kilograms)   [p]That is, about 375 tons (about 345 metric tons)   [q]That is, about 675 tons (about 610 metric tons)   [r]That is, about 3,750 tons (about 3,450 metric tons)

"Praise be to you, O LORD,
     God of our father Israel,
     from everlasting to everlasting.
Yours, O LORD, is the greatness and the power
     and the glory and the majesty and the splendor,
     for everything in heaven and earth is yours.
Yours, O LORD, is the kingdom;
     you are exalted as head over all.
Wealth and honor come from you;
     you are the ruler of all things.
In your hands are strength and power
     to exalt and give strength to all.
Now, our God, we give you thanks,
     and praise your glorious name.

"But who am I, and who are my people, that we should be able to give as generously as this? Everything comes from you, and we have given you only what comes from your hand. We are aliens and strangers in your sight, as were all our forefathers. Our days on earth are like a shadow, without hope. O LORD our God, as for all this abundance that we have provided for building you a temple for your Holy Name, it comes from your hand, and all of it belongs to you. I know, my God, that you test the heart and are pleased with integrity. All these things have I given willingly and with honest intent. And now I have seen with joy how willingly your people who are here have given to you. O LORD, God of our fathers Abraham, Isaac and Israel, keep this desire in the hearts of your people forever, and keep their hearts loyal to you. And give my son Solomon the wholehearted devotion to keep your commands, requirements and decrees and to do everything to build the palatial structure for which I have provided."

Then David said to the whole assembly, "Praise the LORD your God." So they all praised the LORD, the God of their fathers; they bowed low and fell prostrate before the LORD and the king.

1 Chron.
29:21,22

CLOSE OF ASSEMBLY.   The next day they made sacrifices to the LORD and presented burnt offerings to him: a thousand bulls, a thousand rams and a thousand male lambs, together with their drink offerings, and other sacrifices in abundance for all Israel. They ate and drank with great joy in the presence of the LORD that day.

Then they acknowledged Solomon son of David as king a second time, anointing him before the LORD to be ruler and Zadok to be priest.

The Book of Psalms

*I*mperfect as he is, David has a pure heart. This is perhaps best seen in the many songs (or psalms) which he writes. The contents of his songs reveal a wide-ranging spiritual sensitivity, from deepest sorrow to highest joy. Several psalms which demonstrate the breadth of David's emotions have already been presented. There were the soul-wrenching laments at the deaths of Saul, Jonathan, and Abner. There was the keen sense of relief when David was delivered from Saul and other enemies. There was the sheer celebration and thanksgiving when the ark was being brought into Jerusalem. And there were the many ardent prayers for his own safety.

Songs of praise, supplication, and thanksgiving are clearly a significant part of Israel's worship, as evidenced by David's recent appointment of singers to minister through songs and prophecy at the temple. All of those appointed are trained and skilled in music. They and their descendants after them will continue to propagate the songs of David and to write other songs themselves.

A collection of 150 of these songs, known as the Psalms, contains songs not only by David and Solomon but also by the sons of Korah—Asaph, Heman, and Ethan—who were assigned to the ministry of songs. Even a song of Moses is included (Psalm 90). Because of David's significant contributions to the Psalms, both personally and through his ministers of song, most of that collection is presented here at this point.

Based upon the specific indications accompanying particular psalms, 17 of the psalms have either already been included in the historical record or will soon be presented. Another 21 psalms, which are apparently written in a later period, will be presented in two separate groupings within their appropriate historical contexts. The remaining 112 psalms are presented at this time. Although the original collection was divided into five books, the psalms which follow are taken from all of those books and rearranged within five major topical groupings.

Psalms of the Troubled Soul

*I*n the first grouping of 35 psalms, the fears of one whose enemies beset him on every hand are reflected. The enemy not only threatens physical harm but also brings mockery, jeers, slander, and lies. Often the enemy is a former friend or companion of the one oppressed. At times the writer even doubts that God hears his prayers; at other times he gives thanks to God for having heard his supplications. At times there is doubt that anything lives beyond the grave; at other times there is a clear message of resurrection. There is a harsh attitude against the enemy, with prayers for not only the enemy's destruction but the destruction of the enemy's family as well. Yet David himself has repeatedly forgiven Saul, the one who has most directly threatened his life. The apparent harshness, then, may be simply the exaggeration of a pursued and fearful soul. In all, these psalms speak to anyone who has ever known persecution for righteousness, or anyone who feels betrayed or alone in the midst of a hostile world.

Prayer for protection of the righteous.   Psa. 5

For the director of music. For flutes. A psalm of David.

Give ear to my words, O LORD,
    consider my sighing.
Listen to my cry for help,
    my King and my God,
    for to you I pray.
In the morning, O LORD, you hear my voice;
    in the morning I lay my requests before you

and wait in expectation.

You are not a God who takes pleasure in evil;
   with you the wicked cannot dwell.
The arrogant cannot stand in your presence;
   you hate all who do wrong.
You destroy those who tell lies;
   bloodthirsty and deceitful men
   the LORD abhors.

But I, by your great mercy,
   will come into your house;
in reverence will I bow down
   toward your holy temple.
Lead me, O LORD, in your righteousness
   because of my enemies—
   make straight your way before me.

Not a word from their mouth can betrusted;
   their heart is filled with destruction.
Their throat is an open grave;
   with their tongue they speak deceit.
Declare them guilty, O God!
   Let their intrigues be their downfall.
Banish them for their many sins,
   for they have rebelled against you.

But let all who take refuge in you beglad;
   let them ever sing for joy.
Spread your protection over them,
   that those who love your name may rejoice in you.
For surely, O LORD, you bless the righteous;
   you surround them with your favor as with a shield.

Psa. 6   **Prayer for deliverance from enemies.**

For the director of music. With stringed instruments. According to *sheminith.*[s]
A psalm of David.

O LORD, do not rebuke me in your anger
   or discipline me in your wrath.
Be merciful to me, LORD, for I am faint;
   O LORD, heal me, for my bones are in agony.
My soul is in anguish.
   How long, O LORD, how long?

Turn, O LORD, and deliver me;
   save me because of your unfailing love.
No one remembers you when he is dead.
   Who praises you from the grave[t]?

I am worn out from groaning;
   all night long I flood my bed with weeping
   and drench my couch with tears.
My eyes grow weak with sorrow;

[s]Title: Probably a musical term   [t]Hebrew *Sheol*

they fail because of all my foes.

Away from me, all you who do evil,
for the LORD has heard my weeping.
The LORD has heard my cry for mercy;
the LORD accepts my prayer.
All my enemies will be ashamed and dismayed;
they will turn back in sudden disgrace.

Prayer for refuge from enemies.   Psa. 7

A *shiggaion*[u] of David, which he sang to the LORD concerning Cush, a Benjamite.

O LORD my God, I take refuge in you;
save and deliver me from all who pursue me,
or they will tear me like a lion
and rip me to pieces with no one to rescue me.

O LORD my God, if I have done this
and there is guilt on my hands—
if I have done evil to him who is at peace with me
or without cause have robbed my foe—
then let my enemy pursue and overtake me;
let him trample my life to the ground
and make me sleep in the dust.   *Selah*

Arise, O LORD, in your anger;
rise up against the rage of my enemies.
Awake, my God; decree justice.
Let the assembled peoples gather around you.
Rule over them from on high;
let the LORD judge the peoples.
Judge me, O LORD, according to my righteousness,
according to my integrity, O Most High.
O righteous God,
who searches minds and hearts,
bring to an end the violence of the wicked
and make the righteous secure.

My shield[v] is God Most High,
who saves the upright in heart.
God is a righteous judge,
a God who expresses his wrath every day.
If he does not relent,
he[w] will sharpen his sword;
he will bend and string his bow.
He has prepared his deadly weapons;
he makes ready his flaming arrows.

He who is pregnant with evil
and conceives trouble gives birth to disillusionment.
He who digs a hole and scoops it out
falls into the pit he has made.

[u]Title: Probably a literary or musical term   [v]Or *sovereign*   [w]Or *If a man does not repent, / God*

The trouble he causes recoils on himself;
  his violence comes down on his own head.

I will give thanks to the LORD because of his righteousness
  and will sing praise to the name of the LORD Most High.

Psa. 10   **Prayer for relief from oppression by the wicked.**

Why,[x] O LORD, do you stand far off?
  Why do you hide yourself in times of trouble?

In his arrogance the wicked man hunts down the weak,
  who are caught in the schemes he devises.
He boasts of the cravings of his heart;
  he blesses the greedy and reviles the LORD.
In his pride the wicked does not seek him;
  in all his thoughts there is no room for God.
His ways are always prosperous;
  he is haughty and your laws are far from him;
  he sneers at all his enemies.
He says to himself, "Nothing will shake me;
  I'll always be happy and never have trouble."
His mouth is full of curses and lies and threats;
  trouble and evil are under his tongue.
He lies in wait near the villages;
  from ambush he murders the innocent,
  watching in secret for his victims.
He lies in wait like a lion in cover;
  he lies in wait to catch the helpless;
  he catches the helpless and drags them off in his net.
His victims are crushed, they collapse;
  they fall under his strength.
He says to himself, "God has forgotten;
  he covers his face and never sees."

Arise, LORD! Lift up your hand, O God.
  Do not forget the helpless.
Why does the wicked man revile God?
  Why does he say to himself,
  "He won't call me to account"?
But you, O God, do see trouble and grief;
  you consider it to take it in hand.
The victim commits himself to you;
  you are the helper of the fatherless.
Break the arm of the wicked and evil man;
  call him to account for his wickedness
  that would not be found out.

The LORD is King for ever and ever;
  the nations will perish from his land.
You hear, O LORD, the desire of the afflicted;

---

[x]Psalms 9 and 10 may have been originally a single acrostic poem, the stanzas of which
begin with the successive letters of the Hebrew alphabet. In the Septuagint they constitute
one psalm.

you encourage them, and you listen to their cry,
defending the fatherless and the oppressed,
in order that man, who is of the earth, may terrify no more.

Security of righteous from threats of the wicked.

Psa. 11

For the director of music. Of David.

In the LORD I take refuge.
How then can you say to me:
"Flee like a bird to your mountain.
For look, the wicked bend their bows;
they set their arrows against the strings
to shoot from the shadows
at the upright in heart.
When the foundations are being destroyed,
what can the righteous do*y*?"

The LORD is in his holy temple;
the LORD is on his heavenly throne.
He observes the sons of men;
his eyes examine them.
The LORD examines the righteous,
but the wicked*z* and those who love violence
his soul hates.
On the wicked he will rain
fiery coals and burning sulfur;
a scorching wind will be their lot.

For the LORD is righteous,
he loves justice;
upright men will see his face.

Prayer for salvation from enemies.

Psa. 13

For the director of music. A psalm of David.

How long, O LORD? Will you forget me forever?
How long will you hide your face from me?
How long must I wrestle with my thoughts
and every day have sorrow in my heart?
How long will my enemy triumph over me?

Look on me and answer, O LORD my God.
Give light to my eyes, or I will sleep in death;
my enemy will say, "I have overcome him,"
and my foes will rejoice when I fall.

But I trust in your unfailing love;
my heart rejoices in your salvation.
I will sing to the LORD,
for he has been good to me.

*y*Or *what is the Righteous One doing*   *z*Or *The* LORD, *the Righteous One, examines the*
wicked, |

Psa. 17   **Prayer for rescue from enemies.**

A prayer of David.

Hear, O LORD, my righteous plea;
　　listen to my cry.
Give ear to my prayer—
　　it does not rise from deceitful lips.
May my vindication come from you;
　　may your eyes see what is right.

Though you probe my heart and examine me at night,
　　though you test me, you will find nothing;
　　I have resolved that my mouth will not sin.
As for the deeds of men—
　　by the word of your lips
I have kept myself
　　from the ways of the violent.
My steps have held to your paths;
　　my feet have not slipped.

I call on you, O God, for you will answer me;
　　give ear to me and hear my prayer.
Show the wonder of your great love,
　　you who save by your right hand
　　those who take refuge in you from their foes.
Keep me as the apple of your eye;
　　hide me in the shadow of your wings
from the wicked who assail me,
　　from my mortal enemies who surround me.

They close up their callous hearts,
　　and their mouths speak with arrogance.
They have tracked me down, they now surround me,
　　with eyes alert, to throw me to the ground.
They are like a lion hungry for prey,
　　like a great lion crouching in cover.

Rise up, O LORD, confront them, bring them down;
　　rescue me from the wicked by your sword.
O LORD, by your hand save me from such men,
　　from men of this world whose reward is in this life.

You still the hunger of those you cherish;
　　their sons have plenty,
　　and they store up wealth for their children.
And I—in righteousness I will see your face;
　　when I awake, I will be satisfied with seeing your likeness.

Psa. 23   **The Lord as a protective Shepherd.**

A psalm of David.

The LORD is my shepherd, I shall not be in want.
　　He makes me lie down in green pastures,

he leads me beside quiet waters,
 he restores my soul.
He guides me in paths of righteousness
 for his name's sake.
Even though I walk
 through the valley of the shadow of death,[a]
I will fear no evil,
 for you are with me;
your rod and your staff,
 they comfort me.

You prepare a table before me
 in the presence of my enemies.
You anoint my head with oil;
 my cup overflows.
Surely goodness and love will follow me
 all the days of my life,
and I will dwell in the house of the LORD
 forever.

Prayer for redemption of the righteous.   Psa. 26

Of David.

Vindicate me, O LORD,
 for I have led a blameless life;
I have trusted in the LORD
 without wavering.
Test me, O LORD, and try me,
 examine my heart and my mind;
for your love is ever before me,
 and I walk continually in your truth.
I do not sit with deceitful men,
 nor do I consort with hypocrites;
I abhor the assembly of evildoers
 and refuse to sit with the wicked.
I wash my hands in innocence,
 and go about your altar, O LORD,
proclaiming aloud your praise
 and telling of all your wonderful deeds.
I love the house where you live, O LORD,
 the place where your glory dwells.

Do not take away my soul along with sinners,
 my life with bloodthirsty men,
in whose hands are wicked schemes,
 whose right hands are full of bribes.
But I lead a blameless life;
 redeem me and be merciful to me.

My feet stand on level ground;
 in the great assembly I will praise the LORD.

[a] *Or through the darkest valley*

Psa. 28 **Prayer for salvation of righteous and punishment of wicked.**

Of David.

To you I call, O LORD my Rock;
    do not turn a deaf ear to me.
For if you remain silent,
    I will be like those who have gone down to the pit.
Hear my cry for mercy
    as I call to you for help,
as I lift up my hands
    toward your Most Holy Place.

Do not drag me away with the wicked,
    with those who do evil,
who speak cordially with their neighbors
    but harbor malice in their hearts.
Repay them for their deeds
    and for their evil work;
repay them for what their hands have done
    and bring back upon them what they deserve.
Since they show no regard for the works of the LORD
    and what his hands have done,
he will tear them down
    and never build them up again.

Praise be to the LORD,
    for he has heard my cry for mercy.
The LORD is my strength and my shield;
    my heart trusts in him, and I am helped.
My heart leaps for joy
    and I will give thanks to him in song.

The LORD is the strength of his people,
    a fortress of salvation for his anointed one.
Save your people and bless your inheritance;
    be their shepherd and carry them forever.

Psa. 31 **Prayer for relief from pursuers and slanderers.**

For the director of music. A psalm of David.

In you, O LORD, I have taken refuge;
    let me never be put to shame;
    deliver me in your righteousness.
Turn your ear to me,
    come quickly to my rescue;
be my rock of refuge,
    a strong fortress to save me.
Since you are my rock and my fortress,
    for the sake of your name lead and guide me.
Free me from the trap that is set for me,
    for you are my refuge.
Into your hands I commit my spirit;
    redeem me, O LORD, the God of truth.

I hate those who cling to worthless idols;

I trust in the LORD.
I will be glad and rejoice in your love,
    for you saw my affliction
    and knew the anguish of my soul.
You have not handed me over to the enemy
    but have set my feet in a spacious place.

Be merciful to me, O LORD, for I am in distress;
    my eyes grow weak with sorrow,
    my soul and my body with grief.
My life is consumed by anguish
    and my years by groaning;
my strength fails because of my affliction,[b]
    and my bones grow weak.
Because of all my enemies,
    I am the utter contempt of my neighbors;
I am a dread to my friends—
    those who see me on the street flee from me.
I am forgotten by them as though I were dead;
    I have become like broken pottery.
For I hear the slander of many;
    there is terror on every side;
they conspire against me
    and plot to take my life.

But I trust in you, O LORD;
    I say, "You are my God."
My times are in your hands;
    deliver me from my enemies
    and from those who pursue me.
Let your face shine on your servant;
    save me in your unfailing love.
Let me not be put to shame, O LORD,
    for I have cried out to you;
but let the wicked be put to shame
    and lie silent in the grave.[c]
Let their lying lips be silenced,
    for with pride and contempt
    they speak arrogantly against the righteous.

How great is your goodness,
    which you have stored up for those who fear you,
which you bestow in the sight of men
    on those who take refuge in you.
In the shelter of your presence you hide them
    from the intrigues of men;
in your dwelling you keep them safe
    from accusing tongues.

Praise be to the LORD,
    for he showed his wonderful love to me
    when I was in a besieged city.

[b]Or guilt   [c]Hebrew Sheol

In my alarm I said,
  "I am cut off from your sight!"
Yet you heard my cry for mercy
  when I called to you for help.

Love the LORD, all his saints!
  The LORD preserves the faithful,
  but the proud he pays back in full.
Be strong and take heart,
  all you who hope in the LORD.

Psa. 35

Prayer for vindication in the eyes of enemies who gloat.

Of David.

Contend, O LORD, with those who contend with me;
  fight against those who fight against me.
Take up shield and buckler;
  arise and come to my aid.
Brandish spear and javelin[d]
  against those who pursue me.
Say to my soul,
  "I am your salvation."

May those who seek my life
  be disgraced and put to shame;
may those who plot my ruin
  be turned back in dismay.
May they be like chaff before the wind,
  with the angel of the LORD driving them away;
may their path be dark and slippery,
  with the angel of the LORD pursuing them.
Since they hid their net for me without cause
  and without cause dug a pit for me,
may ruin overtake them by surprise—
  may the net they hid entangle them,
  may they fall into the pit, to their ruin.
Then my soul will rejoice in the LORD
  and delight in his salvation.
My whole being will exclaim,
  "Who is like you, O LORD?
You rescue the poor from those too strong for them,
  the poor and needy from those who rob them."

Ruthless witnesses come forward;
  they question me on things I know nothing about.
They repay me evil for good
  and leave my soul forlorn.
Yet when they were ill, I put on sackcloth
  and humbled myself with fasting.
When my prayers returned to me unanswered,
  I went about mourning
  as though for my friend or brother.

[d]Or *and block the way*

I bowed my head in grief
    as though weeping for my mother.
But when I stumbled, they gathered in glee;
    attackers gathered against me when I was unaware.
    They slandered me without ceasing.
Like the ungodly they maliciously mocked[e];
    they gnashed their teeth at me.
O Lord, how long will you look on?
    Rescue my life from their ravages,
    my precious life from these lions.
I will give you thanks in the great assembly;
    among throngs of people I will praise you.

Let not those gloat over me
    who are my enemies without cause;
let not those who hate me without reason
    maliciously wink the eye.
They do not speak peaceably,
    but devise false accusations
    against those who live quietly in the land.
They gape at me and say, "Aha! Aha!
    With our own eyes we have seen it."

O LORD, you have seen this; be not silent.
    Do not be far from me, O Lord.
Awake, and rise to my defense!
    Contend for me, my God and Lord.
Vindicate me in your righteousness, O LORD my God;
    do not let them gloat over me.
Do not let them think, "Aha, just what we wanted!"
    or say, "We have swallowed him up."

May all who gloat over my distress
    be put to shame and confusion;
may all who exalt themselves over me
    be clothed with shame and disgrace.
May those who delight in my vindication
    shout for joy and gladness;
may they always say, "The LORD be exalted,
    who delights in the well-being of his servant."
My tongue will speak of your righteousness
    and of your praises all day long.

Prayer for weak and those who suffer betrayal by friends.   Psa. 41

For the director of music. A psalm of David.

Blessed is he who has regard for the weak;
    the LORD delivers him in times of trouble.
The LORD will protect him and preserve his life;
    he will bless him in the land
    and not surrender him to the desire of his foes.
The LORD will sustain him on his sickbed

[e]Septuagint; Hebrew may mean *ungodly circle of mockers.*

and restore him from his bed of illness.

I said, "O LORD, have mercy on me;
   heal me, for I have sinned against you."
My enemies say of me in malice,
   "When will he die and his name perish?"
Whenever one comes to see me,
   he speaks falsely, while his heart gathers slander;
   then he goes out and spreads it abroad.

All my enemies whisper together against me;
   they imagine the worst for me, saying,
"A vile disease has beset him;
   he will never get up from the place where he lies."
Even my close friend, whom I trusted,
   he who shared my bread,
   has lifted up his heel against me.

But you, O LORD, have mercy on me;
   raise me up, that I may repay them.
I know that you are pleased with me,
   for my enemy does not triumph over me.
In my integrity you uphold me
   and set me in your presence forever.

Praise be to the LORD, the God of Israel,
   from everlasting to everlasting.

                Amen and Amen.

Psa. 43   **Prayer for insight in the face of opposition.**

Vindicate *f* me, O God,
   and plead my cause against an ungodly nation;
   rescue me from deceitful and wicked men.
You are God my stronghold.
   Why have you rejected me?
Why must I go about mourning,
   oppressed by the enemy?
Send forth your light and your truth,
   let them guide me;
let them bring me to your holy mountain,
   to the place where you dwell.
Then will I go to the altar of God,
   to God, my joy and my delight.
I will praise you with the harp,
   O God, my God.

Why are you downcast, O my soul?
   Why so disturbed within me?
Put your hope in God,
   for I will yet praise him,
   my Savior and my God.

f In many Hebrew manuscripts Psalms 42 and 43 constitute one psalm.

Refuge and strength in the God who rules over nations.

For the director of music. Of the Sons of Korah. According to *alamoth*.g A song.

God is our refuge and strength,
    an ever-present help in trouble.
Therefore we will not fear, though the earth give way
    and the mountains fall into the heart of the sea,
though its waters roar and foam
    and the mountains quake with their surging.   *Selah*

There is a river whose streams make glad the city of God,
    the holy place where the Most High dwells.
God is within her, she will not fall;
    God will help her at break of day.
Nations are in uproar, kingdoms fall;
    he lifts his voice, the earth melts.

The LORD Almighty is with us;
    the God of Jacob is our fortress.   *Selah*

Come and see the works of the LORD,
    the desolations he has brought on the earth.
He makes wars cease to the ends of the earth;
    he breaks the bow and shatters the spear,
    he burns the shieldsh with fire.
"Be still, and know that I am God;
    I will be exalted among the nations,
    I will be exalted in the earth."

The LORD Almighty is with us;
    the God of Jacob is our fortress.   *Selah*

The anguish of having disloyal companions.

For the director of music. With stringed instruments. A *maskil*i of David.

Listen to my prayer, O God,
    do not ignore my plea;
    hear me and answer me.
My thoughts trouble me and I am distraught
    at the voice of the enemy,
    at the stares of the wicked;
for they bring down suffering upon me
    and revile me in their anger.

My heart is in anguish within me;
    the terrors of death assail me.
Fear and trembling have beset me;
    horror has overwhelmed me.
I said, "Oh, that I had the wings of a dove!
    I would fly away and be at rest—
I would flee far away
    and stay in the desert;   *Selah*
I would hurry to my place of shelter,

gTitle: Probably a musical term   hOr *chariots*   iTitle: Probably a literary or musical
term

far from the tempest and storm."

Confuse the wicked, O Lord, confound their speech,
    for I see violence and strife in the city.
Day and night they prowl about on its walls;
    malice and abuse are within it.
Destructive forces are at work in the city;
    threats and lies never leave its streets.

If an enemy were insulting me,
    I could endure it;
if a foe were raising himself against me,
    I could hide from him.
But it is you, a man like myself,
    my companion, my close friend,
with whom I once enjoyed sweet fellowship
    as we walked with the throng at the house of God.

Let death take my enemies by surprise;
    let them go down alive to the grave,*j*
    for evil finds lodging among them.

But I call to God,
    and the LORD saves me.
Evening, morning and noon
    I cry out in distress,
    and he hears my voice.
He ransoms me unharmed
    from the battle waged against me,
    even though many oppose me.
God, who is enthroned forever,
    will hear them and afflict them—   *Selah*
men who never change their ways
    and have no fear of God.

My companion attacks his friends;
    he violates his covenant.
His speech is smooth as butter,
    yet war is in his heart;
his words are more soothing than oil,
    yet they are drawn swords.

Cast your cares on the LORD
    and he will sustain you;
    he will never let the righteous fall.
But you, O God, will bring down the wicked
    into the pit of corruption;
bloodthirsty and deceitful men
    will not live out half their days.

But as for me, I trust in you.

j Hebrew *Sheol*

Prayer for God's defense and shelter.   Psa. 61

> For the director of music. With stringed instruments. Of David.

Hear my cry, O God;
  listen to my prayer.

From the ends of the earth I call to you,
  I call as my heart grows faint;
  lead me to the rock that is higher than I.
For you have been my refuge,
  a strong tower against the foe.

I long to dwell in your tent forever
  and take refuge in the shelter of your wings.   *Selah*
For you have heard my vows, O God;
  you have given me the heritage of those who fear your
    name.

Increase the days of the king's life,
  his years for many generations.
May he be enthroned in God's presence forever;
  appoint your love and faithfulness to protect him.

Then will I ever sing praise to your name
  and fulfill my vows day after day.

God is our only strength, whose love excels all others'.   Psa. 62

> For the director of music. For Jeduthun. A psalm of David.

My soul finds rest in God alone;
  my salvation comes from him.
He alone is my rock and my salvation;
  he is my fortress, I will never be shaken.

How long will you assault a man?
  Would all of you throw him down—
  this leaning wall, this tottering fence?
They fully intend to topple him
  from his lofty place;
  they take delight in lies.
With their mouths they bless,
  but in their hearts they curse.   *Selah*

Find rest, O my soul, in God alone;
  my hope comes from him.
He alone is my rock and my salvation;
  he is my fortress, I will not be shaken.
My salvation and my honor depend on God[k];
  he is my mighty rock, my refuge.
Trust in him at all times, O people;
  pour out your hearts to him,
  for God is our refuge.   *Selah*

Lowborn men are but a breath,
  the highborn are but a lie;

[k]Or / *God Most High is my salvation and my honor*

if weighed on a balance, they are nothing;
 together they are only a breath.
Do not trust in extortion
 or take pride in stolen goods;
though your riches increase,
 do not set your heart on them.

One thing God has spoken,
 two things have I heard:
that you, O God, are strong,
 and that you, O Lord, are loving.
Surely you will reward each person
 according to what he has done.

Psa. 64 **Plea against conspirators who scheme evil deeds.**

For the director of music. A psalm of David.

Hear me, O God, as I voice my complaint;
 protect my life from the threat of the enemy.
Hide me from the conspiracy of the wicked,
 from that noisy crowd of evildoers.

They sharpen their tongues like swords
 and aim their words like deadly arrows.
They shoot from ambush at the innocent man;
 they shoot at him suddenly, without fear.

They encourage each other in evil plans,
 they talk about hiding their snares;
 they say, "Who will see them[1]?"
They plot injustice and say,
 "We have devised a perfect plan!"
 Surely the mind and heart of man are cunning.

But God will shoot them with arrows;
 suddenly they will be struck down.
He will turn their own tongues against them
 and bring them to ruin;
 all who see them will shake their heads in scorn.

All mankind will fear;
 they will proclaim the works of God
 and ponder what he has done.
Let the righteous rejoice in the LORD
 and take refuge in him;
 let all the upright in heart praise him!

Psa. 69 **Prayer for end of scorn.**

For the director of music. To ˌthe tune ofˌ "Lilies." Of David.

Save me, O God,
 for the waters have come up to my neck.
I sink in the miry depths,
 where there is no foothold.

[1]Or *us*

I have come into the deep waters;
    the floods engulf me.
I am worn out calling for help;
    my throat is parched.
My eyes fail,
    looking for my God.
Those who hate me without reason
    outnumber the hairs of my head;
many are my enemies without cause,
    those who seek to destroy me.
I am forced to restore
    what I did not steal.

You know my folly, O God;
    my guilt is not hidden from you.

May those who hope in you
    not be disgraced because of me,
    O Lord, the LORD Almighty;
may those who seek you
    not be put to shame because of me,
    O God of Israel.
For I endure scorn for your sake,
    and shame covers my face.
I am a stranger to my brothers,
    an alien to my own mother's sons;
for zeal for your house consumes me,
    and the insults of those who insult you fall on me.
When I weep and fast,
    I must endure scorn;
when I put on sackcloth,
    people make sport of me.
Those who sit at the gate mock me,
    and I am the song of the drunkards.

But I pray to you, O LORD,
    in the time of your favor;
in your great love, O God,
    answer me with your sure salvation.
Rescue me from the mire,
    do not let me sink;
deliver me from those who hate me,
    from the deep waters.
Do not let the floodwaters engulf me
    or the depths swallow me up
    or the pit close its mouth over me.
Answer me, O LORD, out of the goodness of your love;
    in your great mercy turn to me.
Do not hide your face from your servant;
    answer me quickly, for I am in trouble.
Come near and rescue me;
    redeem me because of my foes.

You know how I am scorned, disgraced and shamed;

all my enemies are before you.
Scorn has broken my heart
    and has left me helpless;
I looked for sympathy, but there was none,
    for comforters, but I found none.
They put gall in my food
    and gave me vinegar for my thirst.

May the table set before them become a snare;
    may it become retribution and^m a trap.
May their eyes be darkened so they cannot see,
    and their backs be bent forever.
Pour out your wrath on them;
    let your fierce anger overtake them.
May their place be deserted;
    let there be no one to dwell in their tents.
For they persecute those you wound
    and talk about the pain of those you hurt.
Charge them with crime upon crime;
    do not let them share in your salvation.
May they be blotted out of the book of life
    and not be listed with the righteous.

I am in pain and distress;
    may your salvation, O God, protect me.

I will praise God's name in song
    and glorify him with thanksgiving.
This will please the LORD more than an ox,
    more than a bull with its horns and hoofs.
The poor will see and be glad—
    you who seek God, may your hearts live!
The LORD hears the needy
    and does not despise his captive people.

Let heaven and earth praise him,
    the seas and all that move in them,
for God will save Zion
    and rebuild the cities of Judah.
Then people will settle there and possess it;
    the children of his servants will inherit it,
    and those who love his name will dwell there.

Psa. 70   **Urgency of the need for God's deliverance.**

For the director of music. Of David. A petition.

Hasten, O God, to save me;
    O LORD, come quickly to help me.
May those who seek my life
    be put to shame and confusion;
may all who desire my ruin
    be turned back in disgrace.
May those who say to me, "Aha! Aha!"

―――――――――

^mOr snare / and their fellowship become

turn back because of their shame.
But may all who seek you
    rejoice and be glad in you;
may those who love your salvation always say,
    "Let God be exalted!"

Yet I am poor and needy;
    come quickly to me, O God.
You are my help and my deliverer;
    O LORD, do not delay.

Prayer for God's presence even in old age.   Psa. 71

In you, O LORD, I have taken refuge;
    let me never be put to shame.
Rescue me and deliver me in your righteousness;
    turn your ear to me and save me.
Be my rock of refuge,
    to which I can always go;
give the command to save me,
    for you are my rock and my fortress.
Deliver me, O my God, from the hand of the wicked,
    from the grasp of evil and cruel men.

For you have been my hope, O Sovereign LORD,
    my confidence since my youth.
From birth I have relied on you;
    you brought me forth from my mother's womb.
    I will ever praise you.
I have become like a portent to many,
    but you are my strong refuge.
My mouth is filled with your praise,
    declaring your splendor all day long.

Do not cast me away when I am old;
    do not forsake me when my strength is gone.
For my enemies speak against me;
    those who wait to kill me conspire together.
They say, "God has forsaken him;
    pursue him and seize him,
    for no one will rescue him."
Be not far from me, O God;
    come quickly, O my God, to help me.
May my accusers perish in shame;
    may those who want to harm me
    be covered with scorn and disgrace.

But as for me, I will always have hope;
    I will praise you more and more.
My mouth will tell of your righteousness,
    of your salvation all day long,
    though I know not its measure.
I will come and proclaim your mighty acts, O Sovereign
    LORD;
    I will proclaim your righteousness, yours alone.

Since my youth, O God, you have taught me,
　　and to this day I declare your marvelous deeds.
Even when I am old and gray,
　　do not forsake me, O God,
till I declare your power to the next generation,
　　your might to all who are to come.

Your righteousness reaches to the skies, O God,
　　you who have done great things.
　　Who, O God, is like you?
Though you have made me see troubles, many and bitter,
　　you will restore my life again;
from the depths of the earth
　　you will again bring me up.
You will increase my honor
　　and comfort me once again.

I will praise you with the harp
　　for your faithfulness, O my God;
I will sing praise to you with the lyre,
　　O Holy One of Israel.
My lips will shout for joy
　　when I sing praise to you—
　　I, whom you have redeemed.
My tongue will tell of your righteous acts
　　all day long,
for those who wanted to harm me
　　have been put to shame and confusion.

Psa. 77   **The comfort of knowing God's record of deliverance.**

For the director of music. For Jeduthun. Of Asaph. A psalm.

I cried out to God for help;
　　I cried out to God to hear me.
When I was in distress, I sought the Lord;
　　at night I stretched out untiring hands
　　and my soul refused to be comforted.

I remembered you, O God, and I groaned;
　　I mused, and my spirit grew faint.   *Selah*
You kept my eyes from closing;
　　I was too troubled to speak.
I thought about the former days,
　　the years of long ago;
I remembered my songs in the night.
　　My heart mused and my spirit inquired:

"Will the Lord reject forever?
　　Will he never show his favor again?
Has his unfailing love vanished forever?
　　Has his promise failed for all time?
Has God forgotten to be merciful?
　　Has he in anger withheld his compassion?"   *Selah*

Then I thought, "To this I will appeal:

the years of the right hand of the Most High."
I will remember the deeds of the LORD;
    yes, I will remember your miracles of long ago.
I will meditate on all your works
    and consider all your mighty deeds.

Your ways, O God, are holy.
    What god is so great as our God?
You are the God who performs miracles;
    you display your power among the peoples.
With your mighty arm you redeemed your people,
    the descendants of Jacob and Joseph.   *Selah*

The waters saw you, O God,
    the waters saw you and writhed;
    the very depths were convulsed.
The clouds poured down water,
    the skies resounded with thunder;
    your arrows flashed back and forth.
Your thunder was heard in the whirlwind,
    your lightning lit up the world;
    the earth trembled and quaked.
Your path led through the sea,
    your way through the mighty waters,
    though your footprints were not seen.

You led your people like a flock
    by the hand of Moses and Aaron.

Prayer for punishment of oppressing nations.   Psa. 83

A song. A psalm of Asaph.

O God, do not keep silent;
    be not quiet, O God, be not still.
See how your enemies are astir,
    how your foes rear their heads.
With cunning they conspire against your people;
    they plot against those you cherish.
"Come," they say, "let us destroy them as a nation,
    that the name of Israel be remembered no more."

With one mind they plot together;
    they form an alliance against you—
the tents of Edom and the Ishmaelites,
    of Moab and the Hagrites,
Gebal,[n] Ammon and Amalek,
    Philistia, with the people of Tyre.
Even Assyria has joined them
    to lend strength to the descendants of Lot.   *Selah*

Do to them as you did to Midian,
    as you did to Sisera and Jabin at the river Kishon,
who perished at Endor

[n] That is, Byblos

and became like refuse on the ground.
Make their nobles like Oreb and Zeeb,
  all their princes like Zebah and Zalmunna,
who said, "Let us take possession
  of the pasturelands of God."

Make them like tumbleweed, O my God,
  like chaff before the wind.
As fire consumes the forest
  or a flame sets the mountains ablaze,
so pursue them with your tempest
  and terrify them with your storm.
Cover their faces with shame
  so that men will seek your name, O LORD.

May they ever be ashamed and dismayed;
  may they perish in disgrace.
Let them know that you, whose name is the LORD—
  that you alone are the Most High over all the earth.

Psa. 86 **Prayer for mercy in face of enemies.**

A prayer of David.

Hear, O LORD, and answer me,
  for I am poor and needy.
Guard my life, for I am devoted to you.
  You are my God; save your servant
  who trusts in you.
Have mercy on me, O Lord,
  for I call to you all day long.
Bring joy to your servant,
  for to you, O Lord,
  I lift up my soul.

You are forgiving and good, O Lord,
  abounding in love to all who call to you.
Hear my prayer, O LORD;
  listen to my cry for mercy.
In the day of my trouble I will call to you,
  for you will answer me.

Among the gods there is none like you, O Lord;
  no deeds can compare with yours.
All the nations you have made
  will come and worship before you, O Lord;
  they will bring glory to your name.
For you are great and do marvelous deeds;
  you alone are God.

Teach me your way, O LORD,
  and I will walk in your truth;
give me an undivided heart,
  that I may fear your name.
I will praise you, O Lord my God, with all my heart;
  I will glorify your name forever.

For great is your love toward me;
   you have delivered me from the depths of the grave.[o]

The arrogant are attacking me, O God;
   a band of ruthless men seeks my life—
   men without regard for you.
But you, O Lord, are a compassionate and gracious God,
   slow to anger, abounding in love and faithfulness.
Turn to me and have mercy on me;
   grant your strength to your servant
   and save the son of your maidservant.[p]
Give me a sign of your goodness,
   that my enemies may see it and be put to shame,
   for you, O LORD, have helped me and comforted me.

The fear of one who is dying and wonders if God hears him.   **Psa. 88**

A song. A psalm of the Sons of Korah. For the director of music. According to
   mahalath leannoth.[q] A *maskil*[r] of Heman the Ezrahite.

O LORD, the God who saves me,
   day and night I cry out before you.
May my prayer come before you;
   turn your ear to my cry.

For my soul is full of trouble
   and my life draws near the grave.[o]
I am counted among those who go down to the pit;
   I am like a man without strength.
I am set apart with the dead,
   like the slain who lie in the grave,
whom you remember no more,
   who are cut off from your care.

You have put me in the lowest pit,
   in the darkest depths.
Your wrath lies heavily upon me;
   you have overwhelmed me with all your waves.   *Selah*
You have taken from me my closest friends
   and have made me repulsive to them.
I am confined and cannot escape;
   my eyes are dim with grief.

I call to you, O LORD, every day;
   I spread out my hands to you.
Do you show your wonders to the dead?
   Do those who are dead rise up and praise you?   *Selah*
Is your love declared in the grave,
   your faithfulness in Destruction[s]?
Are your wonders known in the place of darkness,
   or your righteous deeds in the land of oblivion?

But I cry to you for help, O LORD;
   in the morning my prayer comes before you.

---

[o]Hebrew *Sheol*   [p]Or *save your faithful son*   [q]Title: Possibly a tune, "The Suffering of
Affliction"   [r]Title: Probably a literary or musical term   [s]Hebrew *Abaddon*

Why, O LORD, do you reject me
and hide your face from me?

From my youth I have been afflicted and close to death;
I have suffered your terrors and am in despair.
Your wrath has swept over me;
your terrors have destroyed me.
All day long they surround me like a flood;
they have completely engulfed me.
You have taken my companions and loved ones from me;
the darkness is my closest friend.

Psa. 91 **The personal protection of one who trusts in God.**

He who dwells in the shelter of the Most High
will rest in the shadow of the Almighty.[t]
I will say[u] of the LORD, "He is my refuge and my fortress,
my God, in whom I trust."

Surely he will save you from the fowler's snare
and from the deadly pestilence.
He will cover you with his feathers,
and under his wings you will find refuge;
his faithfulness will be your shield and rampart.
You will not fear the terror of night,
nor the arrow that flies by day,
nor the pestilence that stalks in the darkness,
nor the plague that destroys at midday.
A thousand may fall at your side,
ten thousand at your right hand,
but it will not come near you.
You will only observe with your eyes
and see the punishment of the wicked.

If you make the Most High your dwelling—
even the LORD, who is my refuge—
then no harm will befall you,
no disaster will come near your tent.
For he will command his angels concerning you
to guard you in all your ways;
they will lift you up in their hands,
so that you will not strike your foot against a stone.
You will tread upon the lion and the cobra;
you will trample the great lion and the serpent.

"Because he loves me," says the LORD, "I will rescue him;
I will protect him, for he acknowledges my name.
He will call upon me, and I will answer him;
I will be with him in trouble,
I will deliver him and honor him.
With long life will I satisfy him
and show him my salvation."

[t]Hebrew *Shaddai*   [u]*Or He says*

The God of creation as a personal Shepherd.   Psa. 95

> Come, let us sing for joy to the LORD;
>> let us shout aloud to the Rock of our salvation.
> Let us come before him with thanksgiving
>> and extol him with music and song.
>
> For the LORD is the great God,
>> the great King above all gods.
> In his hand are the depths of the earth,
>> and the mountain peaks belong to him.
> The sea is his, for he made it,
>> and his hands formed the dry land.
>
> Come, let us bow down in worship,
>> let us kneel before the LORD our Maker;
> for he is our God
>> and we are the people of his pasture,
>> the flock under his care.
>
> Today, if you hear his voice,
>> do not harden your hearts as you did at Meribah,[v]
>> as you did that day at Massah[w] in the desert,
> where your fathers tested and tried me,
>> though they had seen what I did.
> For forty years I was angry with that generation;
>> I said, "They are a people whose hearts go astray,
>> and they have not known my ways."
> So I declared on oath in my anger,
>> "They shall never enter my rest."

Prayer for victory over enemies.   Psa. 108

> A song. A psalm of David.

> My heart is steadfast, O God;
>> I will sing and make music with all my soul.
> Awake, harp and lyre!
>> I will awaken the dawn.
> I will praise you, O LORD, among the nations;
>> I will sing of you among the peoples.
> For great is your love, higher than the heavens;
>> your faithfulness reaches to the skies.
> Be exalted, O God, above the heavens,
>> and let your glory be over all the earth.
>
> Save us and help us with your right hand,
>> that those you love may be delivered.
> God has spoken from his sanctuary:
>> "In triumph I will parcel out Shechem
>> and measure off the Valley of Succoth.
> Gilead is mine, Manasseh is mine;
>> Ephraim is my helmet,
>> Judah my scepter.
> Moab is my washbasin,

---

[v]*Meribah means quarreling.*   [w]*Massah means testing.*

upon Edom I toss my sandal;
over Philistia I shout in triumph."

Who will bring me to the fortified city?
Who will lead me to Edom?
Is it not you, O God, you who have rejected us
and no longer go out with our armies?
Give us aid against the enemy,
for the help of man is worthless.
With God we will gain the victory,
and he will trample down our enemies.

Psa. 109   **Prayer that one's accusers suffer punishment.**

For the director of music. Of David. A psalm.

O God, whom I praise,
do not remain silent,
for wicked and deceitful men
have opened their mouths against me;
they have spoken against me with lying tongues.
With words of hatred they surround me;
they attack me without cause.
In return for my friendship they accuse me,
but I am a man of prayer.
They repay me evil for good,
and hatred for my friendship.

Appoint[x] an evil man[y] to oppose him;
let an accuser[z] stand at his right hand.
When he is tried, let him be found guilty,
and may his prayers condemn him.
May his days be few;
may another take his place of leadership.
May his children be fatherless
and his wife a widow.
May his children be wandering beggars;
may they be driven[a] from their ruined homes.
May a creditor seize all he has;
may strangers plunder the fruits of his labor.
May no one extend kindness to him
or take pity on his fatherless children.
May his descendants be cut off,
their names blotted out from the next generation.
May the iniquity of his fathers be remembered before the LORD;
may the sin of his mother never be blotted out.
May their sins always remain before the LORD,
that he may cut off the memory of them from the earth.

For he never thought of doing a kindness,
but hounded to death the poor

---

[x]Or ⌐They say:⌐ "Appoint (with quotation marks at the end of verse 19)   [y]Or the Evil One
[z]Or let Satan   [a]Septuagint; Hebrew sought

and the needy and the brokenhearted.
He loved to pronounce a curse—
    may it[b] come on him;
he found no pleasure in blessing—
    may it be[c] far from him.
He wore cursing as his garment;
    it entered into his body like water,
    into his bones like oil.
May it be like a cloak wrapped about him,
    like a belt tied forever around him.
May this be the LORD's payment to my accusers,
    to those who speak evil of me.

But you, O Sovereign LORD,
    deal well with me for your name's sake;
    out of the goodness of your love, deliver me.
For I am poor and needy,
    and my heart is wounded within me.
I fade away like an evening shadow;
    I am shaken off like a locust.
My knees give way from fasting;
    my body is thin and gaunt.
I am an object of scorn to my accusers;
    when they see me, they shake their heads.

Help me, O LORD my God;
    save me in accordance with your love.
Let them know that it is your hand,
    that you, O LORD, have done it.
They may curse, but you will bless;
    when they attack they will be put to shame,
    but your servant will rejoice.
My accusers will be clothed with disgrace
    and wrapped in shame as in a cloak.

With my mouth I will greatly extol the LORD;
    in the great throng I will praise him.
For he stands at the right hand of the needy one,
    to save his life from those who condemn him.

Prayer for deliverance from lying Gentiles who press war.   Psa. 120

A song of ascents.

I call on the LORD in my distress,
    and he answers me.
Save me, O LORD, from lying lips
    and from deceitful tongues.

What will he do to you,
    and what more besides, O deceitful tongue?
He will punish you with a warrior's sharp arrows,
    with burning coals of the broom tree.

[b]Or curse, / and it has   [c]Or blessing, / and it is

Woe to me that I dwell in Meshech,
    that I live among the tents of Kedar!
Too long have I lived
    among those who hate peace.
I am a man of peace;
    but when I speak, they are for war.

Psa. 121   **The Lord watches over his people.**

A song of ascents.

I lift up my eyes to the hills—
    where does my help come from?
My help comes from the LORD,
    the Maker of heaven and earth.

He will not let your foot slip—
    he who watches over you will not slumber;
indeed, he who watches over Israel
    will neither slumber nor sleep.

The LORD watches over you—
    the LORD is your shade at your right hand;
the sun will not harm you by day,
    nor the moon by night.

The LORD will keep you from all harm—
    he will watch over your life;
the LORD will watch over your coming and going
    both now and forevermore.

Psa. 140   **Prayer for protection from violent persons.**

For the director of music. A psalm of David.

Rescue me, O LORD, from evil men;
    protect me from men of violence,
who devise evil plans in their hearts
    and stir up war every day.
They make their tongues as sharp as a serpent's;
    the poison of vipers is on their lips.   *Selah*

Keep me, O LORD, from the hands of the wicked;
    protect me from men of violence
    who plan to trip my feet.
Proud men have hidden a snare for me;
    they have spread out the cords of their net
    and have set traps for me along my path.   *Selah*

O LORD, I say to you, "You are my God."
    Hear, O LORD, my cry for mercy.
O Sovereign LORD, my strong deliverer,
    who shields my head in the day of battle—
do not grant the wicked their desires, O LORD;
    do not let their plans succeed,
    or they will become proud.   *Selah*

Let the heads of those who surround me
    be covered with the trouble their lips have caused.

Let burning coals fall upon them;
    may they be thrown into the fire,
    into miry pits, never to rise.
Let slanderers not be established in the land;
    may disaster hunt down men of violence.

I know that the LORD secures justice for the poor
    and upholds the cause of the needy.
Surely the righteous will praise your name
    and the upright will live before you.

Prayer for preservation of life and protection against trouble.   Psa. 143

A psalm of David.

O LORD, hear my prayer,
    listen to my cry for mercy;
in your faithfulness and righteousness
    come to my relief.
Do not bring your servant into judgment,
    for no one living is righteous before you.

The enemy pursues me,
    he crushes me to the ground;
he makes me dwell in darkness
    like those long dead.
So my spirit grows faint within me;
    my heart within me is dismayed.

I remember the days of long ago;
    I meditate on all your works
    and consider what your hands have done.
I spread out my hands to you;
    my soul thirsts for you like a parched land.   *Selah*

Answer me quickly, O LORD;
    my spirit fails.
Do not hide your face from me
    or I will be like those who go down to the pit.
Let the morning bring me word of your unfailing love,
    for I have put my trust in you.
Show me the way I should go,
    for to you I lift up my soul.
Rescue me from my enemies, O LORD,
    for I hide myself in you.
Teach me to do your will,
    for you are my God;
may your good Spirit
    lead me on level ground.

For your name's sake, O LORD, preserve my life;
    in your righteousness, bring me out of trouble.
In your unfailing love, silence my enemies;
    destroy all my foes,
    for I am your servant.

Psa. 144 **Prayer for God's power.**

Of David.

Praise be to the LORD my Rock,
　　who trains my hands for war,
　　my fingers for battle.
He is my loving God and my fortress,
　　my stronghold and my deliverer,
my shield, in whom I take refuge,
　　who subdues peoples[d] under me.

O LORD, what is man that you care for him,
　　the son of man that you think of him?
Man is like a breath;
　　his days are like a fleeting shadow.

Part your heavens, O LORD, and come down;
　　touch the mountains, so that they smoke.
Send forth lightning and scatter ⌊the enemies⌋;
　　shoot your arrows and rout them.
Reach down your hand from on high;
　　deliver me and rescue me
from the mighty waters,
　　from the hands of foreigners
whose mouths are full of lies,
　　whose right hands are deceitful.

I will sing a new song to you, O God;
　　on the ten-stringed lyre I will make music to you,
to the One who gives victory to kings,
　　who delivers his servant David from the deadly sword.

Deliver me and rescue me
　　from the hands of foreigners
whose mouths are full of lies,
　　whose right hands are deceitful.

Then our sons in their youth
　　will be like well-nurtured plants,
and our daughters will be like pillars
　　carved to adorn a palace.
Our barns will be filled
　　with every kind of provision.
Our sheep will increase by thousands,
　　by tens of thousands in our fields;
　　our oxen will draw heavy loads.[e]
There will be no breaching of walls,
　　no going into captivity,
　　no cry of distress in our streets.

Blessed are the people of whom this is true;
　　blessed are the people whose God is the LORD.

[d]Many manuscripts of the Masoretic Text, Dead Sea Scrolls, Aquila, Jerome and Syriac; most manuscripts of the Masoretic Text *subdues my people*　　[e]Or *our chieftains will be firmly established*

*Psalms About Righteousness and Wickedness*_____

*O*ne of the consistent themes of the Scriptures is the inherent superiority of righteousness over wickedness. But often the wicked appear to prosper more than the righteous, and often it seems that the wicked escape punishment. When such inequity appears, is it enough for the righteous simply to know they are doing God's will and to be satisfied with the crumbs from the table? Or is it even true that the righteous are second-class citizens? Behind the facades of wealth and power might there not be untold discontent and misery? And, in any event, will not the wicked receive their just reward in due time, at least at the final judgment of mankind? These are many of the questions and themes addressed in the following 17 psalms.

Vitality of righteousness and vulnerability of the wicked.　　　Psa. 1

Blessed is the man
　　who does not walk in the counsel of the wicked
or stand in the way of sinners
　　or sit in the seat of mockers.
But his delight is in the law of the LORD,
　　and on his law he meditates day and night.
He is like a tree planted by streams of water,
　　which yields its fruit in season
and whose leaf does not wither.
　　Whatever he does prospers.

Not so the wicked!
　　They are like chaff
　　that the wind blows away.
Therefore the wicked will not stand in the judgment,
　　nor sinners in the assembly of the righteous.

For the LORD watches over the way of the righteous,
　　but the way of the wicked will perish.

Foolishness of disbelief and misery of evildoers.　　　Psa. 14

For the director of music. Of David.

The fool*f* says in his heart,
　　"There is no God."
They are corrupt, their deeds are vile;
　　there is no one who does good.

The LORD looks down from heaven
　　on the sons of men
to see if there are any who understand,
　　any who seek God.
All have turned aside,
　　they have together become corrupt;
there is no one who does good,
　　not even one.

f The Hebrew words rendered *fool* in Psalms denote one who is morally deficient.

Will evildoers never learn—
    those who devour my people as men eat bread
    and who do not call on the LORD?
There they are, overwhelmed with dread,
    for God is present in the company of the righteous.
You evildoers frustrate the plans of the poor,
    but the LORD is their refuge.

Oh, that salvation for Israel would come out of Zion!
    When the LORD restores the fortunes of his people,
    let Jacob rejoice and Israel be glad!

Psa. 15   ## Characteristics of a righteous person.

A psalm of David.

LORD, who may dwell in your sanctuary?
    Who may live on your holy hill?

He whose walk is blameless
    and who does what is righteous,
who speaks the truth from his heart
    and has no slander on his tongue,
who does his neighbor no wrong
    and casts no slur on his fellowman,
who despises a vile man
    but honors those who fear the LORD,
who keeps his oath
    even when it hurts,
who lends his money without usury
    and does not accept a bribe against the innocent.

He who does these things
    will never be shaken.

Psa. 36   ## Depravity of the wicked and favor of the righteous.

For the director of music. Of David the servant of the LORD.

An oracle is within my heart
    concerning the sinfulness of the wicked:[g]
There is no fear of God
    before his eyes.
For in his own eyes he flatters himself
    too much to detect or hate his sin.
The words of his mouth are wicked and deceitful;
    he has ceased to be wise and to do good.
Even on his bed he plots evil;
    he commits himself to a sinful course
    and does not reject what is wrong.

Your love, O LORD, reaches to the heavens,
    your faithfulness to the skies.
Your righteousness is like the mighty mountains,
    your justice like the great deep.
O LORD, you preserve both man and beast.

gOr heart: / Sin proceeds from the wicked.

How priceless is your unfailing love!
Both high and low among men
find[h] refuge in the shadow of your wings.
They feast on the abundance of your house;
you give them drink from your river of delights.
For with you is the fountain of life;
in your light we see light.

Continue your love to those who know you,
your righteousness to the upright in heart.
May the foot of the proud not come against me,
nor the hand of the wicked drive me away.
See how the evildoers lie fallen—
thrown down, not able to rise!

The righteous poor have no cause to envy wicked.

Psa. 37

Of David.

Do[i] not fret because of evil men
or be envious of those who do wrong;
for like the grass they will soon wither,
like green plants they will soon die away.

Trust in the LORD and do good;
dwell in the land and enjoy safe pasture.
Delight yourself in the LORD
and he will give you the desires of your heart.

Commit your way to the LORD;
trust in him and he will do this;
He will make your righteousness shine like the dawn,
the justice of your cause like the noonday sun.

Be still before the LORD and wait patiently for him;
do not fret when men succeed in their ways,
when they carry out their wicked schemes.

Refrain from anger and turn from wrath;
do not fret—it leads only to evil.
For evil men will be cut off,
but those who hope in the LORD will inherit the land.

A little while, and the wicked will be no more;
though you look for them, they will not be found.
But the meek will inherit the land
and enjoy great peace.

The wicked plot against the righteous
and gnash their teeth at them;
but the Lord laughs at the wicked,
for he knows their day is coming.

The wicked draw the sword

[h] *Or love, O God! | Men find;* or *love! | Both heavenly beings and men | find* [i] This psalm is
an acrostic poem, the stanzas of which begin with the successive letters of the Hebrew
alphabet.

and bend the bow
to bring down the poor and needy,
  to slay those whose ways are upright.
But their swords will pierce their own hearts,
  and their bows will be broken.

Better the little that the righteous have
  than the wealth of many wicked;
for the power of the wicked will be broken,
  but the LORD upholds the righteous.

The days of the blameless are known to the LORD,
  and their inheritance will endure forever.
In times of disaster they will not wither;
  in days of famine they will enjoy plenty.

But the wicked will perish:
  The LORD's enemies will be like the beauty of the fields,
  they will vanish—vanish like smoke.

The wicked borrow and do not repay,
  but the righteous give generously;
those the LORD blesses will inherit the land,
  but those he curses will be cut off.

If the LORD delights in a man's way,
  he makes his steps firm;
though he stumble, he will not fall,
  for the LORD upholds him with his hand.

I was young and now I am old,
  yet I have never seen the righteous forsaken
  or their children begging bread.
They are always generous and lend freely;
  their children will be blessed.

Turn from evil and do good;
  then you will dwell in the land forever.
For the LORD loves the just
  and will not forsake his faithful ones.

They will be protected forever,
  but the offspring of the wicked will be cut off;
the righteous will inherit the land
  and dwell in it forever.

The mouth of the righteous man utters wisdom,
  and his tongue speaks what is just.
The law of his God is in his heart;
  his feet do not slip.

The wicked lie in wait for the righteous,
  seeking their very lives;
but the LORD will not leave them in their power
  or let them be condemned when brought to trial.

Wait for the LORD
        and keep his way.
He will exalt you to inherit the land;
        when the wicked are cut off, you will see it.

I have seen a wicked and ruthless man
        flourishing like a green tree in its native soil,
but he soon passed away and was no more;
        though I looked for him, he could not be found.

Consider the blameless, observe the upright;
        there is a future[j] for the man of peace.
But all sinners will be destroyed;
        the future[k] of the wicked will be cut off.

The salvation of the righteous comes from the LORD;
        he is their stronghold in time of trouble.
The LORD helps them and delivers them;
        he delivers them from the wicked and saves them,
        because they take refuge in him.

                                                                                      Psa. 39

Difficulty withholding outrage; reminder of life's brevity.

        For the director of music. For Jeduthun. A psalm of David.

I said, "I will watch my ways
        and keep my tongue from sin;
I will put a muzzle on my mouth
        as long as the wicked are in my presence."
But when I was silent and still,
        not even saying anything good,
        my anguish increased.
My heart grew hot within me,
        and as I meditated, the fire burned;
        then I spoke with my tongue:

"Show me, O LORD, my life's end
        and the number of my days;
        let me know how fleeting is my life.
You have made my days a mere handbreadth;
        the span of my years is as nothing before you.
        Each man's life is but a breath.   *Selah*
Man is a mere phantom as he goes to and fro:
        He bustles about, but only in vain;
        he heaps up wealth, not knowing who will get it.

"But now, Lord, what do I look for?
        My hope is in you.
Save me from all my transgressions;
        do not make me the scorn of fools.
I was silent; I would not open my mouth,
        for you are the one who has done this.
Remove your scourge from me;
        I am overcome by the blow of your hand.

---

[j]*Or there will be posterity*   [k]*Or posterity*

You rebuke and discipline men for their sin;
    you consume their wealth like a moth—
    each man is but a breath.   *Selah*

"Hear my prayer, O LORD,
    listen to my cry for help;
    be not deaf to my weeping.
For I dwell with you as an alien,
    a stranger, as all my fathers were.
Look away from me, that I may rejoice again
    before I depart and am no more."

Psa. 40

Recognition of true religion in righteous living.

For the director of music. Of David. A psalm.

I waited patiently for the LORD;
    he turned to me and heard my cry.
He lifted me out of the slimy pit,
    out of the mud and mire;
he set my feet on a rock
    and gave me a firm place to stand.
He put a new song in my mouth,
    a hymn of praise to our God.
Many will see and fear
    and put their trust in the LORD.

Blessed is the man
    who makes the LORD his trust,
who does not look to the proud,
    to those who turn aside to false gods.[l]
Many, O LORD my God,
    are the wonders you have done.
The things you planned for us
    no one can recount to you;
were I to speak and tell of them,
    they would be too many to declare.

Sacrifice and offering you did not desire,
    but my ears you have pierced[m][n];
burnt offerings and sin offerings
    you did not require.
Then I said, "Here I am, I have come—
    it is written about me in the scroll.[o]
I desire to do your will, O my God;
    your law is within my heart."

I proclaim righteousness in the great assembly;
    I do not seal my lips,
    as you know, O LORD.
I do not hide your righteousness in my heart;
    I speak of your faithfulness and salvation.
I do not conceal your love and your truth
    from the great assembly.

[l]Or *to falsehood*   [m]Hebrew; Septuagint *but a body you have prepared for me* (see also
Symmachus and Theodotion)   [n]Or *opened*   [o]Or *come / with the scroll written for me*

Do not withhold your mercy from me, O LORD;
    may your love and your truth always protect me.
For troubles without number surround me;
    my sins have overtaken me, and I cannot see.
They are more than the hairs of my head,
    and my heart fails within me.

Be pleased, O LORD, to save me;
    O LORD, come quickly to help me.
May all who seek to take my life
    be put to shame and confusion;
may all who desire my ruin
    be turned back in disgrace.
May those who say to me, "Aha! Aha!"
    be appalled at their own shame.
But may all who seek you
    rejoice and be glad in you;
may those who love your salvation always say,
    "The LORD be exalted!"

Yet I am poor and needy;
    may the Lord think of me.
You are my help and my deliverer;
    O my God, do not delay.

Spiritual insight better than wealth robbed by death.   Psa. 49

    For the director of music. Of the Sons of Korah. A psalm.

Hear this, all you peoples;
    listen, all who live in this world,
both low and high,
    rich and poor alike:
My mouth will speak words of wisdom;
    the utterance from my heart will give understanding.
I will turn my ear to a proverb;
    with the harp I will expound my riddle:

Why should I fear when evil days come,
    when wicked deceivers surround me—
those who trust in their wealth
    and boast of their great riches?
No man can redeem the life of another
    or give to God a ransom for him—
the ransom for a life is costly,
    no payment is ever enough—
that he should live on forever
    and not see decay.

For all can see that wise men die;
    the foolish and the senseless alike perish
    and leave their wealth to others.
Their tombs will remain their houses*p* forever,
    their dwellings for endless generations,

*p*Septuagint and Syriac; Hebrew *In their thoughts their houses will remain*

though they had^q named lands after themselves.

But man, despite his riches, does not endure;
    he is^r like the beasts that perish.

This is the fate of those who trust in themselves,
    and of their followers, who approve their sayings.   *Selah*
Like sheep they are destined for the grave,^s
    and death will feed on them.
The upright will rule over them in the morning;
    their forms will decay in the grave,^t
    far from their princely mansions.
But God will redeem my life^u from the grave;
    he will surely take me to himself.   *Selah*

Do not be overawed when a man grows rich,
    when the splendor of his house increases;
for he will take nothing with him when he dies,
    his splendor will not descend with him.
Though while he lived he counted himself blessed—
    and men praise you when you prosper—
he will join the generation of his fathers,
    who will never see the light ⌊of life⌋.

A man who has riches without understanding
    is like the beasts that perish.

Psa. 50   **True significance of sacrificing; jeopardy of wicked.**

A psalm of Asaph.

The Mighty One, God, the LORD,
    speaks and summons the earth
    from the rising of the sun to the place where it sets.
From Zion, perfect in beauty,
    God shines forth.
Our God comes and will not be silent;
    a fire devours before him,
    and around him a tempest rages.
He summons the heavens above,
    and the earth, that he may judge his people:
"Gather to me my consecrated ones,
    who made a covenant with me by sacrifice."
And the heavens proclaim his righteousness,
    for God himself is judge.   *Selah*

"Hear, O my people, and I will speak,
    O Israel, and I will testify against you:
    I am God, your God.
I do not rebuke you for your sacrifices
    or your burnt offerings, which are ever before me.
I have no need of a bull from your stall
    or of goats from your pens,

---

^qOr / *for they have*   ^rHebrew; Septuagint and Syriac read verse 12 the same as verse 20.
^sHebrew *Sheol*; also in verse 15   ^tHebrew *Sheol*   ^uOr *soul*

for every animal of the forest is mine,
  and the cattle on a thousand hills.
I know every bird in the mountains,
  and the creatures of the field are mine.
If I were hungry I would not tell you,
  for the world is mine, and all that is in it.
Do I eat the flesh of bulls
  or drink the blood of goats?
Sacrifice thank offerings to God,
  fulfill your vows to the Most High,
and call upon me in the day of trouble;
  I will deliver you, and you will honor me."

But to the wicked, God says:

"What right have you to recite my laws
  or take my covenant on your lips?
You hate my instruction
  and cast my words behind you.
When you see a thief, you join with him;
  you throw in your lot with adulterers.
You use your mouth for evil
  and harness your tongue to deceit.
You speak continually against your brother
  and slander your own mother's son.
These things you have done and I kept silent;
  you thought I was altogether[v] like you.
But I will rebuke you
  and accuse you to your face.

"Consider this, you who forget God,
  or I will tear you to pieces, with none to rescue:
He who sacrifices thank offerings honors me,
  and he prepares the way
so that I may show him[w] the salvation of God."

Folly of riches compared with blessings of righteous.   Psa. 73

A psalm of Asaph.

Surely God is good to Israel,
  to those who are pure in heart.

But as for me, my feet had almost slipped;
  I had nearly lost my foothold.
For I envied the arrogant
  when I saw the prosperity of the wicked.

They have no struggles;
  their bodies are healthy and strong.[x]
They are free from the burdens common to man;
  they are not plagued by human ills.
Therefore pride is their necklace;

[v]Or thought the 'I AM' was   [w]Or and to him who considers his way / I will show   [x]With
a different word division of the Hebrew; Masoretic Text struggles at their death; / their
bodies are healthy

they clothe themselves with violence.
From their callous hearts comes iniquity[y];
    the evil conceits of their minds know no limits.
They scoff, and speak with malice;
    in their arrogance they threaten oppression.
Their mouths lay claim to heaven,
    and their tongues take possession of the earth.
Therefore their people turn to them
    and drink up waters in abundance.[z]
They say, "How can God know?
    Does the Most High have knowledge?"

This is what the wicked are like—
    always carefree, they increase in wealth.

Surely in vain have I kept my heart pure;
    in vain have I washed my hands in innocence.
All day long I have been plagued;
    I have been punished every morning.

If I had said, "I will speak thus,"
    I would have betrayed your children.
When I tried to understand all this,
    it was oppressive to me
till I entered the sanctuary of God;
    then I understood their final destiny.

Surely you place them on slippery ground;
    you cast them down to ruin.
How suddenly are they destroyed,
    completely swept away by terrors!
As a dream when one awakes,
    so when you arise, O Lord,
    you will despise them as fantasies.

When my heart was grieved
    and my spirit embittered,
I was senseless and ignorant;
    I was a brute beast before you.

Yet I am always with you;
    you hold me by my right hand.
You guide me with your counsel,
    and afterward you will take me into glory.
Whom have I in heaven but you?
    And earth has nothing I desire besides you.
My flesh and my heart may fail,
    but God is the strength of my heart
    and my portion forever.

Those who are far from you will perish;
    you destroy all who are unfaithful to you.

[y]Syriac (see also Septuagint); Hebrew *Their eyes bulge with fat*   [z]The meaning of the Hebrew for this verse is uncertain.

But as for me, it is good to be near God.
I have made the Sovereign LORD my refuge;
I will tell of all your deeds.

God's wrath against evil to be greatly feared.

Psa. 76

For the director of music. With stringed instruments. A psalm of Asaph. A song.

In Judah God is known;
his name is great in Israel.
His tent is in Salem,
his dwelling place in Zion.
There he broke the flashing arrows,
the shields and the swords, the weapons of war.   *Selah*

You are resplendent with light,
more majestic than mountains rich with game.
Valiant men lie plundered,
they sleep their last sleep;
not one of the warriors
can lift his hands.
At your rebuke, O God of Jacob,
both horse and chariot lie still.
You alone are to be feared.
Who can stand before you when you are angry?
From heaven you pronounced judgment,
and the land feared and was quiet—
when you, O God, rose up to judge,
to save all the afflicted of the land.   *Selah*
Surely your wrath against men brings you praise,
and the survivors of your wrath are restrained.[a]

Make vows to the LORD your God and fulfill them;
let all the neighboring lands
bring gifts to the One to be feared.
He breaks the spirit of rulers;
he is feared by the kings of the earth.

Though all are "gods," the wicked will nevertheless die.

Psa. 82

A psalm of Asaph.

God presides in the great assembly;
he gives judgment among the "gods":

"How long will you[b] defend the unjust
and show partiality to the wicked?   *Selah*
Defend the cause of the weak and fatherless;
maintain the rights of the poor and oppressed.
Rescue the weak and needy;
deliver them from the hand of the wicked.

---

[a]Or *Surely the wrath of men brings you praise, / and with the remainder of wrath you arm yourself*   [b]The Hebrew is plural.

"They know nothing, they understand nothing.
　　They walk about in darkness;
　　all the foundations of the earth are shaken.
"I said, 'You are "gods";
　　you are all sons of the Most High.'
But you will die like mere men;
　　you will fall like every other ruler."

Rise up, O God, judge the earth,
　　for all the nations are your inheritance.

Psa. 84　**Superiority of the house of God over dwellings of the wicked.**

For the director of music. According to *gittith*.[c] Of the Sons of Korah. A psalm.

How lovely is your dwelling place,
　　O LORD Almighty!
My soul yearns, even faints,
　　for the courts of the LORD;
my heart and my flesh cry out
　　for the living God.

Even the sparrow has found a home,
　　and the swallow a nest for herself,
　　where she may have her young—
a place near your altar,
　　O LORD Almighty, my King and my God.
Blessed are those who dwell in your house;
　　they are ever praising you.   *Selah*

Blessed are those whose strength is in you,
　　who have set their hearts on pilgrimage.
As they pass through the Valley of Baca,
　　they make it a place of springs;
　　the autumn rains also cover it with pools.[d]
They go from strength to strength,
　　till each appears before God in Zion.

Hear my prayer, O LORD God Almighty;
　　listen to me, O God of Jacob.   *Selah*
Look upon our shield,[e] O God;
　　look with favor on your anointed one.

Better is one day in your courts
　　than a thousand elsewhere;
I would rather be a doorkeeper in the house of my God
　　than dwell in the tents of the wicked.
For the LORD God is a sun and shield;
　　the LORD bestows favor and honor;
no good thing does he withhold
　　from those whose walk is blameless.

O LORD Almighty,
　　blessed is the man who trusts in you.

---

[c]Title: Probably a musical term　　[d]Or *blessings*　　[e]Or *sovereign*

Importance of remembering life's brevity.

A prayer of Moses the man of God.

Lord, you have been our dwelling place
    throughout all generations.
Before the mountains were born
    or you brought forth the earth and the world,
    from everlasting to everlasting you are God.

You turn men back to dust,
    saying, "Return to dust, O sons of men."
For a thousand years in your sight
    are like a day that has just gone by,
    or like a watch in the night.
You sweep men away in the sleep of death;
    they are like the new grass of the morning—
though in the morning it springs up new,
    by evening it is dry and withered.

We are consumed by your anger
    and terrified by your indignation.
You have set our iniquities before you,
    our secret sins in the light of your presence.
All our days pass away under your wrath;
    we finish our years with a moan.
The length of our days is seventy years—
    or eighty, if we have the strength;
yet their span*f* is but trouble and sorrow,
    for they quickly pass, and we fly away.

Who knows the power of your anger?
    For your wrath is as great as the fear that is due you.
Teach us to number our days aright,
    that we may gain a heart of wisdom.

Relent, O LORD! How long will it be?
    Have compassion on your servants.
Satisfy us in the morning with your unfailing love,
    that we may sing for joy and be glad all our days.
Make us glad for as many days as you have afflicted us,
    for as many years as we have seen trouble.
May your deeds be shown to your servants,
    your splendor to their children.

May the favor*g* of the Lord our God rest upon us;
    establish the work of our hands for us—
    yes, establish the work of our hands.

Only the righteous will truly flourish.

A psalm. A song. For the Sabbath day.

It is good to praise the LORD
    and make music to your name, O Most High,
to proclaim your love in the morning

f Or yet the best of them   *g Or beauty*

and your faithfulness at night,
to the music of the ten-stringed lyre
and the melody of the harp.

For you make me glad by your deeds, O LORD;
I sing for joy at the works of your hands.
How great are your works, O LORD,
how profound your thoughts!
The senseless man does not know,
fools do not understand,
that though the wicked spring up like grass
and all evildoers flourish,
they will be forever destroyed.

But you, O LORD, are exalted forever.

For surely your enemies, O LORD,
surely your enemies will perish;
all evildoers will be scattered.
You have exalted my horn[h] like that of a wild ox;
fine oils have been poured upon me.
My eyes have seen the defeat of my adversaries;
my ears have heard the rout of my wicked foes.

The righteous will flourish like a palm tree,
they will grow like a cedar of Lebanon;
planted in the house of the LORD,
they will flourish in the courts of our God.
They will still bear fruit in old age,
they will stay fresh and green,
proclaiming, "The LORD is upright;
he is my Rock, and there is no wickedness in him."

Psa. 112 **Benefits accruing to a righteous person.**

Praise[i] the LORD.[j]

Blessed is the man who fears the LORD,
who finds great delight in his commands.

His children will be mighty in the land;
the generation of the upright will be blessed.
Wealth and riches are in his house,
and his righteousness endures forever.
Even in darkness light dawns for the upright,
for the gracious and compassionate and righteous man.[k]
Good will come to him who is generous and lends freely,
who conducts his affairs with justice.
Surely he will never be shaken;
a righteous man will be remembered forever.
He will have no fear of bad news;
his heart is steadfast, trusting in the LORD.

[h]*Horn* here symbolizes strength.   [i]This psalm is an acrostic poem, the verses of which
begin with the successive letters of the Hebrew alphabet.   [j]Hebrew *Hallelu Yah*
[k]Or / for ⌊the LORD⌋ *is gracious and compassionate and righteous*

His heart is secure, he will have no fear;
    in the end he will look in triumph on his foes.
He has scattered abroad his gifts to the poor,
    his righteousness endures forever;
    his horn[1] will be lifted high in honor.

The wicked man will see and be vexed,
    he will gnash his teeth and waste away;
    the longings of the wicked will come to nothing.

Idolaters have no source of trust as do believers.   Psa. 115

Not to us, O LORD, not to us
    but to your name be the glory,
    because of your love and faithfulness.

Why do the nations say,
    "Where is their God?"
Our God is in heaven;
    he does whatever pleases him.
But their idols are silver and gold,
    made by the hands of men.
They have mouths, but cannot speak,
    eyes, but they cannot see;
they have ears, but cannot hear,
    noses, but they cannot smell;
they have hands, but cannot feel,
    feet, but they cannot walk;
    nor can they utter a sound with their throats.
Those who make them will be like them,
    and so will all who trust in them.

O house of Israel, trust in the LORD—
    he is their help and shield.
O house of Aaron, trust in the LORD—
    he is their help and shield.
You who fear him, trust in the LORD—
    he is their help and shield.

The LORD remembers us and will bless us:
    He will bless the house of Israel,
    he will bless the house of Aaron,
he will bless those who fear the LORD—
    small and great alike.

May the LORD make you increase,
    both you and your children.
May you be blessed by the LORD,
    the Maker of heaven and earth.

The highest heavens belong to the LORD,
    but the earth he has given to man.
It is not the dead who praise the LORD,
    those who go down to silence;

[1]*Horn* here symbolizes dignity.

it is we who extol the LORD,
both now and forevermore.

Praise the LORD.[m]

Psalms of Joy and Praise

*T*n the following group of 36 psalms there is unbounded praise for the
Lord of creation and the many wonders he has performed. There is
profound gratitude for man's own elevated glory and for the many
blessings bestowed upon him. There is exaltation of the King who rules over
nations and throughout all of nature. But most importantly, there is thanksgiving for the personal concern this loving God has for each individual and his
special needs.

Psa. 8   **Praise for man's glory and status in God's sight.**

For the director of music. According to *gittith*.[n] A psalm of David.

O LORD, our Lord,
how majestic is your name in all the earth!

You have set your glory
above the heavens.
From the lips of children and infants
you have ordained praise[o]
because of your enemies,
to silence the foe and the avenger.

When I consider your heavens,
the work of your fingers,
the moon and the stars,
which you have set in place,
what is man that you are mindful of him,
the son of man that you care for him?
You made him a little lower than the heavenly beings[p]
and crowned him with glory and honor.

You made him ruler over the works of your hands;
you put everything under his feet:
all flocks and herds,
and the beasts of the field,
the birds of the air,
and the fish of the sea,
all that swim the paths of the seas.

O LORD, our Lord,
how majestic is your name in all the earth!

---

[m] Hebrew *Hallelu Yah*
God
[n] Title: Probably a musical term
[o] Or *strength*
[p] Or *than*

Praise for God's judgment against wicked nations.

Psa. 9

For[q] the director of music. To the tune of, "The Death of the Son." A psalm of David.

I will praise you, O LORD, with all my heart;
  I will tell of all your wonders.
I will be glad and rejoice in you;
  I will sing praise to your name, O Most High.

My enemies turn back;
  they stumble and perish before you.
For you have upheld my right and my cause;
  you have sat on your throne, judging righteously.
You have rebuked the nations and destroyed the wicked;
  you have blotted out their name for ever and ever.
Endless ruin has overtaken the enemy,
  you have uprooted their cities;
  even the memory of them has perished.

The LORD reigns forever;
  he has established his throne for judgment.
He will judge the world in righteousness;
  he will govern the peoples with justice.
The LORD is a refuge for the oppressed,
  a stronghold in times of trouble.
Those who know your name will trust in you,
  for you, LORD, have never forsaken those who seek you.

Sing praises to the LORD, enthroned in Zion;
  proclaim among the nations what he has done.
For he who avenges blood remembers;
  he does not ignore the cry of the afflicted.

O LORD, see how my enemies persecute me!
  Have mercy and lift me up from the gates of death,
that I may declare your praises
  in the gates of the Daughter of Zion
  and there rejoice in your salvation.
The nations have fallen into the pit they have dug;
  their feet are caught in the net they have hidden.
The LORD is known by his justice;
  the wicked are ensnared by the work of their hands.
                                                    Higgaion.[r] *Selah*

The wicked return to the grave,[s]
  all the nations that forget God.
But the needy will not always be forgotten,
  nor the hope of the afflicted ever perish.

Arise, O LORD, let not man triumph;
  let the nations be judged in your presence.
Strike them with terror, O LORD;
  let the nations know they are but men.   *Selah*

[q]Psalms 9 and 10 may have been originally a single acrostic poem, the stanzas of which
begin with the successive letters of the Hebrew alphabet. In the Septuagint they
constitute one psalm.   [r]Or *Meditation*; possibly a musical notation   [s]Hebrew *Sheol*

Psa. 16   **Praise for joy and security of the righteous.**

A *miktam*[t] of David.

Keep me safe, O God,
    for in you I take refuge.

I said to the LORD, "You are my Lord;
    apart from you I have no good thing."
As for the saints who are in the land,
    they are the glorious ones in whom is all my delight.[u]
The sorrows of those will increase
    who run after other gods.
I will not pour out their libations of blood
    or take up their names on my lips.

LORD, you have assigned me my portion and my cup;
    you have made my lot secure.
The boundary lines have fallen for me in pleasant places;
    surely I have a delightful inheritance.

I will praise the LORD, who counsels me;
    even at night my heart instructs me.
I have set the LORD always before me.
    Because he is at my right hand,
    I will not be shaken.

Therefore my heart is glad and my tongue rejoices;
    my body also will rest secure,
because you will not abandon me to the grave,[v]
    nor will you let your Holy One[w] see decay.
You have made[x] known to me the path of life;
    you will fill me with joy in your presence,
    with eternal pleasures at your right hand.

Psa. 19   **Praise for God's creation and for his laws.**

For the director of music. A psalm of David.

The heavens declare the glory of God;
    the skies proclaim the work of his hands.
Day after day they pour forth speech;
    night after night they display knowledge.
There is no speech or language
    where their voice is not heard.[y]
Their voice[z] goes out into all the earth,
    their words to the ends of the world.

In the heavens he has pitched a tent for the sun,
    which is like a bridegroom coming forth from his
        pavilion,
    like a champion rejoicing to run his course.
It rises at one end of the heavens

---

[t]Title: Probably a literary or musical term   [u]Or *As for the pagan priests who are in the
land / and the nobles in whom all delight, I said:*   [v]Hebrew *Sheol*   [w]Or *your faithful one*
[x]Or *You will make*   [y]Or *They have no speech, there are no words; / no sound is heard from
them*   [z]Septuagint, Jerome and Syriac; Hebrew *line*

and makes its circuit to the other;
  nothing is hidden from its heat.

The law of the LORD is perfect,
  reviving the soul.
The statutes of the LORD are trustworthy,
  making wise the simple.
The precepts of the LORD are right,
  giving joy to the heart.
The commands of the LORD are radiant,
  giving light to the eyes.
The fear of the LORD is pure,
  enduring forever.
The ordinances of the LORD are sure
  and altogether righteous.
They are more precious than gold,
  than much pure gold;
they are sweeter than honey,
  than honey from the comb.
By them is your servant warned;
  in keeping them there is great reward.

Who can discern his errors?
  Forgive my hidden faults.
Keep your servant also from willful sins;
  may they not rule over me.
Then will I be blameless,
  innocent of great transgression.

May the words of my mouth and the meditation of my
      heart
  be pleasing in your sight,
  O LORD, my Rock and my Redeemer.

Praise for the king's blessings and reminder of God's wrath.   Psa. 21

For the director of music. A psalm of David.

O LORD, the king rejoices in your strength.
  How great is his joy in the victories you give!
You have granted him the desire of his heart
  and have not withheld the request of his lips.   *Selah*
You welcomed him with rich blessings
  and placed a crown of pure gold on his head.
He asked you for life, and you gave it to him—
  length of days, for ever and ever.
Through the victories you gave, his glory is great;
  you have bestowed on him splendor and majesty.
Surely you have granted him eternal blessings
  and made him glad with the joy of your presence.
For the king trusts in the LORD;
  through the unfailing love of the Most High
  he will not be shaken.

Your hand will lay hold on all your enemies;
  your right hand will seize your foes.

At the time of your appearing
you will make them like a fiery furnace.
In his wrath the LORD will swallow them up,
and his fire will consume them.
You will destroy their descendants from the earth,
their posterity from mankind.
Though they plot evil against you
and devise wicked schemes, they cannot succeed;
for you will make them turn their backs
when you aim at them with drawn bow.

Be exalted, O LORD, in your strength;
we will sing and praise your might.

Psa. 24

The earth belongs to the King of glory.

Of David. A psalm.

The earth is the LORD's, and everything in it,
the world, and all who live in it;
for he founded it upon the seas
and established it upon the waters.

Who may ascend the hill of the LORD?
Who may stand in his holy place?
He who has clean hands and a pure heart,
who does not lift up his soul to an idol
or swear by what is false.*a*
He will receive blessing from the LORD
and vindication from God his Savior.
Such is the generation of those who seek him,
who seek your face, O God of Jacob.*b*   *Selah*

Lift up your heads, O you gates;
be lifted up, you ancient doors,
that the King of glory may come in.
Who is this King of glory?
The LORD strong and mighty,
the LORD mighty in battle.
Lift up your heads, O you gates;
lift them up, you ancient doors,
that the King of glory may come in.
Who is he, this King of glory?
The LORD Almighty—
he is the King of glory.   *Selah*

Psa. 29

God's power and glory as seen in the lightning.

A psalm of David.

Ascribe to the LORD, O mighty ones,
ascribe to the LORD glory and strength.
Ascribe to the LORD the glory due his name;
worship the LORD in the splendor of his*c* holiness.

---

*a*Or *swear falsely*   *b*Two Hebrew manuscripts and Syriac (see also Septuagint); most
Hebrew manuscripts *face, Jacob*   *c*Or LORD *with the splendor of*

The voice of the LORD is over the waters;
 the God of glory thunders,
 the LORD thunders over the mighty waters.
The voice of the LORD is powerful;
 the voice of the LORD is majestic.
The voice of the LORD breaks the cedars;
 the LORD breaks in pieces the cedars of Lebanon.
He makes Lebanon skip like a calf,
 Sirion[d] like a young wild ox.
The voice of the LORD strikes
 with flashes of lightning.
The voice of the LORD shakes the desert;
 the LORD shakes the Desert of Kadesh.
The voice of the LORD twists the oaks[e]
 and strips the forests bare.
And in his temple all cry, "Glory!"

The LORD sits[f] enthroned over the flood;
 the LORD is enthroned as King forever.
The LORD gives strength to his people;
 the LORD blesses his people with peace.

Sing praises to God for his power, purpose, and love.

Psa. 33

Sing joyfully to the LORD, you righteous;
 it is fitting for the upright to praise him.
Praise the LORD with the harp;
 make music to him on the ten-stringed lyre.
Sing to him a new song;
 play skillfully, and shout for joy.

For the word of the LORD is right and true;
 he is faithful in all he does.
The LORD loves righteousness and justice;
 the earth is full of his unfailing love.

By the word of the LORD were the heavens made,
 their starry host by the breath of his mouth.
He gathers the waters of the sea into jars[g];
 he puts the deep into storehouses.
Let all the earth fear the LORD;
 let all the people of the world revere him.
For he spoke, and it came to be;
 he commanded, and it stood firm.
The LORD foils the plans of the nations;
 he thwarts the purposes of the peoples.
But the plans of the LORD stand firm forever,
 the purposes of his heart through all generations.

Blessed is the nation whose God is the LORD,
 the people he chose for his inheritance.
From heaven the LORD looks down

[d] That is, Mount Hermon   [e] Or LORD *makes the deer give birth*   [f] Or *sat*   [g] Or *sea as into a heap*

and sees all mankind;
from his dwelling place he watches
    all who live on earth—
he who forms the hearts of all,
    who considers everything they do.
No king is saved by the size of his army;
    no warrior escapes by his great strength.
A horse is a vain hope for deliverance;
    despite all its great strength it cannot save.
But the eyes of the LORD are on those who fear him,
    on those whose hope is in his unfailing love,
to deliver them from death
    and keep them alive in famine.

We wait in hope for the LORD;
    he is our help and our shield.
In him our hearts rejoice,
    for we trust in his holy name.
May your unfailing love rest upon us, O LORD,
    even as we put our hope in you.

Psa. 65   **Praise for God's forgiveness, power, and physical blessings.**

For the director of music. A psalm of David. A song.

Praise awaits[h] you, O God, in Zion;
    to you our vows will be fulfilled.
O you who hear prayer,
    to you all men will come.
When we were overwhelmed by sins,
    you forgave[i] our transgressions.
Blessed are those you choose
    and bring near to live in your courts!
We are filled with the good things of your house,
    of your holy temple.

You answer us with awesome deeds of righteousness,
    O God our Savior,
the hope of all the ends of the earth
    and of the farthest seas,
who formed the mountains by your power,
    having armed yourself with strength,
who stilled the roaring of the seas,
    the roaring of their waves,
    and the turmoil of the nations.
Those living far away fear your wonders;
    where morning dawns and evening fades
    you call forth songs of joy.

You care for the land and water it;
    you enrich it abundantly.
The streams of God are filled with water

---

[h]Or *befits;* the meaning of the Hebrew for this word is uncertain.   [i]Or *made atonement for*

to provide the people with grain,
for so you have ordained it.[j]
You drench its furrows
and level its ridges;
you soften it with showers
and bless its crops.
You crown the year with your bounty,
and your carts overflow with abundance.
The grasslands of the desert overflow;
the hills are clothed with gladness.
The meadows are covered with flocks
and the valleys are mantled with grain;
they shout for joy and sing.

Praise for God's deliverance from the oppression of sin.   Psa. 66

For the director of music. A song. A psalm.

Shout with joy to God, all the earth!
Sing the glory of his name;
make his praise glorious!
Say to God, "How awesome are your deeds!
So great is your power
that your enemies cringe before you.
All the earth bows down to you;
they sing praise to you,
they sing praise to your name."   *Selah*

Come and see what God has done,
how awesome his works in man's behalf!
He turned the sea into dry land,
they passed through the waters on foot—
come, let us rejoice in him.
He rules forever by his power,
his eyes watch the nations—
let not the rebellious rise up against him.   *Selah*

Praise our God, O peoples,
let the sound of his praise be heard;
he has preserved our lives
and kept our feet from slipping.
For you, O God, tested us;
you refined us like silver.
You brought us into prison
and laid burdens on our backs.
You let men ride over our heads;
we went through fire and water,
but you brought us to a place of abundance.

I will come to your temple with burnt offerings
and fulfill my vows to you—
vows my lips promised and my mouth spoke
when I was in trouble.

jOr for that is how you prepare the land

I will sacrifice fat animals to you
and an offering of rams;
I will offer bulls and goats.   *Selah*

Come and listen, all you who fear God;
let me tell you what he has done for me.
I cried out to him with my mouth;
his praise was on my tongue.
If I had cherished sin in my heart,
the Lord would not have listened;
but God has surely listened
and heard my voice in prayer.
Praise be to God,
who has not rejected my prayer
or withheld his love from me!

Psa. 67   **Praise and prayer for God's blessings.**

For the director of music. With stringed instruments. A psalm. A song.

May God be gracious to us and bless us
and make his face shine upon us,   *Selah*
that your ways may be known on earth,
your salvation among all nations.

May the peoples praise you, O God;
may all the peoples praise you.
May the nations be glad and sing for joy,
for you rule the peoples justly
and guide the nations of the earth.   *Selah*
May the peoples praise you, O God;
may all the peoples praise you.

Then the land will yield its harvest,
and God, our God, will bless us.
God will bless us,
and all the ends of the earth will fear him.

Psa. 68   **Praise for a God of power who cares about individual problems.**

For the director of music. Of David. A psalm. A song.

May God arise, may his enemies be scattered;
may his foes flee before him.
As smoke is blown away by the wind,
may you blow them away;
as wax melts before the fire,
may the wicked perish before God.
But may the righteous be glad
and rejoice before God;
may they be happy and joyful.

Sing to God, sing praise to his name,
extol him who rides on the clouds[k]—
his name is the LORD—
and rejoice before him.

---

[k]Or / *prepare the way for him who rides through the deserts*

A father to the fatherless, a defender of widows,
　　is God in his holy dwelling.
God sets the lonely in families,[1]
　　he leads forth the prisoners with singing;
　　but the rebellious live in a sun-scorched land.

When you went out before your people, O God,
　　when you marched through the wasteland,　　　　　*Selah*
the earth shook,
　　the heavens poured down rain,
before God, the One of Sinai,
　　before God, the God of Israel.
You gave abundant showers, O God;
　　you refreshed your weary inheritance.
Your people settled in it,
　　and from your bounty, O God, you provided for the
　　　　poor.

The Lord announced the word,
　　and great was the company of those who proclaimed it:
"Kings and armies flee in haste;
　　in the camps men divide the plunder.
Even while you sleep among the campfires,[m]
　　the wings of ⌐my⌐ dove are sheathed with silver,
　　its feathers with shining gold."
When the Almighty[n] scattered the kings in the land,
　　it was like snow fallen on Zalmon.

The mountains of Bashan are majestic mountains;
　　rugged are the mountains of Bashan.
Why gaze in envy, O rugged mountains,
　　at the mountain where God chooses to reign,
　　where the LORD himself will dwell forever?
The chariots of God are tens of thousands
　　and thousands of thousands;
　　the Lord ⌐has come⌐ from Sinai into his sanctuary.
When you ascended on high,
　　you led captives in your train;
　　you received gifts from men,
even from[o] the rebellious—
　　that you,[p] O LORD God, might dwell there.

Praise be to the Lord, to God our Savior,
　　who daily bears our burdens.　　　　　　　　　*Selah*
Our God is a God who saves;
　　from the Sovereign LORD comes escape from death.

Surely God will crush the heads of his enemies,
　　the hairy crowns of those who go on in their sins.
The Lord says, "I will bring them from Bashan;
　　I will bring them from the depths of the sea,

---

[1]Or *the desolate in a homeland*　　[m]Or *saddlebags*　　[n]Hebrew *Shaddai*　　[o]Or *gifts for*
men, / even　　[p]Or *they*

that you may plunge your feet in the blood of your foes,
while the tongues of your dogs have their share."

Your procession has come into view, O God,
the procession of my God and King into the sanctuary.
In front are the singers, after them the musicians;
with them are the maidens playing tambourines.
Praise God in the great congregation;
praise the LORD in the assembly of Israel.
There is the little tribe of Benjamin, leading them,
there the great throng of Judah's princes,
and there the princes of Zebulun and of Naphtali.

Summon your power, O God[q];
show us your strength, O God, as you have done before.
Because of your temple at Jerusalem
kings will bring you gifts.
Rebuke the beast among the reeds,
the herd of bulls among the calves of the nations.
Humbled, may it bring bars of silver.
Scatter the nations who delight in war.
Envoys will come from Egypt;
Cush[r] will submit herself to God.

Sing to God, O kingdoms of the earth,
sing praise to the Lord,   *Selah*
to him who rides the ancient skies above,
who thunders with mighty voice.
Proclaim the power of God,
whose majesty is over Israel,
whose power is in the skies.
You are awesome, O God, in your sanctuary;
the God of Israel gives power and strength to his people.

Praise be to God!

Psa. 75 **Praise to the great Judge of the earth.**

For the director of music. ⌊To the tune of⌋ "Do Not Destroy." A psalm of Asaph. A song.

We give thanks to you, O God,
we give thanks, for your Name is near;
men tell of your wonderful deeds.

You say, "I choose the appointed time;
it is I who judge uprightly.
When the earth and all its people quake,
it is I who hold its pillars firm.   *Selah*
To the arrogant I say, 'Boast no more,'
and to the wicked, 'Do not lift up your horns.
Do not lift your horns against heaven;
do not speak with outstretched neck.'"

No one from the east or the west

---

[q]Many Hebrew manuscripts, Septuagint and Syriac; most Hebrew manuscripts *Your God has summoned power for you*   [r]That is, the upper Nile region

or from the desert can exalt a man.
But it is God who judges:
He brings one down, he exalts another.
In the hand of the LORD is a cup
full of foaming wine mixed with spices;
he pours it out, and all the wicked of the earth
drink it down to its very dregs.

As for me, I will declare this forever;
I will sing praise to the God of Jacob.
I will cut off the horns of all the wicked,
but the horns of the righteous will be lifted up.

Praise for God's majesty and holiness.　　Psa. 93

The LORD reigns, he is robed in majesty;
the LORD is robed in majesty
and is armed with strength.
The world is firmly established;
it cannot be moved.
Your throne was established long ago;
you are from all eternity.

The seas have lifted up, O LORD,
the seas have lifted up their voice;
the seas have lifted up their pounding waves.
Mightier than the thunder of the great waters,
mightier than the breakers of the sea—
the LORD on high is mighty.

Your statutes stand firm;
holiness adorns your house
for endless days, O LORD.

Praise for God's discipline of man and nations.　　Psa. 94

O LORD, the God who avenges,
O God who avenges, shine forth.
Rise up, O Judge of the earth;
pay back to the proud what they deserve.
How long will the wicked, O LORD,
how long will the wicked be jubilant?

They pour out arrogant words;
all the evildoers are full of boasting.
They crush your people, O LORD;
they oppress your inheritance.
They slay the widow and the alien;
they murder the fatherless.
They say, "The LORD does not see;
the God of Jacob pays no heed."

Take heed, you senseless ones among the people;
you fools, when will you become wise?
Does he who implanted the ear not hear?
Does he who formed the eye not see?
Does he who disciplines nations not punish?

Does he who teaches man lack knowledge?
The LORD knows the thoughts of man;
   he knows that they are futile.

Blessed is the man you discipline, O LORD,
   the man you teach from your law;
you grant him relief from days of trouble,
   till a pit is dug for the wicked.
For the LORD will not reject his people;
   he will never forsake his inheritance.
Judgment will again be founded on righteousness,
   and all the upright in heart will follow it.

Who will rise up for me against the wicked?
   Who will take a stand for me against evildoers?
Unless the LORD had given me help,
   I would soon have dwelt in the silence of death.
When I said, "My foot is slipping,"
   your love, O LORD, supported me.
When anxiety was great within me,
   your consolation brought joy to my soul.

Can a corrupt throne be allied with you—
   one that brings on misery by its decrees?
They band together against the righteous
   and condemn the innocent to death.
But the LORD has become my fortress,
   and my God the rock in whom I take refuge.
He will repay them for their sins
   and destroy them for their wickedness;
   the LORD our God will destroy them.

Psa. 97   **Rejoicing because of God's righteousness and justice.**

The LORD reigns, let the earth be glad;
   let the distant shores rejoice.

Clouds and thick darkness surround him;
   righteousness and justice are the foundation of his
      throne.
Fire goes before him
   and consumes his foes on every side.
His lightning lights up the world;
   the earth sees and trembles.
The mountains melt like wax before the LORD,
   before the Lord of all the earth.
The heavens proclaim his righteousness,
   and all the peoples see his glory.

All who worship images are put to shame,
   those who boast in idols—
   worship him, all you gods!

Zion hears and rejoices
   and the villages of Judah are glad
   because of your judgments, O LORD.

For you, O Lord, are the Most High over all the earth;
   you are exalted far above all gods.

Let those who love the Lord hate evil,
   for he guards the lives of his faithful ones
   and delivers them from the hand of the wicked.
Light is shed upon the righteous
   and joy on the upright in heart.
Rejoice in the Lord, you who are righteous,
   and praise his holy name.

A song of praise for the salvation of the Lord.   Psa. 98

A psalm.

Sing to the Lord a new song,
   for he has done marvelous things;
his right hand and his holy arm
   have worked salvation for him.
The Lord has made his salvation known
   and revealed his righteousness to the nations.
He has remembered his love
   and his faithfulness to the house of Israel;
all the ends of the earth have seen
   the salvation of our God.

Shout for joy to the Lord, all the earth,
   burst into jubilant song with music;
make music to the Lord with the harp,
   with the harp and the sound of singing,
with trumpets and the blast of the ram's horn—
   shout for joy before the Lord, the King.

Let the sea resound, and everything in it,
   the world, and all who live in it.
Let the rivers clap their hands,
   let the mountains sing together for joy;
let them sing before the Lord,
   for he comes to judge the earth.
He will judge the world in righteousness
   and the peoples with equity.

Exaltation of the God who is holy and just.   Psa. 99

The Lord reigns,
   let the nations tremble;
he sits enthroned between the cherubim,
   let the earth shake.
Great is the Lord in Zion;
   he is exalted over all the nations.
Let them praise your great and awesome name—
   he is holy.

The King is mighty, he loves justice—
   you have established equity;
in Jacob you have done
   what is just and right.

Exalt the LORD our God
and worship at his footstool;
he is holy.

Moses and Aaron were among his priests,
Samuel was among those who called on his name;
they called on the LORD
and he answered them.
He spoke to them from the pillar of cloud;
they kept his statutes and the decrees he gave them.

O LORD our God,
you answered them;
you were to Israel[s] a forgiving God,
though you punished their misdeeds.[t]
Exalt the LORD our God
and worship at his holy mountain,
for the LORD our God is holy.

Psa. 100 **Joy of being children of a loving and faithful God.**

A psalm. For giving thanks.

Shout for joy to the LORD, all the earth.
Worship the LORD with gladness;
come before him with joyful songs.
Know that the LORD is God.
It is he who made us, and we are his[u];
we are his people, the sheep of his pasture.

Enter his gates with thanksgiving
and his courts with praise;
give thanks to him and praise his name.
For the LORD is good and his love endures forever;
his faithfulness continues through all generations.

Psa. 103 **Praise for a compassionate God.**

Of David.

Praise the LORD, O my soul;
all my inmost being, praise his holy name.
Praise the LORD, O my soul,
and forget not all his benefits—
who forgives all your sins
and heals all your diseases,
who redeems your life from the pit
and crowns you with love and compassion,
who satisfies your desires with good things
so that your youth is renewed like the eagle's.

The LORD works righteousness
and justice for all the oppressed.

He made known his ways to Moses,
his deeds to the people of Israel:

[s]Hebrew them [t]Or / an avenger of the wrongs done to them [u]Or and not we ourselves

The LORD is compassionate and gracious,
    slow to anger, abounding in love.
He will not always accuse,
    nor will he harbor his anger forever;
he does not treat us as our sins deserve
    or repay us according to our iniquities.
For as high as the heavens are above the earth,
    so great is his love for those who fear him;
as far as the east is from the west,
    so far has he removed our transgressions from us.
As a father has compassion on his children,
    so the LORD has compassion on those who fear him;
for he knows how we are formed,
    he remembers that we are dust.
As for man, his days are like grass,
    he flourishes like a flower of the field;
the wind blows over it and it is gone,
    and its place remembers it no more.
But from everlasting to everlasting
    the LORD's love is with those who fear him,
    and his righteousness with their children's children—
with those who keep his covenant
    and remember to obey his precepts.

The LORD has established his throne in heaven,
    and his kingdom rules over all.

Praise the LORD, you his angels,
    you mighty ones who do his bidding,
    who obey his word.
Praise the LORD, all his heavenly hosts,
    you his servants who do his will.
Praise the LORD, all his works
    everywhere in his dominion.

Praise the LORD, O my soul.

Praise for the wonders of God's creation.   Psa. 104

Praise the LORD, O my soul.

O LORD my God, you are very great;
    you are clothed with splendor and majesty.
He wraps himself in light as with a garment;
    he stretches out the heavens like a tent
    and lays the beams of his upper chambers on their
        waters.
He makes the clouds his chariot
    and rides on the wings of the wind.
He makes winds his messengers,[v]
    flames of fire his servants.

He set the earth on its foundations;

[v] Or *angels*

it can never be moved.
You covered it with the deep as with a garment;
    the waters stood above the mountains.
But at your rebuke the waters fled,
    at the sound of your thunder they took to flight;
they flowed over the mountains,
        they went down into the valleys,
        to the place you assigned for them.
You set a boundary they cannot cross;
    never again will they cover the earth.

He makes springs pour water into the ravines;
    it flows between the mountains.
They give water to all the beasts of the field;
    the wild donkeys quench their thirst.
The birds of the air nest by the waters;
    they sing among the branches.
He waters the mountains from his upper chambers;
    the earth is satisfied by the fruit of his work.
He makes grass grow for the cattle,
        and plants for man to cultivate—
        bringing forth food from the earth:
wine that gladdens the heart of man,
        oil to make his face shine,
        and bread that sustains his heart.
The trees of the LORD are well watered,
    the cedars of Lebanon that he planted.
There the birds make their nests;
    the stork has its home in the pine trees.
The high mountains belong to the wild goats;
    the crags are a refuge for the coneys.[w]

The moon marks off the seasons,
    and the sun knows when to go down.
You bring darkness, it becomes night,
    and all the beasts of the forest prowl.
The lions roar for their prey
    and seek their food from God.
The sun rises, and they steal away;
    they return and lie down in their dens.
Then man goes out to his work,
    to his labor until evening.

How many are your works, O LORD!
    In wisdom you made them all;
    the earth is full of your creatures.
There is the sea, vast and spacious,
        teeming with creatures beyond number—
        living things both large and small.
There the ships go to and fro,
    and the leviathan, which you formed to frolic there.

[w]That is, the hyrax or rock badger

These all look to you
  to give them their food at the proper time.
When you give it to them,
  they gather it up;
when you open your hand,
  they are satisfied with good things.
When you hide your face,
  they are terrified;
when you take away their breath,
  they die and return to the dust.
When you send your Spirit,
  they are created,
  and you renew the face of the earth.

May the glory of the LORD endure forever;
  may the LORD rejoice in his works—
he who looks at the earth, and it trembles,
  who touches the mountains, and they smoke.

I will sing to the LORD all my life;
  I will sing praise to my God as long as I live.
May my meditation be pleasing to him,
  as I rejoice in the LORD.
But may sinners vanish from the earth
  and the wicked be no more.

Praise the LORD, O my soul.

Praise the LORD.x

Praise for a Lord of heaven who is sensitive.   Psa. 113

Praise the LORD.y

Praise, O servants of the LORD,
  praise the name of the LORD.
Let the name of the LORD be praised,
  both now and forevermore.
From the rising of the sun to the place where it sets,
  the name of the LORD is to be praised.

The LORD is exalted over all the nations,
  his glory above the heavens.
Who is like the LORD our God,
  the One who sits enthroned on high,
who stoops down to look
  on the heavens and the earth?

He raises the poor from the dust
  and lifts the needy from the ash heap;
he seats them with princes,
  with the princes of their people.
He settles the barren woman in her home
  as a happy mother of children.

xHebrew Hallelu Yah; in the Septuagint this line stands at the beginning of Psalm 105.
yHebrew Hallelu Yah

Praise the LORD.

Psa. 114 **How God's wonders ought to bring trembling.**

When Israel came out of Egypt,
    the house of Jacob from a people of foreign tongue,
Judah became God's sanctuary,
    Israel his dominion.

The sea looked and fled,
    the Jordan turned back;
the mountains skipped like rams,
    the hills like lambs.

Why was it, O sea, that you fled,
    O Jordan, that you turned back,
you mountains, that you skipped like rams,
    you hills, like lambs?

Tremble, O earth, at the presence of the Lord,
    at the presence of the God of Jacob,
who turned the rock into a pool,
    the hard rock into springs of water.

Psa. 117 **Praise for God's love and faithfulness.**

Praise the LORD, all you nations;
    extol him, all you peoples.
For great is his love toward us,
    and the faithfulness of the LORD endures forever.

Praise the LORD.[z]

Psa. 119 **Praise for the insight and guidance of God's laws.**

א Aleph

Blessed[a] are they whose ways are blameless,
    who walk according to the law of the LORD.
Blessed are they who keep his statutes
    and seek him with all their heart.
They do nothing wrong;
    they walk in his ways.
You have laid down precepts
    that are to be fully obeyed.
Oh, that my ways were steadfast
    in obeying your decrees!
Then I would not be put to shame
    when I consider all your commands.
I will praise you with an upright heart
    as I learn your righteous laws.
I will obey your decrees;
    do not utterly forsake me.

[z] Hebrew *Hallelu Yah*   [a] This psalm is an acrostic poem; the verses of each stanza begin with the same letter of the Hebrew alphabet.

ב Beth

How can a young man keep his way pure?
    By living according to your word.
I seek you with all my heart;
    do not let me stray from your commands.
I have hidden your word in my heart
    that I might not sin against you.
Praise be to you, O LORD;
    teach me your decrees.
With my lips I recount
    all the laws that come from your mouth.
I rejoice in following your statutes
    as one rejoices in great riches.
I meditate on your precepts
    and consider your ways.
I delight in your decrees;
    I will not neglect your word.

ג Gimel

Do good to your servant, and I will live;
    I will obey your word.
Open my eyes that I may see
    wonderful things in your law.
I am a stranger on earth;
    do not hide your commands from me.
My soul is consumed with longing
    for your laws at all times.
You rebuke the arrogant, who are cursed
    and who stray from your commands.
Remove from me scorn and contempt,
    for I keep your statutes.
Though rulers sit together and slander me,
    your servant will meditate on your decrees.
Your statutes are my delight;
    they are my counselors.

ד Daleth

I am laid low in the dust;
    preserve my life according to your word.
I recounted my ways and you answered me;
    teach me your decrees.
Let me understand the teaching of your precepts;
    then I will meditate on your wonders.
My soul is weary with sorrow;
    strengthen me according to your word.
Keep me from deceitful ways;
    be gracious to me through your law.
I have chosen the way of truth;
    I have set my heart on your laws.
I hold fast to your statutes, O LORD;
    do not let me be put to shame.

I run in the path of your commands,
    for you have set my heart free.

ה   He

Teach me, O LORD, to follow your decrees;
    then I will keep them to the end.
Give me understanding, and I will keep your law
    and obey it with all my heart.
Direct me in the path of your commands,
    for there I find delight.
Turn my heart toward your statutes
    and not toward selfish gain.
Turn my eyes away from worthless things;
    preserve my life according to your word.[b]
Fulfill your promise to your servant,
    so that you may be feared.
Take away the disgrace I dread,
    for your laws are good.
How I long for your precepts!
    Preserve my life in your righteousness.

ו   Waw

May your unfailing love come to me, O LORD,
    your salvation according to your promise;
then I will answer the one who taunts me,
    for I trust in your word.
Do not snatch the word of truth from my mouth,
    for I have put my hope in your laws.
I will always obey your law,
    for ever and ever.
I will walk about in freedom,
    for I have sought out your precepts.
I will speak of your statutes before kings
    and will not be put to shame,
for I delight in your commands
    because I love them.
I lift up my hands to[c] your commands, which I love,
    and I meditate on your decrees.

ז   Zayin

Remember your word to your servant,
    for you have given me hope.
My comfort in my suffering is this:
    Your promise preserves my life.
The arrogant mock me without restraint,
    but I do not turn from your law.
I remember your ancient laws, O LORD,
    and I find comfort in them.
Indignation grips me because of the wicked,

[b]Two manuscripts of the Masoretic Text and Dead Sea Scrolls; most manuscripts of the
Masoretic Text *life in your way*   [c]Or *for*

who have forsaken your law.
Your decrees are the theme of my song
    wherever I lodge.
In the night I remember your name, O LORD,
    and I will keep your law.
This has been my practice:
    I obey your precepts.

ח Heth

You are my portion, O LORD;
    I have promised to obey your words.
I have sought your face with all my heart;
    be gracious to me according to your promise.
I have considered my ways
    and have turned my steps to your statutes.
I will hasten and not delay
    to obey your commands.
Though the wicked bind me with ropes,
    I will not forget your law.
At midnight I rise to give you thanks
    for your righteous laws.
I am a friend to all who fear you,
    to all who follow your precepts.
The earth is filled with your love, O LORD;
    teach me your decrees.

ט Teth

Do good to your servant
    according to your word, O LORD.
Teach me knowledge and good judgment,
    for I believe in your commands.
Before I was afflicted I went astray,
    but now I obey your word.
You are good, and what you do is good;
    teach me your decrees.
Though the arrogant have smeared me with lies,
    I keep your precepts with all my heart.
Their hearts are callous and unfeeling,
    but I delight in your law.
It was good for me to be afflicted
    so that I might learn your decrees.
The law from your mouth is more precious to me
    than thousands of pieces of silver and gold.

י Yodh

Your hands made me and formed me;
    give me understanding to learn your commands.
May those who fear you rejoice when they see me,
    for I have put my hope in your word.
I know, O LORD, that your laws are righteous,
    and in faithfulness you have afflicted me.
May your unfailing love be my comfort,

according to your promise to your servant.
Let your compassion come to me that I may live,
    for your law is my delight.
May the arrogant be put to shame for wronging me without
      cause;
    but I will meditate on your precepts.
May those who fear you turn to me,
    those who understand your statutes.
May my heart be blameless toward your decrees,
    that I may not be put to shame.

כ Kaph

My soul faints with longing for your salvation,
    but I have put my hope in your word.
My eyes fail, looking for your promise;
    I say, "When will you comfort me?"
Though I am like a wineskin in the smoke,
    I do not forget your decrees.
How long must your servant wait?
    When will you punish my persecutors?
The arrogant dig pitfalls for me,
    contrary to your law.
All your commands are trustworthy;
    help me, for men persecute me without cause.
They almost wiped me from the earth,
    but I have not forsaken your precepts.
Preserve my life according to your love,
    and I will obey the statutes of your mouth.

ל Lamedh

Your word, O LORD, is eternal;
    it stands firm in the heavens.
Your faithfulness continues through all generations;
    you established the earth, and it endures.
Your laws endure to this day,
    for all things serve you.
If your law had not been my delight,
    I would have perished in my affliction.
I will never forget your precepts,
    for by them you have preserved my life.
Save me, for I am yours;
    I have sought out your precepts.
The wicked are waiting to destroy me,
    but I will ponder your statutes.
To all perfection I see a limit;
    but your commands are boundless.

מ Mem

Oh, how I love your law!
    I meditate on it all day long.

Your commands make me wiser than my enemies,
    for they are ever with me.
I have more insight than all my teachers,
    for I meditate on your statutes.
I have more understanding than the elders,
    for I obey your precepts.
I have kept my feet from every evil path
    so that I might obey your word.
I have not departed from your laws,
    for you yourself have taught me.
How sweet are your words to my taste,
    sweeter than honey to my mouth!
I gain understanding from your precepts;
    therefore I hate every wrong path.

‏נ‎ Nun

Your word is a lamp to my feet
    and a light for my path.
I have taken an oath and confirmed it,
    that I will follow your righteous laws.
I have suffered much;
    preserve my life, O LORD, according to your word.
Accept, O LORD, the willing praise of my mouth,
    and teach me your laws.
Though I constantly take my life in my hands,
    I will not forget your law.
The wicked have set a snare for me,
    but I have not strayed from your precepts.
Your statutes are my heritage forever;
    they are the joy of my heart.
My heart is set on keeping your decrees
    to the very end.

‏ס‎ Samekh

I hate double-minded men,
    but I love your law.
You are my refuge and my shield;
    I have put my hope in your word.
Away from me, you evildoers,
    that I may keep the commands of my God!
Sustain me according to your promise, and I will live;
    do not let my hopes be dashed.
Uphold me, and I will be delivered;
    I will always have regard for your decrees.
You reject all who stray from your decrees,
    for their deceitfulness is in vain.
All the wicked of the earth you discard like dross;
    therefore I love your statutes.
My flesh trembles in fear of you;
    I stand in awe of your laws.

ע   Ayin

I have done what is righteous and just;
    do not leave me to my oppressors.
Ensure your servant's well-being;
    let not the arrogant oppress me.
My eyes fail, looking for your salvation,
    looking for your righteous promise.
Deal with your servant according to your love
    and teach me your decrees.
I am your servant; give me discernment
    that I may understand your statutes.
It is time for you to act, O LORD;
    your law is being broken.
Because I love your commands
    more than gold, more than pure gold,
and because I consider all your precepts right,
    I hate every wrong path.

פ   Pe

Your statutes are wonderful;
    therefore I obey them.
The unfolding of your words gives light;
    it gives understanding to the simple.
I open my mouth and pant,
    longing for your commands.
Turn to me and have mercy on me,
    as you always do to those who love your name.
Direct my footsteps according to your word;
    let no sin rule over me.
Redeem me from the oppression of men,
    that I may obey your precepts.
Make your face shine upon your servant
    and teach me your decrees.
Streams of tears flow from my eyes,
    for your law is not obeyed.

צ   Tsadhe

Righteous are you, O LORD,
    and your laws are right.
The statutes you have laid down are righteous;
    they are fully trustworthy.
My zeal wears me out,
    for my enemies ignore your words.
Your promises have been thoroughly tested,
    and your servant loves them.
Though I am lowly and despised,
    I do not forget your precepts.
Your righteousness is everlasting
    and your law is true.
Trouble and distress have come upon me,
    but your commands are my delight.

Your statutes are forever right;
  give me understanding that I may live.

ק Qoph

I call with all my heart; answer me, O LORD,
  and I will obey your decrees.
I call out to you; save me
  and I will keep your statutes.
I rise before dawn and cry for help;
  I have put my hope in your word.
My eyes stay open through the watches of the night,
  that I may meditate on your promises.
Hear my voice in accordance with your love;
  preserve my life, O LORD, according to your laws.
Those who devise wicked schemes are near,
  but they are far from your law.
Yet you are near, O LORD,
  and all your commands are true.
Long ago I learned from your statutes
  that you established them to last forever.

ר Resh

Look upon my suffering and deliver me,
  for I have not forgotten your law.
Defend my cause and redeem me;
  preserve my life according to your promise.
Salvation is far from the wicked,
  for they do not seek out your decrees.
Your compassion is great, O LORD;
  preserve my life according to your laws.
Many are the foes who persecute me,
  but I have not turned from your statutes.
I look on the faithless with loathing,
  for they do not obey your word.
See how I love your precepts;
  preserve my life, O LORD, according to your love.
All your words are true;
  all your righteous laws are eternal.

שׁ Sin and Shin

Rulers persecute me without cause,
  but my heart trembles at your word.
I rejoice in your promise
  like one who finds great spoil.
I hate and abhor falsehood
  but I love your law.
Seven times a day I praise you
  for your righteous laws.
Great peace have they who love your law,
  and nothing can make them stumble.
I wait for your salvation, O LORD,
  and I follow your commands.

I obey your statutes,
    for I love them greatly.
I obey your precepts and your statutes,
    for all my ways are known to you.

ת   Taw

May my cry come before you, O Lord;
    give me understanding according to your word.
May my supplication come before you;
    deliver me according to your promise.
May my lips overflow with praise,
    for you teach me your decrees.
May my tongue sing of your word,
    for all your commands are righteous.
May your hand be ready to help me,
    for I have chosen your precepts.
I long for your salvation, O Lord,
    and your law is my delight.
Let me live that I may praise you,
    and may your laws sustain me.
I have strayed like a lost sheep.
    Seek your servant,
    for I have not forgotten your commands.

Psa. 122

Praise for Jerusalem and the house of the Lord.

A song of ascents. Of David.

I rejoiced with those who said to me,
    "Let us go to the house of the Lord."
Our feet are standing
    in your gates, O Jerusalem.

Jerusalem is built like a city
    that is closely compacted together.
That is where the tribes go up,
    the tribes of the Lord,
to praise the name of the Lord
    according to the statute given to Israel.
There the thrones for judgment stand,
    the thrones of the house of David.

Pray for the peace of Jerusalem:
    "May those who love you be secure.
May there be peace within your walls
    and security within your citadels."
For the sake of my brothers and friends,
    I will say, "Peace be within you."
For the sake of the house of the Lord our God,
    I will seek your prosperity.

Psa. 124

Praise for escape from enemies.

A song of ascents. Of David.

If the Lord had not been on our side—
    let Israel say—

if the LORD had not been on our side
    when men attacked us,
when their anger flared against us,
    they would have swallowed us alive;
the flood would have engulfed us,
    the torrent would have swept over us,
the raging waters
    would have swept us away.

Praise be to the LORD,
    who has not let us be torn by their teeth.
We have escaped like a bird
    out of the fowler's snare;
the snare has been broken,
    and we have escaped.
Our help is in the name of the LORD,
    the Maker of heaven and earth.

Joy of brothers living harmoniously.   Psa. 133

A song of ascents. Of David.

How good and pleasant it is
    when brothers live together in unity!
It is like precious oil poured on the head,
    running down on the beard,
running down on Aaron's beard,
    down upon the collar of his robes.
It is as if the dew of Hermon
    were falling on Mount Zion.
For there the LORD bestows his blessing,
    even life forevermore.

A call for temple servants to praise God.   Psa. 134

A song of ascents.

Praise the LORD, all you servants of the LORD
    who minister by night in the house of the LORD.
Lift up your hands in the sanctuary
    and praise the LORD.

May the LORD, the Maker of heaven and earth,
    bless you from Zion.

The many things for which temple servants can give praise.   Psa. 135

Praise the LORD.[d]

Praise the name of the LORD;
    praise him, you servants of the LORD,
you who minister in the house of the LORD,
    in the courts of the house of our God.

Praise the LORD, for the LORD is good;
    sing praise to his name, for that is pleasant.
For the LORD has chosen Jacob to be his own,
    Israel to be his treasured possession.

[d]Hebrew *Hallelu Yah*

I know that the LORD is great,
  that our Lord is greater than all gods.
The LORD does whatever pleases him,
  in the heavens and on the earth,
  in the seas and all their depths.
He makes clouds rise from the ends of the earth;
  he sends lightning with the rain
  and brings out the wind from his storehouses.

He struck down the firstborn of Egypt,
  the firstborn of men and animals.
He sent his signs and wonders into your midst, O Egypt,
  against Pharaoh and all his servants.
He struck down many nations
  and killed mighty kings—
Sihon king of the Amorites,
    Og king of Bashan
    and all the kings of Canaan—
and he gave their land as an inheritance,
    an inheritance to his people Israel.

Your name, O LORD, endures forever,
  your renown, O LORD, through all generations.
For the LORD will vindicate his people
  and have compassion on his servants.

The idols of the nations are silver and gold,
  made by the hands of men.
They have mouths, but cannot speak,
  eyes, but they cannot see;
they have ears, but cannot hear,
  nor is there breath in their mouths.
Those who make them will be like them,
  and so will all who trust in them.

O house of Israel, praise the LORD;
  O house of Aaron, praise the LORD;
O house of Levi, praise the LORD;
  you who fear him, praise the LORD.
Praise be to the LORD from Zion,
  to him who dwells in Jerusalem.

Praise the LORD.

Psa. 136 **Special poem of thanksgiving for all things.**

Give thanks to the LORD, for he is good.

His love endures forever.

Give thanks to the God of gods.

His love endures forever.

Give thanks to the Lord of lords:

His love endures forever.

to him who alone does great wonders,

His love endures forever.

who by his understanding made the heavens,
His love endures forever.

who spread out the earth upon the waters,
His love endures forever.

who made the great lights—
His love endures forever.

the sun to govern the day,
His love endures forever.

the moon and stars to govern the night;
His love endures forever.

to him who struck down the firstborn of Egypt
His love endures forever.

and brought Israel out from among them
His love endures forever.

with a mighty hand and outstretched arm;
His love endures forever.

to him who divided the Red Sea*ᵉ* asunder
His love endures forever.

and brought Israel through the midst of it,
His love endures forever.

but swept Pharaoh and his army into the Red Sea;
His love endures forever.

to him who led his people through the desert,
His love endures forever.

who struck down great kings,
His love endures forever.

and killed mighty kings—
His love endures forever.

Sihon king of the Amorites
His love endures forever.

and Og king of Bashan—
His love endures forever.

and gave their land as an inheritance,
His love endures forever.

an inheritance to his servant Israel;
His love endures forever.

to the One who remembered us in our low estate
His love endures forever.

and freed us from our enemies,
His love endures forever.

and who gives food to every creature.
His love endures forever.

Give thanks to the God of heaven.
His love endures forever.

ᵉHebrew *Yam Suph;* that is, Sea of Reeds

Psa. 138 **Praise to the faithful God.**

Of David.

I will praise you, O Lᴏʀᴅ, with all my heart;
before the "gods" I will sing your praise.
I will bow down toward your holy temple
and will praise your name
for your love and your faithfulness,
for you have exalted above all things
your name and your word.
When I called, you answered me;
you made me bold and stouthearted.

May all the kings of the earth praise you, O Lᴏʀᴅ,
when they hear the words of your mouth.
May they sing of the ways of the Lᴏʀᴅ,
for the glory of the Lᴏʀᴅ is great.

Though the Lᴏʀᴅ is on high, he looks upon the lowly,
but the proud he knows from afar.
Though I walk in the midst of trouble,
you preserve my life;
you stretch out your hand against the anger of my foes,
with your right hand you save me.
The Lᴏʀᴅ will fulfill ˌhis purposeˌ for me;
your love, O Lᴏʀᴅ, endures forever—
do not abandon the works of your hands.

Psa. 139 **The wonder of God's total familiarity with each life.**

For the director of music. Of David. A psalm.

O Lᴏʀᴅ, you have searched me
and you know me.
You know when I sit and when I rise;
you perceive my thoughts from afar.
You discern my going out and my lying down;
you are familiar with all my ways.
Before a word is on my tongue
you know it completely, O Lᴏʀᴅ.

You hem me in—behind and before;
you have laid your hand upon me.
Such knowledge is too wonderful for me,
too lofty for me to attain.

Where can I go from your Spirit?
Where can I flee from your presence?
If I go up to the heavens, you are there;
if I make my bed in the depths,ᶠ you are there.
If I rise on the wings of the dawn,
if I settle on the far side of the sea,
even there your hand will guide me,
your right hand will hold me fast.

ᶠHebrew *Sheol*

If I say, "Surely the darkness will hide me
    and the light become night around me,"
even the darkness will not be dark to you;
    the night will shine like the day,
    for darkness is as light to you.

For you created my inmost being;
    you knit me together in my mother's womb.
I praise you because I am fearfully and wonderfully made;
    your works are wonderful,
    I know that full well.
My frame was not hidden from you
    when I was made in the secret place.
When I was woven together in the depths of the earth,
    your eyes saw my unformed body.
All the days ordained for me
    were written in your book
    before one of them came to be.

How precious to[g] me are your thoughts, O God!
    How vast is the sum of them!
Were I to count them,
    they would outnumber the grains of sand.
When I awake,
    I am still with you.

If only you would slay the wicked, O God!
    Away from me, you bloodthirsty men!
They speak of you with evil intent;
    your adversaries misuse your name.
Do I not hate those who hate you, O Lord,
    and abhor those who rise up against you?
I have nothing but hatred for them;
    I count them my enemies.

Search me, O God, and know my heart;
    test me and know my anxious thoughts.
See if there is any offensive way in me,
    and lead me in the way everlasting.

Praise to a faithful, loving, and righteous God.   Psa. 145

A psalm of praise. Of David.

I[h] will exalt you, my God the King;
    I will praise your name for ever and ever.
Every day I will praise you
    and extol your name for ever and ever.

Great is the Lord and most worthy of praise;
    his greatness no one can fathom.
One generation will commend your works to another;
    they will tell of your mighty acts.

[g]Or concerning   [h]This psalm is an acrostic poem, the verses of which (including verse 13b) begin with the successive letters of the Hebrew alphabet.

They will speak of the glorious splendor of your majesty,
    and I will meditate on your wonderful works.[i]
They will tell of the power of your awesome works,
    and I will proclaim your great deeds.
They will celebrate your abundant goodness
    and joyfully sing of your righteousness.

The LORD is gracious and compassionate,
    slow to anger and rich in love.
The LORD is good to all;
    he has compassion on all he has made.
All you have made will praise you, O LORD;
    your saints will extol you.
They will tell of the glory of your kingdom
    and speak of your might,
so that all men may know of your mighty acts
    and the glorious splendor of your kingdom.
Your kingdom is an everlasting kingdom,
    and your dominion endures through all generations.

The LORD is faithful to all his promises
    and loving toward all he has made.[j]
The LORD upholds all those who fall
    and lifts up all who are bowed down.
The eyes of all look to you,
    and you give them their food at the proper time.
You open your hand
    and satisfy the desires of every living thing.

The LORD is righteous in all his ways
    and loving toward all he has made.
The LORD is near to all who call on him,
    to all who call on him in truth.
He fulfills the desires of those who fear him;
    he hears their cry and saves them.
The LORD watches over all who love him,
    but all the wicked he will destroy.

My mouth will speak in praise of the LORD.
    Let every creature praise his holy name
    for ever and ever.

Psa. 148   **All creatures praise the God of creation.**

Praise the LORD.[k]

Praise the LORD from the heavens,
    praise him in the heights above.
Praise him, all his angels,
    praise him, all his heavenly hosts.
Praise him, sun and moon,

---

[i]Dead Sea Scrolls and Syriac (see also Septuagint); Masoretic Text *On the glorious splendor of your majesty / and on your wonderful works I will meditate*   [j]One manuscript of the Masoretic Text, Dead Sea Scrolls and Syriac (see also Septuagint); most manuscripts of the Masoretic Text do not have the last two lines of verse 13.   [k]Hebrew *Hallelu Yah*

praise him, all you shining stars.
Praise him, you highest heavens
    and you waters above the skies.
Let them praise the name of the LORD,
    for he commanded and they were created.
He set them in place for ever and ever;
    he gave a decree that will never pass away.

Praise the LORD from the earth,
    you great sea creatures and all ocean depths,
lightning and hail, snow and clouds,
    stormy winds that do his bidding,
you mountains and all hills,
    fruit trees and all cedars,
wild animals and all cattle,
    small creatures and flying birds,
kings of the earth and all nations,
    you princes and all rulers on earth,
young men and maidens,
    old men and children.

Let them praise the name of the LORD,
    for his name alone is exalted;
    his splendor is above the earth and the heavens.
He has raised up for his people a horn,[l]
    the praise of all his saints,
    of Israel, the people close to his heart.

Praise the LORD.

A call for all things to praise the Lord.

Psa. 150

Praise the LORD.[m]

Praise God in his sanctuary;
    praise him in his mighty heavens.
Praise him for his acts of power;
    praise him for his surpassing greatness.
Praise him with the sounding of the trumpet,
    praise him with the harp and lyre,
praise him with tambourine and dancing,
    praise him with the strings and flute,
praise him with the clash of cymbals,
    praise him with resounding cymbals.

Let everything that has breath praise the LORD.

Praise the LORD.

◇
---

[l]Horn here symbolizes strong one, that is, king.   [m]Hebrew Hallelu Yah

Psalms Expressing a Variety of Sentiments

The next 16 psalms contain a variety of sentiments from the heart of a believer to his God. In this grouping is an indication of the complexity of human nature and the acknowledgment of a God who answers every need.

Psa. 4   **Mercy demands obedience.**

For the director of music. With stringed instruments. A psalm of David.

Answer me when I call to you,
  O my righteous God.
Give me relief from my distress;
  be merciful to me and hear my prayer.

How long, O men, will you turn my glory into shame[n]?
  How long will you love delusions and seek false gods[o]?
                                                                    Selah

Know that the LORD has set apart the godly for himself;
  the LORD will hear when I call to him.

In your anger do not sin;
  when you are on your beds,
  search your hearts and be silent.
                                                                    Selah
Offer right sacrifices
  and trust in the LORD.

Many are asking, "Who can show us any good?"
  Let the light of your face shine upon us, O LORD.
You have filled my heart with greater joy
  than when their grain and new wine abound.
I will lie down and sleep in peace,
  for you alone, O LORD,
  make me dwell in safety.

Psa. 12   **Misuse of the gift of speech.**

For the director of music. According to *sheminith*.[p] A psalm of David.

Help, LORD, for the godly are no more;
  the faithful have vanished from among men.
Everyone lies to his neighbor;
  their flattering lips speak with deception.

May the LORD cut off all flattering lips
  and every boastful tongue
that says, "We will triumph with our tongues;
  we own our lips[q]—who is our master?"

"Because of the oppression of the weak
  and the groaning of the needy,
I will now arise," says the LORD.
  "I will protect them from those who malign them."
And the words of the LORD are flawless,

[n]*Or you dishonor my Glorious One*   [o]*Or seek lies*   [p]Title: Probably a musical term
[q]*Or / our lips are our plowshares*

like silver refined in a furnace of clay,
purified seven times.

O LORD, you will keep us safe
and protect us from such people forever.
The wicked freely strut about
when what is vile is honored among men.

Prayer for others' welfare, and expression of trust. Psa. 20

For the director of music. A psalm of David.

May the LORD answer you when you are in distress;
may the name of the God of Jacob protect you.
May he send you help from the sanctuary
and grant you support from Zion.
May he remember all your sacrifices
and accept your burnt offerings. *Selah*
May he give you the desire of your heart
and make all your plans succeed.
We will shout for joy when you are victorious
and will lift up our banners in the name of our God.
May the LORD grant all your requests.

Now I know that the LORD saves his anointed;
he answers him from his holy heaven
with the saving power of his right hand.
Some trust in chariots and some in horses,
but we trust in the name of the LORD our God.
They are brought to their knees and fall,
but we rise up and stand firm.

O LORD, save the king!
Answer[r] us when we call!

Expression of trust in God and his instruction. Psa. 25

Of David.

To[s] you, O LORD, I lift up my soul;
in you I trust, O my God.
Do not let me be put to shame,
nor let my enemies triumph over me.
No one whose hope is in you
will ever be put to shame,
but they will be put to shame
who are treacherous without excuse.

Show me your ways, O LORD,
teach me your paths;
guide me in your truth and teach me,
for you are God my Savior,
and my hope is in you all day long.
Remember, O LORD, your great mercy and love,
for they are from of old.

[r]Or *save! | O King, answer*   [s]This psalm is an acrostic poem, the verses of which begin
with the successive letters of the Hebrew alphabet.

Remember not the sins of my youth
   and my rebellious ways;
according to your love remember me,
   for you are good, O LORD.

Good and upright is the LORD;
   therefore he instructs sinners in his ways.
He guides the humble in what is right
   and teaches them his way.
All the ways of the LORD are loving and faithful
   for those who keep the demands of his covenant.
For the sake of your name, O LORD,
   forgive my iniquity, though it is great.
Who, then, is the man that fears the LORD?
   He will instruct him in the way chosen for him.
He will spend his days in prosperity,
   and his descendants will inherit the land.
The LORD confides in those who fear him;
   he makes his covenant known to them.
My eyes are ever on the LORD,
   for only he will release my feet from the snare.

Turn to me and be gracious to me,
   for I am lonely and afflicted.
The troubles of my heart have multiplied;
   free me from my anguish.
Look upon my affliction and my distress
   and take away all my sins.
See how my enemies have increased
   and how fiercely they hate me!
Guard my life and rescue me;
   let me not be put to shame,
   for I take refuge in you.
May integrity and uprightness protect me,
   because my hope is in you.

Redeem Israel, O God,
   from all their troubles!

Psa. 32   **Blessedness of confession and forgiveness of sins.**

Of David. A *maskil.*[t]

Blessed is he
   whose transgressions are forgiven,
   whose sins are covered.
Blessed is the man
   whose sin the LORD does not count against him
   and in whose spirit is no deceit.

When I kept silent,
   my bones wasted away
   through my groaning all day long.
For day and night

[t]Title: Probably a literary or musical term

your hand was heavy upon me;
my strength was sapped
    as in the heat of summer.   *Selah*
Then I acknowledged my sin to you
    and did not cover up my iniquity.
I said, "I will confess
    my transgressions to the LORD"—
and you forgave
    the guilt of my sin.   *Selah*

Therefore let everyone who is godly pray to you
    while you may be found;
surely when the mighty waters rise,
    they will not reach him.
You are my hiding place;
    you will protect me from trouble
    and surround me with songs of deliverance.   *Selah*

I will instruct you and teach you in the way you should go;
    I will counsel you and watch over you.
Do not be like the horse or the mule,
    which have no understanding
but must be controlled by bit and bridle
    or they will not come to you.
Many are the woes of the wicked,
    but the LORD's unfailing love
    surrounds the man who trusts in him.

Rejoice in the LORD and be glad, you righteous;
    sing, all you who are upright in heart!

Agonizing confession of sin.   Psa. 38

A psalm of David. A petition.

O LORD, do not rebuke me in your anger
    or discipline me in your wrath.
For your arrows have pierced me,
    and your hand has come down upon me.
Because of your wrath there is no health in my body;
    my bones have no soundness because of my sin.
My guilt has overwhelmed me
    like a burden too heavy to bear.

My wounds fester and are loathsome
    because of my sinful folly.
I am bowed down and brought very low;
    all day long I go about mourning.
My back is filled with searing pain;
    there is no health in my body.
I am feeble and utterly crushed;
    I groan in anguish of heart.

All my longings lie open before you, O Lord;
    my sighing is not hidden from you.
My heart pounds, my strength fails me;

even the light has gone from my eyes.
My friends and companions avoid me because of my
wounds;
my neighbors stay far away.
Those who seek my life set their traps,
those who would harm me talk of my ruin;
all day long they plot deception.

I am like a deaf man, who cannot hear,
like a mute, who cannot open his mouth;
I have become like a man who does not hear,
whose mouth can offer no reply.
I wait for you, O LORD;
you will answer, O Lord my God.
For I said, "Do not let them gloat
or exalt themselves over me when my foot slips."

For I am about to fall,
and my pain is ever with me.
I confess my iniquity;
I am troubled by my sin.
Many are those who are my vigorous enemies;
those who hate me without reason are numerous.
Those who repay my good with evil
slander me when I pursue what is good.

O LORD, do not forsake me;
be not far from me, O my God.
Come quickly to help me,
O Lord my Savior.

Psa. 42   **Importance of hoping in God when one is depressed.**

For[u] the director of music. A *maskil*[v] of the Sons of Korah.

As the deer pants for streams of water,
so my soul pants for you, O God.
My soul thirsts for God, for the living God.
When can I go and meet with God?
My tears have been my food
day and night,
while men say to me all day long,
"Where is your God?"
These things I remember
as I pour out my soul:
how I used to go with the multitude,
leading the procession to the house of God,
with shouts of joy and thanksgiving
among the festive throng.

Why are you downcast, O my soul?
Why so disturbed within me?
Put your hope in God,

---

[u] In many Hebrew manuscripts Psalms 42 and 43 constitute one psalm.   [v] Title: Probably a literary or musical term

> for I will yet praise him,
>   my Savior and my God.

My[w] soul is downcast within me;
  therefore I will remember you
from the land of the Jordan,
  the heights of Hermon—from Mount Mizar.
Deep calls to deep
  in the roar of your waterfalls;
all your waves and breakers
  have swept over me.

By day the LORD directs his love,
  at night his song is with me—
  a prayer to the God of my life.

I say to God my Rock,
  "Why have you forgotten me?
Why must I go about mourning,
  oppressed by the enemy?"
My bones suffer mortal agony
  as my foes taunt me,
saying to me all day long,
  "Where is your God?"

Why are you downcast, O my soul?
  Why so disturbed within me?
Put your hope in God,
  for I will yet praise him,
  my Savior and my God.

Universality of sin and its consequences.   Psa. 53

For the director of music. According to *mahalath*.[x] A *maskil*[y] of David.

The fool says in his heart,
  "There is no God."
They are corrupt, and their ways are vile;
  there is no one who does good.

God looks down from heaven
  on the sons of men
to see if there are any who understand,
  any who seek God.
Everyone has turned away,
  they have together become corrupt;
there is no one who does good,
  not even one.

Will the evildoers never learn—
  those who devour my people as men eat bread
  and who do not call on God?
There they were, overwhelmed with dread,

[w]A few Hebrew manuscripts, Septuagint and Syriac; most Hebrew manuscripts *praise him for his saving help.* / [6]*O my God, my*   [x]Title: Probably a musical term   [y]Title: Probably a literary or musical term

where there was nothing to dread.
God scattered the bones of those who attacked you;
  you put them to shame, for God despised them.

Oh, that salvation for Israel would come out of Zion!
  When God restores the fortunes of his people,
  let Jacob rejoice and Israel be glad!

Psa. 58   ## Outrage against leaders who promote injustice.

For the director of music. ⌞To the tune of⌟ "Do Not Destroy." Of David. A *miktam*.[z]

Do you rulers indeed speak justly?
  Do you judge uprightly among men?
No, in your heart you devise injustice,
  and your hands mete out violence on the earth.
Even from birth the wicked go astray;
  from the womb they are wayward and speak lies.
Their venom is like the venom of a snake,
  like that of a cobra that has stopped its ears,
that will not heed the tune of the charmer,
  however skillful the enchanter may be.

Break the teeth in their mouths, O God;
  tear out, O LORD, the fangs of the lions!
Let them vanish like water that flows away;
  when they draw the bow, let their arrows be blunted.
Like a slug melting away as it moves along,
  like a stillborn child, may they not see the sun.

Before your pots can feel ⌞the heat of⌟ the thorns—
  whether they be green or dry—the wicked will be swept
    away.[a]
The righteous will be glad when they are avenged,
  when they bathe their feet in the blood of the wicked.
Then men will say,
  "Surely the righteous still are rewarded;
  surely there is a God who judges the earth."

Psa. 81   ## The continual stubbornness of Israel.

For the director of music. According to *gittith*.[b] Of Asaph.

Sing for joy to God our strength;
  shout aloud to the God of Jacob!
Begin the music, strike the tambourine,
  play the melodious harp and lyre.

Sound the ram's horn at the New Moon,
  and when the moon is full, on the day of our Feast;
this is a decree for Israel,
  an ordinance of the God of Jacob.
He established it as a statute for Joseph
  when he went out against Egypt,

---

[z] Title: Probably a literary or musical term   [a] The meaning of the Hebrew for this verse is
uncertain.   [b] Title: Probably a musical term

where we heard a language we did not understand.[c]

He says, "I removed the burden from their shoulders;
 their hands were set free from the basket.
In your distress you called and I rescued you,
 I answered you out of a thundercloud;
 I tested you at the waters of Meribah.   *Selah*

"Hear, O my people, and I will warn you—
 if you would but listen to me, O Israel!
You shall have no foreign god among you;
 you shall not bow down to an alien god.
I am the LORD your God,
 who brought you up out of Egypt.
 Open wide your mouth and I will fill it.

"But my people would not listen to me;
 Israel would not submit to me.
So I gave them over to their stubborn hearts
 to follow their own devices.

"If my people would but listen to me,
 if Israel would follow my ways,
how quickly would I subdue their enemies
 and turn my hand against their foes!
Those who hate the LORD would cringe before him,
 and their punishment would last forever.
But you would be fed with the finest of wheat;
 with honey from the rock I would satisfy you."

Expression of commitment to righteous living.   Psa. 101

Of David. A psalm.

I will sing of your love and justice;
 to you, O LORD, I will sing praise.
I will be careful to lead a blameless life—
 when will you come to me?

I will walk in my house
 with blameless heart.
I will set before my eyes
 no vile thing.

The deeds of faithless men I hate;
 they will not cling to me.
Men of perverse heart shall be far from me;
 I will have nothing to do with evil.

Whoever slanders his neighbor in secret,
 him will I put to silence;
whoever has haughty eyes and a proud heart,
 him will I not endure.

My eyes will be on the faithful in the land,
 that they may dwell with me;

[c] Or / *and we heard a voice we had not known*

he whose walk is blameless
will minister to me.
No one who practices deceit
will dwell in my house;
no one who speaks falsely
will stand in my presence.

Every morning I will put to silence
all the wicked in the land;
I will cut off every evildoer
from the city of the LORD.

Psa. 111   **Fearing a loving God is the beginning of understanding.**

Praise[d] the LORD.[e]

I will extol the LORD with all my heart
in the council of the upright and in the assembly.

Great are the works of the LORD;
they are pondered by all who delight in them.
Glorious and majestic are his deeds,
and his righteousness endures forever.
He has caused his wonders to be remembered;
the LORD is gracious and compassionate.
He provides food for those who fear him;
he remembers his covenant forever.
He has shown his people the power of his works,
giving them the lands of other nations.
The works of his hands are faithful and just;
all his precepts are trustworthy.
They are steadfast for ever and ever,
done in faithfulness and uprightness.
He provided redemption for his people;
he ordained his covenant forever—
holy and awesome is his name.

The fear of the LORD is the beginning of wisdom;
all who follow his precepts have good understanding.
To him belongs eternal praise.

Psa. 130   **Only hope of redemption is in God's forgiveness.**

A song of ascents.

Out of the depths I cry to you, O LORD;
O Lord, hear my voice.
Let your ears be attentive
to my cry for mercy.

If you, O LORD, kept a record of sins,
O Lord, who could stand?
But with you there is forgiveness;
therefore you are feared.

[d]This psalm is an acrostic poem, the lines of which begin with the successive letters of
the Hebrew alphabet.   [e]Hebrew *Hallelu Yah*

I wait for the LORD, my soul waits,
    and in his word I put my hope.
My soul waits for the Lord
    more than watchmen wait for the morning,
    more than watchmen wait for the morning.

O Israel, put your hope in the LORD,
    for with the LORD is unfailing love
    and with him is full redemption.
He himself will redeem Israel
    from all their sins.

Expression of quiet humility.   Psa. 131

A song of ascents. Of David.

My heart is not proud, O LORD,
    my eyes are not haughty;
I do not concern myself with great matters
    or things too wonderful for me.
But I have stilled and quieted my soul;
    like a weaned child with its mother,
    like a weaned child is my soul within me.

O Israel, put your hope in the LORD
    both now and forevermore.

Prayer for wise use of one's speech.   Psa. 141

A psalm of David.

O LORD, I call to you; come quickly to me.
    Hear my voice when I call to you.
May my prayer be set before you like incense;
    may the lifting up of my hands be like the evening
        sacrifice.

Set a guard over my mouth, O LORD;
    keep watch over the door of my lips.
Let not my heart be drawn to what is evil,
    to take part in wicked deeds
with men who are evildoers;
    let me not eat of their delicacies.

Let a righteous man[f] strike me—it is a kindness;
    let him rebuke me—it is oil on my head.
    My head will not refuse it.

Yet my prayer is ever against the deeds of evildoers;
    their rulers will be thrown down from the cliffs,
    and the wicked will learn that my words were well
        spoken.
⌊They will say,⌋ "As one plows and breaks up the earth,
    so our bones have been scattered at the mouth of the
        grave.[g]"

But my eyes are fixed on you, O Sovereign LORD;

---

f Or *Let the Righteous One*   g Hebrew *Sheol*

in you I take refuge—do not give me over to death.
Keep me from the snares they have laid for me,
    from the traps set by evildoers.
Let the wicked fall into their own nets,
    while I pass by in safety.

Psa. 146   **The God who cares is the God to trust.**

Praise the LORD.[h]

Praise the LORD, O my soul.
    I will praise the LORD all my life;
    I will sing praise to my God as long as I live.

Do not put your trust in princes,
    in mortal men, who cannot save.
When their spirit departs, they return to the ground;
    on that very day their plans come to nothing.

Blessed is he whose help is the God of Jacob,
    whose hope is in the LORD his God,
the Maker of heaven and earth,
    the sea, and everything in them—
    the LORD, who remains faithful forever.
He upholds the cause of the oppressed
    and gives food to the hungry.
The LORD sets prisoners free,
    the LORD gives sight to the blind,
the LORD lifts up those who are bowed down,
    the LORD loves the righteous.
The LORD watches over the alien
    and sustains the fatherless and the widow,
    but he frustrates the ways of the wicked.

The LORD reigns forever,
    your God, O Zion, for all generations.

Praise the LORD.

Psalms of the Messiah

*I*n the historical record there have already been hints of One who will come as Savior of the world. This Savior, or Messiah, is also referred to indirectly in many of the psalms, several of which have already been presented. In the eight psalms which follow, the coming Messiah is the central subject. More messianic psalms will also be presented in later periods. While those who write them and those who sing them probably believe that the messianic psalms refer primarily to a great political king to come, later events will show that the Messiah comes as the spiritual leader of his people.

Psa. 2   **The coming Messiah and a warning to earthly rulers.**

Why do the nations conspire[i]
    and the peoples plot in vain?

[h]Hebrew *Hallelu Yah*   [i]Hebrew; Septuagint *rage*

The kings of the earth take their stand
    and the rulers gather together
against the LORD
    and against his Anointed One.[j]
"Let us break their chains," they say,
    "and throw off their fetters."

The One enthroned in heaven laughs;
    the Lord scoffs at them.
Then he rebukes them in his anger
    and terrifies them in his wrath, saying,
"I have installed my King [k]
    on Zion, my holy hill."

I will proclaim the decree of the LORD:

He said to me, "You are my Son[l];
    today I have become your Father.[m]
Ask of me,
    and I will make the nations your inheritance,
    the ends of the earth your possession.
You will rule them with an iron scepter[n];
    you will dash them to pieces like pottery."

Therefore, you kings, be wise;
    be warned, you rulers of the earth.
Serve the LORD with fear
    and rejoice with trembling.
Kiss the Son, lest he be angry
    and you be destroyed in your way,
for his wrath can flare up in a moment.
    Blessed are all who take refuge in him.

Prayer for God's presence and praise for the Messiah.   Psa. 22

For the director of music. To ⌊the tune of⌋ "The Doe of the Morning." A psalm of David.

My God, my God, why have you forsaken me?
    Why are you so far from saving me,
    so far from the words of my groaning?
O my God, I cry out by day, but you do not answer,
    by night, and am not silent.

Yet you are enthroned as the Holy One;
    you are the praise of Israel.[o]
In you our fathers put their trust;
    they trusted and you delivered them.
They cried to you and were saved;
    in you they trusted and were not disappointed.

But I am a worm and not a man,
    scorned by men and despised by the people.
All who see me mock me;
    they hurl insults, shaking their heads:

---

[j]Or *anointed one*   [k]Or *king*   [l]Or *son*   [m]Or *have begotten you*   [n]Or *will break them*
with a rod of iron   [o]Or *Yet you are holy, / enthroned on the praises of Israel*

"He trusts in the LORD;
    let the LORD rescue him.
Let him deliver him,
    since he delights in him."

Yet you brought me out of the womb;
    you made me trust in you
    even at my mother's breast.
From birth I was cast upon you;
    from my mother's womb you have been my God.
Do not be far from me,
    for trouble is near
    and there is no one to help.

Many bulls surround me;
    strong bulls of Bashan encircle me.
Roaring lions tearing their prey
    open their mouths wide against me.
I am poured out like water,
    and all my bones are out of joint.
My heart has turned to wax;
    it has melted away within me.
My strength is dried up like a potsherd,
    and my tongue sticks to the roof of my mouth;
    you lay me[p] in the dust of death.
Dogs have surrounded me;
    a band of evil men has encircled me,
    they have pierced[q] my hands and my feet.
I can count all my bones;
    people stare and gloat over me.
They divide my garments among them
    and cast lots for my clothing.

But you, O LORD, be not far off;
    O my Strength, come quickly to help me.
Deliver my life from the sword,
    my precious life from the power of the dogs.
Rescue me from the mouth of the lions;
    save[r] me from the horns of the wild oxen.

I will declare your name to my brothers;
    in the congregation I will praise you.
You who fear the LORD, praise him!
    All you descendants of Jacob, honor him!
    Revere him, all you descendants of Israel!
For he has not despised or disdained
    the suffering of the afflicted one;
he has not hidden his face from him
    but has listened to his cry for help.
From you comes the theme of my praise in the great
    assembly;

[p]Or / I am laid   [q]Some Hebrew manuscripts, Septuagint and Syriac; most Hebrew
manuscripts / like the lion,   [r]Or / you have heard

before those who fear you[s] will I fulfill my vows.
The poor will eat and be satisfied;
    they who seek the LORD will praise him—
    may your hearts live forever!
All the ends of the earth
    will remember and turn to the LORD,
and all the families of the nations
    will bow down before him,
for dominion belongs to the LORD
    and he rules over the nations.

All the rich of the earth will feast and worship;
    all who go down to the dust will kneel before him—
    those who cannot keep themselves alive.
Posterity will serve him;
    future generations will be told about the Lord.
They will proclaim his righteousness
    to a people yet unborn—
    for he has done it.

Confidence in the resurrection of the righteous.   Psa. 27

Of David.

The LORD is my light and my salvation—
    whom shall I fear?
The LORD is the stronghold of my life—
    of whom shall I be afraid?
When evil men advance against me
    to devour my flesh,[t]
when my enemies and my foes attack me,
    they will stumble and fall.
Though an army besiege me,
    my heart will not fear;
though war break out against me,
    even then will I be confident.

One thing I ask of the LORD,
    this is what I seek:
that I may dwell in the house of the LORD
    all the days of my life,
to gaze upon the beauty of the LORD
    and to seek him in his temple.
For in the day of trouble
    he will keep me safe in his dwelling;
he will hide me in the shelter of his tabernacle
    and set me high upon a rock.
Then my head will be exalted
    above the enemies who surround me;
at his tabernacle will I sacrifice with shouts of joy;
    I will sing and make music to the LORD.

[s] Hebrew *him*   [t] Or *to slander me*

Hear my voice when I call, O LORD;
  be merciful to me and answer me.
My heart says of you, "Seek his[u] face!"
  Your face, LORD, I will seek.
Do not hide your face from me,
  do not turn your servant away in anger;
  you have been my helper.
Do not reject me or forsake me,
  O God my Savior.
Though my father and mother forsake me,
  the LORD will receive me.
Teach me your way, O LORD;
  lead me in a straight path
  because of my oppressors.
Do not turn me over to the desire of my foes,
  for false witnesses rise up against me,
  breathing out violence.

I am still confident of this:
  I will see the goodness of the LORD
  in the land of the living.
Wait for the LORD;
  be strong and take heart
  and wait for the LORD.

Psa. 45 **Majesty of the eternal King and the beauty of his kingdom.**

For the director of music. To the tune of "Lilies." Of the Sons of Korah. A *maskil.*[v]
A wedding song.

My heart is stirred by a noble theme
  as I recite my verses for the king;
  my tongue is the pen of a skillful writer.

You are the most excellent of men
  and your lips have been anointed with grace,
  since God has blessed you forever.
Gird your sword upon your side, O mighty one;
  clothe yourself with splendor and majesty.
In your majesty ride forth victoriously
  in behalf of truth, humility and righteousness;
  let your right hand display awesome deeds.
Let your sharp arrows pierce the hearts of the king's
      enemies;
  let the nations fall beneath your feet.
Your throne, O God, will last for ever and ever;
  a scepter of justice will be the scepter of your kingdom.
You love righteousness and hate wickedness;
  therefore God, your God, has set you above your
      companions

---

[u]Or *To you, O my heart, he has said, "Seek my*   [v]Title: Probably a literary or musical term

by anointing you with the oil of joy.
All your robes are fragrant with myrrh and aloes and cassia;
   from palaces adorned with ivory
   the music of the strings makes you glad.
Daughters of kings are among your honored women;
   at your right hand is the royal bride in gold of Ophir.

Listen, O daughter, consider and give ear:
   Forget your people and your father's house.
The king is enthralled by your beauty;
   honor him, for he is your lord.
The Daughter of Tyre will come with a gift,^{w}
   men of wealth will seek your favor.

All glorious is the princess within ⌊her chamber⌋;
   her gown is interwoven with gold.
In embroidered garments she is led to the king;
   her virgin companions follow her
   and are brought to you.
They are led in with joy and gladness;
   they enter the palace of the king.

Your sons will take the place of your fathers;
   you will make them princes throughout the land.
I will perpetuate your memory through all generations;
   therefore the nations will praise you for ever and ever.

Exaltation of the King of Kings.   Psa. 47

   For the director of music. Of the Sons of Korah. A psalm.

Clap your hands, all you nations;
   shout to God with cries of joy.
How awesome is the LORD Most High,
   the great King over all the earth!
He subdued nations under us,
   peoples under our feet.
He chose our inheritance for us,
   the pride of Jacob, whom he loved.   *Selah*

God has ascended amid shouts of joy,
   the LORD amid the sounding of trumpets.
Sing praises to God, sing praises;
   sing praises to our King, sing praises.

For God is the King of all the earth;
   sing to him a psalm^x of praise.
God reigns over the nations;
   God is seated on his holy throne.
The nobles of the nations assemble
   as the people of the God of Abraham,
for the kings^y of the earth belong to God;
   he is greatly exalted.

---

^{w}Or *A Tyrian robe is among the gifts* ^{x}Or *a maskil* (probably a literary or musical term)
^{y}Or *shields*

Psa. 48   **The glory of Zion.**

A song. A psalm of the Sons of Korah.

Great is the LORD, and most worthy of praise,
   in the city of our God, his holy mountain.
It is beautiful in its loftiness,
   the joy of the whole earth.
Like the utmost heights of Zaphon[z] is Mount Zion,
   the[a] city of the Great King.
God is in her citadels;
   he has shown himself to be her fortress.

When the kings joined forces,
   when they advanced together,
they saw ⌊her⌋ and were astounded;
   they fled in terror.
Trembling seized them there,
   pain like that of a woman in labor.
You destroyed them like ships of Tarshish
   shattered by an east wind.

As we have heard,
   so have we seen
in the city of the LORD Almighty,
   in the city of our God:
   God makes her secure forever.   *Selah*

Within your temple, O God,
   we meditate on your unfailing love.
Like your name, O God,
   your praise reaches to the ends of the earth;
   your right hand is filled with righteousness.
Mount Zion rejoices,
   the villages of Judah are glad
   because of your judgments.

Walk about Zion, go around her,
   count her towers,
consider well her ramparts,
   view her citadels,
   that you may tell of them to the next generation.
For this God is our God for ever and ever;
   he will be our guide even to the end.

Psa. 87   **Messiah to be born in Zion.**

Of the Sons of Korah. A psalm. A song.

He has set his foundation on the holy mountain;
   the LORD loves the gates of Zion
   more than all the dwellings of Jacob.
Glorious things are said of you,
   O city of God: *Selah*
"I will record Rahab[b] and Babylon

---

[z]Zaphon can refer to a sacred mountain or the direction north.   [a]Or *earth,* / *Mount Zion,*
on the northern side / *of the*   [b]A poetic name for Egypt

among those who acknowledge me—
Philistia too, and Tyre, along with Cush[c]—
and will say, 'This[d] one was born in Zion.'"

Indeed, of Zion it will be said,
"This one and that one were born in her,
and the Most High himself will establish her."
The LORD will write in the register of the peoples:
"This one was born in Zion."   *Selah*
As they make music they will sing,
"All my fountains are in you."

The Messiah will be priest and king.   Psa. 110

Of David. A psalm.

The LORD says to my Lord:
"Sit at my right hand
until I make your enemies
a footstool for your feet."

The LORD will extend your mighty scepter from Zion;
you will rule in the midst of your enemies.
Your troops will be willing
on your day of battle.
Arrayed in holy majesty,
from the womb of the dawn
you will receive the dew of your youth.[e]

The LORD has sworn
and will not change his mind:
"You are a priest forever,
in the order of Melchizedek."

The Lord is at your right hand;
he will crush kings on the day of his wrath.
He will judge the nations, heaping up the dead
and crushing the rulers of the whole earth.
He will drink from a brook beside the way[f];
therefore he will lift up his head.

This concludes the prayers of David son of Jesse.   Psa. 72:20

Solomon Becomes King

All preparations having now been made, it is only a matter of time before David dies and Solomon takes the throne as king. But when power hangs in the balance, it is not unusual for power-seekers to attempt to grab it for themselves. Such is the case with Adonijah, who attempts a bloodless coup. However, a quick response from Nathan and Bathsheba prevents the attempt from being successful.

[c]That is, the upper Nile region   [d]Or "O Rahab and Babylon, / Philistia, Tyre and Cush, /
I will record concerning those who acknowledge me: / 'This   [e]Or / your young men will come
to you like the dew   [f]Or / The One who grants succession will set him in authority

1 Kgs.
1:1-4
Jerusalem

DAVID'S HEALTH FAILS.   When King David was old and well advanced in years, he could not keep warm even when they put covers over him. So his servants said to him, "Let us look for a young virgin to attend the king and take care of him. She can lie beside him so that our lord the king may keep warm."

Then they searched throughout Israel for a beautiful girl and found Abishag, a Shunammite, and brought her to the king. The girl was very beautiful; she took care of the king and waited on him, but the king had no intimate relations with her.

1 Kgs.
1:5-10

ADONIJAH ATTEMPTS COUP.   Now Adonijah, whose mother was Haggith, put himself forward and said, "I will be king." So he got chariots and horses*g* ready, with fifty men to run ahead of him. (His father had never interfered with him by asking, "Why do you behave as you do?" He was also very handsome and was born next after Absalom.)

Adonijah conferred with Joab son of Zeruiah and with Abiathar the priest, and they gave him their support. But Zadok the priest, Benaiah son of Jehoiada, Nathan the prophet, Shimei and Rei*h* and David's special guard did not join Adonijah.

Adonijah then sacrificed sheep, cattle and fattened calves at the Stone of Zoheleth near En Rogel. He invited all his brothers, the king's sons, and all the men of Judah who were royal officials, but he did not invite Nathan the prophet or Benaiah or the special guard or his brother Solomon.

1 Kgs.
1:11-14

NATHAN ADVISES BATHSHEBA.   Then Nathan asked Bathsheba, Solomon's mother, "Have you not heard that Adonijah, the son of Haggith, has become king without our lord David's knowing it? Now then, let me advise you how you can save your own life and the life of your son Solomon. Go in to King David and say to him, 'My lord the king, did you not swear to me your servant: "Surely Solomon your son shall be king after me, and he will sit on my throne"? Why then has Adonijah become king?' While you are still there talking to the king, I will come in and confirm what you have said."

1 Kgs.
1:15-27

BATHSHEBA COUNSELS DAVID.   So Bathsheba went to see the aged king in his room, where Abishag the Shunammite was attending him. Bathsheba bowed low and knelt before the king.

"What is it you want?" the king asked.

She said to him, "My lord, you yourself swore to me your servant by the LORD your God: 'Solomon your son shall be king after me, and he will sit on my throne.' But now Adonijah has become king, and you, my lord the king, do not know about it. He has sacrificed great numbers of cattle, fattened calves, and sheep, and has invited all the king's sons, Abiathar the priest and Joab the commander of the army, but he has not invited Solomon your servant. My lord the king, the eyes of all Israel are on you, to learn from you who will sit on the throne of my lord the king after him. Otherwise, as soon as my lord the king is laid to rest with his fathers, I and my son Solomon will be treated as criminals."

While she was still speaking with the king, Nathan the prophet arrived. And they told the king, "Nathan the prophet is here." So he went before the king and bowed with his face to the ground.

Nathan said, "Have you, my lord the king, declared that Adonijah shall

---

*g*Or *charioteers*   *h*Or *and his friends*

be king after you, and that he will sit on your throne? Today he has gone down and sacrificed great numbers of cattle, fattened calves, and sheep. He has invited all the king's sons, the commanders of the army and Abiathar the priest. Right now they are eating and drinking with him and saying, 'Long live King Adonijah!' But me your servant, and Zadok the priest, and Benaiah son of Jehoiada, and your servant Solomon he did not invite. Is this something my lord the king has done without letting his servants know who should sit on the throne of my lord the king after him?'"

PROMISE TO BATHSHEBA.   Then King David said, "Call in Bathsheba." So she came into the king's presence and stood before him.

1 Kgs.
1:28-31

The king then took an oath: "As surely as the LORD lives, who has delivered me out of every trouble, I will surely carry out today what I swore to you by the LORD, the God of Israel: Solomon your son shall be king after me, and he will sit on my throne in my place."

Then Bathsheba bowed low with her face to the ground and, kneeling before the king, said, "May my lord King David live forever!"

ZADOK GIVEN INSTRUCTIONS.   King David said, "Call in Zadok the priest, Nathan the prophet and Benaiah son of Jehoiada." When they came before the king, he said to them: "Take your lord's servants with you and set Solomon my son on my own mule and take him down to Gihon. There have Zadok the priest and Nathan the prophet anoint him king over Israel. Blow the trumpet and shout, 'Long live King Solomon!' Then you are to go up with him, and he is to come and sit on my throne and reign in my place. I have appointed him ruler over Israel and Judah."

1 Kgs.
1:32-37

Benaiah son of Jehoiada answered the king, "Amen! May the LORD, the God of my lord the king, so declare it. As the LORD was with my lord the king, so may he be with Solomon to make his throne even greater than the throne of my lord King David!"

SOLOMON IS MADE KING.   So Zadok the priest, Nathan the prophet, Benaiah son of Jehoiada, the Kerethites and the Pelethites went down and put Solomon on King David's mule and escorted him to Gihon. Zadok the priest took the horn of oil from the sacred tent and anointed Solomon. Then they sounded the trumpet and all the people shouted, "Long live King Solomon!" And all the people went up after him, playing flutes and rejoicing greatly, so that the ground shook with the sound.

1 Kgs.
1:38-40

ADONIJAH HEARS OF CORONATION.   Adonijah and all the guests who were with him heard it as they were finishing their feast. On hearing the sound of the trumpet, Joab asked, "What's the meaning of all the noise in the city?"

1 Kgs.
1:41-48

Even as he was speaking, Jonathan son of Abiathar the priest arrived. Adonijah said, "Come in. A worthy man like you must be bringing good news."

"Not at all!" Jonathan answered. "Our lord King David has made Solomon king. The king has sent with him Zadok the priest, Nathan the prophet, Benaiah son of Jehoiada, the Kerethites and the Pelethites, and they have put him on the king's mule, and Zadok the priest and Nathan the prophet have anointed him king at Gihon. From there they have gone up cheering, and the city resounds with it. That's the noise you hear. Moreover, Solomon has taken his seat on the royal throne. Also, the royal officials have come to congratulate our lord King David, saying, 'May your God make Solomon's name more famous than yours and his throne greater than yours!' And the king bowed in worship on his bed and said, 'Praise be to the LORD, the God of Israel, who has allowed my eyes to see a successor on my throne today.'"

1 Kgs.
1:49-53

ADONIJAH SUBMITS TO SOLOMON.　At this, all Adonijah's guests rose in alarm and dispersed. But Adonijah, in fear of Solomon, went and took hold of the horns of the altar. Then Solomon was told, "Adonijah is afraid of King Solomon and is clinging to the horns of the altar. He says, 'Let King Solomon swear to me today that he will not put his servant to death with the sword.'"

Solomon replied, "If he shows himself to be a worthy man, not a hair of his head will fall to the ground; but if evil is found in him, he will die." Then King Solomon sent men, and they brought him down from the altar. And Adonijah came and bowed down to King Solomon, and Solomon said, "Go to your home."

2 Sam.
23:1-7

DAVID'S LAST PROPHECY.　These are the last words of David:

"The oracle of David son of Jesse,
　　the oracle of the man exalted by the Most High,
　　the man anointed by the God of Jacob,
　　Israel's singer of songs[i]:

"The Spirit of the LORD spoke through me;
　　his word was on my tongue.
The God of Israel spoke,
　　the Rock of Israel said to me:
'When one rules over men in righteousness,
　　when he rules in the fear of God,
he is like the light of morning at sunrise
　　on a cloudless morning,
like the brightness after rain
　　that brings the grass from the earth.'

"Is not my house right with God?
　　Has he not made with me an everlasting covenant,
　　arranged and secured in every part?
Will he not bring to fruition my salvation
　　and grant me my every desire?
But evil men are all to be cast aside like thorns,
　　which are not gathered with the hand.
Whoever touches thorns
　　uses a tool of iron or the shaft of a spear;
　　they are burned up where they lie."

1 Kgs.
2:1-9

LAST WORDS TO SOLOMON.　When the time drew near for David to die, he gave a charge to Solomon his son.

"I am about to go the way of all the earth," he said. "So be strong, show yourself a man, and observe what the LORD your God requires: Walk in his ways, and keep his decrees and commands, his laws and requirements, as written in the Law of Moses, so that you may prosper in all you do and

_____
[i]Or Israel's beloved singer

wherever you go, and that the LORD may keep his promise to me: 'If your descendants watch how they live, and if they walk faithfully before me with all their heart and soul, you will never fail to have a man on the throne of Israel.'

"Now you yourself know what Joab son of Zeruiah did to me—what he did to the two commanders of Israel's armies, Abner son of Ner and Amasa son of Jether. He killed them, shedding their blood in peacetime as if in battle, and with that blood stained the belt around his waist and the sandals on his feet. Deal with him according to your wisdom, but do not let his gray head go down to the grave[j] in peace.

"But show kindness to the sons of Barzillai of Gilead and let them be among those who eat at your table. They stood by me when I fled from your brother Absalom.

"And remember, you have with you Shimei son of Gera, the Benjamite from Bahurim, who called down bitter curses on me the day I went to Mahanaim. When he came down to meet me at the Jordan, I swore to him by the LORD: 'I will not put you to death by the sword.' But now, do not consider him innocent. You are a man of wisdom; you will know what to do to him. Bring his gray head down to the grave in blood."

DAVID DIES. [Kg] Then David rested with his fathers and was buried in the City of David. [Ch] He died at a good old age, having enjoyed long life, wealth and honor. His son Solomon succeeded him as king.

1 Kgs. 2:10
1 Chron. 29:28
(Ca. 971 B.C.)

RECORDS OF DAVID'S REIGN. As for the events of King David's reign, from beginning to end, they are written in the records of Samuel the seer, the records of Nathan the prophet and the records of Gad the seer, together with the details of his reign and power, and the circumstances that surrounded him and Israel and the kingdoms of all the other lands.

1 Chron. 29:29,30

SOLOMON'S KINGSHIP. So Solomon sat on the throne of the LORD as king in place of his father David. He prospered and all Israel obeyed him. All the officers and mighty men, as well as all of King David's sons, pledged their submission to King Solomon.

The LORD highly exalted Solomon in the sight of all Israel and bestowed on him royal splendor such as no king over Israel ever had before.

1 Kgs. 2:12
1 Chron. 29:23-25
2 Chron. 1:1
(Ca. 971 B.C.)

Solomon Secures His Kingship

Solomon no sooner ascends to the throne than he takes drastic measures to secure his position as king. The first is initiated by its ultimate victim, Adonijah, who had tried unsuccessfully to steal the throne from Solomon. When Adonijah requests to marry Abishag, the young woman chosen to attend David in his last days, Solomon interprets the request as a conspiratorial move on the part of Adonijah, Abiathar, and Joab—and orders Adonijah's execution.

Then, in keeping with his father's parting advice regarding Joab, Solomon has the former army chief executed. While it seems strange that David himself would not have felt more loyalty for his comrade-in-arms, Solomon makes it

[j]Hebrew *Sheol*; also in verse 9

clear that the death of Joab is necessary in order to requite the shedding of innocent blood when Joab killed Abner and Amasa.

Finally, Shimei, the descendant of Saul who cursed David during Absalom's rebellion, violates an agreement to remain in Jerusalem under protective custody, and he too is eventually executed.

Solomon not only solidifies his position from potential internal opponents but also judiciously forms a peaceful alliance with one of his potential foreign adversaries by marrying the daughter of Egypt's ruling Pharaoh. Because of these various political steps, Solomon's reign begins with a calm hardly known by the former king.

1 Kgs.
2:13-18
(Ca. 971
B.C.)
Jerusalem

ADONIJAH ASKS FOR WIFE. Now Adonijah, the son of Haggith, went to Bathsheba, Solomon's mother. Bathsheba asked him, "Do you come peacefully?"

He answered, "Yes, peacefully." Then he added, "I have something to say to you."

"You may say it," she replied.

"As you know," he said, "the kingdom was mine. All Israel looked to me as their king. But things changed, and the kingdom has gone to my brother; for it has come to him from the LORD. Now I have one request to make of you. Do not refuse me."

"You may make it," she said.

So he continued, "Please ask King Solomon—he will not refuse you—to give me Abishag the Shunammite as my wife."

"Very well," Bathsheba replied, "I will speak to the king for you."

1 Kgs.
2:19-25

ADONIJAH EXECUTED. When Bathsheba went to King Solomon to speak to him for Adonijah, the king stood up to meet her, bowed down to her and sat down on his throne. He had a throne brought for the king's mother, and she sat down at his right hand.

"I have one small request to make of you," she said. "Do not refuse me."

The king replied, "Make it, my mother; I will not refuse you."

So she said, "Let Abishag the Shunammite be given in marriage to your brother Adonijah."

King Solomon answered his mother, "Why do you request Abishag the Shunammite for Adonijah? You might as well request the kingdom for him—after all, he is my older brother—yes, for him and for Abiathar the priest and Joab son of Zeruiah!"

Then King Solomon swore by the LORD: "May God deal with me, be it ever so severely, if Adonijah does not pay with his life for this request! And now, as surely as the LORD lives—he who has established me securely on the throne of my father David and has founded a dynasty for me as he promised—Adonijah shall be put to death today!" So King Solomon gave orders to Benaiah son of Jehoiada, and he struck down Adonijah and he died.

1 Kgs.
2:26,27

ABIATHAR REMOVED AS PRIEST. To Abiathar the priest the king said, "Go back to your fields in Anathoth. You deserve to die, but I will not put you to death now, because you carried the ark of the Sovereign LORD before my father David and shared all my father's hardships." So Solomon removed Abiathar from the priesthood of the LORD, fulfilling the word the LORD had spoken at Shiloh about the house of Eli.

JOAB EXECUTED.   When the news reached Joab, who had conspired with Adonijah though not with Absalom, he fled to the tent of the LORD and took hold of the horns of the altar. King Solomon was told that Joab had fled to the tent of the LORD and was beside the altar. Then Solomon ordered Benaiah son of Jehoiada, "Go, strike him down!"

1 Kgs.
2:28-34

So Benaiah entered the tent of the LORD and said to Joab, "The king says, 'Come out!' "

But he answered, "No, I will die here."

Benaiah reported to the king, "This is how Joab answered me."

Then the king commanded Benaiah, "Do as he says. Strike him down and bury him, and so clear me and my father's house of the guilt of the innocent blood that Joab shed. The LORD will repay him for the blood he shed, because without the knowledge of my father David he attacked two men and killed them with the sword. Both of them—Abner son of Ner, commander of Israel's army, and Amasa son of Jether, commander of Judah's army—were better men and more upright than he. May the guilt of their blood rest on the head of Joab and his descendants forever. But on David and his descendants, his house and his throne, may there be the LORD's peace forever."

So Benaiah son of Jehoiada went up and struck down Joab and killed him, and he was buried on his own land^k in the desert.

BENAIAH AND ZADOK ELEVATED.   The king put Benaiah son of Jehoiada over the army in Joab's position and replaced Abiathar with Zadok the priest.

1 Kgs. 2:35

SHIMEI CONFINED TO CITY.   Then the king sent for Shimei and said to him, "Build yourself a house in Jerusalem and live there, but do not go anywhere else. The day you leave and cross the Kidron Valley, you can be sure you will die; your blood will be on your own head."

1 Kgs.
2:36-38

Shimei answered the king, "What you say is good. Your servant will do as my lord the king has said." And Shimei stayed in Jerusalem for a long time.

SHIMEI EXECUTED.   But three years later, two of Shimei's slaves ran off to Achish son of Maacah, king of Gath, and Shimei was told, "Your slaves are in Gath." At this, he saddled his donkey and went to Achish at Gath in search of his slaves. So Shimei went away and brought the slaves back from Gath.

1 Kgs.
2:39-46

When Solomon was told that Shimei had gone from Jerusalem to Gath and had returned, the king summoned Shimei and said to him, "Did I not make you swear by the LORD and warn you, 'On the day you leave to go anywhere else, you can be sure you will die'? At that time you said to me, 'What you say is good. I will obey.' Why then did you not keep your oath to the LORD and obey the command I gave you?"

The king also said to Shimei, "You know in your heart all the wrong you did to my father David. Now the LORD will repay you for your wrongdoing. But King Solomon will be blessed, and David's throne will remain secure before the LORD forever."

Then the king gave the order to Benaiah son of Jehoiada, and he went out and struck Shimei down and killed him.

The kingdom was now firmly established in Solomon's hands.

^{k}Or *buried in his tomb*

1 Kgs. 3:1	ROYAL MARRIAGE. Solomon made an alliance with Pharaoh king of Egypt and married his daughter. He brought her to the City of David until he finished building his palace and the temple of the LORD, and the wall around Jerusalem.
1 Kgs. 9:16	WIFE'S WEDDING GIFT. (Pharaoh king of Egypt had attacked and captured Gezer. He had set it on fire. He killed its Canaanite inhabitants and then gave it as a wedding gift to his daughter, Solomon's wife.

Solomon Blessed with Wisdom

*A*lthough Solomon's reign begins with bloodshed, it can be seen even in the executions—and more so in the marriage alliance with Egypt— that Solomon is a judicious and farsighted ruler. He will soon receive a special gift of wisdom—a wisdom that is perhaps unparalleled in history. And it speaks well of Solomon that, when the opportunity presents itself, he refuses to ask for wealth or power, preferring wisdom instead. The record of this special bestowment upon Solomon begins with a notation about the worship of Solomon and his people prior to the erection of the temple. The section concludes with one of the most famous stories of all time—the story of Solomon deciding the fate of an infant claimed by two mothers.

1 Kgs. 3:2,3	WORSHIP PRIOR TO TEMPLE. The people, however, were still sacrificing at the high places, because a temple had not yet been built for the Name of the LORD. Solomon showed his love for the LORD by walking according to the statutes of his father David, except that he offered sacrifices and burned incense on the high places.
1 Kgs. 3:4 2 Chron. 1:2-6 Gibeon	SACRIFICES AT GIBEON. Then Solomon spoke to all Israel—to the commanders of thousands and commanders of hundreds, to the judges and to all the leaders in Israel, the heads of families—and Solomon and the whole assembly went to the high place at Gibeon, for God's Tent of Meeting was there, which Moses the LORD's servant had made in the desert. Now David had brought up the ark of God from Kiriath Jearim to the place he had prepared for it, because he had pitched a tent for it in Jerusalem. But the bronze altar that Bezalel son of Uri, the son of Hur, had made was in Gibeon in front of the tabernacle of the LORD; so Solomon and the assembly inquired of him there. Solomon went up to the bronze altar before the LORD in the Tent of Meeting and offered a thousand burnt offerings on it.
1 Kgs. 3:5-14 2 Chron. 1:7-12	SOLOMON ASKS FOR WISDOM. At Gibeon the LORD appeared to Solomon during the night in a dream, and God said, "Ask for whatever you want me to give you."

Solomon answered, "You have shown great kindness to your servant, my father David, because he was faithful to you and righteous and upright in heart. You have continued this great kindness to him and have given him a son to sit on his throne this very day.

"Now, O LORD my God, you have made your servant king in place of my father David. But I am only a little child and do not know how to carry out my duties. Your servant is here among the people you have chosen, a great people, too numerous to count or number. So give your servant a discerning heart to govern your people and to distinguish between right and wrong. For who is able to govern this great people of yours?"

The Lord was pleased that Solomon had asked for this. So God said to him, "Since you have asked for this and not for long life or wealth for yourself, nor have asked for the death of your enemies but for discernment in administering justice, I will do what you have asked. I will give you a wise and discerning heart, so that there will never have been anyone like you, nor will there ever be. Moreover, I will give you what you have not asked for—both riches and honor—so that in your lifetime you will have no equal among kings. And if you walk in my ways and obey my statutes and commands as David your father did, I will give you a long life."

CELEBRATION UPON RETURN.   Then Solomon awoke—and he realized it had been a dream.   **1 Kgs. 3:15 / 2 Chron. 1:13**

He returned to Jerusalem, stood before the ark of the Lord's covenant and sacrificed burnt offerings and fellowship offerings.[1] Then he gave a feast for all his court.

DISPUTE OVER INFANT.   Now two prostitutes came to the king and stood before him. One of them said, "My lord, this woman and I live in the   **1 Kgs. 3:16-28** same house. I had a baby while she was there with me. The third day after my child was born, this woman also had a baby. We were alone; there was no one in the house but the two of us.

"During the night this woman's son died because she lay on him. So she got up in the middle of the night and took my son from my side while I your servant was asleep. She put him by her breast and put her dead son by my breast. The next morning, I got up to nurse my son—and he was dead! But when I looked at him closely in the morning light, I saw that it wasn't the son I had borne."

The other woman said, "No! The living one is my son; the dead one is yours."

But the first one insisted, "No! The dead one is yours; the living one is mine." And so they argued before the king.

The king said, "This one says, 'My son is alive and your son is dead,' while that one says, 'No! Your son is dead and mine is alive.'"

Then the king said, "Bring me a sword." So they brought a sword for the king. He then gave an order: "Cut the living child in two and give half to one and half to the other."

The woman whose son was alive was filled with compassion for her son and said to the king, "Please, my lord, give her the living baby! Don't kill him!"

But the other said, "Neither I nor you shall have him. Cut him in two!"

Then the king gave his ruling: "Give the living baby to the first woman. Do not kill him; she is his mother."

When all Israel heard the verdict the king had given, they held the king in awe, because they saw that he had wisdom from God to administer justice.

◇

---

[1]Traditionally *peace offerings*

Building of the Temple

*P*erhaps Solomon's best-known achievement is the building of the magnificent temple in Jerusalem. A temple unsurpassed in beauty, it would become a national monument symbolic of Israel's special relationship with God. King David had drawn up the initial plans, and it is now left to Solomon to oversee the construction. The detail with which the temple is described is reminiscent of that which accompanied the building of the tabernacle in the wilderness. Even the two structures themselves are similar in design, though multiple stories and a grand porch are two major additions in the case of the temple.

Much of the work is to be done with materials provided by the skilled workmen from Tyre. The record begins with the making of a contract between Solomon and King Hiram of Tyre. Sometime later, another man by the same name of Hiram will be brought from Tyre to do the brasswork for the temple furnishings. The completed work is magnificent beyond description.

1 Kgs.
5:1-9
2 Chron.
2:1,3-16
Jerusalem

CONTRACT WITH KING HIRAM. ^{Ch} Solomon gave orders to build a temple for the Name of the LORD and a royal palace for himself. ^{Kg} When Hiram king of Tyre heard that Solomon had been anointed king to succeed his father David, he sent his envoys to Solomon, because he had always been on friendly terms with David. Solomon sent back this message to Hiram:

"You know that because of the wars waged against my father David from all sides, he could not build a temple for the Name of the LORD his God until the LORD put his enemies under his feet. But now the LORD my God has given me rest on every side, and there is no adversary or disaster. I intend, therefore, to build a temple for the Name of the LORD my God, as the LORD told my father David, when he said, 'Your son whom I will put on the throne in your place will build the temple for my Name.' ^{Ch} Solomon sent this message to Hiram^m king of Tyre:

"Send me cedar logs as you did for my father David when you sent him cedar to build a palace to live in. Now I am about to build a temple for the Name of the LORD my God and to dedicate it to him for burning fragrant incense before him, for setting out the consecrated bread regularly, and for making burnt offerings every morning and evening and on Sabbaths and New Moons and at the appointed feasts of the LORD our God. This is a lasting ordinance for Israel.

"The temple I am going to build will be great, because our God is greater than all other gods. But who is able to build a temple for him, since the heavens, even the highest heavens, cannot contain him? Who then am I to build a temple for him, except as a place to burn sacrifices before him?

"Send me, therefore, a man skilled to work in gold and silver, bronze and iron, and in purple, crimson and blue yarn, and experienced in the art of engraving, to work in Judah and Jerusalem with my skilled craftsmen, whom my father David provided.

"Send me also cedar, pine and algum^n logs from Lebanon, for I know that your men are skilled in cutting timber there. My men will work with

---

^{m}Hebrew *Huram,* a variant of *Hiram* ^{n}Probably a variant of *almug;* possibly juniper

yours to provide me with plenty of lumber, because the temple I build must be large and magnificent. I will give your servants, the woodsmen who cut the timber, twenty thousand cors[o] of ground wheat, twenty thousand cors of barley, twenty thousand baths[p] of wine and twenty thousand baths of olive oil."

Hiram king of Tyre replied by letter to Solomon:

"Because the LORD loves his people, he has made you their king."

And Hiram added:

"Praise be to the LORD, the God of Israel, who made heaven and earth! He has given King David a wise son, endowed with intelligence and discernment, who will build a temple for the LORD and a palace for himself.

"I am sending you Huram-Abi, a man of great skill, whose mother was from Dan and whose father was from Tyre. He is trained to work in gold and silver, bronze and iron, stone and wood, and with purple and blue and crimson yarn and fine linen. He is experienced in all kinds of engraving and can execute any design given to him. He will work with your craftsmen and with those of my lord, David your father.

"Now let my lord send his servants the wheat and barley and the olive oil and wine he promised, and we will cut all the logs from Lebanon that you need and will float them in rafts by sea down to Joppa. You can then take them up to Jerusalem."

MUTUALLY PROFITABLE TREATY. In this way Hiram kept Solomon supplied with all the cedar and pine logs he wanted, and Solomon gave Hiram twenty thousand cors[o] of wheat as food for his household, in addition to twenty thousand baths[q r] of pressed olive oil. Solomon continued to do this for Hiram year after year. The LORD gave Solomon wisdom, just as he had promised him. There were peaceful relations between Hiram and Solomon, and the two of them made a treaty. **1 Kgs. 5:10-12**

LABORERS CONSCRIPTED. [Kg] King Solomon conscripted laborers from all Israel—thirty thousand men. He sent them off to Lebanon in shifts of ten thousand a month, so that they spent one month in Lebanon and two months at home. Adoniram was in charge of the forced labor. [Ch] Solomon took a census of all the aliens who were in Israel, after the census his father David had taken; and they were found to be 153,600. He assigned 70,000 of them to be carriers and 80,000 to be stonecutters in the hills, with 3,600 foremen over them to keep the people working. [Kg] At the king's command they removed from the quarry large blocks of quality stone to provide a foundation of dressed stone for the temple. The craftsmen of Solomon and Hiram and the men of Gebal[s] cut and prepared the timber and stone for the building of the temple. **1 Kgs. 5:13-18 2 Chron. 2:2,17,18**

CONSTRUCTION BEGINS. [Kg] In the four hundred and eightieth[t] year after the Israelites had come out of Egypt, in the fourth year of Solomon's reign over Israel, in the month of Ziv, the second month, he began to build **1 Kgs. 6:1 2 Chron. 3:1,2 (Ca. 967 B.C.) Mount Moriah**

[o]That is, probably about 125,000 bushels (about 4,400 kiloliters) [p]That is, probably about 115,000 gallons (about 440 kiloliters) [q]Septuagint (see also 2Chron. 2:10); Hebrew *twenty cors* [r]That is, about 115,000 gallons (about 440 kiloliters) [s]That is, Byblos [t]Hebrew; Septuagint *four hundred and fortieth*

the temple of the LORD.   Ch Then Solomon began to build the temple of the LORD in Jerusalem on Mount Moriah, where the LORD had appeared to his father David. It was on the threshing floor of Araunah[u] the Jebusite, the place provided by David.

1 Kgs. 6:11-13 GOD'S PROMISE TO SOLOMON.   The word of the LORD came to Solomon: "As for this temple you are building, if you follow my decrees, carry out my regulations and keep all my commands and obey them, I will fulfill through you the promise I gave to David your father. And I will live among the Israelites and will not abandon my people Israel."

1 Kgs. 6:2 2 Chron. 3:3 DIMENSIONS OF TEMPLE.   The temple that King Solomon built for the LORD was sixty cubits long, twenty wide and thirty high.[v]

1 Kgs. 6:9b,18 2 Chron. 3:5-7a MATERIAL USED.   Ch He paneled the main hall with pine and covered it with fine gold and decorated it with palm tree and chain designs. He adorned the temple with precious stones. And the gold he used was gold of Parvaim. He overlaid the ceiling beams, doorframes, walls and doors of the temple with gold . . . Kg The inside of the temple was cedar, carved with gourds and open flowers. Everything was cedar; no stone was to be seen.

1 Kgs. 6:7 PREFABRICATED STONES.   In building the temple, only blocks dressed at the quarry were used, and no hammer, chisel or any other iron tool was heard at the temple site while it was being built.

1 Kgs. 6:3 2 Chron. 3:4 THE PORCH.   The portico at the front of the temple was twenty cubits[w] long across the width of the building and twenty cubits[x] high.
He overlaid the inside with pure gold.

1 Kgs. 6:4 THE WINDOWS.   He made narrow clerestory windows in the temple.

1 Kgs. 6:5,6,8,10 2 Chron. 3:9b MULTIPLE STORIES.   Kg Against the walls of the main hall and inner sanctuary he built a structure around the building, in which there were side rooms. The lowest floor was five cubits[y] wide, the middle floor six cubits[z] and the third floor seven.[a] He made offset ledges around the outside of the temple so that nothing would be inserted into the temple walls.
The entrance to the lowest[b] floor was on the south side of the temple; a stairway led up to the middle level and from there to the third. And he built the side rooms all along the temple. The height of each was five cubits, and they were attached to the temple by beams of cedar. Ch He also overlaid the upper parts with gold.

1 Kgs. 6:16,17,19-22 2 Chron. 3:8,9a MOST HOLY PLACE.   Kg He partitioned off twenty cubits[c] at the rear of the temple with cedar boards from floor to ceiling to form within the temple an inner sanctuary, the Most Holy Place. The main hall in front of this room was forty cubits[d] long.
He prepared the inner sanctuary within the temple to set the ark of the covenant of the LORD there. The inner sanctuary was twenty cubits long,

[u]Hebrew *Ornan,* a variant of *Araunah*   [v]That is, about 90 feet (about 27 meters) long and 30 feet (about 9 meters) wide and 45 feet (about 13.5 meters) high   [w]That is, about 30 feet (about 9 meters)   [x]Some Septuagint and Syriac manuscripts; Hebrew *and a hundred and twenty*   [y]That is, about 7 1/2 feet (about 2.3 meters)   [z]That is, about 9 feet (about 2.7 meters)   [a]That is, about 10 1/2 feet (about 3.1 meters)   [b]Septuagint; Hebrew *middle*   [c]That is, about 30 feet (about 9 meters)   [d]That is, about 60 feet (about 18 meters)

twenty wide and twenty high.[e] He overlaid the inside with pure gold, and he also overlaid the altar of cedar. Solomon covered the inside of the temple with pure gold, and he extended gold chains across the front of the inner sanctuary, which was overlaid with gold. So he overlaid the whole interior with gold. [Ch] The gold nails weighed fifty shekels.[f]

THE CHERUBIM. [Kg] In the inner sanctuary he made a pair of cherubim of olive wood, each ten cubits[g] high. One wing of the first cherub was five cubits long, and the other wing five cubits—ten cubits from wing tip to wing tip. The second cherub also measured ten cubits, for the two cherubim were identical in size and shape. The height of each cherub was ten cubits. He placed the cherubim inside the innermost room of the temple, with their wings spread out. The wing of one cherub touched one wall, while the wing of the other touched the other wall, and their wings touched each other in the middle of the room. He overlaid the cherubim with gold. [Ch] The wings of these cherubim extended twenty cubits. They stood on their feet, facing the main hall.[h]

1 Kgs.
6:23-28
2 Chron.
3:10-13

THE VEIL. He made the curtain of blue, purple and crimson yarn and fine linen, with cherubim worked into it.

2 Chron.
3:14

THE WALLS AND FLOOR. He lined its interior walls with cedar boards, paneling them from the floor of the temple to the ceiling, and covered the floor of the temple with planks of pine.

On the walls all around the temple, in both the inner and outer rooms, he carved cherubim, palm trees and open flowers. He also covered the floors of both the inner and outer rooms of the temple with gold.

1 Kgs.
6:15,29,30
2 Chron.
3:7b

THE DOORS. For the entrance of the inner sanctuary he made doors of olive wood with five-sided jambs. And on the two olive wood doors he carved cherubim, palm trees and open flowers, and overlaid the cherubim and palm trees with beaten gold. In the same way he made four-sided jambs of olive wood for the entrance to the main hall. He also made two pine doors, each having two leaves that turned in sockets. He carved cherubim, palm trees and open flowers on them and overlaid them with gold hammered evenly over the carvings.

1 Kgs.
6:31-35

COMPLETION OF CONSTRUCTION. The foundation of the temple of the LORD was laid in the fourth year, in the month of Ziv. In the eleventh year in the month of Bul, the eighth month, the temple was finished in all its details according to its specifications. He had spent seven years building it.

1 Kgs.
6:9a,14
6:37,38
(Ca. 960
B.C.)

HIRAM THE ARTISAN. King Solomon sent to Tyre and brought Huram[i], whose mother was a widow from the tribe of Naphtali and whose father was a man of Tyre and a craftsman in bronze. Huram was highly skilled and experienced in all kinds of bronze work. He came to King Solomon and did all the work assigned to him.

1 Kgs.
7:13,14

THE TWO PILLARS. He cast two bronze pillars, each eighteen cubits high and twelve cubits around,[j] by line. He also made two capitals of cast

1 Kgs.
7:15-22
2 Chron.
3:15-17

[e]That is, about 30 feet (about 9 meters) long, wide and high   [f]That is, about 1 1/4 pounds (about 0.6 kilogram)   [g]That is, about 15 feet (about 4.5 meters)   [h]Or *facing inward*   [i]Hebrew *Hiram*, a variant of *Huram*   [j]That is, about 27 feet (about 8.1 meters) high and 18 feet (about 5.4 meters) around

bronze to set on the tops of the pillars; each capital was five cubits[k] high. A network of interwoven chains festooned the capitals on top of the pillars, seven for each capital. He made pomegranates in two rows[l] encircling each network to decorate the capitals on top of the pillars.[m] He did the same for each capital. The capitals on top of the pillars in the portico were in the shape of lilies, four cubits[n] high. On the capitals of both pillars, above the bowl-shaped part next to the network, were the two hundred pomegranates in rows all around. He erected the pillars at the portico of the temple. The pillar to the south he named Jakin[o] and the one to the north Boaz.[p] The capitals on top were in the shape of lilies. And so the work on the pillars was completed.

**2 Chron.
4:1**

ALTAR OF BRASS.   He made a bronze altar twenty cubits long, twenty cubits wide and ten cubits high.[q]

**1 Kgs.
7:23-26,39b
2 Chron.
4:2-5,10,6c**

THE SEA.   He made the Sea of cast metal, circular in shape, measuring ten cubits from rim to rim and five cubits[r] high. It took a line of thirty cubits[s] to measure around it. Below the rim, figures of bulls encircled it— ten to a cubit.[t] The bulls were cast in two rows in one piece with the Sea.

The Sea stood on twelve bulls, three facing north, three facing west, three facing south and three facing east. The Sea rested on top of them, and their hindquarters were toward the center. It was a handbreadth[u] in thickness, and its rim was like the rim of a cup, like a lily blossom. It held three thousand baths.[v] He placed the Sea on the south side, at the southeast corner... to be used by the priests for washing.

**1 Kgs.
7:27-37**

THE STANDS.   He also made ten movable stands of bronze; each was four cubits long, four wide and three high.[w] This is how the stands were made: They had side panels attached to uprights. On the panels between the uprights were lions, bulls and cherubim—and on the uprights as well. Above and below the lions and bulls were wreaths of hammered work. Each stand had four bronze wheels with bronze axles, and each had a basin resting on four supports, cast with wreaths on each side. On the inside of the stand there was an opening that had a circular frame one cubit[t] deep. This opening was round, and with its basework it measured a cubit and a half.[x] Around its opening there was engraving. The panels of the stands were square, not round. The four wheels were under the panels, and the axles of the wheels were attached to the stand. The diameter of each wheel was a cubit and a half. The wheels were made like chariot wheels; the axles, rims, spokes and hubs were all of cast metal.

Each stand had four handles, one on each corner, projecting from the stand. At the top of the stand there was a circular band half a cubit[y] deep. The supports and panels were attached to the top of the stand. He engraved

---

[k]That is, about 7 1/2 feet (about 2.3 meters)   [l]Two Hebrew manuscripts and Septuagint; most Hebrew manuscripts *made the pillars, and there were two rows*   [m]Many Hebrew manuscripts and Syriac; most Hebrew manuscripts *pomegranates*   [n]That is, about 6 feet (about 1.8 meters)   [o]*Jakin* probably means *he establishes.*   [p]*Boaz* probably means *in him is strength.*   [q]That is, about 30 feet (about 9 meters) long and wide, and about 15 feet (about 4.5 meters) high   [r]That is, about 7 1/2 feet (about 2.3 meters)   [s]That is, about 45 feet (about 13.5 meters).   [t]That is, about 1 1/2 feet (about 0.5 meter)   [u]That is, about 3 inches (about 8 centimeters)   [v]That is, about 17,500 gallons (about 66 kiloliters)   [w]That is, about 6 feet (about 1.8 meters) long and wide and about 4 1/2 feet (about 1.3 meters) high   [x]That is, about 2 1/4 feet (about 0.7 meter)   [y]That is, about 3/4 foot (about 0.2 meter)

cherubim, lions and palm trees on the surfaces of the supports and on the panels, in every available space, with wreaths all around. This is the way he made the ten stands. They were all cast in the same molds and were identical in size and shape.

THE BRONZE BASINS.　Kg He then made ten bronze basins, each holding forty baths[z] and measuring four cubits across, one basin to go on each of the ten stands. He placed five of the stands on the south side of the temple and five on the north. Ch In them the things to be used for the burnt offerings were rinsed...

1 Kgs. 7:38,39a
2 Chron. 4:6a,b

THE COURTYARDS.　Kg And he built the inner courtyard of three courses of dressed stone and one course of trimmed cedar beams. Ch He made the courtyard of the priests, and the large court and the doors for the court, and overlaid the doors with bronze.

1 Kgs. 6:36
2 Chron. 4:9

HIRAM'S BRASSWORKS.　He also made the basins and shovels and sprinkling bowls.
So Huram finished all the work he had undertaken for King Solomon in the temple of the LORD:

1 Kgs. 7:40-47
2 Chron. 4:11-18

the two pillars;
the two bowl-shaped capitals on top of the pillars;
the two sets of network decorating the two bowl-shaped capitals on
　　top of the pillars;
the four hundred pomegranates for the two sets of network (two rows
　　of pomegranates for each network, decorating the bowl-shaped
　　capitals on top of the pillars);
the ten stands with their ten basins;
the Sea and the twelve bulls under it;
the pots, shovels and sprinkling bowls.

All these objects that Huram made for King Solomon for the temple of the LORD were of burnished bronze. The king had them cast in clay molds in the plain of the Jordan between Succoth and Zarethan. Solomon left all these things unweighed, because there were so many; the weight of the bronze was not determined.

THE GOLDEN VESSELS.　Kg Solomon also made all the furnishings that were in the LORD's temple:

1 Kgs. 7:48-50
2 Chron. 4:7,8,19-22

the golden altar;
the golden table on which was the bread of the Presence;
the lampstands of pure gold (five on the right and five on the left, in
　　front of the inner sanctuary);
the gold floral work and lamps and tongs;
the pure gold basins, wick trimmers, sprinkling bowls, dishes and
　　censers;
and the gold sockets for the doors of the innermost room, the Most
　　Holy Place, and also for the doors of the main hall of the temple.
　　Ch He made ten tables and placed them in the temple, five on the
　　south side and five on the north. He also made a hundred gold
　　sprinkling bowls.

[z]That is, about 230 gallons (about 880 liters)

1 Kgs. 7:51
2 Chron.
5:1

COMPLETION OF FURNISHINGS.   When all the work King Solomon had done for the temple of the LORD was finished, he brought in the things his father David had dedicated—the silver and gold and the furnishings—and he placed them in the treasuries of the LORD's temple.

1 Kgs. 9:25
2 Chron.
8:12-16

CONTINUAL WORSHIP.   On the altar of the LORD that he had built in front of the portico, Solomon sacrificed burnt offerings to the LORD, according to the daily requirement for offerings commanded by Moses for Sabbaths, New Moons and the three annual feasts—the Feast of Unleavened Bread, the Feast of Weeks and the Feast of Tabernacles. In keeping with the ordinance of his father David, he appointed the divisions of the priests for their duties, and the Levites to lead the praise and to assist the priests according to each day's requirement. He also appointed the gatekeepers by divisions for the various gates, because this was what David the man of God had ordered. They did not deviate from the king's commands to the priests or to the Levites in any matter, including that of the treasuries.

All Solomon's work was carried out, from the day the foundation of the temple of the LORD was laid until its completion. So the temple of the LORD was finished.

Dedication of the Temple

*T*he temple and its furnishings now complete, Solomon brings the people together for a solemn dedication of the temple to God's use and glory. Solomon reminds his people of the covenant relationship signified by the temple, and thus of their obligation to remain faithful to God. Solomon's dedicatory prayer asks that God will hear the people's prayers and bless them in times of special need. As the dedication begins, the old tabernacle is brought to the temple site.

1 Kgs.
8:1-11
2 Chron.
5:2-14
(Ca. 960
B.C.)
Jerusalem

TABERNACLE MOVED. Then Solomon summoned to Jerusalem the elders of Israel, all the heads of the tribes and the chiefs of the Israelite families, to bring up the ark of the LORD's covenant from Zion, the City of David. And all the men of Israel came together to the king at the time of the festival in the seventh month.

When all the elders of Israel had arrived, the Levites took up the ark, and they brought up the ark and the Tent of Meeting and all the sacred furnishings in it. The priests, who were Levites, carried them up; and King Solomon and the entire assembly of Israel that had gathered about him were before the ark, sacrificing so many sheep and cattle that they could not be recorded or counted.

The priests then brought the ark of the LORD's covenant to its place in the inner sanctuary of the temple, the Most Holy Place, and put it beneath the wings of the cherubim. The cherubim spread their wings over the place of the ark and covered the ark and its carrying poles. These poles were so long that their ends, extending from the ark, could be seen from in front of the inner sanctuary, but not from outside the Holy Place; and they are still there today. There was nothing in the ark except the two tablets that Moses had placed in it at Horeb, where the LORD made a covenant with the Israelites after they came out of Egypt.

The priests then withdrew from the Holy Place. All the priests who were there had consecrated themselves, regardless of their divisions. All the Levites who were musicians—Asaph, Heman, Jeduthun and their sons and relatives—stood on the east side of the altar, dressed in fine linen and playing cymbals, harps and lyres. They were accompanied by 120 priests sounding trumpets. The trumpeters and singers joined in unison, as with one voice, to give praise and thanks to the LORD. Accompanied by trumpets, cymbals and other instruments, they raised their voices in praise to the LORD and sang:

> "He is good;
>   his love endures forever."

Then the temple of the LORD was filled with a cloud, and the priests could not perform their service because of the cloud, for the glory of the LORD filled the temple of God.

DEDICATORY ADDRESS.   Then Solomon said, "The LORD has said that he would dwell in a dark cloud; I have built a magnificent temple for you, a place for you to dwell forever."

1 Kgs.
8:12-21
2 Chron.
6:1-11

While the whole assembly of Israel was standing there, the king turned around and blessed them. Then he said:

"Praise be to the LORD, the God of Israel, who with his hands has fulfilled what he promised with his mouth to my father David. For he said, 'Since the day I brought my people out of Egypt, I have not chosen a city in any tribe of Israel to have a temple built for my Name to be there, nor have I chosen anyone to be the leader over my people Israel. But now I have chosen Jerusalem for my Name to be there, and I have chosen David to rule my people Israel.'

"My father David had it in his heart to build a temple for the Name of the LORD, the God of Israel. But the LORD said to my father David, 'Because it was in your heart to build a temple for my Name, you did well to have this in your heart. Nevertheless, you are not the one to build the temple, but your son, who is your own flesh and blood—he is the one who will build the temple for my Name.'

"The LORD has kept the promise he made. I have succeeded David my father and now I sit on the throne of Israel, just as the LORD promised, and I have built the temple for the Name of the LORD, the God of Israel. There I have placed the ark, in which is the covenant of the LORD that he made with the people of Israel."

DEDICATORY PRAYER.   Then Solomon stood before the altar of the LORD in front of the whole assembly of Israel and spread out his hands. Now he had made a bronze platform, five cubits[a] long, five cubits wide and three cubits[b] high, and had placed it in the center of the outer court. He stood on the platform and then knelt down before the whole assembly of Israel and spread out his hands toward heaven. He said:

1 Kgs.
8:22-30
2 Chron.
6:12-21

"O LORD, God of Israel, there is no God like you in heaven or on earth— you who keep your covenant of love with your servants who continue wholeheartedly in your way. You have kept your promise to your servant

[a]That is, about 7 1/2 feet (about 2.3 meters)   [b]That is, about 4 1/2 feet (about 1.3 meters)

David my father; with your mouth you have promised and with your hand you have fulfilled it—as it is today.

"Now LORD, God of Israel, keep for your servant David my father the promises you made to him when you said, 'You shall never fail to have a man to sit before me on the throne of Israel, if only your sons are careful in all they do to walk before me according to my law, as you have done.' And now, O LORD, God of Israel, let your word that you promised your servant David come true.

"But will God really dwell on earth with men? The heavens, even the highest heavens, cannot contain you. How much less this temple I have built! Yet give attention to your servant's prayer and his plea for mercy, O LORD my God. Hear the cry and the prayer that your servant is praying in your presence. May your eyes be open toward this temple day and night, this place of which you said you would put your Name there. May you hear the prayer your servant prays toward this place. Hear the supplications of your servant and of your people Israel when they pray toward this place. Hear from heaven, your dwelling place; and when you hear, forgive.

1 Kgs.
8:31,32
2 Chron.
6:22,23

OATHS UPON ALTAR.   "When a man wrongs his neighbor and is required to take an oath and he comes and swears the oath before your altar in this temple, then hear from heaven and act. Judge between your servants, repaying the guilty by bringing down on his own head what he has done. Declare the innocent not guilty and so establish his innocence.

1 Kgs.
8:33,34
2 Chron.
6:24,25

IN DEFEAT.   "When your people Israel have been defeated by an enemy because they have sinned against you and when they turn back and confess your name, praying and making supplication before you in this temple, then hear from heaven and forgive the sin of your people Israel and bring them back to the land you gave to them and their fathers.

1 Kgs.
8:35,36
2 Chron.
6:26,27

IN DROUGHTS.   "When the heavens are shut up and there is no rain because your people have sinned against you, and when they pray toward this place and confess your name and turn from their sin because you have afflicted them, then hear from heaven and forgive the sin of your servants, your people Israel. Teach them the right way to live, and send rain on the land you gave your people for an inheritance.

1 Kgs.
8:37-40
2 Chron.
6:28-31

IN FAMINE OR PLAGUE.   "When famine or plague comes to the land, or blight or mildew, locusts or grasshoppers, or when enemies besiege them in any of their cities, whatever disaster or disease may come, and when a prayer or plea is made by any of your people Israel—each one aware of his afflictions and pains, and spreading out his hands toward this temple—then hear from heaven, your dwelling place. Forgive, and deal with each man according to all he does, since you know his heart (for you alone know the hearts of men), so that they will fear you and walk in your ways all the time they live in the land you gave our fathers.

1 Kgs.
8:41-43
2 Chron.
6:32,33

FOR STRANGERS.   "As for the foreigner who does not belong to your people Israel but has come from a distant land because of your great name and your mighty hand and your outstretched arm—when he comes and prays toward this temple, then hear from heaven, your dwelling place, and do whatever the foreigner asks of you, so that all the peoples of the earth may know your name and fear you, as do your own people Israel, and may know that this house I have built bears your Name.

IN BATTLE.   "When your people go to war against their enemies, wherever you send them, and when they pray to you toward the city you have chosen and the temple I have built for your Name, then hear from heaven their prayer and their plea, and uphold their cause.

1 Kgs.
8:44,45
2 Chron.
6:34,35

IN CAPTIVITY.   "When they sin against you—for there is no one who does not sin—and you become angry with them and give them over to the enemy, who takes them captive to his own land, far away or near; and if they have a change of heart in the land where they are held captive, and repent and plead with you in the land of their conquerors and say, 'We have sinned, we have done wrong, we have acted wickedly'; and if they turn back to you with all their heart and soul in the land of their enemies who took them captive, and pray to you toward the land you gave their fathers, toward the city you have chosen and the temple I have built for your Name; then from heaven, your dwelling place, hear their prayer and their plea, and uphold their cause. And forgive your people, who have sinned against you; forgive all the offenses they have committed against you, and cause their conquerors to show them mercy; for they are your people and your inheritance, whom you brought out of Egypt, out of that iron-smelting furnace.

1 Kgs.
8:46-53
2 Chron.
6:36-39

"May your eyes be open to your servant's plea and to the plea of your people Israel, and may you listen to them whenever they cry out to you. For you singled them out from all the nations of the world to be your own inheritance, just as you declared through your servant Moses when you, O Sovereign LORD, brought our fathers out of Egypt."

CLOSE OF PRAYER.   "Now, my God, may your eyes be open and your ears attentive to the prayers offered in this place.

2 Chron.
6:40-42

"Now arise, O LORD God, and come to your resting place,
you and the ark of your might.
May your priests, O LORD God, be clothed with salvation,
may your saints rejoice in your goodness.
O LORD God, do not reject your anointed one.
Remember the great love promised to David your
servant."

SOLOMON'S BENEDICTION.   When Solomon had finished all these prayers and supplications to the LORD, he rose from before the altar of the LORD, where he had been kneeling with his hands spread out toward heaven. He stood and blessed the whole assembly of Israel in a loud voice, saying:

1 Kgs.
8:54-61

"Praise be to the LORD, who has given rest to his people Israel just as he promised. Not one word has failed of all the good promises he gave through his servant Moses. May the LORD our God be with us as he was with our fathers; may he never leave us nor forsake us. May he turn our hearts to him, to walk in all his ways and to keep the commands, decrees and regulations he gave our fathers. And may these words of mine, which I have prayed before the LORD, be near to the LORD our God day and night, that he may uphold the cause of his servant and the cause of his people Israel according to each day's need, so that all the peoples of the earth may know that the LORD is God and that there is no other. But your hearts must be fully committed to the LORD our God, to live by his decrees and obey his commands, as at this time."

**2 Chron.
7:1-3**

GLORY FILLS TEMPLE.   When Solomon finished praying, fire came down from heaven and consumed the burnt offering and the sacrifices, and the glory of the LORD filled the temple. The priests could not enter the temple of the LORD because the glory of the LORD filled it. When all the Israelites saw the fire coming down and the glory of the LORD above the temple, they knelt on the pavement with their faces to the ground, and they worshiped and gave thanks to the LORD, saying,

> "He is good;
>   his love endures forever."

**1 Kgs.
8:62-66
2 Chron.
7:4-10**

SACRIFICE AND FESTIVAL.   Then the king and all the people offered sacrifices before the LORD. And King Solomon offered a sacrifice of twenty-two thousand head of cattle and a hundred and twenty thousand sheep and goats. So the king and all the people dedicated the temple of God. The priests took their positions, as did the Levites with the LORD's musical instruments, which King David had made for praising the LORD and which were used when he gave thanks, saying, "His love endures forever." Opposite the Levites, the priests blew their trumpets, and all the Israelites were standing.

Solomon consecrated the middle part of the courtyard in front of the temple of the LORD, and there he offered burnt offerings and the fat of the fellowship offerings,^{c} because the bronze altar he had made could not hold the burnt offerings, the grain offerings and the fat portions.

So Solomon observed the festival at that time for seven days, and all Israel with him—a vast assembly, people from Lebo^d Hamath to the Wadi of Egypt. On the eighth day they held an assembly, for they had celebrated the dedication of the altar for seven days and the festival for seven days more. On the twenty-third day of the seventh month he sent the people to their homes, joyful and glad in heart for the good things the LORD had done for David and Solomon and for his people Israel.

Construction of Cities and Royal Palace

*W*hile the temple has been under construction, so too has been a royal palace for Solomon. The palace actually requires six more years to complete than the temple itself and includes separate dwellings for both Solomon and Pharaoh's daughter (whom he had married). Solomon's building program includes the construction or repair of many cities throughout his kingdom, a task accomplished through the use of forced labor by captives living within the country.

1 Kgs. 7:1

THIRTEEN YEARS IN BUILDING.   It took Solomon thirteen years, however, to complete the construction of his palace.

**1 Kgs.
7:2-12**

DESCRIPTION OF PALACE.   He built the Palace of the Forest of Lebanon a hundred cubits long, fifty wide and thirty high,^{e} with four rows of cedar columns supporting trimmed cedar beams. It was roofed with

---

^{c}Traditionally *peace offerings* ^{d}Or *from the entrance to* ^{e}That is, about 150 feet (about 46 meters) long, 75 feet (about 23 meters) wide and 45 feet (about 13.5 meters) high

cedar above the beams that rested on the columns—forty-five beams, fifteen to a row. Its windows were placed high in sets of three, facing each other. All the doorways had rectangular frames; they were in the front part in sets of three, facing each other.*f*

He made a colonnade fifty cubits long and thirty wide.*g* In front of it was a portico, and in front of that were pillars and an overhanging roof.

He built the throne hall, the Hall of Justice, where he was to judge, and he covered it with cedar from floor to ceiling.*h* And the palace in which he was to live, set farther back, was similar in design. Solomon also made a palace like this hall for Pharaoh's daughter, whom he had married.

All these structures, from the outside to the great courtyard and from foundation to eaves, were made of blocks of high-grade stone cut to size and trimmed with a saw on their inner and outer faces. The foundations were laid with large stones of good quality, some measuring ten cubits*i* and some eight.*j* Above were high-grade stones, cut to size, and cedar beams. The great courtyard was surrounded by a wall of three courses of dressed stone and one course of trimmed cedar beams, as was the inner courtyard of the temple of the LORD with its portico.

GOD COVENANTS WITH SOLOMON. When Solomon had finished the temple of the LORD and the royal palace, and had succeeded in carrying out all he had in mind to do in the temple of the LORD and in his own palace, the LORD appeared to him at night and said:

> 1 Kgs.
> 9:1-9
> 2 Chron.
> 7:11-22

"I have heard your prayer and have chosen this place for myself as a temple for sacrifices.

"When I shut up the heavens so that there is no rain, or command locusts to devour the land or send a plague among my people, if my people, who are called by my name, will humble themselves and pray and seek my face and turn from their wicked ways, then will I hear from heaven and will forgive their sin and will heal their land. Now my eyes will be open and my ears attentive to the prayers offered in this place. I have chosen and consecrated this temple so that my Name may be there forever. My eyes and my heart will always be there.

"As for you, if you walk before me as David your father did, and do all I command, and observe my decrees and laws, I will establish your royal throne, as I covenanted with David your father when I said, 'You shall never fail to have a man to rule over Israel.'

"But if you*k* turn away and forsake the decrees and commands I have given you*k* and go off to serve other gods and worship them, then I will uproot Israel from my land, which I have given them, and will reject this temple I have consecrated for my Name. I will make it a byword and an object of ridicule among all peoples. And though this temple is now so imposing, all who pass by will be appalled and say, 'Why has the LORD done such a thing to this land and to this temple?' People will answer, 'Because they have forsaken the LORD, the God of their fathers, who brought them out of Egypt, and have embraced other gods, worshiping and serving them—that is why he brought all this disaster on them.'"

---

*f*The meaning of the Hebrew for this clause is uncertain.   *g*That is, about 75 feet
(about 23 meters) long and 45 feet (about 13.5 meters) wide   *h*Vulgate and Syriac;
Hebrew *floor*   *i*That is, about 15 feet (about 4.5 meters)   *j*That is, about 12 feet
(about 3.6 meters)   *k*The Hebrew is plural.

1 Kgs. 9:10-14 Galilee

HIRAM DISPLEASED.   At the end of twenty years, during which Solomon built these two buildings—the temple of the LORD and the royal palace—King Solomon gave twenty towns in Galilee to Hiram king of Tyre, because Hiram had supplied him with all the cedar and pine and gold he wanted. But when Hiram went from Tyre to see the towns that Solomon had given him, he was not pleased with them. "What kind of towns are these you have given me, my brother?" he asked. And he called them the Land of Cabul,[l] a name they have to this day. Now Hiram had sent to the king 120 talents[m] of gold.

2 Chron. 8:1,2

HIRAM RETURNS CITIES.   At the end of twenty years, during which Solomon built the temple of the LORD and his own palace, Solomon rebuilt the villages that Hiram[n] had given him, and settled Israelites in them.

2 Chron. 8:3

CAPTURE OF HAMATH.   Solomon then went to Hamath Zobah and captured it.

1 Kgs. 9:17-19 2 Chron. 8:4-6

BUILDING OF CITIES.   He also built up Tadmor in the desert and all the store cities he had built in Hamath. He rebuilt Upper Beth Horon and Lower Beth Horon as fortified cities, with walls and with gates and bars, as well as Baalath and all his store cities, and all the cities for his chariots and for his horses[o]—whatever he desired to build in Jerusalem, in Lebanon and throughout all the territory he ruled.

1 Kgs. 9:20-23,15 2 Chron. 8:7-10

USE OF FORCED LABOR.   All the people left from the Amorites, Hittites, Perizzites, Hivites and Jebusites (these peoples were not Israelites), that is, their descendants remaining in the land, whom the Israelites could not exterminate[p]—these Solomon conscripted for his slave labor force, as it is to this day. But Solomon did not make slaves of any of the Israelites; they were his fighting men, his government officials, his officers, his captains, and the commanders of his chariots and charioteers. They were also the chief officials in charge of Solomon's projects—550 officials supervising the men who did the work.

Here is the account of the forced labor King Solomon conscripted to build the LORD's temple, his own palace, the supporting terraces,[q] the wall of Jerusalem, and Hazor, Megiddo and Gezer.

1 Kgs. 9:24 2 Chron. 8:11 Jerusalem

NEW HOUSE FOR WIFE.   Solomon brought Pharaoh's daughter up from the City of David to the palace he had built for her, for he said, "My wife must not live in the palace of David king of Israel, because the places the ark of the LORD has entered are holy."

1 Kgs. 9:26-28 10:22 2 Chron. 8:17,18 9:21

NAVY FORMED WITH HIRAM.   King Solomon also built ships at Ezion Geber, which is near Elath in Edom, on the shore of the Red Sea.[r] And Hiram sent his men—sailors who knew the sea—to serve in the fleet with Solomon's men. They sailed to Ophir and brought back 420 talents[s] of gold, which they delivered to King Solomon. The king had a fleet of trading ships[t] at sea along with the ships of Hiram. Once every three years it returned, carrying gold, silver and ivory, and apes and baboons.

---

[l]Cabul sounds like the Hebrew for good-for-nothing.   [m]That is, about 4 1/2 tons (about 4 metric tons)   [n]Hebrew Huram, a variant of Hiram; also in verse 18   [o]Or charioteers [p]The Hebrew term refers to the irrevocable giving over of things or persons to the LORD, often by totally destroying them.   [q]Or the Millo   [r]Hebrew Yam Suph; that is, Sea of Reeds   [s]That is, about 16 tons (about 14.5 metric tons)   [t]Hebrew of ships of Tarshish

Extent of Solomon's Glory

*B*ecause Solomon had asked for wisdom instead of wealth, God promised to give him both—wisdom beyond all men, and untold riches. Over the years of Solomon's reign, God's promise has become reality. Solomon's kingdom has developed into the most peaceful and prosperous kingdom ever known. Solomon's glory is documented not only by official statistics but also by the visit of the Queen of Sheba. The visit itself is altogether remarkable, particularly because the queen's home in southern Arabia (perhaps the modern country of Yemen) is a 1200-mile camel ride across hot desert territories inhabited by roving groups of bandits ready to relieve the queen of the treasure which she carries. What motivates her to come so great a distance is far more than mere curiosity at Solomon's wealth. It is the search for wisdom and insight which compels her (as it has compelled people of all times), and she is not in the least disappointed.

SOLOMON'S WISDOM.   God gave Solomon wisdom and very great insight, and a breadth of understanding as measureless as the sand on the seashore. Solomon's wisdom was greater than the wisdom of all the men of the East, and greater than all the wisdom of Egypt. He was wiser than any other man, including Ethan the Ezrahite—wiser than Heman, Calcol and Darda, the sons of Mahol. And his fame spread to all the surrounding nations. He spoke three thousand proverbs and his songs numbered a thousand and five. He described plant life, from the cedar of Lebanon to the hyssop that grows out of walls. He also taught about animals and birds, reptiles and fish. Men of all nations came to listen to Solomon's wisdom, sent by all the kings of the world, who had heard of his wisdom.

1 Kgs. 4:29-34

SOLOMON'S WEALTH.   The weight of the gold that Solomon received yearly was 666 talents,[u] not including the revenues from merchants and traders and from all the Arabian kings and the governors of the land.

King Solomon made two hundred large shields of hammered gold; six hundred bekas[v] of gold went into each shield. He also made three hundred small shields of hammered gold, with three minas[w] of gold in each shield. The king put them in the Palace of the Forest of Lebanon.

Then the king made a great throne inlaid with ivory and overlaid with fine gold. The throne had six steps, and its back had a rounded top. On both sides of the seat were armrests, with a lion standing beside each of them. Twelve lions stood on the six steps, one at either end of each step. Nothing like it had ever been made for any other kingdom. All King Solomon's goblets were gold, and all the household articles in the Palace of the Forest of Lebanon were pure gold. Nothing was made of silver, because silver was considered of little value in Solomon's days. The king made silver as common in Jerusalem as stones, and cedar as plentiful as sycamore-fig trees in the foothills.

King Solomon was greater in riches and wisdom than all the other kings of the earth. The whole world sought audience with Solomon to hear the wisdom God had put in his heart. Year after year, everyone who came

1 Kgs. 10:14-21 10:27,23-25 2 Chron. 1:15 9:13-20, 27, 22-24

---

[u]That is, about 25 tons (about 23 metric tons)   [v]That is, about 7 1/2 pounds (about 3.5 kilograms)   [w]That is, about 3 3/4 pounds (about 1.7 kilograms)

brought a gift—articles of silver and gold, robes, weapons and spices, and horses and mules.

1 Kgs. 4:26
10:26,28,29
2 Chron.
1:14,16,17
9:25,28

HORSES AND CHARIOTS.   Solomon accumulated chariots and horses; he had fourteen hundred chariots and twelve thousand horses,[x] which he kept in the chariot cities and also with him in Jerusalem. Solomon had four[y] thousand stalls for chariot horses . . . Solomon's horses were imported from Egypt[z] and from Kue[a]—the royal merchants purchased them from Kue. They imported a chariot from Egypt for six hundred shekels[b] of silver, and a horse for a hundred and fifty.[c] They also exported them to all the kings of the Hittites and of the Arameans.

1 Kgs.
4:21,24
2 Chron.
9:26

EXTENT OF KINGDOM.   And Solomon ruled over all the kingdoms from the River[d] to the land of the Philistines, as far as the border of Egypt. These countries brought tribute and were Solomon's subjects all his life. For he ruled over all the kingdoms west of the River, from Tiphsah to Gaza, and had peace on all sides.

1 Kgs.
4:20,25

SECURITY OF KINGDOM.   The people of Judah and Israel were as numerous as the sand on the seashore; they ate, they drank and they were happy. During Solomon's lifetime Judah and Israel, from Dan to Beersheba, lived in safety, each man under his own vine and fig tree.

1 Kgs.
4:1-6

SOLOMON'S PRINCES.   So King Solomon ruled over all Israel. And these were his chief officials:

> Azariah son of Zadok—the priest;
> Elihoreph and Ahijah, sons of Shisha—secretaries;
> Jehoshaphat son of Ahilud—recorder;
> Benaiah son of Jehoiada—commander in chief;
> Zadok and Abiathar—priests;
> Azariah son of Nathan—in charge of the district officers;
> Zabud son of Nathan—a priest and personal adviser to the king;
> Ahishar—in charge of the palace;
> Adoniram son of Abda—in charge of forced labor.

1 Kgs.
4:7-19

SOLOMON'S COMMISSARIES.   Solomon also had twelve district governors over all Israel, who supplied provisions for the king and the royal household. Each one had to provide supplies for one month in the year. These are their names:

> Ben-Hur—in the hill country of Ephraim;
> Ben-Deker—in Makaz, Shaalbim, Beth Shemesh and Elon Bethhanan;
> Ben-Hesed—in Arubboth (Socoh and all the land of Hepher were his);
> Ben-Abinadab—in Naphoth Dor[e] (he was married to Taphath daughter of Solomon);
> Baana son of Ahilud—in Taanach and Megiddo, and in all of Beth Shan next to Zarethan below Jezreel, from Beth Shan to Abel Meholah across to Jokmeam;
> Ben-Geber—in Ramoth Gilead (the settlements of Jair son of Manasseh in Gilead were his, as well as the district of Argob in

[x]Or *charioteers*   [y]Some Septuagint manuscripts (see also 2 Chron. 9:25); Hebrew *forty*   [z]Or possibly *Muzur*, a region in Cilicia   [a]Probably *Cilicia*   [b]That is, about 15 pounds (about 7 kilograms)   [c]That is, about 3 3/4 pounds (about 1.7 kilograms)   [d]That is, the Euphrates   [e]Or *in the heights of Dor*

Bashan and its sixty large walled cities with bronze gate bars);

Ahinadab son of Iddo—in Mahanaim;

Ahimaaz—in Naphtali (he had married Basemath daughter of Solomon);

Baana son of Hushai—in Asher and in Aloth;

Jehoshaphat son of Paruah—in Issachar;

Shimei son of Ela—in Benjamin;

Geber son of Uri—in Gilead (the country of Sihon king of the Amorites and the country of Og king of Bashan). He was the only governor over the district.

PROVISIONS FOR SOLOMON.   Solomon's daily provisions were thirty cors*f* of fine flour and sixty cors*g* of meal, ten head of stall-fed cattle, twenty of pasture-fed cattle and a hundred sheep and goats, as well as deer, gazelles, roebucks and choice fowl.

The district officers, each in his month, supplied provisions for King Solomon and all who came to the king's table. They saw to it that nothing was lacking. They also brought to the proper place their quotas of barley and straw for the chariot horses and the other horses.

1 Kgs.
4:22,23-27,
28

VISIT BY QUEEN OF SHEBA.   When the queen of Sheba heard about the fame of Solomon and his relation to the name of the LORD, she came to test him with hard questions. Arriving at Jerusalem with a very great caravan—with camels carrying spices, large quantities of gold, and precious stones—she came to Solomon and talked with him about all that she had on her mind. Solomon answered all her questions; nothing was too hard for the king to explain to her. When the queen of Sheba saw all the wisdom of Solomon and the palace he had built, the food on his table, the seating of his officials, the attending servants in their robes, his cupbearers, and the burnt offerings he made at*h* the temple of the LORD, she was overwhelmed.

1 Kgs.
10:1-13
2 Chron.
9:1-12
Jerusalem

She said to the king, "The report I heard in my own country about your achievements and your wisdom is true. But I did not believe these things until I came and saw with my own eyes. Indeed, not even half was told me; in wisdom and wealth you have far exceeded the report I heard. How happy your men must be! How happy your officials, who continually stand before you and hear your wisdom! Praise be to the LORD your God, who has delighted in you and placed you on the throne of Israel. Because of the LORD's eternal love for Israel, he has made you king, to maintain justice and righteousness."

And she gave the king 120 talents*i* of gold, large quantities of spices, and precious stones. Never again were so many spices brought in as those the queen of Sheba gave to King Solomon.

(Hiram's ships brought gold from Ophir; and from there they brought great cargoes of almugwood*j* and precious stones. The king used the almugwood to make supports for the temple of the LORD and for the royal palace, and to make harps and lyres for the musicians. So much almugwood has never been imported or seen since that day.)

King Solomon gave the queen of Sheba all she desired and asked for,

---

*f*That is, probably about 185 bushels (about 6.6 kiloliters)   *g*That is, probably about 375 bushels (about 13.2 kiloliters)   *h*Or *the ascent by which he went up to*   *i*That is, about 4 1/2 tons (about 4 metric tons)   *j*Probably a variant of *algumwood*

besides what he had given her out of his royal bounty. Then she left and returned with her retinue to her own country.

**Psa.
72:1-19**

Solomon celebrates his blessings.

Of Solomon.

Endow the king with your justice, O God,
    the royal son with your righteousness.
He will[k] judge your people in righteousness,
    your afflicted ones with justice.
The mountains will bring prosperity to the people,
    the hills the fruit of righteousness.
He will defend the afflicted among the people
    and save the children of the needy;
    he will crush the oppressor.

He will endure[l] as long as the sun,
    as long as the moon, through all generations.
He will be like rain falling on a mown field,
    like showers watering the earth.
In his days the righteous will flourish;
    prosperity will abound till the moon is no more.

He will rule from sea to sea
    and from the River[m] to the ends of the earth.[n]
The desert tribes will bow before him
    and his enemies will lick the dust.
The kings of Tarshish and of distant shores
    will bring tribute to him;
the kings of Sheba and Seba
    will present him gifts.
All kings will bow down to him
    and all nations will serve him.

For he will deliver the needy who cry out,
    the afflicted who have no one to help.
He will take pity on the weak and the needy
    and save the needy from death.
He will rescue them from oppression and violence,
    for precious is their blood in his sight.

Long may he live!
    May gold from Sheba be given him.
May people ever pray for him
    and bless him all day long.
Let grain abound throughout the land;
    on the tops of the hills may it sway.
Let its fruit flourish like Lebanon;
    let it thrive like the grass of the field.
May his name endure forever;
    may it continue as long as the sun.

---

[k]Or *May he*; similarly in verses 3–11 and 17   [l]Septuagint; Hebrew *You will be feared*
[m]That is, the Euphrates   [n]Or *the end of the land*

> All nations will be blessed through him,
> and they will call him blessed.
>
> Praise be to the LORD God, the God of Israel,
> who alone does marvelous deeds.
> Praise be to his glorious name forever;
> may the whole earth be filled with his glory.
>
> Amen and Amen.

Proverbs of Solomon

As the historical record has indicated, Solomon the wise king is the author of literally thousands of proverbs. The proverbs are short poems, usually in the form of couplets, which set high ethical standards and give practical advice for daily living through the use of comparative, or perhaps antithetical, imagery. For example:

> A word aptly spoken
> is like apples of gold in settings of silver.
> or:
> The kisses of an enemy may be profuse,
> but faithful are the wounds of a friend.

Such poetic verses place high value on wisdom and sharply contrast good and evil, righteousness and wickedness, justice and injustice. Both in style and content the proverbs are somewhat typical of the wisdom literature prevalent during this time, not only in Israel but in other countries as well, including Mesopotamia and Egypt. Of particular similarity is the Egyptian "Teachings of Amen-em-opet." It is not known which culture influenced the other, if indeed there is any connection at all. However, the Hebrew proverbs are distinct in that all wisdom is seen as flowing from the true God, rather than being a mere accumulation of human observation and experience.

Many of the proverbs and other wise sayings recorded in Scripture may have been written either earlier or even later than Solomon's time—including several by Agur and Lemuel, whose further identities are not revealed. Putting aside questions of specific authorship, and simply recognizing that a substantial number of the sayings are written by Solomon, the entire collection is presented at this point.

The various proverbs and wise sayings, which number more than 600, fall amid several discourses and narratives on wisdom. To facilitate understanding, the proverbs and wise sayings are presented here under appropriate topic headings. (Many of the proverbs could easily be placed under more than one topic, and therefore the topics themselves are necessarily arbitrary.) By seeing the individual proverbs in the context of others dealing with the same subject, one can gain a richer appreciation for "the wisdom which comes from above."

The Book of Proverbs——— ARRANGED TOPICALLY ———

Introduction to wisdom

The Call of Wisdom

Prov.
8:1-11

Does not wisdom call out?
　　Does not understanding raise her voice?
On the heights along the way,
　　where the paths meet, she takes her stand;
beside the gates leading into the city,
　　at the entrances, she cries aloud:
"To you, O men, I call out;
　　I raise my voice to all mankind.
You who are simple, gain prudence;
　　you who are foolish, gain understanding.
Listen, for I have worthy things to say;
　　I open my lips to speak what is right.
My mouth speaks what is true,
　　for my lips detest wickedness.
All the words of my mouth are just;
　　none of them is crooked or perverse.
To the discerning all of them are right;
　　they are faultless to those who have knowledge.
Choose my instruction instead of silver,
　　knowledge rather than choice gold,
for wisdom is more precious than rubies,
　　and nothing you desire can compare with her.

Prov.
8:12-31

"I, wisdom, dwell together with prudence;
　　I possess knowledge and discretion.
To fear the LORD is to hate evil;
　　I hate pride and arrogance,
　　evil behavior and perverse speech.
Counsel and sound judgment are mine;
　　I have understanding and power.
By me kings reign
　　and rulers make laws that are just;
by me princes govern,
　　and all nobles who rule on earth.[o]
I love those who love me,
　　and those who seek me find me.
With me are riches and honor,
　　enduring wealth and prosperity.
My fruit is better than fine gold;
　　what I yield surpasses choice silver.
I walk in the way of righteousness,
　　along the paths of justice,
bestowing wealth on those who love me
　　and making their treasuries full.

[o]Many Hebrew manuscripts and Septuagint; most Hebrew manuscripts *and nobles—all
righteous rulers*

"The LORD brought me forth as the first of his works,[p, q]
    before his deeds of old;
I was appointed[r] from eternity,
    from the beginning, before the world began.
When there were no oceans, I was given birth,
    when there were no springs abounding with water;
before the mountains were settled in place,
    before the hills, I was given birth,
before he made the earth or its fields
    or any of the dust of the world.
I was there when he set the heavens in place,
    when he marked out the horizon on the face of the deep,
when he established the clouds above
    and fixed securely the fountains of the deep,
when he gave the sea its boundary
    so the waters would not overstep his command,
and when he marked out the foundations of the earth.
    Then I was the craftsman at his side.
I was filled with delight day after day,
    rejoicing always in his presence,
rejoicing in his whole world
    and delighting in mankind.

"Now then, my sons, listen to me;
    blessed are those who keep my ways.
                        Prov. 8:32-36
Listen to my instruction and be wise;
    do not ignore it.
Blessed is the man who listens to me,
    watching daily at my doors,
    waiting at my doorway.
For whoever finds me finds life
    and receives favor from the LORD.
But whoever fails to find me harms himself;
    all who hate me love death."
Wisdom has built her house;
    she has hewn out its seven pillars.   **Prov. 9:1-6**
She has prepared her meat and mixed her wine;
    she has also set her table.
She has sent out her maids, and she calls
    from the highest point of the city.
"Let all who are simple come in here!"
    she says to those who lack judgment.
"Come, eat my food
    and drink the wine I have mixed.
Leave your simple ways and you will live;
    walk in the way of understanding.

Benefits of Following Wisdom

My son, if you accept my words
    and store up my commands within you,   **Prov. 2:1-22**

[p]Or way; or dominion   [q]Or The LORD possessed me at the beginning of his work; or The LORD brought me forth at the beginning of his work   [r]Or fashioned

turning your ear to wisdom
    and applying your heart to understanding,
and if you call out for insight
    and cry aloud for understanding,
and if you look for it as for silver
    and search for it as for hidden treasure,
then you will understand the fear of the LORD
    and find the knowledge of God.
For the LORD gives wisdom,
    and from his mouth come knowledge and understanding.
He holds victory in store for the upright,
    he is a shield to those whose walk is blameless,
for he guards the course of the just
    and protects the way of his faithful ones.

Then you will understand what is right and just
    and fair—every good path.
For wisdom will enter your heart,
    and knowledge will be pleasant to your soul.
Discretion will protect you,
    and understanding will guard you.

Wisdom will save you from the ways of wicked men,
    from men whose words are perverse,
who leave the straight paths
    to walk in dark ways,
who delight in doing wrong
    and rejoice in the perverseness of evil,
whose paths are crooked
    and who are devious in their ways.

It will save you also from the adulteress,
    from the wayward wife with her seductive words,
who has left the partner of her youth
    and ignored the covenant she made before God.[s]
For her house leads down to death
    and her paths to the spirits of the dead.
None who go to her return
    or attain the paths of life.

Thus you will walk in the ways of good men
    and keep to the paths of the righteous.
For the upright will live in the land,
    and the blameless will remain in it;
but the wicked will be cut off from the land,
    and the unfaithful will be torn from it.

Prov.
3:13-24

Blessed is the man who finds wisdom,
    the man who gains understanding,
for she is more profitable than silver
    and yields better returns than gold.
She is more precious than rubies;

[s]Or *covenant of her God*

nothing you desire can compare with her.
Long life is in her right hand;
 in her left hand are riches and honor.
Her ways are pleasant ways,
 and all her paths are peace.
She is a tree of life to those who embrace her;
 those who lay hold of her will be blessed.

By wisdom the LORD laid the earth's foundations,
 by understanding he set the heavens in place;
by his knowledge the deeps were divided,
 and the clouds let drop the dew.

My son, preserve sound judgment and discernment,
 do not let them out of your sight;
they will be life for you,
 an ornament to grace your neck.
Then you will go on your way in safety,
 and your foot will not stumble;
when you lie down, you will not be afraid;
 when you lie down, your sleep will be sweet.

Dangers of Rejecting Wisdom

Wisdom calls aloud in the street,
 she raises her voice in the public squares;
at the head of the noisy streets*ᵗ* she cries out,
 in the gateways of the city she makes her speech:

"How long will you simple ones*ᵘ* love your simple ways?
 How long will mockers delight in mockery
 and fools hate knowledge?
If you had responded to my rebuke,
 I would have poured out my heart to you
 and made my thoughts known to you.
But since you rejected me when I called
 and no one gave heed when I stretched out my hand,
since you ignored all my advice
 and would not accept my rebuke,
I in turn will laugh at your disaster;
 I will mock when calamity overtakes you—
when calamity overtakes you like a storm,
 when disaster sweeps over you like a whirlwind,
 when distress and trouble overwhelm you.

"Then they will call to me but I will not answer;
 they will look for me but will not find me.
Since they hated knowledge
 and did not choose to fear the LORD,
since they would not accept my advice
 and spurned my rebuke,
they will eat the fruit of their ways

**Prov.
1:20-33**

---

*ᵗ*Hebrew; Septuagint / *on the tops of the walls*   *ᵘ*The Hebrew word rendered *simple* in
Proverbs generally denotes one without moral direction and inclined to evil.

and be filled with the fruit of their schemes.
For the waywardness of the simple will kill them,
    and the complacency of fools will destroy them;
but whoever listens to me will live in safety
    and be at ease, without fear of harm."

**Prov.
9:13-18**

The woman Folly is loud;
    she is undisciplined and without knowledge.
She sits at the door of her house,
    on a seat at the highest point of the city,
calling out to those who pass by,
    who go straight on their way.
"Let all who are simple come in here!"
    she says to those who lack judgment.
"Stolen water is sweet;
    food eaten in secret is delicious!"
But little do they know that the dead are there,
    that her guests are in the depths of the grave.[v]

Solomon's Personal Plea

**Prov.
4:1-27**

Listen, my sons, to a father's instruction;
    pay attention and gain understanding.
I give you sound learning,
    so do not forsake my teaching.
When I was a boy in my father's house,
    still tender, and an only child of my mother,
he taught me and said,
    "Lay hold of my words with all your heart;
    keep my commands and you will live.
Get wisdom, get understanding;
    do not forget my words or swerve from them.
Do not forsake wisdom, and she will protect you;
    love her, and she will watch over you.
Wisdom is supreme; therefore get wisdom.
    Though it cost all you have,[w] get understanding.
Esteem her, and she will exalt you;
    embrace her, and she will honor you.
She will set a garland of grace on your head
    and present you with a crown of splendor."

Listen, my son, accept what I say,
    and the years of your life will be many.
I guide you in the way of wisdom
    and lead you along straight paths.
When you walk, your steps will not be hampered;
    when you run, you will not stumble.
Hold on to instruction, do not let it go;
    guard it well, for it is your life.
Do not set foot on the path of the wicked
    or walk in the way of evil men.

[v]Hebrew *Sheol*   [w]Or *Whatever else you get*

Avoid it, do not travel on it;
 turn from it and go on your way.
For they cannot sleep till they do evil;
 they are robbed of slumber till they make someone fall.
They eat the bread of wickedness
 and drink the wine of violence.

The path of the righteous is like the first gleam of dawn,
 shining ever brighter till the full light of day.
But the way of the wicked is like deep darkness;
 they do not know what makes them stumble.

My son, pay attention to what I say;
 listen closely to my words.
Do not let them out of your sight,
 keep them within your heart;
for they are life to those who find them
 and health to a man's whole body.
Above all else, guard your heart,
 for it is the wellspring of life.
Put away perversity from your mouth;
 keep corrupt talk far from your lips.
Let your eyes look straight ahead,
 fix your gaze directly before you.
Make level[x] paths for your feet
 and take only ways that are firm.
Do not swerve to the right or the left;
 keep your foot from evil.

Proverbs of Solomon and Sayings of the Wise

Value of Wise Sayings

Pay attention and listen to the sayings of the wise;
 apply your heart to what I teach,
for it is pleasing when you keep them in your heart
 and have all of them ready on your lips.
So that your trust may be in the LORD,
 I teach you today, even you.
Have I not written thirty[y] sayings for you,
 sayings of counsel and knowledge,
teaching you true and reliable words,
 so that you can give sound answers
 to him who sent you?

Prov.
22:17-21

Purpose of the Proverbs

The proverbs of Solomon son of David, king of Israel:

Prov. 1:1-7

for attaining wisdom and discipline;
 for understanding words of insight;
for acquiring a disciplined and prudent life,
 doing what is right and just and fair;

---

[x] Or *Consider the*   [y] Or *not formerly written;* or *not written excellent*

for giving prudence to the simple,
knowledge and discretion to the young—
let the wise listen and add to their learning,
and let the discerning get guidance—
for understanding proverbs and parables,
the sayings and riddles of the wise.

The fear of the LORD is the beginning of knowledge,
but fools[z] despise wisdom and discipline.

Prov. 25:1 These are more proverbs of Solomon, copied by the men of Hezekiah king of Judah:

Preeminence of God

Fear of the Lord

Prov. 9:10-12 "The fear of the LORD is the beginning of wisdom,
and knowledge of the Holy One is understanding.
For through me your days will be many,
and years will be added to your life.
If you are wise, your wisdom will reward you;
if you are a mocker, you alone will suffer."

10:27 The fear of the LORD adds length to life,
but the years of the wicked are cut short.

14:2 He whose walk is upright fears the LORD,
but he whose ways are devious despises him.

14:26,27 He who fears the LORD has a secure fortress,
and for his children it will be a refuge.

The fear of the LORD is a fountain of life,
turning a man from the snares of death.

15:33 The fear of the LORD teaches a man wisdom,[a]
and humility comes before honor.

19:23 The fear of the LORD leads to life:
Then one rests content, untouched by trouble.

28:14 Blessed is the man who always fears the LORD,
but he who hardens his heart falls into trouble.

Trust in God or self

Prov. 3:5-8 Trust in the LORD with all your heart
and lean not on your own understanding;
in all your ways acknowledge him,
and he will make your paths straight.[b]

Do not be wise in your own eyes;
fear the LORD and shun evil.
This will bring health to your body
and nourishment to your bones.

[z]The Hebrew words rendered *fool* in Proverbs, and often elsewhere in the Old Testament, denote one who is morally deficient.   [a]Or *Wisdom teaches the fear of the LORD*   [b]Or *will direct your paths*

There is a way that seems right to a man,
    but in the end it leads to death.
14:12
16:25

Commit to the LORD whatever you do,
    and your plans will succeed.
16:3

Whoever gives heed to instruction prospers,
    and blessed is he who trusts in the LORD.
16:20

A fool finds no pleasure in understanding
    but delights in airing his own opinions.
18:2

The words of a man's mouth are deep waters,
    but the fountain of wisdom is a bubbling brook.
18:4

The name of the LORD is a strong tower;
    the righteous run to it and are safe.
18:10

A man's own folly ruins his life,
    yet his heart rages against the LORD.
19:3

A man's steps are directed by the LORD.
    How then can anyone understand his own way?
20:24

A wise man attacks the city of the mighty
    and pulls down the stronghold in which they trust.
21:22

Do you see a man wise in his own eyes?
    There is more hope for a fool than for him.
26:12

He who trusts in himself is a fool,
    but he who walks in wisdom is kept safe.
28:26

Fear of man will prove to be a snare,
    but whoever trusts in the LORD is kept safe.
29:25

Divine providence

The eyes of the LORD are everywhere,
    keeping watch on the wicked and the good.
Prov. 15:3

To man belong the plans of the heart,
    but from the LORD comes the reply of the tongue.
16:1

The LORD works out everything for his own ends—
    even the wicked for a day of disaster.
16:4

In his heart a man plans his course,
    but the LORD determines his steps.
16:9

The lot is cast into the lap,
    but its every decision is from the LORD.
16:33

Many are the plans in a man's heart,
    but it is the LORD's purpose that prevails.
19:21

There is no wisdom, no insight, no plan
    that can succeed against the LORD.
21:30,31

The horse is made ready for the day of battle,
    but victory rests with the LORD.

22:12	The eyes of the LORD keep watch over knowledge,
	but he frustrates the words of the unfaithful.
27:1	Do not boast about tomorrow,
	for you do not know what a day may bring forth.

Insight and Ignorance

Wisdom and folly

Prov. 13:14	The teaching of the wise is a fountain of life,
	turning a man from the snares of death.
14:24	The wealth of the wise is their crown,
	but the folly of fools yields folly.
15:24	The path of life leads upward for the wise
	to keep him from going down to the grave.[c]
16:22	Understanding is a fountain of life to those who have it,
	but folly brings punishment to fools.
17:12	Better to meet a bear robbed of her cubs
	than a fool in his folly.
24:7	Wisdom is too high for a fool;
	in the assembly at the gate he has nothing to say.
24:13,14	Eat honey, my son, for it is good;
	honey from the comb is sweet to your taste.
	Know also that wisdom is sweet to your soul;
	if you find it, there is a future hope for you,
	and your hope will not be cut off.

Dealing with fools

Prov.
26:4-11	Do not answer a fool according to his folly,
	or you will be like him yourself.
	Answer a fool according to his folly,
	or he will be wise in his own eyes.
	Like cutting off one's feet or drinking violence
	is the sending of a message by the hand of a fool.
	Like a lame man's legs that hang limp
	is a proverb in the mouth of a fool.
	Like tying a stone in a sling
	is the giving of honor to a fool.
	Like a thornbush in a drunkard's hand
	is a proverb in the mouth of a fool.
	Like an archer who wounds at random
	is he who hires a fool or any passer-by.
	As a dog returns to its vomit,
	so a fool repeats his folly.

[c]Hebrew *Sheol*

Though you grind a fool in a mortar,   27:22
   grinding him like grain with a pestle,
   you will not remove his folly from him.

If a wise man goes to court with a fool,   29:9
   the fool rages and scoffs, and there is no peace.

Discernment and understanding

Wisdom is found on the lips of the discerning,   Prov. 10:13
   but a rod is for the back of him who lacks judgment.

A fool finds pleasure in evil conduct,   10:23
   but a man of understanding delights in wisdom.

Good understanding wins favor,   13:15
   but the way of the unfaithful is hard.*d*

The mocker seeks wisdom and finds none,   14:6
   but knowledge comes easily to the discerning.

The wisdom of the prudent is to give thought to their ways,   14:8
   but the folly of fools is deception.

A simple man believes anything,   14:15
   but a prudent man gives thought to his steps.

Wisdom reposes in the heart of the discerning   14:33
   and even among fools she lets herself be known.*e*

Folly delights a man who lacks judgment,   15:21
   but a man of understanding keeps a straight course.

How much better to get wisdom than gold,   16:16
   to choose understanding rather than silver!

A discerning man keeps wisdom in view,   17:24
   but a fool's eyes wander to the ends of the earth.

He who gets wisdom loves his own soul;   19:8
   he who cherishes understanding prospers.

The purposes of a man's heart are deep waters,   20:5
   but a man of understanding draws them out.

Ears that hear and eyes that see—   20:12
   the LORD has made them both.

Knowledge

Wise men store up knowledge,   Prov. 10:14
   but the mouth of a fool invites ruin.

Every prudent man acts out of knowledge,   13:16
   but a fool exposes his folly.

The simple inherit folly,   14:18
   but the prudent are crowned with knowledge.

The discerning heart seeks knowledge,   15:14

*d*Or *unfaithful does not endure*   *e*Hebrew; Septuagint and Syriac / *but in the heart of fools*
she is not known

but the mouth of a fool feeds on folly.

18:15 The heart of the discerning acquires knowledge;
the ears of the wise seek it out.

19:2 It is not good to have zeal without knowledge,
nor to be hasty and miss the way.

20:15 Gold there is, and rubies in abundance,
but lips that speak knowledge are a rare jewel.

21:11 When a mocker is punished, the simple gain wisdom;
when a wise man is instructed, he gets knowledge.

23:12 Apply your heart to instruction
and your ears to words of knowledge.

24:3,4 By wisdom a house is built,
and through understanding it is established;
through knowledge its rooms are filled
with rare and beautiful treasures.

Sharing and Responding to Wisdom

Advice and rebuke

Prov. 3:1,2 My son, do not forget my teaching,
but keep my commands in your heart,
for they will prolong your life many years
and bring you prosperity.

9:7-9 "Whoever corrects a mocker invites insult;
whoever rebukes a wicked man incurs abuse.
Do not rebuke a mocker or he will hate you;
rebuke a wise man and he will love you.
Instruct a wise man and he will be wiser still;
teach a righteous man and he will add to his learning.

10:8 The wise in heart accept commands,
but a chattering fool comes to ruin.

12:15 The way of a fool seems right to him,
but a wise man listens to advice.

13:1 A wise son heeds his father's instruction,
but a mocker does not listen to rebuke.

13:13 He who scorns instruction will pay for it,
but he who respects a command is rewarded.

15:31 He who listens to a life-giving rebuke
will be at home among the wise.

17:10 A rebuke impresses a man of discernment
more than a hundred lashes a fool.

19:16 He who obeys instructions guards his life,
but he who is contemptuous of his ways will die.

19:20 Listen to advice and accept instruction,
and in the end you will be wise.

Flog a mocker, and the simple will learn prudence;
    rebuke a discerning man, and he will gain knowledge.
                           19:25

Stop listening to instruction, my son,
    and you will stray from the words of knowledge.
                           19:27

Do not speak to a fool,
    for he will scorn the wisdom of your words.
                           23:9

Like an earring of gold or an ornament of fine gold
    is a wise man's rebuke to a listening ear.
                           25:12

Better is open rebuke
    than hidden love.
                           27:5,6

Wounds from a friend can be trusted,
    but an enemy multiplies kisses.

As iron sharpens iron,
    so one man sharpens another.
                           27:17

A man who remains stiff-necked after many rebukes
    will suddenly be destroyed—without remedy.
                           29:1

Value of advisers

For lack of guidance a nation falls,
    but many advisers make victory sure.
                     Prov. 11:14

Plans fail for lack of counsel,
    but with many advisers they succeed.
                           15:22

Make plans by seeking advice;
    if you wage war, obtain guidance.
                           20:18

A wise man has great power,
    and a man of knowledge increases strength;
for waging war you need guidance,
    and for victory many advisers.
                           24:5,6

Discipline

My son, do not despise the LORD's discipline
    and do not resent his rebuke,
because the LORD disciplines those he loves,
    as a father*f* the son he delights in.
                     Prov.
                     3:11,12

He who heeds discipline shows the way to life,
    but whoever ignores correction leads others astray.
                           10:17

Whoever loves discipline loves knowledge,
    but he who hates correction is stupid.
                           12:1

He who ignores discipline comes to poverty and shame,
    but whoever heeds correction is honored.
                           13:18

He who spares the rod hates his son,
    but he who loves him is careful to discipline him.
                           13:24

f Hebrew; Septuagint / *and he punishes*

15:5	A fool spurns his father's discipline, 　but whoever heeds correction shows prudence.
15:10	Stern discipline awaits him who leaves the path; 　he who hates correction will die.
15:12	A mocker resents correction; 　he will not consult the wise.
15:32	He who ignores discipline despises himself, 　but whoever heeds correction gains understanding.
19:18	Discipline your son, for in that there is hope; 　do not be a willing party to his death.
20:30	Blows and wounds cleanse away evil, 　and beatings purge the inmost being.
22:6	Train*g* a child in the way he should go, 　and when he is old he will not turn from it.
22:15	Folly is bound up in the heart of a child, 　but the rod of discipline will drive it far from him.
23:13,14	Do not withhold discipline from a child; 　if you punish him with the rod, he will not die. Punish him with the rod 　and save his soul from death.*h*
29:15	The rod of correction imparts wisdom, 　but a child left to himself disgraces his mother.
29:17	Discipline your son, and he will give you peace; 　he will bring delight to your soul.
29:19	A servant cannot be corrected by mere words; 　though he understands, he will not respond.
29:21	If a man pampers his servant from youth, 　he will bring grief*i* in the end.

Lawkeeping

Prov. 28:4	Those who forsake the law praise the wicked, 　but those who keep the law resist them.
28:7	He who keeps the law is a discerning son, 　but a companion of gluttons disgraces his father.
28:9	If anyone turns a deaf ear to the law, 　even his prayers are detestable.
29:18	Where there is no revelation, the people cast off restraint; 　but blessed is he who keeps the law.

Repentance

Prov. 14:9	Fools mock at making amends for sin, 　but goodwill is found among the upright.

---

*g*Or *Start*　　*h*Hebrew *Sheol*　　*i*The meaning of the Hebrew for this word is uncertain.

He who conceals his sins does not prosper,   28:13
  but whoever confesses and renounces them finds mercy.

Good and Evil

Righteousness and wickedness

Blessings crown the head of the righteous,   Prov.
  but violence overwhelms the mouth of the wicked.*j*   10:6,7

The memory of the righteous will be a blessing,
  but the name of the wicked will rot.

The wages of the righteous bring them life,   10:16
  but the income of the wicked brings them punishment.

The prospect of the righteous is joy,   10:28-30
  but the hopes of the wicked come to nothing.

The way of the LORD is a refuge for the righteous,
  but it is the ruin of those who do evil.

The righteous will never be uprooted,
  but the wicked will not remain in the land.

The righteousness of the blameless makes a straight way for   11:3-10
    them,
  but the wicked are brought down by their own wickedness.

The righteousness of the upright delivers them,
  but the unfaithful are trapped by evil desires.

When a wicked man dies, his hope perishes;
  all he expected from his power comes to nothing.

The righteous man is rescued from trouble,
  and it comes on the wicked instead.

With his mouth the godless destroys his neighbor,
  but through knowledge the righteous escape.

When the righteous prosper, the city rejoices;
  when the wicked perish, there are shouts of joy.

The wicked man earns deceptive wages,   11:18-20
  but he who sows righteousness reaps a sure reward.

The truly righteous man attains life,
  but he who pursues evil goes to his death.

The LORD detests men of perverse heart
  but he delights in those whose ways are blameless.

The desire of the righteous ends only in good,   11:23
  but the hope of the wicked only in wrath.

A good man obtains favor from the LORD,   12:2,3
  but the LORD condemns a crafty man.

j Or but the mouth of the wicked conceals violence

A man cannot be established through wickedness,
    but the righteous cannot be uprooted.

12:5-8   The plans of the righteous are just,
    but the advice of the wicked is deceitful.

The words of the wicked lie in wait for blood,
    but the speech of the upright rescues them.

Wicked men are overthrown and are no more,
    but the house of the righteous stands firm.

A man is praised according to his wisdom,
    but men with warped minds are despised.

12:12   The wicked desire the plunder of evil men,
    but the root of the righteous flourishes.

12:21   No harm befalls the righteous,
    but the wicked have their fill of trouble.

12:28   In the way of righteousness there is life;
    along that path is immortality.

13:9   The light of the righteous shines brightly,
    but the lamp of the wicked is snuffed out.

13:21   Misfortune pursues the sinner,
    but prosperity is the reward of the righteous.

13:25   The righteous eat to their hearts' content,
    but the stomach of the wicked goes hungry.

14:11   The house of the wicked will be destroyed,
    but the tent of the upright will flourish.

14:19   Evil men will bow down in the presence of the good,
    and the wicked at the gates of the righteous.

14:34   Righteousness exalts a nation,
    but sin is a disgrace to any people.

15:6   The house of the righteous contains great treasure,
    but the income of the wicked brings them trouble.

15:9   The LORD detests the way of the wicked
    but he loves those who pursue righteousness.

20:7   The righteous man leads a blameless life;
    blessed are his children after him.

21:18   The wicked become a ransom for the righteous,
    and the unfaithful for the upright.

24:15,16   Do not lie in wait like an outlaw against a righteous man's
       house,
    do not raid his dwelling place;
for though a righteous man falls seven times, he rises again,
    but the wicked are brought down by calamity.

When the righteous triumph, there is great elation;   28:12
    but when the wicked rise to power, men go into hiding.

When the wicked rise to power, people go into hiding;   28:28
    but when the wicked perish, the righteous thrive.

When the righteous thrive, the people rejoice;   29:2
    when the wicked rule, the people groan.

When the wicked thrive, so does sin,   29:16
    but the righteous will see their downfall.

The righteous detest the dishonest;   29:27
    the wicked detest the upright.

Integrity and perversion

The man of integrity walks securely,   Prov. 10:9
    but he who takes crooked paths will be found out.

Righteousness guards the man of integrity,   13:6
    but wickedness overthrows the sinner.

The LORD detests the thoughts of the wicked,   15:26
    but those of the pure are pleasing to him.

The way of the guilty is devious,   21:8
    but the conduct of the innocent is upright.

He who plots evil   24:8,9
    will be known as a schemer.
The schemes of folly are sin,
    and men detest a mocker.

He whose walk is blameless is kept safe,   28:18
    but he whose ways are perverse will suddenly fall.

Bloodthirsty men hate a man of integrity   29:10
    and seek to kill the upright.

Appropriate consequences

The LORD's curse is on the house of the wicked,   Prov.
    but he blesses the home of the righteous.   3:33-35
He mocks proud mockers
    but gives grace to the humble.
The wise inherit honor,
    but fools he holds up to shame.
The LORD does not let the righteous go hungry   10:3
    but he thwarts the craving of the wicked.

The blessing of the LORD brings wealth,   10:22
    and he adds no trouble to it.

What the wicked dreads will overtake him;   10:24,25
    what the righteous desire will be granted.

When the storm has swept by, the wicked are gone,
    but the righteous stand firm forever.

Be sure of this: The wicked will not go unpunished,   11:21

but those who are righteous will go free.

11:27
He who seeks good finds goodwill,
but evil comes to him who searches for it.

11:30,31
The fruit of the righteous is a tree of life,
and he who wins souls is wise.

If the righteous receive their due on earth,
how much more the ungodly and the sinner!

14:14
The faithless will be fully repaid for their ways,
and the good man rewarded for his.

14:22
Do not those who plot evil go astray?
But those who plan what is good find*k* love and faithfulness.

16:7
When a man's ways are pleasing to the LORD,
he makes even his enemies live at peace with him.

17:13
If a man pays back evil for good,
evil will never leave his house.

18:3
When wickedness comes, so does contempt,
and with shame comes disgrace.

19:29
Penalties are prepared for mockers,
and beatings for the backs of fools.

21:12
The Righteous One*l* takes note of the house of the wicked
and brings the wicked to ruin.

21:16
A man who strays from the path of understanding
comes to rest in the company of the dead.

21:21
He who pursues righteousness and love
finds life, prosperity*m* and honor.

22:8
He who sows wickedness reaps trouble,
and the rod of his fury will be destroyed.

26:1
Like snow in summer or rain in harvest,
honor is not fitting for a fool.

26:3
A whip for the horse, a halter for the donkey,
and a rod for the backs of fools!

26:27
If a man digs a pit, he will fall into it;
if a man rolls a stone, it will roll back on him.

Sincere Motivation

Motive and the heart

Prov. 15:11
Death and Destruction*n* lie open before the LORD—
how much more the hearts of men!

16:2
All a man's ways seem innocent to him,
but motives are weighed by the LORD.

---

*k*Or *show*   *l*Or *The righteous man*   *m*Or *righteousness*   *n*Hebrew *Sheol and Abaddon*

The crucible for silver and the furnace for gold,   17:3
    but the LORD tests the heart.

Even a child is known by his actions,   20:11
    by whether his conduct is pure and right.

The lamp of the LORD searches the spirit of a man^o;   20:27
    it searches out his inmost being.

All a man's ways seem right to him,   21:2
    but the LORD weighs the heart.

As water reflects a face,   27:19
    so a man's heart reflects the man.

False worship

The LORD detests the sacrifice of the wicked,   **Prov. 15:8**
    but the prayer of the upright pleases him.

The LORD is far from the wicked   15:29
    but he hears the prayer of the righteous.

To do what is right and just   21:3
    is more acceptable to the LORD than sacrifice.

The sacrifice of the wicked is detestable—   21:27
    how much more so when brought with evil intent!

Duplicity

A scoundrel and villain,   **Prov.**
    who goes about with a corrupt mouth,   **6:12-15**
    who winks with his eye,
    signals with his feet
    and motions with his fingers,
    who plots evil with deceit in his heart—
    he always stirs up dissension.
Therefore disaster will overtake him in an instant;
    he will suddenly be destroyed—without remedy.

He who winks maliciously causes grief,   10:10,11
    and a chattering fool comes to ruin.

The mouth of the righteous is a fountain of life,
    but violence overwhelms the mouth of the wicked.

The integrity of the upright guides them,   11:3
    but the unfaithful are destroyed by their duplicity.

He who winks with his eye is plotting perversity;   16:30
    he who purses his lips is bent on evil.

"It's no good, it's no good!" says the buyer;   20:14
    then off he goes and boasts about his purchase.

Do not eat the food of a stingy man,   23:6-8
    do not crave his delicacies;

---

^oOr *The spirit of man is the LORD's lamp*

for he is the kind of man
who is always thinking about the cost.*p*
"Eat and drink," he says to you,
but his heart is not with you.
You will vomit up the little you have eaten
and will have wasted your compliments.

26:23-26
Like a coating of glaze*q* over earthenware
are fervent lips with an evil heart.

A malicious man disguises himself with his lips,
but in his heart he harbors deceit.
Though his speech is charming, do not believe him,
for seven abominations fill his heart.
His malice may be concealed by deception,
but his wickedness will be exposed in the assembly.

Concern for Others

Love and faithfulness

Prov. 3:3,4
Let love and faithfulness never leave you;
bind them around your neck,
write them on the tablet of your heart.
Then you will win favor and a good name
in the sight of God and man.

16:6
Through love and faithfulness sin is atoned for;
through the fear of the LORD a man avoids evil.

20:6
Many a man claims to have unfailing love,
but a faithful man who can find?

25:19
Like a bad tooth or a lame foot
is reliance on the unfaithful in times of trouble.

Love, hatred, and compassion

Prov. 10:12
Hatred stirs up dissension,
but love covers over all wrongs.

15:17
Better a meal of vegetables where there is love
than a fattened calf with hatred.

17:5
He who mocks the poor shows contempt for their Maker;
whoever gloats over disaster will not go unpunished.

24:17,18
Do not gloat when your enemy falls;
when he stumbles, do not let your heart rejoice,
or the LORD will see and disapprove
and turn his wrath away from him.

25:21,22
If your enemy is hungry, give him food to eat;
if he is thirsty, give him water to drink.
In doing this, you will heap burning coals on his head,
and the LORD will reward you.

---

*p*Or *for as he thinks within himself, / so he is;* or *for as he puts on a feast, / so he is*   *q*With
a different word division of the Hebrew; Masoretic Text *of silver dross*

Kindness and mercy

A kindhearted woman gains respect,
but ruthless men gain only wealth.

Prov.
11:16,17

A kind man benefits himself,
but a cruel man brings trouble on himself.

A righteous man cares for the needs of his animal,
but the kindest acts of the wicked are cruel.

12:10

An anxious heart weighs a man down,
but a kind word cheers him up.

12:25

The wicked man craves evil;
his neighbor gets no mercy from him.

21:10

Overstaying welcome

If you find honey, eat just enough—
too much of it, and you will vomit.
Seldom set foot in your neighbor's house—
too much of you, and he will hate you.

Prov.
25:16,17

Concern for Self

Pride and humility

When pride comes, then comes disgrace,
but with humility comes wisdom.

Prov. 11:2

Better to be a nobody and yet have a servant
than pretend to be somebody and have no food.

12:9

One man pretends to be rich, yet has nothing;
another pretends to be poor, yet has great wealth.

13:7

Pride only breeds quarrels,
but wisdom is found in those who take advice.

13:10

The LORD tears down the proud man's house
but he keeps the widow's boundaries intact.

15:25

The LORD detests all the proud of heart.
Be sure of this: They will not go unpunished.

16:5

Pride goes before destruction,
a haughty spirit before a fall.

16:18,19

Better to be lowly in spirit and among the oppressed
than to share plunder with the proud.

Before his downfall a man's heart is proud,
but humility comes before honor.

18:12

It is not fitting for a fool to live in luxury—
how much worse for a slave to rule over princes!

19:10

Who can say, "I have kept my heart pure;
I am clean and without sin"?

20:9

Haughty eyes and a proud heart,

21:4

the lamp of the wicked, are sin!

21:24 The proud and arrogant man— "Mocker" is his name;
  he behaves with overweening pride.

22:4 Humility and the fear of the LORD
  bring wealth and honor and life.

25:27 It is not good to eat too much honey,
  nor is it honorable to seek one's own honor.

26:16 The sluggard is wiser in his own eyes
  than seven men who answer discreetly.

27:2 Let another praise you, and not your own mouth;
  someone else, and not your own lips.

27:21 The crucible for silver and the furnace for gold,
  but man is tested by the praise he receives.

29:23 A man's pride brings him low,
  but a man of lowly spirit gains honor.

Selfishness

Prov. 18:1 An unfriendly man pursues selfish ends;
  he defies all sound judgment.

Jealousy

Prov. 27:4 Anger is cruel and fury overwhelming,
  but who can stand before jealousy?

Envy

Prov. 14:30 A heart at peace gives life to the body,
  but envy rots the bones.

24:19,20 Do not fret because of evil men
  or be envious of the wicked,
  for the evil man has no future hope,
  and the lamp of the wicked will be snuffed out.

Greed

Prov. 28:25 A greedy man stirs up dissension,
  but he who trusts in the LORD will prosper.

Control of Self

Self-control

Prov. 25:28 Like a city whose walls are broken down
  is a man who lacks self-control.

29:11 A fool gives full vent to his anger,
  but a wise man keeps himself under control.

Rashness

Prov. 20:25 It is a trap for a man to dedicate something rashly
  and only later to consider his vows.

21:5 The plans of the diligent lead to profit

as surely as haste leads to poverty.

What you have seen with your eyes   25:8
    do not bring[r] hastily to court,
for what will you do in the end
    if your neighbor puts you to shame?

Do you see a man who speaks in haste?   29:20
    There is more hope for a fool than for him.

Temper and patience

A fool shows his annoyance at once,   Prov. 12:16
    but a prudent man overlooks an insult.

A wise man fears the LORD and shuns evil,   14:16,17
    but a fool is hotheaded and reckless.

A quick-tempered man does foolish things,
    and a crafty man is hated.

A patient man has great understanding,   14:29
    but a quick-tempered man displays folly.

A hot-tempered man stirs up dissension,   15:18
    but a patient man calms a quarrel.

Better a patient man than a warrior,   16:32
    a man who controls his temper than one who takes a city.

A man's wisdom gives him patience;   19:11
    it is to his glory to overlook an offense.

A hot-tempered man must pay the penalty;   19:19
    if you rescue him, you will have to do it again.

Do not make friends with a hot-tempered man,   22:24,25
    do not associate with one easily angered,
or you may learn his ways
    and get yourself ensnared.

Mockers stir up a city,   29:8
    but wise men turn away anger.

An angry man stirs up dissension,   29:22
    and a hot-tempered one commits many sins.

Drunkenness and gluttony

Wine is a mocker and beer a brawler;   Prov. 20:1
    whoever is led astray by them is not wise.

Listen, my son, and be wise,   23:19-21
    and keep your heart on the right path.
Do not join those who drink too much wine
    or gorge themselves on meat,
for drunkards and gluttons become poor,
    and drowsiness clothes them in rags.

[r]Or nobleman / on whom you had set your eyes. / [8]Do not go

23:29-35
Who has woe? Who has sorrow?
　　Who has strife? Who has complaints?
　　Who has needless bruises? Who has bloodshot eyes?
Those who linger over wine,
　　who go to sample bowls of mixed wine.
Do not gaze at wine when it is red,
　　when it sparkles in the cup,
　　when it goes down smoothly!
In the end it bites like a snake
　　and poisons like a viper.
Your eyes will see strange sights
　　and your mind imagine confusing things.
You will be like one sleeping on the high seas,
　　lying on top of the rigging.
"They hit me," you will say, "but I'm not hurt!
　　They beat me, but I don't feel it!
When will I wake up
　　so I can find another drink?"

Adultery

Prov. 5:1-6
My son, pay attention to my wisdom,
　　listen well to my words of insight,
that you may maintain discretion
　　and your lips may preserve knowledge.
For the lips of an adulteress drip honey,
　　and her speech is smoother than oil;
but in the end she is bitter as gall,
　　sharp as a double-edged sword.
Her feet go down to death;
　　her steps lead straight to the grave.[s]
She gives no thought to the way of life;
　　her paths are crooked, but she knows it not.

5:7-14
Now then, my sons, listen to me;
　　do not turn aside from what I say.
Keep to a path far from her,
　　do not go near the door of her house,
lest you give your best strength to others
　　and your years to one who is cruel,
lest strangers feast on your wealth
　　and your toil enrich another man's house.
At the end of your life you will groan,
　　when your flesh and body are spent.
You will say, "How I hated discipline!
　　How my heart spurned correction!
I would not obey my teachers
　　or listen to my instructors.
I have come to the brink of utter ruin
　　in the midst of the whole assembly."

5:15:20
Drink water from your own cistern,

[s]Hebrew *Sheol*

running water from your own well.
Should your springs overflow in the streets,
    your streams of water in the public squares?
Let them be yours alone,
    never to be shared with strangers.
May your fountain be blessed,
    and may you rejoice in the wife of your youth.
A loving doe, a graceful deer—
    may her breasts satisfy you always,
    may you ever be captivated by her love.
Why be captivated, my son, by an adulteress?
    Why embrace the bosom of another man's wife?

For a man's ways are in full view of the LORD,   5:21-23
    and he examines all his paths.
The evil deeds of a wicked man ensnare him;
    the cords of his sin hold him fast.
He will die for lack of discipline,
    led astray by his own great folly.

My son, keep your father's commands   6:20-29
    and do not forsake your mother's teaching.
Bind them upon your heart forever;
    fasten them around your neck.
When you walk, they will guide you;
    when you sleep, they will watch over you;
    when you awake, they will speak to you.
For these commands are a lamp,
    this teaching is a light,
and the corrections of discipline
    are the way to life,
keeping you from the immoral woman,
    from the smooth tongue of the wayward wife.
Do not lust in your heart after her beauty
    or let her captivate you with her eyes,
for the prostitute reduces you to a loaf of bread,
    and the adulteress preys upon your very life.
Can a man scoop fire into his lap
    without his clothes being burned?
Can a man walk on hot coals
    without his feet being scorched?
So is he who sleeps with another man's wife;
    no one who touches her will go unpunished.

Men do not despise a thief if he steals   6:30-35
    to satisfy his hunger when he is starving.
Yet if he is caught, he must pay sevenfold,
    though it costs him all the wealth of his house.
But a man who commits adultery lacks judgment;
    whoever does so destroys himself.
Blows and disgrace are his lot,
    and his shame will never be wiped away;
for jealousy arouses a husband's fury,

and he will show no mercy when he takes revenge.
He will not accept any compensation;
   he will refuse the bribe, however great it is.

7:1-5

My son, keep my words
   and store up my commands within you.
Keep my commands and you will live;
   guard my teachings as the apple of your eye.
Bind them on your fingers;
   write them on the tablet of your heart.
Say to wisdom, "You are my sister,"
   and call understanding your kinsman;
they will keep you from the adulteress,
   from the wayward wife with her seductive words.

7:6-9

At the window of my house
   I looked out through the lattice.
I saw among the simple,
   I noticed among the young men,
   a youth who lacked judgment.
He was going down the street near her corner,
   walking along in the direction of her house
at twilight, as the day was fading,
   as the dark of night set in.

7:10-13

Then out came a woman to meet him,
   dressed like a prostitute and with crafty intent.
(She is loud and defiant,
   her feet never stay at home;
now in the street, now in the squares,
   at every corner she lurks.)
She took hold of him and kissed him
   and with a brazen face she said:

7:14-20

"I have fellowship offerings[t] at home;
   today I fulfilled my vows.
So I came out to meet you;
   I looked for you and have found you!
I have covered my bed
   with colored linens from Egypt.
I have perfumed my bed
   with myrrh, aloes and cinnamon.
Come, let's drink deep of love till morning;
   let's enjoy ourselves with love!
My husband is not at home;
   he has gone on a long journey.
He took his purse filled with money
   and will not be home till full moon."

7:21-23

With persuasive words she led him astray;
   she seduced him with her smooth talk.
All at once he followed her

---

[t]Tradionally *peace offerings*

> like an ox going to the slaughter,
> like a deer[u] stepping into a noose[v]
> > till an arrow pierces his liver,
> like a bird darting into a snare,
> > little knowing it will cost him his life.

> Now then, my sons, listen to me;
> > pay attention to what I say.
> Do not let your heart turn to her ways
> > or stray into her paths.
> Many are the victims she has brought down;
> > her slain are a mighty throng.
> Her house is a highway to the grave,[w]
> > leading down to the chambers of death.

7:24-27

> The mouth of an adulteress is a deep pit;
> > he who is under the LORD's wrath will fall into it.

22:14

Prostitution

> My son, give me your heart
> > and let your eyes keep to my ways,
> for a prostitute is a deep pit
> > and a wayward wife is a narrow well.
> Like a bandit she lies in wait,
> > and multiplies the unfaithful among men.

Prov.
23:26-28

> A man who loves wisdom brings joy to his father,
> > but a companion of prostitutes squanders his wealth.

29:3

Control of the Tongue

Wise and foolish talk

> A fool's talk brings a rod to his back,
> > but the lips of the wise protect them.

Prov. 14:3

> The tongue of the wise commends knowledge,
> > but the mouth of the fool gushes folly.

15:2

> The lips of the wise spread knowledge;
> > not so the hearts of fools.

15:7

> A wise man's heart guides his mouth,
> > and his lips promote instruction.[x]

16:23

> A fool's lips bring him strife,
> > and his mouth invites a beating.

18:6,7

> A fool's mouth is his undoing,
> > and his lips are a snare to his soul.

> Better a poor man whose walk is blameless
> > than a fool whose lips are perverse.

19:1

> My son, if your heart is wise,

23:15,16

[u]Syriac (see also Septuagint); Hebrew *fool*   [v]The meaning of the Hebrew for this line is uncertain.   [w]Hebrew *Sheol*   [x]Or *mouth / and makes his lips persuasive*

then my heart will be glad;
  my inmost being will rejoice
    when your lips speak what is right.

Righteous and wicked talk

Prov.
10:20,21

The tongue of the righteous is choice silver,
  but the heart of the wicked is of little value.

The lips of the righteous nourish many,
  but fools die for lack of judgment.

10:31,32

The mouth of the righteous brings forth wisdom,
  but a perverse tongue will be cut out.

The lips of the righteous know what is fitting,
  but the mouth of the wicked only what is perverse.

11:11

Through the blessing of the upright a city is exalted,
  but by the mouth of the wicked it is destroyed.

12:13,14

An evil man is trapped by his sinful talk,
  but a righteous man escapes trouble.

From the fruit of his lips a man is filled with good things
  as surely as the work of his hands rewards him.

13:2

From the fruit of his lips a man enjoys good things,
  but the unfaithful have a craving for violence.

15:28

The heart of the righteous weighs its answers,
  but the mouth of the wicked gushes evil.

17:4

A wicked man listens to evil lips;
  a liar pays attention to a malicious tongue.

Appropriate speech

Prov. 15:23

A man finds joy in giving an apt reply—
  and how good is a timely word!

16:21

The wise in heart are called discerning,
  and pleasant words promote instruction.ʸ

16:24

Pleasant words are a honeycomb,
  sweet to the soul and healing to the bones.

25:11

A word aptly spoken
  is like apples of gold in settings of silver.

27:14

If a man loudly blesses his neighbor early in the morning,
  it will be taken as a curse.

Maintaining silence

Prov. 10:19

When words are many, sin is not absent,
  but he who holds his tongue is wise.

12:23

A prudent man keeps his knowledge to himself,
  but the heart of fools blurts out folly.

ʸOr *words make a man persuasive*

He who guards his lips guards his life,
    but he who speaks rashly will come to ruin.   13:3

Even a fool is thought wise if he keeps silent,
    and discerning if he holds his tongue.   17:28

He who answers before listening—
    that is his folly and his shame.   18:13

He who guards his mouth and his tongue
    keeps himself from calamity.   21:23

Controlled speech

A gentle answer turns away wrath,
    but a harsh word stirs up anger.   Prov. 15:1

A man of knowledge uses words with restraint,
    and a man of understanding is even-tempered.   17:27

Through patience a ruler can be persuaded,
    and a gentle tongue can break a bone.   25:15

Flattery

A lying tongue hates those it hurts,
    and a flattering mouth works ruin.   Prov. 26:28

He who rebukes a man will in the end gain more favor
    than he who has a flattering tongue.   28:23

Whoever flatters his neighbor
    is spreading a net for his feet.   29:5

Slander and gossip

He who conceals his hatred has lying lips,
    and whoever spreads slander is a fool.   Prov. 10:18

A gossip betrays a confidence,
    but a trustworthy man keeps a secret.   11:13

A perverse man stirs up dissension,
    and a gossip separates close friends.   16:28

He who covers over an offense promotes love,
    but whoever repeats the matter separates close friends.   17:9

The words of a gossip are like choice morsels;
    they go down to a man's inmost parts.   18:8
                                                         26:22

A gossip betrays a confidence;
    so avoid a man who talks too much.   20:19

Without wood a fire goes out;
    without gossip a quarrel dies down.   26:20

Hurtful talk

A man who lacks judgment derides his neighbor,
    but a man of understanding holds his tongue.   Prov. 11:12

Reckless words pierce like a sword,   12:18

but the tongue of the wise brings healing.

15:4   The tongue that brings healing is a tree of life,
            but a deceitful tongue crushes the spirit.

16:27   A scoundrel plots evil,
            and his speech is like a scorching fire.

25:23   As a north wind brings rain,
            so a sly tongue brings angry looks.

26:2   Like a fluttering sparrow or a darting swallow,
            an undeserved curse does not come to rest.

Quarreling

Prov. 17:14   Starting a quarrel is like breaching a dam;
                   so drop the matter before a dispute breaks out.

17:19   He who loves a quarrel loves sin;
            he who builds a high gate invites destruction.

20:3   It is to a man's honor to avoid strife,
            but every fool is quick to quarrel.

22:10   Drive out the mocker, and out goes strife;
            quarrels and insults are ended.

26:21   As charcoal to embers and as wood to fire,
            so is a quarrelsome man for kindling strife.

Lying

Prov. 12:19   Truthful lips endure forever,
                   but a lying tongue lasts only a moment.

12:22   The LORD detests lying lips,
            but he delights in men who are truthful.

17:20   A man of perverse heart does not prosper;
            he whose tongue is deceitful falls into trouble.

19:5   A false witness will not go unpunished,
            and he who pours out lies will not go free.

19:22   What a man desires is unfailing love z;
            better to be poor than a liar.

21:6   A fortune made by a lying tongue
            is a fleeting vapor and a deadly snare. a

Power of tongue

Prov.   From the fruit of his mouth a man's stomach is filled;
18:20,21   with the harvest from his lips he is satisfied.

The tongue has the power of life and death,
     and those who love it will eat its fruit.

z Or *A man's greed is his shame*   a Some Hebrew manuscripts, Septuagint and Vulgate;
most Hebrew manuscripts *vapor for those who seek death*

Disharmony and Strife

Solicitation to evil

My son, if sinners entice you,
  do not give in to them.
If they say, "Come along with us;
  let's lie in wait for someone's blood,
  let's waylay some harmless soul;
let's swallow them alive, like the grave,[b]
  and whole, like those who go down to the pit;
we will get all sorts of valuable things
  and fill our houses with plunder;
throw in your lot with us,
  and we will share a common purse"—
my son, do not go along with them,
  do not set foot on their paths;
for their feet rush into sin,
  they are swift to shed blood.
How useless to spread a net
  in full view of all the birds!
These men lie in wait for their own blood;
  they waylay only themselves!
Such is the end of all who go after ill-gotten gain;
  it takes away the lives of those who get it.

Prov. 1:10-19

A violent man entices his neighbor
  and leads him down a path that is not good.

16:29

Like a muddied spring or a polluted well
  is a righteous man who gives way to the wicked.

25:26

Stone is heavy and sand a burden,
  but provocation by a fool is heavier than both.

27:3

He who leads the upright along an evil path
  will fall into his own trap,
  but the blameless will receive a good inheritance.

28:10

Violence

Do not envy a violent man
  or choose any of his ways,
for the LORD detests a perverse man
  but takes the upright into his confidence.

Prov. 3:31,32

The violence of the wicked will drag them away,
  for they refuse to do what is right.

21:7

A wicked man puts up a bold front,
  but an upright man gives thought to his ways.

21:29

Murderers

A man tormented by the guilt of murder
  will be a fugitive till death;
  let no one support him.

Prov. 28:17

[b]Hebrew *Sheol*

Causing others harm

Prov.
3:29,30
	Do not plot harm against your neighbor,
	  who lives trustfully near you.
	Do not accuse a man for no reason—
	  when he has done you no harm.

Revenge

Prov. 20:22	Do not say, "I'll pay you back for this wrong!" Wait for the LORD, and he will deliver you.

24:28,29	Do not testify against your neighbor without cause,
	  or use your lips to deceive.
	Do not say, "I'll do to him as he has done to me;
	  I'll pay that man back for what he did."

Dissension and strife

Prov.
6:16-19
	There are six things the LORD hates,
	  seven that are detestable to him:
	    haughty eyes,
	    a lying tongue,
	    hands that shed innocent blood,
	    a heart that devises wicked schemes,
	    feet that are quick to rush into evil,
	    a false witness who pours out lies
	    and a man who stirs up dissension among brothers.

17:1	Better a dry crust with peace and quiet than a house full of feasting,[c] with strife.
18:18	Casting the lot settles disputes and keeps strong opponents apart.
18:19	An offended brother is more unyielding than a fortified city, and disputes are like the barred gates of a citadel.

Meddling

Prov. 26:17	Like one who seizes a dog by the ears is a passer-by who meddles in a quarrel not his own.

Honesty

Truthfulness

Prov. 12:20	There is deceit in the hearts of those who plot evil, but joy for those who promote peace.
13:5	The righteous hate what is false, but the wicked bring shame and disgrace.
24:26	An honest answer is like a kiss on the lips.
26:18,19	Like a madman shooting firebrands or deadly arrows is a man who deceives his neighbor

[c]Hebrew *sacrifices*

and says, "I was only joking!"

Accurate weights

The LORD abhors dishonest scales
  but accurate weights are his delight.   Prov. 11:1

Honest scales and balances are from the LORD;   16:11
  all the weights in the bag are of his making.

Differing weights and differing measures—   20:10
  the LORD detests them both.

The LORD detests differing weights,   20:23
  and dishonest scales do not please him.

Boundary stones

Do not move an ancient boundary stone   Prov. 22:28
  set up by your forefathers.

Do not move an ancient boundary stone   23:10,11
  or encroach on the fields of the fatherless,
for their Defender is strong;
  he will take up their case against you,

Wrongfully obtained gains

Ill-gotten treasures are of no value,   Prov. 10:2
  but righteousness delivers from death.

Dishonest money dwindles away,   13:11
  but he who gathers money little by little makes it grow.

Food gained by fraud tastes sweet to a man,   20:17
  but he ends up with a mouth full of gravel.

An inheritance quickly gained at the beginning   20:21
  will not be blessed at the end.

Bribery

A greedy man brings trouble to his family,   Prov. 15:27
  but he who hates bribes will live.

A bribe is a charm to the one who gives it;   17:8
  wherever he turns, he succeeds.

A wicked man accepts a bribe in secret   17:23
  to pervert the course of justice.

A gift given in secret soothes anger,   21:14
  and a bribe concealed in the cloak pacifies great wrath.

Justice

False witnesses

A truthful witness gives honest testimony,   Prov. 12:17
  but a false witness tells lies.

A truthful witness does not deceive,   14:5
  but a false witness pours out lies.

14:25	A truthful witness saves lives, but a false witness is deceitful.
19:9	A false witness will not go unpunished, and he who pours out lies will not go free.
19:28	A corrupt witness mocks at justice, and the mouth of the wicked gulps down evil.
21:28	A false witness will perish, and whoever listens to him will be destroyed forever.[d]

25:18	Like a club or a sword or a sharp arrow
	    is the man who gives false testimony against his
	        neighbor.

Open-mindedness

Prov. 18:17	The first to present his case seems right, till another comes forward and questions him.

Judicial justice

Prov. 17:15	Acquitting the guilty and condemning the innocent— the LORD detests them both.
17:26	It is not good to punish an innocent man, or to flog officials for their integrity.
18:5	It is not good to be partial to the wicked or to deprive the innocent of justice.
21:15	When justice is done, it brings joy to the righteous but terror to evildoers.

24:11,12	Rescue those being led away to death;
	    hold back those staggering toward slaughter.
	If you say, "But we knew nothing about this,"
	    does not he who weighs the heart perceive it?
	Does not he who guards your life know it?
	    Will he not repay each person according to what he has
	        done?

24:23-25	These also are sayings of the wise:
	
	To show partiality in judging is not good:
	Whoever says to the guilty, "You are innocent"—
	    peoples will curse him and nations denounce him.
	But it will go well with those who convict the guilty,
	    and rich blessing will come upon them.

28:5	Evil men do not understand justice, but those who seek the LORD understand it fully.
29:26	Many seek an audience with a ruler, but it is from the LORD that man gets justice.

---

[d]Or / *but the words of an obedient man will live on*

Economic Well-Being

Wealth and poverty

Honor the LORD with your wealth,
    with the firstfruits of all your crops;
then your barns will be filled to overflowing,
    and your vats will brim over with new wine.

Prov.
3:9,10

The wealth of the rich is their fortified city,
    but poverty is the ruin of the poor.

10:15

Wealth is worthless in the day of wrath,
    but righteousness delivers from death.

11:4

Whoever trusts in his riches will fall,
    but the righteous will thrive like a green leaf.

11:28

A man's riches may ransom his life,
    but a poor man hears no threat.

13:8

The poor are shunned even by their neighbors,
    but the rich have many friends.

14:20

Better a little with the fear of the LORD
    than great wealth with turmoil.

15:16

Of what use is money in the hand of a fool,
    since he has no desire to get wisdom?

17:16

The wealth of the rich is their fortified city;
    they imagine it an unscalable wall.

18:11

A poor man pleads for mercy,
    but a rich man answers harshly.

18:23

Wealth brings many friends,
    but a poor man's friend deserts him.

19:4

Many curry favor with a ruler,
    and everyone is the friend of a man who gives gifts.

19:6

A poor man is shunned by all his relatives—
    how much more do his friends avoid him!
Though he pursues them with pleading,
    they are nowhere to be found.[e]

19:7

Rich and poor have this in common:
    The LORD is the Maker of them all.

22:2

The rich rule over the poor,
    and the borrower is servant to the lender.

22:7

Do not wear yourself out to get rich;
    have the wisdom to show restraint.
Cast but a glance at riches, and they are gone,
    for they will surely sprout wings
    and fly off to the sky like an eagle.

23:4,5

[e]The meaning of the Hebrew for this sentence is uncertain.

27:7	He who is full loathes honey, but to the hungry even what is bitter tastes sweet.
28:6	Better a poor man whose walk is blameless than a rich man whose ways are perverse.
28:8	He who increases his wealth by exorbitant interest amasses it for another, who will be kind to the poor.
28:11	A rich man may be wise in his own eyes, but a poor man who has discernment sees through him.
28:20-22	A faithful man will be richly blessed, but one eager to get rich will not go unpunished.
	To show partiality is not good— yet a man will do wrong for a piece of bread.
	A stingy man is eager to get rich and is unaware that poverty awaits him.

Benevolence and generosity

Prov. 3:27,28	Do not withhold good from those who deserve it, when it is in your power to act. Do not say to your neighbor, "Come back later; I'll give it tomorrow"— when you now have it with you.
11:24-26	One man gives freely, yet gains even more; another withholds unduly, but comes to poverty.
	A generous man will prosper; he who refreshes others will himself be refreshed.
	People curse the man who hoards grain, but blessing crowns him who is willing to sell.
13:22	A good man leaves an inheritance for his children's children, but a sinner's wealth is stored up for the righteous.
14:21	He who despises his neighbor sins, but blessed is he who is kind to the needy.
18:16	A gift opens the way for the giver and ushers him into the presence of the great.
19:17	He who is kind to the poor lends to the LORD, and he will reward him for what he has done.
21:13	If a man shuts his ears to the cry of the poor, he too will cry out and not be answered.
22:9	A generous man will himself be blessed, for he shares his food with the poor.
25:14	Like clouds and wind without rain is a man who boasts of gifts he does not give.
28:27	He who gives to the poor will lack nothing,

but he who closes his eyes to them receives many curses.

Oppression of the poor

A poor man's field may produce abundant food,
  but injustice sweeps it away.   Prov. 13:23

He who oppresses the poor shows contempt for their Maker,   14:31
  but whoever is kind to the needy honors God.

All the days of the oppressed are wretched,   15:15
  but the cheerful heart has a continual feast.

Better a little with righteousness   16:8
  than much gain with injustice.

He who oppresses the poor to increase his wealth   22:16
  and he who gives gifts to the rich—both come to poverty.
Do not exploit the poor because they are poor   22:22,23
  and do not crush the needy in court,
for the LORD will take up their case
  and will plunder those who plunder them.

The righteous care about justice for the poor,   29:7
  but the wicked have no such concern.

The poor man and the oppressor have this in common: 29:13
  The LORD gives sight to the eyes of both.

Industriousness

Go to the ant, you sluggard;   Prov. 6:6-8
  consider its ways and be wise!
It has no commander,
  no overseer or ruler,
yet it stores its provisions in summer
  and gathers its food at harvest.

How long will you lie there, you sluggard?   6:9-11
  When will you get up from your sleep?
A little sleep, a little slumber,
  a little folding of the hands to rest—
and poverty will come on you like a bandit
  and scarcity like an armed man.*f*

Lazy hands make a man poor,   10:4,5
  but diligent hands bring wealth.

He who gathers crops in summer is a wise son,
  but he who sleeps during harvest is a disgraceful son.

As vinegar to the teeth and smoke to the eyes,   10:26
  so is a sluggard to those who send him.

He who works his land will have abundant food,   12:11
  but he who chases fantasies lacks judgment.

f Or like a vagrant / and scarcity like a beggar

12:24	Diligent hands will rule, but laziness ends in slave labor.
12:27	The lazy man does not roast$ his game, but the diligent man prizes his possessions.
13:4	The sluggard craves and gets nothing, but the desires of the diligent are fully satisfied.

14:4	Where there are no oxen, the manger is empty,
	    but from the strength of an ox comes an abundant
	        harvest.

14:23	All hard work brings a profit, but mere talk leads only to poverty.
15:19	The way of the sluggard is blocked with thorns, but the path of the upright is a highway.
16:26	The laborer's appetite works for him; his hunger drives him on.
18:9	One who is slack in his work is brother to one who destroys.
19:15	Laziness brings on deep sleep, and the shiftless man goes hungry.
19:24 **26:15**	The sluggard buries his hand in the dish; he will not even bring it back to his mouth!
20:4	A sluggard does not plow in season; so at harvest time he looks but finds nothing.
20:13	Do not love sleep or you will grow poor; stay awake and you will have food to spare.
21:17	He who loves pleasure will become poor; whoever loves wine and oil will never be rich.

21:25,26	The sluggard's craving will be the death of him,
	    because his hands refuse to work.
	All day long he craves for more,
	    but the righteous give without sparing.

22:29	Do you see a man skilled in his work?
	    He will serve before kings;
	    he will not serve before obscure men.

24:27	Finish your outdoor work
	    and get your fields ready;
	    after that, build your house.

24:30-34	I went past the field of the sluggard,
	    past the vineyard of the man who lacks judgment;
	thorns had come up everywhere,
	    the ground was covered with weeds,
	    and the stone wall was in ruins.

$The meaning of the Hebrew for this word is uncertain.

I applied my heart to what I observed
    and learned a lesson from what I saw:
A little sleep, a little slumber,
    a little folding of the hands to rest—
and poverty will come on you like a bandit
    and scarcity like an armed man.*h*

As a door turns on its hinges,   **26:14**
    so a sluggard turns on his bed.

He who tends a fig tree will eat its fruit,   **27:18**
    and he who looks after his master will be honored.

Be sure you know the condition of your flocks,   **27:23-27**
    give careful attention to your herds;
for riches do not endure forever,
    and a crown is not secure for all generations.
When the hay is removed and new growth appears
    and the grass from the hills is gathered in,
the lambs will provide you with clothing,
    and the goats with the price of a field.
You will have plenty of goats' milk
    to feed you and your family
    and to nourish your servant girls.

He who works his land will have abundant food,   **28:19**
    but the one who chases fantasies will have his fill of
        poverty.

Conservation

In the house of the wise are stores of choice food and oil, **Prov. 21:20**
    but a foolish man devours all he has.

Surety for another

My son, if you have put up security for your neighbor, **Prov. 6:1-5**
    if you have struck hands in pledge for another,
if you have been trapped by what you said,
    ensnared by the words of your mouth,
then do this, my son, to free yourself,
    since you have fallen into your neighbor's hands:
Go and humble yourself;
    press your plea with your neighbor!
Allow no sleep to your eyes,
    no slumber to your eyelids.
Free yourself, like a gazelle from the hand of the hunter,
    like a bird from the snare of the fowler.

He who puts up security for another will surely suffer, **11:15**
    but whoever refuses to strike hands in pledge is safe.

A man lacking in judgment strikes hands in pledge **17:18**
    and puts up security for his neighbor.

*h*Or *like a vagrant / and scarcity like a beggar*

20:16
27:13
	Take the garment of one who puts up security for a
	    stranger;
	  hold it in pledge if he does it for a wayward woman.

22:26,17	Do not be a man who strikes hands in pledge
	  or puts up security for debts;
	if you lack the means to pay,
	  your very bed will be snatched from under you.

Persons and Attributes

Parents and children

Prov. 1:8,9	Listen, my son, to your father's instruction
	  and do not forsake your mother's teaching.
	They will be a garland to grace your head
	  and a chain to adorn your neck.

10:1	The Proverbs of Solomon
	A wise son brings joy to his father, but a foolish son grief to his mother.
11:29	He who brings trouble on his family will inherit only wind, and the fool will be servant to the wise.
15:20	A wise son brings joy to his father, but a foolish man despises his mother.
17:2	A wise servant will rule over a disgraceful son, and will share the inheritance as one of the brothers.
17:6	Children's children are a crown to the aged, and parents are the pride of their children.
17:21	To have a fool for a son brings grief; there is no joy for the father of a fool.
17:25	A foolish son brings grief to his father and bitterness to the one who bore him.
19:26	He who robs his father and drives out his mother is a son who brings shame and disgrace.
20:20	If a man curses his father or mother, his lamp will be snuffed out in pitch darkness.

23:22-25	Listen to your father, who gave you life,
	  and do not despise your mother when she is old.
	Buy the truth and do not sell it;
	  get wisdom, discipline and understanding.
	The father of a righteous man has great joy;
	  he who has a wise son delights in him.
	May your father and mother be glad;
	  may she who gave you birth rejoice!

28:24	He who robs his father or mother and says, "It's not wrong"— he is partner to him who destroys.

The elderly

Gray hair is a crown of splendor;   Prov. 16:31
  it is attained by a righteous life.

The glory of young men is their strength,   20:29
  gray hair the splendor of the old.

Women and wives

Like a gold ring in a pig's snout   Prov. 11:22
  is a beautiful woman who shows no discretion.

A wife of noble character is her husband's crown,   12:4
  but a disgraceful wife is like decay in his bones.

The wise woman builds her house,   14:1
  but with her own hands the foolish one tears hers down.

He who finds a wife finds what is good   18:22
  and receives favor from the LORD.

A foolish son is his father's ruin,   19:13,14
  and a quarrelsome wife is like a constant dripping.

Houses and wealth are inherited from parents,
  but a prudent wife is from the LORD.

Better to live on a corner of the roof   21:9
  than share a house with a quarrelsome wife.   25:24

Better to live in a desert   21:19
  than with a quarrelsome and ill-tempered wife.

A quarrelsome wife is like   27:15,16
  a constant dripping on a rainy day;
restraining her is like restraining the wind
  or grasping oil with the hand.

Kings and rulers

A large population is a king's glory,   Prov. 14:28
  but without subjects a prince is ruined.

A king delights in a wise servant,   14:35
  but a shameful servant incurs his wrath.

The lips of a king speak as an oracle,   16:10
  and his mouth should not betray justice.

Kings detest wrongdoing,   16:12-15
  for a throne is established through righteousness.

Kings take pleasure in honest lips;
  they value a man who speaks the truth.

A king's wrath is a messenger of death,
  but a wise man will appease it.

When a king's face brightens, it means life;
  his favor is like a rain cloud in spring.

17:7	Arrogant[i] lips are unsuited to a fool— how much worse lying lips to a ruler!
17:11	An evil man is bent only on rebellion; a merciless official will be sent against him.
19:12	A king's rage is like the roar of a lion, but his favor is like dew on the grass.
20:2	A king's wrath is like the roar of a lion; he who angers him forfeits his life.
20:8	When a king sits on his throne to judge, he winnows out all evil with his eyes.
20:26	A wise king winnows out the wicked; he drives the threshing wheel over them.
20:28	Love and faithfulness keep a king safe; through love his throne is made secure.
21:1	The king's heart is in the hand of the LORD; he directs it like a watercourse wherever he pleases.
22:11	He who loves a pure heart and whose speech is gracious will have the king for his friend.

23:1-3	When you sit to dine with a ruler,
	   note well what[j] is before you,
	and put a knife to your throat
	   if you are given to gluttony.
	Do not crave his delicacies,
	   for that food is deceptive.

24:21,22	Fear the LORD and the king, my son,
	   and do not join with the rebellious,
	for those two will send sudden destruction upon them,
	   and who knows what calamities they can bring?

25:2-7	It is the glory of God to conceal a matter;
	   to search out a matter is the glory of kings.
	
	As the heavens are high and the earth is deep,
	   so the hearts of kings are unsearchable.
	
	Remove the dross from the silver,
	   and out comes material for[k] the silversmith;
	remove the wicked from the king's presence,
	   and his throne will be established through righteousness.
	
	Do not exalt yourself in the king's presence,
	   and do not claim a place among great men;
	it is better for him to say to you, "Come up here,"
	   than for him to humiliate you before a nobleman.

28:2,3	When a country is rebellious, it has many rulers,

[i]Or Eloquent   [j]Or who   [k]Or comes a vessel from

but a man of understanding and knowledge maintains
  order.

A ruler[l] who oppresses the poor
  is like a driving rain that leaves no crops.

Like a roaring lion or a charging bear   28:15,16
  is a wicked man ruling over a helpless people.

A tyrannical ruler lacks judgment,
  but he who hates ill-gotten gain will enjoy a long life.

By justice a king gives a country stability,   29:4
  but one who is greedy for bribes tears it down.

If a ruler listens to lies,   29:12
  all his officials become wicked.

If a king judges the poor with fairness,   29:14
  his throne will always be secure.

Messengers

A wicked messenger falls into trouble,   Prov. 13:17
  but a trustworthy envoy brings healing.

Like the coolness of snow at harvest time   25:13
  is a trustworthy messenger to those who send him;
  he refreshes the spirit of his masters.

Companions

A righteous man is cautious in friendship,[m]   Prov. 12:26
  but the way of the wicked leads them astray.

He who walks with the wise grows wise,   13:20
  but a companion of fools suffers harm.

Stay away from a foolish man,   14:7
  for you will not find knowledge on his lips.

A friend loves at all times,   17:17
  and a brother is born for adversity.

A man of many companions may come to ruin,   18:24
  but there is a friend who sticks closer than a brother.

Do not envy wicked men,   24:1,2
  do not desire their company;
for their hearts plot violence,
  and their lips talk about making trouble.

Like a bird that strays from its nest   27:8-10
  is a man who strays from his home.

Perfume and incense bring joy to the heart,
  and the pleasantness of one's friend springs from his
    earnest counsel.

---

[l]Or *A poor man*   [m]Or *man is a guide to his neighbor*

Do not forsake your friend and the friend of your father,
    and do not go to your brother's house when disaster strikes
        you—
    better a neighbor nearby than a brother far away.

29:24 The accomplice of a thief is his own enemy;
    he is put under oath and dare not testify.

Various Concerns

Caution

Prov. 16:17 The highway of the upright avoids evil;
    he who guards his way guards his life.

22:3
27:12 A prudent man sees danger and takes refuge,
    but the simple keep going and suffer for it.

22:5 In the paths of the wicked lie thorns and snares,
    but he who guards his soul stays far from them.

Reputation

Prov. 22:1 A good name is more desirable than great riches;
    to be esteemed is better than silver or gold.

25:9,10 If you argue your case with a neighbor,
    do not betray another man's confidence,
or he who hears it may shame you
    and you will never lose your bad reputation.

Courage

Prov.
3:25,26 Have no fear of sudden disaster
    or of the ruin that overtakes the wicked,
for the LORD will be your confidence
    and will keep your foot from being snared.

14:32 When calamity comes, the wicked are brought down,
    but even in death the righteous have a refuge.

22:13 The sluggard says, "There is a lion outside!"
    or, "I will be murdered in the streets!"

24:10 If you falter in times of trouble,
    how small is your strength!

26:13 The sluggard says, "There is a lion in the road,
    a fierce lion roaming the streets!"

28:1 The wicked man flees though no one pursues,
    but the righteous are as bold as a lion.

Hope

Prov. 13:12 Hope deferred makes the heart sick,
    but a longing fulfilled is a tree of life.

13:19 A longing fulfilled is sweet to the soul,
    but fools detest turning from evil.

23:17,18 Do not let your heart envy sinners,

but always be zealous for the fear of the LORD.
There is surely a future hope for you,
    and your hope will not be cut off.

Various Observations

Joy and grief

Each heart knows its own bitterness,
    and no one else can share its joy.   Prov. 14:10

Even in laughter the heart may ache,   14:13
    and joy may end in grief.

A happy heart makes the face cheerful,   15:13
    but heartache crushes the spirit.

A cheerful heart is good medicine,   17:22
    but a crushed spirit dries up the bones.

A man's spirit sustains him in sickness,   18:14
    but a crushed spirit who can bear?

Like one who takes away a garment on a cold day,   25:20
    or like vinegar poured on soda,
    is one who sings songs to a heavy heart.

Be wise, my son, and bring joy to my heart;   27:11
    then I can answer anyone who treats me with contempt.

An evil man is snared by his own sin,   29:6
    but a righteous one can sing and be glad.

Good news

A cheerful look brings joy to the heart,   Prov. 15:30
    and good news gives health to the bones.

Like cold water to a weary soul   25:25
    is good news from a distant land.

Curiosity

Death and Destruction[n] are never satisfied,   Prov. 27:20
    and neither are the eyes of man.

Sayings of Agur

The sayings of Agur son of Jakeh—an oracle[o]:   Prov.
                                                               30:1-4
This man declared to Ithiel,
    to Ithiel and to Ucal:[p]

"I am the most ignorant of men;
    I do not have a man's understanding.
I have not learned wisdom,
    nor have I knowledge of the Holy One.
Who has gone up to heaven and come down?

[n]Hebrew *Sheol* and *Abaddon*   [o]Or *Jakeh of Massa*   [p]Masoretic Text; with a different
word division of the Hebrew *declared, "I am weary, O God; / I am weary, O God, and faint.*

Who has gathered up the wind in the hollow of his
    hands?
Who has wrapped up the waters in his cloak?
Who has established all the ends of the earth?
What is his name, and the name of his son?
    Tell me if you know!

30:5,6

"Every word of God is flawless;
    he is a shield to those who take refuge in him.
Do not add to his words,
    or he will rebuke you and prove you a liar.

30:7-9

"Two things I ask of you, O LORD;
    do not refuse me before I die:
Keep falsehood and lies far from me;
    give me neither poverty nor riches,
    but give me only my daily bread.
Otherwise, I may have too much and disown you
    and say, 'Who is the LORD?'
Or I may become poor and steal,
    and so dishonor the name of my God.

30:10

"Do not slander a servant to his master,
    or he will curse you, and you will pay for it.

30:11-14

"There are those who curse their fathers
    and do not bless their mothers;
those who are pure in their own eyes
    and yet are not cleansed of their filth;
those whose eyes are ever so haughty,
    whose glances are so disdainful;
those whose teeth are swords
    and whose jaws are set with knives
to devour the poor from the earth,
    the needy from among mankind.

30:15a

"The leech has two daughters.
    'Give! Give!' they cry.

30:15b,16

"There are three things that are never satisfied,
    four that never say, 'Enough!':
the grave,*q* the barren womb,
    land, which is never satisfied with water,
    and fire, which never says, 'Enough!'

30:17

"The eye that mocks a father,
    that scorns obedience to a mother,
will be pecked out by the ravens of the valley,
    will be eaten by the vultures.

30:18,19

"There are three things that are too amazing for me,
    four that I do not understand:

q Hebrew *Sheol*

the way of an eagle in the sky,
    the way of a snake on a rock,
the way of a ship on the high seas,
    and the way of a man with a maiden.

"This is the way of an adulteress: 30:20
    She eats and wipes her mouth
    and says, 'I've done nothing wrong.'

"Under three things the earth trembles,   30:21-23
    under four it cannot bear up:
a servant who becomes king,
    a fool who is full of food,
an unloved woman who is married,
    and a maidservant who displaces her mistress.

"Four things on earth are small,   30:24-28
    yet they are extremely wise:
Ants are creatures of little strength,
    yet they store up their food in the summer;
coneys[r] are creatures of little power,
    yet they make their home in the crags;
locusts have no king,
    yet they advance together in ranks;
a lizard can be caught with the hand,
    yet it is found in kings' palaces.

"There are three things that are stately in their stride,   30:29-31
    four that move with stately bearing:
a lion, mighty among beasts,
    who retreats before nothing;
a strutting rooster, a he-goat,
    and a king with his army around him.[s]

"If you have played the fool and exalted yourself,   30:32,33
    or if you have planned evil,
    clap your hand over your mouth!
For as churning the milk produces butter,
    and as twisting the nose produces blood,
    so stirring up anger produces strife."

Sayings of King Lemuel

The sayings of King Lemuel—an oracle[t] his mother taught him: Prov.
                                                                        31:1-3
    "O my son, O son of my womb,
        O son of my vows,[u]
    do not spend your strength on women,
        your vigor on those who ruin kings.

    "It is not for kings, O Lemuel—   31:4-7
        not for kings to drink wine,
        not for rulers to crave beer,

---

[r]That is, the hyrax or rock badger   [s]Or *king secure against revolt*   [t]Or *of Lemuel king*
of Massa, which   [u]Or / *the answer to my prayers*

lest they drink and forget what the law decrees,
    and deprive all the oppressed of their rights.
Give beer to those who are perishing,
    wine to those who are in anguish;
let them drink and forget their poverty
    and remember their misery no more.

31:8,9
       "Speak up for those who cannot speak for themselves,
          for the rights of all who are destitute.
       Speak up and judge fairly;
          defend the rights of the poor and needy."

The Wife of Noble Character

Prov.
31:10-31

*v*A wife of noble character who can find?
    She is worth far more than rubies.
Her husband has full confidence in her
    and lacks nothing of value.
She brings him good, not harm,
    all the days of her life.
She selects wool and flax
    and works with eager hands.
She is like the merchant ships,
    bringing her food from afar.
She gets up while it is still dark;
    she provides food for her family
    and portions for her servant girls.
She considers a field and buys it;
    out of her earnings she plants a vineyard.
She sets about her work vigorously;
    her arms are strong for her tasks.
She sees that her trading is profitable,
    and her lamp does not go out at night.
In her hand she holds the distaff
    and grasps the spindle with her fingers.
She opens her arms to the poor
    and extends her hands to the needy.
When it snows, she has no fear for her household;
    for all of them are clothed in scarlet.
She makes coverings for her bed;
    she is clothed in fine linen and purple.
Her husband is respected at the city gate,
    where he takes his seat among the elders of the land.
She makes linen garments and sells them,
    and supplies the merchants with sashes.
She is clothed with strength and dignity;
    she can laugh at the days to come.
She speaks with wisdom,
    and faithful instruction is on her tongue.
She watches over the affairs of her household

---

*v*Verses 10–31 are an acrostic, each verse beginning with a successive letter of the
Hebrew alphabet.

and does not eat the bread of idleness.
Her children arise and call her blessed;
    her husband also, and he praises her:
"Many women do noble things,
    but you surpass them all."
Charm is deceptive, and beauty is fleeting;
    but a woman who fears the LORD is to be praised.
Give her the reward she has earned,
    and let her works bring her praise at the city gate.

Songs of Solomon

*I*n addition to the proverbs which he authored and inspired, Solomon also wrote the lyrics of over a thousand songs. As a psalmist, Solomon may have been surpassed only by his father, David. Yet, unlike the many recorded psalms of David, only two, or perhaps three, of Solomon's psalms are preserved. One of these (Psalm 72) refers to a visit by the Queen of Sheba and has already been presented in an earlier section. The second song attributed to Solomon (Psalm 127) does not easily fit into any single historical context and is therefore presented here as a further example of Solomon's lyrical work.

Solomon acknowledges the Giver of all things.   Psa. 127

A song of ascents. Of Solomon.

Unless the LORD builds the house,
    its builders labor in vain.
Unless the LORD watches over the city,
    the watchmen stand guard in vain.
In vain you rise early
    and stay up late,
toiling for food to eat—
    for he grants sleep to^w those he loves.

Sons are a heritage from the LORD,
    children a reward from him.
Like arrows in the hands of a warrior
    are sons born in one's youth.
Blessed is the man
    whose quiver is full of them.
They will not be put to shame
    when they contend with their enemies in the gate.

Another special collection of lyrics which may also be Solomon's work is included at this time. The collection is known in most English versions as the "Song of Solomon" and in the Greek as the "Song of Songs." The title "Song of Songs" would suggest acceptance of the song as the most beautiful of all the songs or psalms. Unlike most of the preceding literature, the "Song of Songs" deals more with love than with wisdom, prayer, or praise.

^{w}Or *eat—/ for while they sleep he provides for*

Because the speakers are not easily identifiable, it is difficult to make the writing unfold as any kind of drama. Furthermore, since the various parts of the song focus upon the speaker's innermost thoughts and passions rather than portraying what is actually happening to the people involved, it is not even a love story in the usual sense.

The song reflects the feelings of a lover and his beloved—that is, a bridegroom and his bride. Despite language which is unusually graphic and sensual in description, there is no hint of improper lust. And while the song dispels notions of celibacy and asceticism as an ideal, it does not presume sexual relations outside a marriage relationship.

On its face, the Song of Songs is a beautiful and striking statement about human love. It suggests that all life, including human sexuality, is holy because God has created it. There is in the song a celebration of life simply for its own beauty and experience.

Although the writing itself makes no reference to history, purpose, religion, sin, salvation, or even God himself, many have seen in its celebration an allegory representing the love relationship between God and man. For many Jews it presents God as the lover and the nation of Israel as the beloved. With the coming of the Messiah, it will be seen by many as an allegory of Christ and his church. Whatever else its purpose may serve, the Song of Songs expresses unrestricted joy in a relationship of love.

*The Song of Songs*_____

Song of Songs 1:1	Solomon's Song of Songs.

1:2-4a *Beloved*

> Let him kiss me with the kisses of his mouth—
>   for your love is more delightful than wine.
> Pleasing is the fragrance of your perfumes;
>   your name is like perfume poured out.
> No wonder the maidens love you!
> Take me away with you—let us hurry!
> Let the king bring me into his chambers.

1:4b *Friends*

> We rejoice and delight in you*x*;
>   we will praise your love more than wine.

1:4c-7 *Beloved*

> How right they are to adore you!
>
> Dark am I, yet lovely,
>   O daughters of Jerusalem,
>   dark like the tents of Kedar,
>   like the tent curtains of Solomon.*y*
> Do not stare at me because I am dark,

---

*x*The Hebrew is masculine singular.   *y*Or *Salma*

because I am darkened by the sun.
My mother's sons were angry with me
    and made me take care of the vineyards;
    my own vineyard I have neglected.
Tell me, you whom I love, where you graze your flock
    and where you rest your sheep at midday.
Why should I be like a veiled woman
    beside the flocks of your friends?

Lover   1:8-11

If you do not know, most beautiful of women,
    follow the tracks of the sheep
and graze your young goats
    by the tents of the shepherds.
I liken you, my darling, to a mare
    harnessed to one of the chariots of Pharaoh.
Your cheeks are beautiful with earrings,
    your neck with strings of jewels.
We will make you earrings of gold,
    studded with silver.

Beloved   1:12-14

While the king was at his table,
    my perfume spread its fragrance.
My lover is to me a sachet of myrrh
    resting between my breasts.
My lover is to me a cluster of henna blossoms
    from the vineyards of En Gedi.

Lover   1:15

How beautiful you are, my darling!
    Oh, how beautiful!
    Your eyes are doves.

Beloved   1:16

How handsome you are, my lover!
    Oh, how charming!
    And our bed is verdant.

Lover   1:17

The beams of our house are cedars;
    our rafters are firs.

Beloved   2:1

I am a rose[z] of Sharon,
    a lily of the valleys.

[z]Possibly a member of the crocus family

2:2   *Lover*

           Like a lily among thorns
              is my darling among the maidens.

2:3-13   *Beloved*

           Like an apple tree among the trees of the forest
              is my lover among the young men.
           I delight to sit in his shade,
              and his fruit is sweet to my taste.
           He has taken me to the banquet hall,
              and his banner over me is love.
           Strengthen me with raisins,
              refresh me with apples,
              for I am faint with love.
           His left arm is under my head,
              and his right arm embraces me.
           Daughters of Jerusalem, I charge you
              by the gazelles and by the does of the field:
           Do not arouse or awaken love
              until it so desires.

           Listen! My lover!
              Look! Here he comes,
           leaping across the mountains,
              bounding over the hills.
           My lover is like a gazelle or a young stag.
              Look! There he stands behind our wall,
           gazing through the windows,
              peering through the lattice.
           My lover spoke and said to me,
              "Arise, my darling,
              my beautiful one, and come with me.
           See! The winter is past;
              the rains are over and gone.
           Flowers appear on the earth;
              the season of singing has come,
           the cooing of doves
              is heard in our land.
           The fig tree forms its early fruit;
              the blossoming vines spread their fragrance.
           Arise, come, my darling;
              my beautiful one, come with me."

2:14,15   *Lover*

           My dove in the clefts of the rock,
              in the hiding places on the mountainside,
           show me your face,
              let me hear your voice;
           for your voice is sweet,
              and your face is lovely.
           Catch for us the foxes,

the little foxes
that ruin the vineyards,
    our vineyards that are in bloom.

Beloved   2:16-3:11

My lover is mine and I am his;
    he browses among the lilies.
Until the day breaks
    and the shadows flee,
turn, my lover,
    and be like a gazelle
or like a young stag
    on the rugged hills.[a]

All night long on my bed
    I looked for the one my heart loves;
    I looked for him but did not find him.
I will get up now and go about the city,
    through its streets and squares;
I will search for the one my heart loves.
    So I looked for him but did not find him.
The watchmen found me
    as they made their rounds in the city.
    "Have you seen the one my heart loves?"
Scarcely had I passed them
    when I found the one my heart loves.
I held him and would not let him go
    till I had brought him to my mother's house,
    to the room of the one who conceived me.
Daughters of Jerusalem, I charge you
    by the gazelles and by the does of the field:
Do not arouse or awaken love
    until it so desires.

Who is this coming up from the desert
    like a column of smoke,
perfumed with myrrh and incense
    made from all the spices of the merchant?
Look! It is Solomon's carriage,
    escorted by sixty warriors,
    the noblest of Israel,
all of them wearing the sword,
    all experienced in battle,
each with his sword at his side,
    prepared for the terrors of the night.
King Solomon made for himself the carriage;
    he made it of wood from Lebanon.
Its posts he made of silver,
    its base of gold.
Its seat was upholstered with purple,

---

[a]Or *the hills of Bether*

its interior lovingly inlaid
by[b] the daughters of Jerusalem.
Come out, you daughters of Zion,
and look at King Solomon wearing the crown,
the crown with which his mother crowned him
on the day of his wedding,
the day his heart rejoiced.

4:1-15 *Lover*

How beautiful you are, my darling!
Oh, how beautiful!
Your eyes behind your veil are doves.
Your hair is like a flock of goats
descending from Mount Gilead.
Your teeth are like a flock of sheep just shorn,
coming up from the washing.
Each has its twin;
not one of them is alone.
Your lips are like a scarlet ribbon;
your mouth is lovely.
Your temples behind your veil
are like the halves of a pomegranate.
Your neck is like the tower of David,
built with elegance[c];
on it hang a thousand shields,
all of them shields of warriors.
Your two breasts are like two fawns,
like twin fawns of a gazelle
that browse among the lilies.
Until the day breaks
and the shadows flee,
I will go to the mountain of myrrh
and to the hill of incense.
All beautiful you are, my darling;
there is no flaw in you.

Come with me from Lebanon, my bride,
come with me from Lebanon.
Descend from the crest of Amana,
from the top of Senir, the summit of Hermon,
from the lions' dens
and the mountain haunts of the leopards.
You have stolen my heart, my sister, my bride;
you have stolen my heart
with one glance of your eyes,
with one jewel of your necklace.
How delightful is your love, my sister, my bride!
How much more pleasing is your love than wine,
and the fragrance of your perfume than any spice!

[b]Or *its inlaid interior a gift of love / from* [c]The meaning of the Hebrew for this word is
uncertain.

Your lips drop sweetness as the honeycomb, my bride;
  milk and honey are under your tongue.
The fragrance of your garments is like that of Lebanon.
You are a garden locked up, my sister, my bride;
  you are a spring enclosed, a sealed fountain.
Your plants are an orchard of pomegranates
  with choice fruits,
  with henna and nard,
  nard and saffron,
  calamus and cinnamon,
  with every kind of incense tree,
  with myrrh and aloes
  and all the finest spices.
You are[d] a garden fountain,
  a well of flowing water
  streaming down from Lebanon.

Beloved   4:16

  Awake, north wind,
    and come, south wind!
  Blow on my garden,
    that its fragrance may spread abroad.
  Let my lover come into his garden
    and taste its choice fruits.

Lover   5:1a

  I have come into my garden, my sister, my bride;
    I have gathered my myrrh with my spice.
  I have eaten my honeycomb and my honey;
    I have drunk my wine and my milk.

Friends   5:1b

  Eat, O friends, and drink;
    drink your fill, O lovers.

Beloved   5:2-8

  I slept but my heart was awake.
    Listen! My lover is knocking:
  "Open to me, my sister, my darling,
    my dove, my flawless one.
  My head is drenched with dew,
    my hair with the dampness of the night."
  I have taken off my robe—
    must I put it on again?
  I have washed my feet—
    must I soil them again?
  My lover thrust his hand through the latch-opening;
    my heart began to pound for him.
  I arose to open for my lover,

[d]Or *I am* (spoken by the *Beloved*)

and my hands dripped with myrrh,
my fingers with flowing myrrh,
    on the handles of the lock.
I opened for my lover,
    but my lover had left; he was gone.
    My heart sank at his departure.[e]
I looked for him but did not find him.
    I called him but he did not answer.
The watchmen found me
    as they made their rounds in the city.
They beat me, they bruised me;
    they took away my cloak,
    those watchmen of the walls!
O daughters of Jerusalem, I charge you—
    if you find my lover,
what will you tell him?
    Tell him I am faint with love.

5:9   *Friends*

How is your beloved better than others,
    most beautiful of women?
How is your beloved better than others,
    that you charge us so?

5:10-16   *Beloved*

My lover is radiant and ruddy,
    outstanding among ten thousand.
His head is purest gold;
    his hair is wavy
    and black as a raven.
His eyes are like doves
    by the water streams,
washed in milk,
    mounted like jewels.
His cheeks are like beds of spice
    yielding perfume.
His lips are like lilies
    dripping with myrrh.
His arms are rods of gold
    set with chrysolite.
His body is like polished ivory
    decorated with sapphires.[f]
His legs are pillars of marble
    set on bases of pure gold.
His appearance is like Lebanon,
    choice as its cedars.
His mouth is sweetness itself;
    he is altogether lovely.
This is my lover, this my friend,

[e]*Or heart had gone out to him when he spoke*   [f]*Or lapis lazuli*

O daughters of Jerusalem.

Friends

Where has your lover gone,
  most beautiful of women?
Which way did your lover turn,
  that we may look for him with you?

Beloved

My lover has gone down to his garden,
  to the beds of spices,
to browse in the gardens
  and to gather lilies.
I am my lover's and my lover is mine;
  he browses among the lilies.

Lover

You are beautiful, my darling, as Tirzah,
  lovely as Jerusalem,
  majestic as troops with banners.
Turn your eyes from me;
  they overwhelm me.
Your hair is like a flock of goats
  descending from Gilead.
Your teeth are like a flock of sheep
  coming up from the washing.
Each has its twin,
  not one of them is alone.
Your temples behind your veil
  are like the halves of a pomegranate.
Sixty queens there may be,
  and eighty concubines,
  and virgins beyond number;
but my dove, my perfect one, is unique,
  the only daughter of her mother,
  the favorite of the one who bore her.
The maidens saw her and called her blessed;
  the queens and concubines praised her.
Who is this that appears like the dawn,
  fair as the moon, bright as the sun,
  majestic as the stars in procession?
I went down to the grove of nut trees
  to look at the new growth in the valley,
to see if the vines had budded
  or the pomegranates were in bloom.
Before I realized it,
  my desire set me among the royal chariots of my
    people.[8]

---

[8] Or *among the chariots of Amminadab;* or *among the chariots of the people of the prince*

6:13a   *Friends*

> Come back, come back, O Shulammite;
>> come back, come back, that we may gaze on you!

6:13b-7:9a   *Lover*

> Why would you gaze on the Shulammite
>> as on the dance of Mahanaim?
>
> How beautiful your sandaled feet,
>> O prince's daughter!
> Your graceful legs are like jewels,
>> the work of a craftsman's hands.
> Your navel is a rounded goblet
>> that never lacks blended wine.
> Your waist is a mound of wheat
>> encircled by lilies.
> Your breasts are like two fawns,
>> twins of a gazelle.
> Your neck is like an ivory tower.
> Your eyes are the pools of Heshbon
>> by the gate of Bath Rabbim.
> Your nose is like the tower of Lebanon
>> looking toward Damascus.
> Your head crowns you like Mount Carmel.
>> Your hair is like royal tapestry;
>> the king is held captive by its tresses.
> How beautiful you are and how pleasing,
>> O love, with your delights!
> Your stature is like that of the palm,
>> and your breasts like clusters of fruit.
> I said, "I will climb the palm tree;
>> I will take hold of its fruit."
> May your breasts be like the clusters of the vine,
>> the fragrance of your breath like apples,
>> and your mouth like the best wine.

7-9b-8:4   *Beloved*

> May the wine go straight to my lover,
>> flowing gently over lips and teeth.[h]
> I belong to my lover,
>> and his desire is for me.
> Come, my lover, let us go to the countryside,
>> let us spend the night in the villages.[i]
> Let us go early to the vineyards
>> to see if the vines have budded,
> if their blossoms have opened,
>> and if the pomegranates are in bloom—
>> there I will give you my love.
> The mandrakes send out their fragrance,

[h]Septuagint, Aquila, Vulgate and Syriac; Hebrew *lips of sleepers*   [i]Or *henna bushes*

and at our door is every delicacy,
both new and old,
> that I have stored up for you, my lover.

If only you were to me like a brother,
> who was nursed at my mother's breasts!
Then, if I found you outside,
> I would kiss you,
> and no one would despise me.
I would lead you
> and bring you to my mother's house—
> she who has taught me.
I would give you spiced wine to drink,
> the nectar of my pomegranates.
His left arm is under my head
> and his right arm embraces me.
Daughters of Jerusalem, I charge you:
> Do not arouse or awaken love
> until it so desires.

Friends
8:5a

Who is this coming up from the desert
> leaning on her lover?

Beloved
8:5b-7

Under the apple tree I roused you;
> there your mother conceived you,
> there she who was in labor gave you birth.
Place me like a seal over your heart,
> like a seal on your arm;
for love is as strong as death,
> its jealousy[j] unyielding as the grave.[k]
It burns like blazing fire,
> like a mighty flame.[l]
Many waters cannot quench love;
> rivers cannot wash it away.
If one were to give
> all the wealth of his house for love,
> it[m] would be utterly scorned.

Friends
8:8,9

We have a young sister,
> and her breasts are not yet grown.
What shall we do for our sister
> for the day she is spoken for?
If she is a wall,
> we will build towers of silver on her.
If she is a door,
> we will enclose her with panels of cedar.

---

[j] Or ardor   [k] Hebrew *Sheol*   [l] Or / *like the very flame of the* LORD   [m] Or he

| 8:10-12 | *Beloved* |

I am a wall,
  and my breasts are like towers.
Thus I have become in his eyes
  like one bringing contentment.
Solomon had a vineyard in Baal Hamon;
  he let out his vineyard to tenants.
Each was to bring for its fruit
  a thousand shekels[n] of silver.
But my own vineyard is mine to give;
  the thousand shekels are for you, O Solomon,
  and two hundred[o] are for those who tend its fruit.

| 8:13 | *Lover* |

You who dwell in the gardens
  with friends in attendance,
  let me hear your voice!

| 8:14 | *Beloved* |

Come away, my lover,
  and be like a gazelle
or like a young stag
  on the spice-laden mountains.

Solomon's Glory Fades

An inspired writer of a later time will issue the warning, "If you think you are standing firm, be careful that you don't fall!" It is an appropriate warning for both men and nations. Because the wisdom of the message seems readily apparent, it is surprising that the wisest man of the age could so easily ignore the danger. Yet how often do men fall at the height of success, and the greater the height, the greater the fall! So it is that the picture-perfect story of Solomon comes to a lamentable end. Ignoring the history of earlier Israelites, Solomon enters into forbidden marriages with women of foreign extract and is soon influenced to worship their foreign gods. Solomon's fall stands as a powerful reminder of how easy it is to turn from adoration to idolatry.

| 1 Kgs. 11:1-3 | MARRIAGES TO FOREIGN WIVES. |

King Solomon, however, loved many foreign women besides Pharaoh's daughter—Moabites, Ammonites, Edomites, Sidonians and Hittites. They were from nations about which the LORD had told the Israelites, "You must not intermarry with them, because they will surely turn your hearts after their gods." Nevertheless, Solomon held fast to them in love. He had seven hundred wives of royal birth and three hundred concubines, and his wives led him astray.

| 1 Kgs. 11:4-8 | SOLOMON TURNS TO IDOLATRY. |

As Solomon grew old, his wives turned his heart after other gods, and his heart was not fully devoted to

[n] That is, about 25 pounds (about 11.5 kilograms)   [o] That is, about 5 pounds (about 2.3 kilograms)

the LORD his God, as the heart of David his father had been. He followed Ashtoreth the goddess of the Sidonians, and Molech[p] the detestable god of the Ammonites. So Solomon did evil in the eyes of the LORD; he did not follow the LORD completely, as David his father had done.

On a hill east of Jerusalem, Solomon built a high place for Chemosh the detestable god of Moab, and for Molech the detestable god of the Ammonites. He did the same for all his foreign wives, who burned incense and offered sacrifices to their gods.

GOD'S ANGRY RESPONSE.   The LORD became angry with Solomon because his heart had turned away from the LORD, the God of Israel, who had appeared to him twice. Although he had forbidden Solomon to follow other gods, Solomon did not keep the LORD's command. So the LORD said to Solomon, "Since this is your attitude and you have not kept my covenant and my decrees, which I commanded you, I will most certainly tear the kingdom away from you and give it to one of your subordinates. Nevertheless, for the sake of David your father, I will not do it during your lifetime. I will tear it out of the hand of your son. Yet I will not tear the whole kingdom from him, but will give him one tribe for the sake of David my servant and for the sake of Jerusalem, which I have chosen." *1 Kgs. 11:9-13*

HADAD TO BE ADVERSARY.   Then the LORD raised up against Solomon an adversary, Hadad the Edomite, from the royal line of Edom. Earlier when David was fighting with Edom, Joab the commander of the army, who had gone up to bury the dead, had struck down all the men in Edom. Joab and all the Israelites stayed there for six months, until they had destroyed all the men in Edom. But Hadad, still only a boy, fled to Egypt with some Edomite officials who had served his father. They set out from Midian and went to Paran. Then taking men from Paran with them, they went to Egypt, to Pharaoh king of Egypt, who gave Hadad a house and land and provided him with food. *1 Kgs. 11:14-22*

Pharaoh was so pleased with Hadad that he gave him a sister of his own wife, Queen Tahpenes, in marriage. The sister of Tahpenes bore him a son named Genubath, whom Tahpenes brought up in the royal palace. There Genubath lived with Pharaoh's own children.

While he was in Egypt, Hadad heard that David rested with his fathers and that Joab the commander of the army was also dead. Then Hadad said to Pharaoh, "Let me go, that I may return to my own country."

"What have you lacked here that you want to go back to your own country?" Pharaoh asked.

"Nothing," Hadad replied, "but do let me go!"

REZON TO BE ADVERSARY.   And God raised up against Solomon another adversary, Rezon son of Eliada, who had fled from his master, Hadadezer king of Zobah. He gathered men around him and became the leader of a band of rebels when David destroyed the forces[q] of Zobah; the rebels went to Damascus, where they settled and took control. Rezon was Israel's adversary as long as Solomon lived, adding to the trouble caused by Hadad. So Rezon ruled in Aram and was hostile toward Israel. *1 Kgs. 11:23-25*

JEROBOAM REBELS.   Also, Jeroboam son of Nebat rebelled against the king. He was one of Solomon's officials, an Ephraimite from Zeredah, and his mother was a widow named Zeruah. *1 Kgs. 11:26-40*

_____

[p]Hebrew *Milcom*   [q]Hebrew *destroyed them*

Here is the account of how he rebelled against the king: Solomon had built the supporting terraces[r] and had filled in the gap in the wall of the city of David his father. Now Jeroboam was a man of standing, and when Solomon saw how well the young man did his work, he put him in charge of the whole labor force of the house of Joseph.

About that time Jeroboam was going out of Jerusalem, and Ahijah the prophet of Shiloh met him on the way, wearing a new cloak. The two of them were alone out in the country, and Ahijah took hold of the new cloak he was wearing and tore it into twelve pieces. Then he said to Jeroboam, "Take ten pieces for yourself, for this is what the LORD, the God of Israel, says: 'See, I am going to tear the kingdom out of Solomon's hand and give you ten tribes. But for the sake of my servant David and the city of Jerusalem, which I have chosen out of all the tribes of Israel, he will have one tribe. I will do this because they have[s] forsaken me and worshiped Ashtoreth the goddess of the Sidonians, Chemosh the god of the Moabites, and Molech the god of the Ammonites, and have not walked in my ways, nor done what is right in my eyes, nor kept my statutes and laws as David, Solomon's father, did.

" 'But I will not take the whole kingdom out of Solomon's hand; I have made him ruler all the days of his life for the sake of David my servant, whom I chose and who observed my commands and statutes. I will take the kingdom from his son's hands and give you ten tribes. I will give one tribe to his son so that David my servant may always have a lamp before me in Jerusalem, the city where I chose to put my Name. However, as for you, I will take you, and you will rule over all that your heart desires; you will be king over Israel. If you do whatever I command you and walk in my ways and do what is right in my eyes by keeping my statutes and commands, as David my servant did, I will be with you. I will build you a dynasty as enduring as the one I built for David and will give Israel to you. I will humble David's descendants because of this, but not forever.' "

Solomon tried to kill Jeroboam, but Jeroboam fled to Egypt, to Shishak the king, and stayed there until Solomon's death.

Solomon's Reflections on Life

*D*espite his great sin—or perhaps because of it—Solomon may ultimately have gained the most valuable wisdom of all: a full appreciation of the emptiness of all that he had—even his own wisdom—when compared to things eternal. The book traditionally known as Ecclesiastes, meaning the Preacher or the Teacher, may have been written either personally by King Solomon or sometime later by a scribe in Solomon's honor as the patron of the wisdom movement. In either case, Solomon appears to be the Teacher, and the observations about life which are the basis for the writing seem to be drawn from Solomon's own experiences. The central frame of reference indicates that the author has experienced the consequence of great sin, such as that into which Solomon fell.

In this writing, Solomon's wisdom challenges the wisdom literature of other cultures in which truth is sought by empirical observation of life without

[r] Or *the Millo*   [s] Hebrew; Septuagint, Vulgate and Syriac *because he has*

reference to a creative God. The premise of Solomon's wisdom is that only the Creator of the universe can know the true needs of his creatures and provide for their ultimate fulfillment.

Ecclesiastes is a critical essay about the meaning of life. In its original organization several themes are woven together in an overlapping collage. For purposes of this presentation, the book has been organized according to topics in order to highlight the obvious themes of the Teacher.

As thus organized, the book begins by posing man's ultimate question: what is the meaning of life? The Teacher first observes the cyclical flow of life, in which human nature—like physical nature—never seems to change. The Teacher then explores death—its certainty and unexpectedness. If Solomon is writing these reflections in his last years, it is not at all surprising that he confronts the issue of death. To Solomon the fact of death brings home the transience of life and gives urgency to the ultimate question: what is life's meaning? When measured against eternity, the brevity of life makes it more important than ever to utilize the present time in the most meaningful way possible. The Teacher then considers what there is in this "life under the sun" that has any real or lasting meaning, and his search is both unproductive and discouraging. None of the things in which man normally puts his trust for happiness and fulfillment can really achieve those goals. In the final analysis, such things as wealth, power, pleasure, popularity, and human wisdom are all sheer vanity—meaningless and empty.

Human insight cannot give a clue as to what is meaningful; only "the wisdom which is from above" can imbue one's life with lasting purpose. To illustrate the value of divine wisdom, the Teacher then gives several proverbs and wise sayings of the type contained in the more complete book of Proverbs. In one of the most beautiful poems in the Scriptures, the Teacher shows that there is purpose and balance to all things, even in this present life. Just as there is a time to die, there is a time to live. Just as there is a time for sorrow, there is a time for joy. And everyday life takes on significance in the enjoyment of one's work and the happiness of human love. The message is aimed directly at the young people for whom much of the wisdom literature is intended. In conclusion the Teacher urges that all things find their fulfillment in acknowledging the Creator's purpose for mankind and in obeying his will.

Ecclesiastes———— ARRANGED TOPICALLY ————

The Search for Meaning

The words of the Teacher,[t] son of David, king in Jerusalem: Eccl. 1:1

THE ULTIMATE QUESTION.   Eccl. 1:2,3

> "Meaningless! Meaningless!"
>   says the Teacher.
> "Utterly meaningless!
>   Everything is meaningless."

[t]Or *leader of the assembly*; also in verses 2 and 12

> What does man gain from all his labor
>   at which he toils under the sun?

Eccl. 1:4-11   CYCLICAL NATURE OF LIFE.

> Generations come and generations go,
>   but the earth remains forever.
> The sun rises and the sun sets,
>   and hurries back to where it rises.
> The wind blows to the south
>   and turns to the north;
> round and round it goes,
>   ever returning on its course.
> All streams flow into the sea,
>   yet the sea is never full.
> To the place the streams come from,
>   there they return again.
> All things are wearisome,
>   more than one can say.
> The eye never has enough of seeing,
>   nor the ear its fill of hearing.
> What has been will be again,
>   what has been done will be done again;
>   there is nothing new under the sun.
> Is there anything of which one can say,
>   "Look! This is something new"?
> It was here already, long ago;
>   it was here before our time.
> There is no remembrance of men of old,
>   and even those who are yet to come
> will not be remembered
>   by those who follow.

**Eccl.
6:10-12**   MAN'S SEARCH FOR MEANING.

> Whatever exists has already been named,
>   and what man is has been known;
> no man can contend
>   with one who is stronger than he.
> The more the words,
>   the less the meaning,
>   and how does that profit anyone?

For who knows what is good for a man in life, during the few and mean-ingless days he passes through like a shadow? Who can tell him what will happen under the sun after he is gone?

Importance of Finding Meaning

**Eccl.
3:18-22**   MORTALITY OF ANIMALS AND MAN.
I also thought, "As for men, God tests them so that they may see that they are like the animals. Man's fate is like that of the animals; the same fate awaits them both: As one dies, so dies the other. All have the same

breath[u]; man has no advantage over the animal. Everything is meaningless. All go to the same place; all come from dust, and to dust all return.
Who knows if the spirit of man rises upward and if the spirit of the
animal[v] goes down into the earth?"

So I saw that there is nothing better for a man than to enjoy his work,
because that is his lot. For who can bring him to see what will happen after
him?

MORTALITY OF FOOLISH AND WISE.

Eccl.
2:12-16

> Then I turned my thoughts to consider wisdom,
> and also madness and folly.
> What more can the king's successor do
> than what has already been done?
> I saw that wisdom is better than folly,
> just as light is better than darkness.
> The wise man has eyes in his head,
> while the fool walks in the darkness;
> but I came to realize
> that the same fate overtakes them both.

Then I thought in my heart,

> "The fate of the fool will overtake me also.
> What then do I gain by being wise?"
> I said in my heart,
> "This too is meaningless."
> For the wise man, like the fool, will not be long
> remembered;
> in days to come both will be forgotten.
> Like the fool, the wise man too must die!

MORTALITY OF RIGHTEOUS AND WICKED.

Eccl. 9:1-3

So I reflected on all this and concluded that the righteous and the wise
and what they do are in God's hands, but no man knows whether love or
hate awaits him. All share a common destiny—the righteous and the
wicked, the good and the bad,[w] the clean and the unclean, those who offer
sacrifices and those who do not.

> As it is with the good man,
> so with the sinner;
> as it is with those who take oaths,
> so with those who are afraid to take them.

This is the evil in everything that happens under the sun: The same destiny overtakes all. The hearts of men, moreover, are full of evil and there is
madness in their hearts while they live, and afterward they join the dead.

IMPORTANCE OF THE PRESENT.

Eccl. 9:4-10

Anyone who is among the living has hope[x]—even a live dog is better off
than a dead lion!

[u]Or spirit   [v]Or *Who knows the spirit of man, which rises upward, or the spirit of the animal,*
which   [w]Septuagint (Aquila), Vulgate and Syriac; Hebrew does not have *and the bad.*
[x]Or *What then is to be chosen? With all who live, there is hope*

For the living know that they will die,
　　but the dead know nothing;
they have no further reward,
　　and even the memory of them is forgotten.
Their love, their hate
　　and their jealousy have long since vanished;
never again will they have a part
　　in anything that happens under the sun.

Go, eat your food with gladness, and drink your wine with a joyful heart, for it is now that God favors what you do. Always be clothed in white, and always anoint your head with oil. Enjoy life with your wife, whom you love, all the days of this meaningless life that God has given you under the sun—all your meaningless days. For this is your lot in life and in your toilsome labor under the sun. Whatever your hand finds to do, do it with all your might, for in the grave,ʸ where you are going, there is neither working nor planning nor knowledge nor wisdom.

**Eccl.
9:11,12**

THE UNEXPECTANCY OF DEATH.
　　I have seen something else under the sun:

The race is not to the swift
　　or the battle to the strong,
nor does food come to the wise
　　or wealth to the brilliant
　　or favor to the learned;
but time and chance happen to them all.

Moreover, no man knows when his hour will come:

As fish are caught in a cruel net,
　　or birds are taken in a snare,
so men are trapped by evil times
　　that fall unexpectedly upon them.

**Eccl.
8:16,17**

LIFE'S MEANING INSCRUTABLE.
　　When I applied my mind to know wisdom and to observe man's labor on earth—his eyes not seeing sleep day or night—then I saw all that God has done. No one can comprehend what goes on under the sun. Despite all his efforts to search it out, man cannot discover its meaning. Even if a wise man claims he knows, he cannot really comprehend it.

Meaninglessness of Human Pursuits

**Eccl.
1:12-18**

EMPTINESS OF HUMAN WISDOM.
　　I, the Teacher, was king over Israel in Jerusalem. I devoted myself to study and to explore by wisdom all that is done under heaven. What a heavy burden God has laid on men! I have seen all the things that are done under the sun; all of them are meaningless, a chasing after the wind.

What is twisted cannot be straightened;
　　what is lacking cannot be counted.

I thought to myself, "Look, I have grown and increased in wisdom more than anyone who has ruled over Jerusalem before me; I have experienced

ʸHebrew *Sheol*

much of wisdom and knowledge." Then I applied myself to the understanding of wisdom, and also of madness and folly, but I learned that this,
too, is a chasing after the wind.

> For with much wisdom comes much sorrow;
> the more knowledge, the more grief.

EMPTINESS OF PLEASURE.

Eccl. 2:1-3

I thought in my heart, "Come now, I will test you with pleasure to find
out what is good." But that also proved to be meaningless. "Laughter," I
said, "is foolish. And what does pleasure accomplish?" I tried cheering
myself with wine, and embracing folly—my mind still guiding me with
wisdom. I wanted to see what was worthwhile for men to do under heav-
en during the few days of their lives.

EMPTINESS OF ACHIEVEMENT.

Eccl. 2:4-11

I undertook great projects: I built houses for myself and planted vineyards. I made gardens and parks and planted all kinds of fruit trees in
them. I made reservoirs to water groves of flourishing trees. I bought male
and female slaves and had other slaves who were born in my house. I also
owned more herds and flocks than anyone in Jerusalem before me. I
amassed silver and gold for myself, and the treasure of kings and
provinces. I acquired men and women singers, and a harem[z] as well—the
delights of the heart of man. I became greater by far than anyone in
Jerusalem before me. In all this my wisdom stayed with me.

> I denied myself nothing my eyes desired;
> I refused my heart no pleasure.
> My heart took delight in all my work,
> and this was the reward for all my labor.
> Yet when I surveyed all that my hands had done
> and what I had toiled to achieve,
> everything was meaningless, a chasing after the wind;
> nothing was gained under the sun.

EMPTINESS OF LABOR.

Eccl.
2:17-26

So I hated life, because the work that is done under the sun was grievous to me. All of it is meaningless, a chasing after the wind. I hated all the
things I had toiled for under the sun, because I must leave them to the one
who comes after me. And who knows whether he will be a wise man or a
fool? Yet he will have control over all the work into which I have poured
my effort and skill under the sun. This too is meaningless. So my heart
began to despair over all my toilsome labor under the sun. For a man may
do his work with wisdom, knowledge and skill, and then he must leave all
he owns to someone who has not worked for it. This too is meaningless
and a great misfortune. What does a man get for all the toil and anxious
striving with which he labors under the sun? All his days his work is pain
and grief; even at night his mind does not rest. This too is meaningless.

A man can do nothing better than to eat and drink and find satisfaction
in his work. This too, I see, is from the hand of God, for without him, who
can eat or find enjoyment? To the man who pleases him, God gives wisdom, knowledge and happiness, but to the sinner he gives the task of

---

[z]The meaning of the Hebrew for this phrase is uncertain.

gathering and storing up wealth to hand it over to the one who pleases God. This too is meaningless, a chasing after the wind.

Eccl. 4:1-3   EMPTINESS OF HUMAN CONDITION.
Again I looked and saw all the oppression that was taking place under the sun:

> I saw the tears of the oppressed—
>   and they have no comforter;
> power was on the side of their oppressors—
>   and they have no comforter.
> And I declared that the dead,
>   who had already died,
> are happier than the living,
>   who are still alive.
> But better than both
>   is he who has not yet been,
> who has not seen the evil
>   that is done under the sun.

Eccl. 4:4-6   EMPTINESS OF ACCUMULATION.
And I saw that all labor and all achievement spring from man's envy of his neighbor. This too is meaningless, a chasing after the wind.

> The fool folds his hands
>   and ruins himself.
> Better one handful with tranquillity
>   than two handfuls with toil
>   and chasing after the wind.

Eccl. 4:7-12   EMPTINESS OF UNSHARED LIVES.
Again I saw something meaningless under the sun:

> There was a man all alone;
>   he had neither son nor brother.
> There was no end to his toil,
>   yet his eyes were not content with his wealth.
> "For whom am I toiling," he asked,
>   "and why am I depriving myself of enjoyment?"
> This too is meaningless—
>   a miserable business!
>
> Two are better than one,
>   because they have a good return for their work:
> If one falls down,
>   his friend can help him up.
> But pity the man who falls
>   and has no one to help him up!
> Also, if two lie down together, they will keep warm.
>   But how can one keep warm alone?
> Though one may be overpowered,
>   two can defend themselves.
> A cord of three strands is not quickly broken.

Eccl. 4:13-16   EMPTINESS OF POLITICS.
Better a poor but wise youth than an old but foolish king who no longer

knows how to take warning. The youth may have come from prison to the kingship, or he may have been born in poverty within his kingdom. I saw that all who lived and walked under the sun followed the youth, the king's successor. There was no end to all the people who were before them. But those who came later were not pleased with the successor. This too is meaningless, a chasing after the wind.

EMPTINESS OF FALSE WORSHIP.   Eccl. 5:1-7

Guard your steps when you go to the house of God. Go near to listen rather than to offer the sacrifice of fools, who do not know that they do wrong.

> Do not be quick with your mouth,
>   do not be hasty in your heart
>   to utter anything before God.
> God is in heaven
>   and you are on earth,
>   so let your words be few.
> As a dream comes when there are many cares,
>   so the speech of a fool when there are many words.

When you make a vow to God, do not delay in fulfilling it. He has no pleasure in fools; fulfill your vow. It is better not to vow than to make a vow and not fulfill it. Do not let your mouth lead you into sin. And do not protest to the ₗtemple₎ messenger, "My vow was a mistake." Why should God be angry at what you say and destroy the work of your hands? Much dreaming and many words are meaningless. Therefore stand in awe of God.

EMPTINESS OF WEALTH.   Eccl. 5:8-20

If you see the poor oppressed in a district, and justice and rights denied, do not be surprised at such things; for one official is eyed by a higher one, and over them both are others higher still. The increase from the land is taken by all; the king himself profits from the fields.

> Whoever loves money never has money enough;
>   whoever loves wealth is never satisfied with his income.
>   This too is meaningless.
>
> As goods increase,
>   so do those who consume them.
> And what benefit are they to the owner
>   except to feast his eyes on them?
>
> The sleep of a laborer is sweet,
>   whether he eats little or much,
> but the abundance of a rich man
>   permits him no sleep.

I have seen a grievous evil under the sun:

> wealth hoarded to the harm of its owner,
>   or wealth lost through some misfortune,
> so that when he has a son
>   there is nothing left for him.
> Naked a man comes from his mother's womb,
>   and as he comes, so he departs.

> He takes nothing from his labor
>   that he can carry in his hand.

This too is a grievous evil:

> As a man comes, so he departs,
>   and what does he gain,
>   since he toils for the wind?
> All his days he eats in darkness,
>   with great frustration, affliction and anger.

Then I realized that it is good and proper for a man to eat and drink, and to find satisfaction in his toilsome labor under the sun during the few days of life God has given him—for this is his lot. Moreover, when God gives any man wealth and possessions, and enables him to enjoy them, to accept his lot and be happy in his work—this is a gift of God. He seldom reflects on the days of his life, because God keeps him occupied with gladness of heart.

Eccl. 6:1-9   **EMPTINESS OF MATERIALISM.**

    I have seen another evil under the sun, and it weighs heavily on men: God gives a man wealth, possessions and honor, so that he lacks nothing his heart desires, but God does not enable him to enjoy them, and a stranger enjoys them instead. This is meaningless, a grievous evil.

    A man may have a hundred children and live many years; yet no matter how long he lives, if he cannot enjoy his prosperity and does not receive proper burial, I say that a stillborn child is better off than he. It comes without meaning, it departs in darkness, and in darkness its name is shrouded. Though it never saw the sun or knew anything, it has more rest than does that man—even if he lives a thousand years twice over but fails to enjoy his prosperity. Do not all go to the same place?

> All man's efforts are for his mouth,
>   yet his appetite is never satisfied.
> What advantage has a wise man
>   over a fool?
> What does a poor man gain
>   by knowing how to conduct himself before others?
> Better what the eye sees
>   than the roving of the appetite.
> This too is meaningless,
>   a chasing after the wind.

Eccl.   **EMPTINESS OF PROSPERITY.**
7:13,14

    Consider what God has done:

> Who can straighten
>   what he has made crooked?
> When times are good, be happy;
>   but when times are bad, consider:
> God has made the one
>   as well as the other.
> Therefore, a man cannot discover
>   anything about his future.

EMPTINESS OF DEFIANCE.   Eccl. 8:2-6

Obey the king's command, I say, because you took an oath before God.
Do not be in a hurry to leave the king's presence. Do not stand up for a bad
cause, for he will do whatever he pleases. Since a king's word is supreme,
who can say to him, "What are you doing?"

> Whoever obeys his command will come to no harm,
>   and the wise heart will know the proper time and
>   procedure.
> For there is a proper time and procedure for every matter,
>   though a man's misery weighs heavily upon him.

EMPTINESS OF WICKEDNESS.   Eccl. 8:7-13

> Since no man knows the future,
>   who can tell him what is to come?
> No man has power over the wind to contain it[a];
>   so no one has power over the day of his death.
> As no one is discharged in time of war,
>   so wickedness will not release those who practice it.

All this I saw, as I applied my mind to everything done under the sun.
There is a time when a man lords it over others to his own[b] hurt. Then too,
I saw the wicked buried—those who used to come and go from the holy
place and receive praise[c] in the city where they did this. This too is meaningless.

When the sentence for a crime is not quickly carried out, the hearts of
the people are filled with schemes to do wrong. Although a wicked man
commits a hundred crimes and still lives a long time, I know that it will go
better with God-fearing men, who are reverent before God. Yet because
the wicked do not fear God, it will not go well with them, and their days
will not lengthen like a shadow.

EMPTINESS OF INJUSTICE.   Eccl.
                                                                                     8:14,15
There is something else meaningless that occurs on earth: righteous men
who get what the wicked deserve, and wicked men who get what the
righteous deserve. This too, I say, is meaningless. So I commend the enjoyment of life, because nothing is better for a man under the sun than to eat
and drink and be glad. Then joy will accompany him in his work all the
days of the life God has given him under the sun.

EMPTINESS OF STRENGTH.   Eccl.
                                                                                     9:13-18
I also saw under the sun this example of wisdom that greatly impressed
me: There was once a small city with only a few people in it. And a powerful king came against it, surrounded it and built huge siegeworks
against it. Now there lived in that city a man poor but wise, and he saved
the city by his wisdom. But nobody remembered that poor man. So I said,
"Wisdom is better than strength." But the poor man's wisdom is despised,
and his words are no longer heeded.

> The quiet words of the wise are more to be heeded
>   than the shouts of a ruler of fools.

---

[a]Or over his spirit to retain it   [b]Or to their   [c]Some Hebrew manuscripts and
Septuagint (Aquila); most Hebrew manuscripts and are forgotten

> Wisdom is better than weapons of war,
> but one sinner destroys much good.

Value of Wisdom

Eccl.
12:9,10

PROVERBS OF THE TEACHER.

Not only was the Teacher wise, but also he imparted knowledge to the people. He pondered and searched out and set in order many proverbs. The Teacher searched to find just the right words, and what he wrote was upright and true.

Eccl.
7:7-12

VARIOUS PROVERBS.

> Extortion turns a wise man into a fool,
> and a bribe corrupts the heart.

> The end of a matter is better than its beginning,
> and patience is better than pride.
> Do not be quickly provoked in your spirit,
> for anger resides in the lap of fools.

> Do not say, "Why were the old days better than these?"
> For it is not wise to ask such questions.

> Wisdom, like an inheritance, is a good thing
> and benefits those who see the sun.
> Wisdom is a shelter
> as money is a shelter,
> but the advantage of knowledge is this:
> that wisdom preserves the life of its possessor.

Eccl.
7:19-26

> Wisdom makes one wise man more powerful
> than ten rulers in a city.

> There is not a righteous man on earth
> who does what is right and never sins.

> Do not pay attention to every word people say,
> or you may hear your servant cursing you—
> for you know in your heart
> that many times you yourself have cursed others.

All this I tested by wisdom and I said,

> "I am determined to be wise"—
> but this was beyond me.
> Whatever wisdom may be,
> it is far off and most profound—
> who can discover it?
> So I turned my mind to understand,
> to investigate and to search out wisdom and the scheme
> of things
> and to understand the stupidity of wickedness
> and the madness of folly.

> I find more bitter than death
> the woman who is a snare,
> whose heart is a trap
> and whose hands are chains.

The man who pleases God will escape her,
  but the sinner she will ensnare.

As dead flies give perfume a bad smell,
  so a little folly outweighs wisdom and honor.
The heart of the wise inclines to the right,
  but the heart of the fool to the left.
Even as he walks along the road,
    the fool lacks sense
    and shows everyone how stupid he is.
If a ruler's anger rises against you,
    do not leave your post;
    calmness can lay great errors to rest.

Eccl.
10:1-11:6

There is an evil I have seen under the sun,
  the sort of error that arises from a ruler:
Fools are put in many high positions,
  while the rich occupy the low ones.
I have seen slaves on horseback,
  while princes go on foot like slaves.

Whoever digs a pit may fall into it;
  whoever breaks through a wall may be bitten by a snake.
Whoever quarries stones may be injured by them;
  whoever splits logs may be endangered by them.

If the ax is dull
    and its edge unsharpened,
more strength is needed
    but skill will bring success.

If a snake bites before it is charmed,
  there is no profit for the charmer.

Words from a wise man's mouth are gracious,
  but a fool is consumed by his own lips.
At the beginning his words are folly;
    at the end they are wicked madness—
    and the fool multiplies words.

No one knows what is coming—
  who can tell him what will happen after him?

A fool's work wearies him;
  he does not know the way to town.

Woe to you, O land whose king was a servant[d]
  and whose princes feast in the morning.
Blessed are you, O land whose king is of noble birth
    and whose princes eat at a proper time—
    for strength and not for drunkenness.

If a man is lazy, the rafters sag;
  if his hands are idle, the house leaks.

[d]Or *king is a child*

A feast is made for laughter,
    and wine makes life merry,
    but money is the answer for everything.

Do not revile the king even in your thoughts,
    or curse the rich in your bedroom,
because a bird of the air may carry your words,
    and a bird on the wing may report what you say.

Cast your bread upon the waters,
    for after many days you will find it again.
Give portions to seven, yes to eight,
    for you do not know what disaster may come upon the
        land.

If clouds are full of water,
    they pour rain upon the earth.
Whether a tree falls to the south or to the north,
    in the place where it falls, there will it lie.
Whoever watches the wind will not plant;
    whoever looks at the clouds will not reap.

As you do not know the path of the wind,
    or how the body is formed[e] in a mother's womb,
so you cannot understand the work of God,
    the Maker of all things.

Sow your seed in the morning,
    and at evening let not your hands be idle,
for you do not know which will succeed,
    whether this or that,
    or whether both will do equally well.

**Eccl.
12:11,12**

SAYINGS OF THE WISE.
    The words of the wise are like goads, their collected sayings like firmly
embedded nails—given by one Shepherd. Be warned, my son, of anything
in addition to them.
    Of making many books there is no end, and much study wearies the
body.

Eccl. 7:1-6

WISDOM COMES FROM SORROW.

A good name is better than fine perfume,
    and the day of death better than the day of birth.
It is better to go to a house of mourning
    than to go to a house of feasting,
for death is the destiny of every man;
    the living should take this to heart.
Sorrow is better than laughter,
    because a sad face is good for the heart.
The heart of the wise is in the house of mourning,
    but the heart of fools is in the house of pleasure.
It is better to heed a wise man's rebuke
    than to listen to the song of fools.
Like the crackling of thorns under the pot,

---

[e]Or *know how life* (or *the spirit*) / *enters the body being formed*

so is the laughter of fools.
This too is meaningless.

DANGER OF EXTREMISM.
In this meaningless life of mine I have seen both of these:

Eccl.
7:15-18

a righteous man perishing in his righteousness,
and a wicked man living long in his wickedness.
Do not be overrighteous,
neither be overwise—
why destroy yourself?
Do not be overwicked,
and do not be a fool—
why die before your time?
It is good to grasp the one
and not let go of the other.
The man who fears God will avoid all ⌐extremes⌐.*f*

FEW CHOOSE WISDOM.
"Look," says the Teacher,*g* "this is what I have discovered:

Eccl.
7:27-29

"Adding one thing to another to discover the scheme of
things—
while I was still searching
but not finding—
I found one ⌐upright⌐ man among a thousand,
but not one ⌐upright⌐ woman among them all.
This only have I found:
God made mankind upright,
but men have gone in search of many schemes."

ENRICHING NATURE OF WISDOM.

Eccl. 8:1

Who is like the wise man?
Who knows the explanation of things?
Wisdom brightens a man's face
and changes its hard appearance.

Life's True Meaning

PURPOSE AND BALANCE IN LIFE.

Eccl. 3:1-17

There is a time for everything,
and a season for every activity under heaven:

a time to be born and a time to die,
a time to plant and a time to uproot,
a time to kill and a time to heal,
a time to tear down and a time to build,
a time to weep and a time to laugh,
a time to mourn and a time to dance,
a time to scatter stones and a time to gather them,
a time to embrace and a time to refrain,
a time to search and a time to give up,
a time to keep and a time to throw away,
a time to tear and a time to mend,
a time to be silent and a time to speak,

*f*Or will follow them both   *g*Or leader of the assembly

a time to love and a time to hate,
a time for war and a time for peace.

What does the worker gain from his toil? I have seen the burden God has laid on men. He has made everything beautiful in its time. He has also set eternity in the hearts of men; yet they cannot fathom what God has done from beginning to end. I know that there is nothing better for men than to be happy and do good while they live. That everyone may eat and drink, and find satisfaction in all his toil—this is the gift of God. I know that everything God does will endure forever; nothing can be added to it and nothing taken from it. God does it so that men will revere him.

Whatever is has already been,
and what will be has been before;
and God will call the past to account.[h]

And I saw something else under the sun:

In the place of judgment—wickedness was there,
in the place of justice—wickedness was there.

I thought in my heart,

"God will bring to judgment
both the righteous and the wicked,
for there will be a time for every activity,
a time for every deed."

Eccl.
11:7-12:8

ADVICE TO YOUNG PEOPLE.

Light is sweet,
and it pleases the eyes to see the sun.
However many years a man may live,
let him enjoy them all.
But let him remember the days of darkness,
for they will be many.
Everything to come is meaningless.

Be happy, young man, while you are young,
and let your heart give you joy in the days of your youth.
Follow the ways of your heart
and whatever your eyes see,
but know that for all these things
God will bring you to judgment.
So then, banish anxiety from your heart
and cast off the troubles of your body,
for youth and vigor are meaningless.

Remember your Creator
in the days of your youth,
before the days of trouble come
and the years approach when you will say,
"I find no pleasure in them"—
before the sun and the light
and the moon and the stars grow dark,
and the clouds return after the rain;
when the keepers of the house tremble,
and the strong men stoop,

[h]Or *God calls back the past*

when the grinders cease because they are few,
    and those looking through the windows grow dim;
when the doors to the street are closed
    and the sound of grinding fades;
when men rise up at the sound of birds,
    but all their songs grow faint;
when men are afraid of heights
    and of dangers in the streets;
when the almond tree blossoms
    and the grasshopper drags himself along
    and desire no longer is stirred.
Then man goes to his eternal home
    and mourners go about the streets.

Remember him—before the silver cord is severed,
    or the golden bowl is broken;
before the pitcher is shattered at the spring,
    or the wheel broken at the well,
and the dust returns to the ground it came from,
    and the spirit returns to God who gave it.

"Meaningless! Meaningless!" says the Teacher.[i]
    "Everything is meaningless!"

WHERE LIFE FINDS ITS MEANING.   Eccl.
                                                                                                                     12:13,14
    Now all has been heard;
        here is the conclusion of the matter:
    Fear God and keep his commandments,
        for this is the whole duty of man.
    For God will bring every deed into judgment,
        including every hidden thing,
        whether it is good or evil.

End of Solomon's Reign

With that parting advice to those who would follow him in these "days under the sun," Solomon himself falls prey to the "same destiny which overtakes all men." After a rather obscure reference to other historical records pertaining to Solomon (perhaps the record of Samuel and the Kings), the end of Solomon's life is given only brief mention.

OTHER RECORDS OF SOLOMON.   As for the other events of Solomon's   1 Kgs.
reign, from beginning to end, are they not written in the records of Nathan   11:41
the prophet, in the prophecy of Ahijah the Shilonite and in the visions of   2 Chron.
Iddo the seer concerning Jeroboam son of Nebat?   9:29

SOLOMON'S DEATH.   Solomon reigned in Jerusalem over all Israel forty   1 Kgs. 11:42,43
years. Then he rested with his fathers and was buried in the city of David   2 Chron.
his father.   9:30,31a
                                                                                                                  (Ca. 931 B.C.)

SOLOMON'S SUCCESSOR.   And Rehoboam his son succeeded him as   2 Chron.
king.   9:31b

[i]Or the leader of the assembly

THE DIVIDED KINGDOM

(Ca. 930-725 B.C.)

Division Between Israel and Judah

*J*ust as Solomon experienced a rise to unprecedented heights of personal prosperity and security, only to fall victim to moral weakness and political conflict, so too his kingdom, in the hands of his son Rehoboam, is headed toward certain disaster. By attempting to levy even greater burdens than his father had apparently ordered in his later years, Rehoboam will cause rebellion among the people of Israel. Only the tribes of Judah and Benjamin will remain with Rehoboam, while the rest of Israel—all of the northern tribes—will appoint a man by the name of Jeroboam as their king.

Ironically, even under such a king as Rehoboam it is the nation of Judah which remains somewhat faithful to God. In the north, Jeroboam quickly leads Israel into idolatry, and over the next 25 years Israel will prove to be so wicked that even self-proclaimed prophets of God will be seen lying to each other. The Levites, and others who are righteous in Israel, are forced southward to join with the people of Judah.

The division is permanent, and the fall is great. Civil conflict will last for years, as will wars with foreign enemies, who are quick to notice the vulnerability of this once-unified but now-broken people. And Judah, as well as Israel, will turn its face to idolatry.

1 Kgs. 12:1-5 2 Chron. 10:1-5 (Ca. 931 B.C.) Shechem

PEOPLE REQUEST FREEDOM.   Rehoboam went to Shechem, for all the Israelites had gone there to make him king. When Jeroboam son of Nebat heard this (he was still in Egypt, where he had fled from King Solomon), he returned from*ᵃ* Egypt. So they sent for Jeroboam, and he and the whole assembly of Israel went to Rehoboam and said to him: "Your father put a heavy yoke on us, but now lighten the harsh labor and the heavy yoke he put on us, and we will serve you."

Rehoboam answered, "Go away for three days and then come back to me." So the people went away.

1 Kgs. 12:6-11 2 Chron. 10:6-11

REHOBOAM ASKS ADVICE.   Then King Rehoboam consulted the elders who had served his father Solomon during his lifetime. "How would you advise me to answer these people?" he asked.

They replied, "If today you will be a servant to these people and serve

ᵃOr he remained in

them and give them a favorable answer, they will always be your servants."

But Rehoboam rejected the advice the elders gave him and consulted the young men who had grown up with him and were serving him. He asked them, "What is your advice? How should we answer these people who say to me, 'Lighten the yoke your father put on us'?"

The young men who had grown up with him replied, "Tell these people who have said to you, 'Your father put a heavy yoke on us, but make our yoke lighter'—tell them, 'My little finger is thicker than my father's waist. My father laid on you a heavy yoke; I will make it even heavier. My father scourged you with whips; I will scourge you with scorpions.'"

GREATER BURDENS LEVIED.   Three days later Jeroboam and all the people returned to Rehoboam, as the king had said, "Come back to me in three days." The king answered the people harshly. Rejecting the advice given him by the elders, he followed the advice of the young men and said, "My father made your yoke heavy; I will make it even heavier. My father scourged you with whips; I will scourge you with scorpions." So the king did not listen to the people, for this turn of events was from the LORD, to fulfill the word the LORD had spoken to Jeroboam son of Nebat through Ahijah the Shilonite.

1 Kgs.
12:12-15
2 Chron.
10:12-15

ALL BUT JUDAH REBEL.   When all Israel saw that the king refused to listen to them, they answered the king:

1 Kgs.
12:16-19
2 Chron.
10:16-19

> "What share do we have in David,
>   what part in Jesse's son?
> To your tents, O Israel!
>   Look after your own house, O David!"

So the Israelites went home. But as for the Israelites who were living in the towns of Judah, Rehoboam still ruled over them.

King Rehoboam sent out Adoniram,[b] who was in charge of forced labor, but all Israel stoned him to death. King Rehoboam, however, managed to get into his chariot and escape to Jerusalem. So Israel has been in rebellion against the house of David to this day.

In Israel

JEROBOAM KING OF ISRAEL.   When all the Israelites heard that Jeroboam had returned, they sent and called him to the assembly and made him king over all Israel. Only the tribe of Judah remained loyal to the house of David.

1 Kgs.
12:20
(931 B.C.)

In Judah

PROPHET THWARTS CIVIL WAR.   When Rehoboam arrived in Jerusalem, he mustered the whole house of Judah and the tribe of Benjamin—a hundred and eighty thousand fighting men—to make war against the house of Israel and to regain the kingdom for Rehoboam son of Solomon.

1 Kgs.
12:21-24
2 Chron.
11:1-4
Jerusalem

But this word of God came to Shemaiah the man of God: "Say to Rehoboam son of Solomon king of Judah, to the whole house of Judah and Benjamin, and to the rest of the people, 'This is what the LORD says: Do not go up to fight against your brothers, the Israelites. Go home, every one of

---

[b]Some Septuagint manuscripts and Syriac (see also 1 Kings 4:6 and 5:14); Hebrew *Adoram*

you, for this is my doing.' " So they obeyed the word of the LORD and went
home again, as the LORD had ordered.

In Israel

1 Kgs.
12:25-33
2 Chron.
11:15
Shechem

ALTARS AT DAN AND BETHEL.   Then Jeroboam fortified Shechem in
the hill country of Ephraim and lived there. From there he went out and
built up Peniel.[c]

Jeroboam thought to himself, "The kingdom will now likely revert to
the house of David. If these people go up to offer sacrifices at the temple
of the LORD in Jerusalem, they will again give their allegiance to their
lord, Rehoboam king of Judah. They will kill me and return to King
Rehoboam."

After seeking advice, the king made two golden calves. He said to the
people, "It is too much for you to go up to Jerusalem. Here are your gods,
O Israel, who brought you up out of Egypt." One he set up in Bethel, and
the other in Dan. And this thing became a sin; the people went even as far
as Dan to worship the one there.

Jeroboam built shrines on high places and appointed priests from all
sorts of people, even though they were not Levites. He instituted a festival
on the fifteenth day of the eighth month, like the festival held in Judah,
and offered sacrifices on the altar. This he did in Bethel, sacrificing to the
calves he had made. And at Bethel he also installed priests at the high
places he had made. On the fifteenth day of the eighth month, a month of
his own choosing, he offered sacrifices on the altar he had built at Bethel.
So he instituted the festival for the Israelites and went up to the altar to
make offerings.

In Judah

2 Chron.
11:13,14

LEVITES FLEE TO JUDAH.   The priests and Levites from all their districts throughout Israel sided with him. The Levites even abandoned their
pasturelands and property, and came to Judah and Jerusalem because
Jeroboam and his sons had rejected them as priests of the LORD.

2 Chron.
11:16,17
Jerusalem

ORTHODOX FLEE TO JUDAH.   Those from every tribe of Israel who set
their hearts on seeking the LORD, the God of Israel, followed the Levites to
Jerusalem to offer sacrifices to the LORD, the God of their fathers. They
strengthened the kingdom of Judah and supported Rehoboam son of
Solomon three years, walking in the ways of David and Solomon during
this time.

In Israel

1 Kgs.
13:1-3
Bethel

PROPHECY AGAINST ALTAR.   By the word of the LORD a man of God
came from Judah to Bethel, as Jeroboam was standing by the altar to make
an offering. He cried out against the altar by the word of the LORD: "O
altar, altar! This is what the LORD says: 'A son named Josiah will be born
to the house of David. On you he will sacrifice the priests of the high
places who now make offerings here, and human bones will be burned on
you.' " That same day the man of God gave a sign: "This is the sign the
LORD has declared: The altar will be split apart and the ashes on it will be
poured out."

[c]Hebrew *Penuel*, a variant of *Peniel*

JEROBOAM'S HAND WITHERED.   When King Jeroboam heard what the man of God cried out against the altar at Bethel, he stretched out his hand from the altar and said, "Seize him!" But the hand he stretched out toward the man shriveled up, so that he could not pull it back. Also, the altar was split apart and its ashes poured out according to the sign given by the man of God by the word of the LORD.

*1 Kgs.
13:4-6*

Then the king said to the man of God, "Intercede with the LORD your God and pray for me that my hand may be restored." So the man of God interceded with the LORD, and the king's hand was restored and became as it was before.

PROPHET REFUSES HOSPITALITY.   The king said to the man of God, "Come home with me and have something to eat, and I will give you a gift."

*1 Kgs.
13:7-10*

But the man of God answered the king, "Even if you were to give me half your possessions, I would not go with you, nor would I eat bread or drink water here. For I was commanded by the word of the LORD: 'You must not eat bread or drink water or return by the way you came.'" So he took another road and did not return by the way he had come to Bethel.

PROPHET LIES.   Now there was a certain old prophet living in Bethel, whose sons came and told him all that the man of God had done there that day. They also told their father what he had said to the king. Their father asked them, "Which way did he go?" And his sons showed him which road the man of God from Judah had taken. So he said to his sons, "Saddle the donkey for me." And when they had saddled the donkey for him, he mounted it and rode after the man of God. He found him sitting under an oak tree and asked, "Are you the man of God who came from Judah?"

*1 Kgs.
13:11-19*

"I am," he replied.

So the prophet said to him, "Come home with me and eat."

The man of God said, "I cannot turn back and go with you, nor can I eat bread or drink water with you in this place. I have been told by the word of the LORD: 'You must not eat bread or drink water there or return by the way you came.'"

The old prophet answered, "I too am a prophet, as you are. And an angel said to me by the word of the LORD: 'Bring him back with you to your house so that he may eat bread and drink water.'" (But he was lying to him.) So the man of God returned with him and ate and drank in his house.

MAN OF GOD IS KILLED.   While they were sitting at the table, the word of the LORD came to the old prophet who had brought him back. He cried out to the man of God who had come from Judah, "This is what the LORD says: 'You have defied the word of the LORD and have not kept the command the LORD your God gave you. You came back and ate bread and drank water in the place where he told you not to eat or drink. Therefore your body will not be buried in the tomb of your fathers.'"

*1 Kgs.
13:20-24*

When the man of God had finished eating and drinking, the prophet who had brought him back saddled his donkey for him. As he went on his way, a lion met him on the road and killed him, and his body was thrown down on the road, with both the donkey and the lion standing beside it.

1 Kgs.
13:25-32

PROPHET BURIES HIS VICTIM.   Some people who passed by saw the body thrown down there, with the lion standing beside the body, and they went and reported it in the city where the old prophet lived.

When the prophet who had brought him back from his journey heard of it, he said, "It is the man of God who defied the word of the LORD. The LORD has given him over to the lion, which has mauled him and killed him, as the word of the LORD had warned him."

The prophet said to his sons, "Saddle the donkey for me," and they did so. Then he went out and found the body thrown down on the road, with the donkey and the lion standing beside it. The lion had neither eaten the body nor mauled the donkey. So the prophet picked up the body of the man of God, laid it on the donkey, and brought it back to his own city to mourn for him and bury him. Then he laid the body in his own tomb, and they mourned over him and said, "Oh, my brother!"

After burying him, he said to his sons, "When I die, bury me in the grave where the man of God is buried; lay my bones beside his bones. For the message he declared by the word of the LORD against the altar in Bethel and against all the shrines on the high places in the towns of Samaria will certainly come true."

1 Kgs.
13:33,34

JEROBOAM CONTINUES IDOLATRY.   Even after this, Jeroboam did not change his evil ways, but once more appointed priests for the high places from all sorts of people. Anyone who wanted to become a priest he consecrated for the high places. This was the sin of the house of Jeroboam that led to its downfall and to its destruction from the face of the earth.

1 Kgs.
14:1-4

JEROBOAM'S SON SICK.   At that time Abijah son of Jeroboam became ill, and Jeroboam said to his wife, "Go, disguise yourself, so you won't be recognized as the wife of Jeroboam. Then go to Shiloh. Ahijah the prophet is there—the one who told me I would be king over this people. Take ten loaves of bread with you, some cakes and a jar of honey, and go to him. He will tell you what will happen to the boy." So Jeroboam's wife did what he said and went to Ahijah's house in Shiloh.

Now Ahijah could not see; his sight was gone because of his age.

1 Kgs.
14:5-16

PROPHECY AGAINST JEROBOAM.   But the LORD had told Ahijah, "Jeroboam's wife is coming to ask you about her son, for he is ill, and you are to give her such and such an answer. When she arrives, she will pretend to be someone else."

So when Ahijah heard the sound of her footsteps at the door, he said, "Come in, wife of Jeroboam. Why this pretense? I have been sent to you with bad news. Go, tell Jeroboam that this is what the LORD, the God of Israel, says: 'I raised you up from among the people and made you a leader over my people Israel. I tore the kingdom away from the house of David and gave it to you, but you have not been like my servant David, who kept my commands and followed me with all his heart, doing only what was right in my eyes. You have done more evil than all who lived before you. You have made for yourself other gods, idols made of metal; you have provoked me to anger and thrust me behind your back.

" 'Because of this, I am going to bring disaster on the house of Jeroboam. I will cut off from Jeroboam every last male in Israel—slave or free. I will burn up the house of Jeroboam as one burns dung, until it is all gone. Dogs will eat those belonging to Jeroboam who die in the city, and the birds of the air will feed on those who die in the country. The Lord has spoken!'

"As for you, go back home. When you set foot in your city, the boy will die. All Israel will mourn for him and bury him. He is the only one belonging to Jeroboam who will be buried, because he is the only one in the house of Jeroboam in whom the Lord, the God of Israel, has found anything good.

"The Lord will raise up for himself a king over Israel who will cut off the family of Jeroboam. This is the day! What? Yes, even now.[d] And the Lord will strike Israel, so that it will be like a reed swaying in the water. He will uproot Israel from this good land that he gave to their forefathers and scatter them beyond the River,[e] because they provoked the Lord to anger by making Asherah poles.[f] And he will give Israel up because of the sins Jeroboam has committed and has caused Israel to commit."

JEROBOAM'S SON DIES.   Then Jeroboam's wife got up and left and went to Tirzah. As soon as she stepped over the threshold of the house, the boy died. They buried him, and all Israel mourned for him, as the Lord had said through his servant the prophet Ahijah.

In Judah

REHOBOAM FORTIFIES JUDAH.   Rehoboam lived in Jerusalem and built up towns for defense in Judah: Bethlehem, Etam, Tekoa, Beth Zur, Soco, Adullam, Gath, Mareshah, Ziph, Adoraim, Lachish, Azekah, Zorah, Aijalon and Hebron. These were fortified cities in Judah and Benjamin. He strengthened their defenses and put commanders in them, with supplies of food, olive oil and wine. He put shields and spears in all the cities, and made them very strong. So Judah and Benjamin were his.

REHOBOAM'S FAMILY.   Rehoboam married Mahalath, who was the daughter of David's son Jerimoth and of Abihail, the daughter of Jesse's son Eliab. She bore him sons: Jeush, Shemariah and Zaham. Then he married Maacah daughter of Absalom, who bore him Abijah, Attai, Ziza and Shelomith. Rehoboam loved Maacah daughter of Absalom more than any of his other wives and concubines. In all, he had eighteen wives and sixty concubines, twenty-eight sons and sixty daughters.

Rehoboam appointed Abijah son of Maacah to be the chief prince among his brothers, in order to make him king. He acted wisely, dispersing some of his sons throughout the districts of Judah and Benjamin, and to all the fortified cities. He gave them abundant provisions and took many wives for them.

JUDAH TURNS TO IDOLATRY.   [Ch] After Rehoboam's position as king was established and he had become strong, he and all Israel[g] with him abandoned the law of the Lord. He did evil because he had not set his heart on seeking the Lord. [Kg] Judah did evil in the eyes of the Lord. By the sins they committed they stirred up his jealous anger more than their fathers had done. They also set up for themselves high places, sacred stones and Asherah poles on every high hill and under every spreading tree. There were even male shrine prostitutes in the land; the people

Margin references:
1 Kgs. 14:17,18

2 Chron. 11:5-12
Jerusalem

2 Chron. 11:18-23

1 Kgs. 14:22-24
2 Chron. 12:1,14

---

[d]The meaning of the Hebrew for this sentence is uncertain.   [e]That is, the Euphrates
[f]That is, symbols of the goddess Asherah; here and elsewhere in 1 Kings   [g]That is, Judah, as frequently in 2 Chron.

engaged in all the detestable practices of the nations the LORD had driven out before the Israelites.

1 Kgs. 14:25 2 Chron. 12:2-4

INVASION FROM EGYPT.   Because they had been unfaithful to the LORD, Shishak king of Egypt attacked Jerusalem in the fifth year of King Rehoboam. With twelve hundred chariots and sixty thousand horsemen and the innumerable troops of Libyans, Sukkites and Cushites[h] that came with him from Egypt, he captured the fortified cities of Judah and came as far as Jerusalem.

2 Chron. 12:5-8

SHEMAIAH EXPLAINS REASON.   Then the prophet Shemaiah came to Rehoboam and to the leaders of Judah who had assembled in Jerusalem for fear of Shishak, and he said to them, "This is what the LORD says, 'You have abandoned me; therefore, I now abandon you to Shishak.'"

The leaders of Israel and the king humbled themselves and said, "The LORD is just."

When the LORD saw that they humbled themselves, this word of the LORD came to Shemaiah: "Since they have humbled themselves, I will not destroy them but will soon give them deliverance. My wrath will not be poured out on Jerusalem through Shishak. They will, however, become subject to him, so that they may learn the difference between serving me and serving the kings of other lands."

1 Kgs. 14:26-28 2 Chron. 12:9-11

GOLD SHIELDS TAKEN.   When Shishak king of Egypt attacked Jerusalem, he carried off the treasures of the temple of the LORD and the treasures of the royal palace. He took everything, including the gold shields Solomon had made. So King Rehoboam made bronze shields to replace them and assigned these to the commanders of the guard on duty at the entrance to the royal palace. Whenever the king went to the LORD's temple, the guards went with him, bearing the shields, and afterward they returned them to the guardroom.

2 Chron. 12:12

JUDAH NOT ALL BAD.   Because Rehoboam humbled himself, the LORD's anger turned from him, and he was not totally destroyed. Indeed, there was some good in Judah.

1 Kgs. 14:30 15:6; 2 Chron. 12:15b

CONSTANT WAR WITH ISRAEL.   There was continual warfare between Rehoboam and Jeroboam.

1 Kgs. 14:21,29 2 Chron. 12:13,15a

RECORD OF REHOBOAM'S REIGN.   King Rehoboam established himself firmly in Jerusalem and continued as king. He was forty-one years old when he became king, and he reigned seventeen years in Jerusalem, the city the LORD had chosen out of all the tribes of Israel in which to put his Name. His mother's name was Naamah; she was an Ammonite.

As for the events of Rehoboam's reign, from beginning to end, are they not written in the records of Shemaiah the prophet and of Iddo the seer that deal with genealogies?

1 Kgs. 14:31 2 Chron. 12:16

DEATH OF REHOBOAM.   Rehoboam rested with his fathers and was buried in the City of David. And Abijah his son succeeded him as king.

1 Kgs. 15:1,2 2 Chron. 13:1,2a (914 B.C.)

ABIJAH KING OF JUDAH.   In the eighteenth year of the reign of Jeroboam son of Nebat, Abijah[i] became king of Judah, and he reigned in

[h]That is, people from the upper Nile region   [i]Some Hebrew manuscripts and Septuagint (see also 2 Chron. 12:16); most Hebrew manuscripts *Abijam*

Jerusalem three years. His mother's name was Maacah a daughter of Abishalom.[j]

WAR BETWEEN JUDAH AND ISRAEL.. There was war between Abijah and Jeroboam. Abijah went into battle with a force of four hundred thousand able fighting men, and Jeroboam drew up a battle line against him with eight hundred thousand able troops.

1 Kgs. 15:7b
2 Chron. 13:2b,3

ABIJAH'S MESSAGE TO JEROBOAM. Abijah stood on Mount Zemaraim, in the hill country of Ephraim, and said, "Jeroboam and all Israel, listen to me! Don't you know that the LORD, the God of Israel, has given the kingship of Israel to David and his descendants forever by a covenant of salt? Yet Jeroboam son of Nebat, an official of Solomon son of David, rebelled against his master. Some worthless scoundrels gathered around him and opposed Rehoboam son of Solomon when he was young and indecisive and not strong enough to resist them.

2 Chron. 13:4-12
Hill country of Ephraim

"And now you plan to resist the kingdom of the LORD, which is in the hands of David's descendants. You are indeed a vast army and have with you the golden calves that Jeroboam made to be your gods. But didn't you drive out the priests of the LORD, the sons of Aaron, and the Levites, and make priests of your own as the peoples of other lands do? Whoever comes to consecrate himself with a young bull and seven rams may become a priest of what are not gods.

"As for us, the LORD is our God, and we have not forsaken him. The priests who serve the LORD are sons of Aaron, and the Levites assist them. Every morning and evening they present burnt offerings and fragrant incense to the LORD. They set out the bread on the ceremonially clean table and light the lamps on the gold lampstand every evening. We are observing the requirements of the LORD our God. But you have forsaken him. God is with us; he is our leader. His priests with their trumpets will sound the battle cry against you. Men of Israel, do not fight against the LORD, the God of your fathers, for you will not succeed."

JUDAH SURVIVES AMBUSH. Now Jeroboam had sent troops around to the rear, so that while he was in front of Judah the ambush was behind them. Judah turned and saw that they were being attacked at both front and rear. Then they cried out to the LORD. The priests blew their trumpets and the men of Judah raised the battle cry. At the sound of their battle cry, God routed Jeroboam and all Israel before Abijah and Judah. The Israelites fled before Judah, and God delivered them into their hands. Abijah and his men inflicted heavy losses on them, so that there were five hundred thousand casualties among Israel's able men. The men of Israel were subdued on that occasion, and the men of Judah were victorious because they relied on the LORD, the God of their fathers.

2 Chron. 13:13-20a

Abijah pursued Jeroboam and took from him the towns of Bethel, Jeshanah and Ephron, with their surrounding villages. Jeroboam did not regain power during the time of Abijah.

ABIJAH'S FAMILY. But Abijah grew in strength. He married fourteen wives and had twenty-two sons and sixteen daughters.

2 Chron. 13:21

ABIJAH'S CHARACTER. He committed all the sins his father had done before him; his heart was not fully devoted to the LORD his God, as the

1 Kgs. 15:3-5
Jerusalem

[j]A variant of *Absalom*

heart of David his forefather had been. Nevertheless, for David's sake the LORD his God gave him a lamp in Jerusalem by raising up a son to succeed him and by making Jerusalem strong. For David had done what was right in the eyes of the LORD and had not failed to keep any of the LORD's commands all the days of his life—except in the case of Uriah the Hittite.

1 Kgs.
15:7a,8a
2 Chron.
13:22; 14:1a
(911 B.C.)

DEATH OF ABIJAH. The other events of Abijah's reign, what he did and what he said, are written in the annotations of the prophet Iddo. And Abijah rested with his fathers and was buried in the City of David.

Two Kingdoms in Contrast

Now that almost a quarter of a century has passed since the once-powerful nation of Israel divided into two kingdoms, the character of each becomes fairly set for the remaining three-quarters of a century. Judah, blessed with two good leaders in Asa and his son Jehoshaphat, will remain largely faithful to God. Both men will bring about reforms in Judah and reinstate appreciation for the law.

In Israel, by contrast, none of the next seven kings will bring moral enlightenment to an idolatrous nation, and civil war will continue to divide God's people. It is a sober reminder that God's people will, through the ages, face division and strife when they forsake their God.

In Judah

1 Kgs.
15:8b-10
2 Chron.
14:1b

PEACE UNDER ASA. Asa his son succeeded him as king, and in his days the country was at peace for ten years.

1 Kgs.
15:11
2 Chron.
14:2-5

ASA REFORMS JUDAH. Asa did what was good and right in the eyes of the LORD his God. He removed the foreign altars and the high places, smashed the sacred stones and cut down the Asherah poles.[k] He commanded Judah to seek the LORD, the God of their fathers, and to obey his laws and commands. He removed the high places and incense altars in every town in Judah, and the kingdom was at peace under him.

2 Chron.
14:6-8

ASA REFORTIFIES JUDAH. He built up the fortified cities of Judah, since the land was at peace. No one was at war with him during those years, for the LORD gave him rest.

"Let us build up these towns," he said to Judah, "and put walls around them, with towers, gates and bars. The land is still ours, because we have sought the LORD our God; we sought him and he has given us rest on every side." So they built and prospered.

Asa had an army of three hundred thousand men from Judah, equipped with large shields and with spears, and two hundred and eighty thousand from Benjamin, armed with small shields and with bows. All these were brave fighting men.

[k]That is, symbols of the goddess Asherah; here and elsewhere in 2 Chron.

In Israel

JEROBOAM DIES.   The other events of Jeroboam's reign, his wars and how he ruled, are written in the book of the annals of the kings of Israel. He reigned for twenty-two years and then rested with his fathers.

1 Kgs.
14:19,20a
2 Chron.
13:20b

NADAB KING OF ISRAEL.   And Nadab his son succeeded him as king.
   Nadab son of Jeroboam became king of Israel in the second year of Asa king of Judah, and he reigned over Israel two years.

1 Kgs.
14:20b
15:25
(910 B.C.)

NADAB'S CHARACTER.   He did evil in the eyes of the LORD, walking in the ways of his father and in his sin, which he had caused Israel to commit.

1 Kgs.
15:26

NADAB ASSASSINATED.   As for the other events of Nadab's reign, and all he did, are they not written in the book of the annals of the kings of Israel?
   Baasha son of Ahijah of the house of Issachar plotted against him, and he struck him down at Gibbethon, a Philistine town, while Nadab and all Israel were besieging it.

1 Kgs.
15:31,27
(909 B.C.)

BAASHA KING OF ISRAEL.   Baasha killed Nadab in the third year of Asa king of Judah and succeeded him as king.

1 Kgs.
15:28
(909 B.C.)

JEROBOAM'S FAMILY KILLED.   As soon as he began to reign, he killed Jeroboam's whole family. He did not leave Jeroboam anyone that breathed, but destroyed them all, according to the word of the LORD given through his servant Ahijah the Shilonite—because of the sins Jeroboam had committed and had caused Israel to commit, and because he provoked the LORD, the God of Israel, to anger.

1 Kgs.
15:29,30

BAASHA'S CHARACTER.   In the third year of Asa king of Judah, Baasha son of Ahijah became king of all Israel in Tirzah, and he reigned twenty-four years. He did evil in the eyes of the LORD, walking in the ways of Jeroboam and in his sin, which he had caused Israel to commit.

1 Kgs.
15:33,34
Tirzah

In Judah

JUDAH REPELS ETHIOPIANS.   Zerah the Cushite marched out against them with a vast army[1] and three hundred chariots, and came as far as Mareshah. Asa went out to meet him, and they took up battle positions in the Valley of Zephathah near Mareshah.

2 Chron.
14:9-15
Mareshah

   Then Asa called to the LORD his God and said, "LORD, there is no one like you to help the powerless against the mighty. Help us, O LORD our God, for we rely on you, and in your name we have come against this vast army. O LORD, you are our God; do not let man prevail against you."

   The LORD struck down the Cushites before Asa and Judah. The Cushites fled, and Asa and his army pursued them as far as Gerar. Such a great number of Cushites fell that they could not recover; they were crushed before the LORD and his forces. The men of Judah carried off a large amount of plunder. They destroyed all the villages around Gerar, for the terror of the LORD had fallen upon them. They plundered all these villages, since there was much booty there. They also attacked the camps of the herdsmen and carried off droves of sheep and goats and camels. Then they returned to Jerusalem.

[1]Hebrew *with an army of a thousand thousands* or *with an army of thousands upon thousands*

2 Chron. 15:1-7	**WARNING FROM AZARIAH.** The Spirit of God came upon Azariah son of Oded. He went out to meet Asa and said to him, "Listen to me, Asa and all Judah and Benjamin. The LORD is with you when you are with him. If you seek him, he will be found by you, but if you forsake him, he will forsake you. For a long time Israel was without the true God, without a priest to teach and without the law. But in their distress they turned to the LORD, the God of Israel, and sought him, and he was found by them. In those days it was not safe to travel about, for all the inhabitants of the lands were in great turmoil. One nation was being crushed by another and one city by another, because God was troubling them with every kind of distress. But as for you, be strong and do not give up, for your work will be rewarded."

1 Kgs. 15:12,14,15 2 Chron. 15:8,17,18	**ASA REFORMS JUDAH AGAIN.** When Asa heard these words and the prophecy of Azariah son of ^{m} Oded the prophet, he took courage. He removed the detestable idols from the whole land of Judah and Benjamin and from the towns he had captured in the hills of Ephraim. He repaired the altar of the LORD that was in front of the portico of the LORD's temple. Although he did not remove the high places from Israel, Asa's heart was fully committed ⌊to the LORD⌋ all his life. He brought into the temple of God the silver and gold and the articles that he and his father had dedicated.

2 Chron. 15:19	**FOUR MORE PEACEFUL YEARS.** There was no more war until the thirty-fifth year of Asa's reign.

2 Chron. 15:9-15 Jerusalem	**RENEWAL OF COVENANT.** Then he assembled all Judah and Benjamin and the people from Ephraim, Manasseh and Simeon who had settled among them, for large numbers had come over to him from Israel when they saw that the LORD his God was with him. They assembled at Jerusalem in the third month of the fifteenth year of Asa's reign. At that time they sacrificed to the LORD seven hundred head of cattle and seven thousand sheep and goats from the plunder they had brought back. They entered into a covenant to seek the LORD, the God of their fathers, with all their heart and soul. All who would not seek the LORD, the God of Israel, were to be put to death, whether small or great, man or woman. They took an oath to the LORD with loud acclamation, with shouting and with trumpets and horns. All Judah rejoiced about the oath because they had sworn it wholeheartedly. They sought God eagerly, and he was found by them. So the LORD gave them rest on every side.

1 Kgs. 15:13 2 Chron. 15:16	**MOTHER REMOVED AS QUEEN.** King Asa also deposed his grandmother Maacah from her position as queen mother, because she had made a repulsive Asherah pole. Asa cut the pole down, broke it up and burned it in the Kidron Valley.

1 Kgs. 15:16,17 1 Kgs. 15:32 2 Chron. 16:1	**BAASHA THREATENS WAR.** There was war between Asa and Baasha king of Israel throughout their reigns. Baasha king of Israel went up against Judah and fortified Ramah to prevent anyone from leaving or entering the territory of Asa king of Judah.

1 Kgs. 15:18-21 2 Chron. 16:2-5	**ASA ENLISTS SYRIA'S AID.** Asa then took all the silver and gold that was left in the treasuries of the LORD's temple and of his own palace. He entrusted it to his officials and sent them to Ben-Hadad son of Tabrimmon,

^{m}Vulgate and Syriac (see also Septuagint and verse 1); Hebrew does not have *Azariah son of*.

the son of Hezion, the king of Aram, who was ruling in Damascus. "Let there be a treaty between me and you," he said, "as there was between my father and your father. See, I am sending you a gift of silver and gold. Now break your treaty with Baasha king of Israel so he will withdraw from me."

Ben-Hadad agreed with King Asa and sent the commanders of his forces against the towns of Israel. He conquered Ijon, Dan, Abel Beth Maacah and all Kinnereth in addition to Naphtali. When Baasha heard this, he stopped building Ramah and withdrew to Tirzah.

RAMAH DISMANTLED.   Then King Asa issued an order to all Judah— no one was exempt—and they carried away from Ramah the stones and timber Baasha had been using there. With them King Asa built up Geba in Benjamin, and also Mizpah.

1 Kgs.
15:22
2 Chron.
16:6

HANANI REBUKES ASA.   At that time Hanani the seer came to Asa king of Judah and said to him: "Because you relied on the king of Aram and not on the LORD your God, the army of the king of Aram has escaped from your hand. Were not the Cushites[n] and Libyans a mighty army with great numbers of chariots and horsemen[o]? Yet when you relied on the LORD, he delivered them into your hand. For the eyes of the LORD range throughout the earth to strengthen those whose hearts are fully committed to him. You have done a foolish thing, and from now on you will be at war."

2 Chron.
16:7-9

ASA RESPONDS ANGRILY.   Asa was angry with the seer because of this; he was so enraged that he put him in prison. At the same time Asa brutally oppressed some of the people.

2 Chron.
16:10

In Israel

JEHU WARNS BAASHA.   Moreover, the word of the LORD came through the prophet Jehu son of Hanani to Baasha and his house, because of all the evil he had done in the eyes of the LORD, provoking him to anger by the things he did, and becoming like the house of Jeroboam—and also because he destroyed it. Then the word of the LORD came to Jehu son of Hanani against Baasha: "I lifted you up from the dust and made you leader of my people Israel, but you walked in the ways of Jeroboam and caused my people Israel to sin and to provoke me to anger by their sins. So I am about to consume Baasha and his house, and I will make your house like that of Jeroboam son of Nebat. Dogs will eat those belonging to Baasha who die in the city, and the birds of the air will feed on those who die in the country."

1 Kgs.
16:7,1-4

BAASHA DIES.   As for the other events of Baasha's reign, what he did and his achievements, are they not written in the book of the annals of the kings of Israel? Baasha rested with his fathers and was buried in Tirzah.

1 Kgs.
16:5,6a
(886 B.C.)

ELAH KING OF ISRAEL.   And Elah his son succeeded him as king.

In the twenty-sixth year of Asa king of Judah, Elah son of Baasha became king of Israel, and he reigned in Tirzah two years. As for the other events of Elah's reign, and all he did, are they not written in the book of the annals of the kings of Israel?

1 Kgs.
16:6b,8,14
(886 B.C.)

ELAH ASSASSINATED.   Zimri, one of his officials, who had command of half his chariots, plotted against him. Elah was in Tirzah at the time,

1 Kgs.
16:9,10
(885 B.C.)
Tirzah

[n]That is, people from the upper Nile region   [o]Or charioteers

getting drunk in the home of Arza, the man in charge of the palace at Tirzah. Zimri came in, struck him down and killed him in the twenty-seventh year of Asa king of Judah. Then he succeeded him as king.

1 Kgs.
16:15a
Tirzah

ZIMRI KING FOR WEEK.   In the twenty-seventh year of Asa king of Judah, Zimri reigned in Tirzah seven days.

1 Kgs.
16:11-13,20

BAASHA'S FAMILY KILLED.   As soon as he began to reign and was seated on the throne, he killed off Baasha's whole family. He did not spare a single male, whether relative or friend. So Zimri destroyed the whole family of Baasha, in accordance with the word of the LORD spoken against Baasha through the prophet Jehu—because of all the sins Baasha and his son Elah had committed and had caused Israel to commit, so that they provoked the LORD, the God of Israel, to anger by their worthless idols.

As for the other events of Zimri's reign, and the rebellion he carried out, are they not written in the book of the annals of the kings of Israel?

1 Kgs.
16:15b-19

ZIMRI COMMITS SUICIDE.   The army was encamped near Gibbethon, a Philistine town. When the Israelites in the camp heard that Zimri had plotted against the king and murdered him, they proclaimed Omri, the commander of the army, king over Israel that very day there in the camp. Then Omri and all the Israelites with him withdrew from Gibbethon and laid siege to Tirzah. When Zimri saw that the city was taken, he went into the citadel of the royal palace and set the palace on fire around him. So he died, because of the sins he had committed, doing evil in the eyes of the LORD and walking in the ways of Jeroboam and in the sin he had committed and had caused Israel to commit.

1 Kgs.
16:21
(885 B.C.)

OMRI AND TIBNI COMPETE.   Then the people of Israel were split into two factions; half supported Tibni son of Ginath for king, and the other half supported Omri.

1 Kgs.
16:31a
(885 B.C.)

OMRI ARRANGES MARRIAGE.   He not only considered it trivial to commit the sins of Jeroboam son of Nebat, but he also married [his son, Ahab, to (?)] Jezebel daughter of Ethbaal king of the Sidonians...

1 Kgs.
16:22,23
(880 B.C.)

OMRI GAINS FULL CONTROL.   But Omri's followers proved stronger than those of Tibni son of Ginath. So Tibni died and Omri became king.

In the thirty-first year of Asa king of Judah, Omri became king of Israel, and he reigned twelve years, six of them in Tirzah.

1 Kgs.
16:24
Samaria

SAMARIA MADE CAPITAL.   He bought the hill of Samaria from Shemer for two talents*p* of silver and built a city on the hill, calling it Samaria, after Shemer, the name of the former owner of the hill.

1 Kgs.
16:25,26

OMRI'S CHARACTER.   But Omri did evil in the eyes of the LORD and sinned more than all those before him. He walked in all the ways of Jeroboam son of Nebat and in his sin, which he had caused Israel to commit, so that they provoked the LORD, the God of Israel, to anger by their worthless idols.

1 Kgs.
16:27,28a
(874 B.C.)

OMRI DIES.   As for the other events of Omri's reign, what he did and the things he achieved, are they not written in the book of the annals of the kings of Israel? Omri rested with his fathers and was buried in Samaria.

*p*That is, about 150 pounds (about 70 kilograms)

AHAB KING OF ISRAEL.   And Ahab his son succeeded him as king.

In the thirty-eighth year of Asa king of Judah, Ahab son of Omri became king of Israel, and he reigned in Samaria over Israel twenty-two years.

1 Kgs.
16:28b,29
(874 B.C.)

AHAB WORST KING.   (There was never a man like Ahab, who sold himself to do evil in the eyes of the LORD, urged on by Jezebel his wife. He behaved in the vilest manner by going after idols, like the Amorites the LORD drove out before Israel.) [Ahab] began to serve Baal and worship him. He set up an altar for Baal in the temple of Baal that he built in Samaria. Ahab also made an Asherah pole and did more to provoke the LORD, the God of Israel, to anger than did all the kings of Israel before him.

1 Kgs.
21:25,26
16:31b-33

JERICHO REBUILT.   In Ahab's time, Hiel of Bethel rebuilt Jericho. He laid its foundations at the cost of his firstborn son Abiram, and he set up its gates at the cost of his youngest son Segub, in accordance with the word of the LORD spoken by Joshua son of Nun.

1 Kgs.
16:34
Jericho

In Judah

ASA'S DISEASED FEET.   In the thirty-ninth year of his reign Asa was afflicted with a disease in his feet. Though his disease was severe, even in his illness he did not seek help from the LORD, but only from the physicians.

1 Kgs.
15:23b
2 Chron.
16:12

DEATH OF ASA.   The events of Asa's reign, from beginning to end, are written in the book of the kings of Judah and Israel. Then in the forty-first year of his reign Asa died and rested with his fathers. They buried him in the tomb that he had cut out for himself in the City of David. They laid him on a bier covered with spices and various blended perfumes, and they made a huge fire in his honor.

1 Kgs.
15:23a,24a
2 Chron.
16:11,13,14
(870 B.C.)
Jerusalem

JEHOSHAPHAT KING OF JUDAH.   And Jehoshaphat his son succeeded him as king.

Jehoshaphat son of Asa became king of Judah in the fourth year of Ahab king of Israel. Jehoshaphat was thirty-five years old when he became king, and he reigned in Jerusalem twenty-five years. His mother's name was Azubah daughter of Shilhi.

1 Kgs.
15:24b
22:41,42
2 Chron.
17:1; 20:31
(870 B.C.)

CHARACTER OF JEHOSHAPHAT.   ChHe walked in the ways of his father Asa and did not stray from them; he did what was right in the eyes of the LORD. KgHe rid the land of the rest of the male shrine prostitutes who remained there even after the reign of his father Asa. There was then no king in Edom; a deputy ruled. ChThe high places, however, were not removed, and the people still had not set their hearts on the God of their fathers.

1 Kgs.
22:43,46,47
2 Chron.
20:32,33

JUDAH PROSPERS.   He stationed troops in all the fortified cities of Judah and put garrisons in Judah and in the towns of Ephraim that his father Asa had captured.

The LORD was with Jehoshaphat because in his early years he walked in the ways his father David had followed. He did not consult the Baals but sought the God of his father and followed his commands rather than the practices of Israel. The LORD established the kingdom under his control; and all Judah brought gifts to Jehoshaphat, so that he had great wealth and honor. His heart was devoted to the ways of the LORD; furthermore, he removed the high places and the Asherah poles from Judah.

2 Chron.
17:2-6

2 Chron. 17:7-9	**LAW TAUGHT IN JUDAH.** In the third year of his reign he sent his officials Ben-Hail, Obadiah, Zechariah, Nethanel and Micaiah to teach in the towns of Judah. With them were certain Levites—Shemaiah, Nethaniah, Zebadiah, Asahel, Shemiramoth, Jehonathan, Adonijah, Tobijah and Tob-Adonijah—and the priests Elishama and Jehoram. They taught throughout Judah, taking with them the Book of the Law of the LORD; they went around to all the towns of Judah and taught the people.
2 Chron. 17:10-13a;18:1a	**JEHOSHAPHAT BECOMES WEALTHY.** The fear of the LORD fell on all the kingdoms of the lands surrounding Judah, so that they did not make war with Jehoshaphat. Some Philistines brought Jehoshaphat gifts and silver as tribute, and the Arabs brought him flocks: seven thousand seven hundred rams and seven thousand seven hundred goats.

Jehoshaphat became more and more powerful; he built forts and store cities in Judah and had large supplies in the towns of Judah. Now Jehoshaphat had great wealth and honor...

2 Chron. 17:13b-19	**STRONG MILITARY POWER.** He also kept experienced fighting men in Jerusalem. Their enrollment by families was as follows:

> From Judah, commanders of units of 1,000:
> Adnah the commander, with 300,000 fighting men;
> next, Jehohanan the commander, with 280,000;
> next, Amasiah son of Zicri, who volunteered himself for the service of the LORD, with 200,000.
> From Benjamin:
> Eliada, a valiant soldier, with 200,000 men armed with bows and shields;
> next, Jehozabad, with 180,000 men armed for battle.

These were the men who served the king, besides those he stationed in the fortified cities throughout Judah.

1 Kgs. 22:44 2 Chron. 18:1b	**TREATY WITH AHAB.** Jehoshaphat was also at peace with the king of Israel.

Elijah the Prophet

When Israel is in a time of great crisis, it is predictable that God will raise up a spokesman to call out to his people and to perform special miracles to confirm his message. (It happened, for example, when Moses spoke God's message of deliverance in both words and miracles.) Israel is clearly in another crisis of character and direction, and God's man of the day is the prophet Elijah. While ministering spiritually to his people, Elijah himself is ministered to physically by a widow whose meal must be miraculously multiplied, and also by birds who are sent by God to feed Elijah. Elijah's own miraculous power from God is so great that he is able to raise a young boy from the dead. Indeed there is great similarity between Elijah's miracles and the miracles of the Messiah centuries later.

Elijah is perhaps best-known for his dramatic mountaintop encounter with the prophets of Baal. On the heights of Mount Carmel Elijah throws out a challenge to test the power of this pagan god, and, having completely devastated the pagan priests, he demonstrates beyond question the unlimited power of the one true and living God of the universe.

Yet immediately after this great demonstration of God's power, Elijah shows himself to be like other men of God who come down from "mountain-top" experiences only to face self-doubt and to forget God's power and concern. In his period of retreat Elijah is led to Mount Sinai, where he encounters God (as Moses had done before him) and is given his mission—to call out to God's wayward people. Elijah begins his ministry with a special message for King Ahab.

In Israel

ELIJAH FORETELLS DROUGHT. Now Elijah the Tishbite, from Tishbe[q] in Gilead, said to Ahab, "As the LORD, the God of Israel, lives, whom I serve, there will be neither dew nor rain in the next few years except at my word."

1 Kgs. 17:1

ELIJAH FED BY RAVENS. Then the word of the LORD came to Elijah: "Leave here, turn eastward and hide in the Kerith Ravine, east of the Jordan. You will drink from the brook, and I have ordered the ravens to feed you there."

1 Kgs. 17:2-7 Brook Kerith

So he did what the LORD had told him. He went to the Kerith Ravine, east of the Jordan, and stayed there. The ravens brought him bread and meat in the morning and bread and meat in the evening, and he drank from the brook.

Some time later the brook dried up because there had been no rain in the land.

WIDOW'S UNLIMITED MEAL. Then the word of the LORD came to him: "Go at once to Zarephath of Sidon and stay there. I have commanded a widow in that place to supply you with food." So he went to Zarephath. When he came to the town gate, a widow was there gathering sticks. He called to her and asked, "Would you bring me a little water in a jar so I may have a drink?" As she was going to get it, he called, "And bring me, please, a piece of bread."

1 Kgs. 17:8-16 Zarephath

"As surely as the LORD your God lives," she replied, "I don't have any bread—only a handful of flour in a jar and a little oil in a jug. I am gathering a few sticks to take home and make a meal for myself and my son, that we may eat it—and die."

Elijah said to her, "Don't be afraid. Go home and do as you have said. But first make a small cake of bread for me from what you have and bring it to me, and then make something for yourself and your son. For this is what the LORD, the God of Israel, says: 'The jar of flour will not be used up and the jug of oil will not run dry until the day the LORD gives rain on the land.'"

She went away and did as Elijah had told her. So there was food every day for Elijah and for the woman and her family. For the jar of flour was not used up and the jug of oil did not run dry, in keeping with the word of the LORD spoken by Elijah.

WIDOW'S SON RAISED. Some time later the son of the woman who owned the house became ill. He grew worse and worse, and finally

1 Kgs. 17:17-24

q Or Tishbite, of the settlers

stopped breathing. She said to Elijah, "What do you have against me, man of God? Did you come to remind me of my sin and kill my son?"

"Give me your son," Elijah replied. He took him from her arms, carried him to the upper room where he was staying, and laid him on his bed. Then he cried out to the LORD, "O LORD my God, have you brought tragedy also upon this widow I am staying with, by causing her son to die?" Then he stretched himself out on the boy three times and cried to the LORD, "O LORD my God, let this boy's life return to him!"

The LORD heard Elijah's cry, and the boy's life returned to him, and he lived. Elijah picked up the child and carried him down from the room into the house. He gave him to his mother and said, "Look, your son is alive!"

Then the woman said to Elijah, "Now I know that you are a man of God and that the word of the LORD from your mouth is the truth."

1 Kgs.
18:1,2a
Samaria

ELIJAH SENT TO AHAB.   After a long time, in the third year, the word of the LORD came to Elijah: "Go and present yourself to Ahab, and I will send rain on the land." So Elijah went to present himself to Ahab.

1 Kgs.
18:2b-6

OBADIAH GIVEN MISSION.   Now the famine was severe in Samaria, and Ahab had summoned Obadiah, who was in charge of his palace. (Obadiah was a devout believer in the LORD. While Jezebel was killing off the LORD's prophets, Obadiah had taken a hundred prophets and hidden them in two caves, fifty in each, and had supplied them with food and water.) Ahab had said to Obadiah, "Go through the land to all the springs and valleys. Maybe we can find some grass to keep the horses and mules alive so we will not have to kill any of our animals." So they divided the land they were to cover, Ahab going in one direction and Obadiah in another.

1 Kgs.
18:7-15

ELIJAH AND OBADIAH MEET.   As Obadiah was walking along, Elijah met him. Obadiah recognized him, bowed down to the ground, and said, "Is it really you, my lord Elijah?"

"Yes," he replied. "Go tell your master, 'Elijah is here.'"

"What have I done wrong," asked Obadiah, "that you are handing your servant over to Ahab to be put to death? As surely as the LORD your God lives, there is not a nation or kingdom where my master has not sent someone to look for you. And whenever a nation or kingdom claimed you were not there, he made them swear they could not find you. But now you tell me to go to my master and say, 'Elijah is here.' I don't know where the Spirit of the LORD may carry you when I leave you. If I go and tell Ahab and he doesn't find you, he will kill me. Yet I your servant have worshiped the LORD since my youth. Haven't you heard, my lord, what I did while Jezebel was killing the prophets of the LORD? I hid a hundred of the LORD's prophets in two caves, fifty in each, and supplied them with food and water. And now you tell me to go to my master and say, 'Elijah is here.' He will kill me!"

Elijah said, "As the LORD Almighty lives, whom I serve, I will surely present myself to Ahab today."

1 Kgs.
18:16-21
Mount
Carmel

PRIESTS OF BAAL SUMMONED.   So Obadiah went to meet Ahab and told him, and Ahab went to meet Elijah. When he saw Elijah, he said to him, "Is that you, you troubler of Israel?"

"I have not made trouble for Israel," Elijah replied. "But you and your father's family have. You have abandoned the LORD's commands and have followed the Baals. Now summon the people from all over Israel to meet me on Mount Carmel. And bring the four hundred and fifty prophets of Baal and the four hundred prophets of Asherah, who eat at Jezebel's table."

So Ahab sent word throughout all Israel and assembled the prophets on Mount Carmel. Elijah went before the people and said, "How long will you waver between two opinions? If the LORD is God, follow him; but if Baal is God, follow him."

But the people said nothing.

ELIJAH PROPOSES TEST.   Then Elijah said to them, "I am the only one of the LORD's prophets left, but Baal has four hundred and fifty prophets. Get two bulls for us. Let them choose one for themselves, and let them cut it into pieces and put it on the wood but not set fire to it. I will prepare the other bull and put it on the wood but not set fire to it. Then you call on the name of your god, and I will call on the name of the LORD. The god who answers by fire—he is God." **1 Kgs. 18:22-25**

Then all the people said, "What you say is good."

Elijah said to the prophets of Baal, "Choose one of the bulls and prepare it first, since there are so many of you. Call on the name of your god, but do not light the fire."

ELIJAH MOCKS PRIESTS.   So they took the bull given them and prepared it. **1 Kgs. 18:26-29**

Then they called on the name of Baal from morning till noon. "O Baal, answer us!" they shouted. But there was no response; no one answered. And they danced around the altar they had made.

At noon Elijah began to taunt them. "Shout louder!" he said. "Surely he is a god! Perhaps he is deep in thought, or busy, or traveling. Maybe he is sleeping and must be awakened." So they shouted louder and slashed themselves with swords and spears, as was their custom, until their blood flowed. Midday passed, and they continued their frantic prophesying until the time for the evening sacrifice. But there was no response, no one answered, no one paid attention.

GOD'S POWER DEMONSTRATED.   Then Elijah said to all the people, "Come here to me." They came to him, and he repaired the altar of the LORD, which was in ruins. Elijah took twelve stones, one for each of the tribes descended from Jacob, to whom the word of the LORD had come, saying, "Your name shall be Israel." With the stones he built an altar in the name of the LORD, and he dug a trench around it large enough to hold two seahs[r] of seed. He arranged the wood, cut the bull into pieces and laid it on the wood. Then he said to them, "Fill four large jars with water and pour it on the offering and on the wood." **1 Kgs. 18:30-39**

"Do it again," he said, and they did it again.

"Do it a third time," he ordered, and they did it the third time. The water ran down around the altar and even filled the trench.

At the time of sacrifice, the prophet Elijah stepped forward and prayed: "O LORD, God of Abraham, Isaac and Israel, let it be known today that you are God in Israel and that I am your servant and have done all these things at your command. Answer me, O LORD, answer me, so these people will

[r]That is, probably about 13 quarts (about 15 liters)

know that you, O LORD, are God, and that you are turning their hearts back again."

Then the fire of the LORD fell and burned up the sacrifice, the wood, the stones and the soil, and also licked up the water in the trench.

When all the people saw this, they fell prostrate and cried, "The LORD—he is God! The LORD—he is God!"

1 Kgs.
18:40

BAAL'S PRIESTS SLAIN.   Then Elijah commanded them, "Seize the prophets of Baal. Don't let anyone get away!" They seized them, and Elijah had them brought down to the Kishon Valley and slaughtered there.

1 Kgs.
18:41-45

RAIN ENDS DROUGHT.   And Elijah said to Ahab, "Go, eat and drink, for there is the sound of a heavy rain." So Ahab went off to eat and drink, but Elijah climbed to the top of Carmel, bent down to the ground and put his face between his knees.

"Go and look toward the sea," he told his servant. And he went up and looked.

"There is nothing there," he said.

Seven times Elijah said, "Go back."

The seventh time the servant reported, "A cloud as small as a man's hand is rising from the sea."

So Elijah said, "Go and tell Ahab, 'Hitch up your chariot and go down before the rain stops you.'"

Meanwhile, the sky grew black with clouds, the wind rose, a heavy rain came on and Ahab rode off to Jezreel.

1 Kgs.
18:46
19:1,2
Jezreel

JEZEBEL THREATENS ELIJAH.   The power of the LORD came upon Elijah and, tucking his cloak into his belt, he ran ahead of Ahab all the way to Jezreel. Now Ahab told Jezebel everything Elijah had done and how he had killed all the prophets with the sword. So Jezebel sent a messenger to Elijah to say, "May the gods deal with me, be it ever so severely, if by this time tomorrow I do not make your life like that of one of them."

1 Kgs.
19:3,4
Beersheba

ELIJAH PRAYS TO DIE.   Elijah was afraid[s] and ran for his life. When he came to Beersheba in Judah, he left his servant there, while he himself went a day's journey into the desert. He came to a broom tree, sat down under it and prayed that he might die. "I have had enough, LORD," he said. "Take my life; I am no better than my ancestors."

1 Kgs.
19:5-8
Mt. Horeb

ELIJAH SENT TO HOREB.   Then he lay down under the tree and fell asleep.

All at once an angel touched him and said, "Get up and eat." He looked around, and there by his head was a cake of bread baked over hot coals, and a jar of water. He ate and drank and then lay down again.

The angel of the LORD came back a second time and touched him and said, "Get up and eat, for the journey is too much for you." So he got up and ate and drank. Strengthened by that food, he traveled forty days and forty nights until he reached Horeb, the mountain of God.

1 Kgs.
19:9-12

GOD APPEARS ON HOREB.   There he went into a cave and spent the night.

And the word of the LORD came to him: "What are you doing here, Elijah?"

He replied, "I have been very zealous for the LORD God Almighty. The

[s]Or *Elijah saw*

Israelites have rejected your covenant, broken down your altars, and put your prophets to death with the sword. I am the only one left, and now they are trying to kill me too."

The LORD said, "Go out and stand on the mountain in the presence of the LORD, for the LORD is about to pass by."

Then a great and powerful wind tore the mountains apart and shattered the rocks before the LORD, but the LORD was not in the wind. After the wind there was an earthquake, but the LORD was not in the earthquake. After the earthquake came a fire, but the LORD was not in the fire. And after the fire came a gentle whisper.

ELIJAH'S MISSION TOLD.   When Elijah heard it, he pulled his cloak   1 Kgs.
over his face and went out and stood at the mouth of the cave.   19:13-18

Then a voice said to him, "What are you doing here, Elijah?"

He replied, "I have been very zealous for the LORD God Almighty. The Israelites have rejected your covenant, broken down your altars, and put your prophets to death with the sword. I am the only one left, and now they are trying to kill me too."

The LORD said to him, "Go back the way you came, and go to the Desert of Damascus. When you get there, anoint Hazael king over Aram. Also, anoint Jehu son of Nimshi king over Israel, and anoint Elisha son of Shaphat from Abel Meholah to succeed you as prophet. Jehu will put to death any who escape the sword of Hazael, and Elisha will put to death any who escape the sword of Jehu. Yet I reserve seven thousand in Israel— all whose knees have not bowed down to Baal and all whose mouths have not kissed him."

ELISHA CALLED AS PROPHET.   So Elijah went from there and found   1 Kgs.
Elisha son of Shaphat. He was plowing with twelve yoke of oxen, and   19:19-21
he himself was driving the twelfth pair. Elijah went up to him and threw his cloak around him. Elisha then left his oxen and ran after Elijah. "Let me kiss my father and mother good-by," he said, "and then I will come with you."

"Go back," Elijah replied. "What have I done to you?"

So Elisha left him and went back. He took his yoke of oxen and slaughtered them. He burned the plowing equipment to cook the meat and gave it to the people, and they ate. Then he set out to follow Elijah and became his attendant.

Ahab and Jezebel

Two of the most wicked people who ever lived just happen to be married to each other—King Ahab of Israel, already described as the most evil king to rule Israel, and his wife, Jezebel, whose name even centuries later will be used to describe a treacherous woman. Ahab, however, is now seen in one of his best lights, as Israel is attacked by the Syrians of Aram under the leadership of Ben-Hadad. In an effort to get Ahab's attention, God gives him the victory, only to rebuke him for what is an uncharacteristically merciful act on Ahab's part. King Jehoshaphat of Judah is also rebuked for joining in alliance with his northern brethren. Apparently the lesson to be learned is that God demands strict obedience even when certain acts seem entirely appropriate—

perhaps even righteous—according to human notions. But God also shows his readiness to forgive a penitent King Ahab.

In Israel

1 Kgs. 20:1
Samaria
(Ca. 857
B.C.)

SYRIA BESIEGES SAMARIA.   Now Ben-Hadad king of Aram mustered his entire army. Accompanied by thirty-two kings with their horses and chariots, he went up and besieged Samaria and attacked it.

1 Kgs.
20:2-12

NEGOTIATIONS FAIL.   He sent messengers into the city to Ahab king of Israel, saying, "This is what Ben-Hadad says: 'Your silver and gold are mine, and the best of your wives and children are mine.'"

The king of Israel answered, "Just as you say, my lord the king. I and all I have are yours."

The messengers came again and said, "This is what Ben-Hadad says: 'I sent to demand your silver and gold, your wives and your children. But about this time tomorrow I am going to send my officials to search your palace and the houses of your officials. They will seize everything you value and carry it away.'"

The king of Israel summoned all the elders of the land and said to them, "See how this man is looking for trouble! When he sent for my wives and my children, my silver and my gold, I did not refuse him."

The elders and the people all answered, "Don't listen to him or agree to his demands."

So he replied to Ben-Hadad's messengers, "Tell my lord the king, 'Your servant will do all you demanded the first time, but this demand I cannot meet.'" They left and took the answer back to Ben-Hadad.

Then Ben-Hadad sent another message to Ahab: "May the gods deal with me, be it ever so severely, if enough dust remains in Samaria to give each of my men a handful."

The king of Israel answered, "Tell him: 'One who puts on his armor should not boast like one who takes it off.'"

Ben-Hadad heard this message while he and the kings were drinking in their tents,[t] and he ordered his men: "Prepare to attack." So they prepared to attack the city.

1 Kgs.
20:13,14

GOD ASSURES AHAB.   Meanwhile a prophet came to Ahab king of Israel and announced, "This is what the LORD says: 'Do you see this vast army? I will give it into your hand today, and then you will know that I am the LORD.'"

"But who will do this?" asked Ahab.

The prophet replied, "This is what the LORD says: 'The young officers of the provincial commanders will do it.'"

"And who will start the battle?" he asked.

The prophet answered, "You will."

1 Kgs.
20:15-22

AHAB DEFEATS SYRIANS.   So Ahab summoned the young officers of the provincial commanders, 232 men. Then he assembled the rest of the Israelites, 7,000 in all. They set out at noon while Ben-Hadad and the 32 kings allied with him were in their tents getting drunk. The young officers of the provincial commanders went out first.

Now Ben-Hadad had dispatched scouts, who reported, "Men are advancing from Samaria."

[t]Or *in Succoth*

He said, "If they have come out for peace, take them alive; if they have come out for war, take them alive."

The young officers of the provincial commanders marched out of the city with the army behind them and each one struck down his opponent. At that, the Arameans fled, with the Israelites in pursuit. But Ben-Hadad king of Aram escaped on horseback with some of his horsemen. The king of Israel advanced and overpowered the horses and chariots and inflicted heavy losses on the Arameans.

Afterward, the prophet came to the king of Israel and said, "Strengthen your position and see what must be done, because next spring the king of Aram will attack you again."

ISRAEL PREVAILS AGAIN.   Meanwhile, the officials of the king of Aram advised him, "Their gods are gods of the hills. That is why they were too strong for us. But if we fight them on the plains, surely we will be stronger than they. Do this: Remove all the kings from their commands and replace them with other officers. You must also raise an army like the one you lost—horse for horse and chariot for chariot—so we can fight Israel on the plains. Then surely we will be stronger than they." He agreed with them and acted accordingly. *1 Kgs. 20:23-30a (Ca. 856 B.C.) Aphek*

The next spring Ben-Hadad mustered the Arameans and went up to Aphek to fight against Israel. When the Israelites were also mustered and given provisions, they marched out to meet them. The Israelites camped opposite them like two small flocks of goats, while the Arameans covered the countryside.

The man of God came up and told the king of Israel, "This is what the LORD says: 'Because the Arameans think the LORD is a god of the hills and not a god of the valleys, I will deliver this vast army into your hands, and you will know that I am the LORD.'"

For seven days they camped opposite each other, and on the seventh day the battle was joined. The Israelites inflicted a hundred thousand casualties on the Aramean foot soldiers in one day. The rest of them escaped to the city of Aphek, where the wall collapsed on twenty-seven thousand of them.

AHAB SPARES BEN-HADAD.   And Ben-Hadad fled to the city and hid in an inner room. *1 Kgs. 20:30b-34*

His officials said to him, "Look, we have heard that the kings of the house of Israel are merciful. Let us go to the king of Israel with sackcloth around our waists and ropes around our heads. Perhaps he will spare your life."

Wearing sackcloth around their waists and ropes around their heads, they went to the king of Israel and said, "Your servant Ben-Hadad says: 'Please let me live.'"

The king answered, "Is he still alive? He is my brother."

The men took this as a good sign and were quick to pick up his word. "Yes, your brother Ben-Hadad!" they said.

"Go and get him," the king said. When Ben-Hadad came out, Ahab had him come up into his chariot.

"I will return the cities my father took from your father," Ben-Hadad offered. "You may set up your own market areas in Damascus, as my father did in Samaria."

⌊Ahab said,⌋ "On the basis of a treaty I will set you free." So he made a treaty with him, and let him go.

**1 Kgs.
20:35-43**

PROPHET REBUKES AHAB.   By the word of the LORD one of the sons of the prophets said to his companion, "Strike me with your weapon," but the man refused.

So the prophet said, "Because you have not obeyed the LORD, as soon as you leave me a lion will kill you." And after the man went away, a lion found him and killed him.

The prophet found another man and said, "Strike me, please." So the man struck him and wounded him. Then the prophet went and stood by the road waiting for the king. He disguised himself with his headband down over his eyes. As the king passed by, the prophet called out to him, "Your servant went into the thick of the battle, and someone came to me with a captive and said, 'Guard this man. If he is missing, it will be your life for his life, or you must pay a talent*u* of silver.' While your servant was busy here and there, the man disappeared."

"That is your sentence," the king of Israel said. "You have pronounced it yourself."

Then the prophet quickly removed the headband from his eyes, and the king of Israel recognized him as one of the prophets. He said to the king, "This is what the LORD says: 'You have set free a man I had determined should die.*v* Therefore it is your life for his life, your people for his people.'" Sullen and angry, the king of Israel went to his palace in Samaria.

1 Kgs. 22:1

PEACE WITH SYRIA.   For three years there was no war between Aram and Israel.

**1 Kgs.
21:1-3
Samaria**

AHAB COVETS VINEYARD.   Some time later there was an incident involving a vineyard belonging to Naboth the Jezreelite. The vineyard was in Jezreel, close to the palace of Ahab king of Samaria. Ahab said to Naboth, "Let me have your vineyard to use for a vegetable garden, since it is close to my palace. In exchange I will give you a better vineyard or, if you prefer, I will pay you whatever it is worth."

But Naboth replied, "The LORD forbid that I should give you the inheritance of my fathers."

**1 Kgs.
21:4-16**

JEZEBEL'S DEADLY SCHEME.   So Ahab went home, sullen and angry because Naboth the Jezreelite had said, "I will not give you the inheritance of my fathers." He lay on his bed sulking and refused to eat.

His wife Jezebel came in and asked him, "Why are you so sullen? Why won't you eat?"

He answered her, "Because I said to Naboth the Jezreelite, 'Sell me your vineyard; or if you prefer, I will give you another vineyard in its place.' But he said, 'I will not give you my vineyard.'"

Jezebel his wife said, "Is this how you act as king over Israel? Get up and eat! Cheer up. I'll get you the vineyard of Naboth the Jezreelite."

So she wrote letters in Ahab's name, placed his seal on them, and sent

---

*u*That is, about 75 pounds (about 34 kilograms)   *v*The Hebrew term refers to the irrevocable giving over of things or persons to the LORD, often by totally destroying them.

them to the elders and nobles who lived in Naboth's city with him. In those letters she wrote:

"Proclaim a day of fasting and seat Naboth in a prominent place among the people. But seat two scoundrels opposite him and have them testify that he has cursed both God and the king. Then take him out and stone him to death."

So the elders and nobles who lived in Naboth's city did as Jezebel directed in the letters she had written to them. They proclaimed a fast and seated Naboth in a prominent place among the people. Then two scoundrels came and sat opposite him and brought charges against Naboth before the people, saying, "Naboth has cursed both God and the king." So they took him outside the city and stoned him to death. Then they sent word to Jezebel: "Naboth has been stoned and is dead."

As soon as Jezebel heard that Naboth had been stoned to death, she said to Ahab, "Get up and take possession of the vineyard of Naboth the Jezreelite that he refused to sell you. He is no longer alive, but dead." When Ahab heard that Naboth was dead, he got up and went down to take possession of Naboth's vineyard.

ELIJAH TELLS PUNISHMENT.   Then the word of the LORD came to Elijah the Tishbite: "Go down to meet Ahab king of Israel, who rules in Samaria. He is now in Naboth's vineyard, where he has gone to take possession of it. Say to him, 'This is what the LORD says: Have you not murdered a man and seized his property?' Then say to him, 'This is what the LORD says: In the place where dogs licked up Naboth's blood, dogs will lick up your blood—yes, yours!' "

1 Kgs. 21:17-24

Ahab said to Elijah, "So you have found me, my enemy!"

"I have found you," he answered, "because you have sold yourself to do evil in the eyes of the LORD. 'I am going to bring disaster on you. I will consume your descendants and cut off from Ahab every last male in Israel— slave or free. I will make your house like that of Jeroboam son of Nebat and that of Baasha son of Ahijah, because you have provoked me to anger and have caused Israel to sin.'

"And also concerning Jezebel the LORD says: 'Dogs will devour Jezebel by the wall of*w* Jezreel.'

"Dogs will eat those belonging to Ahab who die in the city, and the birds of the air will feed on those who die in the country."

REPENTANCE BRINGS STAY.   When Ahab heard these words, he tore his clothes, put on sackcloth and fasted. He lay in sackcloth and went around meekly.

1 Kgs. 21:27-29

Then the word of the LORD came to Elijah the Tishbite: "Have you noticed how Ahab has humbled himself before me? Because he has humbled himself, I will not bring this disaster in his day, but I will bring it on his house in the days of his son."

AHAZIAH BECOMES CO-REGENT.   Ahaziah son of Ahab became king of Israel in Samaria in the seventeenth year of Jehoshaphat king of Judah, and he reigned over Israel two years.

1 Kgs. 22:51 Samaria

JEHOSHAPHAT JOINS AHAB.   *Kg*But in the third year Jehoshaphat king of Judah went down to see the king of Israel. *Ch*Ahab slaughtered many

1 Kgs. 22:2-4 2 Chron. 18:2,3 (853 B.C.)

*w*Most Hebrew manuscripts; a few Hebrew manuscripts, Vulgate and Syriac (see also 2 Kings 9:26) *the plot of ground at*

sheep and cattle for him and the people with him and urged him to attack Ramoth Gilead. ^{Kg}The king of Israel had said to his officials, "Don't you know that Ramoth Gilead belongs to us and yet we are doing nothing to retake it from the king of Aram?"

So he asked Jehoshaphat, "Will you go with me to fight against Ramoth Gilead?"

Jehoshaphat replied to the king of Israel, "I am as you are, my people as your people, my horses as your horses."

1 Kgs.
22:5,6,10-12
2 Chron.
18:4,5,9-11

PROPHETS PROMISE VICTORY.   But Jehoshaphat also said to the king of Israel, "First seek the counsel of the LORD."

So the king of Israel brought together the prophets—about four hundred men—and asked them, "Shall I go to war against Ramoth Gilead, or shall I refrain?"

"Go," they answered, "for the Lord will give it into the king's hand."

Dressed in their royal robes, the king of Israel and Jehoshaphat king of Judah were sitting on their thrones at the threshing floor by the entrance of the gate of Samaria, with all the prophets prophesying before them. Now Zedekiah son of Kenaanah had made iron horns and he declared, "This is what the LORD says: 'With these you will gore the Arameans until they are destroyed.'"

All the other prophets were prophesying the same thing. "Attack Ramoth Gilead and be victorious," they said, "for the LORD will give it into the king's hand."

1 Kgs.
22:7-9,13-28
2 Chron.
18:6-8,12-27

MICAIAH'S PROPHECY.   But Jehoshaphat asked, "Is there not a prophet of the LORD here whom we can inquire of?"

The king of Israel answered Jehoshaphat, "There is still one man through whom we can inquire of the LORD, but I hate him because he never prophesies anything good about me, but always bad. He is Micaiah son of Imlah."

"The king should not say that," Jehoshaphat replied.

So the king of Israel called one of his officials and said, "Bring Micaiah son of Imlah at once."

The messenger who had gone to summon Micaiah said to him, "Look, as one man the other prophets are predicting success for the king. Let your word agree with theirs, and speak favorably."

But Micaiah said, "As surely as the LORD lives, I can tell him only what the LORD tells me."

When he arrived, the king asked him, "Micaiah, shall we go to war against Ramoth Gilead, or shall I refrain?"

"Attack and be victorious," he answered, "for the LORD will give it into the king's hand."

The king said to him, "How many times must I make you swear to tell me nothing but the truth in the name of the LORD?"

Then Micaiah answered, "I saw all Israel scattered on the hills like sheep without a shepherd, and the LORD said, 'These people have no master. Let each one go home in peace.'"

The king of Israel said to Jehoshaphat, "Didn't I tell you that he never prophesies anything good about me, but only bad?"

Micaiah continued, "Therefore hear the word of the LORD: I saw the LORD sitting on his throne with all the host of heaven standing around him on his right and on his left. And the LORD said, 'Who will entice Ahab into attacking Ramoth Gilead and going to his death there?'

"One suggested this, and another that. Finally, a spirit came forward, stood before the LORD and said, 'I will entice him.'

" 'By what means?' the LORD asked.

" 'I will go out and be a lying spirit in the mouths of all his prophets,' he said.

" 'You will succeed in enticing him,' said the LORD. 'Go and do it.'

"So now the LORD has put a lying spirit in the mouths of all these prophets of yours. The LORD has decreed disaster for you."

Then Zedekiah son of Kenaanah went up and slapped Micaiah in the face. "Which way did the spirit from^x the LORD go when he went from me to speak to you?" he asked.

Micaiah replied, "You will find out on the day you go to hide in an inner room."

The king of Israel then ordered, "Take Micaiah and send him back to Amon the ruler of the city and to Joash the king's son and say, 'This is what the king says: Put this fellow in prison and give him nothing but bread and water until I return safely.' "

Micaiah declared, "If you ever return safely, the LORD has not spoken through me." Then he added, "Mark my words, all you people!"

AHAB KILLED IN BATTLE.   So the king of Israel and Jehoshaphat king of Judah went up to Ramoth Gilead. The king of Israel said to Jehoshaphat, "I will enter the battle in disguise, but you wear your royal robes." So the king of Israel disguised himself and went into battle.

1 Kgs. 22:29-36 2 Chron. 18:28-34 Ramoth Gilead (853 B.C.)

Now the king of Aram had ordered his thirty-two chariot commanders, "Do not fight with anyone, small or great, except the king of Israel." When the chariot commanders saw Jehoshaphat, they thought, "Surely this is the king of Israel." So they turned to attack him, but when Jehoshaphat cried out, the chariot commanders saw that he was not the king of Israel and stopped pursuing him.

But someone drew his bow at random and hit the king of Israel between the sections of his armor. The king told his chariot driver, "Wheel around and get me out of the fighting. I've been wounded." All day long the battle raged, and the king was propped up in his chariot facing the Arameans. The blood from his wound ran onto the floor of the chariot, and that evening he died. As the sun was setting, a cry spread through the army: "Every man to his town; everyone to his land!"

JEHOSHAPHAT REBUKED.   When Jehoshaphat king of Judah returned safely to his palace in Jerusalem, Jehu the seer, the son of Hanani, went out to meet him and said to the king, "Should you help the wicked and love^y those who hate the LORD? Because of this, the wrath of the LORD is upon you. There is, however, some good in you, for you have rid the land of the Asherah poles and have set your heart on seeking God."

2 Chron. 19:1-3 Jerusalem

AHAB BURIED.   So the king died and was brought to Samaria, and they buried him there. They washed the chariot at a pool in Samaria (where the prostitutes bathed),^z and the dogs licked up his blood, as the word of the LORD had declared.

1 Kgs. 22:37-40a Samaria

As for the other events of Ahab's reign, including all he did, the palace

---

^xOr *Spirit of*   ^yOr *and make alliances with*   ^zOr *Samaria and cleaned the weapons*

he built and inlaid with ivory, and the cities he fortified, are they not written in the book of the annals of the kings of Israel? Ahab rested with his fathers.

1 Kgs.
22:40b
(853 B.C.)

AHAZIAH RULES ALONE.   And Ahaziah his son succeeded him as king.

1 Kgs.
22:52,53

AHAZIAH'S CHARACTER.   He did evil in the eyes of the LORD, because he walked in the ways of his father and mother and in the ways of Jeroboam son of Nebat, who caused Israel to sin. He served and worshiped Baal and provoked the LORD, the God of Israel, to anger, just as his father had done.

2 Kgs. 3:4,5

MOAB REVOLTS.   Now Mesha king of Moab raised sheep, and he had to supply the king of Israel with a hundred thousand lambs and with the wool of a hundred thousand rams. But after Ahab died, the king of Moab rebelled against the king of Israel.

In Judah

2 Chron.
19:4-11
Jerusalem

JUSTICE SYSTEM REFORMED.   Jehoshaphat lived in Jerusalem, and he went out again among the people from Beersheba to the hill country of Ephraim and turned them back to the LORD, the God of their fathers. He appointed judges in the land, in each of the fortified cities of Judah. He told them, "Consider carefully what you do, because you are not judging for man but for the LORD, who is with you whenever you give a verdict. Now let the fear of the LORD be upon you. Judge carefully, for with the LORD our God there is no injustice or partiality or bribery."

In Jerusalem also, Jehoshaphat appointed some of the Levites, priests and heads of Israelite families to administer the law of the LORD and to settle disputes. And they lived in Jerusalem. He gave them these orders: "You must serve faithfully and wholeheartedly in the fear of the LORD. In every case that comes before you from your fellow countrymen who live in the cities—whether bloodshed or other concerns of the law, commands, decrees or ordinances—you are to warn them not to sin against the LORD; otherwise his wrath will come on you and your brothers. Do this, and you will not sin.

"Amariah the chief priest will be over you in any matter concerning the LORD, and Zebadiah son of Ishmael, the leader of the tribe of Judah, will be over you in any matter concerning the king, and the Levites will serve as officials before you. Act with courage, and may the LORD be with those who do well."

2 Chron.
20:1,2

MOABITES INVADE JUDAH.   After this, the Moabites and Ammonites with some of the Meunites[a] came to make war on Jehoshaphat.

Some men came and told Jehoshaphat, "A vast army is coming against you from Edom,[b] from the other side of the Sea.[c] It is already in Hazazon Tamar" (that is, En Gedi).

2 Chron.
20:3-12

JEHOSHAPHAT PRAYS.   Alarmed, Jehoshaphat resolved to inquire of the LORD, and he proclaimed a fast for all Judah. The people of Judah came together to seek help from the LORD; indeed, they came from every town in Judah to seek him.

[a]Some Septuagint manuscripts; Hebrew *Ammonites*   [b]One Hebrew manuscript; most
Hebrew manuscripts, Septuagint and Vulgate *Aram*   [c]That is, the Dead Sea

Then Jehoshaphat stood up in the assembly of Judah and Jerusalem at the temple of the LORD in the front of the new courtyard and said:

"O LORD, God of our fathers, are you not the God who is in heaven? You rule over all the kingdoms of the nations. Power and might are in your hand, and no one can withstand you. O our God, did you not drive out the inhabitants of this land before your people Israel and give it forever to the descendants of Abraham your friend? They have lived in it and have built in it a sanctuary for your Name, saying, 'If calamity comes upon us, whether the sword of judgment, or plague or famine, we will stand in your presence before this temple that bears your Name and will cry out to you in our distress, and you will hear us and save us.'

"But now here are men from Ammon, Moab and Mount Seir, whose territory you would not allow Israel to invade when they came from Egypt; so they turned away from them and did not destroy them. See how they are repaying us by coming to drive us out of the possession you gave us as an inheritance. O our God, will you not judge them? For we have no power to face this vast army that is attacking us. We do not know what to do, but our eyes are upon you."

GOD'S SPIRIT ANSWERS.   All the men of Judah, with their wives and children and little ones, stood there before the LORD.

2 Chron.
20:13-19

Then the Spirit of the LORD came upon Jahaziel son of Zechariah, the son of Benaiah, the son of Jeiel, the son of Mattaniah, a Levite and descendant of Asaph, as he stood in the assembly.

He said: "Listen, King Jehoshaphat and all who live in Judah and Jerusalem! This is what the LORD says to you: 'Do not be afraid or discouraged because of this vast army. For the battle is not yours, but God's. Tomorrow march down against them. They will be climbing up by the Pass of Ziz, and you will find them at the end of the gorge in the Desert of Jeruel. You will not have to fight this battle. Take up your positions; stand firm and see the deliverance the LORD will give you, O Judah and Jerusalem. Do not be afraid; do not be discouraged. Go out to face them tomorrow, and the LORD will be with you.'"

Jehoshaphat bowed with his face to the ground, and all the people of Judah and Jerusalem fell down in worship before the LORD. Then some Levites from the Kohathites and Korahites stood up and praised the LORD, the God of Israel, with a very loud voice.

MOABITES DESTROYED.   Early in the morning they left for the Desert of Tekoa. As they set out, Jehoshaphat stood and said, "Listen to me, Judah and people of Jerusalem! Have faith in the LORD your God and you will be upheld; have faith in his prophets and you will be successful." After consulting the people, Jehoshaphat appointed men to sing to the LORD and to praise him for the splendor of his[d] holiness as they went out at the head of the army, saying:

2 Chron.
20:20-24
Desert of
Tekoa

"Give thanks to the LORD,
for his love endures forever."

As they began to sing and praise, the LORD set ambushes against the men of Ammon and Moab and Mount Seir who were invading Judah, and

[d]Or *him with the splendor of*

they were defeated. The men of Ammon and Moab rose up against the men from Mount Seir to destroy and annihilate them. After they finished slaughtering the men from Seir, they helped to destroy one another.

When the men of Judah came to the place that overlooks the desert and looked toward the vast army, they saw only dead bodies lying on the ground; no one had escaped.

2 Chron.
20:25-30
Valley of
Beracah

TRIUMPHANT RETURN.   So Jehoshaphat and his men went to carry off their plunder, and they found among them a great amount of equipment and clothing^e and also articles of value—more than they could take away. There was so much plunder that it took three days to collect it. On the fourth day they assembled in the Valley of Beracah, where they praised the LORD. This is why it is called the Valley of Beracah^f to this day.

Then, led by Jehoshaphat, all the men of Judah and Jerusalem returned joyfully to Jerusalem, for the LORD had given them cause to rejoice over their enemies. They entered Jerusalem and went to the temple of the LORD with harps and lutes and trumpets.

The fear of God came upon all the kingdoms of the countries when they heard how the LORD had fought against the enemies of Israel. And the kingdom of Jehoshaphat was at peace, for his God had given him rest on every side.

2 Chron.
20:35-37
1 Kgs.
22:48,49
Jerusalem

LIMITED SHIPPING ALLIANCE.   ^ChLater, Jehoshaphat king of Judah made an alliance with Ahaziah king of Israel, who was guilty of wickedness. He agreed with him to construct a fleet of trading ships.^g ^KgNow Jehoshaphat built a fleet of trading ships^h to go to Ophir for gold... ^ChAfter these were built at Ezion Geber, Eliezer son of Dodavahu of Mareshah prophesied against Jehoshaphat, saying, "Because you have made an alliance with Ahaziah, the LORD will destroy what you have made." The ships were wrecked and were not able to set sail to trade.^i ^KgAt that time Ahaziah son of Ahab said to Jehoshaphat, "Let my men sail with your men," but Jehoshaphat refused.

In Israel

2 Kgs. 1:2
Samaria

AHAZIAH FALLS ILL.   Now Ahaziah had fallen through the lattice of his upper room in Samaria and injured himself. So he sent messengers, saying to them, "Go and consult Baal-Zebub, the god of Ekron, to see if I will recover from this injury."

2 Kgs.
1:3-8

ELIJAH BRINGS PROPHECY.   But the angel of the LORD said to Elijah the Tishbite, "Go up and meet the messengers of the king of Samaria and ask them, 'Is it because there is no God in Israel that you are going off to consult Baal-Zebub, the god of Ekron?' Therefore this is what the LORD says: 'You will not leave the bed you are lying on. You will certainly die!'" So Elijah went.

When the messengers returned to the king, he asked them, "Why have you come back?"

"A man came to meet us," they replied. "And he said to us, 'Go back to the king who sent you and tell him, "This is what the LORD says: Is it because there is no God in Israel that you are sending men to consult

^eSome Hebrew manuscripts and Vulgate; most Hebrew manuscripts *corpses*   ^fBeracah means *praise*.   ^gHebrew *of ships that could go to Tarshish*   ^hHebrew *of ships of Tarshish*   ^iHebrew *sail for Tarshish*

Baal-Zebub, the god of Ekron? Therefore you will not leave the bed you are lying on. You will certainly die!"'"

The king asked them, "What kind of man was it who came to meet you and told you this?"

They replied, "He was a man with a garment of hair and with a leather belt around his waist."

The king said, "That was Elijah the Tishbite."

MESSENGERS KILLED.   Then he sent to Elijah a captain with his company of fifty men. The captain went up to Elijah, who was sitting on the top of a hill, and said to him, "Man of God, the king says, 'Come down!'"

Elijah answered the captain, "If I am a man of God, may fire come down from heaven and consume you and your fifty men!" Then fire fell from heaven and consumed the captain and his men.

At this the king sent to Elijah another captain with his fifty men. The captain said to him, "Man of God, this is what the king says, 'Come down at once!'"

"If I am a man of God," Elijah replied, "may fire come down from heaven and consume you and your fifty men!" Then the fire of God fell from heaven and consumed him and his fifty men.

So the king sent a third captain with his fifty men. This third captain went up and fell on his knees before Elijah. "Man of God," he begged, "please have respect for my life and the lives of these fifty men, your servants! See, fire has fallen from heaven and consumed the first two captains and all their men. But now have respect for my life!"

2 Kgs. 1:9-14

AHAZIAH TOLD OF DEATH.   The angel of the LORD said to Elijah, "Go down with him; do not be afraid of him." So Elijah got up and went down with him to the king.

He told the king, "This is what the LORD says: Is it because there is no God in Israel for you to consult that you have sent messengers to consult Baal-Zebub, the god of Ekron? Because you have done this, you will never leave the bed you are lying on. You will certainly die!"

2 Kgs. 1:15,16

AHAZIAH DIES.   So he died, according to the word of the LORD that Elijah had spoken. As for all the other events of Ahaziah's reign, and what he did, are they not written in the book of the annals of the kings of Israel?

2 Kgs. 1:17a,18 (853 B.C.)

JORAM (JEHORAM) BECOMES KING.   Because Ahaziah had no son, Joram *j* [son of Ahab] succeeded him as king [of Israel in Samaria in the eighteenth year of Jehoshaphat] in the second year of Jehoram son of Jehoshaphat king of Judah, and he reigned twelve years.

2 Kgs. 1:17b 3:1 (853-852 B.C.)

JORAM'S CHARACTER.   He did evil in the eyes of the LORD, but not as his father and mother had done. He got rid of the sacred stone of Baal that his father had made. Nevertheless he clung to the sins of Jeroboam son of Nebat, which he had caused Israel to commit; he did not turn away from them.

2 Kgs. 3:2,3

*j*Hebrew *Jehoram,* a variant of *Joram*

Elisha the Prophet

*S*ometime earlier God had directed Elijah to enlist the services of Elisha to help him in the ministry of prophecy. Since then, Elisha has been Elijah's protégé, following him about and learning the work of a prophet. Like his teacher, Elisha will also work wonderful miracles. In fact, while only five of Elijah's miracles are recorded, at least 12 of Elisha's will be forthcoming. Like Elijah, Elisha will perform several miracles similar in nature to those performed by the Messiah to come.

But Elisha's ministry must await the end of Elijah's. And what an end it is to be! Elijah apparently knows that God is about to take him. He is now seen traveling from Gilgal to the Jordan River, where he is taken up in a whirlwind. The clear implication is that Elijah never dies in a physical sense, but is in some special way translated into another realm. Perhaps it is the same way in which Enoch "was no more." However it happens, Elisha is so excited about it that he can hardly contain himself.

2 Kgs.
2:1-11

ELIJAH TAKEN UP.   When the LORD was about to take Elijah up to heaven in a whirlwind, Elijah and Elisha were on their way from Gilgal. Elijah said to Elisha, "Stay here; the LORD has sent me to Bethel."

But Elisha said, "As surely as the LORD lives and as you live, I will not leave you." So they went down to Bethel.

The company of the prophets at Bethel came out to Elisha and asked, "Do you know that the LORD is going to take your master from you today?"

"Yes, I know," Elisha replied, "but do not speak of it."

Then Elijah said to him, "Stay here, Elisha; the LORD has sent me to Jericho."

And he replied, "As surely as the LORD lives and as you live, I will not leave you." So they went to Jericho.

The company of the prophets at Jericho went up to Elisha and asked him, "Do you know that the LORD is going to take your master from you today?"

"Yes, I know," he replied, "but do not speak of it."

Then Elijah said to him, "Stay here; the LORD has sent me to the Jordan."

And he replied, "As surely as the LORD lives and as you live, I will not leave you." So the two of them walked on.

Fifty men of the company of the prophets went and stood at a distance, facing the place where Elijah and Elisha had stopped at the Jordan. Elijah took his cloak, rolled it up and struck the water with it. The water divided to the right and to the left, and the two of them crossed over on dry ground.

When they had crossed, Elijah said to Elisha, "Tell me, what can I do for you before I am taken from you?"

"Let me inherit a double portion of your spirit," Elisha replied.

"You have asked a difficult thing," Elijah said, "yet if you see me when I am taken from you, it will be yours—otherwise not."

As they were walking along and talking together, suddenly a chariot of fire and horses of fire appeared and separated the two of them, and Elijah went up to heaven in a whirlwind.

ELISHA RECEIVES SPIRIT.   Elisha saw this and cried out, "My father! My father! The chariots and horsemen of Israel!" And Elisha saw him no more. Then he took hold of his own clothes and tore them apart.

2 Kgs. 2:12-15

He picked up the cloak that had fallen from Elijah and went back and stood on the bank of the Jordan. Then he took the cloak that had fallen from him and struck the water with it. "Where now is the LORD, the God of Elijah?" he asked. When he struck the water, it divided to the right and to the left, and he crossed over.

The company of the prophets from Jericho, who were watching, said, "The spirit of Elijah is resting on Elisha." And they went to meet him and bowed to the ground before him.

NO TRACE OF ELIJAH.   "Look," they said, "we your servants have fifty able men. Let them go and look for your master. Perhaps the Spirit of the LORD has picked him up and set him down on some mountain or in some valley."

2 Kgs. 2:16-18 Jericho

"No," Elisha replied, "do not send them."

But they persisted until he was too ashamed to refuse. So he said, "Send them." And they sent fifty men, who searched for three days but did not find him. When they returned to Elisha, who was staying in Jericho, he said to them, "Didn't I tell you not to go?"

ELISHA PURIFIES WATER.   The men of the city said to Elisha, "Look, our lord, this town is well situated, as you can see, but the water is bad and the land is unproductive."

2 Kgs. 2:19-22

"Bring me a new bowl," he said, "and put salt in it." So they brought it to him.

Then he went out to the spring and threw the salt into it, saying, "This is what the LORD says: 'I have healed this water. Never again will it cause death or make the land unproductive.'" And the water has remained wholesome to this day, according to the word Elisha had spoken.

CHILDREN JEER ELISHA.   From there Elisha went up to Bethel. As he was walking along the road, some youths came out of the town and jeered at him. "Go on up, you baldhead!" they said. "Go on up, you baldhead!" He turned around, looked at them and called down a curse on them in the name of the LORD. Then two bears came out of the woods and mauled forty-two of the youths. And he went on to Mount Carmel and from there returned to Samaria.

2 Kgs. 2:23-25 Samaria

MIRACLE OF INCREASED OIL.   The wife of a man from the company of the prophets cried out to Elisha, "Your servant my husband is dead, and you know that he revered the LORD. But now his creditor is coming to take my two boys as his slaves."

2 Kgs. 4:1-7

Elisha replied to her, "How can I help you? Tell me, what do you have in your house?"

"Your servant has nothing there at all," she said, "except a little oil."

Elisha said, "Go around and ask all your neighbors for empty jars. Don't ask for just a few. Then go inside and shut the door behind you and your sons. Pour oil into all the jars, and as each is filled, put it to one side."

She left him and afterward shut the door behind her and her sons. They brought the jars to her and she kept pouring. When all the jars were full, she said to her son, "Bring me another one."

But he replied, "There is not a jar left." Then the oil stopped flowing.

She went and told the man of God, and he said, "Go, sell the oil and pay your debts. You and your sons can live on what is left."

2 Kgs. 4:8-17 Shunem

SON PROMISED TO SHUNAMMITE.   One day Elisha went to Shunem. And a well-to-do woman was there, who urged him to stay for a meal. So whenever he came by, he stopped there to eat. She said to her husband, "I know that this man who often comes our way is a holy man of God. Let's make a small room on the roof and put in it a bed and a table, a chair and a lamp for him. Then he can stay there whenever he comes to us."

One day when Elisha came, he went up to his room and lay down there. He said to his servant Gehazi, "Call the Shunammite." So he called her, and she stood before him. Elisha said to him, "Tell her, 'You have gone to all this trouble for us. Now what can be done for you? Can we speak on your behalf to the king or the commander of the army?'"

She replied, "I have a home among my own people."

"What can be done for her?" Elisha asked.

Gehazi said, "Well, she has no son and her husband is old."

Then Elisha said, "Call her." So he called her, and she stood in the doorway. "About this time next year," Elisha said, "you will hold a son in your arms."

"No, my lord," she objected. "Don't mislead your servant, O man of God!"

But the woman became pregnant, and the next year about that same time she gave birth to a son, just as Elisha had told her.

2 Kgs. 4:38-41 Gilgal

ELISHA PURIFIES STEW.   Elisha returned to Gilgal and there was a famine in that region. While the company of the prophets was meeting with him, he said to his servant, "Put on the large pot and cook some stew for these men."

One of them went out into the fields to gather herbs and found a wild vine. He gathered some of its gourds and filled the fold of his cloak. When he returned, he cut them up into the pot of stew, though no one knew what they were. The stew was poured out for the men, but as they began to eat it, they cried out, "O man of God, there is death in the pot!" And they could not eat it.

Elisha said, "Get some flour." He put it into the pot and said, "Serve it to the people to eat." And there was nothing harmful in the pot.

2 Kgs. 4:42-44

HUNDRED FED WITH LOAVES.   A man came from Baal Shalishah, bringing the man of God twenty loaves of barley bread baked from the first ripe grain, along with some heads of new grain. "Give it to the people to eat," Elisha said.

"How can I set this before a hundred men?" his servant asked.

But Elisha answered, "Give it to the people to eat. For this is what the LORD says: 'They will eat and have some left over.'" Then he set it before them, and they ate and had some left over, according to the word of the LORD.

2 Kgs. 4:18-37 Shunem

SHUNAMMITE'S SON RAISED.   The child grew, and one day he went out to his father, who was with the reapers. "My head! My head!" he said to his father.

His father told a servant, "Carry him to his mother." After the servant had lifted him up and carried him to his mother, the boy sat on her lap until noon, and then he died. She went up and laid him on the bed of the man of God, then shut the door and went out.

She called her husband and said, "Please send me one of the servants and a donkey so I can go to the man of God quickly and return."

"Why go to him today?" he asked. "It's not the New Moon or the Sabbath."

"It's all right," she said.

She saddled the donkey and said to her servant, "Lead on; don't slow down for me unless I tell you." So she set out and came to the man of God at Mount Carmel.

When he saw her in the distance, the man of God said to his servant Gehazi, "Look! There's the Shunammite! Run to meet her and ask her, 'Are you all right? Is your husband all right? Is your child all right?'"

"Everything is all right," she said.

When she reached the man of God at the mountain, she took hold of his feet. Gehazi came over to push her away, but the man of God said, "Leave her alone! She is in bitter distress, but the LORD has hidden it from me and has not told me why."

"Did I ask you for a son, my lord?" she said. "Didn't I tell you, 'Don't raise my hopes'?"

Elisha said to Gehazi, "Tuck your cloak into your belt, take my staff in your hand and run. If you meet anyone, do not greet him, and if anyone greets you, do not answer. Lay my staff on the boy's face."

But the child's mother said, "As surely as the LORD lives and as you live, I will not leave you." So he got up and followed her.

Gehazi went on ahead and laid the staff on the boy's face, but there was no sound or response. So Gehazi went back to meet Elisha and told him, "The boy has not awakened."

When Elisha reached the house, there was the boy lying dead on his couch. He went in, shut the door on the two of them and prayed to the LORD. Then he got on the bed and lay upon the boy, mouth to mouth, eyes to eyes, hands to hands. As he stretched himself out upon him, the boy's body grew warm. Elisha turned away and walked back and forth in the room and then got on the bed and stretched out upon him once more. The boy sneezed seven times and opened his eyes.

Elisha summoned Gehazi and said, "Call the Shunammite." And he did. When she came, he said, "Take your son." She came in, fell at his feet and bowed to the ground. Then she took her son and went out.

FAMINE FORETOLD.   Now Elisha had said to the woman whose son he had restored to life, "Go away with your family and stay for a while wherever you can, because the LORD has decreed a famine in the land that will last seven years." The woman proceeded to do as the man of God said. She and her family went away and stayed in the land of the Philistines seven years.

2 Kgs.
8:1,2

AXHEAD MADE TO FLOAT.   The company of the prophets said to Elisha, "Look, the place where we meet with you is too small for us. Let us go to the Jordan, where each of us can get a pole; and let us build a place there for us to live."

And he said, "Go."

Then one of them said, "Won't you please come with your servants?"

"I will," Elisha replied. And he went with them.

2 Kgs.
6:1-7

They went to the Jordan and began to cut down trees. As one of them was cutting down a tree, the iron axhead fell into the water. "Oh, my lord," he cried out, "it was borrowed!"

The man of God asked, "Where did it fall?" When he showed him the place, Elisha cut a stick and threw it there, and made the iron float. "Lift it out," he said. Then the man reached out his hand and took it.

Miracles and Massacres

God works so hard to get his people's attention! Even when man is at his worst, God does not forsake him. In fact, it is frequently during times of spiritual crises that God shows his power most dramatically. Surely this is true for both Judah and Israel during the reigns of Jehoshaphat and Jehoram in the south and Joram in the north, for God brings wonder after wonder upon his people.

God defeats the Moabites by making water appear as blood. Jehoram receives a mysterious letter from the prophet Elijah, who was taken miraculously from the earth sometime earlier. Syrian troops are divinely blinded. A leader of the Syrians is cured of leprosy. And an entire army flees at the sound of chariots which never existed.

Yet through all of this God is largely ignored by his people. So it is that punishment comes—first through invasions by foreign forces and revolt by the Edomites, then in the deaths of Jehoram and his successor Ahaziah in Judah, as well as King Joram of Israel. And God's executioner, Jehu, the anointed king of Israel, does not stop until all of former King Ahab's princes and other family members—including Queen Jezebel—are totally destroyed. The eradication of sin is seen as a terrifying force. The consequences are certain, even if sometimes delayed. And the same principle is true for the Edomites, against whom God will bring Obadiah to prophesy.

In Judah

2 Kgs. 8:16,17
2 Chron. 21:5
(853 B.C.?)

JEHORAM CO-REGENT AGAIN. In the fifth year of Joram[k] son of Ahab king of Israel, when Jehoshaphat was king of Judah, Jehoram son of Jehoshaphat began his reign as king of Judah. He was thirty-two years old when he became king, and he reigned in Jerusalem eight years.

2 Chron. 21:2-4

JEHORAM KILLS BROTHERS. Jehoram's brothers, the sons of Jehoshaphat, were Azariah, Jehiel, Zechariah, Azariahu, Michael and Shephatiah. All these were sons of Jehoshaphat king of Israel.[l] Their father had given them many gifts of silver and gold and articles of value, as well as fortified cities in Judah, but he had given the kingdom to Jehoram because he was his firstborn son.

When Jehoram established himself firmly over his father's kingdom, he put all his brothers to the sword along with some of the princes of Israel.

2 Kgs. 3:6-9

JUDAH JOINS AGAINST MOAB. So at that time King Joram set out from Samaria and mobilized all Israel. He also sent this message to Jehoshaphat king of Judah: "The king of Moab has rebelled against me. Will you go with me to fight against Moab?"

[k]Hebrew *Jehoram*, a variant of *Joram*   [l]That is, Judah, as frequently in 2 Chron.

"I will go with you," he replied. "I am as you are, my people as your people, my horses as your horses."

"By what route shall we attack?" he asked.

"Through the Desert of Edom," he answered.

So the king of Israel set out with the king of Judah and the king of Edom. After a roundabout march of seven days, the army had no more water for themselves or for the animals with them.

WATER AND VICTORY PROMISED. "What!" exclaimed the king of Israel. "Has the LORD called us three kings together only to hand us over to Moab?"

2 Kgs. 3:10-20

But Jehoshaphat asked, "Is there no prophet of the LORD here, that we may inquire of the LORD through him?"

An officer of the king of Israel answered, "Elisha son of Shaphat is here. He used to pour water on the hands of Elijah.*m*"

Jehoshaphat said, "The word of the LORD is with him." So the king of Israel and Jehoshaphat and the king of Edom went down to him.

Elisha said to the king of Israel, "What do we have to do with each other? Go to the prophets of your father and the prophets of your mother."

"No," the king of Israel answered, "because it was the LORD who called us three kings together to hand us over to Moab."

Elisha said, "As surely as the LORD Almighty lives, whom I serve, if I did not have respect for the presence of Jehoshaphat king of Judah, I would not look at you or even notice you. But now bring me a harpist."

While the harpist was playing, the hand of the LORD came upon Elisha and he said, "This is what the LORD says: Make this valley full of ditches. For this is what the LORD says: You will see neither wind nor rain, yet this valley will be filled with water, and you, your cattle and your other animals will drink. This is an easy thing in the eyes of the LORD; he will also hand Moab over to you. You will overthrow every fortified city and every major town. You will cut down every good tree, stop up all the springs, and ruin every good field with stones."

The next morning, about the time for offering the sacrifice, there it was—water flowing from the direction of Edom! And the land was filled with water.

MOABITES DEFEATED. Now all the Moabites had heard that the kings had come to fight against them; so every man, young and old, who could bear arms was called up and stationed on the border. When they got up early in the morning, the sun was shining on the water. To the Moabites across the way, the water looked red—like blood. "That's blood!" they said. "Those kings must have fought and slaughtered each other. Now to the plunder, Moab!"

2 Kgs. 3:21-27

But when the Moabites came to the camp of Israel, the Israelites rose up and fought them until they fled. And the Israelites invaded the land and slaughtered the Moabites. They destroyed the towns, and each man threw a stone on every good field until it was covered. They stopped up all the springs and cut down every good tree. Only Kir Hareseth was left with its stones in place, but men armed with slings surrounded it and attacked it as well.

When the king of Moab saw that the battle had gone against him, he

---

*m*That is, he was Elijah's personal servant.

took with him seven hundred swordsmen to break through to the king of Edom, but they failed. Then he took his firstborn son, who was to succeed him as king, and offered him as a sacrifice on the city wall. The fury against Israel was great; they withdrew and returned to their own land.

1 Kgs.
22:45,50a
2 Chron.
20:34; 21:1a
(848 B.C.?)

DEATH OF JEHOSHAPHAT.   The other events of Jehoshaphat's reign, from beginning to end, are written in the annals of Jehu son of Hanani, which are recorded in the book of the kings of Israel. Then Jehoshaphat rested with his fathers and was buried with them in the City of David.

1 Kgs.
22:50b
2 Chron.
21:1b,20a
(848 B.C.)

JEHORAM (JORAM) REIGNS ALONE.   And Jehoram his son succeeded him as king. Jehoram was thirty-two years old when he became king, and he reigned in Jerusalem eight years.

2 Kgs.
8:18,19
2 Chron.
21:6,7,11

CHARACTER OF JEHORAM.   He walked in the ways of the kings of Israel, as the house of Ahab had done, for he married a daughter of Ahab. He did evil in the eyes of the LORD. Nevertheless, because of the covenant the LORD had made with David, the LORD was not willing to destroy the house of David. He had promised to maintain a lamp for him and his descendants forever. He had also built high places on the hills of Judah and had caused the people of Jerusalem to prostitute themselves and had led Judah astray.

2 Chron.
21:12-15

MYSTERIOUS LETTER FROM ELIJAH.   Jehoram received a letter from Elijah the prophet, which said:

"This is what the LORD, the God of your father David, says: 'You have not walked in the ways of your father Jehoshaphat or of Asa king of Judah. But you have walked in the ways of the kings of Israel, and you have led Judah and the people of Jerusalem to prostitute themselves, just as the house of Ahab did. You have also murdered your own brothers, members of your father's house, men who were better than you. So now the LORD is about to strike your people, your sons, your wives and everything that is yours, with a heavy blow. You yourself will be very ill with a lingering disease of the bowels, until the disease causes your bowels to come out.'"

2 Chron.
21:16,17

FOREIGN ARMIES INVADE.   The LORD aroused against Jehoram the hostility of the Philistines and of the Arabs who lived near the Cushites. They attacked Judah, invaded it and carried off all the goods found in the king's palace, together with his sons and wives. Not a son was left to him except Ahaziah,[n] the youngest.

2 Kgs.
8:20-22
2 Chron.
21:8-10

EDOM AND LIBNAH REVOLT.   In the time of Jehoram, Edom rebelled against Judah and set up its own king. So Jehoram went there with his officers and all his chariots. The Edomites surrounded him and his chariot commanders, but he rose up and broke through by night. To this day Edom has been in rebellion against Judah.

Libnah revolted at the same time, because Jehoram had forsaken the LORD, the God of his fathers.

[n]Hebrew *Jehoahaz*, a variant of *Ahaziah*

Obadiah's Prophecy Against Edom

he history of God's miraculous working in the affairs of Israel and Judah is the context for the prophecy of Obadiah, perhaps the first of several written prophecies later collected in Scripture. Little is known about Obadiah except that his name means "servant of God." Some believe that Obadiah belongs to a much later period, possibly 250 years later. Others suggest the present historical context, based on his strongly worded attack against Edom, which has recently revolted and apparently given aid to the Philistine and Arab invaders of Judah. Obadiah has two concerns: first, the haughty pride of the Edomites, whose mountain strongholds in Mount Seir, south of Judah, have given them a false sense of security; and second, their quickness to aid those who would destroy Judah.

This matter is a particularly sensitive one to the descendants of Israel. It is important to remember that the Edomites are the descendants of Esau, with whom Jacob (Israel) had struggled for supremacy. In the centuries since the brothers themselves reconciled, there has been much friction between these nations. The Edomites refused the Israelites passage on their march to Canaan; both Saul and David fought with and finally subdued Edom; and Solomon put down an attempted revolt during his reign. So when the Edomites liberate themselves from Judah's control during the reign of Jehoram, and give aid to foreign enemies, it is cause for angry reaction.

Obadiah predicts that Edom will reap what it sows and will itself be brought to ruin. History will confirm the accuracy of the prediction. In addition to its immediate relevance, the prophecy stands as a warning to all enemies of God's people, especially those who ought to be "brothers."

PREFACE. The vision of Obadiah.   Obad. 1

This is what the Sovereign LORD says about Edom—

> We have heard a message from the LORD:
>   An envoy was sent to the nations to say,
>   "Rise, and let us go against her for battle"—

PRIDE REBUKED.   Obad. 2-4

> "See, I will make you small among the nations;
>   you will be utterly despised.
> The pride of your heart has deceived you,
>   you who live in the clefts of the rocks[o]
>   and make your home on the heights,
> you who say to yourself,
>   'Who can bring me down to the ground?'
> Though you soar like the eagle
>   and make your nest among the stars,
>   from there I will bring you down,"
>   declares the LORD.

oOr of Sela

**Obad.
5-7**

VULNERABILITY EXPOSED.

"If thieves came to you,
     if robbers in the night—
Oh, what a disaster awaits you—
     would they not steal only as much as they wanted?
If grape pickers came to you,
     would they not leave a few grapes?
But how Esau will be ransacked,
     his hidden treasures pillaged!
All your allies will force you to the border;
     your friends will deceive and overpower you;
those who eat your bread will set a trap for you,*p*
     but you will not detect it.

**Obad.
8-14**

REASON FOR PUNISHMENT.

"In that day," declares the LORD,
     "will I not destroy the wise men of Edom,
     men of understanding in the mountains of Esau?
Your warriors, O Teman, will be terrified,
     and everyone in Esau's mountains
     will be cut down in the slaughter.
Because of the violence against your brother Jacob,
     you will be covered with shame;
     you will be destroyed forever.
On the day you stood aloof
     while strangers carried off his wealth
and foreigners entered his gates
     and cast lots for Jerusalem,
     you were like one of them.
You should not look down on your brother
     in the day of his misfortune,
nor rejoice over the people of Judah
     in the day of their destruction,
nor boast so much
     in the day of their trouble.
You should not march through the gates of my people
     in the day of their disaster,
nor look down on them in their calamity
     in the day of their disaster,
nor seize their wealth
     in the day of their disaster.
You should not wait at the crossroads
     to cut down their fugitives,
nor hand over their survivors
     in the day of their trouble.

**Obad.
15-18**

FUTURE DESTRUCTION.

"The day of the LORD is near
     for all nations.

----

*p*The meaning of the Hebrew for this clause is uncertain.

As you have done, it will be done to you;
  your deeds will return upon your own head.
Just as you drank on my holy hill,
  so all the nations will drink continually;
they will drink and drink
  and be as if they had never been.
But on Mount Zion will be deliverance;
  it will be holy,
and the house of Jacob
  will possess its inheritance.
The house of Jacob will be a fire
  and the house of Joseph a flame;
the house of Esau will be stubble,
  and they will set it on fire and consume it.
There will be no survivors
  from the house of Esau."

                                        The LORD has spoken.

GOD'S PEOPLE RESTORED.   Obad.
                                                                        19-21

People from the Negev will occupy
  the mountains of Esau,
and people from the foothills will possess
  the land of the Philistines.
They will occupy the fields of Ephraim and Samaria,
  and Benjamin will possess Gilead.
This company of Israelite exiles who are in Canaan
  will possess ˌthe landˌ as far as Zarephath;
the exiles from Jerusalem who are in Sepharad
  will possess the towns of the Negev.
Deliverers will go up onᵍ Mount Zion
  to govern the mountains of Esau.
And the kingdom will be the LORD's.

The historical record of the many miracles and massacres of this period continues now with the record of Jehoram's being struck ill, just as Elijah's letter had predicted.

JEHORAM STRUCK ILL.   After all this, the LORD afflicted Jehoram with   2 Chron.
an incurable disease of the bowels.   21:18

In Israel

SYRIA'S PLANS THWARTED.   Now the king of Aram was at war with   2 Kgs.
Israel. After conferring with his officers, he said, "I will set up my camp in   6:8-12
such and such a place."
    The man of God sent word to the king of Israel: "Beware of passing that place, because the Arameans are going down there." So the king of Israel checked on the place indicated by the man of God. Time and again Elisha warned the king, so that he was on his guard in such places.
    This enraged the king of Aram. He summoned his officers and demanded of them, "Will you not tell me which of us is on the side of the king of Israel?"

ᵍOr *from*

"None of us, my lord the king," said one of his officers, "but Elisha, the prophet who is in Israel, tells the king of Israel the very words you speak in your bedroom."

**2 Kgs.
6:13-18
Dothan**

SYRIANS BLINDED. "Go, find out where he is," the king ordered, "so I can send men and capture him." The report came back: "He is in Dothan." Then he sent horses and chariots and a strong force there. They went by night and surrounded the city.

When the servant of the man of God got up and went out early the next morning, an army with horses and chariots had surrounded the city. "Oh, my lord, what shall we do?" the servant asked.

"Don't be afraid," the prophet answered. "Those who are with us are more than those who are with them."

And Elisha prayed, "O LORD, open his eyes so he may see." Then the LORD opened the servant's eyes, and he looked and saw the hills full of horses and chariots of fire all around Elisha.

As the enemy came down toward him, Elisha prayed to the LORD, "Strike these people with blindness." So he struck them with blindness, as Elisha had asked.

**2 Kgs.
6:19-23
Samaria**

SYRIANS RELEASED IN SAMARIA. Elisha told them, "This is not the road and this is not the city. Follow me, and I will lead you to the man you are looking for." And he led them to Samaria.

After they entered the city, Elisha said, "LORD, open the eyes of these men so they can see." Then the LORD opened their eyes and they looked, and there they were, inside Samaria.

When the king of Israel saw them, he asked Elisha, "Shall I kill them, my father? Shall I kill them?"

"Do not kill them," he answered. "Would you kill men you have captured with your own sword or bow? Set food and water before them so that they may eat and drink and then go back to their master." So he prepared a great feast for them, and after they had finished eating and drinking, he sent them away, and they returned to their master. So the bands from Aram stopped raiding Israel's territory.

**2 Kgs.
8:3-6**

WOMAN'S LAND RESTORED. At the end of the seven years she came back from the land of the Philistines and went to the king to beg for her house and land. The king was talking to Gehazi, the servant of the man of God, and had said, "Tell me about all the great things Elisha has done." Just as Gehazi was telling the king how Elisha had restored the dead to life, the woman whose son Elisha had brought back to life came to beg the king for her house and land.

Gehazi said, "This is the woman, my lord the king, and this is her son whom Elisha restored to life." The king asked the woman about it, and she told him.

Then he assigned an official to her case and said to him, "Give back everything that belonged to her, including all the income from her land from the day she left the country until now."

**2 Kgs.
5:1-14
Jordan
River**

NAAMAN HEALED OF LEPROSY. Now Naaman was commander of the army of the king of Aram. He was a great man in the sight of his master and highly regarded, because through him the LORD had given victory to Aram. He was a valiant soldier, but he had leprosy.[r]

Now bands from Aram had gone out and had taken captive a young girl from Israel, and she served Naaman's wife. She said to her mistress, "If only my master would see the prophet who is in Samaria! He would cure him of his leprosy."

Naaman went to his master and told him what the girl from Israel had said. "By all means, go," the king of Aram replied. "I will send a letter to the king of Israel." So Naaman left, taking with him ten talents[s] of silver, six thousand shekels[t] of gold and ten sets of clothing. The letter that he took to the king of Israel read: "With this letter I am sending my servant Naaman to you so that you may cure him of his leprosy."

As soon as the king of Israel read the letter, he tore his robes and said, "Am I God? Can I kill and bring back to life? Why does this fellow send someone to me to be cured of his leprosy? See how he is trying to pick a quarrel with me!"

When Elisha the man of God heard that the king of Israel had torn his robes, he sent him this message: "Why have you torn your robes? Have the man come to me and he will know that there is a prophet in Israel." So Naaman went with his horses and chariots and stopped at the door of Elisha's house. Elisha sent a messenger to say to him, "Go, wash yourself seven times in the Jordan, and your flesh will be restored and you will be cleansed."

But Naaman went away angry and said, "I thought that he would surely come out to me and stand and call on the name of the LORD his God, wave his hand over the spot and cure me of my leprosy. Are not Abana and Pharpar, the rivers of Damascus, better than any of the waters of Israel? Couldn't I wash in them and be cleansed?" So he turned and went off in a rage.

Naaman's servants went to him and said, "My father, if the prophet had told you to do some great thing, would you not have done it? How much more, then, when he tells you, 'Wash and be cleansed'!" So he went down and dipped himself in the Jordan seven times, as the man of God had told him, and his flesh was restored and became clean like that of a young boy.

NAAMAN EXPRESSES FAITH.   Then Naaman and all his attendants went back to the man of God. He stood before him and said, "Now I know that there is no God in all the world except in Israel. Please accept now a gift from your servant."

2 Kgs.
5:15-19a

The prophet answered, "As surely as the LORD lives, whom I serve, I will not accept a thing." And even though Naaman urged him, he refused.

"If you will not," said Naaman, "please let me, your servant, be given as much earth as a pair of mules can carry, for your servant will never again make burnt offerings and sacrifices to any other god but the LORD. But may the LORD forgive your servant for this one thing: When my master enters the temple of Rimmon to bow down and he is leaning on my arm and I bow there also—when I bow down in the temple of Rimmon, may the LORD forgive your servant for this."

"Go in peace," Elisha said.

[r] The Hebrew word was used for various diseases affecting the skin—not necessarily leprosy.   [s] That is, about 750 pounds (about 340 kilograms)   [t] That is, about 150 pounds (about 70 kilograms)

**2 Kgs.
5:19b-27**

GEHAZI'S SIN.   After Naaman had traveled some distance, Gehazi, the servant of Elisha the man of God, said to himself, "My master was too easy on Naaman, this Aramean, by not accepting from him what he brought. As surely as the LORD lives, I will run after him and get something from him."

So Gehazi hurried after Naaman. When Naaman saw him running toward him, he got down from the chariot to meet him. "Is everything all right?" he asked.

"Everything is all right," Gehazi answered. "My master sent me to say, 'Two young men from the company of the prophets have just come to me from the hill country of Ephraim. Please give them a talent[u] of silver and two sets of clothing.'"

"By all means, take two talents," said Naaman. He urged Gehazi to accept them, and then tied up the two talents of silver in two bags, with two sets of clothing. He gave them to two of his servants, and they carried them ahead of Gehazi. When Gehazi came to the hill, he took the things from the servants and put them away in the house. He sent the men away and they left. Then he went in and stood before his master Elisha.

"Where have you been, Gehazi?" Elisha asked.

"Your servant didn't go anywhere," Gehazi answered.

But Elisha said to him, "Was not my spirit with you when the man got down from his chariot to meet you? Is this the time to take money, or to accept clothes, olive groves, vineyards, flocks, herds, or menservants and maidservants? Naaman's leprosy will cling to you and to your descendants forever." Then Gehazi went from Elisha's presence and he was leprous, as white as snow.

**2 Kgs. 6:24
Samaria**

SECOND SIEGE OF SAMARIA.   Some time later, Ben-Hadad king of Aram mobilized his entire army and marched up and laid siege to Samaria.

**2 Kgs.
6:25-31**

FAMINE BRINGS SUFFERINGS.   There was a great famine in the city; the siege lasted so long that a donkey's head sold for eighty shekels[v] of silver, and a quarter of a cab[w] of seed pods[x] for five shekels.[y]

As the king of Israel was passing by on the wall, a woman cried to him, "Help me, my lord the king!"

The king replied, "If the LORD does not help you, where can I get help for you? From the threshing floor? From the winepress?" Then he asked her, "What's the matter?"

She answered, "This woman said to me, 'Give up your son so we may eat him today, and tomorrow we'll eat my son.' So we cooked my son and ate him. The next day I said to her, 'Give up your son so we may eat him,' but she had hidden him."

When the king heard the woman's words, he tore his robes. As he went along the wall, the people looked, and there, underneath, he had sackcloth on his body. He said, "May God deal with me, be it ever so severely, if the head of Elisha son of Shaphat remains on his shoulders today!"

**2 Kgs.
6:32-7:2**

PROMISE OF PLENTY.   Now Elisha was sitting in his house, and the elders were sitting with him. The king sent a messenger ahead, but before he arrived, Elisha said to the elders, "Don't you see how this murderer is

---

[u]That is, about 75 pounds (about 34 kilograms)   [v]That is, about 2 pounds (about 1 kilogram)   [w]That is, probably about 1/2 pint (about 0.3 liter)   [x]Or of doves' dung [y]That is, about 2 ounces (about 55 grams)

sending someone to cut off my head? Look, when the messenger comes, shut the door and hold it shut against him. Is not the sound of his master's footsteps behind him?"

While he was still talking to them, the messenger came down to him. And ⌊the king⌋ said, "This disaster is from the LORD. Why should I wait for the LORD any longer?" Elisha said, "Hear the word of the LORD. This is what the LORD says: About this time tomorrow, a seah[z] of flour will sell for a shekel[a] and two seahs[b] of barley for a shekel at the gate of Samaria."

The officer on whose arm the king was leaning said to the man of God, "Look, even if the LORD should open the floodgates of the heavens, could this happen?"

"You will see it with your own eyes," answered Elisha, "but you will not eat any of it!"

DISCOVERY BY LEPERS.   Now there were four men with leprosy[c] at the entrance of the city gate. They said to each other, "Why stay here until we die? If we say, 'We'll go into the city'—the famine is there, and we will die. And if we stay here, we will die. So let's go over to the camp of the Arameans and surrender. If they spare us, we live; if they kill us, then we die."

2 Kgs. 7:3-8

At dusk they got up and went to the camp of the Arameans. When they reached the edge of the camp, not a man was there, for the Lord had caused the Arameans to hear the sound of chariots and horses and a great army, so that they said to one another, "Look, the king of Israel has hired the Hittite and Egyptian kings to attack us!" So they got up and fled in the dusk and abandoned their tents and their horses and donkeys. They left the camp as it was and ran for their lives.

The men who had leprosy reached the edge of the camp and entered one of the tents. They ate and drank, and carried away silver, gold and clothes, and went off and hid them. They returned and entered another tent and took some things from it and hid them also.

DISCOVERY REPORTED.   Then they said to each other, "We're not doing right. This is a day of good news and we are keeping it to ourselves. If we wait until daylight, punishment will overtake us. Let's go at once and report this to the royal palace."

2 Kgs. 7:9-11

So they went and called out to the city gatekeepers and told them, "We went into the Aramean camp and not a man was there—not a sound of anyone—only tethered horses and donkeys, and the tents left just as they were." The gatekeepers shouted the news, and it was reported within the palace.

DISCOVERY CONFIRMED.   The king got up in the night and said to his officers, "I will tell you what the Arameans have done to us. They know we are starving; so they have left the camp to hide in the countryside, thinking, 'They will surely come out, and then we will take them alive and get into the city.'"

2 Kgs. 7:12-16

One of his officers answered, "Have some men take five of the horses that are left in the city. Their plight will be like that of all the Israelites left

---

[z]That is, probably about 7 quarts (about 7.3 liters)   [a]That is, about 2/5 ounce (about 11 grams)   [b]That is, probably about 13 quarts (about 15 liters)   [c]The Hebrew word is used for various diseases affecting the skin—not necessarily leprosy.

here—yes, they will only be like all these Israelites who are doomed. So let us send them to find out what happened."

So they selected two chariots with their horses, and the king sent them after the Aramean army. He commanded the drivers, "Go and find out what has happened." They followed them as far as the Jordan, and they found the whole road strewn with the clothing and equipment the Arameans had thrown away in their headlong flight. So the messengers returned and reported to the king. Then the people went out and plundered the camp of the Arameans. So a seah of flour sold for a shekel, and two seahs of barley sold for a shekel, as the LORD had said.

| 2 Kgs. 7:17-20 | **PROPHECIES FULFILLED.** Now the king had put the officer on whose arm he leaned in charge of the gate, and the people trampled him in the gateway, and he died, just as the man of God had foretold when the king came down to his house. It happened as the man of God had said to the king: "About this time tomorrow, a seah of flour will sell for a shekel and two seahs of barley for a shekel at the gate of Samaria."

The officer had said to the man of God, "Look, even if the LORD should open the floodgates of the heavens, could this happen?" The man of God had replied, "You will see it with your own eyes, but you will not eat any of it!" And that is exactly what happened to him, for the people trampled him in the gateway, and he died.

In Judah

2 Kgs.
8:23,24a
2 Chron.
21:19,20b
(841 B.C.)
Jerusalem

JEHORAM DIES. ᴷᵍAs for the other events of Jehoram's reign, and all he did, are they not written in the book of the annals of the kings of Judah?

ᶜʰIn the course of time, at the end of the second year, his bowels came out because of the disease, and he died in great pain. His people made no fire in his honor, as they had for his fathers.

He passed away, to no one's regret, and was buried in the City of David, but not in the tombs of the kings.

2 Kgs.
8:24b-26
9:29
2 Chron.
22:1,2
(841 B.C.)

AHAZIAH (JEHOAHAZ) KING. ᴷᵍAnd Ahaziah his son succeeded him as king.

In the twelfth*ᵈ* year of Joram son of Ahab king of Israel, Ahaziah son of Jehoram king of Judah began to reign. ᶜʰThe people of Jerusalem made Ahaziah, Jehoram's youngest son, king in his place, since the raiders, who came with the Arabs into the camp, had killed all the older sons. So Ahaziah son of Jehoram king of Judah began to reign.

Ahaziah was twenty-two*ᵉ* years old when he became king, and he reigned in Jerusalem one year. His mother's name was Athaliah, a granddaughter of Omri.

2 Kgs. 8:27
2 Chron.
22:3,4

CHARACTER OF AHAZIAH. He too walked in the ways of the house of Ahab, for his mother encouraged him in doing wrong. He did evil in the eyes of the LORD, as the house of Ahab had done, for after his father's death they became his advisers, to his undoing.

In Israel

2 Kgs.
8:7-13
Damascus

ELISHA MEETS WITH HAZAEL. Elisha went to Damascus, and Ben-Hadad king of Aram was ill. When the king was told, "The man of God

---

ᵈ[eleventh (?)]   ᵉSome Septuagint manuscripts and Syriac (see also 2 Kings 8:26); Hebrew *forty-two*

has come all the way up here," he said to Hazael, "Take a gift with you and go to meet the man of God. Consult the LORD through him; ask him, 'Will I recover from this illness?'"

Hazael went to meet Elisha, taking with him as a gift forty camel-loads of all the finest wares of Damascus. He went in and stood before him, and said, "Your son Ben-Hadad king of Aram has sent me to ask, 'Will I recover from this illness?'"

Elisha answered, "Go and say to him, 'You will certainly recover'; but*f* the LORD has revealed to me that he will in fact die." He stared at him with a fixed gaze until Hazael felt ashamed. Then the man of God began to weep.

"Why is my lord weeping?" asked Hazael.

"Because I know the harm you will do to the Israelites," he answered. "You will set fire to their fortified places, kill their young men with the sword, dash their little children to the ground, and rip open their pregnant women."

Hazael said, "How could your servant, a mere dog, accomplish such a feat?"

"The LORD has shown me that you will become king of Aram," answered Elisha.

HAZAEL KILLS BEN-HADAD. Then Hazael left Elisha and returned to his master. When Ben-Hadad asked, "What did Elisha say to you?" Hazael replied, "He told me that you would certainly recover." But the next day he took a thick cloth, soaked it in water and spread it over the king's face, so that he died. Then Hazael succeeded him as king.

2 Kgs. 8:14,15

AHAZIAH AIDS JORAM. Ahaziah went with Joram son of Ahab to war against Hazael king of Aram at Ramoth Gilead. The Arameans wounded Joram;

2 Kgs. 8:28
2 Chron. 22:5
(841 B.C.)

JORAM WOUNDED. (Now Joram and all Israel had been defending Ramoth Gilead against Hazael king of Aram, but King Joram*g* had returned to Jezreel to recover from the wounds the Arameans had inflicted on him in the battle with Hazael king of Aram.)

2 Kgs. 8:29a
9:14b,15a
2 Chron. 22:6a

AHAZIAH VISITS JORAM. Then Ahaziah son of Jehoram king of Judah went down to Jezreel to see Joram son of Ahab, because he had been wounded.

2 Kgs. 8:29b
2 Chron. 22:6b

JEHU ANOINTED ISRAEL'S KING. The prophet Elisha summoned a man from the company of the prophets and said to him, "Tuck your cloak into your belt, take this flask of oil with you and go to Ramoth Gilead. When you get there, look for Jehu son of Jehoshaphat, the son of Nimshi. Go to him, get him away from his companions and take him into an inner room. Then take the flask and pour the oil on his head and declare, 'This is what the LORD says: I anoint you king over Israel.' Then open the door and run; don't delay!"

2 Kgs. 9:1-13
Ramoth Gilead
(841 B.C.)

So the young man, the prophet, went to Ramoth Gilead. When he arrived, he found the army officers sitting together. "I have a message for you, commander," he said.

"For which of us?" asked Jehu.

*f*The Hebrew may also be read *Go and say, 'You will certainly not recover,' for.*   *g*Hebrew *Jehoram,* a variant of *Joram*

"For you, commander," he replied.

Jehu got up and went into the house. Then the prophet poured the oil on Jehu's head and declared, "This is what the LORD, the God of Israel, says: 'I anoint you king over the LORD's people Israel. You are to destroy the house of Ahab your master, and I will avenge the blood of my servants the prophets and the blood of all the LORD's servants shed by Jezebel. The whole house of Ahab will perish. I will cut off from Ahab every last male in Israel—slave or free. I will make the house of Ahab like the house of Jeroboam son of Nebat and like the house of Baasha son of Ahijah. As for Jezebel, dogs will devour her on the plot of ground at Jezreel, and no one will bury her.'" Then he opened the door and ran.

When Jehu went out to his fellow officers, one of them asked him, "Is everything all right? Why did this madman come to you?"

"You know the man and the sort of things he says," Jehu replied.

"That's not true!" they said. "Tell us."

Jehu said, "Here is what he told me: 'This is what the LORD says: I anoint you king over Israel.'"

They hurried and took their cloaks and spread them under him on the bare steps. Then they blew the trumpet and shouted, "Jehu is king!"

2 Kgs. 9:14a, 15b-26

JEHU KILLS JORAM.   So Jehu son of Jehoshaphat, the son of Nimshi, conspired against Joram. Jehu said, "If this is the way you feel, don't let anyone slip out of the city to go and tell the news in Jezreel." Then he got into his chariot and rode to Jezreel, because Joram was resting there and Ahaziah king of Judah had gone down to see him.

When the lookout standing on the tower in Jezreel saw Jehu's troops approaching, he called out, "I see some troops coming."

"Get a horseman," Joram ordered. "Send him to meet them and ask, 'Do you come in peace?'"

The horseman rode off to meet Jehu and said, "This is what the king says: 'Do you come in peace?'"

"What do you have to do with peace?" Jehu replied. "Fall in behind me."

The lookout reported, "The messenger has reached them, but he isn't coming back."

So the king sent out a second horseman. When he came to them he said, "This is what the king says: 'Do you come in peace?'"

Jehu replied, "What do you have to do with peace? Fall in behind me."

The lookout reported, "He has reached them, but he isn't coming back either. The driving is like that of Jehu son of Nimshi—he drives like a madman."

"Hitch up my chariot," Joram ordered. And when it was hitched up, Joram king of Israel and Ahaziah king of Judah rode out, each in his own chariot, to meet Jehu. They met him at the plot of ground that had belonged to Naboth the Jezreelite. When Joram saw Jehu he asked, "Have you come in peace, Jehu?"

"How can there be peace," Jehu replied, "as long as all the idolatry and witchcraft of your mother Jezebel abound?"

Joram turned about and fled, calling out to Ahaziah, "Treachery, Ahaziah!"

Then Jehu drew his bow and shot Joram between the shoulders. The arrow pierced his heart and he slumped down in his chariot. Jehu said to

Bidkar, his chariot officer, "Pick him up and throw him on the field that belonged to Naboth the Jezreelite. Remember how you and I were riding together in chariots behind Ahab his father when the LORD made this prophecy about him: 'Yesterday I saw the blood of Naboth and the blood of his sons, declares the LORD, and I will surely make you pay for it on this plot of ground, declares the LORD.'[h] Now then, pick him up and throw him on that plot, in accordance with the word of the LORD."

AHAZIAH ALSO WOUNDED.   [ch]Through Ahaziah's visit to Joram, God brought about Ahaziah's downfall. When Ahaziah arrived, he went out with Joram to meet Jehu son of Nimshi, whom the LORD had anointed to destroy the house of Ahab. [kg]When Ahaziah king of Judah saw what had happened, he fled up the road to Beth Haggan.[i] Jehu chased him, shouting, "Kill him too!" They wounded him in his chariot on the way up to Gur near Ibleam, but he escaped to Megiddo...

2 Kgs. 9:27
2 Chron. 22:7

JEZEBEL KILLED.   Then Jehu went to Jezreel. When Jezebel heard about it, she painted her eyes, arranged her hair and looked out of a window. As Jehu entered the gate, she asked, "Have you come in peace, Zimri, you murderer of your master?"[j]

He looked up at the window and called out, "Who is on my side? Who?" Two or three eunuchs looked down at him. "Throw her down!" Jehu said. So they threw her down, and some of her blood spattered the wall and the horses as they trampled her underfoot.

Jehu went in and ate and drank. "Take care of that cursed woman," he said, "and bury her, for she was a king's daughter." But when they went out to bury her, they found nothing except her skull, her feet and her hands. They went back and told Jehu, who said, "This is the word of the LORD that he spoke through his servant Elijah the Tishbite: On the plot of ground at Jezreel dogs will devour Jezebel's flesh.[k] Jezebel's body will be like refuse on the ground in the plot at Jezreel, so that no one will be able to say, 'This is Jezebel.'"

2 Kgs. 9:30-37
Jezreel

AHAB'S PRINCES MASSACRED.   Now there were in Samaria seventy sons of the house of Ahab. So Jehu wrote letters and sent them to Samaria: to the officials of Jezreel,[l] to the elders and to the guardians of Ahab's children. He said, "As soon as this letter reaches you, since your master's sons are with you and you have chariots and horses, a fortified city and weapons, choose the best and most worthy of your master's sons and set him on his father's throne. Then fight for your master's house."

But they were terrified and said, "If two kings could not resist him, how can we?"

So the palace administrator, the city governor, the elders and the guardians sent this message to Jehu: "We are your servants and we will do anything you say. We will not appoint anyone as king; you do whatever you think best."

Then Jehu wrote them a second letter, saying, "If you are on my side and will obey me, take the heads of your master's sons and come to me in Jezreel by this time tomorrow."

Now the royal princes, seventy of them, were with the leading men of

2 Kgs. 10:1-11
Samaria

---

[h]See 1 Kings 21:19.   [i]Or *fled by way of the garden house*   [j]Or *"Did Zimri have peace, who murdered his master?"*   [k]See 1 Kings 21:23.   [l]Hebrew; some Septuagint manuscripts and Vulgate *of the city*

the city, who were rearing them. When the letter arrived, these men took the princes and slaughtered all seventy of them. They put their heads in baskets and sent them to Jehu in Jezreel. When the messenger arrived, he told Jehu, "They have brought the heads of the princes."

Then Jehu ordered, "Put them in two piles at the entrance of the city gate until morning."

The next morning Jehu went out. He stood before all the people and said, "You are innocent. It was I who conspired against my master and killed him, but who killed all these? Know then, that not a word the LORD has spoken against the house of Ahab will fail. The LORD has done what he promised through his servant Elijah." So Jehu killed everyone in Jezreel who remained of the house of Ahab, as well as all his chief men, his close friends and his priests, leaving him no survivor.

2 Kgs. 10:12-14
2 Chron. 22:8
Beth Eked

AHAZIAH'S PRINCES MASSACRED.   ChWhile Jehu was executing judgment on the house of Ahab, he found the princes of Judah and the sons of Ahaziah's relatives, who had been attending Ahaziah, and he killed them. Jehu then set out and went toward Samaria. At Beth Eked of the Shepherds, he met some relatives of Ahaziah king of Judah and asked, "Who are you?"

They said, "We are relatives of Ahaziah, and we have come down to greet the families of the king and of the queen mother."

"Take them alive!" he ordered. So they took them alive and slaughtered them by the well of Beth Eked—forty-two men. He left no survivor.

2 Kgs. 9:28
2 Chron. 22:9
Jerusalem

AHAZIAH FOUND AND KILLED.   ChHe then went in search of Ahaziah, and his men captured him while he was hiding in Samaria. He was brought to Jehu and put to death. KgHis servants took him by chariot to Jerusalem and buried him with his fathers in his tomb in the City of David. ChThey buried him, for they said, "He was a son of Jehoshaphat, who sought the LORD with all his heart." So there was no one in the house of Ahaziah powerful enough to retain the kingdom.

2 Kgs. 10:15,16

JEHONADAB JOINS JEHU.   After he left there, he came upon Jehonadab son of Recab, who was on his way to meet him. Jehu greeted him and said, "Are you in accord with me, as I am with you?"

"I am," Jehonadab answered.

"If so," said Jehu, "give me your hand." So he did, and Jehu helped him up into the chariot. Jehu said, "Come with me and see my zeal for the LORD." Then he had him ride along in his chariot.

2 Kgs. 10:17
Samaria

AHAB'S FAMILY KILLED.   When Jehu came to Samaria, he killed all who were left there of Ahab's family; he destroyed them, according to the word of the LORD spoken to Elijah.

The Era of Joash in Judah

*U*ntil this time all the kings of Israel and Judah have been old enough to rule for themselves. Due to unusual circumstances, Judah will soon have its first child-king. This occurs when Jehoram's widow, Athaliah, rises to power in a way that would have pleased her mother, Jezebel: she kills all the royal offspring, including her own. Having done this, she usurps the throne for six years. However, one child, Joash, has been saved and hidden. At the age of seven he is presented to the people as king by Jehoiada the priest.

With Joash obviously unable to rule at such an early age, the affairs of state are conducted by the priests and military leaders.

While there is some spiritual renewal during this period, paganism still remains—so much so that God calls the prophet Joel to cry out against it. Joel does so, using a locust infestation as the basis for a stinging attack and a bold warning of God's judgment.

As he comes of age, Joash brings credit to his rule by ordering repairs of the once-beautiful temple of Solomon, now in partial ruin. He later discredits himself by accepting paganism along with the others who ignore Joel's prophecy.

In Israel, meanwhile, King Jehu destroys the worship of Baal, only to worship the calves set up initially by Jeroboam. After Jehu's death, both Israel and Judah are oppressed by the ever-menacing Syrians out of Aram, but Joash eventually buys them off in Judah. On his deathbed, Elisha predicts Israel's later success against the Syrians.

In Judah

ATHALIAH USURPS THRONE. When Athaliah the mother of Ahaziah saw that her son was dead, she proceeded to destroy the whole royal family of the house of Judah.

2 Kgs. 11:1
2 Chron. 22:10
(841 B.C.)

JOASH SAVED FROM COUP. But Jehosheba,*m* the daughter of King Jehoram, took Joash son of Ahaziah and stole him away from among the royal princes who were about to be murdered and put him and his nurse in a bedroom. Because Jehosheba,*m* the daughter of King Jehoram and wife of the priest Jehoiada, was Ahaziah's sister, she hid the child from Athaliah so she could not kill him. He remained hidden with them at the temple of God for six years while Athaliah ruled the land.

2 Kgs. 11:2,3
2 Chron. 22:11,12

In Israel

JEHU DESTROYS BAAL WORSHIP. Then Jehu brought all the people together and said to them, "Ahab served Baal a little; Jehu will serve him much. Now summon all the prophets of Baal, all his ministers and all his priests. See that no one is missing, because I am going to hold a great sacrifice for Baal. Anyone who fails to come will no longer live." But Jehu was acting deceptively in order to destroy the ministers of Baal.

2 Kgs. 10:18-28

Jehu said, "Call an assembly in honor of Baal." So they proclaimed it. Then he sent word throughout Israel, and all the ministers of Baal came; not one stayed away. They crowded into the temple of Baal until it was full from one end to the other. And Jehu said to the keeper of the wardrobe, "Bring robes for all the ministers of Baal." So he brought out robes for them.

Then Jehu and Jehonadab son of Recab went into the temple of Baal. Jehu said to the ministers of Baal, "Look around and see that no servants of the LORD are here with you—only ministers of Baal." So they went in to make sacrifices and burnt offerings. Now Jehu had posted eighty men outside with this warning: "If one of you lets any of the men I am placing in your hands escape, it will be your life for his life."

As soon as Jehu had finished making the burnt offering, he ordered the

---

*m*Hebrew *Jehoshabeath*, a variant of *Jehosheba*

guards and officers: "Go in and kill them; let no one escape." So they cut them down with the sword. The guards and officers threw the bodies out and then entered the inner shrine of the temple of Baal. They brought the sacred stone out of the temple of Baal and burned it. They demolished the sacred stone of Baal and tore down the temple of Baal, and people have used it for a latrine to this day.

So Jehu destroyed Baal worship in Israel.

2 Kgs.
10:30

GOD'S PROMISE TO JEHU. The LORD said to Jehu, "Because you have done well in accomplishing what is right in my eyes and have done to the house of Ahab all I had in mind to do, your descendants will sit on the throne of Israel to the fourth generation."

2 Kgs.
10:29,31

JEHU LIKE JEROBOAM. However, he did not turn away from the sins of Jeroboam son of Nebat, which he had caused Israel to commit—the worship of the golden calves at Bethel and Dan. Yet Jehu was not careful to keep the law of the LORD, the God of Israel, with all his heart. He did not turn away from the sins of Jeroboam, which he had caused Israel to commit.

In Judah

2 Kgs.
11:4-11
2 Chron.
23:1-10
Jerusalem

JEHOIADA PLANS FOR JOASH. In the seventh year Jehoiada showed his strength. He made a covenant with the commanders of units of a hundred: Azariah son of Jeroham, Ishmael son of Jehohanan, Azariah son of Obed, Maaseiah son of Adaiah, and Elishaphat son of Zicri. They went throughout Judah and gathered the Levites and the heads of Israelite families from all the towns. When they came to Jerusalem, the whole assembly made a covenant with the king at the temple of God.

Jehoiada said to them, "The king's son shall reign, as the LORD promised concerning the descendants of David. Now this is what you are to do: A third of you priests and Levites who are going on duty on the Sabbath are to keep watch at the doors, a third of you at the royal palace and a third at the Foundation Gate, and all the other men are to be in the courtyards of the temple of the LORD. No one is to enter the temple of the LORD except the priests and Levites on duty; they may enter because they are consecrated, but all the other men are to guard what the LORD has assigned to them.[n] The Levites are to station themselves around the king, each man with his weapons in his hand. Anyone who enters the temple must be put to death. Stay close to the king wherever he goes."

The Levites and all the men of Judah did just as Jehoiada the priest ordered. Each one took his men—those who were going on duty on the Sabbath and those who were going off duty—for Jehoiada the priest had not released any of the divisions. Then he gave the commanders of units of a hundred the spears and the large and small shields that had belonged to King David and that were in the temple of God. He stationed all the men, each with his weapon in his hand, around the king—near the altar and the temple, from the south side to the north side of the temple.

2 Kgs.
11:12
2 Chron.
23:11
(835 B.C.)

JOASH CROWNED. Jehoiada and his sons brought out the king's son and put the crown on him; they presented him with a copy of the covenant and proclaimed him king. They anointed him and shouted, "Long live the king!"

---

[n] Or *to observe the* LORD's *command ¸not to enter¸*

ATHALIAH KILLED.   When Athaliah heard the noise made by the
guards and the people, she went to the people at the temple of the LORD.
She looked and there was the king, standing by the pillar, as the custom
was. The officers and the trumpeters were beside the king, and all the people of the land were rejoicing and blowing trumpets. Then Athaliah tore
her robes and called out, "Treason! Treason!"

    Jehoiada the priest ordered the commanders of units of a hundred, who
were in charge of the troops: "Bring her out between the ranks*o* and put to
the sword anyone who follows her." For the priest had said, "She must not
be put to death in the temple of the LORD." So they seized her as she
reached the place where the horses enter the palace grounds, and there she
was put to death.

2 Kgs.
11:13-16
2 Chron.
23:12-15
(835 B.C.)

JOASH BECOMES CHILD-KING.   Joash*p* was seven years old when he
began to reign. In the seventh year of Jehu, Joash*q* became king, and he
reigned in Jerusalem forty years. His mother's name was Zibiah; she was
from Beersheba.

2 Kgs.
11:21; 12:1
2 Chron.
24:1

PEOPLE FEEL RENEWAL.   Jehoiada then made a covenant that he and
the people and the king*r* would be the LORD's people. All the people went
to the temple of Baal and tore it down. They smashed the altars and idols
and killed Mattan the priest of Baal in front of the altars.

2 Kgs.
11:17-20
2 Chron.
23:16-21

    Then Jehoiada placed the oversight of the temple of the LORD in the
hands of the priests, who were Levites, to whom David had made assign-
ments in the temple, to present the burnt offerings of the LORD as written
in the Law of Moses, with rejoicing and singing, as David had ordered. He
also stationed doorkeepers at the gates of the LORD's temple so that no one
who was in any way unclean might enter.

    He took with him the commanders of hundreds, the nobles, the rulers
of the people and all the people of the land and brought the king down
from the temple of the LORD. They went into the palace through the Upper
Gate and seated the king on the royal throne, and all the people of the land
rejoiced. And the city was quiet, because Athaliah had been slain with the
sword.

JEHOIDA'S INFLUENCE.   Joash did what was right in the eyes of the
LORD all the years Jehoiada the priest instructed him.

2 Kgs. 12:2
2 Chron.
24:2

TRACES OF PAGANISM.   The high places, however, were not removed;
the people continued to offer sacrifices and burn incense there.

2 Kgs. 12:3

The Prophecy of Joel

    *J*t is apparently during the very early years of Joash's reign as a child-
king that a great disaster befalls Judah. Although the people have previously experienced threats from invading armies, they are evidently
not prepared for the army of locusts which swarms over Judah, completely
devastating crops and food supplies. Seizing the occasion to draw a parallel,

---

*o*Or *out from the precincts*   *p*Hebrew *Jehoash,* a variant of *Joash*   *q*Hebrew *Jehoash,* a
variant of *Joash*   *r*Or *covenant between ˌthe* LORDˌ *and the people and the king that they*
(see 2 Kings 11:17)

the prophet Joel vividly describes another invasion which is to come. Like many prophecies, it has both primary and secondary applications.

On one level, Joel warns a spiritually ambivalent Judah that anything less than total devotion to the one true God will result in punishment—namely, invasion and destruction by marauding forces from the north.

He further warns that the day of the Lord is coming, when God will bring all mankind to an ultimate accounting for their lives and deeds. The vivid imagery of Joel's prophecy is similar to that of later prophecies which will also speak of that great day of judgment—the day of the Lord.

Joel urges the people to pray, to fast, and to repent in order to stay God's judgment. In addition to Joel's serious warnings are words of assurance that God will one day pour out his Spirit upon all nations—a promise of hope which will be remembered when the Messiah comes and God sends his Spirit in a special demonstration to the Messiah's followers.

Joel begins his prophecy with reference to the recent invasion of the locusts.

Joel 1:1   PREFACE.   The word of the LORD that came to Joel son of Pethuel.

Joel 1:2-12   DEVASTATION BY LOCUSTS.

> Hear this, you elders;
>> listen, all who live in the land.
> Has anything like this ever happened in your days
>> or in the days of your forefathers?
> Tell it to your children,
>> and let your children tell it to their children,
>> and their children to the next generation.
> What the locust swarm has left
>> the great locusts have eaten;
> what the great locusts have left
>> the young locusts have eaten;
> what the young locusts have left
>> other locusts[s] have eaten.

> Wake up, you drunkards, and weep!
>> Wail, all you drinkers of wine;
> wail because of the new wine,
>> for it has been snatched from your lips.
> A nation has invaded my land,
>> powerful and without number;
> it has the teeth of a lion,
>> the fangs of a lioness.
> It has laid waste my vines
>> and ruined my fig trees.
> It has stripped off their bark
>> and thrown it away,
>> leaving their branches white.

[s]The precise meaning of the four Hebrew words used here for locusts is uncertain.

Mourn like a virgin[t] in sackcloth
    grieving for the husband[u] of her youth.
Grain offerings and drink offerings
    are cut off from the house of the LORD.
The priests are in mourning,
    those who minister before the LORD.
The fields are ruined,
    the ground is dried up[v];
the grain is destroyed,
    the new wine is dried up,
    the oil fails.
Despair, you farmers,
    wail, you vine growers;
grieve for the wheat and the barley,
    because the harvest of the field is destroyed.
The vine is dried up
    and the fig tree is withered;
the pomegranate, the palm and the apple tree—
    all the trees of the field—are dried up.
Surely the joy of mankind
    is withered away.

CALL FOR REPENTANCE.

Joel
1:13-20

Put on sackcloth, O priests, and mourn;
    wail, you who minister before the altar.
Come, spend the night in sackcloth,
    you who minister before my God;
for the grain offerings and drink offerings
    are withheld from the house of your God.
Declare a holy fast;
    call a sacred assembly.
Summon the elders
    and all who live in the land
to the house of the LORD your God,
    and cry out to the LORD.

Alas for that day!
    For the day of the LORD is near;
    it will come like destruction from the Almighty.[w]

Has not the food been cut off
    before our very eyes—
joy and gladness
    from the house of our God?
The seeds are shriveled
    beneath the clods.[x]
The storehouses are in ruins,
    the granaries have been broken down,
    for the grain has dried up.
How the cattle moan!

[t]Or *young woman*   [u]Or *betrothed*   [v]Or *ground mourns*   [w]Hebrew *Shaddai*   [x]The meaning of the Hebrew for this word is uncertain.

The herds mill about
because they have no pasture;
    even the flocks of sheep are suffering.

To you, O LORD, I call,
    for fire has devoured the open pastures
    and flames have burned up all the trees of the field.
Even the wild animals pant for you;
    the streams of water have dried up
    and fire has devoured the open pastures.

Joel 2:1-11   DAY OF THE LORD.

Blow the trumpet in Zion;
    sound the alarm on my holy hill.
Let all who live in the land tremble,
    for the day of the LORD is coming.
It is close at hand—
    a day of darkness and gloom,
    a day of clouds and blackness.
Like dawn spreading across the mountains
    a large and mighty army comes,
such as never was of old
    nor ever will be in ages to come.

Before them fire devours,
    behind them a flame blazes.
Before them the land is like the garden of Eden,
    behind them, a desert waste—
    nothing escapes them.
They have the appearance of horses;
    they gallop along like cavalry.
With a noise like that of chariots
    they leap over the mountaintops,
like a crackling fire consuming stubble,
    like a mighty army drawn up for battle.

At the sight of them, nations are in anguish;
    every face turns pale.
They charge like warriors;
    they scale walls like soldiers.
They all march in line,
    not swerving from their course.
They do not jostle each other;
    each marches straight ahead.
They plunge through defenses
    without breaking ranks.
They rush upon the city;
    they run along the wall.
They climb into the houses;
    like thieves they enter through the windows.

Before them the earth shakes,
    the sky trembles,
the sun and moon are darkened,

and the stars no longer shine.
The LORD thunders
　　at the head of his army;
his forces are beyond number,
　　and mighty are those who obey his command.
The day of the LORD is great;
　　it is dreadful.
　　Who can endure it?

CALL FOR REDEDICATION.

Joel
2:12-17

"Even now," declares the LORD,
　　"return to me with all your heart,
　　with fasting and weeping and mourning."

Rend your heart
　　and not your garments.
Return to the LORD your God,
　　for he is gracious and compassionate,
slow to anger and abounding in love,
　　and he relents from sending calamity.
Who knows? He may turn and have pity
　　and leave behind a blessing—
grain offerings and drink offerings
　　for the LORD your God.

Blow the trumpet in Zion,
　　declare a holy fast,
　　call a sacred assembly.
Gather the people,
　　consecrate the assembly;
bring together the elders,
　　gather the children,
　　those nursing at the breast.
Let the bridegroom leave his room
　　and the bride her chamber.
Let the priests, who minister before the LORD,
　　weep between the temple porch and the altar.
Let them say, "Spare your people, O LORD.
　　Do not make your inheritance an object of scorn,
　　a byword among the nations.
Why should they say among the peoples,
　　'Where is their God?'"

PROMISE OF BLESSING.

Joel
2:18-27

Then the LORD will be jealous for his land
　　and take pity on his people.

The LORD will reply*y* to them:

"I am sending you grain, new wine and oil,
　　enough to satisfy you fully;
never again will I make you

---

*y*Or LORD was jealous . . . / and took pity . . . / *19*The LORD replied

an object of scorn to the nations.

"I will drive the northern army far from you,
    pushing it into a parched and barren land,
with its front columns going into the eastern sea[z]
    and those in the rear into the western sea.[a]
And its stench will go up;
    its smell will rise."

Surely he has done great things.[b]
    Be not afraid, O land;
    be glad and rejoice.
Surely the LORD has done great things.
    Be not afraid, O wild animals,
    for the open pastures are becoming green.
The trees are bearing their fruit;
    the fig tree and the vine yield their riches.
Be glad, O people of Zion,
    rejoice in the LORD your God,
for he has given you
    the autumn rains in righteousness.[c]
He sends you abundant showers,
    both autumn and spring rains, as before.
The threshing floors will be filled with grain;
    the vats will overflow with new wine and oil.

"I will repay you for the years the locusts have eaten—
    the great locust and the young locust,
    the other locusts and the locust swarm[d]—
my great army that I sent among you.
You will have plenty to eat, until you are full,
    and you will praise the name of the LORD your God,
    who has worked wonders for you;
never again will my people be shamed.
Then you will know that I am in Israel,
    that I am the LORD your God,
    and that there is no other;
never again will my people be shamed.

PROMISE OF GOD'S SPIRIT.

Joel
2:28-32

"And afterward,
    I will pour out my Spirit on all people.
Your sons and daughters will prophesy,
    your old men will dream dreams,
    your young men will see visions.
Even on my servants, both men and women,
    I will pour out my Spirit in those days.
I will show wonders in the heavens
    and on the earth,
    blood and fire and billows of smoke.

---

[z]That is, the Dead Sea   [a]That is, the Mediterranean   [b]Or rise. / Surely it has done great
things."   [c]Or / the teacher for righteousness: [d]The precise meaning of the four Hebrew
words used here for locusts is uncertain.

The sun will be turned to darkness
    and the moon to blood
        before the coming of the great and dreadful day of the
            LORD.
And everyone who calls
    on the name of the LORD will be saved;
for on Mount Zion and in Jerusalem
    there will be deliverance,
    as the LORD has said,
among the survivors
    whom the LORD calls.

PUNISHMENT OF ENEMIES.   Joel 3:1-8

"In those days and at that time,
    when I restore the fortunes of Judah and Jerusalem,
I will gather all nations
    and bring them down to the Valley of Jehoshaphat.[e]
There I will enter into judgment against them
    concerning my inheritance, my people Israel,
for they scattered my people among the nations
    and divided up my land.
They cast lots for my people
    and traded boys for prostitutes;
they sold girls for wine
    that they might drink.

"Now what have you against me, O Tyre and Sidon and all you regions of Philistia? Are you repaying me for something I have done? If you are paying me back, I will swiftly and speedily return on your own heads what you have done. For you took my silver and my gold and carried off my finest treasures to your temples. You sold the people of Judah and Jerusalem to the Greeks, that you might send them far from their homeland.

"See, I am going to rouse them out of the places to which you sold them, and I will return on your own heads what you have done. I will sell your sons and daughters to the people of Judah, and they will sell them to the Sabeans, a nation far away." The LORD has spoken.

PROMISE OF VICTORY.   Joel 3:9-17

Proclaim this among the nations:
    Prepare for war!
Rouse the warriors!
    Let all the fighting men draw near and attack.
Beat your plowshares into swords
    and your pruning hooks into spears.
Let the weakling say,
    "I am strong!"
Come quickly, all you nations from every side,
    and assemble there.

    Bring down your warriors, O LORD!

"Let the nations be roused;

[e]*Jehoshaphat* means *the LORD judges*; also in verse 12.

let them advance into the Valley of Jehoshaphat,
for there I will sit
to judge all the nations on every side.
Swing the sickle,
for the harvest is ripe.
Come, trample the grapes,
for the winepress is full
and the vats overflow—
so great is their wickedness!"

Multitudes, multitudes
in the valley of decision!
For the day of the LORD is near
in the valley of decision.
The sun and moon will be darkened,
and the stars no longer shine.
The LORD will roar from Zion
and thunder from Jerusalem;
the earth and the sky will tremble.
But the LORD will be a refuge for his people,
a stronghold for the people of Israel.
"Then you will know that I, the LORD your God,
dwell in Zion, my holy hill.
Jerusalem will be holy;
never again will foreigners invade her.

**Joel
3:18-21**

RESTORATION OF JUDAH.

"In that day the mountains will drip new wine,
and the hills will flow with milk;
all the ravines of Judah will run with water.
A fountain will flow out of the LORD's house
and will water the valley of acacias.^{f}
But Egypt will be desolate,
Edom a desert waste,
because of violence done to the people of Judah,
in whose land they shed innocent blood.
Judah will be inhabited forever
and Jerusalem through all generations.
Their bloodguilt, which I have not pardoned,
I will pardon."

The LORD dwells in Zion!

The account of the era of Joash continues as Joash begins his own family.

In Judah

**2 Chron.
24:3**

JOASH TAKES WIVES.   Jehoiada chose two wives for him, and he had
sons and daughters.

**2 Kgs.
12:4,5
2 Chron.
24:4,5
Jerusalem**

ORDER TO REPAIR TEMPLE.   ᶜʰSome time later Joash decided to restore
the temple of the LORD. ᴷᵍJoash said to the priests, "Collect all the money
that is brought as sacred offerings to the temple of the LORD—the money

^{f}Or *Valley of Shittim*

collected in the census, the money received from personal vows and the
money brought voluntarily to the temple. Let every priest receive the
money from one of the treasurers, and let it be used to repair whatever
damage is found in the temple." ᶜʰHe called together the priests and
Levites and said to them, "Go to the towns of Judah and collect the money
due annually from all Israel, to repair the temple of your God. Do it now."
But the Levites did not act at once.

In Israel

FOREIGN ARMIES ATTACK.   In those days the Lᴏʀᴅ began to reduce the
size of Israel. Hazael overpowered the Israelites throughout their territory
east of the Jordan in all the land of Gilead (the region of Gad, Reuben and
Manasseh), from Aroer by the Arnon Gorge through Gilead to Bashan.

2 Kgs.
10:32,33

JEHU DIES.   As for the other events of Jehu's reign, all he did, and all his
achievements, are they not written in the book of the annals of the kings
of Israel?
   Jehu rested with his fathers and was buried in Samaria. The time that
Jehu reigned over Israel in Samaria was twenty-eight years.

2 Kgs.
10:34,
35a,36
(814 B.C.)

JEHOAHAZ KING OF ISRAEL.   And Jehoahaz his son succeeded him as
king. In the twenty-third year of Joash son of Ahaziah king of Judah,
Jehoahaz son of Jehu became king of Israel in Samaria, and he reigned seventeen years.

2 Kgs.
10:35b;13:1
(814 B.C.)

CHARACTER OF JEHOAHAZ.   He did evil in the eyes of the Lᴏʀᴅ by
following the sins of Jeroboam son of Nebat, which he had caused Israel
to commit, and he did not turn away from them.

2 Kgs. 13:2

In Judah

REPAIRING OF THE TEMPLE.   ᴷᵍBut by the twenty-third year of King
Joash the priests still had not repaired the temple. ᶜʰTherefore the king
summoned Jehoiada the chief priest and said to him, "Why haven't you
required the Levites to bring in from Judah and Jerusalem the tax imposed
by Moses the servant of the Lᴏʀᴅ and by the assembly of Israel for the Tent
of the Testimony?"
   Now the sons of that wicked woman Athaliah had broken into the temple of God and had used even its sacred objects for the Baals. ᴷᵍTherefore
King Joash summoned Jehoiada the priest and the other priests and asked
them, "Why aren't you repairing the damage done to the temple? Take no
more money from your treasurers, but hand it over for repairing the temple." The priests agreed that they would not collect any more money from
the people and that they would not repair the temple themselves.
   Jehoiada the priest took a chest and bored a hole in its lid. He placed it
beside the altar, on the right side as one enters the temple of the Lᴏʀᴅ. The
priests who guarded the entrance put into the chest all the money that was
brought to the temple of the Lᴏʀᴅ. ᶜʰA proclamation was then issued in
Judah and Jerusalem that they should bring to the Lᴏʀᴅ the tax that Moses
the servant of God had required of Israel in the desert. All the officials and
all the people brought their contributions gladly, dropping them into the
chest until it was full. Whenever the chest was brought in by the Levites

2 Kgs.
12:6-16
2 Chron.
24:6-14

to the king's officials and they saw that there was a large amount of money, the royal secretary and the officer of the chief priest would come and empty the chest and carry it back to its place. They did this regularly and collected a great amount of money. The king and Jehoiada gave it to the men who carried out the work required for the temple of the LORD. They hired masons and carpenters to restore the LORD's temple, and also workers in iron and bronze to repair the temple.

^{Kg}The money brought into the temple was not spent for making silver basins, wick trimmers, sprinkling bowls, trumpets or any other articles of gold or silver for the temple of the LORD; it was paid to the workmen, who used it to repair the temple. They did not require an accounting from those to whom they gave the money to pay the workers, because they acted with complete honesty. The money from the guilt offerings and sin offerings was not brought into the temple of the LORD; it belonged to the priests.

^{Ch}The men in charge of the work were diligent, and the repairs progressed under them. They rebuilt the temple of God according to its original design and reinforced it. When they had finished, they brought the rest of the money to the king and Jehoiada, and with it were made articles for the LORD's temple: articles for the service and for the burnt offerings, and also dishes and other objects of gold and silver. As long as Jehoiada lived, burnt offerings were presented continually in the temple of the LORD.

2 Chron. 24:15,16

DEATH OF JEHOIDA.   Now Jehoiada was old and full of years, and he died at the age of a hundred and thirty. He was buried with the kings in the City of David, because of the good he had done in Israel for God and his temple.

2 Chron. 24:17-19 Jerusalem

JOASH ACCEPTS PAGANISM.   After the death of Jehoiada, the officials of Judah came and paid homage to the king, and he listened to them. They abandoned the temple of the LORD, the God of their fathers, and worshiped Asherah poles and idols. Because of their guilt, God's anger came upon Judah and Jerusalem. Although the LORD sent prophets to the people to bring them back to him, and though they testified against them, they would not listen.

2 Chron. 24:20-22

JEHOIDA'S SON KILLED.   Then the Spirit of God came upon Zechariah son of Jehoiada the priest. He stood before the people and said, "This is what God says: 'Why do you disobey the LORD's commands? You will not prosper. Because you have forsaken the LORD, he has forsaken you.'"

But they plotted against him, and by order of the king they stoned him to death in the courtyard of the LORD's temple. King Joash did not remember the kindness Zechariah's father Jehoiada had shown him but killed his son, who said as he lay dying, "May the LORD see this and call you to account."

In Israel

2 Kgs. 13:3

ISRAEL OPPRESSED BY SYRIANS.   So the LORD's anger burned against Israel, and for a long time he kept them under the power of Hazael king of Aram and Ben-Hadad his son.

JEHOAHAZ REPENTS. Then Jehoahaz sought the LORD's favor, and the LORD listened to him, for he saw how severely the king of Aram was oppressing Israel.

2 Kgs. 13:4

ISRAEL SUFFERS GREATLY. Nothing had been left of the army of Jehoahaz except fifty horsemen, ten chariots and ten thousand foot soldiers, for the king of Aram had destroyed the rest and made them like the dust at threshing time.

2 Kgs. 13:7

In Judah

JUDAH PUNISHED BY SYRIANS. At the turn of the year,^{g} the army of Aram marched against Joash; it invaded Judah and Jerusalem and killed all the leaders of the people. They sent all the plunder to their king in Damascus. Although the Aramean army had come with only a few men, the LORD delivered into their hands a much larger army. Because Judah had forsaken the LORD, the God of their fathers, judgment was executed on Joash.

2 Chron. 24:23,24

SYRIANS BOUGHT OFF. About this time Hazael king of Aram went up and attacked Gath and captured it. Then he turned to attack Jerusalem. But Joash king of Judah took all the sacred objects dedicated by his fathers—Jehoshaphat, Jehoram and Ahaziah, the kings of Judah—and the gifts he himself had dedicated and all the gold found in the treasuries of the temple of the LORD and of the royal palace, and he sent them to Hazael king of Aram, who then withdrew from Jerusalem.

2 Kgs. 12:17,18

In Israel

JEHOAHAZ DIES. As for the other events of the reign of Jehoahaz, all he did and his achievements, are they not written in the book of the annals of the kings of Israel? Jehoahaz rested with his fathers and was buried in Samaria.

2 Kgs. 13:8,9a (798 B.C.) Samaria

JEHOASH KING OF ISRAEL. And Jehoash^h his son succeeded him as king.
In the thirty-seventh year of Joash king of Judah, Jehoash son of Jehoahaz became king of Israel in Samaria, and he reigned sixteen years.

2 Kgs. 13:9b,10 (798 B.C.)

CHARACTER OF JEHOASH. He did evil in the eyes of the LORD and did not turn away from any of the sins of Jeroboam son of Nebat, which he had caused Israel to commit; he continued in them.

2 Kgs. 13:11

ELISHA'S DEATHBED PROPHECY. Now Elisha was suffering from the illness from which he died. Jehoash king of Israel went down to see him and wept over him. "My father! My father!" he cried. "The chariots and horsemen of Israel!"
Elisha said, "Get a bow and some arrows," and he did so. "Take the bow in your hands," he said to the king of Israel. When he had taken it, Elisha put his hands on the king's hands.
"Open the east window," he said, and he opened it. "Shoot!" Elisha said, and he shot. "The LORD's arrow of victory, the arrow of victory over Aram!" Elisha declared. "You will completely destroy the Arameans at Aphek."
Then he said, "Take the arrows," and the king took them. Elisha told

2 Kgs. 13:14-19

^{g}That is, in the spring ^{h}Hebrew *Joash*, a variant of *Jehoash* him, "Strike the ground." He struck it three times and stopped. The man of God was angry with him and said, "You should have struck the ground five or six times; then you would have defeated Aram and completely destroyed it. But now you will defeat it only three times."

2 Kgs.
13:20a

ELISHA DIES.   Elisha died and was buried.

In Judah

2 Kgs.
12:20,
21a,19
2 Chron.
24:25-27a
(796 B.C.)
Beth Millo

JOASH ASSASSINATED.   KgHis officials conspired against him and assassinated him at Beth Millo, on the road down to Silla. ChWhen the Arameans withdrew, they left Joash severely wounded. His officials conspired against him for murdering the son of Jehoiada the priest, and they killed him in his bed. So he died and was buried in the City of David, but not in the tombs of the kings.

Those who conspired against him were Zabad,*i* son of Shimeath an Ammonite woman, and Jehozabad, son of Shimrith *j* a Moabite woman. The account of his sons, the many prophecies about him, and the record of the restoration of the temple of God are written in the annotations on the book of the kings.

Era of Jeroboam II in Israel _____

Over the next 60 years the kingdoms of Israel and Judah will continue their spiritual decline. Nothing, it seems, can stop their headlong rush to disaster—particularly Israel, with its love affair with Baal and idol worship. In the south, Amaziah reigns well enough, but he too sets up idols on his return from successful campaigns against the Edomites.

Under the leadership of Jeroboam II, Israel will experience great military success and resulting prosperity. But Jeroboam's reign will see at least three prophets crying out against increased spiritual and moral decay. Jonah will be sent by God as a special messenger to the Assyrians in Nineveh; Hosea will attack the problem of idolatry in Israel; and Amos will speak out against religious formalism and social injustice. It is increasingly clear that God's patience is running out and that captivity is in sight for the people of Israel.

One event in this period occurs at the site of Elisha's tomb and proves to be quite a humorous experience—at least for those not actually involved! The event's more serious message probably has something to do with the fact that Elisha's prophecy concerning victory over the Syrians is about to be fulfilled and a dead nation brought back to life.

In Judah

2 Kgs.
12:21b
14:1,2
2 Chron.
24:27b;25:1
Jerusalem

AMAZIAH KING OF JUDAH.   And Amaziah his son succeeded him as king. In the second year of Jehoash*k* son of Jehoahaz king of Israel, Amaziah son of Joash king of Judah began to reign. He was twenty-five years old when he became king, and he reigned in Jerusalem twenty-nine years. His mother's name was Jehoaddin; she was from Jerusalem.

2 Kgs.
14:3-6
2 Chron.
25:2-4

AMAZIAH'S CHARACTER.   He did what was right in the eyes of the LORD, but not as his father David had done. In everything he followed the

*i*A variant of *Jozabad*   *j*A variant of *Shomer*   *k*Hebrew *Joash,* a variant of *Jehoash* example of his father Joash. The high places, however, were not removed; the people continued to offer sacrifices and burn incense there.

After the kingdom was firmly in his grasp, he executed the officials who had murdered his father the king. Yet he did not put the sons of the assassins to death, in accordance with what is written in the Book of the Law of Moses where the LORD commanded: "Fathers shall not be put to death for their children, nor children put to death for their fathers; each is to die for his own sins."[l]

In Israel

SURPRISE IN ELISHA'S TOMB.   Now Moabite raiders used to enter the country every spring. Once while some Israelites were burying a man, suddenly they saw a band of raiders; so they threw the man's body into Elisha's tomb. When the body touched Elisha's bones, the man came to life and stood up on his feet.

2 Kgs. 13:20b,21

SUCCESS AGAINST SYRIANS.   Hazael king of Aram oppressed Israel throughout the reign of Jehoahaz. But the LORD was gracious to them and had compassion and showed concern for them because of his covenant with Abraham, Isaac and Jacob. To this day he has been unwilling to destroy them or banish them from his presence.

2 Kgs. 13:22-25

Hazael king of Aram died, and Ben-Hadad his son succeeded him as king. Then Jehoash son of Jehoahaz recaptured from Ben-Hadad son of Hazael the towns he had taken in battle from his father Jehoahaz. Three times Jehoash defeated him, and so he recovered the Israelite towns.

In Judah

AMAZIAH PLANS EDOM CAMPAIGN.   Amaziah called the people of Judah together and assigned them according to their families to commanders of thousands and commanders of hundreds for all Judah and Benjamin. He then mustered those twenty years old or more and found that there were three hundred thousand men ready for military service, able to handle the spear and shield.

2 Chron. 25:5

MERCENARIES SENT BACK.   He also hired a hundred thousand fighting men from Israel for a hundred talents[m] of silver.

2 Chron. 25:6-10

But a man of God came to him and said, "O king, these troops from Israel must not march with you, for the LORD is not with Israel—not with any of the people of Ephraim. Even if you go and fight courageously in battle, God will overthrow you before the enemy, for God has the power to help or to overthrow."

Amaziah asked the man of God, "But what about the hundred talents I paid for these Israelite troops?"

The man of God replied, "The LORD can give you much more than that."

So Amaziah dismissed the troops who had come to him from Ephraim and sent them home. They were furious with Judah and left for home in a great rage.

EDOMITES DESTROYED.   Amaziah then marshaled his strength and led his army to the Valley of Salt, where he killed ten thousand men of Seir. The army of Judah also captured ten thousand men alive, took them to the top of a cliff and threw them down so that all were dashed to pieces.

2 Kgs. 14:7
2 Chron. 25:11,12

[l]Deut. 24:16   [m]That is, about 3 3/4 tons (about 3.4 metric tons)

2 Chron.
25:13

MERCENARIES WREAK HAVOC. Meanwhile the troops that Amaziah had sent back and had not allowed to take part in the war raided Judean towns from Samaria to Beth Horon. They killed three thousand people and carried off great quantities of plunder.

2 Chron.
25:14-16

AMAZIAH SETS UP IDOLS. When Amaziah returned from slaughtering the Edomites, he brought back the gods of the people of Seir. He set them up as his own gods, bowed down to them and burned sacrifices to them. The anger of the LORD burned against Amaziah, and he sent a prophet to him, who said, "Why do you consult this people's gods, which could not save their own people from your hand?"

While he was still speaking, the king said to him, "Have we appointed you an adviser to the king? Stop! Why be struck down?"

So the prophet stopped but said, "I know that God has determined to destroy you, because you have done this and have not listened to my counsel."

2 Kgs.
14:8-14
2 Chron.
25:17-24

JUDAH BEATEN BY ISRAEL. After Amaziah king of Judah consulted his advisers, he sent this challenge to Jehoash[n] son of Jehoahaz, the son of Jehu, king of Israel: "Come, meet me face to face."

But Jehoash king of Israel replied to Amaziah king of Judah: "A thistle in Lebanon sent a message to a cedar in Lebanon, 'Give your daughter to my son in marriage.' Then a wild beast in Lebanon came along and trampled the thistle underfoot. You say to yourself that you have defeated Edom, and now you are arrogant and proud. But stay at home! Why ask for trouble and cause your own downfall and that of Judah also?"

Amaziah, however, would not listen, for God so worked that he might hand them over to ⌊Jehoash⌋, because they sought the gods of Edom. So Jehoash king of Israel attacked. He and Amaziah king of Judah faced each other at Beth Shemesh in Judah. Judah was routed by Israel, and every man fled to his home. Jehoash king of Israel captured Amaziah king of Judah, the son of Joash, the son of Ahaziah,[o] at Beth Shemesh. Then Jehoash brought him to Jerusalem and broke down the wall of Jerusalem from the Ephraim Gate to the Corner Gate—a section about six hundred feet[p] long. He took all the gold and silver and all the articles found in the temple of God that had been in the care of Obed-Edom, together with the palace treasures and the hostages, and returned to Samaria.

In Israel

2 Kgs.
13:12,13a,c
2 Kgs.
14:15,16a
(782 B.C.)

JEHOASH DIES. As for the other events of the reign of Jehoash, what he did and his achievements, including his war against Amaziah king of Judah, are they not written in the book of the annals of the kings of Israel? Jehoash rested with his fathers and was buried in Samaria with the kings of Israel.

2 Kgs.
13:13b
2 Kgs.
14:16b,23
(781 B.C.)

JEROBOAM II BEGINS SOLE RULE. And Jeroboam his son succeeded him as king.

In the fifteenth year of Amaziah son of Joash king of Judah, Jeroboam son of Jehoash king of Israel became king in Samaria, and he reigned forty-one years.

[n]Hebrew *Joash*, a variant of *Jehoash*   [o]Hebrew *Jehoahaz*, a variant of *Ahaziah*
[p]Hebrew *four hundred cubits* (about 180 meters)

JEROBOAM'S CHARACTER. He did evil in the eyes of the LORD and did not turn away from any of the sins of Jeroboam son of Nebat, which he had caused Israel to commit.

2 Kgs. 14:24

The Preaching of Jonah Against Nineveh

*H*ere in the midst of Jeroboam II's reign, sometime around 780-775 B.C., is found one of the most interesting ministries ever recorded. God selects a man from southern Galilee by the name of Jonah to take a special message of repentance to the heathen Assyrians living in the great metropolitan area of Nineveh. Nineveh is one of the most ancient of the large cities, having been established by the great warrior Nimrod back in the days of the patriarchs. Located east of the Tigris River, it is the royal residence of the Assyrian kings. Jonah's mission takes place between the reigns of Shalmaneser III (860-824 B.C.) and Tiglath-Pileser III (745-727 B.C.), during the rule of a lesser-known king.

The basic improbability of the mission, as viewed through human eyes, is underscored when Jonah attempts to evade his special responsibility and is swallowed by a large fish which God miraculously provides for the occasion. Thereby convinced of God's limitless power, Jonah proceeds to deliver the message that Nineveh is about to be destroyed and that repentance is in order. To his surprise, and even disappointment, Nineveh's inhabitants repent and are saved from the threatened destruction.

All in all, the account is an amazing demonstration of God's universal grace and divine concern at a time when a rather exclusivistic Israel is in great need of a reminder that, despite being God's chosen people, their failure to repent actually lowers them to a level of spirituality beneath even penitent pagans.

GOD CALLS JONAH. The word of the LORD came to Jonah son of Amittai: "Go to the great city of Nineveh and preach against it, because its wickedness has come up before me."

Jonah 1:1,2

JONAH RUNS AWAY. But Jonah ran away from the LORD and headed for Tarshish. He went down to Joppa, where he found a ship bound for that port. After paying the fare, he went aboard and sailed for Tarshish to flee from the LORD.

Jonah 1:3

THROWN INTO SEA. Then the LORD sent a great wind on the sea, and such a violent storm arose that the ship threatened to break up. All the sailors were afraid and each cried out to his own god. And they threw the cargo into the sea to lighten the ship.

Jonah 1:4-16

But Jonah had gone below deck, where he lay down and fell into a deep sleep. The captain went to him and said, "How can you sleep? Get up and call on your god! Maybe he will take notice of us, and we will not perish."

Then the sailors said to each other, "Come, let us cast lots to find out who is responsible for this calamity." They cast lots and the lot fell on Jonah.

So they asked him, "Tell us, who is responsible for making all this trouble for us? What do you do? Where do you come from? What is your country? From what people are you?"

He answered, "I am a Hebrew and I worship the LORD, the God of heaven, who made the sea and the land."

This terrified them and they asked, "What have you done?" (They knew he was running away from the LORD, because he had already told them so.)

The sea was getting rougher and rougher. So they asked him, "What should we do to you to make the sea calm down for us?"

"Pick me up and throw me into the sea," he replied, "and it will become calm. I know that it is my fault that this great storm has come upon you."

Instead, the men did their best to row back to land. But they could not, for the sea grew even wilder than before. Then they cried to the LORD, "O LORD, please do not let us die for taking this man's life. Do not hold us accountable for killing an innocent man, for you, O LORD, have done as you pleased." Then they took Jonah and threw him overboard, and the raging sea grew calm. At this the men greatly feared the LORD, and they offered a sacrifice to the LORD and made vows to him.

Jonah 1:17   SWALLOWED BY FISH.   But the LORD provided a great fish to swallow Jonah, and Jonah was inside the fish three days and three nights.

Jonah 2:1-9   JONAH'S PRAYER.   From inside the fish Jonah prayed to the LORD his God. He said:

> "In my distress I called to the LORD,
>   and he answered me.
> From the depths of the grave*q* I called for help,
>   and you listened to my cry.
> You hurled me into the deep,
>   into the very heart of the seas,
>   and the currents swirled about me;
> all your waves and breakers
>   swept over me.
> I said, 'I have been banished
>   from your sight;
> yet I will look again
>   toward your holy temple.'
> The engulfing waters threatened me,*r*
>   the deep surrounded me;
>   seaweed was wrapped around my head.
> To the roots of the mountains I sank down;
>   the earth beneath barred me in forever.
> But you brought my life up from the pit,
>   O LORD my God.
>
> "When my life was ebbing away,
>   I remembered you, LORD,
> and my prayer rose to you,
>   to your holy temple.
>
> "Those who cling to worthless idols
>   forfeit the grace that could be theirs.
> But I, with a song of thanksgiving,
>   will sacrifice to you.

---

*q*Hebrew *Sheol*   *r*Or *waters were at my throat*

What I have vowed I will make good.
Salvation comes from the LORD."

JONAH PUT ON LAND.   And the LORD commanded the fish, and it vomited Jonah onto dry land.

Jonah 2:10

MISSION ORDERED AGAIN.   Then the word of the LORD came to Jonah a second time: "Go to the great city of Nineveh and proclaim to it the message I give you."

Jonah 3:1,2

NINEVITES REPENT.   Jonah obeyed the word of the LORD and went to Nineveh. Now Nineveh was a very important city—a visit required three days. On the first day, Jonah started into the city. He proclaimed: "Forty more days and Nineveh will be overturned." The Ninevites believed God. They declared a fast, and all of them, from the greatest to the least, put on sackcloth.

Jonah 3:3-5

KING ORDERS RIGHTEOUSNESS.   When the news reached the king of Nineveh, he rose from his throne, took off his royal robes, covered himself with sackcloth and sat down in the dust. Then he issued a proclamation in Nineveh:

Jonah 3:6-9

"By the decree of the king and his nobles:

Do not let any man or beast, herd or flock, taste anything; do not let them eat or drink. But let man and beast be covered with sackcloth. Let everyone call urgently on God. Let them give up their evil ways and their violence. Who knows? God may yet relent and with compassion turn from his fierce anger so that we will not perish."

GOD HAS COMPASSION.   When God saw what they did and how they turned from their evil ways, he had compassion and did not bring upon them the destruction he had threatened.

Jonah 3:10

JONAH ANGRY AT GOD.   But Jonah was greatly displeased and became angry. He prayed to the LORD, "O LORD, is this not what I said when I was still at home? That is why I was so quick to flee to Tarshish. I knew that you are a gracious and compassionate God, slow to anger and abounding in love, a God who relents from sending calamity. Now, O LORD, take away my life, for it is better for me to die than to live."
But the LORD replied, "Have you any right to be angry?"

Jonah 4:1-4

VINE SHOWS GOD'S CONCERN.   Jonah went out and sat down at a place east of the city. There he made himself a shelter, sat in its shade and waited to see what would happen to the city. Then the LORD God provided a vine and made it grow up over Jonah to give shade for his head to ease his discomfort, and Jonah was very happy about the vine. But at dawn the next day God provided a worm, which chewed the vine so that it withered. When the sun rose, God provided a scorching east wind, and the sun blazed on Jonah's head so that he grew faint. He wanted to die, and said, "It would be better for me to die than to live."
But God said to Jonah, "Do you have a right to be angry about the vine?"
"I do," he said. "I am angry enough to die."
But the LORD said, "You have been concerned about this vine, though you did not tend it or make it grow. It sprang up overnight and died overnight. But Nineveh has more than a hundred and twenty thousand

Jonah 4:5-11

people who cannot tell their right hand from their left, and many cattle as well. Should I not be concerned about that great city?"

The historical record now confirms Jonah's mission and tells how God gives Jeroboam great military success and prosperity.

In Israel

2 Kgs. 13:5
14:25-27

ISRAEL RESTORED.   The LORD provided a deliverer for Israel, and they escaped from the power of Aram. So the Israelites lived in their own homes as they had before. He [Jeroboam] was the one who restored the boundaries of Israel from Lebo^s Hamath to the Sea of the Arabah,^{t} in accordance with the word of the LORD, the God of Israel, spoken through his servant Jonah son of Amittai, the prophet from Gath Hepher.

The LORD had seen how bitterly everyone in Israel, whether slave or free, was suffering; there was no one to help them. And since the LORD had not said he would blot out the name of Israel from under heaven, he saved them by the hand of Jeroboam son of Jehoash.

2 Kgs. 13:6

ISRAEL CONTINUES SIN.   But they did not turn away from the sins of the house of Jeroboam, which he had caused Israel to commit; they continued in them. Also, the Asherah pole^u remained standing in Samaria.

The Prophecies of Hosea

The foregoing passage is only a brief reference in the historical account, but it is a forceful reminder that after a century-and-a-half as part of a broken kingdom the people of Israel have not been willing to put away their idols or forget their pagan Baal. If there is anything which especially affronts God, it must surely be the sight of men and women (whom he has created) bowing in worship to sticks and stones (which he has also created and which, therefore, have no intrinsic power). This is especially true because God has repeatedly and patiently demonstrated his concern, love, and protection to each generation of this nation to whom he has specially chosen to reveal himself.

To God, the people of Israel have been as a wife in covenant relationship with him. And yet their continual idolatry is a constant reminder of their unfaithfulness to the covenant. Each generation has been adulterous in its wickedness and idolatry, and now the time is swiftly approaching when God is going to put Israel away as an adulterous spouse.

In an effort to draw Israel away from her spiritual lovers and to show her the danger of her infidelity, God calls upon the prophet Hosea to bring his message and warnings—through both hard preaching and prophecy, and in another (and most unusual) way as well.

God calls upon Hosea to marry a woman whom God knows will be unfaithful to Hosea and bear children of her unfaithfulness. Even the children's names pronounce God's prophecy. Jezreel, the firstborn, predicts that the people of Israel will be "scattered by God," in clear reference to the eventual

---

^{s}Or *from the entrance to* ^{t}That is, the Dead Sea ^{u}That is, a symbol of the goddess Asherah; here and elsewhere in 2 Kings

conquering of Israel by foreign invaders, who will take them out of the land of Canaan. The second child, Lo-ruhamah, warns that when this time comes God will be "without mercy." And, as if that were not enough, the third child, Lo-ammi, signifies God's total rejection of Israel, of whom he will say, "not my people."

When Hosea's wife, Gomer, consorts with other lovers, she only typifies Israel's unfaithfulness in playing the harlot with other gods. And yet, as always, God speaks a message of hope through Hosea. Just as Hosea redeems Gomer from literal slavery, God stands ready to redeem his people from sin. And yet this time God will not renew his love so easily as he has in the past. This time Israel will know real suffering and discipline before being restored to God's love and favor.

The prophet Hosea begins his ministry during Jeroboam's reign, and will continue his work for the next 60 or 65 years. His ministry will span the reigns of the next two or three kings of Israel as well as Jeroboam's. It is not known exactly when he delivers his various rebukes, admonitions, and warnings, but they are all collected at this point to show the central thrust of his message.

Hosea's prophecies against Israel, to which he sometimes refers as Ephraim, begin with a reference to his own disastrous marriage and the anger and anguish which he himself feels. No message has more impact than one growing out of the messenger's own experience. Perhaps that accounts for the power of Hosea's prophecies.

PREFACE. The word of the LORD that came to Hosea son of Beeri during the reigns of Uzziah, Jotham, Ahaz and Hezekiah, kings of Judah, and during the reign of Jeroboam son of Jehoash[v] king of Israel:

Hosea 1:1

HOSEA'S OWN FAMILY. When the LORD began to speak through Hosea, the LORD said to him, "Go, take to yourself an adulterous wife and children of unfaithfulness, because the land is guilty of the vilest adultery in departing from the LORD." So he married Gomer daughter of Diblaim, and she conceived and bore him a son.

Hosea 1:2-9

Then the LORD said to Hosea, "Call him Jezreel, because I will soon punish the house of Jehu for the massacre at Jezreel, and I will put an end to the kingdom of Israel. In that day I will break Israel's bow in the Valley of Jezreel."

Gomer conceived again and gave birth to a daughter. Then the LORD said to Hosea, "Call her Lo-Ruhamah,[w] for I will no longer show love to the house of Israel, that I should at all forgive them. Yet I will show love to the house of Judah; and I will save them—not by bow, sword or battle, or by horses and horsemen, but by the LORD their God."

After she had weaned Lo-Ruhamah, Gomer had another son. Then the LORD said, "Call him Lo-Ammi,[x] for you are not my people, and I am not your God.

HOPE FOR FUTURE. "Yet the Israelites will be like the sand on the seashore, which cannot be measured or counted. In the place where it was said to them, 'You are not my people,' they will be called 'sons of the living

Hosea 1:10-2:1

[v]Hebrew *Joash*, a variant of *Jehoash*   [w]*Lo-Ruhamah* means *not loved.*   [x]*Lo-Ammi* means *not my people.*

God.' The people of Judah and the people of Israel will be reunited, and they will appoint one leader and will come up out of the land, for great will be the day of Jezreel. "Say of your brothers, 'My people,' and of your sisters, 'My loved one.'

Hosea
2:2-13

ANGER AGAINST WIFE.

"Rebuke your mother, rebuke her,
    for she is not my wife,
    and I am not her husband.
Let her remove the adulterous look from her face
    and the unfaithfulness from between her breasts.
Otherwise I will strip her naked
    and make her as bare as on the day she was born;
I will make her like a desert,
    turn her into a parched land,
    and slay her with thirst.
I will not show my love to her children,
    because they are the children of adultery.
Their mother has been unfaithful
    and has conceived them in disgrace.
She said, 'I will go after my lovers,
    who give me my food and my water,
    my wool and my linen, my oil and my drink.'
Therefore I will block her path with thornbushes;
    I will wall her in so that she cannot find her way.
She will chase after her lovers but not catch them;
    she will look for them but not find them.
Then she will say,
    'I will go back to my husband as at first,
    for then I was better off than now.'
She has not acknowledged that I was the one
    who gave her the grain, the new wine and oil,
who lavished on her the silver and gold—
    which they used for Baal.

"Therefore I will take away my grain when it ripens,
    and my new wine when it is ready.
I will take back my wool and my linen,
    intended to cover her nakedness.
So now I will expose her lewdness
    before the eyes of her lovers;
    no one will take her out of my hands.
I will stop all her celebrations:
    her yearly festivals, her New Moons,
    her Sabbath days—all her appointed feasts.
I will ruin her vines and her fig trees,
    which she said were her pay from her lovers;
I will make them a thicket,
    and wild animals will devour them.
I will punish her for the days
    she burned incense to the Baals;
she decked herself with rings and jewelry,

and went after her lovers,
but me she forgot,"

declares the LORD.

FORGIVENESS AND ACCEPTANCE.

"Therefore I am now going to allure her;
I will lead her into the desert
and speak tenderly to her.
There I will give her back her vineyards,
and will make the Valley of Achor^y a door of hope.
There she will sing^z as in the days of her youth,
as in the day she came up out of Egypt.

"In that day," declares the LORD,
"you will call me 'my husband';
you will no longer call me 'my master.$^{a'}$
I will remove the names of the Baals from her lips;
no longer will their names be invoked.
In that day I will make a covenant for them
with the beasts of the field and the birds of the air
and the creatures that move along the ground.
Bow and sword and battle
I will abolish from the land,
so that all may lie down in safety.
I will betroth you to me forever;
I will betroth you in^b righteousness and justice,
in^c love and compassion.
I will betroth you in faithfulness,
and you will acknowledge the LORD.

"In that day I will respond,"
declares the LORD—
"I will respond to the skies,
and they will respond to the earth;
and the earth will respond to the grain,
the new wine and oil,
and they will respond to Jezreel.^{d}
I will plant her for myself in the land;
I will show my love to the one I called 'Not my loved
one.$^{e'}$
I will say to those called 'Not my people,$^{f'}$ 'You are my
people';
and they will say, 'You are my God.'"

HOSEA TAKES BACK GOMER.
The LORD said to me, "Go, show your
love to your wife again, though she is loved by another and is an adulteress. Love her as the LORD loves the Israelites, though they turn to other
gods and love the sacred raisin cakes."

So I bought her for fifteen shekels^g of silver and about a homer and a

---

^{y}*Achor* means *trouble.* ^{z}Or *respond* ^{a}Hebrew *baal* ^{b}Or *with* ^{c}Or *with*
^{d}*Jezreel* means *God plants.* ^{e}Hebrew *Lo-Ruhamah* ^{f}Hebrew *Lo-Ammi* ^{g}That is,
about 6 ounces (about 170 grams)

lethek[h] of barley. Then I told her, "You are to live with[i] me many days; you must not be a prostitute or be intimate with any man, and I will live with[i] you."

Hosea 3:4,5

ISRAEL'S OWN REDEMPTION.   For the Israelites will live many days without king or prince, without sacrifice or sacred stones, without ephod or idol. Afterward the Israelites will return and seek the LORD their God and David their king. They will come trembling to the LORD and to his blessings in the last days.

Hosea 4:1-6a

CHARGE AGAINST ISRAEL.

> Hear the word of the LORD, you Israelites,
>> because the LORD has a charge to bring
>> against you who live in the land:
> "There is no faithfulness, no love,
>> no acknowledgment of God in the land.
> There is only cursing,[j] lying and murder,
>> stealing and adultery;
> they break all bounds,
>> and bloodshed follows bloodshed.
> Because of this the land mourns,[k]
>> and all who live in it waste away;
> the beasts of the field and the birds of the air
>> and the fish of the sea are dying.

> "But let no man bring a charge,
>> let no man accuse another,
> for your people are like those
>> who bring charges against a priest.
> You stumble day and night,
>> and the prophets stumble with you.
> So I will destroy your mother—
>> my people are destroyed from lack of knowledge.

Hosea 4:6b-9

SINS OF THE PRIESTS.

> "Because you have rejected knowledge,
>> I also reject you as my priests;
> because you have ignored the law of your God,
>> I also will ignore your children.
> The more the priests increased,
>> the more they sinned against me;
>> they exchanged[l] their[m] Glory for something disgraceful.
> They feed on the sins of my people
>> and relish their wickedness.
> And it will be: Like people, like priests.
>> I will punish both of them for their ways
>> and repay them for their deeds.

---

[h]That is, probably about 10 bushels (about 330 liters)   [i]Or *wait for*   [j]That is, to pronounce a curse upon   [k]Or *dries up*   [l]Syriac and an ancient Hebrew scribal tradition; Masoretic Text *I will exchange*   [m]Masoretic Text; an ancient Hebrew scribal tradition *my*

ADULTERY OF IDOLATRY.

Hosea
4:10-19

"They will eat but not have enough;
    they will engage in prostitution but not increase,
because they have deserted the LORD
    to give themselves to prostitution,
to old wine and new,
    which take away the understanding of my people.
They consult a wooden idol
    and are answered by a stick of wood.
A spirit of prostitution leads them astray;
    they are unfaithful to their God.
They sacrifice on the mountaintops
    and burn offerings on the hills,
under oak, poplar and terebinth,
    where the shade is pleasant.
Therefore your daughters turn to prostitution
    and your daughters-in-law to adultery.

"I will not punish your daughters
    when they turn to prostitution,
nor your daughters-in-law
    when they commit adultery,
because the men themselves consort with harlots
    and sacrifice with shrine prostitutes—
    a people without understanding will come to ruin!

"Though you commit adultery, O Israel,
    let not Judah become guilty.

"Do not go to Gilgal;
    do not go up to Beth Aven.[n]
    And do not swear, 'As surely as the LORD lives!'
The Israelites are stubborn,
    like a stubborn heifer.
How then can the LORD pasture them
    like lambs in a meadow?
Ephraim is joined to idols;
    leave him alone!
Even when their drinks are gone,
    they continue their prostitution;
    their rulers dearly love shameful ways.
A whirlwind will sweep them away,
    and their sacrifices will bring them shame.

JUDGMENT PRONOUNCED.

Hosea
5:1-15

"Hear this, you priests!
    Pay attention, you Israelites!
Listen, O royal house!
    This judgment is against you:
You have been a snare at Mizpah,
    a net spread out on Tabor.

[n]*Beth Aven* means *house of wickedness* (a name for Bethel, which means *house of God*).

The rebels are deep in slaughter.
    I will discipline all of them.
I know all about Ephraim;
    Israel is not hidden from me.
Ephraim, you have now turned to prostitution;
    Israel is corrupt.

"Their deeds do not permit them
    to return to their God.
A spirit of prostitution is in their heart;
    they do not acknowledge the LORD.
Israel's arrogance testifies against them;
    the Israelites, even Ephraim, stumble in their sin;
    Judah also stumbles with them.
When they go with their flocks and herds
    to seek the LORD,
they will not find him;
    he has withdrawn himself from them.
They are unfaithful to the LORD;
    they give birth to illegitimate children.
Now their New Moon festivals
    will devour them and their fields.

"Sound the trumpet in Gibeah,
    the horn in Ramah.
Raise the battle cry in Beth Aven[o];
    lead on, O Benjamin.
Ephraim will be laid waste
    on the day of reckoning.
Among the tribes of Israel
    I proclaim what is certain.
Judah's leaders are like those
    who move boundary stones.
I will pour out my wrath on them
    like a flood of water.
Ephraim is oppressed,
    trampled in judgment,
    intent on pursuing idols.[p]
I am like a moth to Ephraim,
    like rot to the people of Judah.

"When Ephraim saw his sickness,
    and Judah his sores,
then Ephraim turned to Assyria,
    and sent to the great king for help.
But he is not able to cure you,
    not able to heal your sores.
For I will be like a lion to Ephraim,
    like a great lion to Judah.
I will tear them to pieces and go away;

[o]*Beth Aven* means *house of wickedness* (a name for Bethel, which means *house of God*).
[p]The meaning of the Hebrew for this word is uncertain.

I will carry them off, with no one to rescue them.
Then I will go back to my place
until they admit their guilt.
And they will seek my face;
in their misery they will earnestly seek me."

ISRAEL EXPRESSES REPENTANCE.

Hosea
6:1-3

"Come, let us return to the LORD.
He has torn us to pieces
but he will heal us;
he has injured us
but he will bind up our wounds.
After two days he will revive us;
on the third day he will restore us,
that we may live in his presence.
Let us acknowledge the LORD;
let us press on to acknowledge him.
As surely as the sun rises,
he will appear;
he will come to us like the winter rains,
like the spring rains that water the earth."

REPENTANCE SHORT-LIVED.

Hosea
6:4-11

"What can I do with you, Ephraim?
What can I do with you, Judah?
Your love is like the morning mist,
like the early dew that disappears.
Therefore I cut you in pieces with my prophets,
I killed you with the words of my mouth;
my judgments flashed like lightning upon you.
For I desire mercy, not sacrifice,
and acknowledgment of God rather than burnt offerings.
Like Adam,*q* they have broken the covenant—
they were unfaithful to me there.
Gilead is a city of wicked men,
stained with footprints of blood.
As marauders lie in ambush for a man,
so do bands of priests;
they murder on the road to Shechem,
committing shameful crimes.
I have seen a horrible thing
in the house of Israel.
There Ephraim is given to prostitution
and Israel is defiled.

"Also for you, Judah,
a harvest is appointed.

ISRAEL'S WICKEDNESS.

Hosea
7:1-7

"Whenever I would restore the fortunes of my people,

q Or As at Adam; or Like men

whenever I would heal Israel,
the sins of Ephraim are exposed
    and the crimes of Samaria revealed.
They practice deceit,
    thieves break into houses,
    bandits rob in the streets;
but they do not realize
    that I remember all their evil deeds.
Their sins engulf them;
    they are always before me.

"They delight the king with their wickedness,
    the princes with their lies.
They are all adulterers,
    burning like an oven
whose fire the baker need not stir
    from the kneading of the dough till it rises.
On the day of the festival of our king
    the princes become inflamed with wine,
    and he joins hands with the mockers.
Their hearts are like an oven;
    they approach him with intrigue.
Their passion smolders all night;
    in the morning it blazes like a flaming fire.
All of them are hot as an oven;
    they devour their rulers.
All their kings fall,
    and none of them calls on me.

**Hosea
7:8-16**

FOREIGN RELATIONS.

"Ephraim mixes with the nations;
    Ephraim is a flat cake not turned over.
Foreigners sap his strength,
    but he does not realize it.
His hair is sprinkled with gray,
    but he does not notice.
Israel's arrogance testifies against him,
    but despite all this
he does not return to the LORD his God
    or search for him.

"Ephraim is like a dove,
    easily deceived and senseless—
now calling to Egypt,
    now turning to Assyria.
When they go, I will throw my net over them;
    I will pull them down like birds of the air.
When I hear them flocking together,
    I will catch them.
Woe to them,
    because they have strayed from me!
Destruction to them,
    because they have rebelled against me!

I long to redeem them
 but they speak lies against me.
They do not cry out to me from their hearts
 but wail upon their beds.
They gather together[r] for grain and new wine
 but turn away from me.
I trained them and strengthened them,
 but they plot evil against me.
They do not turn to the Most High;
 they are like a faulty bow.
Their leaders will fall by the sword
 because of their insolent words.
For this they will be ridiculed
 in the land of Egypt.

CENSURE FOR CALF IDOLS.

Hosea
8:1-14

"Put the trumpet to your lips!
 An eagle is over the house of the LORD
because the people have broken my covenant
 and rebelled against my law.
Israel cries out to me,
 'O our God, we acknowledge you!'
But Israel has rejected what is good;
 an enemy will pursue him.
They set up kings without my consent;
 they choose princes without my approval.
With their silver and gold
 they make idols for themselves
 to their own destruction.
Throw out your calf-idol, O Samaria!
 My anger burns against them.
How long will they be incapable of purity?
 They are from Israel!
This calf—a craftsman has made it;
 it is not God.
It will be broken in pieces,
 that calf of Samaria.

"They sow the wind
 and reap the whirlwind.
The stalk has no head;
 it will produce no flour.
Were it to yield grain,
 foreigners would swallow it up.
Israel is swallowed up;
 now she is among the nations
 like a worthless thing.
For they have gone up to Assyria
 like a wild donkey wandering alone.

[r]Most Hebrew manuscripts; some Hebrew manuscripts and Septuagint *They slash themselves*

Ephraim has sold herself to lovers.
Although they have sold themselves among the nations,
    I will now gather them together.
They will begin to waste away
    under the oppression of the mighty king.

"Though Ephraim built many altars for sin offerings,
    these have become altars for sinning.
I wrote for them the many things of my law,
    but they regarded them as something alien.
They offer sacrifices given to me
    and they eat the meat,
    but the LORD is not pleased with them.
Now he will remember their wickedness
    and punish their sins:
    They will return to Egypt.
Israel has forgotten his Maker
    and built palaces;
    Judah has fortified many towns.
But I will send fire upon their cities
    that will consume their fortresses."

Hosea 9:1-17

PUNISHMENT IN STORE.

Do not rejoice, O Israel;
    do not be jubilant like the other nations.
For you have been unfaithful to your God;
    you love the wages of a prostitute
    at every threshing floor.
Threshing floors and winepresses will not feed the people;
    the new wine will fail them.
They will not remain in the LORD's land;
    Ephraim will return to Egypt
    and eat unclean[s] food in Assyria.
They will not pour out wine offerings to the LORD,
    nor will their sacrifices please him.
Such sacrifices will be to them like the bread of mourners;
    all who eat them will be unclean.
This food will be for themselves;
    it will not come into the temple of the LORD.

What will you do on the day of your appointed feasts,
    on the festival days of the LORD?
Even if they escape from destruction,
    Egypt will gather them,
    and Memphis will bury them.
Their treasures of silver will be taken over by briers,
    and thorns will overrun their tents.
The days of punishment are coming,
    the days of reckoning are at hand.
    Let Israel know this.

[s]That is, ceremonially unclean

Because your sins are so many
    and your hostility so great,
the prophet is considered a fool,
    the inspired man a maniac.
The prophet, along with my God,
    is the watchman over Ephraim,[t]
yet snares await him on all his paths,
    and hostility in the house of his God.
They have sunk deep into corruption,
    as in the days of Gibeah.
God will remember their wickedness
    and punish them for their sins.

"When I found Israel,
    it was like finding grapes in the desert;
when I saw your fathers,
    it was like seeing the early fruit on the fig tree.
But when they came to Baal Peor,
    they consecrated themselves to that shameful idol
    and became as vile as the thing they loved.
Ephraim's glory will fly away like a bird—
    no birth, no pregnancy, no conception.
Even if they rear children,
    I will bereave them of every one.
Woe to them
    when I turn away from them!
I have seen Ephraim, like Tyre,
    planted in a pleasant place.
But Ephraim will bring out
    their children to the slayer."

Give them, O LORD—
    what will you give them?
Give them wombs that miscarry
    and breasts that are dry.

"Because of all their wickedness in Gilgal,
    I hated them there.
Because of their sinful deeds,
    I will drive them out of my house.
I will no longer love them;
    all their leaders are rebellious.
Ephraim is blighted,
    their root is withered,
    they yield no fruit.
Even if they bear children,
    I will slay their cherished offspring."

My God will reject them
    because they have not obeyed him;
    they will be wanderers among the nations.

[t]Or *The prophet is the watchman over Ephraim, / the people of my God*

JUNE 19

**Hosea
10:1-15**

PREDICTION OF CAPTIVITY.

Israel was a spreading vine;
   he brought forth fruit for himself.
As his fruit increased,
   he built more altars;
as his land prospered,
   he adorned his sacred stones.
Their heart is deceitful,
   and now they must bear their guilt.
The LORD will demolish their altars
   and destroy their sacred stones.

Then they will say, "We have no king
   because we did not revere the LORD.
But even if we had a king,
   what could he do for us?"
They make many promises,
   take false oaths
   and make agreements;
therefore lawsuits spring up
   like poisonous weeds in a plowed field.
The people who live in Samaria fear
   for the calf-idol of Beth Aven.[u]
Its people will mourn over it,
   and so will its idolatrous priests,
those who had rejoiced over its splendor,
   because it is taken from them into exile.
It will be carried to Assyria
   as tribute for the great king.
Ephraim will be disgraced;
   Israel will be ashamed of its wooden idols.[v]
Samaria and its king will float away
   like a twig on the surface of the waters.
The high places of wickedness[w] will be destroyed—
   it is the sin of Israel.
Thorns and thistles will grow up
   and cover their altars.
Then they will say to the mountains, "Cover us!"
   and to the hills, "Fall on us!"

"Since the days of Gibeah, you have sinned, O Israel,
   and there you have remained.[x]
Did not war overtake
   the evildoers in Gibeah?
When I please, I will punish them;
   nations will be gathered against them
to put them in bonds for their double sin.
Ephraim is a trained heifer
   that loves to thresh;

[u]*Beth Aven* means *house of wickedness* (a name for Bethel, which means *house of God*).
[v]Or *its counsel*   [w]Hebrew *aven*, a reference to Beth Aven (a derogatory name for Bethel)   [x]Or *there a stand was taken*

so I will put a yoke
   on her fair neck.
I will drive Ephraim,
   Judah must plow,
   and Jacob must break up the ground.
Sow for yourselves righteousness,
   reap the fruit of unfailing love,
and break up your unplowed ground;
   for it is time to seek the LORD,
until he comes
   and showers righteousness on you.
But you have planted wickedness,
   you have reaped evil,
   you have eaten the fruit of deception.
Because you have depended on your own strength
   and on your many warriors,
the roar of battle will rise against your people,
   so that all your fortresses will be devastated—
as Shalman devastated Beth Arbel on the day of battle,
   when mothers were dashed to the ground with their
      children.
Thus will it happen to you, O Bethel,
   because your wickedness is great.
When that day dawns,
   the king of Israel will be completely destroyed.

GOD'S LOVE FOR ISRAEL.

Hosea
11:1-11

"When Israel was a child, I loved him,
   and out of Egypt I called my son.
But the more I*y* called Israel,
   the further they went from me.*z*
They sacrificed to the Baals
   and they burned incense to images.
It was I who taught Ephraim to walk,
   taking them by the arms;
but they did not realize
   it was I who healed them.
I led them with cords of human kindness,
   with ties of love;
I lifted the yoke from their neck
   and bent down to feed them.

"Will they not return to Egypt
   and will not Assyria rule over them
   because they refuse to repent?
Swords will flash in their cities,
   will destroy the bars of their gates
   and put an end to their plans.
My people are determined to turn from me.
   Even if they call to the Most High,

---

*y*Some Septuagint manuscripts; Hebrew *they*   *z*Septuagint; Hebrew *them*

> he will by no means exalt them.
>
> "How can I give you up, Ephraim?
>> How can I hand you over, Israel?
> How can I treat you like Admah?
>> How can I make you like Zeboiim?
> My heart is changed within me;
>> all my compassion is aroused.
> I will not carry out my fierce anger,
>> nor will I turn and devastate Ephraim.
> For I am God, and not man—
>> the Holy One among you.
>> I will not come in wrath.*a*
> They will follow the LORD;
>> he will roar like a lion.
> When he roars,
>> his children will come trembling from the west.
> They will come trembling
>> like birds from Egypt,
>> like doves from Assyria.
> I will settle them in their homes,"
>> declares the LORD.

Hosea
11:12-13:3

RECITATION OF ISRAEL'S SINS.

> Ephraim has surrounded me with lies,
>> the house of Israel with deceit.
> And Judah is unruly against God,
>> even against the faithful Holy One.
> Ephraim feeds on the wind;
>> he pursues the east wind all day
>> and multiplies lies and violence.
> He makes a treaty with Assyria
>> and sends olive oil to Egypt.
> The LORD has a charge to bring against Judah;
>> he will punish Jacob*b* according to his ways
>> and repay him according to his deeds.
> In the womb he grasped his brother's heel;
>> as a man he struggled with God.
> He struggled with the angel and overcame him;
>> he wept and begged for his favor.
> He found him at Bethel
>> and talked with him there—
> the LORD God Almighty,
>> the LORD is his name of renown!
> But you must return to your God;
>> maintain love and justice,
>> and wait for your God always.
>
> The merchant uses dishonest scales;
>> he loves to defraud.
> Ephraim boasts,

---

*a*Or *come against any city*   *b*Jacob means *he grasps the heel* (figuratively, *he deceives*).

"I am very rich; I have become wealthy.
With all my wealth they will not find in me
    any iniquity or sin."

"I am the Lord your God,
    ⌊who brought you⌋ out of[c] Egypt;
I will make you live in tents again,
    as in the days of your appointed feasts.
I spoke to the prophets,
    gave them many visions
    and told parables through them."

Is Gilead wicked?
    Its people are worthless!
Do they sacrifice bulls in Gilgal?
    Their altars will be like piles of stones
    on a plowed field.
Jacob fled to the country of Aram[d];
    Israel served to get a wife,
    and to pay for her he tended sheep.
The Lord used a prophet to bring Israel up from Egypt,
    by a prophet he cared for him.
But Ephraim has bitterly provoked him to anger;
    his Lord will leave upon him the guilt of his bloodshed
    and will repay him for his contempt.

When Ephraim spoke, men trembled;
    he was exalted in Israel.
But he became guilty of Baal worship and died.
Now they sin more and more;
    they make idols for themselves from their silver,
cleverly fashioned images,
    all of them the work of craftsmen.
It is said of these people,
    "They offer human sacrifice
    and kiss[e] the calf-idols."
Therefore they will be like the morning mist,
    like the early dew that disappears,
    like chaff swirling from a threshing floor,
    like smoke escaping through a window.

THE WRATH OF GOD.

Hosea
13:4-16

"But I am the Lord your God,
    ⌊who brought you⌋ out of[c] Egypt.
You shall acknowledge no God but me,
    no Savior except me.
I cared for you in the desert,
    in the land of burning heat.
When I fed them, they were satisfied;
    when they were satisfied, they became proud;

[c]Or God / ever since you were in
sacrifice / kiss
    [d]That is, Northwest Mesopotamia
    [e]"Men who

then they forgot me.
So I will come upon them like a lion,
   like a leopard I will lurk by the path.
Like a bear robbed of her cubs,
   I will attack them and rip them open.
Like a lion I will devour them;
   a wild animal will tear them apart.

"You are destroyed, O Israel,
   because you are against me, against your helper.
Where is your king, that he may save you?
   Where are your rulers in all your towns,
of whom you said,
   'Give me a king and princes'?
So in my anger I gave you a king,
   and in my wrath I took him away.
The guilt of Ephraim is stored up,
   his sins are kept on record.
Pains as of a woman in childbirth come to him,
   but he is a child without wisdom;
when the time arrives,
   he does not come to the opening of the womb.

"I will ransom them from the power of the grave^f;
   I will redeem them from death.
Where, O death, are your plagues?
   Where, O grave,^{f} is your destruction?

"I will have no compassion,
   even though he thrives among his brothers.
An east wind from the LORD will come,
   blowing in from the desert;
his spring will fail
   and his well dry up.
His storehouse will be plundered
   of all its treasures.
The people of Samaria must bear their guilt,
   because they have rebelled against their God.
They will fall by the sword;
   their little ones will be dashed to the ground,
   their pregnant women ripped open."

Hosea
14:1-9

PROMISE OF FORGIVENESS.

Return, O Israel, to the LORD your God.
   Your sins have been your downfall!
Take words with you
   and return to the LORD.
Say to him:
   "Forgive all our sins
and receive us graciously,
   that we may offer the fruit of our lips.^{g}

^{f} Hebrew *Sheol* ^{g} Or *offer our lips as sacrifices of bulls*

> Assyria cannot save us;
> > we will not mount war-horses.
> We will never again say 'Our gods'
> > to what our own hands have made,
> > for in you the fatherless find compassion."

> "I will heal their waywardness
> > and love them freely,
> > for my anger has turned away from them.
> I will be like the dew to Israel;
> > he will blossom like a lily.
> Like a cedar of Lebanon
> > he will send down his roots;
> > his young shoots will grow.
> His splendor will be like an olive tree,
> > his fragrance like a cedar of Lebanon.
> Men will dwell again in his shade.
> > He will flourish like the grain.
> He will blossom like a vine,
> > and his fame will be like the wine from Lebanon.
> O Ephraim, what more have I[h] to do with idols?
> > I will answer him and care for him.
> I am like a green pine tree;
> > your fruitfulness comes from me."

> Who is wise? He will realize these things.
> > Who is discerning? He will understand them.
> The ways of the LORD are right;
> > the righteous walk in them,
> > but the rebellious stumble in them.

> Despite the warnings of Hosea, the people remain entrenched in idolatry:
> The focus now turns to Judah, which, though affected less than Israel, has problems of its own.

In Judah

AMAZIAH RENEWS REIGN.   Amaziah son of Joash king of Judah lived for fifteen years after the death of Jehoash son of Jehoahaz king of Israel.

2 Kgs. 14:17
2 Chron. 25:25

AMAZIAH ASSASSINATED.   As for the other events of Amaziah's reign, from beginning to end, are they not written in the book of the kings of Judah and Israel? From the time that Amaziah turned away from following the LORD, they conspired against him in Jerusalem and he fled to Lachish, but they sent men after him to Lachish and killed him there. He was brought back by horse and was buried with his fathers in the City of Judah.

2 Kgs.
14:18-20
2 Chron.
25:26-28
(767 B.C.)

UZZIAH (AZARIAH) MADE KING.   ChThen all the people of Judah took Uzziah,[i] who was sixteen years old, and made him king in place of his father Amaziah.

> Uzziah was sixteen years old when he became king, and he reigned in Jerusalem fifty-two years. His mother's name was Jecoliah; she was from

2 Kgs.
14:21; 15:1,2
2 Chron.
26:1,3
Jerusalem

[h]Or *What more has Ephraim*   [i]Also called *Azariah*

Jerusalem. ^{kg}In the twenty-seventh year of Jeroboam king of Israel, Azariah son of Amaziah king of Judah began to reign.

2 Kgs. 15:3
2 Chron. 26:4,5

UZZIAH'S CHARACTER.   He did what was right in the eyes of the LORD, just as his father Amaziah had done. He sought God during the days of Zechariah, who instructed him in the fear^j of God. As long as he sought the LORD, God gave him success.

2 Kgs. 15:4

HIGH PLACES REMAIN.   The high places, however, were not removed, and the people continued to offer sacrifices and burn incense there.

2 Kgs. 14:22
2 Chron. 26:2

ELATH REBUILT.   He was the one who rebuilt Elath and restored it to Judah after Amaziah rested with his fathers.

2 Chron. 26:6-8

SUCCESS AGAINST PHILISTINES.   He went to war against the Philistines and broke down the walls of Gath, Jabneh and Ashdod. He then rebuilt towns near Ashdod and elsewhere among the Philistines. God helped him against the Philistines and against the Arabs who lived in Gur Baal and against the Meunites. The Ammonites brought tribute to Uzziah, and his fame spread as far as the border of Egypt, because he had become very powerful.

2 Chron. 26:9,10,15

UZZIAH'S INDUSTRIES.   Uzziah built towers in Jerusalem at the Corner Gate, at the Valley Gate and at the angle of the wall, and he fortified them. He also built towers in the desert and dug many cisterns, because he had much livestock in the foothills and in the plain. He had people working his fields and vineyards in the hills and in the fertile lands, for he loved the soil. In Jerusalem he made machines designed by skillful men for use on the towers and on the corner defenses to shoot arrows and hurl large stones. His fame spread far and wide, for he was greatly helped until he became powerful.

2 Chron. 26:11-14

UZZIAH'S MILITARY STRENGTH.   Uzziah had a well-trained army, ready to go out by divisions according to their numbers as mustered by Jeiel the secretary and Maaseiah the officer under the direction of Hananiah, one of the royal officials. The total number of family leaders over the fighting men was 2,600. Under their command was an army of 307,500 men trained for war, a powerful force to support the king against his enemies. Uzziah provided shields, spears, helmets, coats of armor, bows and slingstones for the entire army.

The Prophecies of Amos

*I*n the days of Uzziah and Jeroboam II, God calls a lowly shepherd from Tekoa, near Bethlehem in Judah, to prophesy against several nations, but principally against Israel. Amos comes to Israel at a time when Jeroboam's great military successes have brought unparalleled prosperity, and with it selfishness, greed, and immorality. Although he comes to the center of calf worship at Bethel, he does not attack idolatry as such (as does his contemporary, Hosea). He concentrates instead on rebuking both Israel and Judah for the meaninglessness of their worship, whatever its form. He calls for consistency in one's religious exercises and daily ethical conduct, and cries out

---

^jMany Hebrew manuscripts, Septuagint and Syriac; other Hebrew manuscripts *vision*

against a people who honor deity with their many sacrifices yet refuse justice and mercy to the oppressed and needy.

Amos' message comes first in the form of eight "burdens" against various nations. Three sermons of judgment then follow, and an oracle containing five visions: of locusts, fire, a plumb line, ripe fruit, and the altar. Amos ends his writing with a message of hope and a promise of restoration.

It is not at all surprising that Amos is rebuked by Amaziah, the high priest, for it is, after all, the selfish religious establishment which has led the people into this institutionalized and meaningless form of religion.

PREFACE. The words of Amos, one of the shepherds of Tekoa—what he saw concerning Israel two years before the earthquake, when Uzziah was king of Judah and Jeroboam son of Jehoash[k] was king of Israel.

Amos 1:1

JUDGMENT AGAINST NATIONS. He said:

Amos 1:2

> "The LORD roars from Zion
>   and thunders from Jerusalem;
> the pastures of the shepherds dry up,[l]
>   and the top of Carmel withers."

AGAINST SYRIANS. This is what the LORD says:

Amos 1:3-5

> "For three sins of Damascus,
>   even for four, I will not turn back ⌐my wrath⌐.
> Because she threshed Gilead
>   with sledges having iron teeth,
> I will send fire upon the house of Hazael
>   that will consume the fortresses of Ben-Hadad.
> I will break down the gate of Damascus;
>   I will destroy the king who is in[m] the Valley of Aven[n]
> and the one who holds the scepter in Beth Eden.
>   The people of Aram will go into exile to Kir,"
>   says the LORD.

AGAINST PHILISTINES. This is what the LORD says:

Amos 1:6-8

> "For three sins of Gaza,
>   even for four, I will not turn back ⌐my wrath⌐.
> Because she took captive whole communities
>   and sold them to Edom,
> I will send fire upon the walls of Gaza
>   that will consume her fortresses.
> I will destroy the king[o] of Ashdod
>   and the one who holds the scepter in Ashkelon.
> I will turn my hand against Ekron,
>   till the last of the Philistines is dead,"
>   says the Sovereign LORD.

AGAINST TYRE. This is what the LORD says:

Amos 1:9,10

> "For three sins of Tyre,
>   even for four, I will not turn back ⌐my wrath⌐.

---

[k]Hebrew *Joash*, a variant of *Jehoash*   [l]Or *shepherds mourn*   [m]Or *the inhabitants of*
[n]*Aven* means *wickedness*.   [o]Or *inhabitants*

Because she sold whole communities of captives to Edom,
disregarding a treaty of brotherhood,
I will send fire upon the walls of Tyre
that will consume her fortresses."

Amos 1:11,12 AGAINST EDOMITES. This is what the LORD says:

"For three sins of Edom,
even for four, I will not turn back ⌊my wrath⌋.
Because he pursued his brother with a sword,
stifling all compassion,[p]
because his anger raged continually
and his fury flamed unchecked,
I will send fire upon Teman
that will consume the fortresses of Bozrah."

Amos 1:13-15 AGAINST AMMONITES. This is what the LORD says:

"For three sins of Ammon,
even for four, I will not turn back ⌊my wrath⌋.
Because he ripped open the pregnant women of Gilead
in order to extend his borders,
I will set fire to the walls of Rabbah
that will consume her fortresses
amid war cries on the day of battle,
amid violent winds on a stormy day.
Her king[q] will go into exile,
he and his officials together,"
says the LORD.

Amos 2:1-3 AGAINST MOABITES. This is what the LORD says:

"For three sins of Moab,
even for four, I will not turn back ⌊my wrath⌋.
Because he burned, as if to lime,
the bones of Edom's king,
I will send fire upon Moab
that will consume the fortresses of Kerioth.[r]
Moab will go down in great tumult
amid war cries and the blast of the trumpet.
I will destroy her ruler
and kill all her officials with him,"
says the LORD.

Amos 2:4,5 AGAINST JUDAH. This is what the LORD says:

"For three sins of Judah,
even for four, I will not turn back ⌊my wrath⌋.
Because they have rejected the law of the LORD
and have not kept his decrees,
because they have been led astray by false gods,[s]
the gods[t] their ancestors followed,

[p]Or *sword / and destroyed his allies* [q]Or / *Molech;* Hebrew *malcam* [r]Or *of her cities*
[s]Or *by lies* [t]Or *lies*

I will send fire upon Judah
    that will consume the fortresses of Jerusalem."

AGAINST ISRAEL.   This is what the LORD says:

Amos
2:6-16

"For three sins of Israel,
    even for four, I will not turn back my wrath.
They sell the righteous for silver,
    and the needy for a pair of sandals.
They trample on the heads of the poor
    as upon the dust of the ground
    and deny justice to the oppressed.
Father and son use the same girl
    and so profane my holy name.
They lie down beside every altar
    on garments taken in pledge.
In the house of their god
    they drink wine taken as fines.

"I destroyed the Amorite before them,
    though he was tall as the cedars
    and strong as the oaks.
I destroyed his fruit above
    and his roots below.

"I brought you up out of Egypt,
    and I led you forty years in the desert
    to give you the land of the Amorites.
I also raised up prophets from among your sons
    and Nazirites from among your young men.
Is this not true, people of Israel?"

declares the LORD.

"But you made the Nazirites drink wine
    and commanded the prophets not to prophesy.

"Now then, I will crush you
    as a cart crushes when loaded with grain.
The swift will not escape,
    the strong will not muster their strength,
    and the warrior will not save his life.
The archer will not stand his ground,
    the fleet-footed soldier will not get away,
    and the horseman will not save his life.
Even the bravest warriors
    will flee naked on that day,"

declares the LORD.

GOD'S PLANS REVEALED.   Hear this word the LORD has spoken against you, O people of Israel—against the whole family I brought up out of Egypt:

Amos
3:1-10

"You only have I chosen
    of all the families of the earth;
    therefore I will punish you
    for all your sins."

Do two walk together
    unless they have agreed to do so?
Does a lion roar in the thicket
    when he has no prey?
Does he growl in his den
    when he has caught nothing?
Does a bird fall into a trap on the ground
    where no snare has been set?
Does a trap spring up from the earth
    when there is nothing to catch?
When a trumpet sounds in a city,
    do not the people tremble?
When disaster comes to a city,
    has not the LORD caused it?

Surely the Sovereign LORD does nothing
    without revealing his plan
    to his servants the prophets.

The lion has roared—
    who will not fear?
The Sovereign LORD has spoken—
    who can but prophesy?

Proclaim to the fortresses of Ashdod
    and to the fortresses of Egypt:
"Assemble yourselves on the mountains of Samaria;
    see the great unrest within her
    and the oppression among her people."

"They do not know how to do right," declares the LORD,
    "who hoard plunder and loot in their fortresses."

Amos
3:11-15
PROMISE OF PUNISHMENT.   Therefore this is what the Sovereign LORD
says:

"An enemy will overrun the land;
    he will pull down your strongholds
    and plunder your fortresses."

This is what the LORD says:

"As a shepherd saves from the lion's mouth
    only two leg bones or a piece of an ear,
    so will the Israelites be saved,
those who sit in Samaria
    on the edge of their beds
    and in Damascus on their couches.ᵘ"

"Hear this and testify against the house of Jacob," declares the Lord, the
LORD God Almighty.

"On the day I punish Israel for her sins,
    I will destroy the altars of Bethel;
the horns of the altar will be cut off
    and fall to the ground.

ᵘThe meaning of the Hebrew for this line is uncertain.

I will tear down the winter house
 along with the summer house;
the houses adorned with ivory will be destroyed
 and the mansions will be demolished,"
declares the LORD.

GOD'S MANY WARNINGS.
Amos
4:1-11

Hear this word, you cows of Bashan on Mount Samaria,
 you women who oppress the poor and crush the needy
and say to your husbands, "Bring us some drinks!"
The Sovereign LORD has sworn by his holiness:
 "The time will surely come
when you will be taken away with hooks,
 the last of you with fishhooks.
You will each go straight out
 through breaks in the wall,
 and you will be cast out toward Harmon,*v*"
declares the LORD.

"Go to Bethel and sin;
 go to Gilgal and sin yet more.
Bring your sacrifices every morning,
 your tithes every three years,*w*
Burn leavened bread as a thank offering
 and brag about your freewill offerings—
boast about them, you Israelites,
 for this is what you love to do,"
declares the Sovereign LORD.

"I gave you empty stomachs*x* in every city
 and lack of bread in every town,
 yet you have not returned to me,"
declares the LORD.

"I also withheld rain from you
 when the harvest was still three months away.
I sent rain on one town,
 but withheld it from another.
One field had rain;
 another had none and dried up.
People staggered from town to town for water
 but did not get enough to drink,
 yet you have not returned to me,"
declares the LORD.

"Many times I struck your gardens and vineyards,
 I struck them with blight and mildew.
Locusts devoured your fig and olive trees,
 yet you have not returned to me,"
declares the LORD.

"I sent plagues among you

---

*v*Masoretic Text; with a different word division of the Hebrew (see Septuagint) *out, O
mountain of oppression* *w*Or *tithes on the third day* *x*Hebrew *you cleanness of teeth*

as I did to Egypt.
I killed your young men with the sword,
along with your captured horses.
I filled your nostrils with the stench of your camps,
yet you have not returned to me,"

declares the LORD.

"I overthrew some of you
as I[y] overthrew Sodom and Gomorrah.
You were like a burning stick snatched from the fire,
yet you have not returned to me,"

declares the LORD.

Amos 4:12,13

NEED TO PREPARE.

"Therefore this is what I will do to you, Israel,
and because I will do this to you,
prepare to meet your God, O Israel."

He who forms the mountains,
creates the wind,
and reveals his thoughts to man,
he who turns dawn to darkness,
and treads the high places of the earth—
the LORD God Almighty is his name.

Amos 5:1-15

CRY AGAINST INJUSTICE.

Hear this word, O house of Israel, this lament I take up concerning you:

"Fallen is Virgin Israel,
never to rise again,
deserted in her own land,
with no one to lift her up."

This is what the Sovereign LORD says:

"The city that marches out a thousand strong for Israel
will have only a hundred left;
the town that marches out a hundred strong
will have only ten left."

This is what the LORD says to the house of Israel:

"Seek me and live;
do not seek Bethel,
do not go to Gilgal,
do not journey to Beersheba.
For Gilgal will surely go into exile,
and Bethel will be reduced to nothing.[z]"
Seek the LORD and live,
or he will sweep through the house of Joseph like a fire;
it will devour,
and Bethel will have no one to quench it.

You who turn justice into bitterness

---

[y]Hebrew *God*   [z]Or *grief;* or *wickedness;* Hebrew *aven,* a reference to Beth Aven (a derogatory name for Bethel)

and cast righteousness to the ground
(he who made the Pleiades and Orion,
    who turns blackness into dawn
    and darkens day into night,
who calls for the waters of the sea
    and pours them out over the face of the land—
    the LORD is his name—
he flashes destruction on the stronghold
    and brings the fortified city to ruin),
you hate the one who reproves in court
    and despise him who tells the truth.

You trample on the poor
    and force him to give you grain.
Therefore, though you have built stone mansions,
    you will not live in them;
though you have planted lush vineyards,
    you will not drink their wine.
For I know how many are your offenses
    and how great your sins.

You oppress the righteous and take bribes
    and you deprive the poor of justice in the courts.
Therefore the prudent man keeps quiet in such times,
    for the times are evil.

Seek good, not evil,
    that you may live.
Then the LORD God Almighty will be with you,
    just as you say he is.
Hate evil, love good;
    maintain justice in the courts.
Perhaps the LORD God Almighty will have mercy
    on the remnant of Joseph.

DAY OF THE LORD.   Therefore this is what the Lord, the LORD God   Amos
Almighty, says: 5:16-20

"There will be wailing in all the streets
    and cries of anguish in every public square.
The farmers will be summoned to weep
    and the mourners to wail.
There will be wailing in all the vineyards,
    for I will pass through your midst,"

                                                                says the LORD.

Woe to you who long
    for the day of the LORD!
Why do you long for the day of the LORD?
    That day will be darkness, not light.
It will be as though a man fled from a lion
    only to meet a bear,
as though he entered his house
    and rested his hand on the wall
    only to have a snake bite him.

> Will not the day of the LORD be darkness, not light—
>   pitch-dark, without a ray of brightness?

Amos
5:21-26 EMPTINESS OF RITUAL.

> "I hate, I despise your religious feasts;
>   I cannot stand your assemblies.
> Even though you bring me burnt offerings and grain
>   offerings,
>   I will not accept them.
> Though you bring choice fellowship offerings,[a]
>   I will have no regard for them.
> Away with the noise of your songs!
>   I will not listen to the music of your harps.
> But let justice roll on like a river,
>   righteousness like a never-failing stream!

> "Did you bring me sacrifices and offerings
>   forty years in the desert, O house of Israel?
> You have lifted up the shrine of your king,
>   the pedestal of your idols,
>   the star of your god[b]—
>   which you made for yourselves.

Amos 5:27 PREDICTION OF CAPTIVITY.

> Therefore I will send you into exile beyond Damascus,"
>   says the LORD, whose name is God Almighty.

Amos 6:1-7 REBUKE FOR COMPLACENCY.

> Woe to you who are complacent in Zion,
>   and to you who feel secure on Mount Samaria,
> you notable men of the foremost nation,
>   to whom the people of Israel come!
> Go to Calneh and look at it;
>   go from there to great Hamath,
>   and then go down to Gath in Philistia.
> Are they better off than your two kingdoms?
>   Is their land larger than yours?
> You put off the evil day
>   and bring near a reign of terror.
> You lie on beds inlaid with ivory
>   and lounge on your couches.
> You dine on choice lambs
>   and fattened calves.
> You strum away on your harps like David
>   and improvise on musical instruments.
> You drink wine by the bowlful
>   and use the finest lotions,
>   but you do not grieve over the ruin of Joseph.
> Therefore you will be among the first to go into exile;
>   your feasting and lounging will end.

---

[a]Traditionally *peace offerings*   [b]*Or lifted up Sakkuth your king / and Kaiwan your idols, /
your star-gods*; Septuagint *lifted up the shrine of Molech / and the star of your god Rephan, /
their idols*

REBUKE FOR PRIDE.   The Sovereign LORD has sworn by himself—the
LORD God Almighty declares:

> "I abhor the pride of Jacob
>   and detest his fortresses;
> I will deliver up the city
>   and everything in it."

If ten men are left in one house, they too will die. And if a relative who
is to burn the bodies comes to carry them out of the house and asks anyone still hiding there, "Is anyone with you?" and he says, "No," then he
will say, "Hush! We must not mention the name of the LORD."

> For the LORD has given the command,
>   and he will smash the great house into pieces
>   and the small house into bits.
>
> Do horses run on the rocky crags?
>   Does one plow there with oxen?
> But you have turned justice into poison
>   and the fruit of righteousness into bitterness—
> you who rejoice in the conquest of Lo Debar^c
>   and say, "Did we not take Karnaim^d by our own
>   strength?"
>
> For the LORD God Almighty declares,
>   "I will stir up a nation against you, O house of Israel,
> that will oppress you all the way
>   from Lebo^e Hamath to the valley of the Arabah."

VISION OF LOCUSTS.   This is what the Sovereign LORD showed me: He
was preparing swarms of locusts after the king's share had been harvested and just as the second crop was coming up. When they had stripped the
land clean, I cried out, "Sovereign LORD, forgive! How can Jacob survive?
He is so small!"
  So the LORD relented.
  "This will not happen," the LORD said.

VISION OF FIRE.   This is what the Sovereign LORD showed me: The
Sovereign LORD was calling for judgment by fire; it dried up the great deep
and devoured the land. Then I cried out, "Sovereign LORD, I beg you, stop!
How can Jacob survive? He is so small!"
  So the LORD relented.
  "This will not happen either," the Sovereign LORD said.

VISION OF PLUMB LINE.   This is what he showed me: The Lord was
standing by a wall that had been built true to plumb, with a plumb line in
his hand. And the LORD asked me, "What do you see, Amos?"
  "A plumb line," I replied.
  Then the Lord said, "Look, I am setting a plumb line among my people
Israel; I will spare them no longer.

---

^cLo Debar means nothing.   ^dKarnaim means horns; horn here symbolizes strength.
^eOr from the entrance to

> "The high places of Isaac will be destroyed
> and the sanctuaries of Israel will be ruined;
> with my sword I will rise against the house of Jeroboam."

Amos 8:1-3   VISION OF RIPE FRUIT.   This is what the Sovereign LORD showed me: a
basket of ripe fruit. "What do you see, Amos?" he asked.
"A basket of ripe fruit," I answered.
Then the LORD said to me, "The time is ripe for my people Israel; I will
spare them no longer.
"In that day," declares the Sovereign LORD, "the songs in the temple will
turn to wailing.*f* Many, many bodies—flung everywhere! Silence!"

Amos 8:4-6   UNETHICAL RELIGION.

> Hear this, you who trample the needy
> and do away with the poor of the land,

saying,

> "When will the New Moon be over
> that we may sell grain,
> and the Sabbath be ended
> that we may market wheat?"—
> skimping the measure,
> boosting the price
> and cheating with dishonest scales,
> buying the poor with silver
> and the needy for a pair of sandals,
> selling even the sweepings with the wheat.

Amos
8:7-14   PROMISE OF PUNISHMENT.   The LORD has sworn by the Pride of Jacob:
"I will never forget anything they have done.

> "Will not the land tremble for this,
> and all who live in it mourn?
> The whole land will rise like the Nile;
> it will be stirred up and then sink
> like the river of Egypt.

"In that day," declares the Sovereign LORD,

> "I will make the sun go down at noon
> and darken the earth in broad daylight.
> I will turn your religious feasts into mourning
> and all your singing into weeping.
> I will make all of you wear sackcloth
> and shave your heads.
> I will make that time like mourning for an only son
> and the end of it like a bitter day.

> "The days are coming," declares the Sovereign LORD,
> "when I will send a famine through the land—
> not a famine of food or a thirst for water,
> but a famine of hearing the words of the LORD.
> Men will stagger from sea to sea

*f*Or *"the temple singers will wail*

and wander from north to east,
searching for the word of the LORD,
but they will not find it.

"In that day

"the lovely young women and strong young men
will faint because of thirst.
They who swear by the shame*g* of Samaria,
or say, 'As surely as your god lives, O Dan,'
or, 'As surely as the god*h* of Beersheba lives'—
they will fall,
never to rise again."

VISION OF THE ALTAR.   I saw the Lord standing by the altar, and he said:

Amos
9:1-10

"Strike the tops of the pillars
so that the thresholds shake.
Bring them down on the heads of all the people;
those who are left I will kill with the sword.
Not one will get away,
none will escape.
Though they dig down to the depths of the grave,*i*
from there my hand will take them.
Though they climb up to the heavens,
from there I will bring them down.
Though they hide themselves on the top of Carmel,
there I will hunt them down and seize them.
Though they hide from me at the bottom of the sea,
there I will command the serpent to bite them.
Though they are driven into exile by their enemies,
there I will command the sword to slay them.
I will fix my eyes upon them
for evil and not for good."

The Lord, the LORD Almighty,
he who touches the earth and it melts,
and all who live in it mourn—
the whole land rises like the Nile,
then sinks like the river of Egypt—
he who builds his lofty palace*j* in the heavens
and sets its foundation*k* on the earth,
who calls for the waters of the sea
and pours them out over the face of the land—
the LORD is his name.

"Are not you Israelites
the same to me as the Cushites*l*?"

declares the LORD.

"Did I not bring Israel up from Egypt,

*g*Or *by Ashima*; or *by the idol*   *h*Or *power*   *i*Hebrew *to Sheol*   *j*The meaning of the
Hebrew for this phrase is uncertain.   *k*The meaning of the Hebrew for this word is
uncertain.   *l*That is, people from the upper Nile region

  the Philistines from Caphtor[m]
  and the Arameans from Kir?

"Surely the eyes of the Sovereign LORD
  are on the sinful kingdom.
I will destroy it
  from the face of the earth—
yet I will not totally destroy
  the house of Jacob,"

declares the LORD.

"For I will give the command,
  and I will shake the house of Israel
   among all the nations
as grain is shaken in a sieve,
  and not a pebble will reach the ground.
All the sinners among my people
  will die by the sword,
all those who say,
  'Disaster will not overtake or meet us.'

**Amos
9:11-15**

PROMISE OF RESTORATION.

"In that day I will restore
  David's fallen tent.
I will repair its broken places,
  restore its ruins,
  and build it as it used to be,
so that they may possess the remnant of Edom
  and all the nations that bear my name,[n]"

declares the LORD, who will do these things.

"The days are coming," declares the LORD,

"when the reaper will be overtaken by the plowman
  and the planter by the one treading grapes.
New wine will drip from the mountains
  and flow from all the hills.
I will bring back my exiled[o] people Israel;
  they will rebuild the ruined cities and live in them.
They will plant vineyards and drink their wine;
  they will make gardens and eat their fruit.
I will plant Israel in their own land,
  never again to be uprooted
  from the land I have given them,"

says the LORD your God.

**Amos
7:10-13**

PRIEST'S ANGRY RESPONSE.

Then Amaziah the priest of Bethel sent a message to Jeroboam king of Israel: "Amos is raising a conspiracy against you in the very heart of Israel. The land cannot bear all his words. For this is what Amos is saying:

  " 'Jeroboam will die by the sword,

[m]That is, Crete [n]Hebrew; Septuagint *so that the remnant of men / and all the nations that bear my name may seek ⌊the Lord⌋* [o]Or *will restore the fortunes of my*

and Israel will surely go into exile,
away from their native land.' "

Then Amaziah said to Amos, "Get out, you seer! Go back to the land of Judah. Earn your bread there and do your prophesying there. Don't prophesy anymore at Bethel, because this is the king's sanctuary and the temple of the kingdom."

AMOS' ANSWER. Amos answered Amaziah, "I was neither a prophet nor a prophet's son, but I was a shepherd, and I also took care of sycamore-fig trees. But the LORD took me from tending the flock and said to me, 'Go, prophesy to my people Israel.' Now then, hear the word of the LORD. You say,

> Amos
> 7:14-17

" 'Do not prophesy against Israel,
    and stop preaching against the house of Isaac.'

"Therefore this is what the LORD says:

" 'Your wife will become a prostitute in the city,
    and your sons and daughters will fall by the sword.
Your land will be measured and divided up,
    and you yourself will die in a pagan[p] country.
And Israel will certainly go into exile,
    away from their native land.' "

The wickedness against which Amos speaks is also seen in the political chaos which comes following Jeroboam's death.

In Israel

DEATH OF JEROBOAM II. As for the other events of Jeroboam's reign, all he did, and his military achievements, including how he recovered for Israel both Damascus and Hamath, which had belonged to Yaudi,[q] are they not written in the book of the annals of the kings of Israel? Jeroboam rested with his fathers, the kings of Israel.

> 2 Kgs.
> 14:28,29a
> (753 B.C.)

ZECHARIAH KING OF ISRAEL. And Zechariah his son succeeded him as king.
   In the thirty-eighth year of Azariah king of Judah, Zechariah son of Jeroboam became king of Israel in Samaria, and he reigned six months.

> 2 Kgs.
> 14:29b;15:8
> Samaria

ZECHARIAH'S CHARACTER. He did evil in the eyes of the LORD, as his fathers had done. He did not turn away from the sins of Jeroboam son of Nebat, which he had caused Israel to commit.

> 2 Kgs. 15:9

ZECHARIAH ASSASSINATED. Shallum son of Jabesh conspired against Zechariah. He attacked him in front of the people,[r] assassinated him and succeeded him as king. The other events of Zechariah's reign are written in the book of the annals of the kings of Israel.

> 2 Kgs.
> 15:10,11
> (752 B.C.)

PROMISE TO JEHU FULFILLED. So the word of the LORD spoken to Jehu was fulfilled: "Your descendants will sit on the throne of Israel to the fourth generation."[s]

> 2 Kgs.
> 15:12

SHALLUM ASSASSINATED. Shallum son of Jabesh became king in the thirty-ninth year of Uzziah king of Judah, and he reigned in Samaria one

> 2 Kgs.
> 15:13-15
> (752 B.C.)

---

[p]Hebrew an unclean   [q]Or Judah   [r]Hebrew; some Septuagint manuscripts in Ibleam
[s]2 Kings 10:30

month. Then Menahem son of Gadi went from Tirzah up to Samaria. He attacked Shallum son of Jabesh in Samaria, assassinated him and succeeded him as king.

The other events of Shallum's reign, and the conspiracy he led, are written in the book of the annals of the kings of Israel.

2 Kgs.
15:16,17
(752 B.C.)

MENAHEM KING OF ISRAEL.   At that time Menahem, starting out from Tirzah, attacked Tiphsah and everyone in the city and its vicinity, because they refused to open their gates. He sacked Tiphsah and ripped open all the pregnant women.

In the thirty-ninth year of Azariah king of Judah, Menahem son of Gadi became king of Israel, and he reigned in Samaria ten years.

2 Kgs.
15:18

MENAHEM'S CHARACTER.   He did evil in the eyes of the LORD. During his entire reign he did not turn away from the sins of Jeroboam son of Nebat, which he had caused Israel to commit.

Era of Uzziah and Jotham in Judah

Since at least 767 B.C., King Uzziah, also known as Azariah, has reigned over Judah with great success. But his good fortune is about to go to his head, and he will suffer serious illness for his presumptuousness. Uzziah's illness will necessitate a co-regent to run the day-to-day affairs of state. In filling that role, Uzziah's son Jotham is a good leader. But he is not the religious man needed by this materialistic, immoral, unjust, and complacent people.

In Judah

2 Kgs.
15:5a
2 Chron.
26:16-21a
Jerusalem

SIN MAKES UZZIAH LEPROUS.   But after Uzziah became powerful, his pride led to his downfall. He was unfaithful to the LORD his God, and entered the temple of the LORD to burn incense on the altar of incense. Azariah the priest with eighty other courageous priests of the LORD followed him in. They confronted him and said, "It is not right for you, Uzziah, to burn incense to the LORD. That is for the priests, the descendants of Aaron, who have been consecrated to burn incense. Leave the sanctuary, for you have been unfaithful; and you will not be honored by the LORD God."

Uzziah, who had a censer in his hand ready to burn incense, became angry. While he was raging at the priests in their presence before the incense altar in the LORD's temple, leprosy[t] broke out on his forehead. When Azariah the chief priest and all the other priests looked at him, they saw that he had leprosy on his forehead, so they hurried him out. Indeed, he himself was eager to leave, because the LORD had afflicted him.

King Uzziah had leprosy until the day he died. He lived in a separate house[u]—leprous, and excluded from the temple of the LORD.

2 Kgs. 15:5b
2 Chron.
26:21b

JOTHAM CO-REGENT.   Jotham his son had charge of the palace and governed the people of the land.

[t]The Hebrew word was used for various diseases affecting the skin—not necessarily leprosy.   [u]Or *in a house where he was relieved of responsibilities*

The Prophecies of Isaiah

uring Uzziah's reign, and in the year immediately following his death, perhaps the greatest evangelistic prophet ever known to God's people begins an active ministry which will last some 40 years. Isaiah will do for Judah what Joel, Hosea, and Amos have done for Israel: he will tell the people about God's judgment against religious formalism, idolatry, oppression, immorality, and pride, and also warn them of the captivity they are about to face. Throughout his prophecies Isaiah repeatedly refers to the final day of the Lord, when all people will face judgment like that being brought against Israel and Judah. The imagery is exciting and visionary. Isaiah also looks forward to the coming of the Messiah and Savior, who will redeem all mankind from their sins. For this reason, much of what Isaiah has to say will be as meaningful to future generations as it is to those who live in Judah at this time.

Isaiah's message begins with a condemnation of Judah's many sins. He insists that Judah's sins will bring severe punishment, from which neither Judah's idols nor its leaders can save the people. He challenges the people to come to their senses before it is too late, and to look forward to the last days, when there will be a spiritual renewal and everlasting peace.

PREFACE. The vision concerning Judah and Jerusalem that Isaiah son of Amoz saw during the reigns of Uzziah, Jotham, Ahaz and Hezekiah, kings of Judah.

Isa. 1:1

JUDAH'S SINFUL STATE.

Isa. 1:2-9

Hear, O heavens! Listen, O earth!
For the LORD has spoken:
"I reared children and brought them up,
but they have rebelled against me.
The ox knows his master,
the donkey his owner's manger,
but Israel does not know,
my people do not understand."

Ah, sinful nation,
a people loaded with guilt,
a brood of evildoers,
children given to corruption!
They have forsaken the LORD;
they have spurned the Holy One of Israel
and turned their backs on him.

Why should you be beaten anymore?
Why do you persist in rebellion?
Your whole head is injured,
your whole heart afflicted.
From the sole of your foot to the top of your head
there is no soundness—
only wounds and welts
and open sores,

not cleansed or bandaged
    or soothed with oil.

Your country is desolate,
    your cities burned with fire;
your fields are being stripped by foreigners
    right before you,
       laid waste as when overthrown by strangers.
The Daughter of Zion is left
    like a shelter in a vineyard,
like a hut in a field of melons,
    like a city under siege.
Unless the LORD Almighty
    had left us some survivors,
we would have become like Sodom,
    we would have been like Gomorrah.

Isa. 5:1-7   PARABLE OF VINEYARD.

I will sing for the one I love
    a song about his vineyard:
My loved one had a vineyard
    on a fertile hillside.
He dug it up and cleared it of stones
    and planted it with the choicest vines.
He built a watchtower in it
    and cut out a winepress as well.
Then he looked for a crop of good grapes,
    but it yielded only bad fruit.

"Now you dwellers in Jerusalem and men of Judah,
    judge between me and my vineyard.
What more could have been done for my vineyard
    than I have done for it?
When I looked for good grapes,
    why did it yield only bad?
Now I will tell you
    what I am going to do to my vineyard:
I will take away its hedge,
    and it will be destroyed;
I will break down its wall,
    and it will be trampled.
I will make it a wasteland,
    neither pruned nor cultivated,
    and briers and thorns will grow there.
I will command the clouds
    not to rain on it."

The vineyard of the LORD Almighty
    is the house of Israel,
and the men of Judah
    are the garden of his delight.
And he looked for justice, but saw bloodshed;
    for righteousness, but heard cries of distress.

SIN OF RELIGIOUS FORMALISM.

Isa. 1:10-17

Hear the word of the LORD,
    you rulers of Sodom;
listen to the law of our God,
    you people of Gomorrah!
"The multitude of your sacrifices—
    what are they to me?" says the LORD.
"I have more than enough of burnt offerings,
    of rams and the fat of fattened animals;
I have no pleasure
    in the blood of bulls and lambs and goats.
When you come to appear before me,
    who has asked this of you,
    this trampling of my courts?
Stop bringing meaningless offerings!
    Your incense is detestable to me.
New Moons, Sabbaths and convocations—
    I cannot bear your evil assemblies.
Your New Moon festivals and your appointed feasts
    my soul hates.
They have become a burden to me;
    I am weary of bearing them.
When you spread out your hands in prayer,
    I will hide my eyes from you;
even if you offer many prayers,
    I will not listen.
Your hands are full of blood;
    wash and make yourselves clean.
Take your evil deeds
    out of my sight!
Stop doing wrong,
    learn to do right!
Seek justice,
    encourage the oppressed.^{v}
Defend the cause of the fatherless,
    plead the case of the widow.

SIN OF INJUSTICE.

Isa. 1:21-26

See how the faithful city
    has become a harlot!
She once was full of justice;
    righteousness used to dwell in her—
    but now murderers!
Your silver has become dross,
    your choice wine is diluted with water.
Your rulers are rebels,
    companions of thieves;
they all love bribes
    and chase after gifts.

^{v}Or / rebuke the oppressor

They do not defend the cause of the fatherless;
the widow's case does not come before them.
Therefore the Lord, the LORD Almighty,
the Mighty One of Israel, declares:
"Ah, I will get relief from my foes
and avenge myself on my enemies.
I will turn my hand against you;
I will thoroughly purge away your dross
and remove all your impurities.
I will restore your judges as in days of old,
your counselors as at the beginning.
Afterward you will be called
the City of Righteousness,
the Faithful City."

Isa. 2:6-9   SIN OF IDOLATRY.

You have abandoned your people,
the house of Jacob.
They are full of superstitions from the East;
they practice divination like the Philistines
and clasp hands with pagans.
Their land is full of silver and gold;
there is no end to their treasures.
Their land is full of horses;
there is no end to their chariots.
Their land is full of idols;
they bow down to the work of their hands,
to what their fingers have made.
So man will be brought low
and mankind humbled—
do not forgive them.*w*

Isa. 2:10-18   SIN OF PRIDE.

Go into the rocks,
hide in the ground
from dread of the LORD
and the splendor of his majesty!
The eyes of the arrogant man will be humbled
and the pride of men brought low;
the LORD alone will be exalted in that day.

The LORD Almighty has a day in store
for all the proud and lofty,
for all that is exalted
(and they will be humbled),
for all the cedars of Lebanon, tall and lofty,
and all the oaks of Bashan,
for all the towering mountains
and all the high hills,
for every lofty tower

*w*Or *not raise them up*

and every fortified wall,
for every trading ship[x]
and every stately vessel.
The arrogance of man will be brought low
and the pride of men humbled;
the LORD alone will be exalted in that day,
and the idols will totally disappear.

SIN OF THE LEADERS.

Isa. 3:8-15

Jerusalem staggers,
Judah is falling;
their words and deeds are against the LORD,
defying his glorious presence.
The look on their faces testifies against them;
they parade their sin like Sodom;
they do not hide it.
Woe to them!
They have brought disaster upon themselves.

Tell the righteous it will be well with them,
for they will enjoy the fruit of their deeds.
Woe to the wicked! Disaster is upon them!
They will be paid back for what their hands have done.

Youths oppress my people,
women rule over them.
O my people, your guides lead you astray;
they turn you from the path.

The LORD takes his place in court;
he rises to judge the people.
The LORD enters into judgment
against the elders and leaders of his people:
"It is you who have ruined my vineyard;
the plunder from the poor is in your houses.
What do you mean by crushing my people
and grinding the faces of the poor?"
                                 declares the Lord, the LORD Almighty.

SIN OF THE WOMEN.

Isa.
3:16-4:1
32:9-11

The LORD says,
"The women of Zion are haughty,
walking along with outstretched necks,
flirting with their eyes,
tripping along with mincing steps,
with ornaments jingling on their ankles.
Therefore the Lord will bring sores on the heads of the
women of Zion;
the LORD will make their scalps bald."

In that day the Lord will snatch away their finery: the bangles and headbands and crescent necklaces, the earrings and bracelets and veils, the

[x]Hebrew *every ship of Tarshish*

headdresses and ankle chains and sashes, the perfume bottles and charms,
the signet rings and nose rings, the fine robes and the capes and cloaks, the
purses and mirrors, and the linen garments and tiaras and shawls.

> Instead of fragrance there will be a stench;
>   instead of a sash, a rope;
> instead of well-dressed hair, baldness;
>   instead of fine clothing, sackcloth;
>   instead of beauty, branding.
> Your men will fall by the sword,
>   your warriors in battle.
> The gates of Zion will lament and mourn;
>   destitute, she will sit on the ground.
> In that day seven women
>   will take hold of one man
> and say, "We will eat our own food
>   and provide our own clothes;
> only let us be called by your name.
>   Take away our disgrace!"
> You women who are so complacent,
>   rise up and listen to me;
> you daughters who feel secure,
>   hear what I have to say!
> In little more than a year
>   you who feel secure will tremble;
> the grape harvest will fail,
>   and the harvest of fruit will not come.
> Tremble, you complacent women;
>   shudder, you daughters who feel secure!
> Strip off your clothes,
>   put sackcloth around your waists.

Isa. 5:8-10   SIN OF GREED.

> Woe to you who add house to house
>   and join field to field
> till no space is left
>   and you live alone in the land.

The LORD Almighty has declared in my hearing:

> "Surely the great houses will become desolate,
>   the fine mansions left without occupants.
> A ten-acre^y vineyard will produce only a bath^z of wine,
>   a homer^a of seed only an ephah^b of grain."

Isa. 5:11-14   SIN OF REVELRY.

> Woe to those who rise early in the morning
>   to run after their drinks,
> who stay up late at night

^yHebrew *ten-yoke*, that is, the land plowed by 10 yoke of oxen in one day   ^zThat is, probably about 6 gallons (about 22 liters)   ^aThat is, probably about 6 bushels (about 220 liters)   ^bThat is, probably about 3/5 bushel (about 22 liters)

till they are inflamed with wine.
They have harps and lyres at their banquets,
    tambourines and flutes and wine,
but they have no regard for the deeds of the LORD,
    no respect for the work of his hands.
Therefore my people will go into exile
    for lack of understanding;
their men of rank will die of hunger
    and their masses will be parched with thirst.
Therefore the grave[c] enlarges its appetite
    and opens its mouth without limit;
into it will descend their nobles and masses
    with all their brawlers and revelers.

SIN OF ARROGANCE.   Isa. 5:15-17

So man will be brought low
    and mankind humbled,
    the eyes of the arrogant humbled.
But the LORD Almighty will be exalted by his justice,
    and the holy God will show himself holy by his
        righteousness.
Then sheep will graze as in their own pasture;
    lambs will feed[d] among the ruins of the rich.

SIN OF RATIONALIZATION.   Isa. 5:18-21

Woe to those who draw sin along with cords of deceit,
    and wickedness as with cart ropes,
to those who say, "Let God hurry,
    let him hasten his work
    so we may see it.
Let it approach,
    let the plan of the Holy One of Israel come,
    so we may know it."

Woe to those who call evil good
    and good evil,
who put darkness for light
    and light for darkness,
who put bitter for sweet
    and sweet for bitter.

Woe to those who are wise in their own eyes
    and clever in their own sight.

SIN OF DRUNKENNESS.   Isa. 5:22

Woe to those who are heroes at drinking wine
    and champions at mixing drinks,

SIN OF INJUSTICE.   Isa. 5:23

who acquit the guilty for a bribe,
    but deny justice to the innocent.

[c]Hebrew *Sheol*   [d]Septuagint; Hebrew / *strangers will eat*

Isa. 5:24,25 ANGER OF GOD.

Therefore, as tongues of fire lick up straw
and as dry grass sinks down in the flames,
so their roots will decay
and their flowers blow away like dust;
for they have rejected the law of the LORD Almighty
and spurned the word of the Holy One of Israel.
Therefore the LORD's anger burns against his people;
his hand is raised and he strikes them down.
The mountains shake,
and the dead bodies are like refuse in the streets.

Yet for all this, his anger is not turned away,
his hand is still upraised.

Isa. 5:26-30 DESTRUCTIVE FORCES SUMMONED.

He lifts up a banner for the distant nations,
he whistles for those at the ends of the earth.
Here they come,
swiftly and speedily!
Not one of them grows tired or stumbles,
not one slumbers or sleeps;
not a belt is loosened at the waist,
not a sandal thong is broken.
Their arrows are sharp,
all their bows are strung;
their horses' hoofs seem like flint,
their chariot wheels like a whirlwind.
Their roar is like that of the lion,
they roar like young lions;
they growl as they seize their prey
and carry it off with no one to rescue.
In that day they will roar over it
like the roaring of the sea.
And if one looks at the land,
he will see darkness and distress;
even the light will be darkened by the clouds.

Isa. 1:27-31 PUNISHMENTS FOR UNREPENTANT.

Zion will be redeemed with justice,
her penitent ones with righteousness.
But rebels and sinners will both be broken,
and those who forsake the LORD will perish.

"You will be ashamed because of the sacred oaks
in which you have delighted;
you will be disgraced because of the gardens
that you have chosen.
You will be like an oak with fading leaves,
like a garden without water.
The mighty man will become tinder
and his work a spark;

        both will burn together,
            with no one to quench the fire."

IDOLS CANNOT SAVE.   Isa. 2:19-21

        Men will flee to caves in the rocks
            and to holes in the ground
        from dread of the LORD
            and the splendor of his majesty,
            when he rises to shake the earth.
        In that day men will throw away
            to the rodents and bats
        their idols of silver and idols of gold,
            which they made to worship.
        They will flee to caverns in the rocks
            and to the overhanging crags
        from dread of the LORD
            and the splendor of his majesty,
            when he rises to shake the earth.

MEN CANNOT SAVE.   Isa.
                                                         2:22-3:7

        Stop trusting in man,
            who has but a breath in his nostrils.
        Of what account is he?
        See now, the Lord,
            the LORD Almighty,
        is about to take from Jerusalem and Judah
            both supply and support:
        all supplies of food and all supplies of water,
            the hero and warrior,
        the judge and prophet,
            the soothsayer and elder,
        the captain of fifty and man of rank,
            the counselor, skilled craftsman and clever enchanter.

        I will make boys their officials;
            mere children will govern them.
        People will oppress each other—
            man against man, neighbor against neighbor.
        The young will rise up against the old,
            the base against the honorable.

        A man will seize one of his brothers
            at his father's home, and say,
        "You have a cloak, you be our leader;
            take charge of this heap of ruins!"
        But in that day he will cry out,
            "I have no remedy.
        I have no food or clothing in my house;
            do not make me the leader of the people."

A CALL FOR REASON.   Isa. 1:18-20

        "Come now, let us reason together,"
            says the LORD.

"Though your sins are like scarlet,
    they shall be as white as snow;
though they are red as crimson,
    they shall be like wool.
If you are willing and obedient,
    you will eat the best from the land;
but if you resist and rebel,
    you will be devoured by the sword."
                    For the mouth of the LORD has spoken.

Isa. 4:2-6   A SPIRITUAL RESTORATION.   In that day the Branch of the LORD will be beautiful and glorious, and the fruit of the land will be the pride and glory of the survivors in Israel. Those who are left in Zion, who remain in Jerusalem, will be called holy, all who are recorded among the living in Jerusalem. The Lord will wash away the filth of the women of Zion; he will cleanse the bloodstains from Jerusalem by a spirit[e] of judgment and a spirit[e] of fire. Then the LORD will create over all of Mount Zion and over those who assemble there a cloud of smoke by day and a glow of flaming fire by night; over all the glory will be a canopy. It will be a shelter and shade from the heat of the day, and a refuge and hiding place from the storm and rain.

Isa. 2:1-5   THE LAST DAYS.   This is what Isaiah son of Amoz saw concerning Judah and Jerusalem:

In the last days

        the mountain of the LORD's temple will be established
            as chief among the mountains;
        it will be raised above the hills,
            and all nations will stream to it.

Many peoples will come and say,

    "Come, let us go up to the mountain of the LORD,
        to the house of the God of Jacob.
    He will teach us his ways,
        so that we may walk in his paths."
    The law will go out from Zion,
        the word of the LORD from Jerusalem.
    He will judge between the nations
        and will settle disputes for many peoples.
    They will beat their swords into plowshares
        and their spears into pruning hooks.
    Nation will not take up sword against nation,
        nor will they train for war anymore.

    Come, O house of Jacob,
        let us walk in the light of the LORD.

The focus turns back temporarily to Israel and to the political upheaval there at this time.

[e]Or *the Spirit*

In Israel

TIGLATH-PILESER CHALLENGES.   Then Pul*f* king of Assyria invaded
the land, and Menahem gave him a thousand talents*g* of silver to gain his
support and strengthen his own hold on the kingdom. Menahem exacted
this money from Israel. Every wealthy man had to contribute fifty shekels*h*
of silver to be given to the king of Assyria. So the king of Assyria withdrew
and stayed in the land no longer.

**2 Kgs.
15:19,20**

DEATH OF MENAHEM.   As for the other events of Menahem's reign,
and all he did, are they not written in the book of the annals of the kings
of Israel? Menahem rested with his fathers.

**2 Kgs.
15:21,22a
(742 B.C.)**

PEKAHIAH KING OF ISRAEL.   And Pekahiah his son succeeded him as
king.
    In the fiftieth year of Azariah king of Judah, Pekahiah son of Menahem
became king of Israel in Samaria, and he reigned two years.

**2 Kgs.
15:22b,23
(742 B.C.)**

PEKAHIAH'S CHARACTER.   Pekahiah did evil in the eyes of the LORD.
He did not turn away from the sins of Jeroboam son of Nebat, which he
had caused Israel to commit.

**2 Kgs.
15:24**

PEKAHIAH ASSASSINATED.   One of his chief officers, Pekah son of
Remaliah, conspired against him. Taking fifty men of Gilead with him, he
assassinated Pekahiah, along with Argob and Arieh, in the citadel of the
royal palace at Samaria. So Pekah killed Pekahiah and succeeded him as
king.
    The other events of Pekahiah's reign, and all he did, are written in the
book of the annals of the kings of Israel.

**2 Kgs.
15:25,26
(741 B.C.)**

PEKAH BEGINS SOLE RULE.   In the fifty-second year of Azariah king
of Judah, Pekah son of Remaliah became king of Israel in Samaria, and he
reigned twenty years.

**2 Kgs.
15:27
(741 B.C.)**

PEKAH'S CHARACTER.   He did evil in the eyes of the LORD. He did not
turn away from the sins of Jeroboam son of Nebat, which he had caused
Israel to commit.

**2 Kgs.
15:28**

In Judah

DEATH OF UZZIAH.   The other events of Uzziah's reign, from beginning to end, are recorded by the prophet Isaiah son of Amoz. Uzziah rested with his fathers and was buried near them in a field for burial that
belonged to the kings, for people said, "He had leprosy."

2 Kgs.
15:6,7a
2 Chron.
26:22,23a
(739 B.C.)

JOTHAM BEGINS SOLE REIGN.   And Jotham his son succeeded him as
king.
    In the second year of Pekah son of Remaliah king of Israel, Jotham son
of Uzziah king of Judah began to reign. He was twenty-five years old
when he became king, and he reigned in Jerusalem sixteen years. His
mother's name was Jerusha daughter of Zadok.

2 Kgs.
15:7b,32,33
2 Chron.
26:23b
27:1,8
(739 B.C.)

JOTHAM'S CHARACTER.   He did what was right in the eyes of the
LORD, just as his father Uzziah had done, but unlike him he did not enter
the temple of the LORD.

2 Kgs.
15:34
2 Chron.
27:2a

---

*f*Also called *Tiglath-Pileser*   *g*That is, about 37 tons (about 34 metric tons)   *h*That is,
about 1 1/4 pounds (about 0.6 kilogram)

2 Kgs.
15:35a
2 Chron.
27:2b

JUDAH'S SPIRITUAL CONDITION.   The people, however, continued their corrupt practices.

Isaiah's Mission Told in Vision

As Jotham assumes full control upon the death of Uzziah, the prophet Isaiah receives a vision in which he sees himself in the heavenly presence of God. Isaiah is told to go to the people of Judah with a message which God knows the people will not accept. Nevertheless Isaiah is told to keep on preaching even until their rejection has brought them utter ruin.

Isa. 6:1-13   ISAIAH'S VISION.   In the year that King Uzziah died, I saw the Lord seated on a throne, high and exalted, and the train of his robe filled the temple. Above him were seraphs, each with six wings: With two wings they covered their faces, with two they covered their feet, and with two they were flying. And they were calling to one another:

> "Holy, holy, holy is the LORD Almighty;
> the whole earth is full of his glory."

At the sound of their voices the doorposts and thresholds shook and the temple was filled with smoke.

"Woe to me!" I cried. "I am ruined! For I am a man of unclean lips, and I live among a people of unclean lips, and my eyes have seen the King, the LORD Almighty."

Then one of the seraphs flew to me with a live coal in his hand, which he had taken with tongs from the altar. With it he touched my mouth and said, "See, this has touched your lips; your guilt is taken away and your sin atoned for."

Then I heard the voice of the Lord saying, "Whom shall I send? And who will go for us?"

And I said, "Here am I. Send me!"

He said, "Go and tell this people:

> "'Be ever hearing, but never understanding;
>   be ever seeing, but never perceiving.'
> Make the heart of this people calloused;
>   make their ears dull
>   and close their eyes.[i]
> Otherwise they might see with their eyes,
>   hear with their ears,
>   understand with their hearts,
>   and turn and be healed."

Then I said, "For how long, O Lord?"

And he answered:

> "Until the cities lie ruined
>   and without inhabitant,

[i]Hebrew; Septuagint 'You will be ever hearing, but never understanding; / you will be ever seeing, but never perceiving.' / [10]This people's heart has become calloused; / they hardly hear with their ears, / and they have closed their eyes

until the houses are left deserted
and the fields ruined and ravaged,
until the LORD has sent everyone far away
and the land is utterly forsaken.
And though a tenth remains in the land,
it will again be laid waste.
But as the terebinth and oak
leave stumps when they are cut down,
so the holy seed will be the stump in the land."

A brief record of Jotham's administration follows.

JOTHAM'S BUILDINGS.   Jotham rebuilt the Upper Gate of the temple of the LORD and did extensive work on the wall at the hill of Ophel. He built towns in the Judean hills and forts and towers in the wooded areas.

2 Kgs.
15:35b
2 Chron.
27:3,4

AMMONITES SUBJUGATED.   Jotham made war on the king of the Ammonites and conquered them. That year the Ammonites paid him a hundred talents[j] of silver, ten thousand cors[k] of wheat and ten thousand cors of barley. The Ammonites brought him the same amount also in the second and third years.

2 Chron.
27:5,6

Jotham grew powerful because he walked steadfastly before the LORD his God.

The Prophecies of Micah

s Amos went to the people of the north, so the prophet Micah comes to the people of Judah, and the message is the same: God does not appreciate empty worship from those whose lives are morally and ethically bankrupt. He desires righteous thoughts and deeds, and not just a show of traditional formal worship. This is also the message of Micah's contemporary, Isaiah, whose writings are often strikingly similar in content. God's message through all of his prophets is unmistakably the same message—of sin, destruction, exile, restoration, and the coming of a Messiah to save the world.

Micah's predictions of future events are more numerous and specific than those of other prophets. For example, Micah predicts the fall of Samaria, the invasion of Judah by Sennacherib, the fall of Jerusalem, the destruction of the temple, the exile in Babylon, the return from captivity to peace and prosperity, and the birth of the Messiah in the city of Bethlehem.

The three major discourses which follow are representative of Micah's preaching to the people of Judah.

PREFACE.   The word of the LORD that came to Micah of Moresheth during the reigns of Jotham, Ahaz and Hezekiah, kings of Judah—the vision he saw concerning Samaria and Jerusalem.

Micah 1:1

---

[j]That is, about 3 3/4 tons (about 3.4 metric tons)   [k]That is, probably about 62,000 bushels (about 2,200 kiloliters)

First Discourse

**Micah
1:2-7**

JUDGMENT AGAINST ISRAEL.

> Hear, O peoples, all of you,
>> listen, O earth and all who are in it,
> that the Sovereign LORD may witness against you,
>> the Lord from his holy temple.
>
> Look! The LORD is coming from his dwelling place;
>> he comes down and treads the high places of the earth.
> The mountains melt beneath him
>> and the valleys split apart,
> like wax before the fire,
>> like water rushing down a slope.
> All this is because of Jacob's transgression,
>> because of the sins of the house of Israel.
> What is Jacob's transgression?
>> Is it not Samaria?
> What is Judah's high place?
>> Is it not Jerusalem?
>
> "Therefore I will make Samaria a heap of rubble,
>> a place for planting vineyards.
> I will pour her stones into the valley
>> and lay bare her foundations.
> All her idols will be broken to pieces;
>> all her temple gifts will be burned with fire;
>> I will destroy all her images.
> Since she gathered her gifts from the wages of prostitutes,
>> as the wages of prostitutes they will again be used."

**Micah
1:8-16**

JUDAH LIKE ISRAEL.

> Because of this I will weep and wail;
>> I will go about barefoot and naked.
> I will howl like a jackal
>> and moan like an owl.
> For her wound is incurable;
>> it has come to Judah.
> It[l] has reached the very gate of my people,
>> even to Jerusalem itself.
> Tell it not in Gath[m];
>> weep not at all.[n]
> In Beth Ophrah[o]
>> roll in the dust.
> Pass on in nakedness and shame,
>> you who live in Shaphir.[p]
> Those who live in Zaanan[q]
>> will not come out.
> Beth Ezel is in mourning;

---

[l]Or *He*   [m]*Gath* sounds like the Hebrew for *tell*.   [n]Hebrew; Septuagint may suggest *not in Acco*. The Hebrew for *in Acco* sounds like the Hebrew for *weep*.   [o]*Beth Ophrah* means *house of dust*.   [p]*Shaphir* means *pleasant*.   [q]*Zaanan* sounds like the Hebrew for *come out.*

its protection is taken from you.
Those who live in Maroth[r] writhe in pain,
    waiting for relief,
because disaster has come from the LORD,
    even to the gate of Jerusalem.
You who live in Lachish,[s]
    harness the team to the chariot.
You were the beginning of sin
    to the Daughter of Zion,
for the transgressions of Israel
    were found in you.
Therefore you will give parting gifts
    to Moresheth Gath.
The town of Aczib[t] will prove deceptive
    to the kings of Israel.
I will bring a conqueror against you
    who live in Mareshah.[u]
He who is the glory of Israel
    will come to Adullam.
Shave your heads in mourning
    for the children in whom you delight;
make yourselves as bald as the vulture,
    for they will go from you into exile.

SIN OF COVETOUSNESS.

Micah
2:1,2

Woe to those who plan iniquity,
    to those who plot evil on their beds!
At morning's light they carry it out
    because it is in their power to do it.
They covet fields and seize them,
    and houses, and take them.
They defraud a man of his home,
    a fellowman of his inheritance.

REWARD OF GREED.   Therefore, the LORD says:

Micah
2:3-5

"I am planning disaster against this people,
    from which you cannot save yourselves.
You will no longer walk proudly,
    for it will be a time of calamity.
In that day men will ridicule you;
    they will taunt you with this mournful song:
'We are utterly ruined;
    my people's possession is divided up.
He takes it from me!
    He assigns our fields to traitors.'"

Therefore you will have no one in the assembly of the LORD
    to divide the land by lot.

---

[r]*Maroth* sounds like the Hebrew for *bitter.*   [s]*Lachish* sounds like the Hebrew for *team.*
[t]*Aczib* means *deception.*   [u]*Mareshah* sounds like the Hebrew for *conqueror.*

Micah 2:6-11   DESIRE FOR FALSE PROPHETS.

"Do not prophesy," their prophets say.
"Do not prophesy about these things;
    disgrace will not overtake us."
Should it be said, O house of Jacob:
"Is the Spirit of the LORD angry?
    Does he do such things?"

"Do not my words do good
    to him whose ways are upright?
Lately my people have risen up
    like an enemy.
You strip off the rich robe
    from those who pass by without a care,
    like men returning from battle.
You drive the women of my people
    from their pleasant homes.
You take away my blessing
    from their children forever.
Get up, go away!
    For this is not your resting place,
because it is defiled,
    it is ruined, beyond all remedy.
If a liar and deceiver comes and says,
    'I will prophesy for you plenty of wine and beer,'
    he would be just the prophet for this people!

Micah 2:12,13   DELIVERANCE PROMISED.

"I will surely gather all of you, O Jacob;
    I will surely bring together the remnant of Israel.
I will bring them together like sheep in a pen,
    like a flock in its pasture;
    the place will throng with people.
One who breaks open the way will go up before them;
    they will break through the gate and go out.
Their king will pass through before them,
    the LORD at their head."

Second Discourse

Micah 3:1-4   LEADERS REBUKED.   Then I said,

"Listen, you leaders of Jacob,
    you rulers of the house of Israel.
Should you not know justice,
    you who hate good and love evil;
who tear the skin from my people
    and the flesh from their bones;
who eat my people's flesh,
    strip off their skin
    and break their bones in pieces;
who chop them up like meat for the pan,
    like flesh for the pot?"

Then they will cry out to the LORD,
    but he will not answer them.
At that time he will hide his face from them
    because of the evil they have done.

FALSE PROPHETS REBUKED.   This is what the LORD says:

Micah
3:5-7

"As for the prophets
    who lead my people astray,
if one feeds them,
    they proclaim 'peace';
if he does not,
    they prepare to wage war against him.
Therefore night will come over you, without visions,
    and darkness, without divination.
The sun will set for the prophets,
    and the day will go dark for them.
The seers will be ashamed
    and the diviners disgraced.
They will all cover their faces
    because there is no answer from God."

MICAH HAS GOD'S SPIRIT.

Micah 3:8

But as for me, I am filled with power,
    with the Spirit of the LORD,
    and with justice and might,
to declare to Jacob his transgression,
    to Israel his sin.

SINS OF THE RULERS.

Micah
3:9-12

Hear this, you leaders of the house of Jacob,
    you rulers of the house of Israel,
who despise justice
    and distort all that is right;
who build Zion with bloodshed,
    and Jerusalem with wickedness.
Her leaders judge for a bribe,
    her priests teach for a price,
    and her prophets tell fortunes for money.
Yet they lean upon the LORD and say,
    "Is not the LORD among us?
    No disaster will come upon us."
Therefore because of you,
    Zion will be plowed like a field,
Jerusalem will become a heap of rubble,
    the temple hill a mound overgrown with thickets.

COMING OF MESSIAH.   In the last days

Micah
4:1-5

the mountain of the LORD's temple will be established
    as chief among the mountains;
it will be raised above the hills,
    and peoples will stream to it.

Many nations will come and say,

"Come, let us go up to the mountain of the LORD,
　to the house of the God of Jacob.
He will teach us his ways,
　so that we may walk in his paths."
The law will go out from Zion,
　the word of the LORD from Jerusalem.
He will judge between many peoples
　and will settle disputes for strong nations far and wide.
They will beat their swords into plowshares
　and their spears into pruning hooks.
Nation will not take up sword against nation,
　nor will they train for war anymore.
Every man will sit under his own vine
　and under his own fig tree,
and no one will make them afraid,
　for the LORD Almighty has spoken.
All the nations may walk
　in the name of their gods;
we will walk in the name of the LORD
　our God for ever and ever.

**Micah
4:6-13**

RESTORATION OF REMNANT.　"In that day," declares the LORD,

"I will gather the lame;
　I will assemble the exiles
　and those I have brought to grief.
I will make the lame a remnant,
　those driven away a strong nation.
The LORD will rule over them in Mount Zion
　from that day and forever.
As for you, O watchtower of the flock,
　O stronghold[v] of the Daughter of Zion,
the former dominion will be restored to you;
　kingship will come to the Daughter of Jerusalem."

Why do you now cry aloud—
　have you no king?
Has your counselor perished,
　that pain seizes you like that of a woman in labor?
Writhe in agony, O Daughter of Zion,
　like a woman in labor,
for now you must leave the city
　to camp in the open field.
You will go to Babylon;
　there you will be rescued.
There the LORD will redeem you
　out of the hand of your enemies.

But now many nations
　are gathered against you.

[v]Or *hill*

They say, "Let her be defiled,
let our eyes gloat over Zion!"
But they do not know
the thoughts of the LORD;
they do not understand his plan,
he who gathers them like sheaves to the threshing floor.

"Rise and thresh, O Daughter of Zion,
for I will give you horns of iron;
I will give you hoofs of bronze
and you will break to pieces many nations."

You will devote their ill-gotten gains to the LORD,
their wealth to the Lord of all the earth.

BIRTHPLACE OF MESSIAH.   Micah 5:1-5a

Marshal your troops, O city of troops,*w*
for a siege is laid against us.
They will strike Israel's ruler
on the cheek with a rod.

"But you, Bethlehem Ephrathah,
though you are small among the clans*x* of Judah,
out of you will come for me
one who will be ruler over Israel,
whose origins*y* are from of old,
from ancient times.*z*"

Therefore Israel will be abandoned
until the time when she who is in labor gives birth
and the rest of his brothers return
to join the Israelites.

He will stand and shepherd his flock
in the strength of the LORD,
in the majesty of the name of the LORD his God.
And they will live securely, for then his greatness
will reach to the ends of the earth.
And he will be their peace.

JUDGMENT AGAINST ASSYRIA.   Micah 5:5b-9

When the Assyrian invades our land
and marches through our fortresses,
we will raise against him seven shepherds,
even eight leaders of men.
They will rule*a* the land of Assyria with the sword,
the land of Nimrod with drawn sword.*b*
He will deliver us from the Assyrian
when he invades our land
and marches into our borders.

The remnant of Jacob will be

*w*Or *Strengthen your walls, O walled city*   *x*Or *rulers*   *y*Hebrew *goings out*   *z*Or
from days of eternity   *a*Or *crush*   *b*Or *Nimrod in its gates*

in the midst of many peoples
like dew from the LORD,
 like showers on the grass,
which do not wait for man
 or linger for mankind.
The remnant of Jacob will be among the nations,
 in the midst of many peoples,
like a lion among the beasts of the forest,
 like a young lion among flocks of sheep,
which mauls and mangles as it goes,
 and no one can rescue.
Your hand will be lifted up in triumph over your enemies,
 and all your foes will be destroyed.

Micah 5:10-15

PAGANISM TO BE DESTROYED. "In that day," declares the LORD,

"I will destroy your horses from among you
 and demolish your chariots.
I will destroy the cities of your land
 and tear down all your strongholds.
I will destroy your witchcraft
 and you will no longer cast spells.
I will destroy your carved images
 and your sacred stones from among you;
you will no longer bow down
 to the work of your hands.
I will uproot from among you your Asherah poles[c]
 and demolish your cities.
I will take vengeance in anger and wrath
 upon the nations that have not obeyed me."

Third Discourse

Micah 6:1-5

GOD'S CHARGE AGAINST JUDAH. Listen to what the LORD says:

"Stand up, plead your case before the mountains;
 let the hills hear what you have to say.
Hear, O mountains, the LORD's accusation;
 listen, you everlasting foundations of the earth.
For the LORD has a case against his people;
 he is lodging a charge against Israel.

"My people, what have I done to you?
 How have I burdened you? Answer me.
I brought you up out of Egypt
 and redeemed you from the land of slavery.
I sent Moses to lead you,
 also Aaron and Miriam.
My people, remember
 what Balak king of Moab counseled
 and what Balaam son of Beor answered.
Remember ⌊your journey⌋ from Shittim to Gilgal,
 that you may know the righteous acts of the LORD."

---

[c] That is, symbols of the goddess Asherah

WHAT GOD REALLY WANTS.

With what shall I come before the LORD
    and bow down before the exalted God?
Shall I come before him with burnt offerings,
    with calves a year old?
Will the LORD be pleased with thousands of rams,
    with ten thousand rivers of oil?
Shall I offer my firstborn for my transgression,
    the fruit of my body for the sin of my soul?
He has showed you, O man, what is good.
    And what does the LORD require of you?
To act justly and to love mercy
    and to walk humbly with your God.

JUDAH'S SIN AND PUNISHMENT.

Listen! The LORD is calling to the city—
    and to fear your name is wisdom—
    "Heed the rod and the One who appointed it.*d*
Am I still to forget, O wicked house,
    your ill-gotten treasures
    and the short ephah,*e* which is accursed?
Shall I acquit a man with dishonest scales,
    with a bag of false weights?
Her rich men are violent;
    her people are liars
    and their tongues speak deceitfully.
Therefore, I have begun to destroy you,
    to ruin you because of your sins.
You will eat but not be satisfied;
    your stomach will still be empty.*f*
You will store up but save nothing,
    because what you save I will give to the sword.
You will plant but not harvest;
    you will press olives but not use the oil on yourselves,
    you will crush grapes but not drink the wine.
You have observed the statutes of Omri
    and all the practices of Ahab's house,
    and you have followed their traditions.
Therefore I will give you over to ruin
    and your people to derision;
    you will bear the scorn of the nations.*g*"

MISERY OF JUDAH'S SIN.

What misery is mine!
I am like one who gathers summer fruit
    at the gleaning of the vineyard;
there is no cluster of grapes to eat,
    none of the early figs that I crave.

---

d The meaning of the Hebrew for this line is uncertain.   *e* An ephah was a dry
measure.   *f* The meaning of the Hebrew for this word is uncertain.   *g* Septuagint;
Hebrew *scorn due my people*

The godly have been swept from the land;
  not one upright man remains.
All men lie in wait to shed blood;
  each hunts his brother with a net.
Both hands are skilled in doing evil;
  the ruler demands gifts,
the judge accepts bribes,
  the powerful dictate what they desire—
  they all conspire together.
The best of them is like a brier,
  the most upright worse than a thorn hedge.
The day of your watchmen has come,
  the day God visits you.
  Now is the time of their confusion.
Do not trust a neighbor;
  put no confidence in a friend.
Even with her who lies in your embrace
  be careful of your words.
For a son dishonors his father,
  a daughter rises up against her mother,
a daughter-in-law against her mother-in-law—
  a man's enemies are the members of his own household.

But as for me, I watch in hope for the LORD,
  I wait for God my Savior;
  my God will hear me.

**Micah
7:8-13**

THE RENEWAL OF ISRAEL.

Do not gloat over me, my enemy!
  Though I have fallen, I will rise.
Though I sit in darkness,
  the LORD will be my light.
Because I have sinned against him,
  I will bear the LORD's wrath,
until he pleads my case
  and establishes my right.
He will bring me out into the light;
  I will see his righteousness.
Then my enemy will see it
  and will be covered with shame,
she who said to me,
  "Where is the LORD your God?"
My eyes will see her downfall;
  even now she will be trampled underfoot
  like mire in the streets.

The day for building your walls will come,
  the day for extending your boundaries.
In that day people will come to you
  from Assyria and the cities of Egypt,
even from Egypt to the Euphrates
  and from sea to sea
  and from mountain to mountain.

The earth will become desolate because of its inhabitants,
    as the result of their deeds.

PRAYER AND PRAISE.

Micah
7:14-20

Shepherd your people with your staff,
    the flock of your inheritance,
which lives by itself in a forest,
    in fertile pasturelands.[h]
Let them feed in Bashan and Gilead
    as in days long ago.

"As in the days when you came out of Egypt,
    I will show them my wonders."

Nations will see and be ashamed,
    deprived of all their power.
They will lay their hands on their mouths
    and their ears will become deaf.
They will lick dust like a snake,
    like creatures that crawl on the ground.
They will come trembling out of their dens;
    they will turn in fear to the LORD our God
    and will be afraid of you.
Who is a God like you,
    who pardons sin and forgives the transgression
    of the remnant of his inheritance?
You do not stay angry forever
    but delight to show mercy.
You will again have compassion on us;
    you will tread our sins underfoot
    and hurl all our iniquities into the depths of the sea.
You will be true to Jacob,
    and show mercy to Abraham,
as you pledged on oath to our fathers
    in days long ago.

Early Beginnings of Captivity

*T*he warnings of the prophets that Israel would fall into Assyrian captivity are already starting to come true. It will be several more years before total collapse takes place, but the record indicates that even now, during Pekah's reign, many of the people of Reuben, Gad, and Manasseh are taken captive by Tiglath-Pileser (King Pul).

In Israel

FIRST CAPTIVES TAKEN. ᴷᵍIn the time of Pekah king of Israel, Tiglath-Pileser king of Assyria came and took Ijon, Abel Beth Maacah, Janoah, Kedesh and Hazor. He took Gilead and Galilee, including all the land of Naphtali, and deported the people to Assyria. ᶜʰThe people of the half-

2 Kgs.
15:29
1 Chron.
5:23-26
Assyria

[h]Or *in the middle of Carmel*

tribe of Manasseh were numerous; they settled in the land from Bashan to Baal Hermon, that is, to Senir (Mount Hermon).

These were the heads of their families: Epher, Ishi, Eliel, Azriel, Jeremiah, Hodaviah and Jahdiel. They were brave warriors, famous men, and heads of their families. But they were unfaithful to the God of their fathers and prostituted themselves to the gods of the peoples of the land, whom God had destroyed before them. So the God of Israel stirred up the spirit of Pul king of Assyria (that is, Tiglath-Pileser king of Assyria), who took the Reubenites, the Gadites and the half-tribe of Manasseh into exile. He took them to Halah, Habor, Hara and the river of Gozan, where they are to this day.

War Between Syria, Israel, and Judah

*T*his shocking turn of events causes both Israel and Syria to fear the Assyrians. They draw together in an unusual alliance and even call upon Judah to join them. When Judah refuses to become involved, Syria and Israel turn against Judah in an effort to force her support. This strange conflict begins when Jotham is in power, and continues during the reign of his son Ahaz, who has apparently been a co-regent for nine years.

In Judah

2 Kgs.
15:37

SYRIA AND ISRAEL THREATEN.   (In those days the LORD began to send Rezin king of Aram and Pekah son of Remaliah against Judah.)

In Israel

2 Kgs.
15:31,30
(732 B.C.)

PEKAH ASSASSINATED.   As for the other events of Pekah's reign, and all he did, are they not written in the book of the annals of the kings of Israel? Then Hoshea son of Elah conspired against Pekah son of Remaliah. He attacked and assassinated him, and then succeeded him as king in the twentieth year of Jotham son of Uzziah.

2 Kgs. 17:1
(732 B.C.)

HOSHEA KING OF ISRAEL.   In the twelfth year of Ahaz king of Judah, Hoshea son of Elah became king of Israel in Samaria, and he reigned nine years.

2 Kgs. 17:2

HOSHEA'S CHARACTER.   He did evil in the eyes of the LORD, but not like the kings of Israel who preceded him.

In Judah

2 Kgs.
15:36,38a
2 Chron.
27:7,9a
(730 B.C.)

DEATH OF JOTHAM.   As for the other events of Jotham's reign, and what he did, are they not written in the book of the annals of the kings of Judah? Jotham rested with his fathers and was buried with them in the City of David, the city of his father.

2 Kgs.
15:38b
16:1,2a
2 Chron.
27:9b; 28:1a

AHAZ BEGINS SOLE REIGN.   And Ahaz his son succeeded him as king. In the seventeenth year of Pekah son of Remaliah, Ahaz son of Jotham king of Judah began to reign. Ahaz was twenty years old when he became king, and he reigned in Jerusalem sixteen years.

2 Kgs.
16:2b-4
2 Chron.
28:1b-4

CHARACTER OF AHAZ.   Unlike David his father, he did not do what was right in the eyes of the LORD. He walked in the ways of the kings of Israel and also made cast idols for worshiping the Baals. He burned sacrifices in the Valley of Ben Hinnom and sacrificed his sons in the fire, following the detestable ways of the nations the LORD had driven out before the Israelites. He offered sacrifices and burned incense at the high places, on the hilltops and under every spreading tree.

Isaiah Prophesies About a Savior

*I*saiah records the challenge made to Ahaz by King Rezin of Aram and King Pekah of Israel, and then relates his own peculiar exchange with Ahaz. God is ready to defend Judah despite her wickedness, and tells Ahaz to request a sign. This he arrogantly refuses to do. Isaiah then says that the Lord himself will give Ahaz a sign, whether he likes it or not. The sign evidently has nothing to do with the pending battle, but rather with the coming Messiah, or Savior. At first it appears that Isaiah is merely telling of impending political and military events: Assyria is bringing destruction and, after some time, Syria and Israel will be captured. Assyria herself will then be destroyed, and a remnant of God's people will be brought back to reestablish a Jewish nation.

Laced throughout that narrative, however, are messianic prophecies. The Savior will be called Immanuel at his birth. He will be a descendant of King David, whose father's name was Jesse. He will establish a kingdom and draw to himself a remnant of those who love God. And in the last days there will be justice, peace, and rejoicing in the Savior's kingdom.

AHAZ LEARNS OF ALLIANCE.　When Ahaz son of Jotham, the son of Uzziah, was king of Judah, King Rezin of Aram and Pekah son of Remaliah king of Israel marched up to fight against Jerusalem, but they could not overpower it.

Isa. 7:1,2

Now the house of David was told, "Aram has allied itself with*[i]* Ephraim"; so the hearts of Ahaz and his people were shaken, as the trees of the forest are shaken by the wind.

GOD'S MESSAGE TO AHAZ.　Then the LORD said to Isaiah, "Go out, you and your son Shear-Jashub,*[j]* to meet Ahaz at the end of the aqueduct of the Upper Pool, on the road to the Washerman's Field. Say to him, 'Be careful, keep calm and don't be afraid. Do not lose heart because of these two smoldering stubs of firewood—because of the fierce anger of Rezin and Aram and of the son of Remaliah. Aram, Ephraim and Remaliah's son have plotted your ruin, saying, "Let us invade Judah; let us tear it apart and divide it among ourselves, and make the son of Tabeel king over it." Yet this is what the Sovereign LORD says:

Isa. 7:3-9

" 'It will not take place,
　　it will not happen,
　for the head of Aram is Damascus,
　　and the head of Damascus is only Rezin.
　Within sixty-five years
　　Ephraim will be too shattered to be a people.
　The head of Ephraim is Samaria,
　　and the head of Samaria is only Remaliah's son.
　If you do not stand firm in your faith,

---

[i]Or has set up camp in　　[j]Shear-Jashub means a remnant will return.

you will not stand at all.' "

Isa. 7:10-12 AHAZ REFUSES A SIGN.   Again the LORD spoke to Ahaz, "Ask the LORD your God for a sign, whether in the deepest depths or in the highest heights."

But Ahaz said, "I will not ask; I will not put the LORD to the test."

Isa. 7:13-15 SAVIOR TO BE IMMANUEL.   Then Isaiah said, "Hear now, you house of David! Is it not enough to try the patience of men? Will you try the patience of my God also? Therefore the Lord himself will give you[k] a sign: The virgin will be with child and will give birth to a son, and[l] will call him Immanuel.[m] He will eat curds and honey when he knows enough to reject the wrong and choose the right.

Isa. 7:16-25 ASSYRIA TO DESTROY.   But before the boy knows enough to reject the wrong and choose the right, the land of the two kings you dread will be laid waste. The LORD will bring on you and on your people and on the house of your father a time unlike any since Ephraim broke away from Judah—he will bring the king of Assyria."

In that day the LORD will whistle for flies from the distant streams of Egypt and for bees from the land of Assyria. They will all come and settle in the steep ravines and in the crevices in the rocks, on all the thornbushes and at all the water holes. In that day the Lord will use a razor hired from beyond the River[n]—the king of Assyria—to shave your head and the hair of your legs, and to take off your beards also. In that day, a man will keep alive a young cow and two goats. And because of the abundance of the milk they give, he will have curds to eat. All who remain in the land will eat curds and honey. In that day, in every place where there were a thousand vines worth a thousand silver shekels,[o] there will be only briers and thorns. Men will go there with bow and arrow, for the land will be covered with briers and thorns. As for all the hills once cultivated by the hoe, you will no longer go there for fear of the briers and thorns; they will become places where cattle are turned loose and where sheep run.

Isa. 8:1-10 SYRIA AND ISRAEL TO FALL.   The LORD said to me, "Take a large scroll and write on it with an ordinary pen: Maher-Shalal-Hash-Baz.[p] And I will call in Uriah the priest and Zechariah son of Jeberekiah as reliable witnesses for me."

Then I went to the prophetess, and she conceived and gave birth to a son. And the LORD said to me, "Name him Maher-Shalal-Hash-Baz. Before the boy knows how to say 'My father' or 'My mother,' the wealth of Damascus and the plunder of Samaria will be carried off by the king of Assyria."

The LORD spoke to me again:

> "Because this people has rejected
>   the gently flowing waters of Shiloah
>   and rejoices over Rezin
>   and the son of Remaliah,
>   therefore the Lord is about to bring against them

---

[k]The Hebrew is plural.   [l]Masoretic Text; Dead Sea Scrolls *and he* or *and they*
[m]*Immanuel* means *God with us.*   [n]That is, the Euphrates   [o]That is, about 25 pounds
(about 11.5 kilograms)   [p]*Maher-Shalal-Hash-Baz* means *quick to the plunder, swift to the spoil*

the mighty floodwaters of the River*q*—
   the king of Assyria with all his pomp.
It will overflow all its channels,
   run over all its banks
and sweep on into Judah, swirling over it,
   passing through it and reaching up to the neck.
Its outspread wings will cover the breadth of your land,
   O Immanuel*r*!"

Raise the war cry,*s* you nations, and be shattered!
   Listen, all you distant lands.
Prepare for battle, and be shattered!
   Prepare for battle, and be shattered!
Devise your strategy, but it will be thwarted;
   propose your plan, but it will not stand,
for God is with us.*t*

CALL TO TRUST GOD.   The LORD spoke to me with his strong hand   Isa. 8:11-18
upon me, warning me not to follow the way of this people. He said:

"Do not call conspiracy
   everything that these people call conspiracy*u*;
do not fear what they fear,
   and do not dread it.
The LORD Almighty is the one you are to regard as holy,
   he is the one you are to fear,
   he is the one you are to dread,
and he will be a sanctuary;
   but for both houses of Israel he will be
a stone that causes men to stumble
   and a rock that makes them fall.
And for the people of Jerusalem he will be
   a trap and a snare.
Many of them will stumble;
   they will fall and be broken,
   they will be snared and captured."

Bind up the testimony
   and seal up the law among my disciples.
I will wait for the LORD,
   who is hiding his face from the house of Jacob.
I will put my trust in him.

Here am I, and the children the LORD has given me. We are signs and
symbols in Israel from the LORD Almighty, who dwells on Mount Zion.

OTHERS CANNOT BE TRUSTED.   When men tell you to consult medi-   Isa. 8:19-22
ums and spiritists, who whisper and mutter, should not a people inquire
of their God? Why consult the dead on behalf of the living? To the law and
to the testimony! If they do not speak according to this word, they have no
light of dawn. Distressed and hungry, they will roam through the land;
when they are famished, they will become enraged and, looking upward,

*q*That is, the Euphrates   *r*Immanuel* means *God with us*.   *s*Or *Do your worst*
*t*Hebrew *Immanuel*   *u*Or *Do not call for a treaty / every time these people call for a treaty

will curse their king and their God. Then they will look toward the earth and see only distress and darkness and fearful gloom, and they will be thrust into utter darkness.

Isa. 9:1-7 SAVIOR'S KINGDOM COMING.   Nevertheless, there will be no more gloom for those who were in distress. In the past he humbled the land of Zebulun and the land of Naphtali, but in the future he will honor Galilee of the Gentiles, by the way of the sea, along the Jordan—

> The people walking in darkness
>> have seen a great light;
> on those living in the land of the shadow of death[v]
>> a light has dawned.
> You have enlarged the nation
>> and increased their joy;
> they rejoice before you
>> as people rejoice at the harvest,
> as men rejoice
>> when dividing the plunder.
> For as in the day of Midian's defeat,
>> you have shattered
> the yoke that burdens them,
>> the bar across their shoulders,
>> the rod of their oppressor.
> Every warrior's boot used in battle
>> and every garment rolled in blood
> will be destined for burning,
>> will be fuel for the fire.
> For to us a child is born,
>> to us a son is given,
>> and the government will be on his shoulders.
> And he will be called
>> Wonderful Counselor,[w] Mighty God,
>> Everlasting Father, Prince of Peace.
> Of the increase of his government and peace
>> there will be no end.
> He will reign on David's throne
>> and over his kingdom,
> establishing and upholding it
>> with justice and righteousness
>> from that time on and forever.
> The zeal of the LORD Almighty
>> will accomplish this.

Isa. 9:8-21 GOD'S WRATH AGAINST ISRAEL.

> The Lord has sent a message against Jacob;
>> it will fall on Israel.
> All the people will know it—
>> Ephraim and the inhabitants of Samaria—
> who say with pride
>> and arrogance of heart,

vOr land of darkness   *wOr Wonderful, Counselor*

"The bricks have fallen down,
    but we will rebuild with dressed stone;
the fig trees have been felled,
    but we will replace them with cedars."
But the LORD has strengthened Rezin's foes against them
    and has spurred their enemies on.
Arameans from the east and Philistines from the west
    have devoured Israel with open mouth.

Yet for all this, his anger is not turned away,
    his hand is still upraised.

But the people have not returned to him who struck them,
    nor have they sought the LORD Almighty.
So the LORD will cut off from Israel both head and tail,
    both palm branch and reed in a single day;
the elders and prominent men are the head,
    the prophets who teach lies are the tail.
Those who guide this people mislead them,
    and those who are guided are led astray.
Therefore the Lord will take no pleasure in the young men,
    nor will he pity the fatherless and widows,
for everyone is ungodly and wicked,
    every mouth speaks vileness.

Yet for all this, his anger is not turned away,
    his hand is still upraised.

Surely wickedness burns like a fire;
    it consumes briers and thorns,
it sets the forest thickets ablaze,
    so that it rolls upward in a column of smoke.
By the wrath of the LORD Almighty
    the land will be scorched
and the people will be fuel for the fire;
    no one will spare his brother.
On the right they will devour,
    but still be hungry;
on the left they will eat,
    but not be satisfied.
Each will feed on the flesh of his own offspring[x]:
    Manasseh will feed on Ephraim, and Ephraim on
        Manasseh;
    together they will turn against Judah.

Yet for all this, his anger is not turned away,
    his hand is still upraised.

ANGER AGAINST INJUSTICE.

Isa. 10:1-4

Woe to those who make unjust laws,
    to those who issue oppressive decrees,
to deprive the poor of their rights

[x]Or *arm*

and withhold justice from the oppressed of my people,
  making widows their prey
    and robbing the fatherless.
What will you do on the day of reckoning,
  when disaster comes from afar?
To whom will you run for help?
  Where will you leave your riches?
Nothing will remain but to cringe among the captives
  or fall among the slain.

Yet for all this, his anger is not turned away,
  his hand is still upraised.

Isa. 10:5-19 ASSYRIA'S PUNISHMENT.

"Woe to the Assyrian, the rod of my anger,
  in whose hand is the club of my wrath!
I send him against a godless nation,
  I dispatch him against a people who anger me,
to seize loot and snatch plunder,
  and to trample them down like mud in the streets.
But this is not what he intends,
  this is not what he has in mind;
his purpose is to destroy,
  to put an end to many nations.
'Are not my commanders all kings?' he says.
  'Has not Calno fared like Carchemish?
Is not Hamath like Arpad,
  and Samaria like Damascus?
As my hand seized the kingdoms of the idols,
  kingdoms whose images excelled those of Jerusalem and
    Samaria—
shall I not deal with Jerusalem and her images
  as I dealt with Samaria and her idols?'"

When the Lord has finished all his work against Mount Zion and
Jerusalem, he will say, "I will punish the king of Assyria for the willful
pride of his heart and the haughty look in his eyes. For he says:

" 'By the strength of my hand I have done this,
  and by my wisdom, because I have understanding.
I removed the boundaries of nations,
  I plundered their treasures;
  like a mighty one I subdued[y] their kings.
As one reaches into a nest,
  so my hand reached for the wealth of the nations;
as men gather abandoned eggs,
  so I gathered all the countries;
not one flapped a wing,
  or opened its mouth to chirp.'"

Does the ax raise itself above him who swings it,
  or the saw boast against him who uses it?

[y]Or / I subdued the mighty,

As if a rod were to wield him who lifts it up,
 or a club brandish him who is not wood!
Therefore, the Lord, the LORD Almighty,
 will send a wasting disease upon his sturdy warriors;
under his pomp a fire will be kindled
 like a blazing flame.
The Light of Israel will become a fire,
 their Holy One a flame;
in a single day it will burn and consume
 his thorns and his briers.
The splendor of his forests and fertile fields
 it will completely destroy,
 as when a sick man wastes away.
And the remaining trees of his forests will be so few
 that a child could write them down.

REMNANT TO BE SAVED.

Isa.
10:20-23

In that day the remnant of Israel,
 the survivors of the house of Jacob,
will no longer rely on him
 who struck them down
but will truly rely on the LORD,
 the Holy One of Israel.
A remnant will return,[z] a remnant of Jacob
 will return to the Mighty God.
Though your people, O Israel, be like the sand by the sea,
 only a remnant will return.
Destruction has been decreed,
 overwhelming and righteous.
The Lord, the LORD Almighty, will carry out
 the destruction decreed upon the whole land.

CAPTIVITY WILL BE OVERCOME.   Therefore, this is what the Lord, the LORD Almighty, says:

Isa.
10:24-34

"O my people who live in Zion,
 do not be afraid of the Assyrians,
who beat you with a rod
 and lift up a club against you, as Egypt did.
Very soon my anger against you will end
 and my wrath will be directed to their destruction."

The LORD Almighty will lash them with a whip,
 as when he struck down Midian at the rock of Oreb;
and he will raise his staff over the waters,
 as he did in Egypt.
In that day their burden will be lifted from your shoulders,
 their yoke from your neck;
the yoke will be broken
 because you have grown so fat.[a]

They enter Aiath;

---

[z]Hebrew *shear-jashub*   [a]Hebrew; Septuagint *broken / from your shoulders*

they pass through Migron;
they store supplies at Micmash.
They go over the pass, and say,
"We will camp overnight at Geba."
Ramah trembles;
Gibeah of Saul flees.
Cry out, O Daughter of Gallim!
Listen, O Laishah!
Poor Anathoth!
Madmenah is in flight;
the people of Gebim take cover.
This day they will halt at Nob;
they will shake their fist
at the mount of the Daughter of Zion,
at the hill of Jerusalem.

See, the Lord, the LORD Almighty,
will lop off the boughs with great power.
The lofty trees will be felled,
the tall ones will be brought low.
He will cut down the forest thickets with an ax;
Lebanon will fall before the Mighty One.

Isa. 11:1-9   SAVIOR'S LINEAGE FROM DAVID.

A shoot will come up from the stump of Jesse;
from his roots a Branch will bear fruit.
The Spirit of the LORD will rest on him—
the Spirit of wisdom and of understanding,
the Spirit of counsel and of power,
the Spirit of knowledge and of the fear of the LORD—
and he will delight in the fear of the LORD.

He will not judge by what he sees with his eyes,
or decide by what he hears with his ears;
but with righteousness he will judge the needy,
with justice he will give decisions for the poor of the
earth.
He will strike the earth with the rod of his mouth;
with the breath of his lips he will slay the wicked.
Righteousness will be his belt
and faithfulness the sash around his waist.

The wolf will live with the lamb,
the leopard will lie down with the goat,
the calf and the lion and the yearling*b* together;
and a little child will lead them.
The cow will feed with the bear,
their young will lie down together,
and the lion will eat straw like the ox.
The infant will play near the hole of the cobra,
and the young child put his hand into the viper's nest.

*b*Hebrew; Septuagint *lion will feed*

They will neither harm nor destroy
on all my holy mountain,
for the earth will be full of the knowledge of the LORD
as the waters cover the sea.

SAVIOR TO GATHER REMNANT.   In that day the Root of Jesse will   Isa.
stand as a banner for the peoples; the nations will rally to him, and his   11:10-16
place of rest will be glorious. In that day the Lord will reach out his hand
a second time to reclaim the remnant that is left of his people from Assyria,
from Lower Egypt, from Upper Egypt, *c* from Cush,*d* from Elam, from Babylonia, *e* from Hamath and from the islands of the sea.

He will raise a banner for the nations
and gather the exiles of Israel;
he will assemble the scattered people of Judah
from the four quarters of the earth.
Ephraim's jealousy will vanish,
and Judah's enemies *f* will be cut off;
Ephraim will not be jealous of Judah,
nor Judah hostile toward Ephraim.
They will swoop down on the slopes of Philistia to the
west;
together they will plunder the people to the east.
They will lay hands on Edom and Moab,
and the Ammonites will be subject to them.
The LORD will dry up
the gulf of the Egyptian sea;
with a scorching wind he will sweep his hand
over the Euphrates River.*g*
He will break it up into seven streams
so that men can cross over in sandals.
There will be a highway for the remnant of his people
that is left from Assyria,
as there was for Israel
when they came up from Egypt.

PRAISE FOR DELIVERANCE.   In that day you will say: Isa. 12:1-6

"I will praise you, O LORD.
Although you were angry with me,
your anger has turned away
and you have comforted me.
Surely God is my salvation;
I will trust and not be afraid.
The LORD, the LORD, is my strength and my song;
he has become my salvation."
With joy you will draw water
from the wells of salvation.

In that day you will say:

"Give thanks to the LORD, call on his name;

*c*Hebrew *from Pathros*   *d*That is, the upper Nile region   *e*Hebrew *Shinar*   *f*Or
hostility   *g*Hebrew *the River*

make known among the nations what he has done,
   and proclaim that his name is exalted.
Sing to the LORD, for he has done glorious things;
   let this be known to all the world.
Shout aloud and sing for joy, people of Zion,
   for great is the Holy One of Israel among you."

Ahaz must surely consider Isaiah a crazy dreamer. He probably does not even begin to understand Isaiah's message regarding the coming Messiah. Moreover, he does not have enough faith in God to believe that he could actually defeat Israel and Syria (and even Assyria, if necessary) simply by trusting God. Foolishly, Ahaz will trust his own military strength instead.

So, having rejected God's support and having ignored Isaiah's warnings, Ahaz joins in battle against Pekah and Rezin. The historical account records the predictable results.

2 Kgs. 16:5,6
2 Chron. 28:5-8

JUDAH DEFEATED BY ALLIES.   Therefore the LORD his God handed him over to the king of Aram. The Arameans defeated him and took many of his people as prisoners and brought them to Damascus.

He was also given into the hands of the king of Israel, who inflicted heavy casualties on him. In one day Pekah son of Remaliah killed a hundred and twenty thousand soldiers in Judah—because Judah had forsaken the LORD, the God of their fathers. Zicri, an Ephraimite warrior, killed Maaseiah the king's son, Azrikam the officer in charge of the palace, and Elkanah, second to the king. The Israelites took captive from their kinsmen two hundred thousand wives, sons and daughters. They also took a great deal of plunder, which they carried back to Samaria.

2 Chron. 28:9-15

CAPTIVES' RELEASE SECURED.   But a prophet of the LORD named Oded was there, and he went out to meet the army when it returned to Samaria. He said to them, "Because the LORD, the God of your fathers, was angry with Judah, he gave them into your hand. But you have slaughtered them in a rage that reaches to heaven. And now you intend to make the men and women of Judah and Jerusalem your slaves. But aren't you also guilty of sins against the LORD your God? Now listen to me! Send back your fellow countrymen you have taken as prisoners, for the LORD's fierce anger rests on you."

Then some of the leaders in Ephraim—Azariah son of Jehohanan, Berekiah son of Meshillemoth, Jehizkiah son of Shallum, and Amasa son of Hadlai—confronted those who were arriving from the war. "You must not bring those prisoners here," they said, "or we will be guilty before the LORD. Do you intend to add to our sin and guilt? For our guilt is already great, and his fierce anger rests on Israel."

So the soldiers gave up the prisoners and plunder in the presence of the officials and all the assembly. The men designated by name took the prisoners, and from the plunder they clothed all who were naked. They provided them with clothes and sandals, food and drink, and healing balm. All those who were weak they put on donkeys. So they took them back to their fellow countrymen at Jericho, the City of Palms, and returned to Samaria.

AHAZ SEEKS ASSYRIAN SUPPORT.   At that time King Ahaz sent to the
king[h] of Assyria for help. The Edomites had again come and attacked
Judah and carried away prisoners, while the Philistines had raided towns
in the foothills and in the Negev of Judah. They captured and occupied
Beth Shemesh, Aijalon and Gederoth, as well as Soco, Timnah and Gimzo,
with their surrounding villages. The LORD had humbled Judah because of
Ahaz king of Israel,[i] for he had promoted wickedness in Judah and had
been most unfaithful to the LORD. Tiglath-Pileser[j] king of Assyria came to
him, but he gave him trouble instead of help. Ahaz took some of the
things from the temple of the LORD and from the royal palace and from
the princes and presented them to the king of Assyria, but that did not
help him.

*2 Chron.
28:16-21*

Isaiah Prophesies Against Nations

*U*nder Ahaz, Judah has become a vassal to Assyria, paying tribute and
doing in effect whatever Assyria demands. Dependence upon Assyria
has become necessary because Judah is once again vulnerable to the
Edomites and Philistines. Although Isaiah knows that invasions by foreign
nations are part of God's plan for punishing Judah, he is also aware that these
nations are acting from their own wicked motivations, and that God will ultimately bring about their destruction as well. Therefore Isaiah pronounces
God's judgment against several nations at this and later times. Here are some
of those pronouncements.

WRATH AGAINST NATIONS.   *Isa. 34:1-4*

> Come near, you nations, and listen;
>   pay attention, you peoples!
> Let the earth hear, and all that is in it,
>   the world, and all that comes out of it!
> The LORD is angry with all nations;
>   his wrath is upon all their armies.
> He will totally destroy[k] them,
>   he will give them over to slaughter.
> Their slain will be thrown out,
>   their dead bodies will send up a stench;
>   the mountains will be soaked with their blood.
> All the stars of the heavens will be dissolved
>   and the sky rolled up like a scroll;
> all the starry host will fall
>   like withered leaves from the vine,
>   like shriveled figs from the fig tree.

JUDGMENT AGAINST ASSYRIA.   The LORD Almighty has sworn,   *Isa.
14:24-27*

> "Surely, as I have planned, so it will be,
>   and as I have purposed, so it will stand.

[h]One Hebrew manuscript, Septuagint and Vulgate (see also 2 Kings 16:7); most Hebrew
manuscripts *kings*   [i]That is, Judah, as frequently in 2 Chron.   [j]Hebrew
Tilgath-Pilneser, a variant of *Tiglath-Pileser*   [k]The Hebrew term refers to the irrevocable
giving over of things or persons to the LORD, often by totally destroying them.

I will crush the Assyrian in my land;
   on my mountains I will trample him down.
His yoke will be taken from my people,
   and his burden removed from their shoulders."

This is the plan determined for the whole world;
   this is the hand stretched out over all nations.
For the LORD Almighty has purposed, and who can thwart
      him?
   His hand is stretched out, and who can turn it back?

Isa. 15:1-9   **JUDGMENT AGAINST MOAB.**   An oracle concerning Moab:

Ar in Moab is ruined,
   destroyed in a night!
Kir in Moab is ruined,
   destroyed in a night!
Dibon goes up to its temple,
   to its high places to weep;
Moab wails over Nebo and Medeba.
Every head is shaved
   and every beard cut off.
In the streets they wear sackcloth;
   on the roofs and in the public squares
they all wail,
   prostrate with weeping.
Heshbon and Elealeh cry out,
   their voices are heard all the way to Jahaz.
Therefore the armed men of Moab cry out,
   and their hearts are faint.

My heart cries out over Moab;
   her fugitives flee as far as Zoar,
   as far as Eglath Shelishiyah.
They go up the way to Luhith,
   weeping as they go;
on the road to Horonaim
   they lament their destruction.
The waters of Nimrim are dried up
   and the grass is withered;
the vegetation is gone
   and nothing green is left.
So the wealth they have acquired and stored up
   they carry away over the Ravine of the Poplars.
Their outcry echoes along the border of Moab;
   their wailing reaches as far as Eglaim,
   their lamentation as far as Beer Elim.
Dimon's[1] waters are full of blood,
   but I will bring still more upon Dimon[1]—
a lion upon the fugitives of Moab
   and upon those who remain in the land.

[1]Masoretic Text; Dead Sea Scrolls, some Septuagint manuscripts and Vulgate *Dibon*

Send lambs as tribute   Isa. 16:1-5
    to the ruler of the land,
from Sela, across the desert,
    to the mount of the Daughter of Zion.
Like fluttering birds
    pushed from the nest,
so are the women of Moab
    at the fords of the Arnon.

"Give us counsel,
    render a decision.
Make your shadow like night—
    at high noon.
Hide the fugitives,
    do not betray the refugees.
Let the Moabite fugitives stay with you;
    be their shelter from the destroyer."

The oppressor will come to an end,
    and destruction will cease;
    the aggressor will vanish from the land.
In love a throne will be established;
    in faithfulness a man will sit on it—
    one from the house*m* of David—
one who in judging seeks justice
    and speeds the cause of righteousness.

We have heard of Moab's pride—   Isa. 16:6-14
    her overweening pride and conceit,
her pride and her insolence—
    but her boasts are empty.
Therefore the Moabites wail,
    they wail together for Moab.
Lament and grieve
    for the men*n* of Kir Hareseth.
The fields of Heshbon wither,
    the vines of Sibmah also.
The rulers of the nations
    have trampled down the choicest vines,
which once reached Jazer
    and spread toward the desert.
Their shoots spread out
    and went as far as the sea.
So I weep, as Jazer weeps,
    for the vines of Sibmah.
O Heshbon, O Elealeh,
    I drench you with tears!
The shouts of joy over your ripened fruit
    and over your harvests have been stilled.
Joy and gladness are taken away from the orchards;
    no one sings or shouts in the vineyards;

---

*m*Hebrew *tent*   *n*Or *"raisin cakes,"* a wordplay

no one treads out wine at the presses,
    for I have put an end to the shouting.
My heart laments for Moab like a harp,
    my inmost being for Kir Hareseth.
When Moab appears at her high place,
    she only wears herself out;
when she goes to her shrine to pray,
    it is to no avail.

This is the word the LORD has already spoken concerning Moab. But now the LORD says: "Within three years, as a servant bound by contract would count them, Moab's splendor and all her many people will be despised, and her survivors will be very few and feeble."

Isa. 17:1-14   JUDGMENT AGAINST DAMASCUS.   An oracle concerning Damascus:

"See, Damascus will no longer be a city
    but will become a heap of ruins.
The cities of Aroer will be deserted
    and left to flocks, which will lie down,
    with no one to make them afraid.
The fortified city will disappear from Ephraim,
    and royal power from Damascus;
the remnant of Aram will be
    like the glory of the Israelites,"

                          declares the LORD Almighty.

"In that day the glory of Jacob will fade;
    the fat of his body will waste away.
It will be as when a reaper gathers the standing grain
    and harvests the grain with his arm—
as when a man gleans heads of grain
    in the Valley of Rephaim.
Yet some gleanings will remain,
    as when an olive tree is beaten,
leaving two or three olives on the topmost branches,
    four or five on the fruitful boughs,"

                    declares the LORD, the God of Israel.

In that day men will look to their Maker
    and turn their eyes to the Holy One of Israel.
They will not look to the altars,
    the work of their hands,
and they will have no regard for the Asherah poles[o]
    and the incense altars their fingers have made.

In that day their strong cities, which they left because of the Israelites, will be like places abandoned to thickets and undergrowth. And all will be desolation.

You have forgotten God your Savior;
    you have not remembered the Rock, your fortress.
Therefore, though you set out the finest plants
    and plant imported vines,

[o]That is, symbols of the goddess Asherah

though on the day you set them out, you make them grow,
and on the morning when you plant them, you bring
them to bud,
yet the harvest will be as nothing
in the day of disease and incurable pain.

Oh, the raging of many nations—
they rage like the raging sea!
Oh, the uproar of the peoples—
they roar like the roaring of great waters!
Although the peoples roar like the roar of surging waters,
when he rebukes them they flee far away,
driven before the wind like chaff on the hills,
like tumbleweed before a gale.
In the evening, sudden terror!
Before the morning, they are gone!
This is the portion of those who loot us,
the lot of those who plunder us.

JUDGMENT AGAINST EDOM.   An oracle concerning Dumah*p*:   Isa.
21:11,12

Someone calls to me from Seir,
"Watchman, what is left of the night?
Watchman, what is left of the night?"
The watchman replies,
"Morning is coming, but also the night.
If you would ask, then ask;
and come back yet again."

SECOND JUDGMENT AGAINST EDOM.   Isa. 34:5-17

My sword has drunk its fill in the heavens;
see, it descends in judgment on Edom,
the people I have totally destroyed.
The sword of the LORD is bathed in blood,
it is covered with fat—
the blood of lambs and goats,
fat from the kidneys of rams.
For the LORD has a sacrifice in Bozrah
and a great slaughter in Edom.
And the wild oxen will fall with them,
the bull calves and the great bulls.
Their land will be drenched with blood,
and the dust will be soaked with fat.

For the LORD has a day of vengeance,
a year of retribution, to uphold Zion's cause.
Edom's streams will be turned into pitch,
her dust into burning sulfur;
her land will become blazing pitch!
It will not be quenched night and day;
its smoke will rise forever.
From generation to generation it will lie desolate;

---

p Dumah means *silence* or *stillness*, a word play on *Edom.*

no one will ever pass through it again.
The desert owl^q and screech owl^q will possess it;
   the great owl^q and the raven will nest there.
God will stretch out over Edom
   the measuring line of chaos
   and the plumb line of desolation.
Her nobles will have nothing there to be called a kingdom,
   all her princes will vanish away.
Thorns will overrun her citadels,
   nettles and brambles her strongholds.
She will become a haunt for jackals,
   a home for owls.
Desert creatures will meet with hyenas,
   and wild goats will bleat to each other;
there the night creatures will also repose
   and find for themselves places of rest.
The owl will nest there and lay eggs,
   she will hatch them, and care for her young under the
      shadow of her wings;
there also the falcons will gather,
   each with its mate.

Look in the scroll of the LORD and read:

None of these will be missing,
   not one will lack her mate.
For it is his mouth that has given the order,
   and his Spirit will gather them together.
He allots their portions;
   his hand distributes them by measure.
They will possess it forever
   and dwell there from generation to generation.

Isa.
21:13-17   JUDGMENT AGAINST ARABIA.   An oracle concerning Arabia:

You caravans of Dedanites,
   who camp in the thickets of Arabia,
   bring water for the thirsty;
you who live in Tema,
   bring food for the fugitives.
They flee from the sword,
   from the drawn sword,
from the bent bow
   and from the heat of battle.

This is what the Lord says to me: "Within one year, as a servant bound by contract would count it, all the pomp of Kedar will come to an end. The survivors of the bowmen, the warriors of Kedar, will be few." The LORD, the God of Israel, has spoken.

Isa. 23:1-18   JUDGMENT AGAINST TYRE.   An oracle concerning Tyre:

Wail, O ships of Tarshish!
   For Tyre is destroyed

^qThe precise identification of these birds is uncertain.

and left without house or harbor.
From the land of Cyprus[r]
    word has come to them.

Be silent, you people of the island
    and you merchants of Sidon,
    whom the seafarers have enriched.
On the great waters
    came the grain of the Shihor;
the harvest of the Nile[s] was the revenue of Tyre,
    and she became the marketplace of the nations.

Be ashamed, O Sidon, and you, O fortress of the sea,
    for the sea has spoken:
"I have neither been in labor nor given birth;
    I have neither reared sons nor brought up daughters."
When word comes to Egypt,
    they will be in anguish at the report from Tyre.

Cross over to Tarshish;
    wail, you people of the island.
Is this your city of revelry,
    the old, old city,
whose feet have taken her
    to settle in far-off lands?
Who planned this against Tyre,
    the bestower of crowns,
whose merchants are princes,
    whose traders are renowned in the earth?
The LORD Almighty planned it,
    to bring low the pride of all glory
    and to humble all who are renowned on the earth.

Till[t] your land as along the Nile,
    O Daughter of Tarshish,
    for you no longer have a harbor.
The LORD has stretched out his hand over the sea
    and made its kingdoms tremble.
He has given an order concerning Phoenicia[u]
    that her fortresses be destroyed.
He said, "No more of your reveling,
    O Virgin Daughter of Sidon, now crushed!

"Up, cross over to Cyprus[r];
    even there you will find no rest."
Look at the land of the Babylonians,[v]
    this people that is now of no account!
The Assyrians have made it
    a place for desert creatures;
they raised up their siege towers,

[r]Hebrew *Kittim*   [s]Masoretic Text; one Dead Sea Scroll *Sidon, / who cross over the sea; /
your envoys ³are on the great waters. / The grain of the Shihor, / the harvest of the Nile,*
[t]Dead Sea Scrolls and some Septuagint manuscripts; Masoretic Text *Go through*
[u]Hebrew *Canaan*   [v]Or *Chaldeans*

> they stripped its fortresses bare
> and turned it into a ruin.

> Wail, you ships of Tarshish;
> your fortress is destroyed!

At that time Tyre will be forgotten for seventy years, the span of a king's life. But at the end of these seventy years, it will happen to Tyre as in the song of the prostitute:

> "Take up a harp, walk through the city,
> O prostitute forgotten;
> play the harp well, sing many a song,
> so that you will be remembered."

At the end of seventy years, the LORD will deal with Tyre. She will return to her hire as a prostitute and will ply her trade with all the kingdoms on the face of the earth. Yet her profit and her earnings will be set apart for the LORD; they will not be stored up or hoarded. Her profits will go to those who live before the LORD, for abundant food and fine clothes.

It is not long before some of the judgments begin to be fulfilled, just as Isaiah has prophesied.

In Judah

2 Kgs.
16:7,8

AHAZ PROMOTES SYRIA'S FALL.   Ahaz sent messengers to say to Tiglath-Pileser king of Assyria, "I am your servant and vassal. Come up and save me out of the hand of the king of Aram and of the king of Israel, who are attacking me." And Ahaz took the silver and gold found in the temple of the LORD and in the treasuries of the royal palace and sent it as a gift to the king of Assyria.

2 Kgs.
16:9,10a
(732 B.C.)
Damascus

TIGLATH-PILESER TAKES DAMASCUS.   The king of Assyria complied by attacking Damascus and capturing it. He deported its inhabitants to Kir and put Rezin to death.

Then King Ahaz went to Damascus to meet Tiglath-Pileser king of Assyria.

2 Kgs.
16:10b,11

AHAZ ORDERS SYRIAN ALTAR.   He saw an altar in Damascus and sent to Uriah the priest a sketch of the altar, with detailed plans for its construction. So Uriah the priest built an altar in accordance with all the plans that King Ahaz had sent from Damascus and finished it before King Ahaz returned.

2 Kgs.
16:12-14
Jerusalem

SACRIFICES ON NEW ALTAR.   When the king came back from Damascus and saw the altar, he approached it and presented offerings[w] on it. He offered up his burnt offering and grain offering, poured out his drink offering, and sprinkled the blood of his fellowship offerings[x] on the altar. The bronze altar that stood before the LORD he brought from the front of the temple—from between the new altar and the temple of the LORD—and put it on the north side of the new altar.

2 Kgs.
16:15,16

INSTRUCTIONS FOR USE.   King Ahaz then gave these orders to Uriah the priest: "On the large new altar, offer the morning burnt offering and the evening grain offering, the king's burnt offering and his grain offering,

[w]Or and went up   [x]Traditionally peace offerings

and the burnt offering of all the people of the land, and their grain offering and their drink offering. Sprinkle on the altar all the blood of the burnt offerings and sacrifices. But I will use the bronze altar for seeking guidance." And Uriah the priest did just as King Ahaz had ordered.

USE OF OLD ALTAR.   King Ahaz took away the side panels and removed the basins from the movable stands. He removed the Sea from the bronze bulls that supported it and set it on a stone base. He took away the Sabbath canopy*y* that had been built at the temple and removed the royal entryway outside the temple of the LORD, in deference to the king of Assyria.

2 Kgs.
16:17,18

EXTENT OF AHAZ'S CORRUPTION.   In his time of trouble King Ahaz became even more unfaithful to the LORD. He offered sacrifices to the gods of Damascus, who had defeated him; for he thought, "Since the gods of the kings of Aram have helped them, I will sacrifice to them so they will help me." But they were his downfall and the downfall of all Israel.

Ahaz gathered together the furnishings from the temple of God and took them away.*z* He shut the doors of the LORD's temple and set up altars at every street corner in Jerusalem. In every town in Judah he built high places to burn sacrifices to other gods and provoked the LORD, the God of his fathers, to anger.

2 Chron.
28:22-25

DEATH OF AHAZ.   The other events of his reign and all his ways, from beginning to end, are written in the book of the kings of Judah and Israel. Ahaz rested with his fathers and was buried in the city of Jerusalem, but he was not placed in the tombs of the kings of Israel.

2 Kgs.
16:19,20a
2 Chron.
28:26,27a
(725 B.C.?)

HEZEKIAH BEGINS SOLE REIGN.   And Hezekiah his son succeeded him as king. In the third year of Hoshea son of Elah king of Israel, Hezekiah son of Ahaz king of Judah began to reign. He was twenty-five years old when he became king, and he reigned in Jerusalem twenty-nine years. His mother's name was Abijah*a* daughter of Zechariah.

2 Kgs.
16:20b
18:1,2
2 Chron.
28:27b;29:1
(725 B.C.?)

HEZEKIAH'S CHARACTER.   He did what was right in the eyes of the LORD, just as his father David had done. He removed the high places, smashed the sacred stones and cut down the Asherah poles. He broke into pieces the bronze snake Moses had made, for up to that time the Israelites had been burning incense to it. (It was called*b* Nehushtan.*c*)

Hezekiah trusted in the LORD, the God of Israel. There was no one like him among all the kings of Judah, either before him or after him. He held fast to the LORD and did not cease to follow him; he kept the commands the LORD had given Moses. And the LORD was with him; he was successful in whatever he undertook.

2 Kgs.
18:3-7a
2 Chron.
29:2

◇

---

*y*Or *the dais of his throne* (see Septuagint)   *z*Or *and cut them up*   *a*Hebrew *Abi*, a variant of *Abijah*   *b*Or *He called it*   *c*Nehushtan *sounds like the Hebrew for* bronze *and* snake *and* unclean thing.

More of Isaiah's Prophecies Against Nations

*W*ith the death of Ahaz, Judah has a final opportunity for spiritual renewal. Hezekiah will do what he can to revive Judah, but Isaiah already knows the ultimate outcome and continues to prophesy against the nations who either have brought, or will bring, suffering to God's people. Babylonia in particular is singled out because it is the nation which will carry Judah away into captivity in just a few years. The king of Babylon has the dubious distinction of sharing in Isaiah's oblique references to Satan, the one who has fallen from heaven. Isaiah predicts that Babylon itself will be conquered by the Medo-Persian empire, a fact to which history will later attest. And because they have for years been a threat to Israel, the Philistines are also judged.

Isa. 14:28-32

JUDGMENT AGAINST PHILISTINES. This oracle came in the year King Ahaz died:

> Do not rejoice, all you Philistines,
>> that the rod that struck you is broken;
> from the root of that snake will spring up a viper,
>> its fruit will be a darting, venomous serpent.
> The poorest of the poor will find pasture,
>> and the needy will lie down in safety.
> But your root I will destroy by famine;
>> it will slay your survivors.
>
> Wail, O gate! Howl, O city!
>> Melt away, all you Philistines!
> A cloud of smoke comes from the north,
>> and there is not a straggler in its ranks.
> What answer shall be given
>> to the envoys of that nation?
> "The LORD has established Zion,
>> and in her his afflicted people will find refuge."

Isa. 13:1-8

JUDGMENT AGAINST BABYLON. An oracle concerning Babylon that Isaiah son of Amoz saw:

> Raise a banner on a bare hilltop,
>> shout to them;
> beckon to them
>> to enter the gates of the nobles.
> I have commanded my holy ones;
>> I have summoned my warriors to carry out my wrath—
>> those who rejoice in my triumph.
>
> Listen, a noise on the mountains,
>> like that of a great multitude!
> Listen, an uproar among the kingdoms,
>> like nations massing together!
> The LORD Almighty is mustering
>> an army for war.
> They come from faraway lands,

from the ends of the heavens—
the LORD and the weapons of his wrath—
    to destroy the whole country.

Wail, for the day of the LORD is near;
    it will come like destruction from the Almighty.[d]
Because of this, all hands will go limp,
    every man's heart will melt.
Terror will seize them,
    pain and anguish will grip them;
    they will writhe like a woman in labor.
They will look aghast at each other,
    their faces aflame.

See, the day of the LORD is coming   Isa. 13:9-16
    —a cruel day, with wrath and fierce anger—
to make the land desolate
    and destroy the sinners within it.
The stars of heaven and their constellations
    will not show their light.
The rising sun will be darkened
    and the moon will not give its light.
I will punish the world for its evil,
    the wicked for their sins.
I will put an end to the arrogance of the haughty
    and will humble the pride of the ruthless.
I will make man scarcer than pure gold,
    more rare than the gold of Ophir.
Therefore I will make the heavens tremble;
    and the earth will shake from its place
at the wrath of the LORD Almighty,
    in the day of his burning anger.

Like a hunted gazelle,
    like sheep without a shepherd,
each will return to his own people,
    each will flee to his native land.
Whoever is captured will be thrust through;
    all who are caught will fall by the sword.
Their infants will be dashed to pieces before their eyes;
    their houses will be looted and their wives ravished.

See, I will stir up against them the Medes,   Isa.
    who do not care for silver   13:17-22
    and have no delight in gold.
Their bows will strike down the young men;
    they will have no mercy on infants
    nor will they look with compassion on children.
Babylon, the jewel of kingdoms,
    the glory of the Babylonians'[e] pride,
will be overthrown by God
    like Sodom and Gomorrah.

[d]Hebrew *Shaddai*   [e]*Or Chaldeans'*

She will never be inhabited
　　or lived in through all generations;
no Arab will pitch his tent there,
　　no shepherd will rest his flocks there.
But desert creatures will lie there,
　　jackals will fill her houses;
there the owls will dwell,
　　and there the wild goats will leap about.
Hyenas will howl in her strongholds,
　　jackals in her luxurious palaces.
Her time is at hand,
　　and her days will not be prolonged.

Isa. 14:1,2

The LORD will have compassion on Jacob;
　　once again he will choose Israel
　　and will settle them in their own land.
Aliens will join them
　　and unite with the house of Jacob.
Nations will take them
　　and bring them to their own place.
And the house of Israel will possess the nations
　　as menservants and maidservants in the LORD's land.
They will make captives of their captors
　　and rule over their oppressors.

Isa. 14:3-11

BABYLON'S SATANLIKE FALL.   On the day the LORD gives you relief
from suffering and turmoil and cruel bondage, you will take up this taunt
against the king of Babylon:

How the oppressor has come to an end!
　　How his fury[f] has ended!
The LORD has broken the rod of the wicked,
　　the scepter of the rulers,
which in anger struck down peoples
　　with unceasing blows,
and in fury subdued nations
　　with relentless aggression.
All the lands are at rest and at peace;
　　they break into singing.
Even the pine trees and the cedars of Lebanon
　　exult over you and say,
"Now that you have been laid low,
　　no woodsman comes to cut us down."

The grave[g] below is all astir
　　to meet you at your coming;
it rouses the spirits of the departed to greet you—
　　all those who were leaders in the world;
it makes them rise from their thrones—
　　all those who were kings over the nations.

---

[f] Dead Sea Scrolls, Septuagint and Syriac; the meaning of the word in the Masoretic Text
is uncertain.   [g] Hebrew *Sheol*

They will all respond,
   they will say to you,
"You also have become weak, as we are;
   you have become like us."
All your pomp has been brought down to the grave,
   along with the noise of your harps;
maggots are spread out beneath you
   and worms cover you.

How you have fallen from heaven,   Isa.
   O morning star, son of the dawn!   14:12-23
You have been cast down to the earth,
   you who once laid low the nations!
You said in your heart,
   "I will ascend to heaven;
I will raise my throne
   above the stars of God;
I will sit enthroned on the mount of assembly,
   on the utmost heights of the sacred mountain.*h*
I will ascend above the tops of the clouds;
   I will make myself like the Most High."
But you are brought down to the grave,
   to the depths of the pit.

Those who see you stare at you,
   they ponder your fate:
"Is this the man who shook the earth
   and made kingdoms tremble,
the man who made the world a desert,
   who overthrew its cities
   and would not let his captives go home?"

All the kings of the nations lie in state,
   each in his own tomb.
But you are cast out of your tomb
   like a rejected branch;
you are covered with the slain,
   with those pierced by the sword,
   those who descend to the stones of the pit.
Like a corpse trampled underfoot,
   you will not join them in burial,
for you have destroyed your land
   and killed your people.

The offspring of the wicked
   will never be mentioned again.
Prepare a place to slaughter his sons
   for the sins of their forefathers;
they are not to rise to inherit the land
   and cover the earth with their cities.

"I will rise up against them,"

*h*Or *the north;* Hebrew *Zaphon*

> declares the LORD Almighty.
> "I will cut off from Babylon her name and survivors,
>   her offspring and descendants,"
>   declares the LORD.
> "I will turn her into a place for owls
>   and into swampland;
> I will sweep her with the broom of destruction,"
>   declares the LORD Almighty.

Isa. 21:1-10   ANOTHER BABYLON JUDGMENT.   An oracle concerning the Desert by the Sea:

> Like whirlwinds sweeping through the southland,
>   an invader comes from the desert,
>   from a land of terror.
>
> A dire vision has been shown to me:
>   The traitor betrays, the looter takes loot.
> Elam, attack! Media, lay siege!
>   I will bring to an end all the groaning she caused.
>
> At this my body is racked with pain,
>   pangs seize me, like those of a woman in labor;
> I am staggered by what I hear,
>   I am bewildered by what I see.
> My heart falters,
>   fear makes me tremble;
> the twilight I longed for
>   has become a horror to me.
>
> They set the tables,
>   they spread the rugs,
>   they eat, they drink!
> Get up, you officers,
>   oil the shields!

This is what the Lord says to me:

> "Go, post a lookout
>   and have him report what he sees.
> When he sees chariots
>   with teams of horses,
> riders on donkeys
>   or riders on camels,
> let him be alert,
>   fully alert."

And the lookout[i] shouted,

> "Day after day, my lord, I stand on the watchtower;
>   every night I stay at my post.
> Look, here comes a man in a chariot
>   with a team of horses.
> And he gives back the answer:

[i]Dead Sea Scrolls and Syriac; Masoretic Text *A lion*

'Babylon has fallen, has fallen!
All the images of its gods
lie shattered on the ground!' "

O my people, crushed on the threshing floor,
I tell you what I have heard
from the LORD Almighty,
from the God of Israel.

The Reforms of Hezekiah

*P*erhaps there is hope after all. Now in full control, King Hezekiah will accomplish the most far-reaching religious reforms since the days of Jehoshaphat. Working primarily through the Levites, who have more zeal than do the priests, Hezekiah will cleanse the temple and restore proper worship and religious observance among his people. In a grand gesture of brotherhood, Hezekiah will offer to include the people of the northern tribes in Passover celebrations. Most will refuse the invitation, but some will join in the spiritual renewal.

In Judah

TEMPLE ORDERED CLEANSED. In the first month of the first year of his reign, he opened the doors of the temple of the LORD and repaired them. He brought in the priests and the Levites, assembled them in the square on the east side and said: "Listen to me, Levites! Consecrate yourselves now and consecrate the temple of the LORD, the God of your fathers. Remove all defilement from the sanctuary. Our fathers were unfaithful; they did evil in the eyes of the LORD our God and forsook him. They turned their faces away from the LORD's dwelling place and turned their backs on him. They also shut the doors of the portico and put out the lamps. They did not burn incense or present any burnt offerings at the sanctuary to the God of Israel. Therefore, the anger of the LORD has fallen on Judah and Jerusalem; he has made them an object of dread and horror and scorn, as you can see with your own eyes. This is why our fathers have fallen by the sword and why our sons and daughters and our wives are in captivity. Now I intend to make a covenant with the LORD, the God of Israel, so that his fierce anger will turn away from us. My sons, do not be negligent now, for the LORD has chosen you to stand before him and serve him, to minister before him and to burn incense."

2 Chron.
29:3-11
Jerusalem

LEVITES OBEY ORDER.
Then these Levites set to work:
from the Kohathites,
Mahath son of Amasai and Joel son of Azariah;
from the Merarites,
Kish son of Abdi and Azariah son of Jehallelel;
from the Gershonites,
Joah son of Zimmah and Eden son of Joah;
from the descendants of Elizaphan,
Shimri and Jeiel;
from the descendants of Asaph,
Zechariah and Mattaniah;

2 Chron.
29:12-19

from the descendants of Heman,
   Jehiel and Shimei;
from the descendants of Jeduthun,
   Shemaiah and Uzziel.

When they had assembled their brothers and consecrated themselves, they went in to purify the temple of the LORD, as the king had ordered, following the word of the LORD. The priests went into the sanctuary of the LORD to purify it. They brought out to the courtyard of the LORD's temple everything unclean that they found in the temple of the LORD. The Levites took it and carried it out to the Kidron Valley. They began the consecration on the first day of the first month, and by the eighth day of the month they reached the portico of the LORD. For eight more days they consecrated the temple of the LORD itself, finishing on the sixteenth day of the first month.

Then they went in to King Hezekiah and reported: "We have purified the entire temple of the LORD, the altar of burnt offering with all its utensils, and the table for setting out the consecrated bread, with all its articles. We have prepared and consecrated all the articles that King Ahaz removed in his unfaithfulness while he was king. They are now in front of the LORD's altar."

2 Chron.
29:20-36

TEMPLE RECONSECRATED.   Early the next morning King Hezekiah gathered the city officials together and went up to the temple of the LORD. They brought seven bulls, seven rams, seven male lambs and seven male goats as a sin offering for the kingdom, for the sanctuary and for Judah. The king commanded the priests, the descendants of Aaron, to offer these on the altar of the LORD. So they slaughtered the bulls, and the priests took the blood and sprinkled it on the altar; next they slaughtered the rams and sprinkled their blood on the altar; then they slaughtered the lambs and sprinkled their blood on the altar. The goats for the sin offering were brought before the king and the assembly, and they laid their hands on them. The priests then slaughtered the goats and presented their blood on the altar for a sin offering to atone for all Israel, because the king had ordered the burnt offering and the sin offering for all Israel.

He stationed the Levites in the temple of the LORD with cymbals, harps and lyres in the way prescribed by David and Gad the king's seer and Nathan the prophet; this was commanded by the LORD through his prophets. So the Levites stood ready with David's instruments, and the priests with their trumpets.

Hezekiah gave the order to sacrifice the burnt offering on the altar. As the offering began, singing to the LORD began also, accompanied by trumpets and the instruments of David king of Israel. The whole assembly bowed in worship, while the singers sang and the trumpeters played. All this continued until the sacrifice of the burnt offering was completed.

When the offerings were finished, the king and everyone present with him knelt down and worshiped. King Hezekiah and his officials ordered the Levites to praise the LORD with the words of David and of Asaph the seer. So they sang praises with gladness and bowed their heads and worshiped.

Then Hezekiah said, "You have now dedicated yourselves to the LORD. Come and bring sacrifices and thank offerings to the temple of the LORD." So the assembly brought sacrifices and thank offerings, and all whose hearts were willing brought burnt offerings.

The number of burnt offerings the assembly brought was seventy bulls, a hundred rams and two hundred male lambs—all of them for burnt offerings to the LORD. The animals consecrated as sacrifices amounted to six hundred bulls and three thousand sheep and goats. The priests, however, were too few to skin all the burnt offerings; so their kinsmen the Levites helped them until the task was finished and until other priests had been consecrated, for the Levites had been more conscientious in consecrating themselves than the priests had been. There were burnt offerings in abundance, together with the fat of the fellowship offerings*ʲ* and the drink offerings that accompanied the burnt offerings.

So the service of the temple of the LORD was reestablished. Hezekiah and all the people rejoiced at what God had brought about for his people, because it was done so quickly.

ISRAEL INVITED TO PASSOVER.   Hezekiah sent word to all Israel and Judah and also wrote letters to Ephraim and Manasseh, inviting them to come to the temple of the LORD in Jerusalem and celebrate the Passover to the LORD, the God of Israel. The king and his officials and the whole assembly in Jerusalem decided to celebrate the Passover in the second month. They had not been able to celebrate it at the regular time because not enough priests had consecrated themselves and the people had not assembled in Jerusalem. The plan seemed right both to the king and to the whole assembly. They decided to send a proclamation throughout Israel, from Beersheba to Dan, calling the people to come to Jerusalem and celebrate the Passover to the LORD, the God of Israel. It had not been celebrated in large numbers according to what was written.

At the king's command, couriers went throughout Israel and Judah with letters from the king and from his officials, which read:

2 Chron. 30:1-9

"People of Israel, return to the LORD, the God of Abraham, Isaac and Israel, that he may return to you who are left, who have escaped from the hand of the kings of Assyria. Do not be like your fathers and brothers, who were unfaithful to the LORD, the God of their fathers, so that he made them an object of horror, as you see. Do not be stiff-necked, as your fathers were; submit to the LORD. Come to the sanctuary, which he has consecrated forever. Serve the LORD your God, so that his fierce anger will turn away from you. If you return to the LORD, then your brothers and your children will be shown compassion by their captors and will come back to this land, for the LORD your God is gracious and compassionate. He will not turn his face from you if you return to him."

SOME COME FROM ISRAEL.   The couriers went from town to town in Ephraim and Manasseh, as far as Zebulun, but the people scorned and ridiculed them. Nevertheless, some men of Asher, Manasseh and Zebulun humbled themselves and went to Jerusalem. Also in Judah the hand of God was on the people to give them unity of mind to carry out what the king and his officials had ordered, following the word of the LORD.

2 Chron. 30:10-12

PASSOVER OBSERVED.   A very large crowd of people assembled in Jerusalem to celebrate the Feast of Unleavened Bread in the second month. They removed the altars in Jerusalem and cleared away the incense altars and threw them into the Kidron Valley.

2 Chron. 30:13-22

ʲ Traditionally *peace offerings*

They slaughtered the Passover lamb on the fourteenth day of the second month. The priests and the Levites were ashamed and consecrated themselves and brought burnt offerings to the temple of the LORD. Then they took up their regular positions as prescribed in the Law of Moses the man of God. The priests sprinkled the blood handed to them by the Levites. Since many in the crowd had not consecrated themselves, the Levites had to kill the Passover lambs for all those who were not ceremonially clean and could not consecrate their lambs, to the LORD. Although most of the many people who came from Ephraim, Manasseh, Issachar and Zebulun had not purified themselves, yet they ate the Passover, contrary to what was written. But Hezekiah prayed for them, saying, "May the LORD, who is good, pardon everyone who sets his heart on seeking God—the LORD, the God of his fathers—even if he is not clean according to the rules of the sanctuary." And the LORD heard Hezekiah and healed the people.

The Israelites who were present in Jerusalem celebrated the Feast of Unleavened Bread for seven days with great rejoicing, while the Levites and priests sang to the LORD every day, accompanied by the LORD's instruments of praise.[k]

Hezekiah spoke encouragingly to all the Levites, who showed good understanding of the service of the LORD. For the seven days they ate their assigned portion and offered fellowship offerings[l] and praised the LORD, the God of their fathers.

2 Chron. 30:23-27

SECOND WEEK OBSERVED.   The whole assembly then agreed to celebrate the festival seven more days; so for another seven days they celebrated joyfully. Hezekiah king of Judah provided a thousand bulls and seven thousand sheep and goats for the assembly, and the officials provided them with a thousand bulls and ten thousand sheep and goats. A great number of priests consecrated themselves. The entire assembly of Judah rejoiced, along with the priests and Levites and all who had assembled from Israel, including the aliens who had come from Israel and those who lived in Judah. There was great joy in Jerusalem, for since the days of Solomon son of David king of Israel there had been nothing like this in Jerusalem. The priests and the Levites stood to bless the people, and God heard them, for their prayer reached heaven, his holy dwelling place.

2 Chron. 31:1

IDOLATRY ATTACKED.   When all this had ended, the Israelites who were there went out to the towns of Judah, smashed the sacred stones and cut down the Asherah poles. They destroyed the high places and the altars throughout Judah and Benjamin and in Ephraim and Manasseh. After they had destroyed all of them, the Israelites returned to their own towns and to their own property.

2 Chron. 31:2-8

OTHER RELIGIOUS REFORMS.   Hezekiah assigned the priests and Levites to divisions—each of them according to their duties as priests or Levites—to offer burnt offerings and fellowship offerings, [l] to minister, to give thanks and to sing praises at the gates of the LORD's dwelling. The king contributed from his own possessions for the morning and evening burnt offerings and for the burnt offerings on the Sabbaths, New Moons and appointed feasts as written in the Law of the LORD. He ordered the people living in Jerusalem to give the portion due the priests and Levites

---

[k]Or *priests praised the LORD every day with resounding instruments belonging to the LORD*
[l]Traditionally *peace offerings*

so they could devote themselves to the Law of the LORD. As soon as the
order went out, the Israelites generously gave the firstfruits of their grain,
new wine, oil and honey and all that the fields produced. They brought a
great amount, a tithe of everything. The men of Israel and Judah who lived
in the towns of Judah also brought a tithe of their herds and flocks and a
tithe of the holy things dedicated to the LORD their God, and they piled
them in heaps. They began doing this in the third month and finished in
the seventh month. When Hezekiah and his officials came and saw the
heaps, they praised the LORD and blessed his people Israel.

Hezekiah asked the priests and Levites about the heaps; and Azariah   2 Chron.
the chief priest, from the family of Zadok, answered, "Since the people   31:9-13
began to bring their contributions to the temple of the LORD, we have had
enough to eat and plenty to spare, because the LORD has blessed his people, and this great amount is left over."

Hezekiah gave orders to prepare storerooms in the temple of the LORD,
and this was done. Then they faithfully brought in the contributions, tithes
and dedicated gifts. Conaniah, a Levite, was in charge of these things, and
his brother Shimei was next in rank. Jehiel, Azaziah, Nahath, Asahel,
Jerimoth, Jozabad, Eliel, Ismakiah, Mahath and Benaiah were supervisors
under Conaniah and Shimei his brother, by appointment of King Hezekiah
and Azariah the official in charge of the temple of God.

Kore son of Imnah the Levite, keeper of the East Gate, was in charge of   2 Chron.
the freewill offerings given to God, distributing the contributions made to   31:14-19
the LORD and also the consecrated gifts. Eden, Miniamin, Jeshua, Shemaiah, Amariah and Shecaniah assisted him faithfully in the towns of the
priests, distributing to their fellow priests according to their divisions, old
and young alike.

In addition, they distributed to the males three years old or more whose
names were in the genealogical records—all who would enter the temple
of the LORD to perform the daily duties of their various tasks, according to
their responsibilities and their divisions. And they distributed to the
priests enrolled by their families in the genealogical records and likewise
to the Levites twenty years old or more, according to their responsibilities
and their divisions. They included all the little ones, the wives, and the
sons and daughters of the whole community listed in these genealogical
records. For they were faithful in consecrating themselves.

As for the priests, the descendants of Aaron, who lived on the farm
lands around their towns or in any other towns, men were designated by
name to distribute portions to every male among them and to all who
were recorded in the genealogies of the Levites.

This is what Hezekiah did throughout Judah, doing what was good and   2 Chron.
right and faithful before the LORD his God. In everything that he under-   31:20,21
took in the service of God's temple and in obedience to the law and the
commands, he sought his God and worked wholeheartedly. And so he
prospered.

Isaiah Tells of "Last Days" _____

*P*erhaps it is during this time of jubilant rededication that Isaiah shares with excitement the visions he has received about the coming of the Messiah and the ultimate triumph of good over evil. Using vivid and powerful imagery, Isaiah describes the time when the wicked will be punished and the righteous blessed forever.

Isa. 24:1-23   THE EARTH'S DEVASTATION.

See, the LORD is going to lay waste the earth
    and devastate it;
he will ruin its face
    and scatter its inhabitants—
it will be the same
    for priest as for people,
    for master as for servant,
    for mistress as for maid,
    for seller as for buyer,
    for borrower as for lender,
    for debtor as for creditor.
The earth will be completely laid waste
    and totally plundered.
                    The LORD has spoken this word.

The earth dries up and withers,
    the world languishes and withers,
    the exalted of the earth languish.
The earth is defiled by its people;
    they have disobeyed the laws,
violated the statutes
    and broken the everlasting covenant.
Therefore a curse consumes the earth;
    its people must bear their guilt.
Therefore earth's inhabitants are burned up,
    and very few are left.
The new wine dries up and the vine withers;
    all the merrymakers groan.
The gaiety of the tambourines is stilled,
    the noise of the revelers has stopped,
    the joyful harp is silent.
No longer do they drink wine with a song;
    the beer is bitter to its drinkers.
The ruined city lies desolate;
    the entrance to every house is barred.
In the streets they cry out for wine;
    all joy turns to gloom,
    all gaiety is banished from the earth.
The city is left in ruins,
    its gate is battered to pieces.
So will it be on the earth
    and among the nations,

as when an olive tree is beaten,
   or as when gleanings are left after the grape harvest.

They raise their voices, they shout for joy;
   from the west they acclaim the LORD's majesty.
Therefore in the east give glory to the LORD;
   exalt the name of the LORD, the God of Israel,
   in the islands of the sea.
From the ends of the earth we hear singing:
  "Glory to the Righteous One."

But I said, "I waste away, I waste away!
   Woe to me!
The treacherous betray!
   With treachery the treacherous betray!"
Terror and pit and snare await you,
   O people of the earth.
Whoever flees at the sound of terror
   will fall into a pit;
whoever climbs out of the pit
   will be caught in a snare.

The floodgates of the heavens are opened,
   the foundations of the earth shake.
The earth is broken up,
   the earth is split asunder,
   the earth is thoroughly shaken.
The earth reels like a drunkard,
   it sways like a hut in the wind;
so heavy upon it is the guilt of its rebellion
   that it falls—never to rise again.

In that day the LORD will punish
   the powers in the heavens above
   and the kings on the earth below.
They will be herded together
   like prisoners bound in a dungeon;
they will be shut up in prison
   and be punished[m] after many days.
The moon will be abashed, the sun ashamed;
   for the LORD Almighty will reign
on Mount Zion and in Jerusalem,
   and before its elders, gloriously.

PRAISE FOR SALVATION.   Isa. 25:1-9

O LORD, you are my God;
   I will exalt you and praise your name,
for in perfect faithfulness
   you have done marvelous things,
   things planned long ago.
You have made the city a heap of rubble,
   the fortified town a ruin,

[m]Or released

the foreigners' stronghold a city no more;
  it will never be rebuilt.
Therefore strong peoples will honor you;
  cities of ruthless nations will revere you.
You have been a refuge for the poor,
  a refuge for the needy in his distress,
a shelter from the storm
  and a shade from the heat.
For the breath of the ruthless
  is like a storm driving against a wall
  and like the heat of the desert.
You silence the uproar of foreigners;
  as heat is reduced by the shadow of a cloud,
  so the song of the ruthless is stilled.

On this mountain the LORD Almighty will prepare
  a feast of rich food for all peoples,
a banquet of aged wine—
  the best of meats and the finest of wines.
On this mountain he will destroy
  the shroud that enfolds all peoples,
the sheet that covers all nations;
  he will swallow up death forever.
The Sovereign LORD will wipe away the tears
  from all faces;
he will remove the disgrace of his people
  from all the earth.

                                    The LORD has spoken.

In that day they will say,

    "Surely this is our God;
      we trusted in him, and he saved us.
    This is the LORD, we trusted in him;
      let us rejoice and be glad in his salvation."

Isa. 26:1-7   PRAISE FOR DELIVERANCE.   In that day this song will be sung in the
land of Judah:

        We have a strong city;
          God makes salvation
          its walls and ramparts.
        Open the gates
          that the righteous nation may enter,
          the nation that keeps faith.
        You will keep in perfect peace
          him whose mind is steadfast,
          because he trusts in you.
        Trust in the LORD forever,
          for the LORD, the LORD, is the Rock eternal.
        He humbles those who dwell on high,
          he lays the lofty city low;
        he levels it to the ground
          and casts it down to the dust.

Feet trample it down—
    the feet of the oppressed,
    the footsteps of the poor.

The path of the righteous is level;
    O upright One, you make the way of the righteous
        smooth.

COMMITMENT OF BELIEVERS.   Isa. 26:8,9

Yes, LORD, walking in the way of your laws,[n]
    we wait for you;
your name and renown
    are the desire of our hearts.
My soul yearns for you in the night;
    in the morning my spirit longs for you.
When your judgments come upon the earth,
    the people of the world learn righteousness.

CONDEMNATION OF WICKED.   Isa.
                                                              26:10,11

Though grace is shown to the wicked,
    they do not learn righteousness;
even in a land of uprightness they go on doing evil
    and regard not the majesty of the LORD.
O LORD, your hand is lifted high,
    but they do not see it.
Let them see your zeal for your people and be put to
        shame;
    let the fire reserved for your enemies consume them.

THE ONE GOD.   Isa.
                                                              26:12,13

LORD, you establish peace for us;
    all that we have accomplished you have done for us.
O LORD, our God, other lords besides you have ruled
        over us,
    but your name alone do we honor.

ETERNAL DEATH OF WICKED.   Isa.
                                                              26:14-18

They are now dead, they live no more;
    those departed spirits do not rise.
You punished them and brought them to ruin;
    you wiped out all memory of them.
You have enlarged the nation, O LORD;
    you have enlarged the nation.
You have gained glory for yourself;
    you have extended all the borders of the land.

LORD, they came to you in their distress;
    when you disciplined them,
    they could barely whisper a prayer.[o]
As a woman with child and about to give birth
    writhes and cries out in her pain,

[n]Or judgments   [o]The meaning of the Hebrew for this clause is uncertain.

so were we in your presence, O LORD.
We were with child, we writhed in pain,
　　but we gave birth to wind.
We have not brought salvation to the earth;
　　we have not given birth to people of the world.

Isa. 26:19　　RESURRECTION OF FAITHFUL.

But your dead will live;
　　their bodies will rise.
You who dwell in the dust,
　　wake up and shout for joy.
Your dew is like the dew of the morning;
　　the earth will give birth to her dead.

Isa.
26:20-27:1　　DESTRUCTION OF WICKED.

Go, my people, enter your rooms
　　and shut the doors behind you;
hide yourselves for a little while
　　until his wrath has passed by.
See, the LORD is coming out of his dwelling
　　to punish the people of the earth for their sins.
The earth will disclose the blood shed upon her;
　　she will conceal her slain no longer. In that day,
the LORD will punish with his sword,
　　his fierce, great and powerful sword,
Leviathan the gliding serpent,
　　Leviathan the coiling serpent;
he will slay the monster of the sea.

Isa. 32:1,2　　KINGDOM OF RIGHTEOUSNESS.

See, a king will reign in righteousness
　　and rulers will rule with justice.
Each man will be like a shelter from the wind
　　and a refuge from the storm,
like streams of water in the desert
　　and the shadow of a great rock in a thirsty land.

Isa. 32:3-8　　NO PLACE FOR WICKED.

Then the eyes of those who see will no longer be closed,
　　and the ears of those who hear will listen.
The mind of the rash will know and understand,
　　and the stammering tongue will be fluent and clear.
No longer will the fool be called noble
　　nor the scoundrel be highly respected.
For the fool speaks folly,
　　his mind is busy with evil:
He practices ungodliness
　　and spreads error concerning the LORD;
the hungry he leaves empty
　　and from the thirsty he withholds water.

The scoundrel's methods are wicked,
    he makes up evil schemes
to destroy the poor with lies,
    even when the plea of the needy is just.
But the noble man makes noble plans,
    and by noble deeds he stands.

REJOICING OF THE SAVED.   Isa. 35:1-10

The desert and the parched land will be glad;
    the wilderness will rejoice and blossom.
Like the crocus, it will burst into bloom;
    it will rejoice greatly and shout for joy.
The glory of Lebanon will be given to it,
    the splendor of Carmel and Sharon;
they will see the glory of the LORD,
    the splendor of our God.

Strengthen the feeble hands,
    steady the knees that give way;
say to those with fearful hearts,
  "Be strong, do not fear;
your God will come,
    he will come with vengeance;
with divine retribution
    he will come to save you."

Then will the eyes of the blind be opened
    and the ears of the deaf unstopped.
Then will the lame leap like a deer,
    and the mute tongue shout for joy.
Water will gush forth in the wilderness
    and streams in the desert.
The burning sand will become a pool,
    the thirsty ground bubbling springs.
In the haunts where jackals once lay,
    grass and reeds and papyrus will grow.

And a highway will be there;
    it will be called the Way of Holiness.
The unclean will not journey on it;
    it will be for those who walk in that Way;
    wicked fools will not go about on it.ᵖ
No lion will be there,
    nor will any ferocious beast get up on it;
    they will not be found there.
But only the redeemed will walk there,
    and the ransomed of the LORD will return.
They will enter Zion with singing;
    everlasting joy will crown their heads.
Gladness and joy will overtake them,
    and sorrow and sighing will flee away.

ᵖOr / *the simple will not stray from it*

Isaiah Warns Against Relapse

ell aware of their spiritual fickleness, Isaiah continues to warn the people against their sinful ways, and urges them not to let the excitement of this period of renewal diminish. Once again he rehearses the basic message: if they abandon their newfound dedication, they will be destroyed. And knowing already that they will indeed fail, Isaiah tells them again of Jerusalem's fall, the foreign exile in captivity, the day of restoration, and the punishment of their oppressors. The message is always the same, but the hardness of their hearts keeps them from hearing it.

Isa. 28:1-6   EPHRAIM LIKE FADING WREATH.

Woe to that wreath, the pride of Ephraim's drunkards,
    to the fading flower, his glorious beauty,
set on the head of a fertile valley—
    to that city, the pride of those laid low by wine!
See, the Lord has one who is powerful and strong.
    Like a hailstorm and a destructive wind,
like a driving rain and a flooding downpour,
    he will throw it forcefully to the ground.
That wreath, the pride of Ephraim's drunkards,
    will be trampled underfoot.
That fading flower, his glorious beauty,
    set on the head of a fertile valley,
will be like a fig ripe before harvest—
    as soon as someone sees it and takes it in his hand,
    he swallows it.

In that day the LORD Almighty
    will be a glorious crown,
a beautiful wreath
    for the remnant of his people.
He will be a spirit of justice
    to him who sits in judgment,
a source of strength
    to those who turn back the battle at the gate.

Isa. 28:7-15   SPIRITUAL LEADERS JUDGED.

And these also stagger from wine
    and reel from beer:
Priests and prophets stagger from beer
    and are befuddled with wine;
they reel from beer,
    they stagger when seeing visions,
    they stumble when rendering decisions.
All the tables are covered with vomit
    and there is not a spot without filth.

"Who is it he is trying to teach?
    To whom is he explaining his message?
To children weaned from their milk,
    to those just taken from the breast?

For it is:
    Do and do, do and do,
    rule on rule, rule on rule*q*;
    a little here, a little there."

Very well then, with foreign lips and strange tongues
    God will speak to this people,
to whom he said,
    "This is the resting place, let the weary rest";
and, "This is the place of repose"—
    but they would not listen.
So then, the word of the LORD to them will become:
    Do and do, do and do,
    rule on rule, rule on rule;
    a little here, a little there—
so that they will go and fall backward,
    be injured and snared and captured.

Therefore hear the word of the LORD, you scoffers
    who rule this people in Jerusalem.
You boast, "We have entered into a covenant with death,
    with the grave*r* we have made an agreement.
When an overwhelming scourge sweeps by,
    it cannot touch us,
for we have made a lie our refuge
    and falsehood*s* our hiding place."

WORSHIP IS MEANINGLESS.   The Lord says:

Isa. 29:13

"These people come near to me with their mouth
    and honor me with their lips,
    but their hearts are far from me.
Their worship of me
    is made up only of rules taught by men.*t*

JUSTICE IS COMING.   So this is what the Sovereign LORD says:

Isa.
28:16-22

"See, I lay a stone in Zion,
    a tested stone,
a precious cornerstone for a sure foundation;
    the one who trusts will never be dismayed.
I will make justice the measuring line
    and righteousness the plumb line;
hail will sweep away your refuge, the lie,
    and water will overflow your hiding place.
Your covenant with death will be annulled;
    your agreement with the grave will not stand.
When the overwhelming scourge sweeps by,
    you will be beaten down by it.
As often as it comes it will carry you away;
    morning after morning, by day and by night,

*q*Hebrew / *sav lasav sav lasav / kav lakav kav lakav* (possibly meaningless sounds; perhaps a
mimicking of the prophet's words)   *r*Hebrew *Sheol*   *s*Or *false gods*   *t*Hebrew;
Septuagint *They worship me in vain; / their teachings are but rules taught by men*

it will sweep through."

The understanding of this message
    will bring sheer terror.
The bed is too short to stretch out on,
    the blanket too narrow to wrap around you.
The LORD will rise up as he did at Mount Perazim,
    he will rouse himself as in the Valley of Gibeon—
to do his work, his strange work,
    and perform his task, his alien task.
Now stop your mocking,
    or your chains will become heavier;
the Lord, the LORD Almighty, has told me
    of the destruction decreed against the whole land.

Isa.   REASONABLE PUNISHMENT.
28:23-29

Listen and hear my voice;
    pay attention and hear what I say.
When a farmer plows for planting, does he plow
        continually?
    Does he keep on breaking up and harrowing the soil?
When he has leveled the surface,
    does he not sow caraway and scatter cummin?
Does he not plant wheat in its place,[u]
    barley in its plot, [u]
    and spelt in its field?
His God instructs him
    and teaches him the right way.

Caraway is not threshed with a sledge,
    nor is a cartwheel rolled over cummin;
caraway is beaten out with a rod,
    and cummin with a stick.
Grain must be ground to make bread;
    so one does not go on threshing it forever.
Though he drives the wheels of his threshing cart over it,
    his horses do not grind it.
All this also comes from the LORD Almighty,
    wonderful in counsel and magnificent in wisdom.

Isa. 22:1-14   JERUSALEM WARNINGS IGNORED.   An oracle concerning the Valley
                of Vision:

What troubles you now,
    that you have all gone up on the roofs,
O town full of commotion,
    O city of tumult and revelry?
Your slain were not killed by the sword,
    nor did they die in battle.
All your leaders have fled together;
    they have been captured without using the bow.
All you who were caught were taken prisoner together,

[u]The meaning of the Hebrew for this word is uncertain.

having fled while the enemy was still far away.
Therefore I said, "Turn away from me;
 let me weep bitterly.
Do not try to console me
 over the destruction of my people."

The Lord, the LORD Almighty, has a day
 of tumult and trampling and terror
 in the Valley of Vision,
a day of battering down walls
 and of crying out to the mountains.
Elam takes up the quiver,
 with her charioteers and horses;
 Kir uncovers the shield.
Your choicest valleys are full of chariots,
 and horsemen are posted at the city gates;
 the defenses of Judah are stripped away.

And you looked in that day
 to the weapons in the Palace of the Forest;
you saw that the City of David
 had many breaches in its defenses;
you stored up water
 in the Lower Pool.
You counted the buildings in Jerusalem
 and tore down houses to strengthen the wall.
You built a reservoir between the two walls
 for the water of the Old Pool,
but you did not look to the One who made it,
 or have regard for the One who planned it long ago.

The Lord, the LORD Almighty,
 called you on that day
to weep and to wail,
 to tear out your hair and put on sackcloth.
But see, there is joy and revelry,
 slaughtering of cattle and killing of sheep,
 eating of meat and drinking of wine!
"Let us eat and drink," you say,
 "for tomorrow we die!"

 The LORD Almighty has revealed this in my hearing: "Till your dying
day this sin will not be atoned for," says the Lord, the LORD Almighty.

JERUSALEM WILL FALL.   Isa. 29:1-4

Woe to you, Ariel, Ariel,
 the city where David settled!
Add year to year
 and let your cycle of festivals go on.
Yet I will besiege Ariel;
 she will mourn and lament,
 she will be to me like an altar hearth.^{v}

^{v}The Hebrew for *hearth* sounds like the Hebrew for *Ariel*.

> I will encamp against you all around;
>> I will encircle you with towers
>> and set up my siege works against you.
> Brought low, you will speak from the ground;
>> your speech will mumble out of the dust.
> Your voice will come ghostlike from the earth;
>> out of the dust your speech will whisper.

Isa. 29:5-8   JUDGMENT AGAINST OPPRESSORS.

> But your many enemies will become like fine dust,
>> the ruthless hordes like blown chaff.
> Suddenly, in an instant,
>> the LORD Almighty will come
> with thunder and earthquake and great noise,
>> with windstorm and tempest and flames of a devouring
>>> fire.
> Then the hordes of all the nations that fight against Ariel,
>> that attack her and her fortress and besiege her,
> will be as it is with a dream,
>> with a vision in the night—
> as when a hungry man dreams that he is eating,
>> but he awakens, and his hunger remains;
> as when a thirsty man dreams that he is drinking,
>> but he awakens faint, with his thirst unquenched.
> So will it be with the hordes of all the nations
>> that fight against Mount Zion.

Isa. 33:1   OPPRESSORS TO BE DESTROYED.

> Woe to you, O destroyer,
>> you who have not been destroyed!
> Woe to you, O traitor,
>> you who have not been betrayed!
> When you stop destroying,
>> you will be destroyed;
> when you stop betraying,
>> you will be betrayed.

Isa. 29:9-12   UNDERSTANDING IS LOST.

> Be stunned and amazed,
>> blind yourselves and be sightless;
> be drunk, but not from wine,
>> stagger, but not from beer.
> The LORD has brought over you a deep sleep:
>> He has sealed your eyes (the prophets);
>> he has covered your heads (the seers).

For you this whole vision is nothing but words sealed in a scroll. And if you give the scroll to someone who can read, and say to him, "Read this, please," he will answer, "I can't; it is sealed." Or if you give the scroll to someone who cannot read, and say, "Read this, please," he will answer, "I don't know how to read."

MAN'S WISDOM FAILS.　　　　　　　　　　　　　　Isa.
29:14-16

> Therefore once more I will astound these people
>   with wonder upon wonder;
> the wisdom of the wise will perish,
>   the intelligence of the intelligent will vanish."
> Woe to those who go to great depths
>   to hide their plans from the LORD,
> who do their work in darkness and think,
>   "Who sees us? Who will know?"
> You turn things upside down,
>   as if the potter were thought to be like the clay!
> Shall what is formed say to him who formed it,
>   "He did not make me"?
> Can the pot say of the potter,
>   "He knows nothing"?

UNDERSTANDING WILL COME.　　　　　　　　　　　Isa.
29:17-21

> In a very short time, will not Lebanon be turned into a
>   fertile field
>   and the fertile field seem like a forest?
> In that day the deaf will hear the words of the scroll,
>   and out of gloom and darkness
>   the eyes of the blind will see.
> Once more the humble will rejoice in the LORD;
>   the needy will rejoice in the Holy One of Israel.
> The ruthless will vanish,
>   the mockers will disappear,
>   and all who have an eye for evil will be cut down—
> those who with a word make a man out to be guilty,
>   who ensnare the defender in court
>   and with false testimony deprive the innocent of justice.

A SPIRITUAL REAWAKENING.　　Therefore this is what the LORD, who　　Isa.
redeemed Abraham, says to the house of Jacob:　　　　　　　　　　29:22-24

> "No longer will Jacob be ashamed;
>   no longer will their faces grow pale.
> When they see among them their children,
>   the work of my hands,
> they will keep my name holy;
>   they will acknowledge the holiness of the Holy One of
>   Jacob,
>   and will stand in awe of the God of Israel.
> Those who are wayward in spirit will gain understanding;
>   those who complain will accept instruction."

VINEYARD TO BE RESTORED.　　In that day—　　　　Isa. 27:2-13

> "Sing about a fruitful vineyard:
>   I, the LORD, watch over it;
>   I water it continually.
> I guard it day and night
>   so that no one may harm it.

I am not angry.
If only there were briers and thorns confronting me!
    I would march against them in battle;
    I would set them all on fire.
Or else let them come to me for refuge;
    let them make peace with me,
    yes, let them make peace with me."

In days to come Jacob will take root,
    Israel will bud and blossom
    and fill all the world with fruit.

Has ⌊the LORD⌋ struck her
    as he struck down those who struck her?
Has she been killed
    as those were killed who killed her?
By warfare[w] and exile you contend with her—
    with his fierce blast he drives her out,
    as on a day the east wind blows.
By this, then, will Jacob's guilt be atoned for,
    and this will be the full fruitage of the removal of his sin:
When he makes all the altar stones
    to be like chalk stones crushed to pieces,
no Asherah poles[x] or incense altars
    will be left standing.
The fortified city stands desolate,
    an abandoned settlement, forsaken like the desert;
there the calves graze,
    there they lie down;
    they strip its branches bare.
When its twigs are dry, they are broken off
    and women come and make fires with them.
For this is a people without understanding;
    so their Maker has no compassion on them,
    and their Creator shows them no favor.

In that day the LORD will thresh from the flowing Euphrates[y] to the Wadi of Egypt, and you, O Israelites, will be gathered up one by one. And in that day a great trumpet will sound. Those who were perishing in Assyria and those who were exiled in Egypt will come and worship the LORD on the holy mountain in Jerusalem.

Isa.
32:12-20

BLESSINGS WILL RETURN.

Beat your breasts for the pleasant fields,
    for the fruitful vines
and for the land of my people,
    a land overgrown with thorns and briers—
yes, mourn for all houses of merriment
    and for this city of revelry.
The fortress will be abandoned,
    the noisy city deserted;

---

[w]See Septuagint; the meaning of the Hebrew for this word is uncertain.   [x]That is, symbols of the goddess Asherah   [y]Hebrew *River*

citadel and watchtower will become a wasteland forever,
    the delight of donkeys, a pasture for flocks,
till the Spirit is poured upon us from on high,
    and the desert becomes a fertile field,
    and the fertile field seems like a forest.
Justice will dwell in the desert
    and righteousness live in the fertile field.
The fruit of righteousness will be peace;
    the effect of righteousness will be quietness and
        confidence forever.
My people will live in peaceful dwelling places,
    in secure homes,
    in undisturbed places of rest.
Though hail flattens the forest
    and the city is leveled completely,
how blessed you will be,
    sowing your seed by every stream,
    and letting your cattle and donkeys range free.

SINS WILL BE FORGIVEN.   Isa. 33:2-16

O LORD, be gracious to us;
    we long for you.
Be our strength every morning,
    our salvation in time of distress.
At the thunder of your voice, the peoples flee;
    when you rise up, the nations scatter.
Your plunder, O nations, is harvested as by young locusts;
    like a swarm of locusts men pounce on it.

The LORD is exalted, for he dwells on high;
    he will fill Zion with justice and righteousness.
He will be the sure foundation for your times,
    a rich store of salvation and wisdom and knowledge;
    the fear of the LORD is the key to this treasure. [z]

Look, their brave men cry aloud in the streets;
    the envoys of peace weep bitterly.
The highways are deserted,
    no travelers are on the roads.
The treaty is broken,
    its witnesses [a] are despised,
    no one is respected.
The land mourns [b] and wastes away,
    Lebanon is ashamed and withers;
Sharon is like the Arabah,
    and Bashan and Carmel drop their leaves.

"Now will I arise," says the LORD.
    "Now will I be exalted;
    now will I be lifted up.
You conceive chaff,

[z] Or *is a treasure from him*   [a] Dead Sea Scrolls; Masoretic Text / *the cities*   [b] Or *dries up*

you give birth to straw;
   your breath is a fire that consumes you.
The peoples will be burned as if to lime;
   like cut thornbushes they will be set ablaze."

You who are far away, hear what I have done;
   you who are near, acknowledge my power!
The sinners in Zion are terrified;
   trembling grips the godless:
"Who of us can dwell with the consuming fire?
   Who of us can dwell with everlasting burning?"
He who walks righteously
   and speaks what is right,
who rejects gain from extortion
   and keeps his hand from accepting bribes,
who stops his ears against plots of murder
   and shuts his eyes against contemplating evil—
this is the man who will dwell on the heights,
   whose refuge will be the mountain fortress.
His bread will be supplied,
   and water will not fail him.

Isa.
33:17-24

Your eyes will see the king in his beauty
   and view a land that stretches afar.
In your thoughts you will ponder the former terror:
   "Where is that chief officer?
   Where is the one who took the revenue?
   Where is the officer in charge of the towers?"
You will see those arrogant people no more,
   those people of an obscure speech,
   with their strange, incomprehensible tongue.

Look upon Zion, the city of our festivals;
   your eyes will see Jerusalem,
   a peaceful abode, a tent that will not be moved;
its stakes will never be pulled up,
   nor any of its ropes broken.
There the LORD will be our Mighty One.
   It will be like a place of broad rivers and streams.
No galley with oars will ride them,
   no mighty ship will sail them.
For the LORD is our judge,
   the LORD is our lawgiver,
the LORD is our king;
   it is he who will save us.

Your rigging hangs loose:
   The mast is not held secure,
   the sail is not spread.
Then an abundance of spoils will be divided
   and even the lame will carry off plunder.
No one living in Zion will say, "I am ill";
   and the sins of those who dwell there will be forgiven.

Isaiah takes time out from his public preaching to bring a special message to just one man. It is not known fully why Shebna is singled out, but his breach of trust in ordering his own burial sepulcher while serving as master of Hezekiah's household will cause his demotion to a lesser rank. The historical record will soon confirm his replacement by Eliakim, just as Isaiah now prophesies.

SHEBNA TO LOSE POSITION.   This is what the Lord, the LORD Almighty, says:

Isa.
22:15-19

> "Go, say to this steward,
>   to Shebna, who is in charge of the palace:
>   What are you doing here and who gave you permission
>   to cut out a grave for yourself here,
>   hewing your grave on the height
>   and chiseling your resting place in the rock?
>
> "Beware, the LORD is about to take firm hold of you
>   and hurl you away, O you mighty man.
> He will roll you up tightly like a ball
>   and throw you into a large country.
> There you will die
>   and there your splendid chariots will remain—
>   you disgrace to your master's house!
> I will depose you from your office,
>   and you will be ousted from your position.

ELIAKIM TO REPLACE HIM.   "In that day I will summon my servant, Eliakim son of Hilkiah. I will clothe him with your robe and fasten your sash around him and hand your authority over to him. He will be a father to those who live in Jerusalem and to the house of Judah. I will place on his shoulder the key to the house of David; what he opens no one can shut, and what he shuts no one can open. I will drive him like a peg into a firm place; he will be a seat[c] of honor for the house of his father. All the glory of his family will hang on him: its offspring and offshoots—all its lesser vessels, from the bowls to all the jars.

Isa.
22:20-25

"In that day," declares the LORD Almighty, "the peg driven into the firm place will give way; it will be sheared off and will fall, and the load hanging on it will be cut down." The LORD has spoken.

The Fall of Israel

*D*espite prophetic warnings, Israel still rejects God, and the end is at hand for the northern tribes. Last-minute desperation will lead to an alliance with Egypt in an effort to stave off Assyria, but the cause is hopeless. After a three-year siege, Samaria will fall and many of the people of Israel will be led captive to Assyria. Their lands and homes will be occupied by settlers sent in from Babylonia and other Eastern countries. These new Samaritans will become a hybrid people and will develop an unusual mixed religion.

[c]Or *throne*

The Assyrian king at the time of the siege is Shalmaneser V. Upon Shalmaneser's death, in 722 B.C., Sargon II takes credit for the capture of Israel, but the fall itself is probably accomplished in 723 B.C. Here is the extremely brief account of one of the darkest hours in the history of God's chosen nation.

In Israel

2 Kgs. 17:3 VASSAL TO SHALMANESER.   Shalmaneser king of Assyria came up to attack Hoshea, who had been Shalmaneser's vassal and had paid him tribute.

2 Kgs. 17:4a ALLIANCE DISCOVERED.   But the king of Assyria discovered that Hoshea was a traitor, for he had sent envoys to So^d king of Egypt, and he no longer paid tribute to the king of Assyria, as he had done year by year.

2 Kgs. 17:4b HOSHEA IMPRISONED.   Therefore Shalmaneser seized him and put him in prison.

2 Kgs. 17:5 18:9 (726-723 B.C.) THREE-YEAR SIEGE.   In King Hezekiah's fourth year, which was the seventh year of Hoshea son of Elah king of Israel, Shalmaneser king of Assyria marched against Samaria and laid siege to it. The king of Assyria invaded the entire land, marched against Samaria and laid siege to it for three years.

2 Kgs. 18:10 (723 B.C.) Samaria SAMARIA FALLS.   At the end of three years the Assyrians took it. So Samaria was captured in Hezekiah's sixth year, which was the ninth year of Hoshea king of Israel.

2 Kgs. 17:6 18:11 (723-721 B.C.) ISRAEL TAKEN CAPTIVE.   The king of Assyria deported Israel to Assyria and settled them in Halah, in Gozan on the Habor River and in towns of the Medes.

2 Kgs. 17:7-12 18:12 REASON FOR ISRAEL'S FALL.   All this took place because the Israelites had sinned against the LORD their God, who had brought them up out of Egypt from under the power of Pharaoh king of Egypt. They worshiped other gods and followed the practices of the nations the LORD had driven out before them, as well as the practices that the kings of Israel had introduced. The Israelites secretly did things against the LORD their God that were not right. From watchtower to fortified city they built themselves high places in all their towns. They set up sacred stones and Asherah poles on every high hill and under every spreading tree. At every high place they burned incense, as the nations whom the LORD had driven out before them had done. They did wicked things that provoked the LORD to anger. They worshiped idols, though the LORD had said, "You shall not do this."^{e}

2 Kgs. 17:13,14 PROPHETS' WARNINGS IGNORED.   The LORD warned Israel and Judah through all his prophets and seers: "Turn from your evil ways. Observe my commands and decrees, in accordance with the entire Law that I commanded your fathers to obey and that I delivered to you through my servants the prophets."

But they would not listen and were as stiff-necked as their fathers, who did not trust in the LORD their God.

---

^{d}Or *to Sais, to the; So* is possibly an abbreviation for *Osorkon.* ^{e}Exodus 20:4, 5

ISRAEL'S SINS. They rejected his decrees and the covenant he had made with their fathers and the warnings he had given them. They followed worthless idols and themselves became worthless. They imitated the nations around them although the LORD had ordered them, "Do not do as they do," and they did the things the LORD had forbidden them to do.

2 Kgs. 17:15-17

They forsook all the commands of the LORD their God and made for themselves two idols cast in the shape of calves, and an Asherah pole. They bowed down to all the starry hosts, and they worshiped Baal. They sacrificed their sons and daughters in*f* the fire. They practiced divination and sorcery and sold themselves to do evil in the eyes of the LORD, provoking him to anger.

JUDAH NOT PERFECT. So the LORD was very angry with Israel and removed them from his presence. Only the tribe of Judah was left, and even Judah did not keep the commands of the LORD their God. They followed the practices Israel had introduced. Therefore the LORD rejected all the people of Israel; he afflicted them and gave them into the hands of plunderers, until he thrust them from his presence.

2 Kgs. 17:18-20

JEROBOAM'S GUILT. When he tore Israel away from the house of David, they made Jeroboam son of Nebat their king. Jeroboam enticed Israel away from following the LORD and caused them to commit a great sin. The Israelites persisted in all the sins of Jeroboam and did not turn away from them until the LORD removed them from his presence, as he had warned through all his servants the prophets. So the people of Israel were taken from their homeland into exile in Assyria, and they are still there.

2 Kgs. 17:21-23

FOREIGNERS INHABIT SAMARIA. The king of Assyria brought people from Babylon, Cuthah, Avva, Hamath and Sepharvaim and settled them in the towns of Samaria to replace the Israelites. They took over Samaria and lived in its towns.

2 Kgs. 17:24 Samaria

LIONS ATTACK SETTLERS. When they first lived there, they did not worship the LORD; so he sent lions among them and they killed some of the people. It was reported to the king of Assyria: "The people you deported and resettled in the towns of Samaria do not know what the god of that country requires. He has sent lions among them, which are killing them off, because the people do not know what he requires."

2 Kgs. 17:25,26

SAMARITANS MIX RELIGION. Then the king of Assyria gave this order: "Have one of the priests you took captive from Samaria go back to live there and teach the people what the god of the land requires." So one of the priests who had been exiled from Samaria came to live in Bethel and taught them how to worship the LORD.

2 Kgs. 17:27-41

Nevertheless, each national group made its own gods in the several towns where they settled, and set them up in the shrines the people of Samaria had made at the high places. The men from Babylon made Succoth Benoth, the men from Cuthah made Nergal, and the men from Hamath made Ashima; the Avvites made Nibhaz and Tartak, and the Sepharvites burned their children in the fire as sacrifices to Adrammelech and Anammelech, the gods of Sepharvaim. They worshiped the LORD, but they also appointed all sorts of their own people to officiate for them as

*f*Or *They made their sons and daughters pass through*

priests in the shrines at the high places. They worshiped the LORD, but they also served their own gods in accordance with the customs of the nations from which they had been brought.

To this day they persist in their former practices. They neither worship the LORD nor adhere to the decrees and ordinances, the laws and commands that the LORD gave the descendants of Jacob, whom he named Israel. When the LORD made a covenant with the Israelites, he commanded them: "Do not worship any other gods or bow down to them, serve them or sacrifice to them. But the LORD, who brought you up out of Egypt with mighty power and outstretched arm, is the one you must worship. To him you shall bow down and to him offer sacrifices. You must always be careful to keep the decrees and ordinances, the laws and commands he wrote for you. Do not worship other gods. Do not forget the covenant I have made with you, and do not worship other gods. Rather, worship the LORD your God; it is he who will deliver you from the hand of all your enemies."

They would not listen, however, but persisted in their former practices. Even while these people were worshiping the LORD, they were serving their idols. To this day their children and grandchildren continue to do as their fathers did.

In Judah, meanwhile, Hezekiah holds his own against Assyria and wages a successful campaign against the ever-present Philistines.

In Judah

2 Kgs. 18:7b REBELLION AGAINST ASSYRIA.   He rebelled against the king of
(721 B.C.?)   Assyria and did not serve him.

2 Kgs. 18:8   DEFEAT OF PHILISTINES.   From watchtower to fortified city, he defeated the Philistines, as far as Gaza and its territory.

JUDAH AFTER ISRAEL'S FALL

(Ca. 725-585 B.C.)

Isaiah Warns About Egypt and Ethiopia

ith Assyria threatening conquest, Judah begins to look for help wherever it can be found. Some are urging an alliance with Egypt, which at present is ruled by Cushites from Ethiopia. Since Egypt's military strength lies in its many horses and chariots, Isaiah is displeased with the thought that God's people also wish to rely on horses and chariots, instead of on God's unlimited power. Therefore Isaiah speaks out in judgment against Egypt and Cush. Not only does Isaiah preach his warnings, but at God's direction—and at what must be great embarrassment to himself—Isaiah actually goes about "naked" for three years. (It may be that Isaiah is only stripped of his outer garments, but even that must surely be an affront to his dignity.) God chooses the occasion of Sargon's attack against Ashdod in 711 B.C. to explain further why his respected prophet has seemingly disgraced himself. The timing is particularly appropriate because Ashdod, a Philistine city, has been allied with Egypt against Assyria.

Word of Isaiah's message apparently reaches even as far as Assyria, because Sennacherib's field commander will refer to it some ten years later when he ridicules Judah both for trusting in God (little as it did) and for relying on Egypt's military strength.

Both Isaiah and this Assyrian officer will be proved correct in their assessment of Egypt. In fact, instead of saving Judah from Assyria, Egypt under Pharaoh Neco II will actually become one of Judah's oppressors. Therefore Isaiah's judgments against Egypt are well warranted.

JUDGMENT AGAINST CUSH.

Isa. 18:1-7
(Ca. 714
B.C.)

> Woe to the land of whirring wings [a]
>   along the rivers of Cush,[b]
> which sends envoys by sea
>   in papyrus boats over the water.
>
> Go, swift messengers,
>   to a people tall and smooth-skinned,
>   to a people feared far and wide,
> an aggressive nation of strange speech,

[a] Or *of locusts*   [b] That is, the upper Nile region

whose land is divided by rivers.

All you people of the world,
    you who live on the earth,
when a banner is raised on the mountains,
    you will see it,
and when a trumpet sounds,
    you will hear it.
This is what the LORD says to me:
    "I will remain quiet and will look on from my dwelling
        place,
like shimmering heat in the sunshine,
    like a cloud of dew in the heat of harvest."
For, before the harvest, when the blossom is gone
    and the flower becomes a ripening grape,
he will cut off the shoots with pruning knives,
    and cut down and take away the spreading branches.
They will all be left to the mountain birds of prey
    and to the wild animals;
the birds will feed on them all summer,
    the wild animals all winter.

At that time gifts will be brought to the LORD Almighty

from a people tall and smooth-skinned,
    from a people feared far and wide,
an aggressive nation of strange speech,
    whose land is divided by rivers—

the gifts will be brought to Mount Zion, the place of the Name of the LORD
Almighty.

Isa. 19:1-15 JUDGMENT AGAINST EGYPT.   An oracle concerning Egypt:

See, the LORD rides on a swift cloud
    and is coming to Egypt.
The idols of Egypt tremble before him,
    and the hearts of the Egyptians melt within them.

"I will stir up Egyptian against Egyptian—
    brother will fight against brother,
    neighbor against neighbor,
    city against city,
    kingdom against kingdom.
The Egyptians will lose heart,
    and I will bring their plans to nothing;
they will consult the idols and the spirits of the dead,
    the mediums and the spiritists.
I will hand the Egyptians over
    to the power of a cruel master,
and a fierce king will rule over them,"
    declares the Lord, the LORD Almighty.

The waters of the river will dry up,
    and the riverbed will be parched and dry.
The canals will stink;

the streams of Egypt will dwindle and dry up.
The reeds and rushes will wither,
    also the plants along the Nile,
    at the mouth of the river.
Every sown field along the Nile
    will become parched, will blow away and be no more.
The fishermen will groan and lament,
    all who cast hooks into the Nile;
those who throw nets on the water
    will pine away.
Those who work with combed flax will despair,
    the weavers of fine linen will lose hope.
The workers in cloth will be dejected,
    and all the wage earners will be sick at heart.

The officials of Zoan are nothing but fools;
    the wise counselors of Pharaoh give senseless advice.
How can you say to Pharaoh,
    "I am one of the wise men,
    a disciple of the ancient kings"?

Where are your wise men now?
    Let them show you and make known
what the LORD Almighty
    has planned against Egypt.
The officials of Zoan have become fools,
    the leaders of Memphis[c] are deceived;
the cornerstones of her peoples
    have led Egypt astray.
The LORD has poured into them
    a spirit of dizziness;
they make Egypt stagger in all that she does,
    as a drunkard staggers around in his vomit.
There is nothing Egypt can do—
    head or tail, palm branch or reed.

JUDAH WILL SUBJUGATE EGYPT. In that day the Egyptians will be like women. They will shudder with fear at the uplifted hand that the LORD Almighty raises against them. And the land of Judah will bring terror to the Egyptians; everyone to whom Judah is mentioned will be terrified, because of what the LORD Almighty is planning against them.

In that day five cities in Egypt will speak the language of Canaan and swear allegiance to the LORD Almighty. One of them will be called the City of Destruction.[d]

Isa. 19:16-18

EGYPT WILL ACKNOWLEDGE GOD. In that day there will be an altar to the LORD in the heart of Egypt, and a monument to the LORD at its border. It will be a sign and witness to the LORD Almighty in the land of Egypt. When they cry out to the LORD because of their oppressors, he will send them a savior and defender, and he will rescue them. So the LORD will make himself known to the Egyptians, and in that day they will

Isa. 19:19-22

[c]Hebrew *Noph*   [d]Most manuscripts of the Masoretic Text; some manuscripts of the Masoretic Text, Dead Sea Scrolls and Vulgate *City of the Sun* (that is, Heliopolis)

acknowledge the LORD. They will worship with sacrifices and grain offerings; they will make vows to the LORD and keep them. The LORD will strike Egypt with a plague; he will strike them and heal them. They will turn to the LORD, and he will respond to their pleas and heal them.

Isa. 19:23-25

SPIRITUAL RESTORATION.   In that day there will be a highway from Egypt to Assyria. The Assyrians will go to Egypt and the Egyptians to Assyria. The Egyptians and Assyrians will worship together. In that day Israel will be the third, along with Egypt and Assyria, a blessing on the earth. The LORD Almighty will bless them, saying, "Blessed be Egypt my people, Assyria my handiwork, and Israel my inheritance."

Isa. 20:1,2 (711 B.C.)

ISAIAH'S NAKEDNESS A SIGN.   In the year that the supreme commander, sent by Sargon king of Assyria, came to Ashdod and attacked and captured it—at that time the LORD spoke through Isaiah son of Amoz. He said to him, "Take off the sackcloth from your body and the sandals from your feet." And he did so, going around stripped and barefoot.

Isa. 20:3-6

OPPRESSION OF EGYPT AND CUSH.   Then the LORD said, "Just as my servant Isaiah has gone stripped and barefoot for three years, as a sign and portent against Egypt and Cush,[e] so the king of Assyria will lead away stripped and barefoot the Egyptian captives and Cushite exiles, young and old, with buttocks bared—to Egypt's shame. Those who trusted in Cush and boasted in Egypt will be afraid and put to shame. In that day the people who live on this coast will say, 'See what has happened to those we relied on, those we fled to for help and deliverance from the king of Assyria! How then can we escape?'"

Isa. 30:1-7

EGYPT CANNOT SAVE JUDAH.

> "Woe to the obstinate children,"
>   declares the LORD,
> "to those who carry out plans that are not mine,
>   forming an alliance, but not by my Spirit,
>   heaping sin upon sin;
> who go down to Egypt
>   without consulting me;
> who look for help to Pharaoh's protection,
>   to Egypt's shade for refuge.
> But Pharaoh's protection will be to your shame,
>   Egypt's shade will bring you disgrace.
> Though they have officials in Zoan
>   and their envoys have arrived in Hanes,
> everyone will be put to shame
>   because of a people useless to them,
> who bring neither help nor advantage,
>   but only shame and disgrace."

An oracle concerning the animals of the Negev:

> Through a land of hardship and distress,
>   of lions and lionesses,
>   of adders and darting snakes,
> the envoys carry their riches on donkeys' backs,

[e]That is, the upper Nile region

their treasures on the humps of camels,
to that unprofitable nation,
to Egypt, whose help is utterly useless.
Therefore I call her
Rahab the Do-Nothing.

JUDAH REJECTS TRUTH.   Isa. 30:8-14

Go now, write it on a tablet for them,
inscribe it on a scroll,
that for the days to come
it may be an everlasting witness.
These are rebellious people, deceitful children,
children unwilling to listen to the LORD's instruction.
They say to the seers,
"See no more visions!"
and to the prophets,
"Give us no more visions of what is right!
Tell us pleasant things,
prophesy illusions.
Leave this way,
get off this path,
and stop confronting us
with the Holy One of Israel!"

Therefore, this is what the Holy One of Israel says:

"Because you have rejected this message,
relied on oppression
and depended on deceit,
this sin will become for you
like a high wall, cracked and bulging,
that collapses suddenly, in an instant.
It will break in pieces like pottery,
shattered so mercilessly
that among its pieces not a fragment will be found
for taking coals from a hearth
or scooping water out of a cistern."

GOD IS STRENGTH.   This is what the Sovereign LORD, the Holy One of   Isa.
Israel, says: 30:15-18

"In repentance and rest is your salvation,
in quietness and trust is your strength,
but you would have none of it.
You said, 'No, we will flee on horses.'
Therefore you will flee!
You said, 'We will ride off on swift horses.'
Therefore your pursuers will be swift!
A thousand will flee
at the threat of one;
at the threat of five
you will all flee away,
till you are left
like a flagstaff on a mountaintop,

like a banner on a hill."

Yet the LORD longs to be gracious to you;
    he rises to show you compassion.
For the LORD is a God of justice.
    Blessed are all who wait for him!

Isa.
30:19-26

GOD WILL RESTORE NATION.   O people of Zion, who live in Jerusalem, you will weep no more. How gracious he will be when you cry for help! As soon as he hears, he will answer you. Although the Lord gives you the bread of adversity and the water of affliction, your teachers will be hidden no more; with your own eyes you will see them. Whether you turn to the right or to the left, your ears will hear a voice behind you, saying, "This is the way; walk in it." Then you will defile your idols overlaid with silver and your images covered with gold; you will throw them away like a menstrual cloth and say to them, "Away with you!"

He will also send you rain for the seed you sow in the ground, and the food that comes from the land will be rich and plentiful. In that day your cattle will graze in broad meadows. The oxen and donkeys that work the soil will eat fodder and mash, spread out with fork and shovel. In the day of great slaughter, when the towers fall, streams of water will flow on every high mountain and every lofty hill. The moon will shine like the sun, and the sunlight will be seven times brighter, like the light of seven full days, when the LORD binds up the bruises of his people and heals the wounds he inflicted.

Isa.
30:27-33

ASSYRIA WILL BE PUNISHED.

See, the Name of the LORD comes from afar,
    with burning anger and dense clouds of smoke;
his lips are full of wrath,
    and his tongue is a consuming fire.
His breath is like a rushing torrent,
    rising up to the neck.
He shakes the nations in the sieve of destruction;
    he places in the jaws of the peoples
    a bit that leads them astray.
And you will sing
    as on the night you celebrate a holy festival;
your hearts will rejoice
    as when people go up with flutes
to the mountain of the LORD,
    to the Rock of Israel.
The LORD will cause men to hear his majestic voice
    and will make them see his arm coming down
with raging anger and consuming fire,
    with cloudburst, thunderstorm and hail.
The voice of the LORD will shatter Assyria;
    with his scepter he will strike them down.
Every stroke the LORD lays on them
    with his punishing rod
will be to the music of tambourines and harps,
    as he fights them in battle with the blows of his arm.

Topheth has long been prepared;
  it has been made ready for the king.
Its fire pit has been made deep and wide,
  with an abundance of fire and wood;
the breath of the LORD,
    like a stream of burning sulfur,
    sets it ablaze.

FUTILE RELIANCE ON EGYPT.   Isa. 31:1-3

Woe to those who go down to Egypt for help,
  who rely on horses,
who trust in the multitude of their chariots
    and in the great strength of their horsemen,
but do not look to the Holy One of Israel,
    or seek help from the LORD.
Yet he too is wise and can bring disaster;
    he does not take back his words.
He will rise up against the house of the wicked,
    against those who help evildoers.
But the Egyptians are men and not God;
    their horses are flesh and not spirit.
When the LORD stretches out his hand,
    he who helps will stumble,
    he who is helped will fall;
    both will perish together.

GOD WILL PUNISH ASSYRIA.   This is what the LORD says to me: Isa. 31:4-9

"As a lion growls,
    a great lion over his prey—
and though a whole band of shepherds
    is called together against him,
he is not frightened by their shouts
    or disturbed by their clamor—
so the LORD Almighty will come down
    to do battle on Mount Zion and on its heights.
Like birds hovering overhead,
    the LORD Almighty will shield Jerusalem;
he will shield it and deliver it,
    he will 'pass over' it and will rescue it."

Return to him you have so greatly revolted against, O Israelites. For in
that day every one of you will reject the idols of silver and gold your sinful hands have made.

"Assyria will fall by a sword that is not of man;
    a sword, not of mortals, will devour them.
They will flee before the sword
    and their young men will be put to forced labor.
Their stronghold will fall because of terror;
    at sight of the battle standard their commanders will
        panic,"
declares the LORD,
    whose fire is in Zion,
    whose furnace is in Jerusalem.

Last Years of Hezekiah's Reign

*H*ezekiah must truly have won God's favor by his earlier reforms of worship in Judah, for when it comes time for him to die, his prayer for longer life is answered by an extension of 15 years. Even that most unusual gesture is confirmed by another equally amazing miracle: God turns back the shadow on a stairway-type sun dial.

During Hezekiah's last 15 years he is forced for a time to pay tribute to Sennacherib, before God miraculously causes the deaths of thousands of Assyrian troops and forces Sennacherib to return home in disgrace. Yet even as the Assyrian threat dwindles, a visit by envoys of Babylon portends new trouble for Judah from that increasingly powerful nation.

2 Kgs.
18:13
Isa. 36:1
(701 B.C.)

SENNACHERIB INVADES JUDAH. In the fourteenth *f* year of King Hezekiah's reign, Sennacherib king of Assyria attacked all the fortified cities of Judah and captured them.

2 Kgs.
18:14-16
Jerusalem

JUDAH PAYS TRIBUTE. So Hezekiah king of Judah sent this message to the king of Assyria at Lachish: "I have done wrong. Withdraw from me, and I will pay whatever you demand of me." The king of Assyria exacted from Hezekiah king of Judah three hundred talents *g* of silver and thirty talents *h* of gold. So Hezekiah gave him all the silver that was found in the temple of the LORD and in the treasuries of the royal palace.

At this time Hezekiah king of Judah stripped off the gold with which he had covered the doors and doorposts of the temple of the LORD, and gave it to the king of Assyria.

2 Kgs.
20:1-11
2 Chron.
32-24
Isa.
38:1-8,21,22

HEZEKIAH'S LIFE EXTENDED. In those days Hezekiah became ill and was at the point of death. The prophet Isaiah son of Amoz went to him and said, "This is what the LORD says: Put your house in order, because you are going to die; you will not recover."

Hezekiah turned his face to the wall and prayed to the LORD, "Remember, O LORD, how I have walked before you faithfully and with wholehearted devotion and have done what is good in your eyes." And Hezekiah wept bitterly.

Before Isaiah had left the middle court, the word of the LORD came to him: "Go back and tell Hezekiah, the leader of my people, 'This is what the LORD, the God of your father David, says: I have heard your prayer and seen your tears; I will heal you. On the third day from now you will go up to the temple of the LORD. I will add fifteen years to your life. And I will deliver you and this city from the hand of the king of Assyria. I will defend this city for my sake and for the sake of my servant David.'"

Then Isaiah said, "Prepare a poultice of figs." They did so and applied it to the boil, and he recovered.

Hezekiah had asked Isaiah, "What will be the sign that the LORD will heal me and that I will go up to the temple of the LORD on the third day from now?"

Isaiah answered, "This is the LORD's sign to you that the LORD will do

---

f [24th (?)]   *g* That is, about 11 tons (about 10 metric tons)   *h* That is, about 1 ton
(about 1 metric ton)

what he has promised: Shall the shadow go forward ten steps, or shall it go back ten steps?"

"It is a simple matter for the shadow to go forward ten steps," said Hezekiah. "Rather, have it go back ten steps."

Then the prophet Isaiah called upon the LORD, and the LORD made the shadow go back the ten steps it had gone down on the stairway of Ahaz.

HEZEKIAH'S THANKSGIVING.   A writing of Hezekiah king of Judah   Isa. 38:9-20
after his illness and recovery:

> I said, "In the prime of my life
>   must I go through the gates of death[i]
>   and be robbed of the rest of my years?"
> I said, "I will not again see the LORD,
>   the LORD, in the land of the living;
> no longer will I look on mankind,
>   or be with those who now dwell in this world.[j]
> Like a shepherd's tent my house
>   has been pulled down and taken from me.
> Like a weaver I have rolled up my life,
>   and he has cut me off from the loom;
>   day and night you made an end of me.
> I waited patiently till dawn,
>   but like a lion he broke all my bones;
>   day and night you made an end of me.
> I cried like a swift or thrush,
>   I moaned like a mourning dove.
> My eyes grew weak as I looked to the heavens.
>   I am troubled; O Lord, come to my aid!"
>
> But what can I say?
>   He has spoken to me, and he himself has done this.
> I will walk humbly all my years
>   because of this anguish of my soul.
> Lord, by such things men live;
>   and my spirit finds life in them too.
> You restored me to health
>   and let me live.
> Surely it was for my benefit
>   that I suffered such anguish.
> In your love you kept me
>   from the pit of destruction;
> you have put all my sins
>   behind your back.
> For the grave[i] cannot praise you,
>   death cannot sing your praise;
> those who go down to the pit
>   cannot hope for your faithfulness.
> The living, the living—they praise you,
>   as I am doing today;
> fathers tell their children

[i]Hebrew *Sheol*   [j]A few Hebrew manuscripts; most Hebrew manuscripts *in the place of cessation*

about your faithfulness.

The LORD will save me,
    and we will sing with stringed instruments
all the days of our lives
    in the temple of the LORD.

2 Chron.
32:25,26

HEZEKIAH'S PRIDE.   But Hezekiah's heart was proud and he did not respond to the kindness shown him; therefore the LORD's wrath was on him and on Judah and Jerusalem. Then Hezekiah repented of the pride of his heart, as did the people of Jerusalem; therefore the LORD's wrath did not come upon them during the days of Hezekiah.

2 Chron.
32:27-30

JUDAH'S PROSPERITY.   Hezekiah had very great riches and honor, and he made treasuries for his silver and gold and for his precious stones, spices, shields and all kinds of valuables. He also made buildings to store the harvest of grain, new wine and oil; and he made stalls for various kinds of cattle, and pens for the flocks. He built villages and acquired great numbers of flocks and herds, for God had given him very great riches.

It was Hezekiah who blocked the upper outlet of the Gihon spring and channeled the water down to the west side of the City of David. He succeeded in everything he undertook.

2 Kgs.
20:12-19
Isa. 39:1-8

ENVOYS FROM BABYLON.   At that time Merodach-Baladan son of Baladan king of Babylon sent Hezekiah letters and a gift, because he had heard of Hezekiah's illness. Hezekiah received the messengers and showed them all that was in his storehouses—the silver, the gold, the spices, the fine oil, his armory and everything found among his treasures. There was nothing in his palace or in all his kingdom that Hezekiah did not show them.

Then Isaiah the prophet went to King Hezekiah and asked, "What did those men say, and where did they come from?"

"From a distant land," Hezekiah replied. "They came from Babylon."

The prophet asked, "What did they see in your palace?"

"They saw everything in my palace," Hezekiah said. "There is nothing among my treasures that I did not show them."

Then Isaiah said to Hezekiah, "Hear the word of the LORD: The time will surely come when everything in your palace, and all that your fathers have stored up until this day, will be carried off to Babylon. Nothing will be left, says the LORD. And some of your descendants, your own flesh and blood, that will be born to you, will be taken away, and they will become eunuchs in the palace of the king of Babylon."

"The word of the LORD you have spoken is good," Hezekiah replied. For he thought, "Will there not be peace and security in my lifetime?"

2 Chron.
32:31

ENVOYS A TEST.   But when envoys were sent by the rulers of Babylon to ask him about the miraculous sign that had occurred in the land, God left him to test him and to know everything that was in his heart.

2 Chron.
32:1

SENNACHERIB INVADES AGAIN.   After all that Hezekiah had so faithfully done, Sennacherib king of Assyria came and invaded Judah. He laid siege to the fortified cities, thinking to conquer them for himself.

2 Chron.
32:2-8

HEZEKIAH'S PREPARATIONS.   When Hezekiah saw that Sennacherib had come and that he intended to make war on Jerusalem, he consulted with his officials and military staff about blocking off the water from the

springs outside the city, and they helped him. A large force of men assembled, and they blocked all the springs and the stream that flowed through
the land. "Why should the kings*k* of Assyria come and find plenty of
water?" they said. Then he worked hard repairing all the broken sections
of the wall and building towers on it. He built another wall outside that
one and reinforced the supporting terraces*l* of the City of David. He also
made large numbers of weapons and shields.

He appointed military officers over the people and assembled them
before him in the square at the city gate and encouraged them with these
words: "Be strong and courageous. Do not be afraid or discouraged
because of the king of Assyria and the vast army with him, for there is a
greater power with us than with him. With him is only the arm of flesh,
but with us is the LORD our God to help us and to fight our battles." And
the people gained confidence from what Hezekiah the king of Judah said.

FIELD COMMANDER'S MESSAGE.   ᶜʰLater, when Sennacherib king of
Assyria and all his forces were laying siege to Lachish, he sent his officers
to Jerusalem with this message for Hezekiah king of Judah and for all the
people of Judah who were there:

ᴷᵍThe king of Assyria sent his supreme commander, his chief officer and
his field commander with a large army, from Lachish to King Hezekiah at
Jerusalem. They came up to Jerusalem and stopped at the aqueduct of the
Upper Pool, on the road to the Washerman's Field. They called for the
king; and Eliakim son of Hilkiah the palace administrator, Shebna the secretary, and Joah son of Asaph the recorder went out to them.

The field commander said to them, "Tell Hezekiah:

" 'This is what the great king, the king of Assyria, says: On what are you
basing this confidence of yours? You say you have strategy and military
strength—but you speak only empty words. On whom are you depending, that you rebel against me? Look now, you are depending on Egypt,
that splintered reed of a staff, which pierces a man's hand and wounds
him if he leans on it! Such is Pharaoh king of Egypt to all who depend on
him. And if you say to me, "We are depending on the LORD our God"—
isn't he the one whose high places and altars Hezekiah removed, saying to
Judah and Jerusalem, "You must worship before this altar in Jerusalem"?
ᶜʰWhen Hezekiah says, 'The LORD our God will save us from the hand of
the king of Assyria,' he is misleading you, to let you die of hunger and
thirst.

"Do you not know what I and my fathers have done to all the peoples
of the other lands? Were the gods of those nations ever able to deliver their
land from my hand? Who of all the gods of these nations that my fathers
destroyed has been able to save his people from me? How then can your
god deliver you from my hand? Now do not let Hezekiah deceive you and
mislead you like this. Do not believe him, for no god of any nation or kingdom has been able to deliver his people from my hand or the hand of my
fathers. How much less will your god deliver you from my hand!"
ᴷᵍ" 'Come now, make a bargain with my master, the king of Assyria: I will
give you two thousand horses—if you can put riders on them! How then
can you repulse one officer of the least of my master's officials, even

2 Kgs.
18:17-25
2 Chron.
32:9-15
Isa. 36:2-10
Lachish

---

*k*Hebrew; Septuagint and Syriac *king*   *l*Or *the Millo* though you are depending on Egypt for chariots and horsemen[m]? Furthermore, have I come to attack and destroy this land without word from the LORD? The LORD himself told me to march against this country and destroy it.'"

2 Kgs.
18:26
Isa. 36:11

REQUEST BY MINISTERS. Then Eliakim son of Hilkiah, and Shebna and Joah said to the field commander, "Please speak to your servants in Aramaic, since we understand it. Don't speak to us in Hebrew in the hearing of the people on the wall."

2 Kgs.
18:27-35
2 Chron.
32:16,18,19
Isa.
36:12-20

FIELD COMMANDER INSOLENT. [Kg]But the commander replied, "Was it only to your master and you that my master sent me to say these things, and not to the men sitting on the wall—who, like you, will have to eat their own filth and drink their own urine?"

Then the commander stood and called out in Hebrew: "Hear the word of the great king, the king of Assyria! This is what the king says: Do not let Hezekiah deceive you. He cannot deliver you from my hand. Do not let Hezekiah persuade you to trust in the LORD when he says, 'The LORD will surely deliver us; this city will not be given into the hand of the king of Assyria.'

"Do not listen to Hezekiah. This is what the king of Assyria says: Make peace with me and come out to me. Then every one of you will eat from his own vine and fig tree and drink water from his own cistern, until I come and take you to a land like your own, a land of grain and new wine, a land of bread and vineyards, a land of olive trees and honey. Choose life and not death!

"Do not listen to Hezekiah, for he is misleading you when he says, 'The LORD will deliver us.' Has the god of any nation ever delivered his land from the hand of the king of Assyria? Where are the gods of Hamath and Arpad? Where are the gods of Sepharvaim, Hena and Ivvah? Have they rescued Samaria from my hand? Who of all the gods of these countries has been able to save his land from me? How then can the LORD deliver Jerusalem from my hand?" [Ch]Sennacherib's officers spoke further against the LORD God and against his servant Hezekiah. Then they called out in Hebrew to the people of Jerusalem who were on the wall, to terrify them and make them afraid in order to capture the city. They spoke about the God of Jerusalem as they did about the gods of the other peoples of the world—the work of men's hands.

2 Kgs.
18:36,37
Isa.
36:21,22

REACTION TO TAUNTS. But the people remained silent and said nothing in reply, because the king had commanded, "Do not answer him."

Then Eliakim son of Hilkiah the palace administrator, Shebna the secretary and Joah son of Asaph the recorder went to Hezekiah, with their clothes torn, and told him what the field commander had said.

2 Kgs.
19:1-4
Isa. 37:1-4
Jerusalem

HEZEKIAH CONSULTS ISAIAH. When King Hezekiah heard this, he tore his clothes and put on sackcloth and went into the temple of the LORD. He sent Eliakim the palace administrator, Shebna the secretary and the leading priests, all wearing sackcloth, to the prophet Isaiah son of Amoz. They told him, "This is what Hezekiah says: This day is a day of distress and rebuke and disgrace, as when children come to the point of birth and there is no strength to deliver them. It may be that the LORD your God will hear all the words of the field commander, whom his master, the king of

[m]Or *charioteers*

Assyria, has sent to ridicule the living God, and that he will rebuke him for the words the LORD your God has heard. Therefore pray for the remnant that still survives."

ISAIAH PREDICTS RELIEF. When King Hezekiah's officials came to Isaiah, Isaiah said to them, "Tell your master, 'This is what the LORD says: Do not be afraid of what you have heard—those words with which the underlings of the king of Assyria have blasphemed me. Listen! I am going to put such a spirit in him that when he hears a certain report, he will return to his own country, and there I will have him cut down with the sword.' "

2 Kgs. 19:5-7
Isa. 37:5-7

FIELD COMMANDER WITHDRAWS. When the field commander heard that the king of Assyria had left Lachish, he withdrew and found the king fighting against Libnah.

2 Kgs. 19:8
Isa. 37:8

SENNACHERIB WRITES HEZEKIAH. Now Sennacherib received a report that Tirhakah, the Cushite[n] king of Egypt, was marching out to fight against him. So he again sent messengers to Hezekiah with this word: "Say to Hezekiah king of Judah: Do not let the god you depend on deceive you when he says, 'Jerusalem will not be handed over to the king of Assyria.' Surely you have heard what the kings of Assyria have done to all the countries, destroying them completely. And will you be delivered? Did the gods of the nations that were destroyed by my forefathers deliver them: the gods of Gozan, Haran, Rezeph and the people of Eden who were in Tel Assar? Where is the king of Hamath, the king of Arpad, the king of the city of Sepharvaim, or of Hena or Ivvah?"

2 Kgs. 19:9-13
2 Chron. 32:17
Isa. 37:9-13

HEZEKIAH PRAYS. Hezekiah received the letter from the messengers and read it. Then he went up to the temple of the LORD and spread it out before the LORD. And Hezekiah prayed to the LORD: "O LORD, God of Israel, enthroned between the cherubim, you alone are God over all the kingdoms of the earth. You have made heaven and earth. Give ear, O LORD, and hear; open your eyes, O LORD, and see; listen to the words Sennacherib has sent to insult the living God.

2 Kgs. 19:14-19
2 Chron. 32:20
Isa. 37:14-20

"It is true, O LORD, that the Assyrian kings have laid waste all these nations and their lands. They have thrown their gods into the fire and destroyed them, for they were not gods but only wood and stone, fashioned by men's hands. Now, O LORD our God, deliver us from his hand, so that all kingdoms on earth may know that you alone, O LORD, are God."

GOD ANSWERS THROUGH ISAIAH. Then Isaiah son of Amoz sent a message to Hezekiah: "This is what the LORD, the God of Israel, says: I have heard your prayer concerning Sennacherib king of Assyria. This is the word that the LORD has spoken against him:

2 Kgs. 19:20-34
Isa. 37:21-35

" 'The Virgin Daughter of Zion
        despises you and mocks you.
    The Daughter of Jerusalem
        tosses her head as you flee.
    Who is it you have insulted and blasphemed?
        Against whom have you raised your voice
    and lifted your eyes in pride?
        Against the Holy One of Israel!

[n]That is, from the upper Nile region

By your messengers
    you have heaped insults on the Lord.
And you have said,
   "With my many chariots
I have ascended the heights of the mountains,
    the utmost heights of Lebanon.
I have cut down its tallest cedars,
    the choicest of its pines.
I have reached its remotest parts,
    the finest of its forests.
I have dug wells in foreign lands
    and drunk the water there.
With the soles of my feet
    I have dried up all the streams of Egypt."

" 'Have you not heard?
    Long ago I ordained it.
In days of old I planned it;
    now I have brought it to pass,
that you have turned fortified cities
    into piles of stone.
Their people, drained of power,
    are dismayed and put to shame.
They are like plants in the field,
    like tender green shoots,
like grass sprouting on the roof,
    scorched before it grows up.

" 'But I know where you stay
    and when you come and go
    and how you rage against me.
Because you rage against me
    and your insolence has reached my ears,
I will put my hook in your nose
    and my bit in your mouth,
and I will make you return
    by the way you came.'

"This will be the sign for you, O Hezekiah:

"This year you will eat what grows by itself,
    and the second year what springs from that.
But in the third year sow and reap,
    plant vineyards and eat their fruit.
Once more a remnant of the house of Judah
    will take root below and bear fruit above.
For out of Jerusalem will come a remnant,
    and out of Mount Zion a band of survivors.

The zeal of the LORD Almighty will accomplish this.

"Therefore this is what the LORD says concerning the king of Assyria:

"He will not enter this city
    or shoot an arrow here.

> He will not come before it with shield
> or build a siege ramp against it.
> By the way that he came he will return;
> he will not enter this city,
>
>   declares the LORD.
>
> I will defend this city and save it,
> for my sake and for the sake of David my servant."

ASSYRIANS FLEE MIRACLE.   ^{Kg}That night the angel of the LORD went out and put to death a hundred and eighty-five thousand men in the Assyrian camp. When the people got up the next morning—there were all the dead bodies! So Sennacherib king of Assyria broke camp and withdrew. ^{Ch}So he withdrew to his own land in disgrace. ^{Kg}He returned to Nineveh and stayed there.

2 Kgs.
19:35,36
2 Chron.
32:21a,b,22
Isa.
37:36,37

JUDAH AGAIN PROSPERS.   Many brought offerings to Jerusalem for the LORD and valuable gifts for Hezekiah king of Judah. From then on he was highly regarded by all the nations.

2 Chron.
32:23

DEATH OF HEZEKIAH.   ^{Kg}As for the other events of Hezekiah's reign, all his achievements and how he made the pool and the tunnel by which he brought water into the city, are they not written in the book of the annals of the kings of Judah? ^{Ch}The other events of Hezekiah's reign and his acts of devotion are written in the vision of the prophet Isaiah son of Amoz in the book of the kings of Judah and Israel. Hezekiah rested with his fathers and was buried on the hill where the tombs of David's descendants are. All Judah and the people of Jerusalem honored him when he died.

2 Kgs.
20:20,21a
2 Chron.
32:32,33a
(696 B.C.)

Spiritual Decline Under Manasseh

*F*or a quarter of a century, under Hezekiah's conscientious leadership, Judah has experienced a spiritual revival. But every generation must determine its own commitment, and the fibers of faith are so fragile that a single misguided leader can entice the hearts of believers to worship lesser gods. Whether it is because Hezekiah was so busy leading his nation to God that he neglected his own children, or because his son, at the age of 12, takes the reins of power at far too early an age, the sad fact is that Manasseh turns the people from God back to idolatry and other pagan practices.

MANASSEH KING OF JUDAH.   And Manasseh his son succeeded him as king. Manasseh was twelve years old when he became king, and he reigned in Jerusalem fifty-five years. His mother's name was Hephzibah.

2 Kgs.
20:21b;21:1
2 Chron.
32:33b;33:1
(696 B.C.)

JUDAH RETURNS TO PAGANISM.   He did evil in the eyes of the LORD, following the detestable practices of the nations the LORD had driven out before the Israelites. He rebuilt the high places his father Hezekiah had destroyed; he also erected altars to Baal and made an Asherah pole, as Ahab king of Israel had done. He bowed down to all the starry hosts and worshiped them. He built altars in the temple of the LORD, of which the LORD had said, "In Jerusalem I will put my Name." In both courts of the temple of the LORD, he built altars to all the starry hosts. He sacrificed his

2 Kgs.
21:2-9
2 Chron.
33:2-9
Jerusalem

own son in⁰ the fire, practiced sorcery and divination, and consulted mediums and spiritists. He did much evil in the eyes of the LORD, provoking him to anger.

He took the carved Asherah pole he had made and put it in the temple, of which the LORD had said to David and to his son Solomon, "In this temple and in Jerusalem, which I have chosen out of all the tribes of Israel, I will put my Name forever. I will not again make the feet of the Israelites wander from the land I gave their forefathers, if only they will be careful to do everything I commanded them and will keep the whole Law that my servant Moses gave them." But the people did not listen. Manasseh led them astray, so that they did more evil than the nations the LORD had destroyed before the Israelites.

2 Kgs. 21:16   RULE BY BLOODSHED.   Moreover, Manasseh also shed so much innocent blood that he filled Jerusalem from end to end—besides the sin that he had caused Judah to commit, so that they did evil in the eyes of the LORD.

2 Kgs. 21:10-15   MESSAGE OF THE PROPHETS.   The LORD said through his servants the prophets: "Manasseh king of Judah has committed these detestable sins. He has done more evil than the Amorites who preceded him and has led Judah into sin with his idols. Therefore this is what the LORD, the God of Israel, says: I am going to bring such disaster on Jerusalem and Judah that the ears of everyone who hears of it will tingle. I will stretch out over Jerusalem the measuring line used against Samaria and the plumb line used against the house of Ahab. I will wipe out Jerusalem as one wipes a dish, wiping it and turning it upside down. I will forsake the remnant of my inheritance and hand them over to their enemies. They will be looted and plundered by all their foes, because they have done evil in my eyes and have provoked me to anger from the day their forefathers came out of Egypt until this day."

Isaiah's Prophecies About Restoration and the Messiah

*I*saiah is one of many prophets who have spoken out against Judah's sins and predicted captivity by foreign nations. Already the northern tribes have been taken away. If there was any cause for optimism during the reign of Hezekiah, it has now been lost amid the paganism which Manasseh has fostered. Therefore Isaiah once again takes to the streets to warn against idolatry, sorcery, and even astrology. But now in his last days, and with most of Israel already in foreign exile, Isaiah shifts his emphasis. He projects himself into the period of Judah's exile. He writes as if he were viewing God's people after Jerusalem's destruction. He sees their despair in Babylonian captivity. But even now, through God's revelation, Isaiah sees the restoration of Israel, their return from captivity to a prosperous nation, and the rebuilt city of Jerusalem.

⁰Or *He made his own son pass through*

Isaiah declares that his mission at this time is to bring comfort to those already in exile and to those about to be taken captive. God has a further purpose in Isaiah's prophecies: he wants to reveal what is about to happen so that, when it does, the people will know that it is God who is punishing them and God who will deliver them. He does not want them to attribute anything to the pagan gods which they worship. To make sure there is no mistake about it, God specifically reveals the name of Cyrus the Persian king, who 150 years later will be God's instrument in bringing about the restoration.

Isaiah's prophecies serve further to help the people look forward to the coming of the Messiah and his everlasting kingdom of justice, righteousness, and salvation. The restoration messages are in an appropriate context for the messianic prophecies. Just as Israel has been a suffering servant of God, so too the Messiah will be a suffering servant for all people, including Gentiles. Just as Israel will be restored in prosperity, so too will the faithful believers of all time be blessed in the Messiah's kingdom. And just as the oppressors of God's people are themselves to be destroyed, so too will God's judgment eternally destroy the wicked. And yet for the righteous, God is preparing a place where all will be eternal joy and peace. So in many ways the present punishment of Israel and her promised restoration are analogous to the Messiah's kingdom, the final judgment at the end of time, and the eternal home of the saved.

In all of Scripture, Isaiah's prophecies concerning Israel's restoration and the coming of the Messiah may be the most marvelous, wonderful, comforting, inspiring, optimistic, and encouraging words ever read by a believer—particularly a believer who has either endured great personal suffering or known the despair of spiritual exile. It continues to be a solemn warning to those who would persist in unrighteousness, but it is a refreshing message of hope to all sinners willing to acknowledge their guilt and lead repentant lives in service to God.

PUNISHMENT COMPLETED.   Isa. 40:1,2

> Comfort, comfort my people,
>   says your God.
> Speak tenderly to Jerusalem,
>   and proclaim to her
> that her hard service has been completed,
>   that her sin has been paid for,
> that she has received from the LORD's hand
>   double for all her sins.

THE COMING MESSIAH.   Isa. 40:3-5

> A voice of one calling:
> "In the desert prepare
>   the way for the LORD^P;
> make straight in the wilderness

^{P}Or *A voice of one calling in the desert:* / *"Prepare the way for the LORD*

a highway for our God. *q*
Every valley shall be raised up,
 every mountain and hill made low;
the rough ground shall become level,
 the rugged places a plain.
And the glory of the LORD will be revealed,
 and all mankind together will see it.
                                                For the mouth of the LORD has spoken."

Isa. 40:6-8   FRAGILITY OF LIFE.

A voice says, "Cry out."
And I said, "What shall I cry?"

"All men are like grass,
 and all their glory is like the flowers of the field.
The grass withers and the flowers fall,
 because the breath of the LORD blows on them.
 Surely the people are grass.
The grass withers and the flowers fall,
 but the word of our God stands forever."

Isa. 40:9-11   GOD'S LOVING CONCERN.

You who bring good tidings to Zion,
 go up on a high mountain.
You who bring good tidings to Jerusalem, *r*
 lift up your voice with a shout,
lift it up, do not be afraid;
 say to the towns of Judah,
 "Here is your God!"
See, the Sovereign LORD comes with power,
 and his arm rules for him.
See, his reward is with him,
 and his recompense accompanies him.
He tends his flock like a shepherd:
 He gathers the lambs in his arms
and carries them close to his heart;
 he gently leads those that have young.

Isa.
40:12-14   GOD'S UNLIMITED POWER.

Who has measured the waters in the hollow of his hand,
 or with the breadth of his hand marked off the heavens?
Who has held the dust of the earth in a basket,
 or weighed the mountains on the scales
 and the hills in a balance?
Who has understood the mind *s* of the LORD,
 or instructed him as his counselor?
Whom did the LORD consult to enlighten him,
 and who taught him the right way?
Who was it that taught him knowledge

*q*Hebrew; Septuagint *make straight the paths of our God*   *r*Or *O Zion, bringer of good
tidings, / go up on a high mountain. / O Jerusalem, bringer of good tidings*   *s*Or *Spirit*; or
spirit

or showed him the path of understanding?

VULNERABILITY OF NATIONS.

> Surely the nations are like a drop in a bucket;
>> they are regarded as dust on the scales;
>> he weighs the islands as though they were fine dust.
> Lebanon is not sufficient for altar fires,
>> nor its animals enough for burnt offerings.
> Before him all the nations are as nothing;
>> they are regarded by him as worthless
>> and less than nothing.

FUTILITY OF IDOLATRY.

> To whom, then, will you compare God?
>> What image will you compare him to?
> As for an idol, a craftsman casts it,
>> and a goldsmith overlays it with gold
>> and fashions silver chains for it.
> A man too poor to present such an offering
>> selects wood that will not rot.
> He looks for a skilled craftsman
>> to set up an idol that will not topple.

CREATOR'S STRENGTH.

> Do you not know?
>> Have you not heard?
> Has it not been told you from the beginning?
>> Have you not understood since the earth was founded?
> He sits enthroned above the circle of the earth,
>> and its people are like grasshoppers.
> He stretches out the heavens like a canopy,
>> and spreads them out like a tent to live in.
> He brings princes to naught
>> and reduces the rulers of this world to nothing.
> No sooner are they planted,
>> no sooner are they sown,
>> no sooner do they take root in the ground,
> than he blows on them and they wither,
>> and a whirlwind sweeps them away like chaff.

> "To whom will you compare me?
>> Or who is my equal?" says the Holy One.
> Lift your eyes and look to the heavens:
>> Who created all these?
> He who brings out the starry host one by one,
>> and calls them each by name.
> Because of his great power and mighty strength,
>> not one of them is missing.

MAN'S STRENGTH IN GOD.

> Why do you say, O Jacob,
>> and complain, O Israel,

"My way is hidden from the LORD;
    my cause is disregarded by my God"?
Do you not know?
    Have you not heard?
The LORD is the everlasting God,
    the Creator of the ends of the earth.
He will not grow tired or weary,
    and his understanding no one can fathom.
He gives strength to the weary
    and increases the power of the weak.
Even youths grow tired and weary,
    and young men stumble and fall;
but those who hope in the LORD
    will renew their strength.
They will soar on wings like eagles;
    they will run and not grow weary,
    they will walk and not be faint.

Isa. 41:1-4   GOD'S PROVIDENTIAL CONTROL.

"Be silent before me, you islands!
    Let the nations renew their strength!
Let them come forward and speak;
    let us meet together at the place of judgment.

"Who has stirred up one from the east,
    calling him in righteousness to his service[t]?
He hands nations over to him
    and subdues kings before him.
He turns them to dust with his sword,
    to windblown chaff with his bow.
He pursues them and moves on unscathed,
    by a path his feet have not traveled before.
Who has done this and carried it through,
    calling forth the generations from the beginning?
I, the LORD—with the first of them
    and with the last—I am he."

Isa. 41:5-10   ISRAEL SPECIALLY CHOSEN.

The islands have seen it and fear;
    the ends of the earth tremble.
They approach and come forward;
    each helps the other
    and says to his brother, "Be strong!"
The craftsman encourages the goldsmith,
    and he who smooths with the hammer
    spurs on him who strikes the anvil.
He says of the welding, "It is good."
    He nails down the idol so it will not topple.

"But you, O Israel, my servant,
    Jacob, whom I have chosen,

[t]Or / *whom victory meets at every step*

you descendants of Abraham my friend,
I took you from the ends of the earth,
from its farthest corners I called you.
I said, 'You are my servant';
I have chosen you and have not rejected you.
So do not fear, for I am with you;
do not be dismayed, for I am your God.
I will strengthen you and help you;
I will uphold you with my righteous right hand.

NOTHING TO FEAR.

Isa.
41:11-16

"All who rage against you
will surely be ashamed and disgraced;
those who oppose you
will be as nothing and perish.
Though you search for your enemies,
you will not find them.
Those who wage war against you
will be as nothing at all.
For I am the LORD, your God,
who takes hold of your right hand
and says to you, Do not fear;
I will help you.
Do not be afraid, O worm Jacob,
O little Israel,
for I myself will help you," declares the LORD,
your Redeemer, the Holy One of Israel.
"See, I will make you into a threshing sledge,
new and sharp, with many teeth.
You will thresh the mountains and crush them,
and reduce the hills to chaff.
You will winnow them, the wind will pick them up,
and a gale will blow them away.
But you will rejoice in the LORD
and glory in the Holy One of Israel.

NEEDS TO BE PROVIDED.

Isa.
41:17-20

"The poor and needy search for water,
but there is none;
their tongues are parched with thirst.
But I the LORD will answer them;
I, the God of Israel, will not forsake them.
I will make rivers flow on barren heights,
and springs within the valleys.
I will turn the desert into pools of water,
and the parched ground into springs.
I will put in the desert
the cedar and the acacia, the myrtle and the olive.
I will set pines in the wasteland,
the fir and the cypress together,
so that people may see and know,
may consider and understand,

that the hand of the LORD has done this,
that the Holy One of Israel has created it.

Isa.
41:21-24

IDOLS CANNOT PROVIDE.

"Present your case," says the LORD.
"Set forth your arguments," says Jacob's King.
"Bring in your idols to tell us
what is going to happen.
Tell us what the former things were,
so that we may consider them
and know their final outcome.
Or declare to us the things to come,
tell us what the future holds,
so we may know that you are gods.
Do something, whether good or bad,
so that we will be dismayed and filled with fear.
But you are less than nothing
and your works are utterly worthless;
he who chooses you is detestable.

Isa.
41:25-29

FALSE PROPHETS FAIL.

"I have stirred up one from the north, and he comes—
one from the rising sun who calls on my name.
He treads on rulers as if they were mortar,
as if he were a potter treading the clay.
Who told of this from the beginning, so we could know,
or beforehand, so we could say, 'He was right'?
No one told of this,
no one foretold it,
no one heard any words from you.
I was the first to tell Zion, 'Look, here they are!'
I gave to Jerusalem a messenger of good tidings.
I look but there is no one—
no one among them to give counsel,
no one to give answer when I ask them.
See, they are all false!
Their deeds amount to nothing;
their images are but wind and confusion.

Isa. 42:1-4

MESSIAH BRINGS JUSTICE.

"Here is my servant, whom I uphold,
my chosen one in whom I delight;
I will put my Spirit on him
and he will bring justice to the nations.
He will not shout or cry out,
or raise his voice in the streets.
A bruised reed he will not break,
and a smoldering wick he will not snuff out.
In faithfulness he will bring forth justice;
he will not falter or be discouraged
till he establishes justice on earth.
In his law the islands will put their hope."

NEW KINGDOM FOR ALL.   Isa. 42:5-7

This is what God the LORD says—
he who created the heavens and stretched them out,
    who spread out the earth and all that comes out of it,
who gives breath to its people,
    and life to those who walk on it:
"I, the LORD, have called you in righteousness;
    I will take hold of your hand.
I will keep you and will make you
    to be a covenant for the people
    and a light for the Gentiles,
to open eyes that are blind,
    to free captives from prison
    and to release from the dungeon those who sit in
        darkness.

PREVIEW OF GOD'S PLANS.   Isa. 42:8,9

"I am the LORD; that is my name!
    I will not give my glory to another
    or my praise to idols.
See, the former things have taken place,
    and new things I declare;
before they spring into being
    I announce them to you."

PRAISE FOR GOD'S TRIUMPH.   Isa.
42:10-13

Sing to the LORD a new song,
    his praise from the ends of the earth,
you who go down to the sea, and all that is in it,
    you islands, and all who live in them.
Let the desert and its towns raise their voices;
    let the settlements where Kedar lives rejoice.
Let the people of Sela sing for joy;
    let them shout from the mountaintops.
Let them give glory to the LORD
    and proclaim his praise in the islands.
The LORD will march out like a mighty man,
    like a warrior he will stir up his zeal;
with a shout he will raise the battle cry
    and will triumph over his enemies.

NEW KINGDOM FOR BELIEVERS.   Isa.
42:14-17

"For a long time I have kept silent,
    I have been quiet and held myself back.
But now, like a woman in childbirth,
    I cry out, I gasp and pant.
I will lay waste the mountains and hills
    and dry up all their vegetation;
I will turn rivers into islands
    and dry up the pools.
I will lead the blind by ways they have not known,

along unfamiliar paths I will guide them;
I will turn the darkness into light before them
    and make the rough places smooth.
These are the things I will do;
    I will not forsake them.
But those who trust in idols,
    who say to images, 'You are our gods,'
    will be turned back in utter shame.

Isa.
42:18-22

ISRAEL BLIND AND DEAF.

"Hear, you deaf;
    look, you blind, and see!
Who is blind but my servant,
    and deaf like the messenger I send?
Who is blind like the one committed to me,
    blind like the servant of the LORD?
You have seen many things, but have paid no attention;
    your ears are open, but you hear nothing."
It pleased the LORD
    for the sake of his righteousness
    to make his law great and glorious.
But this is a people plundered and looted,
    all of them trapped in pits
    or hidden away in prisons.
They have become plunder,
    with no one to rescue them;
they have been made loot,
    with no one to say, "Send them back."

Isa.
42:23-25

PUNISHMENT NOT UNDERSTOOD.

Which of you will listen to this
    or pay close attention in time to come?
Who handed Jacob over to become loot,
    and Israel to the plunderers?
Was it not the LORD,
    against whom we have sinned?
For they would not follow his ways;
    they did not obey his law.
So he poured out on them his burning anger,
    the violence of war.
It enveloped them in flames, yet they did not understand;
    it consumed them, but they did not take it to heart.

Isa. 43:1-7

ISRAEL TO BE REDEEMED.

But now, this is what the LORD says—
    he who created you, O Jacob,
    he who formed you, O Israel:
"Fear not, for I have redeemed you;
    I have summoned you by name; you are mine.
When you pass through the waters,
    I will be with you;
and when you pass through the rivers,

they will not sweep over you.
When you walk through the fire,
    you will not be burned;
    the flames will not set you ablaze.
For I am the LORD, your God,
    the Holy One of Israel, your Savior;
I give Egypt for your ransom,
    Cush[u] and Seba in your stead.
Since you are precious and honored in my sight,
    and because I love you,
I will give men in exchange for you,
    and people in exchange for your life.
Do not be afraid, for I am with you;
    I will bring your children from the east
    and gather you from the west.
I will say to the north, 'Give them up!'
    and to the south, 'Do not hold them back.'
Bring my sons from afar
    and my daughters from the ends of the earth—
everyone who is called by my name,
    whom I created for my glory,
    whom I formed and made."

RESTORATION PROVES POWER.

Isa. 43:8-13

Lead out those who have eyes but are blind,
    who have ears but are deaf.
All the nations gather together
    and the peoples assemble.
Which of them foretold this
    and proclaimed to us the former things?
Let them bring in their witnesses to prove they were right,
    so that others may hear and say, "It is true."
"You are my witnesses," declares the LORD,
    "and my servant whom I have chosen,
so that you may know and believe me
    and understand that I am he.
Before me no god was formed,
    nor will there be one after me.
I, even I, am the LORD,
    and apart from me there is no savior.
I have revealed and saved and proclaimed—
    I, and not some foreign god among you.
You are my witnesses," declares the LORD, "that I am God.
    Yes, and from ancient days I am he.
No one can deliver out of my hand.
    When I act, who can reverse it?"

BABYLON WILL FALL.

Isa.
43:14,15

This is what the LORD says—
    your Redeemer, the Holy One of Israel:

---

[u] That is, the upper Nile region

"For your sake I will send to Babylon
and bring down as fugitives all the Babylonians,[v]
in the ships in which they took pride.
I am the LORD, your Holy One,
Israel's Creator, your King."

Isa.
43:16-21

THE PAST IS PAST.

This is what the LORD says—
he who made a way through the sea,
a path through the mighty waters,
who drew out the chariots and horses,
the army and reinforcements together,
and they lay there, never to rise again,
extinguished, snuffed out like a wick:
"Forget the former things;
do not dwell on the past.
See, I am doing a new thing!
Now it springs up; do you not perceive it?
I am making a way in the desert
and streams in the wasteland.
The wild animals honor me,
the jackals and the owls,
because I provide water in the desert
and streams in the wasteland,
to give drink to my people, my chosen,
the people I formed for myself
that they may proclaim my praise.

Isa.
43:22-25

GOD FORGIVES ISRAEL.

"Yet you have not called upon me, O Jacob,
you have not wearied yourselves for me, O Israel.
You have not brought me sheep for burnt offerings,
nor honored me with your sacrifices.
I have not burdened you with grain offerings
nor wearied you with demands for incense.
You have not bought any fragrant calamus for me,
or lavished on me the fat of your sacrifices.
But you have burdened me with your sins
and wearied me with your offenses.

"I, even I, am he who blots out
your transgressions, for my own sake,
and remembers your sins no more.

Isa.
43:26-28

NEED FOR FORGIVENESS.

Review the past for me,
let us argue the matter together;
state the case for your innocence.
Your first father sinned;
your spokesmen rebelled against me.

[v]Or Chaldeans

So I will disgrace the dignitaries of your temple,
    and I will consign Jacob to destruction[w]
    and Israel to scorn.

SPIRIT TO BE GIVEN.   Isa. 44:1-5

"But now listen, O Jacob, my servant,
    Israel, whom I have chosen.
This is what the LORD says—
    he who made you, who formed you in the womb,
    and who will help you:
Do not be afraid, O Jacob, my servant,
    Jeshurun, whom I have chosen.
For I will pour water on the thirsty land,
    and streams on the dry ground;
I will pour out my Spirit on your offspring,
    and my blessing on your descendants.
They will spring up like grass in a meadow,
    like poplar trees by flowing streams.
One will say, 'I belong to the LORD';
    another will call himself by the name of Jacob;
still another will write on his hand, 'The LORD's,'
    and will take the name Israel.

GOD'S ACTIONS HIS WITNESS.   Isa. 44:6-8

"This is what the LORD says—
    Israel's King and Redeemer, the LORD Almighty:
I am the first and I am the last;
    apart from me there is no God.
Who then is like me? Let him proclaim it.
    Let him declare and lay out before me
what has happened since I established my ancient people,
    and what is yet to come—
    yes, let him foretell what will come.
Do not tremble, do not be afraid.
    Did I not proclaim this and foretell it long ago?
You are my witnesses. Is there any God besides me?
    No, there is no other Rock; I know not one."

FUTILITY OF IDOLATRY.   Isa. 44:9-20

All who make idols are nothing,
    and the things they treasure are worthless.
Those who would speak up for them are blind;
    they are ignorant, to their own shame.
Who shapes a god and casts an idol,
    which can profit him nothing?
He and his kind will be put to shame;
    craftsmen are nothing but men.
Let them all come together and take their stand;
    they will be brought down to terror and infamy.

---

[w]The Hebrew term refers to the irrevocable giving over of things or persons to the LORD, often by totally destroying them.

The blacksmith takes a tool
    and works with it in the coals;
he shapes an idol with hammers,
    he forges it with the might of his arm.
He gets hungry and loses his strength;
    he drinks no water and grows faint.
The carpenter measures with a line
    and makes an outline with a marker;
he roughs it out with chisels
    and marks it with compasses.
He shapes it in the form of man,
    of man in all his glory,
    that it may dwell in a shrine.
He cut down cedars,
    or perhaps took a cypress or oak.
He let it grow among the trees of the forest,
    or planted a pine, and the rain made it grow.
It is man's fuel for burning;
    some of it he takes and warms himself,
    he kindles a fire and bakes bread.
But he also fashions a god and worships it;
    he makes an idol and bows down to it.
Half of the wood he burns in the fire;
    over it he prepares his meal,
    he roasts his meat and eats his fill.
He also warms himself and says,
    "Ah! I am warm; I see the fire."
From the rest he makes a god, his idol;
    he bows down to it and worships.
He prays to it and says,
    "Save me; you are my god."
They know nothing, they understand nothing;
    their eyes are plastered over so they cannot see,
    and their minds closed so they cannot understand.
No one stops to think,
    no one has the knowledge or understanding to say,
"Half of it I used for fuel;
    I even baked bread over its coals,
    I roasted meat and I ate.
Shall I make a detestable thing from what is left?
    Shall I bow down to a block of wood?"
He feeds on ashes, a deluded heart misleads him;
    he cannot save himself, or say,
    "Is not this thing in my right hand a lie?"

Isa.
44:21-23   GREATNESS OF GOD.

"Remember these things, O Jacob,
    for you are my servant, O Israel.
I have made you, you are my servant;
    O Israel, I will not forget you.
I have swept away your offenses like a cloud,
    your sins like the morning mist.

Return to me,
   for I have redeemed you."

Sing for joy, O heavens, for the LORD has done this;
   shout aloud, O earth beneath.
Burst into song, you mountains,
   you forests and all your trees,
for the LORD has redeemed Jacob,
   he displays his glory in Israel.

JERUSALEM TO BE REBUILT.   Isa.
                                                                  44:24-28

"This is what the LORD says—
   your Redeemer, who formed you in the womb:

I am the LORD,
who has made all things,
who alone stretched out the heavens,
who spread out the earth by myself,

who foils the signs of false prophets
   and makes fools of diviners,
who overthrows the learning of the wise
   and turns it into nonsense,
who carries out the words of his servants
   and fulfills the predictions of his messengers,

who says of Jerusalem, 'It shall be inhabited,'
   of the towns of Judah, 'They shall be built,'
   and of their ruins, 'I will restore them,'
who says to the watery deep, 'Be dry,
   and I will dry up your streams,'
who says of Cyrus, 'He is my shepherd
   and will accomplish all that I please;
   he will say of Jerusalem, "Let it be rebuilt,"
   and of the temple, "Let its foundations be laid."'

CYRUS TO BE INSTRUMENT.   Isa. 45:1-7

"This is what the LORD says to his anointed,
   to Cyrus, whose right hand I take hold of
to subdue nations before him
   and to strip kings of their armor,
to open doors before him
   so that gates will not be shut:
I will go before you
   and will level the mountains[x];
I will break down gates of bronze
   and cut through bars of iron.
I will give you the treasures of darkness,
   riches stored in secret places,
so that you may know that I am the LORD,

[x]Dead Sea Scrolls and Septuagint; the meaning of the word in the Masoretic Text is
uncertain.

the God of Israel, who summons you by name.
For the sake of Jacob my servant,
  of Israel my chosen,
I summon you by name
  and bestow on you a title of honor,
  though you do not acknowledge me.
I am the LORD, and there is no other;
  apart from me there is no God.
I will strengthen you,
  though you have not acknowledged me,
so that from the rising of the sun
  to the place of its setting
men may know there is none besides me.
  I am the LORD, and there is no other.
I form the light and create darkness,
  I bring prosperity and create disaster;
  I, the LORD, do all these things.

Isa. 45:8   ABUNDANT RESTORATION.

"You heavens above, rain down righteousness;
  let the clouds shower it down.
Let the earth open wide,
  let salvation spring up,
let righteousness grow with it;
  I, the LORD, have created it.

Isa. 45:9-13   GOD'S RIGHT TO USE CYRUS.

"Woe to him who quarrels with his Maker,
  to him who is but a potsherd among the potsherds on
    the ground.
Does the clay say to the potter,
  'What are you making?'
Does your work say,
  'He has no hands'?
Woe to him who says to his father,
  'What have you begotten?'
or to his mother,
  'What have you brought to birth?'

"This is what the LORD says—
  the Holy One of Israel, and its Maker:
Concerning things to come,
  do you question me about my children,
  or give me orders about the work of my hands?
It is I who made the earth
  and created mankind upon it.
My own hands stretched out the heavens;
  I marshaled their starry hosts.
I will raise up Cyrus *y* in my righteousness:
  I will make all his ways straight.

y Hebrew *him*

He will rebuild my city
   and set my exiles free,
but not for a price or reward,
   says the LORD Almighty."

EGYPTIANS WILL KNOW GOD.   This is what the LORD says:

Isa. 45:14

"The products of Egypt and the merchandise of Cush,[z]
   and those tall Sabeans—
they will come over to you
   and will be yours;
they will trudge behind you,
   coming over to you in chains.
They will bow down before you
   and plead with you, saying,
'Surely God is with you, and there is no other;
   there is no other god.'"

IDOLATERS WILL KNOW GOD.

Isa.
45:15-25

Truly you are a God who hides himself,
   O God and Savior of Israel.
All the makers of idols will be put to shame and disgraced;
   they will go off into disgrace together.
But Israel will be saved by the LORD
   with an everlasting salvation;
you will never be put to shame or disgraced,
   to ages everlasting.

For this is what the LORD says—
he who created the heavens,
   he is God;
he who fashioned and made the earth,
   he founded it;
he did not create it to be empty,
   but formed it to be inhabited—
he says:
"I am the LORD,
   and there is no other.
I have not spoken in secret,
   from somewhere in a land of darkness;
I have not said to Jacob's descendants,
   'Seek me in vain.'
I, the LORD, speak the truth;
   I declare what is right.

"Gather together and come;
   assemble, you fugitives from the nations.
Ignorant are those who carry about idols of wood,
   who pray to gods that cannot save.
Declare what is to be, present it—
   let them take counsel together.
Who foretold this long ago,

[z]That is, the upper Nile region

who declared it from the distant past?
Was it not I, the LORD?
And there is no God apart from me,
a righteous God and a Savior;
there is none but me.

"Turn to me and be saved,
all you ends of the earth;
for I am God, and there is no other.
By myself I have sworn,
my mouth has uttered in all integrity
a word that will not be revoked:
Before me every knee will bow;
by me every tongue will swear.
They will say of me, 'In the LORD alone
are righteousness and strength.'"
All who have raged against him
will come to him and be put to shame.
But in the LORD all the descendants of Israel
will be found righteous and will exult.

Isa. 46:1-7   BABYLONIAN IDOLS POWERLESS.

Bel bows down, Nebo stoops low;
their idols are borne by beasts of burden.[a]
The images that are carried about are burdensome,
a burden for the weary.
They stoop and bow down together;
unable to rescue the burden,
they themselves go off into captivity.

"Listen to me, O house of Jacob,
all you who remain of the house of Israel,
you whom I have upheld since you were conceived,
and have carried since your birth.
Even to your old age and gray hairs
I am he, I am he who will sustain you.
I have made you and I will carry you;
I will sustain you and I will rescue you.

"To whom will you compare me or count me equal?
To whom will you liken me that we may be compared?
Some pour out gold from their bags
and weigh out silver on the scales;
they hire a goldsmith to make it into a god,
and they bow down and worship it.
They lift it to their shoulders and carry it;
they set it up in its place, and there it stands.
From that spot it cannot move.
Though one cries out to it, it does not answer;
it cannot save him from his troubles.

[a]Or are but beasts and cattle

POWER SEEN IN RESTORATION.   Isa. 46:8-13

"Remember this, fix it in mind,
    take it to heart, you rebels.
Remember the former things, those of long ago;
    I am God, and there is no other;
    I am God, and there is none like me.
I make known the end from the beginning,
    from ancient times, what is still to come.
I say: My purpose will stand,
    and I will do all that I please.
From the east I summon a bird of prey;
    from a far-off land, a man to fulfill my purpose.
What I have said, that will I bring about;
    what I have planned, that will I do.
Listen to me, you stubborn-hearted,
    you who are far from righteousness.
I am bringing my righteousness near,
    it is not far away;
    and my salvation will not be delayed.
I will grant salvation to Zion,
    my splendor to Israel.

BABYLON WILL FALL.   Isa. 47:1-11

"Go down, sit in the dust,
    Virgin Daughter of Babylon;
sit on the ground without a throne,
    Daughter of the Babylonians.[b]
No more will you be called
    tender or delicate.
Take millstones and grind flour;
    take off your veil.
Lift up your skirts, bare your legs,
    and wade through the streams.
Your nakedness will be exposed
    and your shame uncovered.
I will take vengeance;
    I will spare no one."

Our Redeemer—the LORD Almighty is his name—
    is the Holy One of Israel.

"Sit in silence, go into darkness,
    Daughter of the Babylonians;
no more will you be called
    queen of kingdoms.
I was angry with my people
    and desecrated my inheritance;
I gave them into your hand,
    and you showed them no mercy.
Even on the aged

[b] Or *Chaldeans*; also in verse 5

you laid a very heavy yoke.
You said, 'I will continue forever—
    the eternal queen!'
But you did not consider these things
    or reflect on what might happen.

"Now then, listen, you wanton creature,
    lounging in your security
and saying to yourself,
    'I am, and there is none besides me.
I will never be a widow
    or suffer the loss of children.'
Both of these will overtake you
    in a moment, on a single day:
    loss of children and widowhood.
They will come upon you in full measure,
    in spite of your many sorceries
    and all your potent spells.
You have trusted in your wickedness
    and have said, 'No one sees me.'
Your wisdom and knowledge mislead you
    when you say to yourself,
    'I am, and there is none besides me.'
Disaster will come upon you,
    and you will not know how to conjure it away.
A calamity will fall upon you
    that you cannot ward off with a ransom;
a catastrophe you cannot foresee
    will suddenly come upon you.

Isa.
47:12-15

FRAUD OF ASTROLOGY.

"Keep on, then, with your magic spells
    and with your many sorceries,
    which you have labored at since childhood.
Perhaps you will succeed,
    perhaps you will cause terror.
All the counsel you have received has only worn you out!
    Let your astrologers come forward,
those stargazers who make predictions month by month,
    let them save you from what is coming upon you.
Surely they are like stubble;
    the fire will burn them up.
They cannot even save themselves
    from the power of the flame.
Here are no coals to warm anyone;
    here is no fire to sit by.
That is all they can do for you—
    these you have labored with
    and trafficked with since childhood.
Each of them goes on in his error;
    there is not one that can save you.

SIN REQUIRED PROPHECIES.

"Listen to this, O house of Jacob,
    you who are called by the name of Israel
    and come from the line of Judah,
you who take oaths in the name of the LORD
    and invoke the God of Israel—
    but not in truth or righteousness—
you who call yourselves citizens of the holy city
    and rely on the God of Israel—
    the LORD Almighty is his name:
I foretold the former things long ago,
    my mouth announced them and I made them known;
    then suddenly I acted, and they came to pass.
For I knew how stubborn you were;
    the sinews of your neck were iron,
    your forehead was bronze.
Therefore I told you these things long ago;
    before they happened I announced them to you
so that you could not say,
    'My idols did them;
    my wooden image and metal god ordained them.'
You have heard these things; look at them all.
    Will you not admit them?

REASON FOR PROPHECIES.

"From now on I will tell you of new things,
    of hidden things unknown to you.
They are created now, and not long ago;
    you have not heard of them before today.
So you cannot say,
    'Yes, I knew of them.'
You have neither heard nor understood;
    from of old your ear has not been open.
Well do I know how treacherous you are;
    you were called a rebel from birth.
For my own name's sake I delay my wrath;
    for the sake of my praise I hold it back from you,
    so as not to cut you off.
See, I have refined you, though not as silver;
    I have tested you in the furnace of affliction.
For my own sake, for my own sake, I do this.
    How can I let myself be defamed?
    I will not yield my glory to another.

GOD'S PLAN FOR BABYLON

"Listen to me, O Jacob,
    Israel, whom I have called:
I am he;
    I am the first and I am the last.

My own hand laid the foundations of the earth,
and my right hand spread out the heavens;
when I summon them,
they all stand up together.

"Come together, all of you, and listen:
Which of the idols has foretold these things?
The LORD's chosen ally
will carry out his purpose against Babylon;
his arm will be against the Babylonians.[c]
I, even I, have spoken;
yes, I have called him.
I will bring him,
and he will succeed in his mission.

Isa. 48:16-19

ISRAEL MUST LISTEN NOW.   "Come near me and listen to this:

"From the first announcement I have not spoken in secret;
at the time it happens, I am there."

And now the Sovereign LORD has sent me,
with his Spirit.

This is what the LORD says—
your Redeemer, the Holy One of Israel:
"I am the LORD your God,
who teaches you what is best for you,
who directs you in the way you should go.
If only you had paid attention to my commands,
your peace would have been like a river,
your righteousness like the waves of the sea.
Your descendants would have been like the sand,
your children like its numberless grains;
their name would never be cut off
nor destroyed from before me."

Isa. 48:20-22

REDEMPTION FOR THE RIGHTEOUS.

Leave Babylon,
flee from the Babylonians!
Announce this with shouts of joy
and proclaim it.
Send it out to the ends of the earth;
say, "The LORD has redeemed his servant Jacob."
They did not thirst when he led them through the deserts;
he made water flow for them from the rock;
he split the rock
and water gushed out.

"There is no peace," says the LORD, "for the wicked."

Isa. 49:1-4

ISRAEL GOD'S SERVANT.

Listen to me, you islands;
hear this, you distant nations:
Before I was born the LORD called me;

[c] Or *Chaldeans*; also in verse 20

from my birth he has made mention of my name.
He made my mouth like a sharpened sword,
in the shadow of his hand he hid me;
he made me into a polished arrow
and concealed me in his quiver.
He said to me, "You are my servant,
Israel, in whom I will display my splendor."
But I said, "I have labored to no purpose;
I have spent my strength in vain and for nothing.
Yet what is due me is in the LORD's hand,
and my reward is with my God."

MESSIAH GOD'S SERVANT.   Isa. 49:5-7

And now the LORD says—
he who formed me in the womb to be his servant
to bring Jacob back to him
and gather Israel to himself,
for I am honored in the eyes of the LORD
and my God has been my strength—
he says:
"It is too small a thing for you to be my servant
to restore the tribes of Jacob
and bring back those of Israel I have kept.
I will also make you a light for the Gentiles,
that you may bring my salvation to the ends of the
earth."

This is what the LORD says—
the Redeemer and Holy One of Israel—
to him who was despised and abhorred by the nation,
to the servant of rulers:
"Kings will see you and rise up,
princes will see and bow down,
because of the LORD, who is faithful,
the Holy One of Israel, who has chosen you."

EXILE WILL END.   This is what the LORD says: Isa. 49:8-13

"In the time of my favor I will answer you,
and in the day of salvation I will help you;
I will keep you and will make you
to be a covenant for the people,
to restore the land
and to reassign its desolate inheritances,
to say to the captives, 'Come out,'
and to those in darkness, 'Be free!'

"They will feed beside the roads
and find pasture on every barren hill.
They will neither hunger nor thirst,
nor will the desert heat or the sun beat upon them.
He who has compassion on them will guide them
and lead them beside springs of water.
I will turn all my mountains into roads,

and my highways will be raised up.
See, they will come from afar—
    some from the north, some from the west,
    some from the region of Aswan.[d]"

Shout for joy, O heavens;
    rejoice, O earth;
    burst into song, O mountains!
For the LORD comforts his people
    and will have compassion on his afflicted ones.

Isa.   EXILES WILL NOT BE FORGOTTEN.
49:14-21

But Zion said, "The LORD has forsaken me,
    the Lord has forgotten me."

"Can a mother forget the baby at her breast
    and have no compassion on the child she has borne?
Though she may forget,
    I will not forget you!
See, I have engraved you on the palms of my hands;
    your walls are ever before me.
Your sons hasten back,
    and those who laid you waste depart from you.
Lift up your eyes and look around;
    all your sons gather and come to you.
As surely as I live," declares the LORD,
    "you will wear them all as ornaments;
    you will put them on, like a bride.

"Though you were ruined and made desolate
    and your land laid waste,
now you will be too small for your people,
    and those who devoured you will be far away.
The children born during your bereavement
    will yet say in your hearing,
'This place is too small for us;
    give us more space to live in.'
Then you will say in your heart,
    'Who bore me these?
I was bereaved and barren;
    I was exiled and rejected.
Who brought these up?
I was left all alone,
    but these—where have they come from?' "

Isa.   CAPTORS WILL HONOR EXILES.   This is what the Sovereign LORD says:
49:22,23

"See, I will beckon to the Gentiles,
    I will lift up my banner to the peoples;
they will bring your sons in their arms
    and carry your daughters on their shoulders.
Kings will be your foster fathers,

[d]Dead Sea Scrolls; Masoretic Text *Sinim*

and their queens your nursing mothers.
They will bow down before you with their faces to the
ground;
they will lick the dust at your feet.
Then you will know that I am the LORD;
those who hope in me will not be disappointed."

DELIVERANCE PROMISED.

Isa.
49:24-26

Can plunder be taken from warriors,
or captives rescued from the fierce[e]?

But this is what the LORD says:

"Yes, captives will be taken from warriors,
and plunder retrieved from the fierce;
I will contend with those who contend with you,
and your children I will save.
I will make your oppressors eat their own flesh;
they will be drunk on their own blood, as with wine.
Then all mankind will know
that I, the LORD, am your Savior,
your Redeemer, the Mighty One of Jacob."

EXILE CAUSED BY SIN.   This is what the LORD says:

Isa. 50:1-3

"Where is your mother's certificate of divorce
with which I sent her away?
Or to which of my creditors
did I sell you?
Because of your sins you were sold;
because of your transgressions your mother was sent
away.
When I came, why was there no one?
When I called, why was there no one to answer?
Was my arm too short to ransom you?
Do I lack the strength to rescue you?
By a mere rebuke I dry up the sea,
I turn rivers into a desert;
their fish rot for lack of water
and die of thirst.
I clothe the sky with darkness
and make sackcloth its covering."

OBEDIENCE OF A SERVANT.

Isa. 50:4-9

The Sovereign LORD has given me an instructed tongue,
to know the word that sustains the weary.
He wakens me morning by morning,
wakens my ear to listen like one being taught.
The Sovereign LORD has opened my ears,
and I have not been rebellious;
I have not drawn back.

[e]Dead Sea Scrolls, Vulgate and Syriac (see also Septuagint and verse 25); Masoretic Text
righteous

I offered my back to those who beat me,
    my cheeks to those who pulled out my beard;
I did not hide my face
    from mocking and spitting.
Because the Sovereign LORD helps me,
    I will not be disgraced.
Therefore have I set my face like flint,
    and I know I will not be put to shame.
He who vindicates me is near.
    Who then will bring charges against me?
    Let us face each other!
Who is my accuser?
    Let him confront me!
It is the Sovereign LORD who helps me.
    Who is he that will condemn me?
They will all wear out like a garment;
    the moths will eat them up.

**Isa.
50:10,11**

CAPTIVES MUST TRUST GOD.

Who among you fears the LORD
    and obeys the word of his servant?
Let him who walks in the dark,
    who has no light,
trust in the name of the LORD
    and rely on his God.
But now, all you who light fires
    and provide yourselves with flaming torches,
go, walk in the light of your fires
    and of the torches you have set ablaze.
This is what you shall receive from my hand:
    You will lie down in torment.

Isa. 51:1-3

HOW ABRAHAM WAS BLESSED.

"Listen to me, you who pursue righteousness
    and who seek the LORD:
Look to the rock from which you were cut
    and to the quarry from which you were hewn;
look to Abraham, your father,
    and to Sarah, who gave you birth.
When I called him he was but one,
    and I blessed him and made him many.
The LORD will surely comfort Zion
    and will look with compassion on all her ruins;
he will make her deserts like Eden,
    her wastelands like the garden of the LORD.
Joy and gladness will be found in her,
    thanksgiving and the sound of singing.

Isa. 51:4-8

SALVATION IS COMING.

"Listen to me, my people;
    hear me, my nation:
The law will go out from me;

my justice will become a light to the nations.
My righteousness draws near speedily,
my salvation is on the way,
and my arm will bring justice to the nations.
The islands will look to me
and wait in hope for my arm.
Lift up your eyes to the heavens,
look at the earth beneath;
the heavens will vanish like smoke,
the earth will wear out like a garment
and its inhabitants die like flies.
But my salvation will last forever,
my righteousness will never fail.

"Hear me, you who know what is right,
you people who have my law in your hearts:
Do not fear the reproach of men
or be terrified by their insults.
For the moth will eat them up like a garment;
the worm will devour them like wool.
But my righteousness will last forever,
my salvation through all generations."

RESTORATION OF RANSOMED.
Isa. 51:9-11

Awake, awake! Clothe yourself with strength,
O arm of the LORD;
awake, as in days gone by,
as in generations of old.
Was it not you who cut Rahab to pieces,
who pierced that monster through?
Was it not you who dried up the sea,
the waters of the great deep,
who made a road in the depths of the sea
so that the redeemed might cross over?
The ransomed of the LORD will return.
They will enter Zion with singing;
everlasting joy will crown their heads.
Gladness and joy will overtake them,
and sorrow and sighing will flee away.

NO NEED TO FEAR.
Isa. 51:12-16

"I, even I, am he who comforts you.
Who are you that you fear mortal men,
the sons of men, who are but grass,
that you forget the LORD your Maker,
who stretched out the heavens
and laid the foundations of the earth,
that you live in constant terror every day
because of the wrath of the oppressor,
who is bent on destruction?
For where is the wrath of the oppressor?
The cowering prisoners will soon be set free;

they will not die in their dungeon,
nor will they lack bread.
For I am the LORD your God,
who churns up the sea so that its waves roar—
the LORD Almighty is his name.
I have put my words in your mouth
and covered you with the shadow of my hand—
I who set the heavens in place,
who laid the foundations of the earth,
and who say to Zion, 'You are my people.' "

Isa.
51:17-23

GOD'S WRATH WILL PASS.

Awake, awake!
Rise up, O Jerusalem,
you who have drunk from the hand of the LORD
the cup of his wrath,
you who have drained to its dregs
the goblet that makes men stagger.
Of all the sons she bore
there was none to guide her;
of all the sons she reared
there was none to take her by the hand.
These double calamities have come upon you—
who can comfort you?—
ruin and destruction, famine and sword—
who can^f console you?
Your sons have fainted;
they lie at the head of every street,
like antelope caught in a net.
They are filled with the wrath of the LORD
and the rebuke of your God.

Therefore hear this, you afflicted one,
made drunk, but not with wine.
This is what your Sovereign LORD says,
your God, who defends his people:
"See, I have taken out of your hand
the cup that made you stagger;
from that cup, the goblet of my wrath,
you will never drink again.
I will put it into the hands of your tormentors,
who said to you,
'Fall prostrate that we may walk over you.'
And you made your back like the ground,
like a street to be walked over."

Isa. 52:1,2

BEAUTY OF RESTORATION.

Awake, awake, O Zion,
clothe yourself with strength.
Put on your garments of splendor,

---

^f Dead Sea Scrolls, Septuagint, Vulgate and Syriac; Masoretic Text / how can I

O Jerusalem, the holy city.
The uncircumcised and defiled
   will not enter you again.
Shake off your dust;
   rise up, sit enthroned, O Jerusalem.
Free yourself from the chains on your neck,
   O captive Daughter of Zion.

EXILE DISTASTEFUL TO GOD.   For this is what the LORD says:

Isa. 52:3-6

"You were sold for nothing,
   and without money you will be redeemed."

For this is what the Sovereign LORD says:

"At first my people went down to Egypt to live;
   lately, Assyria has oppressed them.

"And now what do I have here?" declares the LORD.

"For my people have been taken away for nothing,
   and those who rule them mock,[8]"

declares the LORD.

"And all day long
   my name is constantly blasphemed.
Therefore my people will know my name;
   therefore in that day they will know
that it is I who foretold it.
   Yes, it is I."

JOY OF RESTORATION.

Isa. 52:7-10

How beautiful on the mountains
   are the feet of those who bring good news,
who proclaim peace,
   who bring good tidings,
   who proclaim salvation,
who say to Zion,
   "Your God reigns!"
Listen! Your watchmen lift up their voices;
   together they shout for joy.
When the LORD returns to Zion,
   they will see it with their own eyes.
Burst into songs of joy together,
   you ruins of Jerusalem,
for the LORD has comforted his people,
   he has redeemed Jerusalem.
The LORD will lay bare his holy arm
   in the sight of all the nations,
and all the ends of the earth will see
   the salvation of our God.

PURITY OF RESTORATION.

Isa.
52:11,12

Depart, depart, go out from there!

8Dead Sea Scrolls and Vulgate; Masoretic Text *wail*

> Touch no unclean thing!
> Come out from it and be pure,
> > you who carry the vessels of the LORD.
> But you will not leave in haste
> > or go in flight;
> for the LORD will go before you,
> > the God of Israel will be your rear guard.

**Isa.
52:13-15**

GLORY OF SUFFERING SERVANT.

> See, my servant will act wisely[h];
> > he will be raised and lifted up and highly exalted.
> Just as there were many who were appalled at him[i]—
> > his appearance was so disfigured beyond that of any man
> > and his form marred beyond human likeness—
> so will he sprinkle many nations,[j]
> > and kings will shut their mouths because of him.
> For what they were not told, they will see,
> > and what they have not heard, they will understand.

Isa. 53:1-3

MESSIAH'S APPEARANCE.

> Who has believed our message
> > and to whom has the arm of the LORD been revealed?
> He grew up before him like a tender shoot,
> > and like a root out of dry ground.
> He had no beauty or majesty to attract us to him,
> > nothing in his appearance that we should desire him.
> He was despised and rejected by men,
> > a man of sorrows, and familiar with suffering.
> Like one from whom men hide their faces
> > he was despised, and we esteemed him not.

Isa. 53:4-6

HIS SUFFERING FOR OUR SINS.

> Surely he took up our infirmities
> > and carried our sorrows,
> yet we considered him stricken by God,
> > smitten by him, and afflicted.
> But he was pierced for our transgressions,
> > he was crushed for our iniquities;
> the punishment that brought us peace was upon him,
> > and by his wounds we are healed.
> We all, like sheep, have gone astray,
> > each of us has turned to his own way;
> and the LORD has laid on him
> > the iniquity of us all.

Isa. 53:7-9

HUMILITY OF MESSIAH'S DEATH.

> He was oppressed and afflicted,
> > yet he did not open his mouth;
> he was led like a lamb to the slaughter,

[h]Or *will prosper*   [i]Hebrew *you*   [j]Hebrew; Septuagint *so will many nations marvel at him*

and as a sheep before her shearers is silent,
    so he did not open his mouth.
By oppression[k] and judgment he was taken away.
    And who can speak of his descendants?
For he was cut off from the land of the living;
    for the transgression of my people he was stricken.[l]
He was assigned a grave with the wicked,
    and with the rich in his death,
though he had done no violence,
    nor was any deceit in his mouth.

TRIUMPH OF RESURRECTION.

Isa.
53:10-12

Yet it was the LORD's will to crush him and cause him to
    suffer,
    and though the LORD makes[m] his life a guilt offering,
he will see his offspring and prolong his days,
    and the will of the LORD will prosper in his hand.
After the suffering of his soul,
    he will see the light ⌊of life⌋[n] and be satisfied[o];
by his knowledge[p] my righteous servant will justify many,
    and he will bear their iniquities.
Therefore I will give him a portion among the great,[q]
    and he will divide the spoils with the strong,[r]
because he poured out his life unto death,
    and was numbered with the transgressors.
For he bore the sin of many,
    and made intercession for the transgressors.

DESOLATE TO HAVE LIFE.

Isa. 54:1-3

"Sing, O barren woman,
    you who never bore a child;
burst into song, shout for joy,
    you who were never in labor;
because more are the children of the desolate woman
    than of her who has a husband,"

                          says the LORD.

"Enlarge the place of your tent,
    stretch your tent curtains wide,
    do not hold back;
lengthen your cords,
    strengthen your stakes.
For you will spread out to the right and to the left;
    your descendants will dispossess nations
    and settle in their desolate cities.

---

[k]Or *From arrest*   [l]Or *away. | Yet who of his generation considered | that he was cut off from
the land of the living | for the transgression of my people, | to whom the blow was due?*
[m]Hebrew *though you make*   [n]Dead Sea Scrolls (see also Septuagint); Masoretic Text
does not have *the light ⌊of life⌋*.   [o]Or (with Masoretic Text) [11]*He will see the result of the
suffering of his soul | and be satisfied*   [p]Or *by knowledge of him*   [q]Or *many*   [r]Or
numerous

Isa. 54:4-8 ISRAEL AS GOD'S WIFE.

> "Do not be afraid; you will not suffer shame.
>> Do not fear disgrace; you will not be humiliated.
> You will forget the shame of your youth
>> and remember no more the reproach of your widowhood.
> For your Maker is your husband—
>> the LORD Almighty is his name—
> the Holy One of Israel is your Redeemer;
>> he is called the God of all the earth.
> The LORD will call you back
>> as if you were a wife deserted and distressed in spirit—
> a wife who married young,
>> only to be rejected," says your God.
> "For a brief moment I abandoned you,
>> but with deep compassion I will bring you back.
> In a surge of anger
>> I hid my face from you for a moment,
> but with everlasting kindness
>> I will have compassion on you,"
> says the LORD your Redeemer.

Isa. 54:9,10 COVENANT AS WITH NOAH.

> "To me this is like the days of Noah,
>> when I swore that the waters of Noah would never
>>> again cover the earth.
> So now I have sworn not to be angry with you,
>> never to rebuke you again.
> Though the mountains be shaken
>> and the hills be removed,
> yet my unfailing love for you will not be shaken
>> nor my covenant of peace be removed,"
>> says the LORD, who has compassion on you.

Isa. 54:11-17 ISRAEL'S FUTURE SECURITY.

> "O afflicted city, lashed by storms and not comforted,
>> I will build you with stones of turquoise,[s]
>> your foundations with sapphires.[t]
> I will make your battlements of rubies,
>> your gates of sparkling jewels,
>> and all your walls of precious stones.
> All your sons will be taught by the LORD,
>> and great will be your children's peace.
> In righteousness you will be established:
> Tyranny will be far from you;
>> you will have nothing to fear.
> Terror will be far removed;
>> it will not come near you.
> If anyone does attack you, it will not be my doing;
>> whoever attacks you will surrender to you.

---

[s]The meaning of the Hebrew for this word is uncertain.   [t]Or *lapis lazuli*

"See, it is I who created the blacksmith
    who fans the coals into flame
    and forges a weapon fit for its work.
And it is I who have created the destroyer to work havoc;
    no weapon forged against you will prevail,
    and you will refute every tongue that accuses you.
This is the heritage of the servants of the LORD,
    and this is their vindication from me,"
                                declares the LORD.

SPLENDOR OF RESTORATION.   Isa. 55:1-5

"Come, all you who are thirsty,
    come to the waters;
and you who have no money,
    come, buy and eat!
Come, buy wine and milk
    without money and without cost.
Why spend money on what is not bread,
    and your labor on what does not satisfy?
Listen, listen to me, and eat what is good,
    and your soul will delight in the richest of fare.
Give ear and come to me;
    hear me, that your soul may live.
I will make an everlasting covenant with you,
    my faithful love promised to David.
See, I have made him a witness to the peoples,
    a leader and commander of the peoples.
Surely you will summon nations you know not,
    and nations that do not know you will hasten to you,
because of the LORD your God,
    the Holy One of Israel,
    for he has endowed you with splendor."

CALL FOR OBEDIENCE.   Isa. 55:6,7

Seek the LORD while he may be found;
    call on him while he is near.
Let the wicked forsake his way
    and the evil man his thoughts.
Let him turn to the LORD, and he will have mercy on him,
    and to our God, for he will freely pardon.

CERTAINTY OF RESTORATION.   Isa. 55:8-13

"For my thoughts are not your thoughts,
    neither are your ways my ways,"
                                  declares the LORD.
"As the heavens are higher than the earth,
    so are my ways higher than your ways
    and my thoughts than your thoughts.
As the rain and the snow
    come down from heaven,
and do not return to it
    without watering the earth

and making it bud and flourish,
    so that it yields seed for the sower and bread for the
      eater,
so is my word that goes out from my mouth:
    It will not return to me empty,
but will accomplish what I desire
    and achieve the purpose for which I sent it.
You will go out in joy
    and be led forth in peace;
the mountains and hills
    will burst into song before you,
and all the trees of the field
    will clap their hands.
Instead of the thornbush will grow the pine tree,
    and instead of briers the myrtle will grow.
This will be for the LORD's renown,
    for an everlasting sign,
    which will not be destroyed."

Isa. 56:1,2 **CALL FOR RIGHTEOUSNESS.** This is what the LORD says:

"Maintain justice
    and do what is right,
for my salvation is close at hand
    and my righteousness will soon be revealed.
Blessed is the man who does this,
    the man who holds it fast,
who keeps the Sabbath without desecrating it,
    and keeps his hand from doing any evil."

Isa. 56:3-8 **SALVATION ALSO FOR GENTILES.**

Let no foreigner who has bound himself to the LORD say,
    "The LORD will surely exclude me from his people."
And let not any eunuch complain,
    "I am only a dry tree."

For this is what the LORD says:

"To the eunuchs who keep my Sabbaths,
    who choose what pleases me
    and hold fast to my covenant—
to them I will give within my temple and its walls
    a memorial and a name
    better than sons and daughters;
I will give them an everlasting name
    that will not be cut off.
And foreigners who bind themselves to the LORD
    to serve him,
to love the name of the LORD,
    and to worship him,
all who keep the Sabbath without desecrating it
    and who hold fast to my covenant—
these I will bring to my holy mountain
    and give them joy in my house of prayer.

Their burnt offerings and sacrifices
    will be accepted on my altar;
for my house will be called
    a house of prayer for all nations."
The Sovereign LORD declares—
    he who gathers the exiles of Israel:
"I will gather still others to them
    besides those already gathered."

SPIRITUAL LEADERS CONDEMNED.

Isa. 56:9-12

Come, all you beasts of the field,
    come and devour, all you beasts of the forest!
Israel's watchmen are blind,
    they all lack knowledge;
they are all mute dogs,
    they cannot bark;
they lie around and dream,
    they love to sleep.
They are dogs with mighty appetites;
    they never have enough.
They are shepherds who lack understanding;
    they all turn to their own way,
    each seeks his own gain.
"Come," each one cries, "let me get wine!
    Let us drink our fill of beer!
And tomorrow will be like today,
    or even far better."

WHY RIGHTEOUS DIE.

Isa. 57:1,2

The righteous perish,
    and no one ponders it in his heart;
devout men are taken away,
    and no one understands
that the righteous are taken away
    to be spared from evil.
Those who walk uprightly
    enter into peace;
    they find rest as they lie in death.

RESTORATION NOT FOR WICKED.

Isa. 57:3-13

"But you—come here, you sons of a sorceress,
    you offspring of adulterers and prostitutes!
Whom are you mocking?
    At whom do you sneer
    and stick out your tongue?
Are you not a brood of rebels,
    the offspring of liars?
You burn with lust among the oaks
    and under every spreading tree;
you sacrifice your children in the ravines
    and under the overhanging crags.

⌊The idols⌋ among the smooth stones of the ravines are your
portion;
they, they are your lot.
Yes, to them you have poured out drink offerings
and offered grain offerings.
In the light of these things, should I relent?
You have made your bed on a high and lofty hill;
there you went up to offer your sacrifices.
Behind your doors and your doorposts
you have put your pagan symbols.
Forsaking me, you uncovered your bed,
you climbed into it and opened it wide;
you made a pact with those whose beds you love,
and you looked on their nakedness.
You went to Molech[u] with olive oil
and increased your perfumes.
You sent your ambassadors[v] far away;
you descended to the grave[w] itself!
You were wearied by all your ways,
but you would not say, 'It is hopeless.'
You found renewal of your strength,
and so you did not faint.

"Whom have you so dreaded and feared
that you have been false to me,
and have neither remembered me
nor pondered this in your hearts?
Is it not because I have long been silent
that you do not fear me?
I will expose your righteousness and your works,
and they will not benefit you.
When you cry out for help,
let your collection ⌊of idols⌋ save you!
The wind will carry all of them off,
a mere breath will blow them away.
But the man who makes me his refuge
will inherit the land
and possess my holy mountain."

Isa.
57:14-21
RESTORATION FOR CONTRITE.   And it will be said:

"Build up, build up, prepare the road!
Remove the obstacles out of the way of my people."
For this is what the high and lofty One says—
he who lives forever, whose name is holy:
"I live in a high and holy place,
but also with him who is contrite and lowly in spirit,
to revive the spirit of the lowly
and to revive the heart of the contrite.
I will not accuse forever,
nor will I always be angry,

[u]Or *to the king*   [v]Or *idols*   [w]Hebrew *Sheol*

for then the spirit of man would grow faint before me—
    the breath of man that I have created.
I was enraged by his sinful greed;
    I punished him, and hid my face in anger,
    yet he kept on in his willful ways.
I have seen his ways, but I will heal him;
    I will guide him and restore comfort to him,
    creating praise on the lips of the mourners in Israel.
Peace, peace, to those far and near,"
    says the LORD. "And I will heal them."
But the wicked are like the tossing sea,
    which cannot rest,
    whose waves cast up mire and mud.
"There is no peace," says my God, "for the wicked."

EMPTINESS OF FASTING.   Isa. 58:1-5

"Shout it aloud, do not hold back.
    Raise your voice like a trumpet.
Declare to my people their rebellion
    and to the house of Jacob their sins.
For day after day they seek me out;
    they seem eager to know my ways,
as if they were a nation that does what is right
    and has not forsaken the commands of its God.
They ask me for just decisions
    and seem eager for God to come near them.
'Why have we fasted,' they say,
    'and you have not seen it?
Why have we humbled ourselves,
    and you have not noticed?'

"Yet on the day of your fasting, you do as you please
    and exploit all your workers.
Your fasting ends in quarreling and strife,
    and in striking each other with wicked fists.
You cannot fast as you do today
    and expect your voice to be heard on high.
Is this the kind of fast I have chosen,
    only a day for a man to humble himself?
Is it only for bowing one's head like a reed
    and for lying on sackcloth and ashes?
Is that what you call a fast,
    a day acceptable to the LORD?

TRUE FASTING AND ITS REWARD.   Isa. 58:6-12

"Is not this the kind of fasting I have chosen:
    to loose the chains of injustice
    and untie the cords of the yoke,
to set the oppressed free
    and break every yoke?
Is it not to share your food with the hungry
    and to provide the poor wanderer with shelter—

when you see the naked, to clothe him,
and not to turn away from your own flesh and blood?
Then your light will break forth like the dawn,
and your healing will quickly appear;
then your righteousness^x will go before you,
and the glory of the LORD will be your rear guard.
Then you will call, and the LORD will answer;
you will cry for help, and he will say: Here am I.

"If you do away with the yoke of oppression,
with the pointing finger and malicious talk,
and if you spend yourselves in behalf of the hungry
and satisfy the needs of the oppressed,
then your light will rise in the darkness,
and your night will become like the noonday.
The LORD will guide you always;
he will satisfy your needs in a sun-scorched land
and will strengthen your frame.
You will be like a well-watered garden,
like a spring whose waters never fail.
Your people will rebuild the ancient ruins
and will raise up the age-old foundations;
you will be called Repairer of Broken Walls,
Restorer of Streets with Dwellings.

Isa.
58:13,14

CALL FOR SABBATH OBSERVANCE.

"If you keep your feet from breaking the Sabbath
and from doing as you please on my holy day,
if you call the Sabbath a delight
and the LORD's holy day honorable,
and if you honor it by not going your own way
and not doing as you please or speaking idle words,
then you will find your joy in the LORD,
and I will cause you to ride on the heights of the land
and to feast on the inheritance of your father Jacob."
The mouth of the LORD has spoken.

Isa. 59:1-15

CONFESSION OF SINS.

Surely the arm of the LORD is not too short to save,
nor his ear too dull to hear.
But your iniquities have separated
you from your God;
your sins have hidden his face from you,
so that he will not hear.
For your hands are stained with blood,
your fingers with guilt.
Your lips have spoken lies,
and your tongue mutters wicked things.
No one calls for justice;
no one pleads his case with integrity.

^x Or *your righteous One*

They rely on empty arguments and speak lies;
    they conceive trouble and give birth to evil.
They hatch the eggs of vipers
    and spin a spider's web.
Whoever eats their eggs will die,
    and when one is broken, an adder is hatched.
Their cobwebs are useless for clothing;
    they cannot cover themselves with what they make.
Their deeds are evil deeds,
    and acts of violence are in their hands.
Their feet rush into sin;
    they are swift to shed innocent blood.
Their thoughts are evil thoughts;
    ruin and destruction mark their ways.
The way of peace they do not know;
    there is no justice in their paths.
They have turned them into crooked roads;
    no one who walks in them will know peace.

So justice is far from us,
    and righteousness does not reach us.
We look for light, but all is darkness;
    for brightness, but we walk in deep shadows.
Like the blind we grope along the wall,
    feeling our way like men without eyes.
At midday we stumble as if it were twilight;
    among the strong, we are like the dead.
We all growl like bears;
    we moan mournfully like doves.
We look for justice, but find none;
    for deliverance, but it is far away.

For our offenses are many in your sight,
    and our sins testify against us.
Our offenses are ever with us,
    and we acknowledge our iniquities:
rebellion and treachery against the LORD,
    turning our backs on our God,
fomenting oppression and revolt,
    uttering lies our hearts have conceived.
So justice is driven back,
    and righteousness stands at a distance;
truth has stumbled in the streets,
    honesty cannot enter.
Truth is nowhere to be found,
    and whoever shuns evil becomes a prey.

SALVATION FOR PENITENTS.

Isa.
59:16-20

He saw that there was no one,
    he was appalled that there was no one to intervene;

so his own arm worked salvation for him,
    and his own righteousness sustained him.
He put on righteousness as his breastplate,
    and the helmet of salvation on his head;
he put on the garments of vengeance
    and wrapped himself in zeal as in a cloak.
According to what they have done,
    so will he repay
wrath to his enemies
    and retribution to his foes;
    he will repay the islands their due.
From the west, men will fear the name of the LORD,
    and from the rising of the sun, they will revere his glory.
For he will come like a pent-up flood
    that the breath of the LORD drives along. *y*

"The Redeemer will come to Zion,
    to those in Jacob who repent of their sins,"

                      declares the LORD.

Isa. 59:21   PROMISE OF THE SPIRIT. "As for me, this is my covenant with them,"
says the LORD. "My Spirit, who is on you, and my words that I have put in
your mouth will not depart from your mouth, or from the mouths of your
children, or from the mouths of their descendants from this time on and
forever," says the LORD.

Isa. 60:1-14   THE GLORY OF ZION.

"Arise, shine, for your light has come,
    and the glory of the LORD rises upon you.
See, darkness covers the earth
    and thick darkness is over the peoples,
but the LORD rises upon you
    and his glory appears over you.
Nations will come to your light,
    and kings to the brightness of your dawn.

"Lift up your eyes and look about you:
    All assemble and come to you;
your sons come from afar,
    and your daughters are carried on the arm.
Then you will look and be radiant,
    your heart will throb and swell with joy;
the wealth on the seas will be brought to you,
    to you the riches of the nations will come.
Herds of camels will cover your land,
    young camels of Midian and Ephah.
And all from Sheba will come,
    bearing gold and incense
    and proclaiming the praise of the LORD.
All Kedar's flocks will be gathered to you,
    the rams of Nebaioth will serve you;

y Or When the enemy comes in like a flood, / the Spirit of the LORD will put him to flight

they will be accepted as offerings on my altar,
    and I will adorn my glorious temple.

"Who are these that fly along like clouds,
    like doves to their nests?
Surely the islands look to me;
    in the lead are the ships of Tarshish,[z]
bringing your sons from afar,
    with their silver and gold,
to the honor of the LORD your God,
    the Holy One of Israel,
    for he has endowed you with splendor.

"Foreigners will rebuild your walls,
    and their kings will serve you.
Though in anger I struck you,
    in favor I will show you compassion.
Your gates will always stand open,
    they will never be shut, day or night,
so that men may bring you the wealth of the nations—
    their kings led in triumphal procession.
For the nation or kingdom that will not serve you will
      perish;
    it will be utterly ruined.

"The glory of Lebanon will come to you,
    the pine, the fir and the cypress together,
to adorn the place of my sanctuary;
    and I will glorify the place of my feet.
The sons of your oppressors will come bowing before you;
    all who despise you will bow down at your feet
and will call you the City of the LORD,
    Zion of the Holy One of Israel.

"Although you have been forsaken and hated,
    with no one traveling through,
I will make you the everlasting pride
    and the joy of all generations.
You will drink the milk of nations
    and be nursed at royal breasts.
Then you will know that I, the LORD, am your Savior,
    your Redeemer, the Mighty One of Jacob.
Instead of bronze I will bring you gold,
    and silver in place of iron.
Instead of wood I will bring you bronze,
    and iron in place of stones.
I will make peace your governor
    and righteousness your ruler.
No longer will violence be heard in your land,
    nor ruin or destruction within your borders,
but you will call your walls Salvation

Isa.
60:15-22

[z]Or *the trading ships*

and your gates Praise.
The sun will no more be your light by day,
      nor will the brightness of the moon shine on you,
for the LORD will be your everlasting light,
      and your God will be your glory.
Your sun will never set again,
      and your moon will wane no more;
the LORD will be your everlasting light,
      and your days of sorrow will end.
Then will all your people be righteous
      and they will possess the land forever.
They are the shoot I have planted,
      the work of my hands,
      for the display of my splendor.
The least of you will become a thousand,
      the smallest a mighty nation.
I am the LORD;
      in its time I will do this swiftly."

Isa. 61:1-3a   ISAIAH'S MISSION TO COMFORT.

The Spirit of the Sovereign LORD is on me,
      because the LORD has anointed me
      to preach good news to the poor.
He has sent me to bind up the brokenhearted,
      to proclaim freedom for the captives
      and release from darkness for the prisoners,[a]
to proclaim the year of the LORD's favor
      and the day of vengeance of our God,
to comfort all who mourn,
      and provide for those who grieve in Zion—
to bestow on them a crown of beauty
      instead of ashes,
the oil of gladness
      instead of mourning,
and a garment of praise
      instead of a spirit of despair.

Isa.   THE MESSAGE OF HOPE.
61:3b-9

They will be called oaks of righteousness,
      a planting of the LORD
      for the display of his splendor.

They will rebuild the ancient ruins
      and restore the places long devastated;
they will renew the ruined cities
      that have been devastated for generations.
Aliens will shepherd your flocks;
      foreigners will work your fields and vineyards.
And you will be called priests of the LORD,
      you will be named ministers of our God.

[a]Hebrew; Septuagint *the blind*

You will feed on the wealth of nations,
and in their riches you will boast.

Instead of their shame
my people will receive a double portion,
and instead of disgrace
they will rejoice in their inheritance;
and so they will inherit a double portion in their land,
and everlasting joy will be theirs.

"For I, the LORD, love justice;
I hate robbery and iniquity.
In my faithfulness I will reward them
and make an everlasting covenant with them.
Their descendants will be known among the nations
and their offspring among the peoples.
All who see them will acknowledge
that they are a people the LORD has blessed."

PRAISE FOR SALVATION.

Isa.
61:10,11

I delight greatly in the LORD;
my soul rejoices in my God.
For he has clothed me with garments of salvation
and arrayed me in a robe of righteousness,
as a bridegroom adorns his head like a priest,
and as a bride adorns herself with her jewels.
For as the soil makes the sprout come up
and a garden causes seeds to grow,
so the Sovereign LORD will make righteousness and praise
spring up before all nations.

THE BRIDE'S NEW NAME.

Isa. 62:1-5

For Zion's sake I will not keep silent,
for Jerusalem's sake I will not remain quiet,
till her righteousness shines out like the dawn,
her salvation like a blazing torch.
The nations will see your righteousness,
and all kings your glory;
you will be called by a new name
that the mouth of the LORD will bestow.
You will be a crown of splendor in the LORD's hand,
a royal diadem in the hand of your God.
No longer will they call you Deserted,
or name your land Desolate.
But you will be called Hephzibah,[b]
and your land Beulah[c];
for the LORD will take delight in you,
and your land will be married.
As a young man marries a maiden,
so will your sons[d] marry you;
as a bridegroom rejoices over his bride,

---

[b]*Hephzibah* means *my delight is in her.*   [c]*Beulah* means *married.*   [d]Or *Builder*

so will your God rejoice over you.

Isa. 62:6-12   THE HOLY AND REDEEMED.

I have posted watchmen on your walls, O Jerusalem;
    they will never be silent day or night.
You who call on the LORD,
    give yourselves no rest,
and give him no rest till he establishes Jerusalem
    and makes her the praise of the earth.

The LORD has sworn by his right hand
    and by his mighty arm:
"Never again will I give your grain
    as food for your enemies,
and never again will foreigners drink the new wine
    for which you have toiled;
but those who harvest it will eat it
    and praise the LORD,
and those who gather the grapes will drink it
    in the courts of my sanctuary."

Pass through, pass through the gates!
    Prepare the way for the people.
Build up, build up the highway!
    Remove the stones.
Raise a banner for the nations.

The LORD has made proclamation
    to the ends of the earth:
"Say to the Daughter of Zion,
    'See, your Savior comes!
See, his reward is with him,
    and his recompense accompanies him.'"
They will be called the Holy People,
    the Redeemed of the LORD;
and you will be called Sought After,
    the City No Longer Deserted.

Isa. 63:1-6   VENGEANCE AGAINST WICKED.

Who is this coming from Edom,
    from Bozrah, with his garments stained crimson?
Who is this, robed in splendor,
    striding forward in the greatness of his strength?

"It is I, speaking in righteousness,
    mighty to save."

Why are your garments red,
    like those of one treading the winepress?

"I have trodden the winepress alone;
    from the nations no one was with me.
I trampled them in my anger
    and trod them down in my wrath;
their blood spattered my garments,

        and I stained all my clothing.
For the day of vengeance was in my heart,
        and the year of my redemption has come.
I looked, but there was no one to help,
        I was appalled that no one gave support;
so my own arm worked salvation for me,
        and my own wrath sustained me.
I trampled the nations in my anger;
        in my wrath I made them drunk
        and poured their blood on the ground."

KINDNESS TO RIGHTEOUS.   Isa. 63:7-9

I will tell of the kindnesses of the LORD,
        the deeds for which he is to be praised,
        according to all the LORD has done for us—
yes, the many good things he has done
        for the house of Israel,
        according to his compassion and many kindnesses.
He said, "Surely they are my people,
        sons who will not be false to me";
        and so he became their Savior.
In all their distress he too was distressed,
        and the angel of his presence saved them.
In his love and mercy he redeemed them;
        he lifted them up and carried them
        all the days of old.

WRATH AGAINST REBELLIOUS.   Isa. 63:10

Yet they rebelled
        and grieved his Holy Spirit.
So he turned and became their enemy
        and he himself fought against them.

GOD'S PROTECTION RECALLED.   Isa.
                                                       63:11-14
Then his people recalled[e] the days of old,
        the days of Moses and his people—
where is he who brought them through the sea,
        with the shepherd of his flock?
Where is he who set
        his Holy Spirit among them,
who sent his glorious arm of power
        to be at Moses' right hand,
who divided the waters before them,
        to gain for himself everlasting renown,
who led them through the depths?
Like a horse in open country,
        they did not stumble;
like cattle that go down to the plain,
        they were given rest by the Spirit of the LORD.
This is how you guided your people

---

[e]Or *But may he recall*

to make for yourself a glorious name.

Isa.
63:15-19
ISRAEL'S PRAYER TO GOD.

Look down from heaven and see
   from your lofty throne, holy and glorious.
Where are your zeal and your might?
   Your tenderness and compassion are withheld from us.
But you are our Father,
   though Abraham does not know us
   or Israel acknowledge us;
you, O LORD, are our Father,
   our Redeemer from of old is your name.
Why, O LORD, do you make us wander from your ways
   and harden our hearts so we do not revere you?
Return for the sake of your servants,
   the tribes that are your inheritance.
For a little while your people possessed your holy place,
   but now our enemies have trampled down your
      sanctuary.
We are yours from of old;
   but you have not ruled over them,
   they have not been called by your name.ƒ

Isa. 64:1-12
Oh, that you would rend the heavens and come down,
   that the mountains would tremble before you!
As when fire sets twigs ablaze
   and causes water to boil,
come down to make your name known to your enemies
   and cause the nations to quake before you!
For when you did awesome things that we did not expect,
   you came down, and the mountains trembled before you.
Since ancient times no one has heard,
   no ear has perceived,
no eye has seen any God besides you,
   who acts on behalf of those who wait for him.
You come to the help of those who gladly do right,
   who remember your ways.
But when we continued to sin against them,
   you were angry.
   How then can we be saved?
All of us have become like one who is unclean,
   and all our righteous acts are like filthy rags;
we all shrivel up like a leaf,
   and like the wind our sins sweep us away.
No one calls on your name
   or strives to lay hold of you;
for you have hidden your face from us
   and made us waste away because of our sins.

Yet, O LORD, you are our Father.

ƒOr *We are like those you have never ruled,* / *like those never called by your name*

We are the clay, you are the potter;
    we are all the work of your hand.
Do not be angry beyond measure, O LORD;
    do not remember our sins forever.
Oh, look upon us, we pray,
    for we are all your people.
Your sacred cities have become a desert;
    even Zion is a desert, Jerusalem a desolation.
Our holy and glorious temple, where our fathers praised
        you,
    has been burned with fire,
    and all that we treasured lies in ruins.
After all this, O LORD, will you hold yourself back?
    Will you keep silent and punish us beyond measure?

GOD EXPLAINS JUDGMENT.   Isa. 65:1-7

"I revealed myself to those who did not ask for me;
    I was found by those who did not seek me.
To a nation that did not call on my name,
    I said, 'Here am I, here am I.'
All day long I have held out my hands
    to an obstinate people,
who walk in ways not good,
    pursuing their own imaginations—
a people who continually provoke me
    to my very face,
offering sacrifices in gardens
    and burning incense on altars of brick;
who sit among the graves
    and spend their nights keeping secret vigil;
who eat the flesh of pigs,
    and whose pots hold broth of unclean meat;
who say, 'Keep away; don't come near me,
    for I am too sacred for you!'
Such people are smoke in my nostrils,
    a fire that keeps burning all day.

"See, it stands written before me:
    I will not keep silent but will pay back in full;
    I will pay it back into their laps—
both your sins and the sins of your fathers,"
    says the LORD.
"Because they burned sacrifices on the mountains
    and defied me on the hills,
I will measure into their laps
    the full payment for their former deeds."

SALVATION OF REMNANT.   This is what the LORD says: Isa. 65:8-10

"As when juice is still found in a cluster of grapes
    and men say, 'Don't destroy it,
    there is yet some good in it,'
so will I do in behalf of my servants;

I will not destroy them all.
I will bring forth descendants from Jacob,
and from Judah those who will possess my mountains;
my chosen people will inherit them,
and there will my servants live.
Sharon will become a pasture for flocks,
and the Valley of Achor a resting place for herds,
for my people who seek me.

Isa.
65:11,12

NO MERCY FOR UNREPENTANT.

"But as for you who forsake the LORD
and forget my holy mountain,
who spread a table for Fortune
and fill bowls of mixed wine for Destiny,
I will destine you for the sword,
and you will all bend down for the slaughter;
for I called but you did not answer,
I spoke but you did not listen.
You did evil in my sight
and chose what displeases me."

Isa.
65:13-16

BLESSINGS FOR SERVANTS.   Therefore this is what the Sovereign LORD says:

"My servants will eat,
but you will go hungry;
my servants will drink,
but you will go thirsty;
my servants will rejoice,
but you will be put to shame.
My servants will sing
out of the joy of their hearts,
but you will cry out
from anguish of heart
and wail in brokenness of spirit.
You will leave your name
to my chosen ones as a curse;
the Sovereign LORD will put you to death,
but to his servants he will give another name.
Whoever invokes a blessing in the land
will do so by the God of truth;
he who takes an oath in the land
will swear by the God of truth.
For the past troubles will be forgotten
and hidden from my eyes.

Isa.
65:17-25

NEW HEAVENS AND A NEW EARTH.

"Behold, I will create
new heavens and a new earth.
The former things will not be remembered,
nor will they come to mind.
But be glad and rejoice forever
in what I will create,

for I will create Jerusalem to be a delight
  and its people a joy.
I will rejoice over Jerusalem
  and take delight in my people;
the sound of weeping and of crying
  will be heard in it no more.

"Never again will there be in it
  an infant who lives but a few days,
  or an old man who does not live out his years;
he who dies at a hundred
  will be thought a mere youth;
he who fails to reach^g a hundred
  will be considered accursed.
They will build houses and dwell in them;
  they will plant vineyards and eat their fruit.
No longer will they build houses and others live in them,
  or plant and others eat.
For as the days of a tree,
  so will be the days of my people;
my chosen ones will long enjoy
  the works of their hands.
They will not toil in vain
  or bear children doomed to misfortune;
for they will be a people blessed by the LORD,
  they and their descendants with them.
Before they call I will answer;
  while they are still speaking I will hear.
The wolf and the lamb will feed together,
  and the lion will eat straw like the ox,
  but dust will be the serpent's food.
They will neither harm nor destroy
  on all my holy mountain,"

says the LORD.

GOD'S MAJESTY AND POWER.   This is what the LORD says: Isa. 66:1,2

"Heaven is my throne,
  and the earth is my footstool.
Where is the house you will build for me?
  Where will my resting place be?
Has not my hand made all these things,
  and so they came into being?"

declares the LORD.

"This is the one I esteem:
  he who is humble and contrite in spirit,
  and trembles at my word.

GOD'S ENEMIES WILL FALL.   Isa. 66:3-6

But whoever sacrifices a bull
  is like one who kills a man,

^gOr / *the sinner who reaches*

and whoever offers a lamb,
    like one who breaks a dog's neck;
whoever makes a grain offering
    is like one who presents pig's blood,
and whoever burns memorial incense,
    like one who worships an idol.
They have chosen their own ways,
    and their souls delight in their abominations;
so I also will choose harsh treatment for them
    and will bring upon them what they dread.
For when I called, no one answered,
    when I spoke, no one listened.
They did evil in my sight
    and chose what displeases me."

Hear the word of the LORD,
    you who tremble at his word:
"Your brothers who hate you,
    and exclude you because of my name, have said,
'Let the LORD be glorified,
    that we may see your joy!'
    Yet they will be put to shame.
Hear that uproar from the city,
    hear that noise from the temple!
It is the sound of the LORD
    repaying his enemies all they deserve.

Isa. 66:7-14   BELIEVERS WILL BE REWARDED.

"Before she goes into labor,
    she gives birth;
before the pains come upon her,
    she delivers a son.
Who has ever heard of such a thing?
    Who has ever seen such things?
Can a country be born in a day
    or a nation be brought forth in a moment?
Yet no sooner is Zion in labor
    than she gives birth to her children.
Do I bring to the moment of birth
    and not give delivery?" says the LORD.
"Do I close up the womb
    when I bring to delivery?" says your God.
"Rejoice with Jerusalem and be glad for her,
    all you who love her;
rejoice greatly with her,
    all you who mourn over her.
For you will nurse and be satisfied
    at her comforting breasts;
you will drink deeply
    and delight in her overflowing abundance."

For this is what the LORD says:

"I will extend peace to her like a river,
    and the wealth of nations like a flooding stream;
you will nurse and be carried on her arm
    and dandled on her knees.
As a mother comforts her child,
    so will I comfort you;
and you will be comforted over Jerusalem."

When you see this, your heart will rejoice
    and you will flourish like grass;
the hand of the LORD will be made known to his servants,
    but his fury will be shown to his foes.

DESTRUCTION OF WICKED.   Isa.
                                                                                      66:15-17

See, the LORD is coming with fire,
    and his chariots are like a whirlwind;
he will bring down his anger with fury,
    and his rebuke with flames of fire.
For with fire and with his sword
    the LORD will execute judgment upon all men,
    and many will be those slain by the LORD.

"Those who consecrate and purify themselves to go into the gardens, following the one in the midst of[h] those who eat the flesh of pigs and rats and other abominable things—they will meet their end together," declares the LORD.

SURVIVORS TO BE EVANGELISTS.   "And I, because of their actions and   Isa.
their imaginations, am about to come[i] and gather all nations and tongues,   66:18-21
and they will come and see my glory.

"I will set a sign among them, and I will send some of those who survive to the nations—to Tarshish, to the Libyans[j] and Lydians (famous as archers), to Tubal and Greece, and to the distant islands that have not heard of my fame or seen my glory. They will proclaim my glory among the nations. And they will bring all your brothers, from all the nations, to my holy mountain in Jerusalem as an offering to the LORD—on horses, in chariots and wagons, and on mules and camels," says the LORD. "They will bring them, as the Israelites bring their grain offerings, to the temple of the LORD in ceremonially clean vessels. And I will select some of them also to be priests and Levites," says the LORD.

ETERNAL LIFE AND DEATH.   "As the new heavens and the new earth   Isa.
that I make will endure before me," declares the LORD, "so will your name   66:22-24
and descendants endure. From one New Moon to another and from one Sabbath to another, all mankind will come and bow down before me," says the LORD. "And they will go out and look upon the dead bodies of those who rebelled against me; their worm will not die, nor will their fire be quenched, and they will be loathsome to all mankind."

How anyone could ignore or reject such a powerful message is difficult to fathom. But Isaiah himself speaks of those who will refuse to hear or see.

[h]Or gardens behind one of your temples, and   [i]The meaning of the Hebrew for this clause is uncertain.   [j]Some Septuagint manuscripts Put (Libyans); Hebrew Pul

Some will reject the message because they are willfully stubborn, and others because they are caught up in material pursuits, or pleasurable diversions, or even false religious worship. Perhaps saddest of all, God's message will sometimes be hidden from the common people by the very ones who ought to bring understanding—the religious leaders. Once again Isaiah singles out these leaders for special judgment. It is quite possible that this very condemnation proves to be the death knell for Isaiah, for tradition holds that Isaiah was sawn in two by his enemies during Manasseh's reign.

Spiritual Renewal Under Manasseh

*A*s a result of his wicked leadership, Manasseh is taken captive to Babylon by the army of a now-eclipsing Assyrian empire. There in exile with many of his fellow countrymen, Manasseh is conscience-stricken and sincerely repents. Consequently, God reestablishes Manasseh on the throne in Judah, and Manasseh does what he can to abolish the very idolatry he introduced. The historical record begins with a note about the Assyrian coup in which Sennacherib is assassinated by his own sons.

2 Kgs. 19:37 2 Chron. 32:21c Isa. 37:38 (681 B.C.)	SENNACHERIB ASSASSINATED. One day, while he was worshiping in the temple of his god Nisroch, his sons Adrammelech and Sharezer cut him down with the sword, and they escaped to the land of Ararat. And Esarhaddon his son succeeded him as king.
2 Chron. 33:10,11	MANASSEH TAKEN CAPTIVE. The LORD spoke to Manasseh and his people, but they paid no attention. So the LORD brought against them the army commanders of the king of Assyria, who took Manasseh prisoner, put a hook in his nose, bound him with bronze shackles and took him to Babylon.
2 Chron. 33:12,13	REPENTANCE BRINGS RESTORATION. In his distress he sought the favor of the LORD his God and humbled himself greatly before the God of his fathers. And when he prayed to him, the LORD was moved by his entreaty and listened to his plea; so he brought him back to Jerusalem and to his kingdom. Then Manasseh knew that the LORD is God.
2 Chron. 33:14-17	MANASSEH REFORMS JUDAH. Afterward he rebuilt the outer wall of the City of David, west of the Gihon spring in the valley, as far as the entrance of the Fish Gate and encircling the hill of Ophel; he also made it much higher. He stationed military commanders in all the fortified cities in Judah. He got rid of the foreign gods and removed the image from the temple of the LORD, as well as all the altars he had built on the temple hill and in Jerusalem; and he threw them out of the city. Then he restored the altar of the LORD and sacrificed fellowship offerings*k* and thank offerings on it, and told Judah to serve the LORD, the God of Israel. The people, however, continued to sacrifice at the high places, but only to the LORD their God.

*k*Traditionally *peace offerings*

Nahum's Prophecy Against Nineveh

*J*t is about 650 B.C.—some 50 years after God's miraculous destruction of Sennacherib's army. Sennacherib returned from that defeat, in disgrace, to the Assyrian capital of Nineveh. When he was assassinated in 681 B.C., he was followed by his son Esarhaddon, who reigned for 11 years. (It may have been during Esarhaddon's reign that Manasseh was first taken captive and then released to be a puppet king back in Judah.) Esarhaddon is succeeded (in 669 B.C.) by the barbarous Ashurbanipal, who takes his army deep into Palestine and Egypt in 663 B.C. and destroys the Egyptian city of Thebes (No Amon). The hallmark of the Assyrians at this time is not merely military success but ruthlessness and cruelty. They take great pride in maiming their enemies, and even boiling them in tar or skinning them alive. If the veneer of civilization is thin, Assyria is clearly the last fiber of humanity.

These atrocities are particularly disappointing in view of the fact that, only 125 years before, the people of Assyria had responded penitently to the preaching of Jonah and had been the recipients of God's mercy. Perhaps it is because the Ninevites have not shown appreciation for his mercy that God now displays his wrath. While Manasseh is bringing about reforms in Judah, Nahum prophesies against Judah's archenemy, Nineveh, and predicts her fall.

PREFACE.   An oracle concerning Nineveh. The book of the vision of   Nahum 1:1
Nahum the Elkoshite.

GOD'S WRATH AGAINST ENEMIES.   Nahum
                                                                     1:2-6

> The LORD is a jealous and avenging God;
>   the LORD takes vengeance and is filled with wrath.
> The LORD takes vengeance on his foes
>   and maintains his wrath against his enemies.
> The LORD is slow to anger and great in power;
>   the LORD will not leave the guilty unpunished.
> His way is in the whirlwind and the storm,
>   and clouds are the dust of his feet.
> He rebukes the sea and dries it up;
>   he makes all the rivers run dry.
> Bashan and Carmel wither
>   and the blossoms of Lebanon fade.
> The mountains quake before him
>   and the hills melt away.
> The earth trembles at his presence,
>   the world and all who live in it.
> Who can withstand his indignation?
>   Who can endure his fierce anger?
> His wrath is poured out like fire;
>   the rocks are shattered before him.

NINEVEH HAS REFUSED MERCY.   Nahum
                                                                    1:7,8

> The LORD is good,

a refuge in times of trouble.
He cares for those who trust in him,
    but with an overwhelming flood
he will make an end of ⌊Nineveh⌋;
    he will pursue his foes into darkness.

Nahum 1:9,10   CAPTURE WHILE ARMY DRUNK.

Whatever they plot against the LORD
    he[1] will bring to an end;
    trouble will not come a second time.
They will be entangled among thorns
    and drunk from their wine;
    they will be consumed like dry stubble.[m]

Nahum 1:11   SIN OF SENNACHERIB.

From you, ⌊O Nineveh,⌋ has one come forth
    who plots evil against the LORD
    and counsels wickedness.

Nahum 1:12,13   JUDAH'S VASSALAGE WILL CEASE.   This is what the LORD says:

"Although they have allies and are numerous,
    they will be cut off and pass away.
Although I have afflicted you, ⌊O Judah,⌋
    I will afflict you no more.
Now I will break their yoke from your neck
    and tear your shackles away."

Nahum 1:14   COMPLETENESS OF DESTRUCTION.

The LORD has given a command concerning you, ⌊Nineveh⌋:
    "You will have no descendants to bear your name.
I will destroy the carved images and cast idols
    that are in the temple of your gods.
I will prepare your grave,
    for you are vile."

Nahum 1:15   JUDAH WILL BE SAFE.

Look, there on the mountains,
    the feet of one who brings good news,
    who proclaims peace!
Celebrate your festivals, O Judah,
    and fulfill your vows.
No more will the wicked invade you;
    they will be completely destroyed.

Nahum 2:1,2   DESTRUCTION TO RESTORE ISRAEL.

An attacker advances against you, ⌊Nineveh⌋.
    Guard the fortress,
    watch the road,
    brace yourselves,

[1]Or *What do you foes plot against the LORD? | He*   [m]The meaning of the Hebrew for this
verse is uncertain.

marshal all your strength!

The LORD will restore the splendor of Jacob
  like the splendor of Israel,
though destroyers have laid them waste
  and have ruined their vines.

DETAILS OF THE FALL.   Nahum
                                                                       2:3-10

The shields of his soldiers are red;
  the warriors are clad in scarlet.
The metal on the chariots flashes
  on the day they are made ready;
  the spears of pine are brandished.[n]
The chariots storm through the streets,
  rushing back and forth through the squares.
They look like flaming torches;
  they dart about like lightning.

He summons his picked troops,
  yet they stumble on their way.
They dash to the city wall;
  the protective shield is put in place.
The river gates are thrown open
  and the palace collapses.
It is decreed[o] that the city
  be exiled and carried away.
Its slave girls moan like doves
  and beat upon their breasts.
Nineveh is like a pool,
  and its water is draining away.
"Stop! Stop!" they cry,
  but no one turns back.
Plunder the silver!
  Plunder the gold!
The supply is endless,
  the wealth from all its treasures!
She is pillaged, plundered, stripped!
  Hearts melt, knees give way,
  bodies tremble, every face grows pale.

ATROCITIES WILL CEASE.   Nahum
                                                                       2:11-13

Where now is the lions' den,
  the place where they fed their young,
where the lion and lioness went,
  and the cubs, with nothing to fear?
The lion killed enough for his cubs
  and strangled the prey for his mate,
filling his lairs with the kill
  and his dens with the prey.

[n]Hebrew; Septuagint and Syriac / *the horsemen rush to and fro*   [o]The meaning of the
Hebrew for this word is uncertain.

"I am against you,"
    declares the LORD Almighty.
"I will burn up your chariots in smoke,
    and the sword will devour your young lions.
    I will leave you no prey on the earth.
The voices of your messengers
    will no longer be heard."

Nahum 3:1-4

GUILT OF BLOODSHED.

Woe to the city of blood,
    full of lies,
full of plunder,
    never without victims!
The crack of whips,
    the clatter of wheels,
galloping horses
    and jolting chariots!
Charging cavalry,
    flashing swords
    and glittering spears!
Many casualties,
    piles of dead,
bodies without number,
    people stumbling over the corpses—
all because of the wanton lust of a harlot,
    alluring, the mistress of sorceries,
who enslaved nations by her prostitution
    and peoples by her witchcraft.

Nahum 3:5-7

SHAME AND DISGRACE.

"I am against you," declares the LORD Almighty.
    "I will lift your skirts over your face.
I will show the nations your nakedness
    and the kingdoms your shame.
I will pelt you with filth,
    I will treat you with contempt
    and make you a spectacle.
All who see you will flee from you and say,
    'Nineveh is in ruins—who will mourn for her?'
    Where can I find anyone to comfort you?"

Nahum 3:8-11

FATE SAME AS VICTIMS.

Are you better than Thebes,[p]
    situated on the Nile,
    with water around her?
The river was her defense,
    the waters her wall.
Cush[q] and Egypt were her boundless strength;
    Put and Libya were among her allies.
Yet she was taken captive

    [p]Hebrew *No Amon*   [q]That is, the upper Nile region

and went into exile.
Her infants were dashed to pieces
    at the head of every street.
Lots were cast for her nobles,
    and all her great men were put in chains.
You too will become drunk;
    you will go into hiding
    and seek refuge from the enemy.

ASSYRIA'S VULNERABILITY.   Nahum
                                                  3:12-17

All your fortresses are like fig trees
    with their first ripe fruit;
when they are shaken,
    the figs fall into the mouth of the eater.
Look at your troops—
    they are all women!
The gates of your land
    are wide open to your enemies;
    fire has consumed their bars.

Draw water for the siege,
    strengthen your defenses!
Work the clay,
    tread the mortar,
    repair the brickwork!
There the fire will devour you;
    the sword will cut you down
    and, like grasshoppers, consume you.
Multiply like grasshoppers,
    multiply like locusts!
You have increased the number of your merchants
    till they are more than the stars of the sky,
but like locusts they strip the land
    and then fly away.
Your guards are like locusts,
    your officials like swarms of locusts
    that settle in the walls on a cold day—
but when the sun appears they fly away,
    and no one knows where.

WORLD WILL CELEBRATE FALL.   Nahum
                                                  3:18,19

O king of Assyria, your shepherds[r] slumber;
    your nobles lie down to rest.
Your people are scattered on the mountains
    with no one to gather them.
Nothing can heal your wound;
    your injury is fatal.
Everyone who hears the news about you
    claps his hands at your fall,
for who has not felt
    your endless cruelty?

[r] Or *rulers*

From Manasseh to Josiah

*I*n only 40 years Nahum's predictions will come true in exactly the way he has outlined: the Medes, Babylonians, and Scythians will turn the waters of the Khoser River into the city, causing the bricks to be dissolved. Just as Nahum has prophesied, Nineveh will be destroyed so completely that it will be some 2500 years before archaeological traces of this great city will be found.

Before Nineveh's fall, Manasseh's reign will come to an end with his death. Manasseh's son Amon supports idolatry and wickedness and is assassinated after a brief rule of two years. He is succeeded by Josiah, the most godly king that Judah has ever known. Josiah takes the throne when he is only eight years old and initiates sweeping reforms when he is 16.

2 Kgs. 21:17,18a 2 Chron. 33:18-20a (641 B.C.) Jerusalem	**DEATH OF MANASSEH.** ᶜʰThe other events of Manasseh's reign, including his prayer to his God and the words the seers spoke to him in the name of the LORD, the God of Israel, are written in the annals of the kings of Israel.ˢ His prayer and how God was moved by his entreaty, as well as all his sins and unfaithfulness, and the sites where he built high places and set up Asherah poles and idols before he humbled himself—all are written in the records of the seers.ᵗ ᴷᵍManasseh rested with his fathers and was buried in his palace garden, the garden of Uzza.
2 Kgs. 21:18b,19 2 Chron. 33:20b,21	**AMON KING OF JUDAH.** And Amon his son succeeded him as king. Amon was twenty-two years old when he became king, and he reigned in Jerusalem two years. His mother's name was Meshullemeth daughter of Haruz; she was from Jotbah.
2 Kgs. 21:20-22 2 Chron. 33:22,23	**AMON'S CHARACTER.** He did evil in the eyes of the LORD, as his father Manasseh had done. Amon worshiped and offered sacrifices to all the idols Manasseh had made. But unlike his father Manasseh, he did not humble himself before the LORD; Amon increased his guilt.
2 Kgs. 21:25, 23,26a 2 Chron. 33:24 (639 B.C.)	**AMON ASSASSINATED.** As for the other events of Amon's reign, and what he did, are they not written in the book of the annals of the kings of Judah? Amon's officials conspired against him and assassinated the king in his palace. He was buried in his grave in the garden of Uzza.
2 Kgs. 21:24 21:26b 2 Ch. 33:25	**CONSPIRATORS KILLED.** Then the people of the land killed all who had plotted against King Amon, and they made Josiah his son king in his place.
2 Kgs. 22:1 2 Ch. 34:1 (639 B.C.)	**JOSIAH CHILD-KING OF JUDAH.** Josiah was eight years old when he became king, and he reigned in Jerusalem thirty-one years. His mother's name was Jedidah daughter of Adaiah; she was from Bozkath.
2 Kgs. 22:2;23:25 2 Chron. 34:2	**JOSIAH'S GODLY CHARACTER.** He did what was right in the eyes of the LORD and walked in all the ways of his father David, not turning aside to the right or to the left. Neither before nor after Josiah was there a king like him who turned to the LORD as he did—with all his heart and with

---

ˢThat is, Judah, as frequently in 2 Chron. ᵗOne Hebrew manuscript and Septuagint; most Hebrew manuscripts *of Hozai* all his soul and with all his strength, in accordance with all the Law of Moses.

JUDAH'S JUDGMENT STANDS.　　Nevertheless, the LORD did not turn away from the heat of his fierce anger, which burned against Judah because of all that Manasseh had done to provoke him to anger. So the LORD said, "I will remove Judah also from my presence as I removed Israel, and I will reject Jerusalem, the city I chose, and this temple, about which I said, 'There shall my Name be.'*"

2 Kgs.
23:26,27

Zephaniah Prophesies About The Day of the Lord

With a child for its king, the nation of Judah does not yet have the governmental leadership it needs for spiritual renewal. Spiritual leadership must come from older men; therefore one of the young king's distant relatives is called into God's service as a prophet. Zephaniah, like young King Josiah, is a descendant in the fourth generation from King Hezekiah. Zephaniah's mission and message are the same as that of the prophets before him—bringing judgment against immorality, injustice, and pagan idolatry—and yet his central theme is the coming of "the day of the Lord." In one sense, the day of the Lord is coming rather immediately for Judah, when it will be destroyed because of its sins. The day of the Lord is also coming for all the nations which have oppressed God's people. In another sense, the great day of the Lord is coming at the time when God will bring judgment against all the wicked. In each sense, the day of the Lord will be accompanied by salvation of God's faithful remnant. But it is God's terrible judgment against the unrighteous that really calls Zephaniah to his ministry, apparently between 635 and 625 B.C.

PREFACE.　　The word of the LORD that came to Zephaniah son of Cushi, the son of Gedaliah, the son of Amariah, the son of Hezekiah, during the reign of Josiah son of Amon king of Judah:

Zeph. 1:1

THE GREAT JUDGMENT.

Zeph.
1:2,3

　　"I will sweep away everything
　　　　from the face of the earth,"
　　　　　　　　　　　　declares the LORD.
　　"I will sweep away both men and animals;
　　　　I will sweep away the birds of the air
　　　　and the fish of the sea.
　　The wicked will have only heaps of rubble*
　　　　when I cut off man from the face of the earth,"
　　　　　　　　　　　　declares the LORD.

JUDAH'S JUDGMENT.

Zeph.
1:4-13

　　"I will stretch out my hand against Judah
　　　　and against all who live in Jerusalem.
　　I will cut off from this place every remnant of Baal,

*1 Kings 8:29　　*The meaning of the Hebrew for this line is uncertain.

the names of the pagan and the idolatrous priests—
those who bow down on the roofs
to worship the starry host,
those who bow down and swear by the LORD
and who also swear by Molech,*w*
those who turn back from following the LORD
and neither seek the LORD nor inquire of him.
Be silent before the Sovereign LORD,
for the day of the LORD is near.
The LORD has prepared a sacrifice;
he has consecrated those he has invited.
On the day of the LORD's sacrifice
I will punish the princes
and the king's sons
and all those clad
in foreign clothes.
On that day I will punish
all who avoid stepping on the threshold,*x*
who fill the temple of their gods
with violence and deceit.

"On that day," declares the LORD,
"a cry will go up from the Fish Gate,
wailing from the New Quarter,
and a loud crash from the hills.
Wail, you who live in the market district*y*;
all your merchants will be wiped out,
all who trade with*z* silver will be ruined.
At that time I will search Jerusalem with lamps
and punish those who are complacent,
who are like wine left on its dregs,
who think, 'The LORD will do nothing,
either good or bad.'
Their wealth will be plundered,
their houses demolished.
They will build houses
but not live in them;
they will plant vineyards
but not drink the wine.

Zeph.
1:14-18

THE GREAT DAY OF THE LORD.

"The great day of the LORD is near—
near and coming quickly.
Listen! The cry on the day of the LORD will be bitter,
the shouting of the warrior there.
That day will be a day of wrath,
a day of distress and anguish,
a day of trouble and ruin,
a day of darkness and gloom,
a day of clouds and blackness,

---

*w*Hebrew *Malcam*, that is, Milcom   *x*See 1 Samuel 5:5.   *y*Or *the Mortar*   *z*Or *in*

a day of trumpet and battle cry
 against the fortified cities
 and against the corner towers.
I will bring distress on the people
 and they will walk like blind men,
 because they have sinned against the LORD.
Their blood will be poured out like dust
 and their entrails like filth.
Neither their silver nor their gold
 will be able to save them
 on the day of the LORD's wrath.
In the fire of his jealousy
 the whole world will be consumed,
for he will make a sudden end
 of all who live in the earth."

JUDAH'S DAY OF THE LORD.

Zeph.
2:1-3

Gather together, gather together,
 O shameful nation,
before the appointed time arrives
 and that day sweeps on like chaff,
before the fierce anger of the LORD comes upon you,
 before the day of the LORD's wrath comes upon you.
Seek the LORD, all you humble of the land,
 you who do what he commands.
Seek righteousness, seek humility;
 perhaps you will be sheltered
 on the day of the LORD's anger.

PHILISTIA'S JUDGMENT.

Zeph.
2:4-7

Gaza will be abandoned
 and Ashkelon left in ruins.
At midday Ashdod will be emptied
 and Ekron uprooted.
Woe to you who live by the sea,
 O Kerethite people;
the word of the LORD is against you,
 O Canaan, land of the Philistines.

"I will destroy you,
 and none will be left."

The land by the sea, where the Kerethites[a] dwell,
 will be a place for shepherds and sheep pens.
It will belong to the remnant of the house of Judah;
 there they will find pasture.
In the evening they will lie down
 in the houses of Ashkelon.
The LORD their God will care for them;
 he will restore their fortunes.[b]

---

[a]The meaning of the Hebrew for this word is uncertain. [b]Or *will bring back their captives*

Zeph.
2:8-11

MOAB'S AND AMMON'S JUDGMENT.

"I have heard the insults of Moab
        and the taunts of the Ammonites,
who insulted my people
        and made threats against their land.
Therefore, as surely as I live,"
        declares the LORD Almighty, the God of Israel,
"surely Moab will become like Sodom,
        the Ammonites like Gomorrah—
a place of weeds and salt pits,
        a wasteland forever.
The remnant of my people will plunder them;
        the survivors of my nation will inherit their land."

This is what they will get in return for their pride,
        for insulting and mocking the people of the LORD
                Almighty.
The LORD will be awesome to them
        when he destroys all the gods of the land.
The nations on every shore will worship him,
        every one in its own land.

Zeph. 2:12   CUSH'S JUDGMENT.

"You too, O Cushites,[c]
        will be slain by my sword."

Zeph.
2:13-15

ASSYRIA'S JUDGMENT.

He will stretch out his hand against the north
        and destroy Assyria,
leaving Nineveh utterly desolate
        and dry as the desert.
Flocks and herds will lie down there,
        creatures of every kind.
The desert owl and the screech owl
        will roost on her columns.
Their calls will echo through the windows,
        rubble will be in the doorways,
        the beams of cedar will be exposed.
This is the carefree city
        that lived in safety.
She said to herself,
        "I am, and there is none besides me."
What a ruin she has become,
        a lair for wild beasts!
All who pass by her scoff
        and shake their fists.

Zeph.
3:1-7

JUDAH'S SINS LISTED.

Woe to the city of oppressors,
        rebellious and defiled!

[c]That is, people from the upper Nile region

She obeys no one,
    she accepts no correction.
She does not trust in the LORD,
    she does not draw near to her God.
Her officials are roaring lions,
    her rulers are evening wolves,
    who leave nothing for the morning.
Her prophets are arrogant;
    they are treacherous men.
Her priests profane the sanctuary
    and do violence to the law.
The LORD within her is righteous;
    he does no wrong.
Morning by morning he dispenses his justice,
    and every new day he does not fail,
    yet the unrighteous know no shame.

"I have cut off nations;
    their strongholds are demolished.
I have left their streets deserted,
    with no one passing through.
Their cities are destroyed;
    no one will be left—no one at all.
I said to the city,
    'Surely you will fear me
    and accept correction!'
Then her dwelling would not be cut off,
    nor all my punishments come upon her.
But they were still eager
    to act corruptly in all they did.

PLANS FOR RESTORATION.

Zeph.
3:8-13

Therefore wait for me," declares the LORD,
    "for the day I will stand up to testify.[d]
I have decided to assemble the nations,
    to gather the kingdoms
and to pour out my wrath on them—
    all my fierce anger.
The whole world will be consumed
    by the fire of my jealous anger.

"Then will I purify the lips of the peoples,
    that all of them may call on the name of the LORD
    and serve him shoulder to shoulder.
From beyond the rivers of Cush[e]
    my worshipers, my scattered people,
    will bring me offerings.
On that day you will not be put to shame
    for all the wrongs you have done to me,
because I will remove from this city
    those who rejoice in their pride.

[d]Septuagint and Syriac; Hebrew *will rise up to plunder*   [e]That is, the upper Nile region

Never again will you be haughty
   on my holy hill.
But I will leave within you
   the meek and humble,
   who trust in the name of the LORD.
The remnant of Israel will do no wrong;
   they will speak no lies,
   nor will deceit be found in their mouths.
They will eat and lie down
   and no one will make them afraid."

Zeph. 3:14-17

JOY OF SALVATION.

Sing, O Daughter of Zion;
   shout aloud, O Israel!
Be glad and rejoice with all your heart,
   O Daughter of Jerusalem!
The LORD has taken away your punishment,
   he has turned back your enemy.
The LORD, the King of Israel, is with you;
   never again will you fear any harm.
On that day they will say to Jerusalem,
   "Do not fear, O Zion;
   do not let your hands hang limp.
The LORD your God is with you,
   he is mighty to save.
He will take great delight in you,
   he will quiet you with his love,
   he will rejoice over you with singing."

Zeph. 3:18-20

HONOR FOR THE REDEEMED.

"The sorrows for the appointed feasts
   I will remove from you;
   they are a burden and a reproach to you.*f*
At that time I will deal
   with all who oppressed you;
I will rescue the lame
   and gather those who have been scattered.
I will give them praise and honor
   in every land where they were put to shame.
At that time I will gather you;
   at that time I will bring you home.
I will give you honor and praise
   among all the peoples of the earth
when I restore your fortunes*g*
   before your very eyes,"

says the LORD.

f Or "I will gather you who mourn for the appointed feasts; / your reproach is a burden to you
g Or I bring back your captives

*Josiah's Reforms*_____

*T*he extent to which the people of Judah are persuaded by Zephaniah's preaching is not known, but already Zephaniah's influence may have touched the young king. Within just a few years, at the youthful age of 16, Josiah begins to bring about sweeping reforms against idolatry and other pagan practices. Later rediscovery of a copy of the Law of Moses will lead to a great spiritual revival and further religious reforms.

JOSIAH ATTACKS PAGANISM.   In the eighth year of his reign, while he was still young, he began to seek the God of his father David. In his twelfth year he began to purge Judah and Jerusalem of high places, Asherah poles, carved idols and cast images. Under his direction the altars of the Baals were torn down; he cut to pieces the incense altars that were above them, and smashed the Asherah poles, the idols and the images. These he broke to pieces and scattered over the graves of those who had sacrificed to them. He burned the bones of the priests on their altars, and so he purged Judah and Jerusalem. In the towns of Manasseh, Ephraim and Simeon, as far as Naphtali, and in the ruins around them, he tore down the altars and the Asherah poles and crushed the idols to powder and cut to pieces all the incense altars throughout Israel. Then he went back to Jerusalem.

2 Chron.
34:3-7
(627 B.C.)

*Jeremiah the Weeping Prophet*_____

*H*ow does one become a prophet of God? Although typically by training, this is not the case with some of God's most outstanding servants. From Samuel to Elisha to Amos as well as other prophets, the pattern is always the same: God directly calls his prophets to their special ministry. It should not be surprising, then, that some of these special prophets are reluctant to take on the responsibilities of moral leadership for which they are rarely appreciated and, more often than not, are actually persecuted.

An example of how God calls his prophets, and how they sometimes respond only with great reluctance, is seen in the call of Jeremiah in 626 B.C. In fairness to Jeremiah, he may have good reason to be reluctant: at the time of his call he is still a youth, though his exact age is not known. And had he known exactly how much opposition, persecution, and personal rejection he would face over the next 50 years, he would probably have tried to escape his calling, just as Jonah did. But God appeals to Jeremiah through two visions. The first is a branch of an almond tree by which, through a play on words, God explains that he is "watching" the execution of his purpose on earth. (The Hebrew word for "watching" sounds like the Hebrew word for almond tree.) The second vision is of a boiling pot, which is an Oriental symbol of raging war. Through that symbol God reveals to Jeremiah the destruction coming from the north—that is, the invasion by Babylon. God tells Jeremiah that his mission is to be one of rebuke and judgment on one hand and encouragement on the other. Finally, God promises to be with Jeremiah through the many personal trials he will face.

It may be that the persecutions Jeremiah will experience will be the result of the times in which he prophesies. When he begins his ministry, warning against impending national peril, Judah is resting complacently in an unusual period of peace and is soon to experience a brief period of spiritual revival. While Jeremiah is predicting the fall of Jerusalem, the popular message of the priests and false prophets is "peace, peace." Naturally the people prefer to believe the more optimistic line, and so they turn against the prophet of doom. Little do they realize that the political scene is rapidly changing. Even in this year of Jeremiah's call, Nabopolassar will rebel against Assyria and establish the Neo-Babylonian empire. Within 15 years Nineveh will fall under the Medo-Persian alliance, and seven years later Assyria, Babylonia, and Egypt will clash at Carchemish, with Nebuchadnezzar of Babylon emerging as the victor. Through it all Judah will stand in constant peril, and Jeremiah's thankless job will be to bring the message of judgment and national vulnerability to a people who do not want to hear it. What an awesome responsibility for this young man from the little town of Anathoth, a few miles northeast of Jerusalem! How amazed he must be to learn that he was chosen for this special mission before he was ever born!

Jer. 1:1-3   PREFACE. The words of Jeremiah son of Hilkiah, one of the priests at Anathoth in the territory of Benjamin. The word of the LORD came to him in the thirteenth year of the reign of Josiah son of Amon king of Judah, and through the reign of Jehoiakim son of Josiah king of Judah, down to the fifth month of the eleventh year of Zedekiah son of Josiah king of Judah, when the people of Jerusalem went into exile.

Jer.1:4,5   JEREMIAH'S CALL.   The word of the LORD came to me, saying,

> "Before I formed you in the womb I knew[h] you,
>> before you were born I set you apart;
>> I appointed you as a prophet to the nations."

Jer. 1:6-8   JEREMIAH'S RELUCTANCE.   "Ah, Sovereign LORD," I said, "I do not know how to speak; I am only a child."
But the LORD said to me, "Do not say, 'I am only a child.' You must go to everyone I send you to and say whatever I command you. Do not be afraid of them, for I am with you and will rescue you," declares the LORD.

Jer. 1:9-12   VISION OF ALMOND BRANCH.   Then the LORD reached out his hand and touched my mouth and said to me, "Now, I have put my words in your mouth. See, today I appoint you over nations and kingdoms to uproot and tear down, to destroy and overthrow, to build and to plant."
The word of the LORD came to me: "What do you see, Jeremiah?"
"I see the branch of an almond tree," I replied.
The LORD said to me, "You have seen correctly, for I am watching[i] to see that my word is fulfilled."

Jer. 1:13-16   VISION OF BOILING POT.   The word of the LORD came to me again: "What do you see?"
"I see a boiling pot, tilting away from the north," I answered.

[h]Or *chose*   [i]The Hebrew for *watching* sounds like the Hebrew for *almond tree*.

The LORD said to me, "From the north disaster will be poured out on all who live in the land. I am about to summon all the peoples of the northern kingdoms," declares the LORD.

> "Their kings will come and set up their thrones
>   in the entrance of the gates of Jerusalem;
> they will come against all her surrounding walls
>   and against all the towns of Judah.
> I will pronounce my judgments on my people
>   because of their wickedness in forsaking me,
> in burning incense to other gods
>   and in worshiping what their hands have made.

STRENGTH FOR THE MINISTRY.   "Get yourself ready! Stand up and say to them whatever I command you. Do not be terrified by them, or I will terrify you before them. Today I have made you a fortified city, an iron pillar and a bronze wall to stand against the whole land—against the kings of Judah, its officials, its priests and the people of the land. They will fight against you but will not overcome you, for I am with you and will rescue you," declares the LORD.   `Jer. 1:17-19`

*Jeremiah Rebukes an Unfaithful Nation*_____

*I*t does not take long for Jeremiah to get to the point. Characterizing Israel as an unfaithful bride, Jeremiah brings God's judgment against the people for their lust for foreign gods and calls them to repentance.

ISRAEL A LOVING BRIDE.   The word of the LORD came to me: "Go and proclaim in the hearing of Jerusalem: `Jer. 2:1-3`

> " 'I remember the devotion of your youth,
>   how as a bride you loved me
> and followed me through the desert,
>   through a land not sown.
> Israel was holy to the LORD,
>   the firstfruits of his harvest;
> all who devoured her were held guilty,
>   and disaster overtook them,' "

> > > > declares the LORD.

NO CAUSE FOR INFIDELITY.   `Jer. 2:4-9`

> Hear the word of the LORD, O house of Jacob,
>   all you clans of the house of Israel.

This is what the LORD says:

> "What fault did your fathers find in me,
>   that they strayed so far from me?
> They followed worthless idols
>   and became worthless themselves.
> They did not ask, 'Where is the LORD,
>   who brought us up out of Egypt
> and led us through the barren wilderness,
>   through a land of deserts and rifts,

a land of drought and darkness,[j]
    a land where no one travels and no one lives?'
I brought you into a fertile land
    to eat its fruit and rich produce.
But you came and defiled my land
    and made my inheritance detestable.
The priests did not ask,
    'Where is the LORD?'
Those who deal with the law did not know me;
    the leaders rebelled against me.
The prophets prophesied by Baal,
    following worthless idols.

"Therefore I bring charges against you again,"
                          declares the LORD.
"And I will bring charges against your children's children.

Jer. 2:10-12   **IDOLATERS MORE FAITHFUL.**

Cross over to the coasts of Kittim[k] and look,
    send to Kedar[l] and observe closely;
    see if there has ever been anything like this:
Has a nation ever changed its gods?
    (Yet they are not gods at all.)
But my people have exchanged their[m] Glory
    for worthless idols.
Be appalled at this, O heavens,
    and shudder with great horror,"
                          declares the LORD.

Jer. 2:13-19   **LIVING WATER FORSAKEN.**

"My people have committed two sins:
They have forsaken me,
    the spring of living water,
and have dug their own cisterns,
    broken cisterns that cannot hold water.
Is Israel a servant, a slave by birth?
    Why then has he become plunder?
Lions have roared;
    they have growled at him.
They have laid waste his land;
    his towns are burned and deserted.
Also, the men of Memphis[n] and Tahpanhes
    have shaved the crown of your head.[o]
Have you not brought this on yourselves
    by forsaking the LORD your God
    when he led you in the way?
Now why go to Egypt
    to drink water from the Shihor[p]?

[j]Or *and the shadow of death*   [k]That is, Cyprus and western coastlands   [l]The home of
Bedouin tribes in the Syro-Arabian desert   [m]Masoretic Text; an ancient Hebrew
scribal tradition *my*   [n]Hebrew *Noph*   [o]Or *have cracked your skull*   [p]That is, a
branch of the Nile

And why go to Assyria
    to drink water from the River*q*?
Your wickedness will punish you;
    your backsliding will rebuke you.
Consider then and realize
    how evil and bitter it is for you
when you forsake the LORD your God
    and have no awe of me,"
                declares the Lord, the LORD Almighty.

VINE BECAME CORRUPTED.   Jer. 2:20-22

"Long ago you broke off your yoke
    and tore off your bonds;
    you said, 'I will not serve you!'
Indeed, on every high hill
    and under every spreading tree
    you lay down as a prostitute.
I had planted you like a choice vine
    of sound and reliable stock.
How then did you turn against me
    into a corrupt, wild vine?
Although you wash yourself with soda
    and use an abundance of soap,
    the stain of your guilt is still before me,"
                declares the Sovereign LORD.

LUST FOR FOREIGN GODS.   Jer. 2:23-25

"How can you say, 'I am not defiled;
    I have not run after the Baals'?
See how you behaved in the valley;
    consider what you have done.
You are a swift she-camel
    running here and there,
a wild donkey accustomed to the desert,
    sniffing the wind in her craving—
    in her heat who can restrain her?
Any males that pursue her need not tire themselves;
    at mating time they will find her.
Do not run until your feet are bare
    and your throat is dry.
But you said, 'It's no use!
    I love foreign gods,
    and I must go after them.'

IDOLS SO POWERLESS.   Jer. 2:26-29

"As a thief is disgraced when he is caught,
    so the house of Israel is disgraced—
they, their kings and their officials,
    their priests and their prophets.
They say to wood, 'You are my father,'

*q*That is, the Euphrates

and to stone, 'You gave me birth.'
They have turned their backs to me
    and not their faces;
yet when they are in trouble, they say,
    'Come and save us!'
Where then are the gods you made for yourselves?
    Let them come if they can save you
    when you are in trouble!
For you have as many gods
    as you have towns, O Judah.

"Why do you bring charges against me?
    You have all rebelled against me,"

                            declares the LORD.

Jer. 2:30-32   GOD HAS NOT FORGOTTEN.

"In vain I punished your people;
    they did not respond to correction.
Your sword has devoured your prophets
    like a ravening lion.

"You of this generation, consider the word of the LORD:

"Have I been a desert to Israel
    or a land of great darkness?
Why do my people say, 'We are free to roam;
    we will come to you no more'?
Does a maiden forget her jewelry,
    a bride her wedding ornaments?
Yet my people have forgotten me,
    days without number.

Jer. 2:33-35   SINS ARE DENIED.

How skilled you are at pursuing love!
    Even the worst of women can learn from your ways.
On your clothes men find
    the lifeblood of the innocent poor,
    though you did not catch them breaking in.
Yet in spite of all this
    you say, 'I am innocent;
    he is not angry with me.'
But I will pass judgment on you
    because you say, 'I have not sinned.'

Jer. 2:36,37   ALLIES WILL DISAPPOINT.

Why do you go about so much,
    changing your ways?
You will be disappointed by Egypt
    as you were by Assyria.
You will also leave that place
    with your hands on your head,
for the LORD has rejected those you trust;
    you will not be helped by them.

ISRAEL'S HARLOTRY.   Jer. 3:1-5

"If a man divorces his wife
    and she leaves him and marries another man,
  should he return to her again?
    Would not the land be completely defiled?
But you have lived as a prostitute with many lovers—
    would you now return to me?"
                              declares the LORD.
"Look up to the barren heights and see.
    Is there any place where you have not been ravished?
By the roadside you sat waiting for lovers,
    sat like a nomad[r] in the desert.
You have defiled the land
    with your prostitution and wickedness.
Therefore the showers have been withheld,
    and no spring rains have fallen.
Yet you have the brazen look of a prostitute;
    you refuse to blush with shame.
Have you not just called to me:
  'My Father, my friend from my youth,
will you always be angry?
    Will your wrath continue forever?'
This is how you talk,
    but you do all the evil you can."

JUDAH IGNORES WARNING.   During the reign of King Josiah, the   Jer. 3:6-11
LORD said to me, "Have you seen what faithless Israel has done? She has
gone up on every high hill and under every spreading tree and has committed adultery there. I thought that after she had done all this she
would return to me but she did not, and her unfaithful sister Judah saw
it. I gave faithless Israel her certificate of divorce and sent her away
because of all her adulteries. Yet I saw that her unfaithful sister Judah
had no fear; she also went out and committed adultery. Because Israel's
immorality mattered so little to her, she defiled the land and committed
adultery with stone and wood. In spite of all this, her unfaithful sister
Judah did not return to me with all her heart, but only in pretense,"
declares the LORD.

The LORD said to me, "Faithless Israel is more righteous than unfaithful
Judah.

ISRAEL INVITED TO RETURN.   Go, proclaim this message toward the   Jer.
north: 3:12-22a

" 'Return, faithless Israel,' declares the LORD,
    'I will frown on you no longer,
for I am merciful,' declares the LORD,
    'I will not be angry forever.
Only acknowledge your guilt—
    you have rebelled against the LORD your God,
you have scattered your favors to foreign gods

[r]Or an Arab

under every spreading tree,
and have not obeyed me,' "

declares the LORD.

"Return, faithless people," declares the LORD, "for I am your husband.
I will choose you—one from a town and two from a clan—and bring you
to Zion. Then I will give you shepherds after my own heart, who will lead
you with knowledge and understanding. In those days, when your numbers have increased greatly in the land," declares the LORD, "men will no
longer say, 'The ark of the covenant of the LORD.' It will never enter their
minds or be remembered; it will not be missed, nor will another one be
made. At that time they will call Jerusalem The Throne of the LORD, and
all nations will gather in Jerusalem to honor the name of the LORD. No
longer will they follow the stubbornness of their evil hearts. In those days
the house of Judah will join the house of Israel, and together they will
come from a northern land to the land I gave your forefathers as an
inheritance.

"I myself said,

" 'How gladly would I treat you like sons
       and give you a desirable land,
       the most beautiful inheritance of any nation.'
   I thought you would call me 'Father'
       and not turn away from following me.
   But like a woman unfaithful to her husband,
       so you have been unfaithful to me, O house of Israel,"

declares the LORD.

A cry is heard on the barren heights,
       the weeping and pleading of the people of Israel,
   because they have perverted their ways
       and have forgotten the LORD their God.

"Return, faithless people;
       I will cure you of backsliding."

Jer.
3:22b-25

ISRAEL'S CONFESSION.

"Yes, we will come to you,
       for you are the LORD our God.
   Surely the ⌞idolatrous⌟ commotion on the hills
       and mountains is a deception;
   surely in the LORD our God
       is the salvation of Israel.
   From our youth shameful gods have consumed
       the fruits of our fathers' labor—
   their flocks and herds,
       their sons and daughters.
   Let us lie down in our shame,
       and let our disgrace cover us.
   We have sinned against the LORD our God,
       both we and our fathers;
   from our youth till this day
       we have not obeyed the LORD our God."

CONDITIONS FOR RETURN.   Jer. 4:1,2

> "If you will return, O Israel,
> return to me,"
>   declares the LORD.
> "If you put your detestable idols out of my sight
> and no longer go astray,
> and if in a truthful, just and righteous way
> you swear, 'As surely as the LORD lives,'
> then the nations will be blessed by him
> and in him they will glory."

JUDAH CALLED TO REPENT.   This is what the LORD says to the men of   Jer. 4:3,4
Judah and to Jerusalem:

> "Break up your unplowed ground
> and do not sow among thorns.
> Circumcise yourselves to the LORD,
> circumcise your hearts,
> you men of Judah and people of Jerusalem,
> or my wrath will break out and burn like fire
> because of the evil you have done—
> burn with no one to quench it.

IMPENDING FALL TO BABYLON.   Jer. 4:5-9

> "Announce in Judah and proclaim in Jerusalem and say:
> 'Sound the trumpet throughout the land!'
> Cry aloud and say:
> 'Gather together!
> Let us flee to the fortified cities!'
> Raise the signal to go to Zion!
> Flee for safety without delay!
> For I am bringing disaster from the north,
> even terrible destruction."

> A lion has come out of his lair;
> a destroyer of nations has set out.
> He has left his place
> to lay waste your land.
> Your towns will lie in ruins
> without inhabitant.
> So put on sackcloth,
> lament and wail,
> for the fierce anger of the LORD
> has not turned away from us.

> "In that day," declares the LORD,
> "the king and the officials will lose heart,
> the priests will be horrified,
> and the prophets will be appalled."

It is not long before Jeremiah discloses that he is not merely an instrument through whom God mechanically speaks. Jeremiah has his own feelings, doubts, and questions. He now records the first of many conversations he will have with God throughout his ministry. This one reveals Jeremiah's concern for his hearers.

Jer. 4:10   JEREMIAH QUESTIONS GOD.   Then I said, "Ah, Sovereign LORD, how completely you have deceived this people and Jerusalem by saying, 'You will have peace,' when the sword is at our throats."

Jer. 4:11,12   GOD'S ANSWER.   At that time this people and Jerusalem will be told, "A scorching wind from the barren heights in the desert blows toward my people, but not to winnow or cleanse; a wind too strong for that comes from me.⁵ Now I pronounce my judgments against them."

God reaffirms that there will indeed be peace, but not before judgment and terrible destruction which will bring agony to both God himself and his children in Judah.

Jer. 4:13-17   ADVERSARY IS COMING.

> Look! He advances like the clouds,
>   his chariots come like a whirlwind,
> his horses are swifter than eagles.
>   Woe to us! We are ruined!
> O Jerusalem, wash the evil from your heart and be saved.
>   How long will you harbor wicked thoughts?
> A voice is announcing from Dan,
>   proclaiming disaster from the hills of Ephraim.
> "Tell this to the nations,
>   proclaim it to Jerusalem:
> 'A besieging army is coming from a distant land,
>   raising a war cry against the cities of Judah.
> They surround her like men guarding a field,
>   because she has rebelled against me,'"

                                                                    declares the LORD.

Jer. 4:18-21   GOD'S AGONY.

> "Your own conduct and actions
>   have brought this upon you.
> This is your punishment.
>   How bitter it is!
>   How it pierces to the heart!"
>
> Oh, my anguish, my anguish!
>   I writhe in pain.
> Oh, the agony of my heart!
>   My heart pounds within me,
>   I cannot keep silent.
> For I have heard the sound of the trumpet;
>   I have heard the battle cry.
> Disaster follows disaster;
>   the whole land lies in ruins.
> In an instant my tents are destroyed,
>   my shelter in a moment.

⁵Or *comes at my command*

How long must I see the battle standard
  and hear the sound of the trumpet?

JUDAH'S FOOLISHNESS.   Jer. 4:22

"My people are fools;
  they do not know me.
They are senseless children;
  they have no understanding.
They are skilled in doing evil;
  they know not how to do good."

DISASTROUS CONSEQUENCES.   Jer. 4:23-29

I looked at the earth,
  and it was formless and empty;
and at the heavens,
  and their light was gone.
I looked at the mountains,
  and they were quaking;
  all the hills were swaying.
I looked, and there were no people;
  every bird in the sky had flown away.
I looked, and the fruitful land was a desert;
  all its towns lay in ruins
  before the LORD, before his fierce anger.

This is what the LORD says:

"The whole land will be ruined,
  though I will not destroy it completely.
Therefore the earth will mourn
  and the heavens above grow dark,
because I have spoken and will not relent,
  I have decided and will not turn back."

At the sound of horsemen and archers
  every town takes to flight.
Some go into the thickets;
  some climb up among the rocks.
All the towns are deserted;
  no one lives in them.

JUDAH TO BE BETRAYED.   Jer. 4:30,31

What are you doing, O devastated one?
  Why dress yourself in scarlet
  and put on jewels of gold?
Why shade your eyes with paint?
  You adorn yourself in vain.
Your lovers despise you;
  they seek your life.

I hear a cry as of a woman in labor,
  a groan as of one bearing her first child—
the cry of the Daughter of Zion gasping for breath,
  stretching out her hands and saying,

> "Alas! I am fainting;
>> my life is given over to murderers."

Jer. 5:1,2 DISHONESTY RULES JERUSALEM.

> "Go up and down the streets of Jerusalem,
>> look around and consider,
>> search through her squares.
> If you can find but one person
>> who deals honestly and seeks the truth,
>> I will forgive this city.
> Although they say, 'As surely as the LORD lives,'
>> still they are swearing falsely."

Jer. 5:3-6 EVEN LEADERS UNFAITHFUL.

> O LORD, do not your eyes look for truth?
>> You struck them, but they felt no pain;
>> you crushed them, but they refused correction.
> They made their faces harder than stone
>> and refused to repent.
> I thought, "These are only the poor;
>> they are foolish,
> for they do not know the way of the LORD,
>> the requirements of their God.
> So I will go to the leaders
>> and speak to them;
> surely they know the way of the LORD,
>> the requirements of their God."
> But with one accord they too had broken off the yoke
>> and torn off the bonds.
> Therefore a lion from the forest will attack them,
>> a wolf from the desert will ravage them,
> a leopard will lie in wait near their towns
>> to tear to pieces any who venture out,
> for their rebellion is great
>> and their backslidings many.

Jer. 5:7-9 A LUSTFUL NATION.

> "Why should I forgive you?
>> Your children have forsaken me
>> and sworn by gods that are not gods.
> I supplied all their needs,
>> yet they committed adultery
>> and thronged to the houses of prostitutes.
> They are well-fed, lusty stallions,
>> each neighing for another man's wife.
> Should I not punish them for this?"
>> declares the LORD.
> "Should I not avenge myself
>> on such a nation as this?

Jer. 5:10,11 PUNISHMENT FOR INFIDELITY.

> "Go through her vineyards and ravage them,

but do not destroy them completely.
Strip off her branches,
    for these people do not belong to the LORD.
The house of Israel and the house of Judah
    have been utterly unfaithful to me,"

                                                          declares the LORD.

FALSE PROPHETS LIE.   Jer. 5:12,13

They have lied about the LORD;
    they said, "He will do nothing!
No harm will come to us;
    we will never see sword or famine.
The prophets are but wind
    and the word is not in them;
    so let what they say be done to them."

ADVERSARY WILL DEVOUR.   Therefore this is what the LORD God   Jer. 5:14-17
Almighty says:

"Because the people have spoken these words,
    I will make my words in your mouth a fire
    and these people the wood it consumes.
O house of Israel," declares the LORD,
    "I am bringing a distant nation against you—
an ancient and enduring nation,
    a people whose language you do not know,
    whose speech you do not understand.
Their quivers are like an open grave;
    all of them are mighty warriors.
They will devour your harvests and food,
    devour your sons and daughters;
they will devour your flocks and herds,
    devour your vines and fig trees.
With the sword they will destroy
    the fortified cities in which you trust.

MEANING OF PUNISHMENT.   "Yet even in those days," declares the   Jer. 5:18,19
LORD, "I will not destroy you completely. And when the people ask, 'Why
has the LORD our God done all this to us?' you will tell them, 'As you have
forsaken me and served foreign gods in your own land, so now you will
serve foreigners in a land not your own.'

PEOPLE SHOULD FEAR GOD.   Jer. 5:20-25

"Announce this to the house of Jacob
    and proclaim it in Judah:
Hear this, you foolish and senseless people,
    who have eyes but do not see,
    who have ears but do not hear:
Should you not fear me?" declares the LORD.
    "Should you not tremble in my presence?
I made the sand a boundary for the sea,
    an everlasting barrier it cannot cross.
The waves may roll, but they cannot prevail;

they may roar, but they cannot cross it.
But these people have stubborn and rebellious hearts;
   they have turned aside and gone away.
They do not say to themselves,
   'Let us fear the LORD our God,
who gives autumn and spring rains in season,
   who assures us of the regular weeks of harvest.'
Your wrongdoings have kept these away;
   your sins have deprived you of good.

Jer. 5:26-29   INJUSTICE ABOUNDS.

"Among my people are wicked men
   who lie in wait like men who snare birds
   and like those who set traps to catch men.
Like cages full of birds,
   their houses are full of deceit;
they have become rich and powerful
   and have grown fat and sleek.
Their evil deeds have no limit;
   they do not plead the case of the fatherless to win it,
   they do not defend the rights of the poor.
Should I not punish them for this?"
   declares the LORD.
"Should I not avenge myself
   on such a nation as this?

Jer. 5:30,31   PEOPLE SUPPORT LEADERS.

"A horrible and shocking thing
   has happened in the land:
The prophets prophesy lies,
   the priests rule by their own authority,
and my people love it this way.
   But what will you do in the end?

Jer. 6:1-8   SIEGE OF JERUSALEM.

"Flee for safety, people of Benjamin!
   Flee from Jerusalem!
Sound the trumpet in Tekoa!
   Raise the signal over Beth Hakkerem!
For disaster looms out of the north,
   even terrible destruction.
I will destroy the Daughter of Zion,
   so beautiful and delicate.
Shepherds with their flocks will come against her;
   they will pitch their tents around her,
   each tending his own portion."

"Prepare for battle against her!
   Arise, let us attack at noon!
But, alas, the daylight is fading,
   and the shadows of evening grow long.
So arise, let us attack at night

and destroy her fortresses!"

This is what the LORD Almighty says:

"Cut down the trees
    and build siege ramps against Jerusalem.
This city must be punished;
    it is filled with oppression.
As a well pours out its water,
    so she pours out her wickedness.
Violence and destruction resound in her;
    her sickness and wounds are ever before me.
Take warning, O Jerusalem,
    or I will turn away from you
and make your land desolate
    so no one can live in it."

EVERYONE IN JEOPARDY.   This is what the LORD Almighty says: Jer. 6:9-12

"Let them glean the remnant of Israel
    as thoroughly as a vine;
pass your hand over the branches again,
    like one gathering grapes."

To whom can I speak and give warning?
    Who will listen to me?
Their ears are closed[t]
    so they cannot hear.
The word of the LORD is offensive to them;
    they find no pleasure in it.
But I am full of the wrath of the LORD,
    and I cannot hold it in.

"Pour it out on the children in the street
    and on the young men gathered together;
both husband and wife will be caught in it,
    and the old, those weighed down with years.
Their houses will be turned over to others,
    together with their fields and their wives,
when I stretch out my hand
    against those who live in the land,"
                                                        declares the LORD.

LEADERS DECEIVE.   Jer.6:13,14

"From the least to the greatest,
    all are greedy for gain;
prophets and priests alike,
    all practice deceit.
They dress the wound of my people
    as though it were not serious.
'Peace, peace,' they say,
    when there is no peace.

[t]Hebrew *uncircumcised*

Jer. 6:15   SINNERS UNASHAMED.

> Are they ashamed of their loathsome conduct?
>> No, they have no shame at all;
>> they do not even know how to blush.
> So they will fall among the fallen;
>> they will be brought down when I punish them,"
>>>>>>> says the LORD.

Jer. 6:16-21   ANCIENT PATHS IGNORED.   This is what the LORD says:

> "Stand at the crossroads and look;
>> ask for the ancient paths,
> ask where the good way is, and walk in it,
>> and you will find rest for your souls.
>> But you said, 'We will not walk in it.'
> I appointed watchmen over you and said,
>> 'Listen to the sound of the trumpet!'
>> But you said, 'We will not listen.'
> Therefore hear, O nations;
>> observe, O witnesses,
>> what will happen to them.
> Hear, O earth:
> I am bringing disaster on this people,
>> the fruit of their schemes,
> because they have not listened to my words
>> and have rejected my law.
> What do I care about incense from Sheba
>> or sweet calamus from a distant land?
> Your burnt offerings are not acceptable;
>> your sacrifices do not please me."

Therefore this is what the LORD says:

> "I will put obstacles before this people.
>> Fathers and sons alike will stumble over them;
>> neighbors and friends will perish."

Jer. 6:22-26   CRUELTY OF ADVERSARY.   This is what the LORD says:

> "Look, an army is coming
>> from the land of the north;
> a great nation is being stirred up
>> from the ends of the earth.
> They are armed with bow and spear;
>> they are cruel and show no mercy.
> They sound like the roaring sea
>> as they ride on their horses;
> they come like men in battle formation
>> to attack you, O Daughter of Zion."

> We have heard reports about them,
>> and our hands hang limp.
> Anguish has gripped us,
>> pain like that of a woman in labor.
> Do not go out to the fields

or walk on the roads,
  for the enemy has a sword,
    and there is terror on every side.
O my people, put on sackcloth
  and roll in ashes;
mourn with bitter wailing
  as for an only son,
for suddenly the destroyer
  will come upon us.

JUDAH AS IMPURE METAL.

Jer. 6:27-30

"I have made you a tester of metals
  and my people the ore,
that you may observe
  and test their ways.
They are all hardened rebels,
  going about to slander.
They are bronze and iron;
  they all act corruptly.
The bellows blow fiercely
  to burn away the lead with fire,
but the refining goes on in vain;
  the wicked are not purged out.
They are called rejected silver,
  because the LORD has rejected them."

FALSE RELIGIOSITY CONDEMNED.

Jer. 7:1-11

This is the word that came to Jeremiah from the LORD: "Stand at the gate of the LORD's house and there proclaim this message:

" 'Hear the word of the LORD, all you people of Judah who come through these gates to worship the LORD. This is what the LORD Almighty, the God of Israel, says: Reform your ways and your actions, and I will let you live in this place. Do not trust in deceptive words and say, "This is the temple of the LORD, the temple of the LORD, the temple of the LORD!" If you really change your ways and your actions and deal with each other justly, if you do not oppress the alien, the fatherless or the widow and do not shed innocent blood in this place, and if you do not follow other gods to your own harm, then I will let you live in this place, in the land I gave your forefathers for ever and ever. But look, you are trusting in deceptive words that are worthless.

" 'Will you steal and murder, commit adultery and perjury,^u burn incense to Baal and follow other gods you have not known, and then come and stand before me in this house, which bears my Name, and say, "We are safe"— safe to do all these detestable things? Has this house, which bears my Name, become a den of robbers to you? But I have been watching! declares the LORD.

TEMPLE TO BE DESTROYED.

Jer. 7:12-15

" 'Go now to the place in Shiloh where I first made a dwelling for my Name, and see what I did to it because of the wickedness of my people Israel. While you were doing all these things, declares the LORD, I spoke to you again and again, but you did not listen;

^uOr *and swear by false gods*

I called you, but you did not answer. Therefore, what I did to Shiloh I will now do to the house that bears my Name, the temple you trust in, the place I gave to you and your fathers. I will thrust you from my presence, just as I did all your brothers, the people of Ephraim.'

Jer. 7:16-20   IDOLATERS HARM THEMSELVES.   "So do not pray for this people nor offer any plea or petition for them; do not plead with me, for I will not listen to you. Do you not see what they are doing in the towns of Judah and in the streets of Jerusalem? The children gather wood, the fathers light the fire, and the women knead the dough and make cakes of bread for the Queen of Heaven. They pour out drink offerings to other gods to provoke me to anger. But am I the one they are provoking? declares the LORD. Are they not rather harming themselves, to their own shame?

" 'Therefore this is what the Sovereign LORD says: My anger and my wrath will be poured out on this place, on man and beast, on the trees of the field and on the fruit of the ground, and it will burn and not be quenched.

Jer. 7:21-26   ISRAEL ALWAYS STUBBORN.   " 'This is what the LORD Almighty, the God of Israel, says: Go ahead, add your burnt offerings to your other sacrifices and eat the meat yourselves! For when I brought your forefathers out of Egypt and spoke to them, I did not just give them commands about burnt offerings and sacrifices, but I gave them this command: Obey me, and I will be your God and you will be my people. Walk in all the ways I command you, that it may go well with you. But they did not listen or pay attention; instead, they followed the stubborn inclinations of their evil hearts. They went backward and not forward. From the time your forefathers left Egypt until now, day after day, again and again I sent you my servants the prophets. But they did not listen to me or pay attention. They were stiff-necked and did more evil than their forefathers.'

Jer. 7:27-29   JEREMIAH TO BE REJECTED.   "When you tell them all this, they will not listen to you; when you call to them, they will not answer. Therefore say to them, 'This is the nation that has not obeyed the LORD its God or responded to correction. Truth has perished; it has vanished from their lips. Cut off your hair and throw it away; take up a lament on the barren heights, for the LORD has rejected and abandoned this generation that is under his wrath.

Jer. 7:30-34   THE VALLEY OF SLAUGHTER.   " 'The people of Judah have done evil in my eyes, declares the LORD. They have set up their detestable idols in the house that bears my Name and have defiled it. They have built the high places of Topheth in the Valley of Ben Hinnom to burn their sons and daughters in the fire—something I did not command, nor did it enter my mind. So beware, the days are coming, declares the LORD, when people will no longer call it Topheth or the Valley of Ben Hinnom, but the Valley of Slaughter, for they will bury the dead in Topheth until there is no more room. Then the carcasses of this people will become food for the birds of the air and the beasts of the earth, and there will be no one to frighten them away. I will bring an end to the sounds of joy and gladness and to the voices of bride and bridegroom in the towns of Judah and the streets of Jerusalem, for the land will become desolate.

Jer. 8:1-3   BONES TO BE EXPOSED.   " 'At that time, declares the LORD, the bones of the kings and officials of Judah, the bones of the priests and prophets, and the bones of the people of Jerusalem will be removed from their graves. They will be exposed to the sun and the moon and all the stars of the heavens, which they have loved and served and which they have followed and consulted and worshiped. They will not be gathered up or buried, but will be like refuse lying on the ground. Wherever I banish them, all the survivors of this evil nation will prefer death to life, declares the LORD Almighty.'

ISRAEL REFUSES TO RETURN.   "Say to them, 'This is what the LORD says: `Jer. 8:4-7`

> " 'When men fall down, do they not get up?
>> When a man turns away, does he not return?
> Why then have these people turned away?
>> Why does Jerusalem always turn away?
> They cling to deceit;
>> they refuse to return.
> I have listened attentively,
>> but they do not say what is right.
> No one repents of his wickedness,
>> saying, "What have I done?"
> Each pursues his own course
>> like a horse charging into battle.
> Even the stork in the sky
>> knows her appointed seasons,
> and the dove, the swift and the thrush
>> observe the time of their migration.
> But my people do not know
>> the requirements of the LORD.

SCRIBES HAVE MISHANDLED LAW.   `Jer. 8:8,9`

> " 'How can you say, "We are wise,
>> for we have the law of the LORD,"
> when actually the lying pen of the scribes
>> has handled it falsely?
> The wise will be put to shame;
>> they will be dismayed and trapped.
> Since they have rejected the word of the LORD,
>> what kind of wisdom do they have?

LEADERS AGAIN REBUKED.   `Jer. 8:10-12`

> Therefore I will give their wives to other men
>> and their fields to new owners.
> From the least to the greatest,
>> all are greedy for gain;
> prophets and priests alike,
>> all practice deceit.
> They dress the wound of my people
>> as though it were not serious.
> "Peace, peace," they say,
>> when there is no peace.
> Are they ashamed of their loathsome conduct?
>> No, they have no shame at all;

they do not even know how to blush.
So they will fall among the fallen;
they will be brought down when they are punished,
says the LORD.

Jer. 8:13   DEPRIVATION COMING.

" 'I will take away their harvest,
declares the LORD.
There will be no grapes on the vine.
There will be no figs on the tree,
and their leaves will wither.
What I have given them
will be taken from them.^{v}' "

Jer. 8:14-17   DESTRUCTION FOR SINS.

"Why are we sitting here?
Gather together!
Let us flee to the fortified cities
and perish there!
For the LORD our God has doomed us to perish
and given us poisoned water to drink,
because we have sinned against him.
We hoped for peace
but no good has come,
for a time of healing
but there was only terror.
The snorting of the enemy's horses
is heard from Dan;
at the neighing of their stallions
the whole land trembles.
They have come to devour
the land and everything in it,
the city and all who live there."

"See, I will send venomous snakes among you,
vipers that cannot be charmed,
and they will bite you,"
declares the LORD.

Jer.   GOD'S SORROW.
8:18-9:2
O my Comforter ^{w} in sorrow,
my heart is faint within me.
Listen to the cry of my people
from a land far away:
"Is the LORD not in Zion?
Is her King no longer there?"

"Why have they provoked me to anger with their images,
with their worthless foreign idols?"

^{v}The meaning of the Hebrew for this sentence is uncertain. ^{w}The meaning of the
Hebrew for this word is uncertain.

"The harvest is past,
        the summer has ended,
        and we are not saved."

Since my people are crushed, I am crushed;
        I mourn, and horror grips me.
Is there no balm in Gilead?
        Is there no physician there?

Why then is there no healing
        for the wound of my people?
Oh, that my head were a spring of water
        and my eyes a fountain of tears!
I would weep day and night
        for the slain of my people.
Oh, that I had in the desert
        a lodging place for travelers,
so that I might leave my people
        and go away from them;
for they are all adulterers,
        a crowd of unfaithful people.

NATION OF LIARS.   Jer. 9:3-9

"They make ready their tongue
        like a bow, to shoot lies;
it is not by truth
        that they triumph^x in the land.
They go from one sin to another;
        they do not acknowledge me,"

                                        declares the LORD.

"Beware of your friends;
        do not trust your brothers.
For every brother is a deceiver,^{y}
        and every friend a slanderer.
Friend deceives friend,
        and no one speaks the truth.
They have taught their tongues to lie;
        they weary themselves with sinning.
You^z live in the midst of deception;
        in their deceit they refuse to acknowledge me,"

                                        declares the LORD.

Therefore this is what the LORD Almighty says:

"See, I will refine and test them,
        for what else can I do
        because of the sin of my people?
Their tongue is a deadly arrow;
        it speaks with deceit.
With his mouth each speaks cordially to his neighbor,

^{x}Or *lies; / they are not valiant for truth* ^{y}Or *a deceiving Jacob* ^{z}That is, Jeremiah (the Hebrew is singular)

but in his heart he sets a trap for him.
Should I not punish them for this?"
declares the LORD.
"Should I not avenge myself
on such a nation as this?"

Jer. 9:10,11 THOROUGHNESS OF DESTRUCTION.

I will weep and wail for the mountains
and take up a lament concerning the desert pastures.
They are desolate and untraveled,
and the lowing of cattle is not heard.
The birds of the air have fled
and the animals are gone.

"I will make Jerusalem a heap of ruins,
a haunt of jackals;
and I will lay waste the towns of Judah
so no one can live there."

Jer. 9:12-16 REASON FOR DESTRUCTION.   What man is wise enough to understand this? Who has been instructed by the LORD and can explain it? Why
has the land been ruined and laid waste like a desert that no one can cross?
    The LORD said, "It is because they have forsaken my law, which I set
before them; they have not obeyed me or followed my law. Instead, they
have followed the stubbornness of their hearts; they have followed the
Baals, as their fathers taught them." Therefore, this is what the LORD
Almighty, the God of Israel, says: "See, I will make this people eat bitter
food and drink poisoned water. I will scatter them among nations that neither they nor their fathers have known, and I will pursue them with the
sword until I have destroyed them."

Jer. 9:17-22 WAILING FOR ZION.   This is what the LORD Almighty says:

"Consider now! Call for the wailing women to come;
send for the most skillful of them.
Let them come quickly
and wail over us
till our eyes overflow with tears
and water streams from our eyelids.
The sound of wailing is heard from Zion:
'How ruined we are!
How great is our shame!
We must leave our land
because our houses are in ruins.'"

Now, O women, hear the word of the LORD;
open your ears to the words of his mouth.
Teach your daughters how to wail;
teach one another a lament.
Death has climbed in through our windows
and has entered our fortresses;
it has cut off the children from the streets
and the young men from the public squares.

Say, "This is what the LORD declares:

" 'The dead bodies of men will lie
    like refuse on the open field,
like cut grain behind the reaper,
    with no one to gather them.' "

PROPER BOASTING.   This is what the LORD says: Jer. 9:23,24

"Let not the wise man boast of his wisdom
    or the strong man boast of his strength
    or the rich man boast of his riches,
but let him who boasts boast about this:
    that he understands and knows me,
that I am the LORD, who exercises kindness,
    justice and righteousness on earth,
    for in these I delight,"

                                    declares the LORD.

CIRCUMCISION NO GUARANTEE.   "The days are coming," declares   Jer. 9:25,26
the LORD, "when I will punish all who are circumcised only in the flesh—
Egypt, Judah, Edom, Ammon, Moab and all who live in the desert in distant places.[a] For all these nations are really uncircumcised, and even the
whole house of Israel is uncircumcised in heart."

IMPOTENCE OF IDOLS.   Hear what the LORD says to you, O house of   Jer. 10:1-5
Israel. This is what the LORD says:

"Do not learn the ways of the nations
    or be terrified by signs in the sky,
    though the nations are terrified by them.
For the customs of the peoples are worthless;
    they cut a tree out of the forest,
    and a craftsman shapes it with his chisel.
They adorn it with silver and gold;
    they fasten it with hammer and nails
    so it will not totter.
Like a scarecrow in a melon patch,
    their idols cannot speak;
they must be carried
    because they cannot walk.
Do not fear them;
    they can do no harm
    nor can they do any good."

IDOLS COMPARED WITH GOD.   Jer. 10:6-10

No one is like you, O LORD;
    you are great,
    and your name is mighty in power.
Who should not revere you,
    O King of the nations?
    This is your due.
Among all the wise men of the nations
    and in all their kingdoms,
    there is no one like you.

[a]Or desert and who clip the hair by their foreheads

They are all senseless and foolish;
>> they are taught by worthless wooden idols.
Hammered silver is brought from Tarshish
>> and gold from Uphaz.
What the craftsman and goldsmith have made
>> is then dressed in blue and purple—
>> all made by skilled workers.
But the LORD is the true God;
>> he is the living God, the eternal King.
When he is angry, the earth trembles;
>> the nations cannot endure his wrath.

**Jer.
10:11-13**

JEHOVAH CREATED UNIVERSE.   "Tell them this: 'These gods, who did not make the heavens and the earth, will perish from the earth and from under the heavens.' "[b]

But God made the earth by his power;
>> he founded the world by his wisdom
>> and stretched out the heavens by his understanding.
When he thunders, the waters in the heavens roar;
>> he makes clouds rise from the ends of the earth.
He sends lightning with the rain
>> and brings out the wind from his storehouses.

**Jer.
10:14-16**

IDOLS CREATED BY MAN.

Everyone is senseless and without knowledge;
>> every goldsmith is shamed by his idols.
His images are a fraud;
>> they have no breath in them.
They are worthless, the objects of mockery;
>> when their judgment comes, they will perish.
He who is the Portion of Jacob is not like these,
>> for he is the Maker of all things,
including Israel, the tribe of his inheritance—
>> the LORD Almighty is his name.

**Jer.
10:17-22**

CAPTIVITY IS COMING.

Gather up your belongings to leave the land,
>> you who live under siege.
For this is what the LORD says:
>> "At this time I will hurl out
>> those who live in this land;
I will bring distress on them
>> so that they may be captured."

Woe to me because of my injury!
>> My wound is incurable!
Yet I said to myself,
>> "This is my sickness, and I must endure it."
My tent is destroyed;
>> all its ropes are snapped.

[b]The text of this verse is in Aramaic.

My sons are gone from me and are no more;
    no one is left now to pitch my tent
    or to set up my shelter.
The shepherds are senseless
    and do not inquire of the LORD;
so they do not prosper
    and all their flock is scattered.
Listen! The report is coming—
    a great commotion from the land of the north!
It will make the towns of Judah desolate,
    a haunt of jackals.

PRAYER AGAINST NATIONS.   Jer.
                                                                        10:23-25

I know, O LORD, that a man's life is not his own;
    it is not for man to direct his steps.
Correct me, LORD, but only with justice—
    not in your anger,
    lest you reduce me to nothing.
Pour out your wrath on the nations
    that do not acknowledge you,
    on the peoples who do not call on your name.
For they have devoured Jacob;
    they have devoured him completely
    and destroyed his homeland.

COVENANT HAS BEEN BROKEN.   This is the word that came to Jere-   Jer. 11:1-5
miah from the LORD: "Listen to the terms of this covenant and tell them to
the people of Judah and to those who live in Jerusalem. Tell them that this
is what the LORD, the God of Israel, says: 'Cursed is the man who does not
obey the terms of this covenant—the terms I commanded your forefathers
when I brought them out of Egypt, out of the iron-smelting furnace.' I said,
'Obey me and do everything I command you, and you will be my people,
and I will be your God. Then I will fulfill the oath I swore to your forefathers, to give them a land flowing with milk and honey'—the land you
possess today."
    I answered, "Amen, LORD."

COVENANT'S CURSES INVOKED.   The LORD said to me, "Proclaim all   Jer. 11:6-8
these words in the towns of Judah and in the streets of Jerusalem: 'Listen
to the terms of this covenant and follow them. From the time I brought
your forefathers up from Egypt until today, I warned them again and
again, saying, "Obey me." But they did not listen or pay attention; instead,
they followed the stubbornness of their evil hearts. So I brought on them
all the curses of the covenant I had commanded them to follow but that
they did not keep.' "

IDOLATRY BROKE COVENANT.   Then the LORD said to me, "There is a   Jer. 11:9-13
conspiracy among the people of Judah and those who live in Jerusalem.
They have returned to the sins of their forefathers, who refused to listen to
my words. They have followed other gods to serve them. Both the house
of Israel and the house of Judah have broken the covenant I made with
their forefathers. Therefore this is what the LORD says: 'I will bring on them
a disaster they cannot escape. Although they cry out to me, I will not listen
to them. The towns of Judah and the people of Jerusalem will go and cry

out to the gods to whom they burn incense, but they will not help them at all when disaster strikes. You have as many gods as you have towns, O Judah; and the altars you have set up to burn incense to that shameful god Baal are as many as the streets of Jerusalem.'

Jer. 11:14   TOO LATE TO PRAY.   "Do not pray for this people nor offer any plea or petition for them, because I will not listen when they call to me in the time of their distress.

Jer. 11:15-17   PAGANISM PROVOKES ANGER.

> "What is my beloved doing in my temple
>> as she works out her evil schemes with many?
>> Can consecrated meat avert ⌐your punishment⌐?
> When you engage in your wickedness,
>> then you rejoice.^c"
>
> The LORD called you a thriving olive tree
>> with fruit beautiful in form.
> But with the roar of a mighty storm
>> he will set it on fire,
>> and its branches will be broken.

The LORD Almighty, who planted you, has decreed disaster for you, because the house of Israel and the house of Judah have done evil and provoked me to anger by burning incense to Baal.

All of this "hard preaching" finally brings violent reaction, and there is a plot against Jeremiah by the men of his own hometown. (Surely it is true that "a prophet is not without honor except in his own country.") But God exposes the plot and saves Jeremiah, who recalls his naiveté in not recognizing the plot sooner.

Jer. 11:18-23   PLOT AGAINST JEREMIAH.   Because the LORD revealed their plot to me, I knew it, for at that time he showed me what they were doing. I had been like a gentle lamb led to the slaughter; I did not realize that they had plotted against me, saying,

> "Let us destroy the tree and its fruit;
>> let us cut him off from the land of the living,
>> that his name be remembered no more."
> But, O LORD Almighty, you who judge righteously
>> and test the heart and mind,
> let me see your vengeance upon them,
>> for to you I have committed my cause.

"Therefore this is what the LORD says about the men of Anathoth who are seeking your life and saying, 'Do not prophesy in the name of the LORD or you will die by our hands'—therefore this is what the LORD Almighty says: 'I will punish them. Their young men will die by the sword, their sons and daughters by famine. Not even a remnant will be left to them, because I will bring disaster on the men of Anathoth in the year of their punishment.' "

---

^cOr *Could consecrated meat avert your punishment? / Then you would rejoice*

Perhaps because of this first brush with serious persecution, Jeremiah feels the need to be reassured both of his mission and of God's support. He is probably both frightened and angry at the thought of what almost happened to him. It is possible, therefore, that this experience prompts the following exchange between Jeremiah and God.

JEREMIAH ANGRY AT DELAY.   Jer. 12:1-4

> You are always righteous, O LORD,
>   when I bring a case before you.
> Yet I would speak with you about your justice:
>   Why does the way of the wicked prosper?
>   Why do all the faithless live at ease?
> You have planted them, and they have taken root;
>   they grow and bear fruit.
> You are always on their lips
>   but far from their hearts.
> Yet you know me, O LORD;
>   you see me and test my thoughts about you.
> Drag them off like sheep to be butchered!
>   Set them apart for the day of slaughter!
> How long will the land lie parched[d]
>   and the grass in every field be withered?
> Because those who live in it are wicked,
>   the animals and birds have perished.
> Moreover, the people are saying,
>   "He will not see what happens to us."

GOD ANSWERS JEREMIAH.   Jer. 12:5-17

> "If you have raced with men on foot
>   and they have worn you out,
>   how can you compete with horses?
> If you stumble in safe country,[e]
>   how will you manage in the thickets by[f] the Jordan?
> Your brothers, your own family—
>   even they have betrayed you;
>   they have raised a loud cry against you.
> Do not trust them,
>   though they speak well of you.
>
> "I will forsake my house,
>   abandon my inheritance;
> I will give the one I love
>   into the hands of her enemies.
> My inheritance has become to me
>   like a lion in the forest.
> She roars at me;
>   therefore I hate her.
> Has not my inheritance become to me
>   like a speckled bird of prey
>   that other birds of prey surround and attack?

---

[d]Or land mourn   [e]Or If you put your trust in a land of safety   [f]Or the flooding of

Go and gather all the wild beasts;
  bring them to devour.
Many shepherds will ruin my vineyard
  and trample down my field;
they will turn my pleasant field
  into a desolate wasteland.
It will be made a wasteland,
  parched and desolate before me;
the whole land will be laid waste
  because there is no one who cares.
Over all the barren heights in the desert
  destroyers will swarm,
for the sword of the LORD will devour
  from one end of the land to the other;
  no one will be safe.
They will sow wheat but reap thorns;
  they will wear themselves out but gain nothing.
So bear the shame of your harvest
  because of the LORD's fierce anger."

This is what the LORD says: "As for all my wicked neighbors who seize the inheritance I gave my people Israel, I will uproot them from their lands and I will uproot the house of Judah from among them. But after I uproot them, I will again have compassion and will bring each of them back to his own inheritance and his own country. And if they learn well the ways of my people and swear by my name, saying, 'As surely as the LORD lives'— even as they once taught my people to swear by Baal—then they will be established among my people. But if any nation does not listen, I will completely uproot and destroy it," declares the LORD.

In order to give Jeremiah even further assurance, God now makes a tangible demonstration of his plans.

Jer. 13:1-11 LINEN BELT A SIGN. This is what the LORD said to me: "Go and buy a linen belt and put it around your waist, but do not let it touch water." So I bought a belt, as the LORD directed, and put it around my waist.

Then the word of the LORD came to me a second time: "Take the belt you bought and are wearing around your waist, and go now to Perath[8] and hide it there in a crevice in the rocks." So I went and hid it at Perath, as the LORD told me.

Many days later the LORD said to me, "Go now to Perath and get the belt I told you to hide there." So I went to Perath and dug up the belt and took it from the place where I had hidden it, but now it was ruined and completely useless.

Then the word of the LORD came to me: "This is what the LORD says: 'In the same way I will ruin the pride of Judah and the great pride of Jerusalem. These wicked people, who refuse to listen to my words, who follow the stubbornness of their hearts and go after other gods to serve and worship them, will be like this belt—completely useless! For as a belt is bound around a man's waist, so I bound the whole house of Israel and

8Or possibly *the Euphrates*

the whole house of Judah to me,' declares the LORD, 'to be my people for my renown and praise and honor. But they have not listened.'

Strengthened and encouraged by this demonstration, Jeremiah continues his difficult mission.

WARNING OF WINESKINS.   "Say to them: 'This is what the LORD, the God of Israel, says: Every wineskin should be filled with wine.' And if they say to you, 'Don't we know that every wineskin should be filled with wine?' then tell them, 'This is what the LORD says: I am going to fill with drunkenness all who live in this land, including the kings who sit on David's throne, the priests, the prophets and all those living in Jerusalem. I will smash them one against the other, fathers and sons alike, declares the LORD. I will allow no pity or mercy or compassion to keep me from destroying them.' " Jer.
13:12-14

THREAT OF CAPTIVITY. Jer.
13:15-17

Hear and pay attention,
do not be arrogant,
for the LORD has spoken.
Give glory to the LORD your God
before he brings the darkness,
before your feet stumble
on the darkening hills.
You hope for light,
but he will turn it to thick darkness
and change it to deep gloom.
But if you do not listen,
I will weep in secret
because of your pride;
my eyes will weep bitterly,
overflowing with tears,
because the LORD's flock will be taken captive.

JEHOIACHIN TO BE EXILED. Jer.
13:18,19

Say to the king and to the queen mother,
"Come down from your thrones,
for your glorious crowns
will fall from your heads."
The cities in the Negev will be shut up,
and there will be no one to open them.
All Judah will be carried into exile,
carried completely away.

ALLIES WILL BE CAPTORS. Jer.
13:20,21

Lift up your eyes and see
those who are coming from the north.
Where is the flock that was entrusted to you,
the sheep of which you boasted?
What will you say when ⌊the LORD⌋ sets over you
those you cultivated as your special allies?

Will not pain grip you
  like that of a woman in labor?

Jer.
13:22-27

SINS ARE THE CAUSE.

And if you ask yourself,
  "Why has this happened to me?"—
it is because of your many sins
  that your skirts have been torn off
  and your body mistreated.
Can the Ethiopian[h] change his skin
  or the leopard its spots?
Neither can you do good
  who are accustomed to doing evil.

"I will scatter you like chaff
  driven by the desert wind.
This is your lot,
  the portion I have decreed for you,"
                                    declares the LORD,

"because you have forgotten me
  and trusted in false gods.
I will pull up your skirts over your face
  that your shame may be seen—
your adulteries and lustful neighings,
  your shameless prostitution!
I have seen your detestable acts
  on the hills and in the fields.
Woe to you, O Jerusalem!
  How long will you be unclean?"

Jer. 14:1-6

DESTRUCTION LIKE DROUGHT.   This is the word of the LORD to Jeremiah concerning the drought:

"Judah mourns,
  her cities languish;
they wail for the land,
  and a cry goes up from Jerusalem.
The nobles send their servants for water;
  they go to the cisterns
  but find no water.
They return with their jars unfilled;
  dismayed and despairing,
  they cover their heads.
The ground is cracked
  because there is no rain in the land;
the farmers are dismayed
  and cover their heads.
Even the doe in the field
  deserts her newborn fawn
  because there is no grass.
Wild donkeys stand on the barren heights
  and pant like jackals;

[h]Hebrew *Cushite* (probably a person from the upper Nile region)

their eyesight fails
for lack of pasture."

HOW JUDAH WILL PRAY.   Jer. 14:7-9

Although our sins testify against us,
O LORD, do something for the sake of your name.
For our backsliding is great;
we have sinned against you.
O Hope of Israel,
its Savior in times of distress,
why are you like a stranger in the land,
like a traveler who stays only a night?
Why are you like a man taken by surprise,
like a warrior powerless to save?
You are among us, O LORD,
and we bear your name;
do not forsake us!

PRAYERS USELESS.   This is what the LORD says about this people: Jer.
                                                             14:10-12

"They greatly love to wander;
they do not restrain their feet.
So the LORD does not accept them;
he will now remember their wickedness
and punish them for their sins."

Then the LORD said to me, "Do not pray for the well-being of this people. Although they fast, I will not listen to their cry; though they offer
burnt offerings and grain offerings, I will not accept them. Instead, I will
destroy them with the sword, famine and plague."

When Jeremiah prophesies about Judah's impending peril, the people turn
to other prophets. They undoubtedly want a second opinion. After all, in an age
of prophets, with many speaking in God's name and many claiming to know
his will, it is not that easy to distinguish the true from the false. The people,
therefore, search for a message more favorable and comforting than that
of Jeremiah.
    Perhaps even Jeremiah is once again wavering in his confidence. (Why
should he alone be preaching doom? Could he be misunderstanding God's
revelations? Is it possible that the other prophets are right?) Or perhaps
Jeremiah is fully assured in his own mind but needs to know how to respond
to his opposition. Whatever his reason, Jeremiah puts the question to God and
receives a clear response.

JEREMIAH'S QUESTION.   But I said, "Ah, Sovereign LORD, the prophets   Jer. 14:13
keep telling them, 'You will not see the sword or suffer famine. Indeed, I
will give you lasting peace in this place.'"

GOD'S RESPONSE.   Then the LORD said to me, "The prophets are   Jer.
prophesying lies in my name. I have not sent them or appointed them or   14:14-18
spoken to them. They are prophesying to you false visions, divinations,

idolatries[i] and the delusions of their own minds. Therefore, this is what the LORD says about the prophets who are prophesying in my name: I did not send them, yet they are saying, 'No sword or famine will touch this land.' Those same prophets will perish by sword and famine. And the people they are prophesying to will be thrown out into the streets of Jerusalem because of the famine and sword. There will be no one to bury them or their wives, their sons or their daughters. I will pour out on them the calamity they deserve.

"Speak this word to them:

" 'Let my eyes overflow with tears
    night and day without ceasing;
for my virgin daughter—my people—
    has suffered a grievous wound,
    a crushing blow.
If I go into the country,
    I see those slain by the sword;
if I go into the city,
    I see the ravages of famine.
Both prophet and priest
    have gone to a land they know not.' "

Surely there are some who understand and believe Jeremiah's preaching. Surely there are righteous individuals left in this sinful nation. (King Josiah, for example, has already begun the first of what will be many reforms.) Therefore it is likely that those who are still trying to do God's will are praying fervently for God to refrain from bringing judgment against Judah. Why, they ask, must they be punished at a time of righteous renewal? Jeremiah frames the issue in the form of a prayer, and receives what appears to be a harsh answer.

Jer.
14:19-22

PRAYER OF THE JUST.

Have you rejected Judah completely?
    Do you despise Zion?
Why have you afflicted us
    so that we cannot be healed?
We hoped for peace
    but no good has come,
for a time of healing
    but there is only terror.
O LORD, we acknowledge our wickedness
    and the guilt of our fathers;
    we have indeed sinned against you.
For the sake of your name do not despise us;
    do not dishonor your glorious throne.
Remember your covenant with us
    and do not break it.
Do any of the worthless idols of the nations bring rain?
    Do the skies themselves send down showers?

[i]Or visions, worthless divinations

No, it is you, O LORD our God.
Therefore our hope is in you,
for you are the one who does all this.

SENTENCE ALREADY PASSED.   Then the LORD said to me: "Even if   Jer. 15:1,2
Moses and Samuel were to stand before me, my heart would not go out to
this people. Send them away from my presence! Let them go! And if they
ask you, 'Where shall we go?' tell them, 'This is what the LORD says:

" 'Those destined for death, to death;
    those for the sword, to the sword;
    those for starvation, to starvation;
    those for captivity, to captivity.'

FOUR EXECUTIONS.   "I will send four kinds of destroyers against   Jer. 15:3,4
them," declares the LORD, "the sword to kill and the dogs to drag away
and the birds of the air and the beasts of the earth to devour and destroy.
I will make them abhorrent to all the kingdoms of the earth because of
what Manasseh son of Hezekiah king of Judah did in Jerusalem.

COMPASSION PREVENTED.   Jer. 15:5-9

"Who will have pity on you, O Jerusalem?
    Who will mourn for you?
    Who will stop to ask how you are?
You have rejected me," declares the LORD.
    "You keep on backsliding.
So I will lay hands on you and destroy you;
    I can no longer show compassion.
I will winnow them with a winnowing fork
    at the city gates of the land.
I will bring bereavement and destruction on my people,
    for they have not changed their ways.
I will make their widows more numerous
    than the sand of the sea.
At midday I will bring a destroyer
    against the mothers of their young men;
suddenly I will bring down on them
    anguish and terror.
The mother of seven will grow faint
    and breathe her last.
Her sun will set while it is still day;
    she will be disgraced and humiliated.
I will put the survivors to the sword
    before their enemies,"
                                                        declares the LORD.

How can God be so cruel in his rejection of their plea? His response is that
the nation is condemned for its corporate sins. And judgment against the nation
has been accruing for many years, particularly since Manasseh reintroduced
idolatry in Judah. Moreover, God knows that many people who have sincerely
turned to him for a time will later backslide and turn away. So at this time in
history God's compassion is cautious.

Because of this, Jeremiah finds it necessary not only to rebuke the wicked but also to tell believers that even their prayers may not be answered positively. Jeremiah is obviously exasperated by the weight of it all.

Jer. 15:10   JEREMIAH FEELS PRESSURE.

> Alas, my mother, that you gave me birth,
>   a man with whom the whole land strives and contends!
> I have neither lent nor borrowed,
>   yet everyone curses me.

Jer. 15:11   GOD REASSURES.   The LORD said,

> "Surely I will deliver you for a good purpose;
>   surely I will make your enemies plead with you
>   in times of disaster and times of distress.

Jer. 15:12-14   THE DISASTER SPECIFIED.

> "Can a man break iron—
>   iron from the north—or bronze?
> Your wealth and your treasures
>   I will give as plunder, without charge,
> because of all your sins
>   throughout your country.
> I will enslave you to your enemies
>   in *j* a land you do not know,
> for my anger will kindle a fire
>   that will burn against you."

Jer. 15:15-18   JEREMIAH COMPLAINS.

> You understand, O LORD;
>   remember me and care for me.
>   Avenge me on my persecutors.
> You are long-suffering—do not take me away;
>   think of how I suffer reproach for your sake.
> When your words came, I ate them;
>   they were my joy and my heart's delight,
> for I bear your name,
>   O LORD God Almighty.
> I never sat in the company of revelers,
>   never made merry with them;
> I sat alone because your hand was on me
>   and you had filled me with indignation.
> Why is my pain unending
>   and my wound grievous and incurable?
> Will you be to me like a deceptive brook,
>   like a spring that fails?

Jer. 15:19-21   GOD CHASTISES JEREMIAH.   Therefore this is what the LORD says:

> "If you repent, I will restore you
>   that you may serve me;

*j*Some Hebrew manuscripts, Septuagint and Syriac (see also Jer. 17:4); most Hebrew manuscripts *I will cause your enemies to bring you* / *into*

if you utter worthy, not worthless, words,
>   you will be my spokesman.
> Let this people turn to you,
>   but you must not turn to them.
> I will make you a wall to this people,
>   a fortified wall of bronze;
> they will fight against you
>   but will not overcome you,
> for I am with you
>   to rescue and save you,"
>   declares the LORD.
> "I will save you from the hands of the wicked
>   and redeem you from the grasp of the cruel."

At the very time he is most discouraged, Jeremiah is instructed that more sacrifice is in store. He is not to marry, attend funerals, or join in festive celebrations.

JEREMIAH NOT TO MARRY.   Then the word of the LORD came to me: "You must not marry and have sons or daughters in this place." For this is what the LORD says about the sons and daughters born in this land and about the women who are their mothers and the men who are their fathers: "They will die of deadly diseases. They will not be mourned or buried but will be like refuse lying on the ground. They will perish by sword and famine, and their dead bodies will become food for the birds of the air and the beasts of the earth."   *Jer. 16:1-4*

JEREMIAH NOT TO MOURN.   For this is what the LORD says: "Do not enter a house where there is a funeral meal; do not go to mourn or show sympathy, because I have withdrawn my blessing, my love and my pity from this people," declares the LORD. "Both high and low will die in this land. They will not be buried or mourned, and no one will cut himself or shave his head for them. No one will offer food to comfort those who mourn for the dead—not even for a father or a mother—nor will anyone give them a drink to console them.   *Jer. 16:5-7*

JEREMIAH NOT TO FEAST.   "And do not enter a house where there is feasting and sit down to eat and drink. For this is what the LORD Almighty, the God of Israel, says: Before your eyes and in your days I will bring an end to the sounds of joy and gladness and to the voices of bride and bridegroom in this place.   *Jer. 16:8,9*

MESSAGE TO BE PREACHED.   "When you tell these people all this and they ask you, 'Why has the LORD decreed such a great disaster against us? What wrong have we done? What sin have we committed against the LORD our God?' then say to them, 'It is because your fathers forsook me,' declares the LORD, 'and followed other gods and served and worshiped them. They forsook me and did not keep my law. But you have behaved more wickedly than your fathers. See how each of you is following the stubbornness of his evil heart instead of obeying me. So I will throw you out of this land into a land neither you nor your fathers have known, and there you will serve other gods day and night, for I will show you no favor.'   *Jer. 16:10-21*

"However, the days are coming," declares the LORD, "when men will no longer say, 'As surely as the LORD lives, who brought the Israelites up out of Egypt,' but they will say, 'As surely as the LORD lives, who brought the Israelites up out of the land of the north and out of all the countries where he had banished them.' For I will restore them to the land I gave their fore-fathers.

"But now I will send for many fishermen," declares the LORD, "and they will catch them. After that I will send for many hunters, and they will hunt them down on every mountain and hill and from the crevices of the rocks. My eyes are on all their ways; they are not hidden from me, nor is their sin concealed from my eyes. I will repay them double for their wickedness and their sin, because they have defiled my land with the lifeless forms of their vile images and have filled my inheritance with their detestable idols."

> O LORD, my strength and my fortress,
>   my refuge in time of distress,
> to you the nations will come
>   from the ends of the earth and say,
> "Our fathers possessed nothing but false gods,
>   worthless idols that did them no good.
> Do men make their own gods?
>   Yes, but they are not gods!"

> "Therefore I will teach them—
>   this time I will teach them
>   my power and might.
> Then they will know
>   that my name is the LORD.

To Jeremiah's credit, he rises to the occasion and subordinates his personal feelings. Of course, Jeremiah's persevering character was known to God, and that may be why God called him to this demanding ministry. (Calling one to difficult service may actually be God's way of honoring his servant's strength of character.) So it is that Jeremiah resumes his ministry and brings God's message to his people.

Jer. 17:1-4   GOD'S JUDGMENT CONVEYED.

> "Judah's sin is engraved with an iron tool,
>   inscribed with a flint point,
> on the tablets of their hearts
>   and on the horns of their altars.
> Even their children remember
>   their altars and Asherah poles[k]
> beside the spreading trees
>   and on the high hills.
> My mountain in the land
>   and your[l] wealth and all your treasures
> I will give away as plunder,
>   together with your high places,
>   because of sin throughout your country.

[k]That is, symbols of the goddess Asherah   [l]Or hills / [3]and the mountains of the land. / Your

>Through your own fault you will lose
>>the inheritance I gave you.
>I will enslave you to your enemies
>>in a land you do not know,
>for you have kindled my anger,
>>and it will burn forever."

TRUST IN MAN FUTILE.   This is what the LORD says: Jer. 17:5-8

>"Cursed is the one who trusts in man,
>>who depends on flesh for his strength
>>and whose heart turns away from the LORD.
>He will be like a bush in the wastelands;
>>he will not see prosperity when it comes.
>He will dwell in the parched places of the desert,
>>in a salt land where no one lives.

>"But blessed is the man who trusts in the LORD,
>>whose confidence is in him.
>He will be like a tree planted by the water
>>that sends out its roots by the stream.
>It does not fear when heat comes;
>>its leaves are always green.
>It has no worries in a year of drought
>>and never fails to bear fruit."

GOD KNOWS THE HEART.   Jer. 17:9-11

>The heart is deceitful above all things
>>and beyond cure.
>>Who can understand it?

>"I the LORD search the heart
>>and examine the mind,
>to reward a man according to his conduct,
>>according to what his deeds deserve."

>Like a partridge that hatches eggs it did not lay
>>is the man who gains riches by unjust means.
>When his life is half gone, they will desert him,
>>and in the end he will prove to be a fool.

How often Jeremiah longs for his mission to conclude! The cynics and scoffers mock him by asking when all this wrath is going to happen. They observe nothing but peace and prosperity all around, and view talk of Jerusalem's destruction and Judah's fall as so much nonsense. It is probably such taunting that prompts the following prayer from Jeremiah.

PLEA FOR SWIFT EXECUTION.   Jer.
                                                                     17:12-18

>A glorious throne, exalted from the beginning,
>>is the place of our sanctuary.
>O LORD, the hope of Israel,
>>all who forsake you will be put to shame.
>Those who turn away from you will be written in the dust

because they have forsaken the LORD,
   the spring of living water.

Heal me, O LORD, and I will be healed;
   save me and I will be saved,
   for you are the one I praise.
They keep saying to me,
   "Where is the word of the LORD?
   Let it now be fulfilled!"
I have not run away from being your shepherd;
   you know I have not desired the day of despair.
   What passes my lips is open before you.
Do not be a terror to me;
   you are my refuge in the day of disaster.
Let my persecutors be put to shame,
   but keep me from shame;
let them be terrified,
   but keep me from terror.
Bring on them the day of disaster;
   destroy them with double destruction.

Jeremiah now records a special message which he is instructed to bring to Judah. The Sabbath has been honored mostly in the breach for many years, and God now wants it to be observed. Beyond being a requirement of the law, the Sabbath is symbolic of God's covenant with Israel, and its observance takes on added significance at a time when the covenant relationship has been so shattered.

Jer.
17:19-27

KEEPING THE SABBATH HOLY.   This is what the LORD said to me: "Go and stand at the gate of the people, through which the kings of Judah go in and out; stand also at all the other gates of Jerusalem. Say to them, 'Hear the word of the LORD, O kings of Judah and all people of Judah and everyone living in Jerusalem who come through these gates. This is what the LORD says: Be careful not to carry a load on the Sabbath day or bring it through the gates of Jerusalem. Do not bring a load out of your houses or do any work on the Sabbath, but keep the Sabbath day holy, as I commanded your forefathers. Yet they did not listen or pay attention; they were stiff-necked and would not listen or respond to discipline. But if you are careful to obey me, declares the LORD, and bring no load through the gates of this city on the Sabbath, but keep the Sabbath day holy by not doing any work on it, then kings who sit on David's throne will come through the gates of this city with their officials. They and their officials will come riding in chariots and on horses, accompanied by the men of Judah and those living in Jerusalem, and this city will be inhabited forever. People will come from the towns of Judah and the villages around Jerusalem, from the territory of Benjamin and the western foothills, from the hill country and the Negev, bringing burnt offerings and sacrifices, grain offerings, incense and thank offerings to the house of the LORD. But if you do not obey me to keep the Sabbath day holy by not carrying any load as you come through the gates of Jerusalem on the Sabbath day, then I will kindle an unquenchable fire in the gates of Jerusalem that will consume her fortresses.'"

Another sign is now given to Jeremiah for use as an illustration in his preaching. Repeatedly God has likened his relationship with man to a potter's relationship with his clay. As the potter has power over his clay, so God as the Creator of the universe has unlimited power over men and nations, and the right to rule them as he sees fit. To bring that message home clearly to Jeremiah, God directs him to the house of a potter.

JEREMIAH VISITS POTTER.   This is the word that came to Jeremiah from the LORD: "Go down to the potter's house, and there I will give you my message." So I went down to the potter's house, and I saw him working at the wheel. But the pot he was shaping from the clay was marred in his hands; so the potter formed it into another pot, shaping it as seemed best to him.

Jer. 18:1-4

LESSON OF THE POTTER.   Then the word of the LORD came to me: "O house of Israel, can I not do with you as this potter does?" declares the LORD. "Like clay in the hand of the potter, so are you in my hand, O house of Israel. If at any time I announce that a nation or kingdom is to be uprooted, torn down and destroyed, and if that nation I warned repents of its evil, then I will relent and not inflict on it the disaster I had planned. And if at another time I announce that a nation or kingdom is to be built up and planted, and if it does evil in my sight and does not obey me, then I will reconsider the good I had intended to do for it.

Jer. 18:5-12

"Now therefore say to the people of Judah and those living in Jerusalem, 'This is what the LORD says: Look! I am preparing a disaster for you and devising a plan against you. So turn from your evil ways, each one of you, and reform your ways and your actions.' But they will reply, 'It's no use. We will continue with our own plans; each of us will follow the stubbornness of his evil heart.'"

THE POTTER'S PLANS.   Therefore this is what the LORD says:

Jer.
18:13-17

"Inquire among the nations:
Who has ever heard anything like this?
A most horrible thing has been done
by Virgin Israel.
Does the snow of Lebanon
ever vanish from its rocky slopes?
Do its cool waters from distant sources
ever cease to flow?[m]
Yet my people have forgotten me;
they burn incense to worthless idols,
which made them stumble in their ways
and in the ancient paths.
They made them walk in bypaths
and on roads not built up.
Their land will be laid waste,
an object of lasting scorn;
all who pass by will be appalled
and will shake their heads.
Like a wind from the east,

[m]The meaning of the Hebrew for this sentence is uncertain.

> I will scatter them before their enemies;
> I will show them my back and not my face
> in the day of their disaster."

Once again Jeremiah learns of a plot against him, but this plot seems to be more of a countercampaign than a threat to his physical life. Even so, Jeremiah is incensed and cries out for punishment of his detractors. The weeping prophet has now become the angry prophet.

Jer. 18:18   CONSPIRACY AGAINST JEREMIAH.   They said, "Come, let's make plans against Jeremiah; for the teaching of the law by the priest will not be lost, nor will counsel from the wise, nor the word from the prophets. So come, let's attack him with our tongues and pay no attention to anything he says."

Jer. 18:19-23   JEREMIAH'S ANGER.

> Listen to me, O LORD;
>   hear what my accusers are saying!
> Should good be repaid with evil?
>   Yet they have dug a pit for me.
> Remember that I stood before you
>   and spoke in their behalf
>   to turn your wrath away from them.
> So give their children over to famine;
>   hand them over to the power of the sword.
> Let their wives be made childless and widows;
>   let their men be put to death,
>   their young men slain by the sword in battle.
> Let a cry be heard from their houses
>   when you suddenly bring invaders against them,
> for they have dug a pit to capture me
>   and have hidden snares for my feet.
> But you know, O LORD,
>   all their plots to kill me.
> Do not forgive their crimes
>   or blot out their sins from your sight.
> Let them be overthrown before you;
>   deal with them in the time of your anger.

Angry and impatient as he may be, Jeremiah nevertheless continues to take God's message to the people. Once again God graphically illustrates his message, this time using a clay jar.

Jer. 19:1-9   MESSAGE FOR TOPHETH.   This is what the LORD says: "Go and buy a clay jar from a potter. Take along some of the elders of the people and of the priests and go out to the Valley of Ben Hinnom, near the entrance of the Potsherd Gate. There proclaim the words I tell you, and say, 'Hear the word of the LORD, O kings of Judah and people of Jerusalem. This is what the LORD Almighty, the God of Israel, says: Listen! I am going to bring a disaster on this place that will make the ears of everyone who hears of it tingle. For they have forsaken me and made this a place of foreign gods; they have burned sacrifices in it to gods that neither they nor their fathers nor the kings of Judah ever knew, and they have filled this place with the blood of the innocent. They have built the high places of Baal to burn their sons in the fire as offerings to Baal—something I did not command or mention, nor did it enter my mind. So beware, the days are coming, declares the LORD, when people will no longer call this place Topheth or the Valley of Ben Hinnom, but the Valley of Slaughter.

"'In this place I will ruin[n] the plans of Judah and Jerusalem. I will make them fall by the sword before their enemies, at the hands of those who seek their lives, and I will give their carcasses as food to the birds of the air and the beasts of the earth. I will devastate this city and make it an object of scorn; all who pass by will be appalled and will scoff because of all its wounds. I will make them eat the flesh of their sons and daughters, and they will eat one another's flesh during the stress of the siege imposed on them by the enemies who seek their lives.'

MEANING OF BROKEN JAR.   "Then break the jar while those who go   Jer.
with you are watching, and say to them, 'This is what the LORD Almighty   19:10-13
says: I will smash this nation and this city just as this potter's jar is
smashed and cannot be repaired. They will bury the dead in Topheth until
there is no more room. This is what I will do to this place and to those who
live here, declares the LORD. I will make this city like Topheth. The houses
in Jerusalem and those of the kings of Judah will be defiled like this place,
Topheth—all the houses where they burned incense on the roofs to all the
starry hosts and poured out drink offerings to other gods.'"

Jeremiah has been prophesying for some time now during the reign of Josiah, and although he has angered the religious establishment, no official action or physical harm has been brought against him. But his fortune on both counts is about to change, and when it does Jeremiah will once again expose the inner pain that his outer suffering brings. And yet a new sense of trust in God is revealed: there is actually praise for the one who has gotten Jeremiah into all this trouble.

JEREMIAH PREDICTS DISASTER.   Jeremiah then returned from   Jer.
Topheth, where the LORD had sent him to prophesy, and stood in the court   19:14,15
of the LORD's temple and said to all the people, "This is what the LORD
Almighty, the God of Israel, says: 'Listen! I am going to bring on this city
and the villages around it every disaster I pronounced against them,
because they were stiff-necked and would not listen to my words.'"

BEATING AND IMPRISONMENT.   When the priest Pashhur son of   Jer. 20:1,2
Immer, the chief officer in the temple of the LORD, heard Jeremiah prophesying these things, he had Jeremiah the prophet beaten and put in the
stocks at the Upper Gate of Benjamin at the LORD's temple.

JUDGMENT AGAINST PASHHUR.   The next day, when Pashhur   Jer. 20:3-6
released him from the stocks, Jeremiah said to him, "The LORD's name for
you is not Pashhur, but Magor-Missabib.[o] For this is what the LORD says:
'I will make you a terror to yourself and to all your friends; with your own
eyes you will see them fall by the sword of their enemies. I will hand all
Judah over to the king of Babylon, who will carry them away to Babylon
or put them to the sword. I will hand over to their enemies all the wealth

[n]The Hebrew for *ruin* sounds like the Hebrew for *jar* (see verses 1 and 10).
[o]*Magor-Missabib* means *terror on every side.*

of this city—all its products, all its valuables and all the treasures of the kings of Judah. They will take it away as plunder and carry it off to Babylon. And you, Pashhur, and all who live in your house will go into exile to Babylon. There you will die and be buried, you and all your friends to whom you have prophesied lies.'"

Jer.
20:14-18

JEREMIAH'S SELF-PITY.

Cursed be the day I was born!
    May the day my mother bore me not be blessed!
Cursed be the man who brought my father the news,
    who made him very glad, saying,
    "A child is born to you—a son!"
May that man be like the towns
    the LORD overthrew without pity.
May he hear wailing in the morning,
    a battle cry at noon.
For he did not kill me in the womb,
    with my mother as my grave,
    her womb enlarged forever.
Why did I ever come out of the womb
    to see trouble and sorrow
    and to end my days in shame?

Jer. 20:7-10

JEREMIAH FEELS BETRAYED.

O LORD, you deceived[P] me, and I was deceived[P];
    you overpowered me and prevailed.
I am ridiculed all day long;
    everyone mocks me.
Whenever I speak, I cry out
    proclaiming violence and destruction.
So the word of the LORD has brought me
    insult and reproach all day long.
But if I say, "I will not mention him
    or speak any more in his name,"
his word is in my heart like a fire,
    a fire shut up in my bones.
I am weary of holding it in;
    indeed, I cannot.
I hear many whispering,
    "Terror on every side!
    Report him! Let's report him!"
All my friends
    are waiting for me to slip, saying,
"Perhaps he will be deceived;
    then we will prevail over him
    and take our revenge on him."

Jer.
20:11-13

JEREMIAH PRAISES GOD.

But the LORD is with me like a mighty warrior;
    so my persecutors will stumble and not prevail.

P Or persuaded

They will fail and be thoroughly disgraced;
    their dishonor will never be forgotten.
O LORD Almighty, you who examine the righteous
    and probe the heart and mind,
let me see your vengeance upon them,
    for to you I have committed my cause.

Sing to the LORD!
    Give praise to the LORD!
He rescues the life of the needy
    from the hands of the wicked.

Effect of Jeremiah's Preaching

*I*t is obvious that Jeremiah is maturing both as a young man and as a prophet of God. He has been in the crucible of conflict and has emerged victorious. There will be more opposition and more personal sacrifice, but Jeremiah now has the fortitude to endure. Jeremiah will next be heard from after the reign of Josiah has ended. For now, however, the scene changes to a nation on the brink of a thorough, if brief, spiritual revival. Perhaps Jeremiah's preaching has been more effective than he realizes. (When one plants the seed, he never knows when it will bear fruit.)

TEMPLE IS REPAIRED. ᶜʰIn the eighteenth year of Josiah's reign, to purify the land and the temple, he sent Shaphan son of Azaliah and Maaseiah the ruler of the city, with Joah son of Joahaz, the recorder, to repair the temple of the LORD his God. ᴷᵍ"Go up to Hilkiah the high priest and have him get ready the money that has been brought into the temple of the LORD, which the doorkeepers have collected from the people. Have them entrust it to the men appointed to supervise the work on the temple. And have these men pay the workers who repair the temple of the LORD— the carpenters, the builders and the masons. Also have them purchase timber and dressed stone to repair the temple. But they need not account for the money entrusted to them, because they are acting faithfully." ᶜʰThey went to Hilkiah the high priest and gave him the money that had been brought into the temple of God, which the Levites who were the door-keepers had collected from the people of Manasseh, Ephraim and the entire remnant of Israel and from all the people of Judah and Benjamin and the inhabitants of Jerusalem. Then they entrusted it to the men appointed to supervise the work on the LORD's temple. These men paid the workers who repaired and restored the temple. They also gave money to the carpenters and builders to purchase dressed stone, and timber for joists and beams for the buildings that the kings of Judah had allowed to fall into ruin.

The men did the work faithfully. Over them to direct them were Jahath and Obadiah, Levites descended from Merari, and Zechariah and Meshullam, descended from Kohath. The Levites—all who were skilled in playing musical instruments—had charge of the laborers and supervised all the workers from job to job. Some of the Levites were secretaries, scribes and doorkeepers.

2 Kgs.
22:3-7
2 Chron.
34:8-13
(621 B.C.)
Jerusalem

2 Kgs. 22:8
2 Chron. 34:14,15

BOOK OF THE LAW FOUND. [Ch]While they were bringing out the money that had been taken into the temple of the LORD, Hilkiah the priest found the Book of the Law of the LORD that had been given through Moses. Hilkiah said to Shaphan the secretary, "I have found the Book of the Law in the temple of the LORD." [Kg]He gave it to Shaphan, who read it.

2 Kgs. 22:9,10
2 Chron. 34:16-18

LAW READ TO JOSIAH. Then Shaphan took the book to the king and reported to him: "Your officials are doing everything that has been committed to them. They have paid out the money that was in the temple of the LORD and have entrusted it to the supervisors and workers." Then Shaphan the secretary informed the king, "Hilkiah the priest has given me a book." And Shaphan read from it in the presence of the king.

2 Kgs. 22:11-13
2 Chron. 34:19-21

JOSIAH SEES SIGNIFICANCE. When the king heard the words of the Law, he tore his robes. He gave these orders to Hilkiah, Ahikam son of Shaphan, Abdon son of Micah,[q] Shaphan the secretary and Asaiah the king's attendant: "Go and inquire of the LORD for me and for the remnant in Israel and Judah about what is written in this book that has been found. Great is the LORD's anger that is poured out on us because our fathers have not kept the word of the LORD; they have not acted in accordance with all that is written in this book."

2 Kgs. 22:14-20
2 Chron. 34:22-28

HULDAH THE PROPHETESS. Hilkiah and those the king had sent with him[r] went to speak to the prophetess Huldah, who was the wife of Shallum son of Tokhath,[s] the son of Hasrah,[t] keeper of the wardrobe. She lived in Jerusalem, in the Second District.

She said to them, "This is what the LORD, the God of Israel, says: Tell the man who sent you to me, 'This is what the LORD says: I am going to bring disaster on this place and its people—all the curses written in the book that has been read in the presence of the king of Judah. Because they have forsaken me and burned incense to other gods and provoked me to anger by all that their hands have made,[u] my anger will be poured out on this place and will not be quenched.' Tell the king of Judah, who sent you to inquire of the LORD, 'This is what the LORD, the God of Israel, says concerning the words you heard: Because your heart was responsive and you humbled yourself before God when you heard what he spoke against this place and its people, and because you humbled yourself before me and tore your robes and wept in my presence, I have heard you, declares the LORD. Now I will gather you to your fathers, and you will be buried in peace. Your eyes will not see all the disaster I am going to bring on this place and on those who live here.' "

So they took her answer back to the king.

2 Kgs. 23:1,2
2 Chron. 34:29,30

LAW READ TO THE PEOPLE. Then the king called together all the elders of Judah and Jerusalem. He went up to the temple of the LORD with the men of Judah, the people of Jerusalem, the priests and the Levites—all the people from the least to the greatest. He read in their hearing all the words of the Book of the Covenant, which had been found in the temple of the LORD.

[q]Also called *Acbor son of Micaiah* [r]One Hebrew manuscript, Vulgate and Syriac; most Hebrew manuscripts do not have *had sent with him.* [s]Also called *Tikvah* [t]Also called *Harhas* [u]Or *by everything they have done*

COVENANT RENEWED.   The king stood by his pillar and renewed the
covenant in the presence of the LORD—to follow the LORD and keep his
commands, regulations and decrees with all his heart and all his soul, and
to obey the words of the covenant written in this book.

2 Kgs. 23:3
2 Chron.
34:31,32

Then he had everyone in Jerusalem and Benjamin pledge themselves to
it; the people of Jerusalem did this in accordance with the covenant of
God, the God of their fathers.

JOSIAH'S SWEEPING REFORMS.   Kg The king ordered Hilkiah the high
priest, the priests next in rank and the doorkeepers to remove from the
temple of the LORD all the articles made for Baal and Asherah and all the
starry hosts. He burned them outside Jerusalem in the fields of the Kidron
Valley and took the ashes to Bethel. He did away with the pagan priests
appointed by the kings of Judah to burn incense on the high places of the
towns of Judah and on those around Jerusalem—those who burned
incense to Baal, to the sun and moon, to the constellations and to all the
starry hosts. He took the Asherah pole from the temple of the LORD to the
Kidron Valley outside Jerusalem and burned it there. He ground it to
powder and scattered the dust over the graves of the common people. He
also tore down the quarters of the male shrine prostitutes, which were in
the temple of the LORD and where women did weaving for Asherah.

2 Kgs.
23:4-14;24
2 Chron.
34:33

Josiah brought all the priests from the towns of Judah and desecrated
the high places, from Geba to Beersheba, where the priests had burned
incense. He broke down the shrines^v at the gates—at the entrance to the
Gate of Joshua, the city governor, which is on the left of the city gate.
Although the priests of the high places did not serve at the altar of the
LORD in Jerusalem, they ate unleavened bread with their fellow priests.

He desecrated Topheth, which was in the Valley of Ben Hinnom, so no
one could use it to sacrifice his son or daughter in^w the fire to Molech. He
removed from the entrance to the temple of the LORD the horses that the
kings of Judah had dedicated to the sun. They were in the court near the
room of an official named Nathan-Melech. Josiah then burned the chariots
dedicated to the sun.

He pulled down the altars the kings of Judah had erected on the roof
near the upper room of Ahaz, and the altars Manasseh had built in the two
courts of the temple of the LORD. He removed them from there, smashed
them to pieces and threw the rubble into the Kidron Valley. The king also
desecrated the high places that were east of Jerusalem on the south of the
Hill of Corruption—the ones Solomon king of Israel had built for
Ashtoreth the vile goddess of the Sidonians, for Chemosh the vile god of
Moab, and for Molech^x the detestable god of the people of Ammon. Josiah
smashed the sacred stones and cut down the Asherah poles and covered
the sites with human bones.

Furthermore, Josiah got rid of the mediums and spiritists, the household
gods, the idols and all the other detestable things seen in Judah and
Jerusalem. This he did to fulfill the requirements of the law written in the
book that Hilkiah the priest had discovered in the temple of the LORD.
Ch Josiah removed all the detestable idols from all the territory belonging to
the Israelites, and he had all who were present in Israel serve the LORD

---

^{v}Or high places ^{w}Or to make his son or daughter pass through ^{x}Hebrew Milcom

their God. As long as he lived, they did not fail to follow the LORD, the God of their fathers.

2 Kgs. 23:15-20 Bethel

REFORMS EXTEND TO SAMARIA.   Even the altar at Bethel, the high place made by Jeroboam son of Nebat, who had caused Israel to sin—even that altar and high place he demolished. He burned the high place and ground it to powder, and burned the Asherah pole also. Then Josiah looked around, and when he saw the tombs that were there on the hillside, he had the bones removed from them and burned on the altar to defile it, in accordance with the word of the LORD proclaimed by the man of God who foretold these things.

The king asked, "What is that tombstone I see?"

The men of the city said, "It marks the tomb of the man of God who came from Judah and pronounced against the altar of Bethel the very things you have done to it."

"Leave it alone," he said. "Don't let anyone disturb his bones." So they spared his bones and those of the prophet who had come from Samaria.

Just as he had done at Bethel, Josiah removed and defiled all the shrines at the high places that the kings of Israel had built in the towns of Samaria that had provoked the LORD to anger. Josiah slaughtered all the priests of those high places on the altars and burned human bones on them. Then he went back to Jerusalem.

2 Kgs. 23:21-23 2 Chron. 35:1-19 (621 B.C.) Jerusalem

GREAT PASSOVER CELEBRATION.   Josiah celebrated the Passover to the LORD in Jerusalem, and the Passover lamb was slaughtered on the fourteenth day of the first month. He appointed the priests to their duties and encouraged them in the service of the LORD's temple. He said to the Levites, who instructed all Israel and who had been consecrated to the LORD: "Put the sacred ark in the temple that Solomon son of David king of Israel built. It is not to be carried about on your shoulders. Now serve the LORD your God and his people Israel. Prepare yourselves by families in your divisions, according to the directions written by David king of Israel and by his son Solomon.

"Stand in the holy place with a group of Levites for each subdivision of the families of your fellow countrymen, the lay people. Slaughter the Passover lambs, consecrate yourselves and prepare the lambs for your fellow countrymen, doing what the LORD commanded through Moses."

Josiah provided for all the lay people who were there a total of thirty thousand sheep and goats for the Passover offerings, and also three thousand cattle—all from the king's own possessions.

His officials also contributed voluntarily to the people and the priests and Levites. Hilkiah, Zechariah and Jehiel, the administrators of God's temple, gave the priests twenty-six hundred Passover offerings and three hundred cattle. Also Conaniah along with Shemaiah and Nethanel, his brothers, and Hashabiah, Jeiel and Jozabad, the leaders of the Levites, provided five thousand Passover offerings and five hundred head of cattle for the Levites.

The service was arranged and the priests stood in their places with the Levites in their divisions as the king had ordered. The Passover lambs were slaughtered, and the priests sprinkled the blood handed to them, while the Levites skinned the animals. They set aside the burnt offerings to give them to the subdivisions of the families of the people to offer to the LORD, as is written in the Book of Moses. They did the same with the cattle.

They roasted the Passover animals over the fire as prescribed, and boiled the holy offerings in pots, caldrons and pans and served them quickly to all the people. After this, they made preparations for themselves and for the priests, because the priests, the descendants of Aaron, were sacrificing the burnt offerings and the fat portions until nightfall. So the Levites made preparations for themselves and for the Aaronic priests.

The musicians, the descendants of Asaph, were in the places prescribed by David, Asaph, Heman and Jeduthun the king's seer. The gatekeepers at each gate did not need to leave their posts, because their fellow Levites made the preparations for them.

So at that time the entire service of the LORD was carried out for the celebration of the Passover and the offering of burnt offerings on the altar of the LORD, as King Josiah had ordered. The Israelites who were present celebrated the Passover at that time and observed the Feast of Unleavened Bread for seven days. The Passover had not been observed like this in Israel since the days of the prophet Samuel; and none of the kings of Israel had ever celebrated such a Passover as did Josiah, with the priests, the Levites and all Judah and Israel who were there with the people of Jerusalem. This Passover was celebrated in the eighteenth year of Josiah's reign.

RECORDS OF JOSIAH'S REIGN.   The other events of Josiah's reign and his acts of devotion, according to what is written in the Law of the LORD— all the events, from beginning to end, are written in the book of the kings of Israel and Judah.

2 Kgs. 23:28
2 Chron. 35:26,27

Josiah's reign is truly a high point in the history of Judah, but it will not be enough to atone for three centuries of sinning on the part of Israel. The apparent lesson is that sin sometimes sets in motion certain consequences which even subsequent good intentions cannot forestall.

Assyria Falls and Babylonia Emerges

Already the prophecies about the nations are coming true. There is foreign unrest everywhere. Assyria, Babylonia, and Egypt are all vying for supremacy. Just as Jeremiah was beginning his ministry in 626 B.C., Nabopolassar rebelled against Assyria and established the Babylonian Empire. Now, some 14 years later, the time has come for the prophecies of Nahum and others regarding Nineveh's fall to be fulfilled. It takes only a two-month siege by the allied armies of the Medes, Babylonians, and Scythians (from north of the Black Sea) to bring Nineveh to its knees in 612 B.C. Under Nabopolassar, Babylonia begins its rise to world supremacy. But Babylonia must first contend with what is left of Assyria as well as with Pharaoh Neco of Egypt, who succeeds his father, Psammetichus I, in 610 B.C. When Neco recognizes the growing threat of Babylonia, he decides to bolster what few Assyrian forces remain, and that plan of action brings Neco through Canaan.

The incidental result for Judah is loss of its good king Josiah. Why Josiah decides to attack Egypt is not clear, but he goes to Megiddo, a city on the southern edge of the Plain of Esdraelon, and soon finds himself mortally wounded. Here now is the record of Josiah's untimely death and of the brief reign of his son Jehoahaz before Neco replaces him by Jehoahaz's brother Eliakim, whom the pharaoh calls Jehoiakim. During this time Neco tries to make Judah a buffer state between his own country and Babylonia.

2 Kgs.
23:29,30a
2 Chron.
35:20-25
(609 B.C.)
The Plain
of
Megiddo

JOSIAH KILLED IN BATTLE.   After all this, when Josiah had set the temple in order, Neco king of Egypt went up to fight at Carchemish on the Euphrates, and Josiah marched out to meet him in battle. But Neco sent messengers to him, saying, "What quarrel is there between you and me, O king of Judah? It is not you I am attacking at this time, but the house with which I am at war. God has told me to hurry; so stop opposing God, who is with me, or he will destroy you."

Josiah, however, would not turn away from him, but disguised himself to engage him in battle. He would not listen to what Neco had said at God's command but went to fight him on the plain of Megiddo.

Archers shot King Josiah, and he told his officers, "Take me away; I am badly wounded." So they took him out of his chariot, put him in the other chariot he had and brought him to Jerusalem, where he died. He was buried in the tombs of his fathers, and all Judah and Jerusalem mourned for him.

Jeremiah composed laments for Josiah, and to this day all the men and women singers commemorate Josiah in the laments. These became a tradition in Israel and are written in the Laments.

2 Kgs.
23:30b,31
2 Chron.
36:1,2
Jerusalem

JEHOAHAZ (SHALLUM) KING.   And the people of the land took Jehoahaz son of Josiah and anointed him and made him king in Jerusalem in place of his father.

Jehoahaz was twenty-three years old when he became king, and he reigned in Jerusalem three months. His mother's name was Hamutal daughter of Jeremiah; she was from Libnah.

2 Kgs.
23:32

CHARACTER OF JEHOAHAZ.   He did evil in the eyes of the LORD, just as his fathers had done.

2 Kgs.
23:33
2 Chron.
36:3
(609 B.C.)

NECO TAKES JEHOAHAZ CAPTIVE.   Pharaoh Neco put him in chains at Riblah in the land of Hamath[y] so that he might not reign in Jerusalem, and he imposed on Judah a levy of a hundred talents[z] of silver and a talent [a] of gold.

2 Kgs.
23:34,36
2 Chron.
36:4,5a
(608 B.C.)

JEHOIAKIM MADE PUPPET KING.   Pharaoh Neco made Eliakim son of Josiah king in place of his father Josiah and changed Eliakim's name to Jehoiakim. But he took Jehoahaz and carried him off to Egypt, and there he died.

Jehoiakim was twenty-five years old when he became king, and he reigned in Jerusalem eleven years. His mother's name was Zebidah daughter of Pedaiah; she was from Rumah.

2 Kgs. 23:37
2 Ch.36:5b

JEHOIAKIM'S CHARACTER.   And he did evil in the eyes of the LORD, just as his fathers had done.

2 Kgs.
23:35

TRIBUTE TO NECO.   Jehoiakim paid Pharaoh Neco the silver and gold he demanded. In order to do so, he taxed the land and exacted the silver and gold from the people of the land according to their assessments.

[y]Hebrew; Septuagint (see also 2 Chron. 36:3) *Neco at Riblah in Hamath removed him*
[z]That is, about 3 3/4 tons (about 3.4 metric tons)   [a]That is, about 75 pounds (about 34 kilograms)

PROPHECY ABOUT JEHOAHAZ.

> Do not weep for the dead ˻king˼ or mourn his loss;
> rather, weep bitterly for him who is exiled,
> because he will never return
> nor see his native land again.

For this is what the LORD says about Shallum[b] son of Josiah, who succeeded his father as king of Judah but has gone from this place: "He will never return. He will die in the place where they have led him captive; he will not see this land again."

> "Woe to him who builds his palace by unrighteousness,
> his upper rooms by injustice,
> making his countrymen work for nothing,
> not paying them for their labor.
> He says, 'I will build myself a great palace
> with spacious upper rooms.'
> So he makes large windows in it,
> panels it with cedar
> and decorates it in red.

> "Does it make you a king
> to have more and more cedar?
> Did not your father have food and drink?
> He did what was right and just,
> so all went well with him.
> He defended the cause of the poor and needy,
> and so all went well.
> Is that not what it means to know me?"
> declares the LORD.
> "But your eyes and your heart
> are set only on dishonest gain,
> on shedding innocent blood
> and on oppression and extortion."

Jeremiah Faces Charges

Now that Josiah's good influence is gone and his sons have once again let Judah become corrupt, Jeremiah is in more jeopardy than he might otherwise have been. He is reminded of this by a confrontation in which he barely escapes with his life.

PREDICTION ABOUT JERUSALEM. Early in the reign of Jehoiakim son of Josiah king of Judah, this word came from the LORD: "This is what the LORD says: Stand in the courtyard of the LORD's house and speak to all the people of the towns of Judah who come to worship in the house of the LORD. Tell them everything I command you; do not omit a word. Perhaps they will listen and each will turn from his evil way. Then I will relent and not bring on them the disaster I was planning because of the evil they have done. Say to them, 'This is what the LORD says: If you do not listen to me and follow my law, which I have set before you, and if you do not listen to

[b]Also called *Jehoahaz*

the words of my servants the prophets, whom I have sent to you again and again (though you have not listened), then I will make this house like Shiloh and this city an object of cursing among all the nations of the earth.'"

Jer. 26:7-9   PRIESTS CONFRONT JEREMIAH.   The priests, the prophets and all the people heard Jeremiah speak these words in the house of the LORD. But as soon as Jeremiah finished telling all the people everything the LORD had commanded him to say, the priests, the prophets and all the people seized him and said, "You must die! Why do you prophesy in the LORD's name that this house will be like Shiloh and this city will be desolate and deserted?" And all the people crowded around Jeremiah in the house of the LORD.

Jer. 26:10,11   CHARGE BEFORE OFFICIALS.   When the officials of Judah heard about these things, they went up from the royal palace to the house of the LORD and took their places at the entrance of the New Gate of the LORD's house. Then the priests and the prophets said to the officials and all the people, "This man should be sentenced to death because he has prophesied against this city. You have heard it with your own ears!"

Jer. 26:12-15   JEREMIAH'S DEFENSE.   Then Jeremiah said to all the officials and all the people: "The LORD sent me to prophesy against this house and this city all the things you have heard. Now reform your ways and your actions and obey the LORD your God. Then the LORD will relent and not bring the disaster he has pronounced against you. As for me, I am in your hands; do with me whatever you think is good and right. Be assured, however, that if you put me to death, you will bring the guilt of innocent blood on yourselves and on this city and on those who live in it, for in truth the LORD has sent me to you to speak all these words in your hearing."

Jer. 26:16-19   DEFENSE FROM OTHERS.   Then the officials and all the people said to the priests and the prophets, "This man should not be sentenced to death! He has spoken to us in the name of the LORD our God."

Some of the elders of the land stepped forward and said to the entire assembly of people, "Micah of Moresheth prophesied in the days of Hezekiah king of Judah. He told all the people of Judah, 'This is what the LORD Almighty says:

" 'Zion will be plowed like a field,
      Jerusalem will become a heap of rubble,
         the temple hill a mound overgrown with thickets.'[c]

"Did Hezekiah king of Judah or anyone else in Judah put him to death? Did not Hezekiah fear the LORD and seek his favor? And did not the LORD relent, so that he did not bring the disaster he pronounced against them? We are about to bring a terrible disaster on ourselves!"

Jer. 26:24   JEREMIAH RELEASED.   Furthermore, Ahikam son of Shaphan supported Jeremiah, and so he was not handed over to the people to be put to death.

Jer. 26:20-23   URIAH HAS WORSE FATE.   (Now Uriah son of Shemaiah from Kiriath Jearim was another man who prophesied in the name of the LORD; he prophesied the same things against this city and this land as Jeremiah did.

[c]Micah 3:12

When King Jehoiakim and all his officers and officials heard his words, the king sought to put him to death. But Uriah heard of it and fled in fear to Egypt. King Jehoiakim, however, sent Elnathan son of Acbor to Egypt, along with some other men. They brought Uriah out of Egypt and took him to King Jehoiakim, who had him struck down with a sword and his body thrown into the burial place of the common people.)

Jeremiah's Judgment Against Egypt

*J*eremiah's prophetic ministry extends not only to Judah but also to foreign nations which have been Judah's oppressors. Judah's most recent threat has been from Egypt, but the time is near for Egypt to reap its just reward. Here are Jeremiah's warnings to Egypt, as well as to the Philistines, who will be Egypt's last victim in this era of power.

DEFEAT COMING AT CARCHEMISH. This is the word of the LORD that came to Jeremiah the prophet concerning the nations: Jer. 46:1-11

Concerning Egypt:

This is the message against the army of Pharaoh Neco king of Egypt, which was defeated at Carchemish on the Euphrates River by Nebuchadnezzar king of Babylon in the fourth year of Jehoiakim son of Josiah king of Judah:

> "Prepare your shields, both large and small,
> and march out for battle!
> Harness the horses,
> mount the steeds!
> Take your positions
> with helmets on!
> Polish your spears,
> put on your armor!
> What do I see?
> They are terrified,
> they are retreating,
> their warriors are defeated.
> They flee in haste
> without looking back,
> and there is terror on every side,"
>
> declares the LORD.
> "The swift cannot flee
> nor the strong escape.
> In the north by the River Euphrates
> they stumble and fall.
>
> "Who is this that rises like the Nile,
> like rivers of surging waters?
> Egypt rises like the Nile,
> like rivers of surging waters.
> She says, 'I will rise and cover the earth;
> I will destroy cities and their people.'
> Charge, O horses!

Drive furiously, O charioteers!
March on, O warriors—
    men of Cush[d] and Put who carry shields,
    men of Lydia who draw the bow.
But that day belongs to the Lord, the LORD Almighty—
    a day of vengeance, for vengeance on his foes.
The sword will devour till it is satisfied,
    till it has quenched its thirst with blood.
For the Lord, the LORD Almighty, will offer sacrifice
    in the land of the north by the River Euphrates.

"Go up to Gilead and get balm,
    O Virgin Daughter of Egypt.
But you multiply remedies in vain;
    there is no healing for you.

Jer.
46:12-26

BABYLON WILL SUBDUE EGYPT.

The nations will hear of your shame;
    your cries will fill the earth.
One warrior will stumble over another;
    both will fall down together."

This is the message the LORD spoke to Jeremiah the prophet about the coming of Nebuchadnezzar king of Babylon to attack Egypt:

"Announce this in Egypt, and proclaim it in Migdol;
    proclaim it also in Memphis[e] and Tahpanhes:
'Take your positions and get ready,
    for the sword devours those around you.'
Why will your warriors be laid low?
    They cannot stand, for the LORD will push them down.
They will stumble repeatedly;
    they will fall over each other.
They will say, 'Get up, let us go back
    to our own people and our native lands,
    away from the sword of the oppressor.'
There they will exclaim,
    'Pharaoh king of Egypt is only a loud noise;
    he has missed his opportunity.'

"As surely as I live," declares the King,
    whose name is the LORD Almighty,
"one will come who is like Tabor among the mountains,
    like Carmel by the sea.
Pack your belongings for exile,
    you who live in Egypt,
for Memphis will be laid waste
    and lie in ruins without inhabitant.

"Egypt is a beautiful heifer,
    but a gadfly is coming
    against her from the north.

[d] That is, the upper Nile region   [e] Hebrew *Noph*

The mercenaries in her ranks
    are like fattened calves.
They too will turn and flee together,
    they will not stand their ground,
for the day of disaster is coming upon them,
    the time for them to be punished.
Egypt will hiss like a fleeing serpent
    as the enemy advances in force;
they will come against her with axes,
    like men who cut down trees.
They will chop down her forest,"

                        declares the LORD,
  "dense though it be.
They are more numerous than locusts,
    they cannot be counted.
The Daughter of Egypt will be put to shame,
    handed over to the people of the north."

The LORD Almighty, the God of Israel, says: "I am about to bring punishment on Amon god of Thebes,*f* on Pharaoh, on Egypt and her gods and
her kings, and on those who rely on Pharaoh. I will hand them over to
those who seek their lives, to Nebuchadnezzar king of Babylon and his
officers. Later, however, Egypt will be inhabited as in times past," declares
the LORD.

REASSURANCE TO JUDAH.   Jer.
                                                     46:27,28

"Do not fear, O Jacob my servant;
    do not be dismayed, O Israel.
I will surely save you out of a distant place,
    your descendants from the land of their exile.
Jacob will again have peace and security,
    and no one will make him afraid.
Do not fear, O Jacob my servant,
    for I am with you," declares the LORD.
"Though I completely destroy all the nations
    among which I scatter you,
    I will not completely destroy you.
I will discipline you but only with justice;
    I will not let you go entirely unpunished."

PHILISTINES' JEOPARDY.   This is the word of the LORD that came to   Jer. 47:1-7
Jeremiah the prophet concerning the Philistines before Pharaoh attacked
Gaza:

This is what the LORD says:

"See how the waters are rising in the north;
    they will become an overflowing torrent.
They will overflow the land and everything in it,
    the towns and those who live in them.
The people will cry out;
    all who dwell in the land will wail

f Hebrew *No*

at the sound of the hoofs of galloping steeds,
 at the noise of enemy chariots
 and the rumble of their wheels.
Fathers will not turn to help their children;
 their hands will hang limp.
For the day has come
 to destroy all the Philistines
and to cut off all survivors
 who could help Tyre and Sidon.
The LORD is about to destroy the Philistines,
 the remnant from the coasts of Caphtor.⁸
Gaza will shave her head in mourning;
 Ashkelon will be silenced.
O remnant on the plain,
 how long will you cut yourselves?

 " 'Ah, sword of the LORD,' you cry,
  'how long till you rest?
Return to your scabbard;
 cease and be still.'
But how can it rest
 when the LORD has commanded it,
when he has ordered it
 to attack Ashkelon and the coast?"

Habakkuk's Questioning Prophecy

While Jeremiah is continuing his prophecies against Judah and its oppressors, one of Jeremiah's contemporaries, Habakkuk, poses the profound theological question which must nag at anyone who is seriously listening to the prophets. It may even be a question which the various prophets themselves have considered. Certainly Habakkuk is concerned about it. The question is this: how can a righteous and holy God use a wicked nation like Babylonia to bring punishment against God's own people, rebellious and sinful though they may be? Are not the ruthless Babylonians and the other oppressors of Judah merely acting on their own in great arrogance and with no thought whatever of achieving any divine purpose? How then can God permit these unrighteous nations to succeed in their evil oppressions? And the question stretches beyond even the present conflicts to other related issues. How can God permit the wicked to prosper, often at the expense of the righteous? How can a righteous God permit evil to exist at all?

Although God does not provide all the answers in his dialogue with Habakkuk, he does address the central question. His answer is that evil, wherever it is found, always bears within it the seeds of its own destruction. Judah's sins have condemned it to inevitable destruction. The particular agency by which that destruction comes is of no consequence. The enemy may be a righteous or a wicked nation—it matters not. But likewise, if the

---

⁸ That is, Crete

oppressors themselves are evil—as the Babylonians are—then they too will face their own destruction. Only in righteousness is there life; sin always brings death.

PREFACE.   The oracle that Habakkuk the prophet received.   Hab. 1:1

SHOULD EVIL PREVAIL?   Hab. 1:2-4

> How long, O LORD, must I call for help,
>   but you do not listen?
> Or cry out to you, "Violence!"
>   but you do not save?
> Why do you make me look at injustice?
>   Why do you tolerate wrong?
> Destruction and violence are before me;
>   there is strife, and conflict abounds.
> Therefore the law is paralyzed,
>   and justice never prevails.
> The wicked hem in the righteous,
>   so that justice is perverted.

BABYLON WILL PUNISH.   Hab. 1:5-11

> "Look at the nations and watch—
>   and be utterly amazed.
> For I am going to do something in your days
>   that you would not believe,
>   even if you were told.
> I am raising up the Babylonians,[h]
>   that ruthless and impetuous people,
> who sweep across the whole earth
>   to seize dwelling places not their own.
> They are a feared and dreaded people;
>   they are a law to themselves
>   and promote their own honor.
> Their horses are swifter than leopards,
>   fiercer than wolves at dusk.
> Their cavalry gallops headlong;
>   their horsemen come from afar.
> They fly like a vulture swooping to devour;
>   they all come bent on violence.
> Their hordes[i] advance like a desert wind
>   and gather prisoners like sand.
> They deride kings
>   and scoff at rulers.
> They laugh at all fortified cities;
>   they build earthen ramps and capture them.
> Then they sweep past like the wind and go on—
>   guilty men, whose own strength is their god."

WICKED AS EXECUTIONERS?   Hab. 1:12-2:1

> O LORD, are you not from everlasting?

[h]Or Chaldeans   [i]The meaning of the Hebrew for this word is uncertain.

My God, my Holy One, we will not die.
O LORD, you have appointed them to execute judgment;
    O Rock, you have ordained them to punish.
Your eyes are too pure to look on evil;
    you cannot tolerate wrong.
Why then do you tolerate the treacherous?
    Why are you silent while the wicked
    swallow up those more righteous than themselves?
You have made men like fish in the sea,
    like sea creatures that have no ruler.
The wicked foe pulls all of them up with hooks,
    he catches them in his net,
he gathers them up in his dragnet;
    and so he rejoices and is glad.
Therefore he sacrifices to his net
    and burns incense to his dragnet,
for by his net he lives in luxury
    and enjoys the choicest food.
Is he to keep on emptying his net,
    destroying nations without mercy?

I will stand at my watch
    and station myself on the ramparts;
I will look to see what he will say to me,
    and what answer I am to give to this complaint.[j]

Hab. 2:2-5   WICKED ALWAYS PUNISHED.   Then the LORD replied:

"Write down the revelation
    and make it plain on tablets
    so that a herald[k] may run with it.
For the revelation awaits an appointed time;
    it speaks of the end
    and will not prove false.
Though it linger, wait for it;
    it[l] will certainly come and will not delay.

"See, he is puffed up;
    his desires are not upright—
    but the righteous will live by his faith[m]—
indeed, wine betrays him;
    he is arrogant and never at rest.
Because he is as greedy as the grave[n]
    and like death is never satisfied,
he gathers to himself all the nations
    and takes captive all the peoples.

Hab.
2:6-17   "Will not all of them taunt him with ridicule and scorn, saying,

" 'Woe to him who piles up stolen goods
    and makes himself wealthy by extortion!

---

[j] Or *and what to answer when I am rebuked*   [k] Or *so that whoever reads it*   [l] Or *Though he*
linger, wait for him; | he   [m] Or *faithfulness*   [n] Hebrew *Sheol*

How long must this go on?'
Will not your debtors⁰ suddenly arise?
    Will they not wake up and make you tremble?
    Then you will become their victim.
Because you have plundered many nations,
    the peoples who are left will plunder you.
For you have shed man's blood;
    you have destroyed lands and cities and everyone in
        them.

"Woe to him who builds his realm by unjust gain
    to set his nest on high,
    to escape the clutches of ruin!
You have plotted the ruin of many peoples,
    shaming your own house and forfeiting your life.
The stones of the wall will cry out,
    and the beams of the woodwork will echo it.

"Woe to him who builds a city with bloodshed
    and establishes a town by crime!
Has not the LORD Almighty determined
    that the people's labor is only fuel for the fire,
    that the nations exhaust themselves for nothing?
For the earth will be filled with the knowledge of the glory
        of the LORD,
    as the waters cover the sea.

"Woe to him who gives drink to his neighbors,
    pouring it from the wineskin till they are drunk,
    so that he can gaze on their naked bodies.
You will be filled with shame instead of glory.
    Now it is your turn! Drink and be exposedᵖ!
The cup from the LORD's right hand is coming around to
        you,
    and disgrace will cover your glory.
The violence you have done to Lebanon will overwhelm
        you,
    and your destruction of animals will terrify you.
For you have shed man's blood;
    you have destroyed lands and cities and everyone in
        them.

GOD IS IN CONTROL.

Hab.
2:18-20

"Of what value is an idol, since a man has carved it?
    Or an image that teaches lies?
For he who makes it trusts in his own creation;
    he makes idols that cannot speak.
Woe to him who says to wood, 'Come to life!'
    Or to lifeless stone, 'Wake up!'
Can it give guidance?

⁰Or *creditors*   ᵖMasoretic Text; Dead Sea Scrolls, Aquila, Vulgate and Syriac (see also
Septuagint) *and stagger*

> It is covered with gold and silver;
>   there is no breath in it.
> But the LORD is in his holy temple;
>   let all the earth be silent before him."

Satisfied with God's answer, Habakkuk writes a psalm of praise in which he says he will wait patiently for the vengeance of God to punish Judah's wicked oppressors.

**Hab.
3:1-10**

HABAKKUK'S PRAYER.   A prayer of Habakkuk the prophet. On *shigionoth.*q

> LORD, I have heard of your fame;
>   I stand in awe of your deeds, O LORD.
> Renew them in our day,
>   in our time make them known;
>   in wrath remember mercy.
>
> God came from Teman,
>   the Holy One from Mount Paran.   *Selah*r
> His glory covered the heavens
>   and his praise filled the earth.
> His splendor was like the sunrise;
>   rays flashed from his hand,
>   where his power was hidden.
> Plague went before him;
>   pestilence followed his steps.
> He stood, and shook the earth;
>   he looked, and made the nations tremble.
> The ancient mountains crumbled
>   and the age-old hills collapsed.
>   His ways are eternal.
> I saw the tents of Cushan in distress,
>   the dwellings of Midian in anguish.
>
> Were you angry with the rivers, O LORD?
>   Was your wrath against the streams?
> Did you rage against the sea
>   when you rode with your horses
>   and your victorious chariots?
> You uncovered your bow,
>   you called for many arrows.   *Selah*
> You split the earth with rivers;
>   the mountains saw you and writhed.
> Torrents of water swept by;
>   the deep roared
>   and lifted its waves on high.

**Hab.
3:11-19**

> Sun and moon stood still in the heavens
>   at the glint of your flying arrows,
>   at the lightning of your flashing spear.
> In wrath you strode through the earth

---

q Probably a literary or musical term   r A word of uncertain meaning; possibly a musical term

and in anger you threshed the nations.
You came out to deliver your people,
    to save your anointed one.
You crushed the leader of the land of wickedness,
    you stripped him from head to foot.   *Selah*
With his own spear you pierced his head
    when his warriors stormed out to scatter us,
gloating as though about to devour
    the wretched who were in hiding.
You trampled the sea with your horses,
    churning the great waters.

I heard and my heart pounded,
    my lips quivered at the sound;
decay crept into my bones,
    and my legs trembled.
Yet I will wait patiently for the day of calamity
    to come on the nation invading us.
Though the fig tree does not bud
    and there are no grapes on the vines,
though the olive crop fails
    and the fields produce no food,
though there are no sheep in the pen
    and no cattle in the stalls,
yet I will rejoice in the LORD,
    I will be joyful in God my Savior.

The Sovereign LORD is my strength;
    he makes my feet like the feet of a deer,
    he enables me to go on the heights.

For the director of music. On my stringed instruments.

First Deportation from Judah

*A*s Judah cringes like a frightened child between two fighting bullies, the showdown finally takes place at the city of Carchemish on the Euphrates River in the Mesopotamian region east of Canaan. In one of the greatest battles of the ancient world, Nebuchadnezzar II, who has just succeeded his father, soundly defeats the Egyptians under Pharaoh Neco, just as Jeremiah has prophesied. So in 605 B.C. Judah is left in its most vulnerable position ever, and, as expected, Nebuchadnezzar seizes the opportunity to make Judah a tributary. As later historical records will show, many people of Judah, including a young man by the name of Daniel (who will become a great servant of God) are now taken captive to Babylon along with confiscated temple articles.

This group of captives is only the first of many who will follow. Later Babylonian incursions will result in even more people of Judah being carried away. In a somewhat enigmatic reference, the writer of the Chronicles says that King Jehoiakim is also bound and taken captive. Nebuchadnezzar evidently changes his mind, however, because it is clear that Jehoiakim continues as a puppet king in Jerusalem until his death, some eight years later.

Noteworthy in the historical record is a brief reference to the fact that Egypt is unable to help Judah in its time of crisis, just as the prophets had foretold.

2 Kgs. 24:1a (605 B.C.) JUDAH BABYLONIA'S CAPTIVE. During Jehoiakim's reign, Nebuchadnezzar king of Babylon invaded the land, and Jehoiakim became his vassal for three years.

2 Chron. 36:6 Babylon JEHOIAKIM BOUND. Nebuchadnezzar king of Babylon attacked him and bound him with bronze shackles to take him to Babylon.

2 Chron. 36:7 FIRST CAPTIVES TAKEN. Nebuchadnezzar also took to Babylon articles from the temple of the LORD and put them in his temple[s] there.

2 Kgs. 24:7 EGYPT CANNOT HELP. The king of Egypt did not march out from his own country again, because the king of Babylon had taken all his territory, from the Wadi of Egypt to the Euphrates River.

Jeremiah Tells Length of Captivity

With the first captives already taken away to Babylonia, God sends word to Jeremiah to tell the people exactly how long the period of captivity will last and to let them know that this first strike by Babylonia is by no means the last. Yet God reminds Judah that their oppressors will not escape their own punishment at the end of Judah's captivity. The cup of God's wrath will be poured out against all wicked nations.

Jer. 25:1-7 (604 B.C.) REMINDER OF REJECTION. The word came to Jeremiah concerning all the people of Judah in the fourth year of Jehoiakim son of Josiah king of Judah, which was the first year of Nebuchadnezzar king of Babylon. So Jeremiah the prophet said to all the people of Judah and to all those living in Jerusalem: For twenty-three years—from the thirteenth year of Josiah son of Amon king of Judah until this very day—the word of the LORD has come to me and I have spoken to you again and again, but you have not listened.

And though the LORD has sent all his servants the prophets to you again and again, you have not listened or paid any attention. They said, "Turn now, each of you, from your evil ways and your evil practices, and you can stay in the land the LORD gave to you and your fathers for ever and ever. Do not follow other gods to serve and worship them; do not provoke me to anger with what your hands have made. Then I will not harm you."

"But you did not listen to me," declares the LORD, "and you have provoked me with what your hands have made, and you have brought harm to yourselves."

Jer. 25:8-11 CAPTIVITY TO BE 70 YEARS. Therefore the LORD Almighty says this: "Because you have not listened to my words, I will summon all the peoples of the north and my servant Nebuchadnezzar king of Babylon," declares the LORD, "and I will bring them against this land and its inhabitants and against all the surrounding nations. I will completely destroy[t] them and make them an object of horror and scorn, and an everlasting

[s]Or *palace*   [t]The Hebrew term refers to the irrevocable giving over of things or persons to the LORD, often by totally destroying them.

ruin. I will banish from them the sounds of joy and gladness, the voices of bride and bridegroom, the sound of millstones and the light of the lamp. This whole country will become a desolate wasteland, and these nations will serve the king of Babylon seventy years.

BABYLONIA WILL FALL.   "But when the seventy years are fulfilled, I will punish the king of Babylon and his nation, the land of the Babylonians,[u] for their guilt," declares the LORD, "and will make it desolate forever. I will bring upon that land all the things I have spoken against it, all that are written in this book and prophesied by Jeremiah against all the nations. They themselves will be enslaved by many nations and great kings; I will repay them according to their deeds and the work of their hands."

Jer.
25:12-14

CUP OF GOD'S WRATH.   This is what the LORD, the God of Israel, said to me: "Take from my hand this cup filled with the wine of my wrath and make all the nations to whom I send you drink it. When they drink it, they will stagger and go mad because of the sword I will send among them."

Jer.
25:15-26

So I took the cup from the LORD's hand and made all the nations to whom he sent me drink it: Jerusalem and the towns of Judah, its kings and officials, to make them a ruin and an object of horror and scorn and cursing, as they are today; Pharaoh king of Egypt, his attendants, his officials and all his people, and all the foreign people there; all the kings of Uz; all the kings of the Philistines (those of Ashkelon, Gaza, Ekron, and the people left at Ashdod); Edom, Moab and Ammon; all the kings of Tyre and Sidon; the kings of the coastlands across the sea; Dedan, Tema, Buz and all who are in distant places[v]; all the kings of Arabia and all the kings of the foreign people who live in the desert; all the kings of Zimri, Elam and Media; and all the kings of the north, near and far, one after the other—all the kingdoms on the face of the earth. And after all of them, the king of Sheshach[w] will drink it too.

JUDGMENT AGAINST NATIONS.   "Then tell them, 'This is what the LORD Almighty, the God of Israel, says: Drink, get drunk and vomit, and fall to rise no more because of the sword I will send among you.' But if they refuse to take the cup from your hand and drink, tell them, 'This is what the LORD Almighty says: You must drink it! See, I am beginning to bring disaster on the city that bears my Name, and will you indeed go unpunished? You will not go unpunished, for I am calling down a sword upon all who live on the earth, declares the LORD Almighty.'

Jer.
25:27-32

"Now prophesy all these words against them and say to them:

" 'The LORD will roar from on high;
          he will thunder from his holy dwelling
          and roar mightily against his land.
He will shout like those who tread the grapes,
          shout against all who live on the earth.
The tumult will resound to the ends of the earth,
          for the LORD will bring charges against the nations;
he will bring judgment on all mankind
          and put the wicked to the sword,' "

declares the LORD.

[u]Or *Chaldeans*   [v]Or *who clip the hair by their foreheads*   [w]*Sheshach* is a cryptogram for Babylon.

This is what the LORD Almighty says:

"Look! Disaster is spreading
     from nation to nation;
a mighty storm is rising
     from the ends of the earth."

Jer. 25:33-38   SEVERITY OF THE JUDGMENT.   At that time those slain by the LORD will be everywhere—from one end of the earth to the other. They will not be mourned or gathered up or buried, but will be like refuse lying on the ground.

Weep and wail, you shepherds;
     roll in the dust, you leaders of the flock.
For your time to be slaughtered has come;
     you will fall and be shattered like fine pottery.
The shepherds will have nowhere to flee,
     the leaders of the flock no place to escape.
Hear the cry of the shepherds,
     the wailing of the leaders of the flock,
     for the LORD is destroying their pasture.
The peaceful meadows will be laid waste
     because of the fierce anger of the LORD.
Like a lion he will leave his lair,
     and their land will become desolate
because of the sword[x] of the oppressor
     and because of the LORD's fierce anger.

To illustrate further the cause of his wrath, God calls attention to the clan of Recabites, who for generations have obeyed their forefather's command to live an ascetic and nomadic life. The point is this: if there are those who will remain faithful for generations to a man's commands, then there ought to be more people obeying the commands of God, their very Creator.

Jer. 35:1-5   WINE SET BEFORE RECABITES.   This is the word that came to Jeremiah from the LORD during the reign of Jehoiakim son of Josiah king of Judah: "Go to the Recabite family and invite them to come to one of the side rooms of the house of the LORD and give them wine to drink."

So I went to get Jaazaniah son of Jeremiah, the son of Habazziniah, and his brothers and all his sons—the whole family of the Recabites. I brought them into the house of the LORD, into the room of the sons of Hanan son of Igdaliah the man of God. It was next to the room of the officials, which was over that of Maaseiah son of Shallum the doorkeeper. Then I set bowls full of wine and some cups before the men of the Recabite family and said to them, "Drink some wine."

Jer. 35:6-12   RECABITES TELL OF OBSERVANCE.   But they replied, "We do not drink wine, because our forefather Jonadab son of Recab gave us this command: 'Neither you nor your descendants must ever drink wine. Also you must never build houses, sow seed or plant vineyards; you must never have any of these things, but must always live in tents. Then you will live a long time in the land where you are nomads.' We have obeyed

[x]Some Hebrew manuscripts and Septuagint (see also Jer. 46:16 and 50:16); most Hebrew manuscripts *anger*

everything our forefather Jonadab son of Recab commanded us. Neither we nor our wives nor our sons and daughters have ever drunk wine or built houses to live in or had vineyards, fields or crops. We have lived in tents and have fully obeyed everything our forefather Jonadab command-ed us. But when Nebuchadnezzar king of Babylon invaded this land, we said, 'Come, we must go to Jerusalem to escape the Babylonian[y] and Aramean armies.' So we have remained in Jerusalem."

Then the word of the LORD came to Jeremiah, saying:

MESSAGE FOR JUDAH.   "This is what the LORD Almighty, the God of Israel, says: Go and tell the men of Judah and the people of Jerusalem, 'Will you not learn a lesson and obey my words?' declares the LORD. 'Jonadab son of Recab ordered his sons not to drink wine and this com-mand has been kept. To this day they do not drink wine, because they obey their forefather's command. But I have spoken to you again and again, yet you have not obeyed me. Again and again I sent all my servants the prophets to you. They said, "Each of you must turn from your wicked ways and reform your actions; do not follow other gods to serve them. Then you will live in the land I have given to you and your fathers." But you have not paid attention or listened to me. The descendants of Jonadab son of Recab have carried out the command their forefather gave them, but these people have not obeyed me.'
Jer. 35:13-17

"Therefore, this is what the LORD God Almighty, the God of Israel, says: 'Listen! I am going to bring on Judah and on everyone living in Jerusalem every disaster I pronounced against them. I spoke to them, but they did not listen; I called to them, but they did not answer.'"

RECABITES BLESSED.   Then Jeremiah said to the family of the Recabites, "This is what the LORD Almighty, the God of Israel, says: 'You have obeyed the command of your forefather Jonadab and have followed all his instruc-tions and have done everything he ordered.' Therefore, this is what the LORD Almighty, the God of Israel, says: 'Jonadab son of Recab will never fail to have a man to serve me.'"
Jer. 35:18,19

*Jehoiakim Burns Jeremiah's Scroll*_____

*A*fter 23 years of preaching, none of Jeremiah's many prophecies has yet been recorded. Therefore God now directs Jeremiah to record his words on a scroll, apparently not only to preserve them for ages to come, but also to enable the people of Judah to review all of his messages at one time. After Jeremiah dictates God's words to a scribe named Baruch, he directs Baruch to read the scroll aloud in the temple. When news of this final-ly reaches King Jehoiakim, he brazenly burns the scroll, piece by piece. Not surprisingly, this serves only to bring a special judgment against Jehoiakim and his descendants. The burned scroll is replaced by another which, together with a later supplement, has preserved the history of Jeremiah's ministry even to this day.

SCROLL TO BE WRITTEN.   In the fourth year of Jehoiakim son of Josiah king of Judah, this word came to Jeremiah from the LORD: "Take a scroll
Jer. 36:1-3 (604 B.C.)

[y]Or *Chaldean*

and write on it all the words I have spoken to you concerning Israel, Judah and all the other nations from the time I began speaking to you in the reign of Josiah till now. Perhaps when the people of Judah hear about every disaster I plan to inflict on them, each of them will turn from his wicked way; then I will forgive their wickedness and their sin."

Jer. 36:4   DICTATED TO BARUCH.   So Jeremiah called Baruch son of Neriah, and while Jeremiah dictated all the words the LORD had spoken to him, Baruch wrote them on the scroll.

The writing of the scroll has been no easy task. It has apparently been months in the making. Now that it is finally complete, Baruch expresses his weariness to Jeremiah, and Jeremiah responds with a message from God—a message which Jeremiah could just as profitably have directed to himself.

Jer. 45:1-5   BARUCH GIVEN PERSPECTIVE.   This is what Jeremiah the prophet told Baruch son of Neriah in the fourth year of Jehoiakim son of Josiah king of Judah, after Baruch had written on a scroll the words Jeremiah was then dictating: "This is what the LORD, the God of Israel, says to you, Baruch: You said, 'Woe to me! The LORD has added sorrow to my pain; I am worn out with groaning and find no rest.'"

⌊The LORD said,⌋ "Say this to him: 'This is what the LORD says: I will overthrow what I have built and uproot what I have planted, throughout the land. Should you then seek great things for yourself? Seek them not. For I will bring disaster on all people, declares the LORD, but wherever you go I will let you escape with your life.'"

If encouraged now by God's assurances, how discouraged Baruch will be when he learns that he must do it all over again!

Jer. 36:5-7   BARUCH TO READ SCROLL.   Then Jeremiah told Baruch, "I am restricted; I cannot go to the LORD's temple. So you go to the house of the LORD on a day of fasting and read to the people from the scroll the words of the LORD that you wrote as I dictated. Read them to all the people of Judah who come in from their towns. Perhaps they will bring their petition before the LORD, and each will turn from his wicked ways, for the anger and wrath pronounced against this people by the LORD are great."

Jer. 36:8-10   BARUCH READS SCROLL.   Baruch son of Neriah did everything Jere-
(603 B.C.)   miah the prophet told him to do; at the LORD's temple he read the words of the LORD from the scroll. In the ninth month of the fifth year of Jehoiakim son of Josiah king of Judah, a time of fasting before the LORD was proclaimed for all the people in Jerusalem and those who had come from the towns of Judah. From the room of Gemariah son of Shaphan the secretary, which was in the upper courtyard at the entrance of the New Gate of the temple, Baruch read to all the people at the LORD's temple the words of Jeremiah from the scroll.

Jer.   OFFICIALS HEAR OF SCROLL.   When Micaiah son of Gemariah, the son
36:11-15   of Shaphan, heard all the words of the LORD from the scroll, he went down to the secretary's room in the royal palace, where all the officials were sitting: Elishama the secretary, Delaiah son of Shemaiah, Elnathan son of Acbor, Gemariah son of Shaphan, Zedekiah son of Hananiah, and all the other officials. After Micaiah told them everything he had heard Baruch

read to the people from the scroll, all the officials sent Jehudi son of Nethaniah, the son of Shelemiah, the son of Cushi, to say to Baruch, "Bring the scroll from which you have read to the people and come." So Baruch son of Neriah went to them with the scroll in his hand. They said to him, "Sit down, please, and read it to us."

So Baruch read it to them.

OFFICIALS WARN BARUCH.   When they heard all these words, they looked at each other in fear and said to Baruch, "We must report all these words to the king." Then they asked Baruch, "Tell us, how did you come to write all this? Did Jeremiah dictate it?"

"Yes," Baruch replied, "he dictated all these words to me, and I wrote them in ink on the scroll."

Then the officials said to Baruch, "You and Jeremiah, go and hide. Don't let anyone know where you are."

Jer. 36:16-19

JEHOIAKIM BURNS SCROLL.   After they put the scroll in the room of Elishama the secretary, they went to the king in the courtyard and reported everything to him. The king sent Jehudi to get the scroll, and Jehudi brought it from the room of Elishama the secretary and read it to the king and all the officials standing beside him. It was the ninth month and the king was sitting in the winter apartment, with a fire burning in the firepot in front of him. Whenever Jehudi had read three or four columns of the scroll, the king cut them off with a scribe's knife and threw them into the firepot, until the entire scroll was burned in the fire. The king and all his attendants who heard all these words showed no fear, nor did they tear their clothes. Even though Elnathan, Delaiah and Gemariah urged the king not to burn the scroll, he would not listen to them. Instead, the king commanded Jerahmeel, a son of the king, Seraiah son of Azriel and Shelemiah son of Abdeel to arrest Baruch the scribe and Jeremiah the prophet. But the LORD had hidden them.

Jer. 36:20-26

SCROLL TO BE REWRITTEN.   After the king burned the scroll containing the words that Baruch had written at Jeremiah's dictation, the word of the LORD came to Jeremiah: "Take another scroll and write on it all the words that were on the first scroll, which Jehoiakim king of Judah burned up.

Jer. 36:27,28

JUDGMENT AGAINST JEHOIAKIM.   Also tell Jehoiakim king of Judah, 'This is what the LORD says: You burned that scroll and said, "Why did you write on it that the king of Babylon would certainly come and destroy this land and cut off both men and animals from it?" Therefore, this is what the LORD says about Jehoiakim king of Judah: He will have no one to sit on the throne of David; his body will be thrown out and exposed to the heat by day and the frost by night. I will punish him and his children and his attendants for their wickedness; I will bring on them and those living in Jerusalem and the people of Judah every disaster I pronounced against them, because they have not listened.'"

Jer. 36:29-31

SECOND SCROLL WRITTEN.   So Jeremiah took another scroll and gave it to the scribe Baruch son of Neriah, and as Jeremiah dictated, Baruch wrote on it all the words of the scroll that Jehoiakim king of Judah had burned in the fire. And many similar words were added to them.

Jer. 36:32 (603 B.C.)

Daniel the Faithful Captive

*W*hile Jeremiah is having his problems with Jehoiakim, several captives in Babylon are being singled out for duty in the king's service. The requirements for their selection are unusually demanding, and to be chosen would be considered an honor even under normal circumstances. Among those chosen is a young man by the name of Daniel, who distinguishes himself by refusing to eat food or drink wine from Nebuchadnezzar's royal table. For this act of faith Daniel and three others with him are exceptionally blessed by God. After three years of special training they enter the king's service and are found to excel in understanding whenever Nebuchadnezzar inquires of them.

Dan. 1:3-5 (Ca. 604 B.C.) Babylon	CAPTIVES FOR KING'S SERVICE. Then the king ordered Ashpenaz, chief of his court officials, to bring in some of the Israelites from the royal family and the nobility—young men without any physical defect, handsome, showing aptitude for every kind of learning, well informed, quick to understand, and qualified to serve in the king's palace. He was to teach them the language and literature of the Babylonians.[z] The king assigned them a daily amount of food and wine from the king's table. They were to be trained for three years, and after that they were to enter the king's service.
Dan. 1:6,7	NAMES CHANGED. Among these were some from Judah: Daniel, Hananiah, Mishael and Azariah. The chief official gave them new names: to Daniel, the name Belteshazzar; to Hananiah, Shadrach; to Mishael, Meshach; and to Azariah, Abednego.
Dan. 1:8-16	ROYAL FOOD REFUSED. But Daniel resolved not to defile himself with the royal food and wine, and he asked the chief official for permission not to defile himself this way. Now God had caused the official to show favor and sympathy to Daniel, but the official told Daniel, "I am afraid of my lord the king, who has assigned your[a] food and drink. Why should he see you looking worse than the other young men your age? The king would then have my head because of you." Daniel then said to the guard whom the chief official had appointed over Daniel, Hananiah, Mishael and Azariah, "Please test your servants for ten days: Give us nothing but vegetables to eat and water to drink. Then compare our appearance with that of the young men who eat the royal food, and treat your servants in accordance with what you see." So he agreed to this and tested them for ten days. At the end of the ten days they looked healthier and better nourished than any of the young men who ate the royal food. So the guard took away their choice food and the wine they were to drink and gave them vegetables instead.
Dan. 1:17	SPECIAL ABILITIES. To these four young men God gave knowledge and understanding of all kinds of literature and learning. And Daniel could understand visions and dreams of all kinds.
Dan. 1:18-20 (Ca. 601 B.C.)	FAVOR OF NEBUCHADNEZZAR. At the end of the time set by the king to bring them in, the chief official presented them to Nebuchadnezzar. The

[z]Or *Chaldeans*   [a]The Hebrew for *your* and *you* in this verse is plural.

king talked with them, and he found none equal to Daniel, Hananiah, Mishael and Azariah; so they entered the king's service. In every matter of wisdom and understanding about which the king questioned them, he found them ten times better than all the magicians and enchanters in his whole kingdom.

Nebuchadnezzar's Dream

*J*t is apparently not long after he has entered the king's service that Daniel is elevated to a high position in Nebuchadnezzar's palace as a result of his identifying and interpreting a dream. (The event is said to have taken place in the second year of Nebuchadnezzar's reign, but it obviously must have been in the second year of his sole reign after a time of shared rule with his aging father, Nabopolassar.) Nebuchadnezzar's wise men are willing to interpret the dream if only the king will reveal it to them. But Nebuchadnezzar is smarter than that, so he demands that the dream first be repeated to him. When Daniel learns of the dream, he seizes the occasion as an opportunity to glorify God, and volunteers to tell the king of the dream and its meaning.

The dream is of a statue made of different metals—gold, silver, bronze, and iron—and of a stone which breaks the statue. Daniel's interpretation through God's revelation is that there will be a succession of four kingdoms before the coming of an everlasting kingdom. Later history will reveal that in the symbolism of the statue reference is probably being made to Nebuchadnezzar's own Babylonian Empire, then to a Medo-Persian Empire, followed by a Grecian Empire, and finally by a Roman Empire (East and West) during which time the kingdom of the Messiah will have its beginning.

Here is the account of this marvelous foretelling of events to take place in centuries to come.

NEBUCHADNEZZAR HAS DREAM.   In the second year of his reign, Nebuchadnezzar had dreams; his mind was troubled and he could not sleep. So the king summoned the magicians, enchanters, sorcerers and astrologers[b] to tell him what he had dreamed. When they came in and stood before the king, he said to them, "I have had a dream that troubles me and I want to know what it means.[c]"

Dan. 2:1-3
(Ca. 601
B.C.)

WISE MEN CANNOT REVEAL.   Then the astrologers answered the king in Aramaic,[d] "O king, live forever! Tell your servants the dream, and we will interpret it."

The king replied to the astrologers, "This is what I have firmly decided: If you do not tell me what my dream was and interpret it, I will have you cut into pieces and your houses turned into piles of rubble. But if you tell me the dream and explain it, you will receive from me gifts and rewards and great honor. So tell me the dream and interpret it for me."

Once more they replied, "Let the king tell his servants the dream, and we will interpret it."

Then the king answered, "I am certain that you are trying to gain time, because you realize that this is what I have firmly decided: If you do not

Dan. 2:4-11

[b]Or Chaldeans   [c]Or was   [d]The text from here through chapter 7 is in Aramaic.

tell me the dream, there is just one penalty for you. You have conspired to tell me misleading and wicked things, hoping the situation will change. So then, tell me the dream, and I will know that you can interpret it for me."

The astrologers answered the king, "There is not a man on earth who can do what the king asks! No king, however great and mighty, has ever asked such a thing of any magician or enchanter or astrologer. What the king asks is too difficult. No one can reveal it to the king except the gods, and they do not live among men."

Dan
2:12-16

WISE MEN THREATENED.   This made the king so angry and furious that he ordered the execution of all the wise men of Babylon. So the decree was issued to put the wise men to death, and men were sent to look for Daniel and his friends to put them to death.

When Arioch, the commander of the king's guard, had gone out to put to death the wise men of Babylon, Daniel spoke to him with wisdom and tact. He asked the king's officer, "Why did the king issue such a harsh decree?" Arioch then explained the matter to Daniel. At this, Daniel went in to the king and asked for time, so that he might interpret the dream for him.

Dan.
2:17-23

DANIEL PRAYS ABOUT DREAM.   Then Daniel returned to his house and explained the matter to his friends Hananiah, Mishael and Azariah. He urged them to plead for mercy from the God of heaven concerning this mystery, so that he and his friends might not be executed with the rest of the wise men of Babylon. During the night the mystery was revealed to Daniel in a vision. Then Daniel praised the God of heaven and said:

"Praise be to the name of God for ever and ever;
        wisdom and power are his.
He changes times and seasons;
        he sets up kings and deposes them.
He gives wisdom to the wise
        and knowledge to the discerning.
He reveals deep and hidden things;
        he knows what lies in darkness,
        and light dwells with him.
I thank and praise you, O God of my fathers:
        You have given me wisdom and power,
you have made known to me what we asked of you,
        you have made known to us the dream of the king."

Dan.
2:24-30

GOD TO INTERPRET.   Then Daniel went to Arioch, whom the king had appointed to execute the wise men of Babylon, and said to him, "Do not execute the wise men of Babylon. Take me to the king, and I will interpret his dream for him."

Arioch took Daniel to the king at once and said, "I have found a man among the exiles from Judah who can tell the king what his dream means."

The king asked Daniel (also called Belteshazzar), "Are you able to tell me what I saw in my dream and interpret it?"

Daniel replied, "No wise man, enchanter, magician or diviner can explain to the king the mystery he has asked about, but there is a God in heaven who reveals mysteries. He has shown King Nebuchadnezzar what will happen in days to come. Your dream and the visions that passed through your mind as you lay on your bed are these:

"As you were lying there, O king, your mind turned to things to come, and the revealer of mysteries showed you what is going to happen. As for me, this mystery has been revealed to me, not because I have greater wisdom than other living men, but so that you, O king, may know the interpretation and that you may understand what went through your mind.

THE DREAM REVEALED.   "You looked, O king, and there before you stood a large statue—an enormous, dazzling statue, awesome in appearance. The head of the statue was made of pure gold, its chest and arms of silver, its belly and thighs of bronze, its legs of iron, its feet partly of iron and partly of baked clay. While you were watching, a rock was cut out, but not by human hands. It struck the statue on its feet of iron and clay and smashed them. Then the iron, the clay, the bronze, the silver and the gold were broken to pieces at the same time and became like chaff on a threshing floor in the summer. The wind swept them away without leaving a trace. But the rock that struck the statue became a huge mountain and filled the whole earth. **Dan. 2:31-35**

THE DREAM INTERPRETED.   "This was the dream, and now we will interpret it to the king. You, O king, are the king of kings. The God of heaven has given you dominion and power and might and glory; in your hands he has placed mankind and the beasts of the field and the birds of the air. Wherever they live, he has made you ruler over them all. You are that head of gold. **Dan. 2:36-45**

"After you, another kingdom will rise, inferior to yours. Next, a third kingdom, one of bronze, will rule over the whole earth. Finally, there will be a fourth kingdom, strong as iron—for iron breaks and smashes everything—and as iron breaks things to pieces, so it will crush and break all the others. Just as you saw that the feet and toes were partly of baked clay and partly of iron, so this will be a divided kingdom; yet it will have some of the strength of iron in it, even as you saw iron mixed with clay. As the toes were partly iron and partly clay, so this kingdom will be partly strong and partly brittle. And just as you saw the iron mixed with baked clay, so the people will be a mixture and will not remain united, any more than iron mixes with clay.

"In the time of those kings, the God of heaven will set up a kingdom that will never be destroyed, nor will it be left to another people. It will crush all those kingdoms and bring them to an end, but it will itself endure forever. This is the meaning of the vision of the rock cut out of a mountain, but not by human hands—a rock that broke the iron, the bronze, the clay, the silver and the gold to pieces.

"The great God has shown the king what will take place in the future. The dream is true and the interpretation is trustworthy."

HONORS PAID TO DANIEL.   Then King Nebuchadnezzar fell prostrate before Daniel and paid him honor and ordered that an offering and incense be presented to him. The king said to Daniel, "Surely your God is the God of gods and the Lord of kings and a revealer of mysteries, for you were able to reveal this mystery." **Dan. 2:46-49**

Then the king placed Daniel in a high position and lavished many gifts on him. He made him ruler over the entire province of Babylon and placed him in charge of all its wise men. Moreover, at Daniel's request the king appointed Shadrach, Meshach and Abednego administrators over the province of Babylon, while Daniel himself remained at the royal court.

Nebuchadnezzar is impressed, but he is still not a full believer in the true God. Nor is he going to relent in his oppression of Daniel's kinsmen. Furthermore, it does not appear that Daniel's high position in Babylon enables him to speak forcefully on behalf of his fellow countrymen, because the historical record now reflects further deportations from Judah to Babylonia.

Jehoiakim's Last Years

*J*ehoiakim must have a death wish. He has callously burned God's written Word, and now, with the strength of a mouse pursuing a lion, Jehoiakim has the audacity to rebel against Nebuchadnezzar. Fortunately for Judah, Nebuchadnezzar does not react with immediate military force, at least not directly. However, he may well be the motivating force behind the attacks against Judah by several of its neighbors over a four-year period of inconclusive war. Jehoiakim is destined to live his last days in wearying conflict.

2 Kgs. 24:1b (602 B.C.)	JEHOIAKIM ATTEMPTS REBELLION. But then he changed his mind and rebelled against Nebuchadnezzar.
2 Kgs. 24:2-4 (601-597 B.C.)	JUDAH'S NEIGHBORS HARASS. The LORD sent Babylonian,*e* Aramean, Moabite and Ammonite raiders against him. He sent them to destroy Judah, in accordance with the word of the LORD proclaimed by his servants the prophets. Surely these things happened to Judah according to the LORD's command, in order to remove them from his presence because of the sins of Manasseh and all he had done, including the shedding of innocent blood. For he had filled Jerusalem with innocent blood, and the LORD was not willing to forgive.

Perhaps it is during these years of conflict with old enemies of Judah that Jeremiah brings the following judgments against those enemies.

Jer. 48:1-13   JUDGMENT AGAINST MOAB.   Concerning Moab:

This is what the LORD Almighty, the God of Israel, says:

"Woe to Nebo, for it will be ruined.
        Kiriathaim will be disgraced and captured;
        the stronghold*f* will be disgraced and shattered.
Moab will be praised no more;
        in Heshbon*g* men will plot her downfall:
        'Come, let us put an end to that nation.'
You too, O Madmen,*h* will be silenced;
        the sword will pursue you.
Listen to the cries from Horonaim,

*e*Or *Chaldean*   *f*Or / *Misgab*   *g*The Hebrew for *Heshbon* sounds like the Hebrew for *plot.*   *h*The name of the Moabite town Madmen sounds like the Hebrew for *be silenced.*

cries of great havoc and destruction.
Moab will be broken;
 her little ones will cry out.[i]
They go up the way to Luhith,
 weeping bitterly as they go;
on the road down to Horonaim
 anguished cries over the destruction are heard.
Flee! Run for your lives;
 become like a bush[j] in the desert.
Since you trust in your deeds and riches,
 you too will be taken captive,
and Chemosh will go into exile,
 together with his priests and officials.
The destroyer will come against every town,
 and not a town will escape.
The valley will be ruined
 and the plateau destroyed,
 because the LORD has spoken.
Put salt on Moab,
 for she will be laid waste[k];
her towns will become desolate,
 with no one to live in them.

"A curse on him who is lax in doing the LORD's work!
 A curse on him who keeps his sword from bloodshed!

"Moab has been at rest from youth,
 like wine left on its dregs,
not poured from one jar to another—
 she has not gone into exile.
So she tastes as she did,
 and her aroma is unchanged.
But days are coming,"
 declares the LORD,
"when I will send men who pour from jars,
 and they will pour her out;
they will empty her jars
 and smash her jugs.
Then Moab will be ashamed of Chemosh,
 as the house of Israel was ashamed
 when they trusted in Bethel.

"How can you say, 'We are warriors,
 men valiant in battle'?
Moab will be destroyed and her towns invaded;
 her finest young men will go down in the slaughter,"
 declares the King, whose name is the LORD Almighty.
"The fall of Moab is at hand;
 her calamity will come quickly.
Mourn for her, all who live around her,

Jer.
48:14-28

[i]Hebrew; Septuagint / proclaim it to Zoar   [j]Or like Aroer   [k]Or Give wings to Moab, /
for she will fly away

all who know her fame;
say, 'How broken is the mighty scepter,
how broken the glorious staff!'

"Come down from your glory
and sit on the parched ground,
O inhabitants of the Daughter of Dibon,
for he who destroys Moab
will come up against you
and ruin your fortified cities.
Stand by the road and watch,
you who live in Aroer.
Ask the man fleeing and the woman escaping,
ask them, 'What has happened?'
Moab is disgraced, for she is shattered.
Wail and cry out!
Announce by the Arnon
that Moab is destroyed.
Judgment has come to the plateau—
to Holon, Jahzah and Mephaath,
to Dibon, Nebo and Beth Diblathaim,
to Kiriathaim, Beth Gamul and Beth Meon,
to Kerioth and Bozrah—
to all the towns of Moab, far and near.
Moab's horn[1] is cut off;
her arm is broken,"

declares the LORD.

"Make her drunk,
for she has defied the LORD.
Let Moab wallow in her vomit;
let her be an object of ridicule.
Was not Israel the object of your ridicule?
Was she caught among thieves,
that you shake your head in scorn
whenever you speak of her?
Abandon your towns and dwell among the rocks,
you who live in Moab.
Be like a dove that makes its nest
at the mouth of a cave.

Jer.
48:29-39

"We have heard of Moab's pride—
her overweening pride and conceit,
her pride and arrogance
and the haughtiness of her heart.
I know her insolence but it is futile,"

declares the LORD,

"and her boasts accomplish nothing.
Therefore I wail over Moab,
for all Moab I cry out,
I moan for the men of Kir Hareseth.

[1] Horn here symbolizes strength.

I weep for you, as Jazer weeps,
   O vines of Sibmah.
Your branches spread as far as the sea;
   they reached as far as the sea of Jazer.
The destroyer has fallen
   on your ripened fruit and grapes.
Joy and gladness are gone
   from the orchards and fields of Moab.
I have stopped the flow of wine from the presses;
   no one treads them with shouts of joy.
Although there are shouts,
   they are not shouts of joy.

"The sound of their cry rises
   from Heshbon to Elealeh and Jahaz,
from Zoar as far as Horonaim and Eglath Shelishiyah,
   for even the waters of Nimrim are dried up.
In Moab I will put an end
   to those who make offerings on the high places
   and burn incense to their gods,"
                             declares the LORD.
"So my heart laments for Moab like a flute;
   it laments like a flute for the men of Kir Hareseth.
   The wealth they acquired is gone.
Every head is shaved
   and every beard cut off;
every hand is slashed
   and every waist is covered with sackcloth.
On all the roofs in Moab
   and in the public squares
there is nothing but mourning,
   for I have broken Moab
   like a jar that no one wants,"
                             declares the LORD.
"How shattered she is! How they wail!
   How Moab turns her back in shame!
Moab has become an object of ridicule,
   an object of horror to all those around her."

This is what the LORD says:

                                Jer.
                                48:40-47

"Look! An eagle is swooping down,
   spreading its wings over Moab.
Kerioth^m will be captured
   and the strongholds taken.
In that day the hearts of Moab's warriors
   will be like the heart of a woman in labor.
Moab will be destroyed as a nation
   because she defied the LORD.
Terror and pit and snare await you,

^m Or The cities

O people of Moab,"

declares the LORD.

"Whoever flees from the terror
   will fall into a pit,
whoever climbs out of the pit
   will be caught in a snare;
for I will bring upon Moab
   the year of her punishment,"

declares the LORD.

"In the shadow of Heshbon
      the fugitives stand helpless,
for a fire has gone out from Heshbon,
      a blaze from the midst of Sihon;
it burns the foreheads of Moab,
      the skulls of the noisy boasters.
Woe to you, O Moab!
      The people of Chemosh are destroyed;
your sons are taken into exile
      and your daughters into captivity.

"Yet I will restore the fortunes of Moab
      in days to come,"

declares the LORD.

Here ends the judgment on Moab.

Jer. 49:1-6   AGAINST AMMON.   Concerning the Ammonites:

This is what the LORD says:

"Has Israel no sons?
      Has she no heirs?
Why then has Molech[n] taken possession of Gad?
      Why do his people live in its towns?
But the days are coming,"
      declares the LORD,
"when I will sound the battle cry
      against Rabbah of the Ammonites;
it will become a mound of ruins,
      and its surrounding villages will be set on fire.
Then Israel will drive out
      those who drove her out,"

says the LORD.

"Wail, O Heshbon, for Ai is destroyed!
      Cry out, O inhabitants of Rabbah!
Put on sackcloth and mourn;
      rush here and there inside the walls,
for Molech will go into exile,
      together with his priests and officials.
Why do you boast of your valleys,
      boast of your valleys so fruitful?
O unfaithful daughter,

[n]Or their king; Hebrew malcam; also in verse 3

> you trust in your riches and say,
> 'Who will attack me?'
> I will bring terror on you
> from all those around you,"
> > declares the Lord, the LORD Almighty.
> "Every one of you will be driven away,
> and no one will gather the fugitives.
> "Yet afterward, I will restore the fortunes of the Ammonites,"
> > declares the LORD.

AGAINST EDOM.   Concerning Edom:

Jer. 49:7-22

This is what the LORD Almighty says:

> "Is there no longer wisdom in Teman?
> Has counsel perished from the prudent?
> Has their wisdom decayed?
> Turn and flee, hide in deep caves,
> you who live in Dedan,
> for I will bring disaster on Esau
> at the time I punish him.
> If grape pickers came to you,
> would they not leave a few grapes?
> If thieves came during the night,
> would they not steal only as much as they wanted?
> But I will strip Esau bare;
> I will uncover his hiding places,
> so that he cannot conceal himself.
> His children, relatives and neighbors will perish,
> and he will be no more.
> Leave your orphans; I will protect their lives.
> Your widows too can trust in me."

This is what the LORD says: "If those who do not deserve to drink the cup must drink it, why should you go unpunished? You will not go unpunished, but must drink it. I swear by myself," declares the LORD, "that Bozrah will become a ruin and an object of horror, of reproach and of cursing; and all its towns will be in ruins forever."

> I have heard a message from the LORD:
> An envoy was sent to the nations to say,
> "Assemble yourselves to attack it!
> Rise up for battle!"

> "Now I will make you small among the nations,
> despised among men.
> The terror you inspire
> and the pride of your heart have deceived you,
> you who live in the clefts of the rocks,
> who occupy the heights of the hill.
> Though you build your nest as high as the eagle's,
> from there I will bring you down,"
> > declares the LORD.

"Edom will become an object of horror;
    all who pass by will be appalled and will scoff
    because of all its wounds.
As Sodom and Gomorrah were overthrown,
    along with their neighboring towns,"

                                                            says the LORD,

"so no one will live there;
    no man will dwell in it.

"Like a lion coming up from Jordan's thickets
    to a rich pastureland,
I will chase Edom from its land in an instant.
    Who is the chosen one I will appoint for this?
Who is like me and who can challenge me?
    And what shepherd can stand against me?"
Therefore, hear what the LORD has planned against Edom,
    what he has purposed against those who live in Teman:
The young of the flock will be dragged away;
    he will completely destroy their pasture because of them.
At the sound of their fall the earth will tremble;
    their cry will resound to the Red Sea.[o]
Look! An eagle will soar and swoop down,
    spreading its wings over Bozrah.
In that day the hearts of Edom's warriors
    will be like the heart of a woman in labor.

Jer.
49:23-27

AGAINST DAMASCUS.   Concerning Damascus:

"Hamath and Arpad are dismayed,
    for they have heard bad news.
They are disheartened,
    troubled like[p] the restless sea.
Damascus has become feeble,
    she has turned to flee
    and panic has gripped her;
anguish and pain have seized her,
    pain like that of a woman in labor.
Why has the city of renown not been abandoned,
    the town in which I delight?
Surely, her young men will fall in the streets;
    all her soldiers will be silenced in that day,"

                                                    declares the LORD Almighty.

"I will set fire to the walls of Damascus;
    it will consume the fortresses of Ben-Hadad."

Jer.
49:28-33

AGAINST KEDAR AND HAZOR.   Concerning Kedar and the kingdoms
of Hazor, which Nebuchadnezzar king of Babylon attacked:

This is what the LORD says:

"Arise, and attack Kedar
    and destroy the people of the East.
Their tents and their flocks will be taken;

[o]Hebrew *Yam Suph*; that is, Sea of Reeds   [p]Hebrew *on* or *by*

their shelters will be carried off
  with all their goods and camels.
Men will shout to them,
  'Terror on every side!'

"Flee quickly away!
  Stay in deep caves, you who live in Hazor,"
>   declares the LORD.
"Nebuchadnezzar king of Babylon has plotted against you;
  he has devised a plan against you.

"Arise and attack a nation at ease,
  which lives in confidence,"
>   declares the LORD,

"a nation that has neither gates nor bars;
  its people live alone.
Their camels will become plunder,
  and their large herds will be booty.
I will scatter to the winds those who are in distant places^q
  and will bring disaster on them from every side,"
>   declares the LORD.

"Hazor will become a haunt of jackals,
  a desolate place forever.
No one will live there;
  no man will dwell in it."

> But Jehoiakim will not live to see vengeance brought on his enemies.

JEHOIAKIM'S DEATH SEEN.   Therefore this is what the LORD says about   Jer.
Jehoiakim son of Josiah king of Judah: 22:18-23

"They will not mourn for him:
  'Alas, my brother! Alas, my sister!'
They will not mourn for him:
  'Alas, my master! Alas, his splendor!'
He will have the burial of a donkey—
  dragged away and thrown
  outside the gates of Jerusalem."

"Go up to Lebanon and cry out,
  let your voice be heard in Bashan,
cry out from Abarim,
  for all your allies are crushed.
I warned you when you felt secure,
  but you said, 'I will not listen!'
This has been your way from your youth;
  you have not obeyed me.
The wind will drive all your shepherds away,
  and your allies will go into exile.
Then you will be ashamed and disgraced
  because of all your wickedness.
You who live in 'Lebanon,'^r

---

^qOr *who clip the hair by their foreheads*   ^rThat is, the palace in Jerusalem (see 1 Kings 7:2)

> who are nestled in cedar buildings,
> how you will groan when pangs come upon you,
> pain like that of a woman in labor!

2 Kgs. 24:5,6a
2 Chron. 36:8a
(597 B.C.)

JEHOIAKIM'S DEATH.   As for the other events of Jehoiakim's reign, and all he did, are they not written in the book of the annals of the kings of Judah? Jehoiakim rested with his fathers.

The Great Deportation

*U*pon the death of his father, eighteen-year-old Jehoiachin ascends the throne of Judah, but he reigns for only three months. Nebuchadnezzar is not about to allow a second king of Judah to defy him, so he comes to lead the new king away as a captive. Although the historical record indicates that Jehoiachin's character is as evil as his father's, in all fairness it may simply be that during his brief reign nothing is done by his queen mother or advisors to alter the wicked course which Jehoiakim had taken. But God knows a man's heart long before his actions reveal it, and so it is altogether likely that, given enough time, Jehoiachin would have been just like his father. Therefore Jeremiah forewarns Jehoiachin and his mother of their pending fate.

Jehoiachin's fate is linked to the fate of thousands of God's people. There have been many deportations already, and more will follow, but this is to be by far the greatest deportation of them all. Significant among the royal and priestly captives is a man by the name of Ezekiel, who will soon be called by God to be a prophet among his fellow captives in Babylonia.

2 Kgs. 24:6b,8
2 Chron. 36:8b,9a
(597 B.C.)
Jerusalem

JEHOIACHIN CHILD-KING.   And Jehoiachin his son succeeded him as king.

Jehoiachin was eighteen years old when he became king, and he reigned in Jerusalem three months. His mother's name was Nehushta daughter of Elnathan; she was from Jerusalem.

2 Kgs. 24:9
2 Chron. 36:9b

JEHOIACHIN'S CHARACTER.   He did evil in the eyes of the LORD, just as his father had done.

Jer. 22:24-30

JEREMIAH'S PROPHECY.   "As surely as I live," declares the LORD, "even if you, Jehoiachin[s] son of Jehoiakim king of Judah, were a signet ring on my right hand, I would still pull you off. I will hand you over to those who seek your life, those you fear—to Nebuchadnezzar king of Babylon and to the Babylonians.[t] I will hurl you and the mother who gave you birth into another country, where neither of you was born, and there you both will die. You will never come back to the land you long to return to."

> Is this man Jehoiachin a despised, broken pot,
> an object no one wants?
> Why will he and his children be hurled out,
> cast into a land they do not know?
> O land, land, land,
> hear the word of the LORD!

[s]Hebrew *Coniah*, a variant of *Jehoiachin*   [t]Or *Chaldeans*

> This is what the LORD says:
> "Record this man as if childless,
>   a man who will not prosper in his lifetime,
>   for none of his offspring will prosper,
>   none will sit on the throne of David
>   or rule anymore in Judah."

JEHOIACHIN TAKEN CAPTIVE. ^{Kg}At that time the officers of Nebuchadnezzar king of Babylon advanced on Jerusalem and laid siege to it, and Nebuchadnezzar himself came up to the city while his officers were besieging it. Jehoiachin king of Judah, his mother, his attendants, his nobles and his officials all surrendered to him.

2 Kgs.
24:10-12
2 Chron.
36:10a
Dan 1:1
(597 B.C.)

In the eighth year of the reign of the king of Babylon, he took Jehoiachin prisoner. ^{Ch}In the spring, King Nebuchadnezzar sent for him and brought him to Babylon...

THE GREAT DEPORTATION. ^{Kg}As the LORD had declared, Nebuchadnezzar removed all the treasures from the temple of the LORD and from the royal palace, and took away all the gold articles that Solomon king of Israel had made for the temple of the LORD. ^{Dn}These he carried off to the temple of his god in Babylonia[u] and put in the treasure house of his god. ^{Kg}He carried into exile all Jerusalem: all the officers and fighting men, and all the craftsmen and artisans—a total of ten thousand. Only the poorest people of the land were left.

2 Kgs.
24:13-16
Dan. 1:2
(597 B.C.)

Nebuchadnezzar took Jehoiachin captive to Babylon. He also took from Jerusalem to Babylon the king's mother, his wives, his officials and the leading men of the land. The king of Babylon also deported to Babylon the entire force of seven thousand fighting men, strong and fit for war, and a thousand craftsmen and artisans.

Reign of Zedekiah

ith the great deportation under way and young King Jehoiachin being taken to Babylon, Nebuchadnezzar sets up Jehoiachin's uncle Mattaniah to be a puppet king. Mattaniah is the third son of former King Josiah. Nebuchadnezzar calls Mattaniah by the name of Zedekiah, and that is how he will be remembered throughout history. Zedekiah's character, like that of his people, is unrighteous. Zedekiah has the dubious distinction of being the king of Judah during its final destruction. The 11 years of his reign will come to a disastrous end with the fall of Jerusalem.

ZEDEKIAH A PUPPET KING. ^{Kg}He made Mattaniah, Jehoiachin's uncle, king in his place and changed his name to Zedekiah. ^{Jr}Zedekiah son of Josiah was made king of Judah by Nebuchadnezzar king of Babylon; he reigned in place of Jehoiachin[v] son of Jehoiakim. ^{Kg}Zedekiah was twenty-one years old when he became king, and he reigned in Jerusalem eleven years. His mother's name was Hamutal daughter of Jeremiah; she was from Libnah.

2 Kgs.
24:17,18
2 Chron.
36:10b,11
Jer. 37:1
Jer. 52:1
(597 B.C.)

ZEDEKIAH'S CHARACTER. ^{Kg}He did evil in the eyes of the LORD, just as Jehoiakim had done. ^{Ch}He became stiff-necked and hardened his heart

2 Kgs.
24:19,20a

[u]Hebrew *Shinar*   [v]Hebrew *Coniah*, a variant of *Jehoiachin*

2 Chron.
36:12,
13b-16
Jer. 37:2
Jer. 52:2,3a

and would not turn to the LORD, the God of Israel. Furthermore, all the leaders of the priests and the people became more and more unfaithful, following all the detestable practices of the nations and defiling the temple of the LORD, which he had consecrated in Jerusalem.

The LORD, the God of their fathers, sent word to them through his messengers again and again, because he had pity on his people and on his dwelling place. But they mocked God's messengers, despised his words and scoffed at his prophets until the wrath of the LORD was aroused against his people and there was no remedy. JrNeither he nor his attendants nor the people of the land paid any attention to the words the LORD had spoken through Jeremiah the prophet. KgIt was because of the LORD's anger that all this happened to Jerusalem and Judah, and in the end he thrust them from his presence.

Jeremiah's Prophecies Under Zedekiah

*J*eremiah's chief concern during the early part of Zedekiah's reign is the number of false prophets who are still saying that all is well, and that Babylonia will be broken instead of Judah. Perhaps because of the persecution he faces as a true prophet of God, Jeremiah unleashes a blistering attack against those who are masquerading as God's prophets, even among the captives in Babylonia. Jeremiah is forced to write to the people in exile and tell them to settle in for the duration, which will be 70 years.

Jer. 24:1-10 VISION OF THE FIGS. After Jehoiachinw son of Jehoiakim king of Judah and the officials, the craftsmen and the artisans of Judah were carried into exile from Jerusalem to Babylon by Nebuchadnezzar king of Babylon, the LORD showed me two baskets of figs placed in front of the temple of the LORD. One basket had very good figs, like those that ripen early; the other basket had very poor figs, so bad they could not be eaten.

Then the LORD asked me, "What do you see, Jeremiah?"

"Figs," I answered. "The good ones are very good, but the poor ones are so bad they cannot be eaten."

Then the word of the LORD came to me: "This is what the LORD, the God of Israel, says: 'Like these good figs, I regard as good the exiles from Judah, whom I sent away from this place to the land of the Babylonians.x My eyes will watch over them for their good, and I will bring them back to this land. I will build them up and not tear them down; I will plant them and not uproot them. I will give them a heart to know me, that I am the LORD. They will be my people, and I will be their God, for they will return to me with all their heart.

" 'But like the poor figs, which are so bad they cannot be eaten,' says the LORD, 'so will I deal with Zedekiah king of Judah, his officials and the survivors from Jerusalem, whether they remain in this land or live in Egypt. I will make them abhorrent and an offense to all the kingdoms of the earth, a reproach and a byword, an object of ridicule and cursing, wherever I banish them. I will send the sword, famine and plague against them until they are destroyed from the land I gave to them and their fathers.' "

wHebrew *Jeconiah*, a variant of *Jehoiachin*   xOr *Chaldeans*

Jer. 29:1-23

LETTER TO EXILES.   This is the text of the letter that the prophet Jeremiah sent from Jerusalem to the surviving elders among the exiles and to the priests, the prophets and all the other people Nebuchadnezzar had carried into exile from Jerusalem to Babylon. (This was after King Jehoiachin^y and the queen mother, the court officials and the leaders of Judah and Jerusalem, the craftsmen and the artisans had gone into exile from Jerusalem.) He entrusted the letter to Elasah son of Shaphan and to Gemariah son of Hilkiah, whom Zedekiah king of Judah sent to King Nebuchadnezzar in Babylon. It said:

This is what the LORD Almighty, the God of Israel, says to all those I carried into exile from Jerusalem to Babylon: "Build houses and settle down; plant gardens and eat what they produce. Marry and have sons and daughters; find wives for your sons and give your daughters in marriage, so that they too may have sons and daughters. Increase in number there; do not decrease. Also, seek the peace and prosperity of the city to which I have carried you into exile. Pray to the LORD for it, because if it prospers, you too will prosper." Yes, this is what the LORD Almighty, the God of Israel, says: "Do not let the prophets and diviners among you deceive you. Do not listen to the dreams you encourage them to have. They are prophesying lies to you in my name. I have not sent them," declares the LORD.

This is what the LORD says: "When seventy years are completed for Babylon, I will come to you and fulfill my gracious promise to bring you back to this place. For I know the plans I have for you," declares the LORD, "plans to prosper you and not to harm you, plans to give you hope and a future. Then you will call upon me and come and pray to me, and I will listen to you. You will seek me and find me when you seek me with all your heart. I will be found by you," declares the LORD, "and will bring you back from captivity.^z I will gather you from all the nations and places where I have banished you," declares the LORD, "and will bring you back to the place from which I carried you into exile."

You may say, "The LORD has raised up prophets for us in Babylon," but this is what the LORD says about the king who sits on David's throne and all the people who remain in this city, your countrymen who did not go with you into exile—yes, this is what the LORD Almighty says: "I will send the sword, famine and plague against them and I will make them like poor figs that are so bad they cannot be eaten. I will pursue them with the sword, famine and plague and will make them abhorrent to all the kingdoms of the earth and an object of cursing and horror, of scorn and reproach, among all the nations where I drive them. For they have not listened to my words," declares the LORD, "words that I sent to them again and again by my servants the prophets. And you exiles have not listened either," declares the LORD.

Therefore, hear the word of the LORD, all you exiles whom I have sent away from Jerusalem to Babylon. This is what the LORD Almighty, the God of Israel, says about Ahab son of Kolaiah and Zedekiah son of Maaseiah, who are prophesying lies to you in my name: "I will hand them over to Nebuchadnezzar king of Babylon, and he will put them to death before your very eyes. Because of them, all the exiles from Judah who are in Babylon will use this curse: 'The LORD treat you like Zedekiah and Ahab, whom the king of Babylon burned in the fire.' For they have done outrageous things in Israel; they have committed adultery with their neighbors' wives and in my name have spoken lies, which I did not tell them to do. I know it and am a witness to it," declares the LORD.

Jer.
29:24-32

MESSAGE FOR SHEMAIAH.   Tell Shemaiah the Nehelamite, "This is what the LORD Almighty, the God of Israel, says: You sent letters in your own name to all the people in Jerusalem, to Zephaniah son of Maaseiah the priest, and to all the other priests. You said to Zephaniah, 'The LORD has appointed you priest in place of Jehoiada to be in charge of the house of the LORD; you should put any madman who acts like a prophet into the stocks and neck-irons. So why have you not reprimanded Jeremiah from Anathoth, who poses as a prophet among you? He has sent this message to us in Babylon: It will be a long time. Therefore build houses and settle down; plant gardens and eat what they produce.' "

Zephaniah the priest, however, read the letter to Jeremiah the prophet. Then the word of the LORD came to Jeremiah: "Send this message to all the exiles: 'This is what the LORD says about Shemaiah the Nehelamite: Because Shemaiah has prophesied to you, even though I did not send him, and has led you to believe a lie, this is what the LORD says: I will surely punish Shemaiah the Nehelamite and his descendants. He will have no one left among this people, nor will he see the good things I will do for my people, declares the LORD, because he has preached rebellion against me.' "

Jer. 27:1-3
(593 B.C.)

JEREMIAH TO WEAR YOKE.   Early in the reign of Zedekiah[a] son of Josiah king of Judah, this word came to Jeremiah from the LORD: This is what the LORD said to me: "Make a yoke out of straps and crossbars and put it on your neck. Then send word to the kings of Edom, Moab, Ammon, Tyre and Sidon through the envoys who have come to Jerusalem to Zedekiah king of Judah.

Jer. 27:4-11

MEANING TO THE NATIONS.   Give them a message for their masters and say, 'This is what the LORD Almighty, the God of Israel, says: "Tell this to your masters: With my great power and outstretched arm I made the earth and its people and the animals that are on it, and I give it to anyone I please. Now I will hand all your countries over to my servant Nebuchadnezzar king of Babylon; I will make even the wild animals subject to him. All nations will serve him and his son and his grandson until the time for his land comes; then many nations and great kings will subjugate him.

" ' "If, however, any nation or kingdom will not serve Nebuchadnezzar king of Babylon or bow its neck under his yoke, I will punish that nation with the sword, famine and plague, declares the LORD, until I destroy it by his hand. So do not listen to your prophets, your diviners, your interpreters of dreams, your mediums or your sorcerers who tell you, 'You will not serve the king of Babylon.' They prophesy lies to you that will only serve to remove you far from your lands; I will banish you and you will perish. But if any nation will bow its neck under the yoke of the king of Babylon and serve him, I will let that nation remain in its own land to till it and to live there, declares the LORD." ' "

---

[a]A few Hebrew manuscripts and Syriac (see also Jer. 27:3, 12 and 28:1); most Hebrew manuscripts *Jehoiakim* (Most Septuagint manuscripts do not have this verse.)

MEANING TO JUDAH.   I gave the same message to Zedekiah king of Judah. I said, "Bow your neck under the yoke of the king of Babylon; serve him and his people, and you will live. Why will you and your people die by the sword, famine and plague with which the LORD has threatened any nation that will not serve the king of Babylon? Do not listen to the words of the prophets who say to you, 'You will not serve the king of Babylon,' for they are prophesying lies to you. 'I have not sent them,' declares the LORD. 'They are prophesying lies in my name. Therefore, I will banish you and you will perish, both you and the prophets who prophesy to you.'"

Jer. 27:12-15

FATE OF TEMPLE ARTICLES.   Then I said to the priests and all these people, "This is what the LORD says: Do not listen to the prophets who say, 'Very soon now the articles from the LORD's house will be brought back from Babylon.' They are prophesying lies to you. Do not listen to them. Serve the king of Babylon, and you will live. Why should this city become a ruin? If they are prophets and have the word of the LORD, let them plead with the LORD Almighty that the furnishings remaining in the house of the LORD and in the palace of the king of Judah and in Jerusalem not be taken to Babylon. For this is what the LORD Almighty says about the pillars, the Sea, the movable stands and the other furnishings that are left in this city, which Nebuchadnezzar king of Babylon did not take away when he carried Jehoiachin[b] son of Jehoiakim king of Judah into exile from Jerusalem to Babylon, along with all the nobles of Judah and Jerusalem—yes, this is what the LORD Almighty, the God of Israel, says about the things that are left in the house of the LORD and in the palace of the king of Judah and in Jerusalem: 'They will be taken to Babylon and there they will remain until the day I come for them,' declares the LORD. 'Then I will bring them back and restore them to this place.'"

Jer. 27:16-22

HANANIAH CONTRADICTS JEREMIAH.   In the fifth month of that same year, the fourth year, early in the reign of Zedekiah king of Judah, the prophet Hananiah son of Azzur, who was from Gibeon, said to me in the house of the LORD in the presence of the priests and all the people: "This is what the LORD Almighty, the God of Israel, says: 'I will break the yoke of the king of Babylon. Within two years I will bring back to this place all the articles of the LORD's house that Nebuchadnezzar king of Babylon removed from here and took to Babylon. I will also bring back to this place Jehoiachin[b] son of Jehoiakim king of Judah and all the other exiles from Judah who went to Babylon,' declares the LORD, 'for I will break the yoke of the king of Babylon.'"

Jer. 28:1-4 (593 B.C.)

JEREMIAH'S RESPONSE.   Then the prophet Jeremiah replied to the prophet Hananiah before the priests and all the people who were standing in the house of the LORD. He said, "Amen! May the LORD do so! May the LORD fulfill the words you have prophesied by bringing the articles of the LORD's house and all the exiles back to this place from Babylon. Nevertheless, listen to what I have to say in your hearing and in the hearing of all the people: From early times the prophets who preceded you and me have prophesied war, disaster and plague against many countries and great kingdoms. But the prophet who prophesies peace will be recognized as one truly sent by the LORD only if his prediction comes true."

Jer. 28:5-9

[b]Hebrew *Jeconiah*, a variant of *Jehoiachin*

Jer. 28:10,11

HANANIAH BREAKS YOKE.   Then the prophet Hananiah took the yoke off the neck of the prophet Jeremiah and broke it, and he said before all the people, "This is what the LORD says: 'In the same way will I break the yoke of Nebuchadnezzar king of Babylon off the neck of all the nations within two years.' " At this, the prophet Jeremiah went on his way.

Jer. 28:12-17

HANANIAH'S PUNISHMENT.   Shortly after the prophet Hananiah had broken the yoke off the neck of the prophet Jeremiah, the word of the LORD came to Jeremiah: "Go and tell Hananiah, 'This is what the LORD says: You have broken a wooden yoke, but in its place you will get a yoke of iron. This is what the LORD Almighty, the God of Israel, says: I will put an iron yoke on the necks of all these nations to make them serve Nebuchadnezzar king of Babylon, and they will serve him. I will even give him control over the wild animals.' "

Then the prophet Jeremiah said to Hananiah the prophet, "Listen, Hananiah! The LORD has not sent you, yet you have persuaded this nation to trust in lies. Therefore, this is what the LORD says: 'I am about to remove you from the face of the earth. This very year you are going to die, because you have preached rebellion against the LORD.' "

In the seventh month of that same year, Hananiah the prophet died.

Jer. 23:9-14

ATTACK AGAINST PROPHETS.   Concerning the prophets:

> My heart is broken within me;
>   all my bones tremble.
> I am like a drunken man,
>   like a man overcome by wine,
> because of the LORD
>   and his holy words.
> The land is full of adulterers;
>   because of the curse[c] the land lies parched[d]
>   and the pastures in the desert are withered.
> The ˌprophetsˌ follow an evil course
>   and use their power unjustly.
>
> "Both prophet and priest are godless;
>   even in my temple I find their wickedness,"
>   declares the LORD.
>
> "Therefore their path will become slippery;
>   they will be banished to darkness
>   and there they will fall.
> I will bring disaster on them
>   in the year they are punished,"
>   declares the LORD.
>
> "Among the prophets of Samaria
>   I saw this repulsive thing:
> They prophesied by Baal
>   and led my people Israel astray.
> And among the prophets of Jerusalem
>   I have seen something horrible:
> They commit adultery and live a lie.
> They strengthen the hands of evildoers,

---

[c]Or *because of these things*   [d]Or *land mourns*

so that no one turns from his wickedness.
They are all like Sodom to me;
    the people of Jerusalem are like Gomorrah."

Therefore, this is what the LORD Almighty says concerning the prophets: Jer.
23:15-24

"I will make them eat bitter food
    and drink poisoned water,
because from the prophets of Jerusalem
    ungodliness has spread throughout the land."

This is what the LORD Almighty says:

"Do not listen to what the prophets are prophesying to you;
    they fill you with false hopes.
They speak visions from their own minds,
    not from the mouth of the LORD.
They keep saying to those who despise me,
    'The LORD says: You will have peace.'
And to all who follow the stubbornness of their hearts
    they say, 'No harm will come to you.'
But which of them has stood in the council of the LORD
    to see or to hear his word?
    Who has listened and heard his word?
See, the storm of the LORD
    will burst out in wrath,
a whirlwind swirling down
    on the heads of the wicked.
The anger of the LORD will not turn back
    until he fully accomplishes
    the purposes of his heart.
In days to come
    you will understand it clearly.
I did not send these prophets,
    yet they have run with their message;
I did not speak to them,
    yet they have prophesied.
But if they had stood in my council,
    they would have proclaimed my words to my people
and would have turned them from their evil ways
    and from their evil deeds.

"Am I only a God nearby,"

declares the LORD,

"and not a God far away?
Can anyone hide in secret places
    so that I cannot see him?"

declares the LORD.

"Do not I fill heaven and earth?"

declares the LORD.

DREAMS ARE DELUSIONS.   "I have heard what the prophets say who   Jer.
23:25-32
prophesy lies in my name. They say, 'I had a dream! I had a dream!' How
long will this continue in the hearts of these lying prophets, who prophesy

the delusions of their own minds? They think the dreams they tell one another will make my people forget my name, just as their fathers forgot my name through Baal worship. Let the prophet who has a dream tell his dream, but let the one who has my word speak it faithfully. For what has straw to do with grain?" declares the LORD. "Is not my word like fire," declares the LORD, "and like a hammer that breaks a rock in pieces?

"Therefore," declares the LORD, "I am against the prophets who steal from one another words supposedly from me. Yes," declares the LORD, "I am against the prophets who wag their own tongues and yet declare, 'The LORD declares.' Indeed, I am against those who prophesy false dreams," declares the LORD. "They tell them and lead my people astray with their reckless lies, yet I did not send or appoint them. They do not benefit these people in the least," declares the LORD.

Jer. 23:33-40

FALSE ORACLES. "When these people, or a prophet or a priest, ask you, 'What is the oracle[e] of the LORD?' say to them, 'What oracle?[f] I will forsake you, declares the LORD.' If a prophet or a priest or anyone else claims, 'This is the oracle of the LORD,' I will punish that man and his household. This is what each of you keeps on saying to his friend or relative: 'What is the LORD's answer?' or 'What has the LORD spoken?' But you must not mention 'the oracle of the LORD' again, because every man's own word becomes his oracle and so you distort the words of the living God, the LORD Almighty, our God. This is what you keep saying to a prophet: 'What is the LORD's answer to you?' or 'What has the LORD spoken?' Although you claim, 'This is the oracle of the LORD,' this is what the LORD says: You used the words, 'This is the oracle of the LORD,' even though I told you that you must not claim, 'This is the oracle of the LORD.' Therefore, I will surely forget you and cast you out of my presence along with the city I gave to you and your fathers. I will bring upon you everlasting disgrace—everlasting shame that will not be forgotten."

If God and his servant Jeremiah are outraged against false prophets, their fierce chastisement is only a warm-up for the judgment that Jeremiah will bring against Babylonia. Prophets down through the years have brought many judgments against Babylonia, but none is more specific than Jeremiah's.

With Babylonia now a real threat, and not just the predicted enemy of earlier prophecies, the time is ripe to reassure Judah of the ultimate fate of its oppressor. Of all the people who need this assurance, it is the exiles in Babylonia who need it the most. Therefore this judgment against Babylon is given by Jeremiah to a staff officer named Seraiah, who is being sent to Babylon on behalf of King Zedekiah.

Jer. 51:59 (593 B.C.)

MESSAGE GIVEN TO SERAIAH. This is the message Jeremiah gave to the staff officer Seraiah son of Neriah, the son of Mahseiah, when he went to Babylon with Zedekiah king of Judah in the fourth year of his reign.

Jer. 50:1-3

JUDGMENT AGAINST BABYLON. This is the word the LORD spoke through Jeremiah the prophet concerning Babylon and the land of the Babylonians[g]:

[e]Or *burden* (see Septuagint and Vulgate)   [f]Hebrew; Septuagint and Vulgate *'You are the burden.* (The Hebrew for *oracle* and *burden* is the same.)   [g]Or *Chaldeans*

"Announce and proclaim among the nations,
    lift up a banner and proclaim it;
    keep nothing back, but say,
'Babylon will be captured;
    Bel will be put to shame,
    Marduk filled with terror.
Her images will be put to shame
    and her idols filled with terror.'
A nation from the north will attack her
    and lay waste her land.
No one will live in it;
    both men and animals will flee away.

JUDAH'S EXILE WILL END.   Jer. 50:4-10

"In those days, at that time,"
    declares the LORD,
"the people of Israel and the people of Judah together
    will go in tears to seek the LORD their God.
They will ask the way to Zion
    and turn their faces toward it.
They will come and bind themselves to the LORD
    in an everlasting covenant
    that will not be forgotten.

"My people have been lost sheep;
    their shepherds have led them astray
    and caused them to roam on the mountains.
They wandered over mountain and hill
    and forgot their own resting place.
Whoever found them devoured them;
    their enemies said, 'We are not guilty,
for they sinned against the LORD, their true pasture,
    the LORD, the hope of their fathers.'

"Flee out of Babylon;
    leave the land of the Babylonians,
    and be like the goats that lead the flock.
For I will stir up and bring against Babylon
    an alliance of great nations from the land of the north.
They will take up their positions against her,
    and from the north she will be captured.
Their arrows will be like skilled warriors
    who do not return empty-handed.
So Babylonia[h] will be plundered;
    all who plunder her will have their fill,"
                                        declares the LORD.

BABYLON TO BE DISGRACED.   Jer.
                                                              50:11-13

"Because you rejoice and are glad,
    you who pillage my inheritance,
because you frolic like a heifer threshing grain

[h] Or Chaldea

> and neigh like stallions,
> your mother will be greatly ashamed;
>> she who gave you birth will be disgraced.
> She will be the least of the nations—
>> a wilderness, a dry land, a desert.
> Because of the LORD's anger she will not be inhabited
>> but will be completely desolate.
> All who pass Babylon will be horrified and scoff
>> because of all her wounds.

Jer.
50:14-16

BABYLON'S ENEMIES ENCOURAGED.

> "Take up your positions around Babylon,
>> all you who draw the bow.
> Shoot at her! Spare no arrows,
>> for she has sinned against the LORD.
> Shout against her on every side!
>> She surrenders, her towers fall,
>> her walls are torn down.
> Since this is the vengeance of the LORD,
>> take vengeance on her;
>> do to her as she has done to others.
> Cut off from Babylon the sower,
>> and the reaper with his sickle at harvest.
> Because of the sword of the oppressor
>> let everyone return to his own people,
>> let everyone flee to his own land.

Jer.
50:17,18

NEBUCHADNEZZAR TO BE PUNISHED.

> "Israel is a scattered flock
>> that lions have chased away.
> The first to devour him
>> was the king of Assyria;
> the last to crush his bones
>> was Nebuchadnezzar king of Babylon."

Therefore this is what the LORD Almighty, the God of Israel, says:

> "I will punish the king of Babylon and his land
>> as I punished the king of Assyria.

Jer.
50:19,20

ISRAEL AND JUDAH FORGIVEN.

> But I will bring Israel back to his own pasture
>> and he will graze on Carmel and Bashan;
> his appetite will be satisfied
>> on the hills of Ephraim and Gilead.
> In those days, at that time,"
>> declares the LORD,
> "search will be made for Israel's guilt,
>> but there will be none,
> and for the sins of Judah,
>> but none will be found,
>> for I will forgive the remnant I spare.

ENEMIES CALLED TO WAR.

"Attack the land of Merathaim
and those who live in Pekod.
Pursue, kill and completely destroy[i] them,"

declares the LORD.

"Do everything I have commanded you.
The noise of battle is in the land,
the noise of great destruction!
How broken and shattered
is the hammer of the whole earth!
How desolate is Babylon
among the nations!
I set a trap for you, O Babylon,
and you were caught before you knew it;
you were found and captured
because you opposed the LORD.
The LORD has opened his arsenal
and brought out the weapons of his wrath,
for the Sovereign LORD Almighty has work to do
in the land of the Babylonians.
Come against her from afar.
Break open her granaries;
pile her up like heaps of grain.
Completely destroy her
and leave her no remnant.
Kill all her young bulls;
let them go down to the slaughter!
Woe to them! For their day has come,
the time for them to be punished.
Listen to the fugitives and refugees from Babylon
declaring in Zion
how the LORD our God has taken vengeance,
vengeance for his temple.

"Summon archers against Babylon,
all those who draw the bow.
Encamp all around her;
let no one escape.
Repay her for her deeds;
do to her as she has done.
For she has defied the LORD,
the Holy One of Israel.
Therefore, her young men will fall in the streets;
all her soldiers will be silenced in that day,"

declares the LORD.

ARROGANCE CAUSES DEFEAT.

"See, I am against you, O arrogant one,"
declares the Lord, the LORD Almighty,

---

[i]The Hebrew term refers to the irrevocable giving over of things or persons to the LORD,
often by totally destroying them.

"for your day has come,
the time for you to be punished.
The arrogant one will stumble and fall
and no one will help her up;
I will kindle a fire in her towns
that will consume all who are around her."

Jer.
50:33,34

ISRAEL'S REDEEMER STRONG.   This is what the LORD Almighty says:

"The people of Israel are oppressed,
and the people of Judah as well.
All their captors hold them fast,
refusing to let them go.
Yet their Redeemer is strong;
the LORD Almighty is his name.
He will vigorously defend their cause
so that he may bring rest to their land,
but unrest to those who live in Babylon.

Jer.
50:35-40

BABYLON'S COMING DESOLATION.

"A sword against the Babylonians!"
declares the LORD—
"against those who live in Babylon
and against her officials and wise men!
A sword against her false prophets!
They will become fools.
A sword against her warriors!
They will be filled with terror.
A sword against her horses and chariots
and all the foreigners in her ranks!
They will become women.
A sword against her treasures!
They will be plundered.
A drought on[j] her waters!
They will dry up.
For it is a land of idols,
idols that will go mad with terror.

"So desert creatures and hyenas will live there,
and there the owl will dwell.
It will never again be inhabited
or lived in from generation to generation.
As God overthrew Sodom and Gomorrah
along with their neighboring towns,"

declares the LORD,

"so no one will live there;
no man will dwell in it.

Jer.
50:41-46

ENEMIES FROM THE NORTH.

"Look! An army is coming from the north;
a great nation and many kings

jOr *A sword against*

are being stirred up from the ends of the earth.
They are armed with bows and spears;
    they are cruel and without mercy.
They sound like the roaring sea
    as they ride on their horses;
they come like men in battle formation
    to attack you, O Daughter of Babylon.
The king of Babylon has heard reports about them,
    and his hands hang limp.
Anguish has gripped him,
    pain like that of a woman in labor.
Like a lion coming up from Jordan's thickets
    to a rich pastureland,
I will chase Babylon from its land in an instant.
    Who is the chosen one I will appoint for this?
Who is like me and who can challenge me?
    And what shepherd can stand against me?"
Therefore, hear what the LORD has planned against
        Babylon,
    what he has purposed against the land of the
        Babylonians:
The young of the flock will be dragged away;
    he will completely destroy their pasture because of them.
At the sound of Babylon's capture the earth will tremble;
    its cry will resound among the nations.

ISRAEL NOT FORSAKEN.   This is what the LORD says: Jer. 51:1-5

"See, I will stir up the spirit of a destroyer
    against Babylon and the people of Leb Kamai.[k]
I will send foreigners to Babylon
    to winnow her and to devastate her land;
they will oppose her on every side
    in the day of her disaster.
Let not the archer string his bow,
    nor let him put on his armor.
Do not spare her young men;
    completely destroy[l] her army.
They will fall down slain in Babylon,[m]
    fatally wounded in her streets.
For Israel and Judah have not been forsaken
    by their God, the LORD Almighty,
though their land[n] is full of guilt
    before the Holy One of Israel.

JOY OF CAPTIVES' RELEASE.   Jer. 51:6-10

"Flee from Babylon!
    Run for your lives!
    Do not be destroyed because of her sins.

---

[k]Leb Kamai is a cryptogram for Chaldea, that is, Babylonia.   [l]The Hebrew term refers
to the irrevocable giving over of things or persons to the LORD, often by totally
destroying them.   [m]Or Chaldea   [n]Or / and the land of the Babylonians

It is time for the Lord's vengeance;
    he will pay her what she deserves.
Babylon was a gold cup in the Lord's hand;
    she made the whole earth drunk.
The nations drank her wine;
    therefore they have now gone mad.
Babylon will suddenly fall and be broken.
    Wail over her!
Get balm for her pain;
    perhaps she can be healed.

" 'We would have healed Babylon,
        but she cannot be healed;
    let us leave her and each go to his own land,
        for her judgment reaches to the skies,
        it rises as high as the clouds.'

" 'The Lord has vindicated us;
        come, let us tell in Zion
        what the Lord our God has done.'

Jer.
51:11-14

MEDES WILL SUBDUE BABYLON.

"Sharpen the arrows,
        take up the shields!
The Lord has stirred up the kings of the Medes,
        because his purpose is to destroy Babylon.
The Lord will take vengeance,
        vengeance for his temple.
Lift up a banner against the walls of Babylon!
        Reinforce the guard,
station the watchmen,
        prepare an ambush!
The Lord will carry out his purpose,
        his decree against the people of Babylon.
You who live by many waters
        and are rich in treasures,
your end has come,
        the time for you to be cut off.
The Lord Almighty has sworn by himself:
        I will surely fill you with men, as with a swarm of
            locusts,
        and they will shout in triumph over you.

Jer.
51:15,16

GOD'S CREATIVE POWER.

"He made the earth by his power;
        he founded the world by his wisdom
        and stretched out the heavens by his understanding.
When he thunders, the waters in the heavens roar;
        he makes clouds rise from the ends of the earth.
He sends lightning with the rain
        and brings out the wind from his storehouses.

IDOLS ARE POWERLESS.

Jer.
51:17-19

> "Every man is senseless and without knowledge;
>   every goldsmith is shamed by his idols.
> His images are a fraud;
>   they have no breath in them.
> They are worthless, the objects of mockery;
>   when their judgment comes, they will perish.
> He who is the Portion of Jacob is not like these,
>   for he is the Maker of all things,
> including the tribe of his inheritance—
>   the LORD Almighty is his name.

ISRAEL GOD'S INSTRUMENT.

Jer.
51:20-23

> "You are my war club,
>   my weapon for battle—
> with you I shatter nations,
>   with you I destroy kingdoms,
> with you I shatter horse and rider,
>   with you I shatter chariot and driver,
> with you I shatter man and woman,
>   with you I shatter old man and youth,
>   with you I shatter young man and maiden,
> with you I shatter shepherd and flock,
>   with you I shatter farmer and oxen,
>   with you I shatter governors and officials.

COMPLETENESS OF DESTRUCTION.   "Before your eyes I will repay

Jer.
51:24-26

Babylon and all who live in Babylonia° for all the wrong they have done
in Zion," declares the LORD.

> "I am against you, O destroying mountain,
>   you who destroy the whole earth,"
>
>   declares the LORD.
> "I will stretch out my hand against you,
>   roll you off the cliffs,
>   and make you a burned-out mountain.
> No rock will be taken from you for a cornerstone,
>   nor any stone for a foundation,
>   for you will be desolate forever,"
>
>   declares the LORD.

STRENGTH OF THE MEDES.

Jer.
51:27-33

> "Lift up a banner in the land!
>   Blow the trumpet among the nations!
> Prepare the nations for battle against her;
>   summon against her these kingdoms:
>   Ararat, Minni and Ashkenaz.
> Appoint a commander against her;
>   send up horses like a swarm of locusts.
> Prepare the nations for battle against her—

°Or *Chaldea*; also in verse 35

the kings of the Medes,
their governors and all their officials,
    and all the countries they rule.
The land trembles and writhes,
    for the LORD's purposes against Babylon stand—
to lay waste the land of Babylon
    so that no one will live there.
Babylon's warriors have stopped fighting;
    they remain in their strongholds.
Their strength is exhausted;
    they have become like women.
Her dwellings are set on fire;
    the bars of her gates are broken.
One courier follows another
    and messenger follows messenger
to announce to the king of Babylon
    that his entire city is captured,
the river crossings seized,
    the marshes set on fire,
    and the soldiers terrified."

This is what the LORD Almighty, the God of Israel, says:

"The Daughter of Babylon is like a threshing floor
    at the time it is trampled;
    the time to harvest her will soon come."

Jer.
51:34,35

VENGEANCE ON NEBUCHADNEZZAR.

"Nebuchadnezzar king of Babylon has devoured us,
    he has thrown us into confusion,
    he has made us an empty jar.
Like a serpent he has swallowed us
    and filled his stomach with our delicacies,
    and then has spewed us out.
May the violence done to our flesh*p* be upon Babylon,"
    say the inhabitants of Zion.
"May our blood be on those who live in Babylonia,"
    says Jerusalem.

Jer.
51:36-44

BABYLON'S GREAT FALL.   Therefore, this is what the LORD says:

"See, I will defend your cause
    and avenge you;
I will dry up her sea
    and make her springs dry.
Babylon will be a heap of ruins,
    a haunt of jackals,
an object of horror and scorn,
    a place where no one lives.
Her people all roar like young lions,
    they growl like lion cubs.
But while they are aroused,

*p*Or *done to us and to our children*

I will set out a feast for them
and make them drunk,
so that they shout with laughter—
then sleep forever and not awake,"

declares the LORD.

"I will bring them down
like lambs to the slaughter,
like rams and goats.

"How Sheshach[q] will be captured,
the boast of the whole earth seized!
What a horror Babylon will be
among the nations!
The sea will rise over Babylon;
its roaring waves will cover her.
Her towns will be desolate,
a dry and desert land,
a land where no one lives,
through which no man travels.
I will punish Bel in Babylon
and make him spew out what he has swallowed.
The nations will no longer stream to him.
And the wall of Babylon will fall.

PREPARE FOR RETURN.   Jer.
                                                                51:45-50

"Come out of her, my people!
Run for your lives!
Run from the fierce anger of the LORD.
Do not lose heart or be afraid
when rumors are heard in the land;
one rumor comes this year, another the next,
rumors of violence in the land
and of ruler against ruler.
For the time will surely come
when I will punish the idols of Babylon;
her whole land will be disgraced
and her slain will all lie fallen within her.
Then heaven and earth and all that is in them
will shout for joy over Babylon,
for out of the north
destroyers will attack her,"

declares the LORD.

"Babylon must fall because of Israel's slain,
just as the slain in all the earth
have fallen because of Babylon.
You who have escaped the sword,
leave and do not linger!
Remember the LORD in a distant land,
and think on Jerusalem."

qSheshach is a cryptogram for Babylon.

Jer.
51:51-58

GOD'S RETRIBUTION.

"We are disgraced,
    for we have been insulted
    and shame covers our faces,
because foreigners have entered
    the holy places of the LORD's house."

"But days are coming," declares the LORD,
    "when I will punish her idols,
and throughout her land
    the wounded will groan.
Even if Babylon reaches the sky
    and fortifies her lofty stronghold,
I will send destroyers against her,"

                                        declares the LORD.

"The sound of a cry comes from Babylon,
    the sound of great destruction
    from the land of the Babylonians.[r]
The LORD will destroy Babylon;
    he will silence her noisy din.
Waves ⌊of enemies⌋ will rage like great waters;
    the roar of their voices will resound.
A destroyer will come against Babylon;
    her warriors will be captured,
    and their bows will be broken.
For the LORD is a God of retribution;
    he will repay in full.
I will make her officials and wise men drunk,
    her governors, officers and warriors as well;
they will sleep forever and not awake,"
    declares the King, whose name is the LORD Almighty.

This is what the LORD Almighty says:

"Babylon's thick wall will be leveled
    and her high gates set on fire;
the peoples exhaust themselves for nothing,
    the nations' labor is only fuel for the flames."

Jer.
51:60-64a

SERAIAH'S INSTRUCTIONS.   Jeremiah had written on a scroll about all
the disasters that would come upon Babylon—all that had been recorded
concerning Babylon. He said to Seraiah, "When you get to Babylon, see
that you read all these words aloud. Then say, 'O LORD, you have said you
will destroy this place, so that neither man nor animal will live in it; it will
be desolate forever.' When you finish reading this scroll, tie a stone to it
and throw it into the Euphrates. Then say, 'So will Babylon sink to rise no
more because of the disaster I will bring upon her. And her people will
fall.'"

Jeremiah also brings a brief judgment against Elam, a province in the
south of modern Iran, on the eastern edge of Babylonia. Although Elam and

[r] Or Chaldeans

Babylonia have been bitter enemies over the centuries, it is probable that Elam is at this time a part of Nebuchadnezzar's empire and an ally against Judah.

JUDGMENT AGAINST ELAM.   This is the word of the LORD that came to Jeremiah the prophet concerning Elam, early in the reign of Zedekiah king of Judah:

Jer. 49:34-39

This is what the LORD Almighty says:

"See, I will break the bow of Elam,
    the mainstay of their might.
I will bring against Elam the four winds
    from the four quarters of the heavens;
I will scatter them to the four winds,
    and there will not be a nation
    where Elam's exiles do not go.
I will shatter Elam before their foes,
    before those who seek their lives;
I will bring disaster upon them,
    even my fierce anger,"

declares the LORD.

"I will pursue them with the sword
    until I have made an end of them.
I will set my throne in Elam
    and destroy her king and officials,"

declares the LORD.

"Yet I will restore the fortunes of Elam
    in days to come,"

declares the LORD.

Is it possible that Zedekiah has a remnant of moral consciousness somewhere amid his callous unrighteousness? The following account seems to suggest that he does, at least for a time. For whatever reasons—perhaps sincere, perhaps only practical, perhaps even political—Zedekiah orders his people to free all their Hebrew slaves. The law given to Moses sets strict limitations on when fellow Hebrews can be enslaved, and requires their release at the end of seven years. Zedekiah's order is obeyed at first, but, when the people renege, Jeremiah rebukes their sin.

HEBREW SLAVES RETAKEN.   The word came to Jeremiah from the LORD after King Zedekiah had made a covenant with all the people in Jerusalem to proclaim freedom for the slaves. Everyone was to free his Hebrew slaves, both male and female; no one was to hold a fellow Jew in bondage. So all the officials and people who entered into this covenant agreed that they would free their male and female slaves and no longer hold them in bondage. They agreed, and set them free. But afterward they changed their minds and took back the slaves they had freed and enslaved them again.

Jer. 34:8-11

LAW VIOLATED.   Then the word of the LORD came to Jeremiah: "This is what the LORD, the God of Israel, says: I made a covenant with your forefathers when I brought them out of Egypt, out of the land of slavery. I said, 'Every seventh year each of you must free any fellow Hebrew who has

Jer. 34:12-16

sold himself to you. After he has served you six years, you must let him go free.'[s] Your fathers, however, did not listen to me or pay attention to me. Recently you repented and did what is right in my sight: Each of you proclaimed freedom to his countrymen. You even made a covenant before me in the house that bears my Name. But now you have turned around and profaned my name; each of you has taken back the male and female slaves you had set free to go where they wished. You have forced them to become your slaves again.

Jer.
34:17-20

FATE OF COVENANT-BREAKERS.   "Therefore, this is what the LORD says: You have not obeyed me; you have not proclaimed freedom for your fellow countrymen. So I now proclaim 'freedom' for you, declares the LORD— 'freedom' to fall by the sword, plague and famine. I will make you abhorrent to all the kingdoms of the earth. The men who have violated my covenant and have not fulfilled the terms of the covenant they made before me, I will treat like the calf they cut in two and then walked between its pieces. The leaders of Judah and Jerusalem, the court officials, the priests and all the people of the land who walked between the pieces of the calf, I will hand over to their enemies who seek their lives. Their dead bodies will become food for the birds of the air and the beasts of the earth.

Jer.
34:21,22

PUNISHMENT FOR JUDAH.   "I will hand Zedekiah king of Judah and his officials over to their enemies who seek their lives, to the army of the king of Babylon, which has withdrawn from you. I am going to give the order, declares the LORD, and I will bring them back to this city. They will fight against it, take it and burn it down. And I will lay waste the towns of Judah so no one can live there."

Ezekiel, Prophet in Exile

*W*hat Jeremiah is to the people of Judah in Jerusalem, the prophet Ezekiel is to the captives in Babylonian exile. Ezekiel himself was among those of the priestly aristocracy who were carried away in the great deportation of 597 B.C., along with King Jehoiachin. His designated home is in a place called Tel Abib by the Kebar River in Chaldea. Of priestly heritage through the line of Aaron, Eleazar, and Zadok, Ezekiel brings to his role as prophet a unique acquaintance with the priesthood, the temple, and ceremonial worship, which shows through in many of his prophecies.

If there is a special theme to Ezekiel's prophetic messages, it is that, by both its severe punishment and subsequent restoration, Judah will come to know its God as the true God of the universe, who rules over the affairs of individuals and nations. Like virtually all the prophets of Judah, Ezekiel predicts the fall of Jerusalem due to Judah's many sins; he brings harsh judgment against Judah's oppressors; and he prophesies about the restoration of the nation. Like the other prophets of Israel and Judah, Ezekiel points to the coming Kingdom. Ezekiel's visions and writings are filled with symbolism, allegories, parables, and proverbs.

Ezekiel begins the record of his prophetic office with an account of his call

[s]Deut. 15:12

to ministry. It happens in the fifth year of his exile, when he is 30 years old—the age of recognized maturity at which Levites begin their priestly service and at which other significant figures, including the Messiah and his forerunner, will begin their special missions.

GOD'S HAND ON EZEKIEL.   In the ^{t} thirtieth year, in the fourth month on the fifth day, while I was among the exiles by the Kebar River, the heavens were opened and I saw visions of God.

Ezk. 1:1-3
River
Kebar
(592 B.C.)

On the fifth of the month—it was the fifth year of the exile of King Jehoiachin—the word of the LORD came to Ezekiel the priest, the son of Buzi,^{u} by the Kebar River in the land of the Babylonians.^{v} There the hand of the LORD was upon him.

VISION OF FOUR CREATURES.   I looked, and I saw a windstorm coming out of the north—an immense cloud with flashing lightning and surrounded by brilliant light. The center of the fire looked like glowing metal, and in the fire was what looked like four living creatures. In appearance their form was that of a man, but each of them had four faces and four wings. Their legs were straight; their feet were like those of a calf and gleamed like burnished bronze. Under their wings on their four sides they had the hands of a man. All four of them had faces and wings, and their wings touched one another. Each one went straight ahead; they did not turn as they moved.

Ezk. 1:4-24

Their faces looked like this: Each of the four had the face of a man, and on the right side each had the face of a lion, and on the left the face of an ox; each also had the face of an eagle. Such were their faces. Their wings were spread out upward; each had two wings, one touching the wing of another creature on either side, and two wings covering its body. Each one went straight ahead. Wherever the spirit would go, they would go, without turning as they went. The appearance of the living creatures was like burning coals of fire or like torches. Fire moved back and forth among the creatures; it was bright, and lightning flashed out of it. The creatures sped back and forth like flashes of lightning.

As I looked at the living creatures, I saw a wheel on the ground beside each creature with its four faces. This was the appearance and structure of the wheels: They sparkled like chrysolite, and all four looked alike. Each appeared to be made like a wheel intersecting a wheel. As they moved, they would go in any one of the four directions the creatures faced; the wheels did not turn about^w as the creatures went. Their rims were high and awesome, and all four rims were full of eyes all around.

When the living creatures moved, the wheels beside them moved; and when the living creatures rose from the ground, the wheels also rose. Wherever the spirit would go, they would go, and the wheels would rise along with them, because the spirit of the living creatures was in the wheels. When the creatures moved, they also moved; when the creatures stood still, they also stood still; and when the creatures rose from the ground, the wheels rose along with them, because the spirit of the living creatures was in the wheels.

Spread out above the heads of the living creatures was what looked like

^{t}Or ⌊my⌋ ^{u}Or *Ezekiel son of Buzi the priest* ^{v}Or *Chaldeans* ^{w}Or *aside*

an expanse, sparkling like ice, and awesome. Under the expanse their wings were stretched out one toward the other, and each had two wings covering its body. When the creatures moved, I heard the sound of their wings, like the roar of rushing waters, like the voice of the Almighty,[x] like the tumult of an army. When they stood still, they lowered their wings.

Ezk.
1:25-28

APPEARANCE OF GOD.   Then there came a voice from above the expanse over their heads as they stood with lowered wings. Above the expanse over their heads was what looked like a throne of sapphire,[y] and high above on the throne was a figure like that of a man. I saw that from what appeared to be his waist up he looked like glowing metal, as if full of fire, and that from there down he looked like fire; and brilliant light surrounded him. Like the appearance of a rainbow in the clouds on a rainy day, so was the radiance around him.

This was the appearance of the likeness of the glory of the LORD. When I saw it, I fell facedown, and I heard the voice of one speaking.

Ezk. 2:1,2

GOD CALLS EZEKIEL.   He said to me, "Son of man, stand up on your feet and I will speak to you." As he spoke, the Spirit came into me and raised me to my feet, and I heard him speaking to me.

Ezk. 2:3-8

EZEKIEL'S MISSION TOLD.   He said: "Son of man, I am sending you to the Israelites, to a rebellious nation that has rebelled against me; they and their fathers have been in revolt against me to this very day. The people to whom I am sending you are obstinate and stubborn. Say to them, 'This is what the Sovereign LORD says.' And whether they listen or fail to listen— for they are a rebellious house—they will know that a prophet has been among them. And you, son of man, do not be afraid of them or their words. Do not be afraid, though briers and thorns are all around you and you live among scorpions. Do not be afraid of what they say or terrified by them, though they are a rebellious house. You must speak my words to them, whether they listen or fail to listen, for they are rebellious. But you, son of man, listen to what I say to you. Do not rebel like that rebellious house; open your mouth and eat what I give you."

Ezk.
2:9-3:3

EZEKIEL EATS SCROLL.   Then I looked, and I saw a hand stretched out to me. In it was a scroll, which he unrolled before me. On both sides of it were written words of lament and mourning and woe. And he said to me, "Son of man, eat what is before you, eat this scroll; then go and speak to the house of Israel." So I opened my mouth, and he gave me the scroll to eat.

Then he said to me, "Son of man, eat this scroll I am giving you and fill your stomach with it." So I ate it, and it tasted as sweet as honey in my mouth.

Ezk. 3:4-11

DIFFICULTY OF MINISTRY.   He then said to me: "Son of man, go now to the house of Israel and speak my words to them. You are not being sent to a people of obscure speech and difficult language, but to the house of Israel—not to many peoples of obscure speech and difficult language, whose words you cannot understand. Surely if I had sent you to them, they would have listened to you. But the house of Israel is not willing to listen to you because they are not willing to listen to me, for the whole house of Israel is hardened and obstinate. But I will make you as unyield-

[x]Hebrew *Shaddai*   [y]Or *lapis lazuli*

ing and hardened as they are. I will make your forehead like the hardest stone, harder than flint. Do not be afraid of them or terrified by them, though they are a rebellious house."

And he said to me, "Son of man, listen carefully and take to heart all the words I speak to you. Go now to your countrymen in exile and speak to them. Say to them, 'This is what the Sovereign LORD says,' whether they listen or fail to listen."

VISION ENDS.   Then the Spirit lifted me up, and I heard behind me a loud rumbling sound—May the glory of the LORD be praised in his dwelling place!—the sound of the wings of the living creatures brushing against each other and the sound of the wheels beside them, a loud rumbling sound.

Ezk.
3:12,13

EZEKIEL STUNNED.   The Spirit then lifted me up and took me away, and I went in bitterness and in the anger of my spirit, with the strong hand of the LORD upon me. I came to the exiles who lived at Tel Abib near the Kebar River. And there, where they were living, I sat among them for seven days—overwhelmed.

Ezk.
3:14,15
Tel Abib

ACCOUNTABILITY OF MINISTRY.   At the end of seven days the word of the LORD came to me: "Son of man, I have made you a watchman for the house of Israel; so hear the word I speak and give them warning from me. When I say to a wicked man, 'You will surely die,' and you do not warn him or speak out to dissuade him from his evil ways in order to save his life, that wicked man will die forᶻ his sin, and I will hold you accountable for his blood. But if you do warn the wicked man and he does not turn from his wickedness or from his evil ways, he will die for his sin; but you will have saved yourself.

Ezk.
3:16-21

"Again, when a righteous man turns from his righteousness and does evil, and I put a stumbling block before him, he will die. Since you did not warn him, he will die for his sin. The righteous things he did will not be remembered, and I will hold you accountable for his blood. But if you do warn the righteous man not to sin and he does not sin, he will surely live because he took warning, and you will have saved yourself."

As Ezekiel reels under the weight of his new responsibility, the Holy Spirit leads him to the plain, where God instructs him in five acts which are symbolic of Jerusalem's destruction and Judah's fall. The central message of his ministry follows, couched in a judgment against the mountains of Israel (perhaps because they are often the site of pagan worship) and a prophecy announcing Judah's end.

TAKEN TO PLAIN.   The hand of the LORD was upon me there, and he said to me, "Get up and go out to the plain, and there I will speak to you." So I got up and went out to the plain. And the glory of the LORD was standing there, like the glory I had seen by the Kebar River, and I fell facedown.

Ezk.
3:22,23

SIGN OF CONFINEMENT.   Then the Spirit came into me and raised me to my feet. He spoke to me and said: "Go, shut yourself inside your house. And you, son of man, they will tie with ropes; you will be bound so that you cannot go out among the people. I will make your tongue stick to the

Ezk.
3:24-27

ᶻOr *in*

roof of your mouth so that you will be silent and unable to rebuke them, though they are a rebellious house. But when I speak to you, I will open your mouth and you shall say to them, 'This is what the Sovereign LORD says.' Whoever will listen let him listen, and whoever will refuse let him refuse; for they are a rebellious house.

Ezk. 4:1-3 SIGN OF SIEGE. "Now, son of man, take a clay tablet, put it in front of you and draw the city of Jerusalem on it. Then lay siege to it: Erect siege works against it, build a ramp up to it, set up camps against it and put battering rams around it. Then take an iron pan, place it as an iron wall between you and the city and turn your face toward it. It will be under siege, and you shall besiege it. This will be a sign to the house of Israel.

Ezk. 4:4-8 SIGN OF DISCOMFORT. "Then lie on your left side and put the sin of the house of Israel upon yourself.ᵃ You are to bear their sin for the number of days you lie on your side. I have assigned you the same number of days as the years of their sin. So for 390 days you will bear the sin of the house of Israel.

"After you have finished this, lie down again, this time on your right side, and bear the sin of the house of Judah. I have assigned you 40 days, a day for each year. Turn your face toward the siege of Jerusalem and with bared arm prophesy against her. I will tie you up with ropes so that you cannot turn from one side to the other until you have finished the days of your siege.

Ezk. 4:9-17 SIGN OF DEFILED FOOD. "Take wheat and barley, beans and lentils, millet and spelt; put them in a storage jar and use them to make bread for yourself. You are to eat it during the 390 days you lie on your side. Weigh out twenty shekelsᵇ of food to eat each day and eat it at set times. Also measure out a sixth of a hinᶜ of water and drink it at set times. Eat the food as you would a barley cake; bake it in the sight of the people, using human excrement for fuel." The LORD said, "In this way the people of Israel will eat defiled food among the nations where I will drive them."

Then I said, "Not so, Sovereign LORD! I have never defiled myself. From my youth until now I have never eaten anything found dead or torn by wild animals. No unclean meat has ever entered my mouth."

"Very well," he said, "I will let you bake your bread over cow manure instead of human excrement."

He then said to me: "Son of man, I will cut off the supply of food in Jerusalem. The people will eat rationed food in anxiety and drink rationed water in despair, for food and water will be scarce. They will be appalled at the sight of each other and will waste away because ofᵈ their sin.

Ezk. 5:1-17 SIGN OF EZEKIEL'S HAIR. "Now, son of man, take a sharp sword and use it as a barber's razor to shave your head and your beard. Then take a set of scales and divide up the hair. When the days of your siege come to an end, burn a third of the hair with fire inside the city. Take a third and strike it with the sword all around the city. And scatter a third to the wind. For I will pursue them with drawn sword. But take a few strands of hair and tuck them away in the folds of your garment. Again, take a few of these and throw them into the fire and burn them up. A fire will spread from there to the whole house of Israel.

ᵃOr *your side*   ᵇThat is, about 8 ounces (about 0.2 kilogram)   ᶜThat is, about 2/3 quart (about 0.6 liter)   ᵈOr *away in*

"This is what the Sovereign LORD says: This is Jerusalem, which I have set in the center of the nations, with countries all around her. Yet in her wickedness she has rebelled against my laws and decrees more than the nations and countries around her. She has rejected my laws and has not followed my decrees.

"Therefore this is what the Sovereign LORD says: You have been more unruly than the nations around you and have not followed my decrees or kept my laws. You have not even[e] conformed to the standards of the nations around you.

"Therefore this is what the Sovereign LORD says: I myself am against you, Jerusalem, and I will inflict punishment on you in the sight of the nations. Because of all your detestable idols, I will do to you what I have never done before and will never do again. Therefore in your midst fathers will eat their children, and children will eat their fathers. I will inflict punishment on you and will scatter all your survivors to the winds. Therefore as surely as I live, declares the Sovereign LORD, because you have defiled my sanctuary with all your vile images and detestable practices, I myself will withdraw my favor; I will not look on you with pity or spare you. A third of your people will die of the plague or perish by famine inside you; a third will fall by the sword outside your walls; and a third I will scatter to the winds and pursue with drawn sword.

"Then my anger will cease and my wrath against them will subside, and I will be avenged. And when I have spent my wrath upon them, they will know that I the LORD have spoken in my zeal.

"I will make you a ruin and a reproach among the nations around you, in the sight of all who pass by. You will be a reproach and a taunt, a warning and an object of horror to the nations around you when I inflict punishment on you in anger and in wrath and with stinging rebuke. I the LORD have spoken. When I shoot at you with my deadly and destructive arrows of famine, I will shoot to destroy you. I will bring more and more famine upon you and cut off your supply of food. I will send famine and wild beasts against you, and they will leave you childless. Plague and bloodshed will sweep through you, and I will bring the sword against you. I the LORD have spoken."

PROPHECY AGAINST MOUNTAINS.   The word of the LORD came to me: "Son of man, set your face against the mountains of Israel; prophesy against them and say: 'O mountains of Israel, hear the word of the Sovereign LORD. This is what the Sovereign LORD says to the mountains and hills, to the ravines and valleys: I am about to bring a sword against you, and I will destroy your high places. Your altars will be demolished and your incense altars will be smashed; and I will slay your people in front of your idols. I will lay the dead bodies of the Israelites in front of their idols, and I will scatter your bones around your altars. Wherever you live, the towns will be laid waste and the high places demolished, so that your altars will be laid waste and devastated, your idols smashed and ruined, your incense altars broken down, and what you have made wiped out. Your people will fall slain among you, and you will know that I am the LORD.   Ezk. 6:1-14

" 'But I will spare some, for some of you will escape the sword when

[e]Most Hebrew manuscripts; some Hebrew manuscripts and Syriac *You have*

you are scattered among the lands and nations. Then in the nations where they have been carried captive, those who escape will remember me—how I have been grieved by their adulterous hearts, which have turned away from me, and by their eyes, which have lusted after their idols. They will loathe themselves for the evil they have done and for all their detestable practices. And they will know that I am the LORD; I did not threaten in vain to bring this calamity on them.

" 'This is what the Sovereign LORD says: Strike your hands together and stamp your feet and cry out "Alas!" because of all the wicked and detestable practices of the house of Israel, for they will fall by the sword, famine and plague. He that is far away will die of the plague, and he that is near will fall by the sword, and he that survives and is spared will die of famine. So will I spend my wrath upon them. And they will know that I am the LORD, when their people lie slain among their idols around their altars, on every high hill and on all the mountaintops, under every spreading tree and every leafy oak—places where they offered fragrant incense to all their idols. And I will stretch out my hand against them and make the land a desolate waste from the desert to Diblah *f*—wherever they live. Then they will know that I am the LORD.' "

Ezk. 7:1-9 THE END HAS COME.   The word of the LORD came to me: "Son of man, this is what the Sovereign LORD says to the land of Israel: The end! The end has come upon the four corners of the land. The end is now upon you and I will unleash my anger against you. I will judge you according to your conduct and repay you for all your detestable practices. I will not look on you with pity or spare you; I will surely repay you for your conduct and the detestable practices among you. Then you will know that I am the LORD.

"This is what the Sovereign LORD says: Disaster! An unheard-of *g* disaster is coming. The end has come! The end has come! It has roused itself against you. It has come! Doom has come upon you—you who dwell in the land. The time has come, the day is near; there is panic, not joy, upon the mountains. I am about to pour out my wrath on you and spend my anger against you; I will judge you according to your conduct and repay you for all your detestable practices. I will not look on you with pity or spare you; I will repay you in accordance with your conduct and the detestable practices among you. Then you will know that it is I the LORD who strikes the blow.

Ezk. 7:10-27 "The day is here! It has come! Doom has burst forth, the rod has budded, arrogance has blossomed! Violence has grown into*h* a rod to punish wickedness; none of the people will be left, none of that crowd—no wealth, nothing of value. The time has come, the day has arrived. Let not the buyer rejoice nor the seller grieve, for wrath is upon the whole crowd. The seller will not recover the land he has sold as long as both of them live, for the vision concerning the whole crowd will not be reversed. Because of their sins, not one of them will preserve his life. Though they blow the trumpet and get everything ready, no one will go into battle, for my wrath is upon the whole crowd.

"Outside is the sword, inside are plague and famine; those in the

---

f Most Hebrew manuscripts; a few Hebrew manuscripts *Riblah*   *g* Most Hebrew
manuscripts; some Hebrew manuscripts and Syriac *Disaster after*   *h* Or *The violent one*
has become

country will die by the sword, and those in the city will be devoured by famine and plague. All who survive and escape will be in the mountains, moaning like doves of the valleys, each because of his sins. Every hand will go limp, and every knee will become as weak as water. They will put on sackcloth and be clothed with terror. Their faces will be covered with shame and their heads will be shaved. They will throw their silver into the streets, and their gold will be an unclean thing. Their silver and gold will not be able to save them in the day of the LORD's wrath. They will not satisfy their hunger or fill their stomachs with it, for it has made them stumble into sin. They were proud of their beautiful jewelry and used it to make their detestable idols and vile images. Therefore I will turn these into an unclean thing for them. I will hand it all over as plunder to foreigners and as loot to the wicked of the earth, and they will defile it. I will turn my face away from them, and they will desecrate my treasured place; robbers will enter it and desecrate it.

"Prepare chains, because the land is full of bloodshed and the city is full of violence. I will bring the most wicked of the nations to take possession of their houses; I will put an end to the pride of the mighty, and their sanctuaries will be desecrated. When terror comes, they will seek peace, but there will be none. Calamity upon calamity will come, and rumor upon rumor. They will try to get a vision from the prophet; the teaching of the law by the priest will be lost, as will the counsel of the elders. The king will mourn, the prince will be clothed with despair, and the hands of the people of the land will tremble. I will deal with them according to their conduct, and by their own standards I will judge them. Then they will know that I am the LORD."

Ezekiel's Denunciations of Judah

Over the next five years, from 591 to 586 B.C., Ezekiel brings a number of denunciations against Judah for its idolatry, its false prophets, its corrupt leaders, its rebellious spirit, its religious infidelity, and its sins. An introduction to these denunciations comes in the form of a most unusual occurrence. Ezekiel says that God took him to Jerusalem to show him the idolatry in the temple and the punishment of idolaters and corrupt leaders, and then returned him to his house in Tel Abib. It all happens somehow while Ezekiel is sitting in his house in the presence of a group of elders.

EZEKIEL TAKEN TO JERUSALEM.   In the sixth year, in the sixth month on the fifth day, while I was sitting in my house and the elders of Judah were sitting before me, the hand of the Sovereign LORD came upon me there. I looked, and I saw a figure like that of a man.[i] From what appeared to be his waist down he was like fire, and from there up his appearance was as bright as glowing metal. He stretched out what looked like a hand and took me by the hair of my head. The Spirit lifted me up between earth and heaven and in visions of God he took me to Jerusalem, to the entrance to the north gate of the inner court, where the idol that provokes to

Ezk. 8:1-4
Tel Abib
(591 B.C.)

---

[i] Or *saw a fiery figure*

jealousy stood. And there before me was the glory of the God of Israel, as in the vision I had seen in the plain.

Ezk. 8:5-18 IDOLATRY IN TEMPLE. Then he said to me, "Son of man, look toward the north." So I looked, and in the entrance north of the gate of the altar I saw this idol of jealousy.

And he said to me, "Son of man, do you see what they are doing—the utterly detestable things the house of Israel is doing here, things that will drive me far from my sanctuary? But you will see things that are even more detestable."

Then he brought me to the entrance to the court. I looked, and I saw a hole in the wall. He said to me, "Son of man, now dig into the wall." So I dug into the wall and saw a doorway there.

And he said to me, "Go in and see the wicked and detestable things they are doing here." So I went in and looked, and I saw portrayed all over the walls all kinds of crawling things and detestable animals and all the idols of the house of Israel. In front of them stood seventy elders of the house of Israel, and Jaazaniah son of Shaphan was standing among them. Each had a censer in his hand, and a fragrant cloud of incense was rising.

He said to me, "Son of man, have you seen what the elders of the house of Israel are doing in the darkness, each at the shrine of his own idol? They say, 'The LORD does not see us; the LORD has forsaken the land.'" Again, he said, "You will see them doing things that are even more detestable."

Then he brought me to the entrance to the north gate of the house of the LORD, and I saw women sitting there, mourning for Tammuz. He said to me, "Do you see this, son of man? You will see things that are even more detestable than this."

He then brought me into the inner court of the house of the LORD, and there at the entrance to the temple, between the portico and the altar, were about twenty-five men. With their backs toward the temple of the LORD and their faces toward the east, they were bowing down to the sun in the east.

He said to me, "Have you seen this, son of man? Is it a trivial matter for the house of Judah to do the detestable things they are doing here? Must they also fill the land with violence and continually provoke me to anger? Look at them putting the branch to their nose! Therefore I will deal with them in anger; I will not look on them with pity or spare them. Although they shout in my ears, I will not listen to them."

Ezk. 9:1-11 DEATH OF IDOLATERS. Then I heard him call out in a loud voice, "Bring the guards of the city here, each with a weapon in his hand." And I saw six men coming from the direction of the upper gate, which faces north, each with a deadly weapon in his hand. With them was a man clothed in linen who had a writing kit at his side. They came in and stood beside the bronze altar.

Now the glory of the God of Israel went up from above the cherubim, where it had been, and moved to the threshold of the temple. Then the LORD called to the man clothed in linen who had the writing kit at his side and said to him, "Go throughout the city of Jerusalem and put a mark on the foreheads of those who grieve and lament over all the detestable things that are done in it."

As I listened, he said to the others, "Follow him through the city and kill, without showing pity or compassion. Slaughter old men, young men and maidens, women and children, but do not touch anyone who has the mark. Begin at my sanctuary." So they began with the elders who were in front of the temple.

Then he said to them, "Defile the temple and fill the courts with the slain. Go!" So they went out and began killing throughout the city. While they were killing and I was left alone, I fell facedown, crying out, "Ah, Sovereign LORD! Are you going to destroy the entire remnant of Israel in this outpouring of your wrath on Jerusalem?"

He answered me, "The sin of the house of Israel and Judah is exceedingly great; the land is full of bloodshed and the city is full of injustice. They say, 'The LORD has forsaken the land; the LORD does not see.' So I will not look on them with pity or spare them, but I will bring down on their own heads what they have done."

Then the man in linen with the writing kit at his side brought back word, saying, "I have done as you commanded."

GLORY LEAVES TEMPLE.   I looked, and I saw the likeness of a throne   Ezk.
of sapphire[j] above the expanse that was over the heads of the cherubim.   10:1-22
The LORD said to the man clothed in linen, "Go in among the wheels beneath the cherubim. Fill your hands with burning coals from among the cherubim and scatter them over the city." And as I watched, he went in.

Now the cherubim were standing on the south side of the temple when the man went in, and a cloud filled the inner court. Then the glory of the LORD rose from above the cherubim and moved to the threshold of the temple. The cloud filled the temple, and the court was full of the radiance of the glory of the LORD. The sound of the wings of the cherubim could be heard as far away as the outer court, like the voice of God Almighty[k] when he speaks.

When the LORD commanded the man in linen, "Take fire from among the wheels, from among the cherubim," the man went in and stood beside a wheel. Then one of the cherubim reached out his hand to the fire that was among them. He took up some of it and put it into the hands of the man in linen, who took it and went out. (Under the wings of the cherubim could be seen what looked like the hands of a man.)

I looked, and I saw beside the cherubim four wheels, one beside each of the cherubim; the wheels sparkled like chrysolite. As for their appearance, the four of them looked alike; each was like a wheel intersecting a wheel. As they moved, they would go in any one of the four directions the cherubim faced; the wheels did not turn about[l] as the cherubim went. The cherubim went in whatever direction the head faced, without turning as they went. Their entire bodies, including their backs, their hands and their wings, were completely full of eyes, as were their four wheels. I heard the wheels being called "the whirling wheels." Each of the cherubim had four faces: One face was that of a cherub, the second the face of a man, the third the face of a lion, and the fourth the face of an eagle.

Then the cherubim rose upward. These were the living creatures I had seen by the Kebar River. When the cherubim moved, the wheels beside them moved; and when the cherubim spread their wings to rise from the ground, the wheels did not leave their side. When the cherubim stood still,

---

[j]Or *lapis lazuli*   [k]Hebrew *El-Shaddai*   [l]Or *aside*

they also stood still; and when the cherubim rose, they rose with them, because the spirit of the living creatures was in them.

Then the glory of the LORD departed from over the threshold of the temple and stopped above the cherubim. While I watched, the cherubim spread their wings and rose from the ground, and as they went, the wheels went with them. They stopped at the entrance to the east gate of the LORD's house, and the glory of the God of Israel was above them.

These were the living creatures I had seen beneath the God of Israel by the Kebar River, and I realized that they were cherubim. Each had four faces and four wings, and under their wings was what looked like the hands of a man. Their faces had the same appearance as those I had seen by the Kebar River. Each one went straight ahead.

Ezk.
11:1-13

CORRUPT LEADERS JUDGED.   Then the Spirit lifted me up and brought me to the gate of the house of the LORD that faces east. There at the entrance to the gate were twenty-five men, and I saw among them Jaazaniah son of Azzur and Pelatiah son of Benaiah, leaders of the people. The LORD said to me, "Son of man, these are the men who are plotting evil and giving wicked advice in this city. They say, 'Will it not soon be time to build houses?'[m] This city is a cooking pot, and we are the meat.' Therefore prophesy against them; prophesy, son of man."

Then the Spirit of the LORD came upon me, and he told me to say: "This is what the LORD says: That is what you are saying, O house of Israel, but I know what is going through your mind. You have killed many people in this city and filled its streets with the dead.

"Therefore this is what the Sovereign LORD says: The bodies you have thrown there are the meat and this city is the pot, but I will drive you out of it. You fear the sword, and the sword is what I will bring against you, declares the Sovereign LORD. I will drive you out of the city and hand you over to foreigners and inflict punishment on you. You will fall by the sword, and I will execute judgment on you at the borders of Israel. Then you will know that I am the LORD. This city will not be a pot for you, nor will you be the meat in it; I will execute judgment on you at the borders of Israel. And you will know that I am the LORD, for you have not followed my decrees or kept my laws but have conformed to the standards of the nations around you."

Now as I was prophesying, Pelatiah son of Benaiah died. Then I fell facedown and cried out in a loud voice, "Ah, Sovereign LORD! Will you completely destroy the remnant of Israel?"

Ezk.
11:14-21

PROMISE OF RESTORATION.   The word of the LORD came to me: "Son of man, your brothers—your brothers who are your blood relatives[n] and the whole house of Israel—are those of whom the people of Jerusalem have said, 'They are[o] far away from the LORD; this land was given to us as our possession.'

"Therefore say: 'This is what the Sovereign LORD says: Although I sent them far away among the nations and scattered them among the countries, yet for a little while I have been a sanctuary for them in the countries where they have gone.'

"Therefore say: 'This is what the Sovereign LORD says: I will gather you

---

[m]Or *This is not the time to build houses.*   [n]Or *are in exile with you* (see Septuagint and Syriac)
[o]Or *those to whom the people of Jerusalem have said, 'Stay*

from the nations and bring you back from the countries where you have been scattered, and I will give you back the land of Israel again.'

"They will return to it and remove all its vile images and detestable idols. I will give them an undivided heart and put a new spirit in them; I will remove from them their heart of stone and give them a heart of flesh. Then they will follow my decrees and be careful to keep my laws. They will be my people, and I will be their God. But as for those whose hearts are devoted to their vile images and detestable idols, I will bring down on their own heads what they have done, declares the Sovereign LORD."

EZEKIEL RETURNED TO TEL ABIB.   Then the cherubim, with the wheels beside them, spread their wings, and the glory of the God of Israel was above them. The glory of the LORD went up from within the city and stopped above the mountain east of it. The Spirit lifted me up and brought me to the exiles in Babylonia[p] in the vision given by the Spirit of God.

Ezk. 11:22-25

Then the vision I had seen went up from me, and I told the exiles everything the LORD had shown me.

Sometime after Ezekiel's visionary trip to Jerusalem, God directs him to enact two signs before his people: one depicts the further exile of those still in Judah, while the other shows all the anxiety which will accompany the fall. When Ezekiel actually performs these enactments it must be a curious scene for the onlookers. Presumably there are those who accept Ezekiel as God's prophet and who look sincerely for whatever message is to be derived. Yet there are not many believers among these bitter exiles, and the unbelievers must think Ezekiel is insane. In explaining the significance of the enactment, Ezekiel brings a prophecy about King Zedekiah's final fate that, five years later, will come true in minute detail.

THE EXILE ENACTMENT.   The word of the LORD came to me: "Son of man, you are living among a rebellious people. They have eyes to see but do not see and ears to hear but do not hear, for they are a rebellious people.

Ezk. 12:1-16

"Therefore, son of man, pack your belongings for exile and in the daytime, as they watch, set out and go from where you are to another place. Perhaps they will understand, though they are a rebellious house. During the daytime, while they watch, bring out your belongings packed for exile. Then in the evening, while they are watching, go out like those who go into exile. While they watch, dig through the wall and take your belongings out through it. Put them on your shoulder as they are watching and carry them out at dusk. Cover your face so that you cannot see the land, for I have made you a sign to the house of Israel."

So I did as I was commanded. During the day I brought out my things packed for exile. Then in the evening I dug through the wall with my hands. I took my belongings out at dusk, carrying them on my shoulders while they watched.

In the morning the word of the LORD came to me: "Son of man, did not that rebellious house of Israel ask you, 'What are you doing?'

"Say to them, 'This is what the Sovereign LORD says: This oracle concerns the prince in Jerusalem and the whole house of Israel who are there.' Say to them, 'I am a sign to you.'

[p]Or Chaldea

"As I have done, so it will be done to them. They will go into exile as captives.

"The prince among them will put his things on his shoulder at dusk and leave, and a hole will be dug in the wall for him to go through. He will cover his face so that he cannot see the land. I will spread my net for him, and he will be caught in my snare; I will bring him to Babylonia, the land of the Chaldeans, but he will not see it, and there he will die. I will scatter to the winds all those around him—his staff and all his troops—and I will pursue them with drawn sword.

"They will know that I am the LORD, when I disperse them among the nations and scatter them through the countries. But I will spare a few of them from the sword, famine and plague, so that in the nations where they go they may acknowledge all their detestable practices. Then they will know that I am the LORD."

Ezk.
12:17-20

THE ANXIETY ENACTMENT.   The word of the LORD came to me: "Son of man, tremble as you eat your food, and shudder in fear as you drink your water. Say to the people of the land: 'This is what the Sovereign LORD says about those living in Jerusalem and in the land of Israel: They will eat their food in anxiety and drink their water in despair, for their land will be stripped of everything in it because of the violence of all who live there. The inhabited towns will be laid waste and the land will be desolate. Then you will know that I am the LORD.'"

In order to correct two prevalent misunderstandings about the certainty and timing of God's prophecies, God brings these two messages to Ezekiel.

Ezk.
12:21-25

CERTAINTY OF PROPHECIES.   The word of the LORD came to me: "Son of man, what is this proverb you have in the land of Israel: 'The days go by and every vision comes to nothing'? Say to them, 'This is what the Sovereign LORD says: I am going to put an end to this proverb, and they will no longer quote it in Israel.' Say to them, 'The days are near when every vision will be fulfilled. For there will be no more false visions or flattering divinations among the people of Israel. But I the LORD will speak what I will, and it shall be fulfilled without delay. For in your days, you rebellious house, I will fulfill whatever I say, declares the Sovereign LORD.'"

Ezk.
12:26-28

IMMEDIACY OF FULFILLMENT.   The word of the LORD came to me: "Son of man, the house of Israel is saying, 'The vision he sees is for many years from now, and he prophesies about the distant future.'

"Therefore say to them, 'This is what the Sovereign LORD says: None of my words will be delayed any longer; whatever I say will be fulfilled, declares the Sovereign LORD.'"

One of the primary reasons that people have so little confidence in God's proclamations is that many false messages are being preached by those pretending to be men of God. Over the centuries there will be no end to such men. Therefore God calls Ezekiel to speak out against the false prophets and prophetesses who are deceiving Judah into believing their captivity will soon end with swift victory over Babylonia.

DECEIT OF FALSE PROPHETS. The word of the LORD came to me: "Son of man, prophesy against the prophets of Israel who are now prophesying. Say to those who prophesy out of their own imagination: 'Hear the word of the LORD! This is what the Sovereign LORD says: Woe to the foolish[q] prophets who follow their own spirit and have seen nothing! Your prophets, O Israel, are like jackals among ruins. You have not gone up to the breaks in the wall to repair it for the house of Israel so that it will stand firm in the battle on the day of the LORD. Their visions are false and their divinations a lie. They say, "The LORD declares," when the LORD has not sent them; yet they expect their words to be fulfilled. Have you not seen false visions and uttered lying divinations when you say, "The LORD declares," though I have not spoken?

" 'Therefore this is what the Sovereign LORD says: Because of your false words and lying visions, I am against you, declares the Sovereign LORD. My hand will be against the prophets who see false visions and utter lying divinations. They will not belong to the council of my people or be listed in the records of the house of Israel, nor will they enter the land of Israel. Then you will know that I am the Sovereign LORD.

" 'Because they lead my people astray, saying, "Peace," when there is no peace, and because, when a flimsy wall is built, they cover it with whitewash, therefore tell those who cover it with whitewash that it is going to fall. Rain will come in torrents, and I will send hailstones hurtling down, and violent winds will burst forth. When the wall collapses, will people not ask you, "Where is the whitewash you covered it with?"

" 'Therefore this is what the Sovereign LORD says: In my wrath I will unleash a violent wind, and in my anger hailstones and torrents of rain will fall with destructive fury. I will tear down the wall you have covered with whitewash and will level it to the ground so that its foundation will be laid bare. When it[r] falls, you will be destroyed in it; and you will know that I am the LORD. So I will spend my wrath against the wall and against those who covered it with whitewash. I will say to you, "The wall is gone and so are those who whitewashed it, those prophets of Israel who prophesied to Jerusalem and saw visions of peace for her when there was no peace, declares the Sovereign LORD." '

SIN OF THE PROPHETESSES. "Now, son of man, set your face against the daughters of your people who prophesy out of their own imagination. Prophesy against them and say, 'This is what the Sovereign LORD says: Woe to the women who sew magic charms on all their wrists and make veils of various lengths for their heads in order to ensnare people. Will you ensnare the lives of my people but preserve your own? You have profaned me among my people for a few handfuls of barley and scraps of bread. By lying to my people, who listen to lies, you have killed those who should not have died and have spared those who should not live.

" 'Therefore this is what the Sovereign LORD says: I am against your magic charms with which you ensnare people like birds and I will tear them from your arms; I will set free the people that you ensnare like birds. I will tear off your veils and save my people from your hands, and they will no longer fall prey to your power. Then you will know that I am the LORD. Because you disheartened the righteous with your lies, when I had

Ezk. 13:1-16

Ezk. 13:17-23

---

[q] Or *wicked*   [r] Or *the city*

brought them no grief, and because you encouraged the wicked not to turn from their evil ways and so save their lives, therefore you will no longer see false visions or practice divination. I will save my people from your hands. And then you will know that I am the LORD.'"

One irony of the people's continued idolatry is their practice of seeking God's will from the prophets. They are fascinated and allured by the various idols they have set up in their hearts, but deep down in those same hearts there is evidently the realization that only a much greater God can provide the real answers to life. Yet God considers their dual allegiance an affront and orders Ezekiel not to accommodate their curiosity.

Ezk. 14:1-11

PROPHECY NOT FOR IDOLATERS.   Some of the elders of Israel came to me and sat down in front of me. Then the word of the LORD came to me: "Son of man, these men have set up idols in their hearts and put wicked stumbling blocks before their faces. Should I let them inquire of me at all? Therefore speak to them and tell them, 'This is what the Sovereign LORD says: When any Israelite sets up idols in his heart and puts a wicked stumbling block before his face and then goes to a prophet, I the LORD will answer him myself in keeping with his great idolatry. I will do this to recapture the hearts of the people of Israel, who have all deserted me for their idols.'

"Therefore say to the house of Israel, 'This is what the Sovereign LORD says: Repent! Turn from your idols and renounce all your detestable practices!

" 'When any Israelite or any alien living in Israel separates himself from me and sets up idols in his heart and puts a wicked stumbling block before his face and then goes to a prophet to inquire of me, I the LORD will answer him myself. I will set my face against that man and make him an example and a byword. I will cut him off from my people. Then you will know that I am the LORD.

" 'And if the prophet is enticed to utter a prophecy, I the LORD have enticed that prophet, and I will stretch out my hand against him and destroy him from among my people Israel. They will bear their guilt—the prophet will be as guilty as the one who consults him. Then the people of Israel will no longer stray from me, nor will they defile themselves anymore with all their sins. They will be my people, and I will be their God, declares the Sovereign LORD.'"

How many righteous people does it take to save a nation? It has been 1500 years since Abraham asked that same question concerning Sodom and Gomorrah. Surely at this time there are righteous believers among both the captives and their Jerusalem kinsmen who are asking this same question themselves. God's answer to Ezekiel is that there comes a time when a nation's sins so completely condemn it that not even a remnant of righteous citizens can stop the destruction inherent in evil. God uses as his illustration of a righteous remnant a trio of faithful believers: Noah, who saw all of mankind (except his own family) destroyed by the great flood; Job, the patient patriarch; and Daniel (possibly the Daniel who is one of the chosen captives serving in Nebuchadnezzar's palace, who will distinguish himself among God's exiles even more than he already has).

JUDGMENT INESCAPABLE.   The word of the LORD came to me: "Son of man, if a country sins against me by being unfaithful and I stretch out my hand against it to cut off its food supply and send famine upon it and kill its men and their animals, even if these three men—Noah, Daniel[s] and Job—were in it, they could save only themselves by their righteousness, declares the Sovereign LORD.

Ezk.
14:12-23

"Or if I send wild beasts through that country and they leave it childless and it becomes desolate so that no one can pass through it because of the beasts, as surely as I live, declares the Sovereign LORD, even if these three men were in it, they could not save their own sons or daughters. They alone would be saved, but the land would be desolate.

"Or if I bring a sword against that country and say, 'Let the sword pass throughout the land,' and I kill its men and their animals, as surely as I live, declares the Sovereign LORD, even if these three men were in it, they could not save their own sons or daughters. They alone would be saved.

"Or if I send a plague into that land and pour out my wrath upon it through bloodshed, killing its men and their animals, as surely as I live, declares the Sovereign LORD, even if Noah, Daniel and Job were in it, they could save neither son nor daughter. They would save only themselves by their righteousness.

"For this is what the Sovereign LORD says: How much worse will it be when I send against Jerusalem my four dreadful judgments—sword and famine and wild beasts and plague—to kill its men and their animals! Yet there will be some survivors—sons and daughters who will be brought out of it. They will come to you, and when you see their conduct and their actions, you will be consoled regarding the disaster I have brought upon Jerusalem—every disaster I have brought upon it. You will be consoled when you see their conduct and their actions, for you will know that I have done nothing in it without cause, declares the Sovereign LORD."

Using three allegories, God foretells Judah's imminent destruction. The first allegory shows Judah as a useless vine to be burned. The second is a vitriolic attack against Judah's unfaithfulness, portraying Judah as an adulterous wife, worse than her two sisters, Israel and Edom, and less moral than a prostitute. The third allegory, using two eagles and a vine, calls specific attention to the personal ruin of King Zedekiah.

THE USELESS VINE.   The word of the LORD came to me: "Son of man, how is the wood of a vine better than that of a branch on any of the trees in the forest? Is wood ever taken from it to make anything useful? Do they make pegs from it to hang things on? And after it is thrown on the fire as fuel and the fire burns both ends and chars the middle, is it then useful for anything? If it was not useful for anything when it was whole, how much less can it be made into something useful when the fire has burned it and it is charred?

Ezk. 15:1-8

"Therefore this is what the Sovereign LORD says: As I have given the wood of the vine among the trees of the forest as fuel for the fire, so will I

[s]Or *Danel*; the Hebrew spelling may suggest a person other than the prophet Daniel.

treat the people living in Jerusalem. I will set my face against them.
Although they have come out of the fire, the fire will yet consume them.
And when I set my face against them, you will know that I am the LORD. I
will make the land desolate because they have been unfaithful, declares
the Sovereign LORD."

Ezk.
16:1-14

THE UNFAITHFUL WIFE.   The word of the LORD came to me: "Son of
man, confront Jerusalem with her detestable practices and say, 'This is
what the Sovereign LORD says to Jerusalem: Your ancestry and birth were
in the land of the Canaanites; your father was an Amorite and your mother a Hittite. On the day you were born your cord was not cut, nor were you
washed with water to make you clean, nor were you rubbed with salt or
wrapped in cloths. No one looked on you with pity or had compassion
enough to do any of these things for you. Rather, you were thrown out into
the open field, for on the day you were born you were despised.

" 'Then I passed by and saw you kicking about in your blood, and as
you lay there in your blood I said to you, "Live!"[t] I made you grow like a
plant of the field. You grew up and developed and became the most beautiful of jewels.[u] Your breasts were formed and your hair grew, you who
were naked and bare.

" 'Later I passed by, and when I looked at you and saw that you were
old enough for love, I spread the corner of my garment over you and covered your nakedness. I gave you my solemn oath and entered into a
covenant with you, declares the Sovereign LORD, and you became mine.

" 'I bathed[v] you with water and washed the blood from you and put
ointments on you. I clothed you with an embroidered dress and put
leather sandals on you. I dressed you in fine linen and covered you with
costly garments. I adorned you with jewelry: I put bracelets on your arms
and a necklace around your neck, and I put a ring on your nose, earrings
on your ears and a beautiful crown on your head. So you were adorned
with gold and silver; your clothes were of fine linen and costly fabric and
embroidered cloth. Your food was fine flour, honey and olive oil. You
became very beautiful and rose to be a queen. And your fame spread
among the nations on account of your beauty, because the splendor I had
given you made your beauty perfect, declares the Sovereign LORD.

Ezk.
16:15-22

" 'But you trusted in your beauty and used your fame to become a prostitute. You lavished your favors on anyone who passed by and your beauty became his.[w] You took some of your garments to make gaudy high
places, where you carried on your prostitution. Such things should not
happen, nor should they ever occur. You also took the fine jewelry I gave
you, the jewelry made of my gold and silver, and you made for yourself
male idols and engaged in prostitution with them. And you took your
embroidered clothes to put on them, and you offered my oil and incense
before them. Also the food I provided for you—the fine flour, olive oil and
honey I gave you to eat—you offered as fragrant incense before them. That
is what happened, declares the Sovereign LORD.

" 'And you took your sons and daughters whom you bore to me and
sacrificed them as food to the idols. Was your prostitution not enough?

[t]A few Hebrew manuscripts, Septuagint and Syriac; most Hebrew manuscripts "Live!"
And as you lay there in your blood I said to you, "Live!"   [u]Or became mature   [v]Or I had
bathed   [w]Most Hebrew manuscripts; one Hebrew manuscript (see some Septuagint
manuscripts) by. *Such a thing should not happen*

You slaughtered my children and sacrificed them^x to the idols. In all your detestable practices and your prostitution you did not remember the days of your youth, when you were naked and bare, kicking about in your blood.

" 'Woe! Woe to you, declares the Sovereign LORD. In addition to all your other wickedness, you built a mound for yourself and made a lofty shrine in every public square. At the head of every street you built your lofty shrines and degraded your beauty, offering your body with increasing promiscuity to anyone who passed by. You engaged in prostitution with the Egyptians, your lustful neighbors, and provoked me to anger with your increasing promiscuity. So I stretched out my hand against you and reduced your territory; I gave you over to the greed of your enemies, the daughters of the Philistines, who were shocked by your lewd conduct. You engaged in prostitution with the Assyrians too, because you were insatiable; and even after that, you still were not satisfied. Then you increased your promiscuity to include Babylonia,^y a land of merchants, but even with this you were not satisfied.

Ezk.
16:23-34

" 'How weak-willed you are, declares the Sovereign LORD, when you do all these things, acting like a brazen prostitute! When you built your mounds at the head of every street and made your lofty shrines in every public square, you were unlike a prostitute, because you scorned payment.

" 'You adulterous wife! You prefer strangers to your own husband! Every prostitute receives a fee, but you give gifts to all your lovers, bribing them to come to you from everywhere for your illicit favors. So in your prostitution you are the opposite of others; no one runs after you for your favors. You are the very opposite, for you give payment and none is given to you.

" 'Therefore, you prostitute, hear the word of the LORD! This is what the Sovereign LORD says: Because you poured out your wealth^z and exposed your nakedness in your promiscuity with your lovers, and because of all your detestable idols, and because you gave them your children's blood, therefore I am going to gather all your lovers, with whom you found pleasure, those you loved as well as those you hated. I will gather them against you from all around and will strip you in front of them, and they will see all your nakedness. I will sentence you to the punishment of women who commit adultery and who shed blood; I will bring upon you the blood vengeance of my wrath and jealous anger. Then I will hand you over to your lovers, and they will tear down your mounds and destroy your lofty shrines. They will strip you of your clothes and take your fine jewelry and leave you naked and bare. They will bring a mob against you, who will stone you and hack you to pieces with their swords. They will burn down your houses and inflict punishment on you in the sight of many women. I will put a stop to your prostitution, and you will no longer pay your lovers. Then my wrath against you will subside and my jealous anger will turn away from you; I will be calm and no longer angry.

Ezk.
16:35-43

" 'Because you did not remember the days of your youth but enraged me with all these things, I will surely bring down on your head what you have done, declares the Sovereign LORD. Did you not add lewdness to all your other detestable practices?

---

^xOr *and made them pass through ⸤the fire⸥*   ^yOr *Chaldea*   ^zOr *lust*

Ezk.
16:44-52

" 'Everyone who quotes proverbs will quote this proverb about you: "Like mother, like daughter." You are a true daughter of your mother, who despised her husband and her children; and you are a true sister of your sisters, who despised their husbands and their children. Your mother was a Hittite and your father an Amorite. Your older sister was Samaria, who lived to the north of you with her daughters; and your younger sister, who lived to the south of you with her daughters, was Sodom. You not only walked in their ways and copied their detestable practices, but in all your ways you soon became more depraved than they. As surely as I live, declares the Sovereign LORD, your sister Sodom and her daughters never did what you and your daughters have done.

" 'Now this was the sin of your sister Sodom: She and her daughters were arrogant, overfed and unconcerned; they did not help the poor and needy. They were haughty and did detestable things before me. Therefore I did away with them as you have seen. Samaria did not commit half the sins you did. You have done more detestable things than they, and have made your sisters seem righteous by all these things you have done. Bear your disgrace, for you have furnished some justification for your sisters. Because your sins were more vile than theirs, they appear more righteous than you. So then, be ashamed and bear your disgrace, for you have made your sisters appear righteous.

Ezk.
16:53-58

" 'However, I will restore the fortunes of Sodom and her daughters and of Samaria and her daughters, and your fortunes along with them, so that you may bear your disgrace and be ashamed of all you have done in giving them comfort. And your sisters, Sodom with her daughters and Samaria with her daughters, will return to what they were before; and you and your daughters will return to what you were before. You would not even mention your sister Sodom in the day of your pride, before your wickedness was uncovered. Even so, you are now scorned by the daughters of Edom[a] and all her neighbors and the daughters of the Philistines— all those around you who despise you. You will bear the consequences of your lewdness and your detestable practices, declares the LORD.

Ezk.
16:59-63

" 'This is what the Sovereign LORD says: I will deal with you as you deserve, because you have despised my oath by breaking the covenant. Yet I will remember the covenant I made with you in the days of your youth, and I will establish an everlasting covenant with you. Then you will remember your ways and be ashamed when you receive your sisters, both those who are older than you and those who are younger. I will give them to you as daughters, but not on the basis of my covenant with you. So I will establish my covenant with you, and you will know that I am the LORD. Then, when I make atonement for you for all you have done, you will remember and be ashamed and never again open your mouth because of your humiliation, declares the Sovereign LORD.' "

Ezk.
17:1-18

TWO EAGLES AND A VINE.   The word of the LORD came to me: "Son of man, set forth an allegory and tell the house of Israel a parable. Say to them, 'This is what the Sovereign LORD says: A great eagle with powerful wings, long feathers and full plumage of varied colors came to Lebanon.

---

[a] Many Hebrew manuscripts and Syriac; most Hebrew manuscripts, Septuagint and Vulgate *Aram*

Taking hold of the top of a cedar, he broke off its topmost shoot and carried it away to a land of merchants, where he planted it in a city of traders.

" 'He took some of the seed of your land and put it in fertile soil. He planted it like a willow by abundant water, and it sprouted and became a low, spreading vine. Its branches turned toward him, but its roots remained under it. So it became a vine and produced branches and put out leafy boughs.

" 'But there was another great eagle with powerful wings and full plumage. The vine now sent out its roots toward him from the plot where it was planted and stretched out its branches to him for water. It had been planted in good soil by abundant water so that it would produce branches, bear fruit and become a splendid vine.'

"Say to them, 'This is what the Sovereign LORD says: Will it thrive? Will it not be uprooted and stripped of its fruit so that it withers? All its new growth will wither. It will not take a strong arm or many people to pull it up by the roots. Even if it is transplanted, will it thrive? Will it not wither completely when the east wind strikes it—wither away in the plot where it grew?' "

Then the word of the LORD came to me: "Say to this rebellious house, 'Do you not know what these things mean?' Say to them: 'The king of Babylon went to Jerusalem and carried off her king and her nobles, bringing them back with him to Babylon. Then he took a member of the royal family and made a treaty with him, putting him under oath. He also carried away the leading men of the land, so that the kingdom would be brought low, unable to rise again, surviving only by keeping his treaty. But the king rebelled against him by sending his envoys to Egypt to get horses and a large army. Will he succeed? Will he who does such things escape? Will he break the treaty and yet escape?

" 'As surely as I live, declares the Sovereign LORD, he shall die in Babylon, in the land of the king who put him on the throne, whose oath he despised and whose treaty he broke. Pharaoh with his mighty army and great horde will be of no help to him in war, when ramps are built and siege works erected to destroy many lives. He despised the oath by breaking the covenant. Because he had given his hand in pledge and yet did all these things, he shall not escape.

" 'Therefore this is what the Sovereign LORD says: As surely as I live, I will bring down on his head my oath that he despised and my covenant that he broke. I will spread my net for him, and he will be caught in my snare. I will bring him to Babylon and execute judgment upon him there because he was unfaithful to me. All his fleeing troops will fall by the sword, and the survivors will be scattered to the winds. Then you will know that I the LORD have spoken.

Ezk.
17:19-24

" 'This is what the Sovereign LORD says: I myself will take a shoot from the very top of a cedar and plant it; I will break off a tender sprig from its topmost shoots and plant it on a high and lofty mountain. On the mountain heights of Israel I will plant it; it will produce branches and bear fruit and become a splendid cedar. Birds of every kind will nest in it; they will find shelter in the shade of its branches. All the trees of the field will know that I the LORD bring down the tall tree and make the low tree grow tall. I dry up the green tree and make the dry tree flourish.

" 'I the LORD have spoken, and I will do it.' "

It is only natural in times of pending punishment to place the blame on others, to hide behind prior good conduct, or perhaps to take security in one's family or heritage. In one of the clearest passages in all of prophecy, God discredits any notion that the people of Judah are suffering only because of their predecessors' sins, or that they can claim any immunity as descendants of faithful forefathers such as Abraham. No, each person is accountable for his own sins, says Ezekiel; and God assures his people that, just as the wicked can repent and be saved, the righteous can fall into sin and be destroyed.

Ezk. 18:1-9   PERSONAL ACCOUNTABILITY.   The word of the LORD came to me: "What do you people mean by quoting this proverb about the land of Israel:

> " 'The fathers eat sour grapes,
>   and the children's teeth are set on edge'?

"As surely as I live, declares the Sovereign LORD, you will no longer quote this proverb in Israel. For every living soul belongs to me, the father as well as the son—both alike belong to me. The soul who sins is the one who will die.

> "Suppose there is a righteous man
>   who does what is just and right.
> He does not eat at the mountain shrines
>   or look to the idols of the house of Israel.
> He does not defile his neighbor's wife
>   or lie with a woman during her period.
> He does not oppress anyone,
>   but returns what he took in pledge for a loan.
> He does not commit robbery
>   but gives his food to the hungry
>   and provides clothing for the naked.
> He does not lend at usury
>   or take excessive interest.[b]
> He withholds his hand from doing wrong
>   and judges fairly between man and man.
> He follows my decrees
>   and faithfully keeps my laws.
> That man is righteous;
>   he will surely live,

>   declares the Sovereign LORD.

Ezk. 18:10-20   "Suppose he has a violent son, who sheds blood or does any of these other things[c] (though the father has done none of them):

> "He eats at the mountain shrines.
> He defiles his neighbor's wife.
> He oppresses the poor and needy.
> He commits robbery.
> He does not return what he took in pledge.
> He looks to the idols.
> He does detestable things.

[b]Or *take interest*; similarly in verses 13 and 17   [c]Or *things to a brother*

He lends at usury and takes excessive interest.

Will such a man live? He will not! Because he has done all these detestable things, he will surely be put to death and his blood will be on his own head.

"But suppose this son has a son who sees all the sins his father commits, and though he sees them, he does not do such things:

"He does not eat at the mountain shrines
      or look to the idols of the house of Israel.
He does not defile his neighbor's wife.
He does not oppress anyone
      or require a pledge for a loan.
He does not commit robbery
      but gives his food to the hungry
      and provides clothing for the naked.
He withholds his hand from sin[d]
      and takes no usury or excessive interest.
He keeps my laws and follows my decrees.

He will not die for his father's sin; he will surely live. But his father will die for his own sin, because he practiced extortion, robbed his brother and did what was wrong among his people.

"Yet you ask, 'Why does the son not share the guilt of his father?' Since the son has done what is just and right and has been careful to keep all my decrees, he will surely live. The soul who sins is the one who will die. The son will not share the guilt of the father, nor will the father share the guilt of the son. The righteousness of the righteous man will be credited to him, and the wickedness of the wicked will be charged against him.

REPENTANCE AND REJECTION.   "But if a wicked man turns away from all the sins he has committed and keeps all my decrees and does what is just and right, he will surely live; he will not die. None of the offenses he has committed will be remembered against him. Because of the righteous things he has done, he will live. Do I take any pleasure in the death of the wicked? declares the Sovereign LORD. Rather, am I not pleased when they turn from their ways and live?

**Ezk.
18:21-32**

"But if a righteous man turns from his righteousness and commits sin and does the same detestable things the wicked man does, will he live? None of the righteous things he has done will be remembered. Because of the unfaithfulness he is guilty of and because of the sins he has committed, he will die.

"Yet you say, 'The way of the Lord is not just.' Hear, O house of Israel: Is my way unjust? Is it not your ways that are unjust? If a righteous man turns from his righteousness and commits sin, he will die for it; because of the sin he has committed he will die. But if a wicked man turns away from the wickedness he has committed and does what is just and right, he will save his life. Because he considers all the offenses he has committed and turns away from them, he will surely live; he will not die. Yet the house of Israel says, 'The way of the Lord is not just.' Are my ways unjust, O house of Israel? Is it not your ways that are unjust?

"Therefore, O house of Israel, I will judge you, each one according to his

[d] Septuagint (see also verse 8); Hebrew *from the poor*

ways, declares the Sovereign LORD. Repent! Turn away from all your offenses; then sin will not be your downfall. Rid yourselves of all the offenses you have committed, and get a new heart and a new spirit. Why will you die, O house of Israel? For I take no pleasure in the death of anyone, declares the Sovereign LORD. Repent and live!

As a lasting reminder of how the wicked are brought down, Ezekiel writes a lament for two of Judah's kings who were taken by Judah's oppressors. It has been some 17 years since Pharaoh Neco led King Jehoahaz away to captivity in Egypt, and some six years since Nebuchadnezzar brought a subdued King Jehoiakin to Babylonia. Their capture and exile are witness to Judah's vulnerability to God's judgment.

Ezk. 19:1-9 LAMENT FOR THE KINGS. "Take up a lament concerning the princes of Israel and say:

> " 'What a lioness was your mother
>   among the lions!
> She lay down among the young lions
>   and reared her cubs.
> She brought up one of her cubs,
>   and he became a strong lion.
> He learned to tear the prey
>   and he devoured men.
> The nations heard about him,
>   and he was trapped in their pit.
> They led him with hooks
>   to the land of Egypt.

> " 'When she saw her hope unfulfilled,
>   her expectation gone,
> she took another of her cubs
>   and made him a strong lion.
> He prowled among the lions,
>   for he was now a strong lion.
> He learned to tear the prey
>   and he devoured men.
> He broke down[e] their strongholds
>   and devastated their towns.
> The land and all who were in it
>   were terrified by his roaring.
> Then the nations came against him,
>   those from regions round about.
> They spread their net for him,
>   and he was trapped in their pit.
> With hooks they pulled him into a cage
>   and brought him to the king of Babylon.
> They put him in prison,
>   so his roar was heard no longer
>   on the mountains of Israel.

[e]Targum (see Septuagint); Hebrew *He knew*

" 'Your mother was like a vine in your vineyard^f Ezk.
    planted by the water;   19:10-14
it was fruitful and full of branches
    because of abundant water.
Its branches were strong,
    fit for a ruler's scepter.
It towered high
    above the thick foliage,
conspicuous for its height
    and for its many branches.
But it was uprooted in fury
    and thrown to the ground.
The east wind made it shrivel,
    it was stripped of its fruit;
its strong branches withered
    and fire consumed them.
Now it is planted in the desert,
    in a dry and thirsty land.
Fire spread from one of its main^g branches
    and consumed its fruit.
No strong branch is left on it
    fit for a ruler's scepter.'

This is a lament and is to be used as a lament."

In the following year, 590 B.C., God once again chastises Israel, citing their long history of rebellion and his repeated reluctance to bring ultimate punishment against them. He reminds Israel that they continue to be as sinful as their fathers, but that the day is coming when God's chosen ones will be an obedient and holy people.

HISTORY OF REBELLIOUSNESS.   In the seventh year, in the fifth month   Ezk.
on the tenth day, some of the elders of Israel came to inquire of the LORD,   20:1-12
and they sat down in front of me.   (590 B.C.)
Then the word of the LORD came to me: "Son of man, speak to the elders of Israel and say to them, 'This is what the Sovereign LORD says: Have you come to inquire of me? As surely as I live, I will not let you inquire of me, declares the Sovereign LORD.'
"Will you judge them? Will you judge them, son of man? Then confront them with the detestable practices of their fathers and say to them: 'This is what the Sovereign LORD says: On the day I chose Israel, I swore with uplifted hand to the descendants of the house of Jacob and revealed myself to them in Egypt. With uplifted hand I said to them, "I am the LORD your God." On that day I swore to them that I would bring them out of Egypt into a land I had searched out for them, a land flowing with milk and honey, the most beautiful of all lands. And I said to them, "Each of you, get rid of the vile images you have set your eyes on, and do not defile yourselves with the idols of Egypt. I am the LORD your God."
" 'But they rebelled against me and would not listen to me; they did not get rid of the vile images they had set their eyes on, nor did they forsake

^{f}Two Hebrew manuscripts; most Hebrew manuscripts *your blood* ^{g}Or *from under its*

the idols of Egypt. So I said I would pour out my wrath on them and spend my anger against them in Egypt. But for the sake of my name I did what would keep it from being profaned in the eyes of the nations they lived among and in whose sight I had revealed myself to the Israelites by bringing them out of Egypt. Therefore I led them out of Egypt and brought them into the desert. I gave them my decrees and made known to them my laws, for the man who obeys them will live by them. Also I gave them my Sabbaths as a sign between us, so they would know that I the LORD made them holy.

Ezk.
20:13-29 " 'Yet the people of Israel rebelled against me in the desert. They did not follow my decrees but rejected my laws—although the man who obeys them will live by them—and they utterly desecrated my Sabbaths. So I said I would pour out my wrath on them and destroy them in the desert. But for the sake of my name I did what would keep it from being profaned in the eyes of the nations in whose sight I had brought them out. Also with uplifted hand I swore to them in the desert that I would not bring them into the land I had given them—a land flowing with milk and honey, most beautiful of all lands—because they rejected my laws and did not follow my decrees and desecrated my Sabbaths. For their hearts were devoted to their idols. Yet I looked on them with pity and did not destroy them or put an end to them in the desert. I said to their children in the desert, "Do not follow the statutes of your fathers or keep their laws or defile yourselves with their idols. I am the LORD your God; follow my decrees and be careful to keep my laws. Keep my Sabbaths holy, that they may be a sign between us. Then you will know that I am the LORD your God."

" 'But the children rebelled against me: They did not follow my decrees, they were not careful to keep my laws—although the man who obeys them will live by them—and they desecrated my Sabbaths. So I said I would pour out my wrath on them and spend my anger against them in the desert. But I withheld my hand, and for the sake of my name I did what would keep it from being profaned in the eyes of the nations in whose sight I had brought them out. Also with uplifted hand I swore to them in the desert that I would disperse them among the nations and scatter them through the countries, because they had not obeyed my laws but had rejected my decrees and desecrated my Sabbaths, and their eyes ˌlustedˌ after their fathers' idols. I also gave them over to statutes that were not good and laws they could not live by; I let them become defiled through their gifts—the sacrifice of every firstborn[h]—that I might fill them with horror so they would know that I am the LORD.'

"Therefore, son of man, speak to the people of Israel and say to them, 'This is what the Sovereign LORD says: In this also your fathers blasphemed me by forsaking me: When I brought them into the land I had sworn to give them and they saw any high hill or any leafy tree, there they offered their sacrifices, made offerings that provoked me to anger, presented their fragrant incense and poured out their drink offerings. Then I said to them: What is this high place you go to?' " (It is called Bamah[i] to this day.)

Ezk.
20:30-38 PRESENT REBELLIOUSNESS.   "Therefore say to the house of Israel: 'This is what the Sovereign LORD says: Will you defile yourselves the way

[h]Or—*making every firstborn pass through ˌthe fireˌ*   [i]*Bamah* means *high place.*

your fathers did and lust after their vile images? When you offer your gifts—the sacrifice of your sons in[j] the fire—you continue to defile yourselves with all your idols to this day. Am I to let you inquire of me, O house of Israel? As surely as I live, declares the Sovereign LORD, I will not let you inquire of me.

" 'You say, "We want to be like the nations, like the peoples of the world, who serve wood and stone." But what you have in mind will never happen. As surely as I live, declares the Sovereign LORD, I will rule over you with a mighty hand and an outstretched arm and with outpoured wrath. I will bring you from the nations and gather you from the countries where you have been scattered—with a mighty hand and an outstretched arm and with outpoured wrath. I will bring you into the desert of the nations and there, face to face, I will execute judgment upon you. As I judged your fathers in the desert of the land of Egypt, so I will judge you, declares the Sovereign LORD. I will take note of you as you pass under my rod, and I will bring you into the bond of the covenant. I will purge you of those who revolt and rebel against me. Although I will bring them out of the land where they are living, yet they will not enter the land of Israel. Then you will know that I am the LORD.

TIME OF NO REBELLION. " 'As for you, O house of Israel, this is what the Sovereign LORD says: Go and serve your idols, every one of you! But afterward you will surely listen to me and no longer profane my holy name with your gifts and idols. For on my holy mountain, the high mountain of Israel, declares the Sovereign LORD, there in the land the entire house of Israel will serve me, and there I will accept them. There I will require your offerings and your choice gifts,[k] along with all your holy sacrifices. I will accept you as fragrant incense when I bring you out from the nations and gather you from the countries where you have been scattered, and I will show myself holy among you in the sight of the nations. Then you will know that I am the LORD, when I bring you into the land of Israel, the land I had sworn with uplifted hand to give to your fathers. There you will remember your conduct and all the actions by which you have defiled yourselves, and you will loathe yourselves for all the evil you have done. You will know that I am the LORD, when I deal with you for my name's sake and not according to your evil ways and your corrupt practices, O house of Israel, declares the Sovereign LORD.' "

Ezk.
20:39-44

Because of Israel's rebellion, judgment has already come against the northern tribes, and God's vengeance is poised against Judah. Ezekiel now sees the sword of judgment coming. Ezekiel turns his face southward and brings still other pronouncements against Judah's sin. Perhaps the judgments keep coming for the simple reason that so far few people have believed their message. As Ezekiel complains, they think he is simply bringing nice little parables—interesting sermons from which they derive entertainment. Hence the picture of a sword. Maybe it will get their attention.

VIEW TO THE HOMELAND. The word of the LORD came to me: "Son of man, set your face toward the south; preach against the south and prophesy against the forest of the southland. Say to the southern forest:

Ezk.
20:45-49

[j]Or *making your sons pass through*   [k]Or *and the gifts of your firstfruits*

'Hear the word of the LORD. This is what the Sovereign LORD says: I am about to set fire to you, and it will consume all your trees, both green and dry. The blazing flame will not be quenched, and every face from south to north will be scorched by it. Everyone will see that I the LORD have kindled it; it will not be quenched.'"

Then I said, "Ah, Sovereign LORD! They are saying of me, 'Isn't he just telling parables?'"

Ezk.
21:1-12

SWORD OF JUDGMENT.   The word of the LORD came to me: "Son of man, set your face against Jerusalem and preach against the sanctuary. Prophesy against the land of Israel and say to her: 'This is what the LORD says: I am against you. I will draw my sword from its scabbard and cut off from you both the righteous and the wicked. Because I am going to cut off the righteous and the wicked, my sword will be unsheathed against everyone from south to north. Then all people will know that I the LORD have drawn my sword from its scabbard; it will not return again.'

"Therefore groan, son of man! Groan before them with broken heart and bitter grief. And when they ask you, 'Why are you groaning?' you shall say, 'Because of the news that is coming. Every heart will melt and every hand go limp; every spirit will become faint and every knee become as weak as water.' It is coming! It will surely take place, declares the Sovereign LORD."

The word of the LORD came to me: "Son of man, prophesy and say, 'This is what the Lord says:

" 'A sword, a sword,
    sharpened and polished—
sharpened for the slaughter,
    polished to flash like lightning!

" 'Shall we rejoice in the scepter of my son ⸢Judah⸥? The sword despises every such stick.

" 'The sword is appointed to be polished,
    to be grasped with the hand;
it is sharpened and polished,
    made ready for the hand of the slayer.
Cry out and wail, son of man,
    for it is against my people;
it is against all the princes of Israel.
They are thrown to the sword
    along with my people.
Therefore beat your breast.

Ezk.
21:13-17

" 'Testing will surely come. And what if the scepter ⸢of Judah⸥, which the sword despises, does not continue? declares the Sovereign LORD.'

"So then, son of man, prophesy
    and strike your hands together.
Let the sword strike twice,
    even three times.
It is a sword for slaughter—
    a sword for great slaughter,
    closing in on them from every side.
So that hearts may melt

and the fallen be many,
I have stationed the sword for slaughter[l]
   at all their gates.
Oh! It is made to flash like lightning,
   it is grasped for slaughter.
O sword, slash to the right,
   then to the left,
   wherever your blade is turned.
I too will strike my hands together,
   and my wrath will subside.
I the LORD have spoken."

BABYLONIA IS SWORD. The word of the LORD came to me: "Son of man, mark out two roads for the sword of the king of Babylon to take, both starting from the same country. Make a signpost where the road branches off to the city. Mark out one road for the sword to come against Rabbah of the Ammonites and another against Judah and fortified Jerusalem. For the king of Babylon will stop at the fork in the road, at the junction of the two roads, to seek an omen: He will cast lots with arrows, he will consult his idols, he will examine the liver. Into his right hand will come the lot for Jerusalem, where he is to set up battering rams, to give the command to slaughter, to sound the battle cry, to set battering rams against the gates, to build a ramp and to erect siege works. It will seem like a false omen to those who have sworn allegiance to him, but he will remind them of their guilt and take them captive.   *Ezk. 21:18-24*

"Therefore this is what the Sovereign LORD says: 'Because you people have brought to mind your guilt by your open rebellion, revealing your sins in all that you do—because you have done this, you will be taken captive.

WARNING TO ZEDEKIAH. " 'O profane and wicked prince of Israel, whose day has come, whose time of punishment has reached its climax, this is what the Sovereign LORD says: Take off the turban, remove the crown. It will not be as it was: The lowly will be exalted and the exalted will be brought low. A ruin! A ruin! I will make it a ruin! It will not be restored until he comes to whom it rightfully belongs; to him I will give it.'   *Ezk. 21:25-27*

AMMONITES SHARE FATE. "And you, son of man, prophesy and say, 'This is what the Sovereign LORD says about the Ammonites and their insults: *Ezk. 21:28-32*

" 'A sword, a sword,
   drawn for the slaughter,
polished to consume
   and to flash like lightning!
Despite false visions concerning you
   and lying divinations about you,
it will be laid on the necks
   of the wicked who are to be slain,
whose day has come,
   whose time of punishment has reached its climax.

---

[l]Septuagint; the meaning of the Hebrew for this word is uncertain.

Return the sword to its scabbard.
    In the place where you were created,
in the land of your ancestry,
    I will judge you.
I will pour out my wrath upon you
    and breathe out my fiery anger against you;
I will hand you over to brutal men,
    men skilled in destruction.
You will be fuel for the fire,
    your blood will be shed in your land,
you will be remembered no more;
    for I the LORD have spoken.' "

Ezk.
22:1-16

ENUMERATION OF SINS.   The word of the LORD came to me: "Son of
man, will you judge her? Will you judge this city of bloodshed? Then confront her with all her detestable practices and say: 'This is what the
Sovereign LORD says: O city that brings on herself doom by shedding
blood in her midst and defiles herself by making idols, you have become
guilty because of the blood you have shed and have become defiled by the
idols you have made. You have brought your days to a close, and the end
of your years has come. Therefore I will make you an object of scorn to the
nations and a laughingstock to all the countries. Those who are near and
those who are far away will mock you, O infamous city, full of turmoil.

" 'See how each of the princes of Israel who are in you uses his power
to shed blood. In you they have treated father and mother with contempt;
in you they have oppressed the alien and mistreated the fatherless and the
widow. You have despised my holy things and desecrated my Sabbaths. In
you are slanderous men bent on shedding blood; in you are those who eat
at the mountain shrines and commit lewd acts. In you are those who dishonor their fathers' bed; in you are those who violate women during their
period, when they are ceremonially unclean. In you one man commits a
detestable offense with his neighbor's wife, another shamefully defiles his
daughter-in-law, and another violates his sister, his own father's daughter.
In you men accept bribes to shed blood; you take usury and excessive
interest[m] and make unjust gain from your neighbors by extortion. And
you have forgotten me, declares the Sovereign LORD.

" 'I will surely strike my hands together at the unjust gain you have
made and at the blood you have shed in your midst. Will your courage
endure or your hands be strong in the day I deal with you? I the LORD have
spoken, and I will do it. I will disperse you among the nations and scatter
you through the countries; and I will put an end to your uncleanness.
When you have been defiled[n] in the eyes of the nations, you will know
that I am the LORD.' "

Ezk.
22:17-31

Then the word of the LORD came to me: "Son of man, the house of Israel
has become dross to me; all of them are the copper, tin, iron and lead left
inside a furnace. They are but the dross of silver. Therefore this is what the
Sovereign LORD says: 'Because you have all become dross, I will gather
you into Jerusalem. As men gather silver, copper, iron, lead and tin into a
furnace to melt it with a fiery blast, so will I gather you in my anger and
my wrath and put you inside the city and melt you. I will gather you and

---

[m]Or *usury and interest*   [n]Or *When I have allotted you your inheritance*

I will blow on you with my fiery wrath, and you will be melted inside her. As silver is melted in a furnace, so you will be melted inside her, and you will know that I the LORD have poured out my wrath upon you.'"

Again the word of the LORD came to me: "Son of man, say to the land, 'You are a land that has had no rain or showers*o* in the day of wrath.' There is a conspiracy of her princes*p* within her like a roaring lion tearing its prey; they devour people, take treasures and precious things and make many widows within her. Her priests do violence to my law and profane my holy things; they do not distinguish between the holy and the common; they teach that there is no difference between the unclean and the clean; and they shut their eyes to the keeping of my Sabbaths, so that I am profaned among them. Her officials within her are like wolves tearing their prey; they shed blood and kill people to make unjust gain. Her prophets whitewash these deeds for them by false visions and lying divinations. They say, 'This is what the Sovereign LORD says'—when the LORD has not spoken. The people of the land practice extortion and commit robbery; they oppress the poor and needy and mistreat the alien, denying them justice.

"I looked for a man among them who would build up the wall and stand before me in the gap on behalf of the land so I would not have to destroy it, but I found none. So I will pour out my wrath on them and consume them with my fiery anger, bringing down on their own heads all they have done, declares the Sovereign LORD."

If the picture of a sword fails to get Judah's attention, the following allegory certainly ought to. In all of Scripture there is probably no more graphic an indictment. Modern readers are almost offended by the candid exposure of two promiscuous sisters, representing Israel and Judah. One gets at least some idea of the degree to which God himself is offended by his people's infidelity.

TWO PROMISCUOUS SISTERS. The word of the LORD came to me: "Son of man, there were two women, daughters of the same mother. They became prostitutes in Egypt, engaging in prostitution from their youth. In that land their breasts were fondled and their virgin bosoms caressed. The older was named Oholah, and her sister was Oholibah. They were mine and gave birth to sons and daughters. Oholah is Samaria, and Oholibah is Jerusalem.

"Oholah engaged in prostitution while she was still mine; and she lusted after her lovers, the Assyrians—warriors clothed in blue, governors and commanders, all of them handsome young men, and mounted horsemen. She gave herself as a prostitute to all the elite of the Assyrians and defiled herself with all the idols of everyone she lusted after. She did not give up the prostitution she began in Egypt, when during her youth men slept with her, caressed her virgin bosom and poured out their lust upon her.

"Therefore I handed her over to her lovers, the Assyrians, for whom she lusted. They stripped her naked, took away her sons and daughters and killed her with the sword. She became a byword among women, and punishment was inflicted on her.

Ezk. 23:1-13

*o*Septuagint; Hebrew *has not been cleansed or rained on*   *p*Septuagint; Hebrew *prophets*

"Her sister Oholibah saw this, yet in her lust and prostitution she was more depraved than her sister. She too lusted after the Assyrians—governors and commanders, warriors in full dress, mounted horsemen, all handsome young men. I saw that she too defiled herself; both of them went the same way.

Ezk.
23:14-27
"But she carried her prostitution still further. She saw men portrayed on a wall, figures of Chaldeans*q* portrayed in red, with belts around their waists and flowing turbans on their heads; all of them looked like Babylonian chariot officers, natives of Chaldea.*r* As soon as she saw them, she lusted after them and sent messengers to them in Chaldea. Then the Babylonians came to her, to the bed of love, and in their lust they defiled her. After she had been defiled by them, she turned away from them in disgust. When she carried on her prostitution openly and exposed her nakedness, I turned away from her in disgust, just as I had turned away from her sister. Yet she became more and more promiscuous as she recalled the days of her youth, when she was a prostitute in Egypt. There she lusted after her lovers, whose genitals were like those of donkeys and whose emission was like that of horses. So you longed for the lewdness of your youth, when in Egypt your bosom was caressed and your young breasts fondled.*s*

"Therefore, Oholibah, this is what the Sovereign LORD says: I will stir up your lovers against you, those you turned away from in disgust, and I will bring them against you from every side—the Babylonians and all the Chaldeans, the men of Pekod and Shoa and Koa, and all the Assyrians with them, handsome young men, all of them governors and commanders, chariot officers and men of high rank, all mounted on horses. They will come against you with weapons,*t* chariots and wagons and with a throng of people; they will take up positions against you on every side with large and small shields and with helmets. I will turn you over to them for punishment, and they will punish you according to their standards. I will direct my jealous anger against you, and they will deal with you in fury. They will cut off your noses and your ears, and those of you who are left will fall by the sword. They will take away your sons and daughters, and those of you who are left will be consumed by fire. They will also strip you of your clothes and take your fine jewelry. So I will put a stop to the lewdness and prostitution you began in Egypt. You will not look on these things with longing or remember Egypt anymore.

Ezk.
23:28-45
"For this is what the Sovereign LORD says: I am about to hand you over to those you hate, to those you turned away from in disgust. They will deal with you in hatred and take away everything you have worked for. They will leave you naked and bare, and the shame of your prostitution will be exposed. Your lewdness and promiscuity have brought this upon you, because you lusted after the nations and defiled yourself with their idols. You have gone the way of your sister; so I will put her cup into your hand.

"This is what the Sovereign LORD says:

"You will drink your sister's cup,
    a cup large and deep;

---

*q*Or *Babylonia*   *r*Or *Babylonia*; also in verse 16   *s*Syriac (see also verse 3); Hebrew *caressed because of your young breasts*   *t*The meaning of the Hebrew for this word is uncertain.

> it will bring scorn and derision,
>> for it holds so much.
> You will be filled with drunkenness and sorrow,
>> the cup of ruin and desolation,
>> the cup of your sister Samaria.
> You will drink it and drain it dry;
>> you will dash it to pieces
>> and tear your breasts.

I have spoken, declares the Sovereign LORD.

"Therefore this is what the Sovereign LORD says: Since you have forgotten me and thrust me behind your back, you must bear the consequences of your lewdness and prostitution."

The LORD said to me: "Son of man, will you judge Oholah and Oholibah? Then confront them with their detestable practices, for they have committed adultery and blood is on their hands. They committed adultery with their idols; they even sacrificed their children, whom they bore to me,[u] as food for them. They have also done this to me: At that same time they defiled my sanctuary and desecrated my Sabbaths. On the very day they sacrificed their children to their idols, they entered my sanctuary and desecrated it. That is what they did in my house.

"They even sent messengers for men who came from far away, and when they arrived you bathed yourself for them, painted your eyes and put on your jewelry. You sat on an elegant couch, with a table spread before it on which you had placed the incense and oil that belonged to me.

"The noise of a carefree crowd was around her; Sabeans[v] were brought from the desert along with men from the rabble, and they put bracelets on the arms of the woman and her sister and beautiful crowns on their heads. Then I said about the one worn out by adultery, 'Now let them use her as a prostitute, for that is all she is.' And they slept with her. As men sleep with a prostitute, so they slept with those lewd women, Oholah and Oholibah. But righteous men will sentence them to the punishment of women who commit adultery and shed blood, because they are adulterous and blood is on their hands.

"This is what the Sovereign LORD says: Bring a mob against them and give them over to terror and plunder. The mob will stone them and cut them down with their swords; they will kill their sons and daughters and burn down their houses.

"So I will put an end to lewdness in the land, that all women may take warning and not imitate you. You will suffer the penalty for your lewdness and bear the consequences of your sins of idolatry. Then you will know that I am the Sovereign LORD."

Ezk.
23:46-49

What more can be said? God feels deeply the shame and disgrace that his "bride" has brought him. Her disrespect for his spiritual leadership, her chasing after material satisfaction, and her many adulteries with lesser gods have left him no choice. Israel must be put away until she repents. The time has come. Even now it begins.

---

[u]Or *even made the children they bore to me pass through* ⌞*the fire*⌟   [v]Or *drunkards*

AUGUST 21

Siege of Jerusalem_____

*J*t is not known exactly when Zedekiah first gets the foolish notion to
rebel against Nebuchadnezzar, but it is probably around 590-589 B.C.
When he does rebel, Nebuchadnezzar responds in predictable fashion
about 588 B.C. by entering Judah with his powerful Babylonian army and laying siege to its cities, including Jerusalem. (Have not all the prophets warned
that it would happen?)

2 Kgs. 24:20b REBELLION AGAINST BABYLON.   He also rebelled against King Nebu-
2 Ch. 36:13a chadnezzar, who had made him take an oath in God's name.
Jer. 52:3b
(590-589)   SIEGE OF JERUSALEM.   So in the ninth year of Zedekiah's reign, on the
2 Kgs. 25:1 tenth day of the tenth month, Nebuchadnezzar king of Babylon marched
Jer. 39:1   against Jerusalem with his whole army. They camped outside the city and
52:4   built siege works all around it.
(588 B.C.)

Siege Announced to Ezekiel_____

*A*most amazing thing happens on the very day of the siege, in the ninth
year of Zedekiah's reign, in the tenth month on the tenth day. Some
300 to 700 miles away from Jerusalem, in the city of Tel Abib, near the
Kebar River in Babylonia, the prophet Ezekiel is told about the siege. No messenger of Ezekiel's day can deliver news that quickly! None, that is, except God
himself. And here is what Ezekiel is told.

Ezk. 24:1,2 THE SIEGE ANNOUNCED.   In the ninth year, in the tenth month on the
(588 B.C.)   tenth day, the word of the LORD came to me: "Son of man, record this date,
this very date, because the king of Babylon has laid siege to Jerusalem this
very day.

Ezk.   PARABLE OF COOKING POT.   Tell this rebellious house a parable and
24:3-14   say to them: 'This is what the Sovereign LORD says:

" 'Put on the cooking pot; put it on
and pour water into it.
Put into it the pieces of meat,
all the choice pieces—the leg and the shoulder.
Fill it with the best of these bones;
take the pick of the flock.
Pile wood beneath it for the bones;
bring it to a boil
and cook the bones in it.

" 'For this is what the Sovereign LORD says:

" 'Woe to the city of bloodshed,
to the pot now encrusted,
whose deposit will not go away!
Empty it piece by piece
without casting lots for them.

" 'For the blood she shed is in her midst:
She poured it on the bare rock;
she did not pour it on the ground,

                    where the dust would cover it.
            To stir up wrath and take revenge
            I put her blood on the bare rock,
                    so that it would not be covered.

" 'Therefore this is what the Sovereign LORD says:

    " 'Woe to the city of bloodshed!
            I, too, will pile the wood high.
    So heap on the wood
            and kindle the fire.
    Cook the meat well,
            mixing in the spices;
            and let the bones be charred.
    Then set the empty pot on the coals
            till it becomes hot and its copper glows
    so its impurities may be melted
            and its deposit burned away.
    It has frustrated all efforts;
            its heavy deposit has not been removed,
            not even by fire.

" 'Now your impurity is lewdness. Because I tried to cleanse you but you would not be cleansed from your impurity, you will not be clean again until my wrath against you has subsided.

" 'I the LORD have spoken. The time has come for me to act. I will not hold back; I will not have pity, nor will I relent. You will be judged according to your conduct and your actions, declares the Sovereign LORD.' "

Following this word about the beginning of Jerusalem's siege comes one of the most disturbing accounts in all of recorded Scripture. It is nothing new for God to provide signs of his working. Ezekiel himself has enacted many of these signs in the presence of his people and provided the interpretation for their edification. And it is nothing new for God to require great sacrifice on the part of his prophets. But God now brings a sign which requires the ultimate sacrifice of Ezekiel. As a sign that there is to be no mourning for the loss of life when Jerusalem finally falls, God actually takes the life of Ezekiel's wife!

DEATH OF WIFE.   The word of the LORD came to me: "Son of man, with one blow I am about to take away from you the delight of your eyes. Yet do not lament or weep or shed any tears. Groan quietly; do not mourn for the dead. Keep your turban fastened and your sandals on your feet; do not cover the lower part of your face or eat the customary food ⌊of mourners⌋."   **Ezk. 24:15-24**

So I spoke to the people in the morning, and in the evening my wife died. The next morning I did as I had been commanded.

Then the people asked me, "Won't you tell us what these things have to do with us?"

So I said to them, "The word of the LORD came to me: Say to the house of Israel, 'This is what the Sovereign LORD says: I am about to desecrate my sanctuary—the stronghold in which you take pride, the delight of your eyes, the object of your affection. The sons and daughters you left behind will fall by the sword. And you will do as I have done. You will not cover the lower part of your face or eat the customary food ⌐of mourners⌐. You will keep your turbans on your heads and your sandals on your feet. You will not mourn or weep but will waste away because of[w] your sins and groan among yourselves. Ezekiel will be a sign to you; you will do just as he has done. When this happens, you will know that I am the Sovereign LORD.'

Ezk.
24:25-27

SIGN OF JERUSALEM'S FALL. "And you, son of man, on the day I take away their stronghold, their joy and glory, the delight of their eyes, their heart's desire, and their sons and daughters as well—on that day a fugitive will come to tell you the news. At that time your mouth will be opened; you will speak with him and will no longer be silent. So you will be a sign to them, and they will know that I am the LORD."

Perhaps Ezekiel's wife was dying in any event, and God simply used her death as a way of bringing an important message. But that would be highly coincidental and clearly contrary to Ezekiel's account. Certainly it can be said that Ezekiel is being asked to give up no more than what God himself will give up one day in order to bring a sign to all the world. Perhaps that itself is the very answer: as Creator of the universe God can and does act in ways that confound man. Death undoubtedly has a totally different significance to God than it does to man. But the immediate mystery is how Ezekiel can seemingly take his wife's death in stride and continue his ministry. What testimony to any man's faith this would be!

Jeremiah's Prophecies During Siege

*T*he focus returns to Jerusalem. With Nebuchadnezzar's army just outside the walls, Zedekiah realizes that it is time to consult God. But the answer from Jeremiah is to surrender or be destroyed.

Jer. 21:1,2

ZEDEKIAH INQUIRES OF FATE. The word came to Jeremiah from the LORD when King Zedekiah sent to him Pashhur son of Malkijah and the priest Zephaniah son of Maaseiah. They said: "Inquire now of the LORD for us because Nebuchadnezzar[x] king of Babylon is attacking us. Perhaps the LORD will perform wonders for us as in times past so that he will withdraw from us."

Jer. 21:3-7

FAMINE, PLAGUE, AND SWORD. But Jeremiah answered them, "Tell Zedekiah, 'This is what the LORD, the God of Israel, says: I am about to turn against you the weapons of war that are in your hands, which you are using to fight the king of Babylon and the Babylonians[y] who are outside the wall besieging you. And I will gather them inside this city. I myself will fight against you with an outstretched hand and a mighty arm in anger and fury and great wrath. I will strike down those who live in this city—both men and animals—and they will die of a terrible plague.

[w]Or *away in* [x]Hebrew *Nebuchadrezzar,* of which *Nebuchadnezzar* is a variant; here and often in Jeremiah and Ezekiel [y]Or *Chaldeans*

After that, declares the LORD, I will hand over Zedekiah king of Judah, his officials and the people in this city who survive the plague, sword and famine, to Nebuchadnezzar king of Babylon and to their enemies who seek their lives. He will put them to the sword; he will show them no mercy or pity or compassion.'

CHOICE OF SURRENDER. "Furthermore, tell the people, 'This is what the LORD says: See, I am setting before you the way of life and the way of death. Whoever stays in this city will die by the sword, famine or plague. But whoever goes out and surrenders to the Babylonians who are besieging you will live; he will escape with his life. I have determined to do this city harm and not good, declares the LORD. It will be given into the hands of the king of Babylon, and he will destroy it with fire.'

Jer. 21:8-10

RIGHTEOUSNESS PARAMOUNT. "Moreover, say to the royal house of Judah, 'Hear the word of the LORD; O house of David, this is what the LORD says:

Jer. 21:11-14

> " 'Administer justice every morning;
>> rescue from the hand of his oppressor
>> the one who has been robbed,
> or my wrath will break out and burn like fire
>> because of the evil you have done—
>> burn with no one to quench it.
> I am against you, ⌐Jerusalem,⌐
>> you who live above this valley
>> on the rocky plateau,
>
>>>> declares the LORD—
> you who say, "Who can come against us?
>> Who can enter our refuge?"
> I will punish you as your deeds deserve,
>
>>>> declares the LORD.
> I will kindle a fire in your forests
>> that will consume everything around you.' "

JUDGMENT AGAINST EVIL KINGS. This is what the LORD says: "Go down to the palace of the king of Judah and proclaim this message there: 'Hear the word of the LORD, O king of Judah, you who sit on David's throne—you, your officials and your people who come through these gates. This is what the LORD says: Do what is just and right. Rescue from the hand of his oppressor the one who has been robbed. Do no wrong or violence to the alien, the fatherless or the widow, and do not shed innocent blood in this place. For if you are careful to carry out these commands, then kings who sit on David's throne will come through the gates of this palace, riding in chariots and on horses, accompanied by their officials and their people. But if you do not obey these commands, declares the LORD, I swear by myself that this palace will become a ruin.' "

Jer. 22:1-9

For this is what the LORD says about the palace of the king of Judah:

> "Though you are like Gilead to me,
>> like the summit of Lebanon,
> I will surely make you like a desert,
>> like towns not inhabited.
> I will send destroyers against you,
>> each man with his weapons,

and they will cut up your fine cedar beams
and throw them into the fire.

"People from many nations will pass by this city and will ask one another, 'Why has the LORD done such a thing to this great city?' And the answer
will be: 'Because they have forsaken the covenant of the LORD their God
and have worshiped and served other gods.'"

Zedekiah chooses not to surrender, and the siege continues. All but a few
of the other fortified cities in Judah have been taken when God sends Jeremiah
to Zedekiah with a message about Zedekiah's personal future. Although he is
told that he will die a natural death in Babylon, he is spared the knowledge that
he will lose his eyes in the process.

Jer. 34:1-3   ZEDEKIAH TO BE CAPTIVE. While Nebuchadnezzar king of Babylon
and all his army and all the kingdoms and peoples in the empire he ruled
were fighting against Jerusalem and all its surrounding towns, this word
came to Jeremiah from the LORD: "This is what the LORD, the God of Israel,
says: Go to Zedekiah king of Judah and tell him, 'This is what the LORD
says: I am about to hand this city over to the king of Babylon, and he will
burn it down. You will not escape from his grasp but will surely be captured and handed over to him. You will see the king of Babylon with your
own eyes, and he will speak with you face to face. And you will go to
Babylon.

Jer. 34:4,5   NOT TO BE KILLED.   " 'Yet hear the promise of the LORD, O Zedekiah
king of Judah. This is what the LORD says concerning you: You will not die
by the sword; you will die peacefully. As people made a funeral fire in
honor of your fathers, the former kings who preceded you, so they will
make a fire in your honor and lament, "Alas, O master!" I myself make
this promise, declares the LORD.'"

Jer. 34:6,7   JEREMIAH INFORMS ZEDEKIAH.   Then Jeremiah the prophet told all
this to Zedekiah king of Judah, in Jerusalem, while the army of the king of
Babylon was fighting against Jerusalem and the other cities of Judah that
were still holding out—Lachish and Azekah. These were the only fortified
cities left in Judah.

Zedekiah finds no comfort in these words. In fact he is angered to the point
of having Jeremiah placed under house arrest. It is during his own confinement
in the royal palace, and Jerusalem's confinement as well, that Jeremiah goes to
great lengths to reassure the people of Jerusalem that, after the city's fall and an
appropriate time of national penitence, both Jerusalem and all of Israel will be
restored. Jeremiah begins by using the illustration of a field he has bought. His
point is that there will come a time when everything will return to normal, and
life will go on as usual. So that there is no mistake about it, God reveals the
good news through Jeremiah not once but twice.

Jer. 32:1-5   JEREMIAH'S CONFINEMENT.   This is the word that came to Jeremiah
(587 B.C.)   from the LORD in the tenth year of Zedekiah king of Judah, which was the
eighteenth year of Nebuchadnezzar. The army of the king of Babylon was
then besieging Jerusalem, and Jeremiah the prophet was confined in the
courtyard of the guard in the royal palace of Judah.

Now Zedekiah king of Judah had imprisoned him there, saying, "Why do you prophesy as you do? You say, 'This is what the LORD says: I am about to hand this city over to the king of Babylon, and he will capture it. Zedekiah king of Judah will not escape out of the hands of the Babylonians[z] but will certainly be handed over to the king of Babylon, and will speak with him face to face and see him with his own eyes. He will take Zedekiah to Babylon, where he will remain until I deal with him, declares the LORD. If you fight against the Babylonians, you will not succeed.'"

JEREMIAH RELATES PURCHASE.   Jeremiah said, "The word of the LORD came to me: Hanamel son of Shallum your uncle is going to come to you and say, 'Buy my field at Anathoth, because as nearest relative it is your right and duty to buy it.' | Jer. 32:6-12

"Then, just as the LORD had said, my cousin Hanamel came to me in the courtyard of the guard and said, 'Buy my field at Anathoth in the territory of Benjamin. Since it is your right to redeem it and possess it, buy it for yourself.'

"I knew that this was the word of the LORD; so I bought the field at Anathoth from my cousin Hanamel and weighed out for him seventeen shekels[a] of silver. I signed and sealed the deed, had it witnessed, and weighed out the silver on the scales. I took the deed of purchase—the sealed copy containing the terms and conditions, as well as the unsealed copy—and I gave this deed to Baruch son of Neriah, the son of Mahseiah, in the presence of my cousin Hanamel and of the witnesses who had signed the deed and of all the Jews sitting in the courtyard of the guard.

LIFE WILL GO ON.   "In their presence I gave Baruch these instructions: 'This is what the LORD Almighty, the God of Israel, says: Take these documents, both the sealed and unsealed copies of the deed of purchase, and put them in a clay jar so they will last a long time. For this is what the LORD Almighty, the God of Israel, says: Houses, fields and vineyards will again be bought in this land.' | Jer. 32:13-15

JEREMIAH PRAISES GOD.   "After I had given the deed of purchase to Baruch son of Neriah, I prayed to the LORD: | Jer. 32:16-25

"Ah, Sovereign LORD, you have made the heavens and the earth by your great power and outstretched arm. Nothing is too hard for you. You show love to thousands but bring the punishment for the fathers' sins into the laps of their children after them. O great and powerful God, whose name is the LORD Almighty, great are your purposes and mighty are your deeds. Your eyes are open to all the ways of men; you reward everyone according to his conduct and as his deeds deserve. You performed miraculous signs and wonders in Egypt and have continued them to this day, both in Israel and among all mankind, and have gained the renown that is still yours. You brought your people Israel out of Egypt with signs and wonders, by a mighty hand and an outstretched arm and with great terror. You gave them this land you had sworn to give their forefathers, a land flowing with milk and honey. They came in and took possession of it, but they did not obey you or follow your law; they did not do what you commanded them to do. So you brought all this disaster upon them.

[z]Or *Chaldeans*; also in verses 5, 24, 25, 28, 29 and 43   [a]That is, about 7 ounces (about 200 grams)

"See how the siege ramps are built up to take the city. Because of the sword, famine and plague, the city will be handed over to the Babylonians who are attacking it. What you said has happened, as you now see. And though the city will be handed over to the Babylonians, you, O Sovereign LORD, say to me, 'Buy the field with silver and have the transaction witnessed.'"

Jer.
32:26-35

CHARGE AGAINST JERUSALEM.   Then the word of the LORD came to Jeremiah: "I am the LORD, the God of all mankind. Is anything too hard for me? Therefore, this is what the LORD says: I am about to hand this city over to the Babylonians and to Nebuchadnezzar king of Babylon, who will capture it. The Babylonians who are attacking this city will come in and set it on fire; they will burn it down, along with the houses where the people provoked me to anger by burning incense on the roofs to Baal and by pouring out drink offerings to other gods.

"The people of Israel and Judah have done nothing but evil in my sight from their youth; indeed, the people of Israel have done nothing but provoke me with what their hands have made, declares the LORD. From the day it was built until now, this city has so aroused my anger and wrath that I must remove it from my sight. The people of Israel and Judah have provoked me by all the evil they have done—they, their kings and officials, their priests and prophets, the men of Judah and the people of Jerusalem. They turned their backs to me and not their faces; though I taught them again and again, they would not listen or respond to discipline. They set up their abominable idols in the house that bears my Name and defiled it. They built high places for Baal in the Valley of Ben Hinnom to sacrifice their sons and daughters[b] to Molech, though I never commanded, nor did it enter my mind, that they should do such a detestable thing and so make Judah sin.

Jer.
32:36-41

PROMISE OF RESTORATION.   "You are saying about this city, 'By the sword, famine and plague it will be handed over to the king of Babylon'; but this is what the LORD, the God of Israel, says: I will surely gather them from all the lands where I banish them in my furious anger and great wrath; I will bring them back to this place and let them live in safety. They will be my people, and I will be their God. I will give them singleness of heart and action, so that they will always fear me for their own good and the good of their children after them. I will make an everlasting covenant with them: I will never stop doing good to them, and I will inspire them to fear me, so that they will never turn away from me. I will rejoice in doing them good and will assuredly plant them in this land with all my heart and soul.

Jer.
32:42-44

BUSINESS WILL REVIVE.   "This is what the LORD says: As I have brought all this great calamity on this people, so I will give them all the prosperity I have promised them. Once more fields will be bought in this land of which you say, 'It is a desolate waste, without men or animals, for it has been handed over to the Babylonians.' Fields will be bought for silver, and deeds will be signed, sealed and witnessed in the territory of Benjamin, in the villages around Jerusalem, in the towns of Judah and in

[b]Or *to make their sons and daughters pass through ⌊the fire⌋*

the towns of the hill country, of the western foothills and of the Negev, because I will restore their fortunes,*c* declares the LORD."

SECOND WARNING. While Jeremiah was still confined in the court-yard of the guard, the word of the LORD came to him a second time: "This is what the LORD says, he who made the earth, the LORD who formed it and established it—the LORD is his name: 'Call to me and I will answer you and tell you great and unsearchable things you do not know.' For this is what the LORD, the God of Israel, says about the houses in this city and the royal palaces of Judah that have been torn down to be used against the siege ramps and the sword in the fight with the Babylonians*d*: 'They will be filled with the dead bodies of the men I will slay in my anger and wrath. I will hide my face from this city because of all its wickedness.

Jer. 33:1-5

SECOND PROMISE. " 'Nevertheless, I will bring health and healing to it; I will heal my people and will let them enjoy abundant peace and security. I will bring Judah and Israel back from captivity*e* and will rebuild them as they were before. I will cleanse them from all the sin they have committed against me and will forgive all their sins of rebellion against me. Then this city will bring me renown, joy, praise and honor before all nations on earth that hear of all the good things I do for it; and they will be in awe and will tremble at the abundant prosperity and peace I provide for it.'

Jer. 33:6-9

JOY WILL RETURN. "This is what the LORD says: 'You say about this place, "It is a desolate waste, without men or animals." Yet in the towns of Judah and the streets of Jerusalem that are deserted, inhabited by neither men nor animals, there will be heard once more the sounds of joy and gladness, the voices of bride and bridegroom, and the voices of those who bring thank offerings to the house of the LORD, saying,

Jer. 33:10,11

> "Give thanks to the LORD Almighty,
>   for the LORD is good;
>   his love endures forever."

For I will restore the fortunes of the land as they were before,' says the LORD.

PROSPERITY WILL RETURN. "This is what the LORD Almighty says: 'In this place, desolate and without men or animals—in all its towns there will again be pastures for shepherds to rest their flocks. In the towns of the hill country, of the western foothills and of the Negev, in the territory of Benjamin, in the villages around Jerusalem and in the towns of Judah, flocks will again pass under the hand of the one who counts them,' says the LORD.

Jer. 33:12,13

So that all will know that the eventual release of the people of Israel is due not to mere chance or changing political winds, God directs Jeremiah to record God's promises regarding the restoration. Using the prophetic poetry he often employs, Jeremiah makes it clear that it will be the God of Israel who purposely restores his people—nothing else.

---

*c*Or *will bring them back from captivity* *d*Or *Chaldeans* *e*Or *will restore the fortunes of Judah and Israel*

Jer. 30:1-3 RESTORATION PROMISES.   This is the word that came to Jeremiah from the LORD: "This is what the LORD, the God of Israel, says: 'Write in a book all the words I have spoken to you. The days are coming,' declares the LORD, 'when I will bring my people Israel and Judah back from captivity*f* and restore them to the land I gave their forefathers to possess,' says the LORD."

Jer. 30:4-11 EXILE WILL END.   These are the words the LORD spoke concerning Israel and Judah: "This is what the LORD says:

" 'Cries of fear are heard—
 terror, not peace.
Ask and see:
 Can a man bear children?
Then why do I see every strong man
 with his hands on his stomach like a woman in labor,
 every face turned deathly pale?
How awful that day will be!
 None will be like it.
It will be a time of trouble for Jacob,
 but he will be saved out of it.

" 'In that day,' declares the LORD Almighty,
 'I will break the yoke off their necks
and will tear off their bonds;
 no longer will foreigners enslave them.
Instead, they will serve the LORD their God
 and David their king,
 whom I will raise up for them.

" 'So do not fear, O Jacob my servant;
 do not be dismayed, O Israel,'
             declares the LORD.
'I will surely save you out of a distant place,
 your descendants from the land of their exile.
Jacob will again have peace and security,
 and no one will make him afraid.
I am with you and will save you,'
 declares the LORD.
'Though I completely destroy all the nations
 among which I scatter you,
 I will not completely destroy you.
I will discipline you but only with justice;
 I will not let you go entirely unpunished.'

Jer. 30:12-15 SINS BROUGHT EXILE.   "This is what the LORD says:

" 'Your wound is incurable,
 your injury beyond healing.
There is no one to plead your cause,
 no remedy for your sore,
 no healing for you.
All your allies have forgotten you;

f Or will restore the fortunes of my people Israel and Judah

they care nothing for you.
I have struck you as an enemy would
    and punished you as would the cruel,
because your guilt is so great
    and your sins so many.
Why do you cry out over your wound,
    your pain that has no cure?
Because of your great guilt and many sins
    I have done these things to you.

HEALING COMING.

Jer.
30:16,17

" 'But all who devour you will be devoured;
    all your enemies will go into exile.
Those who plunder you will be plundered;
    all who make spoil of you I will despoil.
But I will restore you to health
    and heal your wounds,'

declares the LORD,

'because you are called an outcast,
    Zion for whom no one cares.'

ALL WILL BE NORMAL.   "This is what the LORD says:

Jer.
30:18-24

" 'I will restore the fortunes of Jacob's tents
    and have compassion on his dwellings;
the city will be rebuilt on her ruins,
    and the palace will stand in its proper place.
From them will come songs of thanksgiving
    and the sound of rejoicing.
I will add to their numbers,
    and they will not be decreased;
I will bring them honor,
    and they will not be disdained.
Their children will be as in days of old,
    and their community will be established before me;
    I will punish all who oppress them.
Their leader will be one of their own;
    their ruler will arise from among them.
I will bring him near and he will come close to me,
    for who is he who will devote himself
    to be close to me?'

declares the LORD.

" 'So you will be my people,
    and I will be your God.' "

See, the storm of the LORD
    will burst out in wrath,
a driving wind swirling down
    on the heads of the wicked.
The fierce anger of the LORD will not turn back
    until he fully accomplishes
    the purposes of his heart.

In days to come
you will understand this.

Jer. 31:1-14   THE JOY OF RESTORATION.   "At that time," declares the LORD, "I will
be the God of all the clans of Israel, and they will be my people."
This is what the LORD says:

"The people who survive the sword
will find favor in the desert;
I will come to give rest to Israel."

The LORD appeared to us in the past, [8] saying:

"I have loved you with an everlasting love;
I have drawn you with loving-kindness.
I will build you up again
and you will be rebuilt, O Virgin Israel.
Again you will take up your tambourines
and go out to dance with the joyful.
Again you will plant vineyards
on the hills of Samaria;
the farmers will plant them
and enjoy their fruit.
There will be a day when watchmen cry out
on the hills of Ephraim,
'Come, let us go up to Zion,
to the LORD our God.' "

This is what the LORD says:

"Sing with joy for Jacob;
shout for the foremost of the nations.
Make your praises heard, and say,
'O LORD, save your people,
the remnant of Israel.'
See, I will bring them from the land of the north
and gather them from the ends of the earth.
Among them will be the blind and the lame,
expectant mothers and women in labor;
a great throng will return.
They will come with weeping;
they will pray as I bring them back.
I will lead them beside streams of water
on a level path where they will not stumble,
because I am Israel's father,
and Ephraim is my firstborn son.

"Hear the word of the LORD, O nations;
proclaim it in distant coastlands:
'He who scattered Israel will gather them
and will watch over his flock like a shepherd.'
For the LORD will ransom Jacob
and redeem them from the hand of those stronger than
they.

[8] *Or* LORD *has appeared to us from afar*

They will come and shout for joy on the heights of Zion;
    they will rejoice in the bounty of the LORD—
the grain, the new wine and the oil,
    the young of the flocks and herds.
They will be like a well-watered garden,
    and they will sorrow no more.
Then maidens will dance and be glad,
    young men and old as well.
I will turn their mourning into gladness;
    I will give them comfort and joy instead of sorrow.
I will satisfy the priests with abundance,
    and my people will be filled with my bounty,"
                      declares the LORD.

To those who languish as captives in the deportation camp at Ramah, God brings this special word of hope.

ENCOURAGEMENT.   This is what the LORD says: Jer.
                                              31:15-17

"A voice is heard in Ramah,
    mourning and great weeping,
Rachel weeping for her children
    and refusing to be comforted,
    because her children are no more."

This is what the LORD says:

"Restrain your voice from weeping
    and your eyes from tears,
for your work will be rewarded,"
                      declares the LORD.
  "They will return from the land of the enemy.
So there is hope for your future,"
                      declares the LORD.
  "Your children will return to their own land.

"I have surely heard Ephraim's moaning: Jer.
  'You disciplined me like an unruly calf,   31:18-25
    and I have been disciplined.
Restore me, and I will return,
    because you are the LORD my God.
After I strayed,
    I repented;
after I came to understand,
    I beat my breast.
I was ashamed and humiliated
    because I bore the disgrace of my youth.'
Is not Ephraim my dear son,
    the child in whom I delight?
Though I often speak against him,
    I still remember him.
Therefore my heart yearns for him;
    I have great compassion for him,"
                      declares the LORD.

"Set up road signs;
   put up guideposts.
Take note of the highway,
   the road that you take.
Return, O Virgin Israel,
   return to your towns.
How long will you wander,
   O unfaithful daughter?
The LORD will create a new thing on earth—
   a woman will surround[h] a man."

This is what the LORD Almighty, the God of Israel, says: "When I bring them back from captivity,[i] the people in the land of Judah and in its towns will once again use these words: 'The LORD bless you, O righteous dwelling, O sacred mountain.' People will live together in Judah and all its towns—farmers and those who move about with their flocks. I will refresh the weary and satisfy the faint."

These words may have come to Jeremiah in a dream, because he indicates that he now awakes from a pleasant sleep.

Jer. 31:26   AWAKENING.   At this I awoke and looked around. My sleep had been pleasant to me.

Jeremiah Sees Spiritual Restoration Under the Messiah

There can be no doubt that God intends to bring the people of Israel back to Canaan from their various places of exile. And there can be no doubt that he intends to reestablish Israel as a united nation. But he says that the new kingdom will last forever, that a son of David will always be on Israel's throne, that Israel will enjoy continuous peace, and that sin will never again separate Israel from God.

All of this will cause great confusion to future generations of Hebrews who read the restoration promises of Jeremiah, Isaiah, and the other prophets, yet continue to see a hostile world about them. Many of them will keep vigil for the coming of a political Israel which will truly have lasting peace and prosperity. Many will look for a mighty king to bring them deliverance from future oppressors. Many will look for a country whose geographical boundaries are clearly delineated and secure. Yet Jeremiah suggests that their attitude toward the coming kingdom is misguided.

Here now are three separate discourses in which Jeremiah appears to reach beyond the end of the 70-year exile to a kingdom of a different nature and to the Messiah who will save his people from their sins. In two of the discourses Jeremiah repeats virtually the same poetic prophecy, which itself is similar to several prophecies brought by Isaiah.

[h]Or will go about ⌊seeking⌋; or will protect   [i]Or I restore their fortunes

First Discourse

REGATHERING OF REMNANT.   "Woe to the shepherds who are de-   Jer. 23:1-4
stroying and scattering the sheep of my pasture!" declares the LORD.
Therefore this is what the LORD, the God of Israel, says to the shepherds
who tend my people: "Because you have scattered my flock and driven
them away and have not bestowed care on them, I will bestow punishment on you for the evil you have done," declares the LORD. "I myself will
gather the remnant of my flock out of all the countries where I have driv-
en them and will bring them back to their pasture, where they will be fruitful and increase in number. I will place shepherds over them who will tend
them, and they will no longer be afraid or terrified, nor will any be missing," declares the LORD.

RIGHTEOUS BRANCH OF DAVID.   Jer. 23:5,6

"The days are coming," declares the LORD,
    "when I will raise up to David[j] a righteous Branch,
a King who will reign wisely
    and do what is just and right in the land.
In his days Judah will be saved
    and Israel will live in safety.
This is the name by which he will be called:
    The LORD Our Righteousness.

RESTORATION WILL BE WITNESS.   "So then, the days are coming,"   Jer. 23:7,8
declares the LORD, "when people will no longer say, 'As surely as the LORD
lives, who brought the Israelites up out of Egypt,' but they will say, 'As
surely as the LORD lives, who brought the descendants of Israel up out of
the land of the north and out of all the countries where he had banished
them.' Then they will live in their own land."

Second Discourse

RIGHTEOUS BRANCH OF DAVID.   " 'The days are coming,' declares   Jer.
the LORD, 'when I will fulfill the gracious promise I made to the house of   33:14-16
Israel and to the house of Judah.

" 'In those days and at that time
    I will make a righteous Branch sprout from David's line;
    he will do what is just and right in the land.
In those days Judah will be saved
    and Jerusalem will live in safety.
This is the name by which it[k] will be called:
    The LORD Our Righteousness.'

SPIRITUAL LEADERSHIP. For this is what the LORD says: 'David will   Jer.
never fail to have a man to sit on the throne of the house of Israel, nor will   33:17,18
the priests, who are Levites, ever fail to have a man to stand before me
continually to offer burnt offerings, to burn grain offerings and to present
sacrifices.' "

CERTAINTY OF THE PROMISE. The word of the LORD came to Jeremiah: Jer.
"This is what the LORD says: 'If you can break my covenant with the day   33:19-22
and my covenant with the night, so that day and night no longer come at

[j]Or *up from David's line*   [k]Or *he*

their appointed time, then my covenant with David my servant—and my covenant with the Levites who are priests ministering before me—can be broken and David will no longer have a descendant to reign on his throne. I will make the descendants of David my servant and the Levites who minister before me as countless as the stars of the sky and as measureless as the sand on the seashore.' "

Jer.
33:23-26

ISRAEL IN THE NEW KINGDOM.   The word of the LORD came to Jeremiah: "Have you not noticed that these people are saying, 'The LORD has rejected the two kingdoms[l] he chose'? So they despise my people and no longer regard them as a nation. This is what the LORD says: 'If I have not established my covenant with day and night and the fixed laws of heaven and earth, then I will reject the descendants of Jacob and David my servant and will not choose one of his sons to rule over the descendants of Abraham, Isaac and Jacob. For I will restore their fortunes[m] and have compassion on them.'"

Third Discourse

Jer.
31:27,28

TIME OF REBUILDING.   "The days are coming," declares the LORD, "when I will plant the house of Israel and the house of Judah with the offspring of men and of animals. Just as I watched over them to uproot and tear down, and to overthrow, destroy and bring disaster, so I will watch over them to build and to plant," declares the LORD.

Jer.
31:29,30

PERSONAL ACCOUNTABILITY.   "In those days people will no longer say,

> 'The fathers have eaten sour grapes,
>   and the children's teeth are set on edge.'

Instead, everyone will die for his own sin; whoever eats sour grapes—his own teeth will be set on edge.

Jer.
31:31-34

A NEW COVENANT.

> "The time is coming," declares the LORD,
>   "when I will make a new covenant
> with the house of Israel
>   and with the house of Judah.
> It will not be like the covenant
>   I made with their forefathers
> when I took them by the hand
>   to lead them out of Egypt,
> because they broke my covenant,
>   though I was a husband to[n] them,[o]"
>   declares the LORD.
> "This is the covenant I will make with the house of Israel
>   after that time," declares the LORD.
> "I will put my law in their minds
>   and write it on their hearts.
> I will be their God,
>   and they will be my people.
> No longer will a man teach his neighbor,

[l]Or *families*   [m]Or *will bring them back from captivity*   [n]Hebrew; Septuagint and Syriac
/ *and I turned away from*   [o]Or *was their master*

> or a man his brother, saying, 'Know the LORD,'
> because they will all know me,
>> from the least of them to the greatest,"
>>>> declares the LORD.
> "For I will forgive their wickedness
>> and will remember their sins no more."

ISRAEL ALWAYS SPECIAL.   This is what the LORD says,

Jer. 31:35-37

> he who appoints the sun
>> to shine by day,
> who decrees the moon and stars
>> to shine by night,
> who stirs up the sea
>> so that its waves roar—
>> the LORD Almighty is his name:
> "Only if these decrees vanish from my sight,"
>> declares the LORD,
> "will the descendants of Israel ever cease
>> to be a nation before me."

> This is what the LORD says:

> "Only if the heavens above can be measured
>> and the foundations of the earth below be searched out
> will I reject all the descendants of Israel
>> because of all they have done,"
>>>> declares the LORD.

A LASTING JERUSALEM.   "The days are coming," declares the LORD, "when this city will be rebuilt for me from the Tower of Hananel to the Corner Gate. The measuring line will stretch from there straight to the hill of Gareb and then turn to Goah. The whole valley where dead bodies and ashes are thrown, and all the terraces out to the Kidron Valley on the east as far as the corner of the Horse Gate, will be holy to the LORD. The city will never again be uprooted or demolished."

Jer. 31:38-40

Ezekiel's Prophecies During Siege

*W*hile Jeremiah is prophesying in Jerusalem about events to happen in centuries to come, Ezekiel is bringing prophecies to his fellow captives in Babylonia concerning events destined for more immediate fulfillment. Over the two-year period of Jerusalem's siege, Ezekiel's prophecies concentrate on Judah's many oppressors: Ammon, Moab, Edom, Philistia, Egypt, and the cities of Tyre and Sidon. Particularly singled out are Egypt, Tyre, and Sidon. Like prophets before him, Ezekiel pronounces scathing judgments against these nations for their own wickedness and their many wars against God's people. During Jehoiakim's reign, only a decade prior to this time, Syrian, Moabite, and Ammonite raiders had harassed Judah for at least four years. Edom, Egypt, and Philistia had been almost-continual enemies of the nation of Israel.

Beyond the various judgments against Israel's enemies which Isaiah, Jeremiah, and others have already brought, Ezekiel's judgments condemn the celebration which will take place over Judah's fall. The prophecies are written prospectively, as if Jerusalem has already fallen, and point out that no tears will come from Judah's neighbors. On the contrary, they will attempt to take advantage of Judah's vulnerability. (Ammon, for example, will prove Ezekiel true by promoting the assassination of the governor appointed by the Babylonians to rule over the remnant not taken captive.) It will be the nations' self-righteous gloating which will draw God's wrath. He will not sit idly by when his people are disgraced in the eyes of their haughty neighbors.

Ezk. 25:1-7
(Ca. 588 B.C.?)

JUDGMENT AGAINST AMMON.   The word of the LORD came to me: "Son of man, set your face against the Ammonites and prophesy against them. Say to them, 'Hear the word of the Sovereign LORD. This is what the Sovereign LORD says: Because you said "Aha!" over my sanctuary when it was desecrated and over the land of Israel when it was laid waste and over the people of Judah when they went into exile, therefore I am going to give you to the people of the East as a possession. They will set up their camps and pitch their tents among you; they will eat your fruit and drink your milk. I will turn Rabbah into a pasture for camels and Ammon into a resting place for sheep. Then you will know that I am the LORD. For this is what the Sovereign LORD says: Because you have clapped your hands and stamped your feet, rejoicing with all the malice of your heart against the land of Israel, therefore I will stretch out my hand against you and give you as plunder to the nations. I will cut you off from the nations and exterminate you from the countries. I will destroy you, and you will know that I am the LORD.'"

Ezk. 25:8-11

JUDGMENT AGAINST MOAB.   "This is what the Sovereign LORD says: 'Because Moab and Seir said, "Look, the house of Judah has become like all the other nations," therefore I will expose the flank of Moab, beginning at its frontier towns—Beth Jeshimoth, Baal Meon and Kiriathaim—the glory of that land. I will give Moab along with the Ammonites to the people of the East as a possession, so that the Ammonites will not be remembered among the nations; and I will inflict punishment on Moab. Then they will know that I am the LORD.'"

Ezk. 25:12-14

JUDGMENT AGAINST EDOM.   "This is what the Sovereign LORD says: 'Because Edom took revenge on the house of Judah and became very guilty by doing so, therefore this is what the Sovereign LORD says: I will stretch out my hand against Edom and kill its men and their animals. I will lay it waste, and from Teman to Dedan they will fall by the sword. I will take vengeance on Edom by the hand of my people Israel, and they will deal with Edom in accordance with my anger and my wrath; they will know my vengeance, declares the Sovereign LORD.'"

Ezk. 25:15-17

JUDGMENT AGAINST PHILISTIA.   "This is what the Sovereign LORD says: 'Because the Philistines acted in vengeance and took revenge with malice in their hearts, and with ancient hostility sought to destroy Judah, therefore this is what the Sovereign LORD says: I am about to stretch out my hand against the Philistines, and I will cut off the Kerethites and destroy those remaining along the coast. I will carry out great vengeance on them and punish them in my wrath. Then they will know that I am the LORD, when I take vengeance on them.'"

JUDGMENT AGAINST EGYPT.   In the tenth year, in the tenth month on
the twelfth day, the word of the LORD came to me: "Son of man, set your
face against Pharaoh king of Egypt and prophesy against him and against
all Egypt. Speak to him and say: 'This is what the Sovereign LORD says:

Ezk.
29:1-16
(587 B.C.)

" 'I am against you, Pharaoh king of Egypt,
    you great monster lying among your streams.
You say, "The Nile is mine;
    I made it for myself."
But I will put hooks in your jaws
    and make the fish of your streams stick to your scales.
I will pull you out from among your streams,
    with all the fish sticking to your scales.
I will leave you in the desert,
    you and all the fish of your streams.
You will fall on the open field
    and not be gathered or picked up.
I will give you as food
    to the beasts of the earth and the birds of the air.

Then all who live in Egypt will know that I am the LORD.

" 'You have been a staff of reed for the house of Israel. When they
grasped you with their hands, you splintered and you tore open their
shoulders; when they leaned on you, you broke and their backs were
wrenched.[p]

" 'Therefore this is what the Sovereign LORD says: I will bring a sword
against you and kill your men and their animals. Egypt will become a desolate wasteland. Then they will know that I am the LORD.

" 'Because you said, "The Nile is mine; I made it," therefore I am against
you and against your streams, and I will make the land of Egypt a ruin and
a desolate waste from Migdol to Aswan, as far as the border of Cush.[q] No
foot of man or animal will pass through it; no one will live there for forty
years. I will make the land of Egypt desolate among devastated lands, and
her cities will lie desolate forty years among ruined cities. And I will disperse the Egyptians among the nations and scatter them through the countries.

" 'Yet this is what the Sovereign LORD says: At the end of forty years I
will gather the Egyptians from the nations where they were scattered. I
will bring them back from captivity and return them to Upper Egypt,[r] the
land of their ancestry. There they will be a lowly kingdom. It will be the
lowliest of kingdoms and will never again exalt itself above the other
nations. I will make it so weak that it will never again rule over the
nations. Egypt will no longer be a source of confidence for the people of
Israel but will be a reminder of their sin in turning to her for help. Then
they will know that I am the Sovereign LORD.' "

LAMENT FOR EGYPT.   The word of the LORD came to me: "Son of man,
prophesy and say: 'This is what the Sovereign LORD says:

Ezk.
30:1-19

" 'Wail and say,

[p]Syriac (see also Septuagint and Vulgate); Hebrew *and you caused their backs to stand*
[q]That is, the upper Nile region   [r]Hebrew *to Pathros*

"Alas for that day!"
For the day is near,
    the day of the LORD is near—
a day of clouds,
    a time of doom for the nations.
A sword will come against Egypt,
    and anguish will come upon Cush.[s]
When the slain fall in Egypt,
    her wealth will be carried away
    and her foundations torn down.

Cush and Put, Lydia and all Arabia, Libya[t] and the people of the covenant land will fall by the sword along with Egypt.

" 'This is what the LORD says:

" 'The allies of Egypt will fall
    and her proud strength will fail.
From Migdol to Aswan
    they will fall by the sword within her,
                                                                declares the Sovereign LORD.
" 'They will be desolate
    among desolate lands,
and their cities will lie
    among ruined cities.
Then they will know that I am the LORD,
    when I set fire to Egypt
    and all her helpers are crushed.

" 'On that day messengers will go out from me in ships to frighten Cush out of her complacency. Anguish will take hold of them on the day of Egypt's doom, for it is sure to come.

" 'This is what the Sovereign LORD says:

" 'I will put an end to the hordes of Egypt
    by the hand of Nebuchadnezzar king of Babylon.
He and his army—the most ruthless of nations—
    will be brought in to destroy the land.
They will draw their swords against Egypt
    and fill the land with the slain.
I will dry up the streams of the Nile
    and sell the land to evil men;
by the hand of foreigners
    I will lay waste the land and everything in it.

I the LORD have spoken.

" 'This is what the Sovereign LORD says:

" 'I will destroy the idols
    and put an end to the images in Memphis.[u]
No longer will there be a prince in Egypt,
    and I will spread fear throughout the land.

---

[s]That is, the upper Nile region   [t]Hebrew *Cub*   [u]Hebrew *Noph*

I will lay waste Upper Egypt,*v*
   set fire to Zoan
   and inflict punishment on Thebes.*w*
I will pour out my wrath on Pelusium,*x*
   the stronghold of Egypt,
   and cut off the hordes of Thebes.
I will set fire to Egypt;
   Pelusium will writhe in agony.
Thebes will be taken by storm;
   Memphis will be in constant distress.
The young men of Heliopolis*y* and Bubastis*z*
   will fall by the sword,
   and the cities themselves will go into captivity.
Dark will be the day at Tahpanhes
   when I break the yoke of Egypt;
   there her proud strength will come to an end.
She will be covered with clouds,
   and her villages will go into captivity.
So I will inflict punishment on Egypt,
   and they will know that I am the LORD.' "

JUDGMENT AGAINST PHARAOH. In the eleventh year, in the first month on the seventh day, the word of the LORD came to me: "Son of man, I have broken the arm of Pharaoh king of Egypt. It has not been bound up for healing or put in a splint so as to become strong enough to hold a sword. Therefore this is what the Sovereign LORD says: I am against Pharaoh king of Egypt. I will break both his arms, the good arm as well as the broken one, and make the sword fall from his hand. I will disperse the Egyptians among the nations and scatter them through the countries. I will strengthen the arms of the king of Babylon and put my sword in his hand, but I will break the arms of Pharaoh, and he will groan before him like a mortally wounded man. I will strengthen the arms of the king of Babylon, but the arms of Pharaoh will fall limp. Then they will know that I am the LORD, when I put my sword into the hand of the king of Babylon and he brandishes it against Egypt. I will disperse the Egyptians among the nations and scatter them through the countries. Then they will know that I am the LORD."

Ezk.
30:20-26
(586 B.C.)

EGYPT COMPARED TO ASSYRIA. In the eleventh year, in the third month on the first day, the word of the LORD came to me: "Son of man, say to Pharaoh king of Egypt and to his hordes:

Ezk.
31:1-18
(586 B.C.)

" 'Who can be compared with you in majesty?
   Consider Assyria, once a cedar in Lebanon,
      with beautiful branches overshadowing the forest;
   it towered on high,
      its top above the thick foliage.
The waters nourished it,
      deep springs made it grow tall;
   their streams flowed
      all around its base

*v*Hebrew *waste Pathros*   *w*Hebrew *No*   *x*Hebrew *Sin*   *y*Hebrew *Awen* (or *On*)
*z*Hebrew *Pi Beseth*

and sent their channels
    to all the trees of the field.
So it towered higher
    than all the trees of the field;
its boughs increased
    and its branches grew long,
    spreading because of abundant waters.
All the birds of the air
    nested in its boughs,
all the beasts of the field
    gave birth under its branches;
all the great nations
    lived in its shade.
It was majestic in beauty,
    with its spreading boughs,
for its roots went down
    to abundant waters.
The cedars in the garden of God
    could not rival it,
nor could the pine trees
    equal its boughs,
nor could the plane trees
    compare with its branches—
no tree in the garden of God
    could match its beauty.
I made it beautiful
    with abundant branches,
the envy of all the trees of Eden
    in the garden of God.

" 'Therefore this is what the Sovereign LORD says: Because it towered on high, lifting its top above the thick foliage, and because it was proud of its height, I handed it over to the ruler of the nations, for him to deal with according to its wickedness. I cast it aside, and the most ruthless of foreign nations cut it down and left it. Its boughs fell on the mountains and in all the valleys; its branches lay broken in all the ravines of the land. All the nations of the earth came out from under its shade and left it. All the birds of the air settled on the fallen tree, and all the beasts of the field were among its branches. Therefore no other trees by the waters are ever to tower proudly on high, lifting their tops above the thick foliage. No other trees so well-watered are ever to reach such a height; they are all destined for death, for the earth below, among mortal men, with those who go down to the pit.

" 'This is what the Sovereign LORD says: On the day it was brought down to the grave[a] I covered the deep springs with mourning for it; I held back its streams, and its abundant waters were restrained. Because of it I clothed Lebanon with gloom, and all the trees of the field withered away. I made the nations tremble at the sound of its fall when I brought it down to the grave with those who go down to the pit. Then all the trees of Eden, the choicest and best of Lebanon, all the trees that were well-watered, were

---

[a]Hebrew *Sheol*

consoled in the earth below. Those who lived in its shade, its allies among the nations, had also gone down to the grave with it, joining those killed by the sword.

" 'Which of the trees of Eden can be compared with you in splendor and majesty? Yet you, too, will be brought down with the trees of Eden to the earth below; you will lie among the uncircumcised, with those killed by the sword.

" 'This is Pharaoh and all his hordes, declares the Sovereign LORD.' "

It will be some 60 years before Egypt will be ruled by a foreign nation, but in 525 B.C., during the reign of Pharaoh Amasis, Egypt will be made a part of the great Persian Empire under Cambyses II.

Ezekiel now turns to the great maritime cities of Tyre and Sidon, whose seaports and trading fleets have made them wealthy. The original city of Tyre was located on the mainland, whereas the new city was built on an island half a mile offshore. Thus Ezekiel describes the destroyed island city as being like a bare rock, and the wicked king of Tyre apparently has such pride that he is compared with Satan himself.

JUDGMENT AGAINST TYRE.   In the eleventh year, on the first day of the month, the word of the LORD came to me: "Son of man, because Tyre has said of Jerusalem, 'Aha! The gate to the nations is broken, and its doors have swung open to me; now that she lies in ruins I will prosper,' therefore this is what the Sovereign LORD says: I am against you, O Tyre, and I will bring many nations against you, like the sea casting up its waves. They will destroy the walls of Tyre and pull down her towers; I will scrape away her rubble and make her a bare rock. Out in the sea she will become a place to spread fishnets, for I have spoken, declares the Sovereign LORD. She will become plunder for the nations, and her settlements on the mainland will be ravaged by the sword. Then they will know that I am the LORD.

Ezk. 26:1-6 (586 B.C.)

"For this is what the Sovereign LORD says: From the north I am going to bring against Tyre Nebuchadnezzar[b] king of Babylon, king of kings, with horses and chariots, with horsemen and a great army. He will ravage your settlements on the mainland with the sword; he will set up siege works against you, build a ramp up to your walls and raise his shields against you. He will direct the blows of his battering rams against your walls and demolish your towers with his weapons. His horses will be so many that they will cover you with dust. Your walls will tremble at the noise of the war horses, wagons and chariots when he enters your gates as men enter a city whose walls have been broken through. The hoofs of his horses will trample all your streets; he will kill your people with the sword, and your strong pillars will fall to the ground. They will plunder your wealth and loot your merchandise; they will break down your walls and demolish your fine houses and throw your stones, timber and rubble into the sea. I will put an end to your noisy songs, and the music of your harps will be heard no more. I will make you a bare rock, and you will become a place to spread fishnets. You will never be rebuilt, for I the LORD have spoken, declares the Sovereign LORD.

Ezk. 26:7-14

[b]Hebrew *Nebuchadrezzar*, of which *Nebuchadnezzar* is a variant; here and often in Ezekiel and Jeremiah

Ezk.
26:15-21

"This is what the Sovereign LORD says to Tyre: Will not the coastlands tremble at the sound of your fall, when the wounded groan and the slaughter takes place in you? Then all the princes of the coast will step down from their thrones and lay aside their robes and take off their embroidered garments. Clothed with terror, they will sit on the ground, trembling every moment, appalled at you. Then they will take up a lament concerning you and say to you:

" 'How you are destroyed, O city of renown,
    peopled by men of the sea!
You were a power on the seas,
    you and your citizens;
you put your terror
    on all who lived there.
Now the coastlands tremble
    on the day of your fall;
the islands in the sea
    are terrified at your collapse.'

"This is what the Sovereign LORD says: When I make you a desolate city, like cities no longer inhabited, and when I bring the ocean depths over you and its vast waters cover you, then I will bring you down with those who go down to the pit, to the people of long ago. I will make you dwell in the earth below, as in ancient ruins, with those who go down to the pit, and you will not return or take your place^c in the land of the living. I will bring you to a horrible end and you will be no more. You will be sought, but you will never again be found, declares the Sovereign LORD."

Ezk.
27:1-11

LAMENT FOR TYRE.   The word of the LORD came to me: "Son of man, take up a lament concerning Tyre. Say to Tyre, situated at the gateway to the sea, merchant of peoples on many coasts, 'This is what the Sovereign LORD says:

" 'You say, O Tyre,
    "I am perfect in beauty."
Your domain was on the high seas;
    your builders brought your beauty to perfection.
They made all your timbers
    of pine trees from Senir^d;
they took a cedar from Lebanon
    to make a mast for you.
Of oaks from Bashan
    they made your oars;
of cypress wood^e from the coasts of Cyprus^f
    they made your deck, inlaid with ivory.
Fine embroidered linen from Egypt was your sail
    and served as your banner;
your awnings were of blue and purple
    from the coasts of Elishah.
Men of Sidon and Arvad were your oarsmen;
    your skilled men, O Tyre, were aboard as your seamen.

---

^{c}Septuagint; Hebrew *return, and I will give glory* ^{d}That is, Hermon ^{e}Targum; the Masoretic Text has a different division of the consonants. ^{f}Hebrew *Kittim*

Veteran craftsmen of Gebal*g* were on board
  as shipwrights to caulk your seams.
All the ships of the sea and their sailors
  came alongside to trade for your wares.

" 'Men of Persia, Lydia and Put
  served as soldiers in your army.
They hung their shields and helmets on your walls,
  bringing you splendor.
Men of Arvad and Helech
  manned your walls on every side;
men of Gammad
  were in your towers.
They hung their shields around your walls;
  they brought your beauty to perfection.

" 'Tarshish did business with you because of your great wealth of goods; they exchanged silver, iron, tin and lead for your merchandise.

" 'Greece, Tubal and Meshech traded with you; they exchanged slaves and articles of bronze for your wares.

" 'Men of Beth Togarmah exchanged work horses, war horses and mules for your merchandise.

" 'The men of Rhodes*h* traded with you, and many coastlands were your customers; they paid you with ivory tusks and ebony.

" 'Aram*i* did business with you because of your many products; they exchanged turquoise, purple fabric, embroidered work, fine linen, coral and rubies for your merchandise.

" 'Judah and Israel traded with you; they exchanged wheat from Minnith and confections,*j* honey, oil and balm for your wares.

" 'Damascus, because of your many products and great wealth of goods, did business with you in wine from Helbon and wool from Zahar.

" 'Danites and Greeks from Uzal bought your merchandise; they exchanged wrought iron, cassia and calamus for your wares.

" 'Dedan traded in saddle blankets with you.

" 'Arabia and all the princes of Kedar were your customers; they did business with you in lambs, rams and goats.

" 'The merchants of Sheba and Raamah traded with you; for your merchandise they exchanged the finest of all kinds of spices and precious stones, and gold.

" 'Haran, Canneh and Eden and merchants of Sheba, Asshur and Kilmad traded with you. In your marketplace they traded with you beautiful garments, blue fabric, embroidered work and multicolored rugs with cords twisted and tightly knotted.

Ezk.
27:12-24

" 'The ships of Tarshish serve
  as carriers for your wares.
You are filled with heavy cargo
  in the heart of the sea.
Your oarsmen take you
  out to the high seas.

Ezk.
27:25-36

*g*That is, Byblos   *h*Septuagint; Hebrew *Dedan*   *i*Most Hebrew manuscripts; some Hebrew manuscripts and Syriac *Edom*   *j*The meaning of the Hebrew for this word is uncertain.

But the east wind will break you to pieces
    in the heart of the sea.
Your wealth, merchandise and wares,
    your mariners, seamen and shipwrights,
your merchants and all your soldiers,
    and everyone else on board
will sink into the heart of the sea
    on the day of your shipwreck.
The shorelands will quake
    when your seamen cry out.
All who handle the oars
    will abandon their ships;
the mariners and all the seamen
    will stand on the shore.
They will raise their voice
    and cry bitterly over you;
they will sprinkle dust on their heads
    and roll in ashes.
They will shave their heads because of you
    and will put on sackcloth.
They will weep over you with anguish of soul
    and with bitter mourning.
As they wail and mourn over you,
    they will take up a lament concerning you:
"Who was ever silenced like Tyre,
    surrounded by the sea?"
When your merchandise went out on the seas,
    you satisfied many nations;
with your great wealth and your wares
    you enriched the kings of the earth.
Now you are shattered by the sea
    in the depths of the waters;
your wares and all your company
    have gone down with you.
All who live in the coastlands
    are appalled at you;
their kings shudder with horror
    and their faces are distorted with fear.
The merchants among the nations hiss at you;
    you have come to a horrible end
    and will be no more.'"

Ezk.
28:1-10

JUDGMENT AGAINST TYRE'S KING.   The word of the LORD came to
me: "Son of man, say to the ruler of Tyre, 'This is what the Sovereign LORD
says:

" 'In the pride of your heart
    you say, "I am a god;
I sit on the throne of a god
    in the heart of the seas."
But you are a man and not a god,
    though you think you are as wise as a god.

Are you wiser than Daniel[k]?
    Is no secret hidden from you?
By your wisdom and understanding
    you have gained wealth for yourself
and amassed gold and silver
    in your treasuries.
By your great skill in trading
    you have increased your wealth,
and because of your wealth
    your heart has grown proud.

" 'Therefore this is what the Sovereign LORD says:

" 'Because you think you are wise,
        as wise as a god,
I am going to bring foreigners against you,
        the most ruthless of nations;
they will draw their swords against your beauty and
            wisdom
    and pierce your shining splendor.
They will bring you down to the pit,
    and you will die a violent death
        in the heart of the seas.
Will you then say, "I am a god,"
    in the presence of those who kill you?
You will be but a man, not a god,
    in the hands of those who slay you.
You will die the death of the uncircumcised
    at the hands of foreigners.

I have spoken, declares the Sovereign LORD.' "

KING'S SATANLIKE RULE.   The word of the LORD came to me: "Son of   Ezk.
man, take up a lament concerning the king of Tyre and say to him: 'This is   28:11-19
what the Sovereign LORD says:

" 'You were the model of perfection,
        full of wisdom and perfect in beauty.
You were in Eden,
        the garden of God;
every precious stone adorned you:
        ruby, topaz and emerald,
        chrysolite, onyx and jasper,
        sapphire,[l] turquoise and beryl.[m]
Your settings and mountings[n] were made of gold;
    on the day you were created they were prepared.
You were anointed as a guardian cherub,
    for so I ordained you.
You were on the holy mount of God;
    you walked among the fiery stones.
You were blameless in your ways

[k]Or *Danel*; the Hebrew spelling may suggest a person other than the prophet Daniel.
[l]Or *lapis lazuli*   [m]The precise identification of some of these precious stones is
uncertain.   [n]The meaning of the Hebrew for this phrase is uncertain.

from the day you were created
till wickedness was found in you.
Through your widespread trade
you were filled with violence,
and you sinned.
So I drove you in disgrace from the mount of God,
and I expelled you, O guardian cherub,
from among the fiery stones.
Your heart became proud
on account of your beauty,
and you corrupted your wisdom
because of your splendor.
So I threw you to the earth;
I made a spectacle of you before kings.
By your many sins and dishonest trade
you have desecrated your sanctuaries.
So I made a fire come out from you,
and it consumed you,
and I reduced you to ashes on the ground
in the sight of all who were watching.
All the nations who knew you
are appalled at you;
you have come to a horrible end
and will be no more.' "

Ezk.
28:20-26

JUDGMENT AGAINST SIDON.   The word of the LORD came to me: "Son of man, set your face against Sidon; prophesy against her and say: 'This is what the Sovereign LORD says:

" 'I am against you, O Sidon,
and I will gain glory within you.
They will know that I am the LORD,
when I inflict punishment on her
and show myself holy within her.
I will send a plague upon her
and make blood flow in her streets.
The slain will fall within her,
with the sword against her on every side.
Then they will know that I am the LORD.

" 'No longer will the people of Israel have malicious neighbors who are painful briers and sharp thorns. Then they will know that I am the Sovereign LORD.

" 'This is what the Sovereign LORD says: When I gather the people of Israel from the nations where they have been scattered, I will show myself holy among them in the sight of the nations. Then they will live in their own land, which I gave to my servant Jacob. They will live there in safety and will build houses and plant vineyards; they will live in safety when I inflict punishment on all their neighbors who maligned them. Then they will know that I am the LORD their God.' "

Sixteen years from now, after Nebuchadnezzar has laid a 13-year siege against Tyre, Ezekiel will record a footnote to this prophecy (Ezk. 29:17-20).

Jeremiah Escapes Death

*A*fter apparently having been released for a time from house arrest in the royal palace, Jeremiah is first imprisoned in a dungeon and then put down into an empty well, before being saved by, of all people, Zedekiah. One gets the feeling that Zedekiah really does fear God and his prophet after all. This is somewhat confirmed when Zedekiah approaches Jeremiah secretly to learn what God's plans are. Unfortunately, Zedekiah never accepts God's words.

It is revealed somewhat incidentally that, before the end of Jerusalem's siege, Nebuchadnezzar temporarily withdraws his forces in order to push the Egyptian army back to its borders. Egypt had hoped to come to Judah's rescue in order to keep Judah as a buffer state between Babylonia and its own territory. But Babylonia prevails and returns to finish off Jerusalem.

Here are the incidents leading to Jeremiah's imprisonment and close brush with death. With famine having set in and bread being scarce, these events evidently take place just prior to Jerusalem's fall.

FUTURE FATE SOUGHT. King Zedekiah, however, sent Jehucal son of Shelemiah with the priest Zephaniah son of Maaseiah to Jeremiah the prophet with this message: "Please pray to the LORD our God for us."   Jer. 37:3-5

Now Jeremiah was free to come and go among the people, for he had not yet been put in prison. Pharaoh's army had marched out of Egypt, and when the Babylonians*⁰* who were besieging Jerusalem heard the report about them, they withdrew from Jerusalem.

BABYLONIANS WILL RETURN. Then the word of the LORD came to Jeremiah the prophet: "This is what the LORD, the God of Israel, says: Tell the king of Judah, who sent you to inquire of me, 'Pharaoh's army, which has marched out to support you, will go back to its own land, to Egypt. Then the Babylonians will return and attack this city; they will capture it and burn it down.'   Jer. 37:6-10

"This is what the LORD says: Do not deceive yourselves, thinking, 'The Babylonians will surely leave us.' They will not! Even if you were to defeat the entire Babylonian*ᵖ* army that is attacking you and only wounded men were left in their tents, they would come out and burn this city down."

JEREMIAH IMPRISONED. After the Babylonian army had withdrawn from Jerusalem because of Pharaoh's army, Jeremiah started to leave the city to go to the territory of Benjamin to get his share of the property among the people there. But when he reached the Benjamin Gate, the captain of the guard, whose name was Irijah son of Shelemiah, the son of Hananiah, arrested him and said, "You are deserting to the Babylonians!"   Jer. 37:11-16

"That's not true!" Jeremiah said. "I am not deserting to the Babylonians." But Irijah would not listen to him; instead, he arrested Jeremiah and brought him to the officials. They were angry with Jeremiah and had him beaten and imprisoned in the house of Jonathan the secretary, which they had made into a prison.

⁰Or Chaldeans; also in verses 8, 9, 13 and 14   ᵖOr Chaldean; also in verse 11

Jeremiah was put into a vaulted cell in a dungeon, where he remained a long time.

Jer. 37:17   ZEDEKIAH WARNED AGAIN.   Then King Zedekiah sent for him and had him brought to the palace, where he asked him privately, "Is there any word from the LORD?"

"Yes," Jeremiah replied, "you will be handed over to the king of Babylon."

Jer.   LIMITED RELEASE.   Then Jeremiah said to King Zedekiah, "What crime
37:18-21   have I committed against you or your officials or this people, that you have put me in prison? Where are your prophets who prophesied to you, 'The king of Babylon will not attack you or this land'? But now, my lord the king, please listen. Let me bring my petition before you: Do not send me back to the house of Jonathan the secretary, or I will die there."

King Zedekiah then gave orders for Jeremiah to be placed in the court-yard of the guard and given bread from the street of the bakers each day until all the bread in the city was gone. So Jeremiah remained in the court-yard of the guard.

Jer. 38:1-3   OFFICIALS CONSPIRE.   Shephatiah son of Mattan, Gedaliah son of Pashhur, Jehucal^q son of Shelemiah, and Pashhur son of Malkijah heard what Jeremiah was telling all the people when he said, "This is what the LORD says: 'Whoever stays in this city will die by the sword, famine or plague, but whoever goes over to the Babylonians^r will live. He will escape with his life; he will live.' And this is what the LORD says: 'This city will certainly be handed over to the army of the king of Babylon, who will capture it.' "

Jer. 38:4-6   JEREMIAH PUT INTO CISTERN.   Then the officials said to the king, "This man should be put to death. He is discouraging the soldiers who are left in this city, as well as all the people, by the things he is saying to them. This man is not seeking the good of these people but their ruin."

"He is in your hands," King Zedekiah answered. "The king can do noth-ing to oppose you."

So they took Jeremiah and put him into the cistern of Malkijah, the king's son, which was in the courtyard of the guard. They lowered Jeremiah by ropes into the cistern; it had no water in it, only mud, and Jeremiah sank down into the mud.

Jer. 38:7-13   JEREMIAH RESCUED.   But Ebed-Melech, a Cushite,^s an official^t in the royal palace, heard that they had put Jeremiah into the cistern. While the king was sitting in the Benjamin Gate, Ebed-Melech went out of the palace and said to him, "My lord the king, these men have acted wickedly in all they have done to Jeremiah the prophet. They have thrown him into a cis-tern, where he will starve to death when there is no longer any bread in the city."

Then the king commanded Ebed-Melech the Cushite, "Take thirty men from here with you and lift Jeremiah the prophet out of the cistern before he dies."

So Ebed-Melech took the men with him and went to a room under the treasury in the palace. He took some old rags and worn-out clothes from

^qHebrew *Jucal*, a variant of *Jehucal*   ^rOr *Chaldeans*   ^sProbably from the upper Nile region   ^tOr *a eunuch*

there and let them down with ropes to Jeremiah in the cistern. Ebed-Melech the Cushite said to Jeremiah, "Put these old rags and worn-out clothes under your arms to pad the ropes." Jeremiah did so, and they pulled him up with the ropes and lifted him out of the cistern. And Jeremiah remained in the courtyard of the guard.

ZEDEKIAH ASKS PRIVATELY.   Then King Zedekiah sent for Jeremiah the prophet and had him brought to the third entrance to the temple of the LORD. "I am going to ask you something," the king said to Jeremiah. "Do not hide anything from me." *Jer. 38:14-16*

Jeremiah said to Zedekiah, "If I give you an answer, will you not kill me? Even if I did give you counsel, you would not listen to me."

But King Zedekiah swore this oath secretly to Jeremiah: "As surely as the LORD lives, who has given us breath, I will neither kill you nor hand you over to those who are seeking your life."

ZEDEKIAH'S OPTIONS.   Then Jeremiah said to Zedekiah, "This is what the LORD God Almighty, the God of Israel, says: 'If you surrender to the officers of the king of Babylon, your life will be spared and this city will not be burned down; you and your family will live. But if you will not surrender to the officers of the king of Babylon, this city will be handed over to the Babylonians and they will burn it down; you yourself will not escape from their hands.'" *Jer. 38:17,18*

ZEDEKIAH FEARS SURRENDER.   King Zedekiah said to Jeremiah, "I am afraid of the Jews who have gone over to the Babylonians, for the Babylonians may hand me over to them and they will mistreat me." *Jer. 38:19-23*

"They will not hand you over," Jeremiah replied. "Obey the LORD by doing what I tell you. Then it will go well with you, and your life will be spared. But if you refuse to surrender, this is what the LORD has revealed to me: All the women left in the palace of the king of Judah will be brought out to the officials of the king of Babylon. Those women will say to you:

> " 'They misled you and overcame you—
>   those trusted friends of yours.
> Your feet are sunk in the mud;
>   your friends have deserted you.'

"All your wives and children will be brought out to the Babylonians. You yourself will not escape from their hands but will be captured by the king of Babylon; and this city will[u] be burned down."

CONVERSATION KEPT SECRET.   Then Zedekiah said to Jeremiah, "Do not let anyone know about this conversation, or you may die. If the officials hear that I talked with you, and they come to you and say, 'Tell us what you said to the king and what the king said to you; do not hide it from us or we will kill you,' then tell them, 'I was pleading with the king not to send me back to Jonathan's house to die there.'" *Jer. 38:24-27*

All the officials did come to Jeremiah and question him, and he told them everything the king had ordered him to say. So they said no more to him, for no one had heard his conversation with the king.

HOUSE ARREST CONTINUES.   And Jeremiah remained in the courtyard of the guard until the day Jerusalem was captured. *Jer. 38:28*

uOr *and you will cause this city to*

Fall of Jerusalem

*T*he end has finally come. Plagued by famine, drought, and pestilence from within, and besieged by the Babylonian hordes from without, the City of David finally falls. The historical record is mercifully brief in its account, as if the shame of it all forbids greater mention. The essential details are these: the wall is breached in the fourth month of 586 B.C.; when Zedekiah and his troops flee the city by night, they are quickly captured; a month later the glorious temple of Solomon and the royal palace are razed; the remaining noblemen are killed and temple treasures are taken as booty; and, over a period of four years, hundreds of people are taken captive and deported to Babylon. With the fall now an undeniable reality, the final chapter of the glorious era of Israel comes to a close, and the prophets of God are regrettably vindicated. Ezekiel in particular is proved correct as to the final fate of Zedekiah and the exact manner in which it happens.

2 Kgs. 25:2-4a
Jer. 39:2,3
Jer. 52:5-7a
(586 B.C.)
Jerusalem

WALL IS BROKEN. ᴷᵍBy the ninth day of the ⌊fourth⌋ᵛ month the famine in the city had become so severe that there was no food for the people to eat. ᴶʳAnd on the ninth day of the fourth month of Zedekiah's eleventh year, the city wall was broken through. Then all the officials of the king of Babylon came and took seats in the Middle Gate: Nergal-Sharezer of Samgar, Nebo-Sarsekimʷ a chief officer, Nergal-Sharezer a high official and all the other officials of the king of Babylon.

2 Kgs. 25:4b-6a
Jer. 39:4,5a
52:7b-9a

KING AND ARMY FLEE. When Zedekiah king of Judah and all the soldiers saw them, they fled; they left the city at night by way of the king's garden, through the gate between the two walls, and headed toward the Arabah.ˣ

But the Babylonianʸ army pursued them and overtook Zedekiah in the plains of Jericho.

2 Kgs. 25:6b,7
Jer. 39:5b-7
52:9b-11
Riblah

ZEDEKIAH HUMILIATED. He was taken to the king of Babylon at Riblah in the land of Hamath, where he pronounced sentence on him. There at Riblah the king of Babylon slaughtered the sons of Zedekiah before his eyes; he also killed all the officials of Judah. Then he put out Zedekiah's eyes, bound him with bronze shackles and took him to Babylon, where he put him in prison till the day of his death.

2 Kgs. 25:8-10
2 Chron. 36:17,19
Jer. 39:8
52:12-14
(586 B.C.)
Jerusalem

DESTRUCTION OF CITY. ᶜʰHe brought up against them the king of the Babylonians,ᶻ who killed their young men with the sword in the sanctuary, and spared neither young man nor young woman, old man or aged. God handed all of them over to Nebuchadnezzar. ᴶʳOn the tenth day of the fifth month, in the nineteenth year of Nebuchadnezzar king of Babylon, Nebuzaradan commander of the imperial guard, who served the king of Babylon, came to Jerusalem. He set fire to the temple of the LORD, the royal palace and all the houses of Jerusalem. Every important building he burned down. The whole Babylonian army under the commander of the imperial guard broke down all the walls around Jerusalem.

ᵛSee Jer. 52:6. ʷOr *Nergal-Sharezer, Samgar-Nebo, Sarsekim* ˣOr *the Jordan Valley*
ʸOr *Chaldean* ᶻOr *Chaldeans*

OFFICIALS EXECUTED. The commander of the guard took as prisoners Seraiah the chief priest, Zephaniah the priest next in rank and the three doorkeepers. Of those still in the city, he took the officer in charge of the fighting men and seven royal advisers. He also took the secretary who was chief officer in charge of conscripting the people of the land and sixty of his men who were found in the city. Nebuzaradan the commander took them all and brought them to the king of Babylon at Riblah. There at Riblah, in the land of Hamath, the king had them executed.

2 Kgs.
25:18-21a
Jer.
52:24-27a

TREASURES TAKEN. The Babylonians broke up the bronze pillars, the movable stands and the bronze Sea that were at the temple of the LORD and they carried all the bronze to Babylon. They also took away the pots, shovels, wick trimmers, sprinkling bowls, dishes and all the bronze articles used in the temple service. The commander of the imperial guard took away the basins, censers, sprinkling bowls, pots, lampstands, dishes and bowls used for drink offerings—all that were made of pure gold or silver.

2 Kgs.
25:13-17
2 Chron.
36:18
Jer.
52:17-23
Jerusalem

The bronze from the two pillars, the Sea and the twelve bronze bulls under it, and the movable stands, which King Solomon had made for the temple of the LORD, was more than could be weighed. Each of the pillars was eighteen cubits high and twelve cubits in circumference*a*; each was four fingers thick, and hollow. The bronze capital on top of the one pillar was five cubits*b* high and was decorated with a network and pomegranates of bronze all around. The other pillar, with its pomegranates, was similar. There were ninety-six pomegranates on the sides; the total number of pomegranates above the surrounding network was a hundred.

FURTHER DEPORTATIONS BEGIN. JrNebuzaradan the commander of the guard carried into exile some of the poorest people and those who remained in the city, along with the rest of the craftsmen*c* and those who had gone over to the king of Babylon. JrBut Nebuzaradan the commander of the guard left behind in the land of Judah some of the poor people, who owned nothing; and at that time he gave them vineyards and fields.

2 Kgs.
25:11,12
Jer. 39:9,10
52:15,16

NUMBER OF FUTURE CAPTIVES. So Judah went into captivity, away from her land. This is the number of the people Nebuchadnezzar carried into exile:

2 Kgs.
25:21b
Jer.
52:27b-30
(598-582
B.C.)

in the seventh year, 3,023 Jews;
in Nebuchadnezzar's eighteenth year,
    832 people from Jerusalem;
in his twenty-third year,
    745 Jews taken into exile by Nebuzaradan
    the commander of the imperial guard.
    There were 4,600 people in all.

PROSPECT FOR CAPTIVES. He carried into exile to Babylon the remnant, who escaped from the sword, and they became servants to him and his sons until the kingdom of Persia came to power. The land enjoyed its sabbath rests; all the time of its desolation it rested, until the seventy years were completed in fulfillment of the word of the LORD spoken by Jeremiah.

2 Chron.
36:20,21
Babylon

*a*That is, about 27 feet (about 8.1 meters) high and 18 feet (about 5.4 meters) in circumference   *b*That is, about 7 1/2 feet (about 2.3 meters)   *c*Or *populace*

Gedaliah and Jeremiah

hile the city that Jeremiah had tried to save was being destroyed and the people to whom he had preached God's words of warning were being killed or taken away captive, God reassured Jeremiah that he would be saved. Working through Nebuchadnezzar and his officers, God now fulfills his promise. Jeremiah's future is about to cross paths with a man named Gedaliah, whom Nebuchadnezzar appoints as governor over the people left behind.

2 Kgs.
25:22
(586 B.C.)

GEDALIAH MADE GOVERNOR.   Nebuchadnezzar king of Babylon appointed Gedaliah son of Ahikam, the son of Shaphan, to be over the people he had left behind in Judah.

Jer.
39:15-18
Jerusalem

JEREMIAH'S PRIOR ASSURANCE.   While Jeremiah had been confined in the courtyard of the guard, the word of the LORD came to him: "Go and tell Ebed-Melech the Cushite, 'This is what the LORD Almighty, the God of Israel, says: I am about to fulfill my words against this city through disaster, not prosperity. At that time they will be fulfilled before your eyes. But I will rescue you on that day, declares the LORD; you will not be handed over to those you fear. I will save you; you will not fall by the sword but will escape with your life, because you trust in me, declares the LORD.'"

Jer.
39:11-14

JEREMIAH SAVED.   Now Nebuchadnezzar king of Babylon had given these orders about Jeremiah through Nebuzaradan commander of the imperial guard: "Take him and look after him; don't harm him but do for him whatever he asks." So Nebuzaradan the commander of the guard, Nebushazban a chief officer, Nergal-Sharezer a high official and all the other officers of the king of Babylon sent and had Jeremiah taken out of the courtyard of the guard. They turned him over to Gedaliah son of Ahikam, the son of Shaphan, to take him back to his home. So he remained among his own people.

Jer. 40:1-5
Ramah

DETAILS OF RELEASE.   The word came to Jeremiah from the LORD after Nebuzaradan commander of the imperial guard had released him at Ramah. He had found Jeremiah bound in chains among all the captives from Jerusalem and Judah who were being carried into exile to Babylon. When the commander of the guard found Jeremiah, he said to him, "The LORD your God decreed this disaster for this place. And now the LORD has brought it about; he has done just as he said he would. All this happened because you people sinned against the LORD and did not obey him. But today I am freeing you from the chains on your wrists. Come with me to Babylon, if you like, and I will look after you; but if you do not want to, then don't come. Look, the whole country lies before you; go wherever you please." However, before Jeremiah turned to go,[d] Nebuzaradan added, "Go back to Gedaliah son of Ahikam, the son of Shaphan, whom the king of Babylon has appointed over the towns of Judah, and live with him among the people, or go anywhere else you please."

Then the commander gave him provisions and a present and let him go.

---

[d]Or *Jeremiah answered*

JEREMIAH WITH THOSE LEFT.　So Jeremiah went to Gedaliah son of　　Jer. 40:6
Ahikam at Mizpah and stayed with him among the people who were left　　Mizpah
behind in the land.

Jeremiah's Lamentations

*I*t would be altogether reasonable for Jeremiah to gloat over the fall of
Jerusalem. After all, he stood virtually alone in predicting its destruction, and suffered a great deal of persecution as a result. Now that his
prophecies have come true, it would be natural enough for him to say, "I told
you so!" But that would not be consistent with Jeremiah's character. Like the
God he serves, Jeremiah is grieved at the loss of Jerusalem and the scattering of
God's people. He is both angry and sad. He is angry at the priests and prophets
whose sins made the destruction necessary. He is angry at the nations which
have either directly overthrown Judah or failed to come to her rescue. But mostly Jeremiah is sad. This weeping prophet, who so many times lamented his own
sufferings, now laments the suffering of his fellow countrymen.

Although its authorship is not specifically indicated, it seems most likely
that Jeremiah is the author of a writing known simply as Lamentations. The
poem expresses the many mixed feelings which this aging and weary man of
God must have. Sometimes he speaks from a personal viewpoint about his own
sufferings and persecutions; sometimes he voices the nation's collective horror,
grief, confusion, and yet hope. So poignant is this beautiful lament that even to
this day it is read by these Hebrews' descendants each year on the anniversary
of the temple's destruction. From a literary standpoint alone, the poem is a
classic. Far beyond that, however, it is one of the most powerful and moving
expressions of human emotions that one will ever read, and it bears a timeless
message which is nothing less than sublime.

How[e] deserted lies the city,　　　　　　　　　　　Lam.
　　once so full of people!　　　　　　　　　　　　1:1-6
How like a widow is she,　　　　　　　　　　　　(586 B.C.)
　　who once was great among the nations!
She who was queen among the provinces
　　has now become a slave.

Bitterly she weeps at night,
　　tears are upon her cheeks.
Among all her lovers
　　there is none to comfort her.
All her friends have betrayed her;
　　they have become her enemies.

After affliction and harsh labor,
　　Judah has gone into exile.
She dwells among the nations;
　　she finds no resting place.

[e]This chapter is an acrostic poem, the verses of which begin with the successive letters of the
Hebrew alphabet.

All who pursue her have overtaken her
    in the midst of her distress.

The roads to Zion mourn,
    for no one comes to her appointed feasts.
All her gateways are desolate,
    her priests groan,
her maidens grieve,
    and she is in bitter anguish.

Her foes have become her masters;
    her enemies are at ease.
The LORD has brought her grief
    because of her many sins.
Her children have gone into exile,
    captive before the foe.

All the splendor has departed
    from the Daughter of Zion.
Her princes are like deer
    that find no pasture;
in weakness they have fled
    before the pursuer.

Lam. 1:7-11

In the days of her affliction and wandering
    Jerusalem remembers all the treasures
    that were hers in days of old.
When her people fell into enemy hands,
    there was no one to help her.
Her enemies looked at her
    and laughed at her destruction.

Jerusalem has sinned greatly
    and so has become unclean.
All who honored her despise her,
    for they have seen her nakedness;
she herself groans
    and turns away.

Her filthiness clung to her skirts;
    she did not consider her future.
Her fall was astounding;
    there was none to comfort her.
"Look, O LORD, on my affliction,
    for the enemy has triumphed."

The enemy laid hands
    on all her treasures;
she saw pagan nations
    enter her sanctuary—
those you had forbidden
    to enter your assembly.

All her people groan
    as they search for bread;
they barter their treasures for food

to keep themselves alive.
"Look, O Lord, and consider,
    for I am despised."

"Is it nothing to you, all you who pass by?   Lam.
    Look around and see.   1:12-17
Is any suffering like my suffering
    that was inflicted on me,
that the Lord brought on me
    in the day of his fierce anger?

"From on high he sent fire,
    sent it down into my bones.
He spread a net for my feet
    and turned me back.
He made me desolate,
    faint all the day long.

"My sins have been bound into a yoke*f*;
    by his hands they were woven together.
They have come upon my neck
    and the Lord has sapped my strength.
He has handed me over
    to those I cannot withstand.

"The Lord has rejected
    all the warriors in my midst;
he has summoned an army against me
    to*g* crush my young men.
In his winepress the Lord has trampled
    the Virgin Daughter of Judah.

"This is why I weep
    and my eyes overflow with tears.
No one is near to comfort me,
    no one to restore my spirit.
My children are destitute
    because the enemy has prevailed."

Zion stretches out her hands,
    but there is no one to comfort her.
The Lord has decreed for Jacob
    that his neighbors become his foes;
Jerusalem has become
    an unclean thing among them.

"The Lord is righteous,   Lam.
    yet I rebelled against his command.   1:18-22
Listen, all you peoples;
    look upon my suffering.
My young men and maidens
    have gone into exile.

---

f Most Hebrew manuscripts; Septuagint *He kept watch over my sins*   *g* Or *has set a time
for me | when he will*

"I called to my allies
    but they betrayed me.
My priests and my elders
    perished in the city
while they searched for food
    to keep themselves alive.

"See, O LORD, how distressed I am!
    I am in torment within,
and in my heart I am disturbed,
    for I have been most rebellious.
Outside, the sword bereaves;
    inside, there is only death.

"People have heard my groaning,
    but there is no one to comfort me.
All my enemies have heard of my distress;
    they rejoice at what you have done.
May you bring the day you have announced
    so they may become like me.

"Let all their wickedness come before you;
    deal with them
as you have dealt with me
    because of all my sins.
My groans are many
    and my heart is faint."

Lam.
2:1-10

How[h] the Lord has covered the Daughter of Zion
    with the cloud of his anger[i]!
He has hurled down the splendor of Israel
    from heaven to earth;
he has not remembered his footstool
    in the day of his anger.

Without pity the Lord has swallowed up
    all the dwellings of Jacob;
in his wrath he has torn down
    the strongholds of the Daughter of Judah.
He has brought her kingdom and its princes
    down to the ground in dishonor.

In fierce anger he has cut off
    every horn[j] of Israel.
He has withdrawn his right hand
    at the approach of the enemy.
He has burned in Jacob like a flaming fire
    that consumes everything around it.

Like an enemy he has strung his bow;
    his right hand is ready.

[h]This chapter is an acrostic poem, the verses of which begin with the successive letters
of the Hebrew alphabet.   [i]Or *How the Lord in his anger / has treated the Daughter of
Zion with contempt*   [j]Or / *all the strength*; or *every king*; horn here symbolizes strength.

Like a foe he has slain
    all who were pleasing to the eye;
he has poured out his wrath like fire
    on the tent of the Daughter of Zion.

The Lord is like an enemy;
    he has swallowed up Israel.
He has swallowed up all her palaces
    and destroyed her strongholds.
He has multiplied mourning and lamentation
    for the Daughter of Judah.

He has laid waste his dwelling like a garden;
    he has destroyed his place of meeting.
The LORD has made Zion forget
    her appointed feasts and her Sabbaths;
in his fierce anger he has spurned
    both king and priest.

The Lord has rejected his altar
    and abandoned his sanctuary.
He has handed over to the enemy
    the walls of her palaces;
they have raised a shout in the house of the LORD
    as on the day of an appointed feast.

The LORD determined to tear down
    the wall around the Daughter of Zion.
He stretched out a measuring line
    and did not withhold his hand from destroying.
He made ramparts and walls lament;
    together they wasted away.

Her gates have sunk into the ground;
    their bars he has broken and destroyed.
Her king and her princes are exiled among the nations,
    the law is no more,
and her prophets no longer find
    visions from the LORD.

The elders of the Daughter of Zion
    sit on the ground in silence;
they have sprinkled dust on their heads
    and put on sackcloth.
The young women of Jerusalem
    have bowed their heads to the ground.

My eyes fail from weeping,
    I am in torment within,
my heart is poured out on the ground
    because my people are destroyed,
because children and infants faint
    in the streets of the city.

They say to their mothers,
    "Where is bread and wine?"

Lam.
2:11-17

as they faint like wounded men
in the streets of the city,
as their lives ebb away
in their mothers' arms.

What can I say for you?
With what can I compare you,
O Daughter of Jerusalem?
To what can I liken you,
that I may comfort you,
O Virgin Daughter of Zion?
Your wound is as deep as the sea.
Who can heal you?

The visions of your prophets
were false and worthless;
they did not expose your sin
to ward off your captivity.
The oracles they gave you
were false and misleading.

All who pass your way
clap their hands at you;
they scoff and shake their heads
at the Daughter of Jerusalem:
"Is this the city that was called
the perfection of beauty,
the joy of the whole earth?"

All your enemies open their mouths
wide against you;
they scoff and gnash their teeth
and say, "We have swallowed her up.
This is the day we have waited for;
we have lived to see it."

The LORD has done what he planned;
he has fulfilled his word,
which he decreed long ago.
He has overthrown you without pity,
he has let the enemy gloat over you,
he has exalted the horn[k] of your foes.

Lam.
2:18-22

The hearts of the people
cry out to the Lord.
O wall of the Daughter of Zion,
let your tears flow like a river
day and night;
give yourself no relief,
your eyes no rest.

Arise, cry out in the night,
as the watches of the night begin;

[k] *Horn* here symbolizes strength.

pour out your heart like water
    in the presence of the Lord.
Lift up your hands to him
    for the lives of your children,
who faint from hunger
    at the head of every street.

"Look, O LORD, and consider:
    Whom have you ever treated like this?
Should women eat their offspring,
    the children they have cared for?
Should priest and prophet be killed
    in the sanctuary of the Lord?

"Young and old lie together
    in the dust of the streets;
my young men and maidens
    have fallen by the sword.
You have slain them in the day of your anger;
    you have slaughtered them without pity.

"As you summon to a feast day,
    so you summoned against me terrors on every side.
In the day of the LORD's anger
    no one escaped or survived;
those I cared for and reared,
    my enemy has destroyed."

I[1] am the man who has seen affliction
    by the rod of his wrath.
He has driven me away and made me walk
    in darkness rather than light;
indeed, he has turned his hand against me
    again and again, all day long.

He has made my skin and my flesh grow old
    and has broken my bones.
He has besieged me and surrounded me
    with bitterness and hardship.
He has made me dwell in darkness
    like those long dead.

He has walled me in so I cannot escape;
    he has weighed me down with chains.
Even when I call out or cry for help,
    he shuts out my prayer.
He has barred my way with blocks of stone;
    he has made my paths crooked.

Like a bear lying in wait,
    like a lion in hiding,

Lam.
3:1-21

---

[1] This chapter is an acrostic poem; the verses of each stanza begin with the successive letters of the Hebrew alphabet, and the verses within each stanza begin with the same letter.

he dragged me from the path and mangled me
and left me without help.
He drew his bow
and made me the target for his arrows.

He pierced my heart
with arrows from his quiver.
I became the laughingstock of all my people;
they mock me in song all day long.
He has filled me with bitter herbs
and sated me with gall.

He has broken my teeth with gravel;
he has trampled me in the dust.
I have been deprived of peace;
I have forgotten what prosperity is.
So I say, "My splendor is gone
and all that I had hoped from the LORD."

I remember my affliction and my wandering,
the bitterness and the gall.
I well remember them,
and my soul is downcast within me.
Yet this I call to mind
and therefore I have hope:

Because of the LORD's great love we are not consumed,
for his compassions never fail.
They are new every morning;
great is your faithfulness.
I say to myself, "The LORD is my portion;
therefore I will wait for him."

The LORD is good to those whose hope is in him,
to the one who seeks him;
it is good to wait quietly
for the salvation of the LORD.
It is good for a man to bear the yoke
while he is young.

Let him sit alone in silence,
for the LORD has laid it on him.
Let him bury his face in the dust—
there may yet be hope.
Let him offer his cheek to one who would strike him,
and let him be filled with disgrace.

For men are not cast off
by the Lord forever.
Though he brings grief, he will show compassion,
so great is his unfailing love.
For he does not willingly bring affliction
or grief to the children of men.

To crush underfoot
all prisoners in the land,

*Lam.
3:22-33*

*Lam.
3:34-54*

to deny a man his rights
    before the Most High,
to deprive a man of justice—
    would not the Lord see such things?

Who can speak and have it happen
    if the Lord has not decreed it?
Is it not from the mouth of the Most High
    that both calamities and good things come?
Why should any living man complain
    when punished for his sins?

Let us examine our ways and test them,
    and let us return to the LORD.
Let us lift up our hearts and our hands
    to God in heaven, and say:
"We have sinned and rebelled
    and you have not forgiven.

"You have covered yourself with anger and pursued us;
    you have slain without pity.
You have covered yourself with a cloud
    so that no prayer can get through.
You have made us scum and refuse
    among the nations.

"All our enemies have opened their mouths
    wide against us.
We have suffered terror and pitfalls,
    ruin and destruction."
Streams of tears flow from my eyes
    because my people are destroyed.

My eyes will flow unceasingly,
    without relief,
until the LORD looks down
    from heaven and sees.
What I see brings grief to my soul
    because of all the women of my city.

Those who were my enemies without cause
    hunted me like a bird.
They tried to end my life in a pit
    and threw stones at me;
the waters closed over my head,
    and I thought I was about to be cut off.

I called on your name, O LORD,
    from the depths of the pit.
You heard my plea: "Do not close your ears
    to my cry for relief."
You came near when I called you,
    and you said, "Do not fear."

O Lord, you took up my case;
    you redeemed my life.

Lam.
3:55-66

You have seen, O LORD, the wrong done to me.
>   Uphold my cause!
You have seen the depth of their vengeance,
>   all their plots against me.

O LORD, you have heard their insults,
>   all their plots against me—
what my enemies whisper and mutter
>   against me all day long.
Look at them! Sitting or standing,
>   they mock me in their songs.

Pay them back what they deserve, O LORD,
>   for what their hands have done.
Put a veil over their hearts,
>   and may your curse be on them!
Pursue them in anger and destroy them
>   from under the heavens of the LORD.

**Lam.
4:1-10**

How[m] the gold has lost its luster,
>   the fine gold become dull!
The sacred gems are scattered
>   at the head of every street.

How the precious sons of Zion,
>   once worth their weight in gold,
are now considered as pots of clay,
>   the work of a potter's hands!

Even jackals offer their breasts
>   to nurse their young,
but my people have become heartless
>   like ostriches in the desert.

Because of thirst the infant's tongue
>   sticks to the roof of its mouth;
the children beg for bread,
>   but no one gives it to them.

Those who once ate delicacies
>   are destitute in the streets.
Those nurtured in purple
>   now lie on ash heaps.

The punishment of my people
>   is greater than that of Sodom,
which was overthrown in a moment
>   without a hand turned to help her.

Their princes were brighter than snow
>   and whiter than milk,
their bodies more ruddy than rubies,
>   their appearance like sapphires.[n]

---

[m]This chapter is an acrostic poem, the verses of which begin with the successive letters of the Hebrew alphabet.   [n]Or *lapis lazuli*

But now they are blacker than soot;
    they are not recognized in the streets.
Their skin has shriveled on their bones;
    it has become as dry as a stick.

Those killed by the sword are better off
    than those who die of famine;
racked with hunger, they waste away
    for lack of food from the field.

With their own hands compassionate women
    have cooked their own children,
who became their food
    when my people were destroyed.

The LORD has given full vent to his wrath;
    he has poured out his fierce anger.
He kindled a fire in Zion
    that consumed her foundations.

Lam.
4:11-22

The kings of the earth did not believe,
    nor did any of the world's people,
that enemies and foes could enter
    the gates of Jerusalem.

But it happened because of the sins of her prophets
    and the iniquities of her priests,
who shed within her
    the blood of the righteous.

Now they grope through the streets
    like men who are blind.
They are so defiled with blood
    that no one dares to touch their garments.

"Go away! You are unclean!" men cry to them.
    "Away! Away! Don't touch us!"
When they flee and wander about,
    people among the nations say,
    "They can stay here no longer."

The LORD himself has scattered them;
    he no longer watches over them.
The priests are shown no honor,
    the elders no favor.

Moreover, our eyes failed,
    looking in vain for help;
from our towers we watched
    for a nation that could not save us.

Men stalked us at every step,
    so we could not walk in our streets.
Our end was near, our days were numbered,
    for our end had come.

Our pursuers were swifter

than eagles in the sky;
they chased us over the mountains
    and lay in wait for us in the desert.

The LORD's anointed, our very life breath,
    was caught in their traps.
We thought that under his shadow
    we would live among the nations.

Rejoice and be glad, O Daughter of Edom,
    you who live in the land of Uz.
But to you also the cup will be passed;
    you will be drunk and stripped naked.

O Daughter of Zion, your punishment will end;
    he will not prolong your exile.
But, O Daughter of Edom, he will punish your sin
    and expose your wickedness.

**Lam.
5:1-18**

Remember, O LORD, what has happened to us;
    look, and see our disgrace.
Our inheritance has been turned over to aliens,
    our homes to foreigners.
We have become orphans and fatherless,
    our mothers like widows.
We must buy the water we drink;
    our wood can be had only at a price.
Those who pursue us are at our heels;
    we are weary and find no rest.
We submitted to Egypt and Assyria
    to get enough bread.
Our fathers sinned and are no more,
    and we bear their punishment.
Slaves rule over us,
    and there is none to free us from their hands.
We get our bread at the risk of our lives
    because of the sword in the desert.
Our skin is hot as an oven,
    feverish from hunger.
Women have been ravished in Zion,
    and virgins in the towns of Judah.
Princes have been hung up by their hands;
    elders are shown no respect.
Young men toil at the millstones;
    boys stagger under loads of wood.
The elders are gone from the city gate;
    the young men have stopped their music.
Joy is gone from our hearts;
    our dancing has turned to mourning.
The crown has fallen from our head.
    Woe to us, for we have sinned!
Because of this our hearts are faint,
    because of these things our eyes grow dim

for Mount Zion, which lies desolate,
    with jackals prowling over it.

You, O LORD, reign forever;
    your throne endures from generation to generation.   Lam.
5:19-22
Why do you always forget us?
    Why do you forsake us so long?
Restore us to yourself, O LORD, that we may return;
    renew our days as of old
unless you have utterly rejected us
    and are angry with us beyond measure.

A Remnant Flees to Egypt

*O*nly two months will pass before there is conflict from within the ranks
of those who have been left desolate in Judah. A contingent of army officers who had not been captured will apparently fall under the influence
of the Ammonites, who will persuade them to assassinate Gedaliah. Their character is further revealed when they murder 70 innocent men, apparently without reason, and take captive their own countrymen at Mizpah.

Just when it appears that other former officers are about to right all the
wrongs, they too exhibit wicked character. After lying to Jeremiah, they lead
away to Egypt a whole remnant of Hebrews, including Jeremiah and Baruch.
Egypt is seemingly chosen for two reasons: first of all, there is fear that
Nebuchadnezzar will punish the former officers for killing his appointed governor, and they therefore believe that they can find safety under Pharaoh
Hophra's protection. Second, they—and particularly their wives—seem drawn
to Egypt's idolatry and worship of the pagan Queen of Heaven.

So it is that in the very country against which he has brought such harsh
judgments, Jeremiah finds himself once again crying out against idolatry and
having to bring more rebuke and judgment.

GEDALIAH WELCOMES OFFICERS.   When all the army officers and   2 Kgs.
25:23,24
Jer. 40:7-10
Mizpah
(586 B.C.)
their men who were still in the open country heard that the king of
Babylon had appointed Gedaliah son of Ahikam as governor over the land
and had put him in charge of the men, women and children who were the
poorest in the land and who had not been carried into exile to Babylon,
they came to Gedaliah at Mizpah—Ishmael son of Nethaniah, Johanan
and Jonathan the sons of Kareah, Seraiah son of Tanhumeth, the sons of
Ephai the Netophathite, and Jaazaniah*o* the son of the Maacathite, and
their men. Gedaliah son of Ahikam, the son of Shaphan, took an oath to
reassure them and their men. "Do not be afraid to serve the Babylonians,*p*"
he said. "Settle down in the land and serve the king of Babylon, and it will
go well with you. I myself will stay at Mizpah to represent you before the
Babylonians who come to us, but you are to harvest the wine, summer
fruit and oil, and put them in your storage jars, and live in the towns you
have taken over."

*o*Hebrew *Jezaniah*, a variant of *Jaazaniah*   *p*Or *Chaldeans*; also in verse 10

Jer. 40:11,12	**REMNANT HARVESTS FRUITS.** When all the Jews in Moab, Ammon, Edom and all the other countries heard that the king of Babylon had left a remnant in Judah and had appointed Gedaliah son of Ahikam, the son of Shaphan, as governor over them, they all came back to the land of Judah, to Gedaliah at Mizpah, from all the countries where they had been scattered. And they harvested an abundance of wine and summer fruit.
Jer. 40:13-16	**WARNING ABOUT ISHMAEL.** Johanan son of Kareah and all the army officers still in the open country came to Gedaliah at Mizpah and said to him, "Don't you know that Baalis king of the Ammonites has sent Ishmael son of Nethaniah to take your life?" But Gedaliah son of Ahikam did not believe them. Then Johanan son of Kareah said privately to Gedaliah in Mizpah, "Let me go and kill Ishmael son of Nethaniah, and no one will know it. Why should he take your life and cause all the Jews who are gathered around you to be scattered and the remnant of Judah to perish?" But Gedaliah son of Ahikam said to Johanan son of Kareah, "Don't do such a thing! What you are saying about Ishmael is not true."
2 Kgs. 25:25 Jer 41:1-3	**GEDALIAH ASSASSINATED.** In the seventh month Ishmael son of Nethaniah, the son of Elishama, who was of royal blood and had been one of the king's officers, came with ten men to Gedaliah son of Ahikam at Mizpah. While they were eating together there, Ishmael son of Nethaniah and the ten men who were with him got up and struck down Gedaliah son of Ahikam, the son of Shaphan, with the sword, killing the one whom the king of Babylon had appointed as governor over the land. Ishmael also killed all the Jews who were with Gedaliah at Mizpah, as well as the Babylonian*q* soldiers who were there.
Jer. 41:4-9	**SEVENTY MURDERED.** The day after Gedaliah's assassination, before anyone knew about it, eighty men who had shaved off their beards, torn their clothes and cut themselves came from Shechem, Shiloh and Samaria, bringing grain offerings and incense with them to the house of the LORD. Ishmael son of Nethaniah went out from Mizpah to meet them, weeping as he went. When he met them, he said, "Come to Gedaliah son of Ahikam." When they went into the city, Ishmael son of Nethaniah and the men who were with him slaughtered them and threw them into a cistern. But ten of them said to Ishmael, "Don't kill us! We have wheat and barley, oil and honey, hidden in a field." So he let them alone and did not kill them with the others. Now the cistern where he threw all the bodies of the men he had killed along with Gedaliah was the one King Asa had made as part of his defense against Baasha king of Israel. Ishmael son of Nethaniah filled it with the dead.
Jer. 41:10	**PEOPLE OF MIZPAH TAKEN.** Ishmael made captives of all the rest of the people who were in Mizpah—the king's daughters along with all the others who were left there, over whom Nebuzaradan commander of the imperial guard had appointed Gedaliah son of Ahikam. Ishmael son of Nethaniah took them captive and set out to cross over to the Ammonites.
Jer. 41:11-15	**JOHANAN RESCUES.** When Johanan son of Kareah and all the army officers who were with him heard about all the crimes Ishmael son of Nethaniah had committed, they took all their men and went to fight

q Or Chaldean

Ishmael son of Nethaniah. They caught up with him near the great pool in Gibeon. When all the people Ishmael had with him saw Johanan son of Kareah and the army officers who were with him, they were glad. All the people Ishmael had taken captive at Mizpah turned and went over to Johanan son of Kareah. But Ishmael son of Nethaniah and eight of his men escaped from Johanan and fled to the Ammonites.

FEAR OF BABYLONIANS.   Then Johanan son of Kareah and all the army officers who were with him led away all the survivors from Mizpah whom he had recovered from Ishmael son of Nethaniah after he had assassinated Gedaliah son of Ahikam: the soldiers, women, children and court officials he had brought from Gibeon. And they went on, stopping at Geruth Kimham near Bethlehem on their way to Egypt to escape the Babylonians.[r] They were afraid of them because Ishmael son of Nethaniah had killed Gedaliah son of Ahikam, whom the king of Babylon had appointed as governor over the land.

2 Kgs. 25:26
Jer. 41:16-18
Near Bethlehem

JEREMIAH ASKS FOR DIRECTION.   Then all the army officers, including Johanan son of Kareah and Jezaniah[s] son of Hoshaiah, and all the people from the least to the greatest approached Jeremiah the prophet and said to him, "Please hear our petition and pray to the LORD your God for this entire remnant. For as you now see, though we were once many, now only a few are left. Pray that the LORD your God will tell us where we should go and what we should do."

"I have heard you," replied Jeremiah the prophet. "I will certainly pray to the LORD your God as you have requested; I will tell you everything the LORD says and will keep nothing back from you."

Jer. 42:1-4

PROMISE OF COMPLIANCE.   Then they said to Jeremiah, "May the LORD be a true and faithful witness against us if we do not act in accordance with everything the LORD your God sends you to tell us. Whether it is favorable or unfavorable, we will obey the LORD our God, to whom we are sending you, so that it will go well with us, for we will obey the LORD our God."

Jer. 42:5,6

REMNANT TO STAY.   Ten days later the word of the LORD came to Jeremiah. So he called together Johanan son of Kareah and all the army officers who were with him and all the people from the least to the greatest. He said to them, "This is what the LORD, the God of Israel, to whom you sent me to present your petition, says: 'If you stay in this land, I will build you up and not tear you down; I will plant you and not uproot you, for I am grieved over the disaster I have inflicted on you. Do not be afraid of the king of Babylon, whom you now fear. Do not be afraid of him, declares the LORD, for I am with you and will save you and deliver you from his hands. I will show you compassion so that he will have compassion on you and restore you to your land.'

"However, if you say, 'We will not stay in this land,' and so disobey the LORD your God, and if you say, 'No, we will go and live in Egypt, where we will not see war or hear the trumpet or be hungry for bread,' then hear the word of the LORD, O remnant of Judah. This is what the LORD Almighty, the God of Israel, says: 'If you are determined to go to Egypt and you do go to settle there, then the sword you fear will overtake you there, and the famine you dread will follow you into Egypt, and there you

Jer. 42:7-18

[r]Or *Chaldeans*   [s]Hebrew; Septuagint (see also 43:2) *Azariah*

will die. Indeed, all who are determined to go to Egypt to settle there will die by the sword, famine and plague; not one of them will survive or escape the disaster I will bring on them.' This is what the LORD Almighty, the God of Israel, says: 'As my anger and wrath have been poured out on those who lived in Jerusalem, so will my wrath be poured out on you when you go to Egypt. You will be an object of cursing and horror, of condemnation and reproach; you will never see this place again.'

Jer. 42:19-22 WARNING AGAINST FLIGHT.   "O remnant of Judah, the LORD has told you, 'Do not go to Egypt.' Be sure of this: I warn you today that you made a fatal mistake[t] when you sent me to the LORD your God and said, 'Pray to the LORD our God for us; tell us everything he says and we will do it.' I have told you today, but you still have not obeyed the LORD your God in all he sent me to tell you. So now, be sure of this: You will die by the sword, famine and plague in the place where you want to go to settle."

Jer. 43:1-3 JEREMIAH CALLED LIAR.   When Jeremiah finished telling the people all the words of the LORD their God—everything the LORD had sent him to tell them—Azariah son of Hoshaiah and Johanan son of Kareah and all the arrogant men said to Jeremiah, "You are lying! The LORD our God has not sent you to say, 'You must not go to Egypt to settle there.' But Baruch son of Neriah is inciting you against us to hand us over to the Babylonians,[u] so they may kill us or carry us into exile to Babylon."

Jer. 43:4-7 REMNANT LED AWAY.   So Johanan son of Kareah and all the army officers and all the people disobeyed the LORD's command to stay in the land of Judah. Instead, Johanan son of Kareah and all the army officers led away all the remnant of Judah who had come back to live in the land of Judah from all the nations where they had been scattered. They also led away all the men, women and children and the king's daughters whom Nebuzaradan commander of the imperial guard had left with Gedaliah son of Ahikam, the son of Shaphan, and Jeremiah the prophet and Baruch son of Neriah. So they entered Egypt in disobedience to the LORD and went as far as Tahpanhes.

Jer. 43:8-13 PROPHECY ABOUT EGYPT.   In Tahpanhes the word of the LORD came to Jeremiah: "While the Jews are watching, take some large stones with you and bury them in clay in the brick pavement at the entrance to Pharaoh's palace in Tahpanhes. Then say to them, 'This is what the LORD Almighty, the God of Israel, says: I will send for my servant Nebuchadnezzar king of Babylon, and I will set his throne over these stones I have buried here; he will spread his royal canopy above them. He will come and attack Egypt, bringing death to those destined for death, captivity to those destined for captivity, and the sword to those destined for the sword. He[v] will set fire to the temples of the gods of Egypt; he will burn their temples and take their gods captive. As a shepherd wraps his garment around him, so will he wrap Egypt around himself and depart from there unscathed. There in the temple of the sun[w] in Egypt he will demolish the sacred pillars and will burn down the temples of the gods of Egypt.' "

Jer. 44:1-14 EGYPTIAN HEBREWS WARNED.   This word came to Jeremiah concerning all the Jews living in Lower Egypt—in Migdol, Tahpanhes and

---

[t]Or *you erred in your hearts*   [u]Or *Chaldeans*   [v]Or *I*   [w]Or *in Heliopolis*

Memphis[x]—and in Upper Egypt[y]: "This is what the LORD Almighty, the God of Israel, says: You saw the great disaster I brought on Jerusalem and on all the towns of Judah. Today they lie deserted and in ruins because of the evil they have done. They provoked me to anger by burning incense and by worshiping other gods that neither they nor you nor your fathers ever knew. Again and again I sent my servants the prophets, who said, 'Do not do this detestable thing that I hate!' But they did not listen or pay attention; they did not turn from their wickedness or stop burning incense to other gods. Therefore, my fierce anger was poured out; it raged against the towns of Judah and the streets of Jerusalem and made them the desolate ruins they are today.

"Now this is what the LORD God Almighty, the God of Israel, says: Why bring such great disaster on yourselves by cutting off from Judah the men and women, the children and infants, and so leave yourselves without a remnant? Why provoke me to anger with what your hands have made, burning incense to other gods in Egypt, where you have come to live? You will destroy yourselves and make yourselves an object of cursing and reproach among all the nations on earth. Have you forgotten the wickedness committed by your fathers and by the kings and queens of Judah and the wickedness committed by you and your wives in the land of Judah and the streets of Jerusalem? To this day they have not humbled themselves or shown reverence, nor have they followed my law and the decrees I set before you and your fathers.

"Therefore, this is what the LORD Almighty, the God of Israel, says: I am determined to bring disaster on you and to destroy all Judah. I will take away the remnant of Judah who were determined to go to Egypt to settle there. They will all perish in Egypt; they will fall by the sword or die from famine. From the least to the greatest, they will die by sword or famine. They will become an object of cursing and horror, of condemnation and reproach. I will punish those who live in Egypt with the sword, famine and plague, as I punished Jerusalem. None of the remnant of Judah who have gone to live in Egypt will escape or survive to return to the land of Judah, to which they long to return and live; none will return except a few fugitives."

PEOPLE'S IMPUDENT RESPONSE.   Then all the men who knew that their wives were burning incense to other gods, along with all the women who were present—a large assembly—and all the people living in Lower and Upper Egypt,[z] said to Jeremiah, "We will not listen to the message you have spoken to us in the name of the LORD! We will certainly do everything we said we would: We will burn incense to the Queen of Heaven and will pour out drink offerings to her just as we and our fathers, our kings and our officials did in the towns of Judah and in the streets of Jerusalem. At that time we had plenty of food and were well off and suffered no harm. But ever since we stopped burning incense to the Queen of Heaven and pouring out drink offerings to her, we have had nothing and have been perishing by sword and famine."

The women added, "When we burned incense to the Queen of Heaven and poured out drink offerings to her, did not our husbands know that we were making cakes like her image and pouring out drink offerings to her?"

Jer.
44:15-19

[x]Hebrew *Noph*   [y]Hebrew *in Pathros*   [z]Hebrew *in Egypt and Pathros*

Jer.
44:20-23
PAGANISM JUDAH'S DOWNFALL.   Then Jeremiah said to all the people, both men and women, who were answering him, "Did not the LORD remember and think about the incense burned in the towns of Judah and the streets of Jerusalem by you and your fathers, your kings and your officials and the people of the land? When the LORD could no longer endure your wicked actions and the detestable things you did, your land became an object of cursing and a desolate waste without inhabitants, as it is today. Because you have burned incense and have sinned against the LORD and have not obeyed him or followed his law or his decrees or his stipulations, this disaster has come upon you, as you now see."

Jer.
44:24-28
JUDGMENT AGAINST IDOLATERS.   Then Jeremiah said to all the people, including the women, "Hear the word of the LORD, all you people of Judah in Egypt. This is what the LORD Almighty, the God of Israel, says: You and your wives have shown by your actions what you promised when you said, 'We will certainly carry out the vows we made to burn incense and pour out drink offerings to the Queen of Heaven.'

"Go ahead then, do what you promised! Keep your vows! But hear the word of the LORD, all Jews living in Egypt: 'I swear by my great name,' says the LORD, 'that no one from Judah living anywhere in Egypt will ever again invoke my name or swear, "As surely as the Sovereign LORD lives." For I am watching over them for harm, not for good; the Jews in Egypt will perish by sword and famine until they are all destroyed. Those who escape the sword and return to the land of Judah from Egypt will be very few. Then the whole remnant of Judah who came to live in Egypt will know whose word will stand—mine or theirs.

Jer.
44:29,30
PHARAOH'S FATE A SIGN.   " 'This will be the sign to you that I will punish you in this place,' declares the LORD, 'so that you will know that my threats of harm against you will surely stand.' This is what the LORD says: 'I am going to hand Pharaoh Hophra king of Egypt over to his enemies who seek his life, just as I handed Zedekiah king of Judah over to Nebuchadnezzar king of Babylon, the enemy who was seeking his life.' "

Jer. 51:64b
END OF JEREMIAH'S MINISTRY.   The words of Jeremiah end here.

What a disheartening experience this must be for Jeremiah—off in a foreign country, separated from his scattered family, and surrounded by idolatrous Hebrews who have not even begun to learn the lesson of Judah's fall. Now in his older years Jeremiah must indeed have a broken heart. But surely in the kingdom of the Messiah about whom he has confidently prophesied he will receive great reward.

THE EXILED NATION

(Ca. 585-535 B.C.)

Ezekiel's Restoration Prophecies

Twenty years have passed since the first captives were deported from Judah and the exile was begun. Now the city of Jerusalem has fallen and the exile of the nation continues with greater magnitude. It will be another fifty years before the exile will end.

It is evidently some six months before one of the survivors of the Jerusalem slaughter finally makes his way to the prophet Ezekiel in Babylonia. Ezekiel gets a few hours' advance warning of Jerusalem's fall when, on the evening before the messenger's arrival, Ezekiel is suddenly unable to speak. Undoubtedly he recalls the day the siege against Jerusalem began—the day of his wife's death—when God told him that his mouth would be opened when the messenger from Jerusalem arrived with news of the fall. Just as promised, Ezekiel's temporary muteness disappears the following morning before the messenger arrives. With this dramatic confirmation of his earlier predictions regarding Jerusalem, Ezekiel sets about once again to take God's word to the people. He reminds them that the desolation has not yet ended, but assures them that it will end soon, and that the promised restoration will begin. The time for healing will come quickly, and so Ezekiel changes his focus to comfort a scattered and defeated people.

JERUSALEM'S FALL ANNOUNCED.   In the twelfth year of our exile, in the tenth month on the fifth day, a man who had escaped from Jerusalem came to me and said, "The city has fallen!" Now the evening before the man arrived, the hand of the LORD was upon me, and he opened my mouth before the man came to me in the morning. So my mouth was opened and I was no longer silent.

Ezk.
33:21,22
(586 B.C.)

REASON FOR DISPOSSESSION.   Then the word of the LORD came to me: "Son of man, the people living in those ruins in the land of Israel are saying, 'Abraham was only one man, yet he possessed the land. But we are many; surely the land has been given to us as our possession.' Therefore say to them, 'This is what the Sovereign LORD says: Since you eat meat with the blood still in it and look to your idols and shed blood, should you then possess the land? You rely on your sword, you do detestable things, and each of you defiles his neighbor's wife. Should you then possess the land?'

Ezk.
33:23-26

Ezk.
33:27-29

DESOLATION NOT ENDED.   "Say this to them: 'This is what the Sovereign LORD says: As surely as I live, those who are left in the ruins will fall by the sword, those out in the country I will give to the wild animals to be devoured, and those in strongholds and caves will die of a plague. I will make the land a desolate waste, and her proud strength will come to an end, and the mountains of Israel will become desolate so that no one will cross them. Then they will know that I am the LORD, when I have made the land a desolate waste because of all the detestable things they have done.'

Ezk.
33:30-33

NOBODY REALLY CARES.   "As for you, son of man, your countrymen are talking together about you by the walls and at the doors of the houses, saying to each other, 'Come and hear the message that has come from the LORD.' My people come to you, as they usually do, and sit before you to listen to your words, but they do not put them into practice. With their mouths they express devotion, but their hearts are greedy for unjust gain. Indeed, to them you are nothing more than one who sings love songs with a beautiful voice and plays an instrument well, for they hear your words but do not put them into practice.

"When all this comes true—and it surely will—then they will know that a prophet has been among them."

Now, in a prophecy about the lost sheep of Israel, Ezekiel summarizes the basic message of his entire ministry: that Israel's spiritual leaders have led the people to slaughter, but that God is going to gather his scattered people back in Palestine (as Canaan will come to be known), and that he will one day raise up a Savior for his people—the Messiah—who will be the Good Shepherd.

Ezk.
34:1-10

LEADERS ACCOUNTABLE.   The word of the LORD came to me: "Son of man, prophesy against the shepherds of Israel; prophesy and say to them: 'This is what the Sovereign LORD says: Woe to the shepherds of Israel who only take care of themselves! Should not shepherds take care of the flock? You eat the curds, clothe yourselves with the wool and slaughter the choice animals, but you do not take care of the flock. You have not strengthened the weak or healed the sick or bound up the injured. You have not brought back the strays or searched for the lost. You have ruled them harshly and brutally. So they were scattered because there was no shepherd, and when they were scattered they became food for all the wild animals. My sheep wandered over all the mountains and on every high hill. They were scattered over the whole earth, and no one searched or looked for them.

" 'Therefore, you shepherds, hear the word of the LORD: As surely as I live, declares the Sovereign LORD, because my flock lacks a shepherd and so has been plundered and has become food for all the wild animals, and because my shepherds did not search for my flock but cared for themselves rather than for my flock, therefore, O shepherds, hear the word of the LORD: This is what the Sovereign LORD says: I am against the shepherds and will hold them accountable for my flock. I will remove them from tending the flock so that the shepherds can no longer feed themselves. I will rescue my flock from their mouths, and it will no longer be food for them.

NATION TO BE RESTORED.   " 'For this is what the Sovereign LORD says: I myself will search for my sheep and look after them. As a shepherd looks after his scattered flock when he is with them, so will I look after my sheep. I will rescue them from all the places where they were scattered on a day of clouds and darkness. I will bring them out from the nations and gather them from the countries, and I will bring them into their own land. I will pasture them on the mountains of Israel, in the ravines and in all the settlements in the land. I will tend them in a good pasture, and the mountain heights of Israel will be their grazing land. There they will lie down in good grazing land, and there they will feed in a rich pasture on the mountains of Israel. I myself will tend my sheep and have them lie down, declares the Sovereign LORD. I will search for the lost and bring back the strays. I will bind up the injured and strengthen the weak, but the sleek and the strong I will destroy. I will shepherd the flock with justice. Ezk. 34:11-16

INDIVIDUAL JUDGMENT.   " 'As for you, my flock, this is what the Sovereign LORD says: I will judge between one sheep and another, and between rams and goats. Is it not enough for you to feed on the good pasture? Must you also trample the rest of your pasture with your feet? Is it not enough for you to drink clear water? Must you also muddy the rest with your feet? Must my flock feed on what you have trampled and drink what you have muddied with your feet? Ezk. 34:17-19

THE GOOD SHEPHERD.   " 'Therefore this is what the Sovereign LORD says to them: See, I myself will judge between the fat sheep and the lean sheep. Because you shove with flank and shoulder, butting all the weak sheep with your horns until you have driven them away, I will save my flock, and they will no longer be plundered. I will judge between one sheep and another. I will place over them one shepherd, my servant David, and he will tend them; he will tend them and be their shepherd. I the LORD will be their God, and my servant David will be prince among them. I the LORD have spoken. Ezk. 34:20-24

THE NEW COVENANT.   " 'I will make a covenant of peace with them and rid the land of wild beasts so that they may live in the desert and sleep in the forests in safety. I will bless them and the places surrounding my hill.[a] I will send down showers in season; there will be showers of blessing. The trees of the field will yield their fruit and the ground will yield its crops; the people will be secure in their land. They will know that I am the LORD, when I break the bars of their yoke and rescue them from the hands of those who enslaved them. They will no longer be plundered by the nations, nor will wild animals devour them. They will live in safety, and no one will make them afraid. I will provide for them a land renowned for its crops, and they will no longer be victims of famine in the land or bear the scorn of the nations. Then they will know that I, the LORD their God, am with them and that they, the house of Israel, are my people, declares the Sovereign LORD. You my sheep, the sheep of my pasture, are people, and I am your God, declares the Sovereign LORD.' " Ezk. 34:25-31

> During the siege Ezekiel brought judgment against Judah's oppressors, particularly for the glee with which they would welcome the fall of Jerusalem.

[a] Or I will make them and the places surrounding my hill a blessing

Using Edom to represent all those nations, Ezekiel again promises that destruction awaits them. He then consoles Israel with more assurances of the national restoration to come.

Ezk.
35:1-15

EDOM'S PUNISHMENT.   The word of the LORD came to me: "Son of man, set your face against Mount Seir; prophesy against it and say: 'This is what the Sovereign LORD says: I am against you, Mount Seir, and I will stretch out my hand against you and make you a desolate waste. I will turn your towns into ruins and you will be desolate. Then you will know that I am the LORD.

" 'Because you harbored an ancient hostility and delivered the Israelites over to the sword at the time of their calamity, the time their punishment reached its climax, therefore as surely as I live, declares the Sovereign LORD, I will give you over to bloodshed and it will pursue you. Since you did not hate bloodshed, bloodshed will pursue you. I will make Mount Seir a desolate waste and cut off from it all who come and go. I will fill your mountains with the slain; those killed by the sword will fall on your hills and in your valleys and in all your ravines. I will make you desolate forever; your towns will not be inhabited. Then you will know that I am the LORD.

" 'Because you have said, "These two nations and countries will be ours and we will take possession of them," even though I the LORD was there, therefore as surely as I live, declares the Sovereign LORD, I will treat you in accordance with the anger and jealousy you showed in your hatred of them and I will make myself known among them when I judge you. Then you will know that I the LORD have heard all the contemptible things you have said against the mountains of Israel. You said, "They have been laid waste and have been given over to us to devour." You boasted against me and spoke against me without restraint, and I heard it. This is what the Sovereign LORD says: While the whole earth rejoices, I will make you desolate. Because you rejoiced when the inheritance of the house of Israel became desolate, that is how I will treat you. You will be desolate, O Mount Seir, you and all of Edom. Then they will know that I am the LORD.' "

Ezk.
36:1-7

SCORN TO REPAY SCORN.   "Son of man, prophesy to the mountains of Israel and say, 'O mountains of Israel, hear the word of the LORD. This is what the Sovereign LORD says: The enemy said of you, "Aha! The ancient heights have become our possession." ' Therefore prophesy and say, 'This is what the Sovereign LORD says: Because they ravaged and hounded you from every side so that you became the possession of the rest of the nations and the object of people's malicious talk and slander, therefore, O mountains of Israel, hear the word of the Sovereign LORD: This is what the Sovereign LORD says to the mountains and hills, to the ravines and valleys, to the desolate ruins and the deserted towns that have been plundered and ridiculed by the rest of the nations around you—this is what the Sovereign LORD says: In my burning zeal I have spoken against the rest of the nations, and against all Edom, for with glee and with malice in their hearts they made my land their own possession so that they might plunder its pastureland.' Therefore prophesy concerning the land of Israel and say to the mountains and hills, to the ravines and valleys: 'This is what the Sovereign LORD says: I speak in my jealous wrath because you have suffered the scorn of the nations. Therefore this is what the Sovereign LORD says: I swear with uplifted hand that the nations around you will also suffer scorn.

ISRAEL TO PROSPER.   " 'But you, O mountains of Israel, will produce branches and fruit for my people Israel, for they will soon come home. I am concerned for you and will look on you with favor; you will be plowed and sown, and I will multiply the number of people upon you, even the whole house of Israel. The towns will be inhabited and the ruins rebuilt. I will increase the number of men and animals upon you, and they will be fruitful and become numerous. I will settle people on you as in the past and will make you prosper more than before. Then you will know that I am the LORD. I will cause people, my people Israel, to walk upon you. They will possess you, and you will be their inheritance; you will never again deprive them of their children.

Ezk. 36:8-12

TAUNTS WILL CEASE.   " 'This is what the Sovereign LORD says: Because people say to you, "You devour men and deprive your nation of its children," therefore you will no longer devour men or make your nation childless, declares the Sovereign LORD. No longer will I make you hear the taunts of the nations, and no longer will you suffer the scorn of the peoples or cause your nation to fall, declares the Sovereign LORD.' "

Ezk. 36:13-15

HOLY NAME HONORED.   Again the word of the LORD came to me: "Son of man, when the people of Israel were living in their own land, they defiled it by their conduct and their actions. Their conduct was like a woman's monthly uncleanness in my sight. So I poured out my wrath on them because they had shed blood in the land and because they had defiled it with their idols. I dispersed them among the nations, and they were scattered through the countries; I judged them according to their conduct and their actions. And wherever they went among the nations they profaned my holy name, for it was said of them, 'These are the LORD's people, and yet they had to leave his land.' I had concern for my holy name, which the house of Israel profaned among the nations where they had gone.

Ezk. 36:16-23

"Therefore say to the house of Israel, 'This is what the Sovereign LORD says: It is not for your sake, O house of Israel, that I am going to do these things, but for the sake of my holy name, which you have profaned among the nations where you have gone. I will show the holiness of my great name, which has been profaned among the nations, the name you have profaned among them. Then the nations will know that I am the LORD, declares the Sovereign LORD, when I show myself holy through you before their eyes.

A NEW SPIRIT.   " 'For I will take you out of the nations; I will gather you from all the countries and bring you back into your own land. I will sprinkle clean water on you, and you will be clean; I will cleanse you from all your impurities and from all your idols. I will give you a new heart and put a new spirit in you; I will remove from you your heart of stone and give you a heart of flesh. And I will put my Spirit in you and move you to follow my decrees and be careful to keep my laws. You will live in the land I gave your forefathers; you will be my people, and I will be your God. I will save you from all your uncleanness. I will call for the grain and make it plentiful and will not bring famine upon you. I will increase the fruit of

Ezk. 36:24-32

the trees and the crops of the field, so that you will no longer suffer disgrace among the nations because of famine. Then you will remember your evil ways and wicked deeds, and you will loathe yourselves for your sins and detestable practices. I want you to know that I am not doing this for your sake, declares the Sovereign LORD. Be ashamed and disgraced for your conduct, O house of Israel!

Ezk.
36:33-36

A GREAT REPLANTING. " 'This is what the Sovereign LORD says: On the day I cleanse you from all your sins, I will resettle your towns, and the ruins will be rebuilt. The desolate land will be cultivated instead of lying desolate in the sight of all who pass through it. They will say, "This land that was laid waste has become like the garden of Eden; the cities that were lying in ruins, desolate and destroyed, are now fortified and inhabited." Then the nations around you that remain will know that I the LORD have rebuilt what was destroyed and have replanted what was desolate. I the LORD have spoken, and I will do it.'

Ezk.
36:37,38

REPOPULATION OF NATION. "This is what the Sovereign LORD says: Once again I will yield to the plea of the house of Israel and do this for them: I will make their people as numerous as sheep, as numerous as the flocks for offerings at Jerusalem during her appointed feasts. So will the ruined cities be filled with flocks of people. Then they will know that I am the LORD."

God brings a fascinating vision to Ezekiel in demonstration of the new life which Israel will have. The visual image—of dry bones coming to life—must bring a smile to Ezekiel's face as he now relates the vision.

Ezk.
37:1-14

VISION OF DRY BONES. The hand of the LORD was upon me, and he brought me out by the Spirit of the LORD and set me in the middle of a valley; it was full of bones. He led me back and forth among them, and I saw a great many bones on the floor of the valley, bones that were very dry. He asked me, "Son of man, can these bones live?"

I said, "O Sovereign LORD, you alone know."

Then he said to me, "Prophesy to these bones and say to them, 'Dry bones, hear the word of the LORD! This is what the Sovereign LORD says to these bones: I will make breath[b] enter you, and you will come to life. I will attach tendons to you and make flesh come upon you and cover you with skin; I will put breath in you, and you will come to life. Then you will know that I am the LORD.'"

So I prophesied as I was commanded. And as I was prophesying, there was a noise, a rattling sound, and the bones came together, bone to bone. I looked, and tendons and flesh appeared on them and skin covered them, but there was no breath in them.

Then he said to me, "Prophesy to the breath; prophesy, son of man, and say to it, 'This is what the Sovereign LORD says: Come from the four winds, O breath, and breathe into these slain, that they may live.'" So I prophesied as he commanded me, and breath entered them; they came to life and stood up on their feet—a vast army.

Then he said to me: "Son of man, these bones are the whole house of Israel. They say, 'Our bones are dried up and our hope is gone; we are cut

[b]The Hebrew for this word can also mean *wind* or *spirit* (see verses 6-14).

off.' Therefore prophesy and say to them: 'This is what the Sovereign LORD says: O my people, I am going to open your graves and bring you up from them; I will bring you back to the land of Israel. Then you, my people, will know that I am the LORD, when I open your graves and bring you up from them. I will put my Spirit in you and you will live, and I will settle you in your own land. Then you will know that I the LORD have spoken, and I have done it, declares the LORD.' "

Another sign is to be shown to the people. Two sticks, one representing the northern tribes and the other depicting the tribe of Judah, are to be held together to signify the reunification of the nation of Israel. This is followed by a messianic prophecy of the new kingdom to come.

SIGN OF TWO STICKS.   The word of the LORD came to me: "Son of man, take a stick of wood and write on it, 'Belonging to Judah and the Israelites associated with him.' Then take another stick of wood, and write on it, 'Ephraim's stick, belonging to Joseph and all the house of Israel associated with him.' Join them together into one stick so that they will become one in your hand.

Ezk. 37:15-23

"When your countrymen ask you, 'Won't you tell us what you mean by this?' say to them, 'This is what the Sovereign LORD says: I am going to take the stick of Joseph—which is in Ephraim's hand—and of the Israelite tribes associated with him, and join it to Judah's stick, making them a single stick of wood, and they will become one in my hand.' Hold before their eyes the sticks you have written on and say to them, 'This is what the Sovereign LORD says: I will take the Israelites out of the nations where they have gone. I will gather them from all around and bring them back into their own land. I will make them one nation in the land, on the mountains of Israel. There will be one king over all of them and they will never again be two nations or be divided into two kingdoms. They will no longer defile themselves with their idols and vile images or with any of their offenses, for I will save them from all their sinful backsliding,c and I will cleanse them. They will be my people, and I will be their God.

THE NEW KINGDOM.   " 'My servant David will be king over them, and they will all have one shepherd. They will follow my laws and be careful to keep my decrees. They will live in the land I gave to my servant Jacob, the land where your fathers lived. They and their children and their children's children will live there forever, and David my servant will be their prince forever. I will make a covenant of peace with them; it will be an everlasting covenant. I will establish them and increase their numbers, and I will put my sanctuary among them forever. My dwelling place will be with them; I will be their God, and they will be my people. Then the nations will know that I the LORD make Israel holy, when my sanctuary is among them forever.' "

Ezk. 37:24-28

The climax of Ezekiel's restoration prophecies takes his hearers not only to the new kingdom of the Good Shepherd but apparently to the time when the forces of evil will be destroyed forever. The language is apocalyptic (that is,

cMany Hebrew manuscripts (see also Septuagint); most Hebrew manuscripts *all their dwelling places where they sinned*

symbolically predictive of future events) and challenging to interpret. The forces of evil are represented by Gog, ruler of a land called Magog, and by Meshech and Tubal. These names correspond to the sons of the patriarch Japheth, who have generally been associated with the warlike Goths, Cretans, and Scythians. God's vision to Ezekiel is that of a great battle on a wide panorama of the universe in which death and destruction are cataclysmic—far beyond anything which either Israel or Judah has experienced. But the reasons for the destruction are the same: rebellion and wickedness. The other difference is that the punishment will be of an eternal nature. At that time there will be no restoration of the wicked—only everlasting peace and joy for the righteous.

Ezk. 38:1-6   JUDGMENT AGAINST EVIL.   The word of the LORD came to me: "Son of man, set your face against Gog, of the land of Magog, the chief prince of[d] Meshech and Tubal; prophesy against him and say: 'This is what the Sovereign LORD says: I am against you, O Gog, chief prince of[e] Meshech and Tubal. I will turn you around, put hooks in your jaws and bring you out with your whole army—your horses, your horsemen fully armed, and a great horde with large and small shields, all of them brandishing their swords. Persia, Cush[f] and Put will be with them, all with shields and helmets, also Gomer with all its troops, and Beth Togarmah from the far north with all its troops—the many nations with you.

Ezk. 38:7-9   HORDES OF EVIL.   " 'Get ready; be prepared, you and all the hordes gathered about you, and take command of them. After many days you will be called to arms. In future years you will invade a land that has recovered from war, whose people were gathered from many nations to the mountains of Israel, which had long been desolate. They had been brought out from the nations, and now all of them live in safety. You and all your troops and the many nations with you will go up, advancing like a storm; you will be like a cloud covering the land.

Ezk. 38:10-13   EVIL COVETS THE RIGHTEOUS.   " 'This is what the Sovereign LORD says: On that day thoughts will come into your mind and you will devise an evil scheme. You will say, "I will invade a land of unwalled villages; I will attack a peaceful and unsuspecting people—all of them living without walls and without gates and bars. I will plunder and loot and turn my hand against the resettled ruins and the people gathered from the nations, rich in livestock and goods, living at the center of the land." Sheba and Dedan and the merchants of Tarshish and all her villages[g] will say to you, "Have you come to plunder? Have you gathered your hordes to loot, to carry off silver and gold, to take away livestock and goods and to seize much plunder?" '

Ezk. 38:14-16   BATTLE TO BE SIGN.   "Therefore, son of man, prophesy and say to Gog: 'This is what the Sovereign LORD says: In that day, when my people Israel are living in safety, will you not take notice of it? You will come from your place in the far north, you and many nations with you, all of them riding on horses, a great horde, a mighty army. You will advance against my people Israel like a cloud that covers the land. In days to come, O Gog, I will

---

*d*Or *the prince of Rosh,*   *e*Or *Gog, prince of Rosh,*   *f*That is, the upper Nile region
*g*Or *her strong lions*

bring you against my land, so that the nations may know me when I show myself holy through you before their eyes.

DESTRUCTION OF EVIL.   " 'This is what the Sovereign LORD says: Are you not the one I spoke of in former days by my servants the prophets of Israel? At that time they prophesied for years that I would bring you against them. This is what will happen in that day: When Gog attacks the land of Israel, my hot anger will be aroused, declares the Sovereign LORD. In my zeal and fiery wrath I declare that at that time there shall be a great earthquake in the land of Israel. The fish of the sea, the birds of the air, the beasts of the field, every creature that moves along the ground, and all the people on the face of the earth will tremble at my presence. The mountains will be overturned, the cliffs will crumble and every wall will fall to the ground. I will summon a sword against Gog on all my mountains, declares the Sovereign LORD. Every man's sword will be against his brother. I will execute judgment upon him with plague and bloodshed; I will pour down torrents of rain, hailstones and burning sulfur on him and on his troops and on the many nations with him. And so I will show my greatness and my holiness, and I will make myself known in the sight of many nations. Then they will know that I am the LORD.' "Son of man, prophesy against Gog and say: 'This is what the Sovereign LORD says: I am against you, O Gog, chief prince of[h] Meshech and Tubal. I will turn you around and drag you along. I will bring you from the far north and send you against the mountains of Israel. Then I will strike your bow from your left hand and make your arrows drop from your right hand. On the mountains of Israel you will fall, you and all your troops and the nations with you. I will give you as food to all kinds of carrion birds and to the wild animals. You will fall in the open field, for I have spoken, declares the Sovereign LORD. I will send fire on Magog and on those who live in safety in the coastlands, and they will know that I am the LORD.

Ezk. 38:17-39:6

THE DAY IS COMING.   " 'I will make known my holy name among my people Israel. I will no longer let my holy name be profaned, and the nations will know that I the LORD am the Holy One in Israel. It is coming! It will surely take place, declares the Sovereign LORD. This is the day I have spoken of.

Ezk. 39:7,8

FINALITY OF DESTRUCTION.   " 'Then those who live in the towns of Israel will go out and use the weapons for fuel and burn them up—the small and large shields, the bows and arrows, the war clubs and spears. For seven years they will use them for fuel. They will not need to gather wood from the fields or cut it from the forests, because they will use the weapons for fuel. And they will plunder those who plundered them and loot those who looted them, declares the Sovereign LORD.

" 'On that day I will give Gog a burial place in Israel, in the valley of those who travel east toward[i] the Sea.[j] It will block the way of travelers, because Gog and all his hordes will be buried there. So it will be called the Valley of Hamon Gog.[k]

" 'For seven months the house of Israel will be burying them in order to cleanse the land. All the people of the land will bury them, and the day

Ezk. 39:9-16

[h]Or Gog, prince of Rosh,   [i]Or of   [j]That is, the Dead Sea   [k]Hamon Gog means hordes of Gog.

I am glorified will be a memorable day for them, declares the Sovereign LORD.

" 'Men will be regularly employed to cleanse the land. Some will go throughout the land and, in addition to them, others will bury those that remain on the ground. At the end of the seven months they will begin their search. As they go through the land and one of them sees a human bone, he will set up a marker beside it until the gravediggers have buried it in the Valley of Hamon Gog. (Also a town called Hamonah¹ will be there.) And so they will cleanse the land.'

Ezk. 39:17-20

CELEBRATION OF RIGHTEOUS.   "Son of man, this is what the Sovereign LORD says: Call out to every kind of bird and all the wild animals: 'Assemble and come together from all around to the sacrifice I am preparing for you, the great sacrifice on the mountains of Israel. There you will eat flesh and drink blood. You will eat the flesh of mighty men and drink the blood of the princes of the earth as if they were rams and lambs, goats and bulls—all of them fattened animals from Bashan. At the sacrifice I am preparing for you, you will eat fat till you are glutted and drink blood till you are drunk. At my table you will eat your fill of horses and riders, mighty men and soldiers of every kind,' declares the Sovereign LORD.

Ezk. 39:21-24

ISRAEL EXAMPLE OF JUDGMENT.   "I will display my glory among the nations, and all the nations will see the punishment I inflict and the hand I lay upon them. From that day forward the house of Israel will know that I am the LORD their God. And the nations will know that the people of Israel went into exile for their sin, because they were unfaithful to me. So I hid my face from them and handed them over to their enemies, and they all fell by the sword. I dealt with them according to their uncleanness and their offenses, and I hid my face from them.

Ezk. 39:25-29

RESTORATION OF SPIRIT.   "Therefore this is what the Sovereign LORD says: I will now bring Jacob back from captivity^m and will have compassion on all the people of Israel, and I will be zealous for my holy name. They will forget their shame and all the unfaithfulness they showed toward me when they lived in safety in their land with no one to make them afraid. When I have brought them back from the nations and have gathered them from the countries of their enemies, I will show myself holy through them in the sight of many nations. Then they will know that I am the LORD their God, for though I sent them into exile among the nations, I will gather them to their own land, not leaving any behind. I will no longer hide my face from them, for I will pour out my Spirit on the house of Israel, declares the Sovereign LORD."

Egypt has the dubious distinction of being singled out among the nations as an example of the forces of evil. Ezekiel first brings a lament for Egypt, then assigns her a place of burial in the same grave with the hordes of evil, including Meshech and Tubal.

Ezk. 32:1-10 (585 B.C.)

LAMENT FOR EGYPT.   In the twelfth year, in the twelfth month on the first day, the word of the LORD came to me: "Son of man, take up a lament concerning Pharaoh king of Egypt and say to him:

---

¹Hamonah means horde.   ^mOr now restore the fortunes of Jacob

" 'You are like a lion among the nations;
　　you are like a monster in the seas
　thrashing about in your streams,
　　churning the water with your feet
　　and muddying the streams.

" 'This is what the Sovereign LORD says:

" 'With a great throng of people
　　I will cast my net over you,
　　and they will haul you up in my net.
I will throw you on the land
　　and hurl you on the open field.
I will let all the birds of the air settle on you
　　and all the beasts of the earth gorge themselves on you.
I will spread your flesh on the mountains
　　and fill the valleys with your remains.
I will drench the land with your flowing blood
　　all the way to the mountains,
　　and the ravines will be filled with your flesh.
When I snuff you out, I will cover the heavens
　　and darken their stars;
I will cover the sun with a cloud,
　　and the moon will not give its light.
All the shining lights in the heavens
　　I will darken over you;
　　I will bring darkness over your land,
　　　　　　　　　　　　　　　　declares the Sovereign LORD.
I will trouble the hearts of many peoples
　　when I bring about your destruction among the nations,
　　among[n] lands you have not known.
I will cause many peoples to be appalled at you,
　　and their kings will shudder with horror because of you
　　when I brandish my sword before them.
On the day of your downfall
　　each of them will tremble
　　every moment for his life.

" 'For this is what the Sovereign LORD says:

Ezk.
32:11-16

" 'The sword of the king of Babylon
　　will come against you.
I will cause your hordes to fall
　　by the swords of mighty men—
　　the most ruthless of all nations.
They will shatter the pride of Egypt,
　　and all her hordes will be overthrown.
I will destroy all her cattle
　　from beside abundant waters
no longer to be stirred by the foot of man
　　or muddied by the hoofs of cattle.
Then I will let her waters settle

[n]Hebrew; Septuagint *bring you into captivity among the nations,* / to

and make her streams flow like oil,
> declares the Sovereign LORD.
When I make Egypt desolate
and strip the land of everything in it,
when I strike down all who live there,
then they will know that I am the LORD.'

"This is the lament they will chant for her. The daughters of the nations will chant it; for Egypt and all her hordes they will chant it, declares the Sovereign LORD."

Ezk. 32:17-32

GRAVES OF EVIL. In the twelfth year, on the fifteenth day of the month, the word of the LORD came to me: "Son of man, wail for the hordes of Egypt and consign to the earth below both her and the daughters of mighty nations, with those who go down to the pit. Say to them, 'Are you more favored than others? Go down and be laid among the uncircumcised.' They will fall among those killed by the sword. The sword is drawn; let her be dragged off with all her hordes. From within the grave[o] the mighty leaders will say of Egypt and her allies, 'They have come down and they lie with the uncircumcised, with those killed by the sword.'

"Assyria is there with her whole army; she is surrounded by the graves of all her slain, all who have fallen by the sword. Their graves are in the depths of the pit and her army lies around her grave. All who had spread terror in the land of the living are slain, fallen by the sword.

"Elam is there, with all her hordes around her grave. All of them are slain, fallen by the sword. All who had spread terror in the land of the living went down uncircumcised to the earth below. They bear their shame with those who go down to the pit. A bed is made for her among the slain, with all her hordes around her grave. All of them are uncircumcised, killed by the sword. Because their terror had spread in the land of the living, they bear their shame with those who go down to the pit; they are laid among the slain.

"Meshech and Tubal are there, with all their hordes around their graves. All of them are uncircumcised, killed by the sword because they spread their terror in the land of the living. Do they not lie with the other uncircumcised warriors who have fallen, who went down to the grave with their weapons of war, whose swords were placed under their heads? The punishment for their sins rested on their bones, though the terror of these warriors had stalked through the land of the living.

"You too, O Pharaoh, will be broken and will lie among the uncircumcised, with those killed by the sword.

"Edom is there, her kings and all her princes; despite their power, they are laid with those killed by the sword. They lie with the uncircumcised, with those who go down to the pit.

"All the princes of the north and all the Sidonians are there; they went down with the slain in disgrace despite the terror caused by their power. They lie uncircumcised with those killed by the sword and bear their shame with those who go down to the pit.

"Pharaoh—he and all his army—will see them and he will be consoled for all his hordes that were killed by the sword, declares the Sovereign LORD. Although I had him spread terror in the land of the living, Pharaoh

---

[o]Hebrew *Sheol*

and all his hordes will be laid among the uncircumcised, with those killed
by the sword, declares the Sovereign LORD."

As a messenger of the eternal destruction to come, Ezekiel sees that God
has made him personally accountable—not for the response of his hearers, but
for his own faithfulness in preaching the word. His role is that of the watchman
seeing the approach of danger.

WATCHMAN'S ACCOUNTABILITY.   The word of the LORD came to me: Ezk. 33:1-9
"Son of man, speak to your countrymen and say to them: 'When I bring
the sword against a land, and the people of the land choose one of their
men and make him their watchman, and he sees the sword coming against
the land and blows the trumpet to warn the people, then if anyone hears
the trumpet but does not take warning and the sword comes and takes his
life, his blood will be on his own head. Since he heard the sound of the
trumpet but did not take warning, his blood will be on his own head. If he
had taken warning, he would have saved himself. But if the watchman
sees the sword coming and does not blow the trumpet to warn the people
and the sword comes and takes the life of one of them, that man will be
taken away because of his sin, but I will hold the watchman accountable
for his blood.'

"Son of man, I have made you a watchman for the house of Israel; so
hear the word I speak and give them warning from me. When I say to the
wicked, 'O wicked man, you will surely die,' and you do not speak out to
dissuade him from his ways, that wicked man will die for[p] his sin, and I
will hold you accountable for his blood. But if you do warn the wicked
man to turn from his ways and he does not do so, he will die for his sin,
but you will have saved yourself.

The response from those he is warning is predictable: they demand to
know what right God has to bring punishment against Israel. Although Ezekiel
has already answered their arguments, he insists one last time that, although
God hates the punishment which must come to the wicked, it must nevertheless come (and furthermore, that no one is in a position to argue the matter). Yet
the promise is equally sure that even the wicked can be saved through sincere
and righteous repentance.

GOD HATES PUNISHMENT.   "Son of man, say to the house of Israel,   Ezk.
'This is what you are saying: "Our offenses and sins weigh us down, and   33:10,11
we are wasting away because of[q] them. How then can we live?" ' Say to
them, 'As surely as I live, declares the Sovereign LORD, I take no pleasure
in the death of the wicked, but rather that they turn from their ways and
live. Turn! Turn from your evil ways! Why will you die, O house of Israel?'

REPENTANCE CAN SAVE.   "Therefore, son of man, say to your coun-   Ezk.
trymen, 'The righteousness of the righteous man will not save him when   33:12-16
he disobeys, and the wickedness of the wicked man will not cause him to
fall when he turns from it. The righteous man, if he sins, will not be
allowed to live because of his former righteousness.' If I tell the righteous
man that he will surely live, but then he trusts in his righteousness and

[p]Or in   [q]Or away in

does evil, none of the righteous things he has done will be remembered; he will die for the evil he has done. And if I say to the wicked man, 'You will surely die,' but he then turns away from his sin and does what is just and right—if he gives back what he took in pledge for a loan, returns what he has stolen, follows the decrees that give life, and does no evil, he will surely live; he will not die. None of the sins he has committed will be remembered against him. He has done what is just and right; he will surely live.

Ezk.
33:17-20

GOD IS JUST.   "Yet your countrymen say, 'The way of the Lord is not just.' But it is their way that is not just. If a righteous man turns from his righteousness and does evil, he will die for it. And if a wicked man turns away from his wickedness and does what is just and right, he will live by doing so. Yet, O house of Israel, you say, 'The way of the Lord is not just.' But I will judge each of you according to his own ways."

Shadrach, Meshach, and Abednego

*W*hile Ezekiel is dealing with the issue of punishment for the wicked, Daniel's three friends, Shadrach, Meshach, and Abednego, are in the capital city of Babylon, about to be punished by King Nebuchadnezzar for being faithful to God. Possibly using the gold recently seized as booty in the capture of Judah, Nebuchadnezzar erects a huge image which he commands all the people to worship. When Daniel's three friends refuse to do so, they are put into a fiery furnace. But they are saved from death by the power of God, and Nebuchadnezzar is once again impressed by the God in whom they place their trust. (Where Daniel is during this episode is not known. Presumably he is away from the capital, for surely he would have interceded on behalf of his friends.)

Dan. 3:1-3
(Ca. 584
B.C.?)

GOLDEN IMAGE ERECTED.   King Nebuchadnezzar made an image of gold, ninety feet high and nine feet[r] wide, and set it up on the plain of Dura in the province of Babylon. He then summoned the satraps, prefects, governors, advisers, treasurers, judges, magistrates and all the other provincial officials to come to the dedication of the image he had set up. So the satraps, prefects, governors, advisers, treasurers, judges, magistrates and all the other provincial officials assembled for the dedication of the image that King Nebuchadnezzar had set up, and they stood before it.

Dan. 3:4-7

MANDATE REQUIRING WORSHIP.   Then the herald loudly proclaimed, "This is what you are commanded to do, O peoples, nations and men of every language: As soon as you hear the sound of the horn, flute, zither, lyre, harp, pipes and all kinds of music, you must fall down and worship the image of gold that King Nebuchadnezzar has set up. Whoever does not fall down and worship will immediately be thrown into a blazing furnace."

Therefore, as soon as they heard the sound of the horn, flute, zither, lyre, harp and all kinds of music, all the peoples, nations and men of every language fell down and worshiped the image of gold that King Nebuchadnezzar had set up.

[r]Aramaic *sixty cubits high and six cubits wide* (about 27 meters high and 2.7 meters wide)

ASTROLOGERS ACCUSE HEBREWS.   At this time some astrologers[s] came forward and denounced the Jews. They said to King Nebuchadnezzar, "O king, live forever! You have issued a decree, O king, that everyone who hears the sound of the horn, flute, zither, lyre, harp, pipes and all kinds of music must fall down and worship the image of gold, and that whoever does not fall down and worship will be thrown into a blazing furnace. But there are some Jews whom you have set over the affairs of the province of Babylon—Shadrach, Meshach and Abednego—who pay no attention to you, O king. They neither serve your gods nor worship the image of gold you have set up." Dan.
3:8-12

NEBUCHADNEZZAR REBUFFED.   Furious with rage, Nebuchadnezzar summoned Shadrach, Meshach and Abednego. So these men were brought before the king, and Nebuchadnezzar said to them, "Is it true, Shadrach, Meshach and Abednego, that you do not serve my gods or worship the image of gold I have set up? Now when you hear the sound of the horn, flute, zither, lyre, harp, pipes and all kinds of music, if you are ready to fall down and worship the image I made, very good. But if you do not worship it, you will be thrown immediately into a blazing furnace. Then what god will be able to rescue you from my hand?" Dan.
3:13-18

Shadrach, Meshach and Abednego replied to the king, "O Nebuchadnezzar, we do not need to defend ourselves before you in this matter. If we are thrown into the blazing furnace, the God we serve is able to save us from it, and he will rescue us from your hand, O king. But even if he does not, we want you to know, O king, that we will not serve your gods or worship the image of gold you have set up."

THREE THROWN INTO FURNACE.   Then Nebuchadnezzar was furious with Shadrach, Meshach and Abednego, and his attitude toward them changed. He ordered the furnace heated seven times hotter than usual and commanded some of the strongest soldiers in his army to tie up Shadrach, Meshach and Abednego and throw them into the blazing furnace. So these men, wearing their robes, trousers, turbans and other clothes, were bound and thrown into the blazing furnace. The king's command was so urgent and the furnace so hot that the flames of the fire killed the soldiers who took up Shadrach, Meshach and Abednego, and these three men, firmly tied, fell into the blazing furnace. Dan.
3:19-23

THREE RESCUED BY ANGEL.   Then King Nebuchadnezzar leaped to his feet in amazement and asked his advisers, "Weren't there three men that we tied up and threw into the fire?" Dan.
3:24-27

They replied, "Certainly, O king."

He said, "Look! I see four men walking around in the fire, unbound and unharmed, and the fourth looks like a son of the gods."

Nebuchadnezzar then approached the opening of the blazing furnace and shouted, "Shadrach, Meshach and Abednego, servants of the Most High God, come out! Come here!"

So Shadrach, Meshach and Abednego came out of the fire, and the satraps, prefects, governors and royal advisers crowded around them. They saw that the fire had not harmed their bodies, nor was a hair of their heads singed; their robes were not scorched, and there was no smell of fire on them.

[s]Or *Chaldeans*

Dan. 3:28-30	THREE ARE HONORED. Then Nebuchadnezzar said, "Praise be to the God of Shadrach, Meshach and Abednego, who has sent his angel and rescued his servants! They trusted in him and defied the king's command and were willing to give up their lives rather than serve or worship any god except their own God. Therefore I decree that the people of any nation or language who say anything against the God of Shadrach, Meshach and Abednego be cut into pieces and their houses be turned into piles of rubble, for no other god can save in this way." Then the king promoted Shadrach, Meshach and Abednego in the province of Babylon.

Just as before, when Daniel had interpreted his dream and Nebuchadnezzar had praised the God of the Hebrews, there is no evidence of any lasting conviction in Nebuchadnezzar's heart. But the concept of a real and powerful God is steadily having its effect on this pagan world leader, and may someday result in true conversion.

Ezekiel's Great Temple Vision

*I*t has been some 12 years since any recorded word of the Lord has come to Ezekiel. In what seems to be a mere continuation of his previous futuristic vision, Ezekiel now sees the great temple. The vision reminds one in many ways (particularly in its attention to detail) of two earlier descriptions—of the tabernacle in the wilderness and of Solomon's magnificent temple in Jerusalem. The similarity suggests that, to the people of Israel, one of the most important features of the restoration is the rebuilding of their now-ruined temple. Ezekiel's prophecy must surely give renewed hope to this downcast nation, yet his vision casts another image far beyond the time when the nation will be reestablished and the temple will be rebuilt. This becomes clear when it is realized that the rebuilt temple will not have the physical beauty of the one which it replaces, and that the dimensions of the great temple described here are on a much grander scale than could possibly be built in the soon-to-be-reconstructed city of Jerusalem.

There are also significant differences to be seen in the religious service of the great temple. Notably missing, for example, are the ark of the covenant, the golden lampstand, the bread of the Presence, and the veil. There is no observance of the Feast of Weeks and no Day of Atonement, that holiest of all days. Nor will the Levites serve as they have served under Moses' Law. Although there will still be priests, there is no high priest. Instead, there will be a "prince," or a succession of "princes," who will offer sacrifices as representatives of the people. What Ezekiel is about to be shown is something far different from anything he or his people have known to this time.

As he was at the beginning of his ministry, Ezekiel is once again taken by the hand of the Lord to the land of Israel. There he is shown symbolically the new temple to come, its worship rituals, its celebrations, its servants and priests, its laws, and the division of the land surrounding it.

Ezk. 40:1-4 (572 B.C.)	EZEKIEL TAKEN TO ISRAEL. In the twenty-fifth year of our exile, at the beginning of the year, on the tenth of the month, in the fourteenth year

after the fall of the city—on that very day the hand of the LORD was upon me and he took me there. In visions of God he took me to the land of Israel and set me on a very high mountain, on whose south side were some buildings that looked like a city. He took me there, and I saw a man whose appearance was like bronze; he was standing in the gateway with a linen cord and a measuring rod in his hand. The man said to me, "Son of man, look with your eyes and hear with your ears and pay attention to everything I am going to show you, for that is why you have been brought here. Tell the house of Israel everything you see."

THE EAST GATE. I saw a wall completely surrounding the temple area. The length of the measuring rod in the man's hand was six long cubits, each of which was a cubit*t* and a handbreadth.*u* He measured the wall; it was one measuring rod thick and one rod high.

Ezk. 40:5-16

Then he went to the gate facing east. He climbed its steps and measured the threshold of the gate; it was one rod deep.*v* The alcoves for the guards were one rod long and one rod wide, and the projecting walls between the alcoves were five cubits thick. And the threshold of the gate next to the portico facing the temple was one rod deep.

Then he measured the portico of the gateway; it*w* was eight cubits deep and its jambs were two cubits thick. The portico of the gateway faced the temple.

Inside the east gate were three alcoves on each side; the three had the same measurements, and the faces of the projecting walls on each side had the same measurements. Then he measured the width of the entrance to the gateway; it was ten cubits and its length was thirteen cubits. In front of each alcove was a wall one cubit high, and the alcoves were six cubits square. Then he measured the gateway from the top of the rear wall of one alcove to the top of the opposite one; the distance was twenty-five cubits from one parapet opening to the opposite one. He measured along the faces of the projecting walls all around the inside of the gateway—sixty cubits. The measurement was up to the portico*x* facing the courtyard.*y* The distance from the entrance of the gateway to the far end of its portico was fifty cubits. The alcoves and the projecting walls inside the gateway were surmounted by narrow parapet openings all around, as was the portico; the openings all around faced inward. The faces of the projecting walls were decorated with palm trees.

THE OUTER COURT. Then he brought me into the outer court. There I saw some rooms and a pavement that had been constructed all around the court; there were thirty rooms along the pavement. It abutted the sides of the gateways and was as wide as they were long; this was the lower pavement. Then he measured the distance from the inside of the lower gateway to the outside of the inner court; it was a hundred cubits on the east side as well as on the north.

Ezk. 40:17-19

THE NORTH GATE. Then he measured the length and width of the gate facing north, leading into the outer court. Its alcoves—three on each side—

Ezk. 40:20-23

*t*The common cubit was about 1 1/2 feet (about 0.5 meter).   *u*That is, about 3 inches (about 8 centimeters)   *v*Septuagint; Hebrew *deep, the first threshold, one rod deep*
*w*Many Hebrew manuscripts, Septuagint, Vulgate and Syriac; most Hebrew manuscripts *gateway facing the temple; it was one rod deep.* *9Then he measured the portico of the gateway; it*
*x*Septuagint; Hebrew *projecting wall*   *y*The meaning of the Hebrew for this verse is uncertain.

its projecting walls and its portico had the same measurements as those of the first gateway. It was fifty cubits long and twenty-five cubits wide. Its openings, its portico and its palm tree decorations had the same measurements as those of the gate facing east. Seven steps led up to it, with its portico opposite them. There was a gate to the inner court facing the north gate, just as there was on the east. He measured from one gate to the opposite one; it was a hundred cubits.

Ezk.
40:24-27

THE SOUTH GATE.   Then he led me to the south side and I saw a gate facing south. He measured its jambs and its portico, and they had the same measurements as the others. The gateway and its portico had narrow openings all around, like the openings of the others. It was fifty cubits long and twenty-five cubits wide. Seven steps led up to it, with its portico opposite them; it had palm tree decorations on the faces of the projecting walls on each side. The inner court also had a gate facing south, and he measured from this gate to the outer gate on the south side; it was a hundred cubits.

Ezk.
40:28-37

GATES TO INNER COURT.   Then he brought me into the inner court through the south gate, and he measured the south gate; it had the same measurements as the others. Its alcoves, its projecting walls and its portico had the same measurements as the others. The gateway and its portico had openings all around. It was fifty cubits long and twenty-five cubits wide. (The porticoes of the gateways around the inner court were twenty-five cubits wide and five cubits deep.) Its portico faced the outer court; palm trees decorated its jambs, and eight steps led up to it.

Then he brought me to the inner court on the east side, and he measured the gateway; it had the same measurements as the others. Its alcoves, its projecting walls and its portico had the same measurements as the others. The gateway and its portico had openings all around. It was fifty cubits long and twenty-five cubits wide. Its portico[z] faced the outer court; palm trees decorated the jambs on either side, and eight steps led up to it.

Then he brought me to the north gate and measured it. It had the same measurements as the others, as did its alcoves, its projecting walls and its portico, and it had openings all around. It was fifty cubits long and twenty-five cubits wide. Its portico[z] faced the outer court; palm trees decorated the jambs on either side, and eight steps led up to it.

Ezk.
40:38-43

ROOMS FOR PREPARATION.   A room with a doorway was by the portico in each of the inner gateways, where the burnt offerings were washed. In the portico of the gateway were two tables on each side, on which the burnt offerings, sin offerings and guilt offerings were slaughtered. By the outside wall of the portico of the gateway, near the steps at the entrance to the north gateway were two tables, and on the other side of the steps were two tables. So there were four tables on one side of the gateway and four on the other—eight tables in all—on which the sacrifices were slaughtered. There were also four tables of dressed stone for the burnt offerings, each a cubit and a half long, a cubit and a half wide and a cubit high. On them were placed the utensils for slaughtering the burnt offerings and the other sacrifices. And double-pronged hooks, each a handbreadth long, were attached to the wall all around. The tables were for the flesh of the offerings.

[z]Septuagint (see also verses 31 and 34); Hebrew *jambs*

ROOMS FOR PRIESTS. Outside the inner gate, within the inner court, were two rooms, one[a] at the side of the north gate and facing south, and another at the side of the south[b] gate and facing north. He said to me, "The room facing south is for the priests who have charge of the temple, and the room facing north is for the priests who have charge of the altar. These are the sons of Zadok, who are the only Levites who may draw near to the LORD to minister before him."

Ezk. 40:44-46

COURT AND ALTAR. Then he measured the court: It was square—a hundred cubits long and a hundred cubits wide. And the altar was in front of the temple.

Ezk. 40:47

THE PORTICO. He brought me to the portico of the temple and measured the jambs of the portico; they were five cubits wide on either side. The width of the entrance was fourteen cubits and its projecting walls were[c] three cubits wide on either side. The portico was twenty cubits wide, and twelve[d] cubits from front to back. It was reached by a flight of stairs,[e] and there were pillars on each side of the jambs.

Ezk. 40:48,49

OUTER SANCTUARY. Then the man brought me to the outer sanctuary and measured the jambs; the width of the jambs was six cubits[f] on each side.[g] The entrance was ten cubits wide, and the projecting walls on each side of it were five cubits wide. He also measured the outer sanctuary; it was forty cubits long and twenty cubits wide.

Ezk. 41:1,2

MOST HOLY PLACE. Then he went into the inner sanctuary and measured the jambs of the entrance; each was two cubits wide. The entrance was six cubits wide, and the projecting walls on each side of it were seven cubits wide. And he measured the length of the inner sanctuary; it was twenty cubits, and its width was twenty cubits across the end of the outer sanctuary. He said to me, "This is the Most Holy Place."

Ezk. 41:3,4

SIDE ROOMS. Then he measured the wall of the temple; it was six cubits thick, and each side room around the temple was four cubits wide. The side rooms were on three levels, one above another, thirty on each level. There were ledges all around the wall of the temple to serve as supports for the side rooms, so that the supports were not inserted into the wall of the temple. The side rooms all around the temple were wider at each successive level. The structure surrounding the temple was built in ascending stages, so that the rooms widened as one went upward. A stairway went up from the lowest floor to the top floor through the middle floor.

Ezk. 41:5-12

I saw that the temple had a raised base all around it, forming the foundation of the side rooms. It was the length of the rod, six long cubits. The outer wall of the side rooms was five cubits thick. The open area between the side rooms of the temple and the priests' rooms was twenty cubits wide all around the temple. There were entrances to the side rooms from the open area, one on the north and another on the south; and the base adjoining the open area was five cubits wide all around.

The building facing the temple courtyard on the west side was seventy

[a]Septuagint; Hebrew *were rooms for singers, which were*   [b]Septuagint; Hebrew *east*
[c]Septuagint; Hebrew *entrance was*   [d]Septuagint; Hebrew *eleven*   [e]Hebrew;
Septuagint *Ten steps led up to it*   [f]The common cubit was about 1 1/2 feet (about 0.5 meter).   [g]One Hebrew manuscript and Septuagint; most Hebrew manuscripts *side, the width of the tent*

cubits wide. The wall of the building was five cubits thick all around, and its length was ninety cubits.

**Ezk.
41:13-15a**

TEMPLE MEASUREMENTS.   Then he measured the temple; it was a hundred cubits long, and the temple courtyard and the building with its walls were also a hundred cubits long. The width of the temple courtyard on the east, including the front of the temple, was a hundred cubits.

Then he measured the length of the building facing the courtyard at the rear of the temple, including its galleries on each side; it was a hundred cubits.

**Ezk.
41:15b-20**

DECORATIONS.   The outer sanctuary, the inner sanctuary and the portico facing the court, as well as the thresholds and the narrow windows and galleries around the three of them—everything beyond and including the threshold was covered with wood. The floor, the wall up to the windows, and the windows were covered. In the space above the outside of the entrance to the inner sanctuary and on the walls at regular intervals all around the inner and outer sanctuary were carved cherubim and palm trees. Palm trees alternated with cherubim. Each cherub had two faces: the face of a man toward the palm tree on one side and the face of a lion toward the palm tree on the other. They were carved all around the whole temple. From the floor to the area above the entrance, cherubim and palm trees were carved on the wall of the outer sanctuary.

**Ezk.
41:21-26**

TABLE AND DOORS.   The outer sanctuary had a rectangular doorframe, and the one at the front of the Most Holy Place was similar. There was a wooden altar three cubits high and two cubits square[h]; its corners, its base[i] and its sides were of wood. The man said to me, "This is the table that is before the LORD." Both the outer sanctuary and the Most Holy Place had double doors. Each door had two leaves—two hinged leaves for each door. And on the doors of the outer sanctuary were carved cherubim and palm trees like those carved on the walls, and there was a wooden overhang on the front of the portico. On the sidewalls of the portico were narrow windows with palm trees carved on each side. The side rooms of the temple also had overhangs.

**Ezk.
42:1-14**

USE OF PRIESTS' ROOMS.   Then the man led me northward into the outer court and brought me to the rooms opposite the temple courtyard and opposite the outer wall on the north side. The building whose door faced north was a hundred cubits[j] long and fifty cubits wide. Both in the section twenty cubits from the inner court and in the section opposite the pavement of the outer court, gallery faced gallery at the three levels. In front of the rooms was an inner passageway ten cubits wide and a hundred cubits[k] long. Their doors were on the north. Now the upper rooms were narrower, for the galleries took more space from them than from the rooms on the lower and middle floors of the building. The rooms on the third floor had no pillars, as the courts had; so they were smaller in floor space than those on the lower and middle floors. There was an outer wall parallel to the rooms and the outer court; it extended in front of the rooms for fifty cubits. While the row of rooms on the side next to the outer court was fifty cubits long, the row on the side nearest the sanctuary was a

---

[h]Septuagint; Hebrew *long*   [i]Septuagint; Hebrew *length*   [j]The common cubit was about 1 1/2 feet (about 0.5 meter).   [k]Septuagint and Syriac; Hebrew *and one cubit*

hundred cubits long. The lower rooms had an entrance on the east side as one enters them from the outer court.

On the south side[l] along the length of the wall of the outer court, adjoining the temple courtyard and opposite the outer wall, were rooms with a passageway in front of them. These were like the rooms on the north; they had the same length and width, with similar exits and dimensions. Similar to the doorways on the north were the doorways of the rooms on the south. There was a doorway at the beginning of the passageway that was parallel to the corresponding wall extending eastward, by which one enters the rooms.

Then he said to me, "The north and south rooms facing the temple courtyard are the priests' rooms, where the priests who approach the LORD will eat the most holy offerings. There they will put the most holy offerings—the grain offerings, the sin offerings and the guilt offerings—for the place is holy. Once the priests enter the holy precincts, they are not to go into the outer court until they leave behind the garments in which they minister, for these are holy. They are to put on other clothes before they go near the places that are for the people."

OUTER TEMPLE AREA.   When he had finished measuring what was inside the temple area, he led me out by the east gate and measured the area all around: He measured the east side with the measuring rod; it was five hundred cubits.[m] He measured the north side; it was five hundred cubits[n] by the measuring rod. He measured the south side; it was five hundred cubits by the measuring rod. Then he turned to the west side and measured; it was five hundred cubits by the measuring rod. So he measured the area on all four sides. It had a wall around it, five hundred cubits long and five hundred cubits wide, to separate the holy from the common. *(Ezk. 42:15-20)*

GLORY ENTERS TEMPLE.   Then the man brought me to the gate facing east, and I saw the glory of the God of Israel coming from the east. His voice was like the roar of rushing waters, and the land was radiant with his glory. The vision I saw was like the vision I had seen when he[o] came to destroy the city and like the visions I had seen by the Kebar River, and I fell facedown. The glory of the LORD entered the temple through the gate facing east. Then the Spirit lifted me up and brought me into the inner court, and the glory of the LORD filled the temple. *(Ezk. 43:1-5)*

HOLINESS OF TEMPLE.   While the man was standing beside me, I heard someone speaking to me from inside the temple. He said: "Son of man, this is the place of my throne and the place for the soles of my feet. This is where I will live among the Israelites forever. The house of Israel will never again defile my holy name—neither they nor their kings—by their prostitution[p] and the lifeless idols[q] of their kings at their high places. When they placed their threshold next to my threshold and their doorposts beside my doorposts, with only a wall between me and them, they defiled my holy name by their detestable practices. So I destroyed them in my anger. Now let them put away from me their prostitution and the lifeless idols of their kings, and I will live among them forever. *(Ezk. 43:6-9)*

---

[l]Septuagint; Hebrew *Eastward*   [m]See Septuagint of verse 17; Hebrew *rods*; also in verses 18 and 19.   [n]Septuagint; Hebrew *rods*   [o]Some Hebrew manuscripts and Vulgate; most Hebrew manuscripts *I*   [p]Or *their spiritual adultery*; also in verse 9   [q]Or *the corpses*; also in verse 9

Ezk. 43:10,11

VISION FOR SINNERS' SHAME. "Son of man, describe the temple to the people of Israel, that they may be ashamed of their sins. Let them consider the plan, and if they are ashamed of all they have done, make known to them the design of the temple—its arrangement, its exits and entrances—its whole design and all its regulations[r] and laws. Write these down before them so that they may be faithful to its design and follow all its regulations.

Ezk. 43:12

SURROUNDING AREA HOLY. "This is the law of the temple: All the surrounding area on top of the mountain will be most holy. Such is the law of the temple.

Ezk. 43:13-17

THE ALTAR. "These are the measurements of the altar in long cubits, that cubit being a cubit[s] and a handbreadth[t]: Its gutter is a cubit deep and a cubit wide, with a rim of one span[u] around the edge. And this is the height of the altar: From the gutter on the ground up to the lower ledge it is two cubits high and a cubit wide, and from the smaller ledge up to the larger ledge it is four cubits high and a cubit wide. The altar hearth is four cubits high, and four horns project upward from the hearth. The altar hearth is square, twelve cubits long and twelve cubits wide. The upper ledge also is square, fourteen cubits long and fourteen cubits wide, with a rim of half a cubit and a gutter of a cubit all around. The steps of the altar face east."

Ezk. 43:18-27

DEDICATION OF ALTAR. Then he said to me, "Son of man, this is what the Sovereign LORD says: These will be the regulations for sacrificing burnt offerings and sprinkling blood upon the altar when it is built: You are to give a young bull as a sin offering to the priests, who are Levites, of the family of Zadok, who come near to minister before me, declares the Sovereign LORD. You are to take some of its blood and put it on the four horns of the altar and on the four corners of the upper ledge and all around the rim, and so purify the altar and make atonement for it. You are to take the bull for the sin offering and burn it in the designated part of the temple area outside the sanctuary.

"On the second day you are to offer a male goat without defect for a sin offering, and the altar is to be purified as it was purified with the bull. When you have finished purifying it, you are to offer a young bull and a ram from the flock, both without defect. You are to offer them before the LORD, and the priests are to sprinkle salt on them and sacrifice them as a burnt offering to the LORD.

"For seven days you are to provide a male goat daily for a sin offering; you are also to provide a young bull and a ram from the flock, both without defect. For seven days they are to make atonement for the altar and cleanse it; thus they will dedicate it. At the end of these days, from the eighth day on, the priests are to present your burnt offerings and fellowship offerings[v] on the altar. Then I will accept you, declares the Sovereign LORD."

Ezk. 44:1-3

PRIVILEGE OF PRINCE. Then the man brought me back to the outer gate of the sanctuary, the one facing east, and it was shut. The LORD said to me, "This gate is to remain shut. It must not be opened; no one may

[r]Some Hebrew manuscripts and Septuagint; most Hebrew manuscripts *regulations and its whole design*   [s]The common cubit was about 1 1/2 feet (about 0.5 meter).   [t]That is, about 3 inches (about 8 centimeters)   [u]That is, about 9 inches (about 22 centimeters)   [v]Traditionally *peace offerings*

enter through it. It is to remain shut because the LORD, the God of Israel, has entered through it. The prince himself is the only one who may sit inside the gateway to eat in the presence of the LORD. He is to enter by way of the portico of the gateway and go out the same way."

UNCIRCUMCISED EXCLUDED.   Then the man brought me by way of the north gate to the front of the temple. I looked and saw the glory of the LORD filling the temple of the LORD, and I fell facedown.

Ezk. 44:4-9

The LORD said to me, "Son of man, look carefully, listen closely and give attention to everything I tell you concerning all the regulations regarding the temple of the LORD. Give attention to the entrance of the temple and all the exits of the sanctuary. Say to the rebellious house of Israel, 'This is what the Sovereign LORD says: Enough of your detestable practices, O house of Israel! In addition to all your other detestable practices, you brought foreigners uncircumcised in heart and flesh into my sanctuary, desecrating my temple while you offered me food, fat and blood, and you broke my covenant. Instead of carrying out your duty in regard to my holy things, you put others in charge of my sanctuary. This is what the Sovereign LORD says: No foreigner uncircumcised in heart and flesh is to enter my sanctuary, not even the foreigners who live among the Israelites.

LIMITATIONS ON LEVITES.   " 'The Levites who went far from me when Israel went astray and who wandered from me after their idols must bear the consequences of their sin. They may serve in my sanctuary, having charge of the gates of the temple and serving in it; they may slaughter the burnt offerings and sacrifices for the people and stand before the people and serve them. But because they served them in the presence of their idols and made the house of Israel fall into sin, therefore I have sworn with uplifted hand that they must bear the consequences of their sin, declares the Sovereign LORD. They are not to come near to serve me as priests or come near any of my holy things or my most holy offerings; they must bear the shame of their detestable practices. Yet I will put them in charge of the duties of the temple and all the work that is to be done in it.

Ezk. 44:10-14

PRIESTS OF ZADOK ANCESTRY.   " 'But the priests, who are Levites and descendants of Zadok and who faithfully carried out the duties of my sanctuary when the Israelites went astray from me, are to come near to minister before me; they are to stand before me to offer sacrifices of fat and blood, declares the Sovereign LORD. They alone are to enter my sanctuary; they alone are to come near my table to minister before me and perform my service.

Ezk. 44:15,16

PRIESTS' GARMENTS.   " 'When they enter the gates of the inner court, they are to wear linen clothes; they must not wear any woolen garment while ministering at the gates of the inner court or inside the temple. They are to wear linen turbans on their heads and linen undergarments around their waists. They must not wear anything that makes them perspire. When they go out into the outer court where the people are, they are to take off the clothes they have been ministering in and are to leave them in the sacred rooms, and put on other clothes, so that they do not consecrate the people by means of their garments.

Ezk. 44:17-19

RESTRICTIONS ON PRIESTS.   " 'They must not shave their heads or let their hair grow long, but they are to keep the hair of their heads trimmed. No priest is to drink wine when he enters the inner court. They must not

Ezk. 44:20-23, 24b, 25-27,31

marry widows or divorced women; they may marry only virgins of Israelite descent or widows of priests. They are to teach my people the difference between the holy and the common and show them how to distinguish between the unclean and the clean.

They are to keep my laws and my decrees for all my appointed feasts, and they are to keep my Sabbaths holy.

" 'A priest must not defile himself by going near a dead person; however, if the dead person was his father or mother, son or daughter, brother or unmarried sister, then he may defile himself. After he is cleansed, he must wait seven days. On the day he goes into the inner court of the sanctuary to minister in the sanctuary, he is to offer a sin offering for himself, declares the Sovereign LORD. The priests must not eat anything, bird or animal, found dead or torn by wild animals.

Ezk. 44:24a — PRIESTS TO BE JUDGES. " 'In any dispute, the priests are to serve as judges and decide it according to my ordinances.

Ezk. 44:28-30 — NO POSSESSION FOR PRIESTS. " 'I am to be the only inheritance the priests have. You are to give them no possession in Israel; I will be their possession. They will eat the grain offerings, the sin offerings and the guilt offerings; and everything in Israel devoted^w to the LORD will belong to them. The best of all the firstfruits and of all your special gifts will belong to the priests. You are to give them the first portion of your ground meal so that a blessing may rest on your household.

Ezk. 45:1-5 — SACRED LAND. " 'When you allot the land as an inheritance, you are to present to the LORD a portion of the land as a sacred district, 25,000 cubits long and 20,000^x cubits wide; the entire area will be holy. Of this, a section 500 cubits square is to be for the sanctuary, with 50 cubits around it for open land. In the sacred district, measure off a section 25,000 cubits^y long and 10,000 cubits^z wide. In it will be the sanctuary, the Most Holy Place. It will be the sacred portion of the land for the priests, who minister in the sanctuary and who draw near to minister before the LORD. It will be a place for their houses as well as a holy place for the sanctuary. An area 25,000 cubits long and 10,000 cubits wide will belong to the Levites, who serve in the temple, as their possession for towns to live in. ^{a}

Ezk. 45:6 — LAND FOR CITY. " 'You are to give the city as its property an area 5,000 cubits wide and 25,000 cubits long, adjoining the sacred portion; it will belong to the whole house of Israel.

Ezk. 45:7,8a — PRINCE'S LAND. " 'The prince will have the land bordering each side of the area formed by the sacred district and the property of the city. It will extend westward from the west side and eastward from the east side, running lengthwise from the western to the eastern border parallel to one of the tribal portions. This land will be his possession in Israel.

Ezk. 45:8b-12 — JUSTICE OF PRINCES. And my princes will no longer oppress my people but will allow the house of Israel to possess the land according to their tribes.

" 'This is what the Sovereign LORD says: You have gone far enough, O princes of Israel! Give up your violence and oppression and do what is just

---

^{w}The Hebrew term refers to the irrevocable giving over of things or persons to the LORD.
^{x}Septuagint (see also verses 3 and 5 and 48:9); Hebrew *10,000* ^{y}That is, about 7 miles (about 12 kilometers) ^{z}That is, about 3 miles (about 5 kilometers) ^{a}Septuagint; Hebrew *temple; they will have as their possession 20 rooms*

and right. Stop dispossessing my people, declares the Sovereign LORD. You are to use accurate scales, an accurate ephah[b] and an accurate bath. [c] The ephah and the bath are to be the same size, the bath containing a tenth of a homer[d] and the ephah a tenth of a homer; the homer is to be the standard measure for both. The shekel[e] is to consist of twenty gerahs. Twenty shekels plus twenty-five shekels plus fifteen shekels equal one mina.[f]

OFFERINGS FROM PEOPLE.   " 'This is the special gift you are to offer: a sixth of an ephah from each homer of wheat and a sixth of an ephah from each homer of barley. The prescribed portion of oil, measured by the bath, is a tenth of a bath from each cor (which consists of ten baths or one homer, for ten baths are equivalent to a homer). Also one sheep is to be taken from every flock of two hundred from the well-watered pastures of Israel. These will be used for the grain offerings, burnt offerings and fellowship offerings[g] to make atonement for the people, declares the Sovereign LORD. All the people of the land will participate in this special gift for the use of the prince in Israel.

Ezk. 45:13-16

PRINCE'S ROLE IN OFFERINGS.   It will be the duty of the prince to provide the burnt offerings, grain offerings and drink offerings at the festivals, the New Moons and the Sabbaths—at all the appointed feasts of the house of Israel. He will provide the sin offerings, grain offerings, burnt offerings and fellowship offerings to make atonement for the house of Israel.

Ezk. 45:17

SIN OFFERINGS.   " 'This is what the Sovereign LORD says: In the first month on the first day you are to take a young bull without defect and purify the sanctuary. The priest is to take some of the blood of the sin offering and put it on the doorposts of the temple, on the four corners of the upper ledge of the altar and on the gateposts of the inner court. You are to do the same on the seventh day of the month for anyone who sins unintentionally or through ignorance; so you are to make atonement for the temple.

Ezk. 45:18-20

PASSOVER.   " 'In the first month on the fourteenth day you are to observe the Passover, a feast lasting seven days, during which you shall eat bread made without yeast. On that day the prince is to provide a bull as a sin offering for himself and for all the people of the land. Every day during the seven days of the Feast he is to provide seven bulls and seven rams without defect as a burnt offering to the LORD, and a male goat for a sin offering. He is to provide as a grain offering an ephah for each bull and an ephah for each ram, along with a hin[h] of oil for each ephah.

" 'During the seven days of the Feast, which begins in the seventh month on the fifteenth day, he is to make the same provision for sin offerings, burnt offerings, grain offerings and oil.

Ezk. 45:21-25

SABBATHS AND NEW MOON.   " 'This is what the Sovereign LORD says: The gate of the inner court facing east is to be shut on the six working days, but on the Sabbath day and on the day of the New Moon it is to be opened. The prince is to enter from the outside through the portico of the

Ezk. 46:1-8

---

[b]An ephah was a dry measure.   [c]A bath was a liquid measure.   [d]A homer was a dry measure.   [e]A shekel weighed about 2/5 ounce (about 11.5 grams).   [f]That is, 60 shekels; the common mina was 50 shekels.   [g]Traditionally *peace offerings*   [h]That is, probably about 4 quarts (about 4 liters)

gateway and stand by the gatepost. The priests are to sacrifice his burnt offering and his fellowship offerings.[i] He is to worship at the threshold of the gateway and then go out, but the gate will not be shut until evening. On the Sabbaths and New Moons the people of the land are to worship in the presence of the LORD at the entrance to that gateway. The burnt offering the prince brings to the LORD on the Sabbath day is to be six male lambs and a ram, all without defect. The grain offering given with the ram is to be an ephah,[j] and the grain offering with the lambs is to be as much as he pleases, along with a hin[k] of oil for each ephah. On the day of the New Moon he is to offer a young bull, six lambs and a ram, all without defect. He is to provide as a grain offering one ephah with the bull, one ephah with the ram, and with the lambs as much as he wants to give, along with a hin of oil with each ephah. When the prince enters, he is to go in through the portico of the gateway, and he is to come out the same way.

Ezk.
46:9,10

ENTRY AND EXIT.   " 'When the people of the land come before the LORD at the appointed feasts, whoever enters by the north gate to worship is to go out the south gate; and whoever enters by the south gate is to go out the north gate. No one is to return through the gate by which he entered, but each is to go out the opposite gate. The prince is to be among them, going in when they go in and going out when they go out.

Ezk.
46:11,12

GRAIN AND FREEWILL OFFERINGS.   " 'At the festivals and the appointed feasts, the grain offering is to be an ephah with a bull, an ephah with a ram, and with the lambs as much as one pleases, along with a hin of oil for each ephah. When the prince provides a freewill offering to the LORD—whether a burnt offering or fellowship offerings—the gate facing east is to be opened for him. He shall offer his burnt offering or his fellowship offerings as he does on the Sabbath day. Then he shall go out, and after he has gone out, the gate will be shut.

Ezk.
46:13-15

GRAIN AND BURNT OFFERINGS.   " 'Every day you are to provide a year-old lamb without defect for a burnt offering to the LORD; morning by morning you shall provide it. You are also to provide with it morning by morning a grain offering, consisting of a sixth of an ephah with a third of a hin of oil to moisten the flour. The presenting of this grain offering to the LORD is a lasting ordinance. So the lamb and the grain offering and the oil shall be provided morning by morning for a regular burnt offering.

Ezk.
46:16-18

INHERITANCE TO PRINCE'S SONS.   " 'This is what the Sovereign LORD says: If the prince makes a gift from his inheritance to one of his sons, it will also belong to his descendants; it is to be their property by inheritance. If, however, he makes a gift from his inheritance to one of his servants, the servant may keep it until the year of freedom; then it will revert to the prince. His inheritance belongs to his sons only; it is theirs. The prince must not take any of the inheritance of the people, driving them off their property. He is to give his sons their inheritance out of his own property, so that none of my people will be separated from his property.' "

Ezk.
46:19,20

PREPARATION OF OFFERINGS.   Then the man brought me through the entrance at the side of the gate to the sacred rooms facing north, which belonged to the priests, and showed me a place at the western end. He

---

[i]Traditionally *peace offerings*   [j]That is, probably about 3/5 bushel (about 22 liters)
[k]That is, probably about 4 quarts (about 4 liters)

said to me, "This is the place where the priests will cook the guilt offering and the sin offering and bake the grain offering, to avoid bringing them into the outer court and consecrating the people."

THE KITCHENS.   He then brought me to the outer court and led me around to its four corners, and I saw in each corner another court. In the four corners of the outer court were enclosed[l] courts, forty cubits long and thirty cubits wide; each of the courts in the four corners was the same size. Around the inside of each of the four courts was a ledge of stone, with places for fire built all around under the ledge. He said to me, "These are the kitchens where those who minister at the temple will cook the sacrifices of the people."

Ezk.
46:21-24

THE TEMPLE'S RIVER.   The man brought me back to the entrance of the temple, and I saw water coming out from under the threshold of the temple toward the east (for the temple faced east). The water was coming down from under the south side of the temple, south of the altar. He then brought me out through the north gate and led me around the outside to the outer gate facing east, and the water was flowing from the south side.

Ezk.
47:1-12

As the man went eastward with a measuring line in his hand, he measured off a thousand cubits[m] and then led me through water that was ankle-deep. He measured off another thousand cubits and led me through water that was knee-deep. He measured off another thousand and led me through water that was up to the waist. He measured off another thousand, but now it was a river that I could not cross, because the water had risen and was deep enough to swim in—a river that no one could cross. He asked me, "Son of man, do you see this?"

Then he led me back to the bank of the river. When I arrived there, I saw a great number of trees on each side of the river. He said to me, "This water flows toward the eastern region and goes down into the Arabah,[n] where it enters the Sea.[o] When it empties into the Sea,[o] the water there becomes fresh. Swarms of living creatures will live wherever the river flows. There will be large numbers of fish, because this water flows there and makes the salt water fresh; so where the river flows everything will live. Fishermen will stand along the shore; from En Gedi to En Eglaim there will be places for spreading nets. The fish will be of many kinds—like the fish of the Great Sea.[p] But the swamps and marshes will not become fresh; they will be left for salt. Fruit trees of all kinds will grow on both banks of the river. Their leaves will not wither, nor will their fruit fail. Every month they will bear, because the water from the sanctuary flows to them. Their fruit will serve for food and their leaves for healing."

EQUAL DIVISION OF LAND.   This is what the Sovereign LORD says: "These are the boundaries by which you are to divide the land for an inheritance among the twelve tribes of Israel, with two portions for Joseph. You are to divide it equally among them. Because I swore with uplifted hand to give it to your forefathers, this land will become your inheritance.

Ezk.
47:13,14

[l]The meaning of the Hebrew for this word is uncertain.   [m]That is, about 1,500 feet (about 450 meters)   [n]Or *the Jordan Valley*   [o]That is, the Dead Sea   [p]That is, the Mediterranean

Ezk. 47:15-20	OUTER BOUNDARIES. "This is to be the boundary of the land:

"On the north side it will run from the Great Sea by the Hethlon road past Lebo[q] Hamath to Zedad, Berothah[r] and Sibraim (which lies on the border between Damascus and Hamath), as far as Hazer Hatticon, which is on the border of Hauran. The boundary will extend from the sea to Hazar Enan,[s] along the northern border of Damascus, with the border of Hamath to the north. This will be the north boundary.

"On the east side the boundary will run between Hauran and Damascus, along the Jordan between Gilead and the land of Israel, to the eastern sea and as far as Tamar.[t] This will be the east boundary.

"On the south side it will run from Tamar as far as the waters of Meribah Kadesh, then along the Wadi ⌊of Egypt⌋ to the Great Sea. This will be the south boundary.

"On the west side, the Great Sea will be the boundary to a point opposite Lebo[u] Hamath. This will be the west boundary.

Ezk. 47:21-23	INHERITANCE OF ALIENS. "You are to distribute this land among

yourselves according to the tribes of Israel. You are to allot it as an inheritance for yourselves and for the aliens who have settled among you and who have children. You are to consider them as native-born Israelites; along with you they are to be allotted an inheritance among the tribes of Israel. In whatever tribe the alien settles, there you are to give him his inheritance," declares the Sovereign LORD.

Ezk. 48:1-7	SEVEN TRIBES' LAND. "These are the tribes, listed by name: At the

northern frontier, Dan will have one portion; it will follow the Hethlon road to Lebo[v] Hamath; Hazar Enan and the northern border of Damascus next to Hamath will be part of its border from the east side to the west side.

"Asher will have one portion; it will border the territory of Dan from east to west.

"Naphtali will have one portion; it will border the territory of Asher from east to west.

"Manasseh will have one portion; it will border the territory of Naphtali from east to west.

"Ephraim will have one portion; it will border the territory of Manasseh from east to west.

"Reuben will have one portion; it will border the territory of Ephraim from east to west.

"Judah will have one portion; it will border the territory of Reuben from east to west.

Ezk. 48:8-14	THE SACRED LANDS. "Bordering the territory of Judah from east to

west will be the portion you are to present as a special gift. It will be 25,000 cubits[w] wide, and its length from east to west will equal one of the tribal portions; the sanctuary will be in the center of it.

"The special portion you are to offer to the LORD will be 25,000 cubits long and 10,000 cubits[x] wide. This will be the sacred portion for the

---

[q]Or *past the entrance to*   [r]See Septuagint and Ezekiel 48:1; Hebrew *road to go into Zedad,* [16]*Hamath, Berothah*   [s]Hebrew *Enon,* a variant of *Enan*   [t]Septuagint and Syriac; Hebrew *Israel. You will measure to the eastern sea*   [u]Or *opposite the entrance to*   [v]Or *to the entrance to*   [w]That is, about 7 miles (about 12 kilometers)   [x]That is, about 3 miles (about 5 kilometers)

priests. It will be 25,000 cubits long on the north side, 10,000 cubits wide on the west side, 10,000 cubits wide on the east side and 25,000 cubits long on the south side. In the center of it will be the sanctuary of the LORD. This will be for the consecrated priests, the Zadokites, who were faithful in serving me and did not go astray as the Levites did when the Israelites went astray. It will be a special gift to them from the sacred portion of the land, a most holy portion, bordering the territory of the Levites.

"Alongside the territory of the priests, the Levites will have an allotment 25,000 cubits long and 10,000 cubits wide. Its total length will be 25,000 cubits and its width 10,000 cubits. They must not sell or exchange any of it. This is the best of the land and must not pass into other hands, because it is holy to the LORD.

COMMON LAND.   "The remaining area, 5,000 cubits wide and 25,000 cubits long, will be for the common use of the city, for houses and for pastureland. The city will be in the center of it and will have these measurements: the north side 4,500 cubits, the south side 4,500 cubits, the east side 4,500 cubits, and the west side 4,500 cubits. The pastureland for the city will be 250 cubits on the north, 250 cubits on the south, 250 cubits on the east, and 250 cubits on the west. What remains of the area, bordering on the sacred portion and running the length of it, will be 10,000 cubits on the east side and 10,000 cubits on the west side. Its produce will supply food for the workers of the city. The workers from the city who farm it will come from all the tribes of Israel. The entire portion will be a square, 25,000 cubits on each side. As a special gift you will set aside the sacred portion, along with the property of the city. | Ezk. 48:15-20

THE PRINCE'S LAND.   "What remains on both sides of the area formed by the sacred portion and the city property will belong to the prince. It will extend eastward from the 25,000 cubits of the sacred portion to the eastern border, and westward from the 25,000 cubits to the western border. Both these areas running the length of the tribal portions will belong to the prince, and the sacred portion with the temple sanctuary will be in the center of them. So the property of the Levites and the property of the city will lie in the center of the area that belongs to the prince. The area belonging to the prince will lie between the border of Judah and the border of Benjamin. | Ezk. 48:21,22

FIVE TRIBES' LAND.   "As for the rest of the tribes: Benjamin will have one portion; it will extend from the east side to the west side. | Ezk. 48:23-29

"Simeon will have one portion; it will border the territory of Benjamin from east to west.

"Issachar will have one portion; it will border the territory of Simeon from east to west.

"Zebulun will have one portion; it will border the territory of Issachar from east to west.

"Gad will have one portion; it will border the territory of Zebulun from east to west.

"The southern boundary of Gad will run south from Tamar to the waters of Meribah Kadesh, then along the Wadi ˌof Egyptˌ to the Great Sea.ʸ

"This is the land you are to allot as an inheritance to the tribes of Israel, and these will be their portions," declares the Sovereign LORD.

ʸ That is, the Mediterranean

Ezk. 48:30-34	**CITY GATES.** "These will be the exits of the city: Beginning on the north side, which is 4,500 cubits long, the gates of the city will be named after the tribes of Israel. The three gates on the north side will be the gate of Reuben, the gate of Judah and the gate of Levi. "On the east side, which is 4,500 cubits long, will be three gates: the gate of Joseph, the gate of Benjamin and the gate of Dan. "On the south side, which measures 4,500 cubits, will be three gates: the gate of Simeon, the gate of Issachar and the gate of Zebulun. "On the west side, which is 4,500 cubits long, will be three gates: the gate of Gad, the gate of Asher and the gate of Naphtali.
Ezk. 48:35a	**TOTAL CIRCUMFERENCE.** "The distance all around will be 18,000 cubits.
Ezk. 48:35b	**CITY'S NAME.** "And the name of the city from that time on will be: THE LORD IS THERE."

> Whatever else it may be, God's temple is for true worshipers only—those whose lives are holy, whose wills are obedient, and whose hearts are pure.

End of Ezekiel's Ministry

fter Ezekiel's great temple vision, it is another two years before the word of the Lord comes to him again. This time it comes as a somewhat strange footnote to a judgment which Ezekiel had brought 16 years earlier against the city of Tyre. Pursuant to the earlier prophecy, Nebuchadnezzar was to destroy Tyre completely, and someday it would be left a "bare rock." Since then Nebuchadnezzar has indeed laid a 13-year siege against Tyre, and the mainland city has evidently been destroyed. But Nebuchadnezzar has apparently not been able to reach the island city itself—at least not profitably enough to make it worth his trouble. Therefore God seems to be telling Ezekiel that he is giving Egypt to Nebuchadnezzar as a consolation prize. For such a brief passage, it raises several interesting questions. It even ends on a mysterious note.

Ezk. 29:17-20 (570 B.C.)	**UNPROFITABLE SIEGE OF TYRE.** In the twenty-seventh year, in the first month on the first day, the word of the LORD came to me: "Son of man, Nebuchadnezzar king of Babylon drove his army in a hard campaign against Tyre; every head was rubbed bare and every shoulder made raw. Yet he and his army got no reward from the campaign he led against Tyre. Therefore this is what the Sovereign LORD says: I am going to give Egypt to Nebuchadnezzar king of Babylon, and he will carry off its wealth. He will loot and plunder the land as pay for his army. I have given him Egypt as a reward for his efforts because he and his army did it for me, declares the Sovereign LORD.
Ezk. 29:21	**EZEKIEL'S FUTURE ROLE.** "On that day I will make a horn[z] grow for the house of Israel, and I will open your mouth among them. Then they will know that I am the LORD."

[z]*Horn* here symbolizes strength.

If, in fact, Nebuchadnezzar was unable to subdue Tyre completely, the city's fate is not yet secure. In 322 B.C. Alexander the Great and his mighty Grecian army will build a causeway to the island and bring about the very degree of destruction which Ezekiel has predicted.

With this enigmatic passage the prophecies of Ezekiel come to an end. At age 55 Ezekiel has had a wonderful ministry lasting 25 years, and perhaps God continues to use him, as the last passage seems to suggest. It will be another 34 years before the first exiles return to Palestine. Ezekiel will be 89 years old if his life continues until that time. So, even if Ezekiel dies in his land of exile, it is altogether possible that he will live long enough to see the beginning of the great restoration about which he has brought such hope.

Nebuchadnezzar's Temporary Insanity

*I*n what appears to be the last two or three years of his reign, King Nebuchadnezzar of Babylonia apparently becomes a true believer in the powerful God of his servant Daniel. The process of belief has been a long one, developing over some 40 years. Nebuchadnezzar was first awed by Daniel's God when Daniel was given the ability to tell the king his dreams and interpret their meaning. He was further amazed when this God of the Hebrews saved Shadrach, Meshach, and Abednego from the fiery furnace. Polytheistic in his beliefs, however, he has yet to confront the singular, exclusive power of a creative and personal God of the universe, and does not at this point recognize his dependence upon such a divine being. He in fact still believes that all his accomplishments have been the result of his own abilities, and he fails to see a purposeful God working through him. As he reflects on his reign, his heart is filled with false pride. Yet, ironically, this very pride makes Nebuchadnezzar an easy target for God's final appeal to him.

In the account that follows, Nebuchadnezzar issues an edict telling the whole world how God first warned him and then proceeded to humble him by bringing on a period of temporary insanity, during which time he roamed outside his palace like the animals among which he lived. His expressed reason for revealing the embarrassing incident is to bring honor to a God powerful enough to so humble a world leader, yet gracious enough to restore him to his throne. In issuing the royal decree Nebuchadnezzar appears to be a sincere believer, even to the point of evangelistically urging all people to turn to this very special King of heaven, the Most High God. What a happy ending to the life of one who has spent years oppressing God's chosen nation!

NEBUCHADNEZZAR ISSUES EDICT.   King Nebuchadnezzar,   Dan. 4:1-3
                                                                   (Ca. 562
To the peoples, nations and men of every language, who live in all the   B.C.?)
world:

May you prosper greatly!

It is my pleasure to tell you about the miraculous signs and wonders that the Most High God has performed for me.

How great are his signs,

> how mighty his wonders!
> His kingdom is an eternal kingdom;
> his dominion endures from generation to generation.

Dan.
4:4-18 DANIEL TOLD OF DREAM.   I, Nebuchadnezzar, was at home in my palace, contented and prosperous. I had a dream that made me afraid. As I was lying in my bed, the images and visions that passed through my mind terrified me. So I commanded that all the wise men of Babylon be brought before me to interpret the dream for me. When the magicians, enchanters, astrologers[a] and diviners came, I told them the dream, but they could not interpret it for me. Finally, Daniel came into my presence and I told him the dream. (He is called Belteshazzar, after the name of my god, and the spirit of the holy gods is in him.)

I said, "Belteshazzar, chief of the magicians, I know that the spirit of the holy gods is in you, and no mystery is too difficult for you. Here is my dream; interpret it for me. These are the visions I saw while lying in my bed: I looked, and there before me stood a tree in the middle of the land. Its height was enormous. The tree grew large and strong and its top touched the sky; it was visible to the ends of the earth. Its leaves were beautiful, its fruit abundant, and on it was food for all. Under it the beasts of the field found shelter, and the birds of the air lived in its branches; from it every creature was fed.

"In the visions I saw while lying in my bed, I looked, and there before me was a messenger,[b] a holy one, coming down from heaven. He called in a loud voice: 'Cut down the tree and trim off its branches; strip off its leaves and scatter its fruit. Let the animals flee from under it and the birds from its branches. But let the stump and its roots, bound with iron and bronze, remain in the ground, in the grass of the field.

" 'Let him be drenched with the dew of heaven, and let him live with the animals among the plants of the earth. Let his mind be changed from that of a man and let him be given the mind of an animal, till seven times[c] pass by for him.

" 'The decision is announced by messengers, the holy ones declare the verdict, so that the living may know that the Most High is sovereign over the kingdoms of men and gives them to anyone he wishes and sets over them the lowliest of men.'

"This is the dream that I, King Nebuchadnezzar, had. Now, Belteshazzar, tell me what it means, for none of the wise men in my kingdom can interpret it for me. But you can, because the spirit of the holy gods is in you."

Dan.
4:19-27 DREAM IS WARNING.   Then Daniel (also called Belteshazzar) was greatly perplexed for a time, and his thoughts terrified him. So the king said, "Belteshazzar, do not let the dream or its meaning alarm you."

Belteshazzar answered, "My lord, if only the dream applied to your enemies and its meaning to your adversaries! The tree you saw, which grew large and strong, with its top touching the sky, visible to the whole earth, with beautiful leaves and abundant fruit, providing food for all, giving shelter to the beasts of the field, and having nesting places in its branches for the birds of the air—you, O king, are that tree! You have become great

---

[a]Or Chaldeans   [b]Or watchman   [c]Or years

and strong; your greatness has grown until it reaches the sky, and your dominion extends to distant parts of the earth.

"You, O king, saw a messenger, a holy one, coming down from heaven and saying, 'Cut down the tree and destroy it, but leave the stump, bound with iron and bronze, in the grass of the field, while its roots remain in the ground. Let him be drenched with the dew of heaven; let him live like the wild animals, until seven times pass by for him.'

"This is the interpretation, O king, and this is the decree the Most High has issued against my lord the king: You will be driven away from people and will live with the wild animals; you will eat grass like cattle and be drenched with the dew of heaven. Seven times will pass by for you until you acknowledge that the Most High is sovereign over the kingdoms of men and gives them to anyone he wishes. The command to leave the stump of the tree with its roots means that your kingdom will be restored to you when you acknowledge that Heaven rules. Therefore, O king, be pleased to accept my advice: Renounce your sins by doing what is right, and your wickedness by being kind to the oppressed. It may be that then your prosperity will continue."

YEAR WITHOUT REPENTANCE.   All this happened to King Nebuchad-nezzar. Twelve months later, as the king was walking on the roof of the royal palace of Babylon, he said, "Is not this the great Babylon I have built as the royal residence, by my mighty power and for the glory of my majesty?"

Dan. 4:28-30

TEMPORARY INSANITY.   The words were still on his lips when a voice came from heaven, "This is what is decreed for you, King Nebuchad-nezzar: Your royal authority has been taken from you. You will be driven away from people and will live with the wild animals; you will eat grass like cattle. Seven times will pass by for you until you acknowledge that the Most High is sovereign over the kingdoms of men and gives them to any-one he wishes."

Immediately what had been said about Nebuchadnezzar was fulfilled. He was driven away from people and ate grass like cattle. His body was drenched with the dew of heaven until his hair grew like the feathers of an eagle and his nails like the claws of a bird.

Dan. 4:31-33

SANITY RESTORED.   At the end of that time, I, Nebuchadnezzar, raised my eyes toward heaven, and my sanity was restored. Then I praised the Most High; I honored and glorified him who lives forever.

Dan. 4:34,35

> His dominion is an eternal dominion;
>   his kingdom endures from generation to generation.
> All the peoples of the earth
>   are regarded as nothing.
> He does as he pleases
>   with the powers of heaven
>   and the peoples of the earth.
> No one can hold back his hand
>   or say to him: "What have you done?"

PRAISE TO THE TRUE GOD. At the same time that my sanity was restored, my honor and splendor were returned to me for the glory of my kingdom. My advisers and nobles sought me out, and I was restored to my throne and became even greater than before. Now I, Nebuchadnezzar,

Dan. 4:36,37

praise and exalt and glorify the King of heaven, because everything he does is right and all his ways are just. And those who walk in pride he is able to humble.

How long Nebuchadnezzar's mental illness lasted is not clear from the phrase "seven times." What is clear is that it was long enough to confront Nebuchadnezzar with his sinful state and his need for a redeeming God. How often it is that God humbles the proud, weakens the powerful, and brings shame to the beautiful in an effort to call all his creatures to know him! Of course not all people respond in penitent belief, but in Nebuchadnezzar God apparently found a fertile conscience that was ripe for conversion.

End of Jeremiah's Ministry

A minor historical footnote brings to a close the record of Jeremiah's ministry. It comes at a time of changing leadership in Babylonia. After a reign of some 45 years, Nebuchadnezzar is succeeded by his son Evil-Merodach (Amel-Marduk in Babylonian). In the first year of his reign he releases Jehoiachin from prison and brings him to a place of honor in Babylonia. Evil-Merodach evidently considers Jehoiachin the legitimate king of Judah and thus accords him an elevated status. (Jehoiachin had been taken captive 37 years earlier in the great deportation of 597 B.C.) At 55 he gets a new lease on life, but he will not figure in Judah's future history.

Jer.
52:31-34
2 Kgs.
25:27-30
(Ca. 561
B.C.)

JEHOIACHIN'S RELEASE.   In the thirty-seventh year of the exile of Jehoiachin king of Judah, in the year Evil-Merodach[d] became king of Babylon, he released Jehoiachin king of Judah and freed him from prison on the twenty-fifth day of the twelfth month. He spoke kindly to him and gave him a seat of honor higher than those of the other kings who were with him in Babylon. So Jehoiachin put aside his prison clothes and for the rest of his life ate regularly at the king's table. Day by day the king of Babylon gave Jehoiachin a regular allowance as long as he lived, till the day of his death.

Whether Jeremiah is still alive at this time is not known. His last prophetic utterance took place in 586 B.C. after he had been taken to Egypt by a renegade band of his own people. At that time his ministry had spanned more than 40 years, and it has been about 25 years since then. Without knowing how old Jeremiah was when he received his prophetic call, in 627 B.C., it is not possible to determine his age at this time. In any event, the record of Jehoiachin's release is probably added to Jeremiah's prophecies by his faithful scribe, Baruch.

Although there will be other prophets and prophecies to come, the era of the great written prophecies of Isaiah, Jeremiah, and Ezekiel now comes to a close.

[d]Also called *Amel-Marduk*

Job and the Problem of Suffering

Now, some 45 years following the first deportation from Judah, God's chosen nation continues to be a dispersed people. By this time many of them must wonder if there is still a God—not a "state God" attached to a nation which has been virtually destroyed, but a personal God who knows their personal misery and still cares. Even the wicked and rebellious exiles, who by now must have bent their knees in prayer for deliverance, are surely thinking that God no longer hears them. For a nation in suffering, there are many questions to be asked: how can they believe in a God who would allow such suffering? On the other hand, how can they curse God in times of adversity when he has previously brought such prosperity? Is their faith to be contingent upon economic well-being?

The ones who must be the most perplexed, however, are the faithful ones who never understood their personal involvement in the first place. After remaining true to God while almost everyone else chased after idolatry and wickedness, their reward has been the same—and sometimes worse. They too were taken captive. They too saw swords enter their children's bodies. In the siege of Jerusalem they had starved and been victims of pestilence and plague. Here in captivity they still often go hungry and are poorly clothed. Whatever happened to the promise that the righteous would be blessed? Why were some of the wicked not taken into exile, but rather allowed to prosper under the same government that has enslaved their fellow countrymen? Where is the justice of God in these circumstances? And if punishment is for the wicked, what sin has led to the suffering of the righteous?

Of course these are the same questions which every generation asks about death, sorrow, pain, and suffering. But because his people are suffering so greatly at this time, it may well be that God chooses this context in which to give at least some insight into both the thorny theological issues and the intense emotional feelings of individual sufferers. Although there is a wide difference of opinion about its date, one of the most outstanding masterpieces in all of literature is possibly written during this period. The writing is in the form of a historical poem. It is historical in that it is based upon the life of one of the early patriarchs named Job. Job's steadfastness following more adversity than most people will ever face has been legendary. Even the prophet Ezekiel referred to Job, along with Noah and Daniel, as a man of great righteousness. And yet Job apparently struggled with the reasons for his adversity before coming to peace about it. Therefore it is altogether fitting that this poem addressing the problem of suffering be based upon Job's personal struggle.

There is still another reason why Job is a most appropriate choice. At this time when people are in search of a personal God, the writer takes them back before their own prophets, before the teaching of the law, before the promises made to Abraham, to a man who is not even one of the children of Israel. He is just a lone human being who finds himself in terrible suffering for no apparent reason.

The first scene of the poem opens with a picture of Job's enviable prosperity, then turns quickly to a conversation between God and Satan. When God points to Job as an example of a righteous man, Satan suggests that Job remains righteous only because of his prosperity. God permits Satan to test this theory by removing Job's prosperity. Job's faith remains intact. So Satan next suggests that his personal suffering will bring curses against God. Once again Job disappoints Satan.

In the second scene, Job still does not curse God, but he does put some hard questions to God. Why must he, a righteous man, suffer? What sins have brought on his pain? Why is God so inconsistent in his punishment of the wicked? Throughout the presentation of Job's case against God, three of Job's friends—Eliphaz, Bildad, and Zophar—argue against him. They try to convince him that the answer lies in a simple syllogism: God always punishes sin; suffering is the result of sin; therefore Job is more of a sinner than he is willing to admit. Throughout it all, Job maintains his innocence and demands to know God's rationale.

The third scene introduces a young man named Elihu who claims that neither Job nor his friends are correct. God does not act capriciously, as Job claims, and suffering is not necessarily the result of sin, as Job's friends claim. Elihu argues that suffering is often used by God to teach lessons and to strengthen a person.

In the final scene God himself speaks to Job and demands to know what right Job has to question the Creator of the universe about his ways. Job's humble response demonstrates the depth of his righteous character, and his prosperity is restored.

Job 1:1-3   PROSPERITY OF JOB.   In the land of Uz there lived a man whose name was Job. This man was blameless and upright; he feared God and shunned evil. He had seven sons and three daughters, and he owned seven thousand sheep, three thousand camels, five hundred yoke of oxen and five hundred donkeys, and had a large number of servants. He was the greatest man among all the people of the East.

Job 1:4,5   RIGHTEOUSNESS OF JOB.   His sons used to take turns holding feasts in their homes, and they would invite their three sisters to eat and drink with them. When a period of feasting had run its course, Job would send and have them purified. Early in the morning he would sacrifice a burnt offering for each of them, thinking, "Perhaps my children have sinned and cursed God in their hearts." This was Job's regular custom.

Job 1:6-12   SATAN PROPOSES CHALLENGE.   One day the angels[e] came to present themselves before the LORD, and Satan[f] also came with them. The LORD said to Satan, "Where have you come from?"

Satan answered the LORD, "From roaming through the earth and going back and forth in it."

Then the LORD said to Satan, "Have you considered my servant Job? There is no one on earth like him; he is blameless and upright, a man who fears God and shuns evil."

"Does Job fear God for nothing?" Satan replied. "Have you not put a

<hr>

[e]Hebrew *the sons of God*   [f]*Satan* means *accuser.*

hedge around him and his household and everything he has? You have blessed the work of his hands, so that his flocks and herds are spread throughout the land. But stretch out your hand and strike everything he has, and he will surely curse you to your face."

The LORD said to Satan, "Very well, then, everything he has is in your hands, but on the man himself do not lay a finger."

Then Satan went out from the presence of the LORD.

JOB LOSES ALL.   One day when Job's sons and daughters were feasting and drinking wine at the oldest brother's house, a messenger came to Job and said, "The oxen were plowing and the donkeys were grazing nearby, and the Sabeans attacked and carried them off. They put the servants to the sword, and I am the only one who has escaped to tell you!"   Job 1:13-19

While he was still speaking, another messenger came and said, "The fire of God fell from the sky and burned up the sheep and the servants, and I am the only one who has escaped to tell you!"

While he was still speaking, another messenger came and said, "The Chaldeans formed three raiding parties and swept down on your camels and carried them off. They put the servants to the sword, and I am the only one who has escaped to tell you!"

While he was still speaking, yet another messenger came and said, "Your sons and daughters were feasting and drinking wine at the oldest brother's house, when suddenly a mighty wind swept in from the desert and struck the four corners of the house. It collapsed on them and they are dead, and I am the only one who has escaped to tell you!"

JOB'S RESPONSE.   At this, Job got up and tore his robe and shaved his head. Then he fell to the ground in worship and said: Job 1:20-22

> "Naked I came from my mother's womb,
>   and naked I will depart.^{g}
> The LORD gave and the LORD has taken away;
>   may the name of the LORD be praised."

In all this, Job did not sin by charging God with wrongdoing.

JOB PERSONALLY AFFLICTED.   On another day the angels^h came to present themselves before the LORD, and Satan also came with them to present himself before him. And the LORD said to Satan, "Where have you come from?"   Job 2:1-9

Satan answered the LORD, "From roaming through the earth and going back and forth in it."

Then the LORD said to Satan, "Have you considered my servant Job? There is no one on earth like him; he is blameless and upright, a man who fears God and shuns evil. And he still maintains his integrity, though you incited me against him to ruin him without any reason."

"Skin for skin!" Satan replied. "A man will give all he has for his own life. But stretch out your hand and strike his flesh and bones, and he will surely curse you to your face."

The LORD said to Satan, "Very well, then, he is in your hands; but you must spare his life."

So Satan went out from the presence of the LORD and afflicted Job with painful sores from the soles of his feet to the top of his head. Then Job took

^{g}Or *will return there* ^{h}Hebrew *the sons of God*

a piece of broken pottery and scraped himself with it as he sat among the ashes.

His wife said to him, "Are you still holding on to your integrity? Curse God and die!"

Job 2:10 JOB'S RESPONSE.   He replied, "You are talking like a foolish[i] woman. Shall we accept good from God, and not trouble?"

In all this, Job did not sin in what he said.

Job 2:11-13 JOB'S THREE FRIENDS.   When Job's three friends, Eliphaz the Temanite, Bildad the Shuhite and Zophar the Naamathite, heard about all the troubles that had come upon him, they set out from their homes and met together by agreement to go and sympathize with him and comfort him. When they saw him from a distance, they could hardly recognize him; they began to weep aloud, and they tore their robes and sprinkled dust on their heads. Then they sat on the ground with him for seven days and seven nights. No one said a word to him, because they saw how great his suffering was.

Job

Job 3:1-26 JOB CURSES BIRTH.   After this, Job opened his mouth and cursed the day of his birth. He said:

"May the day of my birth perish,
  and the night it was said, 'A boy is born!'
That day—may it turn to darkness;
  may God above not care about it;
  may no light shine upon it.
May darkness and deep shadow[j] claim it once more;
  may a cloud settle over it;
  may blackness overwhelm its light.
That night—may thick darkness seize it;
  may it not be included among the days of the year
  nor be entered in any of the months.
May that night be barren;
  may no shout of joy be heard in it.
May those who curse days[k] curse that day,
  those who are ready to rouse Leviathan.
May its morning stars become dark;
  may it wait for daylight in vain
  and not see the first rays of dawn,
for it did not shut the doors of the womb on me
  to hide trouble from my eyes.

"Why did I not perish at birth,
  and die as I came from the womb?
Why were there knees to receive me
  and breasts that I might be nursed?
For now I would be lying down in peace;
  I would be asleep and at rest
with kings and counselors of the earth,

---

[i]The Hebrew word rendered *foolish* denotes moral deficiency.   [j]Or *and the shadow of death*   [k]Or *the sea*

who built for themselves places now lying in ruins,
with rulers who had gold,
who filled their houses with silver.
Or why was I not hidden in the ground like a stillborn
child,
like an infant who never saw the light of day?
There the wicked cease from turmoil,
and there the weary are at rest.
Captives also enjoy their ease;
they no longer hear the slave driver's shout.
The small and the great are there,
and the slave is freed from his master.

"Why is light given to those in misery,
and life to the bitter of soul,
to those who long for death that does not come,
who search for it more than for hidden treasure,
who are filled with gladness
and rejoice when they reach the grave?
Why is life given to a man
whose way is hidden,
whom God has hedged in?
For sighing comes to me instead of food;
my groans pour out like water.
What I feared has come upon me;
what I dreaded has happened to me.
I have no peace, no quietness;
I have no rest, but only turmoil."

Eliphaz

BELIEVE YOUR OWN TEACHING.   Then Eliphaz the Temanite replied: Job 4:1-6

"If someone ventures a word with you, will you be
impatient?
But who can keep from speaking?
Think how you have instructed many,
how you have strengthened feeble hands.
Your words have supported those who stumbled;
you have strengthened faltering knees.
But now trouble comes to you, and you are discouraged;
it strikes you, and you are dismayed.
Should not your piety be your confidence
and your blameless ways your hope?

ONLY WICKED TRULY DESTROYED.   Job 4:7-11

"Consider now: Who, being innocent, has ever perished?
Where were the upright ever destroyed?
As I have observed, those who plow evil
and those who sow trouble reap it.
At the breath of God they are destroyed;
at the blast of his anger they perish.
The lions may roar and growl,
yet the teeth of the great lions are broken.

The lion perishes for lack of prey,
and the cubs of the lioness are scattered.

Job 4:12-16 APPEAL TO MYSTICISM.

"A word was secretly brought to me,
my ears caught a whisper of it.
Amid disquieting dreams in the night,
when deep sleep falls on men,
fear and trembling seized me
and made all my bones shake.
A spirit glided past my face,
and the hair on my body stood on end.
It stopped,
but I could not tell what it was.
A form stood before my eyes,
and I heard a hushed voice:

Job 4:17-21 MAN'S VULNERABILITY.

'Can a mortal be more righteous than God?
Can a man be more pure than his Maker?
If God places no trust in his servants,
if he charges his angels with error,
how much more those who live in houses of clay,
whose foundations are in the dust,
who are crushed more readily than a moth!
Between dawn and dusk they are broken to pieces;
unnoticed, they perish forever.
Are not the cords of their tent pulled up,
so that they die without wisdom?'[1]

Job 5:1-7 EVERYONE HAS TROUBLE.

"Call if you will, but who will answer you?
To which of the holy ones will you turn?
Resentment kills a fool,
and envy slays the simple.
I myself have seen a fool taking root,
but suddenly his house was cursed.
His children are far from safety,
crushed in court without a defender.
The hungry consume his harvest,
taking it even from among thorns,
and the thirsty pant after his wealth.
For hardship does not spring from the soil,
nor does trouble sprout from the ground.
Yet man is born to trouble
as surely as sparks fly upward.

Job 5:8-16 ONLY GOD KNOWS WHY.

"But if it were I, I would appeal to God;
I would lay my cause before him.

[1]Some interpreters end the quotation after verse 17.

He performs wonders that cannot be fathomed,
    miracles that cannot be counted.
He bestows rain on the earth;
    he sends water upon the countryside.
The lowly he sets on high,
    and those who mourn are lifted to safety.
He thwarts the plans of the crafty,
    so that their hands achieve no success.
He catches the wise in their craftiness,
    and the schemes of the wily are swept away.
Darkness comes upon them in the daytime;
    at noon they grope as in the night.
He saves the needy from the sword in their mouth;
    he saves them from the clutches of the powerful.
So the poor have hope,
    and injustice shuts its mouth.

BLESSINGS FOLLOW DISCIPLINE.   Job 5:17-27

"Blessed is the man whom God corrects;
    so do not despise the discipline of the Almighty.*m*
For he wounds, but he also binds up;
    he injures, but his hands also heal.
From six calamities he will rescue you;
    in seven no harm will befall you.
In famine he will ransom you from death,
    and in battle from the stroke of the sword.
You will be protected from the lash of the tongue,
    and need not fear when destruction comes.
You will laugh at destruction and famine,
    and need not fear the beasts of the earth.
For you will have a covenant with the stones of the field,
    and the wild animals will be at peace with you.
You will know that your tent is secure;
    you will take stock of your property and find nothing
        missing.
You will know that your children will be many,
    and your descendants like the grass of the earth.
You will come to the grave in full vigor,
    like sheaves gathered in season.

"We have examined this, and it is true.
    So hear it and apply it to yourself."

Job

CURSES COME FROM ANGUISH.   Then Job replied: Job 6:1-7

"If only my anguish could be weighed
    and all my misery be placed on the scales!
It would surely outweigh the sand of the seas—
    no wonder my words have been impetuous.
The arrows of the Almighty are in me,

*m*Hebrew *Shaddai*; here and throughout Job

> my spirit drinks in their poison;
> God's terrors are marshaled against me.
> Does a wild donkey bray when it has grass,
> or an ox bellow when it has fodder?
> Is tasteless food eaten without salt,
> or is there flavor in the white of an egg[n]?
> I refuse to touch it;
> such food makes me ill.

Job 6:8-13   FEAR OF SINNING IN PAIN.

> "Oh, that I might have my request,
> that God would grant what I hope for,
> that God would be willing to crush me,
> to let loose his hand and cut me off!
> Then I would still have this consolation—
> my joy in unrelenting pain—
> that I had not denied the words of the Holy One.

> "What strength do I have, that I should still hope?
> What prospects, that I should be patient?
> Do I have the strength of stone?
> Is my flesh bronze?
> Do I have any power to help myself,
> now that success has been driven from me?

Job 6:14-23   CANNOT DEPEND ON FRIENDS.

> "A despairing man should have the devotion of his friends,
> even though he forsakes the fear of the Almighty.
> But my brothers are as undependable as intermittent
> streams,
> as the streams that overflow
> when darkened by thawing ice
> and swollen with melting snow,
> but that cease to flow in the dry season,
> and in the heat vanish from their channels.
> Caravans turn aside from their routes;
> they go up into the wasteland and perish.
> The caravans of Tema look for water,
> the traveling merchants of Sheba look in hope.
> They are distressed, because they had been confident;
> they arrive there, only to be disappointed.
> Now you too have proved to be of no help;
> you see something dreadful and are afraid.
> Have I ever said, 'Give something on my behalf,
> pay a ransom for me from your wealth,
> deliver me from the hand of the enemy,
> ransom me from the clutches of the ruthless'?

Job 6:24-27   REBUKE FOR CHIDING.

> "Teach me, and I will be quiet;

[n]The meaning of the Hebrew for this phrase is uncertain.

show me where I have been wrong.
How painful are honest words!
But what do your arguments prove?
Do you mean to correct what I say,
and treat the words of a despairing man as wind?
You would even cast lots for the fatherless
and barter away your friend.

NO MALICE IN CURSES.
Job 6:28-30

"But now be so kind as to look at me.
Would I lie to your face?
Relent, do not be unjust;
reconsider, for my integrity is at stake.[o]
Is there any wickedness on my lips?
Can my mouth not discern malice?

EXPECTANCY OF HARDSHIP.
Job 7:1-5

"Does not man have hard service on earth?
Are not his days like those of a hired man?
Like a slave longing for the evening shadows,
or a hired man waiting eagerly for his wages,
so I have been allotted months of futility,
and nights of misery have been assigned to me.
When I lie down I think, 'How long before I get up?'
The night drags on, and I toss till dawn.
My body is clothed with worms and scabs,
my skin is broken and festering.

BREVITY OF LIFE.
Job 7:6-10

"My days are swifter than a weaver's shuttle,
and they come to an end without hope.
Remember, O God, that my life is but a breath;
my eyes will never see happiness again.
The eye that now sees me will see me no longer;
you will look for me, but I will be no more.
As a cloud vanishes and is gone,
so he who goes down to the grave[p] does not return.
He will never come to his house again;
his place will know him no more.

BITTERNESS OF PAIN.
Job 7:11-16

"Therefore I will not keep silent;
I will speak out in the anguish of my spirit,
I will complain in the bitterness of my soul.
Am I the sea, or the monster of the deep,
that you put me under guard?
When I think my bed will comfort me
and my couch will ease my complaint,
even then you frighten me with dreams
and terrify me with visions,

[o] Or *my righteousness still stands*   [p] Hebrew *Sheol*

> so that I prefer strangling and death,
> > rather than this body of mine.
> I despise my life; I would not live forever.
> Let me alone; my days have no meaning.

Job 7:17-21 WHAT IS MAN'S SIGNIFICANCE?

> "What is man that you make so much of him,
> > that you give him so much attention,
> that you examine him every morning
> > and test him every moment?
> Will you never look away from me,
> > or let me alone even for an instant?
> If I have sinned, what have I done to you,
> > O watcher of men?
> Why have you made me your target?
> > Have I become a burden to you?*q*
> Why do you not pardon my offenses
> > and forgive my sins?
> For I will soon lie down in the dust;
> > you will search for me, but I will be no more."

Bildad

Job 8:1-7 GOD IS JUST.   Then Bildad the Shuhite replied:

> "How long will you say such things?
> > Your words are a blustering wind.
> Does God pervert justice?
> > Does the Almighty pervert what is right?
> When your children sinned against him,
> > he gave them over to the penalty of their sin.
> But if you will look to God
> > and plead with the Almighty,
> if you are pure and upright,
> > even now he will rouse himself on your behalf
> > and restore you to your rightful place.
> Your beginnings will seem humble,
> > so prosperous will your future be.

Job 8:8-10 APPEAL TO SCHOLARSHIP.

> "Ask the former generations
> > and find out what their fathers learned,
> for we were born only yesterday and know nothing,
> > and our days on earth are but a shadow.
> Will they not instruct you and tell you?
> > Will they not bring forth words from their understanding?

Job 8:11-19 SECURITY IS IN GOD.

> Can papyrus grow tall where there is no marsh?
> > Can reeds thrive without water?
> While still growing and uncut,

---

*q*A few manuscripts of the Masoretic Text, an ancient Hebrew scribal tradition and Septuagint; most manuscripts of the Masoretic Text *I have become a burden to myself.*

they wither more quickly than grass.
Such is the destiny of all who forget God;
   so perishes the hope of the godless.
What he trusts in is fragile[r];
   what he relies on is a spider's web.
He leans on his web, but it gives way;
   he clings to it, but it does not hold.
He is like a well-watered plant in the sunshine,
   spreading its shoots over the garden;
it entwines its roots around a pile of rocks
   and looks for a place among the stones.
But when it is torn from its spot,
   that place disowns it and says, 'I never saw you.'
Surely its life withers away,
   and[s] from the soil other plants grow.

MISERY WILL BE AVENGED.   Job 8:20-22

"Surely God does not reject a blameless man
   or strengthen the hands of evildoers.
He will yet fill your mouth with laughter
   and your lips with shouts of joy.
Your enemies will be clothed in shame,
   and the tents of the wicked will be no more."

Job

GOD'S CREATIVE POWER.   Then Job replied: Job 9:1-13

"Indeed, I know that this is true.
   But how can a mortal be righteous before God?
Though one wished to dispute with him,
   he could not answer him one time out of a thousand.
His wisdom is profound, his power is vast.
   Who has resisted him and come out unscathed?
He moves mountains without their knowing it
   and overturns them in his anger.
He shakes the earth from its place
   and makes its pillars tremble.
He speaks to the sun and it does not shine;
   he seals off the light of the stars.
He alone stretches out the heavens
   and treads on the waves of the sea.
He is the Maker of the Bear and Orion,
   the Pleiades and the constellations of the south.
He performs wonders that cannot be fathomed,
   miracles that cannot be counted.
When he passes me, I cannot see him;
   when he goes by, I cannot perceive him.
If he snatches away, who can stop him?
   Who can say to him, 'What are you doing?'

[r]The meaning of the Hebrew for this word is uncertain.   [s]Or Surely all the joy it has /
is that

God does not restrain his anger;
even the cohorts of Rahab cowered at his feet.

Job 9:14-20   NO ARGUMENT AGAINST GOD.

"How then can I dispute with him?
How can I find words to argue with him?
Though I were innocent, I could not answer him;
I could only plead with my Judge for mercy.
Even if I summoned him and he responded,
I do not believe he would give me a hearing.
He would crush me with a storm
and multiply my wounds for no reason.
He would not let me regain my breath
but would overwhelm me with misery.
If it is a matter of strength, he is mighty!
And if it is a matter of justice, who will summon him[t]?
Even if I were innocent, my mouth would condemn me;
if I were blameless, it would pronounce me guilty.

Job 9:21-24   INNOCENCE NO GUARANTEE.

"Although I am blameless,
I have no concern for myself;
I despise my own life.
It is all the same; that is why I say,
'He destroys both the blameless and the wicked.'
When a scourge brings sudden death,
he mocks the despair of the innocent.
When a land falls into the hands of the wicked,
he blindfolds its judges.
If it is not he, then who is it?

Job 9:25-31   SUFFERING REMAINS.

"My days are swifter than a runner;
they fly away without a glimpse of joy.
They skim past like boats of papyrus,
like eagles swooping down on their prey.
If I say, 'I will forget my complaint,
I will change my expression, and smile,'
I still dread all my sufferings,
for I know you will not hold me innocent.
Since I am already found guilty,
why should I struggle in vain?
Even if I washed myself with soap[u]
and my hands with washing soda,
you would plunge me into a slime pit
so that even my clothes would detest me.

Job 9:32-35   NO ADVOCATE FOR MAN.

"He is not a man like me that I might answer him,
that we might confront each other in court.

[t]See Septuagint; Hebrew me.   [u]Or snow

If only there were someone to arbitrate between us,
     to lay his hand upon us both,
someone to remove God's rod from me,
     so that his terror would frighten me no more.
Then I would speak up without fear of him,
     but as it now stands with me, I cannot.

IS MAN'S CONDITION KNOWN?   Job 10:1-7

"I loathe my very life;
     therefore I will give free rein to my complaint
     and speak out in the bitterness of my soul.
I will say to God: Do not condemn me,
     but tell me what charges you have against me.
Does it please you to oppress me,
     to spurn the work of your hands,
     while you smile on the schemes of the wicked?
Do you have eyes of flesh?
     Do you see as a mortal sees?
Are your days like those of a mortal
     or your years like those of a man,
that you must search out my faults
     and probe after my sin—
though you know that I am not guilty
     and that no one can rescue me from your hand?

SHOULD CREATOR DESTROY?   Job 10:8-12

"Your hands shaped me and made me.
     Will you now turn and destroy me?
Remember that you molded me like clay.
     Will you now turn me to dust again?
Did you not pour me out like milk
     and curdle me like cheese,
clothe me with skin and flesh
     and knit me together with bones and sinews?
You gave me life and showed me kindness,
     and in your providence watched over my spirit.

SINFULNESS NOT THE ISSUE.   Job 10:13-17

"But this is what you concealed in your heart,
     and I know that this was in your mind:
If I sinned, you would be watching me
     and would not let my offense go unpunished.
If I am guilty—woe to me!
     Even if I am innocent, I cannot lift my head,
for I am full of shame
     and drowned in^v my affliction.
If I hold my head high, you stalk me like a lion
     and again display your awesome power against me.
You bring new witnesses against me
     and increase your anger toward me;
     your forces come against me wave upon wave.

^{v}Or and aware of

SEPTEMBER 11

Job 10:18-22

SORROWFUL HUMAN CONDITION.

> "Why then did you bring me out of the womb?
> I wish I had died before any eye saw me.
> If only I had never come into being,
> or had been carried straight from the womb to the grave!
> Are not my few days almost over?
> Turn away from me so I can have a moment's joy
> before I go to the place of no return,
> to the land of gloom and deep shadow,[w]
> to the land of deepest night,
> of deep shadow and disorder,
> where even the light is like darkness."

Zophar

Job 11:1-6

APPEAL TO ZOPHAR'S INSIGHT.   Then Zophar the Naamathite replied:

> "Are all these words to go unanswered?
> Is this talker to be vindicated?
> Will your idle talk reduce men to silence?
> Will no one rebuke you when you mock?
> You say to God, 'My beliefs are flawless
> and I am pure in your sight.'
> Oh, how I wish that God would speak,
> that he would open his lips against you
> and disclose to you the secrets of wisdom,
> for true wisdom has two sides.
> Know this: God has even forgotten some of your sin.

Job 11:7-9

GOD'S WISDOM HIDDEN.

> "Can you fathom the mysteries of God?
> Can you probe the limits of the Almighty?
> They are higher than the heavens—what can you do?
> They are deeper than the depths of the grave[x]—what can
> you know?
> Their measure is longer than the earth
> and wider than the sea.

Job 11:10-12

GOD RECOGNIZES SUFFERING.

> "If he comes along and confines you in prison
> and convenes a court, who can oppose him?
> Surely he recognizes deceitful men;
> and when he sees evil, does he not take note?
> But a witless man can no more become wise
> than a wild donkey's colt can be born a man.[y]

Job 11:13-20

TROUBLES WILL PASS.

> "Yet if you devote your heart to him

[w]Or *and the shadow of death*   [x]Hebrew *than Sheol*   [y]Or *wild donkey can be born tame*

and stretch out your hands to him,
if you put away the sin that is in your hand
and allow no evil to dwell in your tent,
then you will lift up your face without shame;
you will stand firm and without fear.
You will surely forget your trouble,
recalling it only as waters gone by.
Life will be brighter than noonday,
and darkness will become like morning.
You will be secure, because there is hope;
you will look about you and take your rest in safety.
You will lie down, with no one to make you afraid,
and many will court your favor.
But the eyes of the wicked will fail,
and escape will elude them;
their hope will become a dying gasp."

Job

TRUTH IN ARGUMENTS.   Then Job replied: Job 12:1-3

"Doubtless you are the people,
and wisdom will die with you!
But I have a mind as well as you;
I am not inferior to you.
Who does not know all these things?

WICKED SCORN OTHERS' TROUBLE.   Job 12:4-6

"I have become a laughingstock to my friends,
though I called upon God and he answered—
a mere laughingstock, though righteous and blameless!
Men at ease have contempt for misfortune
as the fate of those whose feet are slipping.
The tents of marauders are undisturbed,
and those who provoke God are secure—
those who carry their god in their hands.ᶻ

GOD PERMITS SUFFERING.   Job 12:7-12

"But ask the animals, and they will teach you,
or the birds of the air, and they will tell you;
or speak to the earth, and it will teach you,
or let the fish of the sea inform you.
Which of all these does not know
that the hand of the LORD has done this?
In his hand is the life of every creature
and the breath of all mankind.
Does not the ear test words
as the tongue tastes food?
Is not wisdom found among the aged?
Does not long life bring understanding?

ᶻOr secure / in what God's hand brings them

Job
12:13-15

GOD'S PROVIDENTIAL CONTROL.

"To God belong wisdom and power;
    counsel and understanding are his.
What he tears down cannot be rebuilt;
    the man he imprisons cannot be released.
If he holds back the waters, there is drought;
    if he lets them loose, they devastate the land.
To him belong strength and victory;
    both deceived and deceiver are his.
He leads counselors away stripped
    and makes fools of judges.
He takes off the shackles put on by kings
    and ties a loincloth[a] around their waist.
He leads priests away stripped
    and overthrows men long established.
He silences the lips of trusted advisers
    and takes away the discernment of elders.
He pours contempt on nobles
    and disarms the mighty.
He reveals the deep things of darkness
    and brings deep shadows into the light.
He makes nations great, and destroys them;
    he enlarges nations, and disperses them.
He deprives the leaders of the earth of their reason;
    he sends them wandering through a trackless waste.
They grope in darkness with no light;
    he makes them stagger like drunkards.

Job 13:1-5   NEED FOR GOD'S ANSWERS.

"My eyes have seen all this,
    my ears have heard and understood it.
What you know, I also know;
    I am not inferior to you.
But I desire to speak to the Almighty
    and to argue my case with God.
You, however, smear me with lies;
    you are worthless physicians, all of you!
If only you would be altogether silent!
    For you, that would be wisdom.

Job 13:6-12   MAN'S ANSWERS INADEQUATE.

Hear now my argument;
    listen to the plea of my lips.
Will you speak wickedly on God's behalf?
    Will you speak deceitfully for him?
Will you show him partiality?
    Will you argue the case for God?
Would it turn out well if he examined you?
    Could you deceive him as you might deceive men?

[a]Or *shackles of kings / and ties a belt*

He would surely rebuke you
 if you secretly showed partiality.
Would not his splendor terrify you?
 Would not the dread of him fall on you?
Your maxims are proverbs of ashes;
 your defenses are defenses of clay.

CONFIDENCE IN QUESTIONING.

Job
13:13-19

"Keep silent and let me speak;
 then let come to me what may.
Why do I put myself in jeopardy
 and take my life in my hands?
Though he slay me, yet will I hope in him;
 I will surely[b] defend my ways to his face.
Indeed, this will turn out for my deliverance,
 for no godless man would dare come before him!
Listen carefully to my words;
 let your ears take in what I say.
Now that I have prepared my case,
 I know I will be vindicated.
Can anyone bring charges against me?
 If so, I will be silent and die.

JOB'S OPENING STATEMENT.

Job
13:20-22

"Only grant me these two things, O God,
 and then I will not hide from you:
Withdraw your hand far from me,
 and stop frightening me with your terrors.
Then summon me and I will answer,
 or let me speak, and you reply.

WHAT SINS MERIT THIS?

Job
13:23-27

How many wrongs and sins have I committed?
 Show me my offense and my sin.
Why do you hide your face
 and consider me your enemy?
Will you torment a windblown leaf?
 Will you chase after dry chaff?
For you write down bitter things against me
 and make me inherit the sins of my youth.
You fasten my feet in shackles;
 you keep close watch on all my paths
 by putting marks on the soles of my feet.

LIFE IS LIMITED.

Job
13:28-14:6

"So man wastes away like something rotten,
 like a garment eaten by moths.

"Man born of woman
 is of few days and full of trouble.

[b]Or *He will surely slay me; I have no hope—/ yet I will*

He springs up like a flower and withers away;
  like a fleeting shadow, he does not endure.
Do you fix your eye on such a one?
  Will you bring him[c] before you for judgment?
Who can bring what is pure from the impure?
  No one!
Man's days are determined;
  you have decreed the number of his months
  and have set limits he cannot exceed.
So look away from him and let him alone,
  till he has put in his time like a hired man.

Job 14:7-12   MAN LIVES ONLY ONCE.

"At least there is hope for a tree:
  If it is cut down, it will sprout again,
  and its new shoots will not fail.
Its roots may grow old in the ground
  and its stump die in the soil,
yet at the scent of water it will bud
  and put forth shoots like a plant.
But man dies and is laid low;
  he breathes his last and is no more.
As water disappears from the sea
  or a riverbed becomes parched and dry,
so man lies down and does not rise;
  till the heavens are no more, men will not awake
  or be roused from their sleep.

Job
14:13-17   ONLY HOPE IS RESURRECTION.

"If only you would hide me in the grave[d]
  and conceal me till your anger has passed!
If only you would set me a time
  and then remember me!
If a man dies, will he live again?
  All the days of my hard service
  I will wait for my renewal[e] to come.
You will call and I will answer you;
  you will long for the creature your hands have made.
Surely then you will count my steps
  but not keep track of my sin.
My offenses will be sealed up in a bag;
  you will cover over my sin.

Job
14:18-22   SORROW IN MEANTIME.

"But as a mountain erodes and crumbles
  and as a rock is moved from its place,
as water wears away stones
  and torrents wash away the soil,
  so you destroy man's hope.
You overpower him once for all, and he is gone;

---

[c]Septuagint, Vulgate and Syriac; Hebrew *me*   [d]Hebrew *Sheol*   [e]Or *release*

> you change his countenance and send him away.
> If his sons are honored, he does not know it;
>   if they are brought low, he does not see it.
> He feels but the pain of his own body
>   and mourns only for himself."

Eliphaz

REBUKE FOR QUESTIONING GOD.   Then Eliphaz the Temanite replied: **Job 15:1-13**

> "Would a wise man answer with empty notions
>   or fill his belly with the hot east wind?
> Would he argue with useless words,
>   with speeches that have no value?
> But you even undermine piety
>   and hinder devotion to God.
> Your sin prompts your mouth;
>   you adopt the tongue of the crafty.
> Your own mouth condemns you, not mine;
>   your own lips testify against you.
>
> "Are you the first man ever born?
>   Were you brought forth before the hills?
> Do you listen in on God's council?
>   Do you limit wisdom to yourself?
> What do you know that we do not know?
>   What insights do you have that we do not have?
> The gray-haired and the aged are on our side,
>   men even older than your father.
> Are God's consolations not enough for you,
>   words spoken gently to you?
> Why has your heart carried you away,
>   and why do your eyes flash,
> so that you vent your rage against God
>   and pour out such words from your mouth?

MAN MERELY GOD'S PAWN.   **Job 15:14-16**

> "What is man, that he could be pure,
>   or one born of woman, that he could be righteous?
> If God places no trust in his holy ones,
>   if even the heavens are not pure in his eyes,
> how much less man, who is vile and corrupt,
>   who drinks up evil like water!

INEVITABLE FATE OF WICKED.   **Job 15:17-35**

> "Listen to me and I will explain to you;
>   let me tell you what I have seen,
> what wise men have declared,
>   hiding nothing received from their fathers
> (to whom alone the land was given
>   when no alien passed among them):
> All his days the wicked man suffers torment,

the ruthless through all the years stored up for him.
Terrifying sounds fill his ears;
    when all seems well, marauders attack him.
He despairs of escaping the darkness;
    he is marked for the sword.
He wanders about—food for vultures*f*;
    he knows the day of darkness is at hand.
Distress and anguish fill him with terror;
    they overwhelm him, like a king poised to attack,
because he shakes his fist at God
    and vaunts himself against the Almighty,
defiantly charging against him
    with a thick, strong shield.

"Though his face is covered with fat
    and his waist bulges with flesh,
he will inhabit ruined towns
    and houses where no one lives,
    houses crumbling to rubble.
He will no longer be rich and his wealth will not endure,
    nor will his possessions spread over the land.
He will not escape the darkness;
    a flame will wither his shoots,
    and the breath of God's mouth will carry him away.
Let him not deceive himself by trusting what is worthless,
    for he will get nothing in return.
Before his time he will be paid in full,
    and his branches will not flourish.
He will be like a vine stripped of its unripe grapes,
    like an olive tree shedding its blossoms.
For the company of the godless will be barren,
    and fire will consume the tents of those who love bribes.
They conceive trouble and give birth to evil;
    their womb fashions deceit."

Job

Job 16:1-6   SPEECHES NO RELIEF.   Then Job replied:

"I have heard many things like these;
    miserable comforters are you all!
Will your long-winded speeches never end?
    What ails you that you keep on arguing?
I also could speak like you,
    if you were in my place;
I could make fine speeches against you
    and shake my head at you.
But my mouth would encourage you;
    comfort from my lips would bring you relief.

"Yet if I speak, my pain is not relieved;
    and if I refrain, it does not go away.

f Or *about, looking for food*

HOW GOD HAS DEVASTATED.

Job 16:7-14

> Surely, O God, you have worn me out;
>> you have devastated my entire household.
> You have bound me—and it has become a witness;
>> my gauntness rises up and testifies against me.
> God assails me and tears me in his anger
>> and gnashes his teeth at me;
>> my opponent fastens on me his piercing eyes.
> Men open their mouths to jeer at me;
>> they strike my cheek in scorn
>> and unite together against me.
> God has turned me over to evil men
>> and thrown me into the clutches of the wicked.
> All was well with me, but he shattered me;
>> he seized me by the neck and crushed me.
> He has made me his target;
>> his archers surround me.
> Without pity, he pierces my kidneys
>> and spills my gall on the ground.
> Again and again he bursts upon me;
>> he rushes at me like a warrior.

MAINTAINING INNOCENCE.

Job 16:15-17

> "I have sewed sackcloth over my skin
>> and buried my brow in the dust.
> My face is red with weeping,
>> deep shadows ring my eyes;
> yet my hands have been free of violence
>> and my prayer is pure.

SURELY THERE IS ADVOCATE.

Job 16:18-21

> "O earth, do not cover my blood;
>> may my cry never be laid to rest!
> Even now my witness is in heaven;
>> my advocate is on high.
> My intercessor is my friend[g]
>> as my eyes pour out tears to God;
> on behalf of a man he pleads with God
>> as a man pleads for his friend.

FRIENDS MOCK CURIOSITY.

Job 16:22-17:9

> "Only a few years will pass
>> before I go on the journey of no return.
> My spirit is broken,
>> my days are cut short,
>> the grave awaits me.
> Surely mockers surround me;
>> my eyes must dwell on their hostility.

> "Give me, O God, the pledge you demand.

g Or My friends treat me with scorn

Who else will put up security for me?
You have closed their minds to understanding;
    therefore you will not let them triumph.
If a man denounces his friends for reward,
    the eyes of his children will fail.

"God has made me a byword to everyone,
    a man in whose face people spit.
My eyes have grown dim with grief;
    my whole frame is but a shadow.
Upright men are appalled at this;
    the innocent are aroused against the ungodly.
Nevertheless, the righteous will hold to their ways,
    and those with clean hands will grow stronger.

Job 17:10-16

LIMITATIONS ON SYMPATHY.

"But come on, all of you, try again!
    I will not find a wise man among you.
My days have passed, my plans are shattered,
    and so are the desires of my heart.
These men turn night into day;
    in the face of darkness they say, 'Light is near.'
If the only home I hope for is the grave,[h]
    if I spread out my bed in darkness,
if I say to corruption, 'You are my father,'
    and to the worm, 'My mother' or 'My sister,'
where then is my hope?
    Who can see any hope for me?
Will it go down to the gates of death[h]?
    Will we descend together into the dust?"

Bildad

Job 18:1-4

NONSUFFERERS KNOW SOMETHING.   Then Bildad the Shuhite replied:

"When will you end these speeches?
    Be sensible, and then we can talk.
Why are we regarded as cattle
    and considered stupid in your sight?
You who tear yourself to pieces in your anger,
    is the earth to be abandoned for your sake?
Or must the rocks be moved from their place?

Job 18:5-21

SUFFERING FROM WICKEDNESS.

"The lamp of the wicked is snuffed out;
    the flame of his fire stops burning.
The light in his tent becomes dark;
    the lamp beside him goes out.
The vigor of his step is weakened;
    his own schemes throw him down.
His feet thrust him into a net

[h]Hebrew *Sheol*

and he wanders into its mesh.
A trap seizes him by the heel;
    a snare holds him fast.
A noose is hidden for him on the ground;
    a trap lies in his path.
Terrors startle him on every side
    and dog his every step.
Calamity is hungry for him;
    disaster is ready for him when he falls.
It eats away parts of his skin;
    death's firstborn devours his limbs.
He is torn from the security of his tent
    and marched off to the king of terrors.
Fire resides*i* in his tent;
    burning sulfur is scattered over his dwelling.
His roots dry up below
    and his branches wither above.
The memory of him perishes from the earth;
    he has no name in the land.
He is driven from light into darkness
    and is banished from the world.
He has no offspring or descendants among his people,
    no survivor where once he lived.
Men of the west are appalled at his fate;
    men of the east are seized with horror.
Surely such is the dwelling of an evil man;
    such is the place of one who knows not God."

Job

EVEN RIGHTEOUS SUFFER.   Then Job replied: Job 19:1-6

"How long will you torment me
    and crush me with words?
Ten times now you have reproached me;
    shamelessly you attack me.
If it is true that I have gone astray,
    my error remains my concern alone.
If indeed you would exalt yourselves above me
    and use my humiliation against me,
then know that God has wronged me
    and drawn his net around me.

JOB'S DESTRUCTION.   Job 19:7-12

"Though I cry, 'I've been wronged!' I get no response;
    though I call for help, there is no justice.
He has blocked my way so I cannot pass;
    he has shrouded my paths in darkness.
He has stripped me of my honor
    and removed the crown from my head.
He tears me down on every side till I am gone;

*i*Or *Nothing he had remains*

> he uproots my hope like a tree.
> His anger burns against me;
>   he counts me among his enemies.
> His troops advance in force;
>   they build a siege ramp against me
>   and encamp around my tent.

Job
19:13-20

JOB'S ALIENATION.

> "He has alienated my brothers from me;
>   my acquaintances are completely estranged from me.
> My kinsmen have gone away;
>   my friends have forgotten me.
> My guests and my maidservants count me a stranger;
>   they look upon me as an alien.
> I summon my servant, but he does not answer,
>   though I beg him with my own mouth.
> My breath is offensive to my wife;
>   I am loathsome to my own brothers.
> Even the little boys scorn me;
>   when I appear, they ridicule me.
> All my intimate friends detest me;
>   those I love have turned against me.
> I am nothing but skin and bones;
>   I have escaped with only the skin of my teeth.*j*

Job
19:21,22

PLEA FOR PITY.

> "Have pity on me, my friends, have pity,
>   for the hand of God has struck me.
> Why do you pursue me as God does?
>   Will you never get enough of my flesh?

Job
19:23-27

CONFIDENCE IN RESURRECTION.

> "Oh, that my words were recorded,
>   that they were written on a scroll,
> that they were inscribed with an iron tool on*k* lead,
>   or engraved in rock forever!
> I know that my Redeemer*l* lives,
>   and that in the end he will stand upon the earth.*m*
> And after my skin has been destroyed,
>   yet*n* in*o* my flesh I will see God;
> I myself will see him
>   with my own eyes—I, and not another.
>   How my heart yearns within me!

Job
19:28,29

ARGUMENTS CUT BOTH WAYS.

> "If you say, 'How we will hound him,
>   since the root of the trouble lies in him,*p*'
> you should fear the sword yourselves;

*j*Or *only my gums*   *k*Or *and*   *l*Or *defender*   *m*Or *upon my grave*   *n*Or *And after I awake, / though this body has been destroyed, / then*   *o*Or */ apart from*   *p*Many Hebrew manuscripts, Septuagint and Vulgate; most Hebrew manuscripts *me*

for wrath will bring punishment by the sword,
and then you will know that there is judgment. *q*"

Zophar

REBUKE PROMPTS REPLY.   Then Zophar the Naamathite replied: Job 20:1-3

"My troubled thoughts prompt me to answer
because I am greatly disturbed.
I hear a rebuke that dishonors me,
and my understanding inspires me to reply.

WICKED ALWAYS FALL.   Job 20:4-11

"Surely you know how it has been from of old,
ever since man *r* was placed on the earth,
that the mirth of the wicked is brief,
the joy of the godless lasts but a moment.
Though his pride reaches to the heavens
and his head touches the clouds,
he will perish forever, like his own dung;
those who have seen him will say, 'Where is he?'
Like a dream he flies away, no more to be found,
banished like a vision of the night.
The eye that saw him will not see him again;
his place will look on him no more.
His children must make amends to the poor;
his own hands must give back his wealth.
The youthful vigor that fills his bones
will lie with him in the dust.

REPAYMENT FOR SINS.   Job
                                                                    20:12-19

"Though evil is sweet in his mouth
and he hides it under his tongue,
though he cannot bear to let it go
and keeps it in his mouth,
yet his food will turn sour in his stomach;
it will become the venom of serpents within him.
He will spit out the riches he swallowed;
God will make his stomach vomit them up.
He will suck the poison of serpents;
the fangs of an adder will kill him.
He will not enjoy the streams,
the rivers flowing with honey and cream.
What he toiled for he must give back uneaten;
he will not enjoy the profit from his trading.
For he has oppressed the poor and left them destitute;
he has seized houses he did not build.

WICKED HAVE NO DEFENSE.   Job
                                                                    20:20-29

"Surely he will have no respite from his craving;
he cannot save himself by his treasure.

qOr / that you may come to know the Almighty   rOr Adam

Nothing is left for him to devour;
 his prosperity will not endure.
In the midst of his plenty, distress will overtake him;
 the full force of misery will come upon him.
When he has filled his belly,
 God will vent his burning anger against him
 and rain down his blows upon him.
Though he flees from an iron weapon,
 a bronze-tipped arrow pierces him.
He pulls it out of his back,
 the gleaming point out of his liver.
Terrors will come over him;
 total darkness lies in wait for his treasures.
A fire unfanned will consume him
 and devour what is left in his tent.
The heavens will expose his guilt;
 the earth will rise up against him.
A flood will carry off his house,
 rushing waters[s] on the day of God's wrath.
Such is the fate God allots the wicked,
 the heritage appointed for them by God."

Job

Job 21:1-3   LISTEN FURTHER.   Then Job replied:

"Listen carefully to my words;
 let this be the consolation you give me.
Bear with me while I speak,
 and after I have spoken, mock on.

Job 21:4-18   WICKED OFTEN PROSPER.

"Is my complaint directed to man?
 Why should I not be impatient?
Look at me and be astonished;
 clap your hand over your mouth.
When I think about this, I am terrified;
 trembling seizes my body.
Why do the wicked live on,
 growing old and increasing in power?
They see their children established around them,
 their offspring before their eyes.
Their homes are safe and free from fear;
 the rod of God is not upon them.
Their bulls never fail to breed;
 their cows calve and do not miscarry.
They send forth their children as a flock;
 their little ones dance about.
They sing to the music of tambourine and harp;
 they make merry to the sound of the flute.
They spend their years in prosperity

[s]Or *The possessions in his house will be carried off, / washed away*

and go down to the grave[t] in peace.[u]
Yet they say to God, 'Leave us alone!
We have no desire to know your ways.
Who is the Almighty, that we should serve him?
What would we gain by praying to him?'
But their prosperity is not in their own hands,
so I stand aloof from the counsel of the wicked.

"Yet how often is the lamp of the wicked snuffed out?
How often does calamity come upon them,
the fate God allots in his anger?
How often are they like straw before the wind,
like chaff swept away by a gale?

UNFAIR PUNISHMENT.

Job
21:19-21

⌊It is said,⌋ 'God stores up a man's punishment for his sons.'
Let him repay the man himself, so that he will know it!
Let his own eyes see his destruction;
let him drink of the wrath of the Almighty.[v]
For what does he care about the family he leaves behind
when his allotted months come to an end?

INEQUITIES IN DEATH.

Job
21:22-26

"Can anyone teach knowledge to God,
since he judges even the highest?
One man dies in full vigor,
completely secure and at ease,
his body[w] well nourished,
his bones rich with marrow.
Another man dies in bitterness of soul,
never having enjoyed anything good.
Side by side they lie in the dust,
and worms cover them both.

DEATH INADEQUATE PUNISHMENT.

Job
21:27-33

"I know full well what you are thinking,
the schemes by which you would wrong me.
You say, 'Where now is the great man's house,
the tents where wicked men lived?'
Have you never questioned those who travel?
Have you paid no regard to their accounts—
that the evil man is spared from the day of calamity,
that he is delivered from[x] the day of wrath?
Who denounces his conduct to his face?
Who repays him for what he has done?
He is carried to the grave,
and watch is kept over his tomb.
The soil in the valley is sweet to him;
all men follow after him,
and a countless throng goes[y] before him.

[t]Hebrew *Sheol*   [u]Or *in an instant*   [v]Verses 17 and 18 may be taken as exclamations
and 19 and 20 as declarations.   [w]The meaning of the Hebrew for this word is uncertain.
[x]Or *man is reserved for the day of calamity, / that he is brought forth to*   [y]Or */ as a countless
throng went*

Job 21:34   ANSWERS FALL SHORT.

> "So how can you console me with your nonsense?
>   Nothing is left of your answers but falsehood!"

Eliphaz

Job 22:1-3   MAN CANNOT BENEFIT GOD.   Then Eliphaz the Temanite replied:

> "Can a man be of benefit to God?
>   Can even a wise man benefit him?
> What pleasure would it give the Almighty if you were
>   righteous?
>   What would he gain if your ways were blameless?

Job 22:4-11   LESS RIGHTEOUS THAN BELIEVED.

> "Is it for your piety that he rebukes you
>   and brings charges against you?
> Is not your wickedness great?
>   Are not your sins endless?
> You demanded security from your brothers for no reason;
>   you stripped men of their clothing, leaving them naked.
> You gave no water to the weary
>   and you withheld food from the hungry,
> though you were a powerful man, owning land—
>   an honored man, living on it.
> And you sent widows away empty-handed
>   and broke the strength of the fatherless.
> That is why snares are all around you,
>   why sudden peril terrifies you,
> why it is so dark you cannot see,
>   and why a flood of water covers you.

Job 22:12-20   WICKEDNESS CANNOT BE HIDDEN.

> "Is not God in the heights of heaven?
>   And see how lofty are the highest stars!
> Yet you say, 'What does God know?
>   Does he judge through such darkness?
> Thick clouds veil him, so he does not see us
>   as he goes about in the vaulted heavens.'
> Will you keep to the old path
>   that evil men have trod?
> They were carried off before their time,
>   their foundations washed away by a flood.
> They said to God, 'Leave us alone!
>   What can the Almighty do to us?'
> Yet it was he who filled their houses with good things,
>   so I stand aloof from the counsel of the wicked.
>
> "The righteous see their ruin and rejoice;
>   the innocent mock them, saying,

'Surely our foes are destroyed,
  and fire devours their wealth.'

JOB SHOULD REPENT.

Job
22:21-30

"Submit to God and be at peace with him;
  in this way prosperity will come to you.
Accept instruction from his mouth
  and lay up his words in your heart.
If you return to the Almighty, you will be restored:
  If you remove wickedness far from your tent
and assign your nuggets to the dust,
  your gold of Ophir to the rocks in the ravines,
then the Almighty will be your gold,
  the choicest silver for you.
Surely then you will find delight in the Almighty
  and will lift up your face to God.
You will pray to him, and he will hear you,
  and you will fulfill your vows.
What you decide on will be done,
  and light will shine on your ways.
When men are brought low and you say, 'Lift them up!'
  then he will save the downcast.
He will deliver even one who is not innocent,
  who will be delivered through the cleanness of your
    hands."

Job

DESIRE FOR PERSONAL HEARING.   Then Job replied:

Job 23:1-7

"Even today my complaint is bitter;
  his hand ^{z} is heavy in spite of ^{a} my groaning.
If only I knew where to find him;
  if only I could go to his dwelling!
I would state my case before him
  and fill my mouth with arguments.
I would find out what he would answer me,
  and consider what he would say.
Would he oppose me with great power?
  No, he would not press charges against me.
There an upright man could present his case before him,
  and I would be delivered forever from my judge.

RIGHTEOUSNESS REASSERTED.

Job 23:8-12

"But if I go to the east, he is not there;
  if I go to the west, I do not find him.
When he is at work in the north, I do not see him;
  when he turns to the south, I catch no glimpse of him.
But he knows the way that I take;
  when he has tested me, I will come forth as gold.
My feet have closely followed his steps;

---

^{z}Septuagint and Syriac; Hebrew / *the hand on me* ^{a}Or *heavy on me in*

> I have kept to his way without turning aside.
> I have not departed from the commands of his lips;
> I have treasured the words of his mouth more than my
> daily bread.

Job
23:13-17

GOD'S CONTROL IS FEARSOME.

> "But he stands alone, and who can oppose him?
> He does whatever he pleases.
> He carries out his decree against me,
> and many such plans he still has in store.
> That is why I am terrified before him;
> when I think of all this, I fear him.
> God has made my heart faint;
> the Almighty has terrified me.
> Yet I am not silenced by the darkness,
> by the thick darkness that covers my face.

Job 24:1-12 SUFFERING WITHOUT JUDGMENT.

> "Why does the Almighty not set times for judgment?
> Why must those who know him look in vain for such
> days?
> Men move boundary stones;
> they pasture flocks they have stolen.
> They drive away the orphan's donkey
> and take the widow's ox in pledge.
> They thrust the needy from the path
> and force all the poor of the land into hiding.
> Like wild donkeys in the desert,
> the poor go about their labor of foraging food;
> the wasteland provides food for their children.
> They gather fodder in the fields
> and glean in the vineyards of the wicked.
> Lacking clothes, they spend the night naked;
> they have nothing to cover themselves in the cold.
> They are drenched by mountain rains
> and hug the rocks for lack of shelter.
> The fatherless child is snatched from the breast;
> the infant of the poor is seized for a debt.
> Lacking clothes, they go about naked;
> they carry the sheaves, but still go hungry.
> They crush olives among the terraces[b];
> they tread the winepresses, yet suffer thirst.
> The groans of the dying rise from the city,
> and the souls of the wounded cry out for help.
> But God charges no one with wrongdoing.

Job
24:13-17

DEEDS OF DARKNESS.

> "There are those who rebel against the light,
> who do not know its ways
> or stay in its paths.

---

[b]Or *olives between the millstones*; the meaning of the Hebrew for this word is uncertain.

When daylight is gone, the murderer rises up
    and kills the poor and needy;
    in the night he steals forth like a thief.
The eye of the adulterer watches for dusk;
    he thinks, 'No eye will see me,'
    and he keeps his face concealed.
In the dark, men break into houses,
    but by day they shut themselves in;
    they want nothing to do with the light.
For all of them, deep darkness is their morning[c];
    they make friends with the terrors of darkness.[d]

WICKED FACE DEATH.

Job
24:18-25

"Yet they are foam on the surface of the water;
    their portion of the land is cursed,
    so that no one goes to the vineyards.
As heat and drought snatch away the melted snow,
    so the grave[e] snatches away those who have sinned.
The womb forgets them,
    the worm feasts on them;
evil men are no longer remembered
    but are broken like a tree.
They prey on the barren and childless woman,
    and to the widow show no kindness.
But God drags away the mighty by his power;
    though they become established, they have no assurance
        of life.
He may let them rest in a feeling of security,
    but his eyes are on their ways.
For a little while they are exalted, and then they are gone;
    they are brought low and gathered up like all others;
    they are cut off like heads of grain.

"If this is not so, who can prove me false
    and reduce my words to nothing?"

Bildad

RIGHTEOUSNESS IS IMPOSSIBLE.   Then Bildad the Shuhite replied:

Job 25:1-6

"Dominion and awe belong to God;
    he establishes order in the heights of heaven.
Can his forces be numbered?
    Upon whom does his light not rise?
How then can a man be righteous before God?
    How can one born of woman be pure?
If even the moon is not bright
    and the stars are not pure in his eyes,
how much less man, who is but a maggot—
    a son of man, who is only a worm!"

[c]Or *them, their morning is like the shadow of death*   [d]Or *of the shadow of death*
[e]Hebrew *Sheol*

Job

Job 26:1-4   WORDS NO CONSOLATION.   Then Job replied:

> "How you have helped the powerless!
>> How you have saved the arm that is feeble!
> What advice you have offered to one without wisdom!
>> And what great insight you have displayed!
> Who has helped you utter these words?
>> And whose spirit spoke from your mouth?

Job 26:5-14   GOD'S WAYS UNFATHOMABLE.

> "The dead are in deep anguish,
>> those beneath the waters and all that live in them.
> Death*f* is naked before God;
>> Destruction*g* lies uncovered.
> He spreads out the northern ⌞skies⌟ over empty space;
>> he suspends the earth over nothing.
> He wraps up the waters in his clouds,
>> yet the clouds do not burst under their weight.
> He covers the face of the full moon,
>> spreading his clouds over it.
> He marks out the horizon on the face of the waters
>> for a boundary between light and darkness.
> The pillars of the heavens quake,
>> aghast at his rebuke.
> By his power he churned up the sea;
>> by his wisdom he cut Rahab to pieces.
> By his breath the skies became fair;
>> his hand pierced the gliding serpent.
> And these are but the outer fringe of his works;
>> how faint the whisper we hear of him!
>> Who then can understand the thunder of his power?"

Job 27:1-6   JOB'S FAITH WILL CONTINUE.   And Job continued his discourse:

> "As surely as God lives, who has denied me justice,
>> the Almighty, who has made me taste bitterness of soul,
> as long as I have life within me,
>> the breath of God in my nostrils,
> my lips will not speak wickedness,
>> and my tongue will utter no deceit.
> I will never admit you are in the right;
>> till I die, I will not deny my integrity.
> I will maintain my righteousness and never let go of it;
>> my conscience will not reproach me as long as I live.

Job 27:7-12   WICKED ARE NOT HEARD.

> "May my enemies be like the wicked,
>> my adversaries like the unjust!
> For what hope has the godless when he is cut off,
>> when God takes away his life?

f Hebrew *Sheol*   *g* Hebrew *Abaddon*

Does God listen to his cry
    when distress comes upon him?
Will he find delight in the Almighty?
    Will he call upon God at all times?

"I will teach you about the power of God;
    the ways of the Almighty I will not conceal.
You have all seen this yourselves.
    Why then this meaningless talk?

FATE OF WICKED.

Job
27:13-23

"Here is the fate God allots to the wicked,
    the heritage a ruthless man receives from the Almighty:
However many his children, their fate is the sword;
    his offspring will never have enough to eat.
The plague will bury those who survive him,
    and their widows will not weep for them.
Though he heaps up silver like dust
    and clothes like piles of clay,
what he lays up the righteous will wear,
    and the innocent will divide his silver.
The house he builds is like a moth's cocoon,
    like a hut made by a watchman.
He lies down wealthy, but will do so no more;
    when he opens his eyes, all is gone.
Terrors overtake him like a flood;
    a tempest snatches him away in the night.
The east wind carries him off, and he is gone;
    it sweeps him out of his place.
It hurls itself against him without mercy
    as he flees headlong from its power.
It claps its hands in derision
    and hisses him out of his place.

WISDOM IS HIDDEN.

Job 28:1-19

"There is a mine for silver
    and a place where gold is refined.
Iron is taken from the earth,
    and copper is smelted from ore.
Man puts an end to the darkness;
    he searches the farthest recesses
    for ore in the blackest darkness.
Far from where people dwell he cuts a shaft,
    in places forgotten by the foot of man;
    far from men he dangles and sways.
The earth, from which food comes,
    is transformed below as by fire;
sapphires[h] come from its rocks,
    and its dust contains nuggets of gold.
No bird of prey knows that hidden path,

[h] Or *lapis lazuli*

> no falcon's eye has seen it.
> Proud beasts do not set foot on it,
>   and no lion prowls there.
> Man's hand assaults the flinty rock
>   and lays bare the roots of the mountains.
> He tunnels through the rock;
>   his eyes see all its treasures.
> He searches[i] the sources of the rivers
>   and brings hidden things to light.

> "But where can wisdom be found?
>   Where does understanding dwell?
> Man does not comprehend its worth;
>   it cannot be found in the land of the living.
> The deep says, 'It is not in me';
>   the sea says, 'It is not with me.'
> It cannot be bought with the finest gold,
>   nor can its price be weighed in silver.
> It cannot be bought with the gold of Ophir,
>   with precious onyx or sapphires.
> Neither gold nor crystal can compare with it,
>   nor can it be had for jewels of gold.
> Coral and jasper are not worthy of mention;
>   the price of wisdom is beyond rubies.
> The topaz of Cush cannot compare with it;
>   it cannot be bought with pure gold.

Job 28:20-28   WISDOM IN FEAR OF GOD.

> "Where then does wisdom come from?
>   Where does understanding dwell?
> It is hidden from the eyes of every living thing,
>   concealed even from the birds of the air.
> Destruction[j] and Death say,
>   'Only a rumor of it has reached our ears.'
> God understands the way to it
>   and he alone knows where it dwells,
> for he views the ends of the earth
>   and sees everything under the heavens.
> When he established the force of the wind
>   and measured out the waters,
> when he made a decree for the rain
>   and a path for the thunderstorm,
> then he looked at wisdom and appraised it;
>   he confirmed it and tested it.
> And he said to man,
>   'The fear of the Lord—that is wisdom,
>   and to shun evil is understanding.'"

Job 29:1-6   JOB'S FORMER PROSPERITY.   Job continued his discourse:

> "How I long for the months gone by,

---

[i]Septuagint, Aquila and Vulgate; Hebrew *He dams up*   [j]Hebrew *Abaddon*

for the days when God watched over me,
when his lamp shone upon my head
and by his light I walked through darkness!
Oh, for the days when I was in my prime,
when God's intimate friendship blessed my house,
when the Almighty was still with me
and my children were around me,
when my path was drenched with cream
and the rock poured out for me streams of olive oil.

JOB'S FORMER ESTEEM.   **Job 29:7-25**

"When I went to the gate of the city
and took my seat in the public square,
the young men saw me and stepped aside
and the old men rose to their feet;
the chief men refrained from speaking
and covered their mouths with their hands;
the voices of the nobles were hushed,
and their tongues stuck to the roof of their mouths.
Whoever heard me spoke well of me,
and those who saw me commended me,
because I rescued the poor who cried for help,
and the fatherless who had none to assist him.
The man who was dying blessed me;
I made the widow's heart sing.
I put on righteousness as my clothing;
justice was my robe and my turban.
I was eyes to the blind
and feet to the lame.
I was a father to the needy;
I took up the case of the stranger.
I broke the fangs of the wicked
and snatched the victims from their teeth.

"I thought, 'I will die in my own house,
my days as numerous as the grains of sand.
My roots will reach to the water,
and the dew will lie all night on my branches.
My glory will remain fresh in me,
the bow ever new in my hand.'

"Men listened to me expectantly,
waiting in silence for my counsel.
After I had spoken, they spoke no more;
my words fell gently on their ears.
They waited for me as for showers
and drank in my words as the spring rain.
When I smiled at them, they scarcely believed it;
the light of my face was precious to them.[k]
I chose the way for them and sat as their chief;
I dwelt as a king among his troops;
I was like one who comforts mourners.

[k] The meaning of the Hebrew for this clause is uncertain.

Job 30:1-15   ROBBED OF DIGNITY.

> "But now they mock me,
>   men younger than I,
> whose fathers I would have disdained
>   to put with my sheep dogs.
> Of what use was the strength of their hands to me,
>   since their vigor had gone from them?
> Haggard from want and hunger,
>   they roamed[l] the parched land
>   in desolate wastelands at night.
> In the brush they gathered salt herbs,
>   and their food[m] was the root of the broom tree.
> They were banished from their fellow men,
>   shouted at as if they were thieves.
> They were forced to live in the dry stream beds,
>   among the rocks and in holes in the ground.
> They brayed among the bushes
>   and huddled in the undergrowth.
> A base and nameless brood,
>   they were driven out of the land.
>
> "And now their sons mock me in song;
>   I have become a byword among them.
> They detest me and keep their distance;
>   they do not hesitate to spit in my face.
> Now that God has unstrung my bow and afflicted me,
>   they throw off restraint in my presence.
> On my right the tribe[n] attacks;
>   they lay snares for my feet,
>   they build their siege ramps against me.
> They break up my road;
>   they succeed in destroying me—
>   without anyone's helping them.[o]
> They advance as through a gaping breach;
>   amid the ruins they come rolling in.
> Terrors overwhelm me;
>   my dignity is driven away as by the wind,
>   my safety vanishes like a cloud.

Job 30:16-19   ROBBED OF HEALTH.

> "And now my life ebbs away;
>   days of suffering grip me.
> Night pierces my bones;
>   my gnawing pains never rest.
> In his great power ⌊God⌋ becomes like clothing to me[p];
>   he binds me like the neck of my garment.
> He throws me into the mud,
>   and I am reduced to dust and ashes.

---

[l]Or *gnawed*   [m]Or *fuel*   [n]The meaning of the Hebrew for this word is uncertain.
[o]Or *me. | 'No one can help him,' ⌊they say⌋.*   [p]Hebrew; Septuagint ⌊*God*⌋ *grasps my clothing*

NO RESPONSE TO GRIEF.

Job
30:20-26

"I cry out to you, O God, but you do not answer;
 I stand up, but you merely look at me.
You turn on me ruthlessly;
 with the might of your hand you attack me.
You snatch me up and drive me before the wind;
 you toss me about in the storm.
I know you will bring me down to death,
 to the place appointed for all the living.

"Surely no one lays a hand on a broken man
 when he cries for help in his distress.
Have I not wept for those in trouble?
 Has not my soul grieved for the poor?
Yet when I hoped for good, evil came;
 when I looked for light, then came darkness.

HORROR OF PAIN.

Job
30:27-31

The churning inside me never stops;
 days of suffering confront me.
I go about blackened, but not by the sun;
 I stand up in the assembly and cry for help.
I have become a brother of jackals,
 a companion of owls.
My skin grows black and peels;
 my body burns with fever.
My harp is tuned to mourning,
 and my flute to the sound of wailing.

EYES CLOSED TO LUST.

Job 31:1-4

"I made a covenant with my eyes
 not to look lustfully at a girl.
For what is man's lot from God above,
 his heritage from the Almighty on high?
Is it not ruin for the wicked,
 disaster for those who do wrong?
Does he not see my ways
 and count my every step?

DECEIT DISDAINED.

Job 31:5-8

"If I have walked in falsehood
 or my foot has hurried after deceit—
let God weigh me in honest scales
 and he will know that I am blameless—
if my steps have turned from the path,
 if my heart has been led by my eyes,
 or if my hands have been defiled,
then may others eat what I have sown,
 and may my crops be uprooted.

Job 31:9-12   FAITHFUL TO WIFE.

> "If my heart has been enticed by a woman,
>   or if I have lurked at my neighbor's door,
> then may my wife grind another man's grain,
>   and may other men sleep with her.
> For that would have been shameful,
>   a sin to be judged.
> It is a fire that burns to Destruction[q];
>   it would have uprooted my harvest.

Job
31:13-15   SERVANTS TREATED JUSTLY.

> "If I have denied justice to my menservants and
>   maidservants
>   when they had a grievance against me,
> what will I do when God confronts me?
>   What will I answer when called to account?
> Did not he who made me in the womb make them?
>   Did not the same one form us both within our mothers?

Job
31:16-23   BENEVOLENT TO NEEDY.

> "If I have denied the desires of the poor
>   or let the eyes of the widow grow weary,
> if I have kept my bread to myself,
>   not sharing it with the fatherless—
> but from my youth I reared him as would a father,
>   and from my birth I guided the widow—
> if I have seen anyone perishing for lack of clothing,
>   or a needy man without a garment,
> and his heart did not bless me
>   for warming him with the fleece from my sheep,
> if I have raised my hand against the fatherless,
>   knowing that I had influence in court,
> then let my arm fall from the shoulder,
>   let it be broken off at the joint.
> For I dreaded destruction from God,
>   and for fear of his splendor I could not do such things.

Job
31:24,25   NO TRUST IN RICHES.

> "If I have put my trust in gold
>   or said to pure gold, 'You are my security,'
> if I have rejoiced over my great wealth,
>   the fortune my hands had gained,

Job
31:26-28   NO IDOLATRY.

> if I have regarded the sun in its radiance
>   or the moon moving in splendor,
> so that my heart was secretly enticed
>   and my hand offered them a kiss of homage,
> then these also would be sins to be judged,
>   for I would have been unfaithful to God on high.

[q]Hebrew *Abaddon*

NO VENGEFUL GLOATING.　　　　　　　　　　　　　　　Job
　　　　　　　　　　　　　　　　　　　　　　　　　　31:29,30

　　　"If I have rejoiced at my enemy's misfortune
　　　　　　or gloated over the trouble that came to him—
　　　I have not allowed my mouth to sin
　　　　　　by invoking a curse against his life—

HOSPITABLE TO STRANGERS.　　　　　　　　　　　　　　Job
　　　　　　　　　　　　　　　　　　　　　　　　　　31:31,32

　　　if the men of my household have never said,
　　　　　　'Who has not had his fill of Job's meat?'—
　　　but no stranger had to spend the night in the street,
　　　　　　for my door was always open to the traveler—

NO HYPOCRISY.　　　　　　　　　　　　　　　　　　　Job
　　　　　　　　　　　　　　　　　　　　　　　　　　31:33,34

　　　if I have concealed my sin as men do,[r]
　　　　　　by hiding my guilt in my heart
　　　because I so feared the crowd
　　　　　　and so dreaded the contempt of the clans
　　　　　　that I kept silent and would not go outside—

INDICTMENT WELCOMED.　　　　　　　　　　　　　　　Job
　　　　　　　　　　　　　　　　　　　　　　　　　　31:35-37

　　　("Oh, that I had someone to hear me!
　　　　　　I sign now my defense—let the Almighty answer me;
　　　　　　let my accuser put his indictment in writing.
　　　Surely I would wear it on my shoulder,
　　　　　　I would put it on like a crown.
　　　I would give him an account of my every step;
　　　　　　like a prince I would approach him.)—

NO TENANTS MISTREATED.　　　　　　　　　　　　　　Job
　　　　　　　　　　　　　　　　　　　　　　　　　　31:38-40

　　　"if my land cries out against me
　　　　　　and all its furrows are wet with tears,
　　　if I have devoured its yield without payment
　　　　　　or broken the spirit of its tenants,
　　　then let briers come up instead of wheat
　　　　　　and weeds instead of barley."

　　The words of Job are ended.

Elihu　　　　　　　　　　　　　　　　　　　　　　　⬕

ELIHU'S YOUTHFUL ANGER.　　So these three men stopped answering　Job 32:1-5
Job, because he was righteous in his own eyes. But Elihu son of Barakel the
Buzite, of the family of Ram, became very angry with Job for justifying
himself rather than God. He was also angry with the three friends, because
they had found no way to refute Job, and yet had condemned him.[s] Now
Elihu had waited before speaking to Job because they were older than he.
But when he saw that the three men had nothing more to say, his anger
was aroused.

[r]Or *as Adam did*　　　[s]Masoretic Text; an ancient Hebrew scribal tradition *Job, and so had*
condemned God

Job 32:6-9 INSIGHT OF THE YOUNG. So Elihu son of Barakel the Buzite said:

> "I am young in years,
>   and you are old;
> that is why I was fearful,
>   not daring to tell you what I know.
> I thought, 'Age should speak;
>   advanced years should teach wisdom.'
> But it is the spirit*t* in a man,
>   the breath of the Almighty, that gives him understanding.
> It is not only the old*u* who are wise,
>   not only the aged who understand what is right.

Job 32:10-14 PREVIOUS ANSWERS INADEQUATE.

> "Therefore I say: Listen to me;
>   I too will tell you what I know.
> I waited while you spoke,
>   I listened to your reasoning;
> while you were searching for words,
>   I gave you my full attention.
> But not one of you has proved Job wrong;
>   none of you has answered his arguments.
> Do not say, 'We have found wisdom;
>   let God refute him, not man.'
> But Job has not marshaled his words against me,
>   and I will not answer him with your arguments.

Job 32:15-22 COMPULSION TO SPEAK.

> "They are dismayed and have no more to say;
>   words have failed them.
> Must I wait, now that they are silent,
>   now that they stand there with no reply?
> I too will have my say;
>   I too will tell what I know.
> For I am full of words,
>   and the spirit within me compels me;
> inside I am like bottled-up wine,
>   like new wineskins ready to burst.
> I must speak and find relief;
>   I must open my lips and reply.
> I will show partiality to no one,
>   nor will I flatter any man;
> for if I were skilled in flattery,
>   my Maker would soon take me away.

Job 33:1-7 SINCERITY OF CONCERN.

> "But now, Job, listen to my words;
>   pay attention to everything I say.
> I am about to open my mouth;
>   my words are on the tip of my tongue.

*t*Or *Spirit*   *u*Or *many;* or *great*

My words come from an upright heart;
    my lips sincerely speak what I know.
The Spirit of God has made me;
    the breath of the Almighty gives me life.
Answer me then, if you can;
    prepare yourself and confront me.
I am just like you before God;
    I too have been taken from clay.
No fear of me should alarm you,
    nor should my hand be heavy upon you.

WHERE JOB IS WRONG.   Job 33:8-13

"But you have said in my hearing—
    I heard the very words—
'I am pure and without sin;
    I am clean and free from guilt.
Yet God has found fault with me;
    he considers me his enemy.
He fastens my feet in shackles;
    he keeps close watch on all my paths.'

"But I tell you, in this you are not right,
    for God is greater than man.
Why do you complain to him
    that he answers none of man's words[v]?

HOW GOD SPEAKS.   Job 33:14-22

For God does speak—now one way, now another—
    though man may not perceive it.
In a dream, in a vision of the night,
    when deep sleep falls on men
    as they slumber in their beds,
he may speak in their ears
    and terrify them with warnings,
to turn man from wrongdoing
    and keep him from pride,
to preserve his soul from the pit,[w]
    his life from perishing by the sword.[x]
Or a man may be chastened on a bed of pain
    with constant distress in his bones,
so that his very being finds food repulsive
    and his soul loathes the choicest meal.
His flesh wastes away to nothing,
    and his bones, once hidden, now stick out.
His soul draws near to the pit,[y]
    and his life to the messengers of death.[z]

INTERVENTION OF ANGELS.   Job 33:23-28

"Yet if there is an angel on his side

---

[v]Or *that he does not answer for any of his actions*   [w]Or *preserve him from the grave*   [x]Or
from crossing the River   [y]Or *He draws near to the grave*   [z]Or *to the dead*

as a mediator, one out of a thousand,
  to tell a man what is right for him,
to be gracious to him and say,
  'Spare him from going down to the pit[a];
  I have found a ransom for him'—
then his flesh is renewed like a child's;
  it is restored as in the days of his youth.
He prays to God and finds favor with him,
  he sees God's face and shouts for joy;
  he is restored by God to his righteous state.
Then he comes to men and says,
  'I sinned, and perverted what was right,
  but I did not get what I deserved.
He redeemed my soul from going down to the pit,[b]
  and I will live to enjoy the light.'

**Job
33:29,30**

A REASON FOR SUFFERING.

"God does all these things to a man—
  twice, even three times—
to turn back his soul from the pit,[c]
  that the light of life may shine on him.

**Job
33:31-34:4**

PLEA FOR ATTENTION.

"Pay attention, Job, and listen to me;
  be silent, and I will speak.
If you have anything to say, answer me;
  speak up, for I want you to be cleared.
But if not, then listen to me;
  be silent, and I will teach you wisdom."

Then Elihu said:

"Hear my words, you wise men;
  listen to me, you men of learning.
For the ear tests words
  as the tongue tastes food.
Let us discern for ourselves what is right;
  let us learn together what is good.

Job 34:5-9

JOB'S BASIC POSITION.

"Job says, 'I am innocent,
  but God denies me justice.
Although I am right,
  I am considered a liar;
although I am guiltless,
  his arrow inflicts an incurable wound.'
What man is like Job,
  who drinks scorn like water?
He keeps company with evildoers;
  he associates with wicked men.

[a]Or *grave*   [b]Or *redeemed me from going down to the grave*   [c]Or *turn him back from the grave*

For he says, 'It profits a man nothing
    when he tries to please God.'

ALMIGHTY IS JUST.

Job
34:10-20

"So listen to me, you men of understanding.
    Far be it from God to do evil,
    from the Almighty to do wrong.
He repays a man for what he has done;
    he brings upon him what his conduct deserves.
It is unthinkable that God would do wrong,
    that the Almighty would pervert justice.
Who appointed him over the earth?
    Who put him in charge of the whole world?
If it were his intention
    and he withdrew his spirit[d] and breath,
all mankind would perish together
    and man would return to the dust.

"If you have understanding, hear this;
    listen to what I say.
Can he who hates justice govern?
    Will you condemn the just and mighty One?
Is he not the One who says to kings, 'You are worthless,'
    and to nobles, 'You are wicked,'
who shows no partiality to princes
    and does not favor the rich over the poor,
    for they are all the work of his hands?
They die in an instant, in the middle of the night;
    the people are shaken and they pass away;
    the mighty are removed without human hand.

GOD SEES WICKEDNESS.

Job
34:21-30

"His eyes are on the ways of men;
    he sees their every step.
There is no dark place, no deep shadow,
    where evildoers can hide.
God has no need to examine men further,
    that they should come before him for judgment.
Without inquiry he shatters the mighty
    and sets up others in their place.
Because he takes note of their deeds,
    he overthrows them in the night and they are crushed.
He punishes them for their wickedness
    where everyone can see them,
because they turned from following him
    and had no regard for any of his ways.
They caused the cry of the poor to come before him,
    so that he heard the cry of the needy.
But if he remains silent, who can condemn him?
    If he hides his face, who can see him?

[d] Or *Spirit*

> Yet he is over man and nation alike,
>> to keep a godless man from ruling,
>> from laying snares for the people.

**Job
34:31-33**

NOMINAL REPENTANCE.

> "Suppose a man says to God,
>> 'I am guilty but will offend no more.
> Teach me what I cannot see;
>> if I have done wrong, I will not do so again.'
> Should God then reward you on your terms,
>> when you refuse to repent?
> You must decide, not I;
>> so tell me what you know.

**Job
34:34-37**

JOB IS COMPOUNDING SINS.

> "Men of understanding declare,
>> wise men who hear me say to me,
> 'Job speaks without knowledge;
>> his words lack insight.'
> Oh, that Job might be tested to the utmost
>> for answering like a wicked man!
> To his sin he adds rebellion;
>> scornfully he claps his hands among us
>> and multiplies his words against God."

Job 35:1-3   JOB ARGUES INCONSISTENTLY.   Then Elihu said:

> "Do you think this is just?
>> You say, 'I will be cleared by God.^{e}'
> Yet you ask him, 'What profit is it to me,^{f}
>> and what do I gain by not sinning?'

Job 35:4-8   SINS DO NOT AFFECT GOD.

> "I would like to reply to you
>> and to your friends with you.
> Look up at the heavens and see;
>> gaze at the clouds so high above you.
> If you sin, how does that affect him?
>> If your sins are many, what does that do to him?
> If you are righteous, what do you give to him,
>> or what does he receive from your hand?
> Your wickedness affects only a man like yourself,
>> and your righteousness only the sons of men.

Job 35:9-16   TALKING TO GOD IS USELESS.

> "Men cry out under a load of oppression;
>> they plead for relief from the arm of the powerful.
> But no one says, 'Where is God my Maker,
>> who gives songs in the night,
>> who teaches more to us than to^g the beasts of the earth

^{e}Or *My righteousness is more than God's* ^{f}Or *you* ^{g}Or *teaches us by*

and makes us wiser than[h] the birds of the air?'
He does not answer when men cry out
  because of the arrogance of the wicked.
Indeed, God does not listen to their empty plea;
  the Almighty pays no attention to it.
How much less, then, will he listen
  when you say that you do not see him,
that your case is before him
  and you must wait for him,
and further, that his anger never punishes
  and he does not take the least notice of wickedness.[i]
So Job opens his mouth with empty talk;
  without knowledge he multiplies words."

CLAIMED AUTHORITY.   Elihu continued:

Job 36:1-4

"Bear with me a little longer and I will show you
  that there is more to be said in God's behalf.
I get my knowledge from afar;
  I will ascribe justice to my Maker.
Be assured that my words are not false;
  one perfect in knowledge is with you.

GOD RULES RATIONALLY.

Job 36:5-12

"God is mighty, but does not despise men;
  he is mighty, and firm in his purpose.
He does not keep the wicked alive
  but gives the afflicted their rights.
He does not take his eyes off the righteous;
  he enthrones them with kings
  and exalts them forever.
But if men are bound in chains,
  held fast by cords of affliction,
he tells them what they have done—
  that they have sinned arrogantly.
He makes them listen to correction
  and commands them to repent of their evil.
If they obey and serve him,
  they will spend the rest of their days in prosperity
  and their years in contentment.
But if they do not listen,
  they will perish by the sword[j]
  and die without knowledge.

GOD ANSWERS SUFFERERS.

Job
36:13-15

"The godless in heart harbor resentment;
  even when he fetters them, they do not cry for help.
They die in their youth,
  among male prostitutes of the shrines.

---

[h]Or *us wise by*   [i]Symmachus, Theodotion and Vulgate; the meaning of the Hebrew for this word is uncertain.   [j]Or *will cross the River*

But those who suffer he delivers in their suffering;
he speaks to them in their affliction.

Job 36:16-21

WARNING AGAINST WICKEDNESS.

"He is wooing you from the jaws of distress
to a spacious place free from restriction,
to the comfort of your table laden with choice food.
But now you are laden with the judgment due the wicked;
judgment and justice have taken hold of you.
Be careful that no one entices you by riches;
do not let a large bribe turn you aside.
Would your wealth
or even all your mighty efforts
sustain you so you would not be in distress?
Do not long for the night,
to drag people away from their homes.^k
Beware of turning to evil,
which you seem to prefer to affliction.

Job 36:22-26

GOD'S GREATNESS.

"God is exalted in his power.
Who is a teacher like him?
Who has prescribed his ways for him,
or said to him, 'You have done wrong'?
Remember to extol his work,
which men have praised in song.
All mankind has seen it;
men gaze on it from afar.
How great is God—beyond our understanding!
The number of his years is past finding out.

Job 36:27-37:13

LIGHTNING-LIKE POWER.

"He draws up the drops of water,
which distill as rain to the streams^l;
the clouds pour down their moisture
and abundant showers fall on mankind.
Who can understand how he spreads out the clouds,
how he thunders from his pavilion?
See how he scatters his lightning about him,
bathing the depths of the sea.
This is the way he governs^m the nations
and provides food in abundance.
He fills his hands with lightning
and commands it to strike its mark.
His thunder announces the coming storm;
even the cattle make known its approach.^n

"At this my heart pounds
and leaps from its place.

---

^k The meaning of the Hebrew for verses 18-20 is uncertain.   ^l Or *distill from the mist as rain*   ^m Or *nourishes*   ^n Or *announces his coming— / the One zealous against evil*

Listen! Listen to the roar of his voice,
　　to the rumbling that comes from his mouth.
He unleashes his lightning beneath the whole heaven
　　and sends it to the ends of the earth.
After that comes the sound of his roar;
　　he thunders with his majestic voice.
When his voice resounds,
　　he holds nothing back.
God's voice thunders in marvelous ways;
　　he does great things beyond our understanding.
He says to the snow, 'Fall on the earth,'
　　and to the rain shower, 'Be a mighty downpour.'
So that all men he has made may know his work,
　　he stops every man from his labor.º
The animals take cover;
　　they remain in their dens.
The tempest comes out from its chamber,
　　the cold from the driving winds.
The breath of God produces ice,
　　and the broad waters become frozen.
He loads the clouds with moisture;
　　he scatters his lightning through them.
At his direction they swirl around
　　over the face of the whole earth
　　to do whatever he commands them.
He brings the clouds to punish men,
　　or to water his earthᵖ and show his love.

POWER IS INEXPLICABLE.

Job
37:14-18

"Listen to this, Job;
　　stop and consider God's wonders.
Do you know how God controls the clouds
　　and makes his lightning flash?
Do you know how the clouds hang poised,
　　those wonders of him who is perfect in knowledge?
You who swelter in your clothes
　　when the land lies hushed under the south wind,
can you join him in spreading out the skies,
　　hard as a mirror of cast bronze?

NO STANDING BEFORE GOD.

Job
37:19-24

"Tell us what we should say to him;
　　we cannot draw up our case because of our darkness.
Should he be told that I want to speak?
　　Would any man ask to be swallowed up?
Now no one can look at the sun,
　　bright as it is in the skies
　　after the wind has swept them clean.
Out of the north he comes in golden splendor;
　　God comes in awesome majesty.

ºOr / *he fills all men with fear by his power*　　ᵖOr *to favor them*

The Almighty is beyond our reach and exalted in power;
>> in his justice and great righteousness, he does not oppress.
Therefore, men revere him,
>> for does he not have regard for all the wise in heart?[q]"

The Lord

Job 38:1-3 GOD'S TURN TO QUESTION. Then the LORD answered Job out of the storm. He said:

"Who is this that darkens my counsel
>> with words without knowledge?
Brace yourself like a man;
>> I will question you,
>> and you shall answer me.

Job 38:4-15 WHAT POWER DO YOU HAVE?

"Where were you when I laid the earth's foundation?
>> Tell me, if you understand.
Who marked off its dimensions? Surely you know!
>> Who stretched a measuring line across it?
On what were its footings set,
>> or who laid its cornerstone—
while the morning stars sang together
>> and all the angels[r] shouted for joy?

"Who shut up the sea behind doors
>> when it burst forth from the womb,
when I made the clouds its garment
>> and wrapped it in thick darkness,
when I fixed limits for it
>> and set its doors and bars in place,
when I said, 'This far you may come and no farther;
>> here is where your proud waves halt'?

"Have you ever given orders to the morning,
>> or shown the dawn its place,
that it might take the earth by the edges
>> and shake the wicked out of it?
The earth takes shape like clay under a seal;
>> its features stand out like those of a garment.
The wicked are denied their light,
>> and their upraised arm is broken.

Job 3:16-21 WHAT UNDERSTANDING?

"Have you journeyed to the springs of the sea
>> or walked in the recesses of the deep?
Have the gates of death been shown to you?
>> Have you seen the gates of the shadow of death[s]?

---

[q]Or *for he does not have regard for any who think they are wise.*   [r]Hebrew *the sons of God*
[s]Or *gates of deep shadows*

Have you comprehended the vast expanses of the earth?
Tell me, if you know all this.

"What is the way to the abode of light?
And where does darkness reside?
Can you take them to their places?
Do you know the paths to their dwellings?
Surely you know, for you were already born!
You have lived so many years!

WHAT CONTROL?

Job
38:22-30

"Have you entered the storehouses of the snow
or seen the storehouses of the hail,
which I reserve for times of trouble,
for days of war and battle?
What is the way to the place where the lightning is
dispersed,
or the place where the east winds are scattered over
the earth?
Who cuts a channel for the torrents of rain,
and a path for the thunderstorm,
to water a land where no man lives,
a desert with no one in it,
to satisfy a desolate wasteland
and make it sprout with grass?
Does the rain have a father?
Who fathers the drops of dew?
From whose womb comes the ice?
Who gives birth to the frost from the heavens
when the waters become hard as stone,
when the surface of the deep is frozen?

WHAT DOMINION?

Job
38:31-33

"Can you bind the beautiful[t] Pleiades?
Can you loose the cords of Orion?
Can you bring forth the constellations in their seasons[u]
or lead out the Bear[v] with its cubs?
Do you know the laws of the heavens?
Can you set up ⌊God's[w]⌋ dominion over the earth?

WHAT AUTHORITY?

Job
38:34,35

"Can you raise your voice to the clouds
and cover yourself with a flood of water?
Do you send the lightning bolts on their way?
Do they report to you, 'Here we are'?

WHAT WISDOM?

Job
38:36-38

Who endowed the heart[x] with wisdom
or gave understanding to the mind[x]?
Who has the wisdom to count the clouds?

[t]Or *the twinkling;* or *the chains of the*   [u]Or *the morning star in its season*   [v]Or *out Leo*
[w]Or *his;* or *their*   [x]The meaning of the Hebrew for this word is uncertain.

> Who can tip over the water jars of the heavens
> when the dust becomes hard
> and the clods of earth stick together?

Job 38:39-41

WHAT PROVIDENCE?

> "Do you hunt the prey for the lioness
> and satisfy the hunger of the lions
> when they crouch in their dens
> or lie in wait in a thicket?
> Who provides food for the raven
> when its young cry out to God
> and wander about for lack of food?

Job 39:1-4

WHAT KNOWLEDGE?

> "Do you know when the mountain goats give birth?
> Do you watch when the doe bears her fawn?
> Do you count the months till they bear?
> Do you know the time they give birth?
> They crouch down and bring forth their young;
> their labor pains are ended.
> Their young thrive and grow strong in the wilds;
> they leave and do not return.

Job 39:5-12

WHAT FREEDOM?

> "Who let the wild donkey go free?
> Who untied his ropes?
> I gave him the wasteland as his home,
> the salt flats as his habitat.
> He laughs at the commotion in the town;
> he does not hear a driver's shout.
> He ranges the hills for his pasture
> and searches for any green thing.

> "Will the wild ox consent to serve you?
> Will he stay by your manger at night?
> Can you hold him to the furrow with a harness?
> Will he till the valleys behind you?
> Will you rely on him for his great strength?
> Will you leave your heavy work to him?
> Can you trust him to bring in your grain
> and gather it to your threshing floor?

Job 39:13-30

WHAT CREATIVITY?

> "The wings of the ostrich flap joyfully,
> but they cannot compare with the pinions and feathers of
> the stork.
> She lays her eggs on the ground
> and lets them warm in the sand,
> unmindful that a foot may crush them,
> that some wild animal may trample them.
> She treats her young harshly, as if they were not hers;
> she cares not that her labor was in vain,

for God did not endow her with wisdom
    or give her a share of good sense.
Yet when she spreads her feathers to run,
    she laughs at horse and rider.

"Do you give the horse his strength
    or clothe his neck with a flowing mane?
Do you make him leap like a locust,
    striking terror with his proud snorting?
He paws fiercely, rejoicing in his strength,
    and charges into the fray.
He laughs at fear, afraid of nothing;
    he does not shy away from the sword.
The quiver rattles against his side,
    along with the flashing spear and lance.
In frenzied excitement he eats up the ground;
    he cannot stand still when the trumpet sounds.
At the blast of the trumpet he snorts, 'Aha!'
    He catches the scent of battle from afar,
    the shout of commanders and the battle cry.

"Does the hawk take flight by your wisdom
    and spread his wings toward the south?
Does the eagle soar at your command
    and build his nest on high?
He dwells on a cliff and stays there at night;
    a rocky crag is his stronghold.
From there he seeks out his food;
    his eyes detect it from afar.
His young ones feast on blood,
    and where the slain are, there is he."

RESPONSE DEMANDED.   The LORD said to Job: Job 40:1,2

"Will the one who contends with the Almighty correct him?
    Let him who accuses God answer him!"

JOB IS DUMBFOUNDED.   Then Job answered the LORD: Job 40:3-5

"I am unworthy—how can I reply to you?
    I put my hand over my mouth.
I spoke once, but I have no answer—
    twice, but I will say no more."

MORE QUESTIONS.   Then the LORD spoke to Job out of the storm: Job 40:6,7

"Brace yourself like a man;
    I will question you,
    and you shall answer me.

WHAT RIGHT TO ACCUSE GOD?   Job 40:8-14

"Would you discredit my justice?
    Would you condemn me to justify yourself?
Do you have an arm like God's,
    and can your voice thunder like his?

Then adorn yourself with glory and splendor,
and clothe yourself in honor and majesty.
Unleash the fury of your wrath,
look at every proud man and bring him low,
look at every proud man and humble him,
crush the wicked where they stand.
Bury them all in the dust together;
shroud their faces in the grave.
Then I myself will admit to you
that your own right hand can save you.

Job 40:15-24   MAN FEARS LARGE ANIMALS.

"Look at the behemoth,[y]
which I made along with you
and which feeds on grass like an ox.
What strength he has in his loins,
what power in the muscles of his belly!
His tail[z] sways like a cedar;
the sinews of his thighs are close-knit.
His bones are tubes of bronze,
his limbs like rods of iron.
He ranks first among the works of God,
yet his Maker can approach him with his sword.
The hills bring him their produce,
and all the wild animals play nearby.
Under the lotus plants he lies,
hidden among the reeds in the marsh.
The lotuses conceal him in their shadow;
the poplars by the stream surround him.
When the river rages, he is not alarmed;
he is secure, though the Jordan should surge against his
mouth.
Can anyone capture him by the eyes,[a]
or trap him and pierce his nose?

Job 41:1-34   EVEN LARGE REPTILES FEARED.

"Can you pull in the leviathan[b] with a fishhook
or tie down his tongue with a rope?
Can you put a cord through his nose
or pierce his jaw with a hook?
Will he keep begging you for mercy?
Will he speak to you with gentle words?
Will he make an agreement with you
for you to take him as your slave for life?
Can you make a pet of him like a bird
or put him on a leash for your girls?
Will traders barter for him?
Will they divide him up among the merchants?
Can you fill his hide with harpoons

---

[y] Possibly the hippopotamus or the elephant   [z] Possibly trunk   [a] Or *by a water hole*
[b] Possibly the crocodile

or his head with fishing spears?
If you lay a hand on him,
    you will remember the struggle and never do it again!
Any hope of subduing him is false;
    the mere sight of him is overpowering.
No one is fierce enough to rouse him.
    Who then is able to stand against me?
Who has a claim against me that I must pay?
    Everything under heaven belongs to me.

"I will not fail to speak of his limbs,
    his strength and his graceful form.
Who can strip off his outer coat?
    Who would approach him with a bridle?
Who dares open the doors of his mouth,
    ringed about with his fearsome teeth?
His back has[c] rows of shields
    tightly sealed together;
each is so close to the next
    that no air can pass between.
They are joined fast to one another;
    they cling together and cannot be parted.
His snorting throws out flashes of light;
    his eyes are like the rays of dawn.
Firebrands stream from his mouth;
    sparks of fire shoot out.
Smoke pours from his nostrils
    as from a boiling pot over a fire of reeds.
His breath sets coals ablaze,
    and flames dart from his mouth.
Strength resides in his neck;
    dismay goes before him.
The folds of his flesh are tightly joined;
    they are firm and immovable.
His chest is hard as rock,
    hard as a lower millstone.
When he rises up, the mighty are terrified;
    they retreat before his thrashing.
The sword that reaches him has no effect,
    nor does the spear or the dart or the javelin.
Iron he treats like straw
    and bronze like rotten wood.
Arrows do not make him flee;
    slingstones are like chaff to him.
A club seems to him but a piece of straw;
    he laughs at the rattling of the lance.
His undersides are jagged potsherds,
    leaving a trail in the mud like a threshing sledge.
He makes the depths churn like a boiling caldron
    and stirs up the sea like a pot of ointment.

---

[c] Or *His pride is his*

> Behind him he leaves a glistening wake;
> one would think the deep had white hair.
> Nothing on earth is his equal—
> a creature without fear.
> He looks down on all that are haughty;
> he is king over all that are proud."

Job 42:1 JOB'S REPLY.   Then Job replied to the LORD:

Job 42:2,3 JOB'S CONFESSION.

> "I know that you can do all things;
> no plan of yours can be thwarted.
> ⌊You asked,⌋ 'Who is this that obscures my counsel without
> knowledge?'
> Surely I spoke of things I did not understand,
> things too wonderful for me to know.

Job 42:4-6 JOB'S REPENTANCE.

> ⌊"You said,⌋ 'Listen now, and I will speak;
> I will question you,
> and you shall answer me.'
> My ears had heard of you
> but now my eyes have seen you.
> Therefore I despise myself
> and repent in dust and ashes."

Job 42:7-9 JOB'S FRIENDS REBUKED.   After the LORD had said these things to Job, he said to Eliphaz the Temanite, "I am angry with you and your two friends, because you have not spoken of me what is right, as my servant Job has. So now take seven bulls and seven rams and go to my servant Job and sacrifice a burnt offering for yourselves. My servant Job will pray for you, and I will accept his prayer and not deal with you according to your folly. You have not spoken of me what is right, as my servant Job has." So Eliphaz the Temanite, Bildad the Shuhite and Zophar the Naamathite did what the LORD told them; and the LORD accepted Job's prayer.

Job 42:10-17 JOB'S PROSPERITY RESTORED.   After Job had prayed for his friends, the LORD made him prosperous again and gave him twice as much as he had before. All his brothers and sisters and everyone who had known him before came and ate with him in his house. They comforted and consoled him over all the trouble the LORD had brought upon him, and each one gave him a piece of silver[d] and a gold ring.

The LORD blessed the latter part of Job's life more than the first. He had fourteen thousand sheep, six thousand camels, a thousand yoke of oxen and a thousand donkeys. And he also had seven sons and three daughters. The first daughter he named Jemimah, the second Keziah and the third Keren-Happuch. Nowhere in all the land were there found women as beautiful as Job's daughters, and their father granted them an inheritance along with their brothers.

After this, Job lived a hundred and forty years; he saw his children and

---

[d]Hebrew *him a kesitah*; a kesitah was a unit of money of unknown weight and value.

their children to the fourth generation. And so he died, old and full of years.

Even in this literary masterpiece, one does not find all the answers one might wish. But that in itself is part of what Job learned. In this life man will never know all of God's wisdom, and in some respects is not even in a position to ask the question "Why?" But some things are made clear from Job's confrontation. First, although it is not always readily noticeable, the wicked will one day come to judgment. Second, the notion that suffering is always the result of sin is totally destroyed. And finally, man is in no position to justify his own situation by accusing God of injustice.

As Job himself points out, these theological niceties are not likely to stop the tears of one who is languishing in captivity, or suffering persecution, or writhing in pain from a cruel disease. But they do challenge God's people in exile to recognize with humility the sovereignty of God, and to trust that in his wisdom there truly is a time and purpose for all things, including adversity and suffering. Whether or not it is apparent, God is working in the life of each individual, as well as in the lives of nations, to bring his people into a closer relationship with him, and thereby into greater harmony within themselves and with each other.

Psalms of a People in Exile

*M*any of the sentiments expressed by Job are the same feelings contained within a number of psalms written about the people of Israel in exile. Like Job, the people have fallen from prosperity into shame. Like Job, they are facing ridicule and even death. Their prayers in the midst of captivity and exile reveal a people reflecting seriously upon their predicament and the sins which brought it about. Confession is a central theme, and hope for deliverance is their prayer. The following ten psalms expose the agonizing loneliness of not only these captives but anyone who has ever awakened to the harsh realization that he or she is in spiritual exile.

Confession of national sin and prayer for restoration.   Psa. 44

For the director of music. Of the Sons of Korah. A *maskil*.[e]

We have heard with our ears, O God;
    our fathers have told us
what you did in their days,
    in days long ago.
With your hand you drove out the nations
    and planted our fathers;
you crushed the peoples
    and made our fathers flourish.
It was not by their sword that they won the land,
    nor did their arm bring them victory;
it was your right hand, your arm,

[e]Title: Probably a literary or musical term

and the light of your face, for you loved them.

You are my King and my God,
 who decrees *f* victories for Jacob.
Through you we push back our enemies;
 through your name we trample our foes.
I do not trust in my bow,
 my sword does not bring me victory;
but you give us victory over our enemies,
 you put our adversaries to shame.
In God we make our boast all day long,
 and we will praise your name forever. *Selah*

But now you have rejected and humbled us;
 you no longer go out with our armies.
You made us retreat before the enemy,
 and our adversaries have plundered us.
You gave us up to be devoured like sheep
 and have scattered us among the nations.
You sold your people for a pittance,
 gaining nothing from their sale.

You have made us a reproach to our neighbors,
 the scorn and derision of those around us.
You have made us a byword among the nations;
 the peoples shake their heads at us.
My disgrace is before me all day long,
 and my face is covered with shame
at the taunts of those who reproach and revile me,
 because of the enemy, who is bent on revenge.

All this happened to us,
 though we had not forgotten you
 or been false to your covenant.
Our hearts had not turned back;
 our feet had not strayed from your path.
But you crushed us and made us a haunt for jackals
 and covered us over with deep darkness.

If we had forgotten the name of our God
 or spread out our hands to a foreign god,
would not God have discovered it,
 since he knows the secrets of the heart?
Yet for your sake we face death all day long;
 we are considered as sheep to be slaughtered.

Awake, O Lord! Why do you sleep?
 Rouse yourself! Do not reject us forever.
Why do you hide your face
 and forget our misery and oppression?

We are brought down to the dust;
 our bodies cling to the ground.

f Septuagint, Aquila and Syriac; Hebrew *King, O God;* / *command*

Rise up and help us;
　　redeem us because of your unfailing love.

Prayer for God to use limitless power to restore the people.   Psa. 74

A *maskil*⁸ of Asaph.

Why have you rejected us forever, O God?
　　Why does your anger smolder against the sheep of your
　　　　pasture?
Remember the people you purchased of old,
　　the tribe of your inheritance, whom you redeemed—
Mount Zion, where you dwelt.
Turn your steps toward these everlasting ruins,
　　all this destruction the enemy has brought on the
　　　　sanctuary.

Your foes roared in the place where you met with us;
　　they set up their standards as signs.
They behaved like men wielding axes
　　to cut through a thicket of trees.
They smashed all the carved paneling
　　with their axes and hatchets.
They burned your sanctuary to the ground;
　　they defiled the dwelling place of your Name.
They said in their hearts, "We will crush them completely!"
　　They burned every place where God was worshiped in
　　　　the land.
We are given no miraculous signs;
　　no prophets are left,
　　and none of us knows how long this will be.

How long will the enemy mock you, O God?
　　Will the foe revile your name forever?
Why do you hold back your hand, your right hand?
　　Take it from the folds of your garment and destroy them!

But you, O God, are my king from of old;
　　you bring salvation upon the earth.
It was you who split open the sea by your power;
　　you broke the heads of the monster in the waters.
It was you who crushed the heads of Leviathan
　　and gave him as food to the creatures of the desert.
It was you who opened up springs and streams;
　　you dried up the ever flowing rivers.
The day is yours, and yours also the night;
　　you established the sun and moon.
It was you who set all the boundaries of the earth;
　　you made both summer and winter.

Remember how the enemy has mocked you, O Lord,
　　how foolish people have reviled your name.
Do not hand over the life of your dove to wild beasts;
　　do not forget the lives of your afflicted people forever.

⁸Title: Probably a literary or musical term

Have regard for your covenant,
    because haunts of violence fill the dark places of the land.
Do not let the oppressed retreat in disgrace;
    may the poor and needy praise your name.

Rise up, O God, and defend your cause;
    remember how fools mock you all day long.
Do not ignore the clamor of your adversaries,
    the uproar of your enemies, which rises continually.

Psa. 79   **When will God hear the captives' cry and repay enemies?**

A psalm of Asaph.

O God, the nations have invaded your inheritance;
    they have defiled your holy temple,
    they have reduced Jerusalem to rubble.
They have given the dead bodies of your servants
    as food to the birds of the air,
    the flesh of your saints to the beasts of the earth.
They have poured out blood like water
    all around Jerusalem,
    and there is no one to bury the dead.
We are objects of reproach to our neighbors,
    of scorn and derision to those around us.

How long, O LORD? Will you be angry forever?
    How long will your jealousy burn like fire?
Pour out your wrath on the nations
    that do not acknowledge you,
on the kingdoms
    that do not call on your name;
for they have devoured Jacob
    and destroyed his homeland.
Do not hold against us the sins of the fathers;
    may your mercy come quickly to meet us,
    for we are in desperate need.

Help us, O God our Savior,
    for the glory of your name;
deliver us and forgive our sins
    for your name's sake.
Why should the nations say,
    "Where is their God?"
Before our eyes, make known among the nations
    that you avenge the outpoured blood of your servants.
May the groans of the prisoners come before you;
    by the strength of your arm
    preserve those condemned to die.

Pay back into the laps of our neighbors seven times
    the reproach they have hurled at you, O Lord.
Then we your people, the sheep of your pasture,
    will praise you forever;
from generation to generation
    we will recount your praise.

Prayer for restoration of the vine brought out of Egypt.   Psa. 80

For the director of music. To ʲthe tune ofʲ "The Lilies of the Covenant." Of Asaph.
A psalm.

Hear us, O Shepherd of Israel,
    you who lead Joseph like a flock;
you who sit enthroned between the cherubim, shine forth
    before Ephraim, Benjamin and Manasseh.
Awaken your might;
    come and save us.

Restore us, O God;
    make your face shine upon us,
    that we may be saved.

O Lord God Almighty,
    how long will your anger smolder
    against the prayers of your people?
You have fed them with the bread of tears;
    you have made them drink tears by the bowlful.
You have made us a source of contention to our neighbors,
    and our enemies mock us.

Restore us, O God Almighty;
    make your face shine upon us,
    that we may be saved.

You brought a vine out of Egypt;
    you drove out the nations and planted it.
You cleared the ground for it,
    and it took root and filled the land.
The mountains were covered with its shade,
    the mighty cedars with its branches.
It sent out its boughs to the Sea,ʰ
    its shoots as far as the River.ⁱ

Why have you broken down its walls
    so that all who pass by pick its grapes?
Boars from the forest ravage it
    and the creatures of the field feed on it.
Return to us, O God Almighty!
    Look down from heaven and see!
Watch over this vine,
    the root your right hand has planted,
    the son ʲ you have raised up for yourself.

Your vine is cut down, it is burned with fire;
    at your rebuke your people perish.
Let your hand rest on the man at your right hand,
    the son of man you have raised up for yourself.
Then we will not turn away from you;
    revive us, and we will call on your name.

Restore us, O Lord God Almighty;

ʰProbably the Mediterranean   ⁱThat is, the Euphrates   ʲOr *branch*

make your face shine upon us,
that we may be saved.

Psa. 85 **Restoration must be accompanied by righteousness.**

For the director of music. Of the Sons of Korah. A psalm.

You showed favor to your land, O LORD;
you restored the fortunes of Jacob.
You forgave the iniquity of your people
and covered all their sins. *Selah*
You set aside all your wrath
and turned from your fierce anger.

Restore us again, O God our Savior,
and put away your displeasure toward us.
Will you be angry with us forever?
Will you prolong your anger through all generations?
Will you not revive us again,
that your people may rejoice in you?
Show us your unfailing love, O LORD,
and grant us your salvation.

I will listen to what God the LORD will say;
he promises peace to his people, his saints—
but let them not return to folly.
Surely his salvation is near those who fear him,
that his glory may dwell in our land.

Love and faithfulness meet together;
righteousness and peace kiss each other.
Faithfulness springs forth from the earth,
and righteousness looks down from heaven.
The LORD will indeed give what is good,
and our land will yield its harvest.
Righteousness goes before him
and prepares the way for his steps.

Psa. 89 **Call for God to remember his promise to David.**

A *maskil*[k] of Ethan the Ezrahite.

I will sing of the LORD's great love forever;
with my mouth I will make your faithfulness known
through all generations.
I will declare that your love stands firm forever,
that you established your faithfulness in heaven itself.

You said, "I have made a covenant with my chosen one,
I have sworn to David my servant,
'I will establish your line forever
and make your throne firm through all generations.' " *Selah*

The heavens praise your wonders, O LORD,
your faithfulness too, in the assembly of the holy ones.

[k]Title: Probably a literary or musical term

For who in the skies above can compare with the LORD?
>   Who is like the LORD among the heavenly beings?
In the council of the holy ones God is greatly feared;
>   he is more awesome than all who surround him.
O LORD God Almighty, who is like you?
>   You are mighty, O LORD, and your faithfulness surrounds
>   you.

You rule over the surging sea;
>   when its waves mount up, you still them.
You crushed Rahab like one of the slain;
>   with your strong arm you scattered your enemies.
The heavens are yours, and yours also the earth;
>   you founded the world and all that is in it.
You created the north and the south;
>   Tabor and Hermon sing for joy at your name.
Your arm is endued with power;
>   your hand is strong, your right hand exalted.

Righteousness and justice are the foundation of your
>   throne;
>   love and faithfulness go before you.
Blessed are those who have learned to acclaim you,
>   who walk in the light of your presence, O LORD.
They rejoice in your name all day long;
>   they exult in your righteousness.
For you are their glory and strength,
>   and by your favor you exalt our horn.*l*
Indeed, our shield*m* belongs to the LORD,
>   our king to the Holy One of Israel.

Once you spoke in a vision,
>   to your faithful people you said:
"I have bestowed strength on a warrior;
>   I have exalted a young man from among the people.
I have found David my servant;
>   with my sacred oil I have anointed him.
My hand will sustain him;
>   surely my arm will strengthen him.
No enemy will subject him to tribute;
>   no wicked man will oppress him.
I will crush his foes before him
>   and strike down his adversaries.
My faithful love will be with him,
>   and through my name his horn*n* will be exalted.
I will set his hand over the sea,
>   his right hand over the rivers.
He will call out to me, 'You are my Father,
>   my God, the Rock my Savior.'
I will also appoint him my firstborn,
>   the most exalted of the kings of the earth.

l Horn here symbolizes strong one.   *m* Or *sovereign*   *n Horn* here symbolizes strength.

I will maintain my love to him forever,
and my covenant with him will never fail.
I will establish his line forever,
his throne as long as the heavens endure.

"If his sons forsake my law
and do not follow my statutes,
if they violate my decrees
and fail to keep my commands,
I will punish their sin with the rod,
their iniquity with flogging;
but I will not take my love from him,
nor will I ever betray my faithfulness.
I will not violate my covenant
or alter what my lips have uttered.
Once for all, I have sworn by my holiness—
and I will not lie to David—
that his line will continue forever
and his throne endure before me like the sun;
it will be established forever like the moon,
the faithful witness in the sky."   *Selah*

But you have rejected, you have spurned,
you have been very angry with your anointed one.
You have renounced the covenant with your servant
and have defiled his crown in the dust.
You have broken through all his walls
and reduced his strongholds to ruins.
All who pass by have plundered him;
he has become the scorn of his neighbors.
You have exalted the right hand of his foes;
you have made all his enemies rejoice.
You have turned back the edge of his sword
and have not supported him in battle.
You have put an end to his splendor
and cast his throne to the ground.
You have cut short the days of his youth;
you have covered him with a mantle of shame.   *Selah*

How long, O LORD? Will you hide yourself forever?
How long will your wrath burn like fire?
Remember how fleeting is my life.
For what futility you have created all men!
What man can live and not see death,
or save himself from the power of the grave*o*?   *Selah*
O Lord, where is your former great love,
which in your faithfulness you swore to David?
Remember, Lord, how your servant has*p* been mocked,
how I bear in my heart the taunts of all the nations,
the taunts with which your enemies have mocked, O LORD,

*o*Hebrew *Sheol*   *p*Or *your servants have*

with which they have mocked every step of your
   anointed one.

   Praise be to the LORD forever!

      Amen and Amen.

Nation's prayer is like that of an afflicted man.

Psa. 102

A prayer of an afflicted man. When he is faint and pours out his lament before
the LORD.

Hear my prayer, O LORD;
   let my cry for help come to you.
Do not hide your face from me
   when I am in distress.
Turn your ear to me;
   when I call, answer me quickly.

For my days vanish like smoke;
   my bones burn like glowing embers.
My heart is blighted and withered like grass;
   I forget to eat my food.
Because of my loud groaning
   I am reduced to skin and bones.
I am like a desert owl,
   like an owl among the ruins.
I lie awake; I have become
   like a bird alone on a roof.
All day long my enemies taunt me;
   those who rail against me use my name as a curse.
For I eat ashes as my food
   and mingle my drink with tears
because of your great wrath,
   for you have taken me up and thrown me aside.
My days are like the evening shadow;
   I wither away like grass.

But you, O LORD, sit enthroned forever;
   your renown endures through all generations.
You will arise and have compassion on Zion,
   for it is time to show favor to her;
   the appointed time has come.
For her stones are dear to your servants;
   her very dust moves them to pity.
The nations will fear the name of the LORD,
   all the kings of the earth will revere your glory.
For the LORD will rebuild Zion
   and appear in his glory.
He will respond to the prayer of the destitute;
   he will not despise their plea.

Let this be written for a future generation,
   that a people not yet created may praise the LORD:
"The LORD looked down from his sanctuary on high,
   from heaven he viewed the earth,

to hear the groans of the prisoners
  and release those condemned to death."
So the name of the LORD will be declared in Zion
  and his praise in Jerusalem
when the peoples and the kingdoms
  assemble to worship the LORD.

In the course of my life*q* he broke my strength;
  he cut short my days.
So I said:
  "Do not take me away, O my God, in the midst of my
    days;
  your years go on through all generations.
In the beginning you laid the foundations of the earth,
  and the heavens are the work of your hands.
They will perish, but you remain;
  they will all wear out like a garment.
Like clothing you will change them
  and they will be discarded.
But you remain the same,
  and your years will never end.
The children of your servants will live in your presence;
  their descendants will be established before you."

Psa. 106

Israel's history and prayer for people's return.

Praise the LORD.*r*

Give thanks to the LORD, for he is good;
  his love endures forever.
Who can proclaim the mighty acts of the LORD
  or fully declare his praise?
Blessed are they who maintain justice,
  who constantly do what is right.
Remember me, O LORD, when you show favor to your
    people,
  come to my aid when you save them,
that I may enjoy the prosperity of your chosen ones,
  that I may share in the joy of your nation
  and join your inheritance in giving praise.

We have sinned, even as our fathers did;
  we have done wrong and acted wickedly.
When our fathers were in Egypt,
  they gave no thought to your miracles;
they did not remember your many kindnesses,
  and they rebelled by the sea, the Red Sea.*s*
Yet he saved them for his name's sake,
  to make his mighty power known.
He rebuked the Red Sea, and it dried up;
  he led them through the depths as through a desert.

---

*q*Or *By his power*   *r*Hebrew *Hallelu Yah*   *s*Hebrew *Yam Suph*; that is, Sea of Reeds

He saved them from the hand of the foe;
    from the hand of the enemy he redeemed them.
The waters covered their adversaries;
    not one of them survived.
Then they believed his promises
    and sang his praise.

But they soon forgot what he had done
    and did not wait for his counsel.
In the desert they gave in to their craving;
    in the wasteland they put God to the test.
So he gave them what they asked for,
    but sent a wasting disease upon them.

In the camp they grew envious of Moses
    and of Aaron, who was consecrated to the LORD.
The earth opened up and swallowed Dathan;
    it buried the company of Abiram.
Fire blazed among their followers;
    a flame consumed the wicked.

At Horeb they made a calf
    and worshiped an idol cast from metal.
They exchanged their Glory
    for an image of a bull, which eats grass.
They forgot the God who saved them,
    who had done great things in Egypt,
miracles in the land of Ham
    and awesome deeds by the Red Sea.
So he said he would destroy them—
    had not Moses, his chosen one,
stood in the breach before him
    to keep his wrath from destroying them.

Then they despised the pleasant land;
    they did not believe his promise.
They grumbled in their tents
    and did not obey the LORD.
So he swore to them with uplifted hand
    that he would make them fall in the desert,
make their descendants fall among the nations
    and scatter them throughout the lands.

They yoked themselves to the Baal of Peor
    and ate sacrifices offered to lifeless gods;
they provoked the LORD to anger by their wicked deeds,
    and a plague broke out among them.
But Phinehas stood up and intervened,
    and the plague was checked.
This was credited to him as righteousness
    for endless generations to come.

By the waters of Meribah they angered the LORD,
    and trouble came to Moses because of them;
for they rebelled against the Spirit of God,

and rash words came from Moses' lips.[t]

They did not destroy the peoples
    as the LORD had commanded them,
but they mingled with the nations
    and adopted their customs.
They worshiped their idols,
    which became a snare to them.
They sacrificed their sons
    and their daughters to demons.
They shed innocent blood,
    the blood of their sons and daughters,
whom they sacrificed to the idols of Canaan,
    and the land was desecrated by their blood.
They defiled themselves by what they did;
    by their deeds they prostituted themselves.

Therefore the LORD was angry with his people
    and abhorred his inheritance.
He handed them over to the nations,
    and their foes ruled over them.
Their enemies oppressed them
    and subjected them to their power.
Many times he delivered them,
    but they were bent on rebellion
    and they wasted away in their sin.

But he took note of their distress
    when he heard their cry;
for their sake he remembered his covenant
    and out of his great love he relented.
He caused them to be pitied
    by all who held them captive.

Save us, O LORD our God,
    and gather us from the nations,
that we may give thanks to your holy name
    and glory in your praise.

Praise be to the LORD, the God of Israel,
    from everlasting to everlasting.
Let all the people say, "Amen!"

Praise the LORD.

Psa. 123   **Prayer for mercy.**

A song of ascents.

I lift up my eyes to you,
    to you whose throne is in heaven.
As the eyes of slaves look to the hand of their master,
    as the eyes of a maid look to the hand of her mistress,
so our eyes look to the LORD our God,
    till he shows us his mercy.

[t]Or *against his spirit, / and rash words came from his lips*

Have mercy on us, O LORD, have mercy on us,
  for we have endured much contempt.
We have endured much ridicule from the proud,
  much contempt from the arrogant.

Lament in Babylon.   Psa. 137

By the rivers of Babylon we sat and wept
  when we remembered Zion.
There on the poplars
  we hung our harps,
for there our captors asked us for songs,
  our tormentors demanded songs of joy;
  they said, "Sing us one of the songs of Zion!"

How can we sing the songs of the LORD
  while in a foreign land?
If I forget you, O Jerusalem,
  may my right hand forget ⌊its skill⌋.
May my tongue cling to the roof of my mouth
  if I do not remember you,
  if I do not consider Jerusalem
  my highest joy.

Remember, O LORD, what the Edomites did
  on the day Jerusalem fell.
"Tear it down," they cried,
  "tear it down to its foundations!"

O Daughter of Babylon, doomed to destruction,
  happy is he who repays you
  for what you have done to us—
he who seizes your infants
  and dashes them against the rocks.

Daniel's Apocalyptic Visions

*I*t has been perhaps ten to twelve years since anything has been heard from Daniel, God's captive servant who was put into the service of King Nebuchadnezzar as a young man. During this time Daniel has achieved great respect in the royal palace, primarily due to his successful interpretation of various dreams and riddles. Now in his later years, Daniel has served a succession of Babylonian leaders. After Nebuchadnezzar came his son, Evil-Merodach, who reigned only about two years (ca. 561-559 B.C.) before being assassinated by his brother-in-law, Neriglissar. Neriglissar ruled for four years (ca. 559-555 B.C.). His reign was followed very briefly by Labashi-Marduk (ca. 555 B.C.) before a usurper named Nabonidus took the throne (ca. 555 B.C.). Although Nabonidus will technically be the ruler of Babylonia until about 539 B.C., he earlier removed himself to northern Arabia when he was strongly opposed by priests of Marduk, who objected to his introduction of the moon-god, Sin. In 552 B.C. his son Belshazzar became a co-regent and now rules the rapidly declining empire.

During the first and third years of Belshazzar's rule, Daniel has two of the most amazing prophetic dreams since Ezekiel's vision of the great battle against Gog and the hordes of evil. Interestingly, there are events and characters in Daniel's dreams which seem to correspond with things Ezekiel saw in his great temple vision. The first dream shows four beasts which, as Daniel is told, represent the four kingdoms prior to the kingdom of the Most High. The second dream pictures a battle between a ram and a goat. It apparently has to do with the time when one will challenge the Prince of Princes.

Various themes are evident. Throughout the universe, just as between warring nations, there is an ongoing battle between the forces of good and evil, between God and Satan, between justice and injustice, between morality and immorality. And the same battle is waged within every individual. While evil brings about its own destruction even now, there will come a time when the great destruction of evil and its champions will take place. It will be a final destruction, giving way to a permanent state of peace and righteousness in the eternal kingdom of God.

Dan.
7:1-14
(552 B.C.)

DREAM OF FOUR BEASTS.   In the first year of Belshazzar king of Babylon, Daniel had a dream, and visions passed through his mind as he was lying on his bed. He wrote down the substance of his dream.

Daniel said: "In my vision at night I looked, and there before me were the four winds of heaven churning up the great sea. Four great beasts, each different from the others, came up out of the sea.

"The first was like a lion, and it had the wings of an eagle. I watched until its wings were torn off and it was lifted from the ground so that it stood on two feet like a man, and the heart of a man was given to it.

"And there before me was a second beast, which looked like a bear. It was raised up on one of its sides, and it had three ribs in its mouth between its teeth. It was told, 'Get up and eat your fill of flesh!'

"After that, I looked, and there before me was another beast, one that looked like a leopard. And on its back it had four wings like those of a bird. This beast had four heads, and it was given authority to rule.

"After that, in my vision at night I looked, and there before me was a fourth beast—terrifying and frightening and very powerful. It had large iron teeth; it crushed and devoured its victims and trampled underfoot whatever was left. It was different from all the former beasts, and it had ten horns.

"While I was thinking about the horns, there before me was another horn, a little one, which came up among them; and three of the first horns were uprooted before it. This horn had eyes like the eyes of a man and a mouth that spoke boastfully.

"As I looked,

"thrones were set in place,
    and the Ancient of Days took his seat.
His clothing was as white as snow;
    the hair of his head was white like wool.
His throne was flaming with fire,
    and its wheels were all ablaze.
A river of fire was flowing,
    coming out from before him.

Thousands upon thousands attended him;
  ten thousand times ten thousand stood before him.
The court was seated,
  and the books were opened.

"Then I continued to watch because of the boastful words the horn was speaking. I kept looking until the beast was slain and its body destroyed and thrown into the blazing fire. (The other beasts had been stripped of their authority, but were allowed to live for a period of time.)

"In my vision at night I looked, and there before me was one like a son of man, coming with the clouds of heaven. He approached the Ancient of Days and was led into his presence. He was given authority, glory and sovereign power; all peoples, nations and men of every language worshiped him. His dominion is an everlasting dominion that will not pass away, and his kingdom is one that will never be destroyed.

THE INTERPRETATION.   "I, Daniel, was troubled in spirit, and the visions that passed through my mind disturbed me. I approached one of those standing there and asked him the true meaning of all this.

"So he told me and gave me the interpretation of these things: 'The four great beasts are four kingdoms that will rise from the earth. But the saints of the Most High will receive the kingdom and will possess it forever— yes, for ever and ever.'

Dan.
7:15-18

DANIEL'S FURTHER QUESTIONS.   "Then I wanted to know the true meaning of the fourth beast, which was different from all the others and most terrifying, with its iron teeth and bronze claws—the beast that crushed and devoured its victims and trampled underfoot whatever was left. I also wanted to know about the ten horns on its head and about the other horn that came up, before which three of them fell—the horn that looked more imposing than the others and that had eyes and a mouth that spoke boastfully. As I watched, this horn was waging war against the saints and defeating them, until the Ancient of Days came and pronounced judgment in favor of the saints of the Most High, and the time came when they possessed the kingdom.

Dan.
7:19-22

FURTHER EXPLANATION.   "He gave me this explanation: 'The fourth beast is a fourth kingdom that will appear on earth. It will be different from all the other kingdoms and will devour the whole earth, trampling it down and crushing it. The ten horns are ten kings who will come from this kingdom. After them another king will arise, different from the earlier ones; he will subdue three kings. He will speak against the Most High and oppress his saints and try to change the set times and the laws. The saints will be handed over to him for a time, times and half a time.ᵘ

Dan.
7:23-27

" 'But the court will sit, and his power will be taken away and completely destroyed forever. Then the sovereignty, power and greatness of the kingdoms under the whole heaven will be handed over to the saints, the people of the Most High. His kingdom will be an everlasting kingdom, and all rulers will worship and obey him.'

DANIEL TROUBLED.   "This is the end of the matter. I, Daniel, was deeply troubled by my thoughts, and my face turned pale, but I kept the matter to myself."

Dan. 7:28

ᵘOr for a year, two years and half a year

Dan.
8:1-14
(549 B.C.)

VISION OF RAM AND GOAT.   In the third year of King Belshazzar's reign, I, Daniel, had a vision, after the one that had already appeared to me. In my vision I saw myself in the citadel of Susa in the province of Elam; in the vision I was beside the Ulai Canal. I looked up, and there before me was a ram with two horns, standing beside the canal, and the horns were long. One of the horns was longer than the other but grew up later. I watched the ram as he charged toward the west and the north and the south. No animal could stand against him, and none could rescue from his power. He did as he pleased and became great.

As I was thinking about this, suddenly a goat with a prominent horn between his eyes came from the west, crossing the whole earth without touching the ground. He came toward the two-horned ram I had seen standing beside the canal and charged at him in great rage. I saw him attack the ram furiously, striking the ram and shattering his two horns. The ram was powerless to stand against him; the goat knocked him to the ground and trampled on him, and none could rescue the ram from his power. The goat became very great, but at the height of his power his large horn was broken off, and in its place four prominent horns grew up toward the four winds of heaven.

Out of one of them came another horn, which started small but grew in power to the south and to the east and toward the Beautiful Land. It grew until it reached the host of the heavens, and it threw some of the starry host down to the earth and trampled on them. It set itself up to be as great as the Prince of the host; it took away the daily sacrifice from him, and the place of his sanctuary was brought low. Because of rebellion, the host ⸢of the saints⸣^{v} and the daily sacrifice were given over to it. It prospered in everything it did, and truth was thrown to the ground.

Then I heard a holy one speaking, and another holy one said to him, "How long will it take for the vision to be fulfilled—the vision concerning the daily sacrifice, the rebellion that causes desolation, and the surrender of the sanctuary and of the host that will be trampled underfoot?"

He said to me, "It will take 2,300 evenings and mornings; then the sanctuary will be reconsecrated."

Dan.
8:15-26

INTERPRETATION GIVEN.   While I, Daniel, was watching the vision and trying to understand it, there before me stood one who looked like a man. And I heard a man's voice from the Ulai calling, "Gabriel, tell this man the meaning of the vision."

As he came near the place where I was standing, I was terrified and fell prostrate. "Son of man," he said to me, "understand that the vision concerns the time of the end."

While he was speaking to me, I was in a deep sleep, with my face to the ground. Then he touched me and raised me to my feet.

He said: "I am going to tell you what will happen later in the time of wrath, because the vision concerns the appointed time of the end.^{w} The two-horned ram that you saw represents the kings of Media and Persia. The shaggy goat is the king of Greece, and the large horn between his eyes is the first king. The four horns that replaced the one that was broken off represent four kingdoms that will emerge from his nation but will not have the same power.

^{v}Or *rebellion, the armies* ^{w}Or *because the end will be at the appointed time*

"In the latter part of their reign, when rebels have become completely wicked, a stern-faced king, a master of intrigue, will arise. He will become very strong, but not by his own power. He will cause astounding devastation and will succeed in whatever he does. He will destroy the mighty men and the holy people. He will cause deceit to prosper, and he will consider himself superior. When they feel secure, he will destroy many and take his stand against the Prince of princes. Yet he will be destroyed, but not by human power.

"The vision of the evenings and mornings that has been given you is true, but seal up the vision, for it concerns the distant future."

DANIEL MYSTIFIED.   I, Daniel, was exhausted and lay ill for several   Dan. 8:27
days. Then I got up and went about the king's business. I was appalled by
the vision; it was beyond understanding.

Daniel himself did not know exactly what to make of all that he had seen, and any difficult questions which the visions may raise should not obscure the more obvious message of hope which the visions clearly bring.

The Writing on the Wall

Over the next seven years Daniel again slips into obscurity in Belshazzar's palace. Then, on the occasion of a great banquet at which there is excessive drunkenness, praise of lesser gods, and defilement of goblets taken from Solomon's temple, Belshazzar sees a finger writing something unintelligible on the wall. When Daniel is finally called to interpret it, the message is that Belshazzar's arrogance has cost him his life. As if to stave off God's judgment, Belshazzar elevates Daniel to the third-highest position in his government. But by the end of the night Belshazzar is dead.

BANQUET AND REVELRY.   King Belshazzar gave a great banquet for a   Dan. 5:1-4
thousand of his nobles and drank wine with them. While Belshazzar was   (542 B.C.)
drinking his wine, he gave orders to bring in the gold and silver goblets
that Nebuchadnezzar his father[x] had taken from the temple in Jerusalem,
so that the king and his nobles, his wives and his concubines might drink
from them. So they brought in the gold goblets that had been taken from
the temple of God in Jerusalem, and the king and his nobles, his wives and
his concubines drank from them. As they drank the wine, they praised the
gods of gold and silver, of bronze, iron, wood and stone.

WRITING ON WALL.   Suddenly the fingers of a human hand appeared   Dan. 5:5,6
and wrote on the plaster of the wall, near the lampstand in the royal
palace. The king watched the hand as it wrote. His face turned pale and he
was so frightened that his knees knocked together and his legs gave way.

WISE MEN CANNOT INTERPRET.   The king called out for the enchant-   Dan. 5:7-9
ers, astrologers[y] and diviners to be brought and said to these wise men of
Babylon, "Whoever reads this writing and tells me what it means will be
clothed in purple and have a gold chain placed around his neck, and he
will be made the third highest ruler in the kingdom."

[x]Or ancestor; or predecessor   [y]Or Chaldeans

Then all the king's wise men came in, but they could not read the writing or tell the king what it meant. So King Belshazzar became even more terrified and his face grew more pale. His nobles were baffled.

Dan.
5:10-16
DANIEL BROUGHT IN.   The queen,[z] hearing the voices of the king and his nobles, came into the banquet hall. "O king, live forever!" she said. "Don't be alarmed! Don't look so pale! There is a man in your kingdom who has the spirit of the holy gods in him. In the time of your father he was found to have insight and intelligence and wisdom like that of the gods. King Nebuchadnezzar your father—your father the king, I say— appointed him chief of the magicians, enchanters, astrologers and diviners. This man Daniel, whom the king called Belteshazzar, was found to have a keen mind and knowledge and understanding, and also the ability to interpret dreams, explain riddles and solve difficult problems. Call for Daniel, and he will tell you what the writing means."

So Daniel was brought before the king, and the king said to him, "Are you Daniel, one of the exiles my father the king brought from Judah? I have heard that the spirit of the gods is in you and that you have insight, intelligence and outstanding wisdom. The wise men and enchanters were brought before me to read this writing and tell me what it means, but they could not explain it. Now I have heard that you are able to give interpretations and to solve difficult problems. If you can read this writing and tell me what it means, you will be clothed in purple and have a gold chain placed around your neck, and you will be made the third highest ruler in the kingdom."

Dan.
5:17-23
REASON FOR WRITING.   Then Daniel answered the king, "You may keep your gifts for yourself and give your rewards to someone else. Nevertheless, I will read the writing for the king and tell him what it means.

"O king, the Most High God gave your father Nebuchadnezzar sovereignty and greatness and glory and splendor. Because of the high position he gave him, all the peoples and nations and men of every language dreaded and feared him. Those the king wanted to put to death, he put to death; those he wanted to spare, he spared; those he wanted to promote, he promoted; and those he wanted to humble, he humbled. But when his heart became arrogant and hardened with pride, he was deposed from his royal throne and stripped of his glory. He was driven away from people and given the mind of an animal; he lived with the wild donkeys and ate grass like cattle; and his body was drenched with the dew of heaven, until he acknowledged that the Most High God is sovereign over the kingdoms of men and sets over them anyone he wishes.

"But you his son,[a] O Belshazzar, have not humbled yourself, though you knew all this. Instead, you have set yourself up against the Lord of heaven. You had the goblets from his temple brought to you, and you and your nobles, your wives and your concubines drank wine from them. You praised the gods of silver and gold, of bronze, iron, wood and stone, which cannot see or hear or understand. But you did not honor the God who holds in his hand your life and all your ways.

Dan.
5:24-28
WRITING INTERPRETED.   Therefore he sent the hand that wrote the inscription.

[z]Or *queen mother*   [a]Or *descendant*; or *successor*

"This is the inscription that was written:

MENE, MENE, TEKEL, PARSIN[b]

"This is what these words mean:

Mene[c]: God has numbered the days of your reign and brought it to an end.
Tekel[d]: You have been weighed on the scales and found wanting.
Peres[e]: Your kingdom is divided and given to the Medes and Persians."

DANIEL ELEVATED.   Then at Belshazzar's command, Daniel was   Dan. 5:29
clothed in purple, a gold chain was placed around his neck, and he was
proclaimed the third highest ruler in the kingdom.

BELSHAZZAR KILLED.   That very night Belshazzar, king of the Babylo-   Dan.
nians,[f] was slain, and Darius the Mede took over the kingdom, at the age   5:30,31
of sixty-two.

Who actually killed Belshazzar is not known, but presumably it was Darius the Mede. Yet that only compounds the issue, because the identity of Darius is itself unclear. He is definitely not the great Darius of Persia who will come to power some 20 years later. Most speculation centers on a man by the name of Gobryas (or Gubaru), who is sometimes identified as an ally of Cyrus and the governor of the Gutium peoples, who took Babylon from the Babylonians. Whoever he might actually be, this Darius the Mede will have control of the nation for about three years before he sees his own writing on the wall, as it were, and virtually hands Babylonia over to the ascending Persian Empire.

The Seventy "Sevens"

ometime during the first year of Darius the Mede's reign, Daniel reads a copy of Jeremiah's prophecies. Evidently copies have been circulating among the exiles ever since Baruch penned the last words on the third scroll 20 years earlier. Daniel is particularly moved by the recitation of Israel's sins and the 70-year exile which Jeremiah predicted. Here in 542 B.C., 63 years have passed since Daniel and other exiles were taken in the first deportation, in 605 B.C. Realizing that the prophecy indicates still another seven years before the promised restoration is to begin, Daniel turns to God in prayer. Here now is his prayer in which he not only confesses his own sins, but also those of his fellow sons of Israel.

DANIEL READS JEREMIAH.   In the first year of Darius son of Xerxes[g]   Dan. 9:1,2
(a Mede by descent), who was made ruler over the Babylonian[h] king-   (542 B.C.)
dom—in the first year of his reign, I, Daniel, understood from the
Scriptures, according to the word of the LORD given to Jeremiah the
prophet, that the desolation of Jerusalem would last seventy years.

[b]Aramaic *UPARSIN* (that is, *AND PARSIN*)   [c]*Mene* can mean *numbered* or *mina* (a unit of money).   [d]*Tekel* can mean *weighed* or *shekel*.   [e]*Peres* (the singular of *Parsin*) can mean *divided* or *Persia* or *a half mina* or *a half shekel*.   [f]Or *Chaldeans*   [g]Hebrew *Ahasuerus*   [h]Or *Chaldean*

Dan.
9:3-19

DANIEL'S PRAYER.   So I turned to the Lord God and pleaded with him in prayer and petition, in fasting, and in sackcloth and ashes.

I prayed to the LORD my God and confessed:

"O Lord, the great and awesome God, who keeps his covenant of love with all who love him and obey his commands, we have sinned and done wrong. We have been wicked and have rebelled; we have turned away from your commands and laws. We have not listened to your servants the prophets, who spoke in your name to our kings, our princes and our fathers, and to all the people of the land.

"Lord, you are righteous, but this day we are covered with shame—the men of Judah and people of Jerusalem and all Israel, both near and far, in all the countries where you have scattered us because of our unfaithfulness to you. O LORD, we and our kings, our princes and our fathers are covered with shame because we have sinned against you. The Lord our God is merciful and forgiving, even though we have rebelled against him; we have not obeyed the LORD our God or kept the laws he gave us through his servants the prophets. All Israel has transgressed your law and turned away, refusing to obey you.

"Therefore the curses and sworn judgments written in the Law of Moses, the servant of God, have been poured out on us, because we have sinned against you. You have fulfilled the words spoken against us and against our rulers by bringing upon us great disaster. Under the whole heaven nothing has ever been done like what has been done to Jerusalem. Just as it is written in the Law of Moses, all this disaster has come upon us, yet we have not sought the favor of the LORD our God by turning from our sins and giving attention to your truth. The LORD did not hesitate to bring the disaster upon us, for the LORD our God is righteous in everything he does; yet we have not obeyed him.

"Now, O Lord our God, who brought your people out of Egypt with a mighty hand and who made for yourself a name that endures to this day, we have sinned, we have done wrong. O Lord, in keeping with all your righteous acts, turn away your anger and your wrath from Jerusalem, your city, your holy hill. Our sins and the iniquities of our fathers have made Jerusalem and your people an object of scorn to all those around us.

"Now, our God, hear the prayers and petitions of your servant. For your sake, O Lord, look with favor on your desolate sanctuary. Give ear, O God, and hear; open your eyes and see the desolation of the city that bears your Name. We do not make requests of you because we are righteous, but because of your great mercy. O Lord, listen! O Lord, forgive! O Lord, hear and act! For your sake, O my God, do not delay, because your city and your people bear your Name."

One of the most intriguing passages of all Scripture follows this account of Daniel's beautiful prayer of contrition. As Daniel is in his period of prayer, he is approached by the angel Gabriel, whom he recognizes from earlier visions. Gabriel brings a message about seventy "sevens," a message which apparently speaks in response to Daniel's concern about the restoration. There is general consensus that each "seven" represents a week of years—that is, seven years. From that point forward much discussion has ensued.

The first seven "sevens," or 49 years, may well have reference to the time it will take to rebuild the city of Jerusalem. But the particular decree setting that time period into motion is much debated in light of the various decrees which will issue concerning Jerusalem's reconstruction.

The second set of "sevens," the 62 "sevens," has apparent reference to the coming of the Messiah. (The Hebrew text says there are 69 "sevens," whereas the number used in most translations is 62, which may or may not simply be 69 less the first seven "sevens.") This would set the Messiah's coming at roughly 550 years from the time of Daniel.

As with the preceding weeks, the final week, or last seven years, has also been the subject of much discussion. Some believe it represents the beginning of the Messiah's church and the apostolic age. Others believe it foretells a seven-year period during which time God will reestablish Israel as his covenant people prior to the Messiah's second advent. What all agree on is the fact that God is working purposely in history on the behalf of his righteous ones.

GABRIEL APPEARS TO DANIEL.   While I was speaking and praying, confessing my sin and the sin of my people Israel and making my request to the LORD my God for his holy hill—while I was still in prayer, Gabriel, the man I had seen in the earlier vision, came to me in swift flight about the time of the evening sacrifice. He instructed me and said to me, "Daniel, I have now come to give you insight and understanding. As soon as you began to pray, an answer was given, which I have come to tell you, for you are highly esteemed. Therefore, consider the message and understand the vision:

Dan. 9:20-23 (542 B.C.)

THE SEVENTY "SEVENS."   "Seventy 'sevens'[i] are decreed for your people and your holy city to finish[j] transgression, to put an end to sin, to atone for wickedness, to bring in everlasting righteousness, to seal up vision and prophecy and to anoint the most holy.[k]

"Know and understand this: From the issuing of the decree[l] to restore and rebuild Jerusalem until the Anointed One,[m] the ruler, comes, there will be seven 'sevens,' and sixty-two 'sevens.' It will be rebuilt with streets and a trench, but in times of trouble.

Dan. 9:24,25

GABRIEL'S EXPLANATION.   After the sixty-two 'sevens,' the Anointed One will be cut off and will have nothing.[n] The people of the ruler who will come will destroy the city and the sanctuary. The end will come like a flood: War will continue until the end, and desolations have been decreed. He will confirm a covenant with many for one 'seven.'[o] In the middle of the 'seven'[o] he will put an end to sacrifice and offering. And on a wing ˻of the temple˼ he will set up an abomination that causes desolation, until the end that is decreed is poured out on him.[p]" [q]

Dan. 9:26,27

◈

[i]Or 'weeks'   [j]Or restrain   [k]Or Most Holy Place; or most holy One   [l]Or word   [m]Or an anointed one   [n]Or off and will have no one; or off, but not for himself   [o]Or 'week'   [p]Or it   [q]Or And one who causes desolation will come upon the pinnacle of the abominable ˻temple˼, until the end that is decreed is poured out on the desolated ˻city˼

Daniel in the Lions' Den

Sometime later during the reign of Darius the Mede, a plot is laid against Daniel by those opposed to his rise to greater power. The end result is that Daniel is placed in a den of lions but saved from harm by the God to whom he faithfully prays. The incident allows an interesting insight into Darius, who (at least for a time) is even evangelistic on behalf of this marvelous "God of Daniel."

**Dan. 6:1-3
(Ca.
541-540
B.C.)**

DANIEL'S HIGH RANK.   It pleased Darius to appoint 120 satraps to rule throughout the kingdom, with three administrators over them, one of whom was Daniel. The satraps were made accountable to them so that the king might not suffer loss. Now Daniel so distinguished himself among the administrators and the satraps by his exceptional qualities that the king planned to set him over the whole kingdom.

Dan. 6:4,5

CONSPIRATORS PLOT TRAP.   At this, the administrators and the satraps tried to find grounds for charges against Daniel in his conduct of government affairs, but they were unable to do so. They could find no corruption in him, because he was trustworthy and neither corrupt nor negligent. Finally these men said, "We will never find any basis for charges against this man Daniel unless it has something to do with the law of his God."

Dan. 6:6-9

DECREE AGAINST PRAYERS.   So the administrators and the satraps went as a group to the king and said: "O King Darius, live forever! The royal administrators, prefects, satraps, advisers and governors have all agreed that the king should issue an edict and enforce the decree that anyone who prays to any god or man during the next thirty days, except to you, O king, shall be thrown into the lions' den. Now, O king, issue the decree and put it in writing so that it cannot be altered—in accordance with the laws of the Medes and Persians, which cannot be repealed." So King Darius put the decree in writing.

Dan. 6:10

DANIEL PRAYS ANYWAY.   Now when Daniel learned that the decree had been published, he went home to his upstairs room where the windows opened toward Jerusalem. Three times a day he got down on his knees and prayed, giving thanks to his God, just as he had done before.

**Dan.
6:11-15**

KING TOLD ABOUT DANIEL.   Then these men went as a group and found Daniel praying and asking God for help. So they went to the king and spoke to him about his royal decree: "Did you not publish a decree that during the next thirty days anyone who prays to any god or man except to you, O king, would be thrown into the lions' den?"

The king answered, "The decree stands—in accordance with the laws of the Medes and Persians, which cannot be repealed."

Then they said to the king, "Daniel, who is one of the exiles from Judah, pays no attention to you, O king, or to the decree you put in writing. He still prays three times a day." When the king heard this, he was greatly distressed; he was determined to rescue Daniel and made every effort until sundown to save him.

Then the men went as a group to the king and said to him, "Remember, O king, that according to the law of the Medes and Persians no decree or edict that the king issues can be changed."

DANIEL IN LIONS' DEN.   So the king gave the order, and they brought Daniel and threw him into the lions' den. The king said to Daniel, "May your God, whom you serve continually, rescue you!"

Dan. 6:16-18

A stone was brought and placed over the mouth of the den, and the king sealed it with his own signet ring and with the rings of his nobles, so that Daniel's situation might not be changed. Then the king returned to his palace and spent the night without eating and without any entertainment being brought to him. And he could not sleep.

DANIEL UNHARMED.   At the first light of dawn, the king got up and hurried to the lions' den. When he came near the den, he called to Daniel in an anguished voice, "Daniel, servant of the living God, has your God, whom you serve continually, been able to rescue you from the lions?"

Dan. 6:19-23

Daniel answered, "O king, live forever! My God sent his angel, and he shut the mouths of the lions. They have not hurt me, because I was found innocent in his sight. Nor have I ever done any wrong before you, O king."

The king was overjoyed and gave orders to lift Daniel out of the den. And when Daniel was lifted from the den, no wound was found on him, because he had trusted in his God.

CONSPIRATORS KILLED.   At the king's command, the men who had falsely accused Daniel were brought in and thrown into the lions' den, along with their wives and children. And before they reached the floor of the den, the lions overpowered them and crushed all their bones.

Dan. 6:24

KING'S DECREE.   Then King Darius wrote to all the peoples, nations and men of every language throughout the land:

Dan. 6:25-27

"May you prosper greatly!

"I issue a decree that in every part of my kingdom people must fear and reverence the God of Daniel.

> "For he is the living God
>   and he endures forever;
> his kingdom will not be destroyed,
>   his dominion will never end.
> He rescues and he saves;
>   he performs signs and wonders
>   in the heavens and on the earth.
> He has rescued Daniel
>   from the power of the lions."

Darius' enthusiasm for the "God of Daniel" is evidently not long-lived. There is no evidence that Babylon did in fact turn to God. On the contrary, it appears that Darius' character is so unaffected that he betrays his own nation. Realizing Babylonia's now-weakened condition against the power of Persia, Darius deserts to Cyrus and helps bring about the final overthrow of the very nation he has ruled. Since Nabonidus has gotten into such a drunken state while in exile that he cannot raise a defense, Cyrus walks into Babylon without any opposition and is hailed as king of Babylonia.

So ends the power of the great Babylonian Empire, just as the prophets had foretold. Never again will it rise to a position of great power. Concurrent with the change of rule in Babylon, Daniel leaves the palace and his position of governmental prominence.

Dan. 1:21   KING'S SERVICE ENDS.   And Daniel remained there until the first year of King Cyrus.

And yet apparently Daniel finds favor under the new Persian government as well.

Dan. 6:28   DANIEL'S FATE.   So Daniel prospered during the reign of Darius and the reign of Cyrus[r] the Persian.

What Daniel does from this point on is unknown, but presumably he remains in Babylon. He will be heard from once again after a period of two or three years.

[r]Or Darius, that is, the reign of Cyrus

PERIOD OF RESTORATION
(Ca. 535-425 B.C.)

First Return to Jerusalem

*T*he rise of the Persian Empire will prove to be a real blessing to the exiled nation of Israel. Unlike the Assyrians and Babylonians, who believed in the uprooting of their captives, Persia's policy is one of repatriation and maintaining the status quo of the political, social, and religious situation to the extent possible. The idea, apparently, is that a happy people will be less likely to rebel. For that reason, as well as for the fulfillment of God's promised restoration, a very important step is taken by Cyrus the Great in 539-538 B.C. He issues the following decree encouraging volunteers among the Hebrews to return to Jerusalem and rebuild the temple.

CYRUS' DECREE.   In the first year of Cyrus king of Persia, in order to fulfill the word of the LORD spoken by Jeremiah, the LORD moved the heart of Cyrus king of Persia to make a proclamation throughout his realm and to put it in writing:

Ezra 1:1-4
2 Chron.
36:22,23
(539-538 B.C.)

"This is what Cyrus king of Persia says:

" 'The LORD, the God of heaven, has given me all the kingdoms of the earth and he has appointed me to build a temple for him at Jerusalem in Judah. Anyone of his people among you—may his God be with him, and let him go up to Jerusalem in Judah and build the temple of the LORD, the God of Israel, the God who is in Jerusalem. And the people of any place where survivors may now be living are to provide him with silver and gold, with goods and livestock, and with freewill offerings for the temple of God in Jerusalem.' "

Imagine the excitement and celebration which must come when the news of this decree makes its way to all the captives in exile! And yet there is an immediate dilemma. After over six decades away from their homeland, the people of Israel are pretty well entrenched in the Babylonian-turned-Persian society. Those who took Jeremiah's advice have bought or built homes, begun businesses, and learned a new language and way of life. There is also a whole new generation of Jews, as they are now called, who have never even set foot in Palestine. Therefore it will take a real pioneering spirit to leave a prosperous situation for the desolation of the Palestinian landscape.

Despite the hard decision, over 42,000 decide to return under the leadership of Sheshbazzar, who is appointed governor. Relatives and neighbors give what they can to support the resettlement and reconstruction programs. Even Cyrus assists by returning the temple articles which Nebuchadnezzar had looted. All is set, and the great migration takes place in 538 B.C. Within two years, in 536 B.C., the initial resettlement has been completed and the foundation of the temple laid—70 years after the first deportation, in 605 B.C.! And yet, even as they get started, the people are met with opposition. Restoration will not come easily.

Ezra 1:5,6
(538 B.C.)
Babylonia

RESETTLEMENT PREPARATIONS. Then the family heads of Judah and Benjamin, and the priests and Levites—everyone whose heart God had moved—prepared to go up and build the house of the LORD in Jerusalem. All their neighbors assisted them with articles of silver and gold, with goods and livestock, and with valuable gifts, in addition to all the freewill offerings.

Ezra 1:7-11

TEMPLE ARTICLES RETURNED. Moreover, King Cyrus brought out the articles belonging to the temple of the LORD, which Nebuchadnezzar had carried away from Jerusalem and had placed in the temple of his god.[a] Cyrus king of Persia had them brought by Mithredath the treasurer, who counted them out to Sheshbazzar the prince of Judah.

This was the inventory:

gold dishes	30
silver dishes	1,000
silver pans[b]	29
gold bowls	30
matching silver bowls	410
other articles	1,000

In all, there were 5,400 articles of gold and of silver. Sheshbazzar brought all these along when the exiles came up from Babylon to Jerusalem.

Ezra 2:1-35

LIST OF RETURNING EXILES. Now these are the people of the province who came up from the captivity of the exiles, whom Nebuchadnezzar king of Babylon had taken captive to Babylon (they returned to Jerusalem and Judah, each to his own town, in company with Zerubbabel, Jeshua, Nehemiah, Seraiah, Reelaiah, Mordecai, Bilshan, Mispar, Bigvai, Rehum and Baanah):

The list of the men of the people of Israel:

the descendants of Parosh	2,172
of Shephatiah	372
of Arah	775
of Pahath-Moab (through the line of Jeshua and Joab)	2,812
of Elam	1,254
of Zattu	945
of Zaccai	760
of Bani	642
of Bebai	623
of Azgad	1,222
of Adonikam	666

[a]Or gods   [b]The meaning of the Hebrew for this word is uncertain.

of Bigvai	2,056
of Adin	454
of Ater (through Hezekiah)	98
of Bezai	323
of Jorah	112
of Hashum	223
of Gibbar	95

the men of Bethlehem	123
of Netophah	56
of Anathoth	128
of Azmaveth	42
of Kiriath Jearim,[c] Kephirah and Beeroth	743
of Ramah and Geba	621
of Micmash	122
of Bethel and Ai	223
of Nebo	52
of Magbish	156
of the other Elam	1,254
of Harim	320
of Lod, Hadid and Ono	725
of Jericho	345
of Senaah	3,630

The priests:

Ezra 2:36-63

the descendants of Jedaiah (through the family of Jeshua)	973
of Immer	1,052
of Pashhur	1,247
of Harim	1,017

The Levites:

the descendants of Jeshua and Kadmiel (through the line of Hodaviah)	74

The singers:

the descendants of Asaph	128

The gatekeepers of the temple:

the descendants of Shallum, Ater, Talmon, Akkub, Hatita and Shobai	139

The temple servants:

the descendants of
Ziha, Hasupha, Tabbaoth,
Keros, Siaha, Padon,
Lebanah, Hagabah, Akkub,
Hagab, Shalmai, Hanan,
Giddel, Gahar, Reaiah,
Rezin, Nekoda, Gazzam,

[c]See Septuagint (see also Neh. 7:29); Hebrew *Kiriath Arim.*

Uzza, Paseah, Besai,
Asnah, Meunim, Nephusim,
Bakbuk, Hakupha, Harhur,
Bazluth, Mehida, Harsha,
Barkos, Sisera, Temah,
Neziah and Hatipha

The descendants of the servants of Solomon:

the descendants of
Sotai, Hassophereth, Peruda,
Jaala, Darkon, Giddel,
Shephatiah, Hattil,
Pokereth-Hazzebaim and Ami

The temple servants and the descendants of the servants of
Solomon   392

The following came up from the towns of Tel Melah, Tel Harsha, Kerub, Addon and Immer, but they could not show that their families were descended from Israel:

The descendants of
Delaiah, Tobiah and Nekoda   652

And from among the priests:

The descendants of
Hobaiah, Hakkoz and Barzillai (a man who had married a
daughter of Barzillai the Gileadite and was called by that name).
These searched for their family records, but they could not find them and so were excluded from the priesthood as unclean. The governor ordered them not to eat any of the most sacred food until there was a priest ministering with the Urim and Thummim.

Ezra
2:64-67

NUMBER OF COMPANY.   The whole company numbered 42,360, besides their 7,337 menservants and maidservants; and they also had 200 men and women singers. They had 736 horses, 245 mules, 435 camels and 6,720 donkeys.

Ezra
2:68,69
Jerusalem

OFFERINGS AT JERUSALEM.   When they arrived at the house of the LORD in Jerusalem, some of the heads of the families gave freewill offerings toward the rebuilding of the house of God on its site. According to their ability they gave to the treasury for this work 61,000 drachmas[d] of gold, 5,000 minas[e] of silver and 100 priestly garments.

Ezra 2:70

SETTLERS DISPERSE.   The priests, the Levites, the singers, the gatekeepers and the temple servants settled in their own towns, along with some of the other people, and the rest of the Israelites settled in their towns.

Ezra 3:1-6

ALTAR REBUILT.   When the seventh month came and the Israelites had settled in their towns, the people assembled as one man in Jerusalem. Then Jeshua son of Jozadak and his fellow priests and Zerubbabel son of Shealtiel and his associates began to build the altar of the God of Israel to

---

[d]That is, about 1,100 pounds (about 500 kilograms)   [e]That is, about 3 tons (about 2.9
metric tons)

sacrifice burnt offerings on it, in accordance with what is written in the Law of Moses the man of God. Despite their fear of the peoples around them, they built the altar on its foundation and sacrificed burnt offerings on it to the LORD, both the morning and evening sacrifices. Then in accordance with what is written, they celebrated the Feast of Tabernacles with the required number of burnt offerings prescribed for each day. After that, they presented the regular burnt offerings, the New Moon sacrifices and the sacrifices for all the appointed sacred feasts of the LORD, as well as those brought as freewill offerings to the LORD. On the first day of the seventh month they began to offer burnt offerings to the LORD, though the foundation of the LORD's temple had not yet been laid.

PREPARATIONS FOR TEMPLE. Then they gave money to the masons and carpenters, and gave food and drink and oil to the people of Sidon and Tyre, so that they would bring cedar logs by sea from Lebanon to Joppa, as authorized by Cyrus king of Persia.

Ezra 3:7

TEMPLE FOUNDATION LAID. In the second month of the second year after their arrival at the house of God in Jerusalem, Zerubbabel son of Shealtiel, Jeshua son of Jozadak and the rest of their brothers (the priests and the Levites and all who had returned from the captivity to Jerusalem) began the work, appointing Levites twenty years of age and older to supervise the building of the house of the LORD. Jeshua and his sons and brothers and Kadmiel and his sons (descendants of Hodaviah*f*) and the sons of Henadad and their sons and brothers—all Levites—joined together in supervising those working on the house of God.

Ezra 3:8,9

CELEBRATION ENSUES. When the builders laid the foundation of the temple of the LORD, the priests in their vestments and with trumpets, and the Levites (the sons of Asaph) with cymbals, took their places to praise the LORD, as prescribed by David king of Israel. With praise and thanksgiving they sang to the LORD:

Ezra 3:10,11

> "He is good;
>   his love to Israel endures forever."

And all the people gave a great shout of praise to the LORD, because the foundation of the house of the LORD was laid.

MIXED EMOTIONS. But many of the older priests and Levites and family heads, who had seen the former temple, wept aloud when they saw the foundation of this temple being laid, while many others shouted for joy. No one could distinguish the sound of the shouts of joy from the sound of weeping, because the people made so much noise. And the sound was heard far away.

Ezra 3:12,13

ENEMIES FEIGN HELP. When the enemies of Judah and Benjamin heard that the exiles were building a temple for the LORD, the God of Israel, they came to Zerubbabel and to the heads of the families and said, "Let us help you build because, like you, we seek your God and have been sacrificing to him since the time of Esarhaddon king of Assyria, who brought us here."

But Zerubbabel, Jeshua and the rest of the heads of the families of Israel answered, "You have no part with us in building a temple to our God. We

Ezra 4:1-3

---

f Hebrew *Yehudah*, probably a variant of *Hodaviah*

alone will build it for the LORD, the God of Israel, as King Cyrus, the king of Persia, commanded us."

Ezra 4:4,5 ENEMIES DISCOURAGE PLANS.   Then the peoples around them set out to discourage the people of Judah and make them afraid to go on building.⁸ They hired counselors to work against them and frustrate their plans during the entire reign of Cyrus king of Persia and down to the reign of Darius king of Persia.

Daniel's Last Vision

*J*s it just coincidence that, in the same year the temple foundation is laid and the restoration is begun in earnest, God should bring to Daniel another amazing vision of both near and future events? This is a time of great expectations! It is a time for perspective and overview. It is a time for reassurance that God will continue to rule in this world and in the world beyond, even after his promised restoration is complete. It is a time for looking far into the future and having the comfort that all the struggles of this life are going to be vindicated.

As with Daniel's previous visions, this vision too is filled with symbolism—with names apparently having double meanings and with oblique references to future historical events. The first part of the vision calls Daniel's attention to various kings and princes, especially kings of "the North" who do battle with kings of "the South." The four Persian kings may well be Cambyses, Smerdis, Darius, and Xerxes. "The mighty king of Greece" is probably Alexander the Great. If Egypt is the kingdom of the South, then perhaps the kings referred to are the Ptolemies: Soter (ca. 283 B.C.), Philadelphus (ca. 486-285 B.C.) and his daughter Bernice, and Ptolemy Philopator. If the Seleucid kingdom of Syria is the kingdom of the North, then perhaps the kings referred to are Antiochus III (ca. 198-187 B.C.) and almost certainly the contemptible Antiochus Epiphanes, who will desecrate the temple and bring a temporary end to sacrificing (ca. 165 B.C.).

The second part of the vision appears to be much more futuristic. Using the character of "the king of the North" as a springboard, it looks as if the vision jumps ahead to the time when a certain "king" will pretentiously exalt himself. The vision then ends on the most hopeful note of all—resurrection!

Dan.
10:1-3
(536 B.C.) PERIOD OF MOURNING.   In the third year of Cyrus king of Persia, a revelation was given to Daniel (who was called Belteshazzar). Its message was true and it concerned a great war.ʰ The understanding of the message came to him in a vision.

At that time I, Daniel, mourned for three weeks. I ate no choice food; no meat or wine touched my lips; and I used no lotions at all until the three weeks were over.

Dan.
10:4-6 STARTLING VISION.   On the twenty-fourth day of the first month, as I was standing on the bank of the great river, the Tigris, I looked up and there before me was a man dressed in linen, with a belt of the finest gold around his waist. His body was like chrysolite, his face like lightning, his

⁸Or *and troubled them as they built*   ʰOr *true and burdensome*

eyes like flaming torches, his arms and legs like the gleam of burnished bronze, and his voice like the sound of a multitude.

REACTION TO VISION.   I, Daniel, was the only one who saw the vision; the men with me did not see it, but such terror overwhelmed them that they fled and hid themselves. So I was left alone, gazing at this great vision; I had no strength left, my face turned deathly pale and I was helpless. Then I heard him speaking, and as I listened to him, I fell into a deep sleep, my face to the ground.

Dan.
10:7-9

DANIEL COMFORTED.   A hand touched me and set me trembling on my hands and knees. He said, "Daniel, you who are highly esteemed, consider carefully the words I am about to speak to you, and stand up, for I have now been sent to you." And when he said this to me, I stood up trembling.

Dan.
10:10-19

Then he continued, "Do not be afraid, Daniel. Since the first day that you set your mind to gain understanding and to humble yourself before your God, your words were heard, and I have come in response to them. But the prince of the Persian kingdom resisted me twenty-one days. Then Michael, one of the chief princes, came to help me, because I was detained there with the king of Persia. Now I have come to explain to you what will happen to your people in the future, for the vision concerns a time yet to come."

While he was saying this to me, I bowed with my face toward the ground and was speechless. Then one who looked like a man[i] touched my lips, and I opened my mouth and began to speak. I said to the one standing before me, "I am overcome with anguish because of the vision, my lord, and I am helpless. How can I, your servant, talk with you, my lord? My strength is gone and I can hardly breathe."

Again the one who looked like a man touched me and gave me strength. "Do not be afraid, O man highly esteemed," he said. "Peace! Be strong now; be strong."

When he spoke to me, I was strengthened and said, "Speak, my lord, since you have given me strength."

POLITICAL CHANGES.   So he said, "Do you know why I have come to you? Soon I will return to fight against the prince of Persia, and when I go, the prince of Greece will come; but first I will tell you what is written in the Book of Truth. (No one supports me against them except Michael, your prince. And in the first year of Darius the Mede, I took my stand to support and protect him.)

Dan.
10:20-11:4

"Now then, I tell you the truth: Three more kings will appear in Persia, and then a fourth, who will be far richer than all the others. When he has gained power by his wealth, he will stir up everyone against the kingdom of Greece. Then a mighty king will appear, who will rule with great power and do as he pleases. After he has appeared, his empire will be broken up and parceled out toward the four winds of heaven. It will not go to his descendants, nor will it have the power he exercised, because his empire will be uprooted and given to others.

KINGS OF NORTH AND SOUTH.   "The king of the South will become strong, but one of his commanders will become even stronger than he and

Dan.
11:5-20

---

[i]Most manuscripts of the Masoretic Text; one manuscript of the Masoretic Text, Dead Sea Scrolls and Septuagint *Then something that looked like a man's hand*

will rule his own kingdom with great power. After some years, they will become allies. The daughter of the king of the South will go to the king of the North to make an alliance, but she will not retain her power, and he and his power[j] will not last. In those days she will be handed over, together with her royal escort and her father[k] and the one who supported her.

"One from her family line will arise to take her place. He will attack the forces of the king of the North and enter his fortress; he will fight against them and be victorious. He will also seize their gods, their metal images and their valuable articles of silver and gold and carry them off to Egypt. For some years he will leave the king of the North alone. Then the king of the North will invade the realm of the king of the South but will retreat to his own country. His sons will prepare for war and assemble a great army, which will sweep on like an irresistible flood and carry the battle as far as his fortress.

"Then the king of the South will march out in a rage and fight against the king of the North, who will raise a large army, but it will be defeated. When the army is carried off, the king of the South will be filled with pride and will slaughter many thousands, yet he will not remain triumphant. For the king of the North will muster another army, larger than the first; and after several years, he will advance with a huge army fully equipped.

"In those times many will rise against the king of the South. The violent men among your own people will rebel in fulfillment of the vision, but without success. Then the king of the North will come and build up siege ramps and will capture a fortified city. The forces of the South will be powerless to resist; even their best troops will not have the strength to stand. The invader will do as he pleases; no one will be able to stand against him. He will establish himself in the Beautiful Land and will have the power to destroy it. He will determine to come with the might of his entire kingdom and will make an alliance with the king of the South. And he will give him a daughter in marriage in order to overthrow the kingdom, but his plans[l] will not succeed or help him. Then he will turn his attention to the coastlands and will take many of them, but a commander will put an end to his insolence and will turn his insolence back upon him. After this, he will turn back toward the fortresses of his own country but will stumble and fall, to be seen no more.

"His successor will send out a tax collector to maintain the royal splendor. In a few years, however, he will be destroyed, yet not in anger or in battle.

Dan. 11:21-35

THE CONTEMPTIBLE KING.   "He will be succeeded by a contemptible person who has not been given the honor of royalty. He will invade the kingdom when its people feel secure, and he will seize it through intrigue. Then an overwhelming army will be swept away before him; both it and a prince of the covenant will be destroyed. After coming to an agreement with him, he will act deceitfully, and with only a few people he will rise to power. When the richest provinces feel secure, he will invade them and will achieve what neither his fathers nor his forefathers did. He will distribute plunder, loot and wealth among his followers. He will plot the overthrow of fortresses—but only for a time.

[j]Or *offspring*   [k]Or *child* (see Vulgate and Syriac)   [l]Or *but she*

"With a large army he will stir up his strength and courage against the king of the South. The king of the South will wage war with a large and very powerful army, but he will not be able to stand because of the plots devised against him. Those who eat from the king's provisions will try to destroy him; his army will be swept away, and many will fall in battle. The two kings, with their hearts bent on evil, will sit at the same table and lie to each other, but to no avail, because an end will still come at the appointed time. The king of the North will return to his own country with great wealth, but his heart will be set against the holy covenant. He will take action against it and then return to his own country.

"At the appointed time he will invade the South again, but this time the outcome will be different from what it was before. Ships of the western coastlands[m] will oppose him, and he will lose heart. Then he will turn back and vent his fury against the holy covenant. He will return and show favor to those who forsake the holy covenant.

"His armed forces will rise up to desecrate the temple fortress and will abolish the daily sacrifice. Then they will set up the abomination that causes desolation. With flattery he will corrupt those who have violated the covenant, but the people who know their God will firmly resist him.

"Those who are wise will instruct many, though for a time they will fall by the sword or be burned or captured or plundered. When they fall, they will receive a little help, and many who are not sincere will join them. Some of the wise will stumble, so that they may be refined, purified and made spotless until the time of the end, for it will still come at the appointed time.

KING WHO EXALTS HIMSELF. "The king will do as he pleases. He will exalt and magnify himself above every god and will say unheard-of things against the God of gods. He will be successful until the time of wrath is completed, for what has been determined must take place. He will show no regard for the gods of his fathers or for the one desired by women, nor will he regard any god, but will exalt himself above them all. Instead of them, he will honor a god of fortresses; a god unknown to his fathers he will honor with gold and silver, with precious stones and costly gifts. He will attack the mightiest fortresses with the help of a foreign god and will greatly honor those who acknowledge him. He will make them rulers over many people and will distribute the land at a price.[n] **Dan. 11:36-45**

"At the time of the end the king of the South will engage him in battle, and the king of the North will storm out against him with chariots and cavalry and a great fleet of ships. He will invade many countries and sweep through them like a flood. He will also invade the Beautiful Land. Many countries will fall, but Edom, Moab and the leaders of Ammon will be delivered from his hand. He will extend his power over many countries; Egypt will not escape. He will gain control of the treasures of gold and silver and all the riches of Egypt, with the Libyans and Nubians in submission. But reports from the east and the north will alarm him, and he will set out in a great rage to destroy and annihilate many. He will pitch his royal tents between the seas at[o] the beautiful holy mountain. Yet he will come to his end, and no one will help him.

[m]Hebrew of Kittim   [n]Or land for a reward   [o]Or the sea and

Dan. 12:1-4	**END OF TIME.** "At that time Michael, the great prince who protects your people, will arise. There will be a time of distress such as has not happened from the beginning of nations until then. But at that time your people—everyone whose name is found written in the book—will be delivered. Multitudes who sleep in the dust of the earth will awake: some to everlasting life, others to shame and everlasting contempt. Those who are wise*p* will shine like the brightness of the heavens, and those who lead many to righteousness, like the stars for ever and ever. But you, Daniel, close up and seal the words of the scroll until the time of the end. Many will go here and there to increase knowledge."
Dan. 12:5-12	**TIME OF FULFILLMENT.** Then I, Daniel, looked, and there before me stood two others, one on this bank of the river and one on the opposite bank. One of them said to the man clothed in linen, who was above the waters of the river, "How long will it be before these astonishing things are fulfilled?" The man clothed in linen, who was above the waters of the river, lifted his right hand and his left hand toward heaven, and I heard him swear by him who lives forever, saying, "It will be for a time, times and half a time.*q* When the power of the holy people has been finally broken, all these things will be completed." I heard, but I did not understand. So I asked, "My lord, what will the outcome of all this be?" He replied, "Go your way, Daniel, because the words are closed up and sealed until the time of the end. Many will be purified, made spotless and refined, but the wicked will continue to be wicked. None of the wicked will understand, but those who are wise will understand. "From the time that the daily sacrifice is abolished and the abomination that causes desolation is set up, there will be 1,290 days. Blessed is the one who waits for and reaches the end of the 1,335 days.

As with all apocalyptic prophecies, the time when these events are to occur is subject to widely diverse interpretation. The first part of the vision apparently has reference to events to take place over the next four centuries. Because the historical account in Scripture falls mostly silent during the period evidently referred to, this revelation may well be meant to fill that gap, at least in outline form. Moreover, these events would be especially significant in leading up to the time just before the coming of the Messiah.

As for Daniel himself, the vision ends with an assurance that after his death he will rise again to receive his reward.

Dan. 12:13	**PROMISE TO DANIEL.** "As for you, go your way till the end. You will rest, and then at the end of the days you will rise to receive your allotted inheritance."

So ends the record of Daniel's life and marvelous encounters with the world beyond. Challenging as his visions sometimes may be, they are invaluable in stretching one's imagination to the time when all mysteries will be revealed.

---

p Or *who impart wisdom*   *q* Or *a year, two years and half a year*

Opposition to Temple's Construction

rom 536 B.C. until 522 B.C., work on the temple comes to a halt. The opposition of Israel's enemies is in part the problem, but another part is the priority given by the settlers to building their own houses and preparing the land for crops. The record of the opposition contains various correspondence between Israel's enemies and the Persian leaders by whom the resettlement is being permitted. The first formal accusation against Israel is apparently lodged during the reign of Cambyses, who took control of the Persian Empire when his father, Cyrus, died in 530 B.C. Like his father, Cambyses is basically a good man. He is an apt ruler during his seven-year reign. He is referred to in this brief account as Xerxes, a name which applies to his position and is not to be confused with a later Persian ruler better known by that name.

ACCUSATIONS.   At the beginning of the reign of Xerxes,[r] they lodged an accusation against the people of Judah and Jerusalem.

Ezra 4:6
(529-520 B.C.)

There is no indication that Cambyses takes any official action to stop the reconstruction program. In 525 B.C. he leads his forces into Egypt and takes Memphis from Pharaoh Amasis and his son Psamtik II. This Persian dominance must surely be at least the beginning of the fulfillment of the many prophecies concerning Egypt's fall. Egypt will come under complete domination during the next six years. While Cambyses is involved in the Egyptian campaign, back home his half-brother, Smerdis, has been killed by Cambyses' aides to prevent any chance of a coup. However, a Mede by the name of Guamata, claiming to be Smerdis, does in fact lead a revolt and rules for about ten months in 522 B.C. It is this pseudo-Smerdis to whom the historical record evidently refers as Artaxerxes in the following account of the letters between the local commanding officer and this usurper. Again, there should be no confusion between this titular name and the better-known Artaxerxes to come 60 years later.

REHUM'S LETTER.   And in the days of Artaxerxes king of Persia, Bishlam, Mithredath, Tabeel and the rest of his associates wrote a letter to Artaxerxes. The letter was written in Aramaic script and in the Aramaic language.[s] [t]

Ezra 4:7-16
(522 B.C.)

Rehum the commanding officer and Shimshai the secretary wrote a letter against Jerusalem to Artaxerxes the king as follows:

Rehum the commanding officer and Shimshai the secretary, together with the rest of their associates—the judges and officials over the men from Tripolis, Persia,[u] Erech and Babylon, the Elamites of Susa, and the other people whom the great and honorable Ashurbanipal[v] deported and settled in the city of Samaria and elsewhere in Trans-Euphrates.

(This is a copy of the letter they sent him.)

---

[r]Hebrew *Ahasuerus*, a variant of Xerxes' Persian name   [s]Or *written in Aramaic and translated*   [t]The text of Ezra 4:8–6:18 is in Aramaic.   [u]Or *officials, magistrates and governors over the men from*   [v]Aramaic *Osnappar*, a variant of *Ashurbanipal*

To King Artaxerxes,

From your servants, the men of Trans-Euphrates:

The king should know that the Jews who came up to us from you have gone to Jerusalem and are rebuilding that rebellious and wicked city. They are restoring the walls and repairing the foundations.

Furthermore, the king should know that if this city is built and its walls are restored, no more taxes, tribute or duty will be paid, and the royal revenues will suffer. Now since we are under obligation to the palace and it is not proper for us to see the king dishonored, we are sending this message to inform the king, so that a search may be made in the archives of your predecessors. In these records you will find that this city is a rebellious city, troublesome to kings and provinces, a place of rebellion from ancient times. That is why this city was destroyed. We inform the king that if this city is built and its walls are restored, you will be left with nothing in Trans-Euphrates.

Ezra 4:17-22

KING'S REPLY.   The king sent this reply:

To Rehum the commanding officer, Shimshai the secretary and the rest of their associates living in Samaria and elsewhere in Trans-Euphrates:

Greetings.

The letter you sent us has been read and translated in my presence. I issued an order and a search was made, and it was found that this city has a long history of revolt against kings and has been a place of rebellion and sedition. Jerusalem has had powerful kings ruling over the whole of Trans-Euphrates, and taxes, tribute and duty were paid to them. Now issue an order to these men to stop work, so that this city will not be rebuilt until I so order. Be careful not to neglect this matter. Why let this threat grow, to the detriment of the royal interests?

Ezra 4:23,24

TEMPLE CONSTRUCTION HALTED.   As soon as the copy of the letter of King Artaxerxes was read to Rehum and Shimshai the secretary and their associates, they went immediately to the Jews in Jerusalem and compelled them by force to stop.

Thus the work on the house of God in Jerusalem came to a standstill until the second year of the reign of Darius king of Persia.

No sooner has the order to stop construction been given than there is a shake-up in the Persian power structure. When Cambyses dies, near Mount Carmel (possibly by suicide), a distant relative named Darius moves against Guamata and assumes control of the empire here in 522 B.C. Darius moves quickly to pull together his shaky kingdom and creates a code of laws to be enforced throughout his empire. It is not surprising, then, that under circumstances soon to appear Darius is receptive to a plea by the people of Israel to be permitted to continue work on the temple. The issue is raised when the prophets Haggai and Zechariah defy the earlier order of Guamata.

Ezra 5:1,2 (522-521 B.C.)

TEMPLE WORK RESTARTED.   Now Haggai the prophet and Zechariah the prophet, a descendant of Iddo, prophesied to the Jews in Judah and Jerusalem in the name of the God of Israel, who was over them. Then

Zerubbabel son of Shealtiel and Jeshua son of Jozadak set to work to rebuild the house of God in Jerusalem. And the prophets of God were with them, helping them.

AUTHORITY QUESTIONED.   At that time Tattenai, governor of Trans-   Ezra 5:3-5
Euphrates, and Shethar-Bozenai and their associates went to them and asked, "Who authorized you to rebuild this temple and restore this structure?" They also asked, "What are the names of the men constructing this building?"^{w} But the eye of their God was watching over the elders of the Jews, and they were not stopped until a report could go to Darius and his written reply be received.

LETTER TO DARIUS.   This is a copy of the letter that Tattenai, governor   Ezra 5:6-17
of Trans-Euphrates, and Shethar-Bozenai and their associates, the officials of Trans-Euphrates, sent to King Darius. The report they sent him read as follows:

To King Darius:

Cordial greetings.

The king should know that we went to the district of Judah, to the temple of the great God. The people are building it with large stones and placing the timbers in the walls. The work is being carried on with diligence and is making rapid progress under their direction.

We questioned the elders and asked them, "Who authorized you to rebuild this temple and restore this structure?" We also asked them their names, so that we could write down the names of their leaders for your information.

This is the answer they gave us:

"We are the servants of the God of heaven and earth, and we are rebuilding the temple that was built many years ago, one that a great king of Israel built and finished. But because our fathers angered the God of heaven, he handed them over to Nebuchadnezzar the Chaldean, king of Babylon, who destroyed this temple and deported the people to Babylon.

"However, in the first year of Cyrus king of Babylon, King Cyrus issued a decree to rebuild this house of God. He even removed from the temple^x of Babylon the gold and silver articles of the house of God, which Nebuchadnezzar had taken from the temple in Jerusalem and brought to the temple^x in Babylon.

"Then King Cyrus gave them to a man named Sheshbazzar, whom he had appointed governor, and he told him, 'Take these articles and go and deposit them in the temple in Jerusalem. And rebuild the house of God on its site.' So this Sheshbazzar came and laid the foundations of the house of God in Jerusalem. From that day to the present it has been under construction but is not yet finished."

Now if it pleases the king, let a search be made in the royal archives of Babylon to see if King Cyrus did in fact issue a decree to rebuild this house of God in Jerusalem. Then let the king send us his decision in this matter.

---

^{w}See Septuagint; Aramaic ^{4}*We told them the names of the men constructing this building.*
^{x}Or *palace*

Ezra 6:1-5   MEMO OF CYRUS' DECREE.   King Darius then issued an order, and they searched in the archives stored in the treasury at Babylon. A scroll was found in the citadel of Ecbatana in the province of Media, and this was written on it:

Memorandum:

In the first year of King Cyrus, the king issued a decree concerning the temple of God in Jerusalem:

Let the temple be rebuilt as a place to present sacrifices, and let its foundations be laid. It is to be ninety feet[y] high and ninety feet wide, with three courses of large stones and one of timbers. The costs are to be paid by the royal treasury. Also, the gold and silver articles of the house of God, which Nebuchadnezzar took from the temple in Jerusalem and brought to Babylon, are to be returned to their places in the temple in Jerusalem; they are to be deposited in the house of God.

Ezra 6:6-12
(521-520
B.C.)   DARIUS' DECREE.   Now then, Tattenai, governor of Trans-Euphrates, and Shethar-Bozenai and you, their fellow officials of that province, stay away from there. Do not interfere with the work on this temple of God. Let the governor of the Jews and the Jewish elders rebuild this house of God on its site.

Moreover, I hereby decree what you are to do for these elders of the Jews in the construction of this house of God:

The expenses of these men are to be fully paid out of the royal treasury, from the revenues of Trans-Euphrates, so that the work will not stop. Whatever is needed—young bulls, rams, male lambs for burnt offerings to the God of heaven, and wheat, salt, wine and oil, as requested by the priests in Jerusalem—must be given them daily without fail, so that they may offer sacrifices pleasing to the God of heaven and pray for the well-being of the king and his sons.

Furthermore, I decree that if anyone changes this edict, a beam is to be pulled from his house and he is to be lifted up and impaled on it. And for this crime his house is to be made a pile of rubble. May God, who has caused his Name to dwell there, overthrow any king or people who lifts a hand to change this decree or to destroy this temple in Jerusalem.

I Darius have decreed it. Let it be carried out with diligence.

Ezra 6:13   TATTENAI COMPLIES.   Then, because of the decree King Darius had sent, Tattenai, governor of Trans-Euphrates, and Shethar-Bozenai and their associates carried it out with diligence.

Once again God works through a Persian ruler to implement the promised restoration. The Persian government is even supplying funds for the temple's construction and the sacrifices to be made in it! This sounds highly unusual, but it is consistent with the Persian policy of promoting polytheism throughout the empire. Darius' decree suggests that he welcomes the goodwill of any god, including this "God of heaven."

◇

[y]Aramaic *sixty cubits* (about 27 meters)

Preaching of Haggai and Zechariah

From this point on, finishing the temple ought to be easy. But the cessation of official opposition does not eliminate all the problems besetting the project. The people of Israel themselves are still part of the problem. They are having droughts and famine and are putting off work on the temple until they are prosperous enough to give it their attention.

The two men who come to the rescue of the temple project are Haggai and Zechariah, both prophets of God. Little is known about Haggai, but it is surmised that he is one of the exiles who remembers the former temple before its destruction. If so, he is probably at least 75 years old. His very young associate, Zechariah, was evidently born in Babylonia into the priestly family of Iddo, his grandfather. It was Haggai and Zechariah, of course, who had initiated the renewal of the work which led to Tattenai's letter and Darius' decree. Now, over a four-month period, they will continue to encourage the construction effort.

Through Haggai, God tells the people why they have been facing such economic problems. It is because they have set their own selfish interests as the highest priority rather than totally committing themselves to construction of the temple. This message comes to Haggai in the summer of 520 B.C. It is addressed to Zerubbabel, who has become governor, and Joshua (Jeshua) the high priest, but it is meant for all the people.

PRIORITIES CHASTISED. In the second year of King Darius, on the first day of the sixth month, the word of the LORD came through the prophet Haggai to Zerubbabel son of Shealtiel, governor of Judah, and to Joshua[z] son of Jehozadak, the high priest: **Haggai 1:1-11 (520 B.C.)**

This is what the LORD Almighty says: "These people say, 'The time has not yet come for the LORD's house to be built.'"

Then the word of the LORD came through the prophet Haggai: "Is it a time for you yourselves to be living in your paneled houses, while this house remains a ruin?"

Now this is what the LORD Almighty says: "Give careful thought to your ways. You have planted much, but have harvested little. You eat, but never have enough. You drink, but never have your fill. You put on clothes, but are not warm. You earn wages, only to put them in a purse with holes in it."

This is what the LORD Almighty says: "Give careful thought to your ways. Go up into the mountains and bring down timber and build the house, so that I may take pleasure in it and be honored," says the LORD. "You expected much, but see, it turned out to be little. What you brought home, I blew away. Why?" declares the LORD Almighty. "Because of my house, which remains a ruin, while each of you is busy with his own house. Therefore, because of you the heavens have withheld their dew and the earth its crops. I called for a drought on the fields and the mountains, on the grain, the new wine, the oil and whatever the ground produces, on men and cattle, and on the labor of your hands."

[z]A variant of *Jeshua;* here and elsewhere in Haggai

Within three weeks the people respond favorably to Haggai's preaching and the work is renewed in earnest.

Haggai 1:12,13   PEOPLE RESPOND POSITIVELY.   Then Zerubbabel son of Shealtiel, Joshua son of Jehozadak, the high priest, and the whole remnant of the people obeyed the voice of the LORD their God and the message of the prophet Haggai, because the LORD their God had sent him. And the people feared the LORD.

Then Haggai, the LORD's messenger, gave this message of the LORD to the people: "I am with you," declares the LORD.

Haggai 1:14,15   WORK BEGUN AGAIN.   So the LORD stirred up the spirit of Zerubbabel son of Shealtiel, governor of Judah, and the spirit of Joshua son of Jehozadak, the high priest, and the spirit of the whole remnant of the people. They came and began to work on the house of the LORD Almighty, their God, on the twenty-fourth day of the sixth month in the second year of King Darius.

A month later God asks Haggai to address the concern of the older exiles, who had wept when the temple foundation was laid. Remembering the beauty of the great temple of Solomon, they know that its replacement will be smaller and less ornate. God's words of comfort are perhaps messianic in nature. He promises that, even though the architectural appointments will not compare with those of Solomon's temple, God will one day fill this new temple with an even greater glory. Perhaps the message alludes symbolically to another temple, or possibly to the fact that the Messiah will personally walk through the very building they are now erecting.

Haggai 2:1-9 (520 B.C.)   TEMPLE'S FUTURE GLORY.   On the twenty-first day of the seventh month, the word of the LORD came through the prophet Haggai: "Speak to Zerubbabel son of Shealtiel, governor of Judah, to Joshua son of Jehozadak, the high priest, and to the remnant of the people. Ask them, 'Who of you is left who saw this house in its former glory? How does it look to you now? Does it not seem to you like nothing? But now be strong, O Zerubbabel,' declares the LORD. 'Be strong, O Joshua son of Jehozadak, the high priest. Be strong, all you people of the land,' declares the LORD, 'and work. For I am with you,' declares the LORD Almighty. 'This is what I covenanted with you when you came out of Egypt. And my Spirit remains among you. Do not fear.'

"This is what the LORD Almighty says: 'In a little while I will once more shake the heavens and the earth, the sea and the dry land. I will shake all nations, and the desired of all nations will come, and I will fill this house with glory,' says the LORD Almighty. 'The silver is mine and the gold is mine,' declares the LORD Almighty. 'The glory of this present house will be greater than the glory of the former house,' says the LORD Almighty. 'And in this place I will grant peace,' declares the LORD Almighty."

In the next month Zechariah is given a brief message for the people to remind them how their forefathers had fallen time and again into sinful practices. Now that the work on the temple is underway, there can be no turning back, except a turning back to God.

LESSON FROM FOREFATHERS.   In the eighth month of the second year Zech. 1:1-6
of Darius, the word of the LORD came to the prophet Zechariah son of (520 B.C.)
Berekiah, the son of Iddo:

"The LORD was very angry with your forefathers. Therefore tell the people: This is what the LORD Almighty says: 'Return to me,' declares the LORD Almighty, 'and I will return to you,' says the LORD Almighty. Do not be like your forefathers, to whom the earlier prophets proclaimed: This is what the LORD Almighty says: 'Turn from your evil ways and your evil practices.' But they would not listen or pay attention to me, declares the LORD. Where are your forefathers now? And the prophets, do they live forever? But did not my words and my decrees, which I commanded my servants the prophets, overtake your forefathers?

"Then they repented and said, 'The LORD Almighty has done to us what our ways and practices deserve, just as he determined to do.'"

At the end of the following month Haggai continues Zechariah's theme. Haggai contends that the temple workers cannot claim to be righteous simply because they are working on the house of the Lord. In fact, if their personal lives are not holy, their involvement in the temple's construction will actually desecrate the holy sanctuary. Haggai brings his lessons in the form of two hypothetical questions to the priests.

HYPOTHETICAL QUESTIONS.   On the twenty-fourth day of the ninth Haggai
month, in the second year of Darius, the word of the LORD came to the 2:10-14
prophet Haggai: "This is what the LORD Almighty says: 'Ask the priests (520 B.C.)
what the law says: If a person carries consecrated meat in the fold of his garment, and that fold touches some bread or stew, some wine, oil or other food, does it become consecrated?'"

The priests answered, "No."

Then Haggai said, "If a person defiled by contact with a dead body touches one of these things, does it become defiled?"

"Yes," the priests replied, "it becomes defiled."

Then Haggai said, " 'So it is with this people and this nation in my sight,' declares the LORD. 'Whatever they do and whatever they offer there is defiled.

PROSPERITY FROM COMMITMENT.   " 'Now give careful thought to Haggai
this from this day on[a]—consider how things were before one stone was 2:15-19
laid on another in the LORD's temple. When anyone came to a heap of twenty measures, there were only ten. When anyone went to a wine vat to draw fifty measures, there were only twenty. I struck all the work of your hands with blight, mildew and hail, yet you did not turn to me,' declares the LORD. 'From this day on, from this twenty-fourth day of the ninth month, give careful thought to the day when the foundation of the LORD's temple was laid. Give careful thought: Is there yet any seed left in the barn? Until now, the vine and the fig tree, the pomegranate and the olive tree have not borne fruit.

" 'From this day on I will bless you.'"

[a]Or to the days past

Later in the same day God brings a special message, ostensibly for Zerubbabel the governor. However, there is reason to believe that Zerubbabel himself is not being referred to in the prophetic wording, but rather another leader of God's people—the coming Messiah.

Haggai
2:20-23
(520 B.C.)

SPECIAL PROPHECY.   The word of the LORD came to Haggai a second time on the twenty-fourth day of the month: "Tell Zerubbabel governor of Judah that I will shake the heavens and the earth. I will overturn royal thrones and shatter the power of the foreign kingdoms. I will overthrow chariots and their drivers; horses and their riders will fall, each by the sword of his brother.

" 'On that day,' declares the LORD Almighty, 'I will take you, my servant Zerubbabel son of Shealtiel,' declares the LORD, 'and I will make you like my signet ring, for I have chosen you,' declares the LORD Almighty."

The work on the temple now fully underway, Haggai slips from further notice in the historical record. Brief as his recorded ministry may have been, it has filled a most significant need in the restoration of the nation and its religious life.

Zechariah's Visions

$\mathcal{E}$xactly two months after Haggai's last prophecy, Zechariah is shown a series of eight graphic visions, not unlike those shown to Daniel. They refer to many of the people and events of the present time but repeatedly appear to have dual significance, either messianic or apocalyptic. These visions are then followed by a symbolic occurrence involving Joshua the high priest. If there is one theme to all of the visions, it may be the theme of assurance.

In the first vision is assurance that Israel will be restored in prosperity.

Zech.
1:7-17
(520 B.C.)

ANGEL AND HORSEMEN.   On the twenty-fourth day of the eleventh month, the month of Shebat, in the second year of Darius, the word of the LORD came to the prophet Zechariah son of Berekiah, the son of Iddo.

During the night I had a vision—and there before me was a man riding a red horse! He was standing among the myrtle trees in a ravine. Behind him were red, brown and white horses.

I asked, "What are these, my lord?"

The angel who was talking with me answered, "I will show you what they are."

Then the man standing among the myrtle trees explained, "They are the ones the LORD has sent to go throughout the earth."

And they reported to the angel of the LORD, who was standing among the myrtle trees, "We have gone throughout the earth and found the whole world at rest and in peace."

Then the angel of the LORD said, "LORD Almighty, how long will you withhold mercy from Jerusalem and from the towns of Judah, which you have been angry with these seventy years?" So the LORD spoke kind and comforting words to the angel who talked with me.

Then the angel who was speaking to me said, "Proclaim this word: This is what the LORD Almighty says: 'I am very jealous for Jerusalem and Zion, but I am very angry with the nations that feel secure. I was only a little angry, but they added to the calamity.'

"Therefore, this is what the LORD says: 'I will return to Jerusalem with mercy, and there my house will be rebuilt. And the measuring line will be stretched out over Jerusalem,' declares the LORD Almighty.

"Proclaim further: This is what the LORD Almighty says: 'My towns will again overflow with prosperity, and the LORD will again comfort Zion and choose Jerusalem.' "

In the second vision is assurance that Israel's oppressors will indeed be punished.

HORNS AND CRAFTSMEN.   Then I looked up—and there before me were four horns! I asked the angel who was speaking to me, "What are these?"

Zech. 1:18-21

He answered me, "These are the horns that scattered Judah, Israel and Jerusalem."

Then the LORD showed me four craftsmen. I asked, "What are these coming to do?"

He answered, "These are the horns that scattered Judah so that no one could raise his head, but the craftsmen have come to terrify them and throw down these horns of the nations who lifted up their horns against the land of Judah to scatter its people."

In the third vision is assurance that God will be among his returning people.

MAN WITH MEASURING LINE.   Then I looked up—and there before me was a man with a measuring line in his hand! I asked, "Where are you going?"

Zech. 2:1-13

He answered me, "To measure Jerusalem, to find out how wide and how long it is."

Then the angel who was speaking to me left, and another angel came to meet him and said to him: "Run, tell that young man, 'Jerusalem will be a city without walls because of the great number of men and livestock in it. And I myself will be a wall of fire around it,' declares the LORD, 'and I will be its glory within.'

"Come! Come! Flee from the land of the north," declares the LORD, "for I have scattered you to the four winds of heaven," declares the LORD.

"Come, O Zion! Escape, you who live in the Daughter of Babylon!" For this is what the LORD Almighty says: "After he has honored me and has sent me against the nations that have plundered you—for whoever touches you touches the apple of his eye—I will surely raise my hand against them so that their slaves will plunder them.[b] Then you will know that the LORD Almighty has sent me.

"Shout and be glad, O Daughter of Zion. For I am coming, and I will live among you," declares the LORD. "Many nations will be joined with the LORD in that day and will become my people. I will live among you and you will know that the LORD Almighty has sent me to you. The LORD will inherit Judah as his portion in the holy land and will again choose

[b]Or says after . . . eye: 9"I . . . plunder them."

Jerusalem. Be still before the LORD, all mankind, because he has roused himself from his holy dwelling."

In the fourth vision is assurance that the sins of the people will be removed by him who is called the Branch.

Zech.
3:1-10

PRIEST'S GARMENTS.   Then he showed me Joshua[c] the high priest standing before the angel of the LORD, and Satan[d] standing at his right side to accuse him. The LORD said to Satan, "The LORD rebuke you, Satan! The LORD, who has chosen Jerusalem, rebuke you! Is not this man a burning stick snatched from the fire?"

Now Joshua was dressed in filthy clothes as he stood before the angel. The angel said to those who were standing before him, "Take off his filthy clothes."

Then he said to Joshua, "See, I have taken away your sin, and I will put rich garments on you."

Then I said, "Put a clean turban on his head." So they put a clean turban on his head and clothed him, while the angel of the LORD stood by.

The angel of the LORD gave this charge to Joshua: "This is what the LORD Almighty says: 'If you will walk in my ways and keep my requirements, then you will govern my house and have charge of my courts, and I will give you a place among these standing here.

" 'Listen, O high priest Joshua and your associates seated before you, who are men symbolic of things to come: I am going to bring my servant, the Branch. See, the stone I have set in front of Joshua! There are seven eyes[e] on that one stone, and I will engrave an inscription on it,' says the LORD Almighty, 'and I will remove the sin of this land in a single day.

" 'In that day each of you will invite his neighbor to sit under his vine and fig tree,' declares the LORD Almighty."

In the fifth vision is assurance that God will complete his temple through his two anointed ones.

Zech.
4:1-14

LAMPSTAND AND OLIVE TREES.   Then the angel who talked with me returned and wakened me, as a man is wakened from his sleep. He asked me, "What do you see?"

I answered, "I see a solid gold lampstand with a bowl at the top and seven lights on it, with seven channels to the lights. Also there are two olive trees by it, one on the right of the bowl and the other on its left."

I asked the angel who talked with me, "What are these, my lord?"

He answered, "Do you not know what these are?"

"No, my lord," I replied.

So he said to me, "This is the word of the LORD to Zerubbabel: 'Not by might nor by power, but by my Spirit,' says the LORD Almighty.

"What[f] are you, O mighty mountain? Before Zerubbabel you will become level ground. Then he will bring out the capstone to shouts of 'God bless it! God bless it!' "

Then the word of the LORD came to me: "The hands of Zerubbabel have

---

[c]A variant of *Jeshua*; here and elsewhere in Zechariah   [d]*Satan* means *accuser*.   [e]Or *facets*   [f]Or *Who*

laid the foundation of this temple; his hands will also complete it. Then you will know that the LORD Almighty has sent me to you.

"Who despises the day of small things? Men will rejoice when they see the plumb line in the hand of Zerubbabel.

"(These seven are the eyes of the LORD, which range throughout the earth.)"

Then I asked the angel, "What are these two olive trees on the right and the left of the lampstand?"

Again I asked him, "What are these two olive branches beside the two gold pipes that pour out golden oil?"

He replied, "Do you not know what these are?"

"No, my lord," I said.

So he said, "These are the two who are anointed to*g* serve the Lord of all the earth."

In the sixth vision is assurance that wickedness will always be punished.

THE FLYING SCROLL.   I looked again—and there before me was a flying scroll!

He asked me, "What do you see?"

I answered, "I see a flying scroll, thirty feet long and fifteen feet wide.*h*"

And he said to me, "This is the curse that is going out over the whole land; for according to what it says on one side, every thief will be banished, and according to what it says on the other, everyone who swears falsely will be banished. The LORD Almighty declares, 'I will send it out, and it will enter the house of the thief and the house of him who swears falsely by my name. It will remain in his house and destroy it, both its timbers and its stones.' "

Zech. 5:1-4

In the seventh vision is assurance that wicked nations will be brought to their knees.

WOMAN IN A BASKET.   Then the angel who was speaking to me came forward and said to me, "Look up and see what this is that is appearing."

I asked, "What is it?"

He replied, "It is a measuring basket.*i*" And he added, "This is the iniquity*j* of the people throughout the land."

Then the cover of lead was raised, and there in the basket sat a woman! He said, "This is wickedness," and he pushed her back into the basket and pushed the lead cover down over its mouth.

Then I looked up—and there before me were two women, with the wind in their wings! They had wings like those of a stork, and they lifted up the basket between heaven and earth.

"Where are they taking the basket?" I asked the angel who was speaking to me.

He replied, "To the country of Babylonia*k* to build a house for it. When it is ready, the basket will be set there in its place."

Zech. 5:5-11

*g*Or *two who bring oil and*   *h*Hebrew *twenty cubits long and ten cubits wide* (about 9 meters long and 4.5 meters wide)   *i*Hebrew *an ephah*   *j*Or *appearance*   *k*Hebrew *Shinar*

In the eighth vision is assurance that there is to be rest at last!

Zech. 6:1-8   FOUR CHARIOTS.   I looked up again—and there before me were four chariots coming out from between two mountains—mountains of bronze! The first chariot had red horses, the second black, the third white, and the fourth dappled—all of them powerful. I asked the angel who was speaking to me, "What are these, my lord?"

The angel answered me, "These are the four spirits[l] of heaven, going out from standing in the presence of the Lord of the whole world. The one with the black horses is going toward the north country, the one with the white horses toward the west,[m] and the one with the dappled horses toward the south."

When the powerful horses went out, they were straining to go throughout the earth. And he said, "Go throughout the earth!" So they went throughout the earth.

Then he called to me, "Look, those going toward the north country have given my Spirit[n] rest in the land of the north."

Zechariah is now told to place a crown on the head of Joshua the high priest, an enactment which is symbolic of the Messiah, who will be both Priest and King over his people. As the office of high priest evolves in postexilic Israel, it will take on kinglike overtones. This change will prove to be significant when the Messiah comes to establish his own kingdom, for his "kingship" will threaten the priestly power structure and will lead ultimately to his death.

Zech.   CROWN FOR JOSHUA.   The word of the LORD came to me: "Take ⌊silver
6:9-15   and gold⌋ from the exiles Heldai, Tobijah and Jedaiah, who have arrived from Babylon. Go the same day to the house of Josiah son of Zephaniah. Take the silver and gold and make a crown, and set it on the head of the high priest, Joshua son of Jehozadak. Tell him this is what the LORD Almighty says: 'Here is the man whose name is the Branch, and he will branch out from his place and build the temple of the LORD. It is he who will build the temple of the LORD, and he will be clothed with majesty and will sit and rule on his throne. And he will be a priest on his throne. And there will be harmony between the two.' The crown will be given to Heldai,[o] Tobijah, Jedaiah and Hen[p] son of Zephaniah as a memorial in the temple of the LORD. Those who are far away will come and help to build the temple of the LORD, and you will know that the LORD Almighty has sent me to you. This will happen if you diligently obey the LORD your God."

Do the carpenters and masons now laboring at the temple site have any idea of the majestic stage upon which they are playing their roles? Perhaps they do. If so, Zechariah's visions must bring both comfort and incredible excitement!

[l]Or winds   [m]Or horses after them   [n]Or spirit   [o]Syriac; Hebrew Helem   [p]Or and
the gracious one, the

The Meaning of Restoration

*A*s Haggai's mission was to construct the temple of God in Jerusalem, Zechariah's mission is to establish the spiritual house of Israel. It is Zechariah's role to interpret the significance of their work and to give them reason to persevere. The temple is still not completed. The city walls have not even begun to be rebuilt. The outlying towns and lands are still in rubble and disarray. And, worst of all, the religious life of the people is slow in developing after the years in exile, during which religious exercise had naturally waned.

Therefore God presents Zechariah with an opportunity to bring encouragement to his people, to explain the essence of true religion and thus to breathe meaning into the noble enterprise in which they are engaged. The opportunity comes two years after Zechariah's eight visions, when the people of Bethel ask Zechariah about observing certain religious days. God's message through Zechariah is like that brought by the prophet Amos: true religion finds its expression in moral lives and social justice.

INQUIRY FROM BETHEL. In the fourth year of King Darius, the word of the LORD came to Zechariah on the fourth day of the ninth month, the month of Kislev. The people of Bethel had sent Sharezer and Regem-Melech, together with their men, to entreat the LORD by asking the priests of the house of the LORD Almighty and the prophets, "Should I mourn and fast in the fifth month, as I have done for so many years?"

Zech. 7:1-3 (518 B.C.)

MOTIVE FOR FASTING. Then the word of the LORD Almighty came to me: "Ask all the people of the land and the priests, 'When you fasted and mourned in the fifth and seventh months for the past seventy years, was it really for me that you fasted? And when you were eating and drinking, were you not just feasting for yourselves? Are these not the words the LORD proclaimed through the earlier prophets when Jerusalem and its surrounding towns were at rest and prosperous, and the Negev and the western foothills were settled?' "

Zech. 7:4-7

ESSENCE OF RELIGION. And the word of the LORD came again to Zechariah: "This is what the LORD Almighty says: 'Administer true justice; show mercy and compassion to one another. Do not oppress the widow or the fatherless, the alien or the poor. In your hearts do not think evil of each other.'

Zech. 7:8-10

FOREFATHERS MISSED POINT. "But they refused to pay attention; stubbornly they turned their backs and stopped up their ears. They made their hearts as hard as flint and would not listen to the law or to the words that the LORD Almighty had sent by his Spirit through the earlier prophets. So the LORD Almighty was very angry.

Zech. 7:11-14

" 'When I called, they did not listen; so when they called, I would not listen,' says the LORD Almighty. 'I scattered them with a whirlwind among all the nations, where they were strangers. The land was left so desolate behind them that no one could come or go. This is how they made the pleasant land desolate.' "

Zech. 8:1-8   RESTORATION HAS COME.   Again the word of the LORD Almighty came to me. This is what the LORD Almighty says: "I am very jealous for Zion; I am burning with jealousy for her."

This is what the LORD says: "I will return to Zion and dwell in Jerusalem. Then Jerusalem will be called the City of Truth, and the mountain of the LORD Almighty will be called the Holy Mountain."

This is what the LORD Almighty says: "Once again men and women of ripe old age will sit in the streets of Jerusalem, each with cane in hand because of his age. The city streets will be filled with boys and girls playing there."

This is what the LORD Almighty says: "It may seem marvelous to the remnant of this people at that time, but will it seem marvelous to me?" declares the LORD Almighty.

This is what the LORD Almighty says: "I will save my people from the countries of the east and the west. I will bring them back to live in Jerusalem; they will be my people, and I will be faithful and righteous to them as their God."

Zech.   MOTIVATION FOR WORKERS.   This is what the LORD Almighty says:
8:9-13   "You who now hear these words spoken by the prophets who were there when the foundation was laid for the house of the LORD Almighty, let your hands be strong so that the temple may be built. Before that time there were no wages for man or beast. No one could go about his business safely because of his enemy, for I had turned every man against his neighbor. But now I will not deal with the remnant of this people as I did in the past," declares the LORD Almighty.

"The seed will grow well, the vine will yield its fruit, the ground will produce its crops, and the heavens will drop their dew. I will give all these things as an inheritance to the remnant of this people. As you have been an object of cursing among the nations, O Judah and Israel, so will I save you, and you will be a blessing. Do not be afraid, but let your hands be strong."

Zech.   CALL FOR TRUE RELIGION.   This is what the LORD Almighty says: "Just
8:14-17   as I had determined to bring disaster upon you and showed no pity when your fathers angered me," says the LORD Almighty, "so now I have determined to do good again to Jerusalem and Judah. Do not be afraid. These are the things you are to do: Speak the truth to each other, and render true and sound judgment in your courts; do not plot evil against your neighbor, and do not love to swear falsely. I hate all this," declares the LORD.

Zech.   JOY OF OBSERVANCES.   Again the word of the LORD Almighty came to
8:18,19   me. This is what the LORD Almighty says: "The fasts of the fourth, fifth, seventh and tenth months will become joyful and glad occasions and happy festivals for Judah. Therefore love truth and peace."

Zech.   FUTURE RESTORATION.   This is what the LORD Almighty says: "Many
8:20-23   peoples and the inhabitants of many cities will yet come, and the inhabitants of one city will go to another and say, 'Let us go at once to entreat the LORD and seek the LORD Almighty. I myself am going.' And many peoples and powerful nations will come to Jerusalem to seek the LORD Almighty and to entreat him."

This is what the LORD Almighty says: "In those days ten men from all languages and nations will take firm hold of one Jew by the hem of his robe and say, 'Let us go with you, because we have heard that God is with you.' "

An Oracle

This encouragement to the workers has its predictable effect, as the historical record indicates.

TEMPLE PROGRESSES.   So the elders of the Jews continued to build and prosper under the preaching of Haggai the prophet and Zechariah, a descendant of Iddo.

Ezra 6:14a

Completion of the Temple

*W*ith the encouragement of Haggai and Zechariah, the work on the temple goes forward to completion in the year 516 B.C. Just as 70 years elapsed from the first deportation to the return of the first settlers, it has been 70 years since the temple of Solomon was destroyed, in 586 B.C. The precision with which God works in the affairs of nations stands as a wonderful witness to his power in the lives of individuals as well. This exact fulfillment of God's promise ought to encourage people everywhere to know that he truly is God—the faithful God who keeps his promises.

Even though this new sanctuary lacks the splendor of the temple it replaces, the people nevertheless greet the day of completion with joyous celebration!

TEMPLE COMPLETED.   They finished building the temple according to the command of the God of Israel and the decrees of Cyrus, Darius and Artaxerxes, kings of Persia. The temple was completed on the third day of the month Adar, in the sixth year of the reign of King Darius.

Ezra 6:14b,15 (516 B.C.)

JOYOUS CELEBRATION.   Then the people of Israel—the priests, the Levites and the rest of the exiles—celebrated the dedication of the house of God with joy. For the dedication of this house of God they offered a hundred bulls, two hundred rams, four hundred male lambs and, as a sin offering for all Israel, twelve male goats, one for each of the tribes of Israel. And they installed the priests in their divisions and the Levites in their groups for the service of God at Jerusalem, according to what is written in the Book of Moses.

Ezra 6:16-18

PASSOVER OBSERVED.   On the fourteenth day of the first month, the exiles celebrated the Passover. The priests and Levites had purified themselves and were all ceremonially clean. The Levites slaughtered the Passover lamb for all the exiles, for their brothers the priests and for themselves. So the Israelites who had returned from the exile ate it, together with all who had separated themselves from the unclean practices of their Gentile neighbors in order to seek the LORD, the God of Israel. For seven days they celebrated with joy the Feast of Unleavened Bread, because the LORD had filled them with joy by changing the attitude of the king of Assyria, so that he assisted them in the work on the house of God, the God of Israel.

Ezra 6:19-22

Psalms of a Nation Restored

The celebration over the completion of the temple is only symbolic of the greater joy that has been brought to the people of this restored nation. There are many struggles still ahead and more opposition to come, but the people are no longer in captivity and those who have chosen to return are no longer in a foreign land. With the house of God now restored, the nation's new life has begun in earnest.

These feelings are reflected in a number of psalms which give praise to God for hearing the people's prayers in captivity and for being faithful in his promises of restoration. The 11 psalms presented here are the last of the 150 psalms (as presented). They are a fitting conclusion to the first group of psalms, which poured out the troubled souls of those who were beset by the threats and scorn of their enemies. Truly God has been just and faithful to his people.

Psa. 78   **God's faithfulness to a rebellious nation.**

A *maskil*[q] of Asaph.

O my people, hear my teaching;
  listen to the words of my mouth.
I will open my mouth in parables,
  I will utter hidden things, things from of old—
what we have heard and known,
  what our fathers have told us.
We will not hide them from their children;
  we will tell the next generation
the praiseworthy deeds of the LORD,
  his power, and the wonders he has done.
He decreed statutes for Jacob
  and established the law in Israel,
which he commanded our forefathers
  to teach their children,
so the next generation would know them,
  even the children yet to be born,
  and they in turn would tell their children.
Then they would put their trust in God
  and would not forget his deeds
  but would keep his commands.
They would not be like their forefathers—
  a stubborn and rebellious generation,
whose hearts were not loyal to God,
  whose spirits were not faithful to him.

The men of Ephraim, though armed with bows,
  turned back on the day of battle;
they did not keep God's covenant
  and refused to live by his law.
They forgot what he had done,
  the wonders he had shown them.

q Title: Probably a literary or musical term

He did miracles in the sight of their fathers
   in the land of Egypt, in the region of Zoan.
He divided the sea and led them through;
   he made the water stand firm like a wall.
He guided them with the cloud by day
   and with light from the fire all night.
He split the rocks in the desert
   and gave them water as abundant as the seas;
he brought streams out of a rocky crag
   and made water flow down like rivers.

But they continued to sin against him,
   rebelling in the desert against the Most High.
They willfully put God to the test
   by demanding the food they craved.
They spoke against God, saying,
   "Can God spread a table in the desert?
When he struck the rock, water gushed out,
   and streams flowed abundantly.
But can he also give us food?
   Can he supply meat for his people?"
When the LORD heard them, he was very angry;
   his fire broke out against Jacob,
   and his wrath rose against Israel,
for they did not believe in God
   or trust in his deliverance.
Yet he gave a command to the skies above
   and opened the doors of the heavens;
he rained down manna for the people to eat,
   he gave them the grain of heaven.
Men ate the bread of angels;
   he sent them all the food they could eat.
He let loose the east wind from the heavens
   and led forth the south wind by his power.
He rained meat down on them like dust,
   flying birds like sand on the seashore.
He made them come down inside their camp,
   all around their tents.
They ate till they had more than enough,
   for he had given them what they craved.
But before they turned from the food they craved,
   even while it was still in their mouths,
God's anger rose against them;
   he put to death the sturdiest among them,
   cutting down the young men of Israel.

In spite of all this, they kept on sinning;
   in spite of his wonders, they did not believe.
So he ended their days in futility
   and their years in terror.
Whenever God slew them, they would seek him;
   they eagerly turned to him again.
They remembered that God was their Rock,

that God Most High was their Redeemer.
But then they would flatter him with their mouths,
  lying to him with their tongues;
their hearts were not loyal to him,
  they were not faithful to his covenant.
Yet he was merciful;
  he forgave their iniquities
  and did not destroy them.
Time after time he restrained his anger
  and did not stir up his full wrath.
He remembered that they were but flesh,
  a passing breeze that does not return.

How often they rebelled against him in the desert
  and grieved him in the wasteland!
Again and again they put God to the test;
  they vexed the Holy One of Israel.
They did not remember his power—
  the day he redeemed them from the oppressor,
the day he displayed his miraculous signs in Egypt,
  his wonders in the region of Zoan.
He turned their rivers to blood;
  they could not drink from their streams.
He sent swarms of flies that devoured them,
  and frogs that devastated them.
He gave their crops to the grasshopper,
  their produce to the locust.
He destroyed their vines with hail
  and their sycamore-figs with sleet.
He gave over their cattle to the hail,
  their livestock to bolts of lightning.
He unleashed against them his hot anger,
  his wrath, indignation and hostility—
  a band of destroying angels.
He prepared a path for his anger;
  he did not spare them from death
  but gave them over to the plague.
He struck down all the firstborn of Egypt,
  the firstfruits of manhood in the tents of Ham.
But he brought his people out like a flock;
  he led them like sheep through the desert.
He guided them safely, so they were unafraid;
  but the sea engulfed their enemies.
Thus he brought them to the border of his holy land,
  to the hill country his right hand had taken.
He drove out nations before them
  and allotted their lands to them as an inheritance;
  he settled the tribes of Israel in their homes.

But they put God to the test
  and rebelled against the Most High;
  they did not keep his statutes.
Like their fathers they were disloyal and faithless,

as unreliable as a faulty bow.
They angered him with their high places;
 they aroused his jealousy with their idols.
When God heard them, he was very angry;
 he rejected Israel completely.
He abandoned the tabernacle of Shiloh,
 the tent he had set up among men.
He sent ⌊the ark of⌋ his might into captivity,
 his splendor into the hands of the enemy.
He gave his people over to the sword;
 he was very angry with his inheritance.
Fire consumed their young men,
 and their maidens had no wedding songs;
their priests were put to the sword,
 and their widows could not weep.

Then the Lord awoke as from sleep,
 as a man wakes from the stupor of wine.
He beat back his enemies;
 he put them to everlasting shame.
Then he rejected the tents of Joseph,
 he did not choose the tribe of Ephraim;
but he chose the tribe of Judah,
 Mount Zion, which he loved.
He built his sanctuary like the heights,
 like the earth that he established forever.
He chose David his servant
 and took him from the sheep pens;
from tending the sheep he brought him
 to be the shepherd of his people Jacob,
 of Israel his inheritance.
And David shepherded them with integrity of heart;
 with skillful hands he led them.

Israel's restoration after punishment.

Psa. 107

Give thanks to the LORD, for he is good;
 his love endures forever.
Let the redeemed of the LORD say this—
 those he redeemed from the hand of the foe,
those he gathered from the lands,
 from east and west, from north and south.[r]

Some wandered in desert wastelands,
 finding no way to a city where they could settle.
They were hungry and thirsty,
 and their lives ebbed away.
Then they cried out to the LORD in their trouble,
 and he delivered them from their distress.
He led them by a straight way
 to a city where they could settle.
Let them give thanks to the LORD for his unfailing love

[r]Hebrew *north and the sea*

and his wonderful deeds for men,
for he satisfies the thirsty
and fills the hungry with good things.

Some sat in darkness and the deepest gloom,
prisoners suffering in iron chains,
for they had rebelled against the words of God
and despised the counsel of the Most High.
So he subjected them to bitter labor;
they stumbled, and there was no one to help.
Then they cried to the LORD in their trouble,
and he saved them from their distress.
He brought them out of darkness and the deepest gloom
and broke away their chains.
Let them give thanks to the LORD for his unfailing love
and his wonderful deeds for men,
for he breaks down gates of bronze
and cuts through bars of iron.

Some became fools through their rebellious ways
and suffered affliction because of their iniquities.
They loathed all food
and drew near the gates of death.
Then they cried to the LORD in their trouble,
and he saved them from their distress.
He sent forth his word and healed them;
he rescued them from the grave.
Let them give thanks to the LORD for his unfailing love
and his wonderful deeds for men.
Let them sacrifice thank offerings
and tell of his works with songs of joy.

Others went out on the sea in ships;
they were merchants on the mighty waters.
They saw the works of the LORD,
his wonderful deeds in the deep.
For he spoke and stirred up a tempest
that lifted high the waves.
They mounted up to the heavens and went down to the
depths;
in their peril their courage melted away.
They reeled and staggered like drunken men;
they were at their wits' end.
Then they cried out to the LORD in their trouble,
and he brought them out of their distress.
He stilled the storm to a whisper;
the waves of the sea were hushed.
They were glad when it grew calm,
and he guided them to their desired haven.
Let them give thanks to the LORD for his unfailing love
and his wonderful deeds for men.
Let them exalt him in the assembly of the people
and praise him in the council of the elders.

He turned rivers into a desert,
  flowing springs into thirsty ground,
and fruitful land into a salt waste,
  because of the wickedness of those who lived there.
He turned the desert into pools of water
  and the parched ground into flowing springs;
there he brought the hungry to live,
  and they founded a city where they could settle.
They sowed fields and planted vineyards
  that yielded a fruitful harvest;
he blessed them, and their numbers greatly increased,
  and he did not let their herds diminish.

Then their numbers decreased, and they were humbled
  by oppression, calamity and sorrow;
he who pours contempt on nobles
  made them wander in a trackless waste.
But he lifted the needy out of their affliction
  and increased their families like flocks.
The upright see and rejoice,
  but all the wicked shut their mouths.

Whoever is wise, let him heed these things
  and consider the great love of the LORD.

Praise for deliverance from the chains and death of captivity.   Psa. 116

I love the LORD, for he heard my voice;
  he heard my cry for mercy.
Because he turned his ear to me,
  I will call on him as long as I live.

The cords of death entangled me,
  the anguish of the grave[s] came upon me;
  I was overcome by trouble and sorrow.
Then I called on the name of the LORD:
  "O LORD, save me!"

The LORD is gracious and righteous;
  our God is full of compassion.
The LORD protects the simplehearted;
  when I was in great need, he saved me.

Be at rest once more, O my soul,
  for the LORD has been good to you.

For you, O LORD, have delivered my soul from death,
  my eyes from tears,
  my feet from stumbling,
that I may walk before the LORD
  in the land of the living.
I believed; therefore[t] I said,
  "I am greatly afflicted."
And in my dismay I said,

[s]Hebrew Sheol   [t]Or believed even when

"All men are liars."

How can I repay the LORD
   for all his goodness to me?
I will lift up the cup of salvation
   and call on the name of the LORD.
I will fulfill my vows to the LORD
   in the presence of all his people.

Precious in the sight of the LORD
   is the death of his saints.
O LORD, truly I am your servant;
   I am your servant, the son of your maidservant[u];
   you have freed me from my chains.

I will sacrifice a thank offering to you
   and call on the name of the LORD.
I will fulfill my vows to the LORD
   in the presence of all his people,
in the courts of the house of the LORD—
   in your midst, O Jerusalem.

Praise the LORD.[v]

Psa. 118   **Praise for a renewed life.**

Give thanks to the LORD, for he is good;
   his love endures forever.

Let Israel say:
   "His love endures forever."
Let the house of Aaron say:
   "His love endures forever."
Let those who fear the LORD say:
   "His love endures forever."

In my anguish I cried to the LORD,
   and he answered by setting me free.
The LORD is with me; I will not be afraid.
   What can man do to me?
The LORD is with me; he is my helper.
   I will look in triumph on my enemies.

It is better to take refuge in the LORD
   than to trust in man.
It is better to take refuge in the LORD
   than to trust in princes.

All the nations surrounded me,
   but in the name of the LORD I cut them off.
They surrounded me on every side,
   but in the name of the LORD I cut them off.
They swarmed around me like bees,
   but they died out as quickly as burning thorns;
   in the name of the LORD I cut them off.

[u]Or servant, your faithful son   [v]Hebrew Hallelu Yah

I was pushed back and about to fall,
    but the LORD helped me.
The LORD is my strength and my song;
    he has become my salvation.

Shouts of joy and victory
    resound in the tents of the righteous:
"The LORD's right hand has done mighty things!
    The LORD's right hand is lifted high;
    the LORD's right hand has done mighty things!"

I will not die but live,
    and will proclaim what the LORD has done.
The LORD has chastened me severely,
    but he has not given me over to death.

Open for me the gates of righteousness;
    I will enter and give thanks to the LORD.
This is the gate of the LORD
    through which the righteous may enter.
I will give you thanks, for you answered me;
    you have become my salvation.

The stone the builders rejected
    has become the capstone;
the LORD has done this,
    and it is marvelous in our eyes.
This is the day the LORD has made;
    let us rejoice and be glad in it.

O LORD, save us;
    O LORD, grant us success.
Blessed is he who comes in the name of the LORD.
    From the house of the LORD we bless you.*w*
The LORD is God,
    and he has made his light shine upon us.
With boughs in hand, join in the festal procession
    up*x* to the horns of the altar.

You are my God, and I will give you thanks;
    you are my God, and I will exalt you.

Give thanks to the LORD, for he is good;
    his love endures forever.

Prayer of trust that foreign dominance will end.   Psa. 125

A song of ascents.

Those who trust in the LORD are like Mount Zion,
    which cannot be shaken but endures forever.
As the mountains surround Jerusalem,
    so the LORD surrounds his people
    both now and forevermore.

The scepter of the wicked will not remain

---

*w*The Hebrew is plural.   *x*Or *Bind the festal sacrifice with ropes / and take it*

over the land allotted to the righteous,
for then the righteous might use
    their hands to do evil.

Do good, O LORD, to those who are good,
    to those who are upright in heart.
But those who turn to crooked ways
    the LORD will banish with the evildoers.

Peace be upon Israel.

Psa. 126

Joy of return to Jerusalem.

A song of ascents.

When the LORD brought back the captives to^y Zion,
    we were like men who dreamed.^z
Our mouths were filled with laughter,
    our tongues with songs of joy.
Then it was said among the nations,
    "The LORD has done great things for them."
The LORD has done great things for us,
    and we are filled with joy.

Restore our fortunes,^a O LORD,
    like streams in the Negev.
Those who sow in tears
    will reap with songs of joy.
He who goes out weeping,
    carrying seed to sow,
will return with songs of joy,
    carrying sheaves with him.

Psa. 128

Blessings of righteousness and prosperity of Jerusalem.

A song of ascents.

Blessed are all who fear the LORD,
    who walk in his ways.
You will eat the fruit of your labor;
    blessings and prosperity will be yours.
Your wife will be like a fruitful vine
    within your house;
your sons will be like olive shoots
    around your table.
Thus is the man blessed
    who fears the LORD.

May the LORD bless you from Zion
    all the days of your life;
may you see the prosperity of Jerusalem,
    and may you live to see your children's children.

Peace be upon Israel.

---

^yOr LORD *restored the fortunes of*   ^zOr *men restored to health*   ^aOr *Bring back our captives*

Deliverance will bring shame to scoffers.   Psa. 129

A song of ascents.

They have greatly oppressed me from my youth—
    let Israel say—
they have greatly oppressed me from my youth,
    but they have not gained the victory over me.
Plowmen have plowed my back
    and made their furrows long.
But the LORD is righteous;
    he has cut me free from the cords of the wicked.

May all who hate Zion
    be turned back in shame.
May they be like grass on the roof,
    which withers before it can grow;
with it the reaper cannot fill his hands,
    nor the one who gathers fill his arms.
May those who pass by not say,
    "The blessing of the LORD be upon you;
    we bless you in the name of the LORD."

Call for God's fulfillment of royal promise.   Psa. 132

A song of ascents.

O LORD, remember David
    and all the hardships he endured.

He swore an oath to the LORD
    and made a vow to the Mighty One of Jacob:
"I will not enter my house
    or go to my bed—
I will allow no sleep to my eyes,
    no slumber to my eyelids,
till I find a place for the LORD,
    a dwelling for the Mighty One of Jacob."

We heard it in Ephrathah,
    we came upon it in the fields of Jaar*b:c*
"Let us go to his dwelling place;
    let us worship at his footstool—
arise, O LORD, and come to your resting place,
    you and the ark of your might.
May your priests be clothed with righteousness;
    may your saints sing for joy."

For the sake of David your servant,
    do not reject your anointed one.

The LORD swore an oath to David,
    a sure oath that he will not revoke:
"One of your own descendants
    I will place on your throne—

b That is, Kiriath Jearim   *c* Or *heard of it in Ephrathah, / we found it in the fields of Jaar.*
(And no quotes around verses 7-9)

if your sons keep my covenant
    and the statutes I teach them,
then their sons will sit
    on your throne for ever and ever."

For the LORD has chosen Zion,
    he has desired it for his dwelling:
"This is my resting place for ever and ever;
    here I will sit enthroned, for I have desired it—
I will bless her with abundant provisions;
    her poor will I satisfy with food.
I will clothe her priests with salvation,
    and her saints will ever sing for joy.

"Here I will make a horn^d grow for David
    and set up a lamp for my anointed one.
I will clothe his enemies with shame,
    but the crown on his head will be resplendent."

Psa. 147   **Creator's power has brought restoration.**

Praise the LORD.^{e}

How good it is to sing praises to our God,
    how pleasant and fitting to praise him!

The LORD builds up Jerusalem;
    he gathers the exiles of Israel.
He heals the brokenhearted
    and binds up their wounds.

He determines the number of the stars
    and calls them each by name.
Great is our Lord and mighty in power;
    his understanding has no limit.
The LORD sustains the humble
    but casts the wicked to the ground.

Sing to the LORD with thanksgiving;
    make music to our God on the harp.
He covers the sky with clouds;
    he supplies the earth with rain
    and makes grass grow on the hills.
He provides food for the cattle
    and for the young ravens when they call.

His pleasure is not in the strength of the horse,
    nor his delight in the legs of a man;
the LORD delights in those who fear him,
    who put their hope in his unfailing love.

Extol the LORD, O Jerusalem;
    praise your God, O Zion,
for he strengthens the bars of your gates
    and blesses your people within you.

^{d}*Horn* here symbolizes strong one, that is, king. ^{e}Hebrew *Hallelu Yah*

He grants peace to your borders
    and satisfies you with the finest of wheat.

He sends his command to the earth;
    his word runs swiftly.
He spreads the snow like wool
    and scatters the frost like ashes.
He hurls down his hail like pebbles.
    Who can withstand his icy blast?
He sends his word and melts them;
    he stirs up his breezes, and the waters flow.

He has revealed his word to Jacob,
    his laws and decrees to Israel.
He has done this for no other nation;
    they do not know his laws.

Praise the LORD.

Praise for the King and preparedness to fight for the nation.   Psa. 149

Praise the LORD.*f*

Sing to the LORD a new song,
    his praise in the assembly of the saints.

Let Israel rejoice in their Maker;
    let the people of Zion be glad in their King.
Let them praise his name with dancing
    and make music to him with tambourine and harp.
For the LORD takes delight in his people;
    he crowns the humble with salvation.
Let the saints rejoice in this honor
    and sing for joy on their beds.

May the praise of God be in their mouths
    and a double-edged sword in their hands,
to inflict vengeance on the nations
    and punishment on the peoples,
to bind their kings with fetters,
    their nobles with shackles of iron,
to carry out the sentence written against them.
    This is the glory of all his saints.

Praise the LORD.

Zechariah's Futuristic Prophecies

*T*here is no indication at all as to when the final prophecies of Zechariah are either received or recorded. It is not likely that they would have come later than about 460 B.C. Since the historical record is otherwise virtually silent for about 35 years, Zechariah's last prophecies will be set forth at this point.

f Hebrew *Hallelu Yah*

The prophecies, in the form of two oracles, are once again highly figurative. They are undoubtedly messianic and give some of the clearest details about the life and death of the Messiah. For example, in contrast to the present kings and their chariots of war, this spiritual King will come gently in peace, riding on a donkey. He will be betrayed for 30 pieces of silver, and he will be pierced at the time of his death.

Zechariah addresses a number of themes—past, present, and future—which lead to an apocalyptic view of the great battle between good and evil, the destruction of the wicked, and the salvation of the righteous.

Zech. 9:1-8   DESTRUCTION OF OPPRESSORS.

The word of the LORD is against the land of Hadrach
    and will rest upon Damascus—
for the eyes of men and all the tribes of Israel
    are on the LORD—*g*
and upon Hamath too, which borders on it,
    and upon Tyre and Sidon, though they are very skillful.
Tyre has built herself a stronghold;
    she has heaped up silver like dust,
    and gold like the dirt of the streets.
But the Lord will take away her possessions
    and destroy her power on the sea,
    and she will be consumed by fire.
Ashkelon will see it and fear;
    Gaza will writhe in agony,
    and Ekron too, for her hope will wither.
Gaza will lose her king
    and Ashkelon will be deserted.
Foreigners will occupy Ashdod,
    and I will cut off the pride of the Philistines.
I will take the blood from their mouths,
    the forbidden food from between their teeth.
Those who are left will belong to our God
    and become leaders in Judah,
    and Ekron will be like the Jebusites.
But I will defend my house
    against marauding forces.
Never again will an oppressor overrun my people,
    for now I am keeping watch.

Zech.   COMING OF ZION'S KING.
9:9-13
Rejoice greatly, O Daughter of Zion!
    Shout, Daughter of Jerusalem!
See, your king*h* comes to you,
    righteous and having salvation,
    gentle and riding on a donkey,
    on a colt, the foal of a donkey.
I will take away the chariots from Ephraim

*g*Or *Damascus. / For the eye of the* LORD *is on all mankind, / as well as on the tribes of Israel,*
*h*Or *King*

and the war-horses from Jerusalem,
and the battle bow will be broken.
He will proclaim peace to the nations.
His rule will extend from sea to sea
and from the River[i] to the ends of the earth.[j]
As for you, because of the blood of my covenant with you,
I will free your prisoners from the waterless pit.
Return to your fortress, O prisoners of hope;
even now I announce that I will restore twice as much to
you.
I will bend Judah as I bend my bow
and fill it with Ephraim.
I will rouse your sons, O Zion,
against your sons, O Greece,
and make you like a warrior's sword.

APPEARANCE OF THE LORD.

Zech.
9:14-17

Then the LORD will appear over them;
his arrow will flash like lightning.
The Sovereign LORD will sound the trumpet;
he will march in the storms of the south,
and the LORD Almighty will shield them.
They will destroy
and overcome with slingstones.
They will drink and roar as with wine;
they will be full like a bowl
used for sprinkling[k] the corners of the altar.
The LORD their God will save them on that day
as the flock of his people.
They will sparkle in his land
like jewels in a crown.
How attractive and beautiful they will be!
Grain will make the young men thrive,
and new wine the young women.

RUIN BY LEADERS.

Zech.
10:1-3

Ask the LORD for rain in the springtime;
it is the LORD who makes the storm clouds.
He gives showers of rain to men,
and plants of the field to everyone.
The idols speak deceit,
diviners see visions that lie;
they tell dreams that are false,
they give comfort in vain.
Therefore the people wander like sheep
oppressed for lack of a shepherd.

"My anger burns against the shepherds,
and I will punish the leaders;
for the LORD Almighty will care

---

[i]That is, the Euphrates   [j]Or the end of the land   [k]Or bowl, / like

>
> for his flock, the house of Judah,
> and make them like a proud horse in battle.

Zech.
10:4-12

REDEMPTION OF ISRAEL.

> From Judah will come the cornerstone,
> from him the tent peg,
> from him the battle bow,
> from him every ruler.
> Together they[l] will be like mighty men
> trampling the muddy streets in battle.
> Because the LORD is with them,
> they will fight and overthrow the horsemen.
>
> "I will strengthen the house of Judah
> and save the house of Joseph.
> I will restore them
> because I have compassion on them.
> They will be as though
> I had not rejected them,
> for I am the LORD their God
> and I will answer them.
> The Ephraimites will become like mighty men,
> and their hearts will be glad as with wine.
> Their children will see it and be joyful;
> their hearts will rejoice in the LORD.
> I will signal for them
> and gather them in.
> Surely I will redeem them;
> they will be as numerous as before.
> Though I scatter them among the peoples,
> yet in distant lands they will remember me.
> They and their children will survive,
> and they will return.
> I will bring them back from Egypt
> and gather them from Assyria.
> I will bring them to Gilead and Lebanon,
> and there will not be room enough for them.
> They will pass through the sea of trouble;
> the surging sea will be subdued
> and all the depths of the Nile will dry up.
> Assyria's pride will be brought down
> and Egypt's scepter will pass away.
> I will strengthen them in the LORD
> and in his name they will walk,"

declares the LORD.

Zech.
11:1-3

LAMENT FOR SHEPHERDS.

> Open your doors, O Lebanon,
> so that fire may devour your cedars!
> Wail, O pine tree, for the cedar has fallen;

---

[l]Or *ruler, all of them together.* / [5]*They*

> the stately trees are ruined!
> Wail, oaks of Bashan;
> > the dense forest has been cut down!
> Listen to the wail of the shepherds;
> > their rich pastures are destroyed!
> Listen to the roar of the lions;
> > the lush thicket of the Jordan is ruined!

THE GOOD AND BAD SHEPHERDS.   This is what the LORD my God says: "Pasture the flock marked for slaughter. Their buyers slaughter them and go unpunished. Those who sell them say, 'Praise the LORD, I am rich!' Their own shepherds do not spare them. For I will no longer have pity on the people of the land," declares the LORD. "I will hand everyone over to his neighbor and his king. They will oppress the land, and I will not rescue them from their hands."

Zech.
11:4-17

So I pastured the flock marked for slaughter, particularly the oppressed of the flock. Then I took two staffs and called one Favor and the other Union, and I pastured the flock. In one month I got rid of the three shepherds.

The flock detested me, and I grew weary of them and said, "I will not be your shepherd. Let the dying die, and the perishing perish. Let those who are left eat one another's flesh."

Then I took my staff called Favor and broke it, revoking the covenant I had made with all the nations. It was revoked on that day, and so the afflicted of the flock who were watching me knew it was the word of the LORD.

I told them, "If you think it best, give me my pay; but if not, keep it." So they paid me thirty pieces of silver.

And the LORD said to me, "Throw it to the potter"— the handsome price at which they priced me! So I took the thirty pieces of silver and threw them into the house of the LORD to the potter.

Then I broke my second staff called Union, breaking the brotherhood between Judah and Israel.

Then the LORD said to me, "Take again the equipment of a foolish shepherd. For I am going to raise up a shepherd over the land who will not care for the lost, or seek the young, or heal the injured, or feed the healthy, but will eat the meat of the choice sheep, tearing off their hoofs.

> "Woe to the worthless shepherd,
> > who deserts the flock!
> May the sword strike his arm and his right eye!
> > May his arm be completely withered,
> > his right eye totally blinded!"

An Oracle

SALVATION OF JERUSALEM.   This is the word of the LORD concerning Israel. The LORD, who stretches out the heavens, who lays the foundation of the earth, and who forms the spirit of man within him, declares: "I am going to make Jerusalem a cup that sends all the surrounding peoples reeling. Judah will be besieged as well as Jerusalem. On that day, when all the nations of the earth are gathered against her, I will make Jerusalem an immovable rock for all the nations. All who try to move it will injure themselves. On that day I will strike every horse with panic and its rider with

Zech.
12:1-9

madness," declares the LORD. "I will keep a watchful eye over the house of Judah, but I will blind all the horses of the nations. Then the leaders of Judah will say in their hearts, 'The people of Jerusalem are strong, because the LORD Almighty is their God.'

"On that day I will make the leaders of Judah like a firepot in a wood-pile, like a flaming torch among sheaves. They will consume right and left all the surrounding peoples, but Jerusalem will remain intact in her place.

"The LORD will save the dwellings of Judah first, so that the honor of the house of David and of Jerusalem's inhabitants may not be greater than that of Judah. On that day the LORD will shield those who live in Jerusalem, so that the feeblest among them will be like David, and the house of David will be like God, like the Angel of the LORD going before them. On that day I will set out to destroy all the nations that attack Jerusalem.

Zech.
12:10-14

MOURNING FOR ONE PIERCED.   "And I will pour out on the house of David and the inhabitants of Jerusalem a spirit[m] of grace and supplica-tion. They will look on[n] me, the one they have pierced, and they will mourn for him as one mourns for an only child, and grieve bitterly for him as one grieves for a firstborn son. On that day the weeping in Jerusalem will be great, like the weeping of Hadad Rimmon in the plain of Megiddo. The land will mourn, each clan by itself, with their wives by themselves: the clan of the house of David and their wives, the clan of the house of Nathan and their wives, the clan of the house of Levi and their wives, the clan of Shimei and their wives, and all the rest of the clans and their wives.

Zech.
13:1-6

CLEANSING FROM SIN.   "On that day a fountain will be opened to the house of David and the inhabitants of Jerusalem, to cleanse them from sin and impurity.

"On that day, I will banish the names of the idols from the land, and they will be remembered no more," declares the LORD Almighty. "I will remove both the prophets and the spirit of impurity from the land. And if anyone still prophesies, his father and mother, to whom he was born, will say to him, 'You must die, because you have told lies in the LORD's name.' When he prophesies, his own parents will stab him.

"On that day every prophet will be ashamed of his prophetic vision. He will not put on a prophet's garment of hair in order to deceive. He will say, 'I am not a prophet. I am a farmer; the land has been my livelihood since my youth.[o]' If someone asks him, 'What are these wounds on your body[p]?' he will answer, 'The wounds I was given at the house of my friends.'

Zech.
13:7-9

THE SCATTERED SHEEP.

> "Awake, O sword, against my shepherd,
>   against the man who is close to me!"
>   declares the LORD Almighty.
> "Strike the shepherd,
>   and the sheep will be scattered,
>   and I will turn my hand against the little ones.
> In the whole land," declares the LORD,
>   "two-thirds will be struck down and perish;
>   yet one-third will be left in it.

[m]Or the Spirit   [n]Or to   [o]Or farmer; a man sold me in my youth   [p]Or wounds between your hands

> This third I will bring into the fire;
>   I will refine them like silver
>   and test them like gold.
> They will call on my name
>   and I will answer them;
>   I will say, 'They are my people,'
>   and they will say, 'The LORD is our God.' "

THE GREAT BATTLE.   A day of the LORD is coming when your plunder will be divided among you.

I will gather all the nations to Jerusalem to fight against it; the city will be captured, the houses ransacked, and the women raped. Half of the city will go into exile, but the rest of the people will not be taken from the city.

Then the LORD will go out and fight against those nations, as he fights in the day of battle. On that day his feet will stand on the Mount of Olives, east of Jerusalem, and the Mount of Olives will be split in two from east to west, forming a great valley, with half of the mountain moving north and half moving south. You will flee by my mountain valley, for it will extend to Azel. You will flee as you fled from the earthquake*q* in the days of Uzziah king of Judah. Then the LORD my God will come, and all the holy ones with him.

On that day there will be no light, no cold or frost. It will be a unique day, without daytime or nighttime—a day known to the LORD. When evening comes, there will be light.

Zech. 14:1-7

THE KING'S REIGN.   On that day living water will flow out from Jerusalem, half to the eastern sea*r* and half to the western sea,*s* in summer and in winter.

The LORD will be king over the whole earth. On that day there will be one LORD, and his name the only name.

The whole land, from Geba to Rimmon, south of Jerusalem, will become like the Arabah. But Jerusalem will be raised up and remain in its place, from the Benjamin Gate to the site of the First Gate, to the Corner Gate, and from the Tower of Hananel to the royal winepresses. It will be inhabited; never again will it be destroyed. Jerusalem will be secure.

Zech. 14:8-11

PUNISHMENT OF WICKED.   This is the plague with which the LORD will strike all the nations that fought against Jerusalem: Their flesh will rot while they are still standing on their feet, their eyes will rot in their sockets, and their tongues will rot in their mouths. On that day men will be stricken by the LORD with great panic. Each man will seize the hand of another, and they will attack each other. Judah too will fight at Jerusalem. The wealth of all the surrounding nations will be collected—great quantities of gold and silver and clothing. A similar plague will strike the horses and mules, the camels and donkeys, and all the animals in those camps.

Zech. 14:12-15

CELEBRATION OF RIGHTEOUS.   Then the survivors from all the nations that have attacked Jerusalem will go up year after year to worship the King, the LORD Almighty, and to celebrate the Feast of Tabernacles.

Zech. 14:16

ALL WILL ACKNOWLEDGE KING.   If any of the peoples of the earth do not go up to Jerusalem to worship the King, the LORD Almighty, they will

Zech. 14:17-19

---

*q*Or *5My mountain valley will be blocked and will extend to Azel. It will be blocked as it was blocked because of the earthquake*   *r*That is, the Dead Sea   *s*That is, the Mediterranean

have no rain. If the Egyptian people do not go up and take part, they will have no rain. The LORD[t] will bring on them the plague he inflicts on the nations that do not go up to celebrate the Feast of Tabernacles. This will be the punishment of Egypt and the punishment of all the nations that do not go up to celebrate the Feast of Tabernacles.

Zech.
14:20,21

HOLINESS OF KINGDOM.   On that day HOLY TO THE LORD will be inscribed on the bells of the horses, and the cooking pots in the LORD's house will be like the sacred bowls in front of the altar. Every pot in Jerusalem and Judah will be holy to the LORD Almighty, and all who come to sacrifice will take some of the pots and cook in them. And on that day there will no longer be a Canaanite[u] in the house of the LORD Almighty.

What a grand picture of the age to come! And what a perfect way for Zechariah to end his ministry. Like Daniel, Zechariah undoubtedly will rest for a time, then awake to meet the exciting fulfillment of his own words from God.

Esther and the Feast of Purim

With the temple now completed, the people of Israel are free to go about the job of recultivating the land and reconstructing other buildings in the cities. The resettlement process is laborious, and it will take another 60 years to restore the level of civilization that the nation once knew.

During this time Darius has thoroughly subdued Egypt, but, as with Israel, has permitted life in Egypt to go on pretty much as usual. When Darius dies, in 486 B.C., he is replaced by his son Xerxes I. Xerxes does not share the tolerant policies of his father and grandfather. He offends the Egyptians and Greeks through repressive measures, and offends even his own countrymen by his high taxes and destruction of a statue of the god Marduk. It is not known what kind of relationship Xerxes has with Israel at the outset, but it does not appear that he has any particular animosity against the Jews. There are still many Jews in his own country and, although they do have enemies there, no official opposition is apparent.

If Xerxes is the king referred to in other records as Ahasuerus (and there is considerable disagreement on the issue), then it is during his reign that one of the most fascinating stories in all of Jewish history takes place. It is a story of intrigue at the royal palace in Susa. There is plot and counterplot. There is suspense and danger, and unexpected twists of fate. And the final undoing of the villain is delightfully ironic. It is such a wonderful story that it should not be ruined by any preview. Suffice it to say that it takes place over a period of four years (presumably beginning in 483 B.C., the third year of Xerxes' reign), and features a beautiful Jewish girl whose Persian name is Esther, her father-figure Mordecai, his wicked enemy Haman, and the king himself.

[t]Or part, then the LORD   [u]Or merchant

THE STORY OF ESTHER.   This is what happened during the time of
Xerxes,[v] the Xerxes who ruled over 127 provinces stretching from India to
Cush[w]: At that time King Xerxes reigned from his royal throne in the
citadel of Susa, and in the third year of his reign he gave a banquet for all
his nobles and officials. The military leaders of Persia and Media, the
princes, and the nobles of the provinces were present.

For a full 180 days he displayed the vast wealth of his kingdom and the
splendor and glory of his majesty. When these days were over, the king
gave a banquet, lasting seven days, in the enclosed garden of the king's
palace, for all the people from the least to the greatest, who were in the
citadel of Susa. The garden had hangings of white and blue linen, fastened
with cords of white linen and purple material to silver rings on marble pillars. There were couches of gold and silver on a mosaic pavement of por-
phyry, marble, mother-of-pearl and other costly stones. Wine was served
in goblets of gold, each one different from the other, and the royal wine
was abundant, in keeping with the king's liberality. By the king's command each guest was allowed to drink in his own way, for the king
instructed all the wine stewards to serve each man what he wished.

Queen Vashti also gave a banquet for the women in the royal palace of
King Xerxes.

On the seventh day, when King Xerxes was in high spirits from wine, he
commanded the seven eunuchs who served him—Mehuman, Biztha,
Harbona, Bigtha, Abagtha, Zethar and Carcas—to bring before him Queen
Vashti, wearing her royal crown, in order to display her beauty to the people and nobles, for she was lovely to look at. But when the attendants
delivered the king's command, Queen Vashti refused to come. Then the
king became furious and burned with anger.

Since it was customary for the king to consult experts in matters of law
and justice, he spoke with the wise men who understood the times and
were closest to the king—Carshena, Shethar, Admatha, Tarshish, Meres,
Marsena and Memucan, the seven nobles of Persia and Media who had
special access to the king and were highest in the kingdom.

"According to law, what must be done to Queen Vashti?" he asked. "She
has not obeyed the command of King Xerxes that the eunuchs have taken
to her."

Then Memucan replied in the presence of the king and the nobles,
"Queen Vashti has done wrong, not only against the king but also against
all the nobles and the peoples of all the provinces of King Xerxes. For the
queen's conduct will become known to all the women, and so they will
despise their husbands and say, 'King Xerxes commanded Queen Vashti to
be brought before him, but she would not come.' This very day the Persian
and Median women of the nobility who have heard about the queen's conduct will respond to all the king's nobles in the same way. There will be no
end of disrespect and discord.

"Therefore, if it pleases the king, let him issue a royal decree and let it
be written in the laws of Persia and Media, which cannot be repealed, that
Vashti is never again to enter the presence of King Xerxes. Also let the king
give her royal position to someone else who is better than she. Then when

Esther
1:1-22
(483-479
B.C.?)
Susa

[v]Hebrew *Ahasuerus*, a variant of Xerxes' Persian name; here and throughout Esther
[w]That is, the upper Nile region

the king's edict is proclaimed throughout all his vast realm, all the women will respect their husbands, from the least to the greatest."

The king and his nobles were pleased with this advice, so the king did as Memucan proposed. He sent dispatches to all parts of the kingdom, to each province in its own script and to each people in its own language, proclaiming in each people's tongue that every man should be ruler over his own household.

Esther 2:1-23

Later when the anger of King Xerxes had subsided, he remembered Vashti and what she had done and what he had decreed about her. Then the king's personal attendants proposed, "Let a search be made for beautiful young virgins for the king. Let the king appoint commissioners in every province of his realm to bring all these beautiful girls into the harem at the citadel of Susa. Let them be placed under the care of Hegai, the king's eunuch, who is in charge of the women; and let beauty treatments be given to them. Then let the girl who pleases the king be queen instead of Vashti." This advice appealed to the king, and he followed it.

Now there was in the citadel of Susa a Jew of the tribe of Benjamin, named Mordecai son of Jair, the son of Shimei, the son of Kish, who had been carried into exile from Jerusalem by Nebuchadnezzar king of Babylon, among those taken captive with Jehoiachin[x] king of Judah. Mordecai had a cousin named Hadassah, whom he had brought up because she had neither father nor mother. This girl, who was also known as Esther, was lovely in form and features, and Mordecai had taken her as his own daughter when her father and mother died.

When the king's order and edict had been proclaimed, many girls were brought to the citadel of Susa and put under the care of Hegai. Esther also was taken to the king's palace and entrusted to Hegai, who had charge of the harem. The girl pleased him and won his favor. Immediately he provided her with her beauty treatments and special food. He assigned to her seven maids selected from the king's palace and moved her and her maids into the best place in the harem.

Esther had not revealed her nationality and family background, because Mordecai had forbidden her to do so. Every day he walked back and forth near the courtyard of the harem to find out how Esther was and what was happening to her.

Before a girl's turn came to go in to King Xerxes, she had to complete twelve months of beauty treatments prescribed for the women, six months with oil of myrrh and six with perfumes and cosmetics. And this is how she would go to the king: Anything she wanted was given her to take with her from the harem to the king's palace. In the evening she would go there and in the morning return to another part of the harem to the care of Shaashgaz, the king's eunuch who was in charge of the concubines. She would not return to the king unless he was pleased with her and summoned her by name.

When the turn came for Esther (the girl Mordecai had adopted, the daughter of his uncle Abihail) to go to the king, she asked for nothing other than what Hegai, the king's eunuch who was in charge of the harem, suggested. And Esther won the favor of everyone who saw her. She was

[x]Hebrew *Jeconiah*, a variant of *Jehoiachin*

taken to King Xerxes in the royal residence in the tenth month, the month of Tebeth, in the seventh year of his reign.

Now the king was attracted to Esther more than to any of the other women, and she won his favor and approval more than any of the other virgins. So he set a royal crown on her head and made her queen instead of Vashti. And the king gave a great banquet, Esther's banquet, for all his nobles and officials. He proclaimed a holiday throughout the provinces and distributed gifts with royal liberality.

When the virgins were assembled a second time, Mordecai was sitting at the king's gate. But Esther had kept secret her family background and nationality just as Mordecai had told her to do, for she continued to follow Mordecai's instructions as she had done when he was bringing her up.

During the time Mordecai was sitting at the king's gate, Bigthana[y] and Teresh, two of the king's officers who guarded the doorway, became angry and conspired to assassinate King Xerxes. But Mordecai found out about the plot and told Queen Esther, who in turn reported it to the king, giving credit to Mordecai. And when the report was investigated and found to be true, the two officials were hanged on a gallows.[z] All this was recorded in the book of the annals in the presence of the king.

After these events, King Xerxes honored Haman son of Hammedatha, the Agagite, elevating him and giving him a seat of honor higher than that of all the other nobles. All the royal officials at the king's gate knelt down and paid honor to Haman, for the king had commanded this concerning him. But Mordecai would not kneel down or pay him honor.

Esther
3:1-15

Then the royal officials at the king's gate asked Mordecai, "Why do you disobey the king's command?" Day after day they spoke to him but he refused to comply. Therefore they told Haman about it to see whether Mordecai's behavior would be tolerated, for he had told them he was a Jew.

When Haman saw that Mordecai would not kneel down or pay him honor, he was enraged. Yet having learned who Mordecai's people were, he scorned the idea of killing only Mordecai. Instead Haman looked for a way to destroy all Mordecai's people, the Jews, throughout the whole kingdom of Xerxes.

In the twelfth year of King Xerxes, in the first month, the month of Nisan, they cast the *pur* (that is, the lot) in the presence of Haman to select a day and month. And the lot fell on[a] the twelfth month, the month of Adar.

Then Haman said to King Xerxes, "There is a certain people dispersed and scattered among the peoples in all the provinces of your kingdom whose customs are different from those of all other people and who do not obey the king's laws; it is not in the king's best interest to tolerate them. If it pleases the king, let a decree be issued to destroy them, and I will put ten thousand talents[b] of silver into the royal treasury for the men who carry out this business."

So the king took his signet ring from his finger and gave it to Haman son of Hammedatha, the Agagite, the enemy of the Jews. "Keep the money," the king said to Haman, "and do with the people as you please."

---

[y]Hebrew *Bigthan*, a variant of *Bigthana*   [z]Or *were hung* (or *impaled*) *on poles*; similarly elsewhere in Esther   [a]Septuagint; Hebrew does not have *And the lot fell on.*   [b]That is, about 375 tons (about 345 metric tons)

Then on the thirteenth day of the first month the royal secretaries were summoned. They wrote out in the script of each province and in the language of each people all Haman's orders to the king's satraps, the governors of the various provinces and the nobles of the various peoples. These were written in the name of King Xerxes himself and sealed with his own ring. Dispatches were sent by couriers to all the king's provinces with the order to destroy, kill and annihilate all the Jews—young and old, women and little children—on a single day, the thirteenth day of the twelfth month, the month of Adar, and to plunder their goods. A copy of the text of the edict was to be issued as law in every province and made known to the people of every nationality so they would be ready for that day.

Spurred on by the king's command, the couriers went out, and the edict was issued in the citadel of Susa. The king and Haman sat down to drink, but the city of Susa was bewildered.

Esther 4:1-17

When Mordecai learned of all that had been done, he tore his clothes, put on sackcloth and ashes, and went out into the city, wailing loudly and bitterly. But he went only as far as the king's gate, because no one clothed in sackcloth was allowed to enter it. In every province to which the edict and order of the king came, there was great mourning among the Jews, with fasting, weeping and wailing. Many lay in sackcloth and ashes.

When Esther's maids and eunuchs came and told her about Mordecai, she was in great distress. She sent clothes for him to put on instead of his sackcloth, but he would not accept them. Then Esther summoned Hathach, one of the king's eunuchs assigned to attend her, and ordered him to find out what was troubling Mordecai and why.

So Hathach went out to Mordecai in the open square of the city in front of the king's gate. Mordecai told him everything that had happened to him, including the exact amount of money Haman had promised to pay into the royal treasury for the destruction of the Jews. He also gave him a copy of the text of the edict for their annihilation, which had been published in Susa, to show to Esther and explain it to her, and he told him to urge her to go into the king's presence to beg for mercy and plead with him for her people.

Hathach went back and reported to Esther what Mordecai had said. Then she instructed him to say to Mordecai, "All the king's officials and the people of the royal provinces know that for any man or woman who approaches the king in the inner court without being summoned the king has but one law: that he be put to death. The only exception to this is for the king to extend the gold scepter to him and spare his life. But thirty days have passed since I was called to go to the king."

When Esther's words were reported to Mordecai, he sent back this answer: "Do not think that because you are in the king's house you alone of all the Jews will escape. For if you remain silent at this time, relief and deliverance for the Jews will arise from another place, but you and your father's family will perish. And who knows but that you have come to royal position for such a time as this?"

Then Esther sent this reply to Mordecai: "Go, gather together all the Jews who are in Susa, and fast for me. Do not eat or drink for three days, night or day. I and my maids will fast as you do. When this is done, I will go to the king, even though it is against the law. And if I perish, I perish."

So Mordecai went away and carried out all of Esther's instructions.

On the third day Esther put on her royal robes and stood in the inner court of the palace, in front of the king's hall. The king was sitting on his royal throne in the hall, facing the entrance. When he saw Queen Esther standing in the court, he was pleased with her and held out to her the gold scepter that was in his hand. So Esther approached and touched the tip of the scepter.

Then the king asked, "What is it, Queen Esther? What is your request? Even up to half the kingdom, it will be given you."

"If it pleases the king," replied Esther, "let the king, together with Haman, come today to a banquet I have prepared for him."

"Bring Haman at once," the king said, "so that we may do what Esther asks."

So the king and Haman went to the banquet Esther had prepared. As they were drinking wine, the king again asked Esther, "Now what is your petition? It will be given you. And what is your request? Even up to half the kingdom, it will be granted."

Esther replied, "My petition and my request is this: If the king regards me with favor and if it pleases the king to grant my petition and fulfill my request, let the king and Haman come tomorrow to the banquet I will prepare for them. Then I will answer the king's question."

Haman went out that day happy and in high spirits. But when he saw Mordecai at the king's gate and observed that he neither rose nor showed fear in his presence, he was filled with rage against Mordecai. Nevertheless, Haman restrained himself and went home.

Calling together his friends and Zeresh, his wife, Haman boasted to them about his vast wealth, his many sons, and all the ways the king had honored him and how he had elevated him above the other nobles and officials. "And that's not all," Haman added. "I'm the only person Queen Esther invited to accompany the king to the banquet she gave. And she has invited me along with the king tomorrow. But all this gives me no satisfaction as long as I see that Jew Mordecai sitting at the king's gate."

His wife Zeresh and all his friends said to him, "Have a gallows built, seventy-five feet[c] high, and ask the king in the morning to have Mordecai hanged on it. Then go with the king to the dinner and be happy." This suggestion delighted Haman, and he had the gallows built.

That night the king could not sleep; so he ordered the book of the chronicles, the record of his reign, to be brought in and read to him. It was found recorded there that Mordecai had exposed Bigthana and Teresh, two of the king's officers who guarded the doorway, who had conspired to assassinate King Xerxes.

"What honor and recognition has Mordecai received for this?" the king asked.

"Nothing has been done for him," his attendants answered.

The king said, "Who is in the court?" Now Haman had just entered the outer court of the palace to speak to the king about hanging Mordecai on the gallows he had erected for him.

His attendants answered, "Haman is standing in the court."

"Bring him in," the king ordered.

Esther
5:1-14

Esther
6:1-14

[c]Hebrew *fifty cubits* (about 23 meters)

When Haman entered, the king asked him, "What should be done for the man the king delights to honor?"

Now Haman thought to himself, "Who is there that the king would rather honor than me?" So he answered the king, "For the man the king delights to honor, have them bring a royal robe the king has worn and a horse the king has ridden, one with a royal crest placed on its head. Then let the robe and horse be entrusted to one of the king's most noble princes. Let them robe the man the king delights to honor, and lead him on the horse through the city streets, proclaiming before him, 'This is what is done for the man the king delights to honor!' "

"Go at once," the king commanded Haman. "Get the robe and the horse and do just as you have suggested for Mordecai the Jew, who sits at the king's gate. Do not neglect anything you have recommended."

So Haman got the robe and the horse. He robed Mordecai, and led him on horseback through the city streets, proclaiming before him, "This is what is done for the man the king delights to honor!"

Afterward Mordecai returned to the king's gate. But Haman rushed home, with his head covered in grief, and told Zeresh his wife and all his friends everything that had happened to him.

His advisers and his wife Zeresh said to him, "Since Mordecai, before whom your downfall has started, is of Jewish origin, you cannot stand against him—you will surely come to ruin!" While they were still talking with him, the king's eunuchs arrived and hurried Haman away to the banquet Esther had prepared.

Esther 7:1-10

So the king and Haman went to dine with Queen Esther, and as they were drinking wine on that second day, the king again asked, "Queen Esther, what is your petition? It will be given you. What is your request? Even up to half the kingdom, it will be granted."

Then Queen Esther answered, "If I have found favor with you, O king, and if it pleases your majesty, grant me my life—this is my petition. And spare my people—this is my request. For I and my people have been sold for destruction and slaughter and annihilation. If we had merely been sold as male and female slaves, I would have kept quiet, because no such distress would justify disturbing the king.*d*"

King Xerxes asked Queen Esther, "Who is he? Where is the man who has dared to do such a thing?"

Esther said, "The adversary and enemy is this vile Haman."

Then Haman was terrified before the king and queen. The king got up in a rage, left his wine and went out into the palace garden. But Haman, realizing that the king had already decided his fate, stayed behind to beg Queen Esther for his life.

Just as the king returned from the palace garden to the banquet hall, Haman was falling on the couch where Esther was reclining.

The king exclaimed, "Will he even molest the queen while she is with me in the house?"

As soon as the word left the king's mouth, they covered Haman's face. Then Harbona, one of the eunuchs attending the king, said, "A gallows

d Or quiet, but the compensation our adversary offers cannot be compared with the loss the king would suffer

seventy-five feet*e* high stands by Haman's house. He had it made for Mordecai, who spoke up to help the king."

The king said, "Hang him on it!" So they hanged Haman on the gallows he had prepared for Mordecai. Then the king's fury subsided.

That same day King Xerxes gave Queen Esther the estate of Haman, the enemy of the Jews. And Mordecai came into the presence of the king, for Esther had told how he was related to her. The king took off his signet ring, which he had reclaimed from Haman, and presented it to Mordecai. And Esther appointed him over Haman's estate.

Esther 8:1-17

Esther again pleaded with the king, falling at his feet and weeping. She begged him to put an end to the evil plan of Haman the Agagite, which he had devised against the Jews. Then the king extended the gold scepter to Esther and she arose and stood before him.

"If it pleases the king," she said, "and if he regards me with favor and thinks it the right thing to do, and if he is pleased with me, let an order be written overruling the dispatches that Haman son of Hammedatha, the Agagite, devised and wrote to destroy the Jews in all the king's provinces. For how can I bear to see disaster fall on my people? How can I bear to see the destruction of my family?"

King Xerxes replied to Queen Esther and to Mordecai the Jew, "Because Haman attacked the Jews, I have given his estate to Esther, and they have hanged him on the gallows. Now write another decree in the king's name in behalf of the Jews as seems best to you, and seal it with the king's signet ring—for no document written in the king's name and sealed with his ring can be revoked."

At once the royal secretaries were summoned—on the twenty-third day of the third month, the month of Sivan. They wrote out all Mordecai's orders to the Jews, and to the satraps, governors and nobles of the 127 provinces stretching from India to Cush.*f* These orders were written in the script of each province and the language of each people and also to the Jews in their own script and language. Mordecai wrote in the name of King Xerxes, sealed the dispatches with the king's signet ring, and sent them by mounted couriers, who rode fast horses especially bred for the king.

The king's edict granted the Jews in every city the right to assemble and protect themselves; to destroy, kill and annihilate any armed force of any nationality or province that might attack them and their women and children; and to plunder the property of their enemies. The day appointed for the Jews to do this in all the provinces of King Xerxes was the thirteenth day of the twelfth month, the month of Adar. A copy of the text of the edict was to be issued as law in every province and made known to the people of every nationality so that the Jews would be ready on that day to avenge themselves on their enemies.

The couriers, riding the royal horses, raced out, spurred on by the king's command. And the edict was also issued in the citadel of Susa.

Mordecai left the king's presence wearing royal garments of blue and white, a large crown of gold and a purple robe of fine linen. And the city of Susa held a joyous celebration. For the Jews it was a time of happiness and joy, gladness and honor. In every province and in every city, wherever

---

*e*Hebrew *fifty cubits* (about 23 meters)   *f*That is, the upper Nile region

the edict of the king went, there was joy and gladness among the Jews, with feasting and celebrating. And many people of other nationalities became Jews because fear of the Jews had seized them.

Esther 9:1-17   On the thirteenth day of the twelfth month, the month of Adar, the edict commanded by the king was to be carried out. On this day the enemies of the Jews had hoped to overpower them, but now the tables were turned and the Jews got the upper hand over those who hated them. The Jews assembled in their cities in all the provinces of King Xerxes to attack those seeking their destruction. No one could stand against them, because the people of all the other nationalities were afraid of them. And all the nobles of the provinces, the satraps, the governors and the king's administrators helped the Jews, because fear of Mordecai had seized them. Mordecai was prominent in the palace; his reputation spread throughout the provinces, and he became more and more powerful.

The Jews struck down all their enemies with the sword, killing and destroying them, and they did what they pleased to those who hated them. In the citadel of Susa, the Jews killed and destroyed five hundred men. They also killed Parshandatha, Dalphon, Aspatha, Poratha, Adalia, Aridatha, Parmashta, Arisai, Aridai and Vaizatha, the ten sons of Haman son of Hammedatha, the enemy of the Jews. But they did not lay their hands on the plunder.

The number of those slain in the citadel of Susa was reported to the king that same day. The king said to Queen Esther, "The Jews have killed and destroyed five hundred men and the ten sons of Haman in the citadel of Susa. What have they done in the rest of the king's provinces? Now what is your petition? It will be given you. What is your request? It will also be granted."

"If it pleases the king," Esther answered, "give the Jews in Susa permission to carry out this day's edict tomorrow also, and let Haman's ten sons be hanged on gallows."

So the king commanded that this be done. An edict was issued in Susa, and they hanged the ten sons of Haman. The Jews in Susa came together on the fourteenth day of the month of Adar, and they put to death in Susa three hundred men, but they did not lay their hands on the plunder.

Meanwhile, the remainder of the Jews who were in the king's provinces also assembled to protect themselves and get relief from their enemies. They killed seventy-five thousand of them but did not lay their hands on the plunder. This happened on the thirteenth day of the month of Adar, and on the fourteenth they rested and made it a day of feasting and joy.

This wonderful historical account must surely be an inspiration to Jews all over the Persian Empire whose ancestors have suffered continual persecution. It is a patriotic story and a supreme example of personal courage. Although there is no mention of God or covenant or restoration, there is the clear message that God watches providentially over his people.

The celebration which ensued following the great victory over Haman and his supporters was the beginning of a yearly commemoration observed by Jews even to this day. At each celebration the story of Esther is read as a reminder of God's deliverance of his people. How the tradition of Purim comes about is recorded in an appendix to the story itself, as is a historical footnote about Mordecai's rise to power in Xerxes' government.

INSTITUTION OF PURIM.   The Jews in Susa, however, had assembled on the thirteenth and fourteenth, and then on the fifteenth they rested and made it a day of feasting and joy.

Esther
9:18-32
(479 B.C.?)

That is why rural Jews—those living in villages—observe the fourteenth of the month of Adar as a day of joy and feasting, a day for giving presents to each other.

Mordecai recorded these events, and he sent letters to all the Jews throughout the provinces of King Xerxes, near and far, to have them celebrate annually the fourteenth and fifteenth days of the month of Adar as the time when the Jews got relief from their enemies, and as the month when their sorrow was turned into joy and their mourning into a day of celebration. He wrote them to observe the days as days of feasting and joy and giving presents of food to one another and gifts to the poor.

So the Jews agreed to continue the celebration they had begun, doing what Mordecai had written to them. For Haman son of Hammedatha, the Agagite, the enemy of all the Jews, had plotted against the Jews to destroy them and had cast the *pur* (that is, the lot) for their ruin and destruction. But when the plot came to the king's attention,⁸ he issued written orders that the evil scheme Haman had devised against the Jews should come back onto his own head, and that he and his sons should be hanged on the gallows. (Therefore these days were called Purim, from the word *pur*.) Because of everything written in this letter and because of what they had seen and what had happened to them, the Jews took it upon themselves to establish the custom that they and their descendants and all who join them should without fail observe these two days every year, in the way prescribed and at the time appointed. These days should be remembered and observed in every generation by every family, and in every province and in every city. And these days of Purim should never cease to be celebrated by the Jews, nor should the memory of them die out among their descendants.

So Queen Esther, daughter of Abihail, along with Mordecai the Jew, wrote with full authority to confirm this second letter concerning Purim. And Mordecai sent letters to all the Jews in the 127 provinces of the kingdom of Xerxes—words of goodwill and assurance—to establish these days of Purim at their designated times, as Mordecai the Jew and Queen Esther had decreed for them, and as they had established for themselves and their descendants in regard to their times of fasting and lamentation. Esther's decree confirmed these regulations about Purim, and it was written down in the records.

MORDECAI'S HIGH POSITION.   King Xerxes imposed tribute throughout the empire, to its distant shores. And all his acts of power and might, together with a full account of the greatness of Mordecai to which the king had raised him, are they not written in the book of the annals of the kings of Media and Persia? Mordecai the Jew was second in rank to King Xerxes, preeminent among the Jews, and held in high esteem by his many fellow Jews, because he worked for the good of his people and spoke up for the welfare of all the Jews.

Esther
10:1-3

⁸Or *when Esther came before the king*

Prophecies of Malachi

From the time of Esther's courageous intercession it will be another 20 years before the historical record resumes. In the first 14 years of that time, King Xerxes' fortunes will take a turn for the worse, and he will finally be murdered in his own bedroom in 465 B.C. Xerxes' younger son, Longimanus, will then assume the Persian throne as Artaxerxes I.

Little is known of what happens in the area known as Trans-Euphrates in the 60 years following the completion of the temple. Later history indicates that the excitement surrounding the rebuilding of the temple, and even the incident with Esther and Haman, is not long-lived. Once again in the rollercoaster history of this beleaguered nation, discouragement apparently sets in. Part of the problem is that it simply takes a long time to revitalize a country which has been so totally devastated. But another part of the problem seemingly stems from the very thing that was meant to give the people of Israel hope and encouragement—that is, all the restoration prophecies with their grand visions of the coming Messiah and his powerful kingdom. After many years of slow progress, ongoing opposition, and continued dominance by the Persians, the people are asking the obvious questions: is this the restoration we were promised? Where is this Branch of Jesse, this King of the house of David who is supposed to deliver us from our enemies and establish an everlasting kingdom? When will this city that still lies mostly in ruins be transformed into a glorious Jerusalem? Was the Haman incident only a coincidence? Does God really care about his people? Is there really divine justice?

As discouragement and cynicism set in, the people's spiritual commitment suffers: the temple service is being neglected for lack of tithes and offerings; the priests are offering blemished sacrifices and failing to give instruction in the law; the men are marrying wives who worship foreign gods; and divorce is rampant.

Is there no spiritual leader during this decline—no one to chastise the sinners and bring hope to the disheartened? Although it is not at all certain that this is the context in which his ministry takes place, it is possible that this is the very time when the prophet Malachi comes on the scene. Without a doubt his prophecies speak to the very issues of this period. Malachi's message is powerful in its simplicity: yes, God does still love his people; and, yes, all the grandeur of the ultimate restoration is still coming—in God's own time. In the meantime, it is each person's responsibility to lead the kind of life that will be fit for God's holy kingdom.

Nothing much is known about who this prophet of God really is. Malachi's style of prophecy is distinctive by its use of affirmations, questions, and answers. After first presenting a given affirmation, Malachi asks the questions a doubter would ask, then proceeds to demonstrate the foolishness of the doubter and the wisdom of the stated affirmation. Throughout it all is Malachi's assurance that "the day of the Lord" is definitely coming.

Mal. 1:1   PREFACE.   An oracle: The word of the LORD to Israel through Malachi.[h]

[h]Malachi means *my messenger.*

GOD'S LOVE CONTINUES.   "I have loved you," says the LORD.   Mal. 1:2-5
  "But you ask, 'How have you loved us?'   (500-460
  "Was not Esau Jacob's brother?" the LORD says. "Yet I have loved Jacob,   B.C.?)
but Esau I have hated, and I have turned his mountains into a wasteland
and left his inheritance to the desert jackals."
  Edom may say, "Though we have been crushed, we will rebuild the
ruins."
  But this is what the LORD Almighty says: "They may build, but I will
demolish. They will be called the Wicked Land, a people always under the
wrath of the LORD. You will see it with your own eyes and say, 'Great is the
LORD—even beyond the borders of Israel!'

BLEMISHED SACRIFICES.   "A son honors his father, and a servant his   Mal. 1:6-14
master. If I am a father, where is the honor due me? If I am a master, where
is the respect due me?" says the LORD Almighty. "It is you, O priests, who
show contempt for my name.
  "But you ask, 'How have we shown contempt for your name?'
  "You place defiled food on my altar.
  "But you ask, 'How have we defiled you?'
  "By saying that the LORD's table is contemptible. When you bring blind
animals for sacrifice, is that not wrong? When you sacrifice crippled or
diseased animals, is that not wrong? Try offering them to your governor!
Would he be pleased with you? Would he accept you?" says the LORD
Almighty.
  "Now implore God to be gracious to us. With such offerings from your
hands, will he accept you?"—says the LORD Almighty.
  "Oh, that one of you would shut the temple doors, so that you would
not light useless fires on my altar! I am not pleased with you," says the
LORD Almighty, "and I will accept no offering from your hands. My name
will be great among the nations, from the rising to the setting of the sun.
In every place incense and pure offerings will be brought to my name,
because my name will be great among the nations," says the LORD
Almighty.
  "But you profane it by saying of the Lord's table, 'It is defiled,' and of its
food, 'It is contemptible.' And you say, 'What a burden!' and you sniff at
it contemptuously," says the LORD Almighty.
  "When you bring injured, crippled or diseased animals and offer them
as sacrifices, should I accept them from your hands?" says the LORD.
"Cursed is the cheat who has an acceptable male in his flock and vows to
give it, but then sacrifices a blemished animal to the Lord. For I am a great
king," says the LORD Almighty, "and my name is to be feared among the
nations.

NO PRIESTLY TEACHING.   "And now this admonition is for you, O   Mal. 2:1-9
priests. If you do not listen, and if you do not set your heart to honor my
name," says the LORD Almighty, "I will send a curse upon you, and I will
curse your blessings. Yes, I have already cursed them, because you have
not set your heart to honor me.
  "Because of you I will rebukeⁱ your descendants^j; I will spread on your
faces the offal from your festival sacrifices, and you will be carried off with

_iOr *cut off* (see Septuagint)   _jOr *will blight your grain*

it. And you will know that I have sent you this admonition so that my covenant with Levi may continue," says the LORD Almighty. "My covenant was with him, a covenant of life and peace, and I gave them to him; this called for reverence and he revered me and stood in awe of my name. True instruction was in his mouth and nothing false was found on his lips. He walked with me in peace and uprightness, and turned many from sin.

"For the lips of a priest ought to preserve knowledge, and from his mouth men should seek instruction—because he is the messenger of the LORD Almighty. But you have turned from the way and by your teaching have caused many to stumble; you have violated the covenant with Levi," says the LORD Almighty. "So I have caused you to be despised and humiliated before all the people, because you have not followed my ways but have shown partiality in matters of the law."

Mal. 2:10-12

INTERMARRIAGES.   Have we not all one Father[k]? Did not one God create us? Why do we profane the covenant of our fathers by breaking faith with one another?

Judah has broken faith. A detestable thing has been committed in Israel and in Jerusalem: Judah has desecrated the sanctuary the LORD loves, by marrying the daughter of a foreign god. As for the man who does this, whoever he may be, may the LORD cut him off from the tents of Jacob[l]— even though he brings offerings to the LORD Almighty.

Mal. 2:13-16

RAMPANT DIVORCE.   Another thing you do: You flood the LORD's altar with tears. You weep and wail because he no longer pays attention to your offerings or accepts them with pleasure from your hands. You ask, "Why?" It is because the LORD is acting as the witness between you and the wife of your youth, because you have broken faith with her, though she is your partner, the wife of your marriage covenant.

Has not ⌊the LORD⌋ made them one? In flesh and spirit they are his. And why one? Because he was seeking godly offspring.[m] So guard yourself in your spirit, and do not break faith with the wife of your youth.

"I hate divorce," says the LORD God of Israel, "and I hate a man's covering himself[n] with violence as well as with his garment," says the LORD Almighty.

So guard yourself in your spirit, and do not break faith.

Mal. 2:17-3:4

LORD OF JUSTICE COMING.   You have wearied the LORD with your words.

"How have we wearied him?" you ask.

By saying, "All who do evil are good in the eyes of the LORD, and he is pleased with them" or "Where is the God of justice?" "See, I will send my messenger, who will prepare the way before me. Then suddenly the Lord you are seeking will come to his temple; the messenger of the covenant, whom you desire, will come," says the LORD Almighty.

But who can endure the day of his coming? Who can stand when he appears? For he will be like a refiner's fire or a launderer's soap. He will sit as a refiner and purifier of silver; he will purify the Levites and refine them like gold and silver. Then the LORD will have men who will bring

---

[k]Or father   [l]Or 12May the LORD cut off from the tents of Jacob anyone who gives testimony in behalf of the man who does this   [m]Or 15But the one ⌊who is our father⌋ did not do this, not as long as life remained in him. And what was he seeking? An offspring from God   [n]Or his wife

offerings in righteousness, and the offerings of Judah and Jerusalem will be acceptable to the LORD, as in days gone by, as in former years.

WICKED TO BE JUDGED.   "So I will come near to you for judgment. I   Mal. 3:5
will be quick to testify against sorcerers, adulterers and perjurers, against those who defraud laborers of their wages, who oppress the widows and the fatherless, and deprive aliens of justice, but do not fear me," says the LORD Almighty.

ROBBING GOD.   "I the LORD do not change. So you, O descendants of   Mal. 3:6-12
Jacob, are not destroyed. Ever since the time of your forefathers you have turned away from my decrees and have not kept them. Return to me, and I will return to you," says the LORD Almighty.
    "But you ask, 'How are we to return?'
    "Will a man rob God? Yet you rob me.
    "But you ask, 'How do we rob you?'
    "In tithes and offerings. You are under a curse—the whole nation of you—because you are robbing me. Bring the whole tithe into the store-house, that there may be food in my house. Test me in this," says the LORD Almighty, "and see if I will not throw open the floodgates of heaven and pour out so much blessing that you will not have room enough for it. I will prevent pests from devouring your crops, and the vines in your fields will not cast their fruit," says the LORD Almighty. "Then all the nations will call you blessed, for yours will be a delightful land," says the LORD Almighty.

DAY OF THE LORD COMING.   "You have said harsh things against me,"   Mal.
says the LORD.   3:13-4:3
    "Yet you ask, 'What have we said against you?'
    "You have said, 'It is futile to serve God. What did we gain by carrying out his requirements and going about like mourners before the LORD Almighty? But now we call the arrogant blessed. Certainly the evildoers prosper, and even those who challenge God escape.' "
    Then those who feared the LORD talked with each other, and the LORD listened and heard. A scroll of remembrance was written in his presence concerning those who feared the LORD and honored his name.
    "They will be mine," says the LORD Almighty, "in the day when I make up my treasured possession.º I will spare them, just as in compassion a man spares his son who serves him. And you will again see the distinction between the righteous and the wicked, between those who serve God and those who do not. "Surely the day is coming; it will burn like a furnace. All the arrogant and every evildoer will be stubble, and that day that is com-ing will set them on fire," says the LORD Almighty. "Not a root or a branch will be left to them. But for you who revere my name, the sun of righ-teousness will rise with healing in its wings. And you will go out and leap like calves released from the stall. Then you will trample down the wicked; they will be ashes under the soles of your feet on the day when I do these things," says the LORD Almighty.

PEOPLE'S RESPONSIBILITY.   "Remember the law of my servant Moses,   Mal. 4:4
the decrees and laws I gave him at Horeb for all Israel.

ºOr Almighty, "my treasured possession, in the day when I act

Mal. 4:5,6   MESSIAH COMING.   "See, I will send you the prophet Elijah before that great and dreadful day of the LORD comes. He will turn the hearts of the fathers to their children, and the hearts of the children to their fathers; or else I will come and strike the land with a curse."

Ezra and the Second Return

*J*f in fact Malachi prophesied during the prior 40 to 60 years, he paved the way for a time of renewed interest in the law and in the work of two men whose joint leadership brings about a time of religious reform. It happens during the reign of Artaxerxes, who took over the Persian rule upon the death of his father, in 465 B.C. Like Xerxes' final years, Artaxerxes' reign is also troublesome, with revolts to be quelled in Egypt and Greece, where his father had been so insensitive. It is somewhat surprising, then, that any attempt by the Jews to strengthen their own nation would not be viewed with more suspicion. However, it may well be that Artaxerxes sees Israel as a peaceful nation minding its own business, and geographically suited to be a buffer against Egypt if sufficiently redeveloped. Therefore Artaxerxes actually promotes further development of Israel and particularly the promulgation of its unique law, which he greatly admires.

With Artaxerxes' blessings, a great teacher of the law named Ezra, along with a company of over 1500 Jews, leave Babylon in 458 B.C. to be the second contingent of Jews to return to Palestine since the exile. After a rushed four-month trek, they arrive in Jerusalem with more treasures for the temple service and the ongoing redevelopment project.

Ezra 7:1-7   EZRA PREPARES RETURN.   After these things, during the reign of Ar-
(458 B.C.)   taxerxes king of Persia, Ezra son of Seraiah, the son of Azariah, the son of Hilkiah, the son of Shallum, the son of Zadok, the son of Ahitub, the son of Amariah, the son of Azariah, the son of Meraioth, the son of Zerahiah, the son of Uzzi, the son of Bukki, the son of Abishua, the son of Phinehas, the son of Eleazar, the son of Aaron the chief priest—this Ezra came up from Babylon. He was a teacher well versed in the Law of Moses, which the LORD, the God of Israel, had given. The king had granted him everything he asked, for the hand of the LORD his God was on him. Some of the Israelites, including priests, Levites, singers, gatekeepers and temple servants, also came up to Jerusalem in the seventh year of King Artaxerxes.

Ezra   ARTAXERXES' AUTHORIZATION.   This is a copy of the letter King Ar-
7:11-26   taxerxes had given to Ezra the priest and teacher, a man learned in matters
Babylon   concerning the commands and decrees of the LORD for Israel:

*p*Artaxerxes, king of kings,

To Ezra the priest, a teacher of the Law of the God of heaven:

Greetings.

    Now I decree that any of the Israelites in my kingdom, including priests and Levites, who wish to go to Jerusalem with you, may go. You are sent

*p*The text of Ezra 7:12-26 is in Aramaic.

by the king and his seven advisers to inquire about Judah and Jerusalem with regard to the Law of your God, which is in your hand. Moreover, you are to take with you the silver and gold that the king and his advisers have freely given to the God of Israel, whose dwelling is in Jerusalem, together with all the silver and gold you may obtain from the province of Babylon, as well as the freewill offerings of the people and priests for the temple of their God in Jerusalem. With this money be sure to buy bulls, rams and male lambs, together with their grain offerings and drink offerings, and sacrifice them on the altar of the temple of your God in Jerusalem.

You and your brother Jews may then do whatever seems best with the rest of the silver and gold, in accordance with the will of your God. Deliver to the God of Jerusalem all the articles entrusted to you for worship in the temple of your God. And anything else needed for the temple of your God that you may have occasion to supply, you may provide from the royal treasury.

Now I, King Artaxerxes, order all the treasurers of Trans-Euphrates to provide with diligence whatever Ezra the priest, a teacher of the Law of the God of heaven, may ask of you—up to a hundred talents^q of silver, a hundred cors^r of wheat, a hundred baths^s of wine, a hundred baths^s of olive oil, and salt without limit. Whatever the God of heaven has prescribed, let it be done with diligence for the temple of the God of heaven. Why should there be wrath against the realm of the king and of his sons? You are also to know that you have no authority to impose taxes, tribute or duty on any of the priests, Levites, singers, gatekeepers, temple servants or other workers at this house of God.

And you, Ezra, in accordance with the wisdom of your God, which you possess, appoint magistrates and judges to administer justice to all the people of Trans-Euphrates—all who know the laws of your God. And you are to teach any who do not know them. Whoever does not obey the law of your God and the law of the king must surely be punished by death, banishment, confiscation of property, or imprisonment.

EZRA'S GRATITUDE.   Praise be to the LORD, the God of our fathers, who has put it into the king's heart to bring honor to the house of the LORD in Jerusalem in this way and who has extended his good favor to me before the king and his advisers and all the king's powerful officials. Because the hand of the LORD my God was on me, I took courage and gathered leading men from Israel to go up with me.

Ezra
7:27,28

LEVITES SUMMONED.   I assembled them at the canal that flows toward Ahava, and we camped there three days. When I checked among the people and the priests, I found no Levites there. So I summoned Eliezer, Ariel, Shemaiah, Elnathan, Jarib, Elnathan, Nathan, Zechariah and Meshullam, who were leaders, and Joiarib and Elnathan, who were men of learning, and I sent them to Iddo, the leader in Casiphia. I told them what to say to Iddo and his kinsmen, the temple servants in Casiphia, so that they might bring attendants to us for the house of our God. Because the gracious hand of our God was on us, they brought us Sherebiah, a capable man, from the descendants of Mahli son of Levi, the son of Israel, and Sherebiah's sons

Ezra
8:15-20
Ahava
Canal

---

^{q}That is, about 3 3/4 tons (about 3.4 metric tons) ^{r}That is, probably about 600 bushels (about 22 kiloliters) ^{s}That is, probably about 600 gallons (about 2.2 kiloliters)

and brothers, 18 men; and Hashabiah, together with Jeshaiah from the descendants of Merari, and his brothers and nephews, 20 men. They also brought 220 of the temple servants—a body that David and the officials had established to assist the Levites. All were registered by name.

Ezra 8:21-23

PRAYER FOR SAFETY.   There, by the Ahava Canal, I proclaimed a fast, so that we might humble ourselves before our God and ask him for a safe journey for us and our children, with all our possessions. I was ashamed to ask the king for soldiers and horsemen to protect us from enemies on the road, because we had told the king, "The gracious hand of our God is on everyone who looks to him, but his great anger is against all who forsake him." So we fasted and petitioned our God about this, and he answered our prayer.

Ezra 8:24-30

VALUABLES ENTRUSTED.   Then I set apart twelve of the leading priests, together with Sherebiah, Hashabiah and ten of their brothers, and I weighed out to them the offering of silver and gold and the articles that the king, his advisers, his officials and all Israel present there had donated for the house of our God. I weighed out to them 650 talents*[t]* of silver, silver articles weighing 100 talents,*[u]* 100 talents*[u]* of gold, 20 bowls of gold valued at 1,000 darics,*[v]* and two fine articles of polished bronze, as precious as gold.

I said to them, "You as well as these articles are consecrated to the LORD. The silver and gold are a freewill offering to the LORD, the God of your fathers. Guard them carefully until you weigh them out in the chambers of the house of the LORD in Jerusalem before the leading priests and the Levites and the family heads of Israel." Then the priests and Levites received the silver and gold and sacred articles that had been weighed out to be taken to the house of our God in Jerusalem.

Ezra 8:31,32; 7:8-10 Jerusalem

JOURNEY TO JERUSALEM.   On the twelfth day of the first month we set out from the Ahava Canal to go to Jerusalem. The hand of our God was on us, and he protected us from enemies and bandits along the way. So we arrived in Jerusalem, where we rested three days.

Ezra arrived in Jerusalem in the fifth month of the seventh year of the king. He had begun his journey from Babylon on the first day of the first month, and he arrived in Jerusalem on the first day of the fifth month, for the gracious hand of his God was on him. For Ezra had devoted himself to the study and observance of the Law of the LORD, and to teaching its decrees and laws in Israel.

Ezra 8:1-14

ENUMERATION OF RETURNEES.   These are the family heads and those registered with them who came up with me from Babylon during the reign of King Artaxerxes:

of the descendants of Phinehas, Gershom;
of the descendants of Ithamar, Daniel;
of the descendants of David, Hattush of the descendants of Shecaniah;

of the descendants of Parosh, Zechariah, and with him were registered 150 men;

*[t]*That is, about 25 tons (about 22 metric tons)   *[u]*That is, about 3 3/4 tons (about 3.4 metric tons)   *[v]*That is, about 19 pounds (about 8.5 kilograms)

of the descendants of Pahath-Moab, Eliehoenai son of Zerahiah, and with him 200 men;

of the descendants of Zattu,^w Shecaniah son of Jahaziel, and with him 300 men;

of the descendants of Adin, Ebed son of Jonathan, and with him 50 men;

of the descendants of Elam, Jeshaiah son of Athaliah, and with him 70 men;

of the descendants of Shephatiah, Zebadiah son of Michael, and with him 80 men;

of the descendants of Joab, Obadiah son of Jehiel, and with him 218 men;

of the descendants of Bani,^x Shelomith son of Josiphiah, and with him 160 men;

of the descendants of Bebai, Zechariah son of Bebai, and with him 28 men;

of the descendants of Azgad, Johanan son of Hakkatan, and with him 110 men;

of the descendants of Adonikam, the last ones, whose names were Eliphelet, Jeuel and Shemaiah, and with them 60 men;

of the descendants of Bigvai, Uthai and Zaccur, and with them 70 men.

ACCOUNTING AND SACRIFICE. On the fourth day, in the house of our God, we weighed out the silver and gold and the sacred articles into the hands of Meremoth son of Uriah, the priest. Eleazar son of Phinehas was with him, and so were the Levites Jozabad son of Jeshua and Noadiah son of Binnui. Everything was accounted for by number and weight, and the entire weight was recorded at that time.

Then the exiles who had returned from captivity sacrificed burnt offerings to the God of Israel: twelve bulls for all Israel, ninety-six rams, seventy-seven male lambs, and as a sin offering, twelve male goats. All this was a burnt offering to the LORD. They also delivered the king's orders to the royal satraps and to the governors of Trans-Euphrates, who then gave assistance to the people and to the house of God.

_{Ezra
8:33-36}

Problem of Intermarriage

*U*pon Ezra's arrival in Palestine, he is informed that many of the men of Israel have married wives of foreign extract, in violation of the law given to Moses. Ezra is distressed at the news because he knows the reason behind the rule and fears the consequences of disobedience. Marriage to foreign wives was prohibited because of the danger that the women would influence their husbands and children to worship their strange gods and idols. And history had proved the wisdom of the rule. Disastrous results came when the rule was violated during the wilderness wanderings, and Solomon himself fell spiritually as a result of his many foreign wives. Therefore Ezra takes immediate and drastic steps to remedy the problem. The

---

^wSome Septuagint manuscripts (also 1 Esdras 8:32); Hebrew does not have *Zattu*.
^xSome Septuagint manuscripts (also 1 Esdras 8:36); Hebrew does not have *Bani*.

men who are guilty are called upon to put away their wives, which most of them do after special hearings are set up to decide individual cases. This move is probably representative of Ezra's broader role in bringing back the teaching of the law and setting up courts of justice to enforce it.

Ezra 9:1-4
(458 B.C.)

INTERMARRIAGES TOLD.   After these things had been done, the leaders came to me and said, "The people of Israel, including the priests and the Levites, have not kept themselves separate from the neighboring peoples with their detestable practices, like those of the Canaanites, Hittites, Perizzites, Jebusites, Ammonites, Moabites, Egyptians and Amorites. They have taken some of their daughters as wives for themselves and their sons, and have mingled the holy race with the peoples around them. And the leaders and officials have led the way in this unfaithfulness."

When I heard this, I tore my tunic and cloak, pulled hair from my head and beard and sat down appalled. Then everyone who trembled at the words of the God of Israel gathered around me because of this unfaithfulness of the exiles. And I sat there appalled until the evening sacrifice.

Ezra 9:5-15

EZRA'S PRAYER.   Then, at the evening sacrifice, I rose from my self-abasement, with my tunic and cloak torn, and fell on my knees with my hands spread out to the LORD my God and prayed:

"O my God, I am too ashamed and disgraced to lift up my face to you, my God, because our sins are higher than our heads and our guilt has reached to the heavens. From the days of our forefathers until now, our guilt has been great. Because of our sins, we and our kings and our priests have been subjected to the sword and captivity, to pillage and humiliation at the hand of foreign kings, as it is today.

"But now, for a brief moment, the LORD our God has been gracious in leaving us a remnant and giving us a firm place in his sanctuary, and so our God gives light to our eyes and a little relief in our bondage. Though we are slaves, our God has not deserted us in our bondage. He has shown us kindness in the sight of the kings of Persia: He has granted us new life to rebuild the house of our God and repair its ruins, and he has given us a wall of protection in Judah and Jerusalem.

"But now, O our God, what can we say after this? For we have disregarded the commands you gave through your servants the prophets when you said: 'The land you are entering to possess is a land polluted by the corruption of its peoples. By their detestable practices they have filled it with their impurity from one end to the other. Therefore, do not give your daughters in marriage to their sons or take their daughters for your sons. Do not seek a treaty of friendship with them at any time, that you may be strong and eat the good things of the land and leave it to your children as an everlasting inheritance.'

"What has happened to us is a result of our evil deeds and our great guilt, and yet, our God, you have punished us less than our sins have deserved and have given us a remnant like this. Shall we again break your commands and intermarry with the peoples who commit such detestable practices? Would you not be angry enough with us to destroy us, leaving us no remnant or survivor? O LORD, God of Israel, you are righteous! We are left this day as a remnant. Here we are before you in our guilt, though because of it not one of us can stand in your presence."

SHECANIAH'S SUGGESTION.   While Ezra was praying and confessing,   Ezra 10:1-4
weeping and throwing himself down before the house of God, a large
crowd of Israelites—men, women and children—gathered around him.
They too wept bitterly. Then Shecaniah son of Jehiel, one of the descendants of Elam, said to Ezra, "We have been unfaithful to our God by marrying foreign women from the peoples around us. But in spite of this, there
is still hope for Israel. Now let us make a covenant before our God to send
away all these women and their children, in accordance with the counsel
of my lord and of those who fear the commands of our God. Let it be done
according to the Law. Rise up; this matter is in your hands. We will support you, so take courage and do it."

CALL FOR ASSEMBLY.   So Ezra rose up and put the leading priests and   Ezra 10:5-8
Levites and all Israel under oath to do what had been suggested. And they
took the oath. Then Ezra withdrew from before the house of God and went
to the room of Jehohanan son of Eliashib. While he was there, he ate no
food and drank no water, because he continued to mourn over the unfaithfulness of the exiles.

A proclamation was then issued throughout Judah and Jerusalem for all
the exiles to assemble in Jerusalem. Anyone who failed to appear within
three days would forfeit all his property, in accordance with the decision
of the officials and elders, and would himself be expelled from the assembly of the exiles.

EZRA'S PLEA.   Within the three days, all the men of Judah and Benjamin   Ezra
10:9-11
had gathered in Jerusalem. And on the twentieth day of the ninth month,
all the people were sitting in the square before the house of God, greatly
distressed by the occasion and because of the rain. Then Ezra the priest
stood up and said to them, "You have been unfaithful; you have married
foreign women, adding to Israel's guilt. Now make confession to the LORD,
the God of your fathers, and do his will. Separate yourselves from the peoples around you and from your foreign wives."

PLAN FOR RESOLUTION.   The whole assembly responded with a loud   Ezra
10:12-15
voice: "You are right! We must do as you say. But there are many people
here and it is the rainy season; so we cannot stand outside. Besides, this
matter cannot be taken care of in a day or two, because we have sinned
greatly in this thing. Let our officials act for the whole assembly. Then let
everyone in our towns who has married a foreign woman come at a set
time, along with the elders and judges of each town, until the fierce anger
of our God in this matter is turned away from us." Only Jonathan son of
Asahel and Jahzeiah son of Tikvah, supported by Meshullam and
Shabbethai the Levite, opposed this.

CASES DECIDED.   So the exiles did as was proposed. Ezra the priest   Ezra
10:16,17
selected men who were family heads, one from each family division, and
all of them designated by name. On the first day of the tenth month they
sat down to investigate the cases, and by the first day of the first month
they finished dealing with all the men who had married foreign women.

LIST OF THE GUILTY.   Ezra
10:18-44

Among the descendants of the priests, the following had married foreign women:

From the descendants of Jeshua son of Jozadak, and his brothers:

Maaseiah, Eliezer, Jarib and Gedaliah. (They all gave their hands in pledge to put away their wives, and for their guilt they each presented a ram from the flock as a guilt offering.)

From the descendants of Immer:
Hanani and Zebadiah.

From the descendants of Harim:
Maaseiah, Elijah, Shemaiah, Jehiel and Uzziah.

From the descendants of Pashhur:
Elioenai, Maaseiah, Ishmael, Nethanel, Jozabad and Elasah.

Among the Levites:

Jozabad, Shimei, Kelaiah (that is, Kelita), Pethahiah, Judah and Eliezer.

From the singers:
Eliashib.

From the gatekeepers:
Shallum, Telem and Uri.

And among the other Israelites:

From the descendants of Parosh:
Ramiah, Izziah, Malkijah, Mijamin, Eleazar, Malkijah and Benaiah.

From the descendants of Elam:
Mattaniah, Zechariah, Jehiel, Abdi, Jeremoth and Elijah.

From the descendants of Zattu:
Elioenai, Eliashib, Mattaniah, Jeremoth, Zabad and Aziza.

From the descendants of Bebai:
Jehohanan, Hananiah, Zabbai and Athlai.

From the descendants of Bani:
Meshullam, Malluch, Adaiah, Jashub, Sheal and Jeremoth.

From the descendants of Pahath-Moab:
Adna, Kelal, Benaiah, Maaseiah, Mattaniah, Bezalel, Binnui and Manasseh.

From the descendants of Harim:
Eliezer, Ishijah, Malkijah, Shemaiah, Shimeon, Benjamin, Malluch and Shemariah.

From the descendants of Hashum:
Mattenai, Mattattah, Zabad, Eliphelet, Jeremai, Manasseh and Shimei.

From the descendants of Bani:
Maadai, Amram, Uel, Benaiah, Bedeiah, Keluhi, Vaniah, Meremoth, Eliashib, Mattaniah, Mattenai and Jaasu.

From the descendants of Binnui:*y*
Shimei, Shelemiah, Nathan, Adaiah, Macnadebai, Shashai, Sharai, Azarel, Shelemiah, Shemariah, Shallum, Amariah and Joseph.

From the descendants of Nebo:
Jeiel, Mattithiah, Zabad, Zebina, Jaddai, Joel and Benaiah.

All these had married foreign women, and some of them had children by these wives.*z*

---

*y*See Septuagint (also 1 Esdras 9:34); Hebrew *Jaasu* *38and Bani and Binnui,*   *z*Or *and they sent them away with their children*

Nehemiah Rebuilds the Wall_____

hile Ezra is proceeding with the revitalization of the law in Israel, a man soon to be his closest associate is back in the Persian palace at Susa in the position of the king's cupbearer. That may not sound like a probable stepping-stone to political greatness, or even a very noteworthy position at all, but considering the fact that many kings have met their deaths by poisoning, being a royal cupbearer is a position of great trust. The man who holds that position in Artaxerxes' house is a Jew named Nehemiah. The relationship between Artaxerxes and Nehemiah is evidently much closer than one might normally expect. It is both a compliment to Nehemiah and a good insight into the character of Artaxerxes.

It has been some 14 years since Artaxerxes authorized Ezra to lead the second group of exiles back to Jerusalem. In the interim, the further construction of the city and its wall has been hampered by a number of problems, apparently including sabotage by those who wish to see Israel remain weak. Israel's principal opponents are certain secular-minded and fearful nobles, as well as Sanballat and other leaders of Samaria, who still harbor resentment from the time that Zerubbabel refused their help in building the temple.

Now, in 445 B.C., a report of this delay comes to Nehemiah through one of his brothers who has just arrived from Palestine. The report so upsets Nehemiah that Artaxerxes notices his sadness and inquires as to its cause. When Nehemiah explains his concern, Artaxerxes agrees to appoint Nehemiah as temporary governor and commissions him to go to Jerusalem to rebuild the wall. It takes little time to see that Nehemiah is a man of action. He immediately travels to Jerusalem, assesses the situation firsthand, devises an ingenious plan for working on the wall, sidesteps his opponents, and completes his primary mission within six months of receiving his commission from the king! Here is how it all happens.

NEWS FROM JERUSALEM.   The words of Nehemiah son of Hacaliah: Neh. 1:1-3
(445-444
In the month of Kislev in the twentieth year, while I was in the citadel of   B.C.)
Susa, Hanani, one of my brothers, came from Judah with some other men, and I questioned them about the Jewish remnant that survived the exile, and also about Jerusalem.

They said to me, "Those who survived the exile and are back in the province are in great trouble and disgrace. The wall of Jerusalem is broken down, and its gates have been burned with fire."

NEHEMIAH'S PRAYER.   When I heard these things, I sat down and   Neh.
wept. For some days I mourned and fasted and prayed before the God of   1:4-11a
heaven. Then I said:

"O LORD, God of heaven, the great and awesome God, who keeps his covenant of love with those who love him and obey his commands, let your ear be attentive and your eyes open to hear the prayer your servant is praying before you day and night for your servants, the people of Israel. I confess the sins we Israelites, including myself and my father's house, have committed against you. We have acted very wickedly toward you.

We have not obeyed the commands, decrees and laws you gave your servant Moses.

"Remember the instruction you gave your servant Moses, saying, 'If you are unfaithful, I will scatter you among the nations, but if you return to me and obey my commands, then even if your exiled people are at the farthest horizon, I will gather them from there and bring them to the place I have chosen as a dwelling for my Name.'

"They are your servants and your people, whom you redeemed by your great strength and your mighty hand. O Lord, let your ear be attentive to the prayer of this your servant and to the prayer of your servants who delight in revering your name. Give your servant success today by granting him favor in the presence of this man."

Neh.
1:11b-2:3
KING NOTICES SADNESS.   I was cupbearer to the king. In the month of Nisan in the twentieth year of King Artaxerxes, when wine was brought for him, I took the wine and gave it to the king. I had not been sad in his presence before; so the king asked me, "Why does your face look so sad when you are not ill? This can be nothing but sadness of heart."

I was very much afraid, but I said to the king, "May the king live forever! Why should my face not look sad when the city where my fathers are buried lies in ruins, and its gates have been destroyed by fire?"

Neh. 2:4-6
NEHEMIAH COMMISSIONED.   The king said to me, "What is it you want?"

Then I prayed to the God of heaven, and I answered the king, "If it pleases the king and if your servant has found favor in his sight, let him send me to the city in Judah where my fathers are buried so that I can rebuild it."

Then the king, with the queen sitting beside him, asked me, "How long will your journey take, and when will you get back?" It pleased the king to send me; so I set a time.

Neh. 2:7,8
ADDITIONAL AUTHORITY.   I also said to him, "If it pleases the king, may I have letters to the governors of Trans-Euphrates, so that they will provide me safe-conduct until I arrive in Judah? And may I have a letter to Asaph, keeper of the king's forest, so he will give me timber to make beams for the gates of the citadel by the temple and for the city wall and for the residence I will occupy?" And because the gracious hand of my God was upon me, the king granted my requests.

Neh.
2:9,10
Samaria
SAMARITANS UPSET.   So I went to the governors of Trans-Euphrates and gave them the king's letters. The king had also sent army officers and cavalry with me.

When Sanballat the Horonite and Tobiah the Ammonite official heard about this, they were very much disturbed that someone had come to promote the welfare of the Israelites.

Neh.
2:11-16
Jerusalem
NIGHTTIME INSPECTION.   I went to Jerusalem, and after staying there three days I set out during the night with a few men. I had not told anyone what my God had put in my heart to do for Jerusalem. There were no mounts with me except the one I was riding on.

By night I went out through the Valley Gate toward the Jackal[a] Well and the Dung Gate, examining the walls of Jerusalem, which had been broken

[a]Or *Serpent* or *Fig*

down, and its gates, which had been destroyed by fire. Then I moved on toward the Fountain Gate and the King's Pool, but there was not enough room for my mount to get through; so I went up the valley by night, examining the wall. Finally, I turned back and reentered through the Valley Gate. The officials did not know where I had gone or what I was doing, because as yet I had said nothing to the Jews or the priests or nobles or officials or any others who would be doing the work.

PLANS REVEALED.   Then I said to them, "You see the trouble we are in: Jerusalem lies in ruins, and its gates have been burned with fire. Come, let us rebuild the wall of Jerusalem, and we will no longer be in disgrace." I also told them about the gracious hand of my God upon me and what the king had said to me.
 They replied, "Let us start rebuilding." So they began this good work.

**Neh.
2:17,18**

PLANS RIDICULED.   But when Sanballat the Horonite, Tobiah the Ammonite official and Geshem the Arab heard about it, they mocked and ridiculed us. "What is this you are doing?" they asked. "Are you rebelling against the king?"
 I answered them by saying, "The God of heaven will give us success. We his servants will start rebuilding, but as for you, you have no share in Jerusalem or any claim or historic right to it."

**Neh.
2:19,20**

DIVISION OF LABOR.   Eliashib the high priest and his fellow priests went to work and rebuilt the Sheep Gate. They dedicated it and set its doors in place, building as far as the Tower of the Hundred, which they dedicated, and as far as the Tower of Hananel. The men of Jericho built the adjoining section, and Zaccur son of Imri built next to them.

**Neh.
3:1-32**

 The Fish Gate was rebuilt by the sons of Hassenaah. They laid its beams and put its doors and bolts and bars in place. Meremoth son of Uriah, the son of Hakkoz, repaired the next section. Next to him Meshullam son of Berekiah, the son of Meshezabel, made repairs, and next to him Zadok son of Baana also made repairs. The next section was repaired by the men of Tekoa, but their nobles would not put their shoulders to the work under their supervisors.[b]

 The Jeshanah[c] Gate was repaired by Joiada son of Paseah and Meshullam son of Besodeiah. They laid its beams and put its doors and bolts and bars in place. Next to them, repairs were made by men from Gibeon and Mizpah—Melatiah of Gibeon and Jadon of Meronoth—places under the authority of the governor of Trans-Euphrates. Uzziel son of Harhaiah, one of the goldsmiths, repaired the next section; and Hananiah, one of the perfume-makers, made repairs next to that. They restored[d] Jerusalem as far as the Broad Wall. Rephaiah son of Hur, ruler of a half-district of Jerusalem, repaired the next section. Adjoining this, Jedaiah son of Harumaph made repairs opposite his house, and Hattush son of Hashabneiah made repairs next to him. Malkijah son of Harim and Hasshub son of Pahath-Moab repaired another section and the Tower of the Ovens. Shallum son of Hallohesh, ruler of a half-district of Jerusalem, repaired the next section with the help of his daughters.

 The Valley Gate was repaired by Hanun and the residents of Zanoah.

bOr their Lord or the governor   cOr Old   dOr They left out part of

They rebuilt it and put its doors and bolts and bars in place. They also repaired five hundred yards[e] of the wall as far as the Dung Gate.

The Dung Gate was repaired by Malkijah son of Recab, ruler of the district of Beth Hakkerem. He rebuilt it and put its doors and bolts and bars in place.

The Fountain Gate was repaired by Shallun son of Col-Hozeh, ruler of the district of Mizpah. He rebuilt it, roofing it over and putting its doors and bolts and bars in place. He also repaired the wall of the Pool of Siloam,[f] by the King's Garden, as far as the steps going down from the City of David. Beyond him, Nehemiah son of Azbuk, ruler of a half-district of Beth Zur, made repairs up to a point opposite the tombs[g] of David, as far as the artificial pool and the House of the Heroes.

Next to him, the repairs were made by the Levites under Rehum son of Bani. Beside him, Hashabiah, ruler of half the district of Keilah, carried out repairs for his district. Next to him, the repairs were made by their countrymen under Binnui[h] son of Henadad, ruler of the other half-district of Keilah. Next to him, Ezer son of Jeshua, ruler of Mizpah, repaired another section, from a point facing the ascent to the armory as far as the angle. Next to him, Baruch son of Zabbai zealously repaired another section, from the angle to the entrance of the house of Eliashib the high priest. Next to him, Meremoth son of Uriah, the son of Hakkoz, repaired another section, from the entrance of Eliashib's house to the end of it.

The repairs next to him were made by the priests from the surrounding region. Beyond them, Benjamin and Hasshub made repairs in front of their house; and next to them, Azariah son of Maaseiah, the son of Ananiah, made repairs beside his house. Next to him, Binnui son of Henadad repaired another section, from Azariah's house to the angle and the corner, and Palal son of Uzai worked opposite the angle and the tower projecting from the upper palace near the court of the guard. Next to him, Pedaiah son of Parosh and the temple servants living on the hill of Ophel made repairs up to a point opposite the Water Gate toward the east and the projecting tower. Next to them, the men of Tekoa repaired another section, from the great projecting tower to the wall of Ophel.

Above the Horse Gate, the priests made repairs, each in front of his own house. Next to them, Zadok son of Immer made repairs opposite his house. Next to him, Shemaiah son of Shecaniah, the guard at the East Gate, made repairs. Next to him, Hananiah son of Shelemiah, and Hanun, the sixth son of Zalaph, repaired another section. Next to them, Meshullam son of Berekiah made repairs opposite his living quarters. Next to him, Malkijah, one of the goldsmiths, made repairs as far as the house of the temple servants and the merchants, opposite the Inspection Gate, and as far as the room above the corner; and between the room above the corner and the Sheep Gate the goldsmiths and merchants made repairs.

Neh. 4:1-3 **TAUNTS OF SAMARITANS.**   When Sanballat heard that we were rebuilding the wall, he became angry and was greatly incensed. He ridiculed

---

[e]Hebrew *a thousand cubits* (about 450 meters)   [f]Hebrew *Shelah,* a variant of *Shiloah,* that is, Siloam   [g]Hebrew; Septuagint, some Vulgate manuscripts and Syriac *tomb*
[h]Two Hebrew manuscripts and Syriac (see also Septuagint and verse 24); most Hebrew manuscripts *Bavvai*

the Jews, and in the presence of his associates and the army of Samaria, he said, "What are those feeble Jews doing? Will they restore their wall? Will they offer sacrifices? Will they finish in a day? Can they bring the stones back to life from those heaps of rubble—burned as they are?"

Tobiah the Ammonite, who was at his side, said, "What they are building—if even a fox climbed up on it, he would break down their wall of stones!"

PRAYER ABOUT TAUNTS.   Hear us, O our God, for we are despised. Turn their insults back on their own heads. Give them over as plunder in a land of captivity. Do not cover up their guilt or blot out their sins from your sight, for they have thrown insults in the face of^i the builders. Neh. 4:4,5

OPPOSITION BECOMES VIOLENT.   So we rebuilt the wall till all of it reached half its height, for the people worked with all their heart. Neh. 4:6-9

But when Sanballat, Tobiah, the Arabs, the Ammonites and the men of Ashdod heard that the repairs to Jerusalem's walls had gone ahead and that the gaps were being closed, they were very angry. They all plotted together to come and fight against Jerusalem and stir up trouble against it. But we prayed to our God and posted a guard day and night to meet this threat.

WORKERS DISCOURAGED.   Meanwhile, the people in Judah said, "The strength of the laborers is giving out, and there is so much rubble that we cannot rebuild the wall." Neh. 4:10-12

Also our enemies said, "Before they know it or see us, we will be right there among them and will kill them and put an end to the work."

Then the Jews who lived near them came and told us ten times over, "Wherever you turn, they will attack us."

NEHEMIAH'S PLAN.   Therefore I stationed some of the people behind the lowest points of the wall at the exposed places, posting them by families, with their swords, spears and bows. After I looked things over, I stood up and said to the nobles, the officials and the rest of the people, "Don't be afraid of them. Remember the Lord, who is great and awesome, and fight for your brothers, your sons and your daughters, your wives and your homes." Neh. 4:13-23

When our enemies heard that we were aware of their plot and that God had frustrated it, we all returned to the wall, each to his own work.

From that day on, half of my men did the work, while the other half were equipped with spears, shields, bows and armor. The officers posted themselves behind all the people of Judah who were building the wall. Those who carried materials did their work with one hand and held a weapon in the other, and each of the builders wore his sword at his side as he worked. But the man who sounded the trumpet stayed with me.

Then I said to the nobles, the officials and the rest of the people, "The work is extensive and spread out, and we are widely separated from each other along the wall. Wherever you hear the sound of the trumpet, join us there. Our God will fight for us!"

So we continued the work with half the men holding spears, from the first light of dawn till the stars came out. At that time I also said to the people, "Have every man and his helper stay inside Jerusalem at night, so

---

^{i}Or *have provoked you to anger before*

they can serve us as guards by night and workmen by day." Neither I nor my brothers nor my men nor the guards with me took off our clothes; each had his weapon, even when he went for water.[j]

Neh. 5:1-5 **USURY PROBLEM ARISES.**   Now the men and their wives raised a great outcry against their Jewish brothers. Some were saying, "We and our sons and daughters are numerous; in order for us to eat and stay alive, we must get grain."

Others were saying, "We are mortgaging our fields, our vineyards and our homes to get grain during the famine."

Still others were saying, "We have had to borrow money to pay the king's tax on our fields and vineyards. Although we are of the same flesh and blood as our countrymen and though our sons are as good as theirs, yet we have to subject our sons and daughters to slavery. Some of our daughters have already been enslaved, but we are powerless, because our fields and our vineyards belong to others."

Neh. 5:6-11 **NEHEMIAH CHASTISES NOBLES.**   When I heard their outcry and these charges, I was very angry. I pondered them in my mind and then accused the nobles and officials. I told them, "You are exacting usury from your own countrymen!" So I called together a large meeting to deal with them and said: "As far as possible, we have bought back our Jewish brothers who were sold to the Gentiles. Now you are selling your brothers, only for them to be sold back to us!" They kept quiet, because they could find nothing to say.

So I continued, "What you are doing is not right. Shouldn't you walk in the fear of our God to avoid the reproach of our Gentile enemies? I and my brothers and my men are also lending the people money and grain. But let the exacting of usury stop! Give back to them immediately their fields, vineyards, olive groves and houses, and also the usury you are charging them—the hundredth part of the money, grain, new wine and oil."

Neh. 5:12,13 **NOBLES PROMISE CESSATION.**   "We will give it back," they said. "And we will not demand anything more from them. We will do as you say."

Then I summoned the priests and made the nobles and officials take an oath to do what they had promised. I also shook out the folds of my robe and said, "In this way may God shake out of his house and possessions every man who does not keep this promise. So may such a man be shaken out and emptied!"

At this the whole assembly said, "Amen," and praised the LORD. And the people did as they had promised.

Neh. 5:14-16 **NO ABUSE OF OFFICE.**   Moreover, from the twentieth year of King Artaxerxes, when I was appointed to be their governor in the land of Judah, until his thirty-second year—twelve years—neither I nor my brothers ate the food allotted to the governor. But the earlier governors—those preceding me—placed a heavy burden on the people and took forty shekels[k] of silver from them in addition to food and wine. Their assistants also lorded it over the people. But out of reverence for God I did not act like that.

[j]The meaning of the Hebrew for this clause is uncertain.   [k]That is, about 1 pound (about 0.5 kilogram)

Instead, I devoted myself to the work on this wall. All my men were assembled there for the work; we*l* did not acquire any land.

NEHEMIAH'S BENEVOLENCE.   Furthermore, a hundred and fifty Jews and officials ate at my table, as well as those who came to us from the surrounding nations. Each day one ox, six choice sheep and some poultry were prepared for me, and every ten days an abundant supply of wine of all kinds. In spite of all this, I never demanded the food allotted to the governor, because the demands were heavy on these people.

Neh. 5:17-19

Remember me with favor, O my God, for all I have done for these people.

SANBALLAT SCHEMES.   When word came to Sanballat, Tobiah, Geshem the Arab and the rest of our enemies that I had rebuilt the wall and not a gap was left in it—though up to that time I had not set the doors in the gates—Sanballat and Geshem sent me this message: "Come, let us meet together in one of the villages *m* on the plain of Ono."

Neh. 6:1-4

But they were scheming to harm me; so I sent messengers to them with this reply: "I am carrying on a great project and cannot go down. Why should the work stop while I leave it and go down to you?" Four times they sent me the same message, and each time I gave them the same answer.

VEILED THREAT.   Then, the fifth time, Sanballat sent his aide to me with the same message, and in his hand was an unsealed letter in which was written:

Neh. 6:5-9

"It is reported among the nations—and Geshem*n* says it is true—that you and the Jews are plotting to revolt, and therefore you are building the wall. Moreover, according to these reports you are about to become their king and have even appointed prophets to make this proclamation about you in Jerusalem: 'There is a king in Judah!' Now this report will get back to the king; so come, let us confer together."

I sent him this reply: "Nothing like what you are saying is happening; you are just making it up out of your head."

They were all trying to frighten us, thinking, "Their hands will get too weak for the work, and it will not be completed."

But I prayed, "Now strengthen my hands."

PLOY TO DISCREDIT.   One day I went to the house of Shemaiah son of Delaiah, the son of Mehetabel, who was shut in at his home. He said, "Let us meet in the house of God, inside the temple, and let us close the temple doors, because men are coming to kill you—by night they are coming to kill you."

Neh. 6:10-13

But I said, "Should a man like me run away? Or should one like me go into the temple to save his life? I will not go!" I realized that God had not sent him, but that he had prophesied against me because Tobiah and Sanballat had hired him. He had been hired to intimidate me so that I would commit a sin by doing this, and then they would give me a bad name to discredit me.

*l*Most Hebrew manuscripts; some Hebrew manuscripts, Septuagint, Vulgate and Syriac *I*
*m*Or *in Kephirim*   *n*Hebrew *Gashmu*, a variant of *Geshem*

| Neh. 6:17-19 | **LETTERS OF INTIMIDATION.** Also, in those days the nobles of Judah were sending many letters to Tobiah, and replies from Tobiah kept coming to them. For many in Judah were under oath to him, since he was son-in-law to Shecaniah son of Arah, and his son Jehohanan had married the daughter of Meshullam son of Berekiah. Moreover, they kept reporting to me his good deeds and then telling him what I said. And Tobiah sent letters to intimidate me. |

| Neh. 6:14 | **PRAYER ABOUT ENEMIES.** Remember Tobiah and Sanballat, O my God, because of what they have done; remember also the prophetess Noadiah and the rest of the prophets who have been trying to intimidate me. |

| Neh. 6:15 (444 B.C.) | **COMPLETION OF WALL.** So the wall was completed on the twenty-fifth of Elul, in fifty-two days. |

| Neh. 6:16 | **ENEMIES GIVE UP.** When all our enemies heard about this, all the surrounding nations were afraid and lost their self-confidence, because they realized that this work had been done with the help of our God. |

Redistribution of Population

Now that the wall has been completed, it occurs to Nehemiah that the city is too large for the number of people inhabiting it; it would take a larger population to defend it properly and to maintain it. Therefore Nehemiah first reviews the record of the initial group of exiles to return and then devises a plan by which 10 percent of the population of Judah and Benjamin will be asked to move into Jerusalem. The record begins with some administrative details.

| Neh. 7:1,2 (444 B.C.) | **HANANI APPOINTED.** After the wall had been rebuilt and I had set the doors in place, the gatekeepers and the singers and the Levites were appointed. I put in charge of Jerusalem my brother Hanani, along with^o Hananiah the commander of the citadel, because he was a man of integrity and feared God more than most men do. |

| Neh. 7:3 | **GATE REGULATIONS.** I said to them, "The gates of Jerusalem are not to be opened until the sun is hot. While the gatekeepers are still on duty, have them shut the doors and bar them. Also appoint residents of Jerusalem as guards, some at their posts and some near their own houses." |

| Neh. 7:4 | **UNDERPOPULATION PROBLEM.** Now the city was large and spacious, but there were few people in it, and the houses had not yet been rebuilt. |

| Neh. 7:5-73 | **GENEALOGICAL RECORD.** So my God put it into my heart to assemble the nobles, the officials and the common people for registration by families. I found the genealogical record of those who had been the first to return. This is what I found written there: |

These are the people of the province who came up from the captivity of the exiles whom Nebuchadnezzar king of Babylon had taken captive (they returned to Jerusalem and Judah, each to his own town, in company with Zerubbabel, Jeshua, Nehemiah, Azariah, Raamiah, Nahamani, Mordecai, Bilshan, Mispereth, Bigvai, Nehum and Baanah):

^oOr Hanani, that is,

The list of the men of Israel:

the descendants of Parosh	2,172
of Shephatiah	372
of Arah	652
of Pahath-Moab (through the line of Jeshua and Joab)	2,818
of Elam	1,254
of Zattu	845
of Zaccai	760
of Binnui	648
of Bebai	628
of Azgad	2,322
of Adonikam	667
of Bigvai	2,067
of Adin	655
of Ater (through Hezekiah)	98
of Hashum	328
of Bezai	324
of Hariph	112
of Gibeon	95
the men of Bethlehem and Netophah	188
of Anathoth	128
of Beth Azmaveth	42
of Kiriath Jearim, Kephirah and Beeroth	743
of Ramah and Geba	621
of Micmash	122
of Bethel and Ai	123
of the other Nebo	52
of the other Elam	1,254
of Harim	320
of Jericho	345
of Lod, Hadid and Ono	721
of Senaah	3,930

The priests:

the descendants of Jedaiah (through the family of Jeshua)	973
of Immer	1,052
of Pashhur	1,247
of Harim	1,017

The Levites:

the descendants of Jeshua (through Kadmiel through the line of Hodaviah)	74

The singers:

the descendants of Asaph	148

The gatekeepers:

the descendants of Shallum, Ater, Talmon, Akkub, Hatita and Shobai	138

The temple servants:

the descendants of
Ziha, Hasupha, Tabbaoth,
Keros, Sia, Padon,
Lebana, Hagaba, Shalmai,
Hanan, Giddel, Gahar,
Reaiah, Rezin, Nekoda,
Gazzam, Uzza, Paseah,
Besai, Meunim, Nephusim,
Bakbuk, Hakupha, Harhur,
Bazluth, Mehida, Harsha,
Barkos, Sisera, Temah,
Neziah and Hatipha

The descendants of the servants of Solomon:

the descendants of
Sotai, Sophereth, Perida,
Jaala, Darkon, Giddel,
Shephatiah, Hattil,
Pokereth-Hazzebaim and Amon

The temple servants and the descendants of the servants of
Solomon   392

The following came up from the towns of Tel Melah, Tel Harsha, Kerub, Addon and Immer, but they could not show that their families were descended from Israel:

the descendants of
Delaiah, Tobiah and Nekoda   642

And from among the priests:

the descendants of
Hobaiah, Hakkoz and Barzillai (a man who had married a
daughter of Barzillai the Gileadite and was called by that name).
These searched for their family records, but they could not find them and so were excluded from the priesthood as unclean. The governor, therefore, ordered them not to eat any of the most sacred food until there should be a priest ministering with the Urim and Thummim.

The whole company numbered 42,360, besides their 7,337 menservants and maidservants; and they also had 245 men and women singers. There were 736 horses, 245 mules,[p] 435 camels and 6,720 donkeys.

Some of the heads of the families contributed to the work. The governor gave to the treasury 1,000 drachmas[q] of gold, 50 bowls and 530 garments for priests. Some of the heads of the families gave to the treasury for the work 20,000 drachmas[r] of gold and 2,200 minas[s] of silver. The total given by the rest of the people was 20,000 drachmas of gold, 2,000 minas[t] of silver and 67 garments for priests.

The priests, the Levites, the gatekeepers, the singers and the temple

---

[p]Some Hebrew manuscripts (see also Ezra 2:66); most Hebrew manuscripts do not have this verse.   [q]That is, about 19 pounds (about 8.5 kilograms)   [r]That is, about 375 pounds (about 170 kilograms)   [s]That is, about 1 1/3 tons (about 1.2 metric tons)   [t]That is, about 1 1/4 tons (about 1.1 metric tons)

servants, along with certain of the people and the rest of the Israelites, settled in their own towns.

When the seventh month came and the Israelites had settled in their towns,

REDISTRIBUTION PLAN.   Now the leaders of the people settled in Jerusalem, and the rest of the people cast lots to bring one out of every ten to live in Jerusalem, the holy city, while the remaining nine were to stay in their own towns. The people commended all the men who volunteered to live in Jerusalem.

Neh.
11:1,2

RESETTLED LEADERS.   These are the provincial leaders who settled in Jerusalem (now some Israelites, priests, Levites, temple servants and descendants of Solomon's servants lived in the towns of Judah, each on his own property in the various towns, while other people from both Judah and Benjamin lived in Jerusalem):

Neh.
11:3-19

From the descendants of Judah:

Athaiah son of Uzziah, the son of Zechariah, the son of Amariah, the son of Shephatiah, the son of Mahalalel, a descendant of Perez; and Maaseiah son of Baruch, the son of Col-Hozeh, the son of Hazaiah, the son of Adaiah, the son of Joiarib, the son of Zechariah, a descendant of Shelah. The descendants of Perez who lived in Jerusalem totaled 468 able men.

From the descendants of Benjamin:

Sallu son of Meshullam, the son of Joed, the son of Pedaiah, the son of Kolaiah, the son of Maaseiah, the son of Ithiel, the son of Jeshaiah, and his followers, Gabbai and Sallai—928 men. Joel son of Zicri was their chief officer, and Judah son of Hassenuah was over the Second District of the city.

From the priests:

Jedaiah; the son of Joiarib; Jakin; Seraiah son of Hilkiah, the son of Meshullam, the son of Zadok, the son of Meraioth, the son of Ahitub, supervisor in the house of God, and their associates, who carried on work for the temple—822 men; Adaiah son of Jeroham, the son of Pelaliah, the son of Amzi, the son of Zechariah, the son of Pashhur, the son of Malkijah, and his associates, who were heads of families—242 men; Amashsai son of Azarel, the son of Ahzai, the son of Meshillemoth, the son of Immer, and his*u* associates, who were able men—128. Their chief officer was Zabdiel son of Haggedolim.

From the Levites:

Shemaiah son of Hasshub, the son of Azrikam, the son of Hashabiah, the son of Bunni; Shabbethai and Jozabad, two of the heads of the Levites, who had charge of the outside work of the house of God; Mattaniah son of Mica, the son of Zabdi, the son of Asaph, the director who led in thanksgiving and prayer; Bakbukiah, second among his associates; and Abda son of Shammua, the son of Galal, the son of Jeduthun. The Levites in the holy city totaled 284.

u Most Septuagint manuscripts; Hebrew *their*

The gatekeepers:

Akkub, Talmon and their associates, who kept watch at the gates—172 men.

**Neh.
11:20-36**

RECORD OF OTHER SETTLEMENTS.   The rest of the Israelites, with the priests and Levites, were in all the towns of Judah, each on his ancestral property.

The temple servants lived on the hill of Ophel, and Ziha and Gishpa were in charge of them.

The chief officer of the Levites in Jerusalem was Uzzi son of Bani, the son of Hashabiah, the son of Mattaniah, the son of Mica. Uzzi was one of Asaph's descendants, who were the singers responsible for the service of the house of God. The singers were under the king's orders, which regulated their daily activity.

Pethahiah son of Meshezabel, one of the descendants of Zerah son of Judah, was the king's agent in all affairs relating to the people.

As for the villages with their fields, some of the people of Judah lived in Kiriath Arba and its surrounding settlements, in Dibon and its settlements, in Jekabzeel and its villages, in Jeshua, in Moladah, in Beth Pelet, in Hazar Shual, in Beersheba and its settlements, in Ziklag, in Meconah and its settlements, in En Rimmon, in Zorah, in Jarmuth, Zanoah, Adullam and their villages, in Lachish and its fields, and in Azekah and its settlements. So they were living all the way from Beersheba to the Valley of Hinnom.

The descendants of the Benjamites from Geba lived in Micmash, Aija, Bethel and its settlements, in Anathoth, Nob and Ananiah, in Hazor, Ramah and Gittaim, in Hadid, Zeboim and Neballat, in Lod and Ono, and in the Valley of the Craftsmen.

Some of the divisions of the Levites of Judah settled in Benjamin.

At this time of record-keeping the following four lists are given for historical purposes.

**Neh.
12:1-9**

PRIESTS AND LEVITES.   These were the priests and Levites who returned with Zerubbabel son of Shealtiel and with Jeshua:

Seraiah, Jeremiah, Ezra,
Amariah, Malluch, Hattush,
Shecaniah, Rehum, Meremoth,
Iddo, Ginnethon,[v] Abijah,
Mijamin,[w] Moadiah, Bilgah,
Shemaiah, Joiarib, Jedaiah,
Sallu, Amok, Hilkiah and Jedaiah.

These were the leaders of the priests and their associates in the days of Jeshua.

The Levites were Jeshua, Binnui, Kadmiel, Sherebiah, Judah, and also Mattaniah, who, together with his associates, was in charge of the songs of thanksgiving. Bakbukiah and Unni, their associates, stood opposite them in the services.

---

[v]Many Hebrew manuscripts and Vulgate (see also Neh. 12:16); most Hebrew manuscripts *Ginnethoi*   [w]A variant of *Miniamin*

HIGH PRIESTS FROM JESHUA.   Jeshua was the father of Joiakim, Joiakim the father of Eliashib, Eliashib the father of Joiada, Joiada the father of Jonathan, and Jonathan the father of Jaddua.

Neh. 12:10,11

HEADS OF PRIESTLY FAMILIES.   In the days of Joiakim, these were the heads of the priestly families:

Neh. 12:12-21

    of Seraiah's family, Meraiah;
    of Jeremiah's, Hananiah;
    of Ezra's, Meshullam;
    of Amariah's, Jehohanan;
    of Malluch's, Jonathan;
    of Shecaniah's,[x] Joseph;
    of Harim's, Adna;
    of Meremoth's,[y] Helkai;
    of Iddo's, Zechariah;
    of Ginnethon's, Meshullam;
    of Abijah's, Zicri;
    of Miniamin's and of Moadiah's, Piltai;
    of Bilgah's, Shammua;
    of Shemaiah's, Jehonathan;
    of Joiarib's, Mattenai;
    of Jedaiah's, Uzzi;
    of Sallu's, Kallai;
    of Amok's, Eber;
    of Hilkiah's, Hashabiah;
    of Jedaiah's, Nethanel.

CHIEF LEVITICAL HEADS.   The family heads of the Levites in the days of Eliashib, Joiada, Johanan and Jaddua, as well as those of the priests, were recorded in the reign of Darius the Persian. The family heads among the descendants of Levi up to the time of Johanan son of Eliashib were recorded in the book of the annals. And the leaders of the Levites were Hashabiah, Sherebiah, Jeshua son of Kadmiel, and their associates, who stood opposite them to give praise and thanksgiving, one section responding to the other, as prescribed by David the man of God.

Neh. 12:22-26

    Mattaniah, Bakbukiah, Obadiah, Meshullam, Talmon and Akkub were gatekeepers who guarded the storerooms at the gates. They served in the days of Joiakim son of Jeshua, the son of Jozadak, and in the days of Nehemiah the governor and of Ezra the priest and scribe.

Law and Covenant

*O*nce settled, the people are called together for a reading of the law on the first day of the civil year. Ezra, Nehemiah, and the Levites spend long hours reading and interpreting the law. When the people mourn for all the sins they have committed under the law, they are reminded that it is a festival day to be celebrated. And the people soon join in the reinstitution of the Feast of Tabernacles, which commemorates the Israelites' living in tents during the wilderness wanderings.

[x] Very many Hebrew manuscripts, some Septuagint manuscripts and Syriac (see also Neh. 12:3); most Hebrew manuscripts *Shebaniah's*   [y] Some Septuagint manuscripts (see also Neh. 12:3); Hebrew *Meraioth's*

Some three weeks later the law is read again, and the people respond with a great national confession and a written covenant with God. Truly it is one of the finest hours in the history of God's people. Perhaps the years of exile have served to purge much of the rebelliousness of earlier generations.

Neh. 8:1-6
(444 B.C.)

EZRA READS LAW.   When the seventh month came and the Israelites had settled in their towns, all the people assembled as one man in the square before the Water Gate. They told Ezra the scribe to bring out the Book of the Law of Moses, which the LORD had commanded for Israel.

So on the first day of the seventh month Ezra the priest brought the Law before the assembly, which was made up of men and women and all who were able to understand. He read it aloud from daybreak till noon as he faced the square before the Water Gate in the presence of the men, women and others who could understand. And all the people listened attentively to the Book of the Law.

Ezra the scribe stood on a high wooden platform built for the occasion. Beside him on his right stood Mattithiah, Shema, Anaiah, Uriah, Hilkiah and Maaseiah; and on his left were Pedaiah, Mishael, Malkijah, Hashum, Hashbaddanah, Zechariah and Meshullam.

Ezra opened the book. All the people could see him because he was standing above them; and as he opened it, the people all stood up. Ezra praised the LORD, the great God; and all the people lifted their hands and responded, "Amen! Amen!" Then they bowed down and worshiped the LORD with their faces to the ground.

Neh. 8:7,8

LEVITES INTERPRET LAW.   The Levites—Jeshua, Bani, Sherebiah, Jamin, Akkub, Shabbethai, Hodiah, Maaseiah, Kelita, Azariah, Jozabad, Hanan and Pelaiah—instructed the people in the Law while the people were standing there. They read from the Book of the Law of God, making it clear[z] and giving the meaning so that the people could understand what was being read.

Neh.
8:9-12

MOURNERS TO CELEBRATE.   Then Nehemiah the governor, Ezra the priest and scribe, and the Levites who were instructing the people said to them all, "This day is sacred to the LORD your God. Do not mourn or weep." For all the people had been weeping as they listened to the words of the Law.

Nehemiah said, "Go and enjoy choice food and sweet drinks, and send some to those who have nothing prepared. This day is sacred to our Lord. Do not grieve, for the joy of the LORD is your strength."

The Levites calmed all the people, saying, "Be still, for this is a sacred day. Do not grieve."

Then all the people went away to eat and drink, to send portions of food and to celebrate with great joy, because they now understood the words that had been made known to them.

Neh.
8:13-18

FEAST OF TABERNACLES.   On the second day of the month, the heads of all the families, along with the priests and the Levites, gathered around Ezra the scribe to give attention to the words of the Law. They found written in the Law, which the LORD had commanded through Moses, that the Israelites were to live in booths during the feast of the seventh month and that they should proclaim this word and spread it throughout their towns

[z]Or *God, translating it*

and in Jerusalem: "Go out into the hill country and bring back branches from olive and wild olive trees, and from myrtles, palms and shade trees, to make booths"—as it is written.[a]

So the people went out and brought back branches and built themselves booths on their own roofs, in their courtyards, in the courts of the house of God and in the square by the Water Gate and the one by the Gate of Ephraim. The whole company that had returned from exile built booths and lived in them. From the days of Joshua son of Nun until that day, the Israelites had not celebrated it like this. And their joy was very great.

Day after day, from the first day to the last, Ezra read from the Book of the Law of God. They celebrated the feast for seven days, and on the eighth day, in accordance with the regulation, there was an assembly.

DAY OF CONFESSION.   On the twenty-fourth day of the same month, the Israelites gathered together, fasting and wearing sackcloth and having dust on their heads. Those of Israelite descent had separated themselves from all foreigners. They stood in their places and confessed their sins and the wickedness of their fathers. They stood where they were and read from the Book of the Law of the LORD their God for a quarter of the day, and spent another quarter in confession and in worshiping the LORD their God. Standing on the stairs were the Levites—Jeshua, Bani, Kadmiel, Shebaniah, Bunni, Sherebiah, Bani and Kenani—who called with loud voices to the LORD their God.

Neh. 9:1-4

CONFESSIONAL PRAYER.   And the Levites—Jeshua, Kadmiel, Bani, Hashabneiah, Sherebiah, Hodiah, Shebaniah and Pethahiah—said: "Stand up and praise the LORD your God, who is from everlasting to everlasting.[b]"

Neh. 9:5-12

"Blessed be your glorious name, and may it be exalted above all blessing and praise. You alone are the LORD. You made the heavens, even the highest heavens, and all their starry host, the earth and all that is on it, the seas and all that is in them. You give life to everything, and the multitudes of heaven worship you.

"You are the LORD God, who chose Abram and brought him out of Ur of the Chaldeans and named him Abraham. You found his heart faithful to you, and you made a covenant with him to give to his descendants the land of the Canaanites, Hittites, Amorites, Perizzites, Jebusites and Girgashites. You have kept your promise because you are righteous.

"You saw the suffering of our forefathers in Egypt; you heard their cry at the Red Sea.[c] You sent miraculous signs and wonders against Pharaoh, against all his officials and all the people of his land, for you knew how arrogantly the Egyptians treated them. You made a name for yourself, which remains to this day. You divided the sea before them, so that they passed through it on dry ground, but you hurled their pursuers into the depths, like a stone into mighty waters. By day you led them with a pillar of cloud, and by night with a pillar of fire to give them light on the way they were to take.

"You came down on Mount Sinai; you spoke to them from heaven. You gave them regulations and laws that are just and right, and decrees and commands that are good. You made known to them your holy Sabbath

Neh. 9:13-25

---

[a]See Lev. 23:37-40.   [b]Or *God for ever and ever*   [c]Hebrew *Yam Suph*; that is, Sea of Reeds

and gave them commands, decrees and laws through your servant Moses. In their hunger you gave them bread from heaven and in their thirst you brought them water from the rock; you told them to go in and take possession of the land you had sworn with uplifted hand to give them.

"But they, our forefathers, became arrogant and stiff-necked, and did not obey your commands. They refused to listen and failed to remember the miracles you performed among them. They became stiff-necked and in their rebellion appointed a leader in order to return to their slavery. But you are a forgiving God, gracious and compassionate, slow to anger and abounding in love. Therefore you did not desert them, even when they cast for themselves an image of a calf and said, 'This is your god, who brought you up out of Egypt,' or when they committed awful blasphemies.

"Because of your great compassion you did not abandon them in the desert. By day the pillar of cloud did not cease to guide them on their path, nor the pillar of fire by night to shine on the way they were to take. You gave your good Spirit to instruct them. You did not withhold your manna from their mouths, and you gave them water for their thirst. For forty years you sustained them in the desert; they lacked nothing, their clothes did not wear out nor did their feet become swollen.

"You gave them kingdoms and nations, allotting to them even the remotest frontiers. They took over the country of Sihon[d] king of Heshbon and the country of Og king of Bashan. You made their sons as numerous as the stars in the sky, and you brought them into the land that you told their fathers to enter and possess. Their sons went in and took possession of the land. You subdued before them the Canaanites, who lived in the land; you handed the Canaanites over to them, along with their kings and the peoples of the land, to deal with them as they pleased. They captured fortified cities and fertile land; they took possession of houses filled with all kinds of good things, wells already dug, vineyards, olive groves and fruit trees in abundance. They ate to the full and were well-nourished; they reveled in your great goodness.

"But they were disobedient and rebelled against you; they put your law behind their backs. They killed your prophets, who had admonished them in order to turn them back to you; they committed awful blasphemies. So you handed them over to their enemies, who oppressed them. But when they were oppressed they cried out to you. From heaven you heard them, and in your great compassion you gave them deliverers, who rescued them from the hand of their enemies.

Neh.
9:26-38
"But as soon as they were at rest, they again did what was evil in your sight. Then you abandoned them to the hand of their enemies so that they ruled over them. And when they cried out to you again, you heard from heaven, and in your compassion you delivered them time after time.

"You warned them to return to your law, but they became arrogant and disobeyed your commands. They sinned against your ordinances, by which a man will live if he obeys them. Stubbornly they turned their backs on you, became stiff-necked and refused to listen. For many years you were patient with them. By your Spirit you admonished them through your prophets. Yet they paid no attention, so you handed them over to the

[d]One Hebrew manuscript and Septuagint; most Hebrew manuscripts *Sihon, that is, the country of the*

neighboring peoples. But in your great mercy you did not put an end to them or abandon them, for you are a gracious and merciful God.

"Now therefore, O our God, the great, mighty and awesome God, who keeps his covenant of love, do not let all this hardship seem trifling in your eyes—the hardship that has come upon us, upon our kings and leaders, upon our priests and prophets, upon our fathers and all your people, from the days of the kings of Assyria until today. In all that has happened to us, you have been just; you have acted faithfully, while we did wrong. Our kings, our leaders, our priests and our fathers did not follow your law; they did not pay attention to your commands or the warnings you gave them. Even while they were in their kingdom, enjoying your great goodness to them in the spacious and fertile land you gave them, they did not serve you or turn from their evil ways.

"But see, we are slaves today, slaves in the land you gave our forefathers so they could eat its fruit and the other good things it produces. Because of our sins, its abundant harvest goes to the kings you have placed over us. They rule over our bodies and our cattle as they please. We are in great distress.

"In view of all this, we are making a binding agreement, putting it in writing, and our leaders, our Levites and our priests are affixing their seals to it."

COVENANT SEALERS.   Those who sealed it were: Neh.
                                                                       10:1-27

Nehemiah the governor, the son of Hacaliah.

Zedekiah, Seraiah, Azariah, Jeremiah,
Pashhur, Amariah, Malkijah,
Hattush, Shebaniah, Malluch,
Harim, Meremoth, Obadiah,
Daniel, Ginnethon, Baruch,
Meshullam, Abijah, Mijamin,
Maaziah, Bilgai and Shemaiah.
These were the priests.

The Levites:

Jeshua son of Azaniah, Binnui of the sons of Henadad, Kadmiel,
and their associates: Shebaniah,
Hodiah, Kelita, Pelaiah, Hanan,
Mica, Rehob, Hashabiah,
Zaccur, Sherebiah, Shebaniah,
Hodiah, Bani and Beninu.

The leaders of the people:

Parosh, Pahath-Moab, Elam, Zattu, Bani,
Bunni, Azgad, Bebai,
Adonijah, Bigvai, Adin,
Ater, Hezekiah, Azzur,
Hodiah, Hashum, Bezai,
Hariph, Anathoth, Nebai,
Magpiash, Meshullam, Hezir,
Meshezabel, Zadok, Jaddua,
Pelatiah, Hanan, Anaiah,

Hoshea, Hananiah, Hasshub,
Hallohesh, Pilha, Shobek,
Rehum, Hashabnah, Maaseiah,
Ahiah, Hanan, Anan,
Malluch, Harim and Baanah.

Neh.
10:28-39

THE WRITTEN COVENANT.   "The rest of the people—priests, Levites, gatekeepers, singers, temple servants and all who separated themselves from the neighboring peoples for the sake of the Law of God, together with their wives and all their sons and daughters who are able to under-stand—all these now join their brothers the nobles, and bind themselves with a curse and an oath to follow the Law of God given through Moses the servant of God and to obey carefully all the commands, regulations and decrees of the LORD our Lord.

"We promise not to give our daughters in marriage to the peoples around us or take their daughters for our sons.

"When the neighboring peoples bring merchandise or grain to sell on the Sabbath, we will not buy from them on the Sabbath or on any holy day. Every seventh year we will forgo working the land and will cancel all debts.

"We assume the responsibility for carrying out the commands to give a third of a shekel[e] each year for the service of the house of our God: for the bread set out on the table; for the regular grain offerings and burnt offer-ings; for the offerings on the Sabbaths, New Moon festivals and appoint-ed feasts; for the holy offerings; for sin offerings to make atonement for Israel; and for all the duties of the house of our God.

"We—the priests, the Levites and the people—have cast lots to deter-mine when each of our families is to bring to the house of our God at set times each year a contribution of wood to burn on the altar of the LORD our God, as it is written in the Law.

"We also assume responsibility for bringing to the house of the LORD each year the firstfruits of our crops and of every fruit tree.

"As it is also written in the Law, we will bring the firstborn of our sons and of our cattle, of our herds and of our flocks to the house of our God, to the priests ministering there.

"Moreover, we will bring to the storerooms of the house of our God, to the priests, the first of our ground meal, of our grain, offerings, of the fruit of all our trees and of our new wine and oil. And we will bring a tithe of our crops to the Levites, for it is the Levites who collect the tithes in all the towns where we work. A priest descended from Aaron is to accompany the Levites when they receive the tithes, and the Levites are to bring a tenth of the tithes up to the house of our God, to the storerooms of the treasury. The people of Israel, including the Levites, are to bring their con-tributions of grain, new wine and oil to the storerooms where the articles for the sanctuary are kept and where the ministering priests, the gate-keepers and the singers stay.

"We will not neglect the house of our God."

⸻⸻⸻⸻⸻◇⸻⸻⸻⸻⸻

[e] That is, about 1/8 ounce (about 4 grams)

Nehemiah's Religious Reforms

Nehemiah continues to govern Israel over the next 11 years, and then, in 432 B.C., at the end of his term of appointment, returns to Artaxerxes in Susa. What Nehemiah does while there is not indicated, but presumably he reports on his work and makes plans for a return. One thing which he has never done, but which he has probably wanted to do for some time, is to dedicate the wall which he was so instrumental in building. Evidently Nehemiah has not wished to proceed without Artaxerxes' approval for such a celebration. If that is the case, Artaxerxes' permission is presumably granted. The king also gives permission for Nehemiah to return, perhaps this time for an indefinite period or even permanently.

It is not known how long Nehemiah stayed in Susa, but it was long enough for some of the people back in Palestine to forget the covenant they made when Nehemiah was with them. Since then, they have neglected and desecrated the temple, violated the Sabbath, failed to continue temple offerings, and begun again to marry foreign wives. When Nehemiah sees what has happened in his absence, he is furious! Nehemiah's fierce anger is evident in the way he calls down divine curses upon, and even physically abuses, those who have been violating the law. Here is a man of God who is not content with pious preaching while sin runs rampant about him. Nehemiah's personal involvement in cleansing the temple puts him in good company. Centuries from now, the Messiah (about whom Nehemiah undoubtedly has read) will himself angrily throw offenders out of this very same house of God.

Nehemiah is anxious to have his overdue dedication of the wall, but the celebration will have to wait until the people's sinful ways are corrected.

TEMPLE DESECRATION.   Before this, Eliashib the priest had been put in charge of the storerooms of the house of our God. He was closely associated with Tobiah, and he had provided him with a large room formerly used to store the grain offerings and incense and temple articles, and also the tithes of grain, new wine and oil prescribed for the Levites, singers and gatekeepers, as well as the contributions for the priests.

Neh. 13:4-9 (Ca. 425 B.C.?)

But while all this was going on, I was not in Jerusalem, for in the thirty-second year of Artaxerxes king of Babylon I had returned to the king. Some time later I asked his permission and came back to Jerusalem. Here I learned about the evil thing Eliashib had done in providing Tobiah a room in the courts of the house of God. I was greatly displeased and threw all Tobiah's household goods out of the room. I gave orders to purify the rooms, and then I put back into them the equipment of the house of God, with the grain offerings and the incense.

TEMPLE SUPPORT NEGLECTED.   I also learned that the portions assigned to the Levites had not been given to them, and that all the Levites and singers responsible for the service had gone back to their own fields. So I rebuked the officials and asked them, "Why is the house of God neglected?" Then I called them together and stationed them at their posts.

Neh. 13:10,11

SABBATH VIOLATED.   In those days I saw men in Judah treading wine-presses on the Sabbath and bringing in grain and loading it on donkeys,

Neh. 13:15-22

together with wine, grapes, figs and all other kinds of loads. And they were bringing all this into Jerusalem on the Sabbath. Therefore I warned them against selling food on that day. Men from Tyre who lived in Jerusalem were bringing in fish and all kinds of merchandise and selling them in Jerusalem on the Sabbath to the people of Judah. I rebuked the nobles of Judah and said to them, "What is this wicked thing you are doing—desecrating the Sabbath day? Didn't your forefathers do the same things, so that our God brought all this calamity upon us and upon this city? Now you are stirring up more wrath against Israel by desecrating the Sabbath."

When evening shadows fell on the gates of Jerusalem before the Sabbath, I ordered the doors to be shut and not opened until the Sabbath was over. I stationed some of my own men at the gates so that no load could be brought in on the Sabbath day. Once or twice the merchants and sellers of all kinds of goods spent the night outside Jerusalem. But I warned them and said, "Why do you spend the night by the wall? If you do this again, I will lay hands on you." From that time on they no longer came on the Sabbath. Then I commanded the Levites to purify themselves and go and guard the gates in order to keep the Sabbath day holy.

Remember me for this also, O my God, and show mercy to me according to your great love.

Neh. 13:23-31 FOREIGN MARRIAGES.   Moreover, in those days I saw men of Judah who had married women from Ashdod, Ammon and Moab. Half of their children spoke the language of Ashdod or the language of one of the other peoples, and did not know how to speak the language of Judah. I rebuked them and called curses down on them. I beat some of the men and pulled out their hair. I made them take an oath in God's name and said: "You are not to give your daughters in marriage to their sons, nor are you to take their daughters in marriage for your sons or for yourselves. Was it not because of marriages like these that Solomon king of Israel sinned? Among the many nations there was no king like him. He was loved by his God, and God made him king over all Israel, but even he was led into sin by foreign women. Must we hear now that you too are doing all this terrible wickedness and are being unfaithful to our God by marrying foreign women?"

One of the sons of Joiada son of Eliashib the high priest was son-in-law to Sanballat the Horonite. And I drove him away from me.

Remember them, O my God, because they defiled the priestly office and the covenant of the priesthood and of the Levites.

So I purified the priests and the Levites of everything foreign, and assigned them duties, each to his own task. I also made provision for contributions of wood at designated times, and for the firstfruits.

Remember me with favor, O my God.

◆

Dedication of the Wall_____

*W*ith these religious reforms behind him, Nehemiah can get on with his plans for dedicating the wall. And it is only appropriate for him to have such a celebration, because it is the rebuilding of the wall for which Nehemiah will be most remembered in the centuries to come. When the day set for dedication finally arrives, there is a great choral procession by two choirs marching in opposite directions on top of the wall. This is followed by sacrifices, offerings, and a reading of the law. The account of this day of celebration begins with the call for Levites and singers. Then follows, in Nehemiah's own words, the record of the happy events which follow.

CALL FOR PARTICIPANTS.   At the dedication of the wall of Jerusalem, the Levites were sought out from where they lived and were brought to Jerusalem to celebrate joyfully the dedication with songs of thanksgiving and with the music of cymbals, harps and lyres. The singers also were brought together from the region around Jerusalem—from the villages of the Netophathites, from Beth Gilgal, and from the area of Geba and Azmaveth, for the singers had built villages for themselves around Jerusalem.

Neh. 12:27-29 (Ca. 425 B.C.?)

CEREMONIAL PURIFICATION.   When the priests and Levites had purified themselves ceremonially, they purified the people, the gates and the wall.

Neh. 12:30

TWO CHORAL PROCESSIONS.   I had the leaders of Judah go up on top[f] of the wall. I also assigned two large choirs to give thanks. One was to proceed on top[g] of the wall to the right, toward the Dung Gate. Hoshaiah and half the leaders of Judah followed them, along with Azariah, Ezra, Meshullam, Judah, Benjamin, Shemaiah, Jeremiah, as well as some priests with trumpets, and also Zechariah son of Jonathan, the son of Shemaiah, the son of Mattaniah, the son of Micaiah, the son of Zaccur, the son of Asaph, and his associates—Shemaiah, Azarel, Milalai, Gilalai, Maai, Nethanel, Judah and Hanani—with musical instruments ⌐prescribed by⌐ David the man of God. Ezra the scribe led the procession. At the Fountain Gate they continued directly up the steps of the City of David on the ascent to the wall and passed above the house of David to the Water Gate on the east.

Neh. 12:31-39

The second choir proceeded in the opposite direction. I followed them on top[h] of the wall, together with half the people—past the Tower of the Ovens to the Broad Wall, over the Gate of Ephraim, the Jeshanah[i] Gate, the Fish Gate, the Tower of Hananel and the Tower of the Hundred, as far as the Sheep Gate. At the Gate of the Guard they stopped.

CHOIRS IN TEMPLE.   The two choirs that gave thanks then took their places in the house of God; so did I, together with half the officials, as well as the priests—Eliakim, Maaseiah, Miniamin, Micaiah, Elioenai, Zechariah and Hananiah with their trumpets—and also Maaseiah, Shemaiah, Eleazar, Uzzi, Jehohanan, Malkijah, Elam and Ezer. The choirs sang under the direction of Jezrahiah.

Neh. 12:40-42

f Or go alongside   g Or proceed alongside   h Or them alongside   i Or Old

Neh. 12:43	**SACRIFICES AND REJOICING.** And on that day they offered great sacrifices, rejoicing because God had given them great joy. The women and children also rejoiced. The sound of rejoicing in Jerusalem could be heard far away.
Neh. 12:44-47 13:12-14	**FILLING THE STOREROOMS.** All Judah brought the tithes of grain, new wine and oil into the storerooms.

At that time men were appointed to be in charge of the storerooms for the contributions, firstfruits and tithes. From the fields around the towns they were to bring into the storerooms the portions required by the Law for the priests and the Levites, for Judah was pleased with the ministering priests and Levites. I put Shelemiah the priest, Zadok the scribe, and a Levite named Pedaiah in charge of the storerooms and made Hanan son of Zaccur, the son of Mattaniah, their assistant, because these men were considered trustworthy. They were made responsible for distributing the supplies to their brothers.

They performed the service of their God and the service of purification, as did also the singers and gatekeepers, according to the commands of David and his son Solomon. For long ago, in the days of David and Asaph, there had been directors for the singers and for the songs of praise and thanksgiving to God. So in the days of Zerubbabel and of Nehemiah, all Israel contributed the daily portions for the singers and gatekeepers. They also set aside the portion for the other Levites, and the Levites set aside the portion for the descendants of Aaron.

Remember me for this, O my God, and do not blot out what I have so faithfully done for the house of my God and its services.

Neh. 13:1,2	**READING OF LAW.** On that day the Book of Moses was read aloud in the hearing of the people and there it was found written that no Ammonite or Moabite should ever be admitted into the assembly of God, because they had not met the Israelites with food and water but had hired Balaam to call a curse down on them. (Our God, however, turned the curse into a blessing.)
Neh. 13:3	**PEOPLE'S RESPONSE.** When the people heard this law, they excluded from Israel all who were of foreign descent.

Official Records of Israel

This passage brings to an end any further account of either Ezra or Nehemiah. Presumably they both remain in Palestine exercising their respective responsibilities until their deaths. On several occasions Ezra is referred to as a scribe. Consistent with that role, it is thought that he is one of several scribes who may have compiled chronicles of Israel's history. To a nation whose history has been so turbulent, and whose people are even now scattered throughout many nations, it is vitally important that a record of their existence be preserved. Undoubtedly a man of God such as Ezra would be particularly concerned that future generations be made aware of Israel's unique status as a chosen nation through which God has revealed himself to the whole world.

An important part of any nation's history is the preservation of national archives. Genealogical records are particularly vital to the division and ownership of property, to marriages and inheritance, to right of office, and to royal privilege. Perhaps one of the most important reasons for the genealogies will not be fully appreciated until the Messiah is born. At that time one of the many proofs of his messiahship will be that he is of the lineage of King David and the house of Judah, just as the prophets have foretold.

Therefore it may well be that Ezra spends part of his final years recording Israel's history, particularly through the eras of the monarchy, the divided kingdom, the exile, and the initial period of restoration. If so, one might speculate that Ezra also compiles the national archives and major genealogical lists. Although they do not make particularly exciting reading, their importance to the nation at this time cannot be overstated. Throughout these genealogies and other related records are various historical footnotes, many of which have already been included where appropriate in the historical record. Several of the genealogical lists have also been seen in the earlier Genesis accounts, but additional names often appear in the present listings.

Included in the following records are: genealogies from Adam to Noah to Abraham and Isaac; the descendants of Esau (the Edomites); and the 12 tribes descending from Jacob (Israel), with the exception of Dan and Zebulun. Special emphasis is given to the royal tribe of Judah, the priestly line of Levi, and the Benjamite genealogy of King Saul.

TO NOAH'S SONS.   Adam, Seth, Enosh, Kenan, Mahalalel, Jared, Enoch, Methuselah, Lamech, Noah.

1 Chron.
1:1-4

> The sons of Noah: [j]
> Shem, Ham and Japheth.

THE JAPHETHITES.
> The sons [k] of Japheth:
> Gomer, Magog, Madai, Javan, Tubal, Meshech and Tiras.
> The sons of Gomer:
> Ashkenaz, Riphath [l] and Togarmah.
> The sons of Javan:
> Elishah, Tarshish, the Kittim and the Rodanim.

1 Chron.
1:5-7

THE HAMITES.
> The sons of Ham:
> Cush, Mizraim, [m] Put and Canaan.
> The sons of Cush:
> Seba, Havilah, Sabta, Raamah and Sabteca.
> The sons of Raamah:
> Sheba and Dedan.
> Cush was the father [n] of
> Nimrod, who grew to be a mighty warrior on earth.
> Mizraim was the father of
> the Ludites, Anamites, Lehabites, Naphtuhites, Pathrusites, Caslu-
> hites (from whom the Philistines came) and Caphtorites.

1 Chron.
1:8-16

---

[j] Septuagint; Hebrew does not have this line.   [k] *Sons* may mean *descendants* or *successors* or *nations*; also in verses 6-10, 17 and 20.   [l] Many Hebrew manuscripts and Vulgate (see also Septuagint and Gen. 10:3); most Hebrew manuscripts *Diphath*   [m] That is, Egypt   [n] *Father* may mean *ancestor* or *predecessor* or *founder*; also in verses 11, 13, 18 and 20.

Canaan was the father of
    Sidon his firstborn,[o] and of the Hittites, Jebusites, Amorites, Girga-
        shites, Hivites, Arkites, Sinites, Arvadites, Zemarites and Ha-
        mathites.

1 Chron.
1:17-27
THE SHEMITES.
    The sons of Shem:
    Elam, Asshur, Arphaxad, Lud and Aram.
    The sons of Aram:[p]
    Uz, Hul, Gether and Meshech.
    Arphaxad was the father of Shelah,
    and Shelah the father of Eber.
    Two sons were born to Eber:
        One was named Peleg,[q] because in his time the earth was divided;
        his brother was named Joktan.
    Joktan was the father of
        Almodad, Sheleph, Hazarmaveth, Jerah, Hadoram, Uzal, Diklah,
        Obal,[r] Abimael, Sheba, Ophir, Havilah and Jobab. All these were
        sons of Joktan.

    Shem, Arphaxad,[s] Shelah,
    Eber, Peleg, Reu,
    Serug, Nahor, Terah
    and Abram (that is, Abraham).

1 Chron.
1:28
ABRAHAM'S FAMILY.
    The sons of Abraham:
    Isaac and Ishmael.

1 Chron.
1:29-31
ISHMAEL'S DESCENDANTS.
    These were their descendants:
        Nebaioth the firstborn of Ishmael, Kedar, Adbeel, Mibsam,
        Mishma, Dumah, Massa, Hadad, Tema, Jetur, Naphish and
        Kedemah. These were the sons of Ishmael.

1 Chron.
1:32,33
DESCENDANTS BY KETURAH.
    The sons born to Keturah, Abraham's concubine:
    Zimran, Jokshan, Medan, Midian, Ishbak and Shuah.
    The sons of Jokshan:
    Sheba and Dedan.
    The sons of Midian:
    Ephah, Epher, Hanoch, Abida and Eldaah.
    All these were descendants of Keturah.

1 Chron.
1:34-37
ISAAC'S DESCENDANTS.
    Abraham was the father of Isaac.
    The sons of Isaac:
    Esau and Israel.
    The sons of Esau:
    Eliphaz, Reuel, Jeush, Jalam and Korah.

---

[o]Or *of the Sidonians, the foremost*   [p]One Hebrew manuscript and some Septuagint
manuscripts (see also Gen. 10:23); most Hebrew manuscripts do not have this line.
[q]*Peleg* means *division.*   [r]Some Hebrew manuscripts and Syriac (see also Gen. 10:28);
most Hebrew manuscripts *Ebal*   [s]Hebrew; some Septuagint manuscripts *Arphaxad,
Cainan* (see also note at Gen. 11:10)

The sons of Eliphaz:
Teman, Omar, Zepho,[t] Gatam and Kenaz;
by Timna: Amalek.[u]
The sons of Reuel:
Nahath, Zerah, Shammah and Mizzah.

ESAU'S EDOMITE DESCENDANTS.

1 Chron.
1:38-42

The sons of Seir:
Lotan, Shobal, Zibeon, Anah, Dishon, Ezer and Dishan.
The sons of Lotan:
Hori and Homam. Timna was Lotan's sister.
The sons of Shobal:
Alvan,[v] Manahath, Ebal, Shepho and Onam.
The sons of Zibeon:
Aiah and Anah.
The son of Anah:
Dishon.
The sons of Dishon:
Hemdan,[w] Eshban, Ithran and Keran.
The sons of Ezer:
Bilhan, Zaavan and Akan.[x]
The sons of Dishan[y]:
Uz and Aran.

RULERS OF EDOM.

1 Chron.
1:43-54

These were the kings who reigned in Edom before any Israelite king
reigned[z]:
Bela son of Beor, whose city was named Dinhabah.
When Bela died, Jobab son of Zerah from Bozrah succeeded him as
king.
When Jobab died, Husham from the land of the Temanites succeeded
him as king.
When Husham died, Hadad son of Bedad, who defeated Midian in
the country of Moab, succeeded him as king. His city was named
Avith.
When Hadad died, Samlah from Masrekah succeeded him as king.
When Samlah died, Shaul from Rehoboth on the river[a] succeeded him
as king.
When Shaul died, Baal-Hanan son of Acbor succeeded him as king.
When Baal-Hanan died, Hadad succeeded him as king. His city was
named Pau,[b] and his wife's name was Mehetabel daughter of
Matred, the daughter of Me-Zahab. Hadad also died.

The chiefs of Edom were:

[t]Many Hebrew manuscripts, some Septuagint manuscripts and Syriac (see also Gen.
36:11); most Hebrew manuscripts *Zephi*   [u]Some Septuagint manuscripts (see also Gen.
36:12); Hebrew *Gatam, Kenaz, Timna and Amalek*   [v]Many Hebrew manuscripts and
some Septuagint manuscripts (see also Gen. 36:23); most Hebrew manuscripts *Alian*
[w]Many Hebrew manuscripts and some Septuagint manuscripts (see also Gen. 36:26);
most Hebrew manuscripts *Hamran*   [x]Many Hebrew and Septuagint manuscripts (see
also Gen. 36:27); most Hebrew manuscripts *Zaavan, Jaakan*   [y]Hebrew *Dishon,* a variant
of *Dishan*   [z]Or *before an Israelite king reigned over them*   [a]Possibly the Euphrates
[b]Many Hebrew manuscripts, some Septuagint manuscripts, Vulgate and Syriac (see also
Gen. 36:39); most Hebrew manuscripts *Pai*

Timna, Alvah, Jetheth, Oholibamah, Elah, Pinon, Kenaz, Teman, Mibzar, Magdiel and Iram. These were the chiefs of Edom.

1 Chron.
2:1,2

JACOB'S (ISRAEL'S) SONS.   These were the sons of Israel: Reuben, Simeon, Levi, Judah, Issachar, Zebulun, Dan, Joseph, Benjamin, Naphtali, Gad and Asher.

(2:3-4:23)

(JUDAH'S DESCENDANTS FOLLOW.)

1 Chron.
2:3-9

TO HEZRON'S THREE SONS.
The sons of Judah:
Er, Onan and Shelah. These three were born to him by a Canaanite woman, the daughter of Shua. Er, Judah's firstborn, was wicked in the LORD's sight; so the LORD put him to death. Tamar, Judah's daughter-in-law, bore him Perez and Zerah. Judah had five sons in all.

The sons of Perez:
Hezron and Hamul.
The sons of Zerah:
Zimri, Ethan, Heman, Calcol and Darda^c—five in all.
The son of Carmi:
Achar,^{d} who brought trouble on Israel by violating the ban on taking devoted things.^{e}
The son of Ethan:
Azariah.
The sons born to Hezron were:
Jerahmeel, Ram and Caleb.^{f}

1 Chron.
2:10-17

RAM'S DESCENDANTS.
Ram was the father of
Amminadab, and Amminadab the father of Nahshon, the leader of the people of Judah. Nahshon was the father of Salmon,^{g} Salmon the father of Boaz, Boaz the father of Obed and Obed the father of Jesse.
Jesse was the father of
Eliab his firstborn; the second son was Abinadab, the third Shimea, the fourth Nethanel, the fifth Raddai, the sixth Ozem and the seventh David. Their sisters were Zeruiah and Abigail. Zeruiah's three sons were Abishai, Joab and Asahel. Abigail was the mother of Amasa, whose father was Jether the Ishmaelite.

1 Chron.
2:18-24

CALEB'S DESCENDANTS.
Caleb son of Hezron had children by his wife Azubah (and by Jerioth). These were her sons: Jesher, Shobab and Ardon. When Azubah died, Caleb married Ephrath, who bore him Hur. Hur was the father of Uri, and Uri the father of Bezalel.
Later, Hezron lay with the daughter of Makir the father of Gilead (he had married her when he was sixty years old), and she bore him Segub. Segub was the father of Jair, who controlled twenty-three

---

^{c}Many Hebrew manuscripts, some Septuagint manuscripts and Syriac (see also 1 Kings 4:31); most Hebrew manuscripts *Dara* ^{d}*Achar* means *trouble; Achar* is called *Achan* in Joshua. ^{e}The Hebrew term refers to the irrevocable giving over of things or persons to the LORD, often by totally destroying them. ^{f}Hebrew *Kelubai,* a variant of *Caleb* ^{g}Septuagint (see also Ruth 4:21); Hebrew *Salma*

towns in Gilead. (But Geshur and Aram captured Havvoth Jair,[h] as well as Kenath with its surrounding settlements—sixty towns.) All these were descendants of Makir the father of Gilead.

After Hezron died in Caleb Ephrathah, Abijah the wife of Hezron bore him Ashhur the father[i] of Tekoa.

CALEB'S CLANS.

1 Chron.
2:42-55

The sons of Caleb the brother of Jerahmeel:
Mesha his firstborn, who was the father of Ziph, and his son Mareshah,[j] who was the father of Hebron.
The sons of Hebron:
Korah, Tappuah, Rekem and Shema. Shema was the father of Raham, and Raham the father of Jorkeam. Rekem was the father of Shammai. The son of Shammai was Maon, and Maon was the father of Beth Zur.
Caleb's concubine Ephah was the mother of Haran, Moza and Gazez. Haran was the father of Gazez.
The sons of Jahdai:
Regem, Jotham, Geshan, Pelet, Ephah and Shaaph.
Caleb's concubine Maacah was the mother of Sheber and Tirhanah. She also gave birth to Shaaph the father of Madmannah and to Sheva the father of Macbenah and Gibea. Caleb's daughter was Acsah. These were the descendants of Caleb.

The sons of Hur the firstborn of Ephrathah:
Shobal the father of Kiriath Jearim, Salma the father of Bethlehem, and Hareph the father of Beth Gader.
The descendants of Shobal the father of Kiriath Jearim were:
Haroeh, half the Manahathites, and the clans of Kiriath Jearim: the Ithrites, Puthites, Shumathites and Mishraites. From these descended the Zorathites and Eshtaolites.
The descendants of Salma:
Bethlehem, the Netophathites, Atroth Beth Joab, half the Manaha-thites, the Zorites, and the clans of scribes[k] who lived at Jabez: the Tirathites, Shimeathites and Sucathites. These are the Kenites who came from Hammath, the father of the house of Recab.[l]

JERAHMEEL'S DESCENDANTS.

1 Chron.
2:25-41

The sons of Jerahmeel the firstborn of Hezron:
Ram his firstborn, Bunah, Oren, Ozem and[m] Ahijah. Jerahmeel had another wife, whose name was Atarah; she was the mother of Onam.
The sons of Ram the firstborn of Jerahmeel:
Maaz, Jamin and Eker.
The sons of Onam:
Shammai and Jada.
The sons of Shammai:
Nadab and Abishur.
Abishur's wife was named Abihail, who bore him Ahban and Molid.

---

[h]Or captured the settlements of Jair   [i]Father may mean civic leader or military leader; also in verses 42, 45, 49-52 and possibly elsewhere.   [j]The meaning of the Hebrew for this phrase is uncertain.   [k]Or of the Sopherites   [l]Or father of Beth Recab   [m]Or Oren and Ozem, by

The sons of Nadab:
Seled and Appaim. Seled died without children.
The son of Appaim:
Ishi, who was the father of Sheshan.
Sheshan was the father of Ahlai.
The sons of Jada, Shammai's brother:
Jether and Jonathan. Jether died without children.
The sons of Jonathan:
Peleth and Zaza.
These were the descendants of Jerahmeel.
Sheshan had no sons—only daughters.
He had an Egyptian servant named Jarha. Sheshan gave his daugh-
ter in marriage to his servant Jarha, and she bore him Attai.
Attai was the father of Nathan,
Nathan the father of Zabad,
Zabad the father of Ephlal,
Ephlal the father of Obed,
Obed the father of Jehu,
Jehu the father of Azariah,
Azariah the father of Helez,
Helez the father of Eleasah,
Eleasah the father of Sismai,
Sismai the father of Shallum,
Shallum the father of Jekamiah,
and Jekamiah the father of Elishama.

1 Chron.
4:1-23

OTHER CLANS OF JUDAH.   The descendants of Judah:
Perez, Hezron, Carmi, Hur and Shobal.
Reaiah son of Shobal was the father of Jahath, and Jahath the father of
Ahumai and Lahad. These were the clans of the Zorathites.
These were the sons[n] of Etam:
Jezreel, Ishma and Idbash. Their sister was named Hazzelelponi.
Penuel was the father of Gedor, and Ezer the father of Hushah.
These were the descendants of Hur, the firstborn of Ephrathah and
father[o] of Bethlehem.
Ashhur the father of Tekoa had two wives, Helah and Naarah.
Naarah bore him Ahuzzam, Hepher, Temeni and Haahashtari. These
were the descendants of Naarah.
The sons of Helah:
Zereth, Zohar, Ethnan, and Koz, who was the father of Anub and
Hazzobebah and of the clans of Aharhel son of Harum.

Jabez was more honorable than his brothers. His mother had named
him Jabez,[p] saying, "I gave birth to him in pain." Jabez cried out to the
God of Israel, "Oh, that you would bless me and enlarge my territory! Let
your hand be with me, and keep me from harm so that I will be free from
pain." And God granted his request.

Kelub, Shuhah's brother, was the father of Mehir, who was the father
of Eshton. Eshton was the father of Beth Rapha, Paseah and

[n]Some Septuagint manuscripts (see also Vulgate); Hebrew *father*   [o]*Father* may mean
civic leader or *military leader*; also in verses 12, 14, 17, 18 and possibly elsewhere.
[p]*Jabez* sounds like the Hebrew for *pain*.

Tehinnah the father of Ir Nahash.*q* These were the men of Recah.

The sons of Kenaz:
　Othniel and Seraiah.
The sons of Othniel:
　Hathath and Meonothai.*r* Meonothai was the father of Ophrah.
Seraiah was the father of Joab,
　the father of Ge Harashim.*s* It was called this because its people
　were craftsmen.
The sons of Caleb son of Jephunneh:
　Iru, Elah and Naam.
The son of Elah:
　Kenaz.
The sons of Jehallelel:
　Ziph, Ziphah, Tiria and Asarel.
The sons of Ezrah:
　Jether, Mered, Epher and Jalon. One of Mered's wives gave birth to
　Miriam, Shammai and Ishbah the father of Eshtemoa. (His
　Judean wife gave birth to Jered the father of Gedor, Heber the
　father of Soco, and Jekuthiel the father of Zanoah.) These were
　the children of Pharaoh's daughter Bithiah, whom Mered had
　married.
The sons of Hodiah's wife, the sister of Naham:
　the father of Keilah the Garmite, and Eshtemoa the Maacathite.
The sons of Shimon:
　Amnon, Rinnah, Ben-Hanan and Tilon.
The descendants of Ishi:
　Zoheth and Ben-Zoheth.
The sons of Shelah son of Judah:
　Er the father of Lecah, Laadah the father of Mareshah and the clans
　of the linen workers at Beth Ashbea, Jokim, the men of Cozeba,
　and Joash and Saraph, who ruled in Moab and Jashubi Lehem.
　(These records are from ancient times.) They were the potters
　who lived at Netaim and Gederah; they stayed there and worked
　for the king.

THE KINGS OF JUDAH.　　　　　　　　　　　　　　　　　　　1 Chron.
　Solomon's son was Rehoboam,　　　　　　　　　　　　　　　3:10-16
　　Abijah his son,
　　Asa his son,
　　Jehoshaphat his son,
　　Jehoram*t* his son,
　　Ahaziah his son,
　　Joash his son,
　　Amaziah his son,
　　Azariah his son,
　　Jotham his son,
　　Ahaz his son,

---

q Or *of the city of Nahash*　　*r* Some Septuagint manuscripts and Vulgate; Hebrew does
not have *and Meonothai.*　　*s* *Ge Harashim* means *valley of craftsmen.*　　*t* Hebrew *Joram,* a
variant of *Jehoram*

Hezekiah his son,
Manasseh his son,
Amon his son,
Josiah his son.
The sons of Josiah:
Johanan the firstborn,
Jehoiakim the second son,
Zedekiah the third,
Shallum the fourth.
The successors of Jehoiakim:
Jehoiachin[u] his son,
and Zedekiah.

1 Chron.
3:17-24

ROYAL LINE AFTER EXILE.
The descendants of Jehoiachin the captive:
Shealtiel his son, Malkiram, Pedaiah, Shenazzar, Jekamiah, Hosha-
ma and Nedabiah.
The sons of Pedaiah:
Zerubbabel and Shimei.
The sons of Zerubbabel:
Meshullam and Hananiah.
Shelomith was their sister.
There were also five others:
Hashubah, Ohel, Berekiah, Hasadiah and Jushab-Hesed.
The descendants of Hananiah:
Pelatiah and Jeshaiah, and the sons of Rephaiah, of Arnan, of
Obadiah and of Shecaniah.
The descendants of Shecaniah:
Shemaiah and his sons:
Hattush, Igal, Bariah, Neariah and Shaphat—six in all.
The sons of Neariah:
Elioenai, Hizkiah and Azrikam—three in all.
The sons of Elioenai:
Hodaviah, Eliashib, Pelaiah, Akkub, Johanan, Delaiah and Anani—
seven in all.

1 Chron.
4:24-43

SIMEON.
The descendants of Simeon:
Nemuel, Jamin, Jarib, Zerah and Shaul;
Shallum was Shaul's son, Mibsam his son and Mishma his son.
The descendants of Mishma:
Hammuel his son, Zaccur his son and Shimei his son.
Shimei had sixteen sons and six daughters, but his brothers did not have
many children; so their entire clan did not become as numerous as the peo-
ple of Judah. They lived in Beersheba, Moladah, Hazar Shual, Bilhah,
Ezem, Tolad, Bethuel, Hormah, Ziklag, Beth Marcaboth, Hazar Susim,
Beth Biri and Shaaraim. These were their towns until the reign of David.
Their surrounding villages were Etam, Ain, Rimmon, Token and Ashan—
five towns—and all the villages around these towns as far as Baalath.[v]
These were their settlements. And they kept a genealogical record.

[u]Hebrew *Jeconiah*, a variant of *Jehoiachin*   [v]Some Septuagint manuscripts (see also Joshua
19:8); Hebrew *Baal*

Meshobab, Jamlech, Joshah son of Amaziah, Joel, Jehu son of Joshibiah, the son of Seraiah, the son of Asiel, also Elioenai, Jaakobah, Jeshohaiah, Asaiah, Adiel, Jesimiel, Benaiah, and Ziza son of Shiphi, the son of Allon, the son of Jedaiah, the son of Shimri, the son of Shemaiah.

The men listed above by name were leaders of their clans. Their families increased greatly, and they went to the outskirts of Gedor to the east of the valley in search of pasture for their flocks. They found rich, good pasture, and the land was spacious, peaceful and quiet. Some Hamites had lived there formerly.

The men whose names were listed came in the days of Hezekiah king of Judah. They attacked the Hamites in their dwellings and also the Meunites who were there and completely destroyed[w] them, as is evident to this day. Then they settled in their place, because there was pasture for their flocks. And five hundred of these Simeonites, led by Pelatiah, Neariah, Rephaiah and Uzziel, the sons of Ishi, invaded the hill country of Seir. They killed the remaining Amalekites who had escaped, and they have lived there to this day.

REUBEN.   The sons of Reuben the firstborn of Israel (he was the firstborn, but when he defiled his father's marriage bed, his rights as firstborn were given to the sons of Joseph son of Israel; so he could not be listed in the genealogical record in accordance with his birthright, and though Judah was the strongest of his brothers and a ruler came from him, the rights of the firstborn belonged to Joseph)—the sons of Reuben the firstborn of Israel: *(1 Chron. 5:1-9)*

Hanoch, Pallu, Hezron and Carmi.
The descendants of Joel:
　Shemaiah his son, Gog his son,
　Shimei his son, Micah his son,
　Reaiah his son, Baal his son,
　and Beerah his son, whom Tiglath-Pileser[x] king of Assyria took into exile. Beerah was a leader of the Reubenites.
Their relatives by clans, listed according to their genealogical records:
　Jeiel the chief, Zechariah, and Bela son of Azaz, the son of Shema, the son of Joel. They settled in the area from Aroer to Nebo and Baal Meon. To the east they occupied the land up to the edge of the desert that extends to the Euphrates River, because their livestock had increased in Gilead.

GAD.   *(1 Chron. 5:11-17)*
The Gadites lived next to them in Bashan, as far as Salecah:
　Joel was the chief, Shapham the second, then Janai and Shaphat, in Bashan.
Their relatives, by families, were:
　Michael, Meshullam, Sheba, Jorai, Jacan, Zia and Eber—seven in all.
　These were the sons of Abihail son of Huri, the son of Jaroah, the son of Gilead, the son of Michael, the son of Jeshishai, the son of Jahdo, the son of Buz.

---

[w]The Hebrew term refers to the irrevocable giving over of things or persons to the LORD, often by totally destroying them.　[x]Hebrew *Tilgath-Pilneser*, a variant of *Tiglath-Pileser;* also in verse 26

Ahi son of Abdiel, the son of Guni, was head of their family.

The Gadites lived in Gilead, in Bashan and its outlying villages, and on all the pasturelands of Sharon as far as they extended.

All these were entered in the genealogical records during the reigns of Jotham king of Judah and Jeroboam king of Israel.

1 Chron. 6:1	**LEVI.** The sons of Levi: Gershon, Kohath and Merari.

1 Chron. 6:2-15	**KOHATH TO AARON'S DESCENDANTS.** The sons of Kohath: Amram, Izhar, Hebron and Uzziel.

The children of Amram:

Aaron, Moses and Miriam.

The sons of Aaron:

Nadab, Abihu, Eleazar and Ithamar.

Eleazar was the father of Phinehas,

Phinehas the father of Abishua,

Abishua the father of Bukki,

Bukki the father of Uzzi,

Uzzi the father of Zerahiah,

Zerahiah the father of Meraioth,

Meraioth the father of Amariah,

Amariah the father of Ahitub,

Ahitub the father of Zadok,

Zadok the father of Ahimaaz,

Ahimaaz the father of Azariah,

Azariah the father of Johanan,

Johanan the father of Azariah (it was he who served as priest in the temple Solomon built in Jerusalem),

Azariah the father of Amariah,

Amariah the father of Ahitub,

Ahitub the father of Zadok,

Zadok the father of Shallum,

Shallum the father of Hilkiah,

Hilkiah the father of Azariah,

Azariah the father of Seraiah,

and Seraiah the father of Jehozadak.

Jehozadak was deported when the LORD sent Judah and Jerusalem into exile by the hand of Nebuchadnezzar.

1 Chron. 6:16-19a	**LEVI'S SONS AND GRANDSONS.** The sons of Levi: Gershon,y Kohath and Merari.

These are the names of the sons of Gershon:

Libni and Shimei.

The sons of Kohath:

Amram, Izhar, Hebron and Uzziel.

The sons of Merari:

Mahli and Mushi.

---

y Hebrew *Gershom,* a variant of *Gershon;* also in verses 17, 20, 43, 62 and 71

CLANS OF LEVITES.

These are the clans of the Levites listed according to their fathers:
Of Gershon:

Libni his son, Jehath his son,
Zimmah his son, Joah his son,
Iddo his son, Zerah his son
and Jeatherai his son.

The descendants of Kohath:

Amminadab his son, Korah his son,
Assir his son, Elkanah his son,
Ebiasaph his son, Assir his son,
Tahath his son, Uriel his son,
Uzziah his son and Shaul his son.

The descendants of Elkanah:

Amasai, Ahimoth,
Elkanah his son,^{z} Zophai his son,
Nahath his son, Eliab his son,
Jeroham his son, Elkanah his son
and Samuel his son. ^{a}

The sons of Samuel:

Joel^b the firstborn
and Abijah the second son.

The descendants of Merari:

Mahli, Libni his son,
Shimei his son, Uzzah his son,
Shimea his son, Haggiah his son
and Asaiah his son.

TEMPLE MUSICIANS.   These are the men David put in charge of the
music in the house of the LORD after the ark came to rest there. They ministered with music before the tabernacle, the Tent of Meeting, until
Solomon built the temple of the LORD in Jerusalem. They performed their
duties according to the regulations laid down for them.

Here are the men who served, together with their sons:
From the Kohathites:

Heman, the musician,
the son of Joel, the son of Samuel,
the son of Elkanah, the son of Jeroham,
the son of Eliel, the son of Toah,
the son of Zuph, the son of Elkanah,
the son of Mahath, the son of Amasai,
the son of Elkanah, the son of Joel,
the son of Azariah, the son of Zephaniah,
the son of Tahath, the son of Assir,
the son of Ebiasaph, the son of Korah,
the son of Izhar, the son of Kohath,
the son of Levi, the son of Israel;

^{z}Some Hebrew manuscripts, Septuagint and Syriac; most Hebrew manuscripts *Ahimoth*
^{26}*and Elkanah. The sons of Elkanah:* ^{a}Some Septuagint manuscripts (see also 1 Samuel
1:19,20 and 1 Chron. 6:33,34); Hebrew does not have *and Samuel his son.* ^{b}Some
Septuagint manuscripts and Syriac (see also 1 Samuel 8:2 and 1 Chron. 6:33); Hebrew
does not have *Joel.*

and Heman's associate Asaph, who served at his right hand:
    Asaph son of Berekiah, the son of Shimea,
    the son of Michael, the son of Baaseiah,[c]
    the son of Malkijah, the son of Ethni,
    the son of Zerah, the son of Adaiah,
    the son of Ethan, the son of Zimmah,
    the son of Shimei, the son of Jahath,
    the son of Gershon, the son of Levi;
and from their associates, the Merarites, at his left hand:
    Ethan son of Kishi, the son of Abdi,
    the son of Malluch, the son of Hashabiah,
    the son of Amaziah, the son of Hilkiah,
    the son of Amzi, the son of Bani,
    the son of Shemer, the son of Mahli,
    the son of Mushi, the son of Merari,
    the son of Levi.

1 Chron.
6:48-53

HIGH PRIESTS.   Their fellow Levites were assigned to all the other duties of the tabernacle, the house of God. But Aaron and his descendants were the ones who presented offerings on the altar of burnt offering and on the altar of incense in connection with all that was done in the Most Holy Place, making atonement for Israel, in accordance with all that Moses the servant of God had commanded.

These were the descendants of Aaron:
    Eleazar his son, Phinehas his son,
    Abishua his son, Bukki his son,
    Uzzi his son, Zerahiah his son,
    Meraioth his son, Amariah his son,
    Ahitub his son, Zadok his son
    and Ahimaaz his son.

1 Chron.
6:54-81

CITIES AND LANDS.   These were the locations of their settlements allotted as their territory (they were assigned to the descendants of Aaron who were from the Kohathite clan, because the first lot was for them):

They were given Hebron in Judah with its surrounding pasturelands. But the fields and villages around the city were given to Caleb son of Jephunneh.

So the descendants of Aaron were given Hebron (a city of refuge), and Libnah,[d] Jattir, Eshtemoa, Hilen, Debir, Ashan, Juttah[e] and Beth Shemesh, together with their pasturelands. And from the tribe of Benjamin they were given Gibeon,[f] Geba, Alemeth and Anathoth, together with their pasturelands.

These towns, which were distributed among the Kohathite clans, were thirteen in all.

The rest of Kohath's descendants were allotted ten towns from the clans of half the tribe of Manasseh.

The descendants of Gershon, clan by clan, were allotted thirteen towns

[c]Most Hebrew manuscripts; some Hebrew manuscripts, one Septuagint manuscript and Syriac *Maaseiah*   [d]See Joshua 21:13; Hebrew *given the cities of refuge: Hebron, Libnah*.
[e]Syriac (see also Septuagint and Joshua 21:16); Hebrew does not have *Juttah*.   [f]See Joshua 21:17; Hebrew does not have *Gibeon*.

from the tribes of Issachar, Asher and Naphtali, and from the part of the tribe of Manasseh that is in Bashan.

The descendants of Merari, clan by clan, were allotted twelve towns from the tribes of Reuben, Gad and Zebulun.

So the Israelites gave the Levites these towns and their pasturelands. From the tribes of Judah, Simeon and Benjamin they allotted the previously named towns.

Some of the Kohathite clans were given as their territory towns from the tribe of Ephraim.

In the hill country of Ephraim they were given Shechem (a city of refuge), and Gezer,[g] Jokmeam, Beth Horon, Aijalon and Gath Rimmon, together with their pasturelands.

And from half the tribe of Manasseh the Israelites gave Aner and Bileam, together with their pasturelands, to the rest of the Kohathite clans.

The Gershonites received the following:
From the clan of the half-tribe of Manasseh
    they received Golan in Bashan and also Ashtaroth, together with
    their pasturelands;
from the tribe of Issachar
    they received Kedesh, Daberath, Ramoth and Anem, together with
    their pasturelands;
from the tribe of Asher
    they received Mashal, Abdon, Hukok and Rehob, together with
    their pasturelands;
and from the tribe of Naphtali
    they received Kedesh in Galilee, Hammon and Kiriathaim, together
    with their pasturelands.

The Merarites (the rest of the Levites) received the following:
From the tribe of Zebulun
    they received Jokneam, Kartah,[h] Rimmono and Tabor, together
    with their pasturelands;
from the tribe of Reuben across the Jordan east of Jericho
    they received Bezer in the desert, Jahzah, Kedemoth and Mephaath,
    together with their pasturelands;
and from the tribe of Gad
    they received Ramoth in Gilead, Mahanaim, Heshbon and Jazer,
    together with their pasturelands.

ISSACHAR.   The sons of Issachar: 1 Chron.
    Tola, Puah, Jashub and Shimron—four in all.   7:1-5
The sons of Tola:
    Uzzi, Rephaiah, Jeriel, Jahmai, Ibsam and Samuel—heads of their
    families. During the reign of David, the descendants of Tola listed
    as fighting men in their genealogy numbered 22,600.
The son of Uzzi:
    Izrahiah.
The sons of Izrahiah:
    Michael, Obadiah, Joel and Isshiah. All five of them were chiefs.

---

[g] See Joshua 21:21; Hebrew *given the cities of refuge: Shechem, Gezer*.   [h] See Septuagint
and Joshua 21:34; Hebrew does not have *Jokneam, Kartah*.

According to their family genealogy, they had 36,000 men ready for battle, for they had many wives and children.

The relatives who were fighting men belonging to all the clans of Issachar, as listed in their genealogy, were 87,000 in all.

1 Chron. 7:6-12

BENJAMIN.

Three sons of Benjamin:

Bela, Beker and Jediael.

The sons of Bela:

Ezbon, Uzzi, Uzziel, Jerimoth and Iri, heads of families—five in all. Their genealogical record listed 22,034 fighting men.

The sons of Beker:

Zemirah, Joash, Eliezer, Elioenai, Omri, Jeremoth, Abijah, Anathoth and Alemeth. All these were the sons of Beker. Their genealogical record listed the heads of families and 20,200 fighting men.

The son of Jediael:

Bilhan.

The sons of Bilhan:

Jeush, Benjamin, Ehud, Kenaanah, Zethan, Tarshish and Ahishahar. All these sons of Jediael were heads of families. There were 17,200 fighting men ready to go out to war.

The Shuppites and Huppites were the descendants of Ir, and the Hushites the descendants of Aher.

1 Chron. 8:1-40

GENEALOGY OF SAUL. Benjamin was the father of Bela his firstborn, Ashbel the second son, Aharah the third,

Nohah the fourth and Rapha the fifth.

The sons of Bela were:

Addar, Gera, Abihud,[i] Abishua, Naaman, Ahoah, Gera, Shephuphan and Huram.

These were the descendants of Ehud, who were heads of families of those living in Geba and were deported to Manahath:

Naaman, Ahijah, and Gera, who deported them and who was the father of Uzza and Ahihud.

Sons were born to Shaharaim in Moab after he had divorced his wives Hushim and Baara. By his wife Hodesh he had Jobab, Zibia, Mesha, Malcam, Jeuz, Sakia and Mirmah. These were his sons, heads of families. By Hushim he had Abitub and Elpaal.

The sons of Elpaal:

Eber, Misham, Shemed (who built Ono and Lod with its surrounding villages), and Beriah and Shema, who were heads of families of those living in Aijalon and who drove out the inhabitants of Gath.

Ahio, Shashak, Jeremoth, Zebadiah, Arad, Eder, Michael, Ishpah and Joha were the sons of Beriah.

Zebadiah, Meshullam, Hizki, Heber, Ishmerai, Izliah and Jobab were the sons of Elpaal.

Jakim, Zicri, Zabdi, Elienai, Zillethai, Eliel, Adaiah, Beraiah and Shimrath were the sons of Shimei.

Ishpan, Eber, Eliel, Abdon, Zicri, Hanan, Hananiah, Elam, Anthothijah, Iphdeiah and Penuel were the sons of Shashak.

---

[i]Or *Gera the father of Ehud*

Shamsherai, Shehariah, Athaliah, Jaareshiah, Elijah and Zicri were the
    sons of Jeroham.
All these were heads of families, chiefs as listed in their genealogy, and
they lived in Jerusalem.

Jeiel[j] the father[k] of Gibeon lived in Gibeon.
    His wife's name was Maacah, and his firstborn son was Abdon, fol-
        lowed by Zur, Kish, Baal, Ner,[l] Nadab, Gedor, Ahio, Zeker and
        Mikloth, who was the father of Shimeah. They too lived near
        their relatives in Jerusalem.
Ner was the father of Kish, Kish the father of Saul, and Saul the father
    of Jonathan, Malki-Shua, Abinadab and Esh-Baal.[m]
The son of Jonathan:
    Merib-Baal,[n] who was the father of Micah.
The sons of Micah:
    Pithon, Melech, Tarea and Ahaz.
    Ahaz was the father of Jehoaddah, Jehoaddah was the father of
        Alemeth, Azmaveth and Zimri, and Zimri was the father of
        Moza. Moza was the father of Binea; Raphah was his son, Eleasah
        his son and Azel his son.
Azel had six sons, and these were their names:
    Azrikam, Bokeru, Ishmael, Sheariah, Obadiah and Hanan. All these
        were the sons of Azel.
The sons of his brother Eshek:
    Ulam his firstborn, Jeush the second son and Eliphelet the third.
        The sons of Ulam were brave warriors who could handle the
        bow. They had many sons and grandsons—150 in all.
All these were the descendants of Benjamin.

NAPHTALI.

The sons of Naphtali:
    Jahziel, Guni, Jezer and Shillem[o]—the descendants of Bilhah.

1 Chron.
7:13

MANASSEH (JOSEPH).

The descendants of Manasseh:
    Asriel was his descendant through his Aramean concubine. She
        gave birth to Makir the father of Gilead. Makir took a wife from
        among the Huppites and Shuppites. His sister's name was Maacah.
        Another descendant was named Zelophehad, who had only
        daughters.
        Makir's wife Maacah gave birth to a son and named him Peresh.
    His brother was named Sheresh, and his sons were Ulam and Rakem.
The son of Ulam:
    Bedan.
These were the sons of Gilead son of Makir, the son of Manasseh. His
    sister Hammoleketh gave birth to Ishhod, Abiezer and Mahlah.
The sons of Shemida were:
    Ahian, Shechem, Likhi and Aniam.

1 Chron.
7:14-19

---

[j]Some Septuagint manuscripts (see also 1 Chron. 9:35); Hebrew does not have *Jeiel*.
[k]*Father* may mean *civic leader* or *military leader*.   [l]Some Septuagint manuscripts (see
also 1 Chron. 9:36); Hebrew does not have *Ner*.   [m]Also known as *Ish-Bosheth*
[n]Also known as *Mephibosheth*   [o]Some Hebrew and Septuagint manuscripts (see also
Gen. 46:24 and Num. 26:49); most Hebrew manuscripts *Shallum*

1 Chron.
7:20-29

EPHRAIM (JOSEPH).
  The descendants of Ephraim:
    Shuthelah, Bered his son,
    Tahath his son, Eleadah his son,
    Tahath his son, Zabad his son
    and Shuthelah his son.
        Ezer and Elead were killed by the native-born men of Gath, when they went down to seize their livestock. Their father Ephraim mourned for them many days, and his relatives came to comfort him. Then he lay with his wife again, and she became pregnant and gave birth to a son. He named him Beriah,*p* because there had been misfortune in his family. His daughter was Sheerah, who built Lower and Upper Beth Horon as well as Uzzen Sheerah.
    Rephah was his son, Resheph his son,*q*
    Telah his son, Tahan his son,
    Ladan his son, Ammihud his son,
    Elishama his son, Nun his son
    and Joshua his son.
  Their lands and settlements included Bethel and its surrounding villages, Naaran to the east, Gezer and its villages to the west, and Shechem and its villages all the way to Ayyah and its villages. Along the borders of Manasseh were Beth Shan, Taanach, Megiddo and Dor, together with their villages. The descendants of Joseph son of Israel lived in these towns.

1 Chron.
7:30-40

ASHER.
  The sons of Asher:
    Imnah, Ishvah, Ishvi and Beriah. Their sister was Serah.
  The sons of Beriah:
    Heber and Malkiel, who was the father of Birzaith.
  Heber was the father of Japhlet, Shomer and Hotham and of their sister Shua.
  The sons of Japhlet:
    Pasach, Bimhal and Ashvath.
    These were Japhlet's sons.
  The sons of Shomer:
    Ahi, Rohgah,*r* Hubbah and Aram.
  The sons of his brother Helem:
    Zophah, Imna, Shelesh and Amal.
  The sons of Zophah:
    Suah, Harnepher, Shual, Beri, Imrah, Bezer, Hod, Shamma, Shilshah, Ithran*s* and Beera.
  The sons of Jether:
    Jephunneh, Pispah and Ara.
  The sons of Ulla:
    Arah, Hanniel and Rizia.
  All these were descendants of Asher—heads of families, choice men, brave warriors and outstanding leaders. The number of men ready for battle, as listed in their genealogy, was 26,000.

p Beriah sounds like the Hebrew for *misfortune.*   *q*Some Septuagint manuscripts; Hebrew does not have *his son.*   *r*Or *of his brother Shomer: Rohgah*   *s*Possibly a variant of *Jether*

CONCLUSION.   All Israel was listed in the genealogies recorded in the   1 Chron.
book of the kings of Israel.   9:1a

Following these genealogies is a record of the people of Jerusalem, but the
specific time, either before or after the exile, is not entirely clear. It does seem to
correspond most closely, however, to similar listings in Nehemiah's accounts. If
so, these are the families living in Jerusalem at the very time that these national archives are being compiled.

INHABITANTS OF JERUSALEM.   The people of Judah were taken cap-   1 Chron.
tive to Babylon because of their unfaithfulness. Now the first to resettle on   9:1b-9
their own property in their own towns were some Israelites, priests,
Levites and temple servants.
    Those from Judah, from Benjamin, and from Ephraim and Manasseh
who lived in Jerusalem were:
    Uthai son of Ammihud, the son of Omri, the son of Imri, the son of
        Bani, a descendant of Perez son of Judah.
    Of the Shilonites:
    Asaiah the firstborn and his sons.
    Of the Zerahites:
    Jeuel.
    The people from Judah numbered 690.
    Of the Benjamites:
    Sallu son of Meshullam, the son of Hodaviah, the son of Hassenuah;
    Ibneiah son of Jeroham; Elah son of Uzzi, the son of Micri; and
        Meshullam son of Shephatiah, the son of Reuel, the son of Ib-
        nijah.
    The people from Benjamin, as listed in their genealogy, numbered
        956. All these men were heads of their families.
    Of the priests: 1 Chron.
    Jedaiah; Jehoiarib; Jakin;   9:10-16
    Azariah son of Hilkiah, the son of Meshullam, the son of Zadok, the
        son of Meraioth, the son of Ahitub, the official in charge of the
        house of God;
    Adaiah son of Jeroham, the son of Pashhur, the son of Malkijah; and
        Maasai son of Adiel, the son of Jahzerah, the son of Meshullam,
        the son of Meshillemith, the son of Immer.
    The priests, who were heads of families, numbered 1,760. They
        were able men, responsible for ministering in the house of God.
    Of the Levites:
    Shemaiah son of Hasshub, the son of Azrikam, the son of
        Hashabiah, a Merarite; Bakbakkar, Heresh, Galal and Mattaniah
        son of Mica, the son of Zicri, the son of Asaph; Obadiah son of
        Shemaiah, the son of Galal, the son of Jeduthun; and Berekiah son
        of Asa, the son of Elkanah, who lived in the villages of the
        Netophathites.
    The gatekeepers: 1 Chron.
    Shallum, Akkub, Talmon, Ahiman and their brothers, Shallum their   9:17-32
        chief being stationed at the King's Gate on the east, up to the
        present time. These were the gatekeepers belonging to the camp
        of the Levites. Shallum son of Kore, the son of Ebiasaph, the son

of Korah, and his fellow gatekeepers from his family (the Korahites) were responsible for guarding the thresholds of the Tent[t]
just as their fathers had been responsible for guarding the entrance to the dwelling of the LORD. In earlier times Phinehas son
of Eleazar was in charge of the gatekeepers, and the LORD was
with him. Zechariah son of Meshelemiah was the gatekeeper at
the entrance to the Tent of Meeting.

Altogether, those chosen to be gatekeepers at the thresholds numbered
212. They were registered by genealogy in their villages. The gatekeepers
had been assigned to their positions of trust by David and Samuel the seer.
They and their descendants were in charge of guarding the gates of the
house of the LORD—the house called the Tent. The gatekeepers were on the
four sides: east, west, north and south. Their brothers in their villages had
to come from time to time and share their duties for seven-day periods.
But the four principal gatekeepers, who were Levites, were entrusted with
the responsibility for the rooms and treasuries in the house of God. They
would spend the night stationed around the house of God, because they
had to guard it; and they had charge of the key for opening it each morning.

Some of them were in charge of the articles used in the temple service;
they counted them when they were brought in and when they were taken
out. Others were assigned to take care of the furnishings and all the other
articles of the sanctuary, as well as the flour and wine, and the oil, incense
and spices. But some of the priests took care of mixing the spices. A Levite
named Mattithiah, the firstborn son of Shallum the Korahite, was entrusted with the responsibility for baking the offering bread. Some of their
Kohathite brothers were in charge of preparing for every Sabbath the
bread set out on the table.

1 Chron.
9:33,34

Those who were musicians, heads of Levite families, stayed in the
rooms of the temple and were exempt from other duties because they were
responsible for the work day and night.

All these were heads of Levite families, chiefs as listed in their genealogy, and they lived in Jerusalem.

[t]That is, the temple

OCTOBER 15

HISTORICAL INTERLUDE
(Ca. 425-5 B.C.)

End of Old Testament Record

*A*s the historical record of the Old Testament comes to a close, the curtain falls on the early centuries of mankind's existence. From Adam and Eve to Ezra and Nehemiah, God has revealed himself in the affairs of both individuals and nations. From the earliest days of the patriarchs, a divine master plan has been unfolding to teach mankind the nature of God, and to prepare the world for a Savior who will transform man's sinful condition and bring true life. God's instrumentality in this plan has been the relatively obscure Hebrew nation of Israel. Some 650 years before it came into being, God promised the faithful patriarch Abraham that his descendants would become a great nation and have a land of their own—and that through them all the people of the earth would be blessed.

When the 12 tribes of Israel were delivered out of Egyptian bondage and brought to Mount Sinai, the first promise was fulfilled. God covenanted with the new nation of Israel that he would be their God and they in turn covenanted that they would be his people. Among other symbols of the covenant was the law given through Moses. In its divine origin and theocratic nature it was like no other law ever given. Through that law, God elevated moral consciousness and established a whole new religion, with a tabernacle, priests, sacrifices, offerings, Sabbaths, and holy festivals. It was a great beginning. But in the very week of its inception, the nation exhibited a spirit of rebellion which would continue generation after generation. This rebellion brought 40 years of wandering in the wilderness as punishment. But God in his mercy forgave his people and led them to the promised land of Canaan. After the local inhabitants were substantially subdued over the period of the judges, the nation finally had its own land, and God's second promise to Abraham was fulfilled.

From that point on, it remained only for the nation of Israel to become a blessing to the whole world. In the 120-year-long monarchy of Saul, David, and Solomon it seemed that the nation's rise to prominence and power was the beginning of the third fulfillment. But upon Solomon's death the rebellion of the people once again brought disaster—this time civil war and a divided kingdom. For 325 years the people became more and more rebellious, turning away from their God, the Creator of the universe, to pagan gods and idols of man's own making. Because sin always brings death, the people's sins were a death knell to the nation itself. God used Israel's territorial enemies as his agents of judgment, and both segments of the kingdom were taken captive and carried away into exile. Throughout the period of spiritual and political decline, God had sent one messenger after another, crying out against the people's sins and warning of impending punishment. And yet, without exception, every message had ended with a note of hope and a promise of restoration. Exile would end within 70 years, and the temple would be rebuilt. Even beyond that were prophecies of a Messiah who would come and establish an everlasting kingdom of peace and joy.

Faithful as always, God fulfilled his promise when he brought his people back into their land, exactly as he had foretold—70 years after the first deportation. And when the temple was rebuilt, some 20 years later, God's word was once again proved true. But when foreign dominance and local oppression continued over the next century, disillusionment and cynicism set in—and with it, renewed spiritual rebellion.

Despite the message of Malachi that the day of the Lord was coming, and despite the temporary spiritual revival under Ezra and Nehemiah, the Old Testament record does not end on a note of great optimism or confidence. The people of Israel continue even now in their willful violation of God's laws; the nation is still at the mercy of the Persian Empire; and, as far as the Jews can tell, there is no sign that any super-king is about to establish the ideal kingdom which they have come to expect. Never mind that every other promise that God has made in over 40 centuries has been faithfully fulfilled. Where is this great Messiah of which the prophets have spoken? Has God finally gone too far in an effort to hold his people's attention? Is this a promise that is too difficult for even the God of heaven to fulfill?

Although comfortable retrospect might chide the Jews for their lack of faith, it is easy to understand their true discouragement. Others in later centuries—Jew and non-Jew alike—whose primary focus is on a physical rather than a spiritual kingdom, or the coming of the end when they mistakenly expect it, will suffer the same disillusionment. And saddest of all, when the Messiah finally does come, he will be so unlike the Jews' preconceived image of him that most of them will not even recognize him.

How long will it be before the Messiah comes? How long must the Jews—indeed the whole world—wait for this glorious day of promise? If Daniel has given a clue in his vision of the seventy "sevens," the Messiah's coming will not be before some 400 years from now. Indeed this is approximately the same period during which the historical record of Scripture will lie silent.

But why would there be such a historical interlude? Certainly one can only speculate, but perhaps it is simply to dramatize the most important event in the history of mankind. Perhaps there is something to be said for disassociating the Messiah from any exclusive ties to this small Hebrew nation so that his kingdom may be seen as truly universal. Perhaps the political situation in a later time will be more conducive to the Messiah's mission. Or perhaps the delay is to insure against any possibility that fulfillment of relatively recent prophecies is merely contrived by wishful believers. Whatever God's reasons, it is clear that the nation of Israel will have to wait further for the promised Messiah and for the day when, through their race, all the nations of the earth will be blessed.

Writings of the Apocrypha

*T*he historical record of the Old Testament, as presently divided, is composed of 39 separate writings. In the presentation thus far, the contents of these various writings have been integrated into one continuous narrative—arranged, to the degree possible, in the chronological order of their occurrence. The events span the period from creation to approximately 425 B.C. Not until approximately 5 B.C. will any further events be recorded in any scriptural writings. These accounts will be contained in the New Testament, which is itself a collection of 27 different writings.

Over the next four to six centuries, many other historical and religious documents pertaining to the Jews will be written. Therefore it cannot be said that there are no historical records of the Jews arising out of this period. When it is said that the historical record of Scripture lies silent during this time, emphasis is being placed on the word *Scripture*. The so-called apocryphal or "hidden" writings of this period are not accepted as Scripture by all believers.

Jumping several centuries ahead, the inclusion of these writings will begin with the Greek version of the Old Testament—the Septuagint—which will be widely used in the first century. The Apocrypha will then be adopted as part of the Latin Vulgate, edited by Jerome in about A.D. 400. In more modern times, all English versions of the Bible from A.D. 1382 down to and including the original King James Version of A.D. 1611 will contain the apocryphal writings. In the earlier Greek and Latin versions, the apocryphal writings are interspersed with the other Old Testament writings. In his German Bible of 1534, Luther will collect them into a unified supplement and present them at the end of the Old Testament. The Catholic English version retains the more scattered format even until now, but most Protestant versions will drop the Apocrypha altogether, beginning about A.D. 1629.

In the view of those who reject their inclusion in scriptural canon, the apocryphal writings do not meet the test of having originated from divine inspiration. The Apocrypha are never included in the Hebrew Old Testament, and the Jews do not accept these writings as part of their approved Scriptures. In fact, Hebrew manuscripts of most of the apocryphal writings are not even to be found. It is perhaps significant that several of the writings reflect notions of mysticism and demonology apparently traceable to Persian influences during the Jewish dispersion and arguably inconsistent with either Jewish or later Christian beliefs.

Despite their current lack of credibility among a large segment of believers, these disputed writings are generally moral in nature and do give insight into some of the history, customs, and religious developments of the Jews during this intertestamental period. The following 14 writings, briefly summarized at this point, comprise the so-called Apocrypha. Although most of them emerge from 300 B.C. to A.D. 100, several refer back to earlier times and assume various specific historical contexts.

FIRST ESDRAS, the Greek name for Ezra, is a historical record from the end of the exile until the completion of the temple. It is a compilation which virtually duplicates portions of Ezra, Nehemiah, and the Chronicles. One additional story purports to explain Zerubbabel's leading role in the rebuilding of the temple. According to the story, Zerubbabel argued successfully against two other guards of King Darius that women and truth are stronger than kings and wine.

SECOND ESDRAS is of Latin origin in the first three centuries A.D. and purports to record a series of apocalyptic visions about the future of the world. In that regard it is similar to the apocalyptic visions of the leading prophets, particularly those of Daniel. A major portion of the writing addresses many of the hard issues confronted in the book of Job: how can God permit the suffering of his people? Why should God choose nations more wicked than Israel itself to punish Israel? Why live righteously when the wicked seem to be more prosperous? How long will it be before the righteous finally get their reward? How will the wicked be punished? And, just as in Job, although some answers are provided, the basic response is that there are simply many things which man cannot yet know.

THE BOOK OF TOBIT is a piece of religious fiction about a pious Jew named Tobit and his son Tobias. The story itself is primarily about Tobias' journey from Nineveh to a city called Ecbatana to retrieve money which his father has deposited there. On his journey Tobias meets and marries a distant cousin, Sarah, who has lost seven husbands, each on the night of the wedding before the marriage was consummated. A central figure in the story introduces elements of Persian mysticism and demonism. This figure purports to be an archangel by the name of Raphael who is disguised as Tobias' guide. Apart from the story line, the moral message is a promotion of unselfishness and charity, particularly as seen in the life of Tobit and in the principles which he instills in his son.

THE BOOK OF JUDITH is another piece of religious fiction, about a beautiful Jewish woman named Judith who saves her city, and indeed the entire nation of Israel, by deceiving an Assyrian general and cutting off his head. The general, whose name is Holofernes, is supposedly under the command of Nebuchadnezzar, king over the Assyrians in Nineveh. That obvious historical miscue only further confirms the fictional nature of the tale and draws attention more clearly to the author's apparent purpose in writing it. That purpose seems to be the promotion of strict observance of the Jewish law, particularly the ceremonial and dietary laws. The story may well be a product of the Jewish Pharisees, who will be further described in following narrative.

THE ADDITIONS TO THE BOOK OF ESTHER are supplements to the canonical account of Esther. Those supplements are found scattered throughout the Greek translations of the book of Esther. Because there are no direct references in Esther to God or the Jewish religion, it may well be that the translators decided to add the various supplements in order to bolster the book's religious impact. Among the additions are a dream by Mordecai about the events recorded in Esther; the purported contents of King Artaxerxes' edict authorizing the massacre of the Jews; a supposed account of Esther's prayer to God before approaching the king unsummoned; the purported contents of the letter which permitted the Jews to defend themselves; and finally an epilogue in which Mordecai demonstrates how his dream had been fulfilled in all the prior events.

THE WISDOM OF SOLOMON is a poem similar in style to Ecclesiastes and is characteristic of the literature in the wisdom movement of Solomon. Therefore, although it is written apparently as late as 50-40 B.C., it sometimes bears Solomon's name. The poem speaks beautifully of God's omniscience, the nature of death, the security of the upright, the superiority of virtue, and the destruction of the wicked. As all wisdom literature, it eloquently exalts the value of wisdom. And, reminiscent of the prophets, the writer launches a vicious assault against idolatry and pagan perversion. The writing concludes with a review of God's dealings with Israel and his perpetual care for his people, even in the times of their unfaithfulness.

ECCLESIASTICUS is the longest book of the Apocrypha and is most similar in content and style to the book of Proverbs. It was originally written in Hebrew about 180 B.C. in the city of Jerusalem, and then translated into Greek some 50 years later in the city of Alexandria. The last section of the book contains a review of all the great men in Jewish history, ending with Simon the high priest, who dies in 199 B.C. A prologue indicates that the author is a man by the name of Jeshua and that he has derived his thoughts from many years of studying the law, the prophets, and other Old Testament wisdom literature. It is not surprising that Ecclesiasticus, also known as the Wisdom of Sirach (after Jeshua's father) should begin with the words, "All wisdom comes from the Lord and remains with him forever."

Like the book of Proverbs, Ecclesiasticus finds wisdom in the fear of the Lord and also in self-control, particularly of the tongue. Charity and humility are encouraged, and there are warnings against improper desires and excessive use of wine. The brevity of life and punishment of the wicked are seen as motivations for proper living. Wicked women and woeful wives are bitterly denounced, as are adulterous husbands. Unlike any of the wisdom literature found in the canonical Scriptures, Ecclesiasticus includes such mundane advice as proper dining etiquette and basic health habits. There is praise for various occupations, from physicians to ordinary tradesmen, of whom it is said, "They support the fabric of the world" and "Their prayer is in the practice of their trade." In all, Ecclesiasticus covers a broad scope of wise sayings reflective of the wisdom literature already presented.

THE BOOK OF BARUCH, supposed to have been written by Jeremiah's scribe, purportedly accompanied a donation of money to support the worship in the temple in 582 B.C. However, the fact that the temple was in ruins at that time casts doubt upon the historical accuracy of the writing. It appears that the writing actually emerges near the end of the first century at a time when Jerusalem and the reconstructed temple are once again threatened. In the

writing is a confession of national sin, a plea for mercy, a call for wisdom, and words of encouragement to a nation under oppression. These are followed by "The Letter of Jeremiah," purportedly from the great weeping prophet to the captives in Babylon, warning them against involvement in idolatry. The supposed letter is one of the most insightful and scathing attacks against idolatry ever written.

THE STORY OF SUSANNA is a short story about a virtuous woman named Susanna who is falsely accused of infidelity by two evil Jewish elders when she spurns their lustful advances. As she is being led away for execution, following a trial in which her accusers have perjured themselves, Daniel—presumably the Daniel of the Old Testament—urges that the two elders be questioned outside each other's presence. That move results in conflicting testimony which confirms Susanna's innocence. The story may well be simply a hypothetical case used to bring about reform of a rule of evidence in capital cases. While under the law it takes two witnesses to establish guilt, it remains possible for the two to conspire to bring about the death of an innocent person. The new rule of procedure would help to expose any such conspiracy and provide the death penalty for the conspirators instead.

THE SONG OF THE THREE CHILDREN is a writing of the period 170-150 B.C. which is meant for integration with the book of Daniel (at 3:23). It purports to record the miracle which saved Shadrach, Meshach, and Abednego as they were in the fiery furnace, along with a prayer by Azariah (Abednego), which is really a confession of Israel's sin and a plea for the nation's salvation. There is also a song of praise to the God who has delivered the three men from the fires of death.

THE STORY OF BEL AND THE DRAGON is the third story attached to the book of Daniel and is an attack against idolatry, especially the worship of serpents, or "dragons," as is prevalent in 100 B.C., when the story is written. The story sets Daniel in a controversy with King Cyrus as to whether the Babylonian god Bel actually eats the food offered to it daily. Through simple ingenuity, Daniel is able to demonstrate that the food is consumed by the priests of Bel. Daniel then causes the death of a revered serpent, which so angers its Babylonian worshipers that they throw Daniel into a lions' den. In this fictional version of the lions' den, Daniel is ministered to by the prophet Habakkuk, who is supposedly whisked, in some miraculous fashion, from Judea to Babylon for the occasion.

THE PRAYER OF MANASSES is a brief but excellent example of a pious penitent prayer, perhaps Pharisaic in origin.

THE FIRST BOOK OF MACCABEES contains the history of the Jewish people in Judea in the period from 175-132 B.C. It details much of the history which will appear in summary form in later narrative. The principal kings of the period—the Seleucids in Syria and the Ptolemies in Egypt—are seen in a seesaw struggle, with the Jews caught in the middle. Reference is made to a later Roman power, but during this period there is no direct Roman rule affecting Judea. The historical account begins primarily with the Seleucid king, Antiochus Epiphanes, who brings great persecution against the Jews and their religion. Militant reaction comes from those Jews who would rather die than see the law suppressed. Those Jews are led in battle after battle over several decades by a man named Mattathias and three of his sons.

The first son to take over his father's leadership is named Judas, but is called Maccabeus. It is this man after whom the historical record is named. Judas Maccabeus is followed by his two brothers Jonathan and Simon, and later by Simon's son John Hyrcanus. The military exploits of the Jews against Syrians, Greeks, Egyptians, and Edomites, as well as a number of more local enemies, are reminiscent of the wars of King David. But the almost-constant fighting finally brings Judea and the Jews a brief period of peace in the midst of centuries of conflict. Jonathan and Simon are appointed as both high priests and governors, which indicates an evolution in the traditional roles of Jewish leadership. The First Book of Maccabees is the most important and trustworthy history of the Jews during its time.

THE SECOND BOOK OF MACCABEES presumes to cover the period from 175-160 B.C. but is less historical than patriotic. The book professes to be a readable summary of a much-detailed, five-volume work by Jason of Cyrene. Most notable in the book are the graphic accounts of violent atrocities which Antiochus Epiphanes allegedly brought against the Jews.

From these writings and the historical records of other nations over the next four centuries, something of the Jews' continued development, as both a nation and a dispersed people, can be pieced together.

Influences on a Dispersed People

*J*t is easy to think that after the exile all the Jews in Babylonia return to Palestine. That is by no means the case. Many Jews choose not to return and are still living in Babylonia, Egypt, and other areas as well. Those who have been assimilated into other cultures have been influenced in a number of ways, including their religious beliefs and practices. With the Hebrew language rapidly giving way to Aramaic and other languages, there is waning interest in reading the Torah, as the Law of Moses has come to be known. Thus the law's influence itself has diminished. That fact, combined with local eating habits, has led many Jews to ignore the strict dietary rules imposed on them by the law.

Of course local religious beliefs have a profound effect, as already seen when the Jews intermarried with those involved in idolatry and various pagan practices. Also of significant impact are the Persian beliefs in astrology and the occult. As a result, when many Jews read their Scriptures in this postexilic period, they attach special meanings to any passage dealing with demons and angels, or light and darkness. The Torah is gradually being mystified in the eyes of many. A good example is found in the apocryphal book of Tobit, in which Persian Zoroastrianism and pagan demons are promoted.

One of the most disastrous influences of Persian origin is the belief that God is an aloof, impersonal god. It does not take long for any Jew, or non-Jew for that matter, who accepts this notion to have difficulty with Isaiah's prophecy that the Messiah would be called Immanuel—that is, God with us.

With these and other cultural threats becoming increasingly apparent, the more orthodox Jews take steps to combat the pagan influences. And yet, ironically, the steps they take are not particularly in the direction of the very law they are trying to preserve. They too are victims of their strange environment. Under the law, the temple is to be the center of their sacrificial form of worship, and priests have the responsibility of teaching the law to each generation. Yet during the exile, and even after its end in areas other than Palestine, there is no temple, and sacrificing is often politically impossible. Substituting as best they can, the faithful begin to emphasize prayer and the inward sacrifice of the heart. The temple is replaced by an institution known as the synagogue, where the people gather for singing, prayer, and discussion of God's laws. Ezekiel's house in Tel Abib of Babylonia may have been a prototype, and Ezra's assembly for the reading of the law may have given impetus to the synagogue movement even in the shadow of the reconstructed temple. And the further away from Jerusalem one might go at this time, the more synagogues he would find.

The synagogues themselves foster changes in the Jewish religion. First to be noticed is the declining role of the priest, and his replacement by those known as rabbis. The rabbis are men whose superior knowledge of the law has set them in positions of great respect as the teachers in the synagogues. The fact that they gain such respect, oddly enough, leads to a second, and most significant, link in the evolution of Judaism. That link is the rise of sectarianism. The synagogues lend themselves readily to both special-interest groups and different schools of thought which are no longer under the direct influence of the priestly line of authority.

Another extension of the rabbinical movement is the development of the many written interpretations of the rabbis and the often greater importance attached to these writings than to those of the Torah itself. The first collections of these writings, known as the Midrash, is closely linked to the Torah. However, later collections will begin to incorporate oral traditions without such direct ties.

One final important development at this time is the beginning of so-called remnant theology. With paganism and secularism bringing about a compromised theology, the more orthodox are beginning to think the unthinkable. Perhaps there are Jews who are "erring Jews"—which, when interpreted, really means they are not true Jews at all! Of course this radical idea hardly touches ground before the next logical question is asked: who then is the faithful remnant? Predictably enough, each of the sects believes that its own special teachings and understandings of the law qualify them—and perhaps only them. The irony of it all is that there are those in Palestine who also take up the faithful-remnant cry. They in turn condemn even the more orthodox Jews in Babylonia for not returning to the land of promise and, presumably, for abandoning temple worship in favor of these unauthorized synagogues!

As all these changes are starting to have their impact on Judaism, the Persian Empire is slowly crumbling around the Jews in Palestine and those who are dispersed. From the time of Artaxerxes' death, in 424 B.C., the Persian throne is both shaky and bloodstained. Over the following century, intrigue, assassinations, and coup after coup will take place in Susa. The final fall of the empire will come in 330 B.C. at the hands of Alexander the Great of Macedonia. Under Persian dominance they have had both relative peace and official cooperation—even encouragement. In the years to come they will not always be so blessed.

Hellenism and the Jews

*E*ven before the fall of the Persian forces under Darius III at the great Battle of Arbela, Alexander sweeps through Syria, Palestine, and Egypt. It is during this time that he finally and completely destroys the city of Tyre, ending any doubt as to whether Ezekiel's prophecy would be fulfilled. He also establishes a new city on the Nile to take its place. That city, appropriately named Alexandria, will become a significant center of Greek influence. And because a large number of Jews will eventually be citizens of Alexandria, the Greek Hellenistic culture will have a profound effect on both the Jewish people and their religion for centuries to come. Therefore, by 332 B.C. Jews in both Egypt and Palestine are feeling the effects of still another foreign dominance. Apparently Alexander permits the Jews in Palestine a measure of self-rule, and generally views them with favor.

In later centuries, Alexander's military victories will become legendary. After crushing the Persians, Alexander pushes on as far as the Ganges River in India, thus linking together for the first time the cultures of both East and West. For a God who works through history, this may well be a providential step in the divine plan, because along with Alexander's military dominance goes the Hellenistic culture, and along with the culture goes the *koine* Greek language. Its universality in future years will be of inestimable value in spreading to the known world the good news of the Messiah's coming.

When Alexander dies, in 323 B.C., there is a classic power struggle and land grab among his generals. In brief, the Ptolemies take control over Egypt and the Seleucids end up with Syria. It does not take long to realize who is caught in the middle—the Jews in Palestine. Ptolemy I captures Jerusalem and takes a number of Jews to colonize Alexandria. He gives them full citizenship and encourages Jewish scholarship. Here for the first time many Jewish intellectuals come under the influence of Greek philosophy with its logic and abstract concepts. The effects will soon be seen. In addition, Alexandria becomes the source of several of the apocryphal writings. Perhaps the most significant outgrowth of this intellectual community comes during the reign of Ptolemy II, who commissions a Greek translation of the Old Testament for the great library at Alexandria. Over the next 300 years this Greek version, known as the Septuagint, will virtually replace the use of the Hebrew manuscripts.

While the Ptolemies and their Hellenism are proving to be in many ways advantageous to the Jews, the Seleucids have an altogether different view of how Hellenism ought to be used. And unfortunately they manage to take Palestine away from the Ptolemies, at least from time to time. Throughout the second century B.C. there is a tug-of-war over Palestine which gives the Seleucids on-again, off-again control over the Jews there. In 190 B.C. the Seleucid king, Antiochus III, is defeated by an emerging world power—Rome. Rome has just emerged from 65 years of Punic wars with Carthage and a magnificent victory in 201 B.C. over the famed General Hannibal. Now it has cast greedy eyes on Greece. In order to concentrate entirely on Greece itself, Rome makes a pact with Antiochus IV and permits continued rule over Syria and Palestine. This Seleucid ruler, whose name is Epiphanes, is one of the cruelest men ever to hold public office. His idea of extending Greek influence and paying the heavy tribute he owes the Roman emperor is not exactly the friendliest gesture to a conquered nation. He begins by selling the office of high priest, then builds a gymnasium for naked athletes, confiscates property, loots the temple, and haughtily sacrifices a pig on a pagan altar he has erected there.

The pig may have been the last straw for a group of Jews called Maccabeans, under the leadership of Mattathias. They begin a running guerilla warfare which lasts from 163 to 143 B.C. Ephiphanes' response is to massacre 1000 Jewish soldiers in his army who refuse to fight on the Sabbath. With the help of the pious Hasidim sect, the Maccabeans finally achieve a Jewish dynasty under John Hyrcanus in 135 B.C. Of course they exercise a fairly tenuous self-rule under the watchful eye of Rome, but for the next three-quarters of a century at least it will be a refreshing break in the action for a beleaguered nation of Jews.

As they savor the temporary return to power which they have achieved, and reflect on some 50 years of brutal persecution, the Jews surely must be thinking more and more about their national destiny. At this point they have come a long way from the early days of restoration and its hope of a politically strong kingdom. If there were ever any doubts about what kind of Messiah is needed, they are all gone now. It is clear that what Israel needs now is a strong political and military leader—perhaps someone like Alexander the Great. After all, it is only a matter of time before the Romans are free to turn their attention to Palestine. And when they do, even the brave Maccabeans will be no match for the Roman legions. Without doubt, the Jews' only hope is the coming of the conquering king they have been promised, and what better time than now? It may be this very thinking which, just over a century from now, will be a significant factor in how the Jews of that day react to an unassuming man of peace who claims to be their king.

Judaism Under Roman Rule

*I*n 63 B.C. the inevitable happens. Under General Pompey the Romans invade Palestine and capture Jerusalem. But a measure of self-rule remains while Pompey and his former ally, Julius Caesar, turn against each other in a power struggle. Pompey is defeated in 48 B.C. In the next year Caesar appoints Antipater as procurator over all Judea, as Palestine is now known, and is himself assassinated in 44 B.C. After Caesar's friend Antony appoints Antipater's son Herod as tetrarch of Galilee, the Hasmoneans briefly revolt and force Herod to his fortress at Masada, near the Dead Sea. When Herod manages to get to Rome, Antony names him king of Judea and proceeds to resubdue the province so that Herod can establish his rule.

Between 37 B.C. and 30 B.C. political intrigue and more wars will bring to the Egyptian stage the last and most famous of all the Ptolemies—Cleopatra. As a Greek ruler she poses the last real threat to Roman dominance. Her marriage to Antony is legendary, along with their battle of Actium in 31 B.C., where both lose their lives to Caesar's nephew and adopted son, Octavian.

Judea is not greatly affected by these Roman infightings, and Herod retains his control of Judea under Octavian. In 27 B.C. the Roman Senate gives Octavian the title of Augustus, and it is this Augustus Caesar who gets credit for founding the Roman Empire with its Pax Romana, or Roman Peace. For the next two centuries the civilized world will enjoy unprecedented peace, prosperity, and, for the most part, good civil government under Roman rule. It causes one to think again of a God who is working through history to achieve his eternal purposes. A century later one would be able to look back and see what an ideal time this was for the divine events about to happen in Judea, and later throughout the whole empire.

Meanwhile, Herod curries Jewish favor by restoring the temple in Jerusalem, which had been virtually destroyed by King Epiphanes. Despite this, Herod will not prove to be a true friend to the Jews. In fact, he orders that when he dies a number of prominent Jews are to be killed so that there will be a time of national mourning! In the meantime he is so obsessed with the security of his throne that he virtually eliminates any possible contenders. He has his favorite wife executed, and "playfully" drowns his young brother-in-law, Aristobulus. It is no wonder, then, that news of the birth of a Jewish "king" will not be received with enthusiasm.

Herod will not be the only one to greet any such news with distress. Ironically, many of the Jews themselves will have serious doubts. To understand their doubts, it is necessary to understand who the Jews are religiously at this point in history. The sectarianism which began after the exile has increased and solidified at this time. The sects are as much political and cultural as they are religious.

The Pharisees have become masters of the oral traditions which have come down from the rabbis over the past four centuries. They are enamored with interpretations and legalistic hypotheticals which do not necessarily have to be answered with reference to the Torah. Although they probably would not acknowledge it, apparently for the Pharisees tradition is on a par with the law itself. That fact takes on added significance when it is coupled with the belief that one earns merit with God by scrupulously observing every technicality of law and tradition. And yet the Pharisees have broad support among the common people, particularly because they hold to a belief in life after death, which some of the other sects now deny. With this popular support, many Pharisees have been chosen for high government positions, including the Sanhedrin, which is the highest tribunal of the Jews.

The second major sect is known as the Sadducees. They are closely associated with the Greek intellectual movement arising earlier out of the Alexandrian community, and have adopted the Epicurean belief that the soul dies with the body. They do not believe in a resurrection. Somewhat curiously, the Sadducees reject oral tradition and accept only the written law, but they readily apply their Hellenistic logic to their understanding of the Torah.

Many more sects also have come into being, including the radically pious ones, called Essenes, the openly rebellious Zealots, the politically active Herodians, and the Samaritans, whose hybrid religion continues from centuries past. Found throughout several of the sects are traces of Persian mysticism, Greek humanism, patriotic Judaism, and time-honored ritualistic traditions. In their religious beliefs and practices, the Jews have come a long way from Mount Sinai.

JESUS THE CHRIST
(Ca. 5 B.C.-A.D. 30)

The Coming of the Messiah

*A*ll is now ready for the most important event in human history. It is an event planned even before the creation of the world. It is the keeping of a promise made to Abraham over 2000 years earlier. It is the fulfillment of a host of prophecies regarding a Messiah who would come to establish his kingdom. Most importantly, it is the beginning of a dynamically new relationship between God and man. The event is the coming of the Savior of the world, the Messiah—or, as referred to in the Greek, the Christ.

This Christ is not to be just another world leader, as Cyrus, Alexander, or Caesar. He is not to be just another great man of God, as Abraham, Moses, or David. He is to be God himself in human flesh! The Lord of heaven is to become a servant of the earth. God, who has previously made himself known through a nation and a law, is now to reveal himself in the most personal way possible—in the form of a man. Until now God's blessings have been reserved mostly for a chosen people, but now they are to become available to all people in every generation.

Who is this Christ, this Messiah? His name is Jesus. His symbolic name, Immanuel (meaning "God with us"), signifies his deity. He is man, to be sure, but God as well; and he is God—the God of Creation—but man as well. God lowers himself so that man might be elevated. He leaves heaven so that man might enter it. To man, who cannot begin to understand the ways of God, it is clearly a great mystery. But what a marvelous and wonderful mystery it is!

As the New Testament record now begins, the Scriptures proclaim the good news about the salvation of mankind which comes through obedient faith in Jesus the Christ. The good news begins with the miraculous birth of Jesus to a virgin of Galilee in the days of Herod, King of Judea. Then, as Jesus grows into manhood, his coming as the promised Messiah and Savior is announced by John the Baptist. As Jesus begins his own ministry, he confirms his deity with miraculous healings and other signs and wonders, and proclaims the imminent coming of the kingdom of God. His teaching calls men and women to new spiritual heights in their worship of God and in their relationships with one another.

But because his teaching challenges traditional practices of the Jewish religion of his day, and because he claims divine authority, Jesus meets strong opposition from religious leaders. That opposition ultimately leads to arrest and trial before Jewish and Roman authorities. Although falsely accused, Jesus is condemned and sentenced to die by crucifixion—an event which is intended to silence both the man and his message. Instead, the good news comes to a powerful climax when, on the third day after his death, Jesus rises from the grave and shows himself alive, proving his own miraculous resurrection. The Christian hope which derives from the gospel message is that, just as Jesus is raised from the dead, so also the righteous in Christ will be raised to eternal life!

The Gospel Accounts

*A*lthough secular history attests to his ministry and influence, the details of Jesus' life were never preserved in an explicitly biographical form. What is known about the historical Jesus comes primarily from the Gospel accounts of Matthew, Mark, Luke, and John—four of Jesus' disciples. However, none of the accounts purports to be a biography of Jesus, as such, despite the fact that certain aspects of his life are covered in great detail and are usually set within specific historical contexts. The Gospel accounts, while clearly historic in nature, are principally documents of faith— the record of those events and teachings upon which Jesus' followers based their belief and hope. Therefore, the exact times and places of those events are not always recorded, and the actual sequence of events can be traced with only limited certainty.

The Gospel accounts vary in the order in which the record of Jesus' ministry is presented. Apart from the fact that the Gospel accounts were never intended as chronological records, the differences in sequential order may be attributed to several factors. First of all, each account was written by a different author, each having a unique perspective. Each writer also focused upon different events, either because he was writing primarily to a particular audience or because he wished to achieve a particular purpose in his writing. This is especially true, for example, of John's account. This also explains why some events are recorded by only one, or perhaps two, of the Gospel writers, and why one account will include certain particulars not included in other accounts of the same event. Although a cursory reading of the different accounts can seem somewhat confusing, careful study discloses a striking harmony not expected of purely human documents which might have been written under the same diversity of time and circumstances.

What follows is a combination of the four Gospel accounts with an integration of the recorded events as nearly as possible in their proper chronological sequence. As previously indicated, any such attempt necessarily involves a degree of speculation, because it is simply not revealed when certain events actually occurred. It is not even certain whether Jesus' entire ministry lasted for 2 1/2 years or for 3 1/2 years. Each position has its supporters. Much of the problem of dating depends upon which feasts Jesus attended, and upon references to certain seasons of the year. The harmony which follows assumes a 3 1/2-year ministry.

While major areas of Jesus' ministry can be ascertained fairly easily, it is not always easy to know which events occurred within which major ministry. Sometimes it is also difficult to judge whether two very similar events actually occurred twice or whether there was only one such event which was recorded in a somewhat different context by a different writer. Examples of this problem are the cleansings of the temple and the laments over Jerusalem.

Despite these difficulties, however, the record of Jesus' life and work can be seen very well from a careful study of the four accounts. Any individual perspective which might be lost in attempting to combine the four separate accounts is far outweighed, at least for the purpose of this presentation of the Bible, by a new sense of context and an added appreciation of the significance of each separate event within that context.

In developing this particular harmony of the Gospels, the usual approach is to take the single account which most completely records a particular event and use it as a basis for the full text. To that account is added any significant additional aspects of the event which are recorded by any other writer. As often as possible, a particular account is followed as long as practicable in order to maintain a given literary style and continuity of authorship. This approach becomes increasingly difficult to maintain at the end of Jesus' ministry, since all four accounts recorded most of the final events, often from different perspectives.

The following scheme is used to alert the reader to the composition of the harmony. In the margin beside each paragraph is an indication of all accounts which record the events within that paragraph. Repetitive verses are indicated by light-face type. Where more than one account is used in the text, the text itself will indicate which account is being cited at the time.

In addition, there are also marginal indications of the geographic location of particular occurrences and the dates or times of given events as best as can be determined. Attempts to assign exact times, dates, and locations often depend solely upon a generally assumed framework which cannot be verified with complete accuracy. However, having some frame of reference seems desirable as an aid to better understanding the wonderful life and ministry of Jesus.

Introductions by the Gospel Writers

Mark's account begins simply,

The beginning of the gospel about Jesus Christ, the Son of God.[a]   Mk. 1:1

Mark introduces the reader to the good news about Jesus the Christ which is about to be told. That good news is beautifully summarized by John in a prologue to his account. It begins, as does the first book of Old Testament

[a]Some manuscripts do not have *the Son of God*.

Scripture, with the creation of man, and shows that the Word (a designation for God as Christ) was not only the source through which all things were made, but also came into this world in human form as the man, Jesus. It also shows that through Jesus, mankind has received the grace of God unto salvation, as attested to during Christ's ministry by John the Baptist, a special messenger of God.

Jn. 1:1-18   In the beginning was the Word, and the Word was with God, and the Word was God. He was with God in the beginning.

Through him all things were made; without him nothing was made that has been made. In him was life, and that life was the light of men. The light shines in the darkness, but the darkness has not understood[b] it.

There came a man who was sent from God; his name was John. He came as a witness to testify concerning that light, so that through him all men might believe. He himself was not the light; he came only as a witness to the light. The true light that gives light to every man was coming into the world.[c]

He was in the world, and though the world was made through him, the world did not recognize him. He came to that which was his own, but his own did not receive him. Yet to all who received him, to those who believed in his name, he gave the right to become children of God—children born not of natural descent,[d] nor of human decision or a husband's will, but born of God.

The Word became flesh and made his dwelling among us. We have seen his glory, the glory of the One and Only, [e] who came from the Father, full of grace and truth.

John testifies concerning him. He cries out, saying, "This was he of whom I said, 'He who comes after me has surpassed me because he was before me.'" From the fullness of his grace we have all received one blessing after another. For the law was given through Moses; grace and truth came through Jesus Christ. No one has ever seen God, but God the One and Only,[e][f] who is at the Father's side, has made him known.

In his own introduction, Luke writes to a man by the name of Theophilus in order to provide a more complete narrative of the life and work of this incarnate Word, Jesus the Christ, and of the things accomplished by Jesus' followers. Luke points out that, prior to his own account, other writers had already undertaken to record the events surrounding Jesus' coming and the work of his disciples during his ministry. Thus the records of Christ began to be compiled soon after his death and resurrection.

Lk. 1:1-4   Many have undertaken to draw up an account of the things that have been fulfilled[g] among us, just as they were handed down to us by those who from the first were eyewitnesses and servants of the word. Therefore, since I myself have carefully investigated everything from the beginning, it seemed good also to me to write an orderly account for you, most excellent Theophilus, so that you may know the certainty of the things you have been taught.

[b]Or darkness, and the darkness has not overcome   [c]Or This was the true light that gives light to every man who comes into the world   [d]Greek of bloods   [e]Or the Only Begotten   [f]Some manuscripts but the only (or only begotten) Son   [g]Or been surely believed

The Genealogies of Jesus

*M*atthew's account has no formal introduction, but rather begins with a genealogy tracing the descent of Jesus from his ancestor, Abraham, through the royal lineage of David the King. Matthew lists 42 of the known generations and divides these into three groups of 14 each. The genealogy is traced through Jesus' legal father, Joseph, as the husband of the virgin Mary, to whom Jesus was born.

Matthew's genealogy contains several happy surprises. Back in Jesus' early roots are not only such notable righteous men as Abraham and David, but also several who stand out in history as being particularly unrighteous, including wicked King Manasseh. Not only are there Jews, as would be expected, but also Gentiles, including a Canaanite and a Moabite, whose respective countrymen have been notorious enemies of God's people. Also somewhat surprising, in view of their social status at this time, is the listing of women as well as men. Furthermore, at least two of the women are known best for sins which they had committed.

A record of the genealogy of Jesus Christ the son of David, the son of Abraham: Mt. 1:1-17

Abraham was the father of Isaac,
  Isaac the father of Jacob,
  Jacob the father of Judah and his brothers,
  Judah the father of Perez and Zerah, whose mother was Tamar,
  Perez the father of Hezron,
  Hezron the father of Ram,
  Ram the father of Amminadab,
  Amminadab the father of Nahshon,
  Nahshon the father of Salmon,
  Salmon the father of Boaz, whose mother was Rahab,
  Boaz the father of Obed, whose mother was Ruth,
  Obed the father of Jesse,
  and Jesse the father of King David.

David was the father of Solomon, whose mother had been Uriah's wife,
  Solomon the father of Rehoboam,
  Rehoboam the father of Abijah,
  Abijah the father of Asa,
  Asa the father of Jehoshaphat,
  Jehoshaphat the father of Jehoram,
  Jehoram the father of Uzziah,
  Uzziah the father of Jotham,
  Jotham the father of Ahaz,
  Ahaz the father of Hezekiah,
  Hezekiah the father of Manasseh,
  Manasseh the father of Amon,
  Amon the father of Josiah,
  and Josiah the father of Jeconiah[h] and his brothers at the time of the
      exile to Babylon.

[h] That is, Jehoiachin

After the exile to Babylon:
> Jeconiah was the father of Shealtiel,
> Shealtiel the father of Zerubbabel,
> Zerubbabel the father of Abiud,
> Abiud the father of Eliakim,
> Eliakim the father of Azor,
> Azor the father of Zadok,
> Zadok the father of Akim,
> Akim the father of Eliud,
> Eliud the father of Eleazar,
> Eleazar the father of Matthan,
> Matthan the father of Jacob,
> and Jacob the father of Joseph, the husband of Mary, of whom was
> born Jesus, who is called Christ.

Thus there were fourteen generations in all from Abraham to David, fourteen from David to the exile to Babylon, and fourteen from the exile to the Christ. [i]

Luke also provides a genealogy of Jesus, but his account traces the lineage directly through Jesus' mother, Mary. This explains the difference in ancestors from Heli (assumed to be the father-in-law of Mary's husband, Joseph) to David. Luke's genealogy also goes beyond Abraham, all the way back through Noah, Enoch, Seth, and Adam to God himself, who created the human race.

Lk. 3:23b-38   He was the son, so it was thought, of Joseph,

> the son of Heli, the son of Matthat,
> the son of Levi, the son of Melki,
> the son of Jannai, the son of Joseph,
> the son of Mattathias, the son of Amos,
> the son of Nahum, the son of Esli,
> the son of Naggai, the son of Maath,
> the son of Mattathias, the son of Semein,
> the son of Josech, the son of Joda,
> the son of Joanan, the son of Rhesa,
> the son of Zerubbabel, the son of Shealtiel,
> the son of Neri, the son of Melki,
> the son of Addi, the son of Cosam,
> the son of Elmadam, the son of Er,
> the son of Joshua, the son of Eliezer,
> the son of Jorim, the son of Matthat,
> the son of Levi, the son of Simeon,
> the son of Judah, the son of Joseph,
> the son of Jonam, the son of Eliakim,
> the son of Melea, the son of Menna,
> the son of Mattatha, the son of Nathan,
> the son of David, the son of Jesse,
> the son of Obed, the son of Boaz,
> the son of Salmon, [j] the son of Nahshon,

[i] Or Messiah. "The Christ" (Greek) and "the Messiah" (Hebrew) both mean "the Anointed One."   [j] Some early manuscripts Sala

the son of Amminadab, the son of Ram,[k]
the son of Hezron, the son of Perez,
the son of Judah, the son of Jacob,
the son of Isaac, the son of Abraham,
the son of Terah, the son of Nahor,
the son of Serug, the son of Reu,
the son of Peleg, the son of Eber,
the son of Shelah, the son of Cainan,
the son of Arphaxad, the son of Shem,
the son of Noah, the son of Lamech,
the son of Methuselah, the son of Enoch,
the son of Jared, the son of Mahalalel,
the son of Kenan, the son of Enosh,
the son of Seth, the son of Adam,
the son of God.

Perhaps the most significant aspect of these genealogies is the connection between Jesus and his ancestor, King David. The prophets of old had repeatedly foretold that the Messiah would be of the house of David, and a branch of Jesse, David's father. Therefore, from the Jews' perspective, Jesus is of the royal lineage and worthy to be king of Israel. While this brings comfort to many, it brings confusion to others, who are expecting the Messiah to be the same kind of political king as those who reigned before him.

The Births of Jesus and John the Baptist

*J*esus is to be born in Judea approximately 747 years after the foundation of Rome. Now in the time of Herod the Great, who has been granted the title "King of the Jews" by the Roman senate under Emperor Caesar Augustus, the former land of Palestine is divided into the provinces of Judea, Samaria, and Galilee to the west of the Jordan River, and Perea and Decapolis to the east. The cities of Jerusalem and Bethlehem are both in Judea, while Nazareth is in Galilee. That Jesus is born in the province of Judea is surprising because his family's home is in Nazareth, some 75 miles north. But, due to a decree by Caesar Augustus requiring everyone to return to his own city, Jesus' birth takes place in Bethlehem—the very city named by the prophet Micah over 700 years earlier!

If that fulfillment is not enough to catch the attention of those familiar with earlier prophecies, an even more amazing fulfillment is involved—namely, Jesus' virgin birth. Isaiah had prophesied that the Messiah would be born of a virgin. Certainly there have been miraculous births before, as when couples were beyond the normal age of childbearing. Abraham and Sarah are the foremost example, and Zechariah and Elizabeth are soon to become another. However, never before nor since has a woman conceived without the seed of man. Not only is Mary a virgin in the sense of being a young woman, but, more importantly, she is a virgin in the fact that she has not had sexual relations with

[k]Some manuscripts *Amminadab, the son of Admin, the son of Arni*; other manuscripts vary widely.

either her fiancé, Joseph, or any other man. The Gospel accounts state unequiv-
ocally that Jesus is miraculously conceived in Mary by the Holy Spirit of God.

The divine nature of Jesus' birth is both wonderful and exciting, but the
human side of the story is touching in and of itself. Although she is told in
advance about the miraculous birth, Mary must surely feel the embarrassment
of being thought unchaste by her family and friends. She must surely feel the
weight of concern in the mind of Joseph. When the two of them find themselves
far from home at the time of delivery, they must both feel a terrible isolation
and awesome expectation about this special child from God. Yet Mary's confident faith and Joseph's loving support are both rewarded with more celebration than any other human family has ever known at the arrival of a new child.
From lowly shepherds on the earth to the highest halls of heaven, the majesty
of the occasion is heralded with songs of joy!

As the account of Jesus' birth begins, there is another birth announced as
well—that of God's special messenger, John, who, because of his ministry of
repentance and baptism, will later be known as John the Baptist. Luke and
Matthew tell the story of the two births and of the early events which follow in
the young life of Jesus.

Lk. 1:5-17
(Ca. 6-4
B.C.)
JOHN'S BIRTH FORETOLD.   In the time of Herod king of Judea there
was a priest named Zechariah, who belonged to the priestly division of
Abijah; his wife Elizabeth was also a descendant of Aaron. Both of them
were upright in the sight of God, observing all the Lord's commandments
and regulations blamelessly. But they had no children, because Elizabeth
was barren; and they were both well along in years.

Once when Zechariah's division was on duty and he was serving as
priest before God, he was chosen by lot, according to the custom of the
priesthood, to go into the temple of the Lord and burn incense. And when
the time for the burning of incense came, all the assembled worshipers
were praying outside.

Then an angel of the Lord appeared to him, standing at the right side of
the altar of incense. When Zechariah saw him, he was startled and was
gripped with fear. But the angel said to him: "Do not be afraid, Zechariah;
your prayer has been heard. Your wife Elizabeth will bear you a son, and
you are to give him the name John. He will be a joy and delight to you, and
many will rejoice because of his birth, for he will be great in the sight of
the Lord. He is never to take wine or other fermented drink, and he will
be filled with the Holy Spirit even from birth.[1] Many of the people of Israel
will he bring back to the Lord their God. And he will go on before the
Lord, in the spirit and power of Elijah, to turn the hearts of the fathers to
their children and the disobedient to the wisdom of the righteous—to
make ready a people prepared for the Lord."

Lk. 1:18-25   ZECHARIAH MADE SPEECHLESS.   Zechariah asked the angel, "How
can I be sure of this? I am an old man and my wife is well along in years."

The angel answered, "I am Gabriel. I stand in the presence of God, and
I have been sent to speak to you and to tell you this good news. And now
you will be silent and not able to speak until the day this happens, because

---

[1]Or *from his mother's womb*

you did not believe my words, which will come true at their proper time."

Meanwhile, the people were waiting for Zechariah and wondering why he stayed so long in the temple. When he came out, he could not speak to them. They realized he had seen a vision in the temple, for he kept making signs to them but remained unable to speak.

When his time of service was completed, he returned home. After this his wife Elizabeth became pregnant and for five months remained in seclusion. "The Lord has done this for me," she said. "In these days he has shown his favor and taken away my disgrace among the people."

MARY TOLD OF CONCEPTION. In the sixth month, God sent the angel Gabriel to Nazareth, a town in Galilee, to a virgin pledged to be married to a man named Joseph, a descendant of David. The virgin's name was Mary. The angel went to her and said, "Greetings, you who are highly favored! The Lord is with you."

Mary was greatly troubled at his words and wondered what kind of greeting this might be. But the angel said to her, "Do not be afraid, Mary, you have found favor with God. You will be with child and give birth to a son, and you are to give him the name Jesus. He will be great and will be called the Son of the Most High. The Lord God will give him the throne of his father David, and he will reign over the house of Jacob forever; his kingdom will never end."

"How will this be," Mary asked the angel, "since I am a virgin?"

The angel answered, "The Holy Spirit will come upon you, and the power of the Most High will overshadow you. So the holy one to be born will be called[m] the Son of God. Even Elizabeth your relative is going to have a child in her old age, and she who was said to be barren is in her sixth month. For nothing is impossible with God."

"I am the Lord's servant," Mary answered. "May it be to me as you have said." Then the angel left her.

Lk. 1:26-38
Nazareth

MARY VISITS ELIZABETH. At that time Mary got ready and hurried to a town in the hill country of Judea, where she entered Zechariah's home and greeted Elizabeth. When Elizabeth heard Mary's greeting, the baby leaped in her womb, and Elizabeth was filled with the Holy Spirit. In a loud voice she exclaimed: "Blessed are you among women, and blessed is the child you will bear! But why am I so favored, that the mother of my Lord should come to me? As soon as the sound of your greeting reached my ears, the baby in my womb leaped for joy. Blessed is she who has believed that what the Lord has said to her will be accomplished!"

Lk. 1:39-45
A city of
Judah

MARY PRAISES GOD. And Mary said:

Lk. 1:46-56

"My soul glorifies the Lord
and my spirit rejoices in God my Savior,
for he has been mindful
of the humble state of his servant.
From now on all generations will call me blessed,
for the Mighty One has done great things for me—
holy is his name.
His mercy extends to those who fear him,
from generation to generation.

[m] *Or So the child to be born will be called holy,*

> He has performed mighty deeds with his arm;
> > he has scattered those who are proud in their inmost
> > thoughts.
> He has brought down rulers from their thrones
> > but has lifted up the humble.
> He has filled the hungry with good things
> > but has sent the rich away empty.
> He has helped his servant Israel,
> > remembering to be merciful
> to Abraham and his descendants forever,
> > even as he said to our fathers."

Mary stayed with Elizabeth for about three months and then returned home.

Lk. 1:57-66   JOHN THE BAPTIST IS BORN.   When it was time for Elizabeth to have her baby, she gave birth to a son. Her neighbors and relatives heard that the Lord had shown her great mercy, and they shared her joy.

On the eighth day they came to circumcise the child, and they were going to name him after his father Zechariah, but his mother spoke up and said, "No! He is to be called John."

They said to her, "There is no one among your relatives who has that name."

Then they made signs to his father, to find out what he would like to name the child. He asked for a writing tablet, and to everyone's astonishment he wrote, "His name is John." Immediately his mouth was opened and his tongue was loosed, and he began to speak, praising God. The neighbors were all filled with awe, and throughout the hill country of Judea people were talking about all these things. Everyone who heard this wondered about it, asking, "What then is this child going to be?" For the Lord's hand was with him.

Lk. 1:67-80   ZECHARIAH PROPHESIES.   His father Zechariah was filled with the Holy Spirit and prophesied:

> "Praise be to the Lord, the God of Israel,
> > because he has come and has redeemed his people.
> He has raised up a horn[n] of salvation for us
> > in the house of his servant David
> (as he said through his holy prophets of long ago),
> > salvation from our enemies
> > and from the hand of all who hate us—
> to show mercy to our fathers
> > and to remember his holy covenant,
> > the oath he swore to our father Abraham:
> to rescue us from the hand of our enemies,
> > and to enable us to serve him without fear
> > in holiness and righteousness before him all our days.
>
> And you, my child, will be called a prophet of the Most
> > High;

---

[n]*Horn* here symbolizes strength.

for you will go on before the Lord to prepare the way for
    him,
to give his people the knowledge of salvation
    through the forgiveness of their sins,
because of the tender mercy of our God,
    by which the rising sun will come to us from heaven
to shine on those living in darkness
    and in the shadow of death,
    to guide our feet into the path of peace."

And the child grew and became strong in spirit; and he lived in the desert until he appeared publicly to Israel.

JOSEPH TOLD OF CONCEPTION. This is how the birth of Jesus Christ came about: His mother Mary was pledged to be married to Joseph, but before they came together, she was found to be with child through the Holy Spirit. Because Joseph her husband was a righteous man and did not want to expose her to public disgrace, he had in mind to divorce her quietly.

Mt.
1:18-25a

But after he had considered this, an angel of the Lord appeared to him in a dream and said, "Joseph son of David, do not be afraid to take Mary home as your wife, because what is conceived in her is from the Holy Spirit. She will give birth to a son, and you are to give him the name Jesus,[o] because he will save his people from their sins."

All this took place to fulfill what the Lord had said through the prophet: "The virgin will be with child and will give birth to a son, and they will call him Immanuel"[p]—which means, "God with us."

When Joseph woke up, he did what the angel of the Lord had commanded him and took Mary home as his wife. But he had no union with her until she gave birth to a son.

JESUS THE CHRIST IS BORN. In those days Caesar Augustus issued a decree that a census should be taken of the entire Roman world. (This was the first census that took place while Quirinius was governor of Syria.) And everyone went to his own town to register.

Lk. 2:1-7
Bethlehem
(Ca. 5-3
B.C.)

So Joseph also went up from the town of Nazareth in Galilee to Judea, to Bethlehem the town of David, because he belonged to the house and line of David. He went there to register with Mary, who was pledged to be married to him and was expecting a child. While they were there, the time came for the baby to be born, and she gave birth to her firstborn, a son. She wrapped him in cloths and placed him in a manger, because there was no room for them in the inn.

ANGELS PROCLAIM BIRTH. And there were shepherds living out in the fields nearby, keeping watch over their flocks at night. An angel of the Lord appeared to them, and the glory of the Lord shone around them, and they were terrified. But the angel said to them, "Do not be afraid. I bring you good news of great joy that will be for all the people. Today in the town of David a Savior has been born to you; he is Christ[q] the Lord. This will be a sign to you: You will find a baby wrapped in cloths and lying in a manger."

Lk. 2:8-14

---

[o]*Jesus* is the Greek form of *Joshua*, which means *the LORD saves.*   [p]Isaiah 7:14   [q]Or *Messiah.* "The Christ" (Greek) and "the Messiah" (Hebrew) both mean "the Anointed One."

Suddenly a great company of the heavenly host appeared with the angel, praising God and saying,

"Glory to God in the highest,
and on earth peace to men on whom his favor rests."

Lk. 2:15-20 SHEPHERDS VISIT BABY. When the angels had left them and gone into heaven, the shepherds said to one another, "Let's go to Bethlehem and see this thing that has happened, which the Lord has told us about."

So they hurried off and found Mary and Joseph, and the baby, who was lying in the manger. When they had seen him, they spread the word concerning what had been told them about this child, and all who heard it were amazed at what the shepherds said to them. But Mary treasured up all these things and pondered them in her heart. The shepherds returned, glorifying and praising God for all the things they had heard and seen, which were just as they had been told.

Mt. 1:25b
Lk. 2:21 JESUS CIRCUMCISED AND NAMED. On the eighth day, when it was time to circumcise him, he was named Jesus, the name the angel had given him before he had been conceived.

Lk. 2:22-24
Jerusalem JESUS PRESENTED IN TEMPLE. When the time of their purification according to the Law of Moses had been completed, Joseph and Mary took him to Jerusalem to present him to the Lord (as it is written in the Law of the Lord, "Every firstborn male is to be consecrated to the Lord"ʳ), and to offer a sacrifice in keeping with what is said in the Law of the Lord: "a pair of doves or two young pigeons."ˢ

Lk. 2:25-35 SIMEON EXPRESSES HIS JOY. Now there was a man in Jerusalem called Simeon, who was righteous and devout. He was waiting for the consolation of Israel, and the Holy Spirit was upon him. It had been revealed to him by the Holy Spirit that he would not die before he had seen the Lord's Christ. Moved by the Spirit, he went into the temple courts. When the parents brought in the child Jesus to do for him what the custom of the Law required, Simeon took him in his arms and praised God, saying:

"Sovereign Lord, as you have promised,
you now dismissᵗ your servant in peace.
For my eyes have seen your salvation,
which you have prepared in the sight of all people,
a light for revelation to the Gentiles
and for glory to your people Israel."

The child's father and mother marveled at what was said about him. Then Simeon blessed them and said to Mary, his mother: "This child is destined to cause the falling and rising of many in Israel, and to be a sign that will be spoken against, so that the thoughts of many hearts will be revealed. And a sword will pierce your own soul too."

Lk. 2:36-38 ANNA THE PROPHETESS. There was also a prophetess, Anna, the daughter of Phanuel, of the tribe of Asher. She was very old; she had lived with her husband seven years after her marriage, and then was a widow until she was eighty-four.ᵘ She never left the temple but worshiped night and day, fasting and praying. Coming up to them at that very moment, she

ʳExodus 13:2,12   ˢLev. 12:8   ᵗOr promised, / now dismiss   ᵘOr widow for eighty-four years gave thanks to God and spoke about the child to all who were looking forward to the redemption of Jerusalem.

Visit of the Magi and Flight into Egypt

*T*he rite of purification takes place 40 days after Jesus' birth and ordinarily would have required the offering of a yearling lamb and a pigeon. However, the law permits poor parents, such as Joseph and Mary are, to offer a second pigeon or dove instead of the lamb, which they cannot afford. Thus, even by his parents' offering of purification, it can be seen that Jesus comes humbly into the world.

Despite these lowly beginnings, news of Jesus' birth spreads quickly throughout Judea and even beyond its borders. Matthew records the account of a visit to Bethlehem by certain philosopher-priests who, interestingly enough, may even be pagan Zoroastrians from Persia. Their presumed contact with Jews of the Dispersion has undoubtedly made them familiar with the Jewish Messiah of prophecy. The Magi are prompted to travel the great distance to Jerusalem because of a star which appeared at the time of Jesus' birth. It is not known how many make the long journey (certainly no compelling evidence exists for the traditional three), but they apparently arrive some six months after Jesus' birth and inquire as to the child's whereabouts. By this time Joseph and Mary have found accommodations in a house, and it is in this house that the Magi's gifts are offered to the newborn "King of the Jews."

King Herod is alarmed by the Magi's visit because he believes Jesus' birth poses a political threat to his reign. Because of this, Herod sends his soldiers to Bethlehem to kill all male children who might have been born within the timeframe suggested by the Magi's calculations. By Jewish reckoning, any child over 12 months is considered two years old. Since apparently six months have passed following Jesus' birth, Herod makes his order broad enough to prevent any mistake by including all of the estimated 40 to 50 baby boys in Bethlehem who would be up to 12 or 13 months old at this time.

As will be seen, however, Joseph will be warned about the slaughter and will quickly depart for Egypt, where he and Mary and the child Jesus will stay until after Herod's own death.

WISE MEN SEEK JESUS.   After Jesus was born in Bethlehem in Judea, during the time of King Herod, Magi[v] from the east came to Jerusalem and asked, "Where is the one who has been born king of the Jews? We saw his star in the east[w] and have come to worship him."

When King Herod heard this he was disturbed, and all Jerusalem with him. When he had called together all the people's chief priests and teachers of the law, he asked them where the Christ[x] was to be born. "In Bethlehem in Judea," they replied, "for this is what the prophet has written:

" 'But you, Bethlehem, in the land of Judah,
    are by no means least among the rulers of Judah;
    for out of you will come a ruler

Mt. 2:1-8
Jerusalem
(Ca. 4-2
B.C.)

---

[v]Traditionally *Wise Men*   [w]Or *star when it rose*   [x]Or *Messiah*

who will be the shepherd of my people Israel.'*y*"

Then Herod called the Magi secretly and found out from them the exact time the star had appeared. He sent them to Bethlehem and said, "Go and make a careful search for the child. As soon as you find him, report to me, so that I too may go and worship him."

Mt. 2:9-12
Bethlehem
WISE MEN VISIT JESUS.   After they had heard the king, they went on their way, and the star they had seen in the east*z* went ahead of them until it stopped over the place where the child was. When they saw the star, they were overjoyed. On coming to the house, they saw the child with his mother Mary, and they bowed down and worshiped him. Then they opened their treasures and presented him with gifts of gold and of incense and of myrrh. And having been warned in a dream not to go back to Herod, they returned to their country by another route.

Mt. 2:13-15
Egypt
FLIGHT TO EGYPT.   When they had gone, an angel of the Lord appeared to Joseph in a dream. "Get up," he said, "take the child and his mother and escape to Egypt. Stay there until I tell you, for Herod is going to search for the child to kill him."

So he got up, took the child and his mother during the night and left for Egypt, where he stayed until the death of Herod. And so was fulfilled what the Lord had said through the prophet: "Out of Egypt I called my son."*a*

Mt. 2:16-18
HEROD ORDERS SLAUGHTER.   When Herod realized that he had been outwitted by the Magi, he was furious, and he gave orders to kill all the boys in Bethlehem and its vicinity who were two years old and under, in accordance with the time he had learned from the Magi. Then what was said through the prophet Jeremiah was fulfilled:

> "A voice is heard in Ramah,
>   weeping and great mourning,
> Rachel weeping for her children
>   and refusing to be comforted,
> because they are no more."*b*

From Infancy to Manhood

*A*fter their brief stay in Egypt, Joseph and Mary return to their home in Nazareth of Galilee, where Joseph resumes his trade as a carpenter. Over the next ten years Jesus continues to grow physically, mentally, and spiritually. There is no further record of Jesus until, at the age of 12, he is taken to Jerusalem for the Passover celebration. At age 12, Jesus has reached the point at which a Jewish boy is soon to become a "son of the law," which law he is expected to learn and obey. But Jesus' understanding of the law is far greater than that of other boys his age. After the Passover celebration is completed, Jesus' parents lose track of his whereabouts until they discover him in profound conversation with the learned rabbis. When his parents express their concern

*y*Micah 5:2   *z*Or *seen when it rose*   *a*Hosea 11:1   *b*Jer. 31:15

about his leaving them, Jesus gives a response which indicates that, even now, he is aware of his divine sonship and role as the Messiah.

RETURN TO NAZARETH.   ^MtAfter Herod died, an angel of the Lord appeared in a dream to Joseph in Egypt and said, "Get up, take the child and his mother and go to the land of Israel, for those who were trying to take the child's life are dead."

Mt. 2:19-23
Lk. 2:39,40
Nazareth

So he got up, took the child and his mother and went to the land of Israel. But when he heard that Archelaus was reigning in Judea in place of his father Herod, he was afraid to go there. Having been warned in a dream, he withdrew to the district of Galilee, and he went and lived in a town called Nazareth. So was fulfilled what was said through the prophets: "He will be called a Nazarene." ^LkAnd the child grew and became strong; he was filled with wisdom, and the grace of God was upon him.

JESUS VISITS JERUSALEM.   Every year his parents went to Jerusalem for the Feast of the Passover. When he was twelve years old, they went up to the Feast, according to the custom. After the Feast was over, while his parents were returning home, the boy Jesus stayed behind in Jerusalem, but they were unaware of it. Thinking he was in their company, they traveled on for a day. Then they began looking for him among their relatives and friends. When they did not find him, they went back to Jerusalem to look for him. After three days they found him in the temple courts, sitting among the teachers, listening to them and asking them questions. Everyone who heard him was amazed at his understanding and his answers. When his parents saw him, they were astonished. His mother said to him, "Son, why have you treated us like this? Your father and I have been anxiously searching for you."

Lk. 2:41-50
Jerusalem

"Why were you searching for me?" he asked. "Didn't you know I had to be in my Father's house?" But they did not understand what he was saying to them.

GROWING UP IN NAZARETH.   Then he went down to Nazareth with them and was obedient to them. But his mother treasured all these things in her heart. And Jesus grew in wisdom and stature, and in favor with God and men.

Lk. 2:51,52
Nazareth

Little more is known of Jesus' first 30 years. It is known that Jesus has at least four brothers—James, Joses, Judas (Jude), and Simon—and also some sisters, who are not named. Because there is no further reference to Joseph, it appears that he probably died while Jesus was still a relatively young man. The support of his mother and younger brothers and sisters, therefore, would naturally fall upon Jesus as the firstborn. For many years, then, Jesus evidently has provided for his family by working as a carpenter, having learned the trade from his father.

Now at about the age of 30—the Jewish age of spiritual leadership—Jesus turns from the work of supporting his earthly family to the task of spiritually feeding the whole family of man.

◇

The Ministry of John the Baptist

hen it comes time for Jesus to carry out his divine commission, the ground has already been broken by the successful ministry of John the Baptist, who proclaims Jesus to be "the Lamb of God." John thereby sets the stage for Jesus' own claim that he is the Messiah. As seen so many times before, the Jews have been awaiting the coming of the prophesied Messiah, believing that he will deliver them from political bondage and be an ideal national leader. What they have not expected is a leader arising from among the common people—yet divine in nature—and establishing a spiritual rather than a political kingdom. Perhaps because of this very misconception, John the Baptist is called to prepare the way for Jesus and to testify on his behalf. It is with this announcement of Jesus' special ministry that the gospel message begins its central focus, as seen by the fact that only at this point do Mark and John begin their Gospel accounts.

Jesus' forerunner, John, is a prophet of priestly descent, as were several of the prophets of old. Like Elijah, John is not a writer, but an evangelist and a spokesman for God whose outspoken preaching of repentance and baptism brings him multitudes of disciples. Some of these disciples will be so devoted to John and his teaching that they will not accept even the deity of Jesus, which John is sent to proclaim. As with most of his fellow prophets, John's teaching of spiritual purity is accompanied by strong appeals for practical ethical conduct toward one's fellowman.

Living much of his time in desert areas and existing on a diet of locusts and honey, John strikes an image of being some kind of ascetic wild man. However, his lifestyle is probably dictated more out of necessity than eccentricity, and is by no means offensive to the throngs who come from the cities to hear him. The more intriguing question is why sophisticated city people would go out of their way to be taught by a rough man of the wilderness whose preaching is unusually harsh and demanding. Could it be, ironically, that John's appeal lies in the very strictness of his message, which is in sharp contrast to the soft religiosity peddled by religious leaders seeking popular support? Could it be that John's call for personal purity and individual righteousness is seen as a refreshing change from the ritualistic and institutional religion which has developed over the centuries? Whatever his appeal, John's ministry is given the highest possible honor when even Jesus himself comes to receive John's baptism. Although it is not for sins that Jesus is baptized, his exemplary act of ceremonial washing gives occasion for a dramatic confirmation of his deity.

Mt. 3:1-3
Mk. 1:2-4
Lk. 3:1-6
Wilderness,
Jordan
region
A.D. 27)

JOHN DECLARES HIS MISSION.   In the fifteenth year of the reign of Tiberius Caesar—when Pontius Pilate was governor of Judea, Herod tetrarch of Galilee, his brother Philip tetrarch of Iturea and Traconitis, and Lysanias tetrarch of Abilene—during the high priesthood of Annas and Caiaphas, the word of God came to John son of Zechariah in the desert. He went into all the country around the Jordan, preaching a baptism of repentance for the forgiveness of sins. As is written in the book of the words of Isaiah the prophet:

"A voice of one calling in the desert,
'Prepare the way for the Lord,
    make straight paths for him.
Every valley shall be filled in,
    every mountain and hill made low.
The crooked roads shall become straight,
    the rough ways smooth.
And all mankind will see God's salvation.' "*c*

JOHN BAPTIZES THE PEOPLE.   John's clothes were made of camel's hair, and he had a leather belt around his waist. His food was locusts and wild honey. People went out to him from Jerusalem and all Judea and the whole region of the Jordan. Confessing their sins, they were baptized by him in the Jordan River.

Mt. 3:4-6
Mk. 1:5,6

JOHN PREACHES REPENTANCE.   John said to the crowds coming out to be baptized by him, "You brood of vipers! Who warned you to flee from the coming wrath? Produce fruit in keeping with repentance. And do not begin to say to yourselves, 'We have Abraham as our father.' For I tell you that out of these stones God can raise up children for Abraham. The ax is already at the root of the trees, and every tree that does not produce good fruit will be cut down and thrown into the fire."

Mt. 3:7-10
Lk. 3:7-14

"What should we do then?" the crowd asked.

John answered, "The man with two tunics should share with him who has none, and the one who has food should do the same."

Tax collectors also came to be baptized. "Teacher," they asked, "what should we do?"

"Don't collect any more than you are required to," he told them.

Then some soldiers asked him, "And what should we do?"

He replied, "Don't extort money and don't accuse people falsely—be content with your pay."

JOHN ANNOUNCES CHRIST.   The people were waiting expectantly and were all wondering in their hearts if John might possibly be the Christ.*d* John answered them all, "I baptize you with*e* water. But one more powerful than I will come, the thongs of whose sandals I am not worthy to untie. He will baptize you with the Holy Spirit and with fire. His winnowing fork is in his hand to clear his threshing floor and to gather the wheat into his barn, but he will burn up the chaff with unquenchable fire." And with many other words John exhorted the people and preached the good news to them.

Mt. 3:11,12
Mk. 1:7,8
Lk. 3:15-18

JESUS IS BAPTIZED.   *Mt*Then Jesus came from Galilee to the Jordan to be baptized by John. But John tried to deter him, saying, "I need to be baptized by you, and do you come to me?"

Jesus replied, "Let it be so now; it is proper for us to do this to fulfill all righteousness." Then John consented.

As soon as Jesus was baptized, he went up out of the water. At that moment heaven was opened, and he saw the Spirit of God descending like a dove and lighting on him. And a voice from heaven said, "This is my Son, whom I love; with him I am well pleased." *Lk*Now Jesus himself was about thirty years old when he began his ministry.

Mt. 3:13-17
Mk. 1:9-11
Lk. 3:21-23a
From Galilee to Jordan

c Isaiah 40:3-5   *d* Or *Messiah*   *e* Or *in*

Jesus Faces Temptations

One of the big, as-yet-unanswered questions about Jesus' identity is whether he, as God in the flesh, is vulnerable to the same temptations which all other people face. Although not every temptation which Jesus may encounter will be found in the Gospel accounts, the writers do record a series of temptations which are representative of most of the temptations faced by man. In various encounters with Satan, Jesus must deal with the need to satisfy fleshly appetites, the urge to acquire that which pleases the eye, and the desire to give vent to pride.

This is no academic exercise. As he does with everyone else, Satan confronts Jesus when he is most vulnerable. Jesus has just had a mountaintop spiritual experience: he has been honored by the voice from heaven. How tempting it would be to flaunt his deity in some dramatic way! He is just beginning his mission to a world looking desperately for a leader. How tempting it would be to acquire the whole world's allegiance in one fell swoop! And at the time of the first temptation, Jesus is physically weakened from a 40-day fast. How tempting it would be to produce that which would satisfy normal human hunger!

In every case Jesus' response to temptation is the same. Alone in the desert of temptation, Jesus—divine though he is—recognizes the value of prayer and fasting, and with every temptation he recalls the words of Scripture, which are a reminder of truth and wisdom in the face of Satan's lies.

Mt. 4:1-11
Mk.
1:12-13
Lk. 4:1-13
Mountain
in wilder-
ness

DEVIL TEMPTS JESUS.   Then Jesus was led by the Spirit into the desert to be tempted by the devil. After fasting forty days and forty nights, he was hungry. The tempter came to him and said, "If you are the Son of God, tell these stones to become bread."

Jesus answered, "It is written: 'Man does not live on bread alone, but on every word that comes from the mouth of God.'*f*"

Then the devil took him to the holy city and had him stand on the highest point of the temple. "If you are the Son of God," he said, "throw yourself down. For it is written:

" 'He will command his angels concerning you,
        and they will lift you up in their hands,
    so that you will not strike your foot against a stone.'*g*"

Jesus answered him, "It is also written: 'Do not put the Lord your God to the test.'*h*"

Again, the devil took him to a very high mountain and showed him all the kingdoms of the world and their splendor. "All this I will give you," he said, "if you will bow down and worship me."

Jesus said to him, "Away from me, Satan! For it is written: 'Worship the Lord your God, and serve him only.'*i*"

Then the devil left him, and angels came and attended him.

Throughout his life Jesus will continue to resist all temptation and remain sinless. It is his perfect righteousness—beyond the righteousness of even such

*f*Deut. 8:3   *g*Psalm 91:11,12   *h*Deut. 6:16   *i*Deut. 6:13

great prophets as Elijah and now John the Baptist—that shows Jesus to be the Messiah. By virtue of the heavenly annunciation which he witnesses, John is convinced that Jesus is not only incomparably righteous, but also truly God's Anointed One, the Christ. John therefore repudiates any possibility of himself being viewed as the Messiah, and forcefully proclaims Jesus as the messianic Lamb of God.

JOHN EXPLAINS HIS MINISTRY.   Now this was John's testimony when the Jews of Jerusalem sent priests and Levites to ask him who he was. He did not fail to confess, but confessed freely, "I am not the Christ.j"   Jn. 1:19-28
Bethany

They asked him, "Then who are you? Are you Elijah?"

He said, "I am not."

"Are you the Prophet?"

He answered, "No."

Finally they said, "Who are you? Give us an answer to take back to those who sent us. What do you say about yourself?"

John replied in the words of Isaiah the prophet, "I am the voice of one calling in the desert, 'Make straight the way for the Lord.' "k

Now some Pharisees who had been sent questioned him, "Why then do you baptize if you are not the Christ, nor Elijah, nor the Prophet?"

"I baptize withl water," John replied, "but among you stands one you do not know. He is the one who comes after me, the thongs of whose sandals I am not worthy to untie."

This all happened at Bethany on the other side of the Jordan, where John was baptizing.

JOHN SAYS JESUS IS CHRIST.   The next day John saw Jesus coming toward him and said, "Look, the Lamb of God, who takes away the sin of the world! This is the one I meant when I said, 'A man who comes after me has surpassed me because he was before me.' I myself did not know him, but the reason I came baptizing with water was that he might be revealed to Israel."   Jn. 1:29-34

Then John gave this testimony: "I saw the Spirit come down from heaven as a dove and remain on him. I would not have known him, except that the one who sent me to baptize with water told me, 'The man on whom you see the Spirit come down and remain is he who will baptize with the Holy Spirit.' I have seen and I testify that this is the Son of God."

Jesus' Early Work in Judea, Samaria, and Galilee

The early ministry of Jesus is reported solely by the apostle John. His account shows that Jesus' teaching quickly appeals to the common people and results in many faithful disciples. It is during this time that Jesus also performs his first miracles. And just as Nehemiah had done centuries before, Jesus wastes no time in confronting those who profane the sanctity of the temple worship. Jesus also makes it clear from the beginning that his

jOr Messiah. "The Christ" (Greek) and "the Messiah" (Hebrew) both mean "the Anointed One."   kIsaiah 40:3   lOr in

message of salvation will extend beyond the Jewish nation to all people. As if to emphasize the universality of his spiritual kingdom, Jesus takes his ministry to the Samaritans. This people of mixed nationality and religion have been archenemies of the Jews ever since their ancestors were brought in from Assyria to repopulate northern Israel after the first Jews were taken into Assyrian captivity. So Jesus' outreach to Gentiles could not begin more pointedly.

The ministry of John the Baptist will come to an end when he is imprisoned by Herod Antipas, the second son of Herod the Great, who became tetrarch over the provinces of Galilee and Perea upon his father's death. The reason for John's imprisonment will subsequently appear, but for now the Gospel accounts resume with John the Baptist pointing his own disciples to the true Lamb of God.

Jn. 1:35-42 ANDREW AND SIMON PETER. The next day John was there again with two of his disciples. When he saw Jesus passing by, he said, "Look, the Lamb of God!"

When the two disciples heard him say this, they followed Jesus. Turning around, Jesus saw them following and asked, "What do you want?"

They said, "Rabbi" (which means Teacher), "where are you staying?"

"Come," he replied, "and you will see."

So they went and saw where he was staying, and spent that day with him. It was about the tenth hour.

Andrew, Simon Peter's brother, was one of the two who heard what John had said and who had followed Jesus. The first thing Andrew did was to find his brother Simon and tell him, "We have found the Messiah" (that is, the Christ). And he brought him to Jesus.

Jesus looked at him and said, "You are Simon son of John. You will be called Cephas" (which, when translated, is Peter[m]).

Jn. 1:43-51 PHILIP AND NATHANAEL. The next day Jesus decided to leave for Galilee. Finding Philip, he said to him, "Follow me."

Philip, like Andrew and Peter, was from the town of Bethsaida. Philip found Nathanael and told him, "We have found the one Moses wrote about in the Law, and about whom the prophets also wrote—Jesus of Nazareth, the son of Joseph."

"Nazareth! Can anything good come from there?" Nathanael asked.

"Come and see," said Philip.

When Jesus saw Nathanael approaching, he said of him, "Here is a true Israelite, in whom there is nothing false."

"How do you know me?" Nathanael asked.

Jesus answered, "I saw you while you were still under the fig tree before Philip called you."

Then Nathanael declared, "Rabbi, you are the Son of God; you are the King of Israel."

Jesus said, "You believe[n] because I told you I saw you under the fig tree. You shall see greater things than that." He then added, "I tell you[o] the truth, you[o] shall see heaven open, and the angels of God ascending and descending on the Son of Man."

[m]Both *Cephas* (Aramaic) and *Peter* (Greek) mean *rock*.   [n]Or *Do you believe . . . ?*
[o]The Greek is plural.

JESUS TURNS WATER INTO WINE.   On the third day a wedding took place at Cana in Galilee. Jesus' mother was there, and Jesus and his disciples had also been invited to the wedding. When the wine was gone, Jesus' mother said to him, "They have no more wine."

Jn. 2:1-12
Cana

"Dear woman, why do you involve me?" Jesus replied. "My time has not yet come."

His mother said to the servants, "Do whatever he tells you."

Nearby stood six stone water jars, the kind used by the Jews for ceremonial washing, each holding from twenty to thirty gallons.[P]

Jesus said to the servants, "Fill the jars with water"; so they filled them to the brim.

Then he told them, "Now draw some out and take it to the master of the banquet."

They did so, and the master of the banquet tasted the water that had been turned into wine. He did not realize where it had come from, though the servants who had drawn the water knew. Then he called the bridegroom aside and said, "Everyone brings out the choice wine first and then the cheaper wine after the guests have had too much to drink; but you have saved the best till now."

This, the first of his miraculous signs, Jesus performed at Cana in Galilee. He thus revealed his glory, and his disciples put their faith in him.

After this he went down to Capernaum with his mother and brothers and his disciples. There they stayed for a few days.

MERCHANTS DRIVEN FROM TEMPLE.   When it was almost time for the Jewish Passover, Jesus went up to Jerusalem. In the temple courts he found men selling cattle, sheep and doves, and others sitting at tables exchanging money. So he made a whip out of cords, and drove all from the temple area, both sheep and cattle; he scattered the coins of the money changers and overturned their tables. To those who sold doves he said, "Get these out of here! How dare you turn my Father's house into a market!"

[First
Passover
April,
A.D. 27]
Jn. 2:13-25
Jerusalem

His disciples remembered that it is written: "Zeal for your house will consume me."[q]

Then the Jews demanded of him, "What miraculous sign can you show us to prove your authority to do all this?"

Jesus answered them, "Destroy this temple, and I will raise it again in three days."

The Jews replied, "It has taken forty-six years to build this temple, and you are going to raise it in three days?" But the temple he had spoken of was his body. After he was raised from the dead, his disciples recalled what he had said. Then they believed the Scripture and the words that Jesus had spoken.

Now while he was in Jerusalem at the Passover Feast, many people saw the miraculous signs he was doing and believed in his name.[r] But Jesus would not entrust himself to them, for he knew all men. He did not need man's testimony about man, for he knew what was in a man.

JESUS TEACHES NICODEMUS.   Now there was a man of the Pharisees named Nicodemus, a member of the Jewish ruling council. He came to

Jn. 3:1-21

[P]Greek *two to three metretes* (probably about 75 to 115 liters)   [q]Psalm 69:9   [r]Or *and believed in him*

Jesus at night and said, "Rabbi, we know you are a teacher who has come from God. For no one could perform the miraculous signs you are doing if God were not with him."

In reply Jesus declared, "I tell you the truth, no one can see the kingdom of God unless he is born again.[s]"

"How can a man be born when he is old?" Nicodemus asked. "Surely he cannot enter a second time into his mother's womb to be born!"

Jesus answered, "I tell you the truth, no one can enter the kingdom of God unless he is born of water and the Spirit. Flesh gives birth to flesh, but the Spirit[t] gives birth to spirit. You should not be surprised at my saying, 'You[u] must be born again.' The wind blows wherever it pleases. You hear its sound, but you cannot tell where it comes from or where it is going. So it is with everyone born of the Spirit."

"How can this be?" Nicodemus asked.

"You are Israel's teacher," said Jesus, "and do you not understand these things? I tell you the truth, we speak of what we know, and we testify to what we have seen, but still you people do not accept our testimony. I have spoken to you of earthly things and you do not believe; how then will you believe if I speak of heavenly things? No one has ever gone into heaven except the one who came from heaven—the Son of Man.[v] Just as Moses lifted up the snake in the desert, so the Son of Man must be lifted up, that everyone who believes in him may have eternal life.[w]

"For God so loved the world that he gave his one and only Son,[x] that whoever believes in him shall not perish but have eternal life. For God did not send his Son into the world to condemn the world, but to save the world through him. Whoever believes in him is not condemned, but whoever does not believe stands condemned already because he has not believed in the name of God's one and only Son.[y] This is the verdict: Light has come into the world, but men loved darkness instead of light because their deeds were evil. Everyone who does evil hates the light, and will not come into the light for fear that his deeds will be exposed. But whoever lives by the truth comes into the light, so that it may be seen plainly that what he has done has been done through God."[z]

Jn. 3:22-24
Judea

JESUS AND JOHN BAPTIZE.   After this, Jesus and his disciples went out into the Judean countryside, where he spent some time with them, and baptized. Now John also was baptizing at Aenon near Salim, because there was plenty of water, and people were constantly coming to be baptized. (This was before John was put in prison.)

Jn. 3:25-36

JOHN TESTIFIES ABOUT JESUS.   An argument developed between some of John's disciples and a certain Jew[a] over the matter of ceremonial washing. They came to John and said to him, "Rabbi, that man who was with you on the other side of the Jordan—the one you testified about—well, he is baptizing, and everyone is going to him."

To this John replied, "A man can receive only what is given him from heaven. You yourselves can testify that I said, 'I am not the Christ[b] but am sent ahead of him.' The bride belongs to the bridegroom. The friend who attends the bridegroom waits and listens for him, and is full of joy when

---

[s]Or *born from above*   [t]Or *but spirit*   [u]The Greek is plural.   [v]Some manuscripts *Man, who is in heaven*   [w]Or *believes may have eternal life in him*   [x]Or *his only begotten Son*   [y]Or *God's only begotten Son*   [z]Some interpreters end the quotation after verse 15.   [a]Some manuscripts *and certain Jews*   [b]Or *Messiah*

he hears the bridegroom's voice. That joy is mine, and it is now complete. He must become greater; I must become less.

"The one who comes from above is above all; the one who is from the earth belongs to the earth, and speaks as one from the earth. The one who comes from heaven is above all. He testifies to what he has seen and heard, but no one accepts his testimony. The man who has accepted it has certified that God is truthful. For the one whom God has sent speaks the words of God, for God[c] gives the Spirit without limit. The Father loves the Son and has placed everything in his hands. Whoever believes in the Son has eternal life, but whoever rejects the Son will not see life, for God's wrath remains on him."[d]

JESUS LEAVES FOR GALILEE. The Pharisees heard that Jesus was gaining and baptizing more disciples than John, although in fact it was not Jesus who baptized, but his disciples. When the Lord learned of this, he left Judea and went back once more to Galilee.

Jn. 4:1-3
Judea

WOMAN AT THE WELL. Now he had to go through Samaria. So he came to a town in Samaria called Sychar, near the plot of ground Jacob had given to his son Joseph. Jacob's well was there, and Jesus, tired as he was from the journey, sat down by the well. It was about the sixth hour.

Jn. 4:4-26
Sychar

When a Samaritan woman came to draw water, Jesus said to her, "Will you give me a drink?" (His disciples had gone into the town to buy food.)

The Samaritan woman said to him, "You are a Jew and I am a Samaritan woman. How can you ask me for a drink?" (For Jews do not associate with Samaritans.[e])

Jesus answered her, "If you knew the gift of God and who it is that asks you for a drink, you would have asked him and he would have given you living water."

"Sir," the woman said, "you have nothing to draw with and the well is deep. Where can you get this living water? Are you greater than our father Jacob, who gave us the well and drank from it himself, as did also his sons and his flocks and herds?"

Jesus answered, "Everyone who drinks this water will be thirsty again, but whoever drinks the water I give him will never thirst. Indeed, the water I give him will become in him a spring of water welling up to eternal life."

The woman said to him, "Sir, give me this water so that I won't get thirsty and have to keep coming here to draw water."

He told her, "Go, call your husband and come back."

"I have no husband," she replied.

Jesus said to her, "You are right when you say you have no husband. The fact is, you have had five husbands, and the man you now have is not your husband. What you have just said is quite true."

"Sir," the woman said, "I can see that you are a prophet. Our fathers worshiped on this mountain, but you Jews claim that the place where we must worship is in Jerusalem."

Jesus declared, "Believe me, woman, a time is coming when you will worship the Father neither on this mountain nor in Jerusalem. You Samaritans worship what you do not know; we worship what we do

[c]Greek *he*   [d]Some interpreters end the quotation after verse 30.   [e]Or *do not use dishes Samaritans have used*

know, for salvation is from the Jews. Yet a time is coming and has now come when the true worshipers will worship the Father in spirit and truth, for they are the kind of worshipers the Father seeks. God is spirit, and his worshipers must worship in spirit and in truth."

The woman said, "I know that Messiah" (called Christ) "is coming. When he comes, he will explain everything to us."

Then Jesus declared, "I who speak to you am he."

Jn. 4:27-38
(Dec.,
A.D. 27)

SPIRITUAL FOOD.   Just then his disciples returned and were surprised to find him talking with a woman. But no one asked, "What do you want?" or "Why are you talking with her?"

Then, leaving her water jar, the woman went back to the town and said to the people, "Come, see a man who told me everything I ever did. Could this be the Christ *f*?" They came out of the town and made their way toward him.

Meanwhile his disciples urged him, "Rabbi, eat something."

But he said to them, "I have food to eat that you know nothing about."

Then his disciples said to each other, "Could someone have brought him food?"

"My food," said Jesus, "is to do the will of him who sent me and to finish his work. Do you not say, 'Four months more and then the harvest'? I tell you, open your eyes and look at the fields! They are ripe for harvest. Even now the reaper draws his wages, even now he harvests the crop for eternal life, so that the sower and the reaper may be glad together. Thus the saying 'One sows and another reaps' is true. I sent you to reap what you have not worked for. Others have done the hard work, and you have reaped the benefits of their labor."

Jn. 4:39-42

MANY SAMARITANS CONVERTED.   Many of the Samaritans from that town believed in him because of the woman's testimony, "He told me everything I ever did." So when the Samaritans came to him, they urged him to stay with them, and he stayed two days. And because of his words many more became believers.

They said to the woman, "We no longer believe just because of what you said; now we have heard for ourselves, and we know that this man really is the Savior of the world."

Jn. 4:43-45
Galilee

JESUS RETURNS TO GALILEE.   After the two days he left for Galilee. (Now Jesus himself had pointed out that a prophet has no honor in his own country.) When he arrived in Galilee, the Galileans welcomed him. They had seen all that he had done in Jerusalem at the Passover Feast, for they also had been there.

Jn. 4:46-54
Cana

BOY IN CAPERNAUM HEALED.   Once more he visited Cana in Galilee, where he had turned the water into wine. And there was a certain royal official whose son lay sick at Capernaum. When this man heard that Jesus had arrived in Galilee from Judea, he went to him and begged him to come and heal his son, who was close to death.

"Unless you people see miraculous signs and wonders," Jesus told him, "you will never believe."

The royal official said, "Sir, come down before my child dies."

Jesus replied, "You may go. Your son will live."

The man took Jesus at his word and departed. While he was still on the

f Or *Messiah*

way, his servants met him with the news that his boy was living. When he inquired as to the time when his son got better, they said to him, "The fever left him yesterday at the seventh hour."

Then the father realized that this was the exact time at which Jesus had said to him, "Your son will live." So he and all his household believed.

This was the second miraculous sign that Jesus performed, having come from Judea to Galilee.

JOHN THE BAPTIST IMPRISONED. But when John rebuked Herod the tetrarch because of Herodias, his brother's wife, and all the other evil things he had done, Herod added this to them all: He locked John up in prison.

Lk. 3:19,20

Beginning of the Great Galilean Ministry

*A*pparently in order to emphasize the nature of his ministry, Jesus does not come as a religious leader in any traditional sense. He holds no official position, nor is he specially trained to be a priest or other cleric. Instead, he takes his ministry to the city streets and roads of Palestine, to homes and fields, and wherever else the common people might be found. He is particularly fond of attending the Jewish synagogues, where the common man is permitted to discuss the meaning of Jewish Scripture.

Rejected by those closest to him in Nazareth, Jesus takes his ministry elsewhere. Surprisingly, though, it is not to Jerusalem and surrounding Judea that Jesus goes, despite the fact that Jerusalem is the Holy City—capital of ancient Israel, site of the temple, and surely, as the Jews anticipate it, the seat of the coming Messiah's government. Contrary to their expectation, Jesus takes his ministry primarily to Galilee. Using the city of Capernaum as a base for his travels, Jesus teaches and performs miracles around the Sea of Galilee (Lake of Gennesaret) and throughout the entire province. It is here that Jesus gains popularity among the people and begins to see the crowds swell. Matthew begins his account of the Galilean ministry by observing that this phase of Jesus' ministry is a fulfillment of Isaiah's prophecy.

COMING OF KINGDOM PREACHED. ᴹᵗWhen Jesus heard that John had been put in prison, he returned to Galilee. Leaving Nazareth, he went and lived in Capernaum, which was by the lake in the area of Zebulun and Naphtali—to fulfill what was said through the prophet Isaiah:

Mt. 4:12-17
Mk.
1:14,15
Lk. 4:14,15
Capernaum

> "Land of Zebulun and land of Naphtali,
>   the way to the sea, along the Jordan,
>   Galilee of the Gentiles—
> the people living in darkness
>   have seen a great light;
> on those living in the land of the shadow of death
>   a light has dawned."[8]

From that time on Jesus began to preach, "Repent, for the kingdom of heaven is near." ᴸᵏ[And] news about him spread through the whole countryside. He taught in their synagogues, and everyone praised him.

[8]Isaiah 9:1,2

Lk. 4:16-30
Nazareth

JESUS REJECTED AT NAZARETH.   He went to Nazareth, where he had been brought up, and on the Sabbath day he went into the synagogue, as was his custom. And he stood up to read. The scroll of the prophet Isaiah was handed to him. Unrolling it, he found the place where it is written:

> "The Spirit of the Lord is on me,
>> because he has anointed me
>> to preach good news to the poor.
> He has sent me to proclaim freedom for the prisoners
>> and recovery of sight for the blind,
> to release the oppressed,
>> to proclaim the year of the Lord's favor."[h]

Then he rolled up the scroll, gave it back to the attendant and sat down. The eyes of everyone in the synagogue were fastened on him, and he began by saying to them, "Today this scripture is fulfilled in your hearing."

All spoke well of him and were amazed at the gracious words that came from his lips. "Isn't this Joseph's son?" they asked.

Jesus said to them, "Surely you will quote this proverb to me: 'Physician, heal yourself! Do here in your hometown what we have heard that you did in Capernaum.'"

"I tell you the truth," he continued, "no prophet is accepted in his hometown. I assure you that there were many widows in Israel in Elijah's time, when the sky was shut for three and a half years and there was a severe famine throughout the land. Yet Elijah was not sent to any of them, but to a widow in Zarephath in the region of Sidon. And there were many in Israel with leprosy[i] in the time of Elisha the prophet, yet not one of them was cleansed—only Naaman the Syrian."

All the people in the synagogue were furious when they heard this. They got up, drove him out of the town, and took him to the brow of the hill on which the town was built, in order to throw him down the cliff. But he walked right through the crowd and went on his way.

Lk. 5:1-10a
Lake of
Gennesaret

GREAT CATCH OF FISH.   One day as Jesus was standing by the Lake of Gennesaret,[j] with the people crowding around him and listening to the word of God, he saw at the water's edge two boats, left there by the fishermen, who were washing their nets. He got into one of the boats, the one belonging to Simon, and asked him to put out a little from shore. Then he sat down and taught the people from the boat.

When he had finished speaking, he said to Simon, "Put out into deep water, and let down[k] the nets for a catch."

Simon answered, "Master, we've worked hard all night and haven't caught anything. But because you say so, I will let down the nets."

When they had done so, they caught such a large number of fish that their nets began to break. So they signaled their partners in the other boat to come and help them, and they came and filled both boats so full that they began to sink.

When Simon Peter saw this, he fell at Jesus' knees and said, "Go away from me, Lord; I am a sinful man!" For he and all his companions were

---

[h]Isaiah 61:1,2   [i] The Greek word was used for various diseases affecting the skin—not necessarily leprosy.   [j] That is, Sea of Galilee   [k]The Greek verb is plural.

astonished at the catch of fish they had taken, and so were James and John, the sons of Zebedee, Simon's partners.

SIMON, ANDREW, JAMES, AND JOHN.
 ᴸᵏThen Jesus said to Simon, "Don't be afraid; from now on you will catch men." ᴹᵗCome, follow me," Jesus said, "and I will make you fishers of men." At once they left their nets and followed him.

Going on from there, he saw two other brothers, James son of Zebedee and his brother John. They were in a boat with their father Zebedee, preparing their nets. Jesus called them, and immediately they left the boat and their father and followed him.

Mt. 4:18-22
Mk. 1:16-20
Lk. **5:10b,11**

JESUS TEACHES AT CAPERNAUM.   They went to Capernaum, and when the Sabbath came, Jesus went into the synagogue and began to teach. The people were amazed at his teaching, because he taught them as one who had authority, not as the teachers of the law.

Mk. **1:21,22**
Lk. 4:31,32
Capernaum

UNCLEAN SPIRIT HEALED.   Just then a man in their synagogue who was possessed by an evil[l] spirit cried out, "What do you want with us, Jesus of Nazareth? Have you come to destroy us? I know who you are— the Holy One of God!"

"Be quiet!" said Jesus sternly. "Come out of him!" The evil spirit shook the man violently and came out of him with a shriek.

The people were all so amazed that they asked each other, "What is this? A new teaching—and with authority! He even gives orders to evil spirits and they obey him." News about him spread quickly over the whole region of Galilee.

Mk. **1:23-28**
Lk. 4:33-37

PETER'S MOTHER-IN-LAW HEALED.   As soon as they left the synagogue, they went with James and John to the home of Simon and Andrew. Simon's mother-in-law was in bed with a fever, and they told Jesus about her. So he went to her, took her hand and helped her up. The fever left her and she began to wait on them.

Mt. 8:14,15
Mk. **1:29-31**
Lk. 4:38,39

OTHERS HEALED.   That evening after sunset the people brought to Jesus all the sick and demon-possessed. The whole town gathered at the door, and Jesus healed many who had various diseases. He also drove out many demons, but he would not let the demons speak because they knew who he was.

Mt. 8:16,17
Mk. **1:32-34**
Lk. 4:40,41

JESUS GOES OUT TO PRAY.   Very early in the morning, while it was still dark, Jesus got up, left the house and went off to a solitary place, where he prayed. Simon and his companions went to look for him, and when they found him, they exclaimed: "Everyone is looking for you!"

Jesus replied, "Let us go somewhere else—to the nearby villages—so I can preach there also. That is why I have come."

Mk. **1:35-38**
Lk. 4:42,43

JESUS TRAVELS ABOUT.   Jesus went throughout Galilee, teaching in their synagogues, preaching the good news of the kingdom, and healing every disease and sickness among the people. News about him spread all over Syria, and people brought to him all who were ill with various diseases, those suffering severe pain, the demon-possessed, those having seizures, and the paralyzed, and he healed them. Large crowds from Galilee, the Decapolis,[m] Jerusalem, Judea and the region across the Jordan followed him.

Mt. 4:23-25
Mk. 1:39
Lk. 4:44
Galilee

[l]Greek *unclean*   [m]That is, the Ten Cities

Mt. 8:1-4
Mk.
1:40-45
Lk. 5:12-16

LEPER CLEANSED.   A man with leprosy[n] came to him and begged him on his knees, "If you are willing, you can make me clean."

Filled with compassion, Jesus reached out his hand and touched the man. "I am willing," he said. "Be clean!" Immediately the leprosy left him and he was cured.

Jesus sent him away at once with a strong warning: "See that you don't tell this to anyone. But go, show yourself to the priest and offer the sacrifices that Moses commanded for your cleansing, as a testimony to them." Instead he went out and began to talk freely, spreading the news. As a result, Jesus could no longer enter a town openly but stayed outside in lonely places. Yet the people still came to him from everywhere.

Mt. 9:1,2
Mk. 2:1-5
Lk. 5:17-20
Capernaum

PARALYTIC HEALED.   A few days later, when Jesus again entered Capernaum, the people heard that he had come home. So many gathered that there was no room left, not even outside the door, and he preached the word to them. Some men came, bringing to him a paralytic, carried by four of them. Since they could not get him to Jesus because of the crowd, they made an opening in the roof above Jesus and, after digging through it, lowered the mat the paralyzed man was lying on. When Jesus saw their faith, he said to the paralytic, "Son, your sins are forgiven."

Mt. 9:3-8
Mk. 2:6-12
Lk. 5:21-26

SCRIBES QUESTION AUTHORITY.   Now some teachers of the law were sitting there, thinking to themselves, "Why does this fellow talk like that? He's blaspheming! Who can forgive sins but God alone?"

Immediately Jesus knew in his spirit that this was what they were thinking in their hearts, and he said to them, "Why are you thinking these things? Which is easier: to say to the paralytic, 'Your sins are forgiven,' or to say, 'Get up, take your mat and walk'? But that you may know that the Son of Man has authority on earth to forgive sins..." He said to the paralytic, "I tell you, get up, take your mat and go home." He got up, took his mat and walked out in full view of them all. This amazed everyone and they praised God, saying, "We have never seen anything like this!"

The Rise of Opposition

*T*his confrontation is but the first of many which will take place between Jesus and the religious leaders of his day. By indicating that he has the divine authority to forgive sins, Jesus naturally arouses immediate reaction from the Scribes and Pharisees. Since they correctly believe that only God can forgive sins, they reject the possibility that Jesus himself is divine and conclude instead that he is guilty of blasphemy.

In addition to the written law given through Moses, the Pharisees accept as equally binding the oral traditions of the rabbis, which traditions have evolved into a highly ritualistic set of religious observances. So when Jesus and his disciples violate some of these traditional rules, the Pharisees are highly offended. Through two parables Jesus tells them that their system of legalistic observances simply will not substitute for the true righteousness which God has always demanded.

[n]The Greek word was used for various diseases affecting the skin—not necessarily leprosy.

John alone records what is apparently a brief trip to Jerusalem, where Jesus attends "a feast of the Jews." Although the exact feast is not indicated, there is strong evidence that it is the Passover of A.D. 28. (Some believe it was Pentecost or the Feast of Tabernacles.) While in Jerusalem, Jesus is once again criticized, this time for healing a man on the Sabbath, the day on which no work is to be done. If there was ever a perfect example of the fallacy of legalism, surely this is it. The incident also raises some fundamental questions: what is at stake—the law itself, or only interpretations of the law? Under what circumstances, if any, may the letter of the law be disregarded in favor of higher concerns consistent with the spirit of the law? Does Jesus consider the law given through Moses to be binding upon his disciples? These very legitimate questions are clearly on the minds of the religious establishment.

Despite growing opposition, Jesus continues to go about teaching and performing miracles, yet almost consciously without fanfare. As if to underscore the urgency of his mission in the face of opposition, Jesus appoints 12 of his disciples as specially chosen apostles to aid him in his ministry. With their added support, Jesus continues to attract even greater crowds from among the common people.

MATTHEW (LEVI) IS CALLED. Once again Jesus went out beside the lake. A large crowd came to him, and he began to teach them. As he walked along, he saw Levi son of Alphaeus sitting at the tax collector's booth. "Follow me," Jesus told him, and Levi got up and followed him.

Mt. 9:9
Mk. 2:13,14
Lk. 5:27,28
Galilee

EATING WITH SINNERS. ᴸᵏThen Levi held a great banquet for Jesus at his house, and a large crowd of tax collectors and others were eating with them. But the Pharisees and the teachers of the law who belonged to their sect complained to his disciples, "Why do you eat and drink with tax collectors and 'sinners'?" ᴹᵗOn hearing this, Jesus said, "It is not the healthy who need a doctor, but the sick. But go and learn what this means: 'I desire mercy, not sacrifice.'ᵒ For I have not come to call the righteous, but sinners."

Mt. 9:10-13
Mk. 2:15-17
Lk. 5:29-32

DISCIPLES NOT FASTING. They said to him, "John's disciples often fast and pray, and so do the disciples of the Pharisees, but yours go on eating and drinking."

Mt. 9:14-17
Mk. 2:18-22
Lk. 5:33-39

Jesus answered, "Can you make the guests of the bridegroom fast while he is with them? But the time will come when the bridegroom will be taken from them; in those days they will fast."

He told them this parable: "No one tears a patch from a new garment and sews it on an old one. If he does, he will have torn the new garment, and the patch from the new will not match the old. And no one pours new wine into old wineskins. If he does, the new wine will burst the skins, the wine will run out and the wineskins will be ruined. No, new wine must be poured into new wineskins. And no one after drinking old wine wants the new, for he says, 'The old is better.' "

HEALING AT POOL OF BETHESDA. Some time later, Jesus went up to Jerusalem for a feast of the Jews. Now there is in Jerusalem near the Sheep Gate a pool, which in Aramaic is called Bethesdaᵖ and which is

[Second Passover April, A.D. 28]

ᵒHosea 6:6   ᵖSome manuscripts *Bethzatha*; other manuscripts *Bethsaida*

Jn.
5:1-3,5-9a
Jerusalem

surrounded by five covered colonnades. Here a great number of disabled people used to lie—the blind, the lame, the paralyzed.[q] One who was there had been an invalid for thirty-eight years. When Jesus saw him lying there and learned that he had been in this condition for a long time, he asked him, "Do you want to get well?"

"Sir," the invalid replied, "I have no one to help me into the pool when the water is stirred. While I am trying to get in, someone else goes down ahead of me."

Then Jesus said to him, "Get up! Pick up your mat and walk." At once the man was cured; he picked up his mat and walked.

Jn. 5:9b-15

HEALED MAN QUESTIONED.   The day on which this took place was a Sabbath, and so the Jews said to the man who had been healed, "It is the Sabbath; the law forbids you to carry your mat."

But he replied, "The man who made me well said to me, 'Pick up your mat and walk.' "

So they asked him, "Who is this fellow who told you to pick it up and walk?"

The man who was healed had no idea who it was, for Jesus had slipped away into the crowd that was there.

Later Jesus found him at the temple and said to him, "See, you are well again. Stop sinning or something worse may happen to you." The man went away and told the Jews that it was Jesus who had made him well.

Jn. 5:16-29

RESURRECTION AND LIFE.   So, because Jesus was doing these things on the Sabbath, the Jews persecuted him. Jesus said to them, "My Father is always at his work to this very day, and I, too, am working." For this reason the Jews tried all the harder to kill him; not only was he breaking the Sabbath, but he was even calling God his own Father, making himself equal with God.

Jesus gave them this answer: "I tell you the truth, the Son can do nothing by himself; he can do only what he sees his Father doing, because whatever the Father does the Son also does. For the Father loves the Son and shows him all he does. Yes, to your amazement he will show him even greater things than these. For just as the Father raises the dead and gives them life, even so the Son gives life to whom he is pleased to give it. Moreover, the Father judges no one, but has entrusted all judgment to the Son, that all may honor the Son just as they honor the Father. He who does not honor the Son does not honor the Father, who sent him.

"I tell you the truth, whoever hears my word and believes him who sent me has eternal life and will not be condemned; he has crossed over from death to life. I tell you the truth, a time is coming and has now come when the dead will hear the voice of the Son of God and those who hear will live. For as the Father has life in himself, so he has granted the Son to have life in himself. And he has given him authority to judge because he is the Son of Man.

"Do not be amazed at this, for a time is coming when all who are in their graves will hear his voice and come out—those who have done good will rise to live, and those who have done evil will rise to be condemned.

[q]Some less important manuscripts *paralyzed—and they waited for the moving of the waters.*
[4]*From time to time an angel of the Lord would come down and stir up the waters. The first one into the pool after each such disturbance would be cured of whatever disease he had.*

DISCUSSION OF AUTHORITY.   By myself I can do nothing; I judge only   Jn. 5:30-47
as I hear, and my judgment is just, for I seek not to please myself but him
who sent me.

"If I testify about myself, my testimony is not valid. There is another
who testifies in my favor, and I know that his testimony about me is valid.

"You have sent to John and he has testified to the truth. Not that I accept
human testimony; but I mention it that you may be saved. John was a
lamp that burned and gave light, and you chose for a time to enjoy his
light.

"I have testimony weightier than that of John. For the very work that the
Father has given me to finish, and which I am doing, testifies that the
Father has sent me. And the Father who sent me has himself testified concerning me. You have never heard his voice nor seen his form, nor does his
word dwell in you, for you do not believe the one he sent. You diligently
study[r] the Scriptures because you think that by them you possess eternal
life. These are the Scriptures that testify about me, yet you refuse to come
to me to have life.

"I do not accept praise from men, but I know you. I know that you do
not have the love of God in your hearts. I have come in my Father's name,
and you do not accept me; but if someone else comes in his own name, you
will accept him. How can you believe if you accept praise from one another, yet make no effort to obtain the praise that comes from the only God[s]?

"But do not think I will accuse you before the Father. Your accuser is
Moses, on whom your hopes are set. If you believed Moses, you would
believe me, for he wrote about me. But since you do not believe what he
wrote, how are you going to believe what I say?"

PLUCKING GRAIN ON SABBATH.   Mt At that time Jesus went through   Mt. 12:1-8
Mk.
2:23-28
Lk. 6:1-5
Galilee
the grainfields on the Sabbath. His disciples were hungry and began to
pick some heads of grain and eat them. When the Pharisees saw this, they
said to him, "Look! Your disciples are doing what is unlawful on the
Sabbath."

He answered, "Haven't you read what David did when he and his companions were hungry? He entered the house of God, and he and his companions ate the consecrated bread—which was not lawful for them to do,
but only for the priests. Or haven't you read in the Law that on the
Sabbath the priests in the temple desecrate the day and yet are innocent?
I tell you that one[t] greater than the temple is here. If you had known what
these words mean, 'I desire mercy, not sacrifice,'[u] you would not have condemned the innocent. Mk Then he said to them, "The Sabbath was made for
man, not man for the Sabbath. So the Son of Man is Lord even of the
Sabbath."

HEALING ON SABBATH.   Lk On another Sabbath he went into the syna-   Mt. 12:9-14
Mk. 3:1-6
Lk. 6:6-11
gogue and was teaching, and a man was there whose right hand was
shriveled. The Pharisees and the teachers of the law were looking for a
reason to accuse Jesus, so they watched him closely to see if he would heal
on the Sabbath. Mt Looking for a reason to accuse Jesus, they asked him, "Is
it lawful to heal on the Sabbath?"

He said to them, "If any of you has a sheep and it falls into a pit on the

[r]Or *Study diligently* (the imperative)   [s]Some early manuscripts *the Only One*   [t]Or
something; also in verses 41 and 42   [u]Hosea 6:6

Sabbath, will you not take hold of it and lift it out? How much more valuable is a man than a sheep! Therefore it is lawful to do good on the Sabbath." ᴹᵏJesus said to the man with the shriveled hand, "Stand up in front of everyone."

Then Jesus asked them, "Which is lawful on the Sabbath: to do good or to do evil, to save life or to kill?" But they remained silent.

He looked around at them in anger and, deeply distressed at their stubborn hearts, said to the man, "Stretch out your hand." He stretched it out, and his hand was completely restored. ᴸᵏBut they were furious and began to discuss with one another what they might do to Jesus. ᴹᵏThen the Pharisees went out and began to plot with the Herodians how they might kill Jesus.

Mt.
12:15-21
Mk. 3:7-12
By the sea

JESUS HEALS OTHERS. ᴹᵏJesus withdrew with his disciples to the lake, and a large crowd from Galilee followed. When they heard all he was doing, many people came to him from Judea, Jerusalem, Idumea, and the regions across the Jordan and around Tyre and Sidon. Because of the crowd he told his disciples to have a small boat ready for him, to keep the people from crowding him. For he had healed many, so that those with diseases were pushing forward to touch him. Whenever the evilᵛ spirits saw him, they fell down before him and cried out, "You are the Son of God." But he gave them strict orders not to tell who he was. ᴹᵗThis was to fulfill what was spoken through the prophet Isaiah:

> "Here is my servant whom I have chosen,
> the one I love, in whom I delight;
> I will put my Spirit on him,
> and he will proclaim justice to the nations.
> He will not quarrel or cry out;
> no one will hear his voice in the streets.
> A bruised reed he will not break,
> and a smoldering wick he will not snuff out,
> till he leads justice to victory.
> In his name the nations will put their hope."ʷ

Mk.
3:13-19
Lk. 6:12-16
Hills near
sea

JESUS APPOINTS 12 APOSTLES. One of those days Jesus went out to a mountainside to pray, and spent the night praying to God. When morning came, he called his disciples to him and chose twelve of them, whom he also designated apostles: Simon (whom he named Peter), his brother Andrew, James, John, Philip, Bartholomew, Matthew, Thomas, James son of Alphaeus, Simon who was called the Zealot, Judas son of James, and Judas Iscariot, who became a traitor.

Lk. 6:17-19

GREAT CROWD GATHERS. He went down with them and stood on a level place. A large crowd of his disciples was there and a great number of people from all over Judea, from Jerusalem, and from the coast of Tyre and Sidon, who had come to hear him and to be healed of their diseases. Those troubled by evilˣ spirits were cured, and the people all tried to touch him, because power was coming from him and healing them all.

ᵛGreek *unclean*   ʷIsaiah 42:1-4   ˣGreek *unclean*

The Sermon on the Mount

*T*he "Sermon on the Mount" is perhaps the most familiar and instructive sermon ever presented by Jesus. Matthew and Luke may record Jesus' teaching in two different settings, although the content appears much the same. Just as many of Jesus' sermons are apparently never recorded, so too some of his sermons are probably repeated from place to place. In any event, this collection of Jesus' teachings brings one to the heart of his message concerning the kingdom of God.

Covering a broad spectrum of spiritual topics, Jesus speaks of the nature of the kingdom, of repentance, of faith, and of worship—and particularly of prayer and humility. Always demonstrating a concern for human welfare, Jesus deals specifically with family and social relationships and discusses at length the effect of possessions on one's faith and peace of mind. The discourse begins beautifully with the blessings in store for the righteous, and harshly with the woes which will befall those whose lives are spiritually rebellious.

BEATITUDES PROCLAIMED.   Now when he saw the crowds, he went up on a mountainside and sat down. His disciples came to him, and he began to teach them, saying:

Mt. 5:1-12
Lk. 6:20-23
**Mountain
near
Capernaum**

> "Blessed are the poor in spirit,
>> for theirs is the kingdom of heaven.
> Blessed are those who mourn,
>> for they will be comforted.
> Blessed are the meek,
>> for they will inherit the earth.
> Blessed are those who hunger and thirst for righteousness,
>> for they will be filled.
> Blessed are the merciful,
>> for they will be shown mercy.
> Blessed are the pure in heart,
>> for they will see God.
> Blessed are the peacemakers,
>> for they will be called sons of God.
> Blessed are those who are persecuted because of
>> righteousness,
>> for theirs is the kingdom of heaven.

"Blessed are you when people insult you, persecute you and falsely say all kinds of evil against you because of me. Rejoice and be glad, because great is your reward in heaven, for in the same way they persecuted the prophets who were before you.

WOES PRONOUNCED.

Lk. 6:24-26

> "But woe to you who are rich,
>> for you have already received your comfort.
> Woe to you who are well fed now,
>> for you will go hungry.
> Woe to you who laugh now,
>> for you will mourn and weep.

Woe to you when all men speak well of you,
for that is how their fathers treated the false prophets.

Mt. 5:13-16   NATURE OF BELIEVERS.   "You are the salt of the earth. But if the salt loses its saltiness, how can it be made salty again? It is no longer good for anything, except to be thrown out and trampled by men.

"You are the light of the world. A city on a hill cannot be hidden. Neither do people light a lamp and put it under a bowl. Instead they put it on its stand, and it gives light to everyone in the house. In the same way, let your light shine before men, that they may see your good deeds and praise your Father in heaven.

Mt. 5:17-20   LAW AND GOSPEL.   "Do not think that I have come to abolish the Law or the Prophets; I have not come to abolish them but to fulfill them. I tell you the truth, until heaven and earth disappear, not the smallest letter, not the least stroke of a pen, will by any means disappear from the Law until everything is accomplished. Anyone who breaks one of the least of these commandments and teaches others to do the same will be called least in the kingdom of heaven, but whoever practices and teaches these commands will be called great in the kingdom of heaven. For I tell you that unless your righteousness surpasses that of the Pharisees and the teachers of the law, you will certainly not enter the kingdom of heaven.

Mt. 5:21-26   THE SIXTH COMMANDMENT.   "You have heard that it was said to the people long ago, 'Do not murder,[y] and anyone who murders will be subject to judgment.' But I tell you that anyone who is angry with his brother[z] will be subject to judgment. Again, anyone who says to his brother, 'Raca,[a]' is answerable to the Sanhedrin. But anyone who says, 'You fool!' will be in danger of the fire of hell.

"Therefore, if you are offering your gift at the altar and there remember that your brother has something against you, leave your gift there in front of the altar. First go and be reconciled to your brother; then come and offer your gift.

"Settle matters quickly with your adversary who is taking you to court. Do it while you are still with him on the way, or he may hand you over to the judge, and the judge may hand you over to the officer, and you may be thrown into prison. I tell you the truth, you will not get out until you have paid the last penny.[b]

Mt. 5:27-30   THE SEVENTH COMMANDMENT.   "You have heard that it was said, 'Do not commit adultery.'[c] But I tell you that anyone who looks at a woman lustfully has already committed adultery with her in his heart. If your right eye causes you to sin, gouge it out and throw it away. It is better for you to lose one part of your body than for your whole body to be thrown into hell. And if your right hand causes you to sin, cut it off and throw it away. It is better for you to lose one part of your body than for your whole body to go into hell.

Mt. 5:31,32   MARRIAGE AND DIVORCE.   "It has been said, 'Anyone who divorces his wife must give her a certificate of divorce.'[d] But I tell you that anyone who divorces his wife, except for marital unfaithfulness, causes her to

---

[y]Exodus 20:13   [z]Some manuscripts *brother without cause*   [a]An Aramaic term of contempt   [b]Greek *kodrantes*   [c]Exodus 20:14   [d]Deut. 24:1

become an adulteress, and anyone who marries the divorced woman commits adultery.

HONESTY WITHOUT OATHS.   "Again, you have heard that it was said to the people long ago, 'Do not break your oath, but keep the oaths you have made to the Lord.' But I tell you, Do not swear at all: either by heaven, for it is God's throne; or by the earth, for it is his footstool; or by Jerusalem, for it is the city of the Great King. And do not swear by your head, for you cannot make even one hair white or black. Simply let your 'Yes' be 'Yes,' and your 'No,' 'No'; anything beyond this comes from the evil one.

Mt. 5:33-37

REGARDING RETALIATION.   Mt"You have heard that it was said, 'Eye for eye, and tooth for tooth.'ᵉ But I tell you, Do not resist an evil person. If someone strikes you on the right cheek, turn to him the other also. And if someone wants to sue you and take your tunic, let him have your cloak as well. If someone forces you to go one mile, go with him two miles. Give to the one who asks you, and do not turn away from the one who wants to borrow from you. ᴸᵏDo to others as you would have them do to you.

Mt. 5:38-42
Lk. 6:27-31

LOVE FOR ENEMIES.   Mt"You have heard that it was said, 'Love your neighborᶠ and hate your enemy.' But I tell you: Love your enemiesᵍ and pray for those who persecute you, that you may be sons of your Father in heaven. He causes his sun to rise on the evil and the good, and sends rain on the righteous and the unrighteous. If you love those who love you, what reward will you get? Are not even the tax collectors doing that? And if you greet only your brothers, what are you doing more than others? Do not even pagans do that? ᴸᵏAnd if you lend to those from whom you expect repayment, what credit is that to you? Even 'sinners' lend to 'sinners,' expecting to be repaid in full. But love your enemies, do good to them, and lend to them without expecting to get anything back. Then your reward will be great, and you will be sons of the Most High, because he is kind to the ungrateful and wicked. Be merciful, just as your Father is merciful.

Mt. 5:43-48
Lk. 6:32-36

ON GIVING.   "Be careful not to do your 'acts of righteousness' before men, to be seen by them. If you do, you will have no reward from your Father in heaven.

"So when you give to the needy, do not announce it with trumpets, as the hypocrites do in the synagogues and on the streets, to be honored by men. I tell you the truth, they have received their reward in full. But when you give to the needy, do not let your left hand know what your right hand is doing, so that your giving may be in secret. Then your Father, who sees what is done in secret, will reward you.

Mt. 6:1-4

ON PRAYING.   "And when you pray, do not be like the hypocrites, for they love to pray standing in the synagogues and on the street corners to be seen by men. I tell you the truth, they have received their reward in full. But when you pray, go into your room, close the door and pray to your Father, who is unseen. Then your Father, who sees what is done in secret, will reward you. And when you pray, do not keep on babbling like pagans, for they think they will be heard because of their many words.

Mt. 6:5-15

ᵉExodus 21:24; Lev. 24:20; Deut. 19:21   ᶠLev. 19:18   ᵍSome late manuscripts *enemies, bless those who curse you, do good to those who hate you*

Do not be like them, for your Father knows what you need before you ask him.

"This, then, is how you should pray:

" 'Our Father in heaven,
hallowed be your name,
your kingdom come,
your will be done
    on earth as it is in heaven.
Give us today our daily bread.
Forgive us our debts,
    as we also have forgiven our debtors.
And lead us not into temptation,
but deliver us from the evil one.*h*

For if you forgive men when they sin against you, your heavenly Father will also forgive you. But if you do not forgive men their sins, your Father will not forgive your sins.

Mt. 6:16-18   ON FASTING.   "When you fast, do not look somber as the hypocrites do, for they disfigure their faces to show men they are fasting. I tell you the truth, they have received their reward in full. But when you fast, put oil on your head and wash your face, so that it will not be obvious to men that you are fasting, but only to your Father, who is unseen; and your Father, who sees what is done in secret, will reward you.

Mt. 6:19-21   SPIRITUAL TREASURES.   "Do not store up for yourselves treasures on earth, where moth and rust destroy, and where thieves break in and steal. But store up for yourselves treasures in heaven, where moth and rust do not destroy, and where thieves do not break in and steal. For where your treasure is, there your heart will be also.

Mt. 6:22,23   VALUE OF SPIRITUAL INSIGHT.   "The eye is the lamp of the body. If your eyes are good, your whole body will be full of light. But if your eyes are bad, your whole body will be full of darkness. If then the light within you is darkness, how great is that darkness!

Mt. 6:24   NEED FOR UNDIVIDED LOYALTY.   "No one can serve two masters. Either he will hate the one and love the other, or he will be devoted to the one and despise the other. You cannot serve both God and Money.

Mt. 6:25-34   AVOIDING ANXIETY.   "Therefore I tell you, do not worry about your life, what you will eat or drink; or about your body, what you will wear. Is not life more important than food, and the body more important than clothes? Look at the birds of the air; they do not sow or reap or store away in barns, and yet your heavenly Father feeds them. Are you not much more valuable than they? Who of you by worrying can add a single hour to his life*i*?

"And why do you worry about clothes? See how the lilies of the field grow. They do not labor or spin. Yet I tell you that not even Solomon in all his splendor was dressed like one of these. If that is how God clothes the grass of the field, which is here today and tomorrow is thrown into the fire, will he not much more clothe you, O you of little faith? So do not worry, saying, 'What shall we eat?' or 'What shall we drink?' or 'What

---

*h*Or *from evil*; some late manuscripts *one, | for yours is the kingdom and the power and the glory forever. Amen.*   *i*Or *single cubit to his height*

shall we wear?' For the pagans run after all these things, and your heavenly Father knows that you need them. But seek first his kingdom and his righteousness, and all these things will be given to you as well. Therefore do not worry about tomorrow, for tomorrow will worry about itself. Each day has enough trouble of its own.

HYPOCRITICAL JUDGING.   "Do not judge, and you will not be judged. Do not condemn, and you will not be condemned. Forgive, and you will be forgiven. Give, and it will be given to you. A good measure, pressed down, shaken together and running over, will be poured into your lap. For with the measure you use, it will be measured to you." Mt. 7:1-5 / Lk. 6:37-42

He also told them this parable: "Can a blind man lead a blind man? Will they not both fall into a pit? A student is not above his teacher, but everyone who is fully trained will be like his teacher.

"Why do you look at the speck of sawdust in your brother's eye and pay no attention to the plank in your own eye? How can you say to your brother, 'Brother, let me take the speck out of your eye,' when you yourself fail to see the plank in your own eye? You hypocrite, first take the plank out of your eye, and then you will see clearly to remove the speck from your brother's eye.

INAPPROPRIATE CONCERN.   "Do not give dogs what is sacred; do not throw your pearls to pigs. If you do, they may trample them under their feet, and then turn and tear you to pieces. Mt. 7:6

SEEKING GRACE.   "Ask and it will be given to you; seek and you will find; knock and the door will be opened to you. For everyone who asks receives; he who seeks finds; and to him who knocks, the door will be opened. Mt. 7:7-12

"Which of you, if his son asks for bread, will give him a stone? Or if he asks for a fish, will give him a snake? If you, then, though you are evil, know how to give good gifts to your children, how much more will your Father in heaven give good gifts to those who ask him! So in everything, do to others what you would have them do to you, for this sums up the Law and the Prophets.

UNPOPULAR DISCIPLESHIP.   "Enter through the narrow gate. For wide is the gate and broad is the road that leads to destruction, and many enter through it. But small is the gate and narrow the road that leads to life, and only a few find it. Mt. 7:13,14

TESTING RELIGIOUS LEADERS.   Mt"Watch out for false prophets. They come to you in sheep's clothing, but inwardly they are ferocious wolves. By their fruit you will recognize them. Do people pick grapes from thornbushes, or figs from thistles? Likewise every good tree bears good fruit, but a bad tree bears bad fruit. A good tree cannot bear bad fruit, and a bad tree cannot bear good fruit. Every tree that does not bear good fruit is cut down and thrown into the fire. Thus, by their fruit you will recognize them. LkThe good man brings good things out of the good stored up in his heart, and the evil man brings evil things out of the evil stored up in his heart. For out of the overflow of his heart his mouth speaks. Mt"Not everyone who says to me, 'Lord, Lord,' will enter the kingdom of heaven, but only he who does the will of my Father who is in heaven. Many will say to me on that day, 'Lord, Lord, did we not prophesy in your name, and in your name drive out demons and perform many miracles?' Then I will tell Mt. 7:15-23 / Lk. 6:43-45 them plainly, 'I never knew you. Away from me, you evildoers!'

Mt. 7:24-27
Lk. 6:46-49

FAITH AND DEEDS. Lk"Why do you call me, 'Lord, Lord,' and do not do what I say? Mt"Therefore everyone who hears these words of mine and puts them into practice is like a wise man who built his house on the rock. The rain came down, the streams rose, and the winds blew and beat against that house; yet it did not fall, because it had its foundation on the rock. But everyone who hears these words of mine and does not put them into practice is like a foolish man who built his house on sand. The rain came down, the streams rose, and the winds blew and beat against that house, and it fell with a great crash."

Mt. 7:28,29

CROWD IS ASTONISHED. When Jesus had finished saying these things, the crowds were amazed at his teaching, because he taught as one who had authority, and not as their teachers of the law.

The Ministry Continues

Such perceptive and authoritative teaching has obviously won the attention of the multitudes, who have long been disillusioned by the empty ritualism and superficiality of their present religious system. As Jesus' fame continues to spread, John the Baptist sends a message to Jesus asking for final confirmation of his messiahship. John is perhaps sensing an impending death and undoubtedly wants to reassure himself that his own ministry has not been in vain. Jesus sends a message of reassurance and praises John for his courage and dedication as a servant of God.

No doubt by this time the religious leaders are also becoming increasingly aware of Jesus' extraordinary power. Instead of accepting it as divine, they accuse Jesus of having power from Satan. What follows is a scathing rebuke of the Pharisees for their disbelief and hypocrisy, and an urgent call for repentance. The events leading to this confrontation begin to unfold as Jesus makes his way from the mountain back to Capernaum.

Mt. 8:5-13
Lk. 7:1-10
Capernaum

CENTURION'S SLAVE HEALED. LkWhen Jesus had finished saying all this in the hearing of the people, he entered Capernaum. There a centurion's servant, whom his master valued highly, was sick and about to die. The centurion heard of Jesus and sent some elders of the Jews to him, asking him to come and heal his servant. When they came to Jesus, they pleaded earnestly with him, "This man deserves to have you do this, because he loves our nation and has built our synagogue." So Jesus went with them.

He was not far from the house when the centurion sent friends to say to him: "Lord, don't trouble yourself, for I do not deserve to have you come under my roof. That is why I did not even consider myself worthy to come to you. But say the word, and my servant will be healed. For I myself am a man under authority, with soldiers under me. I tell this one, 'Go,' and he goes; and that one, 'Come,' and he comes. I say to my servant, 'Do this,' and he does it."

When Jesus heard this, he was amazed at him, and turning to the crowd following him, he said, "I tell you, I have not found such great faith even in Israel." MtI say to you that many will come from the east and the west, and will take their places at the feast with Abraham, Isaac and Jacob in the

kingdom of heaven. But the subjects of the kingdom will be thrown outside, into the darkness, where there will be weeping and gnashing of
teeth."

Then Jesus said to the centurion, "Go! It will be done just as you
believed it would." And his servant was healed at that very hour. LkThen
the men who had been sent returned to the house and found the servant
well.

WIDOW'S SON RAISED. Soon afterward, Jesus went to a town called
Nain, and his disciples and a large crowd went along with him. As he
approached the town gate, a dead person was being carried out—the only
son of his mother, and she was a widow. And a large crowd from the town
was with her. When the Lord saw her, his heart went out to her and he
said, "Don't cry."

Then he went up and touched the coffin, and those carrying it stood still.
He said, "Young man, I say to you, get up!" The dead man sat up and
began to talk, and Jesus gave him back to his mother.

They were all filled with awe and praised God. "A great prophet has
appeared among us," they said. "God has come to help his people." This
news about Jesus spread throughout Judea *j* and the surrounding country.

Lk. 7:11-17
Nain

JOHN THE BAPTIST QUESTIONS. John's disciples told him about all
these things. Calling two of them, he sent them to the Lord to ask, "Are
you the one who was to come, or should we expect someone else?"

When the men came to Jesus, they said, "John the Baptist sent us to you
to ask, 'Are you the one who was to come, or should we expect someone
else?' "

At that very time Jesus cured many who had diseases, sicknesses and
evil spirits, and gave sight to many who were blind. So he replied to the
messengers, "Go back and report to John what you have seen and heard:
The blind receive sight, the lame walk, those who have leprosy*k* are cured,
the deaf hear, the dead are raised, and the good news is preached to the
poor. Blessed is the man who does not fall away on account of me."

Mt. 11:2-6
Lk. 7:18-23

JESUS PRAISES JOHN. LkAfter John's messengers left, Jesus began to
speak to the crowd about John: "What did you go out into the desert to
see? A reed swayed by the wind? If not, what did you go out to see? A
man dressed in fine clothes? No, those who wear expensive clothes and
indulge in luxury are in palaces. But what did you go out to see? A
prophet? Yes, I tell you, and more than a prophet. This is the one about
whom it is written:

Mt. 11:7-15
Lk. 7:24-30

" 'I will send my messenger ahead of you,
           who will prepare your way before you.'*l*

I tell you, among those born of women there is no one greater than John;
yet the one who is least in the kingdom of God is greater than he."

MtFrom the days of John the Baptist until now, the kingdom of heaven
has been forcefully advancing, and forceful men lay hold of it. For all the
Prophets and the Law prophesied until John. And if you are willing to

---

*j*Or *the land of the Jews*   *k*The Greek word was used for various diseases affecting the
skin—not necessarily leprosy.   *l*Mal. 3:1

accept it, he is the Elijah who was to come. He who has ears, let him hear. ᴸᵏ(All the people, even the tax collectors, when they heard Jesus' words, acknowledged that God's way was right, because they had been baptized by John. But the Pharisees and experts in the law rejected God's purpose for themselves, because they had not been baptized by John.)

Mt.
11:16-19
Lk. 7:31-35

JESUS REPROVES REJECTION.   "To what, then, can I compare the people of this generation? What are they like? They are like children sitting in the marketplace and calling out to each other:

> " 'We played the flute for you,
>   and you did not dance;
>   we sang a dirge,
>   and you did not cry.'

For John the Baptist came neither eating bread nor drinking wine, and you say, 'He has a demon.' The Son of Man came eating and drinking, and you say, 'Here is a glutton and a drunkard, a friend of tax collectors and "sinners." ' But wisdom is proved right by all her children."

Lk. 7:36-50

ANNOINTING BY SINFUL WOMAN.   Now one of the Pharisees invited Jesus to have dinner with him, so he went to the Pharisee's house and reclined at the table. When a woman who had lived a sinful life in that town learned that Jesus was eating at the Pharisee's house, she brought an alabaster jar of perfume, and as she stood behind him at his feet weeping, she began to wet his feet with her tears. Then she wiped them with her hair, kissed them and poured perfume on them.

When the Pharisee who had invited him saw this, he said to himself, "If this man were a prophet, he would know who is touching him and what kind of woman she is—that she is a sinner."

Jesus answered him, "Simon, I have something to tell you."

"Tell me, teacher," he said.

"Two men owed money to a certain moneylender. One owed him five hundred denarii,ᵐ and the other fifty. Neither of them had the money to pay him back, so he canceled the debts of both. Now which of them will love him more?"

Simon replied, "I suppose the one who had the bigger debt canceled."

"You have judged correctly," Jesus said.

Then he turned toward the woman and said to Simon, "Do you see this woman? I came into your house. You did not give me any water for my feet, but she wet my feet with her tears and wiped them with her hair. You did not give me a kiss, but this woman, from the time I entered, has not stopped kissing my feet. You did not put oil on my head, but she has poured perfume on my feet. Therefore, I tell you, her many sins have been forgiven—for she loved much. But he who has been forgiven little loves little."

Then Jesus said to her, "Your sins are forgiven."

The other guests began to say among themselves, "Who is this who even forgives sins?"

Jesus said to the woman, "Your faith has saved you; go in peace."

ᵐA denarius was a coin worth about a day's wages.

WOMEN PROVIDE SUPPORT.   After this, Jesus traveled about from one   Lk. 8:1-3
town and village to another, proclaiming the good news of the kingdom of   Galilee
God. The Twelve were with him, and also some women who had been
cured of evil spirits and diseases: Mary (called Magdalene) from whom
seven demons had come out; Joanna the wife of Cuza, the manager of
Herod's household; Susanna; and many others. These women were helping to support them out of their own means.

JESUS ACCUSED.   ^{Mk}Then Jesus entered a house, and again a crowd   Mt.
gathered, so that he and his disciples were not even able to eat. ^{Mt}Then   12:22-30
they brought him a demon-possessed man who was blind and mute, and   Mk.
Jesus healed him, so that he could both talk and see. All the people were   3:20;22-27
astonished and said, "Could this be the Son of David?"   Lk.
11:14-23
But when the Pharisees heard this, they said, "It is only by Beelzebub,[n]   Capernaum
the prince of demons, that this fellow drives out demons."

Jesus knew their thoughts and said to them, "Every kingdom divided
against itself will be ruined, and every city or household divided against
itself will not stand. If Satan drives out Satan, he is divided against himself. How then can his kingdom stand? And if I drive out demons by
Beelzebub, by whom do your people drive them out? So then, they will be
your judges. But if I drive out demons by the Spirit of God, then the kingdom of God has come upon you.

"Or again, how can anyone enter a strong man's house and carry off his
possessions unless he first ties up the strong man? Then he can rob his
house.

"He who is not with me is against me, and he who does not gather with
me scatters.

BLASPHEMY CONDEMNED.   ^{Mt}And so I tell you, every sin and blas-   Mt.
phemy will be forgiven men, but the blasphemy against the Spirit will not   12:31-37
be forgiven. Anyone who speaks a word against the Son of Man will be   Mk.
forgiven, but anyone who speaks against the Holy Spirit will not be for-   3:21;28-30
given, either in this age or in the age to come. ^{Mk}He said this because they
were saying, "He has an evil spirit." ^{Mt}"Make a tree good and its fruit will
be good, or make a tree bad and its fruit will be bad, for a tree is recognized by its fruit. You brood of vipers, how can you who are evil say anything good? For out of the overflow of the heart the mouth speaks. The
good man brings good things out of the good stored up in him, and the
evil man brings evil things out of the evil stored up in him. But I tell you
that men will have to give account on the day of judgment for every careless word they have spoken. For by your words you will be acquitted, and
by your words you will be condemned." ^{Mk}When his family heard about
this, they went to take charge of him, for they said, "He is out of his mind."

REQUEST FOR PROOF REBUKED.   Then some of the Pharisees and   Mt.
teachers of the law said to him, "Teacher, we want to see a miraculous sign   12:38-42
from you."   Lk.
11:29-32
He answered, "A wicked and adulterous generation asks for a miraculous sign! But none will be given it except the sign of the prophet Jonah.
For as Jonah was three days and three nights in the belly of a huge fish, so
the Son of Man will be three days and three nights in the heart of the earth.

[n]Greek *Beezeboul* or *Beelzeboul*

The men of Nineveh will stand up at the judgment with this generation and condemn it; for they repented at the preaching of Jonah, and now one[o] greater than Jonah is here. The Queen of the South will rise at the judgment with this generation and condemn it; for she came from the ends of the earth to listen to Solomon's wisdom, and now one greater than Solomon is here.

Mt.
12:43-45
Lk.
11:24-28

NEED FOR MORAL REFORM. [Mt]"When an evil[p] spirit comes out of a man, it goes through arid places seeking rest and does not find it. Then it says, 'I will return to the house I left.' When it arrives, it finds the house unoccupied, swept clean and put in order. Then it goes and takes with it seven other spirits more wicked than itself, and they go in and live there. And the final condition of that man is worse than the first. That is how it will be with this wicked generation." [Lk]As Jesus was saying these things, a woman in the crowd called out, "Blessed is the mother who gave you birth and nursed you."

He replied, "Blessed rather are those who hear the word of God and obey it."

Mt.
12:46-50
Mk.
3:31-35
Lk. 8:19-21

JESUS TELLS TRUE KINSHIP. While Jesus was still talking to the crowd, his mother and brothers stood outside, wanting to speak to him. Someone told him, "Your mother and brothers are standing outside, wanting to speak to you."[q]

He replied to him, "Who is my mother, and who are my brothers?" Pointing to his disciples, he said, "Here are my mother and my brothers. For whoever does the will of my Father in heaven is my brother and sister and mother."

Lk.
11:33-36

INNER RIGHTEOUSNESS. "No one lights a lamp and puts it in a place where it will be hidden, or under a bowl. Instead he puts it on its stand, so that those who come in may see the light. Your eye is the lamp of your body. When your eyes are good, your whole body also is full of light. But when they are bad, your body also is full of darkness. See to it, then, that the light within you is not darkness. Therefore, if your whole body is full of light, and no part of it dark, it will be completely lighted, as when the light of a lamp shines on you."

Lk.
11:37-44

HYPOCRISY CONDEMNED. When Jesus had finished speaking, a Pharisee invited him to eat with him; so he went in and reclined at the table. But the Pharisee, noticing that Jesus did not first wash before the meal, was surprised.

Then the Lord said to him, "Now then, you Pharisees clean the outside of the cup and dish, but inside you are full of greed and wickedness. You foolish people! Did not the one who made the outside make the inside also? But give what is inside ⌊the dish⌋[r] to the poor, and everything will be clean for you.

"Woe to you Pharisees, because you give God a tenth of your mint, rue and all other kinds of garden herbs, but you neglect justice and the love of God. You should have practiced the latter without leaving the former undone.

"Woe to you Pharisees, because you love the most important seats in the synagogues and greetings in the marketplaces.

[o]Or *something*   [p]Greek *unclean*   [q]Some manuscripts do not have verse 47.   [r]Or *what you have*

"Woe to you, because you are like unmarked graves, which men walk over without knowing it."

LAWYERS CONDEMNED.   One of the experts in the law answered him, "Teacher, when you say these things, you insult us also."

Lk.
11:45-52

Jesus replied, "And you experts in the law, woe to you, because you load people down with burdens they can hardly carry, and you yourselves will not lift one finger to help them.

"Woe to you, because you build tombs for the prophets, and it was your forefathers who killed them. So you testify that you approve of what your forefathers did; they killed the prophets, and you build their tombs. Because of this, God in his wisdom said, 'I will send them prophets and apostles, some of whom they will kill and others they will persecute.' Therefore this generation will be held responsible for the blood of all the prophets that has been shed since the beginning of the world, from the blood of Abel to the blood of Zechariah, who was killed between the altar and the sanctuary. Yes, I tell you, this generation will be held responsible for it all.

"Woe to you experts in the law, because you have taken away the key to knowledge. You yourselves have not entered, and you have hindered those who were entering."

LEADERS TRY TO TRAP JESUS.   When Jesus left there, the Pharisees and the teachers of the law began to oppose him fiercely and to besiege him with questions, waiting to catch him in something he might say.

Lk.
11:53,54

WARNING AGAINST HYPOCRISY.   Meanwhile, when a crowd of many thousands had gathered, so that they were trampling on one another, Jesus began to speak first to his disciples, saying: "Be on your guard against the yeast of the Pharisees, which is hypocrisy. There is nothing concealed that will not be disclosed, or hidden that will not be made known. What you have said in the dark will be heard in the daylight, and what you have whispered in the ear in the inner rooms will be proclaimed from the roofs.

Lk. 12:1-3

FEARING GOD, NOT MAN.   "I tell you, my friends, do not be afraid of those who kill the body and after that can do no more. But I will show you whom you should fear: Fear him who, after the killing of the body, has power to throw you into hell. Yes, I tell you, fear him. Are not five sparrows sold for two pennies[s]? Yet not one of them is forgotten by God. Indeed, the very hairs of your head are all numbered. Don't be afraid; you are worth more than many sparrows.

Lk. 12:4-12

"I tell you, whoever acknowledges me before men, the Son of Man will also acknowledge him before the angels of God. But he who disowns me before men will be disowned before the angels of God. And everyone who speaks a word against the Son of Man will be forgiven, but anyone who blasphemes against the Holy Spirit will not be forgiven.

"When you are brought before synagogues, rulers and authorities, do not worry about how you will defend yourselves or what you will say, for the Holy Spirit will teach you at that time what you should say."

FOOLISH RICH MAN.   Someone in the crowd said to him, "Teacher, tell my brother to divide the inheritance with me."

Lk.
12:13-21

[s]Greek *two assaria*

Jesus replied, "Man, who appointed me a judge or an arbiter between you?" Then he said to them, "Watch out! Be on your guard against all kinds of greed; a man's life does not consist in the abundance of his possessions."

And he told them this parable: "The ground of a certain rich man produced a good crop. He thought to himself, 'What shall I do? I have no place to store my crops.'

"Then he said, 'This is what I'll do. I will tear down my barns and build bigger ones, and there I will store all my grain and my goods. And I'll say to myself, "You have plenty of good things laid up for many years. Take life easy; eat, drink and be merry." '

"But God said to him, 'You fool! This very night your life will be demanded from you. Then who will get what you have prepared for yourself?'

"This is how it will be with anyone who stores up things for himself but is not rich toward God."

Lk.
12:22-34

TRUSTING GOD'S PROVIDENCE.   Then Jesus said to his disciples: "Therefore I tell you, do not worry about your life, what you will eat; or about your body, what you will wear. Life is more than food, and the body more than clothes. Consider the ravens: They do not sow or reap, they have no storeroom or barn; yet God feeds them. And how much more valuable you are than birds! Who of you by worrying can add a single hour to his life[t]? Since you cannot do this very little thing, why do you worry about the rest?

"Consider how the lilies grow. They do not labor or spin. Yet I tell you, not even Solomon in all his splendor was dressed like one of these. If that is how God clothes the grass of the field, which is here today, and tomorrow is thrown into the fire, how much more will he clothe you, O you of little faith! And do not set your heart on what you will eat or drink; do not worry about it. For the pagan world runs after all such things, and your Father knows that you need them. But seek his kingdom, and these things will be given to you as well.

"Do not be afraid, little flock, for your Father has been pleased to give you the kingdom. Sell your possessions and give to the poor. Provide purses for yourselves that will not wear out, a treasure in heaven that will not be exhausted, where no thief comes near and no moth destroys. For where your treasure is, there your heart will be also.

Lk.
12:35-40

PARABLE OF WATCHFUL SERVANTS.   "Be dressed ready for service and keep your lamps burning, like men waiting for their master to return from a wedding banquet, so that when he comes and knocks they can immediately open the door for him. It will be good for those servants whose master finds them watching when he comes. I tell you the truth, he will dress himself to serve, will have them recline at the table and will come and wait on them. It will be good for those servants whose master finds them ready, even if he comes in the second or third watch of the night. But understand this: If the owner of the house had known at what hour the thief was coming, he would not have let his house be broken into. You also must be ready, because the Son of Man will come at an hour when you do not expect him."

[t]Or *single cubit to his height*

EXHORTATION TO WATCHFULNESS.   Peter asked, "Lord, are you | Lk.
telling this parable to us, or to everyone?" | 12:41-48

The Lord answered, "Who then is the faithful and wise manager, whom the master puts in charge of his servants to give them their food allowance at the proper time? It will be good for that servant whom the master finds doing so when he returns. I tell you the truth, he will put him in charge of all his possessions. But suppose the servant says to himself, 'My master is taking a long time in coming,' and he then begins to beat the menservants and maidservants and to eat and drink and get drunk. The master of that servant will come on a day when he does not expect him and at an hour he is not aware of. He will cut him to pieces and assign him a place with the unbelievers.

"That servant who knows his master's will and does not get ready or does not do what his master wants will be beaten with many blows. But the one who does not know and does things deserving punishment will be beaten with few blows. From everyone who has been given much, much will be demanded; and from the one who has been entrusted with much, much more will be asked.

DIVISION PREDICTED.   "I have come to bring fire on the earth, and how | Lk.
I wish it were already kindled! But I have a baptism to undergo, and how | 12:49-53
distressed I am until it is completed! Do you think I came to bring peace on earth? No, I tell you, but division. From now on there will be five in one family divided against each other, three against two and two against three. They will be divided, father against son and son against father, mother against daughter and daughter against mother, mother-in-law against daughter-in-law and daughter-in-law against mother-in-law."

TIMELY ACCEPTANCE URGED.   He said to the crowd: "When you see | Lk.
a cloud rising in the west, immediately you say, 'It's going to rain,' and it | 12:54-59
does. And when the south wind blows, you say, 'It's going to be hot,' and it is. Hypocrites! You know how to interpret the appearance of the earth and the sky. How is it that you don't know how to interpret this present time?

"Why don't you judge for yourselves what is right? As you are going with your adversary to the magistrate, try hard to be reconciled to him on the way, or he may drag you off to the judge, and the judge turn you over to the officer, and the officer throw you into prison. I tell you, you will not get out until you have paid the last penny.[u]"

URGENCY OF REPENTANCE.   Now there were some present at that | Lk. 13:1-5
time who told Jesus about the Galileans whose blood Pilate had mixed with their sacrifices. Jesus answered, "Do you think that these Galileans were worse sinners than all the other Galileans because they suffered this way? I tell you, no! But unless you repent, you too will all perish. Or those eighteen who died when the tower in Siloam fell on them—do you think they were more guilty than all the others living in Jerusalem? I tell you, no! But unless you repent, you too will all perish."

UNFRUITFUL FIG TREE.   Then he told this parable: "A man had a fig | Lk. 13:6-9
tree, planted in his vineyard, and he went to look for fruit on it, but did not find any. So he said to the man who took care of the vineyard, 'For three

[u]Greek lepton

years now I've been coming to look for fruit on this fig tree and haven't found any. Cut it down! Why should it use up the soil?'

" 'Sir,' the man replied, 'leave it alone for one more year, and I'll dig around it and fertilize it. If it bears fruit next year, fine! If not, then cut it down.' "

Lk. 13:10-17

STOOPED WOMAN HEALED.   On a Sabbath Jesus was teaching in one of the synagogues, and a woman was there who had been crippled by a spirit for eighteen years. She was bent over and could not straighten up at all. When Jesus saw her, he called her forward and said to her, "Woman, you are set free from your infirmity." Then he put his hands on her, and immediately she straightened up and praised God.

Indignant because Jesus had healed on the Sabbath, the synagogue ruler said to the people, "There are six days for work. So come and be healed on those days, not on the Sabbath."

The Lord answered him, "You hypocrites! Doesn't each of you on the Sabbath untie his ox or donkey from the stall and lead it out to give it water? Then should not this woman, a daughter of Abraham, whom Satan has kept bound for eighteen long years, be set free on the Sabbath day from what bound her?"

When he said this, all his opponents were humiliated, but the people were delighted with all the wonderful things he was doing.

Teaching Through Parables

*B*etween the many heated confrontations, Jesus continues to teach his disciples quietly concerning the kingdom of God. As the Great Teacher, Jesus uses numerous methods of instructing his disciples. He employs hyperbole, warnings, laments, and denunciations. He presents truth through beatitudes, proverbs, and dialogue. Of all his methods, however, perhaps the most interesting and distinctive mode of teaching is his use of parables. These illustrations of a moral truth or principle are usually in the form of a simple comparison. As often as not, Jesus' parables are comparisons with things either found in nature or known through human experience.

Although Jesus says the parables will have the effect of concealing truth, he must have in mind those hearers whose hearts are closed to his teaching. Most of the lessons are fairly simple to understand and especially well-suited for the common man, to whom Jesus directs his teaching.

Many parables are recorded by the Gospel writers throughout Jesus' ministry, but a particular series has been collected, principally by Matthew, which gives unique insight into Jesus' use of these simple illustrations.

Mt. 13:1-9
Mk. 4:1-9
Lk. 8:4-8
Sea of Galilee

PARABLE OF THE SOWER.   That same day Jesus went out of the house and sat by the lake. Such large crowds gathered around him that he got into a boat and sat in it, while all the people stood on the shore. Then he told them many things in parables, saying: "A farmer went out to sow his seed. As he was scattering the seed, some fell along the path, and the birds came and ate it up. Some fell on rocky places, where it did not have much soil. It sprang up quickly, because the soil was shallow. But when the sun came up, the plants were scorched, and they withered because they had no root. Other seed fell among thorns, which grew up and choked the plants. Still other seed fell on good soil, where it produced a crop—a hundred, sixty or thirty times what was sown. He who has ears, let him hear."

PURPOSE OF PARABLES.   The disciples came to him and asked, "Why do you speak to the people in parables?"

He replied, "The knowledge of the secrets of the kingdom of heaven has been given to you, but not to them. Whoever has will be given more, and he will have an abundance. Whoever does not have, even what he has will be taken from him. This is why I speak to them in parables:

> "Though seeing, they do not see;
> though hearing, they do not hear or understand.

In them is fulfilled the prophecy of Isaiah:

> " 'You will be ever hearing but never understanding;
>   you will be ever seeing but never perceiving.
> For this people's heart has become calloused;
>   they hardly hear with their ears,
>   and they have closed their eyes.
> Otherwise they might see with their eyes,
>   hear with their ears,
>   understand with their hearts
> and turn, and I would heal them.'[v]

But blessed are your eyes because they see, and your ears because they hear. For I tell you the truth, many prophets and righteous men longed to see what you see but did not see it, and to hear what you hear but did not hear it.

PARABLE OF SOWER EXPLAINED.   "Listen then to what the parable of the sower means: When anyone hears the message about the kingdom and does not understand it, the evil one comes and snatches away what was sown in his heart. This is the seed sown along the path. The one who received the seed that fell on rocky places is the man who hears the word and at once receives it with joy. But since he has no root, he lasts only a short time. When trouble or persecution comes because of the word, he quickly falls away. The one who received the seed that fell among the thorns is the man who hears the word, but the worries of this life and the deceitfulness of wealth choke it, making it unfruitful. But the one who received the seed that fell on good soil is the man who hears the word and understands it. He produces a crop, yielding a hundred, sixty or thirty times what was sown."

PARABLE OF THE WEEDS.   Jesus told them another parable: "The kingdom of heaven is like a man who sowed good seed in his field. But while everyone was sleeping, his enemy came and sowed weeds among the wheat, and went away. When the wheat sprouted and formed heads, then the weeds also appeared.

"The owner's servants came to him and said, 'Sir, didn't you sow good seed in your field? Where then did the weeds come from?'

Mt.
13:10-17
Mk.
4:10-12
Lk. 8:9,10

Mt.
13:18-23
Mk.
4:13-20
Lk. 8:11-15

Mt.
13:24-30

[v]Isaiah 6:9, 10

" 'An enemy did this,' he replied.

"The servants asked him, 'Do you want us to go and pull them up?'

" 'No,' he answered, 'because while you are pulling the weeds, you may root up the wheat with them. Let both grow together until the harvest. At that time I will tell the harvesters: First collect the weeds and tie them in bundles to be burned; then gather the wheat and bring it into my barn.' "

Mt.
13:36-43
PARABLE OF THE WEEDS EXPLAINED.   Then he left the crowd and went into the house. His disciples came to him and said, "Explain to us the parable of the weeds in the field."

He answered, "The one who sowed the good seed is the Son of Man. The field is the world, and the good seed stands for the sons of the kingdom. The weeds are the sons of the evil one, and the enemy who sows them is the devil. The harvest is the end of the age, and the harvesters are angels.

"As the weeds are pulled up and burned in the fire, so it will be at the end of the age. The Son of Man will send out his angels, and they will weed out of his kingdom everything that causes sin and all who do evil. They will throw them into the fiery furnace, where there will be weeping and gnashing of teeth. Then the righteous will shine like the sun in the kingdom of their Father. He who has ears, let him hear.

Mk.
4:21-25
Lk. 8:16-18
PARABLE OF THE LIGHTED LAMP.   He said to them, "Do you bring in a lamp to put it under a bowl or a bed? Instead, don't you put it on its stand? For whatever is hidden is meant to be disclosed, and whatever is concealed is meant to be brought out into the open. If anyone has ears to hear, let him hear."

"Consider carefully what you hear," he continued. "With the measure you use, it will be measured to you—and even more. Whoever has will be given more; whoever does not have, even what he has will be taken from him."

Mk.
4:26-29
PARABLE OF THE SEED GROWING.   He also said, "This is what the kingdom of God is like. A man scatters seed on the ground. Night and day, whether he sleeps or gets up, the seed sprouts and grows, though he does not know how. All by itself the soil produces grain—first the stalk, then the head, then the full kernel in the head. As soon as the grain is ripe, he puts the sickle to it, because the harvest has come."

Mt.
13:31,32
Mk.
4:30-32
Lk.
13:18,19
PARABLE OF THE MUSTARD SEED.   He told them another parable: "The kingdom of heaven is like a mustard seed, which a man took and planted in his field. Though it is the smallest of all your seeds, yet when it grows, it is the largest of garden plants and becomes a tree, so that the birds of the air come and perch in its branches."

Mt. 13:33
Lk.
13:20,21
PARABLE OF THE YEAST.   He told them still another parable: "The kingdom of heaven is like yeast that a woman took and mixed into a large amount ^{w} of flour until it worked all through the dough."

Mt. 13:44
PARABLE OF HIDDEN TREASURE.   "The kingdom of heaven is like treasure hidden in a field. When a man found it, he hid it again, and then in his joy went and sold all he had and bought that field.

^{w}Greek *three satas* (probably about 1/2 bushel or 22 liters)

PARABLE OF VALUABLE PEARL.   "Again, the kingdom of heaven is like a merchant looking for fine pearls. When he found one of great value, he went away and sold everything he had and bought it.   Mt. 13:45,46

PARABLE OF THE NET.   "Once again, the kingdom of heaven is like a net that was let down into the lake and caught all kinds of fish. When it was full, the fishermen pulled it up on the shore. Then they sat down and collected the good fish in baskets, but threw the bad away. This is how it will be at the end of the age. The angels will come and separate the wicked from the righteous and throw them into the fiery furnace, where there will be weeping and gnashing of teeth.   Mt. 13:47-50

PARABLE OF TREASURES.   "Have you understood all these things?" Jesus asked.   Mt. 13:51,52
    "Yes," they replied.
    He said to them, "Therefore every teacher of the law who has been instructed about the kingdom of heaven is like the owner of a house who brings out of his storeroom new treasures as well as old."

PARABLES FULFILL PROPHECY.   Mk With many similar parables Jesus spoke the word to them, as much as they could understand. He did not say anything to them without using a parable. But when he was alone with his own disciples, he explained everything. MtSo was fulfilled what was spoken through the prophet: Mt. 13:34,35 Mk. 4:33,34

> "I will open my mouth in parables,
>   I will utter things hidden since the creation of the
>   world."ˣ

Performing Miracles

t is one thing for a man to teach what he claims is truth; it is quite another thing to demonstrate one's authority to claim that truth. That is why the miracles which Jesus performs are such a vital part of his ministry. They are not being performed merely to entertain, or to show off his divine power, or even to convince the skeptical. Nor does Jesus heal the sick and raise the dead simply because of his great compassion for those who suffer.

More than this, the miracles are a means of confirming the message that the kingdom of God is now being established with power! God is establishing his rule through Christ, and proving it with the miraculous power which Jesus exercises over the forces of nature, over the spirit world, and over death and disease. Mark's account takes Jesus from his teaching in parables and follows him throughout Galilee as he confirms the authority of his teaching with miraculous works.

CHALLENGING FOLLOWERS.   Mt When Jesus saw the crowd around him, he gave orders to cross to the other side of the lake. Then a teacher of the law came to him and said, "Teacher, I will follow you wherever you go." Lk Jesus replied, "Foxes have holes and birds of the air have nests, but the Son of Man has no place to lay his head."   Mt. 8:18-22 Lk. 9:57-62

ˣPsalm 78:2

He said to another man, "Follow me."

But the man replied, "Lord, first let me go and bury my father."

Jesus said to him, "Let the dead bury their own dead, but you go and proclaim the kingdom of God."

Still another said, "I will follow you, Lord; but first let me go back and say good-by to my family."

Jesus replied, "No one who puts his hand to the plow and looks back is fit for service in the kingdom of God."

Mt. 8:23-27
Mk. 4:35-41
Lk. 8:22-25
Sea of Galilee

JESUS CALMS THE SEA.   That day when evening came, he said to his disciples, "Let us go over to the other side." Leaving the crowd behind, they took him along, just as he was, in the boat. There were also other boats with him. A furious squall came up, and the waves broke over the boat, so that it was nearly swamped. Jesus was in the stern, sleeping on a cushion. The disciples woke him and said to him, "Teacher, don't you care if we drown?"

He got up, rebuked the wind and said to the waves, "Quiet! Be still!" Then the wind died down and it was completely calm.

He said to his disciples, "Why are you so afraid? Do you still have no faith?"

They were terrified and asked each other, "Who is this? Even the wind and the waves obey him!"

Mt. 8:28-34
Mk. 5:1-20
Lk. 8:26-39
Gerasa

DEMON-POSSESSED GERASENE.   They went across the lake to the region of the Gerasenes.[y] When Jesus got out of the boat, a man with an evil[z] spirit came from the tombs to meet him. This man lived in the tombs, and no one could bind him any more, not even with a chain. For he had often been chained hand and foot, but he tore the chains apart and broke the irons on his feet. No one was strong enough to subdue him. Night and day among the tombs and in the hills he would cry out and cut himself with stones.

When he saw Jesus from a distance, he ran and fell on his knees in front of him. He shouted at the top of his voice, "What do you want with me, Jesus, Son of the Most High God? Swear to God that you won't torture me!" For Jesus had said to him, "Come out of this man, you evil spirit!"

Then Jesus asked him, "What is your name?"

"My name is Legion," he replied, "for we are many." And he begged Jesus again and again not to send them out of the area.

A large herd of pigs was feeding on the nearby hillside. The demons begged Jesus, "Send us among the pigs; allow us to go into them." He gave them permission, and the evil spirits came out and went into the pigs. The herd, about two thousand in number, rushed down the steep bank into the lake and were drowned.

Those tending the pigs ran off and reported this in the town and countryside, and the people went out to see what had happened. When they came to Jesus, they saw the man who had been possessed by the legion of demons, sitting there, dressed and in his right mind; and they were afraid. Those who had seen it told the people what had happened to the demon-possessed man—and told about the pigs as well. Then the people began to plead with Jesus to leave their region.

As Jesus was getting into the boat, the man who had been demon-

[y]Some manuscripts *Gadarenes*; other manuscripts *Gergesenes*   [z]Greek *unclean*

possessed begged to go with him. Jesus did not let him, but said, "Go home to your family and tell them how much the Lord has done for you, and how he has had mercy on you." So the man went away and began to tell in the Decapolis[a] how much Jesus had done for him. And all the people were amazed.

JAIRUS BEGS JESUS TO HEAL.   When Jesus had again crossed over by boat to the other side of the lake, a large crowd gathered around him while he was by the lake. Then one of the synagogue rulers, named Jairus, came there. Seeing Jesus, he fell at his feet and pleaded earnestly with him, "My little daughter is dying. Please come and put your hands on her so that she will be healed and live." So Jesus went with him.

Mt. 9:18,19
Mk.
5:21-24a
Lk. 8:40-42

WOMAN TOUCHES GARMENT.   A large crowd followed and pressed around him. And a woman was there who had been subject to bleeding for twelve years. She had suffered a great deal under the care of many doctors and had spent all she had, yet instead of getting better she grew worse. When she heard about Jesus, she came up behind him in the crowd and touched his cloak, because she thought, "If I just touch his clothes, I will be healed." Immediately her bleeding stopped and she felt in her body that she was freed from her suffering.

Mt. 9:20-22
Mk.
5:24b-34
Lk. 8:43-48

At once Jesus realized that power had gone out from him. He turned around in the crowd and asked, "Who touched my clothes?"

"You see the people crowding against you," his disciples answered, "and yet you can ask, 'Who touched me?' "

But Jesus kept looking around to see who had done it. Then the woman, knowing what had happened to her, came and fell at his feet and, trembling with fear, told him the whole truth. He said to her, "Daughter, your faith has healed you. Go in peace and be freed from your suffering."

JAIRUS' DAUGHTER RAISED.   While Jesus was still speaking, some men came from the house of Jairus, the synagogue ruler. "Your daughter is dead," they said. "Why bother the teacher any more?"

Mt. 9:23-26
Mk.
5:35-43
Lk. 8:49-56
Capernaum

Ignoring what they said, Jesus told the synagogue ruler, "Don't be afraid; just believe."

He did not let anyone follow him except Peter, James and John the brother of James. When they came to the home of the synagogue ruler, Jesus saw a commotion, with people crying and wailing loudly. He went in and said to them, "Why all this commotion and wailing? The child is not dead but asleep." But they laughed at him.

After he put them all out, he took the child's father and mother and the disciples who were with him, and went in where the child was. He took her by the hand and said to her, *"Talitha koum!"* (which means, "Little girl, I say to you, get up!"). Immediately the girl stood up and walked around (she was twelve years old). At this they were completely astonished. He gave strict orders not to let anyone know about this, and told them to give her something to eat.

TWO BLIND MEN HEALED.   As Jesus went on from there, two blind men followed him, calling out, "Have mercy on us, Son of David!"

Mt. 9:27-31

When he had gone indoors, the blind men came to him, and he asked them, "Do you believe that I am able to do this?"

"Yes, Lord," they replied.

[a]That is, the Ten Cities

Then he touched their eyes and said, "According to your faith will it be done to you"; and their sight was restored. Jesus warned them sternly, "See that no one knows about this." But they went out and spread the news about him all over that region.

Mt. 9:32-34 MUTE MADE TO SPEAK.   While they were going out, a man who was demon-possessed and could not talk was brought to Jesus. And when the demon was driven out, the man who had been mute spoke. The crowd was amazed and said, "Nothing like this has ever been seen in Israel."

But the Pharisees said, "It is by the prince of demons that he drives out demons."

Mt.
13:53-58
Mk. 6:1-6a
Nazareth
JESUS REJECTED AGAIN.   Jesus left there and went to his hometown, accompanied by his disciples. When the Sabbath came, he began to teach in the synagogue, and many who heard him were amazed.

"Where did this man get these things?" they asked. "What's this wisdom that has been given him, that he even does miracles! Isn't this the carpenter? Isn't this Mary's son and the brother of James, Joseph,[b] Judas and Simon? Aren't his sisters here with us?" And they took offense at him.

Jesus said to them, "Only in his hometown, among his relatives and in his own house is a prophet without honor." He could not do any miracles there, except lay his hands on a few sick people and heal them. And he was amazed at their lack of faith.

Sending Out Apostles

*A*fter his second rejection in his hometown of Nazareth, Jesus gains renewed encouragement as he is met by crowds in other parts of Galilee. Keenly aware of their need for spiritual guidance, Jesus calls for those who are willing to work among the multitudes for the sake of his kingdom. The time is especially appropriate, then, for sending out the 12 apostles on a special mission of teaching and performing miracles with the power he gives them. He warns them that they, like all who would work in the Lord's name, will be persecuted and will face the need for sacrifice.

Perhaps for that reason, or perhaps to provide a stronger witness of his messiahship, Jesus sends the apostles out in pairs. Interestingly, Jesus does not appear to place particular emphasis on organization, methods of evangelism, or academic religious training. The 12 apostles are mostly of simple education, but the power of Christ is with them.

As the apostles are away carrying out their mission, Jesus will hear that John the Baptist has been put to death by Herod.

Mt. 9:35-38
Mk. 6:6b
NEED FOR WORKERS.   Jesus went through all the towns and villages, teaching in their synagogues, preaching the good news of the kingdom and healing every disease and sickness. When he saw the crowds, he had compassion on them, because they were harassed and helpless, like sheep without a shepherd. Then he said to his disciples, "The harvest is plentiful but the workers are few. Ask the Lord of the harvest, therefore, to send out workers into his harvest field."

---

[b]Greek *Joses*, a variant of *Joseph*

APOSTLES GIVEN POWER TO HEAL.   MkCalling the Twelve to him, he sent them out two by two... Mtand gave them authority to drive out evilc spirits and to heal every disease and sickness.

Mt. 10:1-4
Mk. 6:7
Lk. 9:1,2

APOSTLES INSTRUCTED.   These twelve Jesus sent out with the following instructions: "Do not go among the Gentiles or enter any town of the Samaritans. Go rather to the lost sheep of Israel. As you go, preach this message: 'The kingdom of heaven is near.' Heal the sick, raise the dead, cleanse those who have leprosy,d drive out demons. Freely you have received, freely give. Do not take along any gold or silver or copper in your belts; take no bag for the journey, or extra tunic, or sandals or a staff; for the worker is worth his keep.

Mt. 10:5-15
Mk. 6:8-11
Lk. 9:3-5

"Whatever town or village you enter, search for some worthy person there and stay at his house until you leave. As you enter the home, give it your greeting. If the home is deserving, let your peace rest on it; if it is not, let your peace return to you. If anyone will not welcome you or listen to your words, shake the dust off your feet when you leave that home or town. I tell you the truth, it will be more bearable for Sodom and Gomorrah on the day of judgment than for that town.

APOSTLES WARNED.   I am sending you out like sheep among wolves. Therefore be as shrewd as snakes and as innocent as doves.

Mt.
10:16-33

"Be on your guard against men; they will hand you over to the local councils and flog you in their synagogues. On my account you will be brought before governors and kings as witnesses to them and to the Gentiles. But when they arrest you, do not worry about what to say or how to say it. At that time you will be given what to say, for it will not be you speaking, but the Spirit of your Father speaking through you.

"Brother will betray brother to death, and a father his child; children will rebel against their parents and have them put to death. All men will hate you because of me, but he who stands firm to the end will be saved. When you are persecuted in one place, flee to another. I tell you the truth, you will not finish going through the cities of Israel before the Son of Man comes.

"A student is not above his teacher, nor a servant above his master. It is enough for the student to be like his teacher, and the servant like his master. If the head of the house has been called Beelzebub,e how much more the members of his household!

"So do not be afraid of them. There is nothing concealed that will not be disclosed, or hidden that will not be made known. What I tell you in the dark, speak in the daylight; what is whispered in your ear, proclaim from the roofs. Do not be afraid of those who kill the body but cannot kill the soul. Rather, be afraid of the One who can destroy both soul and body in hell. Are not two sparrows sold for a pennyf? Yet not one of them will fall to the ground apart from the will of your Father. And even the very hairs of your head are all numbered. So don't be afraid; you are worth more than many sparrows.

"Whoever acknowledges me before men, I will also acknowledge him before my Father in heaven. But whoever disowns me before men, I will disown him before my Father in heaven.

cGreek *unclean*   dThe Greek word was used for various diseases affecting the skin—not necessarily leprosy.   eGreek *Beezeboul* or *Beelzeboul*   fGreek *an assarion*

Mt.
10: 34-39
	CONFLICT AND SACRIFICE. "Do not suppose that I have come to bring peace to the earth. I did not come to bring peace, but a sword. For I have come to turn
	
	   " 'a man against his father,
	      a daughter against her mother,
	       a daughter-in-law against her mother-in-law—
	        a man's enemies will be the members of his own
	           household.'[g]
	
	"Anyone who loves his father or mother more than me is not worthy of me; anyone who loves his son or daughter more than me is not worthy of me; and anyone who does not take his cross and follow me is not worthy of me. Whoever finds his life will lose it, and whoever loses his life for my sake will find it.

Mt. 10:40-42	**RECEIVING APOSTLES.** "He who receives you receives me, and he who receives me receives the one who sent me. Anyone who receives a prophet because he is a prophet will receive a prophet's reward, and anyone who receives a righteous man because he is a righteous man will receive a righteous man's reward. And if anyone gives even a cup of cold water to one of these little ones because he is my disciple, I tell you the truth, he will certainly not lose his reward."
Mt. 11:1 Mk. 6:12,13 Lk. 9:6	**APOSTLES IN ACTION.** [Mt]After Jesus had finished instructing his twelve disciples, he went on from there to teach and preach in the towns of Galilee.[h] [Lk]So they set out and went from village to village, preaching the gospel and healing people everywhere.

Mt. 14:1,2
Mk.
6:14-16
Lk. 9:7-9
Perea
	HEROD CURIOUS ABOUT JESUS. [Mk]King Herod heard about this, for Jesus' name had become well known. Some were saying,[i] "John the Baptist has been raised from the dead, and that is why miraculous powers are at work in him."
	    Others said, "He is Elijah."
	    And still others claimed, "He is a prophet, like one of the prophets of long ago."
	    But when Herod heard this, he said, "John, the man I beheaded, has been raised from the dead!" [Lk]. . ."I beheaded John. Who, then, is this I hear such things about?" And he tried to see him.

Mt.
14:3-12a
Mk.
6:17-29
	DEATH OF JOHN THE BAPTIST. [Mk]For Herod himself had given orders to have John arrested, and he had him bound and put in prison. He did this because of Herodias, his brother Philip's wife, whom he had married. For John had been saying to Herod, "It is not lawful for you to have your brother's wife." So Herodias nursed a grudge against John and wanted to kill him. But she was not able to, because Herod feared John and protected him, knowing him to be a righteous and holy man. When Herod heard John, he was greatly puzzled[j]; yet he liked to listen to him.
	    Finally the opportune time came. On his birthday Herod gave a banquet for his high officials and military commanders and the leading men of Galilee. When the daughter of Herodias came in and danced, she pleased Herod and his dinner guests.
	    The king said to the girl, "Ask me for anything you want, and I'll give it

[g]Micah 7:6   [h]Greek *in their towns*   [i]Some early manuscripts *He was saying*
[j]Some early manuscripts *he did many things*

to you." And he promised her with an oath, "Whatever you ask I will give you, up to half my kingdom."

She went out and said to her mother, "What shall I ask for?"

"The head of John the Baptist," she answered.

At once the girl hurried in to the king with the request: "I want you to give me right now the head of John the Baptist on a platter."

The king was greatly distressed, but because of his oaths and his dinner guests, he did not want to refuse her. So he immediately sent an executioner with orders to bring John's head. The man went, beheaded John in the prison, and brought back his head on a platter. He presented it to the girl, and she gave it to her mother. ᴹᵗJohn's disciples came and took his body and buried it.

APOSTLES' RETURN AND REPORT. ᴸᵏWhen the apostles returned, they reported to Jesus what they had done. ᴹᵏThen, because so many people were coming and going that they did not even have a chance to eat, he said to them, "Come with me by yourselves to a quiet place and get some rest."

So they went away by themselves in a boat . . . ᴶⁿto the far shore of the Sea of Galilee (that is, the Sea of Tiberias), ᴹᵏto a solitary place. But many who saw them leaving recognized them and ran on foot from all the towns and got there ahead of them.

Mt.
14:12b,13
Mk.
6:30-33
Lk.
9:10,11a
Jn. 6:1

Miracles and Multitudes

As his ministry nears its second year, Jesus reaches a peak of popularity among the multitudes. He amazes a crowd of over 5000 by feeding them all, using just a few loaves of bread and some fish. Upon that demonstration they are ready to make him king, but of course they have misunderstood the nature of his kingdom. When Jesus says that he is the true bread of life and that they must eat his flesh, many are offended and turn away. They can accept Jesus as a popular hero who works wonders, but they are unwilling to accept the demands of discipleship.

Jesus continues his dialogue with the Pharisees, pointing out the danger of legalism, especially regarding traditional doctrinal rules which are not a part of the law. Naturally, Jesus' condemnation of their institutionalized religion, as well as his threat to their political power base, evokes their hostility. Opposition in Judea grows to such a point that the political and religious leaders there are seeking to kill Jesus. Therefore Jesus remains in Galilee for a while longer, apparently not even leaving to attend the Passover Feast in Jerusalem, which takes place during this time.

Despite his opposition, what is so impressive about Jesus is the extent to which he has won the hearts of the common people. The prophets of old had also preached righteousness and brought judgment against false religious leaders, but none of them ever had the popular following of Jesus. Which of the prophets could match Jesus' insight? Which of the prophets could approach Jesus' personal righteousness? And which of the prophets did the people want to make their king? This Jesus is not just another prophet, but rather the Messiah about whom all the other prophets have prophesied.

Mt. 14:14
Mk. 6:34
Lk. 9:11b
Jn. 6:2-4

JESUS TEACHES MULTITUDE. ᴹᵏWhen Jesus landed and saw a large crowd, he had compassion on them, because they were like sheep without a shepherd. So he began teaching them many things. ᴸᵏHe welcomed them and spoke to them about the kingdom of God, and healed those who needed healing. ᴶⁿThe Jewish Passover Feast was near.

[Third
Passover
April,
A.D. 29]
Mt.
14:15-21
Mk.
6:35-44
Lk. 9:12-17
Jn. 6:5-14

FIVE THOUSAND FED. ᴹᵏBy this time it was late in the day, so his disciples came to him. "This is a remote place," they said, "and it's already very late. Send the people away so they can go to the surrounding countryside and villages and buy themselves something to eat." ᴶⁿWhen Jesus looked up and saw a great crowd coming toward him, he said to Philip, "Where shall we buy bread for these people to eat?" He asked this only to test him, for he already had in mind what he was going to do.

Philip answered him, "Eight months' wagesᵏ would not buy enough bread for each one to have a bite!"

Another of his disciples, Andrew, Simon Peter's brother, spoke up, "Here is a boy with five small barley loaves and two small fish, but how far will they go among so many?" ᴹᵏThen Jesus directed them to have all the people sit down in groups on the green grass. So they sat down in groups of hundreds and fifties. Taking the five loaves and the two fish and looking up to heaven, he gave thanks and broke the loaves. Then he gave them to his disciples to set before the people. He also divided the two fish among them all. They all ate and were satisfied, and the disciples picked up twelve basketfuls of broken pieces of bread and fish. The number of the men who had eaten was five thousand. ᴶⁿAfter the people saw the miraculous sign that Jesus did, they began to say, "Surely this is the Prophet who is to come into the world."

Mt.
14:22,23a
Mk.
6:45,46
Jn. 6:15-17a

KINGSHIP AVOIDED. ᴹᵏImmediately Jesus made his disciples get into the boat and go on ahead of him to Bethsaida, while he dismissed the crowd. ᴶⁿJesus, knowing that they intended to come and make him king by force, withdrew again to a mountain by himself.

Mt.
14:23b-27
Mk.
6:47-50
Jn.
6:17b-21

JESUS WALKS ON WATER. ᴶⁿBy now it was dark, and Jesus had not yet joined them. A strong wind was blowing and the waters grew rough. ᴹᵏHe saw the disciples straining at the oars, because the wind was against them. About the fourth watch of the night he went out to them, walking on the lake. ᴶⁿWhen they had rowed three or three and a half miles,ˡ they saw Jesus approaching the boat, walking on the water . . . ᴹᵏHe was about to pass by them, but when they saw him walking on the lake, they thought he was a ghost. They cried out, because they all saw him and were terrified.

Immediately he spoke to them and said, "Take courage! It is I. Don't be afraid."

Mt.
14:28-33
Mk.
6:51,52
Sea of
Galilee

PETER WALKS ON WATER. ᴹᵗ"Lord, if it's you," Peter replied, "tell me to come to you on the water."

"Come," he said.

Then Peter got down out of the boat, walked on the water and came toward Jesus. But when he saw the wind, he was afraid and, beginning to sink, cried out, "Lord, save me!"

ᵏGreek *two hundred denarii*   ˡGreek *rowed twenty-five or thirty stadia* (about 5 or 6 kilometers)

Immediately Jesus reached out his hand and caught him. "You of little faith," he said, "why did you doubt?"

And when they climbed into the boat, the wind died down. Mk They were completely amazed, for they had not understood about the loaves; their hearts were hardened. Mt Then those who were in the boat worshiped him, saying, "Truly you are the Son of God."

MIRACLES AT GENNESARET.   When they had crossed over, they land-ed at Gennesaret and anchored there. As soon as they got out of the boat, people recognized Jesus. They ran throughout that whole region and car-ried the sick on mats to wherever they heard he was. And wherever he went—into villages, towns or countryside—they placed the sick in the marketplaces. They begged him to let them touch even the edge of his cloak, and all who touched him were healed.

Mt.
14:34-36
Mk.
6:53-56
Plain of
Gennesaret

JESUS' CROSSING IS MYSTERY.   The next day the crowd that had stayed on the opposite shore of the lake realized that only one boat had been there, and that Jesus had not entered it with his disciples, but that they had gone away alone. Then some boats from Tiberias landed near the place where the people had eaten the bread after the Lord had given thanks. Once the crowd realized that neither Jesus nor his disciples were there, they got into the boats and went to Capernaum in search of Jesus.

Jn. 6:22-24

DISCOURSE ON BREAD OF LIFE.   When they found him on the other side of the lake, they asked him, "Rabbi, when did you get here?"

Jn. 6:25-40
Capernaum

Jesus answered, "I tell you the truth, you are looking for me, not because you saw miraculous signs but because you ate the loaves and had your fill. Do not work for food that spoils, but for food that endures to eternal life, which the Son of Man will give you. On him God the Father has placed his seal of approval."

Then they asked him, "What must we do to do the works God re-quires?"

Jesus answered, "The work of God is this: to believe in the one he has sent."

So they asked him, "What miraculous sign then will you give that we may see it and believe you? What will you do? Our forefathers ate the manna in the desert; as it is written: 'He gave them bread from heaven to eat.' m "

Jesus said to them, "I tell you the truth, it is not Moses who has given you the bread from heaven, but it is my Father who gives you the true bread from heaven. For the bread of God is he who comes down from heaven and gives life to the world."

"Sir," they said, "from now on give us this bread."

Then Jesus declared, "I am the bread of life. He who comes to me will never go hungry, and he who believes in me will never be thirsty. But as I told you, you have seen me and still you do not believe. All that the Father gives me will come to me, and whoever comes to me I will never drive away. For I have come down from heaven not to do my will but to do the will of him who sent me. And this is the will of him who sent me, that I shall lose none of all that he has given me, but raise them up at the last day. For my Father's will is that everyone who looks to the Son and

m Exodus 16:4; Neh. 9:15; Psalm 78:24,25

believes in him shall have eternal life, and I will raise him up at the last day."

Jn. 6:41-51 JEWS CHALLENGE JESUS' CLAIM.   At this the Jews began to grumble about him because he said, "I am the bread that came down from heaven." They said, "Is this not Jesus, the son of Joseph, whose father and mother we know? How can he now say, 'I came down from heaven'?"

"Stop grumbling among yourselves," Jesus answered. "No one can come to me unless the Father who sent me draws him, and I will raise him up at the last day. It is written in the Prophets: 'They will all be taught by God.'[n] Everyone who listens to the Father and learns from him comes to me. No one has seen the Father except the one who is from God; only he has seen the Father. I tell you the truth, he who believes has everlasting life. I am the bread of life. Your forefathers ate the manna in the desert, yet they died. But here is the bread that comes down from heaven, which a man may eat and not die. I am the living bread that came down from heaven. If anyone eats of this bread, he will live forever. This bread is my flesh, which I will give for the life of the world."

Jn. 6:52-59 JEWS QUESTION EATING FLESH.   Then the Jews began to argue sharply among themselves, "How can this man give us his flesh to eat?"

Jesus said to them, "I tell you the truth, unless you eat the flesh of the Son of Man and drink his blood, you have no life in you. Whoever eats my flesh and drinks my blood has eternal life, and I will raise him up at the last day. For my flesh is real food and my blood is real drink. Whoever eats my flesh and drinks my blood remains in me, and I in him. Just as the living Father sent me and I live because of the Father, so the one who feeds on me will live because of me. This is the bread that came down from heaven. Your forefathers ate manna and died, but he who feeds on this bread will live forever." He said this while teaching in the synagogue in Capernaum.

Jn. 6:60-66 OFFENDED DISCIPLES TURN AWAY.   On hearing it, many of his disciples said, "This is a hard teaching. Who can accept it?"

Aware that his disciples were grumbling about this, Jesus said to them, "Does this offend you? What if you see the Son of Man ascend to where he was before! The Spirit gives life; the flesh counts for nothing. The words I have spoken to you are spirit[o] and they are life. Yet there are some of you who do not believe." For Jesus had known from the beginning which of them did not believe and who would betray him. He went on to say, "This is why I told you that no one can come to me unless the Father has enabled him."

From this time many of his disciples turned back and no longer followed him.

Jn. 6:67-71 PETER AFFIRMS FAITH.   "You do not want to leave too, do you?" Jesus
Capernaum asked the Twelve.

Simon Peter answered him, "Lord, to whom shall we go? You have the words of eternal life. We believe and know that you are the Holy One of God."

Then Jesus replied, "Have I not chosen you, the Twelve? Yet one of you is a devil!" (He meant Judas, the son of Simon Iscariot, who, though one of the Twelve, was later to betray him.)

[n] Isaiah 54:13   [o] Or Spirit

TRADITION CONDEMNED. The Pharisees and some of the teachers of the law who had come from Jerusalem gathered around Jesus and saw some of his disciples eating food with hands that were "unclean," that is, unwashed. (The Pharisees and all the Jews do not eat unless they give their hands a ceremonial washing, holding to the tradition of the elders. When they come from the marketplace they do not eat unless they wash. And they observe many other traditions, such as the washing of cups, pitchers and kettles.*p*)

So the Pharisees and teachers of the law asked Jesus, "Why don't your disciples live according to the tradition of the elders instead of eating their food with 'unclean' hands?"

He replied, "Isaiah was right when he prophesied about you hypocrites; as it is written:

" 'These people honor me with their lips,
        but their hearts are far from me.
    They worship me in vain;
        their teachings are but rules taught by men.'*q*

You have let go of the commands of God and are holding on to the traditions of men."

And he said to them: "You have a fine way of setting aside the commands of God in order to observe*r* your own traditions! For Moses said, 'Honor your father and your mother,'*s* and, 'Anyone who curses his father or mother must be put to death.'*t* But you say that if a man says to his father or mother: 'Whatever help you might otherwise have received from me is Corban' (that is, a gift devoted to God), then you no longer let him do anything for his father or mother. Thus you nullify the word of God by your tradition that you have handed down. And you do many things like that."

Mt. 15:1-9
Mk. 7:1-13
(Spring,
A.D. 29)

DEFILEMENT CONTRASTED. *Mk*Again Jesus called the crowd to him and said, "Listen to me, everyone, and understand this. Nothing outside a man can make him 'unclean' by going into him. Rather, it is what comes out of a man that makes him 'unclean.'*u*" *Mt*Then the disciples came to him and asked, "Do you know that the Pharisees were offended when they heard this?"

He replied, "Every plant that my heavenly Father has not planted will be pulled up by the roots. Leave them; they are blind guides.*v* If a blind man leads a blind man, both will fall into a pit."

Peter said, "Explain the parable to us."

"Are you still so dull?" Jesus asked them. *Mk*"Don't you see that nothing that enters a man from the outside can make him 'unclean'? For it doesn't go into his heart but into his stomach, and then out of his body." (In saying this, Jesus declared all foods "clean.")

He went on: "What comes out of a man is what makes him 'unclean.' For from within, out of men's hearts, come evil thoughts, sexual immorality, theft, murder, adultery, greed, malice, deceit, lewdness, envy, slander,

Mt.
15:10-20
Mk.
7:14-23

---

*p*Some early manuscripts *pitchers, kettles and dining couches*   *q*Isaiah 29:13   *r*Some manuscripts *set up*   *s*Exodus 20:12; Deut. 5:16   *t*Exodus 21:17; Lev. 20:9   *u*Some early manuscripts *'unclean.' 16If anyone has ears to hear, let him hear.*   *v*Some manuscripts *guides of the blind*

arrogance and folly. All these evils come from inside and make a man 'unclean.'"

Jn. 7:1 MINISTRY ONLY IN GALILEE. After this, Jesus went around in Galilee, purposely staying away from Judea because the Jews there were waiting to take his life.

Extensive Tour Throughout Galilee

*P*erhaps in an act of withdrawal from the Jews, or perhaps as part of a plan for wider evangelism, Jesus turns his ministry now to Phoenicia and the area around Tyre and Sidon. Here he encounters a Canaanite woman who begs Jesus to heal her daughter. As descendants of Noah's son Ham, against whom a curse had been directed, the Canaanites are looked down upon by the Jews as unworthy of God's blessings. So the woman's request is an excellent opportunity for Jesus to teach his disciples once again about the universality of his kingdom. At first it appears that Jesus rebuffs the woman, but the end result demonstrates Jesus' concern for all people, and also provides an excellent example of persistent faith on the part of a believer.

Returning to the Sea of Galilee, Jesus will perform more miracles and chastise the Pharisees for demanding signs of his deity. After that, Jesus will continue his extensive tour by going north into Caesarea Philippi.

Mt.
15:21-28
Mk.
7:24-30
Tyre and
Sidon

CANAANITE WOMAN PLEADS. ᴹᵗLeaving that place, Jesus withdrew to the region of Tyre and Sidon. ᴹᵏHe entered a house and did not want anyone to know it; yet he could not keep his presence secret. ᴹᵗA Canaanite woman from that vicinity came to him, crying out, "Lord, Son of David, have mercy on me! My daughter is suffering terribly from demon-possession."

Jesus did not answer a word. So his disciples came to him and urged him, "Send her away, for she keeps crying out after us."

He answered, "I was sent only to the lost sheep of Israel."

The woman came and knelt before him. "Lord, help me!" she said.

He replied, "It is not right to take the children's bread and toss it to their dogs."

"Yes, Lord," she said, "but even the dogs eat the crumbs that fall from their masters' table."

Then Jesus answered, "Woman, you have great faith! Your request is granted." And her daughter was healed from that very hour.

Mt.
15:29-31
Mk.
7:31-37

DEAF MUTE HEALED. ᴹᵗThen Jesus left the vicinity of Tyre and went through Sidon, down to the Sea of Galilee and into the region of the Decapolis. ʷ There some people brought to him a man who was deaf and could hardly talk, and they begged him to place his hand on the man.

After he took him aside, away from the crowd, Jesus put his fingers into the man's ears. Then he spit and touched the man's tongue. He looked up to heaven and with a deep sigh said to him, *"Ephphatha!"* (which means, "Be opened!"). At this, the man's ears were opened, his tongue was loosened and he began to speak plainly.

ʷThat is, the Ten Cities

Jesus commanded them not to tell anyone. But the more he did so, the more they kept talking about it. People were overwhelmed with amazement. "He has done everything well," they said. "He even makes the deaf hear and the mute speak." Mt Great crowds came to him, bringing the lame, the blind, the crippled, the mute and many others, and laid them at his feet; and he healed them. The people were amazed when they saw the mute speaking, the crippled made well, the lame walking and the blind seeing. And they praised the God of Israel.

FOUR THOUSAND FED.   During those days another large crowd gathered. Since they had nothing to eat, Jesus called his disciples to him and said, "I have compassion for these people; they have already been with me three days and have nothing to eat. If I send them home hungry, they will collapse on the way, because some of them have come a long distance."

His disciples answered, "But where in this remote place can anyone get enough bread to feed them?"

"How many loaves do you have?" Jesus asked.

"Seven," they replied.

He told the crowd to sit down on the ground. When he had taken the seven loaves and given thanks, he broke them and gave them to his disciples to set before the people, and they did so. They had a few small fish as well; he gave thanks for them also and told the disciples to distribute them. The people ate and were satisfied. Afterward the disciples picked up seven basketfuls of broken pieces that were left over. About four thousand men were present. And having sent them away, he got into the boat with his disciples and went to the region of Dalmanutha.

Mt. 15:32-39 Mk. 8:1-10 Hills by sea

PHARISEES ASK FOR SIGN.   Mt The Pharisees and Sadducees came to Jesus and tested him by asking him to show them a sign from heaven.

He replied,x "When evening comes, you say, 'It will be fair weather, for the sky is red,' and in the morning, 'Today it will be stormy, for the sky is red and overcast.' You know how to interpret the appearance of the sky, but you cannot interpret the signs of the times. A wicked and adulterous generation looks for a miraculous sign, but none will be given it except the sign of Jonah." Mk Then he left them, got back into the boat and crossed to the other side.

Mt. 16:1-4 Mk. 8:11-13 Magadan

WARNING ABOUT LEADERS.   Mk The disciples had forgotten to bring bread, except for one loaf they had with them in the boat. Mt "Be careful," Jesus said to them. "Be on your guard against the yeast of the Pharisees and Sadducees." Mk They discussed this with one another and said, "It is because we have no bread."

Aware of their discussion, Jesus asked them: "Why are you talking about having no bread? Do you still not see or understand? Are your hearts hardened? Do you have eyes but fail to see, and ears but fail to hear? And don't you remember? When I broke the five loaves for the five thousand, how many basketfuls of pieces did you pick up?"

"Twelve," they replied.

"And when I broke the seven loaves for the four thousand, how many basketfuls of pieces did you pick up?"

They answered, "Seven."

Mt. 16:5-12 Mk. 8:14-21

xSome early manuscripts do not have the rest of verse 2 and all of verse 3.

He said to them, "Do you still not understand?" ᴹᵗHow is it you don't understand that I was not talking to you about bread? But be on your guard against the yeast of the Pharisees and Sadducees." Then they understood that he was not telling them to guard against the yeast used in bread, but against the teaching of the Pharisees and Sadducees.

Mk.
8:22-26
Bethsaida

BLIND MAN NEAR BETHSAIDA.   They came to Bethsaida, and some people brought a blind man and begged Jesus to touch him. He took the blind man by the hand and led him outside the village. When he had spit on the man's eyes and put his hands on him, Jesus asked, "Do you see anything?"

He looked up and said, "I see people; they look like trees walking around."

Once more Jesus put his hands on the man's eyes. Then his eyes were opened, his sight was restored, and he saw everything clearly. Jesus sent him home, saying, "Don't go into the village.ʸ"

Preparation of Apostles for the End

s Jesus now continues his extensive tour north through Caesarea Philippi and then south again into Galilee, he uses this time to prepare his chosen disciples for his death and to strengthen their ministry in carrying on his work. At this point in Jesus' ministry the apostles are truly convinced that Jesus is the Messiah, but apparently they too have notions of a political Messiah. Realizing that their understanding of his messiahship is still very limited, and that their somewhat simplistic faith will be tested, Jesus begins to tell the apostles about his death, as well as the burdens which they themselves will face. Talk of their Leader's imminent death must surely confuse these men, who have hopes of playing key roles in a wholly different kind of kingdom.

The highlight of this period of preparation comes when Jesus takes Peter, James, and John (who seem to be the inner circle of the disciples) to (apparently) Mount Hermon. There Jesus is transfigured. In what is evidently more than a mere vision, Moses and Elijah appear with Jesus as representatives of the law and the prophets. The subsequent disappearance of Moses and Elijah, as well as words of confirmation spoken from heaven, indicate to the three disciples the demise of the former dispensation and the supremacy of the kingdom of God in Christ Jesus.

Even with this demonstration to the inner three, and despite Jesus' warning about humility in the use of their miraculous power, it is not long before all the disciples begin to dispute among themselves as to who among them is the greatest. Jesus sets a young child before them as an example of humility and teaches them about temptation, discipline, and forgiveness.

The Gospel accounts record here a confession by Peter that Jesus is the Christ. Using the word "rock" symbolically (since Peter's name means "rock"), Jesus says that it is upon the rock of Peter's confession of Christ that Jesus' kingdom will be established.

ʸSome manuscripts *Don't go and tell anyone in the village*

PETER ACKNOWLEDGES CHRIST.   When Jesus came to the region of
Caesarea Philippi, he asked his disciples, "Who do people say the Son of
Man is?"

They replied, "Some say John the Baptist; others say Elijah; and still others, Jeremiah or one of the prophets."

"But what about you?" he asked. "Who do you say I am?"

Simon Peter answered, "You are the Christ,^{z} the Son of the living God."

Jesus replied, "Blessed are you, Simon son of Jonah, for this was not
revealed to you by man, but by my Father in heaven. And I tell you that
you are Peter,^{a} and on this rock I will build my church, and the gates of
Hades ^{b} will not overcome it.^{c} I will give you the keys of the kingdom of
heaven; whatever you bind on earth will be ^{d} bound in heaven, and whatever you loose on earth will be ^{d} loosed in heaven." Then he warned his
disciples not to tell anyone that he was the Christ.

Mt.
16:13-20
Mk.
8:27-30
Lk. 9:18-20
Caesarea
Philippi

SUFFERING FORETOLD.   From that time on Jesus began to explain to
his disciples that he must go to Jerusalem and suffer many things at the
hands of the elders, chief priests and teachers of the law, and that he must
be killed and on the third day be raised to life.

Peter took him aside and began to rebuke him. "Never, Lord!" he said.
"This shall never happen to you!"

Jesus turned and said to Peter, "Get behind me, Satan! You are a stumbling block to me; you do not have in mind the things of God, but the
things of men."

Mt.
16:21-23
Mk.
8:31-33
Lk. 9:21,22

BURDENS OF DISCIPLESHIP.   Then he called the crowd to him along
with his disciples and said: "If anyone would come after me, he must deny
himself and take up his cross and follow me. For whoever wants to save
his life^e will lose it, but whoever loses his life for me and for the gospel will
save it. What good is it for a man to gain the whole world, yet forfeit his
soul? Or what can a man give in exchange for his soul? If anyone is
ashamed of me and my words in this adulterous and sinful generation, the
Son of Man will be ashamed of him when he comes in his Father's glory
with the holy angels."

Mt.
16:24-27
Mk.
8:34-38
Lk. 9:23-26

KINGDOM WITHIN LIFETIME.   And he said to them, "I tell you the
truth, some who are standing here will not taste death before they see the
kingdom of God come with power."

Mt. 16:28
Mk. 9:1
Lk. 9:27

JESUS IS TRANSFIGURED.   After six days Jesus took with him Peter,
James and John the brother of James, and led them up a high mountain by
themselves. There he was transfigured before them. His face shone like the
sun, and his clothes became as white as the light. Just then there appeared
before them Moses and Elijah, talking with Jesus.

Peter said to Jesus, "Lord, it is good for us to be here. If you wish, I will
put up three shelters—one for you, one for Moses and one for Elijah."

While he was still speaking, a bright cloud enveloped them, and a voice
from the cloud said, "This is my Son, whom I love; with him I am well
pleased. Listen to him!"

When the disciples heard this, they fell facedown to the ground, terrified.

Mt. 17:1-8
Mk. 9:2-8
Lk.
9:28-36a
Mount
Hermon?

^{z}Or Messiah ^{a}Peter means rock. ^{b}Or hell ^{c}Or not prove stronger than it ^{d}Or
have been ^{e}The Greek word means either life or soul

But Jesus came and touched them. "Get up," he said. "Don't be afraid." When they looked up, they saw no one except Jesus.

Mt. 17:9-13
Mk. 9:9-13
Lk. 9:36b
APOSTLES ASK ABOUT ELIJAH.   ^{Mt}As they were coming down the mountain, Jesus instructed them, "Don't tell anyone what you have seen, until the Son of Man has been raised from the dead."

The disciples asked him, "Why then do the teachers of the law say that Elijah must come first?"

Jesus replied, "To be sure, Elijah comes and will restore all things. But I tell you, Elijah has already come, and they did not recognize him, but have done to him everything they wished. In the same way the Son of Man is going to suffer at their hands." Then the disciples understood that he was talking to them about John the Baptist. ^{Lk}The disciples kept this to themselves, and told no one at that time what they had seen.

Mt.
17:14-21
Mk.
9:14-29
Lk.
9:37-43a;
17:5,6
Near the
mountain
EPILEPTIC BOY HEALED.   ^{Mk}When they came to the other disciples, they saw a large crowd around them and the teachers of the law arguing with them. As soon as all the people saw Jesus, they were overwhelmed with wonder and ran to greet him.

"What are you arguing with them about?" he asked.

A man in the crowd answered, "Teacher, I brought you my son, who is possessed by a spirit that has robbed him of speech. Whenever it seizes him, it throws him to the ground. He foams at the mouth, gnashes his teeth and becomes rigid. I asked your disciples to drive out the spirit, but they could not."

"O unbelieving generation," Jesus replied, "how long shall I stay with you? How long shall I put up with you? Bring the boy to me."

So they brought him. When the spirit saw Jesus, it immediately threw the boy into a convulsion. He fell to the ground and rolled around, foaming at the mouth.

Jesus asked the boy's father, "How long has he been like this?"

"From childhood," he answered. "It has often thrown him into fire or water to kill him. But if you can do anything, take pity on us and help us."

"'If you can'?" said Jesus. "Everything is possible for him who believes."

Immediately the boy's father exclaimed, "I do believe; help me overcome my unbelief!"

When Jesus saw that a crowd was running to the scene, he rebuked the evil^f spirit. "You deaf and mute spirit," he said, "I command you, come out of him and never enter him again."

The spirit shrieked, convulsed him violently and came out. The boy looked so much like a corpse that many said, "He's dead." But Jesus took him by the hand and lifted him to his feet, and he stood up.

After Jesus had gone indoors, his disciples asked him privately, "Why couldn't we drive it out?" ^{Mt}He replied, "Because you have so little faith. I tell you the truth, if you have faith as small as a mustard seed, you can say to this mountain, 'Move from here to there' and it will move. Nothing will be impossible for you.^g" ^{Mk}"This kind can come out only by prayer.^h"

^fGreek *unclean*   ^gSome manuscripts *you.* ²¹*But this kind does not go out except by prayer and fasting.*   ^hSome manuscripts *prayer and fasting*

DEATH AGAIN FORETOLD.   They left that place and passed through Galilee. Jesus did not want anyone to know where they were, because he was teaching his disciples. He said to them, "The Son of Man is going to be betrayed into the hands of men. They will kill him, and after three days he will rise." But they did not understand what he meant and were afraid to ask him about it.

Mt.
17:22,23
Mk.
9:30-32
Lk.
9:43b-45
Galilee

COIN FROM FISH'S MOUTH.   After Jesus and his disciples arrived in Capernaum, the collectors of the two-drachma tax came to Peter and asked, "Doesn't your teacher pay the temple tax[i]?"

Mt.
17:24-27
Capernaum

"Yes, he does," he replied.

When Peter came into the house, Jesus was the first to speak. "What do you think, Simon?" he asked. "From whom do the kings of the earth collect duty and taxes—from their own sons or from others?"

"From others," Peter answered.

"Then the sons are exempt," Jesus said to him. "But so that we may not offend them, go to the lake and throw out your line. Take the first fish you catch; open its mouth and you will find a four-drachma coin. Take it and give it to them for my tax and yours."

APOSTLES DISPUTE ABOUT RANK.   [Mk]They came to Capernaum. When he was in the house, he asked them, "What were you arguing about on the road?" But they kept quiet because on the way they had argued about who was the greatest.

Sitting down, Jesus called the Twelve and said, "If anyone wants to be first, he must be the very last, and the servant of all." [Lk]"Suppose one of you had a servant plowing or looking after the sheep. Would he say to the servant when he comes in from the field, 'Come along now and sit down to eat'? Would he not rather say, 'Prepare my supper, get yourself ready and wait on me while I eat and drink; after that you may eat and drink'? Would he thank the servant because he did what he was told to do? So you also, when you have done everything you were told to do, should say, 'We are unworthy servants; we have only done our duty.' " [Mt]He called a little child and had him stand among them. And he said: "I tell you the truth, unless you change and become like little children, you will never enter the kingdom of heaven. Therefore, whoever humbles himself like this child is the greatest in the kingdom of heaven.

Mt. 18:1-4
Mk.
9:33-35
Lk.
9:46-48;
17:7-10

CONCERN FOR THE YOUNG.   [Mk]"Whoever welcomes one of these little children in my name welcomes me; and whoever welcomes me does not welcome me but the one who sent me." [Mt]But if anyone causes one of these little ones who believe in me to sin, it would be better for him to have a large millstone hung around his neck and to be drowned in the depths of the sea.

Mt.
18:5,6,10-14
Mk.
9:36,37,42
Lk. 17:2,3a

"See that you do not look down on one of these little ones. For I tell you that their angels in heaven always see the face of my Father in heaven.[j]

"What do you think? If a man owns a hundred sheep, and one of them wanders away, will he not leave the ninety-nine on the hills and go to look for the one that wandered off? And if he finds it, I tell you the truth, he is happier about that one sheep than about the ninety-nine that did not

[i]Greek *the two drachmas*   [j]Some manuscripts *heaven.* [11]*The Son of Man came to save what was lost.*

wander off. In the same way your Father in heaven is not willing that any of these little ones should be lost.

Mt. 18:7-9
Mk. 9:43-50
Lk. 17:1

WARNING ABOUT TEMPTATION.   Mt "Woe to the world because of the things that cause people to sin! Such things must come, but woe to the man through whom they come! If your hand or your foot causes you to sin, cut it off and throw it away. It is better for you to enter life maimed or crippled than to have two hands or two feet and be thrown into eternal fire. Mk And if your eye causes you to sin, pluck it out. It is better for you to enter the kingdom of God with one eye than to have two eyes and be thrown into hell, where

" 'their worm does not die,
            and the fire is not quenched.'k

Everyone will be salted with fire.

"Salt is good, but if it loses its saltiness, how can you make it salty again? Have salt in yourselves, and be at peace with each other."

Mk. 9:38-41
Lk. 9:49,50

WORKS DONE IN JESUS' NAME.   "Teacher," said John, "we saw a man driving out demons in your name and we told him to stop, because he was not one of us."

"Do not stop him," Jesus said. "No one who does a miracle in my name can in the next moment say anything bad about me, for whoever is not against us is for us. I tell you the truth, anyone who gives you a cup of water in my name because you belong to Christ will certainly not lose his reward.

Mt. 18:15-17

REBUKE AND DISCIPLINE.   "If your brother sins against you,l go and show him his fault, just between the two of you. If he listens to you, you have won your brother over. But if he will not listen, take one or two others along, so that 'every matter may be established by the testimony of two or three witnesses.'m If he refuses to listen to them, tell it to the church; and if he refuses to listen even to the church, treat him as you would a pagan or a tax collector.

Mt. 18:18-20

APOSTLES GIVEN AUTHORITY.   "I tell you the truth, whatever you bind on earth will be n bound in heaven, and whatever you loose on earth will be n loosed in heaven.

"Again, I tell you that if two of you on earth agree about anything you ask for, it will be done for you by my Father in heaven. For where two or three come together in my name, there am I with them."

Mt. 18:21,22
Lk. 17:3b,4

PETER ASKS ABOUT FORGIVENESS.   Mt Then Peter came to Jesus and asked, "Lord, how many times shall I forgive my brother when he sins against me? Up to seven times?"

Jesus answered, "I tell you, not seven times, but seventy-seven times.o Lk "If your brother sins, rebuke him, and if he repents, forgive him. If he sins against you seven times in a day, and seven times comes back to you and says, 'I repent,' forgive him."

Mt. 18:23-35

PARABLE OF SERVANTS IN DEBT.   "Therefore, the kingdom of heaven is like a king who wanted to settle accounts with his servants. As he began the settlement, a man who owed him ten thousand talentsp was brought

kIsaiah 66:24   lSome manuscripts do not have *against you*.   mDeut. 19:15   nOr *have been*   oOr *seventy times seven*   pThat is, millions of dollars to him. Since he was not able to pay, the master ordered that he and his wife and his children and all that he had be sold to repay the debt.

"The servant fell on his knees before him. 'Be patient with me,' he begged, 'and I will pay back everything.' The servant's master took pity on him, canceled the debt and let him go.

"But when that servant went out, he found one of his fellow servants who owed him a hundred denarii.*9* He grabbed him and began to choke him. 'Pay back what you owe me!' he demanded.

"His fellow servant fell to his knees and begged him, 'Be patient with me, and I will pay you back.'

"But he refused. Instead, he went off and had the man thrown into prison until he could pay the debt. When the other servants saw what had happened, they were greatly distressed and went and told their master everything that had happened.

"Then the master called the servant in. 'You wicked servant,' he said, 'I canceled all that debt of yours because you begged me to. Shouldn't you have had mercy on your fellow servant just as I had on you?' In anger his master turned him over to the jailers to be tortured, until he should pay back all he owed.

"This is how my heavenly Father will treat each of you unless you forgive your brother from your heart."

In Jerusalem for Feast of Tabernacles

*I*t has been six months since the last Passover, which Jesus evidently did not attend because of threats on his life. However, as the time arrives for the annual Feast of Tabernacles, held for eight days in late September and early October, apparently Jesus feels that he can once again journey safely to Jerusalem. The Feast of Tabernacles, one of three national festivals (along with Passover and Pentecost) which all males are obliged to attend, is a commemoration of the ancient wilderness journey, during which the Israelites had lived in tents. Accordingly, during the festival the people live in improvised booths made of tree branches. For this reason the feast is also known as the Festival of Booths. More anciently, the feast was referred to as the Feast of the Harvest, or the Feast of the Ingathering, since it was celebrated after the vintage and harvest were gathered.

Though some of Jesus' brothers will later become leaders in the church, apparently at this point they cannot bring themselves to believe that their brother is the Messiah. Almost tauntingly, it seems, they urge him to go up to Jerusalem to celebrate the feast. Jesus puts them off, however, perhaps realizing that their intentions for him are not sincere. For his own reasons he prefers to go up quietly and therefore tells them that he is not yet ready to go. Jesus will follow them after they have gone, but only after some delay.

When Jesus finally arrives in Jerusalem he will spend his time teaching and confronting the religious leaders who have assembled. It is a time of mixed feelings among the Jews. Some are busy trying to have Jesus arrested,

9That is, a few dollars

while others are convinced by his teaching and miraculous works that he is the Messiah.

Jn. 7:2-9
Capernaum
(Sept./
Oct., A.D.
29)

BROTHERS TAUNT JESUS.   But when the Jewish Feast of Tabernacles was near, Jesus' brothers said to him, "You ought to leave here and go to Judea, so that your disciples may see the miracles you do. No one who wants to become a public figure acts in secret. Since you are doing these things, show yourself to the world." For even his own brothers did not believe in him.

Therefore Jesus told them, "The right time for me has not yet come; for you any time is right. The world cannot hate you, but it hates me because I testify that what it does is evil. You go to the Feast. I am not yet[r] going up to this Feast, because for me the right time has not yet come." Having said this, he stayed in Galilee.

Jn. 7:10-13
Jerusalem
(Oct.,
A.D. 29)

JESUS GOES PRIVATELY.   However, after his brothers had left for the Feast, he went also, not publicly, but in secret. Now at the Feast the Jews were watching for him and asking, "Where is that man?"

Among the crowds there was widespread whispering about him. Some said, "He is a good man."

Others replied, "No, he deceives the people." But no one would say anything publicly about him for fear of the Jews.

Jn. 7:14-24

JESUS TEACHES IN TEMPLE.   Not until halfway through the Feast did Jesus go up to the temple courts and begin to teach. The Jews were amazed and asked, "How did this man get such learning without having studied?"

Jesus answered, "My teaching is not my own. It comes from him who sent me. If anyone chooses to do God's will, he will find out whether my teaching comes from God or whether I speak on my own. He who speaks on his own does so to gain honor for himself, but he who works for the honor of the one who sent him is a man of truth; there is nothing false about him. Has not Moses given you the law? Yet not one of you keeps the law. Why are you trying to kill me?"

"You are demon-possessed," the crowd answered. "Who is trying to kill you?"

Jesus said to them, "I did one miracle, and you are all astonished. Yet, because Moses gave you circumcision (though actually it did not come from Moses, but from the patriarchs), you circumcise a child on the Sabbath. Now if a child can be circumcised on the Sabbath so that the law of Moses may not be broken, why are you angry with me for healing the whole man on the Sabbath? Stop judging by mere appearances, and make a right judgment."

Jn. 7:25-31

JEWS DISCUSS CHRIST.   At that point some of the people of Jerusalem began to ask, "Isn't this the man they are trying to kill? Here he is, speaking publicly, and they are not saying a word to him. Have the authorities really concluded that he is the Christ[s]? But we know where this man is from; when the Christ comes, no one will know where he is from."

Then Jesus, still teaching in the temple courts, cried out, "Yes, you know me, and you know where I am from. I am not here on my own, but he who

[r]Some early manuscripts do not have *yet*.   [s]Or *Messiah*

sent me is true. You do not know him, but I know him because I am from him and he sent me."

At this they tried to seize him, but no one laid a hand on him, because his time had not yet come. Still, many in the crowd put their faith in him. They said, "When the Christ comes, will he do more miraculous signs than this man?"

GUARDS SENT TO ARREST.   The Pharisees heard the crowd whispering such things about him. Then the chief priests and the Pharisees sent temple guards to arrest him.

Jn. 7:32-36

Jesus said, "I am with you for only a short time, and then I go to the one who sent me. You will look for me, but you will not find me; and where I am, you cannot come."

The Jews said to one another, "Where does this man intend to go that we cannot find him? Will he go where our people live scattered among the Greeks, and teach the Greeks? What did he mean when he said, 'You will look for me, but you will not find me,' and 'Where I am, you cannot come'?"

SPIRITUAL DRINK.   On the last and greatest day of the Feast, Jesus stood and said in a loud voice, "If anyone is thirsty, let him come to me and drink. Whoever believes in me, as ^{t} the Scripture has said, streams of living water will flow from within him." By this he meant the Spirit, whom those who believed in him were later to receive. Up to that time the Spirit had not been given, since Jesus had not yet been glorified.

Jn. 7:37-39

MORE DIVISION AMONG JEWS.   On hearing his words, some of the people said, "Surely this man is the Prophet."

Jn. 7:40-44

Others said, "He is the Christ."

Still others asked, "How can the Christ come from Galilee? Does not the Scripture say that the Christ will come from David's family ^{u} and from Bethlehem, the town where David lived?" Thus the people were divided because of Jesus. Some wanted to seize him, but no one laid a hand on him.

NICODEMUS COUNSELS CAUTION.   Finally the temple guards went back to the chief priests and Pharisees, who asked them, "Why didn't you bring him in?"

Jn. 7:45-52

"No one ever spoke the way this man does," the guards declared.

"You mean he has deceived you also?" the Pharisees retorted. "Has any of the rulers or of the Pharisees believed in him? No! But this mob that knows nothing of the law—there is a curse on them."

Nicodemus, who had gone to Jesus earlier and who was one of their own number, asked, "Does our law condemn anyone without first hearing him to find out what he is doing?"

They replied, "Are you from Galilee, too? Look into it, and you will find that a prophet ^{v} does not come out of Galilee."

[The earliest manuscripts and many other ancient witnesses do not have John 7:53–8:11.]

^{t}Or / If anyone is thirsty, let him come to me. / And let him drink, ^{38}who believes in me. / As
^{u}Greek seed ^{v}Two early manuscripts the Prophet

NOVEMBER 5

Jn.
7:53-8:11
In temple

WOMAN CAUGHT IN ADULTERY.   Then each went to his own home. But Jesus went to the Mount of Olives. At dawn he appeared again in the temple courts, where all the people gathered around him, and he sat down to teach them. The teachers of the law and the Pharisees brought in a woman caught in adultery. They made her stand before the group and said to Jesus, "Teacher, this woman was caught in the act of adultery. In the Law Moses commanded us to stone such women. Now what do you say?" They were using this question as a trap, in order to have a basis for accusing him.

But Jesus bent down and started to write on the ground with his finger. When they kept on questioning him, he straightened up and said to them, "If any one of you is without sin, let him be the first to throw a stone at her." Again he stooped down and wrote on the ground.

At this, those who heard began to go away one at a time, the older ones first, until only Jesus was left, with the woman still standing there. Jesus straightened up and asked her, "Woman, where are they? Has no one condemned you?"

"No one, sir," she said.

"Then neither do I condemn you," Jesus declared. "Go now and leave your life of sin."

Jn. 8:12-20

LIGHT OF THE WORLD.   When Jesus spoke again to the people, he said, "I am the light of the world. Whoever follows me will never walk in darkness, but will have the light of life."

The Pharisees challenged him, "Here you are, appearing as your own witness; your testimony is not valid."

Jesus answered, "Even if I testify on my own behalf, my testimony is valid, for I know where I came from and where I am going. But you have no idea where I come from or where I am going. You judge by human standards; I pass judgment on no one. But if I do judge, my decisions are right, because I am not alone. I stand with the Father, who sent me. In your own Law it is written that the testimony of two men is valid. I am one who testifies for myself; my other witness is the Father, who sent me."

Then they asked him, "Where is your father?"

"You do not know me or my Father," Jesus replied. "If you knew me, you would know my Father also." He spoke these words while teaching in the temple area near the place where the offerings were put. Yet no one seized him, because his time had not yet come.

Jn. 8:21-30

WARNING AGAINST UNBELIEF.   Once more Jesus said to them, "I am going away, and you will look for me, and you will die in your sin. Where I go, you cannot come."

This made the Jews ask, "Will he kill himself? Is that why he says, 'Where I go, you cannot come'?"

But he continued, "You are from below; I am from above. You are of this world; I am not of this world. I told you that you would die in your sins; if you do not believe that I am ˻the one I claim to be˼,[w] you will indeed die in your sins."

---

[w]Or I am he

"Who are you?" they asked.

"Just what I have been claiming all along," Jesus replied. "I have much to say in judgment of you. But he who sent me is reliable, and what I have heard from him I tell the world."

They did not understand that he was telling them about his Father. So Jesus said, "When you have lifted up the Son of Man, then you will know that I am ⌊the one I claim to be⌋ and that I do nothing on my own but speak just what the Father has taught me. The one who sent me is with me; he has not left me alone, for I always do what pleases him." Even as he spoke, many put their faith in him.

ON SPIRITUAL FREEDOM.   To the Jews who had believed him, Jesus   Jn. 8:31-38
said, "If you hold to my teaching, you are really my disciples. Then you will know the truth, and the truth will set you free."

They answered him, "We are Abraham's descendants[x] and have never been slaves of anyone. How can you say that we shall be set free?"

Jesus replied, "I tell you the truth, everyone who sins is a slave to sin. Now a slave has no permanent place in the family, but a son belongs to it forever. So if the Son sets you free, you will be free indeed. I know you are Abraham's descendants. Yet you are ready to kill me, because you have no room for my word. I am telling you what I have seen in the Father's presence, and you do what you have heard from your father.[y]"

TRUE CHILDREN OF ABRAHAM.   "Abraham is our father," they an-   Jn. 8:39-47
swered.

"If you were Abraham's children," said Jesus, "then you would[z] do the things Abraham did. As it is, you are determined to kill me, a man who has told you the truth that I heard from God. Abraham did not do such things. You are doing the things your own father does."

"We are not illegitimate children," they protested. "The only Father we have is God himself."

Jesus said to them, "If God were your Father, you would love me, for I came from God and now am here. I have not come on my own; but he sent me. Why is my language not clear to you? Because you are unable to hear what I say. You belong to your father, the devil, and you want to carry out your father's desire. He was a murderer from the beginning, not holding to the truth, for there is no truth in him. When he lies, he speaks his native language, for he is a liar and the father of lies. Yet because I tell the truth, you do not believe me! Can any of you prove me guilty of sin? If I am telling the truth, why don't you believe me? He who belongs to God hears what God says. The reason you do not hear is that you do not belong to God."

DECLARES ETERNAL EXISTENCE.   The Jews answered him, "Aren't   Jn. 8:48-59
we right in saying that you are a Samaritan and demon-possessed?"

"I am not possessed by a demon," said Jesus, "but I honor my Father and you dishonor me. I am not seeking glory for myself; but there is one who seeks it, and he is the judge. I tell you the truth, if anyone keeps my word, he will never see death."

At this the Jews exclaimed, "Now we know that you are demon-possessed! Abraham died and so did the prophets, yet you say that if

---

[x]Greek *seed*; also in verse 37   [y]Or *presence. Therefore do what you have heard from the Father.*   [z]Some early manuscripts *"If you are Abraham's children," said Jesus, "then*

anyone keeps your word, he will never taste death. Are you greater than our father Abraham? He died, and so did the prophets. Who do you think you are?"

Jesus replied, "If I glorify myself, my glory means nothing. My Father, whom you claim as your God, is the one who glorifies me. Though you do not know him, I know him. If I said I did not, I would be a liar like you, but I do know him and keep his word. Your father Abraham rejoiced at the thought of seeing my day; he saw it and was glad."

"You are not yet fifty years old," the Jews said to him, "and you have seen Abraham!"

"I tell you the truth," Jesus answered, "before Abraham was born, I am!" At this, they picked up stones to stone him, but Jesus hid himself, slipping away from the temple grounds.

Jn. 9:1-12   **HEALING OF MAN BORN BLIND.**   As he went along, he saw a man blind from birth. His disciples asked him, "Rabbi, who sinned, this man or his parents, that he was born blind?"

"Neither this man nor his parents sinned," said Jesus, "but this happened so that the work of God might be displayed in his life. As long as it is day, we must do the work of him who sent me. Night is coming, when no one can work. While I am in the world, I am the light of the world."

Having said this, he spit on the ground, made some mud with the saliva, and put it on the man's eyes. "Go," he told him, "wash in the Pool of Siloam" (this word means Sent). So the man went and washed, and came home seeing.

His neighbors and those who had formerly seen him begging asked, "Isn't this the same man who used to sit and beg?" Some claimed that he was.

Others said, "No, he only looks like him."

But he himself insisted, "I am the man."

"How then were your eyes opened?" they demanded.

He replied, "The man they call Jesus made some mud and put it on my eyes. He told me to go to Siloam and wash. So I went and washed, and then I could see."

"Where is this man?" they asked him.

"I don't know," he said.

Jn. 9:13-17   **PHARISEES QUESTION MAN.**   They brought to the Pharisees the man who had been blind. Now the day on which Jesus had made the mud and opened the man's eyes was a Sabbath. Therefore the Pharisees also asked him how he had received his sight. "He put mud on my eyes," the man replied, "and I washed, and now I see."

Some of the Pharisees said, "This man is not from God, for he does not keep the Sabbath."

But others asked, "How can a sinner do such miraculous signs?" So they were divided.

Finally they turned again to the blind man, "What have you to say about him? It was your eyes he opened."

The man replied, "He is a prophet."

Jn. 9:18-23   **PARENTS ARE QUESTIONED.**   The Jews still did not believe that he had been blind and had received his sight until they sent for the man's parents. "Is this your son?" they asked. "Is this the one you say was born blind? How is it that now he can see?"

"We know he is our son," the parents answered, "and we know he was born blind. But how he can see now, or who opened his eyes, we don't know. Ask him. He is of age; he will speak for himself." His parents said this because they were afraid of the Jews, for already the Jews had decided that anyone who acknowledged that Jesus was the Christ*a* would be put out of the synagogue. That was why his parents said, "He is of age; ask him."

MAN QUESTIONED AGAIN.   A second time they summoned the man who had been blind. "Give glory to God,*b*" they said. "We know this man is a sinner."

Jn. 9:24-34

He replied, "Whether he is a sinner or not, I don't know. One thing I do know. I was blind but now I see!"

Then they asked him, "What did he do to you? How did he open your eyes?"

He answered, "I have told you already and you did not listen. Why do you want to hear it again? Do you want to become his disciples, too?"

Then they hurled insults at him and said, "You are this fellow's disciple! We are disciples of Moses! We know that God spoke to Moses, but as for this fellow, we don't even know where he comes from."

The man answered, "Now that is remarkable! You don't know where he comes from, yet he opened my eyes. We know that God does not listen to sinners. He listens to the godly man who does his will. Nobody has ever heard of opening the eyes of a man born blind. If this man were not from God, he could do nothing."

To this they replied, "You were steeped in sin at birth; how dare you lecture us!" And they threw him out.

JESUS CONFRONTS HEALED MAN.   Jesus heard that they had thrown him out, and when he found him, he said, "Do you believe in the Son of Man?"

Jn. 9:35-41

"Who is he, sir?" the man asked. "Tell me so that I may believe in him."

Jesus said, "You have now seen him; in fact, he is the one speaking with you."

Then the man said, "Lord, I believe," and he worshiped him.

Jesus said, "For judgment I have come into this world, so that the blind will see and those who see will become blind."

Some Pharisees who were with him heard him say this and asked, "What? Are we blind too?"

Jesus said, "If you were blind, you would not be guilty of sin; but now that you claim you can see, your guilt remains.

SHEEP AND THEIR SHEPHERD.   "I tell you the truth, the man who does not enter the sheep pen by the gate, but climbs in by some other way, is a thief and a robber. The man who enters by the gate is the shepherd of his sheep. The watchman opens the gate for him, and the sheep listen to his voice. He calls his own sheep by name and leads them out. When he has brought out all his own, he goes on ahead of them, and his sheep follow him because they know his voice. But they will never follow a stranger; in fact, they will run away from him because they do not recognize a stranger's voice." Jesus used this figure of speech, but they did not understand what he was telling them.

Jn. 10:1-6

*a*Or *Messiah*   *b*A solemn charge to tell the truth (see Joshua 7:19)

Jn. 10:7-10

THE GATE FOR THE SHEEP.   Therefore Jesus said again, "I tell you the truth, I am the gate for the sheep. All who ever came before me were thieves and robbers, but the sheep did not listen to them. I am the gate; whoever enters through me will be saved.[c] He will come in and go out, and find pasture. The thief comes only to steal and kill and destroy; I have come that they may have life, and have it to the full.

Jn. 10:11-18

THE GOOD SHEPHERD.   "I am the good shepherd. The good shepherd lays down his life for the sheep. The hired hand is not the shepherd who owns the sheep. So when he sees the wolf coming, he abandons the sheep and runs away. Then the wolf attacks the flock and scatters it. The man runs away because he is a hired hand and cares nothing for the sheep.

"I am the good shepherd; I know my sheep and my sheep know me—just as the Father knows me and I know the Father—and I lay down my life for the sheep. I have other sheep that are not of this sheep pen. I must bring them also. They too will listen to my voice, and there shall be one flock and one shepherd. The reason my Father loves me is that I lay down my life—only to take it up again. No one takes it from me, but I lay it down of my own accord. I have authority to lay it down and authority to take it up again. This command I received from my Father."

Jn. 10:19-21

JEWS STILL DIVIDED.   At these words the Jews were again divided. Many of them said, "He is demon-possessed and raving mad. Why listen to him?"

But others said, "These are not the sayings of a man possessed by a demon. Can a demon open the eyes of the blind?"

Ministry from Galilee to Judea

After the Feast of Dedication, Jesus apparently returns to Capernaum for the final two months of his Galilean ministry. He not only feels growing opposition from the people there who want a political leader, but also knows that it is nearing the time for him to be delivered up. From this time forward, Jesus resolutely faces his final suffering. As he sets out on his journey to Jerusalem, in Samaria he again encounters immediate rejection. Making what amounts to a final appeal to the northern region, Jesus sends out 72 of his disciples, to whom he gives the power to heal in his name, with the mission of proclaiming the coming of his kingdom.

As Jesus proceeds down through Judea, he is apparently near Jericho when he tells the parable of the Good Samaritan, an illustration all the more remarkable in view of Jesus' own rejection by the Samaritans just a short time before. Jesus will then travel on to Bethany, visiting in the home of Martha and Mary, and later proceed to Jerusalem for the Feast of Dedication.

This is a time of transition for the Master. Initial excitement among the masses is followed by doubt and even hostility as Jesus refuses to accept the role that most

[c] Or *kept safe*

people want him to play. In a way it is characteristic of the turnabout which inevitably comes when people accept Jesus into their lives for any number of wrong reasons: the excitement can give way to disappointment.

GALILEAN MINISTRY ENDS.   As the time approached for him to be taken up to heaven, Jesus resolutely set out for Jerusalem. And he sent messengers on ahead, who went into a Samaritan village to get things ready for him; but the people there did not welcome him, because he was heading for Jerusalem. When the disciples James and John saw this, they asked, "Lord, do you want us to call fire down from heaven to destroy them*d*?" But Jesus turned and rebuked them, and*e* they went to another village.

Mt. 19:1,2
Mk. 10:1
Lk. 9:51-56
Samaria
to Judea

TEN LEPERS HEALED.   Now on his way to Jerusalem, Jesus traveled along the border between Samaria and Galilee. As he was going into a village, ten men who had leprosy*f* met him. They stood at a distance and called out in a loud voice, "Jesus, Master, have pity on us!"

Lk.
17:11-19

When he saw them, he said, "Go, show yourselves to the priests." And as they went, they were cleansed.

One of them, when he saw he was healed, came back, praising God in a loud voice. He threw himself at Jesus' feet and thanked him—and he was a Samaritan.

Jesus asked, "Were not all ten cleansed? Where are the other nine? Was no one found to return and give praise to God except this foreigner?" Then he said to him, "Rise and go; your faith has made you well."

SEVENTY-TWO SENT OUT.   After this the Lord appointed seventy-two*g* others and sent them two by two ahead of him to every town and place where he was about to go. He told them, "The harvest is plentiful, but the workers are few. Ask the Lord of the harvest, therefore, to send out workers into his harvest field. Go! I am sending you out like lambs among wolves. Do not take a purse or bag or sandals; and do not greet anyone on the road.

Mt.
11:20-24
Lk. 10:1-16

"When you enter a house, first say, 'Peace to this house.' If a man of peace is there, your peace will rest on him; if not, it will return to you. Stay in that house, eating and drinking whatever they give you, for the worker deserves his wages. Do not move around from house to house.

"When you enter a town and are welcomed, eat what is set before you. Heal the sick who are there and tell them, 'The kingdom of God is near you.' But when you enter a town and are not welcomed, go into its streets and say, 'Even the dust of your town that sticks to our feet we wipe off against you. Yet be sure of this: The kingdom of God is near.' I tell you, it will be more bearable on that day for Sodom than for that town.

"Woe to you, Korazin! Woe to you, Bethsaida! For if the miracles that were performed in you had been performed in Tyre and Sidon, they would have repented long ago, sitting in sackcloth and ashes. But it will be more bearable for Tyre and Sidon at the judgment than for you. And you, Capernaum, will you be lifted up to the skies? No, you will go down to the depths.*h*

*d*Some manuscripts *them, even as Elijah did*   *e*Some manuscripts *them. And he said,*
"You do not know what kind of spirit you are of, for the Son of Man did not come to destroy
men's lives, but to save them." 56And   *f*The Greek word was used for various diseases
affecting the skin—not necessarily leprosy.   *g*Some manuscripts *seventy*   *h*Greek
Hades

"He who listens to you listens to me; he who rejects you rejects me; but he who rejects me rejects him who sent me."

Lk.
10:17-20

SEVENTY-TWO RETURN.   The seventy-two returned with joy and said, "Lord, even the demons submit to us in your name."

He replied, "I saw Satan fall like lightning from heaven. I have given you authority to trample on snakes and scorpions and to overcome all the power of the enemy; nothing will harm you. However, do not rejoice that the spirits submit to you, but rejoice that your names are written in heaven."

Mt.
11:25-27
Lk.
10:21-24

THANKS GIVEN FOR REVELATION.   At that time Jesus, full of joy through the Holy Spirit, said, "I praise you, Father, Lord of heaven and earth, because you have hidden these things from the wise and learned, and revealed them to little children. Yes, Father, for this was your good pleasure.

"All things have been committed to me by my Father. No one knows who the Son is except the Father, and no one knows who the Father is except the Son and those to whom the Son chooses to reveal him."

Then he turned to his disciples and said privately, "Blessed are the eyes that see what you see. For I tell you that many prophets and kings wanted to see what you see but did not see it, and to hear what you hear but did not hear it."

Mt.
11:28-30

REST FOR THE WEARY.   "Come to me, all you who are weary and burdened, and I will give you rest. Take my yoke upon you and learn from me, for I am gentle and humble in heart, and you will find rest for your souls. For my yoke is easy and my burden is light."

Lk.
10:25-37
Jericho?

PARABLE OF GOOD SAMARITAN.   On one occasion an expert in the law stood up to test Jesus. "Teacher," he asked, "what must I do to inherit eternal life?"

"What is written in the Law?" he replied. "How do you read it?"

He answered: " 'Love the Lord your God with all your heart and with all your soul and with all your strength and with all your mind'[i]; and, 'Love your neighbor as yourself.'[j]"

"You have answered correctly," Jesus replied. "Do this and you will live."

But he wanted to justify himself, so he asked Jesus, "And who is my neighbor?"

In reply Jesus said: "A man was going down from Jerusalem to Jericho, when he fell into the hands of robbers. They stripped him of his clothes, beat him and went away, leaving him half dead. A priest happened to be going down the same road, and when he saw the man, he passed by on the other side. So too, a Levite, when he came to the place and saw him, passed by on the other side. But a Samaritan, as he traveled, came where the man was; and when he saw him, he took pity on him. He went to him and bandaged his wounds, pouring on oil and wine. Then he put the man on his own donkey, took him to an inn and took care of him. The next day he took out two silver coins[k] and gave them to the innkeeper. 'Look after him,' he said, 'and when I return, I will reimburse you for any extra expense you may have.'

[i]Deut. 6:5   [j]Lev. 19:18   [k]Greek *two denarii*

"Which of these three do you think was a neighbor to the man who fell into the hands of robbers?"

The expert in the law replied, "The one who had mercy on him."

Jesus told him, "Go and do likewise."

WITH MARTHA AND MARY.   As Jesus and his disciples were on their way, he came to a village where a woman named Martha opened her home to him. She had a sister called Mary, who sat at the Lord's feet listening to what he said. But Martha was distracted by all the preparations that had to be made. She came to him and asked, "Lord, don't you care that my sister has left me to do the work by myself? Tell her to help me!"

"Martha, Martha," the Lord answered, "you are worried and upset about many things, but only one thing is needed.[l] Mary has chosen what is better, and it will not be taken away from her."

Lk. 10:38-42 Bethany?

TEACHING HOW TO PRAY.   One day Jesus was praying in a certain place. When he finished, one of his disciples said to him, "Lord, teach us to pray, just as John taught his disciples."

He said to them, "When you pray, say:

Lk. 11:1-4 Mount of Olives?

" 'Father,[m]
   hallowed be your name,
   your kingdom come.[n]
Give us each day our daily bread.
Forgive us our sins,
    for we also forgive everyone who sins against us.[o]
And lead us not into temptation.[p]' "

PARABLE OF PERSISTENCE.   Then he said to them, "Suppose one of you has a friend, and he goes to him at midnight and says, 'Friend, lend me three loaves of bread, because a friend of mine on a journey has come to me, and I have nothing to set before him.'

"Then the one inside answers, 'Don't bother me. The door is already locked, and my children are with me in bed. I can't get up and give you anything.' I tell you, though he will not get up and give him the bread because he is his friend, yet because of the man's boldness[q] he will get up and give him as much as he needs.

Lk. 11:5-8

PRAYING WITH FAITH.   "So I say to you: Ask and it will be given to you; seek and you will find; knock and the door will be opened to you. For everyone who asks receives; he who seeks finds; and to him who knocks, the door will be opened.

"Which of you fathers, if your son asks for[r] a fish, will give him a snake instead? Or if he asks for an egg, will give him a scorpion? If you then, though you are evil, know how to give good gifts to your children, how much more will your Father in heaven give the Holy Spirit to those who ask him!"

Lk. 11:9-13

[l]Some manuscripts *but few things are needed—or only one*   [m]Some manuscripts *Our Father in heaven*   [n]Some manuscripts *come. May your will be done on earth as it is in heaven.*   [o]Greek *everyone who is indebted to us*   [p]Some manuscripts *temptation but deliver us from the evil one*   [q]Or *persistence*   [r]Some manuscripts *for bread, will give him a stone; or if he asks for*

*In Jerusalem for Feast of Dedication*_____

hether intentionally present for the feast or there for other reasons, Jesus is in Jerusalem in December during the eight-day Feast of Dedication, known more modernly as Hanukkah. This feast was instituted as recently as 164 B.C. by Judas Maccabaeus in commemoration of the refurbishing of the temple after it had been profaned for idolatrous use in 168 B.C. by Antiochus Epiphanes. Faithful Jews are gathering in Jerusalem in order to celebrate the rededication of the temple, and Jesus takes this opportunity to reach out to the large number of people present.

When various Jewish leaders ask Jesus whether he is the Christ, he reminds them of his miraculous works as proof of his deity. He then says that he and the Father are one, thereby infuriating the Jews, who see this as rank blasphemy. They take up rocks to stone Jesus and try to have him arrested, but Jesus escapes.

Jn.
10:22-30
Jerusalem
(Nov./
Dec., A.D.
29)

JESUS AFFIRMS OWN DEITY.   Then came the Feast of Dedication[s] at Jerusalem. It was winter, and Jesus was in the temple area walking in Solomon's Colonnade. The Jews gathered around him, saying, "How long will you keep us in suspense? If you are the Christ,[t] tell us plainly."

Jesus answered, "I did tell you, but you do not believe. The miracles I do in my Father's name speak for me, but you do not believe because you are not my sheep. My sheep listen to my voice; I know them, and they follow me. I give them eternal life, and they shall never perish; no one can snatch them out of my hand. My Father, who has given them to me, is greater than all[u]; no one can snatch them out of my Father's hand. I and the Father are one."

Jn.
10:31-39

ATTEMPT TO STONE JESUS.   Again the Jews picked up stones to stone him, but Jesus said to them, "I have shown you many great miracles from the Father. For which of these do you stone me?"

"We are not stoning you for any of these," replied the Jews, "but for blasphemy, because you, a mere man, claim to be God."

Jesus answered them, "Is it not written in your Law, 'I have said you are gods'[v]? If he called them 'gods,' to whom the word of God came—and the Scripture cannot be broken—what about the one whom the Father set apart as his very own and sent into the world? Why then do you accuse me of blasphemy because I said, 'I am God's Son'? Do not believe me unless I do what my Father does. But if I do it, even though you do not believe me, believe the miracles, that you may know and understand that the Father is in me, and I in the Father." Again they tried to seize him, but he escaped their grasp.

Jn.
10:40-42
Perea

TO PEREA.   Then Jesus went back across the Jordan to the place where John had been baptizing in the early days. Here he stayed and many people came to him. They said, "Though John never performed a miraculous sign, all that John said about this man was true." And in that place many believed in Jesus.

---

[s]That is, Hanukkah   [t]Or *Messiah*   [u]Many early manuscripts *What my Father has given me is greater than all*   [v]Psalm 82:6

The Perean Ministry

hen Jesus goes into the area beyond the Jordan River, he is entering the Perean province ruled by the tetrarch Herod Antipas, who also rules Galilee. It is this same Herod who had earlier beheaded John the Baptist, and he probably now fears a popular uprising of the people in response to Jesus' presence in that territory. Jesus does not fear Herod, however, because he knows that his end will come only in Jerusalem. It is unclear whether a warning about Herod comes from Pharisees who really believe in Jesus or whether they are simply trying to get Jesus to leave their area.

During this period of his ministry Jesus once again teaches through numerous parables. His parables cover a wide range of subjects, including the cost of discipleship, the value of lost souls, the rejection of his kingdom, the need for humility, and the unrighteousness of hypocritical religion.

NUMBER TO BE SAVED.   Then Jesus went through the towns and villages, teaching as he made his way to Jerusalem. Someone asked him, "Lord, are only a few people going to be saved?"

Lk.
13:22-30
Perea

He said to them, "Make every effort to enter through the narrow door, because many, I tell you, will try to enter and will not be able to. Once the owner of the house gets up and closes the door, you will stand outside knocking and pleading, 'Sir, open the door for us.'

"But he will answer, 'I don't know you or where you come from.'

"Then you will say, 'We ate and drank with you, and you taught in our streets.'

"But he will reply, 'I don't know you or where you come from. Away from me, all you evildoers!'

"There will be weeping there, and gnashing of teeth, when you see Abraham, Isaac and Jacob and all the prophets in the kingdom of God, but you yourselves thrown out. People will come from east and west and north and south, and will take their places at the feast in the kingdom of God. Indeed there are those who are last who will be first, and first who will be last."

JESUS WARNED ABOUT HEROD.   At that time some Pharisees came to Jesus and said to him, "Leave this place and go somewhere else. Herod wants to kill you."

Lk.
13:31-33

He replied, "Go tell that fox, 'I will drive out demons and heal people today and tomorrow, and on the third day I will reach my goal.' In any case, I must keep going today and tomorrow and the next day—for surely no prophet can die outside Jerusalem!

LAMENT OVER JERUSALEM.   "O Jerusalem, Jerusalem, you who kill the prophets and stone those sent to you, how often I have longed to gather your children together, as a hen gathers her chicks under her wings, but you were not willing! Look, your house is left to you desolate. I tell you, you will not see me again until you say, 'Blessed is he who comes in the name of the Lord.'*w*"

Lk.
13:34,35

*w*Psalm 118:26

Lk. 14:1-6 MAN HEALED OF DROPSY. One Sabbath, when Jesus went to eat in the house of a prominent Pharisee, he was being carefully watched. There in front of him was a man suffering from dropsy. Jesus asked the Pharisees and experts in the law, "Is it lawful to heal on the Sabbath or not?" But they remained silent. So taking hold of the man, he healed him and sent him away.

Then he asked them, "If one of you has a son[x] or an ox that falls into a well on the Sabbath day, will you not immediately pull him out?" And they had nothing to say.

Lk. 14:7-11 PARABLE OF PLACE OF HONOR. When he noticed how the guests picked the places of honor at the table, he told them this parable: "When someone invites you to a wedding feast, do not take the place of honor, for a person more distinguished than you may have been invited. If so, the host who invited both of you will come and say to you, 'Give this man your seat.' Then, humiliated, you will have to take the least important place. But when you are invited, take the lowest place, so that when your host comes, he will say to you, 'Friend, move up to a better place.' Then you will be honored in the presence of all your fellow guests. For everyone who exalts himself will be humbled, and he who humbles himself will be exalted."

Lk. 14:12-14 URGING UNSELFISHNESS. Then Jesus said to his host, "When you give a luncheon or dinner, do not invite your friends, your brothers or relatives, or your rich neighbors; if you do, they may invite you back and so you will be repaid. But when you give a banquet, invite the poor, the crippled, the lame, the blind, and you will be blessed. Although they cannot repay you, you will be repaid at the resurrection of the righteous."

Lk. 14:15-24 PARABLE OF GREAT BANQUET. When one of those at the table with him heard this, he said to Jesus, "Blessed is the man who will eat at the feast in the kingdom of God."

Jesus replied: "A certain man was preparing a great banquet and invited many guests. At the time of the banquet he sent his servant to tell those who had been invited, 'Come, for everything is now ready.'

"But they all alike began to make excuses. The first said, 'I have just bought a field, and I must go and see it. Please excuse me.'

"Another said, 'I have just bought five yoke of oxen, and I'm on my way to try them out. Please excuse me.'

"Still another said, 'I just got married, so I can't come.'

"The servant came back and reported this to his master. Then the owner of the house became angry and ordered his servant, 'Go out quickly into the streets and alleys of the town and bring in the poor, the crippled, the blind and the lame.'

"'Sir,' the servant said, 'what you ordered has been done, but there is still room.'

"Then the master told his servant, 'Go out to the roads and country lanes and make them come in, so that my house will be full. I tell you, not one of those men who were invited will get a taste of my banquet.'"

Lk. 14:25-33 COST OF DISCIPLESHIP. Large crowds were traveling with Jesus, and turning to them he said: "If anyone comes to me and does not hate his father and mother, his wife and children, his brothers and sisters—yes,

[x]Some manuscripts *donkey*

even his own life—he cannot be my disciple. And anyone who does not carry his cross and follow me cannot be my disciple.

"Suppose one of you wants to build a tower. Will he not first sit down and estimate the cost to see if he has enough money to complete it? For if he lays the foundation and is not able to finish it, everyone who sees it will ridicule him, saying, 'This fellow began to build and was not able to finish.'

"Or suppose a king is about to go to war against another king. Will he not first sit down and consider whether he is able with ten thousand men to oppose the one coming against him with twenty thousand? If he is not able, he will send a delegation while the other is still a long way off and will ask for terms of peace. In the same way, any of you who does not give up everything he has cannot be my disciple.

PARABLE OF THE SALT.   "Salt is good, but if it loses its saltiness, how can it be made salty again? It is fit neither for the soil nor for the manure pile; it is thrown out.

"He who has ears to hear, let him hear."

Lk.
14:34,35

PARABLE OF LOST SHEEP.   Now the tax collectors and "sinners" were all gathering around to hear him. But the Pharisees and the teachers of the law muttered, "This man welcomes sinners and eats with them."

Then Jesus told them this parable: "Suppose one of you has a hundred sheep and loses one of them. Does he not leave the ninety-nine in the open country and go after the lost sheep until he finds it? And when he finds it, he joyfully puts it on his shoulders and goes home. Then he calls his friends and neighbors together and says, 'Rejoice with me; I have found my lost sheep.' I tell you that in the same way there will be more rejoicing in heaven over one sinner who repents than over ninety-nine righteous persons who do not need to repent.

Lk. 15:1-7

PARABLE OF LOST COIN.   "Or suppose a woman has ten silver coins^y and loses one. Does she not light a lamp, sweep the house and search carefully until she finds it? And when she finds it, she calls her friends and neighbors together and says, 'Rejoice with me; I have found my lost coin.' In the same way, I tell you, there is rejoicing in the presence of the angels of God over one sinner who repents."

Lk. 15:8-10

PARABLE OF LOST SON.   Jesus continued: "There was a man who had two sons. The younger one said to his father, 'Father, give me my share of the estate.' So he divided his property between them.

"Not long after that, the younger son got together all he had, set off for a distant country and there squandered his wealth in wild living. After he had spent everything, there was a severe famine in that whole country, and he began to be in need. So he went and hired himself out to a citizen of that country, who sent him to his fields to feed pigs. He longed to fill his stomach with the pods that the pigs were eating, but no one gave him anything.

"When he came to his senses, he said, 'How many of my father's hired men have food to spare, and here I am starving to death! I will set out and go back to my father and say to him: Father, I have sinned against heaven and against you. I am no longer worthy to be called your son; make me like one of your hired men.' So he got up and went to his father.

Lk. 15:11-32

^{y}Greek *ten drachmas*, each worth about a day's wages

"But while he was still a long way off, his father saw him and was filled with compassion for him; he ran to his son, threw his arms around him and kissed him.

"The son said to him, 'Father, I have sinned against heaven and against you. I am no longer worthy to be called your son.^{z}'

"But the father said to his servants, 'Quick! Bring the best robe and put it on him. Put a ring on his finger and sandals on his feet. Bring the fattened calf and kill it. Let's have a feast and celebrate. For this son of mine was dead and is alive again; he was lost and is found.' So they began to celebrate.

"Meanwhile, the older son was in the field. When he came near the house, he heard music and dancing. So he called one of the servants and asked him what was going on. 'Your brother has come,' he replied, 'and your father has killed the fattened calf because he has him back safe and sound.'

"The older brother became angry and refused to go in. So his father went out and pleaded with him. But he answered his father, 'Look! All these years I've been slaving for you and never disobeyed your orders. Yet you never gave me even a young goat so I could celebrate with my friends. But when this son of yours who has squandered your property with prostitutes comes home, you kill the fattened calf for him!'

"'My son,' the father said, 'you are always with me, and everything I have is yours. But we had to celebrate and be glad, because this brother of yours was dead and is alive again; he was lost and is found.'"

Lk. 16:1-13 PARABLE OF DISHONEST MANAGER.   Jesus told his disciples: "There was a rich man whose manager was accused of wasting his possessions. So he called him in and asked him, 'What is this I hear about you? Give an account of your management, because you cannot be manager any longer.'

"The manager said to himself, 'What shall I do now? My master is taking away my job. I'm not strong enough to dig, and I'm ashamed to beg— I know what I'll do so that, when I lose my job here, people will welcome me into their houses.'

"So he called in each one of his master's debtors. He asked the first, 'How much do you owe my master?'

"'Eight hundred gallons^a of olive oil,' he replied.

"The manager told him, 'Take your bill, sit down quickly, and make it four hundred.'

"Then he asked the second, 'And how much do you owe?'

"'A thousand bushels^b of wheat,' he replied.

"He told him, 'Take your bill and make it eight hundred.'

"The master commended the dishonest manager because he had acted shrewdly. For the people of this world are more shrewd in dealing with their own kind than are the people of the light. I tell you, use worldly wealth to gain friends for yourselves, so that when it is gone, you will be welcomed into eternal dwellings.

"Whoever can be trusted with very little can also be trusted with much, and whoever is dishonest with very little will also be dishonest with much.

^{z}Some early manuscripts *son. Make me like one of your hired men.* ^{a}Greek *one hundred batous* (probably about 3 kiloliters) ^{b}Greek *one hundred korous* (probably about 35 kiloliters)

So if you have not been trustworthy in handling worldly wealth, who will trust you with true riches? And if you have not been trustworthy with someone else's property, who will give you property of your own?

"No servant can serve two masters. Either he will hate the one and love the other, or he will be devoted to the one and despise the other. You cannot serve both God and Money."

PHARISEES SCOFF AT PARABLE.   The Pharisees, who loved money, heard all this and were sneering at Jesus. He said to them, "You are the ones who justify yourselves in the eyes of men, but God knows your hearts. What is highly valued among men is detestable in God's sight.

Lk.
16:14,15

SUBSTANCE OF LAW.   "The Law and the Prophets were proclaimed until John. Since that time, the good news of the kingdom of God is being preached, and everyone is forcing his way into it. It is easier for heaven and earth to disappear than for the least stroke of a pen to drop out of the Law.

"Anyone who divorces his wife and marries another woman commits adultery, and the man who marries a divorced woman commits adultery.

Lk.
16:16-18

RICH MAN AND LAZARUS.   "There was a rich man who was dressed in purple and fine linen and lived in luxury every day. At his gate was laid a beggar named Lazarus, covered with sores and longing to eat what fell from the rich man's table. Even the dogs came and licked his sores.

"The time came when the beggar died and the angels carried him to Abraham's side. The rich man also died and was buried. In hell,[c] where he was in torment, he looked up and saw Abraham far away, with Lazarus by his side. So he called to him, 'Father Abraham, have pity on me and send Lazarus to dip the tip of his finger in water and cool my tongue, because I am in agony in this fire.'

"But Abraham replied, 'Son, remember that in your lifetime you received your good things, while Lazarus received bad things, but now he is comforted here and you are in agony. And besides all this, between us and you a great chasm has been fixed, so that those who want to go from here to you cannot, nor can anyone cross over from there to us.'

"He answered, 'Then I beg you, father, send Lazarus to my father's house, for I have five brothers. Let him warn them, so that they will not also come to this place of torment.'

"Abraham replied, 'They have Moses and the Prophets; let them listen to them.'

"'No, father Abraham,' he said, 'but if someone from the dead goes to them, they will repent.'

"He said to him, 'If they do not listen to Moses and the Prophets, they will not be convinced even if someone rises from the dead.'"

Lk.
16:19-31

COMING OF KINGDOM.   Once, having been asked by the Pharisees when the kingdom of God would come, Jesus replied, "The kingdom of God does not come with your careful observation, nor will people say, 'Here it is,' or 'There it is,' because the kingdom of God is within[d] you."

Then he said to his disciples, "The time is coming when you will long to see one of the days of the Son of Man, but you will not see it. Men will tell you, 'There he is!' or 'Here he is!' Do not go running off after them. For the Son of Man in his day[e] will be like the lightning, which flashes and lights

Lk.
17:20-35,37

[c]Greek *Hades*   [d]Or *among*   [e]Some manuscripts do not have *in his day.*

up the sky from one end to the other. But first he must suffer many things and be rejected by this generation.

"Just as it was in the days of Noah, so also will it be in the days of the Son of Man. People were eating, drinking, marrying and being given in marriage up to the day Noah entered the ark. Then the flood came and destroyed them all.

"It was the same in the days of Lot. People were eating and drinking, buying and selling, planting and building. But the day Lot left Sodom, fire and sulfur rained down from heaven and destroyed them all.

"It will be just like this on the day the Son of Man is revealed. On that day no one who is on the roof of his house, with his goods inside, should go down to get them. Likewise, no one in the field should go back for anything. Remember Lot's wife! Whoever tries to keep his life will lose it, and whoever loses his life will preserve it. I tell you, on that night two people will be in one bed; one will be taken and the other left. Two women will be grinding grain together; one will be taken and the other left.*f*"

"Where, Lord?" they asked.

He replied, "Where there is a dead body, there the vultures will gather."

Lk. 18:1-8 PERSISTENT WIDOW.   Then Jesus told his disciples a parable to show them that they should always pray and not give up. He said: "In a certain town there was a judge who neither feared God nor cared about men. And there was a widow in that town who kept coming to him with the plea, 'Grant me justice against my adversary.'

"For some time he refused. But finally he said to himself, 'Even though I don't fear God or care about men, yet because this widow keeps bothering me, I will see that she gets justice, so that she won't eventually wear me out with her coming!'"

And the Lord said, "Listen to what the unjust judge says. And will not God bring about justice for his chosen ones, who cry out to him day and night? Will he keep putting them off? I tell you, he will see that they get justice, and quickly. However, when the Son of Man comes, will he find faith on the earth?"

Lk. 18:9-14 PHARISEE AND TAX COLLECTOR.   To some who were confident of their own righteousness and looked down on everybody else, Jesus told this parable: "Two men went up to the temple to pray, one a Pharisee and the other a tax collector. The Pharisee stood up and prayed about*g* himself: 'God, I thank you that I am not like other men—robbers, evildoers, adulterers—or even like this tax collector. I fast twice a week and give a tenth of all I get.'

"But the tax collector stood at a distance. He would not even look up to heaven, but beat his breast and said, 'God, have mercy on me, a sinner.'

"I tell you that this man, rather than the other, went home justified before God. For everyone who exalts himself will be humbled, and he who humbles himself will be exalted."

Mt. 20:1-16 VINEYARD WORKERS.   "For the kingdom of heaven is like a landowner who went out early in the morning to hire men to work in his vineyard. He agreed to pay them a denarius for the day and sent them into his vineyard.

---

*f*Some manuscripts *left.* *36Two men will be in the field; one will be taken and the other left.*
*g*Or *to*

"About the third hour he went out and saw others standing in the marketplace doing nothing. He told them, 'You also go and work in my vineyard, and I will pay you whatever is right.' So they went.

"He went out again about the sixth hour and the ninth hour and did the same thing. About the eleventh hour he went out and found still others standing around. He asked them, 'Why have you been standing here all day long doing nothing?'

" 'Because no one has hired us,' they answered.

"He said to them, 'You also go and work in my vineyard.'

"When evening came, the owner of the vineyard said to his foreman, 'Call the workers and pay them their wages, beginning with the last ones hired and going on to the first.'

"The workers who were hired about the eleventh hour came and each received a denarius. So when those came who were hired first, they expected to receive more. But each one of them also received a denarius. When they received it, they began to grumble against the landowner. 'These men who were hired last worked only one hour,' they said, 'and you have made them equal to us who have borne the burden of the work and the heat of the day.'

"But he answered one of them, 'Friend, I am not being unfair to you. Didn't you agree to work for a denarius? Take your pay and go. I want to give the man who was hired last the same as I gave you. Don't I have the right to do what I want with my own money? Or are you envious because I am generous?'

"So the last will be first, and the first will be last."

Return to Judea to Raise Lazarus

John records one of the most poignant events found in all of the Gospel accounts. While Jesus is in Perea he learns that his friend Lazarus is seriously ill in Bethany, near Jerusalem. Jesus, of course, wants to be with Lazarus, despite his fearful disciples' counsel against returning that close to Jerusalem. Knowing that Lazarus has died, Jesus immediately sets out for Bethany.

What follows is a touching account of Jesus meeting Lazarus' sisters, Martha and Mary, and being moved to tears. Then, although it has been four days since Lazarus died, Jesus goes to the tomb and raises Lazarus from the dead. This, of course, is such a dramatic and conclusive demonstration of Jesus' power that his opponents call a hasty conference and immediately plot to kill him. Aware of the danger, Jesus withdraws northward to the town of Ephraim, near the wilderness.

LAZARUS' ILLNESS TOLD. Now a man named Lazarus was sick. He was from Bethany, the village of Mary and her sister Martha. This Mary, whose brother Lazarus now lay sick, was the same one who poured perfume on the Lord and wiped his feet with her hair. So the sisters sent word to Jesus, "Lord, the one you love is sick." **Jn. 11:1-4 Perea**

When he heard this, Jesus said, "This sickness will not end in death. No, it is for God's glory so that God's Son may be glorified through it."

Jn. 11:5-16   DISCIPLES FEAR RETURN.   Jesus loved Martha and her sister and Lazarus. Yet when he heard that Lazarus was sick, he stayed where he was two more days.

Then he said to his disciples, "Let us go back to Judea."

"But Rabbi," they said, "a short while ago the Jews tried to stone you, and yet you are going back there?"

Jesus answered, "Are there not twelve hours of daylight? A man who walks by day will not stumble, for he sees by this world's light. It is when he walks by night that he stumbles, for he has no light."

After he had said this, he went on to tell them, "Our friend Lazarus has fallen asleep; but I am going there to wake him up."

His disciples replied, "Lord, if he sleeps, he will get better." Jesus had been speaking of his death, but his disciples thought he meant natural sleep.

So then he told them plainly, "Lazarus is dead, and for your sake I am glad I was not there, so that you may believe. But let us go to him."

Then Thomas (called Didymus) said to the rest of the disciples, "Let us also go, that we may die with him."

Jn. 11:17-27 Near Bethany   JESUS TALKS WITH MARTHA.   On his arrival, Jesus found that Lazarus had already been in the tomb for four days. Bethany was less than two miles[h] from Jerusalem, and many Jews had come to Martha and Mary to comfort them in the loss of their brother. When Martha heard that Jesus was coming, she went out to meet him, but Mary stayed at home.

"Lord," Martha said to Jesus, "if you had been here, my brother would not have died. But I know that even now God will give you whatever you ask."

Jesus said to her, "Your brother will rise again."

Martha answered, "I know he will rise again in the resurrection at the last day."

Jesus said to her, "I am the resurrection and the life. He who believes in me will live, even though he dies; and whoever lives and believes in me will never die. Do you believe this?"

"Yes, Lord," she told him, "I believe that you are the Christ,[i] the Son of God, who was to come into the world."

Jn. 11:28-37   JESUS TALKS WITH MARY.   And after she had said this, she went back and called her sister Mary aside. "The Teacher is here," she said, "and is asking for you." When Mary heard this, she got up quickly and went to him. Now Jesus had not yet entered the village, but was still at the place where Martha had met him. When the Jews who had been with Mary in the house, comforting her, noticed how quickly she got up and went out, they followed her, supposing she was going to the tomb to mourn there.

When Mary reached the place where Jesus was and saw him, she fell at his feet and said, "Lord, if you had been here, my brother would not have died."

When Jesus saw her weeping, and the Jews who had come along with her also weeping, he was deeply moved in spirit and troubled. "Where have you laid him?" he asked.

"Come and see, Lord," they replied.

Jesus wept.

[h]Greek *fifteen stadia* (about 3 kilometers)   [i]Or *Messiah*

Then the Jews said, "See how he loved him!"

But some of them said, "Could not he who opened the eyes of the blind man have kept this man from dying?"

LAZARUS RAISED.   Jesus, once more deeply moved, came to the tomb. **Jn. 11:38-44** It was a cave with a stone laid across the entrance. "Take away the stone," he said.

"But, Lord," said Martha, the sister of the dead man, "by this time there is a bad odor, for he has been there four days."

Then Jesus said, "Did I not tell you that if you believed, you would see the glory of God?"

So they took away the stone. Then Jesus looked up and said, "Father, I thank you that you have heard me. I knew that you always hear me, but I said this for the benefit of the people standing here, that they may believe that you sent me."

When he had said this, Jesus called in a loud voice, "Lazarus, come out!" The dead man came out, his hands and feet wrapped with strips of linen, and a cloth around his face.

Jesus said to them, "Take off the grave clothes and let him go."

COUNCIL PLOTS TO KILL JESUS.   Therefore many of the Jews who had **Jn. 11:45-53** come to visit Mary, and had seen what Jesus did, put their faith in him. But some of them went to the Pharisees and told them what Jesus had done. Then the chief priests and the Pharisees called a meeting of the Sanhedrin.

"What are we accomplishing?" they asked. "Here is this man performing many miraculous signs. If we let him go on like this, everyone will believe in him, and then the Romans will come and take away both our place[j] and our nation."

Then one of them, named Caiaphas, who was high priest that year, spoke up, "You know nothing at all! You do not realize that it is better for you that one man die for the people than that the whole nation perish."

He did not say this on his own, but as high priest that year he prophesied that Jesus would die for the Jewish nation, and not only for that nation but also for the scattered children of God, to bring them together and make them one. So from that day on they plotted to take his life.

JESUS GOES TO EPHRAIM.   Therefore Jesus no longer moved about **Jn. 11:54** publicly among the Jews. Instead he withdrew to a region near the desert, **Ephraim** to a village called Ephraim, where he stayed with his disciples.

The Final Journey

*F*rom Ephraim, the final days of Jesus' life and ministry begin to count down. What occurs during this period, probably between January and the end of March, is a microcosm of his entire ministry. There is more teaching to be done and, as always, the need for dialogue and confrontation with the Pharisees. Jesus once again blesses little children and once again reminds those who would follow him of the burdens they must bear. As he has done twice before, Jesus again tells of his impending death. And there are more parables to be taught and still more people to be healed.

*j*Or temple

Surely it is a constant source of discouragement to Jesus—even in these last days, and after repeated lessons on humility—that his disciples are still seeking personal glory in the kingdom. Even now the apostles continue to think only in terms of an earthly kingdom. James and John, prompted by their mother, ask that they be given special positions. Jesus admonishes them once again, pointing to the spiritual nature of his kingdom and to the need for humility and service. Yet the time is short now, and Jesus knows that they will soon understand.

There is at least one person who already seems to understand about Jesus' mission and his call for humility. That person is Mary, the sister of Lazarus. As Jesus' journey to Jerusalem comes to an end, the Gospel accounts tell the beautiful story of Mary anointing Jesus with precious ointments. It will be a touching prelude to the brutal events of the final week.

Mt. 19:3-9
Mk. 10:2-9

PHARISEES QUESTION DIVORCE.   Some Pharisees came to him to test him. They asked, "Is it lawful for a man to divorce his wife for any and every reason?"

"Haven't you read," he replied, "that at the beginning the Creator 'made them male and female,'^{k} and said, 'For this reason a man will leave his father and mother and be united to his wife, and the two will become one flesh'^{l}? So they are no longer two, but one. Therefore what God has joined together, let man not separate."

"Why then," they asked, "did Moses command that a man give his wife a certificate of divorce and send her away?"

Jesus replied, "Moses permitted you to divorce your wives because your hearts were hard. But it was not this way from the beginning. I tell you that anyone who divorces his wife, except for marital unfaithfulness, and marries another woman commits adultery."

Mt.
19:10-12
Mk.
10:10-12

DISCIPLES QUESTION JESUS. ^{Mk}When they were in the house again, the disciples asked Jesus about this. He answered, "Anyone who divorces his wife and marries another woman commits adultery against her. And if she divorces her husband and marries another man, she commits adultery." ^{Mt}The disciples said to him, "If this is the situation between a husband and wife, it is better not to marry."

Jesus replied, "Not everyone can accept this word, but only those to whom it has been given. For some are eunuchs because they were born that way; others were made that way by men; and others have renounced marriage^m because of the kingdom of heaven. The one who can accept this should accept it."

Mt.
19:13-15
Mk.
10:13-16
Lk.
18:15-17

JESUS BLESSES CHILDREN.   People were bringing little children to Jesus to have him touch them, but the disciples rebuked them. When Jesus saw this, he was indignant. He said to them, "Let the little children come to me, and do not hinder them, for the kingdom of God belongs to such as these. I tell you the truth, anyone who will not receive the kingdom of God like a little child will never enter it." And he took the children in his arms, put his hands on them and blessed them.

^{k}Gen. 1:27 ^{l}Gen. 2:24 ^{m}Or *have made themselves eunuchs*

RICH YOUNG MAN.   As Jesus started on his way, a man ran up to him and fell on his knees before him. "Good teacher," he asked, "what must I do to inherit eternal life?"

"Why do you call me good?" Jesus answered. "No one is good—except God alone. You know the commandments: 'Do not murder, do not commit adultery, do not steal, do not give false testimony, do not defraud, honor your father and mother.'*n*"

"Teacher," he declared, "all these I have kept since I was a boy."

Jesus looked at him and loved him. "One thing you lack," he said. "Go, sell everything you have and give to the poor, and you will have treasure in heaven. Then come, follow me."

At this the man's face fell. He went away sad, because he had great wealth.

Mt.
19:16-22
Mk.
10:17-22
Lk.
18:18-23

LOVE OF POSSESSIONS.   Jesus looked around and said to his disciples, "How hard it is for the rich to enter the kingdom of God!"

The disciples were amazed at his words. But Jesus said again, "Children, how hard it is*o* to enter the kingdom of God! It is easier for a camel to go through the eye of a needle than for a rich man to enter the kingdom of God."

The disciples were even more amazed, and said to each other, "Who then can be saved?"

Jesus looked at them and said, "With man this is impossible, but not with God; all things are possible with God."

Mt.
19:23-26
Mk.
10:23-27
Lk.
18:24-27

FORSAKING EARTHLY ATTACHMENTS.   Peter answered him, "We have left everything to follow you! What then will there be for us?"

Jesus said to them, "I tell you the truth, at the renewal of all things, when the Son of Man sits on his glorious throne, you who have followed me will also sit on twelve thrones, judging the twelve tribes of Israel. And everyone who has left houses or brothers or sisters or father or mother*p* or children or fields for my sake will receive a hundred times as much and will inherit eternal life. But many who are first will be last, and many who are last will be first.

Mt.
19:27-30
Mk.
10:28-31
Lk.
18:28-30

DEATH FORETOLD THIRD TIME.   *Mk*They were on their way up to Jerusalem, with Jesus leading the way, and the disciples were astonished, while those who followed were afraid. Again he took the Twelve aside and told them what was going to happen to him. "We are going up to Jerusalem," he said, "and the Son of Man will be betrayed to the chief priests and teachers of the law. They will condemn him to death and will hand him over to the Gentiles, who will mock him and spit on him, flog him and kill him. Three days later he will rise." *Lk*The disciples did not understand any of this. Its meaning was hidden from them, and they did not know what he was talking about.

Mt.
20:17-19
Mk.
10:32-34
Lk.
18:31-34
On road to
Jerusalem

REQUEST BY JAMES AND JOHN.   *Mt*Then the mother of Zebedee's sons came to Jesus with her sons and, kneeling down, asked a favor of him.

"What is it you want?" he asked.

She said, "Grant that one of these two sons of mine may sit at your right and the other at your left in your kingdom." *Mk*Then James and John, the

Mt.
20:20-23
Mk.
10:35-40

---

*n*Exodus 20:12-16; Deut. 5:16-20   *o*Some manuscripts *is for those who trust in riches*
*p*Some manuscripts *mother or wife*

sons of Zebedee, came to him. "Teacher," they said, "we want you to do for us whatever we ask."

"What do you want me to do for you?" he asked.

They replied, "Let one of us sit at your right and the other at your left in your glory."

"You don't know what you are asking," Jesus said. "Can you drink the cup I drink or be baptized with the baptism I am baptized with?"

"We can," they answered.

Jesus said to them, "You will drink the cup I drink and be baptized with the baptism I am baptized with, but to sit at my right or left is not for me to grant. These places belong to those for whom they have been prepared."

Mt.
20:24-28
Mk.
10:41-45

JESUS TEACHES HUMILITY.   When the ten heard about this, they became indignant with James and John. Jesus called them together and said, "You know that those who are regarded as rulers of the Gentiles lord it over them, and their high officials exercise authority over them. Not so with you. Instead, whoever wants to become great among you must be your servant, and whoever wants to be first must be slave of all. For even the Son of Man did not come to be served, but to serve, and to give his life as a ransom for many."

Lk. 19:1-10
In Jericho

ZACCHAEUS RECEIVES JESUS.   Jesus entered Jericho and was passing through. A man was there by the name of Zacchaeus; he was a chief tax collector and was wealthy. He wanted to see who Jesus was, but being a short man he could not, because of the crowd. So he ran ahead and climbed a sycamore-fig tree to see him, since Jesus was coming that way.

When Jesus reached the spot, he looked up and said to him, "Zacchaeus, come down immediately. I must stay at your house today." So he came down at once and welcomed him gladly.

All the people saw this and began to mutter, "He has gone to be the guest of a 'sinner.'"

But Zacchaeus stood up and said to the Lord, "Look, Lord! Here and now I give half of my possessions to the poor, and if I have cheated anybody out of anything, I will pay back four times the amount."

Jesus said to him, "Today salvation has come to this house, because this man, too, is a son of Abraham. For the Son of Man came to seek and to save what was lost."

Mt.
20:29-34
Mk.
10:46-52
Lk.
18:35-43

BLIND BARTIMAEUS HEALED.   MkAs Jesus and his disciples, together with a large crowd, were leaving the city, a blind man, Bartimaeus (that is, the Son of Timaeus), was sitting by the roadside begging. When he heard that it was Jesus of Nazareth, he began to shout, "Jesus, Son of David, have mercy on me!"

Many rebuked him and told him to be quiet, but he shouted all the more, "Son of David, have mercy on me!"

Jesus stopped and said, "Call him."

So they called to the blind man, "Cheer up! On your feet! He's calling you." Throwing his cloak aside, he jumped to his feet and came to Jesus.

"What do you want me to do for you?" Jesus asked him.

The blind man said, "Rabbi, I want to see."

"Go," said Jesus, "your faith has healed you." LkImmediately he received his sight and followed Jesus, praising God. When all the people saw it, they also praised God.

PARABLE OF THE TEN MINAS.   While they were listening to this, he
went on to tell them a parable, because he was near Jerusalem and the people thought that the kingdom of God was going to appear at once. He said:
"A man of noble birth went to a distant country to have himself appointed king and then to return. So he called ten of his servants and gave them
ten minas.⁹ 'Put this money to work,' he said, 'until I come back.'

"But his subjects hated him and sent a delegation after him to say, 'We
don't want this man to be our king.'

"He was made king, however, and returned home. Then he sent for the
servants to whom he had given the money, in order to find out what they
had gained with it.

"The first one came and said, 'Sir, your mina has earned ten more.'

"'Well done, my good servant!' his master replied. 'Because you have
been trustworthy in a very small matter, take charge of ten cities.'

"The second came and said, 'Sir, your mina has earned five more.'

"His master answered, 'You take charge of five cities.'

"Then another servant came and said, 'Sir, here is your mina; I have kept
it laid away in a piece of cloth. I was afraid of you, because you are a hard
man. You take out what you did not put in and reap what you did not
sow.'

"His master replied, 'I will judge you by your own words, you wicked
servant! You knew, did you, that I am a hard man, taking out what I did
not put in, and reaping what I did not sow? Why then didn't you put my
money on deposit, so that when I came back, I could have collected it with
interest?'

"Then he said to those standing by, 'Take his mina away from him and
give it to the one who has ten minas.'

"'Sir,' they said, 'he already has ten!'

"He replied, 'I tell you that to everyone who has, more will be given, but
as for the one who has nothing, even what he has will be taken away. But
those enemies of mine who did not want me to be king over them—bring
them here and kill them in front of me.'"

Lk.
19:11-27

TRAVELING TOWARD JERUSALEM.   After Jesus had said this, he went
on ahead, going up to Jerusalem.

Lk. 19:28

ARREST PLANNED FOR PASSOVER.   When it was almost time for the
Jewish Passover, many went up from the country to Jerusalem for their
ceremonial cleansing before the Passover. They kept looking for Jesus, and
as they stood in the temple area they asked one another, "What do you
think? Isn't he coming to the Feast at all?" But the chief priests and
Pharisees had given orders that if anyone found out where Jesus was, he
should report it so that they might arrest him.

Jn.
11:55-57

MARY ANOINTS JESUS.   ᴶⁿSix days before the Passover, Jesus arrived at
Bethany, where Lazarus lived, whom Jesus had raised from the dead. Here
[ᴹᵗin the home of a man known as Simon the Leper] a dinner was given in
Jesus' honor. Martha served, while Lazarus was among those reclining at
the table with him. Then Mary took about a pintʳ of pure nard, an expensive perfume; she poured it on Jesus' feet and wiped his feet with her hair.
And the house was filled with the fragrance of the perfume.

Mt. 26:6-13
Mk. 14:3-9
Jn. 12:1-8

⁹A mina was about three months' wages.   ʳGreek *a litra* (probably about 0.5 liter)

But one of his disciples, Judas Iscariot, who was later to betray him, objected, "Why wasn't this perfume sold and the money given to the poor? It was worth a year's wages.ˢ" He did not say this because he cared about the poor but because he was a thief; as keeper of the money bag, he used to help himself to what was put into it.

"Leave her alone," Jesus replied. "˩It was intended˩ that she should save this perfume for the day of my burial. You will always have the poor among you, but you will not always have me." ᴹᵏI tell you the truth, wherever the gospel is preached throughout the world, what she has done will also be told, in memory of her."

Jn. 12:9-11
(Saturday?)
PLOT TO KILL LAZARUS.   Meanwhile a large crowd of Jews found out that Jesus was there and came, not only because of him but also to see Lazarus, whom he had raised from the dead. So the chief priests made plans to kill Lazarus as well, for on account of him many of the Jews were going over to Jesus and putting their faith in him.

The Triumphant Entry—Sunday

*J*t is late March and the Feast of the Passover is near. The time has come for Jesus to be delivered up. No Jewish feast is more important to the people, and no feast could be more appropriate for the culmination of Jesus' life and ministry. Passover comes at the beginning of the Feast of Unleavened Bread, which lasts for seven days. It commemorates the exodus of the people of ancient Israel from their captivity in Egypt. On the Passover, the paschal lamb is slain, just as it was at the beginning of the exodus, at which time its blood was sprinkled over the doors of the Israelites. When death passed over Egypt and the firstborn of each household was killed, God spared only those households whose doors were covered by the blood. As the perfect Lamb of God, Jesus himself is about to be slain for the salvation of all who would recognize and accept the power in his blood.

Even as Jesus approaches Jerusalem, his enemies are plotting his death. But the suffering will not come until Jesus has entered the city in triumph. Riding on a lowly colt, Jesus is met by multitudes who shout praise to God for having sent this "great prophet" in whom they now believe. Jesus knows, however, that most of them still do not understand the true nature of his messiahship and deity, and that there are many more who still do not believe in him at all. As Jesus is now given the greatest welcome of his ministry, his enemies fear his popularity and let him have his day of glory.

Jn.
12:12,13
(Sunday)
CROWD GOES TO MEET JESUS.   The next day the great crowd that had come for the Feast heard that Jesus was on his way to Jerusalem. They took palm branches and went out to meet him, shouting,

"Hosanna!ᵗ"

"Blessed is he who comes in the name of the Lord!"ᵘ

"Blessed is the King of Israel!"

ˢGreek *three hundred denarii*   ᵗA Hebrew expression meaning "Save!" which became an exclamation of praise   ᵘPsalm 118:25,26

JESUS SENDS FOR COLT.   Lk As he approached Bethphage and Bethany at the hill called the Mount of Olives, he sent two of his disciples, saying to them, "Go to the village ahead of you, and as you enter it, you will find a colt tied there, which no one has ever ridden. Untie it and bring it here. If anyone asks you, 'Why are you untying it?' tell him, 'The Lord needs it.'" Mt This took place to fulfill what was spoken through the prophet:

> "Say to the Daughter of Zion,
>   'See, your king comes to you,
>   gentle and riding on a donkey,
>   on a colt, the foal of a donkey.' "v

Mt. 21:1-7
Mk. 11:1-7
Lk.
19:29-35
Jn.
12:14-16

Jn At first his disciples did not understand all this. Only after Jesus was glorified did they realize that these things had been written about him and that they had done these things to him. Mk They went and found a colt outside in the street, tied at a doorway. As they untied it, some people standing there asked, "What are you doing, untying that colt?" They answered as Jesus had told them to, and the people let them go. When they brought the colt to Jesus and threw their cloaks over it, he sat on it.

JESUS ENTERS JERUSALEM.   Lk When he came near the place where the road goes down the Mount of Olives, the whole crowd of disciples began joyfully to praise God in loud voices for all the miracles they had seen:

> "Blessed is the king who comes in the name of the Lord!"w

> "Peace in heaven and glory in the highest!"

Mt. 21:8,9
Mk.
11:8-10
Lk.
19:36-40
Jerusalem
(Sunday)

Some of the Pharisees in the crowd said to Jesus, "Teacher, rebuke your disciples!"
"I tell you," he replied, "if they keep quiet, the stones will cry out." Mk Many people spread their cloaks on the road, while others spread branches they had cut in the fields.

JESUS FORESEES DESTRUCTION.   As he approached Jerusalem and saw the city, he wept over it and said, "If you, even you, had only known on this day what would bring you peace—but now it is hidden from your eyes. The days will come upon you when your enemies will build an embankment against you and encircle you and hem you in on every side. They will dash you to the ground, you and the children within your walls. They will not leave one stone on another, because you did not recognize the time of God's coming to you."

Lk.
19:41-44

JESUS' POPULARITY RECOGNIZED.   Mt When Jesus entered Jerusalem, the whole city was stirred and asked, "Who is this?"
The crowds answered, "This is Jesus, the prophet from Nazareth in Galilee." Jn Now the crowd that was with him when he called Lazarus from the tomb and raised him from the dead continued to spread the word. Many people, because they had heard that he had given this miraculous sign, went out to meet him. So the Pharisees said to one another, "See, this is getting us nowhere. Look how the whole world has gone after him!"

Mt.
21:10,11
Jn.
12:17-19

RETURN TO BETHANY.   Jesus entered Jerusalem and went to the temple. He looked around at everything, but since it was already late, he went out to Bethany with the Twelve.

Mt. 21:17
Mk. 11:11
Bethany

vZech. 9:9   wPsalm 118:26

Final Week—Monday

O n the next day, Jesus' popularity is still at a high peak, and children sing his praises as if to thank him for his continual remembrance of them. In a contrasting mood of the day, Matthew, Mark, and Luke each record an incident almost identical to one recorded by John at the beginning of Jesus' ministry—that is, the throwing out of the temple merchants. If this is in fact a separate incident, it just may be that Jesus is taking this last opportunity to purify the temple. Enraged as they must be, the merchants and the money changers, like the religious leaders, fear the people and will bide their time.

Jesus now speaks freely of his impending crucifixion and makes a special effort to explain its purpose. There are many who still disbelieve, but, as John observes, even their disbelief is the fulfillment of prophecy.

Now Jesus leaves Bethany and places a curse on an unfruitful fig tree, an incident which he will later use to illustrate a lesson on the power of faith.

Mt. 21:18,19 Mk. 11:12-14	**UNFRUITFUL FIG TREE.** The next day as they were leaving Bethany, Jesus was hungry. Seeing in the distance a fig tree in leaf, he went to find out if it had any fruit. When he reached it, he found nothing but leaves, because it was not the season for figs. Then he said to the tree, "May no one ever eat fruit from you again." And his disciples heard him say it.
Mt. 21:12,13 Mk. 11:15-17 Lk. 19:45,46 At temple	**JESUS CLEANSES TEMPLE.** On reaching Jerusalem, Jesus entered the temple area and began driving out those who were buying and selling there. He overturned the tables of the money changers and the benches of those selling doves, and would not allow anyone to carry merchandise through the temple courts. And as he taught them, he said, "Is it not written:

> " 'My house will be called
>   a house of prayer for all nations'[x]?

But you have made it 'a den of robbers.'[y]"

Mk. 11:18 Lk. 19:47,48	**PLOT DELAYED.** [Mk]The chief priests and the teachers of the law heard this and began looking for a way to kill him, for they feared him, because the whole crowd was amazed at his teaching. [Lk]Yet they could not find any way to do it, because all the people hung on his words.
Mt. 21:14-16	**CHILDREN PRAISE JESUS.** The blind and the lame came to him at the temple, and he healed them. But when the chief priests and the teachers of the law saw the wonderful things he did and the children shouting in the temple area, "Hosanna to the Son of David," they were indignant.

"Do you hear what these children are saying?" they asked him.

"Yes," replied Jesus, "have you never read,

> " 'From the lips of children and infants
>   you have ordained praise'[z]?"

Jn. 12:20-26	**PURPOSE OF CHRIST'S DEATH.** Now there were some Greeks among those who went up to worship at the Feast. They came to Philip, who was from Bethsaida in Galilee, with a request. "Sir," they said, "we would like

[x]Isaiah 56:7   [y]Jer. 7:11   [z]Psalm 8:2

to see Jesus." Philip went to tell Andrew; Andrew and Philip in turn told Jesus.

Jesus replied, "The hour has come for the Son of Man to be glorified. I tell you the truth, unless a kernel of wheat falls to the ground and dies, it remains only a single seed. But if it dies, it produces many seeds. The man who loves his life will lose it, while the man who hates his life in this world will keep it for eternal life. Whoever serves me must follow me; and where I am, my servant also will be. My Father will honor the one who serves me.

FORETELLING CRUCIFIXION.   "Now my heart is troubled, and what shall I say? 'Father, save me from this hour'? No, it was for this very reason I came to this hour. Father, glorify your name!"

Jn.
12:27-33

Then a voice came from heaven, "I have glorified it, and will glorify it again." The crowd that was there and heard it said it had thundered; others said an angel had spoken to him.

Jesus said, "This voice was for your benefit, not mine. Now is the time for judgment on this world; now the prince of this world will be driven out. But I, when I am lifted up from the earth, will draw all men to myself." He said this to show the kind of death he was going to die.

CALL FOR WALKING IN LIGHT.   The crowd spoke up, "We have heard from the Law that the Christ *a* will remain forever, so how can you say, 'The Son of Man must be lifted up'? Who is this 'Son of Man'?"

Jn.
12:34-36

Then Jesus told them, "You are going to have the light just a little while longer. Walk while you have the light, before darkness overtakes you. The man who walks in the dark does not know where he is going. Put your trust in the light while you have it, so that you may become sons of light." When he had finished speaking, Jesus left and hid himself from them.

RETURN TO BETHANY.   When evening came, they *b* went out of the city.

Mk. 11:19
Bethany

Final Week—Tuesday Morning

*T*uesday comes as a day of great confrontation with the religious leaders assembled in Jerusalem. By way of parables, Jesus points out that the leaders' predecessors have always rejected God's messengers and that now they themselves are rejecting even the Son of God. This obviously angers the Pharisees, and they attempt to trap Jesus into making some statement by which they can have him arrested. His answer takes them by surprise, and they are left with no basis for a charge.

The Pharisees are then joined in their questioning by the Sadducees. Although the Sadducees often clash politically and religiously with the Pharisees, the Sadducees are equally threatened by Jesus' teaching. So they are willing to join with the Pharisees to rid themselves of this Galilean troublemaker. Since the Sadducees deny any resurrection from the dead, it is only natural that they try to catch Jesus by posing a potentially embarrassing hypothetical situation concerning any supposed life after death. To their

---

*a*Or *Messiah*   *b*Some early manuscripts *he*

dismay Jesus, as the Son of God, once again responds with superior spiritual insight.

When a Pharisee questioned Jesus concerning the greatest commandment, he delivers a response that goes to the heart of his message and ministry. He then sharply chastises both sects for having failed to grasp the true meaning of worship and service before God. Observing a widow contributing all that she has—although it was only two small coins—Jesus points to her as an example of true spirituality.

Mt.
21:20-22
Mk.
11:20-26
From
Bethany to
Jerusalem

LESSON FROM FIG TREE. ᴹᵏIn the morning, as they went along, they saw the fig tree withered from the roots. Peter remembered and said to Jesus, "Rabbi, look! The fig tree you cursed has withered!" ᴹᵗWhen the disciples saw this, they were amazed. "How did the fig tree wither so quickly?" they asked.

Jesus replied, "I tell you the truth, if you have faith and do not doubt, not only can you do what was done to the fig tree, but also you can say to this mountain, 'Go, throw yourself into the sea,' and it will be done. If you believe, you will receive whatever you ask for in prayer." ᴹᵏAnd when you stand praying, if you hold anything against anyone, forgive him, so that your Father in heaven may forgive you your sins.ᶜ"

Mt.
21:23-27
Mk.
11:27-33
Lk. 20:1-8

JESUS' AUTHORITY QUESTIONED. They arrived again in Jerusalem, and while Jesus was walking in the temple courts, the chief priests, the teachers of the law and the elders came to him. "By what authority are you doing these things?" they asked. "And who gave you authority to do this?"

Jesus replied, "I will ask you one question. Answer me, and I will tell you by what authority I am doing these things. John's baptism—was it from heaven, or from men? Tell me!"

They discussed it among themselves and said, "If we say, 'From heaven,' he will ask, 'Then why didn't you believe him?' But if we say, 'From men'. . ." (They feared the people, for everyone held that John really was a prophet.)

So they answered Jesus, "We don't know."

Jesus said, "Neither will I tell you by what authority I am doing these things."

Mt.
21:28-32

PARABLE OF TWO SONS. "What do you think? There was a man who had two sons. He went to the first and said, 'Son, go and work today in the vineyard.'

"'I will not,' he answered, but later he changed his mind and went.

"Then the father went to the other son and said the same thing. He answered, 'I will, sir,' but he did not go.

"Which of the two did what his father wanted?"

"The first," they answered.

Jesus said to them, "I tell you the truth, the tax collectors and the prostitutes are entering the kingdom of God ahead of you. For John came to you to show you the way of righteousness, and you did not believe him, but the tax collectors and the prostitutes did. And even after you saw this, you did not repent and believe him.

ᶜSome manuscripts sins. ²⁶But if you do not forgive, neither will your Father who is in heaven forgive your sins.

PARABLE OF MURDEROUS TENANTS.   ᴹᵏHe then began to speak to
them in parables: "A man planted a vineyard. He put a wall around it, dug
a pit for the winepress and built a watchtower. Then he rented the vineyard to some farmers and went away on a journey. At harvest time he sent
a servant to the tenants to collect from them some of the fruit of the vineyard. But they seized him, beat him and sent him away empty-handed.
Then he sent another servant to them; they struck this man on the head
and treated him shamefully. He sent still another, and that one they killed.
He sent many others; some of them they beat, others they killed.

"He had one left to send, a son, whom he loved. He sent him last of all,
saying, 'They will respect my son.'

"But the tenants said to one another, 'This is the heir. Come, let's kill
him, and the inheritance will be ours.' So they took him and killed him,
and threw him out of the vineyard.

"What then will the owner of the vineyard do? He will come and kill
those tenants and give the vineyard to others.

ᴸᵏWhen the people heard this, they said, "May this never be!"

Mt.
21:33-41
Mk. 12:1-9
Lk. 20:9-16

THE REJECTED STONE.   Jesus said to them, "Have you never read in the
Scriptures:

" 'The stone the builders rejected
    has become the capstoneᵈ;
  the Lord has done this,
    and it is marvelous in our eyes'ᵉ?

"Therefore I tell you that the kingdom of God will be taken away from
you and given to a people who will produce its fruit. He who falls on this
stone will be broken to pieces, but he on whom it falls will be crushed."ᶠ

Mt.
21:42-44
Mk.
12:10,11
Lk.
20:17,18

RELIGIOUS LEADERS ANGERED.   When the chief priests and the Pharisees heard Jesus' parables, they knew he was talking about them. They
looked for a way to arrest him, but they were afraid of the crowd because
the people held that he was a prophet.

Mt.
21:45,46
Mk. 12:12
Lk. 20:19

PARABLE OF WEDDING BANQUET.   Jesus spoke to them again in parables, saying: "The kingdom of heaven is like a king who prepared a wedding banquet for his son. He sent his servants to those who had been invited to the banquet to tell them to come, but they refused to come.

"Then he sent some more servants and said, 'Tell those who have been
invited that I have prepared my dinner: My oxen and fattened cattle have
been butchered, and everything is ready. Come to the wedding banquet.'

"But they paid no attention and went off—one to his field, another to his
business. The rest seized his servants, mistreated them and killed them.
The king was enraged. He sent his army and destroyed those murderers
and burned their city.

"Then he said to his servants, 'The wedding banquet is ready, but those
I invited did not deserve to come. Go to the street corners and invite to the
banquet anyone you find.' So the servants went out into the streets and
gathered all the people they could find, both good and bad, and the wedding hall was filled with guests.

"But when the king came in to see the guests, he noticed a man there

Mt. 22:1-14

ᵈOr *cornerstone*   ᵉPsalm 118:22,23   ᶠSome manuscripts do not have verse 44.

who was not wearing wedding clothes. 'Friend,' he asked, 'how did you get in here without wedding clothes?' The man was speechless.

"Then the king told the attendants, 'Tie him hand and foot, and throw him outside, into the darkness, where there will be weeping and gnashing of teeth.'

"For many are invited, but few are chosen."

Mt.
22:15-22
Mk.
12:13-17
Lk.
20:20-26

LEADERS ASK ABOUT TAXES.   ᴹᵗThen the Pharisees went out and laid plans to trap him in his words. They sent their disciples to him along with the Herodians. . . ᴸᵏspies, who pretended to be honest. They hoped to catch Jesus in something he said so that they might hand him over to the power and authority of the governor. So the spies questioned him: "Teacher, we know that you speak and teach what is right, and that you do not show partiality but teach the way of God in accordance with the truth. Is it right for us to pay taxes to Caesar or not?"

He saw through their duplicity and said to them, "Show me a denarius. Whose portrait and inscription are on it?"

"Caesar's," they replied.

He said to them, "Then give to Caesar what is Caesar's, and to God what is God's."

They were unable to trap him in what he had said there in public. And astonished by his answer, they became silent.

Mt.
22:23-33
Mk.
12:18-27
Lk.
20:27-28

RESURRECTION QUESTIONED.   That same day the Sadducees, who say there is no resurrection, came to him with a question. "Teacher," they said, "Moses told us that if a man dies without having children, his brother must marry the widow and have children for him. Now there were seven brothers among us. The first one married and died, and since he had no children, he left his wife to his brother. The same thing happened to the second and third brother, right on down to the seventh. Finally, the woman died. Now then, at the resurrection, whose wife will she be of the seven, since all of them were married to her?"

Jesus replied, "You are in error because you do not know the Scriptures or the power of God. At the resurrection people will neither marry nor be given in marriage; they will be like the angels in heaven. But about the resurrection of the dead—have you not read what God said to you, 'I am the God of Abraham, the God of Isaac, and the God of Jacob'ᵍ? He is not the God of the dead but of the living."

When the crowds heard this, they were astonished at his teaching.

Mt.
22:34-40
Mk.
12:28-34
Lk.
20:39,40

THE GREATEST COMMANDMENT.   One of the teachers of the law came and heard them debating. Noticing that Jesus had given them a good answer, he asked him, "Of all the commandments, which is the most important?"

"The most important one," answered Jesus, "is this: 'Hear, O Israel, the Lord our God, the Lord is one.ʰ Love the Lord your God with all your heart and with all your soul and with all your mind and with all your strength.'ⁱ The second is this: 'Love your neighbor as yourself.'ʲ There is no commandment greater than these."

"Well said, teacher," the man replied. "You are right in saying that God is one and there is no other but him. To love him with all your heart, with all your understanding and with all your strength, and to love your

ᵍExodus 3:6   ʰOr *the Lord our God is one Lord*   ⁱDeut. 6:4,5   ʲLev. 19:18

neighbor as yourself is more important than all burnt offerings and sacrifices."

When Jesus saw that he had answered wisely, he said to him, "You are not far from the kingdom of God."

JESUS ASKS ABOUT ANCESTRY.   ^MtWhile the Pharisees were gathered together, Jesus asked them, "What do you think about the Christ^k? Whose son is he?"

"The son of David," they replied.

He said to them, "How is it then that David, speaking by the Spirit, calls him 'Lord'? For he says,

Mt.
22:41-46
Mk.
12:35-37
Lk.
20:41-44

" 'The Lord said to my Lord:
"Sit at my right hand
until I put your enemies
under your feet." '^l

If then David calls him 'Lord,' how can he be his son?"

^MkThe large crowd listened to him with delight. ^MtNo one could say a word in reply, and from that day on no one dared to ask him any more questions.

SELF-RIGHTEOUSNESS CONDEMNED.   Then Jesus said to the crowds and to his disciples: "The teachers of the law and the Pharisees sit in Moses' seat. So you must obey them and do everything they tell you. But do not do what they do, for they do not practice what they preach. They tie up heavy loads and put them on men's shoulders, but they themselves are not willing to lift a finger to move them.

Mt. 23:1-12
Mk.
12:38-40
Lk.
20:45-47

"Everything they do is done for men to see: They make their phylacteries^m wide and the tassels on their garments long; they love the place of honor at banquets and the most important seats in the synagogues; they love to be greeted in the marketplaces and to have men call them 'Rabbi.'

"But you are not to be called 'Rabbi,' for you have only one Master and you are all brothers. And do not call anyone on earth 'father,' for you have one Father, and he is in heaven. Nor are you to be called 'teacher,' for you have one Teacher, the Christ.^k The greatest among you will be your servant. For whoever exalts himself will be humbled, and whoever humbles himself will be exalted.

FALSE RELIGION CONDEMNED.   "Woe to you, teachers of the law and Pharisees, you hypocrites! You shut the kingdom of heaven in men's faces. You yourselves do not enter, nor will you let those enter who are trying to.^n

Mt.
23:13-15

"Woe to you, teachers of the law and Pharisees, you hypocrites! You travel over land and sea to win a single convert, and when he becomes one, you make him twice as much a son of hell as you are.

LEGALISM CONDEMNED.   "Woe to you, blind guides! You say, 'If anyone swears by the temple, it means nothing; but if anyone swears by the gold of the temple, he is bound by his oath.' You blind fools! Which is greater: the gold, or the temple that makes the gold sacred? You also say,

Mt.
23:16-22

^kOr Messiah   ^lPsalm 110:1   ^mThat is, boxes containing Scripture verses, worn on forehead and arm   ^nSome manuscripts to. ^14Woe to you, teachers of the law and Pharisees, you hypocrites! You devour widows' houses and for a show make lengthy prayers. Therefore you will be punished more severely.

'If anyone swears by the altar, it means nothing; but if anyone swears by the gift on it, he is bound by his oath.' You blind men! Which is greater: the gift, or the altar that makes the gift sacred? Therefore, he who swears by the altar swears by it and by everything on it. And he who swears by the temple swears by it and by the one who dwells in it. And he who swears by heaven swears by God's throne and by the one who sits on it.

Mt.
23:23,24

INJUSTICE CONDEMNED. "Woe to you, teachers of the law and Pharisees, you hypocrites! You give a tenth of your spices—mint, dill and cummin. But you have neglected the more important matters of the law—justice, mercy and faithfulness. You should have practiced the latter, without neglecting the former. You blind guides! You strain out a gnat but swallow a camel.

Mt.
23:25-28

HYPOCRISY CONDEMNED. "Woe to you, teachers of the law and Pharisees, you hypocrites! You clean the outside of the cup and dish, but inside they are full of greed and self-indulgence. Blind Pharisee! First clean the inside of the cup and dish, and then the outside also will be clean.

"Woe to you, teachers of the law and Pharisees, you hypocrites! You are like whitewashed tombs, which look beautiful on the outside but on the inside are full of dead men's bones and everything unclean. In the same way, on the outside you appear to people as righteous but on the inside you are full of hypocrisy and wickedness.

Mt.
23:29-36

PERSECUTION CONDEMNED. "Woe to you, teachers of the law and Pharisees, you hypocrites! You build tombs for the prophets and decorate the graves of the righteous. And you say, 'If we had lived in the days of our forefathers, we would not have taken part with them in shedding the blood of the prophets.' So you testify against yourselves that you are the descendants of those who murdered the prophets. Fill up, then, the measure of the sin of your forefathers!

"You snakes! You brood of vipers! How will you escape being condemned to hell? Therefore I am sending you prophets and wise men and teachers. Some of them you will kill and crucify; others you will flog in your synagogues and pursue from town to town. And so upon you will come all the righteous blood that has been shed on earth, from the blood of righteous Abel to the blood of Zechariah son of Berekiah, whom you murdered between the temple and the altar. I tell you the truth, all this will come upon this generation.

Mt.
23:37-39

LAMENT OVER JERUSALEM. "O Jerusalem, Jerusalem, you who kill the prophets and stone those sent to you, how often I have longed to gather your children together, as a hen gathers her chicks under her wings, but you were not willing. Look, your house is left to you desolate. For I tell you, you will not see me again until you say, 'Blessed is he who comes in the name of the Lord.'[o]"

Mk.
12:41-44
Lk. 21:1-4

WIDOW AN EXAMPLE. Jesus sat down opposite the place where the offerings were put and watched the crowd putting their money into the temple treasury. Many rich people threw in large amounts. But a poor widow came and put in two very small copper coins,[p] worth only a fraction of a penny.[q]

Calling his disciples to him, Jesus said, "I tell you the truth, this poor

[o]Psalm 118:26   [p]Greek *two lepta*   [q]Greek *kodrantes*

widow has put more into the treasury than all the others. They all gave out of their wealth; but she, out of her poverty, put in everything—all she had to live on."

Discourse of Future Events

*A*t the end of this indicting exposé, Jesus and his disciples make their way out of the temple. When one of the disciples comments on the beauty of the temple and its stones, Jesus makes the cryptic observation that there will come a time when the temple will be destroyed. Jesus and his disciples then go to the Mount of Olives, just outside the city. Peter, Andrew, James, and John come to Jesus privately, wanting to know more about the temple's destruction, the signs of his coming, and the end of the age. From their Jewish apocalyptic perspective, they apparently anticipate that the end of the age will coincide with Jesus' imminent political ascendancy. Even now, they misunderstand the nature of his kingdom. Like many of the ancient prophecies, Jesus' answer has been the source of much discussion.

There is general agreement regarding Jesus' reference to the destruction of the temple. In retrospect, it is known that only 40 years later, in A.D. 70, the Roman legions laid siege to Jerusalem, thoroughly sacking it and completely destroying the temple. Most would agree that Jesus describes events which precede that destruction. Some feel that Jesus' entire discourse is made with reference to Jerusalem's destruction by the Romans, while others see in it additional apocalyptic prophecy concerning future events. Still others view it as one prophecy having a dual significance.

In order to underscore the need for watchfulness, faithfulness, and spiritual readiness, Jesus will conclude his prophecies by telling two parables and describing the final judgment.

TEMPLE TO BE DESTROYED. As he was leaving the temple, one of his disciples said to him, "Look, Teacher! What massive stones! What magnificent buildings!"

"Do you see all these great buildings?" replied Jesus. "Not one stone here will be left on another; every one will be thrown down."

Mt. 24:1,2
Mk. 13:1,2
Lk. 21:5,6
Leaving
temple
(Tuesday)

DISCIPLES ASK QUESTIONS. ᴹᵏAs Jesus was sitting on the Mount of Olives opposite the temple, Peter, James, John and Andrew asked him privately, ᴹᵗ"Tell us," they said, "when will this happen, and what will be the sign of your coming and of the end of the age?"

Mt. 24:3
Mk. 13:3,4
Lk. 21:7
Mount of
Olives
(Tuesday)

JESUS TELLS OF SIGNS. ᴹᵗJesus answered: "Watch out that no one deceives you. For many will come in my name, claiming, 'I am the Christ,ʳ' and will deceive many. You will hear of wars and rumors of wars, but see to it that you are not alarmed. Such things must happen, but the end is still to come. Nation will rise against nation, and kingdom against kingdom. There will be famines and earthquakes in various places. All these are the beginning of birth pains. ᴹᵏYou must be on your guard. You will be handed over to the local councils and flogged in the synagogues.

Mt. 24:4-35
Mk.
13:5-31
Lk. 21:8-33

ʳOr *Messiah*

On account of me you will stand before governors and kings as witnesses to them. And the gospel must first be preached to all nations. Whenever you are arrested and brought to trial, do not worry beforehand about what to say. Just say whatever is given you at the time, for it is not you speaking, but the Holy Spirit.

"Brother will betray brother to death, and a father his child. Children will rebel against their parents and have them put to death. MtBecause of the increase of wickedness, the love of most will grow cold, ... MkAll men will hate you because of me, but he who stands firm to the end will be saved. MtAnd this gospel of the kingdom will be preached in the whole world as a testimony to all nations, and then the end will come.

"So when you see standing in the holy place 'the abomination that causes desolation,'s spoken of through the prophet Daniel—let the reader understand—then let those who are in Judea flee to the mountains. Let no one on the roof of his house go down to take anything out of the house. Let no one in the field go back to get his cloak. LkWhen you see Jerusalem being surrounded by armies, you will know that its desolation is near. Then let those who are in Judea flee to the mountains, let those in the city get out, and let those in the country not enter the city. For this is the time of punishment in fulfillment of all that has been written. MtHow dreadful it will be in those days for pregnant women and nursing mothers! Pray that your flight will not take place in winter or on the Sabbath. For then there will be great distress, unequaled from the beginning of the world until now—and never to be equaled again. LkThere will be great distress in the land and wrath against this people. They will fall by the sword and will be taken as prisoners to all the nations. Jerusalem will be trampled on by the Gentiles until the times of the Gentiles are fulfilled. MtIf those days had not been cut short, no one would survive, but for the sake of the elect those days will be shortened. At that time if anyone says to you, 'Look, here is the Christ!' or, 'There he is!' do not believe it. For false Christs and false prophets will appear and perform great signs and miracles to deceive even the elect—if that were possible. See, I have told you ahead of time.

"So if anyone tells you, 'There he is, out in the desert,' do not go out; or, 'Here he is, in the inner rooms,' do not believe it. For as lightning that comes from the east is visible even in the west, so will be the coming of the Son of Man. Wherever there is a carcass, there the vultures will gather.

"Immediately after the distress of those days

> " 'the sun will be darkened,
>   and the moon will not give its light;
>   the stars will fall from the sky,
>   and the heavenly bodies will be shaken.'t

"At that time the sign of the Son of Man will appear in the sky, and all the nations of the earth will mourn. They will see the Son of Man coming on the clouds of the sky, with power and great glory. And he will send his angels with a loud trumpet call, and they will gather his elect from the four winds, from one end of the heavens to the other. Lk"There will be signs in the sun, moon and stars. On the earth, nations will be in anguish and perplexity at the roaring and tossing of the sea. Men will faint from

sDaniel 9:27; 11:31; 12:11   tIsaiah 13:10; 34:4

terror, apprehensive of what is coming on the world, for the heavenly bodies will be shaken. At that time they will see the Son of Man coming in a cloud with power and great glory. When these things begin to take place, stand up and lift up your heads, because your redemption is drawing near." Mt"Now learn this lesson from the fig tree: As soon as its twigs get tender and its leaves come out, you know that summer is near. Even so, when you see all these things, you know that it^u is near, right at the door. I tell you the truth, this generation^v will certainly not pass away until all these things have happened. Heaven and earth will pass away, but my words will never pass away.

EXACT TIMES UNKNOWN.   "No one knows about that day or hour, not even the angels in heaven, nor the Son,^{w} but only the Father. As it was in the days of Noah, so it will be at the coming of the Son of Man. For in the days before the flood, people were eating and drinking, marrying and giving in marriage, up to the day Noah entered the ark; and they knew nothing about what would happen until the flood came and took them all away. That is how it will be at the coming of the Son of Man. Two men will be in the field; one will be taken and the other left. Two women will be grinding with a hand mill; one will be taken and the other left.

"Therefore keep watch, because you do not know on what day your Lord will come. But understand this: If the owner of the house had known at what time of night the thief was coming, he would have kept watch and would not have let his house be broken into. So you also must be ready, because the Son of Man will come at an hour when you do not expect him.

Mt.
24:36-44
Mk.
13:32,33

JESUS URGES WATCHFULNESS.   Lk"Be careful, or your hearts will be weighed down with dissipation, drunkenness and the anxieties of life, and that day will close on you unexpectedly like a trap. For it will come upon all those who live on the face of the whole earth. Be always on the watch, and pray that you may be able to escape all that is about to happen, and that you may be able to stand before the Son of Man." Mk It's like a man going away: He leaves his house and puts his servants in charge, each with his assigned task, and tells the one at the door to keep watch. Mt"Who then is the faithful and wise servant, whom the master has put in charge of the servants in his household to give them their food at the proper time? It will be good for that servant whose master finds him doing so when he returns. I tell you the truth, he will put him in charge of all his possessions. But suppose that servant is wicked and says to himself, 'My master is staying away a long time,' and he then begins to beat his fellow servants and to eat and drink with drunkards. The master of that servant will come on a day when he does not expect him and at an hour he is not aware of. He will cut him to pieces and assign him a place with the hypocrites, where there will be weeping and gnashing of teeth. Mk"Therefore keep watch because you do not know when the owner of the house will come back— whether in the evening, or at midnight, or when the rooster crows, or at dawn. If he comes suddenly, do not let him find you sleeping. What I say to you, I say to everyone: 'Watch!' "

Mt.
24:45-51
Mk.
13:34-37
Lk.
21:34-36

WISE AND FOOLISH VIRGINS.   "At that time the kingdom of heaven will be like ten virgins who took their lamps and went out to meet the

Mt. 25:1-13

^{u}Or he ^{v}Or race ^{w}Some manuscripts do not have nor the Son.

bridegroom. Five of them were foolish and five were wise. The foolish ones took their lamps but did not take any oil with them. The wise, however, took oil in jars along with their lamps. The bridegroom was a long time in coming, and they all became drowsy and fell asleep.

"At midnight the cry rang out: 'Here's the bridegroom! Come out to meet him!'

"Then all the virgins woke up and trimmed their lamps. The foolish ones said to the wise, 'Give us some of your oil; our lamps are going out.'

"'No,' they replied, 'there may not be enough for both us and you. Instead, go to those who sell oil and buy some for yourselves.'

"But while they were on their way to buy the oil, the bridegroom arrived. The virgins who were ready went in with him to the wedding banquet. And the door was shut.

"Later the others also came. 'Sir! Sir!' they said. 'Open the door for us!'

"But he replied, 'I tell you the truth, I don't know you.'

"Therefore keep watch, because you do not know the day or the hour.

Mt.
25:14-30

PARABLE OF TALENTS. "Again, it will be like a man going on a journey, who called his servants and entrusted his property to them. To one he gave five talents[x] of money, to another two talents, and to another one talent, each according to his ability. Then he went on his journey. The man who had received the five talents went at once and put his money to work and gained five more. So also, the one with the two talents gained two more. But the man who had received the one talent went off, dug a hole in the ground and hid his master's money.

"After a long time the master of those servants returned and settled accounts with them. The man who had received the five talents brought the other five. 'Master,' he said, 'you entrusted me with five talents. See, I have gained five more.'

"His master replied, 'Well done, good and faithful servant! You have been faithful with a few things; I will put you in charge of many things. Come and share your master's happiness!'

"The man with the two talents also came. 'Master,' he said, 'you entrusted me with two talents; see, I have gained two more.'

"His master replied, 'Well done, good and faithful servant! You have been faithful with a few things; I will put you in charge of many things. Come and share your master's happiness!'

"Then the man who had received the one talent came. 'Master,' he said, 'I knew that you are a hard man, harvesting where you have not sown and gathering where you have not scattered seed. So I was afraid and went out and hid your talent in the ground. See, here is what belongs to you.'

"His master replied, 'You wicked, lazy servant! So you knew that I harvest where I have not sown and gather where I have not scattered seed? Well then, you should have put my money on deposit with the bankers, so that when I returned I would have received it back with interest.

"'Take the talent from him and give it to the one who has the ten talents. For everyone who has will be given more, and he will have an abundance. Whoever does not have, even what he has will be taken from him. And throw that worthless servant outside, into the darkness, where there will be weeping and gnashing of teeth.'

[x]A talent was worth more than a thousand dollars.

CONCERNING LAST JUDGMENT. "When the Son of Man comes in his
glory, and all the angels with him, he will sit on his throne in heavenly
glory. All the nations will be gathered before him, and he will separate the
people one from another as a shepherd separates the sheep from the goats.
He will put the sheep on his right and the goats on his left.

Mt.
25:31-46

"Then the King will say to those on his right, 'Come, you who are
blessed by my Father; take your inheritance, the kingdom prepared for
you since the creation of the world. For I was hungry and you gave me
something to eat, I was thirsty and you gave me something to drink, I was
a stranger and you invited me in, I needed clothes and you clothed me, I
was sick and you looked after me, I was in prison and you came to visit
me.'

"Then the righteous will answer him, 'Lord, when did we see you hungry and feed you, or thirsty and give you something to drink? When did
we see you a stranger and invite you in, or needing clothes and clothe
you? When did we see you sick or in prison and go to visit you?'

"The King will reply, 'I tell you the truth, whatever you did for one of
the least of these brothers of mine, you did for me.'

"Then he will say to those on his left, 'Depart from me, you who are
cursed, into the eternal fire prepared for the devil and his angels. For I was
hungry and you gave me nothing to eat, I was thirsty and you gave me
nothing to drink, I was a stranger and you did not invite me in, I needed
clothes and you did not clothe me, I was sick and in prison and you did
not look after me.'

"They also will answer, 'Lord, when did we see you hungry or thirsty or
a stranger or needing clothes or sick or in prison, and did not help you?'

"He will reply, 'I tell you the truth, whatever you did not do for one of
the least of these, you did not do for me.'

"Then they will go away to eternal punishment, but the righteous to
eternal life."

Final Week—Tuesday Afternoon

*A*s the long day of confrontation and teaching comes to an end, Jesus
tells his disciples that his death is only two days away. Already the
chief priests and elders are conspiring against him in the palace of
the high priest. Aware that the feast is almost upon them, the conspirators
are anxious to have Jesus killed before that time. Even as they plot how to
snare Jesus, they are approached by Judas Iscariot, one of Christ's chosen
disciples.

For his own reasons, Judas has decided to betray Jesus, and has therefore come to bargain with the members of the council. Of course they are
delighted at this unexpected assistance. The amount agreed to is 30 pieces
of silver (which at this time is the approximate price of a slave). It is not
clear whether Judas knows fully the serious consequences of the betrayal.
Later evidence indicates that he may not have anticipated that Jesus would
actually die as a result. Be that as it may, Judas is apparently both covetous
and dishonest—this despite the fact that he has been acting as a kind of
treasurer for the disciples.

Mt. 26:1,2   JESUS FORESEES CRUCIFIXION.   When Jesus had finished saying all
these things, he said to his disciples, "As you know, the Passover is two
days away—and the Son of Man will be handed over to be crucified."

Mt. 26:3-5   PRIESTS AND ELDERS CONSPIRE.   Then the chief priests and the elders
Mk. 14:1,2   of the people assembled in the palace of the high priest, whose name was
Lk. 22:1,2   Caiaphas, and they plotted to arrest Jesus in some sly way and kill him.
"But not during the Feast," they said, "or there may be a riot among the
people."

Mt.   JUDAS BARGAINS TO BETRAY.   ᴸᵏThen Satan entered Judas, called
26:14-16   Iscariot, one of the Twelve. And Judas went to the chief priests and the offi-
Mk.   cers of the temple guard and discussed with them how he might betray
14:10,11   Jesus. ᴹᵗand asked, "What are you willing to give me if I hand him over to
Lk. 22:3-6   you?" So they counted out for him thirty silver coins. ᴸᵏHe consented, and
watched for an opportunity to hand Jesus over to them when no crowd
was present.

Final Week—Wednesday

*T*he preceding events of this final week appear to be accounted for by
the Gospel writers within the clear context of either Sunday, Monday,
or Tuesday, just as they have been presented. The exact timing of what
happens after those events, however, appears less certain. John in particular
touches only lightly upon the events between Jesus' triumphant entry and the
so-called "last supper" which Jesus shares with his disciples. Referring to various public reactions during that time, John notes that, despite Jesus' teaching
and miraculous works, there are still many people who either disbelieve or are
afraid to acknowledge their belief. Then John records what is apparently Jesus'
last public appeal before his subsequent arrest. As there is no evidence that
these events occurred on any of the prior three days, they are set forth here as
occurring on Wednesday, though that time frame is only speculative.

Of far greater significance at this point is the chronology related to the last
supper, Jesus' crucifixion, and his subsequent resurrection. Traditionally the
last supper is believed to have occurred on Thursday evening, followed by the
crucifixion on Friday afternoon and the resurrection on Sunday morning.
However, such reckoning raises at least two questions. First, in an action-
packed final week, what reason is there to believe that there would be a whole
day of either actual inactivity or activity which is left unrecorded? Second, and
far more important—if Jesus is crucified on Friday afternoon and thereafter
hurriedly put into the tomb, how can there be sufficient time to match Jesus'
own prediction that he would remain in the tomb for three days and three
nights before being resurrected? Even if one stretches imagination within the
traditional time frame in order to find parts of three days, it is not possible to
find three nights.

The resolution of both questions appears to be found in recognizing
that the last supper took place on Wednesday evening, followed by the crucifixion and burial on Thursday. Acceptance of that assumption requires an

understanding of the Passover, the Feast of Unleavened Bread, and the way in which the Jews reckon time. As for the reckoning of time, the Jewish day begins at sunset on the previous evening. This means, for example, that our Wednesday night is actually Thursday, and our Thursday night is actually Friday.

Passover is observed on the 14th day of the month of Nisan, corresponding to March-April. As noted earlier, Passover is observed in commemoration of the deliverance of the ancient Israelites from their Egyptian bondage. The name derives from the "passing over" of the Israelites when death came to the firstborn of each Egyptian family. As part of that same commemoration, Passover is followed by the seven-day Feast of Unleavened Bread, which reminds the Jews of their forefathers' flight from Egypt, during which time the Israelites ate unleavened bread only. (It is common among the Jews of Jesus' day to refer to both celebrations by only one name, either as "Passover" or as the "Feast of Unleavened Bread.") By God's direction (Leviticus 23), a lamb is to be slaughtered late on the 14th day (Passover) and the Passover meal eaten that evening, which would be the beginning of the 15th day, the first day of the Feast of Unleavened Bread. The entire 15th day is then to be observed as a special Sabbath, or high holy day, regardless of the day of the week on which it might fall in any given year. (If the 15th day is a Friday, then both that Friday and the next day, Saturday, are observed as Sabbaths.)

With that background the picture begins to come clear. Matthew, Mark, and Luke record the disciples' preparation for the Passover on the first day of the Feast of Unleavened Bread on which the Passover lamb had to be sacrificed. That would place their preparations, then, at the beginning of the 14th day, which, of course, begins on the evening of the 13th day. (Among the preparations common on the evening of the 13th day is the removal of all leaven from the house.) Therefore it appears that the disciples assume they are preparing the upper room primarily for the special paschal meal which they expect to share with Jesus the following evening, and they apparently do not contemplate that the regular meal on the first night will in fact be their "last supper" with Jesus.

Although generally referring to the occasion as a part of the Passover celebration, Jesus seems to explain why it is important for him to eat with them on the night before the actual Passover meal. As will be seen, Jesus' words are: "I have eagerly desired to eat this Passover with you before I suffer. For I tell you, I will not eat it again until it finds fulfillment in the kingdom of God. In referring to his suffering, Jesus is obviously anticipating that his own sacrificial death will take place later that day, preventing him from participating in the actual Passover supper.

John's account eliminates any doubt that this supper occurred prior to the actual Passover meal. When Jesus tells Judas during the supper to do what he is about to do, some of the other disciples "thought Jesus was telling him to buy what was needed for the Feast." Furthermore, the Jews who have obtained Jesus' arrest will not enter Pilate's palace for fear that they will be ceremonially unclean, and therefore unable to eat the Passover. Most convincing is the fact that the day of Jesus' crucifixion is plainly stated to be "the day of Preparation of Passover Week"—the day on which the paschal lamb is slain for the Passover meal taken during the evening of that day.

The most meaningful result of moving away from the traditional time frame is seeing how Jesus' crucifixion becomes the perfect "type" of the Passover Lamb. Under Hebrew law, the paschal lamb is chosen on the tenth day and then "kept up" until the 14th day, when it is sacrificed for the sins of the people. If Jesus' triumphant entry into Jerusalem is counted as the tenth day, Thursday would be the 14th day, and thus the day on which Jesus is crucified. Far more important than this possible parallel is the fact that Jesus, as the perfect Lamb of God, does not celebrate the Passover with some other ordinary sacrificial lamb, but rather becomes himself the Lamb who is slain—precisely at the appropriate hour!

There is therefore strong evidence that the last supper takes place on the evening prior to the Day of Preparation, which by modern reckoning would be Wednesday night. Proceeding upon that assumption, the events associated with this final Wednesday include not only Jesus' last public teaching, but also the account of Peter and John finding the upper room and making preparations for the Passover celebration.

Lk. 21:37,38 At temple (Wednesday morning)	JESUS TEACHES AT TEMPLE. Each day Jesus was teaching at the temple, and each evening he went out to spend the night on the hill called the Mount of Olives, and all the people came early in the morning to hear him at the temple.
Jn. 12:37	MANY STILL DISBELIEVE. Even after Jesus had done all these miraculous signs in their presence, they still would not believe in him.
Jn. 12:38-41	DISBELIEF FULFILLS PROPHECY. This was to fulfill the word of Isaiah the prophet:

> "Lord, who has believed our message
>   and to whom has the arm of the Lord been revealed?"[y]

For this reason they could not believe, because, as Isaiah says elsewhere:

> "He has blinded their eyes
>   and deadened their hearts,
> so they can neither see with their eyes,
>   nor understand with their hearts,
>   nor turn—and I would heal them."[z]

Isaiah said this because he saw Jesus' glory and spoke about him.

Jn. 12:42,43	SOME ARE AFRAID. Yet at the same time many even among the leaders believed in him. But because of the Pharisees they would not confess their faith for fear they would be put out of the synagogue; for they loved praise from men more than praise from God.
Jn. 12:44-50	FINAL PUBLIC APPEAL. Then Jesus cried out, "When a man believes in me, he does not believe in me only, but in the one who sent me. When he looks at me, he sees the one who sent me. I have come into the world as a light, so that no one who believes in me should stay in darkness.

"As for the person who hears my words but does not keep them, I do not judge him. For I did not come to judge the world, but to save it. There is a judge for the one who rejects me and does not accept my words; that

[y]Isaiah 53:1   [z]Isaiah 6:10

very word which I spoke will condemn him at the last day. For I did not speak of my own accord, but the Father who sent me commanded me what to say and how to say it. I know that his command leads to eternal life. So whatever I say is just what the Father has told me to say."

DISCIPLES MAKE PREPARATIONS.   Then came the day of Unleavened Bread on which the Passover lamb had to be sacrificed. Jesus sent Peter and John, saying, "Go and make preparations for us to eat the Passover."

"Where do you want us to prepare for it?" they asked.

He replied, "As you enter the city, a man carrying a jar of water will meet you. Follow him to the house that he enters, and say to the owner of the house, 'The Teacher asks: Where is the guest room, where I may eat the Passover with my disciples?' He will show you a large upper room, all furnished. Make preparations there."

They left and found things just as Jesus had told them. So they prepared the Passover.

Mt. 26:17-19
Mk. 14:12-16
Lk. 22:7-13
Upper room
(Wednesday afternoon)

The Upper Room

*W*ith the plot to kill Jesus taking its final form, and with the clamor for his life reaching a crescendo, an upper room in Jerusalem becomes the calm at the center of the storm. Here Jesus and his chosen disciples withdraw to themselves to await participation in the Passover Feast. Undoubtedly because Jesus has indicated that the coming of his kingdom is imminent, the apostles begin to discuss who among themselves is the greatest. Is it conceivable that, after having been with Jesus throughout his ministry, and having listened to all his teaching about the nature of the kingdom, his chosen 12 still have political aspirations for power and rank within an earthly kingdom? What must Jesus do to convince them otherwise? Taking on the role of a servant, Jesus begins to wash the feet of his disciples in order to teach them the need, not for power and position, but for humility and service to others.

As the supper progresses, Jesus takes the bread and wine and tells his disciples to partake of them as symbols of his body and blood, thereby instituting his special memorial and covenant with all his disciples. Then, as if to prepare for the sealing of that covenant, Jesus reveals Judas as his betrayer and sends him out to complete the betrayal, now near at hand.

What follows is a call for mutual love, not only because of the petty rivalries which continue to divide the disciples, but also because Jesus knows they will need each other's support in order to endure the challenges soon to come their way.

When Jesus tells them that he is going away, Peter replies that he wants to follow. And when Jesus responds that Peter cannot go with him at this time, Peter insists that, if necessary, he is willing to die for Jesus. Luke and John record the first of two warnings to Peter that he will deny Jesus before the coming of daylight. Matthew and Mark show that Jesus repeats the warning a little later in a different setting as the disciples make their way toward the Mount of Olives.

The events in the upper room begin now with Jesus expressing his love for his disciples.

Lk.
22:14-16
Upper
room

IMPORTANCE OF OCCASION.   When the hour came, Jesus and his apostles reclined at the table. And he said to them, "I have eagerly desired to eat this Passover with you before I suffer. For I tell you, I will not eat it again until it finds fulfillment in the kingdom of God."

Mt.
26:26-29
Mk.
14:22-25
Lk.
22:17-20

INSTITUTION OF MEMORIAL.   After taking the cup, he gave thanks and said, "Take this and divide it among you. For I tell you I will not drink again of the fruit of the vine until the kingdom of God comes."

And he took bread, gave thanks and broke it, and gave it to them, saying, "This is my body given for you; do this in remembrance of me."

In the same way, after the supper he took the cup, saying, "This cup is the new covenant in my blood, which is poured out for you.

Lk.
22:21,23

JESUS HINTS OF BETRAYER.   But the hand of him who is going to betray me is with mine on the table. They began to question among themselves which of them it might be who would do this.

Lk.
22:24-30

APOSTLES DISPUTE.   Also a dispute arose among them as to which of them was considered to be greatest. Jesus said to them, "The kings of the Gentiles lord it over them; and those who exercise authority over them call themselves Benefactors. But you are not to be like that. Instead, the greatest among you should be like the youngest, and the one who rules like the one who serves. For who is greater, the one who is at the table or the one who serves? Is it not the one who is at the table? But I am among you as one who serves. You are those who have stood by me in my trials. And I confer on you a kingdom, just as my Father conferred one on me, so that you may eat and drink at my table in my kingdom and sit on thrones, judging the twelve tribes of Israel.

Jn. 13:1-5

JESUS WASHES APOSTLES' FEET.   Jesus knew that the time had come for him to leave this world and go to the Father. Having loved his own who were in the world, he now showed them the full extent of his love.[a]

The evening meal was being served, and the devil had already prompted Judas Iscariot, son of Simon, to betray Jesus. Jesus knew that the Father had put all things under his power, and that he had come from God and was returning to God; so he got up from the meal, took off his outer clothing, and wrapped a towel around his waist. After that, he poured water into a basin and began to wash his disciples' feet, drying them with the towel that was wrapped around him.

Jn. 13:6-11

PETER IS HESITANT.   He came to Simon Peter, who said to him, "Lord, are you going to wash my feet?"

Jesus replied, "You do not realize now what I am doing, but later you will understand."

"No," said Peter, "you shall never wash my feet."

Jesus answered, "Unless I wash you, you have no part with me."

"Then, Lord," Simon Peter replied, "not just my feet but my hands and my head as well!"

Jesus answered, "A person who has had a bath needs only to wash his feet; his whole body is clean. And you are clean, though not every one of

[a]Or *he loved them to the last*

you." For he knew who was going to betray him, and that was why he said not every one was clean.

JESUS EXPLAINS WASHING.   When he had finished washing their feet, he put on his clothes and returned to his place. "Do you understand what I have done for you?" he asked them. "You call me 'Teacher' and 'Lord,' and rightly so, for that is what I am. Now that I, your Lord and Teacher, have washed your feet, you also should wash one another's feet. I have set you an example that you should do as I have done for you. I tell you the truth, no servant is greater than his master, nor is a messenger greater than the one who sent him. Now that you know these things, you will be blessed if you do them.

Jn.
13:12-17

JESUS PREDICTS BETRAYAL.   "I am not referring to all of you; I know those I have chosen. But this is to fulfill the scripture: 'He who shares my bread has lifted up his heel against me.'[b]

"I am telling you now before it happens, so that when it does happen you will believe that I am He. I tell you the truth, whoever accepts anyone I send accepts me; and whoever accepts me accepts the one who sent me."

After he had said this, Jesus was troubled in spirit and testified, "I tell you the truth, one of you is going to betray me."

Mt.
26:20,21
Mk.
14:17,18
Jn.
13:18-21

BETRAYER IDENTIFIED.   [Mt]They were very sad and began to say to him one after the other, "Surely not I, Lord?"

Jesus replied, "The one who has dipped his hand into the bowl with me will betray me. The Son of Man will go just as it is written about him. But woe to that man who betrays the Son of Man! It would be better for him if he had not been born." [Jn]His disciples stared at one another, at a loss to know which of them he meant. One of them, the disciple whom Jesus loved, was reclining next to him. Simon Peter motioned to this disciple and said, "Ask him which one he means."

Leaning back against Jesus, he asked him, "Lord, who is it?"

Jesus answered, "It is the one to whom I will give this piece of bread when I have dipped it in the dish." Then, dipping the piece of bread, he gave it to Judas Iscariot, son of Simon. As soon as Judas took the bread, Satan entered into him. [Mt]Then Judas, the one who would betray him, said, "Surely not I, Rabbi?"

Jesus answered, "Yes, it is you."[c]

Mt.
26:22-25
Mk.
14:19-21
Lk. 22:22
Jn.
13:22-27a

JESUS SENDS JUDAS OUT.   "What you are about to do, do quickly," Jesus told him, but no one at the meal understood why Jesus said this to him. Since Judas had charge of the money, some thought Jesus was telling him to buy what was needed for the Feast, or to give something to the poor. As soon as Judas had taken the bread, he went out. And it was night.

Jn.
13:27b-30

JESUS CALLS FOR LOVE.   When he was gone, Jesus said, "Now is the Son of Man glorified and God is glorified in him. If God is glorified in him,[d] God will glorify the Son in himself, and will glorify him at once.

"My children, I will be with you only a little longer. You will look for me, and just as I told the Jews, so I tell you now: Where I am going, you cannot come.

"A new command I give you: Love one another. As I have loved you, so

Jn.
13:31-35

[b]Psalm 41:9   [c]Or "You yourself have said it   [d]Many early manuscripts do not have If God is glorified in him.

you must love one another. By this all men will know that you are my disciples, if you love one another."

Lk.
22:31-34
Jn.
13:36-38

PETER MAKES REQUEST.   ᴶⁿSimon Peter asked him, "Lord, where are you going?"

Jesus replied, "Where I am going, you cannot follow now, but you will follow later."

Peter asked, "Lord, why can't I follow you now? I will lay down my life for you." ᴸᵏ"Simon, Simon, Satan has asked to sift you*ᵉ* as wheat. But I have prayed for you, Simon, that your faith may not fail. And when you have turned back, strengthen your brothers."

But he replied, "Lord, I am ready to go with you to prison and to death."

Jesus answered, "I tell you, Peter, before the rooster crows today, you will deny three times that you know me."

Jn. 14:1-4

JESUS TO PREPARE PLACE.   "Do not let your hearts be troubled. Trust in God*ᶠ*; trust also in me. In my Father's house are many rooms; if it were not so, I would have told you. I am going there to prepare a place for you. And if I go and prepare a place for you, I will come back and take you to be with me that you also may be where I am. You know the way to the place where I am going."

Jn. 14:5-7

THOMAS WANTS TO KNOW WAY.   Thomas said to him, "Lord, we don't know where you are going, so how can we know the way?"

Jesus answered, "I am the way and the truth and the life. No one comes to the Father except through me. If you really knew me, you would know*ᵍ* my Father as well. From now on, you do know him and have seen him."

Jn. 14:8-15

PHILIP WANTS TO SEE FATHER.   Philip said, "Lord, show us the Father and that will be enough for us."

Jesus answered: "Don't you know me, Philip, even after I have been among you such a long time? Anyone who has seen me has seen the Father. How can you say, 'Show us the Father'? Don't you believe that I am in the Father, and that the Father is in me? The words I say to you are not just my own. Rather, it is the Father, living in me, who is doing his work. Believe me when I say that I am in the Father and the Father is in me; or at least believe on the evidence of the miracles themselves. I tell you the truth, anyone who has faith in me will do what I have been doing. He will do even greater things than these, because I am going to the Father. And I will do whatever you ask in my name, so that the Son may bring glory to the Father. You may ask me for anything in my name, and I will do it.

"If you love me, you will obey what I command.

Jn.
14:16-21

JESUS PROMISES HOLY SPIRIT.   And I will ask the Father, and he will give you another Counselor to be with you forever—the Spirit of truth. The world cannot accept him, because it neither sees him nor knows him. But you know him, for he lives with you and will be*ʰ* in you. I will not leave you as orphans; I will come to you. Before long, the world will not see me anymore, but you will see me. Because I live, you also will live. On that day you will realize that I am in my Father, and you are in me, and I am in you. Whoever has my commands and obeys them, he is the one who

---

*ᵉ*The Greek is plural.   *ᶠ*Or *You trust in God*   *ᵍ*Some early manuscripts *If you really have known me, you will know*   *ʰ*Some early manuscripts *and is*

loves me. He who loves me will be loved by my Father, and I too will love him and show myself to him."

JUDAS IS PUZZLED.   Then Judas (not Judas Iscariot) said, "But, Lord, why do you intend to show yourself to us and not to the world?"
    Jesus replied, "If anyone loves me, he will obey my teaching. My Father will love him, and we will come to him and make our home with him. He who does not love me will not obey my teaching. These words you hear are not my own; they belong to the Father who sent me.

Jn.
14:22-24

JESUS PREDICTS RETURN.   "All this I have spoken while still with you. But the Counselor, the Holy Spirit, whom the Father will send in my name, will teach you all things and will remind you of everything I have said to you. Peace I leave with you; my peace I give you. I do not give to you as the world gives. Do not let your hearts be troubled and do not be afraid.
    "You heard me say, 'I am going away and I am coming back to you.' If you loved me, you would be glad that I am going to the Father, for the Father is greater than I. I have told you now before it happens, so that when it does happen you will believe. I will not speak with you much longer, for the prince of this world is coming. He has no hold on me, but the world must learn that I love the Father and that I do exactly what my Father has commanded me.

Jn.
14:25-31a

FULFILLMENT OF PROPHECY.   Then Jesus asked them, "When I sent you without purse, bag or sandals, did you lack anything?"
    "Nothing," they answered.
    He said to them, "But now if you have a purse, take it, and also a bag; and if you don't have a sword, sell your cloak and buy one. It is written: 'And he was numbered with the transgressors'[i]; and I tell you that this must be fulfilled in me. Yes, what is written about me is reaching its fulfillment."
    The disciples said, "See, Lord, here are two swords."
    "That is enough," he replied.

Lk.
22:35-38

TO MOUNT OF OLIVES.   [Jn]"Come now; let us leave." [Mt]When they had sung a hymn, they went out to the Mount of Olives.

Mt. 26:30
Mk. 14:26
Lk. 22:39
Jn. 14:31b

WARNING ABOUT FORSAKING.   Then Jesus told them, "This very night you will all fall away on account of me, for it is written:

    " 'I will strike the shepherd,
        and the sheep of the flock will be scattered.'[j]

But after I have risen, I will go ahead of you into Galilee."

Mt.
26:31,32
Mk.
14:27,28

PETER BOASTS LOYALTY.   Peter replied, "Even if all fall away on account of you, I never will."
    "I tell you the truth," Jesus answered, "this very night, before the rooster crows, you will disown me three times."
    But Peter declared, "Even if I have to die with you, I will never disown you." And all the other disciples said the same.

Mt.
26:33-35
Mk.
14:29-31

[i]Isaiah 53:12   [j]Zech. 13:7

Final Discourse

*J*ohn alone records the final discourse of Jesus with his chosen disciples. It comes as Jesus and his disciples continue toward the Mount of Olives, just before they cross the Kidron Valley, which forms the eastern border of Jerusalem. Each word Jesus speaks reflects the burden which he feels in leaving these men to finish the work which he has begun. Jesus encourages them in their faith and promises that in his name they will perform great works. Again he calls them to mutual love in order to withstand the inevitable persecution which awaits them. Explaining the necessity of his going away, Jesus promises that they will not be left wholly on their own. Jesus reassures them that the Holy Spirit will be with them and will guide them in their mission.

After reminding them that joy will come from the sorrow they are about to bear, Jesus offers up a prayer. In that prayer Jesus asks first for glorification that God himself might be glorified, then prays for the 11 disciples, and finally for all his disciples, that they might love one another and thereby be a continuing witness to the world.

The final discourse begins with an allegory about the vine and its branches as a lesson in fruitfulness through Christ.

Jn. 15:1-8   VINE AND BRANCHES.   "I am the true vine, and my Father is the gardener. He cuts off every branch in me that bears no fruit, while every branch that does bear fruit he prunes[k] so that it will be even more fruitful. You are already clean because of the word I have spoken to you. Remain in me, and I will remain in you. No branch can bear fruit by itself; it must remain in the vine. Neither can you bear fruit unless you remain in me.

"I am the vine; you are the branches. If a man remains in me and I in him, he will bear much fruit; apart from me you can do nothing. If anyone does not remain in me, he is like a branch that is thrown away and withers; such branches are picked up, thrown into the fire and burned. If you remain in me and my words remain in you, ask whatever you wish, and it will be given you. This is to my Father's glory, that you bear much fruit, showing yourselves to be my disciples.

Jn. 15:9-17   TO LOVE ONE ANOTHER.   "As the Father has loved me, so have I loved you. Now remain in my love. If you obey my commands, you will remain in my love, just as I have obeyed my Father's commands and remain in his love. I have told you this so that my joy may be in you and that your joy may be complete. My command is this: Love each other as I have loved you. Greater love has no one than this, that he lay down his life for his friends. You are my friends if you do what I command. I no longer call you servants, because a servant does not know his master's business. Instead, I have called you friends, for everything that I learned from my Father I have made known to you. You did not choose me, but I chose you and appointed you to go and bear fruit—fruit that will last. Then the Father will give you whatever you ask in my name. This is my command: Love each other.

[k]The Greek for *prunes* also means *cleans*.

PREPARATION FOR PERSECUTION.   "If the world hates you, keep in

Jn.
15:18-16:4

mind that it hated me first. If you belonged to the world, it would love you
as its own. As it is, you do not belong to the world, but I have chosen you
out of the world. That is why the world hates you. Remember the words I
spoke to you: 'No servant is greater than his master.'[l] If they persecuted
me, they will persecute you also. If they obeyed my teaching, they will
obey yours also. They will treat you this way because of my name, for they
do not know the One who sent me. If I had not come and spoken to them,
they would not be guilty of sin. Now, however, they have no excuse for
their sin. He who hates me hates my Father as well. If I had not done
among them what no one else did, they would not be guilty of sin. But
now they have seen these miracles, and yet they have hated both me and
my Father. But this is to fulfill what is written in their Law: 'They hated me
without reason.'[m]

"When the Counselor comes, whom I will send to you from the Father,
the Spirit of truth who goes out from the Father, he will testify about me.
And you also must testify, for you have been with me from the beginning.

"All this I have told you so that you will not go astray. They will put you
out of the synagogue; in fact, a time is coming when anyone who kills you
will think he is offering a service to God. They will do such things because
they have not known the Father or me. I have told you this, so that when
the time comes you will remember that I warned you. I did not tell you
this at first because I was with you.

NECESSITY OF GOING AWAY.   "Now I am going to him who sent me,

Jn. 16:5-11

yet none of you asks me, 'Where are you going?' Because I have said these
things, you are filled with grief. But I tell you the truth: It is for your good
that I am going away. Unless I go away, the Counselor will not come to you;
but if I go, I will send him to you. When he comes, he will convict the world
of guilt[n] in regard to sin and righteousness and judgment: in regard to sin,
because men do not believe in me; in regard to righteousness, because I am
going to the Father, where you can see me no longer; and in regard to judgment, because the prince of this world now stands condemned.

HOLY SPIRIT'S GUIDANCE.   "I have much more to say to you, more

Jn.
16:12-15

than you can now bear. But when he, the Spirit of truth, comes, he will
guide you into all truth. He will not speak on his own; he will speak only
what he hears, and he will tell you what is yet to come. He will bring glory
to me by taking from what is mine and making it known to you. All that
belongs to the Father is mine. That is why I said the Spirit will take from
what is mine and make it known to you.

DISCIPLES PERPLEXED.   "In a little while you will see me no more, and

Jn.
16:16-18

then after a little while you will see me."

Some of his disciples said to one another, "What does he mean by saying, 'In a little while you will see me no more, and then after a little while
you will see me,' and 'Because I am going to the Father'?" They kept asking, "What does he mean by 'a little while'? We don't understand what he
is saying."

JOY OUT OF SORROW.   Jesus saw that they wanted to ask him about

Jn.
16:19-24

this, so he said to them, "Are you asking one another what I meant when

[l]John 13:16   [m]Psalms 35:19; 69:4   [n]Or will expose the guilt of the world

I said, 'In a little while you will see me no more, and then after a little while you will see me'? I tell you the truth, you will weep and mourn while the world rejoices. You will grieve, but your grief will turn to joy. A woman giving birth to a child has pain because her time has come; but when her baby is born she forgets the anguish because of her joy that a child is born into the world. So with you: Now is your time of grief, but I will see you again and you will rejoice, and no one will take away your joy. In that day you will no longer ask me anything. I tell you the truth, my Father will give you whatever you ask in my name. Until now you have not asked for anything in my name. Ask and you will receive, and your joy will be complete.

Jn.
16:25-28

SPEECH WILL BE MADE CLEAR. "Though I have been speaking figuratively, a time is coming when I will no longer use this kind of language but will tell you plainly about my Father. In that day you will ask in my name. I am not saying that I will ask the Father on your behalf. No, the Father himself loves you because you have loved me and have believed that I came from God. I came from the Father and entered the world; now I am leaving the world and going back to the Father."

Jn.
16:29-33

DISCIPLES EXPRESS BELIEF. Then Jesus' disciples said, "Now you are speaking clearly and without figures of speech. Now we can see that you know all things and that you do not even need to have anyone ask you questions. This makes us believe that you came from God."

"You believe at last!"[o] Jesus answered. "But a time is coming, and has come, when you will be scattered, each to his own home. You will leave me all alone. Yet I am not alone, for my Father is with me.

"I have told you these things, so that in me you may have peace. In this world you will have trouble. But take heart! I have overcome the world."

Jn. 17:1-5

JESUS PRAYS FOR HIMSELF. After Jesus said this, he looked toward heaven and prayed:

"Father, the time has come. Glorify your Son, that your Son may glorify you. For you granted him authority over all people that he might give eternal life to all those you have given him. Now this is eternal life: that they may know you, the only true God, and Jesus Christ, whom you have sent. I have brought you glory on earth by completing the work you gave me to do. And now, Father, glorify me in your presence with the glory I had with you before the world began.

Jn. 17:6-19

JESUS PRAYS FOR DISCIPLES. "I have revealed you[p] to those whom you gave me out of the world. They were yours; you gave them to me and they have obeyed your word. Now they know that everything you have given me comes from you. For I gave them the words you gave me and they accepted them. They knew with certainty that I came from you, and they believed that you sent me. I pray for them. I am not praying for the world, but for those you have given me, for they are yours. All I have is yours, and all you have is mine. And glory has come to me through them. I will remain in the world no longer, but they are still in the world, and I am coming to you. Holy Father, protect them by the power of your name—the name you gave me—so that they may be one as we are one. While I was with them, I protected them and kept them safe by that name

---

[o]Or *"Do you now believe?"*   [p]Greek *your name*; also in verse 26

you gave me. None has been lost except the one doomed to destruction so that Scripture would be fulfilled.

"I am coming to you now, but I say these things while I am still in the world, so that they may have the full measure of my joy within them. I have given them your word and the world has hated them, for they are not of the world any more than I am of the world. My prayer is not that you take them out of the world but that you protect them from the evil one. They are not of the world, even as I am not of it. Sanctify^q them by the truth; your word is truth. As you sent me into the world, I have sent them into the world. For them I sanctify myself, that they too may be truly sanctified.

JESUS PRAYS FOR BELIEVERS. "My prayer is not for them alone. I pray also for those who will believe in me through their message, that all of them may be one, Father, just as you are in me and I am in you. May they also be in us so that the world may believe that you have sent me. I have given them the glory that you gave me, that they may be one as we are one: I in them and you in me. May they be brought to complete unity to let the world know that you sent me and have loved them even as you have loved me.

Jn. 17:20-26

"Father, I want those you have given me to be with me where I am, and to see my glory, the glory you have given me because you loved me before the creation of the world.

"Righteous Father, though the world does not know you, I know you, and they know that you have sent me. I have made you known to them, and will continue to make you known in order that the love you have for me may be in them and that I myself may be in them."

Betrayal and Arrest

*A*t the end of this parting discourse, there is little time remaining for solitude or reflection. The time of betrayal is near. Very soon now Judas will lead the officers of the chief priests to Jesus and betray him in the presence of the other apostles. So the stage is now set, and the arrest is soon to take place. As the hour of betrayal fast approaches, the record begins now with Jesus leading his disciples to an olive grove known as Gethsemane, on the Mount of Olives, just east of Jerusalem. As they arrive in the quiet garden, Jesus' heart is clearly heavy with the prospect of the events soon to take place. Taking Peter, James, and John beyond the others, Jesus goes still further to a quiet place alone, where he agonizes in prayer with the Father. And his aloneness during this critical time is all the more reinforced when three times Jesus returns to the disciples only to find them asleep.

TO GETHSEMANE.   ^{Jn}When he had finished praying, Jesus left with his disciples and crossed the Kidron Valley. On the other side there was an olive grove, and he and his disciples went into it. ^{Mk}They went to a place called Gethsemane, and Jesus said to his disciples, "Sit here while I pray." He took Peter, James and John along with him, and he began to be deeply

Mt. 26:36-38
Mk. 14:32-34
Lk. 22:40
Jn. 18:1
(Wednesday night)

^qGreek *hagiazo* (set apart for sacred use or make holy)

distressed and troubled. "My soul is overwhelmed with sorrow to the point of death," he said to them. "Stay here and keep watch."

Mt. 26:39
Mk. 14:35,36
Lk. 22:41-45

JESUS PRAYS IN AGONY.   He withdrew about a stone's throw beyond them, knelt down and prayed, "Father, if you are willing, take this cup from me; yet not my will, but yours be done." An angel from heaven appeared to him and strengthened him. And being in anguish, he prayed more earnestly, and his sweat was like drops of blood falling to the ground.[r]

When he rose from prayer and went back to the disciples, he found them asleep, exhausted from sorrow.

Mt. 26:40-42
Mk. 14:37-39
Lk. 22:46

JESUS PRAYS A SECOND TIME.   "Could you men not keep watch with me for one hour?" he asked Peter. "Watch and pray so that you will not fall into temptation. The spirit is willing, but the body is weak."

He went away a second time and prayed, "My Father, if it is not possible for this cup to be taken away unless I drink it, may your will be done."

Mt. 26:43-46
Mk. 14:40-42

JESUS PRAYS A THIRD TIME.   When he came back, he again found them sleeping, because their eyes were heavy. So he left them and went away once more and prayed the third time, saying the same thing.

Then he returned to the disciples and said to them, "Are you still sleeping and resting? Look, the hour is near, and the Son of Man is betrayed into the hands of sinners. Rise, let us go! Here comes my betrayer!"

Mt. 26:47-50a
Mk. 14:43-45
Lk. 22:47,48
Jn. 18:2,3

JUDAS BETRAYS JESUS.   [Jn]Now Judas, who betrayed him, knew the place, because Jesus had often met there with his disciples. So Judas came to the grove, guiding a detachment of soldiers and some officials from the chief priests and Pharisees. They were carrying torches, lanterns and weapons. [Mk]Now the betrayer had arranged a signal with them: "The one I kiss is the man; arrest him and lead him away under guard." [Lk]He approached Jesus to kiss him, but Jesus asked him, "Judas, are you betraying the Son of Man with a kiss?" [Mk]Going at once to Jesus, Judas said, "Rabbi!" and kissed him.

Jn. 18:4-9

DISCIPLES' SAFETY INSURED.   Jesus, knowing all that was going to happen to him, went out and asked them, "Who is it you want?"

"Jesus of Nazareth," they replied.

"I am he," Jesus said. (And Judas the traitor was standing there with them.) When Jesus said, "I am he," they drew back and fell to the ground.

Again he asked them, "Who is it you want?"

And they said, "Jesus of Nazareth."

"I told you that I am he," Jesus answered. "If you are looking for me, then let these men go." This happened so that the words he had spoken would be fulfilled: "I have not lost one of those you gave me."[s]

Mt. 26:50b-54
Mk. 14:46,47
Lk. 22:49-51
Jn. 18:10,11

PETER CUTS OFF EAR.   [Mk]The men seized Jesus and arrested him. [Lk]When Jesus' followers saw what was going to happen, they said, "Lord, should we strike with our swords?" [Jn]Then Simon Peter, who had a sword, drew it and struck the high priest's servant, cutting off his right ear. (The servant's name was Malchus.) [Mt]"Put your sword back in its place," Jesus said to him, "for all who draw the sword will die by the sword. Do you think I cannot call on my Father, and he will at once put at my disposal

[r]Some early manuscripts do not have verses 43 and 44.   [s]John 6:39

more than twelve legions of angels? But how then would the Scriptures be fulfilled that say it must happen in this way?" ᴸᵏBut Jesus answered, "No more of this!" And he touched the man's ear and healed him.

JESUS CHIDES ARREST.   Then Jesus said to the chief priests, the officers of the temple guard, and the elders, who had come for him, "Am I leading a rebellion, that you have come with swords and clubs? Every day I was with you in the temple courts, and you did not lay a hand on me. But this is your hour—when darkness reigns."

Mt.
26:55,56a
Mk.
14:48,49
Lk.
22:52,53

JESUS ARRESTED.   ᴶⁿThen the detachment of soldiers with its commander and the Jewish officials arrested Jesus. ᴹᵗThen all the disciples deserted him and fled. ᴹᵏA young man, wearing nothing but a linen garment, was following Jesus. When they seized him, he fled naked, leaving his garment behind.

Mt. 26:56b
Mk.
14:50-52
Jn. 18:12a

Trial Before Sanhedrin

ollowing Jesus' arrest, John records that Jesus is first taken before Annas, who had been high priest from A.D. 6-15, before being deposed by the Roman procurator Valerius Gratus. It appears that Annas continued to exercise great influence among the Jews, and so it is no surprise that Jesus is brought before him for questioning. Jesus is sent next to Annas' son-in-law, Caiaphas, who has served as high priest since A.D. 18. Caiaphas presides over the Sanhedrin (also known as The Council), which is the Jewish Supreme Court, composed of 71 elders drawn from among the chief priests and scribes. Some of the members of the Sanhedrin apparently join Caiaphas at his house in the late hours of the night in order to interrogate Jesus regarding his claims of messiahship. Then, as day breaks on Thursday morning, the entire council is called together in order to vote official condemnation.

Laced throughout the record of Jesus' trial before the Jewish leaders is a moving account of Peter's personal struggle with loyalty to Jesus. In the garden Peter had been characteristically impulsive in rushing to Jesus' defense. But now, as he comes to understand the seriousness of Jesus' arrest, Peter realizes his own potential jeopardy. When confronted with charges that he is one of Jesus' disciples, Peter weakens and denies any such association. On three separate occasions throughout this long night, and to a number of different accusers, Peter will make vehement and even profane denials in order to shield himself. His later feelings of remorse and his subsequent leadership in the establishment of the church will stand in clear contrast to Judas, who on this same day will be consumed by his guilt and take his own life.

JESUS LED TO ANNAS.   They bound him and brought him first to Annas, who was the father-in-law of Caiaphas, the high priest that year. Caiaphas was the one who had advised the Jews that it would be good if one man died for the people.

Jn.
18:12b-14
Jerusalem

PETER'S FIRST DENIAL.   Simon Peter and another disciple were following Jesus. Because this disciple was known to the high priest, he went with Jesus into the high priest's courtyard, but Peter had to wait outside

Jn.
18:15-17

at the door. The other disciple, who was known to the high priest, came back, spoke to the girl on duty there and brought Peter in.

"You are not one of his disciples, are you?" the girl at the door asked Peter.

He replied, "I am not."

Jn.
18:19-23
JESUS BEFORE ANNAS.   Meanwhile, the high priest questioned Jesus about his disciples and his teaching.

"I have spoken openly to the world," Jesus replied. "I always taught in synagogues or at the temple, where all the Jews come together. I said nothing in secret. Why question me? Ask those who heard me. Surely they know what I said."

When Jesus said this, one of the officials nearby struck him in the face. "Is this the way you answer the high priest?" he demanded.

"If I said something wrong," Jesus replied, "testify as to what is wrong. But if I spoke the truth, why did you strike me?"

Mt. 26:57,58
Mk. 14:53,54
Lk. 22:54
Jn. 18:18,24
TO CAIAPHAS, HIGH PRIEST.   ᴶⁿThen Annas sent him, still bound, to Caiaphas the high priest.ᵗ ᴸᵏThen seizing him, they led him away and took him into the house of the high priest. Peter followed at a distance.

Mt.
26:69-72
Mk.
14:66-70a
Lk.
22:55-58
Jn. 18:25
PETER AGAIN DENIES.   ᴸᵏBut when they had kindled a fire in the middle of the courtyard and had sat down together, Peter sat down with them. A servant girl saw him seated there in the firelight. She looked closely at him and said, "This man was with him."

But he denied it. "Woman, I don't know him," he said. ᴹᵗThen he went out to the gateway, where another girl saw him and said to the people there, "This fellow was with Jesus of Nazareth."

He denied it again, with an oath: "I don't know the man!" ᴸᵏA little later someone else saw him and said, "You also are one of them."

"Man, I am not!" Peter replied.

Mt.
26:59-66
Mk.
14:55-64
BEFORE CAIAPHAS AND COUNCIL.   The chief priests and the whole Sanhedrin were looking for evidence against Jesus so that they could put him to death, but they did not find any. Many testified falsely against him, but their statements did not agree.

Then some stood up and gave this false testimony against him: "We heard him say, 'I will destroy this man-made temple and in three days will build another, not made by man.'" Yet even then their testimony did not agree.

Then the high priest stood up before them and asked Jesus, "Are you not going to answer? What is this testimony that these men are bringing against you?" But Jesus remained silent and gave no answer.

Again the high priest asked him, "Are you the Christ,ᵘ the Son of the Blessed One?"

"I am," said Jesus. "And you will see the Son of Man sitting at the right hand of the Mighty One and coming on the clouds of heaven."

The high priest tore his clothes. "Why do we need any more witnesses?" he asked. "You have heard the blasphemy. What do you think?"

They all condemned him as worthy of death.

ᵗOr *(Now Annas had sent him, still bound, to Caiaphas the high priest.)*   ᵘOr *Messiah*

JESUS IS ABUSED.   The men who were guarding Jesus began mocking and beating him. They blindfolded him and demanded, "Prophesy! Who hit you?" And they said many other insulting things to him.

Mt. 26:67,68
Mk. 14:65
Lk. 22:63-65

PETER DENIES STILL AGAIN.   ᴹᵗAfter a little while [ᴸᵏabout an hour later], those standing there went up to Peter and said, "Surely you are one of them, for your accent gives you away."

Then he began to call down curses on himself and he swore to them, "I don't know the man!" ᴶⁿOne of the high priest's servants, a relative of the man whose ear Peter had cut off, challenged him, "Didn't I see you with him in the olive grove?" ᴸᵏPeter replied, "Man, I don't know what you're talking about!"

Mt. 26:73,74a
Mk. 14:70b,71
Lk. 22:59,60a
Jn. 18:26,27

PETER WEEPS.   Just as he was speaking, the rooster crowed. The Lord turned and looked straight at Peter. Then Peter remembered the word the Lord had spoken to him: "Before the rooster crows today, you will disown me three times." And he went outside and wept bitterly.

Mt. 26:74b,75
Mk. 14:72
Lk. 22:60b-62

COUNCIL CONDEMNS JESUS.   ᴸᵏAt daybreak the council of the elders of the people, both the chief priests and teachers of the law, met together, and Jesus was led before them. "If you are the Christ,ᵛ" they said, "tell us."

Jesus answered, "If I tell you, you will not believe me, and if I asked you, you would not answer. But from now on, the Son of Man will be seated at the right hand of the mighty God."

They all asked, "Are you then the Son of God?"

He replied, "You are right in saying I am."

Then they said, "Why do we need any more testimony? We have heard it from his own lips." ᴹᵗEarly in the morning, all the chief priests and the elders of the people came to the decision to put Jesus to death.

Mt. 27:1
Mk. 15:1a
Lk. 22:66-71
(Early Thursday morning)

JUDAS COMMITS SUICIDE.   When Judas, who had betrayed him, saw that Jesus was condemned, he was seized with remorse and returned the thirty silver coins to the chief priests and the elders. "I have sinned," he said, "for I have betrayed innocent blood."

"What is that to us?" they replied. "That's your responsibility."

So Judas threw the money into the temple and left. Then he went away and hanged himself.

The chief priests picked up the coins and said, "It is against the law to put this into the treasury, since it is blood money." So they decided to use the money to buy the potter's field as a burial place for foreigners. That is why it has been called the Field of Blood to this day. Then what was spoken by Jeremiah the prophet was fulfilled: "They took the thirty silver coins, the price set on him by the people of Israel, and they used them to buy the potter's field, as the Lord commanded me."ʷ

Mt. 27:3-10

------------◇------------

ᵛOr *Messiah*   ʷSee Zech. 11:12,13; Jer. 19:1-13; 32:6-9.

Trial Before Pilate

he significance of what is about to happen can only be understood in the context of the political relationship between the Jews and their Roman rulers. The Jews have condemned Jesus to death on the basis of their own religious laws against blasphemy, in response to Jesus' claim to be the Son of God. But the Sanhedrin has no power to execute condemned prisoners without approval of the Roman government. Yet clearly such a pagan government will not regard a charge of blasphemy with the same degree of seriousness as do the Jews. Therefore more appropriate charges will have to be laid before the governor. Being politically astute, the Jewish leaders will accuse Jesus of sedition in allegedly urging refusal to pay taxes and in claiming to be the king of the Jews.

The man to hear these charges is the Roman procurator and governor, Pontius Pilate, who rules over Judea, Idumea, and Samaria. Pilate began his rule about the time John the Baptist began his ministry. Although his primary responsibility is that of financial administration and collection of taxes for the Roman Empire, Pilate is also burdened with the responsibility of approving and carrying out the execution of anyone sentenced to death by the people's own government—in this case the Sanhedrin. Pilate has a reputation for unprincipled capriciousness, and the manner in which he handles Jesus' case gives no reason to doubt the truth of that reputation. Apparently convinced of Jesus' innocence, Pilate initially takes every available step to avoid personal responsibility. He sends Jesus to Herod Antipas (beheader of John the Baptist), but Herod wants no part of it either. Pilate then tries to release Jesus, but the mob insists that a notorious insurrectionist by the name of Barabbas be released instead. When even a scourging of Jesus fails to placate the crowd, Pilate finally washes his hands of the matter and orders that Jesus be put to death.

Matthew's account begins the record of these tense hours as Jesus is first led to Pilate.

[Fourth Passover April, A.D. 30] Mt. 27:2 Mk. 15:1b Lk. 23:1,2 Jn. 18:28-32 Praetorium (Thursday morning)	JESUS TAKEN TO PILATE. ᴹᵗThey bound him, led him away and handed him over to Pilate, the governor. ᴶⁿBy now it was early morning, and to avoid ceremonial uncleanness the Jews did not enter the palace; they wanted to be able to eat the Passover. So Pilate came out to them and asked, "What charges are you bringing against this man?" "If he were not a criminal," they replied, "we would not have handed him over to you." ᴸᵏAnd they began to accuse him, saying, "We have found this man subverting our nation. He opposes payment of taxes to Caesar and claims to be Christ,ˣ a king." ᴶⁿPilate said, "Take him yourselves and judge him by your own law." "But we have no right to execute anyone," the Jews objected. This happened so that the words Jesus had spoken indicating the kind of death he was going to die would be fulfilled.
Mt.27:11-14 Mk. 15:2-5 Lk. 23:3,4 Jn.18:33-38	PILATE QUESTIONS JESUS. ᴶⁿPilate then went back inside the palace, summoned Jesus and asked him, "Are you the king of the Jews?"

ˣOr *Messiah*

"Is that your own idea," Jesus asked, "or did others talk to you about me?"

"Am I a Jew?" Pilate replied. "It was your people and your chief priests who handed you over to me. What is it you have done?"

Jesus said, "My kingdom is not of this world. If it were, my servants would fight to prevent my arrest by the Jews. But now my kingdom is from another place."

"You are a king, then!" said Pilate.

Jesus answered, "You are right in saying I am a king. In fact, for this reason I was born, and for this I came into the world, to testify to the truth. Everyone on the side of truth listens to me."

"What is truth?" Pilate asked. With this he went out again to the Jews and said, "I find no basis for a charge against him. ᴹᵗWhen he was accused by the chief priests and the elders, he gave no answer. Then Pilate asked him, "Don't you hear the testimony they are bringing against you?" But Jesus made no reply, not even to a single charge—to the great amazement of the governor.

PILATE SENDS JESUS TO HEROD. But they insisted, "He stirs up the people all over Judea ʸ by his teaching. He started in Galilee and has come all the way here."   Lk. 23:5-7

On hearing this, Pilate asked if the man was a Galilean. When he learned that Jesus was under Herod's jurisdiction, he sent him to Herod, who was also in Jerusalem at that time.

JESUS BEFORE HEROD ANTIPAS. When Herod saw Jesus, he was greatly pleased, because for a long time he had been wanting to see him. From what he had heard about him, he hoped to see him perform some miracle. He plied him with many questions, but Jesus gave him no answer. The chief priests and the teachers of the law were standing there, vehemently accusing him. Then Herod and his soldiers ridiculed and mocked him. Dressing him in an elegant robe, they sent him back to Pilate. That day Herod and Pilate became friends—before this they had been enemies.   Lk. 23:8-12
Palace of
Herod
(Thursday
morning)

PILATE'S WIFE SENDS WARNING. While Pilate was sitting on the judge's seat, his wife sent him this message: "Don't have anything to do with that innocent man, for I have suffered a great deal today in a dream because of him."   Mt. 27:19

PILATE SEEKS TO RELEASE. Pilate called together the chief priests, the rulers and the people, and said to them, "You brought me this man as one who was inciting the people to rebellion. I have examined him in your presence and have found no basis for your charges against him. Neither has Herod, for he sent him back to us; as you can see, he has done nothing to deserve death. Therefore, I will punish him and then release him.ᶻ"   Lk.
23:13-16
Praetorium
(Thursday
morning)

JESUS OR BARABBAS. Now it was the custom at the Feast to release a prisoner whom the people requested. A man called Barabbas was in prison with the insurrectionists who had committed murder in the uprising. The crowd came up and asked Pilate to do for them what he usually did.   Mt.
27:15-18
Mk.
15:6-10
Jn. 18:39

"Do you want me to release to you the king of the Jews?" asked Pilate,

---

ʸOr *over the land of the Jews*   ᶻSome manuscripts *him.*" ¹⁷*Now he was obliged to release one man to them at the Feast.*

knowing it was out of envy that the chief priests had handed Jesus over to him.

Mt.
27:20,21
Mk. 15:11
Lk.
23:18,19
Jn. 18:40

CROWD DEMANDS BARABBAS. MkBut the chief priests stirred up the crowd to have Pilate release Barabbas instead. JnThey shouted back, "No, not him! Give us Barabbas!" LkWith one voice they cried out, "Away with this man! Release Barabbas to us!" Mt"Which of the two do you want me to release to you?" asked the governor.

"Barabbas," they answered.

Mt.
27:22,23
Mk.
15:12-14
Lk.
23:20-23

JESUS' CRUCIFIXION DEMANDED. Mt"What shall I do, then, with Jesus who is called Christ?" Pilate asked.

They all answered, "Crucify him!"

"Why? What crime has he committed?" asked Pilate.

But they shouted all the louder, "Crucify him!" LkWanting to release Jesus, Pilate appealed to them again. But they kept shouting, "Crucify him! Crucify him!"

For the third time he spoke to them: "Why? What crime has this man committed? I have found in him no grounds for the death penalty. Therefore I will have him punished and then release him."

But with loud shouts they insistently demanded that he be crucified, and their shouts prevailed.

Mt.
27:27-30
Mk.
15:16-19
Jn. 19:1-3

CROWN OF THORNS. JnThen Pilate took Jesus and had him flogged. MtThen the governor's soldiers took Jesus into the Praetorium and gathered the whole company of soldiers around him. They stripped him and put a scarlet robe on him, and then twisted together a crown of thorns and set it on his head. They put a staff in his right hand and knelt in front of him and mocked him. "Hail, king of the Jews!" they said. They spit on him, and took the staff and struck him on the head again and again.

Jn. 19:4-6

PILATE PRESENTS JESUS. Once more Pilate came out and said to the Jews, "Look, I am bringing him out to you to let you know that I find no basis for a charge against him." When Jesus came out wearing the crown of thorns and the purple robe, Pilate said to them, "Here is the man!"

As soon as the chief priests and their officials saw him, they shouted, "Crucify! Crucify!"

But Pilate answered, "You take him and crucify him. As for me, I find no basis for a charge against him."

Jn. 19:7-11

JESUS QUESTIONED AGAIN. The Jews insisted, "We have a law, and according to that law he must die, because he claimed to be the Son of God."

When Pilate heard this, he was even more afraid, and he went back inside the palace. "Where do you come from?" he asked Jesus, but Jesus gave him no answer. "Do you refuse to speak to me?" Pilate said. "Don't you realize I have power either to free you or to crucify you?"

Jesus answered, "You would have no power over me if it were not given to you from above. Therefore the one who handed me over to you is guilty of a greater sin."

Jn.
19:12-15

PLAY ON PILATE'S LOYALTY. From then on, Pilate tried to set Jesus free, but the Jews kept shouting, "If you let this man go, you are no friend of Caesar. Anyone who claims to be a king opposes Caesar."

When Pilate heard this, he brought Jesus out and sat down on the judge's seat at a place known as the Stone Pavement (which in Aramaic is

Gabbatha). It was the day of Preparation of Passover Week, about the sixth hour.

"Here is your king," Pilate said to the Jews.

But they shouted, "Take him away! Take him away! Crucify him!"

"Shall I crucify your king?" Pilate asked.

"We have no king but Caesar," the chief priests answered.

PILATE WASHES HANDS. When Pilate saw that he was getting nowhere, but that instead an uproar was starting, he took water and washed his hands in front of the crowd. "I am innocent of this man's blood," he said. "It is your responsibility!"

All the people answered, "Let his blood be on us and on our children!"

Mt. 27:24,25

BARABBAS IS RELEASED. So Pilate decided to grant their demand. He released the man who had been thrown into prison for insurrection and murder, the one they asked for, and surrendered Jesus to their will.

Mt. 27:26
Mk. 15:15
Lk. 23:24,25
Jn. 19:16

JESUS IS LED OUT. Mk And when they had mocked him, they took off the purple robe and put his own clothes on him. Then they led him out to crucify him. Jn Carrying his own cross, he went out...

Mt. 27:31
Mk. 15:20
Jn. 19:17

SIMON OF CYRENE. A certain man from Cyrene, Simon, the father of Alexander and Rufus, was passing by on his way in from the country, and they forced him to carry the cross. They brought Jesus to the place called Golgotha (which means The Place of the Skull).

Mt. 27:32
Mk. 15:21,22
Lk. 23:26

WOMEN WEEP FOR JESUS. A large number of people followed him, including women who mourned and wailed for him. Jesus turned and said to them, "Daughters of Jerusalem, do not weep for me; weep for yourselves and for your children. For the time will come when you will say, 'Blessed are the barren women, the wombs that never bore and the breasts that never nursed!' Then

Lk. 23:27-31

" 'they will say to the mountains, "Fall on us!"
and to the hills, "Cover us!" ' [a]

For if men do these things when the tree is green, what will happen when it is dry?"

The Crucifixion of Jesus

*I*t is sometime before noon when the procession reaches the outskirts of Jerusalem and the crowd gathers on a craggy little hill which is known as Golgotha—that is, The Skull. As Jesus is nailed to the wooden cross and lifted up, the scene below him becomes a strange mixture of emotions. On one hand he sees the bitter sorrow of his family and followers, and on the other hand he sees the carnival-like atmosphere of the soldiers and those who have demanded his death. As he awaits his death with increasing pain and agony, Jesus speaks briefly with one of the two robbers crucified with him. Then, seeing his mother, Mary, he directs John to care for her. By early afternoon the end is near. As unusual darkness covers the land, Jesus cries out his

[a] Hosea 10:8

last words and gives up his spirit in death. The significance of the hour is marked by a series of miraculous events which fill the people with awe.

Mt.
27:33,34,38
Mk. 15:23,
25,27,28
Lk.
23:32-34a
Jn. 19:18
(9 A.M.-
noon)

JESUS IS CRUCIFIED.   ᴸᵏTwo other men, both criminals, were also led out with him to be executed. When they came to the place called the Skull, there they crucified him, along with the criminals—one on his right, the other on his left. Jesus said, "Father, forgive them, for they do not know what they are doing."ᵇ ᴹᵏThen they offered him wine mixed with myrrh, but he did not take it.

It was the third hour when they crucified him.

Mt. 27:37
Mk. 15:26
Lk. 23:38
Jn.
19:19-22

INSCRIPTION ON CROSS.   Pilate had a notice prepared and fastened to the cross. It read: JESUS OF NAZARETH, THE KING OF THE JEWS. Many of the Jews read this sign, for the place where Jesus was crucified was near the city, and the sign was written in Aramaic, Latin and Greek. The chief priests of the Jews protested to Pilate, "Do not write 'The King of the Jews,' but that this man claimed to be king of the Jews."

Pilate answered, "What I have written, I have written."

Mt.
27:35,36
Mk. 15:24
Lk. 23:34b
Jn.
19:23,24

SOLDIERS CAST LOTS.   When the soldiers crucified Jesus, they took his clothes, dividing them into four shares, one for each of them, with the undergarment remaining. This garment was seamless, woven in one piece from top to bottom.

"Let's not tear it," they said to one another. "Let's decide by lot who will get it."

This happened that the scripture might be fulfilled which said,

"They divided my garments among them
and cast lots for my clothing."ᶜ

So this is what the soldiers did.

Mt.
27:39-44
Mk.
15:29-32
Lk.
23:35-37

CROWD MOCKS JESUS.   ᴹᵗThose who passed by hurled insults at him, shaking their heads and saying, "You who are going to destroy the temple and build it in three days, save yourself! Come down from the cross, if you are the Son of God!"

In the same way the chief priests, the teachers of the law and the elders mocked him. "He saved others," they said, "but he can't save himself! He's the King of Israel! Let him come down now from the cross, and we will believe in him. He trusts in God. Let God rescue him now if he wants him, for he said, 'I am the Son of God.'" ᴸᵏThe soldiers also came up and mocked him. They offered him wine vinegar and said, "If you are the king of the Jews, save yourself."

Lk.
23:39-43

THIEF ASKS REMEMBRANCE.   One of the criminals who hung there hurled insults at him: "Aren't you the Christ? Save yourself and us!"

But the other criminal rebuked him. "Don't you fear God," he said, "since you are under the same sentence? We are punished justly, for we are getting what our deeds deserve. But this man has done nothing wrong."

Then he said, "Jesus, remember me when you come into your kingdom.ᵈ"

ᵇSome early manuscripts do not have this sentence.   ᶜPsalm 22:18   ᵈSome manuscripts *come with your kingly power*

Jesus answered him, "I tell you the truth, today you will be with me in paradise."

JESUS PROVIDES FOR MARY.   Near the cross of Jesus stood his mother, his mother's sister, Mary the wife of Clopas, and Mary Magdalene. When Jesus saw his mother there, and the disciple whom he loved standing nearby, he said to his mother, "Dear woman, here is your son," and to the disciple, "Here is your mother." From that time on, this disciple took her into his home.

Jn. 19:25-27

JESUS CRIES OUT.   From the sixth hour until the ninth hour darkness came over all the land. About the ninth hour Jesus cried out in a loud voice, "Eloi, Eloi,[e] lama sabachthani?"—which means, "My God, my God, why have you forsaken me?"[f]

When some of those standing there heard this, they said, "He's calling Elijah."

Mt. 27:45-47
Mk. 15:33-35
Lk. 23:44,45a
(About 3 P.M.)

JESUS IS GIVEN DRINK.   [Jn]Later, knowing that all was now completed, and so that the Scripture would be fulfilled, Jesus said, "I am thirsty." [Mt]Immediately one of them ran and got a sponge. He filled it with wine vinegar, put it on a stick, and offered it to Jesus to drink. The rest said, "Now leave him alone. Let's see if Elijah comes to save him."

Mt. 27:48,49
Mk. 15:36
Jn. 19:28,29

JESUS DIES.   [Jn]When he had received the drink, Jesus said, "It is finished." [Lk]Jesus called out with a loud voice, "Father, into your hands I commit my spirit." [Jn]With that, he bowed his head and gave up his spirit.

Mt. 27:50
Mk. 15:37
Lk. 23:46
Jn. 19:30

MIRACULOUS EVENTS.   At that moment the curtain of the temple was torn in two from top to bottom. The earth shook and the rocks split. The tombs broke open and the bodies of many holy people who had died were raised to life. They came out of the tombs, and after Jesus' resurrection they went into the holy city and appeared to many people.

Mt. 27:51-53
Mk. 15:38
Lk. 23:45b

PEOPLE STRUCK WITH AWE.   [Mt]When the centurion and those with him who were guarding Jesus saw the earthquake and all that had happened, they were terrified, and exclaimed, "Surely he was the Son[g] of God!" [Mk]Some women were watching from a distance. Among them were Mary Magdalene, Mary the mother of James the younger and of Joses, and Salome. In Galilee these women had followed him and cared for his needs. Many other women who had come up with him to Jerusalem were also there. [Lk]When all the people who had gathered to witness this sight saw what took place, they beat their breasts and went away. But all those who knew him, including the women who had followed him from Galilee, stood at a distance, watching these things.

Mt. 27:54-56
Mk. 15:39-41
Lk. 23:47-49

JESUS IS PIERCED.   Now it was the day of Preparation, and the next day was to be a special Sabbath. Because the Jews did not want the bodies left on the crosses during the Sabbath, they asked Pilate to have the legs broken and the bodies taken down. The soldiers therefore came and broke the legs of the first man who had been crucified with Jesus, and then those of the other. But when they came to Jesus and found that he was already dead, they did not break his legs. Instead, one of the soldiers pierced Jesus' side with a spear, bringing a sudden flow of blood and water. The man who saw it has given testimony, and his testimony is true. He knows that he tells the truth, and he testifies so that you also may believe. These

Jn. 19:31-37

[e]Some manuscripts *Eli, Eli*   [f]Psalm 22:1   [g]Or *a son*

things happened so that the scripture would be fulfilled: "Not one of his bones will be broken,"[h] and, as another scripture says, "They will look on the one they have pierced."[i]

The Burial of Jesus

*E*ven in Jesus' burial a remarkable story unfolds involving two men whose names will live throughout history: Nicodemus and Joseph of Arimathea. That anyone outside Jesus' family would have sufficient courage to ask for his body would be curious enough. The real surprise, however, is that it should be a member of the very council which had called for Jesus' execution. Yet the record notes that Joseph of Arimathea, a respected member of the council, is also a believer, and it is he who will bury Jesus' body in his own tomb. Joseph will be aided by Nicodemus, the Pharisee and Jewish ruler who had come to Jesus by night asking how one is to be born again. Although the record of that visit did not disclose the result of their discussion, the happy ending is that apparently Nicodemus has become a believer. It is fitting, therefore, that two men whose lives have been so touched by Jesus should now express their gratitude in this final tribute.

Mt. 27:57,58
Mk. 15:42-45
Lk. 23:50-52
Jn. 19:38a
Garden near Golgotha

JOSEPH ASKS FOR BODY.   It was Preparation Day (that is, the day before the Sabbath). So as evening approached, Joseph of Arimathea, a prominent member of the Council, who was himself waiting for the kingdom of God, went boldly to Pilate and asked for Jesus' body. Pilate was surprised to hear that he was already dead. Summoning the centurion, he asked him if Jesus had already died. When he learned from the centurion that it was so, he gave the body to Joseph.

Mt. 27:59,60
Mk. 15:46
Lk. 23:53,54
Jn. 19:38b-42

JESUS BURIED.   [Jn]With Pilate's permission, he came and took the body away. He was accompanied by Nicodemus, the man who earlier had visited Jesus at night. Nicodemus brought a mixture of myrrh and aloes, about seventy-five pounds.[j] Taking Jesus' body, the two of them wrapped it, with the spices, in strips of linen. This was in accordance with Jewish burial customs. [Mt]Joseph took the body, wrapped it in a clean linen cloth, and placed it in his own new tomb that he had cut out of the rock. [Jn]Because it was the Jewish day of Preparation and since the tomb was nearby, they laid Jesus there. [Mt]He rolled a big stone in front of the entrance to the tomb and went away.

Mt. 27:61
Mk. 15:47
Lk. 23:55,56

WOMEN PREPARE ANOINTMENT.   The women who had come with Jesus from Galilee followed Joseph and saw the tomb and how his body was laid in it. Then they went home and prepared spices and perfumes. But they rested on the Sabbath in obedience to the commandment.

Mt. 27:62-66
(Thursday night, or early Friday)

SOLDIERS GUARD TOMB.   The next day, the one after Preparation Day, the chief priests and the Pharisees went to Pilate. "Sir," they said, "we remember that while he was still alive that deceiver said, 'After three days I will rise again.' So give the order for the tomb to be made secure until the third day. Otherwise, his disciples may come and steal the body and tell

[h]Exodus 12:46; Num. 9:12; Psalm 34:20   [i]Zech. 12:10   [j]Greek *a hundred litrai* (about 34 kilograms)

the people that he has been raised from the dead. This last deception will be worse than the first."

"Take a guard," Pilate answered. "Go, make the tomb as secure as you know how." So they went and made the tomb secure by putting a seal on the stone and posting the guard.

Jesus' Resurrection and Appearances

*T*he importance of Jesus' death is surpassed only by the good news of his resurrection! Jesus has prophesied that he will live again, and therefore his credibility is in jeopardy if he is now unable to demonstrate power over his own death. That very claim, and its obvious implications, has already prompted the Jewish leaders to demand a Roman guard at the tomb.

The events which follow are nothing short of marvelous. They not only confirm Jesus' credibility but also provide for believers the assurance of life after death. The drama of Jesus' reappearance unfolds with initial fear, amazement, and outright disbelief on the part of the disciples, but thereafter turns to both belief and joyous celebration. His reappearance is not merely an apparition from the spirit world. Jesus eats in their presence and invites them to touch the wounds where his hands were nailed to the cross. He appears not only in Jerusalem immediately after his resurrection but also later in Galilee. Jesus' appearance is no mere figment of their imagination. This is Jesus himself!

The Gospel writers begin their accounts of the resurrection as the stone sealing the tomb is rolled away. Several of the women come to the tomb early Sunday morning, only to find it empty. When angels at the tomb tell them that Jesus has been raised from the dead, the women react with both fear and joy. At that point the chronology of events becomes somewhat complex, but it appears that Mary Magdalene runs ahead of the other women to find Peter and John, who, upon being told of the body's disappearance, rush with Mary to the empty tomb. As Peter and John go away greatly perplexed, Jesus himself appears to Mary Magdalene there by the tomb, and then to the other women who are still on their way back from the tomb to tell of the resurrection. Of course Jesus' appearance to Mary and the other women gives them even more to tell about, but when the disciples hear it, they simply cannot bring themselves to believe it.

Although there is no direct record of it, apparently Jesus makes a special appearance to Peter sometime on Sunday. The other apostles make reference to that appearance as they are discussing the resurrection later that night with a disciple named Cleopas, to whom Jesus had appeared during the same day. Finally, on this day of resurrection, Jesus will be seen to appear to all the other apostles except for Thomas, who is not present at the time. Thomas' subsequent disbelief is dispelled a week later, when Jesus again appears to the apostles and Thomas views Jesus in person. The apostles will be with Jesus on several occasions, both in Jerusalem and further north in Galilee, before he gives them their apostolic commission and parting instructions.

Sense now the quietness and anticipation on the morning of this ultimate miracle—the resurrection of Jesus the Christ!

Mt. 28:2-4
(Sunday morning)

STONE ROLLED AWAY.   There was a violent earthquake, for an angel of the Lord came down from heaven and, going to the tomb, rolled back the stone and sat on it. His appearance was like lightning, and his clothes were white as snow. The guards were so afraid of him that they shook and became like dead men.

Mt. 28:1
Mk. 16:1-4
Lk. 24:1-3
Jn. 20:1
At the tomb (Sunday morning)

WOMEN COME TO TOMB.   When the Sabbath was over, Mary Magdalene, Mary the mother of James, and Salome bought spices so that they might go to anoint Jesus' body. Very early on the first day of the week, just after sunrise, they were on their way to the tomb and they asked each other, "Who will roll the stone away from the entrance of the tomb?"

But when they looked up, they saw that the stone, which was very large, had been rolled away.

Mt. 28:5-7
Mk. 16:5-7

RESURRECTION ANNOUNCED.   As they entered the tomb, they saw a young man dressed in a white robe sitting on the right side, and they were alarmed.

"Don't be alarmed," he said. "You are looking for Jesus the Nazarene, who was crucified. He has risen! He is not here. See the place where they laid him. But go, tell his disciples and Peter, 'He is going ahead of you into Galilee. There you will see him, just as he told you.'"

Lk. 24:4-8

WOMEN REMINDED OF PROPHECY.   While they were wondering about this, suddenly two men in clothes that gleamed like lightning stood beside them. In their fright the women bowed down with their faces to the ground, but the men said to them, "Why do you look for the living among the dead? He is not here; he has risen! Remember how he told you, while he was still with you in Galilee: 'The Son of Man must be delivered into the hands of sinful men, be crucified and on the third day be raised again.'" Then they remembered his words.

Mk. 16:8

WOMEN GO AWAY FEARFUL.   Trembling and bewildered, the women went out and fled from the tomb. They said nothing to anyone, because they were afraid.

Jn. 20:2

PETER AND JOHN TOLD.   So [Mary of Magdala] came running to Simon Peter and the other disciple, the one Jesus loved, and said, "They have taken the Lord out of the tomb, and we don't know where they have put him!"

Lk. 24:12
Jn. 20:3-10
At tomb

PETER AND JOHN VIEW TOMB.   So Peter and the other disciple started for the tomb. Both were running, but the other disciple outran Peter and reached the tomb first. He bent over and looked in at the strips of linen lying there but did not go in. Then Simon Peter, who was behind him, arrived and went into the tomb. He saw the strips of linen lying there, as well as the burial cloth that had been around Jesus' head. The cloth was folded up by itself, separate from the linen. Finally the other disciple, who had reached the tomb first, also went inside. He saw and believed. (They still did not understand from Scripture that Jesus had to rise from the dead.)

Then the disciples went back to their homes,

Mk. 16:9
Jn. 20:11-17

JESUS WITH MARY MAGDALENE.   Mk[When Jesus rose early on the first day of the week, he appeared first to Mary Magdalene, out of whom he had driven seven demons.] ᴶⁿMary stood outside the tomb crying. As she wept, she bent over to look into the tomb and saw two angels in white, seated where Jesus' body had been, one at the head and the other at the foot.

They asked her, "Woman, why are you crying?"

"They have taken my Lord away," she said, "and I don't know where they have put him." At this, she turned around and saw Jesus standing there, but she did not realize that it was Jesus.

"Woman," he said, "why are you crying? Who is it you are looking for?"

Thinking he was the gardener, she said, "Sir, if you have carried him away, tell me where you have put him, and I will get him."

Jesus said to her, "Mary."

She turned toward him and cried out in Aramaic, "Rabboni!" (which means Teacher).

Jesus said, "Do not hold on to me, for I have not yet returned to the Father. Go instead to my brothers and tell them, 'I am returning to my Father and your Father, to my God and your God.' "

JESUS APPEARS TO WOMEN.   So the women hurried away from the tomb, afraid yet filled with joy, and ran to tell his disciples. Suddenly Jesus met them. "Greetings," he said. They came to him, clasped his feet and worshiped him. Then Jesus said to them, "Do not be afraid. Go and tell my brothers to go to Galilee; there they will see me."

Mt. 28:8-10

CHIEF PRIESTS COVER UP.   While the women were on their way, some of the guards went into the city and reported to the chief priests everything that had happened. When the chief priests had met with the elders and devised a plan, they gave the soldiers a large sum of money, telling them, "You are to say, 'His disciples came during the night and stole him away while we were asleep.' If this report gets to the governor, we will satisfy him and keep you out of trouble." So the soldiers took the money and did as they were instructed. And this story has been widely circulated among the Jews to this very day.

Mt. 28:11-15

WOMEN TELL OF APPEARANCE.   When they came back from the tomb, they told all these things to the Eleven and to all the others. It was Mary Magdalene, Joanna, Mary the mother of James, and the others with them who told this to the apostles. But they did not believe the women, because their words seemed to them like nonsense.

Mk. 16:10,11
Lk. 24:9-11
Jn. 20:18

JESUS APPEARS TO CLEOPAS.   Now that same day two of them were going to a village called Emmaus, about seven milesᵏ from Jerusalem. They were talking with each other about everything that had happened. As they talked and discussed these things with each other, Jesus himself came up and walked along with them; but they were kept from recognizing him.

Mk. 16:12
Lk. 24:13-27
Road to Emmaus (Sunday afternoon)

He asked them, "What are you discussing together as you walk along?"

They stood still, their faces downcast. One of them, named Cleopas, asked him, "Are you only a visitor to Jerusalem and do not know the things that have happened there in these days?"

"What things?" he asked.

"About Jesus of Nazareth," they replied. "He was a prophet, powerful in word and deed before God and all the people. The chief priests and our

ᵏGreek *sixty stadia* (about 11 kilometers)

rulers handed him over to be sentenced to death, and they crucified him; but we had hoped that he was the one who was going to redeem Israel. And what is more, it is the third day since all this took place. In addition, some of our women amazed us. They went to the tomb early this morning but didn't find his body. They came and told us that they had seen a vision of angels, who said he was alive. Then some of our companions went to the tomb and found it just as the women had said, but him they did not see."

He said to them, "How foolish you are, and how slow of heart to believe all that the prophets have spoken! Did not the Christ[1] have to suffer these things and then enter his glory?" And beginning with Moses and all the Prophets, he explained to them what was said in all the Scriptures concerning himself.

Lk.
24:28-32
Emmaus
(Sunday
evening)

JESUS' IDENTITY REVEALED.   As they approached the village to which they were going, Jesus acted as if he were going farther. But they urged him strongly, "Stay with us, for it is nearly evening; the day is almost over." So he went in to stay with them.

When he was at the table with them, he took bread, gave thanks, broke it and began to give it to them. Then their eyes were opened and they recognized him, and he disappeared from their sight. They asked each other, "Were not our hearts burning within us while he talked with us on the road and opened the Scriptures to us?"

Mk. 16:13
Lk.
24:33-35
Jn. 20:19

CLEOPAS TELLS OF APPEARANCE.   LkThey got up and returned at once to Jerusalem. There [Jnon the evening of that first day of the week, when the disciples were together, with the doors locked for fear of the Jews,] they found the Eleven and those with them, assembled together and saying, "It is true! The Lord has risen and has appeared to Simon." Then the two told what had happened on the way, and how Jesus was recognized by them when he broke the bread.

Mk. 16:14
Lk.
24:36-44
Jn. 20:20
(Sunday
night)

JESUS APPEARS TO DISCIPLES.   While they were still talking about this, Jesus himself stood among them and said to them, "Peace be with you."

They were startled and frightened, thinking they saw a ghost. He said to them, "Why are you troubled, and why do doubts rise in your minds? Look at my hands and my feet. It is I myself! Touch me and see; a ghost does not have flesh and bones, as you see I have."

When he had said this, he showed them his hands and feet. And while they still did not believe it because of joy and amazement, he asked them, "Do you have anything here to eat?" They gave him a piece of broiled fish, and he took it and ate it in their presence.

He said to them, "This is what I told you while I was still with you: Everything must be fulfilled that is written about me in the Law of Moses, the Prophets and the Psalms."

Jn.
20:21-23

APOSTLES RECEIVE AUTHORITY.   Again Jesus said, "Peace be with you! As the Father has sent me, I am sending you." And with that he breathed on them and said, "Receive the Holy Spirit. If you forgive anyone his sins, they are forgiven; if you do not forgive them, they are not forgiven."

[1]Or Messiah

THOMAS DOUBTS.   Now Thomas (called Didymus), one of the Twelve, was not with the disciples when Jesus came. So the other disciples told him, "We have seen the Lord!"

But he said to them, "Unless I see the nail marks in his hands and put my finger where the nails were, and put my hand into his side, I will not believe it."

Jn.
20:24,25

JESUS APPEARS TO THOMAS.   A week later his disciples were in the house again, and Thomas was with them. Though the doors were locked, Jesus came and stood among them and said, "Peace be with you!" Then he said to Thomas, "Put your finger here; see my hands. Reach out your hand and put it into my side. Stop doubting and believe."

Thomas said to him, "My Lord and my God!"

Then Jesus told him, "Because you have seen me, you have believed; blessed are those who have not seen and yet have believed."

Jn.
20:26-29
(Week
after
resurrec-
tion)

JESUS APPEARS TO DISCIPLES.   Afterward Jesus appeared again to his disciples, by the Sea of Tiberias.*m* It happened this way: Simon Peter, Thomas (called Didymus), Nathanael from Cana in Galilee, the sons of Zebedee, and two other disciples were together. "I'm going out to fish," Simon Peter told them, and they said, "We'll go with you." So they went out and got into the boat, but that night they caught nothing.

Early in the morning, Jesus stood on the shore, but the disciples did not realize that it was Jesus.

He called out to them, "Friends, haven't you any fish?"

"No," they answered.

He said, "Throw your net on the right side of the boat and you will find some." When they did, they were unable to haul the net in because of the large number of fish.

Then the disciple whom Jesus loved said to Peter, "It is the Lord!" As soon as Simon Peter heard him say, "It is the Lord," he wrapped his outer garment around him (for he had taken it off) and jumped into the water. The other disciples followed in the boat, towing the net full of fish, for they were not far from shore, about a hundred yards.*n* When they landed, they saw a fire of burning coals there with fish on it, and some bread.

Jesus said to them, "Bring some of the fish you have just caught."

Simon Peter climbed aboard and dragged the net ashore. It was full of large fish, 153, but even with so many the net was not torn. Jesus said to them, "Come and have breakfast." None of the disciples dared ask him, "Who are you?" They knew it was the Lord. Jesus came, took the bread and gave it to them, and did the same with the fish. This was now the third time Jesus appeared to his disciples after he was raised from the dead.

Jn. 21:1-14
Sea of
Galilee
(Some
later time)

PETER REINSTATED.   When they had finished eating, Jesus said to Simon Peter, "Simon son of John, do you truly love me more than these?"

"Yes, Lord," he said, "you know that I love you."

Jesus said, "Feed my lambs."

Again Jesus said, "Simon son of John, do you truly love me?"

He answered, "Yes, Lord, you know that I love you."

Jesus said, "Take care of my sheep."

The third time he said to him, "Simon son of John, do you love me?"

Peter was hurt because Jesus asked him the third time, "Do you love

Jn.
21:15-17

---

*m*That is, Sea of Galilee   *n*Greek *about two hundred cubits* (about 90 meters)

me?" He said, "Lord, you know all things; you know that I love you." Jesus said, "Feed my sheep.

Jn.
21:18,19

PETER'S DEATH FORETOLD.   I tell you the truth, when you were younger you dressed yourself and went where you wanted; but when you are old you will stretch out your hands, and someone else will dress you and lead you where you do not want to go." Jesus said this to indicate the kind of death by which Peter would glorify God. Then he said to him, "Follow me!"

Jn.
21:20-24

JOHN'S DEATH QUESTIONED.   Peter turned and saw that the disciple whom Jesus loved was following them. (This was the one who had leaned back against Jesus at the supper and had said, "Lord, who is going to betray you?") When Peter saw him, he asked, "Lord, what about him?"

Jesus answered, "If I want him to remain alive until I return, what is that to you? You must follow me." Because of this, the rumor spread among the brothers that this disciple would not die. But Jesus did not say that he would not die; he only said, "If I want him to remain alive until I return, what is that to you?"

This is the disciple who testifies to these things and who wrote them down. We know that his testimony is true.

_____

[The earliest manuscripts and some other ancient witnesses do not have Mark 16:9-20.]

Final Instructions and Ascension

After these wonderful events, Jesus is next seen again with his 11 apostles on a mountain in Galilee. There they are given the special mission of evangelizing the world, a task to be accomplished through their personal testimonies regarding Jesus' life, death, and resurrection. Even as they are receiving this commission, some among them still have doubts about their mission. But the time is soon to come when, filled with God's Holy Spirit, each will stand strong in his faith and become a vibrant force in changing the hearts of men and women throughout the world.

Some time passes before Jesus makes his final appearance with the apostles, and the scene changes to Jerusalem. There Jesus directs the apostles to remain in the city until they receive a special power which he promises will come from the Father. Later he gives them their final instructions, promises them the Holy Spirit, and then is caught up into heaven as two angels stand by to comfort the apostles with the grand promise of his second coming.

Mt.
28:16-20
Mk.
16:15-18
On
mountain
in Galilee

JESUS COMMISSIONS APOSTLES.   ᴹᵗThen Jesus came to them and said, "All authority in heaven and on earth has been given to me. Therefore go and make disciples of all nations, baptizing them in⁰ the name of the Father and of the Son and of the Holy Spirit, and teaching them to obey everything I have commanded you. And surely I am with you always, to

⁰Or *into*; see Acts 8:16; 19:5; Romans 6:3; 1 Cor. 1:13; 10:2 and Gal. 3:27.

the very end of the age." [Mk]Whoever believes and is baptized will be saved, but whoever does not believe will be condemned. [Mk]And these signs will accompany those who believe: In my name they will drive out demons; they will speak in new tongues; they will pick up snakes with their hands; and when they drink deadly poison, it will not hurt them at all; they will place their hands on sick people, and they will get well."

PARTING INSTRUCTIONS. Then he opened their minds so they could understand the Scriptures. He told them, "This is what is written: The Christ will suffer and rise from the dead on the third day, and repentance and forgiveness of sins will be preached in his name to all nations, beginning at Jerusalem. You are witnesses of these things. I am going to send you what my Father has promised; but stay in the city until you have been clothed with power from on high." **Lk. 24:45-49 Jerusalem (Before Pentecost)**

JESUS ASCENDS. [Lk]When he had led them out to the vicinity of Bethany, he lifted up his hands and blessed them. [Ac][They] asked him, "Lord, are you at this time going to restore the kingdom to Israel?" **Mk. 16:19 Lk. 24:50,51 Acts 1:6-11**

He said to them: "It is not for you to know the times or dates the Father has set by his own authority. But you will receive power when the Holy Spirit comes on you; and you will be my witnesses in Jerusalem, and in all Judea and Samaria, and to the ends of the earth."

After he said this, he was taken up before their very eyes, and a cloud hid him from their sight.

They were looking intently up into the sky as he was going, when suddenly two men dressed in white stood beside them. "Men of Galilee," they said, "why do you stand here looking into the sky? This same Jesus, who has been taken from you into heaven, will come back in the same way you have seen him go into heaven."

DISCIPLES RETURN JOYFULLY. [Lk]Then they worshiped him and returned to Jerusalem with great joy. [Ac]When they arrived, they went upstairs to the room where they were staying. Those present were Peter, John, James and Andrew; Philip and Thomas, Bartholomew and Matthew; James son of Alphaeus and Simon the Zealot, and Judas son of James. They all joined together constantly in prayer, along with the women and Mary the mother of Jesus, and with his brothers. **Lk. 24:52,53 Acts 1:12-14 Jerusalem**

CALL FOR JUDAS' REPLACEMENT. In those days Peter stood up among the believers[p] (a group numbering about a hundred and twenty) and said, "Brothers, the Scripture had to be fulfilled which the Holy Spirit spoke long ago through the mouth of David concerning Judas, who served as guide for those who arrested Jesus—he was one of our number and shared in this ministry." **Acts 1:15-22**

(With the reward he got for his wickedness, Judas bought a field; there he fell headlong, his body burst open and all his intestines spilled out. Everyone in Jerusalem heard about this, so they called that field in their language Akeldama, that is, Field of Blood.)

"For," said Peter, "it is written in the book of Psalms,

" 'May his place be deserted;
let there be no one to dwell in it,'[q]

[p]Greek *brothers* [q]Psalm 69:25

and,

" 'May another take his place of leadership.'ʳ

Therefore it is necessary to choose one of the men who have been with us the whole time the Lord Jesus went in and out among us, beginning from John's baptism to the time when Jesus was taken up from us. For one of these must become a witness with us of his resurrection."

Acts
1:23-26

MATTHIAS CHOSEN AS APOSTLE.   So they proposed two men: Joseph called Barsabbas (also known as Justus) and Matthias. Then they prayed, "Lord, you know everyone's heart. Show us which of these two you have chosen to take over this apostolic ministry, which Judas left to go where he belongs." Then they cast lots, and the lot fell to Matthias; so he was added to the eleven apostles.

Mk. 16:20

JESUS PREACHED.   Then the disciples went out and preached everywhere, and the Lord worked with them and confirmed his word by the signs that accompanied it.

Conclusion to the Gospel Accounts _____

John's account includes this statement as to his purpose in recording the events of Jesus' ministry:

Jn.
20:30,31

Jesus did many other miraculous signs in the presence of his disciples, which are not recorded in this book. But these are written that you mayˢ believe that Jesus is the Christ, the Son of God, and that by believing you may have life in his name.

Indeed, each of the other accounts unquestionably has the same purpose—the preservation of Jesus' life, teaching, and miraculous works so that all who read may acknowledge him as Lord and Savior.

John concludes his account by indicating that he and the other Gospel writers had been able to capture in written words only a small fraction of all the miracles, healings, praying, and preaching that Jesus did while on this earth.

Jn. 21:25

Jesus did many other things as well. If every one of them were written down, I suppose that even the whole world would not have room for the books that would be written.

Even with only these four brief accounts of his life, the story of Jesus has been preserved throughout the centuries for every generation, translated into major languages throughout the earth, and believed by countless millions who have responded in obedient faith to God through his Son, Jesus the Christ.

ʳPsalm 109:8   ˢSome manuscripts *may continue to*

CHRIST'S CHURCH AND THE APOSTLES

(Ca. A.D. 30-100)

Acts of the Apostles

*A*s the Gospel accounts come to a close with Jesus' ascension, the focus of Scripture turns to the work of the apostles and others in their efforts to spread the good news about Jesus throughout the world, and to the beginning of the church, which comprises Christ's faithful disciples. The historical record of the church in the first 30 years of its history, commonly known as the Acts of the Apostles, is evidently written by Luke. Luke's writing records many of the acts of some of the apostles, principally those of Peter and of Paul (who will become a special apostle), and also includes the work of others, such as Stephen, Philip, Barnabas, and Silas. More importantly, Luke records the work of the Holy Spirit in the church of the first century. After a brief introduction to his writing, Luke stresses the powerful manifestation of the Holy Spirit in the confirmation and spread of the gospel message.

INTRODUCTION TO BOOK.   In my former book, Theophilus, I wrote about all that Jesus began to do and to teach until the day he was taken up to heaven, after giving instructions through the Holy Spirit to the apostles he had chosen. After his suffering, he showed himself to these men and gave many convincing proofs that he was alive. He appeared to them over a period of forty days and spoke about the kingdom of God. On one occasion, while he was eating with them, he gave them this command: "Do not leave Jerusalem, but wait for the gift my Father promised, which you have heard me speak about. For John baptized with*ᵃ* water, but in a few days you will be baptized with the Holy Spirit."

**Acts 1:1-5
Jerusalem
(Ca. A.D. 30)**

Power of the Holy Spirit

*A*s recorded in the Gospel accounts, Jesus had told the apostles to wait in Jerusalem until they should receive power from on high, a reference undoubtedly to the power of God's Holy Spirit, which he had promised they would receive. Luke begins his historical record with the account of a special demonstration of God's power in the ministry of the apostles. The occasion is the Feast of Pentecost, which is celebrated by the

ᵃOr in

Jews each year 50 days after Passover. Also known as the Feast of Weeks, the feast was originally given in celebration of the firstfruits of the harvest. As one of the three major Jewish feasts, Pentecost attracts large numbers of Jews to Jerusalem from throughout the world.

Here in the midst of a throng of Pentecost celebrants, the Holy Spirit descends in power upon the small band of Galilean men whom Jesus has chosen to be his spokesmen. Amazingly, they are heard speaking in all the native languages represented in Jerusalem, declaring the wonders of God. Luke records the sermon preached by Peter, which is a stirring call for the Jews to see Jesus both as the Messiah of prophecy and as the resurrected Lord. When Peter strongly indicts his audience for having played a part in crucifying their Messiah, thousands immediately repent and are baptized. This occasion heralds not only the special power of the Holy Spirit in the ministry of the apostles, but also the formal beginning of Christ's spiritual body, the church.

Acts 2:1-4 THE HOLY SPIRIT. When the day of Pentecost came, they were all together in one place. Suddenly a sound like the blowing of a violent wind came from heaven and filled the whole house where they were sitting. They saw what seemed to be tongues of fire that separated and came to rest on each of them. All of them were filled with the Holy Spirit and began to speak in other tongues[b] as the Spirit enabled them.

Acts 2:5-13 SPEAKING IN OTHER LANGUAGES. Now there were staying in Jerusalem God-fearing Jews from every nation under heaven. When they heard this sound, a crowd came together in bewilderment, because each one heard them speaking in his own language. Utterly amazed, they asked: "Are not all these men who are speaking Galileans? Then how is it that each of us hears them in his own native language? Parthians, Medes and Elamites; residents of Mesopotamia, Judea and Cappadocia, Pontus and Asia, Phrygia and Pamphylia, Egypt and the parts of Libya near Cyrene; visitors from Rome (both Jews and converts to Judaism); Cretans and Arabs—we hear them declaring the wonders of God in our own tongues!" Amazed and perplexed, they asked one another, "What does this mean?"

Some, however, made fun of them and said, "They have had too much wine.[c]"

Acts 2:14-36 PETER PROCLAIMS JESUS AS CHRIST. Then Peter stood up with the Eleven, raised his voice and addressed the crowd: "Fellow Jews and all of you who live in Jerusalem, let me explain this to you; listen carefully to what I say. These men are not drunk, as you suppose. It's only nine in the morning! No, this is what was spoken by the prophet Joel:

" 'In the last days, God says,
    I will pour out my Spirit on all people.
Your sons and daughters will prophesy,
    your young men will see visions,
    your old men will dream dreams.
Even on my servants, both men and women,
    I will pour out my Spirit in those days,

[b]Or *languages*   [c]Or *sweet wine*

> and they will prophesy.
> I will show wonders in the heaven above
>   and signs on the earth below,
>   blood and fire and billows of smoke.
> The sun will be turned to darkness
>   and the moon to blood
>   before the coming of the great and glorious day of the
>   Lord.
> And everyone who calls
>   on the name of the Lord will be saved.'^{d}

"Men of Israel, listen to this: Jesus of Nazareth was a man accredited by God to you by miracles, wonders and signs, which God did among you through him, as you yourselves know. This man was handed over to you by God's set purpose and foreknowledge; and you, with the help of wicked men,^{e} put him to death by nailing him to the cross. But God raised him from the dead, freeing him from the agony of death, because it was impossible for death to keep its hold on him. David said about him:

> " 'I saw the Lord always before me.
>   Because he is at my right hand,
>   I will not be shaken.
> Therefore my heart is glad and my tongue rejoices;
>   my body also will live in hope,
> because you will not abandon me to the grave,
>   nor will you let your Holy One see decay.
> You have made known to me the paths of life;
>   you will fill me with joy in your presence.'^{f}

"Brothers, I can tell you confidently that the patriarch David died and was buried, and his tomb is here to this day. But he was a prophet and knew that God had promised him on oath that he would place one of his descendants on his throne. Seeing what was ahead, he spoke of the resurrection of the Christ,^{g} that he was not abandoned to the grave, nor did his body see decay. God has raised this Jesus to life, and we are all witnesses of the fact. Exalted to the right hand of God, he has received from the Father the promised Holy Spirit and has poured out what you now see and hear. For David did not ascend to heaven, and yet he said,

> " 'The Lord said to my Lord:
> "Sit at my right hand
> until I make your enemies
>   a footstool for your feet." ' ^{h}

"Therefore let all Israel be assured of this: God has made this Jesus, whom you crucified, both Lord and Christ."

FIRST BELIEVERS BAPTIZED.   When the people heard this, they were cut to the heart and said to Peter and the other apostles, "Brothers, what shall we do?"

Peter replied, "Repent and be baptized, every one of you, in the name of

Acts
2:37-41

---

^{d}Joel 2:28-32 ^{e}Or *of those not having the law* (that is, Gentiles) ^{f}Psalm 16:8-11
^{g}Or *Messiah.* "The Christ" (Greek) and "the Messiah" (Hebrew) both mean "the Anointed One" ^{h}Psalm 110:1

Jesus Christ for the forgiveness of your sins. And you will receive the gift of the Holy Spirit. The promise is for you and your children and for all who are far off—for all whom the Lord our God will call."

With many other words he warned them; and he pleaded with them, "Save yourselves from this corrupt generation." Those who accepted his message were baptized, and about three thousand were added to their number that day.

Acts 2:42-47　FELLOWSHIP OF BELIEVERS.　They devoted themselves to the apostles' teaching and to the fellowship, to the breaking of bread and to prayer. Everyone was filled with awe, and many wonders and miraculous signs were done by the apostles. All the believers were together and had everything in common. Selling their possessions and goods, they gave to anyone as he had need. Every day they continued to meet together in the temple courts. They broke bread in their homes and ate together with glad and sincere hearts, praising God and enjoying the favor of all the people. And the Lord added to their number daily those who were being saved.

Growth of the Early Church

*T*he fellowship and brotherhood of the early church continues to attract more and more believers. As news of the gospel message and the miracles which accompany its proclamation spread throughout Jerusalem, the church grows rapidly. In fact, the growth is so astounding that the Jewish leaders become alarmed and have the apostles arrested repeatedly. The Sanhedrin elders possibly realize, however, that they are in no position to make martyrs of the apostles, and are therefore forced to postpone any harsher treatment.

But persecution from without is not the only challenge facing the early church. Problems arise even within the church itself. Luke records, for example, that on one occasion some rather drastic discipline befalls a husband and wife who lie about a contribution they are making to the church. But not even such weaknesses of individual believers can slow the pace of this revolutionary spiritual movement. Not less than a dozen times throughout the historical record, Luke carefully notes the incredible growth of the church. Acting without formal organization and prompted only by their commitment to Christ, these early Christians repeatedly multiply their number by sharing the good news of Christ with all who will listen.

The historical record of this period of growth begins now with the account of the healing and teaching done by Peter and John, activities which will eventually lead to their first arrest.

Acts 3:1-10 Near the temple (Ca. A.D. 30-31)　PETER HEALS CRIPPLED BEGGAR.　One day Peter and John were going up to the temple at the time of prayer—at three in the afternoon. Now a man crippled from birth was being carried to the temple gate called Beautiful, where he was put every day to beg from those going into the temple courts. When he saw Peter and John about to enter, he asked them for money. Peter looked straight at him, as did John. Then Peter said, "Look at us!" So the man gave them his attention, expecting to get something from them.

Then Peter said, "Silver or gold I do not have, but what I have I give you. In the name of Jesus Christ of Nazareth, walk." Taking him by the right hand, he helped him up, and instantly the man's feet and ankles became strong. He jumped to his feet and began to walk. Then he went with them into the temple courts, walking and jumping, and praising God. When all the people saw him walking and praising God, they recognized him as the same man who used to sit begging at the temple gate called Beautiful, and they were filled with wonder and amazement at what had happened to him.

MIRACULOUS POWER EXPLAINED.   While the beggar held on to Peter and John, all the people were astonished and came running to them in the place called Solomon's Colonnade. When Peter saw this, he said to them: "Men of Israel, why does this surprise you? Why do you stare at us as if by our own power or godliness we had made this man walk? The God of Abraham, Isaac and Jacob, the God of our fathers, has glorified his servant Jesus. You handed him over to be killed, and you disowned him before Pilate, though he had decided to let him go. You disowned the Holy and Righteous One and asked that a murderer be released to you. You killed the author of life, but God raised him from the dead. We are witnesses of this. By faith in the name of Jesus, this man whom you see and know was made strong. It is Jesus' name and the faith that comes through him that has given this complete healing to him, as you can all see.

Acts 3:11-16

PETER PREACHES REPENTANCE.   "Now, brothers, I know that you acted in ignorance, as did your leaders. But this is how God fulfilled what he had foretold through all the prophets, saying that his Christ*i* would suffer. Repent, then, and turn to God, so that your sins may be wiped out, that times of refreshing may come from the Lord, and that he may send the Christ, who has been appointed for you—even Jesus. He must remain in heaven until the time comes for God to restore everything, as he promised long ago through his holy prophets. For Moses said, 'The Lord your God will raise up for you a prophet like me from among your own people; you must listen to everything he tells you. Anyone who does not listen to him will be completely cut off from among his people.'*j*

Acts 3:17-26

"Indeed, all the prophets from Samuel on, as many as have spoken, have foretold these days. And you are heirs of the prophets and of the covenant God made with your fathers. He said to Abraham, 'Through your offspring all peoples on earth will be blessed.'*k* When God raised up his servant, he sent him first to you to bless you by turning each of you from your wicked ways."

PETER AND JOHN ARRESTED.   The priests and the captain of the temple guard and the Sadducees came up to Peter and John while they were speaking to the people. They were greatly disturbed because the apostles were teaching the people and proclaiming in Jesus the resurrection of the dead. They seized Peter and John, and because it was evening, they put them in jail until the next day. But many who heard the message believed, and the number of men grew to about five thousand.

Acts 4:1-4

DEFENSE BEFORE SANHEDRIN.   The next day the rulers, elders and teachers of the law met in Jerusalem. Annas the high priest was there, and so were Caiaphas, John, Alexander and the other men of the high priest's

Acts 4:5-12

i Or *Messiah*   *j* Deut. 18:15,18,19   *k* Gen. 22:18; 26:4

family. They had Peter and John brought before them and began to question them: "By what power or what name did you do this?"

Then Peter, filled with the Holy Spirit, said to them: "Rulers and elders of the people! If we are being called to account today for an act of kindness shown to a cripple and are asked how he was healed, then know this, you and all the people of Israel: It is by the name of Jesus Christ of Nazareth, whom you crucified but whom God raised from the dead, that this man stands before you healed. He is

> " 'the stone you builders rejected,
> which has become the capstone.[l]'[m]

Salvation is found in no one else, for there is no other name under heaven given to men by which we must be saved."

Acts
4:13-22

APOSTLES WARNED AND FREED. When they saw the courage of Peter and John and realized that they were unschooled, ordinary men, they were astonished and they took note that these men had been with Jesus. But since they could see the man who had been healed standing there with them, there was nothing they could say. So they ordered them to withdraw from the Sanhedrin and then conferred together. "What are we going to do with these men?" they asked. "Everybody living in Jerusalem knows they have done an outstanding miracle, and we cannot deny it. But to stop this thing from spreading any further among the people, we must warn these men to speak no longer to anyone in this name."

Then they called them in again and commanded them not to speak or teach at all in the name of Jesus. But Peter and John replied, "Judge for yourselves whether it is right in God's sight to obey you rather than God. For we cannot help speaking about what we have seen and heard."

After further threats they let them go. They could not decide how to punish them, because all the people were praising God for what had happened. For the man who was miraculously healed was over forty years old.

Acts
4:23-31
Jerusalem

PRAYER OF CHURCH. On their release, Peter and John went back to their own people and reported all that the chief priests and elders had said to them. When they heard this, they raised their voices together in prayer to God. "Sovereign Lord," they said, "you made the heaven and the earth and the sea, and everything in them. You spoke by the Holy Spirit through the mouth of your servant, our father David:

> " 'Why do the nations rage
> and the peoples plot in vain?
> The kings of the earth take their stand
> and the rulers gather together
> against the Lord
> and against his Anointed One.[n] [o]'

Indeed Herod and Pontius Pilate met together with the Gentiles and the people[p] of Israel in this city to conspire against your holy servant Jesus, whom you anointed. They did what your power and will had decided beforehand should happen. Now, Lord, consider their threats and enable

[l]Or *cornerstone*   [m]Psalm 118:22   [n]That is, Christ or Messiah   [o]Psalm 2:1,2
[p]The Greek is plural.

your servants to speak your word with great boldness. Stretch out your hand to heal and perform miraculous signs and wonders through the name of your holy servant Jesus."

After they prayed, the place where they were meeting was shaken. And they were all filled with the Holy Spirit and spoke the word of God boldly.

SHARING OF POSSESSIONS.   All the believers were one in heart and mind. No one claimed that any of his possessions was his own, but they shared everything they had. With great power the apostles continued to testify to the resurrection of the Lord Jesus, and much grace was upon them all. There were no needy persons among them. For from time to time those who owned lands or houses sold them, brought the money from the sales and put it at the apostles' feet, and it was distributed to anyone as he had need.

Joseph, a Levite from Cyprus, whom the apostles called Barnabas (which means Son of Encouragement), sold a field he owned and brought the money and put it at the apostles' feet.

Acts 4:32-37

PUNISHMENT OF ANANIAS.   Now a man named Ananias, together with his wife Sapphira, also sold a piece of property. With his wife's full knowledge he kept back part of the money for himself, but brought the rest and put it at the apostles' feet.

Then Peter said, "Ananias, how is it that Satan has so filled your heart that you have lied to the Holy Spirit and have kept for yourself some of the money you received for the land? Didn't it belong to you before it was sold? And after it was sold, wasn't the money at your disposal? What made you think of doing such a thing? You have not lied to men but to God."

When Ananias heard this, he fell down and died. And great fear seized all who heard what had happened. Then the young men came forward, wrapped up his body, and carried him out and buried him.

Acts 5:1-6

PUNISHMENT OF SAPPHIRA.   About three hours later his wife came in, not knowing what had happened. Peter asked her, "Tell me, is this the price you and Ananias got for the land?"

"Yes," she said, "that is the price."

Peter said to her, "How could you agree to test the Spirit of the Lord? Look! The feet of the men who buried your husband are at the door, and they will carry you out also."

At that moment she fell down at his feet and died. Then the young men came in and, finding her dead, carried her out and buried her beside her husband. Great fear seized the whole church and all who heard about these events.

Acts 5:7-11

SIGNS AND WONDERS.   The apostles performed many miraculous signs and wonders among the people. And all the believers used to meet together in Solomon's Colonnade. No one else dared join them, even though they were highly regarded by the people. Nevertheless, more and more men and women believed in the Lord and were added to their number. As a result, people brought the sick into the streets and laid them on beds and mats so that at least Peter's shadow might fall on some of them as he passed by. Crowds gathered also from the towns around Jerusalem,

Acts 5:12-16

bringing their sick and those tormented by evil⁹ spirits, and all of them were healed.

**Acts
5:17-21a**

APOSTLES IMPRISONED.   Then the high priest and all his associates, who were members of the party of the Sadducees, were filled with jealousy. They arrested the apostles and put them in the public jail. But during the night an angel of the Lord opened the doors of the jail and brought them out. "Go, stand in the temple courts," he said, "and tell the people the full message of this new life."

At daybreak they entered the temple courts, as they had been told, and began to teach the people.

**Acts
5:21b-26**

APOSTLES' RELEASE DISCOVERED.   When the high priest and his associates arrived, they called together the Sanhedrin—the full assembly of the elders of Israel—and sent to the jail for the apostles. But on arriving at the jail, the officers did not find them there. So they went back and reported, "We found the jail securely locked, with the guards standing at the doors; but when we opened them, we found no one inside." On hearing this report, the captain of the temple guard and the chief priests were puzzled, wondering what would come of this.

Then someone came and said, "Look! The men you put in jail are standing in the temple courts teaching the people." At that, the captain went with his officers and brought the apostles. They did not use force, because they feared that the people would stone them.

**Acts
5:27-32**

APOSTLES REJECT WARNING.   Having brought the apostles, they made them appear before the Sanhedrin to be questioned by the high priest. "We gave you strict orders not to teach in this name," he said. "Yet you have filled Jerusalem with your teaching and are determined to make us guilty of this man's blood."

Peter and the other apostles replied: "We must obey God rather than men! The God of our fathers raised Jesus from the dead—whom you had killed by hanging him on a tree. God exalted him to his own right hand as Prince and Savior that he might give repentance and forgiveness of sins to Israel. We are witnesses of these things, and so is the Holy Spirit, whom God has given to those who obey him."

**Acts
5:33-39**

GAMALIEL'S ADVICE.   When they heard this, they were furious and wanted to put them to death. But a Pharisee named Gamaliel, a teacher of the law, who was honored by all the people, stood up in the Sanhedrin and ordered that the men be put outside for a little while. Then he addressed them: "Men of Israel, consider carefully what you intend to do to these men. Some time ago Theudas appeared, claiming to be somebody, and about four hundred men rallied to him. He was killed, all his followers were dispersed, and it all came to nothing. After him, Judas the Galilean appeared in the days of the census and led a band of people in revolt. He too was killed, and all his followers were scattered. Therefore, in the present case I advise you: Leave these men alone! Let them go! For if their purpose or activity is of human origin, it will fail. But if it is from God, you will not be able to stop these men; you will only find yourselves fighting against God."

⁹Greek *unclean*

APOSTLES RELEASED.   His speech persuaded them. They called the Acts
5:40-42
apostles in and had them flogged. Then they ordered them not to speak in
the name of Jesus, and let them go.

The apostles left the Sanhedrin, rejoicing because they had been counted worthy of suffering disgrace for the Name. Day after day, in the temple
courts and from house to house, they never stopped teaching and proclaiming the good news that Jesus is the Christ.*

SEVEN CHOSEN.   In those days when the number of disciples was Acts 6:1-7
Jerusalem
increasing, the Grecian Jews among them complained against the Hebraic
Jews because their widows were being overlooked in the daily distribution of food. So the Twelve gathered all the disciples together and said, "It
would not be right for us to neglect the ministry of the word of God in
order to wait on tables. Brothers, choose seven men from among you who
are known to be full of the Spirit and wisdom. We will turn this responsibility over to them and will give our attention to prayer and the ministry
of the word."

This proposal pleased the whole group. They chose Stephen, a man full
of faith and of the Holy Spirit; also Philip, Procorus, Nicanor, Timon,
Parmenas, and Nicolas from Antioch, a convert to Judaism. They presented these men to the apostles, who prayed and laid their hands on them.

So the word of God spread. The number of disciples in Jerusalem
increased rapidly, and a large number of priests became obedient to the
faith.

Martyrdom of Stephen

*T*hroughout the centuries since the death of Jesus, thousands of
Christians have died as martyrs to the cause of Christ. It is only fitting,
then, that Luke should record the events surrounding the very first
martyrdom, that of Stephen. This Stephen had been one of the seven men chosen to resolve the problems which arose with regard to distribution of assistance to the Grecian widows. He is a man known for his faith and his ability
to do great wonders through the Holy Spirit. But it is his boldness and wisdom
that finally prompt his adversaries to bring him before The Council on a
charge of blasphemy.

Stephen's defense is a classic review of the history of God's dealing with
the Jewish people, and a reminder to The Council that leaders such as themselves have always rejected and persecuted God's prophets and teachers.
When he accuses them of murdering the Son of God, they angrily condemn
him to death by stoning. Stephen's dying words echo down through time as
the prayer of other martyrs and all believers as well.

CHARGES AGAINST STEPHEN.   Now Stephen, a man full of God's Acts 6:8-15
grace and power, did great wonders and miraculous signs among the people. Opposition arose, however, from members of the Synagogue of the
Freedmen (as it was called)—Jews of Cyrene and Alexandria as well as
the provinces of Cilicia and Asia. These men began to argue with Stephen,

*Or Messiah

but they could not stand up against his wisdom or the Spirit by whom he spoke.

Then they secretly persuaded some men to say, "We have heard Stephen speak words of blasphemy against Moses and against God."

So they stirred up the people and the elders and the teachers of the law. They seized Stephen and brought him before the Sanhedrin. They produced false witnesses, who testified, "This fellow never stops speaking against this holy place and against the law. For we have heard him say that this Jesus of Nazareth will destroy this place and change the customs Moses handed down to us."

All who were sitting in the Sanhedrin looked intently at Stephen, and they saw that his face was like the face of an angel.

Acts 7:1-19   STEPHEN'S DEFENSE.   Then the high priest asked him, "Are these charges true?"

To this he replied: "Brothers and fathers, listen to me! The God of glory appeared to our father Abraham while he was still in Mesopotamia, before he lived in Haran. 'Leave your country and your people,' God said, 'and go to the land I will show you.'[s]

"So he left the land of the Chaldeans and settled in Haran. After the death of his father, God sent him to this land where you are now living. He gave him no inheritance here, not even a foot of ground. But God promised him that he and his descendants after him would possess the land, even though at that time Abraham had no child. God spoke to him in this way: 'Your descendants will be strangers in a country not their own, and they will be enslaved and mistreated four hundred years. But I will punish the nation they serve as slaves,' God said, 'and afterward they will come out of that country and worship me in this place.'[t] Then he gave Abraham the covenant of circumcision. And Abraham became the father of Isaac and circumcised him eight days after his birth. Later Isaac became the father of Jacob, and Jacob became the father of the twelve patriarchs.

"Because the patriarchs were jealous of Joseph, they sold him as a slave into Egypt. But God was with him and rescued him from all his troubles. He gave Joseph wisdom and enabled him to gain the goodwill of Pharaoh king of Egypt; so he made him ruler over Egypt and all his palace.

"Then a famine struck all Egypt and Canaan, bringing great suffering, and our fathers could not find food. When Jacob heard that there was grain in Egypt, he sent our fathers on their first visit. On their second visit, Joseph told his brothers who he was, and Pharaoh learned about Joseph's family. After this, Joseph sent for his father Jacob and his whole family, seventy-five in all. Then Jacob went down to Egypt, where he and our fathers died. Their bodies were brought back to Shechem and placed in the tomb that Abraham had bought from the sons of Hamor at Shechem for a certain sum of money.

"As the time drew near for God to fulfill his promise to Abraham, the number of our people in Egypt greatly increased. Then another king, who knew nothing about Joseph, became ruler of Egypt. He dealt treacherously with our people and oppressed our forefathers by forcing them to throw out their newborn babies so that they would die.

Acts 7:20-38   "At that time Moses was born, and he was no ordinary child.[u] For three

---

[s]Gen. 12:1   [t]Gen. 15:13,14   [u]Or *was fair in the sight of God*

months he was cared for in his father's house. When he was placed outside, Pharaoh's daughter took him and brought him up as her own son. Moses was educated in all the wisdom of the Egyptians and was powerful in speech and action.

"When Moses was forty years old, he decided to visit his fellow Israelites. He saw one of them being mistreated by an Egyptian, so he went to his defense and avenged him by killing the Egyptian. Moses thought that his own people would realize that God was using him to rescue them, but they did not. The next day Moses came upon two Israelites who were fighting. He tried to reconcile them by saying, 'Men, you are brothers; why do you want to hurt each other?'

"But the man who was mistreating the other pushed Moses aside and said, 'Who made you ruler and judge over us? Do you want to kill me as you killed the Egyptian yesterday?'^{v} When Moses heard this, he fled to Midian, where he settled as a foreigner and had two sons.

"After forty years had passed, an angel appeared to Moses in the flames of a burning bush in the desert near Mount Sinai. When he saw this, he was amazed at the sight. As he went over to look more closely, he heard the Lord's voice: 'I am the God of your fathers, the God of Abraham, Isaac and Jacob.'^{w} Moses trembled with fear and did not dare to look.

"Then the Lord said to him, 'Take off your sandals; the place where you are standing is holy ground. I have indeed seen the oppression of my people in Egypt. I have heard their groaning and have come down to set them free. Now come, I will send you back to Egypt.'^{x}

"This is the same Moses whom they had rejected with the words, 'Who made you ruler and judge?' He was sent to be their ruler and deliverer by God himself, through the angel who appeared to him in the bush. He led them out of Egypt and did wonders and miraculous signs in Egypt, at the Red Sea ^{y} and for forty years in the desert.

"This is that Moses who told the Israelites, 'God will send you a prophet like me from your own people.'^{z} He was in the assembly in the desert, with the angel who spoke to him on Mount Sinai, and with our fathers; and he received living words to pass on to us.

"But our fathers refused to obey him. Instead, they rejected him and in their hearts turned back to Egypt. They told Aaron, 'Make us gods who will go before us. As for this fellow Moses who led us out of Egypt—we don't know what has happened to him!'^{a} That was the time they made an idol in the form of a calf. They brought sacrifices to it and held a celebration in honor of what their hands had made. But God turned away and gave them over to the worship of the heavenly bodies. This agrees with what is written in the book of the prophets:

    Acts
    7:39-53

" 'Did you bring me sacrifices and offerings
    forty years in the desert, O house of Israel?
You have lifted up the shrine of Molech
    and the star of your god Rephan,
    the idols you made to worship.
Therefore I will send you into exile' ^{b} beyond Babylon.

"Our forefathers had the tabernacle of the Testimony with them in the

^{v}Exodus 2:14 ^{w}Exodus 3:6 ^{x}Exodus 3:5,7,8,10 ^{y}That is, Sea of Reeds
^{z}Deut. 18:15 ^{a}Exodus 32:1 ^{b}Amos 5:25–27

desert. It had been made as God directed Moses, according to the pattern he had seen. Having received the tabernacle, our fathers under Joshua brought it with them when they took the land from the nations God drove out before them. It remained in the land until the time of David, who enjoyed God's favor and asked that he might provide a dwelling place for the God of Jacob.[c] But it was Solomon who built the house for him.

"However, the Most High does not live in houses made by men. As the prophet says:

" 'Heaven is my throne,
  and the earth is my footstool.
What kind of house will you build for me?

says the Lord.

  Or where will my resting place be?
  Has not my hand made all these things?'[d]

"You stiff-necked people, with uncircumcised hearts and ears! You are just like your fathers: You always resist the Holy Spirit! Was there ever a prophet your fathers did not persecute? They even killed those who predicted the coming of the Righteous One. And now you have betrayed and murdered him—you who have received the law that was put into effect through angels but have not obeyed it."

Acts 7:54-8:1a   STEPHEN STONED TO DEATH.   When they heard this, they were furious and gnashed their teeth at him. But Stephen, full of the Holy Spirit, looked up to heaven and saw the glory of God, and Jesus standing at the right hand of God. "Look," he said, "I see heaven open and the Son of Man standing at the right hand of God."

At this they covered their ears and, yelling at the top of their voices, they all rushed at him, dragged him out of the city and began to stone him. Meanwhile, the witnesses laid their clothes at the feet of a young man named Saul.

While they were stoning him, Stephen prayed, "Lord Jesus, receive my spirit." Then he fell on his knees and cried out, "Lord, do not hold this sin against them." When he had said this, he fell asleep. And Saul was there, giving approval to his death.

Persecution and Preaching

*J*t is no surprise that the growing church encounters opposition. Some people are annoyed by the efforts being made to teach them; others are enraged when presented with the truth of Christ. Many are apparently jealous of the joyous fellowship which can be seen among the disciples. There are also rulers and religious leaders who fear loss of power or influence as so many people turn to follow the teaching of the Man from Nazareth. So it is not surprising that the apostles have been put into prison so often, or that Stephen has now been killed.

Yet the early Christians are probably caught by surprise when a more widespread, organized persecution arises. Reacting swiftly, these new converts leave Jerusalem and flee to cities throughout Judea and Samaria. Yet

[c]Some early manuscripts *the house of Jacob*   [d]Isaiah 66:1,2

despite the personal tragedies involved, their persecution actually becomes a blessing. Because of their zeal in sharing the gospel with others, the church thereby expands its boundaries far beyond Jerusalem.

Two examples of this preaching are given in the historical record, both involving the evangelist Philip. He is first seen in Samaria with a magician named Simon, and sometime later he is seen on the road from Jerusalem to Gaza teaching an Ethiopian government official.

Throughout this period of persecution, the apostles stay in Jerusalem at the core of the church, except for a brief trip to Samaria made by Peter and John to take care of a matter of special concern.

As the account of this general period of persecution begins, Luke notes that an influential Jew by the name of Saul is among those in charge of imprisoning the Christians. It will not be long before Saul will face a crisis of conscience in which he must answer the call of Christ.

CHURCH SCATTERED.   On that day a great persecution broke out against the church at Jerusalem, and all except the apostles were scattered throughout Judea and Samaria. Godly men buried Stephen and mourned deeply for him. But Saul began to destroy the church. Going from house to house, he dragged off men and women and put them in prison.
Acts 8:1b-3
Jerusalem

PHILIP'S SAMARIAN MINISTRY.   Those who had been scattered preached the word wherever they went. Philip went down to a city in Samaria and proclaimed the Christ*e* there. When the crowds heard Philip and saw the miraculous signs he did, they all paid close attention to what he said. With shrieks, evil*f* spirits came out of many, and many paralytics and cripples were healed. So there was great joy in that city.
Acts 8:4-8
Samaria

SIMON THE SORCERER.   Now for some time a man named Simon had practiced sorcery in the city and amazed all the people of Samaria. He boasted that he was someone great, and all the people, both high and low, gave him their attention and exclaimed, "This man is the divine power known as the Great Power." They followed him because he had amazed them for a long time with his magic. But when they believed Philip as he preached the good news of the kingdom of God and the name of Jesus Christ, they were baptized, both men and women. Simon himself believed and was baptized. And he followed Philip everywhere, astonished by the great signs and miracles he saw.
Acts 8:9-13

PRAYER FOR HOLY SPIRIT.   When the apostles in Jerusalem heard that Samaria had accepted the word of God, they sent Peter and John to them. When they arrived, they prayed for them that they might receive the Holy Spirit, because the Holy Spirit had not yet come upon any of them; they had simply been baptized into*g* the name of the Lord Jesus. Then Peter and John placed their hands on them, and they received the Holy Spirit.
Acts
8:14-17

SIMON REBUKED BY PETER.   When Simon saw that the Spirit was given at the laying on of the apostles' hands, he offered them money and said, "Give me also this ability so that everyone on whom I lay my hands may receive the Holy Spirit."

Peter answered: "May your money perish with you, because you thought you could buy the gift of God with money! You have no part or
Acts
8:18-24

*e*Or Messiah   *f*Greek unclean   *g*Or in

share in this ministry, because your heart is not right before God. Repent of this wickedness and pray to the Lord. Perhaps he will forgive you for having such a thought in your heart. For I see that you are full of bitterness and captive to sin."

Then Simon answered, "Pray to the Lord for me so that nothing you have said may happen to me."

Acts 8:25 **RETURN TO JERUSALEM.** When they had testified and proclaimed the word of the Lord, Peter and John returned to Jerusalem, preaching the gospel in many Samaritan villages.

Acts 8:26-35 Road to Gaza **PHILIP TEACHES ETHIOPIAN.** Now an angel of the Lord said to Philip, "Go south to the road—the desert road—that goes down from Jerusalem to Gaza." So he started out, and on his way he met an Ethiopian[h] eunuch, an important official in charge of all the treasury of Candace, queen of the Ethiopians. This man had gone to Jerusalem to worship, and on his way home was sitting in his chariot reading the book of Isaiah the prophet. The Spirit told Philip, "Go to that chariot and stay near it."

Then Philip ran up to the chariot and heard the man reading Isaiah the prophet. "Do you understand what you are reading?" Philip asked.

"How can I," he said, "unless someone explains it to me?" So he invited Philip to come up and sit with him.

The eunuch was reading this passage of Scripture:

> "He was led like a sheep to the slaughter,
>   and as a lamb before the shearer is silent,
>   so he did not open his mouth.
> In his humiliation he was deprived of justice.
>   Who can speak of his descendants?
>   For his life was taken from the earth."[i]

The eunuch asked Philip, "Tell me, please, who is the prophet talking about, himself or someone else?" Then Philip began with that very passage of Scripture and told him the good news about Jesus.

Acts 8:36-39 **ETHIOPIAN BAPTIZED.** As they traveled along the road, they came to some water and the eunuch said, "Look, here is water. Why shouldn't I be baptized?"[j] And he gave orders to stop the chariot. Then both Philip and the eunuch went down into the water and Philip baptized him. When they came up out of the water, the Spirit of the Lord suddenly took Philip away, and the eunuch did not see him again, but went on his way rejoicing.

Acts 8:40 Caesarea **PHILIP CONTINUES PREACHING.** Philip, however, appeared at Azotus and traveled about, preaching the gospel in all the towns until he reached Caesarea.

◇

---

[h]That is, from the upper Nile region   [i]Isaiah 53:7,8   [j]Some late manuscripts baptized?" [37]Philip said, "If you believe with all your heart, you may." The eunuch answered, "I believe that Jesus Christ is the Son of God."

Conversion of Saul

Saul will later become one of the most widely known and widely read of all the apostles. He will make three major missionary journeys, establishing churches throughout what is known today as Turkey, Greece, and Italy. He will write at least 13 inspired letters of Scripture and preach Christ to high government officials. And he will suffer perhaps as much persecution for the sake of the Lord as any other who has defended Jesus' name. But for now Saul is known only as the great persecutor of the Lord's church. He is feared by all who regard the name of Jesus as precious.

The events which lead to the radical change in this man Saul are truly remarkable. In one sense his conversion experience is like that of any other believer who commits his life in faithful obedience to Christ. But Saul is destined to become a special apostle for the Lord, and that necessitates his ability to testify to the resurrection of Jesus. Therefore Saul's conversion involves a personal appearance by Jesus himself. Later in his ministry, in response to those who will question his apostleship, Saul (then to be known as Paul) will refer to this experience as the basis for his apostleship and the beginning of his special mission for Christ.

Unaware at this point of what the future holds for his life, Saul is seen now relentlessly searching out believers in Jesus (whose sect is known at this time simply as "The Way") in order to arrest and persecute them.

JESUS APPEARS TO SAUL. Meanwhile, Saul was still breathing out murderous threats against the Lord's disciples. He went to the high priest and asked him for letters to the synagogues in Damascus, so that if he found any there who belonged to the Way, whether men or women, he might take them as prisoners to Jerusalem. As he neared Damascus on his journey, suddenly a light from heaven flashed around him. He fell to the ground and heard a voice say to him, "Saul, Saul, why do you persecute me?" *Acts 9:1-9 / Near Damascus*

"Who are you, Lord?" Saul asked.

"I am Jesus, whom you are persecuting," he replied. "Now get up and go into the city, and you will be told what you must do."

The men traveling with Saul stood there speechless; they heard the sound but did not see anyone. Saul got up from the ground, but when he opened his eyes he could see nothing. So they led him by the hand into Damascus. For three days he was blind, and did not eat or drink anything.

ANANIAS SENT TO SAUL. In Damascus there was a disciple named Ananias. The Lord called to him in a vision, "Ananias!" *Acts 9:10-16 / Damascus*

"Yes, Lord," he answered.

The Lord told him, "Go to the house of Judas on Straight Street and ask for a man from Tarsus named Saul, for he is praying. In a vision he has seen a man named Ananias come and place his hands on him to restore his sight."

"Lord," Ananias answered, "I have heard many reports about this man and all the harm he has done to your saints in Jerusalem. And he has come here with authority from the chief priests to arrest all who call on your name."

But the Lord said to Ananias, "Go! This man is my chosen instrument to carry my name before the Gentiles and their kings and before the people of Israel. I will show him how much he must suffer for my name."

Acts 9:17-19

SAUL BAPTIZED BY ANANIAS.   Then Ananias went to the house and entered it. Placing his hands on Saul, he said, "Brother Saul, the Lord— Jesus, who appeared to you on the road as you were coming here—has sent me so that you may see again and be filled with the Holy Spirit." Immediately, something like scales fell from Saul's eyes, and he could see again. He got up and was baptized, and after taking some food, he regained his strength.

Saul spent several days with the disciples in Damascus.

Acts 9:20-22

SAUL PROCLAIMS JESUS.   At once he began to preach in the synagogues that Jesus is the Son of God. All those who heard him were astonished and asked, "Isn't he the man who raised havoc in Jerusalem among those who call on this name? And hasn't he come here to take them as prisoners to the chief priests?" Yet Saul grew more and more powerful and baffled the Jews living in Damascus by proving that Jesus is the Christ.[k]

Acts 9:23-25

CONSPIRACY TO KILL SAUL.   After many days had gone by, the Jews conspired to kill him, but Saul learned of their plan. Day and night they kept close watch on the city gates in order to kill him. But his followers took him by night and lowered him in a basket through an opening in the wall.

Acts 9:26-30

MIXED RECEPTION IN JERUSALEM.   When he came to Jerusalem, he tried to join the disciples, but they were all afraid of him, not believing that he really was a disciple. But Barnabas took him and brought him to the apostles. He told them how Saul on his journey had seen the Lord and that the Lord had spoken to him, and how in Damascus he had preached fearlessly in the name of Jesus. So Saul stayed with them and moved about freely in Jerusalem, speaking boldly in the name of the Lord. He talked and debated with the Grecian Jews, but they tried to kill him. When the brothers learned of this, they took him down to Caesarea and sent him off to Tarsus.

Acts 9:31

PEACE AND CONTINUED GROWTH.   Then the church throughout Judea, Galilee and Samaria enjoyed a time of peace. It was strengthened; and encouraged by the Holy Spirit, it grew in numbers, living in the fear of the Lord.

First Gentile Converts

*A*s the church enters this period of peace and continued growth, the time is ripe for God's eternal plan to be implemented in still another major dimension—the extension of God's grace to the Gentiles. For hundreds of years God's dealings with man have focused upon the small nation of Israel and its Jewish people. Yet God had promised their father Abraham that through his seed all nations would be blessed. And Jesus himself continually proclaimed and demonstrated that his saving power was for

[k]Or *Messiah*

all. But neither the apostles nor the early Jewish Christians have as yet comprehended the full implications of that message.

God's eternal plan all along has been that all people of the world—Jew and non-Jew alike—should come to know him through Christ Jesus. Until this time, however, only Jews, or Gentile converts known as proselytes, have been the subjects of early evangelistic efforts. To approach "pagan" Gentiles has seemed unthinkable. Even the apostle Peter still shares this narrow view. Thus it will take a special vision from the Lord to convince him that the Gentiles are also included within God's plan.

The first Gentile recipient of the gospel message is a devout Roman military leader by the name of Cornelius. Because of Cornelius' continual prayers, God arranges for Peter to preach to Cornelius the good news of Jesus. Peter's initial reluctance is overcome by an outpouring of the Holy Spirit upon Cornelius and his household—a fact which Peter will later use in defense of his actions to his Jewish brethren who question his association with Gentiles. With this event, the new era of God's grace for all mankind is boldly proclaimed. Shortly thereafter, other Christians begin teaching Greeks in Antioch, north of Jerusalem. Then the Jerusalem church sends Barnabas to Antioch to work among the Gentiles, and he in turn enlists the aid of Saul. So the church's Gentile ministry and fellowship grows steadily, even to the point that when the Jewish Christians in Judea have a special financial need, the Gentile Christians in Antioch volunteer to supply that need.

Luke begins now with the account of Peter raising a woman from the dead, not realizing that he is soon to become involved in an even more significant event.

AENEAS HEALED OF PARALYSIS. As Peter traveled about the country, he went to visit the saints in Lydda. There he found a man named Aeneas, a paralytic who had been bedridden for eight years. "Aeneas," Peter said to him, "Jesus Christ heals you. Get up and take care of your mat." Immediately Aeneas got up. All those who lived in Lydda and Sharon saw him and turned to the Lord.

Acts 9:32-35 Lydda, Sharon

DORCAS RAISED FROM DEAD. In Joppa there was a disciple named Tabitha (which, when translated, is Dorcas[1]), who was always doing good and helping the poor. About that time she became sick and died, and her body was washed and placed in an upstairs room. Lydda was near Joppa; so when the disciples heard that Peter was in Lydda, they sent two men to him and urged him, "Please come at once!"

Acts 9:36-43 Joppa

Peter went with them, and when he arrived he was taken upstairs to the room. All the widows stood around him, crying and showing him the robes and other clothing that Dorcas had made while she was still with them.

Peter sent them all out of the room; then he got down on his knees and prayed. Turning toward the dead woman, he said, "Tabitha, get up." She opened her eyes, and seeing Peter she sat up. He took her by the hand and helped her to her feet. Then he called the believers and the widows and

[1]Both *Tabitha* (Aramaic) and *Dorcas* (Greek) mean *gazelle*.

presented her to them alive. This became known all over Joppa, and many people believed in the Lord. Peter stayed in Joppa for some time with a tanner named Simon.

Acts 10:1-8
Caesarea

CORNELIUS HAS VISION.   At Caesarea there was a man named Cornelius, a centurion in what was known as the Italian Regiment. He and all his family were devout and God-fearing; he gave generously to those in need and prayed to God regularly. One day at about three in the afternoon he had a vision. He distinctly saw an angel of God, who came to him and said, "Cornelius!"

Cornelius stared at him in fear. "What is it, Lord?" he asked.

The angel answered, "Your prayers and gifts to the poor have come up as a memorial offering before God. Now send men to Joppa to bring back a man named Simon who is called Peter. He is staying with Simon the tanner, whose house is by the sea."

When the angel who spoke to him had gone, Cornelius called two of his servants and a devout soldier who was one of his attendants. He told them everything that had happened and sent them to Joppa.

Acts
10:9-16
Joppa

PETER HAS VISION.   About noon the following day as they were on their journey and approaching the city, Peter went up on the roof to pray. He became hungry and wanted something to eat, and while the meal was being prepared, he fell into a trance. He saw heaven opened and something like a large sheet being let down to earth by its four corners. It contained all kinds of four-footed animals, as well as reptiles of the earth and birds of the air. Then a voice told him, "Get up, Peter. Kill and eat."

"Surely not, Lord!" Peter replied. "I have never eaten anything impure or unclean."

The voice spoke to him a second time, "Do not call anything impure that God has made clean."

This happened three times, and immediately the sheet was taken back to heaven.

Acts
10:17-23a

CORNELIUS SENDS FOR PETER.   While Peter was wondering about the meaning of the vision, the men sent by Cornelius found out where Simon's house was and stopped at the gate. They called out, asking if Simon who was known as Peter was staying there.

While Peter was still thinking about the vision, the Spirit said to him, "Simon, three*m* men are looking for you. So get up and go downstairs. Do not hesitate to go with them, for I have sent them."

Peter went down and said to the men, "I'm the one you're looking for. Why have you come?"

The men replied, "We have come from Cornelius the centurion. He is a righteous and God-fearing man, who is respected by all the Jewish people. A holy angel told him to have you come to his house so that he could hear what you have to say." Then Peter invited the men into the house to be his guests.

Acts
10:23b-29
Caesarea

PETER GOES TO CORNELIUS.   The next day Peter started out with them, and some of the brothers from Joppa went along. The following day he arrived in Caesarea. Cornelius was expecting them and had called together his relatives and close friends. As Peter entered the house, Cor-

---

*m*One early manuscript *two*; other manuscripts do not have the number.

nelius met him and fell at his feet in reverence. But Peter made him get up. "Stand up," he said, "I am only a man myself."

Talking with him, Peter went inside and found a large gathering of people. He said to them: "You are well aware that it is against our law for a Jew to associate with a Gentile or visit him. But God has shown me that I should not call any man impure or unclean. So when I was sent for, I came without raising any objection. May I ask why you sent for me?"

CORNELIUS TELLS OF VISION. Cornelius answered: "Four days ago I was in my house praying at this hour, at three in the afternoon. Suddenly a man in shining clothes stood before me and said, 'Cornelius, God has heard your prayer and remembered your gifts to the poor. Send to Joppa for Simon who is called Peter. He is a guest in the home of Simon the tanner, who lives by the sea.' So I sent for you immediately, and it was good of you to come. Now we are all here in the presence of God to listen to everything the Lord has commanded you to tell us."

Acts 10:30-33

PETER PROCLAIMS JESUS. Then Peter began to speak: "I now realize how true it is that God does not show favoritism but accepts men from every nation who fear him and do what is right. You know the message God sent to the people of Israel, telling the good news of peace through Jesus Christ, who is Lord of all. You know what has happened throughout Judea, beginning in Galilee after the baptism that John preached—how God anointed Jesus of Nazareth with the Holy Spirit and power, and how he went around doing good and healing all who were under the power of the devil, because God was with him.

Acts 10:34-43

"We are witnesses of everything he did in the country of the Jews and in Jerusalem. They killed him by hanging him on a tree, but God raised him from the dead on the third day and caused him to be seen. He was not seen by all the people, but by witnesses whom God had already chosen—by us who ate and drank with him after he rose from the dead. He commanded us to preach to the people and to testify that he is the one whom God appointed as judge of the living and the dead. All the prophets testify about him that everyone who believes in him receives forgiveness of sins through his name."

CORNELIUS BAPTIZED. While Peter was still speaking these words, the Holy Spirit came on all who heard the message. The circumcised believers who had come with Peter were astonished that the gift of the Holy Spirit had been poured out even on the Gentiles. For they heard them speaking in tongues[n] and praising God.

Acts 10:44-48

Then Peter said, "Can anyone keep these people from being baptized with water? They have received the Holy Spirit just as we have." So he ordered that they be baptized in the name of Jesus Christ. Then they asked Peter to stay with them for a few days.

PETER RESPONDS TO QUESTIONS. The apostles and the brothers throughout Judea heard that the Gentiles also had received the word of God. So when Peter went up to Jerusalem, the circumcised believers criticized him and said, "You went into the house of uncircumcised men and ate with them."

Acts 11:1-18 Jerusalem

Peter began and explained everything to them precisely as it had happened: "I was in the city of Joppa praying, and in a trance I saw a vision.

[n] Or other languages

I saw something like a large sheet being let down from heaven by its four corners, and it came down to where I was. I looked into it and saw four-footed animals of the earth, wild beasts, reptiles, and birds of the air. Then I heard a voice telling me, 'Get up, Peter. Kill and eat.'

"I replied, 'Surely not, Lord! Nothing impure or unclean has ever entered my mouth.'

"The voice spoke from heaven a second time, 'Do not call anything impure that God has made clean.' This happened three times, and then it was all pulled up to heaven again.

"Right then three men who had been sent to me from Caesarea stopped at the house where I was staying. The Spirit told me to have no hesitation about going with them. These six brothers also went with me, and we entered the man's house. He told us how he had seen an angel appear in his house and say, 'Send to Joppa for Simon who is called Peter. He will bring you a message through which you and all your household will be saved.'

"As I began to speak, the Holy Spirit came on them as he had come on us at the beginning. Then I remembered what the Lord had said: 'John baptized with⁰ water, but you will be baptized with the Holy Spirit.' So if God gave them the same gift as he gave us, who believed in the Lord Jesus Christ, who was I to think that I could oppose God?"

When they heard this, they had no further objections and praised God, saying, "So then, God has granted even the Gentiles repentance unto life."

Acts
11:19-21
GOSPEL PREACHED IN ANTIOCH.   Now those who had been scattered by the persecution in connection with Stephen traveled as far as Phoenicia, Cyprus and Antioch, telling the message only to Jews. Some of them, however, men from Cyprus and Cyrene, went to Antioch and began to speak to Greeks also, telling them the good news about the Lord Jesus. The Lord's hand was with them, and a great number of people believed and turned to the Lord.

Acts
11:22-26
Antioch
BARNABAS AND SAUL IN ANTIOCH.   News of this reached the ears of the church at Jerusalem, and they sent Barnabas to Antioch. When he arrived and saw the evidence of the grace of God, he was glad and encouraged them all to remain true to the Lord with all their hearts. He was a good man, full of the Holy Spirit and faith, and a great number of people were brought to the Lord.

Then Barnabas went to Tarsus to look for Saul, and when he found him, he brought him to Antioch. So for a whole year Barnabas and Saul met with the church and taught great numbers of people. The disciples were called Christians first at Antioch.

Acts
11:27-28
Antioch
AGABUS PREDICTS FAMINE.   During this time some prophets came down from Jerusalem to Antioch. One of them, named Agabus, stood up and through the Spirit predicted that a severe famine would spread over the entire Roman world. (This happened during the reign of Claudius.)

Acts
11:29,30
Jerusalem
GIFT TAKEN TO JERUSALEM.   The disciples, each according to his ability, decided to provide help for the brothers living in Judea. This they did, sending their gift to the elders by Barnabas and Saul.

⁰Or *in*

Persecution by Herod Agrippa I

*T*he period of calm which permitted the church to reach out to Gentiles is not to continue for long. King Herod Agrippa I will soon find it politically advantageous to instigate a new period of persecution against these believers, who are now called Christians. To Agrippa, persecution must be a familiar practice. It was Agrippa's grandfather, Herod the Great, who had ordered the killing of infants near the time of Jesus' birth, and it was his uncle, Herod Antipas, who had beheaded John the Baptist and joined with Pontius Pilate in mocking Jesus. Agrippa himself is the son of Aristobulus, who was killed by order of his own father, Herod the Great. Agrippa's uncles—Archelaus, Philip, and Antipas—had ruled various provinces of the kingdom, but have now either died or been banished from their rule. Their departure has left Herod Agrippa in control of all the territory formerly ruled by Herod the Great.

Among his other acts of persecution, Agrippa seizes James, the brother of John, and puts him to death. Peter too is imprisoned, and probably destined for the same fate. But Peter will be spared by a miracle. Ironically, Herod's wickedness will result in his own death, and the church will continue to grow despite his attempt at oppression.

JAMES KILLED.   It was about this time that King Herod arrested some who belonged to the church, intending to persecute them. He had James, the brother of John, put to death with the sword. When he saw that this pleased the Jews, he proceeded to seize Peter also. This happened during the Feast of Unleavened Bread. After arresting him, he put him in prison, handing him over to be guarded by four squads of four soldiers each. Herod intended to bring him out for public trial after the Passover. $\quad$ Acts 12:1-5 Jerusalem

So Peter was kept in prison, but the church was earnestly praying to God for him.

ANGEL RESCUES PETER.   The night before Herod was to bring him to trial, Peter was sleeping between two soldiers, bound with two chains, and sentries stood guard at the entrance. Suddenly an angel of the Lord appeared and a light shone in the cell. He struck Peter on the side and woke him up. "Quick, get up!" he said, and the chains fell off Peter's wrists. $\quad$ Acts 12:6-11

Then the angel said to him, "Put on your clothes and sandals." And Peter did so. "Wrap your cloak around you and follow me," the angel told him. Peter followed him out of the prison, but he had no idea that what the angel was doing was really happening; he thought he was seeing a vision. They passed the first and second guards and came to the iron gate leading to the city. It opened for them by itself, and they went through it. When they had walked the length of one street, suddenly the angel left him.

Then Peter came to himself and said, "Now I know without a doubt that the Lord sent his angel and rescued me from Herod's clutches and from everything the Jewish people were anticipating."

PETER TELLS OF DELIVERANCE.   When this had dawned on him, he went to the house of Mary the mother of John, also called Mark, where many people had gathered and were praying. Peter knocked at the outer $\quad$ Acts 12:12-17

entrance, and a servant girl named Rhoda came to answer the door. When she recognized Peter's voice, she was so overjoyed she ran back without opening it and exclaimed, "Peter is at the door!"

"You're out of your mind," they told her. When she kept insisting that it was so, they said, "It must be his angel."

But Peter kept on knocking, and when they opened the door and saw him, they were astonished. Peter motioned with his hand for them to be quiet and described how the Lord had brought him out of prison. "Tell James and the brothers about this," he said, and then he left for another place.

Acts 12:18,19a — HEROD HAS GUARDS KILLED.   In the morning, there was no small commotion among the soldiers as to what had become of Peter. After Herod had a thorough search made for him and did not find him, he cross-examined the guards and ordered that they be executed.

Acts 12:19b-23 Caesarea — HEROD DIES BECAUSE OF PRIDE.   Then Herod went from Judea to Caesarea and stayed there a while. He had been quarreling with the people of Tyre and Sidon; they now joined together and sought an audience with him. Having secured the support of Blastus, a trusted personal servant of the king, they asked for peace, because they depended on the king's country for their food supply.

On the appointed day Herod, wearing his royal robes, sat on his throne and delivered a public address to the people. They shouted, "This is the voice of a god, not of a man." Immediately, because Herod did not give praise to God, an angel of the Lord struck him down, and he was eaten by worms and died.

Acts 12:24,25 Antioch — JOHN MARK TAKEN TO ANTIOCH.   But the word of God continued to increase and spread.

When Barnabas and Saul had finished their mission, they returned from*ᵖ* Jerusalem, taking with them John, also called Mark.

First Missionary Journey

*I*n order to evangelize more effectively the world outside Judea and Samaria, the Holy Spirit now directs Barnabas and Saul (from this time on referred to as Paul) to set out on a tour of what is known today as Cyprus and central Turkey. Leaving from Antioch in northern Syria and sailing from the port of Seleucia, Paul and Barnabas land at Salamis, on the Mediterranean island of Cyprus. After crossing the island to Paphos, they then sail for the region of Pamphylia, on the southern Turkish coast, where they spend some time in the city of Perga. It is here that John Mark, who will later write one of the four Gospel accounts and who has apparently been traveling with them, returns to Jerusalem. Later in the historical record it will be seen that John's return causes some problems in the relationship between Paul and the young evangelist, but a reconciliation will ultimately prevail.

From Perga, Paul's group travels to the city of Antioch in the region of Pisidia. Luke records Paul's sermon there, a sermon that is perhaps representative of Paul's preaching throughout the entire tour. Similar in some respects

ᵖSome manuscripts to

to Peter's sermon on Pentecost, it is principally aimed at Jews who gather in the synagogues on the Sabbath. It recites a history of God's dealings with the nation of Israel, notes the many prophecies about the coming Messiah, and sets forth Jesus as that resurrected Lord. But Paul is quick to add that even the Gentiles are now recipients of God's grace.

Thereafter in Antioch, and in the cities of Iconium, Lystra, and Derbe, many Jews and Gentiles believe in Jesus. But certain ones among the Jews who are jealous of Paul's success stir up the people and instigate persecution against him. Withstanding even stoning, Paul then begins the return trip to Syria. Along the way he will visit the newly established congregations of Christians and appoint elders as spiritual shepherds in each congregation.

BARNABAS AND SAUL CALLED.   In the church at Antioch there were prophets and teachers: Barnabas, Simeon called Niger, Lucius of Cyrene, Manaen (who had been brought up with Herod the tetrarch) and Saul. While they were worshiping the Lord and fasting, the Holy Spirit said, "Set apart for me Barnabas and Saul for the work to which I have called them." So after they had fasted and prayed, they placed their hands on them and sent them off.

Acts 13:1-3 Antioch

JOURNEY BEGINS IN CYPRUS.   The two of them, sent on their way by the Holy Spirit, went down to Seleucia and sailed from there to Cyprus. When they arrived at Salamis, they proclaimed the word of God in the Jewish synagogues. John was with them as their helper.

Acts 13:4,5 Cyprus

ELYMAS BLINDED.   They traveled through the whole island until they came to Paphos. There they met a Jewish sorcerer and false prophet named Bar-Jesus, who was an attendant of the proconsul, Sergius Paulus. The proconsul, an intelligent man, sent for Barnabas and Saul because he wanted to hear the word of God. But Elymas the sorcerer (for that is what his name means) opposed them and tried to turn the proconsul from the faith. Then Saul, who was also called Paul, filled with the Holy Spirit, looked straight at Elymas and said, "You are a child of the devil and an enemy of everything that is right! You are full of all kinds of deceit and trickery. Will you never stop perverting the right ways of the Lord? Now the hand of the Lord is against you. You are going to be blind, and for a time you will be unable to see the light of the sun."

Acts 13:6-12 Paphos on Cyprus

Immediately mist and darkness came over him, and he groped about, seeking someone to lead him by the hand. When the proconsul saw what had happened, he believed, for he was amazed at the teaching about the Lord.

JOHN MARK RETURNS.   From Paphos, Paul and his companions sailed to Perga in Pamphylia, where John left them to return to Jerusalem. From Perga they went on to Pisidian Antioch.

Acts 13:13,14a Perga in Pamphylia

PAUL'S FIRST RECORDED SERMON.   On the Sabbath they entered the synagogue and sat down. After the reading from the Law and the Prophets, the synagogue rulers sent word to them, saying, "Brothers, if you have a message of encouragement for the people, please speak."

Acts 13:14b-25 Antioch in Pisidia

Standing up, Paul motioned with his hand and said: "Men of Israel and you Gentiles who worship God, listen to me! The God of the people of Israel chose our fathers; he made the people prosper during their stay in Egypt, with mighty power he led them out of that country, he endured their conduct[q] for about forty years in the desert, he overthrew seven nations in Canaan and gave their land to his people as their inheritance. All this took about 450 years.

"After this, God gave them judges until the time of Samuel the prophet. Then the people asked for a king, and he gave them Saul son of Kish, of the tribe of Benjamin, who ruled forty years. After removing Saul, he made David their king. He testified concerning him: 'I have found David son of Jesse a man after my own heart; he will do everything I want him to do.'

"From this man's descendants God has brought to Israel the Savior Jesus, as he promised. Before the coming of Jesus, John preached repentance and baptism to all the people of Israel. As John was completing his work, he said: 'Who do you think I am? I am not that one. No, but he is coming after me, whose sandals I am not worthy to untie.'

Acts
13:26-41

"Brothers, children of Abraham, and you God-fearing Gentiles, it is to us that this message of salvation has been sent. The people of Jerusalem and their rulers did not recognize Jesus, yet in condemning him they fulfilled the words of the prophets that are read every Sabbath. Though they found no proper ground for a death sentence, they asked Pilate to have him executed. When they had carried out all that was written about him, they took him down from the tree and laid him in a tomb. But God raised him from the dead, and for many days he was seen by those who had traveled with him from Galilee to Jerusalem. They are now his witnesses to our people.

"We tell you the good news: What God promised our fathers he has fulfilled for us, their children, by raising up Jesus. As it is written in the second Psalm:

" 'You are my Son;
     today I have become your Father.'[r][s]

The fact that God raised him from the dead, never to decay, is stated in these words:

" 'I will give you the holy and sure blessings promised to
     David.'[t]

So it is stated elsewhere:

" 'You will not let your Holy One see decay.'[u]

"For when David had served God's purpose in his own generation, he fell asleep; he was buried with his fathers and his body decayed. But the one whom God raised from the dead did not see decay.

"Therefore, my brothers, I want you to know that through Jesus the forgiveness of sins is proclaimed to you. Through him everyone who believes is justified from everything you could not be justified from by the law of Moses. Take care that what the prophets have said does not happen to you:

" 'Look, you scoffers,
     wonder and perish,
   for I am going to do something in your days
     that you would never believe,
     even if someone told you.'[v]"

---

[q]Some manuscripts *and cared for them*   [r]Or *have begotten you*   [s]Psalm 2:7   [t]Isaiah 55:3   [u]Psalm 16:10   [v]Hab. 1:5

SERMON WELL-RECEIVED.   As Paul and Barnabas were leaving the   Acts 13:42,43
synagogue, the people invited them to speak further about these things on
the next Sabbath. When the congregation was dismissed, many of the Jews
and devout converts to Judaism followed Paul and Barnabas, who talked
with them and urged them to continue in the grace of God.

JEALOUSY AND OPPOSITION.   On the next Sabbath almost the whole   Acts 13:44-47
city gathered to hear the word of the Lord. When the Jews saw the crowds,
they were filled with jealousy and talked abusively against what Paul was
saying.

Then Paul and Barnabas answered them boldly: "We had to speak the
word of God to you first. Since you reject it and do not consider yourselves
worthy of eternal life, we now turn to the Gentiles. For this is what the
Lord has commanded us:

" 'I have made you^w a light for the Gentiles,
that you^w may bring salvation to the ends of the
earth.'^{x}"

GENTILES BELIEVE.   When the Gentiles heard this, they were glad and   Acts 13:48-52
honored the word of the Lord; and all who were appointed for eternal life
believed.

The word of the Lord spread through the whole region. But the Jews
incited the God-fearing women of high standing and the leading men of
the city. They stirred up persecution against Paul and Barnabas, and
expelled them from their region. So they shook the dust from their feet in
protest against them and went to Iconium. And the disciples were filled
with joy and with the Holy Spirit.

MIXED RESPONSE IN ICONIUM.   At Iconium Paul and Barnabas went   Acts 14:1-7 Iconium
as usual into the Jewish synagogue. There they spoke so effectively that a
great number of Jews and Gentiles believed. But the Jews who refused to
believe stirred up the Gentiles and poisoned their minds against the brothers. So Paul and Barnabas spent considerable time there, speaking boldly
for the Lord, who confirmed the message of his grace by enabling them to
do miraculous signs and wonders. The people of the city were divided;
some sided with the Jews, others with the apostles. There was a plot afoot
among the Gentiles and Jews, together with their leaders, to mistreat them
and stone them. But they found out about it and fled to the Lycaonian
cities of Lystra and Derbe and to the surrounding country, where they continued to preach the good news.

CRIPPLED MAN HEALED.   In Lystra there sat a man crippled in his feet,   Acts 14:8-10 Lystra
who was lame from birth and had never walked. He listened to Paul as he
was speaking. Paul looked directly at him, saw that he had faith to be
healed and called out, "Stand up on your feet!" At that, the man jumped
up and began to walk.

BARNABAS AND PAUL WORSHIPED.   When the crowd saw what Paul   Acts 14:11-18
had done, they shouted in the Lycaonian language, "The gods have come
down to us in human form!" Barnabas they called Zeus, and Paul they
called Hermes because he was the chief speaker. The priest of Zeus, whose
temple was just outside the city, brought bulls and wreaths to the city
gates because he and the crowd wanted to offer sacrifices to them.

^{w}The Greek is singular. ^{x}Isaiah 49:6

But when the apostles Barnabas and Paul heard of this, they tore their clothes and rushed out into the crowd, shouting: "Men, why are you doing this? We too are only men, human like you. We are bringing you good news, telling you to turn from these worthless things to the living God, who made heaven and earth and sea and everything in them. In the past, he let all nations go their own way. Yet he has not left himself without testimony: He has shown kindness by giving you rain from heaven and crops in their seasons; he provides you with plenty of food and fills your hearts with joy." Even with these words, they had difficulty keeping the crowd from sacrificing to them.

Acts 14:19,20

PAUL STONED.   Then some Jews came from Antioch and Iconium and won the crowd over. They stoned Paul and dragged him outside the city, thinking he was dead. But after the disciples had gathered around him, he got up and went back into the city. The next day he and Barnabas left for Derbe.

Acts 14:21-23 Antioch in Pisidia

STRENGTHENING CHURCHES.   They preached the good news in that city and won a large number of disciples. Then they returned to Lystra, Iconium and Antioch, strengthening the disciples and encouraging them to remain true to the faith. "We must go through many hardships to enter the kingdom of God," they said. Paul and Barnabas appointed elders*y* for them in each church and, with prayer and fasting, committed them to the Lord, in whom they had put their trust.

Acts 14:24-28 Antioch in Syria

REPORT TO CHURCH IN ANTIOCH.   After going through Pisidia, they came into Pamphylia, and when they had preached the word in Perga, they went down to Attalia.

From Attalia they sailed back to Antioch, where they had been committed to the grace of God for the work they had now completed. On arriving there, they gathered the church together and reported all that God had done through them and how he had opened the door of faith to the Gentiles. And they stayed there a long time with the disciples.

The Jerusalem Conference

*T*he tour through ancient Asia Minor apparently ends somewhere around A.D. 47. Paul and Barnabas probably settle back into concentrated efforts at teaching in the local area, but their respite is not to last for long. By A.D. 48 there is trouble in the church. Certain Jewish Christians from Jerusalem go north to Antioch, teaching the Gentile Christians that they must be circumcised, in addition to being baptized, in order to be obedient to God. To the Jews the rite of circumcision is a sign of the covenant relationship which they have with God, so it is only natural that they should think the same act would be required of Gentile Christians. But their more serious misconception lies in their belief that circumcision is required as part of keeping the Law of Moses. They are not only urging Gentiles to be circumcised, but demanding that they keep the entire law, just as the Jewish Christians are continuing to do.

*y*Or *Barnabas ordained elders;* or *Barnabas had elders elected*

The problem posed by these so-called "Judaizing teachers" will continue to divide the church in the ensuing years, and it will be a subject for discussion in several of Paul's later letters. For now, however, the problem is temporarily solved by a conference at Jerusalem in which Paul and Barnabas meet with the apostles and elders. After reviewing the work of the Holy Spirit in leading the way to Gentile evangelism, and after consulting Scripture for prophecy concerning the Gentiles, they all agree that circumcision (and by implication the law itself) is not binding on the Gentiles. This message is sent to Gentile Christians, along with a warning that they avoid certain idolatrous practices common among pagan Gentiles. As a result of this agreement, unity will finally prevail, at least temporarily.

JUDAIZERS PROMPT MEETING. Some men came down from Judea to Antioch and were teaching the brothers: "Unless you are circumcised, according to the custom taught by Moses, you cannot be saved." This brought Paul and Barnabas into sharp dispute and debate with them. So Paul and Barnabas were appointed, along with some other believers, to go up to Jerusalem to see the apostles and elders about this question. The church sent them on their way, and as they traveled through Phoenicia and Samaria, they told how the Gentiles had been converted. This news made all the brothers very glad. When they came to Jerusalem, they were welcomed by the church and the apostles and elders, to whom they reported everything God had done through them. *(Acts 15:1-5 Antioch (Ca. A.D. 48-50))*

Then some of the believers who belonged to the party of the Pharisees stood up and said, "The Gentiles must be circumcised and required to obey the law of Moses."

GENTILE EVANGELISM RECOUNTED. The apostles and elders met to consider this question. After much discussion, Peter got up and addressed them: "Brothers, you know that some time ago God made a choice among you that the Gentiles might hear from my lips the message of the gospel and believe. God, who knows the heart, showed that he accepted them by giving the Holy Spirit to them, just as he did to us. He made no distinction between us and them, for he purified their hearts by faith. Now then, why do you try to test God by putting on the necks of the disciples a yoke that neither we nor our fathers have been able to bear? No! We believe it is through the grace of our Lord Jesus that we are saved, just as they are." *(Acts 15:6-12 Jerusalem)*

The whole assembly became silent as they listened to Barnabas and Paul telling about the miraculous signs and wonders God had done among the Gentiles through them.

JAMES SUGGESTS RESOLUTION. When they finished, James spoke up: "Brothers, listen to me. Simon[z] has described to us how God at first showed his concern by taking from the Gentiles a people for himself. The words of the prophets are in agreement with this, as it is written: *(Acts 15:13-21)*

" 'After this I will return
    and rebuild David's fallen tent.
Its ruins I will rebuild,
    and I will restore it,

---

[z]Greek *Simeon*, a variant of *Simon*; that is, Peter

that the remnant of men may seek the Lord,
  and all the Gentiles who bear my name,
says the Lord, who does these things'[a]
  that have been known for ages.[b]

"It is my judgment, therefore, that we should not make it difficult for the Gentiles who are turning to God. Instead we should write to them, telling them to abstain from food polluted by idols, from sexual immorality, from the meat of strangled animals and from blood. For Moses has been preached in every city from the earliest times and is read in the synagogues on every Sabbath."

**Acts
15:22-29**

LETTER SENT TO GENTILES.   Then the apostles and elders, with the whole church, decided to choose some of their own men and send them to Antioch with Paul and Barnabas. They chose Judas (called Barsabbas) and Silas, two men who were leaders among the brothers. With them they sent the following letter:

The apostles and elders, your brothers,

To the Gentile believers in Antioch, Syria and Cilicia:

Greetings.

We have heard that some went out from us without our authorization and disturbed you, troubling your minds by what they said. So we all agreed to choose some men and send them to you with our dear friends Barnabas and Paul—men who have risked their lives for the name of our Lord Jesus Christ. Therefore we are sending Judas and Silas to confirm by word of mouth what we are writing. It seemed good to the Holy Spirit and to us not to burden you with anything beyond the following requirements: You are to abstain from food sacrificed to idols, from blood, from the meat of strangled animals and from sexual immorality. You will do well to avoid these things.

Farewell.

**Acts
15:30-35
Antioch**

GENTILES REJOICE.   The men were sent off and went down to Antioch, where they gathered the church together and delivered the letter. The people read it and were glad for its encouraging message. Judas and Silas, who themselves were prophets, said much to encourage and strengthen the brothers. After spending some time there, they were sent off by the brothers with the blessing of peace to return to those who had sent them.[c] But Paul and Barnabas remained in Antioch, where they and many others taught and preached the word of the Lord.

◇

[a]Amos 9:11,12   [b]Some manuscripts *things'* —/ [18]*known to the Lord for ages is his work*
[c]Some manuscripts *them,* [34]*but Silas decided to remain there*

Letter to the Galatians

*A*lthough there is no consensus on the matter, it appears that while Paul and Barnabas were in Antioch, Paul may have written his letter to the Galatian Christians among whom he and Barnabas had worked during their recent travels to Antioch of Pisidia, Iconium, Lystra, and Derbe. If this assumption is correct, the letter would have been written about A.D. 50, shortly following the Jerusalem conference. The subject of Paul's letter parallels that of the conference itself, which pertained to the problems created by those Jewish Christians who were insisting that Gentile converts submit to the rite of circumcision and observe other rituals to which the Jews were accustomed. Again, the real issue is undoubtedly the contention by the Judaizers that Christians should be required to continue obeying the Law of Moses. In his letter Paul strongly defends the Christian's freedom from the law, and proclaims the new covenant relationship which Christians have through God's grace.

Paul begins this letter by defending his own apostleship, which apparently has been questioned by the Judaizers in Galatia in their attempt to discredit Paul's teaching. The main thrust of his defense is that he did not receive his gospel from the other apostles. As proof, he carefully outlines his limited contact with the apostles in Jerusalem. (The one contact to which Paul makes no reference is his brief trip to Jerusalem to deliver the gift from the brethren in Antioch.) Paul urges that, as a specially chosen apostle, he received directly from God the good news of freedom in Christ.

SALUTATION.   Paul, an apostle—sent not from men nor by man, but by Jesus Christ and God the Father, who raised him from the dead—and all the brothers with me,   Gal. 1:1-5

To the churches in Galatia:

Grace and peace to you from God our Father and the Lord Jesus Christ, who gave himself for our sins to rescue us from the present evil age, according to the will of our God and Father, to whom be glory for ever and ever. Amen.

Authority As an Apostle

PERVERSION OF GOSPEL.   I am astonished that you are so quickly deserting the one who called you by the grace of Christ and are turning to a different gospel—which is really no gospel at all. Evidently some people are throwing you into confusion and are trying to pervert the gospel of Christ. But even if we or an angel from heaven should preach a gospel other than the one we preached to you, let him be eternally condemned! As we have already said, so now I say again: If anybody is preaching to you a gospel other than what you accepted, let him be eternally condemned!   Gal. 1:6-9

GOSPEL'S DIVINE ORIGIN.   Am I now trying to win the approval of men, or of God? Or am I trying to please men? If I were still trying to please men, I would not be a servant of Christ.   Gal. 1:10-12

I want you to know, brothers, that the gospel I preached is not something that man made up. I did not receive it from any man, nor was I taught it; rather, I received it by revelation from Jesus Christ.

Gal. 1:13-17

TEACHING DIVINELY REVEALED.   For you have heard of my previous way of life in Judaism, how intensely I persecuted the church of God and tried to destroy it. I was advancing in Judaism beyond many Jews of my own age and was extremely zealous for the traditions of my fathers. But when God, who set me apart from birth[d] and called me by his grace, was pleased to reveal his Son in me so that I might preach him among the Gentiles, I did not consult any man, nor did I go up to Jerusalem to see those who were apostles before I was, but I went immediately into Arabia and later returned to Damascus.

Gal. 1:18-24

DOCTRINE NOT FROM APOSTLES.   Then after three years, I went up to Jerusalem to get acquainted with Peter[e] and stayed with him fifteen days. I saw none of the other apostles—only James, the Lord's brother. I assure you before God that what I am writing you is no lie. Later I went to Syria and Cilicia. I was personally unknown to the churches of Judea that are in Christ. They only heard the report: "The man who formerly persecuted us is now preaching the faith he once tried to destroy." And they praised God because of me.

Gal. 2:1-10

GENTILE EVANGELISM ACCEPTED.   Fourteen years later I went up again to Jerusalem, this time with Barnabas. I took Titus along also. I went in response to a revelation and set before them the gospel that I preach among the Gentiles. But I did this privately to those who seemed to be leaders, for fear that I was running or had run my race in vain. Yet not even Titus, who was with me, was compelled to be circumcised, even though he was a Greek. This matter arose because some false brothers had infiltrated our ranks to spy on the freedom we have in Christ Jesus and to make us slaves. We did not give in to them for a moment, so that the truth of the gospel might remain with you.

As for those who seemed to be important—whatever they were makes no difference to me; God does not judge by external appearance—those men added nothing to my message. On the contrary, they saw that I had been entrusted with the task of preaching the gospel to the Gentiles,[f] just as Peter had been to the Jews.[g] For God, who was at work in the ministry of Peter as an apostle to the Jews, was also at work in my ministry as an apostle to the Gentiles. James, Peter [h] and John, those reputed to be pillars, gave me and Barnabas the right hand of fellowship when they recognized the grace given to me. They agreed that we should go to the Gentiles, and they to the Jews. All they asked was that we should continue to remember the poor, the very thing I was eager to do.

Gal. 2:11-14

PAUL REBUKED PETER.   When Peter came to Antioch, I opposed him to his face, because he was clearly in the wrong. Before certain men came from James, he used to eat with the Gentiles. But when they arrived, he began to draw back and separate himself from the Gentiles because he was afraid of those who belonged to the circumcision group. The other Jews joined him in his hypocrisy, so that by their hypocrisy even Barnabas was led astray.

When I saw that they were not acting in line with the truth of the gospel,

---

*d*Or *from my mother's womb*   *e*Greek *Cephas*   *f*Greek *uncircumcised*   *g*Greek
circumcised   *h*Greek *Cephas*

I said to Peter in front of them all, "You are a Jew, yet you live like a Gentile and not like a Jew. How is it, then, that you force Gentiles to follow Jewish customs?"

Doctrine of Justification

LAW AND CHRIST.   "We who are Jews by birth and not 'Gentile sinners' know that a man is not justified by observing the law, but by faith in Jesus Christ. So we, too, have put our faith in Christ Jesus that we may be justified by faith in Christ and not by observing the law, because by observing the law no one will be justified.

Gal. 2:15-21

"If, while we seek to be justified in Christ, it becomes evident that we ourselves are sinners, does that mean that Christ promotes sin? Absolutely not! If I rebuild what I destroyed, I prove that I am a lawbreaker. For through the law I died to the law so that I might live for God. I have been crucified with Christ and I no longer live, but Christ lives in me. The life I live in the body, I live by faith in the Son of God, who loved me and gave himself for me. I do not set aside the grace of God, for if righteousness could be gained through the law, Christ died for nothing!"[i]

LAW AND FAITH.   You foolish Galatians! Who has bewitched you? Before your very eyes Jesus Christ was clearly portrayed as crucified. I would like to learn just one thing from you: Did you receive the Spirit by observing the law, or by believing what you heard? Are you so foolish? After beginning with the Spirit, are you now trying to attain your goal by human effort? Have you suffered so much for nothing—if it really was for nothing? Does God give you his Spirit and work miracles among you because you observe the law, or because you believe what you heard?

Gal. 3:1-5

ABRAHAM'S FAITH.   Consider Abraham: "He believed God, and it was credited to him as righteousness."[j] Understand, then, that those who believe are children of Abraham. The Scripture foresaw that God would justify the Gentiles by faith, and announced the gospel in advance to Abraham: "All nations will be blessed through you."[k] So those who have faith are blessed along with Abraham, the man of faith.

Gal. 3:6-9

CHRIST SAVES, NOT WORKS.   All who rely on observing the law are under a curse, for it is written: "Cursed is everyone who does not continue to do everything written in the Book of the Law."[l] Clearly no one is justified before God by the law, because, "The righteous will live by faith."[m] The law is not based on faith; on the contrary, "The man who does these things will live by them."[n] Christ redeemed us from the curse of the law by becoming a curse for us, for it is written: "Cursed is everyone who is hung on a tree."[o] He redeemed us in order that the blessing given to Abraham might come to the Gentiles through Christ Jesus, so that by faith we might receive the promise of the Spirit.

Gal. 3:10-14

INHERITANCE BY PROMISE.   Brothers, let me take an example from everyday life. Just as no one can set aside or add to a human covenant that has been duly established, so it is in this case. The promises were spoken to Abraham and to his seed. The Scripture does not say "and to seeds," meaning many people, but "and to your seed,"[p] meaning one person, who

Gal. 3:15-18

[i]Some interpreters end the quotation after verse 14.   [j]Gen. 15:6   [k]Gen. 12:3; 18:18; 22:18   [l]Deut. 27:26   [m]Hab. 2:4   [n]Lev. 18:5   [o]Deut. 21:23   [p]Gen. 12:7; 13:15; 24:7

is Christ. What I mean is this: The law, introduced 430 years later, does not set aside the covenant previously established by God and thus do away with the promise. For if the inheritance depends on the law, then it no longer depends on a promise; but God in his grace gave it to Abraham through a promise.

Gal.
3:19-22

PURPOSE OF LAW.   What, then, was the purpose of the law? It was added because of transgressions until the Seed to whom the promise referred had come. The law was put into effect through angels by a mediator. A mediator, however, does not represent just one party; but God is one.

Is the law, therefore, opposed to the promises of God? Absolutely not! For if a law had been given that could impart life, then righteousness would certainly have come by the law. But the Scripture declares that the whole world is a prisoner of sin, so that what was promised, being given through faith in Jesus Christ, might be given to those who believe.

Gal.
3:23-29

HEIRS THROUGH FAITH.   Before this faith came, we were held prisoners by the law, locked up until faith should be revealed. So the law was put in charge to lead us to Christ*q* that we might be justified by faith. Now that faith has come, we are no longer under the supervision of the law.

You are all sons of God through faith in Christ Jesus, for all of you who were baptized into Christ have clothed yourselves with Christ. There is neither Jew nor Greek, slave nor free, male nor female, for you are all one in Christ Jesus. If you belong to Christ, then you are Abraham's seed, and heirs according to the promise.

Gal. 4:1-7

ADOPTION AS SONS.   What I am saying is that as long as the heir is a child, he is no different from a slave, although he owns the whole estate. He is subject to guardians and trustees until the time set by his father. So also, when we were children, we were in slavery under the basic principles of the world. But when the time had fully come, God sent his Son, born of a woman, born under law, to redeem those under law, that we might receive the full rights of sons. Because you are sons, God sent the Spirit of his Son into our hearts, the Spirit who calls out, "*Abba,r* Father." So you are no longer a slave, but a son; and since you are a son, God has made you also an heir.

Gal. 4:8-11

RETURN TO LEGALISM.   Formerly, when you did not know God, you were slaves to those who by nature are not gods. But now that you know God—or rather are known by God—how is it that you are turning back to those weak and miserable principles? Do you wish to be enslaved by them all over again? You are observing special days and months and seasons and years! I fear for you, that somehow I have wasted my efforts on you.

Gal.
4:12-20

PAUL CALLS ON THEIR LOVE.   I plead with you, brothers, become like me, for I became like you. You have done me no wrong. As you know, it was because of an illness that I first preached the gospel to you. Even though my illness was a trial to you, you did not treat me with contempt or scorn. Instead, you welcomed me as if I were an angel of God, as if I were Christ Jesus himself. What has happened to all your joy? I can testify that, if you could have done so, you would have torn out your eyes and

*q*Or *charge until Christ came*   *r*Aramaic for *Father*

given them to me. Have I now become your enemy by telling you the truth?

Those people are zealous to win you over, but for no good. What they want is to alienate you ⌊from us⌋, so that you may be zealous for them. It is fine to be zealous, provided the purpose is good, and to be so always and not just when I am with you. My dear children, for whom I am again in the pains of childbirth until Christ is formed in you, how I wish I could be with you now and change my tone, because I am perplexed about you!

ALLEGORY OF SARAH AND HAGAR. Tell me, you who want to be under the law, are you not aware of what the law says? For it is written that Abraham had two sons, one by the slave woman and the other by the free woman. His son by the slave woman was born in the ordinary way; but his son by the free woman was born as the result of a promise. Gal. 4:21-5:1

These things may be taken figuratively, for the women represent two covenants. One covenant is from Mount Sinai and bears children who are to be slaves: This is Hagar. Now Hagar stands for Mount Sinai in Arabia and corresponds to the present city of Jerusalem, because she is in slavery with her children. But the Jerusalem that is above is free, and she is our mother. For it is written:

"Be glad, O barren woman,
    who bears no children;
break forth and cry aloud,
    you who have no labor pains;
because more are the children of the desolate woman
    than of her who has a husband."[s]

Now you, brothers, like Isaac, are children of promise. At that time the son born in the ordinary way persecuted the son born by the power of the Spirit. It is the same now. But what does the Scripture say? "Get rid of the slave woman and her son, for the slave woman's son will never share in the inheritance with the free woman's son."[t] Therefore, brothers, we are not children of the slave woman, but of the free woman. It is for freedom that Christ has set us free. Stand firm, then, and do not let yourselves be burdened again by a yoke of slavery.

Christian Liberty

CIRCUMCISION A MATTER OF LAW. Mark my words! I, Paul, tell you that if you let yourselves be circumcised, Christ will be of no value to you at all. Again I declare to every man who lets himself be circumcised that he is obligated to obey the whole law. You who are trying to be justified by law have been alienated from Christ; you have fallen away from grace. But by faith we eagerly await through the Spirit the righteousness for which we hope. For in Christ Jesus neither circumcision nor uncircumcision has any value. The only thing that counts is faith expressing itself through love. Gal. 5:2-12

You were running a good race. Who cut in on you and kept you from obeying the truth? That kind of persuasion does not come from the one who calls you. "A little yeast works through the whole batch of dough." I am confident in the Lord that you will take no other view. The one who is

[s]Isaiah 54:1   [t]Gen. 21:10

throwing you into confusion will pay the penalty, whoever he may be. Brothers, if I am still preaching circumcision, why am I still being persecuted? In that case the offense of the cross has been abolished. As for those agitators, I wish they would go the whole way and emasculate themselves!

Gal.
5:13-15

LAW FULFILLED IN LOVE.   You, my brothers, were called to be free. But do not use your freedom to indulge the sinful nature[u]; rather, serve one another in love. The entire law is summed up in a single command: "Love your neighbor as yourself."[v] If you keep on biting and devouring each other, watch out or you will be destroyed by each other.

Gal.
5:16-26

FLESH AND SPIRIT.   So I say, live by the Spirit, and you will not gratify the desires of the sinful nature. For the sinful nature desires what is contrary to the Spirit, and the Spirit what is contrary to the sinful nature. They are in conflict with each other, so that you do not do what you want. But if you are led by the Spirit, you are not under law.

The acts of the sinful nature are obvious: sexual immorality, impurity and debauchery; idolatry and witchcraft; hatred, discord, jealousy, fits of rage, selfish ambition, dissensions, factions and envy; drunkenness, orgies, and the like. I warn you, as I did before, that those who live like this will not inherit the kingdom of God.

But the fruit of the Spirit is love, joy, peace, patience, kindness, goodness, faithfulness, gentleness and self-control. Against such things there is no law. Those who belong to Christ Jesus have crucified the sinful nature with its passions and desires. Since we live by the Spirit, let us keep in step with the Spirit. Let us not become conceited, provoking and envying each other.

Gal. 6:1-6

MUTUAL RESPONSIBILITY.   Brothers, if someone is caught in a sin, you who are spiritual should restore him gently. But watch yourself, or you also may be tempted. Carry each other's burdens, and in this way you will fulfill the law of Christ. If anyone thinks he is something when he is nothing, he deceives himself. Each one should test his own actions. Then he can take pride in himself, without comparing himself to somebody else, for each one should carry his own load.

Anyone who receives instruction in the word must share all good things with his instructor.

Gal. 6:7-10

LIVING BY THE SPIRIT.   Do not be deceived: God cannot be mocked. A man reaps what he sows. The one who sows to please his sinful nature, from that nature[w] will reap destruction; the one who sows to please the Spirit, from the Spirit will reap eternal life. Let us not become weary in doing good, for at the proper time we will reap a harvest if we do not give up. Therefore, as we have opportunity, let us do good to all people, especially to those who belong to the family of believers.

Gal.
6:11-16

NEITHER CIRCUMCISION NOR LAW.   See what large letters I use as I write to you with my own hand!

Those who want to make a good impression outwardly are trying to compel you to be circumcised. The only reason they do this is to avoid being persecuted for the cross of Christ. Not even those who are circumcised obey the law, yet they want you to be circumcised that they may

uOr the flesh; also in verses 16, 17, 19 and 24   vLev. 19:18   wOr his flesh, from the flesh

boast about your flesh. May I never boast except in the cross of our Lord Jesus Christ, through which[x] the world has been crucified to me, and I to the world. Neither circumcision nor uncircumcision means anything; what counts is a new creation. Peace and mercy to all who follow this rule, even to the Israel of God.

BENEDICTION.   Finally, let no one cause me trouble, for I bear on my body the marks of Jesus.

Gal. 6:17,18

The grace of our Lord Jesus Christ be with your spirit, brothers. Amen.

Second Missionary Journey

*A*pparently not long after writing his letter to the churches in Galatia, Paul decides that it is an appropriate time for a personal visit. Through such a visit Paul hopes to observe how the churches are developing and lend the weight of his actual presence to resolving the circumcision question about which he has written. Accompanying Paul from Antioch is his fellow minister, Silas, who was one of the two representatives sent to Antioch following the Jerusalem conference. After traveling through northern Syria and Cilicia, they proceed to Derbe and then on to Lystra, where they find a disciple named Timothy. Their meeting is the beginning of a close and productive relationship between the older apostle and this young man, who is to become Paul's protégé.

With Timothy now added to their number, Paul and Silas continue traveling through the regions of Phrygia and Galatia. Being directed by the Holy Spirit, Paul passes by Mysia and spends some time in Troas, where Luke indicates that he joins Paul's company. Then, through a vision, Paul is again given directions—this time to go to Macedonia, a province in what today is northern Greece. There, in the city of Philippi, Paul converts a godly woman named Lydia and establishes a congregation with which Paul will have perhaps one of his closest associations over the ensuing years. Some of that great mutual affection undoubtedly arises from an experience in which Paul and Silas are imprisoned, only to be released miraculously from their chains and thereby given opportunity to convert both their jailer and his household.

Apparently leaving Luke behind at Philippi, Paul, Silas, and Timothy travel on to Thessalonica, where they spend three weeks with only marginal results, and then go on to Berea, where their preaching is received with great eagerness by both Jews and Greeks. But opposition stirred up by Jews from Thessalonica forces Paul to leave Silas and Timothy temporarily and proceed alone to Athens, the capital of ancient Greece. There Paul engages the Epicurean and Stoic philosophers in discussion and, standing among their pagan altars, gives a classic discourse concerning the true and living God. Thereafter Silas and Timothy apparently join Paul in Athens for a brief time, but are then sent to Thessalonica.

After remaining alone for some time in Athens, Paul journeys west to Corinth, where he spends over a year-and-a-half teaching the gospel. While in Corinth, Paul supports himself in the trade of tentmaking, together with

[x]Or *whom*

Aquila and his wife, Priscilla, who have recently come from Italy. Paul is rejoined by Silas and Timothy, who bring news from Macedonia. In response to questions which have been raised, Paul writes two letters to the brethren in Thessalonica before leaving Corinth. Thereafter he returns to Antioch by way of Ephesus, Caesarea, and Jerusalem.

Luke's record of this second missionary journey begins on a discordant note as Paul has a dispute with Barnabas, who was initially planning to join Paul on the tour.

Acts
15:36-41
Antioch

PAUL AND BARNABAS SEPARATE.   Some time later Paul said to Barnabas, "Let us go back and visit the brothers in all the towns where we preached the word of the Lord and see how they are doing." Barnabas wanted to take John, also called Mark, with them, but Paul did not think it wise to take him, because he had deserted them in Pamphylia and had not continued with them in the work. They had such a sharp disagreement that they parted company. Barnabas took Mark and sailed for Cyprus, but Paul chose Silas and left, commended by the brothers to the grace of the Lord. He went through Syria and Cilicia, strengthening the churches.

Acts 16:1-3
Lystra

TIMOTHY JOINS PAUL AND SILAS.   He came to Derbe and then to Lystra, where a disciple named Timothy lived, whose mother was a Jewess and a believer, but whose father was a Greek. The brothers at Lystra and Iconium spoke well of him. Paul wanted to take him along on the journey, so he circumcised him because of the Jews who lived in that area, for they all knew that his father was a Greek.

Acts 16:4,5
Phrygia
and
Galatia

CHURCHES ARE STRENGTHENED.   As they traveled from town to town, they delivered the decisions reached by the apostles and elders in Jerusalem for the people to obey. So the churches were strengthened in the faith and grew daily in numbers.

Acts
16:6-10
Troas

VISION OF MACEDONIAN CALL.   Paul and his companions traveled throughout the region of Phrygia and Galatia, having been kept by the Holy Spirit from preaching the word in the province of Asia. When they came to the border of Mysia, they tried to enter Bithynia, but the Spirit of Jesus would not allow them to. So they passed by Mysia and went down to Troas. During the night Paul had a vision of a man of Macedonia standing and begging him, "Come over to Macedonia and help us." After Paul had seen the vision, we got ready at once to leave for Macedonia, concluding that God had called us to preach the gospel to them.

Acts
16:11-15
Philippi

LYDIA CONVERTED IN PHILIPPI.   From Troas we put out to sea and sailed straight for Samothrace, and the next day on to Neapolis. From there we traveled to Philippi, a Roman colony and the leading city of that district of Macedonia. And we stayed there several days.

On the Sabbath we went outside the city gate to the river, where we expected to find a place of prayer. We sat down and began to speak to the women who had gathered there. One of those listening was a woman named Lydia, a dealer in purple cloth from the city of Thyatira, who was a worshiper of God. The Lord opened her heart to respond to Paul's message. When she and the members of her household were baptized, she invited us to her home. "If you consider me a believer in the Lord," she said, "come and stay at my house." And she persuaded us.

EVIL SPIRIT REMOVED. Once when we were going to the place of prayer, we were met by a slave girl who had a spirit by which she predicted the future. She earned a great deal of money for her owners by fortune-telling. This girl followed Paul and the rest of us, shouting, "These men are servants of the Most High God, who are telling you the way to be saved." She kept this up for many days. Finally Paul became so troubled that he turned around and said to the spirit, "In the name of Jesus Christ I command you to come out of her!" At that moment the spirit left her.

Acts 16:16-18

PAUL AND SILAS IMPRISONED. When the owners of the slave girl realized that their hope of making money was gone, they seized Paul and Silas and dragged them into the marketplace to face the authorities. They brought them before the magistrates and said, "These men are Jews, and are throwing our city into an uproar by advocating customs unlawful for us Romans to accept or practice."

The crowd joined in the attack against Paul and Silas, and the magistrates ordered them to be stripped and beaten. After they had been severely flogged, they were thrown into prison, and the jailer was commanded to guard them carefully. Upon receiving such orders, he put them in the inner cell and fastened their feet in the stocks.

Acts 16:19-24

PHILIPPIAN JAILER CONVERTED. About midnight Paul and Silas were praying and singing hymns to God, and the other prisoners were listening to them. Suddenly there was such a violent earthquake that the foundations of the prison were shaken. At once all the prison doors flew open, and everybody's chains came loose. The jailer woke up, and when he saw the prison doors open, he drew his sword and was about to kill himself because he thought the prisoners had escaped. But Paul shouted, "Don't harm yourself! We are all here!"

The jailer called for lights, rushed in and fell trembling before Paul and Silas. He then brought them out and asked, "Sirs, what must I do to be saved?"

They replied, "Believe in the Lord Jesus, and you will be saved—you and your household." Then they spoke the word of the Lord to him and to all the others in his house. At that hour of the night the jailer took them and washed their wounds; then immediately he and all his family were baptized. The jailer brought them into his house and set a meal before them; he was filled with joy because he had come to believe in God—he and his whole family.

Acts 16:25-34

PAUL AND SILAS RELEASED. When it was daylight, the magistrates sent their officers to the jailer with the order: "Release those men." The jailer told Paul, "The magistrates have ordered that you and Silas be released. Now you can leave. Go in peace."

But Paul said to the officers: "They beat us publicly without a trial, even though we are Roman citizens, and threw us into prison. And now do they want to get rid of us quietly? No! Let them come themselves and escort us out."

The officers reported this to the magistrates, and when they heard that Paul and Silas were Roman citizens, they were alarmed. They came to appease them and escorted them from the prison, requesting them to leave the city. After Paul and Silas came out of the prison, they went to Lydia's house, where they met with the brothers and encouraged them. Then they left.

Acts 16:35-40

Acts 17:1-4
Thessa-
lonica

TEACHING IN THESSALONICA. When they had passed through Amphipolis and Apollonia, they came to Thessalonica, where there was a Jewish synagogue. As his custom was, Paul went into the synagogue, and on three Sabbath days he reasoned with them from the Scriptures, explaining and proving that the Christ[y] had to suffer and rise from the dead. "This Jesus I am proclaiming to you is the Christ,[y]" he said. Some of the Jews were persuaded and joined Paul and Silas, as did a large number of God-fearing Greeks and not a few prominent women.

Acts 17:5-9

ATTACK ON JASON'S HOUSE. But the Jews were jealous; so they rounded up some bad characters from the marketplace, formed a mob and started a riot in the city. They rushed to Jason's house in search of Paul and Silas in order to bring them out to the crowd.[z] But when they did not find them, they dragged Jason and some other brothers before the city officials, shouting: "These men who have caused trouble all over the world have now come here, and Jason has welcomed them into his house. They are all defying Caesar's decrees, saying that there is another king, one called Jesus." When they heard this, the crowd and the city officials were thrown into turmoil. Then they made Jason and the others post bond and let them go.

Acts
17:10-12
Berea

GOOD RECEPTION AT BEREA. As soon as it was night, the brothers sent Paul and Silas away to Berea. On arriving there, they went to the Jewish synagogue. Now the Bereans were of more noble character than the Thessalonians, for they received the message with great eagerness and examined the Scriptures every day to see if what Paul said was true. Many of the Jews believed, as did also a number of prominent Greek women and many Greek men.

Acts
17:13-15

AGITATORS FORCE DEPARTURE. When the Jews in Thessalonica learned that Paul was preaching the word of God at Berea, they went there too, agitating the crowds and stirring them up. The brothers immediately sent Paul to the coast, but Silas and Timothy stayed at Berea. The men who escorted Paul brought him to Athens and then left with instructions for Silas and Timothy to join him as soon as possible.

Acts
17:16-21
Athens

WITH PHILOSOPHERS IN ATHENS. While Paul was waiting for them in Athens, he was greatly distressed to see that the city was full of idols. So he reasoned in the synagogue with the Jews and the God-fearing Greeks, as well as in the marketplace day by day with those who happened to be there. A group of Epicurean and Stoic philosophers began to dispute with him. Some of them asked, "What is this babbler trying to say?" Others remarked, "He seems to be advocating foreign gods." They said this because Paul was preaching the good news about Jesus and the resurrection. Then they took him and brought him to a meeting of the Areopagus, where they said to him, "May we know what this new teaching is that you are presenting? You are bringing some strange ideas to our ears, and we want to know what they mean." (All the Athenians and the foreigners who lived there spent their time doing nothing but talking about and listening to the latest ideas.)

Acts
17:22-31
Areopagus

SERMON ABOUT "UNKNOWN GOD." Paul then stood up in the meeting of the Areopagus and said: "Men of Athens! I see that in every way

*y*Or *Messiah*   *z*Or *the assembly of the people*

you are very religious. For as I walked around and looked carefully at your objects of worship, I even found an altar with this inscription: TO AN UNKNOWN GOD. Now what you worship as something unknown I am going to proclaim to you.

"The God who made the world and everything in it is the Lord of heaven and earth and does not live in temples built by hands. And he is not served by human hands, as if he needed anything, because he himself gives all men life and breath and everything else. From one man he made every nation of men, that they should inhabit the whole earth; and he determined the times set for them and the exact places where they should live. God did this so that men would seek him and perhaps reach out for him and find him, though he is not far from each one of us. 'For in him we live and move and have our being.' As some of your own poets have said, 'We are his offspring.'

"Therefore since we are God's offspring, we should not think that the divine being is like gold or silver or stone—an image made by man's design and skill. In the past God overlooked such ignorance, but now he commands all people everywhere to repent. For he has set a day when he will judge the world with justice by the man he has appointed. He has given proof of this to all men by raising him from the dead."

CROWD'S REACTION. When they heard about the resurrection of the dead, some of them sneered, but others said, "We want to hear you again on this subject." At that, Paul left the Council. A few men became followers of Paul and believed. Among them was Dionysius, a member of the Areopagus, also a woman named Damaris, and a number of others. — Acts 17:32-34

AQUILA AND PRISCILLA. After this, Paul left Athens and went to Corinth. There he met a Jew named Aquila, a native of Pontus, who had recently come from Italy with his wife Priscilla, because Claudius had ordered all the Jews to leave Rome. Paul went to see them, and because he was a tentmaker as they were, he stayed and worked with them. Every Sabbath he reasoned in the synagogue, trying to persuade Jews and Greeks. — Acts 18:1-4 Corinth

UNBELIEVING JEWS. When Silas and Timothy came from Macedonia, Paul devoted himself exclusively to preaching, testifying to the Jews that Jesus was the Christ.[a] But when the Jews opposed Paul and became abusive, he shook out his clothes in protest and said to them, "Your blood be on your own heads! I am clear of my responsibility. From now on I will go to the Gentiles." — Acts 18:5-7

Then Paul left the synagogue and went next door to the house of Titius Justus, a worshiper of God.

MANY JEWS ACCEPT GOSPEL. Crispus, the synagogue ruler, and his entire household believed in the Lord; and many of the Corinthians who heard him believed and were baptized. — Acts 18:8-11

One night the Lord spoke to Paul in a vision: "Do not be afraid; keep on speaking, do not be silent. For I am with you, and no one is going to attack and harm you, because I have many people in this city." So Paul stayed for a year and a half, teaching them the word of God.

[a]Or *Messiah*; also in verse 28

First Letter to the Thessalonians

*D*uring this time, somewhere around A.D. 51, it seems likely that Paul writes two letters to the Christians in Thessalonica, through which Paul has passed on his way to Corinth. At some point Paul has sent Timothy back to Thessalonica in order to establish more fully the Thessalonians' faith and to exhort them to steadfastness in the face of persecution. Paul's letter takes on the same purpose. Although Luke's historical record of Paul's visit to Thessalonica mentions only three weeks of confrontation with the Jews in the synagogue, Paul's letter clearly addresses Gentile Christians, probably Greeks, who had been converted from paganism. Paul reminds these new converts that they have turned from idols to worship the true and living God, and he exhorts them to continue in purity, love, and labor for the Lord. He also answers questions which have arisen in their minds regarding the second coming of Christ. As a basis for his many exhortations, Paul begins his letter by referring to Timothy, Silas, and himself as examples of sacrifice and suffering.

1 Thess. 1:1	SALUTATION. Paul, Silas[b] and Timothy,
	To the church of the Thessalonians in God the Father and the Lord Jesus Christ:
	Grace and peace to you.[c]
1 Thess. 1:2-10	THANKS FOR THEIR FAITH. We always thank God for all of you, mentioning you in our prayers. We continually remember before our God and Father your work produced by faith, your labor prompted by love, and your endurance inspired by hope in our Lord Jesus Christ.

For we know, brothers loved by God, that he has chosen you, because our gospel came to you not simply with words, but also with power, with the Holy Spirit and with deep conviction. You know how we lived among you for your sake. You became imitators of us and of the Lord; in spite of severe suffering, you welcomed the message with the joy given by the Holy Spirit. And so you became a model to all the believers in Macedonia and Achaia. The Lord's message rang out from you not only in Macedonia and Achaia—your faith in God has become known everywhere. Therefore we do not need to say anything about it, for they themselves report what kind of reception you gave us. They tell how you turned to God from idols to serve the living and true God, and to wait for his Son from heaven, whom he raised from the dead—Jesus, who rescues us from the coming wrath.

1 Thess. 2:1-12	PAUL'S MINISTRY AMONG THEM. You know, brothers, that our visit to you was not a failure. We had previously suffered and been insulted in Philippi, as you know, but with the help of our God we dared to tell you his gospel in spite of strong opposition. For the appeal we make does not spring from error or impure motives, nor are we trying to trick you. On the contrary, we speak as men approved by God to be entrusted with the gospel. We are not trying to please men but God, who tests our hearts.

[b]Greek *Silvanus*, a variant of *Silas*   [c]Some early manuscripts *you from God our Father*
and the Lord Jesus Christ

You know we never used flattery, nor did we put on a mask to cover up greed—God is our witness. We were not looking for praise from men, not from you or anyone else.

As apostles of Christ we could have been a burden to you, but we were gentle among you, like a mother caring for her little children. We loved you so much that we were delighted to share with you not only the gospel of God but our lives as well, because you had become so dear to us. Surely you remember, brothers, our toil and hardship; we worked night and day in order not to be a burden to anyone while we preached the gospel of God to you.

You are witnesses, and so is God, of how holy, righteous and blameless we were among you who believed. For you know that we dealt with each of you as a father deals with his own children, encouraging, comforting and urging you to live lives worthy of God, who calls you into his kingdom and glory.

EAGER RECEPTION APPRECIATED.   And we also thank God continually because, when you received the word of God, which you heard from us, you accepted it not as the word of men, but as it actually is, the word of God, which is at work in you who believe. For you, brothers, became imitators of God's churches in Judea, which are in Christ Jesus: You suffered from your own countrymen the same things those churches suffered from the Jews, who killed the Lord Jesus and the prophets and also drove us out. They displease God and are hostile to all men in their effort to keep us from speaking to the Gentiles so that they may be saved. In this way they always heap up their sins to the limit. The wrath of God has come upon them at last.[d]

1 Thess. 2:13-16

DESIRE TO BE WITH THEM.   But, brothers, when we were torn away from you for a short time (in person, not in thought), out of our intense longing we made every effort to see you. For we wanted to come to you—certainly I, Paul, did, again and again—but Satan stopped us. For what is our hope, our joy, or the crown in which we will glory in the presence of our Lord Jesus when he comes? Is it not you? Indeed, you are our glory and joy.

1 Thess. 2:17-20

TIMOTHY'S MISSION.   So when we could stand it no longer, we thought it best to be left by ourselves in Athens. We sent Timothy, who is our brother and God's fellow worker[e] in spreading the gospel of Christ, to strengthen and encourage you in your faith, so that no one would be unsettled by these trials. You know quite well that we were destined for them. In fact, when we were with you, we kept telling you that we would be persecuted. And it turned out that way, as you well know. For this reason, when I could stand it no longer, I sent to find out about your faith. I was afraid that in some way the tempter might have tempted you and our efforts might have been useless.

1 Thess. 3:1-5

GOOD NEWS COMFORTING.   But Timothy has just now come to us from you and has brought good news about your faith and love. He has told us that you always have pleasant memories of us and that you long to see us, just as we also long to see you. Therefore, brothers, in all our distress and persecution we were encouraged about you because of your

1 Thess. 3:6-10

[d]Or *them fully*   [e]Some manuscripts *brother and fellow worker*; other manuscripts *brother and God's servant*

faith. For now we really live, since you are standing firm in the Lord. How can we thank God enough for you in return for all the joy we have in the presence of our God because of you? Night and day we pray most earnestly that we may see you again and supply what is lacking in your faith.

1 Thess. 3:11-13

PAUL'S PRAYER FOR THEM. Now may our God and Father himself and our Lord Jesus clear the way for us to come to you. May the Lord make your love increase and overflow for each other and for everyone else, just as ours does for you. May he strengthen your hearts so that you will be blameless and holy in the presence of our God and Father when our Lord Jesus comes with all his holy ones.

1 Thess. 4:1-8

EXHORTATION TO CHASTITY. Finally, brothers, we instructed you how to live in order to please God, as in fact you are living. Now we ask you and urge you in the Lord Jesus to do this more and more. For you know what instructions we gave you by the authority of the Lord Jesus.

It is God's will that you should be sanctified: that you should avoid sexual immorality; that each of you should learn to control his own body*f* in a way that is holy and honorable, not in passionate lust like the heathen, who do not know God; and that in this matter no one should wrong his brother or take advantage of him. The Lord will punish men for all such sins, as we have already told you and warned you. For God did not call us to be impure, but to live a holy life. Therefore, he who rejects this instruction does not reject man but God, who gives you his Holy Spirit.

1 Thess. 4:9-12

EXHORTATION TOWARD LOVE. Now about brotherly love we do not need to write to you, for you yourselves have been taught by God to love each other. And in fact, you do love all the brothers throughout Macedonia. Yet we urge you, brothers, to do so more and more.

Make it your ambition to lead a quiet life, to mind your own business and to work with your hands, just as we told you, so that your daily life may win the respect of outsiders and so that you will not be dependent on anybody.

1 Thess. 4:13-18

NATURE OF THE RESURRECTION. Brothers, we do not want you to be ignorant about those who fall asleep, or to grieve like the rest of men, who have no hope. We believe that Jesus died and rose again and so we believe that God will bring with Jesus those who have fallen asleep in him. According to the Lord's own word, we tell you that we who are still alive, who are left till the coming of the Lord, will certainly not precede those who have fallen asleep. For the Lord himself will come down from heaven, with a loud command, with the voice of the archangel and with the trumpet call of God, and the dead in Christ will rise first. After that, we who are still alive and are left will be caught up together with them in the clouds to meet the Lord in the air. And so we will be with the Lord forever. Therefore encourage each other with these words.

1 Thess. 5:1-11

READINESS FOR SECOND COMING. Now, brothers, about times and dates we do not need to write to you, for you know very well that the day of the Lord will come like a thief in the night. While people are saying, "Peace and safety," destruction will come on them suddenly, as labor pains on a pregnant woman, and they will not escape.

But you, brothers, are not in darkness so that this day should surprise

f Or learn to live with his own wife; or learn to acquire a wife you like a thief. You are all sons of the light and sons of the day. We do not belong to the night or to the darkness. So then, let us not be like others, who are asleep, but let us be alert and self-controlled. For those who sleep, sleep at night, and those who get drunk, get drunk at night. But since we belong to the day, let us be self-controlled, putting on faith and love as a breastplate, and the hope of salvation as a helmet. For God did not appoint us to suffer wrath but to receive salvation through our Lord Jesus Christ. He died for us so that, whether we are awake or asleep, we may live together with him. Therefore encourage one another and build each other up, just as in fact you are doing.

VARIOUS EXHORTATIONS. Now we ask you, brothers, to respect those who work hard among you, who are over you in the Lord and who admonish you. Hold them in the highest regard in love because of their work. Live in peace with each other. And we urge you, brothers, warn those who are idle, encourage the timid, help the weak, be patient with everyone. Make sure that nobody pays back wrong for wrong, but always try to be kind to each other and to everyone else.

1 Thess.
5:12-22

Be joyful always; pray continually; give thanks in all circumstances, for this is God's will for you in Christ Jesus.

Do not put out the Spirit's fire; do not treat prophecies with contempt. Test everything. Hold on to the good. Avoid every kind of evil.

BENEDICTION. May God himself, the God of peace, sanctify you through and through. May your whole spirit, soul and body be kept blameless at the coming of our Lord Jesus Christ. The one who calls you is faithful and he will do it.

1 Thess.
5:23-28

Brothers, pray for us. Greet all the brothers with a holy kiss. I charge you before the Lord to have this letter read to all the brothers.

The grace of our Lord Jesus Christ be with you.

Second Letter to the Thessalonians

*P*aul's first letter seemingly causes some misunderstanding among the Thessalonians, many of whom interpreted it as saying that the second coming would be taking place right away. Therefore Paul sends a second letter to clarify this misunderstanding. He points to some of the events which will precede the second coming and admonishes them to continue working both for their own support and for the Lord.

SALUTATION. Paul, Silas[8] and Timothy,

2 Thess.
1:1,2

To the church of the Thessalonians in God our Father and the Lord Jesus Christ:

Grace and peace to you from God the Father and the Lord Jesus Christ.

PRAISING STEADFASTNESS. We ought always to thank God for you, brothers, and rightly so, because your faith is growing more and more, and the love every one of you has for each other is increasing. Therefore,

2 Thess.
1:3,4

[8]Greek *Silvanus*, a variant of *Silas*

among God's churches we boast about your perseverance and faith in all the persecutions and trials you are enduring.

2 Thess. 1:5-10

ENDURANCE TO BE REWARDED.   All this is evidence that God's judgment is right, and as a result you will be counted worthy of the kingdom of God, for which you are suffering. God is just: He will pay back trouble to those who trouble you and give relief to you who are troubled, and to us as well. This will happen when the Lord Jesus is revealed from heaven in blazing fire with his powerful angels. He will punish those who do not know God and do not obey the gospel of our Lord Jesus. They will be punished with everlasting destruction and shut out from the presence of the Lord and from the majesty of his power on the day he comes to be glorified in his holy people and to be marveled at among all those who have believed. This includes you, because you believed our testimony to you.

2 Thess. 1:11,12

PAUL'S PRAYER FOR THEM.   With this in mind, we constantly pray for you, that our God may count you worthy of his calling, and that by his power he may fulfill every good purpose of yours and every act prompted by your faith. We pray this so that the name of our Lord Jesus may be glorified in you, and you in him, according to the grace of our God and the Lord Jesus Christ.[h]

2 Thess. 2:1-12

EVENTS BEFORE SECOND COMING.   Concerning the coming of our Lord Jesus Christ and our being gathered to him, we ask you, brothers, not to become easily unsettled or alarmed by some prophecy, report or letter supposed to have come from us, saying that the day of the Lord has already come. Don't let anyone deceive you in any way, for ⌐that day will not come⌐ until the rebellion occurs and the man of lawlessness[i] is revealed, the man doomed to destruction. He will oppose and will exalt himself over everything that is called God or is worshiped, so that he sets himself up in God's temple, proclaiming himself to be God.

Don't you remember that when I was with you I used to tell you these things? And now you know what is holding him back, so that he may be revealed at the proper time. For the secret power of lawlessness is already at work; but the one who now holds it back will continue to do so till he is taken out of the way. And then the lawless one will be revealed, whom the Lord Jesus will overthrow with the breath of his mouth and destroy by the splendor of his coming. The coming of the lawless one will be in accordance with the work of Satan displayed in all kinds of counterfeit miracles, signs and wonders, and in every sort of evil that deceives those who are perishing. They perish because they refused to love the truth and so be saved. For this reason God sends them a powerful delusion so that they will believe the lie and so that all will be condemned who have not believed the truth but have delighted in wickedness.

2 Thess. 2:13-17

CALL TO STAND FIRM.   But we ought always to thank God for you, brothers loved by the Lord, because from the beginning God chose you[j] to be saved through the sanctifying work of the Spirit and through belief in the truth. He called you to this through our gospel, that you might share in the glory of our Lord Jesus Christ. So then, brothers, stand firm and

---

[h]Or *God and Lord, Jesus Christ*   [i]Some manuscripts *sin*   [j]Some manuscripts *because God chose you as his firstfruits*

hold to the teachings[k] we passed on to you, whether by word of mouth or by letter.

May our Lord Jesus Christ himself and God our Father, who loved us and by his grace gave us eternal encouragement and good hope, encourage your hearts and strengthen you in every good deed and word.

REQUEST FOR PRAYER. Finally, brothers, pray for us that the message of the Lord may spread rapidly and be honored, just as it was with you. And pray that we may be delivered from wicked and evil men, for not everyone has faith. But the Lord is faithful, and he will strengthen and protect you from the evil one. We have confidence in the Lord that you are doing and will continue to do the things we command. May the Lord direct your hearts into God's love and Christ's perseverance.

2 Thess. 3:1-5

WARNING AGAINST IDLENESS. In the name of the Lord Jesus Christ, we command you, brothers, to keep away from every brother who is idle and does not live according to the teaching[l] you received from us. For you yourselves know how you ought to follow our example. We were not idle when we were with you, nor did we eat anyone's food without paying for it. On the contrary, we worked night and day, laboring and toiling so that we would not be a burden to any of you. We did this, not because we do not have the right to such help, but in order to make ourselves a model for you to follow. For even when we were with you, we gave you this rule: "If a man will not work, he shall not eat."

2 Thess. 3:6-15

We hear that some among you are idle. They are not busy; they are busybodies. Such people we command and urge in the Lord Jesus Christ to settle down and earn the bread they eat. And as for you, brothers, never tire of doing what is right.

If anyone does not obey our instruction in this letter, take special note of him. Do not associate with him, in order that he may feel ashamed. Yet do not regard him as an enemy, but warn him as a brother.

BENEDICTION. Now may the Lord of peace himself give you peace at all times and in every way. The Lord be with all of you.

2 Thess. 3:16-18

I, Paul, write this greeting in my own hand, which is the distinguishing mark in all my letters. This is how I write.

The grace of our Lord Jesus Christ be with you all.

The historical record continues with this account of Paul being persecuted in Corinth.

CHARGES BEFORE GALLIO. While Gallio was proconsul of Achaia, the Jews made a united attack on Paul and brought him into court. "This man," they charged, "is persuading the people to worship God in ways contrary to the law."

Acts 18:12-17

Just as Paul was about to speak, Gallio said to the Jews, "If you Jews were making a complaint about some misdemeanor or serious crime, it would be reasonable for me to listen to you. But since it involves questions about words and names and your own law—settle the matter yourselves. I will not be a judge of such things." So he had them ejected from the court. Then they all turned on Sosthenes the synagogue ruler and beat him in front of the court. But Gallio showed no concern whatever.

[k]Or *traditions*   [l]Or *tradition*

Acts 18:18-22 Antioch	RETURN TO ANTIOCH. Paul stayed on in Corinth for some time. Then he left the brothers and sailed for Syria, accompanied by Priscilla and Aquila. Before he sailed, he had his hair cut off at Cenchrea because of a vow he had taken. They arrived at Ephesus, where Paul left Priscilla and Aquila. He himself went into the synagogue and reasoned with the Jews. When they asked him to spend more time with them, he declined. But as he left, he promised, "I will come back if it is God's will." Then he set sail from Ephesus. When he landed at Caesarea, he went up and greeted the church and then went down to Antioch.

Third Missionary Journey

*L*uke does not indicate how long Paul stays in Antioch after returning from his second missionary journey. But it is probably not long before Paul is once again preparing for an extended evangelistic tour. He begins his third journey by passing north and west through Galatia and Phrygia. It is clear that Paul continues to be concerned about the spiritual growth of those whom he had converted several years earlier.

Paul then travels on through Asia to its capital, Ephesus, and thereby fulfills a desire he first felt on his second tour, when he was directed by the Holy Spirit to Macedonia instead. It appears that Paul relishes the opportunity to be in this important city, because he stays here for approximately three years. Of special significance during this time are letters which Paul writes to the church in Corinth—a church which has developed some serious problems since Paul last visited with them.

Acts 18:23 Galatia and Phrygia	BEGINNING OF JOURNEY. After spending some time in Antioch, Paul set out from there and traveled from place to place throughout the region of Galatia and Phrygia, strengthening all the disciples.
Acts 18:24-28 Ephesus and Achaia	APOLLOS IS TAUGHT. Meanwhile a Jew named Apollos, a native of Alexandria, came to Ephesus. He was a learned man, with a thorough knowledge of the Scriptures. He had been instructed in the way of the Lord, and he spoke with great fervor[m] and taught about Jesus accurately, though he knew only the baptism of John. He began to speak boldly in the synagogue. When Priscilla and Aquila heard him, they invited him to their home and explained to him the way of God more adequately. When Apollos wanted to go to Achaia, the brothers encouraged him and wrote to the disciples there to welcome him. On arriving, he was a great help to those who by grace had believed. For he vigorously refuted the Jews in public debate, proving from the Scriptures that Jesus was the Christ.
Acts 19:1-7 Ephesus	DISCIPLES REBAPTIZED. While Apollos was at Corinth, Paul took the road through the interior and arrived at Ephesus. There he found some disciples and asked them, "Did you receive the Holy Spirit when[n] you believed?" They answered, "No, we have not even heard that there is a Holy Spirit." So Paul asked, "Then what baptism did you receive?"

[m] Or with fervor in the Spirit   [n] Or after

"John's baptism," they replied.

Paul said, "John's baptism was a baptism of repentance. He told the people to believe in the one coming after him, that is, in Jesus." On hearing this, they were baptized into[o] the name of the Lord Jesus. When Paul placed his hands on them, the Holy Spirit came on them, and they spoke in tongues[p] and prophesied. There were about twelve men in all.

Acts 19:8-10 (From A.D. 53 to 55)

MINISTRY IN EPHESUS. Paul entered the synagogue and spoke boldly there for three months, arguing persuasively about the kingdom of God. But some of them became obstinate; they refused to believe and publicly maligned the Way. So Paul left them. He took the disciples with him and had discussions daily in the lecture hall of Tyrannus. This went on for two years, so that all the Jews and Greeks who lived in the province of Asia heard the word of the Lord.

Acts 19:11-16

EXORCISTS USE JESUS' NAME. God did extraordinary miracles through Paul, so that even handkerchiefs and aprons that had touched him were taken to the sick, and their illnesses were cured and the evil spirits left them.

Some Jews who went around driving out evil spirits tried to invoke the name of the Lord Jesus over those who were demon-possessed. They would say, "In the name of Jesus, whom Paul preaches, I command you to come out." Seven sons of Sceva, a Jewish chief priest, were doing this. ⌞One day⌟ the evil spirit answered them, "Jesus I know, and I know about Paul, but who are you?" Then the man who had the evil spirit jumped on them and overpowered them all. He gave them such a beating that they ran out of the house naked and bleeding.

Acts 19:17-20

SORCERY GIVEN UP. When this became known to the Jews and Greeks living in Ephesus, they were all seized with fear, and the name of the Lord Jesus was held in high honor. Many of those who believed now came and openly confessed their evil deeds. A number who had practiced sorcery brought their scrolls together and burned them publicly. When they calculated the value of the scrolls, the total came to fifty thousand drachmas.[q] In this way the word of the Lord spread widely and grew in power.

Acts 19:21,22

PAUL ANTICIPATES JOURNEY. After all this had happened, Paul decided to go to Jerusalem, passing through Macedonia and Achaia. "After I have been there," he said, "I must visit Rome also." He sent two of his helpers, Timothy and Erastus, to Macedonia, while he stayed in the province of Asia a little longer.

First Letter to the Corinthians

Paul has apparently sent a letter to the church in Corinth by the hands of Timothy, who recently would have passed through Corinth on his way to Macedonia. In a second letter, written perhaps A.D. 55-56, Paul mentions the previous Corinthian letter and indicates that he has received a return letter from the Corinthians which has been brought to Ephesus by a group including Stephanas, Fortunatus, and Achaicus. Although the content of Paul's first letter is unknown, the letter

[o]Or *in* [p]Or *other languages* [q]A drachma was a silver coin worth about a day's wages.

which Paul received from the Corinthians evidently posed specific questions regarding marriage and singleness, food sacrificed to idols, spiritual gifts, and certain special contributions which the Corinthians were making. Paul answers these questions in his second letter (traditionally referred to as 1 Corinthians) and expresses concern about various divisions among the Corinthians which have been reported to Paul by members of Chloe's family. Additionally, Paul addresses some of the particular problems which these Christians are facing in the pagan city of Corinth, including matters pertaining to sexual morality and modesty, and the issue of fellowship with pagans.

1 Cor.
1:1-3

SALUTATION.   Paul, called to be an apostle of Christ Jesus by the will of God, and our brother Sosthenes,

To the church of God in Corinth, to those sanctified in Christ Jesus and called to be holy, together with all those everywhere who call on the name of our Lord Jesus Christ—their Lord and ours:

Grace and peace to you from God our Father and the Lord Jesus Christ.

1 Cor.
1:4-9

THANKSGIVING FOR GRACE.   I always thank God for you because of his grace given you in Christ Jesus. For in him you have been enriched in every way—in all your speaking and in all your knowledge—because our testimony about Christ was confirmed in you. Therefore you do not lack any spiritual gift as you eagerly wait for our Lord Jesus Christ to be revealed. He will keep you strong to the end, so that you will be blameless on the day of our Lord Jesus Christ. God, who has called you into fellowship with his Son Jesus Christ our Lord, is faithful.

Regarding Divisions Within the Church

1 Cor.
1:10-17

WARNING AGAINST DIVISIONS.   I appeal to you, brothers, in the name of our Lord Jesus Christ, that all of you agree with one another so that there may be no divisions among you and that you may be perfectly united in mind and thought. My brothers, some from Chloe's household have informed me that there are quarrels among you. What I mean is this: One of you says, "I follow Paul"; another, "I follow Apollos"; another, "I follow Cephas^r^"; still another, "I follow Christ."

Is Christ divided? Was Paul crucified for you? Were you baptized into^s the name of Paul? I am thankful that I did not baptize any of you except Crispus and Gaius, so no one can say that you were baptized into my name. (Yes, I also baptized the household of Stephanas; beyond that, I don't remember if I baptized anyone else.) For Christ did not send me to baptize, but to preach the gospel—not with words of human wisdom, lest the cross of Christ be emptied of its power.

1 Cor.
1:18-25

GOD'S WISDOM.   For the message of the cross is foolishness to those who are perishing, but to us who are being saved it is the power of God. For it is written:

"I will destroy the wisdom of the wise;
    the intelligence of the intelligent I will frustrate." ^t

Where is the wise man? Where is the scholar? Where is the philosopher of this age? Has not God made foolish the wisdom of the world? For since

^rThat is, Peter   ^sOr *in*   ^tIsaiah 29:14

in the wisdom of God the world through its wisdom did not know him, God was pleased through the foolishness of what was preached to save those who believe. Jews demand miraculous signs and Greeks look for wisdom, but we preach Christ crucified: a stumbling block to Jews and foolishness to Gentiles, but to those whom God has called, both Jews and Greeks, Christ the power of God and the wisdom of God. For the foolishness of God is wiser than man's wisdom, and the weakness of God is stronger than man's strength.

EXAMPLE OF LOWLINESS.   Brothers, think of what you were when you were called. Not many of you were wise by human standards; not many were influential; not many were of noble birth. But God chose the foolish things of the world to shame the wise; God chose the weak things of the world to shame the strong. He chose the lowly things of this world and the despised things—and the things that are not—to nullify the things that are, so that no one may boast before him. It is because of him that you are in Christ Jesus, who has become for us wisdom from God—that is, our righteousness, holiness and redemption. Therefore, as it is written: "Let him who boasts boast in the Lord."[u]

1 Cor.
1:26-31

PREACHING NOT ELOQUENT.   When I came to you, brothers, I did not come with eloquence or superior wisdom as I proclaimed to you the testimony about God.[v] For I resolved to know nothing while I was with you except Jesus Christ and him crucified. I came to you in weakness and fear, and with much trembling. My message and my preaching were not with wise and persuasive words, but with a demonstration of the Spirit's power, so that your faith might not rest on men's wisdom, but on God's power.

1 Cor.
2:1-5

WISDOM FROM THE SPIRIT.   We do, however, speak a message of wisdom among the mature, but not the wisdom of this age or of the rulers of this age, who are coming to nothing. No, we speak of God's secret wisdom, a wisdom that has been hidden and that God destined for our glory before time began. None of the rulers of this age understood it, for if they had, they would not have crucified the Lord of glory. However, as it is written:

1 Cor.
2:6-13

> "No eye has seen,
>   no ear has heard,
>   no mind has conceived
>   what God has prepared for those who love him" [w]—

but God has revealed it to us by his Spirit.
   The Spirit searches all things, even the deep things of God. For who among men knows the thoughts of a man except the man's spirit within him? In the same way no one knows the thoughts of God except the Spirit of God. We have not received the spirit of the world but the Spirit who is from God, that we may understand what God has freely given us. This is what we speak, not in words taught us by human wisdom but in words taught by the Spirit, expressing spiritual truths in spiritual words.[x]

WISDOM FOR SPIRITUALLY MINDED.   The man without the Spirit does not accept the things that come from the Spirit of God, for they are

1 Cor.
2:14-16

---

[u]Jer. 9:24   [v]Some manuscripts *as I proclaimed to you God's mystery*   [w]Isaiah 64:4
[x]Or *Spirit, interpreting spiritual truths to spiritual men*

foolishness to him, and he cannot understand them, because they are spiritually discerned. The spiritual man makes judgments about all things, but he himself is not subject to any man's judgment:

> "For who has known the mind of the Lord
> that he may instruct him?"[y]

But we have the mind of Christ.

1 Cor.
3:1-4

DIVISIONS PREVENT GROWTH.   Brothers, I could not address you as spiritual but as worldly—mere infants in Christ. I gave you milk, not solid food, for you were not yet ready for it. Indeed, you are still not ready. You are still worldly. For since there is jealousy and quarreling among you, are you not worldly? Are you not acting like mere men? For when one says, "I follow Paul," and another, "I follow Apollos," are you not mere men?

1 Cor.
3:5-9

MINISTERS ARE SERVANTS.   What, after all, is Apollos? And what is Paul? Only servants, through whom you came to believe—as the Lord has assigned to each his task. I planted the seed, Apollos watered it, but God made it grow. So neither he who plants nor he who waters is anything, but only God, who makes things grow. The man who plants and the man who waters have one purpose, and each will be rewarded according to his own labor. For we are God's fellow workers; you are God's field, God's building.

1 Cor.
3:10-15

CHRIST IS FOUNDATION.   By the grace God has given me, I laid a foundation as an expert builder, and someone else is building on it. But each one should be careful how he builds. For no one can lay any foundation other than the one already laid, which is Jesus Christ. If any man builds on this foundation using gold, silver, costly stones, wood, hay or straw, his work will be shown for what it is, because the Day will bring it to light. It will be revealed with fire, and the fire will test the quality of each man's work. If what he has built survives, he will receive his reward. If it is burned up, he will suffer loss; he himself will be saved, but only as one escaping through the flames.

1 Cor.
3:16,17

DIVISION DESTROYS TEMPLE.   Don't you know that you yourselves are God's temple and that God's Spirit lives in you? If anyone destroys God's temple, God will destroy him; for God's temple is sacred, and you are that temple.

1 Cor.
3:18-23

LOYALTY TO CHRIST ALONE.   Do not deceive yourselves. If any one of you thinks he is wise by the standards of this age, he should become a "fool" so that he may become wise. For the wisdom of this world is foolishness in God's sight. As it is written: "He catches the wise in their craftiness"[z]; and again, "The Lord knows that the thoughts of the wise are futile."[a] So then, no more boasting about men! All things are yours, whether Paul or Apollos or Cephas[b] or the world or life or death or the present or the future—all are yours, and you are of Christ, and Christ is of God.

1 Cor.
4:1-5

MINISTERS TO BE JUDGED.   So then, men ought to regard us as servants of Christ and as those entrusted with the secret things of God. Now it is required that those who have been given a trust must prove faithful. I care very little if I am judged by you or by any human court; indeed, I do

---

[y]Isaiah 40:13   [z]Job 5:13   [a]Psalm 94:11   [b]That is, Peter

not even judge myself. My conscience is clear, but that does not make me innocent. It is the Lord who judges me. Therefore judge nothing before the appointed time; wait till the Lord comes. He will bring to light what is hidden in darkness and will expose the motives of men's hearts. At that time each will receive his praise from God.

WARNING AGAINST PRIDE.   Now, brothers, I have applied these things to myself and Apollos for your benefit, so that you may learn from us the meaning of the saying, "Do not go beyond what is written." Then you will not take pride in one man over against another. For who makes you different from anyone else? What do you have that you did not receive? And if you did receive it, why do you boast as though you did not?

1 Cor. 4:6-8

Already you have all you want! Already you have become rich! You have become kings—and that without us! How I wish that you really had become kings so that we might be kings with you!

EVEN APOSTLES ARE DEBASED.   For it seems to me that God has put us apostles on display at the end of the procession, like men condemned to die in the arena. We have been made a spectacle to the whole universe, to angels as well as to men. We are fools for Christ, but you are so wise in Christ! We are weak, but you are strong! You are honored, we are dishonored! To this very hour we go hungry and thirsty, we are in rags, we are brutally treated, we are homeless. We work hard with our own hands. When we are cursed, we bless; when we are persecuted, we endure it; when we are slandered, we answer kindly. Up to this moment we have become the scum of the earth, the refuse of the world.

1 Cor. 4:9-13

PAUL APPEALS AS FATHER.   I am not writing this to shame you, but to warn you, as my dear children. Even though you have ten thousand guardians in Christ, you do not have many fathers, for in Christ Jesus I became your father through the gospel. Therefore I urge you to imitate me. For this reason I am sending to you Timothy, my son whom I love, who is faithful in the Lord. He will remind you of my way of life in Christ Jesus, which agrees with what I teach everywhere in every church.

1 Cor. 4:14-21

Some of you have become arrogant, as if I were not coming to you. But I will come to you very soon, if the Lord is willing, and then I will find out not only how these arrogant people are talking, but what power they have. For the kingdom of God is not a matter of talk but of power. What do you prefer? Shall I come to you with a whip, or in love and with a gentle spirit?

Regarding Immorality

CALL FOR DISCIPLINE.   It is actually reported that there is sexual immorality among you, and of a kind that does not occur even among pagans: A man has his father's wife. And you are proud! Shouldn't you rather have been filled with grief and have put out of your fellowship the man who did this? Even though I am not physically present, I am with you in spirit. And I have already passed judgment on the one who did this, just as if I were present. When you are assembled in the name of our Lord Jesus and I am with you in spirit, and the power of our Lord Jesus is present,

1 Cor. 5:1-5

hand this man over to Satan, so that the sinful nature[c] may be destroyed and his spirit saved on the day of the Lord.

1 Cor.
5:6-8

DANGER OF TOLERATING SIN.   Your boasting is not good. Don't you know that a little yeast works through the whole batch of dough? Get rid of the old yeast that you may be a new batch without yeast—as you really are. For Christ, our Passover lamb, has been sacrificed. Therefore let us keep the Festival, not with the old yeast, the yeast of malice and wickedness, but with bread without yeast, the bread of sincerity and truth.

1 Cor.
5:9-13

DUTY OF SELF-POLICING.   I have written you in my letter not to associate with sexually immoral people—not at all meaning the people of this world who are immoral, or the greedy and swindlers, or idolaters. In that case you would have to leave this world. But now I am writing you that you must not associate with anyone who calls himself a brother but is sexually immoral or greedy, an idolater or a slanderer, a drunkard or a swindler. With such a man do not even eat.

What business is it of mine to judge those outside the church? Are you not to judge those inside? God will judge those outside. "Expel the wicked man from among you."[d]

1 Cor.
6:1-8

JUDGMENT AMONG SELVES.   If any of you has a dispute with another, dare he take it before the ungodly for judgment instead of before the saints? Do you not know that the saints will judge the world? And if you are to judge the world, are you not competent to judge trivial cases? Do you not know that we will judge angels? How much more the things of this life! Therefore, if you have disputes about such matters, appoint as judges even men of little account in the church![e] I say this to shame you. Is it possible that there is nobody among you wise enough to judge a dispute between believers? But instead, one brother goes to law against another—and this in front of unbelievers!

The very fact that you have lawsuits among you means you have been completely defeated already. Why not rather be wronged? Why not rather be cheated? Instead, you yourselves cheat and do wrong, and you do this to your brothers.

1 Cor.
6:9-11

SIN PREVENTS INHERITANCE.   Do you not know that the wicked will not inherit the kingdom of God? Do not be deceived: Neither the sexually immoral nor idolaters nor adulterers nor male prostitutes nor homosexual offenders nor thieves nor the greedy nor drunkards nor slanderers nor swindlers will inherit the kingdom of God. And that is what some of you were. But you were washed, you were sanctified, you were justified in the name of the Lord Jesus Christ and by the Spirit of our God.

1 Cor.
6:12-20

BODIES NOT MEANT FOR SIN.   "Everything is permissible for me"—but not everything is beneficial. "Everything is permissible for me"—but I will not be mastered by anything. "Food for the stomach and the stomach for food"—but God will destroy them both. The body is not meant for sexual immorality, but for the Lord, and the Lord for the body. By his power God raised the Lord from the dead, and he will raise us also. Do you not know that your bodies are members of Christ himself? Shall I then take the members of Christ and unite them with a prostitute? Never! Do

---

[c]Or that his body; or that the flesh   [d]Deut. 17:7; 19:19; 21:21; 22:21,24; 24:7   [e]Or matters, do you appoint as judges men of little account in the church?

you not know that he who unites himself with a prostitute is one with her in body? For it is said, "The two will become one flesh."*f* But he who unites himself with the Lord is one with him in spirit.

Flee from sexual immorality. All other sins a man commits are outside his body, but he who sins sexually sins against his own body. Do you not know that your body is a temple of the Holy Spirit, who is in you, whom you have received from God? You are not your own; you were bought at a price. Therefore honor God with your body.

Regarding Marriage and Singleness

MARITAL RELATIONS.   Now for the matters you wrote about: It is good for a man not to marry.*g* But since there is so much immorality, each man should have his own wife, and each woman her own husband. The husband should fulfill his marital duty to his wife, and likewise the wife to her husband. The wife's body does not belong to her alone but also to her husband. In the same way, the husband's body does not belong to him alone but also to his wife. Do not deprive each other except by mutual consent and for a time, so that you may devote yourselves to prayer. Then come together again so that Satan will not tempt you because of your lack of self-control. I say this as a concession, not as a command. I wish that all men were as I am. But each man has his own gift from God; one has this gift, another has that.

1 Cor. 7:1-7

SINGLENESS.   Now to the unmarried and the widows I say: It is good for them to stay unmarried, as I am. But if they cannot control themselves, they should marry, for it is better to marry than to burn with passion.

1 Cor. 7:8,9

REGARDING SEPARATION.   To the married I give this command (not I, but the Lord): A wife must not separate from her husband. But if she does, she must remain unmarried or else be reconciled to her husband. And a husband must not divorce his wife.

1 Cor. 7:10,11

UNBELIEVING SPOUSES.   To the rest I say this (I, not the Lord): If any brother has a wife who is not a believer and she is willing to live with him, he must not divorce her. And if a woman has a husband who is not a believer and he is willing to live with her, she must not divorce him. For the unbelieving husband has been sanctified through his wife, and the unbelieving wife has been sanctified through her believing husband. Otherwise your children would be unclean, but as it is, they are holy.

But if the unbeliever leaves, let him do so. A believing man or woman is not bound in such circumstances; God has called us to live in peace. How do you know, wife, whether you will save your husband? Or, how do you know, husband, whether you will save your wife?

1 Cor. 7:12-16

REMAINING IN PRESENT STATE.   Nevertheless, each one should retain the place in life that the Lord assigned to him and to which God has called him. This is the rule I lay down in all the churches. Was a man already circumcised when he was called? He should not become uncircumcised. Was a man uncircumcised when he was called? He should not be circumcised. Circumcision is nothing and uncircumcision is nothing. Keeping God's commands is what counts. Each one should remain in the situation which he was in when God called him. Were you a slave when

1 Cor. 7:17-24

*f*Gen. 2:24   *g*Or "It is good for a man not to have sexual relations with a woman."

you were called? Don't let it trouble you—although if you can gain your freedom, do so. For he who was a slave when he was called by the Lord is the Lord's freedman; similarly, he who was a free man when he was called is Christ's slave. You were bought at a price; do not become slaves of men. Brothers, each man, as responsible to God, should remain in the situation God called him to.

1 Cor.
7:25-31

REASON FOR ADVICE.   Now about virgins: I have no command from the Lord, but I give a judgment as one who by the Lord's mercy is trustworthy. Because of the present crisis, I think that it is good for you to remain as you are. Are you married? Do not seek a divorce. Are you unmarried? Do not look for a wife. But if you do marry, you have not sinned; and if a virgin marries, she has not sinned. But those who marry will face many troubles in this life, and I want to spare you this.

What I mean, brothers, is that the time is short. From now on those who have wives should live as if they had none; those who mourn, as if they did not; those who are happy, as if they were not; those who buy something, as if it were not theirs to keep; those who use the things of the world, as if not engrossed in them. For this world in its present form is passing away.

1 Cor.
7:32-35

ADVANTAGES OF SINGLENESS.   I would like you to be free from concern. An unmarried man is concerned about the Lord's affairs—how he can please the Lord. But a married man is concerned about the affairs of this world—how he can please his wife—and his interests are divided. An unmarried woman or virgin is concerned about the Lord's affairs: Her aim is to be devoted to the Lord in both body and spirit. But a married woman is concerned about the affairs of this world—how she can please her husband. I am saying this for your own good, not to restrict you, but that you may live in a right way in undivided devotion to the Lord.

1 Cor.
7:36-38

REGARDING MARRIAGE.   If anyone thinks he is acting improperly toward the virgin he is engaged to, and if she is getting along in years and he feels he ought to marry, he should do as he wants. He is not sinning. They should get married. But the man who has settled the matter in his own mind, who is under no compulsion but has control over his own will, and who has made up his mind not to marry the virgin—this man also does the right thing. So then, he who marries the virgin does right, but he who does not marry her does even better.[h]

1 Cor.
7:39,40

REGARDING WIDOWS.   A woman is bound to her husband as long as he lives. But if her husband dies, she is free to marry anyone she wishes, but he must belong to the Lord. In my judgment, she is happier if she stays as she is—and I think that I too have the Spirit of God.

Regarding Mutual Submission

1 Cor.
8:1-3

KNOWLEDGE WITH LOVE.   Now about food sacrificed to idols: We know that we all possess knowledge.[i] Knowledge puffs up, but love

[h]Or [36]If anyone thinks he is not treating his daughter properly, and if she is getting along in years, and he feels she ought to marry, he should do as he wants. He is not sinning. He should let her get married. [37]But the man who has settled the matter in his own mind, who is under no compulsion but has control over his own will, and who has made up his mind to keep the virgin unmarried—this man also does the right thing. [38]So then, he who gives his virgin in marriage does right, but he who does not give her in marriage does even better.   [i]Or "We all possess knowledge," as you say

builds up. The man who thinks he knows something does not yet know as he ought to know. But the man who loves God is known by God.

KNOWLEDGE REGARDING IDOLS. So then, about eating food sacrificed to idols: We know that an idol is nothing at all in the world and that there is no God but one. For even if there are so-called gods, whether in heaven or on earth (as indeed there are many "gods" and many "lords"), yet for us there is but one God, the Father, from whom all things came and for whom we live; and there is but one Lord, Jesus Christ, through whom all things came and through whom we live.

1 Cor.
8:4-6

WEAK WITHOUT KNOWLEDGE. But not everyone knows this. Some people are still so accustomed to idols that when they eat such food they think of it as having been sacrificed to an idol, and since their conscience is weak, it is defiled. But food does not bring us near to God; we are no worse if we do not eat, and no better if we do.

1 Cor.
8:7,8

RESPONSIBILITY TOWARD WEAK. Be careful, however, that the exercise of your freedom does not become a stumbling block to the weak. For if anyone with a weak conscience sees you who have this knowledge eating in an idol's temple, won't he be emboldened to eat what has been sacrificed to idols? So this weak brother, for whom Christ died, is destroyed by your knowledge. When you sin against your brothers in this way and wound their weak conscience, you sin against Christ. Therefore, if what I eat causes my brother to fall into sin, I will never eat meat again, so that I will not cause him to fall.

1 Cor.
8:9-13

FREEDOM IS NOT THE ISSUE. Am I not free? Am I not an apostle? Have I not seen Jesus our Lord? Are you not the result of my work in the Lord? Even though I may not be an apostle to others, surely I am to you! For you are the seal of my apostleship in the Lord.

1 Cor.
9:1,2

RIGHTS ARE NOT THE ISSUE. This is my defense to those who sit in judgment on me. Don't we have the right to food and drink? Don't we have the right to take a believing wife along with us, as do the other apostles and the Lord's brothers and Cephas[j]? Or is it only I and Barnabas who must work for a living?

Who serves as a soldier at his own expense? Who plants a vineyard and does not eat of its grapes? Who tends a flock and does not drink of the milk?

1 Cor.
9:3-7

EXAMPLE OF A LAWFUL CLAIM. Do I say this merely from a human point of view? Doesn't the Law say the same thing? For it is written in the Law of Moses: "Do not muzzle an ox while it is treading out the grain."[k] Is it about oxen that God is concerned? Surely he says this for us, doesn't he? Yes, this was written for us, because when the plowman plows and the thresher threshes, they ought to do so in the hope of sharing in the harvest. If we have sown spiritual seed among you, is it too much if we reap a material harvest from you? If others have this right of support from you, shouldn't we have it all the more?

1 Cor.
9:8-12a

FORGOING RIGHTS. But we did not use this right. On the contrary, we put up with anything rather than hinder the gospel of Christ. Don't you know that those who work in the temple get their food from the temple, and those who serve at the altar share in what is offered on the altar? In

1 Cor.
9:12b-14

---

[j] That is, Peter   [k] Deut. 25:4

the same way, the Lord has commanded that those who preach the gospel should receive their living from the gospel.

1 Cor. 9:15-18

REWARDS FOR GIVING UP RIGHTS.   But I have not used any of these rights. And I am not writing this in the hope that you will do such things for me. I would rather die than have anyone deprive me of this boast. Yet when I preach the gospel, I cannot boast, for I am compelled to preach. Woe to me if I do not preach the gospel! If I preach voluntarily, I have a reward; if not voluntarily, I am simply discharging the trust committed to me. What then is my reward? Just this: that in preaching the gospel I may offer it free of charge, and so not make use of my rights in preaching it.

1 Cor. 9:19-23

CONCESSION VERSUS ASSERTION.   Though I am free and belong to no man, I make myself a slave to everyone, to win as many as possible. To the Jews I became like a Jew, to win the Jews. To those under the law I became like one under the law (though I myself am not under the law), so as to win those under the law. To those not having the law I became like one not having the law (though I am not free from God's law but am under Christ's law), so as to win those not having the law. To the weak I became weak, to win the weak. I have become all things to all men so that by all possible means I might save some. I do all this for the sake of the gospel, that I may share in its blessings.

1 Cor. 9:24-27

VALUE OF SELF-DISCIPLINE.   Do you not know that in a race all the runners run, but only one gets the prize? Run in such a way as to get the prize. Everyone who competes in the games goes into strict training. They do it to get a crown that will not last; but we do it to get a crown that will last forever. Therefore I do not run like a man running aimlessly; I do not fight like a man beating the air. No, I beat my body and make it my slave so that after I have preached to others, I myself will not be disqualified for the prize.

1 Cor. 10:1-5

EXAMPLE OF OVERCONFIDENCE.   For I do not want you to be ignorant of the fact, brothers, that our forefathers were all under the cloud and that they all passed through the sea. They were all baptized into Moses in the cloud and in the sea. They all ate the same spiritual food and drank the same spiritual drink; for they drank from the spiritual rock that accompanied them, and that rock was Christ. Nevertheless, God was not pleased with most of them; their bodies were scattered over the desert.

1 Cor. 10:6-10

EXAMPLE OF SELF-INDULGENCE.   Now these things occurred as examples[l] to keep us from setting our hearts on evil things as they did. Do not be idolaters, as some of them were; as it is written: "The people sat down to eat and drink and got up to indulge in pagan revelry."[m] We should not commit sexual immorality, as some of them did—and in one day twenty-three thousand of them died. We should not test the Lord, as some of them did—and were killed by snakes. And do not grumble, as some of them did—and were killed by the destroying angel.

1 Cor. 10:11-13

EXAMPLES ARE WARNING.   These things happened to them as examples and were written down as warnings for us, on whom the fulfillment of the ages has come. So, if you think you are standing firm, be careful that you don't fall! No temptation has seized you except what is common to man. And God is faithful; he will not let you be tempted beyond what you

[l]Or *types*   [m]Exodus 32:6

can bear. But when you are tempted, he will also provide a way out so that you can stand up under it.

ACTIONS INDICATE LOYALTIES. Therefore, my dear friends, flee from idolatry. I speak to sensible people; judge for yourselves what I say. Is not the cup of thanksgiving for which we give thanks a participation in the blood of Christ? And is not the bread that we break a participation in the body of Christ? Because there is one loaf, we, who are many, are one body, for we all partake of the one loaf.

1 Cor.
10:14-22

Consider the people of Israel: Do not those who eat the sacrifices participate in the altar? Do I mean then that a sacrifice offered to an idol is anything, or that an idol is anything? No, but the sacrifices of pagans are offered to demons, not to God, and I do not want you to be participants with demons. You cannot drink the cup of the Lord and the cup of demons too; you cannot have a part in both the Lord's table and the table of demons. Are we trying to arouse the Lord's jealousy? Are we stronger than he?

LIBERTY YIELDS FORBEARANCE. "Everything is permissible"—but not everything is beneficial. "Everything is permissible"—but not everything is constructive. Nobody should seek his own good, but the good of others.

1 Cor.
10:23-30

Eat anything sold in the meat market without raising questions of conscience, for, "The earth is the Lord's, and everything in it."[n]

If some unbeliever invites you to a meal and you want to go, eat whatever is put before you without raising questions of conscience. But if anyone says to you, "This has been offered in sacrifice," then do not eat it, both for the sake of the man who told you and for conscience' sake[o]—the other man's conscience, I mean, not yours. For why should my freedom be judged by another's conscience? If I take part in the meal with thankfulness, why am I denounced because of something I thank God for?

YIELD SELF FOR OTHERS' SAKE. So whether you eat or drink or whatever you do, do it all for the glory of God. Do not cause anyone to stumble, whether Jews, Greeks or the church of God—even as I try to please everybody in every way. For I am not seeking my own good but the good of many, so that they may be saved. Follow my example, as I follow the example of Christ.

1 Cor.
10:31-11:1

Regarding Role Distinctions

VEILS AS SYMBOL. I praise you for remembering me in everything and for holding to the teachings,[p] just as I passed them on to you.

1 Cor.
11:2-10

Now I want you to realize that the head of every man is Christ, and the head of the woman is man, and the head of Christ is God. Every man who prays or prophesies with his head covered dishonors his head. And every woman who prays or prophesies with her head uncovered dishonors her head—it is just as though her head were shaved. If a woman does not cover her head, she should have her hair cut off; and if it is a disgrace for a woman to have her hair cut or shaved off, she should cover her head.

---

[n]Psalm 24:1   [o]Some manuscripts conscience' sake, for "the earth is the Lord's and everything in it"   [p]Or traditions

A man ought not to cover his head,[q] since he is the image and glory of God; but the woman is the glory of man. For man did not come from woman, but woman from man; neither was man created for woman, but woman for man. For this reason, and because of the angels, the woman ought to have a sign of authority on her head.

1 Cor.
11:11-16

EQUALITY DESPITE DISTINCTIONS.   In the Lord, however, woman is not independent of man, nor is man independent of woman. For as woman came from man, so also man is born of woman. But everything comes from God. Judge for yourselves: Is it proper for a woman to pray to God with her head uncovered? Does not the very nature of things teach you that if a man has long hair, it is a disgrace to him, but that if a woman has long hair, it is her glory? For long hair is given to her as a covering. If anyone wants to be contentious about this, we have no other practice—nor do the churches of God.

Regarding Body Unity and Fellowship

1 Cor.
11:17-22

PROBLEM WITH FELLOWSHIP.   In the following directives I have no praise for you, for your meetings do more harm than good. In the first place, I hear that when you come together as a church, there are divisions among you, and to some extent I believe it. No doubt there have to be differences among you to show which of you have God's approval. When you come together, it is not the Lord's Supper you eat, for as you eat, each of you goes ahead without waiting for anybody else. One remains hungry, another gets drunk. Don't you have homes to eat and drink in? Or do you despise the church of God and humiliate those who have nothing? What shall I say to you? Shall I praise you for this? Certainly not!

1 Cor.
11:23-26

SUPPER AS REMINDER OF UNITY.   For I received from the Lord what I also passed on to you: The Lord Jesus, on the night he was betrayed, took bread, and when he had given thanks, he broke it and said, "This is my body, which is for you; do this in remembrance of me." In the same way, after supper he took the cup, saying, "This cup is the new covenant in my blood; do this, whenever you drink it, in remembrance of me." For whenever you eat this bread and drink this cup, you proclaim the Lord's death until he comes.

1 Cor.
11:27-34

EATING WITH VIEW TO UNITY.   Therefore, whoever eats the bread or drinks the cup of the Lord in an unworthy manner will be guilty of sinning against the body and blood of the Lord. A man ought to examine himself before he eats of the bread and drinks of the cup. For anyone who eats and drinks without recognizing the body of the Lord eats and drinks judgment on himself. That is why many among you are weak and sick, and a number of you have fallen asleep. But if we judged ourselves, we would not come under judgment. When we are judged by the Lord, we are being disciplined so that we will not be condemned with the world.

So then, my brothers, when you come together to eat, wait for each other.

[q]Or [4]Every man who prays or prophesies with long hair dishonors his head. [5]And every woman who prays or prophesies with no covering of hair, on her head dishonors her head—she is just like one of the "shorn women." [6]If a woman has no covering, let her be for now with short hair, but since it is a disgrace for a woman to have her hair shorn or shaved, she should grow it again. [7]A man ought not to have long hair

If anyone is hungry, he should eat at home, so that when you meet together it may not result in judgment.

And when I come I will give further directions.

Regarding Spiritual Gifts

SOURCE OF GIFTS.   Now about spiritual gifts, brothers, I do not want you to be ignorant. You know that when you were pagans, somehow or other you were influenced and led astray to mute idols. Therefore I tell you that no one who is speaking by the Spirit of God says, "Jesus be cursed," and no one can say, "Jesus is Lord," except by the Holy Spirit.

1 Cor.
12:1-3

DESPITE VARIETY, SAME SOURCE.   There are different kinds of gifts, but the same Spirit. There are different kinds of service, but the same Lord. There are different kinds of working, but the same God works all of them in all men.

Now to each one the manifestation of the Spirit is given for the common good. To one there is given through the Spirit the message of wisdom, to another the message of knowledge by means of the same Spirit, to another faith by the same Spirit, to another gifts of healing by that one Spirit, to another miraculous powers, to another prophecy, to another distinguishing between spirits, to another speaking in different kinds of tongues,[r] and to still another the interpretation of tongues.[r] All these are the work of one and the same Spirit, and he gives them to each one, just as he determines.

1 Cor.
12:4-11

BODY HAS MANY MEMBERS.   The body is a unit, though it is made up of many parts; and though all its parts are many, they form one body. So it is with Christ. For we were all baptized by[s] one Spirit into one body— whether Jews or Greeks, slave or free—and we were all given the one Spirit to drink.

Now the body is not made up of one part but of many.

1 Cor.
12:12-14

BODY IS DIVERSE.   If the foot should say, "Because I am not a hand, I do not belong to the body," it would not for that reason cease to be part of the body. And if the ear should say, "Because I am not an eye, I do not belong to the body," it would not for that reason cease to be part of the body. If the whole body were an eye, where would the sense of hearing be? If the whole body were an ear, where would the sense of smell be? But in fact God has arranged the parts in the body, every one of them, just as he wanted them to be. If they were all one part, where would the body be? As it is, there are many parts, but one body.

The eye cannot say to the hand, "I don't need you!" And the head cannot say to the feet, "I don't need you!"

1 Cor.
12:15-21

EVERY MEMBER IMPORTANT.   On the contrary, those parts of the body that seem to be weaker are indispensable, and the parts that we think are less honorable we treat with special honor. And the parts that are unpresentable are treated with special modesty, while our presentable parts need no special treatment. But God has combined the members of the body and has given greater honor to the parts that lacked it, so that there should be no division in the body, but that its parts should have equal

1 Cor.
12:22-26

[r]Or *languages*   [s]Or *with; or in*

concern for each other. If one part suffers, every part suffers with it; if one part is honored, every part rejoices with it.

1 Cor.
12:27-31

CHURCH NEEDS DIVERSITY.   Now you are the body of Christ, and each one of you is a part of it. And in the church God has appointed first of all apostles, second prophets, third teachers, then workers of miracles, also those having gifts of healing, those able to help others, those with gifts of administration, and those speaking in different kinds of tongues. Are all apostles? Are all prophets? Are all teachers? Do all work miracles? Do all have gifts of healing? Do all speak in tongues[t]? Do all interpret? But eagerly desire[u] the greater gifts.

And now I will show you the most excellent way.

1 Cor.
13:1-3

LOVE IS GREATEST GIFT.   If I speak in the tongues[v] of men and of angels, but have not love, I am only a resounding gong or a clanging cymbal. If I have the gift of prophecy and can fathom all mysteries and all knowledge, and if I have a faith that can move mountains, but have not love, I am nothing. If I give all I possess to the poor and surrender my body to the flames,[w] but have not love, I gain nothing.

1 Cor.
13:4-7

THE QUALITIES OF LOVE.   Love is patient, love is kind. It does not envy, it does not boast, it is not proud. It is not rude, it is not self-seeking, it is not easily angered, it keeps no record of wrongs. Love does not delight in evil but rejoices with the truth. It always protects, always trusts, always hopes, always perseveres.

1 Cor.
13:8-13

LOVE WILL OUTLAST GIFTS.   Love never fails. But where there are prophecies, they will cease; where there are tongues, they will be stilled; where there is knowledge, it will pass away. For we know in part and we prophesy in part, but when perfection comes, the imperfect disappears. When I was a child, I talked like a child, I thought like a child, I reasoned like a child. When I became a man, I put childish ways behind me. Now we see but a poor reflection as in a mirror; then we shall see face to face. Now I know in part; then I shall know fully, even as I am fully known.

And now these three remain: faith, hope and love. But the greatest of these is love.

1 Cor.
14:1-5

PROPHECY VERSUS TONGUES.   Follow the way of love and eagerly desire spiritual gifts, especially the gift of prophecy. For anyone who speaks in a tongue[x] does not speak to men but to God. Indeed, no one understands him; he utters mysteries with his spirit.[y] But everyone who prophesies speaks to men for their strengthening, encouragement and comfort. He who speaks in a tongue edifies himself, but he who prophesies edifies the church. I would like every one of you to speak in tongues,[z] but I would rather have you prophesy. He who prophesies is greater than one who speaks in tongues,[z] unless he interprets, so that the church may be edified.

1 Cor.
14:6-12

TONGUES NEED INTERPRETATION.   Now, brothers, if I come to you and speak in tongues, what good will I be to you, unless I bring you some revelation or knowledge or prophecy or word of instruction? Even in the case of lifeless things that make sounds, such as the flute or harp, how will

---

[t]Or *other languages*   [u]Or *But you are eagerly desiring*   [v]Or *languages*   [w]Some early manuscripts *body that I may boast*   [x]Or *another language*; also in verses 4, 13, 14, 19, 26 and 27   [y]Or *by the Spirit*   [z]Or *other languages*; also in verses 6, 18, 22, 23 and 39

anyone know what tune is being played unless there is a distinction in the notes? Again, if the trumpet does not sound a clear call, who will get ready for battle? So it is with you. Unless you speak intelligible words with your tongue, how will anyone know what you are saying? You will just be speaking into the air. Undoubtedly there are all sorts of languages in the world, yet none of them is without meaning. If then I do not grasp the meaning of what someone is saying, I am a foreigner to the speaker, and he is a foreigner to me. So it is with you. Since you are eager to have spiritual gifts, try to excel in gifts that build up the church.

TONGUES CANNOT EDIFY.   For this reason anyone who speaks in a tongue should pray that he may interpret what he says. For if I pray in a tongue, my spirit prays, but my mind is unfruitful. So what shall I do? I will pray with my spirit, but I will also pray with my mind; I will sing with my spirit, but I will also sing with my mind. If you are praising God with your spirit, how can one who finds himself among those who do not understand[a] say "Amen" to your thanksgiving, since he does not know what you are saying? You may be giving thanks well enough, but the other man is not edified.

1 Cor. 14:13-19

I thank God that I speak in tongues more than all of you. But in the church I would rather speak five intelligible words to instruct others than ten thousand words in a tongue.

TONGUES ARE SIGN.   Brothers, stop thinking like children. In regard to evil be infants, but in your thinking be adults. In the Law it is written:

1 Cor. 14:20-22

> "Through men of strange tongues
>   and through the lips of foreigners
> I will speak to this people,
>   but even then they will not listen to me," [b]

says the Lord.
Tongues, then, are a sign, not for believers but for unbelievers; prophecy, however, is for believers, not for unbelievers.

PROPHECY TEACHES.   So if the whole church comes together and everyone speaks in tongues, and some who do not understand[c] or some unbelievers come in, will they not say that you are out of your mind? But if an unbeliever or someone who does not understand[d] comes in while everybody is prophesying, he will be convinced by all that he is a sinner and will be judged by all, and the secrets of his heart will be laid bare. So he will fall down and worship God, exclaiming, "God is really among you!"

1 Cor. 14:23-25

ORDERLY USE OF GIFTS.   What then shall we say, brothers? When you come together, everyone has a hymn, or a word of instruction, a revelation, a tongue or an interpretation. All of these must be done for the strengthening of the church. If anyone speaks in a tongue, two—or at the most three—should speak, one at a time, and someone must interpret. If there is no interpreter, the speaker should keep quiet in the church and speak to himself and God.

1 Cor. 14:26-33a

Two or three prophets should speak, and the others should weigh carefully what is said. And if a revelation comes to someone who is sitting down, the first speaker should stop. For you can all prophesy in turn so

---

[a]Or among the inquirers   [b]Isaiah 28:11,12   [c]Or some inquirers   [d]Or or some inquirer

that everyone may be instructed and encouraged. The spirits of prophets are subject to the control of prophets. For God is not a God of disorder but of peace.

1 Cor.
14:33b-36

WOMEN NOT TO LEAD.   As in all the congregations of the saints, women should remain silent in the churches. They are not allowed to speak, but must be in submission, as the Law says. If they want to inquire about something, they should ask their own husbands at home; for it is disgraceful for a woman to speak in the church.

Did the word of God originate with you? Or are you the only people it has reached?

1 Cor.
14:37-40

DIRECTIONS ARE LORD'S COMMAND.   If anybody thinks he is a prophet or spiritually gifted, let him acknowledge that what I am writing to you is the Lord's command. If he ignores this, he himself will be ignored.*e*

Therefore, my brothers, be eager to prophesy, and do not forbid speaking in tongues. But everything should be done in a fitting and orderly way.

Regarding the Resurrection

1 Cor.
15:1-11

RESURRECTION A PROVABLE FACT.   Now, brothers, I want to remind you of the gospel I preached to you, which you received and on which you have taken your stand. By this gospel you are saved, if you hold firmly to the word I preached to you. Otherwise, you have believed in vain.

For what I received I passed on to you as of first importance*f*: that Christ died for our sins according to the Scriptures, that he was buried, that he was raised on the third day according to the Scriptures, and that he appeared to Peter,*g* and then to the Twelve. After that, he appeared to more than five hundred of the brothers at the same time, most of whom are still living, though some have fallen asleep. Then he appeared to James, then to all the apostles, and last of all he appeared to me also, as to one abnormally born.

For I am the least of the apostles and do not even deserve to be called an apostle, because I persecuted the church of God. But by the grace of God I am what I am, and his grace to me was not without effect. No, I worked harder than all of them—yet not I, but the grace of God that was with me. Whether, then, it was I or they, this is what we preach, and this is what you believed.

1 Cor.
15:12-19

RESURRECTION IS CENTRAL.   But if it is preached that Christ has been raised from the dead, how can some of you say that there is no resurrection of the dead? If there is no resurrection of the dead, then not even Christ has been raised. And if Christ has not been raised, our preaching is useless and so is your faith. More than that, we are then found to be false witnesses about God, for we have testified about God that he raised Christ from the dead. But he did not raise him if in fact the dead are not raised. For if the dead are not raised, then Christ has not been raised either. And if Christ has not been raised, your faith is futile; you are still in your sins. Then those also who have fallen asleep in Christ are lost. If only for this life we have hope in Christ, we are to be pitied more than all men.

---

*e*Some manuscripts *If he is ignorant of this, let him be ignorant*   *f*Or *you at the first*
*g*Greek *Cephas*

OUR RESURRECTION CERTAIN.   But Christ has indeed been raised   1 Cor.
from the dead, the firstfruits of those who have fallen asleep. For since   15:20-28
death came through a man, the resurrection of the dead comes also
through a man. For as in Adam all die, so in Christ all will be made alive.
But each in his own turn: Christ, the firstfruits; then, when he comes,
those who belong to him. Then the end will come, when he hands over
the kingdom to God the Father after he has destroyed all dominion,
authority and power. For he must reign until he has put all his enemies
under his feet. The last enemy to be destroyed is death. For he "has put
everything under his feet."[h] Now when it says that "everything" has been
put under him, it is clear that this does not include God himself, who put
everything under Christ. When he has done this, then the Son himself
will be made subject to him who put everything under him, so that God
may be all in all.

CONDUCT BASED UPON HOPE.   Now if there is no resurrection, what   1 Cor.
will those do who are baptized for the dead? If the dead are not raised at   15:29-34
all, why are people baptized for them? And as for us, why do we endanger ourselves every hour? I die every day—I mean that, brothers—just as
surely as I glory over you in Christ Jesus our Lord. If I fought wild beasts
in Ephesus for merely human reasons, what have I gained? If the dead are
not raised,

> "Let us eat and drink,
>   for tomorrow we die." [i]

Do not be misled: "Bad company corrupts good character." Come back
to your senses as you ought, and stop sinning; for there are some who are
ignorant of God—I say this to your shame.

NEW BODIES IN RESURRECTION.   But someone may ask, "How are   1 Cor.
the dead raised? With what kind of body will they come?" How foolish!   15:35-41
What you sow does not come to life unless it dies. When you sow, you do
not plant the body that will be, but just a seed, perhaps of wheat or of
something else. But God gives it a body as he has determined, and to each
kind of seed he gives its own body. All flesh is not the same: Men have
one kind of flesh, animals have another, birds another and fish another.
There are also heavenly bodies and there are earthly bodies; but the
splendor of the heavenly bodies is one kind, and the splendor of the
earthly bodies is another. The sun has one kind of splendor, the moon
another and the stars another; and star differs from star in splendor.

BODIES TO BE SPIRITUAL.   So will it be with the resurrection of the   1 Cor.
dead. The body that is sown is perishable, it is raised imperishable; it is   15:42-50
sown in dishonor, it is raised in glory; it is sown in weakness, it is raised
in power; it is sown a natural body, it is raised a spiritual body.
    If there is a natural body, there is also a spiritual body. So it is written:
"The first man Adam became a living being"[j]; the last Adam, a life-giving
spirit. The spiritual did not come first, but the natural, and after that the
spiritual. The first man was of the dust of the earth, the second man from
heaven. As was the earthly man, so are those who are of the earth; and as
is the man from heaven, so also are those who are of heaven. And just as

---

[h]Psalm 8:6   [i]Isaiah 22:13   [j]Gen. 2:7

we have borne the likeness of the earthly man, so shall we[k] bear the likeness of the man from heaven.

I declare to you, brothers, that flesh and blood cannot inherit the kingdom of God, nor does the perishable inherit the imperishable.

**1 Cor.
15:51-53**

RESURRECTION AND GLORIFICATION.   Listen, I tell you a mystery: We will not all sleep, but we will all be changed—in a flash, in the twinkling of an eye, at the last trumpet. For the trumpet will sound, the dead will be raised imperishable, and we will be changed. For the perishable must clothe itself with the imperishable, and the mortal with immortality.

**1 Cor.
15:54-58**

CONFIDENCE IN DEATH.   When the perishable has been clothed with the imperishable, and the mortal with immortality, then the saying that is written will come true: "Death has been swallowed up in victory."[l]

"Where, O death, is your victory?
Where, O death, is your sting?"[m]

The sting of death is sin, and the power of sin is the law. But thanks be to God! He gives us the victory through our Lord Jesus Christ.

Therefore, my dear brothers, stand firm. Let nothing move you. Always give yourselves fully to the work of the Lord, because you know that your labor in the Lord is not in vain.

Closing Personal Thoughts

**1 Cor.
16:1-4**

COLLECTION FOR JERUSALEM.   Now about the collection for God's people: Do what I told the Galatian churches to do. On the first day of every week, each one of you should set aside a sum of money in keeping with his income, saving it up, so that when I come no collections will have to be made. Then, when I arrive, I will give letters of introduction to the men you approve and send them with your gift to Jerusalem. If it seems advisable for me to go also, they will accompany me.

**1 Cor.
16:5-9**

PAUL'S FUTURE PLANS.   After I go through Macedonia, I will come to you—for I will be going through Macedonia. Perhaps I will stay with you awhile, or even spend the winter, so that you can help me on my journey, wherever I go. I do not want to see you now and make only a passing visit; I hope to spend some time with you, if the Lord permits. But I will stay on at Ephesus until Pentecost, because a great door for effective work has opened to me, and there are many who oppose me.

**1 Cor.
16:10-12**

ABOUT TIMOTHY AND APOLLOS.   If Timothy comes, see to it that he has nothing to fear while he is with you, for he is carrying on the work of the Lord, just as I am. No one, then, should refuse to accept him. Send him on his way in peace so that he may return to me. I am expecting him along with the brothers.

Now about our brother Apollos: I strongly urged him to go to you with the brothers. He was quite unwilling to go now, but he will go when he has the opportunity.

**1 Cor.
16:13,14**

GENERAL EXHORTATIONS.   Be on your guard; stand firm in the faith; be men of courage; be strong. Do everything in love.

[k]Some early manuscripts *so let us*   [l]Isaiah 25:8   [m]Hosea 13:14

REGARD FOR FELLOW WORKERS.   You know that the household of
Stephanas were the first converts in Achaia, and they have devoted themselves to the service of the saints. I urge you, brothers, to submit to such as
these and to everyone who joins in the work, and labors at it. I was glad
when Stephanas, Fortunatus and Achaicus arrived, because they have
supplied what was lacking from you. For they refreshed my spirit and
yours also. Such men deserve recognition.

1 Cor.
16:15-18

GREETINGS.   The churches in the province of Asia send you greetings.
Aquila and Priscilla[n] greet you warmly in the Lord, and so does the
church that meets at their house. All the brothers here send you greetings.
Greet one another with a holy kiss.

1 Cor.
16:19,20

BENEDICTION.   I, Paul, write this greeting in my own hand.
    If anyone does not love the Lord—a curse be on him. Come, O Lord[o]!
    The grace of the Lord Jesus be with you.
    My love to all of you in Christ Jesus. Amen.[p]

1 Cor.
16:21-24

>   If Paul expects a quick response to his letter, apparently it does not come.
> In the meantime, the historical record in Acts returns to Paul's final days in
> Ephesus.

SILVERSMITHS INCITED.   About that time there arose a great disturbance about the Way. A silversmith named Demetrius, who made silver
shrines of Artemis, brought in no little business for the craftsmen. He
called them together, along with the workmen in related trades, and said:
"Men, you know we receive a good income from this business. And you
see and hear how this fellow Paul has convinced and led astray large numbers of people here in Ephesus and in practically the whole province of
Asia. He says that man-made gods are no gods at all. There is danger not
only that our trade will lose its good name, but also that the temple of the
great goddess Artemis will be discredited, and the goddess herself, who is
worshiped throughout the province of Asia and the world, will be robbed
of her divine majesty."

Acts
19:23-27
Ephesus

RIOT ENSUES.   When they heard this, they were furious and began
shouting: "Great is Artemis of the Ephesians!" Soon the whole city was in
an uproar. The people seized Gaius and Aristarchus, Paul's traveling companions from Macedonia, and rushed as one man into the theater. Paul
wanted to appear before the crowd, but the disciples would not let him.
Even some of the officials of the province, friends of Paul, sent him a message begging him not to venture into the theater.
    The assembly was in confusion: Some were shouting one thing, some
another. Most of the people did not even know why they were there. The
Jews pushed Alexander to the front, and some of the crowd shouted
instructions to him. He motioned for silence in order to make a defense
before the people. But when they realized he was a Jew, they all shouted
in unison for about two hours: "Great is Artemis of the Ephesians!"

Acts
19:28-34

TOWN CLERK CALMS CROWD.   The city clerk quieted the crowd and
said: "Men of Ephesus, doesn't all the world know that the city of Ephesus
is the guardian of the temple of the great Artemis and of her image, which

Acts
19:35-41

[n]Greek *Prisca*, a variant of *Priscilla*   [o]In Aramaic the expression *Come, O Lord* is
Marana tha.   [p]Some manuscripts do not have *Amen*.

fell from heaven? Therefore, since these facts are undeniable, you ought to be quiet and not do anything rash. You have brought these men here, though they have neither robbed temples nor blasphemed our goddess. If, then, Demetrius and his fellow craftsmen have a grievance against anybody, the courts are open and there are proconsuls. They can press charges. If there is anything further you want to bring up, it must be settled in a legal assembly. As it is, we are in danger of being charged with rioting because of today's events. In that case we would not be able to account for this commotion, since there is no reason for it." After he had said this, he dismissed the assembly.

Acts 20:1 To Macedonia PAUL LEAVES EPHESUS. When the uproar had ended, Paul sent for the disciples and, after encouraging them, said good-by and set out for Macedonia.

Second Letter to the Corinthians

*T*he confrontation with Demetrius and the other craftsmen is undoubtedly not the only reason Paul left Ephesus. Understandably, Paul must be anxious to hear from Titus regarding the Corinthians' reaction to his previous letter, so it appears that Paul decides to go on to Troas, where he hopes to meet Titus. Perhaps disappointed at not finding Titus there, Paul goes on to Macedonia, where Titus joins him. There Paul writes his final letter to the Corinthians, probably about A.D. 56-57. In the letter he explains why he has not visited them a third time, as he had hoped, and shares with them at great length the sense of fulfillment he has in both his ministry and in them personally. At the end of his letter (10-13), Paul's tone changes abruptly as he once again defends his apostleship and personal character. This letter is sent with Titus and others who are returning to Corinth to receive funds being given for relief of the brethren in Judea who are in need of financial assistance.

2 Cor. 1:1,2 SALUTATION. Paul, an apostle of Christ Jesus by the will of God, and Timothy our brother,

To the church of God in Corinth, together with all the saints throughout Achaia:

Grace and peace to you from God our Father and the Lord Jesus Christ.

2 Cor. 1:3-7 GRATITUDE FOR GOD'S COMFORT. Praise be to the God and Father of our Lord Jesus Christ, the Father of compassion and the God of all comfort, who comforts us in all our troubles, so that we can comfort those in any trouble with the comfort we ourselves have received from God. For just as the sufferings of Christ flow over into our lives, so also through Christ our comfort overflows. If we are distressed, it is for your comfort and salvation; if we are comforted, it is for your comfort, which produces in you patient endurance of the same sufferings we suffer. And our hope for you is firm, because we know that just as you share in our sufferings, so also you share in our comfort.

2 Cor. 1:8-11 EARLIER DESPAIR DISSIPATED. We do not want you to be uninformed, brothers, about the hardships we suffered in the province of Asia. We were under great pressure, far beyond our ability to endure, so that we despaired even of life. Indeed, in our hearts we felt the sentence of death. But this happened that we might not rely on ourselves but on God, who raises the dead. He has delivered us from such a deadly peril, and he will deliver us. On him we have set our hope that he will continue to deliver us, as you help us by your prayers. Then many will give thanks on our[q] behalf for the gracious favor granted us in answer to the prayers of many.

HOPE FOR POSITIVE VIEW.   Now this is our boast: Our conscience testifies that we have conducted ourselves in the world, and especially in our relations with you, in the holiness and sincerity that are from God. We have done so not according to worldly wisdom but according to God's grace. For we do not write you anything you cannot read or understand. And I hope that, as you have understood us in part, you will come to understand fully that you can boast of us just as we will boast of you in the day of the Lord Jesus.

2 Cor.
1:12-14

TRAVEL PLANS NOT WHIMSICAL.   Because I was confident of this, I planned to visit you first so that you might benefit twice. I planned to visit you on my way to Macedonia and to come back to you from Macedonia, and then to have you send me on my way to Judea. When I planned this, did I do it lightly? Or do I make my plans in a worldly manner so that in the same breath I say, "Yes, yes" and "No, no"?

2 Cor.
1:15-22

But as surely as God is faithful, our message to you is not "Yes" and "No." For the Son of God, Jesus Christ, who was preached among you by me and Silas[r] and Timothy, was not "Yes" and "No," but in him it has always been "Yes." For no matter how many promises God has made, they are "Yes" in Christ. And so through him the "Amen" is spoken by us to the glory of God. Now it is God who makes both us and you stand firm in Christ. He anointed us, set his seal of ownership on us, and put his Spirit in our hearts as a deposit, guaranteeing what is to come.

REASONS FOR LETTER.   I call God as my witness that it was in order to spare you that I did not return to Corinth. Not that we lord it over your faith, but we work with you for your joy, because it is by faith you stand firm. So I made up my mind that I would not make another painful visit to you. For if I grieve you, who is left to make me glad but you whom I have grieved? I wrote as I did so that when I came I should not be distressed by those who ought to make me rejoice. I had confidence in all of you, that you would all share my joy. For I wrote you out of great distress and anguish of heart and with many tears, not to grieve you but to let you know the depth of my love for you.

2 Cor.
1:23-2:4

TROUBLEMAKERS TO BE FORGIVEN.   If anyone has caused grief, he has not so much grieved me as he has grieved all of you, to some extent—not to put it too severely. The punishment inflicted on him by the majority is sufficient for him. Now instead, you ought to forgive and comfort him, so that he will not be overwhelmed by excessive sorrow. I urge you, therefore, to reaffirm your love for him. The reason I wrote you was to see if you would stand the test and be obedient in everything. If you forgive anyone, I also forgive him. And what I have forgiven—if there was anything to forgive—I have forgiven in the sight of Christ for your sake, in

2 Cor.
2:5-11

[q]Many manuscripts *your*   [r]Greek *Silvanus*, a variant of *Silas*

order that Satan might not outwit us. For we are not unaware of his schemes.

2 Cor. 2:12,13

EAGERNESS FOR TITUS' REPORT.   Now when I went to Troas to preach the gospel of Christ and found that the Lord had opened a door for me, I still had no peace of mind, because I did not find my brother Titus there. So I said good-by to them and went on to Macedonia.

Regarding Paul's Ministry

2 Cor. 2:14-17

SUCCESS OF MINISTRY.   But thanks be to God, who always leads us in triumphal procession in Christ and through us spreads everywhere the fragrance of the knowledge of him. For we are to God the aroma of Christ among those who are being saved and those who are perishing. To the one we are the smell of death; to the other, the fragrance of life. And who is equal to such a task? Unlike so many, we do not peddle the word of God for profit. On the contrary, in Christ we speak before God with sincerity, like men sent from God.

2 Cor. 3:1-3

THEY ARE PAUL'S PROOF.   Are we beginning to commend ourselves again? Or do we need, like some people, letters of recommendation to you or from you? You yourselves are our letter, written on our hearts, known and read by everybody. You show that you are a letter from Christ, the result of our ministry, written not with ink but with the Spirit of the living God, not on tablets of stone but on tablets of human hearts.

2 Cor. 3:4-6

SOURCE OF PAUL'S COMPETENCE.   Such confidence as this is ours through Christ before God. Not that we are competent in ourselves to claim anything for ourselves, but our competence comes from God. He has made us competent as ministers of a new covenant—not of the letter but of the Spirit; for the letter kills, but the Spirit gives life.

2 Cor. 3:7-11

SPLENDOR OF GOSPEL MESSAGE.   Now if the ministry that brought death, which was engraved in letters on stone, came with glory, so that the Israelites could not look steadily at the face of Moses because of its glory, fading though it was, will not the ministry of the Spirit be even more glorious? If the ministry that condemns men is glorious, how much more glorious is the ministry that brings righteousness! For what was glorious has no glory now in comparison with the surpassing glory. And if what was fading away came with glory, how much greater is the glory of that which lasts!

2 Cor. 3:12-18

UNVEILING OF THE SPIRIT.   Therefore, since we have such a hope, we are very bold. We are not like Moses, who would put a veil over his face to keep the Israelites from gazing at it while the radiance was fading away. But their minds were made dull, for to this day the same veil remains when the old covenant is read. It has not been removed, because only in Christ is it taken away. Even to this day when Moses is read, a veil covers their hearts. But whenever anyone turns to the Lord, the veil is taken away. Now the Lord is the Spirit, and where the Spirit of the Lord is, there is freedom. And we, who with unveiled faces all reflect[s] the Lord's glory, are being transformed into his likeness with ever-increasing glory, which comes from the Lord, who is the Spirit.

[s]Or *contemplate*

GOSPEL PREACHED HONESTLY.   Therefore, since through God's mercy we have this ministry, we do not lose heart. Rather, we have renounced secret and shameful ways; we do not use deception, nor do we distort the word of God. On the contrary, by setting forth the truth plainly we commend ourselves to every man's conscience in the sight of God. And even if our gospel is veiled, it is veiled to those who are perishing. The god of this age has blinded the minds of unbelievers, so that they cannot see the light of the gospel of the glory of Christ, who is the image of God. For we do not preach ourselves, but Jesus Christ as Lord, and ourselves as your servants for Jesus' sake. For God, who said, "Let light shine out of darkness," [t] made his light shine in our hearts to give us the light of the knowledge of the glory of God in the face of Christ.

2 Cor. 4:1-6

PERSECUTION IS PROOF.   But we have this treasure in jars of clay to show that this all-surpassing power is from God and not from us. We are hard pressed on every side, but not crushed; perplexed, but not in despair; persecuted, but not abandoned; struck down, but not destroyed. We always carry around in our body the death of Jesus, so that the life of Jesus may also be revealed in our body. For we who are alive are always being given over to death for Jesus' sake, so that his life may be revealed in our mortal body. So then, death is at work in us, but life is at work in you.

2 Cor. 4:7-12

PREACHING FROM FAITH.   It is written: "I believed; therefore I have spoken." [u] With that same spirit of faith we also believe and therefore speak, because we know that the one who raised the Lord Jesus from the dead will also raise us with Jesus and present us with you in his presence. All this is for your benefit, so that the grace that is reaching more and more people may cause thanksgiving to overflow to the glory of God.

2 Cor. 4:13-15

INNER STRENGTH.   Therefore we do not lose heart. Though outwardly we are wasting away, yet inwardly we are being renewed day by day. For our light and momentary troubles are achieving for us an eternal glory that far outweighs them all. So we fix our eyes not on what is seen, but on what is unseen. For what is seen is temporary, but what is unseen is eternal.

2 Cor. 4:16-18

LONGING FOR ETERNAL DWELLING.   Now we know that if the earthly tent we live in is destroyed, we have a building from God, an eternal house in heaven, not built by human hands. Meanwhile we groan, longing to be clothed with our heavenly dwelling, because when we are clothed, we will not be found naked. For while we are in this tent, we groan and are burdened, because we do not wish to be unclothed but to be clothed with our heavenly dwelling, so that what is mortal may be swallowed up by life. Now it is God who has made us for this very purpose and has given us the Spirit as a deposit, guaranteeing what is to come.

2 Cor. 5:1-5

COURAGE FACING DEATH.   Therefore we are always confident and know that as long as we are at home in the body we are away from the Lord. We live by faith, not by sight. We are confident, I say, and would prefer to be away from the body and at home with the Lord. So we make it our goal to please him, whether we are at home in the body or away from it. For we must all appear before the judgment seat of Christ, that each one may receive what is due him for the things done while in the body, whether good or bad.

2 Cor. 5:6-10

[t]Gen. 1:3   [u]Psalm 116:10

2 Cor.
5:11-15

BOASTING FOR THEIR SAKE. Since, then, we know what it is to fear the Lord, we try to persuade men. What we are is plain to God, and I hope it is also plain to your conscience. We are not trying to commend ourselves to you again, but are giving you an opportunity to take pride in us, so that you can answer those who take pride in what is seen rather than in what is in the heart. If we are out of our mind, it is for the sake of God; if we are in our right mind, it is for you. For Christ's love compels us, because we are convinced that one died for all, and therefore all died. And he died for all, that those who live should no longer live for themselves but for him who died for them and was raised again.

2 Cor.
5:16-6:2

MINISTRY OF RECONCILIATION. So from now on we regard no one from a worldly point of view. Though we once regarded Christ in this way, we do so no longer. Therefore, if anyone is in Christ, he is a new creation; the old has gone, the new has come! All this is from God, who reconciled us to himself through Christ and gave us the ministry of reconciliation: that God was reconciling the world to himself in Christ, not counting men's sins against them. And he has committed to us the message of reconciliation. We are therefore Christ's ambassadors, as though God were making his appeal through us. We implore you on Christ's behalf: Be reconciled to God. God made him who had no sin to be sin^v for us, so that in him we might become the righteousness of God. As God's fellow workers we urge you not to receive God's grace in vain. For he says,

> "In the time of my favor I heard you,
>   and in the day of salvation I helped you."^{w}

I tell you, now is the time of God's favor, now is the day of salvation.

2 Cor.
6:3-10

SUBMISSION WHERE AFFLICTION. We put no stumbling block in anyone's path, so that our ministry will not be discredited. Rather, as servants of God we commend ourselves in every way: in great endurance; in troubles, hardships and distresses; in beatings, imprisonments and riots; in hard work, sleepless nights and hunger; in purity, understanding, patience and kindness; in the Holy Spirit and in sincere love; in truthful speech and in the power of God; with weapons of righteousness in the right hand and in the left; through glory and dishonor, bad report and good report; genuine, yet regarded as impostors; known, yet regarded as unknown; dying, and yet we live on; beaten, and yet not killed; sorrowful, yet always rejoicing; poor, yet making many rich; having nothing, and yet possessing everything.

2 Cor.
6:11-13

CALL FOR FULL ACCEPTANCE. We have spoken freely to you, Corinthians, and opened wide our hearts to you. We are not withholding our affection from you, but you are withholding yours from us. As a fair exchange—I speak as to my children—open wide your hearts also.

2 Cor.
6:14-7:1

THOSE WHO OPPOSE GOSPEL. Do not be yoked together with unbelievers. For what do righteousness and wickedness have in common? Or what fellowship can light have with darkness? What harmony is there between Christ and Belial^x? What does a believer have in common with an unbeliever? What agreement is there between the temple of God and idols? For we are the temple of the living God. As God has said: "I will live

---

^{v}Or *be a sin offering* ^{w}Isaiah 49:8 ^{x}Greek *Beliar*, a variant of *Belial*

with them and walk among them, and I will be their God, and they will be my people."*y*

> "Therefore come out from them
>   and be separate,
>   says the Lord.
> Touch no unclean thing,
>   and I will receive you."*z*
> "I will be a Father to you,
>   and you will be my sons and daughters,
>   says the Lord Almighty."*a*

Since we have these promises, dear friends, let us purify ourselves from everything that contaminates body and spirit, perfecting holiness out of reverence for God.

PLEADING FOR FELLOWSHIP.   Make room for us in your hearts. We have wronged no one, we have corrupted no one, we have exploited no one. I do not say this to condemn you; I have said before that you have such a place in our hearts that we would live or die with you. I have great confidence in you; I take great pride in you. I am greatly encouraged; in all our troubles my joy knows no bounds.

2 Cor. 7:2-4

JOY AT NEWS OF ATTITUDE.   For when we came into Macedonia, this body of ours had no rest, but we were harassed at every turn—conflicts on the outside, fears within. But God, who comforts the downcast, comforted us by the coming of Titus, and not only by his coming but also by the comfort you had given him. He told us about your longing for me, your deep sorrow, your ardent concern for me, so that my joy was greater than ever.

2 Cor. 7:5-7

JOY IN THEIR ZEAL.   Even if I caused you sorrow by my letter, I do not regret it. Though I did regret it—I see that my letter hurt you, but only for a little while—yet now I am happy, not because you were made sorry, but because your sorrow led you to repentance. For you became sorrowful as God intended and so were not harmed in any way by us. Godly sorrow brings repentance that leads to salvation and leaves no regret, but worldly sorrow brings death. See what this godly sorrow has produced in you: what earnestness, what eagerness to clear yourselves, what indignation, what alarm, what longing, what concern, what readiness to see justice done. At every point you have proved yourselves to be innocent in this matter. So even though I wrote to you, it was not on account of the one who did the wrong or of the injured party, but rather that before God you could see for yourselves how devoted to us you are. By all this we are encouraged.

2 Cor. 7:8-13a

JOY REGARDING TITUS.   In addition to our own encouragement, we were especially delighted to see how happy Titus was, because his spirit has been refreshed by all of you. I had boasted to him about you, and you have not embarrassed me. But just as everything we said to you was true, so our boasting about you to Titus has proved to be true as well. And his affection for you is all the greater when he remembers that you were all

2 Cor. 7 :13b-16

*y*Lev. 26:12; Jer. 32:38; Ezek. 37:27   *z*Isaiah 52:11; Ezek. 20:34,41   *a*2 Samuel 7:14; 7:8

obedient, receiving him with fear and trembling. I am glad I can have complete confidence in you.

Regarding Collection for Brethren in Judea

2 Cor.
8:1-5

LIBERALITY OF MACEDONIANS.   And now, brothers, we want you to know about the grace that God has given the Macedonian churches. Out of the most severe trial, their overflowing joy and their extreme poverty welled up in rich generosity. For I testify that they gave as much as they were able, and even beyond their ability. Entirely on their own, they urgently pleaded with us for the privilege of sharing in this service to the saints. And they did not do as we expected, but they gave themselves first to the Lord and then to us in keeping with God's will.

2 Cor.
8:6-9

GIFT A PROOF OF LOVE.   So we urged Titus, since he had earlier made a beginning, to bring also to completion this act of grace on your part. But just as you excel in everything—in faith, in speech, in knowledge, in complete earnestness and in your love for us[b]—see that you also excel in this grace of giving.

I am not commanding you, but I want to test the sincerity of your love by comparing it with the earnestness of others. For you know the grace of our Lord Jesus Christ, that though he was rich, yet for your sakes he became poor, so that you through his poverty might become rich.

2 Cor.
8:10-15

LIBERALITY MAKES EQUALITY.   And here is my advice about what is best for you in this matter: Last year you were the first not only to give but also to have the desire to do so. Now finish the work, so that your eager willingness to do it may be matched by your completion of it, according to your means. For if the willingness is there, the gift is acceptable according to what one has, not according to what he does not have.

Our desire is not that others might be relieved while you are hard pressed, but that there might be equality. At the present time your plenty will supply what they need, so that in turn their plenty will supply what you need. Then there will be equality, as it is written: "He who gathered much did not have too much, and he who gathered little did not have too little."[c]

2 Cor.
8:16-24

MEN TO CONVEY GIFT.   I thank God, who put into the heart of Titus the same concern I have for you. For Titus not only welcomed our appeal, but he is coming to you with much enthusiasm and on his own initiative. And we are sending along with him the brother who is praised by all the churches for his service to the gospel. What is more, he was chosen by the churches to accompany us as we carry the offering, which we administer in order to honor the Lord himself and to show our eagerness to help. We want to avoid any criticism of the way we administer this liberal gift. For we are taking pains to do what is right, not only in the eyes of the Lord but also in the eyes of men.

In addition, we are sending with them our brother who has often proved to us in many ways that he is zealous, and now even more so because of his great confidence in you. As for Titus, he is my partner and fellow worker among you; as for our brothers, they are representatives of the churches and an honor to Christ. Therefore show these men the proof

[b]Some manuscripts *in our love for you*   [c]Exodus 16:18

of your love and the reason for our pride in you, so that the churches can see it.

READINESS OF GIFT. There is no need for me to write to you about this service to the saints. For I know your eagerness to help, and I have been boasting about it to the Macedonians, telling them that since last year you in Achaia were ready to give; and your enthusiasm has stirred most of them to action. But I am sending the brothers in order that our boasting about you in this matter should not prove hollow, but that you may be ready, as I said you would be. For if any Macedonians come with me and find you unprepared, we—not to say anything about you—would be ashamed of having been so confident. So I thought it necessary to urge the brothers to visit you in advance and finish the arrangements for the generous gift you had promised. Then it will be ready as a generous gift, not as one grudgingly given.

2 Cor. 9:1-5

CHEERFUL, ABUNDANT GIVING. Remember this: Whoever sows sparingly will also reap sparingly, and whoever sows generously will also reap generously. Each man should give what he has decided in his heart to give, not reluctantly or under compulsion, for God loves a cheerful giver. And God is able to make all grace abound to you, so that in all things at all times, having all that you need, you will abound in every good work. As it is written:

2 Cor. 9:6-9

> "He has scattered abroad his gifts to the poor;
>   his righteousness endures forever."[d]

GENEROSITY GLORIFIES GOD. Now he who supplies seed to the sower and bread for food will also supply and increase your store of seed and will enlarge the harvest of your righteousness. You will be made rich in every way so that you can be generous on every occasion, and through us your generosity will result in thanksgiving to God.

2 Cor. 9:10-15

This service that you perform is not only supplying the needs of God's people but is also overflowing in many expressions of thanks to God. Because of the service by which you have proved yourselves, men will praise God for the obedience that accompanies your confession of the gospel of Christ, and for your generosity in sharing with them and with everyone else. And in their prayers for you their hearts will go out to you, because of the surpassing grace God has given you. Thanks be to God for his indescribable gift!

Defense of Paul's Apostleship

PAUL'S RESPONSE TO CHARGE. By the meekness and gentleness of Christ, I appeal to you—I, Paul, who am "timid" when face to face with you, but "bold" when away! I beg you that when I come I may not have to be as bold as I expect to be toward some people who think that we live by the standards of this world. For though we live in the world, we do not wage war as the world does. The weapons we fight with are not the weapons of the world. On the contrary, they have divine power to demolish strongholds. We demolish arguments and every pretension that sets itself up against the knowledge of God, and we take captive every thought to make it obedient to Christ. And we will be ready to punish every act of disobedience, once your obedience is complete.

2 Cor. 10:1-6

[d]Psalm 112:9

2 Cor.
10:7-11

APPEARANCES AND LETTERS.   You are looking only on the surface of things.*e* If anyone is confident that he belongs to Christ, he should consider again that we belong to Christ just as much as he. For even if I boast somewhat freely about the authority the Lord gave us for building you up rather than pulling you down, I will not be ashamed of it. I do not want to seem to be trying to frighten you with my letters. For some say, "His letters are weighty and forceful, but in person he is unimpressive and his speaking amounts to nothing." Such people should realize that what we are in our letters when we are absent, we will be in our actions when we are present.

2 Cor.
10:12-18

COMPARISONS WITH OTHERS.   We do not dare to classify or compare ourselves with some who commend themselves. When they measure themselves by themselves and compare themselves with themselves, they are not wise. We, however, will not boast beyond proper limits, but will confine our boasting to the field God has assigned to us, a field that reaches even to you. We are not going too far in our boasting, as would be the case if we had not come to you, for we did get as far as you with the gospel of Christ. Neither do we go beyond our limits by boasting of work done by others.*f* Our hope is that, as your faith continues to grow, our area of activity among you will greatly expand, so that we can preach the gospel in the regions beyond you. For we do not want to boast about work already done in another man's territory. But, "Let him who boasts boast in the Lord."*g* For it is not the one who commends himself who is approved, but the one whom the Lord commends.

2 Cor.
11:1-6

ORATORY VERSUS KNOWLEDGE.   I hope you will put up with a little of my foolishness; but you are already doing that. I am jealous for you with a godly jealousy. I promised you to one husband, to Christ, so that I might present you as a pure virgin to him. But I am afraid that just as Eve was deceived by the serpent's cunning, your minds may somehow be led astray from your sincere and pure devotion to Christ. For if someone comes to you and preaches a Jesus other than the Jesus we preached, or if you receive a different spirit from the one you received, or a different gospel from the one you accepted, you put up with it easily enough. But I do not think I am in the least inferior to those "super-apostles." I may not be a trained speaker, but I do have knowledge. We have made this perfectly clear to you in every way.

2 Cor.
11:7-11

PREACHING A MATTER OF LOVE.   Was it a sin for me to lower myself in order to elevate you by preaching the gospel of God to you free of charge? I robbed other churches by receiving support from them so as to serve you. And when I was with you and needed something, I was not a burden to anyone, for the brothers who came from Macedonia supplied what I needed. I have kept myself from being a burden to you in any way, and will continue to do so. As surely as the truth of Christ is in me, nobody in the regions of Achaia will stop this boasting of mine. Why? Because I do not love you? God knows I do!

eOr Look at the obvious facts   fOr 13We, however, will not boast about things that cannot be measured, but we will boast according to the standard of measurement that the God of measure has assigned us—a measurement that relates even to you. 14 . . . 15Neither do we boast about things that cannot be measured in regard to the work done by others.   gJer. 9:24

OTHERS' PREACHING A RUSE.   And I will keep on doing what I am
doing in order to cut the ground from under those who want an opportunity to be considered equal with us in the things they boast about.

2 Cor.
11:12-15

For such men are false apostles, deceitful workmen, masquerading as
apostles of Christ. And no wonder, for Satan himself masquerades as an
angel of light. It is not surprising, then, if his servants masquerade as servants of righteousness. Their end will be what their actions deserve.

PAUL FORCED TO BOAST.   I repeat: Let no one take me for a fool. But
if you do, then receive me just as you would a fool, so that I may do a little boasting. In this self-confident boasting I am not talking as the Lord
would, but as a fool. Since many are boasting in the way the world does,
I too will boast. You gladly put up with fools since you are so wise! In fact,
you even put up with anyone who enslaves you or exploits you or takes
advantage of you or pushes himself forward or slaps you in the face. To
my shame I admit that we were too weak for that!

2 Cor.
11:16-21a

BASIS FOR BOASTING.   What anyone else dares to boast about—I am
speaking as a fool—I also dare to boast about. Are they Hebrews? So am I.
Are they Israelites? So am I. Are they Abraham's descendants? So am I.
Are they servants of Christ? (I am out of my mind to talk like this.) I am
more. I have worked much harder, been in prison more frequently, been
flogged more severely, and been exposed to death again and again. Five
times I received from the Jews the forty lashes minus one. Three times I
was beaten with rods, once I was stoned, three times I was shipwrecked, I
spent a night and a day in the open sea, I have been constantly on the
move. I have been in danger from rivers, in danger from bandits, in danger from my own countrymen, in danger from Gentiles; in danger in the
city, in danger in the country, in danger at sea; and in danger from false
brothers. I have labored and toiled and have often gone without sleep; I
have known hunger and thirst and have often gone without food; I have
been cold and naked. Besides everything else, I face daily the pressure of
my concern for all the churches. Who is weak, and I do not feel weak?
Who is led into sin, and I do not inwardly burn?

2 Cor.
11:21b-29

SUFFERINGS INDICATE STRENGTH.   If I must boast, I will boast of the
things that show my weakness. The God and Father of the Lord Jesus, who
is to be praised forever, knows that I am not lying. In Damascus the governor under King Aretas had the city of the Damascenes guarded in order
to arrest me. But I was lowered in a basket from a window in the wall and
slipped through his hands.

2 Cor.
11:30-33

REVELATIONS VERIFY.   I must go on boasting. Although there is nothing to be gained, I will go on to visions and revelations from the Lord. I
know a man in Christ who fourteen years ago was caught up to the third
heaven. Whether it was in the body or out of the body I do not know—
God knows. And I know that this man—whether in the body or apart from
the body I do not know, but God knows—was caught up to paradise. He
heard inexpressible things, things that man is not permitted to tell. I will
boast about a man like that, but I will not boast about myself, except about
my weaknesses. Even if I should choose to boast, I would not be a fool,
because I would be speaking the truth. But I refrain, so no one will think
more of me than is warranted by what I do or say.

2 Cor.
12:1-6

2 Cor. 12:7-10	**WEAKNESS FOR CHRIST'S SAKE.** To keep me from becoming conceited because of these surpassingly great revelations, there was given me a thorn in my flesh, a messenger of Satan, to torment me. Three times I pleaded with the Lord to take it away from me. But he said to me, "My grace is sufficient for you, for my power is made perfect in weakness." Therefore I will boast all the more gladly about my weaknesses, so that Christ's power may rest on me. That is why, for Christ's sake, I delight in weaknesses, in insults, in hardships, in persecutions, in difficulties. For when I am weak, then I am strong.
2 Cor. 12:11-13	**MIRACLES ARE CREDENTIALS.** I have made a fool of myself, but you drove me to it. I ought to have been commended by you, for I am not in the least inferior to the "super-apostles," even though I am nothing. The things that mark an apostle—signs, wonders and miracles—were done among you with great perseverance. How were you inferior to the other churches, except that I was never a burden to you? Forgive me this wrong!
2 Cor. 12:14-18	**NO ULTERIOR ADVANTAGE.** Now I am ready to visit you for the third time, and I will not be a burden to you, because what I want is not your possessions but you. After all, children should not have to save up for their parents, but parents for their children. So I will very gladly spend for you everything I have and expend myself as well. If I love you more, will you love me less? Be that as it may, I have not been a burden to you. Yet, crafty fellow that I am, I caught you by trickery! Did I exploit you through any of the men I sent you? I urged Titus to go to you and I sent our brother with him. Titus did not exploit you, did he? Did we not act in the same spirit and follow the same course?
2 Cor. 12:19-21	**REASON FOR DEFENSE.** Have you been thinking all along that we have been defending ourselves to you? We have been speaking in the sight of God as those in Christ; and everything we do, dear friends, is for your strengthening. For I am afraid that when I come I may not find you as I want you to be, and you may not find me as you want me to be. I fear that there may be quarreling, jealousy, outbursts of anger, factions, slander, gossip, arrogance and disorder. I am afraid that when I come again my God will humble me before you, and I will be grieved over many who have sinned earlier and have not repented of the impurity, sexual sin and debauchery in which they have indulged.
2 Cor. 13:1-4	**REGARDING TROUBLEMAKERS.** This will be my third visit to you. "Every matter must be established by the testimony of two or three witnesses."[h] I already gave you a warning when I was with you the second time. I now repeat it while absent: On my return I will not spare those who sinned earlier or any of the others, since you are demanding proof that Christ is speaking through me. He is not weak in dealing with you, but is powerful among you. For to be sure, he was crucified in weakness, yet he lives by God's power. Likewise, we are weak in him, yet by God's power we will live with him to serve you.
2 Cor. 13:5-10	**EACH TO EXAMINE HIMSELF.** Examine yourselves to see whether you are in the faith; test yourselves. Do you not realize that Christ Jesus is in you—unless, of course, you fail the test? And I trust that you will discover that we have not failed the test. Now we pray to God that you will not

[h]Deut. 19:15

do anything wrong. Not that people will see that we have stood the test but that you will do what is right even though we may seem to have failed. For we cannot do anything against the truth, but only for the truth. We are glad whenever we are weak but you are strong; and our prayer is for your perfection. This is why I write these things when I am absent, that when I come I may not have to be harsh in my use of authority—the authority the Lord gave me for building you up, not for tearing you down.

EXHORTATIONS AND GREETINGS.   Finally, brothers, good-by. Aim for perfection, listen to my appeal, be of one mind, live in peace. And the God of love and peace will be with you.
    Greet one another with a holy kiss. All the saints send their greetings.

2 Cor.
13:11-13

BENEDICTION.   May the grace of the Lord Jesus Christ, and the love of God, and the fellowship of the Holy Spirit be with you all.

2 Cor.
13:14

    It is not long after the writing of this letter that Paul finally is able to make his promised third visit to Corinth and other parts of Achaia.

PAUL ARRIVES IN GREECE.   He traveled through that area, speaking many words of encouragement to the people, and finally arrived in Greece, where he stayed three months.

Acts
20:2-3a
(Ca. A.D.
56,57)

*Letter to the Romans*_____

*D*uring this short time in Corinth, somewhere around A.D. 56-58, Paul writes a letter to the saints in Rome, telling of his desire to visit them, but indicating his inability to do so at this time. He tells them that he must first go to Jerusalem in order to deliver contributions being sent by the brethren in Macedonia and Achaia. Anticipating that he will eventually be able to visit Rome on his way to Spain, and perhaps feeling the need to establish his credentials before his arrival, Paul first explains his understanding of the gospel, carefully contrasting the gospel with the Law of Moses. Paul then concludes with various practical teachings which necessarily flow out of the gospel message.

    The theme of Paul's letter is that those who are righteous through faith will be those who truly live. Paul begins by examining the judgment of God and the righteousness of God. Under God's judgment, even the man who thinks himself "righteous" is a sinner without excuse. Under God's righteousness, even the "sinful" man is justified and reconciled to God through grace. Paul then shows how, through Christ, there is freedom from judgment, sin, the law, and even death. Next, Paul discusses the unique problem faced by certain Jews who are having difficulty believing that the God of the Jews could possibly include the Gentiles in his promises made to Abraham. After laying a deep theological foundation, Paul concludes the letter with practical applications for transforming one's life to Christian service, and for regulating one's conduct in relation to his fellowman, to civil government, and to those brothers and sisters in Christ who may be spiritually weak. The thrust of the letter is the superiority of obedient faith over futile attempts to earn salvation through strict law-keeping. Grace is not seen as a substitute for law, but rather as a higher motivation to obey God's laws.

Rom. 1:1-7   SALUTATION. Paul, a servant of Christ Jesus, called to be an apostle and set apart for the gospel of God—the gospel he promised beforehand through his prophets in the Holy Scriptures regarding his Son, who as to his human nature was a descendant of David, and who through the Spirit[i] of holiness was declared with power to be the Son of God[j] by his resurrection from the dead: Jesus Christ our Lord. Through him and for his name's sake, we received grace and apostleship to call people from among all the Gentiles to the obedience that comes from faith. And you also are among those who are called to belong to Jesus Christ.

To all in Rome who are loved by God and called to be saints:

Grace and peace to you from God our Father and from the Lord Jesus Christ.

Rom. 1:8-15   DESIRE TO BE WITH ROMANS. First, I thank my God through Jesus Christ for all of you, because your faith is being reported all over the world. God, whom I serve with my whole heart in preaching the gospel of his Son, is my witness how constantly I remember you in my prayers at all times; and I pray that now at last by God's will the way may be opened for me to come to you.

I long to see you so that I may impart to you some spiritual gift to make you strong—that is, that you and I may be mutually encouraged by each other's faith. I do not want you to be unaware, brothers, that I planned many times to come to you (but have been prevented from doing so until now) in order that I might have a harvest among you, just as I have had among the other Gentiles.

I am obligated both to Greeks and non-Greeks, both to the wise and the foolish. That is why I am so eager to preach the gospel also to you who are at Rome.

Rom. 1:16,17   THEME OF THE GOSPEL. I am not ashamed of the gospel, because it is the power of God for the salvation of everyone who believes: first for the Jew, then for the Gentile. For in the gospel a righteousness from God is revealed, a righteousness that is by faith from first to last,[k] just as it is written: "The righteous will live by faith."[l]

Judgment of God

Rom. 1:18-23   GENTILES REJECTED GOD. The wrath of God is being revealed from heaven against all the godlessness and wickedness of men who suppress the truth by their wickedness, since what may be known about God is plain to them, because God has made it plain to them. For since the creation of the world God's invisible qualities—his eternal power and divine nature—have been clearly seen, being understood from what has been made, so that men are without excuse.

For although they knew God, they neither glorified him as God nor gave thanks to him, but their thinking became futile and their foolish hearts were darkened. Although they claimed to be wise, they became fools and exchanged the glory of the immortal God for images made to look like mortal man and birds and animals and reptiles.

---

[i]Or who as to his spirit   [j]Or was appointed to be the Son of God with power   [k]Or is from faith to faith   [l]Hab. 2:4

IDOLATRY LED TO IMMORALITY. Therefore God gave them over in the sinful desires of their hearts to sexual impurity for the degrading of their bodies with one another. They exchanged the truth of God for a lie, and worshiped and served created things rather than the Creator—who is forever praised. Amen.

Rom. 1:24,25

UNNATURAL REPLACED NATURAL. Because of this, God gave them over to shameful lusts. Even their women exchanged natural relations for unnatural ones. In the same way the men also abandoned natural relations with women and were inflamed with lust for one another. Men committed indecent acts with other men, and received in themselves the due penalty for their perversion.

Rom. 1:26, 27

SINFULNESS REPLACED PURITY. Furthermore, since they did not think it worthwhile to retain the knowledge of God, he gave them over to a depraved mind, to do what ought not to be done. They have become filled with every kind of wickedness, evil, greed and depravity. They are full of envy, murder, strife, deceit and malice. They are gossips, slanderers, God-haters, insolent, arrogant and boastful; they invent ways of doing evil; they disobey their parents; they are senseless, faithless, heartless, ruthless. Although they know God's righteous decree that those who do such things deserve death, they not only continue to do these very things but also approve of those who practice them.

Rom. 1:28-32

ALL ARE SINNERS. You, therefore, have no excuse, you who pass judgment on someone else, for at whatever point you judge the other, you are condemning yourself, because you who pass judgment do the same things. Now we know that God's judgment against those who do such things is based on truth. So when you, a mere man, pass judgment on them and yet do the same things, do you think you will escape God's judgment? Or do you show contempt for the riches of his kindness, tolerance and patience, not realizing that God's kindness leads you towards repentance?

But because of your stubbornness and your unrepentant heart, you are storing up wrath against yourself for the day of God's wrath, when his righteous judgment will be revealed.

Rom. 2:1-5

GOD'S JUDGMENT IMPARTIAL. God "will give to each person according to what he has done."[m] To those who by persistence in doing good seek glory, honor and immortality, he will give eternal life. But for those who are self-seeking and who reject the truth and follow evil, there will be wrath and anger. There will be trouble and distress for every human being who does evil: first for the Jew, then for the Gentile; but glory, honor and peace for everyone who does good: first for the Jew, then for the Gentile. For God does not show favoritism.

Rom. 2:6-11

THOSE WITHOUT THE LAW. All who sin apart from the law will also perish apart from the law, and all who sin under the law will be judged by the law. For it is not those who hear the law who are righteous in God's sight, but it is those who obey the law who will be declared righteous. (Indeed, when Gentiles, who do not have the law, do by nature things required by the law, they are a law for themselves, even though they do not have the law, since they show that the requirements of the law are

Rom. 2:12-16

---

[m]Psalm 62:12; Prov. 24:12

written on their hearts, their consciences also bearing witness, and their thoughts now accusing, now even defending them.) This will take place on the day when God will judge men's secrets through Jesus Christ, as my gospel declares.

**Rom.
2:17-24**

LAW CANNOT JUSTIFY.   Now you, if you call yourself a Jew; if you rely on the law and brag about your relationship to God; if you know his will and approve of what is superior because you are instructed by the law; if you are convinced that you are a guide for the blind, a light for those who are in the dark, an instructor of the foolish, a teacher of infants, because you have in the law the embodiment of knowledge and truth—you, then, who teach others, do you not teach yourself? You who preach against stealing, do you steal? You who say that people should not commit adultery, do you commit adultery? You who abhor idols, do you rob temples? You who brag about the law, do you dishonor God by breaking the law? As it is written: "God's name is blasphemed among the Gentiles because of you."[n]

**Rom.
2:25-29**

CIRCUMCISION CANNOT JUSTIFY.   Circumcision has value if you observe the law, but if you break the law, you have become as though you had not been circumcised. If those who are not circumcised keep the law's requirements, will they not be regarded as though they were circumcised? The one who is not circumcised physically and yet obeys the law will condemn you who, even though you have the[o] written code and circumcision, are a lawbreaker.

A man is not a Jew if he is only one outwardly, nor is circumcision merely outward and physical. No, a man is a Jew if he is one inwardly; and circumcision is circumcision of the heart, by the Spirit, not by the written code. Such a man's praise is not from men, but from God.

Rom. 3:1-4

PRIDE IN HERITAGE.   What advantage, then, is there in being a Jew, or what value is there in circumcision? Much in every way! First of all, they have been entrusted with the very words of God.

What if some did not have faith? Will their lack of faith nullify God's faithfulness? Not at all! Let God be true, and every man a liar. As it is written:

"So that you may be proved right when you speak
and prevail when you judge."[p]

Rom. 3:5-8

GOD'S JUDGMENT IS JUST.   But if our unrighteousness brings out God's righteousness more clearly, what shall we say? That God is unjust in bringing his wrath on us? (I am using a human argument.) Certainly not! If that were so, how could God judge the world? Someone might argue, "If my falsehood enhances God's truthfulness and so increases his glory, why am I still condemned as a sinner?" Why not say—as we are being slanderously reported as saying and as some claim that we say—"Let us do evil that good may result"? Their condemnation is deserved.

**Rom.
3:9-18**

ALL ARE UNDER JUDGMENT.   What shall we conclude then? Are we any better[q]? Not at all! We have already made the charge that Jews and Gentiles alike are all under sin. As it is written:

[n]Isaiah 52:5; Ezek. 36:22   [o]Or who, by means of a   [p]Psalm 51:4   [q]Or worse

"There is no one righteous, not even one;
  there is no one who understands,
  no one who seeks God.
All have turned away,
  they have together become worthless;
there is no one who does good,
  not even one."[r]
"Their throats are open graves;
  their tongues practice deceit."[s]
"The poison of vipers is on their lips."[t]
  "Their mouths are full of cursing and bitterness."[u]
"Their feet are swift to shed blood;
  ruin and misery mark their ways,
and the way of peace they do not know."[v]
  "There is no fear of God before their eyes."[w]

LAW FOR EDUCATION.   Now we know that whatever the law says, it says to those who are under the law, so that every mouth may be silenced and the whole world held accountable to God. Therefore no one will be declared righteous in his sight by observing the law; rather, through the law we become conscious of sin.

Rom. 3:19,20

Righteousness of God

JUSTIFICATION THROUGH FAITH.   But now a righteousness from God, apart from law, has been made known, to which the Law and the Prophets testify. This righteousness from God comes through faith in Jesus Christ to all who believe. There is no difference, for all have sinned and fall short of the glory of God, and are justified freely by his grace through the redemption that came by Christ Jesus. God presented him as a sacrifice of atonement,[x] through faith in his blood. He did this to demonstrate his justice, because in his forbearance he had left the sins committed beforehand unpunished—he did it to demonstrate his justice at the present time, so as to be just and the one who justifies those who have faith in Jesus.

Rom. 3:21-26

LAWKEEPING NOT EFFECTUAL.   Where, then, is boasting? It is excluded. On what principle? On that of observing the law? No, but on that of faith. For we maintain that a man is justified by faith apart from observing the law. Is God the God of Jews only? Is he not the God of Gentiles too? Yes, of Gentiles too, since there is only one God, who will justify the circumcised by faith and the uncircumcised through that same faith. Do we, then, nullify the law by this faith? Not at all! Rather, we uphold the law.

Rom. 3:27-31

RIGHTEOUSNESS WITHOUT LAW.   What then shall we say that Abraham, our forefather, discovered in this matter? If, in fact, Abraham was justified by works, he had something to boast about—but not before God. What does the Scripture say? "Abraham believed God, and it was credited to him as righteousness."[y]

Now when a man works, his wages are not credited to him as a gift, but

Rom. 4:1-5

---

[r]Psalms 14:1-3; 53:1-3; Eccles. 7:20   [s]Psalm 5:9   [t]Psalm 140:3   [u]Psalm 10:7
[v]Isaiah 59:7,8   [w]Psalm 36:1   [x]Or *as the one who would turn aside his wrath, taking away sin*   [y]Gen. 15:6

as an obligation. However, to the man who does not work but trusts God who justifies the wicked, his faith is credited as righteousness.

Rom. 4:6-8 DAVID RECOGNIZED GRACE. David says the same thing when he speaks of the blessedness of the man to whom God credits righteousness apart from works:

> "Blessed are they
>> whose transgressions are forgiven,
>> whose sins are covered.
> Blessed is the man
>> whose sin the Lord will never count against him."[z]

Rom. 4:9-12 CIRCUMCISION'S VALUE. Is this blessedness only for the circumcised, or also for the uncircumcised? We have been saying that Abraham's faith was credited to him as righteousness. Under what circumstances was it credited? Was it after he was circumcised, or before? It was not after, but before! And he received the sign of circumcision, a seal of the righteousness that he had by faith while he was still uncircumcised. So then, he is the father of all who believe but have not been circumcised, in order that righteousness might be credited to them. And he is also the father of the circumcised who not only are circumcised but who also walk in the footsteps of the faith that our father Abraham had before he was circumcised.

Rom. 4:13-15 PROMISE BASED UPON FAITH. It was not through law that Abraham and his offspring received the promise that he would be heir of the world, but through the righteousness that comes by faith. For if those who live by law are heirs, faith has no value and the promise is worthless, because law brings wrath. And where there is no law there is no transgression.

Rom. 4:16-18 PROMISE IS FOR ALL PEOPLE. Therefore, the promise comes by faith, so that it may be by grace and may be guaranteed to all Abraham's offspring—not only to those who are of the law but also to those who are of the faith of Abraham. He is the father of us all. As it is written: "I have made you a father of many nations."[a] He is our father in the sight of God, in whom he believed—the God who gives life to the dead and calls things that are not as though they were.

Against all hope, Abraham in hope believed and so became the father of many nations, just as it had been said to him, "So shall your offspring be."[b]

Rom. 4:19-25 ABRAHAM'S FAITH AN EXAMPLE. Without weakening in his faith, he faced the fact that his body was as good as dead—since he was about a hundred years old—and that Sarah's womb was also dead. Yet he did not waver through unbelief regarding the promise of God, but was strengthened in his faith and gave glory to God, being fully persuaded that God had power to do what he had promised. This is why "it was credited to him as righteousness." The words "it was credited to him" were written not for him alone, but also for us, to whom God will credit righteousness—for us who believe in him who raised Jesus our Lord from the dead. He was delivered over to death for our sins and was raised to life for our justification.

[z]Psalm 32:1,2   [a]Gen. 17:5   [b]Gen. 15:5

Freedom from Condemnation

JUSTIFICATION BRINGS PEACE.   Therefore, since we have been justi- Rom. 5:1-5
fied through faith, we[c] have peace with God through our Lord Jesus
Christ, through whom we have gained access by faith into this grace in
which we now stand. And we[c] rejoice in the hope of the glory of God.
Not only so, but we[c] also rejoice in our sufferings, because we know that
suffering produces perseverance; perseverance, character; and character,
hope. And hope does not disappoint us, because God has poured out his
love into our hearts by the Holy Spirit, whom he has given us.

CHRIST'S BLOOD SAVES.   You see, at just the right time, when we were Rom. 5:6-11
still powerless, Christ died for the ungodly. Very rarely will anyone die
for a righteous man, though for a good man someone might possibly dare
to die. But God demonstrates his own love for us in this: While we were
still sinners, Christ died for us.

Since we have now been justified by his blood, how much more shall
we be saved from God's wrath through him! For if, when we were God's
enemies, we were reconciled to him through the death of his Son, how
much more, having been reconciled, shall we be saved through his life!
Not only is this so, but we also rejoice in God through our Lord Jesus
Christ, through whom we have now received reconciliation.

ALL DIE FROM SIN.   Therefore, just as sin entered the world through Rom. 5:12-14
one man, and death through sin, and in this way death came to all men,
because all sinned—for before the law was given, sin was in the world. But
sin is not taken into account when there is no law. Nevertheless, death
reigned from the time of Adam to the time of Moses, even over those who
did not sin by breaking a command, as did Adam, who was a pattern of
the one to come.

ALL CAN BE JUSTIFIED.   But the gift is not like the trespass. For if the Rom. 5:15-19
many died by the trespass of the one man, how much more did God's
grace and the gift that came by the grace of the one man, Jesus Christ,
overflow to the many! Again, the gift of God is not like the result of the one
man's sin: The judgment followed one sin and brought condemnation, but
the gift followed many trespasses and brought justification. For if, by the
trespass of the one man, death reigned through that one man, how much
more will those who receive God's abundant provision of grace and of the
gift of righteousness reign in life through the one man, Jesus Christ.

Consequently, just as the result of one trespass was condemnation for all
men, so also the result of one act of righteousness was justification that
brings life for all men. For just as through the disobedience of the one man
the many were made sinners, so also through the obedience of the one
man the many will be made righteous.

GRACE INCREASED.   The law was added so that the trespass might Rom. 5:20,21
increase. But where sin increased, grace increased all the more, so that, just
as sin reigned in death, so also grace might reign through righteousness to
bring eternal life through Jesus Christ our Lord.

[c]Or let us

Freedom from Sin

Rom. 6:1-4 GRACE NO EXCUSE TO SIN.   What shall we say, then? Shall we go on sinning so that grace may increase? By no means! We died to sin; how can we live in it any longer? Or don't you know that all of us who were baptized into Christ Jesus were baptized into his death? We were therefore buried with him through baptism into death in order that, just as Christ was raised from the dead through the glory of the Father, we too may live a new life.

Rom. 6:5-11 DEAD TO SIN.   If we have been united with him like this in his death, we will certainly also be united with him in his resurrection. For we know that our old self was crucified with him so that the body of sin might be done away with,^{d} that we should no longer be slaves to sin—because anyone who has died has been freed from sin.

Now if we died with Christ, we believe that we will also live with him. For we know that since Christ was raised from the dead, he cannot die again; death no longer has mastery over him. The death he died, he died to sin once for all; but the life he lives, he lives to God.

In the same way, count yourselves dead to sin but alive to God in Christ Jesus.

Rom. 6:12-14 GRACE REQUIRES SUBMISSION.   Therefore do not let sin reign in your mortal body so that you obey its evil desires. Do not offer the parts of your body to sin, as instruments of wickedness, but rather offer yourselves to God, as those who have been brought from death to life; and offer the parts of your body to him as instruments of righteousness. For sin shall not be your master, because you are not under law, but under grace.

Rom. 6:15-19 SLAVERY TO RIGHTEOUSNESS.   What then? Shall we sin because we are not under law but under grace? By no means! Don't you know that when you offer yourselves to someone to obey him as slaves, you are slaves to the one whom you obey—whether you are slaves to sin, which leads to death, or to obedience, which leads to righteousness? But thanks be to God that, though you used to be slaves to sin, you wholeheartedly obeyed the form of teaching to which you were entrusted. You have been set free from sin and have become slaves to righteousness.

I put this in human terms because you are weak in your natural selves. Just as you used to offer the parts of your body in slavery to impurity and to ever-increasing wickedness, so now offer them in slavery to righteousness leading to holiness.

Rom. 6:20-23 GRACE BRINGS LIFE.   When you were slaves to sin, you were free from the control of righteousness. What benefit did you reap at that time from the things you are now ashamed of? Those things result in death! But now that you have been set free from sin and have become slaves to God, the benefit you reap leads to holiness, and the result is eternal life. For the wages of sin is death, but the gift of God is eternal life in^e Christ Jesus our Lord.

Freedom from the Law

Rom. 7:1-3 LAW BINDING DURING LIFETIME.   Do you not know, brothers—for I am speaking to men who know the law—that the law has authority over

---

^{d}Or *be rendered powerless* ^{e}Or *through*

a man only as long as he lives? For example, by law a married woman is bound to her husband as long as he is alive, but if her husband dies, she is released from the law of marriage. So then, if she marries another man while her husband is still alive, she is called an adulteress. But if her husband dies, she is released from that law and is not an adulteress, even though she marries another man.

NOW MARRIED TO CHRIST. So, my brothers, you also died to the law through the body of Christ, that you might belong to another, to him who was raised from the dead, in order that we might bear fruit to God. For when we were controlled by the sinful nature,^{f} the sinful passions aroused by the law were at work in our bodies, so that we bore fruit for death. But now, by dying to what once bound us, we have been released from the law so that we serve in the new way of the Spirit, and not in the old way of the written code. — Rom. 7:4-6

LAW GAVE OPPORTUNITY TO SIN. What shall we say, then? Is the law sin? Certainly not! Indeed I would not have known what sin was except through the law. For I would not have known what coveting really was if the law had not said, "Do not covet."^{g} But sin, seizing the opportunity afforded by the commandment, produced in me every kind of covetous desire. For apart from law, sin is dead. Once I was alive apart from law; but when the commandment came, sin sprang to life and I died. I found that the very commandment that was intended to bring life actually brought death. For sin, seizing the opportunity afforded by the commandment, deceived me, and through the commandment put me to death. So then, the law is holy, and the commandment is holy, righteous and good. — Rom. 7:7-12

LAW DID NOT CAUSE SIN. Did that which is good, then, become death to me? By no means! But in order that sin might be recognized as sin, it produced death in me through what was good, so that through the commandment sin might become utterly sinful.

We know that the law is spiritual; but I am unspiritual, sold as a slave to sin. — Rom. 7:13,14

LAW IS GOOD; MAN IS SINFUL. I do not understand what I do. For what I want to do I do not do, but what I hate I do. And if I do what I do not want to do, I agree that the law is good. As it is, it is no longer I myself who do it, but it is sin living in me. I know that nothing good lives in me, that is, in my sinful nature.^{h} For I have the desire to do what is good, but I cannot carry it out. For what I do is not the good I want to do; no, the evil I do not want to do—this I keep on doing. Now if I do what I do not want to do, it is no longer I who do it, but it is sin living in me that does it. — Rom. 7:15-20

FLESH AND SPIRIT STRUGGLE. So I find this law at work: When I want to do good, evil is right there with me. For in my inner being I delight in God's law; but I see another law at work in the members of my body, waging war against the law of my mind and making me a prisoner of the law of sin at work within my members. What a wretched man I am! Who will rescue me from this body of death? Thanks be to God—through Jesus Christ our Lord! — Rom. 7:21-25

^{f} Or *the flesh*; also in verse 25 ^{g} Exodus 20:17; Deut. 5:21 ^{h} Or *my flesh*

So then, I myself in my mind am a slave to God's law, but in the sinful nature a slave to the law of sin.

Freedom from Death

Rom. 8:1-8   NO CONDEMNATION.   Therefore, there is now no condemnation for those who are in Christ Jesus,[i] because through Christ Jesus the law of the Spirit of life set me free from the law of sin and death. For what the law was powerless to do in that it was weakened by the sinful nature,[j] God did by sending his own Son in the likeness of sinful man to be a sin offering.[k] And so he condemned sin in sinful man,[l] in order that the righteous requirements of the law might be fully met in us, who do not live according to the sinful nature but according to the Spirit.

Those who live according to the sinful nature have their minds set on what that nature desires; but those who live in accordance with the Spirit have their minds set on what the Spirit desires. The mind of sinful man[m] is death, but the mind controlled by the Spirit is life and peace; the sinful mind[n] is hostile to God. It does not submit to God's law, nor can it do so. Those controlled by the sinful nature cannot please God.

Rom. 8:9-11   SPIRIT GIVES LIFE.   You, however, are controlled not by the sinful nature but by the Spirit, if the Spirit of God lives in you. And if anyone does not have the Spirit of Christ, he does not belong to Christ. But if Christ is in you, your body is dead because of sin, yet your spirit is alive because of righteousness. And if the Spirit of him who raised Jesus from the dead is living in you, he who raised Christ from the dead will also give life to your mortal bodies through his Spirit, who lives in you.

Rom. 8:12-17   DUTY TO LIVE BY SPIRIT.   Therefore, brothers, we have an obligation—but it is not to the sinful nature, to live according to it. For if you live according to the sinful nature, you will die; but if by the Spirit you put to death the misdeeds of the body, you will live, because those who are led by the Spirit of God are sons of God. For you did not receive a spirit that makes you a slave again to fear, but you received the Spirit of sonship.[o] And by him we cry, "Abba,[p] Father." The Spirit himself testifies with our spirit that we are God's children. Now if we are children, then we are heirs—heirs of God and co-heirs with Christ, if indeed we share in his sufferings in order that we may also share in his glory.

Rom. 8:18-25   SUFFERINGS DIMINISH IN HOPE.   I consider that our present sufferings are not worth comparing with the glory that will be revealed in us. The creation waits in eager expectation for the sons of God to be revealed. For the creation was subjected to frustration, not by its own choice, but by the will of the one who subjected it, in hope that[q] the creation itself will be liberated from its bondage to decay and brought into the glorious freedom of the children of God.

We know that the whole creation has been groaning as in the pains of childbirth right up to the present time. Not only so, but we ourselves, who have the firstfruits of the Spirit, groan inwardly as we wait eagerly for our adoption as sons, the redemption of our bodies. For in this hope we were

[i]Some later manuscripts *Jesus, who do not live according to the sinful nature but according to the Spirit,*   [j]Or *the flesh;* also in verses 4, 5, 8, 9, 12 and 13   [k]Or *man, for sin*   [l]Or *in the flesh*   [m]Or *mind set on the flesh*   [n]Or *the mind set on the flesh*   [o]Or *adoption*   [p]Aramaic for *Father*   [q]Or *subjected it in hope.* 21For

saved. But hope that is seen is no hope at all. Who hopes for what he already has? But if we hope for what we do not yet have, we wait for it patiently.

SPIRIT BRIDGES GAP.   In the same way, the Spirit helps us in our weakness. We do not know what we ought to pray for, but the Spirit himself intercedes for us with groans that words cannot express. And he who searches our hearts knows the mind of the Spirit, because the Spirit intercedes for the saints in accordance with God's will. Rom. 8:26,27

ETERNAL PLAN FOR BELIEVERS.   And we know that in all things God works for the good of those who love him,[r] who[s] have been called according to his purpose. For those God foreknew he also predestined to be conformed to the likeness of his Son, that he might be the firstborn among many brothers. And those he predestined, he also called; those he called, he also justified; those he justified, he also glorified. Rom. 8:28-34

What, then, shall we say in response to this? If God is for us, who can be against us? He who did not spare his own Son, but gave him up for us all—how will he not also, along with him, graciously give us all things? Who will bring any charge against those whom God has chosen? It is God who justifies. Who is he that condemns? Christ Jesus, who died—more than that, who was raised to life—is at the right hand of God and is also interceding for us.

GOD'S LOVE UNFAILING.   Who shall separate us from the love of Christ? Shall trouble or hardship or persecution or famine or nakedness or danger or sword? As it is written: Rom. 8:35-39

"For your sake we face death all day long;
    we are considered as sheep to be slaughtered."[t]

No, in all these things we are more than conquerors through him who loved us. For I am convinced that neither death nor life, neither angels nor demons,[u] neither the present nor the future, nor any powers, neither height nor depth, nor anything else in all creation, will be able to separate us from the love of God that is in Christ Jesus our Lord.

Regarding the Jewish Experience

CONCERN FOR JEWISH HERITAGE.   I speak the truth in Christ—I am not lying, my conscience confirms it in the Holy Spirit—I have great sorrow and unceasing anguish in my heart. For I could wish that I myself were cursed and cut off from Christ for the sake of my brothers, those of my own race, the people of Israel. Theirs is the adoption as sons; theirs the divine glory, the covenants, the receiving of the law, the temple worship and the promises. Theirs are the patriarchs, and from them is traced the human ancestry of Christ, who is God over all, forever praised![v] Amen. Rom. 9:1-5

BASIS OF GOD'S PROMISE.   It is not as though God's word had failed. For not all who are descended from Israel are Israel. Nor because they are Rom. 9:6-13

---

[r]Some manuscripts *And we know that all things work together for good to those who love God*
[s]Or *works together with those who love him to bring about what is good—with those who*
[t]Psalm 44:22   [u]Or *nor heavenly rulers*   [v]Or *Christ, who is over all. God be forever praised! Or Christ. God who is over all be forever praised!*

his descendants are they all Abraham's children. On the contrary, "It is through Isaac that your offspring will be reckoned."*w* In other words, it is not the natural children who are God's children, but it is the children of the promise who are regarded as Abraham's offspring. For this was how the promise was stated: "At the appointed time I will return, and Sarah will have a son."*x*

Not only that, but Rebekah's children had one and the same father, our father Isaac. Yet, before the twins were born or had done anything good or bad—in order that God's purpose in election might stand: not by works but by him who calls—she was told, "The older will serve the younger."*y* Just as it is written: "Jacob I loved, but Esau I hated."*z*

Rom. 9:14-18

GOD CAN HAVE MERCY ON ANYONE.   What then shall we say? Is God unjust? Not at all! For he says to Moses,

> "I will have mercy on whom I have mercy,
> and I will have compassion on whom I have compassion."*a*

It does not, therefore, depend on man's desire or effort, but on God's mercy. For the Scripture says to Pharaoh: "I raised you up for this very purpose, that I might display my power in you and that my name might be proclaimed in all the earth."*b* Therefore God has mercy on whom he wants to have mercy, and he hardens whom he wants to harden.

Rom. 9:19-24

MAN CANNOT LIMIT GOD'S GRACE.   One of you will say to me: "Then why does God still blame us? For who resists his will?" But who are you, O man, to talk back to God? "Shall what is formed say to him who formed it, 'Why did you make me like this?' "*c* Does not the potter have the right to make out of the same lump of clay some pottery for noble purposes and some for common use?

What if God, choosing to show his wrath and make his power known, bore with great patience the objects of his wrath—prepared for destruction? What if he did this to make the riches of his glory known to the objects of his mercy, whom he prepared in advance for glory—even us, whom he also called, not only from the Jews but also from the Gentiles?

Rom. 9:25-29

PROPHETS TOLD OF GRACE.   As he says in Hosea:

> "I will call them 'my people' who are not my people;
> and I will call her 'my loved one' who is not my loved
> one,"*d*

and,

> "It will happen that in the very place where it was said to
> them,
> 'You are not my people,'
> they will be called 'sons of the living God.' "*e*

Isaiah cries out concerning Israel:

> "Though the number of the Israelites be like the sand by the
> sea,
> only the remnant will be saved.

*w*Gen. 21:12   *x*Gen. 18:10,14   *y*Gen. 25:23   *z*Mal. 1:2,3   *a*Exodus 33:19
*b*Exodus 9:16   *c*Isaiah 29:16; 45:9   *d*Hosea 2:23   *e*Hosea 1:10

> For the Lord will carry out
>   his sentence on earth with speed and finality."*f*

It is just as Isaiah said previously:

> "Unless the Lord Almighty
>   had left us descendants,
> we would have become like Sodom,
>   we would have been like Gomorrah."*g*

JEWS DID NOT SEE GRACE.   What then shall we say? That the Gentiles, who did not pursue righteousness, have obtained it, a righteousness that is by faith; but Israel, who pursued a law of righteousness, has not attained it. Why not? Because they pursued it not by faith but as if it were by works. They stumbled over the "stumbling stone." As it is written:

Rom.
9:30-33

> "See, I lay in Zion a stone that causes men to stumble
>   and a rock that makes them fall,
> and the one who trusts in him will never be put to
>   shame."*h*

JEWS TRIED TO EARN SALVATION.   Brothers, my heart's desire and prayer to God for the Israelites is that they may be saved. For I can testify about them that they are zealous for God, but their zeal is not based on knowledge. Since they did not know the righteousness that comes from God and sought to establish their own, they did not submit to God's righteousness. Christ is the end of the law so that there may be righteousness for everyone who believes.

Rom.
10:1-4

SALVATION FOR ALL.   Moses describes in this way the righteousness that is by the law: "The man who does these things will live by them."*i* But the righteousness that is by faith says: "Do not say in your heart, 'Who will ascend into heaven?'*j*" (that is, to bring Christ down) "or 'Who will descend into the deep?'*k*" (that is, to bring Christ up from the dead). But what does it say? "The word is near you; it is in your mouth and in your heart,"*l* that is, the word of faith we are proclaiming: That if you confess with your mouth, "Jesus is Lord," and believe in your heart that God raised him from the dead, you will be saved. For it is with your heart that you believe and are justified, and it is with your mouth that you confess and are saved. As the Scripture says, "Anyone who trusts in him will never be put to shame."*m* For there is no difference between Jew and Gentile—the same Lord is Lord of all and richly blesses all who call on him, for, "Everyone who calls on the name of the Lord will be saved."*n*

Rom.
10:5-13

GOSPEL PRODUCES FAITH.   How, then, can they call on the one they have not believed in? And how can they believe in the one of whom they have not heard? And how can they hear without someone preaching to them? And how can they preach unless they are sent? As it is written, "How beautiful are the feet of those who bring good news!"*o*

Rom.
10:14-17

But not all the Israelites accepted the good news. For Isaiah says, "Lord, who has believed our message?"*p* Consequently, faith comes from hearing the message, and the message is heard through the word of Christ.

f Isaiah 10:22,23   *g* Isaiah 1:9   *h* Isaiah 8:14; 28:16   *i* Lev. 18:5   *j* Deut. 30:12
k Deut. 30:13   *l* Deut. 30:14   *m* Isaiah 28:16   *n* Joel 2:32   *o* Isaiah 52:7   *p* Isaiah
53:1

Rom.
10:18-21

ISRAEL REJECTED PREACHING.   But I ask: Did they not hear? Of course they did:

> "Their voice has gone out into all the earth,
>   their words to the ends of the world."q

Again I ask: Did Israel not understand? First, Moses says,

> "I will make you envious by those who are not a nation;
>   I will make you angry by a nation that has no
>   understanding."r

And Isaiah boldly says,

> "I was found by those who did not seek me;
>   I revealed myself to those who did not ask for me."s

But concerning Israel he says,

> "All day long I have held out my hands
>   to a disobedient and obstinate people."t

Rom.
11:1-6

ALWAYS A FAITHFUL REMNANT.   I ask then: Did God reject his people? By no means! I am an Israelite myself, a descendant of Abraham, from the tribe of Benjamin. God did not reject his people, whom he foreknew. Don't you know what the Scripture says in the passage about Elijah—how he appealed to God against Israel: "Lord, they have killed your prophets and torn down your altars; I am the only one left, and they are trying to kill me"u? And what was God's answer to him? "I have reserved for myself seven thousand who have not bowed the knee to Baal."v So too, at the present time there is a remnant chosen by grace. And if by grace, then it is no longer by works; if it were, grace would no longer be grace.w

Rom.
11:7-10

UNRIGHTEOUS BLINDED TO TRUTH.   What then? What Israel sought so earnestly it did not obtain, but the elect did. The others were hardened, as it is written:

> "God gave them a spirit of stupor,
>   eyes so that they could not see
>   and ears so that they could not hear,
>   to this very day."x

And David says:

> "May their table become a snare and a trap,
>   a stumbling block and a retribution for them.
> May their eyes be darkened so they cannot see,
>   and their backs be bent forever."y

Rom.
11:11,12

JEWS BROUGHT GRACE TO GENTILES.   Again I ask: Did they stumble so as to fall beyond recovery? Not at all! Rather, because of their transgression, salvation has come to the Gentiles to make Israel envious. But if their transgression means riches for the world, and their loss means riches for the Gentiles, how much greater riches will their fullness bring!

Rom.
11:13-16

GENTILES MAY WIN BACK JEWS.   I am talking to you Gentiles. Inasmuch as I am the apostle to the Gentiles, I make much of my ministry in the hope that I may somehow arouse my own people to envy and save some of them. For if their rejection is the reconciliation of the world, what will their acceptance be but life from the dead? If the part of the dough

qPsalm 19:4   rDeut. 32:21   sIsaiah 65:1   tIsaiah 65:2   u1 Kings 19:10,14
v1 Kings 19:18   wSome manuscripts be grace. But if by works, then it is no longer grace; if it were, work would no longer be work.   xDeut. 29:4; Isaiah 29:10   yPsalm 69:22,23

offered as firstfruits is holy, then the whole batch is holy; if the root is holy, so are the branches.

GENTILES NOT TO BOAST.   If some of the branches have been broken off, and you, though a wild olive shoot, have been grafted in among the others and now share in the nourishing sap from the olive root, do not boast over those branches. If you do, consider this: You do not support the root, but the root supports you. You will say then, "Branches were broken off so that I could be grafted in." Granted. But they were broken off because of unbelief, and you stand by faith. Do not be arrogant, but be afraid. For if God did not spare the natural branches, he will not spare you either.

Consider therefore the kindness and sternness of God: sternness to those who fell, but kindness to you, provided that you continue in his kindness. Otherwise, you also will be cut off. And if they do not persist in unbelief, they will be grafted in, for God is able to graft them in again. After all, if you were cut out of an olive tree that is wild by nature, and contrary to nature were grafted into a cultivated olive tree, how much more readily will these, the natural branches, be grafted into their own olive tree!

GRACE EXTENDS TO ALL.   I do not want you to be ignorant of this mystery, brothers, so that you may not be conceited: Israel has experienced a hardening in part until the full number of the Gentiles has come in. And so all Israel will be saved, as it is written:

> "The deliverer will come from Zion;
> he will turn godlessness away from Jacob.
> And this is[z] my covenant with them
> when I take away their sins."[a]

As far as the gospel is concerned, they are enemies on your account; but as far as election is concerned, they are loved on account of the patriarchs, for God's gifts and his call are irrevocable. Just as you who were at one time disobedient to God have now received mercy as a result of their disobedience, so they too have now become disobedient in order that they too may now[b] receive mercy as a result of God's mercy to you. For God has bound all men over to disobedience so that he may have mercy on them all.

SONG OF PRAISE.

> Oh, the depth of the riches of the wisdom and[c] knowledge
> of God!
> How unsearchable his judgments,
> and his paths beyond tracing out!
> "Who has known the mind of the Lord?
> Or who has been his counselor?"[d]
> "Who has ever given to God,
> that God should repay him?"[e]
> For from him and through him and to him are all things.
> To him be the glory forever! Amen.

Rom.
11:17-24

Rom.
11:25-32

Rom.
11:33-36

[z]Or *will be now.*   [a]Isaiah 59:20,21; 27:9; Jer. 31:33,34   [b]Some manuscripts do not have now.   [c]Or *riches and the wisdom and the*   [d]Isaiah 40:13   [e]Job 41:11

Christian Life and Conduct

Rom.
12:1,2

CALL TO HOLINESS.   Therefore, I urge you, brothers, in view of God's mercy, to offer your bodies as living sacrifices, holy and pleasing to God—this is your spiritual*f* act of worship. Do not conform any longer to the pattern of this world, but be transformed by the renewing of your mind. Then you will be able to test and approve what God's will is—his good, pleasing and perfect will.

Rom.
12:3-8

USE OF GIFTS.   For by the grace given me I say to every one of you: Do not think of yourself more highly than you ought, but rather think of yourself with sober judgment, in accordance with the measure of faith God has given you. Just as each of us has one body with many members, and these members do not all have the same function, so in Christ we who are many form one body, and each member belongs to all the others. We have different gifts, according to the grace given us. If a man's gift is prophesying, let him use it in proportion to his*g* faith. If it is serving, let him serve; if it is teaching, let him teach; if it is encouraging, let him encourage; if it is contributing to the needs of others, let him give generously; if it is leadership, let him govern diligently; if it is showing mercy, let him do it cheerfully.

Rom.
12:9-13

SHOW LOVE THROUGH DEEDS.   Love must be sincere. Hate what is evil; cling to what is good. Be devoted to one another in brotherly love. Honor one another above yourselves. Never be lacking in zeal, but keep your spiritual fervor, serving the Lord. Be joyful in hope, patient in affliction, faithful in prayer. Share with God's people who are in need. Practice hospitality.

Rom.
12:14-21

SHOW LOVE IN RELATIONSHIPS.   Bless those who persecute you; bless and do not curse. Rejoice with those who rejoice; mourn with those who mourn. Live in harmony with one another. Do not be proud, but be willing to associate with people of low position.*h* Do not be conceited.

Do not repay anyone evil for evil. Be careful to do what is right in the eyes of everybody. If it is possible, as far as it depends on you, live at peace with everyone. Do not take revenge, my friends, but leave room for God's wrath, for it is written: "It is mine to avenge; I will repay,"*i* says the Lord. On the contrary:

> "If your enemy is hungry, feed him;
>   if he is thirsty, give him something to drink.
>   In doing this, you will heap burning coals on his head."*j*

Do not be overcome by evil, but overcome evil with good.

Rom.
13:1-7

DUTY TOWARD CIVIL AUTHORITY.   Everyone must submit himself to the governing authorities, for there is no authority except that which God has established. The authorities that exist have been established by God. Consequently, he who rebels against the authority is rebelling against what God has instituted, and those who do so will bring judgment on themselves. For rulers hold no terror for those who do right, but for those who do wrong. Do you want to be free from fear of the one in authority? Then do what is right and he will commend you. For he is God's servant

---

f Or *reasonable*   *g* Or *in agreement with the*   *h* Or *willing to do menial work*   *i* Deut. 32:35   *j* Prov. 25:21,22

to do you good. But if you do wrong, be afraid, for he does not bear the sword for nothing. He is God's servant, an agent of wrath to bring punishment on the wrongdoer. Therefore, it is necessary to submit to the authorities, not only because of possible punishment but also because of conscience.

This is also why you pay taxes, for the authorities are God's servants, who give their full time to governing. Give everyone what you owe him: If you owe taxes, pay taxes; if revenue, then revenue; if respect, then respect; if honor, then honor.

LOVE IS KEY TO OBLIGATIONS.   Let no debt remain outstanding, except the continuing debt to love one another, for he who loves his fellowman has fulfilled the law. The commandments, "Do not commit adultery," "Do not murder," "Do not steal," "Do not covet,"[k] and whatever other commandment there may be, are summed up in this one rule: "Love your neighbor as yourself."[l] Love does no harm to its neighbor. Therefore love is the fulfillment of the law.

Rom. 13:8-10

HOPE IS KEY TO MOTIVATION.   And do this, understanding the present time. The hour has come for you to wake up from your slumber, because our salvation is nearer now than when we first believed. The night is nearly over; the day is almost here. So let us put aside the deeds of darkness and put on the armor of light. Let us behave decently, as in the daytime, not in orgies and drunkenness, not in sexual immorality and debauchery, not in dissension and jealousy. Rather, clothe yourselves with the Lord Jesus Christ, and do not think about how to gratify the desires of the sinful nature.[m]

Rom. 13:11-14

Regarding Mutual Responsibility

NOT TO JUDGE CONSCIENCE.   Accept him whose faith is weak, without passing judgment on disputable matters. One man's faith allows him to eat everything, but another man, whose faith is weak, eats only vegetables. The man who eats everything must not look down on him who does not, and the man who does not eat everything must not condemn the man who does, for God has accepted him. Who are you to judge someone else's servant? To his own master he stands or falls. And he will stand, for the Lord is able to make him stand.

Rom. 14:1-4

MATTERS OF CONSCIENCE.   One man considers one day more sacred than another; another man considers every day alike. Each one should be fully convinced in his own mind. He who regards one day as special, does so to the Lord. He who eats meat, eats to the Lord, for he gives thanks to God; and he who abstains, does so to the Lord and gives thanks to God. For none of us lives to himself alone and none of us dies to himself alone. If we live, we live to the Lord; and if we die, we die to the Lord. So, whether we live or die, we belong to the Lord.

For this very reason, Christ died and returned to life so that he might be the Lord of both the dead and the living.

Rom. 14:5-9

EACH MUST ANSWER.   You, then, why do you judge your brother? Or why do you look down on your brother? For we will all stand before God's judgment seat. It is written:

Rom. 14:10-12

[k]Exodus 20:13-15,17; Deut. 5:17-19,21   [l]Lev. 19:18   [m]Or the flesh

" 'As surely as I live,' says the Lord,
'every knee will bow before me;
every tongue will confess to God.' " [n]

So then, each of us will give an account of himself to God.

**Rom.
14:13-21**

CAUSING BROTHER TO STUMBLE.   Therefore let us stop passing judgment on one another. Instead, make up your mind not to put any stumbling block or obstacle in your brother's way. As one who is in the Lord Jesus, I am fully convinced that no food[o] is unclean in itself. But if anyone regards something as unclean, then for him it is unclean. If your brother is distressed because of what you eat, you are no longer acting in love. Do not by your eating destroy your brother for whom Christ died. Do not allow what you consider good to be spoken of as evil. For the kingdom of God is not a matter of eating and drinking, but of righteousness, peace and joy in the Holy Spirit, because anyone who serves Christ in this way is pleasing to God and approved by men.

Let us therefore make every effort to do what leads to peace and to mutual edification. Do not destroy the work of God for the sake of food. All food is clean, but it is wrong for a man to eat anything that causes someone else to stumble. It is better not to eat meat or drink wine or to do anything else that will cause your brother to fall.

**Rom.
14:22,23**

BASE ACTIONS UPON CONVICTION.   So whatever you believe about these things keep between yourself and God. Blessed is the man who does not condemn himself by what he approves. But the man who has doubts is condemned if he eats, because his eating is not from faith; and everything that does not come from faith is sin.

**Rom.
15:1-6**

EXAMPLE OF FORBEARANCE.   We who are strong ought to bear with the failings of the weak and not to please ourselves. Each of us should please his neighbor for his good, to build him up. For even Christ did not please himself but, as it is written: "The insults of those who insult you have fallen on me."[p] For everything that was written in the past was written to teach us, so that through endurance and the encouragement of the Scriptures we might have hope.

May the God who gives endurance and encouragement give you a spirit of unity among yourselves as you follow Christ Jesus, so that with one heart and mouth you may glorify the God and Father of our Lord Jesus Christ.

**Rom.
15:7-13**

CALL FOR MUTUAL ACCEPTANCE.   Accept one another, then, just as Christ accepted you, in order to bring praise to God. For I tell you that Christ has become a servant of the Jews[q] on behalf of God's truth, to confirm the promises made to the patriarchs so that the Gentiles may glorify God for his mercy, as it is written:

"Therefore I will praise you among the Gentiles;
I will sing hymns to your name."[r]

Again, it says,

"Rejoice, O Gentiles, with his people."[s]

And again,

"Praise the Lord, all you Gentiles,
and sing praises to him, all you peoples."[t]

And again, Isaiah says,

[n]Isaiah 45:23   [o]Or *that nothing*   [p]Psalm 69:9   [q]Greek *circumcision*   [r]2 Samuel
22:50; Psalm 18:49   [s]Deut. 32:43   [t]Psalm 117:1

"The Root of Jesse will spring up,
    one who will arise to rule over the nations;
  the Gentiles will hope in him."[u]

May the God of hope fill you with all joy and peace as you trust in him,
so that you may overflow with hope by the power of the Holy Spirit.

Closing Remarks

REASON FOR WRITING.   I myself am convinced, my brothers, that you
yourselves are full of goodness, complete in knowledge and competent to
instruct one another. I have written you quite boldly on some points, as if
to remind you of them again, because of the grace God gave me to be a
minister of Christ Jesus to the Gentiles with the priestly duty of proclaiming the gospel of God, so that the Gentiles might become an offering
acceptable to God, sanctified by the Holy Spirit.

Rom.
15:14-16

PRIDE IN GENTILE MINISTRY.   Therefore I glory in Christ Jesus in my
service to God. I will not venture to speak of anything except what Christ
has accomplished through me in leading the Gentiles to obey God by what
I have said and done—by the power of signs and miracles, through the
power of the Spirit. So from Jerusalem all the way around to Illyricum, I
have fully proclaimed the gospel of Christ. It has always been my ambition to preach the gospel where Christ was not known, so that I would not
be building on someone else's foundation. Rather, as it is written:

Rom.
15:17-21

"Those who were not told about him will see,
    and those who have not heard will understand."[v]

FUTURE TRAVEL PLANS.   This is why I have often been hindered from
coming to you.
  But now that there is no more place for me to work in these regions, and
since I have been longing for many years to see you, I plan to do so when
I go to Spain. I hope to visit you while passing through and to have you
assist me on my journey there, after I have enjoyed your company for a
while. Now, however, I am on my way to Jerusalem in the service of the
saints there. For Macedonia and Achaia were pleased to make a contribution for the poor among the saints in Jerusalem. They were pleased to do
it, and indeed they owe it to them. For if the Gentiles have shared in the
Jews' spiritual blessings, they owe it to the Jews to share with them their
material blessings. So after I have completed this task and have made sure
that they have received this fruit, I will go to Spain and visit you on the
way. I know that when I come to you, I will come in the full measure of the
blessing of Christ.

Rom.
15:22-29

REQUEST FOR PRAYERS.   I urge you, brothers, by our Lord Jesus Christ
and by the love of the Spirit, to join me in my struggle by praying to God
for me. Pray that I may be rescued from the unbelievers in Judea and that
my service in Jerusalem may be acceptable to the saints there, so that by
God's will I may come to you with joy and together with you be refreshed.
The God of peace be with you all. Amen.

Rom.
15:30-33

COMMENDATION OF PHOEBE.   I commend to you our sister Phoebe,
a servant[w] of the church in Cenchrea. I ask you to receive her in the Lord

Rom.
16:1,2

[u]Isaiah 11:10   [v]Isaiah 52:15   [w]Or deaconess

in a way worthy of the saints and to give her any help she may need from you, for she has been a great help to many people, including me.

Rom.
16:3-16

SPECIAL GREETINGS.   Greet Priscilla[x] and Aquila, my fellow workers in Christ Jesus. They risked their lives for me. Not only I but all the churches of the Gentiles are grateful to them.

Greet also the church that meets at their house.

Greet my dear friend Epenetus, who was the first convert to Christ in the province of Asia.

Greet Mary, who worked very hard for you.

Greet Andronicus and Junias, my relatives who have been in prison with me. They are outstanding among the apostles, and they were in Christ before I was.

Greet Ampliatus, whom I love in the Lord.

Greet Urbanus, our fellow worker in Christ, and my dear friend Stachys.

Greet Apelles, tested and approved in Christ.

Greet those who belong to the household of Aristobulus.

Greet Herodion, my relative.

Greet those in the household of Narcissus who are in the Lord.

Greet Tryphena and Tryphosa, those women who work hard in the Lord.

Greet my dear friend Persis, another woman who has worked very hard in the Lord.

Greet Rufus, chosen in the Lord, and his mother, who has been a mother to me, too.

Greet Asyncritus, Phlegon, Hermes, Patrobas, Hermas and the brothers with them.

Greet Philologus, Julia, Nereus and his sister, and Olympas and all the saints with them.

Greet one another with a holy kiss.

All the churches of Christ send greetings.

Rom.
16:17-20

WARNING ABOUT TROUBLEMAKERS.   I urge you, brothers, to watch out for those who cause divisions and put obstacles in your way that are contrary to the teaching you have learned. Keep away from them. For such people are not serving our Lord Christ, but their own appetites. By smooth talk and flattery they deceive the minds of naive people. Everyone has heard about your obedience, so I am full of joy over you; but I want you to be wise about what is good, and innocent about what is evil.

The God of peace will soon crush Satan under your feet.

The grace of our Lord Jesus be with you.

Rom.
16:21-23

GREETINGS FROM OTHER BRETHREN.   Timothy, my fellow worker, sends his greetings to you, as do Lucius, Jason and Sosipater, my relatives.

I, Tertius, who wrote down this letter, greet you in the Lord.

Gaius, whose hospitality I and the whole church here enjoy, sends you his greetings.

Erastus, who is the city's director of public works, and our brother Quartus send you their greetings.[y]

---

[x]Greek *Prisca*, a variant of *Priscilla*   [y]Some manuscripts *their greetings.* [24]*May the grace of our Lord Jesus Christ be with all of you. Amen.*

PRAISE TO GOD.   Now to him who is able to establish you by my gospel and the proclamation of Jesus Christ, according to the revelation of the mystery hidden for long ages past, but now revealed and made known through the prophetic writings by the command of the eternal God, so that all nations might believe and obey him—to the only wise God be glory forever through Jesus Christ! Amen.

Rom. 16:25-27

As the historical record continues, Paul's plans to leave directly for Jerusalem are abruptly changed, and a detour is made necessary. Paul begins his return to Syria through Philippi, Troas, and Miletus (near Ephesus). While at Miletus, Paul addresses the elders from the church at Ephesus and tells them that he anticipates possible imprisonment and persecution upon his return to Jerusalem. Paul undoubtedly also warns them of the danger of falling away from the teaching of Christ—a concern which he will address at length in various letters later in his life. Sadly, concluding his close association with the church in Ephesus, Paul leaves resolutely to face whatever outcome awaits him in Syria.

FROM GREECE TO TROAS.   Because the Jews made a plot against him just as he was about to sail for Syria, he decided to go back through Macedonia. He was accompanied by Sopater son of Pyrrhus from Berea, Aristarchus and Secundus from Thessalonica, Gaius from Derbe, Timothy also, and Tychicus and Trophimus from the province of Asia. These men went on ahead and waited for us at Troas. But we sailed from Philippi after the Feast of Unleavened Bread, and five days later joined the others at Troas, where we stayed seven days.

Acts 20:3b-6 (Spring, A.D. 58)

EUTYCHUS REVIVED.   On the first day of the week we came together to break bread. Paul spoke to the people and, because he intended to leave the next day, kept on talking until midnight. There were many lamps in the upstairs room where we were meeting. Seated in a window was a young man named Eutychus, who was sinking into a deep sleep as Paul talked on and on. When he was sound asleep, he fell to the ground from the third story and was picked up dead. Paul went down, threw himself on the young man and put his arms around him. "Don't be alarmed," he said. "He's alive!" Then he went upstairs again and broke bread and ate. After talking until daylight, he left. The people took the young man home alive and were greatly comforted.

Acts 20:7-12 Troas

FROM TROAS TO MILETUS.   We went on ahead to the ship and sailed for Assos, where we were going to take Paul aboard. He had made this arrangement because he was going there on foot. When he met us at Assos, we took him aboard and went on to Mitylene. The next day we set sail from there and arrived off Kios. The day after that we crossed over to Samos, and on the following day arrived at Miletus. Paul had decided to sail past Ephesus to avoid spending time in the province of Asia, for he was in a hurry to reach Jerusalem, if possible, by the day of Pentecost.

Acts 20:13-16

DISCOURSE TO EPHESIAN ELDERS.   From Miletus, Paul sent to Ephesus for the elders of the church. When they arrived, he said to them: "You know how I lived the whole time I was with you, from the first day I came into the province of Asia. I served the Lord with great humility and with tears, although I was severely tested by the plots of the Jews. You know

Acts 20:17-35 Miletus

that I have not hesitated to preach anything that would be helpful to you but have taught you publicly and from house to house. I have declared to both Jews and Greeks that they must turn to God in repentance and have faith in our Lord Jesus.

"And now, compelled by the Spirit, I am going to Jerusalem, not knowing what will happen to me there. I only know that in every city the Holy Spirit warns me that prison and hardships are facing me. However, I consider my life worth nothing to me, if only I may finish the race and complete the task the Lord Jesus has given me—the task of testifying to the gospel of God's grace.

"Now I know that none of you among whom I have gone about preaching the kingdom will ever see me again. Therefore, I declare to you today that I am innocent of the blood of all men. For I have not hesitated to proclaim to you the whole will of God. Keep watch over yourselves and all the flock of which the Holy Spirit has made you overseers.^{z} Be shepherds of the church of God,^{a} which he bought with his own blood. I know that after I leave, savage wolves will come in among you and will not spare the flock. Even from your own number men will arise and distort the truth in order to draw away disciples after them. So be on your guard! Remember that for three years I never stopped warning each of you night and day with tears.

"Now I commit you to God and to the word of his grace, which can build you up and give you an inheritance among all those who are sanctified. I have not coveted anyone's silver or gold or clothing. You yourselves know that these hands of mine have supplied my own needs and the needs of my companions. In everything I did, I showed you that by this kind of hard work we must help the weak, remembering the words the Lord Jesus himself said: 'It is more blessed to give than to receive.'"

Acts 20:36-38

SAD FAREWELL.   When he had said this, he knelt down with all of them and prayed. They all wept as they embraced him and kissed him. What grieved them most was his statement that they would never see his face again. Then they accompanied him to the ship.

Acts 21:1-6 Tyre

VISITING DISCIPLES AT TYRE. After we had torn ourselves away from them, we put out to sea and sailed straight to Cos. The next day we went to Rhodes and from there to Patara. We found a ship crossing over to Phoenicia, went on board and set sail. After sighting Cyprus and passing to the south of it, we sailed on to Syria. We landed at Tyre, where our ship was to unload its cargo. Finding the disciples there, we stayed with them seven days. Through the Spirit they urged Paul not to go on to Jerusalem. But when our time was up, we left and continued on our way. All the disciples and their wives and children accompanied us out of the city, and there on the beach we knelt to pray. After saying good-by to each other, we went aboard the ship, and they returned home.

Acts 21:7-14 Caesarea

AGABUS PROPHESIES IMPRISONMENT.   We continued our voyage from Tyre and landed at Ptolemais, where we greeted the brothers and stayed with them for a day. Leaving the next day, we reached Caesarea and stayed at the house of Philip the evangelist, one of the Seven. He had four unmarried daughters who prophesied.

After we had been there a number of days, a prophet named Agabus

^{z}Traditionally *bishops* ^{a}Many manuscripts *of the Lord* came down from Judea. Coming over to us, he took Paul's belt, tied his own hands and feet with it and said, "The Holy Spirit says, 'In this way the Jews of Jerusalem will bind the owner of this belt and will hand him over to the Gentiles.'"

When we heard this, we and the people there pleaded with Paul not to go up to Jerusalem. Then Paul answered, "Why are you weeping and breaking my heart? I am ready not only to be bound, but also to die in Jerusalem for the name of the Lord Jesus." When he would not be dissuaded, we gave up and said, "The Lord's will be done."

JOURNEY ENDS IN JERUSALEM.   After this, we got ready and went up to Jerusalem. Some of the disciples from Caesarea accompanied us and brought us to the home of Mnason, where we were to stay. He was a man from Cyprus and one of the early disciples.

Acts
21:15,16
Jerusalem
(Ca. A.D. 58)

Paul's Arrest and Trial

*T*he prophecy of Agabus is soon to be fulfilled. Upon his return to Jerusalem, Paul now finds himself being arrested and attacked by local Jews who have been stirred up by certain men from Asia. Fortunately, however, Paul will be rescued by Roman soldiers acting under Claudius Lysias, the local Roman commander. The historical record sets forth Paul's attempt to defend himself before a mob which is demanding his death, and indicates a fair reception to his discourse until he mentions being God's messenger to the Gentiles. Angry crowd reaction to that assertion forces Claudius Lysias to take Paul into protective custody.

On the following day, the record reveals that Paul is put on trial before the Sanhedrin Council, in much the same way that Jesus himself had been tried years earlier. By referring to his own heritage as a Pharisee, and to his belief in a resurrection after death, Paul adroitly sets the Pharisees in controversy against the Sadducees, who do not believe in a resurrection. In the debate which ensues, no charges are brought and Paul is returned to custody. When a plot to kill Paul is uncovered, Paul is secreted away by night to Caesarea, where he will later be brought before the governor, Felix.

Now, as Luke records Paul's arrival in Jerusalem before his arrest, an effort is made by James and the elders at Jerusalem to calm the anxiety of Jewish Christians, who are uncertain about Paul's teaching.

PLAN FOR UNITY.   When we arrived at Jerusalem, the brothers received us warmly. The next day Paul and the rest of us went to see James, and all the elders were present. Paul greeted them and reported in detail what God had done among the Gentiles through his ministry.

Acts
21:17-26
Jerusalem
(Pentecost,
A.D. 58?)

When they heard this, they praised God. Then they said to Paul: "You see, brother, how many thousands of Jews have believed, and all of them are zealous for the law. They have been informed that you teach all the Jews who live among the Gentiles to turn away from Moses, telling them not to circumcise their children or live according to our customs. What shall we do? They will certainly hear that you have come, so do what we tell you. There are four men with us who have made a vow. Take these men, join in their purification rites and pay their expenses, so that they can have their heads shaved. Then everybody will know there is no truth in these reports about you, but that you yourself are living in obedience to the law. As for the Gentile believers, we have written to them our decision that they should abstain from food sacrificed to idols, from blood, from the meat of strangled animals and from sexual immorality."

The next day Paul took the men and purified himself along with them. Then he went to the temple to give notice of the date when the days of purification would end and the offering would be made for each of them.

Acts
21:27-30

JEWS SEIZE PAUL IN TEMPLE.   When the seven days were nearly over, some Jews from the province of Asia saw Paul at the temple. They stirred up the whole crowd and seized him, shouting, "Men of Israel, help us! This is the man who teaches all men everywhere against our people and our law and this place. And besides, he has brought Greeks into the temple area and defiled this holy place." (They had previously seen Trophimus the Ephesian in the city with Paul and assumed that Paul had brought him into the temple area.)

The whole city was aroused, and the people came running from all directions. Seizing Paul, they dragged him from the temple, and immediately the gates were shut.

Acts
21:31-36

PAUL ARRESTED.   While they were trying to kill him, news reached the commander of the Roman troops that the whole city of Jerusalem was in an uproar. He at once took some officers and soldiers and ran down to the crowd. When the rioters saw the commander and his soldiers, they stopped beating Paul.

The commander came up and arrested him and ordered him to be bound with two chains. Then he asked who he was and what he had done. Some in the crowd shouted one thing and some another, and since the commander could not get at the truth because of the uproar, he ordered that Paul be taken into the barracks. When Paul reached the steps, the violence of the mob was so great he had to be carried by the soldiers. The crowd that followed kept shouting, "Away with him!"

Acts
21:37-39

PAUL ASKS TO SPEAK.   As the soldiers were about to take Paul into the barracks, he asked the commander, "May I say something to you?"

"Do you speak Greek?" he replied. "Aren't you the Egyptian who started a revolt and led four thousand terrorists out into the desert some time ago?"

Paul answered, "I am a Jew, from Tarsus in Cilicia, a citizen of no ordinary city. Please let me speak to the people."

Acts
21:40-22:21

DEFENSE TO THE CROWD.   Having received the commander's permission, Paul stood on the steps and motioned to the crowd. When they were all silent, he said to them in Aramaic[b]: "Brothers and fathers, listen now to my defense."

When they heard him speak to them in Aramaic, they became very quiet. Then Paul said: "I am a Jew, born in Tarsus of Cilicia, but brought up in this city. Under Gamaliel I was thoroughly trained in the law of our fathers and was just as zealous for God as any of you are today. I persecuted the followers of this Way to their death, arresting both men and women and throwing them into prison, as also the high priest and all the Council can testify. I even obtained letters from them to their brothers in

[b]Or possibly *Hebrew*; also in 22:2

Damascus, and went there to bring these people as prisoners to Jerusalem to be punished.

"About noon as I came near Damascus, suddenly a bright light from heaven flashed around me. I fell to the ground and heard a voice say to me, 'Saul! Saul! Why do you persecute me?'

" 'Who are you, Lord?' I asked.

" 'I am Jesus of Nazareth, whom you are persecuting,' he replied. My companions saw the light, but they did not understand the voice of him who was speaking to me.

" 'What shall I do, Lord?' I asked.

" 'Get up,' the Lord said, 'and go into Damascus. There you will be told all that you have been assigned to do.' My companions led me by the hand into Damascus, because the brilliance of the light had blinded me.

"A man named Ananias came to see me. He was a devout observer of the law and highly respected by all the Jews living there. He stood beside me and said, 'Brother Saul, receive your sight!' And at that very moment I was able to see him.

"Then he said: 'The God of our fathers has chosen you to know his will and to see the Righteous One and to hear words from his mouth. You will be his witness to all men of what you have seen and heard. And now what are you waiting for? Get up, be baptized and wash your sins away, calling on his name.'

"When I returned to Jerusalem and was praying at the temple, I fell into a trance and saw the Lord speaking. 'Quick!' he said to me. 'Leave Jerusalem immediately, because they will not accept your testimony about me.'

" 'Lord,' I replied, 'these men know that I went from one synagogue to another to imprison and beat those who believe in you. And when the blood of your martyr[c] Stephen was shed, I stood there giving my approval and guarding the clothes of those who were killing him.'

"Then the Lord said to me, 'Go; I will send you far away to the Gentiles.' "

ROMAN CITIZENSHIP ASSERTED. The crowd listened to Paul until he said this. Then they raised their voices and shouted, "Rid the earth of him! He's not fit to live!"

Acts 22:22-29

As they were shouting and throwing off their cloaks and flinging dust into the air, the commander ordered Paul to be taken into the barracks. He directed that he be flogged and questioned in order to find out why the people were shouting at him like this. As they stretched him out to flog him, Paul said to the centurion standing there, "Is it legal for you to flog a Roman citizen who hasn't even been found guilty?"

When the centurion heard this, he went to the commander and reported it. "What are you going to do?" he asked. "This man is a Roman citizen."

The commander went to Paul and asked, "Tell me, are you a Roman citizen?"

"Yes, I am," he answered.

Then the commander said, "I had to pay a big price for my citizenship."

"But I was born a citizen," Paul replied.

Those who were about to question him withdrew immediately. The commander himself was alarmed when he realized that he had put Paul, a Roman citizen, in chains.

[c]Or *witness*

Acts
22:30-23:5

ON TRIAL BEFORE SANHEDRIN.   The next day, since the commander wanted to find out exactly why Paul was being accused by the Jews, he released him and ordered the chief priests and all the Sanhedrin to assemble. Then he brought Paul and had him stand before them. Paul looked straight at the Sanhedrin and said, "My brothers, I have fulfilled my duty to God in all good conscience to this day." At this the high priest Ananias ordered those standing near Paul to strike him on the mouth. Then Paul said to him, "God will strike you, you whitewashed wall! You sit there to judge me according to the law, yet you yourself violate the law by commanding that I be struck!"

Those who were standing near Paul said, "You dare to insult God's high priest?"

Paul replied, "Brothers, I did not realize that he was the high priest; for it is written: 'Do not speak evil about the ruler of your people.' [d]"

Acts
23:6-11

CONTENTION ARISES.   Then Paul, knowing that some of them were Sadducees and the others Pharisees, called out in the Sanhedrin, "My brothers, I am a Pharisee, the son of a Pharisee. I stand on trial because of my hope in the resurrection of the dead." When he said this, a dispute broke out between the Pharisees and the Sadducees, and the assembly was divided. (The Sadducees say that there is no resurrection, and that there are neither angels nor spirits, but the Pharisees acknowledge them all.)

There was a great uproar, and some of the teachers of the law who were Pharisees stood up and argued vigorously. "We find nothing wrong with this man," they said. "What if a spirit or an angel has spoken to him?" The dispute became so violent that the commander was afraid Paul would be torn to pieces by them. He ordered the troops to go down and take him away from them by force and bring him into the barracks.

The following night the Lord stood near Paul and said, "Take courage! As you have testified about me in Jerusalem, so you must also testify in Rome."

Acts
23:12-15

CONSPIRACY TO KILL PAUL.   The next morning the Jews formed a conspiracy and bound themselves with an oath not to eat or drink until they had killed Paul. More than forty men were involved in this plot. They went to the chief priests and elders and said, "We have taken a solemn oath not to eat anything until we have killed Paul. Now then, you and the Sanhedrin petition the commander to bring him before you on the pretext of wanting more accurate information about his case. We are ready to kill him before he gets here."

Acts
23:16-22

PAUL'S NEPHEW GIVES WARNING.   But when the son of Paul's sister heard of this plot, he went into the barracks and told Paul.

Then Paul called one of the centurions and said, "Take this young man to the commander; he has something to tell him." So he took him to the commander.

The centurion said, "Paul, the prisoner, sent for me and asked me to bring this young man to you because he has something to tell you."

[d]Exodus 22:28

The commander took the young man by the hand, drew him aside and asked, "What is it you want to tell me?"

He said: "The Jews have agreed to ask you to bring Paul before the Sanhedrin tomorrow on the pretext of wanting more accurate information about him. Don't give in to them, because more than forty of them are waiting in ambush for him. They have taken an oath not to eat or drink until they have killed him. They are ready now, waiting for your consent to their request."

The commander dismissed the young man and cautioned him, "Don't tell anyone that you have reported this to me."

PREPARATIONS FOR TRANSFER.   Then he called two of his centurions and ordered them, "Get ready a detachment of two hundred soldiers, seventy horsemen and two hundred spearmen*e* to go to Caesarea at nine tonight. Provide mounts for Paul so that he may be taken safely to Governor Felix."

Acts
23:23-30

He wrote a letter as follows:

Claudius Lysias,

To His Excellency, Governor Felix:

Greetings.

This man was seized by the Jews and they were about to kill him, but I came with my troops and rescued him, for I had learned that he is a Roman citizen. I wanted to know why they were accusing him, so I brought him to their Sanhedrin. I found that the accusation had to do with questions about their law, but there was no charge against him that deserved death or imprisonment. When I was informed of a plot to be carried out against the man, I sent him to you at once. I also ordered his accusers to present to you their case against him.

PAUL REMOVED TO CAESAREA.   So the soldiers, carrying out their orders, took Paul with them during the night and brought him as far as Antipatris. The next day they let the cavalry go on with him, while they returned to the barracks. When the cavalry arrived in Caesarea, they delivered the letter to the governor and handed Paul over to him. The governor read the letter and asked what province he was from. Learning that he was from Cilicia, he said, "I will hear your case when your accusers get here." Then he ordered that Paul be kept under guard in Herod's palace.

Acts
23:31-35
Caesarea
(Ca. A.D.
58)

Paul Before Felix, Festus, and Agrippa

*A*t Caesarea, Paul has three opportunities to present his defense and to preach the gospel to the Roman authorities who now hold him under arrest. The first appearance is before Felix, the governor and procurator of Judea. Felix had been appointed initially by Claudius Caesar and then confirmed by Claudius' successor, Nero. Felix's wife, Drusilla, who is mentioned by Luke, is the daughter of Herod Agrippa I and the sister of

---

*e*The meaning of the Greek for this word in uncertain.

Herod Agrippa II, before whom Paul will also appear. Felix knows enough about "The Way" to realize that there is no substance to the charges being brought against Paul, and Luke's account hints that Felix is even somewhat troubled by Paul's teaching. But he is primarily motivated by greed and therefore is angered when Paul fails to offer a bribe. Luke's record notes that Paul is forced to remain in jail for two years, at the end of which time Felix is removed from office. (Secular history indicates that serious riots and charges against Felix by the Jews prompted his recall to Rome.)

Felix is succeeded by Porcius Festus, about whom little is known. Festus also finds no fault in Paul and suggests that Paul once again be taken before the Sanhedrin in Jerusalem. But Paul (who, though a Jew, is also a Roman citizen by birth) exercises his right to appeal his case to Caesar.

Shortly after Paul seeks an appeal, Festus is visited by King Herod Agrippa II and his sister Bernice. (It was their father, Herod Agrippa I, who had persecuted the church and killed James the brother of John.) When Festus expresses frustration regarding Paul's case, Agrippa asks if he can hear Paul's story for himself. Paul's presentation before Agrippa summarizes his personal conversion and subsequent ministry. At the conclusion of Paul's discourse Luke relates a memorable conversation between Agrippa and Paul in which Agrippa appears to be uncomfortably vulnerable to the gospel message presented by Paul. But if Agrippa is touched at all, there is no record that he ever responds in full belief.

Acts 24:1-9
Caesarea
(Ca. A.D. 58)

INDICTMENT AGAINST PAUL.   Five days later the high priest Ananias went down to Caesarea with some of the elders and a lawyer named Tertullus, and they brought their charges against Paul before the governor. When Paul was called in, Tertullus presented his case before Felix: "We have enjoyed a long period of peace under you, and your foresight has brought about reforms in this nation. Everywhere and in every way, most excellent Felix, we acknowledge this with profound gratitude. But in order not to weary you further, I would request that you be kind enough to hear us briefly.

"We have found this man to be a troublemaker, stirring up riots among the Jews all over the world. He is a ringleader of the Nazarene sect and even tried to desecrate the temple; so we seized him. By^f examining him yourself you will be able to learn the truth about all these charges we are bringing against him." The Jews joined in the accusation, asserting that these things were true.

Acts 24:10-21

STATEMENT IN DEFENSE.   When the governor motioned for him to speak, Paul replied: "I know that for a number of years you have been a judge over this nation; so I gladly make my defense. You can easily verify that no more than twelve days ago I went up to Jerusalem to worship. My accusers did not find me arguing with anyone at the temple, or stirring up a crowd in the synagogues or anywhere else in the city. And they cannot prove to you the charges they are now making against me. However, I admit that I worship the God of our fathers as a follower of the Way,

^{f}Some manuscripts *him and wanted to judge him according to our law.* ^{7}*But the commander, Lysias, came and with the use of much force snatched him from our hands* ^{8}*and ordered his accusers to come before you. By*

which they call a sect. I believe everything that agrees with the Law and that is written in the Prophets, and I have the same hope in God as these men, that there will be a resurrection of both the righteous and the wicked. So I strive always to keep my conscience clear before God and man.

"After an absence of several years, I came to Jerusalem to bring my people gifts for the poor and to present offerings. I was ceremonially clean when they found me in the temple courts doing this. There was no crowd with me, nor was I involved in any disturbance. But there are some Jews from the province of Asia, who ought to be here before you and bring charges if they have anything against me. Or these who are here should state what crime they found in me when I stood before the Sanhedrin— unless it was this one thing I shouted as I stood in their presence: 'It is concerning the resurrection of the dead that I am on trial before you today.' "

FELIX POSTPONES DECISION. Then Felix, who was well acquainted with the Way, adjourned the proceedings. "When Lysias the commander comes," he said, "I will decide your case." He ordered the centurion to keep Paul under guard but to give him some freedom and permit his friends to take care of his needs. Acts 24:22,23

IN PRISON TWO YEARS. Several days later Felix came with his wife Drusilla, who was a Jewess. He sent for Paul and listened to him as he spoke about faith in Christ Jesus. As Paul discoursed on righteousness, self-control and the judgment to come, Felix was afraid and said, "That's enough for now! You may leave. When I find it convenient, I will send for you." At the same time he was hoping that Paul would offer him a bribe, so he sent for him frequently and talked with him. Acts 24:24-27 (From A.D. 58 to 60)

When two years had passed, Felix was succeeded by Porcius Festus, but because Felix wanted to grant a favor to the Jews, he left Paul in prison.

JEWS ASK FOR PAUL. Three days after arriving in the province, Festus went up from Caesarea to Jerusalem, where the chief priests and Jewish leaders appeared before him and presented the charges against Paul. They urgently requested Festus, as a favor to them, to have Paul transferred to Jerusalem, for they were preparing an ambush to kill him along the way. Festus answered, "Paul is being held at Caesarea, and I myself am going there soon. Let some of your leaders come with me and press charges against the man there, if he has done anything wrong." Acts 25:1-5 Jerusalem

FESTUS HEARS PAUL'S CASE. After spending eight or ten days with them, he went down to Caesarea, and the next day he convened the court and ordered that Paul be brought before him. When Paul appeared, the Jews who had come down from Jerusalem stood around him, bringing many serious charges against him, which they could not prove. Acts 25:6-8 Caesarea

Then Paul made his defense: "I have done nothing wrong against the law of the Jews or against the temple or against Caesar."

PAUL APPEALS TO CAESAR. Festus, wishing to do the Jews a favor, said to Paul, "Are you willing to go up to Jerusalem and stand trial before me there on these charges?" Acts 25:9-12

Paul answered: "I am now standing before Caesar's court, where I ought to be tried. I have not done any wrong to the Jews, as you yourself know very well. If, however, I am guilty of doing anything deserving death, I do not refuse to die. But if the charges brought against me by these Jews are not true, no one has the right to hand me over to them. I appeal to Caesar!"

After Festus had conferred with his council, he declared: "You have appealed to Caesar. To Caesar you will go!"

Acts
25:13-22

FESTUS AND AGRIPPA.   A few days later King Agrippa and Bernice arrived at Caesarea to pay their respects to Festus. Since they were spending many days there, Festus discussed Paul's case with the king. He said: "There is a man here whom Felix left as a prisoner. When I went to Jerusalem, the chief priests and elders of the Jews brought charges against him and asked that he be condemned.

"I told them that it is not the Roman custom to hand over any man before he has faced his accusers and has had an opportunity to defend himself against their charges. When they came here with me, I did not delay the case, but convened the court the next day and ordered the man to be brought in. When his accusers got up to speak, they did not charge him with any of the crimes I had expected. Instead, they had some points of dispute with him about their own religion and about a dead man named Jesus who Paul claimed was alive. I was at a loss how to investigate such matters; so I asked if he would be willing to go to Jerusalem and stand trial there on these charges. When Paul made his appeal to be held over for the Emperor's decision, I ordered him held until I could send him to Caesar."

Then Agrippa said to Festus, "I would like to hear this man myself."

He replied, "Tomorrow you will hear him."

Acts
25:23-27

PAUL PRESENTED TO AUDIENCE.   The next day Agrippa and Bernice came with great pomp and entered the audience room with the high ranking officers and the leading men of the city. At the command of Festus, Paul was brought in. Festus said: "King Agrippa, and all who are present with us, you see this man! The whole Jewish community has petitioned me about him in Jerusalem and here in Caesarea, shouting that he ought not to live any longer. I found he had done nothing deserving of death, but because he made his appeal to the Emperor I decided to send him to Rome. But I have nothing definite to write to His Majesty about him. Therefore I have brought him before all of you, and especially before you, King Agrippa, so that as a result of this investigation I may have something to write. For I think it is unreasonable to send on a prisoner without specifying the charges against him."

Acts
26:1-23

PAUL TELLS OF MISSION.   Then Agrippa said to Paul, "You have permission to speak for yourself."

So Paul motioned with his hand and began his defense: "King Agrippa, I consider myself fortunate to stand before you today as I make my defense against all the accusations of the Jews, and especially so because you are well acquainted with all the Jewish customs and controversies. Therefore, I beg you to listen to me patiently.

"The Jews all know the way I have lived ever since I was a child, from the beginning of my life in my own country, and also in Jerusalem. They have known me for a long time and can testify, if they are willing, that according to the strictest sect of our religion, I lived as a Pharisee. And now it is because of my hope in what God has promised our fathers that I am on trial today. This is the promise our twelve tribes are hoping to see fulfilled as they earnestly serve God day and night. O king, it is because of this hope that the Jews are accusing me. Why should any of you consider it incredible that God raises the dead?

"I too was convinced that I ought to do all that was possible to oppose the name of Jesus of Nazareth. And that is just what I did in Jerusalem. On the authority of the chief priests I put many of the saints in prison, and when they were put to death, I cast my vote against them. Many a time I went from one synagogue to another to have them punished, and I tried to force them to blaspheme. In my obsession against them, I even went to foreign cities to persecute them.

"On one of these journeys I was going to Damascus with the authority and commission of the chief priests. About noon, O king, as I was on the road, I saw a light from heaven, brighter than the sun, blazing around me and my companions. We all fell to the ground, and I heard a voice saying to me in Aramaic,*8* 'Saul, Saul, why do you persecute me? It is hard for you to kick against the goads.'

"Then I asked, 'Who are you, Lord?'

"'I am Jesus, whom you are persecuting,' the Lord replied. 'Now get up and stand on your feet. I have appeared to you to appoint you as a servant and as a witness of what you have seen of me and what I will show you. I will rescue you from your own people and from the Gentiles. I am sending you to them to open their eyes and turn them from darkness to light, and from the power of Satan to God, so that they may receive forgiveness of sins and a place among those who are sanctified by faith in me.'

"So then, King Agrippa, I was not disobedient to the vision from heaven. First to those in Damascus, then to those in Jerusalem and in all Judea, and to the Gentiles also, I preached that they should repent and turn to God and prove their repentance by their deeds. That is why the Jews seized me in the temple courts and tried to kill me. But I have had God's help to this very day, and so I stand here and testify to small and great alike. I am saying nothing beyond what the prophets and Moses said would happen—that the Christ*h* would suffer and, as the first to rise from the dead, would proclaim light to his own people and to the Gentiles."

AGRIPPA'S RESPONSE.   At this point Festus interrupted Paul's defense. "You are out of your mind, Paul!" he shouted. "Your great learning is driving you insane."

"I am not insane, most excellent Festus," Paul replied. "What I am saying is true and reasonable. The king is familiar with these things, and I can speak freely to him. I am convinced that none of this has escaped his notice, because it was not done in a corner. King Agrippa, do you believe the prophets? I know you do."

Then Agrippa said to Paul, "Do you think that in such a short time you can persuade me to be a Christian?"

Paul replied, "Short time or long—I pray God that not only you but all who are listening to me today may become what I am, except for these chains."
Acts
26:24-29

INNOCENCE ACKNOWLEDGED.   The king rose, and with him the governor and Bernice and those sitting with them. They left the room, and
Acts
26:30-32

8Or Hebrew   *hOr Messiah*

while talking with one another, they said, "This man is not doing anything that deserves death or imprisonment."

Agrippa said to Festus, "This man could have been set free if he had not appealed to Caesar."

Voyage to Rome

*T*he time now approaches for Paul to be sent to Rome to make his appeal to Caesar. Paul is placed in the custody of a Roman officer named Julius, and is accompanied by Luke and Aristarchus, a brother in the Lord from Thessalonica. What follows is Luke's account of their almost-disastrous voyage from Caesarea to Rome. Leaving Caesarea, they sail north along the Syrian coast to Sidon, then west along the southern coast of what is known today as Turkey, past the ancient provinces of Cilicia and Pamphylia, to the port city of Myra in Lycia.

At Myra, Paul's entourage obtains passage on an Egyptian ship bound for Italy with both cargo and 276 persons on board. Despite a warning from Paul that trouble awaits them, the crew sets sail and they soon find themselves in difficulty off the east coast of the island of Crete. Attempting to make a safe harbor at Phoenix, on the west coast, the ship is blown off course during a two-week storm and finally breaks apart as it approaches the small island of Malta (Melita), south of Sicily. By God's grace, however, all lives are spared. During the next three months Paul works among the people of Malta and heals many of their diseases. When it is once again safe to sail, the group sets out for Italy on another Egyptian ship which has been waiting out winter storms in the harbor at Malta. The remainder of the voyage is happily uneventful, and Luke records the warm welcome which they receive from the brethren in Italy.

Acts 27:1-8
Leaving
Caesarea
(Ca. A.D.
60)

FROM CAESAREA TO CRETE. When it was decided that we would sail for Italy, Paul and some other prisoners were handed over to a centurion named Julius, who belonged to the Imperial Regiment. We boarded a ship from Adramyttium about to sail for ports along the coast of the province of Asia, and we put out to sea. Aristarchus, a Macedonian from Thessalonica, was with us.

The next day we landed at Sidon; and Julius, in kindness to Paul, allowed him to go to his friends so they might provide for his needs. From there we put out to sea again and passed to the lee of Cyprus because the winds were against us. When we had sailed across the open sea off the coast of Cilicia and Pamphylia, we landed at Myra in Lycia. There the centurion found an Alexandrian ship sailing for Italy and put us on board. We made slow headway for many days and had difficulty arriving off Cnidus. When the wind did not allow us to hold our course, we sailed to the lee of Crete, opposite Salmone. We moved along the coast with difficulty and came to a place called Fair Havens, near the town of Lasea.

Acts
27:9-12
Crete

WARNING AGAINST VOYAGE. Much time had been lost, and sailing had already become dangerous because by now it was after the Fast.[i] So Paul warned them, "Men, I can see that our voyage is going to be disas-

---

[i] That is, the Day of Atonement (Yom Kippur)

trous and bring great loss to ship and cargo, and to our own lives also."
But the centurion, instead of listening to what Paul said, followed the
advice of the pilot and of the owner of the ship. Since the harbor was
unsuitable to winter in, the majority decided that we should sail on, hoping to reach Phoenix and winter there. This was a harbor in Crete, facing
both southwest and northwest.

SHIP BLOWN BY STORM.   When a gentle south wind began to blow,
they thought they had obtained what they wanted; so they weighed
anchor and sailed along the shore of Crete. Before very long, a wind of
hurricane force, called the "northeaster," swept down from the island.
The ship was caught by the storm and could not head into the wind; so
we gave way to it and were driven along. As we passed to the lee of a
small island called Cauda, we were hardly able to make the lifeboat
secure. When the men had hoisted it aboard, they passed ropes under the
ship itself to hold it together. Fearing that they would run aground on the
sandbars of Syrtis, they lowered the sea anchor and let the ship be driven
along. We took such a violent battering from the storm that the next day
they began to throw the cargo overboard. On the third day, they threw the
ship's tackle overboard with their own hands. When neither sun nor stars
appeared for many days and the storm continued raging, we finally gave
up all hope of being saved.

Acts
27:13-20

PAUL PROMISES SAFE PASSAGE.   After the men had gone a long time
without food, Paul stood up before them and said: "Men, you should
have taken my advice not to sail from Crete; then you would have spared
yourselves this damage and loss. But now I urge you to keep up your
courage, because not one of you will be lost; only the ship will be
destroyed. Last night an angel of the God whose I am and whom I serve
stood beside me and said, 'Do not be afraid, Paul. You must stand trial
before Caesar; and God has graciously given you the lives of all who sail
with you.' So keep up your courage, men, for I have faith in God that it
will happen just as he told me. Nevertheless, we must run aground on
some island."

Acts
27:21-26

SAILORS ATTEMPT ESCAPE.   On the fourteenth night we were still
being driven across the Adriatic[j] Sea, when about midnight the sailors
sensed they were approaching land. They took soundings and found that
the water was a hundred and twenty feet[k] deep. A short time later they
took soundings again and found it was ninety feet[l] deep. Fearing that we
would be dashed against the rocks, they dropped four anchors from the
stern and prayed for daylight. In an attempt to escape from the ship, the
sailors let the lifeboat down into the sea, pretending they were going to
lower some anchors from the bow. Then Paul said to the centurion and
the soldiers, "Unless these men stay with the ship, you cannot be saved."
So the soldiers cut the ropes that held the lifeboat and let it fall away.

Acts
27:27-32

PASSENGERS EAT LAST MEAL.   Just before dawn Paul urged them all
to eat. "For the last fourteen days," he said, "you have been in constant
suspense and have gone without food—you haven't eaten anything. Now
I urge you to take some food. You need it to survive. Not one of you will
lose a single hair from his head." After he said this, he took some bread

Acts
27:33-38

---

[j]In ancient times the name referred to an area extending well south of Italy.   [k]Greek
twenty orguias (about 37 meters)   [l]Greek *fifteen orguias* (about 27 meters)

and gave thanks to God in front of them all. Then he broke it and began to eat. They were all encouraged and ate some food themselves. Altogether there were 276 of us on board. When they had eaten as much as they wanted, they lightened the ship by throwing the grain into the sea.

Acts
27:39-44
Malta

SHIPWRECKED.   When daylight came, they did not recognize the land, but they saw a bay with a sandy beach, where they decided to run the ship aground if they could. Cutting loose the anchors, they left them in the sea and at the same time untied the ropes that held the rudders. Then they hoisted the foresail to the wind and made for the beach. But the ship struck a sandbar and ran aground. The bow stuck fast and would not move, and the stern was broken to pieces by the pounding of the surf.

The soldiers planned to kill the prisoners to prevent any of them from swimming away and escaping. But the centurion wanted to spare Paul's life and kept them from carrying out their plan. He ordered those who could swim to jump overboard first and get to land. The rest were to get there on planks or on pieces of the ship. In this way everyone reached land in safety.

Acts 28:1-6

PAUL SEEN AS A GOD.   Once safely on shore, we found out that the island was called Malta. The islanders showed us unusual kindness. They built a fire and welcomed us all because it was raining and cold. Paul gathered a pile of brushwood and, as he put it on the fire, a viper, driven out by the heat, fastened itself on his hand. When the islanders saw the snake hanging from his hand, they said to each other, "This man must be a murderer; for though he escaped from the sea, Justice has not allowed him to live." But Paul shook the snake off into the fire and suffered no ill effects. The people expected him to swell up or suddenly fall dead, but after waiting a long time and seeing nothing unusual happen to him, they changed their minds and said he was a god.

Acts
28:7-10

SICK HEALED ON MALTA.   There was an estate nearby that belonged to Publius, the chief official of the island. He welcomed us to his home and for three days entertained us hospitably. His father was sick in bed, suffering from fever and dysentery. Paul went in to see him and, after prayer, placed his hands on him and healed him. When this had happened, the rest of the sick on the island came and were cured. They honored us in many ways and when we were ready to sail, they furnished us with the supplies we needed.

Acts
28:11-15

FINAL VOYAGE TO ROME.   After three months we put out to sea in a ship that had wintered in the island. It was an Alexandrian ship with the figurehead of the twin gods Castor and Pollux. We put in at Syracuse and stayed there three days. From there we set sail and arrived at Rhegium. The next day the south wind came up, and on the following day we reached Puteoli. There we found some brothers who invited us to spend a week with them. And so we came to Rome. The brothers there had heard that we were coming, and they traveled as far as the Forum of Appius and the Three Taverns to meet us. At the sight of these men Paul thanked God and was encouraged.

House Arrest in Rome

*A*s Paul arrives in Rome, there is no indication that he appears before any court or government official to press his appeal. Instead, it appears that he is placed under house arrest, being permitted to maintain his own living quarters while being guarded by a Roman soldier. Paul is given the freedom to continue preaching from his place of lodging. Luke thereafter records that Paul invites the local Jewish leaders to his house in order to tell them about Jesus and the kingdom of God. Characteristically, some believe while others do not, a result which Paul attributes to the openness of mind with which a person might listen to the good news about Jesus.

PAUL UNDER HOUSE ARREST.   When we got to Rome, Paul was allowed to live by himself, with a soldier to guard him.

Acts 28:16
Rome

JEWISH LEADERS VISIT.   Three days later he called together the leaders of the Jews. When they had assembled, Paul said to them: "My brothers, although I have done nothing against our people or against the customs of our ancestors, I was arrested in Jerusalem and handed over to the Romans. They examined me and wanted to release me, because I was not guilty of any crime deserving death. But when the Jews objected, I was compelled to appeal to Caesar—not that I had any charge to bring against my own people. For this reason I have asked to see you and talk with you. It is because of the hope of Israel that I am bound with this chain."

They replied, "We have not received any letters from Judea concerning you, and none of the brothers who have come from there has reported or said anything bad about you. But we want to hear what your views are, for we know that people everywhere are talking against this sect."

Acts
28:17-22

PAUL PROCLAIMS JESUS.   They arranged to meet Paul on a certain day, and came in even larger numbers to the place where he was staying. From morning till evening he explained and declared to them the kingdom of God and tried to convince them about Jesus from the Law of Moses and from the Prophets. Some were convinced by what he said, but others would not believe. They disagreed among themselves and began to leave after Paul had made this final statement: "The Holy Spirit spoke the truth to your forefathers when he said through Isaiah the prophet:

Acts
28:23-28

" 'Go to this people and say,
"You will be ever hearing but never understanding;
    you will be ever seeing but never perceiving."
For this people's heart has become calloused;
    they hardly hear with their ears,
    and they have closed their eyes.
Otherwise they might see with their eyes,
    hear with their ears,
    understand with their hearts
and turn, and I would heal them.' *m*

*m*Isaiah 6:9,10

"Therefore I want you to know that God's salvation has been sent to the Gentiles, and they will listen!"[n]

Acts 28:30,31 (A.D. 61 to 63) TWO YEARS OF MINISTRY. For two whole years Paul stayed there in his own rented house and welcomed all who came to see him. Boldly and without hindrance he preached the kingdom of God and taught about the Lord Jesus Christ.

Letter to the Colossians

*D*uring these two years of house arrest, generally believed to be about A.D. 61-63, Paul writes four letters which have come to be known as the Prison Epistles. Two of them, the letter to the Colossians and the letter to Philemon, are probably written at the same time. Although Paul has never visited Colosse, one of his companions during this time, Epaphras, has been preaching in the towns of Colosse, Laodicea, and Hierapolis. Epaphras has evidently informed Paul of the pagan secularism which threatens the churches in that region.

In paganism, virtue is not associated with religion. Religious practice is for the purpose of warding off demons and evil ancestors—not for the purpose of becoming a better person. Paul sees that this notion of religion can influence even Christian worship in which slavish adherence to supposed spiritual standards misses the point of one's being transformed into the likeness of Christ. To Paul, the Christian life is more than simply giving up bad habits. It is acquiring a newness of mind which comes from setting your heart and mind on Christ Jesus—who, as Paul says, is the image of the invisible God. Only a person with the mind of Christ can truly overcome the sins of the flesh and live according to the Spirit.

Col. 1:1,2 SALUTATION. Paul, an apostle of Christ Jesus by the will of God, and Timothy our brother,

To the holy and faithful[o] brothers in Christ at Colosse:

Grace and peace to you from God our Father.[p]

Col. 1:3-8 THANKS FOR THEIR FAITH. We always thank God, the Father of our Lord Jesus Christ, when we pray for you, because we have heard of your faith in Christ Jesus and of the love you have for all the saints—the faith and love that spring from the hope that is stored up for you in heaven and that you have already heard about in the word of truth, the gospel that has come to you. All over the world this gospel is bearing fruit and growing, just as it has been doing among you since the day you heard it and understood God's grace in all its truth. You learned it from Epaphras, our dear fellow servant, who is a faithful minister of Christ on our[q] behalf, and who also told us of your love in the Spirit.

Col. 1:9-14 PRAYER FOR THE COLOSSIANS. For this reason, since the day we heard about you, we have not stopped praying for you and asking God to fill you with the knowledge of his will through all spiritual wisdom and

[n]Some manuscripts listen!" 29After he said this, the Jews left, arguing vigorously among themselves. [o]Or believing [p]Some manuscripts Father and the Lord Jesus Christ [q]Some manuscripts your

understanding. And we pray this in order that you may live a life worthy of the Lord and may please him in every way: bearing fruit in every good work, growing in the knowledge of God, being strengthened with all power according to his glorious might so that you may have great endurance and patience, and joyfully giving thanks to the Father, who has qualified you[r] to share in the inheritance of the saints in the kingdom of light. For he has rescued us from the dominion of darkness and brought us into the kingdom of the Son he loves, in whom we have redemption,[s] the forgiveness of sins.

The Preeminence of Christ

THE PERSON OF CHRIST.　　He is the image of the invisible God, the firstborn over all creation. For by him all things were created: things in heaven and on earth, visible and invisible, whether thrones or powers or rulers or authorities; all things were created by him and for him. He is before all things, and in him all things hold together. And he is the head of the body, the church; he is the beginning and the firstborn from among the dead, so that in everything he might have the supremacy. For God was pleased to have all his fullness dwell in him, and through him to reconcile to himself all things, whether things on earth or things in heaven, by making peace through his blood, shed on the cross.

Col.
1:15-20

RELATIONSHIP WITH CHRIST.　　Once you were alienated from God and were enemies in your minds because of[t] your evil behavior. But now he has reconciled you by Christ's physical body through death to present you holy in his sight, without blemish and free from accusation—if you continue in your faith, established and firm, not moved from the hope held out in the gospel. This is the gospel that you heard and that has been proclaimed to every creature under heaven, and of which I, Paul, have become a servant.

Col.
1:21-23

PROCLAIMING CHRIST.　　Now I rejoice in what was suffered for you, and I fill up in my flesh what is still lacking in regard to Christ's afflictions, for the sake of his body, which is the church. I have become its servant by the commission God gave me to present to you the word of God in its fullness—the mystery that has been kept hidden for ages and generations, but is now disclosed to the saints. To them God has chosen to make known among the Gentiles the glorious riches of this mystery, which is Christ in you, the hope of glory.

We proclaim him, admonishing and teaching everyone with all wisdom, so that we may present everyone perfect in Christ. To this end I labor, struggling with all his energy, which so powerfully works in me.

Col.
1:24-29

CONCERN FOR THEIR FAITH.　　I want you to know how much I am struggling for you and for those at Laodicea, and for all who have not met me personally. My purpose is that they may be encouraged in heart and united in love, so that they may have the full riches of complete understanding, in order that they may know the mystery of God, namely, Christ, in whom are hidden all the treasures of wisdom and knowledge. I tell you this so that no one may deceive you by fine-sounding arguments. For though I am absent from you in body, I am present with

Col. 2:1-5

[r]Some manuscripts *us*　　[s]A few late manuscripts *redemption through his blood*　　[t]Or *minds, as shown by*

you in spirit and delight to see how orderly you are and how firm your faith in Christ is.

Col. 2:6-8 WARNING OF FALSE TEACHING.   So then, just as you received Christ Jesus as Lord, continue to live in him, rooted and built up in him, strengthened in the faith as you were taught, and overflowing with thankfulness.

See to it that no one takes you captive through hollow and deceptive philosophy, which depends on human tradition and the basic principles of this world rather than on Christ.

Col. 2:9-15 CHRIST IS ALL-SUFFICIENT.   For in Christ all the fullness of the Deity lives in bodily form, and you have been given fullness in Christ, who is the head over every power and authority. In him you were also circumcised, in the putting off of the sinful nature,^{u} not with a circumcision done by the hands of men but with the circumcision done by Christ, having been buried with him in baptism and raised with him through your faith in the power of God, who raised him from the dead.

When you were dead in your sins and in the uncircumcision of your sinful nature,^{v} God made you^w alive with Christ. He forgave us all our sins, having canceled the written code, with its regulations, that was against us and that stood opposed to us; he took it away, nailing it to the cross. And having disarmed the powers and authorities, he made a public spectacle of them, triumphing over them by the cross.^{x}

Carnality and Spirituality

Col. 2:16-19 CHRIST SHOULD BE FOCUS.   Therefore do not let anyone judge you by what you eat or drink, or with regard to a religious festival, a New Moon celebration or a Sabbath day. These are a shadow of the things that were to come; the reality, however, is found in Christ. Do not let anyone who delights in false humility and the worship of angels disqualify you for the prize. Such a person goes into great detail about what he has seen, and his unspiritual mind puffs him up with idle notions. He has lost connection with the Head, from whom the whole body, supported and held together by its ligaments and sinews, grows as God causes it to grow.

Col. 2:20-23 DOCTRINES MISS SPIRIT.   Since you died with Christ to the basic principles of this world, why, as though you still belonged to it, do you submit to its rules: "Do not handle! Do not taste! Do not touch!"? These are all destined to perish with use, because they are based on human commands and teachings. Such regulations indeed have an appearance of wisdom, with their self-imposed worship, their false humility and their harsh treatment of the body, but they lack any value in restraining sensual indulgence.

Col. 3:1-4 TO BE SPIRITUALLY MINDED.   Since, then, you have been raised with Christ, set your hearts on things above, where Christ is seated at the right hand of God. Set your minds on things above, not on earthly things. For you died, and your life is now hidden with Christ in God. When Christ, who is your^y life, appears, then you also will appear with him in glory.

Col. 3:5-11 LIVES TO BE TRANSFORMED.   Put to death, therefore, whatever belongs to your earthly nature: sexual immorality, impurity, lust, evil desires

---

^{u}Or *the flesh* ^{v}Or *your flesh* ^{w}Some manuscripts *us* ^{x}Or *them in him* ^{y}Some manuscripts *our*

and greed, which is idolatry. Because of these, the wrath of God is coming.[z] You used to walk in these ways, in the life you once lived. But now you must rid yourselves of all such things as these: anger, rage, malice, slander, and filthy language from your lips. Do not lie to each other, since you have taken off your old self with its practices and have put on the new self, which is being renewed in knowledge in the image of its Creator. Here there is no Greek or Jew, circumcised or uncircumcised, barbarian, Scythian, slave or free, but Christ is all, and is in all.

PUTTING ON CHRIST.   Therefore, as God's chosen people, holy and dearly loved, clothe yourselves with compassion, kindness, humility, gentleness and patience. Bear with each other and forgive whatever grievances you may have against one another. Forgive as the Lord forgave you. And over all these virtues put on love, which binds them all together in perfect unity.

Col.
3:12-17

Let the peace of Christ rule in your hearts, since as members of one body you were called to peace. And be thankful. Let the word of Christ dwell in you richly as you teach and admonish one another with all wisdom, and as you sing psalms, hymns and spiritual songs with gratitude in your hearts to God. And whatever you do, whether in word or deed, do it all in the name of the Lord Jesus, giving thanks to God the Father through him.

Christlikeness in Relationships

IN THE FAMILY.   Wives, submit to your husbands, as is fitting in the Lord.

Col.
3:18-21

Husbands, love your wives and do not be harsh with them.

Children, obey your parents in everything, for this pleases the Lord.

Fathers, do not embitter your children, or they will become discouraged.

AMONG MASTERS AND SLAVES.   Slaves, obey your earthly masters in everything; and do it, not only when their eye is on you and to win their favor, but with sincerity of heart and reverence for the Lord. Whatever you do, work at it with all your heart, as working for the Lord, not for men, since you know that you will receive an inheritance from the Lord as a reward. It is the Lord Christ you are serving. Anyone who does wrong will be repaid for his wrong, and there is no favoritism. Masters, provide your slaves with what is right and fair, because you know that you also have a Master in heaven.

Col.
3:22-4:1

Concluding Thoughts

CALL FOR PRAYER.   Devote yourselves to prayer, being watchful and thankful. And pray for us, too, that God may open a door for our message, so that we may proclaim the mystery of Christ, for which I am in chains. Pray that I may proclaim it clearly, as I should.

Col. 4:2-4

WORDS OF CAUTION.   Be wise in the way you act toward outsiders; make the most of every opportunity. Let your conversation be always full of grace, seasoned with salt, so that you may know how to answer everyone.

Col. 4:5,6

---

[z]Some early manuscripts *coming on those who are disobedient*

Col. 4:7-9   REPORT TO BE GIVEN.   Tychicus will tell you all the news about me. He is a dear brother, a faithful minister and fellow servant in the Lord. I am sending him to you for the express purpose that you may know about our [a] circumstances and that he may encourage your hearts. He is coming with Onesimus, our faithful and dear brother, who is one of you. They will tell you everything that is happening here.

Col. 4:10-17   GREETINGS AMONG BRETHREN.   My fellow prisoner Aristarchus sends you his greetings, as does Mark, the cousin of Barnabas. (You have received instructions about him; if he comes to you, welcome him.) Jesus, who is called Justus, also sends greetings. These are the only Jews among my fellow workers for the kingdom of God, and they have proved a comfort to me. Epaphras, who is one of you and a servant of Christ Jesus, sends greetings. He is always wrestling in prayer for you, that you may stand firm in all the will of God, mature and fully assured. I vouch for him that he is working hard for you and for those at Laodicea and Hierapolis. Our dear friend Luke, the doctor, and Demas send greetings. Give my greetings to the brothers at Laodicea, and to Nympha and the church in her house.

After this letter has been read to you, see that it is also read in the church of the Laodiceans and that you in turn read the letter from Laodicea.

Tell Archippus: "See to it that you complete the work you have received in the Lord."

Col. 4:18   BENEDICTION.   I, Paul, write this greeting in my own hand. Remember my chains. Grace be with you.

Letter to Philemon

*A*s Paul indicated, the letter to the Colossians was to be delivered by Tychicus and Onesimus. Another letter, of special significance to Onesimus, is also being sent. Before coming to Rome and being converted by Paul, Onesimus had been a slave of a Christian named Philemon. Onesimus (whose name means "useful") had run away from Philemon and had evidently taken some money or property belonging to his master. Paul now writes to Philemon on behalf of Onesimus and asks that Philemon accept Onesimus back as a brother in Christ. The letter is an insightful study in personal relationships among Christians and contrasts the freedoms that come when one is under bondage to Christ.

Philemon 1-3   SALUTATION.   Paul, a prisoner of Christ Jesus, and Timothy our brother,

To Philemon our dear friend and fellow worker, to Apphia our sister, to Archippus our fellow soldier and to the church that meets in your home:

Grace to you and peace from God our Father and the Lord Jesus Christ.

Philemon 4-7   PAUL'S LOVE FOR PHILEMON.   I always thank my God as I remember you in my prayers, because I hear about your faith in the Lord Jesus and your love for all the saints. I pray that you may be active in sharing your faith, so that you will have a full understanding of every good thing

[a]Some manuscripts *that he may know about your*

we have in Christ. Your love has given me great joy and encouragement, because you, brother, have refreshed the hearts of the saints.

APPEAL ON BEHALF OF ONESIMUS.   Therefore, although in Christ I could be bold and order you to do what you ought to do, yet I appeal to you on the basis of love. I then, as Paul—an old man and now also a prisoner of Christ Jesus—I appeal to you for my son Onesimus,[b] who became my son while I was in chains. Formerly he was useless to you, but now he has become useful both to you and to me.

Philemon
8-14

I am sending him—who is my very heart—back to you. I would have liked to keep him with me so that he could take your place in helping me while I am in chains for the gospel. But I did not want to do anything without your consent, so that any favor you do will be spontaneous and not forced.

ONESIMUS RETURNING AS BROTHER.   Perhaps the reason he was separated from you for a little while was that you might have him back for good—no longer as a slave, but better than a slave, as a dear brother. He is very dear to me but even dearer to you, both as a man and as a brother in the Lord.

Philemon
15-17

So if you consider me a partner, welcome him as you would welcome me.

OFFER TO REPAY ANY LOSS.   If he has done you any wrong or owes you anything, charge it to me. I, Paul, am writing this with my own hand. I will pay it back—not to mention that you owe me your very self. I do wish, brother, that I may have some benefit from you in the Lord; refresh my heart in Christ.

Philemon
18-20

PAUL'S HOPE TO SEE PHILEMON.   Confident of your obedience, I write to you, knowing that you will do even more than I ask.

Philemon
21,22

And one thing more: Prepare a guest room for me, because I hope to be restored to you in answer to your prayers.

GREETINGS AND BENEDICTION.   Epaphras, my fellow prisoner in Christ Jesus, sends you greetings. And so do Mark, Aristarchus, Demas and Luke, my fellow workers.

Philemon
23-25

The grace of the Lord Jesus Christ be with your spirit.

Letter to the Ephesians

A second letter was also to be delivered by Tychicus, but much less is known about its intended destination. Because there is some textual evidence that it was written to the church in Ephesus, the writing has been regarded traditionally as Paul's letter to the Ephesians. That would certainly be consistent with the direction of Tychicus' travel from Rome to Colosse, and of course Paul is no stranger to the Ephesians. But because there are no personal greetings (as might be expected, since the believers in the church there are well-known to Paul), it may be that the letter is one for general circulation to all the churches throughout the region.

---

[b]*Onesimus* means *useful.*

Whatever its intended destination, the message is universal. Paul writes about the exalted relationship between Christ and the church and the practical results which that knowledge ought to bring into the lives of individual Christians. He begins by summarizing how God's eternal plan is revealed through Christ, then proceeds to teach various lessons regarding the church, personal righteousness, earthly relationships, and the Christian's relationship with God.

Eph. 1:1,2   SALUTATION.   Paul, an apostle of Christ Jesus by the will of God,

To the saints in Ephesus,[c] the faithful[d] in Christ Jesus:

Grace and peace to you from God our Father and the Lord Jesus Christ.

Revelation of God's Mystery

Eph. 1:3-10   PRAISE FOR GOD'S GRACE.   Praise be to the God and Father of our Lord Jesus Christ, who has blessed us in the heavenly realms with every spiritual blessing in Christ. For he chose us in him before the creation of the world to be holy and blameless in his sight. In love he[e] predestined us to be adopted as his sons through Jesus Christ, in accordance with his pleasure and will—to the praise of his glorious grace, which he has freely given us in the One he loves. In him we have redemption through his blood, the forgiveness of sins, in accordance with the riches of God's grace that he lavished on us with all wisdom and understanding. And he[f] made known to us the mystery of his will according to his good pleasure, which he purposed in Christ, to be put into effect when the times will have reached their fulfillment—to bring all things in heaven and on earth together under one head, even Christ.

Eph. 1:11-14   HOPE IN CHRIST IS SEALED.   In him we were also chosen,[g] having been predestined according to the plan of him who works out everything in conformity with the purpose of his will, in order that we, who were the first to hope in Christ, might be for the praise of his glory. And you also were included in Christ when you heard the word of truth, the gospel of your salvation. Having believed, you were marked in him with a seal, the promised Holy Spirit, who is a deposit guaranteeing our inheritance until the redemption of those who are God's possession—to the praise of his glory.

Eph. 1:15-23   CHRIST'S POWER AND POSITION.   For this reason, ever since I heard about your faith in the Lord Jesus and your love for all the saints, I have not stopped giving thanks for you, remembering you in my prayers. I keep asking that the God of our Lord Jesus Christ, the glorious Father, may give you the Spirit[h] of wisdom and revelation, so that you may know him better. I pray also that the eyes of your heart may be enlightened in order that you may know the hope to which he has called you, the riches of his glorious inheritance in the saints, and his incomparably great power for us who believe. That power is like the working of his mighty strength, which he exerted in Christ when he raised him from the dead and seated him at his right hand in the heavenly realms, far above

---

[c]Some early manuscripts do not have *in Ephesus.*   [d]Or *believers who are*   [e]Or *sight in love.* [5]He   [f]Or *us. With all wisdom and understanding,* [9]he   [g]Or *were made heirs*   [h]Or *a spirit*

all rule and authority, power and dominion, and every title that can be given, not only in the present age but also in the one to come. And God placed all things under his feet and appointed him to be head over everything for the church, which is his body, the fullness of him who fills everything in every way.

RAISED FROM SPIRITUAL DEATH.   As for you, you were dead in your transgressions and sins, in which you used to live when you followed the ways of this world and of the ruler of the kingdom of the air, the spirit who is now at work in those who are disobedient. All of us also lived among them at one time, gratifying the cravings of our sinful nature[i] and following its desires and thoughts. Like the rest, we were by nature objects of wrath. But because of his great love for us, God, who is rich in mercy, made us alive with Christ even when we were dead in transgressions—it is by grace you have been saved. And God raised us up with Christ and seated us with him in the heavenly realms in Christ Jesus, in order that in the coming ages he might show the incomparable riches of his grace, expressed in his kindness to us in Christ Jesus.

Eph. 2:1-7

GRACE TO LIVE RIGHTEOUSLY.   For it is by grace you have been saved, through faith—and this not from yourselves, it is the gift of God— not by works, so that no one can boast. For we are God's workmanship, created in Christ Jesus to do good works, which God prepared in advance for us to do.

Eph. 2:8-10

BARRIER BROKEN.   Therefore, remember that formerly you who are Gentiles by birth and called "uncircumcised" by those who call themselves "the circumcision" (that done in the body by the hands of men)— remember that at that time you were separate from Christ, excluded from citizenship in Israel and foreigners to the covenants of the promise, without hope and without God in the world. But now in Christ Jesus you who once were far away have been brought near through the blood of Christ.

For he himself is our peace, who has made the two one and has destroyed the barrier, the dividing wall of hostility, by abolishing in his flesh the law with its commandments and regulations. His purpose was to create in himself one new man out of the two, thus making peace, and in this one body to reconcile both of them to God through the cross, by which he put to death their hostility. He came and preached peace to you who were far away and peace to those who were near. For through him we both have access to the Father by one Spirit.

Eph. 2:11-18

CHRIST AS CORNERSTONE.   Consequently, you are no longer foreigners and aliens, but fellow citizens with God's people and members of God's household, built on the foundation of the apostles and prophets, with Christ Jesus himself as the chief cornerstone. In him the whole building is joined together and rises to become a holy temple in the Lord. And in him you too are being built together to become a dwelling in which God lives by his Spirit.

Eph. 2:19-22

REVELATION OF FORMER MYSTERY.   For this reason I, Paul, the prisoner of Christ Jesus for the sake of you Gentiles—

Surely you have heard about the administration of God's grace that was given to me for you, that is, the mystery made known to me by revelation,

Eph. 3:1-6

[i]Or *our flesh*

as I have already written briefly. In reading this, then, you will be able to understand my insight into the mystery of Christ, which was not made known to men in other generations as it has now been revealed by the Spirit to God's holy apostles and prophets. This mystery is that through the gospel the Gentiles are heirs together with Israel, members together of one body, and sharers together in the promise in Christ Jesus.

Eph. 3:7-13   WISDOM SEEN IN CHURCH.   I became a servant of this gospel by the gift of God's grace given me through the working of his power. Although I am less than the least of all God's people, this grace was given me: to preach to the Gentiles the unsearchable riches of Christ, and to make plain to everyone the administration of this mystery, which for ages past was kept hidden in God, who created all things. His intent was that now, through the church, the manifold wisdom of God should be made known to the rulers and authorities in the heavenly realms, according to his eternal purpose which he accomplished in Christ Jesus our Lord. In him and through faith in him we may approach God with freedom and confidence. I ask you, therefore, not to be discouraged because of my sufferings for you, which are your glory.

Eph. 3:14-19   PRAYER FOR STRENGTH.   For this reason I kneel before the Father, from whom his whole family[j] in heaven and on earth derives its name. I pray that out of his glorious riches he may strengthen you with power through his Spirit in your inner being, so that Christ may dwell in your hearts through faith. And I pray that you, being rooted and established in love, may have power, together with all the saints, to grasp how wide and long and high and deep is the love of Christ, and to know this love that surpasses knowledge—that you may be filled to the measure of all the fullness of God.

Eph. 3:20,21   PRAISE TO GOD.   Now to him who is able to do immeasurably more than all we ask or imagine, according to his power that is at work within us, to him be glory in the church and in Christ Jesus throughout all generations, for ever and ever! Amen.

Exhortation Regarding the Church

Eph. 4:1-6   UNITY AMONG SAINTS.   As a prisoner for the Lord, then, I urge you to live a life worthy of the calling you have received. Be completely humble and gentle; be patient, bearing with one another in love. Make every effort to keep the unity of the Spirit through the bond of peace. There is one body and one Spirit—just as you were called to one hope when you were called—one Lord, one faith, one baptism; one God and Father of all, who is over all and through all and in all.

Eph. 4:7-13   GIFTS FOR ACHIEVING UNITY.   But to each one of us grace has been given as Christ apportioned it. This is why it[k] says:

> "When he ascended on high,
>   he led captives in his train
>   and gave gifts to men."[l]

(What does "he ascended" mean except that he also descended to the lower, earthly regions[m]? He who descended is the very one who ascended

---

[j]Or *whom all fatherhood*   [k]Or *God*   [l]Psalm 68:18   [m]Or *the depths of the earth*

higher than all the heavens, in order to fill the whole universe.) It was he who gave some to be apostles, some to be prophets, some to be evangelists, and some to be pastors and teachers, to prepare God's people for works of service, so that the body of Christ may be built up until we all reach unity in the faith and in the knowledge of the Son of God and become mature, attaining to the whole measure of the fullness of Christ.

MATURING AS A BODY.   Then we will no longer be infants, tossed back and forth by the waves, and blown here and there by every wind of teaching and by the cunning and craftiness of men in their deceitful scheming. Instead, speaking the truth in love, we will in all things grow up into him who is the Head, that is, Christ. From him the whole body, joined and held together by every supporting ligament, grows and builds itself up in love, as each part does its work.

Eph. 4:14-16

Exhortation Regarding Personal Righteousness

RENOUNCE SENSUALITY.   So I tell you this, and insist on it in the Lord, that you must no longer live as the Gentiles do, in the futility of their thinking. They are darkened in their understanding and separated from the life of God because of the ignorance that is in them due to the hardening of their hearts. Having lost all sensitivity, they have given themselves over to sensuality so as to indulge in every kind of impurity, with a continual lust for more.

Eph. 4:17-19

RENEW HOLINESS.   You, however, did not come to know Christ that way. Surely you heard of him and were taught in him in accordance with the truth that is in Jesus. You were taught, with regard to your former way of life, to put off your old self, which is being corrupted by its deceitful desires; to be made new in the attitude of your minds; and to put on the new self, created to be like God in true righteousness and holiness.

Eph. 4:20-24

DISCARD UNRIGHTEOUSNESS.   Therefore each of you must put off falsehood and speak truthfully to his neighbor, for we are all members of one body. "In your anger do not sin"[n]: Do not let the sun go down while you are still angry, and do not give the devil a foothold. He who has been stealing must steal no longer, but must work, doing something useful with his own hands, that he may have something to share with those in need.

Do not let any unwholesome talk come out of your mouths, but only what is helpful for building others up according to their needs, that it may benefit those who listen. And do not grieve the Holy Spirit of God, with whom you were sealed for the day of redemption. Get rid of all bitterness, rage and anger, brawling and slander, along with every form of malice. Be kind and compassionate to one another, forgiving each other, just as in Christ God forgave you.

Eph. 4:25-32

IMITATE GOD IN LOVE.   Be imitators of God, therefore, as dearly loved children and live a life of love, just as Christ loved us and gave himself up for us as a fragrant offering and sacrifice to God.

Eph. 5:1,2

BE MORALLY PURE.   But among you there must not be even a hint of sexual immorality, or of any kind of impurity, or of greed, because these

Eph. 5:3-6

[n]Psalm 4:4

are improper for God's holy people. Nor should there be obscenity, foolish talk or coarse joking, which are out of place, but rather thanksgiving. For of this you can be sure: No immoral, impure or greedy person—such a man is an idolater—has any inheritance in the kingdom of Christ and of God.[o] Let no one deceive you with empty words, for because of such things God's wrath comes on those who are disobedient.

Eph. 5:7-14   WALK AS CHILDREN OF LIGHT.   Therefore do not be partners with them.

For you were once darkness, but now you are light in the Lord. Live as children of light (for the fruit of the light consists in all goodness, righteousness and truth) and find out what pleases the Lord. Have nothing to do with the fruitless deeds of darkness, but rather expose them. For it is shameful even to mention what the disobedient do in secret. But everything exposed by the light becomes visible, for it is light that makes everything visible. This is why it is said:

> "Wake up, O sleeper,
>   rise from the dead,
>   and Christ will shine on you."

Eph. 5:15-20   LIVE SPIRIT-FILLED LIVES.   Be very careful, then, how you live—not as unwise but as wise, making the most of every opportunity, because the days are evil. Therefore do not be foolish, but understand what the Lord's will is. Do not get drunk on wine, which leads to debauchery. Instead, be filled with the Spirit. Speak to one another with psalms, hymns and spiritual songs. Sing and make music in your heart to the Lord, always giving thanks to God the Father for everything, in the name of our Lord Jesus Christ.

Exhortation Regarding Relationships

Eph. 5:21-33   MUTUAL SUBMISSION.   Submit to one another out of reverence for Christ.

Wives, submit to your husbands as to the Lord. For the husband is the head of the wife as Christ is the head of the church, his body, of which he is the Savior. Now as the church submits to Christ, so also wives should submit to their husbands in everything.

Husbands, love your wives, just as Christ loved the church and gave himself up for her to make her holy, cleansing[p] her by the washing with water through the word, and to present her to himself as a radiant church, without stain or wrinkle or any other blemish, but holy and blameless. In this same way, husbands ought to love their wives as their own bodies. He who loves his wife loves himself. After all, no one ever hated his own body, but he feeds and cares for it, just as Christ does the church—for we are members of his body. "For this reason a man will leave his father and mother and be united to his wife, and the two will become one flesh."[q] This is a profound mystery—but I am talking about Christ and the church. However, each one of you also must love his wife as he loves himself, and the wife must respect her husband.

Eph. 6:1-4   PARENT-CHILD RELATIONSHIPS.   Children, obey your parents in the Lord, for this is right. "Honor your father and mother"—which is the first

---

[o]Or kingdom of the Christ and God   [p]Or having cleansed   [q]Gen. 2:24

commandment with a promise—"that it may go well with you and that you may enjoy long life on the earth."*r*

Fathers, do not exasperate your children; instead, bring them up in the training and instruction of the Lord.

MASTER-SERVANT ATTITUDES.   Slaves, obey your earthly masters with respect and fear, and with sincerity of heart, just as you would obey Christ. Obey them not only to win their favor when their eye is on you, but like slaves of Christ, doing the will of God from your heart. Serve whole-heartedly, as if you were serving the Lord, not men, because you know that the Lord will reward everyone for whatever good he does, whether he is slave or free.

`Eph. 6:5-9`

And masters, treat your slaves in the same way. Do not threaten them, since you know that he who is both their Master and yours is in heaven, and there is no favoritism with him.

Exhortation Regarding Relationship with God

SPIRITUAL STRUGGLES.   Finally, be strong in the Lord and in his mighty power. Put on the full armor of God so that you can take your stand against the devil's schemes. For our struggle is not against flesh and blood, but against the rulers, against the authorities, against the powers of this dark world and against the spiritual forces of evil in the heavenly realms. Therefore put on the full armor of God, so that when the day of evil comes, you may be able to stand your ground, and after you have done everything, to stand. Stand firm then, with the belt of truth buckled around your waist, with the breastplate of righteousness in place, and with your feet fitted with the readiness that comes from the gospel of peace. In addition to all this, take up the shield of faith, with which you can extinguish all the flaming arrows of the evil one. Take the helmet of salvation and the sword of the Spirit, which is the word of God.

`Eph. 6:10-17`

REQUEST FOR PRAYER.   And pray in the Spirit on all occasions with all kinds of prayers and requests. With this in mind, be alert and always keep on praying for all the saints.

`Eph. 6:18-20`

Pray also for me, that whenever I open my mouth, words may be given me so that I will fearlessly make known the mystery of the gospel, for which I am an ambassador in chains. Pray that I may declare it fearlessly, as I should.

FURTHER REPORT.   Tychicus, the dear brother and faithful servant in the Lord, will tell you everything, so that you also may know how I am and what I am doing. I am sending him to you for this very purpose, that you may know how we are, and that he may encourage you.

`Eph. 6:21,22`

BENEDICTION.   Peace to the brothers, and love with faith from God the Father and the Lord Jesus Christ. Grace to all who love our Lord Jesus Christ with an undying love.

`Eph. 6:23,24`

◇

---

r Deut. 5:16

Letter to the Philippians

$\mathcal{W}$hile still imprisoned, Paul also reaches out to the Christians in Philippi, with whom he has maintained close ties since his three visits to their city. Paul clearly feels a special relationship to the Philippians, not only because of his close association with them in past years but also because they have often generously contributed to his support. Their latest gifts were brought by Epaphroditus, who had become seriously ill after staying to work with Paul. Paul is sending him back now with this letter to his Philippian brethren.

In this letter Paul is writing to a small-town congregation in which two women, Euodia and Syntyche, have had a falling out. As is so often the case when personality conflicts develop, their personal animosity is splitting the whole church. Therefore Paul pleads with the two women—and indeed all Christians—to learn to love each other more.

Paul bases his appeal on the bedrock example of Christ's own humility in putting others' interests first, even at great personal cost. The apostle urges them to sacrifice their selfish feelings and to commit themselves to working out their problems, particularly in light of the fact that their pagan neighbors are watching their behavior. He points out that his appeal is not based upon any credentials that he himself might have, but upon the compelling love of Christ which was demonstrated in his life and sacrificial death. This love, says Paul, is true, noble, right, pure, lovely, admirable, excellent, and praiseworthy—and the only basis upon which fractured groups or interpersonal relations may be healed.

Phil. 1:1,2   SALUTATION. Paul and Timothy, servants of Christ Jesus,

To all the saints in Christ Jesus at Philippi, together with the overseers[s] and deacons:

Grace and peace to you from God our Father and the Lord Jesus Christ.

Reflections upon Imprisonment

Phil. 1:3-11   EXPRESSION OF LOVE. I thank my God every time I remember you. In all my prayers for all of you, I always pray with joy because of your partnership in the gospel from the first day until now, being confident of this, that he who began a good work in you will carry it on to completion until the day of Christ Jesus.

It is right for me to feel this way about all of you, since I have you in my heart; for whether I am in chains or defending and confirming the gospel, all of you share in God's grace with me. God can testify how I long for all of you with the affection of Christ Jesus.

And this is my prayer: that your love may abound more and more in knowledge and depth of insight, so that you may be able to discern what is best and may be pure and blameless until the day of Christ, filled with the fruit of righteousness that comes through Jesus Christ—to the glory and praise of God.

[s] Traditionally *bishops*

IMPRISONMENT A BLESSING.   Now I want you to know, brothers, that what has happened to me has really served to advance the gospel. As a result, it has become clear throughout the whole palace guard[t] and to everyone else that I am in chains for Christ. Because of my chains, most of the brothers in the Lord have been encouraged to speak the word of God more courageously and fearlessly.

Phil.
1:12-14

JOY OVER PREACHING.   It is true that some preach Christ out of envy and rivalry, but others out of goodwill. The latter do so in love, knowing that I am put here for the defense of the gospel. The former preach Christ out of selfish ambition, not sincerely, supposing that they can stir up trouble for me while I am in chains.[u] But what does it matter? The important thing is that in every way, whether from false motives or true, Christ is preached. And because of this I rejoice.

Phil.
1:15-18a

PAUL'S DILEMMA.   Yes, and I will continue to rejoice, for I know that through your prayers and the help given by the Spirit of Jesus Christ, what has happened to me will turn out for my deliverance.[v] I eagerly expect and hope that I will in no way be ashamed, but will have sufficient courage so that now as always Christ will be exalted in my body, whether by life or by death. For to me, to live is Christ and to die is gain. If I am to go on living in the body, this will mean fruitful labor for me. Yet what shall I choose? I do not know! I am torn between the two: I desire to depart and be with Christ, which is better by far; but it is more necessary for you that I remain in the body. Convinced of this, I know that I will remain, and I will continue with all of you for your progress and joy in the faith, so that through my being with you again your joy in Christ Jesus will overflow on account of me.

Phil.
1:18b-26

Various Exhortations

STAND UNITED.   Whatever happens, conduct yourselves in a manner worthy of the gospel of Christ. Then, whether I come and see you or only hear about you in my absence, I will know that you stand firm in one spirit, contending as one man for the faith of the gospel without being frightened in any way by those who oppose you. This is a sign to them that they will be destroyed, but that you will be saved—and that by God. For it has been granted to you on behalf of Christ not only to believe on him, but also to suffer for him, since you are going through the same struggle you saw I had, and now hear that I still have. If you have any encouragement from being united with Christ, if any comfort from his love, if any fellowship with the Spirit, if any tenderness and compassion, then make my joy complete by being like-minded, having the same love, being one in spirit and purpose.

Phil.
1:27-2:2

IMITATE CHRIST'S HUMILITY.   Do nothing out of selfish ambition or vain conceit, but in humility consider others better than yourselves. Each of you should look not only to your own interests, but also to the interests of others.

Phil.
2:3-11

Your attitude should be the same as that of Christ Jesus:

Who, being in very nature[w] God,

---

[t]Or *whole palace*   [u]Some late manuscripts have verses 16 and 17 in reverse order.
[v]Or *salvation*   [w]Or *in the form of*

did not consider equality with God something to be
grasped,
but made himself nothing,
taking the very nature[x] of a servant,
being made in human likeness.
And being found in appearance as a man,
he humbled himself
and became obedient to death—
even death on a cross!
Therefore God exalted him to the highest place
and gave him the name that is above every name,
that at the name of Jesus every knee should bow,
in heaven and on earth and under the earth,
and every tongue confess that Jesus Christ is Lord,
to the glory of God the Father.

**Phil.
2:12,13**

WORK AT RIGHTEOUSNESS.   Therefore, my dear friends, as you have always obeyed—not only in my presence, but now much more in my absence—continue to work out your salvation with fear and trembling, for it is God who works in you to will and to act according to his good purpose.

**Phil.
2:14-18**

BE EXAMPLES OF PEACE.   Do everything without complaining or arguing, so that you may become blameless and pure, children of God without fault in a crooked and depraved generation, in which you shine like stars in the universe as you hold out[y] the word of life—in order that I may boast on the day of Christ that I did not run or labor for nothing. But even if I am being poured out like a drink offering on the sacrifice and service coming from your faith, I am glad and rejoice with all of you. So you too should be glad and rejoice with me.

**Phil.
2:19-24**

TIMOTHY TO COME SOON.   I hope in the Lord Jesus to send Timothy to you soon, that I also may be cheered when I receive news about you. I have no one else like him, who takes a genuine interest in your welfare. For everyone looks out for his own interests, not those of Jesus Christ. But you know that Timothy has proved himself, because as a son with his father he has served with me in the work of the gospel. I hope, therefore, to send him as soon as I see how things go with me. And I am confident in the Lord that I myself will come soon.

**Phil.
2:25-30**

COMMENDATION OF EPAPHRODITUS.   But I think it is necessary to send back to you Epaphroditus, my brother, fellow worker and fellow soldier, who is also your messenger, whom you sent to take care of my needs. For he longs for all of you and is distressed because you heard he was ill. Indeed he was ill, and almost died. But God had mercy on him, and not on him only but also on me, to spare me sorrow upon sorrow. Therefore I am all the more eager to send him, so that when you see him again you may be glad and I may have less anxiety. Welcome him in the Lord with great joy, and honor men like him, because he almost died for the work of Christ, risking his life to make up for the help you could not give me.

[x]Or *the form*   [y]Or *hold on to*

CHRISTIANS SHOULD BE JOYFUL. Finally, my brothers, rejoice in the Lord! It is no trouble for me to write the same things to you again, and it is a safeguard for you.

Various Warnings

OVERCONFIDENCE IN HERITAGE. Watch out for those dogs, those men who do evil, those mutilators of the flesh. For it is we who are the circumcision, we who worship by the Spirit of God, who glory in Christ Jesus, and who put no confidence in the flesh—though I myself have reasons for such confidence.

Phil. 3:2-4a

PAUL'S JEWISH HERITAGE. If anyone else thinks he has reasons to put confidence in the flesh, I have more: circumcised on the eighth day, of the people of Israel, of the tribe of Benjamin, a Hebrew of Hebrews; in regard to the law, a Pharisee; as for zeal, persecuting the church; as for legalistic righteousness, faultless.

Phil. 3:4b-6

EXCHANGING HUMAN CONFIDENCE. But whatever was to my profit I now consider loss for the sake of Christ. What is more, I consider everything a loss compared to the surpassing greatness of knowing Christ Jesus my Lord, for whose sake I have lost all things. I consider them rubbish, that I may gain Christ and be found in him, not having a righteousness of my own that comes from the law, but that which is through faith in Christ—the righteousness that comes from God and is by faith. I want to know Christ and the power of his resurrection and the fellowship of sharing in his sufferings, becoming like him in his death, and so, somehow, to attain to the resurrection from the dead.

Phil. 3:7-11

RIGHTEOUSNESS A STRUGGLE. Not that I have already obtained all this, or have already been made perfect, but I press on to take hold of that for which Christ Jesus took hold of me. Brothers, I do not consider myself yet to have taken hold of it. But one thing I do: Forgetting what is behind and straining toward what is ahead, I press on toward the goal to win the prize for which God has called me heavenward in Christ Jesus.

Phil. 3:12-16

All of us who are mature should take such a view of things. And if on some point you think differently, that too God will make clear to you. Only let us live up to what we have already attained.

WARNING AGAINST WORLDLINESS. Join with others in following my example, brothers, and take note of those who live according to the pattern we gave you. For, as I have often told you before and now say again even with tears, many live as enemies of the cross of Christ. Their destiny is destruction, their god is their stomach, and their glory is in their shame. Their mind is on earthly things. But our citizenship is in heaven. And we eagerly await a Savior from there, the Lord Jesus Christ, who, by the power that enables him to bring everything under his control, will transform our lowly bodies so that they will be like his glorious body. Therefore, my brothers, you whom I love and long for, my joy and crown, that is how you should stand firm in the Lord, dear friends!

Phil. 3:17-4:1

Concluding Thoughts

WOMEN TO RECONCILE. I plead with Euodia and I plead with Syntyche to agree with each other in the Lord. Yes, and I ask you, loyal

Phil. 4:2,3

yokefellow,[z] help these women who have contended at my side in the cause of the gospel, along with Clement and the rest of my fellow workers, whose names are in the book of life.

Phil. 4:4-7   TO SEEK PEACEFULNESS.   Rejoice in the Lord always. I will say it again: Rejoice! Let your gentleness be evident to all. The Lord is near. Do not be anxious about anything, but in everything, by prayer and petition, with thanksgiving, present your requests to God. And the peace of God, which transcends all understanding, will guard your hearts and your minds in Christ Jesus.

Phil. 4:8,9   THINK ON THINGS SPIRITUAL.   Finally, brothers, whatever is true, whatever is noble, whatever is right, whatever is pure, whatever is lovely, whatever is admirable—if anything is excellent or praiseworthy—think about such things. Whatever you have learned or received or heard from me, or seen in me—put it into practice. And the God of peace will be with you.

Phil. 4:10-13   PAUL CONTENT.   I rejoice greatly in the Lord that at last you have renewed your concern for me. Indeed, you have been concerned, but you had no opportunity to show it. I am not saying this because I am in need, for I have learned to be content whatever the circumstances. I know what it is to be in need, and I know what it is to have plenty. I have learned the secret of being content in any and every situation, whether well fed or hungry, whether living in plenty or in want. I can do everything through him who gives me strength.

Phil. 4:14-20   GIFTS FRUITFUL TO THEM.   Yet it was good of you to share in my troubles. Moreover, as you Philippians know, in the early days of your acquaintance with the gospel, when I set out from Macedonia, not one church shared with me in the matter of giving and receiving, except you only; for even when I was in Thessalonica, you sent me aid again and again when I was in need. Not that I am looking for a gift, but I am looking for what may be credited to your account. I have received full payment and even more; I am amply supplied, now that I have received from Epaphroditus the gifts you sent. They are a fragrant offering, an acceptable sacrifice, pleasing to God. And my God will meet all your needs according to his glorious riches in Christ Jesus.

To our God and Father be glory for ever and ever. Amen.

Phil. 4:21-23   GREETINGS AND BENEDICTION.   Greet all the saints in Christ Jesus. The brothers who are with me send greetings. All the saints send you greetings, especially those who belong to Caesar's household.

The grace of the Lord Jesus Christ be with your spirit. Amen.[a]

The historical record of Acts comes to an end with Paul's two years in Rome. What is known after this time about the work of Paul and other church leaders must be pieced together from other accounts. However, it appears that Paul may have been released from house arrest and permitted to be free for a period of time, perhaps up to two or three years. During this time Paul evidently travels to Crete, where he leaves Titus, and also again to Ephesus, where he leaves Timothy. Thereafter, Paul apparently goes, by way of Miletus and Troas, on to the region of Macedonia, perhaps by A.D. 63-64.

[z] Or *loyal Syzygus*   [a] Some manuscripts do not have *Amen.*

First Letter to Timothy

*J*t is probably from Macedonia that Paul writes to Timothy, who as a young evangelist is facing serious challenges to faith and doctrine within the church at Ephesus. Paul therefore deals with matters of church organization and conduct, particularly regarding prayer; the role of women; qualifications of elders and deacons; support of widows; and proper attitudes for Christian slaves. Paul gives Timothy personal instruction and advice on a variety of matters and warns him concerning both false doctrine and those who would teach false doctrine, whose only goal in teaching is either making money or achieving popularity. The entire letter reflects the tone of a father writing to his son, as indeed Paul apparently regards this young man, Timothy.

SALUTATION.   Paul, an apostle of Christ Jesus by the command of God our Savior and of Christ Jesus our hope,

1 Tim.
1:1,2

To Timothy my true son in the faith:

Grace, mercy and peace from God the Father and Christ Jesus our Lord.

Instructions for the Church

UNSOUND DOCTRINE.   As I urged you when I went into Macedonia, stay there in Ephesus so that you may command certain men not to teach false doctrines any longer nor to devote themselves to myths and endless genealogies. These promote controversies rather than God's work—which is by faith. The goal of this command is love, which comes from a pure heart and a good conscience and a sincere faith. Some have wandered away from these and turned to meaningless talk. They want to be teachers of the law, but they do not know what they are talking about or what they so confidently affirm.

1 Tim.
1:3-7

LAW TO BE USED PROPERLY.   We know that the law is good if one uses it properly. We also know that law *b* is made not for the righteous but for lawbreakers and rebels, the ungodly and sinful, the unholy and irreligious; for those who kill their fathers or mothers, for murderers, for adulterers and perverts, for slave traders and liars and perjurers—and for whatever else is contrary to the sound doctrine that conforms to the glorious gospel of the blessed God, which he entrusted to me.

1 Tim.
1:8-11

PAUL AN EXAMPLE.   I thank Christ Jesus our Lord, who has given me strength, that he considered me faithful, appointing me to his service. Even though I was once a blasphemer and a persecutor and a violent man, I was shown mercy because I acted in ignorance and unbelief. The grace of our Lord was poured out on me abundantly, along with the faith and love that are in Christ Jesus.

1 Tim.
1:12-17

Here is a trustworthy saying that deserves full acceptance: Christ Jesus came into the world to save sinners—of whom I am the worst. But for that very reason I was shown mercy so that in me, the worst of sinners, Christ Jesus might display his unlimited patience as an example for those who would believe on him and receive eternal life. Now to the King eternal,

*b*Or *that the law*

immortal, invisible, the only God, be honor and glory for ever and ever. Amen.

**1 Tim.
1:18-20**

TIMOTHY TO KEEP FAITH.   Timothy, my son, I give you this instruction in keeping with the prophecies once made about you, so that by following them you may fight the good fight, holding on to faith and a good conscience. Some have rejected these and so have shipwrecked their faith. Among them are Hymenaeus and Alexander, whom I have handed over to Satan to be taught not to blaspheme.

**1 Tim.
2:1-8**

CALL FOR MEN TO PRAY.   I urge, then, first of all, that requests, prayers, intercession and thanksgiving be made for everyone—for kings and all those in authority, that we may live peaceful and quiet lives in all godliness and holiness. This is good, and pleases God our Savior, who wants all men to be saved and to come to a knowledge of the truth. For there is one God and one mediator between God and men, the man Christ Jesus, who gave himself as a ransom for all men—the testimony given in its proper time. And for this purpose I was appointed a herald and an apostle—I am telling the truth, I am not lying—and a teacher of the true faith to the Gentiles.

I want men everywhere to lift up holy hands in prayer, without anger or disputing.

**1 Tim.
2:9,10**

WOMEN TO BE MODEST.   I also want women to dress modestly, with decency and propriety, not with braided hair or gold or pearls or expensive clothes, but with good deeds, appropriate for women who profess to worship God.

**1 Tim.
2:11-15**

THE ROLE OF WOMEN.   A woman should learn in quietness and full submission. I do not permit a woman to teach or to have authority over a man; she must be silent. For Adam was formed first, then Eve. And Adam was not the one deceived; it was the woman who was deceived and became a sinner. But women[c] will be saved[d] through childbearing—if they continue in faith, love and holiness with propriety.

**1 Tim.
3:1-7**

QUALIFICATIONS OF ELDERS.   Here is a trustworthy saying: If anyone sets his heart on being an overseer,[e] he desires a noble task. Now the overseer must be above reproach, the husband of but one wife, temperate, self-controlled, respectable, hospitable, able to teach, not given to drunkenness, not violent but gentle, not quarrelsome, not a lover of money. He must manage his own family well and see that his children obey him with proper respect. (If anyone does not know how to manage his own family, how can he take care of God's church?) He must not be a recent convert, or he may become conceited and fall under the same judgment as the devil. He must also have a good reputation with outsiders, so that he will not fall into disgrace and into the devil's trap.

**1 Tim.
3:8-13**

QUALIFICATIONS OF DEACONS.   Deacons, likewise, are to be men worthy of respect, sincere, not indulging in much wine, and not pursuing dishonest gain. They must keep hold of the deep truths of the faith with a clear conscience. They must first be tested; and then if there is nothing against them, let them serve as deacons.

In the same way, their wives[f] are to be women worthy of respect, not malicious talkers but temperate and trustworthy in everything.

[c]Greek *she*   [d]Or *restored*   [e]Traditionally *bishop*   [f]Or *way, deaconesses*

A deacon must be the husband of but one wife and must manage his children and his household well. Those who have served well gain an excellent standing and great assurance in their faith in Christ Jesus.

REASON FOR INSTRUCTIONS.   Although I hope to come to you soon, I am writing you these instructions so that, if I am delayed, you will know how people ought to conduct themselves in God's household, which is the church of the living God, the pillar and foundation of the truth. Beyond all question, the mystery of godliness is great:

1 Tim.
3:14-16

> He[g] appeared in a body,[h]
>   was vindicated by the Spirit,
> was seen by angels,
>   was preached among the nations,
> was believed on in the world,
>   was taken up in glory.

HUMAN DOCTRINES.   The Spirit clearly says that in later times some will abandon the faith and follow deceiving spirits and things taught by demons. Such teachings come through hypocritical liars, whose consciences have been seared as with a hot iron. They forbid people to marry and order them to abstain from certain foods, which God created to be received with thanksgiving by those who believe and who know the truth. For everything God created is good, and nothing is to be rejected if it is received with thanksgiving, because it is consecrated by the word of God and prayer.

1 Tim.
4:1-5

Instructions to Timothy

STRIVE FOR GODLINESS.   If you point these things out to the brothers, you will be a good minister of Christ Jesus, brought up in the truths of the faith and of the good teaching that you have followed. Have nothing to do with godless myths and old wives' tales; rather, train yourself to be godly. For physical training is of some value, but godliness has value for all things, holding promise for both the present life and the life to come.

This is a trustworthy saying that deserves full acceptance (and for this we labor and strive), that we have put our hope in the living God, who is the Savior of all men, and especially of those who believe.

1 Tim.
4:6-10

TEACHING AND EXAMPLE.   Command and teach these things. Don't let anyone look down on you because you are young, but set an example for the believers in speech, in life, in love, in faith and in purity. Until I come, devote yourself to the public reading of Scripture, to preaching and to teaching. Do not neglect your gift, which was given you through a prophetic message when the body of elders laid their hands on you.

Be diligent in these matters; give yourself wholly to them, so that everyone may see your progress. Watch your life and doctrine closely. Persevere in them, because if you do, you will save both yourself and your hearers.

1 Tim.
4:11-16

HOW TO TREAT OTHERS.   Do not rebuke an older man harshly, but exhort him as if he were your father. Treat younger men as brothers, older women as mothers, and younger women as sisters, with absolute purity.

1 Tim.
5:1,2

[g]Some manuscripts *God*   [h]Or *in the flesh*

Concerning Widows

1 Tim.
5:3-8

OBLIGATION TOWARD WIDOWS.   Give proper recognition to those widows who are really in need. But if a widow has children or grand-children, these should learn first of all to put their religion into practice by caring for their own family and so repaying their parents and grand-parents, for this is pleasing to God. The widow who is really in need and left all alone puts her hope in God and continues night and day to pray and to ask God for help. But the widow who lives for pleasure is dead even while she lives. Give the people these instructions, too, so that no one may be open to blame. If anyone does not provide for his relatives, and especially for his immediate family, he has denied the faith and is worse than an unbeliever.

1 Tim.
5:9,10

CHURCH'S SUPPORT OF WIDOWS.   No widow may be put on the list of widows unless she is over sixty, has been faithful to her husband,[i] and is well known for her good deeds, such as bringing up children, showing hospitality, washing the feet of the saints, helping those in trouble and devoting herself to all kinds of good deeds.

1 Tim.
5:11-15

REGARDING YOUNGER WIDOWS.   As for younger widows, do not put them on such a list. For when their sensual desires overcome their dedication to Christ, they want to marry. Thus they bring judgment on themselves, because they have broken their first pledge. Besides, they get into the habit of being idle and going about from house to house. And not only do they become idlers, but also gossips and busybodies, saying things they ought not to. So I counsel younger widows to marry, to have children, to manage their homes and to give the enemy no opportunity for slander. Some have in fact already turned away to follow Satan.

1 Tim.
5:16

RESPONSIBILITY OF WOMEN.   If any woman who is a believer has widows in her family, she should help them and not let the church be burdened with them, so that the church can help those widows who are really in need.

Concerning Elders

1 Tim.
5:17-20

HONOR AND SUPPORT OF ELDERS.   The elders who direct the affairs of the church well are worthy of double honor, especially those whose work is preaching and teaching. For the Scripture says, "Do not muzzle the ox while it is treading out the grain,"[j] and "The worker deserves his wages."[k] Do not entertain an accusation against an elder unless it is brought by two or three witnesses. Those who sin are to be rebuked pub-licly, so that the others may take warning.

1 Tim.
5:21,22

CAUTION REGARDING ELDERS.   I charge you, in the sight of God and Christ Jesus and the elect angels, to keep these instructions without par-tiality, and to do nothing out of favoritism.

Do not be hasty in the laying on of hands, and do not share in the sins of others. Keep yourself pure.

Advice to Timothy

1 Tim.
5:23

REGARDING HEALTH.   Stop drinking only water, and use a little wine because of your stomach and your frequent illnesses.

[i]Or has had but one husband   [j]Deut. 25:4   [k]Luke 10:7

REGARDING APPEARANCES.   The sins of some men are obvious, | 1 Tim.
reaching the place of judgment ahead of them; the sins of others trail | 5:24,25
behind them. In the same way, good deeds are obvious, and even those
that are not cannot be hidden.

Instructions to Slaves

TO RESPECT MASTERS.   All who are under the yoke of slavery should | 1 Tim.
consider their masters worthy of full respect, so that God's name and our | 6:1,2
teaching may not be slandered. Those who have believing masters are not
to show less respect for them because they are brothers. Instead, they are
to serve them even better, because those who benefit from their service
are believers, and dear to them. These are the things you are to teach and
urge on them.

Concerning Mercenary Teachers

FALSE MOTIVATIONS.   If anyone teaches false doctrines and does not | 1 Tim.
agree to the sound instruction of our Lord Jesus Christ and to godly | 6:3-5
teaching, he is conceited and understands nothing. He has an unhealthy
interest in controversies and quarrels about words that result in envy,
strife, malicious talk, evil suspicions and constant friction between men of
corrupt mind, who have been robbed of the truth and who think that
godliness is a means to financial gain.

ATTITUDE TOWARD MONEY.   But godliness with contentment is great | 1 Tim.
gain. For we brought nothing into the world, and we can take nothing out | 6:6-10
of it. But if we have food and clothing, we will be content with that. People
who want to get rich fall into temptation and a trap and into many foolish
and harmful desires that plunge men into ruin and destruction. For the
love of money is a root of all kinds of evil. Some people, eager for money,
have wandered from the faith and pierced themselves with many griefs.

TIMOTHY'S MOTIVATION.   But you, man of God, flee from all this, and | 1 Tim.
pursue righteousness, godliness, faith, love, endurance and gentleness. | 6:11-16
Fight the good fight of the faith. Take hold of the eternal life to which you
were called when you made your good confession in the presence of many
witnesses. In the sight of God, who gives life to everything, and of Christ
Jesus, who while testifying before Pontius Pilate made the good confession, I charge you to keep this command without spot or blame until the
appearing of our Lord Jesus Christ, which God will bring about in his own
time—God, the blessed and only Ruler, the King of kings and Lord of
lords, who alone is immortal and who lives in unapproachable light,
whom no one has seen or can see. To him be honor and might forever.
Amen.

PROPER USE OF WEALTH.   Command those who are rich in this pres- | 1 Tim.
ent world not to be arrogant nor to put their hope in wealth, which is so | 6:17-19
uncertain, but to put their hope in God, who richly provides us with
everything for our enjoyment. Command them to do good, to be rich in
good deeds, and to be generous and willing to share. In this way they will
lay up treasure for themselves as a firm foundation for the coming age, so
that they may take hold of the life that is truly life.

Concluding Remarks

1 Tim.
6:20,21 BENEDICTION.   Timothy, guard what has been entrusted to your care. Turn away from godless chatter and the opposing ideas of what is falsely called knowledge, which some have professed and in so doing have wandered from the faith.

Grace be with you.

Letter to Titus

*F*rom Macedonia, Paul is about to leave for Nicopolis in Greece, where he has decided to spend the winter and where he expects Titus to join him. Before leaving, he writes a letter to Titus, whom he had earlier left in Crete. Titus is apparently facing some of the same challenges as Timothy in his efforts to preserve doctrinal purity and to establish effective local congregations. Therefore, Paul's letter to Titus bears a resemblance to his letter to Timothy in its emphasis on false teaching, church organization, and instruction in Christian living.

Titus 1:1-4   SALUTATION.   Paul, a servant of God and an apostle of Jesus Christ for the faith of God's elect and the knowledge of the truth that leads to godliness—a faith and knowledge resting on the hope of eternal life, which God, who does not lie, promised before the beginning of time, and at his appointed season he brought his word to light through the preaching entrusted to me by the command of God our Savior,

To Titus, my true son in our common faith:

Grace and peace from God the Father and Christ Jesus our Savior.

Concerning Church Leaders

Titus 1:5-9   QUALIFICATIONS FOR ELDERS.   The reason I left you in Crete was that you might straighten out what was left unfinished and appoint[l] elders in every town, as I directed you. An elder must be blameless, the husband of but one wife, a man whose children believe and are not open to the charge of being wild and disobedient. Since an overseer[m] is entrusted with God's work, he must be blameless—not overbearing, not quick-tempered, not given to drunkenness, not violent, not pursuing dishonest gain. Rather he must be hospitable, one who loves what is good, who is self-controlled, upright, holy and disciplined. He must hold firmly to the trustworthy message as it has been taught, so that he can encourage others by sound doctrine and refute those who oppose it.

Titus 1:10-2:1   WARNING OF FALSE TEACHERS.   For there are many rebellious people, mere talkers and deceivers, especially those of the circumcision group. They must be silenced, because they are ruining whole households by teaching things they ought not to teach—and that for the sake of dishonest gain. Even one of their own prophets has said, "Cretans are always liars, evil brutes, lazy gluttons." This testimony is true. Therefore, rebuke them sharply, so that they will be sound in the faith and will pay no attention to Jewish myths or to the commands of those who reject the

---

[l]Or *ordain*   [m]Traditionally *bishop*

truth. To the pure, all things are pure, but to those who are corrupted and do not believe, nothing is pure. In fact, both their minds and consciences are corrupted. They claim to know God, but by their actions they deny him. They are detestable, disobedient and unfit for doing anything good. You must teach what is in accord with sound doctrine.

Teaching Various Groups

REGARDING OLDER MEN.   Teach the older men to be temperate, worthy of respect, self-controlled, and sound in faith, in love and in endurance. —*Titus 2:2*

REGARDING OLDER WOMEN.   Likewise, teach the older women to be reverent in the way they live, not to be slanderers or addicted to much wine, but to teach what is good. Then they can train the younger women to love their husbands and children, to be self-controlled and pure, to be busy at home, to be kind, and to be subject to their husbands, so that no one will malign the word of God. —*Titus 2:3-5*

REGARDING YOUNGER MEN.   Similarly, encourage the young men to be self-controlled. In everything set them an example by doing what is good. In your teaching show integrity, seriousness and soundness of speech that cannot be condemned, so that those who oppose you may be ashamed because they have nothing bad to say about us. —*Titus 2:6-8*

REGARDING SLAVES.   Teach slaves to be subject to their masters in everything, to try to please them, not to talk back to them, and not to steal from them, but to show that they can be fully trusted, so that in every way they will make the teaching about God our Savior attractive. —*Titus 2:9,10*

BASIS FOR INSTRUCTIONS.   For the grace of God that brings salvation has appeared to all men. It teaches us to say "No" to ungodliness and worldly passions, and to live self-controlled, upright and godly lives in this present age, while we wait for the blessed hope—the glorious appearing of our great God and Savior, Jesus Christ, who gave himself for us to redeem us from all wickedness and to purify for himself a people that are his very own, eager to do what is good. —*Titus 2:11-15*

These, then, are the things you should teach. Encourage and rebuke with all authority. Do not let anyone despise you.

The Christian Life

NEED FOR RIGHTEOUS LIVING.   Remind the people to be subject to rulers and authorities, to be obedient, to be ready to do whatever is good, to slander no one, to be peaceable and considerate, and to show true humility toward all men. —*Titus 3:1,2*

GRACE DEMANDS GOOD DEEDS.   At one time we too were foolish, disobedient, deceived and enslaved by all kinds of passions and pleasures. We lived in malice and envy, being hated and hating one another. But when the kindness and love of God our Savior appeared, he saved us, not because of righteous things we had done, but because of his mercy. He saved us through the washing of rebirth and renewal by the Holy Spirit, whom he poured out on us generously through Jesus Christ our Savior, so that, having been justified by his grace, we might become heirs having the hope of eternal life. This is a trustworthy saying. And I want you to stress these things, so that those who have trusted in God may be —*Titus 3:3-8* careful to devote themselves to doing what is good. These things are excellent and profitable for everyone.

**Titus
3:9-11**

QUARRELING UNPROFITABLE.   But avoid foolish controversies and genealogies and arguments and quarrels about the law, because these are unprofitable and useless. Warn a divisive person once, and then warn him a second time. After that, have nothing to do with him. You may be sure that such a man is warped and sinful; he is self-condemned.

Concluding Thoughts

**Titus
3:12-14**

PERSONAL MATTERS.   As soon as I send Artemas or Tychicus to you, do your best to come to me at Nicopolis, because I have decided to winter there. Do everything you can to help Zenas the lawyer and Apollos on their way and see that they have everything they need. Our people must learn to devote themselves to doing what is good, in order that they may provide for daily necessities and not live unproductive lives.

Titus 3:15

BENEDICTION.   Everyone with me sends you greetings. Greet those who love us in the faith.

Grace be with you all.

Second Letter to Timothy

*A*lthough there is no direct biblical record which sheds light on the matter, it appears that Paul may have been rearrested in either Nicopolis or Troas and returned to Rome under a sentence of death. This seems likely, because in a second letter to Timothy, written perhaps A.D. 64-67, Paul once again refers to himself as a prisoner and also mentions having made what was apparently a legal defense.

The tone of Paul's last known letter indicates that Paul knows his time is short. Several of his supporters have deserted him in the face of persecution, and Paul wants Timothy to come to him as soon as possible. Tychicus, who has been Paul's messenger on other occasions, is being sent to Ephesus perhaps to carry this letter and also to relieve Timothy so that Timothy can travel to be with Paul. Paul warns Timothy about the coming of opposition and encourages him to be strong in defense of the faith. There is a sense of urgency in his exhortations, as if Timothy is Paul's last link with future generations of those to whom the gospel will be entrusted.

**2 Tim.
1:1,2**

SALUTATION.   Paul, an apostle of Christ Jesus by the will of God, according to the promise of life that is in Christ Jesus,

To Timothy, my dear son:

Grace, mercy and peace from God the Father and Christ Jesus our Lord.

Exhortations to Timothy

**2 Tim.
1:3-7**

CONCERN FOR TIMOTHY.   I thank God, whom I serve, as my forefathers did, with a clear conscience, as night and day I constantly remember you in my prayers. Recalling your tears, I long to see you, so that I may be filled with joy. I have been reminded of your sincere faith, which first lived in your grandmother Lois and in your mother Eunice and, I am persuaded, now lives in you also. For this reason I remind you to fan into flame the gift of God, which is in you through the laying on of my hands. For God did not give us a spirit of timidity, but a spirit of power, of love and of self-discipline.

ENCOURAGEMENT FOR MINISTRY.   So do not be ashamed to testify about our Lord, or ashamed of me his prisoner. But join with me in suffering for the gospel, by the power of God, who has saved us and called us to a holy life—not because of anything we have done but because of his own purpose and grace. This grace was given us in Christ Jesus before the beginning of time, but it has now been revealed through the appearing of our Savior, Christ Jesus, who has destroyed death and has brought life and immortality to light through the gospel. And of this gospel I was appointed a herald and an apostle and a teacher. That is why I am suffering as I am. Yet I am not ashamed, because I know whom I have believed, and am convinced that he is able to guard what I have entrusted to him for that day.

2 Tim.
1:8-12

IMPORTANCE OF DOCTRINE.   What you heard from me, keep as the pattern of sound teaching, with faith and love in Christ Jesus. Guard the good deposit that was entrusted to you—guard it with the help of the Holy Spirit who lives in us.

2 Tim.
1:13,14

MANY HAVE TURNED AWAY.   You know that everyone in the province of Asia has deserted me, including Phygelus and Hermogenes.

2 Tim.
1:15

ONESIPHORUS' FAITH.   May the Lord show mercy to the household of Onesiphorus, because he often refreshed me and was not ashamed of my chains. On the contrary, when he was in Rome, he searched hard for me until he found me. May the Lord grant that he will find mercy from the Lord on that day! You know very well in how many ways he helped me in Ephesus.

2 Tim.
1:16-18

DEDICATION AND DISCIPLINE.   You then, my son, be strong in the grace that is in Christ Jesus. And the things you have heard me say in the presence of many witnesses entrust to reliable men who will also be qualified to teach others. Endure hardship with us like a good soldier of Christ Jesus. No one serving as a soldier gets involved in civilian affairs— he wants to please his commanding officer. Similarly, if anyone competes as an athlete, he does not receive the victor's crown unless he competes according to the rules. The hardworking farmer should be the first to receive a share of the crops. Reflect on what I am saying, for the Lord will give you insight into all this.

2 Tim.
2:1-7

REMEMBERING CHRIST.   Remember Jesus Christ, raised from the dead, descended from David. This is my gospel, for which I am suffering even to the point of being chained like a criminal. But God's word is not chained. Therefore I endure everything for the sake of the elect, that they too may obtain the salvation that is in Christ Jesus, with eternal glory.

2 Tim.
2:8-13

Here is a trustworthy saying:

> If we died with him,
>   we will also live with him;
> if we endure,
>   we will also reign with him.
> If we disown him,
>   he will also disown us;

> if we are faithless,
> he will remain faithful,
> for he cannot disown himself.

**2 Tim.
2:14-19**

HANDLING TRUTH CAREFULLY. Keep reminding them of these things. Warn them before God against quarreling about words; it is of no value, and only ruins those who listen. Do your best to present yourself to God as one approved, a workman who does not need to be ashamed and who correctly handles the word of truth. Avoid godless chatter, because those who indulge in it will become more and more ungodly. Their teaching will spread like gangrene. Among them are Hymenaeus and Philetus, who have wandered away from the truth. They say that the resurrection has already taken place, and they destroy the faith of some. Nevertheless, God's solid foundation stands firm, sealed with this inscription: "The Lord knows those who are his,"[n] and, "Everyone who confesses the name of the Lord must turn away from wickedness."

**2 Tim.
2:20-26**

TEACHING ABOVE QUARRELING. In a large house there are articles not only of gold and silver, but also of wood and clay; some are for noble purposes and some for ignoble. If a man cleanses himself from the latter, he will be an instrument for noble purposes, made holy, useful to the Master and prepared to do any good work.

Flee the evil desires of youth, and pursue righteousness, faith, love and peace, along with those who call on the Lord out of a pure heart. Don't have anything to do with foolish and stupid arguments, because you know they produce quarrels. And the Lord's servant must not quarrel; instead, he must be kind to everyone, able to teach, not resentful. Those who oppose him he must gently instruct, in the hope that God will grant them repentance leading them to a knowledge of the truth, and that they will come to their senses and escape from the trap of the devil, who has taken them captive to do his will.

**2 Tim.
3:1-5**

PREDICTION OF GODLESS TIMES. But mark this: There will be terrible times in the last days. People will be lovers of themselves, lovers of money, boastful, proud, abusive, disobedient to their parents, ungrateful, unholy, without love, unforgiving, slanderous, without self-control, brutal, not lovers of the good, treacherous, rash, conceited, lovers of pleasure rather than lovers of God—having a form of godliness but denying its power. Have nothing to do with them.

**2 Tim.
3:6-9**

EVIL TEACHERS TO BE EXPOSED. They are the kind who worm their way into homes and gain control over weak-willed women, who are loaded down with sins and are swayed by all kinds of evil desires, always learning but never able to acknowledge the truth. Just as Jannes and Jambres opposed Moses, so also these men oppose the truth—men of depraved minds, who, as far as the faith is concerned, are rejected. But they will not get very far because, as in the case of those men, their folly will be clear to everyone.

**2 Tim.
3:10-17**

RESPECT FOR SCRIPTURE. You, however, know all about my teaching, my way of life, my purpose, faith, patience, love, endurance, persecutions, sufferings—what kinds of things happened to me in Antioch, Iconium and Lystra, the persecutions I endured. Yet the Lord rescued me

[n]Num. 16:5 (see Septuagint)

from all of them. In fact, everyone who wants to live a godly life in Christ
Jesus will be persecuted, while evil men and impostors will go from bad
to worse, deceiving and being deceived. But as for you, continue in what
you have learned and have become convinced of, because you know
those from whom you learned it, and how from infancy you have known
the holy Scriptures, which are able to make you wise for salvation
through faith in Christ Jesus. All Scripture is God-breathed and is useful
for teaching, rebuking, correcting and training in righteousness, so that
the man of God may be thoroughly equipped for every good work.

PREACH THE WORD.   In the presence of God and of Christ Jesus, who
will judge the living and the dead, and in view of his appearing and his
kingdom, I give you this charge: Preach the Word; be prepared in season
and out of season; correct, rebuke and encourage—with great patience and
careful instruction. For the time will come when men will not put up with
sound doctrine. Instead, to suit their own desires, they will gather around
them a great number of teachers to say what their itching ears want to
hear. They will turn their ears away from the truth and turn aside to
myths. But you, keep your head in all situations, endure hardship, do the
work of an evangelist, discharge all the duties of your ministry.

*2 Tim.
4:1-5*

REWARD FOR FAITHFUL MINISTRY.   For I am already being poured
out like a drink offering, and the time has come for my departure. I have
fought the good fight, I have finished the race, I have kept the faith. Now
there is in store for me the crown of righteousness, which the Lord, the
righteous Judge, will award to me on that day—and not only to me, but
also to all who have longed for his appearing.

*2 Tim.
4:6-8*

Concluding Thoughts

PAUL ASKS TIMOTHY TO JOIN HIM.   Do your best to come to me
quickly, for Demas, because he loved this world, has deserted me and has
gone to Thessalonica. Crescens has gone to Galatia, and Titus to Dalmatia.
Only Luke is with me. Get Mark and bring him with you, because he is
helpful to me in my ministry. I sent Tychicus to Ephesus. When you come,
bring the cloak that I left with Carpus at Troas, and my scrolls, especially
the parchments.

*2 Tim.
4:9-13*

HOW ALEXANDER OPPOSED HIM.   Alexander the metalworker did
me a great deal of harm. The Lord will repay him for what he has done.
You too should be on your guard against him, because he strongly
opposed our message.

*2 Tim.
4:14,15*

PAUL ALONE IN HIS DEFENSE.   At my first defense, no one came to
my support, but everyone deserted me. May it not be held against them.
But the Lord stood at my side and gave me strength, so that through me
the message might be fully proclaimed and all the Gentiles might hear it.
And I was delivered from the lion's mouth. The Lord will rescue me from
every evil attack and will bring me safely to his heavenly kingdom. To
him be glory for ever and ever. Amen.

*2 Tim.
4:16-18*

GREETINGS AND BENEDICTION.   Greet Priscilla*ᵒ* and Aquila and the
household of Onesiphorus. Erastus stayed in Corinth, and I left Trophimus

*2 Tim.
4:19-22*

ᵒGreek Prisca, a variant of Priscilla

sick in Miletus. Do your best to get here before winter. Eubulus greets you, and so do Pudens, Linus, Claudia and all the brothers.

The Lord be with your spirit. Grace be with you.

No records indicate whether Timothy was ever able to be with Paul before Paul died. Although the exact date and circumstances of Paul's death are unknown, early historical consensus establishes that Paul died a martyr's death. In any event, the second letter to Timothy apparently was Paul's last.

Letter by James

Despite the importance of Paul's ministry and the emphasis given to his work in the historical record of the early church, there are other leaders whose influence cannot be overlooked. At least four of these leaders are the authors of writings which are preserved as part of the New Testament. Two of the authors, James and Jude, are believed to be brothers of Jesus. In the Gospel accounts there is an indication that Jesus' brothers initially rejected his deity and lordship, but the historical record later includes his brothers as being among the disciples in Jerusalem following Christ's ascension.

In addition to the two apostles who are named "James" (one the son of Zebedee, one the son of Alphaeus), there is still another James of great significance in the church. In his Galatian letter, Paul refers to this James as "the Lord's brother," and he indicates that he is a leader in the Jerusalem church. So it would not be surprising that James, "the Lord's brother," would be the author of one of the inspired letters.

If the traditional date of James' death is accurate, then his letter must have been written prior to A.D. 62. It may have been as early as A.D. 50-60, but the exact date is not certain. Addressed to "the twelve tribes scattered among the nations" (a designation for the postexilic Jews and, by extension, all Christians everywhere), the letter probably is intended for general distribution among the scattered churches of Christ. Unlike Paul, James does not struggle with deep issues of doctrine or comment upon any specific problems which a particular local church might be facing. Rather, he addresses himself to the crisis of persecution facing all the churches during this time.

After discussing the nature of temptation, James writes at length concerning the need for consistency between faith and conduct. In context, James appears to be saying that only those who demonstrate true faith can endure the sufferings of the times, and that faith can be measured by conduct. It is also possible that James is urging consistency between belief and action as a source of strength against temptation. James closes his letter with various exhortations for saints having to endure suffering. Despite its immediate relevance to times of widespread persecution, James' writing contains words of practical advice for every Christian's daily walk.

James 1:1   SALUTATION.   James, a servant of God and of the Lord Jesus Christ,

To the twelve tribes scattered among the nations:

Greetings.

Preparation for Oppression

TRIALS HELP DEVELOPMENT.   Consider it pure joy, my brothers,   James
whenever you face trials of many kinds, because you know that the test-   1:2-4
ing of your faith develops perseverance. Perseverance must finish its work
so that you may be mature and complete, not lacking anything.

SEEKING WISDOM.   If any of you lacks wisdom, he should ask God,   James
who gives generously to all without finding fault, and it will be given to   1:5-8
him. But when he asks, he must believe and not doubt, because he who
doubts is like a wave of the sea, blown and tossed by the wind. That man
should not think he will receive anything from the Lord; he is a double-
minded man, unstable in all he does.

RICHES WILL FADE.   The brother in humble circumstances ought to take   James
pride in his high position. But the one who is rich should take pride in his   1:9-11
low position, because he will pass away like a wild flower. For the sun
rises with scorching heat and withers the plant; its blossom falls and its
beauty is destroyed. In the same way, the rich man will fade away even
while he goes about his business.

TEMPTATION COMES FROM WITHIN.   Blessed is the man who per-   James
severes under trial, because when he has stood the test, he will receive the   1:12-15
crown of life that God has promised to those who love him.
    When tempted, no one should say, "God is tempting me." For God
cannot be tempted by evil, nor does he tempt anyone; but each one is
tempted when, by his own evil desire, he is dragged away and enticed.
Then, after desire has conceived, it gives birth to sin; and sin, when it is
full-grown, gives birth to death.

GOODNESS COMES FROM GOD.   Don't be deceived, my dear brothers.   James
Every good and perfect gift is from above, coming down from the Father   1:16-18
of the heavenly lights, who does not change like shifting shadows. He
chose to give us birth through the word of truth, that we might be a kind
of firstfruits of all he created.

Consistency Between Faith and Conduct

WORD PRODUCES RIGHTEOUSNESS.   My dear brothers, take note of   James
this: Everyone should be quick to listen, slow to speak and slow to become   1:19-21
angry, for man's anger does not bring about the righteous life that God
desires. Therefore, get rid of all moral filth and the evil that is so prevalent
and humbly accept the word planted in you, which can save you.

KNOWLEDGE IS NOT ENOUGH.   Do not merely listen to the word, and   James
so deceive yourselves. Do what it says. Anyone who listens to the word   1:22-25
but does not do what it says is like a man who looks at his face in a mirror
and, after looking at himself, goes away and immediately forgets what he
looks like. But the man who looks intently into the perfect law that gives
freedom, and continues to do this, not forgetting what he has heard, but
doing it—he will be blessed in what he does.

TRUE RELIGION.   If anyone considers himself religious and yet does not   James
keep a tight rein on his tongue, he deceives himself and his religion is   1:26,27
worthless. Religion that God our Father accepts as pure and faultless is

this: to look after orphans and widows in their distress and to keep oneself from being polluted by the world.

James 2:1-7

PARTIALITY NOT OF FAITH.   My brothers, as believers in our glorious Lord Jesus Christ, don't show favoritism. Suppose a man comes into your meeting wearing a gold ring and fine clothes, and a poor man in shabby clothes also comes in. If you show special attention to the man wearing fine clothes and say, "Here's a good seat for you," but say to the poor man, "You stand there" or "Sit on the floor by my feet," have you not discriminated among yourselves and become judges with evil thoughts?

Listen, my dear brothers: Has not God chosen those who are poor in the eyes of the world to be rich in faith and to inherit the kingdom he promised those who love him? But you have insulted the poor. Is it not the rich who are exploiting you? Are they not the ones who are dragging you into court? Are they not the ones who are slandering the noble name of him to whom you belong?

James 2:8-13

ANY VIOLATION DISRESPECTS.   If you really keep the royal law found in Scripture, "Love your neighbor as yourself,"[p] you are doing right. But if you show favoritism, you sin and are convicted by the law as lawbreakers. For whoever keeps the whole law and yet stumbles at just one point is guilty of breaking all of it. For he who said, "Do not commit adultery,"[q] also said, "Do not murder."[r] If you do not commit adultery but do commit murder, you have become a lawbreaker.

Speak and act as those who are going to be judged by the law that gives freedom, because judgment without mercy will be shown to anyone who has not been merciful. Mercy triumphs over judgment!

James 2:14-17

CHANGED LIFE EVIDENCES FAITH.   What good is it, my brothers, if a man claims to have faith but has no deeds? Can such faith save him? Suppose a brother or sister is without clothes and daily food. If one of you says to him, "Go, I wish you well; keep warm and well fed," but does nothing about his physical needs, what good is it? In the same way, faith by itself, if it is not accompanied by action, is dead.

James 2:18-20

FAITH WITHOUT WORKS.   But someone will say, "You have faith; I have deeds."

Show me your faith without deeds, and I will show you my faith by what I do. You believe that there is one God. Good! Even the demons believe that—and shudder.

You foolish man, do you want evidence that faith without deeds is useless[s]?

James 2:21-26

EXAMPLES OF OBEDIENT FAITH.   Was not our ancestor Abraham considered righteous for what he did when he offered his son Isaac on the altar? You see that his faith and his actions were working together, and his faith was made complete by what he did. And the scripture was fulfilled that says, "Abraham believed God, and it was credited to him as righteousness,"[t] and he was called God's friend. You see that a person is justified by what he does and not by faith alone.

[p]Lev. 19:18   [q]Exodus 20:14; Deut. 5:18   [r]Exodus 20:13; Deut. 5:17   [s]Some early manuscripts *dead*   [t]Gen. 15:6

In the same way, was not even Rahab the prostitute considered righteous for what she did when she gave lodging to the spies and sent them off in a different direction? As the body without the spirit is dead, so faith without deeds is dead.

PRACTICING WHAT IS PREACHED.   Not many of you should presume to be teachers, my brothers, because you know that we who teach will be judged more strictly. We all stumble in many ways. If anyone is never at fault in what he says, he is a perfect man, able to keep his whole body in check.

James 3:1-5

When we put bits into the mouths of horses to make them obey us, we can turn the whole animal. Or take ships as an example. Although they are so large and are driven by strong winds, they are steered by a very small rudder wherever the pilot wants to go. Likewise the tongue is a small part of the body, but it makes great boasts. Consider what a great forest is set on fire by a small spark.

SPEECH TO REFLECT PURITY.   The tongue also is a fire, a world of evil among the parts of the body. It corrupts the whole person, sets the whole course of his life on fire, and is itself set on fire by hell.

James 3:6-12

All kinds of animals, birds, reptiles and creatures of the sea are being tamed and have been tamed by man, but no man can tame the tongue. It is a restless evil, full of deadly poison.

With the tongue we praise our Lord and Father, and with it we curse men, who have been made in God's likeness. Out of the same mouth come praise and cursing. My brothers, this should not be. Can both fresh water and salt *u* water flow from the same spring? My brothers, can a fig tree bear olives, or a grapevine bear figs? Neither can a salt spring produce fresh water.

WISDOM SHOWN BY GOOD LIFE.   Who is wise and understanding among you? Let him show it by his good life, by deeds done in the humility that comes from wisdom. But if you harbor bitter envy and selfish ambition in your hearts, do not boast about it or deny the truth. Such "wisdom" does not come down from heaven but is earthly, unspiritual, of the devil. For where you have envy and selfish ambition, there you find disorder and every evil practice.

James 3:13-18

But the wisdom that comes from heaven is first of all pure; then peace-loving, considerate, submissive, full of mercy and good fruit, impartial and sincere. Peacemakers who sow in peace raise a harvest of righteousness.

MATERIALISM BRINGS CONFLICT.   What causes fights and quarrels among you? Don't they come from your desires that battle within you? You want something but don't get it. You kill and covet, but you cannot have what you want. You quarrel and fight. You do not have, because you do not ask God. When you ask, you do not receive, because you ask with wrong motives, that you may spend what you get on your pleasures.

James 4:1-4

You adulterous people, don't you know that friendship with the world is hatred toward God? Anyone who chooses to be a friend of the world becomes an enemy of God.

*u*Greek *bitter* (see also verse 14)

James
4:5-10
GODLINESS BRINGS JOY.   Or do you think Scripture says without reason that the spirit he caused to live in us envies intensely?^{v} But he gives us more grace. That is why Scripture says:

> "God opposes the proud
> but gives grace to the humble."^{w}

Submit yourselves, then, to God. Resist the devil, and he will flee from you. Come near to God and he will come near to you. Wash your hands, you sinners, and purify your hearts, you double-minded. Grieve, mourn and wail. Change your laughter to mourning and your joy to gloom. Humble yourselves before the Lord, and he will lift you up.

James
4:11-12
OBEYING VERSUS JUDGING.   Brothers, do not slander one another. Anyone who speaks against his brother or judges him speaks against the law and judges it. When you judge the law, you are not keeping it, but sitting in judgment on it. There is only one Lawgiver and Judge, the one who is able to save and destroy. But you—who are you to judge your neighbor?

Exhortations for Suffering Saints

James
4:13-17
PERSPECTIVE AND PRIORITIES.   Now listen, you who say, "Today or tomorrow we will go to this or that city, spend a year there, carry on business and make money." Why, you do not even know what will happen tomorrow. What is your life? You are a mist that appears for a little while and then vanishes. Instead, you ought to say, "If it is the Lord's will, we will live and do this or that." As it is, you boast and brag. All such boasting is evil. Anyone, then, who knows the good he ought to do and doesn't do it, sins.

James
5:1-6
JUDGMENT AGAINST OPPRESSORS.   Now listen, you rich people, weep and wail because of the misery that is coming upon you. Your wealth has rotted, and moths have eaten your clothes. Your gold and silver are corroded. Their corrosion will testify against you and eat your flesh like fire. You have hoarded wealth in the last days. Look! The wages you failed to pay the workmen who mowed your fields are crying out against you. The cries of the harvesters have reached the ears of the Lord Almighty. You have lived on earth in luxury and self-indulgence. You have fattened yourselves in the day of slaughter.^{x} You have condemned and murdered innocent men, who were not opposing you.

James
5:7-11
STEADFASTNESS IN SUFFERING.   Be patient, then, brothers, until the Lord's coming. See how the farmer waits for the land to yield its valuable crop and how patient he is for the autumn and spring rains. You too, be patient and stand firm, because the Lord's coming is near. Don't grumble against each other, brothers, or you will be judged. The Judge is standing at the door!

Brothers, as an example of patience in the face of suffering, take the prophets who spoke in the name of the Lord. As you know, we consider blessed those who have persevered. You have heard of Job's perseverance and have seen what the Lord finally brought about. The Lord is full of compassion and mercy.

^{v}Or that God jealously longs for the spirit that he made to live in us; or that the Spirit he caused to live in us longs jealously ^{w}Prov. 3:34 ^{x}Or yourselves as in a day of feasting

RASH OATHS.   Above all, my brothers, do not swear—not by heaven or   James 5:12
by earth or by anything else. Let your "Yes" be yes, and your "No," no, or
you will be condemned.

PRAYER AMID SUFFERING.   Is any one of you in trouble? He should   James
pray. Is anyone happy? Let him sing songs of praise. Is any one of you   5:13-18
sick? He should call the elders of the church to pray over him and anoint
him with oil in the name of the Lord. And the prayer offered in faith will
make the sick person well; the Lord will raise him up. If he has sinned, he
will be forgiven. Therefore confess your sins to each other and pray for
each other so that you may be healed. The prayer of a righteous man is
powerful and effective.

   Elijah was a man just like us. He prayed earnestly that it would not rain,
and it did not rain on the land for three and a half years. Again he prayed,
and the heavens gave rain, and the earth produced its crops.

MUTUAL WATCHFULNESS.   My brothers, if one of you should wander   James
from the truth and someone should bring him back, remember this: 5:19,20
Whoever turns a sinner from the error of his way will save him from death
and cover over a multitude of sins.

Letter by Jude

*R*eferring to himself as a brother of James, Jude also addresses a
general audience through a brief writing in which he warns them of
false teachers and encourages them to keep the faith. Estimates of
the letter's date vary from A.D. 60 to perhaps A.D. 80. Little is known of Jude
(Judas) or his work, although some believe he is mentioned on two occasions,
not only as a brother of Jesus, but also as a church leader and prophet in
Jerusalem. In his letter, Jude is trying to combat a widely believed philosophy
which denies that the sins of the flesh can affect the soul—a philosophy
which, naturally enough, has led to flagrant immorality. In order to stress the
potentially dangerous consequences of such teaching, Jude uses both Old
Testament and extrabiblical writings (the book of Enoch) to remind his
readers of God's judgment upon the ungodly.

SALUTATION.   Jude, a servant of Jesus Christ and a brother of James,   Jude 1,2

   To those who have been called, who are loved by God the Father and
kept by*y* Jesus Christ:

   Mercy, peace and love be yours in abundance.

CONTEND FOR THE FAITH.   Dear friends, although I was very eager   Jude 3,4
to write to you about the salvation we share, I felt I had to write and urge
you to contend for the faith that was once for all entrusted to the saints.
For certain men whose condemnation was written about*z* long ago have
secretly slipped in among you. They are godless men, who change the
grace of our God into a license for immorality and deny Jesus Christ our
only Sovereign and Lord.

y Or for; or in   *z Or men who were marked out for condemnation*

Jude 5-7   JUDGMENT UPON UNGODLY.   Though you already know all this, I want to remind you that the Lord[a] delivered his people out of Egypt, but later destroyed those who did not believe. And the angels who did not keep their positions of authority but abandoned their own home—these he has kept in darkness, bound with everlasting chains for judgment on the great Day. In a similar way, Sodom and Gomorrah and the surrounding towns gave themselves up to sexual immorality and perversion. They serve as an example of those who suffer the punishment of eternal fire.

Jude 8-13   FALSE TEACHERS.   In the very same way, these dreamers pollute their own bodies, reject authority and slander celestial beings. But even the archangel Michael, when he was disputing with the devil about the body of Moses, did not dare to bring a slanderous accusation against him, but said, "The Lord rebuke you!" Yet these men speak abusively against whatever they do not understand; and what things they do understand by instinct, like unreasoning animals—these are the very things that destroy them.

Woe to them! They have taken the way of Cain; they have rushed for profit into Balaam's error; they have been destroyed in Korah's rebellion.

These men are blemishes at your love feasts, eating with you without the slightest qualm—shepherds who feed only themselves. They are clouds without rain, blown along by the wind; autumn trees, without fruit and uprooted—twice dead. They are wild waves of the sea, foaming up their shame; wandering stars, for whom blackest darkness has been reserved forever.

Jude 14-16   PROPHECY OF JUDGMENT.   Enoch, the seventh from Adam, prophesied about these men: "See, the Lord is coming with thousands upon thousands of his holy ones to judge everyone, and to convict all the ungodly of all the ungodly acts they have done in the ungodly way, and of all the harsh words ungodly sinners have spoken against him." These men are grumblers and faultfinders; they follow their own evil desires; they boast about themselves and flatter others for their own advantage.

Jude 17-21   ADMONITION TO BE FAITHFUL.   But, dear friends, remember what the apostles of our Lord Jesus Christ foretold. They said to you, "In the last times there will be scoffers who will follow their own ungodly desires." These are the men who divide you, who follow mere natural instincts and do not have the Spirit.

But you, dear friends, build yourselves up in your most holy faith and pray in the Holy Spirit. Keep yourselves in God's love as you wait for the mercy of our Lord Jesus Christ to bring you to eternal life.

Jude 22,23   OBLIGATIONS TOWARD THE ERRING.   Be merciful to those who doubt; snatch others from the fire and save them; to others show mercy, mixed with fear—hating even the clothing stained by corrupted flesh.

Jude 24,25   BENEDICTION.   To him who is able to keep you from falling and to present you before his glorious presence without fault and with great joy—to the only God our Savior be glory, majesty, power and authority, through Jesus Christ our Lord, before all ages, now and forevermore! Amen.

[a]Some early manuscripts *Jesus*

First Letter by Peter

*T*he historical record of Acts does not mention the apostle Peter after the Jerusalem conference, but it appears that his ministry proceeded in the same time period as the missionary efforts of the apostle Paul. It is also evident that their paths must have crossed, perhaps in Rome, and that they were acquainted with each other's work. They even labored together with some of the same brethren—Silas (Silvanus) and Mark (John Mark). Therefore it comes as no surprise that, in the two letters written by Peter, he uses Silas as his scribe, refers to Mark as "my son," and mentions Paul's letters in a way that indicates his familiarity with their contents.

Both of Peter's letters are evidently addressed to the same audience, principally Gentile Christians throughout Asia, Bithynia, Pontus, Galatia, and Cappadocia. These are some of the same areas where Paul had established churches on his preaching tours and include the same Christians to whom Paul had addressed some of his letters. Peter's letters may have been written from either Rome or Jerusalem, as indicated by Peter's reference to the apparently pseudonymous "Babylon." As with other epistles, the exact dates of Peter's two letters are uncertain. If the traditional dating of Peter's death is accurate, the letters would have been written sometime prior to A.D. 64.

Without doubt this is a time of hostility, if not actual physical persecution, against all Christians. Therefore, the subject of Peter's first letter is suffering, and the thrust of the letter is an exhortation to steadfastness. Peter begins by recounting for his readers the blessings which they have in their redemption, and then encourages them in the fact that in Christ they are God's special people. But Peter also reminds them that, as God's redeemed ones, they have a responsibility to glorify God in their lives. He concludes by noting the blessings which come through persecution and by urging steadfastness through faith and godliness.

SALUTATION.   Peter, an apostle of Jesus Christ,   1 Pet. 1:1,2

To God's elect, strangers in the world, scattered throughout Pontus, Galatia, Cappadocia, Asia and Bithynia, who have been chosen according to the foreknowledge of God the Father, through the sanctifying work of the Spirit, for obedience to Jesus Christ and sprinkling by his blood:

Grace and peace be yours in abundance.

The Blessings of Redemption

PRAISE FOR LIVING HOPE.   Praise be to the God and Father of our   1 Pet. 1:3-5
Lord Jesus Christ! In his great mercy he has given us new birth into a living hope through the resurrection of Jesus Christ from the dead, and into an inheritance that can never perish, spoil or fade—kept in heaven for you, who through faith are shielded by God's power until the coming of the salvation that is ready to be revealed in the last time.

SUFFERING BEFORE SALVATION.   In this you greatly rejoice, though   1 Pet. 1:6,7
now for a little while you may have had to suffer grief in all kinds of trials. These have come so that your faith—of greater worth than gold,

which perishes even though refined by fire—may be proved genuine and may result in praise, glory and honor when Jesus Christ is revealed.

1 Pet. 1:8,9 FAITH IN UNSEEN.   Though you have not seen him, you love him; and even though you do not see him now, you believe in him and are filled with an inexpressible and glorious joy, for you are receiving the goal of your faith, the salvation of your souls.

1 Pet. 1:10-12 GOD'S GRACE FORETOLD.   Concerning this salvation, the prophets, who spoke of the grace that was to come to you, searched intently and with the greatest care, trying to find out the time and circumstances to which the Spirit of Christ in them was pointing when he predicted the sufferings of Christ and the glories that would follow. It was revealed to them that they were not serving themselves but you, when they spoke of the things that have now been told you by those who have preached the gospel to you by the Holy Spirit sent from heaven. Even angels long to look into these things.

The Nature of Redemption

1 Pet. 1:13-17 HOLINESS RESPONSIVE TO GRACE.   Therefore, prepare your minds for action; be self-controlled; set your hope fully on the grace to be given you when Jesus Christ is revealed. As obedient children, do not conform to the evil desires you had when you lived in ignorance. But just as he who called you is holy, so be holy in all you do; for it is written: "Be holy, because I am holy."[b]

Since you call on a Father who judges each man's work impartially, live your lives as strangers here in reverent fear.

1 Pet. 1:18-21 CHRIST AS RANSOM.   For you know that it was not with perishable things such as silver or gold that you were redeemed from the empty way of life handed down to you from your forefathers, but with the precious blood of Christ, a lamb without blemish or defect. He was chosen before the creation of the world, but was revealed in these last times for your sake. Through him you believe in God, who raised him from the dead and glorified him, and so your faith and hope are in God.

1 Pet. 1:22-25 NEW CREATURES.   Now that you have purified yourselves by obeying the truth so that you have sincere love for your brothers, love one another deeply, from the heart.[c] For you have been born again, not of perishable seed, but of imperishable, through the living and enduring word of God. For,

> "All men are like grass,
>   and all their glory is like the flowers of the field;
> the grass withers and the flowers fall,
>   but the word of the Lord stands forever."[d]

And this is the word that was preached to you.

1 Pet. 2:1-3 SPIRITUAL MATURITY.   Therefore, rid yourselves of all malice and all deceit, hypocrisy, envy, and slander of every kind. Like newborn babies, crave pure spiritual milk, so that by it you may grow up in your salvation, now that you have tasted that the Lord is good.

[b]Lev. 11:44,45; 19:2   [c]Some early manuscripts *from a pure heart*   [d]Isaiah 40:6-8

STRENGTH AND ACCESS.   As you come to him, the living Stone—   1 Pet. 2:4,5
rejected by men but chosen by God and precious to him—you also, like
living stones, are being built into a spiritual house to be a holy priesthood,
offering spiritual sacrifices acceptable to God through Jesus Christ.

CHRIST THE CORNERSTONE.   For in Scripture it says: 1 Pet. 2:6-8

> "See, I lay a stone in Zion,
> a chosen and precious cornerstone,
> and the one who trusts in him
> will never be put to shame."[e]

Now to you who believe, this stone is precious. But to those who do not
believe,

> "The stone the builders rejected
> has become the capstone,[f]"[g]

and,

> "A stone that causes men to stumble
> and a rock that makes them fall."[h]

They stumble because they disobey the message—which is also what they
were destined for.

GOD'S CHOSEN PEOPLE.   But you are a chosen people, a royal priest-   1 Pet.
hood, a holy nation, a people belonging to God, that you may declare the   2:9,10
praises of him who called you out of darkness into his wonderful light.
Once you were not a people, but now you are the people of God; once you
had not received mercy, but now you have received mercy.

Glorifying God for Redemption

IN CONDUCT.   Dear friends, I urge you, as aliens and strangers in the   1 Pet.
world, to abstain from sinful desires, which war against your soul. Live   2:11,12
such good lives among the pagans that, though they accuse you of doing
wrong, they may see your good deeds and glorify God on the day he
visits us.

AS A CITIZEN.   Submit yourselves for the Lord's sake to every authori-   1 Pet.
ty instituted among men: whether to the king, as the supreme authority, or   2:13-17
to governors, who are sent by him to punish those who do wrong and to
commend those who do right. For it is God's will that by doing good you
should silence the ignorant talk of foolish men. Live as free men, but do
not use your freedom as a cover-up for evil; live as servants of God. Show
proper respect to everyone: Love the brotherhood of believers, fear God,
honor the king.

AS A SLAVE.   Slaves, submit yourselves to your masters with all respect,   1 Pet.
not only to those who are good and considerate, but also to those who are   2:18-25
harsh. For it is commendable if a man bears up under the pain of unjust
suffering because he is conscious of God. But how is it to your credit if you
receive a beating for doing wrong and endure it? But if you suffer for
doing good and you endure it, this is commendable before God. To this
you were called, because Christ suffered for you, leaving you an example,
that you should follow in his steps.

[e]Isaiah 28:16   [f]Or *cornerstone*   [g]Psalm 118:22   [h]Isaiah 8:14

> "He committed no sin,
> and no deceit was found in his mouth."[i]

When they hurled their insults at him, he did not retaliate; when he suffered, he made no threats. Instead, he entrusted himself to him who judges justly. He himself bore our sins in his body on the tree, so that we might die to sins and live for righteousness; by his wounds you have been healed. For you were like sheep going astray, but now you have returned to the Shepherd and Overseer of your souls.

1 Pet. 3:1-6 AS A WIFE.   Wives, in the same way be submissive to your husbands so that, if any of them do not believe the word, they may be won over without words by the behavior of their wives, when they see the purity and reverence of your lives. Your beauty should not come from outward adornment, such as braided hair and the wearing of gold jewelry and fine clothes. Instead, it should be that of your inner self, the unfading beauty of a gentle and quiet spirit, which is of great worth in God's sight. For this is the way the holy women of the past who put their hope in God used to make themselves beautiful. They were submissive to their own husbands, like Sarah, who obeyed Abraham and called him her master. You are her daughters if you do what is right and do not give way to fear.

1 Pet. 3:7 AS A HUSBAND.   Husbands, in the same way be considerate as you live with your wives, and treat them with respect as the weaker partner and as heirs with you of the gracious gift of life, so that nothing will hinder your prayers.

**1 Pet.
3:8-12** IN LOVE AND UNITY.   Finally, all of you, live in harmony with one another; be sympathetic, love as brothers, be compassionate and humble. Do not repay evil with evil or insult with insult, but with blessing, because to this you were called so that you may inherit a blessing. For,

> "Whoever would love life
> and see good days
> must keep his tongue from evil
> and his lips from deceitful speech.
> He must turn from evil and do good;
> he must seek peace and pursue it.
> For the eyes of the Lord are on the righteous
> and his ears are attentive to their prayer,
> but the face of the Lord is against those who do evil."[j]

Steadfastness in Persecution

**1 Pet.
3:13-17** CONFIDENCE IN TRIALS.   Who is going to harm you if you are eager to do good? But even if you should suffer for what is right, you are blessed. "Do not fear what they fear[k]; do not be frightened."[l] But in your hearts set apart Christ as Lord. Always be prepared to give an answer to everyone who asks you to give the reason for the hope that you have. But do this with gentleness and respect, keeping a clear conscience, so that those who speak maliciously against your good behavior in Christ may be ashamed of their slander. It is better, if it is God's will, to suffer for doing good than for doing evil.

---

[i] Isaiah 53:9   [j] Psalm 34:12-16   [k] Or *not fear their threats*   [l] Isaiah 8:12

EFFICACY OF CHRIST'S DEATH.   For Christ died for sins once for all, the righteous for the unrighteous, to bring you to God. He was put to death in the body but made alive by the Spirit, through whom*m* also he went and preached to the spirits in prison who disobeyed long ago when God waited patiently in the days of Noah while the ark was being built. In it only a few people, eight in all, were saved through water,

1 Pet.
3:18-20

MEANING OF BAPTISM.   and this water symbolizes baptism that now saves you also—not the removal of dirt from the body but the pledge*n* of a good conscience toward God. It saves you by the resurrection of Jesus Christ, who has gone into heaven and is at God's right hand—with angels, authorities and powers in submission to him.

1 Pet.
3:21,22

SUFFERING WITHOUT SIN.   Therefore, since Christ suffered in his body, arm yourselves also with the same attitude, because he who has suffered in his body is done with sin. As a result, he does not live the rest of his earthly life for evil human desires, but rather for the will of God. For you have spent enough time in the past doing what pagans choose to do— living in debauchery, lust, drunkenness, orgies, carousing and detestable idolatry. They think it strange that you do not plunge with them into the same flood of dissipation, and they heap abuse on you. But they will have to give account to him who is ready to judge the living and the dead. For this is the reason the gospel was preached even to those who are now dead, so that they might be judged according to men in regard to the body, but live according to God in regard to the spirit.

1 Pet. 4:1-6

BROTHERLY LOVE.   The end of all things is near. Therefore be clear minded and self-controlled so that you can pray. Above all, love each other deeply, because love covers over a multitude of sins. Offer hospitality to one another without grumbling. Each one should use whatever gift he has received to serve others, faithfully administering God's grace in its various forms. If anyone speaks, he should do it as one speaking the very words of God. If anyone serves, he should do it with the strength God provides, so that in all things God may be praised through Jesus Christ. To him be the glory and the power for ever and ever. Amen.

1 Pet.
4:7-11

SUFFERING AS CHRISTIANS.   Dear friends, do not be surprised at the painful trial you are suffering, as though something strange were happening to you. But rejoice that you participate in the sufferings of Christ, so that you may be overjoyed when his glory is revealed. If you are insulted because of the name of Christ, you are blessed, for the Spirit of glory and of God rests on you. If you suffer, it should not be as a murderer or thief or any other kind of criminal, or even as a meddler. However, if you suffer as a Christian, do not be ashamed, but praise God that you bear that name. For it is time for judgment to begin with the family of God; and if it begins with us, what will the outcome be for those who do not obey the gospel of God? And,

1 Pet.
4:12-19

> "If it is hard for the righteous to be saved,
>   what will become of the ungodly and the sinner?"*o*

So then, those who suffer according to God's will should commit themselves to their faithful Creator and continue to do good.

---

*m*Or *alive in the spirit,* [19]*through which*   *n*Or *response*   *o*Prov. 11:31

1 Pet. 5:1-4 RESPONSIBILITY OF ELDERS.   To the elders among you, I appeal as a fellow elder, a witness of Christ's sufferings and one who also will share in the glory to be revealed: Be shepherds of God's flock that is under your care, serving as overseers—not because you must, but because you are willing, as God wants you to be; not greedy for money, but eager to serve; not lording it over those entrusted to you, but being examples to the flock. And when the Chief Shepherd appears, you will receive the crown of glory that will never fade away.

1 Pet. 5:5-7 RESPECT AND HUMILITY.   Young men, in the same way be submissive to those who are older. All of you, clothe yourselves with humility toward one another, because,

> "God opposes the proud
> but gives grace to the humble."[p]

Humble yourselves, therefore, under God's mighty hand, that he may lift you up in due time. Cast all your anxiety on him because he cares for you.

1 Pet. 5:8-11 EXHORTATION FOR PERSECUTION.   Be self-controlled and alert. Your enemy the devil prowls around like a roaring lion looking for someone to devour. Resist him, standing firm in the faith, because you know that your brothers throughout the world are undergoing the same kind of sufferings.

And the God of all grace, who called you to his eternal glory in Christ, after you have suffered a little while, will himself restore you and make you strong, firm and steadfast. To him be the power for ever and ever. Amen.

Concluding Thoughts

1 Pet. 5:12-14 BENEDICTION.   With the help of Silas,[q] whom I regard as a faithful brother, I have written to you briefly, encouraging you and testifying that this is the true grace of God. Stand fast in it.

She who is in Babylon, chosen together with you, sends you her greetings, and so does my son Mark. Greet one another with a kiss of love.

Peace to all of you who are in Christ.

Second Letter by Peter

One of the interesting aspects of Peter's second letter is the prediction of his own imminent death. This seems to indicate that the letter is written very near the end of Peter's life, perhaps after the death of Paul and possibly about A.D. 64. The letter is similar in content both to Jude's letter, which warned against false teachers, and to Paul's discussion of the second coming in his two letters to the Thessalonians.

The error being taught by these false teachers presumably is in regard to the second coming. Evidently their teaching concerning the actual time of the Lord's reappearance is leading some not only to a life of idleness (against which Paul had warned) but also to worldliness and immorality. It is exactly the same problem which the prophet Malachi addressed. When the promised

---

[p]Prov. 3:34   [q]Greek *Silvanus*, a variant of *Silas*

Messiah did not appear soon after his coming was foretold, many Jews became cynical and turned away from God altogether. Here now, some five centuries later, some Christians who have not been blessed with an immediate second coming of the Messiah are also giving up and living lives unbefitting Christians.

It is to this situation that Peter now addresses his own warnings. Peter begins his letter by stressing the importance of true spiritual knowledge. He warns his readers to beware of those who might pervert the gospel of Christ by teaching a counterfeit doctrine. Like Malachi, Peter concludes by clarifying once again that, although Christ has not reappeared as quickly as some have expected, both his coming and the judgment of man are as certain as God's Word itself. The strong implication is that some of his readers ought to be thankful that the Lord has not yet come again, because if he had, they would not have been ready!

SALUTATION.   Simon Peter, a servant and apostle of Jesus Christ,   2 Pet. 1:1,2

To those who through the righteousness of our God and Savior Jesus Christ have received a faith as precious as ours:

Grace and peace be yours in abundance through the knowledge of God and of Jesus our Lord.

Value of True Knowledge

KNOWLEDGE BRINGS GODLINESS.   His divine power has given us   2 Pet. 1:3,4
everything we need for life and godliness through our knowledge of him who called us by his own glory and goodness. Through these he has given us his very great and precious promises, so that through them you may participate in the divine nature and escape the corruption in the world caused by evil desires.

BEYOND KNOWLEDGE INTO LOVE.   For this very reason, make every   2 Pet. 1:5-9
effort to add to your faith goodness; and to goodness, knowledge; and to knowledge, self-control; and to self-control, perseverance; and to perseverance, godliness; and to godliness, brotherly kindness; and to brotherly kindness, love. For if you possess these qualities in increasing measure, they will keep you from being ineffective and unproductive in your knowledge of our Lord Jesus Christ. But if anyone does not have them, he is nearsighted and blind, and has forgotten that he has been cleansed from his past sins.

NEED TO AFFIRM CALLING.   Therefore, my brothers, be all the more   2 Pet.
eager to make your calling and election sure. For if you do these things,   1:10,11
you will never fall, and you will receive a rich welcome into the eternal kingdom of our Lord and Savior Jesus Christ.

REMINDER IN FACE OF DEATH.   So I will always remind you of these   2 Pet.
things, even though you know them and are firmly established in the   1:12-15
truth you now have. I think it is right to refresh your memory as long as I live in the tent of this body, because I know that I will soon put it aside, as our Lord Jesus Christ has made clear to me. And I will make every effort to see that after my departure you will always be able to remember these things.

2 Pet. 1:16-18	FACTUAL NATURE OF GOSPEL. We did not follow cleverly invented stories when we told you about the power and coming of our Lord Jesus Christ, but we were eyewitnesses of his majesty. For he received honor and glory from God the Father when the voice came to him from the Majestic Glory, saying, "This is my Son, whom I love; with him I am well pleased." [r] We ourselves heard this voice that came from heaven when we were with him on the sacred mountain.
2 Pet. 1:19-21	FULFILLMENT OF PROPHECY. And we have the word of the prophets made more certain, and you will do well to pay attention to it, as to a light shining in a dark place, until the day dawns and the morning star rises in your hearts. Above all, you must understand that no prophecy of Scripture came about by the prophet's own interpretation. For prophecy never had its origin in the will of man, but men spoke from God as they were carried along by the Holy Spirit.

Danger of False Teachers

2 Pet. 2:1-3	FALSE TEACHERS. But there were also false prophets among the people, just as there will be false teachers among you. They will secretly introduce destructive heresies, even denying the sovereign Lord who bought them—bringing swift destruction on themselves. Many will follow their shameful ways and will bring the way of truth into disrepute. In their greed these teachers will exploit you with stories they have made up. Their condemnation has long been hanging over them, and their destruction has not been sleeping.
2 Pet. 2:4-10a	GOD WILL PUNISH WICKED. For if God did not spare angels when they sinned, but sent them to hell,[s] putting them into gloomy dungeons[t] to be held for judgment; if he did not spare the ancient world when he brought the flood on its ungodly people, but protected Noah, a preacher of righteousness, and seven others; if he condemned the cities of Sodom and Gomorrah by burning them to ashes, and made them an example of what is going to happen to the ungodly; and if he rescued Lot, a righteous man, who was distressed by the filthy lives of lawless men (for that righteous man, living among them day after day, was tormented in his righteous soul by the lawless deeds he saw and heard)—if this is so, then the Lord knows how to rescue godly men from trials and to hold the unrighteous for the day of judgment, while continuing their punishment.[u] This is especially true of those who follow the corrupt desire of the sinful nature[v] and despise authority.
2 Pet. 2:10b-16	DESCRIPTION OF FALSE TEACHERS. Bold and arrogant, these men are not afraid to slander celestial beings; yet even angels, although they are stronger and more powerful, do not bring slanderous accusations against such beings in the presence of the Lord. But these men blaspheme in matters they do not understand. They are like brute beasts, creatures of instinct, born only to be caught and destroyed, and like beasts they too will perish. They will be paid back with harm for the harm they have done. Their idea of pleasure is to carouse in broad daylight. They are blots and blemishes,

---

[r]Matt. 17:5; Mark 9:7; Luke 9:35   [s]Greek *Tartarus*   [t]Some manuscripts *into chains of darkness*   [u]Or *unrighteous for punishment until the day of judgment*   [v]Or *the flesh*

reveling in their pleasures while they feast with you.*w* With eyes full of adultery, they never stop sinning; they seduce the unstable; they are experts in greed—an accursed brood! They have left the straight way and wandered off to follow the way of Balaam son of Beor, who loved the wages of wickedness. But he was rebuked for his wrongdoing by a donkey—a beast without speech—who spoke with a man's voice and restrained the prophet's madness.

RESULTS OF THEIR TEACHING.   These men are springs without water and mists driven by a storm. Blackest darkness is reserved for them. For they mouth empty, boastful words and, by appealing to the lustful desires of sinful human nature, they entice people who are just escaping from those who live in error. They promise them freedom, while they themselves are slaves of depravity—for a man is a slave to whatever has mastered him. If they have escaped the corruption of the world by knowing our Lord and Savior Jesus Christ and are again entangled in it and overcome, they are worse off at the end than they were at the beginning. It would have been better for them not to have known the way of righteousness, than to have known it and then to turn their backs on the sacred command that was passed on to them. Of them the proverbs are true: "A dog returns to its vomit,"*x* and, "A sow that is washed goes back to her wallowing in the mud."

2 Pet. 2:17-22

Regarding the Second Coming

REASON FOR LETTER.   Dear friends, this is now my second letter to you. I have written both of them as reminders to stimulate you to wholesome thinking. I want you to recall the words spoken in the past by the holy prophets and the command given by our Lord and Savior through your apostles.

2 Pet. 3:1,2

SECOND COMING CERTAIN.   First of all, you must understand that in the last days scoffers will come, scoffing and following their own evil desires. They will say, "Where is this 'coming' he promised? Ever since our fathers died, everything goes on as it has since the beginning of creation." But they deliberately forget that long ago by God's word the heavens existed and the earth was formed out of water and by water. By these waters also the world of that time was deluged and destroyed. By the same word the present heavens and earth are reserved for fire, being kept for the day of judgment and destruction of ungodly men.

2 Pet. 3:3-7

REASON FOR DELAY.   But do not forget this one thing, dear friends: With the Lord a day is like a thousand years, and a thousand years are like a day. The Lord is not slow in keeping his promise, as some understand slowness. He is patient with you, not wanting anyone to perish, but everyone to come to repentance.

2 Pet. 3:8,9

DESCRIPTION OF SECOND COMING.   But the day of the Lord will come like a thief. The heavens will disappear with a roar; the elements will be destroyed by fire, and the earth and everything in it will be laid bare.*y*

2 Pet. 3:10

HOPE SHOULD PROMPT GODLINESS.   Since everything will be destroyed in this way, what kind of people ought you to be? You ought to

2 Pet. 3:11-13

*w*Some manuscripts *in their love feasts*   *x*Prov. 26:11   *y*Some manuscripts *be burned up* live holy and godly lives as you look forward to the day of God and speed its coming.[z] That day will bring about the destruction of the heavens by fire, and the elements will melt in the heat. But in keeping with his promise we are looking forward to a new heaven and a new earth, the home of righteousness.

2 Pet. 3:14-16

AGREEMENT WITH PAUL.   So then, dear friends, since you are looking forward to this, make every effort to be found spotless, blameless and at peace with him. Bear in mind that our Lord's patience means salvation, just as our dear brother Paul also wrote you with the wisdom that God gave him. He writes the same way in all his letters, speaking in them of these matters. His letters contain some things that are hard to understand, which ignorant and unstable people distort, as they do the other Scriptures, to their own destruction.

2 Pet. 3:17,18

FINAL WARNING.   Therefore, dear friends, since you already know this, be on your guard so that you may not be carried away by the error of lawless men and fall from your secure position. But grow in the grace and knowledge of our Lord and Savior Jesus Christ. To him be glory both now and forever! Amen.

Letter to the Hebrews

*T*he writing traditionally referred to as the letter to the Hebrews takes that designation from the fact that it is undoubtedly directed toward Christians having a Jewish background. However, the exact location of those particular Jewish Christians is nowhere indicated. Although many have attributed the writing to Paul, there is reason to believe that it may have been written between A.D. 65 and A.D. 70, sometime after Paul's death but prior to the destruction of the temple, when Jerusalem was sacked. One indication that the writing may have occurred after Paul's death is a reference to the release of Timothy. Neither in the historical record nor in any of Paul's letters is there any indication that Timothy was ever imprisoned. It is quite possible that, if Timothy had traveled to Rome to be with Paul, as Paul had urged him to do, Timothy himself might have been imprisoned at that time or shortly thereafter.

With Paul's authorship left in doubt, it is not clear who the writer might have been. Some believe him to be Luke, while others believe the writer may have been Paul's colleague Barnabas, or perhaps Apollos. Whoever it was, the letter reveals that the author is personally acquainted with those to whom he is writing and is familiar with the persecution which they are enduring.

Obviously having that suffering in mind, and with an awareness that many of the Jewish Christians are being urged to return to Judaism, the writer sets forth a tremendous defense of the Christian faith, drawing forcefully from a Jewish context in urging continued faith in Jesus as the Christ. Moving logically and systematically from one argument to another, the writer shows the superiority of Christ over all that is held to be important to the Jewish

[z]Or as you wait eagerly for the day of God to come

religion—prophets, angels, Moses, Joshua, the Levitical priesthood, the covenant, and the sacrifices. Midway through his letter the writer makes a particularly profound argument based upon the character of a high priest named Melchizedek, to whom Abraham had given an offering. Anticipating that some of his readers might miss the point of his argument concerning Christ's superiority, the writer pauses parenthetically to tell his readers that they need to be more mature in their spiritual understanding. Finally, the writer lists a group of faithful people of God as examples of steadfastness and endurance. He exhorts his readers to imitate the faithful lives of these men and women.

As the writing begins, Christ's majesty is declared with beauty and power.

The Majesty of Christ

GOD SPEAKS THROUGH CHRIST.   In the past God spoke to our fore-fathers through the prophets at many times and in various ways, but in these last days he has spoken to us by his Son, whom he appointed heir of all things, and through whom he made the universe. The Son is the radiance of God's glory and the exact representation of his being, sustaining all things by his powerful word. After he had provided purification for sins, he sat down at the right hand of the Majesty in heaven.

Heb. 1:1-3

CHRIST GREATER THAN ANGELS.   So he became as much superior to the angels as the name he has inherited is superior to theirs.
    For to which of the angels did God ever say,

Heb.
1:4-14

> "You are my Son;
>   today I have become your Father*a*"*b*?

Or again,

> "I will be his Father,
>   and he will be my Son"*c*?

And again, when God brings his firstborn into the world, he says,

> "Let all God's angels worship him."*d*

In speaking of the angels he says,

> "He makes his angels winds,
>   his servants flames of fire."*e*

But about the Son he says,

> "Your throne, O God, will last for ever and ever,
>   and righteousness will be the scepter of your kingdom.
> You have loved righteousness and hated wickedness;
>   therefore God, your God, has set you above your
>   companions
>   by anointing you with the oil of joy."*f*

He also says,

*a*Or *have begotten you*   *b*Psalm 2:7   *c*2 Samuel 7:14; 1 Chron. 17:13   *d*Deut. 32:43
(see Dead Sea Scrolls and Septuagint)   *e*Psalm 104:4   *f*Psalm 45:6,7

"In the beginning, O Lord, you laid the foundations of the
    earth,
and the heavens are the work of your hands.
They will perish, but you remain;
    they will all wear out like a garment.
You will roll them up like a robe;
    like a garment they will be changed.
But you remain the same,
    and your years will never end."[g]

To which of the angels did God ever say,

"Sit at my right hand
until I make your enemies
    a footstool for your feet"[h]?

Are not all angels ministering spirits sent to serve those who will inherit
salvation?

Heb. 2:1-4   WARNING AGAINST REJECTION.   We must pay more careful attention, therefore, to what we have heard, so that we do not drift away. For
if the message spoken by angels was binding, and every violation and
disobedience received its just punishment, how shall we escape if we
ignore such a great salvation? This salvation, which was first announced
by the Lord, was confirmed to us by those who heard him. God also
testified to it by signs, wonders and various miracles, and gifts of the
Holy Spirit distributed according to his will.

Heb.   ALL THINGS SUBJECT TO CHRIST.   It is not to angels that he has
2:5-8a   subjected the world to come, about which we are speaking. But there is a
place where someone has testified:

"What is man that you are mindful of him,
    the son of man that you care for him?
You made him a little[i] lower than the angels;
    you crowned him with glory and honor
    and put everything under his feet."[j]

In putting everything under him, God left nothing that is not subject to
him.

Heb.   CHRIST'S DEATH SHOWS GRACE.   Yet at present we do not see every-
2:8b-13   thing subject to him. But we see Jesus, who was made a little lower than
the angels, now crowned with glory and honor because he suffered death,
so that by the grace of God he might taste death for everyone.

In bringing many sons to glory, it was fitting that God, for whom and
through whom everything exists, should make the author of their salvation perfect through suffering. Both the one who makes men holy and
those who are made holy are of the same family. So Jesus is not ashamed
to call them brothers. He says,

"I will declare your name to my brothers;
    in the presence of the congregation I will sing your
        praises."[k]

And again,

"I will put my trust in him." [l]

[g]Psalm 102:25-27   [h]Psalm 110:1   [i]Or *him for a little while*; also in verse 9   [j]Psalm
8:4-6   [k]Psalm 22:22   [l]Isaiah 8:17

And again he says,

> "Here am I, and the children God has given me."[m]

CHRIST'S HUMANITY GIVES HOPE.   Since the children have flesh and blood, he too shared in their humanity so that by his death he might destroy him who holds the power of death—that is, the devil—and free those who all their lives were held in slavery by their fear of death. For surely it is not angels he helps, but Abraham's descendants. For this reason he had to be made like his brothers in every way, in order that he might become a merciful and faithful high priest in service to God, and that he might make atonement for [n] the sins of the people. Because he himself suffered when he was tempted, he is able to help those who are being tempted.

Heb.
2:14-18

Christ Superior to Moses

JESUS IS GREATER THAN MOSES.   Therefore, holy brothers, who share in the heavenly calling, fix your thoughts on Jesus, the apostle and high priest whom we confess. He was faithful to the one who appointed him, just as Moses was faithful in all God's house. Jesus has been found worthy of greater honor than Moses, just as the builder of a house has greater honor than the house itself. For every house is built by someone, but God is the builder of everything. Moses was faithful as a servant in all God's house, testifying to what would be said in the future. But Christ is faithful as a son over God's house. And we are his house, if we hold on to our courage and the hope of which we boast.

Heb. 3:1-6

SCRIPTURE CALLS FOR BELIEF.   So, as the Holy Spirit says:

> "Today, if you hear his voice,
>> do not harden your hearts
> as you did in the rebellion,
>> during the time of testing in the desert,
> where your fathers tested and tried me
>> and for forty years saw what I did.
> That is why I was angry with that generation,
>> and I said, 'Their hearts are always going astray,
>> and they have not known my ways.'
> So I declared on oath in my anger,
>> 'They shall never enter my rest.' " [o]

Heb.
3:7-11

SIN OF UNBELIEF.   See to it, brothers, that none of you has a sinful, unbelieving heart that turns away from the living God. But encourage one another daily, as long as it is called Today, so that none of you may be hardened by sin's deceitfulness. We have come to share in Christ if we hold firmly till the end the confidence we had at first. As has just been said:

> "Today, if you hear his voice,
>> do not harden your hearts
>> as you did in the rebellion." [p]

Heb.
3:12-15

ISRAELITES' UNBELIEF.   Who were they who heard and rebelled? Were they not all those Moses led out of Egypt? And with whom was he angry

Heb.
3:16-19

---

[m]Isaiah 8:18   [n]Or *and that he might turn aside God's wrath, taking away*   [o]Psalm 95:7-11
[p]Psalm 95:7,8

for forty years? Was it not with those who sinned, whose bodies fell in the desert? And to whom did God swear that they would never enter his rest if not to those who disobeyed *q*? So we see that they were not able to enter, because of their unbelief.

Christ Superior to Joshua

Heb. 4:1-5

PROMISED REST FOR FAITHFUL.   Therefore, since the promise of entering his rest still stands, let us be careful that none of you be found to have fallen short of it. For we also have had the gospel preached to us, just as they did; but the message they heard was of no value to them, because those who heard did not combine it with faith.*r* Now we who have believed enter that rest, just as God has said,

> "So I declared on oath in my anger,
>   'They shall never enter my rest.'"*s*

And yet his work has been finished since the creation of the world. For somewhere he has spoken about the seventh day in these words: "And on the seventh day God rested from all his work."*t* And again in the passage above he says, "They shall never enter my rest."

Heb. 4:6-10

CHRIST'S REST SUPERIOR.   It still remains that some will enter that rest, and those who formerly had the gospel preached to them did not go in, because of their disobedience. Therefore God again set a certain day, calling it Today, when a long time later he spoke through David, as was said before:

> "Today, if you hear his voice,
>   do not harden your hearts."*u*

For if Joshua had given them rest, God would not have spoken later about another day. There remains, then, a Sabbath-rest for the people of God; for anyone who enters God's rest also rests from his own work, just as God did from his.

Heb. 4:11-13

NEED FOR OBEDIENCE.   Let us, therefore, make every effort to enter that rest, so that no one will fall by following their example of disobedience.

For the word of God is living and active. Sharper than any double-edged sword, it penetrates even to dividing soul and spirit, joints and marrow; it judges the thoughts and attitudes of the heart. Nothing in all creation is hidden from God's sight. Everything is uncovered and laid bare before the eyes of him to whom we must give account.

Jesus as High Priest

Heb. 4:14-16

JESUS BRINGS ACCESS TO GOD.   Therefore, since we have a great high priest who has gone through the heavens,*v* Jesus the Son of God, let us hold firmly to the faith we profess. For we do not have a high priest who is unable to sympathize with our weaknesses, but we have one who has been tempted in every way, just as we are—yet was without sin. Let us then approach the throne of grace with confidence, so that we may receive mercy and find grace to help us in our time of need.

q Or disbelieved   r Many manuscripts because they did not share in the faith of those who obeyed   s Psalm 95:11   t Gen. 2:2   u Psalm 95:7,8   v Or gone into heaven

HIGH PRIESTS INTERCEDE.   Every high priest is selected from among   Heb. 5:1-3
men and is appointed to represent them in matters related to God, to offer
gifts and sacrifices for sins. He is able to deal gently with those who are
ignorant and are going astray, since he himself is subject to weakness.
This is why he has to offer sacrifices for his own sins, as well as for the
sins of the people.

JESUS A SPECIAL HIGH PRIEST.   No one takes this honor upon himself;   Heb.
he must be called by God, just as Aaron was. So Christ also did not take   5:4-10
upon himself the glory of becoming a high priest. But God said to him,

> "You are my Son;
> today I have become your Father."*w* " *x*

And he says in another place,

> "You are a priest forever,
> in the order of Melchizedek."*y*

During the days of Jesus' life on earth, he offered up prayers and
petitions with loud cries and tears to the one who could save him from
death, and he was heard because of his reverent submission. Although he
was a son, he learned obedience from what he suffered and, once made
perfect, he became the source of eternal salvation for all who obey him and
was designated by God to be high priest in the order of Melchizedek.

Parenthetical Thoughts Regarding Readers

EXPLANATION DIFFICULT.   We have much to say about this, but it is   Heb.
hard to explain because you are slow to learn. In fact, though by this time   5:11-14
you ought to be teachers, you need someone to teach you the elementary
truths of God's word all over again. You need milk, not solid food! Anyone
who lives on milk, being still an infant, is not acquainted with the teaching about righteousness. But solid food is for the mature, who by constant
use have trained themselves to distinguish good from evil.

NEED TO MATURE.   Therefore let us leave the elementary teachings   Heb. 6:1-3
about Christ and go on to maturity, not laying again the foundation of
repentance from acts that lead to death, *z* and of faith in God, instruction
about baptisms, the laying on of hands, the resurrection of the dead, and
eternal judgment. And God permitting, we will do so.

WARNING AGAINST FALLING AWAY.   It is impossible for those who   Heb. 6:4-8
have once been enlightened, who have tasted the heavenly gift, who have
shared in the Holy Spirit, who have tasted the goodness of the word of
God and the powers of the coming age, if they fall away, to be brought
back to repentance, because *a* to their loss they are crucifying the Son of
God all over again and subjecting him to public disgrace.

Land that drinks in the rain often falling on it and that produces a crop
useful to those for whom it is farmed receives the blessing of God. But
land that produces thorns and thistles is worthless and is in danger of
being cursed. In the end it will be burned.

CONFIDENCE IN CONTINUED FAITH.   Even though we speak like   Heb.
this, dear friends, we are confident of better things in your case—things   6:9-12
that accompany salvation. God is not unjust; he will not forget your work

---

*w*Or *have begotten you*   *x*Psalm 2:7   *y*Psalm 110:4   *z*Or *from useless rituals*   *a*Or
repentance while

and the love you have shown him as you have helped his people and continue to help them. We want each of you to show this same diligence to the very end, in order to make your hope sure. We do not want you to become lazy, but to imitate those who through faith and patience inherit what has been promised.

Christ Superior to Priesthood

Heb.
6:13-20

CHRIST'S SACRIFICE.   When God made his promise to Abraham, since there was no one greater for him to swear by, he swore by himself, saying, "I will surely bless you and give you many descendants."[b] And so after waiting patiently, Abraham received what was promised.

Men swear by someone greater than themselves, and the oath confirms what is said and puts an end to all argument. Because God wanted to make the unchanging nature of his purpose very clear to the heirs of what was promised, he confirmed it with an oath. God did this so that, by two unchangeable things in which it is impossible for God to lie, we who have fled to take hold of the hope offered to us may be greatly encouraged. We have this hope as an anchor for the soul, firm and secure. It enters the inner sanctuary behind the curtain, where Jesus, who went before us, has entered on our behalf. He has become a high priest forever, in the order of Melchizedek.

Heb. 7:1-3

PRIEST LIKE MELCHIZEDEK.   This Melchizedek was king of Salem and priest of God Most High. He met Abraham returning from the defeat of the kings and blessed him, and Abraham gave him a tenth of everything. First, his name means "king of righteousness"; then also, "king of Salem" means "king of peace." Without father or mother, without genealogy, without beginning of days or end of life, like the Son of God he remains a priest forever.

Heb.
7:4-10

MELCHIZEDEK'S SUPERIORITY.   Just think how great he was: Even the patriarch Abraham gave him a tenth of the plunder! Now the law requires the descendants of Levi who become priests to collect a tenth from the people—that is, their brothers—even though their brothers are descended from Abraham. This man, however, did not trace his descent from Levi, yet he collected a tenth from Abraham and blessed him who had the promises. And without doubt the lesser person is blessed by the greater. In the one case, the tenth is collected by men who die; but in the other case, by him who is declared to be living. One might even say that Levi, who collects the tenth, paid the tenth through Abraham, because when Melchizedek met Abraham, Levi was still in the body of his ancestor.

Heb.
7:11-19

CHRIST'S PRIESTHOOD.   If perfection could have been attained through the Levitical priesthood (for on the basis of it the law was given to the people), why was there still need for another priest to come—one in the order of Melchizedek, not in the order of Aaron? For when there is a change of the priesthood, there must also be a change of the law. He of whom these things are said belonged to a different tribe, and no one from that tribe has ever served at the altar. For it is clear that our Lord descended from Judah, and in regard to that tribe Moses said nothing about priests. And what we have said is even more clear if another priest like

[b]Gen. 22:17

Melchizedek appears, one who has become a priest not on the basis of a regulation as to his ancestry but on the basis of the power of an indestructible life. For it is declared:

"You are a priest forever,
    in the order of Melchizedek."[c]

The former regulation is set aside because it was weak and useless (for the law made nothing perfect), and a better hope is introduced, by which we draw near to God.

GUARANTEE OF COVENANT.   And it was not without an oath! Others became priests without any oath, but he became a priest with an oath when God said to him:

Heb.
7:20-22

"The Lord has sworn
    and will not change his mind:
'You are a priest forever.' " [c]

Because of this oath, Jesus has become the guarantee of a better covenant.

CHRIST A PERMANENT PRIEST.   Now there have been many of those priests, since death prevented them from continuing in office; but because Jesus lives forever, he has a permanent priesthood. Therefore he is able to save completely[d] those who come to God through him, because he always lives to intercede for them.

Heb.
7:23-25

CHRIST A PERFECT PRIEST.   Such a high priest meets our need—one who is holy, blameless, pure, set apart from sinners, exalted above the heavens. Unlike the other high priests, he does not need to offer sacrifices day after day, first for his own sins, and then for the sins of the people. He sacrificed for their sins once for all when he offered himself. For the law appoints as high priests men who are weak; but the oath, which came after the law, appointed the Son, who has been made perfect forever.

Heb.
7:26-28

Superiority of Christ's Covenant and Sacrifice

TABERNACLE A PATTERN.   The point of what we are saying is this: We do have such a high priest, who sat down at the right hand of the throne of the Majesty in heaven, and who serves in the sanctuary, the true tabernacle set up by the Lord, not by man.

Heb. 8:1-5

Every high priest is appointed to offer both gifts and sacrifices, and so it was necessary for this one also to have something to offer. If he were on earth, he would not be a priest, for there are already men who offer the gifts prescribed by the law. They serve at a sanctuary that is a copy and shadow of what is in heaven. This is why Moses was warned when he was about to build the tabernacle: "See to it that you make everything according to the pattern shown you on the mountain." [e]

CHRIST'S COVENANT GREATER.   But the ministry Jesus has received is as superior to theirs as the covenant of which he is mediator is superior to the old one, and it is founded on better promises.

Heb. 8:6,7

For if there had been nothing wrong with that first covenant, no place would have been sought for another.

[c]Psalm 110:4   [d]Or forever   [e]Exodus 25:40

Heb.
8:8-13

COVENANT NEEDED REPLACING.   But God found fault with the people and said^f:

> "The time is coming, declares the Lord,
>   when I will make a new covenant
> with the house of Israel
>   and with the house of Judah.
> It will not be like the covenant
>   I made with their forefathers
> when I took them by the hand
>   to lead them out of Egypt,
> because they did not remain faithful to my covenant,
>   and I turned away from them,
>   declares the Lord.
> This is the covenant I will make with the house of Israel
>   after that time, declares the Lord.
> I will put my laws in their minds
>   and write them on their hearts.
> I will be their God,
>   and they will be my people.
> No longer will a man teach his neighbor,
>   or a man his brother, saying, 'Know the Lord,'
> because they will all know me,
>   from the least of them to the greatest.
> For I will forgive their wickedness
>   and will remember their sins no more."^{g}

By calling this covenant "new," he has made the first one obsolete; and what is obsolete and aging will soon disappear.

Heb. 9:1-5

OLD COVENANT'S TABERNACLE.   Now the first covenant had regulations for worship and also an earthly sanctuary. A tabernacle was set up. In its first room were the lampstand, the table and the consecrated bread; this was called the Holy Place. Behind the second curtain was a room called the Most Holy Place, which had the golden altar of incense and the gold-covered ark of the covenant. This ark contained the gold jar of manna, Aaron's staff that had budded, and the stone tablets of the covenant. Above the ark were the cherubim of the Glory, overshadowing the atonement cover.^{h} But we cannot discuss these things in detail now.

Heb.
9:6-10

SACRIFICES ONLY TEMPORARY.   When everything had been arranged like this, the priests entered regularly into the outer room to carry on their ministry. But only the high priest entered the inner room, and that only once a year, and never without blood, which he offered for himself and for the sins the people had committed in ignorance. The Holy Spirit was showing by this that the way into the Most Holy Place had not yet been disclosed as long as the first tabernacle was still standing. This is an illustration for the present time, indicating that the gifts and sacrifices being offered were not able to clear the conscience of the worshiper. They are only a matter of food and drink and various ceremonial washings— external regulations applying until the time of the new order.

^{f}Some manuscripts may be translated *fault and said to the people.* ^{g}Jer. 31:31-34
^{h}Traditionally *the mercy seat*

CHRIST IS PERFECT SACRIFICE.　When Christ came as high priest of the good things that are already here,[i] he went through the greater and more perfect tabernacle that is not man-made, that is to say, not a part of this creation. He did not enter by means of the blood of goats and calves; but he entered the Most Holy Place once for all by his own blood, having obtained eternal redemption. The blood of goats and bulls and the ashes of a heifer sprinkled on those who are ceremonially unclean sanctify them so that they are outwardly clean. How much more, then, will the blood of Christ, who through the eternal Spirit offered himself unblemished to God, cleanse our consciences from acts that lead to death,[j] so that we may serve the living God!

Heb. 9:11-14

DEATH VALIDATES COVENANT.　For this reason Christ is the mediator of a new covenant, that those who are called may receive the promised eternal inheritance—now that he has died as a ransom to set them free from the sins committed under the first covenant.

In the case of a will,[k] it is necessary to prove the death of the one who made it, because a will is in force only when somebody has died; it never takes effect while the one who made it is living. This is why even the first covenant was not put into effect without blood. When Moses had proclaimed every commandment of the law to all the people, he took the blood of calves, together with water, scarlet wool and branches of hyssop, and sprinkled the scroll and all the people. He said, "This is the blood of the covenant, which God has commanded you to keep."[l] In the same way, he sprinkled with the blood both the tabernacle and everything used in its ceremonies. In fact, the law requires that nearly everything be cleansed with blood, and without the shedding of blood there is no forgiveness.

Heb. 9:15-22

SANCTUARY ENTERED ONCE.　It was necessary, then, for the copies of the heavenly things to be purified with these sacrifices, but the heavenly things themselves with better sacrifices than these. For Christ did not enter a man-made sanctuary that was only a copy of the true one; he entered heaven itself, now to appear for us in God's presence. Nor did he enter heaven to offer himself again and again, the way the high priest enters the Most Holy Place every year with blood that is not his own. Then Christ would have had to suffer many times since the creation of the world. But now he has appeared once for all at the end of the ages to do away with sin by the sacrifice of himself. Just as man is destined to die once, and after that to face judgment, so Christ was sacrificed once to take away the sins of many people; and he will appear a second time, not to bear sin, but to bring salvation to those who are waiting for him.

Heb. 9:23-28

SACRIFICES WERE INEFFECTUAL.　The law is only a shadow of the good things that are coming—not the realities themselves. For this reason it can never, by the same sacrifices repeated endlessly year after year, make perfect those who draw near to worship. If it could, would they not have stopped being offered? For the worshipers would have been cleansed once for all, and would no longer have felt guilty for their sins. But those sacrifices are an annual reminder of sins, because it is impossible for the blood of bulls and goats to take away sins.

Heb. 10:1-4

---

[i]Some early manuscripts *are to come*　　[j]Or *from useless rituals*　　[k]Same Greek word as *covenant*　　[l]Exodus 24:8

Heb. 10:5-10	CHRIST REPLACED SACRIFICES. Therefore, when Christ came into the world, he said:

> "Sacrifice and offering you did not desire,
>   but a body you prepared for me;
> with burnt offerings and sin offerings
>   you were not pleased.
> Then I said, 'Here I am—it is written about me in the scroll—
>   I have come to do your will, O God.' " *m*

First he said, "Sacrifices and offerings, burnt offerings and sin offerings you did not desire, nor were you pleased with them" (although the law required them to be made). Then he said, "Here I am, I have come to do your will." He sets aside the first to establish the second. And by that will, we have been made holy through the sacrifice of the body of Jesus Christ once for all.

**Heb.
10:11-14**

CHRIST BOTH PRIEST AND SACRIFICE. Day after day every priest stands and performs his religious duties; again and again he offers the same sacrifices, which can never take away sins. But when this priest had offered for all time one sacrifice for sins, he sat down at the right hand of God. Since that time he waits for his enemies to be made his footstool, because by one sacrifice he has made perfect forever those who are being made holy.

**Heb.
10:15-18**

GREAT SACRIFICE FORESEEN. The Holy Spirit also testifies to us about this. First he says:

> "This is the covenant I will make with them
>   after that time, says the Lord.
> I will put my laws in their hearts,
>   and I will write them on their minds." *n*

Then he adds:

> "Their sins and lawless acts
>   I will remember no more." *o*

And where these have been forgiven, there is no longer any sacrifice for sin.

Exhortation to Continue Faith in Christ

**Heb.
10:19-25**

PROPER RESPONSE TO ACCESS. Therefore, brothers, since we have confidence to enter the Most Holy Place by the blood of Jesus, by a new and living way opened for us through the curtain, that is, his body, and since we have a great priest over the house of God, let us draw near to God with a sincere heart in full assurance of faith, having our hearts sprinkled to cleanse us from a guilty conscience and having our bodies washed with pure water. Let us hold unswervingly to the hope we profess, for he who promised is faithful. And let us consider how we may spur one another on toward love and good deeds. Let us not give up meeting together, as some are in the habit of doing, but let us encourage one another—and all the more as you see the Day approaching.

**Heb.
10:26-31**

CONSEQUENCES OF REJECTION. If we deliberately keep on sinning after we have received the knowledge of the truth, no sacrifice for sins is

*m*Psalm 40:6-8 (see Septuagint)   *n*Jer. 31:33   *o*Jer. 31:34

left, but only a fearful expectation of judgment and of raging fire that will consume the enemies of God. Anyone who rejected the law of Moses died without mercy on the testimony of two or three witnesses. How much more severely do you think a man deserves to be punished who has trampled the Son of God under foot, who has treated as an unholy thing the blood of the covenant that sanctified him, and who has insulted the Spirit of grace? For we know him who said, "It is mine to avenge; I will repay,"*p* and again, "The Lord will judge his people."*q* It is a dreadful thing to fall into the hands of the living God.

STRENGTH IN PERSECUTION.   Remember those earlier days after you had received the light, when you stood your ground in a great contest in the face of suffering. Sometimes you were publicly exposed to insult and persecution; at other times you stood side by side with those who were so treated. You sympathized with those in prison and joyfully accepted the confiscation of your property, because you knew that you yourselves had better and lasting possessions.

Heb. 10:32-34

NEED FOR STRENGTH IN FAITH.   So do not throw away your confidence; it will be richly rewarded. You need to persevere so that when you have done the will of God, you will receive what he has promised. For in just a very little while,

Heb. 10:35-39

> "He who is coming will come and will not delay.
>   But my righteous one*r* will live by faith.
>   And if he shrinks back,
>   I will not be pleased with him."*s*

But we are not of those who shrink back and are destroyed, but of those who believe and are saved.

Examples of Great Faith

ASSURANCE AND HOPE.   Now faith is being sure of what we hope for and certain of what we do not see. This is what the ancients were commended for.

By faith we understand that the universe was formed at God's command, so that what is seen was not made out of what was visible.

Heb. 11:1-3

FAITH OF THE PATRIARCHS.   By faith Abel offered God a better sacrifice than Cain did. By faith he was commended as a righteous man, when God spoke well of his offerings. And by faith he still speaks, even though he is dead.

By faith Enoch was taken from this life, so that he did not experience death; he could not be found, because God had taken him away. For before he was taken, he was commended as one who pleased God. And without faith it is impossible to please God, because anyone who comes to him must believe that he exists and that he rewards those who earnestly seek him.

By faith Noah, when warned about things not yet seen, in holy fear built an ark to save his family. By his faith he condemned the world and became heir of the righteousness that comes by faith.

Heb. 11:4-7

*p*Deut. 32:35   *q*Deut. 32:36; Psalm 135:14   *r*One early manuscript *But the righteous*
*s*Hab. 2:3,4

Heb. 11:8-12	**FAITH OF ABRAHAM.** By faith Abraham, when called to go to a place he would later receive as his inheritance, obeyed and went, even though he did not know where he was going. By faith he made his home in the promised land like a stranger in a foreign country; he lived in tents, as did Isaac and Jacob, who were heirs with him of the same promise. For he was looking forward to the city with foundations, whose architect and builder is God. By faith Abraham, even though he was past age—and Sarah herself was barren—was enabled to become a father because he*t* considered him faithful who had made the promise. And so from this one man, and he as good as dead, came descendants as numerous as the stars in the sky and as countless as the sand on the seashore.
Heb. 11:13-16	**FAITH IN UNSEEN COUNTRY.** All these people were still living by faith when they died. They did not receive the things promised; they only saw them and welcomed them from a distance. And they admitted that they were aliens and strangers on earth. People who say such things show that they are looking for a country of their own. If they had been thinking of the country they had left, they would have had opportunity to return. Instead, they were longing for a better country—a heavenly one. Therefore God is not ashamed to be called their God, for he has prepared a city for them.
Heb. 11:17-19	**ABRAHAM'S FAITH.** By faith Abraham, when God tested him, offered Isaac as a sacrifice. He who had received the promises was about to sacrifice his one and only son, even though God had said to him, "It is through Isaac that your offspring*u* will be reckoned."*v* Abraham reasoned that God could raise the dead, and figuratively speaking, he did receive Isaac back from death.

Heb.
11:20-22
	ISAAC, JACOB, AND JOSEPH. By faith Isaac blessed Jacob and Esau in regard to their future.
	      By faith Jacob, when he was dying, blessed each of Joseph's sons, and worshiped as he leaned on the top of his staff.
	      By faith Joseph, when his end was near, spoke about the exodus of the Israelites from Egypt and gave instructions about his bones.

Heb. 11:23-28	**FAITH OF MOSES.** By faith Moses' parents hid him for three months after he was born, because they saw he was no ordinary child, and they were not afraid of the king's edict. By faith Moses, when he had grown up, refused to be known as the son of Pharaoh's daughter. He chose to be mistreated along with the people of God rather than to enjoy the pleasures of sin for a short time. He regarded disgrace for the sake of Christ as of greater value than the treasures of Egypt, because he was looking ahead to his reward. By faith he left Egypt, not fearing the king's anger; he persevered because he saw him who is invisible. By faith he kept the Passover and the sprinkling of blood, so that the destroyer of the firstborn would not touch the firstborn of Israel.

*t*Or *By faith even Sarah, who was past age, was enabled to bear children because she*   *u*Greek
seed   *v*Gen. 21:12

FAITH OF ISRAELITES.   By faith the people passed through the Red Sea[w] as on dry land; but when the Egyptians tried to do so, they were drowned.

Heb. 11:29-31

By faith the walls of Jericho fell, after the people had marched around them for seven days.

By faith the prostitute Rahab, because she welcomed the spies, was not killed with those who were disobedient.[x]

JUDGES, KINGS, AND PROPHETS.   And what more shall I say? I do not have time to tell about Gideon, Barak, Samson, Jephthah, David, Samuel and the prophets, who through faith conquered kingdoms, administered justice, and gained what was promised; who shut the mouths of lions, quenched the fury of the flames, and escaped the edge of the sword; whose weakness was turned to strength; and who became powerful in battle and routed foreign armies. Women received back their dead, raised to life again. Others were tortured and refused to be released, so that they might gain a better resurrection. Some faced jeers and flogging, while still others were chained and put in prison. They were stoned[y]; they were sawed in two; they were put to death by the sword. They went about in sheepskins and goatskins, destitute, persecuted and mistreated—the world was not worthy of them. They wandered in deserts and mountains, and in caves and holes in the ground.

Heb. 11:32-38

FAITH'S REWARD IN CHRIST.   These were all commended for their faith, yet none of them received what had been promised. God had planned something better for us so that only together with us would they be made perfect.

Heb. 11:39,40

A Call for Steadfast Faith

EXAMPLE DEMANDS PERSEVERANCE.   Therefore, since we are surrounded by such a great cloud of witnesses, let us throw off everything that hinders and the sin that so easily entangles, and let us run with perseverance the race marked out for us. Let us fix our eyes on Jesus, the author and perfecter of our faith, who for the joy set before him endured the cross, scorning its shame, and sat down at the right hand of the throne of God. Consider him who endured such opposition from sinful men, so that you will not grow weary and lose heart.

Heb. 12:1-3

STRUGGLES ARE DISCIPLINE.   In your struggle against sin, you have not yet resisted to the point of shedding your blood. And you have forgotten that word of encouragement that addresses you as sons:

Heb. 12:4-6

> "My son, do not make light of the Lord's discipline,
>   and do not lose heart when he rebukes you,
>   because the Lord disciplines those he loves,
>   and he punishes everyone he accepts as a son."[z]

DISCIPLINE SHOWS SONSHIP.   Endure hardship as discipline; God is treating you as sons. For what son is not disciplined by his father? If you are not disciplined (and everyone undergoes discipline), then you are illegitimate children and not true sons. Moreover, we have all had human fathers who disciplined us and we respected them for it. How much more

Heb. 12:7-11

[w]That is, Sea of Reeds   [x]Or *unbelieving*   [y]Some early manuscripts *stoned; they were put to the test;*   [z]Prov. 3:11,12

should we submit to the Father of our spirits and live! Our fathers disciplined us for a little while as they thought best; but God disciplines us for our good, that we may share in his holiness. No discipline seems pleasant at the time, but painful. Later on, however, it produces a harvest of righteousness and peace for those who have been trained by it.

Heb.
12:12-17

FAITH REQUIRES HOLY LIVES.   Therefore, strengthen your feeble arms and weak knees. "Make level paths for your feet," [a] so that the lame may not be disabled, but rather healed.

Make every effort to live in peace with all men and to be holy; without holiness no one will see the Lord. See to it that no one misses the grace of God and that no bitter root grows up to cause trouble and defile many. See that no one is sexually immoral, or is godless like Esau, who for a single meal sold his inheritance rights as the oldest son. Afterward, as you know, when he wanted to inherit this blessing, he was rejected. He could bring about no change of mind, though he sought the blessing with tears.

Heb.
12:18-21

JUDGMENT UNDER LAW.   You have not come to a mountain that can be touched and that is burning with fire; to darkness, gloom and storm; to a trumpet blast or to such a voice speaking words that those who heard it begged that no further word be spoken to them, because they could not bear what was commanded: "If even an animal touches the mountain, it must be stoned." [b] The sight was so terrifying that Moses said, "I am trembling with fear." [c]

Heb.
12:22-24

GREATER COVENANT; GREATER JUDGMENT.   But you have come to Mount Zion, to the heavenly Jerusalem, the city of the living God. You have come to thousands upon thousands of angels in joyful assembly, to the church of the firstborn, whose names are written in heaven. You have come to God, the judge of all men, to the spirits of righteous men made perfect, to Jesus the mediator of a new covenant, and to the sprinkled blood that speaks a better word than the blood of Abel.

Heb.
12:25-29

GOD TO BE WORSHIPED WITH AWE.   See to it that you do not refuse him who speaks. If they did not escape when they refused him who warned them on earth, how much less will we, if we turn away from him who warns us from heaven? At that time his voice shook the earth, but now he has promised, "Once more I will shake not only the earth but also the heavens." [d] The words "once more" indicate the removing of what can be shaken—that is, created things—so that what cannot be shaken may remain.

Therefore, since we are receiving a kingdom that cannot be shaken, let us be thankful, and so worship God acceptably with reverence and awe, for our God is a consuming fire.

Various Exhortations

Heb.
13:1-3

LOVE EVEN STRANGERS.   Keep on loving each other as brothers. Do not forget to entertain strangers, for by so doing some people have entertained angels without knowing it. Remember those in prison as if you were their fellow prisoners, and those who are mistreated as if you yourselves were suffering.

[a]Prov. 4:26   [b]Exodus 19:12,13   [c]Deut. 9:19   [d]Haggai 2:6

MAINTAIN SEXUAL PURITY.   Marriage should be honored by all, and the marriage bed kept pure, for God will judge the adulterer and all the sexually immoral.

Heb. 13:4

DO NOT TRUST WEALTH.   Keep your lives free from the love of money and be content with what you have, because God has said,

Heb. 13:5,6

> "Never will I leave you;
>   never will I forsake you."*e*

So we say with confidence,

> "The Lord is my helper; I will not be afraid.
>   What can man do to me?"*f*

IMITATE LIVES OF LEADERS.   Remember your leaders, who spoke the word of God to you. Consider the outcome of their way of life and imitate their faith.

Heb. 13:7

AVOID DEMEANING TEACHINGS.   Jesus Christ is the same yesterday and today and forever.

Heb. 13:8-10

Do not be carried away by all kinds of strange teachings. It is good for our hearts to be strengthened by grace, not by ceremonial foods, which are of no value to those who eat them. We have an altar from which those who minister at the tabernacle have no right to eat.

LEAVE WORLD SYSTEM FOR CHRIST.   The high priest carries the blood of animals into the Most Holy Place as a sin offering, but the bodies are burned outside the camp. And so Jesus also suffered outside the city gate to make the people holy through his own blood. Let us, then, go to him outside the camp, bearing the disgrace he bore. For here we do not have an enduring city, but we are looking for the city that is to come.

Heb. 13:11-14

OFFER SACRIFICES OF PRAISE.   Through Jesus, therefore, let us continually offer to God a sacrifice of praise—the fruit of lips that confess his name. And do not forget to do good and to share with others, for with such sacrifices God is pleased.

Heb. 13:15,16

SUBMIT TO CHURCH LEADERS.   Obey your leaders and submit to their authority. They keep watch over you as men who must give an account. Obey them so that their work will be a joy, not a burden, for that would be of no advantage to you.

Heb. 13:17

Closing Thoughts

REQUEST FOR PRAYERS.   Pray for us. We are sure that we have a clear conscience and desire to live honorably in every way. I particularly urge you to pray so that I may be restored to you soon.

Heb. 13:18,19

PRAYER FOR RECIPIENTS.   May the God of peace, who through the blood of the eternal covenant brought back from the dead our Lord Jesus, that great Shepherd of the sheep, equip you with everything good for doing his will, and may he work in us what is pleasing to him, through Jesus Christ, to whom be glory for ever and ever. Amen.

Heb. 13:20,21

FINAL THOUGHTS.   Brothers, I urge you to bear with my word of exhortation, for I have written you only a short letter.

Heb. 13:22-25

I want you to know that our brother Timothy has been released. If he arrives soon, I will come with him to see you.

*e*Deut. 31:6   *f*Psalm 118:6,7

Greet all your leaders and all God's people. Those from Italy send you their greetings.

Grace be with you all.

First Letter by John

oward the end of the first century the church begins to face serious challenges both from without and from within. Persecution and suffering are the shared fate of Christians everywhere. Yet an even greater enemy has come from within—the enemy of false teaching. The Gnostic philosophy, popular at this time, teaches that matter is inherently evil, and that human flesh is therefore evil. This philosophy has led not only to flagrant immorality in exercise of fleshly desires but also to the conclusion that God himself could not possibly become flesh. That, of course, is clearly a threat to the Christian belief that Jesus appeared in human flesh. Who might better be fitted to warn of this error than one who had personally known Jesus and who had witnessed the evidences of his deity? Who might have occupied such a position of respect and authority that Christians everywhere would accept his word as truth? Perhaps none other than the now-aging apostle John. Although he does not directly name himself, John is undoubtedly the author of three brief letters which appear to have been written about A.D. 90-95, perhaps from Ephesus.

The first of John's letters is not addressed to any one church or individual in particular. It is probably intended for widespread circulation. As if he were their father, John writes to his "little children" about the need to continue walking in the light of God's righteousness. He warns his readers about the antichrists—those who teach that Jesus was not God in the flesh. Concerned with their daily walk, as well as their belief in Jesus' deity, John exhorts them to lead lives befitting children of God. He points out that true believers can be distinguished from unbelievers by their mutual love, godly lives, and obedience to God's commands. John concludes his letter by noting the assurance and security which God's children have in Jesus Christ.

1 Jn. 1:1-4   JOHN'S EYEWITNESS TESTIMONY.   That which was from the beginning, which we have heard, which we have seen with our eyes, which we have looked at and our hands have touched—this we proclaim concerning the Word of life. The life appeared; we have seen it and testify to it, and we proclaim to you the eternal life, which was with the Father and has appeared to us. We proclaim to you what we have seen and heard, so that you also may have fellowship with us. And our fellowship is with the Father and with his Son, Jesus Christ. We write this to make our[g] joy complete.

Walking in Light of Righteousness

1 Jn. 1:5-7   BASIS FOR FELLOWSHIP.   This is the message we have heard from him and declare to you: God is light; in him there is no darkness at all. If we claim to have fellowship with him yet walk in the darkness, we lie and do

[g]Some manuscripts your

not live by the truth. But if we walk in the light, as he is in the light, we have fellowship with one another, and the blood of Jesus, his Son, purifies us from all[h] sin.

SINS MUST BE CONFESSED.   If we claim to be without sin, we deceive ourselves and the truth is not in us. If we confess our sins, he is faithful and just and will forgive us our sins and purify us from all unrighteousness. If we claim we have not sinned, we make him out to be a liar and his word has no place in our lives.

1 Jn. 1:8-10

CHRIST IS ADVOCATE.   My dear children, I write this to you so that you will not sin. But if anybody does sin, we have one who speaks to the Father in our defense—Jesus Christ, the Righteous One. He is the atoning sacrifice for our sins, and not only for ours but also for[i] the sins of the whole world.

1 Jn. 2:1,2

ONLY OBEDIENT KNOW GOD.   We know that we have come to know him if we obey his commands. The man who says, "I know him," but does not do what he commands is a liar, and the truth is not in him. But if anyone obeys his word, God's love[j] is truly made complete in him. This is how we know we are in him: Whoever claims to live in him must walk as Jesus did.

1 Jn. 2:3-6

LOVE IS TEST.   Dear friends, I am not writing you a new command but an old one, which you have had since the beginning. This old command is the message you have heard. Yet I am writing you a new command; its truth is seen in him and you, because the darkness is passing and the true light is already shining.

1 Jn. 2:7-11

Anyone who claims to be in the light but hates his brother is still in the darkness. Whoever loves his brother lives in the light, and there is nothing in him[k] to make him stumble. But whoever hates his brother is in the darkness and walks around in the darkness; he does not know where he is going, because the darkness has blinded him.

REASONS FOR WRITING.

1 Jn. 2:12-14

> I write to you, dear children,
>> because your sins have been forgiven on account of his
>>> name.
> I write to you, fathers,
>> because you have known him who is from the beginning.
> I write to you, young men,
>> because you have overcome the evil one.
> I write to you, dear children,
>> because you have known the Father.
> I write to you, fathers,
>> because you have known him who is from the beginning.
> I write to you, young men,
>> because you are strong,
>> and the word of God lives in you,
>> and you have overcome the evil one.

LOVE GOD, NOT THE WORLD.   Do not love the world or anything in the world. If anyone loves the world, the love of the Father is not in him.

1 Jn. 2:15-17

[h]Or *every*   [i]Or *He is the one who turns aside God's wrath, taking away our sins, and not only ours but also*   [j]Or *word, love for God*   [k]Or *it*

For everything in the world—the cravings of sinful man, the lust of his eyes and the boasting of what he has and does—comes not from the Father but from the world. The world and its desires pass away, but the man who does the will of God lives forever.

Warning About Antichrists

1 Jn.
2:18,19

BEWARE OF ANTICHRISTS.   Dear children, this is the last hour; and as you have heard that the antichrist is coming, even now many antichrists have come. This is how we know it is the last hour. They went out from us, but they did not really belong to us. For if they had belonged to us, they would have remained with us; but their going showed that none of them belonged to us.

1 Jn.
2:20-23

ANTICHRISTS DENY DEITY.   But you have an anointing from the Holy One, and all of you know the truth.[l] I do not write to you because you do not know the truth, but because you do know it and because no lie comes from the truth. Who is the liar? It is the man who denies that Jesus is the Christ. Such a man is the antichrist—he denies the Father and the Son. No one who denies the Son has the Father; whoever acknowledges the Son has the Father also.

1 Jn.
2:24-28

CONTINUE YOUR FAITH.   See that what you have heard from the beginning remains in you. If it does, you also will remain in the Son and in the Father. And this is what he promised us—even eternal life.

I am writing these things to you about those who are trying to lead you astray. As for you, the anointing you received from him remains in you, and you do not need anyone to teach you. But as his anointing teaches you about all things and as that anointing is real, not counterfeit—just as it has taught you, remain in him.

And now, dear children, continue in him, so that when he appears we may be confident and unashamed before him at his coming.

Living As Children of God

1 Jn.
2:29-3:3

BE RIGHTEOUS AS CHILDREN.   If you know that he is righteous, you know that everyone who does what is right has been born of him. How great is the love the Father has lavished on us, that we should be called children of God! And that is what we are! The reason the world does not know us is that it did not know him. Dear friends, now we are children of God, and what we will be has not yet been made known. But we know that when he appears,[m] we shall be like him, for we shall see him as he is. Everyone who has this hope in him purifies himself, just as he is pure.

1 Jn. 3:4-6

SINNING IS CONTRARY TO FAITH.   Everyone who sins breaks the law; in fact, sin is lawlessness. But you know that he appeared so that he might take away our sins. And in him is no sin. No one who lives in him keeps on sinning. No one who continues to sin has either seen him or known him.

1 Jn.
3:7-10

GOD'S CHILDREN LIVE RIGHTEOUSLY.   Dear children, do not let anyone lead you astray. He who does what is right is righteous, just as he is righteous. He who does what is sinful is of the devil, because the devil has been sinning from the beginning. The reason the Son of God

---

[l]Some manuscripts *and you know all things*   [m]Or *when it is made known*

appeared was to destroy the devil's work. No one who is born of God will continue to sin, because God's seed remains in him; he cannot go on sinning, because he has been born of God. This is how we know who the children of God are and who the children of the devil are: Anyone who does not do what is right is not a child of God; nor is anyone who does not love his brother.

GOD'S CHILDREN LOVE EACH OTHER. This is the message you heard from the beginning: We should love one another. Do not be like Cain, who belonged to the evil one and murdered his brother. And why did he murder him? Because his own actions were evil and his brother's were righteous. Do not be surprised, my brothers, if the world hates you. We know that we have passed from death to life, because we love our brothers. Anyone who does not love remains in death. Anyone who hates his brother is a murderer, and you know that no murderer has eternal life in him.

1 Jn. 3:11-15

LOVE EVIDENCED BY ACTIONS. This is how we know what love is: Jesus Christ laid down his life for us. And we ought to lay down our lives for our brothers. If anyone has material possessions and sees his brother in need but has no pity on him, how can the love of God be in him? Dear children, let us not love with words or tongue but with actions and in truth.

1 Jn. 3:16-18

OBEYING BRINGS CONFIDENCE. This then is how we know that we belong to the truth, and how we set our hearts at rest in his presence whenever our hearts condemn us. For God is greater than our hearts, and he knows everything.

Dear friends, if our hearts do not condemn us, we have confidence before God and receive from him anything we ask, because we obey his commands and do what pleases him.

1 Jn. 3:19-22

MUST BELIEVE AND LOVE. And this is his command: to believe in the name of his Son, Jesus Christ, and to love one another as he commanded us. Those who obey his commands live in him, and he in them. And this is how we know that he lives in us: We know it by the Spirit he gave us.

1 Jn. 3:23,24

Distinguishing Unbelievers from Believers

ANTICHRISTS DENY INCARNATION. Dear friends, do not believe every spirit, but test the spirits to see whether they are from God, because many false prophets have gone out into the world. This is how you can recognize the Spirit of God: Every spirit that acknowledges that Jesus Christ has come in the flesh is from God, but every spirit that does not acknowledge Jesus is not from God. This is the spirit of the antichrist, which you have heard is coming and even now is already in the world.

1 Jn. 4:1-3

ANTICHRISTS' WORLDLY DOCTRINES. You, dear children, are from God and have overcome them, because the one who is in you is greater than the one who is in the world. They are from the world and therefore speak from the viewpoint of the world, and the world listens to them. We are from God, and whoever knows God listens to us; but whoever is not from God does not listen to us. This is how we recognize the Spirit[n] of truth and the spirit of falsehood.

1 Jn. 4:4-6

[n]Or spirit

1 Jn. 4:7-12	**BELIEVERS REFLECT GOD'S LOVE.** Dear friends, let us love one another, for love comes from God. Everyone who loves has been born of God and knows God. Whoever does not love does not know God, because God is love. This is how God showed his love among us: He sent his one and only Son° into the world that we might live through him. This is love: not that we loved God, but that he loved us and sent his Son as an atoning sacrifice for^p our sins. Dear friends, since God so loved us, we also ought to love one another. No one has ever seen God; but if we love one another, God lives in us and his love is made complete in us.
1 Jn. 4:13-15	**BELIEVERS HAVE GOD'S SPIRIT.** We know that we live in him and he in us, because he has given us of his Spirit. And we have seen and testify that the Father has sent his Son to be the Savior of the world. If anyone acknowledges that Jesus is the Son of God, God lives in him and he in God.

1 Jn.
4:16-19
	SPIRIT OF LOVE. And so we know and rely on the love God has for us.
	    God is love. Whoever lives in love lives in God, and God in him. In this way, love is made complete among us so that we will have confidence on the day of judgment, because in this world we are like him. There is no fear in love. But perfect love drives out fear, because fear has to do with punishment. The one who fears is not made perfect in love.
	    We love because he first loved us.

1 Jn. 4:20-5:1	**LOVING GOD REQUIRES LOVING MAN.** If anyone says, "I love God," yet hates his brother, he is a liar. For anyone who does not love his brother, whom he has seen, cannot love God, whom he has not seen. And he has given us this command: Whoever loves God must also love his brother. Everyone who believes that Jesus is the Christ is born of God, and everyone who loves the father loves his child as well.
1 Jn. 5:2-5	**LOVING GOD REQUIRES OBEDIENCE.** This is how we know that we love the children of God: by loving God and carrying out his commands. This is love for God: to obey his commands. And his commands are not burdensome, for everyone born of God overcomes the world. This is the victory that has overcome the world, even our faith. Who is it that overcomes the world? Only he who believes that Jesus is the Son of God.
1 Jn. 5:6-9	**TESTIMONY TO JESUS.** This is the one who came by water and blood—Jesus Christ. He did not come by water only, but by water and blood. And it is the Spirit who testifies, because the Spirit is the truth. For there are three that testify: the^q Spirit, the water and the blood; and the three are in agreement. We accept man's testimony, but God's testimony is greater because it is the testimony of God, which he has given about his Son.
1 Jn. 5:10-12	**BELIEVERS' LIVES TESTIFY.** Anyone who believes in the Son of God has this testimony in his heart. Anyone who does not believe God has made him out to be a liar, because he has not believed the testimony God has given about his Son. And this is the testimony: God has given us eternal life, and this life is in his Son. He who has the Son has life; he who does not have the Son of God does not have life.

°Or *his only begotten Son*   ^pOr *as the one who would turn aside his wrath, taking away*
^qLate manuscripts of the Vulgate *testify in heaven: the Father, the Word and the Holy Spirit,
and these three are one.* ⁸*And there are three that testify on earth: the* (not found in any Greek
manuscript before the fourteenth century)

Assurances in Christ

ASSURANCE IN ETERNAL LIFE.   I write these things to you who believe in the name of the Son of God so that you may know that you have eternal life.

1 Jn. 5:13

ASSURANCE IN PROPER PRAYER.   This is the confidence we have in approaching God: that if we ask anything according to his will, he hears us. And if we know that he hears us—whatever we ask—we know that we have what we asked of him.

1 Jn.
5:14-17

　　If anyone sees his brother commit a sin that does not lead to death, he should pray and God will give him life. I refer to those whose sin does not lead to death. There is a sin that leads to death. I am not saying that he should pray about that. All wrongdoing is sin, and there is sin that does not lead to death.

SECURITY IN JESUS CHRIST.   We know that anyone born of God does not continue to sin; the one who was born of God keeps him safe, and the evil one cannot harm him. We know that we are children of God, and that the whole world is under the control of the evil one. We know also that the Son of God has come and has given us understanding, so that we may know him who is true. And we are in him who is true—even in his Son Jesus Christ. He is the true God and eternal life.

1 Jn.
5:18-20

NO SECURITY IN IDOLS.   Dear children, keep yourselves from idols.

1 Jn. 5:21

*Second Letter by John*_____

　　*J*ohn's second and third letters appear to have been written together, near the same time as the first. These, however, are more personal in nature. Calling himself simply "the elder," John addresses his second letter somewhat mysteriously to "the chosen lady and her children." Whether that means a particular woman and her family or refers symbolically to a given church is not wholly clear, but it is probably the former, since no other symbolic language appears in the letter. In content this letter is a brief summary of John's more general letter, together with a personal note at the end.

SALUTATION.   The elder,

2 Jn. 1-3

　　To the chosen lady and her children, whom I love in the truth—and not I only, but also all who know the truth—because of the truth, which lives in us and will be with us forever:

　　Grace, mercy and peace from God the Father and from Jesus Christ, the Father's Son, will be with us in truth and love.

CALL FOR LOVE AND OBEDIENCE.   It has given me great joy to find some of your children walking in the truth, just as the Father commanded us. And now, dear lady, I am not writing you a new command but one we have had from the beginning. I ask that we love one another. And this is love: that we walk in obedience to his commands. As you have heard from the beginning, his command is that you walk in love.

2 Jn. 4-6

2 Jn. 7-11   WARNING AGAINST ANTICHRISTS.   Many deceivers, who do not
acknowledge Jesus Christ as coming in the flesh, have gone out into the
world. Any such person is the deceiver and the antichrist. Watch out that
you do not lose what you have worked for, but that you may be rewarded fully. Anyone who runs ahead and does not continue in the teaching
of Christ does not have God; whoever continues in the teaching has both
the Father and the Son. If anyone comes to you and does not bring this
teaching, do not take him into your house or welcome him. Anyone who
welcomes him shares in his wicked work.

2 Jn. 12   HOPE FOR PERSONAL VISIT.   I have much to write to you, but I do not
want to use paper and ink. Instead, I hope to visit you and talk with you
face to face, so that our joy may be complete.

2 Jn. 13   GREETINGS.   The children of your chosen sister send their greetings.

Third Letter by John

*T*he third short letter of John is addressed to a Christian named
Gaius, apparently a leader in the church—perhaps the church to
which the second letter was addressed. In this letter John commends
Gaius for his hospitality and for having been supportive of itinerant
evangelists. He also notes his displeasure toward a man by the name of
Diotrephes, who had been antagonistic both to these traveling evangelists
and to John's own teaching. It may well be that Diotrephes has come to accept
some of the Gnostic teaching which John is trying to combat, or perhaps he
is attempting to prevent any threat to his personal influence in the local
congregation. In contrast to Diotrephes, a brother named Demetrius is highly
commended. Although brief in content, the letter is a good example of
Christian relationships and individual concern.

3 Jn. 1   SALUTATION.   The elder,

To my dear friend Gaius, whom I love in the truth.

3 Jn. 2-4   JOY IN GAIUS' FAITHFULNESS.   Dear friend, I pray that you may enjoy
good health and that all may go well with you, even as your soul is
getting along well. It gave me great joy to have some brothers come and
tell about your faithfulness to the truth and how you continue to walk in
the truth. I have no greater joy than to hear that my children are walking
in the truth.

3 Jn. 5-8   COMMENDATION OF GAIUS.   Dear friend, you are faithful in what you
are doing for the brothers, even though they are strangers to you. They
have told the church about your love. You will do well to send them on
their way in a manner worthy of God. It was for the sake of the Name that
they went out, receiving no help from the pagans. We ought therefore to
show hospitality to such men so that we may work together for the truth.

3 Jn. 9,10   REPROOF OF DIOTREPHES.   I wrote to the church, but Diotrephes, who
loves to be first, will have nothing to do with us. So if I come, I will call
attention to what he is doing, gossiping maliciously about us. Not satisfied
with that, he refuses to welcome the brothers. He also stops those who
want to do so and puts them out of the church.

EXHORTATION TO DO GOOD.   Dear friend, do not imitate what is evil   3 Jn. 11
but what is good. Anyone who does what is good is from God. Anyone
who does what is evil has not seen God.

COMMENDATION OF DEMETRIUS.   Demetrius is well spoken of by   3 Jn. 12
everyone—and even by the truth itself. We also speak well of him, and you
know that our testimony is true.

HOPE FOR PERSONAL VISIT.   I have much to write you, but I do not   3 Jn.
want to do so with pen and ink. I hope to see you soon, and we will talk   13,14a
face to face.

GREETINGS.   Peace to you. The friends here send their greetings. Greet   3 Jn. 14b
the friends there by name.

The Revelation to John

O ne of the most unique and intriguing writings of all Scripture comes
as a fitting conclusion to God's revelation to man. It is a writing
reminiscent of the recorded visions of Ezekiel and Daniel. Its true
Author by revelation is Jesus Christ, and the apostle John simply acts as
scribe. In his last years, perhaps around A.D. 95-96, the aging apostle is found
exiled on the Greek Island of Patmos during the reign of the Roman Emperor
Domitian. On a particular Lord's day, as John relates the experience, he
receives through an angel a revelation from the Spirit of God in which he is
directed to write what he sees and to send it to seven churches in Asia. Those
churches, as well as others at this time, are facing severe persecution and
suffering because of their faith in Christ. The circumstances therefore warrant
both admonition and encouragement.

What John sees and records is a prophecy, both strange and moving, in
which Christ as sovereign Lord engages in battle with the forces of evil and is
clearly the Victor. The account is couched in figurative language, supernatural
imagery, and verbal and numerical symbolism that is not easy to fully
comprehend. Yet it stirs an excitement about the future for all Christians and
gives hope that present sufferings will be lost in a victory so wonderful that
the mind of man can only begin to grasp it.

The Revelation is the consummation of God's scheme of redemption for
man, as presented systematically throughout the Bible. In the early Genesis
account, God was declared to be the omnipotent Creator of the universe,
worthy of praise for his majesty and power. The created universe was wholly
good until penetrated by the power of Satan, who acquainted man with the evil
of sin and its consequences. Because of man's sin, man came to need redemption and reconciliation with God. Through his chosen nation of Israel,
God provided for that redemption. The Old Testament records God's power of
judgment which was made known through Moses, the law, and the prophets.
Then, as recorded in the Gospel accounts, came the good news that man's
Redeemer had come to earth in fulfillment of the law and prophecy. Jesus the
Christ brought a new righteousness of faith, a faith having the power of
salvation. In dying on the cross and in being resurrected from the grave, Jesus
triumphed over Satan's power of death. Based upon that demonstration of his

lordship and power, the church was born and grew to swelling numbers and influence. When the church was met with opposition and persecution, the apostles and other inspired writers penned their various epistles to encourage their fellow Christians to persevere, in prospect of their final redemption in the life to come.

God's scheme of redemption thus becomes the theme of his revelation to John. The revelation unfolds now as the aging apostle begins to relate with unmatched excitement the glorious vision which he has been called to share.

Rev. 1:1-3   REVELATION FROM JESUS CHRIST.   The revelation of Jesus Christ, which God gave him to show his servants what must soon take place. He made it known by sending his angel to his servant John, who testifies to everything he saw—that is, the word of God and the testimony of Jesus Christ. Blessed is the one who reads the words of this prophecy, and blessed are those who hear it and take to heart what is written in it, because the time is near.

Rev. 1:4-5a   SALUTATION TO SEVEN CHURCHES.   John,

> To the seven churches in the province of Asia:

> Grace and peace to you from him who is, and who was, and who is to come, and from the seven spirits[r] before his throne, and from Jesus Christ, who is the faithful witness, the firstborn from the dead, and the ruler of the kings of the earth.

Rev. 1:5b-8   PRAISE TO ALMIGHTY GOD.   To him who loves us and has freed us from our sins by his blood, and has made us to be a kingdom and priests to serve his God and Father—to him be glory and power for ever and ever! Amen.

> Look, he is coming with the clouds,
>   and every eye will see him,
> even those who pierced him;
>   and all the peoples of the earth will mourn because of
>   him.

>   So shall it be! Amen.

"I am the Alpha and the Omega," says the Lord God, "who is, and who was, and who is to come, the Almighty."

Origin and Purpose of Revelation

Rev. 1:9-11   DESCRIPTION OF VOICE.   I, John, your brother and companion in the suffering and kingdom and patient endurance that are ours in Jesus, was on the island of Patmos because of the word of God and the testimony of Jesus. On the Lord's Day I was in the Spirit, and I heard behind me a loud voice like a trumpet, which said: "Write on a scroll what you see and send it to the seven churches: to Ephesus, Smyrna, Pergamum, Thyatira, Sardis, Philadelphia and Laodicea."

Rev. 1:12-16   VISION OF ONE LIKE SON OF MAN.   I turned around to see the voice that was speaking to me. And when I turned I saw seven golden lampstands, and among the lampstands was someone "like a son of man,"[s]

---

[r] Or *the sevenfold Spirit*   [s] Daniel 7:13

dressed in a robe reaching down to his feet and with a golden sash around his chest. His head and hair were white like wool, as white as snow, and his eyes were like blazing fire. His feet were like bronze glowing in a furnace, and his voice was like the sound of rushing waters. In his right hand he held seven stars, and out of his mouth came a sharp double-edged sword. His face was like the sun shining in all its brilliance.

IDENTITY OF VOICE AND VISION.   When I saw him, I fell at his feet as though dead. Then he placed his right hand on me and said: "Do not be afraid. I am the First and the Last. I am the Living One; I was dead, and behold I am alive for ever and ever! And I hold the keys of death and Hades.

Rev.
1:17,18

JOHN'S MANDATE TO WRITE.   "Write, therefore, what you have seen, what is now and what will take place later. The mystery of the seven stars that you saw in my right hand and of the seven golden lampstands is this: The seven stars are the angels[t] of the seven churches, and the seven lampstands are the seven churches.

Rev.
1:19,20

Letters to the Seven Churches

EPHESUS.   "To the angel[u] of the church in Ephesus write:

Rev. 2:1-7

These are the words of him who holds the seven stars in his right hand and walks among the seven golden lampstands: I know your deeds, your hard work and your perseverance. I know that you cannot tolerate wicked men, that you have tested those who claim to be apostles but are not, and have found them false. You have persevered and have endured hardships for my name, and have not grown weary.

Yet I hold this against you: You have forsaken your first love. Remember the height from which you have fallen! Repent and do the things you did at first. If you do not repent, I will come to you and remove your lampstand from its place. But you have this in your favor: You hate the practices of the Nicolaitans, which I also hate.

He who has an ear, let him hear what the Spirit says to the churches. To him who overcomes, I will give the right to eat from the tree of life, which is in the paradise of God.

SMYRNA.   "To the angel of the church in Smyrna write:

Rev. 2:8-11

These are the words of him who is the First and the Last, who died and came to life again. I know your afflictions and your poverty—yet you are rich! I know the slander of those who say they are Jews and are not, but are a synagogue of Satan. Do not be afraid of what you are about to suffer. I tell you, the devil will put some of you in prison to test you, and you will suffer persecution for ten days. Be faithful, even to the point of death, and I will give you the crown of life.

He who has an ear, let him hear what the Spirit says to the churches. He who overcomes will not be hurt at all by the second death.

PERGAMUM.   "To the angel of the church in Pergamum write:

Rev.
2:12-17

These are the words of him who has the sharp, double-edged sword. I know where you live—where Satan has his throne. Yet you remain true to my name. You did not renounce your faith in me, even in the days of

---

[t]Or *messengers*   [u]Or *messenger;* also in verses 8, 12 and 18

Antipas, my faithful witness, who was put to death in your city—where Satan lives.

Nevertheless, I have a few things against you: You have people there who hold to the teaching of Balaam, who taught Balak to entice the Israelites to sin by eating food sacrificed to idols and by committing sexual immorality. Likewise you also have those who hold to the teaching of the Nicolaitans. Repent therefore! Otherwise, I will soon come to you and will fight against them with the sword of my mouth.

He who has an ear, let him hear what the Spirit says to the churches. To him who overcomes, I will give some of the hidden manna. I will also give him a white stone with a new name written on it, known only to him who receives it.

Rev.
2:18-29

THYATIRA.   "To the angel of the church in Thyatira write:

These are the words of the Son of God, whose eyes are like blazing fire and whose feet are like burnished bronze. I know your deeds, your love and faith, your service and perseverance, and that you are now doing more than you did at first.

Nevertheless, I have this against you: You tolerate that woman Jezebel, who calls herself a prophetess. By her teaching she misleads my servants into sexual immorality and the eating of food sacrificed to idols. I have given her time to repent of her immorality, but she is unwilling. So I will cast her on a bed of suffering, and I will make those who commit adultery with her suffer intensely, unless they repent of her ways. I will strike her children dead. Then all the churches will know that I am he who searches hearts and minds, and I will repay each of you according to your deeds. Now I say to the rest of you in Thyatira, to you who do not hold to her teaching and have not learned Satan's so-called deep secrets (I will not impose any other burden on you): Only hold on to what you have until I come.

To him who overcomes and does my will to the end, I will give authority over the nations—

'He will rule them with an iron scepter;
   he will dash them to pieces like pottery'ᵛ—

just as I have received authority from my Father. I will also give him the morning star. He who has an ear, let him hear what the Spirit says to the churches.

Rev. 3:1-6

SARDIS.   "To the angelʷ of the church in Sardis write:

These are the words of him who holds the seven spiritsˣ of God and the seven stars. I know your deeds; you have a reputation of being alive, but you are dead. Wake up! Strengthen what remains and is about to die, for I have not found your deeds complete in the sight of my God. Remember, therefore, what you have received and heard; obey it, and repent. But if you do not wake up, I will come like a thief, and you will not know at what time I will come to you.

Yet you have a few people in Sardis who have not soiled their clothes. They will walk with me, dressed in white, for they are worthy. He who overcomes will, like them, be dressed in white. I will never blot out his

ᵛPsalm 2:9   ʷOr *messenger*; also in verses 7 and 14   ˣOr *the sevenfold Spirit*

name from the book of life, but will acknowledge his name before my Father and his angels. He who has an ear, let him hear what the Spirit says to the churches.

PHILADELPHIA. "To the angel of the church in Philadelphia write: Rev. 3:7-13

These are the words of him who is holy and true, who holds the key of David. What he opens no one can shut, and what he shuts no one can open. I know your deeds. See, I have placed before you an open door that no one can shut. I know that you have little strength, yet you have kept my word and have not denied my name. I will make those who are of the synagogue of Satan, who claim to be Jews though they are not, but are liars—I will make them come and fall down at your feet and acknowledge that I have loved you. Since you have kept my command to endure patiently, I will also keep you from the hour of trial that is going to come upon the whole world to test those who live on the earth.

I am coming soon. Hold on to what you have, so that no one will take your crown. Him who overcomes I will make a pillar in the temple of my God. Never again will he leave it. I will write on him the name of my God and the name of the city of my God, the new Jerusalem, which is coming down out of heaven from my God; and I will also write on him my new name. He who has an ear, let him hear what the Spirit says to the churches.

LAODICEA. "To the angel of the church in Laodicea write: Rev. 3:14-22

These are the words of the Amen, the faithful and true witness, the ruler of God's creation. I know your deeds, that you are neither cold nor hot. I wish you were either one or the other! So, because you are lukewarm—neither hot nor cold—I am about to spit you out of my mouth. You say, 'I am rich; I have acquired wealth and do not need a thing.' But you do not realize that you are wretched, pitiful, poor, blind and naked. I counsel you to buy from me gold refined in the fire, so you can become rich; and white clothes to wear, so you can cover your shameful nakedness; and salve to put on your eyes, so you can see.

Those whom I love I rebuke and discipline. So be earnest, and repent. Here I am! I stand at the door and knock. If anyone hears my voice and opens the door, I will come in and eat with him, and he with me.

To him who overcomes, I will give the right to sit with me on my throne, just as I overcame and sat down with my Father on his throne. He who has an ear, let him hear what the Spirit says to the churches."

Majesty and Centrality of God

The vision which John is about to receive begins with praise for God as the Creator of the universe. Through the songs of various creatures, God's great majesty is declared to be worthy of glory, honor, and power. Significantly, sharing in that honor is he who is called "Lion of the tribe of Judah" and also "the Lamb." Both descriptions are obvious references to Jesus the Christ.

DESCRIPTION OF THRONE. After this I looked, and there before me was a door standing open in heaven. And the voice I had first heard speaking to me like a trumpet said, "Come up here, and I will show you what must take place after this." At once I was in the Spirit, and there Rev. 4:1-6 before me was a throne in heaven with someone sitting on it. And the one who sat there had the appearance of jasper and carnelian. A rainbow, resembling an emerald, encircled the throne. Surrounding the throne were twenty-four other thrones, and seated on them were twenty-four elders. They were dressed in white and had crowns of gold on their heads. From the throne came flashes of lightning, rumblings and peals of thunder. Before the throne, seven lamps were blazing. These are the seven spirits*y* of God. Also before the throne there was what looked like a sea of glass, clear as crystal.

In the center, around the throne, were four living creatures, and they were covered with eyes, in front and in back.

Rev. 4:7,8   FOUR LIVING CREATURES.   The first living creature was like a lion, the second was like an ox, the third had a face like a man, the fourth was like a flying eagle. Each of the four living creatures had six wings and was covered with eyes all around, even under his wings. Day and night they never stop saying:

> "Holy, holy, holy
> is the Lord God Almighty,
> who was, and is, and is to come."

Rev. 4:9-11   TWENTY-FOUR ELDERS.   Whenever the living creatures give glory, honor and thanks to him who sits on the throne and who lives for ever and ever, the twenty-four elders fall down before him who sits on the throne, and worship him who lives for ever and ever. They lay their crowns before the throne and say:

> "You are worthy, our Lord and God,
>   to receive glory and honor and power,
>   for you created all things,
>   and by your will they were created
>   and have their being."

Rev. 5:1-4   SCROLL SEALED.   Then I saw in the right hand of him who sat on the throne a scroll with writing on both sides and sealed with seven seals. And I saw a mighty angel proclaiming in a loud voice, "Who is worthy to break the seals and open the scroll?" But no one in heaven or on earth or under the earth could open the scroll or even look inside it. I wept and wept because no one was found who was worthy to open the scroll or look inside.

Rev. 5:5-7   SCROLL TAKEN BY LAMB.   Then one of the elders said to me, "Do not weep! See, the Lion of the tribe of Judah, the Root of David, has triumphed. He is able to open the scroll and its seven seals."

Then I saw a Lamb, looking as if it had been slain, standing in the center of the throne, encircled by the four living creatures and the elders. He had seven horns and seven eyes, which are the seven spirits*y* of God sent out into all the earth. He came and took the scroll from the right hand of him who sat on the throne.

Rev. 5:8-10   ELDERS PRAISE LAMB.   And when he had taken it, the four living creatures and the twenty-four elders fell down before the Lamb. Each one

yOr the sevenfold Spirit

had a harp and they were holding golden bowls full of incense, which are the prayers of the saints. And they sang a new song:

> "You are worthy to take the scroll
>   and to open its seals,
>   because you were slain,
>   and with your blood you purchased men for God
>   from every tribe and language and people and nation.
>   You have made them to be a kingdom and priests to serve
>   our God,
>   and they will reign on the earth."

ANGELS PRAISE LAMB.   Then I looked and heard the voice of many angels, numbering thousands upon thousands, and ten thousand times ten thousand. They encircled the throne and the living creatures and the elders. In a loud voice they sang:

Rev. 5:11,12

> "Worthy is the Lamb, who was slain,
>   to receive power and wealth and wisdom and strength
>   and honor and glory and praise!"

UNIVERSE PRAISES LAMB.   Then I heard every creature in heaven and on earth and under the earth and on the sea, and all that is in them, singing:

Rev. 5:13,14

> "To him who sits on the throne and to the Lamb
>   be praise and honor and glory and power,
>   for ever and ever!"

The four living creatures said, "Amen," and the elders fell down and worshiped.

Destructiveness of Sin

   With the opening now of the seven seals, John sees four symbolic horses, the souls of Christian martyrs, and preparation for the blowing of seven trumpets. In all of this is a reminder that, despite the power of sin, there is always a remnant of God's people who remain faithful, even in the face of martyrdom.

FIRST SEAL.   I watched as the Lamb opened the first of the seven seals. Then I heard one of the four living creatures say in a voice like thunder, "Come!" I looked, and there before me was a white horse! Its rider held a bow, and he was given a crown, and he rode out as a conqueror bent on conquest.

Rev. 6:1,2

SECOND SEAL.   When the Lamb opened the second seal, I heard the second living creature say, "Come!" Then another horse came out, a fiery red one. Its rider was given power to take peace from the earth and to make men slay each other. To him was given a large sword.

Rev. 6:3,4

THIRD SEAL.   When the Lamb opened the third seal, I heard the third living creature say, "Come!" I looked, and there before me was a black horse! Its rider was holding a pair of scales in his hand. Then I heard what sounded like a voice among the four living creatures, saying, "A quart^z of

Rev. 6:5,6

---

^zGreek *a choinix* (probably about a liter)

wheat for a day's wages,[a] and three quarts of barley for a day's wages,[a] and do not damage the oil and the wine!"

Rev. 6:7,8   FOURTH SEAL.   When the Lamb opened the fourth seal, I heard the voice of the fourth living creature say, "Come!" I looked, and there before me was a pale horse! Its rider was named Death, and Hades was following close behind him. They were given power over a fourth of the earth to kill by sword, famine and plague, and by the wild beasts of the earth.

Rev. 6:9-11   FIFTH SEAL.   When he opened the fifth seal, I saw under the altar the souls of those who had been slain because of the word of God and the testimony they had maintained. They called out in a loud voice, "How long, Sovereign Lord, holy and true, until you judge the inhabitants of the earth and avenge our blood?" Then each of them was given a white robe, and they were told to wait a little longer, until the number of their fellow servants and brothers who were to be killed as they had been was completed.

Rev. 6:12-17   SIXTH SEAL.   I watched as he opened the sixth seal. There was a great earthquake. The sun turned black like sackcloth made of goat hair, the whole moon turned blood red, and the stars in the sky fell to earth, as late figs drop from a fig tree when shaken by a strong wind. The sky receded like a scroll, rolling up, and every mountain and island was removed from its place.

Then the kings of the earth, the princes, the generals, the rich, the mighty, and every slave and every free man hid in caves and among the rocks of the mountains. They called to the mountains and the rocks, "Fall on us and hide us from the face of him who sits on the throne and from the wrath of the Lamb! For the great day of their wrath has come, and who can stand?"

Rev. 7:1-3   SEALING OF SERVANTS.   After this I saw four angels standing at the four corners of the earth, holding back the four winds of the earth to prevent any wind from blowing on the land or on the sea or on any tree. Then I saw another angel coming up from the east, having the seal of the living God. He called out in a loud voice to the four angels who had been given power to harm the land and the sea: "Do not harm the land or the sea or the trees until we put a seal on the foreheads of the servants of our God."

Rev. 7:4-8   144,000 SEALED.   Then I heard the number of those who were sealed: 144,000 from all the tribes of Israel.

> From the tribe of Judah 12,000 were sealed,
> from the tribe of Reuben 12,000,
> from the tribe of Gad 12,000,
> from the tribe of Asher 12,000,
> from the tribe of Naphtali 12,000,
> from the tribe of Manasseh 12,000,
> from the tribe of Simeon 12,000,
> from the tribe of Levi 12,000,
> from the tribe of Issachar 12,000,
> from the tribe of Zebulun 12,000,
> from the tribe of Joseph 12,000,
> from the tribe of Benjamin 12,000.

[a] Greek *a denarius*

MULTITUDE SINGS PRAISE.   After this I looked and there before me was a great multitude that no one could count, from every nation, tribe, people and language, standing before the throne and in front of the Lamb. They were wearing white robes and were holding palm branches in their hands. And they cried out in a loud voice: Rev. 7:9,10

> "Salvation belongs to our God,
>   who sits on the throne,
>   and to the Lamb."

ANGELS WORSHIP GOD.   All the angels were standing around the throne and around the elders and the four living creatures. They fell down on their faces before the throne and worshiped God, saying: Rev. 7:11,12

> "Amen!
> Praise and glory
>   and wisdom and thanks and honor
>   and power and strength
>   be to our God for ever and ever.
> Amen!"

MULTITUDE AS VICTIMS.   Then one of the elders asked me, "These in white robes—who are they, and where did they come from?"   Rev. 7:13,14

I answered, "Sir, you know."

And he said, "These are they who have come out of the great tribulation; they have washed their robes and made them white in the blood of the Lamb.

SECURITY OF SAINTS.   Therefore,   Rev. 7:15-17

> "they are before the throne of God
>   and serve him day and night in his temple;
> and he who sits on the throne will spread his tent over
>   them.
> Never again will they hunger;
>   never again will they thirst.
> The sun will not beat upon them,
>   nor any scorching heat.
> For the Lamb at the center of the throne will be their
>   shepherd;
>   he will lead them to springs of living water.
> And God will wipe away every tear from their eyes."

SEVENTH SEAL.   When he opened the seventh seal, there was silence in heaven for about half an hour.   Rev. 8:1-6

And I saw the seven angels who stand before God, and to them were given seven trumpets.

Another angel, who had a golden censer, came and stood at the altar. He was given much incense to offer, with the prayers of all the saints, on the golden altar before the throne. The smoke of the incense, together with the prayers of the saints, went up before God from the angel's hand. Then the angel took the censer, filled it with fire from the altar, and hurled it on the earth; and there came peals of thunder, rumblings, flashes of lightning and an earthquake.

Then the seven angels who had the seven trumpets prepared to sound them.

Wrath of God Against Evil

The Old Testament is filled with accounts of God's dealings with the nation of Israel, and particularly with demonstrations of his power over evil. Striking similarity exists between the trumpets which are about to be blown and the ten plagues brought against Egypt. Hail and fire, water turned to blood, periods of darkness, and the appearance of locusts all seem to complete the parallel. The sixth trumpet will bring death among mankind, just as in the Passover, when death came to the firstborn of each Egyptian family.

Rev. 8:7   FIRST TRUMPET.   The first angel sounded his trumpet, and there came hail and fire mixed with blood, and it was hurled down upon the earth. A third of the earth was burned up, a third of the trees were burned up, and all the green grass was burned up.

Rev. 8:8,9   SECOND TRUMPET.   The second angel sounded his trumpet, and something like a huge mountain, all ablaze, was thrown into the sea. A third of the sea turned into blood, a third of the living creatures in the sea died, and a third of the ships were destroyed.

Rev. 8:10,11   THIRD TRUMPET.   The third angel sounded his trumpet, and a great star, blazing like a torch, fell from the sky on a third of the rivers and on the springs of water—the name of the star is Wormwood.[b] A third of the waters turned bitter, and many people died from the waters that had become bitter.

Rev. 8:12   FOURTH TRUMPET.   The fourth angel sounded his trumpet, and a third of the sun was struck, a third of the moon, and a third of the stars, so that a third of them turned dark. A third of the day was without light, and also a third of the night.

Rev. 8:13   NEXT THREE TRUMPETS.   As I watched, I heard an eagle that was flying in midair call out in a loud voice: "Woe! Woe! Woe to the inhabitants of the earth, because of the trumpet blasts about to be sounded by the other three angels!"

Rev. 9:1-6   FIFTH TRUMPET.   The fifth angel sounded his trumpet, and I saw a star that had fallen from the sky to the earth. The star was given the key to the shaft of the Abyss. When he opened the Abyss, smoke rose from it like the smoke from a gigantic furnace. The sun and sky were darkened by the smoke from the Abyss. And out of the smoke locusts came down upon the earth and were given power like that of scorpions of the earth. They were told not to harm the grass of the earth or any plant or tree, but only those people who did not have the seal of God on their foreheads. They were not given power to kill them, but only to torture them for five months. And the agony they suffered was like that of the sting of a scorpion when it strikes a man. During those days men will seek death, but will not find it; they will long to die, but death will elude them.

Rev. 9:7-12   DESCRIPTION OF LOCUSTS.   The locusts looked like horses prepared for battle. On their heads they wore something like crowns of gold, and their faces resembled human faces. Their hair was like women's hair, and

[b] That is, Bitterness

their teeth were like lions' teeth. They had breastplates like breastplates of iron, and the sound of their wings was like the thundering of many horses and chariots rushing into battle. They had tails and stings like scorpions, and in their tails they had power to torment people for five months. They had as king over them the angel of the Abyss, whose name in Hebrew is Abaddon, and in Greek, Apollyon.[c]

The first woe is past; two other woes are yet to come.

SIXTH TRUMPET. The sixth angel sounded his trumpet, and I heard a voice coming from the horns[d] of the golden altar that is before God. It said to the sixth angel who had the trumpet, "Release the four angels who are bound at the great river Euphrates." And the four angels who had been kept ready for this very hour and day and month and year were released to kill a third of mankind. The number of the mounted troops was two hundred million. I heard their number.

Rev. 9:13-16

DESCRIPTION OF TROOPS. The horses and riders I saw in my vision looked like this: Their breastplates were fiery red, dark blue, and yellow as sulfur. The heads of the horses resembled the heads of lions, and out of their mouths came fire, smoke and sulfur. A third of mankind was killed by the three plagues of fire, smoke and sulfur that came out of their mouths. The power of the horses was in their mouths and in their tails; for their tails were like snakes, having heads with which they inflict injury.

Rev. 9:17-19

SURVIVORS UNREPENTANT. The rest of mankind that were not killed by these plagues still did not repent of the work of their hands; they did not stop worshiping demons, and idols of gold, silver, bronze, stone and wood—idols that cannot see or hear or walk. Nor did they repent of their murders, their magic arts, their sexual immorality or their thefts.

Rev. 9:20,21

ANGEL WITH LITTLE SCROLL. Then I saw another mighty angel coming down from heaven. He was robed in a cloud, with a rainbow above his head; his face was like the sun, and his legs were like fiery pillars. He was holding a little scroll, which lay open in his hand. He planted his right foot on the sea and his left foot on the land, and he gave a loud shout like the roar of a lion. When he shouted, the voices of the seven thunders spoke. And when the seven thunders spoke, I was about to write; but I heard a voice from heaven say, "Seal up what the seven thunders have said and do not write it down."

Rev. 10:1-4

SEVENTH TRUMPET TO REVEAL. Then the angel I had seen standing on the sea and on the land raised his right hand to heaven. And he swore by him who lives for ever and ever, who created the heavens and all that is in them, the earth and all that is in it, and the sea and all that is in it, and said, "There will be no more delay! But in the days when the seventh angel is about to sound his trumpet, the mystery of God will be accomplished, just as he announced to his servants the prophets."

Rev. 10:5-7

JOHN EATS BITTERSWEET SCROLL. Then the voice that I had heard from heaven spoke to me once more: "Go, take the scroll that lies open in the hand of the angel who is standing on the sea and on the land."

So I went to the angel and asked him to give me the little scroll. He said to me, "Take it and eat it. It will turn your stomach sour, but in your mouth it will be as sweet as honey." I took the little scroll from the angel's hand

Rev. 10:8-11

---

[c]*Abaddon* and *Apollyon* mean *Destroyer.*   [d]That is, projections

and ate it. It tasted as sweet as honey in my mouth, but when I had eaten it, my stomach turned sour. Then I was told, "You must prophesy again about many peoples, nations, languages and kings."

Rev. 11:1,2   GENTILES TRAMPLE ON HOLY CITY.   I was given a reed like a measuring rod and was told, "Go and measure the temple of God and the altar, and count the worshipers there. But exclude the outer court; do not measure it, because it has been given to the Gentiles. They will trample on the holy city for 42 months.

Rev. 11:3-6   GOD'S TWO WITNESSES TESTIFY.   And I will give power to my two witnesses, and they will prophesy for 1,260 days, clothed in sackcloth." These are the two olive trees and the two lampstands that stand before the Lord of the earth. If anyone tries to harm them, fire comes from their mouths and devours their enemies. This is how anyone who wants to harm them must die. These men have power to shut up the sky so that it will not rain during the time they are prophesying; and they have power to turn the waters into blood and to strike the earth with every kind of plague as often as they want.

Rev.
11:7-10   WITNESSES KILLED.   Now when they have finished their testimony, the beast that comes up from the Abyss will attack them, and overpower and kill them. Their bodies will lie in the street of the great city, which is figuratively called Sodom and Egypt, where also their Lord was crucified. For three and a half days men from every people, tribe, language and nation will gaze on their bodies and refuse them burial. The inhabitants of the earth will gloat over them and will celebrate by sending each other gifts, because these two prophets had tormented those who live on the earth.

Rev.
11:11-14   WITNESSES RESURRECTED.   But after the three and a half days a breath of life from God entered them, and they stood on their feet, and terror struck those who saw them. Then they heard a loud voice from heaven saying to them, "Come up here." And they went up to heaven in a cloud, while their enemies looked on.

At that very hour there was a severe earthquake and a tenth of the city collapsed. Seven thousand people were killed in the earthquake, and the survivors were terrified and gave glory to the God of heaven.

The second woe has passed; the third woe is coming soon.

Righteousness of God Seen in Coming of Christ

With the blowing of the seventh trumpet comes the announcement of the kingdom of God through Christ. This was the good news of the Gospel writers—that Jesus, the Word who had become flesh, had come into the world to establish his kingdom. The signs of his coming are seen by John as being the opening of the temple, accompanied by earthquakes and various celestial disturbances.

Rev. 11:15   SEVENTH TRUMPET.   The seventh angel sounded his trumpet, and there were loud voices in heaven, which said:

> "The kingdom of the world has become the kingdom of our
> Lord and of his Christ,
> and he will reign for ever and ever."

ELDERS PRAISE GOD.   And the twenty-four elders, who were seated on   Rev.
their thrones before God, fell on their faces and worshiped God, saying: 11:16-18

> "We give thanks to you, Lord God Almighty,
>   the One who is and who was,
> because you have taken your great power
>   and have begun to reign.
> The nations were angry;
>   and your wrath has come.
> The time has come for judging the dead,
>   and for rewarding your servants the prophets
> and your saints and those who reverence your name,
>   both small and great—
> and for destroying those who destroy the earth."

SIGNS HERALDING KINGDOM.   Then God's temple in heaven was   Rev. 11:19
opened, and within his temple was seen the ark of his covenant. And there
came flashes of lightning, rumblings, peals of thunder, an earthquake and
a great hailstorm.

Opposition to Christ's Church

John now sees God's people as a star-crowned woman whose son,
Christ, rules all nations. Rising in opposition to the woman is Satan himself,
who wages war against God's people in two ways. Satan is first seen as a
dragon, which seems to represent political oppression, and then as a beast
coming out of the sea to make war against God's people, which may represent
religious persecution.

WOMAN BEARS CHILD.   A great and wondrous sign appeared in   Rev. 12:1-6
heaven: a woman clothed with the sun, with the moon under her feet and
a crown of twelve stars on her head. She was pregnant and cried out in
pain as she was about to give birth. Then another sign appeared in
heaven: an enormous red dragon with seven heads and ten horns and
seven crowns on his heads. His tail swept a third of the stars out of the
sky and flung them to the earth. The dragon stood in front of the woman
who was about to give birth, so that he might devour her child the
moment it was born. She gave birth to a son, a male child, who will rule
all the nations with an iron scepter. And her child was snatched up to God
and to his throne. The woman fled into the desert to a place prepared for
her by God, where she might be taken care of for 1,260 days.

SATAN DEFEATED BY MICHAEL.   And there was war in heaven.   Rev. 12:7-9
Michael and his angels fought against the dragon, and the dragon and his
angels fought back. But he was not strong enough, and they lost their
place in heaven. The great dragon was hurled down—that ancient serpent
called the devil, or Satan, who leads the whole world astray. He was
hurled to the earth, and his angels with him.

TRIUMPH OF CHRIST OVER SATAN.   Then I heard a loud voice in   Rev.
heaven say: 12:10-12

> "Now have come the salvation and the power and the
>   kingdom of our God,
>   and the authority of his Christ.
> For the accuser of our brothers,

> who accuses them before our God day and night,
> has been hurled down.
> They overcame him
>   by the blood of the Lamb
>   and by the word of their testimony;
> they did not love their lives so much
>   as to shrink from death.
> Therefore rejoice, you heavens
>   and you who dwell in them!
> But woe to the earth and the sea,
>   because the devil has gone down to you!
> He is filled with fury,
>   because he knows that his time is short."

Rev.
12:13-13:1a

DRAGON PURSUES WOMAN.   When the dragon saw that he had been hurled to the earth, he pursued the woman who had given birth to the male child. The woman was given the two wings of a great eagle, so that she might fly to the place prepared for her in the desert, where she would be taken care of for a time, times and half a time, out of the serpent's reach. Then from his mouth the serpent spewed water like a river, to overtake the woman and sweep her away with the torrent. But the earth helped the woman by opening its mouth and swallowing the river that the dragon had spewed out of his mouth. Then the dragon was enraged at the woman and went off to make war against the rest of her offspring—those who obey God's commandments and hold to the testimony of Jesus. And the dragon[e] stood on the shore of the sea.

Rev.
13:1b-4

DRAGON GIVES POWER TO BEAST.   And I saw a beast coming out of the sea. He had ten horns and seven heads, with ten crowns on his horns, and on each head a blasphemous name. The beast I saw resembled a leopard, but had feet like those of a bear and a mouth like that of a lion. The dragon gave the beast his power and his throne and great authority. One of the heads of the beast seemed to have had a fatal wound, but the fatal wound had been healed. The whole world was astonished and followed the beast. Men worshiped the dragon because he had given authority to the beast, and they also worshiped the beast and asked, "Who is like the beast? Who can make war against him?"

Rev.
13:5-10

BEAST PERSECUTES SAINTS.   The beast was given a mouth to utter proud words and blasphemies and to exercise his authority for forty-two months. He opened his mouth to blaspheme God, and to slander his name and his dwelling place and those who live in heaven. He was given power to make war against the saints and to conquer them. And he was given authority over every tribe, people, language and nation. All inhabitants of the earth will worship the beast—all whose names have not been written in the book of life belonging to the Lamb that was slain from the creation of the world.[f]

He who has an ear, let him hear.

> If anyone is to go into captivity,
>   into captivity he will go.

---

[e]Some late manuscripts *And I*   [f]Or *written from the creation of the world in the book of life belonging to the Lamb that was slain*

> If anyone is to be killed[8] with the sword,
> with the sword he will be killed.

This calls for patient endurance and faithfulness on the part of the saints.

SECOND BEAST COMES FROM EARTH.   Then I saw another beast,   Rev.
coming out of the earth. He had two horns like a lamb, but he spoke like   13:11-17
a dragon. He exercised all the authority of the first beast on his behalf, and
made the earth and its inhabitants worship the first beast, whose fatal
wound had been healed. And he performed great and miraculous signs,
even causing fire to come down from heaven to earth in full view of men.
Because of the signs he was given power to do on behalf of the first beast,
he deceived the inhabitants of the earth. He ordered them to set up an
image in honor of the beast who was wounded by the sword and yet lived.
He was given power to give breath to the image of the first beast, so that
it could speak and cause all who refused to worship the image to be killed.
He also forced everyone, small and great, rich and poor, free and slave, to
receive a mark on his right hand or on his forehead, so that no one could
buy or sell unless he had the mark, which is the name of the beast or the
number of his name.

CAUTION REGARDING INTERPRETATION.   This calls for wisdom. If   Rev. 13:18
anyone has insight, let him calculate the number of the beast, for it is
man's number. His number is 666.

Hope of the Faithful

Throughout their epistles, Paul and the other inspired writers had continually reminded their readers of the glorious hope for those who would
remain steadfast in their faith despite whatever pressures might tempt them
to abandon it. The messages now brought by three angels are strikingly
similar in their appeal.

LAMB WITH REDEEMED.   Then I looked, and there before me was the   Rev. 14:1-5
Lamb, standing on Mount Zion, and with him 144,000 who had his name
and his Father's name written on their foreheads. And I heard a sound
from heaven like the roar of rushing waters and like a loud peal of
thunder. The sound I heard was like that of harpists playing their harps.
And they sang a new song before the throne and before the four living
creatures and the elders. No one could learn the song except the 144,000
who had been redeemed from the earth. These are those who did not
defile themselves with women, for they kept themselves pure. They
follow the Lamb wherever he goes. They were purchased from among
men and offered as firstfruits to God and the Lamb. No lie was found in
their mouths; they are blameless.

FIRST ANGEL.   Then I saw another angel flying in midair, and he had   Rev. 14:6,7
the eternal gospel to proclaim to those who live on the earth—to every
nation, tribe, language and people. He said in a loud voice, "Fear God
and give him glory, because the hour of his judgment has come. Worship
him who made the heavens, the earth, the sea and the springs of water."

8Some manuscripts *anyone kills*

Rev. 14:8	**SECOND ANGEL.** A second angel followed and said, "Fallen! Fallen is Babylon the Great, which made all the nations drink the maddening wine of her adulteries."
Rev. 14:9-12	**THIRD ANGEL.** A third angel followed them and said in a loud voice: "If anyone worships the beast and his image and receives his mark on the forehead or on the hand, he, too, will drink of the wine of God's fury, which has been poured full strength into the cup of his wrath. He will be tormented with burning sulfur in the presence of the holy angels and of the Lamb. And the smoke of their torment rises for ever and ever. There is no rest day or night for those who worship the beast and his image, or for anyone who receives the mark of his name." This calls for patient endurance on the part of the saints who obey God's commandments and remain faithful to Jesus.
Rev. 14:13	**REST FOR FAITHFUL.** Then I heard a voice from heaven say, "Write: Blessed are the dead who die in the Lord from now on." "Yes," says the Spirit, "they will rest from their labor, for their deeds will follow them."

Judgment Against Unrighteous

At this point John envisions God's ultimate judgment on mankind. The scene he describes is a harvest of the earth, upon which God's wrath is imposed. With the pouring out of seven terrifying bowls comes a sense of finality. God's righteousness and holiness are manifested through a cleansing of sin from the world. The imagery is awesome.

Rev. 14:14-16	**EARTH BEING HARVESTED.** I looked, and there before me was a white cloud, and seated on the cloud was one "like a son of man"[h] with a crown of gold on his head and a sharp sickle in his hand. Then another angel came out of the temple and called in a loud voice to him who was sitting on the cloud, "Take your sickle and reap, because the time to reap has come, for the harvest of the earth is ripe." So he who was seated on the cloud swung his sickle over the earth, and the earth was harvested.
Rev. 14:17-20	**WRATH IMPOSED UPON HARVEST.** Another angel came out of the temple in heaven, and he too had a sharp sickle. Still another angel, who had charge of the fire, came from the altar and called in a loud voice to him who had the sharp sickle, "Take your sharp sickle and gather the clusters of grapes from the earth's vine, because its grapes are ripe." The angel swung his sickle on the earth, gathered its grapes and threw them into the great winepress of God's wrath. They were trampled in the winepress outside the city, and blood flowed out of the press, rising as high as the horses' bridles for a distance of 1,600 stadia.[i]
Rev. 15:1	**SEVEN PLAGUES OF WRATH.** I saw in heaven another great and marvelous sign: seven angels with the seven last plagues—last, because with them God's wrath is completed.
Rev. 15:2-4	**GOD'S HOLINESS IN WRATH.** And I saw what looked like a sea of glass mixed with fire and, standing beside the sea, those who had been victorious over the beast and his image and over the number of his name.

[h]Daniel 7:13   [i]That is, about 180 miles (about 300 kilometers)

They held harps given them by God and sang the song of Moses the servant of God and the song of the Lamb:

> "Great and marvelous are your deeds,
>   Lord God Almighty.
> Just and true are your ways,
>   King of the ages.
> Who will not fear you, O Lord,
>   and bring glory to your name?
> For you alone are holy.
> All nations will come
>   and worship before you,
> for your righteous acts have been revealed."

BOWLS OF WRATH.   After this I looked and in heaven the temple, that is, the tabernacle of the Testimony, was opened. Out of the temple came the seven angels with the seven plagues. They were dressed in clean, shining linen and wore golden sashes around their chests. Then one of the four living creatures gave to the seven angels seven golden bowls filled with the wrath of God, who lives for ever and ever. And the temple was filled with smoke from the glory of God and from his power, and no one could enter the temple until the seven plagues of the seven angels were completed. Then I heard a loud voice from the temple saying to the seven angels, "Go, pour out the seven bowls of God's wrath on the earth."

Rev. 15:5-16:1

FIRST BOWL.   The first angel went and poured out his bowl on the land, and ugly and painful sores broke out on the people who had the mark of the beast and worshiped his image.

Rev. 16:2

SECOND BOWL.   The second angel poured out his bowl on the sea, and it turned into blood like that of a dead man, and every living thing in the sea died.

Rev. 16:3

THIRD BOWL.   The third angel poured out his bowl on the rivers and springs of water, and they became blood.

Rev. 16:4

PRAISE FOR GOD'S JUSTICE.   Then I heard the angel in charge of the waters say:

Rev. 16:5-7

> "You are just in these judgments,
>   you who are and who were, the Holy One,
>   because you have so judged;
> for they have shed the blood of your saints and prophets,
>   and you have given them blood to drink as they
>   deserve."

And I heard the altar respond:

> "Yes, Lord God Almighty,
>   true and just are your judgments."

FOURTH BOWL.   The fourth angel poured out his bowl on the sun, and the sun was given power to scorch people with fire. They were seared by the intense heat and they cursed the name of God, who had control over these plagues, but they refused to repent and glorify him.

Rev. 16:8,9

FIFTH BOWL.   The fifth angel poured out his bowl on the throne of the beast, and his kingdom was plunged into darkness. Men gnawed their tongues in agony and cursed the God of heaven because of their pains and their sores, but they refused to repent of what they had done.

Rev. 16:10,11

Rev.
16:12-16

SIXTH BOWL. The sixth angel poured out his bowl on the great river Euphrates, and its water was dried up to prepare the way for the kings from the East. Then I saw three evil[j] spirits that looked like frogs; they came out of the mouth of the dragon, out of the mouth of the beast and out of the mouth of the false prophet. They are spirits of demons performing miraculous signs, and they go out to the kings of the whole world, to gather them for the battle on the great day of God Almighty.

"Behold, I come like a thief! Blessed is he who stays awake and keeps his clothes with him, so that he may not go naked and be shamefully exposed."

Then they gathered the kings together to the place that in Hebrew is called Armageddon.

Rev.
16:17-21

SEVENTH BOWL. The seventh angel poured out his bowl into the air, and out of the temple came a loud voice from the throne, saying, "It is done!" Then there came flashes of lightning, rumblings, peals of thunder and a severe earthquake. No earthquake like it has ever occurred since man has been on earth, so tremendous was the quake. The great city split into three parts, and the cities of the nations collapsed. God remembered Babylon the Great and gave her the cup filled with the wine of the fury of his wrath. Every island fled away and the mountains could not be found. From the sky huge hailstones of about a hundred pounds each fell upon men. And they cursed God on account of the plague of hail, because the plague was so terrible.

Special Judgment upon Babylon

In the images of a drunken prostitute and an incredible scarlet beast, John sees the vision of what appears to be a special judgment of God. Whatever might be the true identification of this "Babylon," its destruction is accompanied by terrible lament.

Rev. 17:1-6

DRUNKEN PROSTITUTE. One of the seven angels who had the seven bowls came and said to me, "Come, I will show you the punishment of the great prostitute, who sits on many waters. With her the kings of the earth committed adultery and the inhabitants of the earth were intoxicated with the wine of her adulteries."

Then the angel carried me away in the Spirit into a desert. There I saw a woman sitting on a scarlet beast that was covered with blasphemous names and had seven heads and ten horns. The woman was dressed in purple and scarlet, and was glittering with gold, precious stones and pearls. She held a golden cup in her hand, filled with abominable things and the filth of her adulteries. This title was written on her forehead:

MYSTERY
BABYLON THE GREAT
THE MOTHER OF PROSTITUTES
AND OF THE ABOMINATIONS OF THE EARTH.

I saw that the woman was drunk with the blood of the saints, the blood of those who bore testimony to Jesus.

When I saw her, I was greatly astonished.

*j*Greek *unclean*

BEAST EXPLAINED.   Then the angel said to me: "Why are you aston-   Rev. 17:7,8
ished? I will explain to you the mystery of the woman and of the beast she
rides, which has the seven heads and ten horns. The beast, which you
saw, once was, now is not, and will come up out of the Abyss and go to
his destruction. The inhabitants of the earth whose names have not been
written in the book of life from the creation of the world will be astonished when they see the beast, because he once was, now is not, and yet
will come.

SEVEN HEADS EXPLAINED.   "This calls for a mind with wisdom. The   Rev.
17:9-11
seven heads are seven hills on which the woman sits. They are also seven
kings. Five have fallen, one is, the other has not yet come; but when he
does come, he must remain for a little while. The beast who once was, and
now is not, is an eighth king. He belongs to the seven and is going to his
destruction.

TEN HORNS EXPLAINED.   "The ten horns you saw are ten kings who   Rev.
17:12-14
have not yet received a kingdom, but who for one hour will receive
authority as kings along with the beast. They have one purpose and will
give their power and authority to the beast. They will make war against
the Lamb, but the Lamb will overcome them because he is Lord of lords
and King of kings—and with him will be his called, chosen and faithful
followers."

WATERS EXPLAINED.   Then the angel said to me, "The waters you saw,   Rev.
17:15-17
where the prostitute sits, are peoples, multitudes, nations and languages.
The beast and the ten horns you saw will hate the prostitute. They will
bring her to ruin and leave her naked; they will eat her flesh and burn her
with fire. For God has put it into their hearts to accomplish his purpose
by agreeing to give the beast their power to rule, until God's words are
fulfilled.

WOMAN EXPLAINED.   The woman you saw is the great city that rules   Rev. 17:18
over the kings of the earth."

REJOICING OVER BABYLON'S FALL.   After this I saw another angel   Rev. 18:1-3
coming down from heaven. He had great authority, and the earth was
illuminated by his splendor. With a mighty voice he shouted:

> "Fallen! Fallen is Babylon the Great!
>   She has become a home for demons
> and a haunt for every evil[k] spirit,
>   a haunt for every unclean and detestable bird.
> For all the nations have drunk
>   the maddening wine of her adulteries.
> The kings of the earth committed adultery with her,
>   and the merchants of the earth grew rich from her
>   excessive luxuries."

WARNING ABOUT BABYLON.   Then I heard another voice from heaven   Rev. 18:4-8
say:

> "Come out of her, my people,
>   so that you will not share in her sins,
>   so that you will not receive any of her plagues;

[k]Greek *unclean*

for her sins are piled up to heaven,
    and God has remembered her crimes.
Give back to her as she has given;
    pay her back double for what she has done.
Mix her a double portion from her own cup.
Give her as much torture and grief
    as the glory and luxury she gave herself.
In her heart she boasts,
    'I sit as queen; I am not a widow,
    and I will never mourn.'
Therefore in one day her plagues will overtake her:
    death, mourning and famine.
She will be consumed by fire,
    for mighty is the Lord God who judges her.

Rev.
18:9,10

LAMENT BY KINGS.   "When the kings of the earth who committed adultery with her and shared her luxury see the smoke of her burning, they will weep and mourn over her. Terrified at her torment, they will stand far off and cry:

" 'Woe! Woe, O great city,
    O Babylon, city of power!
In one hour your doom has come!'

Rev.
18:11-17

LAMENT BY MERCHANTS.   "The merchants of the earth will weep and mourn over her because no one buys their cargoes any more—cargoes of gold, silver, precious stones and pearls; fine linen, purple, silk and scarlet cloth; every sort of citron wood, and articles of every kind made of ivory, costly wood, bronze, iron and marble; cargoes of cinnamon and spice, of incense, myrrh and frankincense, of wine and olive oil, of fine flour and wheat; cattle and sheep; horses and carriages; and bodies and souls of men.

"They will say, 'The fruit you longed for is gone from you. All your riches and splendor have vanished, never to be recovered.' The merchants who sold these things and gained their wealth from her will stand far off, terrified at her torment. They will weep and mourn and cry out:

" 'Woe! Woe, O great city,
    dressed in fine linen, purple and scarlet,
    and glittering with gold, precious stones and pearls!
In one hour such great wealth has been brought to ruin!'

"Every sea captain, and all who travel by ship, the sailors, and all who earn their living from the sea, will stand far off.

Rev.
18:18-20

LAMENT BY SAILORS.   When they see the smoke of her burning, they will exclaim, 'Was there ever a city like this great city?' They will throw dust on their heads, and with weeping and mourning cry out:

" 'Woe! Woe, O great city,
    where all who had ships on the sea
    became rich through her wealth!
In one hour she has been brought to ruin!
Rejoice over her, O heaven!
    Rejoice, saints and apostles and prophets!
God has judged her for the way she treated you.' "

EXTENT OF DESTRUCTION.   Then a mighty angel picked up a boulder the size of a large millstone and threw it into the sea, and said:

Rev. 18:21-24

> "With such violence
>> the great city of Babylon will be thrown down,
>> never to be found again.
> The music of harpists and musicians, flute players and
>> trumpeters,
>> will never be heard in you again.
> No workman of any trade
>> will ever be found in you again.
> The sound of a millstone
>> will never be heard in you again.
> The light of a lamp
>> will never shine in you again.
> The voice of bridegroom and bride
>> will never be heard in you again.
> Your merchants were the world's great men.
>> By your magic spell all the nations were led astray.
> In her was found the blood of prophets and of the saints,
>> and of all who have been killed on the earth."

MULTITUDE CELEBRATES.   After this I heard what sounded like the roar of a great multitude in heaven shouting:

Rev. 19:1-5

> "Hallelujah!
> Salvation and glory and power belong to our God,
>> for true and just are his judgments.
> He has condemned the great prostitute
>> who corrupted the earth by her adulteries.
> He has avenged on her the blood of his servants."

And again they shouted:

> "Hallelujah!
> The smoke from her goes up for ever and ever."

The twenty-four elders and the four living creatures fell down and worshiped God, who was seated on the throne. And they cried:

> "Amen, Hallelujah!"

Then a voice came from the throne, saying:

> "Praise our God,
>> all you his servants,
> you who fear him,
>> both small and great!"

Triumph of Christ and His Church

As John nears the end of his vision, he sees the wedding of Jesus, the Lamb, and his bride, the church. There is joy and honor in being invited as a guest to the wedding supper. Yet even in this blissful scene looms the grim reminder of the destruction which awaits those who have been unrighteous. As the father of all unrighteousness, Satan is finally and totally destroyed. It is therefore clear that Christ and his saints will ultimately triumph over both

Satan and his evil power. That knowledge should be more than sufficient to comfort and encourage every believer in his hope for the future.

Rev. 19:6-8   WEDDING OF LAMB AND BRIDE.   Then I heard what sounded like a great multitude, like the roar of rushing waters and like loud peals of thunder, shouting:

> "Hallelujah!
>   For our Lord God Almighty reigns.
> Let us rejoice and be glad
>   and give him glory!
> For the wedding of the Lamb has come,
>   and his bride has made herself ready.
> Fine linen, bright and clean,
>   was given her to wear."

(Fine linen stands for the righteous acts of the saints.)

Rev. 19:9,10   HONOR OF BEING INVITED.   Then the angel said to me, "Write: 'Blessed are those who are invited to the wedding supper of the Lamb!'" And he added, "These are the true words of God."

At this I fell at his feet to worship him. But he said to me, "Do not do it! I am a fellow servant with you and with your brothers who hold to the testimony of Jesus. Worship God! For the testimony of Jesus is the spirit of prophecy."

Rev. 19:11-16   WORD RULES AS LORD AND KING.   I saw heaven standing open and there before me was a white horse, whose rider is called Faithful and True. With justice he judges and makes war. His eyes are like blazing fire, and on his head are many crowns. He has a name written on him that no one knows but he himself. He is dressed in a robe dipped in blood, and his name is the Word of God. The armies of heaven were following him, riding on white horses and dressed in fine linen, white and clean. Out of his mouth comes a sharp sword with which to strike down the nations. "He will rule them with an iron scepter."[1] He treads the winepress of the fury of the wrath of God Almighty. On his robe and on his thigh he has this name written:

KING OF KINGS AND LORD OF LORDS.

Rev. 19:17,18   BIRDS DEVOUR UNRIGHTEOUS.   And I saw an angel standing in the sun, who cried in a loud voice to all the birds flying in midair, "Come, gather together for the great supper of God, so that you may eat the flesh of kings, generals, and mighty men, of horses and their riders, and the flesh of all people, free and slave, small and great."

Rev. 19:19-21   BEAST AND FALSE PROPHET KILLED.   Then I saw the beast and the kings of the earth and their armies gathered together to make war against the rider on the horse and his army. But the beast was captured, and with him the false prophet who had performed the miraculous signs on his behalf. With these signs he had deluded those who had received the mark of the beast and worshiped his image. The two of them were thrown alive into the fiery lake of burning sulfur. The rest of them were killed with the

[1]Psalm 2:9

sword that came out of the mouth of the rider on the horse, and all the birds gorged themselves on their flesh.

SATAN BOUND FOR A TIME.   And I saw an angel coming down out of heaven, having the key to the Abyss and holding in his hand a great chain. He seized the dragon, that ancient serpent, who is the devil, or Satan, and bound him for a thousand years. He threw him into the Abyss, and locked and sealed it over him, to keep him from deceiving the nations anymore until the thousand years were ended. After that, he must be set free for a short time.

Rev. 20:1-3

MARTYRS REIGN WITH CHRIST.   I saw thrones on which were seated those who had been given authority to judge. And I saw the souls of those who had been beheaded because of their testimony for Jesus and because of the word of God. They had not worshiped the beast or his image and had not received his mark on their foreheads or their hands. They came to life and reigned with Christ a thousand years. (The rest of the dead did not come to life until the thousand years were ended.) This is the first resurrection. Blessed and holy are those who have part in the first resurrection. The second death has no power over them, but they will be priests of God and of Christ and will reign with him for a thousand years.

Rev. 20:4-6

SATAN DESTROYED.   When the thousand years are over, Satan will be released from his prison and will go out to deceive the nations in the four corners of the earth—Gog and Magog—to gather them for battle. In number they are like the sand on the seashore. They marched across the breadth of the earth and surrounded the camp of God's people, the city he loves. But fire came down from heaven and devoured them. And the devil, who deceived them, was thrown into the lake of burning sulfur, where the beast and the false prophet had been thrown. They will be tormented day and night for ever and ever.

Rev. 20:7-10

GREAT JUDGMENT OF THE DEAD.   Then I saw a great white throne and him who was seated on it. Earth and sky fled from his presence, and there was no place for them. And I saw the dead, great and small, standing before the throne, and books were opened. Another book was opened, which is the book of life. The dead were judged according to what they had done as recorded in the books. The sea gave up the dead that were in it, and death and Hades gave up the dead that were in them, and each person was judged according to what he had done. Then death and Hades were thrown into the lake of fire. The lake of fire is the second death. If anyone's name was not found written in the book of life, he was thrown into the lake of fire.

Rev. 20:11-15

VISION OF NEW HEAVEN AND EARTH.   Then I saw a new heaven and a new earth, for the first heaven and the first earth had passed away, and there was no longer any sea. I saw the Holy City, the new Jerusalem, coming down out of heaven from God, prepared as a bride beautifully dressed for her husband. And I heard a loud voice from the throne saying, "Now the dwelling of God is with men, and he will live with them. They will be his people, and God himself will be with them and be their God. He will wipe every tear from their eyes. There will be no more death or mourning or crying or pain, for the old order of things has passed away."
     He who was seated on the throne said, "I am making everything new!"

Rev. 21:1-5

Then he said, "Write this down, for these words are trustworthy and true."

Rev. 21:6-8   REWARD AND DESTRUCTION.   He said to me: "It is done. I am the Alpha and the Omega, the Beginning and the End. To him who is thirsty I will give to drink without cost from the spring of the water of life. He who overcomes will inherit all this, and I will be his God and he will be my son. But the cowardly, the unbelieving, the vile, the murderers, the sexually immoral, those who practice magic arts, the idolaters and all liars—their place will be in the fiery lake of burning sulfur. This is the second death."

Glory and Grandeur of Heaven

In bringing to a conclusion both this revelation and the last of his inspired Scripture, God gives John a vision of what heaven will be like. It is pictured as a Holy City, having a river flowing through it with a tree of life on either side. The cares and sorrows of this life will not be known in heaven, and great joy will abound. This vision of a new heaven and a new earth provides an exciting conclusion to a book whose opening lines told of the majesty of God's first creation.

Rev. 21:9-14   VIEW OF HOLY CITY.   One of the seven angels who had the seven bowls full of the seven last plagues came and said to me, "Come, I will show you the bride, the wife of the Lamb." And he carried me away in the Spirit to a mountain great and high, and showed me the Holy City, Jerusalem, coming down out of heaven from God. It shone with the glory of God, and its brilliance was like that of a very precious jewel, like a jasper, clear as crystal. It had a great, high wall with twelve gates, and with twelve angels at the gates. On the gates were written the names of the twelve tribes of Israel. There were three gates on the east, three on the north, three on the south and three on the west. The wall of the city had twelve foundations, and on them were the names of the twelve apostles of the Lamb.

Rev. 21:15-21   DESCRIPTION OF CITY.   The angel who talked with me had a measuring rod of gold to measure the city, its gates and its walls. The city was laid out like a square, as long as it was wide. He measured the city with the rod and found it to be 12,000 stadia[m] in length, and as wide and high as it is long. He measured its wall and it was 144 cubits[n] thick,[o] by man's measurement, which the angel was using. The wall was made of jasper, and the city of pure gold, as pure as glass. The foundations of the city walls were decorated with every kind of precious stone. The first foundation was jasper, the second sapphire, the third chalcedony, the fourth emerald, the fifth sardonyx, the sixth carnelian, the seventh chrysolite, the eighth beryl, the ninth topaz, the tenth chrysoprase, the eleventh jacinth, and the twelfth amethyst.[p] The twelve gates were twelve pearls, each gate made of a single pearl. The great street of the city was of pure gold, like transparent glass.

[m]That is, about 1,400 miles (about 2,200 kilometers)   [n]That is, about 200 feet (about 65 meters)   [o]Or *high*   [p]The precise identification of some of these precious stones is uncertain.

PURITY AND LIGHT OF CITY.   I did not see a temple in the city, because the Lord God Almighty and the Lamb are its temple. The city does not need the sun or the moon to shine on it, for the glory of God gives it light, and the Lamb is its lamp. The nations will walk by its light, and the kings of the earth will bring their splendor into it. On no day will its gates ever be shut, for there will be no night there. The glory and honor of the nations will be brought into it. Nothing impure will ever enter it, nor will anyone who does what is shameful or deceitful, but only those whose names are written in the Lamb's book of life.

Rev. 21:22-27

BLESSINGS IN RIVER AND TREE.   Then the angel showed me the river of the water of life, as clear as crystal, flowing from the throne of God and of the Lamb down the middle of the great street of the city. On each side of the river stood the tree of life, bearing twelve crops of fruit, yielding its fruit every month. And the leaves of the tree are for the healing of the nations. No longer will there be any curse. The throne of God and of the Lamb will be in the city, and his servants will serve him. They will see his face, and his name will be on their foreheads. There will be no more night. They will not need the light of a lamp or the light of the sun, for the Lord God will give them light. And they will reign for ever and ever.

Rev. 22:1-5

Epilogue

ANGEL VERIFIES REVELATION.   The angel said to me, "These words are trustworthy and true. The Lord, the God of the spirits of the prophets, sent his angel to show his servants the things that must soon take place."

"Behold, I am coming soon! Blessed is he who keeps the words of the prophecy in this book."

Rev. 22:6,7

JOHN VERIFIES REVELATION.   I, John, am the one who heard and saw these things. And when I had heard and seen them, I fell down to worship at the feet of the angel who had been showing them to me. But he said to me, "Do not do it! I am a fellow servant with you and with your brothers the prophets and of all who keep the words of this book. Worship God!"

Then he told me, "Do not seal up the words of the prophecy of this book, because the time is near. Let him who does wrong continue to do wrong; let him who is vile continue to be vile; let him who does right continue to do right; and let him who is holy continue to be holy."

Rev. 22:8-11

JESUS VERIFIES REVELATION.   "Behold, I am coming soon! My reward is with me, and I will give to everyone according to what he has done. I am the Alpha and the Omega, the First and the Last, the Beginning and the End.

"Blessed are those who wash their robes, that they may have the right to the tree of life and may go through the gates into the city. Outside are the dogs, those who practice magic arts, the sexually immoral, the murderers, the idolaters and everyone who loves and practices falsehood.

"I, Jesus, have sent my angel to give you[q] this testimony for the churches. I am the Root and the Offspring of David, and the bright Morning Star."

Rev. 22:12-16

[q]The Greek is plural.

Rev. 22:17   INVITATION TO ENJOY BLESSINGS.   The Spirit and the bride say, "Come!" And let him who hears say, "Come!" Whoever is thirsty, let him come; and whoever wishes, let him take the free gift of the water of life.

Rev.   CAUTION AGAINST MISUSE.   I warn everyone who hears the words of
22:18,19   the prophecy of this book: If anyone adds anything to them, God will add to him the plagues described in this book. And if anyone takes words away from this book of prophecy, God will take away from him his share in the tree of life and in the holy city, which are described in this book.

Rev. 22:20   PROMISE OF JESUS.   He who testifies to these things says, "Yes, I am coming soon."
              Amen. Come, Lord Jesus.

Rev. 22:21   BENEDICTION.   The grace of the Lord Jesus be with God's people. Amen.

So ends the revelation to John and the last of Holy Scripture. In the teachings of Jesus there is abundant life; in the example of his divine Person there is love; and in the power of his resurrection there is hope.

CHRONOLOGY OF SIGNIFICANT EVENTS

TOPICAL CONTENTS FOR THE BOOK OF PROVERBS

CROSS REFERENCE INDEX

CHRONOLOGY OF SIGNIFICANT EVENTS

The following chronological listing is provided in order to show the general flow of major events. Although the events recorded by divine revelation are anchored in history, it is not always possible to ascertain precisely when each event occurred.

Where dates are less certain—particularly in the earlier centuries—approximate dates are given in order to maintain a frame of reference for added understanding.

Topical Contents for the Book of Proverbs

CROSS REFERENCE INDEX

PROVERBS—*Cont.*		18:8	**641**	20:12	**623**	22:7	**647**
16:10	**653**	18:9	**650**	20:13	**650**	22:8	**630**
16:11	**645**	18:10	**621**	20:14	**631**	22:9	**648**
16:12-15	**653**	18:11	**647**	20:15	**624**	22:10	**642**
16:16	**623**	18:12	**633**	20:16	**652**	22:11	**654**
16:17	**656**	18:13	**641**	20:17	**645**	22:12	**622**
16:18-19	**633**	18:14	**657**	20:18	**625**	22:13	**656**
16:20	**621**	18:15	**624**	20:19	**641**	22:14	**639**
16:21	**640**	18:16	**648**	20:20	**652**	22:15	**626**
16:22	**622**	18:17	**646**	20:21	**645**	22:16	**649**
16:23	**639**	18:18-19	**644**	20:22	**644**	22:17-21	**619**
16:24	**640**	18:20-21	**642**	20:23	**645**	22:22-23	**649**
16:25	**621**	18:22	**653**	20:24	**621**	22:24-25	**635**
16:26	**650**	18:23	**647**	20:25	**634**	22:26-27	**652**
16:27	**642**	18:24	**655**	20:26	**654**	22:28	**645**
16:28	**641**	19:1	**639**	20:27	**631**	22:29	**650**
16:29	**643**	19:2	**624**	20:28	**654**	23:1-3	**654**
16:30	**631**	19:3	**621**	20:29	**653**	23:4-5	**647**
16:31	**653**	19:4	**647**	20:30	**626**	23:6-8	**631**
16:32	**635**	19:5	**642**	21:1	**654**	23:9	**625**
16:33	**621**	19:6-7	**647**	21:2-3	**631**	23:10-11	**645**
17:1	**644**	19:8	**623**	21:4	**633**	23:12	**624**
17:2	**652**	19:9	**646**	21:5	**634**	23:13-14	**626**
17:3	**631**	19:10	**633**	21:6	**642**	23:15-16	**639**
17:4	**640**	19:11	**635**	21:7	**643**	23:17-18	**656**
17:5	**632**	19:12	**654**	21:8	**629**	23:19-21	**635**
17:6	**652**	19:13-14	**653**	21:9	**653**	23:22-25	**652**
17:7	**654**	19:15	**650**	21:10	**633**	23:26-28	**639**
17:8	**645**	19:16	**624**	21:11	**624**	23:29-35	**636**
17:9	**641**	19:17	**648**	21:12	**630**	24:1-2	**655**
17:10	**624**	19:18	**626**	21:13	**648**	24:3-4	**624**
17:11	**654**	19:19	**635**	21:14	**645**	24:5-6	**625**
17:12	**622**	19:20	**624**	21:15	**646**	24:7	**622**
17:13	**630**	19:21	**621**	21:16	**630**	24:8-9	**629**
17:14	**642**	19:22	**642**	21:17	**650**	24:10	**656**
17:15	**646**	19:23	**620**	21:18	**628**	24:11-12	**646**
17:16	**647**	19:24	**650**	21:19	**653**	24:13-14	**622**
17:17	**655**	19:25	**625**	21:20	**651**	24:15-16	**628**
17:18	**651**	19:26	**652**	21:21	**630**	24:17-18	**632**
17:19-20	**642**	19:27	**625**	21:22	**621**	24:19-20	**634**
17:21	**652**	19:28	**646**	21:23	**641**	24:21-22	**654**
17:22	**657**	19:29	**630**	21:24	**634**	24:23-25	**646**
17:23	**645**	20:1	**635**	21:25-26	**650**	24:26	**644**
17:24	**623**	20:2	**654**	21:27	**631**	24:27	**650**
17:25	**652**	20:3	**642**	21:28	**646**	24:28-29	**644**
17:26	**646**	20:4	**650**	21:29	**643**	24:30-34	**650**
17:27-28	**641**	20:5	**623**	21:30-31	**621**	25:1	**620**
18:1	**634**	20:6	**632**	22:1	**656**	25:2-7	**654**
18:2	**621**	20:7	**628**	22:2	**647**	25:8	**635**
18:3	**630**	20:8	**654**	22:3	**656**	25:9-10	**656**
18:4	**621**	20:9	**633**	22:4	**634**	25:11	**640**
18:5	**646**	20:10	**645**	22:5	**656**	25:12	**625**
18:6-7	**639**	20:11	**631**	22:6	**626**	25:13	**655**

About the Compiler
F. LaGard Smith

As a Bible scholar, attorney, and classroom teacher, Dr. Smith brings a unique blend of thorough biblical research, objective analysis, and personal insight to his writing. A popular lecturer, Dr. Smith often draws from a keen sense of wit and humor to hold the attention of his listening and reading audiences. Yet the seriousness of his mission is evident in both the topics of his books and in their earnest presentation.

Formerly professor of law at Pepperdine University in Malibu, California, and Scholar in Residence for Christian Studies at Lipscomb University in Nashville, Tennessee, Dr. Smith is a prolific author of more than 20 books on a wide variety of topics ranging from doctrinal commentaries to current social and moral issues to books of inspiration and devotion.

Dr. Smith divides his writing time between the States and rural England, where he and his wife, Ruth, live six months each year in the lovely Cotswold village of Buckland. In addition, Dr. Smith lectures and teaches to a wide variety of audiences throughout the world.

This particular work is the outgrowth of a suggestion by Dr. Smith's father, who early on implanted the idea that "somebody ought to put the Bible in the right order." Upon his father's death, Dr. Smith decided to launch just such a project, the result of which you hold in your hands. In the more than two decades since its original publication, *The Daily Bible* has blessed countless readers with its unique chronological approach and informative narrative.